Edwin B. Williams, General Editor

Edwin B. Williams, A.B., A.M., Ph.D., Doct. d'Univ., LL.D., L.H.D., was chairman of the Department of Romance Languages, dean of the Graduate School, and provost of the University of Pennsylvania. He was a member of the American Philosophical Society and the Hispanic Society of America and the author of *The Bantam New College Spanish & English Dictionary* and the Scribner's (formerly the Holt) *Spanish and English Dictionary* and many other works on the Spanish, Portuguese, and French languages.

THE NEW INTERNATIONAL
WEBSTER'S SPANISH & ENGLISH DICTIONARY

BY EDWIN B. WILLIAMS
Professor of Romance Languages
University of Pennsylvania

TRIDENT PRESS INTERNATIONAL
1997 EDITION

TRIDENT PRESS INTERNATIONAL
1997 EDITION

Copyright © 1968, 1987 by Bantam Books.

Reprinted by permission of Bantam Books, a division of Bantam Doubleday Dell Publishing Group, Inc. Paperback edition available from Bantam under the title The Bantam New College Spanish & English Dictionary.

ISBN 1-888777-43-5

CONTENTS

Luego de leer una entrada, vea LA OTRA SECCIÓN del diccionario para encontrar más información sobre el significado de las palabras. Véase, p.ej., **fuerza** y **force.**

PREFACE TO THE FIRST EDITION

This book is based on primary spoken and written sources. It is designed for speakers of either language who wish to find words or the meanings of words in the foreign language. Its purpose is, therefore, fourfold. It gives to the English-speaking users (1) the Spanish words they need to express their thoughts in Spanish and (2) the English meanings of Spanish words they need to understand Spanish, and to the Spanish-speaking users (3) the English words they need to express their thoughts in English and (4) the Spanish meanings of English words they need to understand English.

To accomplish the purpose of (1) and (3), discriminations are provided in the source language except that, because of the special facility with which the subject of the verb can be shown in Spanish and because of the convenience of showing the object with personal **a**, discriminations in the form of subject and/or object are given in Spanish on the English-Spanish side as well as on the Spanish-English side. For the purpose of (2) and (4) discriminations are not needed and are not given because the user will always have the context of what he hears or reads to guide him. However, some glosses whose purpose is not to show discrimination but rather to elaborate on the meaning of what may be judged to be an unfamiliar or obscure word or expression in the user's native language are provided in that language.

All words are treated in a fixed order according to the parts of speech and the functions of verbs; and meanings with subject, usage, and regional labels come after more general meanings.

In order to facilitate the finding of the meaning and use sought for, changes within a vocabulary entry in part of speech and function of verb, in irregular inflection, in the gender of Spanish nouns, and in the pronunciation of English words are marked with parallels instead of the usual semicolons.

Periods are omitted after labels and grammatical abbreviations and at the end of vocabulary entries.

The feminine form of a Spanish adjective used as a noun (or a Spanish feminine noun having identical spelling with the feminine form of an adjective) that falls alphabetically in a separate position from the adjective is treated in that position and is listed again as a cross reference under the adjective.

The gender of Spanish nouns is shown on both sides of the Dictionary except that the gender of masculine nouns ending in **-o**, feminine nouns ending in **-a, -dad, -tad, -tud, -ión**, and **-umbre**, masculine nouns modified by an adjective ending in **-o**, and feminine nouns modified by an adjective ending in **-a** is not shown on the English-Spanish side.

Numbers referring to the conjugations of irregular Spanish verbs are placed before the abbreviations indicating the part of speech. The list at the end of the Spanish-English part of the Dictionary includes models of all verbs that show a combination of two types of irregularity, e.g., **esforzar, seguir, teñir.**

Proper nouns and abbreviations are listed in their alphabetical position in the main body of the Dictionary. Thus **España** and **español** do not have to be looked up in two different parts of the book. And all subentries are listed in strictly alphabetical order.

The centered period is used in vocabulary entries of irregularly inflected words to mark off the final syllable that has to be detached before the syllable showing the inflection is added, e.g., **lá•piz** *m* (*pl* **-pices**) and **falsi•fy** [ˈfɔlsɪ,faɪ] *v* (*pret & pp* **-fied**).

The pronunciation of all English simple words is shown in a new adaptation of the symbols of the International Phonetic Alphabet and in brackets. The pronunciation of English compound words is not shown provided the pronunciation of the components is shown where they appear as independent vocabulary entries.

Since vocabulary entries are not determined on the basis of etymology, homographs are included in a single entry. When the pronunciation of an English homograph changes, this is shown in the proper place after parallels.

PRÓLOGO DE LA PRIMARA EDICIÓN

Hemos basado este libro en fuentes originales del lenguaje hablado y escrito. Está destinado a los hablantes de uno u otro idioma que buscan palabras o significados de palabras en el idioma extranjero. Tiene, por lo tanto, los cuatro siguientes propósitos: al usuario de habla inglesa le suministra (1) las palabras españolas que necesita para expresar su pensamiento en español y (2) los significados ingleses de las palabras españolas que necesita para comprender el español; y al usuario de habla española le suministra (3) las palabras inglesas que necesita para expresar su pensamiento en inglés y (4) los significados españoles de las palabras inglesas que necesita para comprender el inglés.

Para lograr los propósitos indicados bajo los números (1) y (3), se suministran diferenciaciones (es decir, distinciones entre dos o más significados de una palabra) en la lengua-fuente; pero, dada la facilidad con que el sujeto del verbo puede indicarse en español y dada la conveniencia de destacar el objeto del verbo con la preposición **a,** las diferenciaciones consistentes en el sujeto o el objeto, o ambos, se dan en español tanto en la parte de inglés-español como en la parte de español-inglés. Para los propósitos indicados bajo los números (2) y (4) no se necesitan diferenciaciones y no se dan, porque el usuario siempre tendrá como guía el contexto de lo que oye o lee. Con todo, algunas glosas que no tienen por objeto indicar diferenciaciones sino más bien dilucidar el sentido de lo que parece ser una palabra o expresión raras u obscuras en la lengua nativa del usuario, se indican en esta lengua.

Los vocablos se tratan consecutivamente de acuerdo con las partes de la oración y las funciones verbales; y los significados marcados con calificativos de tema, uso y país van después de los significados más generales.

Para facilitar la búsqueda del significado y el uso deseados, los cambios en la parte de la oración y función verbal, en la flexión, en el género de los nombres españoles y en la pronunciación de las palabras inglesas van señalados con doble raya vertical, en vez del punto y coma de costumbre.

Se han omitido los puntos después de los calificativos y abreviaturas gramaticales y al fin de los artículos.

La forma femenina de un adjetivo español usado como sustantivo (o de un sustantivo femenino que se escribe lo mismo que la forma femenina de un adjetivo), que cae alfabéticamente en lugar apartado del adjetivo, se trata en este lugar y se consigna otra vez bajo el adjetivo con una referencia a la palabra traducida anteriormente.

El género de los nombres españoles aparece en ambas partes del Diccionario; pero no aparece en la parte de inglés-español el género de los nombres masculinos que terminan en **-o,** los nombres femeninos que terminan en **-a, -dad, -tad, -tud, -ión,** y **-umbre,** los nombres masculinos modificados por un adjetivo que termina en **-o** ni los nombres femeninos modificados por un adjetivo que termina en **-a.**

Los números que se refieren a los modelos de conjugación de los verbos españoles van antes de las abreviaturas que indican la parte de la oración. La lista completa de los modelos de conjugación incluye muchos que muestran una combinación de dos irregularidades, p.ej., **esforzar, seguir, teñir.**

Los nombres propios y las abreviaturas se consignan en su propio lugar alfabético en el texto del Diccionario. No hay, pues, que buscar **España** y **español** en dos partes distintas del libro. Y todos los artículos secundarios van colocados en riguroso orden alfabético.

Se usa el punto divisorio en los artículos de palabras de flexión irregular para señalar la sílaba final que debe separarse antes de agregar la sílaba que denota la flexión, p.ej., **lá•piz** (*pl* **-pices**) y **falsi•fy** [ˈfɔlsɪˌfaɪ] *v* (*pret & pp* **-fied**).

La pronunciación de todas las palabras inglesas simples se muestra por medio de una nueva adaptación de los símbolos del Alfabeto fonético internacional y entre corchetes. No se muestra la pronunciación de las palabras inglesas compuestas cuando la pronunciación de los componentes consta en los lugares donde aparecen como artículos independientes.

The author wishes to express his gratitude to many persons who have worked with him in lexicographical research and development and who helped him directly in the compilation of this book and particularly to the following: Paul Aguilar, William Beigel, Henry H. Carter, Eugenio Chang-Rodríguez, R. Thomas Douglass, David Louis Gold, Allison Gronberg, James E. Iannucci, Christopher Stavrou, Roger J. Steiner, John C. Traupman, and José Vidal.

Edwin B. Williams

PREFACE TO THE REVISED EDITION

The main objective of this revision has been to add about 3,200 recent words and meanings, primarily from the fields of science and technology (especially computers, medicine, and genetics), communication, environment, and economics and from colloquial speech. To accommodate the new text, we have omitted (1) the repetition of the infinitive particle (**to**) and (2) many alternative pronunciations, especially of British English.

The label (Am) has been deleted in most instances because this Dictionary focuses, in its entirety, on the Spanish of the Americas. The 22 regional labels have been retained.

Credit for work on this revision is due Mario Bernal, Gerald J. Mac Donald, Liliana Montano, Roger J. Steiner, Sol Steinmetz, Carlos Vega, Lawrence Weisburg, and Diane S. Aronson.

Walter D. Glanze

Como la constitución de los artículos no se ha determinado a base de su etimología, se incluyen bajo un mismo artículo todos los homógrafos de una palabra. Cuando varía la pronunciación de un homógrafo inglés, se indica en su propio lugar después de la doble raya vertical.

EDWIN B. WILLIAMS

PRÓLOGO DE LA EDICIÓN AUMENTADA

El objectivo major de esta revisión ha sido agregar aproximadamente 3,200 palabras y significados recientes, principalmente de las áreas de ciencia y tecnología (especialmente computadores, medicina y genética), comunicaciones, medio ambiente y economía, y del idioma de uso común. Para adaptar el texto nuevo, hemos omitido (1) la repetición del signo de infinitivo **(to)** y (2) muchas pronunciaciones alternativas, especialmento del inglés británico.

El calificativo (Am) ha sido omitido generalmente, porque este Diccionario se concentra en el español de las Américas. Los 22 calificativos regionales han sido retenidos.

Por el trabajo rendido en esta revisión, crédito es debido a Mario Bernal, Gerald J. Mac Donald, Liliana Montano, Roger J. Steiner, Sol Steinmentzo, Carlos Vega, Lawrence Weisburg y Diane S. Aronson.

WALTER D. GLANZE

LABELS AND GRAMMATICAL ABBREVIATIONS
CALIFICATIVOS Y ABREVIATURAS GRAMATICALES

abbr abbreviation—abreviatura
(acronym) acrónimo—a word formed from the initial letters or syllables of a series of words—palabra formada de las letras o sílabas iniciales de una serie de palabras
adj adjective—adjetivo
adv adverb—adverbio
(aer) aeronautics—aeronáutica
(agr) agriculture—agricultura
(alg) algebra—álgebra
(Am) Spanish American—hispano-americano
(anat) anatomy—anatomía
(archaic) arcaico
(archeol) archeology—arqueología
(archit) architecture—arquitectura
(Arg) Argentine—argentino
(arith) arithmetic—aritmética
art article—artículo
(arti) artillery—artillería
(astr) astronomy—astronomía
(aut) automobiles—automóviles
(bact) bacteriology—bacteriología
(baseball) beisbol
(bb) bookbinding—encuadernación
(Bib) Biblical—bíblico
(billiards) billar
(biochem) biochemistry—bioquímica
(biol) biology—biología
(Bol) Bolivian—boliviano
(bowling) bolos
(bot) botany—botánica
(box) boxing—boxeo
(Brit) British—británico
(CAm) Central American—centroamericano
(cards) naipes
(carp) carpentry—carpintería
(chem) chemistry—química
(chess) ajedrez
(Chile) Chilean—chileno
(Col) Colombian—colombiano
(coll) colloquial—familiar
(com) commercial—comercial
comp comparative—comparativo
cond conditional—condicional
conj conjunction—conjunción
(C-R) Costa Rican—costarriqueño
(Cuba) Cuban—cubano
(culin) cooking—cocina
def definite—definido
dem demonstrative—demostrativo
(dent) dentistry—odontología
(dial) dialectal—dialectal
(eccl) ecclesiastical—eclesiástico
(econ) economics—economía
(Ecuad) Ecuadorian—ecuatoriano
(educ) education—educación
(elec) electricity—electricidad

(electron) electronics—electrónica
(El Salv) El Salvador
(ent) entomology—entomología
f feminine noun—nombre femenino
(fa) fine arts—bellas artes
fem feminine—femenino
(fencing) esgrima
(feud) feudalism—feudalismo
(fig) figurative—figurado
fpl feminine noun plural—nombre femenino plural
fsg feminine noun singular—nombre femenino singular
fut future—futuro
(geog) geography—geografía
(geol) geology—geología
(geom) geometry—geometría
ger gerund—gerundio
(gram) grammar—gramática
(Guat) Guatemalan—guatemalteco
(heral) heraldry—heráldica
(hist) history—historia
(Hond) Honduran—hondureño
(hort) horticulture—horticultura
(hum) humorous—jocoso
(hunt) hunting—caza
(ichth) ichthyology—ictiología
imperf imperfect—imperfecto
impers impersonal—impersonal
impv imperative—imperativo
ind indicative—indicativo
indecl indeclinable—indeclinable
indef indefinite—indefinido
inf infinitive—infinitivo
(ins) insurance—seguros
interj interjection—interjección
interr interrogative—interrogativo
intr intransitive verb—verbo intransitivo
invar invariable—invariable
(iron) ironical—irónico
(Lat) Latin—latín
(law) derecho
(letterword) a word in the form of an abbreviation which is pronounced by sounding the names of its letters in succession and which functions as a part of speech—palabra en forma de abreviatura la cual se pronuncia haciendo sonar el nombre de cada letra consecutivamente y que funciona como parte del discurso
(log) logic—lógica
m masculine noun—nombre masculino
(mach) machinery—maquinaria
(mas) masonry—albañilería
masc masculine—masculino
(math) mathematics—matemática
(mech) mechanics—mecánica
(med) medicine—medicina
(metal) metallurgy—metalurgia
(meteor) meteorology—meteorología

(Mex) Mexican—mejicano
mf masculine or feminine noun according to sex—nombre masculino o nombre femenino según el sexo
(mil) military—militar
(min) mining—minería
(mineral) mineralogy—mineralogía
(mountaineering) alpinismo
(mov) moving pictures—cine
mpl masculine noun plural—nombre masculino plural
msg masculine noun singular—nombre masculino singular
(mus) music—música
(myth) mythology—mitología
m & f masculine and feminine noun without regard to sex—nombre masculino y femenino sin tener en cuenta el sexo
(naut) nautical—náutico
(nav) naval—naval militar
neut neuter—neutro
(obs) obsolete—desusado
(obstet) obstetrics—obstetricia
(opt) optics—óptica
(orn) ornithology—ornitología
(paint) painting—pintura
(Pan) Panamanian—panameño
(Para) Paraguayan—paraguayo
(pathol) pathology—patología
pers personal—personal
(Peru) Peruvian—peruano
(pharm) pharmacy—farmacia
(philol) philology—filología
(philos) philosophy—filosofía
(phonet) phonetics—fonética
(phot) photography—fotografía
(phys) physics—física
(physiol) physiology—fisiología
pl plural—plural
(poet) poetical—poético
(pol) politics—política
poss possessive—posesivo
pp past participle—participio pasado
(P-R) Puerto Rican—puertorriqueño
prep preposition—preposición
pres present—presente

pret preterit—pretérito
pron pronoun—pronombre
(psychoanalysis) sicoanálisis
(psychol) psychology—sicología
(rad) radio—radio
ref reflexive verb—verbo reflexivo
reflex reflexive—reflexivo
rel relative—relativo
(rhet) rhetoric—retórica
(rr) railway—ferrocarril
s substantive—substantivo
(SAm) South American—sudamericano
(scornful) despreciativo
(sculp) sculpture—escultura
(S-D) Santo Domingo—República Dominicana
(sew) sewing—costura
sg singular—singular
(slang) jerga
spl substantive plural—substantivo plural
(sport) deporte
ssg substantive singular—substantivo singular
subj subjunctive—subjuntivo
super superlative—superlativo
(surg) surgery—cirugía
(surv) surveying—agrimensura
(taur) bullfighting—tauromaquia
(telg) telegraphy—telegrafía
(telp) telephony—telefonía
(telv) television—televisión
(tennis) tenis
(theat) theater—teatro
(theol) theology—teología
tr transitive verb—verbo transitivo
(typ) printing—imprenta
(Urug) Uruguayan—uruguayo
v verb—verbo
var variant—variante
v aux auxiliary verb—verbo auxiliar
(Ven) Venezuelan—venezolano
(vet) veterinary medicine—veterinaria
(vulg) vulgar—grosero
(W-I) West Indian—antillano
(zool) zoology—zoología

ESPAÑOL-INGLÉS
SPANISH-ENGLISH

A

A, a (a) *f* first letter of the Spanish alphabet
a *prep* at; for, to; on, upon; in, into; by; from; **a decir verdad** to tell the truth; **a la española** in the Spanish manner; **a lo que parece** as it seems; **a no ser por** if it weren't for; **a saberlo yo** if I had known it; **oler a** to smell of
abacería *f* grocery store
abace•ro -ra *mf* grocer
abad *m* abbot
abadejo *m* codfish; (orn) kinglet; (ent) Spanish fly
abadesa *f* abbess
abadía *f* abbacy; abbey
abajar *ref* to lower oneself
abaje•ño -ña *adj* (Mex) coastal, lowland ‖ *mf* (Mex) lowlander
abaje•ro -ra *adj* (Arg) lower, under ‖ *f* (Arg) bellyband, bellystrap; (Arg) saddlecloth
abaji•no -na *adj* (Col, Chile) northern ‖ *mf* (Col, Chile) northerner
abajo *adv* down, underneath; downwards; downstairs; **abajo de** down; **más abajo** lower down; **río abajo** downstream ‖ *interj* down with. . . !
abalanzar §60 *tr* to hurl ‖ *ref* to rush; venture; (*un caballo*) rear
abalear *tr* (SAm) to shoot
abalizar §60 *tr* to mark with buoys ‖ *ref* (naut) to take bearings
abalorio *m* glass bead
abaluartar *tr* to bulwark
abanar *tr* to fan
abanderado *m* colorbearer
abanderar *tr* (*un buque*) to register
abanderizar §60 *tr* to organize into bands ‖ *ref* to band together; (Chile, Peru) to join up
abandona•do -da *adj* lonely
abandonar *tr* to abandon, forsake ‖ *intr* to give up ‖ *ref* to abandon oneself; give up
abandonismo *m* defeatism
abandonista *adj* & *mf* defeatist
abandono *m* abandon, abandonment; neglect; forlornness; yielding
abanicar §73 *tr* to fan
abanico *m* fan; fanlight; sword; **abanico de chimenea** fire screen
abaniquear *tr* to fan
abaniqueo *m* fanning; gesticulations
abanto *adj* skittish (*bull*)
abaratamiento *m* cheapening

abaratar *tr* to cheapen; (*precios*) lower ‖ *intr* & *ref* to get cheap
abarca *f* sandal
abarcar §73 *tr* to embrace; encompass; surround; corner, monopolize
abarloar *tr* (naut) to bring alongside ‖ *ref* to snuggle up
abarquillar *tr* & *ref* to curl up
abarraganamiento *m* illicit cohabitation
abarrancar *ref* to get into a difficult situation
abarrota•do -da *adj* overcrowded
abarrotar *tr* to bar; bind, fasten; jam, pack, stuff; overstock ‖ *ref* to become a glut on the market
abarrote *m* (naut) packing; **abarrotes** groceries; hardware
abarrotería *f* (Guat) grocery store; (CAm) hardware store
abarrote•ro -ra *mf* grocer
abastecer §22 *tr* to supply, provide
abastecimiento *m* supplying; supplies, provisions
abasto *m* supply; abundance; **dar abasto** to be sufficient
abatanar *tr* to full
abatí *m* (Arg, Para) corn; corn whiskey
abatible *adj* collapsible, folding
abati•do -da *adj* downcast; abject, contemptible ‖ *f* abatis
abatimiento *m* discouragement; descent
abatir *tr* to lower; knock down; shoot down; take apart; humble; discourage ‖ *intr* (aer) to drift; (naut) to have leeway ‖ *ref* to be discouraged; be humbled; drop, fall; swoop down
abdicar §73 *tr* & *intr* to abdicate
abdomen *m* abdomen
abecé *m* A B C
abecedario *m* A B C's
abedul *m* birch
abeja *f* bee; **abeja maestra** or **abeja reina** queen bee
abejar *m* apiary, beehive
abejarrón *m* bumblebee
abeje•ro -ra *mf* beekeeper
abejorro *m* bumblebee
aberración *f* aberration; deviation
abertura *f* aperture; opening, crack, slit; cove; openness, frankness
abeto *m* fir tree; hemlock; **abeto del Norte, abeto falso** spruce tree
abier•to -ta *adj* open; frank
abigarra•do -da *adj* motley, variegated

abigeo *m* horse thief, cattle thief
abijar *tr* (Col) to sic
abiselar *tr* to bevel
abisma•do -da *adj* absorbed, lost in thought; mysterious
abismar *tr* to cast down; humble; spoil, ruin ‖ *ref* to sink; cave in; be humbled; give in; lose oneself; be surprised
abismo *m* abyss, chasm
abjurar *tr* to abjure; renounce
ablandabre•vas *m* (*pl* **-vas**) or **ablandahi•gos** *m* (*pl* **-gos**) good-for-nothing
ablandar *tr* to soften; soften up; · soothe; loosen ‖ *intr* (*el tiempo*) to moderate ‖ *ref* to soften; relent; (*el tiempo*) moderate
ablativo *m* ablative
abnegación *f* abnegation; self-denial
abnega•do -da *adj* self-denying
abnegar *ref* to deny oneself; sacrifice oneself
aboba•do -da *adj* stupid, stupid-looking
abobar *tr* to make stupid ‖ *ref* to grow stupid
aboca•do -da *adj* (*vino*) mild, smooth; vulnerable; **abocado a** verging on
abocar §73 *tr* to bite; pour; bring near ‖ *intr* to enter ‖ *ref* to approach; have an interview
abocinar *tr* to give a flare to ‖ *intr* to fall on the face ‖ *ref* to flare
abochornar *tr* to overheat; make blush ‖ *ref* to blush; wilt
abofa•do -da *adj* (Cuba, Mex) swollen
abofetear *tr* to slap in the face
abogacía *f* law, legal profession
abogaderas *fpl* (CAm) specious arguments
abogado *m* lawyer; **abogado criminalista** criminal lawyer; **abogado de secano** quack lawyer; **abogado firmón** lawyer who will sign anything; **abogado trampista** shyster
abogar §44 *intr* to plead; **abogar por** to advocate, back
abolengo *m* ancestry, descent; inheritance
abolición *f* abolition
abolir §1 *tr* to revoke, repeal
abolorio *m* ancestry
abolladura *f* dent; bump, bruise; embossing
abollar *tr* to bump, bruise; dent; stun; emboss ‖ *ref* to get bumped, get bruised; dent, be dented
abollonar *tr* to emboss
abombar *tr* to make convex; stun, confound ‖ *ref* to rot, decompose
abominable *adj* abominable, very bad
abominación *f* abomination
abominar *tr* to detest, abominate ‖ *intr* — **abominar de** to abominate
abona•do -da *adj* trustworthy; apt, likely ‖ *mf* subscriber; (*al gas, electricidad, etc.*) consumer; (*a una localidad en el teatro*) season-ticket holder; (*al ferrocarril*) commuter
abonanzar §60 *intr* (*el tiempo*) to clear up; (*el viento*) abate
abonar *tr* to vouch for; certify; improve; fertilize; **abonar en cuenta a** to credit to the account of ‖ *intr* (*el tiempo*) to clear up ‖ *ref* to subscribe
abonaré *m* promissory note

abono *m* subscription; credit; installment; voucher; fertilizer; manure
abordar *tr* to approach; accost; undertake, plan; (naut) to board; (naut) to run afoul of; (naut) to dock ‖ *intr* to run afoul; (naut) to put into port
aborigen *adj invar* aboriginal, native; **aborígenes** *mpl* aborigines, natives
aborrascar §73 *ref* to get stormy
aborrecer §22 *tr* to abhor, detest, hate; bore ‖ *ref* to get bored
aborrecible *adj* abhorrent, hateful
aborrega•do -da *adj* (*nubes*) fleecy; (*cielo*) mackerel
aborregar *ref* (SAm) to become stupid
abortar *tr* & *intr* to abort
abortista *mf* abortionist
aborto *m* abortion; miscarriage; **aborto despenalizado** legalized abortion
abotagar §44 *ref* to become bloated, swell up
abotonador *m* buttonhook
abotonar *tr* to button ‖ *intr* to bud
abovedar *tr* to arch, vault
abozalar *tr* to muzzle
abra *f* cove; vale; fissure; (Mex) clearing
abrasa•dor -dora *adj* burning, hot
abrasar *tr* to set fire to, burn; parch; nip; squander; shame ‖ *intr* to burn ‖ *ref* to burn; become parched; (fig) to be burning up
abrasi•vo -va *adj* & *m* abrasive
abrazadera *f* clasp, clip, clamp; (typ) bracket
abrazar §60 *tr* to embrace, clasp; include; take in ‖ *ref* (*dos personas*) to embrace
abrazo *m* embrace, hug
abrebo•cas *m* (*pl* **-cas**) mouth prop, mouth gag
abrebote•llas *m* (*pl* **-llas**) bottle opener
abrecar•tas *m* (*pl* **-tas**) knife, letter opener
abreco•ches *m* (*pl* **-ches**) doorman
abrela•tas *m* (*pl* **-tas**) can opener
abreos•tras *m* (*pl* **-tras**) oyster knife
abrevadero *m* watering place, drinking trough
abrevar *tr* to water; wet, soak; irrigate; size ‖ *ref* to drink
abreviación *f* abridgment, abbreviation, shortening; hastening
abreviar *tr* to abridge; abbreviate; shorten; hasten ‖ *intr* to be quick; **abreviar con** to make short work of
abreviatura *f* abbreviation; **en abreviatura** in a hurry
abridero *m* (Mex, P-R) dive, joint
abridor *m* opener; grafting knife; **abridor de guantes** glove stretcher
abridura *f* (act of) opening
abrigadero *m* windbreak
abrigar §44 *tr* to shelter; protect; (*esperanzas, sospechas*) harbor ‖ *ref* to take shelter; wrap oneself up
abrigo *m* shelter; aid, support; cover, wrap; overcoat; (naut) harbor; **abrigo antiaéreo** air-raid shelter; **abrigo de entretiempo** topcoat, spring-and-fall coat; **al abrigo de** sheltered from, protected from; sheltered

by, protected by; (*ropa*) **de mucho abrigo** heavy

abril *m* April

abrillantar *tr* to polish; glaze

abrir *m* opening; **en un abrir y cerrar de ojos** in the twinkling of an eye || §83 *tr* to open; unlock, unfasten; (*el apetito*) whet; (*el bosque*) clear || *intr* to open || *ref* to open; **abrirse a** or **con** to unbosom oneself to

abrochador *m* buttonhook

abrochar *tr* to button, hook, fasten

abrogación *f* repeal; abrogation

abrogar *tr* to repeal; abrogate; annul

abrojo *m* thistle, thorn; **abrojos** reef, hidden rocks

abrótano *m* southernwood

abruma•do -da *adj* hazy; foggy

abruma•dor -dora *adj* crushing, oppressing; overwhelming

abrumar *tr* to crush, oppress; overwhelm; annoy || *ref* to become foggy

abrup•to -ta *adj* abrupt, steep; rough, rugged

absceso *m* abscess

absenta *f* absinth

ábsida *f* or **ábside** *m* apse

absolución *f* absolution; acquittal

absoluta *f* dogmatic statement; (mil) discharge

absolutamente *adv* absolutely; by no means

absolu•to -ta *adj* absolute; arbitrary || *m* absolute; **en absoluto** absolutely not || *f* see **absoluta**

absolvederas *fpl* — **tener buenas absolvederas** to be an indulgent confessor

absolver §47 & §83 *tr* to absolve; to solve, to answer

absorbente *adj* absorbent; (*interesante*) absorbing

absorber *tr* to absorb; use up; attract

absorción *f* absorption

absor•to -ta *adj* absorbed; entranced

abste•mio -mia *adj* abstemious

abstener §71 *ref* to abstain

abstensionismo *m* nonparticipation

abstinente *adj* abstinent

abstracción *f* abstraction; absorption, deep thought; **hacer abstracción de** to leave out, disregard

abstrac•to -ta *adj* abstract

abstraer §75 *tr* to abstract || *intr* — **abstraer de** to do without, leave aside || *ref* to be abstracted or absorbed; **abstraerse de** to do without, leave aside

abstraí•do -da *adj* absorbed in thought; withdrawn

abstru•so -sa *adj* abstruse

absurdidad *f* absurdity

absur•do -da *adj* absurd || *m* absurdity

abuchear *tr* & *intr* to boo, hoot

abuela *f* grandmother; **cuéntaselo a su abuela** tell that to the marines

abuelo *m* grandparent; grandfather; **abuelos** grandparents; ancestors

abulta•do -da *adj* bulky, massive

abultar *tr* to enlarge; exaggerate || *intr* to be bulky

abundamiento *m* abundance; **a mayor abundamiento** with greater reason

abundancia *f* abundance, plenty

abundante *adj* abundant

abundar *intr* to abound

abur *interj* good-bye!, so long!

aburguesa•do -da *adj* middle-class, bourgeois

aburguesar *ref* to become middle-class, become bourgeois

aburri•do -da *adj* bored; tiresome

aburrimiento *m* weariness, fatigue; dullness

aburrir *tr* to bore, tire || *ref* to become bored

abusar *intr* to go too far; **abusar de** to abuse; impose on; overindulge in

abusión *f* superstition

abusi•vo -va *adj* abusive

abuso *m* abuse; imposition

abyec•to -ta *adj* abject

A.C. *abbr* **año de Cristo**

acá *adv* here, around here; **acá y allá** here and there; **de ayer acá** since yesterday; **¿de cuándo acá?** since when?; **desde entonces acá** since then; **más acá** here closer; **muy acá** right here

acaba•do -da *adj* complete, perfect; worn-out, exhausted || *m* finish

acabamiento *m* end; completion; death; decline

acabar *tr* to end, finish, complete || *intr* to end; die; **acabar con** to put an end to; end in; **acabar de** to finish; have just, e.g., **acaba de salir** he has just left; **acababa de salir** he had just left; **acabar por** to end in; end by; **no acabar de decidirse** to be unable to make up one's mind || *ref* to end; be exhausted; be all over; run out of, e.g., **se me acabó el café** I have run out of coffee

acabóse *m* limit, last straw

acacia *f* acacia; **acacia falsa** locust tree

academia *f* academy

académi•co -ca *adj* academic || *mf* academician

acaecer §22 *intr* to happen, occur

acaecimiento *m* happening, occurrence

acalenturar *ref* to get a fever

acalora•do -da *adj* heated; warm; fiery, excited

acaloramiento *m* ardor; passion

acalorar *tr* to heat, warm; incite, encourage; stir up || *ref* to become heated; warm up

acallar *tr* to quiet, silence; pacify

acampada *f* camp

acamar *tr* (*las mieses la lluvia o el viento*) to beat down, blow over

acampamento *m* camp, encampment

acampana•do -da *adj* bell-shaped

acampar *tr*, *intr* & *ref* to encamp

acanalar *tr* to groove; flute; channel; corrugate

acantila•do -da *adj* rocky; steep, precipitous || *m* cliff, bluff

acantonamiento *m* cantonment

acantonar *tr* to canton, quarter || *ref* to be quartered; **acantonarse en** to limit one's activities to

acaparar *tr* to corner; monopolize; hoard

acaramela·do -da *adj* candied; smooth, honey-tongued

acarar *tr* to bring face to face

acarear *tr* to bring face to face; face, brave

acariciar *tr* to caress; (*una ilusión*) cherish

acarraladura *f* (Chile, Peru) run (*in stockings*)

acarreadi·zo -za *adj* transportable

acarrear *tr* to cart, transport, carry along; cause, occasion ‖ *ref* to incur, bring upon oneself

acarreo *m* cartage, drayage; conveyance

acartonar *ref* to shrivel up, become wizened

acasera·do -da *adj* (Chile, Peru) homeloving; (*parroquiano*) (Chile, Peru) regular ‖ *mf* (Chile, Peru) stay-at-home, homebody; (Chile, Peru) regular customer

acaso *m* chance, accident; **al acaso** at random ‖ *adv* maybe, perhaps; **por si acaso** in case of need, just in case

acatamiento *m* homage; respect

acatar *tr* to respect, hold in awe; observe

acatarrar *tr* to chill, give a cold to; (Chile, Mex) to bother, annoy ‖ *ref* to catch cold; get tipsy

acaudala·do -da *adj* rich, well-to-do

acaudalar *tr* to acquire, accumulate

acaudillar *tr* to lead, command; direct

acceder *intr* to accede; agree

accesible *adj* accessible

accesión *f* accession; acquiescence; access, entry

accésit *m* second prize, honorable mention

acceso *m* access, approach; attack, fit, spell; **acceso prohibido** no admittance

acceso·rio -ria *adj* accessory ‖ *m* accessory, fixture, attachment; **accesorios** (theat) properties

accidenta·do -da *adj* agitated; restless; rough, uneven ‖ *mf* victim, casualty

accidental *adj* accidental; acting, protempore, temporary

accidentar *tr* to injure, hurt ‖ *ref* to faint

accidente *m* accident; (*del terreno*) roughness, unevenness; fainting spell

acción *f* action; gesture; (*parte del capital de una sociedad*) share; stock certificate; **acción crecedera** growth stock; **acción de gracias** thanksgiving; **acción liberada** stock dividend; **poner en acción** to set in motion

accionar *tr* to drive ‖ *intr* to gesticulate

accionista *mf* shareholder, stockholder

acebo *m* holly tree

acebuche *m* wild olive

acecinar *tr* to dry-cure, dry-salt; (*el salmón o el arenque*) kipper ‖ *ref* to shrivel up

acechar *tr* to watch, to spy on

acecho *m* watching, spying; **al acecho** or **en acecho** on the watch, spying

acedar *tr* to turn sour; embitter ‖ *ref* to turn sour; wither

acedía *f* sourness; crabbedness; heartburn

ace·do -da *adj* sour, tart; crabbed

aceitar *tr* to oil; grease

aceite *m* oil; olive oil; **aceite de hígado de**

bacalao cod-liver oil; **aceite de linaza** linseed oil; **aceite de pie de buey** neat's-foot oil; **aceite de ricino** castor oil; **aceite mineral** coal oil

aceite·ro -ra *adj* oil ‖ *mf* oiler; oil dealer ‖ *f* oilcan; oil cup; **aceiteras** cruet stand

aceito·so -sa *adj* oily, greasy

aceituna *f* olive

aceituno *m* olive tree

aceleración *f* acceleration

acelerador *m* accelerator

acelerar *tr* & *ref* to accelerate; hasten, hurry

acelga *f* Swiss chard

acémila *f* beast of burden, pack animal; dolt; drudge

acendra·do -da *adj* refined; stainless, spotless

acendrar *tr* to refine; purify, make stainless

acento *m* accent; **acento de altura** pitch accent; **acento ortográfico** written accent, accent mark; **acento prosódico** stress accent, tonic accent

acentuar §21 *tr* to accent; accentuate, emphasize

aceña *f* water-driven flour mill

acepción *f* meaning

acepillar *tr* to plane; brush; smooth

aceptable *adj* acceptable

aceptación *f* acceptance; **aceptación de personas** discrimination; partiality

aceptar *tr* to accept

acequia *f* irrigation ditch; (Bol, Col, Peru) stream, rivulet

acera *f* sidewalk

acera·do -da *adj* steel, steely; (fig) cutting, biting, sharp

acerar *tr* to steel, harden; line with a sidewalk ‖ *ref* to harden; steel oneself

acer·bo -ba *adj* sour, bitter; harsh

acerca *adv* — **acerca de** about, with regard to

acercamiento *m* approach, rapprochement

acercar §73 *tr* to bring near or nearer ‖ *ref* to approach, come near or nearer

acería *f* steel mill

acerico *m* small cushion; pincushion

acero *m* steel; sword; courage, spirit

acérri·mo -ma *adj* all-out; (*enemigo*) bitter

acerrojar *tr* to bolt

acerta·do -da *adj* fit, right; skillful, sure; well-aimed

acertante *mf* winner

acertar §2 *tr* to hit; hit upon; figure out correctly; find; do right ‖ *intr* to be right; succeed; guess right; **acertar a** to happen to; succeed in; **acertar con** to come upon; find

acertijo *m* conundrum, riddle

acervo *m* heap; assets, estate; shoal; store, fund, hoard

acetato *m* acetate

acéti·co -ca *adj* acetic

acetificar §73 *tr* & *ref* to acetify

acetileno *m* acetylene

acetona *f* acetone

acia·go -ga *adj* unlucky, ill-fated, evil

acial *m* (CAm, Ecuad) whip

acíbar *m* aloes; bitterness, sorrow

acicalar *tr* to polish, burnish; dress, dress up ‖ *ref* to get all dressed up

acicate *m* long-pointed spur; incentive, stimulus

acicatear *tr* to spur, urge

acidez *f* acidity

acidificar §73 *tr* & *ref* to acidify

áci•do -da *adj* acid, tart, sour ‖ *m* acid

acierto *m* lucky hit, good shot; good guess; tact, prudence; ability, skill; accuracy; success

aci•mut *m* (*pl* **-muts**) azimut

aclamación *f* acclaim, applause

aclamar *tr* & *intr* to acclaim, to hail, to cheer

aclarar *tr* to brighten, clear; rinse; explain ‖ *intr* to get bright; clear up; dawn

aclarato•rio -ria *adj* explanatory

aclimatar *tr* & *ref* to acclimate

acne *f* acne

acobardar *tr* to cow, intimidate ‖ *ref* to be frightened

acocear *tr* to kick; trample upon, ill-treat

acocil *m* Mexican crayfish; **estar como un acocil** (Mex) to blush, be abashed

acoda•do -da *adj* elbow-shaped

acodar *tr* (*el brazo*) to lean; prop; (hort) to layer ‖ *ref* to lean

acodillar *tr* to bend at an angle ‖ *ref* to double up; to bend, to crumple

acogencia *f* (CAm) acceptance; reception

acoger §17 *tr* to receive, welcome; accept ‖ *ref* to take refuge; resort

acogida *f* reception, welcome; meeting place, confluence; refuge, shelter; **dar acogida a** (com) to honor

acolada *f* accolade

acolchar *tr* to quilt, pad

acolchí *m* (Mex) red-winged blackbird

acólito *m* acolyte; altar boy

acollador *m* (naut) lanyard

acomedi•do -da *adj* obliging

acometer *tr* to attack; undertake; (*el sueño, la enfermedad, el deseo a una persona*) overcome

acometida *f* attack; (*p.ej., de una línea eléctrica*) house connection

acomodación *f* accommodation

acomodadi•zo -za *adj* accommodating, obliging

acomoda•do -da *adj* convenient, suitable; comfort-loving; well-to-do

acomoda•dor -dora *adj* accommodating, obliging ‖ *mf* usher

acomodar *tr* to accommodate; usher; reconcile; suit; furnish, supply ‖ *intr* to be suitable, be convenient ‖ *ref* to comply; come to terms; hire out; make oneself comfortable

acomodo *m* arrangement, adjustment; lodgings; job, position; (Chile) neatness, tidiness

acompañador *m* companion; accompanist

acompañamiento *m* accompaniment; escort, retinue; (theat) extras, supernumeraries

acompañanta *f* female companion or escort; accompanist

acompañante *m* companion; accompanist

acompañar *tr* to accompany; escort; enclose; sympathize with

acompaño *m* (CAm) meeting; encounter

acompasa•do -da *adj* rhythmic; slow; easy-going; cautious

acompleja•do -da *adj* full of complexes

aconchar *tr* to push to safety; (naut) to beach, run aground ‖ *ref* to take shelter; (naut) to run aground; (Chile) to form a deposit

acondiciona•do -da *adj* conditioned; **bien acondicionado** well-disposed; in good condition; **mal acondicionado** ill-disposed; in bad condition

acondicionador *m* conditioner; **acondicionador de aire** air conditioner

acondicionamiento *m* conditioning; **acondicionamiento del aire** air conditioning

acondicionar *tr* to condition; put in condition; repair; season ‖ *ref* to qualify; find a job

acongojar *tr* to grieve, afflict ‖ *ref* to grieve

aconsejable *adj* advisable

aconsejar *tr* to advise, counsel, warn ‖ *ref* to seek advice, get advice

acontecer §22 *intr* to happen, occur

acontecimiento *m* happening, event

acopiar *tr* to gather together

acopio *m* gathering; stock; abundance

acoplado *m* (Arg, Chile, Urug) trailer trolley car

acoplamiento *m* coupling; joint; connection; linkup (in space)

acoplar *tr* to couple; join; connect; hitch; reconcile ‖ *ref* to be reconciled; mate; be intimate

acoquinar *tr* to intimidate

acoraza•do -da *adj* armored, armor-plated; contrary ‖ *m* battleship

acorazar §60 *tr* to armor-plate

acorchar *tr* to line with cork; turn into cork ‖ *ref* to get spongy; wither, shrivel; become corky or pithy; get numb

acorchetar *tr* to bracket

acordar §61 *tr* to agree upon; authorize; reconcile; make level or flush; remind of; tune ‖ *intr* to agree; blend ‖ *ref* to be agreed, come to an agreement; remember; **acordarse de** to remember

acorde *adj* agreed, in accord; in tune ‖ *m* accord; (mus) chord

acordeón *m* accordion

acordonar *tr* to cord, lace; (*monedas*) knurl, mill; rope off

acornar §61 *tr* gore; butt

acornear *tr* to gore; butt

acorralar *tr* to corral, corner; intimidate

acortar *tr* to shorten; reduce; slow down; check, stop ‖ *ref* to become shorter; hold back; be timid; slow down; shrink

acosar *tr* to harass; pester

acosijar *tr* (Mex) to pursue, press, track down

acostar §61 *tr* to lay down; put to bed; (naut) to bring alongside ‖ *ref* to lie down; go to bed; (CAm, Mex) to give birth

acostumbra•do -da *adj* accustomed; customary, usual

acostumbrar *tr* to accustom ‖ *intr* to be accustomed ‖ *ref* to accustom oneself; become accustomed

acotación *f* boundary mark; marginal note; elevation mark

acotamiento *m* boundary mark; marginal note; elevation mark; stage direction

acotar *tr* to mark off, map; annotate; admit, accept; check; vouch for; select; mark elevations on

acotillo *m* sledge hammer

acre *adj* acrid; austere; biting, mordant

acrecentamiento *m* increase, growth; promotion

acrecentar §2 *tr* to increase; promote ‖ *ref* to increase; bud, blossom

acreditar *tr* to accredit; credit; get a reputation for ‖ *ref* to get a reputation, prove oneself

acree•dor -dora *adj* accrediting; deserving ‖ *mf* creditor; **acreedor hipotecario** mortgagee

acribar *tr* to sift; riddle

acribillar *tr* to riddle; harass, plague, pester

acriminar *tr* to incriminate; exaggerate

acrimonio•so -sa *adj* acrid; acrimonious

acriollar *ref* to acquire Spanish American ways

acrisolar *tr* to purify, refine; reveal, bring out

acrobacia *f* acrobatics

acróbata *mf* acrobat

acrobatismo *m* acrobatics

acrónimo *m* acronym

acrópo•lis *adj* (*pl* **-lis**) acropolis

acróstico *m* acrostic

acta *f* minutes; certificate; **acta notarial** affidavit; **actas** proceedings, transactions; **levantar acta** to write up the minutes

actitud *f* attitude; **en actitud de** getting ready to

activar *tr* to activate; hasten, expedite

actividad *f* activity

activista *mf* activist

acti•vo -va *adj* active ‖ *m* (com) assets; (com) credit side

acto *m* act; ceremony, function; commencement; thesis; **acto carnal** sexual intercourse; **acto continuo** right afterward; **acto seguido** right afterward; **acto seguido de** right after; **en acto de servicio** in the line of duty; **hacer acto de presencia** to honor with one's presence

actor *m* actor; agent; **primer actor** leading man

ac•triz *f* (*pl* **-trices**) actress; **primera actriz** leading lady

actuación *f* acting, performance; action; operation; behavior; **actuación en directo** live performance; **actuaciones** legal proceedings

actual *adj* present, present-day; up-to-date ‖ *m* current month

actualidad *f* present time; timeliness; **actualidades** current events; newsreel; **actuali-**

dad escénica theater news; **actualidad gráfica** news in pictures

actualizar §60 *tr* to bring up to date

actualmente *adv* at present, at the present time

actuante *mf* participant

actuar §21 *tr* to actuate ‖ *intr* to act; perform

actua•rio -ria *mf* actuary

acuaplano *m* aquaplane

acuarela *f* water color

acuario *m* aquarium; **Acuario** *m* (astr) Aquarius

acuartelar *tr* to billet, quarter

acuáti•co -ca *adj* aquatic

acuatizaje *m* (aer) alighting on water; (*de nave espacial*) splashdown

acuatizar §60 *intr* (aer) to alight on water

acucia *f* zeal, diligence; yearning

acuciar *tr* to goad, prod; harass; yearn for

acuclillar *ref* to squat, crouch

acuchilla•do -da *adj* knife-shaped; schooled by experience; (*vestido*) slashed

acuchillar *tr* to stab; stab to death; slash

acudir *intr* to come up, respond; apply; hang around; come to the rescue; **acudir a las urnas** to vote

acueducto *m* aqueduct

acuerdo *m* accord; agreement; memory; **de acuerdo con** in accord with; **de común acuerdo** with one accord; **estar en su acuerdo** to be in one's right mind; **ponerse de acuerdo** to come to an agreement; **recobrar su acuerdo** to come to; **tomar un acuerdo** to make a decision; **volver en su acuerdo** to come to; to change one's mind

acuitar *tr & ref* to grieve

acullá *adv* yonder, over there

acumulador *m* storage battery

acumular *tr* to accumulate, gather; store up ‖ *intr & ref* to accumulate, gather

acunar *tr* to rock; cradle

acuñación *f* coining, minting; wedging

acuñar *tr* to coin, mint; wedge; key, lock; (typ) to quoin

acuo•so -sa *adj* watery; juicy

acupuntura *f* acupuncture

acurrucar §73 *ref* to squat, crouch; huddle

acusación *f* accusation

acusa•do -da marked ‖ *mf* accused

acusar *tr* to accuse; show; (*recibo de una carta*) acknowledge ‖ *ref* to confess

acusati•vo -va *adj & m* accusative

acuse *m* acknowledgment

acústi•co -ca *adj* acoustic ‖ *f* acoustics

achacar §73 *tr* to impute, attribute

achaco•so -sa *adj* ailing, sickly

achaparra•do -da *adj* stocky; stubby; chubby

achaparrar *ref* to become stunted

achaque *m* sickliness, indisposition; excuse, pretext; matter, subject; weakness; (coll) monthlies

achatar *tr* to flatten ‖ *ref* (Mex) to become frightened, afraid

achica•do -da *adj* childish; abashed, disconcerted

achicador *m* scoop

ac
ad

achicar §73 *tr* to make smaller; humble; bail, to bail out

achicoria *f* chicory

achicharrar *tr* to scorch; bedevil ‖ *ref* to get scorched

achicharronar *tr* to squash

achín *m* (CAm) peddler; door-to-door salesman

achiquitar *ref* to lose heart, cower

achispa•do -da *adj* tipsy

achispar *tr* to make tipsy ‖ *ref* to get tipsy

achuchar *tr* to incite; crumple, crush; jostle ‖ *ref* (Arg, Urug) to shiver, have a chill

adagio *m* adage

adalid *m* chief; guide, leader; champion

adama•do -da *adj* womanish; chic, stylish

adamar *ref* to become effeminate

adán *m* dirty, ragged fellow; lazy, careless fellow ‖ **Adán** *m* Adam

adaptación *f* adaptation

adaptar *tr* to adapt

adarga *f* oval or heart-shaped leather shield

adarvar *tr* to bewilder, stun

A. de C. *abbr* año de Cristo

adecentar *tr* to clean up, tidy up ‖ *ref* to put on a clean shirt, dress up

adecua•do -da *adj* fitting, suitable

adecuar *tr* to fit, adapt

adefesio *m* nonsense; outlandish outfit; queer-looking fellow

adehala *f* gratuity, extra

adehesar *tr* to convert into pasture

adelanta•do -da *adj* precocious; bold, forward; (*reloj*) fast; **por adelantado** in advance ‖ *m* provincial governor

adelantamiento *m* anticipation; advancement, promotion, progress

adelantar *tr* to move forward; outstrip, get ahead of; advance; promote; improve ‖ *intr* to advance; improve; be fast ‖ *ref* to move forward; gain, be fast

adelante *adv* ahead; forward; **más adelante** farther on; later ‖ *interj* go ahead!; come in!

adelanto *m* advance, progress, improvement; advancement; payment in advance

adelfa *f* oleander

adelgazar §60 *tr* to make thin; taper; purify; argue subtly about; weaken, lessen ‖ *intr* & *ref* to get thin; taper

ademán *m* attitude; gesture; **ademanes** manners; **en ademán de** getting ready to; **hacer ademán de** to make a move to

además *adv* moreover, besides; **además de** in addition to, besides

adentellar *tr* to sink one's teeth into

adentrar *intr* & *ref* to go in; **adentrarse en el mar** to go farther out to sea

adentro *adv* inside; **mar adentro** out at sea; **ser muy de adentro** to be like a member of the family; **tierra adentro** inland ‖ **adentros** *mpl* inmost being, inmost thoughts; **en** or **para sus adentros** to oneself, to himself, etc.

adep•to -ta *adj* initiated ‖ *mf* follower

aderezar §60 *tr* to dress, adorn; cook; (*una tela*) starch; season; repair; lead; (*bebidas*)

mix; (*vinos*) blend ‖ *ref* to dress, get ready

aderezo *m* dressing; seasoning, condiment; starch; finery; equipment; set of jewelry

adestrar §2 *tr* & *ref* var of **adiestrar**

adeuda•do -da *adj* indebted, in debt

adeudar *tr* to owe; to be liable for; charge ‖ *intr* to become related by marriage ‖ *ref* to run into debt

adeudo *m* debt, indebtedness; customs duty; charge, debit

adherencia *f* adhesion; **tener adherencias** to have connections

adherente *adj* adherent ‖ *m* adherent; **adherentes** accessories

adherir §68 *intr* & *ref* to adhere; stick

adhesión *f* adherence, adhesion

adhesi•vo -va *adj* adhesive

adición *f* addition; (*en un café o restaurante*) check

adicionar *tr* to add; add to

adic•to -ta *adj* devoted; supporting ‖ *mf* supporter, follower

adiestramiento *m* training; breaking in

adiestrar *tr* to train; teach; lead, guide ‖ *ref* to train, practice

adietar *tr* to put on a diet

adinera•do -da *adj* wealthy, well-to-do

adiós *m* adieu, good-bye ‖ *interj* adieu!, good-bye!

aditamento *m* addition; accessory

aditi•vo -va *adj* & *m* additive

adivinación *f* prophecy; guessing, divination; **adivinación del pensamiento** mind reading

adivina•dor -dora *mf* guesser; good guesser; **adivinador del pensamiento** mind reader

adivinaja *f* riddle, puzzle

adivinanza *f* riddle; guess

adivinar *tr* to prophesy; guess, divine; (*un enigma*) solve; (*el pensamiento ajeno*) read

adivi•no -na *mf* fortuneteller; guesser

adjetivo *m* adjective

adjudicar §73 *tr* to adjudge, award ‖ *ref* to appropriate

adjuntar *tr* to join, connect; add; enclose

adjun•to -ta *adj* added, attached; enclosed ‖ *mf* associate ‖ *m* adjunct; adjective

adminículo *m* aid, auxiliary; gadget; meddler; **adminículos** emergency equipment

administración *f* administration, management; headquarters

administra•dor -dora *mf* administrator, manager; **administrador de correos** postmaster

administrar *tr* to administer, manage

admiración *f* admiration; wonder; exclamation mark

admira•dor -dora *mf* admirer

admirar *tr* to admire; surprise ‖ *ref* to wonder; **admirarse de** to wonder at

admisible *adj* admissible

admisión *f* admission; (mach) intake

admitir *tr* to admit; allow; accept, recognize; agree to

adobar *tr* to repair, restore; dress, prepare; cook, stew; (*carne, pescado*) pickle; (*pieles*) tan

adobe *m* adobe

adobera *f* (SAm) brick-shaped cheese; mold for brick-shaped cheese

adobo *m* repairing; dressing; cooking; pickling; tanning; pickled meat or fish

adocena•do -da common, ordinary

adoctrinar *tr* to indoctrinate, teach, instruct

adolecer §22 *intr* to fall sick; **adolecer de** to suffer from ‖ *ref —* **adolecerse de** (archaic) to sympathize with, feel sorry for

adolescencia *f* adolescence

adolescente *adj & mf* adolescent

adonde `conj` where, whither

adónde *adv* where, whither

adopción *f* adoption

adoptar *tr* to adopt

adoquín *m* paving stone, paving block; (coll) blockhead

adoquina•do -da *adj* paved with cobblestones ‖ *m* cobblestone paving

adorable *adj* adorable

adoración *f* adoration, worship; **Adoración de los Reyes** Epiphany

adora•dor -dora *mf* adorer, worshiper ‖ *m* suitor

adorar *tr & intr* to adore, worship

adormecer §22 *tr* to put to sleep ‖ *ref* to go to sleep; get sleepy

adormeci•do -da *adj* sleepy, drowsy; numb; calm

adormidera *f* opium poppy

adormilar *ref* to doze, drowse

adornar *tr* to adorn; (*un cuento*) embroider

adornista *mf* decorator

adorno *m* adornment, decoration; **adorno de escaparate** window dressing

adosar *tr* to lean; push close

adquirir §40 *tr* to acquire; **adquirir en propiedad** to buy, purchase

adquisición *f* acquisition

adrede *adv* on purpose

Adriáti•co -ca *adj & m* Adriatic

adscribir §83 *tr* to attribute; assign

adscripción *f* attribution; assignment

aduana *f* customhouse; **aduana seca** inland customhouse; **exento de aduana** duty-free; **sujeto de aduana** dutiable

aduane•ro -ra *adj* customhouse; customs ‖ *m* customhouse officer, customs inspector

aduar *m* Arab settlement; gipsy camp; Indian ranch

adueñar *ref* to take possession

adujar *tr* (naut) to coil ‖ *ref* (naut) to curl up

adular *tr* to flatter, fawn on

adu•lón -lona *adj* fawning, groveling ‖ *mf* fawner

adúltera *f* adulteress

adulterar *tr* to adulterate ‖ *intr* to commit adultery ‖ *ref* to become adulterated, to spoil

adulterio *m* adultery

adúlte•ro -ra *adj* adulterous ‖ *m* adulterer ‖ *f* see **adúltera**

adultez *f* adulthood

adul•to -ta *adj & mf* adult

adulzar §60 *tr* to sweeten; (*metales*) soften

adunar *tr* to join, bring together

adundar *ref* (CAm) to become stupid

adus•to -ta *adj* grim, stern, gloomy; scorching hot

advenedi•zo -za *adj* strange; foreign ‖ *mf* stranger; foreigner; outsider; parvenu, upstart; nouveau riche

advenimiento *m* advent, coming; accession; **esperar el santo advenimiento** to wait in vain

advenir §79 *intr* to come, arrive; happen

adverbio *m* adverb

adversa•rio -ria *mf* adversary

adversidad *f* adversity

advertencia *f* observation; notice, remark; warning; preface

adverti•do -da *adj* capable, clever, wide-awake

advertir §68 *tr* to notice, observe; notify, warn; point out ‖ *ref* to become aware

Adviento *m* (eccl) Advent

adyacente *adj* adjacent

aeración *f* aeration; ventilation; air conditioning

aére•o -a *adj* air, aerial; overhead, elevated; airy, light, fanciful

aerodinámi•co -ca *adj* aerodynamic ‖ *f* aerodynamics

aeródromo *m* aerodrome, airdrome; **aeródromo de urgencia** emergency-landing field

aerofluyente *adj* streamlined

aeroespacial *adj* aerospace

aerofumigación *f* crop dusting

aeromedicina *f* aviation medicine

aeromodelismo *m* model-airplane building

aeromodelista *mf* model-airplane builder

aeromodelo *m* model airplane

aeromotor *m* windmill; airplane motor

aeromoza *f* air hostess, stewardess

aeronáuti•co -ca *adj* aeronautic ‖ *f* aeronautics

aeronave *f* airship; **aeronave cohete** rocket ship

aeropista *f* landing strip

aeroplano *m* aeroplane

aeroposta *f* air mail

aeropostal *adj* air-mail

aeropropulsor *m* airplane engine; **aeropropulsor por reacción** jet engine

aeropuerto *m* airport

aeroscala *f* transit point

aerosol *m* aerosol

aeroste•ro -ra *adj* aviation ‖ *m* flyer; airman

aerotaxi *m* air taxi

aeroterrestre *adj* air-ground

aerovía *f* airway

afable *adj* affable, friendly, agreeable

afama•do -da *adj* noted, famous

afamar *tr* to make famous ‖ *ref* to become famous

afán *m* hard work; eagerness, zeal; task; worry

afanar *tr* to press, hurry ‖ *intr* to strive, toil ‖ *ref* to strive, toil; busy oneself

afano•so -sa *adj* hard, laborious; hard-working

afarolar *ref* to make a fuss, get excited

afear *tr* to deface, disfigure; blame

afeblecer §22 *intr* to grow feeble, get thin

afección *f* affection, fondness; (med) affection

afectación *f* affectation

afecta•do -da *adj* affected; **estar afectado de** (*p.ej., los riñones*) to have (*e.g., kidney*) trouble

afectar *tr* to affect; hurt, injure ‖ *ref* to be moved, be stirred

afecti•vo -va *adj* emotional

afec•to -ta *adj* fond; kind; affected; **afecto a** fond of; (*un empleo, un servicio, etc.*) attached to; **afecto de** suffering from ‖ *m* affection, fondness; emotion

afectuo•so -sa *adj* affectionate; kind

afeitado *m* shave; **afeitado a ras** close shave

afeitar *tr* to shave; adorn; ‖ *ref* to shave; paint

afeite *m* cosmetics, rouge, make-up

afeminación *f* effeminacy

afemina•do -da *adj* effeminate

afeminar *tr* to effeminate ‖ *ref* to become effeminate

aferra•do -da *adj* stubborn, obstinate

aferrar *tr* to seize; catch; hook; (naut) to moor; (naut) to furl ‖ *ref* to interlock, hook together; cling; insist

Afganistán, el Afghanistan

afga•no -na *adj & mf* Afghan

afianzar §60 *tr* to guarantee, vouch for; bail; fasten; prop up; grasp; support ‖ *ref* to hold fast, steady oneself

afición *f* fondness, liking, taste; ardor; zeal; fans, public

aficiona•do -da *adj* fond; amateur; **aficionado a** fond of ‖ *mf* amateur; fan, follower

aficionar *tr* to win, win the attachment of ‖ *ref* — **aficionarse a** or **de** to become fond of; become a follower of, become a fan of

afiebra•do -da *adj* feverish

afiebrar *ref* (SAm) to get a fever

afi•jo -ja *adj* affixed ‖ *m* affix

afila•do -da *adj* sharp; tapering; pointed; peaked

afilador *m* grinder, sharpener; razor strop

afilalápi•ces *m* (*pl* -ces) pencil sharpener

afilar *tr* to grind, sharpen; (*una navaja de afeitar*) strop; (Arg & Urug) to flirt with ‖ *ref* to sharpen, get sharp; taper, get thin

afiliar §77 & **regular** *tr* to affiliate, take in ‖ *ref* — **afiliarse a** to join

afiligranar *tr* to filigree; adorn, embellish

afilón *m* knife sharpener; razor strop

afín *adj* near, bordering; like, similar; related ‖ *mf* relative by marriage

afinador *m* tuner; tuning hammer, tuning key

afinar *tr* to purify, refine, perfect; trim; tune

afincar §73 *intr & ref* to buy up real estate

afinidad *f* affinity; **por afinidad** by marriage

afirmar *tr* to strengthen, secure, fasten; assert ‖ *ref* to hold fast; steady oneself

afirmati•vo -va *adj & f* affirmative

aflicción *f* affliction; sorrow, grief

afligir §27 *tr* to afflict, grieve; (Mex) to beat, whip ‖ *ref* to grieve

aflojar *tr* to slacken, let go; loosen ‖ *intr* to slacken, slow up; abate, lessen ‖ *ref* to come loose; slacken

aflora•do -da *adj* flour; fine, elegant

aflorar *tr* to sift ‖ *intr* to crop out

afluencia *f* flowing; affluence, abundance; crowd, jam, rush; fluency; **horas de afluencia** rush hour

afluente *adj* flowing; abundant; fluent ‖ *m* tributary

afluir §20 *intr* to flow; pour, flock

afmo. *abbr.* **afectísimo**

afofar *tr* to make fluffy, make spongy

afonizar §60 *tr & ref* to unvoice

aforar *tr* to gauge, measure; appraise

aforismo *m* aphorism

afortuna•do -da *adj* fortunate; happy

afrancesa•do -da *adj & mf* Francophile

afrecho *m* bran

afrenta *f* affront

afrentar *tr* to affront ‖ *ref* to be ashamed

afrento•so -sa *adj* outrageous, disgraceful

Africa *f* Africa

africa•no -na *adj & mf* African

afrodisía•co -ca *adj & m* aphrodisiac

afrontamiento *m* confrontation

afrontar *tr* to bring face to face; defy ‖ *ref* — **afrontarse con** to confront, meet face to face

afuera *adv* outside ‖ *interj* clear the way!, look out! ‖ **afueras** *fpl* outskirts, environs

afuetada *f* or **afuetadura** *f* (SAm) beating

agachadiza *f* snipe; **hacer la agachadiza** to duck

agachar *tr* to lower, bend down ‖ *ref* to crouch, squat; cower; (SAm) to give in, yield

agalla *f* gallnut; (*de pez*) gill; (*de ave*) ear lobe; **agallas** courage, guts

ágape *m* banquet, love feast

agarradera *f* hold, grip; handle; **tener agarraderas** to have connections

agarrada *f* brawl, fight, scrap

agarra•do -da *adj* stingy, tight ‖ *f* see **agarrada**

agarrar *tr* to grab, grasp; take hold of; get, obtain ‖ *intr* to take hold; take root; stick ‖ *ref* to grapple; have a good hold; worry; **agarrarse a** to take hold of, cling to

agarro *m* clench, clutch, grip

agarrochar *tr* to jab with a goad

agarrón *m* brawl, fight; grip, tug

agarrotar *tr* to garrote; bind, tie up ‖ *ref* to become numb

agasajar *tr* to regale, lionize, make a fuss over

agasajo *m* kindness, attention; lionization; favor, gift; treat; party

agavillar *tr* to bind or tie in sheaves ‖ *ref* to band together

agazapar *tr* to grab, to nab ‖ *ref* to crouch; to hide

agencia *f* agency; bureau; (Chile) pawn shop; **agencia de noticias** news agency; **agencia matrimonial** marriage broker

agenciar *tr* to manage to bring about; promote ‖ *ref* to manage

agenda *f* notebook

agente *m* agent; policeman; **agente de policía** policeman; **agente viajero** traveling salesman, commercial traveler

agigantar *tr* to make huge ‖ *ref* to become huge

ágil *adj* agile; flexible, light

agilitar *tr & ref* to limber up

agita•do -da *adj* agitated, excited, exalted; (*mar*) rough

agitar *tr* to agitate; shake; wave; stir ‖ *intr* to agitate ‖ *ref* to be agitated; shake; wave; get excited; (*el mar*) get rough

aglomeración *f* agglomeration; crowd; built-up area

aglomerado *m* briquet, coal briquet

aglutinar *tr* to stick together ‖ *ref* to cake

agnósti•co -ca *adj & mf* agnostic

agobiar *tr* to overburden; exhaust, oppress

agolpar *ref* to flock, throng

agonía *f* agony, throes of death; agony, anguish; yearning; craving

agonizar §60 *tr* (*al moribundo*) to assist, attend; harass ‖ *intr* to be in the throes of death

agorar §3 *tr* to augur, foretell

agore•ro -ra *adj* fortunetelling; ill-omened; superstitious ‖ *mf* fortuneteller

agostar *tr* to burn up, to parch ‖ *ref* to dry up; (*la esperanza, la felicidad*) fade away

agostero *m* harvest helper

agosto *m* August; harvest; harvest time; **hacer su agosto** to make hay while the sun shines

agota•do -da *adj* exhausted; sold out; out of print

agotar *tr* to exhaust, wear out, use up ‖ *ref* to become exhausted, be used up; go out of print; run out

agracia•do -da *adj* charming, graceful; nice, pretty ‖ *mf* winner

agradable *adj* agreeable; pleasant

agradar *tr* to please ‖ *intr* to be pleasing ‖ *ref* to be pleased

agradecer §22 *tr* to thank; **agradecerle a uno una cosa** to thank someone for something

agradeci•do -da *adj* thankful, grateful; rewarding

agradecimiento *m* thanks, gratitude

agrado *m* agreeableness, graciousness; pleasure, liking

agrandar *tr* to enlarge ‖ *ref* to grow larger

agranelar *tr* (*cuero*) to grain, pebble

agrapar *tr* to clamp

agrariense *adj & mf* agrarian

agra•rio -ria *adj* agrarian

agravar *tr* to weigh down; aggravate; exaggerate; oppress ‖ *ref* to get worse

agraviar *tr* to wrong, offend ‖ *ref* to take offense

agravio *m* wrong, offense; **agravios de hecho** assault and battery

agravio•so -sa *adj* offensive, insulting

agraz *m* (*pl* **agraces**) sour grape; sour-grape juice; bitterness, displeasure; **en agraz** prematurely

agredir §1 *tr* to attack, assault

agregado *m* aggregate; concrete block; attaché; (*Arg*) tenant farmer

agregar §44 *tr* to add; attach; appoint ‖ *ref* to join

agremiado *m* union member

agremiar *tr* to unionize

agresión *f* aggression

agresi•vo -va *adj* aggressive

agre•sor -sora *adj* aggressive ‖ *mf* aggressor

agreste *adj* country, rustic; wild, rough; uncouth

agriar §77 & *regular tr* to make sour; exasperate ‖ *ref* to turn sour; become exasperated

agrícola *adj* agricultural ‖ *mf* farmer

agricultura *f* agriculture

agridulce *adj* bittersweet

agriera *f* (Chile) heartburn; **agrieras** (Col) cruet stand

agrietar *tr & ref* to crack

agrimensor *m* surveyor

agrimensura *f* surveying

agringar §44 *ref* to act like a gringo

a•grio -gria *adj* sour, acrid; uneven, rough; brittle ‖ **agrios** *mpl* citrus fruit

agronomía *f* agronomy

agropecua•rio -ria *adj* land-and-cattle, farm

agrumar *tr & ref* to curd, clot

agrupar *tr & ref* to group, cluster

agrura *f* sourness; unpleasantness; **agruras** citrus fruit

agua *f* water; (*de un tejado*) slope; **agua abajo** downstream; **agua arriba** upstream; **agua bendita** holy water; **agua corriente** running water; **agua de Colonia** eau de Cologne; **agua de marea** tidewater; **agua gaseosa** carbonated water; **agua oxigenada** hydrogen peroxide; **aguas** mineral springs; (*de sedas; de piedras preciosas*) water, sparkle; **aguas mayores** equinoctial tide; feces; **aguas menores** ordinary tide; urination; **cubrir aguas** to have under roof; **entre dos aguas** under water, under the surface of the water; (coll) undecided

aguacate *m* avocado, alligator pear; pear-shaped emerald

aguacero *m* shower

aguada *f* source of water; water color; watering station

aguade•ro -ra *adj* water ‖ *m* watering place

agua•do -da *adj* watery; thin, watered; weak, washed out, limp; dull, insipid ‖ *f* see **aguada**

agua•dor -dora *mf* water carrier ‖ *m* paddle, bucket

aguafies•tas *mf* (*pl* **-tas**) kill-joy, wet blanket, crapehanger

aguafortista *mf* etcher

aguafuerte *f* etching; **grabar al aguafuerte** to etch

aguaitar *intr* to spy, watch ‖ *tr* to watch, wait for

aguaje *m* watering place; tidal wave; strong current; (*de buque*) wake

aguamala *f* jellyfish

aguamanil *m* ewer, wash pitcher; washstand

aguama•nos *m* (*pl* **-nos**) water for washing hands; washstand

aguamarina *f* aquamarine

aguanie•ves *f* (*pl* **-ves**) wagtail

aguano•so -sa *adj* watery, soaked

aguantada *f* patience, forbearance

aguantar *tr* to hold up, sustain; bear, endure, tolerate; hold back, control ‖ *intr* to last, hold out ‖ *ref* to restrain oneself; keep quiet; **aguantarse las lágrimas** to swallow one's tears

aguante *m* patience, endurance; strength, vigor

aguar §10 *tr* to water; spoil, mar ‖ *ref* to become watery; fill up with water; be spoiled

aguardar *tr* to await, wait for; grant time to ‖ *intr* to wait; **aguardar a que** to wait until

aguardentera *f* liquor bottle, brandy flask

aguardentería *f* liquor store

aguardento•so -sa *adj* brandy; (*voz*) whiskey

aguardiente *m* brandy; spirituous liquor; **aguardiente de caña** rum; **aguardiente de manzana** applejack

aguardo *m* hunter's blind

aguarrás *m* turpentine, oil of turpentine

aguasar *ref* (Arg & Chile) to become countrified

aguazal *m* swamp, pool

agudeza *f* acuteness, acuity; sharpness; witticism; **agudeza visual** visual acuity

agu•do -da *adj* acute; sharp; keen; witty

agüero *m* augury; omen; forecast

aguerri•do -da *adj* inured, hardened

aguijada *f* goad, spur; prod

aguijar *tr* to goad, spur, prod ‖ *intr* to hurry along

aguijón *m* goad, spur; sting; thorn; stimulus; **dar coces contra el aguijón** to kick against the pricks

aguijonear to goad, incite; sting

águila *f* eagle; **¿águila o sol?** (Mex) heads or tails?; **ser un águila** to be wide-awake, be a wizard

aguile•ño -ña *adj* aquiline; sharp-featured

aguilón *m* (*de grúa*) boom, jib; (*del tejado*) gable

aguinaldo *m* Christmas gift, Epiphany gift; Christmas carol

aguja *f* needle; hatpin; steeple, spire; (*del reloj*) hand; **aguja de gancho** crochet needle; **aguja de hacer media** knitting needle; **aguja de zurcir** darning needle; **agujas** (rr) switch; **buscar una aguja en un pajar** to look for a needle in a haystack

agujerear *tr* to make a hole in, pierce, perforate

agujero *m* hole; pincushion; **agujero negro** black hole

agujeta *f* (*de la jeringa*) needle; shoestring; **agujetas** stitches, twinges

agusanar *ref* to get wormy; become worm-eaten

aguzanie•ves *f* (*pl* **-ves**) wagtail

aguzar §60 *tr* to sharpen; incite, stir up; stare at; (*las orejas*) prick up

ah•chís *interj* kerchoo!

aherrojar *tr* to fetter, shackle; oppress

aherrumbrar *tr* & *ref* to rust

ahí *adv* there; **de ahí que** hence; **por ahí** that way

ahija•do -da *mf* godchild; protégé ‖ *m* godson ‖ *f* goddaughter

ahilar *ref* to faint from hunger; waste away; grow poorly; turn sour

ahincar §73 *tr* to urge, press; importune ‖ *ref* to hasten

ahinco *m* earnestness, zeal, eagerness

ahitar *tr* to cloy, surfeit, stuff

ahí•to -ta *adj* surfeited, stuffed; fed up, disgusted ‖ *m* surfeit; indigestion

ahoga•do -da *adj* drowned; smothered; sunk; close, unventilated; **mate ahogado** stalemate; **perecer ahogado** to drown; **verse ahogado** to be swamped

ahogar §44 *tr* to drown; suffocate, smother; (*cal*) slake; (*plantas*) soak; oppress; extinguish; stalemate ‖ *ref* to drown; suffocate; drown oneself

ahogo *m* shortness of breath; great sorrow; stringency

ahondar *tr* to make deeper; go deep into ‖ *intr* to go deep, go deeper

ahora *adv* now; presently; **ahora bien** now then, so then; **ahora mismo** right now; **por ahora** for the present

ahorcajar *ref* to sit astride

ahorcar §73 *tr* to hang ‖ *ref* to hang, be hanged; hang oneself

ahorra•do -da *adj* saving, thrifty

ahorrar *tr* to save; spare ‖ *ref* to save or spare oneself

ahorrati•vo -va *adj* saving, thrifty; stingy ‖ *f* economy

ahorro *m* economy; **ahorros** savings

ahuchar *tr* to hoard

ahuecar §73 *tr* to hollow, hollow out; loosen, fluff up; **ahuecar la voz** to speak in deep and solemn tones ‖ *ref* to be puffed up

ahula•do -da *adj* waterproof, impermeable *m* overshoe

ahumar *tr* to smoke ‖ *intr* to be smoky ‖ *ref* to get smoked up; look or taste smoky; get drunk

ahusar *tr* & *ref* to taper

ahuyentar *tr* to put to flight; scare away ‖ *ref* to flee, run away

aira•do -da *adj* angry; wild; depraved

airar §4 *tr* to anger ‖ *ref* to get angry

aire *m* air; **al aire libre** in the open air; **darse aires** to put on airs

airear *tr* to air, aerate, ventilate ‖ *ref* to get aired; catch cold

airón *m* aigrette, panache; gray heron

airo•so -sa *adj* airy; drafty; graceful, light; resplendent; successful

aislación *f* insulation

aislacionista *adj* & *mf* isolationist

aislador *m* insulator

aislamiento *m* isolation; (elec) insulation

aislar §4 *tr* to isolate; detach, separate; (elec) to insulate ‖ *ref* to live in seclusion

ajar *m* garlic field ‖ *tr* to crumple, muss; (*marchitar*) wither; tamper with; abuse, ill-treat ‖ *ref* to get mussed; wither

ajedrea *f* (bot) savory

ajedrecista *mf* chess player

ajedrez *m* chess; chess set

ajenjo *m* (*Artemisia*) wormwood; (*licor*) absinthe; (*sinsabores y penas*) (fig) wormwood, bitterness; **ajenjo del campo** or **ajenjo mayor** (*Artemisia absinthium*) wormwood

aje•no -na *adj* another's; extraneous, foreign; different; contrary; free; insane; uninformed; **lo ajeno** what belongs to someone else

ajetrear *tr* to drive, harass ‖ *ref* to bustle about; fidget

ajetreo *m* bustle, fuss

ají *m* (*pl* **ajíes**) chili; chili sauce; **ponerse como un ají** (Chile) to turn red as a tomato

aji•mez *m* (*pl* **-meces**) mullioned window

ajo *m* garlic; garlic clove; garlic sauce

ajorca *f* bracelet, anklet

ajornalar *tr* to hire by the day ‖ *ref* to hire out by the day

ajuar *m* housefurnishings; trousseau

ajuiciar *tr* to bring to one's senses ‖ *ref* to come to one's senses

ajustable *adj* adjustable

ajusta•do -da *adj* just, right; tight, close-fitting

ajustar *tr* to adapt, fit, adjust; hire; arrange; reconcile; fasten; settle ‖ *intr* to fit ‖ *ref* to fit; hire out; be hired; come to an agreement

ajuste *m* fit; fitting, adjustment; hiring; arrangement; reconciliation; settlement; agreement

ajusticiar *tr* to execute, put to death

ala *f* wing; (*del sombrero*) brim; (*de puerta, mesa, etc.*) leaf; (*de pez*) fin; (*de hélice*) blade; (football) end; **ahuecar el ala** to beat it; **ala en flecha** (aer) sweptback wing; **alas** boldness, courage; **volar con sus propias alas** to stand on one's own feet

Alá *m* Allah

alabanza *f* praise

alabar *tr* to praise ‖ *ref* to boast

alabarda *f* halberd

alabardero *m* halberdier; hired applauder, claqueur

alabastro *m* alabaster

álabe *m* drooping branch; bucket, paddle; cog

alabear *tr* & *ref* to warp

alacena *f* cupboard, wall closet; (naut) locker; (Mex) booth, stall

alacrán *m* scorpion

ala•do -da *adj* winged

alamar *m* frog (*button and loop on a garment*)

alambica•do -da *adj* precious, oversubtle, fine-spun; begrudged

alambicar §73 *tr* to distill; refine to excess

alambique *m* still, alembic; (*de laboratorio*) retort; **por alambique** sparingly

alambrada *f* chicken wire; wire mesh; (mil) barbed wire; (elec) wiring

alambrado *m* chicken wire; wire mesh; wire fence; (elec) wiring; (mil) wire entanglement

alambraje *m* (elec) wiring

alambrar *tr* to fence with wire; string with wire; wire

alambre *m* wire; **alambre cargado** live wire; **alambre de púas** barbed wire; **alambre sin aislar** bare wire

alambrera *f* wire screen; wire cover

alameda *f* poplar grove; mall, shaded walk

álamo *m* poplar; **álamo de Italia** Lombardy poplar; **álamo negro** black poplar; **álamo temblón** aspen

alampar *ref* to have a craving

alancear *tr* to lance, spear

alano *m* mastiff, great Dane

alarde *m* display, ostentation; (mil) review; **hacer alarde de** to make a show of; boast of

alardear *intr* to boast, brag, show off

alardo•so -sa *adj* showy, ostentatious

alargar §44 *tr* to extend, lengthen, stretch; hand; to increase; let out ‖ *ref* to go away, withdraw; grow longer; be long-winded

alarido *m* howl, shout, yell, whoop

alarma *f* alarm; (aer) alert; **alarma aérea** air-raid warning; **alarma de incendios** fire alarm; **alarma de ladrones** burglar alarm

alarmar *tr* to alarm; alert ‖ *ref* to become alarmed

alarmista *mf* alarmist

alastrar *tr* (*las orejas*) to throw back; (naut) to ballast ‖ *ref* to lie flat, cower

ala•zán -zana *adj* sorrel, reddish-brown ‖ *mf* sorrel horse

alba *f* dawn, daybreak

albacea *m* executor ‖ *f* executrix

albahaquero *m* flowerpot

alba•nés -nesa *adj* & *mf* Albanian

albañal *m* sewer, drain

albañil *m* mason, bricklayer

albañilería *f* masonry

albarán *m* rent sign; bulletin; (com) check list

albarca *f* sandal

albarda *f* packsaddle

albardilla *f* (*tejadillo sobre los muros*) coping; shoulder pad

albaricoque *m* apricot

albaricoquero *m* apricot tree

alba•tros *m* (*pl* **-tros**) albatross

albayalde *m* white lead

albear *intr* to turn white; (Arg) to get up at dawn

albedrío *m* free will; fancy, caprice, pleasure; **libre albedrío** free will

albéitar *m* veterinarian

alberca *f* pond, pool; tank, reservoir; **en alberca** roofless

albérchigo *m* clingstone peach

albergar §44 *tr* to shelter, harbor; house ‖ *intr* & *ref* to take shelter; take lodgings

albergue *m* shelter, refuge; lodging; den, lair

albero *m* dishcloth, dishrag; white earth

al·bo -ba *adj* (poet) white ‖ *f* see **alba**
albóndiga *f* meat ball, fish ball
albor *m* whiteness; dawn
alborada *f* dawn; morning serenade; reveille
alborear *intr* to dawn
albor·noz *m* (*pl* **-noces**) terry cloth; burnoose; cardigan; beach robe
alborota·do -da *adj* hasty, rash; noisy; rough
alborota·dor -dora *mf* agitator, rioter
alborotapue·blos *mf* (*pl* **-blos**) (coll) rabble rouser
alborotar *tr* to agitate, arouse, stir up ‖ *intr* to make a racket ‖ *ref* to get excited; riot; (*la mar*) get rough
alboroto *m* agitation, disturbance; noise, riot; **alborotos** (CAm) candied popcorn; **armar un alboroto** to raise a racket
alborozar §60 *tr* to gladden, cheer, overjoy, elate
alborozo *m* joy, merriment, elation
albricias *fpl* reward for good news; reward given on the occasion of some happy event; **en albricias de** as a token of ‖ *interj* good news!, congratulations!
albufera *f* saltwater lagoon
ál·bum *m* (*pl* **-bumes**) album; **álbum de recortes** scrapbook
albumen *m* albumen
albúmina *f* albumin
albuminar *tr* (phot) to emulsify
albur *m* risk, chance
alcachofa *f* artichoke
alcahue·te -ta *mf* bawd, procurer, go-between; screen, fence; schemer; gossip
alcahuetear *tr* to procure; harbor ‖ *intr* to pander
alcaide *m* governor, warden, jailer
alcalde *m* mayor, chief burgess; **alcalde de monterilla** small-town mayor; **tener el padre alcalde** to have a friend at court
alcaldesa *f* mayoress
álcali *m* alkali
alcali·no -na *adj* alkaline
alcallería *f* pottery
alcana *f* henna
alcance *m* reach, scope, extent; range; pursuit; capacity; late news; import; coverage; brains, intelligence; **al alcance de** within reach of, within range of; **alcance de la vista** eyesight, eyeshot; **alcance del oído** earshot; **dar alcance a** to catch up with
alcancía *f* child's bank; bin, hopper
alcanfor *m* camphor
alcantarilla *f* sewer; culvert
alcantarillar *tr* to sewer
alcanza·do -da *adj* needy, hard up
alcanzar §60 *tr* to reach; overtake, catch up to; grasp; obtain; understand; live through ‖ *intr* to succeed; (*un arma de fuego*) carry; manage; suffice
alcaparrosa *f* vitriol
alcaravea *f* caraway
alcatraz *m* gannet, pelican
alcázar *m* fortress; castle, royal palace; quarterdeck
alce *m* elk, moose
alcista *adj* bullish ‖ *mf* (fig) bull

alcoba *f* bedroom; **alcoba de respeto** master bedroom
alcohol *m* alcohol
alcohóli·co -ca *adj* & *mf* alcoholic
alconafta *f* gasohol
alcor *m* hill, elevation, eminence
alcornoque *m* cork oak; blockhead
alcorque *m* cork-soled shoe; trench for water around a tree
alcorza *f* sugar paste, sugar icing; **ser una alcorza** (Arg) to be highly emotional
alcurnia *f* ancestry, lineage
alcuza *f* olive-oil can
aldaba *f* knocker, door knocker; bolt, crossbar; latch; hitching ring; **aldaba dormida** deadlatch; **tener buenas aldabas** to have pull
aldabonazo *m* knock on the door
aldea *f* village, hamlet
aldea·no -na *adj* village; rustic ‖ *mf* villager
aleación *f* alloy
alear *tr* to alloy ‖ *intr* to flap the wings; to flap one's arms; to convalesce
aleccionar *tr* to teach, instruct; to train, to coach
aleda·ño -ña *adj* bordering ‖ *m* border, boundary
alega·dor -dora *adj* quarrelsome; litigious
alegar §44 *tr* to allege; to declare, assert ‖ *intr* (Col, Hond) to quarrel
alegoría *f* allegory
alegóri·co -ca *adj* allegoric(al)
alegrar *tr* to cheer, gladden; (*un fuego*) to stir ‖ *ref* to be glad, to rejoice; to get tipsy
alegre *adj* glad; bright; cheerful, light-hearted; careless; fast, spicy; **alegre de cascos** scatterbrained
alegría *f* cheer, joy, gladness; brightness, gaiety
aleja·do -da *adj* distant, remote
alejandri·no -na *adj* & *mf* Alexandrine
alejar *tr* & *ref* to move aside, move away
alelar *tr* to make stupid ‖ *ref* to grow stupid
aleluya *m* & *f* hallelujah ‖ *m* Easter time ‖ *f* doggerel; daub; **aleluya navideña** Christmas card ‖ *interj* hallelujah!
ale·mán -mana *adj* & *mf* German
Alemania *f* Germany
alenta·do -da *adj* brave, spirited; proud, haughty; well, healthy ‖ *f* deep breath
alentar §2 *tr* to encourage, cheer up ‖ *intr* to breathe ‖ *ref* to take heart; get well, recover
alerce *m* larch
alergia *f* allergy
alero *m* eaves
alerón *m* aileron
alerta *adv* on the alert ‖ *interj* watch out!, look out! ‖ *m* (mil) alert; (mil) watchword
alertar *tr* to alert
aler·to -ta *adj* alert, watchful, vigilant
alesaje *m* bore
alesna *f* awl
aleta *f* small wing; (*de pez*) fin; (*de hélice*) blade; **aletas** (*natación*) flippers
aletargar §44 *tr* to benumb; put to sleep ‖ *ref* to get drowsy, fall asleep

aletear *intr* to flap the wings; flap, flip, flutter
aleve *adj* treacherous, perfidious
alevosía *f* treachery, perfidy
alevo·so -sa *adj* treacherous, perfidious
alfabetizar §60 *tr* to alphabetize; teach reading and writing to
alfabeto *m* alphabet
alfaneque *m* buzzard
alfanje *m* cutlass
alfarería *f* pottery
alfarero *m* potter
alféizar *m* splay; embrasure
alfeñicar §73 *tr* to candy, ice ‖ *ref* to grow thin; be affected, finical
alfeñique *m* almond-flavored sugar paste; affectation, prudery; thin, delicate person; weakling
alfé·rez *m* (*pl* **-reces**) (mil) second lieutenant; (mil) subaltern (Brit); **alférez de fragata** (nav) ensign; **alférez de navío** (nav) lieutenant (j.g.)
alfil *m* bishop
alfiler *m* pin; **alfiler de corbata** stickpin, scarfpin; **alfiler de madera** clothespin; **alfiler de seguridad** safety pin; **alfileres** pin money
alfilerar *tr* to pin, pin up
alfiletero *m* pincase, needlecase
alfombra *f* carpet; rug
alfombrar *tr* to carpet
alforfón *m* buckwheat
alforja *f* shoulder bag; traveling supplies; **pasarse a la otra alforja** to go too far, take too much liberty
alforza *f* pleat, tuck
al·foz *m* (*pl* **-foces**) outskirts; dependence; mountain pass
alga *f* alga; **alga marina** seaweed; **algas** algae
algaida *f* brush, thicket; sandbank
algalia *f* civet; catheter
algarabía *f* Arabic; (coll) gibberish, jabber; (coll) hubbub, uproar
algarada *f* outcry; uproar
algarroba *f* carob bean
algarrobo *m* carob
algazara *f* Moorish battle cry; din, uproar
álgebra *f* algebra
algebrai·co -ca *adj* algebraic
álgi·do -da *adj* cold, icy, frigid
algo *pron indef* something; anything; **algo por el estilo** something of the sort ‖ *adv* somewhat, a little, rather
algodón *m* cotton; **algodón pólvora** guncotton; **estar criado entre algodones** to be brought up in comfort
algodoncillo *m* milkweed
algodono·so -sa *adj* cottony
alguacil *m* bailiff; mounted police officer at the head of the processional entrance of the bullfighters
alguien *pron indef* somebody, someone
algún *adj indef* apocopated form of **alguno**, used only before masculine singular nouns and adjectives

algu·no -na *adj indef* some, any; not any; **alguna vez** sometimes; ever ‖ *pron indef* someone; **algunos** some
alhaja *f* jewel, gem; **buena alhaja** a bad egg, a sly fellow
alhajera *f* or **alhajero** *m* jewelry box
alharaca *f* fuss, ado, ballyhoo; **hacer alharacas** to make a fuss
alharaquien·to -ta *adj* fussy, noisy
alhe·lí *m* (*pl* **-líes**) gillyflower (*Matthiola incana*); wallflower (*Cheiranthus*)
alheña *f* henna; blight, mildew
alheñar *tr* to henna; blight, mildew ‖ *ref* (*el pelo*) to henna
alhucema *f* lavender
alhumajo *m* pine needles
alia·do -da *adj* allied ‖ *mf* ally
aliaga *f* furze, gorse
alianza *f* alliance; wedding ring; (Bib) covènant
aliar §77 *tr* to ally ‖ *ref* to ally, become allied; form an alliance
alias *adj & m* alias
alicaí·do -da *adj* failing, weak; crestfallen, discouraged
alicates *mpl* pliers
aliciente *m* inducement, incentive
alienar *tr* to alienate; enrapture
aliento *m* breath, breathing; courage, spirit; **dar aliento a** to encourage; **de mucho aliento** arduous, difficult, endless; **nuevo aliento** second wind; **sin aliento** out of breath
alifafe *m* complaint, indisposition
aligerar *tr* to lighten; alleviate, ease; hasten; shorten
aligustre *m* privet
alijador *m* lighter; lighterman; sander
alijar *tr* to unload, lighten; sandpaper
aligeramiento *m* easing; alleviation; **aligeramiento de impuestos** tax relief
alimaña *f* varmint, small predacious animal
alimentante *mf* person obliged to provide child support
alimentar *tr* to feed, nourish; (*p.ej., esperanzas*) to cherish, foster ‖ *ref* to feed, nourish oneself
alimenti·cio -cia *adj* alimentary, nourishing
alimento *m* food, nourishment; encouragement; **alimentos** foodstuffs; allowance; alimony
alindar *tr* to mark off; embellish, prettify ‖ *intr* to border, be contiguous
alinea·do -da *adj* lined up, aligned; **no alineado** nonaligned, Third World
alinear *tr & ref* to align, line up
aliñar *tr* to dress, season
aliño *m* dressing, seasoning
aliquebra·do -da *adj* crestfallen
alisar *tr* to smooth; polish, sleek; iron lightly
aliso *m* alder tree
alistar *tr* to list; enlist, enroll; stripe ‖ *ref* to enlist, enroll; get ready
aliteración *f* alliteration
aliviar *tr* to alleviate, relieve, soothe; remedy; lighten; hasten ‖ *ref* to get better, recover

alivio *m* alleviation, relief; remedy

aljaba *f* quiver

aljama *f* mosque; synagogue; Moorish quarter; ghetto

aljamía *f* Spanish of Moors and Jews; Spanish written in Arabic characters

aljez *m* gypsum

aljibe *m* water tender, tank barge; oil tanker; cistern

aljófar *m* imperfect pearl; (fig) dewdrops

aljofifa *f* floor mop

aljofifar *tr* to mop

alma *f* soul, heart, spirit; (*persona*) living soul; crux, heart; sweetheart; (*de carril*) web; (*de cañón*) bore; (*de escalera*) newel; **dar el alma, entregar el alma, rendir el alma** to give up the ghost

almacén *m* warehouse; store, department store; storehouse; (phot) magazine

almacenaje *m* storage; **almacenaje de datos** (*ordenador*) data storage, memory

almacenamiento *m* storage; (*ordenador*) data storage, memory

almacenar *tr* to store; store up, hoard; to store (electronic) data

almacenista *mf* storekeeper ‖ *m* warehouseman

almáciga *f* seedbed, tree nursery

almádana *f* spalling hammer

almagre *m* red ocher

almajara *f* (hort) hotbed

almanaque *m* almanac; calendar

almeja *f* clam

almena *f* merlon

almenaje *m* battlement

almendra *f* almond; (*de cualquier fruto drupáceo*) kernel; **almendra amarga** bitter almond; **almendra de Málaga** Jordan almond; **almendra tostada** burnt almond

almendrado *m* macaroon

almendro *m* almond tree

almiar *m* haystack, hayrick

almíbar *m* simple syrup; fruit juice; **estar hecho un almíbar** to be as sweet as pie

almibarar *tr* to preserve in syrup; (*sus palabras*) honey ‖ *intr* to candy

almidón *m* starch; paste; **almidón de maíz** cornstarch

almidona·do -da *adj* starched; spruce, dapper; stiff, prim

almidonar *tr* to starch

alminar *m* minaret

almiranta *f* admiral's wife; flagship

almirante *m* admiral

almi·rez *m* (*pl* **-reces**) brass mortar

almizcle *m* musk

almizclera *f* muskrat

almizclero *m* musk deer

almohada *f* pillow; **consultar con la almohada** to sleep it over

almohadilla *f* cushion; pad; (Chile) pincushion

almohaza *f* currycomb

almohazar §60 *tr* to currycomb

almoneda *f* auction; clearance sale

almonedar *tr* to auction

almorranas *fpl* piles, hemorrhoids

almorta *f* grass pea

almorzada *f* double handful, heavy breakfast

almorzar §35 *tr* to lunch on ‖ *intr* to lunch, have lunch

almuecín *m* or **almuédano** *m* muezzin

almuerzo *m* lunch

alna·do -da *mf* stepchild

aloca·do -da *adj* mad, wild, reckless ‖ *mf* madcap

alocar §73 *tr* to drive crazy

alocución *f* address, speech

áloe *m* or **aloe** *m* aloe; aloes

alojar *tr* to lodge; quarter, billet ‖ *intr* & *ref* to lodge; be quartered or billeted

alojo *m* accommodations, lodging

alondra *f* lark

aloquecer §22 *ref* to go crazy, lose one's mind

alosa *f* shad

alpaca *f* alpaca; alpaca wool; alpaca cloth; German silver

alpargata *f* hemp sandal, espadrille

alpende *m* tool shed; lean-to, penthouse

Alpes *mpl* Alps

alpestre *adj* alpine

alpinismo *m* mountain climbing

alpi·no -na *adj* alpine

alpiste *m* canary seed, birdseed; **quedarse alpiste** to be disappointed

alquería *f* farmhouse

alquibla *f* kiblah

alquiladi·zo -za *adj* & *mf* hireling

alquilar *tr* to rent, let, hire ‖ *ref* to hire out; be for rent

alquiler *m* rent, rental, hire; **alquiler de coches** car-rental service; **alquiler sin chófer** drive-yourself service; **de alquiler** for rent, for hire

alquilona *f* cleaning woman, charwoman

alquimia *f* alchemy

alquitarar *tr* to distill

alquitrán *m* tar; **alquitrán de hulla** coal tar

alquitranado *m* tarpaulin

alquitranar *tr* to tar

alrededor *adv* around; **alrededor de** around; about, approximately ‖ **alrededores** *mpl* environs, surroundings, outskirts

Alsacia *f* Alsace

alsacia·no -na *adj* & *mf* Alsatian

alta *f* discharge from hospital; (mil) certificate of induction into active service; **dar de alta** to discharge from the hospital; **darse de alta** to join, be admitted; (mil) to report for duty

altane·ro -ra *adj* towering; arrogant, haughty

altar *m* altar; **altar mayor** high altar; **conducir al altar** to lead to the altar

alta·voz *m* (*pl* **-voces**) loudspeaker

altea *f* (bot) marshmallow

alteración *f* alteration; disturbance; uneven pulse; altercation, quarrel

alterar *tr* to alter; disturb; agitate, upset; falsify; lessen ‖ *ref* to alter; be disturbed; be agitated; lessen; (*el pulso*) flutter

altercación *f* or **altercado** *m* argument, wrangle, bickering

altercar §73 *intr* to argue, bicker, wrangle

alternar *tr & intr* to alternate; **alternar con** to go around with

alternati•vo -va *adj* alternating, alternative; *f* choice, option; admission as a matador; **no tener alternativa** to have no choice

alter•no -na *adj* alternate

alteza *f* sublimity ‖ **Alteza** *f* (*tratamiento*) Highness

altibajo *m* downward thrust; **altibajos** uneven ground; ups and downs

altillo *m* hillock; (*oficina en una tienda o taller*) balcony; (Arg, Ecuad) attic, garret

altimetría *f* altimetry

altiplanicie *f* tableland

altitud *f* altitude; height

altivez *f* or **altiveza** *f* arrogance, haughtiness, pride

alti•vo -va *adj* haughty, proud; high, lofty

al•to -ta *adj* high; upper; top; loud; (*horas*) late; **ponerse tan alto** to take offense, be hoity-toity ‖ *m* height, altitude; story, floor; stop, halt; **de alto a bajo** from top to bottom; **hacer alto** to stop; **pasar por alto** to overlook, disregard ‖ *f* see **alta** ‖ **alto** *adv* high up; loud; aloud; **alto** *interj* halt!

altoparlante *m* loudspeaker

altozanero *m* (Col) public errand boy

altozano *m* hill, knoll; upper part of town; (CAm, Col, Ven) parvis

altruísta *adj* altruistic ‖ *mf* altruist

altura *f* height, altitude; high seas; juncture, point, stage; (mus) pitch; (naut) latitude; **a estas alturas** at this juncture; **a la altura de** (naut) off; **estar a la altura de** to be up to, be equal to; be abreast of; **por estas alturas** around here

alucinación *f* hallucination

alucinante *adj* hallucinogenic

alud *m* avalanche

aludi•do -da *adj* above-mentioned

aludir *intr* to allude

alumbra•do -da *adj* lighted; enlightened; tipsy ‖ *m* lighting; lighting system

alumbramiento *m* lighting; childbirth, accouchement

alumbrar *tr* to light, illuminate; (*a los ciegos*) give sight to; enlighten; (*aguas subterráneas*) discover and bring to the surface ‖ *intr* to have a child ‖ *ref* to get tipsy

alumbre *m* alum

aluminio *m* aluminum

alumnado *m* student body

alum•no -na *mf* (*niño criado como si fuera hijo*) foster child; (*discípulo*) pupil, student; **alumno mimado** teacher's pet

alunizaje *m* lunar landing

alunizar §60 *intr* to land on the moon

alusión *f* allusion

álveo *m* bed of a stream, river bed

alvéolo *m* alveolus; (*de diente*) socket; (*de rueda de agua*) bucket

alza *f* rise, advance. increase; **jugar al alza** to bull the market

alzada *f* height (*e.g., of a horse*)

alza•do -da *adj* (SAm) insolent; rebellious; *m* lump sum, cash settlement; front elevation; (bb) quire, gathering

alzapaño *m* curtain holder; tieback

alzapié *m* snare, trap

alzaprima *f* crowbar, lever; (*de instrumento de arco*) (mus) bridge

alzaprimar *tr* to pry, pry up; arouse, stir up

alzapuer•tas *m* (*pl* **-tas**) (archaic) dumb player, supernumerary

alzar §60 *tr* to raise, lift, hoist; pick up; (*la hostia*) elevate; hide, lock up; (*naipes*) cut; (bb) to gather ‖ *ref* to rise, get up; revolt; **alzarse con** to abscond with

alzaválvu•las *m* (*pl* **-las**) tappet

alzo *m* (CAm) theft

allá *adv* there, over there; back there; **allá en** over in; back in; **el más allá** the beyond; **más allá** farther on, farther away; **más allá de** beyond; **por allá** thereabouts; that way

allanar *tr* to level, smooth, flatten; (*una dificultad*) iron out, overcome, get around; (*una casa*) break into; to subdue ‖ *intr* to level off ‖ *ref* to tumble down; yield, submit; humble oneself

allega•do -da *adj* near, close; related; partisan ‖ *mf* relative; partisan

allegar §44 *tr* to collect, gather; reap ‖ *intr* to approach ‖ *ref* to approach; be attached, be a follower, agree

allende *adv* beyond; **allende.de** besides, in addition to ‖ *prep* beyond

allí *adv* there; **allí dentro** in there; **por allí** that way; around there

ama *f* housekeeper; housewife, lady of the house; landlady, proprietress; **ama de casa** housewife; **ama de cría** or **de leche** wet nurse; **ama de llaves** housekeeper; **ama seca** dry nurse

amable *adj* amiable, kind, obliging; (*digno de ser amado*) lovable

amachinar *ref* to cohabit; get intimate

ama•do -da *adj & mf* beloved

ama•dor -dora *adj* fond, loving ‖ *mf* lover

amadrigar §44 *tr* to welcome, receive with open arms ‖ *ref* to burrow; go into seclusion

amaestrar *tr* to teach, coach; (*a los animales*) train

amagar §44 *tr* to show signs of, threaten; feint ‖ *intr* to look threatening

amago *m* threat, menace; sign, indication; feint

amainar *tr* to lessen; (naut) to lower, shorten ‖ *intr* to subside, die down; lessen; yield ‖ *ref* to lessen; yield

amalgama *f* amalgam

amalgamar *tr & ref* to amalgamate

amamantar *tr* to nurse, to suckle

amancebamiento *m* cohabitation, concubinage, liaison

amancebar *ref* to cohabit, live in concubinage

amancillar *tr* to stain, spot; sully, tarnish

amanecer *m* dawn, daybreak ‖ *v* §22 *intr* to dawn, begin to get light; begin to appear; get awake, start the day

amanecida f dawn, daybreak
amanera•do -da adj mannered, affected
amansar tr (animal) to tame; (caballo) break; soothe, appease
amante adj fond, loving ‖ mf lover
amaño m skill, cleverness, dexterity; trick; **amaños** tools, implements
amapola f poppy
amar tr to love
amaraje m alighting on water
amarar intr to alight on water
amargar §44 tr to make bitter; embitter; (una tertulia, una velada) spoil ‖ intr & ref to become bitter; become embittered
amar•go -ga adj bitter; sour; distressing ‖ **amargos** mpl bitters
amargura f bitterness; sorrow, grief
amarillear intr to turn yellow, show yellow
amarillecer §22 intr to become yellow
amarillen•to -ta adj yellowish
amarillez f yellowness
amari•llo -lla adj & m yellow
amarra f mooring cable; **amarras** support, protection; **soltar las amarras** (naut) to cast off
amarrar tr to moor; lash, tie up; (las cartas) stack
amartelar tr to make love to; make jealous ‖ ref to fall in love; become jealous
amartillar tr to hammer; (un arma de fuego) to cock
amasar tr to knead; mix; massage; (dinero) amass; concoct
amatista f amethyst
Amazonas m Amazon
ambages mpl ambiguity, quibbling; **sin ambages** straight to the point
ámbar m amber
Amberes f Antwerp
ambición f ambition
ambicionar tr to strive for, be eager for
ambicio•so -sa adj ambitious; eager; **ambicioso de figurar** social climber
ambiental adj environmental
ambiente m atmosphere; **medio ambiente** environment; situation
ambi•gú m (pl -gúes) buffet supper; bar, refreshment bar
ambigüedad f ambiguity
ambi•guo -gua adj ambiguous; (género) (gram) common
ámbito m boundary, limit; compass, scope
ambladura f amble
amblar intr to amble
am•bos -bas adj & pron indef both; **ambos a dos** both, both together
ambrosía f ragweed
ambulancia f ambulance; **ambulancia de correos** mail car, railway post office
ambulante adj itinerant, traveling ‖ m railway mail clerk
ambulato•rio -ria adj ambulatory ‖ m welfare center, public clinic; ambulance
amedrentar tr to frighten, scare
amelona•do -da adj melon-shaped; mentally retarded; lovesick

amén interj amen! ‖ m amen ‖ adv — **amén de** aside from; in addition to
amenaza f threat, menace
amenazar §60 tr to threaten, menace
amenguar §10 tr to lessen, diminish; belittle; dishonor
amenidad f amenity
amenizar §60 tr to make pleasant, brighten, cheer
ame•no -na adj agreeable, pleasant
amento m catkin
América f America; **la América Central** Central America; **la América del Norte** North America; **la América del Sur** South America; **la América Latina** Latin America
americana f sack coat, jacket
americanizar §60 tr to Americanize
america•no -na adj & mf American; Spanish American ‖ f see **americana**
amerizar §60 intr to alight on water
ametralladora f machine gun
ametrallar tr to machine-gun
amiba f amoeba
amiga f friend; mistress; schoolmistress; girls' school
amigable adj amicable, friendly
amigacho m chum, crony, pal
amígdala f tonsil
amigdalitis f tonsillitis
ami•go -ga adj friendly; fond ‖ mf friend; sweetheart; **amigo del alma** bosom friend ‖ f see **amiga**
amigote m chum, crony, pal
amilanar tr to terrify, intimidate
aminorar tr to lessen, diminish
amistad f friendship; liaison; **hacer las amistades** to make up; **romper las amistades** to fall out, become enemies
amistar tr to bring together ‖ ref to become friends
amisto•so -sa adj friendly
amniocentesis f amniocentesis
amnistía f amnesty
amnistiar §77 tr to amnesty, grant amnesty to
amo m head of family; landlord, proprietor; boss; **ser el amo del cotarro** to rule the roost
amoblar §61 tr to furnish
amodorrar ref to get drowsy; fall asleep; grow numb
amohinar tr to annoy, irritate, vex
amojonar tr to mark off with landmarks
amoladera f grindstone, whetstone
amolar §61 tr to grind, sharpen; bore, annoy
amoldar tr to mold; model, pattern, fashion; adjust, adapt
amonestación f admonition; marriage banns
amonestar tr to admonish, warn; publish the banns of
amoníaco m ammonia
amontonar tr to heap, pile; accumulate; hoard ‖ ref to collect, gather; crowd; get angry; (Mex) to gang up
amor m love; **al amor del agua** with the current; obligingly; **al amor de la lumbre**

al
am

by the fire, in the warmth of the fire;
amores love affair; **amor propio** amour-
propre; conceit; **por amor de** for the sake
of

amorata•do -da adj livid, black-and-blue

amordazar §60 tr to muzzle; gag

amorío m love-making; love affair

amoro•so -sa adj loving, affectionate, amorous

amortajar tr to shroud; (carp) to mortise

amortecer §22 tr to deaden, muffle || ref to
die away, become faint

amortiguador m shock absorber; door check;
(de automóvil) bumper; **amortiguador de
luz** dimmer; **amortiguador de ruido** muffler

amortiguar §10 tr to deaden, muffle; soften,
tone down; dim; damp; (un golpe) cushion;
(ondas electromagnéticas) damp

amortizar §60 tr to amortize; (una deuda)
pay off

amoscar §73 ref to get peeved; (Mex) to
blush, be embarrassed

amotina•do -da adj mutinous, rebellious ||
mf mutineer, rebel, rioter

amotinar tr to stir up; incite to mutiny || ref
to rise up, mutiny, rebel

amover §47 tr to discharge, dismiss

amovible adj removable, detachable

amparar tr to shelter, protect || ref to seek
shelter; protect oneself

amparo m shelter, protection, refuge; stall;
aid, favor

amperio m ampere

amperio-hora m (pl **amperios-hora**) ampere-
hour

ampliación f amplification; (phot) enlargement

ampliar §77 tr to amplify, enlarge; widen;
(phot) to enlarge

amplificador m amplifier

amplificar §73 tr to amplify; expand, enlarge; magnify

am•plio -plia adj ample; spacious, roomy

amplitud f amplitude; roominess

ampo m dazzling white; snowflake

ampolla f blister; bubble; cruet; bulb, light
bulb

ampollar tr & ref to blister

ampolleta f vial; sandglass, hourglass; bulb,
light bulb; cruet

ampulosidad f bombast, pomposity

ampulo•so -sa adj bombastic, pompous

amputar tr to amputate

amueblar tr to furnish

amujera•do -da adj effeminate

amuleto m amulet, charm

amurallar tr to wall, wall in

amurcar §73 tr to gore

amusgar §44 tr (las orejas el toro, el caballo) to throw back

anacardo m cashew; cashew nut

anacróni•co -ca adj anachronistic

anacronismo m anachronism

ánade mf duck

anadear intr to waddle

anadeo m waddle, waddling

anales mpl annals

analfabetismo m illiteracy

analfabe•to -ta adj & mf illiterate

analgési•co -ca adj analgesic || m painkiller,
analgesic

análi•sis m & f (pl **-sis**) analysis; **análisis
costobeneficio** cost-benefit analysis; **análisis de sistemas** systems analysis; **análisis
gramatical** parsing; **análisis ocupacional**
job analysis

analista mf analyst; annalist

analíti•co -ca adj analytic(al)

analizar §60 tr to analyze; **analizar gramaticalmente** to parse

analogía f analogy; similarity

análo•go -ga adj analogous; similar

ana•ná m (pl **-naes**) pineapple

ananás m pineapple

anaquel m shelf

anaranja•do -da adj & m (color) orange

anarquía f anarchy

anárqui•co -ca adj anarchic(al)

anarquista mf anarch, anarchist

anatema m & f anathema; curse

anatomía f anatomy

anatómi•co -ca adj anatomic(al) || mf anato-
mist

anatomista mf anatomist

anca f croup, haunch; buttock, rump; **a ancas**
or **a las ancas** mounted behind another
person; **anca de rana** frog's leg; **dar ancas vueltas** (Mex) to give odds

ancianidad f old age

ancia•no -na adj old, aged || m old man;
(eccl) elder || f old woman

ancla f anchor; **echar anclas** to cast anchor;
levar anclas to weigh anchor

anclar intr to anchor

anclote m kedge, kedge anchor

ancón m bay, cove

áncora f anchor

ancorar intr to anchor

ancheta f (Arg) foolishness; ridiculous act

an•cho -cha adj wide, broad; full, ample;
loose, loose-fitting || m width, breadth

anchoa f anchovy

anchura f width, breadth; fullness, ample-
ness; looseness; comfort, ease

anchuro•so -sa adj wide, broad; spacious,
roomy

andada f thin, hard-baked cracker; **andadas**
(de conejos y otros animales) tracks; **volver
a las andadas** to revert to one's old tricks

andaderas fpl gocart, walker

anda•do -da adj gone by, elapsed; frequent-
ed, trodden; worn, used; ordinary || m gait
|| f see **andada**

andadores mpl leading strings

andadura f pace, gait; amble; (Mex) mount

Andalucía f Andalusia

anda•luz -luza adj & mf Andalusian

andaluzada f tall story, exaggeration, fish
story

andamiaje m scaffolding

andamio m scaffold; platform

andanada *f* (naut) broadside; (taur) covered upper section; (coll) scolding; (fig) fusillade

andante *adj* walking; errant, wandering

andanza *f* wandering, rambling; fate, fortune

andar *m* gait, pace, walk || §5 *tr* (*p.ej.*, *dos millas*) to go; (*un camino*) go down or up || *intr* to go, walk; run; travel; act, behave; (*p.ej.*, *un reloj*) go, run, work; be, feel; go by, pass, elapse; go (*to bear up, to last*), e.g., **anduve diez horas sin comer** I went ten hours without eating || *ref* to go by, to pass, to elapse; to go away; **andarse sin** to go without

andarie·go -ga *adj* wandering, roving; swift, fleet

andas *fpl* litter; stretcher; bier

andén *m* railway platform; quay; footpath

Andes *mpl* Andes

andinismo *m* mountain climbing in the Andes

andi·no -na *adj* Andean

andraje·ro -ra *mf* ragpicker

andrajo *m* rag, tatter; ragamuffin, scalawag

andrajo·so -sa *adj* ragged, raggedy, in tatters

andurriales *mpl* byways, out-of-the-way place

anea *f* cattail, bulrush

aneblar §2 *tr* to cloud; becloud || *ref* to become clouded; get dark

anécdota *f* anecdote

anegar §44 *tr* to flood; drown || *ref* to become flooded; drown

ane·jo -ja *adj* annexed; accessory || *m* annex; dependency; supplement

anemia *f* anaemia

anémi·co -ca *adj* anaemic

anestesia *f* anaesthesia

anestesiar *tr* anaesthetize

anestési·co -ca *adj & m* anaesthetic

aneurisma *m & f* aneurysm

anexar *tr* to annex

ane·xo -xa *adj* annexed; accessory || *m* annex; dependency

anfi·bio -bia *adj* amphibious

anfiteatro *m* amphitheater

anfitrión *m* host

anfitriona *f* hostess

ánfora *f* voting urn, ballot box

anfractuo·so -sa *adj* winding, tortuous

angarillas *fpl* handbarrow; panniers; cruet stand

ángel *m* angel; **ángel custodio** or **de la guarda** guardian angel; **ángel patudo** wolf in sheep's clothing; **tener ángel** to have great charm

angelical or **angéli·co -ca** *adj* angelic(al)

angina *f* angina; **angina de pecho** angina pectoris

angloparlante *adj* English-speaking || *mf* speaker of English

anglosa·jón -jona *adj & mf* Anglo-Saxon

angos·to -ta *adj* narrow

anguila *f* eel; **anguilas** (*para botar un barco al agua*) ways; **escurrirse como una anguila** to be as slippery as an eel

angular *adj* angular

ángulo *m* angle; corner

angulo·so -sa *adj* (*facciones*) angular

angurria *f* (SAm) raging hunger; greed

angustia *f* anguish, distress, grief

angustia·do -da *adj* distressed, grieved

angustiar *tr* to distress, afflict, grieve

angustio·so -sa *adj* distressed, grieved; worrisome

anhelar *tr* to crave, want badly || *intr* to pant; yearn; **anhelar por** to long for

anhélito *m* hard breathing

anhelo *m* craving; yearning, longing

anhelo·so -sa *adj* eager, yearning; breathless, panting

anhi·dro -dra *adj* anhydrous

Aníbal *m* Hannibal

anidar *tr* to harbor, shelter || *intr & ref* to nestle, make a nest; live

anilina *f* aniline

anilla *f* curtain ring; (*en la gimnasia*) ring; hoop

anillo *m* ring; cigar band; **anillo de compromiso** or **de pedida** engagement ring; **anillo sigilar** signet ring

ánima *f* soul; (*de arma de fuego*) bore

animación *f* animation; liveliness; bustle, movement

anima·do -da *adj* animated, lively

animador *m* (*de un café-cantante*) master of ceremonies

animal *adj & m* animal

animar *tr* to enliven; encourage; strengthen; drive || *ref* to take heart, feel encouraged

ánimo *m* mind, spirit; courage, valor, energy; attention, thought

animosidad *f* animosity, ill will

animo·so -sa *adj* brave, courageous; spirited; ready, disposed

aniña·do -da *adj* babyish, childish

anión *m* anion

aniquilar *tr* to annihilate, destroy || *ref* to be annihilated; decline, waste away; be humbled

anís *m* anise; anise-flavored brandy

aniversa·rio -ria *adj & m* anniversary

anoche *adv* last night

anochecer *m* nightfall, dusk || *v* §22 *intr* to grow dark; arrive or happen at nightfall; end the day; go to sleep || *ref* to get dark; get cloudy; slip away

anochecida *f* nightfall, dusk

anodi·no -na *adj* innocuous, ineffective, harmless

ánodo *m* anode

anomalía *f* anomaly

anóma·lo -la *adj* anomalous

anonadar *tr* to annihilate, destroy; overwhelm; humble

anóni·mo -ma *adj* anonymous || *m* anonymity; **guardar** or **conservar el anónimo** to preserve one's anonymity

anorexia *f* anorexia

anormal *adj* abnormal

anotar *tr* to annotate; note, jot down; point out

anquilosa·do -da *adj* stiff-jointed; old-fashioned

ánsar *m* goose; wild goose

am
an

ansia *f* anxiety, anguish; eagerness; **ansias** (Ven) nausea

ansiar §77 & **regular** *tr* to long for, yearn for ‖ *intr* to be madly in love

ansiedad *f* anxiety, worry; pain

ansio•so -sa *adj* anxious; anguished; longing; covetous

ant. *abbr* anticuado

anta *f* elk

antagonismo *m* antagonism

antaño *adv* last year; of yore, long ago

antárti•co -ca *adj* antarctic

ante *prep* before, in the presence of; in front of; at, with ‖ *m* elk; buff

antea•do -da *adj* buff; (Mex) damaged, shopworn

anteanoche *adv* the night before last

anteayer *adv* the day before yesterday

antebrazo *m* forearm

antecámara *f* antechamber, anteroom

antecedente *adj* antecedent ‖ *m* antecedent; **antecedentes** antecedents

anteceder *tr* to precede, go before

antece•sor -sora *mf* predecessor; ancestor

antedatar *tr* to antedate

antedi•cho -cha *adj* aforesaid, abovementioned

antelación *f* previousness, anticipation

antemano — **de antemano** in advance, beforehand

antena *f* (ent) antenna; (rad) antenna, aerial; **antena de conejo** rabbit ears; **en antena** on the air; **antena interior incorporada** built-in antenna; **llevar a las antenas** to put on the air ·

antenombre *m* title, honorific

anteojera *f* spectacle case; blinker, blinder

anteojo *m* eyeglass; spyglass; **anteojos** eyeglasses, spectacles; binoculars; blinkers

antepasa•do -da *adj* before last ‖ **antepasados** *mpl* ancestors

antepecho *m* railing, guardrail; parapet; window sill

antepenúltima *f* antepenult

anteponer §54 *tr* to place in front; prefer

anteportada *f* half title, bastard title

anteportal *m* porch, vestibule

antepuer!a *f* portière

antepuerto *m* entrance to a mountain pass; (naut) outer harbor

anterior *adj* front; previous; earlier

antes *adv* before; sooner, soonest; rather; previously; **antes bien** rather; on the contrary; **antes de** before; **antes (de) que** before; **cuanto antes** as soon as possible

antesala *f* antechamber; (*p.ej., de médico*) waiting room; **hacer antesala** to dance attendance

antiaére•o -a *adj* antiaircraft

antiartísti•co -ca *adj* inartistic

antibéli•co -ca *adj* antiwar

anticartel *adj* antitrust

anticientífi•co -ca *adj* unscientific

anticipación *f* preparation, anticipation; **con anticipación** in advance

anticipa•do -da *adj* future; advance; **por anticipado** in advance

anticipar *tr* to anticipate, hasten; to move ahead ‖ *ref* to happen early; **anticiparse a** to anticipate, to get ahead of

anticipo *m* anticipation; advance payment, down payment; retaining fee

anticoncepti•vo -va *adj* & *m* contraceptive

anticongelante *m* antifreeze

anticonstitucional *adj* unconstitutional

anticua•do -da *adj* antiquated; old-fashioned; obsolete

anticua•rio -ria *adj* antiquarian ‖ *mf* antiquarian, antiquary; antique dealer

anticuerpo *m* antibody

antideporti•vo -va *adj* unsportsmanlike

antiderrapante or **antideslizante** *adj* nonskid

antideslumbrante *adj* antiglare

antidetonante *adj* & *m* antiknock

antídoto *m* antidote

antieconómi•co -ca *adj* uneconomic(al)

antier *adv* the day before yesterday

antiesclavista *adj* antislavery ‖ *mf* abolitionist

anti•faz *m* (*pl* -faces) veil, mask

antífona *f* anthem

antigás *adj invar* gas (*e.g., mask, shelter*)

antigramatical *adj* ungrammatical

antigravedad *f* weightlessness

antigualla *f* antique; relic, antique; has-been

antiguar §10 *intr* & *ref* to attain seniority

antigüedad *f* antiquity; seniority; (*mueble u otro objeto de arte antiguos*) antique; **antigüedades** antiquities; antiques

anti•guo -gua *adj* old; ancient; antique; former ‖ *mf* veteran; senior

antihigiéni•co -ca *adj* unsanitary

antílope *m* antelope

antilla•no -na *adj* & *mf* West Indian

Antillas *fpl* Antilles

antimateria *f* antimatter

antimonio *m* antimony

antiobre•ro -ra *adj* antilabor

antiparras *spl* spectacles

antipatía *f* dislike, antipathy

antipáti•co -ca *adj* disagreeable, uncongenial

antipatrióti•co -ca *adj* unpatriotic

antiproyectil *adj* antimissile

antirreflejo *adj invar* nonreflecting

antirresbaladi•zo -za *adj* nonskid

antirrobo *adj invar* theft-proof, burglar-proof

antisemíti•co -ca *adj* anti-Semitic

antisépti•co -ca *adj* & *m* antiseptic

antisono•ro -ra *adj* soundproof

antisoviéti•co -ca *adj* anti-Soviet

antitanque *adj* antitank

antiterrorista *adj invar* & *mf* antiterrorist

antíte•sis *f* (*pl* -sis) antithesis

antitóxi•co -ca *adj* antitoxic

antitoxina *f* antitoxin

antojadi•zo -za *adj* capricious, whimsical

antojar *ref* to seem; fancy; seem likely; have a notion to + *inf*; take a fancy to + *inf*

antojo *m* caprice, fancy, whim; snap judgment; birthmark; **antojos** moles, warts; **a su antojo** as one pleases

antología *f* anthology

antónimo *m* antonym

antorcha f torch; **antorcha a soplete** blowtorch

antracita f anthracite

ántrax m anthrax

antro m cave, cavern; (fig) den

antropología f anthropology

antruejo m carnival

anual adj annual

anualidad f annuity; year's pay; annual occurrence

anuario m yearbook; directory; bulletin, catalogue; **anuario telefónico** telephone directory

anublar tr to cloud; dim, darken; blight, wither || ref to become cloudy; be withered; (las esperanzas de uno) fade away

anudar tr to tie, fasten, knot; unite; resume || ref to get knotted; be united; fade away, wilt, fail

anuente adj consenting

anular tr to annul; nullify; remove, discharge || ref to be passed over

anunciar tr to announce; advertise || intr to advertise

anunciante mf advertiser

anuncio m announcement; advertisement

anverso m obverse

anzuelo m fishhook; **picar en el anzuelo** or **tragar el anzuelo** to swallow the bait, swallow the hook

añadi•do -da adj additional || m false hair, switch

añadidura f addition; extra weight, extra measure; **de añadidura** extra, in the bargain; **por añadidura** besides

añadir tr to add; increase

añafil m straight Moorish trumpet

añagaza f bird call; decoy, lure; trap, trick

añe•jo -ja adj aged; stale; musty, rancid

añicos mpl bits, pieces; **hacer añicos** to tear to pieces, break to pieces; **hacerse añicos** to wear oneself out

añil m indigo; bluing

añilar tr to dye with indigo; (la ropa blanca) to blue

año m year; **año bisiesto** leap year; **año económico** fiscal year; **año lectivo** school year; **año luz** (pl **años luz**) light-year; **años birthday; cumplir . . . años** to be . . . years old

añoranza f longing, sorrow

añorar tr to long for, sorrow for; grieve over || intr to yearn; sorrow, grieve

año•so -sa adj aged, old

aojada f (Col) skylight; (Col) transom

aojar tr to cast the evil eye on, jinx

aojo m evil eye, jinx

aovar intr to lay eggs

ap. abbr **aparte, apóstol**

apabilar tr to trim

apabullar tr to mash, crush; squelch

apacentar §2 tr & ref to pasture, graze; feed

apacible adj gentle, mild; calm

apaciguamiento m pacification, appeasement

apaciguar §10 tr to pacify, appease || ref to calm down

apachurrar tr to crush, squash, mash

apadrinar tr to sponsor; act as godfather for; back, support; second

apagabron•cas m (pl **-cas**) bouncer

apagador m extinguisher; (de piano) damper

apagaincen•dios m (pl **-dios**) fire extinguisher

apagar §44 tr to extinguish, put out; (la luz, la radio) turn off; (la cal) slake; (el sonido) damp, muffle; (el fuego del enemigo) silence; (la sed) quench; (el dolor) deaden || ref to go out; subside, calm down, fade away

apagón m blackout

apalabrar tr to bespeak; consider || ref to agree

apalabrear intr (SAm) to make an appointment

apalancar §73 tr to raise with a lever or crowbar

apalear tr to shovel; beat; pile up

apandar tr to steal

apantallar tr to dazzle, amaze; (elec) to shield, screen

apañar tr to grasp; pick up; steal; repair, mend; wrap up || ref to be handy

apañuscar §73 tr to crumple, rumple; steal; (CAm, Col, Ven) to jam, crowd

aparador m sideboard, buffet; showcase; workshop; (Mex) show window, store window

aparar tr to prepare; adorn; block; (las manos, la falda, el pañuelo, la capa) hold out

aparato m apparatus; ostentation, show; exaggeration; radio set; television set; telephone; airplane; camera; bandage, application; (theat) scenery, properties; **aparato auditivo** hearing aid; **aparato de relojería** clockwork; **aparatos sanitarios** bathroom fixtures; **ponerse al aparato** to go or to come to the phone

aparato•so -sa adj showy, pompous, ostentatious

aparcamiento m parking; parking space; **aparcamiento subterraneo** underground garage

aparcar §44 tr & intr to park

aparcería f partnership, sharecropping

aparce•ro -ra mf partner, sharecropper; (Arg) customer

aparear tr to pair, match; mate || ref to pair; mate

aparecer §22 intr & ref to appear; show up

aparecido m ghost, specter

aparejador m builder

aparejar tr to prepare; prime, size; harness

aparejo m preparation; harness; set, kit; priming; sizing; (mas) bond; **aparejos** tools, implements, equipment

aparentar tr to feign, pretend; look, look to be

aparente adj apparent, seeming; evident; right, proper

aparición f apparition

apariencia f appearance, aspect; sign, indication; **salvar las apariencias** to save face

aparqueamiento m parking

aparquear *tr & intr* to park

aparqueo *m* parking

aparragar §44 *ref* to crouch, squat; (CAm) to loll, sprawl

apartadero *m* siding, side track; turnout

aparta•do -da *adj* distant, remote; aloof; (*camino*) side, back; different ‖ *m* side room; post-office box; vocabulary entry; section

apartamento *m* apartment, apartment house

apartar *tr* to take aside; separate; push away; shunt; (*el ganado*) sort ‖ *ref* to separate; move away, keep away, stand aside; withdraw; get divorced; give up

aparte *adv* apart, aside; **aparte de** apart from ‖ *prep* apart from ‖ *m* (theat) aside

apasiona•do -da *adj* passionate; devoted, tender, loving; sore

apasionar *tr* to impassion, appeal deeply to; afflict ‖ *ref* to become impassioned; be stirred up; fall madly in love

apatía *f* apathy

apáti•co -ca *adj* apathetic

apatusco *m* ornament, finery

apdo. *abbr* **apartado**

apeadero *m* horse block; flag stop, wayside station; platform; temporary quarters

apear *tr* to help dismount, help down; bring down; remove; overcome; prop up ‖ *ref* to dismount, get off; back down; stop, put up

apechugar §44 *intr* to push with the chest; **apechugar con** to make the best of

apedazar §60 *tr* to mend, patch; cut or tear to pieces

apedrear *tr* to stone; stone to death; pit; speckle ‖ *intr* to hail ‖ *ref* to be damaged by hail; be pitted

apegar §44 *ref* to become attached, grow fond

apego *m* attachment, fondness

apelación *f* medical consultation; remedy, help; (law) appeal

apelante *adj* appellate

apelar *intr* to appeal, make an appeal; have recourse; refer

apelativo *m* (CAm) surname, family name

apeldar *tr* — **apeldarlas** (coll) to flee, run away

apelmazar §60 *tr* to squeeze, compress ‖ *ref* to cake

apelotonar *tr* to form into a ball ‖ *ref* to form a ball; curl up

apellidar *tr* to call, name; proclaim

apellido *m* name; surname, last name, family name; **apellido de soltera** maiden name

apenar *tr & ref* to grieve

apenas *adv* hardly, scarcely; **apenas si** hardly, scarcely ‖ *conj* no sooner, as soon as

apéndice *m* appendage; (anat) appendix

apendicitis *f* appendicitis

apercancar §73 *ref* (Chile) to get moldy, mildew

apercibir *tr* to prepare; provide; warn; perceive; collect ‖ *ref* to get ready; be provided; **apercibirse de** to notice

apergaminar *ref* to dry up, become yellow and wrinkled

aperitivo *m* appetizer

aperla•do -da *adj* pearly

apero *m* tools, equipment, outfit; riding gear

aperrear *tr* to set the dogs on; harass, plague, pester

apersogar §44 *tr* to tether

apersona•do -da *adj* — **bien apersonado** presentable; **mal apersonado** unpresentable

apersonar *ref* to appear in person; have an interview

apertura *f* opening

apesadumbrar or **apesarar** *tr & ref* to grieve

apestar *tr* to infect with the plague; corrupt; sicken, nauseate; infest ‖ *intr* to stink ‖ *ref* to be infected with the plague

apesto•so -sa *adj* stinking, foul-smelling; pestilent; sickening

apetecer §22 *tr* to hunger for, thirst for, crave

apetecible *adj* desirable, tempting

apetencia *f* hunger, appetite, craving

apetito *m* appetite

apetito•so -sa *adj* tasty; tempting; gourmand

ápex *m* apex

apiadar *tr* to move to pity; take pity on ‖ *ref* to have pity

ápice *m* apex; bit, whit; crux; **estar en los ápices de** to be up in

apilar *tr & ref* to pile, pile up

apimpollar *ref* to sprout, put forth shoots

apiñar *tr & ref* to crowd, jam

apio *m* celery

apisonadora *f* road roller

apisonar *tr* to tamp; roll

aplacar §73 *tr* to placate, appease, pacify; (*la sed*) to quench

aplanacalles *m* (SAm) idler; lazy person

aplanar *tr* to smooth, make even; to astonish; **aplanar las calles** to loaf, bum around ‖ *ref* to collapse; become discouraged

aplanchar *tr* to iron

aplanetizar §60 *intr* to land on another planet

aplastar *tr* to flatten, crush, smash; dumbfound

aplaudida *f* applause

aplaudir *tr & intr* to applaud

aplauso *m* applause; **aplausos** applause

aplazada *f* or **aplazamiento** *m* delay; procrastination

aplazar §60 *tr* to postpone; convene; summon

aplicación *f* appliance, application; diligence

aplica•do -da *adj* industrious, studious; applied

aplicar §73 *tr* to apply; attribute ‖ *ref* to apply; apply oneself

aplomar *tr* to plumb; make straight or vertical ‖ *intr* to be vertical ‖ *ref* to collapse; (Chile) to be embarrassed; (Mex) to be slow, be backward

aplomo *m* aplomb, poise, self-possession; gravity

apoca•do -da *adj* diffident, timid, irresolute; humble, lowly

apocar §73 *tr* to cramp, contract; narrow; humble, belittle

apodar *tr* to nickname; make fun of
apodera•do -da *adj* empowered, authorized
‖ *m* proxy; attorney
apoderamiento *m* authorization; power of
attorney
apoderar *tr* to empower, authorize ‖ *ref* —
apoderarse de to seize, grasp; take possession of
apodo *m* nickname
apofanía *f* ablaut
apogeo *m* apogee; (fig) height, apogee
apolilla•do -da *adj* moth-eaten, mothy
apolilladura *f* moth hole
apolillar *tr* (*la polilla, p.ej., las ropas*) to eat
‖ *ref* to become moth-eaten
apoliti•co -ca *adj* apolitical, nonpolitical
apología *f* eulogy
apoltronar *ref* to loaf around; loll, sprawl
apontizaje *m* deck-landing
apontizar §60 *intr* to deck-land
apoplejía *f* apoplexy
apopléti•co -ca *adj* & *mf* apoplectic
aporcar §73 *tr* (*las hortalizas*) to hill
aporrear *tr* to beat, club, cudgel; annoy ‖ *ref*
to drudge, slave
aportación *f* contribution; dowry
aportar *tr* to contribute; bring; lead; (*como
dote*) bring ‖ *intr* to show up; reach port
aporte *m* contribution
aposentar *tr* to put up, lodge ‖ *ref* to take
lodging
aposento *m* lodging; room; inn
apostadero *m* stand, post; naval station
apostar *tr* to post, station ‖ §61 *tr* to bet,
wager ‖ *intr* to bet; compete
apostilla *f* note, comment
apóstol *m* apostle
apóstrofe *m* & *f* apostrophe (*words addressed
to absent person*)
apóstrofo *m* apostrophe (*written sign*)
apostura *f* neatness, spruceness; bearing,
carriage
apoyabra•zos *m* (*pl* -zos) armrest
apoyali•bros *m* (*pl* -bros) book end
apoyar *tr* to support, hold up; lean, rest;
abet, back ‖ *intr* & *ref* to lean, rest, be
supported
apoyatura *f* (mus) grace note
apoyo *m* support, prop; backing, approval
apreciable *adj* appreciable; estimable
apreciación *f* appraisal
apreciar *tr* to appreciate; appraise; esteem
aprecio *m* appreciation, esteem
aprehender *tr* to apprehend, catch; think,
conceive
aprehensión *f* apprehension
aprehensi•vo -va *adj* apprehensive
aprehensor *m* captor
apremiar *tr* to press, urge; compel, force;
hurry; harass; (*a un deudor*) dun ‖ *intr* to
be urgent
apremio *m* pressure; urgency; compulsion;
oppression; surtax for late payment; (*demanda de pago*)
aprender *tr* & *intr* to learn; aprender haciendo to learn by doing

apren•diz -diza *mf* apprentice; aprendiz de
imprenta printer's devil
aprendizaje *m* apprenticeship; pagar el
aprendizaje to pay for one's inexperience
aprensar *tr* to press; oppress
aprensión *f* apprehension; misgiving, prejudice
aprensi•vo -va *adj* apprehensive
apresar *tr* to grasp, seize; capture
aprestador *m* primer
aprestar *tr* to prepare; (*tejidos*) process;
prime; size ‖ *ref* to get ready
apresto *m* preparation; equipment; priming;
sizing
apresurar *tr* & *ref* to hurry, hasten
apretadera *f* strap, rope; apretaderas pressure
apreta•do -da *adj* compact, tight; close, intimate; dense, thick; difficult, dangerous;
mean, stingy; estar muy apretado to be in
a bad way
apretar §2 *tr* to tighten; squeeze; pinch; hug;
harass, importune; afflict, beset; (*un botón*)
press; (*los puños*) clench; (*los dientes*) grit;
(*la mano*) shake ‖ *intr* to pinch; insist; get
worse; push hard, press forward; apretar a
correr to start running; apretar con to
close in on ‖ *ref* to grieve, be distressed;
crowd
apretón *m* pressure, squeeze; struggle; dash,
run; apretón de manos handshake
apretura *f* crush, jam; tightness; fix, trouble;
need, want
aprietarropa *m* clothespin
¡aprieta! *interj* (coll) baloney!
aprieto *m* crush, jam; fix
aprisa *adv* fast, quickly
aprisco *m* sheepfold
aprisionar *tr* to imprison; bind, tie; shackle
aprobación *f* approbation, approval; pass,
passing grade
aproba•do -da *adj* excellent ‖ *m* pass
aprobar §61 *tr* & *intr* to approve; pass
aprontar *tr* to hand over without delay;
expedite
apropia•do -da *adj* appropriate, fitting,
proper
apropiar *tr* to hand over; fit, adapt ‖ *ref* to
appropriate; preëmpt
aprovechable *adj* available, usable
aprovecha•do -da *adj* thrifty; stingy; diligent; well-spent ‖ *mf* opportunist
aprovechar *tr* to make good use of, take
advantage of; (*una caída de agua*) harness
‖ *intr* to be useful; progress, improve ‖
ref — aprovecharse de to avail oneself of,
take advantage of
aprovisionar *tr* to provision, supply, furnish
aproxima•do -da *adj* approximate, rough
aproximar *tr* to bring near; approximate ‖
ref to come near; approximate
aptitud *f* aptitude; suitability
ap•to -ta *adj* apt; suitable
apuesta *f* bet, wager
apues•to -ta *adj* neat, spruce, elegant ‖ *f* see
apuesta
apulgarar *ref* to become mildewed

apuntador *m* (theat) prompter
apuntalar *tr* to prop up, underpin
apuntar *tr* to point; point at; aim; aim at; take note of; sharpen; stitch, darn, patch; correct; prompt; stake, to put up; (theat) to prompt ‖ *intr* to begin to appear; dawn ‖ *ref* (*el vino*) to begin to turn sour; register; get tipsy
apunte *m* note; rough sketch; stake; rogue, rascal; (theat) cue
apuñalar *tr* & *intr* to stab
apuñear *tr* to punch
apura•do -da *adj* needy, hard up; difficult, dangerous; hurried, rushed
apurar *tr* to purify, refine; clear up, verify; finish; drain, use up, exhaust; hurry, press; annoy ‖ *ref* to worry, grieve; exert oneself, strive
apuro *m* need, want; grief, sorrow; haste, urgency; **apuros** financial embarrassment
aquejar *tr* to grieve, afflict
aquel, aquella *adj dem* (*pl* **aquellos, aquellas**) that, that . . . yonder
aquél, aquélla *pron dem* (*pl* **aquéllos, aquéllas**) that; that one, that one yonder; the one; the former ‖ *m* charm, appeal
aquelarre *m* witches' Sabbath
aquello *pron dem* that; that thing, that matter
aquende *adv* on this side ‖ *prep* on this side of
aquerenciar *ref* to become fond or attached
aquí *adv* here; **aquí dentro** in here; **de aquí en adelante** from now on; **por aquí** this way
aquiescencia *f* acquiescence
aquietar *tr* to quiet, calm
aquilatar *tr* to assay; check; refine
Aquiles *m* Achilles
aquilón *m* north wind
ara *f* altar; altar slab; **en aras de** for the sake of
árabe *adj* Arab, Arabian; (archit) Moresque ‖ *mf* Arab, Arabian ‖ *m* (*idioma*) Arabic **Arabia, la** Arabia
arábi•go -ga *adj* Arabian, Arabic ‖ *m* (*idioma*) Arabic; **estar en arábigo** (coll) to be Greek
arabismo *m* (*estudio, voz, rasgo*) Arabism
aracanga *f* macaw
arado *m* plow
Aragón *m* Aragon
arago•nés -nesa *adj* & *mf* Aragonese
arancel *m* tariff
arancelar *tr* (CAm) to pay
arancela•rio -ria *adj* tariff, customs
arándano *m* whortleberry; **arándano agrio** cranberry
arandela *f* bobèche; (mach) washer
araña *f* spider; chandelier
arañar *tr* to scratch; scrape; scrape together
arañazo *m* scratch
araño *m* scratching
aráquida *f* peanut
arar *tr* to plow
arbitraje *m* arbitration
arbitrar *tr* & *intr* to arbitrate; referee; umpire
arbitra•rio -ria *adj* arbitrary

arbitrio *m* free will; means, ways; **arbitrios** excise taxes
arbitrista *mf* wild-eyed dreamer
árbi•tro -tra *mf* arbiter; referee ‖ *m* umpire
árbol *m* tree; axle, shaft; **árbol del caucho** rubber plant; **árbol de levas** camshaft; **árbol de mando** drive shaft; **árbol de Navidad** Christmas tree; **árbol motor** drive shaft
arbola•do -da *adj* wooded; (*mar*) high ‖ *m* woodland
arboleda *f* grove
arbollón *m* sewer, drain
arbotante *m* flying buttress
arbusto *m* shrub
arca *f* chest, coffer; tank; ark; **arca de agua** water tower; **arca de la alianza** ark of the covenant; **arca de Noé** ark, Noah's ark
arcada *f* arcade; archway; stroke of bow; **arcadas** retching
arcai•co -ca *adj* archaic
arcaísmo *m* archaism
arcaizante *adj* obsolescent
arcángel *m* archangel
arca•no -na *adj* & *m* secret
arcar §73 *tr* to arch
arce *m* maple tree
arcilla *f* clay; **arcilla figulina** potter's clay
arco *m* arch; (*de cuna o mecedor*) rocker; (elec, geom) arc; (mus) bow; **arco iris** rainbow; **arco triunfal** triumphal arch; memorial arch
arcón *m* large chest; bin, bunker
archiduque *m* archduke
archienemigo *m* archenemy
archipiélago *m* archipelago; (coll) maze, entanglement ‖ **Archipiélago** *m* Aegean Sea
archiva•dor -dora *mf* file clerk ‖ *m* filing cabinet; letter file
archivar *tr* to file; file away; hide away
archivero *m* city clerk
archivo *m* archives; files; filing; (Col) office
ardentía *f* heartburn; (*en las olas de la mar*) phosphorescence
arder *tr* to burn ‖ *intr* to burn; blaze; **estar que arde** to be coming to a head ‖ *ref* to burn up
ardid *m* artifice, trick, wile
ardi•do -da *adj* burnt-up; bold, intrepid; angry
ardiendo *adj invar* burning
ardiente *adj* ardent; fiery, passionate; burning, hot
ardilla *f* squirrel; **ardilla de tierra** gopher; **ardilla ladradora** prairie dog; **ardilla listada** chipmunk
ardillón *m* gopher
ardite *m* old Spanish coin of little value; **no me importa un ardite** (coll) I don't care a hang; **no valer un ardite** to be not worth a straw
ardor *m* ardor; eagerness, fervor, zeal; vehemence; courage, dash
ardoro•so -sa *adj* fiery, enthusiastic; balky, restive
ar•duo -dua *adj* arduous, difficult

área *f* area; small plot; **área de descansar** rest area; **área de servicio** service area

arena *f* sand; grit; arena; **arena movediza** quicksand; **arenas** arena; (pathol) stones

arenal *m* sandy place; quicksand

arenga *f* harangue

arengar *tr* & *intr* to harangue

arenis•co -ca *adj* sandy, gritty; sand ‖ *f* sandstone

areno•so -sa *adj* sandy

arenque *m* herring

areómetro *m* hydrometer

arepa *f* corn griddle cake

arete *m* eardrop, earring

arfada *f* (naut) pitching

arfar *intr* (naut) to pitch

argadijo *m* or **argadillo** *m* bobbin, reel; restless fellow

argado *m* prank, trick, artifice

argamasa *f* mortar

argamasar *tr* to mortar, plaster; (*los materiales de construcción*) mix

árgana *f* (mach) crane; **árganas** panniers

Argel *f* Algiers

Argelia *f* Algeria

argeli•no -na *adj* & *mf* Algerian

argentar *tr* to silver

argenti•no -na *adj* & *mf* Argentine, Argentinean ‖ **la Argentina** Argentina, the Argentine

argolla *f* large iron ring; (*que se pone en la nariz a un animal*) ring; engagement ring

argonauta *m* Argonaut

argucia *f* subtlety; trick

argüir §6 *tr* to argue, argue for; prove; accuse ‖ *ref* to argue, dispute

argumenta•dor -dora *adj* argumentative ‖ *mf* arguer

argumentar *tr* to argue for; prove ‖ *intr* & *ref* to argue, dispute

argumento *m* argument

aria *f* (mus) aria

aridez *f* aridity, dryness

ári•do -da *adj* arid; (*aburrido, falto de interés*) dry

Aries *m* Aries

ariete *m* battering ram; **ariete hidráulico** hydraulic ram

arimez *m* projection

a•rio -ria *adj* & *mf* Aryan ‖ *f* see **aria**

aris•co -ca *adj* churlish, surly, evasive; (*caballo*) vicious

arista *f* edge; (*intersección de dos planos*) ridge; (*del grano de trigo*) beard; **arista de encuentro** (archit) groin

aristocracia *f* aristocracy

aristócrata *mf* aristocrat

aristocráti•co -ca *adj* aristocratic

Aristóteles *m* Aristotle

aristotéli•co -ca *adj* & *mf* Aristotelian

aritméti•co -ca *adj* arithmetical ‖ *mf* arithmetician ‖ *f* arithmetic

arlequín *m* harlequin

arma *f* arm, weapon; **alzarse en armas** to rise up, rebel; **arma blanca** steel blade; **arma corta** pistol; **arma de fuego** firearm;

jugar a las armas to fence; **sobre las armas** under arms

armada *f* fleet, armada; navy

armadía *f* raft, float

armadijo *m* trap, snare

arma•do -da *adj* armed; (*hormigón*) reinforced ‖ *f* see **armada**

arma•dor -dora *mf* assembler ‖ *m* recruiter of fishermen and whalers

armadura *f* armor; framework; skeleton; (elec) armature; (*de imán*) keeper

armamentismo *m* military preparedness

armamentis•to -ta *adj* militarist, arms ‖ *mf* arms dealer

armamento *m* armament

armar *tr* to arm; (*un arma*) load; (*una bayoneta*) fix; mount, assemble; build; equip; (*el hormigón*) reinforce; (*una nave*) fit out; (*caballero*) dub; start, stir up; **armarla** to start a row ‖ *ref* to arm oneself; get ready; balk

armario *m* closet, wardrobe; **armario botiquín** medicine cabinet; **armario de luna** wardrobe with mirror; **armario frigorífico** refrigerator

armatoste *m* hulk

armazón *f* frame; assemblage; skeleton

armella *f* screw eye, eyebolt

arme•nio -nia *adj* & *mf* Armenian ‖ **Armenia** *f* Armenia

armería *f* arms shop; arms museum; arms

armero *m* gunsmith; (*para las armas*) rack

armiño *m* ermine

armisticio *m* armistice

armonía *f* harmony

armóni•co -ca *adj* & *m* harmonic ‖ *f* harmonica; **armónica de boca** mouth organ

armonio•so -sa *adj* harmonious

armonizar §60 *tr* & *intr* to harmonize

arnés *m* armor, coat of mail; harness; **arneses** harness, trappings; outfit, equipment; accessories

aro *m* hoop; rim; **aro de émbolo** piston ring

aroma *m* aroma, fragrance

aromáti•co -ca *adj* aromatic

arpa *f* harp

arpar *tr* to claw, scratch; tear, rend

arpegio *m* arpeggio

arpeo *m* grappling iron

arpía *f* harpy; shrew; jade

arpillera *f* burlap, sackcloth

arpista *mf* harpist

arpón *m* harpoon

arponear *tr* & *intr* to harpoon

arqueada *f* (mus) bow

arquear *tr* to arch; (*la lana*) beat; (*una nave*) gauge; to audit ‖ *intr* to retch ‖ *ref* to bow

arqueología *f* archeology

arquería *f* arcade

arquero *m* archer, bowman; goalkeeper, goalie

arquitecto *m* architect

arquitectóni•co -ca *adj* architectural

arquitectura *f* architecture

arrabal *m* suburb; **arrabales** outskirts

arracada *f* earring with pendant

arracimar *ref* to cluster, bunch

ap
ar

arraiga•do -da *adj* deep-rooted; property-owning, landed

arraigar §44 *tr* to establish, strengthen ‖ *intr* to take root ‖ *ref* to take root; become settled

arraigo *m* taking root; stability; property, real estate

arramblar *tr* to cover with sand or gravel; sweep away

arrancadero *m* starting point

arrancar §73 *tr* to root up, pull out, pull up; snatch, wrest; (*lágrimas*) draw forth ‖ *intr* to start; set sail; leave; originate

arranque *m* pull; fit, impulse; jerk, sudden start; sally, outburst; (aut) start, starter; **arranque a mano** (aut) hand cranking; **arranque automático** (aut) self-starter

arrapiezo *m* rag, tatter; whippersnapper

arras *fpl* earnest money, pledge; dowry

arrasar *tr* to level; wreck, demolish; fill to the brim ‖ *intr* to clear up ‖ *ref* to clear up; fill up

arrastra•do -da *adj* mean, crooked ‖ *mf* wretch, crook

arrastrar *tr* to drag, drag along; drag down; impel ‖ *intr* to drag, trail; crawl, creep ‖ *ref* to drag, trail; crawl, creep; drag on; cringe

arrastre *m* drag; crawl; washout; influence; haulage; (*influencia política y social*) (Cuba, Mex) drag

arrayán *m* myrtle

arre *interj* gee!, get up!

arreador *m* muleteer; (SAm) whip

arrear *tr* to drive ‖ *intr* to hurry ‖ *ref* to lose all one's money

arrebata•do -da *adj* rash, reckless; (*color del rostro*) flushed, ruddy

arrebatar *tr* to snatch; carry away; attract; move, stir ‖ *ref* to be carried away, be overcome

arrebatiña *f* scuffle, scramble; **andar a la arrebatiña** to scramble

arrebato *m* rage, fury; ecstasy, rapture

arrebol *m* (*de las nubes*) red; (*de las mejillas*) rosiness; (*afeite*) rouge; **arreboles** red clouds

arrebozar §60 *tr* to muffle ‖ *ref* to muffle one's face

arrebujar *tr* to jumble together; wrap ‖ *ref* to wrap oneself up

arreciar *intr & ref* to grow worse; become more violent; grow stronger

arrecife *m* stone-paved road; dike; reef; **arrecife de coral** coral reef

arredrar *tr* to drive back; frighten ‖ *ref* to draw back; shrink; be frightened

arregazar §60 *tr* to tuck up

arreglar *tr* to adjust, regulate, settle; arrange; fix, repair ‖ *ref* to adjust, settle; arrange; conform; **arreglárselas** to manage, make out

arreglo *m* adjustment, regulation; settlement; arrangement; order, rule; agreement; **con arreglo a** in accordance with

arregostar *ref* to take a liking

arregosto *m* liking, taste

arrellanar *ref* to loll, sprawl; like one's work

arremangar §44 *tr* (*las mangas*) to turn up; (*la ropa*) to tuck up ‖ *ref* to turn up one's sleeves; tuck up one's dress; take a firm stand

arremeter *tr* to attack, assail; (*un caballo*) to spur ‖ *intr* to attack; be offensive to look at; **arremeter contra** to light into, sail into

arremetida *f* attack; (*de un caballo*) sudden start; push; short, wild run

arremolinar *ref* to crowd, mill around; whirl

arrendajo *m* (orn) jay; mimic

arrendar §2 *tr* to rent; (*una caballería*) tie ‖ *ref* to rent, be rented

arreo *m* adornment; (SAm) drove; **arreos** harness, trappings

arrepenti•do -da *adj* repentant ‖ *mf* penitent

arrepentimiento *m* repentance

arrepentir §68 *ref* to repent, be repentant; **arrepentirse de** (*p.ej., un pecado*) to repent

arrequives *mpl* finery; attendant circumstances

arresta•do -da *adj* bold, daring

arrestar *tr* to arrest ‖ *ref* to rush boldly

arresto *m* arrest; boldness, daring; **bajo arresto** under arrest

arrezagar §44 *tr* to tuck up

arriada *f* flood

arriar §77 *tr* to flood; (naut) to lower, strike; slacken ‖ *ref* to be flooded

arriba *adv* up, upward; above; upstairs; uptown; on top; **arriba de** up; **de arriba abajo** from top to bottom; from beginning to end; superciliously; **más arriba** farther up; **río arriba** upstream ‖ *interj* up with . . . !

arribada *f* arrival (*by sea*); **de arribada** (naut) emergency

arribar *intr* to put into port; arrive; to recover, make a comeback; (naut) to fall off to leeward

arribista *adj & mf* parvenu, upstart

arribo *m* arrival

arricete *m* shoal, bar

arriendo *m* rent, rental; lease

arriero *m* muleteer

arriesga•do -da *adj* dangerous, risky; bold, daring

arriesgar §44 *tr* to risk, jeopardize ‖ *ref* to take a risk

arriesgo *m* (SAm) risk; hazard

arrimadillo *m* wainscot

arrimar *tr* to bring close, move up; (*un golpe*) give; abandon, neglect; give up; get rid of ‖ *ref* to come close, move up; snuggle up; lean; depend

arrinconar *tr* to corner; put aside; abandon, neglect; get rid of ‖ *ref* to live in seclusion

arrisca•do -da *adj* enterprising; brisk, spirited; craggy

arriscar §73 *tr* to risk ‖ *ref* to take a risk; (*las reses*) plunge over a cliff

arrisco *m* risk

arritmia *f* arrhythmia

arrivista *adj & mf* parvenu, upstart

arrizar §60 *tr* to reef

arroba *f* Spanish weight of about 25 pounds
arrobar *tr* to entrance, enrapture ‖ *ref* to be enraptured
arrobo *m* ecstasy, rapture
arroce•ro -ra *adj* rice ‖ *mf* rice grower; rice merchant
arrocinar *tr* to bestialize ‖ *ref* to become bestialized; fall madly in love
arrodajar *ref* (CAm) to squat down with one's legs crossed
arrodillar *ref* to kneel, kneel down
arrogancia *f* arrogance
arrogante *adj* arrogant
arrogar §44 *tr* to adopt ‖ *ref* to arrogate to oneself
arrojadi•zo -za *adj* for throwing, projectile
arroja•do -da *adj* bold, fearless, rash
arrojalla•mas *m* (*pl* **-mas**) flame thrower
arrojar *tr* to throw, hurl; emit; bring forth; yield ‖ *ref* to rush, rush forward
arrojo *m* boldness, fearlessness, rashness
arrollado *m* (elec) coil
arrolla•dor -dora *adj* sweeping, devastating
arrollamiento *m* winding
arrollar *tr* to roll; roll up; wind, coil; (*al enemigo*) rout; dumbfound; knock down, run over
arropar *tr* to wrap, wrap up ‖ *ref* to bundle up
arrope *m* grape syrup; honey syrup
arropía *f* taffy
arrostrar *tr* to face; to like ‖ *intr* —**arrostrar con** or **por** to face, resist ‖ *ref* to rush into the fight
arroyada *f* gully; flood, freshet
arroyo *m* stream, brook; gutter; street; (*de lágrimas, sangre, etc.*) stream
arroz *m* rice
arrufar *tr* to sic, incite
arruga *f* wrinkle; crease, rumple
arrugar §44 *tr* to wrinkle; crease, rumple; (*la frente*) to knit; (Cuba, Mex) to bother, annoy ‖ *ref* to wrinkle; crease, rumple; shrink, shrivel; (Cuba, Mex) to lose courage, lose heart
arruinar *tr* to ruin ‖ *ref* to go to ruin
arrullar *tr* to sing to sleep, lull to sleep; to court, woo ‖ *intr* to coo ‖ *ref* to coo; (*las palomas*) to bill
arrullo *m* billing and cooing; lullaby
arrumaje *m* stowage; ballast
arrumar *tr* to stow ‖ *ref* to become overcast
arrumbar *tr* to cast aside, neglect; silence; (*una costa*) determine the lay of ‖ *intr* (naut) to take bearings ‖ *ref* to get seasick; (naut) to take bearings
arsenal *m* arsenal, armory; dockyard, shipyard
arsénico *m* arsenic
art. *abbr* **artículo**
arte *m & f* art; trick; knack; fishing gear; **artes y oficios** arts and crafts; **bellas artes** fine arts; **no tener arte ni parte en** to have nothing to do with
artefacto *m* artifact; appliance, device, contrivance; **artefactos de alumbrado** light-

ing fixtures; **artefactos sanitarios** bathroom fixtures
artemisa *f* sagebrush
arteria *f* artery
artería *f* craftiness, cunning
arte•ro -ra *adj* crafty, cunning, sly
artesa *f* trough; Indian canoe
artesanía *f* craftsmanship
artesa•no -na *mf* artisan, craftsman ‖ *f* craftswoman
artesón *m* kitchen tub; coffer, caisson (*in ceiling*)
árti•co -ca *adj* arctic
articulación *f* articulation; (*de huesos*) joint; **articulación universal** universal joint
articular *tr* to articulate
articulista *mf* feature writer
artículo *m* article; item; joint; (*en un diccionario*) entry; **artículo de fondo** leader, editorial; **artículos de consumo** consumers' goods; **artículos de deporte** sporting goods; **artículos de primera necesidad** basic commodities; **artículos para caballeros** men's furnishings
artífice *mf* artificer; craftsman
artificial *adj* artificial
artificio *m* artifice; workmanship; appliance, device; cunning; trick, ruse
artificio•so -sa *adj* ingenious, skillful; cunning, scheming, deceptive
artilugio *m* contraption, jigger
artillería *f* artillery
artillero *m* artilleryman, gunner
artimaña *f* trap; trick, cunning
artista *mf* artist
artísti•co -ca *adj* artistic
artolas *fpl* mule chair, cacolet
artríti•co -ca *adj & mf* arthritic
artritis *f* arthritis
arúspice *m* diviner, soothsayer
arveja *f* vetch, tare; (Chile) pea
arzobispo *m* archbishop
arzón *m* saddletree; **arzón delantero** saddlebow; **arzón trasero** cantle
as *m* ace; **as de fútbol** football star; **as de la pantalla** movie star; **as del volante** speed king
asa *f* handle; juice; **en asas** with arms akimbo
asa•do -da *adj* roasted; **bien asado** well done; **poco asado** rare ‖ *m* roast
asador *m* spit
asadura *f* entrails
asalaria•do -da *mf* wage earner
asaltar *tr* to assail, assault, storm; overtake, overcome
asalto *m* assault, attack; (box) round; (mil) storm; **tomar por asalto** to take by storm
asamblea *f* assembly
asar *tr* to roast ‖ *ref* to be burning up
asbesto *m* asbestos
ascendencia *f* ancestry
ascendente *adj* ascending; up
ascender §51 *tr* to promote ‖ *intr* to ascend, go up; be promoted; **ascender a** to amount to
ascendiente *adj* ascending; up ‖ *mf* ancestor ‖ *m* ascendancy, upper hand

ascensión *f* ascension, ascent
ascenso *m* ascent; promotion
ascensor *m* elevator; freight elevator
ascensorista *mf* elevator operator
asceta *mf* ascetic
ascéti•co -ca *adj* ascetic
asco *m* disgust, nausea, loathing; **dar asco** to turn the stomach; **estar hecho un asco** to be filthy; **hacer ascos de** to turn one's nose up at; **ser un asco** to be contemptible; be worthless
ascua *f* ember, live coal; **estar sobre ascuas** to be on needles and pins ‖ **ascuas** *interj* ouch!
asea•do -da *adj* clean, neat, tidy
asear *tr* & *ref* to clean up, tidy up; make one's toilet
asechamiento *m* or **asechanza** *f* snare, trap
asechar *tr* to set a trap for
asediar *tr* to besiege; harass
asedio *m* siege
asegundar *tr* to repeat right away
asegurable *adj* insurable
aseguración *f* insurance policy
asegura•dor -dora *mf* insurer, underwriter
asegurar *tr* to fasten, secure; assure; assert; seize; imprison; (*garantizar por un precio contra determinado accidente o pérdida*) insure ‖ *ref* to make sure; take out insurance
asemejar *tr* to make like; compare; resemble ‖ *ref* to be similar
asenso *m* assent; **dar asenso a** to believe
asentada *f* sitting; **de una asentada** at one sitting
asentaderas *fpl* (coll) buttocks
asentadillas — a asentadillas sidesaddle
asenta•do -da *adj* sedate; stable ‖ *f* see **asentada**
asentador *m* strap, razor strop
asentar §2 *tr* to seat; place; establish; tamp down, level; hone, sharpen; note down; (*un golpe*) impart; (*en la mente de uno*) impress; affirm; suppose ‖ *intr* to be becoming ‖ *ref* to sit down; be established, establish oneself; settle
asentimiento *m* assent
asentir §68 *intr* to assent
aseo *m* cleanliness, neatness, tidiness; care; toilet
asépti•co -ca *adj* aseptic
aseptizar §60 *tr* to purify, make aseptic
asequible *adj* accessible, obtainable
aserción *f* assertion
aserradero *m* sawmill
aserra•dor -dora *mf* sawyer; (coll) fiddler ‖ *f* power saw
aserraduras *fpl* sawdust
aserrar §2 *tr* to saw
aserrín *m* sawdust
aserruchar *tr* (SAm) to saw
aserto *m* assertion
asesinar *tr* to assassinate, murder
asesinato *m* assassination, murder
asesi•no -na *adj* murderous ‖ *mf* assassin, murderer

asesorar *tr* to advise ‖ *ref* to seek advice; get advice
asestar *tr* to aim; shoot; (*un golpe*) deal
aseveración *f* assertion, declaration
aseverar *tr* to assert, declare
asfaltar *tr* to asphalt
asfalto *m* asphalt
asfixia *f* asphyxiation
asfixiar *tr* to asphyxiate
así *adv* so, thus; **así . . . como** both . . . and; **así como** as soon as; as well as; **así que** as soon as; with the result that; **así y todo** even so, anyhow; **por decirlo así** so to speak; **y así sucesivamente** and so on
Asia *f* Asia; **el Asia Menor** Asia Minor
asiáti•co -ca *adj* & *mf* Asian, Asiatic
asidero *m* handle; occasion, pretext
asi•duo -dua *adj* assiduous; frequent, persistent
asiento *m* seat; site; (*de un edificio*) settling; (*de una botella, una silla, etc.*) bottom; sediment; list, roll; wisdom, maturity; **asiento abatible** reclining seat; **asiento de rejilla** cane seat; **asiento lanzable** (aer) ejection seat; **asientos** buttocks; **planchar el asiento** to be a wallflower; **tome Vd. asiento** have a seat
asignación *f* assignment; salary; allowance
asignar *tr* to assign
asignatorio *m* heir, inheritor
asignatura *f* course, subject
asila•do -da *mf* inmate
asilar *tr* to shelter; place in an asylum; silo ‖ *ref* to take refuge; be placed in an asylum
asilo *m* asylum; shelter, refuge; (*para menesterosos*) home; **asilo de huérfanos** orphan asylum; **asilo de locos** insane asylum; **asilo de pobres** poorhouse
asilla *f* fastener; collarbone; **asillas** shoulder pole
asimetría *f* asymmetry
asimilar *tr* to compare; take in ‖ *intr* to be alike ‖ *ref* to assimilate; **asimilarse a** to resemble
asimismo *adv* also, likewise
asir §7 *tr* to grasp, seize ‖ *intr* to take root ‖ *ref* to take hold; fight, grapple; **asirse a** or **de** to cling to
Asiria *f* Assyria
asi•rio -ria *adj* & *mf* Assyrian
asistencia *f* attendance; assistance; reward; audience, persons present; welfare, social work; (Mex) sitting room, parlor; **asistencias** allowance, support
asistenta *f* charwoman, cleaning woman
asistente *adj* attendant; present ‖ *m* assistant, helper; bystander, spectator, person present; (mil) orderly
asistir *tr* to assist, help; attend; serve, wait on ‖ *intr* to be present; **asistir a** to be present at, attend
asma *f* asthma
asna *f* she-ass, jenny ass; **asnas** rafters
asnal *adj* donkey; brutish
asno *m* ass, donkey, jackass
asociación *f* association

asocia•do -da *adj* associated; associate ‖ *mf* associate, partner

asociar *tr* to associate; take as partner ‖ *ref* to become associated; become a partner; become partners

asolamiento *m* razing, destruction

asolar *tr* to parch, burn ‖ *ref* to become parched ‖ §61 *tr* to raze, destroy

asoleada *f* or **asoleadura** *f* (SAm) sunstroke

asolear *tr* to sun ‖ *ref* to bask; get sunburned

asomar *tr* (*p.ej., la cabeza*) to show, stick out ‖ *intr* to begin to show or appear; show ‖ *ref* to show, appear; stick out; get tipsy

asombradi•zo -za *adj* timid, shy

asombrar *tr* to shade; (*un color*) darken; frighten; astonish, amaze ‖ *ref* to be frightened; be astonished, amazed

asombro *m* fright; astonishment

asombro•so -sa *adj* astonishing, amazing

asomo *m* mark, token, sign; appearance; **ni por asomo** nothing of the kind, not by a long shot

asordar *tr* to deafen

aspa *f* X-shaped figure; reel; (*de molino de viento*) wheel, vane; propeller blade

aspar *tr* to reel; crucify; annoy, harass ‖ *ref* to writhe; take great pains

aspaviento *m* fuss, excitement

aspecto *m* aspect

aspereza *f* harshness; roughness; bitterness, sourness; gruffness

asperjar *tr* to sprinkle; sprinkle with holy water

áspe•ro -ra *adj* harsh; rough; bitter; gruff

áspid *m* asp

aspirador *m* vacuum cleaner; **aspirador de gasolina** (aut) vacuum tank

aspirante *m* applicant, candidate; **aspirante a cabo** private first class; **aspirante de marina** midshipman

aspirar *tr* to suck in, draw in; inhale ‖ *intr* to aspire; inhale, breathe in

aspirina *f* aspirin

asquear *tr* to loathe ‖ *ref* to be nauseated

asquero•so -sa *adj* disgusting, loathsome; nauseating; squeamish

asta *f* spear; shaft; flagpole, staff, mast; antler; (*de toro*) horn; **a media asta** at half-mast; **dejar en las astas del toro** to leave high and dry

asta•do -da *adj* horned ‖ *m* bull

ástato *m* astatine

aster *m* aster

asterisco *m* asterisk

astil *m* handle; shaft

astilla *f* chip, splinter

astillar *tr* & *ref* to chip, splinter

Astillejos *mpl* (astr) Castor and Pollux

astillero *m* dockyard, shipyard

astro *m* star, heavenly body; (fig) star, leading light

astrofísica *f* astrophysics

astrología *f* astrology

astronauta *m* astronaut

astronáuti•co -ca *adj* astronautic ‖ *f* astronautics

astronave *f* spaceship; **astronave tripulada** manned spaceship

astronavegación *f* space travel

astronomía *f* astronomy

astronómi•co -ca *adj* astronomic(al)

astróno•mo -ma *mf* astronomer

astro•so -sa *adj* ill-fated; vile, contemptible; ragged, shabby

astucia *f* cunning, craftiness; trick

asturia•no -na *adj* & *mf* Asturian

astu•to -ta *adj* astute, cunning; tricky

asueto *m* day off; leisure

asumir *tr* to assume, take on

asunción *f* assumption

asunto *m* subject, matter; affair, business; theme; **asuntos internacionales** world affairs

asurar *tr* to burn; parch; harass, worry

asurcar §73 *tr* to furrow, plow

asustadi•zo -za *adj* scary, skittish

asustar *tr* to scare, frighten

atabal *m* kettledrum; timbrel

ataca•do -da *adj* irresolute, undecided; mean, stingy

atacar §73 *tr* to attack; attach, fasten; pack, jam; (*un barreno*) tamp; corner, contradict ‖ *intr* to attack

ata•do -da *adj* timid, shy; weak, irresolute; insignificant; cramped ‖ *m* pack, bundle, roll

ataguía *f* cofferdam

atajar *tr* to stop, intercept, interrupt; to partition off ‖ *intr* to take a short cut ‖ *ref* to be abashed

atajo *m* short cut; (*en un escrito*) cut

atalaya *m* guard, lookout ‖ *f* watchtower; elevation

atalayar *tr* to watch from a watchtower; spy on

atanquía *f* depilatory ointment

atañer §70 *tr* to concern

ataque *m* attack; **ataque por sorpresa** surprise attack

atar *tr* to tie, fasten

ataracea *f* marquetry, inlaid work

atarantar *tr* to stun, daze

atardecer *m* late afternoon ‖ *v* §22 *intr* to draw toward evening; happen in the late afternoon

atarea•do -da *adj* busy

atarear *tr* to give an assignment to; overload with work ‖ *ref* to toil, work hard, keep busy

atarjea *f* sewer

atarugar §44 *tr* to peg, wedge; plug; stuff, fill; silence, shut up ‖ *ref* to become confused

atasajar *tr* to slash, hack; (*carne*) jerk

atascadero *m* mudhole; pitfall

atascar §73 *tr* to stop, stop up, clog, obstruct ‖ *ref* to get stuck; stuff oneself; clog, get clogged

atasco *m* sticking, clogging; obstruction

ataúd *m* casket, coffin

ataujía *f* damascene work

ataujiar §77 *tr* to damascene

ataviar §77 *tr* to dress, adorn, deck out

atávi-co -ca *adj* atavistic
atavío *m* dress, adornment; **atavíos** finery, frippery, chiffons
atediar *tr* to tire, bore
ateísmo *m* atheism
ateísta *mf* atheist
atelaje *m* harness
atemorizar §60 *tr* to frighten
atemperar *tr* to soften, moderate, temper; adjust, adapt
Atenas *f* Athens
atención *f* attention; **en atención a** in view of
atender §51 *tr* to attend to; heed, pay attention to; take care of; (*a los parroquianos*) wait on
atener §71 *ref* — **atenerse a** to abide by, rely on
ateniense *adj & mf* Athenian
atenta-do -da *adj* moderate, prudent; cautious ‖ *m* attempt, assault
atentar *tr* to attempt, try to commit ‖ *intr* — **atentar a** or **contra** (*p.ej., la vida de una persona*) to attempt ‖ §2 *ref* to grope
aten-to -ta *adj* attentive; courteous, polite ‖ *f* favor (*letter*)
atenuar §21 *tr* to extenuate
ate-o -a *adj & mf* atheist
aterciopela-do -da *adj* velvety
ateri-do -da *adj* stiff, numb with cold
aterrada *f* landfall
aterrajar *tr* to thread, tap
aterraje *m* landing
aterrar *tr* to terrify ‖ §2 *tr* to destroy, demolish; cover with earth ‖ *intr* to land ‖ *ref* to stand inshore
aterrizaje *m* landing; **aterrizaje a ciegas** blind landing; **aterrizaje aplastado** or **en desplome** pancake landing; **aterrizaje forzoso** emergency landing; **aterrizaje sin choque** soft landing
aterrizar §60 *intr* to land
aterronar *tr* to make lumpy ‖ *ref* to cake, lump
aterrorizar §60 *tr* to terrify
atesorar *tr* to treasure; hoard; (*virtudes, perfecciones*) possess
atesta-do -da *adj* stuffed, jammed; obstinate, stubborn ‖ *m* certificate
atestar *tr* (law) to attest ‖ §2 & regular *tr* to jam, pack, stuff, cram; stuff
atestiguar §10 *tr* to attest, testify, depose
atezar §60 *tr* to tan; blacken ‖ *ref* to become tanned, become sunburned
atiborrar *tr* to stuff ‖ *ref* to stuff, stuff oneself
atiesar *tr* to stiffen; tighten ‖ *ref* to become stiff; become tight
atildar *tr* to mark with a tilde, dash, or accent mark: point out; find fault with; tidy up, trim, adorn
atina-do -da *adj* careful, keen, wise
atinar *tr* to find, come upon ‖ *intr* to guess, guess right; be right; manage
atirantar *tr* (Mex) to make taut; brace ‖ *ref* (Mex) to die, pass away
atisbadero *m* peephole
atisbar *tr* to watch, spy on

atisbo *m* glimpse, look, peek
atizar §60 *tr* to stir, poke; snuff; rouse; (*p.ej., un puntapié*) let go
Atlánti-co -ca *adj & m* Atlantic
at-las *m* (*pl* -**las**) atlas
atleta *mf* athlete
atleticismo *m* athletics
atléti-co -ca *adj* athletic ‖ *f* athletics
atmósfera *f* atmosphere
atmosféri-co -ca *adj* atmospheric
atoar *tr* (naut) to tow
atocinar *tr* (*un cerdo*) to cut up; make into bacon; (coll) to murder ‖ *ref* to get angry; fall madly in love
atocha *f* esparto
atolondra-do -da *adj* confused; scatter-brained
atolondrar *tr* to confuse, bewilder
atolladero *m* mudhole; obstacle, difficulty
atollar *intr & ref* to get stuck, get stuck in the mud
atómi-co -ca *adj* atomic
átomo *m* atom
atóni-to -ta *adj* astounded, aghast
atontar *tr* to stun; to confuse, bewilder
atorar *tr* to clog, obstruct ‖ *intr & ref* to stick, get stuck; choke
atormentar *tr* to torment; torture
atornillar *tr* to screw, screw on
atortillar *tr* (SAm) to squash, flatten
atortolar *tr* to rattle, scare, intimidate
atosigar §44 *tr* to poison; harass ‖ *ref* to be in a hurry
atrabanca-do -da *adj* overworked; (Mex) hasty, rash; (Ven) deep in debt
atrabancar §73 *tr & intr* to rush through
atrabilia-rio -ria *adj* irascible, grouchy
atracada *f* quarrel, row
atracador *m* hold-up man
atracar §73 *tr* to hold up; bring up; stuff; (naut) to bring alongside, dock ‖ *intr* (naut) to come alongside, dock ‖ *ref* to stuff; quarrel
atracción *f* attraction; amusement
atraco *m* holdup
atracón *m* stuffing, gluttony; fight; push, shove
atracti-vo -va *adj* attractive ‖ *m* attraction; attractiveness
atraer §75 *tr* to attract
atragantar *tr* to choke down ‖ *ref* to choke; **atragantarse con** to choke on
atraillar §4 *tr* to leash; master, subdue
atrampar *ref* to fall into a trap; be stopped up; stick; get stuck
atrancar §73 *tr* to bar; obstruct ‖ *intr* to stride; read falteringly ‖ *ref* to get stuck; (*una ventana*) stick; (Mex) to stick to one's opinion
atrapamos-cas *m* (*pl* -**cas**) flytrap; (bot) Venus's-flytrap
atrapar *tr* to trap, catch; get, land, net
atrás *adv* back, backward; behind; before; previously; **atrás de** back of, behind; **hacerse atrás** to back up, move back; **hacia atrás** backwards; the other way

atrasa•do -da *adj* late; (*reloj*) slow; needy; back; retarded; in arrears; **atrasado de medios** short of funds; **atrasado de noticias** behind the times

atrasar *tr* to slow down; retard; set back, turn back; delay; leave behind; postdate || *intr* to be slow || *ref* to be slow; lose time; lag, stay behind; be late; be in debt

atraso *m* delay, slowness; backwardness; lag; **atrasos** arrears, delinquency

atravesada *f* (SAm) crossing

atravesar §2 *tr* to cross, go across; pierce; pass through, go through; put crosswise; stake, wager || *ref* to butt in; fight, wrangle; get stuck

atrayente *adj* attractive

atreguar §10 *tr* to give a truce to; grant an extension to || *ref* to agree to a truce

atrever *ref* to dare; **atreverse con** or **contra** to be impudent toward

atrevi•do -da *adj* bold, daring; impudent

atrevimiento *m* boldness, daring; impudence

atribuir §20 *tr* to attribute, ascribe || *ref* to assume

atribular *tr* & *ref* to grieve

atributo *m* attribute

atril *m* lectern; music stand

atrincherar *tr* to entrench || *ref* to dig in

atrio *m* hall, vestibule; court, courtyard; parvis

atri•to -ta *adj* contrite

atrocidad *f* atrocity; enormity

atrofia *f* atrophy

atrofiar *tr* & *ref* to atrophy

atrojar *tr* (*granos*) to garner; (Mex) to befuddle

atrona•do -da *adj* reckless, thoughtless

atronar §61 *tr* to deafen; stun || *intr* to thunder

atropella•do -da *adj* brusk, violent; hasty; tumultuous

atropellar *tr* to trample; knock down; run over; disregard; do hurriedly || *intr* & *ref* to act hastily or recklessly

atropello *m* trampling; knocking down; running over; abuse, insult; outrage

a•troz *adj* (*pl* **-troces**) atrocious; huge, enormous

atto. *abbr* **atento**

atufar *tr* to anger, irritate || *ref* to get angry; (*el vino*) turn sour

atún *m* tuna

aturdi•do -da *adj* reckless, harebrained

aturdir *tr* to stun; perplex, bewilder

atusar *tr* to trim; smooth || *ref* to dress fancily; (*el bigote*) twist

audacia *f* audacity

au•daz *adj* (*pl* **-daces**) audacious

audición *f* audition; hearing; concert; listening

audiencia *f* audience, hearing; audience chamber; royal tribunal; provincial high court

audífono *m* hearing aid; earphone

audiofrecuencia *f* audio frequency

audiómetro *m* audiometer

auditor *m* judge advocate; **auditor de guerra** judge advocate (*in army*); **auditor de marina** judge advocate (*in navy*)

auditorio *m* (*concurso de oyentes*) audience; (*local*) auditorium

auge *m* height, acme; boom; vogue; **estar en auge** to be booming

augur *m* augur

augurar *tr* to augur; wish || *intr* to augur

augurio *m* augury; wish

augus•to -ta *adj* august

aula *f* classroom, lecture room; **aula magna** assembly hall

aulaga *f* gorse, furze

aullar §8 *intr* to howl

aullido *m* howl, howling

aúllo *m* howl

aumentar *tr* to augment, increase, enlarge; promote; exaggerate || *intr* & *ref* to augment, increase

aumento *m* augmentation, increase, enlargement; promotion; (Guat, Mex) postscript, addition; **ir en aumento** to be on the increase

aun *adv* even; **aun cuando** although

aún *adv* still, yet

aunar §8 *tr* & *ref* to join, unite; combine, mix

aunque *conj* although, though

aúpa *interj* up!; **de aúpa** swanky; **los de aúpa** (taur) the picadors

aupar §8 *tr* to help up; extol

aura *f* gentle breeze; breath; popularity; turkey vulture

áure•o -a *adj* gold, golden

aureola *f* halo, aureole

auricular *m* earpiece, receiver; **auricular de casco** headpiece

auriga *m* (poet) coachman, charioteer

aurora *f* aurora, dawn; roseate hue

ausencia *f* absence

ausentar *tr* to send away || *ref* to absent oneself

ausente *adj* absent; absent-minded || *mf* absentee

auspiciar *tr* to sponsor, foster, back

auspicio *m* auspice; **bajo los auspicios de** under the auspices of

auste•ro -ra *adj* austere; harsh; honest; penitent

Australia *f* Australia

australia•no -na *adj* & *mf* Australian

Austria *f* Austria

austría•co -ca *adj* & *mf* Austrian

austro *m* south wind

auténtica *f* certificate; certification

autenticar §73 *tr* to authenticate

autén•ti•co -ca *adj* authentic; real || *f* see **auténtica**

autillo *m* tawny owl

autísti•co -ca *adj* autistic

auto *m* edict; short Biblical play; miracle play; auto; **auto de prisión** commitment, warrant for arrest; **auto sacramental** play in honor of the Sacrament

autoabastecimiento *m* self-sufficiency

autoadhesi•vo -va *adj* self-adhesive

at
au

autoamortizable *adj* self-liquidating
autobanco *m* drive-in bank
autobiografía *f* autobiography
autobombo *m* self-glorification
autobús *m* autobus, bus
autocamión *m* motor truck
autocasa *f* motor home; mobile home; trailer
autocine *m* (Chile, Cuba) drive-in theater
autocinema *f* (Mex) drive-in theater
autocráti•co -ca *adj* autocratic(al)
autócto•no -na *adj* native, indigenous
autodefensa *f* self-defense
autodestrucción *f* self-destruction
autodeterminación *f* self-determination
autodidac•to -ta *adj* self-taught
autodisciplina *f* self-discipline
autodominio *m* self-control
autódromo *m* automobile race track
auto-escuela *f* driving school
autógena *f* welding
autogestión *f* self-administration; independence
autogobierno *m* self-government
autografiar §77 *tr* to autograph
autógra•fo -fa *adj & m* autograph
autoguia•do -da *adj* self-guided, homing
autolimpiador or **autolimpiante** *adj invar* self-cleaning
automación *f* automation
autómata *m* automaton
automáti•co -ca *adj* automatic
automatización *f* automation
automóvil *m* automobile
automovilista *mf* motorist
autonomía *f* autonomy; cruising radius
autóno•mo -ma *adj* autonomous, independent
autopega•do -da *adj* self-sealing
autopiano *m* player piano
autopista *f* turnpike, automobile road
autopsia *f* autopsy
au•tor -tora *mf* author; (*de un crimen*) perpetrator ‖ *f* authoress
autoreactor *m* ramjet (engine)
autoridad *f* authority; pomp, display
autorita•rio -ria *adj & mf* authoritarian
autoriza•do -da *adj* authoritative
autorizar §60 *tr* to authorize; legalize; exalt
autorretrato *m* self-portrait
autoservicio *m* self-service
autostop *m* hitchhiking; **viajar en autostop** to hitchhike
autostopista *mf* hitchhiker
auto-teatro *m* drive-in movie theater
autovía *m* railway motor coach ‖ *f* turnpike, automobile road
auxiliar *adj* auxiliary ‖ *mf* auxiliary; aid, helper; substitute teacher ‖ *v* §77 **& regular** *tr* to aid, help, assist; (*a un moribundo*) attend
auxilio *m* aid, help, assistance; **acudir en auxilio a** or **de** to come to the aid of; **auxilio en carretera** road service; **primeros auxilios** first aid
avahar *tr* to steam; breathe warmth on ‖ *intr* to steam, give off vapor ‖ *ref* to steam,

give off vapor; warm one's hands with one's breath
aval *m* indorsement; countersignature
avalancha *f* avalanche
avalorar *tr* to estimate; encourage
avaluación *f* appraisal, valuation
avaluar §21 *tr* to appraise, estimate
avalúo *m* appraisal, valuation
avance *m* advance; advance payment; (com) balance; (com) estimate; (mov) preview; **avance rápido** (mach, mov) fast forward
avante *adv* (naut) fore
avanza•do -da *adj* advanced; **avanzado de edad** advanced in years ‖ *f* outpost, advance guard
avanzar §60 *tr* to advance, extend; propose ‖ *intr & ref* to advance; approach
avanzo *m* balance sheet; estimate
avaricia *f* avarice
avaricio•so -sa *adj* avaricious
avarien•to -ta *adj* avaricious ‖ *mf* miser
ava•ro -ra *adj* miserly ‖ *mf* miser
avasallar *tr* to subject, subjugate, enslave ‖ *ref* to submit
ave *f* bird; fowl; **ave canora** songbird; **ave de corral** barnyard fowl; **ave de mal agüero** Jonah, jinx; **ave de paso** bird of passage; **ave de rapiña** bird of prey; **ave fría** lapwing; **ave zancuda** wading bird
avecinar *tr* to bring near ‖ *ref* to approach; take up residence
avecindar *tr* to domicile ‖ *ref* to become a resident
avejentar *tr & ref* to age prematurely
avejigar §44 *tr, intr & ref* to blister
avellana *f* hazelnut
avellanar *tr* to countersink ‖ *ref* to shrivel, shrivel up
avellano *m* hazel, hazel tree
avemaría *f* Hail Mary, Ave Maria; **al avemaría** at sunset; **en un avemaría** in a jiffy; **saber como el avemaría** to have a thorough knowledge of
avena *f* oats
avenar *tr* to drain
avenate *m* gruel, oatmeal gruel
avenencia *f* agreement; deal, bargain
avenida *f* avenue; allée; flood, freshet; gathering, assemblage
aveni•do -da *adj* — **bien avenido** in agreement; **mal avenido** in disagreement ‖ *f* see **avenida**
avenimiento *m* agreement; reconciliation
avenir §79 *tr* to reconcile, bring together ‖ *ref* to be reconciled, agree; compromise; correspond
aventa•dor -dora *mf* winnower ‖ *m* fan
aventaja•do -da *adj* excellent, outstanding; advantageous
aventajar *tr* to advance; put ahead; excel ‖ *ref* to advance, win an advantage; excel
aventar §2 *tr* to fan; winnow; scatter to the winds; blow; drive away ‖ *ref* to swell up; flee, run away
aventón *m* (Guat, Mex, Peru) push, shove; (*llevada gratuita*) (Mex) free ride; **pedir aventón** (Mex) to hitchhike

aventura *f* adventure; danger, risk

aventura•do -da *adj* hazardous, venturesome

aventurar *tr* to adventure, venture, hazard ‖ *ref* to adventure, take a risk; venture, to risk

aventure•ro -ra *adj* adventuresome, adventurous ‖ *m* adventurer, soldier of fortune ‖ *f* adventuress

avergonzar §9 *tr* to shame; embarrass ‖ *ref* to be ashamed; be embarrassed

avería *f* aviary; breakdown, failure; (com) damage; (naut) average

averiar §77 *tr* to damage ‖ *ref* to suffer damage; break down

averiguable *adj* ascertainable

averiguar §10 *tr* to ascertain, find out

aversión *f* aversion, dislike; **cobrar aversión a** to take a dislike for

aves•truz *m* (*pl* **-truces**) ostrich

avezar §60 *tr* to accustom ‖ *ref* to become accustomed

aviación *f* aviation

avia•dor -dora *mf* aviator, flyer ‖ *m* aviator, airman; (mil) airman; **aviador postal** air-mail pilot ‖ *f* aviatrix, airwoman

aviar §77 *tr* to make ready, prepare; equip, provide; **estar, encontrarse** or **quedar aviado** to be in a mess, be in a jam ‖ *ref* to hurry; (aer) to take off

avia•triz (*pl* **-trices**) aviatrix

avidez *f* avidity, greediness

ávi•do -da *adj* avid, greedy, eager

aviejar *tr* & *ref* to age prematurely

aviento *m* winnowing fork, pitchfork

avie•so -sa *adj* crooked, distorted; evil-minded, perverse

avilantar *ref* to be insolent

avilantez *f* insolence; meanness

avillana•do -da *adj* rustic, boorish

avillanar *tr* to debase, make boorish ‖ *ref* to become boorish

avinagra•do -da *adj* vinegarish, sour, crabbed

avinagrar *tr* to sour ‖ *ref* to become sour; turn into vinegar

avío *m* provision; arrangement; load; **¡al avío!** let's go!; **avíos** equipment, tools, outfit; **avíos de pescar** fishing tackle

avión *m* airplane; (orn) martin; **avión bi-rreactor** twin-jet plane; **avión de caza** pursuit plane; **avión a chorro, avión de propulsión a chorro** or **a reacción** jet plane; **avión de travesía** airliner; **avión supersónico** supersonic aircraft

avión-correo *m* mailplane

avioneta *f* small plane; **avioneta de alquiler** taxiplane

avisaco•ches *m* (*pl* **-ches**) car caller

avisa•do -da *adj* prudent, wise; **mal avisado** rash, thoughtless

avisa•dor -dora *adj* warning ‖ *mf* informer; adviser ‖ *m* electric bell; **avisador de incendio** fire alarm

avisar *tr* to advise, inform; warn; report on

aviso *m* advice, information; warning; care, prudence; dispatch boat; advertisement; **sobre aviso** on the lookout

avispa *f* wasp

avispa•do -da *adj* brisk, wide-awake; (SAm) startled, scared

avispar *tr* to spur; to stir up ‖ *ref* to fret, worry

avispón *m* hornet

avistar *tr* to descry ‖ *ref* to meet, have an interview

avitaminosis *f* vitamin deficiency

avituallar *tr* to supply, provision ‖ *ref* to take in supplies

avivar *tr* to brighten, enlive, revive ‖ *intr* & *ref* to brighten, revive

avizor *adj* watchful, alert ‖ *m* watcher; **avizores** (slang) eyes

avizorar *tr* to watch, spy on ‖ *ref* to hide and watch, spy

ax *interj* ouch!, ow!

axioma *m* axiom

axiomáti•co -ca *adj* axiomatic

ay *interj* ay!, alas! **¡ay de mí!** woe is me! ‖ *m* sigh

aya *f* nurse, governess

ayer *adj* & *m* yesterday

ayo *m* tutor

ayuda *m* valet; **ayuda de cámera** valet de chambre ‖ *f* help, aid; enema

ayudanta *f* assistant; **ayudanta de cocina** kitchenmaid

ayudante *m* aid, assistant; adjutant; **ayudante de campo** aide-de-camp

ayudantía *f* (*universidad*) assistantship

ayudar *tr* to aid, help, assist

ayunar *intr* to fast

ayu•no -na *adj* fasting; uninformed; **en ayunas** or **en ayuno** fasting; before breakfast; uninformed; missing the point ‖ *m* fast, fasting

ayuntamiento *m* town or city council; town or city hall; sexual intercourse

azabacha•do -da *adj* jet, jet-black

azabache *m* jet; **azabaches** jet trinkets

aza•cán -cana *adj* menial ‖ *mf* drudge ‖ *m* water carrier

azada *f* hoe

azadón *m* hoe; grub hoe; **azadón de peto** or **de pico** mattock

azadonar *tr* to hoe

azafata *f* air hostess, stewardess; lady of the queen's wardrobe

azafate *m* wicker tray

azafrán *m* saffron

azafrana•do -da *adj* saffron

azafranar *tr* to saffron

azahar *m* orange or lemon blossom

azar *m* chance, hazard; accident, misfortune; fate, destiny; losing card; losing throw; (*persona o cosa que traen mala suerte*) Jonah

azarar *ref* to go awry; get rattled

azaro•so -sa *adj* hazardous, risky; unlucky

ázi•mo -ma *adj* unleavened

azófar *m* brass

azoga•do da *adj* fidgety, restless ‖ *m* quicksilver foil; **temblar como un azogado** to shake like a leaf

azogar §44 *tr* (*un espejo*) to silver ‖ *ref* to have mercury poisoning; shake, become agitated

azogue *m* quicksilver; market place; (coll) mirror

azonza•do -da *adj* stupid, dumb

azor *m* goshawk

azorar *tr* to abash; excite, stir up

Azores *fpl* Azores

azotar *tr* to whip, scourge; beat; flail; beat down upon

azote *m* whip; lash; (fig) scourge; **azotes y galeras** tiresome fare

azotea *f* flat roof, roof terrace

azteca *adj & mf* Aztec

azúcar *m* sugar; **azúcar de caña** cane sugar; **azúcar de remolacha** beet sugar

azucarar *tr* to sugar, sugarcoat; sugar over

azucare•ro -ra *adj* sugar ‖ *m* sugar bowl

azucena *f* Madonna lily, white lily

azufrar *tr* to sulfur

azufre *m* sulfur; brimstone

azul *adj & m* blue; **azul marino** navy blue

azular *tr* to color blue, dye blue

azulear *intr* to turn blue

azulejar *tr* to tile, cover with tiles

azulejo *m* glazed colored tile (orn) roller; (orn) indigo bunting; (orn) bee eater

azulones *mpl* blue jeans

azuzar §60 *tr* to sic; tease, incite

B

B, b (be) *f* second letter of the Spanish alphabet

B. *abbr* **Beato, Bueno**

baba *f* drivel, spittle, slobber; (*de culebras, peces, etc.*) slime

babear *intr* to slobber; froth

babel *m & f* (coll) bedlam, confusion; **estar en babel** to be daydreaming

babero *m* bib

Babia *f* — **estar en Babia** to be daydreaming

babieca *adj* silly, simple ‖ *mf* simpleton

Babilonia *f* (*imperio*) Babylonia; (*ciudad*) Babylon

babilóni•co -ca *adj* Babylonian

babilo•nio -nia *adj & mf* Babylonian ‖ *f* see **Babilonia**

bable *m* Asturian dialect; patois

babor *m* (naut) port

babosa *f* slug

babosada *f* (CAm, Mex) stupidity; foolish act

babosear *tr* to slobber over ‖ *intr* to slobber

babo•so -sa *adj* slobbery; (*con las damas*) (coll) mushy ‖ *m* (CAm) scoundrel ‖ *f* see **babosa**

babucha *f* slipper, mule

babuino *m* baboon

bacalao or **bacallao** *m* codfish

baceta *f* (cards) widow

bacía *f* basin, vessel; shaving dish

bacilo *m* bacillus

bacín *m* chamber pot

Baco *m* Bacchus

bacteria *f* bacterium

bacteria•no -na *adj* bacterial

bacteriología *f* bacteriology

bacteriólo•go -ga *mf* bacteriologist

báculo *m* staff; crook; (fig) staff, comfort; **báculo pastoral** crozier

bacha *f* (Mex) (cigarette) butt

bache *m* hole, rut; blip; **bache aéreo** air pocket

bachi•ller -llera *adj* garrulous ‖ *mf* garrulous person ‖ **bachiller** *mf* bachelor

bachillerar *tr* to confer the bachelor's degree on ‖ *ref* to receive the bachelor's degree

bachillerato *m* baccalaureate, bachelor's degree

bachillerear *intr* to babble, prattle

bachillería *f* babble, prattle; gossip

badajo *m* clapper

badana *f* (dressed) sheepskin; **zurrarle a uno la badana** to tan someone's hide

badén *m* gully, gutter

badil *m* fire shovel

badulaque *m* nincompoop

bagaje *m* beast of burden; (mil) baggage

bagatela *f* trinket; triviality; (Chile, Peru) pinball

bagazo *m* waste pulp, bagasse

bagre *adj* (Bol, Col) showy, gaudy; (CAm) sly, slick; (SAm) coarse, ill-bred; (Mex) stupid ‖ *m* catfish

bahareque *m* (CAm, Col, Ven) small hut

bahía *f* bay

bahorrina *f* slop; riffraff

bailable *adj* for dancing ‖ *m* ballet

bailadero *m* dance floor, dance hall

baila•dor -dora *mf* dancer

bailar *tr* (*p.ej., un vals*) to dance; (*un trompo*) spin ‖ *intr* to dance; spin; wobble

baila•rín -rina *mf* dancer ‖ *f* ballerina; **bailarina ombliguista** belly dancer

baile *m* dance; ball; ballet; **baile de etiqueta** dress ball, formal dance; **baile de los globos** bubble dance; **baile de máscaras** masked ball, masquerade ball; **baile de San Vito** (pathol) Saint Vitus's dance; **baile de trajes** costume ball, fancy-dress ball

baja *f* (*de los precios*) fall, drop; (*en la guerra*) casualty; **dar baja** to go down, decline; **dar de baja** to drop; (mil) to mark absent; **darse de baja** to drop out; **jugar a la baja** to bear the market

bajaca *f* (Ecuad) hair ribbon
bajada *f* descent; slope; downspout; (rad) lead-in wire
bajagua *f* (Mex) cheap tobacco
bajamar *f* low tide
bajar *tr* to lower, take down; bring down; (*la escalera*) go down, descend; humble ‖ *intr* to come down, go down; get off ‖ *ref* to bend down; get off; humble oneself
bajel *m* ship, vessel
bajeza *f* humbleness, lowliness; meanness, baseness
bajío *m* shoal, sandbank; pitfall; lowland
bajista *adj* bearish ‖ *mf* (fig) bear
ba•jo -ja *adj* low, under, lower; short; mean, base; lowly, humble; (mus) bass ‖ *m* shoal, sandbank; (mus) bass ‖ *f* see **baja** ‖ **bajo** *adv* down; low, in a low voice ‖ **bajo** *prep* under
bajón *m* bassoon; (*en el caudal, la salud, etc.*) decline, loss
bajonista *mf* bassoon player
bajorrelieve *m* bas-relief
bala *f* bullet; bale; **bala fría** spent bullet; **bala perdida** stray bullet; **ni a bala** (SAm) under no circumstances
balaca *f* boasting, show
balaceo *m* or **balacera** *f* (SAm) shooting; shootout
balada *f* ballad; (mus) ballade
bala•dí *adj* (*pl* **-díes**) trivial, paltry, cheap
baladro *m* scream, shout, outcry
baladronada *f* boast, boasting
baladronear *intr* to boast, brag
bálago *m* chaff
balance *m* balance, balance sheet; rocking, swinging; hesitation, doubt; (*de una nave*) rolling
balancear *tr* to balance ‖ *intr* & *ref* to rock, swing; hesitate, waver; (*la nave*) roll
balancín *m* balance beam; singletree; rocker arm; seesaw
balandra *f* sloop
balandrán *m* cassock
balanza *f* scales, balance; comparison, judgment; **balanza de pagos** balance of payments
balar *intr* to bleat; (coll) to pine
balastar *tr* to ballast
balasto *m* ballast
balaustre *m* baluster, banister
balay *m* wicker basket
balazo *m* shot; bullet wound
balbucear *tr* to stammer ‖ *intr* to stammer, stutter; to babble, to prattle
balbucir §1 *tr* & *intr* var of **balbucear**
Balcanes, los the Balkans
balcarrotas *fpl* (SAm) sideburns; (Mex) locks falling over sides of face
balcón *m* balcony
baldar *tr* to cripple; incapacitate; inconvenience; trump
balde *m* bucket, pail; **de balde** free, gratis; over, in excess; **en balde** in vain
baldear *tr* to wash with pails of water; (*una excavación*) bail out
baldí•o -a *adj* uncultivated; idle, lazy; care-

less; useless, vain; unfounded ‖ *m* untilled land
baldón *m* insult; blot, disgrace
baldonar *tr* to insult; stain, disgrace
baldosa *f* floor tile, paving tile; flagstone
baldra•gas *m* (*pl* **-gas**) jellyfish
balduque *s* red tape, wrapping tape
balear *tr* to shoot at, shoot, shoot to death
baleo *m* (SAm) shooting
balido *m* bleat, bleating
balísti•co -ca *adj* ballistic
baliza *f* buoy, beacon; danger signal
balizaje *m* (aer) airway lighting; (naut) buoys
balizar §60 *tr* to mark with buoys; mark off
balnea•rio -ria *adj* bathing ‖ *m* watering place, spa
balompié *m* football, soccer
balón *m* football; bale; balloon
baloncesto *m* basketball
balota *f* ballot
balotar *intr* to ballot
balsa *f* pool, puddle; raft; float; corkwood; **balsa salvavidas** life float
bálsamo *m* balsam, balm
balsear *tr* to cross by raft; ferry across
balsero *m* ferryman
bálti•co -ca *adj* Baltic
baluarte *m* bulwark
balumba *f* confusion; row
ballena *f* whale; whalebone, (*de corsé*) stay
ballesta *f* crossbow; spring, auto spring
ba•llet *m* (*pl* **-llets**) ballet
bambalinas *fpl* (theat) flies, borders
bambolear *intr* to sway, reel, wobble
bambolla *f* hulk; show, sham; show-off
bam•bú *m* (*pl* **-búes**) bamboo
banana *f* banana; (rad) plug
banane•ro -ra *adj* banana ‖ *m* banana tree
banano *m* banana tree
banas *fpl* (Mex) banns
banasta *f* hamper, large basket
banca *f* bench; banking; stand, fruit stand; (*en el juego*) bank; **banca de hielo** iceberg; **hacer saltar la banca** to break the bank
banca•rio -ria *adj* banking, bank
bancarrota *f* bankruptcy; **hacer bancarrota** to go bankrupt
bancarrote•ro -ra *adj* & *mf* bankrupt
banco *m* bench; bank; (*de peces*) school; **banco de ahorros** savings bank; **banco de datos** (*ordenador*) data bank; memory; **banco de hielo** iceberg; **banco de liquidación** clearing house
banda *f* band; ribbon; faction, party; flock; border, edge; bank, shore; (*de la mesa de billar*) cushion; **banda ciudadana** citizens band, CB; **banda de rodamiento** (aut) tread; **banda de tambores** drum corps; **irse a la banda** (naut) to list
bandada *f* flock, covey; (*de gente*) (coll) flock
bandaje *m* tire
bandazo *m* swerving; (naut) lurch
bandear *tr* to go through, pierce; to pursue; to make love to ‖ *ref* to manage
bandeja *f* tray; dish, platter

bandera f flag, banner; **con banderas desplegadas** with flying colors

banderilla f (taur) banderilla; **poner una banderilla a** to taunt; hit for a loan

banderín m (mil) color corporal; recruiting post

banderola f streamer, pennant; transom

bandido m bandit

bando m proclamation; faction, side

bandolera f bandoleer; female bandit; **en bandolera** across the shoulders

bandolero m highwayman, brigand

bandurria f Spanish lute

banquero m banker

banqueta stool, footstool; (Guat, Mex) sidewalk

banquete m banquet

banquetear tr, intr & ref to banquet

banquisa f floe, iceberg

bañadera f bathtub

bañado m chamber pot; marshland

baña•dor -dora adj bathing || mf bather || m bathing suit

bañar tr to bathe; dip; coat by dipping || ref to bathe

bañera f bathtub

bañista mf bather; frequenter of a spa or seaside resort

baño m bath; bathing; bathroom; bathtub; **baño de asiento** sitz bath; **baño de ducha** shower bath; **baños** bathing place; spa

bao m (naut) beam

baptista adj & mf Baptist

baptisterio m baptistery

baque m thud, thump; bump, bruise

baquelita f bakelite

ba•quet m (pl **-quets**) bucket seat

baqueta f ramrod; drumstick; **correr baquetas** or **pasar por baquetas** to run the gauntlet

baquía f knowledge of the road, paths, rivers, etc. of a region; manual skill

baquia•no -na adj skillful, expert || mf scout, pathfinder, guide

báqui•co -ca adj Bacchic

bar m bar; cocktail bar

barahunda f uproar, tumult

baraja f (de naipes) deck, pack; gang, mob; confusion, mix-up

barajadura f shuffling; dispute, quarrel

barajar tr (naipes) to shuffle; jumble, to mix || intr to shuffle; fight, quarrel || ref to get jumbled or mixed

baranda f railing; (de la mesa de billar) cushion

barandilla f balustrade, railing

barata f cheapness; barter; (Mex) bargain sale; (Chile, Peru) cockroach; (Col, Mex) junk store

baratero m shopkeeper

baratía f (SAm) cheapness

baratija f trinket

baratillo m second-hand goods; second-hand shop; bargain counter

baratío m (CAm) junk store

bara•to -ta adj cheap || m bargain sale; **dar de barato** to admit for the sake of argu-

ment; **de barato** gratis, free || f see **barata** || **barato** adv cheap

báratro m (poet) hell

baratura f cheapness

baraúnda f uproar, tumult

barba f (parte de la cara) chin; (pelo en ella) beard; (del papel) deckle edge; (de ave) gill, wattle; **barba española** Spanish moss; **barbas** whiskers; **hacer la barba a** to shave; to bore, annoy; (Mex) to fawn on; **llevar por la barba** to lead by the nose; **mentir por la barba** (coll) to tell fish stories || m (theat) old man

barbacoa f barbecue; (Col) kitchen cupboard; (Peru) attic

barbada f lower jaw of horse; bridle curb || **la Barbada** Barbados

barbar intr to grow a beard; strike root

barbaridad f barbarism; outrage; piece of folly; large amount; **¡qué barbaridad!** how awful!, what nonsense!

barbarie f barbarity, barbarism

barbarismo m illiteracy; outrage; (gram) barbarism

bárba•ro -ra adj barbaric; barbarous || mf barbarian

barbear tr to reach with the chin; be as high as || intr to reach the same height; **barbear con** to be as high as

barbechar tr to plow for seeding; fallow

barbecho m fallow; **firmar como en un barbecho** to sign with one's eyes closed

barbería f barber shop

barberil adj barber

barbe•ro -ra mf barber; (Mex) flatterer

barbilampi•ño -ña adj smooth-faced, beardless; beginning, green

barbilla f tip of chin; (de pluma) barb; (de pez) wattle

bar•bón -bona adj bearded || m graybeard; solemn old fellow; billy goat

barboquejo m chin strap

barbotar tr & intr to mutter, mumble

barbuchas adj beardless

barbu•do -da adj bearded, long-bearded, heavy-bearded || m shoot, sucker

barbullar tr & intr to blabber

barca f small boat; bark; **barca perforador** offshore (oil) rig

barcia f chaff

barco m boat, ship; **barco cisternas** or **barco tanque** tanker; **barco de carga** cargo boat; **barco náufrago** shipwreck

barchi•lón -lona mf (Ecuad, Peru) nurse, orderly; (Arg, Bol, Peru) quack

barda f thatch; bard, horse armor

bardana f burdock

bardar tr to thatch; (caballo) bard

bardo m bard

baremo m (escala) scale; rate table

bargueño m carved inlaid secretary

bario m barium

barjuleta f haversack

barloventear intr to wander around; turn to windward

barlovento m windward

barman m bartender

bar·niz *m* (*pl* **-nices**) varnish; (*de la loza, la porcelana, etc.*) glaze; gloss, polish; (*conocimientos superficiales*) smattering; (aer) dope

barnizar §60 *tr* to varnish

barómetro *m* barometer; **barómetro aneroide** aneroid barometer

barón *m* baron

baronesa *f* baroness

barquero *m* boatman

barquilla *f* (naut) log; (naut) log chip; (aer) nacelle

barquillero *m* waffle iron; harbor boatman

barquillo *m* cone; waffle

barquín *m* bellows

barra *f* bar; (*de dinamita*) stick; (*en el tribunal*) bar, railing; **barra colectora** (elec) bus bar; **barra de labios** or **para los labios** lipstick; **barra imantada** bar magnet; **barras paralelas** (sport) parallel bars

barrabasada *f* fiendish prank, mean trick

barraca *f* cabin, hut; cottage; storage shed

barracón *m* barracks; fair booth

barragana *f* concubine

barranca *f* gorge, ravine, gully

barranco *m* gorge, ravine, gully; difficulty, obstruction; cliff, precipice

barrar *tr* to daub, smear

barrear *tr* to barricade; bar shut

barredera *f* street sweeper

barre·dor -dora *mf* sweeper; **barredora de alfombras** carpet sweeper; **barredora de nieve** snowplow

barredura *f* sweeping; **barreduras** sweepings

barremi·nas *m* (*pl* **-nas**) mine sweeper

barrena *f* auger, drill, gimlet; (*espiga para taladrar*) bit; (aer) spin; **barrena picada** (aer) tail spin; **entrar en barrena** (aer) to go into a spin

barrenar *tr* to drill; (*un buque*) to scuttle; blast; upset, frustrate; violate

barrende·ro -ra *mf* sweeper

barreno *m* large drill; drill hole; blast hole; pride, vanity; (Chile) mania, pet idea; **dar barreno a** (*un buque*) to scuttle

barreño *m* earthen dishpan

barrer *tr* to sweep, sweep away; graze ‖ *intr* to sweep; **barrer hacia dentro** to look out for oneself

barrera *f* barrier; barricade; (mil) barrage; crockery cupboard; tollgate; (rr) crossing gate; (taur) fence around inside of ring; (taur) first row of seats; **barrera de arrecifes** barrier reef; **barrera de paso a nivel** (rr) crossing gate; **barrera de sonido** or **barrera sónica** sound barrier

barriada *f* district, quarter

barrial *m* (SAm) mudhole; muddy ground

barrica *f* cask, barrel

barriga *f* belly; (*de una vasija, una pared, etc.*) bulge

barri·gón -gona or **barrigu·do -da** *adj* big-bellied

barril *m* barrel

barrilero *m* cooper, barrel maker

barrio *m* ward, quarter; suburb; **barrio bajo** slums; **barrio comercial** shopping district, business district; **el otro barrio** the other world; **estar vestido de barrio** to be dressed in house clothes

barro *m* mud; clay; earthenware; pimple; (coll) money; (Arg, Urug) blunder

barro·co -ca *adj & m* baroque

barro·so -sa *adj* muddy; pimply

barrote *m* heavy bar; bolt; cross brace

barruntar *tr* to guess; to sense

barrunto *m* guess, conjecture; sign, token, foreboding

bartola *f* belly; **a la bartola** lazily

bartolina *f* (CAm, W-I) jail, dungeon

bártulos *mpl* household tools; **liar los bártulos** to pack up one's belongings

barullo *m* confusion, tumult

basar *tr* to base; build ‖ *ref* — **basarse en** to base one's judgment on, rely on

basca *f* nausea, squeamishness; fit of temper, tantrum

basco·so -sa *adj* nauseated, squeamish

báscula *f* scales; platform scale

base *f* base; basis; **a base de** on the basis of

bási·co -ca *adj* basic

Basilea *f* Basle, Basel

basílica *f* basilica

basilisco *m* basilisk; **estar hecho un basilisco** to be in a rage

basquear *intr* to be nauseated

basquetbol *m* basketball

bastante *adj* enough ‖ *adv* enough; fairly, rather ‖ *m* enough

bastar *intr* to be enough, suffice; abound, be more than enough ‖ *ref* to be self-sufficient

bastardilla *f* italics

bastar·do -da *adj & mf* bastard

bastedad *f* coarseness; roughness; (CAm) abundance; excess

bastidor *m* frame; stretcher; (theat) wing; **entre bastidores** behind the scenes

bastilla *f* hem

bastillar *tr* to hem

bas·to -ta *adj* coarse, rough; uncouth ‖ *m* packsaddle; (*naipe*) club; **el basto** the ace of clubs

bastón *m* stick, staff; cane, walking stick; baton; **bastón de esquiar** ski pole or stick

bastoncillo *m* small stick; (*de la retina*) rod

bastonear *tr* to cane, beat

basura *f* sweepings; rubbish, litter, refuse; horse manure

basural *m* (SAm) dump; trash pile

basurero *m* trash can; rubbish dump; rubbish collector

basurita *f* trifle

bata *f* smock; dressing gown, wrapper; **bata de baño** bathrobe

batacazo *m* thud, bump

bataclán *m* (Cuba) burlesque show

bataclana *f* (Cuba) showgirl, stripteaser

batahola *f* racket, hubbub

batalla *f* battle; (*de un vehículo*) wheel base; (*de la silla de montar*) seat; (paint) battle piece; **batalla campal** pitched battle; **librar batalla** to do battle

batallar *intr* to battle, fight; hesitate, waver

bata•llón -llona *adj* (*cuestión*) controversial, moot ‖ *m* battalion

batata *f* sweet potato; (Arg) timidity

bate *m* baseball bat

batea *f* tray; flat-bottomed boat; (rr) flatcar

bateador *m* batter

batear *tr & intr* to bat

batel *m* small boat

batelero *m* boatman

batería *f* battery; footlights; **batería de cocina** kitchen utensils

baterista *mf* drummer

batiboleo *m* (Cuba, Mex) noise; confusion

bati•do -da *adj* (*camino*) beaten; (*tejido*) moiré ‖ *m* batter; milk shake; (rad) beat ‖ *f* battue; combing, search

batidor *m* beater; scout, ranger; **batidor de huevos** egg beater; **batidor de oro** goldbeater

batidora • beater, mixer

batiente *m* jamb; (*hoja de puerta*) leaf, door; (*de piano*) damper; wash, place where surf breaks

batihoja *m* goldbeater; sheet-metal worker

batimiento *m* beating; (phys) beat

batín *m* smoking jacket

batintín *m* Chinese gong

batir *tr* to beat; batter, beat down; (*las alas*) flap; (*manos*) clap; (*las olas*) ply; **batir tiendas** (mil) to strike camp

batiscafo *m* bathyscaphe

bato *m* simpleton, rustic

batuque *m* (Arg) uproar, rumpus, jamboree; **armar un batuque** (Arg) to raise a rumpus

baturrillo *m* hodgepodge

batuta *f* (mus) baton; **llevar la batuta** to boss the show

baúl *m* trunk; **baúl mundo** large trunk; **baúl ropero** wardrobe trunk

bauprés *m* bowsprit

bautismo *m* baptism; **bautismo de aire** first flight

bautista *adj* Baptist ‖ *mf* Baptist; baptizer; **el Bautista** John the Baptist

bautisterio *m* baptistery

bautizar §60 *tr* to baptize; (*el vino*) water

bautizo *m* baptism; christening party

báva•ro -ra *adj & mf* Bavarian

Baviera *f* Bavaria

baya *f* berry

bayeta *f* baize

ba•yo -ya *adj* bay ‖ *m* bay horse ‖ *f* see **baya**

bayoneta *f* bayonet

bayonetear *tr* to bayonet

bayunca *f* or **bayuna** *f* (CAm) bar; tavern

baza *f* trick; **meter baza en** to butt into

bazar *m* bazaar

ba•zo -za *adj* yellowish-brown ‖ *m* yellowish brown; spleen ‖ *f* see **baza**

bazofia *f* refuse, offal, garbage

bazuca *f* bazooka

bazucar §73 *tr* to stir, shake; tamper with

be *m* baa

beata *f* lay sister

beatería *f* cant, hypocrisy

beatificar §73 *tr* to beatify

beatísi•mo -ma *adj* most holy

bea•to -ta *adj* blessed; pious, devout; bigoted, prudish ‖ *mf* beatified person; devout person; bigot; churchgoer ‖ *f* see **beata**

bebé *m* baby; doll

bebede•ro -ra *adj* (archaic) drinkable ‖ *m* watering place; (Col, Ecuad, Mex) watering trough

bebedi•zo -za *adj* drinkable ‖ *m* potion, philter

bebe•dor -dora *adj* drinking ‖ *mf* drinker; hard drinker

beber *m* drink, drinking ‖ *tr & intr* to drink; **beber de** or **en** to drink out of ‖ *ref* to drink, drink up; (*p.ej., un libro*) to drink in

bebestible *adj* drinkable ‖ *m* drink

bebezón *f* (Col) drunk, spree

bebible *adj* drinkable

bebi•do -da *adj* tipsy, unsteady ‖ *f* drink

bebistrajo *m* dose, mixture

beborrotear *intr* to tipple

beca *f* scholarship, fellowship; (*de los colegiales*) sash

becacín *m* snipe, whole snipe

becacina *f* snipe, great snipe

becada *f* woodcock

beca•rio -ria *mf* scholar, fellow

becerra *f* snapdragon

becerrillo *m* calfskin

bece•rro -rra *mf* yearling calf ‖ *m* calfskin ‖ *f* see **becerra**

becuadro *m* (mus) natural sign

bedel *m* beadle

befa *f* jeer, flout, scoff

befar *tr* to jeer at, to scoff at ‖ *intr* (*un caballo*) to move the lips

be•fo -fa *adj* blobber-lipped; knock-kneed ‖ *m* (*de animal*) lip ‖ *f* see **befa**

beisbol *m* baseball

beisbolero *m* or **beisbolista** *m* baseball player

bejuco *m* cane, liana

beldad *f* beauty

beldar §2 *tr* to winnow

belén *m* crèche; bedlam, confusion; madhouse; gossip ‖ **Belén** Bethlehem

bel•fo -fa *adj* (*labio*) blobber; blobber-lipped ‖ *m* (*de animal*) lip; blobber lip

belga *adj & mf* Belgian

Bélgica *f* Belgium

bélgi•co -ca *adj* Belgian ‖ *f* see **Bélgica**

belicista *mf* warmonger

béli•co -ca *adj* warlike

belico•so -sa *adj* bellicose

beligerante *adj & mf* belligerent

belitre *adj* low, mean ‖ *m* scoundrel

bella•co -ca *adj* cunning, sly; wicked ‖ *mf* scoundrel

bellaquear *intr* to cheat, be crooked; (SAm) to be stubborn; rear

bellaquería *f* cunning, slyness; wickedness

belleza *f* beauty; **belleza exótica** glamour girl

be•llo -lla *adj* beautiful, fair

bellota *f* acorn; carnation bud

bem•bo -ba *adj* thick-lipped; (Mex) simple, silly ‖ *mf* (*persona*) thicklips

bemol *adj & m* (mus) flat; **tener bemoles** to be a tough job

bencedrina f benzedrine
bencina f benzine
bendecir §11 tr to bless; consecrate; **bendecir la mesa** to say grace
bendición f benediction, blessing; godsend; (en la mesa) grace; **bendiciones** wedding ceremony; **echar la bendicióna** to have nothing more to do with
bendi•to -ta adj blessed, saintly; simple, silly; happy; (agua) holy; **como el pan bendito** as easy as pie ‖ m simple-minded soul
benedícite m grace; **rezar el benedícite** to say grace
benedicti•no -na adj & mf Benedictine ‖ m benedictine
beneficencia f beneficience; charity, welfare; social service
beneficia•do -da mf person or charity receiving the proceeds of a benefit performance
beneficiar tr to benefit; (la tierra) cultivate; (una mina) work, exploit; (minerales) process, reduce; (una región del país) serve; season; slaughter ‖ ref — **beneficiarse de** to take advantage of
beneficia•rio -ria mf beneficiary
beneficio m benefit; profit, gain, yield; (de una mina) exploitation; smelting, ore reduction; benefit performance; **a beneficio de** for the benefit of; on the strength of; **beneficios sociales** fringe benefits
beneficio•so -sa adj beneficial, profitable
benéfi•co -ca adj charitable, benevolent
benemé•ri•to -ta adj & mf worthy; **benemérito de la patria** national hero
beneplácito m approval, consent
benevolencia f benevolence
benévo•lo -la adj benevolent, kind-hearted
bengala f Bengal light; (aer) flare
benignidad f benignity, mildness, kindness; (del tiempo) mildness
benig•no -na adj benign, mild, kind; (tiempo) clement, mild
benjamín m baby (the youngest child)
beodez f drunkenness
beo•do -da adj & mf drunk
bequista mf (CAm, Cuba) scholarship holder; grant winner
berbi•quí m (pl -quíes) brace; **berbiquí y barrena** brace and bit
berenjena f eggplant
berenjenal m eggplant patch; (coll) predicament, jam, fix
bergante m scoundrel, rascal
bergantín m (naut) brig; **bergantín goleta** (naut) brigantine
berilio m beryllium
berkelio m berkelium
berli•nés -nesa adj Berlin ‖ mf Berliner
bermejear intr to turn bright red; look bright red
berme•jo -ja adj vermilion, bright-red
berme•jón -jona adj red, reddish
bermellón m vermilion
berrear intr to bellow, low; bawl, yowl
berrenchín m rage, tantrum
berrido m bellow; scream, yowl

berrín m touchy person, cross child
berrinche m tantrum, conniption
berro m water cress
berza f cabbage
berzal m cabbage patch
berzas m or **berzotas** m dunderhead, flop
besalamano m (obs) announcement, written in the third person and marked B.L.M. (kisses your hand)
besamanos m levee, reception at court; throwing kisses
besar tr to kiss; to graze ‖ ref to bump heads together
beso m kiss; **beso sonado** buss
bestia adj stupid ‖ mf dunce ‖ f beast; **bestia de carga** beast of burden
bestial adj beastly; (coll) terrific
besucar §73 tr & intr to keep on kissing
besu•cón -cona adj kissing ‖ mf kisser
besuquear tr & intr to keep on kissing
betabel m (Mex) beet
betún m bitumen, pitch; shoe polish
bezo m blubber lip; proud flesh
bezu•do -da adj thick-lipped
biberón m nursing bottle
Biblia f Bible
bíbli•co -ca adj Biblical
bibliófi•lo -la mf bibliophile
bibliografía f bibliography
bibliógra•fo -fa mf bibliographer
biblioteca f library; **biblioteca de consulta** reference library; **biblioteca de préstamo** lending library
biblioteca•rio -ria mf librarian
bibliotecnia f bookmaking; library science
biblioteconomía f library science
bicameral adj bicameral
bicarbonato m bicarbonate
bicicleta f bicycle
bicherío m (SAm) vermin
bichero m boat hook
bicho m bug, insect; vermin; animal; fighting bull; simpleton; brat; **bicho viviente** living soul; **mal bicho** scoundrel; ferocious bull
bidón m (bote, lata) can; (tonel de metal) drum
biela f connecting rod
bielda f winnowing rack; winnowing
bieldar tr to winnow
bieldo m winnowing pitch rake
bien adv well; readily; very; indeed; **ahora bien** now then; **bien como** just as; **bien que** although; **más bien** rather; somewhat; **no bien** as soon as; scarcely ‖ s welfare; property; darling; **bienes** wealth, riches, possessions; **bienes de fortuna** worldly possessions; **bienes dotales** dower; **bienes inmuebles** real estate; **bienes muebles** personal property; **bienes raíces** real estate; **bienes relictos** estate; **bienes semovientes** livestock; **bien público** commonweal; **en bien de** for the sake of
bienal adj biennial
bienama•do -da adj dearly beloved
bienandanza f happiness, prosperity
bienaventura•do -da adj happy, blissful; blessed; simple

bienaventuranza *f* happiness, bliss; blessedness

bienestar *m* well-being, welfare

bienhabla•do -da *adj* well-spoken

bienhada•do -da *adj* fortunate, lucky

bienhe•chor -chora *adj* beneficent ‖ *m* benefactor ‖ *f* benefactress

bienintenciona•do -da *adj* well-meaning

bienio *m* biennium

bienquerencia *f* affection, fondness

bienquistar *tr* to bring together, reconcile

bienvenida *f* safe arrival; welcome; **dar la bienvenida a** to welcome

bienveni•do -da *adj* welcome ‖ *f* see **bienvenida**

bienvivir *intr* to live in comfort; live decently, properly

bif•tec *m* (*pl* **-tecs**) beefsteak

bifurcar §73 *ref* to branch, fork

bigamia *f* bigamy

bíga•mo -ma *adj* bigamous ‖ *mf* bigamist

bigornia *f* two-horn anvil

bigote *m* mustache; **bigotes** (*del gato*) whiskers; **tener bigotes** to have a mind of one's own

bigudí *m* hair curler

bikini *m* bikini (swimsuit)

bilingüe *adj* bilingual

bilis *f* bile; **descargar la bilis** to vent one's spleen

bilma *f* (med) compress

billar *m* billiards; billiard table; billiard room; **billar romano** pinball

billete *m* ticket; note, bill; **billete de abono** season ticket; commutation ticket; **billete de banco** bank note; **billete de ida y vuelta** round-trip ticket; **billete kilométrico** mileage ticket; **medio billete** half fare

billetero *m* billfold; ticket agent

billón *m* (U.S.A.) trillion; (Brit) billion

bimba *f* top hat; (Mex) drinking spree

bimotor *adj* twin-motor ‖ *m* twin-motor plane

biodegradable *adj* biodegradable

biofísi•co -ca *adj* biophysical ‖ *f* biophysics

biografía *f* biography

biógra•fo -fa *mf* biographer

biología *f* biology

biólo•go -ga *mf* biologist

biombo *m* folding screen

bioplasma *f* bioplasm

biopsia *f* biopsy

bióxido *m* dioxide

bioquími•co -ca *adj* biochemical ‖ *mf* biochemist ‖ *f* biochemistry

bipartición *f* fission, splitting

bípe•do -da *adj & mf* biped; human

biplano *m* biplane

biplaza *m* (aer) two-seater

birimbao *m* jews'-harp

birlar *tr* to knock down, shoot down; outwit; **birlar algo a alguien** to snitch something from someone

birlocha *f* kite

Birmania *f* Burma

birma•no -na *adj & mf* Burmese

biro *m* or **birome** *f* (Arg) ball-point pen

birreta *f* biretta, red biretta

birrete *m* mortarboard, academic cap

bis *interj* encore! ‖ *m* encore

bisabue•lo -la *mf* great-grandparent ‖ *m* great-grandfather ‖ *f* great-grandmother

bisagra *f* hinge

bisar *tr* to repeat

bisbisar *tr* to mutter, mumble

bisecar §73 *tr* to bisect

bisel *m* bevel edge

biselar *tr* to bevel

bisies•to -ta *adj* leap

bismuto *m* bismuth

bisnie•to -ta *mf* great-grandchild ‖ *m* great-grandson ‖ *f* great-granddaughter

biso•jo -ja *adj* squint-eyed, cross-eyed

bisonte *m* bison; buffalo

biso•ño -ña *adj* green, inexperienced ‖ *mf* greenhorn, rookie

bisté *m* or **bistec** *m* beefsteak

bisun•to -ta *adj* dirty, greasy

bisutería *f* costume jewelry

bitácora *f* binnacle

bitoque *m* bung; (CAm) sewer; (Mex) spigot

Bizancio Byzantium

bizanti•no -na *adj & mf* Byzantine

bizarría *f* gallantry, bravery; magnanimity

biza•rro -rra *adj* gallant, brave; magnanimous

bizcar §73 *tr* to wink ‖ *intr* to squint

biz•co -ca *adj* squint-eyed, cross-eyed

bizcocho *m* biscuit; cake, sponge cake; hardtack; bisque

bizma *f* poultice

bizmar *tr* to poultice

biznie•to -ta *mf* var of **bisnieto**

bizquear *intr* to squint

bizquera *f* squint

blanca *f* steel blade; **sin blanca** penniless

blanca•zo -za *adj* whitish

blan•co -ca *adj* white; (*tez*) fair; (*fuerza*) water; (*arma*) steel; (*cobarde*) yellow; blank ‖ *mf* (*persona*) white; coward ‖ *m* (*color*) white; blank; target; aim, object; interval; white heat; blank form; **dar en el blanco** to hit the mark; **en blanco** (*hoja*) blank; **hacer blanco** to hit the mark; **quedarse en blanco** to not get the point; to be disappointed ‖ *f* see **blanca**

blancor *m* whiteness

blancura *f* whiteness; purity

blancuz•co -ca *adj* whitish; dirty-white

blandear *tr* to persuade; brandish ‖ *intr & ref* to yield, give in

blandengue *adj* soft, colorless

blandir §1 *tr, intr & ref* to brandish

blan•do -da *adj* bland, soft; indulgent; flabby; sensual; cowardly; (*ojos*) tender

blandón *m* wax candle; candlestick

blandura *f* blandness, softness; tolerance; flabbiness; sensuality; flattery; mild weather; cowardice

blanqueadura *f* whitening; bleaching; whitewash

blanquear *tr* to whiten, bleach; blanch; whitewash; tin ‖ *intr* to turn white

blanqueci•no -na *adj* whitish

blanqui•llo -lla *adj* white, whitish ‖ *m* (Guat, Mex) egg; (Chile, Peru) white peach
blasfemar *tr* to blaspheme, curse
blasfemia *f* blasphemy
blasfe•mo -ma *adj* blasphemous ‖ *mf* blasphemer
blasón *m* (*ciencia de los escudos de armas; escudo de armas*) heraldry; (heral) charge; (fig) glory, honor
blasonar *tr* to emblazon; (fig) to emblazon, extol ‖ *intr* to boast; **blasonar de** to boast of being
bledo *m* straw; **no me importa un bledo** or **no se me da un bledo de ello** that doesn't matter a rap to me
blindaje *m* armor; (elec) shield
blindar *tr* to armor, armor-plate; (elec) to shield
B.L.M. *abbr* **besalamano**
bloc *m* (*pl* **bloques**) pad
blof *m* bluff
blofear *intr* to bluff
blon•do -da *adj* blond, fair, flaxen, light; (Arg) curly ‖ *f* blond lace
bloque *m* block; (*de papel*) pad; **bloque de hormigón** concrete block
bloquear *tr* to blockade; (*un coche, un tren*) brake; (*créditos*) freeze
bloqueo *m* blockade; (*de crédito*) freezing; **bloqueo vertical** (telv) vertical hold
b.l.p. *abbr* **besa los pies**
blujins *mpl* blue jeans
blusa *f* blouse, smock; (*de mujer*) shirtwaist; (Col) jacket
boardilla *f* dormer window; garret
boato *m* show, pomp
bobada *f* folly, piece of folly
bobalías *mf* simpleton, dunce
bobali•cón -cona *adj* simple, silly ‖ *mf* simpleton, nitwit
bobear *intr* to talk nonsense; to dawdle, loiter around
bobería *f* folly, nonsense
bóbilis—de bóbilis free, for nothing; without effort
bobina *f* bobbin; (elec) coil; **bobina de chispas** spark coil; **bobina de encendido** ignition coil, spark coil; **bobina de sintonía** tuning coil
bobinar *tr* to wind
bo•bo -ba *adj* simple, foolish, stupid ‖ *mf* simpleton, fool ‖ *m* (archaic) clown, jester
boca *f* mouth; speech; taste, flavor; (*del estómago*) pit; **a boca de jarro** immoderately; at close range; **boca de agua** hydrant; **boca de dragón** (bot) snapdragon; **boca de riego** hydrant; **buscarle a uno la boca** to draw someone out; **decir con la boca chica** to offer as a mere formality; **no decir esta boca es mía** to not say a word
bocacalle *f* street entrance; intersection
boca•caz *m* (*pl* **-caces**) spillway
bocadillo *m* tape, ribbon; snack, bite; farmer's snack in the field; sandwich
bocadito *m* little bit; (Cuba) cigarillo (*cigaret wrapped in tobacco*)

bocado *m* bite, morsel; bit; **bocado de Adán** Adam's apple; **no tener para un bocado** to not have a cent
bocal *m* narrow-mouthed pitcher; (*de un puerto*) narrows
bocallave *f* keyhole
bocamanga *f* cuff, wristband
bocanada *f* (*de líquido*) swallow; (*de humo*) puff; (*de viento*) gust; boasting
bocartear *tr* to crush, stamp
bocaza *f* loudmouth; gossip
bocera *f* smear on lips
boceto *m* sketch, outline; wax model, clay model
bocina *f* horn, trumpet; auto horn; phonograph horn; ear trumpet
bocio *m* goiter
bocoy *m* large barrel
bocha *f* bowling ball
bochar *tr* (Mex, Ven) to turn down; (Mex, Ven) insult
boche *m* small hole in ground for boys' game; (Ven) slight, snub
bochinche *m* uproar, tumult, row
bochorno *m* sultry weather; blush, embarrassment, shame
bochorno•so -sa *adj* sultry, stuffy; embarrassing, shameful
boda *f* marriage, wedding; **bodas de Camacho** banquet, lavish feast
bodega *f* wine cellar; dock warehouse; granary; grocery store; (*de nave*) hold; cellar; (*hombre que bebe mucho*) tank
bodegón *m* hash house, beanery; saloon; still life
bodegue•ro -ra *mf* cellarer; grocer
bodijo *m* unequal match; simple wedding
bodoque *m* lump; dunce, dolt; (Mex) bump, lump
bodoquera *f* peashooter
bóer *mf* Boer
bofe *adj invar* (CAm) unpleasant, disgusting ‖ *m* (coll) lung; (P-R) cinch, snap; **echar el bofe** or **los bofes** to drudge, to grind; **bofes** lights (*of sheep, etc.*)
bofetada *f* slap in the face
boga *mf* rower ‖ *f* vogue, fashion; rowing
bogar §44 *intr* to row
bogavante *m* lobster
bohardilla *f* dormer window; garret
bohe•mio -mia *adj* & *mf* Bohemian
bohío *m* hut, shack
boicotear *tr* to boycott
boicoteo *m* boycott, boycotting
boina *f* beret
boj *m* boxwood
boja *f* southernwood
bojar *tr* to measure the perimeter of; (*el cuero*) scrape clean ‖ *intr* to measure
bola *f* ball; marble; bowling; shoe polish; shoeshine; (cards) slam; lie, deceit; (Mex) brawl, riot; **bola de alcanfor** moth ball; **bola de cristal** crystal ball; **bola de nieve** snowball; **bola rompedora** wrecking ball; **bolas** Gaucho lasso tipped with balls; **dejar que ruede la bola** to let things take

bi
bo

their course; **raspar la bola** (Chile) to clear out, beat it

bolada f (de una bola) throw; luck, opportunity; (Arg) billiard stroke; (Chile) dainty, tidbit; (Guat, Mex) lie, fib

bolado m (CAm) rumor

bolazo m hit with a ball; **de bolazo** (coll) hurriedly, right away; (Mex) at random

bolchevique adj & mf Bolshevik

bolchevismo m Bolshevism

boleada f (Arg) hunting with bolas; (Mex) shoeshine; (Peru) flunking

bolear tr to throw; (Arg) to catch with bolas; (zapatos) (Mex) to shine; (SAm) to kick out, flunk ‖ intr to play for fun; lie; boast ‖ ref (Arg, Urug) to rear and fall backwards; upset; blush

bole•ro -ra mf bolero dancer ‖ m bolero (dance; music; jacket); (Mex) bootblack ‖ f bowling alley; **bolera encespada** bowling green

boleta f pass, permit, admission ticket; (mil) billet; ballot

boletería f ticket office

boletín m bulletin; ticket; form; press release

boleto m ticket

boliche m bowling; bowling alley; (SAm) hash house

bólido m fireball, bolide

bolígrafo m ball-point pen

bolilápiz m (Mex) ball-point pen

bolillo m bobbin for making lace; frame for stiffening lace cuffs

Bolivia f Bolivia

bolivia•no -na adj & mf Bolivian

bo•lo -la adj (CAm, Mex) drunk; m ninepin, tenpin; dunce, blockhead; (de escalera) newel; (cards) slam; **bolos** bowling, ninepins, tenpins; **jugar a los bolos** to bowl

Bolonia f Bologna

bolsa f purse, pocketbook; pouch; stock exchange, stock market; (en el vestido) bag, pucker; grant, award; **bolsa de agua caliente** hotwater bottle; **bolsa de aire** (aut) air bag; **bolsa de hielo** ice bag; **bolsa de trabajo** employment bureau; **bolsa isotérmica** Thermos bottle; **hacer bolsa** (un vestido) to bag; **jugar a la bolsa** to play the market

bolsear tr to pick the pocket of; (Arg, Bol, Urug) to jilt; (Chile) to sponge on

bolsero m (SAm) sponger; (Mex) pickpocket

bolsicalculadora f pocket calculator

bolsillo m pocket; purse, pocketbook

bolsista m broker, stockbroker; (CAm, Mex) pickpocket

bolso m purse, pocketbook; **bolso de mano** handbag

bollo m bun, roll; bump, lump; dent; (en un vestido) puff; (en adorno de tapicería) tuft; **bollo de crema** cream puff

bomba f pump; bomb; fire engine; lamp globe; high hat; firecracker; soap bubble; bombshell; **a prueba de bombas** bombproof; **bomba atómica** atomic bomb; **bomba coche** car bomb; **bomba cohete** rocket bomb; **bomba de engrase** grease

gun; **bomba de hidrógeno** hydrogen bomb; **bomba de incendios** fire engine; **bomba de profundidad** depth bomb; **bomba de sentina** bilge pump; **bomba estomacal** stomach pump; **bomba neutrónica** neutron bomb; **bomba rompedora** blockbuster; **bomba volante** buzz bomb; **caer como una bomba** to fall like a bombshell; to burst in unexpectedly

bombachas fpl loose-fitting baggy trousers

bombardear tr & intr to bomb; bombard; **bombardear en picado** to dive-bomb

bombardeo m bombing; bombarding; **bombardeo en picado** dive bombing

bombardero m bomber; bombardier

bomba-reloj f time bomb

bombazo m bomb explosion; bomb hit; bomb damage

bombear tr to bomb; ballyhoo, puff up; pump; (SAm) to reconnoiter; (Col) to fire, dismiss ‖ ref to camber, bulge

bombero m fireman; pumpman

bombilla f bulb, light bulb; lamp chimney; tube for sucking up maté; **bombilla de destello** flash bulb

bombillo m trap, stench trap; (naut) pump

bombista m lamp maker; (el que da bombos) booster

bom•bo -ba adj astounded, stunned; (W-I) lukewarm ‖ m bass drum; ballyhoo; (naut) barge, lighter; **dar bombo a** to ballyhoo, puff up; **irse al bombo** (Arg) to fail ‖ f see **bomba**

bombón m bonbon, candy

bombona f carboy

bombonera f candy box

bona•chón -chona adj goodnatured, kind, simple

bonancible adj (tiempo) fair; (mar) calm; (viento) moderate

bonanza f fair weather, calm seas; prosperity, boom; rich ore pocket

bona•zo -za adj kind-hearted

bondad f kindness; favor; **tener la bondad de** to have the kindness to

bondado•so -sa adj kind, generous

bonete m cap, hat; candy bowl

bonetería f hat shop; notion store

bongo m (SAm) barge; canoe

boniato m sweet potato

bonificar §73 tr to improve; give a discount on

boni•to -ta adj pretty, nice; pretty good

bono m bond; food voucher

boñiga f manure, cow dung

boom m (mercado, bolsa) boom

boqueada f gasp of death

boquear tr to pronounce, utter ‖ intr to gasp

boquerel m nozzle

boquete m gap, breach, opening

boquiabier•to -ta adj open-mouthed

boquian•cho -cha adj wide-mouthed

boquiangos•to -ta adj narrow-mouthed

boquihundi•do -da adj hollow-mouthed

boquilla f (de instrumento de viento) mouthpiece; (de pipa) stem; (de cigarro) tip; (de aparato de alumbrado) burner; cigar holder, cigarette holder; (*de manguera*) nozzle; opening in irrigation canal; opening at bottom of trouser leg

boquirro•to -ta *adj* garrulous

boquiverde *adj* obscene, smutty

bórax *m* borax

borbollar or **borbollear** *intr* to bubble up

borbollón *m* bubbling; **a borbollones** impetuously

borborigmos *mpl* rumbling of the bowels

borbotar *intr* to bubble up, bubble over

borce•guí *m* (*pl* **-guíes**) high shoe

borda *f* hut; (naut) gunwale; **arrojar, echar** or **tirar por la borda** to throw overboard

bordada *f* (naut) tack; **dar bordadas** (naut) to tack; pace to and fro

bordado *m* embroidery

bordadura *f* embroidery

bordar *tr* to embroider

borde *m* border, edge; fringe; rim; **borde de la acera** curb; **borde del mar** seaside

bordear *tr* to border || *intr* to go on the edge; (naut) to tack

bordo *m* (naut) board; (naut) side; (naut) tack; (Guat, Mex) dam, dike; **a bordo** (naut) on board; **al bordo** (naut) alongside; **de alto bordo** seagoing; distinguished, important

bordón *m* (*de tambor*) snare; pilgrim's staff; pet word; burden, refrain

bordonear *intr* to grope along with a stick; to go around begging

borgoña *m* Burgundy (*wine*) || **la Borgoña** Burgundy

borgo•ñón -ñona *adj* & *mf* Burgundian

boricua or **borinque•ño -ña** *adj* & *mf* Puerto Rican

borla *f* tassel; powder puff; **tomar la borla** to take a higher degree, take the doctor's degree

borne *m* binding post; (*de la lanza*) tip

bornear *tr* to bend, twist; (*sillares pesados*) set in place || *intr* to swing at anchor || *ref* to warp

borra *f* fuzz, nap, lint

borrachera *f* drunkenness; spree, binge; great exaltation; (coll) piece of folly; **pegarse una borrachera** to go on a binge

borrachería *f* (Mex) bar, tavern

borrachín *m* drunkard

borra•cho -cha *adj* drunk; (*habitualmente*) drinking || *mf* drunkard

borrador *m* blotter, day book; rough draft; eraser

borradura *f* striking out, scratching out

borraj *m* borax

borrajear *tr* & *intr* to scribble; doodle

borrar *tr* to scratch out, cross out; erase, rub out; darken, obscure; blot, smear

borrasca *f* storm, tempest; upset, setback

borrasco•so -sa *adj* stormy

borregos *mpl* fleecy clouds

borrica *f* she-ass; stupid woman

borrico *m* ass, donkey; sawhorse; stupid fellow, ass

borricón *m* or **borricote** *m* drudge

borrón *m* blot; rough draft; blemish; (fig) blot, stain

borronear *tr* to scribble

borro•so -sa *adj* blurred, smudgy, fuzzy; muddy, thick

boruca *f* noise, clamor, uproar

borujo *m* lump, clump

boscaje *m* woodland; (paint) woodland scene

bosque *m* forest, woodland; **bosque maderable** timberland

bosquejar *tr* to sketch, outline; make a rough model of

bosquejo *m* sketch, outline; rough model

bostezar §60 *intr* to yawn, gape

bostezo *m* yawn, yawning

bota *f* shoe, boot; leather wine bag; liquid measure (*125 gallons or 516 liters*); **bota de agua** gum boot; **bota de montar** riding boot; **ponerse las botas** (coll) to hit the jack pot, come out on top

botador *m* boat pole; punch, nailset

botadura *f* launching

botafuego *m* hothead, firebrand

botalón *m* (naut) boom; **botalón de foque** (naut) jib boom

botáni•co -ca *adj* botanical || *mf* botanist || *f* botany

botanista *mf* botanist

botar *tr* to throw, hurl; throw away, throw out; (*un buque*) launch; (*el timón*) shift; fire, dismiss; squander || *intr* to jump; bounce || *ref* (*un caballo*) to buck

botarate *m* madcap, wild man; spendthrift

bote *m* boat, small boat; can, jar, pot; bounce; blow, thrust; (Mex) jug, jail; **bote de paso** ferryboat; **bote de porcelana** apothecary's jar; **bote de remos** rowboat; **bote de salvamento** or **bote salvavidas** lifeboat; **de bote en bote** crowded, jammed; **de bote y voleo** thoughtlessly

botella *f* bottle

botica *f* drug store; medicine

botica•rio -ria *mf* druggist, apothecary

botija *f* earthenware jug with short narrow neck; (CAm, Ven) hidden treasure; (SAm) belly; **decirle a uno botija verde** (Cuba) to let someone have it, tell someone off; **estar hecho una botija** (*un niño*) to be cross and scream; (*una persona*) be fat, be pudgy

botijo *m* earthenware jar with spout and handle

botín *m* booty, plunder, spoils; spat, legging; (Chile) sock

botina *f* shoe, high shoe

botiquín *m* medicine kit, first-aid kit; medicine chest; first-aid station; (Ven) saloon

bo•to -ta *adj* (*sin filo o punta*) blunt, dull; (fig) dull, slow || *m* leather bag || *f* see **bota**

botón *m* button; (*de mueble o puerta*) knob; (*de reloj de bolsillo*) stem; (bot) bud; (elec) push button; **botón de oro** buttercup; **botón de puerta** doorknob; **botones** *msg* bellboy, bellhop

bou *m* fishing with a dragnet between two boats

bóveda *f* dome, vault; crypt; (aut) cowl; **bóveda celeste** canopy of heaven
boxeador *m* boxer; (Mex) brass knuckles
boxear *intr* to box
boxeo *m* boxing
bóxer *m* brass knuckles
boxibalón *m* punching bag
boya *f* buoy; **boya salvavidas** life buoy
boyante *adj* buoyant; lucky, successful; (*que no cala lo que debe calar*) (naut) light
boyera *f* or **boyeriza** *f* ox stable
boyerizo *m* or **boyero** *m* ox driver
bozal *adj* simple, stupid ‖ *m* muzzle; headharness bells; headstall
bozo *m* down on upper lip; lips, mouth; headstall
B.p. *abbr* **Bendición papal**
Br. *abbr* **bachiller**
bracear *intr* to swing the arms; swim with overhead strokes; struggle
brace·ro -ra *adj* arm, hand; thrown with the hand ‖ *m* man who offers his arm to a lady; day laborer; migrant worker; **de bracero** arm in arm
bra·co -ca *adj* pug-nosed
braga *f* diaper, clout; hoisting rope; **bragas** panties, step-ins; breeches; **calzarse las bragas** to wear the pants
bragadura *f* crotch
braga·zas *m* (*pl* **-zas**) easy mark, henpecked fellow
braguero *m* (*para hernias*) truss; (*entrepiernas*) crotch
bragueta *f* fly
bragui·llas *m* (*pl* **-llas**) brat
brama *f* rut, mating, mating time
bramante *adj* bellowing, roaring ‖ *m* packthread, twine
bramar *intr* to bellow, roar; (*el viento*) howl; rage, storm
bramido *m* bellow, roar; howling; raging
brasa *f* live coal, red-hot coal
brasero *m* brazier; (Col) bonfire; (Mex) hearth, fireplace
Brasil, el Brazil
brasile·ño -ña *adj & mf* Brazilian
bravata *f* bravado, bragging; **echar bravatas** to talk big
bravatear *intr* to brag, boast
bravear *intr* to talk big, four-flush
braveza *f* bravery; ferocity; (*de los elementos*) fury, violence
braví·o -a *adj* ferocious; wild, untamed, uncultivated; crude, unpolished; (*mar*) rough, wild; (*terreno*) rough, rugged
bra·vo -va *adj* (*valiente*) brave; fine, excellent; fierce, savage, wild; (*mar*) rough; magnificent; angry, mad; (*perro*) vicious; (*toro*) game; boasting; (*chili*) strong ‖ *interj* bravo!
bravu·cón -cona *adj* four-flushing ‖ *mf* fourflusher
bravura *f* bravery; fierceness; gameness; bravado, boasting
braza *f* fathom
brazada *f* stroke, pull (*with the arm*); **brazada de pecho** breast stroke

brazado *m* armful, armload
brazal *m* arm band; **brazal de luto** mourning band
brazalete *m* bracelet
brazo *m* arm; (*de animal*) foreleg; **a brazo partido** hand to hand (*i.e., without weapons*); **asidos del brazo** arm in arm; **brazo derecho** right-hand man; **brazos** hands, workmen; backers; **hecho un brazo de mar** dressed to kill
brea *f* tar, wood tar; calking substance; packing canvas; **brea seca** rosin
brear *tr* to annoy, mistreat, beat; tar
brebaje *m* beverage, drink
brécol *m* or **brécoles** *mpl* broccoli
brecha *f* opening; (*en un muro*) breach; breakthrough
brega *f* fight, struggle, quarrel; trickery; drudgery
bregar §44 *intr* to strive, struggle, toil
breña *f* or **breñal** *m* or **breñar** *m* rocky thicket
breque *m* brake
brequear *tr & intr* to brake
bresca *f* honeycomb
Bretaña *f* Brittany; **la Gran Bretaña** Great Britain
brete *m* fetters, shackles; tight squeeze, fix
bretones *mpl* Brussels sprouts
breva *f* early fig; cinch, snap
breval *m* early-fig tree
breve *adj* brief, short; **en breve** shortly, soon
brevedad *f* brevity, shortness; **a la mayor brevedad** as soon as possible
brevete *m* note, mark
brezal *m* heath, moor
brezo *m* heath, heather
briba *f* loafing; **andar a la briba** to loaf around
bri·bón -bona *adj* loafing, crooked ‖ *mf* loafer, crook
bribonada *f* loafing, crookedness
bribonear *intr* to loaf around, be crooked
brida *f* bridle
brigada *f* brigade; gang, squad; warrant officer
brillante *adj* bright, brilliant, shining ‖ *m* diamond, gem
brillantez *f* brilliance
brillantina *f* brilliantine; metal polish
brillar *intr* to shine; sparkle
brillazón *f* (Arg, Bol, Urug) pampa mirage
brillo *m* brightness, brilliance; sparkle; **sacar brillo a** to shine
brillo·so -sa *adj* (*que brilla por el mucho uso*) shiny; shining, brilliant
brin *m* canvas
brincar §73 *tr* to bounce up and down; skip, skip over ‖ *intr* to jump, leap; be touchy, get angry easily
brinco *m* bounce; jump, leap; **en dos brincos** or **en un brinco** in an instant
brindador *m* toaster
brindar *tr* to invite; offer; **brindar a uno con una cosa** to offer someone something ‖ *intr* — **brindar a** or **por** to drink to, toast ‖ *ref* — **brindarse a** to offer to

brin•dis *m* (*pl* **-dis**) invitation, treat; toast

brío *m* spirit, enterprise; elegance; **cortar los bríos a** to cut the wings of

brio•so -sa *adj* spirited, lively, enterprising; elegant

brisa *f* breeze; residue of pressed grapes

brisera *f* or **brisero** *m* glass lamp shade (*for candles*)

británi•co -ca *adj* British, Britannic

brita•no -na *adj* British ‖ *mf* Briton, Britisher

brizna *f* chip, particle; (Ven) drizzle

brl. *abbr* **barril**

broca *f* reel, spindle; drill, bit

brocado *m* brocade

brocal *m* (*de pozo*) curbstone; (*de bota*) mouthpiece; (*de banqueta*) (Mex) curb

brocamantón *m* diamond brooch

bróculi *m* broccoli

brocha *f* brush; loaded dice; **de brocha gorda** house (*painter*); (coll) crude, heavy-handed

brochada *f* stroke with a brush; rough sketch

brochazo *m* stroke with a brush

broche *m* clasp, clip, fastener; (*conjunto de dos piezas*) hook and eye; (Chile) paper clip; **broche de oro** punch line; **broche de presión** snap, catch; **broches** (Ecuad) cuff buttons

brocheta *f* skewer

broma *f* joke, jest; fun; shipworm; **bromas aparte** joking aside; **en broma** in fun, jokingly; **gastar una broma a** to play a joke on

bromear *intr* & *ref* to joke, jest; have a good time

bromhídri•co -ca *adj* hydrobromic

bromista *adj* joking ‖ *mf* joker

bromo *m* bromine

bromuro *m* bromide

bronca *f* row, quarrel; rough joke, poor joke; **armar una bronca** to start a row

bronce *m* bronze; **bronce de cañón** gun metal

broncea•do -da *adj* bronze; tanned, sunburned ‖ *m* bronzing; bronze finish; tan, sunburn

bronceador *m* suntan lotion

broncear *tr*, *intr* & *ref* to bronze; tan, sunburn

bron•co -ca *adj* coarse, rough; gruff, crude; (*voz*) harsh, hoarse ‖ *f* see **bronca**

bronquitis *f* bronchitis

broquel *m* buckler, shield; (fig) shield

broqueta *f* skewer

brota *f* bud, shoot

brotadura *f* budding, sprouting; gushing; (*de la piel*) eruption, rash

brotar *tr* to bring forth, produce ‖ *intr* to bud, sprout; gush; (*la piel*) break out

brote *m* bud, shoot; outbreak; (*de petróleo*) gush, spurt

broza *f* (*maleza*) underbrush; (*hojas, ramas, cortezas*) brushwood; (*desperdicio*) trash, rubbish; printer's brush

bruces — **dar** or **caer de bruces** to fall on one's face

bruja *f* witch, sorceress; barn owl; (*mujer fea*) hag; (*mujer de mala vida*) prostitute; (W-I) spook

brujear *tr* (*bestias salvajes*) (Ven) to hunt ‖ *intr* to practice witchcraft

brujería *f* witchcraft, sorcery, magic

brujo *m* sorcerer, wizard

brújula *f* (*flechilla*) magnetic needle; (*instrumento*) compass; (*agujero para la puntería*) sight; **perder la brújula** to lose one's touch

brujulear *tr* (*las cartas*) to uncover gradually; suspect

brulote *m* fire ship; (Arg, Chile, Bol) vulgarity, insult

bruma *f* fog, mist

brumo•so -sa *adj* foggy, misty

bruñido *m* burnish, polish; burnishing

bruñir §12 *tr* to burnish, polish; put rouge on; (CAm) to annoy

brus•co -ca *adj* brusque, gruff; sudden; (*curva*) sharp

bruselas *fpl* tweezers ‖ **Bruselas** Brussels

brusquedad *f* brusqueness, gruffness; suddenness; (*de una curva*) sharpness

brutal *adj* brutal; sudden; huge, terrific; stunning

brutalidad *f* brutality; stupidity; tremendous amount

bruteza *f* brutality; (archaic) roughness

bru•to -ta *adj* brute; rough, coarse; stupid; gross ‖ *mf* (*persona*) brute; blockhead ‖ *m* (*animal*) brute

bu *m* (*pl* **búes**) bugaboo; **hacer el bu a** to scare, frighten

buceador *m* or **buceadora** *f* diver

bucear *intr* to dive, be a diver; delve, search

buceo *m* diving

bucle *m* curl, lock

buche *m* (*de ave*) craw, crop, maw; (*de líquido*) mouthful; (*del vestido*) bag, pucker; (*para secretos*) bosom; belly; (Ecuad) high hat; (Guat, Mex) goiter; **sacar el buche a** to make (*someone*) open up

budín *m* pudding

buen *adj* var of **bueno,** used before masculine singular nouns

buenamente *adv* with ease; gladly, willingly; conveniently

buenaventura *f* fortune, good luck; (*adivinación*) fortune; **decirle a uno la buenaventura** to tell someone his fortune

bue•no -na *adj* good; kind; (*sano*) well; (*tiempo*) good, fine; **a buenas** willingly; **¡buena es ésa** (or **ésta**)! that's a good one; **de buenas a primeras** all of a sudden; from the start; **¿de dónde bueno?** where have you been?, what's new?

buey *m* ox, bullock, steer

búfa•lo -la *mf* buffalo

bufanda *f* muffler, scarf

bufar *intr* to snort

bufete *m* writing desk; law office; (*de un abogado*) clients; law practice; refreshment; (Col) bedpan; **abrir bufete** to open a law office

bufido *m* snort

bu·fo -fa *adj* comic; (Ven) spongy ‖ *mf* buffoon
bu·fón -fona *adj* clownish ‖ *m* clown, buffoon; jester; peddler
bufonada *f* buffoonery; sarcasm
bufonería *f* buffoonery; peddling
bufones·co -ca *adj* clownish; coarse, crude
bugui-bugui *m* boogie-woogie
buharda *f* dormer; dormer window; garret
buhardilla *f* dormer window; garret
buho *m* eagle owl; shy fellow
buhonería *f* peddler's kit; peddler's wares
buhonero *m* peddler, hawker
buitre *m* vulture
buje *m* axle box, bushing
bujería *f* gewgaw, trinket
bujía *f* candle; candlestick; candle power; (*de motor de explosión*) spark plug
bulbo *m* bulb
bulevar *m* boulevard
bulevardero *m* boulevardier, man about town
Bulgaria *f* Bulgaria
búlga·ro -ra *adj & mf* Bulgarian
bulimia *f* bulimia
bulto *m* bulk, volume; bust, statue; parcel, piece of baggage; bump, swelling; pillowcase; form, mass; **a bulto** broadly, by guess; **buscar el bulto a** to keep after; **de bulto** evident; **escurrir** or **huir el bulto** to duck
bulla *f* noise; crowd; loud argument
bullaje *m* crush, mob (*of people*)
bullanga *f* racket, disturbance
bullebulle *mf* busybody, bustler
bulle·ro -ra *adj* noisy; inflammatory
bullicio *m* brawl, riot, uprising; (*rumor que hace mucha gente*) rumble
bullicio·so -sa *adj* brawling, riotous; rumbling ‖ *mf* rioter
bullir §13 *tr* to move ‖ *intr* to boil; abound; bustle, hustle; swarm; move, stir; be restless ‖ *ref* to move, stir
buniato *m* sweet potato
buñuelo *m* cruller, fritter, bun; botch, bungle
buque *m* ship, vessel; (*de una nave*) hull; (*de cualquier cosa*) capacity; (C-R) doorframe; **buque almirante** admiral; **buque cisterna** tanker; **buque de guerra** warship; **buque de vapor** steamer, steamship; **buque de vela** sailboat; **buque escucha** vedette; **buque escuela** training ship; **buque fanal** or **buque faro** lightship; **buque mercante** merchantman, merchant vessel; **buque portaminas** mine layer; **buque tanque** tanker; **buque velero** sailing vessel
burbuja *f* bubble
burbujear *intr* to bubble
burdégano *m* hinny
burdel *m* brothel, disorderly house
Burdeos Bordeaux
bur·do -da *adj* coarse, rough
burear *tr* (Col) to fool ‖ *intr* to have fun
burga *f* hot springs
bur·gués -guesa *adj* middle-class, bourgeois; (*antiartístico*) bourgeois ‖ *m* middle-class man ‖ *f* middle-class woman

burguesía *f* middle class, bourgeoisie; **alta burguesía** upper middle class; **pequeña burguesía** lower middle class
burla *f* hoax, trick; joke; ridicule; **burlas aparte** joking aside; **de burlas** in fun, for fun
burladero *m* safety island, safety zone; (*en las plazas de toros*) covert; (*en los túneles*) safety niche; hiding place
burla·dor -dora *adj* joking; deceptive ‖ *mf* wag, prankster, practical joker ‖ *m* seducer, libertine
burlar *tr* to make fun of; deceive; disappoint; outwit, frustrate; (*a una mujer*) seduce ‖ *intr* to scoff ‖ *ref* to joke; **burlarse de** to make fun of
burlería *f* derision, mockery; deception, trick; scorn, derision; fish story
burles·co -ca *adj* funny, comic, burlesque
burlete *m* weather stripping
bur·lón -lona *adj* joking ‖ *mf* joker ‖ *m* mockingbird
bu·ró *m* (*pl* -rós) writing desk; (Mex) night table
burócrata *mf* jobholder, bureaucrat
burra *f* she-ass; stupid woman; drudge (*woman*)
burrajear *tr & intr* to scribble; doodle
burra·jo -ja *adj* (Mex) coarse, stupid ‖ *m* dung (*used as fuel*)
bu·rro -rra *adj* stupid, asinine ‖ *m* donkey, jackass; sawbuck, sawhorse; (Mex) stepladder; **burro cargado de letras** learned jackass; **burro de carga** drudge ‖ *f* see **burra**
bursátil *adj* stock-market
busca *f* search; **en busca de** in search of
buscani·guas *m* (*pl* -guas) (Col) snake
buscapié *m* (*para dar a entender algo*) hint; (*para averiguar algo*) feeler ‖ **busca·piés** *m* (*pl* -piés) snake
buscaplei·tos *mf* (*pl* -tos) troublemaker
buscar §73 *tr* to seek, hunt, look for; (Mex) to provoke; **buscar tres pies al gato** to be looking for trouble ‖ *ref* to take care of oneself; **buscársela** to manage to get along; to ask for it
buscareta *f* wren
buscarrui·dos *mf* (*pl* -dos) troublemaker
buscavi·das *mf* (*pl* -das) snoop, busybody; go-getter
bus·cón -cona *adj* searching; cheating ‖ *mf* seeker; thief, cheat; (min) prospector ‖ *f* loose woman
busi·lis *m* (*pl* -lis) trouble; **ahí está el busilis** that's the trouble; **dar en el busilis** to hit the nail on the head
búsqueda *f* search, hunt
busto *m* bust
butaca *f* armchair, easy chair; orchestra seat
butifarra *f* Catalonian sausage; loose sock, loose stocking; (Peru) ham and salad sandwich
bution·do -da *adj* lewd, lustful
buz *m* (*pl* buces) kiss of gratitude and reverence; lip; **hacer el buz** (archaic) to bow and scrape

buzo *m* diver
buzón *m* plug, stopper; mailbox, letter box; (*agujero para echar las cartas*) slot, letter

drop; **buzón de alcance** special-delivery box; late-collection slot

C

C, c (ce) *f* third letter of the Spanish alphabet
c. *abbr* **capítulo, compañía, corriente, cuenta**
c *abbr* **caja, cargo, contra, corriente**
cabal *adj* exact; full, complete, perfect; **no estar en sus cabales** to be not in one's right mind ‖ *adv* exactly; completely ‖ *interj* right!
cábala *f* intrigue; divination
cabalgada *f* raid on horseback; gathering of riders
cabalgador *m* rider, horseman
cabalgadura *f* mount, horse; beast of burden
cabalgar §44 *intr* to go horseback riding
cabalgata *f* cavalcade
caballa *f* mackerel
caballada *f* drove of horses; nonsense, stupidity
caballaje *m* stud service
caballazo *m* collision of two horses, trampling by a horse; (Chile, Peru) bitter attack
caballerango *m* (Mex) stableman
caballeres·co -ca *adj* chivalric, knightly; gentlemanly
caballerete *m* (coll) dude
caballería *f* mount, horse, mule; cavalry; chivalry, knighthood; **andarse en caballerías** to fall all over oneself in compliments; **caballería andante** knight-errantry; **caballería mayor** horse, mule; **cabellería menor** ass, donkey
caballeriza *f* stable; stable hands
caballerizo *m* groom, stableman
caballe·ro -ra *adj* riding, mounted; stubborn ‖ *m* knight, nobleman; gentleman; mister; horseman, cavalier, rider; **armar caballero** to knight; **caballero andante** knight errant; **caballero de industria** crook, adventurer, sharper; **Caballero de la triste figura** Knight of the Rueful Countenance (*Don Quijote*); **ir caballero en** to ride
caballerosidad *f* chivalry, gentlemanliness
caballerote *m* boorish fellow, cad
caballete *m* (*bastidor para sostener un cuadro o pizarra*) easel; (*de tejado*) ridge, hip; (*lomo de tierra*) ridge; (*artificio usado como soporte*) trestle, sawbuck, horse; (*de la nariz*) bridge; chimney cap; (*del ave*) breastbone; little horse
caballista *m* horseman; mounted smuggler ‖ *f* horsewoman
caballito *m* little horse; merry-go-round; **caballito del diablo** dragonfly
caballo *m* horse; (*en ajedrez*) knight; playing card (*figure on horseback equivalent to*

queen); (slang) heroin; **a caballo** on horseback; **a caballo de** astride; **a caballo regalado no se le mira el diente** never look a gift horse in the mouth; **caballo blanco** (*persona que da dinero para una empresa dudosa*) angel; **caballo de batalla** battle horse; (*de una controversia*) gist, main point; (*aquello en que uno sobresale*) forte, strong point; **caballo de carreras** race horse; **caballo de fuerza** French horsepower, metric horsepower; **caballo de tiro** draft horse; **caballo de Troya** Trojan horse; **caballo de vapor** French horsepower, metric horsepower; **caballo de vapor inglés** horsepower; **caballo mecedor** rocking horse, hobbyhorse; **caballo padre** stallion; **caballo semental** stallion
caballu·no -na *adj* horse, horselike
cabaña *f* cabin, hut; drove, flock; livestock; pastoral scene; (Arg) cattlebreeding ranch
cabañuelas *fpl* (Arg, Bol) first summer rains; (Mex) winter rains
caba·ret *m* (*pl* **-rets**) cabaret
cabecear *tr* (*un libro*) to put a headband on; (*el vino*) head; (*una media*) put a new foot on ‖ *intr* to nod; bob the head; (*en señal de negación*) shake the head; (*los caballos*) toss the head; (*la caja de un carruaje*) lurch; (*un buque*) pitch
cabeceo *m* (*de la cabeza*) nod, bob, shake; (*de la caja del carruaje*) lurching; (*del buque*) pitch, pitching
cabecera *f* (*de cama, mesa, etc.*) head; bedside; headboard; headwaters; (*de una casa, un campo*) end; (*del capítulo de un libro*) heading; (*de periódico*) headline; capital, county seat; bolster, pillow; (typ) headpiece, vignette; **cabecera de cartel** top billing; **cabecera de puente** (mil) bridgehead
cabecilla *mf* scalawag ‖ *m* ringleader ‖ *f* **cabecilla de alfiler** pinhead
cabellar *intr* to grow hair; to put on false hair ‖ *ref* to put on false hair
cabellera *f* head of hair; foliage; (*del cometa*) coma; (bot) mistletoe
cabello *m* hair; **cabello de Venus** maidenhair; **cabellos de ángel** cotton candy; **en cabello** with the hair down; **en cabellos** bareheaded; **traído por los cabellos** farfetched
cabellu·do -da *adj* hairy
caber §14 *intr* to fit, go; have enough room; be possible; happen, befall; **no cabe duda** there is no doubt; **no cabe más** that's the

limit; **no caber de** to be bursting with; **no caber en sí** to be beside oneself; be puffed up with pride; **todo cabe en** anything can be expected of

cabestrar *tr* to put a halter on

cabestrillo *m* sling

cabestro *m* halter; **llevar** or **traer del cabestro** to lead by the halter; (fig) to lead by the nose

cabeza *f* head; chief city, capital; **cabeza de chorlito** scatterbrains; (Arg) forgetful person; **cabeza de motín** ringleader; **cabeza de playa** beachhead; **cabeza de puente** bridgehead; **cabeza de turco** butt, scapegoat; **cabeza mayor** head of cattle; **cabeza menor** head of sheep, goats, etc.; **de cabeza** headfirst; on end; on one's own; by heart; **ir cabeza abajo** to go downhill; **irse de la cabeza** to go out of one's mind; **mala cabeza** headstrong person; **por su cabeza** on one's own; **romperse la cabeza** to rack one's brains

cabezada *f* butt with the head; blow on the head; (de buque) pitch, pitching; (de bota) instep; (de libro) headband; **dar cabezadas** to nod; (un buque) to pitch

cabezal *m* pillow, cushion; bolster

cabezo *m* hillock; summit, peak; reef

cabe·zón -zona *adj* big-headed; stubborn; (licor) (Chile) strong ‖ *m* (en la ropa) hole for the head; tax register

cabezonada *f* stubbornness

cabezu·do -da *adj* big-headed; headstrong; (vino) heady

cabezuela *f* little head; (harina gruesa del trigo) middling; cornflower

cabida *f* room, space, capacity; influence, pull; **tener cabida en** to be included in

cabildear *intr* to lobby

cabildeo *m* lobbying

cabildero *m* lobbyist

cabildo *m* chapter (of a cathedral); chapter meeting; town hall

cabina *f* cabin; (locutorio del teléfono) booth; bathhouse, dressing room

cabio *m* rafter; joist

cabizba·jo -ja *adj* crestfallen, downcast

cable *m* cable; rope, hawser; **cable de remolque** towline; **cable de retén** guy wire

cablegrafiar §77 *tr & intr* to cable

cablegráfi·co -ca *adj* cable

cablegrama *m* cablegram

cabo *m* end, tip; (punta de tierra que penetra en el mar) cape; (mango) handle; small bundle; small piece; boss, foreman; cord, rope, cable; (mil) corporal; **al cabo** finally, at last; **al cabo de** at the end of; **atar cabos** (coll) to put two and two together; **Cabo de Buena Esperanza** Cape of Good Hope; **Cabo de Hornos** Cape Horn; **cabos** (de caballo) paws, nose, and mane; eyes, eyebrows, and hair; clothing; **cabo suelto** loose end; **estar al cabo de** to be well informed about; **llevar a cabo** to carry out, to accomplish

cabotaje *m* coasting trade

cabra *f* goat; nanny goat; (Chile) light two-wheel carriage; (Chile) sawbuck; (Col, Cuba, Ven) trick, gyp, loaded dice; **cabras** light clouds

cabrahigo wild fig

cabrería *f* goat stable; goat-milk dairy

cabre·ro -ra *mf* goatherd

cabrestante *m* capstan

cabrilla *f* sawbuck, sawhorse; (ichth) grouper; **cabrillas** skipping stones; (olas blancas en el mar) whitecaps

cabrillear *intr* (el mar) to be covered with whitecaps; shimmer

cabrio *m* rafter; joist

cabrí·o -a *adj* goat; goatish ‖ *m* herd of goats

cabriola *f* caper; somersault; **dar cabriolas** to cut capers

cabriolear *intr* to caper, frisk, prance

cabritilla *f* kid, kidskin

cabrito *m* kid; **cabritos** (Chile) popcorn

cabrón *m* buck, billy goat; complaisant cuckold; (Chile) pimp

cabronada *f* shamelessness; shameless forbearance

cabru·no -na *adj* goat

cacahuate *adj* (Mex) pocked ‖ *m* peanut

cacahuete *m* peanut

cacahuete·ro -ra *mf* peanut vendor

cacalote *m* (Mex) raven; (CAm, Mex) candied popcorn; (Cuba) break, blunder

cacao *m* chocolate tree; cocoa, chocolate; **pedir cacao** to call quits; **tener mucho cacao** (Guat) to have a lot of pep

cacaraña *f* pit, pock

cacarear *tr* to crow over, boast of ‖ *intr* (la gallina) to cackle; (el gallo) crow

cacareo *m* (de la gallina) cackling; (del gallo) crowing; (de una persona) (coll) crowing, boasting

cacatúa *f* cockatoo

cacea *f* trolling; **pescar a la cacea** to troll

cacear *tr* to stir with a dipper or ladle ‖ *intr* to troll

cacería *f* hunting; hunting party; (animales cobrados en la caza) bag; hunting scene

cacerola *f* casserole, saucepan

cacique *m* Indian chief; bossy fellow; (en asuntos políticos) (coll) boss; (Chile) lazy lummox; **cacique veranero** Baltimore oriole, hangbird

caciquismo *m* bossism

cacle *m* (Mex) sandal

caco *m* thief, pickpocket; coward

cacto *m* cactus

cacumen *m* summit; acumen, keen insight

cacha·co -ca *adj* (SAm) sporty ‖ *m* (SAm) sport, dude

cachada *f* thrust or wound made with the horns

cachalote *m* sperm whale

cachar *tr* to break to pieces; (la madera) slit, split; to butt with the horns; (Arg, Ecuad, Urug) to make fun of; (Chile) to grasp, understand

cacharpari *m* (Arg, Bol, Perú) send-off party

cacharro *m* crock, earthen pot; piece of crockery; piece of junk; (CAm, W-I) jail; (Col) trinket

cachaza *f* sloth, phlegm; rum; first froth on cane juice when boiled

cachazu•do -da *adj* slothful, phlegmatic ‖ *mf* sluggard

cachear *tr* to frisk

cacheo *m* frisking

cachetada *f* box on the ear

cachete *m* slap in the face; cheek, swollen cheek; dagger

cachetear *tr.*to box on the ear

cachetero *m* dagger; dagger man

cachetina *f* brawl, fistfight

cachicuer•no -na *adj* horn-handled

cachillada *f* brood, litter

cachimba *f* (*para fumar*) pipe; (Arg, Urug) well, spring; (Chile) revolver

cachimbo *m* (*para fumar*) pipe; (Cuba) sugar mill; **chupar cachimbo** (Ven) to smoke a pipe; (*un niño*) (Ven) to suck its finger

cachiporra *f* billy, bludgeon

cachivache *m* good-for-nothing; **cachivaches** broken pottery; pots and pans; junk, trash

cacho *m* slice, piece; (*mercadería que no se vende*) (Chile) drug on the market

cachón *m* (*ola de agua*) breaker; splash of water; **cachones** surf

cachon•do -da *adj* (*perra*) in rut; sexy

cacho•rro -rra *mf* cub, whelp, pup ‖ *m* little pistol

cachucha *f* rowboat; cap; Andalusian dance

cachuela *f* gizzard; fricassee of pork

cachu•pín -pina *mf* (CAm, Mex) Spanish settler in Latin America

cada *adj* each; every; **cada vez más** more and more; **cada vez que** whenever

cadalso *m* stand, platform; (*para la ejecución de un reo*) scaffold

cadarzo *m* floss, floss silk

cadáver *m* corpse, cadaver

cadavéri•co -ca *adj* cadaverous

cadena *f* chain; (telv) network; **cadena antirresbaladiza** (aut) skid chain; **cadena de presidiarios** chain gang; **cadena perpetua** life imprisonment

cadencia *f* cadence, rhythm

cadencio•so -sa *adj* rhythmical

cadenero *m* (surv) lineman

cadera *f* hip

cadete *m* (mil) cadet; (Arg, Bol) apprentice (*without pay*), errand boy

cadillo *m* burdock

cadmio *m* cadmium

caducar §73 *intr* to be in one's dotage; be worn out; lapse, expire

caducidad *f* feebleness; expiration

caedi•zo -za *adj* tottery, ready to fall over ‖ *m* lean-to

caer §15 *intr* to fall; droop; fall due; be, be found; fade; (*el sol, el día, el viento*) decline; happen; **caer a** to face, overlook; **caer bien** to fit; be becoming; make a hit; **caer de plano** to fall flat; **caer en** (*cierto día*) to come on, fall on, happen on; (*cierta página*) be found on; **caer en cama** to fall ill; **caer en favor** to be in favor; **caer en la cuenta** to catch on, get the point; **caer en que** to realize that; **caer mal** to fit badly; be unbecoming; fall flat; **no caigo** (coll) I don't get it ‖ *ref* to fall, fall down; be, be found; **caerse de su peso, caerse de suyo** to be self-evident; **caerse muerto de** (*p.ej., alegría, miedo, risa*) to be overcome with

café *adj* tan ‖ *m* coffee; coffee tree; coffee house; café; (Arg) reprimand; (Mex) tantrum; **café cantante** night club; **café de maquinilla** drip coffee; **café solo** black coffee

cafetal *m* coffee plantation

cafetalero *m* (SAm) coffee planter; coffee dealer

cafetear *intr* to drink coffee

cafetera *f* coffee pot; (Arg) jalopy; **cafetera eléctrica** electric percolator

cafetería *f* cafeteria

cafete•ro -ra *adj* coffee ‖ *mf* coffee dealer; coffee-bean picker ‖ *f* see **cafetera**

cafeto *m* coffee tree

cagar §44 *tr* to spot, stain, spoil ‖ *intr* to defecate ‖ *ref* to defecate; be scared

cagatin•ta *m* or **cagatin•tas** *m* (*pl* **-tas**) office drudge, penpusher

ca•gón -gona *adj* cowardly ‖ *mf* coward

caída *f* fall; spill, tumble; drop; failure; blunder, slip; (*de una cortina*) hang; **a la caída de la noche** at nightfall; **a la caída del sol** at sunset; **caída de agua** waterfall; **caída radiactiva** fallout; **caídas** coarse wool; witticisms

caí•do -da *adj* fallen; (*cuello*) turndown; (*párpado, hombro*) drooping; dejected, crestfallen; **caído en desuso** obsolete ‖ **caídos** *mpl* interest due; **los caídos** (*en la guerra*) the fallen ‖ *f* see **caída**

caimán *m* alligator; schemer

Caín *m* Cain; **pasar las de Caín** (coll) to have a frightful time

Cairo, El Cairo

caja *f* box; case, chest, coffer; (*de caudales*) safe, strongbox; (*para dinero contante*) cashbox; (*dinero contante*) cash; (*ataúd*) casket, coffin; (*de reloj de bolsillo*) case; (*donde se pagan las cuentas en los hoteles*) desk; cashier's desk; (*del aparato de radio o televisión*) cabinet; (*de coche*) body; (*tambor*) drum; (*de fusil*) stock; (*de ascensor, de escalera*) shaft, well; (mach) housing; (typ) case; **caja alta** upper case; **caja baja** lower case; **caja clara** snare drum; **caja de ahorros** savings bank; **caja de cambio de marchas** transmission-gear box; **caja de caudales** safe; **caja de cigüeñal** crankcase; **caja de colores** paintbox; **caja de embalaje** packing box or case; **caja de enchufe** (elec) outlet; **caja de engranajes** gear case; **caja de fuego** firebox; **caja de fusibles** fuse box; **caja de ingletes** miter box; **caja de menores** petty cash; **caja de registro** manhole; **caja de reloj** watchcase; **caja de seguridad** safe; safe-deposit box; **caja de sorpresa** jack-in-the-box; **caja de velocidades** transmission-gear box; **caja fuerte** safe, bank vault; **caja postal de ahorros** postal savings bank; **caja registradora** cash register; **despedir** or **echar con cajas destempladas** to send packing, give the gate

caje·ro -ra *mf* boxmaker; (*en un banco*) cashier, teller; (*en un hotel*) desk clerk

cajeta *f* little box; tobacco box; **de cajeta** (CAm, Mex) fine

cajetilla *f* pack (*of cigarettes*)

cajetín *m* rubber stamp; (typ) box

cajista *mf* compositor

cajón *m* large box, bin; (*caja movible de un mueble*) drawer; (*que se cierra con llave*) locker; (*que sirve de tienda*) booth, stall; (Chile) long gully; (Mex) dry-goods store; (SAm) coffin; **cajón de aire comprimido** caisson; **cajón de sastre** (coll) odds and ends; muddlehead; **ser de cajón** to be in vogue, be the thing

cal *f* lime; **cal apagada** slaked lime; **cal viva** quicklime; **de cal y canto** strong, tough

cala *f* calla lily; cove, inlet; (*de fruta*) sample slice; (*de buque*) hold; suppository

calabacear *tr* (*a un alumno*) to flunk; (*una mujer a un pretendiente*) to jilt

calabacera *f* calabash, pumpkin, squash

calabaza *f* calabash, gourd, pumpkin, squash; dolt; **dar calabaza** a (*un alumno*) to flunk; (*un pretendiente*) to jilt

calabo·bos *m* (*pl* **-bos**) steady drizzle

calabocero *m* jailer, warden

calabozo *m* dungeon; cell, prison cell

calada *f* soaking; (*del ave de rapiña*) swoop; scolding

calado *m* openwork, drawn work; fretwork; (*del agua*) depth; (naut) draught

calafatear *tr* to calk

calafateo *m* calking

calamar *m* squid

calambre *m* cramp

calamidad *f* calamity

calamita *f* magnetic needle

calamito·so -sa *adj* calamitous

cálamo *m* reed, stalk; (poet) pen; (poet) flute, reed

calamoca·no -na *adj* (*algo embriagado*) tipsy; (*chocho*) doddering

calaña *f* nature, kind; pattern; fan

calar *tr* to pierce; soak; wedge; cut open work in; (*un melón*) cut a plug in; (*la bayoneta*) fix; (*un puente levadizo*) lower; (*las redes de pesca*) lower in the water; (*un buque cierta profundidad*) draw; (*a una persona o las intenciones de una persona*) size up, see through; (Arg) to stare at ‖ *ref* to get soaked, get drenched; (*introducirse*) slip in; (*el ave de rapiña*) swoop down; miss fire; (*el sombrero*) pull down tight; (*las gafas*) stick on; **calarse hasta los huesos** to get soaked to the skin

cala·to -ta *adj* (Peru) naked; (Peru) penniless

calavera *m* daredevil; libertine ‖ *f* skull; (*imitación de la calavera*) death's-head; (Mex) tail light

calaverada *f* recklessness, daredeviltry; escapade

calaverear *tr* to spoil, make ugly ‖ *intr* to act recklessly; go on a spree

calcado *m* tracing

calcañal *m* or **calcañar** *m* heel

calcar §73 *tr* to trace; copy, imitate; tread on

calce *m* wedge; iron tire; iron tip; (*de un documento*) (CAm, Mex, P-R) bottom, foot

calceta *f* stocking; fetter, shackle; **hacer calceta** to knit

calcetería *f* hosiery; hosiery shop

calcete·ro -ra *mf* hosier; stocking mender

calcetín *m* sock

calcificar §73 *tr* & *ref* to calcify

calcio *m* calcium

calco *m* tracing; copy, imitation

calcula·dor -dora *adj* calculating; (*egoísta, interesado*) (fig) calculating ‖ *mf* calculator ‖ *f* calculating machine; **calculadora de bolsillo** pocket calculator

calcular *tr* & *intr* to calculate; (*suponer*) (fig) calculate

cálculo *m* calculation; (math, pathol) calculus; **cálculo biliar** gallstone; **cálculo renal** kidney stone

calchona *f* (Chile) goblin, bogey; (Chile) witch, old hag

calda *f* heating, warming; **caldas** hot springs

caldeamiento *m* heating

caldear *tr* to heat; weld ‖ *ref* to get hot; get overheated

caldeo *m* heating; welding

caldera *f* boiler; pot, kettle; (Arg) coffee pot, teapot

calderero *m* boilermaker

calderilla *f* holy-water vessel; copper coin; small change; mountain currant

caldero *m* kettle, pot; (*reloj de bolsillo*) (Arg) turnip

calderón *m* caldron; (*signo*) (mus) pause, hold

caldillo *m* light broth; sauce for fricassee; (Mex) meat bits in broth

caldo *m* broth; sauce, gravy, dressing; salad dressing; (Mex) syrup; (Mex) sugar-cane juice; **caldo de la reina** eggnog; **caldos** wet goods

calefacción *f* heating; **calefacción por agua caliente** hot-water heat; **calefacción por aire caliente** hot-air heat

calefactor *m* heater man; (electron) heater, heater element

calefón *m* (Arg) hot-water heater

calendar *tr* to date

calendario *m* calendar; **hacer calendarios** to meditate; to make wild predictions

calenta·dor -dora *adj* heating ‖ *m* heater; warming pan; (*reloj de bolsillo*) turnip; **calentador a gas** gas heater; **calentador de agua** water heater

calentamiento *m* heating

calentar §2 *tr* to heat; warm; beat; (Chile) to bore, annoy; **calentar la silla** (*detenerse demasiado*) to warm a chair ‖ *ref* to heat up, run hot; warm oneself; warm up; (*estar en celo las bestias*) be in heat; (Chile, Ven) to become annoyed, get angry

calentón *m* warm-up; **darse un calentón** to stop and warm up
calentura *f* fever, temperature
calenturien•to -ta *adj* feverish; exalted; (Chile) consumptive
calenturón *m* high fever
calenturo•so -sa *adj* feverish
calera *f* limekiln; limestone quarry
calesa *f* chaise
caleta *f* cove, inlet
caletre *m* judgment, acumen
calibrador *m* calipers; **calibrador de alambre** wire gauge
calibrar *tr* to calibrate; to gauge
calibre *m* caliber; gauge; bore, diameter
calicanto *m* rubble masonry
cali•có *m* (*pl* **-cós**) calico
calidad *f* quality; condition, term; rank, nobility; importance; **a calidad de que** provided that; **calidad de vida** quality of life; **en calidad de** in the capacity of
cáli•do -da *adj* warm, hot
calidoscopio *m* kaleidoscope
calientaca•mas *m* (*pl* **-mas**) bed warmer
calienta•piés *m* (*pl* **-piés**) foot warmer
caliente *adj* hot; fiery, vehement; (*en celo*) hot; **caliente de cascos** hotheaded; **en caliente** while hot; at once
califa *m* caliph
califato *m* caliphate
calificación *f* qualification; (*nota en un examen*) grade, mark; rating, standing
calificar §73 *tr* to qualify; certify; ennoble; (*un examen*) mark; (*en los registros electorales*) (Chile) to register ‖ *ref* (archaic) to prove one's noble birth; (*en los registros electorales*) (Chile) to register
calificati•vo -va *adj* qualifying ‖ *m* (*nota en la escuela*) grade, mark; (*en un diccionario*) usage label
California *f* California; **la Baja California** Lower California
caligrafía *f* penmanship
calina *f* haze
calino•so -sa *adj* hazy
Calíope *f* Calliope
calipso *m* calypso ‖ **Calipso** *f* Calypso
calistenia *f* calisthenics
calisténi•co -ca *adj* calisthenic
cá•liz *m* (*pl* **-lices**) chalice; **cáliz de dolor** cup of sorrow
cali•zo -za *adj* lime, limestone ‖ *f* limestone
calma *f* calm; calm weather; quiet, tranquillity; slowness; (*cesación*) letup, suspension; **calma chicha** dead calm; **calmas ecuatoriales** doldrums; **en calma** in suspension; (*mercado*) steady; (*mar*) calm, smooth
calmante *adj* soothing; pain-relieving ‖ *m* sedative
calmar *tr* to calm, soothe ‖ *intr* to grow calm; abate ‖ *ref* to calm down
calmazo *m* dead calm
cal•mo -ma *adj* barren, treeless; fallow, uncultivated ‖ *f* see **calma**
calmo•so -sa *adj* calm; slow, lazy

calmu•do -da *adj* calm; (*viento*) (naut) light; (*tiempo*) (naut) mild
caló *m* gypsy slang, underworld slang
calofriar §77 *ref* to become chilled
calofrío *m* chill
calor *m* heat; warmth; (fig) warmth, enthusiasm; **hace calor** it is hot, it is warm; **tener calor** (*una persona*) to be hot, be warm
calorífe•ro -ra *adj* heat ‖ *m* heater, furnace; heating system; foot warmer
calorífu•go -ga *adj* heatproof; fireproof
caloro•so -sa *adj* warm, hot; (fig) warm, enthusiastic, hearty
calotear *tr* (Arg) to gyp, cheat
calpul *m* (Guat) gathering, meeting; (Hond) Indian mound
caluma *f* (Peru) gorge in the Andes; (Peru) Indian hamlet
calumnia *f* calumny, slander
calumniar *tr* to slander
calumnio•so -sa *adj* slanderous
caluro•so -sa *adj* warm, hot; (fig) warm, enthusiastic, hearty
calva *f* bald spot; bare spot, clearing; (*en un tejido*) worn spot
calvario *m* (*sufrimiento moral*) cross; series of misfortunes; string of debts ‖ **Calvario** *m* Calvary; Stations of the Cross
calvero *m* clearing; clay pit
calvez *f* or **calvicie** *f* baldness
cal•vo -va *adj* bald; barren, bare ‖ *f* see **calva**
calza *f* wedge; stocking; **calzas** hose, breeches, tights; **en calzas prietas** in a tight fix
calzada *f* highway, causeway; (S-D) sidewalk
calzado *m* footwear, shoes
calzador *m* shoehorn
calzar §60 *tr* to shoe, put shoes on; provide with shoes; (*cierto tamaño de zapatos, guantes, etc.*) wear, take; (*un zapato a una persona*) fit; wedge; (*una rueda*) block, scotch; (*la pata de una mesa*) block up; tip or trim with iron; (*plantas*) (hort) to hill ‖ *intr* (Arg) to get the place sought; **calzar bien** to wear good footwear; **calzar mal** to wear poor footwear ‖ *ref* to get; (*zapatos, guantes*) put on, wear; put one's shoes on; (*a una persona*) dominate, manage
calzo *m* wedge; chock, skid
calzón *m* trousers, pants; **calzones** trousers, breeches; **calzarse los calzones** to wear the pants
calzonarias *fpl* (Col) suspenders
calzona•zos *m* (*pl* **-zos**) jellyfish; henpecked husband
calzoncillos *mpl* underdrawers
callada *f* (naut) abatement, lull; **a las calladas** or **de callada** on the quiet; **dar la callada por respuesta** to give no answer
calla•do -da *adj* silent; mysterious, secret ‖ *f* see **callada**
callampa *f* (Chile) felt hat; (Chile) large ear; (Chile) mushroom
callana *f* (SAm) Indian baking bowl; (*reloj de bolsillo*) (Chile) turnip; (Chile) behind; (Chile, Peru) flowerpot
callao *m* pebble

callar *tr* to silence; not mention; (*un secrèto*) keep; calm, quiet ‖ *intr & ref* to become silent, keep silent; keep quiet, keep still; **callarse la boca** (coll) to shut up, clam up

calle *f* street; **calle de travesía** cross street; **calle mayor** main street; **dejar en la calle** to deprive of one's livelihood

calleja *f* side street, alley; subterfuge, pretext

callejear *intr* to walk around the streets, to ramble around

calleje•ro -ra *adj* street; gadabout ‖ *m* street guide; list of addresses of newspaper subscribers

callejón *m* alley, lane; **callejón sin salida** blind alley

callejuela *f* side street, alley; subterfuge, pretext

callicida *m* corn cure

callo *m* callus; (*en el pie*) corn; **callos** tripe

callo•so -sa *adj* callous

cama *f* bed; (*para las bestias*) bedding, litter; **cama imperial** four-poster; **cama turca** day bed; **guardar cama** to be sick in bed

camachuelo *m* (orn) bullfinch

camada *f* brood, litter; layer, stratum; (*de ladrones*) den

camafeo *m* cameo

camaleón *m* chameleon

cámara *f* chamber; hall; (*cuerpo legislador*) house, chamber; (*aparato fotográfico*) camera; (*tubo de goma del neumático*) inner tube; (*del arma de fuego*) chamber, breech; (*para cartuchos*) magazine; board, council; (*mueble donde se conservan los alimentos*) icebox; (*evacuación*) bowels; (aer) cockpit; **cámara agrícola** grange; **cámara ardiente** funeral chamber; **cámara cinematografica** movie camera; **cámara de combustión** (aut) combustion chamber; **cámara de compensación** clearing house; **cámara de fuelle** folding camera; **cámara de las máquinas** (naut) engine room; **Cámara de los Comunes** House of Commons; **Cámara de los Lores** House of Lords; **cámara de oxígeno** oxygen tent; **Cámara de Representantes** House of Representatives; **cámara frigorífica** cold-storage room; **cámara indiscreta** candid camera; **cámaras** loose bowels

camarada *m* comrade

camarera *f* waitress; chambermaid, maid; (*en los barcos*) stewardess; (*que sirve a una reina o princesa*) lady in waiting

camarero *m* waiter; valet; (*en un barco o avión*) steward

camarilla *f* clique, coterie, cabal; palace coterie

camarín *m* boudoir; (theat) dressing room

cámaro *m* var of **camarón**

camarógrafo *m* cameraman

camarón *m* shrimp, prawn; (CAm, Col) tip, gratuity; (Ven) nap; **ponerse como un camarón** to blush

camarote *m* stateroom, cabin

camasquin•ce *mf* (*pl* **-ce**) meddlesome person, kibitzer

cambalachar *tr & intr* var of **cambalachear**

cambalache *m* exchange, swap; (Arg) second-hand shop

cambalachear *tr* to swap, exchange, trade off ‖ *intr* to swap, exchange

cambiadis•cos *m* (*pl* **-cos**) record changer

cambiante *adj* changing; fickle; iridescent ‖ **cambiantes** *mpl* iridescence

cambiar *tr* to change; exchange ‖ *intr* to change; **cambiar de** (*p.ej., sombreros, ropa, trenes*) change; **cambiar de marcha** to shift gears ‖ *ref* to change

cambiavía *m* switch; switchman

cambio *m* change; exchange; rate of exchange; (aut) shift; (rr) switch; **cambio de marchas, cambio de velocidades** gearshift; **en cambio** on the other hand

cambista *mf* moneychanger; banker ‖ *m* (Arg) switchman

cambullón *m* (Mex, Col, Ven) barter, exchange; (Chile) subversion; (Peru) scheming, trickery

camelar *tr* to flirt with; cajole, tease

camelo *m* flirtation; joke; false rumor

camellero *m* camel driver

camello *m* camel

camellón *m* drinking trough; flower bed

came•ro -ra *adj* bed ‖ *mf* maker of bedding ‖ *m* (Col) highway

camilla *f* stretcher; couch; round table with heater underneath; (Mex) clothing store

camillero *m* stretcher-bearer

caminante *mf* walker; traveler on foot ‖ *m* groom attending his master's horse

caminar *tr* (*cierta distancia*) to walk ‖ *intr* to walk; go; travel, journey; behave

caminata *f* long walk, hike; outing, jaunt

camine•ro -ra *adj* road, highway

camino *m* road, way; (*viaje*) journey; (*tira larga que se pone en mesas o pisos*) (SAm) runner; **a medio camino** (entre) halfway (between); **camino de** on the way to; **camino de herradura** bridle path; **camino de hierro** railway; **camino de ruedas** wagon road; **Camino de Santiago** Way of St. James (*Milky Way*); **camino de sirga** towpath; **camino de tierra** dirt road; **camino real** highroad; **camino trillado** beaten path; **echar camino adelante** to strike out

camión *m* truck, motor truck; (Mex) bus; **camión volquete** dump truck

camionaje *m* trucking

camione•ro -ra *adj* truck ‖ *m* trucker, teamster

camioneta *f* light truck; station wagon

camionetilla *f* (Guat) station wagon

camión-grua *m* tow truck

camionista *m* trucker, teamster

camisa *f* (*de hombre*) shirt; (*de mujer*) chemise; (*de la culebra*) slough; (*de un libro*) jacket; (*para papeles*) folder; (*de una pieza mecánica*) jacket, casing; (*de un horno de fundición*) lining; **camisa de agua** water jacket; **camisa de dormir** nightshirt; **camisa de fuerza** strait jacket; **cambiarse la camisa** to become a turncoat

camisería *f* haberdashery; shirt factory

camise•ro -ra *mf* haberdasher; shirt maker
camiseta *f* undershirt; (*de traje de baño*) top
camisola *f* stiff shirt
camisolín *m* dickey, shirt front
camón *m* bay window; **camón de vidrios** glass partition
camorra *f* quarrel, row; **armar camorra** to raise Cain, raise a row; **buscar camorra** to be looking for trouble
camorrista *adj* quarrelsome || *mf* quarrelsome person
camote *m* onion; (Mex) sweet potato; (Chile) lie, fib; (Chile, Peru) sweetheart; (Arg, Ecuad) blockhead; (Mex) churl; (El Salv) black-and-blue mark; **tomar un camote** to become infatuated
camotear *tr* (Arg) to filch, snitch; (Guat) to bother || *intr* (Mex) to wander around aimlessly
campal *adj* pitched (*battle*)
campamento *m* camp; encampment
campana *f* bell; (*para la protección de plantas*) bell glass, bell jar; (*de las guarniciones de alumbrado eléctrico*) canopy; **campana de buzo** diving bell; **por campana de vacante** (Mex) rarely, seldom
campanada *f* stroke of a bell, ring of a bell; scandal
campanario *m* belfry, steeple
campanear *tr* (*las campanas*) to ring || *intr* to ring the bells || *ref* to strut
campanero *m* bell ringer; bell founder
campanil *adj* bell || *m* belfry, bell tower
campanilla *f* hand bell; door bell; bubble; (anat) uvula; **de (muchas) campanillas** of great importance
campano *m* cowbell
campante *adj* proud, satisfied; outstanding
campanu•do -da *adj* bell-shaped; pompous, high-sounding
campaña *f* campaign; cruise; countryside
campar *intr* to camp; to excel, stand out
campear *intr* to go to pasture; (*las sementeras*) turn green; stand out, excel; reconnoiter; ride through the fields to check the cattle
campecha•no -na *adj* frank, good-natured, cheerful || *f* (Mex) mixed drink; (Ven) hammock
campeche *m* logwood
campeón *m* champion; **campeón de venta** best seller
campeona *f* championess
campeonato *m* championship
campe•ro -ra *adj* unsheltered, in the open
campesi•no -na *adj* country, rural, peasant || *mf* peasant, farmer || *m* countryman || *f* countrywoman
campestre *adj* country, rural
campiña *f* countryside, open country
campo *m* (*terreno sembradío; sitio o foco de varias actividades*) field; (*en oposición a la ciudad*) country; ground, background; (*campamento*) (mil) camp; **a campo traviesa** across country; **campo de batalla** battlefield; **campo de ensayos** proving ground; **campo de juego** playground;

campo de pruebas testing ground; **campo de tiro** range, shooting range; **campo magnético** magnetic field; **campo santo** cemetery; **levantar el campo** (mil) to break camp; **quedar en el campo** to fall in battle
camposanto *m* cemetery
camuesa *f* pippin (*apple*)
camueso *m* pippin (*tree*)
camuflaje *m* camouflage
camuflar *tr* to camouflage
can *m* dog; (*de arma de fuego*) trigger
cana *f* gray hair; **echar una cana al aire** to cut loose, step out; **peinar canas** to be getting old
Canadá, el Canada
canadiense *adj & mf* Canadian
canal *m* (*cauce artificial*) canal; (*estrecho en el mar*) channel; (anat) duct, canal; (telv) channel; **Canal de la Mancha** English Channel; **Canal de Panamá** Panama Canal; **Canal de Suez** Suez Canal; **canal alimenticio** alimentary canal || *f* channel; (*conducto del tejado*) gutter; (*estría*) flute, groove; pipe; (*de un libro*) fore edge
canalización *f* (*de agua o gas*) mains, pipes; ductwork; (elec) wiring; **canalización de consumo** (elec) house current
canalizar §60 to channel; pipe; (elec) to wire
canalizo *m* (naut) waterway, fairway
canalón *m* rain-water spout; shovel hat; **canalones** ravioli
canalla *m* churl, scoundrel || *f* riffraff, canaille
canallada *f* dirty trick, meanness
canana *f* cartridge belt
canapé *m* sofa, couch
Canarias *fpl* Canaries
cana•rio -ria *adj & mf* Canarian || *m* canary, canary bird || *fpl* see **Canarias**
canasta *f* basket, hamper
canastilla *f* basket; (*ropa para el niño que ha de nacer*) layette; (*equipo de novia*) (dial) trousseau
canastillo *m* basket-weave tray
canasto *m* hamper || **canastos** *interj* confound it!
cáncamo *m* eyebolt; **cáncamo de argolla** ringbolt
cancanear *intr* to loaf around; stammer
cancel *m* storm door; folding screen
cancela *f* door of ironwork
cancelar *tr* to cancel; (*una deuda*) pay off
cáncer *m* cancer; **Cáncer** (astr) Cancer; **cáncer pulmonar** lung cancer
cancerología *f* cancer research; oncology
cancero•so -sa *adj* cancerous
cancilla *f* lattice gate
canciller *m* chancellor
cancillería *f* chancellery
canción *f* song; poem, lyric poem; **canción de amor** love song; **canción de cuna** cradlesong, lullaby; **canción típica** folk song; **volver a la misma canción** to sing the same old song
cancionero *m* songbook; anthology
cancionista *mf* popular singer

canco *m* (Chile) flowerpot; (Chile) earthen jug; (Chile) chamber pot; (Bol) buttock; **cancos** (Chile) woman's broad hips

cancón *m* bugaboo; **hacer un cancón a** (Mex) to try to bluff

cancha *f* field, ground; race track; golf links; tennis court; cockpit; (Urug) path, way; **estar en su cancha** (Arg, Chile, Urug) to be in one's element; **tener cancha** (Arg) to have pull ‖ *interj* gangway!

canche *adj* (Col) tasteless, poorly seasoned; (CAm) blond

candado *m* padlock

candar *tr* to lock, padlock

candela *f* candle; candlestick; fire, light; **con la candela en la mano** at death's door

candelabro *m* candelabrum

candelecho *m* elevated hut for watching the vineyard

candelero *m* candlestick; brass olive-oil lamp; fishing torch

candelilla *f* catkin; (Arg, Chile) will-o'-the-wisp; glowworm

candida•to -ta *mf* candidate

candidatura *f* candidacy; list of candidates; voting paper

candidez *f* whiteness; innocence

cándi•do -da white; simple, innocent

candil *m* open olive-oil lamp

candilejas *fpl* footlights

candon•go -ga *adj* fawning, slick; loafing, shirking ‖ *mf* fawner, flatterer; loafer, shirker ‖ *f* fawning; teasing

candonguear *tr* to kid, tease ‖ *intr* to scheme to get out of work

candor *m* innocence, ingenuousness

caneca *f* glazed earthen bottle

cane•co -ca *adj* (Arg, Bol) tipsy ‖ *f* see **caneca**

canela *f* cinnamon; (*cosa fina*) (coll) peach

canela•do -da *adj* cinnamon-colored

cane•lo -la *adj* cinnamon ‖ *m* (*árbol*) cinnamon ‖ *f* see **canela**

canelón *m* rain-water spout; large icicle; cinnamon candy

cane•sú *m* (*pl* -**súes**) (*prenda*) guimpe; (*pieza de una prenda*) yoke

cangilón *m* jug, jar, bucket; (*de draga*) bucket, scoop; rut, track

cangrejo *m* crab

cangrena *f* gangrene

cangrenar *ref* to have gangrene

canguro *m* kangaroo

caníbal *adj & mf* cannibal

canica *f* (*bolita*) marble; (*juego*) marbles

canicie *f* whiteness (*of hair*)

canícula *f* dog days ‖ **Canícula** *f* Dog Star

caniculares *mpl* dog days

cani•jo -ja *adj* (coll) weak, sickly ‖ *mf* (coll) weakling

canilla *f* shank (*of leg*); (*espita, grifo*) tap; bobbin, spool; (Mex) strength

cani•no -na *adj* canine ‖ *m* canine, canine tooth ‖ *f* excrement of dogs

canje *m* exchange

canjear *tr* to exchange

ca•no -na *adj* gray; gray-haired; hoary, old ‖ *f* see **cana**

canoa *f* canoe; launch

canoe•ro -ra *mf* canoeist

canon *m* canon

canóni•co -ca *adj* canonical ‖ *f* rules of canonical life

canóniga *f* nap before eating; drunk

canónigo *m* canon

canonizar §60 *tr* to canonize; approve

canonjía *f* sinecure

cano•ro -ra *adj* (*voz*) melodious; (*ave*) song, sweet-singing

cano•so -sa *adj* gray-haired

canotié *m* straw hat, skimmer

cansa•do -da *adj* tired, weary; exhausted, worn-out; tiresome

cansancio *m* tiredness, fatigue

cansar *tr* to tire, weary; bore ‖ *intr* be tiresome ‖ *ref* to tire, get tired

cantable *adj* tuneful, singable ‖ *m* (*del libreto de una zarzuela*) lyric; (*de una zarzuela*) musical passage

canta•dor -dora *mf* singer of popular songs

cantaletear *tr* to say over and over again; make fun of

cantalupo *m* cantaloupe

cantante *adj* singing ‖ *mf* singer

cantar *m* song, singing; chant; **Cantar de los Cantares** Song of Songs ‖ *tr* to sing; chant; sing of; **cantarlas claras** to speak out ‖ *intr* to sing; chant; creak, squeak; squeal, peach; **cantar de plano** to make a full confession

cántara *f* jug, pitcher

cantárida *f* Spanish fly

canta•rín -rina *adj* (*voz*) melodious; fond of singing ‖ *mf* singer ‖ *m* professional singer

cántaro *m* jug, pitcher; jugful; ballot box; **llover a cántaros** to rain pitchforks

canta•triz *f* (*pl* -**trices**) singer

cantautor *m* song writer

cantera *f* quarry; talent, genius

cántico *m* canticle

cantidad *f* quantity; amount; sum; **cantidad de movimiento** (mech) momentum

cantiga *f* poem of the troubadours

cantilena *f* ballad, song; **salir con la misma cantilena** to sing the same old song

cantimplora *f* siphon; carafe, decanter; (*frasco para llevar bebida*) canteen; (Col) powder flask; (Guat) mumps

cantina *f* cantine; lunchroom, station restaurant; barroom

cantinera *f* camp follower

cantinero *m* bartender

canto *m* song; singing; (*división del poema épico*) canto; (*de notas iguales y uniformes*) chant; (*extremidad*) edge; (*esquina*) corner; (*de cuchillo*) back; (*de pan*) crust; stone, pebble; **canto de corte** cutting edge; **canto del cisne** swan song

cantonera *f* corner reinforcement; corner table, corner shelf; streetwalker

cantonero *m* corner loafer

can•tor -tora *adj* singing; (*pájaro*) song ‖ *mf* singer ‖ *m* chanter; minstrel; poet, bard

canto•so -sa *adj* rocky, stony
canturrear *tr & intr* to hum
canturreo *m* hum, humming
canzonetista *mf* popular singer
caña *f* cane; reed; stalk, stem; (*del brazo o la pierna*) long bone; (*de bota o media*) leg; wineglass; **caña de azúcar** sugar cane; **caña de pescar** fishing rod
cañada *f* glen, ravine, gully; cattle path; brook
cañamazo *m* canvas, burlap; embroidered canvas
cañamiel *f* sugar cane
cáñamo *m* hemp
cañamones *mpl* birdseed
cañaveral *m* canebrake; sugar-cane plantation
cañería *f* pipe; pipe line; piping; **cañería maestra** gas main, water main
cañero *m* pipe fitter, plumber; sugar-cane dealer; (SAm) cheat; (SAm) bluffer
cañista *m* pipe fitter, plumber
caño *m* pipe, tube; gutter, sewer; ditch; (*chorro*) spurt, jet; (*canal angosto*) channel; organ pipe; (*río pequeño*) (Col) stream
cañón *m* (*pieza de artillería*) cannon; (*valle estrecho*) canyon; (*de arma de fuego; de pluma*) barrel; (*pluma de ave*) quill; (*de escalera*) well; (*de columna; de ascensor*) shaft; organ pipe; (Col) trunk of tree; **cañón de campaña** fieldpiece; **cañón de chimenea** flue, chimney flue; **cañón obús** howitzer
cañonear *tr* to cannonade, to shell
cañutazo *m* gossip
caoba *f* mahogany
caos *m* chaos
caóti•co -ca *adj* chaotic
cap. *abbr* **capitán, capítulo**
capa *f* cloak, cape, mantle; (*de pintura*) coat; (*lo que cubre*) bed, layer; (*apariencia, pretexto*) (fig) cloak, mask; **capa del cielo** canopy of heaven; **capa de ozono** ozone layer; **andar de capa caída** to be on the decline, be in a bad way; (*comedia*) **de capa y espada** cloak-and-sword; (*intriga, espionaje*) **de capa y espada** cloak-and-dagger; **so capa de** under the guise of
capacidad *f* capacity; **capacidad competitiva** competitiveness
capacitar *tr* to enable, qualify; to empower ‖ *ref* to become qualified
capacha *f* fruit basket; (SAm) jail
capacho *m* fruit basket; hamper; (*de albañil*) hod
capar *tr* to geld, castrate; curtail
caparazón *m* caparison; horse blanket; nose bag; (*de crustáceo*) shell
caparrosa *f* vitriol
capa•taz *m* (*pl* **-taces**) overseer, foreman, boss
ca•paz *adj* (*pl* **-paces**) (*grande*) capacious, spacious; (*que tiene cierta aptitud; diestro, instruído*) capable; **capaz de** capable of; with a capacity of; **capaz para** competent in; qualified for; with room for
capcio•so -sa *adj* crafty, deceptive

capea *f* amateur free-for-all bullfight
capear *tr* (*al toro*) to challenge; (*el mal tiempo*) weather; deceive, take in ‖ *intr* (naut) to lay to; (Guat) to play hooky
capellán *m* chaplain
capeo *m* capework (*of bullfighter*)
caperucita *f* little pointed hood; **Caperucita Roja** Little Red Ridinghood
caperuza *f* pointed hood; chimney cap
capilla *f* (*parte de una iglesia con altar*) chapel; (*de los reos de muerte*) death house; (*pliego suelto*) proof sheet; cowl, hood, cape; **estar en capilla** to be in the death house; to be on pins and needles; **estar expuesto en capilla ardiente** to be on view, to lie in state
capiller *m* churchwarden, sexton
capillo *m* baby cap; baptismal cap; hood; cocoon; (*del cigarro*) filler
capirotazo *m* fillip
capirote *m* hood; doctor's cap and hood; cardboard or paper cone (*worn on head*); fillip
capitación *f* poll tax
capital *adj* capital; main, principal; paramount; (*enemigo*) mortal ‖ *m* (*dinero que produce renta*) capital; (*dinero que se presta para producir renta*) principal; **capital de inversión** investment capital ‖ *f* capital
capitalismo *m* capitalism
capitalista *adj* capitalistic ‖ *mf* capitalist; shareholder, investor
capitalizar §60 *tr* to capitalize; (*los intereses devengados*) compound
capitán *m* captain; leader; **capitán de bandera** flag captain; **capitán de corbeta** (nav) lieutenant commander; **capitán del puerto** harbor master
capitana *f* flagship
capitanear *tr* to captain; lead, command
capitanía *f* captaincy; (mil) company
capitel *m* (*de una iglesia*) spire; (*de una columna*) capital
capitolio *m* capitol
capitoste *m* big shot
capítula *f* chapter (*of Scriptures*)
capitular *tr* to accuse; agree on ‖ *intr* to capitulate
capitulear *intr* (Arg, Chile, Peru) to lobby
capituleo *m* (Arg, Chile, Peru) lobbying
capitulero *m* (Arg, Chile, Peru) political henchman, lobbyist
capítulo *m* chapter; chapter house; subject, matter; errand; main point; **ganar capítulo** (coll) to win one's point; **llamar a capítulo** to take to task, call to account; **perder capítulo** to lose one's point
ca•pó *m* (*pl* **-pós**) hood (*of auto*)
capolar *tr* to cut to pieces, chop up
ca•pón -pona *adj* castrated ‖ *m* eunuch; (*pollo*) capon; bundle of firewood; (*golpe*) fillip ‖ *f* shoulder strap
caponera *f* coop for fattening capons; place of welcome; (*cárcel*) coop, jail
caporal *m* chief, leader; foreman (*on cattle ranch*)

ca
ca

capota *f* bonnet; (aer) cowling; (aut) top
capotaje *m* (aer) nosing over
capotar *intr* to upset; (aer) to nose over
capote *m* cape, cloak; (coll) frown, scowl; (Chile, Mex) beating; **capote de monte** poncho; **de capote** (Mex) on the sly; **dar capote a** to flabbergast; (*un rezagado*) to leave hungry; **decir para su capote** to say to oneself; **echar un capote** to turn the conversation
capotear *tr* (*al toro*) to challenge; (*dificultades*) evade, duck; beguile, take in; (*una obra teatral*) cut, make cuts in
Capricornio *m* Capricorn
capricho *m* caprice, whim, fancy
capricho•so -sa *adj* capricious, whimsical; willful
caprichu•do -da *adj* capricious, whimsical
cápsula *f* capsule; (*de botella*) cap
capsular *tr* to cap
captación *f* capture; (*de las aguas de un río*) harnessing; (rad) tuning in, picking up
captar *tr* to catch; (*la confianza de una persona*) win; (*las aguas de un río*) harness; (*las ondas radiofónicas*) tune in, pick up; (*lo que uno dice*) get, grasp ‖ *ref* to attract, win
captura *f* capture, catch
capturar *tr* to capture, catch
capucha *f* cowl, hood; circumflex accent
capuchina *f* garden nasturtium, Indian cress; Capuchin nun; confection of egg yolks
capucho *m* cowl, hood
capuchón *m* lady's cloak and hood; (*de una plumafuente*) cap; (aut) valve cap
capullo *m* cocoon; coarse spun silk; bud; **capullo de rosa** rosebud
capuzar §60 *tr* to throw in headfirst; (*un buque*) overload at the bow
caqui *adj* khaki ‖ *m* khaki; Japanese persimmon
caquinos *mpl* (Mex) guffaw, outburst of laughter
cara *f* face; look, countenance; façade; front; (*de disco de fonógrafo*) side; **a cara descubierta** openly; **a cara o cruz** heads or tails; **cara a** facing; **cara al público** with an audience; **cara de acelga** sallow face; **cara de ajo** vinegar face; **cara de hereje** (*persona de feo aspecto*) fright, baboon; **cara de vinagre** vinegar face; **dar la cara** to take the consequences; **de cara** in the face; facing; **echar a cara o cruz** to flip a coin; **hacer cara a** to stand up to; **tener buena cara** to look well, to look good; **tener mala cara** to look ill, to look bad
cárabe *m* amber
carabina *f* carbine; chaperon
caracol *m* snail; snail shell; (*de pelo*) curl; (*trazado en espiral*) spiral; (*del oído*) cochlea
carácter *m* (*pl* **caracteres**) character; (*marca que se pone a las reses*) brand
característi•co -ca *adj* characteristic ‖ *m* (theat) old man ‖ *f* characteristic; (theat) old woman
caracteriza•do -da *adj* distinguished

caracterizar §60 *tr* to characterize; to confer a distinction on; (*un personaje en la escena*) to interpret ‖ *ref* to dress and make up for a role
caradu•ro -ra *adj* brazen; shameless ‖ *f* scoundrel
caramba *interj* confound it!; upon my word!
carámbano *m* icicle
carambola *f* carom; double shot; trick, cheating
carambolear *intr* to carom ‖ *ref* to get tipsy
caramelo *m* caramel; drop, lozenge
carantamaula *f* ugly false face; (*persona*) ugly mug
carantoña *f* ugly false face; **carantoñas** adulation, fawning
carátula *f* mask; (*profesión de actor*) stage, theater; title page; (*de reloj*) (Mex, Guat) face
caravana *f* caravan; (*casa rodante*) trailer
caravanera *f* caravansary
caray *m* var of **carey**
carbohielo *m* dry ice
carbóli•co -ca *adj* carbolic
carbón *m* (*de leña*) charcoal; (*de piedra*) coal; (*electrodo de carbono de la lámpara de arco o la pila*) carbon; black crayon; (*honguillo parásito*) smut; **carbón de bujía** cannel coal, jet coal; **carbón tal como sale** run-of-mine coal
carboncillo *m* charcoal, charcoal pencil
carbonera *f* bunker, coal bunker; coalbin; (Col) coal mine
carbonería *f* coalyard
carbone•ro -ra *adj* coal, charcoal; coaling ‖ *mf* coaldealer; charcoal burner ‖ *f* see **carbonera**
carbonilla *f* fine coal; (*en los cilindros*) carbon
carbonizar §60 *tr* to char
carbono *m* carbon
carbunclo *m* (*piedra*) carbuncle; (pathol) carbuncle
carbunco *m* (pathol) carbuncle
carbúnculo *m* (*piedra*) carbuncle
carburador *m* carburetor
carburo *m* carbide
carcacha *f* (Mex) jalopy
carcaj *m* quiver
carcajada *f* outburst of laughter
cárcel *f* jail, prison; (*para oprimir dos piezas de madera encoladas*) clamp
carcele•ro -ra *adj* jail ‖ *m* jailer, warden
carcinóge•no -na *adj* carcinogenic; cancer-causing ‖ *m* carcinogen
carcinoma *f* carcinoma
carcoma *f* woodworm, borer; anxiety, worry; spendthrift
carcomer *tr* to bore, gnaw away at; undermine, harass ‖ *ref* to become worm-eaten
cardán *m* universal joint
cardenal *m* cardinal; cardinal bird; black-and-blue mark
cardenillo *m* verdigris
cárde•no -na *adj* purple; dapple-gray; (*agua*) opaline

cardía·co -ca adj cardiac ‖ mf (persona que padece del corazón) cardiac ‖ m (remedio) cardiac
cardinal adj cardinal
cardo m thistle
cardume m school (of fish)
carear tr to bring face to face; compare ‖ intr — **carear a** to overlook ‖ ref to meet face to face
carecer §22 intr — **carecer de** to lack, need, be in want of
carecimiento m lack, need, want
carencia f lack, need, want
carente adj — **carente de** lacking
careo m meeting; confrontation
care·ro -ra adj dear, expensive
carestía f scarcity, want, dearth; high prices; **carestía de la vida** high cost of living
careta f mask; **careta antigás** gas mask
carey m hawksbill turtle; tortoise shell
carga f load, loading; (mercancías que se transportan) freight, cargo; (peso u obligación que pesan sobre una persona) burden; (de substancia explosiva, de electricidad, de soldados contra el enemigo) charge; charge, responsibility, obligation; **carga de familia** dependent; **carga de punta** (elec) peak load; **carga por eje** axle load; **carga útil** pay load; **echar la carga a** to put the blame on; **volver a la carga** to keep at it
cargaderas fpl (Col) suspenders
cargadero m loading platform; freight station
carga·do -da adj loaded; (cielo) overcast, cloudy; (atmósfera, tiempo) close, sultry; (alambre eléctrico) hot, charged; (café, té) strong; (rato, hora) busy; **cargado de años** along in years; **cargado de espaldas** round-shouldered, stoop-shouldered
cargador m loader, stevedore; carrier, porter; (de acumulador) charger
cargamento m load; (naut) loading; (naut) cargo, shipment
cargante adj boring, annoying, tiresome
cargar §44 tr (un peso, mercancías; un carro, un mulo, un barco; un horno; un arma de fuego; a una persona) to load; (una persona con un peso u obligación) burden; (un acumulador; al enemigo) charge; (a una persona) charge with; entrust with; annoy, bore, weary; **cargar en cuenta a** (una persona) to charge to the account of; **cargar** (a una persona) **de** to charge with; burden with ‖ intr to load; (el viento) turn; crowd; incline, tip; (el acento) fall; eat too much, drink too much; **cargar con** to pick up; walk away with; (un fusil) shoulder; take on; **cargar sobre** to rest on; bother, pester; **devolve on** ‖ ref (el cielo) to become overcast; (el viento) turn; become annoyed, be bored; **cargarse de** to have a lot of; (lágrimas) be bathed in
cargaréme m receipt, voucher
cargazón f loading; (en el estómago, la cabeza, etc.) heaviness; mass of heavy clouds; (Arg) clumsy job; (Chile) good

crop; **cargazón alta** (coll) high office; high official
cargo m job, position; duty, responsibility; burden, weight; management; (falta que se atribuye a uno; cantidad que uno debe y la acción de anotarla) charge; **a cargo de** in charge of; **cargo de conciencia** sense of guilt; **girar a cargo de** to draw on; **hacerse cargo de** to take charge of; to realize, become aware of; to look into; **librar a cargo de** to draw on; **vestir el cargo** to look the part
cargosear tr (Arg, Chile) to pester
cargo·so -sa adj annoying, bothersome; onerous, costly
carguero m (naut) freighter; (Arg, Urug) beast of burden
cariaconteci·do -da adj downcast, woebegone
cariar §77 tr & intr to decay
cariátide f caryatid
Caribdis f Charybdis
caribe adj Caribbean ‖ m savage, brute
caricatura f (descripción o figura grotescas; retrato festivo) caricature; (retrato festivo) cartoon
caricaturista mf caricaturist; cartoonist
caricaturizar §60 tr to caricature; cartoon
caricia f caress; endearment
caridad f charity; **la caridad bien ordenada empieza por uno mismo** charity begins at home
caries f decay, tooth decay; caries
carilla f (de colmenero) mask; (de libro) page
carille·no -na adj full-faced
carillón m carillon
carine·gro -gra adj swarthy
cariño m love, affection; loved one; (Chile) gift, present; **cariños** caresses, endearments; (Arg) greetings
cariño·so -sa adj loving, affectionate
caripare·jo -ja adj stone-faced, impassive
carirraí·do -da adj brazen-faced, shameless
carisma f charisma
carismáti·co -ca adj charismatic
carita f little face; **dar** or **hacer carita** (una mujer coqueta) (Mex) to smile back
caritati·vo -va adj charitable
cariz m (de la atmósfera, el tiempo) appearance, look; (de un asunto) look, outlook; (de la cara de uno) look; **mal cariz** angry look, scowl
carlinga f (aer) cockpit
Carlomagno m Charlemagne
Carlos m Charles
carlota f pudding; **carlota rusa** charlotte russe ‖ **Carlota** f Charlotte
carmelita f (Hond) station wagon
carmen m song, poem; house and garden (in Granada)
carmesí (pl -síes) adj & m crimson
carnada f bait; (coll) bait, trap
carnal; adj carnal; (hermano) full; (primo) first
carnaval m carnival
carne f (parte blanda del cuerpo humano y del animal) flesh; (la comestible del ani-

mal) meat; **carne de cañón** cannon fodder; **carne de cerdo asada** roast pork; **carne de cordero** lamb; **carne de gallina** goose flesh; **carne de horca** gallows bird; **carne de res** beef; **carne de ternera** veal; **carne de vaca asada** roast of beef; **carne de venado** venison; **carne fiambre** cold meat; **carne sin hueso** cinch, snap; **carne y sangre** flesh and blood; **cobrar carnes** to put on flesh; **echar carnes** (Mex) to swear, curse; **en carnes** naked; **en vivas carnes** stark-naked

carnear *tr* (Arg, Chile, Urug) to butcher, slaughter; (Arg, Urug) to stab; (Chile) to take in, swindle

carnero *m* sheep; (*carne de este animal*) mutton; (*osario*) charnel house; family vault; (*persona que no tiene voluntad propia*) (Arg, Chile) sheep; **cantar para el carnero** (Arg, Bol, Urug) to die; **no hay tales carneros** there's no truth to it

car•net *m* (*pl* **-nets**) notebook; membership card; (Arg) dance card; **carnet de chófer** driver's license; **carnet de identidad** identification card

carnicería *f* butcher shop, meat market; (fig) carnage, massacre

carnice•ro -ra *adj* carnivorous; bloodthirsty ‖ *mf* butcher

carnosidad *f* fleshiness, corpulence; (*excrecencia carnosa anormal*) proud flesh

carno•so -sa *adj* fleshy; meaty, fat

ca•ro -ra *adj* (*de subido precio; amado, querido*) dear ‖ *f* see **cara** ‖ **caro** *adv* dear

carpa *f* carp; awning, tent; stand at a fair; **carpa dorada** goldfish

carpanta *f* raging hunger

carpeta *f* (*cubierta para mesas*) table cover; (*par de cubiertas para documentos*) letter file, portfolio; (*factura*) invoice; (Col) accounting department; (Peru) writing desk

carpintería *f* carpentry; carpenter shop; **carpintería de taller** millwork

carpintero *m* carpenter; woodpecker; **carpintero de carreta** wheelwright

carra•co -ca *adj* old, decrepit ‖ *f* (*barco viejo*) tub, hulk; (*instrumento de madera para producir un ruido desapacible*) rattle; (*berbiquí*) ratchet drill ‖ **la Carraca** Cádiz navy yard

carraspear *intr* to be hoarse

carraspera *f* hoarseness

carrera *f* (*paso del que corre*) run; (*lucha de velocidad*) race; (*sitio para correr*) race track; (*espacio recorrido corriendo*) course, stretch; (*curso de la vida, profesión*) career; (*calle*) avenue, boulevard; (*raya, crencha*) part (*in hair*); (*en las medias*) run; (*hilera*) row, line; (*viga*) rafter, girder; (*movimiento del émbolo del motor*) stroke; **a carrera abierta** at full speed; **carrera a pie** foot race; **carrera armamentista** or **de armamentos** arms race; **carrera ascendente** upstroke; **carrera de baquetas** gauntlet; **carrera de caballos** horse race; **carrera de campanario** steeplechase; **carrera de obstáculos** obstacle

race; steeplechase; **carrera de relevos** relay race; **carrera descendente** downstroke; **carrera de vallas** hurdle race; **carreras** horse racing, turf

carrerista *adj* horsy ‖ *mf* racegoer; auto racer; bicycle racer ‖ *m* outrider ‖ *f* (slang) streetwalker

carreta *f* cart; **carreta de bueyes** oxcart

carrete *m* reel, spool; fishing reel; (elec) coil

carretear *tr* to cart, haul; (*un carro, una carreta*) drive; (aer) to taxi ‖ *intr* (aer) to taxi

carretera *f* highway, road; **carretera de peaje** turnpike; **carretera de vía libre** expressway, limited-access highway

carretería *f* carts; wagon work; carting business; wagon shop

carrete•ro -ra *adj* wagon, carriage ‖ *m* wheelwright; teamster; charioteer; **jurar como un carretero** to swear like a trooper ‖ *f* see **carretera**

carretilla *f* wheelbarrow; baggage truck; (*para enseñar a los niños a andar*) gocart; (*buscapiés*) snake, serpent; (Arg, Chile, Urug) jaw; **carretilla de mano** handcart; **carretilla elevadora** lift truck; **de carretilla** offhand

carretón *m* cart, wagon, dray; gocart; (rr) truck; covered wagon

carricoche *m* covered wagon

carricuba *f* street sprinkler

carril *m* (*barra de acero en el ferrocarril*) rail, track; (*huella*) track, rut; (*hecho por el arado*) furrow; lane, path; (Chile) train; (Chile, P-R) railroad; **carril de toma** third rail

carrilera *f* track, rut

carrilero *m* (Peru) railroader

carrillera *f* jaw; chin strap

carrillo *m* cheek, jowl; pulley; **comer a dos carrillos** to eat like a glutton; have two sources of income; play both sides

carrizo *m* ditch reed

carro *m* cart, wagon; car, auto; (mach) carriage; **carro alegórico** float; **carro blindado** armored car; **carro correo** mail car; **carro de asalto** tank; **carro de combate** combat car, tank; **carro de equipajes** baggage car; **carro de mudanza** moving van; **carro de riego** street sprinkler; **carro frigorífero** refrigerator car; **carro fúnebre** hearse; **Carro mayor** Big Dipper; **Carro menor** Little Dipper; **carro romano** chariot; **pare Vd. el carro** hold your horses

ca•rró *m* (*pl* **-rrós**) diamond

carrocería *f* (*de automóvil*) body

carrocha *f* eggs (*of insect*)

carromato *m* covered wagon

carro•ño -ña *adj* & *f* carrion

carro-patrulla *f* (SAm) patrol car; police car

carroza *f* coach, carriage; **carroza alegórica** float; **carroza fúnebre** hearse

carruaje *m* carriage

carta *f* (*comunicación escrita*) letter; (*constitución escrita de un país*) charter; (*naipe*) card, playing card; map; **carta aérea** airmail letter; **carta blanca** carte blanche;

carta calumniosa poison-pen letter; **carta certificada** registered letter; **carta de marear** (naut) chart; **carta de naturaleza** naturalization papers; **carta general** form letter; **carta por avión** air-mail letter; **poner las cartas boca arriba** to put one's cards on the table

cartabón m carpenter's square

cartagi·nés -nesa adj & mf Carthaginian

Cartago f Carthage

cartapacio m notebook; schoolboy's satchel; writing book; (*papeles contenidos en una carpeta*) file, dossier

cartear intr to play low cards (*in order to see how the game stands*) || ref to write to each other

cartel m show bill, poster, placard; cartel, trust; (*pasquín*) lampoon; (*de toreros*) bill, line-up; (*del torero*) fame, reputation; **cartel de teatro** bill, show bill; **dar cartel a** to headline; **se prohibe fijar carteles** post no bills; **tener cartel** to be the rage

cartela f card; bracket

cartelera f billboard; (*en los periódicos*) amusement page, theater section

cartelero m billposter

cartelón m show bill

carteo m finessing; exchange of letters

cárter m (mach) housing; **cárter de engranajes** gearcase; **cárter del cigüeñal** crankcase

cartera f portfolio; pocket flap; **cartera de bolsillo** billfold, wallet

cartería f sorting room

carterista m pickpocket, purse snatcher

cartero m letter carrier, postman

cartilagino·so -sa adj gristly

cartílago m gristle

cartilla f primer, speller, reader; notebook; (*de la caja de ahorros*) deposit book; **cartilla de racionamiento** ration book

cartivana f (bb) hinge, joint

cartón m cardboard, pasteboard; cardboard box; **cartón de yeso y fieltro** plasterboard; **cartón picado** stencil; **cartón tabla** wallboard

cartoné — **en cartoné** (bb) in boards, bound in boards

cartucho m cartridge

cartulina f fine cardboard

casa f (*edificio para habitar*) house; (*hogar, domicilio*) home; (*establecimiento comercial o industrial*) firm, concern; (*familia*) household; (*escaque*) square; **a casa** home, homeward; **casa consistorial** town hall, city hall; **casa de azotea** penthouse; **casa de campo** country house; **casa de caridad** poorhouse; **casa de citas** house of assignation; **casa de correos** post office; **casa de empeños** pawnshop; **casa de expósitos** foundling home; **casa de fieras** menagerie; **casa de huéspedes** boarding house; **casa de juego** gambling house; **casa de locos** madhouse; **casa de modas** dress shop; **casa de moneda** mint; **casa de préstamos** pawnshop; **casa de salud** private hospital; **casa de socorro** first-aid station; **casa de**

vecindad or **de vecinos** apartment house, tenement house; **casa editorial** publishing house; **casa matriz** main office; **casa pública** brothel; **casa real** royal palace; royal family; **casas baratas** low-cost housing; **casa solar** or **solariega** ancestral mansion, manor house; **casa y comida** board and lodging; **¡convida la casa!** the drinks are on the house!; **en casa** home, at home; **ir a buscar casa** to go house hunting; **poner casa** to set up housekeeping

casabe m var of **cazabe**

casaca f dress coat; marriage contract; (Guat, Hond) lively whispered conversation; **volver la casaca** to become a turncoat

casade·ro -ra adj marriageable

casa·do -da adj married || mf married person; **(los) no casados** (coll) singles

casal m country place; (Arg) pair, couple

casamente·ro -ra adj matchmaking || mf matchmaker

casamiento m marriage; wedding

casapuerta f entrance hall, vestibule

casaquilla f jacket

casar tr to marry; marry off; match; harmonize; (law) to annul, repeal || intr to marry, get married || ref to marry, get married; **no casarse con nadie** to get tied up with nobody

casatienda f store and home combined

cascabel m sleigh bell, jingle bell; rattlesnake; **ponerle cascabel al gato** to bell the cat

cascabelear intr to jingle; to act tactlessly

cascabeleo m jingle

cascabele·ro -ra adj tactless, thoughtless || mf featherbrain || m baby's rattle

cascabillo m jingle bell; chaff, husk; cup of acorn

cascada f cascade, waterfall

cascajo m pebble; gravel, rubble; broken jar; piece of junk; **estar hecho un cascajo** to be old and worn-out, be a wreck

cascanue·ces m (pl -ces) nutcracker

cascar §73 tr to crack, break, split; beat, strike, hit || ref to crack, break, split

cáscara f hull, peel, rind, shell; bark, crust; **cáscara rueda** (Arg) ring-around-a-rosy; **ser de la cáscara amarga** to be wild and flighty; hold advanced views; (Mex) to be determined

cascarón m eggshell

cascarra·bias mf (pl -bias) crab, grouch

casco m (*pieza que sirve para proteger la cabeza del soldado, el bombero, etc.*) helmet; (*uña de las caballerías*) hoof; (*pedazo de vasija rota*) potsherd; (*capa de la cebolla*) coat, shell; (*del sombrero*) crown; (*cuerpo de la nave*) hull; (*de un barco inservible*) hulk; (*barril, pipa*) barrel, tank, cask, vat; (*pieza del teléfono*) headset, headpiece; bottle; (mach) shell, casing; (*gajo de la naranja*) (Arg, Col, Chile) slice; (Peru) chest, breast; **casco de población** or **casco urbano** city limits; **romperse los cascos** to rack one's brain

casera f landlady; housekeeper

casería f country place; customers

caserío *m* country house; small settlement, hamlet

case•ro -ra *adj* homemade; homeloving; (*remedio*) household; house, home; (*sencillo*) homely ‖ *mf* owner, proprietor; renter; caretaker; janitor; huckster; vendor ‖ *m* landlord ‖ *f* see **casera**

caseta *f* (*casa sin piso alto*) cottage; (*de una feria*) stall, booth; bathhouse

casete *m* cassette

casi *adv* almost, nearly; **casi nada** next to nothing; **casi nunca** hardly ever

casilla *f* hut, shack, shed; cabin, lodge; stall, booth; (*escaque*) square; (*compartimiento en un mueble*) pigeonhole; (*división del papel rayado*) column, square; (*taquilla*) ticket office; (*de locomotora o camión*) cab; (Bol, Chile, Peru, Urug) post-office box; (Ecuad) water closet; (Cuba) bird trap; **sacarle a uno de sus casillas** to jolt someone out of his old habits; drive someone crazy

casille•ro -ra *mf* (rr) crossing guard ‖ *m* filing cabinet, set of pigeonholes

casino *m* casino; club; clubhouse

caso *m* case; chance; event; **caso de conformidad** in case you agree; **caso que** in case; **de caso pensado** deliberately, on purpose; **en todo caso** at all events; **hacer al caso** to be to the purpose; **hacer caso de** to take into account, pay attention to; **hacer caso omiso de** to pass over in silence, not mention; **no venir al caso** to be beside the point; **poner por caso** to take as an example; **venir al caso** to be just the thing

casorio *m* hasty marriage, unwise marriage

caspa *f* dandruff; scurf

cáspita *interj* well well!, upon my word!

caspo•so -sa *adj* full of dandruff

casquete *m* (*cubierta que se ajusta al casco de la cabeza*) skullcap; skull, cranium; (*pieza de la armadura que cubre el casco de la cabeza*) helmet; (*pieza del teléfono*) headset

casquillo *m* butt, cap, tip; bushing, sleeve; ferrule; horseshoe

casquiva•no -na *adj* scatterbrained

casta *f* caste; kind, quality; breed, race

castaña *f* chestnut; (*moño*) knot, chignon; demijohn; **castaña de Indias** horse chestnut; **castaña de Pará** Brazil nut

castañeta *f* castanet; snapping of the fingers

castañetear *tr* (*los dedos*) to snap, click; (*p.ej., una seguidilla*) click off with the castanets ‖ *intr* to click; (*los dientes*) chatter

casta•ño -ña *adj* chestnut, chestnut-colored; (*p.ej., pelo*) brown; (*p.ej., ojos*) hazel ‖ *m* chestnut tree; **castaño de Indias** horse chestnut ‖ *f* see **castaña**

castañuela *f* castanet; **estar como unas castañuelas** to be bubbling over with joy

castella•no -na *adj* & *mf* Castilian ‖ *m* Castilian, Spanish (*language*) ‖ *f* chatelaine

casticidad *f* purity, correctness (*in language*)

casticismo *m* purism

castidad *f* chastity

castiga•dor -dora *mf* punisher ‖ *m* seducer, Don Juan

castigar §44 *tr* to punish, chastise; (*la carne*) mortify; (*los gastos*) cut down, curtail; (*obras, escritos*) correct, emend; (*un tornillo*) (Mex) tighten

castigo *m* punishment, chastisement

Castilla *f* Castile; **Castilla la Nueva** New Castile; **Castilla la Vieja** Old Castile

castillete *m* (min) derrick; tower

castillo *m* castle; (*montura sobre un elefante*) howdah; **castillo en el aire** castle in Spain, castle in the air; **castillo de naipes** house of cards; **castillo de proa** forecastle

casti•zo -za *adj* chaste, pure, correct; pureblooded; real, regular

cas•to -ta *adj* chaste, pure ‖ *f* see **casta**

castor *m* beaver

castrar *tr* to castrate; (*una planta*) prune, cut back; weaken

casual *adj* casual, accidental, chance

casualidad *f* accident, chance; chance event; **por casualidad** by chance

casuca or casucha *f* shack, shanty

casulla *f* chasuble

cata *f* tasting; taste, sample

catacal•dos *mf* (*pl* -dos) rolling stone; busybody

catacumba *f* catacomb

catafoto *m* (rear) reflector

cata•lán -lana *adj* & *mf* Catalan, Catalonian

catalejo *m* spyglass

catalogar §44 *tr* to catalogue

catálogo *m* catalogue

Cataluña *f* Catalonia

cataplasma *f* poultice; **cataplasma de mostaza** mustard plaster

catapulta *f* catapult

catapultar *tr* to catapult

catar *tr* to taste, sample; check, examine; be on the lookout for

catarata *f* cataract, waterfall; (pathol) cataract

catarro *m* (*inflamación de las membranas mucosas*) catarrh; (*resfriado*) head cold

catástrofe *f* catastrophe

catavino *m* cup for tasting wine

catavi•nos *m* (*pl* -nos) winetaster; (*borracho*) rounder

catear *tr* to hunt, look for; (*a un alumno*) to flunk; to explore; (*una casa*) to search

catecismo *m* catechism

cátedra *f* chair, professorship; academic subject; teacher's desk; classroom; **poner cátedra** to hold forth

catedral *f* cathedral

catedrático *m* university professor

categoría *f* category; status, standing; class, kind; condition, quality; **de categoría** prominent

caterva *f* throng, crowd

catéter *m* catheter

cateterizar §60 *tr* to catheterize

cátodo *m* cathode

católi•co -ca *adj* catholic; Catholic; **no estar muy católico** to be under the weather ‖ *mf*

Catholic; **católico romano** Roman Catholic

catorce *adj & pron* fourteen ‖ *m* fourteen; (*en las fechas*) fourteenth

catorcea•vo -va *adj & m* fourteenth

catorza•vo -va *adj & m* fourteenth

catre *m* cot; **catre de tijera** folding cot

catrecillo *m* campstool, folding canvas chair

ca•trín -trina *adj* (CAm, Mex) sporty, swell ‖ *mf* (CAm, Mex) sport, dude

caucasia•no -na or **caucási•co -ca** *adj & mf* Caucasian

Cáucaso *m* Caucasus

cauce *m* river bed; channel, ditch, trench

caución *f* precaution; (law) bail, security

caucionar *tr* to guard against; (law) to give bail for

cauchal *m* rubber plantation

caucho *m* rubber; rubber plant; (Col) rubber raincoat; **caucho esponjoso** foam rubber; **cauchos** (*chanclos*) rubbers

caudal *adj* of great volume ‖ *m* (*de agua*) volume; abundance; wealth

caudalo•so -sa *adj* of great volume; abundant; rich, wealthy

caudillo *m* chief, leader; military leader; caudillo, head of state

causa *f* cause; (law) suit, trial; (Chile) bite, snack; (Peru) potato salad; **a** or **por causa de** on account of, because of

causa•dor -dora *adj* causing ‖ *mf* (*persona*) cause

causante *mf* (*persona*) cause; (law) principal, constituent; (Mex) taxpayer

causar *tr* to cause

causear *tr* (Chile) to get the best of ‖ *intr* (Chile) to have a bite

causeo *m* (Chile) bite, snack

cáusti•co -ca *adj* caustic

cautela *f* caution

cautelo•so -sa *adj* cautious, guarded

cauterizar §60 *tr* to cauterize

cautín *m* soldering iron

cautivar *tr* to take prisoner; attract, win over; (*encantar*) captivate

cautiverio *m* or **cautividad** *f* captivity

cauti•vo -va *adj & mf* captive

cau•to -ta *adj* cautious

cavar *tr* to dig, dig up ‖ *intr* (*una herida*) to go deep; (*el caballo*) to paw; **cavar en** to study thoroughly, to delve into

caverna *f* cavern, cave

cavidad *f* cavity

cavilar *tr* to brood over ‖ *intr* to worry, fret

cavilo•so -sa *adj* suspicious, mistrustful; (CAm) gossipy; (Col) touchy

cayado *m* (*de pastor*) crook; (*de obispo*) crozier

cayo *m* key, reef; **Cayo Hueso** Key West; **Cayos de la Florida** Florida Keys

caz *m* (*pl* **caces**) flume, millrace

caza *m* pursuit plane, fighter; **caza de reacción** jet fighter ‖ *f* chase, hunt; hunting; (*animales que se cazan*) game; **a caza de** on the hunt for; **caza al hombre** man hunt; **caza de grillos** fool's errand, wild-goose chase; **ir de caza** to go hunting

cazaautógra•fos *mf* (*pl* **-fos**) autograph seeker

cazabe *m* cassava, manioc; cassava bread

caza•dor -dora *adj* hunting ‖ *m* hunter; huntsman; **cazador de alforja** trapper; **cazador de cabezas** head-hunter; **cazador de dotes** fortune hunter; **cazador furtivo** poacher ‖ *f* huntress; hunting jacket; jacket

cazanoti•cias (*pl* **-cias**) *m* newshawk ‖ *f* newshen

cazasubmarinos *m* sub(marine) chaser

cazar §60 *tr* to chase; hunt; catch; (*en un descuido o error*) catch up; (*un descuido o error*) catch; (*adquirir con maña*) wangle; (*con halagos o engaños*) take in ‖ *intr* to hunt

cazarreactor *m* jet fighter

cazcalear *intr* to buzz around

cazo *m* dipper, ladle; glue pot; (*de cuchillo*) back

cazuela *f* earthen casserole; stew; (archaic) gallery for women; (SAm) chicken stew

cazu•rro -rra *adj* sullen, surly

cazuz *m* ivy

C. de J. *abbr* **Compañía de Jesús**

cebada *f* barley

cebadera *f* nose bag

cebador *m* (mach) primer

cebar *tr* (*a un animal*) to fatten; (*un horno*) feed; (*un arma de fuego, una bomba, un carburador*) prime; (*una pasión, la esperanza*) nourish; (*atraer*) lure; (*un clavo, un tornillo*) make catch, make take hold; (*un anzuelo*) bait ‖ *intr* (*un clavo, un tornillo*) to catch, take hold ‖ *ref* (*una enfermedad, una epidemia*) to rage; **cebarse en** to be absorbed in; vent one's fury on

cebo *m* fattening; feed; bait; lure; (*carga de un arma de fuego*) primer; priming

cebolla *f* onion; bulb; (*del velón*) oil receptacle

cebra *f* zebra

ce•bú *m* (*pl* **-búes**) zebu

ceca *f* mint; **de Ceca en Meca** or **de la Ceca a la Meca** hither and thither, from pillar to post

cecear *intr* to lisp

ceceo *m* lisp, lisping

cecina *f* dried beef

cedazo *m* sieve

ceder *tr* to yield, cede, give up ‖ *intr* to yield, give way, give in; slacken, relax; go down, decline

cedro *m* cedar; **cedro de Virginia** juniper, red cedar

cédula *f* (*de papel*) slip; form, blank; rent sign; certificate, document; **cédula de vecindad** or **cédula personal** identification papers

cedulón *m* proclamation, public notice; (*pasquín*) lampoon

céfiro *m* zephyr

cegar §66 *tr* to blind; (*un agujero*) plug, stop up; (*una puerta, una ventana*) wall up ‖ *intr* to go blind; be blinded ‖ *ref* to be blinded

cega•to -ta *adj* dim-sighted, weak-eyed

ceguedad *f* blindness

ceguera f blindness; blackout
Ceilán Ceylon
ceila•nés -nesa adj & mf Ceylonese
ceja f (pelo sobre la cuenca del ojo) eyebrow; edge, rim; cloud cap; clearing for a road; **arquear las cejas** to raise one's eyebrows; **fruncir las cejas** to knit one's brow; **quemarse las cejas** to burn the midnight oil
cejar intr to back up; turn back; slacken
cejijun•to -ta or **ceju•do -da** adj beetle-browed; scowling
celada f ambush; trap, trick
celador m guard (e.g., in a museum); (elec) lineman; (Urug) policeman
celaje m cloud effect; skylight, transom; ghost
celar tr to see to; watch over, keep an eye on; hide; carve
celda f cell; **celda de castigo** solitary confinement
celdilla f cell; niche
celebración f celebration; applause; (de una reunión) holding
celebrante m (sacerdote) celebrant
celebrar tr to celebrate; (una reunión) hold; (aprobar) welcome; (un matrimonio) perform; (misa) say || intr (decir misa) to celebrate; be glad || ref to take place, be held; be celebrated
célebre adj celebrated, famous; funny, witty; pretty
celebridad f (fama; persona) celebrity
celeridad f speed, swiftness
celeste adj celestial; sky-blue
celestial adj celestial, heavenly; stupid, silly
celestina f procuress, bawd
celestinaje m procuring, pandering
celibato m celibacy; bachelor
célibe adj celibate, single, unmarried || mf celibate, single person || m bachelor || f unmarried woman
celinda f mock orange
celo m zeal; envy; (impulso reproductivo en las bestias) heat, rut; **celos** jealousy
celofán m or **celofana** f cellophane
celosía f (celotipia) jealousy; (enrejado de listoncillos) lattice window, jalousie
celo•so -sa adj (que tiene celo) zealous; (que tiene celos) jealous; fearful, distrustful; (naut) unsteady
celotipia f jealousy
celta adj Celtic || mf Celt || m (idioma) Celtic
célti•co -ca adj Celtic
célula f cell
celuloide m celluloid; **llevar al celuloide** to put on the screen
cellisca f sleet, sleet storm
cellisquear intr to sleet
cementerio m cemetery
cemento m cement; concrete; **cemento armado** reinforced concrete
cena f supper; dinner || **la Cena** the Last Supper
cena•dor -dora mf diner-out || m arbor, bower, summerhouse
cenaduría f (Mex) supper club
cenagal m quagmire
cenago•so -sa adj muddy, miry

cenaoscu•ras mf (pl -ras) recluse; skinflint
cenar tr to have for supper, have for dinner || intr to have supper, have dinner
cencerrada f tin-pan serenade
cencerrear intr to keep jingling; rattle, jangle; play out of tune
cencerro m cowbell; **a cencerros tapados** cautiously
cendal m gauze, sendal
cenefa f edging, trimming, border
cenicero m ash tray
cenicien•to -ta adj ashen, ash-gray || **la Cenicienta** Cinderella
cenit m zenith
ceniza f ash; ashes; **cenizas** ashes; **huir de las cenizas y caer en las brasas** to jump from the frying pan into the fire
ceni•zo -za adj ashen, ash-gray || f see **ceniza**
cenojil m garter
cenote m (Mex) deep underground water reservoir
censo m census; **levantar el censo** to take the census
censor m censor; **censor jurado de cuentas** certified public accountant
censura f censure; censoring; gossip; **censura de cuentas** auditing
censurar tr (criticar, reprobar) to censure; (formar juicio de) censor
centauro m centaur
centa•vo -va adj hundredth || m hundredth; cent
centella f flash of lightning; flash of light; spark; (de ingenio, de ira) (fig) spark, flash
centellar or **centellear** intr to flash, spark; glimmer, gleam, twinkle
centenar m hundred; **a centenares** by the hundreds
centena•rio -ria adj centennial || mf centenarian || m centennial
cente•no -na adj hundredth || m rye
centési•mo -ma adj & m hundredth
centígra•do -da adj centigrade
centímetro m centimeter
cénti•mo -ma adj hundredth || m hundredth; centime
centinela mf (persona) watch, guard || m & f (soldado) sentinel, sentry; **hacer de centinela** to stand sentinel
centípedo m centipede
central adj central || m sugar mill, sugar refinery || f headquarters, main office; powerhouse; (telp) exchange, central; **central de correos** main post office; **central de teléfonos** telephone exchange
centralista mf telephone operator
centralizar §60 tr & ref to centralize
centrar tr to center; hit the center || ref to concentrate; stress
céntri•co -ca adj center, central; (próximo al centro de la ciudad) downtown
centrifugadora f centrifuge; spin-dryer
centro m center; middle; business district, downtown; club; object, goal, purpose; **centro de mesa** centerpiece; **centro docente** educational institution; **pegar centro** (CAm) to hit the bull's-eye

Centro América f Central America
centroamerica•no -na adj & mf Central American
cénts. abbr **céntimos**
ceñi•do -da adj tight, tight-fitting; lithe, svelte; thrifty
ceñidor m belt, girdle, sash
ceñir §72 tr to gird; girdle; fasten around the waist; fasten, tie; abridge, shorten; surround; (la espada) gird on; (mil) to besiege ‖ ref (reducirse en los gastos) to tighten one's belt; (a pocas palabras) restrict oneself; adapt oneself; **ceñirse a** (p.ej., un muro) to hug, keep close to
ceño m frown; (del cielo, las nubes, el mar) threatening look; (cerco, aro) hoop, ring, band; **arrugar el ceño** to knit one's brow; **mirar con ceño** to frown at
ceño•so -sa or **ceñu•do -da** adj beetlebrowed; frowning, grim, gruff
cepa f (de árbol) stump; (de la cola del animal) stub; (de la vid) vinestalk; (de una famila o linaje) strain; **de buena cepa** of well-known quality
cepillar tr to plane; brush; smooth; (SAm) to flatter
cepillo m (instrumento para alisar la madera) plane; (utensilio para limpieza) brush; (cepo para limosnas) charity box, poor box; (CAm, Mex) flatterer; **cepillo de cabeza** hairbrush; **cepillo de dientes** toothbrush; **cepillo de ropa** clothesbrush; **cepillo de uñas** nail brush
cepo m (de limosnas) poor box; (rama de árbol) bough, branch; (trampa) snare, trap; (del yunque) stock; (para devanar la seda) reel; clamp, vise; (para asegurar a un reo) stocks, pillory; **¡cepos quedos!** quiet!, stop it!
cera f wax; **cera de abejas** beeswax; **cera de los oídos** earwax; **cera de lustrar** polishing wax; **cera de pisos** floor wax; **ceras** honeycomb; **ser como una cera** to be wax in one's hands
cerámi•co -ca adj ceramic
cerbatana f peashooter; ear trumpet; spokesperson, go-between
cerca m close-up; **tener buen cerca** to look good at close quarters ‖ f fence, wall; **cerca viva** hedge ‖ adv near; **cerca de** near, close to; about; to, at the court of; **de cerca** closely; at close range
cercado m fence, wall; walled-in garden or field
cercanía f nearness, proximity; **cercanías** neighborhood, vicinity
cerca•no -na adj close, near; adjoining, neighboring; (que debe acontecer en breve) early
cercar §73 tr to fence in, wall in; encircle, surround; crowd around; (mil) to besiege
cercenar tr to clip, trim; curtail; cut off
cerciorar tr to inform, assure ‖ ref to find out; **cerciorarse de** to ascertain, find out about
cerco m (aro, anillo) hoop, ring; (marco de puerta o ventana) casing, frame; (círculo que aparece alrededor del sol o la luna) halo; (reunión de personas) circle, group; fence, wall; (mil) siege; **poner cerco a** (mil) to lay siege to
cerda f bristle, horsehair; (hembra del cerdo) sow
cerdear intr to be weak in the forelegs; (las cuerdas de un instrumento) rasp, grate; hold back, look for excuses
Cerdeña f Sardinia
cerdo m hog; (persona sucia) pig, swine; (hombre sin cortesía) cad, ill-bred fellow; **cerdo de muerte** pig to be slaughtered; **cerdo de vida** pig not old enough to be slaughtered; **cerdo marino** porpoise
cerdo•so -sa adj bristly
cereal adj & m cereal
cerebro m brain; (seso, inteligencia) brain, brains
ceremonia f ceremony; formality; **de ceremonia** formal; **hacer ceremonias** to stand on ceremony; **por ceremonia** as a matter of form
ceremonio•so -sa adj ceremonious, punctilious; (que gusta de ceremonias) formal
cereza f cherry
cerezo m cherry tree
cerilla f wax taper; wax match
cerillera f or **cerillero** m match box
cerneja f fetlock
cerner §51 tr to sift; (el horizonte) scan ‖ intr to bud, blossom; drizzle ‖ ref to waddle; (el ave) soar, hover; (un mal) threaten; **cernerse sobre** (amenazar) to hang over
cernícalo m (orn) sparrow hawk; ignoramus; jag, drunk
cernir §28 tr to sift
cero m zero; **empezar de cero** to start from scratch; **ser un cero a la izquierda** to not count, be a nobody
cerote m shoemaker's wax; fear
cerotear tr (el hilo) to wax ‖ intr (Chile) to drip
cerra•do -da adj closed; close; incomprehensible; (cielo) cloudy, overcast; (barba) thick; (curva) sharp; quiet, reserved, secretive; dense, stupid
cerradura f lock; closing, locking; **cerradura embutida** mortise lock
cerrajería f locksmith business; hardware; hardware store
cerrajero m locksmith; hardware dealer; (el que trabaja el hierro frío) ironworker
cerrar §2 tr to close, shut; lock; bolt; (el puño) clench; enclose; (la radio) turn off; **cerrar con llave** to lock ‖ intr to close, shut; (la noche) fall; **cerrar con** (el enemigo) to close in on; **cerrar en falso** (una puerta, cerradura, etc.) to not catch ‖ ref to close, to shut; lock; **cerrarse en falso** to not heal right
cerrazón f gathering storm clouds; (Arg) heavy fog
cerre•ro -ra adj free, loose; untamed; haughty; (Mex) rough, unpolished; (café) (Ven) bitter

cerril *adj* rough, uneven; wild, untamed; boorish, rough

cerrillar *tr* to knurl, mill

cerro *m* hill, hillock; (*entre dos surcos*) ridge; (*espinazo*) backbone; (*del animal*) neck; **en cerro** bareback; **echar por los cerros de Úbeda** to talk nonsense; **por los cerros de Úbeda** off the beaten path

cerrojo *m* bolt; **cerrojo dormido** dead bolt

certamen *m* literary competition; contest, match

certe•ro -ra *adj* certain, sure, accurate; well-informed; (*tiro*) well-aimed; (*tirador*) good, crack

certeza *f* certainty

certidumbre *f* certainty; sureness

certificación *f* certification; certificate

certifica•do -da *adj* registered ‖ *m* registered letter, registered package; certificate; **certificado de estudios** transcript

certificar §73 *tr* to certify; (*una carta*) register

certitud *f* certainty

cerval *adj* deer; (*miedo*) intense

cervato *m* fawn

cervecería *f* brewery; beer saloon

cervece•ro -ra *adj* beer ‖ *mf* brewer

cerveza *f* beer; **cerveza a presión** draught beer; **cerveza de marzo** bock beer

cer•viz *f* (*pl* **-vices**) cervix; nape of the neck; **bajar** or **doblar la cerviz** to humble oneself; **levantar la cerviz** to raise one's head, become proud; **ser de dura cerviz** to be ungovernable

cesación *f* cessation, suspension

cesante *adj* retired, out of office ‖ *mf* pensioner

cesantía *f* retirement; dismissal (*of a public official*)

cesar *intr* to stop, cease

César *m* Caesar

cese *m* ceasing; notice of retirement; **cese de alarma** all-clear; **cese de fuego** ceasefire

césped *m* lawn, sward; sod, turf

cesta *f* basket; (*para jugar a la pelota*) wicker scoop; **cesta de costura** sewing basket; **cesta para compras** market basket

cesto *m* basket; washbasket; **cesto de la colada** clothesbasket, washbasket; **estar hecho un cesto** to be overcome with sleep; **ser un cesto** to be crude and ignorant

cetrería *f* falconry

cetrero *m* falconer

cetri•no -na *adj* (*tez*) sallow; jaundiced, melancholy

cetro *m* scepter; (*para aves*) perch, roost; (eccl) verge; **cetro de bufón** bauble; **cetro de locura** fool's scepter; **empuñar el cetro** to ascend the throne

cf. *abbr* **confesor**

cg. *abbr* **centigramo**

C.I. *abbr* **cociente intelectual**

cía. *abbr* **compañia**

cía *f* hipbone

cianamida *f* cyanamide

cianuro *m* cyanide

ciar §77 *intr* to back up; back water; ease up

cibernética *f* cybernetics

ciborio *m* ciborium

cicatear *intr* to be stingy

cicate•ro -ra *adj* stingy ‖ *mf* miser, niggard

cica•triz *f* (*pl* **-trices**) scar

cicatrizar §60 *tr* to heal; (*una impresión dolorosa*) (Arg) to heal ‖ *ref* to heal; to scar

Cicerón *m* Cicero

ciclamor *m* Judas tree; **ciclamor del Canadá** redbud

cícli•co -ca *adj* cyclic(al)

ciclismo *m* bicycle racing

ciclista *mf* bicyclist; bicycle racer

ciclo *m* cycle; series (of lectures); (*en las escuelas*) (Arg, Urug) term

ciclón *m* cyclone

cicuta *f* hemlock

cidra *f* citron (*fruit*)

cidrada *f* citron (*candied rind*)

cidro *m* citron (*tree or shrub*)

cie•go -ga *adj* blind; blocked, stopped up; **más ciego que un topo** blind as a bat ‖ *mf* blind person ‖ *m* blind man ‖ *f* blind woman; **a ciegas** blindly; thoughtlessly; without looking

cielo *m* sky, heavens; (*clima, tiempo*) skies, climate, weather; (*de una cama*) canopy; (*mansión de los bienaventurados*) Heaven; **a cielo abierto** in the open air, outdoors; **a cielo descubierto** openly; **a cielo raso** in the open air, outdoors; in the country; **cielo de la boca** roof of the mouth; **cielo máximo** (aer) ceiling; **cielo raso** ceiling; **llovido del cielo** heaven-sent, manna from heaven

cielorraso *m* ceiling

ciem•piés *m* (*pl* **-piés**) centipede

cien *adj* hundred, a hundred, one hundred

ciénaga *f* swamp, marsh, mudhole

ciencia *f* science; knowledge; learning; **a ciencia cierta** with certainty

ciencia-ficción *f* science fiction

cieno *m* mud, mire, silt

cieno•so -sa *adj* muddy, miry, silty

ciento *adj* & *m* hundred, a hundred, one hundred; **por ciento** per cent

cierne *m* budding, blossoming; **en cierne** in blossom; only beginning

cierrarrenglón *m* marginal stop

cierre *m* closing; shutting; snap, clasp, fastener; latch, lock; (*de una tienda, de la Bolsa*) close; (*paro de trabajo*) shutdown; **cierre cremallera** zipper; **cierre de portada** metal shutter (*of store front*); **cierre de puerta** door check; **cierre hermético** weather stripping; **cierre relámpago** zipper

cierro *m* closing; shutting; (Chile) fence, wall; (Chile) envelope

cier•to -ta *adj* certain; a certain; (*acertado, verdadero*) true; (*seguro*) sure; **por cierto** for sure ‖ **cierto** *adv* surely, certainly

cierva *f* hind

ciervo *m* deer, stag, hart

cierzo *m* cold north wind

cifra f (*número*) cipher; (*escritura secreta*) code; (*enlace de dos o más letras empleado en sellos*) device, monogram, emblem; abbreviation; amount, sum; **en cifra** in code; in brief; mysteriously

cifrar tr to cipher, code; abridge; calculate; **cifrar la dicha en** to base one's happiness in; **cifrar la esperanza en** to place one's hope in ‖ *ref* to be abridged; **cifrarse en** to be based on

cifrario m (com) code

cigarra f harvest fly, locust

cigarrera f cigar case; cigar girl

cigarrería f cigar store, tobacco store

cigarre•ro -ra mf cigar maker; cigar dealer ‖ f see **cigarrera**

cigarrillo m cigarette; **cigarrillo con filtro** filter cigarette

cigarro m cigar; **cigarro de papel** cigarette; **cigarro puro** cigar

cigoñal m well sweep; (*del motor de explosión*) crankshaft

cigüeña f stork; crank, winch

cigüeñal m var of **cigoñal**

cilampa f (CAm) drizzle

cilicio m haircloth, hair shirt

cilindrada f piston displacement

cilindrar tr to roll

cilíndri•co -ca adj cylindrical

cilindro m cylinder; roll, roller; (Mex) barrel organ, hand organ

cima f (*de árbol*) top; (*de montaña*), top, summit; **dar cima a** to complete, to carry out; **por cima** (coll) at the very top

cimarra f — **hacer cimarra** (Arg, Chile) to play hooky

cima•rrón -rrona adj (*animal*) wild, untamed; (*planta*) wild; (*esclavo*) fugitive; (*marinero*) lazy; (*maté*) (Arg, Urug) black, bitter

cimarronear intr (Arg, Urug) to drink black maté ‖ *ref* (*el esclavo*) to flee, run away

címbalo m cymbal

cimbel m decoy pigeon, stool pigeon

cimborio or **cimborrio** m dome

cimbrar or **cimbrear** tr to brandish; swing, sway; bend; thrash, beat ‖ *ref* to swing, sway; shake

cimbre•ño -ña adj flexible, pliant; lithe, willowy

cimentar §2 tr to found, establish; lay the foundations of

cime•ro -ra adj top, uppermost

cimiento m foundation, groundwork; basis; source

cimitarra f scimitar

cinabrio m cinnabar

cinanquia f quinsy

cinc m (pl **cinces**) zinc

cincel m chisel, graver

cincelar tr to chisel, engrave

cinco adj & pron five; **las cinco** five o'clock ‖ m five; (*en las fechas*) fifth; **¡choque Vd. esos cinco!** or **¡vengan esos cinco!** put it here!, shake!; **decirle a uno cuántas son cinco** to tell someone what's what

cincograbado m zinc etching

cincuenta adj, pron & m fifty

cincuenta•vo -va adj & m fiftieth

cincha f cinch; **a revienta cinchas** at breakneck speed; reluctantly

cinchar tr to cinch; band, hoop

cincho m girdle, sash; iron hoop; iron tire

cine m movie; **cine en colores** color movies; **cine hablado** talkie; **cine mudo** silent movie; **cine parlante** talkie; **cine sonoro** sound movie

cineasta mf motion-picture producer; movie fan ‖ m movie actor ‖ f movie actress

cinedrama m screenplay

cinelandia f (coll) movieland

cinema m var of **cine**

cinemateca f film library

cinematografiar §77 tr & intr to cinematograph, film

cinematógrafo m cinematograph; motion picture; motion-picture projector; motion-picture theater

cinematurgo m scriptwriter

cinescopio (telv) m kinescope

cineteatro m movie house

cinéti•co -ca adj kinetic ‖ f kinetics

cínga•ro -ra adj & mf gypsy

cíni•co -ca adj cynical; impudent; slovenly, untidy ‖ mf cynic ‖ m Cynic

cinismo m cynicism; impudence

cinta f ribbon; (*tira de papel, celuloide, etc.*) tape; film; measuring tape; (*borde de la acera*) curb; fillet, scroll; **cinta aislante** electric tape, friction tape; **cinta de medir** tape measure; **cinta de teleimpresor** ticker tape; **cinta grabada de televisión** video tape; **cinta perforada** punched tape

cintillo m hatband; fancy hat cord; ring set with a gem; (*borde de la acera*) (P-R) curb; hair ribbon

cinto m belt, girdle; waist

cintura f (*parte estrecha del cuerpo humano sobre las caderas*) waist; waistline; (*de una chimenea*) throat; **meter en cintura** to bring to reason

cinturón m belt, sash; sword belt; **cinturón de asiento** seat belt; **cinturón de seguridad** safety belt; **cinturón retráctil** retractable safety belt; **cinturón salvavidas** safety belt

cíper m (Mex) zipper

cipo m milestone; signpost; memorial pillar

cipote adj (Col, Ven) stupid; (Guat) chubby ‖ mf (Hond, El Salv, Ven) brat

ciprés m cypress

circo m circus

circón m zircon

circonio m zirconium

circuito m circuit; (*de carreteras, ferrocarriles, etc.*) network; race track; **corto circuito** (elec) short circuit

circulación f circulation; traffic; **circulación rodada** vehicular traffic

circular adj circular ‖ f circular, circular letter; **circular noticiera** newsletter ‖ tr & intr to circulate

círculo m circle; club; clubhouse

circuncidar tr to circumcise; clip, curtail

circundante *adj* surrounding
circundar *tr* to surround, go around
circunferencia *f* circumference
circunfle•jo -ja *adj* circumflex
circunlocución *f* or **circunloquio** *m* circumlocution
circunnavegación *f* circumnavigation
circunnavegar §44 *tr* to circumnavigate
circunscribir §83 *tr* to circumscribe || *ref* to hold oneself down; be held down
circunscripción *f* circumscription; district, subdivision
circunspec•to -ta *adj* circumspect
circunstancia *f* circumstance
circunstancia•do -da *adj* circumstantial, detailed
circunstancial *adj* circumstantial
circunstanciar *tr* to circumstantiate, to describe in detail
circunstante *adj* surrounding; present || *mf* bystander, onlooker
circunveci•no -na *adj* neighboring
circunvolar §61 *tr* to fly around
cirial *m* (eccl) processional candlestick
ciriga•llo -lla *mf* gadabout
ciríli•co -ca *adj* Cyrillic
cirio *m* wax candle
Ciro *m* Cyrus
ciruela *f* plum; **ciruela claudia** greengage; **ciruela pasa** prune
ciruelo *m* plum, plum tree; stupid fellow
cirugía *f* surgery; **cirugía cosmética, decorativa** or **estética** face lifting
ciruja•no -na *mf* surgeon
ciscar §73 *tr* to soil, dirty; (Cuba, Mex) to shame; annoy || *ref* to soil one's clothes, have an accident
cisco *m* culm; row, disturbance
cisma *m* schism; discord, disagreement; (Arg) worry, concern; (Col) gossip; (Col) fastidiousness
cismáti•co -ca *adj* schismatic; dissident; (Col) gossipy; (Col) fastidious || *mf* schismatic; dissident
cisne *m* swan; (Arg) powder puff
cisterna *f* cistern; reservoir; toilet tank
cita *f* date, appointment, engagement; (*mención, pasaje textual*) citation, quotation; **cita a ciegas** blind date; **cita previa** by appointment; **darse cita** to make a date
citación *f* citation, quotation; (*ante un juez*) citation, summons
citar *tr* to make a date with, have an appointment with; cite, quote; (*ante un juez*) cite, summon; (*al toro*) incite, provoke || *ref* to make a date, have an appointment
cítara *f* (mus) zither
ciudad *f* city; city council; **la ciudad Condal** Barcelona; **la ciudad del Apóstol** Santiago de Compostela; **la ciudad del Betis** Seville; **la ciudad del Cabo** Capetown or Cape Town; **la ciudad de los Califas** Cordova; **la ciudad de los Reyes** Lima, Peru; **la ciudad de María Santísima** Seville; **la ciudad Imperial** or **Imperial ciudad** Toledo

ciudadanía *f* citizenship
ciudada•no -na *adj* city; citizen; civic || *mf* citizen; urbanite
ciudadela *f* citadel; (Cuba) tenement house
cívi•co -ca *adj* civic; city; domestic; public-spirited
civil *adj* civil; civilian || *mf* civilian || *m* guard, policeman
civilidad *f* civility
civilista *adj* civil-law || *mf* authority on civil law; (Chile) antimilitarist
civilización *f* civilization
civilizar §60 *tr* to civilize
civismo *m* good citizenship
cizalla *f* shears; metal shaving, metal clipping; **cizalla de guillotina** gate shears, guillotine shears; **cizallas** shears
cizallar *tr* to shear
cizaña *f* darnel; contamination, corruption; discord; **sembrar cizaña** to sow discord
clac *m* (*pl* **claques**) opera hat, claque, crush hat; (*sombrero de tres picos*) cocked hat
clamar *tr* to cry out for || *intr* to cry out; **clamar contra** to cry out against; **clamar por** to cry out for
clamor *m* clamor, outcry; (*toque de difuntos*) knell, toll; fame
clamorear *tr* to clamor for || *intr* to clamor; (*tocar a muerto*) toll
clamoreo *m* clamoring; tolling
clamoro•so -sa *adj* clamorous; loud, noisy
clan *m* clan
clandestinista *mf* (Guat) bootlegger
clandesti•no -na *adj* clandestine
claque *f* claque, hired clappers
clara *f* white of egg; bald spot; (*de un trozo de tela*) thin spot; (*en el tiempo lluvioso*) break, let-up
claraboya *f* (*ventana en el techo*) skylight; (*en la parte alta de la pared*) transom; (*esp. en las iglesias la parte superior de la nave que tiene una serie de ventanas*) clerestory
clarear *tr* to brighten, light up || *intr* (*empezar a amanecer*) to get light, dawn; (*el mal tiempo*) clear up || *ref* (*una tela*) to show through; show one's hand
clarecer §22 *ref* to dawn
clarete *m* claret
claridad *f* clarity; clearness; brightness; fame, glory; blunt remark; **claridades** plain language
clarido•so -sa *adj* (CAm, Mex) blunt, rude, plain-spoken
clarificar §73 *tr* to clarify; brighten, light up; (*lo que estaba turbio*) clear
clarín *m* clarion; fine cambric; (Chile) sweet pea
clarinada *f* clarion call; uncalled-for remark
clarinete *m* clarinet
clarión *m* chalk
clarividencia *f* clairvoyance; clear-sightedness
clarividente *adj* clairvoyant; clear-sighted || *mf* clairvoyant

cla•ro -ra *adj* clear; (*de color*) light; (*pelo*) thin, sparse; (*té*) weak; famous, illustrious;· (*cerveza*) light; **a las claras** publicly, openly, frankly ‖ *m* gap; (*en el bosque*) glade, clearing; space, interval; (*ventana u otra abertura*) light; (*claraboya*) skylight; (*en las nubes*) break; **claro de luna** brief moonlight; **de claro en claro** evidently; from one end to the other; **pasar la noche de claro en claro** to not sleep all night; **poner** or **sacar en claro** to explain, clear up; (*un borrador*) to copy ‖ *f* see **clara** ‖ **claro** *adv* clearly ‖ **claro** *interj* sure!, of course!; **¡claro está!, ¡claro que sí!** sure!, of course!

claror *m* brightness; **claror de luna** moonlight, moonglow

claru•cho -cha *adj* watery, thin

clase *f* class; classroom; **clase alta** upper class; **clase baja** lower class; **clase media** middle class; **clase obrera** working class; **clases** noncommissioned officers, warrant officers; **clases pasivas** pensioners

clasicista *mf* classicist

clási•co -ca *adj* classical ‖ *mf* classicist ‖ *m* classic

clasificador *m* filing cabinet

clasificar §73 *tr* to classify; class; sort; file ‖ *ref* to class

clasismo *m* segregation

clasista *mf* segregationist

claudicar §73 *intr* (*cojear*) to limp; (*obrar defectuosamente*) bungle; back down

claustral *adj* cloistral

claustro *m* cloister; (*junta de la universidad*) faculty

cláusula *f* (*de un contrato u otro documento*) clause; (gram) sentence

clausula•do -da *adj* (*estilo*) choppy ‖ *m* series of clauses

clausular *tr* to close, finish, conclude

clausura *f* confinement; seclusion; enclosure; adjournment

clausurar *tr* (*una asamblea, un tribunal, etc.*) to close, adjourn; (*un comercio por orden gubernativa*) suspend, close up

clava *f* club

clavadista *mf* (Mex) diver

clava•do -da *adj* studded with nails; exact, precise; (*reloj*) stopped; sharp, e.g., **a las siete clavadas** at seven o'clock sharp ‖ *m* (Mex) dive

clavar *tr* to nail; (*un clavo*) drive; (*una daga, un punzón*) stick; (*una piedra preciosa*) set; (*los ojos, la atención*) fix; (*a un caballo al herrarlo*) prick; cheat ‖ *ref* to prick oneself; get cheated; (Mex) to dive; **clavárselas** (CAm) to get drunk

clave *m* harpsichord ‖ *f* (*de un enigma, código, etc.*) key; (*piedra con que se cierra el arco*) (archit) keystone; (mus) clef

clavel *m* carnation, pink; **clavel de ramillete** sweet william; **clavel reventón** double-flowered carnation

clavelón *m* marigold

clavellina *f* carnation, pink

clave•ro -ra *mf* keeper of the keys ‖ *m* clove tree ‖ *f* nail hole

claveta *f* peg, wooden peg

clavetear *tr* to stud; tip, put a tip on; wind up, settle

clavicordio *m* clavichord

clavícula *f* clavicle, collarbone

clavija *f* pin, peg, dowel; (elec) plug; (mus) peg; **apretarle a uno las clavijas** to put the screws on someone

clavillo *m* or **clavito** *m* brad, tack; (*que sujeta las hojas de unas tijeras*) pin, rivet; clove

clavo *m* nail; (*capullo seco de la flor del clavero*) clove; migraine; keen sorrow; (*artículo que no se vende*) (Arg, Bol, Chile) drug on the market; (Col) bad deal; (Hond, Mex) rich vein of ore; (Ven) heartburn; **clavo de alambre** wire nail; **clavo de especia** (*flor*) clove; **clavo de herrar** horseshoe nail; **dar en el clavo** to hit the nail on the head

clemátide *f* clematis

clemencia *f* clemency

clemente *adj* clement, merciful

cleptóma•no -na *mf* kleptomaniac

clerecía *f* clergy

clerical *adj & m* clerical

clericato *m* or **clericatura** *f* priesthood

clerigalla *f* (contemptuous) priests

clérigo *m* cleric, priest; **clérigo de misa y olla** priestlet

clerizonte *m* shabby-looking priest; fake priest

clero *m* clergy

cleró•fo•bo -ba *adj* priest-hating ‖ *mf* priest hater

cliché *m* (*lugar común*) cliché

cliente *mf* (*parroquiano de una tienda*) customer; (*de un abogado*) client; (*de un médico*) patient; (*de un hotel*) guest

clientela *f* customers; clientele; patronage, protection; practice

clima *m* climate; country, region; **clima artificial** air conditioning

climatización *f* air conditioning

climatizar §60 *tr* to air-condition

clíni•co -ca *adj* clinical ‖ *mf* clinician ‖ *f* clinic; private hospital; **clínica de reposo** nursing home, convalescent home

clip *m* paper clip

cliqueteo *m* clicking

clisar *tr* (typ) to plate

clisé *m* (*plancha clisada*) cliché, plate; (phot) plate; (*lugar común*) cliché

clo *m* cluck; **decir clo** (Chile) to kick the bucket; **hacer clo clo** (*la gallina clueca*) to cluck

cloaca *f* sewer

clocar §81 *intr* to cluck

cloquear *intr* to cluck

cloqueo *m* cluck, clucking

clorhídri•co -ca *adj* hydrochloric

cloro *m* chlorine

clorofila *f* chlorophyll

cloroformizar §60 *tr* to chloroform

cloroformo *m* chloroform

cloruro *m* chloride

ci
cl

clóset *m* (SAm) (wall) closet

club *m* (*pl* **clubs**) club; **club náutico** yacht club

clubista *mf* club member

clue•co -ca *adj* broody; decrepit

c.m.b., C.M.B. *abbr* **cuyas manos beso**

coa *f* (Mex) hoe; (Chile) thieves' jargon

coacción *f* coercion, compulsion

coaccionar *tr* to coerce, compel

coacervar *tr* to pile up

coactar *tr* to coerce, compel

coadunar *tr* & *ref* to mix together

coadyuvar *tr* & *intr* to help, aid, assist

coagular *tr* & *ref* (*la sangre*) to coagulate; (*la leche*) curdle

coágulo *m* clot

coalición *f* coalition

coalla *f* woodcock

coartada *f* alibi

coartar *tr* to limit, restrict

coba *f* hoax; flattery

cobalto *m* cobalt

cobarde *adj* cowardly; timid; (*vista*) dim, weak ‖ *mf* coward

cobardear *intr* to act cowardly; be timid

cobardía *f* cowardice; timidity

cobayo *m* guinea pig

cobertera *f* lid; bawd, procuress

cobertizo *m* shed; (*tejado saledizo*) covered balcony, penthouse

cobertor *m* bedcover, bedspread; lid

cobertura *f* cover; covering; (*garantía metálica*) coverage

cobija *f* curved tile; top, lid; short mantilla; (W-I) guano roof; **cobijas** bedclothes

cobijar *tr* to cover; shelter, protect

cobijo *m* covering; shelter, protection; (*hospedaje sin manutención*) lodging

cobra *f* team of mares used in threshing; (hunt) retrieval

cobra•dor -dora *adj* (*perro*) retrieving ‖ *mf* collector; trolley conductor

cobranza *f* collecting; (hunt) retrieval

cobrar *tr* (*lo perdido*) to recover; (*lo que otro le debe*) collect; (*un cheque*) cash; (*cierto precio*) charge; acquire, get; (*una cuerda*) pull in; (*pedir, reclamar*) dun; (hunt) to retrieve; **cobrar afición a** to take a liking for; **cobrar al número llamado** (telp) to reverse the charges; **cobrar ánimo** to take courage; **cobrar carnes** to put on flesh; **cobrar fuerzas** to gain strength ‖ *intr* to get hit ‖ *ref* to recover, come to

cobre *m* copper; copper or brass kitchen utensils; **batir el cobre** to hustle, work with a will; **cobres** (mus) brasses

cobre•ño -ña *adj* copper

cobrero *m* coppersmith

cobri•zo -za *adj* coppery

cobro *m* collection; recovery; **cobro contra entrega** collect on delivery; **en cobro** in a safe place

coca *f* (*en una cuerda*) kink; (coll) head; (slang) cocaine; **de coca** (Mex) free; (Mex) in vain

cocaína *f* cocaine

cocción *f* cooking, baking; (*de objetos cerámicos*) baking, burning

cocear *intr* to kick; (*resistir*) balk, rebel

cocer §16 *tr* to cook; boil; (*pan; ladrillos*) bake; digest ‖ *intr* to cook; boil; ferment ‖ *ref* to suffer a long time

coci•do -da *adj* cooked ‖ *m* Spanish stew

cociente *m* quotient; **cociente intelectual** intelligence quotient

cocina *f* (*pieza*) kitchen; (*arte*) cooking, cuisine; (*aparato*) stove; **cocina de presión** pressure cooker; **cocina económica** kitchen range

cocinar *tr* to cook ‖ *intr* to meddle

cocine•ro -ra *mf* cook

cocinilla *m* meddler ‖ *f* kitchenette; chafing dish; **cocinilla sin fuego** fireless cooker

coco *m* cocoanut; (*moño*) topknot, chignon; (*duende*) bogeyman; (*gesto, mueca*) face, grimace; (*sombrero hongo*) (Col, Ecuad) derby hat; **hacer cocos** to make a face; (*los enamorados*) to make eyes

cocodrilo *m* crocodile

cócora *adj* boring, tiresome ‖ *mf* bore, pest

coco•so -sa *adj* worm-eaten

cocotero *m* cocoanut palm or tree

coctel *m* or **cóctel** *m* cocktail; cocktail party

coctelera *f* cocktail shaker

cocuma *f* (Peru) roast corn on the cob

cochambre *m* dirty, stinking thing, pigsty

cochambro•so -sa *adj* dirty, stinking

coche *m* carriage; coach; car; taxi; (*puerco*) hog; **caminar en el coche de San Francisco** to go or to ride on shank's mare; **coche bar** (rr) club car; **coche bomba** fire engine; (coll) car bomb; **coche celular** Black Maria, prison van; **coche de alquiler** cab, hack; **coche de carreras** racing car; **coche de correos** mail car; **coche de plaza** or **de punto** cab, hack; **coche de reparto** (delivery) van; **coche de serie** (aut) stock car; **coche fúnebre** hearse; **coche rural** station wagon

coche-cama *m* (*pl* **coches-camas**) sleeping car

cochecillo *m* baby carriage; **cochecillo para inválidos** wheelchair; **cochecillo para niños** baby carriage

coche-comedor *m* (*pl* **coches-comedores**) (rr) diner, dining car

coche-correo *m* (*pl* **coches-correo**) (rr) mail car

coche-fumador *m* (*pl* **coches-fumadores**) (rr) smoker, smoking car

coche-habitación *m* (*pl* **coches-habitación**) trailer

cochera *f* coach house; livery stable; carbarn; garage

cochería *f* (Arg, Chile) livery stable

coche•ro -ra *adj* easy to cook ‖ *m* coachman, driver; **cochero de punto** cabby, hackman ‖ *f* see **cochera**

cocherón *m* coach house; (*depósito de locomotoras*) roundhouse

coche-salón *m* (*pl* **coches-salón**) (rr) parlor car

cochevira *f* lard

cochina *f* sow; (*mujer sucia y desaliñada*) trollop

cochinada *f* piggishness, filthiness; dirty trick

cochinillo *m* sucking pig

cochi·no -na *adj* piggish, filthy; (*tacaño*) stingy; (Ven) cowardly ‖ *mf* hog; (*persona muy sucia*) (coll) pig, dirty person ‖ *f* see **cochina**

cochite hervite *adj, adv & m* helter-skelter

cochitril *m* pigsty; den, hovel

cochura *f* batch of dough

codadura *f* (hort) layer

codal *adj* elbow ‖ *m* prop, shoring

codazo *m* poke, nudge; **dar codazo a** (Mex) to tip off

codear *tr* (SAm) to sponge on ‖ *intr* to elbow, elbow one's way ‖ *ref* to hobnob, rub elbows

codelincuencia *f* complicity

codelincuente *mf* accomplice

codera *f* elbow patch; elbow itch

códice *m* codex

codicia *f* covetousness, greed, cupidity

codiciar *tr* to covet

codicilo *m* codicil

codicio·so -sa *adj* covetous, greedy; (*laborioso*) hard-working

codificar §73 *tr* to codify

código *m* code; **código penal** criminal code; **código universal de producto** universal product code (UPC)

codillo *m* (*de animal*) knee; (*estribo*) stirrup; (*de un tubo*) elbow; (*de la rama cortada*) stump

codo *m* elbow; (Guat, Mex) miser, tightwad; **dar de codo a** to nudge; to spurn; **empinar el codo** to crook the elbow; **hablar por los codos** to talk too much

codor·niz *f* (*pl* **-nices**) quail

coeducación *f* coeducation

coeficiente *adj & m* coefficient

coetáne·o -a *adj & mf* contemporary

coexistencia *f* coexistence

coexistir *intr* to coexist

cofa *f* (naut) top; **cofa de vigía** (naut) crow's-nest

cofrade *mf* member, fellow member ‖ *m* brother ‖ *f* sister

cofradía *f* brotherhood, sisterhood; association, fraternity

cofre *m* coffer, chest, trunk

cogedor *m* dustpan; coal shovel, ash shovel

coger §17 *tr* to catch, seize, take hold of: collect, gather, pick; overtake; surprise; hold ‖ *intr* to be, be located; fit ‖ *ref* to get caught; cling; get involved

cogida *f* collecting, gathering, picking; (taur) hook

cogollo *m* (*de la lechuga*) heart; (*de la berza*) head; (*de una planta*) shoot; (*del árbol*) top; (*lo mejor*) cream, pick

cogote *m* back of the neck

cogotera *f* havelock

cogotu·do -da *adj* thick-necked; (coll) proud, stiff-necked; (SAm) moneyed

cogulla *f* cowl, frock; **cogulla de fraile** (bot) monkshood

cohabitar *intr* to live together; (*el hombre y la mujer*) cohabit

cohechar *tr* to bribe; plow just before sowing ‖ *intr* to take a bribe

cohecho *m* bribe

coherede·ro -ra *mf* coheir ‖ *f* coheiress

coherente *adj* coherent

cohesión *f* cohesion

cohete *m* (*fuego artificial*) rocket, skyrocket; (*motor a reacción*) rocket; (coll) fidgety person; **cohete de señales** (aer) flare; **cohete intermedio** or **cohete de alcance medio** intermediate-range missile; **cohete lanzador** booster rocket

cohetería *f* missilery

cohibente *adj* (elec) nonconducting

cohibi·do -da *adj* timid, self-conscious

cohibir *tr* to check, restrain, inhibit; (Mex) to oblige

cohombro *m* cucumber

cohonestar *tr* to gloss over, rationalize

coima *f* rake-off paid to operator of a gambling table; concubine; (SAm) bribe

coincidencia *f* coincidence

coincidir *intr* to coincide; happen at the same time; be at the same time (*at a given place*); agree

coito *m* coition, coitus

coja *f* lame woman; lewd woman

cojear *intr* to limp; (*una mesa, una silla*) wobble; (*adolecer de algún vicio*) slip, lapse, have a weakness

cojera *f* (*anormalidad del que cojea*) lameness; (*movimiento del que cojea*) limp

cojijo *m* bug, insect; peeve

cojijo·so -sa *adj* peevish

cojín *m* cushion

cojincillo *m* pad

cojinete *m* cushion; sewing cushion; (mach) bearing; **cojinete de bolas** ball bearing; **cojinete de rodillos** roller bearing

co·jo -ja *adj* lame, crippled; (*mesa, silla*) wobbly; (*pierna*) game ‖ *mf* lame person, cripple ‖ *f* see **coja**

cojón *m* testicle

cok *m* var of **coque**

col. *abbr* **colonia, columna**

col *f* cabbage; **col de Bruselas** Brussels sprouts

cola *f* (*de animal, de ave, de cometa*) tail; (*de un vestido*) train, trail; (*de personas que esperan turno*) queue; (*extremidad posterior*) tail end, rear end; (*de una clase de alumnos*) bottom; (*pasta fuerte*) glue; **cola del pan** bread line; **cola de milano** or **de pato** dovetail; **cola de pescado** isinglass; **cola de retazo** size, sizing; **hacer cola** to queue, to stand in line

colaboración *f* collaboration; (*en un periódico, coloquio, etc.*) contribution

colaboracionista *mf* collaborationist

colabora·dor -dora *adj* collaborating ‖ *mf* collaborator; contributor

colaborar *intr* to collaborate; (*en un periódico, coloquio, etc.*) contribute

colación *f* (*cotejo; refacción ligera*) collation; (*de un grado de universidad*) conferring;

cl
co

parish land; **sacar a colación** to mention, bring up; **traer a colación** to bring up; adduce as proof; bring up irrelevantly

colacionar tr to collate; compare; (un beneficio) confer

colactánea f foster sister

colactáneo m foster brother

colada f washing powder; wash; (garganta entre montañas) gulch; cattle run; **todo saldrá en la colada** it will all come out in the wash; the day of reckoning will come

coladera f strainer; (Mex) sewer

coladero m strainer; cattle run; narrow pass

colador m strainer, colander

colapez f or **colapiscis** f isinglass

colapso m breakdown, collapse; **colapso nervioso** nervous breakdown

colar tr (un grado universitario) to confer ‖ §61 tr (un líquido) to strain; bleach in hot lye, buck; (metales) cast; (una moneda falsa) pass off; **colar el hueso por** (coll) to squeeze through ‖ intr to run, ooze; squeeze through; come in, slip in; drink wine; **colar a fondo** to sink; **no colar** (una cosa) to not be believed ‖ ref to seep, seep through; slip in, slip through; make a slip; lie; **colarse de gorra** to crash the gate

colateral adj collateral ‖ mf (pariente) collateral ‖ m (com) collateral

colcrén m cold cream

colcha f quilt, counterpane, bedspread

colchón m mattress; **colchón de aire** air mattress; **colchón de muelles** bedspring, spring mattress; **colchón de plumas** feather bed

coleada f wag (of the tail); (Mex, Ven) throwing the bull by twisting its tail

colear tr (taur) to grab by the tail; (la res) (Mex, Ven) to throw by twisting the tail; (Col, Ven) to nag, harass; (Guat) to trail after; (reprobar en un examen) (Chile) to flunk ‖ intr to wag the tail; stay alive, keep going; (los últimos vagones de un tren) sway; (aer) to fishtail; **colear en** (cierta edad) (CAm, W-I) to border on, be close to; **todavía colea** it's not over yet

colección f collection

coleccionar tr to collect

coleccionista mf collector

colecta f collection for charity; (eccl) collect

colectar tr to collect; (obras antes sueltas) collect in one volume

colecti•cio -cia adj new, untrained, green; (tomo) omnibus

colecti•vo -va adj collective

colector m collector; catch basin; (elec) commutator; (aut) manifold

colega mf colleague ‖ m confrere

colegial m schoolboy; (Mex) greenhorn, beginner

colegiala f schoolgirl

colegiatura f scholarship; (Mex) tuition

colegio m school, academy; (sociedad de hombres de una misma profesión) college (e.g., of cardinals, electors)

colegir §57 tr to gather; collect; conclude, infer

cólera m cholera‖ f anger, wrath; (bilis) bile; **montar en cólera** to fly into a rage

coléri•co -ca adj choleric, irascible

colesterol m cholesterol

coleta f pigtail; (del torero) cue, queue; (coll) postscript; **cortarse la coleta** to quit the bull ring; to quit, retire; **tener** or **traer coleta** to have serious consequences

coletero m wren

coleto m buff jacket; (coll) body, one's body, oneself; **decir para su coleto** (coll) to say to oneself; **echarse al coleto** to eat up, drink up; read from cover to cover

colgadero m hanger, hook; clothes rack

colgadizo m lean-to, penthouse; projection over a door, canopy

colga•do -da adj pending, unsettled; **dejar colgado** to disappoint, frustrate; **quedarse colgado** to be disappointed, frustrated

colgador m clothes hanger, coat hanger

colgajo m rag, tatter

colgante adj hanging, dangling; (puente) suspension ‖ m drop, pendant; (archit) festoon; (P-R) watch fob

colgar §63 tr to hang; impute, attribute; (a un alumno) flunk; (a un reo) hang ‖ intr to hang, hang down, dangle; droop; (telp) to hang up; **colgar de** to hang from, hang on; depend on

coli•brí m (pl -bríes) humming bird

cóli•co -ca adj & m colic ‖ f upset stomach

coliche m (coll) at-home, open house

coliflor f cauliflower

coligar §44 ref to join forces, make common cause

colilla f butt, stump, stub

co•lín -lina adj (caballo o yegua) bobtailed ‖ m bobwhite; **colín de Virginia** bobwhite ‖ f see **colina**

colina f hill, knoll

colindante adj adjacent, contiguous

colindar intr to be adjacent

colino•so -sa adj hilly

colirio m eyewash

coliseo m coliseum

colisión f collision; bruise, bump

colista mf person standing in line

colitis f colitis

colma•do -da adj abundant, plentiful ‖ m food store, grocery store; seafood restaurant

colmar tr to fill up; (las esperanzas de uno) fulfill; overwhelm; **colmar de** to shower with, overwhelm with

colmena f beehive

colmenar m apiary

colmene•ro -ra mf beekeeper

colmillo m eyetooth, canine tooth; (del elefante) tusk; **tener el colmillo retorcido** to cut one's eyeteeth

col•mo -ma adj brimful, overflowing ‖ m overflow; thatch, thatch roof; (de un sorbete) topping; **eso es el colmo** (coll) that's the limit; **para colmo de** to top off

colocación f (acción de poner una persona o cosa en un lugar) location; (disposición de una cosa respecto del lugar que ocupa) placement; (*inversión de dinero*) investment; (*empleo*) position, employment, job

colocar §73 *tr* to place, put; (*una trampa*) set || *ref* to get placed, find a job; (*venderse*) sell

colodra *f* milk bucket; drinking horn; (*bebedor de vino*) (coll) toper

colofón *m* colophon

colofonia *f* rosin

coloide *adj & m* colloid

colon *m* colon; (gram) main clause

Colón *m* Columbus

colonia *f* colony; cologne; silk ribbon; housing development; (W-I) sugar plantation || **Colonia** *f* Cologne; **la Colonia del Cabo** Cape Colony

colonial *adj* colonial; overseas || **coloniales** *mpl* imported foods

colonizar §60 *tr & intr* to colonize

colono *m* colonist, settler; tenant farmer; (W-I) owner of sugar plantation

coloquial *adj* colloquial

coloquialismo *m* colloquialism

coloquio *m* colloquy, talk, conference

color *m* color; (*substancia para pintar*) paint; (*para pintarse el rostro*) rouge; **colores** (*bandera*) colors; (*persona*) **de color** of color, colored; (*zapatos*) tan; **sacar los colores a** to make blush; **so color de** under color of, under pretext of; **verlo todo de color de rosa** to see everything through rose-colored glasses

colora•do -da *adj* red, reddish; (*libre, obsceno*) off-color; (*aparentemente justo y razonable*) specious; **ponerse colorado** to blush

colorado•te -ta *adj* ruddy, sanguine

colorante *adj & m* coloring

colorar *tr* to color; dye; stain

colorear *tr* to color; (fig) to color, excuse, palliate || *ref* (*la cereza, el tomate, etc.*) to redden, turn red

colorete *m* rouge; **ponerse colorete** to put on rouge

colorir §1 *tr* to color; (fig) to color, palliate || *intr* to take on color

colosal *adj* colossal

coloso *m* colossus

columbrar *tr* to discern, descry, glimpse; to guess

columna *f* column; **columna de dirección** steering column; **quinta columna** fifth column

columnata *f* colonnade

columnista *mf* columnist

columpiar *tr* to swing || *ref* to swing; to seesaw; (coll) to swing, swagger

columpio *m* swing; **columpio de tabla** seesaw

colusión *f* collusion

collada *f* mountain pass; (naut) steady blow

collado *m* hill, height

collar *m* necklace; dog collar, horse collar; (*aro de hierro asegurado al cuello del malhechor*) collar, band; (*plumas del cuello de ciertas aves*) frill, ring; (*cadena que rodea el cuello como insignia*) cord, chain; (mach) collar

collera *f* horse collar; chain gang; **colleras** (Arg, Chile) cuff links

co•llón -llona *adj* cowardly || *mf* coward

coma *m* (pathol) coma || *f* comma; (*en inglés se emplea el punto en aritmética para separar los enteros de las fracciones decimales*) decimal point

comadre *f* mother or godmother (*with respect to each other*); gossip (*woman*); friend, neighbor (*woman*)

comadrear *intr* to gossip, go around gossiping

comadreja *f* weasel

comadrería *f* gossip, idle gossip

comadre•ro -ra *adj* gossipy || *mf* gossip

comadrón *m* accoucheur

comadrona *f* midwife

comandancia *f* command; commander's headquarters; (mil) majority

comandante *m* commander, commandant; (mil) major

comandar *tr* (mil, nav) to command

comando *m* (mil) command; **comando a distancia** remote control

comarca *f* district, region, country

comarcar §73 *tr* to plant in a line at regular intervals || *intr* to border, be contiguous

comato•so -sa *adj* comatose

comba *f* bend, curve; warp, bulge; skipping rope; **saltar a la comba** to jump rope, skip rope

combar *tr* to bend, curve || *ref* to bend, curve; warp, bulge; sag

combate *m* combat, fight; **combate revancha** (box) return bout; **fuera de combate** hors de combat; (box) knockout

combatiente *adj & m* combatant

combatir *tr* to combat, fight; beat, beat upon || *intr & ref* to combat, fight, struggle

combinación *f* combination; (*de trenes*) connection

combinar *tr & ref* to combine

com•bo -ba *adj* bent, curved, crooked; warped || *m* trunk or rock to stand wine casks on || *f* see **comba**

combustible *adj* combustible || *m* (*substancia que arde con facilidad*) combustible; (*substancia que sirve para calentar, cocinar, etc.*) fuel; **combustible alternativo** alternate fuel

combustión *f* combustion

comede•ro -ra *adj* eatable || *m* manger, feed trough; (Mex) haunt, hangout; **limpiarle a uno el comedero** to deprive someone of his bread and butter

comedia *f* drama, play; theater; comedy; (fig) farce; **comedia cómica** (*drama de desenlace festivo*) comedy; **hacer la comedia** to pretend, make believe

comedian•te -ta *mf* hypocrite || *m* actor, comedian || *f* actress. comedienne

comedi•do -da *adj* courteous, polite; moderate; obliging, accommodating

comedimiento *m* courtesy, politeness; moderation

comediógra•fo -fa *mf* playwright
comedir §50 *ref* to be courteous; restrain oneself, be moderate; be obliging; **comedirse a** to offer to, volunteer to
comedón *m* blackhead
come•dor -dora *adj* heavy-eating ‖ *m* dining room; restaurant, eating place; dining-room suite; **comedor de beneficencia** soup kitchen
comején *m* termite
comendador *m* prelate, prior; knight commander; (*de una orden militar*) commander
comensal *mf* dependent, servant; table companion
comentar *tr* to comment on ‖ *intr* to comment; to gossip
comentario *m* comment, commentary; **comentarios** talk, gossip
comentarista *mf* commentator
comento *m* comment, commentary; deceit, falsehood
comenzar §18 *tr* & *intr* to commence, begin, start
comer *m* eating, food ‖ *tr* to eat; to feed on; to gnaw away; to consume; (*alguna renta*) to enjoy; to itch; (*una pieza en el juego de damas*) to take; **comer vivo** to have it in for; **sin comerlo ni beberlo** (coll) without having anything to do with it; **tener qué comer** to have enough to live on ‖ *intr* to eat; to dine, to have dinner; to itch ‖ *ref* to eat up; (*las uñas*) to bite; (*el dinero*) (coll) to consume, eat up; (*omitir*) to skip, skip over; **comerse unos a otros** to be at loggerheads
comerciable *adj* marketable; sociable
comercial *adj* commercial, business
comerciante *mf* merchant, trader, dealer; **comerciante al por mayor** wholesaler; **comerciante al por menor** retailer
comerciar *intr* to trade, deal
comercio *m* commerce, trade, business; store, shop; business center; commerce, intercourse; **comercio de artículos de regalo** gift shop; **comercio exterior** foreign trade
comestible *adj* eatable ‖ *m* food, foodstuff
cometa *m* comet ‖ *f* kite
cometer *tr* (*un crimen, una falta*) to commit; (*un negocio a una persona*) commit, entrust; (*figuras retóricas*) employ
cometido *m* assignment, duty; commitment
comezón *f* itch
comicastro *m* ham, ham actor
comicios *mpl* polls; **acudir a los comicios** to go to the polls
cómi•co -ca *adj* comic, comical; dramatic ‖ *mf* actor; comedian; **cómico de la legua** strolling player, barnstormer ‖ *f* actress; comedienne
comida *f* (*alimento*) food; (*el que se toma a horas señaladas*) meal; (*el principal de cada día*) dinner; **comida corrida** (Mex) table d'hôte
comidilla *f* hobby; **la comidilla del pueblo** the talk of the town

comienzo *m* beginning, start; **a comienzos de** around the beginning of
comilitona *f* spread, feast
comi•lón -lona *adj* heavy-eating ‖ *mf* hearty eater ‖ *f* hearty meal, spread
comillas *fpl* quotation marks
cominear *intr* (*el hombre*) to fuss around like a woman
comiquear *intr* to put on amateur plays
comiquillo *m* ham, ham actor
comisar *tr* to seize, confiscate
comisario *m* commissary; commissioner; **comisario de a bordo** purser
comisión *f* commission; committee; (*recado*) errand
comisiona•do -da *mf* commissioner ‖ *m* committeeman
comisionar *tr* to commission
comiso *m* seizure, confiscation; confiscated goods
comisura *f* corner (*e.g., of lips*)
comité *m* committee; **comité planeador** steering committee
comitente *mf* constituent
comitiva *f* retinue, suite; procession
como *adv* as, like; so to speak, as it were ‖ *conj* as; when; if; so that; as soon as; as long as; inasmuch as; **así como** as well as; **como no** unless; **como que** because, inasmuch as; **como quien dice** so to speak; **tan luego como** as soon as
cómo *adv* how; why; what; **¿a cómo es. . . ?** how much is. . . ?; **¿cómo no?** why not?
cómoda *f* bureau, commode, chest
comodidad *f* comfort; convenience; advantage, interest
comodín *m* joker, wild card; gadget, jigger; excuse, alibi
cómo•do -da *adj* handy, convenient; comfortable ‖ *f* see **cómoda**
como•dón -dona *adj* comfort-loving, self-indulgent, easy-going
compac•to -ta *adj* compact
compadecer §22 *tr* to pity, feel sorry for ‖ *ref* to harmonize; **compadecerse con** to harmonize with; **compadecerse de** to pity, feel sorry for
compadraje *m* clique, cabal
compadrar *intr* to become a godfather; become friends
compadre *m* father or godfather (*with respect to each other*); friend, companion
compadrear *intr* to be close friends; (Arg, Urug) to brag, show off
compadrería *f* close companionship
compadrito *m* (Arg) bully
compaginar *tr* to arrange, put in order ‖ *ref* to fit, agree; blend
companage *m* snacks, cold cuts
compañerismo *m* companionship
compañe•ro -ra *mf* companion; partner; mate; **compañero de cama** bedfellow; **compañero de candidatura** (pol) running mate; **compañero de cuarto** roommate; **compañero de juego** playmate; **compañero de viaje** fellow traveler ‖ *f* (*esposa*) helpmeet

compañía *f* company; society; **compañía de desembarco** (nav) landing force; **compañía matriz** parent company; **hacerle compañía a una persona** to keep someone company

compañón *m* testicle; **compañón de perro** orchid

comparación *f* comparison

comparar *tr* to compare

comparati•vo -va *adj* compárative

comparecencia *f* (law) appearance

comparecer §22 *intr* (law) to appear

comparendo *m* (law) summons

comparsa *mf* (theat) supernumerary, extra ‖ *f* supernumeraries, extras

compartimiento *m* distribution, division; compartment; **compartimiento estanco** watertight compartment

compartir *tr* to distribute, divide; share

compás *m* (*brújula*) compass; (*instrumento para trazar curvas*) compass or compasses; rule, measure; (mus) time, measure; (mus) bar, measure; (mus) beat; **a compás** (mus) in time; **compás de calibres** calipers; **compás de división** dividers; **llevar el compás** (mus) to keep time

compasible *adj* compassionate; pitiful

compasión *f* compassion; **¡por compasión!** for pity's sake!

compasi•vo -va *adj* compassionate

compatri•cio -cia *mf* or **compatriota** *mf* fellow countryman, compatriot

compeler *tr* to compel

compendiar *tr* to condense, summarize

compendio *m* compendium; **en compendio** in a word

compendio•so -sa *adj* compendious

compensación *f* compensation; (com) clearing, clearance

compensar *tr* to compensate; compensate for ‖ *intr* to compensate ‖ *ref* to be compensated for

competencia *f* (*aptitud*) competence; (*rivalidad*) competition; dispute; area, field; **de la competencia de** in the domain of; **sin competencia** unmatched (*prices*)

competente *adj* competent; reliable

competer *intr* to be incumbent

competición *f* competition

competi•dor -dora *adj* competing ‖ *mf* competitor

competir §50 *intr* to compete; **poder competir** to be competitive

compilación *f* compilation

compilar *tr* to compile

compinche *mf* chum, crony, pal

complacencia *f* complacency

complacer §22 *tr* to please, humor ‖ *ref* to be pleased, take pleasure

complaciente *adj* obliging; indulgent

comple•jo -ja *adj & m* complex; **complejo de inferioridad** inferiority complex

complementar *tr* to complement

complemento *m* complement; completion; perfection; accessory; **complemento directo** (gram) direct object

completar *tr* to complete; perfect

comple•to -ta *adj* complete; (*autobús, tranvía*) full

complexión *f* constitution

complexiona•do -da *adj* — **bien complexionado** strong, robust; **mal complexionado** weak, frail

comple•xo -xa *adj* complex

complica•do -da *adj* complicated, complex

complicar §73 *tr* to complicate; involve ‖ *ref* to become complicated; become involved

cómplice *mf* accomplice, accessory

complicidad *f* complicity

com•plot *m* (*pl* **-plots**) plot, intrigue

compone•dor -dora *mf* composer, compositor; typesetter; arbitrator; repairer ‖ *m* stick, composing stick; **amigable componedor** mediator, umpire

componenda *f* compromise, settlement, reconciliation

componente *adj* component, constituent ‖ *m* component, constituent; member ‖ *f* (mech) component

componer §54 *tr* to compose; compound; mend, repair; pacify, reconcile; arrange, put in order; restore, strengthen; (*huesos dislocados*) (Am) to set; (Col) to bewitch ‖ *ref* to compose oneself; get dressed; make up, become friends again; (*pintarse el rostro*) make up; **componérselas** to make out, manage

comportable *adj* bearable, tolerable

comportamentismo *m* behaviorism

comportamiento *m* behavior, conduct

comportar *tr* to support; bring about, entail ‖ *ref* to act, behave

comporte *m* behavior; carriage, bearing

composición *f* composition; agreement; (*circunspección*) composure, restraint; **hacer una composición de lugar** to lay one's plans carefully

compositi•vo -va *adj* (gram) combining

composi•tor -tora *mf* composer ‖ *m* (Arg, Urug) horse trainer, trainer of fighting cocks

compostura *f* composition; agreement; (*circunspección*) composure, restraint; repair, repairing, mending; (*aseo*) neatness; adulteration; (Arg, Urug) training

compota *f* compote, preserves; **compota de frutas** stewed fruit; **compota de manzanas** applesauce

compotera *f* (*vasija*) compote

compra *f* purchase, buy; shopping; **compra al contado** cash purchase; **compra a plazos** installment buying; **hacer compras, ir de compras** to go shopping

compra•dor -dora *mf* purchaser, buyer; shopper

comprar *tr* to purchase, buy; (*sobornar*) buy off ‖ *intr* to shop

compraventa *f* dealing, business, bargain, trading; resale

comprender *tr* (*entender*) to understand; (*entender; abrazar*) comprehend; (*contener, incluir*) comprise

comprensible *adj* comprehensible, understandable

comprensión *f* understanding, comprehension; inclusion

comprensi•vo -va *adj* understanding; comprehensive; **comprensivo de** inclusive of

compresa *f* (med) compress; **compresa higiénica** sanitary napkin

compresión *f* compression

comprimido *m* tablet

comprimir *tr* to compress; restrain, repress; flatten

comprobación *f* checking, verification; proof

comprobante *adj* proving ‖ *m* certificate, voucher, warrant; proof; claim check

comprobar §61 *tr* to check, verify; prove

comprometer *tr* to compromise, endanger, jeopardize; force, oblige; (*un negocio a un tercero*) entrust ‖ *ref* to promise; commit oneself; become engaged

comprometi•do -da *adj* awkward, embarrassing; engaged to be married

comprometimiento *m* commitment, promise; predicament, awkward situation; compromise

compromiso *m* commitment, promise; appointment, engagement; predicament, awkward situation; betrothal

compuerta *f* hatch, half door; floodgate, sluice

compues•to -ta *adj* & *m* composite, compound

compulsar *tr* to collate; make an authentic copy of

compungi•do -da *adj* remorseful

compungir §27 *tr* to make remorseful ‖ *ref* to feel remorse

compurgar §44 *tr* (*el reo la pena*) (Mex) to finish serving

computar *tr* & *intr* to compute

cómputo *m* computation, calculation

comulgante *mf* (eccl) communicant

comulgar §44 *tr* to administer communion to ‖ *intr* to take communion

comulgatorio *m* communion rail, altar rail

común *adj* common ‖ *m* community; water closet; toilet; **el común de las gentes** the general run of people; **por lo común** commonly

comunal *adj* common; community ‖ *m* community

comune•ro -ra *adj* popular ‖ *m* shareholder

comunicación *f* communication; connection

comunicado *m* communiqué; letter to the editor, official announcement

comunica•dor -dora *adj* communicating

comunicante *mf* communicant, informant

comunicar §73 *tr* to communicate; notify, inform; connect, put into communication ‖ *intr* to communicate ‖ *ref* to communicate; communicate with each other

comunicati•vo -va *adj* communicative

comunidad *f* community

comunión *f* communion; political party; sect

comunismo *m* communism

comunista *mf* communist

comunistizar §60 *tr* to convert to communism ‖ *ref* to become communistic

comunizar §60 *tr* to communize

con *prep* with; to, towards; in spite of; **con que** and so; whereupon; **con tal (de) que** provided that; **con todo** however, nevertheless

conato *m* effort, endeavor; (*delito que no llegó a consumarse*) attempt

cónca•vo -va *adj* concave

concebible *adj* conceivable

concebir §50 *tr* & *intr* to conceive

conceder *tr* to concede, admit; grant

concejal *m* alderman, councilman; **concejales** city fathers

concejo *m* town council; town hall; council meeting; (*expósito*) foundling

concentrar *tr* & *ref* to concentrate

concéntri•co -ca *adj* concentric

concepción *f* conception

concepto *m* concept; opinion, judgment; (*dicho ingenioso*) conceit, witticism; point of view; **en concepto de** under the head of; **tener buen concepto de** or **tener en buen concepto** to have a high opinion of, to hold in high esteem

conceptuar §21 *tr* to deem, judge, regard

conceptuo•so -sa *adj* witty, epigrammatic

concerniente *adj* relative

concernir §28 *tr* to concern

concertar §2 *tr* to concert; mend, repair; (*un casamiento; la paz*) arrange; (*huesos dislocados*) set; (*poner de acuerdo*) reconcile; (*un pacto*) conclude; harmonize ‖ *intr* to concert; agree ‖ *ref* to come to terms, become reconciled; agree

concertino *m* concertmaster

concertista *mf* (mus) manager; (mus) performer, soloist

concesión *f* concession, admission; grant

concesionario *m* licensee; (*comerciante*) dealer

concesi•vo -va *adj* concessive

conciencia *f* (*conocimiento que uno tiene de su propia existencia*) consciousness; (*sentimiento del bien y del mal*) conscience; (*conocimiento*) awareness; **cobrar conciencia de** to become aware of; **en conciencia** in all conscience

concienciación *f* consciousness raising

concienzu•do -da *adj* conscientious; thorough

concierto *m* concert, harmony; (*función de música*) concert; (*composición de música*) concerto

concilia•dor -dora *adj* conciliatory

conciliar *tr* to conciliate, reconcile ‖ *ref* (*el respeto, la estima, etc.*) to conciliate, win

concilio *m* (eccl) council

conci•so -sa *adj* concise

concitar *tr* to stir up, incite, agitate

conciudada•no -na *mf* fellow citizen

concluir §20 *tr* to conclude; convince ‖ *intr* & *ref* to conclude, end

conclusión *f* conclusion

concluyente *adj* conclusive, convincing

concomitar *tr* to accompany, go with

concordancia *f* concordance; (gram, mus) concord

concordar §61 *tr* to harmonize; reconcile; make agree ‖ *intr* to agree

concordia *f* concord; **de concordia** by common consent

concre•to -ta *adj* concrete

concubina *f* concubine

concubio *m* (archaic) bedtime

concuñada *f* sister-in-law

concuñado *m* brother-in-law

concurrencia *f* (*acaecimiento de varios sucesos en un mismo tiempo*) concurrence; (*competencia comercial*) competition; (*ayuda*) assistance, crowd, gathering, attendance

concurrente *adj* concurrent; competing ‖ *mf* competitor, contender, entrant

concurri•do -da *adj* crowded, full of people; well-attended

concurrir *intr* to concur; gather, meet, come together; compete, contend; coincide; **concurrir con** (*p.ej., dinero*) to contribute

concursante *mf* contender

concursar *tr* to declare insolvent ‖ *intr* to contend, compete

concurso *m* contest, competition; (*de gente*) concourse, crowd, throng; backing, coöperation; show, exhibition; **concurso de acreedores** meeting of creditors; **concurso de belleza** beauty contest; **concurso hípico** horse show

concusión *f* concussion; extortion, shakedown

concha *f* (*de molusco o crustáceo*) shell; (*cada una de las dos partes del caparazón de los moluscos bivalvos*) half shell; (*en que se sirve el pescado*) scallop; (*carey*) tortoise shell; oyster; shellfish; horseshoe bay; (theat) prompter's box; **concha de peregrino** scallop shell; (zool) scallop; (*ostras*) **en su concha** on the half shell; **tener muchas conchas** to be sly, cunning

conchabanza *f* comfort; collusion, cabal

conchabar *tr* to join, unite; hire ‖ *ref* to gang up; hire out

conchabero *m* (Col) pieceworker

condado *m* county; earldom

conde *m* count, earl; gypsy chief

condecoración *f* decoration

condecorar *tr* to decorate

condena *f* sentence; penalty, jail term; **condena judicial** conviction

condenación *f* condemnation; (*la eterna*) damnation

condena•do -da *adj* condemned; damned; (Chile) shrewd, clever ‖ *mf* sentenced person; **los condenados** the damned

condenar *tr* to condemn; convict; (*a la pena eterna*) damn; (*p.ej., una ventana*) shut off, block up; (*una habitación*) padlock ‖ *ref* to condemn oneself, confess one's guilt; (*a la pena eterna*) be damned

condensar *tr* to condense ‖ *ref* to condense, be condensed

condesa *f* countess

condescendencia *f* acquiescence, compliance

condescender §51 *intr* to acquiesce, comply; **condescender a** to accede to

condescendiente *adj* acquiescent, obliging

condición *f* condition, state; position, situation; standing; nature, character, temperament; **a condición (de) que** on condition that; **en buenas condiciones** in good condition, in good shape; **tener condición** to have a bad temper

condicional *adj* conditional

condimentar *tr* to season

condimento *m* condiment, seasoning

condiscípulo *m* fellow student

condolencia *f* condolence

condoler §47 *ref* to condole; **condolerse de** to sympathize with, feel sorry for, commiserate with

condominio *m* condominium

condonar *tr* to condone, overlook

cóndor *m* condor; (Chile, Ecuad) gold coin

conducción *f* conveyance, transportation; guiding, leading; (aut) drive, driving; **conducción a la derecha** right-hand drive; **conducción a la izquierda** left-hand drive; **conducción interior** closed car

conducente *adj* conducive

conducir §19 *tr* to conduct; manage, direct; guide, lead; convey, transport; drive; employ, hire ‖ *intr* to lead; conduce ‖ *ref* to conduct oneself, behave

conducta *f* conduct; management, direction; guidance; conveyance; conduct, behavior

conducto *m* pipe; conduit; (anat) duct, canal; agency, intermediary, channel; **por conducto de** through

conduc•tor -tora *adj* conducting ‖ *mf* driver, motorist; (*cobrador en un vehículo público*) conductor ‖ *m & f* (elec & phys) conductor; **buen conductor, buena conductora** good conductor; **mal conductor, mala conductora** bad or poor conductor ‖ *m* (rr) engineman, engine driver

conectar *tr* to connect

conecti•vo -va *adj* connective

conejera *f* burrow, warren; (coll) joint, dive

conejillo *m* young rabbit; **conejillo de Indias** guinea pig

conejo *m* rabbit

conexión *f* connection

conexionar *tr* to connect; put in touch ‖ *ref* to connect; make contacts

confabulación *f* collusion, connivance

confabular *ref* to connive, scheme, plot

confección *f* making, preparation, confection; tailoring; ready-made suit; **confección a medida** suit made to order; **de confección** ready-made

confeccionar *tr* (*ropa*) to make; (*una receta*) make up, concoct

confeccionista *mf* ready-made clothier

confederación *f* confederacy; alliance

confedera•do -da *adj & mf* confederate

confederar *tr & ref* to confederate

conferencia *f* (*reunión para tratar asuntos internacionales, etc.*) conference; (*plática para tratar de algún negocio*) interview; (*disertación en público o en la universidad*) lecture; **conferencia telefónica** (telp) long-distance call

conferenciante *mf* conferee; lecturer
conferenciar *intr* .to confer, hold an interview
conferencista *mf* (Arg) lecturer
conferir §68 *tr* to confer, award, bestow; discuss; compare ‖ *intr* to confer
confesante *mf* confessor
confesar §2 *tr*, *intr* & *ref* to confess
confesión *f* confession; denomination, faith, religion
confe•so -sa *adj* confessed; (*judío*) converted ‖ *mf* converted Jew ‖ *m* lay brother
confesonario *m* confessional
confesor *m* confessor
confiable *adj* reliable, dependable
confia•do -da *adj* unsuspecting; haughty, self-confident
confianza *f* confidence; self-confidence, self-assurance; familiarity; secret deal; **de confianza** reliable
confianzu•do -da *adj* overconfident; overfamiliar
confiar §77 *tr* to confide, entrust; strengthen the confidence of ‖ *intr* & *ref* to confide, trust; **confiar** or **confiarse de** or **en** to confide in, trust in; rely on
confidencia *f* confidence; secret; **de mayor confidencia** top secret
confidencial *adj* confidential
confiden•te -ta *adj* trustworthy, faithful ‖ *mf* confident ‖ *m* spy; informer; secret agent; love seat
configurar *tr* to shape, form
confín *m* confine, border, boundary; **los confines** the confines
confina•do -da *adj* exiled ‖ *m* prisoner
confinamiento *m* confinement; abutment
confinar *tr* to exile; confine ‖ *intr* to border
confirmar *tr* to confirm
confiscar §73 *tr* to confiscate
confita•do -da *adj* hopeful, confident; (*bañado de azúcar*) candied
confitar *tr* (*frutas*) to candy; (*en almíbar*) preserve; (*endulzar*) sweeten
confite *m* candy, bonbon, confection; **confites** confectionery
confitera *f* candy box; candy jar
confitería *f* confectionery; confectionery store
confite•ro -ra *mf* confectioner ‖ *f* see **confitera**
confitura *f* preserves, confiture; **confituras** confectionery
conflagración *f* conflagration
conflagrar *tr* to set fire to
conflicti•vo -va *adj* conflicting; anguished
conflicto *m* conflict; (*apuro*) fix, jam
confluencia *f* confluence
confluir §20 *intr* to flow together; crowd, gather
conformador *m* hat block
conformar *tr* to shape; (*un sombrero*) to block ‖ *intr* & *ref* to conform, comply, yield, agree
conforme *adj* in agreement ‖ *adv* depending on circumstances; fine, O.K.; **conforme a** according to ‖ *conj* as, in proportion as; as soon as ‖ *m* approval

conformidad *f* conformance, conformity; resignation
confort *m* comfort
confortable *adj* comfortable; comforting
confortante *adj* comforting; tonic ‖ *mf* comforter ‖ *m* tonic
confr. *abbr* **confesor**
confricar §73 *tr* to rub
confrontar *tr* (*poner en presencia; cotejar*) to confront ‖ *intr* to border; to agree ‖ *ref* to get along, agree; **confrontarse con** (*hacer frente a*) to confront
confundir *tr* to confuse; (*turbar, dejar desarmado*) confound ‖ *ref* to become confused; (*en la muchedumbre*) get lost
confusión *f* confusion
confutar *tr* to confute
congal *m* (Mex) brothel, whorehouse
congelador *m* freezer
congelar *tr* to congeal, freeze; (*créditos*) (fig) to freeze ‖ *ref* to congeal, freeze
congenial *adj* congenial (*having the same nature*)
congeniar *intr* to be congenial, get along well
congéni•to -ta *adj* congenital
congestión *f* congestion
congestionar *tr* to congest ‖ *ref* to congest, become congested
conglobar *tr* to lump together
congoja *f* anguish, grief
congojo•so -sa *adj* distressing; distressed
congosto *m* narrow mountain pass
congraciar *tr* to win over ‖ *ref* to ingratiate oneself; **congraciarse con** to get into the good graces of
congratulación *f* congratulation
congratular *tr* to congratulate ‖ *ref* to congratulate oneself, rejoice
congregación *f* congregation; **la Congregación de los fieles** the Roman Catholic Church
congregar §44 *tr* to bring together ‖ *ref* to congregate, come together
congresal *m* (Arg, Chile) congressman
congresista *mf* delegate; member of congress ‖ *m* congressman ‖ *f* congresswoman
congreso *m* (*asamblea legislativa*) congress; (*reunión para deliberar sobre intereses comunes*) meeting, convention
congrio *m* conger eel
cóni•co -ca *adj* conical
conjetura *f* conjecture, guess
conjeturar *tr* & *intr* to conjecture, guess
conjugación *f* conjugation
conjugar §44 *tr* to conjugate; combine
conjunción *f* conjunction; combination
conjuntamente *adv* together
conjuntista *m* chorus man ‖ *f* chorus girl
conjunti•vo -va *adj* conjunctive; subjunctive
conjun•to -ta *adj* joined, combined, united ‖ *m* whole, entirety, ensemble; unit; group; (theat) chorus; **de conjunto** general; **en conjunto** as a whole; **en su conjunto** in its entirety
conjura or **conjuración** *f* conspiracy, plot

conjuramentar *tr* to swear in ‖ *ref* to take an oath

conjurar *tr* to swear in; conjure, entreat; conjure away, exorcise ‖ *intr* to conspire, plot ‖ *ref* to conspire, join in a conspiracy

conjuro *m* (*invocación supersticiosa*) conjuration; adjuration, entreaty

conllevar *tr* (*los trabajos*) to share in bearing; (*a una persona*) tolerate, stand for; (*las adversidades*) suffer

conmemorar *tr* to commemorate, memorialize

conmigo *pron* with me, with myself

conmilitón *m* fellow soldier

conminar *tr* to threaten

conmoción *f* commotion; concussion, shock

conmove•dor -dora *adj* touching, moving, stirring

conmover §47 *tr* to touch, move, affect; stir, stir up; shake, upset ‖ *ref* to be touched, be moved

conmutación *f* commutation

conmutador *m* (elec) change-over switch; (SAm) telephone exchange

conmutar *tr* to commute

connivencia *f* connivance; **estar en connivencia** to connive

cono *m* cone; **cono de proa** nose cone; **cono de viento** (aer) wind cone, wind sock

conoce•dor -dora *adj* knowledgeable ‖ *mf* expert, connoisseur

conocer §22 *tr* to know; meet, get to know; tell, distinguish; (law) to try ‖ *intr* to know; **conocer de** or **en** to know, have knowledge of ‖ *ref* to know oneself; know each other; meet, meet each other

conoci•do -da *adj* known, well-known, familiar; distinguished, prominent ‖ *mf* acquaintance

conocimiento *m* knowledge; understanding; acquaintance; consciousness; (com) bill of lading; **con conocimiento de causa** knowingly, with full knowledge; **conocimiento de embarque** (com) bill of lading; **conocimientos** knowledge; **hablar con pleno conocimiento de causa** to know what one is talking about; **perder el conocimiento** to lose consciousness; **por su real conocimiento** (Arg) for real money; **recobrar el conocimiento** to regain consciousness; **venir en conocimiento de** to come to know

conque *adv* and so ‖ *m* condition, terms

conquista *f* conquest

conquista•dor -dora *adj* conquering ‖ *m* conqueror; (*ladrón de corazones*) ladykiller

conquistar *tr* to conquer; (*ganar la voluntad de*) win over

consabi•do -da *adj* well-known; above-mentioned

consagrar *tr* to consecrate; devote; dedicate; (*una nueva palabra*) authorize ‖ *ref* to devote oneself; make a name for oneself

consciente *adj* conscious

conscripción *f* conscription

conscripto *m* conscript, draftee

consecución *f* obtaining, getting

consecuencia *f* (*correspondencia lógica entre sus elementos*) consistency; (*acontecimiento que resulta necesariamente de otro*) consequence; **en consecuencia** accordingly; **guardar consecuencia** to remain consistent; **traer a consecuencia** to bring in

consecuente *adj* (*que tiene proporción consigo mismo*) consistent; (*que sigue en orden a otra cosa*) consecutive

consecuti•vo -va *adj* consecutive

conseguir §67 *tr* to get, obtain; **conseguir +** *inf* to succeed in + *ger*

conseja *f* story, fairy tale; cabal

conseje•ro -ra *adj* advisory ‖ *mf* advisor, counselor; councilor

consejo *m* advice, counsel; board; council; **consejos** advice; **un consejo** a piece of advice

consenso *m* consensus

consenti•do -da *adj* spoiled, pampered; (*marido*) indulgent

consenti•dor -dora *adj* acquiescent; pampering ‖ *mf* acquiescent person; (*de niños*) pamperer ‖ *m* cuckold

consentimiento *m* consent

consentir §68 *tr* to allow; admit; pamper, spoil ‖ *intr* to consent; come loose; **consentir +** *inf* to think that + *ind*; **consentir con** to be indulgent toward; **consentir en** to consent to ‖ *ref* to begin to crack up; (Arg) to be proud

conserje *m* janitor, concierge

conserva *f* preserves; preserved food; pickles; (naut) convoy; **conservas alimenticias** canned goods; **llevar en su conserva** (naut) to convoy; **navegar en (la) conserva** (naut) to sail in a convoy

conservación *f* conservation; preservation; self-preservation; maintenance, upkeep

conserva•dor -dora *adj* preservative; (pol) conservative ‖ *mf* conservative ‖ *m* curator

conservar *tr* to conserve, keep, maintain; preserve ‖ *ref* to take good care of oneself; keep

conservati•vo -va *adj* conservative, preservative

conservatorio *m* (*p.ej., de música*) conservatory; (Arg) private school; (Chile) hothouse, greenhouse

conservera *f* cannery; (Mex) preserve dish

conservería *f* canning

conserve•ro -ra *adj* canning ‖ *mf* canner ‖ *f* see **conservera**

considerable *adj* considerable; large, great, important

consideración *f* consideration; **ser de consideración** to be of importance, be of concern; **someter a consideración** to take under advisement

considera•do -da *adj* (*que guarda consideración a los demás*) considerate; (*digno de respeto*) respected, esteemed; (*que obra con reflexión*) cautious, prudent

considerando *conj & m* whereas

considerar *tr* to consider; treat with consideration

consigna *f* slogan; watchword; (mil) orders; (rr) checkroom

consignación *f* consignment

consignar *tr* to consign; assign; state in writing, set forth

consignatario *m* consignee

consigo *pron* with him, with her, with them, with you; with himself, with herself, with themselves, with yourself or yourselves

consiguiente *adj* consequential; **ir** or **proceder consiguiente** to act consistently ‖ *m* consequence; **por consiguiente** consequently, therefore

consilia•rio -ria *mf* advisor, counselor

consistencia *f* consistence, consistency

consistente *adj* consistent

consistir *intr* to consist; **consistir en** (*estar compuesto de*) to consist of; (*residir en*) consist in

consistorio *m* consistory; town council; town hall

conso•cio -cia *mf* copartner; companion, fellow member

consola *f* console, console table; bracket

consolación *f* consolation

consolar §61 *tr* to console

consolidar *tr* to fund, refund; strengthen; repair

consommé *m* consommé

consonancia *f* consonance; rhyme

consonante *adj* consonantal; rhyming ‖ *m* rhyme ‖ *f* consonant

consonar §61 *intr* to be in harmony; rhyme

cónsone *adj* harmonious ‖ *m* (mus) chord

consorcio *m* consortium; partnership; fellowship

consorte *mf* consort, mate, spouse; partner, companion; **consortes** (law) colitigants; (law) accomplices

conspi•cuo -cua *adj* outstanding, prominent

conspiración *f* conspiracy

conspirar *intr* to conspire

constancia *f* constancy; certainty, proof

constante *adj* constant; steady, regular; sure, certain ‖ *f* constant

constar *intr* to be clear, be certain; be on record; have the right rhythm; **constar de** to consist of; **hacer constar** to state, make known; **y para que conste** in witness whereof

constatación *f* proof

constatar *tr* to prove, establish, show

constelación *f* constellation; climate, weather; epidemic

consternar *tr* to depress, dismay

constipación *f* or **constipado** *m* cold, cold in the head

constipar *tr* (*los poros*) to stop up ‖ *ref* to catch cold

constitución *f* constitution

constituir §20 *tr* to constitute; establish, found; **constituir en** to force into ‖ *ref* — **constituirse en** to set oneself up as

constituti•vo -va *adj* & *m* constituent

constituyente *adj* (*para dictar o reformar la constitución*) constituent

constreñir §72 *tr* to constrain, force, compel; constrict, compress

construcción *f* construction; building, structure; **construcción de buques** shipbuilding

construc•tor -tora *adj* construction ‖ *mf* builder, constructor; **constructor de buques** shipbuilder

construir §20 *tr* to build, construct

consuegro *m* fellow father-in-law (*with respect to the father of one's son-in-law or daughter-in-law*), father-in-law of one's child

consuelda *f* comfrey; **consuelda real** field larkspur; **consuelda sarracena** goldenrod

consuelo *m* consolation; joy, delight; **sin consuelo** inconsolably; to excess

consueta *m* (theat) prompter

consuetudina•rio -ria *adj* customary, usual

cónsul *m* consul

consulado *m* consulate, consulship; (*casa u oficina*) consulate

consular *adj* consular

consulta *f* consultation; opinion; reference

consultación *f* consultation

consultar *tr* to consult; take up, discuss; advise ‖ *intr* to consult, confer

consulti•vo -va *adj* advisory

consul•tor -tora *mf* consultant

consultorio *m* dispensary

consuma•do -da *adj* consummate ‖ *m* consommé

consumar *tr* to consummate; fulfill, carry out

consumerismo *m* consumerism

consumición *f* consumption; drink (*in bar or restaurant*)

consumi•do -da *adj* thin, weak, emaciated; fretful

consumi•dor -dora *mf* consumer; customer (*in bar or restaurant*)

consumir *tr* to consume; exhaust; harass, wear down ‖ *ref* to consume, waste away; long, yearn

consumo *m* consumption; drink (*in bar or restaurant*); customers; **consumos** octroi

consunción *f* consumption; (pathol) consumption

consuno *adv* — **de consuno** together, in accord

consunti•vo -va *adj* consumptive; (*crédito*) consumer

contabilidad *f* accounting, bookkeeping

contabilista *mf* accountant, bookkeeper

contabilizadora *f* computer

contabilizar §60 *tr* to enter in the ledger

contable *adj* countable ‖ *mf* accountant, bookkeeper

contactar *intr* to contact, be in contact

contacto *m* contact; **ponerse en contacto con** to get in touch with

conta•do -da *adj* scarce, rare; **al contado** cash, for cash; **contados** a few; **de contado** right away; **por de contado** of course

contador *m* counter; accountant; (*que mide el agua, gas, electricidad*) meter; (law) receiver; **contador de abonado** house meter; **contador de Geiger** Geiger counter; **contador kilométrico** speedometer; **contador**

público titulado certified public accountant

contaduría f accountancy; accountant's office; box office for advanced sales

contagiar tr to infect; corrupt

contagio m contagion

contagio•so -sa adj contagious

contaminación f contamination; **contaminación ambiental** environmental pollution

contaminante m pollutant

contaminar tr to contaminate; (un texto) corrupt; (la ley de Dios) break

contante adj (dinero) ready

contar §61 tr to count; regard, consider; tell, relate; **contar . . . años** to be . . . years old; **dejarse contar diez** (box) to take the count; **tiene sus horas contadas** his days are numbered ‖ intr to count; **a contar desde** beginning with; **contar con** to count on, rely on; reckon with; expect to

contemplación f contemplation; leniency, condescension

contemplar tr to contemplate; be lenient to ‖ intr to contemplate

contemporáne•o -a adj contemporaneous, contemporary ‖ mf contemporary

contemporizar §60 intr to temporize

contención f containment; contention, strife; (law) suit, litigation

contencio•so -sa adj contentious

contender §51 intr to contend

contendiente mf contender, contestant

contenedor m container

contener §71 tr to contain ‖ ref to contain oneself

conteni•do -da adj moderate, restrained ‖ m content, contents

contenta f gift or treat; indorsement; (mil) certificate of good conduct; (law) release

contentadi•zo -za adj easy to please

contentamiento m contentment

contentar tr to content; reconcile; (com) to indorse

conten•to -ta adj content, contented, glad ‖ m content, contentment; **a contento** to one's satisfaction; **no caber de contento** (coll) to be beside oneself with joy ‖ f see **contenta**

conteo m calculation, estimate, count

contera f tip, metal tip

contesta f answer; (Mex) chat

contestación f answer; argument, debate; **mala contestación** back talk

contestar tr to answer ‖ intr to answer; agree

contesto m (Mex) reply

contexto m interweaving; context

conticinio m dead of night

contienda f contest, dispute, fight

contigo pron with thee, with you

conti•guo -gua adj contiguous, adjoining

continencia f continence

continental adj continental

continente adj continent ‖ m (cosa que contiene en sí a otra) container; (aire del semblante, compostura del cuerpo) mien, bearing; (gran extensión de tierra rodeada por los océanos) continent

contingencia f contingency

contingente adj contingent ‖ m contingent; share, quota

continuar §21 tr & intr to continue; **continuará** to be continued

continuidad f continuity

conti•nuo -nua adj continuous, continual; (mach) endless ‖ **continuo** adv continuously

contonear ref to strut, swagger

contoneo m strut, swagger

contorcer §74 ref to writhe

contorno m contour, outline; **contornos** environs, neighborhood

contorsión f contortion

contra prep against; toward, facing ‖ m (concepto opuesto) con ‖ f trouble, inconvenience; (al comprador) (Cuba) gift, extra; (Chile) antidote; **llevar la contra a** to disagree with

contraalmirante m rear admiral

contraatacar §73 tr & intr to counterattack

contraataque m counterattack

contrabajo m contrabass, double bass

contrabajón m double bassoon

contrabalancear tr to counterbalance

contrabalanza f counterbalance

contrabandear intr to smuggle

contrabandista adj smuggling; contraband ‖ mf smuggler, contrabandist

contrabando m smuggling, contraband; **meter de contrabando** to smuggle, smuggle in

contrabarrera f second row of seats (in bull ring)

contracalle f parallel side street

contracarril m (rr) guardrail

contracción f contraction; (reducción del ritmo normal de los negocios) recession; (al estudio) (Chile, Peru) concentration

contracepti•vo -va adj & m contraceptive

contracorriente f countercurrent, crosscurrent; (entre aguas) undertow

contracultura f counterculture

contrachapado m plywood

contradecir §24 (impv sg -dice) tr to contradict

contradicción f contradiction

contradic•tor -tora adj contradictory ‖ mf contradicter

contradicto•rio -ria adj contradictory

contraer §75 tr to contract; (deudas) incur; (el discurso o idea) condense ‖ ref to contract; shrink; (Chile, Peru) to concentrate, apply oneself

contraescalón m riser (of stairway)

contraespía mf counterspy

contraespionaje m counterespionage

contrafallar tr & intr to overtrump

contrafallo m overtrump

contrafigura f counterpart

contrafuero m infringement, violation

contrafuerte m abutment, buttress

contragolpe m counterstroke; kickback; (box) counter

contrahace•dor -dora adj counterfeiting; fake ‖ mf counterfeiter; fake; impersonator

contrahacer §39 *tr* to counterfeit, copy, imitate; fake; impersonate; (*un libro*) pirate || *ref* to pretend to be
contra·haz *f* (*pl* **-haces**) wrong side
contrahe·cho -cha *adj* counterfeit, fake; deformed
contrahechura *f* counterfeit, fake
contrahuella *f* riser (*of stairway*)
contralor *m* comptroller
contralto *mf* contralto (*person*) || *m* contralto (*voice*)
contraluz *f* view against the light; **a contraluz** against the light
contramaestre *m* foreman; (naut) boatswain; **segundo contramaestre** boatswain's mate
contramandar *tr* to countermand
contramandato *m* countermand
contramano *adv* — **a contramano** in the wrong direction, the wrong way
contramarcha *f* countermarch; reverse
contramarchar *intr* to countermarch; to go in reverse
contraofensiva *f* counteroffensive
contraorden *f* cancellation
contraparte *f* counterpart
contrapasar *intr* to go over to the other side
contrapelo *adv* — **a contrapelo** against the hair, against the grain; the wrong way; **a contrapelo de** against, counter to
contrapesar *tr* to offset, counterbalance
contrapeso *m* counterweight; counterbalance; (*para completar el peso de carne, etc.*) makeweight
contraponer §54 *tr* to set opposite; oppose; compare
contraportada *f* (*del disco*) flip side
contraprestación *f* return favor
contraproducente *adj* self-defeating, unproductive
contraprueba *f* second proof
contrapuerta *f* storm door; vestibule door
contrapuntear *tr* to sing in counterpoint; taunt, be sarcastic to || *ref* to taunt each other
contrapunto *m* counterpoint
contrapunzón *m* nailset, punch
contrariar §77 *tr* to counteract, oppose; annoy, provoke
contrariedad *f* opposition; interference; annoyance, bother
contra·rio -ria *adj* opposite, contrary; harmful || *mf* enemy, opponent, rival || *m* opposite, contrary; **al contrario** on the contrary; **de lo contrario** otherwise
contrarreferencia *f* cross reference
Contrarreforma *f* Counter Reformation
contrarregistro *m* (*para comprobar si algún género ha pasado por la frontera*) double check; (*de una experiencia científica*) control
contrarréplica *f* (law) rejoinder
contrarrestar *tr* to resist, counteract; (*la pelota*) return
contrarrevolución *f* counterrevolution
contrasentido *m* misinterpretation; mistranslation; nonsense

contraseña *f* countersign; baggage check; **contraseña de salida** (mov, theat) check
contrastar *tr* to resist; (*las pesas y medidas*) check || *intr* to resist; contrast
contraste *m* resistance; contrast; assayer; assayer's office; (naut) sudden shift in the wind
contratar *tr* to contract for; hire, engage
contratiempo *m* misfortune, disappointment, setback
contratista *mf* contractor
contrato *m* contract
contratreta *f* counterplot
contratuerca *f* lock nut, jam nut
contravalidación *f* (*documento*) validation
contravalidar *tr* to validate; confirm
contraveneno *m* counterpoison, antidote
contravenir §79 *intr* to act contrary; **contravenir a** to contravene, act counter to
contraventana *f* window shutter
contravidriera *f* storm sash
contrayente *mf* contracting party (*to a marriage*)
contribución *f* contribution; tax; **contribución de sangre** military service; **contribución industrial** excise tax; **contribución territorial** land tax
contribui·dor -dora *mf* contributor; taxpayer
contribuir §20 *tr* & *intr* to contribute
contribuyente *mf* contributor; taxpayer
contrición *f* contrition
contrincante *m* competitor, rival; fellow candidate
contristar *tr* to sadden
contri·to -ta *adj* contrite
control *m* control, check; **control de la natalidad** or **de los nacimientos** birth control; **control remoto** remote control
controlador *m* controller; **controlador aéreo** air-traffic controller
controlar *tr* to control, check
controversia *f* controversy
controvertible *adj* controversial, controvertible
controvertir §68 *tr* to controvert
contubernio *m* cohabitation; evil alliance
contumacia *f* contumacy; (law) contempt
contu·maz *adj* (*pl* **-maces**) contumacious; germ-bearing; (law) guilty of contempt of court
contumelia *f* contumely
contundente *adj* bruising; impressive, convincing
contundir *tr* to bruise
conturbar *tr* to trouble, worry, upset
contusión *f* contusion
contusionar *tr* (Chile) to bruise
convalecencia *f* convalescence
convalecer §22 *intr* to convalesce, recover
convaleciente *adj* & *mf* convalescent
convalidar *tr* to confirm
conveci·no -na *adj* neighboring || *mf* neighbor
convencer §78 *tr* to convince
convencimiento *m* conviction
convención *f* (*acuerdo; conformidad; asamblea*) convention; political convention
convencional *adj* conventional

convenible *adj* docile, compliant; (*precio*) fair, reasonable

conveniencia *f* (*comodidad*) convenience; (*acuerdo, convenio*) agreement; fitness, suitability; (*formas sociales*) propriety; domestic employment; **conveniencias** income, property

conveniencie•ro -ra *adj* comfort-loving

conveniente *adj* (*cómodo*) convenient; fit, suitable; advantageous; proper

convenio *m* pact, covenant, treaty

convenir §79 *intr* to agree; (*concurrir, juntarse*) convene; be suitable, be becoming; be important, be necessary; **conviene a saber** to wit, namely ‖ *ref* to agree, come to an agreement

conventillo *m* (SAm) tenement house

convento *m* convent, monastery; **convento de religiosas** convent

converger §17 or **convergir** §27 *intr* to converge; concur

conversa *f* chat, conversation

conversación *f* conversation

conversacional *adj* conversational

conversar *intr* to converse; live, dwell

conversión *f* conversion

conver•so -sa *adj* converted ‖ *mf* convert ‖ *m* lay brother ‖ *f* see **conversa**

convertible *adj* convertible ‖ *m* (aut) convertible

convertir §68 *tr* to convert; turn ‖ *ref* to convert; be converted; **convertirse en** to turn into, become

conve•xo -xa *adj* convex

convic•to -ta *adj* convicted, found guilty

convida•do -da *mf* guest ‖ *f* treat

convidar *tr* to invite; treat; move, incite; **convidarle a uno con alguna cosa** to treat someone to something ‖ *ref* to offer one's services

convincente *adj* convincing

convite *m* invitation; treat, banquet, party; **convite a escote** Dutch treat

convivir *intr* to live together

convocar §73 *tr* to convoke, call together; (*p.ej., una huelga*) call; acclaim

convoy *m* convoy; escort; cruet stand; (rr) train

convoyar *tr* to convoy

convulsionar *tr* to convulse

conyugal *adj* conjugal

cónyuge *mf* spouse, consort ‖ **cónyuges** *mpl* couple, husband and wife

co•ñac *m* (*pl* -ñacs or -ñaques) cognac

cooperación *f* coöperation

cooperar *intr* to coöperate

cooperati•vo -va *adj* coöperative

cooptar *tr* to coöpt

coordena•do -da *adj* coördinate ‖ *f* (math) coördinate

coordinante *adj* (gram) coördinating

coordinar *tr & intr* to coördinate

copa *f* goblet, wineglass; (*del sombrero*) crown; brazier; vase; drink; sundae; playing card, representing a bowl, equivalent to heart; (*del dolor*) (fig) cup; (sport) cup

copar *tr* (*la puesta equivalente a todo el dinero de la banca*) to cover; (*todos los puestos en una elección*) sweep; (mil) to cut off and capture

copartícipe *mf* copartner, joint partner

copear *intr* to sell wine or liquor by the glass; (coll) to tipple

copero *m* cabinet for wineglasses

copete *m* (*cabello levantado sobre la frente*) pompadour; (*de plumas; de una montaña*) crest; (*de un caballo*) forelock; (*de lana, cabello, plumas, etc.*) tuft; (*de un mueble*) top, finial; (*de un sorbete*) topping; **de alto copete** aristocratic, important; **tener mucho copete** to be high-hat

copetu•do -da *adj* tufted; high, lofty; high-hat

copia *f* plenty, abundance; copy; **copia al carbón** carbon copy; **copia fiel** true copy

copiador *m* or **copiadora** *f* copy(ing) machine; duplicator

copiante *mf* copier, copyist

copiar *tr* to copy, copy down

copiloto *m* copilot

copio•so -sa *adj* copious, abundant

copista *mf* copier, copyist

copla *f* couplet; ballad, popular song; **coplas** verse, poetry; **coplas de ciego** doggerel verse

cople•ro -ra *mf* vendor of ballads; poetaster

coplista *mf* poetaster

copo *m* bundle of cotton, flax, hemp, etc. to be spun; **copo de nieve** snowflake; **copos de jabón** soap flakes

copón *m* ciborium, pyx

copo•so -sa *adj* bushy; flaky, woolly

copu•do -da *adj* bushy, thick

copular *ref* to copulate

coque *m* coke

coqueluche *f* whooping cough

coqueta *adj* coquettish ‖ *f* coquette, flirt; (W-I) dressing table

coquetear *intr* to coquette, flirt; try to please everybody

coquetería *f* coquetry, flirting; affectation

coque•tón -tona *adj* coquettish, kittenish ‖ *m* flirt, lady-killer

coracha *f* leather bag

coraje *m* anger; mettle, spirit

coraju•do -da *adj* ill-tempered; (Arg) brave, courageous

coral *adj* (mus) choral ‖ *m* (mus) chorale; (*zoófito; esqueleto calizo del zoófito; color*) coral; **corales** coral beads

corambre *f* hides, skins

Corán *m* Koran

coranvo•bis *m* (*pl* -bis) fat solemn look

coraza *f* armor; cuirass; (sport) guard

corazón *m* heart; (*centro de una cosa*) core; **de corazón** heartily; **hacer de tripas corazón** to pluck up courage

corazonada *f* impulsiveness; hunch, presentiment; entrails

corbata *f* necktie, cravat; scarf; **corbata de mariposa, corbata de lazo** bow tie; **corbata de nudo corredizo** four-in-hand tie

corbatín *m* bow tie

corbeta *f* corvette

CO
CO

Córcega f Corsica
corcel m steed, charger
corcova f hump, hunch
corcova•do -da adj humpbacked, hunchbacked ‖ mf humpback, hunchback
corcovar tr to bend
corcovear intr to buck; grumble; (Mex) to be afraid
corcha f cork bark; cork bucket (for cooling wine)
corchea f (mus) quaver, eighth note
corche•ro -ra adj cork ‖ f cork bucket (for cooling wine)
corcheta f eye (of hook and eye)
corchete m snap; hook and eye; hook (of hook and eye); (signo) bracket; **corchete de presión** snap fastener
corcho m cork; cork, cork stopper; cork wine cooler; cork box; cork mat; **corcho bornizo, corcho virgen** virgin cork
cordada f (mountaineering) party of two or three men roped together
cordaje m cordage; (naut) rigging
cordal adj wisdom (tooth) ‖ m (mus) tailpiece
cordel m cord, string; (distance of) five steps; cattle run; **a cordel** in a straight line
cordelejo m string; **dar cordelejo a** to make fun of; (Mex) to keep putting off
cordera f ewe lamb; (mujer dócil y humilde) (fig) lamb
cordería f cordage
corderillo m lambskin
corderi•no -na adj lamb ‖ f lambskin
cordero m lamb; lambskin; (hombre dócil y humilde) (fig) lamb
corderuna f lambskin
cordial adj cordial; (dedo) middle ‖ m cordial
cordialidad f cordiality
cordillera f chain of mountains
cordobana f — **andar a la cordobana** to go naked
cordón m lace; (de cuerda o alambre) strand; cordon; milled edge of coin; (de monje) rope belt; **cordón umbilical** umbilical cord
cordoncillo m rib, ridge; braid; (de monedas) milling
cordura f prudence, wisdom
Corea f Korea; **la Corea del Norte** North Korea; **la Corea del Sur** South Korea
corea•no -na adj & mf Korean
corear tr to compose for a chorus; accompany with a chorus; join in singing; agree obsequiously with
coreografía f choreography
coriáce•o -a adj leathery
Corinto f Corinth
corista m choir priest; (theat) chorus man ‖ f chorus girl, chorine
cori•to -ta adj naked; bashful, timid
cormorán m cormorant
cor•nac m (pl **-nacs**) or **cornaca** m mahout
cornada f hook with horns; goring; (en la esgrima) upward thrust
cornadura f or **cornamenta** f (del toro, la vaca, etc.) horns; (del ciervo) antlers

cornamusa f bagpipe
córnea f cornea
cornear tr to butt; to gore
corneja f daw, crow
cornejo m dogwood
córne•o -a adj horn, horny ‖ f see **córnea**
corneta f bugle; swineherd's horn; **corneta acústica** ear trumpet; **corneta de llaves** cornet, cornet-à-pistons; **corneta de monte** hunting-horn
cornisa f cornice
cornisamento m (archit) entablature
corno m horn; dogwood; **corno inglés** (mus) English horn
Cornualles Cornwall
cornucopia f cornucopia; sconce with mirror
cornu•do -da adj horned, antlered; cuckold ‖ m cuckold
coro m chorus; choir; choir loft; **a coros** alternately; **de coro** by heart; **hacer coro a** to echo
corolario m corollary
corona f (cerco de metal; moneda; dignidad real; parte visible de una muela) crown; (cerco de flores) garland, wreath; (aureola) halo; (de eclesiástico) tonsure; (la que corresponde a un título nobiliario) coronet; **corona nupcial** bridal wreath
coronación f coronation
coronamento m or **coronamiento** m coronation; completion, termination; (archit) coping; (naut) taffrail
coronar tr to crown; complete, finish; top, surmount; (checkers) to crown
coronel m colonel
coronelía f colonelcy
coronilla f (de la cabeza) crown; **andar** or **bailar de coronilla** to be hard at it; **estar hasta la coronilla** to be fed up
corotos mpl belongings; utensils
corpiño m bodice, waist; (Arg) brassiere
corporación f corporation
corporal adj corporal, bodily
corpu•do -da adj corpulent
corpulen•to -ta adj corpulent
corpúsculo m corpuscle; particle
corral m corral, stockyard; barnyard; fishpond; theater; **corral de madera** lumberyard; **corral de vacas** pigpen; **hacer corrales** to play hooky
correa f strap, thong; (aer, mach) belt; **besar la correa** to eat humble pie; **correa de seguridad** (aer, aut) safety belt
corrección f (acción de corregir; reprensión) correction; (calidad de correcto) correctness
correcti•vo -va adj & m corrective
correc•to -ta adj correct
correc•tor -tora mf corrector; **corrector de pruebas** proofreader
corredera f track, slide; slide valve; (del trombón) slide; (naut) log; (naut) log line; (puerta) **de corredera** sliding
corredi•zo -za adj slide; sliding; (nudo) slip
corre•dor -dora adj running ‖ mf runner ‖ m corridor; porch, gallery; (el que interviene en compras y ventas de efectos comer-

ciales, etc.) broker; (mil) scout; **corredor de apuestas** bookmaker

corregidor *m* Spanish magistrate; chief magistrate of Spanish town

corregir §57 *tr* to correct; temper, moderate ‖ *intr* (W-I) to have a bowel movement ‖ *ref* to mend one's ways

correlación *f* correlation

correlacionar *tr & intr* to correlate

correlati·vo -va *adj & m* correlative

corre·lón -lona *adj* (SAm) fast, swift; (Col, Mex) cowardly

correncia *f* bashfulness; looseness of the bowels

correntí·o -a *adj* running; free, easy ‖ *f* looseness of the bowels

corren·tón -tona *adj* jolly, full of fun

corrento·so -sa *adj* swift, rapid

correo *m* mail; post office; mail train; postman; courier; **correo aéreo** air mail; **correo urgente** special delivery; **echar al correo** to mail, to post

correo·so -sa *adj* leathery, tough

correr *tr* (*un caballo*) to run, race; (*un riesgo*) run; travel over; overrun; (*una cortina*) draw; (*un toro*) fight; chase, pursue; auction; confuse; throw out; **correrla** to run around all night ‖ *intr* to run; race; pass, elapse; circulate, be common talk; be current; **a todo correr** at full speed; **correr a** to sell for; **correr a cargo de** or **por cuenta de** to be the business of; **correr con** to be on good terms with; be in charge of; (*mes*) **que corre** current ‖ *ref* (*a derecha o a izquierda*) to turn; be confused; be embarrassed, be ashamed; slide, glide; (*una bujía, un color*) run; go too far

correría *f* short trip, excursion; foray, raid

correspondencia *f* correspondence; contact, communication; agreement, harmony; (*en el metro*) connection; (*en una carretera*) interchange

corresponder *intr* to correspond; (*dos habitaciones*) communicate; **corresponder a** (*un beneficio, el afecto de una persona*) to return, reciprocate; concern; be up to ‖ *ref* (*comunicarse por escrito*) to correspond; (*dos cosas*) correspond with each other; be in agreement; be attached to each other

correspondiente *adj* corresponding; correspondent; respective ‖ *mf* correspondent

corresponsal *mf* correspondent

corretaje *m* brokerage

corretear *tr* to harass, pursue; (CAm) to drive away; (Chile) to speed up ‖ *intr* to race around

correveidi·le *mf* (*pl* **-le**) gossip; go-between

corrida *f* run; bullfight; (*carrera de entrenamiento de un caballo*) trial run; **corrida de banco** run on the bank; **corrida de toros** bullfight

corri·do -da *adj* (*peso, medida*) in excess; (*letra*) cursive; continued, unbroken; abashed, ashamed; wordly-wise, sophisticated ‖ *m* overhang; street ballad ‖ *f* see **corrida**

corriente *adj* (*agua*) running; (*actual*) current; common, ordinary; regular; well-known; fluent ‖ *adv* all right, O.K. ‖ *m* current month; **al corriente** on time; informed, aware, posted ‖ *f* current, stream; (elec) current; **corriente de aire** draft; **Corriente del Golfo** Gulf Stream; **ir contra la corriente** to go against the tide

corrillo *m* circle, clique

corrimiento *m* running; sliding; watery discharge; embarrassment, shyness; landslide; rheumatism

corro *m* (*cerco de gente; espacio circular*) ring; (*juego de niñas*) ring-around-a-rosy; **corro de brujas** fairy ring; **hacer corro** to make room

corroborar *tr* to corroborate; strengthen

corroer §62 *tr & ref* to corrode

corromper *tr* to corrupt; spoil; rot; seduce; bribe; annoy ‖ *intr* to smell bad ‖ *ref* to become corrupted; spoil; rot

corrosión *f* corrosion

corrosi·vo -va *adj & m* corrosive

corrugar §44 *tr* to shrink; wrinkle

corrupción *f* corruption; seduction; bribery; stench

corruptela *f* corruption

corruptible *adj* corruptible; (*p.ej., frutas*) perishable

corrusco *m* crust of bread

corsa *f* (naut) day's run

corsario *m* corsair

corsé *m* corset

cor·so -sa *adj & mf* Corsican ‖ *m* (naut) privateering; (SAm) drive, promenade ‖ *f* see **corsa**

corta *f* clearing, cutting, felling

cortaalam·bres *m* (*pl* **-bres**) wire cutter

cortabol·sas *m* (*pl* **-sas**) pick-pocket

cortacésped *m* lawn mower

cortaciga·rros *m* (*pl* **-rros**) cigar cutter

cortacircui·tos *m* (*pl* **-tos**) (elec) fuse

cortacorriente *m* (elec) change-over switch

cortada *f* cut, cutting

cortadillo *m* drinking cup

corta·do -da *adj* (*estilo*) choppy; (SAm) hard up ‖ *f* see **cortada**

corta·dor -dora *adj* cutting ‖ *mf* cutter ‖ *m* butcher ‖ *f* cutting machine

cortafrío *m* cold chisel

cortafuego *s* fire wall

cortahie·los *m* (*pl* **-los**) icebreaker

cortalápi·ces *m* (*pl* **-ces**) pencil sharpener

cortante *adj* cutting, sharp ‖ *m* butcher; butcher knife

cortapape·les *m* (*pl* **-les**) paper cutter

cortapi·cos *m* (*pl* **-cos**) (ent) earwig; **cortapicos y callares** little children should be seen and not heard

cortaplu·mas *m* (*pl* **-mas**) penknife

cortapu·ros *m* (*pl* **-ros**) cigar cutter

cortar *tr* to cut; trim; chop; cut off; cut out, omit; cut short; cut up; carve; (*la corriente; la ignición*) cut off ‖ *intr* to cut; (*el viento, el frío*) be cutting; **cortar de vestir** to cut cloth; gossip ‖ *ref* to become speechless;

(*la leche*) curdle, turn sour; (*la piel*) chap, crack

cortarrenglón *m* marginal stop

cortaú·ñas *m* (*pl* **-ñas**) nail clipper

cortavi·drios *m* (*pl* **-drios**) glass cutter

cortaviento *m* windshield

corte *m* cut; cutting; (*filo de un arma, cuchillo, etc.; borde de un libro*) edge; cross section; (*de un vestido*) cut, fit; piece of material; harvest; **corte de pelo** haircut; **corte de pelo a cepillo** crew cut; **corte de traje** suiting || *f* (*de un rey*) court; (*corral*) yard; stable, fold; (*tribunal de justicia*) court; **Cortes** Parliament; **darse cortes** (SAm) to put on airs; **hacer la corte a** to pay court to; **la Corte** the Capital (*Madrid*)

cortedad *f* shortness; smallness; lack; bashfulness

cortejar *tr* to escort, attend, court; court, woo

cortejo *m* courting; courtship; (*séquito*) cortege; gift, treat; (*coll*) beau

cortera *f* (Chile) streetwalker

cortero *m* (Chile) day laborer

cortés *adj* courteous, polite, courtly

cortesana *f* courtesan

cortesana·zo -za *adj* overpolite, obsequious

cortesanía *f* courtliness

cortesa·no -na *adj* courtly, courteous || *m* courtier || *f* see **cortesana**

cortesía *f* courtesy, politeness, courtliness; gift, favor; (*inclinación de la cabeza o el cuerpo en señal de respeto*) curtsy; (*de una carta*) conclusion; **hecer una cortesía** to make a bow; curtsy

corteza *f* bark; peel, rind, skin; (*de pan*) crust; coarseness; (*envoltura exterior de un órgano*) cortex; **corteza cerebral** cortex

cortijo *m* farm, farmhouse

cortil *m* barnyard

cortina *f* curtain; **correr la cortina** to pull the curtain aside; **cortina de hierro** iron curtain; **cortina de humo** smoke screen

cortinal *m* fenced-in field

cortinilla *f* shade, window shade

cortisona *f* cortisone

cor·to -ta *adj* short; dull; bashful, shy; speechless; **a la corta o a la larga** sooner or later; **desde muy corta edad** from earliest childhood || *f* see **corta**

cortocircuitar *tr & ref* (elec) to short-circuit

cortocircuito *m* (elec) short circuit

cortometraje *m* (mov) short

corva *f* ham, back of knee; (vet) curb

corvejón *m* gambrel, hock; (orn) cormorant

cor·vo -va *adj* arched, bent, curved || *m* hook || *f* see **corva**

cor·zo -za *mf* roe deer

cosa *f* thing; **cosa de** a matter of; **cosa de cajón** a matter of course; **cosa de mieles** something fine; **cosa de nunca acabar** endless bore; **cosa de oír** something worth hearing; **cosa de risa** something to laugh at; **cosa de ver** something worth seeing; **cosa nunca vista** something unheard-of; **cosa que** so that; **cosa rara** strange to say; **como si tal cosa** as if nothing had hap-

pened; **en cosa de** in a matter of; **no . . . gran cosa** not much; **no haber tal cosa** to be not so; **otra cosa** something else; **¿qué cosa?** what's new?

cosa·co -ca *adj & mf* Cossack || *m* Cossack (*horseman*)

coscolina *f* (Mex) loose woman

cos·cón -cona *adj* sly, crafty

cosecha *f* crop, harvest; harvest time; **cosecha de vino** vintage; **de su cosecha** (coll) out of one's own head

cosechar *tr* to harvest, reap || *intr* to harvest

coseche·ro -ra *mf* harvester, reaper; vintner

cose-pape·les *m* (*pl* **-les**) stapler

coser *tr* to sew; join, unite closely; **coser a preguntas** to riddle with questions; **coser a puñaladas** to cut to pieces || *intr* to sew; **ser coser y cantar** to be a cinch || *ref* — **coserse con** or **contra** to be closely attached to

cosméti·co -ca *adj & m* cosmetic

cósmi·co -ca *adj* cosmic

cosmonauta *mf* cosmonaut

cosmonave *f* spacecraft

cosmonavegación *f* space travel

cosmopolita *adj & mf* cosmopolitan

cosmos *m* cosmos; (bot) cosmos

coso *m* enclosure for bullfighting

cosquillas *fpl* tickling, ticklishness; **buscarle a uno las cosquillas** to try to irritate a person; **no sufrir cosquillas** or **tener malas cosquillas** to be touchy

cosquillear *tr* to tickle; tease, taunt; stir up the curiosity of; scare || *intr* to tickle || *ref* to be curious; enjoy oneself

cosquilleo *m* tickling, tickling sensation

cosquillo·so -sa *adj* ticklish; (*que se ofende fácilmente*) touchy

costa *f* coast, shore; cost, price; **a toda costa** at all costs; **Costa Brava** Mediterranean coast in province of Gerona, Spain; **Costa Firme** Spanish Main; **costa marítima** seacoast; **costas** (law) costs

costado *m* side; (*del ejército*) flank; (Mex) station platform; **costados** ancestors, stock

costal *m* bag, sack; **costal de los pecados** human body (*full of sin*); **estar hecho un costal de huesos** to be nothing but skin and bones

costanera *f* slope; **costaneras** rafters

costane·ro -ra *adj* sloping; coastal || *f* see **costanera**

costanilla *f* short steep street

costar §61 *intr* to cost; **cueste lo que cueste** cost what it may

costarricense or **costarrique·ño -ña** *adj & mf* Costa Rican

coste *m* cost; **a coste y costas** at cost

costear *tr* to pay for, defray the cost of; sail along the coast of || *intr* to sail along the coast || *ref* to pay; pay one's way

coste·ño -ña *adj* sloping; coastal

coste·ro -ra *adj* coastal

costilla *f* rib; wealth; **costillas** back, shoulders

costillu·do -da *adj* heavy-set, broad-shouldered

costo *m* cost; **costo de la vida** cost of living; **costo, seguro y flete** cost, insurance, and freight

costo•so -sa *adj* costly, expensive; grievous

costra *f* scab, scale; (*moco de una vela*) snuff

costro•so -sa *adj* scabby, scaly

costumbre *f* custom, habit; **de costumbre** usual; usually; **tener por costumbre** to be in the habit of

costumbrista *mf* critic of manners and customs

costura *f* sewing, needlework; dressmaking; (*unión de dos piezas cosidas*) seam; **alta costura** fashion designing, haute couture

costurar or **costurear** *tr* (CAm, Mex) to sew

costurera *f* seamstress, dressmaker

costurero *m* sewing table

cota *f* coat of arms; coat of mail

cotarrera *f* gossipy woman

cotarro *m* night shelter (*for beggars and tramps*); **alborotar el cotarro** to raise a row

cotejar *tr* to compare, collate

cotejo *m* comparison, collation

cotidia•no -na *adj* daily, everyday

cotilla *f* gossip, tattletale

cotín *m* (sport) backstroke

cotización *f* quotation; dues

cotizante *adj* dues-paying

cotizar §60 *tr* to quote; prorate ‖ *intr* to collect dues; pay dues

coto *m* price; fixed price; term, limit

cotón *m* printed cotton

cotona *f* work shirt

cotonía *f* dimity

cotorra *f* parrot; parakeet; magpie; chatterbox; (Mex) night shelter

cotorrear *intr* to gossip, gabble

cotufa *f* Jerusalem artichoke; delicacy, tidbit; **hacer cotufas** (Bol) to be fastidious; **pedir cotufas en el golfo** to ask for the moon

coturno *m* buskin

covacha *f* cave; cubbyhole; shanty; doghouse

covachuelista *m* clerk, government clerk

coxcojita *f* hopscotch; **a coxcojita** hippety-hop

coy *m* (naut) hammock

coyunda *f* strap for yoking oxen; sandal string; marriage; tyranny

coyuntura *f* joint, articulation; (*sazón, oportunidad*) juncture

coz *f* (*pl* **coces**) kick; big end; ebb; (coll) insult; **dar coces contra el aguijón** to kick against the pricks

c.p.b., C.P.B. *abbr* **cuyos pies beso**

cps. *abbr* **compañeros**

crabrón *m* hornet

crac *m* (*ruido seco*) crack; crash; **hacer crac** to crash, fail

cráneo *m* cranium, skull

crápula *f* drunkenness, debauchery; riffraff

crapulo•so -sa *adj* drunken; vicious, evil

crascitar *intr* to crow, croak

cra•so -sa *adj* fat, greasy, thick; (*ignorancia*) crass, gross

cráter *m* crater

creación *f* creation

crea•dor -dora *adj* creative ‖ *mf* creator

crear *tr* to create; appoint; found ‖ *ref* to make for oneself, build up; trump up

creati•vo -va *adj* creative

crecede•ro -ra *adj* growth; large enough to allow for growth

crecepelo *m* hair restorer

crecer §22 *intr* to grow; increase; (*el río*) rise, swell; (*la luna*) wax ‖ *ref* to grow; take on more authority; get bolder

creces *fpl* growth, increase; excess, extra; **con creces** amply, in abundance

crecida *f* freshet, flood

creciente *adj* growing, increasing ‖ *f* —**creciente de la luna** waxing of the moon, crescent; **creciente del mar** high tide, flood tide

crecimiento *m* growth, increase; **crecimiento cero** zero growth

credenciales *fpl* credentials

crédito *m* credit

credo *m* creed; credo; **con el credo en la boca** with one's heart in one's mouth; **en un credo** in a trice

crédu•lo -la *adj* credulous

creederas *fpl* — **tener buenas creederas** to be gullible

creencia *f* belief; (*crédito que se presta a un hecho*) credence; (*secta*) creed

creer §43 *tr* & *intr* to believe; **¡ya lo creo!** I should say so! ‖ *ref* to believe; believe oneself to be

creíble *adj* believable, credible

creí•do -da *adj* credulous; gullible

crema *f* cream; cold cream; shoe polish; (gram) diaeresis; **crema de menta** creme de menthe; **crema dental** or **crema dentífrica** toothpaste; **crema desvanecedora** vanishing cream

cremación *f* cremation

cremallera *f* rack; zipper

cremato•rio -ria *adj* & *m* crematory

crémor *m* cream of tartar

cremo•so -sa *adj* creamy

crencha *f* part (*in hair*); hair on each side of part

crepitar *intr* to crackle

crepuscular *adj* twilight

crepúsculo *m* twilight

cresa *f* maggot

crespar *tr* & *ref* to curl

cres•po -pa *adj* curly; curled; angry, irritated; stylish, conceited; (*estilo*) turgid ‖ *m* curl

crespón *m* crape; **crespón fúnebre** crape; mourning band

cresta *f* crest; **cresta de gallo** cockscomb; (bot) cockscomb

creta *f* chalk ‖ **Creta** *f* Crete

cretense *adj* & *mf* Cretan

cretona *f* cretonne

creyente *adj* believing ‖ *mf* believer

creyón *m* crayon

cría *f* brood, litter; breeding; raising, rearing; nursing

criada *f* female servant, maid; **criada de casa, criada de servir** housemaid

co
cr

criadero *m* nursery, tree nursery; fish hatchery; oyster bed

criadilla *f* testicle; potato

cria•do -da *adj* — **bien criado** well-bred; **mal criado** ill-bred ‖ *mf* servant ‖ *f* see **criada**

cria•dor -dora *mf* breeder ‖ *f* wet nurse

criamiento *m* care, upkeep

crianza *f* raising, rearing; nursing; (*urbanidad*) breeding, manners; **buena crianza** good breeding; **mala crianza** bad breeding

criar §77 *tr* to raise, rear, bring up; breed; grow; nurse, nourish; fatten; create; foster

criatura *f* (*toda cosa creada; persona que debe su cargo o situación a otra*) creature; little child, little creature

criba *f* screen, sieve

cribar *tr* to screen, sieve

cribo *m* screen, sieve

cric *m* (*pl* **crics**) jack

crimen *m* crime; **crimen de lesa majestad** lese majesty; **crímenes de oficinistas** white-collar crime

criminal *adj* & *mf* criminal

criminar *tr* to accuse, incriminate

criminología *f* criminology

crimino•so -sa *adj* & *mf* criminal

crines *fpl* mane

crío *m* (coll) baby, infant

crio•llo -lla *adj* & *mf* Creole

cripta *f* crypt

crisálida *f* chrysalis

crisantemo *m* chrysanthemum

cri•sis *f* (*pl* **-sis**) crisis; (*pánico económico*) depression, slump; mature judgment; **crisis del servicio doméstico** servant problem; **crisis de llanto** crying fit; **crisis de vivienda** housing shortage; **crisis energética** energy crisis; **crisis ministerial** cabinet crisis; **crisis nerviosa** fit of nerves

crisma *f* (coll) head, bean

crisol *m* crucible

crispar *tr* to cause to twitch ‖ *ref* to twitch

crispatura *f* twitch, twitching

crispir *tr* to grain, to marble

cristal *m* crystal; glass; pane of glass; mirror, looking glass; **cristal cilindrado** plate glass; **cristal de reloj** watch crystal; **cristal de roca** rock crystal; **cristal hilado** glass wool, spun glass; **cristal laminado** laminated glass, safety glass; **cristal tallado** cut glass

cristalera *f* China closet; sideboard; glass door

cristalería *f* glassworks, glass store; glassware; glass cabinet

cristali•no -na *adj* crystalline ‖ *m* lens, crystalline lens

cristalizar §60 *tr* & *ref* to crystallize

cristianar *tr* to baptize, christen

cristiandad *f* Christendom

cristianismo *m* Christianity

cristianizar §60 *tr* to Christianize

cristia•no -na *adj* & *mf* Christian ‖ *m* soul, person; Spanish; watered wine

Cristo *m* Christ; crucifix; **donde Cristo dió las tres voces** in the middle of nowhere

Cristóbal *m* Christopher

criterio *m* criterion

crítica *f* (*jucio sobre una obra literaria, etc.; censura de la conducta de alguno*) criticism; (*arte de juzgar una obra literaria, etc.*) critique; gossip

criticar §73 *tr* & *intr* to criticize

críti•co -ca *adj* critical; (*criticón*) critical (*faultfinding*) ‖ *mf* critic ‖ *f* see **crítica**

criti•cón -cona *adj* critical, faultfinding ‖ *mf* critic, faultfinder

critiquizar §60 *tr* to overcriticize

crizneja *f* braid of hair

croar *intr* to croak

croata *adj* & *mf* Croatian

crocante *m* almond brittle, peanut brittle

crocitar *intr* to crow, croak

croco *m* crocus

croché *m* crochet

crochet *m* (box) hook

croma•do -da *adj* chrome ‖ *m* chromium plating

cromar *tr* to chrome

cromo *m* chromium

cromosoma *m* chromosome

crónica *f* chronicle; news chronicle, feature story

cróni•co -ca *adj* chronic; longstanding; (*vicio*) inveterate ‖ *f* see **crónica**

cronista *mf* chronicler; reporter, feature writer; **cronista de radio** newscaster

cronología *f* chronology

cronometra•dor -dora *mf* (sport) timekeeper

cronometraje *m* (sport) clocking, timing

cronómetro *m* chronometer; stop watch

croqueta *f* croquette

cro•quis *m* (*pl* **-quis**) sketch

croscitar *intr* to crow, croak

crótalo *m* rattlesnake; castanet

cruce *m* crossing; crossroads, intersection; exchange (*e.g., of letters*); (*avería*) (elec) crossed wires, short circuit; **cruce a nivel** grade crossing; **cruce en trébol** cloverleaf intersection

crucero *m* crossroads; railroad crossing; (archit) transept; (aer, naut) cruise, cruising; (nav) cruiser; **crucero a nivel** grade crossing

crucial *adj* crucial

crucificar §73 *tr* to crucify

crucifijo *m* crucifix

crucifixión *f* crucifixion

crucigrama *m* crossword puzzle

cruda *f* (Mex) hangover

crudeza *f* crudeness, rawness; (*del agua*) hardness; harshness, roughness; blustering; **crudezas** undigested food

cru•do -da *adj* crude, raw; (*agua*) hard; harsh, rough; (*tiempo*) raw; (*lienzo*) unbleached; **estar crudo** (P-R) to be rusty; (Mex) to have a hangover ‖ *f* see **cruda**

cruel *adj* cruel

crueldad *f* cruelty

cruen•to -ta *adj* bloody

crujía *f* corridor, hall; hospital ward; block of houses; (naut) midship gangway; **crujía de**

piezas suite of rooms; **sufrir una crujía** (coll) to have a hard time of it

crujido *m* creak; crackle; clatter; chatter; rustle

crujir *intr* to creak; crackle; clatter; chatter; rustle; crunch

crup *m* croup

crustáce•o -a *adj* crustaceous ‖ *m* crustacean

cruz *f* (*pl* **cruces**) cross; (*de una moneda*) tails; (*typ*) dagger; **Cruz del Sur** Southern Cross; **¡cruz y raya!** (coll) that's enough!; **de la cruz a la fecha** from beginning to end

cruza *f* (SAm) intersection; crossbreeding

cruzada *f* (*expedición contra los infieles; propaganda contra un vicio*) crusade; crossroads, intersection

cruza•do -da *adj* crossed; (*de raza mixta*) cross; double-breasted ‖ *m* (*el que toma parte en una cruzada*) crusader; (*caballero de una orden militar*) knight; twill ‖ *f* see **cruzada**

cruzar §60 *tr* to cross; (*la tela*) twill; (*cartas*) exchange; crossbreed; (*naut*) to cruise, cruise over ‖ *intr* to cross; cruise ‖ *ref* to cross each other, cross one another's path; (*alistarse para una cruzada*) take the cross; **cruzarse con** (*otro automóvil*) to pass; **cruzarse de brazos** (*estar ocioso*) to cross one's arms

cs. *abbr* **céntimos, cuartos**

cte. *abbr* **corriente**

c/u *abbr* **cada uno**

cuad. *abbr* **cuadrado**

cuaderna *f* (naut) frame

cuaderno *m* notebook; folder; **cuaderno de bitácora** (naut) logbook; **cuaderno de hojas cambiables** or **sueltas** loose-leaf notebook

cuadra *f* hall, large room; stable; dormitory, ward; croup, rump; block

cuadra•do -da *adj* square; square-shouldered; perfect ‖ *m* square; (*regla*) ruler; (*en las medias*) clock; **de cuadrado** perfectly; (*que se mira frente a frente*) full-faced

cuadragési•mo -ma *adj* & *m* fortieth

cuadrangular *adj* quadrangular ‖ *m* home run

cuadrángu•lo -la *adj* quadrangular ‖ *m* quadrangle

cuadrante *m* quadrant; (*de reloj*) face, dial; **cuadrante solar** sundial

cuadrar *tr* to square; please; (*al toro*) (taur) to square off, line up ‖ *ref* to square; stand at attention; take on a serious air

cuadrilla *f* group, party; crew, gang

cuadrillazo *m* (SAm) surprise attack

cuadrillo *m* (*saeta*) bolt (*arrow*)

cuadrimotor *m* four-motor plane

cua•dro -dra *adj* square ‖ *m* square; (*lienzo, pintura*) painting, picture; (*marco de pintura, ventana, etc.*) frame; (*de jardín*) patch, flower bed; staff, personnel; (*mil*) cadre; (*sport*) team; (*theat*) scene; (*coll*) sight, mess; **a cuadros** checked; **cuadro de costumbres** sketch of manners and customs; **cuadro de distribución** switchboard;

cuadro de mando instrument panel; (*aut*) dashboard; **cuadro indicador** score board; **cuadro vivo** tableau; **en cuadro** square, e.g., **ocho pulgadas en cuadro** eight inches square; topsy-turvy; **quedarse en cuadro** to be all alone in the world; (*mil*) to be skeletonized ‖ *f* see **cuadra**

cuadrúpe•do -da *adj* & *m* quadruped

cuádruple *adj* & *m* quadruple

cuadruplicar §73 *tr* & *ref* to quadruple

cuajada *f* curd

cuajado *m* mincemeat

cuajar *tr* to curd, curdle, thicken, jelly; please, suit ‖ *intr* to take hold, catch on, jell, take shape; (*Mex*) to chatter, prattle ‖ *ref* to curd, curdle, thicken, jelly; sleep sound; become crowded

cuajo *m* curd; (*Mex*) chatter, prattle; (*en la escuela*) (*Mex*) recess

cual *adj rel* & *pron rel* such as; **el cual** which; who; **lo cual** which; **por lo cual** for which reason ‖ *adv* as ‖ *prep* like

cuál *adj interr* & *pron interr* which, what; which one

cualidad *f* quality, characteristic, trait

cualquier *adj indef* (*pl* **cualesquier**) apocopated form of **cualquiera,** used only before masculine nouns and adjectives

cualquiera (*pl* **cualesquiera**) *pron indef* anyone; **cualquiera que** whichever; whoever ‖ *adj indef* any ‖ *adj rel* whichever ‖ *m* (*persona poco importante*) nobody

cuan *adv* as

cuán *adv* how, how much

cuando *conj* when; although; in case; since; **aun cuando** even if, even though; **cuando más** at most; **cuando menos** at least; **cuando mucho** at most; **cuando quiera** whenever; **de cuando en cuando** from time to time ‖ *prep* (coll) at the time of

cuándo *adv* when; **cuándo . . . cuándo** sometimes . . . sometimes; **¿de cuándo acá?** since when?; how come?

cuantía *f* quantity; importance; **delito de mayor cuantía** felony; **delito de menor cuantía** misdemeanor; **de mayor cuantía** first-rate; **de menor cuantía** second-rate, of little importance

cuantiar §77 *tr* to estimate, appraise

cuánti•co -ca *adj* quantum

cuantio•so -sa *adj* large, substantial

cuan•to -ta *adj rel* & *pron rel* as much as, whatever, all that which; **cuantos** as many as, all those who, everybody who; **unos cuantos** some few ‖ **cuanto** *adv* as soon as; as long as; **cuanto antes** as soon as possible; **cuanto más . . . tanto más** the more . . . the more; **cuanto más que** all the more because; **en cuanto** as soon as; while; insofar as; **en cuanto a** as to, as for; **por cuanto** inasmuch as; **por cuanto . . . por tanto** inasmuch as . . . therefore ‖ **cuan•to** *m* (*pl* **-ta**) quantum

cuán•to -ta *adj interr* & *pron interr* how much; **cuántos** how many ‖ **cuánto** *adv* how, how much; how long; how long ago; **cada cuánto** how often

cuáque•ro -ra *adj* & *mf* Quaker
cuarenta *adj, pron* & *m* forty
cuarenta•vo -va *adj* & *m* fortieth
cuarentena *f* forty; quarantine; forty days, forty months, forty years; **poner en cuarentena** to quarantine; withhold one's credence in
cuaresma *f* Lent
cuaresmal *adj* Lenten
cuarta *f* fourth, fourth part; (*de la mano*) span; (CAm, W-I) horse whip
cuartago *m* nag, pony
cuartear *tr* to divide in four parts; divide; (*la aguja*) (naut) to box; (CAm, W-I) to whip ‖ *ref* to crack, split; (taur) to step aside, dodge
cuartel *m* quarter; (*de una ciudad*) section, ward; (*terreno*) lot; flower bed; (mil) barracks; (*buen trato*) (mil) quarter; (*armazón de tablas para cerrar la escotilla*) (naut) hatch; (coll) house, home; **cuartel de bomberos** engine house, firehouse; **cuarteles** (mil) quarters; **cuartel general** (mil) headquarters
cuartelada *f* mutiny, military uprising
cuartelazo *m* (mil) coup, putsch; (mil) takeover
cuarte•rón -rona *mf* quadroon ‖ *m* quarter; (*de puerta*) panel; (*de ventana*) shutter
cuarteto *m* quartet
cuartilla *f* sheet of paper
cuar•to -ta *adj* fourth; quarter ‖ *m* fourth; quarter; room, bedroom; quarter-hour; **cuarto creciente** (*de la luna*) first quarter; **cuarto de aseo** lavatory; **cuarto de baño** bathroom; **cuarto de dormir** bedroom; **cuarto de estar** living room; **cuarto delantero** (*de la res*) forequarter; **cuarto de los niños** nursery; **cuarto de luna** quarter; **cuarto menguante** (*de la luna*) last quarter; **cuarto obscuro** (phot) darkroom; **cuartos** money, cash; **cuarto trasero** (*p.ej., de vaca*) rump ‖ *f* see **cuarta**
cuarzo *m* quartz
cuate *adj* (Mex) twin; (Mex) like ‖ *mf* (Mex) twin; (Mex) pal
cuatrilli•zo -za *mf* quadruplet
cuatrinca *f* foursome
cuatro *adj* & *pron* four; (Mex) deceit, swindle; **las cuatro** four o'clock ‖ *m* four; (*en las fechas*) fourth; (*de voces*) quartet; **más de cuatro** (coll) quite a number
cuatrocien•tos -tas *adj* & *pron* four hundred ‖ **cuatrocientos** *m* four hundred
cuba *f* cask, barrel; tub, vat; (*persona de mucho vientre*) (coll) tub; (*persona que bebe mucho*) (coll) toper; **cuba de riego** street sprinkler
cuba•no -na *adj* & *mf* Cuban
cubertería *f* silverware, cutlery
cubeta *f* keg, cask; pail; bowl, toilet bowl; (*del termómetro*) cup; (chem, phot) tray; (Mex) high hat
cubicaje *m* piston displacement, cylinder capacity

cubicar *tr* (*elevar al cubo*) to cube; measure the volume of; have a piston displacement of
cúbi•co -ca *adj* cubic; (*raíz*) cube
cubierta *f* cover; envelope; roof; (*de un libro*) paper cover; (*de un neumático*) casing, shoe; (*del motor de un coche*) hood; (naut) deck; **bajo cubierta separada** under separate cover; **cubierta de aterrizaje** (nav) flight deck; **cubierta de cama** bedcover; **cubierta de mesa** table cover; **cubierta de paseo** (naut) promenade deck; **cubierta de vuelo** (nav) flight deck; **cubierta principal** (naut) main deck; **entre cubiertas** (naut) between decks
cubiertamente *adv* secretly
cubier•to -ta *adj* covered; (*cielo*) overcast ‖ *m* cover, roof, shelter; (*servicio de mesa para una persona*) cover; knife, fork, and spoon; table d'hôte, prix fixe; **a cubierto de** under cover of; protected from; **bajo cubierto** under cover, indoors ‖ *f* see **cubierta**
cubil *m* (*de fieras*) lair, den; (*de arroyo*) bed
cubilete *m* (*de cocinero*) copper mold; dicebox; mince pie; high hat; (SAm) scheming, wirepulling
cubo *m* bucket; (*de rueda*) hub; (*de un candelero; de una llave de caja*) socket; cube; (mach) barrel, drum; (math) cube; (Arg) finger bowl
cubreasiento *m* seat cover
cubrecama *f* counterpane, bedcover
cubrecorsé *m* corset cover
cubrefuego *m* curfew
cubrelibro *m* jacket
cubrenuca *f* havelock
cubrerrueda *f* mudguard
cubresexo *m* G-string
cubretablero *m* (aut) cowl
cubretetera *f* cozy, tea cozy
cubrir §83 *tr* to cover, cover over, cover up ‖ *ref* to cover oneself; be covered; put one's hat on; (*el cielo*) become overcast; (*satisfacer una deuda*) cover
cucaña *f* greased pole to be climbed as a game; (coll) cinch
cucañe•ro -ra *mf* loafer, parasite
cucar §73 *tr* to wink; to make fun of; (*la caza*) to sight; to incite, stir up ‖ *intr* (*el ganado*) to go off on a run (*when bitten by flies*)
cucaracha *f* roach, cockroach
cucarache•ro -ra *adj* (W-I) sly, tricky; (W-I) amorous, lecherous
cucarda *f* cockade
cuclillas — **en cuclillas** squatting, crouching
cuclillo *m* cuckoo; (coll) cuckold
cu•co -ca *adj* sly, tricky; cute ‖ *mf* sly person ‖ *m* bogeyman; cuckoo; **hacer cuco a** to poke fun at
cu•cú *m* (*pl* **-cúes**) cuckoo (*call*)
cuculla *f* cowl, hood
cucurucho *m* paper cone, ice-cream cone; **hacer cucurucho a** (Chile) to deceive, take in

cuchara f spoon; (*cazo*) dipper, ladle; (*para áridos; para achicar el agua en los botes*) scoop; (*de albañil*) trowel; (Mex) pickpocket; **cuchara de sopa** tablespoon; **media cuchara** (Mex) mason's helper; ordinary fellow; fellow with heavy accent; **meter su cuchara** to butt in

cucharada f spoonful; ladleful; scoop

cucharear tr to spoon, ladle out

cucharetear intr to stir the pot, stir with a spoon; to meddle

cucharilla f teaspoon; (*de soldador*) ladle

cucharón m large spoon; soup ladle, dipper; scoop; **despacharse con el cucharón** to look out for number one

cuchichear intr to whisper

cuchilla f knife; (*hoja de arma blanca de corte*) blade; (*de patín de hielo*) runner; (*cerro escarpado*) hogback; (*de interruptor*) (elec) blade; (poet) sword; **cuchilla de carnicero** butcher knife, cleaver

cuchillada f slash, gash, hack; **cuchilladas** fight, quarrel; **dar cuchillada** (*un actor o un teatro*) to be the hit of the town

cuchillería f cutlery; cutler's shop

cuchillero m cutler

cuchillo m knife; (*en un vestido*) gore; (naut) triangular sail; **cuchillo de trinchar** carving knife; **cuchillo de vidriero** putty knife; **pasar a cuchillo** to put to the sword

cuchitril m hovel, den

cuchufleta f joke, fun, wisecrack

cuchufletear intr to joke, make fun, wisecrack

cuelga f fruit hung up for keeping; birthday present

cuelgaca•pas m (*pl* -pas) cloak hanger

cuello m (*del cuerpo*) neck; (*de una prenda*) collar; shirt collar; **cuello almidonado** stiff collar; **cuello de camisa** shirtband; **cuello de cisne** gooseneck; **cuello de pajarita** or **doblado** wing collar; **levantar el cuello** to get back on one's feet again

cuenca f wooden bowl; (*del ojo*) socket; basin, river basin; **cuenca de polvo** dust bowl

cuenco m earthen bowl; hollow

cuenta f count, calculation; account; (*factura*) bill; (*en un restaurante*) check; (*del rosario*) bead; **abonar en cuenta a** to credit to the account of; **a cuenta** or **a buena cuenta** on account; **adeudar en cuenta a** to charge to the account of; **a fin de cuentas** after all; **caer en la cuenta** to get the point; **cargar en cuenta a** to charge to the account of; **correr por cuenta de** to be the responsibility of, to be under the administration of; **cuenta atrás** countdown; **cuenta corriente** current account; **cuenta de gastos** expense account; **cuenta de la vieja** counting on one's fingers; **cuentas del gran capitán** overdrawn account; **cuentas galanas** illusions; **darse cuenta de** to realize, become aware of; **de cuenta** of importance; **más de la cuenta** too long; too much; **pedir cuentas a** to bring to account; **por la cuenta** apparently;

por mi cuenta to my way of thinking; **tomar por su cuenta** to take upon oneself; **vamos a cuentas** (coll) let's settle this

cuentacorrentista mf depositor

cuentago•tas m (*pl* -tas) dropper, medicine dropper

cuentakiló•metros m (*pl* -tros) odometer

cuente•ro -ra adj (coll) gossipy ‖ mf (coll) gossip

cuentista adj (coll) gossipy ‖ mf story teller; short-story writer; (coll) gossip

cuento m story, tale; short story; prop, support; tip, point; (*cómputo*) count; (coll) gossip, evil talk; (coll) disagreement; **cuento de hadas** fairty tale; **cuento del tío** (SAm) gyp, swindle; **cuento de nunca acabar** (coll) endless affair; **cuento de penas** (coll) hard-luck story; **cuento de viejas** old wives' tale; **Cuentos de Calleja** collection of nursery stories; **dejarse de cuentos** (coll) to come to the point; **estar en el cuento** to be well-informed; **¡puro cuento!** pure fiction!; **sin cuento** countless; **traer a cuento** to bring up; **venir a cuento** (coll) to be opportune; **vivir del cuento** to live by one's wits

cuerda f cord, rope; watch spring; winding a watch or clock; (*acción de ahorcar*) hanging; fishing line; (aer, anat, geom) chord; (mus) string; **acabarse la cuerda** to run down, e.g., **se acabó la cuerda** the watch ran down; **bajo cuerda** secretly, underhandedly; **cuerda de presos** chain gang; **cuerda de remolcar** tow rope; **cuerda de tripa** (mus) catgut; **cuerda tirante** tight rope; **dar cuerda a** to give free rein to; (*un reloj*) to wind; **estar en su cuerda** to be in one's element; **sin cuerda** unwound, rundown

cuer•do -da adj wise, prudent; sane ‖ f see **cuerda**

cuerna f antler; horns

cuerno m horn; (mus) horn; **cuerno de caza** huntinghorn; **cuerno inglés** (mus) English horn

cuero m (*pellejo de buey*) hide; (*después de curtido*) leather; wineskin; **cuero cabelludo** scalp; **cuero en verde** rawhide; **en cueros** stark-naked

cuerpear intr (Arg) to duck, dodge

cuerpo m body; (*parte del vestido hasta la cintura*) waist; (*talle, aspecto*) build; (*de escritos, leyes, etc.*) corpus; corps, staff; (mil) corps; **cuerpo a cuerpo** hand to hand; **cuerpo celeste** heavenly body; **cuerpo compuesto** (chem) compound; **cuerpo de aviación** air corps; **cuerpo de baile** corps de ballet; **cuerpo de bomberos** fire brigade, fire company; **cuerpo de ejército** army corps; **Cuerpo de Paz** Peace Corps; **cuerpo de redacción** editorial staff, **cuerpo simple** (chem) simple substance; **dar con el cuerpo en tierra** (coll) to fall flat on the ground; **de cuerpo entero** full-length; **de medio cuerpo** half-length; **descubrir el cuerpo** to drop one's guard; **en cuerpo** or **en cuerpo de camisa** in shirt sleeves; **estar de cuerpo presente** to be on view, to lie in state; **hacer del cuerpo** (coll) to have a movement of the bowels

cueru•do -da *adj* thick-skinned; annoying, boring; bold, shameless

cuervo *m* raven; **cuervo marino** cormorant; **cuervo merendero** rook

cuesco *m* (*de la fruta*) stone; (*del molino de aceite*) millstone; windiness

cuesta *f* hill, slope, grade; charity drive; **cuesta abajo** downhill; **cuesta arriba** uphill; **llevar a cuestas** to be burdened with

cuestión *f* question; dispute, quarrel; matter; **cuestión batallona** much-debated question; **cuestión palpitante** burning question; **en cuestión de** in a matter of

cuestionable *adj* questionable

cuestionar *tr* to question ‖ *intr* (Arg) to argue

cuestionario *m* questionnaire

cuestua•rio -ria or **cuestuo•so -sa** *adj* profitable, lucrative

cuetear *ref* (Col) to blow up, explode; (Col) to die, kick the bucket; (Mex) to get drunk

cueva *f* cave; cellar; (*de ladrones, fieras, etc.*) den

cufi•fo -fa *adj* (Chile) tipsy

cugulla *f* cowl

cui•co -ca *adj* foreign, outside ‖ *m* (Mex) cop, policeman

cuidado *m* care, concern, worry; ¡**cuidado con . . .!** beware of . . .!, look out for!; **de cuidado** dangerously; **estar de cuidado** to be dangerously ill; **pierda Vd. cuidado** don't worry; **salir de su cuidado** (*una mujer*) to be delivered; **tener cuidado** to beware, be careful

cuidadora *f* (Mex) governess, chaperon

cuidado•so -sa *adj* careful, concerned, worried; watchful

cuidar *tr* to take care of, watch over ‖ *intr —* **cuidar de** to take care of, care for; care to ‖ *ref* to take care of oneself; **cuidarse de** to care about; be careful to

cuita *f* trouble, worry; longing, yearning

cuja *f* bedstead

culata *f* buttock, haunch; (*de la escopeta*) butt; (*de imán*) keeper, yoke; **culata de cilindro** cylinder head

culatazo *m* kick, recoil

culebra *f* snake; (*del alambique*) coil; **culebra de anteojos** cobra; **culebra de cascabel** rattlesnake; **saber más que las culebras** to be crafty

culebrear *intr* to wriggle; wind, meander; zigzag

culebrón *m* foxy fellow; (Mex) poor farce

cule•co -ca *adj* self-satisfied; madly in love

cu•lí *m* (*pl* **-líes**) coolie

culina•rio -ria *adj* culinary

culipandear *intr & ref* (CAm, W-I) to welsh, be evasive

culminar *intr* to culminate

culo *m* seat, behind, backside; (*de animal*) buttocks; (*de un vaso*) bottom; **culo de mal asiento** fidgety person; **volver el culo** to run away

culote *m* base

culpa *f* blame, guilt, fault; **echar la culpa a** to put the blame on; **tener la culpa** to be wrong, be to blame

culpable *adj* blamable, guilty, culpable

culpa•do -da *adj* guilty ‖ *mf* culprit

culpar *tr* to blame, censure, accuse ‖ *ref* to take the blame

cultedad *f* fustian, affectation

culteranismo *m* euphuism, Gongorism

cultiparlar *intr* to speak in a euphuistic manner

cultismo *m* learned word; cultism, Gongorism

cultivar *tr* to cultivate; till

cultivo *m* cultivation; **cultivo de secano** dry farming

cul•to -ta *adj* cultivated, cultured; (*vocablo*) learned ‖ *m* worship; cult; **culto a la personalidad** personality cult

cultura *f* culture, cultivation

culturar *tr* to cultivate, till

cumbre *adj* top, greatest ‖ *f* summit; acme, pinnacle; **conferencia en la cumbre** summit meeting

cúmel *m* kümmel

cumiche *m* (CAm) baby (*youngest member of family*)

cumpa *m* (SAm) pal, buddy; comrade

cúmplase *m* approval, O.K.

cumplea•ños *m* (*pl* **-ños**) birthday

cumpli•do -da *adj* full; perfect; (*en muestras de urbanidad*) correct ‖ *m* correctness; courtesy; present

cumplimentar *tr* to compliment; to pay a complimentary visit to; to carry out, execute; (*un cuestionario*) to fill out

cumplimente•ro -ra *adj* effusive, obsequious

cumplimiento *m* (*muestra de urbanidad*) compliment; (*conducta decorosa*) correctness; fulfillment; perfection; **por cumplimiento** as a matter of pure formality

cumplir *tr* to fulfill, perform, execute; **cumplir años** to have a birthday; **cumplir . . . años** to be . . . years old ‖ *intr* to fall due; to expire; to keep one's promise; to finish one's service in the army; **cumplir con** to fulfill; to fulfill one's obligation to; **cumplir por** to act on behalf of; to pay the respects of ‖ *ref* to be fulfilled, to come true; to fall due; **cúmplase** approved

cumquibus *m* wherewithal

cúmulo *m* heap, pile, lot

cuna *f* cradle

cundido *m* olive, vinegar, and salt for shepherds; olive oil, cheese, and honey to make children eat

cundir *intr* to spread; swell, puff up; increase

cunear *tr* to cradle, rock in a cradle ‖ *intr* to rock, swing, sway

cune•co -ca *mf* (Ven) baby (*youngest member of family*)

cuneta *f* gutter, ditch

cuña *f* wedge; (typ) quoin; **ser buena cuña** to take up a lot of room

cuñada *f* sister-in-law

cuñado *m* brother-in-law

cuñete *m* keg

cuño *m* die; stamp; mark

cuota *f* quota, share; fee, dues; tuition fee

cupé *m* coupé

cupo *m* quota, share; (Mex) capacity

cupón *m* coupon; **cupón de racionamiento** ration coupon

cúpula *f* cupola; dome

cuquillo *m* cuckoo

cura *m* curate; (coll) priest; **este cura** (*yo*) (coll) yours truly (*I*) ‖ *f* cure; care, treatment; **cura de aguas** water cure; **cura de almas** care of souls; **cura de hambre** starvation diet; **cura de reposo** rest cure; **cura de urgencia** first aid; **no tener cura** to be hopeless, be incorrigible

curaca *m* (SAm) boss, chief ‖ *f* (Bol, Peru) priest's housekeeper

curación *f* cure, treatment

curade•ro -ra *mf* caretaker ‖ *m* (law) guardian

curande•ro -ra *mf* quack, healer

curar *tr* (*a un enfermo*) to treat; (*sanar*) cure, heal; (*curtir*) cure; (*la madera*) season; (*una herida*) dress ‖ *intr* to cure; recover; **curar de** to take care of; recover from; mind, pay attention to ‖ *ref* to cure; cure oneself; get well, recover; get drunk; **curarse de** to recover from, get over; **curarse en salud** to be forewarned

curati•vo -va *adj & f* curative

curda *f* jag, drunk

cureña *f* gun carriage

curia *f* (hist) curia; (*de rey*) court; (*conjunto de abogados*) bar

curiales•co -ca *adj* hairsplitting, legalistic

curiosear *tr* to pry into ‖ *intr* to snoop; browse around

curiosidad *f* curiosity; (*objeto de arte raro y curioso*) curio; neatness, tidiness; care, carefulness

curio•so -sa *adj* curious; neat, tidy; careful ‖ *mf* busybody ‖ *m* (Ven) healer, medical man

currinche *m* cub reporter; hit playwright

cu•rro -rra *adj* flashy, sporty ‖ *m* sport, dandy

curruca *f* (orn) whitethroat; **curruca de cabeza negra** blackcap, warbler

curruta•co -ca *adj* dudish, sporty; chubby ‖ *m* dude, sport ‖ *f* chic dame

cursa•do -da *adj* skilled, experienced; (*asignatura*) taken

cursante *mf* student

cursar *tr* (*una materia, estudios*) to take, study; (*conferencias*) attend; (*una carta*) forward; (*un paraje*) frequent, to haunt ‖ *intr* to study; be current

cursear *intr* to have diarrhea

cursería *f* cheapness, flashiness, vulgarity; flashy lot of people

cursi *adj* cheap, flashy, vulgar, loud ‖ *m* sporty guy ‖ *f* flashy dame

cursien•to -ta *adj* diarrheic

cursilería *f* cheapness, flashiness, vulgarity; flashy lot of people

cursillo *m* refresher course; short course of lectures

cursi•vo -va *adj* cursive; italic ‖ *f* cursive; italics

curso *m* course; academic year, school year; price, quotation, current rate; **curso académico** academic year; **curso legal** legal tender; **cursos** loose bowels; **dar curso a** to give way to; to forward

cursor *m* slide; sliding contact; **cursor de procesiones** marshal

curtiduría *f* tannery

curtiembre *f* tannery

curtir *tr* (*las pieles*) to tan; (*el cutis de una persona*) tan, sunburn; harden, inure; **estar curtido en** to be skilled in, be expert in ‖ *ref* to become tanned, sunburned; become hardened; be weather-beaten

curva *f* curve; bend

curvadura *f* painful exhaustion

cur•vo -va *adj* curved, bent ‖ *f* see **curva**

cusca *f* (Col) jag, drunk; (Mex) prostitute, slut

cúspide *f* (*de montaña*) peak; (*de diente*) cusp; apex, tip, top

custodia *f* custody, care; (*de un preso*) guard; (eccl) monstrance

custodiar *tr* to guard, watch over

custodio *m* custodian; guard

cususa *f* (CAm) rum

cu•tí *m* (*pl* **-tíes**) bedtick, ticking

cutícula *f* cuticle

cutio *m* work, labor

cu•tis *m* (& *f*) (*pl* **-tis**) skin, complexion; **cutis anserina** goose flesh

cu•yo -ya *adj rel* whose

c/v *abbr* **cuenta de venta**

Ch

Ch, ch (che) *f* fourth letter of the Spanish alphabet

chabacanada or **chabacanería** *f* crudeness, coarseness, vulgarity

chabaca•no -na *adj* crude, coarse, vulgar ‖ *m* (Mex) apricot tree

chabola *f* shack, shanty; (mil) foxhole

chacal *m* jackal

chacanear *tr* (Chile) to spur, goad on; (Chile) to annoy, bother

chacare•ro -ra *mf* (SAm) farm laborer, field worker; (Col) quack doctor; (Urug) gossip

chacarrachaca *f* row, racket

chacolotear *intr* to clatter

chacota *f* laughter, racket; **hacer chacota de** to make fun of

chacotear *intr* to laugh and make a racket
chacra *f* farm house; small farm; sown field
chacua•co -ca *adj* ugly, crude, boorish ‖ *m* (CAm) cigar butt; (CAm) cheap cigar
cháchara *f* chatter, idle talk; **cháchara** trinkets, junk
chacharear *intr* to chatter
chafallar *tr* to botch
chafandín *m* conceited ass
chafar *tr* to rumple, muss; flatten; cut short; (Chile) to dismiss, send off
chafarrinar *tr* to blot, stain
chafarrinón *m* blot, stain; **echar un chafarrinón a** to insult, throw mud at
chaflán *m* chamfer
chaflanar *tr* to chamfer
chal *m* shawl
cha•lán -lana *adj* horse-dealing ‖ *mf* horse dealer; horse trader ‖ *m* broncobuster, horsebreaker ‖ *f* scow, flatboat
chalanear *tr* (*un negocio*) to pull off shrewdly; (*un caballo*) break; (Arg) to take advantage of ‖ *intr* to horse-trade
chalanería *f* horse trading
chalanes•co -ca *adj* horse-trading
chaleco *m* vest, waistcoat; **al chaleco** (Mex) by force; (Mex) for nothing; **chaleco salvavidas** life jacket
chalecón *m* (Mex) crook
chalupa *f* small two-master; launch, lifeboat; (Mex) corncake
chama•co -ca *mf* (Mex) youngster, urchin
chamago•so -sa *adj* (Mex) dirty, filthy; (Mex) botched
chamarasca *f* brushwood; brush fire
chamarille•ro -ra *mf* junk dealer, secondhand dealer ‖ *m* gambler
chamari•llón -llona *mf* poor card player
chamarra *f* sheepskin jacket
chamarreta *f* loose jacket; square poncho
chamba *f* fluke, scratch; (Mex) work
chambelán *m* chamberlain; (Mex) atomizer, spray
chambergo *m* (orn) bobolink; (Arg) soft hat
chambe•rí *adj* (*pl* **-ríes**) (Peru) showy, flashy
cham•bón -bona *adj* awkward, clumsy; lucky
chambonada *f* awkwardness, clumsiness; stroke of luck
chambonear *intr* to foozle
chambra *f* blouse; (Ven) din, uproar
chambrana *f* trim (*around a door*)
chamburgo *m* (Col) stagnant water, puddle
chamico *m* jimson weed; **dar chamico a** (SAm) to bewitch
chamorrar *tr* to shear
champán *m* sampan; (coll) champagne
champaña *m* champagne
cham•pú *m* (*pl* **-púes**) shampoo
chamuchina *f* rabble; populace
chamuscar §73 *tr* to singe, scorch; (Mex) to undersell
chamusco *m* singe, scorch
chamusquina *f* singeing; fight, row, quarrel; **oler a chamusquina** to look like a fight; smack of heresy
chancar §73 *tr* to crush; beat, beat up; botch
chance *m* (SAm) opportunity, chance

chancear *intr* & *ref* to joke, jest
chance•ro -ra *adj* joking, jesting
chanciller *m* chancellor
chancla *f* old shoe; house slipper
chancleta *mf* good-for-nothing ‖ *f* slipper; (Ven) accelerator
chanclo *m* overshoe, rubber
chancha *f* cheat, lie; (Chile) slut; **hacer la chancha** (Bol, Col, Chile) to play hooky
chanche•ro -ra *mf* (Arg, Chile) pork butcher
chan•cho -cha *adj* dirty, filthy ‖ *m* pig ‖ *f* see **chancha**
chanchulle•ro -ra *mf* crook
chandal *m* or **chándal** *m* jump suit, gym suit
changador *m* (SAm) errand boy
changarro *m* (Mex) small shop
chan•go -ga *adj* (Chile) dull, stupid; (Mex) sly, crafty ‖ *mf* (Mex) monkey ‖ *m* (Arg) house boy
chan•guí *m* (*pl* **-güíes**) trick, deception
chantaje *m* blackmail
chantajista *mf* blackmailer
chantar *tr* to put on; (SAm) to throw hard; (Urug) to keep waiting ‖ *ref* (*p.ej., el sombrero*) to clap on
chantre *m* cantor, precentor
chanza *f* joke, jest
chao *interj* (coll) good-by
chapa *f* sheet, plate; (*hoja fina de madera*) veneer; (*en las mejillas*) flush; (coll) good sense, judgment; (Chile) lock, bolt; **chapa de circulación** (aut) license plate; **chapas** flipping coins
chapa•do -da *adj* plated; veneered; **chapado a la antigua** old-fashioned
chapalear *intr* (*el agua; las manos y los pies en el agua*) to splash; (*la herradura floja*) clatter
chapar *tr* to cover or line with sheets of metal; veneer
chaparrear *intr* to pour
chapa•rro -rra *mf* (Mex) child, little one; (Mex) runt ‖ *m* scrub oak
chaparrón *m* downpour
chapea•do -da *adj* lined with sheets of metal; veneered ‖ *m* plywood; veneer
chapear *tr* to cover or line with sheets of metal; veneer
chapista *m* tinsmith, tinman
chapitel *m* (*remate de torre*) spire; (*capitel de columna*) capital
chapodar *tr* to trim, clear of branches; to curtail
chapotear *tr* to sponge, moisten ‖ *intr* to splash
chapucear *tr* & *intr* to botch, bungle
chapuce•ro -ra *adj* crude, rough; clumsy, bungling ‖ *mf* bungler; amateur ‖ *m* blacksmith; junk dealer
chapurrar *tr* & *intr* to jabber
chapurreo *m* jabber
cha•puz *m* (*pl* **-puces**) duck, ducking
chapuzar §60 *tr, intr* & *ref* to duck
chaqué *m* cutaway coat, morning coat
chaqueta *f* jacket
chaquetilla *f* short jacket; (Ecuad) lady's vest
chaquetón *m* reefer, pea jacket

charamusca *f* brushwood, firewood; (Mex) candy twist

charanga *f* (mil) brass band

charangue•ro -ra *adj* crude, rough; bungling, clumsy ‖ *mf* bungler

charca *f* pool

charco *m* puddle

charla *f* talk, chat; talk, lecture; chatter, prattle

charla•dor -dora *adj* garrulous; gossipy ‖ *mf* chatterbox; gossip

charlar *intr* to talk, chat; chatter, prattle

charla•tán -tana *adj* garrulous; gossipy ‖ *mf* chatterbox; gossip; charlatan

charlatanería *f* garrulity, loquacity

charlatanismo *m* charlatanism; garrulity, loquacity

charnela *f* (*de puerta; de molusco*) hinge; (mach) knuckle

charol *m* varnish; patent leather; lacquered tray; **calzarse las de charol** (Arg, Urug) to hit the jackpot; **darse charol** to blow one's own horn

charola•do -da *adj* shiny

charolar *tr* to varnish, lacquer

charpa *f* pistol belt; (*cabestrillo*) sling

charquear *tr* (*carne de vaca*) to jerk; slash, cut to pieces

charqui *m* jerked beef

charrada *f* country dance; boorishness; tawdry ornamentation

charretera *f* epaulet; garter; (*del aguador*) shoulder pad

charriada *f* (Mex) rodeo

cha•rro -rra *adj* coarse, ill-bred; flashy, loud, showy; Salamanca ‖ *mf* peasant; Salamanca peasant ‖ *m* broad-brimmed hat; Mexican cowboy

chasca *f* brushwood

chascar §73 *tr* (*la lengua*) to click; (*algún manjar*) crunch; (*engullir*) swallow ‖ *intr* to crack, crackle

chascarrillo *m* funny story

chas•co -ca *adj* (Arg, Bol) crinkly, crinkly-haired ‖ *m* joke, trick; disappointment; **dar un chasco a** to play a trick on; **llevar** or **llevarse (un) chasco** to be disappointed

chas•cón -cona *adj* (Bol, Chile) disheveled; (Bol, Chile) bushy-haired; (Bol, Chile) clumsy, unskilled

cha•sis *m* (*pl* -sis) chassis

chasquear *tr* (*un látigo*) to crack; play a trick on; disappoint ‖ *intr* to crack ‖ *ref* to be disappointed

chasqui *m* (SAm) messenger, courier

chasquido *m* crack; crackle

chata *f* barge, scow; flatcar; bedpan; (Mex) dear, darling

chatarra *f* iron slag; junk, scrap iron

chatarrería *f* junk yard

chatarre•ro -ra *mf* junk dealer, scrapiron dealer

cha•to -ta *adj* flat; flat-nosed; blunt; commonplace; disappointed ‖ *m* wineglass ‖ *f* see **chata**

chatre *adj* (Chile, Ecuad) all dressed up

chauvinismo *m* chauvinism

cha•val -vala *adj* (coll) young ‖ *m* lad ‖ *f* lass

chaveta *f* cotter pin; **perder la chaveta** to go out of one's head

chayote *m* chayote, vegetable pear; dunce, fool

chazar §60 *tr* (*la pelota*) to stop; (*el sitio donde paró la pelota*) to mark

che *interj* (SAm) say!, hey!

checar *tr* (Mex) to check

che•co -ca *adj* & *mf* Czech

checoeslova•co -ca *adj* & *mf* Czecho-Slovak

Checoeslovaquia *f* Czecho-Slovakia

checoslova•co -ca *adj* & *mf* Czecho-Slovak

Checoslovaquia *f* Czecho-Slovakia

chechén *m* (Mex) poison ivy

chécheres *mpl* trinkets, junk

chelín *m* shilling

cheque *m* check; **cheque de viajeros** traveler's check

chequear *tr* (CAm, W-I) to check

chequeo *m* control; checkup

chequera *f* checkbook

chévere *adj invar* terrific, fabulous; **¡que chévere!** terrific!

chica *f* lass, little girl; girl; my dear; **chica de cita** call girl; **chica de la vida alegre** party girl

chicalote *m* Mexican poppy

chicle *m* chewing gum

chiclear *intr* (Mex) to chew gum

chi•co -ca *adj* small, little; young ‖ *mf* child, youngster ‖ *m* lad, little boy; young fellow; old man; hand, turn ‖ *f* see **chica**

chicolear *intr* to pay compliments, to flirt ‖ *ref* (Arg, Peru) to enjoy oneself

chico•te -ta *mf* husky youngster ‖ *m* cigar; cigar stub; whip

chicotear *tr* to beat up; kill

chicue•lo -la *adj* small, little ‖ *m* little boy ‖ *f* little girl

chicha *f* corn liquor; **no ser ni chicha ni limonada** to be good for nothing

chícharo *m* pea; (Col) poor cigar; (Mex) apprentice

chicharra *f* harvest fly; chatterbox; **cantar la chicharra** (coll) to be hot and sultry

chicharrón *m* residue of hog's fat; burnt meat; sunburned person; wrinkled person

chiche *adj invar* nice, pretty

chichear *tr* & *intr* to hiss

chi•chón -chona *adj* (CAm) easy; (SAm) joking; (Guat) large-breasted ‖ *m* lump, bump on the head

chifla *f* hissing, whistling; paring knife; **estar de chifla** (Mex) to be in a bad humor

chifla•do -da *adj* (coll) daffy, nutty ‖ *mf* crackbrain, nut

chifladura *f* daffiness, nuttiness; whim, wild idea

chiflar *tr* (*a un actor*) to hiss; (*vino o licor*) to gulp down; (*el cuero*) to pare ‖ *intr* to whistle; (*las aves*) (Guat, Mex) to sing ‖ *ref* to go crazy

chifle *m* whistle; (*para cazar aves*) bird call; powder flask

chiflido *m* whistle, hiss

ch
ch

chiflón *m* (SAm) cold blast of air; rapids; slide of loose stone

chilaba *f* jelab, jellaba

Chile *m* Chile

chile•no -na *adj & mf* Chilean

chilote *m* (CAm) ear of corn

chilla *f* fox call, hare call; clapboard; (Chile) small fox; (Mex) top gallery

chillar *intr* to shriek; to squeak; to hiss, sizzle; (*los colores*) to scream || *ref* to take offense

chillido *m* shriek, scream

chi•llón -llona *adj* shrill, high-pitched; screaming; (*color*) loud

chimenea *f* chimney, smokestack; fireplace, hearth; stovepipe hat; (naut) funnel

chimpancé *m* chimpanzee

china *f* Chinese woman; china, porcelain; pebble; nursemaid; (Col) spinning top || **China** *f* China

chinche *mf* bore, tiresome person || *m* (*clavito de cabeza chata*) thumbtack || *f* (*insecto*) bedbug; **caer** or **morir como chinches** to die like flies

chinchorre•ro -ra *adj* gossipy, mischievous

chincho•so -sa *adj* boring, tiresome

chinero *m* china closet

chines•co -ca *adj* Chinese || **chinescos** *mpl* (mus) bell tree

chingar §44 *tr* to tipple; (CAm) to bob, dock; (CAm, Mex) to bother, annoy || *ref* to tipple; fail

chin•go -ga *adj* (CAm) short; (CAm) dull, blunt; (CAm) naked

chinguirito *m* cheap rum; swig of liquor

chi•no -na *adj & mf* Chinese || *m* (*idioma*) Chinese; (Col) boy, newsboy; (Mex) curl || *f* see **china**

chipichipi *m* drizzle, mist

Chipre *f* Cyprus

chiquero *m* pigsty; bull pen

chiquillada *f* childish prank

chiqui•to -ta *adj* small, little || *mf* little one || *m* (*de vino*) snifter; (Arg) moment, instant || *f* five cents; **no andarse con** or **en chiquitas** to talk right off the shoulder

chiquitura *f* trifle, small matter

chiribita *f* spark; daisy; **chiribitas** spots before the eyes

chiribitil *m* garret; cubbyhole

chirimbolos *mpl* utensils, vessels

chirimía *f* hornpipe

chiripa *f* (billiards) fluke, scratch; stroke of luck

chirivía *f* parsnip

chirle *adj* insipid, tasteless

chirlo *m* slash or scar on the face

chirlota *f* (Mex) meadow lark

chirona *f* jail, jug

chirriar §77 *intr* to creak, squeak; shriek; hiss, sizzle; sing or play out of tune || *ref* (Col) to go on a spree; (Col) to shiver

chirrido *m* creak, squeak; shriek; hiss, sizzle

chirrión *m* squeaky cart; (SAm) whip

chis *interj* sh-sh!; ¡chis, chis! pst!

chischás *m* clash of swords

chisguete *m* swig of wine; squirt

chisme *m* piece of gossip; trinket; **chisme de vecindad** idle talker; **chismes** gossip; articles; **chismes de aseo** toilet articles

chismear *intr* to gossip

chismo•so -sa *adj* gossipy, catty || *mf* gossip

chispa *f* spark; (*pequeña cantidad*) drop; lightning; (fig) sparkle, wit; (coll) drunk, spree; (Col) rumor; **coger una chispa** to go on a drunk; **chispa de entrehierro** (elec) jump spark; **chispas** sprinkle (*of rain*); **dar chispa** (Guat, Mex) to work, to click; **echar chispas** to blow up, hit the ceiling

chispeante *adj* sparkling

chispar *tr* to throw (someone) out

chispear *intr* to spark; sparkle; drizzle, sprinkle

chis•po -pa *adj* tipsy || *m* swallow, drink || *f* see **chispa**

chisporrotear *intr* to spark, sputter

chispo•so -sa *adj* sputtering, sparking

chisquero *m* pocket lighter

chistar *intr* to speak, say something; **no chistar** to not say a word

chiste *m* joke; witticism; **caer en el chiste** to get the point; **dar en el chiste** to hit the nail on the head

chistera *f* fish basket; (coll) top hat

chisto•so -sa *adj* funny; witty || *mf* funny person; wit

chita *f* anklebone; quoits; **a la chita callando** quietly, secretly; **dar en la chita** to hit the nail on the head

chiticalla *mf* (*persona que no revela lo que sabe*) (coll) clam || *f* (coll) secret

chito *interj* hush!, sh-sh!

chivato *m* kid, young goat; (*soplón*) squealer; (Bol) apprentice, helper; (Chile) cheap rum

chi•vo -va *mf* kid || *m* billy goat; (Mex) day's wage; (Col, Ecuad, Ven) fit of rage || *f* nanny goat

chocante *adj* shocking; coarse, crude; (Col) annoying; (Mex) disagreeable

chocar §73 *tr* to shock, annoy, irritate; surprise; (*vasos*) clink; please; ¡choque Vd. esos cinco! shake! || *intr* to shock; collide; clash, fight

chocarre•ro -ra *adj* coarse, crude || *mf* crude joker

choclo *m* wooden overshoe; (Mex) low shoe; (SAm) tender ear of corn

chocolate *m* chocolate

chocha *f* woodcock

chochear *intr* to be in one's dotage; dote, be infatuated

chochera *f* dotage; (Arg, Peru) favorite

cho•chez *f* (*pl* -checes) dotage; doting act or remark

cho•cho -cha *adj* doting; doddering || *m* stick of cinnamon candy; **chochos** candy to quiet a child || *f* see **chocha**

chófer *m* chauffeur

chofeta *f* fire pan (*for lighting cigars*)

cho•lo -la *adj* half-breed (*Indian and white*) || *mf* Indian; half-breed; (Chile) coward; (SAm) darling

cholla *f* (coll) noodle, head; (coll) ability, brains

chomite *m* (Mex) coarse wool; (Mex) woolen skirt

chontal *m* uneducated person

chopo *m* black poplar; gun, rifle; **chopo de Italia** Lombardy poplar; **chopo del Canadá** or **de Virginia** cottonwood; **chopo lombardo** Lombardy poplar

choque *m* shock; collision, impact; clash, conflict, skirmish; (elec) choke, choke coil; **choque en cadena** (aut) pileup, mass collision

choricería *f* sausage shop

chorizo *m* smoked pork sausage

chorlito *m* plover, golden plover; scatterbrains

chorrea•do -da *adj* dirty; spotty

chorrear *intr* to gush, spurt, spout; drip; trickle

chorrera spout, channel; cut, gulley; rapids; lace front, jabot; (Arg) string, stream

chorrillo *m* constant stream; **irse por el chorrillo** to follow the current; **tomar el chorrillo de** to get the habit of

chorro *m* jet, spurt; stream, flow; **a chorros** in abundance; **chorro de arena** sandblast

chotaca•bras *m* (*pl* **-bras**) goatsucker

chotear *tr* to make fun of; (Guat) to keep an eye on

choteo *m* jeering, mocking

choza *f* hut, cabin, lodge

chubasco *m* squall, shower; (fig) temporary setback; **chubasco de agua** rainstorm; **chubasco de nieve** blizzard

chubasco•so -sa *adj* stormy, threatening

chucruta *f* sauerkraut

chucha *f* female dog, bitch; drunk, jag; (Col) opossum; (Col) body odor

chuchaque *m* (Ecuad) hangover

chuchear *tr* (*caza menor*) to trap ‖ *intr* to whisper

chuchería *f* knickknack, trinket; delicacy, tidbit

chu•cho -cha *adj* (CAm) mean, stingy; (*fruto*) (Col) watery; (Col) wrinkled ‖ *m* (coll) dog ‖ *f* see **chucha**

chue•co -ca *adj* (Mex) twisted, bent; (SAm) bow-legged; (Mex) crippled ‖ *m* (Mex) dealing in stolen goods ‖ *f* stump; hockey; hockey ball

chufa *f* groundnut

chufletear *intr* to joke, jest

chula *f* flashy dame (*in lower classes of Madrid*)

chulada *f* light-hearted remark; vulgarity

chul•co -ca *mf* (Bol) baby (*youngest child*)

chulear *tr* to tease; (Mex) to flirt with

chuleta *f* chop, cutlet; slap, smack; (*de los estudiantes*) (coll) crib, pony; **chuleta de cerdo** pork chop; **chuleta de ternera** veal chop; **chuletas** sideburns, side whiskers

chu•lo -la *adj* flashy, sporty; foxy, slick; (Guat, Mex) pretty, cute ‖ *m* sporty fellow (*in lower classes of Madrid*); pimp, procurer; gigolo; butcher's helper; (taur) attendant on foot ‖ *f* see **chula**

chumbera *f* prickly pear

chume•ro -ra *mf* (CAm) apprentice

chunches *mpl* (CAm) junk, stuff

chunga *f* jest, fun

chunguear *ref* to jest, joke

chupa *f* frock, coat; (Arg) drunk, jag; (Arg) tobacco pouch

chupa•do -da *adj* thin, skinny; drunk; (*falda*) tight ‖ *f* suck; pull (*on a cigar*)

chupador *m* teething ring, pacifier

chupaflor *m* (Mex, Ven) hummingbird

chupalla *f* straw hat

chupamirto *m* (Mex) hummingbird

chupar *tr* to suck; (*la hacienda ajena*) milk, sap; absorb ‖ *intr* to suck ‖ *ref* to get thin, lose strength; (*los labios*) smack

chupatin•tas *mf* (*pl* **-tas**) (coll) office drudge

chupete *m* (*para un niño*) pacifier; lollipop; **de chupete** fine, splendid

chu•pón -pona *mf* swindler ‖ *m* (bot) sucker, shoot; (mach) plunger; baby bottle; pacifier

chupópte•ro -ra *mf* sponge

chuquisa *f* (Chile, Peru) prostitute

churrasco *m* barbecue

churrasquear *tr* to barbecue

churre *m* filth, dirt, grease

churrete *m* dirty spot (*on hands or face*)

churrigueres•co -ca *adj* churrigueresque; loud, flashy, tawdry

chu•rro -rra *adj* (*lana*) coarse; (*carnero*) coarse-wooled ‖ *m* coarse-wooled sheep; fritter; botch

churrulle•ro -ra *adj* gossipy, loquacious ‖ *mf* gossip, chatterbox

churrusco *m* burnt piece of bread

churumbela *f* hornpipe, flageolet; maté cup; (Col) worry, anxiety; (Col, Ecuad) pipe

churumo *m* (coll) substance (*money, brains, etc.*)

chus *interj* here! (*to call a dog*); **no decir chus ni mus** to not say boo

chus•co -ca *adj* droll, funny; (Peru) illmannered; (*perro*) (Peru) mongrel

chusma *f* galley slaves; mob, rabble

chuza *f* (Mex) strike (*in bowling*)

D

D, d (de) *f* fifth letter of the Spanish alphabet

D. *abbr* **don**

D.ª *abbr* **doña**

daca give me, hand over; **andar al daca y toma** to be at cross purposes

dactilógra•fo -fa *mf* typist ‖ *m* typewriter

dactilograma *m* fingerprint

dádiva *f* gift, present

dadivo•so -sa *adj* liberal, generous

da•do -da *adj* given; **dado que** provided, as

long as ‖ *m* die; **cargar los dados** to load the dice; **dados** dice; **el dado está tirado** the die is cast

daga *f* dagger

dalia *f* dahlia

dama *f* lady, dame; maid-in-waiting; (*en el juego de damas*) king; (*en el ajedrez y los naipes*) queen; (theat) leading lady; concubine, mistress; **dama joven** (theat) young lead; **damas** checkers; **señalar dama** (*en el juego de.damas*) to crown a man

damajuana *f* demijohn

damasquina•do -da *adj & m* damascene

damasquinar *tr* to damascene

damasqui•no -na *adj* damascene

damero *m* checkerboard

damisela *f* young lady; courtesan

damnación *f* damnation

damnificar §73 *tr* to damage, hurt

da•nés -nesa *adj* Danish ‖ *mf* Dane, ‖ *m* (*idioma*) Danish

dáni•co -ca *adj* Danish

Danubio *m* Danube

danza *f* dance; dancing; dance team; **danza de cintas** Maypole dance; **danza de figuras** square dance; **meter en la danza** to drag in, involve

danza•dor -dora *mf* dancer

danzar §60 *tr* to dance ‖ *intr* to dance; butt in

danza•rín -rina *mf* dancer; meddler, scatterbrain

dañable *adj* harmful; reprehensible

daña•do -da *adj* bad, wicked; spoiled

dañar *tr* to hurt, damage, injure; spoil ‖ *ref* to be damaged; spoil

dañi•no -na *adj* harmful, destructive, noxious; wicked

daño *m* damage, harm; (Arg) witchcraft; **a daño de** on the responsibility of; **daños y perjuicios** (law) damages; **en daño de** to the detriment of; **hacer daño** to be harmful; **hacer daño a** to hurt; **hacerse daño** to hurt oneself; to get hurt

daño•so -sa *adj* harmful, injurious

dar §23 *tr* to give; cause; hit, strike; (*el reloj la hora*) strike; (*cartas*) deal; (*un paseo*) take; (*los buenos días*) wish; (*un film*) show; (*una capa de pintura*) put on, apply; **dar a conocer** to make known; **dar a luz** to bring out, publish; **dar cuerda a** (*un reloj*) to wind; **dar curso a** to circulate; **dar de beber a** to give something to drink to; **dar de comer a** to give something to eat to; **dar la razón a** to admit that (*someone*) is right; **dar prestado** to lend; **dar palmadas** to clap the hands; **dar por** to consider as; **dar que hablar** to cause talk; to stir up criticism; **dar que hacer** to cause annoyance or trouble; **dar que pensar** to give food for thought; to give rise to suspicion ‖ *intr* to take place; to hit, strike; (*el reloj; dos, tres, etc. horas*) to strike; to tell, intimate; **dar a** to overlook; **dar con** to run into; **dar contra** to run against, strike against; **dar de sí** to stretch, to give; **dar en** to overlook; to hit; to run into; to fall into; to be bent on; (*un chiste*)

to catch on to; **dar sobre** to overlook; **dar tras** to pursue hotly ‖ *ref* to give oneself up; to give in, yield; to occur, be found; **darse a** to devote oneself to; **darse a conocer** to make a name for oneself, make oneself known; to get to know each other; **darse cuenta de** to realize, become aware of; **darse la mano** to shake hands; **dárselas de** to pose as; **darse por aludido** to take the hint; **darse por entendido** to show an understanding; to show appreciation; **darse por ofendido** to take offense; **darse por vencido** to give up, to acknowledge defeat

dardo *m* dart; cutting remark

dares y tomares *mpl* quarrels, disputes

dársena *f* basin, marina, inner harbor

darvinia•no -na *adj & mf* Darwinian, Darwinist

darvinismo *m* Darwinism

data *f* date; (*en una cuenta*) item; **de larga data** of long standing; **estar de mala data** to be in a bad humor

datar *f & intr* to date; **datar de** to date from

dátil *m* date

datilera *f* date, date palm

dati•vo -va *adj & m* dative

dato *m* datum; basis, foundation

de *prep* of; from; about; **acompañado de** accompanied by; **cubierto de** covered with; **de noche** in the nighttime; **de no llegar nosotros a la hora** if we do not arrive on time; **más de** more than; **tratar de** to try to

deán *m* (eccl) dean

deanato *m* or **deanazgo** *m* deanship

debajo *adv* below, underneath; **debajo de** below, under

debate *m* debate; altercation, argument

debatir *tr & intr* to debate; fight, argue ‖ *ref* to struggle

debe *m* debit

debelar *tr* to conquer, vanquish

deber *m* duty; (*deuda*) debt; homework, school work; **últimos deberes** last rites ‖ *tr* to owe ‖ *v aux* to have to, ought to, must, should; **deber de** must, most likely ‖ *ref* to be committed; **deberse a** to be due to

debidamente *adv* duly

debi•do -da *adj* due, owed; proper, right; **debido a** due to

débil *adj* weak

debilidad *f* weakness, debility

debilitar *tr & ref* to weaken

débito *m* debt, debit; responsibility

debutante *mf* debutant(e), beginner

debutar *intr* to make one's start, appear for the first time

década *f* decade

decadencia *f* decadence

decadente *adj & mf* decadent

decaer §15 *intr* to decay, decline, fail, weaken; (naut) to drift from the course

decampar *intr* (mil) to decamp

decanato *m* deanship

decano *m* dean

decanta•do -da *adj* puffed-up, overrated

decapitar *tr* to decapitate

decelerar *tr, intr. & ref* to decelerate
decencia *f* decency
decenio *m* decade
dece•no -na *adj & m* tenth
decentar §2 *tr* to cut the first slice of; begin to damage || *ref* to get bedsores
decente *adj* decent, proper; decent-looking
decepción *f* disappointment
decepcionar *tr* to disappoint
decidi•do -da *adj* decided, determined
decidir *tr* to decide; persuade || *intr & ref* to decide
deci•dor -dora *adj* facile, fluent, witty
decimal *adj & m* decimal
déci•mo -ma *adj & m* tenth
decimocta•vo -va *adj* eighteenth
decimocuar•to -ta *adj* fourteenth
decimono•no -na *adj* nineteenth
decimonove•no -na *adj* nineteenth
decimoquin•to -ta *adj* fifteenth
decimosépti•mo -ma *adj* seventeenth
decimosex•to -ta *adj* sixteenth
decimoterce•ro -ra *adj* thirteenth
decimoter•cio -cia *adj* thirteenth
decir *m* say-so; **al decir de** according to || §24 *tr* to say; tell; (*disparates*) talk; **como si dijéramos** so to speak, in a manner of speaking; **decir entre sí** to say to oneself; **decirle a uno cuántas son cinco** to tell a person what's what; **decir para sí** to say to oneself; **decir por decir** to talk for talk's sake; **decir que no** to say no; **decir que sí** to say yes; **decírselo a una persona deletreado** to spell it out to a person; **es decir** that is to say; **mejor dicho** rather; **¡por algo te lo dije!** I told you so!; **por decirlo así** so to speak || *intr* to suit, fit; **¡diga!** (*al contestar el teléfono*) hello! || *ref* to be said; be called; **se dice** it is said, they say
decisión *f* decision
decisi•vo -va *adj* decisive
declamar *tr & intr* to declaim
declaración *f* declaration; (*en bridge*) bid; **declaración de renta** tax return
declarante *mf* declarant, deponent; (*en el juego de bridge*) bidder
declarar *tr* to declare; (*en bridge*) bid; (law) to depose || *ref* to declare oneself; break out, take place
declarati•vo -va *adj* declarative
declinación *f* declination; fall, drop; decline; (gram) declension
declinar *tr & intr* to decline
declive *m* descent, declivity, slope
declividad *f* declivity
decodificador *m* (telv) decoder
decollaje *m* (aer) take-off
decollar *intr* (aer) to take off
decomisar *tr* to seize, confiscate
decomiso *m* seizure, confiscation
decoración *f* decoration; memorizing; (theat) set, scenery; **decoraciones** (theat) scenery; **decoración interior** interior decoration
decorado *m* decoration; (theat) décor, scenery; memorizing
decora•dor -dora *mf* decorator
decorar *tr* to decorate; memorize

decoro *m* decorum; honor, respect; decency, propriety
decoro•so -sa *adj* decorous; respectful; decent
decrecer §22 *intr* to decrease, grow smaller, grow shorter
decrepitar *intr* to crackle
decrépi•to -ta *adj* decrepit
decretar *tr* to decree
decreto *m* decree
decurso *m* course; **en el decurso de** in the course of
dechado *m* sample, model, example; (*labor de las niñas*) sampler
dedada *f* touch, spot; **dar una dedada de miel a** to feed the hopes of
dedal *m* thimble
dedalera *f* foxglove
dedeo *m* (mus) finger dexterity
dedicación *f* dedication; (*aplicación*) diligence
dedicar §73 *tr* to dedicate; devote; autograph || *ref* to devote oneself
dedicatoria *f* dedication
dedil *m* fingerstall
dedillo *m* little finger; **saber** or **tener al dedillo** to have at one's finger tips, have a thorough knowledge of
dedo *m* finger; toe; bit; **alzar el dedo** (*en señal de dar palabra*) to raise one's hand; **cogerse los dedos** to burn one's fingers; **dedo auricular** little finger; **dedo cordial, de en medio,** or **del corazón** middle finger; **dedo gordo** thumb; big toe; **dedo índice** index finger, forefinger; **dedo meñique** little finger; **dedo mostrador** forefinger; **dedo pulgar** thumb; big toe; **estar a dos dedos de** to be within an ace of; **irse de entre los dedos** (coll) to slip between the fingers; **tener en la punta de los dedos** to have at one's fingertips
deducción *f* deduction; drawing off
deducir §19 *tr* (*concluir*) to deduce; (*rebajar*) deduct; (law) to allege
defecar §73 *intr* to defecate
defección *f* defection
defeccionar *intr & ref* (Chile) to defect
defecti•vo -va *adj* defective
defecto *m* defect; shortage, lack; **en defecto de** for lack of
defectuo•so -sa *adj* defective; lacking
defender §51 *tr* to defend; protect; delay, interfere with
defensa *f* defense; fender, guard; (*del toro*) horn; (*del elefante*) tusk; (*del automóvil*) bumper; **defensa marítima** (Arg) sea wall; **defensa propia** self-defense
defensi•vo -va *adj & f* defensive
defen•sor -sora *adj* defending || *mf* defender; (law) counsel for the defense
deferencia *f* deference
deferente *adj* deferential
deferir §68 *tr* to delegate || *intr* to defer
deficiencia *f* deficiency
deficiente *adj* deficient
défi•cit *m* (*pl* **-cits**) deficit
deficita•rio -ria *adj* deficit

da
de

definición *f* definition; decision, verdict
defini•do -da *adj* definite; sharp, defined
definir *tr* to define; settle, determine
definiti•vo -va *adj* definitive; **en definitiva** after all, in short
deflación *f* deflation
deflector *m* baffle
deformación *f* deformation; (rad) distortion
deformar *tr* to deform; disfigure; distort
deforme *adj* deformed
deformidad *f* deformity; gross error
defraudar *tr* to defraud, cheat; (*las esperanzas de una persona*) defeat; (*la claridad del día*) cut off
defuera *adv* outside; **por defuera** on the outside
defunción *f* decease, demise
degeneración *f* (*acción y efecto de degenerar*) degeneration; (*estado de degenerado; depravación*) degeneracy
degenera•do -da *adj & mf* degenerate
degenerar *intr* to degenerate
deglutir *tr & intr* to swallow
degollar §3 *tr* to cut the throat of; kill, massacre; (*un vestido*) cut low in the neck; (*el actor una obra dramática*) butcher, murder; become obnoxious to
degradante *adj* degrading
degradar *tr* to degrade; (mil) to break
degüello *m* throat-cutting; massacre; (*de un arma*) neck; **tirar a degüello** to try to harm
degustar *tr* (*probar*) to taste; (*percibir con deleite el sabor de*) to savor
dehesa *f* pasture land, meadow; (taur) range
deidad *f* deity
deificar §73 *tr* to deify
dejación *f* abandonment; (CAm, Chile, Col) negligence
dejadez *f* laziness; negligence; slovenliness; low spirits
deja•do -da *adj* lazy; negligent; slovenly; dejected
dejamiento *m* laziness; negligence; indolence, languor, indifference
dejar *tr* to leave; abandon; let, allow, permit; **dejar caer** to drop, let fall; **dejar feo** to slight; **dejar fresco** to leave in the lurch; **dejar por** + *inf* or **que** + *inf* to leave (*something*) to be + *pp*, e.g., **hemos dejado dos manuscritos por corregir** or **que corregir** we left two manuscripts to be corrected || *intr* to stop; **dejar de** to stop, cease; fail to || *ref* to be slovenly, neglect oneself; (*una barba*) grow; **dejarse de** (*disparates*) to cut out; (*preguntas*) stop asking; (*dudas*) put aside; **dejarse ver** to show up; be evident
dejillo *m* (*gusto que deja alguna comida*) aftertaste; (*acento regional*) local accent
dejo *m* (*gusto que deja alguna comida*) aftertaste; abandonment; slovenliness; neglect; local accent; (*placer o disgusto que queda después de hecha una cosa*) (fig) aftertaste
delación *f* accusation, denunciation
delantal *m* apron

delante *adv* before, ahead, in front; **delante de** before, ahead of, in front of
delantera *f* front; front row; advantage, lead; cowcatcher; **coger** or **tomar la delantera a** to get ahead of; get a start on; **delanteras** overalls
delante•ro -ra *adj* front, foremost, first || *m* — **delantero centro** (*fútbol*) center forward || *f* see **delantera**
delatar *tr* to accuse, denounce
delega•do -da *mf* delegate
delegar §44 *tr* to delegate
deleitable *adj* delectable, enjoyable
deleitar *tr & ref* to delight
deleite *m* delight
deleito•so -sa *adj* delightful
deletrear *tr & intr* to spell; decipher
deletreo *m* spelling
deleznable *adj* (*poco durable*) perishable; (*que se rompe fácilmente*) crumbly, fragile; (*que se desliza con facilidad*) slippery
delfín *m* (*primogénito del rey de Francia*) dauphin; (*mamífero cetáceo*) dolphin
delgadez *f* thinness, leanness; delicateness, lightness; perspicacity
delga•do -da *adj* thin, lean; delicate, light; sharp, perspicacious; (*terreno*) poor, exhausted || *adv* — **hilar delgado** to hew close to the line; split hairs
delgadu•cho -cha *adj* skinny; slight
deliberar *tr & intr* to deliberate
delicadeza *f* delicacy, delicateness; scrupulousness
delica•do -da *adj* delicate; scrupulous
delicia *f* delight
delicio•so -sa *adj* delicious, delightful
delicti•vo -va *adj* punishable; criminal
delincuencia *f* guilt, criminality
delincuente *adj* guilty, criminal || *mf* criminal
delineante *mf* designer || *m* draughtsman
delinquir §25 *intr* to transgress, be guilty
deliquio *m* faint, swoon; weakening
delirante *adj* delirious
delirar *intr* to be delirious, rant, rave; talk nonsense
delirio *m* delirium; nonsense
delito *m* crime; **delito de incendio** arson; **delito de lesa majestad** lese majesty; **delito de mayor cuantía** (law) felony; **delito de menor cuantía** (law) misdemeanor
deludir *tr* to delude
demacra•do -da *adj* emaciated, wasted, thin
demago•go -ga *mf* demagogue
demanda *f* demand, petition; charity box; lawsuit; undertaking; (*del Santo Grial*) quest; **demanda maxima** (elec) peak load; **en demanda de** in search of; **tener demanda** to be in demand
demanda•do -da *mf* (law) defendant
demandante *mf* (law) complainant, plaintiff
demandar *tr* to ask for, request; (law) to sue || *intr* (law) to sue, bring suit
demarcar §73 *tr* to demarcate
demás *adj* — **el demás . . .** the other. . . , the rest of the . . . ; **estar demás** to be useless, to be in the way; **lo demás** the

rest; **por lo demás** furthermore, besides ‖ *pron* others; **los demás** the others, the rest ‖ *adv* besides; **por demás** in vain; too, too much

demasía *f* excess, surplus; daring, boldness; evil, guilt, wrong; insolence; **en demasía** excessively, too much

demasia•do -da *adj & pron* too much; **demasia•dos -das** too many ‖ **demasiado** *adv* too, too much, too hard

demasiar §77 *intr* to go too far

demediar *tr* to divide in half; use up half of; reach the middle of ‖ *intr* to be divided in half

dementa•do -da *adj* insane; demented

demente *adj* insane ‖ *mf* lunatic

democracia *f* democracy

demócrata *mf* democrat

democráti•co -ca *adj* democratic

demoler §47 *tr* to demolish

demolición *f* demolition

demonía•co -ca *adj* demoniacal

demonio *m* demon, devil; **estudiar con el demonio** to be full of devilishness

demora *f* delay

demorar *tr & ref* to delay

demostración *f* demonstration

demostra•dor -dora *mf* demonstrator ‖ *m* hand (*of clock*)

demostrar §61 *tr* to demonstrate

demostrati•vo -va *adj* demonstrative

demudar *tr* to change, alter; disguise, cloak ‖ *ref* to change countenance, color

denegación *f* denial, refusal

denegar §66 *tr* to deny, refuse

denegrecer §22 *tr* to blacken ‖ *ref* to turn black

dengo•so -sa *adj* affected, finicky, overnice; (Col) strutting

dengue *m* affectation, finickiness, overniceness; (Col) strut, swagger

denguear *ref* (Col) to strut, swagger

denigrar *tr* to defame, revile; insult

denominación *f* denomination

denoda•do -da *adj* bold, daring

denostar §61 *tr* to abuse, insult, mistreat

denotar *tr* to denote

densidad *f* density; darkness, confusion

den•so -sa *adj* dense; dark, confused; crowded, thick, close

denta•do -da *adj* toothed; (*sello de correo*) perforated ‖ *m* gear; teeth

dentadura *f* set of teeth; **dentadura artificial** or **postiza** denture

dental *adj & f* dental

dentellada *f* bite; tooth mark

dentellar *intr* (*los dientes*) to chatter

dentellear *tr* to nibble, nibble at

dentera *f* envy; eagerness; **dar dentera** to set the teeth on edge; make the mouth water

dentición *f* teething

dentífri•co -ca *adj* (*pasta, polvos*) tooth ‖ *m* dentifrice

dentista *mf* dentist

dentistería *f* dentistry

dentística *f* (Chile) dentistry

dentro *adv* inside, within; **dentro de** inside,

within; **dentro de poco** shortly; **por dentro** on the inside

denuedo *m* bravery, courage, daring

denuesto *m* abuse, insult, mistreatment

denuncia *f* denunciation; report; proclamation

denunciar *tr* to denounce; report; (*la guerra*) proclaim

deparar *tr* to furnish, provide; offer, present

departamento *m* department; (rr) compartment; (*piso*) apartment; naval district (*in Spain*)

departir *intr* to chat, converse

depauperación *f* impoverishment; exhaustion, weakening

depauperar *tr* to impoverish; exhaust, weaken

dependencia *f* dependence, dependency; branch, branch office; relationship, friendship; accessory; personnel

depender *intr* to depend; **depender de** to depend on; be attached to, belong to

dependienta *f* female employee, clerk

dependiente *adj* dependent; branch ‖ *mf* employee, clerk

deplorable *adj* deplorable

deplorar *tr* to deplore

deponer §54 *tr* to depose; set aside, remove; (*las armas*) lay down ‖ *intr* to depose; (*evacuar el vientre*) have a movement; (CAm, Mex) to vomit

deportación *f* deportation

deporta•do -da *mf* deportee

deportar *tr* to deport

deporte *m* sport; outdoor recreation

deportista *mf* sport fan ‖ *m* sportsman ‖ *f* sportswoman

deporti•vo -va *adj* sport, sports

depositante *mf* depositor

depositar *tr* to deposit; (*la esperanza, la confianza*) put, place; (*el equipaje*) check; (*a una persona en seguro*) commit; store ‖ *ref* to deposit, settle

deposita•rio -ria *mf* trustee; (*de un secreto*) repository ‖ *m* public treasurer

depósito *m* deposit; depot, warehouse; tank, reservoir; (*de libros en una biblioteca*) stack; (mil) depot; **depósito comercial** bonded warehouse; **depósito de agua** reservoir; **depósito de cadáveres** morgue; **depósito de cereales** grain elevator; **depósito de equipajes** (rr) checkroom; **depósito de gasolina** (aut) gas tank; **depósito de locomotoras** roundhouse; **depósito de municiones** munition dump

depravación *f* depravity, depravation

deprava•do -da *adj* depraved

depravar *tr* to deprave ‖ *ref* to become depraved

deprecar §73 *tr* to entreat, implore

depreciación *f* depreciation

depreciar *tr & ref* to depreciate

depresión *f* depression; drop, dip; (*en un muro*) recess

deprimir *tr* to depress; press down; push in; belittle; humiliate ‖ *ref* to be depressed; (*la frente de una persona*) recede

depurar *tr* to purify, cleanse; purge
derecha *f* right hand; right-hand side; (pol) right; **a la derecha** on the right, to the right
derechamente *adv* rightly; straight, direct; properly; wisely
derechazo *m* blow with the right; (box) right
dereche•ro -ra *adj* right, just
derechista *adj* rightist ‖ *mf* rightist, right-winger
dere•cho -cha *adj* right; right-hand; right-handed; straight; upright, standing; (CAm) lucky ‖ *m* right; law; exemption, privilege; road, path; (*de tela, papel, tabla*) right side; **derecho consuetudinario** common law; **derecho de gentes** law of nations, international law; **derecho de subscripción** (*a una nueva emisión de acciones*) (com) right; **derecho de tránsito** or **paso** right of way; **derecho internacional** international law; **derecho penal** criminal law; **derechos** dues, fees, taxes; (*de aduana*) duties; **derechos de almacenaje** storage, cost of storage; **derechos de autor** royalty; **derechos del hombre** rights of man; **derechos de propiedad literaria** or **derechos reservados** copyright; **derechos humanos** human rights; **según derecho** by right, by rights ‖ *f* see **derecha** ‖ **derecho** *adv* straight, direct; rightly
deriva (aer, naut) drift; **ir a la deriva** (naut) to drift, be adrift
derivado *m* by-product
derivar *tr* to derive ‖ *intr & ref* to derive, be derived; (aer, naut) to drift
dermatitis *f* dermatitis
derogar §44 *tr* to abolish, destroy, repeal
derrabar *tr* to dock, cut off the tail of
derrama•do -da *adj* extravagant, lavish
derramamiento *m* pouring, spilling; shedding; spreading; lavishing, wasting
derramar *tr* to pour, spill; (*sangre*) shed; spread, publish abroad; (*dinero*) lavish, waste ‖ *ref* to run over, overflow; spread, scatter; (*una corriente, un río*) open, empty; (*la plumafuente*) leak
derrame *m* pouring, spilling; (*de sangre*) shed, shedding; spread, scattering; lavishing, wasting; overflow; leakage; slope; chamfering; (pathol) discharge, effusion
derrapada *f* or **derrapaje** *f* (aut) skidding
derredor *m* circumference; **al** or **en derredor** around, round about
derrelícto *m* (naut) derelict
derrelínquir §25 *tr* to abandon, forsake
derrenga•do -da *adj* crooked, out of shape; crippled, lame
derrengar §44 or §66 *tr* to bend, make crooked; cripple
derreniego *m* curse
derreti•do -da *adj* madly in love; (*mantequilla*) drawn ‖ *m* concrete
derretimiento *m* thawing, melting; intense love, passion
derretir §50 *tr* to thaw, melt; (*la mantequilla*) draw; (*la hacienda*) squander ‖ *ref* to thaw, melt; fall madly in love; be quite susceptible; be worried, be impatient

derribar *tr* to destroy, tear down, knock down; wreck; (*un árbol*) fell; bring down, shoot down; overthrow; humiliate ‖ *ref* to fall down, tumble down; throw oneself on the ground
derribo *m* demolition, wrecking; (*de un árbol*) felling; overthrow; (*de un avión enemigo*) bringing down; **derribos** debris, rubble
derrocadero *m* rocky precipice
derrocar §73 or §81 *tr* to throw or hurl from a height; ruin, wreck, tear down; bring down, humble, overthrow
derrocha•dor -dora *mf* wastrel, squanderer
derrochar *tr* to waste, squander
derroche *m* wasting, squandering; extravagance
derrota *f* defeat, rout; road, route, way; (*de embarcación*) course
derrotadamente *adv* shabbily, poorly
derrotar *tr* to rout, put to flight; wear out; ruin ‖ *ref* (naut) to drift from the course
derrotero *m* course, route; ship's course
derrotismo *m* defeatism
derrotista *adj & mf* defeatist
derrubiar *tr & ref* to wash away, wear away
derrubio *m* washout
derruir §20 *tr* to tear down, demolish
derrumbadero *m* crag, precipice; hazard, risky business
derrumbamiento *m* headlong plunge; cave-in, collapse; **derrumbamiento de tierra** landslide
derrumbar *tr* to throw headlong ‖ *ref* to plunge headlong; collapse, cave in, crumble
derrumbe *m* precipice; landslide; cave-in
derviche *m* dervish
desabonar *ref* to drop one's subscription
desabono *m* cancellation of subscription; discredit, disparagement
desabor *m* insipidity, tastelessness
desabotonar *tr* to unbutton ‖ *intr* to blossom, bloom
desabri•do -da *adj* insipid, tasteless; gruff, surly; (*tiempo*) unsettled
desabrigar §44 *tr* to uncover, bare ‖ *ref* to bare oneself; undress
desabrir *tr* to give a bad taste to; displease, embitter
desabrochar *tr* to unclasp, unbutton, unfasten ‖ *ref* to unbosom oneself
desacalorar *ref* to cool off
desacatamiento *m* incivility, disrespect
desacatar *tr* to treat disrespectfully
desacato *m* incivility, disrespect, contempt; (*para con las cosas sagradas*) profanation
desacelerar *tr & ref* to decelerate
desacerta•do -da *adj* mistaken, wrong
desacertar §2 *intr* to be mistaken, be wrong
desacierto *m* error, mistake, blunder
desacomoda•do -da *adj* inconvenient; out of work; in straightened circumstances
desacomodar *tr* to inconvenience; discharge, dismiss
desacomodi•do -da *adj* (SAm) rude; impolite
desacomodo *m* discharge, dismissal

desaconseja•do -da *adj* ill-advised

desaconsejar *tr* to dissuade

desacordar §61 *tr* to put out of tune ‖ *ref* to get out of tune; become forgetful

desacorde *adj* out of tune; incongruous

desacostumbra•do -da *adj* unusual

desacostumbrar *tr* to break of a habit

desacreditar *tr* to discredit; disparage

desacuerdo *m* discord, disagreement; error, mistake; unconsciousness; forgetfulness

desadaptación *f* maladjustment

desadeudar *tr* to free of debt ‖ *ref* to get out of debt

desadormecer §22 *tr* to awaken; free of numbness ‖ *ref* to get awake; shake off the numbness

desadorna•do -da *adj* unadorned, plain; bare, uncovered

desadverti•do -da *adj* unnoticed; inattentive

desadvertimiento *m* inadvertence

desafección *f* dislike

desafec•to -ta *adj* adverse, hostile; opposed ‖ *m* dislike

desaferrar *tr* to unfasten, loosen; make (*a person*) change his mind; (*las áncoras*) weigh

desafiar §77 *tr* to challenge, defy, dare; rival, compete with

desafición *f* dislike

desaficionar *tr* to cause to dislike

desafilar *tr* to make dull ‖ *ref* to become dull

desafina•do -da *adj* flat, out of tune

desafío *m* challenge, dare; rivalry, competition

desafora•do -da *adj* colossal, huge; disorderly, outrageous

desafortuna•do -da *adj* unfortunate

desafuero *m* excess, outrage

desagracia•do -da *adj* ungraceful, graceless

desagradable *adj* disagreeable

desagradar *tr & intr* to displease ‖ *ref* to be displeased

desagradeci•do -da *adj* ungrateful

desagradecimiento *m* ungratefulness

desagrado *m* displeasure

desagraviar *tr* to make amends to, indemnify

desagravio *m* amends, indemnification

desagregación *f* disintegration

desagregar §44 *ref* to disintegrate

desaguadero *m* drain, outlet; (*ocasión de continuo gasto*) (fig) drain

desaguar §10 *tr* to drain, empty; squander, waste ‖ *intr* to flow, empty ‖ *ref* to drain, be drained

desagüe *m* drainage, sewerage; drain, outlet

desaguisa•do -da *adj* illegal ‖ *m* offense, outrage, wrong

desahijar *tr* (*las crías del ganado*) to wean ‖ *ref* (*las abejas*) to swarm

desahogadamente *adv* freely; comfortably, easily; impudently

desahoga•do -da *adj* brazen, forward; roomy; in comfortable circumstances

desahogar §44 *tr* to relieve, comfort; (*deseos, pasiones*) give free rein to ‖ *ref* to take it easy, get comfortable; unbosom oneself, open up one's heart; get out of

debt; **desahogarse en** (*denuestos*) to burst forth in

desahogo *m* brazenness; ample room; comfort; outlet, relief; comfortable circumstances

desahuciar *tr* to deprive of hope; evict, oust, dispossess ‖ *ref* to lose all hope

desahucio *m* eviction, ousting, dispossession

desaira•do -da *adj* unattractive, unprepossessing; unsuccessful

desairar *tr* to slight, snub, disregard

desaire *m* slight, snub, disregard; unattractiveness, lack of charm

desajustar *tr* to put out of order ‖ *ref* to get out of order; disagree

desalabanza *f* belittling, disparagement

desalabar *tr* to belittle, disparage

desala•do -da *adj* eager, in a hurry

desalar *tr* to desalt; clip the wings of ‖ *ref* to hasten, rush; **desalarse por** to be eager to

desalentar §2 *tr* to put out of breath; discourage ‖ *ref* to become discouraged

desalforjar *ref* to loosen one's clothing

desaliento *m* discouragement

desalinización *f* desalinization

desaliña•do -da *adj* slovenly, untidy; careless, slipshod

desaliño *m* slovenliness, untidiness; carelessness, neglect

desalma•do -da *adj* cruel, inhuman

desalojar *tr* to oust, evict; (*al enemigo*) to dislodge; (*el camino*) to clear ‖ *intr* to leave, move away, move out

desalquila•do -da *adj* vacant, unrented

desalterar *tr* to calm, quiet

desalumbra•do -da *adj* dazzled, blinded; confused, unsure of oneself

desamable *adj* unlikeable, unlovable

desamar *tr* to dislike, hate, detest

desamarrar *tr* to untie, unfasten; (naut) to unmoor

desamistar *ref* to fall out, become estranged

desamor *m* dislike, coldness; hatred

desamorrar *tr* to make (*a person*) talk

desamparar *tr* to abandon, forsake; give up

desamparo *m* abandonment, desertion; helplessness

desamuebla•do -da *adj* unfurnished

desandar §5 *tr* to retrace, go back over

desandraja•do -da *adj* ragged, in tatters

desangrar *tr* to bleed; drain; (fig) to bleed, impoverish ‖ *ref* to lose a lot of blood

desanimación *f* discouragement, downheartedness

desanima•do -da *adj* discouraged, downhearted; (*reunión*) lifeless, dull

desanimar *tr* to discourage, dishearten ‖ *ref* to become discouraged

desánimo *m* discouragement

desanublar *tr & ref* to clear up, brighten up

desanudar *tr* to untie; disentangle

desapacible *adj* unpleasant, disagreeable

desapadrinar *tr* to disavow; disapprove

desaparecer §22 *intr & ref* to disappear

desapareci•do -da *adj* missing; extinct ‖ **desaparecidos** *mpl* missing persons

desaparecimiento *m* disappearance

desaparejar *tr* to unharness, unhitch; (naut) to unrig

desaparición *f* disappearance; (Ven) death

desapasiona•do -da *adj* dispassionate, impartial

desapego *m* dislike, coolness, indifference

desapercibi•do -da *adj* unprepared; wanting; unnoticed

desapiada•do -da *adj* merciless, pitiless

desaplica•do -da *adj* idle, lazy

desapodera•do -da *adj* headlong, impetuous; violent, wild; excessive

desapoderar *tr* to dispossess; deprive of power ‖ *ref* — **desapoderarse de** to lose possession of, give up possession of

desapolillar *tr* to free of moths ‖ *ref* to expose oneself to the weather

desapreciar *tr* to depreciate

desaprecio *m* depreciation

desaprender *tr* to unlearn

desaprensión *f* composure, nonchalance

desapretar §2 *tr* to slacken, loosen; (typ) to unlock

desaprobación *f* disapproval

desaprobar §61 *tr* & *intr* to disapprove

desapropiar *tr* to divest ‖ *ref* —**desapropiarse de** to divest oneself of

desaprovecha•do -da *adj* unproductive; indifferent, lackadaisical

desaprovechar *tr* to not take advantage of ‖ *intr* to slip back

desarmable *adj* dismountable

desarmador *m* hammer (*of gun*); (Mex) screwdriver

desarmamiento *m* disarmament; arms reduction

desarmar *tr* to disarm; dismount, dismantle, take apart; (*la cólera*) temper, calm ‖ *intr* & *ref* to disarm

desarme *m* disarmament; dismantling, dismounting

desarraigar §44 *tr* to uproot, dig up; expel, drive out

desarregla•do -da *adj* out of order; slovenly, disorderly; intemperate

desarrimo *m* lack of support; stand-offishness

desarrollar *tr* & *intr* to develop; unroll, unfold ‖ *ref* to develop; unroll, unfold; take place

desarrollo *m* development; unrolling, unfolding; **ayuda al desarrollo** developmental aid

desarropar *tr* & *ref* to undress

desarrugar §44 *tr* & *ref* to unwrinkle

desarzonar *tr* to unsaddle, unhorse

desasea•do -da *adj* dirty, unclean, slovenly

desasentar §2 *tr* to remove; displease ‖ *ref* to stand up

desaseo *m* dirtiness, uncleanliness, slovenliness

desasir §7 *tr* to let go, let go of ‖ *ref* to come loose; let go; **desasirse de** to let go of; give up, get free of

desasosegar §66 *tr* to disquiet, worry, disturb

desasosiego *m* disquiet, worry

desastra•do -da *adj* disastrous; unfortunate, wretched; ragged, shabby

desastre *m* disaster; **ir al desastre** to go to rack and ruin

desastro•so -sa *adj* disastrous

desatacar §73 *tr* to unbuckle, untie

desatar *tr* to untie, undo, unfasten; solve, unravel ‖ *ref* to come loose; free oneself; (*la tempestad*) break loose; forget oneself, go too far; **desatarse en** (*denuestos*) to burst forth in

desatascar §73 *tr* to pull out of the mud; (*un conducto obstruído*) unclog; (*a una persona de un apuro*) extricate

desataviar §77 *tr* to disarray, undress

desatavío *m* disarray, undress, slovenliness

desate *m* (*de palabras*) flood; **desate del vientre** loose bowels

desatención *f* inattention; discourtesy, disrespect

desatender §51 *tr* to slight, disregard, pay no attention to

desatenta•do -da *adj* wild, disorderly, extreme

desaten•to -ta *adj* inattentive; discourteous, disrespectful

desatina•do -da *adj* wild, disorderly; foolish, nonsensical ‖ *mf* fool

desatinar *tr* to bewilder, confuse ‖ *intr* to talk nonsense, act foolishly; lose one's bearings

desatino *m* folly, nonsense; awkwardness, loss of touch

desatolondrar *tr* to bring to ‖ *ref* to come to one's senses

desatollar *tr* to pull out of the mud

desatornillador *m* screwdriver

desatornillar *tr* to unscrew

desatraillar §4 *tr* to unleash

desatrampar *tr* to unclog

desatrancar §73 *tr* to unbar, unbolt; unclog

desatufar *ref* to get out of the close air; cool off, quiet down

desautoriza•do -da *adj* unauthorized

desavenencia *f* disagreement, discord

desavenir §79 *tr* to cause disagreement among ‖ *ref* to disagree; **desavenirse con** to differ with, disagree with

desaventura *f* misfortune

desaviar §77 *tr* to mislead, lead astray

desavisa•do -da *adj* unadvised; ill-advised; thoughtless, careless

desayuna•do -da *adj* — **estar desayunado** to have had breakfast

desayunar *intr* to breakfast ‖ *ref* to breakfast; **desayunarse con** to have breakfast on; **desayunarse de** to get the first news of

desayuno *m* breakfast

desazón *f* insipidity, tastelessness; annoyance, displeasure; discomfort

desazonar *tr* to make tasteless; annoy, displease ‖ *ref* to feel ill

desbancar §73 *tr* to win the bank from; cut out, to supplant

desbandada *f* — **a la desbandada** helter-skelter, in confusion

desbandar *ref* to run away; disband; desert

desbarajustar *tr* to put out of order ‖ *ref* to get out of order, break down

desbarata·do -da *adj* debauched, corrupt ‖ *mf* libertine

desbaratar *tr* to destroy, spoil, ruin; squander, waste; (mil) to rout, throw into confusion ‖ *intr* to talk nonsense ‖ *ref* to be unbalanced

desbarrancadero *m* precipice

desbastar *tr* to smooth off; waste, weaken; (*a una persona inculta*) polish ‖ *ref* to become polished

desbautizar §60 *ref* to lose one's temper

desbeber *intr* (coll) to urinate

desbloquear *tr* to relieve the blockade of; (*crédito*) to unfreeze

desboca·do -da *adj* (*pieza de artillería*) wide-mouthed; (*herramienta*) nicked; (*caballo*) runaway; (*persona*) foul-mouthed

desbocar §73 *tr* to break the mouth of, break the spout of ‖ *intr* (*un río*) to empty; (*una calle*) run, open, end ‖ *ref* (*un caballo*) to run away, break loose; curse, swear

desbordamiento *m* overflow

desbordar *tr* to overwhelm ‖ *intr* & *ref* to overflow

desbozalar *tr* to unmuzzle

desbravar *tr* to tame, break in ‖ *intr* & *ref* to abate, moderate; cool off, calm down

desbrozar §60 *tr* to clear of underbrush, clear of rubbish

desbulla *f* oyster shell

desbulla·dor -dora *mf* oyster opener ‖ *m* oyster fork

desbullar *tr* (*la ostra*) to open

descabal *adj* incomplete, imperfect

descabalgar §44 *intr* to dismount, alight from a horse

descabella·do -da *adj* disheveled; rash, wild

descabellar *tr* to muss, dishevel

descabeza·do -da *adj* crazy, rash, wild

descabezar §60 *tr* to behead; (*un árbol*) top; (*una dificultad*) get the best off; **descabezar el sueño** to doze, snooze ‖ *intr* to border ‖ *ref* to rack one's brains

descabullir §13 *ref* to sneak out, slip away; refuse to face the facts

descachalandra·do -da *adj* untidy; tattered

descacharra·do -da *adj* (CAm) dirty, slovenly, ragged

descaecer §22 *intr* to decline, lose ground

descaecimiento *m* weakness; depression, despondency

descalabazar §60 *ref* to rack one's brain

descalabra·do -da *adj* banged on the head; **salir descalabrado** to come out the loser, be worsted

descalabrar *tr* to bang on the head; knock down ‖ *ref* to bang one's head

descalabro *m* misfortune, setback, loss

descalcificar §73 *tr* to decalcify

descalificar §73 *tr* to disqualify

descalzar §60 *tr* (*las botas, los guantes*) to take off; (*a una persona*) take the shoes or stockings off; undermine ‖ *ref* to take one's shoes or stockings off; take one's gloves

off; (*las botas, los guantes*) take off; (*el caballo*) lose a shoe

descal·zo -za *adj* barefooted; seedy, down at the heel

descamar *ref* to scale, scale off

descaminadamente *adv* off the road, on the wrong track

descaminar *tr* to mislead, lead astray ‖ *ref* to get lost; run off the road

descamino *m* going astray; leading astray; nonsense; contraband, smuggled goods

descamisa·do -da *adj* shirtless, ragged ‖ *m* wretch, ragamuffin

descampa·do -da *adj* free, open ‖ *m* open country

descansadero *m* resting place, stopping place

descansa·do -da *adj* rested, refreshed; calm, restful

descansar *tr* to rest, relieve; (*la cabeza, el brazo*) rest, lean ‖ *intr* to rest; lean; not worry; (*yacer en el sepulcro*) rest; **descansar en** to trust in

descanso *m* rest; peace, quiet; (*de la escalera*) landing; (theat) intermission; (Chile) toilet

descantillar *tr* to chip off; deduct

descañonar *tr* to pluck; shave against the grain; gyp

descapiruzar §60 *tr* (Col) to muss, rumple, crumple

descapotable *adj* & *m* (aut) convertible

descara·do -da *adj* barefaced, brazen, saucy

descarar *ref* to be impudent; **descararse a** to have the nerve to

descarga *f* unloading; (*de un arma de fuego*) discharge; (com) discount; (elec) discharge; **descarga de aduana** customhouse clearance

descargar §44 *tr* to unload; (*de una deuda u obligación*) free; (*un arma de fuego*) discharge; (*un golpe*) strike, deal; (elec) to discharge ‖ *intr* to unload; (*un río*) empty; (*una calle, paseo*) open; (*una nube en lluvia*) burst ‖ *ref* to unburden oneself; resign; **descargarse con** or **en uno de algo** to unload something on someone; **descargarse de** to get rid of; resign from; (*una imputación, un cargo*) clear oneself of

descargo *m* unloading; (*de una obligación*) discharge; (*del cargo que se hace a uno*) release, acquittal; receipt

descargue *m* unloading

descariño *m* coolness, indifference

descarnadamente *adv* right off the shoulder, bluntly

descarnar *tr* to remove the flesh from; chip; wear away; detach from earthly matters ‖ *ref* to lose flesh

descaro *m* brazenness, effrontery

descarriar §77 *tr* to mislead, lead astray ‖ *ref* to go wrong, go astray

descarrilamiento *m* derailment

descarrilar *intr* to jump the track; wander from the point ‖ *ref* to jump the track

descartable *adj* disposable

descartar *tr* to cast aside, reject; discard ‖ *ref* to shirk, evade; **descartarse de** (*un compromiso*) to shirk, evade

descarte *m* casting aside, rejection; discarding; (*cartas desechadas*) discard; shirking, evasion

descasar *tr* to divorce; disturb, disarrange

descascar §73 *tr* to husk, shell, peel ‖ *ref* to break to pieces; jabber, talk too much

descascarar *tr* to shell, peel ‖ *ref* to shell off, peel off

descascarillar *tr* & *ref* to shell, peel

descasta•do -da *adj* ungrateful, ungrateful to one's family

descaudala•do -da *adj* ruined, penniless

descendencia *f* descent

descendente *adj* descendent, descending; (*tren*) down

descender §51 *tr* to bring down, lower; (*la escalera*) descend, go down ‖ *intr* to descend, go down; flow, run; decline

descendiente *mf* descendant

descenso *m* descent; (*de temperatura*) drop; decline

descentralizar §60 *tr* to decentralize

desceñi•do -da *adj* loose-fitting, loose

descepar *tr* to pull up by the roots; extirpate, exterminate

descerebrar *tr* to brain

descerraja•do -da *adj* corrupt, evil, wicked

desciframiento *m* deciphering, decoding; resolving

descifrar *tr* to decipher, decode, figure out

desclasificar §73 *tr* to disqualify

descocer §16 *tr* to digest

descoco *m* impudence, insolence

descocholla•do -da *adj* (Chile) ragged

descolar *tr* to dock, crop; (*a un empleado*) (CAm) to discharge, fire; (Mex) to slight, snub

descolgar §63 *tr* to unhook; take down, lower; (*el auricular*) pick up ‖ *ref* to come down, come off; to show up suddenly; **descolgarse con** to blurt out

descolón *m* (Mex) slight, snub

descolorar *tr* & *ref* to discolor, fade

descolori•do -da *adj* faded, off color

descollante *adj* prominent, outstanding; chief, main

descollar §61 *intr* to tower, stand out; (fig) to excel, stand out

descomedi•do -da *adj* immoderate, excessive; rude, discourteous

descomedir §50 *ref* to be rude, be discourteous

descomer *intr* to have a bowel movement

descómo•do -da *adj* inconvenient

descompasa•do -da *adj* extreme, excessive

descompletar *tr* to break (*a set or series*)

descomponer §54 *tr* to decompose; disturb, disorganize; put out of order; set at odds ‖ *ref* to decompose; (*una persona, la salud de una persona*) (*el tiempo*) change for the worse; (*el rostro*) become distorted; (*un aparato*) get out of order; to lose one's temper; **descomponerse con** to get angry with

descomposición *f* decomposition; disorder, disorganization; discord

descompostura *f* decomposition; disorder, untidiness; brazenness

descompresión *f* decompression

descompues•to -ta *adj* out of order; brazen, discourteous; irritated; drunk

descomulgar §44 *tr* to excommunicate

descomunal *adj* huge, colossal, enormous, extraordinary; (coll) humongous

desconcerta•do -da *adj* out of order; disconcerted, baffled, bewildered; slovenly; unbridled

desconcertar §2 *tr* to put out of order; disturb, upset; (*un hueso*) dislocate; disconcert, bewilder

desconcierto *m* disrepair; disorder; mismanagement; confusion; discomfiture; disagreement; lack of restraint; loose bowels

desconchabar *tr* to dislocate ‖ *ref* to become dislocated; disagree, fall out

desconchado *m* scaly part of wall; (*en la porcelana*) chip

desconchar *tr* & *ref* to chip, chip off; scale off

desconectar *tr* to detach; disconnect

desconfia•do -da *adj* distrustful, suspicious

desconfianza *f* distrust

desconfiar §77 *intr* to lose confidence; **desconfiar de** to lose confidence in, to distrust

desconformar *intr* to dissent, disagree ‖ *ref* to not go well together

descongelación *f* thaw, thawing out

descongelador *m* defroster

descongelar *tr* to melt; defrost; (com) to unfreeze

descongestión *f* decongestion; freeing up

descongestionar *tr* to decongest; free up

desconocer §22 *tr* to not know; disavow, disown; not recognize; slight, ignore; not see ‖ *ref* to be unknown; be quite changed, be unrecognizable

desconocidamente *adv* unknowingly

desconoci•do -da *adj* unknown; strange, unfamiliar; ungrateful ‖ *mf* unknown, unknown person

desconsentir §68 *tr* to not consent to

desconsidera•do -da *adj* ill-considered; inconsiderate

desconsola•do -da *adj* disconsolate, downhearted; (*estómago*) weak

desconsuelo *m* disconsolateness, grief; upset stomach

descontaminación *f* decontamination; **descontaminación de radiactividad** radioactive decontamination

descontar §61 *tr* to discount; deduct; take for granted; **dar por descontado que** to take for granted that

descontentadi•zo -za *adj* hard to please

desconten•to -ta *adj* & *m* discontent

descontinuar §21 *tr* to discontinue

descontrola•do -da *adj* uncontrolled; deregulated

descontrolar *tr* (com) deregulate; decontrol

desconvenar *tr* to call off

desconvenir §79 *intr* to disagree; not go together, not match; not be suitable ‖ *ref* to disagree

desconvidar *tr* to cancel an invitation to; (*lo prometido*) take back

descopar *tr* to top (*a tree*)

descorazonar *tr* to discourage

descorchar *tr* to remove the bark from; (*una botella*) uncork; break into

descornar §61 *tr* to dehorn ‖ *ref* to rack one's brains

descorrer *tr* to run back over; (*una cortina, un cerrojo*) draw ‖ *intr & ref* to flow, run off

descortés *adj* discourteous, impolite

descortesía *f* discourtesy, impoliteness

descortezar §60 *tr* to strip the bark from; take the crust off; polish ‖ *ref* to become polished

descoser *tr* to unstitch, rip ‖ *ref* to loose one's tongue; (coll) to break wind

descosi•do -da *adj* disorderly, wild; indiscreet; desultory ‖ *m* wild man; rip, open seam

descote *m* low neck

descoyuntar *tr* to dislocate; bore, annoy ‖ *ref* (*p.ej., el brazo*) to throw out of joint

descrédito *m* discredit

descreer §43 *tr* to disbelieve; discredit ‖ *intr* to disbelieve

descreí•do -da *adj* disbelieving, unbelieving ‖ *mf* disbeliever, unbeliever

descriar §77 *ref* to spoil; waste away

describir §83 to describe

descripción *f* description

descripti•vo -va *adj* descriptive

descto. *abbr* **descuento**

descuadrar *intr* to disagree; **descuadrar con** (Mex) to displease

descuajar *tr* to liquefy, dissolve; uproot; discourage ‖ *ref* to liquefy; drudge

descuartizar §60 *tr* to tear to pieces; quarter

descubierta *f* open pie; inspection; reconnoitering; (naut) scanning the horizon; **a la descubierta** openly; in the open; reconnoitering

descubiertamente *adv* clearly, openly

descubier•to -ta *adj* bareheaded; (*campo*) bare, barren; (*expuesto a reconvenciones*) under fire ‖ *m* deficiency, shortage; exposition of the Holy Sacrament; **al descubierto** in the open; unprotected; (*sin tener disponibles las acciones que se venden*) short, e.g., **vender al descubierto** to sell short ‖ *f* see **descubierta**

descubri•dor -dora *mf* discoverer ‖ *m* (mil) scout

descubrimiento *m* discovery

descubrir §83 *tr* to discover; uncover, lay open, reveal; invent; (*p.ej., una estatua*) unveil ‖ *ref* to take off one's hat, uncover; be discovered; open one's heart

descuello *m* excellence, superiority; great height; haughtiness

descuento *m* discount; deduction, rebate

descuerar *tr* (Chile) to skin, flay; (Chile) to discredit, flay

descuerno *m* slight, snub

descuida•do -da *adj* careless, negligent; slovenly, dirty; off guard

descuidar *tr* to overlook, neglect; divert, distract, relieve ‖ *ref* to be careless, not bother; be diverted

descuide•ro -ra *mf* sneak thief

descuido *m* carelessness, negligence, neglect; slip, mistake, blunder; oversight; **al descuido** with studied carelessness; **en un descuido** when least expected

descuita•do -da *adj* carefree

deschavetar *intr* to get rattled; go mad; flip one's lid

desde *prep* since, from; after; **desde ahora** from now on; **desde entonces** since then, ever since; **desde hace** for, e.g., **estoy aquí desde hace cinco días** I've been here for five days; **desde luego** at once; of course; **desde que** since

desdecir §24 (*impv sg* **-dice**) *intr* to slip back; be out of harmony ‖ *ref* — **desdecirse de** to take back, retract

desdén *m* scorn, disdain; **al desdén** with studied neglect

desdenta•do -da *adj* toothless

desdeñar *tr* to scorn, disdain ‖ *ref* to be disdainful; **desdeñarse de** to loathe, despise; not deign to

desdeño•so -sa *adj* scornful, disdainful

desdicha *f* misfortune; indigence

desdicha•do -da *adj* unfortunate, unlucky; poor, wretched; backward, timid

desdinerar *tr* to impoverish

desdoblar *tr & intr* to unfold, spread open; split, divide

desdorar *tr* to remove the gold or gilt from; tarnish, sully; disparage

desdoro *m* tarnish, blemish, blot; disparagement

deseable *adj* desirable

desear *tr* to desire, wish

desecar §73 *tr & ref* to dry; drain

desechable *adj* disposable

desechar *tr* to discard, throw out, cast aside; underrate; blame, censure; (*la llave de una puerta*) turn

desecho *m* remainder; offal, rubbish; castoff; scorn, contempt; short cut; **desecho de hierro** scrap iron

desegregación *f* desegregation

desellar *tr* to unseal

desembalaje *m* unpacking

desembalar *tr* to unpack

desembarazar §60 *tr* to free, clear, empty, open ‖ *ref* to free oneself; be cleared, emptied; **desembarazarse de** to get rid of

desembarazo *m* naturalness, lack of restraint; delivery, childbirth; **con desembarazo** naturally, readily

desembarcadero *m* wharf, pier, landing

desembarcar §73 *tr* to unload, debark, disembark ‖ *intr* to land, debark, disembark; (*de un carruaje*) get out, alight; (*la escalera al plano bajo*) end ‖ *ref* to land, debark, disembark

desembarco *m* landing, debarkation, disembarkation; (*de la escalera*) landing

desembarque *m* unloading, debarkation, disembarkation

desembocadura *f* (*de una calle*) opening, outlet; (*de un río*) mouth

desembocar §73 *intr* (*una calle*) open, to end; (*un río*) flow, empty

desembolsar *tr* to disburse, pay out

desembolso *m* disbursement, payment

desembragar §44 *tr* (*el motor*) to disengage ‖ *intr* to throw the clutch out

desembrague *m* disengagement, clutch release

desembravecer §22 *tr* to tame; calm, quiet, pacify

desembriagar §44 *tr & ref* to sober up

desembrollar *tr* to untangle, unravel

desemejante *adj* — **desemejante de** dissimilar from or to, unlike; **desemejantes** dissimilar, unlike

desemejar *tr* to change, disfigure ‖ *intr* to be different, not look alike

desempacar §73 *tr* to unpack, unwrap ‖ *ref* to cool off, calm down

desempalagar §44 *tr* to rid of nausea ‖ *ref* to get rid of nausea

desempañar *tr* (*el vidrio*) to wipe the steam or smear from; take the diaper off

desempapelar *tr* to unwrap; (*una pared, una habitación*) scrape the wallpaper from

desempaquetar *tr* to unpack; unwrap

desempatar *tr* to break the tie between; (*los votos*) break the tie in

desempate *m* breaking a tie

desempedrar §2 *tr* to remove the paving stones from; (*un sitio empedrado*) pound; **ir desempedrando la calle** to dash down the street

desempeñar *tr* (*un papel*) to play (*a rôle*); (*un cargo*) fill, perform; (*a uno de un empeño*) disengage; (*un deber*) discharge; free of debt; take out of hock ‖ *ref* to get out of a jam; get out of debt

desempeño *m* acting, performance; disengagement; (*de un deber*) discharge; payment of a debt; taking out of hock

desempernar *tr* to unbolt

desemplea·do -da *adj & mf* unemployed

desempleo *m* unemployment; **desempleo en masa** mass unemployment

desempolvar *tr* to dust; renew, take up again ‖ *ref* to brush up

desempolvorar *tr* to dust, dust off

desenamorar *tr* to alienate; *ref* to grow apart; **desenamorarse de** to get fed up with

desencadenar *tr* to unchain, unleash ‖ *ref* to break loose

desencajar *tr* to dislocate; disconnect ‖ *ref* to get out of joint; (*el rostro*) be contorted

desencaminar *tr* to lead astray, mislead

desencantamiento *m* disenchantment, disillusion

desencantar *tr* to disenchant, disillusion

desencantarar *tr* (*nombres o números*) to draw; (*un nombre o nombres*) exclude from balloting

desencanto *m* disenchantment, disillusion

desencarecer §22 *tr* to lower the price of ‖ *intr & ref* to come down in price

desencerrar §2 *tr* to release, set free; disclose, reveal

desencoger §17 *tr* to unfold, spread out ‖ *ref* to relax, shake off one's timidity

desencolar *tr* to unglue ‖ *ref* to become unglued

desenconar *tr* to take the soreness out of; calm down

desenchufar *tr* to unplug, disconnect

desendiosar *tr* to bring down a peg

desenfadaderas *fpl* — **tener buenas desenfadaderas** to be resourceful

desenfada·do -da *adj* free, easy, unconstrained

desenfado *m* ease, naturalness; relaxation, calmness

desenfoca·do -da *adj* out of focus

desenfrena·do -da *adj* unbridled, wanton, licentious

desenfrenar *tr* to unbridle ‖ *ref* to yield to temptation; fly into a passion; (*la tempestad, el viento*) break loose

desenfreno *m* unruliness, wantonness, licentiousness

desenfundar *tr* to take out of its sheath, bag, pillowcase, etc.

desenganchar *tr* to unhook, uncouple, unfasten, disengage; to unhitch

desenganche *m* unhooking, disengaging; unhitching

desengañar *tr* to disabuse, undeceive; disillusion; disappoint

desengaño *m* disabusing; disillusionment; disappointment; plain fact, plain truth

desengrana·do -da *adj* out of gear

desengranar *tr* to unmesh; disengage, throw out of gear

desengraso *m* (Chile) dessert

desenlace *m* outcome, result; (*de un drama, novela, etc.*) dénouement

desenlazar §60 *tr* to untie; solve; (*el nudo de un drama*) unravel

desenmarañar *tr* to disentangle; (*una cosa obscura*) unravel

desenmascarar *tr* to unmask ‖ *ref* to take one's mask off

desenojar *tr* to appease, free of anger ‖ *ref* to calm down; be amused

desenredar *tr* to disentangle; clear up ‖ *ref* to extricate oneself

desenredo *m* disentanglement; (*de un drama, novela, etc.*) dénouement

desenrollar *tr* to unroll, unwind, unreel

desensartar *tr* to unstring, unthread

desensillar *tr* to unsaddle (*a horse*)

desentablar *tr* to disrupt; break off (*a bargain, friendship, etc.*)

desentender §51 *ref* — **desentenderse de** to take no part in, not participate in; affect ignorance of, pretend to be unaware of

desenterrar §2 *tr* to dig up; disinter; (fig) to unearth, dig up; (fig) to recall to mind

desentona·do -da *adj* out of tune, flat

desentonar tr to humble, bring down a peg ‖ intr to be out of tune; be out of harmony ‖ ref to talk loud and disrespectfully

desentono m dissonance, false note; loud tone of voice

desentornillar tr to unscrew

desentrampar ref to get out of debt

desentrañar tr to disembowel; figure out, unravel ‖ ref to give away all that one has

desentrena·do -da adj out of training

desentronizar §60 tr to dethrone; strip of influence

desentumecer §22 tr to relieve of numbness ‖ ref to be relieved of numbness

desenvainar tr to unsheathe; (las uñas el animal) show, stretch out; bare, uncover

desenvoltura f naturalness, ease of manner, offhandedness; fluency; lewdness, boldness (chiefly in women)

desenvolver §47 & §83 tr to unfold, unroll, unwrap; unwind; unravel, clear up; develop ‖ ref to unroll; unwind; develop, evolve; extricate oneself; be forward

desenvuel·to -ta adj free and easy, offhand; fluent; brazen, bold, lewd

deseo m desire, wish

deseo·so -sa adj desirous, anxious

desequilibra·do -da adj unbalanced

desequilibrar tr to unbalance ‖ ref to become unbalanced

desequilibrio m disequilibrium, imbalance; derangement, mental instability

deserción f desertion

desertar tr & intr to desert

desertor m deserter

deservicio m disservice

desesperación f despair; **ser una desesperación** to be unbearable

desespera·do -da adj despairing, desperate ‖ mf desperate person

desesperanza f hopelessness

desesperanza·do -da adj hopeless

desesperanzar §60 tr to discourage ‖ ref to lose hope

desesperar tr to drive to despair; exasperate ‖ intr to lose hope; be exasperated ‖ ref to be desperate, lose all hope

desestancar §73 tr to open up, unclog; make free of duty; open the market to

desestimar tr to hold in low regard; refuse, reject

deséxito m failure

desfachata·do -da adj brazen, impudent

desfachatez f brazenness, impudence

desfalcar §73 tr & intr to embezzle

desfalco m embezzlement

desfallecer §22 tr to weaken ‖ intr to grow weak; faint, faint away; lose courage

desfalleci·do -da adj weak; faint

desfallecimiento m weakness; fainting; discouragement

desfavorable adj unfavorable

desfigurar tr to disfigure; distort, misrepresent; disguise; change, alter ‖ ref to look different

desfiladero m defile, pass

desfilar intr to defile, parade, file by

desfile m review, parade

desflorar tr to deflower; mention in passing

desfogar §44 tr (un horno) to vent; (la cal) slake; (una pasión) give free rein to ‖ intr (una tempestad) to break into rain and wind ‖ ref to give vent to one's anger

desfondar tr to stave in; (una nave) bilge; (agr) to trench-plow

desforestar tr to deforest

desgaire m slovenliness; disdain, scorn; **al desgaire** scornfully; carelessly, with affected carelessness

desgajar tr to tear off; split off ‖ ref to come off, come loose; arise, originate; separate, break away

desgana f lack of appetite; indifference; boredom; **a desgana** unwillingly, reluctantly

desgarba·do -da adj ungainly, uncouth

desgarrar tr to tear, rend; (la flema) cough up ‖ ref to tear oneself away

desgarro m tear, rent; brazenness, effrontery; boasting, bragging; (Chile, Col) phlegm, mucus

desgasta·do -da adj worn (out); eroded; (llanta) treadless; (tela) threadbare

desgastar tr to wear away, wear down; to weaken, spoil ‖ ref to wear away; grow weak, decline

desgaste m wear, wearing away

desgoberna·do -da adj ungovernable, uncontrollable

desgobernar §2 tr to misgovern; (un hueso) dislocate ‖ intr (naut) to steer poorly ‖ ref to twist and turn in dancing

desgobierno m misgovernment; dislocation

desgonzar §60 tr to unhinge; disconnect

desgracia f misfortune; (acontecimiento adverso) mishap; (pérdida de favor) disfavor, disgrace; (aspereza en el trato) gruffness; (falta de gracia) lack of charm; **correr con desgracia** to have no luck; **por desgracia** unfortunately

desgracia·do -da adj unfortunate; unattractive, unpleasant; disagreeable ‖ mf wretch, unfortunate

desgraciar tr to displease; spoil ‖ ref to spoil; fail; fall out, disagree

desgranar tr (el maíz) to shell; (un racimo) to pick the grapes from ‖ ref (piezas ensartadas) to come loose

desgreñar tr to dishevel ‖ ref to get disheveled; pull each other's hair

deshabita·do -da adj unoccupied

deshabituar §21 tr to break of a habit

deshacer §39 tr to undo; untie; take apart; wear away, consume, destroy; melt; put to flight, rout; (un tratado o negocio) violate ‖ ref to get out of order; vanish, disappear; **deshacerse de** to get rid of; **deshacerse en** (cumplidos) to lavish; (lágrimas) burst into; **deshacerse por** to strive hard to

desharrapa·do -da adj ragged, in rags

deshebillar tr to unbuckle

deshebrar tr to unravel, unthread

deshecha f sham, pretense; dismissal; **hacer la deshecha** to feign, pretend; (Mex) to pretend lack of interest

deshelar §2 *tr* to thaw, melt; defrost; (aer) to deice ‖ *intr* to thaw, melt
deshereda•do -da *adj* disinherited; underprivileged
desheredar *tr* to disinherit ‖ *ref* to be a disgrace to one's family
desherrar §2 *tr* to unchain, unshackle; (*a una caballería*) unshoe
desherrumbrar *tr* to remove the rust from
deshidratar *tr* to dehydrate
deshielo *m* thaw; defrosting; détente
deshilachar *ref* to fray
deshila•do -da *adj* in a file; **a la deshilada** in single file; secretly ‖ *m* openwork, drawn work
deshilar *tr* to unweave; (*reducir a hilos*) shred ‖ *ref* to fray; get thin
deshilvana•do -da *adj* disconnected, desultory
deshincar §73 *tr* to pull up, pull out
deshinchar *tr* to deflate; (*la cólera*) give vent to ‖ *ref* (*un tumor*) to go down; (*una persona orgullosa*) become deflated
deshojar *tr* to strip of leaves; tear the pages out of ‖ *ref* to lose the leaves
deshollejar *tr* (*la uva*) to peel, skin; (*las habichuelas*) shell
deshollina•dor -dora *mf* chimney sweep; curious observer ‖ *m* long-handled brush or broom
deshones•to -ta *adj* immodest, indecent; improper
deshonor *m* dishonor; disgrace
deshonorar *tr* to dishonor; degrade; disfigure
deshonra *f* dishonor; disrespect; **tener a deshonra** to consider improper
deshonrabue•nos *mf* (*pl* **-nos**) slanderer; (coll) black sheep
deshonrar *tr* to disgrace; (*a una mujer*) seduce; insult
deshonro•so -sa *adj* disgraceful, improper, discreditable
deshora *f* wrong time; **a deshora** at the wrong time, inopportunely; suddenly, unexpectedly
deshuesar *tr* (*la carne de un animal*) to bone; (*la fruta*) stone, take the pits out of
deshumedecer §22 *tr* to dehumidify
desidia *f* laziness, indolence
desidio•so -sa *adj* lazy, indolent ‖ *mf* lazy person
desier•to -ta *adj* desert; deserted ‖ *m* desert; wilderness
designar *tr* to designate; (*un trabajo*) plan
designio *m* design, plan, scheme
desigual *adj* unequal; unlike; rough, uneven; difficult; inconstant
desigualar *tr* to make unequal ‖ *ref* to become unequal; (*aventajarse*) get ahead
desigualdad *f* inequality; roughness, unevenness
desilusión *f* disillusionment; disappointment
desilusionar *tr* to disillusion; disappoint ‖ *ref* to become disillusioned; be disappointed
desimanar or **desimantar** *tr* to demagnetize
desimpresionar *tr* to undeceive

desinclina•do -da *adj* disinclined
desinencia *f* (gram) termination, ending
desinfectante *adj* & *m* disinfectant
desinfectar or **desinficionar** *tr* to disinfect
desinflación *f* deflation
desinflamar *tr* to take the soreness out of
desinflar *tr* to deflate; let the air out of; (*a una persona*) deflate
desinhibición *f* loss of inhibitions
desinsectación *f* insect control
desinsectar *intr* to exterminate insects
desintegración *f* disintegration
desintegrar *tr* & *ref* to disintegrate
desinterés *m* disinterestedness
desinteresa•do -da *adj* (*imparcial*) disinterested; (*poco interesado*) uninterested
desinteresar *ref* to lose interest
desintonizar §60 *tr* (rad) to tune out; (rad) to put out of tune
desintoxicación *f* detoxification; sobering (up)
desintoxicar *tr* to detoxify; sober up
desistir *intr* to desist
desjarretar *tr* to hamstring; bleed to excess
desjuicia•do -da *adj* lacking judgment, senseless
desjuntar *tr* to disjoin, separate
deslabonar *tr* to unlink; disconnect ‖ *ref* to come loose; withdraw
deslastrar *tr* to unballast
deslava•do -da *adj* faded, colorless; barefaced ‖ *mf* barefaced person
deslavar *tr* to wash superficially; fade, take the life out of
desleal *adj* disloyal; unfair
deslealtad *f* disloyalty
deslechar *tr* (Col) to milk
desleír §58 *tr* to dissolve; dilute; (*los colores, la pintura*) thin; (*sus pensamientos*) express too diffusely ‖ *ref* to dissolve; become diluted
deslengua•do -da *adj* foul-mouthed, shameless
desliar §77 *tr* to untie, undo; unravel ‖ *ref* to come untied
desligar §44 *tr* to untie, unbind; disentangle; excuse ‖ *ref* to come untied, come loose
deslindar *tr* to mark the boundaries of; distinguish; define, explain
des•liz *m* (*pl* **-lices**) sliding; (*superficie lisa*) slide; slip, blunder; peccadillo, indiscretion
deslizade•ro -ra *adj* slippery ‖ *m* slippery place; launching way
deslizadi•zo -za *adj* slippery
deslizador *m* (aer) glider
deslizar §60 *tr* to slide; (*decir por descuido*) let slip ‖ *intr* to slide; slip; glide ‖ *ref* to slide; slip; glide; slip away, sneak away; (*un reparo*) slip out; (*caer en una flaqueza*) slide back, backslide
deslomar *tr* to break or strain the back of ‖ *ref* to break or strain one's back; **no deslomarse** to not strain oneself
deslucí•do -da *adj* quiet, lackluster; dull, undistinguished
deslucir §45 *tr* to tarnish; deprive of charm, deprive of distinction; discredit

deslumbramiento *m* dazzle, glare; bewilderment, confusion

deslumbrante *adj* dazzling; bewildering, confusing

deslumbrar *tr* to dazzle; bewilder, confuse

deslustra•do -da *adj* dull, flat, dingy; (*vidrio*) ground, frosted

deslustrar *tr* to tarnish; dull, dim; (*el vidrio*) frost; discredit ‖ *ref* to tarnish

deslustre *m* tarnishing; dulling, dimming; discredit; (*del vidrio*) frosting

deslustro•so -sa *adj* ugly, unbecoming

desmadejar *tr* to enervate, weaken

desmagnetizar §60 *tr* to demagnetize

desmán *m* excess, misconduct; misfortune, mishap

desmanchar *tr* (Chile) to clean of spots

desmanda•do -da *adj* disobedient, unruly

desmandar *tr* to cancel, countermand ‖ *ref* to misbehave; go away, keep apart; get out of control

desmanear *tr* to unfetter, unshackle

desmantela•do -do *adj* dilapidated

desmantelar *tr* to dismantle; (naut) to unmast; (naut) to unrig

desmaña *f* awkwardness, clumsiness

desmaña•do -da *adj* awkward, clumsy

desmaquillar *tr & ref* to take makeup off

desmaya•do -da *adj* faint, languid, weak; unconscious; (*color*) dull

desmayar *tr* to depress, discourage ‖ *intr* to lose heart, be discouraged; falter ‖ *ref* to faint

desmayo *m* depression, discouragement; faint, fainting fit; weeping willow

desmedi•do -da *adj* excessive; boundless, limitless

desmedir §50 *ref* to go too far, be impudent

desmedra•do -da *adj* weak, run-down

desmedrar *tr* to impair ‖ *intr & ref* to decline, deteriorate

desmejorar *tr* to impair, spoil ‖ *intr & ref* to decline, go into a decline

desmelenar *tr* to muss, dishevel, rumple

desmembrar §2 *tr* to dismember

desmemoria *f* forgetfulness

desmemoria•do -da *adj* forgetful

desmemoriar *ref* to become forgetful

desmentida *f* contradiction; **dar una desmentida a** to give the lie to

desmentir §68 *tr* to belie, give the lie to; conceal ‖ *intr* to be out of line ‖ *ref* to contradict oneself

desmenudear *tr & intr* (Col) to sell at retail

desmenuzar §60 *tr* to crumble; chop up; examine in detail; criticize harshly ‖ *ref* to crumb, crumble

desmerece•dor -dora *adj* unworthy

desmerecer §22 *tr* to be unworthy of ‖ *intr* to decline in value; **desmerecer de** to compare unfavorably with

desmesura *f* excess, lack of restraint

desmesura•do -da *adj* excessive, disproportionate; insolent ‖ *mf* insolent person

desmigajar *tr & ref* to crumble, break up

desmigar §44 *tr & ref* to crumble, crumb

desmilitarizar §60 *tr* to demilitarize; **zona desmilitarizada** demilitarized zone

desmirria•do -da *adj* exhausted, emaciated, run-down

desmochar *tr* (*un árbol*) to top; (*al toro*) dehorn; (*una obra artística*) cut

desmodular *tr* to demodulate

desmola•do -da *adj* toothless

desmontable *adj* demountable

desmontar *tr* (*un terreno*) to level; (*un bosque*) clear; dismantle, dismount, take apart, knock down; (*las piezas de artillería del enemigo*) knock out; (*al jinete el caballo*) unhorse, to throw; (*un arma de fuego*) uncock ‖ *ref* to dismount, alight

desmoralizar §60 *tr* to demoralize

desmoronadi•zo -za *adj* crumbly

desmoronar *tr* to wear away ‖ *ref* to wear away; crumble, decline

desmotadera *f* burler; **desmotadera de algodón** cotton gin

desmotar *tr* (*la lana*) to burl; (*el algodón*) gin

desmovilizar §60 *tr* to demobilize

desmurador *m* mouser

desnatadora *f* cream separator

desnatar *tr* to skim; remove the slag from; take the choicest part of

desnaturalizar §60 *tr* to denaturalize; (*el alcohol*) denature; alter, pervert

desnivel *m* unevenness; difference of level

desnivelar *tr* to make uneven ‖ *ref* to become uneven

desnudar *tr* to undress; strip, lay bare; (*la espada*) draw ‖ *ref* to undress, get undressed; become evident; **desnudarse de** to get rid of

desnudez *f* nakedness; bareness

desnu•do -da *adj* naked, nude; bare; destitute, penniless ‖ **el desnudo** the nude

desnutrición *f* undernourishment, malnutrition

desnutri•do -da *adj* undernourished

desobedecer *tr & intr* to disobey

desobediencia *f* disobedience

desobediente *adj* disobedient

desocupación *f* unemployment; idleness, leisure

desocupa•do -da *adj* unemployed; idle; free, unoccupied, vacant, empty ‖ *mf* unemployed person

desocupar *tr* to empty, vacate ‖ *intr* (*una mujer*) to be delivered ‖ *ref* to become empty, vacated; become unemployed, become idle

desodorante *adj & m* deodorant

desodorizar §60 *tr* to deodorize

desoír §48 *tr* to not hear, pretend not to hear

desolación *f* desolation

desola•do -da *adj* desolate, disconsolate

desolar §61 *tr* to desolate, lay waste ‖ *ref* to be desolate, be disconsolate

desoldar §61 *tr* to unsolder ‖ *ref* to come unsoldered

desolla•do -da *adj* brazen, impudent

desollar §61 *tr* to skin, flay; harm, hurt; **desollar vivo** (*hacer pagar mucho más de* *lo justo*) fleece, skin alive; (*murmurar acerbamente de*) (coll) to flay

desopilar *ref* to roar with laughter

desopinar *tr* to defame, discredit

desorbita•do -da *adj* popeyed; crazy

desorbitar *tr* to pop wide-open

desorden *m* disorder

desordena•do -da *adj* disorderly, unruly

desordenar *tr* to put out of order ‖ *ref* to get out of order; be unruly; go too far

desoreja•do -da *adj* infamous, degraded; (*que canta mal*) (Peru) off tune; (Cuba) shameless; (Cuba) spendthrift, prodigal; (Guat) stupid; (Chile) without handles

desorganizar §60 *tr* to disorganize

desorientación *f* disorientation; confusedness; going astray

desorientar *tr* to lead astray; confuse

desovar *intr* to spawn

desove *m* spawning; spawning season

desovillar *tr* to unravel, disentangle; encourage

desoxidar *tr* to deoxidize; clean of rust

despabiladeras *fpl* snuffers

despabila•do -da *adj* wide-awake

despabilar *tr* (*una candela*) to snuff, trim; (*la hacienda*) dissipate; (*una còmida*) dispatch; (*robar*) snitch; (*matar*) dispatch ‖ *ref* to brighten up; wake up; leave, disappear

despacio *adv* slow, slowly; at leisure; (Arg, Chile) in a low voice

despacio•so -sa *adj* slow, easy-going

despachaderas *fpl* surly reply; resourcefulness

despacha•do -da *adj* brazen, impudent; quick, resourceful

despachante *m* (Arg) clerk; **despachante te de aduana** (Arg) customhouse broker

despachar *tr* to send, ship; dispatch, expedite; discharge, dismiss; decide, settle; sell; (*a los parroquianos*) wait on; (*la correspondencia*) attend to; hurry; (*matar*) dispatch, kill ‖ *intr* to hurry; make up one's mind; work, be employed ‖ *ref* to hurry; (*una mujer*) be delivered; speak out

despacho *m* shipping; dispatch, expedition; discharge, dismissal; (*tienda*) store, shop; (*aposento para el estudio*) study; (*aposento para los negocios*) office; (*comunicación por telégrafo o teléfono*) dispatch; (Chile) attic; **despacho de billetes** ticket office; **despacho de localidades** box office; **estar al despacho** to be pending; **tener buen despacho** to be expeditious

despachurrar *tr* to crush, smash, squash; (*dejar sin tener que replicar*) squelch; (*lo que uno trata de decir*) butcher, murder

despampanante *adj* stunning, terrific

despampanar *tr* (*las vides*) to prune, trim; astound ‖ *intr* to give vent to one's feelings ‖ *ref* to fall and hurt oneself

despancar §73 *tr* to husk (*corn*)

desparejar *tr* (*dos cosas que forman pareja*) to break, separate (*a pair*)

desparpajar *tr* to tear apart ‖ *intr* to rant, rave ‖ *ref* to rant, rave; (CAm, Mex, W-I) to wake up

desparramar *tr* to scatter, spread; (*el agua*) to spill; (*la hacienda*) squander ‖ *ref* to scatter, spread; make merry

despartir *tr* to divide, part, separate; to reconcile

despatarrada *f* split (*in dancing*); **hacer la despatarrada** to stretch out on the floor pretending to be ill or injured

despatarrar *tr* to dumbfound ‖ *ref* to open one's legs wide, fall down with legs outspread; lie motionless; be dumbfounded

despavori•do -da *adj* terrified

despea•do -da *adj* footsore

despear *ref* to get sore feet

despecti•vo -va *adj* contemptuous; (gram) pejorative

despecha•do -da *adj* spiteful, enraged

despechar *tr* to spite, enrage; (*destetar*) to wean ‖ *ref* to be enraged; despair, lose hope

despecho *m* spite; despair; weaning; **a despecho de** despite, in spite of; **por despecho** out of spite

despechugar §44 *tr* to carve the breast of ‖ *ref* (coll) to go with bare breast, bare one's breast

despedazar §60 *tr* to break to pieces; (*la honra de uno*) to ruin; (*el alma de una persona*) break ‖ *ref* to break to pieces; **despedazarse de risa** to split one's sides laughing

despedida *f* farewell, leave-taking; (*de una carta*) close, conclusion; (*copla final*) envoi

despedir §50 *tr* to throw; emit, send forth; discharge, dismiss; (*al que sale de la casa*) see off; (*un mal pensamiento*) banish; **despedir en la puerta** to see to the door ‖ *ref* to take leave, say good-by; give up one's job; **despedirse a la francesa** to take French leave; **despedirse de** to take leave of, say good-by to

despega•do -da *adj* gruff, surly

despegar §44 *tr* to loosen, unglue, unseal; open; separate, detach ‖ *intr* (aer) to take off ‖ *ref* to come off; **despegarse con** to be unbecoming to

despego *m* dislike, indifference

despegue *m* (aer) take-off; **despegue vertical** vertical take-off

despeina•do -da *adj* unkempt

despeja•do -da *adj* (*frente*) wide; (*día, cielo*) clear, cloudless; bright, sprightly; (*en el trato*) unconstrained

despejar *tr* to clarify, explain; free; (*una incógnita*) (math) to find ‖ *ref* to brighten up, cheer up; (*el cielo, el tiempo; una situación dificultosa*) clear up; (*un borracho*) sober up

despejo *m* ease, naturalness; talent, intelligence, understanding

despelotar *ref* to disrobe

despeluzar §60 *tr* to muss the hair of; make the hair of (*a person*) stand on end ‖ *ref* (*el pelo*) to stand on end

despeluznante *adj* hair-raising, horrifying

despellejar *tr* to skin, flay; slander, malign

despenalización *f* legalization

despenalizar §60 *tr* to legalize; condone

despenar *tr* to console; (coll) to kill; (Chile) to deprive of hope

despender *tr* to spend, squander; (*el tiempo*) to waste

despensa *f* pantry; food supplies; day's marketing; stewardship; (naut) storeroom

despensero *m* butler, steward; (naut) storekeeper

despeñadamente *adv* hastily; boldly

despeñade•ro -ra *adj* precipitous ‖ *m* precipice; danger, risk

despeñadi•zo -za *adj* precipitous

despeñar *tr* to hurl, throw, push ‖ *ref* to hurl oneself, jump; fall headlong; (*en vicios, pecados, pasiones*) plunge downward

despeño *m* plunge; headlong fall; ruin, failure, collapse; (coll) loose bowels

despepitar *tr* to seed, remove the seeds from ‖ *ref* to rush around madly, go around screaming; **despepitarse por** to be mad about

desperdicia•do -da *adj* wasteful, prodigal ‖ *mf* spendthrift, prodigal

desperdiciar *tr* to waste, squander; (*la ocasión de aprovechar una cosa*) miss, lose

desperdicio *m* waste, squandering; **desperdicios** waste; waste products; by-products; rubbish; **no tener desperdicio** to be excellent, be useful

desperdigar §44 *tr* to separate, scatter

desperecer §22 *ref* to long eagerly

desperezar §60 *ref* to stretch, stretch one's arms and legs

desperfecto *m* blemish, flaw, imperfection

desperna•do -da *adj* footsore, weary

desperta•dor -dora *mf* awakener ‖ *m* alarm clock; warning

despertar §2 *tr* to awaken; arouse, stir ‖ *intr & ref* to awaken, wake up

despestañar *tr* to pluck the eyelashes of ‖ *ref* to look hard, strain one's eyes

despiada•do -da *adj* cruel, pitiless

despichar *tr* to squeeze dry; (Col, Chile) to crush, flatten ‖ *intr* (coll) to croak, die

despidiente *m* stick placed between a hanging scaffold and wall; **despidiente de agua** flashing

despido *m* layoff, discharge

despier•to -ta *adj* wide-awake, alert; **soñar despierto** to daydream

despilfarra•do -da *adj* wasteful; ragged ‖ *mf* prodigal; raggedy person

despilfarrar *tr* to squander, waste ‖ *ref* to spend recklessly

despilfarro *m* squandering, waste, extravagance; slovenliness

despintar *tr* to remove the paint from; disfigure, distort, spoil; **no despintarle a uno los ojos** to not take one's eyes from a person ‖ *intr* to decline, slip back; **despintar de** to be unworthy of ‖ *ref* to fade, wash off; **no despintársele a uno** to not fade from one's memory

despiojar *tr* to delouse; (coll) to free from poverty

despique *m* revenge

despistar *tr* to outwit, throw off the track ‖ *ref* to run off the track, run off the road

desplacer *m* displeasure ‖ §22 *tr* to displease

desplantar *tr* to uproot; throw out of plumb ‖ *ref* to get out of plumb; lose one's upright posture

desplaya•do -da *adj* broad, open, wide ‖ *m* (Arg) wide sandy beach

desplayar *tr* to widen, spread out ‖ *ref* (*el mar*) to recede from the beach

desplaza•do -da *adj* displaced ‖ *mf* displaced person

desplazar §60 *tr* (*cierto peso de agua*) to displace; move, transport ‖ *ref* to move

desplegar §66 *tr* to unfold, spread; display; explain; (mil) to deploy ‖ *ref* to unfold, spread out; (mil) to deploy

despliegue *m* unfolding, spreading out; display; (mil) deployment

desplomar *tr* to throw out of plumb ‖ *ref* to get out of plumb; collapse, tumble; fall down in a faint; (*un trono*) crumble; (aer) to pancake

desplome *m* leaning; collapse, tumbling; falling in a faint; downfall; (aer) pancaking

desplumar *tr* to pluck; (*dejar sin dinero*) fleece ‖ *ref* to molt

despoblado *m* wilderness, deserted spot

despoblar §61 *tr* to depopulate; lay waste; clear, lay bare

despojar *tr* to strip, despoil, divest; dispossess ‖ *ref* to undress; **despojarse de** to divest oneself of; (*ropa*) take off

despojo *m* dispoilment; dispossession; booty, plunder, spoils; prey, victim; **despojos** scraps, leavings; mortal remains; secondhand building materials

despolarizar §60 *tr* to depolarize

despolvar *tr* to dust

despolvorear *tr* to dust, dust off; scatter

desportillar *tr* to chip, nick ‖ *ref* to chip, chip off

desposa•do -da *adj* handcuffed; newly married ‖ *mf* newlywed

desposar *tr* to marry ‖ *ref* to be betrothed, get engaged; get married

desposeer §43 *tr* to dispossess ‖ *ref* —**desposeerse de** to divest oneself of

desposorios *mpl* betrothal, engagement; marriage, nuptials

despostar *tr* to cut up, carve; butcher

déspota *m* despot

despóti•co -ca *adj* despotic

despotismo *m* despotism

despotricar §73 *intr & ref* to rave, rant

despreciable *adj* contemptible, despicable

despreciar *tr* to scorn, despise; slight, snub; overlook, forgive; reject ‖ *ref* —**despreciarse de** to not deign to

despreciati•vo -va *adj* contemptuous, scornful

desprecio *m* scorn, contempt; slight, snub

desprender *tr* to loosen, unfasten, detach; emit, give off; (chem) to liberate ‖ *ref* to come loose, come off; issue, come forth;

desprenderse de to give up, part with; be deduced from

desprendi•do -da *adj* generous, disinterested

desprendimiento *m* loosening, detachment; emission, liberation; generosity, disinterestedness; landslide; (chem) liberation

despreocupación *f* relaxation; impartiality; indifference

despreocupa•do -da *adj* relaxed, unconcerned; impartial; indifferent

despreocupante *adj* relaxing

despreocupar *ref* to relax; **despreocuparse de** to forget about, be unconcerned about

desprestigiar *tr* to disparage, run down ‖ *ref* to lose caste, lose one's standing, lose face

desprestigio *m* disparagement; loss of standing, discredit

despreveni•do -da *adj* off one's guard; **coger a uno desprevenido** to catch someone unawares

desproporciona•do -da *adj* disproportionate

despropósito *m* absurdity, nonsense; malapropism

desproveer §43 & §83 *tr* to deprive

desprovis•to -ta *adj* destitute; **desprovisto de** lacking, devoid of

después *adv* after, afterwards; **después de** after; **después (de) que** after

despuli•do -da *adj* ground (*glass*)

despumar *tr* to skim

despuntar *tr* to dull, blunt; (*un cabo o punta*) (naut) to double, round ‖ *intr* to begin to sprout; (*empezar a amanecer*) dawn; stand out ‖ *ref* to get dull

desquiciar *tr* to unhinge; shake loose, upset; unsettle, perturb; overthrow, undermine

desquitar *tr* to recover, retrieve; compensate ‖ *ref* to retrieve a loss; get revenge, get even

desquite *m* recovery, retrieval; retaliation, revenge; (sport) return match

desrazonable *adj* unreasonable

desrielar *intr* to jump the track

destaca•do -da *adj* outstanding, distinguished

destacamiento *m* (mil) detachment; (mil) detail

destacar §73 *tr* to highlight, point up; emphasize; make stand out; (mil) to detach; (mil) to detail ‖ *intr* to stand out, be conspicuous ‖ *ref* to stand out, project; (fig) to stand out

destajar *tr* to arrange for, establish the terms for; (*la baraja*) cut; carve up

destaje•ro -ra or **destajista** *mf* pieceworker; jobber; free lance

destajo *m* piecework; job, contract; **a destajo** by the piece, by the job; freelancing; **hablar a destajo** to talk too much

destapar *tr* to open, uncover, take the lid off; uncock, unplug; reveal ‖ *ref* to get uncovered; throw off the covers; unbosom oneself

destaponar *tr* to uncock, unplug; (*una botella; las fosas nasales*) unstop

destartala•do -da *adj* tumble-down, ramshackle

destazar §60 *tr* to carve up

destechar *tr* to unroof

destejar *tr* to remove the tiles from; leave unprotected

destejer *tr* to unbraid, unknit, unweave; upset, disturb

destellar *tr & intr* to flash

destello *m* flash, beam, sparkle

destempla•do -da *adj* disagreeable, unpleasant; inharmonious, out of tune; indisposed; (*clima; pulso*) irregular

destemplanza *f* unpleasantness; discord; indisposition; (*del pulso*) irregularity; (*del tiempo*) inclemency; excess

destemple *m* dissonance; indisposition; disorder, disturbance

desteñir §72 *tr* to discolor ‖ *intr & ref* to fade

desternillante *adj* sidesplitting

desternillar *ref* — **desternillarse de risa** to split one's sides with laughter

desterra•do -da *adj* exiled ‖ *mf* exile

desterrar §2 *tr* to exile, banish; (fig) to banish

destetar *tr* to wean ‖ *ref* — **destetarse con** to have known since childhood

destete *m* weaning

destiempo *m* — **a destiempo** untimely

destiento *m* surprise, shock

destierro *m* exile; backwoods

destilación *f* distillation

destiladera *f* still; scheme, stratagem

destilar *tr* to distill; filter; exude ‖ *intr* to drip

destilatorio *m* distillery; (*alambique*) still

destilería *f* distillery

destinación *f* destination

destinar *tr* to destine; assign, designate

destinata•rio -ria *mf* addressee; consignee; (*de homenaje, aplausos*) recipient

destino *m* (*lugar a donde va una persona o una remesa*) destination; (*suerte, encadenamiento fatal de los sucesos*) fate, destiny; employment; place of employment; **con destino a** bound for

destituir §20 *tr* to deprive; dismiss, discharge

destorcer §74 *tr* to untwist, straighten ‖ *ref* to become untwisted; (naut) to drift

destornilla•do -da *adj* rash, reckless, out of one's head

destornillador *m* screwdriver

destornillar *tr* to unscrew ‖ *ref* to lose one's head, go berserk

destoser *ref* to cough (*artificially, to attract attention*)

destrabar *tr* to loosen, untie, detach

destraillar §4 *tr* unleash

destral *m* hatchet

destreza *f* skill, dexterity

destripacuen•tos *m* (*pl* -tos) (coll) butter-in

destripar *tr* to disembowel, gut; crush, mangle; spoil (*a story by telling its outcome*)

destripaterro•nes *m* (*pl* -nes) (coll) clodhopper

destriunfar *tr* to force to play trump

destrocar §81 *tr* to swap back again

destronar *tr* to dethrone; overthrow

destroncar §73 *tr* to chop down; chop off; ruin; exhaust, wear out

destrozar §60 *tr* to shatter, break to pieces; destroy; squander; (*al ejército enemigo*) wipe out

destrozo *m* havoc, destruction; rout, annihilation, defeat

destrucción *f* destruction

destructi·vo -va *adj* destructive

destructor *m* (nav) destroyer

destruir §20 *tr* to destroy ‖ *ref* (alg) to cancel each other

desuellaca·ras *m* (*pl* -ras) sloppy barber; scoundrel

desuello *m* skinning, flaying; shamelessness; (*precio excesivo*) (coll) highway robbery

desuncir §36 *tr* to unyoke

desunir *tr* to disunite; take apart ‖ *ref* to disunite; come apart

desusa·do -da *adj* obsolete, out of use; uncommon, unusual; **estar desusado** (*perder la práctica*) to be rusty

desuso *m* disuse; **caído en desuso** obsolete

desvaí·do -da *adj* lank, ungainly; (*color*) dull

desvainar *tr* to shell

desvali·do -da *adj* helpless, destitute

desvalijar *tr* (*una valija, baúl, etc.*) to rifle; rob, wipe out

desvalorar *tr* to devalue

desvalorizar §60 *tr* to devalue

desván *m* garret, loft

desvanecedor *m* (phot) mask

desvanecer §22 *tr* to dispel, dissipate; (*una conspiración*) break up; (*la sospecha*) banish; (phot) to mask ‖ *ref* to disappear, vanish, evanesce; evaporate; faint, faint away, swoon; (rad) to fade

desvanecimiento *m* disappearance, evanescence; dissipation; pride, vanity; faintness, fainting spell; (phot) masking; (rad) fading, fadeout

desvaria·do -da *adj* delirious, raving

desvariar §77 *intr* to be delirious, rave, rant

desvarío *m* delirium, raving; absurdity, nonsense, extravagance; whim, caprice; inconstancy

desvela·do -da *adj* wakeful, sleepless; watchful, vigilant; anxious, worried

desvelar *tr* to keep awake, not let sleep ‖ *ref* to keep awake, go without sleep; be watchful, be vigilant; **desvelarse por** to be anxious about, be worried about

desvelo *m* wakefulness, sleeplessness; watchfulness, vigilance; anxiety, worry, concern

desvenar *tr* to strip (tobacco)

desvencija·do -da *adj* rickety, ramshackle

desvencijar *tr* to break, tear apart ‖ *ref* to go to rack and ruin

desvendar *tr* to unbandage, undress

desventaja *f* disadvantage

desventaja·do -da *adj* disadvantaged; deprived

desventajo·so -sa *adj* disadvantageous

desventura *f* misfortune

desventura·do -da *adj* unfortunate; fainthearted; stingy

desvergonza·do -da *adj* shameless, impudent

desvergüenza *f* shamelessness, impudence

desvestir §50 *tr & ref* to undress

desviación *f* deviation, deflection; detour; (rad, telv) drift

desviacionismo *m* deviationism

desviacionista *mf* deviationist

desviadero *m* (rr) siding, turnout

desvia·do -da *adj* devious; (gone) astray; off track; lost

desviar §77 *tr* to deviate, deflect; turn aside; dissuade; parry, ward off; (rr) to switch ‖ *ref* to deviate, deflect; turn aside; branch off; be dissuaded

desvío *m* deviation, deflection; coldness, indifference; detour; (rr) siding, sidetrack

desvirgar §44 *tr* to deflower, ravish

desvirtuar §21 *tr* to weaken, spoil, impair

desvivir *ref* — **desvivirse por** to be crazy about; **desvivirse por** + *inf* to be eager to + *inf*, to do one's best to + *inf*

desvolvedor *m* wrench

desvolver §47 & §83 *tr* to alter, change; (*la tierra*) turn up; (*una tuerca o tornillo*) loosen, unscrew

detall *m* — **al detall** at retail

detalladamente *adv* in detail

detallar *tr* to detail, tell in detail; retail, sell at retail

detalle *m* detail; retail; **ahí está el detalle** that's the point

detallista *mf* retailer; person fond of details

detección *f* detection

detectar *tr* to detect

detective *m* detective

detector *m* detector; **detector de mentiras** lie detector

detención *f* detention, detainment; delay; care, thoroughness

detener §71 *tr* to detain; stop; arrest; keep, retain; (*el aliento*) hold ‖ *ref* to stop; linger, tarry

detenidamente *adv* carefully, thoroughly

deteni·do -da *adj* careful, thorough; hesitant, timid; stingy, mean ‖ *mf* person held in custody

detenimiento *m* var of **detención**

detergente *adj & m* detergent

deteriorar *tr & ref* to deteriorate

deterioro *m* deterioration

determinación *f* determination; decision

determina·do -da *adj* determined, resolute; (*artículo*) (gram) definite

determinar *tr* to determine; cause, bring about ‖ *ref* to decide

detestar *tr* to detest; curse; **detestar** + *inf* to hate to + *inf*

detonar *intr* to detonate

detraer §75 *tr* to withdraw, take away, detract; defame, vilify

detrás *adv* behind; **detrás de** behind, back of; **por detrás** behind; behind one's back; **por detrás de** behind the back of

detrimento *m* harm, detriment

deuda *f* debt; indebtedness

deu·do -da *mf* relative ‖ *m* kinship ‖ *f* see **deuda**

deu·dor -dora *adj* indebted ‖ *mf* debtor; **deudor hipotecario** mortgagor; **deudor moroso** delinquent (*in payment*)

devalar *intr* (naut) to drift from the course
devaluación *f* devaluation
devanar *tr* to wind, roll; (*un cuento*) to unfold ‖ *ref* (CAm, Mex, W-I) to roll with laughter; (CAm, Mex, W-I) to writhe in pain
devanear *intr* to talk nonsense; loaf around
devaneo *m* nonsense; loafing; flirtation
devastación *f* devastation
devastar *tr* to devastate
develar *tr* to reveal; (*p.ej., una estatua*) unveil
devengar §44 *tr* (*salarios*) to earn; (*intereses*) draw, earn
devoción *f* devotion
devolución *f* return, restitution
devolver §47 & §83 *tr* to return, give back, send back; pay back; (coll) to vomit ‖ *ref* to return, come back
devorar *tr* to devour
devo•to -ta *adj* devout; devoted; devotional ‖ *mf* devotee; devout person; **devoto del volante** car enthusiast ‖ *m* object of worship
D.F. *abbr* **Distrito Federal**
d/f *abbr* **días fecha**
dho. *abbr* **dicho**
día. *m* day; daytime; daylight; **al día** per day; up to date; **al otro día** on the following day; **buenos días** good morning; **dar los días a** to wish (*someone*) many happy returns of the day; **de día** in the daytime, in the daylight; **día de años** birthday; **día de ayuno** fast day; **día de carne** meat day; **día de engañabobos** December 28th, day when practical jokes are played on unsuspecting people; **día de inauguración** (fa) private view; **día de la raza** Columbus Day; **día del juicio** judgment day; **día de los caídos** Memorial Day; **día de los difuntos** All Souls' Day; **día de ramos** Palm Sunday; **día de Reyes** Epiphany; **día de todos los santos** All Saints' Day; **día de trabajo** workday; weekday; **día de vigilia** fast day; **día festivo** holiday; **día inhábil** day off; holiday; **día laborable** workday, weekday; **día lectivo** school day; **día puente** day off between two holidays; **el día de Año Nuevo** New Year's Day; **el día menos pensado** when least expected; **el mejor día** some fine day; **en cuatro días** in a few days; **en pleno día** in broad daylight; **en su día** in due time; **ocho días** a week; **poner al día** to bring up to date; **quince días** two weeks, a fortnight; **tener sus días** to be up in years; **un día sí y otro no** every other day; **vivir al día** to live from hand to mouth
diabetes *f* diabetes
diabéti•co -ca *adj & mf* diabetic
diablillo *m* imp
diablo *m* devil; (Chile) ox-drawn log drag; **ahí será el diablo** (coll) there will be the devil to pay; **diablo cojuelo** tricky devil; **diablos azules** delirium tremens
diablura *f* devilment, deviltry, mischief
diabóli•co -ca *adj* devilish, diabolical

diaconisa *f* deaconess
diácono *m* deacon
diacríti•co -ca *adj* diacritical
diadema *f* diadem; (*adorno femenino*) tiara
diáfa•no -na *adj* diaphanous
diafragma *m* diaphragm
diagno•sis *f* (*pl -sis*) diagnosis
diagnosticar §73 *tr* to diagnose
diagonal *adj* diagonal ‖ *f* diagonal, bias
diagrama *m* diagram
dialecto *m* dialect
dialogar *intr* to talk
diálogo *m* dialogue
diamante *m* diamond
diametral or **diamétri•co -ca** *adj* diametrical
diámetro *m* diameter
diana *f* bull's-eye; (mil) reveille; **hacer diana** to hit the bull's-eye
diantre *m* devil ‖ *interj* the devil!, the deuce!
diapasón *m* tuning fork; pitch pipe; (*p.ej., del violín*) finger board; **bajar el diapasón** to lower one's voice, to change one's tune
diapositiva *f* slide, lantern slide
dia•rio -ria *adj* daily ‖ *m* diary; daily, daily paper; **diario hablado** newscast
diarismo *m* journalism
diarrea *f* diarrhea
diástole *f* diastole
diatermia *f* diathermy
dibujante *mf* sketcher, illustrator ‖ *m* draftsman
dibujar *tr* to draw, sketch, design; outline ‖ *ref* to be outlined; appear, show
dibujo *m* drawing, sketch, design; outline; **dibujo al carbón** charcoal drawing; **dibujo animado** animated cartoon; **no meterse en dibujos** to attend to one's business
di•caz *adj* (*pl -caces*) sarcastic, witty
dicción *f* diction; word
diccionario *m* dictionary
díceres *mpl* sayings; rumor(s)
diciembre *m* December
dicloruro *m* dichloride
dicotomía *f* dichotomy; (*entre médicos*) split fee
dictado *m* dictation; **escribir al dictado** to take dictation; (*lo que otro dicta*) to take down
dictador *m* dictator
dictadura *f* dictatorship
dictáfono *m* dictaphone
dictamen *m* dictum, judgment, opinion
dictar *tr* to dictate; (*una ley*) promulgate; inspire, suggest; (*una conferencia*) give, deliver (*a lecture*)
dicterio *m* taunt, insult
dicha *f* happiness; luck; **por dicha** by chance
dicharache•ro -ra *adj* obscene, vulgar
dicharacho *m* obscenity, vulgarity; wisecrack
di•cho -cha *adj* said; **dicho y hecho** no sooner said than done; **mejor dicho** rather; **tener por dicho** to consider settled ‖ *m* saying; promise of marriage, one's word; witticism; insult; **dicho de las gentes** talk, hearsay, gossip ‖ *f* see **dicha**

dicho•so -sa *adj* happy; lucky, fortunate; annoying, tiresome

didácti•co -ca *adj* didactic

diecinueve *adj & pron* nineteen ‖ *m* nineteen; (*en las fechas*) nineteenth

diecinueva•vo -va *adj & m* nineteenth

dieciocha•vo -va *adj m* eighteenth

dieciocho *adj & pron* eighteen ‖ *m* eighteen; (*en las fechas*) eighteenth

dieciséis *adj & pron* sixteen ‖ *m* sixteen; (*en las fechas*) sixteenth

dieciseisa•vo -va *adj & m* sixteenth

diecisiete *adj & pron* seventeen ‖ *m* seventeen; (*en las fechas*) seventeenth

diecisietea•vo -va *adj & m* seventeenth

diente *m* tooth; (*de elefante y otros animales*) tusk, fang; (*de peine, sierra, rastrillo*) tooth; (*de rueda dentada*) cog; **dar diente con diente** to shake all over; **decir entre dientes** to mutter, to mumble; **diente canino** eyetooth, canine tooth; **diente de león** dandelion; **estar a diente** to be famished; **tener buen diente** to be a hearty eater; **traer entre dientes** to have a grudge against; to talk about

diére•sis *f* (*pl* **-sis**) diaeresis; (*señal que indica la metafonía*) umlaut

diesel *m* diesel motor

dieseléctri•co -ca *adj* diesel-electric

dies•tro -tra *adj* right; handy, skillful; shrewd, sly; favorable; **a diestro y siniestro** wildly, right and left ‖ *m* expert fencer; bullfighter on foot; matador; halter, bridle ‖ *f* right hand; **juntar diestra con diestra** to join forces

dieta *f* diet; **dietas** per diem; **estar a dieta** to diet, be on a diet

dietario *m* family budget

dietista *mf* dietitian

diez *adj & pron* ten; **las diez** ten o'clock ‖ *m* ten; (*en las fechas*) tenth

diezmar *tr* (*causar gran mortandad en*) to decimate; (*pagar el diezmo de*) tithe

diezmo *m* tithe

difamación *f* defamation, vilification

difamar *tr* to defame, vilify

diferencia *f* difference; **a diferencia de** unlike; **partir la diferencia** to split the difference

diferenciar *tr* to differentiate ‖ *intr* (*discordar*) to differ, dissent ‖ *ref* (*distinguirse una cosa de otra*) to differ, be different

diferente *adj* different

diferir §68 *tr* to defer, postpone, put off ‖ *intr* to differ, be different

difícil *adj* difficult, hard; hard to please

difícilmente *adv* with difficulty

dificultad *f* difficulty; (*reparo que se opone a una opinión*) objection

dificultar *tr* to make difficult; consider difficult ‖ *intr* to raise objections ‖ *ref* to become difficult

dificulto•so -sa *adj* difficult, troublesome; objecting; (coll) ugly, homely

difidencia *f* distrust

difidente *adj* distrustful

difteria *f* diphtheria

difundir *tr* to diffuse; spread, disseminate; divulge, publish; broadcast ‖ *ref* to diffuse; spread

difun•to -ta *adj & mf* deceased; **difunto de taberna** dead-drunk ‖ *m* corpse

difu•so -sa *adj* diffuse; extended; wordy

digerible *adj* digestible

digerir §68 *tr* to digest; **no digerir** to not bear, not stand ‖ *intr* to digest

digestible *adj* digestible

digestión *f* digestion

digesti•vo -va *adj & m* digestive

digesto *m* (law) digest

dígito *m* digit

dignación *f* condescension

dignar *ref* to deign, condescend

dignatario *m* dignitary, official

dignidad *f* dignity; bishop, archbishop

dignificar §73 *tr* to dignify

dig•no -na *adj* worthy; fitting, suitable; (*grave, decoroso*) dignified

digresión *f* digression

dije *m* amulet, charm, trinket; (*persona de excelentes cualidades*) jewel; person all dressed-up; handy person

dilacerar *tr* to tear to pieces; (*la honra, el orgullo*) damage

dilación *f* delay

dilapidación *f* waste; squandering

dilapidar *tr* to squander

dilatación *f* expansion; serenity

dilatar *tr* to dilate, expand; defer, postpone; (*p.ej., la fama*) spread ‖ *ref* to dilate, expand; spread; be wordy; delay

dilección *f* true love

dilec•to -ta *adj* dearly beloved

dilema *m* dilemma

diletante *adj & mf* dilettante

diletantismo *m* dilettantism

diligencia *f* diligence; step, démarche; errand; dispatch, speed; stagecoach; **hacer una diligencia** to do an errand; to have a bowel movement

diligente *adj* diligent; quick, ready

dilucidación *f* explanation; enlightenment

dilucidar *tr* to elucidate, explain

dilución *f* dilution

diluí•do -da *adj* dilute

diluir §20 *tr* to dilute; thin ‖ *ref* to dilute; melt; dissolve

diluviar *intr* to rain hard, pour

diluvio *m* deluge

dimanar *intr* to spring up; **dimanar de** to spring from, originate in

dimensión *f* dimension

dimes *mpl* — **andar en dimes y diretes con** to bicker with

diminuti•vo -va *adj & m* (gram) diminutive

diminu•to -ta *adj* tiny, diminutive; defective

dimisión *f* resignation

dimisorias *fpl* — **dar dimisorias a** to discharge, fire

dimitir *tr* to resign, resign from ‖ *intr* to resign

din *m* (coll) dough, money

Dinamarca *f* Denmark

de
di

dinamar·qués -quesa *adj* Danish || *mf* Dane || *m* Danish (*language*)

dinámi·co -ca *adj* dynamic

dinamita *f* dynamite

dinamitar *tr* to dynamite

dínamo *f* dynamo

dinasta *m* dynast

dinastía *f* dynasty

dindán *m* ding-dong

dinerada *f* or **dineral** *m* large sum of money

dinero *m* money; currency; wealth; **dinero contante** cash; **dinero contante y sonante** ready cash, spot cash; **dinero de bolsillo** pocket money

dinero·so -sa *adj* moneyed, wealthy

dintel *m* lintel, doorhead

dióce·si *f* or **dióce·sis** *f* (*pl* -sis) diocese

diodo *m* diode

dios *m* god; **Dios mediante** God willing; **¡por Dios!** goodness!, for heaven's sake; **¡válgame Dios!** bless me!; **¡vaya con Dios!** off with you!

diosa *f* goddess

diploma *m* diploma

diplomacia *f* diplomacy

diploma·do -da *adj & mf* graduate

diplomar *tr & ref* to graduate

diplomáti·co -ca *adj* diplomatic || *mf* diplomat

diptongar §44 *tr & ref* to diphthongize

diptongo *m* diphthong

diputación *f* congress; commission

diputa·do -da *mf* deputy, representative

diputar *tr* to commission, delegate; designate

dique *m* dike, jetty; dry dock; check, stop; **dique seco** dry dock

dirección *f* direction; (*señas en una carta*) address; administration, management; directorship; (aut) steering; **de dirección única** one-way; **dirección a la derecha** right-hand drive; **dirección a la izquierda** left-hand drive; **perder la dirección** to lose control of the car

directi·vo -va *adj* managing || *mf* director, manager || *f* management

direc·to -ta *adj* direct; straight

direc·tor -tora *adj* directing, guiding; managing, governing || *mf* director, manager; (*de un periódico*) editor; (*de una escuela*) principal; (*de una orquesta*) conductor; **director de escena** stage manager; **director de funeraria** funeral director; **director gerente** managing director

directorio *m* directorship; directory

dirigente *mf* leader, head, executive

dirigible *adj & m* dirigible

dirigir §27 *tr* to direct; manage; (*un automóvil*) steer; (*una carta; la palabra*) address; (*una obra*) dedicate || *ref* to go, betake oneself; turn; **dirigirse a** to address; apply to

dirimir *tr* to dissolve, annul; (*una dificultad*) solve; (*una controversia*) settle, mediate

discar §73 *tr & intr* to dial

disceptar *intr* to discuss, debate

discerniente *adj* discerning

discernir §28 *tr* to discern; distinguish

disciplina *f* discipline; **disiplinas** scourge, whip

disciplina·do -da *adj* disciplined; (*flores*) many-colored

disciplinar *tr* to discipline; teach; scourge, whip

disciplinazo *m* lash

discípu·lo -la *mf* disciple; pupil

disco *m* disk; (*del gramófono*) record, disk; (sport) discus; **disco de cola** (rr) taillight; **disco de goma** (*para un grifo*) washer (*for a spigot*); **disco de identificación** identification tag; **disco de larga duración** long-playing record; **disco de señales** (rr) semaphore; **disco selector** (telp) dial; **disco vertebral** spinal disk; **siempre el mismo disco** the same old song

discóbolo *m* discus thrower

discófi·lo -la *mf* record lover, discophile

dísco·lo -la *adj* ungovernable, wayward

disconforme *adj* disagreeing

discontinuar §21 *tr* to discontinue

discordancia *f* discordance

discordar §61 *intr* to be out of tune; disagree

discorde *adj* discordant, disagreeing; (mus) discordant, out of tune

discordia *f* discord

discoteca *f* discothèque, disco; record cabinet; record library

discreción *f* discretion; wit; witticism; **a discreción** at discretion; (mil) unconditionally

discrepancia *f* discrepancy; dissent

discrepar *intr* to differ, disagree

discretear *intr* to try to be clever, try to sparkle

discre·to -ta *adj* (*juicioso*) discreet; (*discontinuo*) discrete; witty

discrimen *m* risk, hazard; difference

discriminación *f* discrimination

discriminar *tr* to discriminate against || *intr* to discriminate

discriminato·rio -ria *adj* discriminatory

disculpa *f* excuse, apology

disculpar *tr* to excuse; pardon, overlook || *ref* to apologize; **disculparse con** to apologize to; **disculparse de** to apologize for

discurrir *tr* to contrive, invent; guess, conjecture || *intr* to ramble, roam; occur, take place; discourse; reason; pass, elapse

discursis·to -ta *adj* long-winded; (coll) windy; *mf* windbag; big talker

discursi·vo -va *adj* meditative

discurso *m* discourse, speech; (*paso del tiempo*) course; **discurso de sobremesa** after-dinner speech

discusión *f* discussion

discutible *adj* debatable

discutir *tr* to discuss || *intr* to discuss; argue

disecar §73 *tr* to dissect; (*un animal muerto*) stuff; (*una planta*) mount

diseminar *tr* to disseminate; scatter || *ref* to scatter

disensión *f* (*oposición*) dissent; (*contienda*) dissension

disentería *f* dysentery

disentir §68 *intr* to dissent

diseñar *tr* to draw, sketch; design, outline

diseño m drawing, sketch; design, outline
disertar intr to discourse, discuss
diser•to -ta adj fluent, eloquent
disfavor m disfavor
disforme adj formless; monstrous, ugly
disforzar §35 ref (Peru) to be prudish, be finical
dis•fraz m (pl **-fraces**) disguise; (traje de máscara) costume, fancy dress
disfrazar §60 tr to disguise || ref to disguise oneself; wear fancy dress, masquerade, dress in costume
disfrutar tr to enjoy, to use || intr —**disfrutar de** to enjoy, use; **disfrutar con** to enjoy, take enjoyment in
disfrute m enjoyment, use
disfunción f dysfunction
disgregar §44 tr & intr to disintegrate, break up
disgusta•do -da adj tasteless, insipid; sad, sorrowful; disagreeable; (Mex) hard to please
disgustar tr to displease || ref to be displeased; fall out, become estranged
disgusto m displeasure; annoyance, unpleasantness; grief, sorrow; difference, quarrel; **a disgusto** against one's will
disidencia f dissidence; (de una doctrina) dissent
disidente adj dissident || mf dissident, dissenter
disidir intr to dissent
disíla•bo -ba adj dissyllabic || m dissyllable
disímil adj dissimilar
disimilar tr & ref to dissimilate
disimula•do -da adj sly, underhanded; **a lo disimulado** or **a la disimulada** underhandedly; **hacer la disimulada** to feign ignorance
disimular tr to dissemble, dissimulate, hide, conceal; overlook, pardon || intr to dissemble, dissimulate
disimulo m dissembling, dissimulation; indulgence
disipación f dissipation
disipa•do -da adj dissipated; spendthrift || mf debauchee; spendthrift
disipar tr to dissipate || ref to be dissipated; disappear, evanesce
dislate m nonsense
dislocar §73 tr to dislocate || ref to dislocate; be dislocated
disloque m tops, top notch
disminución f diminution; decrease; **disminución física** handicap, disability
disminuir §20 tr, intr & ref to diminish
disociar tr to dissociate
disolución f dissolution; disbandment; (relajación de costumbres) dissoluteness, dissipation
disolu•to -ta adj dissolute || mf debauchee
disolver §47 & §83 tr to dissolve; disband; destroy, ruin || intr & ref to dissolve
disonancia f dissonance
disonar §61 intr to be dissonant, lack harmony, disagree; cause surprise; sound bad

dispar adj unlike, different; (que no hace juego) odd
disparada f sudden flight; **a la disparada** like a shot, in mad haste; **de una disparada** (Arg) right away; **tomar la disparada** (Arg) to take to one's heels
disparadero m trigger
disparador m trigger; (de reloj) escapement; **poner en el disparador** to drive mad
disparar tr to throw, hurl; shoot, fire || intr to rant, talk nonsense || ref to dash away, rush away; (un caballo) run away; (una escopeta) to go off; be beside oneself
disparata•do -da adj absurd, nonsensical; frightful
disparatar intr to talk nonsense; act foolishly
disparate m folly, nonsense; blunder, mistake; outrage
dispare•jo -ja adj unequal, different, uneven, disparate; rough, broken
disparidad f disparity
disparo m shot, discharge; nonsense; (mach) release, trip; **cambiar disparos** to exchange shots
dispendio m waste, extravagance
dispendio•so -sa adj expensive
dispensar tr to excuse, pardon; exempt; dispense; dispense with
dispensario m dispensary; **dispensario de alimentos** soup kitchen
dispepsia f dyspepsia
dispersar tr & ref to disperse
displicente adj disagreeable; cross, fretful, peevish
disponer §54 tr to dispose, arrange; direct, order || intr to dispose; **disponer de** to dispose of, have at one's disposal || ref to prepare, get ready; get ready to die, make one's will
disponible adj available, disposable
disposición f disposition, arrangement, layout; inclination; preparation; disposal; predisposition; state of health; elegance; **estar a la disposición de** to be at the disposal of, be at the service of; **última disposición** last will and testament
dispositivo m appliance, device
dispues•to -ta adj ready, prepared; comely, graceful; clever, skillful; **bien dispuesto** well-disposed; well, in good health; **mal dispuesto** ill-disposed, unfavorable; ill, indisposed
disputa f dispute; fight, struggle; **sin disputa** beyond dispute
disputar tr to dispute, question; argue over; fight for || intr to dispute; debate, argue; fight
disquería f record shop
disque•ro -ra mf record dealer
distancia f distance; **a distancia** at a distance; **a larga distancia** long-distance; **tomar distancia** to stand aside, stand off
distante adj distant
distar intr to be distant, be far; be different
distender §51 tr to distend; (p.ej., las piernas) stretch || ref to distend; relax; (un reloj) run down

di
di

distensión f distension; relaxation of tension

distinción f (*honor, prerrogativa*) distinction; (*diferencia*) distinctness; **a distinción de** unlike

distingui•do -da adj distinguished; refined, urbane, smooth

distinguir §29 tr to distinguish; give distinction to; make out

distinti•vo -va adj distinctive ‖ m badge, insignia; distinction; distinctive mark

distin•to -ta adj distinct; different; **distintos** various, several

distorsión f distortion

distorsionar tr to distort, twist, bend

distracción f distraction; (*licencia en las costumbres*) dissipation; (*substracción de fondos*) embezzlement

distraer §75 tr to distract; amuse, divert, entertain; seduce; embezzle

distraí•do -da adj absent-minded, distracted; licentious, dissolute; (Chile, Mex) untidy, careless

distribución f distribution; electric supply system; timing gears, valve gears

distribui•dor -dora adj distributing ‖ mf distributor ‖ m (aut) distributor; slide valve; **distribuidor automático** vending machine

distribuir §20 tr to distribute

distrito m district; (rr) section; **distrito electoral** precinct; **distrito postal** zone, postal zone

disturbar tr to disturb

disturbio m disturbance

disuadir tr to dissuade

disyunti•vo -va adj disjunctive ‖ f dilemma

disyuntor m circuit breaker

dita f bond, surety

diuca m (Arg, Chile) teacher's pet ‖ f (Arg, Chile) finch (*Fringilla diuca*)

diuréti•co -ca adj & m diuretic

diur•no -na adj day, daytime

diva f goddess; (mus) diva

divagación f digression; wandering

divagar §44 intr to digress; ramble, wander

diván m divan; **diván cama** day bed

divergir §27 intr to diverge

diversidad f diversity; abundance

diversificación f diversification

diversificar §73 tr & ref to diversify

diversión f diversion

diver•so -sa adj diverse, different; **diversos** several, various, divers

diverti•do -da adj amusing, funny; (Am) tipsy

divertimiento m diversion, amusement

divertir §68 tr to divert; amuse ‖ ref to enjoy oneself, have a good time

dividendo m dividend

dividir tr to divide ‖ ref to divide, be divided; separate

divieso m boil

divinidad f divinity; (*persona dotada de gran belleza*) beauty

divinizar §60 tr to deify; exalt, extol

divi•no -na adj divine

divisa f badge; emblem; motto; goal, ideal; currency, foreign exchange

divisar tr to descry, espy

división f division; (*deportes*) class, category; league

divisor m (math) divisor; **máximo común divisor** greatest common divisor; **divisor de voltaje** (rad) voltage divider

divisoria f dividing line; (geog) divide

di•vo -va adj godlike, divine ‖ m god; (mus) opera star ‖ f see **diva**

divorciar tr to divorce ‖ ref to divorce, get divorced

divorcio m divorce; divergency (*in opinion*); (Col) jail for women

divulgación f divulging, disclosure; popularization

divulgar §44 tr to divulge, disclose; popularize

D.ⁿ abbr **don**

dobladillar tr to hem

dobladillo m hem

dobla•do -da adj rough, uneven; stocky, thickset; double-dealing ‖ m (mov) dubbing

doblaje m (mov) dubbing

doblar tr to double; fold, crease; bend; (*una esquina*) turn, round; (*un promontorio*) double; (*una película, generalmente en otro idioma*) dub; (bridge) to double; (Mex) to shoot down ‖ intr to turn; (*tocar a muerto*) toll; (mov, theat) to double, stand in; (bridge) to double ‖ ref to double; fold, crease; bend; bow, stoop; give in, yield

doble adj double; heavy, thick; stocky, thickset; deceitful, two-faced ‖ adv double, doubly ‖ mf (mov, theat) double, stand-in ‖ m double; fold, crease; (*toque de difuntos*) toll, knell; (*suma que se paga por la prórroga de una operación a plazos en la bolsa*) margin; **al doble** doubly

doblegar §44 tr to fold; bend; (*una espada*) brandish, flourish; sway, dominate ‖ ref to fold; bend; give in, yield

doblete adj medium ‖ m (*piedra falsa; cada una de dos palabras que poseen un mismo origen*) doublet; (bridge) doubleton

do•blez m (pl **-bleces**) fold, crease; (*del pantalón*) cuff; duplicity, double-dealing

doce adj & pron twelve; **las doce** twelve o'clock ‖ m twelve; (*en las fechas*) twelfth

docea•vo -va adj & m twelfth

docena f dozen; **docena del fraile** baker's dozen

docencia f (Arg) teaching; (Arg) teaching staff

docente adj educational, teaching

dócil adj docile; soft, ductile

doc•to -ta adj learned ‖ mf scholar

doc•tor -tora mf doctor ‖ f (coll) bluestocking

doctorado m doctorate

doctoran•do -da mf candidate for the doctor's degree

doctorar tr to grant the doctor's degree to ‖ ref to get the doctor's degree

doctrina f doctrine; teaching, instruction; learning; catechism; preaching the Gospel

doctrinar tr to teach, instruct

doctrino *m* orphan (*in orphanage*); **parecer un doctrino** to look scared

documentación *f* documentation; **documentación del buque** ship's papers

documental *adj* documentary ‖ *m* (mov) documentary

documentar *tr* to document

documento *m* document; **documento de prueba** (law) exhibit

dogal *m* (*para atar las caballerías*) halter; (*para ahorcar a un reo*) noose, halter, hangman's rope; **estar con el dogal a la garganta** or **al cuello** to be in a tight spot

dogmáti·co -ca *adj* dogmatic

do·go -ga *mf* bulldog

dolamas *fpl* or **dolames** *mpl* hidden defects of a horse; complaints, aches and pains

dolar §61 *tr* to hew

dólar *m* dollar

dolencia *f* ailment, complaint

doler §47 *tr* to ache, pain; grieve, distress; **dolerle a uno el dinero** to hate to spend money ‖ *intr* to ache, hurt, pain ‖ *ref* to complain; feel sorry; repent

doliente *adj* sick, ill; aching, suffering; sad, sorrowful ‖ *mf* sufferer, patient ‖ *m* mourner

dolo *m* deceit, fraud, guile

dolor *m* ache, pain; grief, sorrow; regret, repentance; **dolor de cabeza** headache; **dolor de muelas** toothache; **dolor de oído** earache; **dolor de yegua** (CAm) lumbago; **estar con dolores** to be in labor

dolori·do -da *adj* sore, painful; grieving, disconsolate

doloro·so -sa *adj* painful; sorrowful, sad

dolo·so -sa *adj* deceitful, guileful

domador *m* horsebreaker; animal tamer

domar *tr* to tame, break; master

domeñar *tr* to master, subdue

domesticar §73 *tr* to domesticate; tame

domésti·co -ca *adj* domestic, household ‖ *mf* domestic, servant

domiciliar *tr* to domicile, settle; (*una carta*) (Mex) to address ‖ *ref* to be domiciled, take up one's residence

domicilio *m* domicile, home; dwelling, house; **domicilio social** home office, company office

dominación *f* domination; (mil) eminence, high ground

dominante *adj* dominant; (*mandón*) domineering ‖ *f* (mus) dominant

dominar *tr* to dominate; check, restrain, subdue; (*una ciencia, un idioma*) master ‖ *intr* to dominate; (*mandar imperiosamente*) domineer ‖ *ref* to restrain oneself

dómine *m* schoolmaster, Latin teacher; pedant

domingo *m* Sunday; **domingo de ramos** Palm Sunday; **domingo de resurrección** Easter Sunday; **guardar el domingo** to keep the Sabbath

dominguillo *m* tumbler

dominica·no -na *adj & mf* Dominican

dominio *m* dominion; domain; (*de una ciencia, de un idioma*) mastery; (*del aire*) supremacy

domi·nó *m* (*pl* **-nós**) (*traje*) domino; (*juego*) dominoes; (*fichas*) set of dominoes

dom.° *abbr* **domingo**

domo *m* dome

dompedro *m* four-o'clock

don *m* gift, present; talent, natural gift; Don (*Spanish title used before masculine Christian names*); **don de acierto** knack for doing the right thing; **don de errar** knack for doing the wrong thing; **don de gentes** charm, social grace; **don de lenguas** linguistic facility; **don de mando** ability to lead, generalship

dona *f* gift, present; **donas** wedding presents from the bridegroom to the bride

donación *f* gift, bequest; endowment

donada *f* lay sister

donado *m* lay brother

dona·dor -dora *mf* donor

donaire *m* charm, grace; witticism; cleverness

donairo·so -sa *adj* charming, graceful; witty; clever

donar *tr* to donate, give

doncel *adj* mild, mellow ‖ *m* (*joven noble aun no armado caballero*) bachelor; (*hombre virgen*) virgin

doncella *f* maiden, virgin; housemaid; lady's maid; maid of honor; (Col, Ven) felon, whitlow

doncellez *f* maidenhood, virginity

doncellona *f* or **doncellueca** *f* unmarried woman, maiden lady

donde *conj* where; wherever; in which; **donde no** otherwise; **por donde quiera** anywhere, everywhere ‖ *prep* at or to the house, office, or store of

dónde *adv* where; **a dónde** where, whither; **de dónde** from where, whence; **por dónde** which way; for what cause, for what reason

dondequiera *adv* anywhere; **dondequiera que** wherever

dondiego *m* four-o'clock; **dondiego de día** morning-glory; **dondiego de noche** four-o'clock

donillero *m* sharper, smoothy

donjuán *m* four-o'clock

donosidad *f* charm, grace, wit

dono·so -sa *adj* charming, graceful, witty

donostiarra *adj* San Sebastian ‖ *mf* native or inhabitant of San Sebastian

donosura *f* charm, grace, wit

doña *f* Doña (*Spanish title used before feminine Christian names*)

doñear *intr* (coll) to hang around women

doquier or **doquiera** *conj* wherever; **por doquier** everywhere

dorada *f* (ichth) gilthead

doradillo *m* fine brass wire

dora·do -da *adj* golden; gilt ‖ *m* gilt, gilding; **dorados** bronze trimmings (*on furniture*) ‖ *f* see **dorada**

di
do

dorar *tr* to gold-plate; gild; (*tostar ligeramente*) brown; (*paliar*) sugar-coat ‖ *ref* to turn golden; turn brown

dormi•lón -lona *adj* sleepy ‖ *mf* sleepyhead ‖ *f* reclining armchair; mimosa; (Mex) headrest; (Ven) sleeping gown; **dormilonas** pearl earrings

dormir §30 *tr* to put to sleep; (*p.ej., una borrachera*) sleep off ‖ *intr* to sleep; spend the night ‖ *ref* to sleep; fall asleep; (*entorpecerse, p.ej., el pie*) go to sleep

dormirlas *m* hide-and-seek

dormitar *intr* to doze, nap

dormitorio *m* bedroom; (*muebles propios de esta habitación*) bedroom suit

dorsal *m* (sport) number (*worn on shirt*)

dorso *m* back

dos *adj & pron* two; **las dos** two o'clock ‖ *m* two; (*en las fechas*) second

dosal•bo -ba *adj* (*horse*) with two white feet

doscien•tos -tas *adj & pron* two hundred ‖ **doscientos** *m* two hundred

dosel *m* canopy, dais

doselera *f* valance, drapery

dosificación *f* dosage

dosificar §73 *tr* (*un medicamento*) to dose, give in doses

do•sis *f* (*pl* **-sis**) dose

dos-pie•zas *m* (*pl* **-zas**) two-piece bathing suit

dotación *f* (*de una mujer; de una fundación*) endowment; (nav) complement; (aer) crew; (*de remeros*) (sport) crew; staff, personnel

dotar *tr* to give a dowry to; endow; (*un buque*) staff, man; (*una oficina*) staff; equip; fix the wages for

dote *m & f* dowry, marriage portion ‖ *m* (*en el juego de naipes*) stack of chips ‖ *f* endowment, talent, gift; **dotes de mando** leadership

dovela *f* voussoir

doza•vo -va *adj & m* twelfth

d/p *abbr* **días plazo**

dracma *f* (*moneda griega*) drachma; (*peso farmacéutico*) dram

draga *f* dredge; (*barco*) dredger

dragado *m* dredging

dragami•nas *m* (*pl* **-nas**) mine sweeper

dragar §44 *tr* to dredge

dragón *m* dragon; (*planta*) snapdragon; (*soldado*) dragoon

dragonear *intr* to flirt; boast; **dragonear de** to boast of being; pretend to be, pass oneself off as

drama *m* drama

dramáti•co -ca *adj* dramatic ‖ *mf* (*autor*) dramatist; actor ‖ *f* (*arte y género*) drama

dramatizar §60 *tr* to dramatize

dramaturgo *m* dramatist

drásti•co -ca *adj* drastic

dren *m* drain

drenaje *m* drainage

drenar *tr* to drain

driblar *tr & intr* to dribble

dril *m* drill; duck; **dril de algodón** denim

driza *f* (naut) halyard

dro. *abbr* **derecho**

droga *f* drug; annoyance, bother; deceit, trick; (Chile, Mex, Peru) bad debt; (Cuba) drug on the market; **drogas milagrosas** wonder drugs

drogadic•to -ta *adj* drug-addicted ‖ *mf* drug addict

drogado *m* doping

drogar §44 *tr* to dope

droguería *f* drug store; drug business; (*comercio de substancias usadas en química, industria, medicina, bellas artes*) drysaltery (Brit)

drogue•ro -ra *mf* druggist; drysalter (Brit)

droguista *mf* druggist; (coll) crook, cheat; (Arg) toper, drunk

drolátí•co -ca *adj* droll, snappy

dromedario *m* dromedary; big heavy animal; brute (*person*)

druida *m* druid

dúa *f* (min) gang of workmen

dual *adj & m* dual

dualidad *f* duality; (Chile) tie vote

ducado *m* duchy, dukedom; (*moneda antigua*) ducat; **gran ducado** grand duchy

dúctil *adj* ductile; easy to handle

ducha *f* (*chorro de agua en una cavidad del cuerpo*) douche; (*chorro de agua sobre el cuerpo entero*) shower bath; (*lista en los tejidos*) stripe; **ducha en alfileres** needle bath

duchar *tr* to douche; give a shower bath to ‖ *ref* to douche; take a shower bath

du•cho -cha *adj* experienced, expert, skillful ‖ *f* see **ducha**

duda *f* doubt; **sin duda** doubtless, no doubt, without doubt

dudable *adj* doubtful

dudar *tr* to doubt; question ‖ *intr* to hesitate; **dudar de** to doubt

dudo•so -sa *adj* doubtful; dubious

duela *f* stave (*of barrel*)

duelista *m* duelist

duelo *m* (*combate entre dos*) duel; grief, sorrow; bereavement, mourning; (*los que asisten a los funerales*) mourners; **batirse en duelo** to duel, to fight a duel; **duelos** hardships; **sin duelo** in abundance

duende *m* elf, goblin; gold cloth, silver cloth; (coll) restless daemon; **tener duende** to be burning within

due•ño -ña *mf* owner, proprietor; **dueño de sí mismo** one's own master; **ser dueño de** to be master of; be at liberty to, be free to ‖ *m* master, landlord ‖ *f* mistress, landlady, housekeeper; duenna; matron; **dueña de casa** housewife

duermevela *f* doze, light sleep; (*sueño fatigoso e interrumpido*) fitful sleep

dula *f* common pasture land; land irrigated from common ditch

dulce *adj* sweet; (*agua*) fresh; (*metal*) soft, ductile; gentle, mild, pleasant; (*manjar*) tasteless, insipid ‖ *m* candy; piece of candy; preserves; **dulce de almíbar** preserved fruit; **dulces** candy

dulcera *f* candy dish, preserve dish

dulcería *f* candy store, confectionery store

dulce•ro -ra *adj* sweet-toothed ‖ *mf* confectioner ‖ *f* see **dulcera**

dulcificar §73 *tr* to sweeten; appease, mollify ‖ *ref* to sweeten, turn sweet

dulcinea *f* sweetheart; ideal

dulzaina *f* flageolet

dulza•rrón -rrona *adj* cloying, sickening

dulzo•so -sa *adj* sweetish

dulzura *f* sweetness; pleasantness, kindliness; (*del clima*) mildness; endearment, sweet word

duna *f* dune

dun•do -da *adj* (CAm, Col) simple, stupid ‖ *mf* (CAm, Col) simpleton

dúo *m* duet, duo

duodéci•mo -ma *adj & m* twelfth

duodeno *m* duodenum

duplica•do -da *adj & m* duplicate; **por duplicado** in duplicate

duplicar §73 *tr* to duplicate; double; repeat

duplicata *f* duplicate

duplicidad *f* (*falsedad*) duplicity; (*calidad de doble*) doubleness

du•plo -pla *adj & m* double

duque *m* duke; **gran duque** grand duke

duquesa *f* duchess; **gran duquesa** grand duchess

dura *f* durability; **de dura** or **de mucha dura** strong, durable

durable *adj* durable, lasting

duración *f* duration, endurance; (*espacio de tiempo del uso de una cosa*) life

durade•ro -ra *adj* durable, lasting

durante *prep* during, for

durar *intr* to last; remain; (*la ropa*) last, wear, wear well

durazno *m* peach; peach tree

dureza *f* hardness; harshness, roughness; **dureza de corazón** hardheartedness; **dureza de oído** hardness of hearing; **dureza de vientre** constipation

durmiente *adj* sleeping; **la Bella Durmiente** Sleeping Beauty ‖ *mf* sleeper ‖ *m* girder, sleeper, stringer; tie, railroad tie; (Ven) steel bar

du•ro -ra *adj* hard; (*huevo*) hard-boiled; harsh, rough; cruel; stubborn, obstinate; unbearable; strong, tough; stingy; (*tiempo*) stormy; **duro de corazón** hard-hearted; **duro de oído** hard of hearing; **duro de película** movie hero; **estar muy duro con** to be hard on; **ser duro de pelar** to be hard to put across; be hard to deal with ‖ *m* dollar (*Spanish coin worth five pesetas*) ‖ *f* see **dura** ‖ **duro** *adv* hard

dux *m* (*pl* **dux**) doge

d/v *abbr* **días vista**

E

E, e (e) *f* sixth letter of the Spanish alphabet

e *conj* (used before words beginning with *i* or *hi* not followed by a vowel) and

ea *interj* hey!

ebanista *m* cabinetmaker, woodworker

ebanistería *f* cabinetmaking, woodwork; cabinetmaker's shop

ébano *m* ebony

ebriedad *f* drunkenness

e•brio -bria *adj* drunk; (*p.ej.*, *de ira*) blind ‖ *mf* drunk

ebrio•so -sa *adj* drinking ‖ *mf* drinker

ebullición *f* boiling

eclécti•co -ca *adj & mf* eclectic

eclesiásti•co -ca *adj & m* ecclesiastic

eclipsar *tr* to eclipse; (fig) to outshine ‖ *ref* to be in eclipse; (fig) to disappear

eclipse *m* eclipse

eclip•sis *f* (*pl* **-sis**) var of **elipsis**

eclisa *f* (rr) fishplate

eco *m* echo; (*del tambor*) rumbling; **hacer eco** to echo; attract attention; **tener eco** to be well received, catch on

ecología *f* ecology

ecológi•co -ca *adj* ecologic(al)

ecologista *mf* or **ecólogo** *m* ecologist

economato *m* stewardship; commissary, company store, coöperative store

economía *f* economy; want, poverty; **economía política** economics; **economías** savings

económi•co -ca *adj* economic; (*que gasta poco; poco costoso*) economical; cheap; miserly, niggardly

economista *mf* economist

economizar §60 *tr* to economize, save; avoid ‖ *intr* to economize, save; skimp

ecónomo *m* steward, trustee; supply priest

ecuación *f* equation

ecuador *m* equator ‖ **el Ecuador** Ecuador

ecuánime *adj* calm, composed; impartial

ecuanimidad *f* equanimity; impartiality

ecuatoria•no -na *adj & mf* Ecuadoran, Ecuadorian

ecuestre *adj* equestrian

eculcorante *adj* sweetening ‖ *m* sweetener

ecuméni•co -ca *adj* ecumenic(al)

eczema *m & f* eczema

echacan•tos *m* (*pl* **-tos**) good-for-nothing

echacher•vos *m* (*pl* **-vos**) pimp, procurer; cheat

echada *f* cast, throw; man's length; (Arg, Mex) boast, hoax

echadero *m* place to stretch out

echadi•zo -za *adj* discarded, waste; spying ‖ *mf* foundling ‖ *m* spy

echa•do -da *adj* stretched out; (C-R) lazy, indolent; **estar echado** (CAm, Mex, P-R) to have an easy job (or easy life) ‖ *f* see **echada**

echar *tr* to throw, throw away, throw out; issue, emit; publish; discharge, dismiss; swallow; (*p.ej., agua*) pour; (*p.ej., un cigarrillo*) smoke; (*la baraja*) deal; (*una partida de cartas*) play; (*una llave*) turn; (*un discurso*) deliver; (*un drama*) put on; (*maldiciones*) utter; (*pelo, dientes, renuevos*) grow, put forth; (*impuestos*) impose, levy; (*la buenaventura*) tell; (*precio, distancia, edad, etc.*) ascribe, attribute; (*una mirada*) cast; (*sangre*) shed; (*la culpa*) lay; (*una mano*) lend; **echar abajo** to demolish, destroy; overthrow; **echar a pasear** to dismiss unceremoniously; **echar a perder** to spoil, ruin; **echar a pique** to sink; **echar de menos** to miss; **echarla de** to claim to be, boast of being; **echarlo todo a rodar** to upset everything; hit the ceiling ‖ *intr* — **echar a** to begin to; burst out (*e.g., crying*); **echar a perder** to spoil, ruin; **echar de ver** to notice, happen to see; **echar por** (*un empleo, un oficio*) to go into, take up; (*la derecha, la izquierda*) turn toward; (*un camino*) go down ‖ *ref* to throw oneself; lie down, stretch out; (*el viento*) fall; (*un abrigo*) throw on; (*una gallina*) set; **echarse a** to begin to; **echarse a morir** to give up in despair; **echarse a perder** to spoil, be ruined; **echarse atrás** to back out; **echarse de ver** to be easy to see; **echárselas de** to claim to be, boast of being; **echarse sobre** to rush at, fall upon

echazón *f* jettison, jetsam

echiquier *m* Exchequer

edad *f* age; **edad crítica** change of life; **edad de quintas** draft age; **edad escolar** school age; **Edad Media** Middle Ages; **edad viril** prime of life; **mayor edad** majority; **menor edad** minority

edecán *m* aide-de-camp

edema *f* edema

edición *f* edition; publication; **la segunda edición de** the spit and image of

edicto *m* edict

edificación *f* construction, building; buildings; (*inspiración con el buen ejemplo*) edification, uplift

edificante *adj* edifying

edificar §73 *tr* to construct, build; (*dar buen ejemplo a*) edify, uplift

edificio *m* edifice, building

editar *tr* to publish

edi•tor -tora *adj* publishing ‖ *mf* publisher

editorial *adj* publishing; editorial ‖ *m* editorial ‖ *f* publishing house

editorialista *mf* editorial writer

editorializar §60 *intr* (Urug) to editorialize

edredón *m* eider down

educación *f* education

educacional *adj* educational

educa•dor -dora *mf* educator

educan•do -da *mf* pupil, student

educar §73 *tr* to educate; (*los sentidos*) train; (*al niño o el adolescente*) rear, bring up

educati•vo -va *adj* educational

EE.UU. *abbr* **Estados Unidos**

efectismo *m* sensationalism

efectista *adj* sensational, theatrical ‖ *mf* sensationalist

efectivamente *adv* actually, really; as a matter of fact

efecti•vo -va *adj* actual, real; (*empleo, cargo*) regular, permanent; (*vigente*) effective; **hacer efectivo** to carry out; (*un cheque*) to cash; **hacerse efectivo** to become effective ‖ *m* cash; **efectivo en caja** cash on hand

efecto *m* effect; end, purpose; article; (*en el juego de billar*) English; **a ese efecto** for that purpose; **al efecto** for the purpose; **con efecto** or **en efecto** indeed, as a matter of fact; **efecto útil** efficiency, output; **llevar a efecto** or **poner en efecto** to put into effect, carry out; **surtir efecto** to work, have the desired effect

efectuar §21 *tr* to carry out, effect, effectuate ‖ *ref* to take place

efervescencia *f* effervescence

efervescente *adj* effervescent

eficacia *f* efficacy

efi•caz *adj* (*pl* **-caces**) efficacious, effectual; efficient

eficiencia *f* efficiency

eficiente *adj* efficient

efigie *f* effigy

efíme•ro -ra *adj* ephemeral

efugio *m* evasion, subterfuge

efusión *f* effusion; (*manifestación de afectos muy viva*) warmth, effusiveness; **efusión de sangre** bloodshed

efusi•vo -va *adj* effusive

égida *f* aegis

egip•cio -cia *adj* & *mf* Egyptian

Egipto *m* Egypt

eglantina *f* sweetbriar

eglefino *m* haddock

égloga *f* eclogue

egoísmo *m* egoism

egoísta *adj* egoistic ‖ *mf* egoist

egolatría *f* self-worship, self-glorification

egotismo *m* egotism

egotista *adj* egotistic(al) ‖ *mf* egotist

egre•gio -gia *adj* distinguished, eminent

egresar *intr* to graduate

egreso *m* departure; graduation

eje *m* (*pieza alrededor de la cual gira un cuerpo*) axle, shaft; (*línea que divide en dos mitades; línea recta alrededor de la cual se supone que gira un cuerpo*) axis; (fig) core, crux; **eje de balancín** rocker, rockershaft; **eje de carretón** axletree; **eje motor** drive shaft; **eje tándem** dual axle; dual rear

ejecución *f* execution

ejecutante *mf* performer

ejecutar *tr* to execute; perform

ejecutivamente *adv* expeditiously

ejecuti•vo -va *adj* urgent, pressing; insistent; executive ‖ *m* executive

ejecu•tor -tora *adj* executive ‖ *mf* executor;

ejecutor de la justicia executioner; **ejecutor testamentario** executor (*of a will*) ‖ *f* — **ejecutora testamentaria** executrix

ejemplar *adj* exemplary ‖ *m* pattern, model; (*de una obra impresa*) copy; precedent; (*caso que sirve de escarmiento*) example; **ejemplar de cortesía** complimentary copy; **ejemplar muestra** sample copy; **sin ejemplar** unprecedented; as a special case

ejemplarizar §60 *tr* to set an example to; exemplify

ejemplificar §73 *tr* to exemplify

ejemplo *m* example, instance; **por ejemplo** for example, for instance; **sin ejemplo** unexampled

ejercer §78 *tr* (*la medicina*) to practice; (*la caridad*) show, exercise; (*una fuerza*) exert ‖ *intr* to practice; **ejercer de** to practice as, work as

ejercicio *m* exercise; drill, practice; (*de un cargo u oficio*) tenure; (*uso constante*) exertion; (*año económico*) fiscal year; **hacer ejercicio** to take exercise; (mil) to drill

ejercitar *tr* to exercise; practice; drill, train ‖ *ref* to exercise; practice

ejército *m* army; **ejército permanente** standing army; **los tres ejércitos** the three arms of the service

ejido *m* commons

ejote *m* (CAm, Mex) string bean

el, la (*pl* **los, las**) *art def* the ‖ *pron dem* that, the one; **el que** who, which, that; he who, the one that

él *pron pers masc* he, it; him, it

elabora•do -da *adj* elaborate; finished

elaborar *tr* to elaborate; (*una teoría*) work out; (*el metal, la madera*) fashion, to work

elación *f* magnanimity, nobility; (*de estilo y lenguaje*) pomposity

elástica *f* knit undershirt; **elásticas** (Ven) suspenders

elasticidad *f* elasticity

elásti•co -ca *adj* elastic ‖ *m* elastic; bedspring ‖ *f* see **elástica**

eléboro *m* hellebore

elección *f* election; choice

electi•vo -va *adj* elective

elec•to -ta *adj* elect

electorado *m* electorate

electorero *m* henchman, heeler

electricidad *f* electricity

electricista *mf* electrician

eléctrico -ca *adj* electric(al)

electrificar §73 *tr* to electrify

electrizar §60 *tr* to electrify

electro *m* electromagnet

electroafeitadora *f* electric shaver

electrocutar *tr* to electrocute

electrodo *m* electrode

electrodomésti•co -ca *adj* electric-appliance ‖ *m* electric appliance

electróge•no -na *adj* generating electricity ‖ *m* electric generator

electroimán *m* electromagnet

electrólisis *f* electrolysis

electrólito *m* electrolyte

electromagnéti•co -ca *adj* electromagnetic

electromo•tor -tora or **-triz** *adj* (*pl* **-tores -toras -trices**) electromotive

electrón *m* electron

electróni•co -ca *adj* electronic ‖ *f* electronics

electrostáti•co -ca *adj* electrostatic

electrotecnia *f* electrical engineering

electrotipar *tr* to electrotype

electrotipo *m* electrotype

elefante *m* elephant; **elefante blanco** (fig) (SAm) white elephant

elegancia *f* elegance; style, stylishness

elegante *adj* elegant; stylish ‖ *mf* fashion plate

eleganto•so -sa *adj* elegant

elegía *f* elegy

elegía•co -ca *adj* elegiac

elegible *adj* eligible

elegir §57 *tr* to elect; choose, select

elemental *adj* (*primordial; simple, no compuesto*) elemental; (*que se refiere a los principios de una ciencia o arte; de fácil comprensión*) elementary

elemento *m* element; (*de una pila o batería*) cell; **elemento de compuestos** (gram) combining form; **elemento en rastro** trace element; **estar en su elemento** to be in one's element

elenco *m* catalogue, list, table; (theat) cast

elepé *adj* (*disco*) long-playing; LP ‖ *m* long-playing record

elevación *f* elevation; **elevación a potencias** (math) involution

eleva•do -da *adj* elevated, high; lofty, sublime

elevador *m* elevator; **elevador de granos** grain elevator

elevar *tr* to elevate, lift; (math) to raise ‖ *ref* to ascend, rise; be exalted; become conceited

elfo *m* elf

elidir *tr* to eliminate; (*una vocal*) elide

eliminar *tr* to eliminate; strike out ‖ *ref* (Mex) to go away, leave

elipse *f* (geom) ellipse

elip•sis *f* (*pl* **-sis**) (gram) ellipsis

elípti•co -ca *adj* (geom & gram) elliptic(al)

elisión *f* elision

elitista *adj* & *mf* elitist

elocución *f* public speaking, elocution

elocuencia *f* eloquence

elocuente *adj* eloquent

elogiable *adj* praiseworthy

elogiar *tr* to praise, eulogize

elogio *m* praise, eulogy

elogio•so -sa *adj* laudatory, glowing

elote *m* (Mex, Guat) ear of corn; **coger asando elotes** (CAm) to catch in the act; **pagar los elotes** (CAm) to be the goat

elucidar *tr* to elucidate

eludir *tr* to elude, evade, avoid

elusi•vo -va *adj* evasive; elusive

ella *pron pers fem* she, it; her, it; (coll) the trouble

ello *pron pers neut* it; (coll) the trouble; **ello es que** the fact is that ‖ *m* (psychoanalysis) id

ec
el

E.M. *abbr* **Estado Mayor**
emancipar *tr* to emancipate
embadurnamiento *m* daub, daubing
embadurnar *tr* to daub
embaír §1 *tr* to deceive, take in, hoax
embajada *f* embassy; ambassadorship; (iron) fine proposition
embajador *m* ambassador; **embajadores** ambassador and wife
embajadora *f* ambassadress
embalaje *m* packing; package; (sport) sprint
embalar *tr* to pack ‖ *intr* (sport) to sprint ‖ *ref* (el motor) to race; (sport) to sprint
embaldosado *m* tile paving
embaldosar *tr* to pave with tile
embalsamar *tr* to embalm; perfume
embalsar *tr* to dam, dam up
embalse *m* dam; damming; backwater
embanastar *tr* to put in a basket; pack, jam, overcrowd
embanquetar *tr* (Mex) to line with sidewalks
embarazada *adj fem* pregnant ‖ *f* pregnant woman
embarazar §60 *tr* (estorbar) to embarrass; obstruct; make pregnant ‖ *ref* to be embarrassed, be encumbered; become pregnant
embarazo *m* embarrassment; obstruction; awkwardness; pregnancy
embarazo•so -sa *adj* embarrassing, troublesome
embarbillar *tr* to rabbet
embarcación *f* boat, ship; embarkation (of passengers)
embarcadero *m* pier, wharf; (rr) platform; **embarcadero de ganado** (Arg) loading chute; **embarcadero flotante** landing stage
embarcador *m* shipper
embarcar §73 *tr* to ship ‖ *intr* to entrain ‖ *ref* to embark, ship; get involved
embarco *m* embarkation (of passengers)
embargar §44 *tr* to embargo; paralyze; (law) to seize, attach
embargo *m* embargo; indigestion; (law) seizure, attachment; **sin embargo** however, nevertheless
embarnizar §60 *tr* to varnish
embarque *m* shipment, embarkation (of freight)
embarrada *f* blunder
embarrancar §73 *tr, intr & ref* to run into a ditch; (una nave) run aground
embarrar *tr* to splash with mud; smear, stain; (CAm, Mex) to involve in a shady deal; **embarrarla** (Arg) to spoil the whole thing
embarrilar *tr* to barrel, put in barrels
embarullar *tr* to muddle, make a mess of; bungle, botch
embastar *tr* to baste, stitch
embate *m* blow, attack; (del mar) beating, dashing; (de viento) gust; **embates de la fortuna** hard knocks
embauca•dor -dora *mf* trickster; impostor; con man
embaucar §73 *tr* to trick, bamboozle, swindle

embaula•do -da *adj* crowded, packed, jammed
embaular §8 *tr* to put in a trunk; jam, pack in
embayar *ref* (Ecuad) to fly into a rage
embazar §60 *tr* to dye brown; hinder, obstruct; astound, dumbfound ‖ *ref* to get bored; be upset, get sick at the stomach
embebecer §22 *tr* to entertain, amuse, fascinate, enchant
embeber *tr* to absorb, soak up; soak; contain, include; embed; contract, shrink ‖ *intr* to contract, shrink ‖ *ref* to be enchanted, be enraptured; become absorbed or immersed; become well versed
embebi•do -da *adj* (vocal) elided; (columna) engaged
embelecar §73 *tr* to cheat, dupe, bamboozle
embeleco *m* cheating, fraud; bore; **embelecos** cuteness
embeleñar *tr* to dope, stupefy; enchant, bewitch
embelequería *f* (Col, Mex, W-I) fraud, swindle
embelesar *tr* to charm, enrapture, fascinate
embeleso *m* charm, fascination, delight
embellece•dor -dora *adj* embellishing, beautifying ‖ *m* (aut) hubcap ‖ *f* beautician
embellecer §22 *tr* to embellish, beautify
embellecimiento *m* embellishment, beautification
embermejecer §22 *tr* to dye red; make blush ‖ *ref* to blush
emberrinchar *ref* to fly into a rage
embestida *f* attack, assault; (detención intempestiva) buttonholing
embesti•dor -dora *mf* beat, sponger
embestir §50 *tr* to attack, assail; to strike; buttonhole, waylay ‖ *intr* to attack, charge, rush
embetunar *tr* to blacken; cover with tar
embicar §73 *tr* (Mex) to turn upside down, tilt ‖ *intr* (Arg, Chile) to run aground
emblandecer §22 *tr* to soften; placate, mollify ‖ *ref* to soften, yield
emblanquecer §22 *tr* to whiten; bleach ‖ *ref* to turn white
emblema *m* emblem
emblemáti•co -ca *adj* emblematic(al)
embobar *tr* to amaze, fascinate ‖ *ref* to stand gaping
embocadero *m* mouth, outlet
embocadura *f* nozzle; (de río) mouth; (del freno; de instrumento de viento) mouthpiece; (de cigarrillo) tip; (del vino) taste; stage entrance
embocar §73 *tr* to catch in the mouth; put in the mouth; take on, undertake; gulp down; try to put over ‖ *intr & ref* to enter, pass
embolada *f* stroke
embolado *m* bull with wooden balls on horns; (theat) minor role; (coll) trick, hoax
embolar *tr* (los cuernos del toro) to put wooden balls on; (el calzado) to shine ‖ *ref* (CAm, Mex) to get drunk
embolia *f* embolism
émbolo *m* (mach) piston; **émbolo buzo** (mach) plunger

embolsar *tr* to pocket, take in

embonar *tr* to fertilize; suit, be becoming to

emboquillar *tr* (*los cigarrillos*) to put tips on; (*una galería o túnel*) cut an entrance in; (*las junturas entre los ladrillos*) (Chile) to point, chink

emborrachar *tr* to intoxicate ‖ *ref* to get drunk; (*los colores de una tela*) run

emborrar *tr* to stuff, pad, wad; gulp down

emborrascar §73 *tr* to stir up, irritate ‖ *ref* to get stormy; (*un negocio*) fail; (*la veta de una mina*) (Arg, CAm, Mex) to peter out

emborronar *tr* to blot; scribble

emboscada *f* ambush, ambuscade

emboscado *m* draft dodger

emboscar §73 *tr* (*tropas para sorprender al enemigo*) to ambush ‖ *ref* to ambush, lie in ambush; shirk, take an easy way out

embota•do -da *adj* blunt, dull; (Chile) black-pawed

embotadura *f* bluntness, dullness

embotar *tr* to blunt, dull; dull, weaken; (*el tabaco*) put in a jar

embotella•do -da *adj* (*discurso*) prepared ‖ *m* bottling; (*del tráfico*) bottleneck

embotellamiento *m* bottling; traffic jam

embotellar *tr* to bottle; (*un negocio*) tie up; (nav) to bottle up

embotijar *tr* (*un suelo*) to underlay with jugs ‖ *ref* to swell up with anger

embovedar *tr* to vault, vault over; put in a vault

emboza•do -da *adj* muffled up ‖ *mf* person muffled up to eyes

embozar §60 *tr* to muffle up to the eyes; (*p.ej., a un perro*) muzzle; disguise ‖ *ref* to muffle oneself up to the eyes

embozo *m* muffler, cloak held over the face; fold back (*of bed sheet*); cunning, dissimulation; **quitarse el embozo** to drop one's mask

embragar §44 *tr* (*el motor*) to engage ‖ *intr* to throw the clutch in

embrague *m* clutch; engagement

embravecer §22 *tr* to enrage, make angry ‖ *ref* to get angry; (*el mar*) get rough

embraveci•do -da *adj* angry; rough, wild

embrear *tr* to tar, cover with tar; calk with tar

embregar §44 *ref* to wrangle

embriagar §44 *tr* to intoxicate, make drunk; enrapture ‖ *ref* to get drunk

embriaguez *f* drunkenness; rapture

embridar *tr* to bridle; check, restrain

embriología *f* embryology

embrión *m* embryo

embroca *f* poultice

embrocar §73 *tr* to empty; (*el toro al torero*) to catch between the horns ‖ *ref* (C-R) to fall on one's face; (Mex) to put on over the head

embrollar *tr* to tangle, muddle, embroil

embrollo *m* entanglement, muddle, embroilment; deception, trick

embromar *tr* to joke with, play jokes on; bore, annoy ‖ *ref* to be bored, be annoyed

embrujar *tr* to bewitch

embrutecer §22 *tr* to brutify, stupefy

embrutecimiento *m* brutalization; coarsening

embuchado *m* pork sausage; subterfuge; (*de la urna electoral*) stuffing (of ballot box)

embudar *tr* to put a funnel in; trick, trap

embudista *adj* tricky, scheming ‖ *mf* schemer

embudo *m* funnel; trick; (mil) shell hole; **embudo de bomba** (mil) bomb crater

embullar *tr* to stir up, excite, key up ‖ *ref* to become excited, keyed up

emburujar *tr* to jumble, pile up ‖ *ref* to wrap oneself up

embuste *m* lie, falsehood, trick; **embustes** baubles, trinkets; (*del niño*) cuteness

embuste•ro -ra *adj* lying, false, tricky ‖ *mf* liar, cheat

embuti•do -da *adj* inlaid, flush ‖ *m* inlay, marquetry; pork sausage; lace insertion

embutir *tr* to stuff, pack tight; insert; inlay; set flush; (*una hoja de metal*) fashion, hammer into shape ‖ *ref* to squeeze in; stuff oneself

emergencia *f* emergence; incident

emerger §17 *intr* to emerge; (*un submarino*) surface

emersión *f* emersion; (*de un submarino*) surfacing

eméti•co -ca *adj & m* emetic

emigración *f* emigration; migration

emigra•do -da *mf* émigré

emigrante *adj & mf* emigrant

emigrar *intr* to emigrate; migrate

eminencia *f* eminence

eminente *adj* eminent

emisa•rio -ria *mf* emissary ‖ *m* outlet

emisión *f* (*acción de exhalar; acción de lanzar ondas luminosas, etc.*) emission; (*títulos creados de una vez*) (com) issue; (*acción de emitir títulos nuevos*) (com) issuance; (rad) broadcast; **emisión seriada** (rad) serial

emi•sor -sora *adj* emitting; broadcasting ‖ *m* (rad) transmitter ‖ *f* broadcasting station

emitir *tr* to emit, send forth; issue, give out; (*p.ej., opiniones*) utter, express; (com) to issue; (rad) to broadcast

emoción *f* emotion

emocional *adj* emotional

emocionante *adj* moving, touching; thrilling, exciting

emocionar *tr* to move, stir; thrill

emoti•vo -va *adj* emotional

empacadi•zo -za *adj* (Arg) touchy

empaca•do -da *adj* (Arg) gruff, grim

empacar §73 *tr* to pack, crate ‖ *ref* to be stubborn; (*un animal*) balk, get balky

empa•cón -cona *adj* stubborn; balky

empacha•do -da *adj* backward, fumbling

empachar *tr* to hinder, embarrass; disguise; surfeit, upset the stomach of ‖ *ref* blush, be embarrassed; be upset, have indigestion

empacho *m* hindrance; embarrassment, bashfulness; indigestion

empacho•so -sa *adj* sickening; shameful

empadronar *tr* to register, take the census of ‖ *ref* to register, be registered in the census

empalagar §44 tr to cloy, pall, surfeit; bore, weary

empalago·so -sa adj cloying, sickening, mawkish; boring, annoying; fawning

empalar tr impale

empalizada f palisade, stockade, fence

empalizar §60 tr to fence in

empalmar tr to splice, connect, join, couple; combine; ‖ intr to connect, make connections; **empalmar con** to connect with; follow, succeed

empalme m splice, connection, joint, coupling; combination; (elec) joint; (rr) connection, junction

empanada f pie; fraud

empanadilla f pie

empana·do -da adj unlighted, unventilated ‖ f see **empanada**

empanar tr to crumb, bread; (las tierras) sow with wheat

empantanar tr to flood; obstruct

empaña·do -da adj dim, misty; blurred, fogged; (voz) flat

empañar tr (a las criaturas) to swaddle; blur, fog, dim, dull; tarnish, sully ‖ ref to blur, fog, dim, dull

empañetar tr to plaster

empapar tr to soak; soak up, absorb; drench ‖ ref to soak; be soaked; to become imbued; be surfeited

empapelado m papering, paper hanging; wallpaper; paper lining

empapela·dor -dora mf paper hanger

empapelar tr to wrap in paper; paper, line with paper; wallpaper; bring a criminal charge against

empaque m packing; look, appearance, mien; stiffness, stuffiness; brazenness

empaquetadura f gasket

empaquetar tr to pack; jam, stuff ‖ ref to pack; pack in; dress up

empareda·do -da mf recluse ‖ m sandwich

emparedar tr to wall in, confine

emparejar tr to pair, match; smooth, make level; even, make even; (una puerta) close flush ‖ intr to come up, come abreast; **emparejar con** to catch up with ‖ ref to pair, match

emparentar §2 intr to become related by marriage; **emparentar con** (buena gente) to marry into the family of; (una familia rica) marry into

emparrado m arbor, bower

emparrillar tr to grill

empasta·dor -dora mf bookbinder

empastadura f binding

empastar tr (un diente) to fill; (un libro) bind with stiff covers; convert into pasture land ‖ ref (Chile) to be overgrown with weeds

empaste m (de diente) filling; stiff binding

empastelar tr (typ) to pie

empatar tr (en la votación y los juegos) to tie; join, connect; tie, fasten ‖ intr to tie ‖ ref to tie; **empatársela a una persona** to be a match for someone; **empatárselo a una persona** (Guat, Hond) to put it over on someone

empate m tie, draw; (Col) penholder; (Ven) waste of time

empatía f empathy

empavar tr (Ecuad) to annoy; (Peru) to kid, razz

empavesado m (naut) dressing, bunting

empavesar tr to bedeck with flags and bunting; (un buque) dress; (un monumento) veil ‖ ref to become overcast

empavonar tr to blue; grease, spread grease over ‖ ref (CAm) to dress up

empecina·do -da adj stubborn

empecinamiento m stubbornness; determination

empecinar tr to tar; dip in pitch ‖ ref to be stubborn; persist

empederni·do -da adj hardened, inveterate; hard-hearted

empedra·do -da adj cloud-flecked; pockmarked; (caballo) dark-spotted ‖ m stone paving

empedrar §2 tr to pave with stones; bespatter

empegado m tarpaulin

empegar §44 tr to coat with pitch, dip in pitch; (el ganado lanar) mark with pitch

empeine m instep; (de la bota) vamp; (enfermedad cutánea) tetter; (región central del hipogastrio) pubes

empelotar ref to get all tangled up; get into a row; take all one's clothes off; (Mex, W-I) to fall madly in love

empella f vamp

empellar tr to push, shove

empeller §31 tr to push, shove

empellón m push, shove; **a empellones** pushing, roughly

empenachar tr to adorn with plumes

empeña·do -da adj (disputa) bitter, heated; **no empeñado** noncommitted

empeñar tr (dar en prenda) to pawn; (una lucha) launch, begin; (prendar, hipotecar) pledge; (la palabra) pledge; force, compel ‖ ref to commit oneself, bind oneself; go into debt; (una lucha, una disputa) begin, start; **empeñarse en** to engage in; persist in, insist on

empeñe·ro -ra mf (Mex) pawnbroker

empeño m pledge, engagement, commitment; (prenda) pawn; pawnshop; persistence, insistence; eagerness, perseverance; effort, endeavor; pledge, backer, patron; favor, protection; **con empeño** eagerly

empeño·so -sa adj eager, persistent

empeorar tr to impair, make worse ‖ intr & ref to get worse, deteriorate

empequeñecer §22 tr (hacer más pequeño) to make smaller, dwarf; (amenguar la importancia de) belittle ‖ ref to get smaller, dwarf

emperador m emperor; **los emperadores** the emperor and empress

empera·triz f (pl -trices) empress

emperchar tr to hang on a clothes rack

emperejilar tr & ref to dress up, spruce up

emperezar §60 tr to delay, put off ‖ intr & ref to get lazy

empericar §73 *ref* (Col, Ecuad) to get drunk; (Mex) to blush

emperifollar *tr & ref* to dress up gaudily

empernar *tr* to bolt

empero *conj* but, however, yet

emperrar *ref* to get stubborn

empezar §18 *tr & intr* to begin

empicar §73 *ref* to become infatuated

empicotar *tr* to pillory

empiema *m* empyema

empina·do -da *adj* high, lofty; steep; stiff, stuck-up || *f* (aer) zoom, zooming; **irse a la empinada** (*un caballo*) to rear

empinar *tr* to raise, lift; tip over; (*el codo*) crook; (aer) to zoom || *intr* to be a toper || *ref* to stand on tiptoe; (*un caballo*) rear; tower, rise high; (aer) to zoom

empingorota·do -da *adj* influential; proud, haughty

empingorotar *tr* to put on top || *ref* to climb up, get up; be stuck-up

empíre·o -a *adj & m* empyrean

empíri·co -ca *adj* empiric(al) || *mf* empiricist

empizarrado *m* slate roof

empizarrar *tr* to roof with slate

emplastar *tr* to put a plaster on; put make-up on; (*un negocio*) tie up, obstruct || *ref* to put make-up on; smear oneself up

emplásti·co -ca *adj* sticky

emplasto *m* plaster, poultice

emplazamiento *m* emplacement, location; (law) summons

emplazar §60 *tr* to place, locate; summon, summons

emplea·do -da *mf* employee; (*de oficina, de tienda*) clerk; **empleado público** civil servant

emplear *tr* to employ; use; (*el dinero*) invest; **estarle a uno bien empleado** to serve someone right || *ref* to be employed; busy oneself; **empleárselo mal** to act up, misbehave

empleo *m* employ, employment; use; job, position, occupation

empleomanía *f* eagerness to hold public office

empleóma·no -na *mf* public officeholder, bureaucrat

emplomar *tr* to lead; line with lead; (*un techo*) cover with lead; put a lead seal on; (*un diente*) (Arg) to fill

emplumar *tr* to put a feather on; adorn with feathers; tar and feather; (Hond) to thrash; **emplumarlas** (Col) to beat it || *intr* to fledge, grow feathers

emplumecer §22 *intr* to fledge, grow feathers

empobrecer §22 *tr* to impoverish || *intr & ref* to become poor

empodrecer §22 *intr & ref* to rot

empolva·do -da *adj* (Mex) rusty

empolvar *tr* to cover with dust; (*el rostro*) powder || *ref* to get dusty; (*el rostro*) powder; (Mex) to get rusty

empolla·do -da *adj* primed for an examination

empollar *tr* (*huevos*) to brood, hatch; (*estudiar con mucha detención*) bone up on || *intr* to grind, be a grind; **empollar sobre** to bone up on || *ref* to hatch; bone up on

empo·llón -llona *mf* (coll) grind

emponcha·do -da *adj* (SAm) poncho-wearing; (SAm) crafty, hypocritical; (SAm) suspicious-looking

emponzoñar *tr* to poison; corrupt

emporcar §81 *tr* to soil, dirty

emporra·do -da *adj* (drogas) high

empotra·do -da *adj* built-in; recessed

empotrar *tr* to embed, recess, fasten in a wall || *intr & ref* to fit, interlock

emprende·dor -dora *adj* enterprising

emprender *tr* to undertake; **emprenderla con** to squabble with, have it out with; **emprenderla para** to set out for

empreñar *tr* to make pregnant || *ref* to become pregnant

empresa *f* enterprise, undertaking; company, concern, firm; device, motto; (*la parte patronal*) management; **empresa anunciadora** advertising agency; **empresa de tranvías** traction company; **pequeña empresa** small business

empresarial *adj* managerial

empresa·rio -ria *mf* contractor; business leader, industrialist; manager; promoter; theatrical manager; **empresario de circo** showman; **empresario de pompas fúnebres** undertaker; **empresario de publicidad** advertising man; **empresario de teatro** impresario, theater manager

emprestar *tr* to borrow

empréstito *m* loan, government loan

empujar *tr* to push, shove; replace || *intr* to push, shove

empujatierra *f* bulldozer

empuje *m* push; (*fuerza o presión ejercidas por una cosa sobre otra*) thrust; (*espíritu emprendedor*) enterprise, push

empujón *m* hard push, shove; **tratar a empujones** to push around

empuñadura *f* (*de la espada*) hilt; first words of a story; (*de bastón o paraguas*) handle

empuñar *tr* to seize, grasp, clutch; (*un empleo o puesto*) obtain; (*la mano*) (Chile) to clench; (Bol) to punch; **empuñar el bastón** (fig) to seize the reins

emular *tr & intr* to emulate; **emular con** to emulate, vie with

ému·lo -la *adj* emulous || *mf* rival

emulsión *f* emulsion

emulsionar *tr* to emulsify

en *prep* at; in; into; by; on; of, e.g., **pensar en** to think of

enaceitar *tr* to oil || *ref* to get oily, get rancid

enagua *f* petticoat; skirt; **enaguas** petticoat

enagüillas *fpl* kilt, short skirt

enajenación *f* alienation; estrangement; rapture; (*distracción*) absent-mindedness; **enajenación mental** mental derangement

enajenar *tr* (*la propiedad, el dominio; a un amigo*) to alienate, estrange; enrapture, transport || *ref* to be enraptured, be transported; **enajenarse de** to dispossess one-

em
en

self of; (*un amigo*) become alienated from

enaltecer §22 *tr* to exalt, extol

enamoradi·zo -za *adj* susceptible

enamora·do -da *adj* lovesick; (*propenso a enamorarse*) susceptible ‖ *mf* sweetheart ‖ *m* lover

enamorar *tr* to make love to; enamor, captivate ‖ *ref* to fall in love

enamoricar §73 *ref* to trifle in love

enangostar *tr & ref* to narrow

ena·no -na *adj* dwarfish ‖ *mf* dwarf

enarbolar *tr* to hoist, hang out; (*una espada*) brandish ‖ *ref* to get angry; (*el caballo*) rear

enarcar §73 *tr* to arch; (*los toneles*) hoop ‖ *ref* to become confused, be bashful; (*el caballo*) (Mex) to rear

enardecer §22 *tr* to inflame, excite ‖ *ref* to get excited; (*una parte del cuerpo*) become inflamed, get sore

enarenar *tr* to throw sand on ‖ *ref* (naut) to run aground

enastar *tr* (*una herramienta*) to put a handle on; (*una bandera*) put a shaft on

encabalgamiento *m* gun carriage; trestlework; (*en el verso*) enjambment

encabalgar §44 *tr* to provide with horses ‖ *intr* to lean, rest

encaballar *tr* to overlap; (typ) to pie

encabezamiento *m* heading; (*fórmula con que comienza un documento*) opening words; tax list; tax rate; **encabezamiento de factura** billhead

encabezar §60 *tr* (*un escrito*) to put a heading or title on; head; register; (*vinos*) fortify

encabritar *ref* (*un caballo*) to rear; (*un buque*) shoot up, pitch up; (*un avión*) nose up

encadenar *tr* to chain, put in chains; brace, buttress; bind, tie together; tie down

encajar *tr* to fit, fit in, make fit; insert, put in; (*un golpe*) give, let go; (*dinero*) put away; (*un chiste*) tell at the wrong time; to palm off; throw, hurl; **encajar una cosa a uno** to foist something on someone, palm something off on someone ‖ *intr* to fit; (*una puerta*) close right ‖ *ref* to squeeze one's way; (*una prenda de vestir*) put on; butt in, intrude

encaje *m* (*tejido de mallas*) lace; (*labor de taracea*) inlay, mosaic; recess, groove; fitting, matching; insertion; appearance, look

encaje·ro -ra *mf* lacemaker; lace dealer

encajonado *m* cofferdam

encajonar *tr* to box, crate, case; squeeze in ‖ *ref* (*un río*) to narrow, narrow down; squeeze in, squeeze through

encalambrar *ref* to get cramps

encalar *tr* (*espolvorear con cal*) to lime, sprinkle with lime; (*blanquear con cal*) whitewash

encalma·do -da *adj* (*mercado de valores*) dull, quiet; (*mar, viento*) becalmed

encalvecer §22 *intr* to get bald

encalladero *m* sand bank, shoal

encallar *intr* to run aground; fail, get stuck

encallecer §22 *intr* (*la piel*) to become callous ‖ *ref* to become callous; (fig) to become callous, become hardened

encamar *tr* to spread out on the ground ‖ *ref* to take to bed; (*el grano*) droop, bend over

encaminar *tr* to direct, show the way to; (*sus esfuerzos, su atención*) direct ‖ *ref* to set out

encanalar *tr* to channel, pipe

encandecer §22 *tr* to make white-hot

encandila·do -da *adj* (*sombrero*) cocked; stiff, erect

encandilar *tr* to daze, befuddle; (*un fuego*) to stir ‖ *ref* (*los ojos*) to flash

encanecer §22 *intr & ref* to turn gray; get old; become moldy

encanta·do -da *adj* absent-minded, distracted; (*casa*) rambling

encanta·dor -dora *adj* charming, enchanting ‖ *mf* charmer ‖ *f* enchantress

encantamiento *m* charm, enchantment

encantar *tr* to charm, enchant, bewitch

encante *m* auction sale; auction house

encanto *m* charm, enchantment, spell

encantusar *tr* to coax, wheedle

encañada *f* gorge, ravine

encañar *tr* (*el agua*) to pipe; (*las tierras*) drain; (*las plantas*) prop up; wind on a spool

encañizada *f* reed fence; weir

encañonar *tr* to pipe; wind on a spool; (*un pliego*) (typ) to tip in

encaperuzar §60 *tr* to put a hood on ‖ *ref* to put on one's hood

encapotar *tr* to cloak ‖ *ref* to frown; cloud over, become overcast

encaprichar *ref* to insist on getting one's way; become infatuated

encaracolado *m* spiral ornament, spiral work

encara·do -da *adj* — **bien encarado** well-featured; **mal encarado** ill-featured

encaramar *tr* to raise up, lift up; praise, extol; elevate, exalt ‖ *ref* to climb, get on top; rise, tower; blush

encarar *tr* to aim, point; (*una dificultad*) face ‖ *intr & ref* to come face to face

encarcelar *tr* to incarcerate, imprison, jail; (*piezas de madera recién encoladas*) clamp; plaster in ‖ *ref* to stay indoors

encarecer §22 *tr* (*el precio*) to raise; raise the price of; extol; urge; overrate ‖ *intr & ref* to rise, rise in price

encarecidamente *adv* earnestly, insistently, eagerly

encarga·do -da *mf* agent, representative; **encargado de negocios** chargé d'affaires

encargamiento *m* duty; obligation; charge

encargar §44 *tr* (*mercancías*) to order; (*confiar*) entrust; urge, warn ‖ *ref* to take charge, be in charge

encargo *m* assignment, job, charge; (*pedido*) order; warning; **como de encargo** or **ni de encargo** just the thing, as if made to order

encariñamiento *m* endearment

encariñar *tr* to awaken love in ‖ *ref* — **encariñarse con** to become fond of, become attached to

encarnación f incarnation, embodiment

encarna•do -da adj red; Caucasian-skin-("flesh")-colored; (de forma humana) incarnate

encarnar tr to incarnate, embody; (el anzuelo) bait ‖ intr to become incarnate; (una herida) heal over

encarnecer §22 intr to put on flesh

encarniza•do -da adj bloodshot; bloody, fierce, bitter, hard-fought

encarnizar §60 tr to anger, provoke ‖ ref to get angry; become fierce; **encarnizarse con** or **en** to be merciless to

encaro m aim; stare; blunderbuss

encarrilar tr to put back on the rails; set right, put on the right track; guide, direct

encarruja•do -da adj wrinkled; (pelo) kinky; (terreno) (Mex) rough

encartar tr to enroll, register; outlaw; (un naipe) slip in ‖ ref to be unable to discard

encartonar tr to cover with cardboard; (libros) bind in boards

encasar tr (un hueso dislocado) to set (a broken bone)

encasillado m set of pigeonholes; (lista de candidatos apoyados por el gobierno) government slate; (SAm) checkerwork

encasillar tr to pigeonhole; sort out, classify; (el gobierno a un candidato) slate

encasquetar tr (un sombrero) to stick on the head; (una idea) drive in; force on

encasquillar tr to put a tip on; (un caballo) shoe ‖ ref to stick, get stuck

encastilla•do -da adj haughty, proud

encastillar tr to fortify with castles; pile up ‖ ref to stick, get stuck; take to the hills; stick to one's opinion

encastrar tr to engage, mesh

encastre m engaging, meshing; groove, socket; insert

encauchar tr to cover with rubber, line with rubber

encausar tr to prosecute, sue, bring to trial

encausticar §73 tr to wax

encáustico m floor wax, furniture polish

encauzar §60 tr (una corriente) to channel; guide, direct

encavar ref to hide, burrow

encebollado m beef stew with onions

encelar tr to make jealous ‖ ref to get jealous; be in rut

encella f cheese mold

encenagar §44 ref to get covered with mud; wallow in vice

encencerrar tr (al ganado) to put a bell on

encendajas fpl kindling, brush

encendedor m lighter; **encendedor de bolsillo** pocket lighter

encender §51 tr to light, kindle; ignite, fire to; (la luz, la radio) turn on; (la lengua) burn; stir up, excite ‖ ref to catch fire, ignite; become excited; blush

encendi•do -da adj bright, high-colored; red, flushed; keen, enthusiastic ‖ m ignition

encenizar §60 tr to cover with ashes ‖ ref to get covered with ashes

encepar tr to put in the stocks ‖ intr & ref to take deep root

encera•do -da adj wax, wax-colored; (huevo) boiled ‖ m oilcloth; tarpaulin; (pizarra) blackboard

encerar tr to wax ‖ intr & ref (el grano) to ripen, turn yellow

encerotar tr (el hilo) to wax

encerradero m sheepfold; (taur) bull pen

encerrar §2 tr to shut in; lock in, lock up; contain, include; encircle; imply ‖ ref to lock oneself in; go into seclusion; **encerrarse con** to be closeted with

encerrona f dilemma; tight spot; (coll) fix

encespedar tr to sod

encestar tr to put in a basket; (coll) to sink (a basketball)

encía f gum

encíclica f encyclical

enciclopedia f encyclopedia

enciclopédi•co -ca adj encyclopedic

encierro m locking up, confinement; inclusion; encirclement; lockup, prison; solitary confinement; retirement, retreat; (taur) bull pen

encima adv above, overhead, on top; at hand, here now; besides, in addition; **de encima** (Chile) in the bargain; **echarse encima** to take upon oneself; **encima de** on, upon; above, over; **por encima** hastily; superficially; **por encima de** above, over; in spite of; **quitarse de encima** to get rid of, shake off

encina f holm oak, evergreen oak

encinta adj pregnant; **dejar encinta** to make pregnant

encintado m curb

encintar tr to trim with ribbons; provide with curbs

enclaustrar tr to cloister; hide away

enclavar tr to nail; pierce, transfix; (el pie del caballo) prick; cheat

enclave m enclave

enclavijar tr to dowel; (un instrumento) to peg

enclenque adj sickly, feeble

enclíti•co -ca adj & m enclitic

enclocar §81 intr & ref to brood

encofrado m planking, timbering; (para el hormigón) form

encoger §17 tr to shrink, shrivel; discourage; draw in ‖ intr to shrink, shrivel ‖ ref to shrink, shrivel; be discouraged; be bashful; (humillarse) cringe; (en la cama) curl up; **encogerse de hombros** to shrug one's shoulders

encogi•do -da adj bashful, timid

encogimiento m shrinkage; crouch; bashfulness, timidity; **encogimiento de hombros** shrug

encojar tr to cripple, lame ‖ ref to become lame; feign illness

encolar tr to glue; (la superficie que ha de pintarse) size; (el vino) clarify; (p.ej., una pelota) throw out of reach

encolerizar §60 tr to anger ‖ ref to get angry

encomendar §2 *tr* to commend, entrust, commit; knight ‖ *ref* to commend oneself; send regards

encomiar *tr* to praise, extol

encomienda *f* charge, commission; commendation, praise; favor, protection; knight's cross; royal land grant (*with Indian inhabitants*); parcel post; (Mex) fruit stand

encomio *m* encomium

enconamiento *m* soreness; rancor, ill will

enconar *tr* to make sore, inflame; aggravate, irritate ‖ *ref* to get sore, become inflamed; (*una herida; el ánimo de uno*) rankle, fester

enconchar *ref* to draw back into one's shell, keep aloof

encono *m* rancor, ill will; (Col, Chile, Mex, W-I) soreness

encono•so -sa *adj* sore, sensitive; harmful; rancorous

encontra•do -da *adj* opposite, facing; contrary; hostile; **estar encontrados** to be at odds

encontrar *tr* to encounter, meet; (*hallar*) find ‖ *intr* to meet; collide ‖ *ref* to meet, meet each other; be, be situated; find oneself; **encontrarse con** to meet, run into

encontrón *m* bump, jolt, collision

encopeta•do -da *adj* aristocratic, of noble descent; conceited, boastful

encorajar *tr* to encourage ‖ *ref* to fly into a rage

encorajinar *ref* to fly into a rage; (Chile) to break up, go to ruin

encorchar *tr* (*botellas*) to cork; (*abejas*) to hive

encordar §61 *tr* (*un violín, una raqueta*) to string; wrap, wind up with rope

encordelar *tr* to string; tie with strings

encornudar *tr* to cuckold, make a cuckold of ‖ *intr* to grow horns

encorralar *tr* to corral

encortinar *tr* to curtain

encorvada *f* stoop, bending over; **hacer la encorvada** to malinger

encorvar *tr* to bend over ‖ *ref* to stoop, bend over; be partial, be biased

encovar §61 *tr & ref* to hide away

encrespar *tr* to curl; (*el pelo*) make stand on end; (*plumas*) ruffle; (*las olas*) stir up; irritate, anger ‖ *ref* to curl; bristle, stand on end; (*el mar, las olas*) get rough; get involved; bristle, get angry

encresta•do -da *adj* proud, haughty

encrucijada *f* crossroads, street intersection; ambush, snare, trap

encrudecer §22 *tr* to make raw; aggravate

encuadernación *f* bookbinding; (*taller*) bindery; **encuadernación a la holandesa** half binding

encuaderna•dor -dora *mf* bookbinder

encuadernar *tr* to bind; **sin encuadernar** unbound

encuadrar *tr* (*encerrar en un marco o cuadro*) to frame; (*incluir dentro de sí*) encompass; (*encajar*) insert, fit in; (Arg) to summarize

encuadre *m* film adaptation; (mov & telv) frame

encubar *tr* to put in a cask or vat; (min) to shore up

encubierta *f* fraud, deception

encubrimiento *m* concealment; (law) complicity

encubrir §83 *tr* to hide, conceal ‖ *ref* to hide; disguise oneself

encuentro *m* encounter, meeting; clash, collision; (*hallazgo*) find; (sport) game, match; **encuentro fronterizo** border clash; **llevarse de encuentro** (CAm, Mex, W-I) to knock down, run over; (CAm, Mex, W-I) to drag down to ruin; **mal encuentro** foul play; **salir al encuentro a** to go to meet; get ahead of; take a stand against

encuerar *tr* to strip of clothes; fleece ‖ *ref* to strip, get undressed

encuesta *f* inquiry; **encuesta demoscópica** opinion poll; survey

encuestador *m* pollster

encuitar *ref* to grieve

encumbra•do -da *adj* high, lofty; sublime; influential

encumbramiento *m* height, elevation; exaltation

encumbrar *tr* to raise, elevate; exalt ‖ *ref* to rise; be exalted; be proud; be flowery, use flowery speech; (*subir una cosa a mucha altura*) tower

encunar *tr* to cradle; catch between the horns

encurtido *m* pickle

encurtir *tr* to pickle

enchapado *m* veneer

enchapar *tr* to veneer

encharcar §73 *tr* to make a puddle of; (*el estómago*) upset ‖ *ref* to turn into a puddle; wallow in vice

enchavetar *tr* to key

enchichar *ref* (SAm) to get drunk; (CAm) to get angry

enchilada *f* (Guat, Mex) corn cake with tomato sauce seasoned with chili

enchilado *m* (Cuba, Mex) shellfish stew with chili sauce

enchilo•so -sa *adj* (CAm, Mex) spicy, hot

enchinar *tr* to pave with pebbles; (Mex) to curl ‖ *ref* (Mex) to get goose flesh

enchispar *tr* to make drunk ‖ *ref* to get drunk

enchivar *ref* (Col, Ecuad, CAm) to fly into a rage

enchufar *tr* (*un tubo o caño*) to fit; (*dos tubos o caños*) connect, connect together; (*dos negocios*) merge; (elec) to connect, plug in ‖ *intr* to fit ‖ *ref* to merge

enchufe *m* fitting; (*de tubo o caño*) male end; (*de dos tubos*) joint; (elec) connector; (elec) plug; (elec) receptacle; sinecure, easy job; **tener enchufe** to have pull, have a drag

enchufismo *m* spoils system; wire pulling

enchufista *m* spoilsman

ende *adv* — **por ende** therefore

endeble *adj* feeble, weak; worthless

endecha *f* dirge

endechadera *f* hired mourner

endemia *f* endemic

endémi•co -ca *adj* endemic
endemonia•do -da *adj* possessed of the devil;· furious, wild; (coll) devilish
endenantes *adv* recently
endentar §2 *tr & intr* to mesh
endentecer §22 *intr* to teethe
enderezar §60 *tr* to stand up; straighten; direct; put in order; regulate ‖ *intr* to go straight ‖ *ref* to stand up, straighten up; head, make one's way; go straight; (aer) to flatten out, level off
endeuda•do -da *adj* indebted
endeudamiento *m* indebtedness
endeudar *ref* to run into debt; acknowledge one's indebtedness
endevota•do -da *adj* pious, devout; fond, devoted
endiabla•do -da *adj* devilish; deformed, ugly; mean, wicked; (Arg) difficult, complicated
endilgar §44 *tr* to send, direct; to spring, unload
endiosar *tr* to deify ‖ *ref* to get stuck-up; get absorbed
endominga•do -da *adj* Sunday; all dressed up
endomingar §44 *ref* to get dressed in one's Sunday best
endosante *mf* endorser
endosar *tr* (*un documento de crédito*) to endorse; (*una cosa poco grata*) unload
endosata•rio -ria *mf* endorsee
endoso *m* endorsement
endriago *m* fabulous monster
endri•no -na *adj* sloe-colored ‖ *m* (*arbusto*) sloe, blackthron ‖ *f* (*fruto*) sloe
endrogar §44 *ref* to run into debt
endulzar §60 *tr* to sweeten; make bearable
endura•dor -dora *adj* saving, stingy
endurar *tr* to harden; delay, put off; (*tolerar*) endure; save, spare ‖ *ref* to get hard
endurecer §22 *tr* to harden; (*robustecer, acostumbrar*) inure
endureci•do -da *adj* hard, strong; inured; hard-hearted; tenacious, obstinate
enebrina *f* juniper berry
enebro *m* juniper
enecha•do -da *adj & mf* foundling
eneldo *m* dill
enema *f* enema
enemiga *f* enmity, hatred
enemi•go -ga *adj* enemy; hostile ‖ *mf* enemy, foe; **el enemigo malo** the Evil One ‖ *f* see **enemiga**
enemistad *f* enmity
enemistar *tr* to make an enemy of; make enemies of ‖ *ref* to become enemies
energéti•co -ca *adj* energy; power
energía *f* energy; power; **energía atómica** atomic power (or energy); **energías alternas** alternate energy sources; **energía solar** solar energy
enérgi•co -ca *adj* energetic
energúme•no -na *adj* fiendish ‖ *mf* crazy person, wild person
enero *m* January
enervar *tr* to enervate; weaken
enési•mo -ma *adj* nth
enfadadi•zo -za *adj* peevish, irritable

enfadar *tr* to annoy, bother; anger
enfado *m* annoyance, bother; anger
enfado•so -sa *adj* annoying, disagreeable
enfaldar *ref* to tuck up one's skirt
enfardar *tr* to bale, pack
énfa•sis *m* (*pl* -sis) emphasis; bombast, affected speech
enfasizar §60 *tr* to emphasize
enfáti•co -ca *adj* emphatic; affected
enfermar *tr* to make sick ‖ *intr* to get sick
enfermedad *f* sickness, illness, disease
enfermera *f* nurse; **enfermera ambulante** visiting nurse
enfermería *f* infirmary
enfermero *m* male nurse
enfermi•zo -za *adj* sickly; (*clima*) unhealthy
enfer•mo -ma *adj* sick, ill; (*enfermizo*) sickly; **enfermo de amor** lovesick ‖ *mf* patient
enfermo•so -sa *adj* sickly
enfiestar *ref* to have a good time
enfilar *tr* to line up; (*p.ej., perlas*) string; aim; go down, go up; (mil) to enfilade ‖ *intr* to bear
enfisema *m* emphysema
enflaquecer §22 *tr* to make thin; weaken ‖ *intr* to get thin; flag, slacken ‖ *ref* to get thin, lose weight
enflauta•do -da *adj* pompous, inflated
enflautar *tr* to blow up, inflate; cheat
enfocar §73 *tr* to focus; (fig) to size up
enfoque *m* focus, focusing; (fig) approach (*to a problem*)
enfoscar §73 *tr* to trim with mortar; patch with mortar; darken, make dark ‖ *ref* to become sullen, become grouchy; become absorbed in business; become overcast
enfrailar *tr* to make a friar or monk of ‖ *ref* to become a friar or monk
enfranque *m* shank
enfrascar §73 *tr* to bottle ‖ *ref* to become involved, intangled; be sunk in work; have a good time
enfrenar *tr* (*un caballo*) to bridle; (*un tren*) brake; check
enfrentamiento *m* (*policía, masas*) confrontation
enfrentar *tr* to put face to face; (*p.ej., al enemigo*) face ‖ *intr* to be facing ‖ *ref* to meet face to face; **enfrentarse con** to stand up to; cope with
enfrente *adv* opposite, in front; **enfrente de** opposite, in front of; opposed to
enfriadera *f* bottle cooler, ice pail
enfriar §77 *tr* to cool, chill; kill ‖ *intr & ref* to cool off
enfundar *tr* to sheathe, put in a case; stuff; (*un tambor*) muffle
enfurecer §22 *tr* to infuriate, anger ‖ *ref* to rage
enfurruñar *ref* to sulk
engalanar *tr* to adorn, deck out, dress
engalla•do -da *adj* straight, erect; haughty
engallador *m* checkrein
enganchar *tr* to hook; (*un caballo*) hitch; (*un coche de ferrocarril*) couple; recruit; inveigle ‖ *intr* to get caught ‖ *ref* to get caught; (mil) to enlist

en
en

enganche *m* hook; hooking; hitching; coupling; inveigling; recruiting; enlisting; (rr) coupler

engañabo•bos *mf* (*pl* **-bos**) bamboozler

engaña•dor -dora *adj* deceptive; (*simpático*) winsome

engañar *tr* to deceive, cheat, fool; (*el tiempo*) while away; (*el sueño, el hambre*) ward off; wheedle ‖ *ref* to be mistaken

engañifa *f* deception, trick

engaño *m* deception, deceit, fraud; mistake; falsehood; **llamarse a engaño** to back out because of fraud

engaño•so -sa *adj* deceptive

engargantar *tr* (*un ave*) to stuff the throat of ‖ *intr & ref* to mesh, engage

engarzar §60 *tr* to link, string, wire; curl; enchase; (Col) to hook

engastar *tr* to enchase, mount, set

engaste *m* enchasing, mounting, setting

engatusar *tr* to coax, wheedle; inveigle

engendrar *tr* to beget, engender; (geom) to generate

engendro *m* foetus; botch, bungle; (*criatura informe*) runt, stunt; **mal engendro** (coll) young tough

engolfar *intr* to go far out in the ocean ‖ *ref* to go far out in the ocean; become deeply involved; be lost in thought

engoma•do -da *adj* (Chile) all dressed up ‖ *m* (CAm) hangover

engomar *tr* to gum ‖ *ref* to have a hangover

engorda *f* fattening; animals being fattened

engordar *tr* to fatten ‖ *intr* to get fat; (coll) to get fat, get rich

engorro *m* bother, nuisance, obstacle

engorro•so -sa *adj* annoying

engoznar *tr* to hinge, to hang on a hinge

engranaje *m* gear, gears, teeth; (fig) link, connection; **engranaje de distribución** (aut) timing gears; **engranaje de tornillo sin fin** worm gear

engranar *tr* to gear, mesh; throw into gear ‖ *intr* to gear, mesh

engrandecer §22 *tr* to amplify, enlarge, magnify; exalt, extol; enhance

engrane *m* gear; mesh

engranerar *tr* (*el grano*) to store

engrapa•dor -dora *mf* stapler

engrapar *tr* to clamp, cramp

engrasador *m* grease cup; **engrasador de pistón** grease gun

engrasar *tr* to grease; smear with grease

engrase *m* greasing; grease

engravar *tr* to spread gravel over

engredar *tr* to chalk, to clay

engreí•do -da *adj* conceited, vain

engreimiento *m* conceit, vanity

engreír §58 *tr* to make conceited; spoil, pamper ‖ *ref* to become conceited

engreña•do -da *adj* disheveled

engrescar §73 *tr* to incite to fight; incite to merriment ‖ *ref* to pick a fight; join in the fun

engrifar *tr* to curl, crisp ‖ *ref* to curl up; stand on end; (*un caballo*) rear

engrillar *tr* to shackle, fetter ‖ *ref* (*las patatas*) to sprout

engringar §44 *ref* to act like a foreigner

engrosar §61 *tr* to broaden; enlarge ‖ *intr* to get fat ‖ *ref* to broaden; swell, get bigger

engrudar *tr* to paste

engrudo *m* paste

engualdrapar *tr* to caparison

enguapear *ref* (Mex) to get drunk

enguirnaldar *tr* to garland, wreathe; trim, bedeck

engullir §13 *tr* to gulp down

engurrio *m* sadness, melancholy

enhebrar *tr* (*una aguja*) to thread; (*perlas*) string; (*mentiras*) rattle off

enhestar §2 *tr* to stand upright, erect; hoist, lift up

enhies•to -ta *adj* upright, straight, erect

enhilar *tr* to thread; direct; line up; (*ideas*) marshal ‖ *intr* to set out

enhorabuena *adv* safely, luckily; **enhorabuena que** thank heavens that ‖ *f* congratulations; **dar la enhorabuena a** to congratulate

enhoramala *adv* unluckily, under an unlucky star; **nacer enhoramala** to be born under an unlucky star; **vete enhoramala** go to the devil

enhornar *tr* to put into the oven

enigma *m* enigma, riddle, puzzle

enigmáti•co -ca *adj* enigmatic(al)

enjabonar *tr* to soap, lather; (*adular*) (coll) to soft-soap; (*reprender*) (coll) to upbraid

enjaezar §60 *tr* to harness, put trappings on

enjalbegado *m* whitewashing

enjalbegar §44 *tr* to whitewash; (*el rostro*) paint ‖ *ref* to paint the face

enjambrar *intr* (*las abejas*) to swarm; to multiply in great numbers

enjambre *m* swarm

enjaretado *m* grating, lattice work

enjarrar *ref* (C-R, Mex) to stand with arms akimbo

enjaular *tr* to cage; jail, lock up

enjergar §44 *tr* to launch, get started, start on a shoestring

enjoyar *tr* to adorn with jewels; set with precious stones; adorn

enjuagadien•tes *m* (*pl* **-tes**) mouthwash

enjuagar §44 *tr* to rinse, rinse out

enjuague *m* rinse; rinsing water; mouthwash; rinsing cup; (coll) plot

enjugador *m* drier; clotheshorse

enjugama•nos *m* (*pl* **-nos**) towel, hand towel

enjugaparabri•sas *m* (*pl* **-sas**) windshield wiper

enjugar §44 *tr* (*secar*) to dry; (*el sudor*) wipe, wipe off; (*lágrimas*) wipe away; (*deudas, un déficit*) wipe out ‖ *ref* to lose weight

enjuiciamiento *m* procedure; prosecution; suit; trial; judgment, sentence

enjuiciar *tr* to prosecute, sue; try; judge

enjundio•so -sa *adj* fatty, greasy; solid, substantial

enju•to -ta *adj* (*tiempo, clima; ojos*) dry; lean, skinny; quiet, stolid ‖ **enjutos** *mpl* brushwood; (*para excitar la gana de beber*) tidbits

enlabiar *tr* to entice, take in; press one's lips against

enlace *m* connection, linking; relationship; betrothal, engagement; marriage; (mil, phonet) liaison; (rr) connection, junction

enlaciar *tr, intr & ref* to wither, wilt, shrivel; rumple

enladrillado *m* brickwork; bricklaying; brick paving

enladrillar *tr* to pave with bricks

enlajado *m* (Ven) flagstone

enlajar *tr* (Ven) to pave with flagstones

enlardar *tr* to baste

enlatado *m* canning

enlatar *tr* to can; roof with tin, line with tin

enlazar §60 *tr* to connect, link; lace; (*un animal con el lazo*) lasso ‖ *intr* (*p.ej., dos trenes*) to connect ‖ *ref* to be connected, be linked; connect; get married; become related by marriage

enlechar *tr* to grout

enlistonado *m* lathing, lath

enlistonar *tr* to lath

enlodar *tr* to muddy, smear with mud; plaster with mud; seal with mud; (fig) to sling mud at

enloquecer §22 *tr* to drive crazy ‖ *intr* to go crazy

enloquecimiento *m* insanity, madness

enlosado *m* flagstone paving

enlosar *tr* to pave with flagstone

enlozar §60 *tr* to enamel

enlozado *m* enamelware

enlucido *m* plaster, coat (*of plaster*)

enlucir §45 *tr* (*una pared*) to plaster; (*la plata*) polish

enlutar *tr* to put in mourning, hang with crape; darken, sadden ‖ *ref* to dress in mourning

enmaderar *tr* to cover with boards; build the framework for

enmagrecer §22 *tr* to make thin ‖ *intr & ref* to get thin

enmalecer §22 *tr* to spoil ‖ *ref* to get full of weeds, be overgrown with weeds

enmarañar *tr* to entangle; confuse ‖ *ref* to become entangled; become overcast, get cloudy

enmarcar §73 *tr* to frame

enmarchitar *tr & ref* to wither

enmaridar *intr & ref* to take a husband

enmarillecer §22 *ref* to turn yellow, turn pale

enmasar *tr* (*tropas*) to mass

enmascarar *tr* to mask; camouflage ‖ *ref* to put on a mask; masquerade

enmasillar *tr* to putty

enmendación *f* emendation

enmendar §2 *tr* (*corregir*) to emend; (*reformar*) amend; (*resarcir*) make amends for ‖ *ref* to amend, mend one's ways, go straight

enmienda *f* (*corrección*) emendation; (*propuesta de variante*) amendment; (*satisfacción del daño hecho*) amends

enmohecer §22 *tr* to make moldy; rust; neglect ‖ *ref* to get moldy; rust; (*la memoria*) get rusty; fade away

enmontar *ref* (CAm, Mex, Col, Ven) to become overgrown with brush

enmudecer §22 *tr* to hush, silence ‖ *intr* to hush up, keep quiet; become dumb, lose one's voice

enmuescar §73 *tr* to notch; (carp) to mortise

ennegrecer §22 *tr* to blacken, dye black ‖ *ref* to turn black; (*el porvenir*) be black

ennoblecer §22 *tr* to ennoble; glorify, enhance

ennoblecimiento *m* ennoblement; glory, splendor; (*grandeza de alma*) nobility

enodio *m* fawn, young deer

enojada *f* (Mex) fit of anger

enojadi•zo -za *adj* irritable, ill-tempered

enojar *tr* to anger; annoy, vex ‖ *ref* to get angry; **enojarse con** or **contra** to get angry with (*a person*); **enojarse de** to get angry at (*a thing*)

enojo *m* anger; annoyance, bother

eno•jón -jona *adj* (Chile, Ecuad, Mex) irritable, ill-tempered

enojo•so -sa *adj* annoying, bothersome

enorgullecer §22 *tr* to fill with pride, make proud ‖ *ref* to be proud; **enorgullecerse de** to pride oneself on

enorme *adj* enormous, huge

enotecnia *f* wine making; oenology

enquiciar *tr* (*una puerta, una ventana*) to hang; fasten, make firm

enrabiar *tr* to enrage ‖ *intr* to have rabies ‖ *ref* to become enraged

enramar *tr* (*ramos*) to intertwine; adorn with branches ‖ *intr* to sprout branches ‖ *ref* to hide in the branches

enranciar *tr* to make rancid ‖ *ref* to get rancid

enrarecer §22 *tr* to rarefy; make scarce ‖ *intr* to become scarce ‖ *ref* to rarefy; become scarce

enrarecimiento *m* (*p.ej., del aire*) thinness; scarceness, scarcity

enrasar *tr* to make flush; grade, level ‖ *intr* to be flush

enratonar *ref* to get sick from eating mice; (Ven) to have a hangover

enredadera *adj* (*planta*) climbing ‖ *f* climbing plant, vine

enreda•dor -dora *mf* gossip, busybody

enredar *tr* to catch in a net; (*redes, una trampa*) set; tangle up; involve, entangle; (*una pelea*) start; intertwine, interweave; endanger, compromise ‖ *intr* to romp around, be frisky ‖ *ref* to get tangled up; get involved, become entangled; (coll) to have an affair

enredijo *m* entanglement

enredo *m* tangle; involvement, entanglement; complication; restlessness; friskiness; mischievous lie; (*de una novela, un drama*) plot; (*trato ilícito de hombre y mujer*) liaison

enre•dón -dona *adj* scheming ‖ *mf* schemer

en
en

enredo·so -sa *adj* entangled, complicated, difficult

enrejado *m* grating, trellis, latticework; iron railing; grill; openwork embroidery

enrejar *tr* to grate, lattice; (*una ventana*) put a grate on; fence with an iron grating; (*ladrillos, tablas*) pile alternately crosswise; (Mex) to darn

enrielar *tr* to make into ingots; lay rails on; put on the tracks; put on the right track

enriquecer §22 *tr* to enrich ‖ *intr & ref* to get rich

enrisca·do -da *adj* craggy, full of cliffs

enrizar §60 *tr & ref* to curl

enrocar §73 *tr & intr* (chess) to castle

enrodrigar §44 *tr* to prop, prop up

enrojar *tr* to redden, make red; (*el horno*) to heat up ‖ *ref* to redden, turn red

enrojecer §22 *tr* to make red; make red-hot; make blush ‖ *intr* to blush ‖ *ref* to turn red; get red-hot; flush; get sore, get inflamed

enromar *tr* to make dull, make blunt

enronquecer §22 *tr* to make hoarse ‖ *intr & ref* to get hoarse

enronquecimiento *m* hoarseness

enroque *m* (chess) castling

enroscar §73 *tr* to coil, twist, screw in ‖ *ref* to coil, twist

enrubiar *tr* to bleach, make blond ‖ *ref* to turn blond

enrubio *m* bleaching; bleaching lotion

enrular *tr & ref* (Arg) to curl

ensacar §73 *tr* to bag, put in a bag

ensaimada *f* twisted coffee cake

ensalada *f* salad; hodgepodge; fiasco, flop

ensaladera *f* salad bowl

ensalmar *tr* (*un hueso*) to set; treat or heal by incantation

ensalmo *m* incantation, spell; **como por ensalmo** as if by magic

ensalzar §60 *tr* to exalt, elevate, extol

ensamblar *tr* to assemble, join, fit together; **ensamblar a cola de milano** or **a cola de pato** to dovetail

ensanchador *m* glove stretcher

ensanchar *tr* to widen, enlarge; (*una prenda ajustada*) ease, let out; (*el corazón*) unburden ‖ *intr & ref* to be proud and haughty

ensanche *m* widening, extension; (*de una calle*) extension; suburban development; allowance (*for enlargement of garment*)

ensandecer §22 *intr* to go crazy

ensangrenta·do -da *adj* bloody, gory

ensangrentar §2 *tr* to bathe in blood; stain with blood ‖ *ref* to rage, go wild; (*p.ej., las manos*) bloody, make bloody

ensañar *tr* to anger, enrage ‖ *ref* to be cruel, be merciless; (*una enfermedad*) rage

ensartar *tr* (*una aguja*) to thread; (*cuentas*) string; stick; rattle off ‖ *ref* to squeeze in

ensayar *tr* to try, try on, try out; (*un espectáculo*) rehearse; (*minerales*) assay; teach, train; test ‖ *ref* to practice

ensaye *m* assay

ensayista *mf* essayist; (Chile) assayer

ensayo *m* trying, trial; testing, test; (*género literario*) essay; (*de minerales*) assay; exercise, practice; (theat) rehearsal; **ensayo de choque** (aut) crash test; **ensayo general** dress rehearsal

ensenada *f* inlet, cove

enseña *f* standard, ensign

enseña·do -da *adj* trained, informed; (*perro de caza*) trained

enseñanza *f* teaching; education, instruction; (*ejemplo que sirve de experiencia*) lesson; **enseñanza superior** higher education

enseñar *tr* to teach; train; show, point out ‖ *intr* to teach

enseñorear *ref* to control oneself; **enseñorearse de** to take possession of

enseres *mpl* utensils, equipment, household goods

enseriar *ref* to become serious

ensillar *tr* to saddle

ensimismamiento *m* absorption in thought, deep thought

ensimismar *ref* to become absorbed in thought; (Chile, Ecuad, Peru) to be proud, be boastful

ensoberbecer §22 to make proud ‖ *ref* to become proud; (*el mar, las olas*) swell, get rough

ensoberbecimiento *m* haughtiness

ensombrecer §22 *tr* to darken ‖ *ref* to get dark; become sad and gloomy

ensoña·dor -dora *adj* dreamy ‖ *mf* dreamer

ensopar *tr* to dip, dunk; soak, drench

ensordece·dor -dora *adj* deafening

ensordecer §22 *tr* to deafen; (*una consonante sonora*) unvoice ‖ *intr* to become deaf; play deaf, not answer ‖ *ref* to unvoice

ensortijar *tr* to curl, make curly; (*la nariz de un animal*) ring, put a ring in ‖ *ref* to curl

ensuciar *tr* to dirty, soil; stain, smear; defile, sully ‖ *ref* to soil oneself; take bribes

ensueño *m* dream; daydream

entablado *m* flooring; wooden framework

entablar *tr* to board, board up; (*un hueso roto*) splint; (*una conversación*) start; (*p.ej., una batalla*) launch; (*un pleito*) bring; (*las piezas del ajedrez y de las damas*) set up ‖ *ref* (*el viento*) to settle

entable *m* boarding; (*en los juegos de ajedrez y damas*) position of men; (Col) business, undertaking

entablillar *tr* (*un hueso roto*) to splint

enta·blón -blona *adj* (Peru) blustering, bragging ‖ *mf* (Peru) bully

entalegar §44 *tr* to bag, put in a bag; (*dinero*) hoard

entalladura *f* carving, sculpture; engraving; slot, groove, mortise; cut, incision (*in a tree*)

entallar *tr* to carve, sculpture; engrave; notch; groove, mortise; (*un traje*) fit, tailor ‖ *intr* to take shape; (*el vestido*) fit; go well, be fitting

entallecer §22 *intr & ref* to shoot, sprout

entapizar §60 *tr* to tapestry, hang with tapestry; cover with a fabric; overgrow, spread over

entarimado *m* parquet, inlaid floor, hardwood floor

entarimar *tr* to parquet, to put an inlaid floor on ‖ *ref* to put on airs

entarugar §44 *tr* to pave with wooden blocks ‖ *ref* (*el sombrero*) (Ven) to stick on

ente *m* being; (coll) guy, odd fellow

enteca•do -da or **ente•co -ca** *adj* sickly, frail

enteleri•do -da *adj* shaking with cold, shaking with fright; sickly, frail

entena *f* lateen yard

entena•do -da *mf* stepchild ‖ *m* stepson ‖ *f* stepdaughter

entendederas *fpl* (coll) brains; **tener malas entendederas** (coll) to have no brains

entende•dor -dora *adj* understanding, intelligent ‖ *mf* understanding person; **al buen entendedor, pocas palabras** a word to the wise is enough

entender *m* understanding, opinion ‖ §51 *tr* to understand; intend, mean ‖ *intr* —**entender de** to be a judge of; be experienced as; **entender de razón** to listen to reason; **entender en** to be familiar with, deal with ‖ *ref* to be understood; be meant; have a secret understanding; **entenderse con** to get along with; concern; (*una mujer*) have an affair with

entendi•do -da *adj* expert, skilled; informed; **no darse por entendido** to take no notice, pretend not to understand; **los entendidos** informed sources; **un entendido en** a well-informed person in

entendimiento *m* understanding

entenebrecer §22 *tr* to darken; confuse ‖ *ref* to get dark; become confused

entera•do -da *adj* informed, posted; (Chile) conceited; (Chile) intrusive, meddlesome ‖ *mf* insider

enterar *tr* to inform, acquaint; to pay; (Arg, Chile) to complete ‖ *intr* (Chile) to get better; (Chile) to drift along ‖ *ref* to find out; to recover; **enterarse de** to find out about, become aware of

entereza *f* entirety, completeness; wholeness; perfection; fairness; constancy, fortitude; strictness

enteri•zo -za *adj* in one piece

enternece•dor -dora *adj* moving, touching

enternecer §22 *tr* to move, touch ‖ *ref* to be moved to pity

enternecimiento *m* pity, compassion

ente•ro -ra *adj* entire, whole, complete; honest, upright; firm, energetic; sound, vigorous; (*tela*) strong, heavy ‖ *m* (arith) integer; payment; (Chile) balance; **por entero** entirely, wholly, completely

enterrador *m* gravedigger

enterramiento *m* burial, interment; (*hoyo*) grave; (*monumento*) tomb

enterrar §2 *tr* to bury, inter; outlive, survive ‖ *ref* to hide away

entesar §2 *tr* to stretch, make taut

entibar *tr* to prop up, shore up ‖ *intr* to rest, lean

entibiar *tr* to cool off; temper, moderate ‖ *ref* to cool off, cool down

entidad *f* entity; importance, consequence, moment; body, organization

entierramuer•tos *m* (*pl* **-tos**) gravedigger

entierro *m* burial, interment; (*hoyo*) grave; (*monumento*) tomb; funeral; funeral cortege; buried treasure

entintar *tr* to ink; ink in; stain with ink; dye

entoldar *tr* to cover with awnings; adorn with hangings ‖ *ref* to get cloudy, become overcast; swell with pride

entomología *f* entomology

entonación *f* intonation; blowing of bellows

entona•do -da *adj* arrogant; haughty; harmonious, in tune

entonar *tr* to intone; sing in tune; (*el órgano*) blow; (*colores*) harmonize; tone, tone up; (*alabanzas*) sound ‖ *intr* to sing in tune ‖ *ref* to be puffed up with pride

entonces *adv* then ‖ *m* — **por aquel entonces** at that time

entonelar *tr* to put in barrels, put in casks

entongar §44 *tr* (Mex, W-I) to pile up, pile in rows; (Col) to drive crazy

entono *m* intoning; arrogance, haughtiness

entontecer §22 *tr* to make foolish, make stupid ‖ *intr & ref* to become foolish, become stupid

entorchado *m* bullion; **ganar los entorchados** to win one's stripes

entorna•do -da *adj* ajar, half-closed

entornar *tr* to half-close; (*los ojos*) squint; (*una puerta*) leave ajar; (*volcar*) upset ‖ *ref* to upset

entornillar *tr* to twist, screw up

entorno *m* environment

entorpecer §22 *tr* to stupefy; obstruct, delay; benumb; (*una cerradura, una ventana*) make stick ‖ *ref* to stick, get stuck

entortar §61 *tr* to bend, make crooked; knock out the eye of ‖ *ref* to bend, get crooked

entrada *f* entrance, entry; admission; arrival; income, receipts; admission ticket; entrance hall; (*número de personas que asisten a un espectáculo*) house; (*producto de cada función*) gate; (*amistad en alguna casa*) entree; (*naipes que guarda un jugador*) hand; (*de una comida*) entree; (*visita breve*) short call; (Col) down payment; (Mex) attack, onslaught; (elec) input; **dar entrada a** to admit; to give an opening to; (*un buque*) to give the right of entry to; **entrada de taquilla** gate; **entrada general** top gallery; **entrada llena** full house; **mucha entrada** good house, good turnout; **se prohibe la entrada** no admittance

entra•do -da *adj* (Chile) officious, self-assertive; **entrado en años** advanced in years ‖ *f* see **entrada**

entra•dor -dora *adj* (*enamoradizo*) susceptible; (Mex) lively, energetic; (Chile) officious, self-assertive

entrama•do -da *adj* half-timbered ‖ *m* timber framework

entram•bos -bas *adj & pron indef* both; **entrambos a dos** both

entrampar *tr* to ensnare, trap; trick, deceive; overload with debt ‖ *ref* to get trapped; be tricked; run into debt

en
en

entrante *adj* entering; (*p.ej., tren*) inbound, incoming; (*próximo, que viene*) next ‖ *mf* entrant; **entrantes y salientes** (coll) hangers-on

entraña *f* internal organ; (fig) heart, center; . **entrañas** entrails; (fig) heart, feeling; (fig) disposition, temper

entrañable *adj* close, intimate

entrañar *tr* to put away deep, bury deep; involve; (*malos pensamientos*) harbor ‖ *ref* to go deep into; be buried deep; be close, be intimate

entrapajar *tr* to wrap up, bandage

entrar *tr* to bring in; overrun, invade; influence ‖ *intr* to enter, go in, come in; (*un río*) empty; (*el viento, la marea*) rise; attack; begin; **entrar a matar** (taur) to go in for the kill; **entrar en** to enter, enter into, go into; fit into; adopt, take up; **que entra** next

entre *prep* (*en medio de*) between; (*en el número de*) among; (*en el intervalo de*) in the course of; **entre manos** at hand; **entre mí** to myself; **entre que** while; **entre tanto** meanwhile; **entre Vd. y yo** between you and me

entreabier·to -ta *adj* half-open; (*puerta*) ajar

entreabrir §83 *tr* to half-open; leave ajar

entreacto *m* entr'acte

entreca·no -na *adj* graying, grayish

entrecarril *m* (Ven) gauge

entrecejo *m* space between the eyebrows; frown; **fruncir el entrecejo** to frown; **mirar con entrecejo** to frown at

entrecoger §17 *tr* to catch, seize; press hard, hold down

entrecoro *m* chancel

entrecorta·do -da *adj* broken, intermittent

entrecortar *tr* to break in on, keep interrupting

entre·cruz *m* (*pl* **-cruces**) interweaving

entrecruzar §60 *tr & ref* to intercross; interweave, interlace; to interbreed

entrecubiertas *fpl* between-decks

entrechocar §73 *ref* to collide, clash

entredicho *m* interdiction, prohibition; (law) injunction; (Bol) alarm bell; **poner en entredicho** to cast doubt upon

entredós *m* (*tira de encaje*) insertion; (typ) long primer

entrefilete *m* short feature, special item

entrefi·no -na *adj* medium

entrega *f* delivery; (*p.ej., de una plaza fuerte*) surrender; (*cuaderno de un libro que se vende suelto*) fascicle; (*de una revista*) issue, number; **por entregas** in instalments

entregar §44 *tr* to deliver; hand over, surrender; fit in, insert; **entregarla** to die ‖ *ref* to give in, surrender; abandon oneself; to devote oneself; **entregarse de** to take possession of, take charge of

entrehierro *m* (elec) spark gap; (phys) air gap

entrelazar §60 *tr* to interlace, interweave

entremediar *tr* to put between

entremedias *adv* in between; in the meantime; **entremedias de** between; among

entremés *m* hors d'œuvre, side dish; short farce (*inserted in an auto or performed between two acts of a comedia*)

entremesear *tr* (*una conversación*) to enliven

entremeter *tr* to put in, insert ‖ *ref* to meddle, intrude, butt in

entremeti·do -da *adj* meddling, meddlesome ‖ *mf* meddler, intruder, busybody

entremezclar *tr & ref* to intermingle, intermix

entremorir §30 & §83 *intr* to flicker, die out

entrenador *m* (sport) coach, trainer, handler

entrenamiento *m* (sport) coaching, training

entrenar *tr & ref* (sport) to coach, train

entrepaño *m* (*de una puerta*) panel; (*espacio entre dos columnas, etc.*) pier; shelf

entreparecer §60 *ref* to show through

entrepiernas *fpl* crotch; patches in the crotch of trousers; (Chile) bathing trunks

entrepuentes *mpl* between-decks; (naut) steerage

entrerrenglón *m* interline; space between the lines

entrerrenglonar *tr* to write between the lines

entrerriel *m* gauge

entrerrisa *f* giggle

entrerrosca *f* (mach) nipple

entresacar §73 *tr* to pick, pick out, select; cull, sift; (*árboles; el pelo*) thin out

entresemana *adv* (SAm) weekdays; workdays

entresijo *m* secret; mystery; **tener muchos entresijos** to be mysterious, be hard to figure out

entresuelo *m* mezzanine, entresol

entretallar *tr* to carve, engrave; carve in bas-relief; do openwork in; intercept

entretanto *adv* meantime, meanwhile ‖ *m* meanwhile; **en el entretanto** in the meantime

entretecho *m* (Arg, Chile, Urug) attic, garret

entretejer *tr* to interweave

entretela *f* interlining

entretelar *tr* to interline

entretención *f* amusement, entertainment

entretener §71 *tr* to amuse, entertain; (*el tiempo*) while away; maintain, keep up; put off, delay; (*el dolor*) allay; (*el hambre*) stave off (*by taking a bite before mealtime*); try to get one's mind off ‖ *ref* to amuse oneself, be amused

entreteni·do -da *adj* amusing, entertaining; (rad) continuous, undamped ‖ *f* kept woman; **dar la entretenida a** or **dar con la entretenida a** to stall off by constant talk

entretenimiento *m* amusement, entertainment; upkeep, maintenance

entretiempo *m* in-between season; **de entretiempo** spring-and-fall (*coat*)

entreventana *f* pier

entrever §80 *tr* to glimpse, descry, catch a glimpse of; guess, suspect

entreverar *tr* to mix ‖ *ref* (Arg) to get all mixed together; (*dos grupos de caballería*) (Arg) to clash in hand-to-hand combat

entrevía *f* gauge

entrevista *f* interview

entrevistar *ref* to have an interview
entristecer §22 *tr* to sadden, make sad ‖ *ref* to sadden, become sad
entrojar *tr* to store in a granary
entrometer *tr & ref* var of **entremeter**
entrometi•do -da *adj & mf* var of **entremetido**
entronar *tr* to enthrone
entroncamiento *m* connection, relationship; (*de caminos, ferrocarriles*) junction
entroncar §73 *tr* to prove relationship between ‖ *intr* to be related; (*dos caminos, ferrocarriles, etc.*) connect
entronerar *tr* (*una bola de billar*) to pocket
entronizar §60 *tr* to enthrone; exalt; popularize ‖ *ref* to be puffed up with pride
entronque *m* connection, relationship; (*caminos, ferrocarriles*) junction
entruchar *tr* to decoy, trick
entru•chón -chona *adj* tricky ‖ *mf* trickster
entuerto *m* wrong, harm, injustice
entumecer §22 *tr* to make numb ‖ *ref* (*un miembro*) to get numb, go to sleep; (*el mar*) swell, get rough
entupir *tr* to stop up, clog; pack tight ‖ *ref* to get stopped up, get clogged
enturbiar *tr* to stir up, make muddy; confuse, upset
entusiasmar *tr* to enthuse, make enthusiastic ‖ *ref* to enthuse, become enthusiastic
entusiasmo *m* enthusiasm; inspiration
entusiasta *adj* enthusiastic ‖ *mf* enthusiast
entusiásti•co -ca *adj* enthusiastic
enumerar *tr* to enumerate
enunciar *tr* to enunciate, enounce
enunciati•vo -va *adj* (gram) declarative
envainar *tr* to sheathe
envalentonar *tr* to embolden, make bold ‖ *ref* to pluck up, take courage
envanecer §22 *tr* to make vain ‖ *ref* to become vain, get conceited
envanecimiento *m* vanity, conceit
envaramiento *m* stiffness
envarar *tr* to make numb, to stiffen ‖ *ref* to get stiff; get numb
envasar *tr* (*p.ej., trigo*) to pack, sack; (*p.ej., vino*) bottle; (*p.ej., pescado*) can; (*una espada*) thrust, poke; (*mucho vino*) put away ‖ *intr* to tipple
envase *m* container; bottle; jar; can; packing; bottling; canning; **envase de hojalata** tin can
envedijar *ref* to get tangled; come to blows
envejecer §22 *tr* to age, make old ‖ *intr & ref* to age, grow old; get out of date
envejeci•do -da *adj* old, aged; experienced, tried
envenenar *tr* to poison; (*llenar de amargura*) envenom, embitter; (*las palabras o conducta de una persona*) put an evil interpretation on ‖ *ref* to take poison
enverdecer §22 *intr* to turn green
envergadura *f* (*de las alas abiertas del ave*) spread; (*ancho de una vela*) breadth; (aer) span, wingspread; (fig) compass, spread, reach

envés *m* wrong side; (*del cuerpo humano*) back
enviado *m* envoy
enviar §77 *tr* to send; (*mercancías*) ship; **enviar a buscar** to send for; **enviar a paseo** to send on his way, dismiss without ceremony; **enviar por** to send for
enviciar *tr* to corrupt, vitiate; (*mimar*) spoil ‖ *intr* to have many leaves and little fruit ‖ *ref* to become addicted; **enviciarse con** or **en** to addict oneself to, become addicted to
envidar *tr* to bid against, bet against ‖ *intr* to bid, bet
envidia *f* envy; desire
envidiable *adj* enviable
envidiar *tr* to envy, begrudge; desire, want
envidio•so -sa *adj* envious; greedy, covetous ‖ *mf* envious person
envilecer §22 *tr* to debase, vilify, revile ‖ *ref* to degrade oneself
envío *m* sending; (*de mercancías*) shipment; (*de dinero*) remittance; (*en una obra*) autograph, inscription
envirota•do -da *adj* stiff, stuck-up
envite *m* bet; bid, offer, invitation; push, shove; (*apuesta adicional a un lance o suerte*) side bet; **al primer envite** right off, at the start
enviudar *intr* (*una mujer*) to become a widow; (*un hombre*) become a widower
envoltorio *m* bundle; (*defecto en el paño*) knot
envoltura *f* cover, wrapper, envelope; swaddling clothes
envolver §47 & §83 *tr* to wrap, wrap up; (*hilo, cinta*) wind, roll up; (*al niño*) swaddle; imply, mean; involve; envelop; (*dejar cortado y sin salida en la disputa*) floor; (mil) to encircle ‖ *ref* to become involved; have an affair
enyerbar *tr* (Col, Chile, Mex) to bewitch ‖ *ref* to be covered with grass; (Mex) to fall madly in love; (Mex) to take poison
enyesar *tr* to plaster; put in a plaster cast; (*la tierra, el vino*) gypsum
enyugar §44 *tr* to yoke
enzima *f* enzyme
enzolvar *tr* (Mex) to clog, stop up
epazote *m* (CAm, Mex) Mexican tea
E.P.D. *abbr* **en paz descanse**
epente•sis *f* (*pl* **-sis**) epenthesis
eperlano *m* smelt
épica *f* epic poetry
epice•no -na *adj* (gram) epicene, common
épi•co -ca *adj* epic ‖ *m* epic poet ‖ *f* see épica
epicúre•o -a *adj* epicurean ‖ *mf* epicurean, epicure
epidemia *f* epidemic
epidémi•co -ca *adj* epidemic
epidemiología *f* epidemiology
epidermis *f* epidermis; **tener la epidermis fina** or **sensible** to be touchy
Epifanía *f* Epiphany, Twelfth-day
epígrafe *m* epigraph; inscription; headline, title; device, motto
epigrama *m* epigram
epilepsia *f* epilepsy

en
ep

epilépti•co -ca *adj & mf* epileptic
epilogar §44 *tr* to sum up, summarize
episcopalista *adj & mf* Episcopalian
episodio *m* episode
epistemología *f* epistemology
epístola *f* epistle
epitafio *m* epitaph
epíteto *m* epithet
epitomar *tr* to epitomize
epítome *m* epitome
E.P.M. *abbr* **en propia mano**
época *f* epoch; **hacer época** to be epoch-making
epopeya *f* epic, epic poem
equidad *f* equity; (*templanza habitual*) equableness; (*moderación en el precio*) reasonableness
equiláte•ro -ra *adj* equilateral
equilibra•do -da *adj* balanced; (fig) sensible, even-tempered
equilibrar *tr* to balance, equilibrate; (*el presupuesto*) balance ‖ *ref* to balance, equilibrate
equilibrio *m* equilibrium, balance, equipoise; (*del presupuesto*) balancing; **equilibrio político** balance of power
equilibrista *mf* balancer, ropedancer
equinoccial *adj* equinoctial
equinoccio *m* equinox
equipaje *m* baggage; piece of baggage; equipment; (naut) crew; **equipaje de mano** hand baggage
equipar *tr* to equip
equiparar *tr* to compare
equi•pier *m* (*pl* **-piers**) teammate
equipo *m* equipment, outfit; crew, gang; (sport) team; **equipo de alta fidelidad** stereo system; hi-fi set; **equipo de novia** trousseau; **equipo de urgencia** first-aid kit
equitación *f* horsemanship, riding
equitati•vo -va *adj* fair, equitable; (*tranquilo*) equable
equivalente *adj & m* equivalent
equivaler §76 *intr* to be equal, be equivalent
equivocación *f* mistake; mistakenness
equivoca•do -da *adj* mistaken, wrong
equivocar §73 *tr* (*una cosa por otra*) to mistake, mix ‖ *ref* to be mistaken, make a mistake; be wrong; **equivocarse con** to be mistaken for; **equivocarse de** to be wrong in, take the wrong . . .
equívo•co -ca *adj* equivocal, ambiguous ‖ *m* equivocation, ambiguity; pun
equivoquista *mf* equivocator; punster
era *f* era, age; threshing floor; vegetable patch, garden bed
eral *m* two-year-old bull
erario *m* state treasury
erección *f* erection; foundation, establishment
eremita *m* hermit
ergástulo *m* dungeon, slave prison
ergio *m* erg
ergotismo *m* argumentativeness; (pathol) ergotism
ergotista *adj invar* argumentative; dogmatic; *mf* dogmatist; know-it-all

erguir §33 *tr* to raise; straighten up ‖ *ref* to straighten up; swell with pride
erial *adj* unplowed, uncultivated ‖ *m* unplowed land, uncultivated land
erigir §27 *tr* to erect, build; found, establish; (*a nueva condición*) elevate ‖ *ref*—**erigirse en** to be elevated to; set oneself up as
eriza•do -da *adj* bristling, bristly, spiny
erizar §60 *tr* to make stand on end, cause to bristle ‖ *ref* to stand on end, to bristle
erizo *m* (*mamífero*) hedgehog; (*zurrón espinoso de la castaña*) bur, thistle; (*púas de hierro que coronan lo alto de una muralla*) cheval-de-frise; (*persona de carácter áspero*) curmudgeon; **erizo de mar** (zool) sea urchin
ermita *f* hermitage
ermita•ño -ña *mf* hermit
erogación *f* (*de bienes o caudales*) distribution; expenditure; (Peru, Ven) gift, charity; (Mex) outlay
erogar §44 *tr* to distribute; (Ecuad) to contribute; (Mex) to cause
erosión *f* erosion
erosionar *tr & ref* to erode
erradicar §73 *tr* to eradicate
erra•do -da *adj* mistaken, wrong
errar §34 *tr* to miss ‖ *intr* to err, be mistaken, be wrong; wander ‖ *ref* to be mistaken, be wrong
errata *f* erratum; printer's error
erróne•o -a *adj* erroneous
error *m* error, mistake; **error de pluma** clerical error; **salvo error u omisión** barring error or omission
eructar *intr* to belch; (coll) to brag
eructo *m* belch, belching
erudición *f* erudition, learning
erudi•to -ta *adj* erudite, learned ‖ *mf* scholar, savant; **erudito a la violeta** egghead, highbrow
erugino•so -sa *adj* rusty
erumpir *intr* (*un volcán*) to erupt
erupción *f* eruption
esbel•to -ta *adj* slender, lithe, willowy
esbirro *m* bailiff, constable; (*el que ejecuta órdenes injustas*) myrmidon, henchman
esbozar §60 *tr* to sketch, outline
esbozo *m* sketch, outline
escabechar *tr* to pickle; (*el pelo, la barba*) dye; (*reprobar en un examen*) flunk; stab to death ‖ *ref* to dye one's hair; (*el pelo, la barba*) dye
escabeche *m* pickle; pickled fish; hair dye
escabel *m* stool; footstool; (*para medrar*) stepping stone
escabio•so -sa *adj* mangy
escabro•so -sa *adj* scabrous, risqué; scabrous, uneven, rough, harsh
escabuche *m* weeding hoe
escabullir §13 *ref* to slip away, sneak away; slip out, wiggle out
escafandra *f* diving suit; **escafandra espacial** space suit
escafandrista *mf* diver

escala f (*escalera de mano*) ladder, stepladder; (*línea graduada de instrumento*) scale; (*de buque*) call; (*de avión*) stop; (*puerto donde toca una embarcación*) port of call; (*serie de las notas musicales*) scale; **en escala de** on a scale of; **en grande escala** on a large scale; **escala móvil** (*de salarios*) sliding scale; **hacer escala** (naut) to call

escalada f scaling, climbing; breaking in; escalation

escalador m climber; (*ladrón*) burglar, housebreaker

escalación f escalation

escalafón m roster, roll, register

escalar tr (*subir, trepar*) to scale; break in, burglarize; (*la compuerta de la acequia*) open ‖ intr to climb; (naut) to call ‖ ref to escalate

escalato•rres m (*pl* **-rres**) steeplejack, human fly

escalda•do -da adj cautious, scared, wary; (*mujer*) lewd, loose

escaldar tr to scald; make red hot ‖ ref to get scalded; chafe

escalera f stairs, stairway; (*la portátil*) ladder; (*de naipes*) sequence; (*en el póker*) straight; **de escalera abajo** from below stairs, from the servants; **escalera de caracol** winding stairway; **escalera de escape** fire escape; **escalera de husillo** winding stairway; **escalera de incendios** fire escape; **escalera de mano** ladder; **escalera de salvamento** fire escape; **escalera de tijera** or **escalera doble** ladder; **escalera excusada** or **falsa** private stairs; **escalera extensible** extension ladder; **escalera hurtada** secret stairway; **escalera mecánica, móvil** or **rodante** escalator, moving stairway

escalerilla f low step; car step; (*en las medias*) runner; (*de naipes*) sequence; thumb index

escalfar tr (*huevos*) to poach; (*el pan*) bake brown

escalinata f stone steps, front steps

escalo m burglary, breaking in

escalofria•do -da adj chilly

escalofrío m chill

escalón m step, rung; (*grada de la escalera*) tread; (fig) step, echelon, grade; (*paso con que uno adelanta sus pretensiones*) (fig) stepping stone; (mil) echelon; (rad) stage

escalonamiento m ranking; gradation

escalonar tr to space out, spread out; (*las horas de trabajo*) stagger; (mil) to echelon

escalope m (*loncha delgada de carne*) scallop (*thin slice of meat*)

escalpar tr to scalp

escalpelo m scalpel

escama f scale; fear, suspicion

escamar tr (*los peces*) to scale; (coll) to frighten ‖ ref to be frightened

escamondar tr to trim, prune

escamo•so -sa adj scaly

escamotea•dor -dora mf prestidigitator; swindler

escamotear tr to whisk out of sight, cause to vanish; (*una carta*) palm; swipe, snitch

escampada f clear spell, break in rain

escampar tr to clear out ‖ intr to stop raining; ease up; **¡ya escampa!** there you go again! ‖ ref — **escamparse del agua** to get in out of the rain

escampavía f (naut) cutter, revenue cutter

escamujar tr (*un árbol, esp. un olivo*) to prune; (*ramas*) clear out

escanciar tr (*vino*) to pour, serve, drink ‖ intr to drink wine

escandalizar §60 tr to scandalize ‖ ref to be scandalized; be outraged, be exasperated

escándalo m scandal; **causar escándalo** to make a scene

escandalo•so -sa adj scandalous; noisy, riotous; loud, flashy

escandallo m (naut) sounding lead; (*del contenido de varios envases*) testing, sampling; cost accounting

escandina•vo -va adj & mf Scandinavian

escandir tr (*versos*) to scan

escansión f scansion; (telv) scanning

escaño m settle, bench with a back; (*en las Cortes*) seat; park bench; (Guat) nag

escañuelo m footstool

escapada f escape, flight; short trip, quick trip

escapar tr to free, save; (*un caballo*) drive hard ‖ intr to escape; flee, run away; **escapar en una tabla** to have a narrow escape ‖ ref to escape; flee, run away; (*el gas, el agua*) leak; **escapársele a uno** to let slip; not notice

escaparate m show window; (*armario con cristales*) cabinet; wardrobe, clothes closet; **escaparete de tienda** shop window

escaparatista mf window dresser

escapatoria f escape, getaway; (*de atenciones, deberes, etc.*) (fig) escape; (*efugio, pretexto*) (coll) evasion, subterfuge

escape m escape; flight; (*de gas, agua*) leak; (*de reloj*) escapement; (aut) exhaust valve; (aut) exhaust, exhaust pipe; **a escape** at full speed, on the run; **escape de rejilla** (rad) grid leak; **escape libre** (aut) cutout

escápula f shoulder blade, scapula

escaque m square; **escaques** chess

escarabajear tr to bother, worry, harass ‖ intr to swarm, crawl; scrawl, scribble

escarabajo m black beetle; (*imperfección en los tejidos*) flaw; (*persona pequeña*) runt

escaramuza f skirmish

escaramuzar §60 intr to skirmish

escarapela f (*divisa en forma de lazo*) cockade; dispute ending in hair pulling

escarapelar intr & ref to quarrel, wrangle

escarbadien•tes m (*pl* **-tes**) toothpick

escarbar tr (*el suelo*) to scratch, scratch up; (*la lumbre*) poke; (*los dientes, los oídos*) pick; pry into

escarcha f frost, hoarfrost

escarchar tr (*confituras*) to frost, put frosting on; (*la tierra del alfarero*) dilute with water; spangle ‖ intr — **escarcha** there is frost

ep
es

escardar or **escardillar** *tr* to weed, weed out

escardillo *m* weeding hoe

escariar *tr* to ream

escarlata *adj* scarlet || *f* scarlet fever

escarlatina *f* scarlet fever

escarmentar §2 *tr* to make an example of || *intr* to learn one's lesson

escarmiento *m* example, lesson, warning; caution, wisdom; punishment

escarnecer §22 *tr* to scoff at, make fun of

escarnio *m* scoff, scoffing

escarola *f* endive

escarpa *f* scarp, escarpment; (Mex) sidewalk

escarpa•do -da *adj* steep; abrupt, craggy

escarpia *f* hooked spike

escarpín *m* pump

escasamente *adv* barely; hardly

escasear *tr* to give sparingly; cut down on, avoid; bevel || *intr* to be scarce

escase•ro -ra *adj* sparing; saving, frugal; stingy || *mf* skinflint

escasez *f* (*falta de una cosa*) scarcity; (*pobreza*) need, want; (*mezquindad*) stinginess

esca•so -sa *adj* (*poco abundante*) scarce; (*no cabal*) scant; (*muy económico*) parsimonious, frugal; (*tacaño*) stingy; (*oportunidad*) dim, slim, slight; **estar escaso de** to be short of

escatimar *tr* & *intr* to scrimp

escena *f* (*parte del teatro donde se representan las obras*) stage; (*subdivisión de un acto*) scene; incident, episode; **poner en escena** to stage

escenario *m* stage; (*disposición de la representación*) setting; (*guión de un cine*) scenario; (*antecedentes de una persona o cosa*) background

escenarista *mf* scenarist

escéni•co -ca *adj* scenic

escenificar §73 *tr* to adapt for the stage

escépti•co -ca *adj* sceptic(al) || *mf* sceptic

Escila *f* Scylla; **entre Escila y Caribdis** between Scylla and Charybdis

Escipión *m* Scipio

escisión *f* (biol) fission; (surg) excision

esclarecer §22 *tr* to light up, brighten; explain, elucidate; ennoble || *intr* to dawn

esclareci•do -da *adj* noble, illustrious

esclavitud *f* slavery

esclavización *f* enslavement

esclavizar §60 *tr* to enslave

escla•vo -va *adj* & *mf* slave

escla•vón -vona *adj* & *mf* Slav

esclerosis múltiple *f* multiple sclerosis

esclusa *f* lock; floodgate; **esclusa de aire** caisson

esclusero *m* lock tender

escoba *f* broom

escobada *f* sweep; sweeping

escobar *tr* to sweep with a broom

escobazar §60 *tr* to sprinkle with a wet broom

escobén *m* (naut) hawse

escobilla *f* brush, whisk; gold and silver sweepings; (elec) brush

escocer §16 *intr* to smart, sting || *ref* to hurt; chafe, become chafed

esco•cés -cesa *adj* Scotch, Scottish || *mf* Scot || *m* Scotchman; (*whisky; dialecto*) Scotch; **los escoceces** the Scotch, the Scottish

Escocia *f* Scotland; **la Nueva Escocia** Nova Scotia

escofina *f* rasp

escofinar *tr* to rasp

escoger §17 *tr* to choose, pick out

escogi•do -da *adj* choice, select

escolar *adj* school || *m* pupil

escolaridad *f* schooling, school attendance; curriculum

escolimo•so -sa *adj* impatient, gruff, restless

escolta *f* escort

escoltar *tr* to escort

escollar *intr* (Arg) to run aground on a reef; (Arg, Chile) to fail

escollera *f* jetty, breakwater

escollo *m* (*peñasco a flor de agua*) reef, rock; (*peligro*) pitfall; (*obstáculo*) stumbling block

escombrar *tr* to clear out

escombro *m* (*pez*) mackerel; **escombros** debris, rubble, rubbish

esconder *tr* to hide, conceal; harbor, contain || *ref* to hide; lurk

escondi•do -da *adj* hidden; **a escondidas** secretly; **a escondidas de** without the knowledge of

escondite *m* hiding place; (*juego de muchachos*) hide-and-seek; **jugar al escondite** to play hide-and-seek

escondrijo *m* hiding place

escopeta *f* shotgun; **escopeta blanca** gentleman hunter; **escopeta de caza** fowling piece; **escopeta de dos cañones** double-barreled shotgun; **escopeta de viento** air rifle; **escopeta negra** professional hunter

escopetazo *m* gunshot; gunshot wound; bad news, blow; (SAm) sarcasm; insult

escoplear *tr* to chisel

escoplo *m* chisel

escorbuto *m* scurvy

escoria *f* dross, scoria, slag; (fig) dross, dregs

escorial *m* cinder bank, slag dump

escorpión *m* scorpion; **Escorpión** *m* (astr) Scorpio

escorzar §60 *tr* to foreshorten

escorzo *m* foreshortening

escota *f* (naut) sheet

escota•do -da *adj* low-neck || *m* low neck

escotadura *f* low neck, low cut in neck

escotar *tr* to cut to fit; draw water from, drain; cut low in the neck || *intr* to go Dutch

escote *m* low neck; (*encajes en el cuello de una vestidura*) tucker; **ir a escote** or **pagar a escote** to go Dutch

escotilla *f* (naut) hatchway, scuttle

escotillón *m* hatch, trap door, scuttle; (theat) trap door

escozor *m* burning, smarting, stinging; grief, sorrow

escriba *m* scribe

escribanía *f* court clerkship; desk; writing materials

escribano *m* court clerk; lawyer's clerk

escribiente *mf* clerk, office clerk; **escribiente a máquina** typist

escribir §83 *tr & intr* to write || *ref* to enroll, enlist; write to each other; **no escribirse** to be impossible to describe

escriño *m* casket, jewel case; straw basket

escri•to -ta *adj* streaked || *m* writing; (law) brief, writ; **poner por escrito** to write down, put in writing

escri•tor -tora *mf* writer

escritorio *m* writing desk; office; **escritorio ministro** kneehole desk, office desk; **escritorio norteamericano** rolltop desk

escritura *f* writing; script, handwriting, longhand; (law) deed, indenture; (law) sworn statement; **escritura al tacto** touch typewriting || **Escritura** *f* Scripture; **Sagrada Escritura** Holy Scripture, Holy Writ

escriturar *tr* to notarize; (*p.ej., a un actor*) book || *ref* (taur) to sign up for a fight

escrnía. *abbr* **escribanía**

escrno. *abbr* **escribano**

escrófula *f* scrofula

escrúpulo *m* scruple

escrupulo•so -sa *adj* scrupulous; exact

escrutar *tr* to scrutinize; (*los votos*) count

escrutinio *m* scrutiny; counting of votes

escuadra *f* (*pequeño número de personas o de soldados*) squad; (*pieza de metal para asegurar las ensambladuras*) angle iron; (*de carpintero*) square; (*de dibujante*) triangle; (nav) squadron

escuadrar *tr* (carp) to square

escuadrilla *f* (aer) squadron

escuadrón *m* (mil) squadron

escualidez *f* squalor

escuáli•do -da *adj* squalid

escualor *m* squalor

escucha *mf* listener || *m* (mil) scout, vedette || *f* listening; (*en un convento*) chaperon; **escuchas telefónicas** listening in on telephone conversations; wiretapping; **estar de escucha** (coll) to eavesdrop

escuchar *tr* to listen to; (*atender a*) heed; (*radiotransmisiones*) monitor || *intr* to listen || *ref* to like the sound of one's own voice

escudar *tr* to shield

escudero *m* esquire; nobleman; lady's page

escudete *m* escutcheon; (*refuerzo en la ropa*) gusset; (*planchuela delante de la cerradura*) escutcheon, escutcheon plate

escudilla *f* bowl

escudo *m* shield; buckler; (*delante de la cerradura*) escutcheon plate; **escudo de armas** coat ·of arms; **escudo térmico** (*de una cápsula espacial*) heat shield

escudriñar *tr* to scrutinize

escuela *f* school; **escuela de artes y oficios** trade school; **escuela de párvulos** kindergarten; **escuela de verano** summer school; **escuela dominical** Sunday school; **Escuela Naval Militar** Naval Academy; **escuela preparatoria** prep school; **hacer escuela** to be the leader of a school (*of thought*)

escuelante *mf* (Mex) schoolteacher || *m* (Mex) schoolboy || *f* (Mex) schoolgirl

escuerzo *m* toad

escue•to -ta *adj* free, unencumbered; bare, unadorned

escuintle *adj* (Mex) sickly || *m* (*perro*) (Mex) mutt; (Mex) brat

esculcar §73 *tr* to frisk

esculpir *tr & intr* to ṣculpture, carve; engrave

escultismo *m* outdoor activities

escultista *m* outdoorsman

escultor *m* sculptor

escultora *f* sculptress

escultura *f* sculpture

escultural *adj* sculptural; statuesque

escupidera *f* cuspidor; chamber pot

escupidura *f* spit; fever blister

escupir *tr & intr* to spit

escurrepla•tos *m* (*pl* -tos) dish rack

escurridero *m* drainpipe; drainboard; slippery spot

escurridi•zo -za *adj* slippery

escurri•do -da *adj* narrow-hipped; abashed, confused

escurridor *m* colander

escurriduras *fpl* dregs, lees

escurrir *tr* (*una vasija; un líquido; la vajilla*) to drain; to wring, wring out; **escurrir el bulto** to duck || *intr* to drip, ooze, trickle; slide, slip || *ref* to drip, ooze, trickle; slide, slip; slip away; (*un reparo*) slip out

esdrúju•lo -la *adj* accented on the antepenult || *m* word or verse accented on the antepenult

ese, esa *adj dem* (*pl* **esos, esas**) that (*near you*) || **ese** *f* sound hole (*of violin*); **hacer eses** to reel, stagger

ése, ésa *pron dem* (*pl* **ésos, ésas**) that (*near you*); **ésa** your city

esencia *f* essence; **esencia de pera** banana oil; **quinta esencia** quintessence

esencial *adj & m* essential

esfera *f* sphere; (*del reloj*) dial

esféri•co -ca *adj* spherical || *m* football

esfero *m* or **esferográfica** *f* (Col) ball-point pen

esfinge *f* sphinx; spiteful woman

esforza•do -da *adj* brave, vigorous, enterprising

esforzar §35 *tr* to strengthen, invigorate; encourage || *ref* to exert oneself; strive

esfuerzo *m* effort, exertion, endeavor; courage, vigor, spirit

esfumar *tr* to stump || *ref* to disappear, fade away

esgarrar *tr* (*la flema*) to try to cough up || *intr* to clear the throat

esgrima *f* fencing

esgrimidura *f* fencing

esgrimir *tr* to wield, brandish; (*un argumento*) swing || *intr* to fence

esgrimista *mf* (Arg, Chile, Peru) fencer; (Chile) swindler, panhandler

esguazar §60 *tr* to ford

esguazo *m* fording; ford

esguince *m* dodge, duck; (*gesto de disgusto*) frown; twist, sprain, wrench

es
es

eslabón m (*de cadena*) link; (*hierro acerado para sacar fuego de un pedernal; cilindro de acero para afilar cuchillos*) steel

eslabonar tr to link; link together, string together ‖ intr to link

eslálom m slalom

esla·vo -va adj Slav, Slavic ‖ mf Slav ‖ m (*idioma*) Slavic

esla·vón -vona adj & mf Slav

eslogan m (*consigna usada en fórmulas publicitarias*) slogan

eslora f (naut) length

eslova·co -ca adj & mf Slovak

esmaltar tr to enamel; embellish

esmalte m enamel; **esmalte para las uñas** nail polish

esmera·do -da adj careful, painstaking

esmeralda f emerald

esmerar tr to polish, shine; examine, check ‖ ref to take pains, do one's best

esmeril m emery

esmeriladora f emery wheel

esmerilar tr to grind or polish with emery

esmero m care, neatness

esmoladera f grindstone

esmoquin m tuxedo, dinner coat

esnifar tr & intr (*heroína*) to sniff

esnob adj snobbish ‖ mf (pl esnobs) snob

esnobismo m snobbery, snobbishness

esnobista adj snobbish

eso pron dem that; **a eso de** about; **eso es** that's it; that is; **por eso** for that reason; therefore

esófago m esophagus

espabila·do -da adj intelligent; bright

espabilar ref to know the ropes; be well informed

espaciador m space bar

espacial adj space, spatial

espaciar §77 (Arg, Chile) & regular tr to space; spread, scatter ‖ ref to expatiate; amuse oneself, relax

espacio m space; **espacio de chispa** spark gap; **espacio exterior** outer space; **espacio libre** (*entre dos cosas*) clearance; **espacio muerto** (*en el cilindro de un motor*) clearance; **por espacio de** in the space of

espacio·so -sa adj spacious, roomy; slow, deliberate

espada m swordsman; (taur) matador ‖ f sword; playing card (*representing a sword*) equivalent to spade; **entre la espada y la pared** between the devil and the deep blue sea

espadachín m swordsman; (*amigo de pendencias*) bully

espadaña f cattail, bulrush, reed mace; (*campanario*) bell gable

espadilla f (*remo que se usa como timón*) scull; (*aguja para sujetar el pelo*) bodkin; red insignia of Order of Santiago

espadín m rapier

espadón m (coll) brass hat

espagueti m spaghetti

espalar tr to shovel

espalda f back; **a espaldas de uno** behind one's back; **de espaldas a** with one's back

to; **tener buenas espaldas** to have broad shoulders; **volver las espaldas a** to turn a cold shoulder to

espaldar m (*de silla*) back; (*enrejado para plantas*) trellis, espalier

espaldarazo m slap on the back; (*ceremonia para armar caballero*) accolade; **dar el espaldarazo a** to accept, approve

espalera f trellis, espalier

espantada f (*de un animal*) sudden flight; (*desistimiento ocasionado por el miedo*) cold feet

espantadi·zo -za adj shy, skittish, scary

espantajo m scarecrow; (*persona fea*) fright

espantamos·cas m (pl -cas) (*para poner a los caballos*) fly net; (*aparato para asustar y alejar las moscas*) fly chaser

espantapája·ros m (pl -ros) scarecrow

espantar tr to scare, frighten; scare away ‖ ref to get scared; be surprised, marvel

espanto m fright, terror; (*amenaza*) threat; ghost

espantosidad f fright; frightfulness; awfulness

espanto·so -sa adj frightening, terrifying

España f Spain; **la Nueva España** New Spain (*Mexico in the early days*)

espa·ñol -ñola adj Spanish; **a la española** in the Spanish manner ‖ mf Spaniard ‖ m (*idioma*) Spanish; **los españoles** the Spanish ‖ f Spanish woman

españolería f Spanishness; hispanophilia

españolada f Spanish mannerism; Spanish remark

españolizar §60 tr to make Spanish, Hispanicize; translate into Spanish ‖ ref to become Spanish

esparadrapo m sticking plaster

esparaván m spavin

esparavel m mortarboard

esparcimiento m spreading, scattering, dissemination; diversion, relaxation; frankness, openness

esparcir §36 tr to spread, scatter; divert, relax ‖ ref to spread, scatter; disperse; take it easy, relax

espárrago m asparagus; (*perno*) stud bolt; awning pole

esparrancar §73 ref to spread one's legs wide apart

esparta·no -na adj & mf Spartan

esparto m esparto grass

espasmo m spasm

espasmódi·co -ca adj spasmodic

espásti·co -ca adj spastic

espato m spar; **espato flúor** fluor spar

espátula f spatula; putty knife

especia f spice

especia·do -da adj spicy

especial adj especial, special

especialidad f speciality; (*ramo a que se consagra una persona o negocio*) specialty

especialista mf specialist

especializar §60 tr, intr & ref to specialize

especiar tr to spice

especie f (*categoría de la clasificación biológica*) species; (*clase, género*) sort, kind;

(*caso, asunto*) matter; (*chisme, cuento*) news, rumor; appearance, pretext, show; remark; **en especie** in kind; **soltar una especie** to try to draw someone out

especie•ro -ra *mf* spice dealer ‖ *m* spice box

especificar §73 *tr* to specify; itemize

especí•co -ca *adj* specific ‖ *m* specific; patent medicine

espécimen *m* (*pl* **especímenes**) specimen

especio•so -sa *adj* (*engañoso*) specious; nice, neat, perfect

especiota *f* hoax, wild idea

espectáculo *m* spectacle; **dar un espectáculo** to make a scene; **espectáculo de atracciones** side show

especta•dor -dora *mf* witness; spectator

espectral *adj* ghostly

espectro *m* specter, phantom, ghost; (*phys*) spectrum

especular *tr* to check, examine; contemplate ‖ *intr* to speculate

espejear *intr* to sparkle

espejismo *m* mirage

espejo *m* mirror, looking glass; model; **espejo de cuerpo entero** full-length mirror, pier glass; **espejo de retrovisión** rear-view mirror; **espejo de vestir** full-length mirror, pier glass; **espejo retrovisor** rear-view mirror

espelunca *f* cave, cavern

espeluznante *adj* hair-raising

espera *f* wait, waiting; (*puesto para cazar*) blind, hunter's blind; composure, patience, respite; delay; (*law*) stay; **no tener espera** to be of the greatest urgency

esperanza *f* hope; **tener puesta su esperanza en** to pin one's faith on

esperanza•do -da *adj* hopeful (*having hope*)

esperanza•dor -dora *adj* hopeful (*giving hope*)

esperanzar §60 *tr* to give hope to

esperanzo•so -sa *adj* hopeful, full of hope

esperar *tr* (*aguardar*) to wait for, await; (*tener esperanza de conseguir*) expect, hope for; **ir a esperar** to go to meet ‖ *intr* to wait; hope; **esperar** + *inf* to hope to + *inf*; **esperar a que** to wait until; **esperar desesperando** to hope against hope; **esperar en** to put one's hope in; **esperar que** to hope that; **esperar sentado** to have a good wait

esperinque *m* smelt

esperma *f* sperm

esperpento *m* monstrosity; freak; nonsense

espesar *m* depth, thickness (*of woods*) ‖ *tr* to thicken; (*un tejido*) weave tighter ‖ *ref* to thicken, get thick or thicker

espe•so -sa *adj* thick; dirty, greasy

espesor *m* thickness; (*de un flúido, gas, masa*) density

espesura *f* thickness; (*matorral*) thicket; (*cabellera muy espesa*) shock of hair; dirtiness, greasiness

espetar *tr* to skewer; pierce, pierce through; **espetar algo a** to spring something on ‖ *ref* to be solemn, be pompous; settle down

espetón *m* (*hurgón*) poker; (*asador*) skewer, spit; jab, poke

espía *mf* spy; squealer ‖ *f* (naut) warping; (*cuerda*) (naut) warp

espiar §77 *tr* to spy on ‖ *intr* to spy; (naut) to warp

espichar *tr* to prick; (*dinero*) (Chile) to cough up; (Chile, Peru) to tap ‖ *intr* (coll) to die ‖ *ref* (Mex, W-I) to get thin

espiche *m* (*arma o instrumento puntiagudo*) prick; (naut) peg, bung

espichón *m* stab, prick

espiga *f* (bot) ear, spike; peg, pin, tenon; (*clavo sin cabeza*) brad; (*badajo*) clapper; (*de una llave*) stem

espigar §44 *tr* to glean; tenon, dowel ‖ *intr* (*los cereales*) to form ears ‖ *ref* to grow tall, shoot up

espigón *m* sharp point, spur; (*mazorca*) ear of corn; (*cerro puntiagudo*) peak; breakwater

espina *f* thorn, spine; (*de los peces*) fishbone; doubt, uncertainty; sorrow; (anat) spine; **dar mala espina a** to worry; **espina de pescado** herringbone; **espina de pez** fishbone; **espina dorsal** spinal column; **estar en espinas** to be on pins and needles

espinaca *f* spinach; **espinacas** spinach

espinal *adj* spinal

espinapez *m* herringbone; thorny matter, difficulty

espinar *m* thorny spot; (fig) thorny matter ‖ *tr* to prick; (*árboles*) protect with thornbushes; hurt, offend

espinazo *m* backbone; (*de un arco*) keystone

espinel *m* trawl, trawl line

espineta *f* spinet

espinilla *f* (*de la pierna*) shin, shinbone; (*granillo en la piel*) blackhead

espino *m* hawthorn; **espino artificial** barbed wire; **espino negro** blackthorn

espinochar *tr* (*el maíz*) to husk

espino•so -sa or **espinu•do -da** *adj* thorny; (*pez*) bony; (*difícil*) (fig) thorny, knotty

espiocha *f* pickaxe

espión *m* spy

espionaje *m* spying, espionage

espira *f* turn

espiración *f* breathing; exhalation

espiral *adj* spiral ‖ *f* (*línea curva que da vueltas alrededor de un punto*) spiral; (*del reloj*) hairspring; (*de humo*) curl, wreath

espirar *tr* to breath; encourage ‖ *intr* to breathe; exhale, expire; (*el viento*) (poet) to blow gently

espiritismo *m* spiritualism

espirito•so -sa *adj* spirited, lively; (*licor*) spirituous

espíritu *m* spirit; (*mente*) mind; (*aparecido, fantasma*) ghost, spirit; **espíritu de equipo** teamwork; **Espíritu Santo** Holy Ghost, Holy Spirit; **dar, despedir, exhalar** or **rendir el espíritu** to give up the ghost

espiritual *adj* spiritual; sharp, witty

espiritualismo *m* spiritualism

espita *f* tap, cock; (coll) tippler

espitar *tr* to tap

esplendidez *f* splendor, magnificence

es
es

espléndi·do -da *adj* splendid, magnificent; generous, open-handed; (poet) brilliant, radiant

esplendor *m* splendor

esplendoro·so -sa *adj* resplendent

espliego *m* lavender

esplín *m* melancholy

espolada *f* prick with spur; **espolada de vino** shot of wine

espolear *tr* to spur, spur on

espoleta *f* fuse; (*hueso*) wishbone

espolón *m* (*del gallo, una montaña, un buque de guerra*) spur; dike, jetty, mole, cutwater; (*prominencia córnea de las caballerías*) fetlock; (*sabañón*) chilblain

espolvorear *tr* (*quitar el polvo de; esparcir el polvo sobre*) dust; (*el azúcar*) sprinkle

esponja *f* sponge; (*sablista*) sponge, sponger; **beber como una esponja** to drink like a fish; **tirar la esponja** to throw in (or up) the sponge

esponja·do -da *adj* proud, puffed-up; fresh, healthy

esponjar *tr* to puff up, make fluffy || *ref* to puff up, become fluffy; be puffed up, be conceited; look fresh and healthy

esponjo·so -sa *adj* spongy

esponsales *mpl* betrothal, engagement

espontanear *ref* to make a clean breast of it; open one's heart

espontáne·o -a *adj* spontaneous || *m* (taur) spectator who jumps into the ring to take on the bull

espora *f* spore

esporádi·co -ca *adj* sporadic

esposa *f* wife; **esposas** handcuffs, manacles

esposar *tr* to handcuff, manacle

espo·so -sa *mf* spouse || *m* husband || *f* see **esposa**

espuela *f* spur; **echar la espuela** (coll) to take a nightcap; **espuela de caballero** delphinium, rocket larkspur; **espuela de galán** nasturtium

espuelar *tr* (SAm) to spur, goad

espuerta *f* two-handled esparto basket

espulgar §44 *tr* to delouse; scrutinize

espuma *f* foam; (*en un vaso de cerveza; saliva parecida a la espuma*) froth; (*película de impurezas en la superficie de un líquido*) scum; **crecer como espuma** to grow like weeds; to have a meteoric rise; **espuma de caucho** foam rubber; **espuma de jabón** lather; **espuma de mar** meerschaum

espumadera *f* skimmer

espumajear *intr* to froth at the mouth

espumajo·so -sa *adj* foamy, frothy

espumante *adj* foaming; (*vino*) sparkling

espumar *tr* to skim || *intr* to foam, froth; (*el jabón*) lather; (*el vino*) sparkle; increase rapidly

espumarajo *m* froth, frothing at the mouth

espumilla *f* voile; (CAm, Ecuad) meringue

espumo·so -sa *adj* foamy, frothy; (*cubierto de una película*) scummy; (*jabonoso*) lathery; (*vino*) sparkling

espu·rio -ria *adj* spurious

espurrear or **espurriar** *tr* to squirt with water from the mouth

esputar *tr* & *intr* to spit

esputo *m* spit, saliva

esq. *abbr* **esquina**

esqueje *m* cutting, slip

esquela *f* note; announcement; death notice; **esquela amorosa** billet-doux

esquelétí·co -ca *adj* skeleton; skeletal, thin, wasted

esqueleto *m* skeleton; (CAm, Mex) blank form; (Chile) sketch, outline

esquema *m* scheme, diagram

es·quí *m* (*pl* **-quís**) ski; skiing; **esquí acuático** water ski; water skiing; **esquí remolcado** ski-joring

esquia·dor -dora *adj* ski || *mf* skier

esquiar §77 *intr* to ski

esquiciar *tr* to sketch

esquicio *m* sketch

esquifar *tr* (naut) to fit out, staff, man

esquife *m* skiff

esquiismo *m* skiing

esquila *f* sheepshearing; hand bell

esquilar *tr* to shear, fleece

esquilimo·so -sa *adj* fastidious, squeamish

esquilmar *tr* to harvest; (*las plantas el jugo de la tierra*) drain, exhaust; (*una fuente de riqueza*) drain, squander, use up; carry away, steal

esquilmo *m* harvest, farm produce; (Mex) farm scrapings

esquilmo·so -sa *adj* fastidious

esquimal *adj* & *mf* Eskimo

esquina *f* corner; (SAm) corner store; **a la vuelta de la esquina** around the corner; **doblar la esquina** to turn the corner; **hacer esquina** (*un edificio*) to be on the corner; **las cuatro esquinas** puss in the corner

esquina·do -da *adj* sharp-cornered; difficult, unsociable

esquinar *tr* to be on the corner of; put in the corner; alienate || *intr* — **esquinar con** to be on the corner of || *ref* — **esquinarse con** to fall out with

esquinazo *m* corner; (Arg, Chile) serenade; **dar esquinazo a** to give the slip to, to shake off

esquinencia *f* quinsy

esquinera *f* corner piece (*of furniture*)

esquirla *f* splinter

esquirol *m* scab, strikebreaker

esquisto *m* schist

esquite *m* (CAm, Mex) popcorn

esquivar *tr* to avoid, evade, shun; dodge || *ref* to withdraw; dodge

esquivez *f* aloofness, gruffness

esqui·vo -va *adj* aloof, gruff

estable *adj* stable, permanent; full-time || *mf* regular guest, permanent guest

establecer §22 *tr* to establish, institute || *ref* to settle, take up residence; start a business, open an office

establecimiento *m* establishment; place of business; decree, ordinance, statute

establo *m* stable

estaca *f* stake, picket, pale; cudgel, club; (*clavo largo*) spike; (hort) cutting

estacada *f* stockade, palisade; dueling ground; **dejar en la estacada** to leave in the lurch; **quedarse en la estacada** to succumb on the field of battle, fall in a duel; fail; lose out

estacar §73 *tr* to stake, stake off; tie to a stake ‖ *ref* to stand stiff

estación *f* (*cada una de las cuatro divisiones del año*) season; (*sitio en que paran los trenes; radioemisora*) station; (*lugar en que se hace alto en un paseo, etc.*) stop; **estación balnearia** bathing resort; **estación de cabeza** (rr) terminal; **estación de carga** freight station; **estación de empalme** junction; **estación de gasolina** gas station, filling station; **estación de la seca** dry season; **estación de paso** (rr) way station; **estación depuradora** sewage-disposal plant; **estación de radiodifusión** broadcasting station; **estación de seguimiento** tracking station; **estación de servicio** service station; **estación difusora** or **emisora** broadcasting station; **estación espacial** space station; **estación gasolinera** gas station, filling station; **estación meteorológica** weather station; **estación telefónica** telephone exchange

estacional *adj* seasonal

estacionamiento *m* stationing; parking; parking lot

estacionar *tr* to station; stand, park ‖ *intr* to stand, park ‖ *ref* to station oneself; be stationary; stand, park; **se prohibe estacionarse** no standing, no parking

estaciona•rio -ria *adj* stationary

estada *f* stay, stop

estadía *f* (*ante un pintor*) sitting; stop, stay; (com) demurrage

estadio *m* stadium; phase, stage; (*longitud*) furlong

estadista *mf* (*perito en estadística*) statistician ‖ *m* statesman

estadística *f* statistics

estadísti•co -ca *adj* statistical ‖ *m* statistician ‖ *f* see **estadística**

estadiunense *adj* American, United States ‖ *mf* American

estadi•zo -za *adj* (*aire*) heavy, stifling; (*agua*) stagnant

estado *m* state; state, condition, status; statement, report; **en estado de buena esperanza** or **en estado interesante** in the family way; **estado asistencial** welfare state; **estado civil** marital status; **estado de ánimo** state of mind; **estado de cuentas** (com) statement; **estado libre asociado** commonwealth; **estado llano** commons, common people; **estado mayor** (mil) staff; **estado mayor conjunto** joint chiefs of staff; **estado mayor general** general staff; **Estados Unidos** *msg* the United States; **estado tapón** buffer state; **estar en estado de guerra** to be under martial law; **los Estados Unidos** *mpl* the United States;

tomar estado to take a wife; to go into the church

estado-policía *m* (*pl* **estados-policías**) police state

estadounidense or **estadunidense** *adj* American, United States ‖ *mf* American

estafa *f* swindle, trick; (*estribo*) stirrup

estafar *tr* to swindle, trick; overcharge

estafeta *f* post, courier; post office; diplomatic mail

estallar *intr* to burst; explode; (*un incendio, una revolución; la guerra*) break out; (*la ira*) break forth

estallido *m* report, crash, explosion; crack; (*p.ej., de la guerra*) outbreak; **dar un estallido** to crash, explode

estambre *m* (*hebras de lana e hilo formado de ellas*) worsted; (bot) stamen; **estambre de la vida** course or thread of life

estampa *f* stamp, print, engraving; press, printing; footstep, track; aspect, appearance; **dar a la estampa** to publish, bring out; **parecer la estampa de la herejía** to be a sight, be a mess; **la propia estampa de** the very image of

estampado *m* printing, stamping; printed fabric, cotton print

estampar *tr* to stamp, print, engrave; (*en al ánimo*) fix, engrave; (*p.ej., el pie*) leave a mark of; (bb) to tool; (*arrojar con fuerza*) (coll) to dash, slam

estampida *f* report, crash, explosion; stampede

estampido *m* report, crash, explosion; **estampido sónico** (aer) sonic boom

estampilla *f* (*sello con letrero para estampar*) stamp; (*sello con una firma en facsímile*) rubber stamp; (*sello de correos o fiscal*) stamp

estampillar *tr* to stamp; rubber-stamp

estanca•do -da *adj* stagnant; (fig) stagnant, dead

estancar §73 *tr* to stanch; stem, check; (*un negocio*) suspend, hold up; corner; monopolize ‖ *ref* to become stagnant, become choked up

estancia *f* stay, sojourn; (*aposento*) living room; day in hospital; cost of day in hospital; (*estrofa*) stanza; (mil) bivouac; (Arg, Urug, Chile) cattle ranch; (Col) small country place; (Ven) truck farm

estanciero *m* rancher, cattle raiser

estan•co -ca *adj* stanch, watertight ‖ *m* government monopoly; cigar store, government store (*for sale of tobacco, matches, postage stamps, etc.*); archives; (Ecuad) liquor store

estándar *m* standard

estandardizar §60 or **estandarizar** §60 *tr* to standardize

estandarte *m* banner, standard

estandartizar §60 *tr* to standardize

estanque *m* basin, reservoir; pond, pool

estanque•ro -ra *mf* storekeeper, tobacconist; (Ecuad) saloonkeeper ‖ *m* reservoir tender

es
es

estanquillo *m* cigar store, government store (*for sale of tobacco, matches, postage stamps, etc.*); (Col, Ecuad) bar, saloon; (Mex) booth, stand

estante *adj* located, being; settled, permanent ‖ *m* shelf; shelving; bookcase, open bookcase

estantería *f* shelves, shelving; book stack

estañar *tr* to tin; tin-plate; solder; (Ven) to hurt, injure; (Ven) to fire

estaño *m* tin

estaquilla *f* peg, dowel, pin; (*clavo pequeño sin cabeza*) brad; (*clavo largo*) spike

estaquillar *tr* to peg, dowel; nail

estar §37 *v aux* (*to form progressive form*) to be, e.g., **están aprendiendo el español** they are learning Spanish ‖ *intr* to be; be in, be home; be ready; **¿a cuántos estamos?** what day of the month is it?; **¡está bien!** O.K.!, all right!; **estar a** to cost, sell at; **estar bien** to be well; **estar bien con** to be on good terms with; **estar de** to be (*on a temporary basis*); **estar de más** to be in the way; be unnecessary; be idle; **estar de viaje** to be on a trip; **estar mal** to be sick, be ill; **estar mal con** to be on bad terms with; **estar para** to be about to; **estar por** to be for, be in favor of; to be about to; to have a mind to; to remain to be + *pp*; **estar sobre sí** to be wary, be on one's guard ‖ *ref* (*p.ej., en casa*) to stay; (*p.ej., quieto*) to keep

estarcido *m* stencil

estarcir §36 *tr* to stencil

estatal *adj* state

estáti•co -ca *adj* static; dumbfounded, speechless

estatificar §73 *tr* to nationalize

estatizar §60 *tr* to nationalize

estatorreactor *m* ramjet (engine)

estatua *f* statue; **quedarse hecho una estatua** to stand aghast

estatuir §20 *tr* to order, decree; establish, prove

estatura *f* stature

estatuta•rio -ria *adj* statutory

estatuto *m* statute

estay *m* (naut) stay; **estay mayor** (naut) mainstay

este, esta *adj dem* (*pl* **estos, estas**) this ‖ *m* east; east wind

éste, ésta *pron dem* (*pl* **éstos, éstas**) this one, this one here; the latter; **ésta** this city

estela *f* (*de un buque*) wake; (*de cohete, humo, cuerpo celeste, etc.*) trail

estenógrafo *m* (Cuba) ball-point pen

estenotipia *f* stenotypy; machine stenography

estepa *f* steppe

estera *f* mat; matting; **cargado de esteras** out of patience

esterar *tr* to cover with matting ‖ *intr* to bundle up for the cold

estercolar *m* dunghill ‖ §61 *tr* to dung, to manure

estercolero *m* manure pile, dunghill; manure collector

estereofóni•co -ca *adj* stereophonic, stereo

estereoscópi•co -ca *adj* stereoscopic, stereo

estereotipa•do -da *adj* stereotyped

estéril *adj* (*que no produce nada*) sterile; (*inútil, vano*) futile

esterilización *f* sterilization

esterilizar §60 *tr* to sterilize ‖ *ref* to become sterile

esterlina *adj fem* (*libra*) sterling (*pound*)

esternón *m* breastbone

estero *m* tideland; estuary; (Arg) swamp, marsh; (Chile) stream; (Col, Ven) pool, puddle

esterto *m* death rattle; (*ruido en ciertas enfermedades, perceptible por la auscultación*) stertor, râle; **estertor agónico** death rattle

esteta *mf* aesthete ‖ *f* beautician

estéti•co -ca *adj* aesthetic ‖ *f* aesthetics

estetoscopio *m* stethoscope

estiaje *m* low water

estiba *f* (naut) stowage

estibador *m* stevedore, longshoreman

estibar *tr* to pack, stuff; (naut) to stow

estiércol *m* dung, manure

esti•gio -gia *adj* Stygian ‖ **Estigia** *f* Styx

estigma *m* stigma

estigmatizar §60 *tr* to stigmatize

estilar *tr* (*una escritura*) to draw up in proper form; be given to ‖ *intr* & *ref* to be in fashion

estilete *m* (*puñal*) stiletto

estilo *m* style; **por el estilo** like that, of the kind; **por el estilo de** like; **estilo directo** (gram) direct discourse; **estilo indirecto** (gram) indirect discourse

estilográfica *f* fountain pen

estima *f* esteem; (naut) dead reckoning

estimable *adj* estimable; considerable; appreciable, computable; esteemed

estimación *f* esteem, estimation; estimate, evaluation

estimar *tr* (*tener en buen concepto*) to esteem; (*apreciar, valuar*) estimate; think, believe; appreciate, thank; be fond of, like; **estimar en poco** to hold in low esteem

estimativa *f* judgment; instinct

estimulante *adj* & *m* stimulant

estimular *tr* to stimulate

estímulo *m* stimulus

estío *m* summer

estipendio *m* stipend; wages

estípti•co -ca *adj* styptic; constipated; mean, stingy

estipular *tr* to stipulate

estiradamente *adv* scarcely, hardly; violently

estira•do -da *adj* conceited, stuck-up; prim, neat; tight, closefisted

estirar *tr* to stretch; (*alambre, metal*) draw; (*planchar ligeramente*) iron lightly; (*un escrito, discurso, cargo, etc.*) (fig) to stretch out; (*el dinero*) (fig) to stretch ‖ *ref* to stretch; put on airs

estirón *m* jerk, tug; **dar un estirón** to grow up in no time

estirpe *f* race, stock, lineage; (*linaje*) strain, pedigree

estitiquez *f* constipation

estival *adj* summer

esto *pron dem* that; **en esto** at this point; **por esto** for this reason

estocada *f* thrust, stab, lunge; (*herida*) stab, stab wound; (*cosa que ocasiona dolor*) blow

Estocolmo *f* Stockholm

estofa *f* brocade; quality, kind

estofado *m* stew

estoi·co -ca *adj & mf* stoic

estóli·do -da *adj* stupid, imbecile

estómago *m* stomach; **estómago de avestruz** iron digestion; **tener buen estómago** or **mucho estómago** to be thick-skinned; have an easy conscience

estopa *f* (*de lino o cáñamo*) tow; (*de calafatear*) (naut) oakum; **estopa de acero** steel wool; **estopa de algodón** cotton waste

estopilla *f* (*tela muy sutil*) lawn; (*tela ordinaria de algodón*) cheesecloth

estoque *m* rapier; sword lily, gladiola

estoquear *tr* to stab with a rapier

estor *m* blind, shade, window shade

estorbar *tr* to hinder, obstruct; inconvenience, bother, annoy ‖ *intr* to be in the way

estorbo *m* hindrance, obstruction; inconvenience, bother, annoyance

estorbo·so -sa *adj* hindering; bothersome, annoying

estornino *m* starling; **estornino de los pastores** grackle, myna

estornudar *intr* to sneeze

estornudo *m* sneeze, sneezing

estrado *m* (*tarima del trono*) dais; lecture platform; (archaic) lady's drawing room; **estrados** courtrooms, law courts; **citar para estrados** to subpoena

estrafala·rio -ria *adj* odd, eccentric; sloppy, sloppily dressed ‖ *mf* screwball

estragar §44 *tr* to spoil, damage, vitiate

estrago *m* damage, ruin, havoc

estrambote *m* tail (*of sonnet*)

estrambóti·co -ca *adj* odd, weird

estrangul *m* (mus) reed, mouthpiece

estrangular *tr & ref* to strangle, choke

estraperlear *intr* to deal in the black market

estraperlista *adj* black-market ‖ *mf* black-market dealer

estraperlo *m* black market

estrapontín *m* folding seat, jump seat

estratagema *f* stratagem; craftiness

estratega *m* strategist

estrategia *f* strategy; **alta estrategia** grand strategy

estratégi·co -ca *adj* strategic(al) ‖ *m* strategist

estratificar §73 *tr & ref* to stratify

estrato *m* stratum, layer

estratosfera *f* stratosphere

estraza *f* rag; brown paper

estrechar *tr* (*reducir a menor ancho*) narrow; (*apretar*) tighten; press, pursue, force, compel; hug, embrace; squeeze; **estrechar la mano a** to shake hands with ‖ *ref* to narrow down; contract; hug, embrace; (*reducir los gastos*) retrench; **estrecharse en**

to squeeze in; **estrecharse la mano** (*dos personas*) to shake hands

estrechez *f* narrowness; rightness; (*amistad íntima*) closeness, intimacy; austerity, strictness; poverty, want, need; trouble, jam; **estrechez de miras** narrow outlook, narrow-mindedness; **hallarse en gran estrechez** to be in dire straits

estre·cho -cha *adj* narrow; tight; close, intimate; austere, strict; stingy, tight; poor, needy; mean ‖ *m* (*paso angosto en el mar*) strait; fix, predicament

estrechura *f* narrowness; tightness; closeness, intimacy; austerity, strictness; trouble, predicament

estregar §66 *tr* to rub hard; scour

estregón *m* hard rub

estrella *f* star; (typ) asterisk, star; (mov & theat) star; (*hado, destino*) (fig) star; **estrella de los Alpes** edelweiss; **estrella de mar** starfish; **estrella de rabo** comet; **estrella filante** or **fugaz** shooting star; **estrella fulgurante** (astr) flare star; **estrella polar** pole-star; **estrella vespertina** evening star; **ver las estrellas** (fig) to see stars

estrella·do -da *adj* (*cielo*) starry; star-spangled; star-shaped; (*huevos*) fried

estrellamar *m* starfish

estrellar *adj* star ‖ *tr* to star, spangle with stars; (*huevos*) fry; shatter, dash to pieces ‖ *ref* to be spangled with stars; crash; **estrellarse con** to clash with

estrellón *m* large star; (*fuego artificial*) star; smash-up

estremecer §22 *tr* to shake; (*el aire*) rend; (fig) to shake, upset ‖ *ref* to shake, tremble, shiver, shudder

estrena *f* (*regalo que se da en señal de agradecimiento*) handsel; first use

estrenar *tr* to use for the first time, wear for the first time; (*un drama*) perform for the first time; (*un cine*) show for the first time; try out for the first time ‖ *ref* to make the day's first transaction; appear for the first time; (*un drama, un cine*) open

estrenista *mf* first-nighter

estreno *m* beginning, debut; première, first performance; first use

estre·nuo -nua *adj* strenuous, vigorous, enterprising

estreñimiento *m* constipation

estreñir §72 *tr* to constipate

estrépito *m* racket, crash; fuss, show

estrepito·so -sa *adj* loud, noisy, boisterous; notorious; shocking

estría *f* flute, groove

estriar §77 *tr* to flute, groove

estribar *intr* to lean, rest; be based, depend

estriberón *m* stepping stone

estribillo *m* (*de un poema*) burden, refrain; pet word, pet phrase

estribo *m* (*de coche*) step; (*de automóvil*) running board; (*apoyo para el pie*) footboard; (*para el pie del jinete*) stirrup; abutment, buttress; (fig) foundation, support;

es
es

perder los estribos to fly off the handle; lose one's head

estribor *m* starboard

estricnina *f* strychnine

estricote *m* (Ven) riotous living; **al estricote** hither and thither

estric·to -ta *adj* strict, severe, rigorous; proper, punctual; (*sentido de una palabra*) narrow

estrictura *f* (pathol) stricture

estrige *f* barn owl; (*Athene noctua*) little owl

estro *m* poetic inspiration; (*de animal*) rut, heat

estrofa *f* strophe

estroncio *m* strontium

estropajo *m* mop; dishcloth; **servir de estropajo** to be forced to do the dirty work; be treated with indifference

estropajo·so -sa *adj* raggedy, slovenly; (*carne*) tough, leathery; spluttering

estropear *tr* to spoil, ruin, damage; abuse, mistreat; cripple, maim ‖ *ref* to spoil, go to ruin; fail

estropicio *m* breakage; havoc, ruin; fracas, rumpus

estructura *f* structure

estruendo *m* noise, crash, boom; confusion, uproar; pomp, show; fame

estruendo·so -sa *adj* noisy, booming

estrujar *tr* to squeeze; press, crush, mash; bruise; rumple; drain, exhaust

estuante *adj* hot, burning

estuario *m* estuary; tideland

estucar §73 *tr* to stucco

estuco *m* stucco; **estuco de París** plaster of Paris

estuche *m* case, box; (*caja y utensilios que se guardan en ella*) kit; casket, jewel case; (*para tijeras*) sheath; **estuche de afeites** compact, vanity case; **ser un estuche** to be a handy fellow

estudia·do -da *adj* affected, studied

estudiantado *m* student body

estudiante *mf* student

estudiantil *adj* student

estudiar *tr* to study; (*la lección a una persona*) to hear (*someone's lesson*) ‖ *intr* to study; **estudiar para . . .** to study to become . . .

estudio *m* study; (*aposento*) studio; (mus) étude; **altos estudios** advanced studies

estudio·so -sa *adj* studious ‖ *m* student, scholar

estufa *f* stove; steam cabinet, steam room; foot stove; (*invernáculo*) hothouse

estul·to -ta *adj* stupid, silly, foolish

estupefac·to -ta *adj* stupefied, dumbfounded

estupen·do -da *adj* stupendous; famous, distinguished

estúpi·do -da *adj* stupid ‖ *mf* dolt

estupor *m* stupor; surprise, amazement

estuprar *tr* to rape, violate

estupro *m* rape, violation

estuque *m* stucco

esturión *m* sturgeon

etapa *f* stage; **a etapas pequeñas** by easy stages

éter *m* ether

etére·o -a *adj* ethereal

eternidad *f* eternity

eternizar §60 *tr* to prolong endlessly ‖ *ref* to be endless, be interminable

eter·no -na *adj* eternal

éti·co -ca *adj* ethical ‖ *f* ethics

etileno *m* ethylene

etilo *m* ethyl

étimo *m* etymon

etimología *f* etymology; **etimología popular** folk etymology

etíope *adj & mf* Ethiopian

etiópi·co -ca *adj & m* Ethiopic

etiqueta *f* (*marbete*) tag, label; (*ceremonial que se debe observar*) etiquette; (*ceremonia en la manera de tratarse*) formality; **de etiqueta** formal, full-dress; **de etiqueta menor** semiformal; **estar de etiqueta** to have become cool toward each other

etiquetar *tr* to tag, label

etiquete·ro -ra *adj* formal, ceremonious; full of compliments

etiquez *f* (pathol) consumption

étni·co -ca *adj* ethnic(al); (gram) gentilic

etnografía *f* ethnography

etnología *f* ethnology

E.U.A. *abbr* **Estados Unidos de América**

eucalipto *m* eucalyptus

Eucaristía *f* Eucharist

eufemismo *m* euphemism

eufemísti·co -ca *adj* euphemistic

eufonía *f* euphony

eufóni·co -ca *adj* euphonic, euphonious

euforia *f* euphoria; endurance, fortitude

eufuísmo *m* euphuism

eufuísti·co -ca *adj* euphuistic

eugenesia *f* eugenics

eunuco *m* eunuch

euritmia *f* regular pulse

euro *m* east wind

Europa *f* Europe

europe·o -a *adj & mf* European

eutanasia *f* euthanasia

eutrapelia *f* moderation; lightheartedness; simple pastime

evacuación *f* evacuation; **evacuación de basuras** garbage disposal

evacuar §21 & regular *tr* to evacuate; (*un trámite*) transact; (*una visita*) pay; (*un encargo, un asunto*) do, carry out; **evacuar el vientre** to have a bowel movement ‖ *intr* to evacuate; have a bowel movement

evadi·do -da *adj* escaped ‖ *mf* escapee

evadir *tr* to avoid, evade, elude ‖ *ref* to evade; escape, flee

evaluar §21 *tr* to evaluate; value

evangéli·co -ca *adj* evangelic(al)

evangelio *m* gospel, gospel truth ‖ **Evangelio** *m* Gospel, Evangel

evangelista *m* Gospel singer or chanter; (Mex) public writer, penman ‖ **Evangelista** *m* Evangelist

evaporar *tr & ref* to evaporate

evaporizar §60 *tr, intr & ref* to vaporize

evasión *f* (*efugio, evasiva*) evasion; (*fuga*) escape

evasi•vo -va *adj* evasive ‖ *f* loophole, pretext, excuse
evento *m* chance, happening, contingency; (Col) sports event; **a todo evento** in any event
eventual *adj* contingent; (*emolumentos; gastos*) incidental
eventualidad *f* eventuality, contingency; uncertainty
evidencia *f* evidence, obviousness; (*prueba judicial*) evidence; **evidencia moral** moral certainty
evidenciar *tr* to show, make evident
evidente *adj* evident, obvious
evitable *adj* avoidable
evitación *f* avoidance; prevention
evitar *tr* to avoid, shun; (*p.ej., el polvo*) keep off; prevent; **evitar** + *inf* to avoid + *ger;* save from + *ger*, e.g., **la luz de la luna nos evitó tener que encender los faroles** the light of the moon saved us from having to light the lights
evo *m* (poet) age, aeon; (theol) eternity
evocar §73 *tr* to evoke; (*p.ej., los demonios*) invoke
evolución *f* evolution; change, development (*of one's point of view, plans, conduct, etc.*)
evolucionar *intr* to evolve; change, develop; (mil & nav) to maneuver
evolucionista *adj & mf* evolutionist; evolutionary
ex *adj* ex- (*former*), e.g., **el ex presidente** the ex-president
ex abrupto *adv* brashly ‖ *m* brash remark
exacción *f* (*de impuestos, deudas, multas, etc.*) exaction, levy; (*cobro injusto*) extortion
exacerbar *tr* to exacerbate, aggravate
exactitud *f* exactness; punctuality
exac•to -ta *adj* exact; punctual, faithful ‖ **exacto** *interj* right!
exactor *m* tax collector
exagerar *tr* to exaggerate
exalta•do -da *adj* exalted; extreme, hotheaded; wrought-up; radical
exaltar *tr* to exalt; extol ‖ *ref* to be wrought-up, get excited
examen *m* examination; **examen de ingreso** entrance examination; **sufrir un examen** to take an examination
examinar *tr* to examine; inspect ‖ *ref* to take an examination; **examinarse de ingreso** to take entrance examinations
exangüe *adj* bloodless; weak, exhausted; dead
exánime *adj* (*sin vida*) lifeless; (*desmayado*) faint, in a faint, lifeless
exasperar *tr* to exasperate
Exc.ª *abbr* **Excelencia**
excandecer §22 *tr* to incense, enrage
excarcelación *f* release
excarcelar *tr* (*a un preso*) to release
excavadora *f* power shovel
excavar *tr* to excavate; loosen soil around

excedente *adj* excess; excessive; on leave ‖ *m* excess, surplus; **excedente de ganancia** profit margin
exceder *tr* (*ser mayor que*) to exceed; (*aventajar*) excel ‖ *ref* to go too far, go to extremes; **excederse a sí mismo** to outdo oneself
excelencia *f* excellence, excellency; **por excelencia** par excellence; **Su Excelencia** Your Excellency
excelente *adj* excellent
excel•so -sa *adj* lofty, sublime ‖ **el Excelso** the Most High
excéntrica *f* eccentric
excentricidad *f* eccentricity
excéntri•co -ca *adj* eccentric; (*barrio*) outlying ‖ *mf* eccentric ‖ *f* see **excéntrica**
excepción *f* exception; **a excepción de** with the exception of
excepcional *adj* exceptional
excepto *prep* except
exceptuar §21 *tr* to except; (*eximir*) exempt
excerpta or **excerta** *adj* excerpt
excesi•vo -va *adj* excessive; excess
exceso *m* excess; **exceso de equipaje** excess baggage; **exceso de peso** excess weight; **exceso de velocidad** speeding
excitable *adj* excitable
excitación *f* excitement; excitation
excitante *adj & m* stimulant
excitar *tr* to excite, stir up, stimulate ‖ *ref* to become excited
exclamación *f* exclamation
exclamar *tr & intr* to exclaim
exclaustrar *tr* (*a un religioso*) to secularize
excluir §20 *tr* to exclude
exclusión *f* exclusion; **con exclusión de** to the exclusion of; **exclusión de contribución** tax deduction
exclusiva *f* rejection, turndown; sole right, monopoly; (*anticipación de una noticia por un periódico*) news beat
exclusive *adv* exclusively ‖ *prep* exclusive of, not counting
exclusivista *adj* exclusive, clannish ‖ *mf* snob
exclusi•vo -va *adj* exclusive ‖ *f* see **exclusiva**
Exc.ᵐᵒ *abbr* **Excelentísimo**
ex combatiente *m* ex-serviceman
excomulgar §44 *tr* to excommunicate; ostracize, banish
excomunión *f* excommunication
excoriar *tr* to skin ‖ *ref* to skin oneself; (*p.ej., el codo*) skin
excrementar *intr* to have a bowel movement
excremento *m* excrement
exculpar *tr* to exculpate, exonerate
excursión *f* excursion, outing
excursionista *mf* excursionist, tourist
excusa *f* excuse; **a excusa** secretly; **excusa es decir** it is unnecessary to say
excusabaraja *f* basket with lid
excusable *adj* excusable; avoidable
excusadamente *adv* unnecessarily
excusa•do -da *adj* exempt; unnecessary; private, set apart; (*puerta*) side ‖ *m* toilet
excusa•lí *m* (*pl* **-líes**) small apron

excusar *tr* to excuse; exempt; avoid; prevent; make unnecessary; **excusar** + *inf* to not have to + *inf* ‖ *ref* to excuse oneself; apologize; **excusarse de** + *inf* to decline to + *inf*

exención *f* exemption

exencionar *tr* to exempt

exentamente *adv* freely; frankly, simply

exentar *tr* to exempt

exen•to -ta *adj* exempt; open, unobstructed; free, disengaged

exequias *fpl* obsequies

exfolia•dor -dora *adj* tear-off

exhalación *f* exhalation; flash of lightning; shooting star; fume, vapor; **como una exhalación** like a flash of lightning

exhalar *tr* to exhale, emit; (*suspiros, quejas*) breathe forth; **exhalar el último suspiro** to breathe one's last ‖ *ref* to exhale; (*con el ejercicio violento del cuerpo*) breathe hard; hurry; crave

exhausti•vo -va *adj* exhaustive

exhaus•to -ta *adj* exhausted; wasted away

exheredar *tr* to disinherit

exhibición *f* exhibition; exhibit; **exhibición repetida** (telv) rerun

exhibición-venta *f* sales exhibit

exhibir *tr* to exhibit; (Mex) to pay ‖ *ref* to make oneself evident

exhilarante *adj* exhilarating; (*gas*) laughing

exhortar *tr* to exhort

exhumar *tr* to exhume

exigencia *f* exigency, requirement

exigente *adj* exigent, demanding

exigir §27 *tr* to exact, require, demand

exi•guo -gua *adj* meager, scanty

exila•do -da *adj & mf* exile

exi•mio -mia *adj* choice, select, superior; distinguished

eximir *tr* to exempt

existencia *f* existence; **en existencia** in stock; **existencias** (com) stock

existente *adj* existing, extant; in stock

existir *intr* to exist

exitazo *m* smash hit

exitista *adj* (Arg) me-too ‖ *mf* (Arg) me-tooer

éxito *m* (*resultado feliz*) success; (*canción, cine, etc. que ha tenido mucho éxito*) hit; (*resultado de un negocio*) outcome, result; **éxito de librería** best seller; **éxito de taquilla** box-office hit, good box office; **éxito de venta** best seller; **éxito rotundo** smash hit

exito•so -sa *adj* (Arg) successful

ex li•bris *m* (*pl* -bris) bookplate

exobiología *f* exobiology

éxodo *m* exodus; **éxodo de técnicos** brain drain

exonerar *tr* to exonerate, relieve; discharge, dismiss; **exonerar el vientre** to have a bowel movement

exorar *tr* to beg, entreat

exorbitante *adj* exorbitant

exorcizar §60 *tr* to exorcise

exornar *tr* to adorn, embellish

exóti•co -ca *adj* exotic; striking, stunning, glamorous

expandir *tr & ref* (Arg, Chile) to expand, extend, spread

expansión *f* expansion; (*manifestación efusiva*) expansiveness; (*difusión de una opinión*) spread; rest, recreation

expansionar *ref* to expand; open one's heart; relax, take it easy

expansi•vo -va *adj* expansive

expatria•do -da *adj & mf* expatriate

expectación *f* expectancy; **expectación de vida** life expectancy

expectativa *f* expectation; **estar en la expectativa de** to be expecting, be on the lookout for

expectorar *tr & intr* to expectorate

expediar *tr* to expedite; handle without delay; rush, speed

expedición *f* (*excursión para realizar una empresa*) expedition; (*remesa*) shipment; (*de un certificado, títulos, etc.*) issuance; (*agilidad, facilidad*) expedition

expedi•dor -dora *mf* sender, shipper

expediente *m* expedient; makeshift, apology; (*agilidad, facilidad*) expedition; (*todos los papeles correspondientes a un asunto*) dossier; (law) action, proceedings; **expediente académico** (educ) record

expedienteo *m* red tape

expedir §50 *tr* to send, ship, remit; (*títulos*) issue; (*despachar, cursar*) expedite

expeditar *tr* to expedite

expediti•vo -va *adj* expeditious

expedi•to -ta *adj* ready; clear, open, unencumbered

expeler *tr* to expel, eject

expende•dor -dora *mf* dealer, retailer; ticket agent; **expendedor de moneda falsa** distributor of counterfeit money

expendeduría *f* cigar store (*for sale of state-monopolized articles*)

expender *tr* to spend; dispense; sell at retail; (*moneda falsa*) circulate

expendio *m* shop, store; retail; (Mex) cigar store

expensar *tr* (Chile, Guat, Mex) to pay the cost of

expensas *fpl* expenses

experiencia *f* (*enseñanza que se adquiere con la práctica o con el vivir; suceso en que uno ha participado, cosa que uno ha experimentado*) experience; (*ensayo, experimento*) experiment

experimenta•do -da *adj* experienced

experimentar *tr* to experience, undergo, feel; test, try, try out ‖ *intr* to experiment

experimento *m* experiment; **experimento piloto** pilot test, pilot run

exper•to -ta *adj & m* expert

expiación *f* expiation, atonement; purification

expiar §77 *tr* to expiate, atone for; purify

expirar *intr* to expire

explanación *f* grading, leveling; explanation

explanada *f* esplanade

explanar *tr* to grade, level; explain

explayar *tr* to enlarge, extend ‖ *ref* to spread out, extend; go for an outing; expatiate, talk at length; **explayarse con** to unbosom oneself to

explicación *f* explanation

explicar §73 *tr* to explain; (*exponer*) expound; (*exculpar*) explain away; (*una clase*) teach ‖ *intr* to explain ‖ *ref* to explain oneself; understand, make out

explicati·vo -va *adj* explanatory

explíci·to -ta *adj* explicit

exploración *f* exploration; (mil) scouting; (telv) scanning

explora·dor -dora *mf* explorer ‖ *m* boy scout; (mil) scout

explorar *tr* to explore; (mil) to scout; (telv) to scan

explosión *f* explosion; (*de gases en un motor*) combustion

explosi·vo -va *adj & m* explosive ‖ *f* (phonet) explosive

explotación *f* operation, running; exploitation; **explotación abusiva** (geol) overexploitation (of resources)

explotar *tr* to operate, run; (*una mina*) work; exploit ‖ *intr* to explode

exponente *m* exponent; (fig) interpreter, apologist

exponer §54 *tr* to expose; (*explicar*) expound; (*a un niño recién nacido*) abandon ‖ *intr* to display, show, exhibit; (eccl) to expose the Host ‖ *ref* to expose oneself; be on view

exportación *f* exportation, export; (*mercaderías que se exportan*) exports

exporta·dor -dora *mf* exporter

exportar *tr & intr* to export

exposición *f* exposition; (*a un peligro; con relación a los puntos cardinales*) exposure; (phot) exposure; (rhet) exposition; **exposición universal** world's fair

exposición-venta *f* sales exhibit

exposímetro *m* light meter

expósi·to -ta *mf* foundling

exposi·tor -tora *mf* exhibitor

exprés *m* express train; (Mex) express company

expresa·do -da *adj* above-mentioned

expresamente *adv* express, expressly

expresar *tr* to express ‖ *ref* to express oneself

expresión *f* expression; (*acción de exprimir*) squeezing; (*zumo exprimido*) juice; **expresiones** regards

expresi·vo -va *adj* expressive; kind, affectionate

expre·so -sa *adj* express ‖ *m* (*tren muy rápido; correo extraordinario*) express; express company

exprimidera *f* squeezer; **exprimidera de naranjas** orange squeezer

exprimi·do -da *adj* lean, skinny; stiff, stuckup; affected, prim, prudish

exprimidor *m* wringer; squeezer; **exprimidor de ropa** clothes wringer

exprimir *tr* to squeeze, press; (*p.ej., la ropa blanca*) wring, wring out; (*extraer apretando*) express

ex profeso *adv* on purpose

expropiar *tr* to expropriate

expues·to -ta *adj* dangerous, hazardous

expugnar *tr* to take by storm

expulsanie·ves *m* (*pl* **-ves**) snowplow

expulsar *tr* to expel

expulsión *f* expulsion

expurgar §44 *tr* to expurgate

exquisi·to -ta *adj* exquisite

extasiar §77 & **regular** *ref* to go into ecstasy

éxta·sis *m* (*pl* **-sis**) ecstasy

extáti·co -ca *adj* ecstatic

extemporal *adj* unseasonable

extemporáne·o -a *adj* unseasonable; untimely, inopportune

extender §51 *tr* to extend, stretch out, spread out; spread; (*un documento*) draw up ‖ *ref* to extend, stretch out; spread; **extenderse a** or **hasta** to amount to

extendidamente *adv* at length, in detail

extensión *f* extension; (*vasta superficie, p.ej., del océano*) expanse; (*alcance, importancia*) extent; extending

extensi·vo -va *adj* extensive; **hacer extensivos a** to extend (*e.g., good wishes*) to

exten·so -sa *adj* extensive, extended, vast; **por extenso** at length, in detail

extenuar §21 *tr* to weaken, emaciate

exterior *adj* exterior, outer, outside; foreign ‖ *m* exterior, outside; appearance, bearing; **al exterior** or **a lo exterior** on the outside; outwardly; **del exterior** from abroad; **en el exterior** on the outside; abroad; **en exteriores** (mov) on location

exterioridad *f* externals, outward appearance; **exterioridades** pomp, show

exteriorista *adj* outgoing, outgiving ‖ *mf* extrovert

exteriorizar §60 *tr* to reveal ‖ *ref* to unbosom one's heart

exterminar *tr* to exterminate

exterminio *m* extermination

exter·no -na *adj* external ‖ *mf* day pupil

extinción *f* extinction; cancellation, elimination

extinguidor *m* (SAm) (*incendios*) fire extinguisher

extinguir §29 *tr* to extinguish, put out; wipe out, put an end to; fulfil, carry out; (*un plazo, un tiempo*) spend, serve ‖ *ref* to be extinguished, go out; come to an end

extin·to -ta *adj* (*volcán*) extinct; deceased ‖ *mf* deceased

extintor *m* fire extinguisher; **extintor de espuma** foam extinguisher; **extintor de granada** fire grenade

extirpar *tr* to extirpate, eradicate

extorno *m* premium adjustment (*based on change in policy*)

extorsión *f* extortion; harm, damage

extorsionar *tr* to harm, damage; extort

extra *adj* extra; **extra de** in addition to, besides ‖ *mf* (theat) extra ‖ *m* (*de un periódico*) extra; extra, bonus

extracción *f* extraction; (*en la lotería*) drawing numbers; **extracción de raíces** (math) evolution

extractar *tr* (*un escrito*) to abstract

extracto *m (de un escrito)* abstract; (pharm) extract

extractor *m* extractor; remover; **extractor de aire** ventilator; **extractor de humos** smoke evacuator

extracurricular *adj* extracurricular

extradición *f* extradition

extraer §75 *tr* to extract; pull; *(la raíz)* (math) to extract

extrafuerte *adj* heavy-duty

extragalácti•co -ca *adj* extragalactic

extralimitar *ref* to go too far

extramural *adj* extramural

extanjerismo *m* borrowing

extranje•ro -ra *adj* foreign, alien ‖ *mf* foreigner, alien; **extranjero enemigo** enemy alien ‖ *m* foreign country; **al extranjero** abroad; **del extranjero** from abroad; **en el extranjero** abroad

extrañar *tr* to banish, expatriate; surprise; find strange; miss ‖ *ref* to be surprised; refuse

extrañeza *f* strangeness, peculiarity; *(desavenencia)* estrangement; wonder, surprise

extra•ño -ña *adj* foreign; *(raro, singular)* strange; extraneous; **extraño a** unconnected with ‖ *mf* foreigner

extraoficial *adj* unofficial

extraordina•rio -ria *adj* extraordinary; extra, special ‖ *m* extra dish; special mail; *(de un periódico)* extra

extrapla•no -na *adj* extra-flat

extrapolar *tr & intr* to extrapolate

extrarradio *m* outer edge of town

extrasensorial *adj* extrasensory

extraterrestre *adj* extraterrestrial; otherworldly

extravagancia *f (singularidad, ridiculez)* extravagance, wildness, folly

extravagante *adj (singular, ridículo)* extravagant, wild, foolish; *(correspondencia en la casa de correos)* in transit

extravia•do -da *adj* lost, misplaced; astray, gone astray; *(lugar)* out-of-the-way

extraviar §77 *tr* to lead astray, mislead; mislay, misplace ‖ *ref* to get lost, go astray; go wrong; get out of line

extravío *m* going astray; loss; misleading; misconduct; misplacement

extrema *f (escasez grande)* extremity; *(de la vida)* end, last moment

extremar *tr* to carry far, carry to the limit ‖ *ref* to strive hard

extremaunción *f* extreme unction; last rites *(Roman Catholic)*

extreme•ño -ña *adj* frontier

extremidad *f* extremity; end, tip; **extremidades** *(pies y manos)* extremities; **la última extremidad** one's last moment

extremismo *m* extremism

extremista *mf* extremist

extre•mo -ma *adj* extreme; utmost; critical, desperate ‖ *m* extremity; *(de la calle)* end; *(del dedo)* tip; *(punto último)* extreme; great care; *(de una conversación, una carta)* point; winter pasture; **al extremo de** to the point of; **de extremo a extremo** from one end to the other; **hacer extremos** to be demonstrative, gush ‖ *f* see **extrema**

extremo•so -sa *adj* extreme, forthright; effusive, gushy, demonstrative

extrínse•co -ca *adj* extrinsic

extroversión *f* extroversion

extroverti•do -da *mf* extrovert

exuberante *adj* exuberant; luxuriant

exudar *tr & intr* to exude

exultante *adj* exultant

exultar *intr* to exult

exvoto *m* votive offering

eyacular *tr & intr* to ejaculate

F

F, f (efe) *f* seventh letter of the Spanish alphabet

f.a.b. *abbr* **franco a bordo**

fabada *f* pork-and-bean stew *(in Asturias)*

fábrica *f* factory, plant; building, masonry; (eccl) vestry

fabricación *f* manufacture; **fabricación en serie** mass production

fabricante *mf* manufacturer

fabricar §73 *tr* to manufacture; devise, invent; fabricate

fabril *adj* factory

fabriquero *m* manufacturer; charcoal burner; churchwarden

fábula *f* fable; *(p.ej., de un drama)* plot, story; rumor, gossip; *(mentira)* story, lie; *(objeto de murmuración)* talk of the town

fabulario *m* book of fables

fabulo•so -sa *adj* fabulous

facción *f* faction; feature; battle; **estar de facción** (mil) to be on duty; **facciones** features

facciona•rio -ria *adj* factional

faceta *f* facet

facetada *f* (Mex) flat joke

face•to -ta *adj* (Mex) affected; (Mex) finicky ‖ *f* see **faceta**

facial *adj* facial

fácil *adj* easy; pliant, yielding; likely; loose, wanton

facilidad *f* facility, ease, easiness; **facilidades de pago** easy payments

facilitar *tr* to facilitate, expedite; furnish, supply

facili•tón -tona *adj* bumbling, brash ‖ *mf* bumbler
facinero•so -sa *adj* wicked ‖ *mf* villain
facistol *m* choir desk
facón *m* (Arg, Urug) gaucho knife
facsimilar *tr* to facsimile; copy
facsímile *m* facsimile
factible *adj* feasible
factor *m* factor; commission merchant; baggageman; freight agent
factoría *f* trading post; (Ecuad, Peru) foundry; (Mex) factory
factura *f* invoice, bill; workmanship; **factura simulada** pro forma invoice; **según factura** as per invoice
facturación *f* invoicing, billing (*del equipaje*) checking
facturar *tr* to invoice, bill; (*el equipaje*) check
facultad *f* faculty; (*de la universidad*) school; knowledge, skill; power; **facultad de altos estudios** graduate school
facultar *tr* to empower, authorize
facultati•vo -va *adj* faculty; optional ‖ *m* doctor, physician
facundia *f* eloquence, fluency
facun•do -da *adj* eloquent, fluent
facha *mf* (*adefesio*) sight ‖ *f* look, appearance; **facha a facha** face to face
fachada *f* façade; (*de un libro*) title page; look, build, bearing; **hacer fachada con** to overlook, to look out on
facha•do -da *adj* — **bien fachado** good-looking ‖ *f* see *fachada*
fachenda *m* boaster, show-off ‖ *f* boasting
fachendear *intr* to boast, show off
fachendista or **fachen•dón -dona** or **fachendo•so -sa** *adj* boastful ‖ *mf* boaster, show-off
fachinal *m* (Arg) marshland
fada *f* fairy, witch
faena *f* work; toil; chore, task, job; (taur) windup; (taur) stunt, trick; (mil) fatigue, fatigue duty; (Guat, Mex, W-I) extra work, overtime; (Ecuad) morning work in the field; (Chile) gang of farm hands
faenero *m* (Chile) farm hand
Faetón *m* Phaëthon
fagot *m* bassoon
faisán *m* pheasant
faja *f* sash, girdle; bandage; band, strip; newspaper wrapper; (*de carretera*) lane; (*de tierra*) strip; **faja central** or **divisoria** median strip; **faja medical** supporter
fajar *tr* to wrap; bandage; swaddle; (*un periódico o revista*) put a wrapper on; beat, thrash; to attack ‖ *ref* to put on a sash
fajardo *m* meat pie
fajín *m* sash
fajina *f* bundle of sticks; fire wood; (mil) call to quarters
fajo *m* bundle; (*de papel moneda*) roll; swig; (Mex) blow; (Mex) leather belt; **fajos** swaddling clothes
falacia *f* deception; deceitfulness
falange *f* phalanx
falangia *f* daddy-longlegs

fa•laz *adj* (*pl* **-laces**) deceitful; deceptive
falba•lá *m* (*pl* **-aes**) gore; flounce, ruffle
falce *m* sickle; falchion
falda *f* skirt, dress; (*regazo*) lap; flap; fold; (*del sombrero*) brim; foothill; (*mujer*) skirt; **cosido a las faldas de** tied to the apron strings of
falde•ro -ra *adj* skirt; (*perro*) lap; lady-loving ‖ *m* lap dog
faldillas *fpl* skirts, coattails
faldón *m* coattail; shirttail; saddle flap
falible *adj* fallible
fáli•co -ca *adj* phallic
falo *m* penis, phallus
falsada *f* swoop (*of bird of prey*)
falsa•rio -ria *adj* lying ‖ *mf* falsifier, crook; liar
falsear *tr* to falsify; counterfeit; forge; (*la verdad*) distort; (*una cerradura*) pick; bevel ‖ *intr* to sag, buckle; give, give way
falsedad *f* falsity; (*mentira*) falsehood
falsete *m* falsetto; plug, tap; door (*between rooms*)
falsetista *f* falsetto
falsía *f* falsity, treachery; unsteadiness
falsificación *f* falsification; fake; counterfeit; forgery
falsificar §73 *tr* to falsify; fake; counterfeit; forge
falsilla *f* guide lines
fal•so -sa *adj* false; counterfeit; (*caballo*) vicious ‖ *m* patch; **coger en falso** (Mex) to catch in a lie; **envidar en falso** to bluff
falta *f* fault; lack, want; misdeed; absence; (*ausencia de la clase*) cut; (sport) fault; **a falta de** for want of; **echar en falta** to miss; **falta de ortografía** misspelling **hacer falta** to be needed; be lacking; **hacerle falta a uno** to need, e.g., **le hacen falta a Juan estos libros** John needs these books; to miss, e.g., **Vd. me hace mucha falta** I miss you very much; **sin falta** without fail
faltar *intr* to be missing, be lacking, be wanting; fall short; run out; be absent; fail; die; lack, need, e.g., **me falta dinero** I lack money, I need money; **faltar a la clase** to cut class; **faltar a la verdad** to fail to tell the truth; **faltar a una cita** to fail to keep an appointment; **faltar . . . para** to be . . . to, e.g., **faltan cinco minutos para las dos** it is five minutes to two; **faltar poco para** to come near; **faltar por** to remain to be, e.g., **faltan por escribir dos cartas** two letters remain to be written
fal•to -ta *adj* short, lacking; (*peso o medida*) short; (Arg) dull, stupid; (Col) proud, vain; **falto de** short of ‖ *f* see **falta**
fal•tón -tona *adj* dilatory, remiss; (Arg) simple-minded
falto•so -sa *adj* addlebrained; (Col) quarrelsome; (CAm, Mex) disrespectful
faltriquera *f* pocket; handbag; **faltriquera de reloj** watch fob; **rascarse la faltriquera** to cough up
falúa *f* barge, tender
falucho *m* felucca

ex
fa

falla f failure, breakdown; defect; (geol) fault; (Mex) baby's bonnet

fallar tr to trump; judge, pass judgment on ‖ intr to fail, miss; misfire; sag, weaken; break down; judge, pass judgment

falleba f espagnolette

fallecer §22 intr to die; fail, expire

falleci·do -da adj deceased, late

falli·do -da adj unsuccessful; bankrupt; (deuda) uncollectible

fallir §13 intr to fail; (Ven) to go bankrupt

fa·llo -lla adj (Chile) silly, simple; **estar fallo a** to be out of (cards of a suit) ‖ m short suit; decision; judgment; verdict; **fallo humano** human error; **tener fallo a** or **de** to be out of ‖ f see **falla**

fama f fame; reputation; rumor; (Chile) bull's-eye; **correr fama** to be rumored; **es fama** it is said, it is rumored

faméli·co -ca adj famished, starving

familia f family

familiar adj familiar; family; (sin ceremonia) informal; (lenguaje, estilo) colloquial ‖ m member of the family; member of the household; acquaintance; **familiar dependiente** dependent

familiaridad f familiarity

familiarizar §60 tr to familiarize ‖ ref to become familiar; become too familiar; familiarize oneself

famo·so -sa adj famous; (excelente) famous; (formidable) some, e.g., **famoso sujeto** some guy

fámu·lo -la mf servant

fanal m beacon, lighthouse; lantern; bell glass, bell jar; lamp shade

fanáti·co -ca adj fanatic(al) ‖ mf fanatic; (sport) fan

fanatismo m fanaticism

fanega f 1.58 bu.; **fanega de tierra** 1.59 acres

fanfarria f fanfare; blustering

fanfa·rrón -rrona adj blustering, bragging; flashy ‖ mf blusterer, braggart

fanfarronada f bluster, bravado

fanfarronnear intr to bluster, brag

fanfarronería f blustering, bragging, sword rattling

fanfurriña f pet, peeve

fango m mud, mire; **llenar de fango** (fig) to sling mud at

fango·so -sa adj muddy; sticky, gooey

fanguero m (Cuba, Mex, P-R) mud, quagmire

fantasear tr to dream of ‖ intr to fancy, to daydream; **fantasear de** to boast of being

fantasía f fantasy; fancy, conceit, vanity; imagery; **con fantasía** (Arg) hard; **de fantasía** fancy, imitation; **tocar por fantasía** (Ven) to play by ear

fantasio·so -sa adj vain, conceited

fantasma m phantom, ghost; stuffed shirt; (telv) ghost; **fantasma magnético** magnetic curves ‖ f scarecrow, hobgoblin

fantas·món -mona adj (coll) conceited ‖ mf conceited person ‖ m stuffed shirt; (coll) scarecrow

fantásti·co -ca adj fantastic; fancy; conceited

fantoche m puppet, marionette; nincompoop, whippersnapper

faquín m street porter, errand boy

fara·lá m (pl -laes) ruffle, flounce; frill

faramalla mf cheat, swindler ‖ f jabber, claptrap; bluff, fake; (Chile) bragging

faramalle·ro -ra or **farama·llón -llona** adj scheming, swindling ‖ mf schemer, swindler

farándula f (baile) farandole; gossip, scheming; theater people; (de gente) (Arg) crush, milling

farandulear intr to boast, to show off

Faraón m Pharaoh

faraute m herald, messenger; interpreter; (actor) prologue; busybody

fardel m bag, bundle; sloppy person

fardo m bundle, package

farero m lighthouse keeper

farfa·lá m (pl -laes) ruffle, flounce

farfullar tr (p.ej., una lección) to sputter through; (p.ej., una tarea) stumble through ‖ intr to sputter

faringe f pharynx

fariseo m pharisee; Pharisee; lanky good-for-nothing

farmacéuti·co -ca adj pharmaceutical ‖ mf pharmacist

farmacia f pharmacy, drug store; **farmacia de guardia** drug store open all night

fármaco m drug, medicine

faro m lighthouse, beacon; floodlight; (aut) headlight; (fig) beacon; **faro piloto** (aut) spotlight; **faros de carretera** (aut) bright lights; **faros de cruce** (aut) dimmers; **faros de población** or **de situación** (aut) parking lights

farol m lamp, light; lantern; street light; (rr) headlight; (coll) conceited fellow; (Bol) bay window; **farol de tope** (naut) headlight

farola f lighthouse; street lamp, lamppost

farolear intr to boast, brag

farole·ro -ra adj boasting ‖ mf boaster ‖ m lamplighter

farolillo m heartseed; Canterbury bell; **farolillo veneciano** Chinese lantern, Japanese lantern

farota f minx, vixen

farotear intr (Col) to romp around, make a racket

faro·tón -tona adj brazen, cheeky ‖ mf cheeky person

farra f salmon trout; (SAm) revelry

fárrago m hodgepodge

farraquista m scatterbrain; muddlehead

farrear intr to celebrate; (coll) to goof off

farro m grits

farru·co -ca adj bold, fearless; ill-humored ‖ mf Galician abroad, Asturian abroad

farru·to -ta adj (Arg, Bol, Chile) sickly

farsa f farce; humbug

farsante adj & mf fake, fraud, humbug

fas — por fas o por nefas rightly or wrongly, in any event

fascinante adj fascinating

fascinar *tr* to fascinate, bewitch; cast a spell on, cast the evil eye on

fascismo *m* fascism

fascista *adj* & *mf* fascist

fase *f* phase

fastidiar *tr* to bore, annoy; cloy, sicken; disappoint ‖ *ref* to get bored; suffer, be a victim

fastidio *m* boredom, annoyance; distaste, nausea

fastidio·so -sa *adj* boring, annoying; cloying, sickening; annoyed, displeased

fas·to -ta *adj* happy, blessed ‖ *m* pomp, show

fastuo·so -sa *adj* vain, pompous; magnificent

fatal *adj* fatal; bad, evil; (law) unextendible

fatalidad *f* fatality; misfortune

fatalismo *m* fatalism

fatalista *mf* fatalist

fatalmente *adv* fatally; inevitably; unfortunately; badly, poorly

fatídi·co -ca *adj* ominous, fateful

fatiga *f* fatigue; hard breathing; **fatigas** hardship

fatigante *adj* tiresome; fatiguing

fatigar §44 *tr* to fatigue, tire, weary; annoy, bother ‖ *ref* to get tired

fatigo·so -sa *adj* fatiguing, tiring; trying, tedious

fa·tuo -tua *adj* fatuous; conceited ‖ *mf* simpleton

fauces *fpl* (anat) fauces; (fig) jaws, mouth

fauna *f* fauna

fauno *m* faun

faus·to -ta *adj* happy, fortunate ‖ *m* pomp, magnificence

fausto·so -sa *adj* magnificent

fau·tor -tora *mf* abettor, accomplice

favor *m* favor; **a favor de** under cover of; by means of; in favor of; **hágame Vd. el favor de** do me the favor to; **por favor** please; **vender favores** to peddle influence

favorable *adj* favorable

favorecer §22 *tr* to favor; flatter

favoritismo *m* favoritism

favori·to -ta *adj* & *mf* favorite

fayanca *f* unstable posture

faz *f* (*pl* **faces**) face; aspect, look; (*de monedas o medallas*) obverse; **faces** cheeks; **faz a faz** face to face

F.C. *abbr* **ferrocarril**

fe *f* faith; testimony, witness; certificate; **¡a fe mía!** upon my faith!; **dar fe de** to certify; **en fe de lo cual** in witness whereof; **fe de erratas** list of errata; **hacer fe** to be valid; **la fe del carbonero** simple faith

fealdad *f* ugliness

Febe *f* Phoebe

feble *adj* weak, sickly; (*moneda, aleación*) lacking in weight or fineness

Febo *m* Phoebus

febrero *m* February

febril *adj* feverish

fécula *f* starch

feculen·to -ta *adj* starchy; fecal

fecundar *tr* to fecundate, to fertilize

fecun·do -da *adj* fecund, fertile

fecha *f* date; **con fecha de** under date of; **de**

larga fecha of long standing; **hasta la fecha** to date

fechador *m* (Chile, Mex) canceler, postmark

fechar *tr* to date

fechoría *f* misdeed, villainy

federación *f* federation

federal *adj* & *mf* federal

federar *tr* & *ref* to federate

feéri·co -ca *adj* fairy

fehaciente *adj* authentic

feldespato *m* feldspar

felicidad *f* felicity, happiness; luck

felicitar *tr* to felicitate, congratulate, wish happiness to

feli·grés -gresa *mf* parishioner, church member

feligresía *f* parish; congregation

Felipe *m* Philip

fe·liz *adj* (*pl* **-lices**) happy; lucky; (*oportuno*) felicitous

fe·lón -lona *adj* perfidious, treacherous ‖ *mf* wicked person

felonía *f* perfidy, treachery

felpa *f* plush; drubbing; severe reprimand

felpu·do -da *adj* plushy, downy ‖ *m* mat, door mat

femenil *adj* feminine, womanly

femeni·no -na *adj* feminine; (*sexo*) female ‖ *m* feminine

fementi·do -da *adj* false, treacherous

feminismo *m* feminism

fenecer §22 *tr* to finish, close ‖ *intr* to come to an end; die

Fenicia *f* Phoenicia

feni·cio -cia *adj* & *mf* Phoenician ‖ *f* see **Fenicia**

fé·nix *m* (*pl* **-nix** or **-nices**) phoenix

fenobarbital *m* phenobarbital

fenomenal *adj* phenomenal

fenómeno *m* phenomenon; monster, freak

fe·o -a *adj* ugly ‖ *m* slight; **hacer un feo a** to slight ‖ **feo** *adv* (Arg, Col, Mex) bad, e.g., **oler feo** to smell bad

feo·te -ta *adj* ugly, hideous

feral *adj* cruel, bloody

fe·raz *adj* (*pl* **-races**) fertile

féretro *m* bier

feria *f* weekday; market; fair; day off; (Mex) small change; (Mex) con man; (CAm, Mex) extra, tip, gratuity; **revolver la feria** to upset the applecart

ferial *adj* week (day); market (day) ‖ *m* market; fair

feriante *adj* fair-going ‖ *mf* fairgoer

feriar *tr* to buy, sell; give, present; (Mex) to give change for

feri·no -na *adj* wild, savage; (*tos*) whooping (*cough*)

fermentación *f* ferment; fermentation

fermentar *tr* & *intr* to ferment

fermento *m* ferment

ferocidad *f* ferocity, fierceness

ferósti·co -ca *adj* irritable; hideous

fe·roz *adj* (*pl* **-roces**) ferocious, fierce

férre·o -a *adj* iron

ferrería *f* ironworks, foundry

ferretear *tr* to trim with iron; work in iron

fa
fe

ferretería *f* ironworks; hardware; hardware store

ferrete•ro -ra *mf* hardware dealer

ferrocarril *m* railroad, railway; **ferrocarril de cremallera** rack railway, mountain railroad

ferrocarrile•ro -ra *adj* railroad, rail ‖ *m* railroader

ferrotipo *m* tintype

ferrovia•rio -ria *adj* railroad, rail ‖ *m* railroader

fértil *adj* fertile

fertilizar §60 *tr* to fertilize

férula *f* flexible splint; ferule; **estar bajo la férula de** to be under the thumb of

férvi•do -da *adj* fervid; (*fiebre; sed*) burning

ferviente *adj* fervent

fervor *m* fervor, zeal

fervoro•so -sa *adj* ardent, zealous

festejar *tr* to fete, honor, entertain; celebrate; court, woo; (Mex) to beat, thrash

festejo *m* feast, entertainment; celebrátion; courting, wooing; (Peru) revelry; **festejos** public festivities

festín *m* feast, banquet

festinar *tr* to hurry through; (CAm) to entertain

festival *m* festival, music festival

festividad *f* festivity; feast day, witticism

festi•vo -va *adj* festive, gay; witty; (*digno no de celebrarse*) solemn

festón *m* festoon

festonear *tr* to festoon

fetiche *m* fetish

féti•do -da *adj* fetid, foul

feto *m* fetus

feú•co -ca or **feú•cho -cha** *adj* hideous, repulsive

feudal *adj* feudal

feudalismo *m* feudalism

feudo *m* fief; **feudo franco** freehold

fiable *adj* trustworthy

fiado *m* — **al fiado** on credit; **en fiado** on bail

fia•dor -dora *mf* bail; **salir fiador por** to go bail for ‖ *m* fastener; catch, pawl; (Chile, Ecuad) chin strap

fiambre *adj* cold, cold-served; (*noticias*) old, stale ‖ *m* cold lunch, cold food; stale news; (Arg) dull party; **fiambres** cold cuts

fiambrera *f* dinner pail, lunch basket

fiambrería *f* (Arg) delicatessen store

fianza *f* guarantee, surety; bond; bail; **fianza carcelera** bail

fiar §77 *tr* to entrust, confide; guarantee; give credit to; sell on credit ‖ *intr & ref* to trust

fiasco *m* fiasco

fibra *f* fiber; (fig) fiber, strength, vigor; **fibras del corazón** heartstrings

fibro•so -sa *adj* fibrous

ficción *f* fiction

ficciona•rio -ria *adj* fictional

fice *m* (ichth) hake

ficti•cio -cia *adj* fictitious

ficha *f* chip; counter; domino; filing card; police record; (elec) plug; **ficha catalográfica** index card; **ficha perforada** punch card; **llevar ficha** to have a police record; **ser una buena ficha** to be a sly fox

ficha•dor -dora *mf* file clerk

fichar *tr* to file; play, move; black-list; (Cuba) to cheat ‖ *intr* (Col) to die

fichero *m* card index, filing cabinet

fidedig•no -na *adj* reliable, trustworthy

fideicomisa•rio -ria *mf* trustee

fideicomiso *m* trusteeship

fidelería *f* (Arg, Ecuad, Peru) vermicelli factory, noodle factory

fidelidad *f* fidelity; punctiliousness; **alta fidelidad** (rad) high fidelity

fideo *m* skinny person; (Arg) joke; (Arg) confusion, disorder; **fideos** vermicelli

Fidias *m* Phidias

fiducia•rio -ria *adj & mf* fiduciary

fiebre *f* fever; **fiebre del heno** hay fever; **fibre tifoidea** typhoid fever

fiel *adj* faithful; exact; punctilious; honest, trustworthy ‖ *m* inspector of weights and measures; (*en las balanzas*) pointer; (*de las tijeras*) pin; **fiel de romana** inspector of weights in a slaughterhouse; **los fieles** the faithful

fielato *m* inspector's office; octroi

fieltro *m* felt; felt hat; felt rug

fiera *f* wild animal; (*persona*) fiend; (taur) bull; **ser una fiera para** to be a fiend for

fierabrás *m* spitfire, little terror

fierecilla *f* shrew

fiereza *f* fierceness; cruelty; deformity

fie•ro -ra *adj* fierce, wild; cruel; deformed, ugly; huge, tremendous; **echar** or **hacer fieros** to bluster ‖ *f* see **fiera**

fierro *m* (SAm) branding iron

fierros *mpl* (Ecuad, Mex) tools

fiesta *f* feast, holy day; holiday; celebration, festivity; **estar de fiesta** (coll) to be in a holiday mood; **fiesta de la hispanidad** or **fiesta de la raza** Columbus Day; **fiesta de todos los santos** All Saints' Day; **fiesta onomástica** saint's day, birthday; **fiestas** holiday, vacation; **hacer fiesta** to take off (*from work*); **hacer fiestas a** to act up to, to fawn on; **la fiesta brava** bullfighting; **no estar para fiestas** to be in no mood for joking; **por fin de fiestas** to top it off; **se acabó la fiesta** let's drop it

fieste•ro -ra *adj* merry, cheerful ‖ *mf* merrymaker, party-goer

figón *m* cheap restaurant

figura *f* figure; face, countenance; (*naipe*) face card; (mus) note; (theat) character; **figura retórica** figure of speech; **hacer figura** to cut a figure

figuración *f* representation; (Arg) status, social standing

figura•do -da *adj* figurative

figurar *tr* to depict, trace, represent; feign ‖ *intr* to figure, be in the limelight ‖ *ref* to figure, imagine

figurati•vo -va *adj* figurative, representative

figurería *f* face, grimace

figurilla *mf* silly little runt ‖ *f* figurine

figurín *m* dummy, model; fashion plate

figurina *f* figurine

figurita *mf* silly little runt

figurón *m* stuffed shirt; **figurón de proa** (naut) figurehead

fija *f* hinge; trowel; *(caballo)* (Peru) sure bet; **la fija** sure thing

fijacarte•les *m* (*pl* **-les**) billposter

fijación *f* fixing, fastening; posting; **fijación de precios** price fixing

fijado *m* (phot) fixing

fija•dor -dora *adj* fixing ‖ *m* carpenter who installs doors and windows; fixing bath; sprayer; (mas) pointer; hair set, hair spray

fijamárge•nes *m* (*pl* **-nes**) margin stop

fijapeína•dos *m* (*pl* **-dos**) hair set, hair spray

fijar *tr* to fix; fasten; *(carteles)* post; *(una fecha; los cabellos; una imagen fotográfica; los precios; la atención; una hora, una cita)* fix; *(residencia)* establish; paste, glue ‖ *ref* to settle; notice; **fijarse en** to notice; pay attention to; be intent on

fijeza *f* firmness, stability; steadfastness; **mirar con fijeza** to stare at

fi•jo -ja *adj* fixed; firm, solid, secure, fast; sure, determined; **de fijo** surely ‖ *f* see **fija**

fil *m* — **estar en fil** or **en un fil** to be alike; **fil derecho** leapfrog

fila *f* row, line; file; *(línea que los soldados forman de frente)* rank; dislike, hatred; **cerrar las filas** (mil) to close ranks; **en fila** in single file; **en filas** (mil) in active service; **fila india** single file, Indian file; **llamar a filas** (mil) to call to the colors; **pasarse a las filas de** to go over to; **romper filas** (mil) to break ranks

filamento *m* filament

filantropía *f* philanthropy

filántrop•po -pa *mf* philanthropist

filar *tr* (naut) to pay out slowly

filarmónica *f* (Mex) accordion

filarmóni•co -ca *adj* philharmonic

filatelia *f* philately

filatelista *mf* philatelist

filatería *f* fast talking; wordiness

filate•ro -ra *adj* fast-talking; wordy ‖ *mf* fast talker; great talker

file•no -na *adj* cute, tiny

filete *m* *(de carne o pescado)* filet or fillet; *(asador)* spit; edge, rim; narrow hem; *(de tornillo)* thread; snaffle bit; (archit, bb) fillet; (typ) rule, fancy rule

filetear *tr* to fillet; *(un tornillo)* thread; (bb) to tool

filiación *f* filiation; description, characteristics; (mil) regimental register

filial *adj* filial ‖ *f* affiliate, branch

filiar §77 *tr* to register ‖ *ref* to enroll

filibustero *m* filibuster, buccaneer

filigrana *f* filigree; *(en el papel)* watermark

filipi•no -na *adj* Filipine, Filipino ‖ *mf* Filipino ‖ **Filipinas** *fpl* Philippines

Filipo *m* Philip *(of Macedonia)*

Filis *f* Phyllis

filiste•o -a *adj* & *mf* Philistine ‖ *m* tall, fat fellow

film *m* (*pl* **-films** or **filmes**) film

filmadora *f* movie camera

filmar *tr* to film, shoot

filo *m* edge; ridge; dividing line; (CAm, Mex) hunger; **al filo de** at, at about; **dar filo a** to sharpen; **filo del viento** direction of the wind; **pasar al filo de la espada** to put to the sword; **por filo** exactly

filobús *m* trolley bus, trackless trolley

filocommunista *adj* & *mf* procommunist

filología *f* philology

filólo•go -ga *mf* philologist

filón *m* seam, vein; (fig) gold mine

filo•so -sa *adj* sharp

filosofía *f* philosophy

filosófi•co -ca *adj* philosophic(al)

filóso•fo -fa *mf* philosopher

filote *m* (Col) corn silk; (Col) ear of green corn

filtración *f* filtering; leak; (fig) leak, loss

filtrado *m* filtrate

filtrar *tr* to filter ‖ *intr* to leak; ooze ‖ *ref* to filter; *(el dinero)* leak away, disappear

filtro *m* filter; *(brebaje para conciliar el amor)* philter, love potion

filu•do -da *adj* (SAm) sharp-edged

filván *m* featheredge

fimo *m* dung, manure

fin *m* end; aim, purpose, end; **a fin de** to, in order to; **a fin de que** in order that, so that; **a fines de** toward the end of, late in; **al fin** finally; **al fin del mundo** far, far away; **al fin y a la postre** or **al fin y al cabo** after all, in the end; **dar fin a** to put an end to; **fin de semana** weekend; **por fin** finally, in short; **sin fin** endless; endlessly; **un sin fin de** no end of

fina•do -da *adj* deceased, late ‖ *mf* deceased

final *adj* final ‖ *m* end; (mus) finale; **por final** finally ‖ *f* (sport) finals; **final de partido** windup

finalidad *f* end, purpose

finalista *mf* finalist

finalizar §60 *tr* to end, terminate; *(una escritura)* (law) to execute ‖ *intr* to end, terminate

financiación *f* financing

financiamiento *m* (SAm) financial backing

financiar *tr* to finance

financie•ro -ra *adj* financial ‖ *mf* financier

finanzas *fpl* finances

finar *intr* to die ‖ *ref* to yearn

finca *f* property, piece of real estate; farm, ranch; **buena finca** sly fellow

fincar §73 *tr* (P-R) to cultivate, farm ‖ *intr* to buy up real estate; (Col) to reside, rest, be based ‖ *ref* to buy up real estate

fincha•do -da *adj* vain, conceited

fi•nés -nesa *adj* Finnic; Finnish ‖ *mf* Finn ‖ *m* *(idioma uraliano)* Finnic; *(idioma de Finlandia)* Finnish

fineza *f* fineness; kindness, courtesy; token of affection, favor

fingi•do -da *adj* fake, sham; false, deceitful

fingir §27 *tr* & *intr* to feign, pretend, fake ‖ *ref* to pretend to be

finiquitar *tr* *(una cuenta)* to settle, to close; finish, wind up

finiquito *m* settlement, closing; **dar finiquito a** to settle, close; finish, wind up

finíti•mo -ma *adj* bordering, neighboring
fini•to -ta *adj* finite
finlan•dés -desa *adj* Finnish ‖ *mf* Finn, Finlander ‖ *m* Finnish
Finlandia *f* Finland
fi•no -na *adj* fine; (*ligero, casi transparente*) sheer; (*esbelto*) thin, slender; (*paño, papel, etc.*) thin; (*agua*) pure; polite, courteous; shrewd, cunning
finta *f* feint
finura *f* fineness, excellence; politeness, courtesy
finústi•co -ca *adj* overobsequious
firma *f* signature; signing; firm; firm name; mail to be signed; **con mi firma** under my hand; **firma en blanco** blank check
firmamento *m* firmament
firmante *adj* signatory ‖ *mf* signer, signatory
firmar *tr & intr* to sign
firme *adj* firm, steady; solid, hard; staunch, unswerving ‖ *adv* firmly, steadily ‖ *m* roadbed; **de firme** hard, e.g., **llover de firme** to rain hard
firmeza *f* firmness; constancy, fortitude
firmón *m* shyster who signs anything
fiscal *adj* fiscal, treasury ‖ *m* treasurer; district attorney; busybody
fiscalizar §60 *tr* to control, inspect; prosecute; pry into
fisco *m* state treasury, exchequer
fisga *f* fish spear; prying, snooping; banter, raillery
fisgar §44 *tr* to harpoon, fish with a spear; pry into ‖ *intr* to pry, snoop; mock, jeer ‖ *ref* to mock, jeer
fis•gón -gona *mf* (coll) mocker, jester; (coll) snooper, busybody
físi•co -ca *adj* physical; (Mex, W-I) finicky, prudish ‖ *mf* physicist ‖ *m* physique ‖ *f* physics; **física de las partículas** particle physics; **física del estado sólido** solid state physics; **física molecular** molecular physics
fisil *adj* fissionable
fisiología *f* physiology
fisiológi•co -ca *adj* physiological
fisión *f* fission
fisionable *adj* fissionable
fisonomía *f* physiognomy
fistol *m* sly fellow; (Mex) necktie pin
fisura *f* (anat, min) fissure; **fisura del paladar** cleft palate
fla•co -ca *adj* thin, skinny; feeble, weak, frail; insecure, unstable ‖ *m* weak spot
flacu•cho -cha *adj* skinny
flagrante *adj* occurring, actual; **en flagrante** in the act
flamante *adj* bright, flaming; brand-new, spick-and-span
flameante *adj* flamboyant
flamear *intr* to flame; flare up (*with anger*); flutter, wave
flamen•co -ca *adj* Flemish; buxom; Andalusian gypsy; flashy, snappy, gypsyish ‖ *mf* Fleming ‖ *m* (*idioma*) Flemish; Andalusian gypsy dance, song, or music; (orn) flamingo

fláme•o -a *adj* flamelike
flamíge•ro -ra *adj* (poet) flaming; (archit) flamboyant
flan *m* custard
flanco *m* side, flank; **coger por el flanco** to catch off guard
Flandes *f* Flanders
flanquear *tr* to flank
flaquear *intr* to weaken, flag; become faint; become discouraged
flaqueza *f* thinness, skinniness; weakness; instability
flashback *m* (*retrospectiva*) flashback
flato *m* gas; gloominess, melancholy
flato•so -sa *adj* flatulent, windy; gloomy, melancholy
flauta *f* flute
flautín *m* piccolo
flautista *mf* flautist, flutist
flebitis *f* phlebitis
fleco *m* fringe; ragged edge; **flecos** bangs
flecha *f* arrow; (aer) sweepback
flechar *tr* (*el arco*) to draw; (*a una persona*) wound with an arrow, kill with an arrow; infatuate
flechero *m* archer, bowman
fleje *m* iron strap, iron hoop
flema *f* phlegm
flemáti•co -ca *adj* phlegmatic(al); (coll) cool
flemón *m* gumboil
flequillo *m* bangs
Flesinga *f* Flushing
fletante *m* shipowner; (Arg, Chile, Ecuad) conveyancer
fletar *tr* (*una nave*) to charter; (*ganado*) load; (*bestias de carga, carros, etc.*) (Arg, Chile, Ecuad, Mex) to hire ‖ *ref* (Arg) to sneak in, slip in; (Cuba, Mex) to beat it, clear out
flete *m* (naut) freight, cargo; (Arg, Bol, Col, Urug) race horse; **salir sin flete** (Col, Ven) to beat it
flexible *adj* flexible; (*sombrero*) soft ‖ *m* soft hat; (elec) flexible cord
flexo *m* gooseneck lamp
flinflanear *intr* to tinkle
flirt *m* or **flirtación** *f* flirting
flirtear *intr* to flirt
flojear *intr* to ease up, idle; flag, weaken
flojedad *f* slackness; looseness; limpness; laziness; weakness
flojel *m* fluff, nap; down, soft feathers
flo•jo -ja *adj* slack, loose; limp; languid; lazy; weak; (*precios*) sagging; (*viento*) light; lax, careless
flor *f* flower; (*de árbol frutal*) blossom; (*del cuero*) grain; (fig) compliment, bouquet; **a flor de** even with, flush with; **a flor de agua** at water level; **decir flores a** to flatter; to flirt with; **flor de la edad** bloom of youth; **flor de la vida** prime of life; **flor del campo** wild flower; **flor de lis** (*escudo de armas de Francia*) lily, fleur-de-lis; **flor de mano** paper flower, artificial flower; **la flor de la canela** the tops; **la flor y nata de** the cream of
flora *f* flora

floral *adj* floral

florcita *f* little flower; **andar de florcita** (Arg, Bol, Chile, Urug) to stroll around with a flower in one's buttonhole, take it easy

florear *tr* to flower, decorate with flowers; (*los naipes*) stack; (*harina*) bolt ‖ *intr* (*la punta de la espada*) to quiver; twang away on a guitar; throw bouquets

florecer §22 *intr* to flower, blossom, bloom; (*prosperar*) flourish ‖ *ref* to become moldy

floreciente *adj* flowering, florescent; flourishing

florenti•no -na *adj & mf* Florentine

floreo *m* idle talk; bright remark; (*de la punta de la espada*) quivering; (*de la guitarra*) twanging; (mus) flourish; **andarse con floreos** to beat about the bush

florera *f* flower girl

florería *f* flower shop

flore•ro -ra *adj* flattering, jesting ‖ *mf* flatterer, jester; florist ‖ *m* (*vaso para flores*) vase; (*maceta con flores*) flowerpot; flower stand, jardiniere; (*cuadro, pintura*) flower piece ‖ *f* see **florera**

florescencia *f* florescence

floresta *f* woods, woodland; grove; rural setting; anthology

florete *m* (*esgrima*) fencing; (*espadín*) foil

floretear *tr* to decorate with flowers ‖ *intr* to fence

flori•do -da *adj* flowery, full of flowers; choice, select

florilegio *m* anthology

floripondio *m* (SAm) angel's-trumpet

florista *mf* florist

floristería *f* flower shop

florón *m* large flower; finial; rosette; (typ) tailpiece, vignette

flota *f* fleet; **flota petrolera** tanker fleet

flotación *f* buoyancy

flotador *m* float

flotaje *m* log driving

flotante *adj* floating; (*barba*) flowing ‖ *m* (Col) braggart

flotar *intr* to float; (*una bandera*) wave

flote *m* floating; **a flote** afloat

fluctuar §21 *intr* to fluctuate; bob up and down; wave; waver; be in danger

fluente *adj* fluent, flowing; (*hemorroides*) bleeding

fluidez *f* fluidity

flúi•do -da *adj* fluid; (*estilo, lenguaje*) fluent ‖ *m* fluid

fluir §20 *intr* to flow

flujo *m* flow, flux; (*acceso de la marea*) floodtide; **flujo de risa** fit of noisy laughter; **flujo de vientre** loose bowels; **flujo y reflujo** ebb and flow

flúor *m* fluorine

fluorescencia *f* fluorescence

fluorescente *adj* fluorescent

fluorhídri•co -ca *adj* hydrofluoric

fluorización *f* fluoridation

fluorizar §60 *tr* to fluoridate

fluoroscopio *m* fluoroscope

fluoruro *m* fluoride

flux *m* (*en el póker*) flush; suit of clothes; **estar en flux** to be penniless; **hacer flux** to blow in everything without settling accounts; **tener flux** to be lucky

fluxión *f* (*acumulación morbosa de humores*) congestion; (*enrojecimiento de la cara y el cuello*) flush; (*constipado de narices*) cold in the head; **fluxión de muelas** swollen cheek; **fluxión de pecho** pneumonia

foca *f* seal

focal *adj* focal

foco *m* focus; (*de vicios*) center; (*de un absceso*) core; electric light

fodo•lí *adj* (*pl* -líes) meddlesome

fodon•go -ga *adj* (Mex) dirty, slovenly

fo•fo -fa *adj* soft, fluffy, spongy

fogaje *m* (*contribución*) hearth money; blush, flush; (Arg) fire, blaze; (Arg, Mex) rash, eruption

fogata *f* blaze, bonfire

fogón *m* cooking stove; (*de máquina de vapor*) firebox

fogonazo *m* powder flash

fogonero *m* fireman, stoker

fogosidad *f* fire, spirit, dash

fogo•so -sa *adj* fiery, spirited

fol. *abbr* folio

folgo *m* foot muff

foliar *tr* to folio

folio *m* folio; **al primer folio** right off; **de a folio** enormous; **en folio** folio

folklore *m* folklore

follaje *m* foliage; gaudy ornament; (*palabrería*) fustian

follar *tr* to shape like a leaf ‖ §61 *tr* to blow with bellows

folletín *m* newspaper serial (*printed at bottom of page*); pamphlet

folleto *m* brochure, pamphlet, tract

fo•llón -llona *adj* careless, indolent, lazy; arrogant, cowardly ‖ *mf* lazy loafer, knave ‖ *m* noiseless rocket

fomentar *tr* to foment; foster, encourage, promote; warm

fonda *f* inn, restaurant; (Chile) refreshment stand

fondeadero *m* anchorage

fondea•do -da *adj* well-heeled

fondear *tr* (*un buque*) to search; scrutinize, examine closely ‖ *intr* to cast anchor ‖ *ref* to save up for a rainy day

fondillos *mpl* seat (*of trousers*)

fondista *mf* innkeeper

fondo *m* bottom; (*de un cuarto, una tienda*) back, rear; (*del mar, de una piscina, etc.*) floor; (*de un cilindro, barril, etc.*) head; background; (*de una casa*) depth; (*de un paño*) ground; (*caudal*) fund; (*lo esencial*) bottom; **a fondo** thoroughly; **bajos fondos sociales** underworld, scum of the earth; **colar a fondo** to sink; **dar fondo** to cast anchor; **echar a fondo** to sink; **en el fondo** at bottom; **estar en fondos** to have funds available; **fondo de amortización** sinking fund; **fondos** (*caudales, dinero*) funds; **irse a fondo** to go to the bottom; (*un negocio*)

fi
fo

to fail; **tener buen fondo** to be good-natured

fonducho *m* cheap eating house
fonéti•co -ca *adj* phonetic
foniatría *f* speech correction
fónica *f* phonics
fono *m* (Chile) earphone
fonoabsorbente *adj* sound-absorbent; sound-deadening
fonocaptor *m* pickup
fonógrafo *m* phonograph; record player
fonología *f* phonology
fontanería *f* plumbing; water-supply system
fontane•ro -ra *adj* fountain ‖ *m* plumber, tinsmith
foque *m* (naut) jib; (coll) piccadilly collar
foraji•do -da *adj* fugitive ‖ *mf* fugitive, outlaw, bandit
foráne•o -a *adj* foreign, strange; offshore
foraste•ro -ra *adj* outside, strange; foreign ‖ *mf* outsider, stranger
forbante *m* freebooter
forcejar or **forcejear** *intr* to struggle, resist, contend
forceju•do -da *adj* strong, husky, robust
fór•ceps *m* (*pl* **-ceps**) forceps
forestal *adj* forest
forja *f* forge; forging; silversmith's forge; foundry, ironworks; mortar
forjar *tr* to forge; build with stone and mortar; roughcast; (*mentiras*) forge ‖ *ref* to forge; hatch, think up
forma *f* form, shape; way; (*de un libro*) format; **de forma que** so that, with the result that; **tener buenas formas** to have a good figure
formación *f* formation; **formación de palabras** word formation
formal *adj* formal, ceremonious; express, definite; reliable; sedate; serious
formalidad *f* formality; reliability; seriousness
formar *tr* to form; to shape, fashion; train, educate ‖ *intr* to form; form a line, stand in line ‖ *ref* to form; form a line, stand in line; take form, grow, develop
formato *m* format
formidable *adj* formidable
formidolo•so -sa *adj* scared, frightened; frightful, horrible
fórmula *f* formula; prescription; **por fórmula** as a matter of form
formular *tr* to formulate
formulario *m* form, blank; **formulario de pedido** order blank
fornicación *f* fornication
fornicar *intr* to fornicate; to have sex
forni•do -da *adj* husky, sturdy, robust
foro *m* forum; (*abogacía*) bar; (*del escenario*) back, rear
forrado *m* lining; padding
forraje *m* forage, fodder
forrajear *tr & intr* to forage
forrar *tr* to line; (*un vestido*) face; (*un libro, un paraguas*) cover; (*un lienzo*) stretch ‖ *ref* (Guat, Mex) to stuff oneself
forro *m* lining; cover, covering; (naut)

sheathing, planking; **forro de freno** brake lining; **ni por el forro** not by a long shot
fortalecer §22 *tr* to fortify, strengthen
fortaleza *f* fortitude; strength, vigor; fortress, stronghold
fortificación *f* fortification
fortificante *m* tonic
fortificar §73 *tr* to fortify
fortín *m* small fort; bunker
fortui•to -ta *adj* fortuitous
fortuna *f* fortune; **correr fortuna** (naut) to ride the storm; **de fortuna** makeshift; **por fortuna** fortunately; **probar fortuna** to try one's luck
fortunón *m* windfall
forza•do -da *adj* forced; (*p.ej., entrada*) forcible; (*sonrisa*) (fig) forced; (*trabajos*) hard ‖ *m* galley slave
forzar §35 *tr* to force
forzo•so -sa *adj* unavoidable; strong, husky; (*trabajos*) hard; (*aterrizaje; marcha*) forced ‖ *f* — **hacer la forzosa a** to put the squeeze on
forzu•do -da *adj* strong, husky, robust
fosa *f* grave; (aut) pit; **fosa de los leones** (Bib) lions' den
fosar *tr* to dig a ditch around
fos•co -ca *adj* dark; cross, sullen; (*tiempo*) threatening
fosfato *m* phosphate
fosforera *f* matchbox
fosforescente *adj* phosphorescent
fósforo *m* (*cuerpo simple*) phosphorus; match; **fósforo de seguridad** safety match
fósil *adj & m* fossil
foso *m* hole, pit; (*que rodea un castillo o fortaleza*) moat; (theat & aut) pit
fotingo *m* jalopy, jitney
foto *f* photo; **foto fija** still
fotocopia *f* photocopy
fotocopiador *m* or **fotocopiadora** *f* photocopier
fotocopiar *tr* to photocopy
fotodrama *m* photoplay
fotofija *m* photo-finish camera
fotogéni•co -ca *adj* photogenic
fotograbado *m* photoengraving
fotografía *f* (*arte*) photography; (*imagen, retrato*) photograph; photograph gallery; **fotografía aérea** aerial photograph(y)
fotografiar §77 *tr & intr* to photograph
fotógra•fo -fa *mf* photographer
fotómetro *m* light meter
fotoperiodismo *m* photojournalism
fotopila *f* solar battery
fotostatar *tr & intr* to photostat
fotóstato *m* photostat
fototubo *m* phototube
fra. *abbr* **factura**
frac *m* (*pl* **-fraques**) full-dress coat, tails; swallow-tailed coat
fracasar *intr* to fail; break to pieces
fracaso *m* failure; breakdown, crash
fracción *f* fraction
fraccionar *tr* to divide up; break up
fracciona•rio -ria *adj* fractional

fractura *f* fracture; breaking open, breaking in

fracturar *tr* to fracture; break open, break in ‖ *ref* (*p.ej., un brazo*) to fracture

fragancia *f* fragrance; good reputation

fragante *adj* fragrant; **en fragante** (archaic) in the act

fragata *f* frigate; **fragata ligera** corvette

frágil *adj* fragile; (*quebradizo; que cae fácilmente en el pecado*) frail; (Mex) poor, needy

fragmento *m* fragment

fragor *m* crash, roar, thunder

fragoro•so -sa *adj* noisy, thundering

fragosidad *f* roughness, unevenness; (*de un bosque*) thickness, denseness; rough road

frago•so -sa *adj* rough, uneven; thick, dense; noisy, thundering

fragua *f* forge

fraguar §10 *tr* to forge; hatch, scheme; (*mentiras*) forge ‖ *intr* to forge; (*la cal, el cemento*) set

fraile *m* friar, monk; **fraile de misa y olla** friarling; **fraile rezador** praying mantis

frambesia *f* (pathol) yaws

frambuesa *f* raspberry

frambueso *m* raspberry bush

francachela *f* feast, spread; carousal, high time; (Arg) excessive familiarity

francalete *m* strap with buckle

fran•cés -cesa *adj* French; **despedirse a la francesa** to take French leave ‖ *m* Frenchman; (*idioma*) French ‖ *f* Frenchwoman

francesada *f* French remark; French invasion of Spain in 1808

francesilla *f* French roll; (bot) turban buttercup

Francia *f* France

francisca•no -na *adj & mf* Franciscan

francmasón *m* Freemason

francmasonería *f* Freemasonry

fran•co -ca *adj* generous, liberal; outspoken, candid, frank; (*camino*) free, open; (*suelo*) loamy; free, gratis; Frankish; **franco a bordo** free on board; **franco de porte** postpaid ‖ *mf* Frank ‖ *m* franc; (*idioma*) Frankish

francolín *m* black partridge

franco•te -ta *adj* frank, wholehearted

francotirador *m* sniper

franela *f* flannel

frangente *m* accident, mishap

frangir §27 *tr* to break up, break to pieces

frangollar *tr* to bungle, to botch

frangollo *m* porridge; mash for cattle; bungle, botch

franja *f* fringe; strip, band; (opt) fringe

franjar *tr* to fringe

franquear *tr* to exempt; cross, go over; grant; free, enfranchise; (*un camino*) open, clear; (*una carta*) frank, pay the postage for; **a franquear en destino** postage will be paid by addressee ‖ *ref* to yield; **franquearse con** to open one's heart to

franqueo *m* freeing, liberation; postage; **franqueo concertado** postage permit

franqueza *f* generosity; candidness, frankness; freedom

franquía *f* (naut) sea room; **en franquía** (naut & fig) in the open

franquicia *f* franchise; exemption, tax exemption; **franquicia postal** franking privilege

franquista *mf* Francoist

frasca *f* leaves, twigs, brush; (Guat, Mex) high jinks

frasco *m* flask; (*p.ej., de aceitunas*) jar

frase *f* phrase; (*oración cabal*) sentence; idiom; **frase hecha** saying, proverb; cliché; **gastar frases** to talk all around the subject

frasear *tr* to phrase ‖ *intr* to talk all around the subject

frasquera *f* bottle frame, liquor case

fratás *m* plastering trowel

fraternal *adj* brotherly, fraternal

fraternidad *f* fraternity, brotherhood

fraternizar §60 *intr* to fraternize

frater•no -na *adj* brotherly, fraternal

fraude *m* fraud; **fraude fiscal** tax evasion

fraudulen•to -ta *adj* fraudulent

fray *m* Fra

frecuencia *f* frequency; **alta frecuencia** high frequency; **baja frecuencia** low frequency; **con frecuencia** frequently

frecuentar *tr* (*ir con frecuencia a*) to frequent; keep up, repeat

frecuente *adj* frequent; (*usual*) common

fregadero *m* sink, kitchen sink

frega•do -da *adj* annoying, bothersome; cunning; (SAm) stubborn; (P-R) brazen ‖ *m* scrubbing; mopping; mess

frega•dor -dora *mf* dishwasher

fregar §66 *tr* (*restregar*) to rub; (*restregar para limpiar*) scrub, scour; (*el pavimento*) mop; (*los platos*) wash; annoy, bother

fregasue•los *m* (*pl* -**los**) mop, floor mop

frega•triz *f* (*pl* -**trices**) var of **fregona**

fre•gón -gona *adj* annoying, bothersome; brazen ‖ *f* (*criada que friega el pavimento*) scrub woman; (*criada que lava la vajilla*) dishwasher, scullery maid

freiduría *f* fried-fish shop

freír §58 & §83 *tr* to fry; bore to death ‖ *intr* to fry; **dejarle a uno freír en su aceite** to let someone stew in his own juice ‖ *ref* to fry; be bored to death; **freírsele a** to try to fool, scheme to deceive

fréjol *m* kidney bean

frenar *tr* to bridle, check, hold back; (*un automóvil, tren*) brake

frene•sí *m* (*pl* -**síes**) frenzy

frenéti•co -ca *adj* frantic; mad, furious; wild

frenillo *m* muzzle; **no tener frenillo en la lengua** to not mince one's words

freno *m* (*parte de la brida*) bit; (*aparato para parar el movimiento de los vehículos*) brake; (fig) brake, check, curb; **freno de contrapedal** coaster brake; **freno de disco** disk brake; **freno de tambor** drum brake; **morder el freno** to champ the bit

frenología *f* phrenology

frentazo *m* (Mex) rebuff

frente *m & f* (*de un edificio*) front ‖ *m* (mil)

front, front line; **al frente de** at the head of, in charge of ‖ *f* brow, forehead; face, front; head; **a frente** straight ahead; **arrugar la frente** to knit the brow; **de frente** straight ahead; abreast; **en frente de** in front of; against, opposed to; **frente a** in front of; compared with

freo *m* channel, strait

fresa *f* strawberry; (*de fresadora*) cutter

fresado *m* milling, millwork

fresadora *f* milling machine

fresal *m* strawberry patch

fresar *tr* to mill

fresca *f* fresh air; cool part of the day; blunt remark, piece of one's mind

fresca•chón -chona *adj* bouncing, buxom; (*viento*) brisk

fresca•les *mf* (*pl* **-les**) forward sort of person

frescamente *adv* recently; cheekily, brazenly

fres•co -ca *adj* (*acabado de hacer o suceder*) fresh; (*moderadamente frío*) cool; (*pintura*) fresh, wet; (*tela, vestido*) light; calm, unruffled; buxom, ruddy; cheeky, fresh; **estar fresco** to be in a fine pinch; **quedarse tan fresco** to show no offense, be indifferent or unconcerned ‖ *m* coolness; fresh air; fresh bacon; (fa) fresco; cool drink; **al fresco** in the open air; in the night air; **hace fresco** it is cool; **tomar el fresco** to go out for some fresh air ‖ *f* see **fresca**

frescor *m* freshness; cool, coolness

fresco•te -ta *adj* plump and rosy

frescura *f* freshness; cool, coolness; unconcern, offhand manner; sharp reply; cheek, impudence

fresno *m* ash tree; (*madera*) ash

fresquera *f* meat closet, food cabinet, icebox

fresquería *f* ice-cream parlor, soft-drink store

fresque•ro -ra *mf* fish dealer; (Peru) softdrink vendor ‖ *f* see **fresquera**

freudismo *m* Freudianism

freza *f* dung; spawning; hole made by game

frialdad *f* coldness; carelessness, laxity; stupidity; (pathol) frigidity; (pathol) impotence; (fig) coolness, coldness

friáti•co -ca *adj* chilly; awkward, stupid; (*ropa*) cold

fricar §73 *tr* to rub

fricasé *m* fricassee

fricción *f* rubbing; massage; (pharm) rubbing liniment; (phys) friction

friccionar *tr* to rub; massage

friega *f* rubbing, massage; annoyance, bother; flogging, whipping

frigidez *f* frigidity; coldness

frigi•do -da *adj* frigid; cold

frigorífero *m* freezing chamber

frigorífi•co -ca *adj* refrigerating; cold-storage ‖ *m* refrigerator; (Arg, Urug) packing house, cold-storage plant

fríjol *m* bean, kidney bean; **fríjol de media luna** Lima bean; **¡fríjoles!** (W-I) absolutely no!

frijolear *tr* (Guat) to annoy, molest

frijolizar §60 *tr* (Peru) to bewitch

fri•o -a *adj* cold; dull, weak, colorless; (fig) cold, cool ‖ *m* cold; **fríos** chills and fever;

coger frío to catch cold; **hace frío** it is cold; **tener frío** (*una persona*) to be cold; **tomar frío** to catch cold

friole•ro -ra *adj* chilly ‖ *f* trifle, trinket; snack, bite

frisar *tr* to rub; to fit, fasten; (naut) to calk ‖ *intr* to agree, get along; **frisar con** or **en** to border on

friso *m* dado, wainscot; (archit) frieze

fri•són -sona *adj & mf* Frisian

fritada *f* fry

fri•to -ta *adj* fried; bored to death ‖ *m* fry; (Ven) daily bread

fritura *f* fry

frívo•lo -la *adj* frivolous; trifling

fronda *f* leaf; (*de helecho*) frond; slingshaped bandage; **frondas** frondage, foliage

frondo•so -sa *adj* leafy; woodsy

frontalera *f* yoke pad

frontera *f* frontier, border; front, façade

fronteri•zo -za *adj* frontier, border; facing, opposite

fronte•ro -ra *adj* frontier, border; facing, opposite; front ‖ *f* see **frontera**

frontín *m* (Mex) flip, fillip

fron•tis *m* (*pl* **-tis**) front, façade

frontispicio *m* frontispiece; (coll) face

frontón *m* (*encima de puertas o ventanas*) gable, pediment; pelota court; pelota wall; handball court

frotamiento *m* rubbing; (phys) friction

frotar *tr* to rub; to chafe ‖ *ref* to rub

fro•tis *m* (*pl* **-tis**) (bact) smear

fructuo•so -sa *adj* fruitful

frugal *adj* (*en comer y beber*) temperate; (*no muy abundante*) frugal

fruición *f* enjoyment, satisfaction; (*del mal ajeno*) evil satisfaction

fruiti•vo -va *adj* enjoyable

frunce *m* shirr, shirring, gathering

frunci•do -da *adj* grim, gruff, stern; (Chile) temperate; (Chile) sad, gloomy ‖ *m* shirr, shirring, gathering

fruncir §36 *tr* to wrinkle, pucker, pleat; (*la frente*) knit; (*los labios*) curl, purse; (*la verdad*) twist, disguise; shirr, gather ‖ *ref* to affect modesty, be shocked

fruslería *f* trifle, trinket; (coll) futility, triviality

frusle•ro -ra *adj* futile, trivial, trifling ‖ *m* rolling pin

frustrar *tr* to frustrate, thwart

fruta *f* fruit; **fruta del tiempo** fruit in season; **fruta de sartén** fritter, pancake; **frutas** fruit; **frutas agrias** citrus fruit

frutal *adj* fruit ‖ *m* fruit tree

frutería *f* fruit store

frute•ro -ra *adj* fruit ‖ *mf* fruit dealer ‖ *m* fruit dish; tray of imitation fruit

frutilla *f* (*del rosario*) bead; Chilean strawberry; gumdrop

fruto *m* (bot & fig) fruit; **fruto de bendición** legitimate offspring; **frutos** produce; **sacar fruto de** to derive benefit from

fu *interj* faugh! fie!; (*del gato*) spit!; **ni fu ni fa** neither this nor that

fucilazo *m* heat lightning, sheet lightning

fuego *m* fire; (*para encender un cigarrillo*) light; (*de arma de fuego*) firing; lighthouse, beacon; hearth, home; rash, eruption; sore, fever blister; **abrir fuego** to open fire; **echar fuego** to blow up, hit the ceiling; **¡fuego!** fire!; **fuego fatuo** will-o'-the-wisp; **fuego graneado** or **nutrido** drumfire; **fuegos artificiales** fireworks; **hacer fuego** to fire, shoot; **marcar a fuego** to brand; **pegar fuego a** to set fire to, set on fire; **poner a fuego y sangre** to lay waste; **prenderse fuego** to catch on fire; **romper fuego** to open fire; stir up a row; **tocar a fuego** to sound the fire alarm

fuelle *m* fold, pucker, wrinkle; (*instrumento para soplar*) bellows; (*cubierta de coche*) folding carriage top; wind clouds; (*persona soplona*) gossip, talebearer

fuente *f* fountain, spring; public hydrant; font, baptismal font; platter, tray; (fig) source; **beber en buenas fuentes** to have good sources of information; **fuente de gasolina** gasoline pump; **fuente de sodas** soda fountain; **fuente para beber** drinking fountain; **fuentes termales** hot springs

fuer *m* — **a fuer de** as a, by way of

fuera *adv* out, outside; away, out of town; **desde fuera** from the outside; **fuera de** outside of; away from; out of; aside from; in addition to; **fuera de que** aside from the fact that; **fuera de sí** beside oneself; **por fuera** on the outside

fuera-bordo *m* outboard motor

fuere-ño -ña *mf* (Mex) hick, stranger

fuero *m* law, statute; code of laws; jurisdiction; exemption, privilege; **fuero interior** conscience, inmost heart; **fueros** pride, arrogance

fuerte *adj* strong; hard; loud; heavy; **hacerse fuerte** to stick to one's guns; (mil) to hole up, to dig in ‖ *adv* hard; loud ‖ *m* fort, fortress; forte, strong point

fuerza *f* force, strength, power; (*de un ejército*) main body; literal meaning; (phys) force; **a fuerza de** by dint of, by force of; **a la fuerza** forcibly, by force; **a viva fuerza** by main strength; **fuerza aérea** air force; **fuerza de agua** water power; **fuerza de sangre** animal power; **fuerza mayor** (law) force majeure, act of God; **fuerza motriz** motive power; **fuerza pública** police; **fuerza viva** kinetic energy; **hacer fuerza** to strain, struggle; to carry weight; **por fuerza** perforce, necessarily; **ser fuerza +** *inf* to be necessary to + *inf*

fuete *m* whip

fufar *intr* (*el gato*) to spit

fuga *f* flight; (*salida de un gas o líquido*) leak; ardor, vigor; (mus) fugue; **darse a la fuga** to take flight, run away; **fuga de capitales** capital flight; **poner en fuga** to put to flight

fugar §44 *ref* to flee, escape, run away

fu-gaz *adj* (*pl* **-gaces**) fleeting, passing; (*estrella*) shooting

fugiti-vo -va *adj & mf* fugitive

fugui-llas *m* (*pl* **-llas**) (coll) hustler

fula-no -na *mf* so-and-so

fulcro *m* fulcrum

fulgor *m* brilliance, radiance

fulgurar *intr* to flash

fulmicotón *m* guncotton

fulminar *tr* to strike with lightning; strike dead; (*censuras, amenazas, etc.*) thunder; (*balas o bombas*) hurl

fullería *f* trickery, cheating

fulle-ro -ra *adj* crooked, cheating ‖ *mf* crook, cheat; **fullero de naipes** cardsharp

fumada *f* puff, whiff

fumadero *m* smoking room; **fumadero de opio** opium den

fuma-dor -dora *adj* smoking ‖ *mf* smoker

fumar *tr* to smoke ‖ *intr* to smoke; **fumar en pipa** to smoke a pipe; **se prohibe fumar** no smoking ‖ *ref* to squander; stay away from; (*la clase*) cut

fumarada *f* (*de humo*) puff; (*de tabaco*) pipeful

fumigación *f* fumigation; **fumigación aérea** crop dusting

fumigar §44 *tr* to fumigate

fumista *m* stove or heater repairman; stove or heater dealer

fumistería *f* stove or heater shop

fumo-so -sa *adj* smoky

funámbu-lo -la *mf* ropewalker

función *f* function; duty, office, function; (*espectáculo teatral*) show, performance; **entrar en funciones** to take office, take up one's duties; **función benéfica** charitable performance; **función de aficionados** amateur performance; **función de títeres** puppet show; **función secundaria** side show

funcional *adj* functional

funcionariado *m* bureaucracy

funcionario *m* functionary, public official, civil servant

funcione-ro -ra *adj* officious, fussy

fund. *abbr* **fundador**

funda *f* case, sheath, envelope, slip; (*para una espada*) scabbard; (*para proteger los muebles*) slip cover; **funda de almohada** pillowcase; **funda de asientos** seat cover; **funda de gafas** spectacle case

fundación *f* foundation

fundadamente *adv* with good reason; on good authority

funda-dor -dora *adj* founding ‖ *mf* founder

fundamental *adj* fundamental

fundamentar *tr* to lay the foundations of

fundamento *m* foundation; (*razón, motivo*) grounds, reason; basis; reliability, sense; (Col) skirt

fundar *tr* to found, base ‖ *ref* — **fundarse en** to be based on; base one's opinion on

fundente *adj* molten ‖ *m* flux

fundería *f* foundry

fundible *adj* fusible

fundición *f* (*acción de fundir*) founding; (*fábrica*) foundry; (*herrería*) forge; (*hierro colado*) cast iron; (typ) font

fundi-do -da *adj* melted; (*individuo*) ruined; (elec) shorted, blown out

fundidor *m* founder, foundryman

fundillo *m* (Cuba, Mex) behind, buttocks

fundir *tr* (*p.ej., metales*) to found; (*campanas, estatuas*) cast; (*derretir para purificar*) smelt; (*colores*) mix; (*un filamento eléctrico*) burn out || *intr* to smelt || *ref* to melt; fuse; (*un filamento eléctrico*) burn out; fail, founder; (fig) to fuse, merge

fúnebre *adj* (*marcha, procesión*) funeral; (*triste*) funereal

funeral *adj* funeral; (*triste, lúgubre*) funereal || *m* funeral; **funerales** funeral

funerala — a la funerala (mil) with arms inverted (*as a token of mourning*)

funera·rio -ria *adj* funeral || *m* mortician, funeral director || *f* (*empresa*) undertaking establishment; (*local*) funeral home, funeral parlor

funes·to -ta *adj* ill-fated; sad, sorrowful; (*p.ej., influencia*) baneful

fungir §27 *intr* (CAm, Mex) to act, function

fungo *m* (pathol) fungus

fungo·so -sa *adj* fungous

funicular *adj & m* funicular

funique *adj* awkward; dull, tiresome

furgón *m* wagon, truck; (rr) freight car, boxcar; (rr) caboose

furgoneta *f* light truck, delivery truck

furia *f* fury

furibun·do -da *adj* furious, frenzied

furio·so -sa *adj* furious; (*muy grande*) terrific, tremendous

furor *m* rage, furor; **causar furor** to make a splash, cause a stir; **hacer furor** to be all the rage

furti·vo -va *adj* furtive; sneaky, poaching

furúnculo *m* boil

fusa *f* (mus) demisemiquaver

fus·co -ca *adj* dark

fusela·do -da *adj* streamlined

fuselaje *m* fuselage

fusible *adj* fusible || *m* (elec) fuse

fusil *m* gun, rifle

fusilar *tr* to shoot, execute; plagiarize

fusilazo *m* (*tiro de fusil*) gunshot, rifle shot; (*relámpago sin ruido*) heat lightning, sheet lightning

fusilería *f* rifle corps; rifles, guns; (*descarga*) fusillade

fusión *f* fusion; melting; **fusión de empresas** (com) merger

fusionar *tr & ref* to fuse, merge

fusta *f* brushwood, twigs; teamster's whip

fustán *m* fustian; cotton petticoat; (Ven) skirt

fuste *m* wood, timber; shaft, stem; (fig) importance, substance

fustigar §44 *tr* to whip, lash; rebuke harshly

fútbol *m* football; soccer, **fútbol asociación** soccer

fútil *adj* futile, trifling, inconsequential

futilidad *f* futility

futre *m* (SAm) dandy, dude

futu·ro -ra *adj* future || *m* future; (gram) future; fiancé; **futuros** (com) futures || *f* fiancée

G

G, g (ge) *f* eighth letter of the Spanish alphabet

G. *abbr* gracia

gaba·cho -cha *adj & mf* Pyrenean; (coll) Frenchy || *m* (coll) Frenchified Spanish (*language*)

gabán *m* overcoat

gabardina *f* gabardine; raincoat with belt

gabarra *f* barge, lighter

gabarro *m* (*en una piedra*) nodule; (*en un tejido*) flaw, defect; mistake

gabinete *m* cabinet; (*de médico, abogado, etc.*) office; studio, study; laboratory; (Col) glassed-in balcony; **de gabinete** armchair, theoretical; **gabinete de aseo** washroom; **gabinete de lectura** reading room

gablete *m* gable

gacela *f* gazelle

gaceta *f* government journal; newspaper; **mentir más que la gaceta** to lie like a trooper

gacetilla *f* town talk, gossip column; short item

gacetillero *m* gossip columnist

gacetista *mf* newspaper reader; newsmonger

gacilla *f* (CAm) safety pin

gacha *f* watery mass; (Col, Ven) earthenware bowl; **gachas** mush, pap; porridge; mud; **gachas de avena** oatmeal; **hacerse unas gachas** to be mushy

ga·cho -cha *adj* turned down; flopping; (*sombrero*) slouch; **a gachas** on all fours || *f* see **gacha**

gachumbo *m* (SAm) hard fruit shell

gachu·pín -pina *mf* (CAm, Mex) Spanish settler in Latin America

gaéli·co -ca *adj* Gaelic || *mf* Gael || *m* Gaelic (*language*)

gafa *f* clamp; (*enganche de los anteojos*) temple; **gafas** glasses; **gafas de sol** or **gafas para sol** sunglasses

gafe *m* jinx, hoodoo

ga·fo -fa *adj* claw-handed; foot-sore || *f* see **gafa**

gaguear *intr* to stutter

gaita *f* hornpipe; hurdy-gurdy; chore, hard task; neck; **gaita gallega** bagpipe

gaite·ro -ra *adj* flashy, gaudy || *m* piper, bagpipe player

gajes *mpl* wages, salary; **gajes del oficio** cares of office, occupational annoyances

gajo *m* broken branch; (*de un racimo de uvas*) small stem; (*división interior de ciertas frutas*) slice; (*de horca*) tine, prong; (*ramal de montes*) spur; curl

gala *f* fine clothes; (*lo más selecto*) choice, cream; tip, fee; **de gala** full-dress; **hacer gala de** to glory in; **llevarse la gala** to win approval

galafate *m* slick thief

galai•co -ca *adj* Galician

galán *m* good-looking fellow; lover, gallant, ladies' man; (*el que sirve de escolta a una dama*) escort, cavalier; (theat) leading man; **galán joven** (theat) juvenile; **primer galán** (theat) leading man

galancete *m* (theat) juvenile

gala•no -na *adj* elegant, graceful; spruce, smartly dressed; rich, tasteful

galante *adj* (*con las damas*) gallant; (*con los caballeros*) flirtatious; (*mujer*) wanton, loose

galantear *tr* to court, woo, make love to; sue, entreat

galantería *f* gallantry; charm, elegance; generosity

galanura *f* charm, elegance

galápago *m* pond tortoise; (*del arado*) moldboard; light saddle; ingot

galardón *m* reward, recompense

galardonar *tr* to reward, recompense

galaxia *f* galaxy

galbana *f* laziness; shiftlessness

galbano•so -sa *adj* lazy; phlegmatic

gale•no -na *adj* gentle; mild ‖ *m* (coll) physician, doctor

galeón *m* (naut) galleon

galeote *m* galley slave

galera *f* covered wagon; women's jail; (*de hospital*) ward; (naut & typ) galley

galerada *f* wagonload; (typ) galley; (typ) galley proof

galería *f* gallery; **galería de tiro** shooting gallery; **galerías** department store; **hablar para la galería** to play to the gallery

galerna *f* stormy wind from the northwest (*on the northern coast of Spain*)

Gales *f* Wales; **el país de Gales** Wales; **la Nueva Gales del Sur** New South Wales

ga•lés -lesa *adj* Welsh ‖ *m* Welshman; Welsh (*language*) ‖ *f* Welsh woman

galguear *intr* (CAm, Mex, Arg) to be hungry

gal•go -ga *adj* (Col) sweet-toothed ‖ *m* greyhound ‖ *f* greyhound bitch; rolling stone; mange; rash

Galia, la Gaul

gálibo *m* template, pattern; (rr) gabarit

galicismo *m* Gallicism

gáli•co -ca *adj* Gallic ‖ *m* syphilis; syphilitic

galillo *m* uvula; gullet

galimatí•as *m* (*pl* **-as**) gibberish, nonsense; confusion

galiparia *f* Frenchified Spanish

ga•lo -la *adj* Gaulish ‖ *mf* Gaul ‖ *m* Gaulish (*language*)

galocha *f* clog, wooden shoe

galón *m* braid, galloon; (*medida para líquidos*) gallon; (mil) chevron, stripe

galopar *intr* to gallop

galope *m* gallop; **a galope** at a gallop; in great haste; **a galope tendido** on the run

galopea•do -da *adj* hasty, sketchy ‖ *m* beating, punching

galopear *intr* to gallop

galopillo *m* scullion, kitchen boy

galopín *m* ragamuffin; (*hombre taimado*) wise guy; (naut) cabin boy

galpón *m* (SAm) iron shed; (Col) tile works

galvanizar §60 *tr* to electroplate; galvanize

galvanoplastia *f* electroplating

galladura *f* tread (*of egg*)

gallardete *m* streamer, pennant

gallardía *f* gallantry; elegance; nobility; generosity

gallar•do -da *adj* gallant; elegant; noble; generous; (*temporal*) fierce

gallear *intr* to stand out, excel; shout, yell, threaten

galle•go -ga *adj* & *mf* Galician

gallera *f* cockpit

galleta *f* hardtack, ship biscuit; cracker; little pitcher; slap

gallina *adj* chicken-hearted ‖ *mf* chicken-hearted person ‖ *f* hen; **estar como gallina en corral ajeno** to be like a fish out of water; **gallina ciega** blindman's buff; **gallina de Guinea** guinea fowl

gallinería *f* poultry shop; cowardice

galline•ro -ra *mf* poultry dealer ‖ *m* hencoop, henhouse; poultry basket; top gallery; babel, madhouse

gallipavo *m* turkey; sour note

gallito *m* (*el que figura sobre los demás*) somebody; **gallito del lugar** cock of the walk

gallo *m* cock, rooster; false note, sour note; boss; frog in the throat; (box) bantamweight; (Col, C-R, Mex) strong man; **gallo de bosque** wood grouse; **gallo de pelea** gamecock; **tener mucho gallo** to be cocky

gallofa *f* vegetables; French roll; talk, gossip

gallofear *intr* to beg, bum, loaf around

gallofe•ro -ra *adj* begging, loafing ‖ *mf* beggar, loafer

gama *f* doe, female fallow deer; (mus & fig) gamut

gamberrismo *m* gangsterism, rowdyism

gambe•rro -rra *adj* & *mf* libertine ‖ *m* hoodlum, tough, rowdy

gambeta *f* crosscaper; caper, prance

gambito *m* gambit

gamo *m* buck, male fallow deer

gamón *m* asphodel

gamonal *m* field of asphodel; boss

gamuza *f* chamois

gana *f* desire; will; **darle a uno la gana de** to feel like, e.g., **le da la gana de trabajar** he feels like working; **de buena gana** willingly; **de gana** in earnest; willingly; **de mala gana** unwillingly; **tener ganas de** to feel like, to have a mind to

ganadería *f* cattle, livestock; brand, stock; cattle raising; cattle ranch

ganade•ro -ra *adj* cattle, livestock ‖ *mf* cattle breeder; cattle dealer ‖ *m* cattleman

fu
ga

ganado *m* cattle, livestock; **ganado caballar** horses; **ganado cabrío** goats; **ganado lanar** sheep; **ganado mayor** large farm animals (*cows, bulls, horses, and mules*); **ganado menor** small farm animals (*sheep, goats, pigs*); **ganado menudo** young cattle; **ganado moreno** swine; **ganado ovejuno** sheep; **ganado porcino** swine; **ganado vacuno** cattle

gana•dor -dora *adj* winning; earning; hard-working ‖ *mf* winner; earner

ganancia *f* gain, profit; (Guat, Mex) extra, bonus; **ganancias y pérdidas** profit and loss

ganancial *adj* profit

ganancio•so -sa *adj* gainful, profitable; earning ‖ *mf* earner

ganapán *m* errand boy; boor

ganapierde *m & f* giveaway

ganar *tr* (*dinero trabajando*) to earn; (*la victoria luchando*) win; (*beneficios en los negocios*) gain; (*a una persona en una contienda*) beat, defeat; (*aventajar*) excel; (*la voluntad de una persona*) win over; (*alcanzar*) reach; **ganar algo a alguien** to win something from someone; **ganar de comer** to earn a living ‖ *intr* to earn; (*mejorar*) improve ‖ *ref* to win over; **ganarse la vida** to earn a livelihood

ganchero *m* log driver; (Chile) odd-jobber; (Ecuad) gentle mount

ganchillo *m* crochet needle; crochet, crochet work; **hacer ganchillo** to crochet

gancho *m* hook; shepherd's crook; coaxer; procurer, pimp; hairpin; (Col, Ecuad) lady's saddle; **gancho de botalones** (naut) gooseneck; **echar el gancho a** to hook in, to land; **tener gancho** (*una mujer*) to have a way with the men

gandaya *f* (coll) bumming, loafing

gandujar *tr* to pleat, shirr

gan•dul -dula *adj* loafing, idling ‖ *mf* loafer, idler

gandulear *intr* to loaf, idle

ganfo•rro -rra *mf* scoundrel

ganga *f* bargain

ganglio *m* ganglion

gangocho *m* burlap

gango•so -sa *adj* snuffling, nasal

gangrena *f* gangrene

gangrenar *tr & ref* to gangrene

gángster *m* gunman, gangster

gangsteril *adj* gangster(like)

gangsterismo *m* gangsterism; mobsterism

ganguear *intr* to snuffle, talk through the nose

gangue•ro -ra *adj* bargain-hunting; self-seeking ‖ *mf* bargain hunter

gano•so -sa *adj* desirous; (*caballo*) (Chile) spirited, fiery

gan•so -sa *mf* dope, dullard ‖ *m* goose; gander; **ganso bravo** wild goose ‖ *f* female goose

Gante Ghent

ganzúa *f* (*garfio*) picklock, lock pick; (*persona*) picklock; pumper (*of secrets*)

gañán *m* farm hand; rough, husky fellow

gañido *m* yelp; croak

gañir §12 *intr* (*el perro*) to yelp; (*p.ej., el cuervo*) croak

garabatear *tr* to scribble ‖ *intr* to hook; beat about the bush; scribble

garabato *m* hook; pothook; scribbling; weeding hoe; (*bozal*) muzzle; (*de una mujer*) winsomeness; **garabato de carnicero** meathook; **garabatos** wiggling of hands and fingers

garabato•so -sa *adj* full of scrawls; winsome

garage *m* or **garaje** *m* garage

garagista *m* garbage man

garambaina *f* gaudy trimming; **garambainas** simpering, smirking; (coll) scribble

garante *adj* responsible ‖ *mf* guarantor, voucher

garantía *f* guarantee, guaranty; warranty; **garantía anticorrosión** antirust warranty

garantir §1 *tr* to guarantee

garantizar §60 *tr* to guarantee

garañón *m* stud jackass; stud camel; stallion

garapiña *f* icing, sugar-coating; iced pineapple drink

garapiñar *tr* to ice, sugar-coat; candy

garapiñera *f* ice-cream freezer

garbanzo *m* chickpea; **garbanzo negro** (fig) black sheep

garbeo *m* walk; promenade

garbillar *tr* to sieve, screen riddle

garbillo *s* sieve, screen; riddled ore

garbo *m* jauntiness, grace, fine bearing; generosity

garbo•so -sa *adj* jaunty, graceful, spruce, sprightly; generous

gardu•ño -ña *mf* (archaic) sneak thief ‖ *f* stone marten, beech marten

garete *m* — **al garete** (naut) adrift

garfa *f* claw

garfio *m* hook, gaff

gargajear *intr* to cough up phlegm, hawk

gargajo *m* phlegm

garganta *f* throat; (*de un río, una vasija, etc.*) neck, throat; (*del pie*) instep; (*entre montañas*) ravine, gorge; (*del arado*) sheath; (*de una polea*) groove; (archit) shaft; **tener buena garganta** to have a good voice

gargantear *intr* to warble

gargantilla *f* necklace

gárgara *f* gargling; **gárgaras** (*líquido*) gargle; **hacer gárgaras** to gargle

gargarear *intr* to gargle

gargarismo *m* gargling; (*líquido*) gargle

gargarizar §60 *intr* to gargle

gárgola *f* gargoyle

garguero *m* gullet; (*caña del pulmón*) windpipe

garita *f* sentry box; porter's lodge; (*de una fortificación*) watchtower; railroad-crossing box; privy (*with one seat*); **garita de centinela** sentry box; **garita de señales** (rr) signal tower

garito *m* gambling den

garlito *m* fish trap; trap, snare

garlopa *f* jack plane, trying plane

garnar *intr* to drizzle

garra _f_ claw, talon; catch, hook; **caer en las garras de** to fall into the clutches of

garrafa _f_ carafe, decanter; **garrafa corchera** demijohn

garrafal _adj_ awful, terrible

garrafiñar _tr_ to snatch

garrafón _m_ carboy, demijohn

garramar _tr_ to snitch

garranchuelo _m_ crab grass

garrapata _f_ cattle tick, sheep tick; (mil) disabled horse; (Chile) little runt; (Mex) slut

garrapatear _intr_ to scrawl, scribble

garrapato _m_ pothook, scrawl; **garrapatos** scrawl

garri•do -da _adj_ handsome, elegant

garroba _f_ carob bean

garrocha _f_ goad; (sport) pole

garrotazo _m_ blow with a club

garrote _m_ club, cudgel; garrote (_method of execution; iron collar used for such execution_); (Mex) brake; **dar garrote a** to garrote

garrote•ro -ra _adj_ (Chile) stingy ‖ _m_ (Mex) brakeman

garrotillo _m_ croup

garrucha _f_ pulley, sheave

gárru•lo -la _adj_ chirping; (_hablador_) garrulous; (_arroyo_) babbling; (_viento_) rustling

garúa drizzle

garuar §21 _intr_ to drizzle

garulla _f_ mob, rabble

garza _f_ heron; **garza real** gray heron

gar•zo -za _adj_ blue ‖ _f_ see **garza**

garzón _m_ boy, youth; suitor; woman chaser

gas _m_ gas; **gas de alumbrado** illuminating gas; **gas exhilarante** or **hilarante** laughing gas; **gas lacrimógeno** tear gas; **gas mostaza** mustard gas

gasa _f_ gauze, chiffon; (_tira de gasa negra con que se rodea el sombrero en señal de luto_) hatband

Gascuña _f_ Gascony

gasear _tr_ to gas

gaseo•so -sa _adj_ gaseous ‖ _f_ soda water, carbonated water

gasificar §73 _tr_ to gasify; exalt, elate ‖ _ref_ to gasify

gasista _m_ gas fitter; (Chile) gasworker

gasoducto _m_ gas pipe line

gasógeno _m_ gas generator, gas producer; mixture of benzine and alcohol used for lighting and cleaning

gas-oil _m_ diesel oil

gasolina _f_ gasoline

gasolinera _f_ motor boat; gas station, filling station

gasómetro _m_ gasholder, gas tank

gastadero _m_ waste

gasta•do -da _adj_ worn-out; used up; spent; (_chiste_) crummy, corny

gasta•dor -dora _adj_ & _mf_ spendthrift ‖ _m_ convict; (mil) sapper, pioneer

gastadura _f_ worn spot

gastar _tr_ (_dinero, tiempo_) to spend; (_en cosas inútiles_) waste; (_echar a perder con el uso_) wear out; (_consumir_) use up; (_p.ej., una_

barba) wear; (_un coche_) keep; **gastarlas** to act, behave ‖ _intr_ to spend ‖ _ref_ to wear; wear out; become used up; waste away

gasto _m_ cost, expense; wear; **gastos de conservación** or **de entretenimiento** upkeep; **gastos de explotación** operating expenses; **gastos menudos** petty expenses; **hacer el gasto** to do most of the talking; to be the subject of conversation; **hacer frente a los gastos** to meet expenses; **meterse en gastos con** to go to the expense of

gasto•so -sa _adj_ wasteful, extravagant

gástri•co -ca _adj_ gastric

gastronomía _f_ gastronomy

gastróno•mo -ma _mf_ gourmet

gata _f_ she-cat; low-hanging cloud; Madrid woman; (Mex) maid, servant girl; **a gatas** on all fours, on hands and knees

gatada _f_ catty act

gatatumba _f_ faked attention, fake emotion, faked pain

gatazo _m_ gyp

gatea•do -da _adj_ catlike; grained, striped ‖ _m_ crawling, climbing; scratching, clawing

gatear _tr_ to scratch, claw; snitch ‖ _intr_ to crawl, climb

gatera _f_ cathole; (naut) hawsehole

gatería _f_ cats; gang of toughs; fake humility

gate•ro -ra _adj_ full of cats ‖ _mf_ cat lover ‖ _f_ see **gatera**

gates•co -ca _adj_ catlike, feline

gatillo _m_ (_de arma de fuego_) trigger; little pickpocket

gato _m_ cat; tomcat; (_instrumento para levantar pesos_) jack, lifting jack; sly fellow; sneak thief; native of Madrid; **gato montés** wildcat; **gato rodante** dolly; **vender gato por liebre** to gyp, cheat

gatopardo _m_ cheetah

gauchada _f_ (SAm) sly trick; (SAm) good turn

gauchaje _m_ (SAm) gathering of Gauchos

gauches•co -ca _adj_ Gaucho

gau•cho -cha _adj_ (SAm) Gaucho; (Arg, Chile) sly, crafty ‖ _m_ (SAm) Gaucho; (SAm) good horseman ‖ _m_ (Arg) mannish woman; (Arg) loose woman

gaulteria _f_ wintergreen

gaveta _f_ drawer, till

gavia _f_ ditch, drain; (_ave_) gull; (min) gang of basket passers; (naut) topsail

gavilán _m_ sparrow hawk; (_de la pluma_) nib; (_en la escritura_) hair stroke; ingrowing nail

gavilla _f_ sheaf, bundle; gang

gaviota _f_ sea gull

gavota _f_ gavotte

gaya _f_ colored stripe; (_ave_) magpie

gayar _tr_ to trim with colored stripes

ga•yo -ya _adj_ cheerful, bright, showy ‖ _m_ (orn) jay ‖ _f_ see **gaya**

gayola _f_ cage; jail

gayomba _f_ Spanish broom

gazapa _f_ lie

gazapatón _m_ blunder, slip

gazapera _f_ rabbit warren; gang, gang of thugs; brawl, row

ga
ga

gazapo *m* young rabbit; sly fellow; slip, boner, blunder; (*de actor*) fluff

gazmiar *tr* (*oliendo*) to sniff; (*comiendo*) nibble ‖ *ref* to complain

gazmoñada *f* or **gazmoñería** *f* prudishness, priggishness

gazmoñe•ro -ra or **gazmo•ño -ña** *adj* prudish, priggish, strait-laced, demure ‖ *mf* prude, prig

gaznápiro *m* gawk, boob, bumpkin

gaznate *m* gullet; (Mex) fritter

gazpacho *m* cold vegetable soup; (Hond) leftovers

gazuza *f* hunger

Gedeón *m* Gideon

gehena *m* Gehenna

géiser *m* geyser

gel *m* gel

gelatina *f* gelatine

gema *f* gem; (bot) bud

geme•lo -la *adj & mf* twin; **gemelos** twins; binoculars; cuff links; **gemelos de campo** field glasses; **gemelos de teatro** opera glasses ‖ **Gemelos** *mpl* (astr) Gemini

gemido *m* moan, groan; wail, whine; howl, roar

Géminis *m* (astr) Gemini

gemiquear *intr* (Chile) to whine

gemir §50 *intr* to moan, groan; wail, whine; howl, roar

gen *m* gene

genciana *f* gentian

gendarme *m* policeman

genealogía *f* genealogy

generación *f* generation

genera•dor -dora *adj* generating ‖ *m* generator

general *adj* general; common, usual; **en general** or **por lo general** in general ‖ *m* general; **capitán general de ejército** five-star general; **general de brigada** brigadier, brigadier general; **general de división** major general ‖ **generales** *fpl* general information, personal data

generala *f* general's wife; call to arms

generalato *m* generalship

generalidad *f* generality; majority; **la generalidad de** the general run of

generalísimo *m* generalissimo

generalizar §60 *tr & intr* to generalize ‖ *ref* to become generalized

generar *tr* to generate

genéri•co -ca *adj* generic; (*artículo*) indefinite; (*nombre*) common; showing gender

género *m* kind, sort; way, manner; cloth, material; (biol, log) genus; (gram) gender; **de género** genre; **género chico** one-act play, one-act operetta; **género de punto** knit goods, knitwear; **género humano** humankind; **género ínfimo** light vaudeville; **género novelístico** fiction; **género picaresco** burlesque; **géneros** goods, merchandise, material; **géneros de pieza** yard goods; **géneros para vestidos** dress goods

genero•so -sa *adj* generous; highborn; noble, magnanimous; (*vino*) rich, full

géne•sis *f* (*pl* **-sis**) genesis ‖ **el Génesis** (Bib) Genesis

genéti•co -ca *adj* genetic ‖ *f* genetics

genial *adj* inspired, geniuslike; pleasant, agreeable; temperamental

geniazo *m* fiery temper

genio *m* (*índole, carácter*) temperament, disposition; (*don altísimo de invención; persona que lo posee; espíritu tutelar, deidad pagana*) genius; fire, spirit

genital *adj* genital ‖ **genitales** *mpl* genitals

geniti•vo -va *adj* genitive

genitourina•rio -ria *adj* genitourinary

genocida *adj* genocidal ‖ *mf* genocide

genocidio *m* genocide

Génova *f* Genoa

geno•vés -vesa *adj & mf* Genoese

gente *f* people; (*parentela, familia*) folks; race, nation; troops; **gente baja** lower classes, rabble; **gente bien** nice people; **gente de bien** decent people; **gente de capa parda** country people; **gente de coleta** bullfighters; **gente de color** colored people; **gente de la cuchilla** butchers; **genta de la vida airada** bullies; underworld; **gente del bronce** bright, lively people; **gente del rey** convicts; **gente de mal vivir** toughs, underworld; **gente de mar** seafaring people; **gente de paz** (*palabras con las cuales se contesta al que pregunta ¿quién?*) friend; **gente de pluma** (coll) clerks; **gente de su majestad** convicts; **gente de trato** tradespeople; **gente forzada** convicts; **gente menuda** small fry; common people

gentecilla *f* mob, rabble

gentil *adj* heathen, gentile; elegant, genteel; noble ‖ *mf* heathen, pagan

gentileza *f* elegance, gentility, courtesy; gallantry; show, splendor; (*hidalguía*) nobility

gentilhombre *m* (*pl* **gentileshombres**) gentleman; messenger to the king; my good man; **gentilhombre de cámara** gentleman in waiting

gentili•cio -cia *adj* national; family; (gram) gentile

gentilidad *f* heathendom

gentío *m* crowd, mob

gentualla *f* or **gentuza** *f* rabble, riffraff

genui•no -na *adj* genuine

geofísi•co -ca *adj* geophysical ‖ *mf* geophysicist ‖ *f* geophysics

geografía *f* geography

geográfi•co -ca *adj* geographic(al)

geógra•fo -fa *mf* geographer

geología *f* geology

geológi•co -ca *adj* geologic(al)

geólo•go -ga *mf* geologist

geómetra *mf* geometrician

geometría *f* geometry; **geometría del espacio** solid geometry

geométri•co -ca *adj* geometric(al)

geopolíti•co -ca *adj* geopolitical ‖ *f* geopolitics

geranio *m* geranium

gerencia *f* management; manager's office

gerente *m* manager, director; **gerente de**

publicidad advertising manager; **gerente de ventas** sales manager

geriatría f geriatry

geriatra adj geriatrical || mf geriatrician

geriátri•co -ca adj geriatrical

germanía f gypsy slang, cant of thieves

germanizar §60 tr to Germanize

germen m germ; **germen plasma** germ plasm

germicida adj germicidal || m germicide

germinal adj germ; germinal

germinar intr to germinate

gerontología f gerontology

gerundio m gerund; present participle; bombastic writer or speaker

gestación f gestation

gestear intr to make faces

gesticular intr to make a face, to make faces; (hacer ademanes) to gesticulate

gestión f step, measure; management; action, proceeding, negotiation

gestionar tr to promote, pursue; manage; negotiate

gesto m face; wry face, grimace; look, appearance; (movimiento, ademán) gesture

ges•tor -tora adj managing || m manager

gestu•do -da adj cross-looking

ghetto m ghetto

giba f hump; annoyance

giga f jig

giganta f giantess

gigante adj giant || m giant; (en las procesiones) giant figure

gigantes•co -ca adj gigantic

gigantez f giant size

gigantilla f large-headed masked figure; little fat woman

gigan•tón -tona mf huge giant || m giant figure

gigote m chopped-meat stew; **hacer gigote** to chop up

gilí adj foolish, stupid

gimnasia f gymnastics; **gimnasia sueca** Swedish movements, setting-up exercises

gimnasio m gymnasium; secondary school, academy

gimnasta mf gymnast

gimnásti•co -ca adj gymnastic || f gymnastics

gimotear intr to whine

gimoteo m whining

ginebra f gin; (de voces) buzz, din; confusion, disorder || **Ginebra** f Geneva

ginebri•no -na adj & mf Genevan

ginecología f gynecology

ginecológi•co -ca adj gynecologic(al)

ginecólo•go -ga mf gynecologist

ginesta f Spanish broom

gira f var of jira

gira•do -da mf drawee

gira•dor -dora mf drawer

giralda f weathercock (in the form of person or animal)

girándula f girandole

girar tr (una visita) to pay; (com) to draw || intr to turn; rotate, gyrate; trade; (com) to draw

girasol m sunflower, sycophant

girato•rio -ria adj revolving || f revolving bookcase

gi•ro -ra adj (Guat) drunk; (Mex) cocky || m turn; rotation; revolution; course, trend, turn; turn of phrase; boast, threat; gash, slash; line of business; trade; (com) draft; **giro a la vista** sight draft; **giro postal** money order || f see **gira**

giroflé m clove

giroscopio m gyroscope

gis m (Col) slate pencil

gitana f gypsy woman, gypsy girl

gitanada f gypsy trick; fawning, flattery

gitanería f band of gypsies; gypsy life; fawning, flattery

gitanes•co -ca adj gypsyish

gita•no -na adj gypsy; flattering; sly, tricky || mf gypsy || m Gypsy (language) || f see **gitana**

glaciación f freezing

glacial adj glacial; (zona) frigid; (fig) cold, indifferent

glaciar m glacier

glándula f gland; **glándula cerrada** ductless gland

glasé m glacé silk

glasea•do -da adj glossy, shiny

glicerina f glycerin

global adj total; global, world-wide

globo m globe; (aparato que, lleno de un gas, se eleva en el aire) balloon; (bomba de lámpara) globe, lamp shade; **globo de aire** (aut) air bag; **globo del ojo** eyeball; **globo sonda** trial balloon; **lanzar un globo sonda** (fig) to send up a trial balloon

glóbulo m globule; (physiol) corpuscle; **glóbulo rojo** red cell

gloria f glory; **ganar la gloria** to go to glory; **oler a gloria** to smell heavenly; **saber a gloria** to taste heavenly

gloriar §77 tr to glorify || intr to recite the rosary || ref to glory

glorieta f arbor, bower, summerhouse; public square; traffic circle

glorificar §73 tr to glorify || ref to glory

glorio•so -sa adj glorious; boastful

glosa f gloss

glosa•dor -dora adj commenting || mf commentator

glosar tr to gloss; audit; (Col) to scold || intr to find fault

glosario m glossary

glóti•co -ca adj glottal

glo•tón -tona adj gluttonous || mf glutton

glotonería f gluttony

glucosa f glucose

gluglú m (del agua) gurgle, glug; (del pavo) gobble; **hacer gluglú** to gurgle, to glug

gluglutear intr to gobble

gnomo m gnome

gob. abbr **gobierno**

gobernación f governing; government; department of the interior; (Arg) territory

gobernad•dor -dora adj governing || m governor

gobernalle m rudder, helm

gobernante *adj* governing ‖ *mf* ruler ‖ *m* self-appointed head

gobernar §2 *tr* to govern; guide, direct; control, rule; (*un buque*) steer ‖ *intr* to govern; steer

goberno·so -sa *adj* orderly

gobierno *m* government; governor's office, governorship; management; control, rule; guidance; (*de un buque*) navigability; **de buen gobierno** (*buque*) navigable; **gobierno de monigotes** puppet government; **gobierno doméstico** housekeeping; **gobierno exilado** government in exile; **para su gobierno** for your guidance; **servir de gobierno** to serve as a guide

goce *m* enjoyment

go·do -da *adj* Gothic ‖ *mf* Goth; Spanish noble; (Arg, Chile) Spaniard

gofio *m* roasted corn meal

gol *m* goal

gola *f* gullet

goldre *m* quiver

goleta *f* schooner

golf *m* golf

golfán *m* white water lily

golfista *mf* golfer

gol·fo -fa *mf* ragamuffin ‖ *m* gulf; open sea; **golfo de Méjico** Gulf of Mexico; **golfo de Vizcaya** Bay of Biscay

Gólgota, el (Bib) Golgotha

golilla *f* gorget, ruff; magistrate's collar; pipe flange; (*de los caños de barro*) collar, sleeve; (*del gallo*) erectile bristles

golondrina *f* swallow; **empresa golondrina** fly-by-night outfit

golosina *f* delicacy, tidbit; eagerness, appetite; trifle

golosinear *intr* to go around eating candy

golo·so -sa *adj* sweet-toothed; (*glotón*) gluttonous; (*apetitoso*) tasty

golpe *m* blow, stroke, hit; bump, bruise; heartbeat; crowd, throng, flock; (*del bolsillo*) flap; (*pestillo*) bolt, latch; (*de licor*) shot; surprise, wonder; (*infortunio*) blow; witticism; **dar golpe** to make a hit; **de golpe** all at once, suddenly; **de golpe y porrazo** slambang; **de un golpe** at one stroke; **golpe de ariete** water hammer; **golpe de calor** heatstroke; **golpe de estado** coup d'état; **golpe de fortuna** stroke of fortune; **golpe de gracia** coup de grâce; **golpe de mano** surprise attack; **golpe de mar** surge; **golpe de ojo** glance; **golpe de teatro** dramatic turn of events; **golpe de tos** fit of coughing; **golpe de vista** glance, look; view; **golpe en vago** miss, flop; **golpe mortal** deathblow; **no dar golpe** to not raise a hand, not do a stroke of work

golpear *tr* to strike, hit, beat; bump, bruise ‖ *intr* to beat, strike; (*el reloj*) tick; (*el motor de combustión interna*) knock

golpete *m* door catch, window catch

golpetear *tr* & *intr* to beat; rattle

golpismo *m* government by coup d'état

gollería *f* delicacy, dainty; **pedir gollerías** to ask for too much

gollete *m* throat, neck; (*de botella*) neck

goma *f* gum, rubber; (*tira de goma elástica*) rubber band; (*neumático*) tire; **goma arábiga** gum arabic; **goma de borrar** eraser, rubber; **goma de mascar** chewing gum; **goma espumosa** foam rubber; **goma laca** shellac

gomecillo *m* blind man's guide

gomia *f* bugaboo; waster; glutton

gomo·so -sa *adj* gum; gummy ‖ *m* dude, dandy

góndola *f* gondola

gondolero *m* gondolier

gongo *m* gong

gonorrea *f* gonorrhea

gordal *adj* large-size

gordia·no -na *adj* Gordian

gordi·flón -flona or **gordin·flón -flona** *adj* chubby, pudgy, fatty ‖ *mf* fatty

gor·do -da *adj* fat, plump; fatty, greasy; coarse; big, large; whopping big; (*agua*) hard ‖ *m* fat, suet; first prize (*in lottery*) ‖ **gordo** *adv* — **hablar gordo** to talk big

gordura *f* fatness, plumpness, stoutness, corpulence; fat, grease

gorgojo *m* grub, weevil; dwarf, runt; **gorgojo del algodón** boll weevil

gorgojo·so -sa *adj* grubby

gorgón *m* (Col) concrete

gorgonear *intr* (*el pavo*) to gobble

gorgoritear *intr* to trill

gorgorito *m* trill

gorgotear *intr* to burble, gurgle

gorgotero *m* peddler, hawker

gorigori *m* lugubrious funeral chant

gorila *f* gorilla; (coll) thug; strong-arm man

gorjear *intr* to warble, trill ‖ *ref* (*el niño*) to gurgle

gorra *f* cap; bumming, sponging; **andar de gorra** to sponge; **colarse de gorra** (coll) to crash the gate; **gorra de visera** cap; **vivir de gorra** to live on other people

gorrada *f* tipping the hat

gorrear *intr* (Ecuad) to sponge

gorretada *f* tipping the hat

gorrión *m* sparrow; **gorrión triguero** bunting

gorrista *adj* sponging ‖ *mf* sponger

gorro *m* cap, bonnet; baby's bonnet; **gorro de dormir** nightcap

go·rrón -rrona *adj* sponging ‖ *mf* sponger ‖ *m* pivot; journal, gudgeon

gota *f* drop; (pathol) gout; **gotas** touch of rum or brandy in coffee; **sudar la gota gorda** to work one's head off

gotear *intr* to drip, dribble; (*llover a gotas espaciadas*) sprinkle

gotera *f* drip, dripping; mark left by dripping; (*en el techo*) leak; (*adorno de una cama*) valance; **estar lleno de goteras** to be full of aches and pains; **es una gotera** it's a constant drain; **goteras** aches, pains; (Col) environs, outskirts

góti·co -ca *adj* Gothic; noble, illustrious ‖ *m* Gothic

goto·so -sa *adj* gouty ‖ *mf* gout sufferer

gozar §60 *tr* (*poseer*) to enjoy ‖ *intr* to enjoy oneself; **gozar de** (*poseer*) to enjoy ‖ *ref* to enjoy oneself; rejoice

gozne *m* hinge

gozo *m* joy, enjoyment; **no caber en sí de gozo** to be beside oneself with joy; **saltar de gozo** to leap with joy

gozo•so -sa *adj* joyful; **gozoso con** or **de** joyful over

gozque *m* or **gozquejo** *m* little yapping dog

grabación *f* (*de disco*) recording; **grabación sobre cinta** tape recording

grabado *m* engraving; print, cut, picture; (*de disco*) recording; **grabado en madera** wood engraving, woodcut; **grabado fuera de texto** inset, insert

graba•dor -dora *adj* recording ‖ *mf* engraver ‖ *f* recorder; **grabadora de cinta** tape recorder

grabador-reproductor *m* cassette recorder

grabadura *f* engraving

grabar *tr* to engrave; (*un sonido, una canción, un disco, etc.*) record; **grabar en** or **sobre cinta** to tape-record ‖ *ref* to become engraved

gracejada *f* (CAm, Mex) cheap comedy, clownishness

gracejar *intr* to be engaging, witty; joke

gracejo *m* lightness, winsome manner, charm; (CAm, Mex) clown

gracia *f* witticism, witty remark, joke; grace; gracefulness; favor; pardon; (*de un chiste*) point; name; **caer en gracia a** to be pleasing to; **de gracia** gratis; **decir dos gracias a** to tell someone a thing or two; **en gracia a** because of; **gracia de Dios** daily bread; air and sunshine; **gracias** thanks; **¡gracias!** thanks!; **gracias a** thanks to; **¡gracias a Dios!** thank heavens!; **hacer gracia** to be pleasing; **hacer gracia de algo a uno** to exempt or free someone from something; **hacerle a uno gracia** to strike someone as funny; **¡linda gracia!** nonsense!; **tener gracia** to be funny, be surprising

graciable *adj* kind, gracious; easy to grant

grácil *adj* thin, small, slender

gracio•so -sa *adj* (*que tiene donaire, gracia*) graceful; (*afable, fino*) gracious; (*agudo, chistoso*) funny, witty; (*que se da de balde*) free, gratis ‖ *mf* comic ‖ *m* gracioso (*gay, comic character in Spanish comedy*)

grada *f* step, stair; row of seats; grandstand; altar step; (agr) harrow; (*plano inclinado sobre el cual se construyen los barcos*) slip; **gradas** stone steps; (Chile, Peru) atrium; **gradas al aire libre** bleachers

gradar *tr* (agr) to harrow

gradería *f* stone steps; row of seats; bleachers; **gradería cubierta** grandstand

gradiente *m* (phys) gradient ‖ *f* slope, gradient

grado *m* step; grade; degree; (*título que se da en las universidades*) degree; (*sección en las escuelas*) grade, form, class; (mil) rank; **de buen grado** willingly; **de grado en grado** by degrees; **de grado o por fuerza** willy-nilly; **de mal grado** unwillingly; **en sumo grado** to a great extent; **mal de mi grado** unwillingly, against my wishes

graduación *f* graduation; (*de las bebidas espirituosas*) strength; (mil) rank

gradual *adj* gradual

graduan•do -da *mf* (*persona próxima a graduarse en la universidad*) graduate (*candidate for a degree*)

graduar §21 *tr* to graduate, grade; (*un grifo, una válvula, etc.*) regulate; appraise, estimate ‖ *ref* to graduate

grafía *f* graph

gráfi•co -ca *adj* graphic(al); printing; illustrated; picture, camera ‖ *m* diagram ‖ *f* graph

grafito *m* graphite

grafospasmo *m* writer's cramp

gragea *f* colored candy; sugar-coated pill

grajear *intr* (*los cuervos*) to caw; (*los niños*) gurgle

grajien•to -ta *adj* foul-smelling

gra•jo -ja *mf* rook, crow; chatterbox ‖ *m* body odor

gral. *abbr* **general**

gramática *f* grammar; **gramática parda** shrewdness, mother wit

gramatical *adj* grammatical

gramáti•co -ca *adj* grammatical ‖ *mf* grammarian ‖ *f* see **gramática**

gramil *m* marking gauge, gauge

gramo *m* gram

gramófono *m* gramophone

gramola *f* console phonograph; portable phonograph

gran *adj* apocopated form of **grande,** used only before nouns of both genders in the singular

grana *f* seed; seeding; seeding time; red; **dar en grana** to go to seed

granada *f* pomegranate; (*proyectil explosivo*) grenade; **granada de mano** hand grenade; **granada de metralla** shrapnel; **granada extintora** fire extinguisher, fire grenade

granadero *m* grenadier

granadilla *f* passionflower

granadina *f* grenadine

grana•do -da *adj* choice, select; mature, expert ‖ *m* pomegranate; **granado blanco** rose of Sharon ‖ *f* see **granada**

granalla *f* filings

granangular *adj* wide-angle

granate *m adj invar & m* garnet

Gran Bretaña, la Great Britain

grande *adj* big, large; great ‖ *m* grandee

grandeza *f* bigness, largeness; greatness; (*tamaño*) size; (*magnificencia*) grandeur; grandees; grandeeship

grandi•llón -llona *adj* oversize, overgrown

grandio•so -sa *adj* grandiose, grand

grandor *m* size

granea•do -da *adj* spattered; (*fuego*) heavy and continuous

granear *tr* to sow; (*la pólvora; una piedra litográfica*) grain; stipple

granel — a granel in bulk, loose; at random; lavishly

granelar *tr* (*el cuero*) to grain

granero *m* granary

granete *m* center punch**

go
gr

granífu•go -ga *adj* hail-dispersing
granito *m* granite
granizada *f* hailstorm; (Arg, Chile) iced drink
granizar §60 *tr* (*p.ej., golpes*) to hail; sprinkle ‖ *intr* to hail
granizo *m* hail
granja *f* farm, grange; dairy; country place
granjear *tr* to earn, gain; win, win over ‖ *ref* to win, win over
granjería *f* husbandry; gain, profit
granje•ro -ra *mf* farmer; merchant, trader
grano *m* grain; (*baya*) berry; (*baya de la uva*) grape; (*tumorcillo en la piel*) pimple; (*peso*) grain; **grano de belleza** beauty spot; **grano de café** coffee bean; **granos** (*fruto de los cereales*) grain; **ir al grano** to come to the point
granuja *m* scoundrel; (*muchacho vagabundo*) waif ‖ *f* loose grape; grapeseed
granujo *m* pimple
granular *adj* granular; pimply ‖ *tr & ref* to granulate
gránulo *m* granule
grapa *f* clamp, clip, staple
grasa *f* fat, grease; (*polvo*) pounce; (Mex) shoe polish; **grasa de ballena** blubber; **grasas** slag
grasien•to -ta *adj* greasy
grasilla *f* pounce
gra•so -sa *adj* fatty, greasy ‖ *m* fattiness, greasiness ‖ *f* see **grasa**
grasones *mpl* wheat porridge
graso•so -sa *adj* greasy; (pathol) fatty
grata *f* wire brush; (*carta*) favor
gratificar §73 *tr* to gratify; reward, recompense; tip, fee
gratín *m* — **al gratín** au gratin
gratis *adv* gratis
gratisda•to -ta *adj* free, gratis
gratitud *f* gratitude
gra•to -ta *adj* pleasing; free; (Bol, Chile) grateful ‖ *f* see **grata**
gratuidad *f* cost exemption; exemption from fees
gratui•to -ta *adj* gratuitous; free, gratis
grava *f* gravel; crushed stone
gravamen *m* burden, obligation; encumbrance, lien; assessment
gravar *tr* to burden, encumber; assess ‖ *ref* to get worse
grave *adj* grave, serious, solemn; hard, difficult; (*que pesa*) heavy; (*sonido*) grave, deep, low; (*música*) majestic, noble; (*negocio*) important; (*enfermedad*) serious; (*acento*) grave; paroxytone
gravedad *f* gravity; seriousness; **de gravedad** seriously; gravely; **gravedad nula** weightlessness, zero gravity
gravedo•so -sa *adj* heavy, pompous
gravidez *f* pregnancy
grávi•do -da *adj* pregnant
gravitación *f* gravitation
gravitar *intr* to gravitate; **gravitar sobre** to weigh down on
gravo•so -sa *adj* burdensome, onerous, costly; boring, tiresome

graznar *intr* to caw, croak; cackle; (*al cantar*) (fig) cackle
graznido *m* caw, croak; cackle; (*canto que disuena mucho*) (fig) cackle
Grecia *f* Greece
grecia•no -na *adj* Grecian
gre•co -ca *adj & mf* Greek
greda *f* clay, fuller's earth
grega•rio -ria *adj* (*que vive confundido con otros*) gregarious; slavish, servile
gregoria•no -na *adj* Gregorian
gremial *adj* guild; trade-union, union ‖ *m* guildsman; union member
gremio *m* guild, corporation; trade union, union; association, society
greña *f* confusion, entanglement; (*de cabello*) shock, tangled mop; **andar a la greña** to get into a hot argument; (*dos mujeres*) to pull each other's hair
greñu•do -da *adj* bushy-headed, shock-headed
gres *m* sandstone; stoneware
gresca *f* tumult, uproar; row, quarrel
grey *f* (*de ganado menor*) flock; group, party; nation, people; (*de fieles*) flock, congregation
grie•go -ga *adj* Greek ‖ *mf* Greek ‖ *m* (*idioma*) Greek; **hablar en griego** to not make sense
grieta *f* crack, crevice, chink; (*en la piel*) chap
grieta•do -da *adj* crackled ‖ *m* crackleware
grietar *ref* to crack, split; (*la piel*) become chapped
gri•fo -fa *adj* (*pelo*) kinky, tangled; (*letra*) script; (W-I) colored; (Mex) drunk; (Col) conceited ‖ *mf* (W-I) person of color; (Mex) drunk ‖ *m* faucet, spigot, tap, cock; (myth) griffin; (Peru) gas station, (Mex) marijuana ‖ *f* (Mex) marijuana
grilla *f* female cricket; (rad) grid; (Col) fight, quarrel; (SAm) annoyance, bother; **¡ésa es grilla!** (coll) you expect me to believe that!
grillar *intr* (*el grillo*) to chirp ‖ *ref* (*las semillas, bulbos, etc.*) to sprout
grillete *m* fetter, shackle
grillo *m* (*insecto*) cricket; (*brote tierno*) sprout, shoot; **grillos** fetters, shackles
grima *f* fright, horror; **dar grima** to grate on the nerves
grin•go -ga *mf* (disparaging) foreigner; (*anglosajón*) gringo ‖ *m* gibberish; **hablar en gringo** to talk nonsense
griñón *m* (*toca de monja*) wimple; (*melocotón*) nectarine
gripe *f* grippe
gris *adj* gray; dull, gloomy ‖ *m* gray; **hacer gris** (*el tiempo*) to be sharp, be brisk
grisáce•o -a *adj* grayish
gri•sú *m* (*pl* -**súes**) firedamp
grita *f* shouting; hubbub, uproar; **dar grita a** to hoot at
gritar *intr* to shout, cry out
gritería *f* shouting, outcry, uproar
grito *m* cry, shout; scream, shriek; **el último grito** the latest thing, all the rage; **poner el**

grito en el cielo to raise the roof, scream wildly

gro. *abbr* **género**

Groenlandia *f* Greenland

grosella *f* currant; **grosella silvestre** gooseberry

grosellero *m* currant bush; **grosellero silvestre** gooseberry bush

grosería *f* grossness, coarseness; churlishness, rudeness; stupidity; vulgarity

grose·ro -ra *adj* gross, coarse; churlish, rude; stupid; vulgar ‖ *mf* churl, boor

grosor *m* thickness, bulk

grosura *f* fat, suet, tallow; meat diet; coarseness, vulgarity

grotes·co -ca *adj* grotesque

grúa *f* crane, derrick; **grúa de bote** (naut) davit; **grúa de auxilio** wrecking crane; **grúa de caballete** gantry crane

grúa-remolque *m* tow truck

grue·so -sa *adj* big, thick, bulky, heavy; coarse, ordinary; stout, fat; (*mar*) rough, heavy; **en grueso** in gross, in bulk ‖ *f* (*doce docenas*) gross

grulla *f* (orn) crane

grumete *m* ship's boy, cabin boy

grumo *m* clot, curd; bunch, cluster

grumo·so -sa *adj* clotty, curdly

gruñido *m* (*de cerdo*) grunt; (*de perro cuando amenaza*) growl; (*de persona*) grumble; (*de puerta*) creak; grumble, scolding

gruñir §12 *intr* (*el cerdo*) to grunt; (*el perro*) growl; (*una persona*) grumble; (*una puerta*) creak

gru·ñón -ñona *adj* grumpy, grumbly ‖ *mf* crosspatch

grupa *f* croup, rump

grupada *f* squall

grupal *adj* group

grupo *m* group; (mach & elec) unit

grupúsculo *m* splinter group

gruta *f* grotto

grutes·co -ca *adj* & *m* (fa) grotesque

Gruyère *m* Swiss cheese

gte. *abbr* **gerente**

guaca *f* (Bol, Peru) Indian tomb; hidden treasure

guacal *m* crate

guacama·yo -ya *adj* (P-R) flashy, sporty ‖ *m* macaw

guachapear *tr* to splash with the feet; bungle, botch ‖ *intr* to clank, clatter

guachinan·go -ga *adj* flattering, sly ‖ *mf* (disparaging term used by Cubans) Mexican

gua·cho -cha *adj* (SAm) homeless, orphan; (SAm) odd, unmatched

guadal *m* bog, swamp; sand hill, dune

Guadalupe *f* Gaudeloupe

guadama·cí *m* (*pl* **-cíes**) embossed leather

guadaña *f* scythe

guadañadora *f* mowing machine

guadañar *tr* to cut with a scythe

guadarnés *m* harness room; harness man

guagua *f* trifle; (SAm) baby; (W-I) bus; (Col) paca

guagüita *f* (Cuba, P-R) station wagon

guajada *f* (Mex) nonsense, folly

guaje *adj* (Hond, Mex) foolish, stupid ‖ *m* (Hond, Mex) calabash, gourd; (CAm) piece of junk

guaji·ro -ra *mf* (W-I) peasant, yokel

guajolote *m* turkey; (Mex) simpleton

gualda *f* (bot) weld, dyer's rocket

gual·do -da *adj* yellow ‖ *f* see **gualda**

gualdrapa *f* housing, trappings; dirty rag hanging from clothes

gualdrapear *tr* to line up head to tail ‖ *intr* (*las velas*) to flap

Gualterio *m* Walter

guanaco *m* (SAm) dope, simpleton; (SAm) tall lanky fellow; (zool) guanaco

guanajo *m* turkey; (W-I) boob, dunce

guano *m* palm tree; bird manure

guante *m* glove; **arrojar el guante** to throw down the gauntlet; **echar un guante** to pass the hat; **guantes** tip, fee; **recoger el guante** to take up the gauntlet; **salvo el guante** excuse my glove

guantelete *m* gauntlet

guantería *f* glove shop

guantón *m* box on the ear

guapear *intr* to bluster, swagger; dress to kill

guape·tón -tona *adj* handsome; flashy, sporty; bold, fearless ‖ *m* bully, tough

guapeza *f* good looks; flashiness, sportiness; (coll) boldness, daring; bravado

gua·po -pa *adj* handsome, good-looking; flashy, sporty; bold, daring ‖ *m* (*hombre pendenciero*) bully; gallant, lady's man

guapura *f* good looks

guarache *m* (Mex) leather sandal; (Mex) tire patch

guarapo *m* sugar-cane juice; fermented juice of sugar cane

guarda *mf* guard, custodian ‖ *m* (Arg) trolley-car conductor; **guarda de la aduana** customhouse officer; **guarda forestal** forest ranger ‖ *f* guard, custody; (*de la ley*) observance; (*de la espada*) guard; (*de la cerradura*) ward; (bb) flyleaf

guardabarrera *mf* (rr) gatekeeper

guardaba·rros *m* (*pl* **-rros**) fender, mudguard, dashboard

guardabosque *m* gamekeeper; forest ranger; shortstop

guardabrisa *m* windshield; (naut) glass candle shade

guardacantón *m* spur stone

guardacarril *m* (rr) railguard

guardacar·tas *m* (*pl* **-tas**) letter file

guardaco·ches *m* (*pl* **-ches**) car watcher

guardacos·tas *m* (*pl* **-tas**) revenue cutter, coast guard cutter; **guardacostas** *mpl* (*servicio*) coast guard

guarda·dor -dora *adj* guarding, protecting; mindful, observant; stingy ‖ *m* guardian, keeper; observer

guardaespal·das *m* (*pl* **-das**) bodyguard

guardafango *m* fender, mudguard

guardafre·nos *m* (*pl* **-nos**) (rr) brakeman, flagman

guardafuego *m* fender, fireguard

guardagu·jas *m* (*pl* **-jas**) (rr) switchman

guardajo•yas *m* (*pl* **-yas**) jewel case
guardalado *m* railing, parapet
guardalmacén *m* warehouseman; (Cuba) country station master
guardamalleta *f* valance
guardameta *m* goalkeeper
guardamue•bles *m* (*pl* **-bles**) warehouse, furniture warehouse
guardanieve *m* snowshed
guardapelo *m* locket
guardapolvo *m* (*sobretodo ligero*) duster; (*resguardo para preservar del polvo*) cover, cloth; (*del reloj*) inner lid; (*sobre una puerta o ventana*) hood
guardapuerta *f* storm door
guardar *tr* to guard; watch over; protect; put away; show, observe; save, e.g., **¡Dios guarde a la Reina!** God save the Queen ‖ *intr* to keep, save; **¡guarda!** look out!, watch out! ‖ *ref* to be on one's guard; **guardarse de** to look out for, watch out for, guard against
guardarraya *f* (CAm, W-I) boundary line, property line
guardarropa *mf* keeper of the wardrobe ‖ *m* (*armario donde se guarda la ropa*) wardrobe; (*local destinado a la custodia de ropa en establecimientos públicos*) checkroom, cloakroom; check boy ‖ *f* check girl, hat girl
guardarropía *f* (theat) wardrobe
guardasilla *f* chair rail
guardaventana *f* storm window
guardavía *m* (rr) trackwalker, lineman
guardavida *m* lifeguard
guardavien•tos *m* (*pl* **-tos**) (*abrigo contra los vientos*) windbreak; (*mitra de chimenea*) chimney pot
guardavivo *m* bead, corner bead
guardería *f* guard, guardship; **guardería infantil** day nursery
guardesa *f* woman guard
guardia *m* guard, guardsman; **guardia civil** rural policeman; **guardia marina** midshipman, middy; **guardia urbano** policeman ‖ *f* (*cuerpo de hombres armados; manera de defenderse en la esgrima*) guard; (naut) watch; **de guardia** on duty; on guard; **guardia civil** rural police; **guardia de asalto** shock troops; **guardia de corps** (mil) bodyguard; **guardia de cuartillo** (naut) dogwatch; **guardia suiza** Swiss Guards
guar•dián -diana *mf* guardian ‖ *m* watchman
guardilla *f* attic; attic room
guardo•so -sa *adj* careful, neat, tidy; (*que ahorra mucho*) thrifty; (*mezquino*) stingy
guarecer §22 *tr* to take in, give shelter to; keep, preserve; (*a un enfermo*) treat ‖ *ref* to take refuge, take shelter
guarida *f* den, lair; shelter; haunt, hangout, hide-out
guarismo *m* cipher, figure

guarnecer §22 *tr* to trim, adorn; equip, provide; bind, edge; (*joyas*) set; stucco, plaster; (*frenos*) line; (*un cojinete*) bush; (*una plaza fuerte*) man, garrison; (culin) garnish
guarnición *f* trimming; equipping; binding, edging; (*de joyas*) setting; stuccoing, plastering; (*de la espada*) guard; (*de frenos*) lining; (*del émbolo*) packing; (*tropa que guarnece un lugar*) garrison; (culin) garnish; **guarniciones** fixtures, fittings; (*de la caballería*) harness
guarnicionar *tr* to garrison
guarnicionero *m* harness maker
guaro *m* (CAm) sugar-cane liquor
gua•rro -rra *mf* hog
guasa *f* heaviness, churlishness; joking, kidding
guasca *f* rawhide; whip; **dar guasca a** to whip, thrash
guasería *f* (SAm) coarseness, crudity; (Chile) timidity
gua•so -sa *adj* (SAm) coarse, crude, uncouth ‖ *mf* (Chile) peasant ‖ *f* see **guasa**
gua•són -sona *adj* heavy, churlish; funny, comical ‖ *mf* dullard, churl; joker, kidder
guata *f* wadding, padding; (Arg, Chile, Peru) belly, paunch; (*de una pared*) (Chile) bulging, warping; (Ecuad) boon companion; **echar guata** (Chile) to prosper
guatemalte•co -ca *adj* & *mf* Guatemalan
guáter *m* toilet, water closet
guau *m* (*ladrido del perro*) bowwow; (bot) woodbine, Virginia creeper; **guau guau** (*perro*) bowwow ‖ *interj* bowwow!
guay *interj* — **¡guay de mí!** (poet) woe is me!
guayaba *f* guava, guava apple
guayabo *m* guava tree; lie, trick
guayaco *m* lignum vitae
Guayana *f* Guyana
gubernamental *adj* governmental; (*defensor*) strong-government
gubernati•vo -va *adj* governmental
gubia *f* gouge
guedeja *f* shock of hair; lion's mane
guerra *f* war, warfare; billiards; **Gran guerra** Great War; **guerra a muerte** war to the death; **guerra bacteriana** or **bacteriológica** germ warfare; **guerra de guerrillas** guerrilla warfare; **guerra de las dos Rosas** War of the Roses; **guerra de los Cien Años** Hundred Years' War; **guerra del Transvaal** Boer War; **guerra de ondas** radio jamming; **guerra de Troya** Trojan War; **guerra fría** cold war; **Guerra Mundial** World War; **guerra nuclear** nuclear war; **guerra relámpago** blitzkrieg; **hacer la guerra** to wage war
guerrea•dor -dora *adj* warring ‖ *mf* warrior
guerrear *intr* to war, wage war, fight; struggle, resist
guerre•ro -ra *adj* war, warlike; warring; mischievous ‖ *mf* fighter ‖ *m* warrior, soldier, fighting man ‖ *f* tight-fitting military jacket

guerrilla *f* band of skirmishers; guerrilla band; guerrilla warfare
guerrillear *intr* to skirmish; wage guerrilla warfare
guerrillero *m* guerrilla
guía *mf* guide, leader; adviser ‖ *m* (mil) guide ‖ *f* guide; guidance; directory; (*del viajero*) guidebook; (*caballo*) leader; (*de la bicicleta*) handle bar; (*del bigote*) turned-up end; (*de la sierra*) fence; marker; shoot, sprout; (mach) guide; (rr) timetable; **guías** reins; **guía sonora** sound track; **guía telefónica** telephone directory; **guía turística** tourist guide
guiadera *f* (mach) guide
guiar §77 *tr* to guide, lead; (*un automóvil*) steer, drive; pilot; (*una planta, una vid*) train ‖ *intr* to shoot, sprout ‖ *ref* — **guiarse por** to be guided by, go by
guija *f* pebble; grass pea
guijarro *m* cobble, cobblestone
guije•ño -ña *adj* pebbly; hard-hearted
guijo *m* gravel
guijo•so -sa *adj* gravelly; pebbly
güila *f* (Mex) prostitute
guillame *m* rabbet plane
Guillermo *m* William
guillotina *f* guillotine; paper cutter
guillotinar *tr* to guillotine
guimbalete *m* pump handle
guinche *m* or **güinche** *m* (mach) crane
guinda *f* sour cherry
guindal *m* sour cherry tree
guindaleza *f* (naut) hawser
guindar *tr* to hoist, raise; win; (*ahorcar*) hang, string up
guindilla *m* policeman, cop; Guinea pepper
guindo *m* sour cherry tree
guindola *f* (naut) boatswain's chair; (naut) life buoy
guinea *f* (*moneda*) guinea
guineo *m* small banana
guinga *f* gingham
guiña *f* (Col, Ven) bad luck
guiñada *f* wink; (naut) yaw
guiñapo *m* rag, tatter; ragamuffin
guiñar *tr* (*el ojo*) to wink ‖ *intr* to wink; (naut) to yaw ‖ *ref* to wink at each other
guiño *m* wink; **hacer guiños a** to make eyes at; **hacerse guiños a** to make faces at each other
guión *m* banner, standard; cross (*carried before prelate in procession*); (*signo ortográfico*) hyphen; (*signo ortográfico largo*)

dash; (mil) guidon; (mov & theat) scenario; (rad & telv) script; (mus) repeat sign; **guión de montaje** (mov) cutter's script; **guión de rodaje** (mov) shooting script
guionista *mf* (mov) scenarist; (mov) scriptwriter; (mov) subtitle writer
guirigay *m* gibberish; confusion, hubbub
guirindola *f* frill, jabot
guirlache *m* almond brittle, peanut brittle
guirnalda *f* garland, wreath
guisa *f* way, manner, wise; **a guisa de** in the manner of, like
guisado *m* stew, meat stew
guisante *m* pea; **guisante de olor** sweet pea
guisar *tr* to cook; stew; arrange, prepare ‖ *intr* to cook
guiso *m* dish
guisote *m* hash
guita *f* twine; (coll) dough, money
guitarra *f* guitar
guitarrista *mf* guitarist
gui•tón -tona *mf* tramp, bum
gula *f* gluttony; gorging, guzzling
gulo•so -sa *adj* gluttonous; guzzling
gumía *f* Moorish poniard
gurrumi•no -na *adj* weak, puny ‖ *m* henpecked husband ‖ *f* uxoriousness
gusanear *intr* to swarm
gusanera *f* nest of worms; ruling passion
gusanien•to -ta *adj* wormy, grubby
gusanillo *m* small worm; twist stitch; (*de la barrena*) spur; **matar el gusanillo** to take a shot of liquor before breakfast
gusano *m* worm; **gusano de luz** glowworm; **gusano de seda** silk worm; **gusano de tierra** earthworm
gusano•so -sa *adj* wormy, grubby
gusarapo *m* waterworm, vinegar worm
gustación *f* tasting; taste
gustar *tr* to taste; try, sample; please, be pleasing to; like, e.g., **me gustan estas peras** I like these pears ‖ *intr* to like e.g., **como Vd. guste** as you like; **gustar de** to like; like to
gustillo *m* slight taste, touch
gusto *m* taste; flavor; liking; caprice, whim; pleasure; **a gusto** as you like it; **con mucho gusto** with pleasure, gladly; **encontrarse a gusto** or **estar a gusto** to like it (*e.g., in the country*); **tanto gusto** so glad to meet you
gusto•so -sa *adj* tasty; agreeable, pleasant; ready, willing, glad
gutapercha *f* gutta-percha
gutural *adj* guttural

gu
ha

H

H, h (hache) *f* ninth letter of the Spanish alphabet
haba *f* bean, broad bean; (*simiente del café y*

el cacao) bean; **ser habas contadas** to be a sure thing
Habana, La Havana

haber *m* salary, wages; credit, credit side; **haberes** property, wealth ‖ *v* §38 *tr* to have; get, get hold of ‖ *v aux* to have, e.g., **lo he visto a menudo** I have seen it often; **haber de** + *inf* to be to + *inf*, e.g., **ha de llegar a mediodía** he is to arrive at noon ‖ *v impers* there to be, e.g., **ha habido tres personas allí** there were three people there; **haber que** + *inf* to be necessary to + *inf*; **no hay de qué** you're welcome, don't mention it ‖ *ref* to behave oneself; **habérselas con** to deal with; to have it out with

habichuela *f* kidney bean; **habichuela verde** string bean

hábil *adj* skillful, capable; (*día*) work

habilidad *f* skill, ability, capability; (*lo que se ejecuta con gracia*) feat; (*enredo, embuste*) scheme, trick

habilido-so -sa *adj* skillful

habilitación *f* qualification; backing, financing; equipping, outfitting; **habilitaciones** fixtures

habilitar *tr* to qualify; back, finance; equip, fit out; (*en un examen*) pass

habitabilidad *f* habitability; (aut) interior (space)

habitable *adj* inhabitable

habitación *f* habitation; (*edificio donde se habita*) house, home, dwelling; (*aposento de la casa o el hotel*) room; (*donde vive una especie vegetal o animal*) habitat

habitante *mf* (*de una casa*) dweller, occupant; (*de una población*) inhabitant

habitar *tr* to inhabit, live in; (*una casa, un piso*) occupy ‖ *intr* to live

hábito *m* garment, dress; habit, custom; **ahorcar los hábitos** to doff the cassock, to leave the priesthood; to change jobs; **el hábito no hace al monje** clothes don't make the man

habitua-do -da *mf* habitué

habitual *adj* habitual; regular, usual

habituar §21 *tr* to accustom ‖ *ref* to become accustomed

habitud *f* relationship, connection; custom, habit

habla *f* speech; **al habla** speaking

hablada *f* talk, talking

habla-dor -dora *adj* talkative; gossipy ‖ *mf* talker, chatterbox; gossip

habladuría *f* cut, sarcasm; **andar con habladurías** to go around gossiping

hablante *adj* speaking ‖ *mf* speaker

hablar *tr* (*una lengua*) to speak, talk; (*disparates*) talk ‖ *intr* to speak, talk; **es hablar por demás** it's wasted talk; **estar hablando** (*una pintura, una estatua*) to be almost alive; **hablar claro** to talk straight from the shoulder

hablilla *f* story, piece of gossip

hablista *mf* speaker, good speaker

hacede-ro -ra *adj* feasible, practicable

hacenda-do -da *adj* landed, property-owning ‖ *mf* landholder, property owner; cattle rancher; plantation owner

hacendar §2 *tr* (*el dominio de bienes raíces*) to pass on ‖ *ref* to buy property in order to settle down

hacende-ro -ra *adj* thrifty

hacendista *m* economist, fiscal expert; man of independent means

hacendo-so -sa *adj* hard-working, thrifty

hacer §39 *tr* (*crear, producir, formar*) to make; (*ejecutar, llevar a cabo*) do; (*un baúl*) pack; (*un papel*) play; (*un mandato*) give; (*un drama*) act, perform; pretend to be; (*una pregunta*) ask; **hace** ago, e.g., **hace un mes** a month ago; **hacer** + *inf* to have + *inf*, e.g., **le hice tomar un libro en la biblioteca** I had him get a book at the library; to make + *inf*, e.g., **el médico me hizo guardar cama** the doctor made me stay in bed; to have + *pp*, e.g., **hará construir una casa** he will have a house built; **hacer . . . que** to be . . . since, e.g., **hace un año que yo estuve aquí** it is a year since I was here; to be for. . . , e.g., **hace un año que estoy aquí** I have been here for a year; for expressions like **hacer frío** to be cold, see the noun ‖ *intr* to act; **hacer a** to fit; **hacer al caso** (coll) to be to the purpose; **hacer como que** + *ind* to pretend to + *inf*; **hacer de** to act as, work as; **hacer por** to try to ‖ *ref* to become, get to be, grow; **hacerse a** to become accustomed to; **hacerse a un lado** to step aside; **hacerse con** to make off with; **hacerse chiquito** to sing small; **hacérsele a uno difícil** to strike one as difficult; **hacerse viejo** to grow old; kill time

hacia *prep* toward; (*cierta hora o época*) about, near; **hacia abajo** downward; **hacia adelante** forward; **hacia arriba** upward; **hacia atrás** backward; the wrong way; **hacia dentro** inward; **hacia fuera** outward

hacienda *f* farmstead, landed estate, country property; property, possessions; ranch; (Arg) cattle, livestock; **hacienda pública** public finance, federal income; **haciendas** household chores

hacina *f* pile, heap; shock, stack

hacinar *tr* to pile, heap, stack

hacha *f* axe; (*hacha pequeña*) hatchet; torch, firebrand; four-wick wax candle; **hacha de armas** battleaxe

hachazo *m* blow with an axe

hachear *tr & intr* to hew, hack, or chop with an axe

hachero *m* torchbearer; (*candelero*) torch stand; (*leñador*) woodcutter

hachich *m* or **hachís** *m* hashish

hacho *m* torch; (*sitio elevado cerca de la costa*) beacon, beacon hill

hada *f* fairy; (*mujer que encanta por su belleza, gracia, etc.*) charmer; **hada madrina** fairy godmother

hadar *tr* (*determinar el hado*) to predestine, foreordain; (*pronosticar*) to foretell; (*encantar*) to charm, cast a spell on

hado *m* fate, destiny

haiga *m* (slang) flashy auto; (slang) sport

halagar §44 *tr* (*lisonjear*) to flatter; (*demostrar cariño a*) cajole, fawn on; (*agradar*) gratify, please

halago *m* flattery; cajolery; gratification; **halagos** flattery, blandishments

halagüe•ño -ña *adj* flattering; fawning; gratifying, pleasing; bright, rosy, promising

halar *tr* (naut) to haul, pull

halcón *m* falcon

halconear *intr* (*la mujer*) to chase after men

halconería *f* falconry

halconero *m* falconer

halda *f* skirt; **poner haldas en cinta** to pull up one's skirts to run; roll up one's sleeves

halieto *m* fish hawk, osprey

hálito *m* breath; vapor; (poet) gentle breeze

halitosis *f* halitosis

halo *m* halo

haló *interj* (*teléfono*) hello!

halógeno *m* halogen

halterio *m* dumbbell

halterofilia *f* weight lifting

halterofilista *mf* weight lifter

haluro *m* halide

hallar *tr* to find; (*averiguar*) find out, discover || *ref* to find oneself; to be; **hallarse bien con** to be satisfied with; **hallárselo todo hecho** to never have to turn a hand; **no hallarse** to feel uncomfortable, not like it

hallazgo *m* (*cosa hallada*) find; (*acción de hallar*) finding, discovery; (*premio al que ha hallado una cosa perdida*) reward, finder's reward, e.g., **diez dólares de hallazgo** ten dollars reward

hallulla *f* bread baked on embers or hot stones; (Chile) fine bread

hamaca *f* hammock

hamamelina *f* witch hazel

hambre *f* hunger; (*escasez general de comestibles*) famine; **matar de hambre** to starve to death; **morir de hambre** to starve to death, die of starvation; **pasar hambre** to go hungry; **tener hambre** to be hungry

hambrear *tr & intr* to starve, famish

hambrien•to -ta *adj* hungry, starving

hambruna *f* (SAm) mad hunger; (Ecuad) starvation

hamburguesa *f* hamburger sandwich

hamo *m* fishhook

hampa *f* underworld life; denizens of the underworld

hampes•co -ca *adj* underworld

hampón *m* bully, tough

hangar *m* (aer) hangar

hara•gán -gana *adj* idling, loafing, lazy || *mf* idler, loafer

haraganear *intr* to idle, loaf, hang around

harapien•to -ta *adj* ragged, tattered

harapo *m* rag, tatter; **andar** or **estar hecho un harapo** (coll) to go around in rags

harapo•so -sa *adj* ragged, tattered

harén *m* harem

harina *f* (*especialmente del trigo*) flour; (*de cualquier grano*) meal; **estar metido en harina** to be deeply absorbed; to be fat and heavy; **harina de avena** oatmeal; **harina**

de maíz corn meal; **ser harina de otro costal** to be a horse of another color

harine•ro -ra *adj* flour || *m* flour dealer; flour bin

harino•so -sa *adj* floury, mealy

harnear *tr* (Col, Chile) to sift

harnero *m* sieve

ha•rón -rona *adj* lazy || *mf* lazy loafer

harpillera *f* burlap, sackcloth

hartar *tr* to stuff, cram; satisfy, satiate; tire, bore; overwhelm, deluge || *intr* to have one's fill || *ref* to stuff; be satiated; tire, be bored

hartazgo *m* or **hartazón** *m* fill, bellyful; **darse un hartazgo** to eat one's fill; **darse un hartazgo de** to have or to get one's fill of

har•to -ta *adj* full, fed up; very much; **harto de** full of, fed up with, sick of || **harto** *adv* enough; very, quite

hartura *f* fill, satiety; full satisfaction; abundance

hasta *adv* even || *prep* until, till; to, as far as; down to, up to; as much as; **hasta ahora** up till now; **hasta aquí** so far; **hasta después** so long, good-by; **hasta la vista** or **hasta luego** so long, good-by; **hasta mañana** see you tomorrow; **hasta más no poder** to the utmost; **hasta no más** to the utmost; **hasta que** until, till

hastial *m* gable end; (*hombrón rústico*) bumpkin

hastiar §77 *tr* to surfeit, sicken, cloy; (*fastidiar*) bother, annoy, bore

hastío *m* surfeit, loathing, disgust; bother, annoyance, boredom

hataca *f* large wooden ladle; (*cilindro para extender la masa*) rolling pin

hatajo *m* small herd, small flock; (*p.ej., de disparates*) lot, flock

hato *m* (*de ganado vacuno*) herd; (*de ovejas*) flock; (*de ropa*) pack, bundle; (*de gente*) clique, ring; (*de gente malvada*) gang; everyday outfit; (*de disparates*) flock, lot; cattle ranch; **liar el hato** to pack up, pack one's baggage; **revolver el hato** to stir up trouble

haya *f* beech tree; (*madera*) beech || **La Haya** The Hague

hayaca *f* (Ven) mince pie

hayo *m* (Col) coca; (Col) coca leaves (*mixed for chewing*)

hayuco *m* beechnut, mast

haz *m* (*pl* **haces**) bunch, bundle; (*de leña*) fagot; (*de mieses*) sheaf; (*de rayos*) beam, pencil; (*de soldados*) file || *f* (*pl* **haces**) face; (*de la tierra*) surface; (*de paño o tela*) right side; (*de un edificio*) façade, front; **a sobre haz** on the surface; **ser de dos haces** to be two-faced

hazaña *f* feat, exploit, deed

hazañería *f* fuss

hazañe•ro -ra *adj* fussy

hazaño•so -sa *adj* gallant, courageous

hazmerreír *m* laughingstock, butt

he *adv* behold, lo and behold; **he aquí** here is, here are; **he allí** there is, there are

ha
he

hebilla *f* buckle

hebra *f* thread; fiber; (*en la madera*) grain;. (*del discurso*) (fig) thread; **de una hebra** (Chile) all at once; **pegar la hebra** to strike up a conversation; to keep on talking

hebre•o -a *adj* & *mf* Hebrew || *m* (*idioma*) Hebrew

hebro•so -sa *adj* fibrous, stringy

hecatombe *f* hecatomb

hechicera *f* witch, sorceress; (*mujer que por su belleza cautiva*) enchantress

hechicería *f* witchcraft, sorcery, wizardry; (fig) fascination, charm

hechice•ro -ra *adj* bewitching, charming, enchanting; magic || *mf* sorcerer, magician; charmer, enchanter || *m* wizard, sorcerer || *f* see **hechicera**

hechizar §60 *tr* to bewitch, cast a spell on; (fig) to bewitch, charm, enchant || *intr* to practice sorcery; (fig) to be charming, enchant

hechi•zo -za *adj* fake, artificial; (*de quita y pon*) detachable; made, manufactured; (*producto*) local, home || *m* spell, charm; magic, sorcery; (fig) magic, sorcery, glamour; (fig) charmer; **hechizos** (*de una mujer*) charms

he•cho -cha *adj* accustomed; finished; turned into; (*traje*) ready-made; (*llegado a la edad adulta*) full-grown || *m* act, deed; fact; event; (*hazaña*) feat; **de hecho** in fact; **en hecho de verdad** as a matter of fact; **estar en el hecho de** to catch on to; **hecho consumado** fait accompli || **hecho** *interj* all right!, OK!

hechura *f* form, shape, cut, build; creation, creature; workmanship; (Chile) drink, treat; **hechuras** cost of making; **no tener hechura** to be impracticable

heder §51 *tr* to bore, annoy, tire || *intr* to stink, reek

hediondez *f* stench, stink

hedion•do -da *adj* stinking, smelly; annoying, boring; obscene, filthy, dirty || *m* bean trefoil; skunk

hedor *m* stench, stink

helada *f* freezing; (*escarcha*) frost; **helada blanca** hoarfrost

heladera *f* refrigerator; (Chile) ice-cream tray

heladería *f* ice-cream parlor

hela•do -da *adj* cold, icy; (*pasmado por el miedo, la sorpresa, etc.*) frozen; (*esquivo, indiferente*) cold, chilly; (*cubierto de azúcar*) (Ven) iced || *m* cold drink; (*manjar*) water ice; (*sorbete*) ice cream; **helado al corte** brick ice cream || *f* see **helada**

hela•dor -dora *adj* freezing || *f* ice-cream freezer

helar §2 *tr* to freeze; harden, congeal; dumbfound; discourage || *intr* to freeze || *ref* to freeze; harden, congeal, set; (*cubrirse de hielo*) to ice

helecho *m* fern

heléni•co -ca *adj* Hellenic

hele•no -na *adj* Hellenic || *mf* Hellene

helero *m* glacier

hélice *f* helix; (*de un buque*) screw, propeller; (*de un avión*) propeller

helicóptero *m* helicopter

helio *m* helium

heliotropo *m* heliotrope

helipuerto *m* heliport

hematíe *m* red cell

hembra *adj invar* (*animal, planta, herramienta*) female; weak, thin, delicate || *f* female; (*del corchete*) eye; (*tuerca*) nut; **hembra de terraja** (mach) die

hembraje *m* (SAm) females of a flock or herd

hembrilla *f* (mach) female part or piece; (*armella*) eyebolt

hemeroteca *f* periodical library

hemiciclo *m* (*semicírculo*) hemicycle; (*gradería semicircular*) amphitheater; (*espacio central del salón de sesiones de las Cortes*) floor

hemisferio *m* hemisphere

hemistiquio *m* hemistich

hemofilia *f* hemophilia

hemoglobina *f* hemoglobin

hemorragia *f* hemorrhage

hemorroides *fpl* hemorrhoids

hemóstato *m* hemostat

henal *m* hayloft

henar *m* hayfield

henchir §50 *tr* to fill; (*un colchón*) stuff; (*a una persona, p.ej., de favores*) heap, shower || *ref* to be filled; stuff, stuff oneself

hendedura *f* crack, split, cleft

hender §51 *tr* to crack, split, cleave; (*el aire, las ondas*) cleave; make one's way through || *ref* to crack, split

hendidura *f* crack, split, cleft

henil *m* hayloft, haymow

henna *f* henna

heno *m* hay

heñir §72 *tr* to knead; **hay mucho que heñir** there's still a lot of work to do

heraldía *f* heraldry

heráldi•co -ca *adj* heraldic || *f* heraldry

heraldo *m* herald

herbáce•o -a *adj* herbaceous

herbajar *tr* & *intr* to graze

herbaje *m* herbage

herba•rio -ria *adj* herbal || *m* (*libro*) herbal; (*colección*) herbarium

herbicida *m* weed killer

herbo•so -sa *adj* grassy

hercúle•o -a *adj* herculean

heredad *f* country estate

heredar *tr* & *intr* to inherit; **heredar a** to inherit from

herede•ro -ra *mf* heir, inheritor; owner of an estate; **heredero forzoso** heir apparent || *m* heir || *f* heiress

heredita•rio -ria *adj* hereditary

hereje *mf* heretic

herejía *f* heresy; insult, outrage; outrageous price

herencia *f* heritage, inheritance; (*transmisión de caracteres biológicos*) heredity; (*patrimonio de un difunto*) estate

heréti•co -ca *adj* heretic(al)

herida *f* injury, wound; insult, outrage; **renovar la herida** to open an old sore; **tocar en la herida** to sting to the quick

heri•do -da *adj* hurt, wounded; (*ofendido*) hurt ‖ *mf* injured person, wounded person; **los heridos** the injured, the wounded ‖ *f* see **herida**

herir §68 *tr* to injure, hurt, wound; (*ofender*) hurt; (*golpear*) strike; (*el sol sobre*) beat down upon; (*un instrumento de cuerda*) play; (*la cuerda de un instrumento*) pluck; touch, move

hermana *f* sister; **hermana de leche** foster sister; **hermana política** sister-in-law; **media hermana** half sister

hermanar *tr* to match, mate; combine, join; harmonize ‖ *ref* to match; become attached as brothers or sisters or brother and sister

hermanastra *f* stepsister

hermanastro *m* stepbrother

hermandad *f* brotherhood; sisterhood; close friendship; close relationship

herma•no -na *adj* (*p.ej., idioma*) sister ‖ *mf* companion, mate ‖ *m* brother; **hermano de leche** foster brother; **hermano político** brother-in-law; **hermanos** brother and sister; brothers and sisters; **hermanos siameses** Siamese twins; **medio hermano** half brother; **primo hermano** first cousin ‖ *f* see **hermana**

herméti•co -ca *adj* hermetic(al); air-tight; impenetrable; tight-lipped

hermosear *tr* to beautify, embellish

hermo•so -sa *adj* beautiful; (*caballero*) handsome

hermosura *f* beauty; (*mujer hermosa*) belle, beauty

hernia *f* hernia

héroe *m* hero

heroi•co -ca *adj* heroic; (*remedio*) desperate

heroína *f* heroine; (*pharm*) heroin

heroinómano *m* heroin addict

heroísmo *m* heroism

herrada *f* wooden bucket

herrador *m* horseshoer

herradura *f* horseshoe; **mostrar las herraduras** (*un caballo*) to kick, be vicious; (coll) to show one's heels

herraje *m* hardware, ironwork

herramental *adj* tool ‖ *m* toolbox, tool bag

herramienta *f* tool; set of tools; (coll) teeth; (coll) horns

herrar §2 *tr* (*guarnecer con hierro*) to fit with hardware; (*un caballo*) to shoe; (*marcar con hierro candente*) to brand; (*un barril*) to hoop

herrería *f* forge, blacksmith shop; blacksmithing; ironworks; rumpus

herrero *m* blacksmith; **herrero de grueso** ironworker; **herrero de obra** steelworker

herrete *m* tip, metal tip

herretear *tr* to tip, put a metal tip on

herrín *m* rust

herón *m* (*tejo de hierro horadado*) quoit; (*arandela*) washer

herrumbre *f* rust; (*honguillo parásito*) rust, plant rot

herrumbro•so -sa *adj* rusty

herventar §2 *tr* to boil

hervidero *m* boiling; bubbling spring; (*en el pecho*) rattle; (*de gente*) swarm

hervidor *m* boiler, cooker

hervir §68 *intr* to boil; (*el mar; una persona encolerizada*) boil, seethe; swarm, teem

hervor *m* boil, boiling; (*de la juventud*) fire, restlessness; **alzar el hervor** to begin to boil

hervoro•so -sa *adj* ardent, fiery, impetuous

heterócli•to -ta *adj* irregular; unconventional

heterodinar *tr* to heterodyne

heterodi•no -na *adj* heterodyne

heterodo•xo -xa *adj* heterodox

heterogeneidad *f* heterogeneity

heterogéne•o -a *adj* heterogeneous

hexámetro *m* hexameter

hez *f* (*pl* **heces**) (fig) scum, dregs; **heces** lees, dregs; feces, excrement

hiato *m* hiatus

hibisco *m* hibiscus

hibridación *f* hybridization

hibridar *tr* & *intr* to hybridize

híbri•do -da *adj* & *m* hybrid

hidal•go -ga *adj* noble, illustrious ‖ *m* nobleman ‖ *f* noblewoman

hidalguez *f* or **hidalguía** *f* nobility

hidra *f* hydra

hidratar *tr* & *ref* to hydrate

hidrato *m* hydrate

hidráuli•co -ca *adj* hydraulic ‖ *f* hydraulics

hidroala *m* (*vehículo mixto de buque y avión*) hydrofoil

hidroaleta *f* (*miembro alar del hidroala*) hydrofoil

hidroavión *m* hydroplane

hidrocarburo *m* hydrocarbon

hidroeléctri•co -ca *adj* hydroelectric

hidrófi•lo -la *adj* (*algodón*) absorbent (*cotton*)

hidrofobia *f* hydrophobia

hidrófu•go -ga *adj* waterproof

hidrógeno *m* hydrogen

hidropesía *f* dropsy

hidróxido *m* hydroxide

hiedra *f* ivy

hiel *f* bile, gall; (fig) gall, bitterness, sorrow; **echar la hiel** to strain, overwork

hielo *m* ice; (fig) coldness, coolness; **hielo flotante** drift ice, ice pack; **hielo seco** dry ice; **romper el hielo** (*quebrantar la reserva*) to break the ice

hiena *f* hyena

hienda *f* dung

hierba *f* grass; (*especialmente la que tiene propiedades medicinales*) herb; **hierba de la plata** honesty; **hierba del asno** evening primrose; **hierba de París** truelove; **hierba gatera** catnip; **hierba pastel** woad; **hierbas** grass, pasture; herb poison; years of age (*said of animals*); **mala hierba** weed; wayward young fellow

he
hi

hierbabuena f mint

hierro m iron; (*marca candente que se pone a los ganados*) brand; **hierro colado** cast iron; **hierro colado en barras** pig iron; **hierro de desecho** scrap iron; **hierro de marcar** branding iron; **hierro dulce** wrought iron; **hierro fundido** cast iron; **hierro galvanizado** galvanized iron; **hierro ondulado** corrugated iron; **hierros** irons, fetters; **llevar hierro a Vizcaya** to carry coals to Newcastle

higa f baby's fist-shaped amulet; scorn, contempt; **dar higa** to misfire; **no dar dos higas por** to not give a rap for

hígado m liver; **echar los hígados** to strain, to overwork; **hígados** guts, courage; **malos hígados** hatred, grudge; **ser un hígado** to be a nuisance

higiene f hygiene

higiéni•co -ca adj hygienic

higo m fig; **higo chumbo** prickly pear; **higo paso** dried fig; **no valer un higo** to be not worth a continental

higuera f fig tree; **higuera chumba** prickly pear

hija f daughter; **hija política** daughter-in-law

hijas•tro -tra mf stepchild ‖ m stepson ‖ f stepdaughter

hi•jo -ja mf child; (*de un animal*) young; **hijo de bendición** legitimate child; good child; **hijo de la cuna** foundling; **hijo del amor** love child; **hijo de leche** foster child ‖ m son; **cada hijo de vecino** every man Jack, every mother's son; **hijo del agua** good sailor; good swimmer; **hijo de su padre** chip off the old block; **hijo de sus propias obras** self-made man; **hijo político** son-in-law; **hijos** children; descendants ‖ f see **hija**

hijodalgo m (*pl* **hijosdalgo**) nobleman

hijuela f little girl, little daughter; (*tira de tela*) gore; branch drain; side path

hijuelero m rural postman

hijuelo m shoot, sucker

hila f row, line; (*acción de hilar*) spinning; **a la hila** in single file; **hilas** (*hebras para curar heridas*) lint

hilacha f shred, fraying; **hilacha de acero** steel wool; **hilacha de algodón** cotton waste; **hilacha de vidrio** spun glass; **hilachas** lint; **mostrar la hilacha** (Arg) to show one's worst side

hilachen•to -ta adj tattered; in rags

hilachos mpl (Mex) rags, tatters

hilacho•so -sa adj frayed, raggedy

hilada f row, line; (mas) course

hilado m spinning; (*hilo*) yarn, thread

hila•dor -dora adj spinning ‖ mf spinner ‖ f spinning machine

hilandería f spinning; spinning mill

hilande•ro -ra adj spinning ‖ m spinning mill

hilar tr & intr to spin; **hilar delgado** to hew close to the line; **hilar largo** to drag on

hilarante adj laughable; (*gas*) laughing

hilaza f yarn, thread; lint; **descubrir la hilaza** to show one's true nature

hilera f row, line; fine thread, fine yarn; (*parhilera*) ridgepole; (mil) file

hilo m thread; (*hebras retorcidas*) yarn; (*alambre*) wire; (*de perlas*) string; (*de agua*) thin stream; (*de luz*) beam; linen, linen fabric; (*de un discurso, de la vida*) (fig) thread; **hilo bramante** twine; **hilo de la muerte** end of life; **hilo de masa** (aut) ground wire; **hilo de medianoche** midnight sharp; **hilo dental** dental floss; **hilo de tierra** (elec) ground wire; **irse al hilo** or **tras el hilo de la gente** to follow the crowd; **manejar los hilos** to pull strings; **perder el hilo de** to lose the thread of

hilván m basting, tacking; basting stitch; (Chile) basting thread; (Ven) hem; **hablar de hilván** to jabber along

hilvanar tr to baste, tack; sketch, outline; (*hacer con precipitación*) hurry; (Ven) to hem ‖ intr to baste, tack

himnario m hymnal, hymn book

himno m hymn; **himno nacional** national anthem

hin m neigh, whinny

hincadura f driving, thrusting, sticking

hincapié m stamping the foot; **hacer hincapié en** to lay great stress on, to emphasize

hincar §73 tr to drive, thrust, stick, sink; (*la rodilla*) go down on, fall on ‖ ref to kneel, kneel down; **hincarse de rodillas** to go down on one's knees

hincha mf (sport) fan, rooter ‖ f grudge, ill will

hinchable adj inflatable; (*goma de mascar*) bubble

hincha•do -da adj swollen; swollen with pride; (*estilo, lenguaje*) pompous, highflown ‖ m (*de un neumático*) inflation ‖ f (sport) fans, rooters

hinchar tr to swell; inflate; (*un neumático*) pump up; exaggerate, embroider ‖ ref to swell; swell up, become puffed up (*with pride*)

hinchazón f swelling; vanity, conceit; (*del estilo, lenguaje*) bombast

hinchismo m (sport) fans, rooters

hin•dú -dúa (*pl* **-dúes -dúas**) adj & mf Hindoo, Hindu

hiniesta f Spanish broom

hinojo m fennel; **de hinojos** on one's knees

hipar intr to hiccup; (*los perros cuando siguen la caza*) pant, snuffle; (*gimotear*) whimper; be worn out; **hipar por** to long for; long to

hiperacidez f hyperacidity

hipérbola f (geom) hyperbola

hipérbole f (rhet) hyperbole

hiperbóli•co -ca adj (geom & rhet) hyperbolic

hipersensible adj (*alérgico*) hypersensitive

hipertensión f hypertension, high blood pressure

hípica f (horseback) riding; equestrianism

hípi•co -ca adj horse, equine

hipnosis f hypnosis

hipnóti•co -ca *adj* hypnotic ‖ *mf* hypnotic ‖ *m* (*medicamento que provoca el sueño*) hypnotic

hipnotismo *m* hypnotism

hipnotista *mf* hypnotist

hipnotizar §60 *tr* to hypnotize

hipo *m* hiccup; longing, desire; **tener hipo contra** to have a grudge against; **tener hipo por** to desire eagerly

hipocondría•co -ca *adj & mf* hypochondriac

hipocresía *f* hypocrisy

hipócrita *adj* hypocritical ‖ *mf* hypocrite

hipodérmi•co -ca *adj* hypodermic

hipódromo *m* hippodrome, race track

hipopótamo *m* hippopotamus

hiposulfito *m* hyposulfite

hipoteca *f* mortgage; **¡buena hipoteca!** you may believe it, if you want to!

hipotecar §73 *tr* to mortgage

hipoteca•rio -ria *adj* mortgage

hipotenusa *f* hypotenuse

hipóte•sis *f* (*pl* -**sis**) hypothesis; **hipótesis de guía** working hypothesis

hipotéti•co -ca *adj* hypothetic(al)

hiriente *adj* cutting, stinging

hirsu•to -ta *adj* hairy, bristly; (fig) brusque, gruff

hirviente *adj* boiling

hisopear *tr* to sprinkle with holy water

hisopo *m* (bot) hyssop; aspergillum, sprinkler of holy water; paint brush, shaving brush

hispalense *adj & mf* Sevillian

hispáni•co -ca *adj & mf* Hispanic

hispanista *mf* Hispanist

hispa•no -na *adj* Spanish; Spanish American ‖ *mf* Spaniard; Spanish American

hispanohablante or **hispanoparlante** *adj* Spanish-speaking ‖ *mf* speaker of Spanish

híspi•do -da *adj* bristly, spiny

histéri•co -ca *adj* hysterical

histerismo *m* hysteria

histología *f* histology

historia *f* history; story, tale; **de historia** notorious, infamous; **dejarse de historias** to come to the point; **historia de lagrimitas** (coll) sob story; **historias** gossip, meddling; **pasar a la historia** to become a thing of the past; **picar en historia** to turn out to be serious

historia•do -da *adj* richly adorned; overadorned; (*cuadro, dibujo*) storied

historial *adj* historical ‖ *m* record, dossier

historiar §77 & regular *tr* to tell the history of; tell the story of; (*un suceso histórico*) (fa) to depict

históri•co -ca *adj* historic(al)

historieta *f* anecdote, brief story; **historieta gráfica** comic strip

histrión *m* actor; juggler, buffoon

histrióni•co -ca *adj* histrionic

hita *f* brad; landmark, milestone

hi•to -ta *adj* fixed, firm; (*casa, calle*) next; (*caballo*) black ‖ *m* (*clavo fijado en la tierra*) peg, hob; (*juego*) quoits; (*blanco*) target; (*mojón*) landmark, milestone; **dar en el hito** to hit the nail on the head; **mirar**

de hito en hito to eye up and down ‖ *f* see **hita**

Hno. *abbr* **Hermano**

hoba•chón -chona *adj* lumpish

hocicar §73 *tr* to nuzzle, root; keep on kissing ‖ *intr* to nuzzle, root; run into a snag; (*la proa*) (naut) to dip

hocico *m* snout; (*de una persona*) snout; sour face; **caer de hocicos** to fall on one's face; **meter el hocico en todo** to poke one's nose into everything; **poner hocico** to make a face

hogaño *adv* this year; at the present time

hogar *m* fireplace, hearth; furnace; home; family life; (*hoguera*) bonfire

hogare•ño -ña *adj* home-loving ‖ *mf* homebody, stay-at-home

hogaza *f* large loaf of bread

hoguera *f* bonfire

hoja *f* (*de planta, libro, mesa, muelle, puerta plegadiza, etc.; pétalo de flor*) leaf; (*de planta acuática*) pad; (*de papel*) sheet; blank sheet; (*de cuchillo, sierra, espada, etc.*) blade; (*hojuela de metal*) foil; (*de persiana*) slat; (*del patín*) runner; **doblar la hoja** to change the subject; **hoja clínica** clinical chart; **hoja de afeitar** razor blade; **hoja de embalaje** packing slip; **hoja de encuadernador** (bb) end paper; **hoja de estaño** tin foil; **hoja de estudios** transcript; **hoja de guarda** (bb) flyleaf; **hoja del anunciante** tear sheet; **hoja de lata** tin, tin plate; **hoja de nenúfar** lily pad; **hoja de paga** pay roll; **hoja de parra** fig leaf; **hoja de pedidos** order blank; **hoja de rodaje** (mov) shooting record; **hoja de ruta** waybill; **hoja de servicios** service record; **hoja de trébol** cloverleaf (*intersection*); **hoja maestra** master blade (*of spring*); **hojas del autor** (typ) advance sheets; **hoja suelta** leaflet, handbill; (bb) flyleaf; **hoja volante** leaflet, handbill

hojalata *f* tin, tin plate

hojalatería *f* tinsmith's shop; tinwork

hojalatero *m* tinsmith, tinner

hojaldre *m & f* puff paste

hojarasca *f* dead leaves; trash, rubbish; bluff, vain show

hojear *tr* to leaf through ‖ *intr* to scale off; (*las hojas de los árboles*) flutter

hojita *f* leaflet; **hojita de afeitar** razor blade

hojo•so -sa *adj* leafy

hojuela *f* (*hoja de otra compuesta*) leaflet; (*fruta de sartén*) pancake; (*hoja muy delgada de metal*) foil; **hojuela de estaño** tin foil

hola *interj* hey!, hello!

Holanda *f* Holland

holan•dés -desa *adj* Dutch; **a la holandesa** (bb) half-bound ‖ *mf* Hollander ‖ *m* Dutchman; (*idioma*) Dutch ‖ *f* Dutch woman

holga•chón -chona *adj* lazy, idle ‖ *mf* loafer, idler

holgadero *m* hangout

holga•do -da *adj* idle, unoccupied; (*vestido*) loose, full, roomy; (*que vive con bienestar*) fairly well-off

hi
ho

holganza *f* idleness, leisure; pleasure, enjoyment

holgar §63 *intr* to idle, be idle; take it easy, rest up; not fit, be too loose; be unnecessary, be of no use; be glad ‖ *ref* to be glad; be amused

holga•zán -zana *adj* idle, lazy ‖ *mf* idler, loafer

holgazanear *intr* to idle, loaf, bum around

hol•gón -gona *adj* pleasure-loving ‖ *mf* loafer, lizard

holgorio *m* fun, merriment

holgura *f* looseness, fulness; enjoyment, merriment; comfort, easy circumstances; (mach) play

holocausto *m* holocaust

hollar §61 *tr* to tread on, to trample on

hollejo *m* hull, peel, skin

hollín *m* soot

hollinar *tr* (Chile) to cover with soot

hollinien•to -ta *adj* sooty

hombracho *m* big husky fellow

hombrada *f* manly act

hombradía *f* manliness, courage

hombre *m* man; husband, man; my boy, old chap; **buen hombre** good-natured fellow; **¡hombre al agua!** or **¡hombre a la mar!** man overboard!; **hombre bueno** arbiter, referee; **hombre de bien** honorable man; **hombre de buenas prendas** man of parts; **hombre de ciencia** scientist; **hombre de dinero** man of means; **hombre de estado** statesman; **hombre de letras** man of letters; **hombre de mundo** man of the world; **hombre de suposición** man of straw; **hombre hecho** grown man ‖ *interj* man alive!, upon my word!

hombre-anuncio *m* sandwich man

hombrear *tr* (Arg) to carry on the shoulders; (Mex) to aid, back ‖ *intr* to try to be somebody; (*una mujer*) to be mannish; **hombrear con** to try to be equal

hombrecillo *m* little man; (*lúpulo*) hop

hombrera *f* (*del vestido*) shoulder; shoulder pad; epaulet

hombre-rana *m* (*pl* **hombres-ranas**) frogman

hombría *f* manliness; **hombría de bien** honor, probity

hombrillo *m* (*de la camisa*) yoke; shoulder piece

hombro *m* shoulder; **arrimar el hombro** to lend a hand, put one's shoulder to the wheel; **encoger los hombros** to let one's shoulders droop; **encogerse de hombros** to shrug one's shoulders; to crouch, to shrink with fear; to not answer; **mirar por encima del hombro** to look down upon; **salir en hombros** to be carried off on the shoulders of the crowd

hombru•no -na *adj* mannish

homenaje *m* homage; (feud) homage; (Chile) gift, favor; **homenaje de boca** lip service; **rendir homenaje a** to swear allegiance to

homeópata *mf* homeopath

homeopatía *f* homeopathy

homicida *adj* homicidal ‖ *mf* homicide

homicidio *m* homicide

homilía *f* homily

homogeneidad *f* homogeneity

homogeneizar §60 *tr* to homogenize

homogéne•o -a *adj* homogeneous

homologación *f* confirmation, ratification; (sport) validation

homologar §44 *tr* to confirm, ratify; (*un récord*) (sport) to validate

homólo•go -ga *adj* homologous ‖ *m* colleague

homóni•mo -ma *adj* homonymous; of the same name ‖ *mf* namesake ‖ *m* homonym

homosexual *adj* & *mf* homosexual; gay

homúnculo *m* guy, little runt

honda *f* sling

hondazo *m* blow with a sling

hondear *tr* (naut) to sound

hondillos *mpl* patches in the crotch of pants

hon•do -da *adj* deep; (*terreno*) low ‖ *m* bottom ‖ *f* see **honda** ‖ **hondo** *adv* deep

hondón *m* (*de la aguja*) eye; (*de un vaso*) bottom; lowland

hondonada *f* lowland, ravine

hondura *f* depth, profundity; **meterse en honduras** to go beyond one's depth

hondure•ño -ña *adj* & *mf* Honduran

honestidad *f* decency; chastity; modesty; honesty, probity; fairness, reasonableness

hones•to -ta *adj* decent; chaste, pure; modest; honest, upright; (*precio*) fair, reasonable

hongo *m* fungus, mushroom; (*sombrero*) bowler, derby

honor *m* honor; **en honor a la verdad** as a matter of fact, to tell the truth; **hacer honor a** to do honor to; (*la firma*) to honor

honorable *adj* honorable

honora•rio -ria *adj* honorary ‖ *s* fee, honorarium

honorífi•co -ca *adj* honorific

honra *f* honor; **tener a mucha honra** to be proud of

honradez *f* honesty, integrity

honra•do -da *adj* honorable

honrar *tr* to honor ‖ *ref* to feel honored

honrilla *f* — **por la negra honrilla** out of concern for what people will say

honro•so -sa *adj* honorable

hopo *m* tuft, shock (*of hair*); bushy tail; **seguir el hopo a** (coll) to keep right after

hora *f* hour; (*momento determinado para algo*) time; **a la hora** on time; **a la hora de ahora** right now; **a la hora en punto** on the hour; **a las pocas horas** within a few hours; **dar hora** to fix a time; **dar la hora** (*el reloj*) to strike; **de última hora** up-to-date; most up-to-date; (*noticias*) late; **en buen hora** or **en hora buena** safely, luckily; all right; **en mal hora** or **en hora mala** unluckily, in an evil hour; **fuera de horas** after hours; **hasta altas horas** until late into the night; **hora de acostarse** bedtime; **hora de aglomeración** rush hour; **hora de cierre** closing time; curfew; **hora de comer** mealtime; **hora deshorada** fatal hour; **hora de verano** daylight-saving time; **hora de verdad** (taur) kill; **hora legal** or

oficial standard time; **hora punta** peak hour; rush hour; **horas de afluencia** rush hour; **horas extra** overtime; **horas de consulta** office hours (*of a doctor*); **horas de ocio** leisure hours; **horas de punta** rush hour; **horas extraordinarias de trabajo** overtime

horadar *tr* to drill, bore, pierce

hora•rio -ria *adj* hour ‖ *m* hour hand; clock; (*de ferrocarriles*) timetable; **horario escolar** roster

horca *f* (*para levantar la paja*) pitchfork; (*para ahorcar a un condenado*) gallows, gibbet; (*de ajos, cebollas, etc.*) string

horcajadas — a horcajadas astride, astraddle

horcajadillas — a horcajadillas astride, astraddle

horcajadura *f* crotch

horcajo *m* (*confluencia de dos ríos*) fork; (*para mulas*) yoke

horcón *m* pitchfork; forked prop (*for fruit trees*); upright, prop

horchata *f* orgeat

horda *f* horde

horero *m* (*reloj*) hour hand

horizontal *adj* & *f* horizontal

horizonte *m* horizon

horma *f* form, mold; shoe tree; hat block; **hallar la horma de su zapato** to meet one's match

hormiga *f* ant; (*enfermedad que causa comezón*) itch

hormigón *m* concrete; **hormigón armado** reinforced concrete

hormigonera *f* concrete mixer

hormigo•so -sa *adj* antlike; full of ants; ant-eaten; (*picante*) itchy

hormiguear *intr* (*ponerse en movimiento gente o animales*) to swarm; (*experimentar una sensación de hormigas corriendo por el cuerpo*) crawl, creep; abound, teem

hormiguero *m* anthill; (*de gente*) swarm, mob

hormillón *m* hat block

hormón *m* or **hormona** *f* hormone

hornacina *f* niche

hornada *f* (*cantidad que se cuece de una vez en un horno*) batch, bake; (*conjunto de individuos de una misma promoción*) crop

hornazo *m* Easter cake filled with hard-boiled eggs; Easter gift to Lenten preacher

horne•ro -ra *mf* baker

hornilla *f* kitchen grate; pigeonhole

hornillo *m* kitchen stove; hot plate; (*de la pipa de fumar*) bowl

horno *m* oven, furnace; (*para cocer ladrillos*) kiln; **alto horno** blast furnace; **horno de cal** limekiln; **horno de fundición** smelting furnace; **horno de ladrillero** brickkiln

horóscopo *m* horoscope; **sacar un horóscopo** to cast a horoscope

horqueta *f* pitchfork; fork, prop; (*ángulo agudo en un río*) (Arg) bend

horquilla *f* pitchfork; (*de bicicleta*) fork; (*de microteléfono*) cradle; (*alfiler para sujetar el pelo*) hairpin

horrar *tr* to save

hórreo *m* granary; (in Asturias and Galicia) crib or granary raised on pillars (*to protect grain from mice and dampness*)

horrible *adj* horrible

horripilante *adj* hair-raising, blood-curdling

horror *m* horror; **tener horror a** to have a horror of

horrorizar §60 *tr* to horrify

horroro•so -sa *adj* horrid; hideous, ugly

hortaliza *f* vegetable

hortela•no -na *adj* garden ‖ *mf* gardener

hortera *m* clerk, helper ‖ *f* wooden bowl

hortícola *adj* horticultural

horticul•tor -tora *mf* horticulturist

horticultura *f* horticulture

hos•co -ca *adj* dark, dark-skinned; sullen, grim, gloomy

hospedaje *m* lodging

hospedar *tr* to lodge ‖ *ref* to lodge, stop, put up

hospedería *f* hospice; inn, hostelry

hospede•ro -ra *mf* innkeeper

hospicio *m* hospice; poorhouse; orphan asylum

hospital *m* hospital; **estar hecho un hospital** (*una persona*) to be full of aches and pains; (*una casa*) to be turned into a hospital; **hospital de la sangre** poor relations; **hospital de primera sangre** (mil) field hospital; **hospital robado** bare house

hospitala•rio -ria *adj* hospitable

hospitalidad *f* hospitality; (*estancia del enfermo en el hospital*) hospitalization

hospitalizar §60 *tr* to hospitalize

hosquedad *f* darkness; sullenness, grimness, gloominess

hostelería *f* restaurant and hotel business

hostería *f* inn, hostelry

hostia *f* sacrificial victim; wafer; (eccl) wafer, Host

hostigar §44 *tr* to scourge; harass; to pester; cloy, surfeit

hostigo•so -sa *adj* cloying, sickening

hostil *adj* hostile

hostilidad *f* hostility

hostilizar §60 *tr* to antagonize; (*al enemigo*) harry, harass

hotel *m* (*establecimiento donde se da comida y alojamiento por dinero*) hotel; (*casa particular lujosa*) mansion

hotele•ro -ra *adj* hotel ‖ *mf* hotelkeeper

hoy *adv* & *s* today; **de hoy a mañana** any time now; **de hoy en adelante** from now on; **hoy día** nowadays

hoya *f* hole, pit, ditch; (*sepultura*) grave; valley; (*almáciga*) seedbed; river basin

hoyanca *f* potter's field

hoyo *m* hole; grave; pockmark

hoyo•so -sa *adj* full of holes

hoyuelo *m* dimple; (*juego de muchachos*) pitching pennies

hoz *f* (*pl* **hoces**) sickle; narrow pass, defile; **de hoz y de coz** headlong, recklessly

hozar §60 *tr* & *intr* to nuzzle, root
hta. *abbr* **hasta**
huacal *m* var of **guacal**
huachinango *m* (Mex) red snapper
hucha *f* workingman's chest; (*alcancía*) toy bank; (*dinero ahorrado*) savings, nest egg
huchear *intr* to cry, shout
hue•co -ca *adj* hollow; (*mullido*) soft, fluffy, spongy; (*voz*) deep, resounding; vain, conceited; (*estilo, lenguaje*) affected, pompous ‖ *m* hollow; interval; (*en un muro, una hilera de coches, etc.*) opening; (*empleo sin proveer*) opening; **hueco de la axila** armpit; **hueco de escalera** stair well
huélfago *m* (vet) heaves
huelga *f* (*ocio*) rest, leisure, idleness; recreation; pleasant spot; (*cesación del trabajo en señal de protesta*) strike; (mach) play; **huelga de brazos caídos** sit-down strike; **huelga de hambre** hunger strike; **huelga general** general strike; **huelga patronal** lockout; **huelga por solidaridad** sympathy strike; **huelga sentada** sit-down strike; **ir a la huelga** or **ponerse en huelga** to go on strike
huelguista *mf* striker
huella *f* track, footprint; trace, mark; rut; (*acción de hollar*) tread, treading; (*peldaño en que se asienta el pie*) tread; **huella dactilar** or **digital** fingerprint; **huella de sonido** sound track; **seguir las huellas de** to follow in the footsteps of
huérfa•no -na *adj* orphan; orphaned; alone, deserted ‖ *mf* orphan; (Chile, Peru) foundling
hue•ro -ra *adj* rotten; (fig) empty, hollow; (Guat, Mex) blond; **salir huero** (coll) to flop, turn out bad ‖ *mf* (Guat, Mex) blond
huerta *f* vegetable garden; fruit garden; irrigated region
huerte•ro -ra *mf* (Arg, Peru) gardener
huerto *m* (*de árboles frutales*) orchard; (*de verduras*) kitchen garden
huesa *f* grave
huesear *intr* to beg (alms)
huesillo *m* (Chile, Peru) sun-dried peach
hueso *m* bone; (*de ciertas frutas*) stone, pit; drudgery; **a otro perro con ese hueso** tell that to the marines; **calarse hasta los huesos** to get soaked to the skin; **hueso de la alegría** crazy bone, funny bone; **hueso de la suerte** wishbone; **hueso duro de roer** a hard nut to crack; **la sin hueso** the tongue; **no dejarle a uno un hueso sano** to beat someone up; to pick someone to pieces; **no poder con sus huesos** to be all in; **soltar la sin hueso** to talk too much; to pour forth insults; **tener los huesos molidos** to be all fagged out
hueso•so -sa *adj* bony
hués•ped -peda *mf* (*persona alojada en casa ajena*) guest; (*persona que hospeda a otra en su casa*) host; (*mesonero*) innkeeper, host
hueste *f* followers; (*ejército*) army, host
huesu•do -da *adj* bony, big-boned
hueva *f* roe, fish roe

hueve•ro -ra *mf* egg dealer ‖ *f* eggcup; oviduct
huevo *m* egg; **huevo a la plancha** fried egg; **huevo al plato** shirred egg; **huevo del té** tea ball; **huevo de zurcir** darning egg or gourd; **huevo duro** hard-boiled egg; **huevo escalfado** poached egg; **huevo estrellado** or **frito** fried egg; **huevo pasado por agua** soft-boiled egg; **huevos revueltos** scrambled eggs
huída *f* flight; (*de un líquido*) leak; (*ensanche en un agujero*) flare, splay; (*de caballo*) shying
huidi•zo -za *adj* fugitive; evasive
huincha *f* (SAm) tape; (SAm) tape measure
huipil *m* (Mex) colorful poncho worn by Indian women
huir §20 *tr* to flee, avoid, shun; (*el cuerpo*) duck ‖ *intr* to flee; (*el tiempo*) fly; (*de la memoria*) to slip ‖ *ref* to flee
hule *m* (*tela impermeable*) oilcloth; rubber; (taur) blood, goring
hulear *intr* (CAm) to gather rubber
hulla *f* coal; **hulla azul** tide power; wind power; **hulla blanca** white power; water power
hullera *f* colliery, coal mine
humanidad *f* humanity; fatness
humanista *adj* & *mf* humanist
humanita•rio -ria *adj* & *mf* humanitarian
huma•no -na *adj* (*perteneciente al hombre*) human; (*compasivo, misericordioso; civilizador*) humane
humareda *f* cloud of smoke
humeante *adj* smoking, smoky; steamy, reeking
humear *tr* (SAm) to fumigate ‖ *intr* to smoke; steam, reek; put on airs; (*reliquias de un alboroto, enemistad, etc.*) last, persist
humectador *m* humidifier
humedad *f* humidity, dampness, moisture
humedecer §22 *tr* to humidify, dampen, moisten, wet
húme•do -da *adj* humid, damp, moist
humero *m* smokestack, chimney
húmero *m* humerus
humidificador *m* air humidifier
humildad *f* humility
humilde *adj* humble
humilladero *m* calvary, road shrine; priedieu
humillante *adj* humiliating
humillar *tr* (*abatir el orgullo de*) to humble; (*avergonzar*) humiliate; (*la cabeza*) bow; (*el cuerpo, las rodillas*) bend ‖ *ref* to humble oneself; cringe, grovel
humo *m* smoke; steam, fume; **a humo de pajas** lightly, thoughtlessly; **bajar los humos a** (coll) to humble, take down a peg; **echar más humo que una chimenea** to smoke like a chimney; **humos** airs, conceit; hearths, homes; **irse todo en humo** to go up in smoke; **tragar el humo** to inhale; **vender humos** to peddle influence

humor *m* humor; **de mal humor** out of humor; **estar de humor para** to be in the humor for; **seguir el humor a** to humor
humorismo *m* humor, humorousness
humorista *mf* humorist
humorísti•co -ca *adj* humorous
humo•so -sa *adj* smoky
hundible *adj* sinkable
hundir *tr* to sink; plunge; (*abrumar*) overwhelm; confound, confute; destroy, ruin ‖ *ref* to sink; collapse; settle, cave in; come to ruin; disappear, vanish
húnga•ro -ra *adj & mf* Hungarian ‖ *m* (*idioma*) Hungarian
Hungría *f* Hungary
hupe *m* punk
huracán *m* hurricane
huraña *f* shyness, unsociability
hura•ño -ña *adj* shy, unsociable
hurgar §44 *tr* to poke; (fig) to stir up, incite; **peor es hurgallo** (i.e., **hurgarlo**) better keep hands off ‖ *intr* to poke ‖ *ref* (*la nariz*) to pick
hurgón *m* poker; thrust, stab
hurgonazo *m* (*con hurgón*) poke; jab, stab, thrust
hurgonear *tr* to poke; to jab, to stab at
hurgonero *m* poker

hu•rón -rona *adj* shy, diffident ‖ *mf* prier, snooper; shy person, diffident person ‖ *m* ferret
huronear *tr* to ferret, hunt with a ferret; to ferret out
huronera *f* ferret hole; lair, hiding place
hurtadillas — **a hurtadillas** by stealth, on the sly; **a hurtadillas de** unbeknown to
hurtar *tr* to steal; (*en pesos y medidas*) cheat; (*el suelo*) wear away; plagiarize; **hurtar el cuerpo** to dodge, duck ‖ *ref* to withdraw, hide
hurto *m* thieving; theft; **a hurto** stealthily, on the sly; **coger con el hurto en las manos** to catch with the goods; **hurto mayor** grand larceny
husma *f* snooping; **andar a la husma** to go around snooping
husmear *tr* to scent, smell out; pry into ‖ *intr* (*la carne*) to smell bad, become gamy
husmo *m* gaminess, high odor; **estar al husmo** to wait for a chance
huso *m* (*para hilar*) spindle; (*para devanar*) bobbin; (*cilindro del torno*) drum; **huso horario** time zone; **ser más derecho que un huso** to be as straight as a ramrod
huta *f* hunter's blind
huy *interj* ouch!
huyente *adj* (*frente*) receding; (*ojeada*) shifty

I

I, i (i) *f* tenth letter of the Spanish alphabet
ib. *abbr* **ibídem**
ibéri•co -ca *adj* Iberian
ibe•ro -ra *adj & mf* Iberian
íbice *m* ibex
ice•berg *m* (*pl* **-bergs**) iceberg
iconoclasia *f* or **iconoclasmo** *m* iconoclasm
iconoclasta *mf* iconoclast
iconoscopio *m* (telv) iconoscope
ictericia *f* jaundice
ictericia•do -da *adj* jaundiced
ictiología *f* ichthyology
ida *f* going; departure; rashness; sally; trail; **de ida y vuelta** round-trip; **idas y venidas** comings and goings
idea *f* idea; **mudar de idea** to change one's mind
ideal *adj & m* ideal
idealista *adj & mf* idealist
idealizar §60 *tr* to idealize
idear *tr* to think up, devise
idemista *adj* yes-saying ‖ *mf* yes sayer
idénti•co -ca *adj* identic(al); (*muy parecido*) very similar
identidad *f* identity, sameness
identificación *f* identification
identificar §73 *tr* to identify
ideología *f* ideology
idíli•co -ca *adj* idyllic

idilio *m* idyll
idioma *m* language; (*modo particular de hablar*) idiom, speech
idiomáti•co -ca *adj* idiomatic; language, linguistic
idiosincrasia *f* idiosyncrasy
idiota *adj* idiotic ‖ *mf* idiot
idiotez *f* idiocy
idiotismo *m* ignorance; (*idiotez*) idiocy; (gram) idiom
i•do -da *adj* wild, scatterbrained; drunk ‖ **los idos** the dead ‖ *f* see **ida**
idolatrar *tr* to idolize
idolatría *f* idolatry; (*amor excesivo a una persona*) idolization
ídolo *m* idol
idoneidad *f* fitness, suitability
idóne•o -a fit, suitable
idus *mpl* ides
iglesia *f* church; **entrar en la iglesia** to go into the church; **llevar a la iglesia** to lead to the altar
iglesie•ro -ra *adj* (Arg) church-going ‖ *mf* (Arg) church goer
igna•ro -ra *adj* ignorant
ignominio•so -sa *adj* ignominious
ignorancia *f* ignorance
ignorante *adj* ignorant ‖ *mf* ignoramus
ignorar *tr* to not know, be ignorant of

igno·to -ta adj unknown

igual adj equal; (liso, llano) smooth, even, level; (no variable) firm, constant, equable; indifferent; **me es igual** it makes no difference to me ‖ m equal; equal sign; **al igual de** like, after the fashion of; **al igual que** as; while, whereas; **en igual de** instead of

iguala f equalization; agreement

igualación f equalization; agreement

igualar tr to equal; (alisar, allanar) smooth, even, level; make equal, match; deem equal ‖ intr & ref to be equal

igualdad f equality; smoothness, evenness; **igualdad de ánimo** equanimity; **igualdad de oportunidades** equal opportunity

igualmente adv likewise; **igualmente que** the same as

ijada f (de animal) flank; (del cuerpo humano) loin; (dolor en estas partes) stitch; **tener su ijada** to have its weak side or point

ijadear intr to pant

ijar m flank; loin

ilegal adj illegal

ilegible adj illegible

ilegíti·mo -ma adj illegitimate

ile·so -sa adj unscathed, unharmed

iletra·do -da adj unlettered, uncultured

ilíci·to -ta adj illicit, unlawful

ilimita·do -da adj limitless

ilitera·to -ta adj illiterate

ilógi·co -ca adj illogical

ilote m ear of corn

iludir tr to elude, evade

iluminación f illumination

iluminador m lighting engineer

iluminar tr to illuminate, light, light up ‖ ref to light up, brighten

ilusión f illusion; (esperanza infundada) delusion; enthusiasm, zeal; dream; **forjarse** or **hacerse ilusiones** to kid oneself, indulge in wishful thinking

ilusionar tr to delude ‖ ref to have illusions, indulge in wishful thinking; be enraptured, be beguiled

ilusionista mf prestidigitator, magician

ilusi·vo -va adj illusive

ilu·so -sa adj deluded, misguided; (propenso a ilusionarse) visionary

iluso·rio -ria adj illusory

ilustración f illustration; enlightenment; illustrated magazine

ilustra·do -da adj illustrated; learned, informed; enlightened

ilustrar tr (adornar con grabados alusivos al texto) to illustrate; make illustrious, make famous; explain, elucidate; enlighten ‖ ref to become famous; be enlightened

ilustre adj illustrious

imagen f image; picture

imaginación f imagination

imaginar tr, intr & ref to imagine

imagina·rio -ria adj imaginary

imaginati·vo -va adj imaginative ‖ f imagination; understanding

imaginería f fancy colored embroidery; carving or painting of religious images

imán m magnet; (fig) lodestone; **imán de herradura** horseshoe magnet; **imán inductor** (elec) field magnet

imanar or **imantar** tr to magnetize

imbatible adj unbeatable

imbécil adj & mf imbecile

imbecilidad f imbecility

imberbe adj beardless

imbíbi·to -ta adj including; included

imbornal m drain hole

imborrable adj indelible; unforgettable

imbuir §20 tr to imbue

imitación adj invar imitation ‖ f imitation; **a imitación de** in imitation of; **de imitación** imitation, fake

imita·do -da adj imitated; mock, sham; imitation

imitar tr to imitate

impaciencia f impatience

impacientar tr to make impatient ‖ ref to get impatient

impaciente adj impatient

impacto m impact, hit; (señal que deja el proyectil) mark; **impacto directo** direct hit

impar adj odd, uneven; (que no tiene igual) unmatched ‖ m odd number

imparcial adj impartial; (que no entra en ningún partido) nonpartisan

impartir tr to distribute, impart; (lecciones) to give

impás m finesse

impasible adj impassible, impassive

impávi·do -da adj dauntless, fearless, intrepid

impecable adj impeccable

impedancia f impedance

impedi·do -da adj disabled, crippled

impedimento m impediment, obstacle, hindrance

impedir §50 tr to hinder, prevent

impeler tr to impel; spur, incite

impenetrable adj impenetrable

impenitente adj & mf impenitent

impensable adj unthinkable

impensa·do -da adj unexpected

imperar intr to rule, reign, command

imperati·vo -va adj & m imperative

imperceptible adj imperceptible

imperdible m safety pin

imperdonable adj unpardonable, unforgivable

imperecede·ro -ra adj imperishable, undying

imperfección f imperfection

imperfec·to -ta adj & m imperfect

imperial adj imperial ‖ f imperial, roof (of a coach or bus)

imperialista adj & mf imperialist

impericia f unskillfulness, inexpertness

imperio m empire; dominion, sway

imperio·so -sa adj (que manda con imperio) imperious; (indispensable) imperative

imperi·to -ta adj unskilled, inexpert

impermeable adj impermeable; water-proof ‖ m raincoat

impersonal adj impersonal

impertérri•to -ta *adj* dauntless, intrepid
impertinencia *f* impertinence; irrelevance; fussiness
impertinente *adj* impertinent; (*que no viene al caso*) irrelevant; (*nimiamente susceptible*) fussy ‖ **impertinentes** *mpl* lorgnette
impetrar *tr* to beg (for); obtain by entreaty
ímpetu *m* impetus; force; haste
impetuo•so -sa *adj* impetuous
impiedad *f* (*falta de religión*) impiety; (*falta de compasión*) pitilessness
impí•o -a *adj* (*irreligioso*) impious; (*falto de compasión*) pitiless
impla *f* wimple
implacable *adj* relentless
implantar *tr* to implant; introduce
implementos *mpl* implements; tools
implicar §73 *tr* (*envolver*) to implicate; (*incluir en esencia*) imply ‖ *intr* to stand in the way
implíci•to -ta *adj* implicit, implied
implorar *tr* to implore
implume *adj* featherless
imponente *adj* imposing ‖ *mf* depositor, investor
imponer §54 *tr* (*la voluntad de uno, silencio, tributos*) to impose; (*dinero a rédito*) invest; (*dinero en depósito*) deposit; instruct; impute falsely ‖ *intr* to dominate, command respect ‖ *ref* (*responsabilidades*) to assume; command attention, command respect; **imponerse a** to dominate, command the respect of; **imponerse de** to learn, to find out
imponible *adj* taxable
impopular *adj* unpopular
impopularidad *f* unpopularity
importación *f* importation; import; imports
importa•dor -dora *mf* importer
importancia *f* importance; (*extensión, tamaño*) size; **ser de la importancia de** to be the concern of
importante *adj* important; large
importar *tr* (*introducir en un país*) to import; amount to; involve, imply; concern ‖ *intr* to import; be important; matter
importe *m* amount
importunar *tr* to importune
importu•no -na *adj* (*molesto*) importunate; (*fuera de sazón*) inopportune
imposibilita•do -da *adj* paralyzed, disabled
imposibilitar *tr* to make impossible ‖ *ref* to become paralyzed, become disabled
imposible *adj* impossible
imposición *f* (*de la voluntad de uno*) imposition; burden; imposture; (*de dinero*) depósit; (*typ*) make-up
impos•tor -tora *mf* impostor; slanderer
impostura *f* imposture
impotable *adj* undrinkable
impotencia *f* impotence
impotente *adj* impotent
impracticable *adj* impracticable, impassable; impractical
impreci•so -sa *adj* imprecise; vague
impregnar *tr* to impregnate, saturate
impremedita•do -da *adj* unpremeditated

imprenta *f* printing; printing shop; (*lo que se publica impreso*) printed matter; (*máquina para imprimir o prensar; conjunto de periódicos o periodistas*) press
imprentar *tr* (*la ropa*) (Chile) to press, iron; (Ecuad) to mark
imprescindible *adj* indispensable, essential
impresentable *adj* unpresentable
impresión *f* (*efecto producido en el ánimo; señal que una cosa deja en otra por presión*) impression; (*acción de imprimir*) printing; (*los ejemplares de una edición*) edition, issue; (phot) print; **impresión dactilar** or **digital** fingerprint
impresionable *adj* impressionable
impresionante *adj* impressive
impresionar *tr* to impress; (*un disco fonográfico*) record; (phot) to expose ‖ *intr* to make an impression ‖ *ref* to be impressed
impreso *m* printed paper or book; **impreso derivado** (*ordenador*) printout; **impresos** printed matter
impre•sor -sora *mf* printer
imprevisible *adj* unforeseeable
imprevisión *f* improvidence, lack of foresight
imprevi•sor -sora *adj* improvident
imprevis•to -ta *adj* unforeseen, unexpected ‖ **imprevistos** *mpl* emergencies, unforeseen expenses
imprimar *tr* to prime
imprimir *tr* (*respeto, miedo; movimiento*) to impart ‖ §83 *tr* to stamp, imprint, impress; (*un disco fonográfico*) press; (typ) to print
improbable *adj* improbable
improbar §61 *tr* to disapprove
improbidad *f* dishonesty; hardness, arduousness
ímpro•bo -ba *adj* dishonest; (*trabajo*) arduous
improcedente *adj* wrong; unfit, untimely
improducti•vo -va *adj* unproductive; unemployed
impronunciable *adj* unpronounceable
improperar *tr* to insult, revile
improperio *m* insult, affront
impropi•cio -cia *adj* unpropitious
impro•pio -pia *adj* improper; (*ajeno*) foreign
impróspe•ro -ra *adj* unsuccessful
imprόvi•do -da *adj* unprepared
improvisación *f* improvisation; meteoric rise; (mus) impromptu
improvisadamente *adv* suddenly, unexpectedly; extempore
improvisar *tr & intr* to improvise
improvi•so -sa *adj* unforeseen, unexpected
imprudencia *f* imprudence; **imprudencia temeraria** criminal negligence
imprudente *adj* imprudent
impudicia *f* immodesty
impúdi•co -ca *adj* immodest
impues•to -ta *adj* informed ‖ *m* tax; **impuesto sobre el valor añadido** or **impuesto al valor agregado** value-added tax; **impuesto sobre la renta** income tax
impugnar *tr* to impugn, contest
impulsar *tr* to impel; drive

ig
im

impulsión *f* impulse, drive
impulsi•vo -va *adj* impulsive
impulso *m* impulse
impune *adj* unpunished
impunidad *f* impunity
impureza *f* impurity
impu•ro -ra *adj* impure
imputar *tr* to impute; credit on account
inabordable *adj* unapproachable
inacabable *adj* endless, interminable
inaccesible *adj* inaccessible
inacción *f* inaction
inacentua•do -da *adj* unaccented
inactividad *f* inactivity
inacti•vo -va *adj* inactive
inadecua•do -da *adj* inadequate; unsuited
inadvertencia *f* inadvertence, oversight
inadverti•do -da *adj* inadvertent, unwitting; careless, thoughtless; unseen, unnoticed
inagotable *adj* inexhaustible
inaguantable *adj* unbearable
inalámbri•co -ca *adj* wireless
inalcanzable *adj* unattainable
inamisto•so -sa *adj* unfriendly
inamovible *adj* irremovable; undetachable; (*incorporado*) built-in
inamovilidad *f* irremovability; tenure, permanent tenure
inane *adj* inane
inanición *f* starvation
inanima•do -da *adj* inanimate, lifeless
inapelable *adj* unappealable; unavoidable
inapetencia *f* loss of appetite
inapreciable *adj* inappreciable; imperceptible
inarmóni•co -ca *adj* unharmonious
inarrugable *adj* wrinkle-free
inarticula•do -da *adj* inarticulate
inartísti•co -ca *adj* inartistic
inasequible *adj* unattainable; unobtainable
inastillable *adj* nonshatterable, shatter-proof
inatacable *adj* unattackable; **inatacable por** resistant to
inaudi•to -ta *adj* unheard-of; outrageous
inauguración *f* inauguration; (*de una estatua*) unveiling
inaugural *adj* inaugural
inaugurar *tr* to inaugurate; (*p.ej., una estatua*) unveil
inaveriguable *adj* unascertainable
inca *mf* Inca
incai•co -ca *adj* Inca, Incan
incalificable *adj* unqualifiable; (*infame, atroz*) unspeakable
incambiable *adj* unchangeable
incandescente *adj* incandescent
incansable *adj* untiring, indefatigable
incapacitar *tr* to incapacitate; (law) to declare incompetent
inca•paz *adj* (*pl* **-paces**) incapable, unable; not large enough; stupid; (law) incompetent; frightful, unbearable
incasable *adj* unmarriageable; opposed to marriage; (*por su fealdad*) unable to find a husband
incautar *ref* — **incautarse de** to hold until claimed; (law) to seize, attach

incau•to -ta *adj* unwary, heedless
incendajas *fpl* kindling
incendiar *tr* to set on fire || *ref* to catch fire
incendia•rio -ria *adj* incendiary || *mf* incendiary, firebug
incendio *m* fire; (fig) fire, passion
incensar §2 *tr* to incense, burn incense before; (fig) to flatter
incensario *m* censer, incense burner
incenti•vo -va *adj* & *m* incentive
inceremonio•so -sa *adj* unceremonious
incertidumbre *f* uncertainty, incertitude
incesante *adj* unceasing
incesto *m* incest
incestuo•so -sa *adj* incestuous
incidencia *f* incidence; **por incidencia** by chance
incidente *adj* incident; incidental || *m* incident
incidir *tr* to make an incision in || *intr* — **incidir en culpa** to fall into guilt; **incidir en** or **sobre** to strike, impinge on
incienso *m* incense; (*olíbano*) frankincense
incier•to -ta *adj* uncertain
incineración *f* incineration; (*de cadáveres*) cremation
incinerar *tr* to incinerate; (*cadáveres*) cremate
incipiente *adj* incipient
incisión *f* incision; (*mordacidad en el lenguaje*) incisiveness, sarcasm
incisi•vo -va *adj* incisive; biting, sarcastic
inci•so -sa *adj* (*estilo del escritor*) choppy || *m* comma; clause; sentence
incitar *tr* to incite
incivil *adj* rude, impolite
inciviliza•do -da *adj* uncivilized
inclemencia *f* inclemency; **a la inclemencia** in the open, without shelter
inclemente *adj* inclement
inclinación *f* inclination; bent, leaning, propensity; nod, bow
inclinar *tr, intr & ref* to incline; bend, bow
ínclito -ta *adj* illustrious, renowned
incluir §20 *tr* to include; (*en una carta*) inclose
inclusa *f* foundling home
incluse•ro -ra *mf* foundling
inclusión *f* inclusion; friendship
inclusive *adv* inclusive, inclusively || *prep* including
inclusi•vo -va *adj* inclusive
inclu•so -sa *adj* inclosed || *f* see **inclusa** || **incluso** *adv* inclusively; (*hasta, aun*) even || **incluso** *prep* including
incobrable *adj* uncollectible; irrecoverable
incógni•to -ta *adj* (*no conocido*) unknown; (*que no se da a conocer*) incognito || *mf* (*persona*) incognito || *m* (*condición de no ser conocido*) incognito; **de incógnito** (*sin ser conocido*) incognito || *f* (math & fig) unknown quantity
incoherente *adj* incoherent
íncola *m* inhabitant
incolo•ro -ra *adj* colorless
incólume *adj* unharmed, safe

incombustible *adj* incombustible, fireproof; cold, indifferent

incomerciable *adj* unmarketable

incomible *adj* uneatable, inedible

incomodar *tr* to inconvenience, disturb

incomodidad *f* inconvenience; annoyance, discomfort

incómo•do -da *adj* inconvenient; annoying, uncomfortable ‖ *m* inconvenience; discomfort

incomparable *adj* incomparable

incompartible *adj* unsharable

incompasi•vo -va *adj* pitiless, unsympathetic

incompatible *adj* incompatible; (*acontecimientos, citas, horas de clase, etc.*) conflicting

incompetente *adj* incompetent

incompetible *adj* unmatchable

incomple•to -ta *adj* incomplete

incomponible *adj* unmendable, beyond repair

incomprable *adj* unpurchasable

incomprensible *adj* incomprehensible

incomprensión *f* incomprehension

incomunicación *f* isolation, solitary confinement

incomunica•do -da *adj* incommunicado; in solitary confinement

inconcebible *adj* inconceivable

inconclu•so -sa *adj* unfinished

inconcluyente *adj* inconclusive

inconcu•so -sa *adj* undeniable

incondicional *adj* unconditional

incone•xo -xa *adj* unconnected; (*inaplicable*) irrelevant

inconfidente *adj* distrustful

inconformidad *f* nonconformity; disagreement

inconformista *mf* nonconformist

inconfundible *adj* unmistakable

incon•gruo -grua *adj* incongruous

inconocible *adj* unknowable

inconquistable *adj* unconquerable; (*que no se deja vencer con ruegos y dádivas*) unbending, unyielding

inconsciencia *f* unconsciousness; unawareness

inconsciente *adj* unconscious; unaware; **lo inconsciente** the unconscious

inconsecuencia *f* (*falta de consecuencia o correspondencia en dichos y hechos*) inconsistency

inconsecuente *adj* inconsistent; (*que no se deduce de otra cosa*) inconsequential

inconsidera•do -da *adj* inconsiderate

inconsiguiente *adj* inconsequential, illogical

inconsistencia *f* (*falta de cohesión*) inconsistency

inconsistente *adj* inconsistent

inconsolable *adj* inconsolable

inconstante *adj* inconstant

inconstitucional *adj* unconstitutional

inconsútil *adj* seamless

incontable *adj* countless, innumerable

incontenible *adj* irrepressible

incontestable *adj* incontestable

incontinente *adj* incontinent ‖ *adv* at once, instantly

incontrastable *adj* invincible; inconvincible; (*argumento*) unanswerable

incontrovertible *adj* incontrovertible

inconveniencia *f* inconvenience; unsuitability; impoliteness; impropriety

inconveniente *adj* inconvenient; unsuitable; impolite; improper ‖ *m* drawback; disadvantage; objection

incordio *m* bore, nuisance

incorporación *f* incorporation, embodiment

incorpora•do -da *adj* (*el que estaba echado*) sitting up; (*montado en la construcción*) built-in

incorporar *tr* to incorporate, embody ‖ *ref* to incorporate; (*el que estaba echado*) sit up; **incorporarse a** to join

incorrec•to -ta *adj* incorrect

incrédu•lo -la *adj* incredulous ‖ *mf* disbeliever, doubter

increíble *adj* incredible

incremento *m* increment, increase

increpar *tr* to chide, rebuke

incriminar *tr* to incriminate; (*un delito, falta, defecto*) exaggerate the gravity of

incruen•to -ta *adj* bloodless

incrustar *tr* to incrust; (*embutir por adorno*) inlay

incubadora *f* incubator

incubar *tr & intr* to incubate ‖ *ref* (fig) to be brewing

incuestionable *adj* unquestionable

inculcar §73 *tr* to inculcate‖ *ref* to become obstinate

inculpable *adj* blameless, guiltless

inculpar *tr* to accuse, blame

incultivable *adj* untillable

incul•to -ta *adj* uncultivated, untilled; uncultured; (*estilo*) coarse, sloppy

incumbencia *f* incumbency, duty, obligation, province

incumbir *intr* — **incumbir a** to be incumbent on

incumplimiento *m* nonfulfillment

incunable *m* incunabulum

incurable *adj & mf* incurable

incuria *f* carelessness, negligence

incurio•so -sa *adj* careless, negligent

incurrir *intr* — **incurrir en** to incur

incursión *f* incursion, inroad, raid

indagación *f* investigation, research

indagatorio *m* deposition of the accused

indagar §44 *tr* to investigate

indebidamente *adv* unduly

indebi•do -da *adj* undue; wrong

indecencia *f* indecency

indecente *adj* indecent

indecible *adj* unspeakable, unutterable

indeci•so -sa *adj* undecided, indecisive; (*contorno, forma*) vague, obscure

indeclinable *adj* unavoidable; (gram) indeclinable

indecoro•so -sa *adj* improper

indefectible *adj* unfailing

indefendible *adj* indefensible

indefen•so -sa *adj* defenseless, undefended

im
in

indefinible *adj* indefinable
indefini•do -da *adj* indefinite; limitless; vague
indeleble *adj* indelible
indelibera•do -da *adj* unpremeditated
indelica•do -da *adj* indelicate
indemne *adj* unharmed, undamaged
indemnidad *f* (*seguridad contra un daño*) indemnity
indemnización *f* (*compensación*) indemnity, indemnification; **indemnización por despido** severance pay
indemnizar §60 *tr* to indemnify
independencia *f* independence
independiente *adj* & *mf* independent
independizar §60 *tr* to free, emancipate ‖ *ref* to become independent
indescriptible *adj* indescribable
indeseable *adj* & *mf* undesirable
indesea•do -da *adj* unwanted
indesmallable *adj* runproof
indestructible *adj* indestructible
indetermina•do -da *adj* indeterminate; (gram) indefinite
indevo•to -ta *adj* impious; not fond, not devoted
india *f* wealth, riches; **Indias Occidentales** West Indies; **la India** India
indiana *f* printed calico
india•no -na *adj* & *mf* Spanish American; East Indian; West Indian ‖ *m* man back from America with great wealth; **indiano de hilo negro** (coll) skinflint ‖ *f* see **indiana**
indicación *f* indication; **por indicación de** at the direction of
indica•do -da *adj* appropriate, advisable; **muy indicado** just the thing, just the person
indica•dor -dora *adj* indicating, pointing ‖ *m* indicator; gauge; (*de tránsito*) traffic signal
indicar §73 *tr* to indicate
indicati•vo -va *adj* & *m* indicative
índice *m* index; **índice de libros prohibidos** (eccl) Index; **índice de materias** table of contents; **índice en el corte** thumb index
indiciar *tr* to betoken, indicate; surmise, suspect
indicio *m* sign, token, indication; **indicios vehementes** circumstantial evidence
indiferente *adj* indifferent; (*que no importa*) immaterial
indígena *adj* indigenous ‖ *mf* native
indigente *adj* indigent
indigestar *ref* to be indigestible; be disliked, be unbearable
indigestible *adj* indigestible
indigestión *f* indigestion
indignación *f* indignation
indigna•do -da *adj* indignant
indignar *tr* to anger, provoke ‖ *ref* to become indignant
indignidad *f* (*falta de mérito*) unworthiness; (*acción reprobable*) indignity
indig•no -na *adj* unworthy
índigo *m* indigo
in•dio -dia *adj* & *mf* Indian ‖ *f* see **india**

indirec•to -ta *adj* indirect ‖ *f* hint, innuendo; **indirecta del padre Cobos** broad hint
indiscernible *adj* indiscernible
indiscre•to -ta *adj* indiscreet
indiscrimina•do -da *adj* indiscriminate; non-discriminating
indisculpable *adj* inexcusable
indiscutible *adj* undeniable
indisoluble *adj* indissoluble
indispensable *adj* unpardonable; indispensable
indisponer §54 *tr* (*alterar la salud de*) to indispose, upset; disturb, upset; **indisponer a uno con** to set someone against, prejudice someone against ‖ *ref* to become indisposed; **indisponerse con** to fall out with
indisponible *adj* unavailable
indispues•to -ta *adj* indisposed
indistintamente *adv* indistinctly; indiscriminately, without distinction
indistin•to -ta *adj* indistinct
individual *adj* individual; (*habitación en un hotel; partido de tenis*) single
individualidad *f* individuality
indivi•duo -dua *adj* individual; indivisible ‖ *mf* (*persona indeterminada*) (coll) individual ‖ *m* (*cada persona*) individual; (*miembro de una corporación*) member, fellow
indócil *adj* unteachable; headstrong, unruly
indocumenta•do -da *adj* unidentified; unqualified ‖ *mf* nobody (*person of no account*)
indochi•no -na *adj* & *mf* Indo-Chinese ‖ **la Indochina** Indochina
indoeurope•o -a *adj* & *m* Indo-European
índole *f* kind, class; nature, disposition, temper
indolente *adj* stolid, impassive; (*perezoso*) indolent
indolo•ro -ra *adj* painless
indoma•do -da *adj* untamed
indone•sio -sia *adj* & *mf* Indonesian ‖ **la Indonesia** Indonesia
inducción *f* induction
inducido *m* (*de dínamo o motor*) (elec) armature
inducir §19 *tr* to induce
inductor *m* (*de dínamo o motor*) (elec) field
indudable *adj* doubtless
indulgente *adj* indulgent
indultar *tr* to pardon; free, exempt
indulto *m* pardon; exemption
indumentaria *f* clothing, dress; historical study of clothing
indumento *m* clothing, dress
industria *f* industry; **de industria** on purpose
industrial *adj* industrial ‖ *m* industrialist
industrializar §60 *tr* to industrialize
industriar *tr* to teach, instruct, train ‖ *ref* to get along, manage
industrio•so -sa *adj* industrious
inédi•to -ta *adj* unpublished; new, novel, unknown
inefable *adj* ineffable
ineficacia *f* inefficacy

inefi•caz *adj* (*pl* **-caces**) inefficacious, ineffectual

inelegible *adj* ineligible

ineludible *adj* inescapable

inenarrable *adj* indescribable

inencogible *adj* unshrinkable

inencontrable *adj* unobtainable

inequidad *f* inequity

inequívo•co -ca *adj* unmistakable

inercia *f* inertia

inerme *adj* unarmed

inerte *adj* inert; slow, sluggish

inescrupulo•so -sa *adj* unscrupulous

inescrutable or **inescudriñable** *adj* inscrutable

inespera•do -da *adj* unexpected, unforeseen; unhoped for

inestable *adj* unstable

inevitable *adj* unavoidable, inevitable

inexactitud *f* inaccuracy, inexactness

inexac•to -ta *adj* inaccurate, inexact

inexcusable *adj* inexcusable, unpardonable; unavoidable; indispensable

inexistencia *f* nonexistence

inexorable *adj* inexorable

inexperiencia *f* inexperience

inexplicable *adj* inexplicable, unexplainable

inexplica•do -da *adj* unexplained, unaccounted for

inexplora•do -da *adj* unexplored; (*mar*) uncharted

inexpresable *adj* inexpressible

inexpues•to -ta *adj* (phot) unexposed

inexpugnable *adj* impregnable; firm, unshakable

inextinguible *adj* unextinguishable; perpetual, lasting; (*sed*) unquenchable; (*risa*) uncontrollable

inextirpable *adj* ineradicable

infalible *adj* infallible

infamación *f* defamation

infamar *tr* to defame, discredit

infame *adj* infamous; vile, frightful ‖ *mf* scoundrel

infamia *f* infamy

infancia *f* infancy

infan•do -da *adj* odious, unmentionable

infanta *f* female child; infanta (*any daughter of a king of Spain; wife of an infante*)

infante *m* male child; infante (*any son of a king of Spain who is not heir to the throne*); (mil) infantryman; **infante de coro** choirboy

infantería *f* infantry; **infantería de marina** marines, marine corps

infantil *adj* infant, infantile, childlike; innocent

infarto *m* (heart) infarct

infatigable *adj* indefatigable

infatuar §21 *tr* to make vain ‖ *ref* to become vain

infaus•to -ta *adj* fatal, unlucky

infección *f* infection

infeccionar *tr* to infect

infeccio•so -sa *adj* infectious

infectar *tr* to infect

infec•to -ta *adj* foul, corrupt; infected; fetid

infecun•do -da *adj* sterile, barren

infe•liz (*pl* **-lices**) *adj* unhappy; simple, goodhearted ‖ *m* wretch, poor soul

inferior *adj* inferior; lower; **inferior a** inferior to; lower than; less than; smaller than ‖ *m* inferior

inferioridad *f* inferiority

inferir §68 *tr* to infer; lead to, entail; (*una herida*) inflict; (*una ofensa*) cause, offer

infernáculo *m* hopscotch

infernal *adj* infernal

infernar §2 *tr* to damn; irritate, annoy

infernillo *m* chafing dish

infestar *tr* to infest ‖ *ref* to become infested

inficionar *tr* to infect ‖ *ref* to become infected

infidelidad *f* infidelity; (*conjunto de infieles*) unbelievers

infidente *adj* faithless, disloyal

infiel *adj* (*falto de fidelidad*) unfaithful; (*no exacto*) inaccurate, inexact; (*no cristiano*) infidel ‖ *mf* infidel

infierno *m* hell; **en el quinto infierno** or **en los quintos infiernos** far, far away

infijo *m* (gram) infix

infiltrar *tr* & *ref* to infiltrate

ínfi•mo -ma *adj* lowest; humblest, most abject; meanest, vilest

infinidad *f* infinity

infiniti•vo -va *adj* & *m* infinitive

infini•to -ta *adj* infinite ‖ *m* infinite; (math) infinity ‖ **infinito** *adv* greatly, very much

infirme *adj* infirm

inflación *f* inflation; (*vanidad*) conceit

infraciona•rio -ria *adj* inflationary

inflado *m* inflation (*of a tire*)

inflamable *adj* inflammable, flammable

inflamación *f* ignition, inflammation; ardor, enthusiasm; (pathol) inflammation

inflamar *tr* to set on fire; inflame ‖ *ref* to catch fire; become inflamed

inflar *tr* to inflate; exaggerate; puff up with pride ‖ *ref* to inflate; be puffed up with pride

inflexible *adj* inflexible; unyielding, unbending

inflexión *f* inflection; **inflexión vocálica** (*metafonía*) umlaut

inflexionar *tr* to umlaut

infligir §27 *tr* to inflict

influencia *f* influence

influenciar *tr* to influence

influenza *f* influenza

influir §20 *intr* to have influence; have great weight; **influir en** or **sobre** to influence

influjo *m* influence; rising tide

influyente *adj* influential

información *f* information; (law) judicial inquiry, investigation; **informaciones** testimonial

informal *adj* (*que no se ajusta a las reglas debidas*) informal; unreliable

informar *tr* & *intr* to inform ‖ *ref* to inquire, find out

informática *f* computer science

informati•vo -va *adj* informational; (*sección de un periódico*) news

informe *adj* shapeless, formless; misshapen ‖ *m* piece of information; report; **informes** information; **informes confidenciales** inside information

infortuna•do -da *adj* unfortunate, unlucky

infortunio *m* misfortune; (*acaecimiento desgraciado*) mishap

infracción *f* infraction, infringement

infraconsumo *m* underconsumption

infrac•to -ta *adj* unperturbable

infraestructura *f* substructure; (rr) roadbed

inframundo *m* underworld

infrarro•jo -ja *adj* & *m* infrared

infrascri•to -ta *adj* undersigned; hereinafter mentioned

infrecuente *adj* infrequent

infringir §27 *tr* to infringe, break, violate

infructuo•so -sa *adj* fruitless, unfruitful

ínfulas *fpl* conceit, airs; **darse ínfulas** to put on airs

infunda•do -da *adj* unfounded, groundless, baseless

infundio *m* lie, fib

infundir *tr* to infuse, instill

infusión *f* infusion; (*acción de echar agua sobre el que se bautiza*) sprinkling; **estar en infusión para** to be all set for

ingeniar *tr* to think up ‖ *ref* to manage; **ingeniarse a** or **para** to manage to; **ingeniarse para ir viviendo** to manage to get along

ingeniería *f* engineering; **ingeniería genética** genetic engineering

ingeniero *m* engineer; **ingeniero de caminos, canales y puertos** government civil engineer

ingenio *m* talent, creative faculty; talented person; cleverness, skill, wit; (*artificio mecánico*) apparatus, device; (*del encuadernador*) paper cutter; engine of war; **afilar** or **aguzar el ingenio** to sharpen one's wits; **ingenio de azúcar** sugar refinery

ingeniosidad *f* ingenuity; wittiness

ingenio•so -sa *adj* (*dotado de ingenio; hecho con ingenio*) ingenious; (*agudo, sutil*) witty

ingéni•to -ta *adj* innate, inborn

ingente *adj* huge, enormous

ingenuidad *f* ingenuousness

inge•nuo -nua *adj* ingenuous

ingerir §68 *tr* & *ref* var of **injerir**

ingestión *f* (food) consumption; ingestion

Inglaterra *f* England

ingle *f* groin

in•glés -glesa *adj* English; **a la inglesa** in the English manner ‖ *m* Englishman; (*idioma*) English; **el inglés medio** Middle English; **los ingleses** the English ‖ *f* Englishwoman

ingramatical *adj* ungrammatical

ingratitud *f* ingratitude, ungratefulness

ingra•to -ta *adj* (*desagradecido*) ungrateful; (*desagradecido; desagradable, áspero; improductivo*) thankless ‖ *mf* ingrate

ingravidez *f* lightness, tenuousness; (*gravedad nula*) weightlessness

ingrávi•do -da *adj* light, tenuous; weightless

ingrediente *m* ingredient

ingresa•do -da *mf* new student

ingresar *tr* to deposit ‖ *intr* to enter, become a member; (*beneficios*) come in ‖ *ref* (Mex) to enlist

ingreso *m* entrance; admission; **ingresos** income, revenue

íngri•mo -ma *adj* solitary, alone

inhábil *adj* unable; unskillful; unfit, unqualified

inhabilidad *f* inability; unskillfulness; unfitness

inhabilitar *tr* to disable, to disqualify, to incapacitate

inhabita•do -da *adj* uninhabited

inhabitua•do -da *adj* unaccustomed

inherente *adj* inherent

inhibir *tr* to inhibit

inhospitala•rio -ria *adj* inhospitable

inhóspi•to -ta *adj* inhospitable

inhumanidad *f* inhumanity

inhuma•no -na *adj* inhuman, inhumane; (Chile) filthy

iniciación *f* initiation

inicial *adj* & *f* initial

iniciar *tr* to initiate ‖ *ref* to be initiated

iniciativa *f* initiative

ini•cuo -cua *adj* wicked, iniquitous

inigualable *adj* incomparable

iniguala•do -da *adj* unequaled

ininteligente *adj* unintelligent

ininteligible *adj* unintelligible

ininterrumpi•do -da *adj* uninterrupted

iniquidad *f* iniquity

injerencia *f* interference, meddling

injerir §68 *tr* to insert, introduce; (*alimentos*) take in; (hort) to graft ‖ *ref* to interfere, meddle, intrude

injertar *tr* (hort & surg) to graft

injerto *m* (hort & surg) graft; transplant

injuria *f* offense, insult; abuse, wrong; damage, harm

injuriar *tr* to offend, insult; abuse, wrong; harm, damage

injurio•so -sa *adj* offensive, insulting; abusive; harmful; (*lenguaje*) profane

injusticia *f* injustice

injustifica•do -da *adj* unjustified

injus•to -ta *adj* unjust

inmacula•do -da *adj* immaculate

inmanejable *adj* unmanageable; unhandy

inmarcesible *adj* unfading

inmaterial *adj* immaterial

inmaturo -ra *adj* immature

inmediación *f* immediacy; proximity, nearness; **inmediaciones** neighborhood, outskirts

inmediatamente *adv* immediately; **inmediatamente que** as soon as

inmedia•to -ta *adj* immediate; close, adjoining, next; next above; next below; (*pago*) prompt; **venir a las inmediatas** to get into the thick of the fight

inmejorable *adj* superb, unsurpassable

inmemorial *adj* immemorial

inmen•so -sa *adj* immense

inmensurable *adj* immeasurable

inmereci•do -da *adj* undeserved

inmergir §27 *tr* to immerse

inmersión _f_ immersion
inmigración _f_ immigration
inmigrante _mf_ immigrant
inmigrar _intr_ to immigrate
inminente _adj_ imminent
inmiscuir §20 **&** regular _tr_ to mix ‖ _ref_ to meddle, interfere
inmobilia•rio -ria _adj_ real-estate
inmoble _adj_ motionless; firm, constant
inmodera•do -da _adj_ immoderate
inmodes•to -ta _adj_ immodest
inmódi•co -ca _adj_ excessive
inmoral _adj_ immoral
inmortal _adj_ immortal, deathless ‖ _mf_ immortal
inmortalizar §60 _tr_ to immortalize
inmotiva•do -da _adj_ groundless; unmotivated
inmovilizar §60 _tr_ to immobilize; (_un caudal_) tie up
inmueble _m_ property, piece of real estate; **inmuebles** real estate
inmun•do -da _adj_ dirty, filthy
inmune _adj_ immune
inmunizar §60 _tr_ to immunize
inmutar _tr_ to change, alter; disturb, upset ‖ _ref_ to change, alter; change countenance; **sin inmutarse** without batting an eye
inna•to -ta _adj_ innate, inborn; natural
innatural _adj_ unnatural
innavegable _adj_ (_río_) unnavigable; (_embarcación_) unseaworthy
innecesa•rio -ria _adj_ unnecessary
innegable _adj_ undeniable
innoble _adj_ ignoble
innocuidad _f_ harmlessness
inno•cuo -cua _adj_ harmless
innovación _f_ innovation
innovar _tr_ to innovate
innumerable _adj_ innumerable
inocencia _f_ innocence
inocentada _f_ simpleness; blunder; (Ecuad) April Fools' joke
inocente _adj_ & _mf_ innocent; **coger por inocente** to make an April fool of
inocen•tón -tona _adj_ simple, gullible ‖ _mf_ gull, dupe
inoculación _f_ inoculation
inocular _tr_ to inoculate; contaminate, pervert
inodo•ro -ra _adj_ odorless ‖ _m_ deodorizer; (_excusado que funciona con agua corriente_) toilet
inofensi•vo -va _adj_ inoffensive
inolvidable _adj_ unforgettable
inope _adj_ impecunious
inopia _f_ indigence
inoportu•no -na _adj_ inopportune, untimely
inorgáni•co -ca _adj_ inorganic
inortodo•xo -xa _adj_ unorthodox
inoxidable _adj_ (_acero_) stainless; inoxidizable
inquietante _adj_ disquieting, upsetting
inquietar _tr_ to disquiet, worry; stir up, excite
inquie•to -ta _adj_ anxious, worried
inquietud _f_ disquiet, worry, concern
inquili•no -na _mf_ tenant, renter
inquina _f_ aversion, dislike, ill will
inquirir §40 _tr_ to inquire, inquire into
inquisición _f_ inquiry; inquisition

insabible _adj_ unknowable
insaciable _adj_ insatiable
insania _f_ insanity
insa•no -na _adj_ insane; imprudent
insatisfacción _f_ dissatisfaction
insatisfe•cho -cha _adj_ unsatisfied
inscribir §83 _tr_ to inscribe; (law) to record ‖ _ref_ to enroll, register
inscripción _f_ inscription; enrollment, registration
insecticida _adj_ & _m_ insecticide
insecto _m_ insect
insegu•ro -ra _adj_ insecure, unsafe; uncertain
insensa•to -ta _adj_ foolish, stupid
insensible _adj_ callous, hard-hearted, unfeeling; imperceptible
inseparable _adj_ inseparable; undetachable ‖ _mf_ inseparable ‖ _m_ lovebird
insepul•to -ta _adj_ unburied
inserción _f_ insertion
inserir §68 _tr_ to insert; (_injertar_) graft, engraft
insertar _tr_ to insert
inservible _adj_ useless
insidia _f_ snare, ambush; plotting
insidiar _tr_ to ambush, waylay; trap, trick
insidio•so -sa _adj_ insidious
insigne _adj_ noted, famous, renowned
insignia _f_ badge, decoration, insignia; banner, standard
insignificante _adj_ insignificant
insince•ro -ra _adj_ insincere
insinuación _f_ insinuation, hint
insinuante _adj_ engaging, slick, crafty
insinuar §21 _tr_ to insinuate; suggest, hint at ‖ _ref_ to creep in, slip in; ingratiate oneself; flow, run; **insinuarse en** to work one's way in
insípi•do -da _adj_ insipid, vapid
insistir _intr_ to insist
ínsi•to -ta _adj_ inbred, innate
insociable _adj_ unsociable
insolencia _f_ insolence
insolentar _tr_ to make insolent ‖ _ref_ to become insolent
insolente _adj_ insolent
insóli•to -ta _adj_ unusual
insoluble _adj_ insoluble
insolvencia _f_ insolvency
insomne _adj_ sleepless
insomnio _m_ insomnia
insondable _adj_ fathomless; inscrutable
insonorización _f_ soundproofing
insonoriza•do -da _adj_ soundproof
insonorizar §60 _tr_ to soundproof
insono•ro -ra _adj_ soundproof
insospecha•do -da _adj_ unsuspected
insostenible _adj_ untenable
inspección _f_ inspection; inspectorship; **inspección técnica de vehículos (I.T.V.)** car inspection
inspeccionar _tr_ to inspect
inspiración _f_ inspiration; inhalation
inspirante _adj_ inspiring
inspirar _tr_ & _intr_ to inspire; (_atraer a los pulmones_) inhale, breathe in ‖ _ref_ to be inspired

instalación f plant, factory; outfit, equipment; arrangements, fittings; installment; **instalación sanitaria** plumbing

instalar tr to install ‖ ref to settle

instantáne•o -a adj instantaneous ‖ f snapshot

instante m instant, moment; **al instante** right away, immediately; **por instantes** uninterruptedly; any time

instantemente adv insistently, urgently

instar tr to press, urge ‖ intr to be pressing, be urgent

instaurar tr to restore; reestablish

instigar §44 tr to instigate

instilar tr to instill

instinti•vo -va adj instinctive

instinto m instinct

institución f institution; **instituciones** (de un Estado) constitution; (de una ciencia, arte, etc.) principles

instituir §20 tr to institute, found

instituto m institute; (de una orden religiosa) rule, constitution; **instituto de segunda enseñanza** or **de enseñanza media** high school

institu•triz f (pl **-trices**) governess

instrucción f instruction; education

instructi•vo -va adj instructive

instruc•tor -tora mf teacher, instructor ‖ m (mil) drillmaster ‖ f instructress

instruí•do -da adj well-educated; well-posted

instruir §20 tr to instruct; (un proceso o expediente) draw up

instrumentar tr to instrument

instrumentista mf instrumentalist

instrumento m instrument; (persona que se emplea para alcanzar un resultado) tool; **instrumento de cuerda** (mus) stringed instrument; **instrumento de viento** (mus) wind instrument

insubordina•do -da adj insubordinate

insubstituíble adj irreplaceable

insudar intr to drudge

insuficiente adj insufficient

insufrible adj insufferable

ínsula f island; one-horse town

insular adj insular ‖ mf islander

insulina f insulin

insulsez f tastelessness; dullness, heaviness

insul•so -sa adj tasteless; dull, heavy

insultada f insult

insultar tr to insult ‖ ref to faint, swoon

insulto m insult; fainting spell

insume adj expensive

insumergible adj unsinkable

insuperable adj insurmountable

insurgente adj & mf insurgent

insurrección f insurrection

intac•to -ta adj intact, untouched

intachable adj blameless, irreproachable

integración f integration

integridad f integrity; virginity

ínte•gro -gra adj integral, whole; honest

intelecto m intellect

intelectual adj & mf intellectual

intelectualidad f intellectuality; (conjunto de los intelectuales de un país o región) intelligentsia

inteligencia f intelligence; **estar en inteligencia con** to be in collusion with

inteligente adj intelligent; trained, skilled

inteligible adj intelligible

intemperancia f intemperance

intemperante adj intemperate

intemperie f inclement weather; **a la intemperie** in the open, unsheltered

intempesti•vo -va adj unseasonable, inopportune, untimely

intención f intention; (cautelosa advertencia) caution; (instinto dañino de un animal) viciousness; **con intención** deliberately, knowingly; **de intención** on purpose

intendencia f intendance; (SAm) mayoralty

intendente m intendant; quartermaster general; (SAm) mayor

intensar tr & ref to intensify

intensidad f intensity

intensificar §73 tr & ref to intensify

intensión f intensity

intensi•vo -va adj intensive

inten•so -sa adj intense

intentar tr to try, to attempt; intend; try out

intento m intent, purpose; **de intento** on purpose

intentona f rash attempt (to rob, escape, etc.)

interacción f interaction

interamerica•no -na adj inter-American

intercalar tr to intercalate, insert

intercambiar tr & ref to interchange

intercambio m interchange, exchange

interceder intr to intercede

interceptar tr to intercept

intercep•tor -tora mf interceptor ‖ m trap; separator; (aer) interceptor

interdecir §24 tr to interdict, forbid

interés m interest; **intereses creados** vested interests; **poner a interés** to put out at interest

interesa•do -da adj interested ‖ mf interested party

interesante adj interesting

interesar tr to interest; involve ‖ intr to be interesting ‖ ref — **interesarse en** or **por** to be interested in, take an interest in

interescolar adj interscholastic, intercollegiate

interfec•to -ta adj murdered ‖ mf victim of murder

interferencia f interference

interferir §68 tr to interfere with ‖ intr to interfere

interfono m intercom

ínterin adv meanwhile ‖ conj while, as long as ‖ m (pl **intérines**) temporary incumbency

interinar tr to fill temporarily, fill in an acting capacity

interi•no -na adj temporary, acting, interim

interior adj interior, inner, inside; home, domestic ‖ m interior, inside; mind, soul; **interiores** entrails, insides

interioridad *f* inside; **interioridades** inside story, private matters
interjección *f* interjection
interlinear *tr* to interline; (typ) to space, lead
interlocu•tor -tora *mf* speaker, party; interviewer
intermedia•rio -ria *adj & mf* intermediary || *m* (com) middleman
interme•dio -dia *adj* intermediate || *m* interval, interim; (mus) intermezzo; (theat) intermission, entr'acte
intermitente *adj* intermittent || *m* (aut) direction light, turning light
internacional *adj* international
internacionalizar §60 *tr* to internationalize
interna•do -da *mf* (mil) internee || *m* boarding school
internamiento *m* internment
internar *tr* to send inland; intern || *intr* to move inland || *ref* to move inland; take refuge, hide; insinuate oneself; **internarse en** to go deeply into
internista *mf* internist
inter•no -na *adj* internal; inside || *mf* boarding-school student; **interno de hospital** intern
interpelar *tr* to seek the protection or aid of; interrogate; interpellate
interpolar *tr* to interpolate; interpose; interrupt briefly
interponer §54 *tr* to interpose; appoint as mediator || *ref* to intervene, intercede
interprender *tr* to take by surprise
interpresa *f* surprise action; surprise seizure
interpretar *tr* to interpret
intérprete *mf* interpreter
interrogación *f* interrogation; question mark
interrogar §44 *tr & intr* to question, interrogate
interrumpir *tr* to interrupt
interruptor *m* (elec) switch; **interruptor automático** (elec) circuit breaker; **interruptor del encendido** (aut) ignition switch; **interruptor de resorte** (elec) snap switch
intersección *f* (geom) intersection
intersticio *m* interstice; interval
intervalo *m* interval
intervención *f* intervention; inspection; (de cuentas) audit, auditing; (surg) operation; **intervención de los precios** price control; **no intervención** nonintervention
intervenir §79 *tr* to take up, work on; inspect, supervise; (cuentas) audit; (un teléfono) tap; (surg) operate on || *intr* to mediate, intervene, intercede; participate; happen
interventor *m* election supervisor; (com) auditor
inter•viev *m* (*pl* -**vievs**) interview
intervievar *tr* to interview
intesta•do -da *adj & mf* intestate
intesti•no -na *adj* internal; domestic || *m* intestine; **intestino delgado** small intestine; **intestino grueso** large intestine
intimación *f* announcement, notification
intimar *tr* to announce || *intr & ref* to become well-acquainted, to become intimate

intimidad *f* intimacy; (parte íntima o personal) privacy
intimidar *tr* to intimidate
inti•mo -ma *adj* intimate; (más interno) innermost
intitular *tr* to entitle || *ref* to use a title; be called
intocable *mf* untouchable
intolerante *adj & mf* intolerant
inton•so -sa *adj* unshorn; ignorant; (libro o revista) uncut || *mf* ignoramus
intoxicación *f* intoxication; poisoning
intoxicar §73 *tr* to poison, intoxicate
intracruzamiento *m* inbreeding
intranquilidad *f* uneasiness, worry
intranquilizar §60 *tr* to make uneasy, worry
intranqui•lo -la *adj* uneasy, worried
intransigente *adj & mf* intransigent, die-hard
intransiti•vo -va *adj* intransitive
intrascendente *adj* unimportant; nonessential
intratable *adj* unmanageable; impassable; unsociable
intrepidez *f* intrepidity
intrépi•do -da *adj* intrepid
intriga *f* intrigue
intrigar §44 *tr* (excitar la curiosidad de) to intrigue || *intr* to intrigue || *ref* to be intrigued
intrinca•do -da *adj* intricate
intrincar §73 *tr* to complicate; confuse, bewilder
intríngu•lis *m* (*pl* -**lis**) hidden motive, mystery
intrínse•co -ca *adj* intrinsic(al)
introducción *f* introduction
introducir §19 *tr* to introduce; insert, put in || *ref* to gain access; meddle, interfere, intrude
introito *m* (de un escrito o una oración) introduction; (de un poema dramático) prologue; (eccl) introit
introspecti•vo -va *adj* introspective
introverti•do -da *mf* introvert
intru•so -sa *adj* intrusive || *mf* intruder, interloper
intuición *f* intuition
intuir §20 *tr* to guess, sense
intuito *m* view, glance, look; **por intuito de** in view of
inundación *f* flood, inundation
inundar *tr* to flood, inundate
inurba•no -na *adj* discourteous, unmannerly
inusita•do -da *adj* (no ordinario) unusual; obsolete, out of use
inusual *adj* unusual
inútil *adj* useless
invadir *tr* to invade
invalidar *tr* to invalidate
invalidez *f* invalidity
inváli•do -da *adj & mf* invalid
invariable *adj* invariable
invasión *f* invasion
inva•sor -sora *mf* invader
invectiva *f* invective
invectivar *tr* to inveigh against
invencible *adj* invincible

in
in

invención *f* invention; finding, discovery; deception

invendible *adj* unsalable

inventar *tr* to invent

inventariar §77 **& regular** *tr* to inventory

inventario *m* inventory

inventi•vo -va *adj* inventive ‖ *f* inventiveness

invento *m* invention

inven•tor -tora *adj* inventive ‖ *mf* inventor

inverecun•do -da *adj* shameless, brazen

inverisímil *adj* improbable, unlikely

invernáculo *m* greenhouse, hothouse, conservatory

invernada *f* wintertime; (SAm) pasture land; (Ven) torrential rain

invernadero *m* greenhouse, hothouse; winter resort; winter pasture

invernal *adj* winter ‖ *m* cattle shed (*in winter-pasture land*)

invernar §2 *intr* to winter; be winter

inverni•zo -za *adj* winter; wintery

inverosímil *adj* improbable, unlikely

inversión *f* inversion; (*de dinero*) investment; (gram) inverted order

inversionista *f* investment ‖ *mf* investor

inver•so -sa *adj* inverse, opposite; **a** or **por la inversa** on the contrary

inversor *m* investor

invertebra•do -da *adj & m* invertebrate

inverti•do -da *adj* inverted ‖ *mf* invert

invertir §68 *tr* to invert; (*dinero*) invest; (*tiempo*) spend; reverse

investidura *f* investment, investiture; station, standing

investigación *f* investigation, research; **investigación mercológica** market research

investigar §44 *tr* to investigate ‖ *intr* to research

investir §50 *tr* — **investir con** or **de** (*poner en posesión de*) to invest with

invetera•do -da *adj* inveterate, confirmed

invic•to -ta *adj* unconquered

invidencia *f* blindness

invidente *adj* blind ‖ *mf* blind person

invierno *m* winter; rainy season

inviolabilidad *f* inviolability; undamageability

invisible *adj* invisible ‖ *m* (Mex) hair net; **en un invisible** in an instant

invitación *f* invitation

invita•do -da *mf* guest

invitar *tr* to invite

invocar §73 *tr* to invoke

involunta•rio -ria *adj* involuntary

invulnerable *adj* invulnerable

inyección *f* injection; **inyección secundaria** booster shot

inyectable *adj* injectable ‖ *m* ampule, phial

inyecta•do -da *adj* bloodshot, inflamed

inyectar *tr* to inject ‖ *ref* to become congested; become inflamed

ionizar §60 *tr* to ionize ‖ *ref* to be ionized

ionosfera *f* ionosphere

ir §41 *intr* to go; be becoming, fit, suit; be at stake; **ir a** + *inf* to be going to + *inf* (*to express futurity*); **ir a buscar** to go get, go for; **ir a parar en** to end up in; **ir con**

cuidado to be careful; **ir con miedo** to be afraid; **ir con tiento** to watch one's step; **ir de caza** to go hunting; **ir de pesca** to go fishing; **lo que va de** so far (as); **¡qué va!** of course not!; **¡vaya!** the deuce!; what a. . . ! ‖ *ref* to go away; leak; wear away; get old; break to pieces

ira *f* anger, wrath, ire

iracun•do -da *adj* angry, wrathful, irate

Irak, el Iraq

Irán, el Iran

ira•nés -nesa or **ira•nio -nia** *adj & mf* Iranian

ira•qués -quesa or **iraquiano -na** *adj & mf* Iraqi

iris *m* (*pl* **iris**) (*del ojo*) iris; rainbow

Irlanda *f* Ireland

irlan•dés -desa *adj* Irish ‖ *m* Irishman; (*idioma*) Irish; **los irlandeses** the Irish ‖ *f* Irishwoman

ironía *f* irony

iróni•co -ca *adj* ironic(al)

ironizar §60 *tr* to ridicule

irracional *adj* irrational

irradiar *tr* to radiate, irradiate; (*difundir*) broadcast ‖ *intr* to radiate

irrazonable *adj* unreasonable

irreal *adj* unreal

irrealidad *f* unreality

irrebatible *adj* irrefutable

irreconocible *adj* unrecognizable

irrecuperable *adj* irretrievable

irrecusable *adj* unimpeachable

irredimible *adj* irredeemable

irreemplazable *adj* irreplaceable

irreflexión *f* rashness, thoughtlessness

irreflexi•vo -va *adj* rash, thoughtless

irregular *adj* irregular ‖ *m* (mil) irregular

irregularidad *f* irregularity; embezzlement

irrelevante *adj* irrelevant

irreligio•so -sa *adj* irreligious

irrellenable *adj* nonrefillable

irremediable *adj* irremediable

irremisible *adj* unpardonable

irreparable *adj* irreparable

irreprimible *adj* irrepressible

irreprochable *adj* irreproachable

irresistible *adj* irresistible

irresoluble *adj* unworkable, unsolvable

irrespetuo•so -sa *adj* disrespectful

irresponsable *adj* irresponsible

irresuel•to -ta *adj* hesitant, wavering

irreverente *adj* irreverent

irrigación *f* irrigation

irrigar §44 *tr* to irrigate

irrisible *adj* laughable, absurd

irrisión *f* derision, ridicule; laughingstock

irritante *adj & m* irritant

irritar *tr* to irritate ‖ *ref* to become exasperated

irrompible *adj* unbreakable

irrumpir *intr* to burst in; **irrumpir en** to burst into

irrupción *f* sudden attack; invasion

isi•dro -dra *mf* hick, jake, yokel

isla *f* island; (*manzana de casas*) block; **isla de peatones** or **isla de seguridad** safety zone (for pedestrians); **islas Baleares** Ba-

learic Islands; **islas Canarias** Canary Islands; **islas de Barlovento** Windward Islands; **islas de Sotavento** Leeward Islands; **islas Filipinas** Philippine Islands
Islam, el Islam
islan•dés -desa *adj* Icelandic || *mf* Icelander || *m* (*idioma*) Icelandic
Islandia *f* Iceland
isle•ño -ña *adj* island || *mf* islander; (Cuba) Canarian
isleta *f* isle
isométri•co -ca *adj* isometric
isométrica *f* isometrics
isósce•les *adj* (*pl* **-les**) isosceles
isótopo *m* isotope
israe•lí (*pl* **-líes**) *adj* & *mf* Israeli

israelita *adj* & *mf* Israelite
istmo *m* isthmus
Italia *f* Italy
italia•no -na *adj* & *mf* Italian
itáli•co -ca *adj* Italic; (typ) italic || *f* (typ) italics
itinera•rio -ria *adj* & *m* itinerary
izar §60 *tr* (naut) to hoist, haul up
izquierda *f* left hand; left-hand side; (pol) left; **a la izquierda** left, on the left, to the left
izquierdear *intr* to go wild, go astray, go awry
izquierdista *adj* leftist || *mf* leftist, leftwinger
izquierdizante *adj* leftish
izquier•do -da *adj* left; left-hand; left-handed; crooked; **levantarse del izquierdo** to get out of bed on the wrong side || *f* see **izquierda**

J

J, j (jota) *f* eleventh letter of the Spanish alphabet
jabalcón *m* strut, brace
jaba•lí *m* (*pl* **-líes**) wild boar
jabalina *f* javelin; wild sow
jabardillo *m* (*de insectos*) noisy swarm; noisy throng
jabeque *m* (naut) xebec; gash in the face
jabón *m* soap; cake of soap; **dar jabón a** to softsoap; **dar un jabón a** (coll) to upbraid, to reprimand; **jabón de afeitar** shaving soap; **jabón de Castilla** Castile soap; **jabón de tocador** or **de olor** toilet soap; **jabón de sastre** soapstone, French chalk; **jabón en polvo** soap powder
jabonado *m* soaping; (*ropa lavada o por lavar*) wash
jabonadura *f* soaping; **dar una jabonadura a** to lambaste, upbraid; **jabonaduras** soapy water; soapsuds
jabonar *tr* to soap; reprimand
jaboncillo *m* cake of toilet soap; **jaboncillo de sastre** soapstone, French chalk
jabone•ro -ra *adj* soap; (*toro*) yellowish, dirty-white || *mf* soapmaker; soap dealer || *f* soap dish
jabonete *m* cake of toilet soap
jabono•so -sa *adj* soapy, lathery
jaca *f* pony, jennet
jacal *m* (Guat, Mex, Ven) hut, shack
jácara *f* merry ballad; cheerful song and dance; night revelers; story, argument; fake, hoax, lie; annoyance, bother
jacarear *intr* to go serenading, go singing in the street; be disagreeable
jáca•ro -ra *adj* & *m* braggart || *f* see **jácara**
jacinto *m* hyacinth
jaco *m* nag, jade; gray parrot
jactancia *f* boasting, bragging
jactancio•so -sa *adj* boastful, bragging

jactar *ref* to boast, brag; **jactarse de** to boast of
jade *m* jade
jadeante *adj* panting
jadear *intr* to pant
jadeo *m* panting
ja•ez *m* (*pl* **-eces**) harness, piece of harness; ilk, stripe, kind; **jaeces** trappings
jaguar *m* jaguar
jagüel *m* (Arg) reservoir
jaharrar *tr* to plaster
jalar *tr* to pull; flirt with || *intr* to get out, beat it || *ref* to get drunk
jalbegar §44 *tr* to whitewash; (*el rostro*) to paint || *ref* to paint the face
jalbegue *m* whitewash; whitewashing; paint, make-up
jalda•do -da *adj* bright-yellow
jalea *f* jelly; **hacerse una jalea** to be madly in love
jalear *tr* (*a los que bailan y cantan*) to animate with clapping and shouting; (*a los perros*) to incite, urge on; (Chile) to tease, pester || *intr* to dance the jaleo || *ref* to have a noisy time; swing and sway
jaleo *m* cheering, shouting; jamboree; jaleo (*vivacious Spanish solo dance*)
jalis•co -ca *adj* (Guat, Mex) drunk || *m* (Mex) straw hat
jalma *f* small packsaddle
jalón *m* surveying rod, range pole; (Guat, Mex) swig of liquor; (CAm) beau; **jalón de mira** leveling rod
jalonar *tr* to stake out, mark out
jalonear *tr* (Mex) to pull, jerk
jalonero *m* (surv) rodman
jamaica *m* Jamaica rum || *f* (Mex) charity fair
jamaica•no -na or **jamaiqui•no -na** *adj* & *mf* Jamaican
jamar *tr* to eat
jamás *adv* never; ever

jamba *f* jamb

jambaje *m* doorframe, window frame

jamelgo *m* jade, nag

jamete *m* samite

jamón *m* ham

jamona *f* fat middle-aged woman

jamugas *fpl* mule chair

jánda•lo -la *adj & mf* Andalusian

Jantipa *f* or **Jantipe** *f* Xanthippe

Japón, el Japan

japo•nés -nesa *adj & mf* Japanese ‖ *m* (*idioma*) Japanese

jaque *m* (*lance del ajedrez*) check; bully; **dar jaque a** to check; **dar jaque mate a** to checkmate; **en jaque** in check; **estar muy jaque** to be full of pep; **jaque mate** checkmate; **tener en jaque** to hold a threat over the head of ‖ *interj* check!

jaquear *tr* to check; (*al enemigo*) harass

jaqueca *f* sick headache; **dar una jaqueca a** to bore to death

jacqueco•so -sa *adj* boring, tiresome

jaquemar *m* jack (*figure that strikes a clock bell*)

jarabe *m* syrup; sweet drink; **jarabe de pico** lip service, idle promise

jarana *f* merrymaking; rumpus; carousal; spree; trick, deceit; jest, joke; small guitar; **ir de jarana** to go on a spree

jaranear *tr* (CAm, Col) to swindle, cheat ‖ *intr* to go on a spree; raise a rumpus; joke

jarane•ro -ra *adj* merrymaking; cheerful, merry ‖ *mf* merrymaker, reveler

jarano *m* sombrero

jarcia *f* fishing tackle; jumble, mess; **jarcias** tackle, rigging; **jarcia trozada** junk (*old cable*)

jardín *m* garden, flower garden; (baseball) field, outfield; (naut) privy, latrine; **jardín central** (baseball) center field; **jardín de la infancia** kindergarten; **jardín derecho** (baseball) right field; **jardín izquierdo** (baseball) left field

jardinera *f* jardiniere, flower stand; basket carriage; summer trolley car, open trolley car

jardinería *f* gardening

jardine•ro -ra *mf* gardener; **jardinero adornista** landscape gardener ‖ *m* (baseball) fielder, outfielder ‖ *f* see **jardinera**

jardinista *mf* landscape gardener

jarea *f* (Mex) hunger

jarear *intr* (Bol) to stop for a rest ‖ *ref* (Mex) to flee, run away; (Mex) to swing, sway; (Mex) to die of starvation

jareta *f* (sew) casing

jari•fo -fa *adj* showy, spruce, natty

jaro•cho -cha *adj* brusk, bluff ‖ *m* insulting fellow; Veracruz peasant

jarope *m* syrup; nasty potion

jarra *f* jug, jar, water pitcher; **de jarras** or **en jarras** with arms akimbo

jarrete *m* hock, gambrel

jarretera *f* garter

jarro *m* pitcher; **echar un jarro de agua (fría) a** to pour cold water on

jarrón *m* (*vaso para adornar chimeneas,* consolas, etc.) vase; (*sobre un pedestal*) urn

jaspe *m* jasper

jaspea•do -da *adj* marbled, speckled ‖ *m* marbling, speckling

jaspear *tr* to marble, speckle

jateo *m* foxhound

ja•to -ta *mf* calf

Jauja *f* Cockaigne; ¿estamos aquí o en Jauja? where do you think you are?; vivir en Jauja to live in the lap of luxury

jaula *m* cage; (*embalaje de listones de madera*) crate; (Mex) open freight car; (Cuba, P-R) police wagon; **jaula de locos** insane asylum, madhouse

jauría *f* pack (*of hounds*)

java•nés -nesa *adj & mf* Javanese ‖ *m* (*idioma*) Javanese

jazmín *m* jasmine; **jasmín de la India** gardenia

jazz *m* jazz

J.C. *abbr* Jesucristo

jebe *m* alum; (SAm) rubber

jedive *m* khedive

jefa *f* female head or leader; **jefa de ruta** hostess (*on a bus*)

jefatura *f* headship, leadership; (*de policía*) headquarters

jefe *m* chief, boss, head, leader; (*de una tribu*) chieftain; **jefe de cocina** chef; **jefe do coro** choirmaster; **jefe de equipajes** (rr) baggage master; **jefe de estación** stationmaster; **jefe del estado** chief of state; **jefe del gobierno** chief executive; **jefe de redacción** editor in chief; **jefe de ruta** guide; **jefe de tren** (rr) conductor; **jefe de tribu** chieftain; **quedar jefe** (Chile) to gamble away everything

jején *m* gnat, sandfly

jenabe *m* or **jenable** *m* mustard

jengibre *m* ginger

Jenofonte *m* Xenophon

jeque *m* sheik

jerarca *m* hierarch, head

jerarquía *f* hierarchy; **de jerarquía** important

jeremiada *f* jeremiad

jeremiquear *intr* to moan; pour out one's troubles

jerez *m* sherry

jerga *f* coarse cloth; straw mattress; (*lenguaje especial de ciertos oficios; lenguaje difícil de entender*) jargon

jergón *m* straw mattress; ill-fitting clothes; (*persona torpe y estúpida*) lummox

Jericó Jericho

jerife *m* shereef

jerigonza *f* (*lenguaje especial de ciertos oficios; lenguaje difícil de entender*) jargon; (*lenguaje vulgar, caló*) slang; piece of folly

jeringa *f* syringe; (*para inyectar materias blandas en una máquina*) gun; annoyance, plague; **jeringa de engrase** or **grasa** grease gun

jeringar §44 *tr* to syringe; inject; give an enema to; plague

jeringazo *m* injection, shot; squirt

jeringuilla f (*jeringa pequeña*) syringe; (bot) mock orange
Jerjes m Xerxes
jeroglífi•co -ca adj & m hieroglyphic
Jerónimo m Jerome
jer•sey m (pl **-seis**) jersey, sweater
Jerusalén Jerusalem
Jesucristo m Jesus Christ
jesuíta adj & m Jesuit
jesuíti•co -ca adj Jesuitic(al)
Jesús m Jesus; (*imagen del niño Jesús*) bambino; **en un decir Jesús** in an instant; **¡Jesús, María y José!** my gracious!
jeta f hog's snout, pig face; (*rostro de una persona*) phiz, mug; **estar con tanta jeta** to make a long face; **poner jeta** to pucker one's lips
jetu•do -da adj thick-lipped; grim, gruff
Jhs. abbr **Jesús**
jíba•ro -ra mf (W-I) white peasant
jibia f cuttlefish
jícara f chocolate cup; (CAm, Mex, W-I) calabash cup
jícaro m calabash (tree)
jifia f swordfish
jilguero m linnet, goldfinch
jilote m (Mex) green ear of corn
jineta f (zool) genet
jinete m rider, horseman
jinetear tr (*caballos cerriles*) to break in ‖ intr to show off one's horsemanship
jinglar intr to swing, to rock
jingoísmo m jingoism
jingoísta adj & mf jingo
jipa•to -ta adj pale, wan; insipid, tasteless; (Guat) drunk
jipijapa m Panama hat ‖ f jipijapa; strip of jipijapa straw
jira f strip of cloth; outing, picnic; trip, tour; swing, political trip
jirón m rag, tatter, shred; (*de una falda*) facing; pennant; bit, drop, shred; **hacer jirones** to tear to shreds
jitomate m (Mex) tomato
joco•so -sa adj jocose, jocular
jocotal m (CAm, Mex) Spanish plum (*tree*)
jocote m (CAm, Mex) Spanish plum (*fruit*)
jocoyote m (Mex) baby (*youngest child*)
jofaina f washbowl, basin
jolgorio m fun, merriment
jonrón m (baseball) home run
Jordán m Jordan (*river*); **ir al Jordán** to be born again
Jordania f Jordan (*country*)
jorda•no -na adj & mf Jordanian
jorguín m sorcerer, wizard
jorguina f sorceress, witch
jorguinería f sorcery, witchcraft
jornada f journey, trip, stage; day's journey; (*horas del trabajo diario del obrero*) workday; (*tiempo que dura la vida de un hombre*) lifetime; battle; (*muerte*) passing; summer residence of diplomat or diplomatic corps; event, occasion; undertaking; (mil) expedition; (*de un drama*) (archaic) act; **a grandes** or **largas jornadas** by forced marches; **al fin de la jornada** in the

end; **caminar por sus jornadas** to proceed with circumspection; **hacer mala jornada** to get nowhere; **jornada ordinaria** full time; **jornada reducida** reduced working hours
jornal m day's work; day's pay; **a jornal** by the day; **jornal mínimo** minimum wage
jornalero m day laborer
joroba f hump; annoyance, bother
joroba•do -da adj humpbacked, hunchbacked; annoyed, bothered ‖ mf humpback, hunchback
jorobar tr to annoy, pester
jorongo m (Mex) poncho; (Mex) woolen blanket
jota f (*letra del alfabeto*) J; jota (*Spanish folk dance and music*); jot, iota, tittle; vegetable soup; **sin faltar una jota** with not a whit left out
joven adj young; **ser joven de esperanzas** to have a bright future ‖ mf youth, young person; **de joven** as a youth, as a young man, as a young woman
jovial adj jovial
joya f jewel; (*brocamantón*) diamond brooch; (*agasajo*) gift, present; (*persona o cosa de mucha valía*) (fig) jewel, gem; **joya de familia** heirloom; **joyas** jewelry; trousseau; **joyas de fantasía** costume jewelry
joyante adj glossy
joyelero m jewel case, casket
joyería f (*conjunto de joyas*) jewelry; jewelry shop; jewelry trade
joye•ro -ra mf jeweler ‖ m jewel case, casket
Juan m John; **Buen Juan** sap, easy mark; **Juan Español** the Spanish people, the typical Spaniard; **San Juan Bautista** John the Baptist
Juana f Jane, Jean, Joan; **Juana de Arco** Joan of Arc, Jeanne d'Arc; **juanas** glove stretcher
juanete m bunion; high cheekbone
jubilación f retirement; (*renta de la persona jubilada*) pension, retirement annuity
jubila•do -da adj retired ‖ mf retired person, pensioner
jubilar tr to retire, pension; throw out ‖ intr to rejoice; retire, be pensioned ‖ ref to rejoice; retire, be pensioned; (Col) to decline, go to pieces; (CAm, Ven) to play hooky; (Cuba, Mex) to become a past master
jubileo m much coming and going, great doings; (eccl) jubilee; **por jubileo** once in a long time
júbilo m jubilation
jubilo•so -sa adj jubilant, joyful
jubón m jerkin
judaísmo m Judaism
judería f (*raza judaica*) Jewry; (*barrio de los judíos*) ghetto
judía f Jewess; kidney bean, string bean; **judía de careta** black-eyed bean; **judía de la peladilla** Lima bean
judicatura f judicature; (*cargo de juez*) judgeship
judicial adj judicial, judiciary

ja
ju

judí•o -a *adj* Jewish ‖ *mf* Jew ‖ *f* see **judía**

juego *m* (*acción de jugar*) play, playing; (*ejercicio recreativo en el cual se gana o se pierde*) game; (*vicio de jugar*) gambling; (*lugar donde se ejecutan ciertos juegos*): (bowling) alley; (tennis) court; (baseball) field; (*tantos necesarios para ganar la partida*) game; (*de muebles*) suit, suite; (*de café*) service; (*de vajilla*) set; (*de luces, colores, aguas*) play; (mach) play; (*p.ej., de diplomacia*) (fig) game; **a juego** to match, e.g., **una silla a juego** a chair to match; **conocer el juego de** to see through, to have the number of; **en juego** at hand; **hacer juego** to match; **hacer juego con** to match, to go with; **juego de alcoba** bedroom suit; **juego de azar** game of chance; **juego de bolas** (mach) ball bearing; **juego de campanas** chimes; **juego de comedor** dining-room suit; **juego de envite** gambling game, game played for money; **juego de escritorio** desk set; **juego de la cuna** cat's cradle; **juego de la pulga** tiddlywinks; **juego del corro** ring-around-a-rosy; **juego del salto** leapfrog; **juego del tres en raya** tick-tack-toe played with movable counters or pebbles; **juego de manos** legerdemain, sleight of hand; roughhousing; **juego de niños** (*cosa muy fácil*) child's play; **juego de palabras** play on words, pun; **juego de pelota** ball game; pelota; **juego de piernas** footwork; **juego de por ver** (Chile) game played for fun; **juego de prendas** game of forfeits, forfeits; **juego de suerte** game of chance; **juego de tejo** shuffleboard; **juego de timbres** glockenspiel; **juego de vocablos** or **voces** play on words, pun; **juego limpio** fair play; **juego público** gambling house; **juegos de sociedad** parlor games; **juegos malabares** juggling; flimflam; **juego sucio** foul play; **no ser cosa de juego** to be no laughing matter; **por juego** in fun, for fun; **verle a uno el juego** to be on to someone

juerga *f* carousal, spree; **juerga de borrachera** drinking bout, binge; **ir de juerga** (coll) to go on a spree

juerguista *mf* carouser, reveler

jue•ves *m* (*pl* **-ves**) Thursday; **Jueves Santo** Maundy Thursday

juez *m* (*pl* **jueces**) judge; **juez de alzadas** appellate judge; **juez de guardia** coroner; **juez de instrucción** examining magistrate; **juez de paz** justice of the peace; **juez de salida** (sport) starter; **juez de tiempo** (sport) timekeeper

jugada *f* (*lance*) play, throw, stroke, move; **mala jugada** dirty trick

juga•dor -dora *mf* player; gambler; **jugador de manos** prestidigitator; **jugador de ventaja** sharper

jugar §42 *tr* (*p.ej., un naipe, una partida de juego*) to play; (*una espada*) wield; (*arriesgar*) stake, risk; (*las manos, los dedos*) move; **jugarle a uno las bebidas** to match someone for the drinks ‖ *intr* to play; to gamble; (*hacer juego dos cosas*) match;

(*intervenir*) figure, participate; **jugar a** (*p.ej., los naipes, el tenis*) to play; **jugar con** (*un contrario*) to play; (*una persona; los sentimientos de una persona*) toy with; match; **jugar en** to have a hand in ‖ *ref* (*p.ej., la vida*) to risk; to be at stake; **jugarse el todo por el todo** to stake all, shoot the works

jugarreta *f* bad play, poor play; mean trick, dirty trick

juglar *m* minstrel, jongleur; (*bufón*) (archaic) juggler

juglaría *f* minstrelsy

jugo *m* (*p.ej., de la naranja*) juice; (*de la carne*) gravy; (*líquido orgánico*) juice; (fig) gist, essence, substance; **en su jugo** (culin) au jus; **jugo de muñeca** elbow grease

jugo•so -sa *adj* juicy; substantial, important

juguete *m* toy, plaything; (*burla*) joke, jest; (theat) skit; **de juguete** toy, e.g., **soldado de juguete** toy soldier; **juguete de movimiento** mechanical toy; **por juguete** for fun, in fun

juguetear *intr* to frolic, romp, sport

juguete•ro -ra *adj* toy ‖ *mf* toy dealer ‖ *m* whatnot, étagère

juguete-sorpresa *m* (*pl* **juguetes-sorpresa**) jack-in-the-box

jugue•tón -tona *adj* playful, frisky

juicio *m* judgment; (law) trial; **estar en su cabal juicio** to be in one's right mind; **estar fuera de juicio** to be out of one's mind; **juicio de Dios** (hist) ordeal; **pedir en juicio** (law) to sue

juicio•so -sa *adj* judicious, wise

julepe *m* julep; scolding; scare, fright

julepear *tr* to scold; whip; (SAm) to scare, frighten; (Mex) to weary, tire out

julio *m* July

julo *m* lead cow, lead mule

jumen•to -ta *mf* ass, donkey

juncal *adj* willowy, rushy; (fig) willowy, lissome

juncia *f* sedge; **vender juncia** to boast, brag

junco *m* (*embarcación china*) junk; (bot) rush, bulrush; **junco de Indias** (bot) rattan; **junco de laguna** (bot) rush, bulrush

junco•so -sa *adj* rushy, full of rushes

jungla *f* jungle

junio *m* June

junípero *m* juniper

junquera *f* rush, bulrush

junquillo *m* jonquil

junta *f* meeting, conference; board, council; junction, union; joint, seam; (*empaquetadura*) gasket; (*arandela*) washer; **junta de comercio** board of trade; **junta de charnela** (mach) knuckle; **junta de sanidad** board of health; **junta universal** (mach) universal joint

juntamente *adv* together; at the same time

juntar *tr* to join, unite; gather, gather together; (*una puerta*) half-close ‖ *ref* to gather together; go along; copulate

jun•to -ta *adj* joined, united; **jun•tos -tas** together ‖ *f* see **junta** ‖ **junto** *adv* together;

at the same time; **junto a** near, close to; **junto con** along with, together with; **todo junto** at the same time, all at once
juntura *f* junction; (*p.ej., de una cañería; de un hueso*) joint; connection, coupling
jura *f* oath
jura•do -da *adj* (*enemigo*) sworn ‖ *m* (*conjunto de cuidadanos encargados de determinar la culpabilidad del acusado; conjunto de examinadores de un certamen*) jury; (*cada uno de los expresados individuous*) juror; juryman
juramentar *tr* to swear in ‖ *ref* to take an oath, be sworn in
juramento *m* oath; (*voto, reniego*) curse, swearword; **prestar juramento a** to swear to; **tomar juramento a** to swear in
jurar *tr* to swear; (*la verdad de una cosa*) swear to; swear allegiance to ‖ *intr* (*pronunciar un juramento*) to swear, take an oath; (*echar votos o reniegos*) swear, curse; **jurar + inf** to swear to + *inf* ‖ *ref* to swear; **jurársela** or **jurárselas a uno** to have it in for someone, swear to get even with someone
jure•ro -ra *mf* (SAm) false witness
jurídi•co -ca *adj* juridical
jurisconsulto *m* (*el que escribe sobre el derecho*) jurist; (*jurisperito*) legal expert
jurisdicción *f* jurisdiction
jurisperito *m* jurist, legal expert
jurisprudencia *f* jurisprudence
jurista *mf* jurist
juro *m* right of perpetual ownership; **de juro** inevitably, for sure
justa *f* joust, tournament
justamente *adv* just, just at that time; justly; (*ajustadamente*) tightly
justar *intr* to joust, to tilt
justicia *f* justice; (*castigo de muerte*) execution; **de justicia** justly, deservedly; **hacer justicia a** to do justice to; **ir por justicia** to go to court, to bring suit
justicie•ro -ra *adj* just, fair; stern, righteous
justificable *adj* justifiable
justifica•do -da *adj* (*hecho*) just, right; (*persona*) just, upright
justificante *m* voucher, proof
justificar §73 *tr* to justify; (typ) to justify
justillo *m* jerkin, waist
justipreciar *tr* to estimate, appraise
jus•to -ta *adj* just; right, exact; (*apretado*) tight ‖ *mf* just person ‖ *f* see **justa** ‖ **justo** *adv* just; right, in tune; tight; (*con estrechez*) in straitened circumstances
Jutlandia *f* Jutland
ju•to -ta *mf* Jute
juvenil *adj* juvenile, youthful
juventud *f* youth; young people
juzgado *m* court of law; courtroom; court of one judge
juzgar §44 *tr & intr* to judge; **a juzgar por** judging by; **juzgar de** to judge, pass judgment on

K

K, k (ka) *f* twelfth letter of the Spanish alphabet
karate *m* or **karaté** *m* karate
karateka *m* karate expert
kermesse *f* var of **quermés**
keroseno *m* kerosene, coal oil
kg. *abbr* **kilogramo**
kilate *m* var of **quilate**
kilo *m* kilo, kilogram
kilociclo *m* kilocycle
kilogramo *m* kilogram
kilometraje *m* kilometrage, distance in kilometers
kilométri•co -ca *adj* kilometric; (coll) interminable, long-drawn-out
kilómetro *m* kilometer
kilovatio *m* kilowatt
kilovatio-hora *m* (*pl* **kilovatios-hora**) kilowatt-hour
kimono *m* var of **quimono**
kinescopio *m* (telv) kinescope
kiosco *m* var of **quiosco**
kirieleisón *m* dirge; **cantar el kirieleisón** to beg mercy
km. *abbr* **kilómetro**
kph. *abbr* **kilómetros por hora**
kv. *abbr* **kilovatio**
kv-h *abbr* **kilovatio-hora**

L

L, l (ele) thirteenth letter of the Spanish alphabet
la *art def fem* of **el** ‖ *pron pers fem* her, it; you ‖ *pron dem* that, the one; **la que** who, which, that; she who, the one that
laberinto *m* labyrinth, maze
labia *f* fluency, smoothness
labial *adj & f* labial
labio *m* lip; (fig) edge, lip; **chuparse los labios** to smack one's lips; **labio leporino** harelip; **leer en los labios** to lip read
labiolectura *f* lip reading

ju
la

labio·so -sa *adj* fluent, smooth

labor *f* labor, work; (*cultivo de los campos*) farming, tilling; (*obra de coser, bordar, etc.*) needlework, fancywork, embroidery; **hacer labor** to match; **labor blanca** linen work, linen embroidery; **labor de ganchillo** crocheting

laborable *adj* workable; arable, tillable; (*dia*) work

laborante *m* journeyman; political henchman

laborar *tr* to work ‖ *intr* to scheme

laboratorio *m* laboratory; **laboratorio de idiomas** language laboratory; **laboratorio espacial** space laboratory; Skylab

laborio·so -sa *adj* (*trabajador*) laborious, industrious; (*trabajoso*) laborious, arduous

laborismo *m* British Labour Party

laborista *adj* Labour ‖ *mf* Labourite

laborterapia *f* work therapy

labra *f* carving

labrada *f* fallow ground (*to be sown the following year*)

labrade·ro -ra *adj* arable, tillable

labra·do -da *adj* wrought, fashioned; carved; figured, embroidered ‖ *m* carving; **labrado de madera** wood carving ‖ *f* see **labrada**

labra·dor -dora *adj* work; farm ‖ *mf* farmer; (*campesino*) peasant ‖ *m* plowman; **el Labrador** Labrador

labrantí·o -a *adj* farm ‖ *m* farmland

labranza *f* farming; farm, farmland

labrar *tr* to work, fashion; (*la piedra, la madera*) carve; (*arar*) plow; (*construir o mandar construir*) build; till, cultivate; cause, bring about ‖ *intr* to make a lasting impression

labrie·go -ga *mf* peasant

laca *f* lacquer; shellac; **laca de uñas** nail polish; **lacas** lacquer ware

lacayo *m* lackey, footman

lacear *tr* to tie with a bow; adorn with bows; (*la caza*) drive within shot; (*la caza menor*) trap, snare

lacería *f* poverty, want; trouble, bother; leprosy

lacerio·so -sa *adj* poor, needy

lacero *m* lassoer; poacher; dogcatcher

la·cio -cia *adj* faded, withered; languid; (*cabello*) lank, straight

lacóni·co -ca *adj* laconic

lacra *f* fault, defect; (*señal dejada por una enfermedad*) mark, remains; sore; scab, scar

lacrimóge·no -na *adj* tear, tear-producing

lacrimo·so -sa *adj* lachrymose, tearful

lactar *tr* to suckle

lácte·o -a *adj* milky

lacustre *adj* lake

ladear *tr* to tip, tilt; bend, lean; (*un avión*) bank ‖ *intr* to tip, tilt; bend, lean; turn away, turn off; (*la aguja de brújula*) deviate ‖ *ref* to tip, tilt; bend, lean; be equal, be even; (Chile) to fall in love; **ladearse a** (*un dictamen, un partido*) to lean to or toward

ladeo *m* tipping, tilting; bending, leaning; inclination, bent

lade·ro -ra *adj* side, lateral ‖ *f* hillside

ladilla *f* crab louse; **pegarse como ladilla** to stick like a leech

ladi·no -na *adj* crafty, sly, cunning; polyglot

lado *m* side; direction; (*del hilo telefónico*) end; **al lado** nearby; **dejar a un lado** to leave aside; **de lado** square, e.g., **diez centímetros de lado** ten centimeters square; **de otro lado** on the other hand; **de un lado** on the one hand; **echar a un lado** to cast aside; to finish up; **hacer lado** to make room; **hacerse a un lado** to step aside; **lados** backers, advisers; **mirar de lado** or **de medio lado** to look askance at; to sneak a look at; **ponerse al lado de** to take sides with; **por el lado de** in the direction of; **tirar por su lado** to pull for oneself

ladrar *tr* (*p.ej., injurias*) to bark ‖ *intr* to bark

ladrido *m* bark, barking; slander, blame

ladrillador *m* bricklayer

ladrillal *m* brickyard

ladrillo *m* brick; (*azulejo*) tile; (*p.ej., de chocolate*) cake; **ladrillo de fuego** or **ladrillo refractario** firebrick

la·drón -drona *adj* thievish, thieving ‖ *mf* thief ‖ *m* sluice gate; **ladrón de corazones** heartbreaker, lady-killer

ladronera *f* den of thieves; thievery; (*alcancía*) child's bank

ladronerío *m* (Arg) gang of thieves; (Arg) wave of thieving

ladronzue·lo -la *mf* petty thief

lagaña *f* var of **legaña**

lagar *m* wine press; olive press; (*establecimiento*) winery

lagarta *f* female lizard; sly woman; (ent) gypsy moth

lagartija *f* green lizard; wall lizard

lagarto *m* lizard; sly fellow; (Mex) fop, dandy; **lagarto de Indias** alligator

lago *m* lake

lagotear *tr & intr* to flatter, wheedle

lágrima *f* tear; (*de cualquier licor*) drop; **beberse las lágrimas** to hold back one's tears; **deshacerse en lágrimas** to weep one's eyes out; **lágrimas de cocodrilo** crocodile tears; **llorar a lágrima viva** to shed bitter tears

lagrimear *intr* to weep easily, be tearful; (*los ojos*) fill

lagrimo·so -sa *adj* tearful; (*ojos*) watery

laguna *f* (*lago pequeño*) lagoon; (*hueco, omisión*) lacuna, gap

laical *adj* lay

laicismo *m* secularism

laja *f* slab, flagstone

lama *f* mud, ooze, slim; pond scum

lambrija *f* earthworm; skinny person

lamedero *m* salt lick

lame·dor -dora *adj* licking ‖ *mf* licker ‖ *m* syrup; **dar lamedor** to lose at first in order to take in one's opponent

lamedura *f* lick, licking

lamentable *adj* lamentable

lamentación *f* lamentation

lamentar *tr, intr & ref* to lament, mourn

lamento *m* lament

lamento•so -sa *adj* lamentable; plaintive

lamer *tr* to lick; lap, lap against; (*las llamas un tejado*) to lick ‖ *ref* (*p.ej., los dedos*) to lick

lame•rón -rona *adj* (coll) sweet-toothed

lametada *f* lap, lick

lámina *f* sheet, plate, strip; (*plancha grabada*) engraving; (*pintura en cobre*) copper plate; (*figura estampada*) cut, picture, illustration

laminador *m* rolling mill

laminar *tr* to laminate; (*el hierro, el acero*) roll

lampadario *m* floor lamp

lámpara *f* lamp, light; (*mancha en la ropa*) grease spot, oil spot; (rad) vacuum tube; **atizar la lámpara** to fill up the glasses again; **lámpara de alcohol** spirit lamp; **lámpara de arco** arc lamp, arc light; **lámpara de bolsillo** flashlight; **lámpara de carretera** (aut) bright light; **lámpara de cruce** (aut) dimmer; **lámpara de pie** floor lamp; **lámpara de sobremesa** table lamp; **lámpara de socorro** trouble light; **lámpara de soldar** blowtorch; **lámpara de techo** ceiling light; (aut) dome light; **lámpara inundante** floodlight; **lámpara testigo** pilot light

lamparilla *f* rushlight; aspen

lampi•ño -ña *adj* beardless; hairless

lampista *mf* lamplighter ‖ *m* tinsmith, plumber, glazier, electrician

lana *f* wool; (CAm) common person; (CAm) swindler; **lana de acero** steel wool; **lana de ceiba** kapoc; **lana de escorias** mineral wool, rock wool; **lana de vidrio** glass wool

lance *m* cast, throw; (*en la red*) catch, haul; (*accidente en el juego*) play, move, stroke; (*ocasión crítica*) chance, pass, juncture; incident, event; (*riña*) row, quarrel; (taur) capework; **de lance** cheap; secondhand; **echar buen lance** to have a break; **lance de honor** affair of honor, duel; **tener pocos lances** to be dull and uninteresting

lancero *m* lancer, spearman, pikeman

lanceta *f* (surg) lancet; (Mex, SAm) sting

lancinante *adj* piercing

lancha *f* barge, lighter; flagstone, slab; (naut) longboat; (nav) launch; (Ecuad) mist, fog; (Ecuad) frost; **lancha automóvil** launch, motor launch; **lancha de auxilio** lifeboat (*stationed on shore*); **lancha de carreras** speedboat; **lancha de desembarco** (nav) landing craft; **lancha salvavidas** lifeboat (*on shipboard*)

lanchar *intr* (Ecuad) to get foggy; (Ecuad) to freeze

lan•dó *m* (*pl* **-dós**) landau

landre *f* swollen gland; hidden pocket

lanería *f* wool shop; **lanerías** woolens, woolen goods

langosta *f* (*insecto*) locust; (*crustáceo*) lobster, spiny lobster

langostera *f* lobster pot

langostín *m* or **langostino** *m* prawn (*Peneus*)

langostón *m* green grasshopper

languidecer §22 *intr* to languish

languidez *f* languor

lángui•do -da *adj* languid, languorous

lano•so -sa *adj* woolly

lanu•do da *adj* woolly; (Ecuad, Ven) coarse, ill-bred

lanza *f* lance, pike; (*de la manguera*) nozzle; (*palo de coche*) wagon pole

lanzabom•bas *m* (*pl* **-bas**) (aer) bomb release; (mil) trench mortar

lanzacohe•tes *m* (*pl* **-tes**) rocket launcher

lanzadera *f* shuttle; **parecer una lanzadera** to buzz around

lanza•do -da *adj* sloping; (*salida de una carrera*) (sport) running (*start*)

lanza•dor -dora *mf* thrower; **lanzador de lodo** (fig) mudslinger ‖ *m* launcher; (aer) jettison gear; (baseball) pitcher

lanzaespu•mas *m* (*pl* **-mas**) foam extinguisher

lanzalla•mas *m* (*pl* **-mas**) flame thrower

lanzamiento *m* throw, hurl, fling, launch; (*de un buque*) launching; (*de un cohete*) shot, launch; (*p.ej., de víveres*) (aer) airdrop; (*de bombas*) (aer) release; (*de paracaidistas*) (aer) jump; (law) dispossession; (naut) steeve

lanzami•nas *m* (*pl* **-nas**) (nav) mine layer

lanzapla•tos *m* (*pl* **-tos**) trap

lanzar §60 *tr* to throw, hurl, fling; (*un proyecto, un cohete, maldiciones, una ofensiva, un producto nuevo, un buque*) launch; (*una mirada*) cast; vomit, throw up; (*flores, hojas una planta*) put forth; (*una advertencia*) toss, toss out; (aer) to airdrop; (*bombas*) (aer) to release; (law) to dispossess ‖ *ref* to launch, launch forth; throw oneself; dash, rush; (aer) to jump; (sport) to sprint

lanzatorpe•dos *m* (*pl* **-dos**) (nav) torpedo tube

laña *f* clamp; rivet

lañar *tr* to clamp; (*objetos de porcelana*) rivet

lapicero *m* pencil holder; mechanical pencil; ball-point pen; **lapicero fuente** fountain pen

lápida *f* tablet, stone; **lápida supulcral** gravestone

lapidar *tr* to stone to death

lá•piz *m* (*pl* **-pices**) (*grafito*) black lead; (*barrita que sirve para escribir*) pencil, lead pencil; **lápiz de bolilla** (Para) ball-point pen; **lápiz de labios** lipstick; **lápiz de pizarra** slate pencil; **lápiz de pasta** (Chile) ball-point pen; **lápiz de plomo** graphite; **lápiz estíptico** styptic pencil; **lápiz labial** lipstick

lapizar §60 *tr* to mark or line with a pencil

la•pón -pona *adj* Lapp ‖ *mf* Lapp, Laplander ‖ *m* (*idioma*) Lapp

Laponia *f* Lapland

lapso *m* lapse

laquear *tr* to lacquer

lardo•so -sa *adj* greasy, fatty

larga *f* long billiard cue; **dar largas a** to postpone, put off

largamente *adv* at length, extensively; in comfort; generously; long, for a long time

largar §44 *tr* to let go, release; ease, slack; utter; (*un golpe*) deal, strike, give; (naut) to unfurl; (Col) to give ‖ *ref* to move away; get away, sneak away, beat it; take to sea; (*el ancla*) to come loose

lar•go -ga *adj* long; abundant; liberal, generous; quick, ready; shrewd, cunning; (naut) loose, slack; **a la larga** in the long run, in the end; **a lo largo** lengthwise; at great length; far away; **a lo largo de** along; along with; throughout; in the course of; (*el mar*) far out in; **a lo más largo** at most; **hacerse a lo largo** to get out in the open sea; **largo de lengua** loose-tongued; **largo de uñas** light-fingered; **pasar de largo** to pass without stopping; take a quick look; miss; **ponerse de largo** to come out, make one's debut; **vestir de largo** to wear long clothes ‖ *m* length ‖ *f* see **larga** ‖ **largo** *adv* at length, at great length; abundantly ‖ **largo** *interj* get out of here!

largometraje *m* full-featured film, full-length movie

largor *m* length

larguero *m* (*palo, madero*) stringer; (*almohada larga*) bolster; (aer) longeron

largueza *f* length; liberality, generosity

larguiru•cho -cha *adj* gangling, lanky

largura *f* length

lárice *m* larch tree

laringe *f* larynx

larínge•o -a *adj* laryngeal

laringitis *f* laryngitis

laringoscopio *m* laryngoscope

larva *f* larva; mask; (*duende*) hobgoblin

lasca *f* advantage, benefit

lascar §73 *tr* (naut) to pay out, slacken; (Mex) to scratch, bruise; (*un objeto de porcelana*) (Mex) to chip

lascivia *f* lasciviousness

lasci•vo -va *adj* lascivious; playful

láser *m* laser

la•so -sa *adj* tired, exhausted; weak, wan

lástima *f* pity; (*quejido*) complaint; **contar lástimas** to tell a hard-luck story; **dar lástima** to be pitiful; **es lástima (que)** it is a pity (that); **estar hecho una lástima** to be a sorry sight; **hacer lástima** to be pitiful; **llorar lástimas** to put on a show of tears; **poner lástima** to be pitiful; **¡qué lástima!** what a pity!, what a shame!; **¡qué lástima de saliva!** what a waste of breath!

lastimar *tr* to hurt, injure; hurt, offend; bruise ‖ *ref* to hurt oneself; bruise oneself; complain

lastime•ro -ra *adj* hurtful, injurious; pitiful, sad, doleful

lastimo•so -sa *adj* pitiful

lastra *f* slab, flagstone

lastrar *tr* (aer & naut) to ballast

lastre *m* (aer & naut) ballast; (fig) wisdom, maturity; (coll) food; (rr) (Chile) ballast

lat. *abrr* **latín, latitud**

lata *f* (*hojalata*) tin, tin plate; (*envase*) tin, tin can; (*madero sin pulir*) log; (*tabla delgada*) lath; annoyance, bore; **dar la lata a** (coll) to pester; **es una lata** that's terribly boring; **estar en la lata** (Col) to be penni-

less; **¡que lata!** what a nuisance! what a curse!

latebra *f* hiding place

latebro•so -sa *adj* furtive, secretive

latente *adj* latent

lateral *adj* lateral

latido *m* (*del perro*) yelp; (*del corazón*) beat, throb; (*dolor*) pang, twinge

latifundio *m* large neglected landed estate

latigazo *m* lash; crack of whip; (*reprensión áspera*) lashing

látigo *m* whip, horsewhip; cinch strap

latiguear *tr* to lash, whip ‖ *intr* crack a whip

latiguillo *m* small whip; (*del actor u orador*) claptrap

latín *m* Latin; **latín de cocina** dog Latin, hog Latin; **latín rústico** or **vulgar** Vulgar Latin; **saber latín** or **mucho latín** to be very shrewd

latinajo *m* dog Latin, hog Latin; Latin word or phrase (*slipped into the vernacular*)

latinar or **latinear** *intr* to use Latin

lati•no -na *adj* Latin; (naut) lateen ‖ *mf* Latin

Latinoamérica *f* Latin America

latinoamerica•no -na *adj* Latin-American ‖ *mf* Latin American

latir *tr* (Ven) to annoy, bore, molest ‖ *intr* (*el perro*) to bark, yelp; (*el corazón*) beat, throb; **me late que** (Mex) I have a hunch that

latitud *f* latitude

la•to -ta *adj* broad ‖ *f* see **lata**

latón *m* brass; (Cuba) garbage pail

lato•so -sa *adj* annoying, boring ‖ *mf* bore

latrocinio *m* thievery; thievishness

laucha *f* (Arg, Chile) mouse

laúd *m* (mus) lute; (zool) leatherback turtle

laudable *adj* laudable

láudano *m* laudanum

laudato•rio -ria *adj* laudatory

laudo *m* (law) finding, decision

láurea *f* laurel wreath

laurea•do -da *adj* & *mf* laureate

laurean•do -da *mf* graduate, candidate for a degree

laurear *tr* to trim or adorn with laurel; crown with laurel; decorate, honor, reward

laurel *m* laurel; (*de la victoria*) laurels; **dormirse sobre sus laureles** to rest or sleep on one's laurels

láure•o -a *adj* laurel ‖ *f* see **láurea**

lauréola *f* crown of laurel, laurel wreath; (*aureola*) halo

lava *f* lava; (min) washing

lavable *adj* washable

lavabo *m* washstand; washroom, lavatory

lavaca•ras *mf* (*pl* **-ras**) fawner, flatterer, bootlicker

lavaco•ches *m* (*pl* **-ches**) car washer

lavada *f* wash(ing)

lavade•dos *m* (*pl* **-dos**) finger bowl

lavadero *m* laundry; (*tabla de lavar*) washboard; (*a orillas de un río*) washing place; (Guat, Mex, SAm) placer

lava•do -da *adj* brazen, fresh, impudent ‖ *m* wash, washing; **lavado a seco** dry cleaning; **lavado cerebral** or **de cerebro** brainwashing; **lavado químico** dry cleaning

lava·dor -dora *mf* washer ‖ *m* (phot) washer ‖ *f* washing machine; **lavadora de platos** or **de vajilla** dishwasher

lavadura *f* washing; (*agua sucia; rozadura de una cuerda*) washings

lavafru·tas *m* (*pl* **-tas**) fruit bowl, finger bowl

lavama·nos *m* (*pl* **-nos**) (*pila con caño y llaῦe*) washstand; (*jofaina*) washbowl

lavanda *f* lavender

lavandera *f* laundress, laundrywoman, washerwoman; (orn) sandpiper

lavandero *m* launderer, laundryman

lavándula *f* lavender

lavao·jos *m* (*pl* **-jos**) eyecup

lavaparabri·sas *m* (*pl* **-sas**) windshield washer

lavapla·tos (*pl* **-tos**) *mf* (*persona*) dishwasher ‖ *m* (*aparato*) dishwasher; (Chile) kitchen sink

lavar *tr & ref* to wash

lavativa *f* enema; annoyance, bore

lavatorio *m* washing; washstand; toilet; washroom; (*ceremonia de lavar los pies*) maundy; (med) wash, lotion

lavavajillas *m* dishwasher

lavazas *fpl* dirty water, wash water

laxante *adj & m* laxative

laxar *tr* to ease, slack; (*el vientre*) loosen

la·xo -xa *adj* lax, slack; (fig) lax, loose

laya *f* spade; kind, quality

layar *tr* to spade, dig with a spade

lazada *f* bowknot

lazar §60 *tr* to lasso

lazarillo *m* blind man's guide

lazari·no -na *adj* leprous ‖ *mf* leper

lázaro *m* raggedy beggar; **estar hecho un lázaro** to be full of sores

lazo *m* bow, knot, tie; lasso, lariat; snare, trap; bond, tie; **armar lazo a** to set a trap for; **caer en el lazo** to fall into the trap; **lazo de amor** truelove knot; **lazo de unión** (fig) tie, bond

Ldo. *abbr* **Licenciado**

le *pron pers* to him, to her, to it; to you; him; you

leal *adj* loyal, faithful; reliable, trustworthy ‖ *m* loyalist

lealtad *f* loyalty; reliability, trustworthiness

le·brel -brela *mf* whippet, small greyhound

lebrillo *m* earthen washtub

lebrón *m* large hare; coward; (Mex) slicker

lección *f* lesson; (*interpretación de un pasaje*) reading; **dar la lección** to recite one's lesson; **echar** or **señalar lección** to assign the lesson; **tomar una lección a** to hear the lesson of

leccionista *mf* private tutor

lecti·vo -va *adj* school (*e.g., day*)

lec·tor -tora *adj* reading ‖ *mf* reader ‖ *m* foreign-language teacher; (*empleado que anota el consumo registrado por el contador de agua, gas o electricidad*) meter reader; **lector mental** mind reader

lectura *f* reading; broad culture; public lecture; college subject; (*interpretación de un pasaje*) reading; (elec) playback; (typ) pica; **lectura de la mente** mind reading

lechada *f* grout; whitewash; (*para hacer papel*) pulp; (CAm, Mex, W-I) whitewash

lechar *tr* to milk; (CAm, Mex, W-I) to whitewash

leche *f* milk; (coll) sperm; **estar con la leche en los labios** to lack experience, to be young and inexperienced; **leche de manteca** buttermilk; **leche desnatada** skim milk; **leche en polvo** milk powder; **tener mala leche** to behave like a cad

lechecillas *fpl* sweetbread

lechera *f* milkmaid, dairymaid; (*vasija para guardar la leche*) milk can; (*vasija para servir la leche*) milk pitcher

lechería *f* dairy, creamery

leche·ro -ra *adj* (*que da leche*) milch; (*perteneciente a la leche*) milk; (*cicatero*) (coll) stingy ‖ *m* milkman, dairyman; (coll) lucky dog ‖ *f* see **lechera**

lecho *m* bed; (*especie de sofá*) couch; (*cauce de río*) bed; layer, stratum; **abandonar el lecho** to get up (*from illness*); **lecho de plumas** (fig) feather bed

le·chón -chona *adj* filthy, sloppy ‖ *mf* suckling pig; (*persona sucia, desaseada*) pig ‖ *m* pig ‖ *f* sow

lecho·so -sa *adj* milky ‖ *m* papaya (*tree*) ‖ *f* papaya (*fruit*)

lechuga *f* lettuce; head of lettuce; (*fuelle formado en la tela*) frill; **lechuga romana** romaine lettuce

lechugui·no -na *adj* stylish, sporty ‖ *m* dandy ‖ *f* stylish young lady

lechuza *f* barn owl, screech owl; owllike woman

lechu·zo -za *adj* owlish; (*muleto*) yearling ‖ *m* bill collector; summons server; owllike fellow ‖ *f* see **lechuza**

leer §43 *tr* to read ‖ *intr* to read; lecture; **leer en** to read (*someone's thoughts*) ‖ *ref* to read, e.g., **este libro se lee con facilidad** this book reads easily

leg. *abbr* **legal, legislatura**

lega *f* lay sister

legación *f* legation

legado *m* (*don que se hace por testamento*) legacy; (*enviado diplomático*) legate

legajo *m* file, docket, dossier

legal *adj* legal; faithful, prompt, right

legalidad *f* legality; faithfulness, promptness

legalizar §60 *tr* to legalize; authenticate

légamo *m* slime, ooze

legamo·so -sa *adj.* slimy, oozy

legaña *f* gum (*on edge of eyelids*)

legaño·so -sa *adj* gummy

legar §44 *tr* to bequeath, will

legata·rio -ria *mf* legatee

legenda·rio -ria *adj* legendary

legible *adj* legible

legión *f* legion

legislación *f* legislation

legisla·dor -dora *adj* legislating ‖ *mf* legislator

legislar *intr* to legislate

legislati·vo -va *adj* legislative

la
le

legislatura f (session of a) legislature
legista m law professor; law student
legitimar tr to legitimate; legitimize
legitimidad f legitimacy
legíti•mo -ma adj legitimate
le•go -ga adj lay; uninformed ‖ m layman; lay brother ‖ f see **lega**
legua f league; **a leguas** far, far away
leguleyo m pettifogger
legumbre f (hortaliza) vegetable; (bot) legume; (Chile) vegetable stew
leíble adj legible, readable
leída f reading
leí•do -da adj well-read; **leído y escribido** (coll) posing as learned ‖ f see **leída**
lejanía f distance, remoteness
leja•no -na adj distant, remote; (pariente) distant
lejía f lye; wash water; severe rebuke
lejiadora f washing machine
lejos adv far; **a lo lejos** in the distance; **de lejos** or **desde lejos** from a distance ‖ m glimpse; look from afar; **tener buen lejos** to look good at a distance
le•lo -la adj stupid, inane
lema m motto, slogan; theme
len adj soft, flossy
lena f spirit, vigor; breathing
lencería f linen goods, dry goods; linen closet; dry-goods store
lence•ro -ra mf linen dealer, dry-goods dealer
lendrera f fine-toothed comb
lendro•so -sa adj nitty, lousy
lene adj (suave al tacto) soft; (ligero) light; kind, agreeable
lengua f (anat) tongue; (idioma) language, tongue; (de tierra, de fuego, de zapato; badajo de campana; lengua de un animal usada como alimento) tongue; **buscar la lengua a** to pick a fight with; **dar la lengua** to chew the rag; **hacerse lenguas de** to rave about; **írsele a** (uno) **la lengua** to blab; **lengua madre** or **matriz** mother tongue (language from which another is derived); **lengua materna** mother tongue (language acquired by reason of nationality); **morderse la lengua** to hold one's tongue; **tener en la lengua** to have on the tip of one's tongue; **tener la lengua gorda** to talk thick; to be drunk; **tener mala lengua** to be blasphemous; to have an evil tongue; **tener mucha lengua** to be a great talker; **tirar de la lengua a** to draw out; **tomar en lenguas** to gossip about; **tomar lengua** or **lenguas** to pick up news
lenguado m sole
lenguaje m language
lengua•raz (pl **-races**) adj foul-mouthed, scurrilous; polyglot ‖ mf linguist
len•guaz adj (pl **-guaces**) garrulous
lengüeta f (de la balanza) pointer, needle; (del zapato) tongue; (anat) epiglottis; (carp) tongue; (de un instrumento de viento) (mus) reed; (Chile) paper cutter; (Mex) petticoat fringe; (SAm) chatterbox
lengüetada f licking, lapping

lengüetear intr to stick the tongue out; flicker, flutter; jabber, rant; lick
lengüilar•go -ga adj foul-mouthed, scurrilous
lengüisu•cio -cia adj (Mex, P-R) foul-mouthed, scurrilous
lenidad f lenience
lenocinio m pandering, procuring
lente m & f lens; **lente de aumento** magnifying glass; **lente de contacto** or **lente invisible** contact lens; **lentes** mpl nose glasses; **lentes de nariz** or **de pinzas** pince-nez; **lente telefotográfica** tele(photo)lens
lenteja f lentil; (del reloj) bob, pendulum bob
lentejuela f sequin, spangle
lentillas fpl contact lenses
lentitud f slowness
len•to -ta adj slow; sticky; (fuego) low
leña f firewood, kindling wood; **cargar de leña** to give a drubbing to; **llevar leña al monte** to carry coals to Newcastle
leña•dor -dora mf woodcutter ‖ m woodsman
leñame m lumber, timber; stock of firewood
leñero m wood merchant; wood purchaser; (sitio donde se guarda la leña) woodshed
leño m (madera) wood; (tronco de árbol, limpio de ramas) log; sap, blockhead; (poet) ship, vessel; **dormir como un leño** to sleep like a log
leño•so -sa adj woody
Leo m (astr) Leo
león m lion
leona f lioness
leona•do -da adj tawny, fulvous
leonera f lion cage, den of lions; dive, gambling joint; junk room, lumber room
leonero m lion keeper; keeper of a gambling joint
leontina f watch chain
leopardo m leopard
leopoldina f watch fob; (mil) Spanish shako
leotardo m leotard
lépa•ro -ra adj (CAm, Mex) indecent, improper
lepe m (Ven) flip in the ear; **saber más que Lepe** to be wide-awake
leperada f (CAm, Mex) coarseness, vulgarity
lepisma f (ent) silver fish, fish moth
lepori•no -na adj hare, harelike
lepra f leprosy
leprosería f leper house
lepro•so -sa adj leprous ‖ mf leper
lerdera f (CAm) laziness, apathy; (CAm) slowness
ler•do -da adj slow, dull; coarse, crude
lesbianismo m lesbianism
les•bio -bia adj & mf Lesbian ‖ f (mujer homosexual) Lesbian, lesbian
lesión f harm, hurt; (pathol) lesion
lesionar tr to harm, hurt, injure
lesi•vo -va adj harmful, injurious
lesna f awl
le•so -sa adj hurt, harmed, injured; wounded; offended; perverted; (SAm) simple, foolish
leste m (naut) east
letal adj lethal, deadly
letame m manure
letanía f litany; (enumeración seguida) litany

letárgi·co -ca *adj* lethargic

letargo *m* lethargy

letargo·so -sa *adj* lethargic

le·tón -tona *adj* Lettish ‖ *mf* Lett ‖ *m* (*idioma*) Lettish, Lett

Letonia *f* Latvia

letra *f* (*del alfabeto*) letter; (*modo de escribir propio de una persona*) hand, handwriting; (*de una canción*) words, lyric; (com) draft; (typ) type; (*sentido material*) (fig) letter; **a la letra** (*al pie de la letra*) to the letter; **a letra vista** (com) at sight; **bellas letras** belles lettres; **cuatro letras** or **dos letras** (*esquela, cartita*) a line; **en letras de molde** in print; **escribir en letra de molde** to print; **las letras y las armas** the pen and the sword; **letra a la vista** (com) sight draft; **letra de cambio** (com) bill of exchange; **letra de imprenta** (typ) type; **letra de mano** handwriting; **letra de molde** printed letter; **letra menuda** fine print; (fig) cunning; **letra muerta** dead letter; **letra negrilla** (typ) boldface; **letra redonda** or **redondilla** (typ) roman; **letras** (*literatura*) letters; (coll) a few words, a line; **primeras letras** elementary education, three R's

letra·do -da *adj* learned, lettered; pedantic ‖ *m* lawyer

letrero *m* sign, notice; (*p.ej., en una botella*) label

letrina *f* privy, latrine; (*cloaca*) sewer; (*cosa sucia*) (fig) cesspool

letrista *mf* lyricist, writer of lyrics (*for songs*); calligrapher, engrosser

leucemia *f* leukemia

leucorrea *f* leucorrhea

leudar *tr* to leaven, ferment with yeast ‖ *ref* (*la masa con la levadura*) to rise

leu·do -da *adj* leavened, fermented

leva *f* weighing anchor; (mach) cam; (mil) levy; (CAm, Col) trick; (CAm, Col) swindle

levada *f* (*de la espada, el florete, etc.*) flourish; (*de los astros*) rise; (*del émbolo*) stroke

levadi·zo -za *adj* (*puente*) lift

levadura *f* leaven; leavening; yeast; (*tabla*) board; **levadura comprimida** yeast cake; **levadura de cerveza** brewer's yeast; **levadura en polvo** baking powder

levantaco·ches *m* (*pl* **-ches**) auto jack

levantada *f* rising, getting up (*from bed or from sickbed*)

levantamiento *m* rise, elevation; insurrection, revolt, uprising; **levantamiento del cadáver** inquest; **levantamiento del censo** census taking; **levantamiento de planos** surveying

levantar *tr* to raise, lift, elevate; agitate, rouse, stir up; (*una sesión*) adjourn; (*la mesa*) clear; (*la voz*) raise; (*el campo*) break; (*gente para el ejército; un sitio; fondos*) raise; (*el ancla*) weigh; straighten up; build, construct, erect; establish, found; **levantar casa** to break up housekeeping; **levantar planos** to make a survey ‖ *ref* to rise; (*de la cama*) get up; (*de una silla*)

stand up; straighten up; (*sublevarse*) rise up, rebel

levantaválvu·las *m* (*pl* **-las**) valve lifter

levantaventana *m* sash lift

levante *m* east; (*viento*) levanter; (CAm, P-R) slander, libel ‖ **Levante** *m* (*países de la parte oriental del Mediterráneo*) Levant; northeastern Mediterranean shores of Spain, especially around Valencia, Alicante, and Murcia

levanti·no -na *adj* Levantine; of the northeastern Mediterranean shores of Spain ‖ *mf* Levantine; native or inhabitant of the northeastern Mediterranean shores of Spain

levar *tr* (*el ancla*) to weigh ‖ *ref* to set sail

leve *adj* (*de poco peso*) light; slight, trivial, trifling

levedad *f* lightness; trivialness

leviatán *m* (Bib & fig) leviathan

levita *m* deacon ‖ *f* coat, frock coat

levitón *m* heavy frock coat

léxi·co -ca *adj* lexical ‖ *m* lexicon; (*caudal de voces de un autor*) vocabulary; (*conjunto de vocablos de una lengua o dialecto*) wordstock

lexicografía *f* lexicography

lexicográfi·co -ca *adj* lexicographic(al)

lexicógra·fo -fa *mf* lexicographer

lexicología *f* lexicology

lexicón *m* lexicon

ley *f* law; loyalty, devotion; norm, standard; (*de un metal*) fineness; **a ley de caballero** on the word of a gentleman; **de buena ley** sterling, genuine; **ley de la selva** law of the jungle; **ley del menor esfuerzo** line of least resistance; **ley marcial** martial law; **ley seca** dry law; **tener** or **tomar ley a** to become devoted to; **venir contra una ley** to break a law

leyenda *f* legend

leyente *adj* reading ‖ *mf* reader

lezna *f* awl

lía *f* plaited esparto rope; **lías** lees, dregs

lianza *f* (Chile) account, credit (*in a store*)

liar §77 *tr* to tie, bind; tie up, wrap up; (*un cigarillo*) roll; embroil, involve; **liarias** to beat it; kick the bucket ‖ *ref* to join together, be associated; have a liaison; become embroiled, become involved; **liárselos** to roll one's own (*i.e., cigarettes*)

libación *f* libation; (*acción de beber vino u otro licor*) libation

liba·nés -nesa *adj* & *mf* Lebanese

Líbano, el Lebanon

libar *tr* to suck; taste, sip ‖ *intr* to pour out a libation; imbibe

libelo *m* lampoon, libel; (law) petition

libélula *f* dragonfly

liberación *f* liberation; (*cancelación de la carga que grava un inmueble*) redemption; (*de una cuenta*) settlement, closing; quittance

liberal *adj* liberal; (*expedito*) quick, ready; (pol) liberal; (*de amplias miras*) (Arg) liberal-minded ‖ *mf* (pol) liberal

liberalidad *f* liberality

liberar *tr* to free

libertad f liberty, freedom; **libertad de cáte-dra** academic freedom; **libertad de cultos** freedom of worship; **libertad de empresa** free enterprise; **libertad de enseñanza** academic freedom; **libertad de imprenta** freedom of the press; **libertad de los mares** freedom of the seas; **libertad de palabra** freedom of speech, free speech; **libertad de reunión** freedom of assembly; **libertad vigilada** probation; **plena libertad** free hand; **tomarse la libertad de** to take the liberty to

liberta·do -da adj bold, daring; free, brash, unrestrained

liberta·dor -dora mf liberator

libertar tr to liberate, set free; (de un peligro, la muerte, etc.) save

liberta·rio -ria adj anarchistic

libertinaje m licentiousness, profligacy; impiety, ungodliness

liberti·no -na adj & mf libertine

liber·to -ta mf (law) probationer ‖ m freedman ‖ f freedwoman

libídine f lewdness, lust; (impulso a las actividades sexuales) libido

libidino·so -sa adj libidinous

libido f libido

libra f pound; **Libra** f (astr) Libra; **libra esterlina** pound sterling

libraco m or **libracho** m trashy book

libra·do -da mf (com) drawee

libra·dor -dora mf (com) drawer

libranza f (com) draft; **libranza postal** money order

librar tr to free; save, spare; (la esperanza) place; (batalla) give, join; (com) to draw ‖ intr to be delivered, give birth; (una religiosa) receive a visitor in the locutory; (com) to draw; **librar bien** to come off well, succeed; **librar mal** to come off badly, fail ‖ ref to free oneself; escape

libre adj free; free, brash, outspoken; free, unmarried; free, loose, licentious; innocent, guiltless; **libre de culpa** (seguro, divorcio) no-fault; **libre de porte** postage prepaid

librea f livery

librecambio m free trade

librecambista mf freetrader

librepensa·dor -dora adj freethinking ‖ mf freethinker

librería f bookstore, bookshop; book business; (mueble) bookshelf; **librería de viejo** second-hand bookshop

libreril adj book

librero m bookseller; (encuadernador) bookbinder; (Cuba, Mex) bookshelf

libres·co -ca adj bookish

libreta f notebook; **libreta de banco** bankbook

libreto m (mus) libretto

librillo m earthen washtub; (de papel de fumar, de sellos, etc.) book

libro m book; **ahorcar los libros** to become a dropout; **a libro abierto** at sight; **hacer libro nuevo** to turn over a new leaf; **libro a la rústica** paperbound book; **libro de**

caballerías romance of chivalry; **libro de cocina** cookbook; **libro de cheques** checkbook; **libro de chistes** joke book; **libro de lance** second-hand book; **libro de mayor venta** best seller; **libro de memoria** memo book; **libro de oro** guest book; **libro de recuerdos** scrapbook; **libro de teléfonos** telephone book; **libro de texto** textbook; **libro diario** day book; **libro en imágenes** picture book; **libro en rústica** paperbound book; **libro mayor** (com) ledger; **libro talonario** checkbook, stub book

libro-registro m (com) book

licencia f license; leave of absence; (mil) furlough; **licencia absoluta** (mil) discharge; **licencia por enfermedad** sick leave

licencia·do -da adj pedantic ‖ mf licenciate ‖ m lawyer; (mil) discharged soldier; university student (wearing the long student gown)

licenciar tr to license; allow, permit; confer the degree of licenciate or master on; (mil) to discharge ‖ ref to receive the degree of licenciate or master; become dissolute; (mil) to be discharged

licenciatura f licenciate, master's degree; graduation with a licenciate or master's degree; work leading to a licenciate or master's degree

licencio·so -sa adj licentious

liceo m (sociedad literaria, establecimiento de enseñanza popular) lyceum; (instituto de segunda enseñanza) (Chile) lycée; (Mex) primary school

licitación f bidding

licita·dor -dora mf bidder

licitar tr to bid on; (Arg) to buy at auction, to sell at auction ‖ intr to bid

líci·to -ta adj fair, just; licit, legal

licor m (bebida espiritosa; cuerpo líquido) liquor; (bebida espiritosa preparada por mezcla de azúcar y substancias aromáticas) liqueur

licorera f cellaret

licorista mf distiller; liquor dealer

licoro·so -sa adj spirituous, alcoholic; (vino) rich, generous

licuar §21 & regular tr to liquefy

lid f fight, combat; dispute, argument; **en buena lid** by fair means

líder adj leading ‖ m leader

liderar tr & intr to lead, be the leader

lidia f fight; bullfight

lidiadera f (Ecuad) quarreling, bickering

lidia·dor -dora mf fighter ‖ ref bullfighter

lidiar tr (un toro) to fight ‖ intr to fight; **lidiar con** to fight with; have to put up with

liebre f hare; (hombre cobarde) coward

liendre f nit

lien·to -ta adj damp, dank

lienza f strip of cloth

lienzo m linen (cloth); linen handkerchief; (de edificio o pared) face, front; (pintura sobre lienzo) canvas

liga *f* (*cinta elástica para asegurar las medias*) garter; (*aleación*) alloy; (*materia pegajosa para cazar pájaros*) birdlime; (*confederación, alianza*) league; (*muérdago*) mistletoe; band; **liga de goma** rubber band

ligado *m* (mus & typ) ligature

ligadura *f* tie, bond; (mus) ligature, glide; (surg) ligature

ligamento *m* ligament

ligar §44 *tr* to tie, bind; join, combine; alloy; (*bebidas*) mix; (surg) to ligate ‖ *ref* to league together; be committed; be bound or attached (*e.g., in friendship*)

ligereza *f* lightness; speed, rapidity; fickleness, inconstancy; tactlessness

lige•ro -ra *adj* light; (*té*) weak; (*tejido*) light, thin; quick; slight; **a la ligera** lightly; quickly; unceremoniously; **de ligero** thoughtlessly, rashly; **ligero de cascos** light-headed, scatter-brained; **ligero de lengua** loose-tongued; **ligero de pies** light-footed; **ligero de ropa** scantily clad ‖ **ligero** *adv* fast, rapidly

lignito *m* lignite

ligustro *m* privet

lija *f* (*pez*) dogfish; (*papel que sirve para pulir*) sandpaper; **darse lija** (W-I) to boast, brag, pat oneself on the back

lijar *tr* to sand, sandpaper

lila *adj* silly, simple ‖ *m* lilac (*color*) ‖ *f* lilac (*plant and flower*)

li•lac *f* (*pl* **-laques**) lilac

liliputiense *adj* & *mf* Lilliputian

lima *f* (*herramienta*) file; sweet lime; sweet-lime tree; (*del tejado*) hip; hip rafter; correcting, polishing; **lima de uñas** nail file; **lima hoya** valley (*of roof*)

limadura *f* filing; (*partecillas*) filings

limalla *f* filings

limar *tr* to file; file down; polish, touch up; smooth, smooth over; (*cercenar*) curtail

limaza *f* (*babosa*) slug; (Ven) large file

limazo *m* slime, sliminess

limbo *m* (*borde*) edge; (theol) limbo; **estar en el limbo** to be quite distraught

limen *m* (physiol, psychol & fig) threshold

limenso *m* (Chile) honeydew melon

lime•ño -ña *adj* & *mf* Limean

limero *m* sweet-lime tree

limita•do -da *adj* limited; dull-witted

limitador *m* — **limitador de corriente** clock meter; slot meter

limitar *tr* to limit; cut down, reduce ‖ *intr* — **limitar con** to border on

límite *m* limit; boundary, border

limítrofe *adj* bordering

limo *m* slime, mud

limón *m* lemon; lemon tree; (*de un coche o carro*) shaft

limonada *f* lemonade

limoncillo *m* citronella

limonera *f* shaft

limonero *m* lemon tree

limosna *f* alms

limosnear *intr* to beg

limosne•ro -ra *adj* almsgiving, charitable ‖ *mf* almsgiver; beggar ‖ *m* alms box

limo•so -sa *adj* slimy, muddy

limpia *f* cleaning

limpiaba•rros *m* (*pl* **-rros**) scraper, foot scraper

limpiabo•tas *m* (*pl* **-tas**) shoeshiner, bootblack; (fig) flatterer

limpiacrista•les *m* (*pl* **-les**) windshield washer

limpiachimene•as *m* (*pl* **-as**) chimney sweep

limpiadien•tes *m* (*pl* **-tes**) toothpick

limpia•dor -dora *adj* cleaning ‖ *mf* cleaner

limpiadura *f* cleaning; **limpiaduras** cleanings, dirt

limpiama•nos *m* (*pl* **-nos**) (Guat, Hond) towel

limpiamente *adv* in a clean manner; with ease, skillfully; simply, sincerely; unselfishly

limpiameta•les *m* (*pl* **-les**) metal polish

limpianieve *m* snowplow

limpiaparabri•sas *m* (*pl* **-sas**) windshield wiper

limpia•piés *m* (*pl* **-piés**) (Mex) door mat

limpiapi•pas *m* (*pl* **-pas**) pipe cleaner

limpiaplu•mas *m* (*pl* **-mas**) penwiper

limpiar *tr* to clean; (*purificar*) cleanse; (*de culpas*) exonerate; (*un árbol*) clean out, prune; (*zapatos*) shine; (*hurtar*) snitch; (*a una persona en el juego*) clean out; (*dinero en el juego*) clean up; (mil) to mop up; **limpiarle a uno de** to clean someone out of ‖ *ref* to clean, clean oneself

limpiaú•ñas *m* (*pl* **-ñas**) nail cleaner, orange stick

limpiaví•as *m* (*pl* **-as**) track cleaner

limpieza *f* (*acción de limpiar*) cleaning; (*calidad de limpio*) cleanness; (*hábito del aseo*) cleanliness; neatness, tidiness; honesty; chastity; ease, skill; (*observancia de las reglas en los juegos*) fair play; **limpieza de bolsa** emptiness of the pocketbook; **limpieza de la casa** house cleaning; **limpieza en seco** dry cleaning

lim•pio -pia *adj* clean; (*que tiene el hábito del aseo*) cleanly; neat, tidy; honest; chaste; clear, free; **dejar limpio** to clean out; **en limpio** (com) net; **estar limpio** to have no (criminal) record; be clean; **limpio de polvo y paja** free, for nothing; net, after deducting expenses; **poner en limpio** to make a clear or fair copy of; **quedar limpio** to be cleaned out; **sacar en limpio** to make a clear or clean copy of; deduce, understand ‖ *f* see **limpia** ‖ **limpio** *adv* fair; cleanly; **jugar limpio** to play fair

limpión *m* (*limpiadura ligera*) lick; (coll) cleaner; (Col) scolding; (Col, Ven) dustcloth; (Ecuad) dishcloth

limusina *f* limousine

lín. *abbr* **línea**

lina *f* (Chile) coarse wool

linaje *m* lineage; class, description; **linaje humano** mankind

linaju•do -da *adj* highborn ‖ *mf* highborn person

linaza *f* flaxseed, linseed

lince *adj* keen, shrewd, discerning; (*ojos*) keen ‖ *m* lynx; (fig) keen person

lincear *tr* to see into

li
li

linchamiento *m* lynching
linchar *tr* to lynch
lindante *adj* bordering, adjoining
lindar *intr* to border, be contiguous; **lindar con** to border on
linde *m* & *f* limit, boundary
linde•ro -ra *adj* bordering, adjoining ‖ *m* edge; boundary stone, landmark ‖ *f* limit, boundary; (bot) spicebush
lindeza *f* prettiness, niceness; elegance; witticism, funny remark; flirting; **lindezas** insults
lin•do -da *adj* pretty, nice; fine, perfect; **de lo lindo** a lot, a great deal; wonderfully ‖ *m* dude, sissy
lindura *f* prettiness, niceness
línea *f* line; (*contorno de una figura, un vestido*) lines; figure, waistline; **conservar la línea** to keep one's figure; **leer entre líneas** to read between the lines; **línea de agua** water line; **línea de batalla** line of battle; **línea de empalme** (rr) branch line; **línea de flotación** water line; **línea de fuego** firing line; **línea de fuerza** (elec) power line; (phys) line of force; **línea del partido** party line; **línea de mira** line of sight; **línea de montaje** assembly line; **línea de puntos** dotted line; **línea de tiro** (mil) line of fire; **línea férrea** railway; **línea internacional de cambio de fecha** international date line; **línea suplementaria** (mus) added line, ledger line
lineal *adj* linear
lineamentos *mpl* lineaments
linfa *f* lymph; (poet) water
linfáti•co -ca *adj* lymphatic
lingote *m* ingot, slug; (naut) ballast bar
lingual *adj* & *f* lingual
lingüista *mf* linguist
lingüísti•co -ca *adj* linguistic ‖ *f* linguistics
linimento *m* liniment
lino *m* flax; (*tela*) linen; (poet) sail
linóleo *m* linoleum
linón *m* lawn
linotipia *f* linotype
linotípi•co -ca *adj* linotype
linotipista *mf* linotype operator
linotipo *m* linotype
linterna *f* lantern; **linterna eléctrica** flashlight
lío *m* bundle; (*de papeles*) batch; muddle, mess; liaison, affair; **armar un lío** to raise a row; **hacerse un lío** to get into a jam
liofilización *f* freeze-drying
liofilizar §60 *tr* to freeze-dry
lionesa — **a la lionesa** (culin) lyonnaise
liorna *f* hubbub, uproar ‖ **Liorna** *f* Leghorn
lio•so -sa *adj* trouble-making; knotty, troublesome
liq.ⁿ *abbr* **liquidación**
líq.° *abbr* **líquido**
liquen *m* lichen
liquidación *f* (*de una cuenta*) sale
liquidar *tr* to liquefy; (com) to liquidate ‖ *intr* (com) to liquidate ‖ *ref* to liquefy
liquidez *f* liquidity

líqui•do -da *adj* & *m* liquid; (com) net ‖ *f* (phonet) liquid
lira *f* (mus) lyre; (*numen de un poeta*) inspiration; poems, poetry
lírica *f* lyric poetry
líri•co -ca *adj* lyric(al); (*músico, operístico*) lyric; fantastic, utopian ‖ *m* lyric poet; (Arg, Ven) visionary ‖ *f* see **lírica**
lirio *m* (bot) iris; **lirio blanco** (*azucena*) Madonna lily; **lirio de agua** (bot) calla, calla lily; **lirio de los valles** (bot) lily of the valley
lirismo *m* lyricism; spellbinding; fancy, illusion
lirón *m* (bot) water plantain; (zool) dormouse; (coll) sleepyhead
lis *m* (bot) lily ‖ *f* (bot) iris; (heral) fleur-de-lis
Lisboa *f* Lisbon
lisia•do -da *adj* hurt, injured; crippled; (*muy deseoso*) eager ‖ *mf* cripple
lisiar *tr* to hurt, injure; cripple ‖ *ref* to become crippled
lisimaquia *f* loosestrife
li•so -sa *adj* even, smooth; (*vestido*) plain, unadorned; (*franco, sincero*) simple, plain-dealing; brash, insolent; **liso y llano** simple, easy
lisonja *f* flattery
lisonjear *tr* to flatter; please ‖ *intr* to flatter
lisonje•ro -ra *adj* flattering; pleasing ‖ *mf* flatterer
lista *f* list; (*tira*) strip; (*en un tejido*) colored stripe; (*recuento en alta voz de las personas que deben estar en un lugar*) roll call; **lista de bajas** casualty list; **lista de comidas** bill of fare; **lista de correos** general delivery; **lista de espera** waiting list; **lista de frecuencia** frequency list; **lista de pagos** pay roll; **pasar lista** to call the roll
listar *tr* to list
listero *m* roll keeper, timekeeper
listín *m* telephone directory; (S-D) newspaper
lis•to -ta *adj* ready; quick, prompt; alert, wide-awake; **estar listo** to be ready; to be finished; **listo de manos** light-fingered; **pasarse de listo** to be shrewd, be clever ‖ *f* see **lista**
listón *m* (*cinta*) ribbon, tape; (*pedazo de tabla angosta*) lath, strip of wood
listonado *m* lath, lathing
lisura *f* evenness, smoothness; plainness; candor; brashness, insolence
lit. *abbr* **literalmente**
lite *f* lawsuit
litera *f* (*vehículo llevado por hombres o por animales*) litter; (*cama fija en los camarotes*) berth; **litera alta** upper berth; **litera baja** lower berth
literal *adj* literal
litera•rio -ria *adj* literary
litera•to -ta *adj* literary ‖ *mf* literary person; **literatos** literati
literatura *f* literature; **literatura de escape** or **de evasión** escape literature
litigación *s* litigation
litigante *adj* & *mf* litigant

litigar §44 *tr & intr* to litigate
litigio *m* litigation, lawsuit; dispute
litigio•so -sa *adj* litigious
litina *s* (chem) lithia
litio *m* (chem) lithium
litisexpensas *fpl* (law) costs
litografía *f* (*arte de grabar en piedra para la reproducción en estampa*) lithography; (*estampa*) lithograph
litografiar §77 *tr* to lithograph
litógra•fo -fa *mf* lithographer
litoral *adj* coastal, littoral ‖ *m* coast, shore
litro *m* liter
liturgia *f* liturgy
litúrgi•co -ca *adj* liturgic(al)
liviandad *f* lightness; inconstancy, fickleness; lewdness
livia•no -na *adj* light; inconstant, fickle; lewd ‖ *m* leading donkey; **livianos** lights, lungs
lívi•do -da *adj* livid
liza *f* combat, fight; (*campo para lidiar*) lists; **entrar en liza** to enter the lists
lo *art def neut* (used with *masc sg* form of *adj*) the, e.g., **lo bueno** the good; what is, e.g., **lo útil** what is useful; **lo mío** what is mine; (used with *adv* or inflected *adj*) the + noun, e.g., **lo aprisa que habla** the speed with which he speaks; **lo tacaños que son** the stinginess of them; how, e.g., **Vd., no sabe lo felices que son** you do not know how happy they are; **lo más** as . . . as, e.g., **lo más temprano posible** as early as possible ‖ *pron pers masc* him, it; you; (with **estar, ser, parecer,** and the like, it stands for an adjective or noun understood and is either not translated or is translated by "so"), e.g., **Vd. está preparado pero ella no lo está** you are ready but she is not ‖ *pron dem* that; **de lo que** + *verb* than + *verb*, e.g., **ese libro ha costado más dinero de lo que vale** that book cost more money than it is worth; **lo de** the matter of, the question of, e.g., **lo de sus deudas** the matter of your debts; **lo de que** the fact that, the statement that; **lo de siempre** the same old story; **lo que** what, that which; **todo lo que** all (that), e.g., **me dió todo lo que tenía** he gave me all he had
loa *f* praise; (*del teatro antiguo*) prologue; short dramatic poem
loable *adj* laudable, praiseworthy
loar *tr* to praise
loba *f* she-wolf; ridge
lobagante *m* lobster (*Homarus*)
lobanillo *m* wen, cyst
lobato *m* wolf cub
lo•bo -ba *adj & mf* (Mex) half-breed ‖ *m* wolf; **coger** or **pillar un lobo** (coll) to go on a jag; **desollar** or **dormir un lobo** to sleep off a drunk; **lobo de mar** (ichth) sea wolf; (coll) old salt, sea dog; **lobo solitario** (fig) lone wolf ‖ *f* see **loba**
lóbre•go -ga *adj* dark, dismal; gloomy
lobreguez *f* darkness; gloominess
lobu•no -na *adj* wolf, wolfish
locación *f* lease
local *adj* local ‖ *m* quarters, place

localidad *f* (*lugar, sitio*) location, locality; (*plaza en un tren*) accommodations; (theat) seat
localización *f* localization; location; **localización de averías** trouble shooting
localizar §60 *tr* (*limitar a un punto determinado*) to localize; (*determinar el lugar de*) locate
locería *f* pottery
loción *f* wash; (pharm) lotion; **loción facial** after-shave lotion
lo•co -ca *adj* crazy, insane, mad; terrific, wonderful; **estar loco por** to be crazy about, to be mad about; **loco de amor** madly in love; **loco de atar** raving mad; **loco perenne** insane, demented; full of fun; **loco rematado** stark-mad; **volver loco** to drive crazy ‖ *mf* crazy person, lunatic ‖ *m* (*bufón*) fool
locomotora *f* engine, locomotive; **locomotora de maniobras** shifting engine
locro *m* (SAm) meat and vegetable stew
lo•cuaz *adj* (*pl* **-cuaces**) loquacious
locución *f* expression, locution; idiomatic phrase, idiom
locuela *f* speech, way of speaking
locue•lo -la *adj* wild, frisky ‖ *f* see **locuela**
locura *f* insanity, madness; folly, madness
locu•tor -tora *mf* announcer, commentator
locutorio *m* (*en un convento de monjas*) parlor, locutory; telephone booth
lodazal *m* mudhole
lodo *m* mud, mire; (*substancia que sirve para cerrar junturas, tapar grietas, etc.*) (chem) lute
lodo•so -sa *adj* muddy
logaritmo *m* logarithm
logia *f* (*p.ej., de francmasones*) lodge; (archit) loggia
lógi•co -ca *adj* logical ‖ *mf* logician ‖ *f* logic
logísti•co -ca *adj* logistic(al) ‖ *f* logistics
logopedia *f* speech correction
logrado -da *adj* successful
lograr *tr* to get, obtain; achieve, attain; **lograr** + *inf* to succeed in + *ger* ‖ *ref* to be successful
logrear *intr* to be a moneylender; profiteer
logre•ro -ra *adj* moneylending; profiteering ‖ *mf* moneylender; profiteer; (Chile) sponger
logro *m* attainment, success; gain, profit; usury; **dar** or **prestar a logro** to lend at usurious rates
loma *f* low hill, elevation
Lombardía *f* Lombardy
lombar•do -da *adj & mf* Lombard
lombriguera *f* wormhole in the ground; (bot) tansy
lom•briz *f* (*pl* **-brices**) worm, earthworm; (pathol) worm; (*persona muy alta y delgada*) beanpole; **lombriz de tierra** earthworm; **lombriz solitaria** tapeworm
lomera *f* (*de la guarnición*) backstrap; (*del tejado*) ridgepole; (bb) backing
lominhies•to -ta *adj* high-backed; conceited
lomo *m* (*de animal, libro, cuchillo*) back; (*tierra que levanta el arado*) ridge; (*carne*

de lomo del animal) loin; (*pliegue del tejido*) crease; (bb) spine; **lomos** ribs
lona *f* canvas; sailcloth; (Mex) burlap
loncha *f* slab, flagstone; slice, strip
lonchería *f* snack bar
londinense *adj* London ‖ *mf* Londoner
Londres *m* London; **el Gran Londres** Greater London
longáni•mo -ma *adj* long-suffering
longaniza *f* pork sausage
longevidad *f* longevity
longe•vo -va *adj* long-lived
longitud *f* length; (astr & geog) longitud
lonja *f* exchange, commodity exchange; grocery store; wool warehouse; (*de carne*) slice; (*de cuero*) strip; (*a la entrada de un edificio*) elevated parvis; (Arg) rawhide
lonjeta *f* bower, summerhouse
lonjista *mf* grocer
lontananza *f* (*de una pintura*) background; **en lontananza** in the distance, on the horizon
loor *m* praise
loquear *intr* to talk nonsense, play the fool; carry on, have a high time
loquera *f* insanity
loquería *f* (Chile) madhouse, insane asylum
loque•ro -ra *mf* guard in a mental hospital ‖ *m* (Arg) confusion, pandemonium; (Arg) insane asylum
loques•co -ca *adj* crazy; funny, jolly
lorán *m* (naut) loran
lord *m* (*pl* **lores**) lord
lo•ro -ra *adj* dark-brown ‖ *m* parrot; cherry laurel; (Chile) spy; (Chile) glass bedpan; (Chile) third degree
losa *f* slab, flagstone; tomb
losange *m* lozenge; (baseball) diamond
lote *m* lot, share, portion; lottery prize; (Cuba, Mex) remnant; (Arg) dunce, simpleton; (Col) swallow, swig; (*de terreno*) (Cuba, Mex) lot
lotear *tr* (Chile) to divide up, divide into lots
lotería *f* lottery; (*juego casero*) lotto; (*cosa insegura, riesgo*) gamble
lote•ro -ra *mf* vendor of lottery tickets
lotizar §60 *tr* (Peru) to divide into lots
loto *m* lotus
loza *f* (*barro cocido y barnizado*) porcelain; crockery, earthenware; **loza fina** china, chinaware
lozanear *intr* to be luxuriant; be full of life ‖ *ref* (*deleitarse*) to luxuriate
lozanía *f* luxuriance, verdure; exuberance, vigor; pride, haughtiness
loza•no -na *adj* luxuriant, verdant; exuberant, vigorous; proud, haughty
lubricante *adj* & *m* lubricant
lubricar §73 *tr* to lubricate
lúbri•co -ca *adj* (*resbaladizo; lascivo*) lubricous (*slippery; lewd*)
lubrificar §73 to lubricate
lucera *f* skylight
lucerna *f* large chandelier; (*abertura, tronera*) loophole
lucero *m* bright star; (*planeta*) Venus; (*ventanillo en un muro*) light; **lucero del alba** or

de la mañana morning star; **lucero de la tarde** evening star; **luceros** (poet) eyes
luci•do -da *adj* generous, magnificent; brilliant, successful; sumptuous; (Arg) striking, dashing
lúci•do -da *adj* lucid
luciente *adj* bright, shining
luciérnaga *f* glowworm, firefly
lucifer *m* overbearing fellow ‖ **Lucifer** *m* Lucifer
lucífe•ro -ra *adj* (poet) bright, dazzling ‖ *m* morning star; (Col) match
lucimiento *m* brilliance, luster; show, dash; success; **quedar** or **salir con lucimiento** to come off with flying colors
lu•cio -cia *adj* shiny ‖ *m* salt pool; (*pez*) pike, luce
lucir §45 *tr* to light, light up; show, display; (*p.ej., un traje nuevo*) sport; help; plaster ‖ *intr* to shine ‖ *ref* to dress up; come off with great success; (*sobresalir, distinguirse*) shine; flop, e.g., **lucido me quedé** I was a flop
lucrar *tr* to get, obtain ‖ *intr* & *ref* to profit, make money
lucrati•vo -va *adj* lucrative
lucro *m* gain, profit; **lucros y daños** profit and loss
lucro•so -sa *adj* lucrative
luctuo•so -sa *adj* sad, mournful, gloomy
lucha *f* fight; (*disputa*) quarrel; (*actividad forzada*) struggle; (*combate cuerpo a cuerpo*) wrestling; **lucha antipolución** antipollution movement (or campaign); **lucha de la cuerda** (sport) tug of war; **lucha por la vida** struggle for existence
lucha•dor -dora *mf* fighter, wrestler
luchar *intr* (*combatir*) to fight; (*disputar*) quarrel; (*esforzarse*) struggle; (*pelear cuerpo a cuerpo*) wrestle
ludibrio *m* derision, mockery, scorn
ludir *tr*, *intr* & *ref* to rub, rub together
luego *adv* next, then; therefore; soon; once in a while; **desde luego** right away; of course; **hasta luego** good-bye, so long; **luego como** as soon as; **luego de** after, right after; **luego que** as soon as
luen•go -ga *adj* long
lúes *f* pestilence; **lúes canina** distemper; **lúes venérea** syphilis
lugano *m* (orn) siskin
lugar *m* place; site, spot; job, position; (*espacio*) room, space; (*asiento*) seat; village, hamlet; (geom) locus; **dar lugar** to make room; **dar lugar a** to give cause for; give rise to; **en lugar de** instead of, in place of; **hacer lugar** to make room; **lugar común** (*expresión trivial*) commonplace; (*retrete*) toilet, water closet; **lugar de cita** tryst; **lugares estrechos** close quarters; **lugar geométrico** locus; **lugar religioso** place of burial
lugarejo *m* hamlet
lugare•ño -ña *adj* village ‖ *mf* villager
lugarteniente *m* lieutenant
luge *m* sled
lúgubre *adj* dismal, gloomy, lugubrious

luir §20 *tr* (naut) to gall, wear; (Chile) to muss, rumple; (*vasijas de barro*) (Chile) to polish ‖ *ref* (Chile) to rub, wear away

luisa *f* (bot) lemon verbena

lujo *m* luxury; **de lujo** de luxe; **gastar mucho lujo** to live in high style; **lujo de** abundance of, excess of

lujo•so -sa *adj* luxurious

lujuria *f* lust, lechery

lujuriante *adj* (*lozano*) luxuriant, lush; (*libidinoso*) lustful

lujuriar *intr* to lust, be lustful; (*los animales*) copulate

lujurio•so -sa *adj* lustful, lecherous ‖ *mf* lecher

lu•lo -la *adj* (Chile) lank, slender ‖ *m* (Chile) bundle

lu•lú *m* (*pl* **-lúes**) spitz dog

lumbago *m* lumbago

lumbre *f* light; fire; (*para encender el cigarrillo*) light; (*hueco en un muro por donde entra la luz*) light; brightness, brilliance; knowledge, learning; **echar lumbre** to blow one's top; **lumbre del agua** surface of the water; **lumbres** tinderbox; **ni por lumbre** not for love or money; **ser la lumbre de los ojos de** to be the light of the eyes of

lumbrera *f* light, source of light; light, lamp; (*abertura por donde entran el aire y la luz*) louver; skylight; dormer window; air duct, ventilating shaft; (*persona insigne*) light, luminary; (mach) port; **lumbreras** eyes

luminar *m* luminary

luminiscente *adj* luminescent

lumino•so -sa *adj* luminous; (*idea*) bright

luminotecnia *f* lighting engineering

lun. *abbr* **lunes**

luna *f* moon; moonlight; (*tabla de cristal*) plate glass; (*espejo*) mirror; (*de los anteojos*) lens, glass; whim; **estar de buena luna** to be in a good mood; **estar de mala luna** to be in a bad mood; **luna de miel** honeymoon; **luna llena** full moon; **luna menguante** waning moon; **luna nueva** new moon; **media luna** half moon; (*figura de cuarto de luna creciente o menguante*) crescent; **quedarse a la luna de Valencia** to be disappointed

lunar *adj* lunar ‖ *m* (*mancha de la piel*) mole; (*punto en un diseño de puntos*) polka dot; (fig) stain, blot, stigma; **lunar postizo** beauty spot

lunáti•co -ca *adj & mf* lunatic

lu•nes *m* (*pl* **-nes**) Monday; **hacer San Lunes** to knock off on Monday

luneta *f* (*de los anteojos*) lens, glass; orchestra seat; (aut) rear window

lunfardo *m* (Arg) thief; underworld slang

lupa *m* magnifying glass

lupanar *m* brothel, bawdyhouse

lupia *mf* (Hond) quack, healer ‖ *f* wen, cyst; **lupias** (Col) small amount of money, small change

lúpulo *m* (vid) hop; (*flores desecadas de la vid*) hops

luquete *m* slice of orange or lemon used to flavor wine; (Chile) bald spot; (*en la ropa*) (Chile) spot, hole

lu•rio -ria *adj* (Mex) mad, crazy

lusitanismo *m* Lusitanism

lusita•no -na *adj & mf* Lusitanian, Portuguese

lustrabo•tas *m* (*pl* **-tas**) shoeshiner

lustrar *tr* to shine, polish ‖ *intr* to wander, roam

lustre *m* shine, polish; luster, gloss; (*fama, gloria*) (fig) luster

lustrina *f* (Chile) shoe polish

lustro *m* five years; chandelier

lustro•so -sa *adj* shining, bright, lustrous

lutera•no -na *adj & mf* Lutheran

luto *m* (*señal exterior de duelo*) mourning; (*duelo, aflicción*) sorrow, bereavement; **estar de luto** to be in mourning; **lutos** crape; **luto riguroso** deep mourning

lutocar *m* (Chile) trash cart

luz *f* (*pl* **luces**) light; window, light; electricity; (*dinero*) money; cash; **a primera luz** at dawn; **a toda luz** or **a todas luces** everywhere; by all means; **dar a luz** to have a child; to give birth to; to bring out; to publish; **entre dos luces** at twilight; half-seas over; **luces de carretera** (aut) bright lights; **luces de cruce** (aut) dimmers; **luz de balizaje** (aer) marker light; **luz de magnesio** magnesium light; flash bulb, flashlight; **luz de matrícula** license-plate light; **luz de parada** stop light; **luz trasera** taillight; **sacar a luz** to bring to light; **salir a luz** to come to light; come out, be published; take place; **ver la luz** to see the light, see the light of day

Luzbel *m* Lucifer

Ll

Ll, ll (elle) *f* fourteenth letter of the Spanish alphabet

llaga *f* sore, ulcer; sorrow, grief; (*entre dos ladrillos*) (mas) seam, joint; (fig) ulcer

llagar §44 *tr* to make sore; hurt

llama *f* flame, blaze; marsh, swamp; (zool) llama; (fig) fire, passion; **saltar de las**

llamas y caer en las brasas to jump out of the frying pan into the fire

llamada *f* call; (*movimiento con que se llama la atención de uno*) sign, signal; knock, ring; reference, reference mark; (mil) call, call to arms; (Mex) cowardice; **batir** or **tocar a llamada** (mil) to sound the call to arms; **llamada a filas** (mil) call to the colors; **llamada a quintas** draft call; **llamada por cobrar** collect call

llamadera f goad

llama·do -da adj so-called || f see **llamada**

llama·dor -dora mf caller || m messenger; door knocker; push button

llamamiento m call; calling, vocation

llamar tr to call; (dar nombre a) name, call; summon; invoke, call upon; (la atención) attract || intr to call; (golpear en la puerta) knock; (hacer sonar la campanilla) ring; (el viento) (naut) to veer || ref to be called, be named; **se llama Juan** his name is John

llamarada f blaze, flare-up; (encendimiento repentino del rostro) flush; (fig) flare-up, outburst

llamarón m flare-up

llamati·vo -va adj showy, loud, flashy, gaudy; (manjar) thirst-raising

llamazar m swamp, marsh

llame m (Chile) bird net, bird trap

llamear intr to blaze, flame, flash

lla·món -mona adj (Mex) cowardly

llampo m (Chile) ore

llana f trowel, float; plain; **dar de llana** to smooth with the trowel

llanada f plain

llanero m ranger, plainsman

llaneza f plainness, simplicity; familiarity; sincerity

lla·no -na adj even, level, smooth; (parecido a un plano geométrico) plane; (sencillo) plain, simple; clear, evident; (palabras) frank; accented on the next to last syllable || m plain; (de la escalera) landing || f see **llana**

llanque m (Peru) rawhide sandal

llanta f (cerco exterior de la rueda) tire (of iron or rubber); (borde exterior de la rueda) rim; (pieza de hierro más ancha que gruesa) iron flat; **llanta de goma** rubber tire; **llanta de invierno** snow tire; **llanta de oruga** (de un tractor de oruga) track

llanto m weeping, crying; **en llanto** in tears

llanura f evenness, level, smoothness; (terreno extenso y llano) plain

llapan·go -ga adj (Ecuad) barefooted

llares m pothanger

llave adj key || f (pieza para abrir y cerrar las cerraduras) key; (herramienta) wrench; (grifo) faucet, spigot, cock; (de arma de fuego) cock; (elec) switch; (de un instrumento de viento) (mus) key; (de un enigma, secreto, traducción, cifra; lugar estratégico más propicio) key; **bajo llave** under lock and key; **echar la llave a** to lock; **llave de caja** socket wrench; **llave de caño** pipe wrench; **llave de cubo** socket wrench; **llave de chispa** flintlock; **llave de estufa** damper; **llave de mandíbulas dentadas** alligator wrench; **llave de paso** stopcock; passkey; **llave de purga** drain cock; **llave espacial** space key; **llave inglesa** monkey wrench; **llave maestra** master key, skeleton key; **llave para tubos** pipe wrench

llave·ro -ra mf keeper of the keys; (carcelero) turnkey || m key ring

llavín m latchkey

llegada f arrival

llegar §44 tr to bring up, bring close || intr to arrive; happen; **llegar a** to arrive at; reach; amount to; be equal to; **llegar a** + inf to come to + inf; succeed in + ger; **llegar a ser** to become || ref to come close

llena f flood

llenado m filling

llena·dor -dora adj (alimento) (Chile) filling

llenar tr to fill; (un formulario) fill out; (ciertas condiciones) fulfill; satisfy; (colmar) overwhelm || intr (la luna) to be full || ref to fill, fill up; stuff oneself; **llenarse a rebosar** to be filled to overflowing

llene m filling; full tank

lle·no -na adj full; **lleno a rebosar** full to overflowing; **lleno de goteras** full of aches and pains || m fill, plenty; fulness, full enjoyment; completeness; full moon; (en el teatro) full house || f see **llena**

lleva or **llevada** f carrying, conveying; ride; **lleva gratuita** free ride

llevade·ro -ra adj bearable, tolerable

llevar tr (transportar) to carry; (traer consigo) take; (conducir) lead; carry away, take away; (cuentas, libros; la anotación en los naipes) keep; (la correspondencia con una persona) carry on; (un drama a la pantalla) put on; (buena o mala vida) lead; (aguantar) bear, stand for; (castigo) suffer; get, obtain; win; (cierto precio) charge; (traje, vestido) wear; (armas) bear; (cierto tiempo) have been, e.g., **llevo ocho días en cama** I have been in bed for a week; (ropa) **a todo llevar** for all kinds of wear; **llevar** (cierto tiempo) **a** (uno) to be older than (someone) by (a certain age); (cierta distancia) **a** (uno) to be ahead of (someone) by (a certain distance); (cierto peso) **a** (uno) to be heavier than (someone) by (a certain weight); **llevar a las antenas** to put on the air; **llevarla hecha** to have it all figured out; **llevar puesto** to wear, to have on; **llevar** + pp to have + pp, e.g., **lleva conseguidas muchas victorias** he has won many victories || ref to carry away; take, take away; carry off; win; get along; **llevarse algo a alguien** to take something away from someone

lloradue·los mf (pl **-los**) crybaby, sniveler

lloralásti·mas mf (pl **-mas**) poverty-crying skinflint

llorar tr to weep over; mourn, lament || intr to weep, cry; (los ojos) water, run

llorera f crying; sobbing

lloriquear intr to whine, to whimper

lloriqueo m whining, whimpering

lloro m weeping, crying; tears

llo·rón -rona adj weeping, crying || mf weeper, crybaby || m weeping willow; pendulous plume || f hired mourner

lloro·so -sa adj weepy; sad, tearful

llovedi·zo -za adj (agua) rain; (techo) leaky

llover §47 tr (enviar como lluvia) to rain

intr to rain; **como llovido** unexpectedly; **llueva o no** rain or shine; **llueve** it is raining || *ref (el techo)* to leak
llovido *m* stowaway
llovizna *f* drizzle
lloviznar *intr* to drizzle

llovizno∙so -sa *adj* moist, damp *(from drizzle)*; drizzly
lluvia *f* rain; rain water; *(copia, muchedumbre)* (fig) shower, downpour; **lluvia ácida** acid rain; **lluvia radiactiva** fallout, radioactive fallout
lluvio∙so -sa *adj* rainy

M

M, m (eme) *f* fifteenth letter of the Spanish alphabet
m. *abbr* **mañana, masculino, meridiano, metro, minuto, muerto**
maca *f* flaw, blemish; bruise *(on fruit)*; spot, stain; hammock
maca∙co -ca *adj* ugly, misshapen || *m* — **macaco de la India** rhesus
macadamizar §60 *tr* to macadamize
macadán *m* macadam
macana *f* cudgel, club; drug on the market; nonsense; (Arg) botch; (Arg) lie, trick
macanear *intr* to fib, lay it on; (Col, Ven) to manage (well)
macanu∙do -da *adj* terrific, swell, grand; (Col, Ecuad) strong, husky
macarrón *m* macaroon; **macarrones** macaroni
macear *tr* to mace, hammer || *intr* to pester, bore
macelo *m* slaughterhouse
macero *m* macebearer
maceta *f* stone hammer; flowerpot; flower vase; *(de herramienta)* handle; *(de cantero)* hammer; (Mex) head
macfarlán *m* inverness cape
macilen∙to -ta *adj* pale, wan, gaunt
macillo *m* hammer *(of piano)*
macis *m* mace *(spice)*
macizar §60 *tr* to fill in, fill up
maci∙zo -za *adj* solid; massive || *m* solid; flower bed; bulk, mass; massif; wall space
macu∙co -ca *adj* (Chile) sly, cunning; (Arg, Chile, Ven) important, notable; (Ecuad) old, worthless; (Arg, Chile, Peru) strong, husky || *m* (Arg, Bol, Col) overgrown boy
mácula *f* spot; stain; blemish; trick, deception
macha *f* (Bol) drunkenness; (Arg) joke; (Bol) mannish woman
machaca *mf* pest, bore || *f* crusher
machacar §73 *tr* to crush, mash, pound || *intr* to pester, bore
macha∙cón -cona *adj* boring, tiresome, importunate || *mf* bore
machada *f* flock of billy goats; stupidity
machado *m* hatchet
machamartillo — **a machamartillo** solidly, firmly, lastingly
machaque∙ro -ra *adj* tiresome, boring || *mf* bore

machar *tr* to crush, grind, pound || *ref* (Bol, Ecuad) to get drunk
machete *m* machete, cane knife
machi *mf* (Chile) quack, healer
machihembrar *tr (ensamblar a ranura y lengüeta)* to feather; *(ensamblar a caja y espiga)* mortise
machina *f* derrick, crane; pile driver; (P-R) merry-go-round
machismo *m* machismo; male chauvinism
machista *m* male chauvinist
macho *adj invar (animal, planta, herramienta)* male; strong, robust; dull, stupid || *m* sledge hammer; abutment, pillar; male; he-mule; dullard; *(del corchete)* hook; (mach) male piece; (coll) he-man; (C-R) blond foreigner; **macho cabrío** he-goat, billy goat; **macho de aterrajar** or **macho de terraja** (mach) tap, screw tap
machona *f* (Arg, Bol, Ecuad, Guat) mannish woman
macho∙rro -rra *adj* barren, sterile || *f* barren woman; (Mex) mannish woman
machucar §73 *tr* to beat, pound, bruise
machu∙cho -cha *adj* sedate, judicious; elderly
madamita *m* (coll) sissy
madeja *f* hank, skein; tangle of hair; *(hombre flojo)* jellyfish; **madeja sin cuenda** hopeless tangle
madera *m* Madeira wine || *f* wood; piece of wood; knack, flair; makings; **madera aserradiza** lumber; **madera contrachapada** plywood; **madera de sierra** lumber; **madera laminada** plywood; **tener madera de** to have what it takes to
maderada *f* raft, float
maderaje *m* or **maderamen** *m* woodwork
maderería *f* lumberyard
madere∙ro -ra *adj* lumber || *m* lumberman; carpenter; log driver
madero *m* log, beam; ship, vessel; blockhead
madrastra *f* stepmother; bother
madraza *f* doting mother
madre *adj* mother || *f* mother; matron; womb; main sewer; river bed; dregs; sediment; **madre adoptiva** foster mother; **madre de leche** wet nurse; **madre patria** mother country, old country; **madre política** mother-in-law; stepmother; **sacar de madre** to annoy, to upset

ll
ma

madreperla f (*molusco*) pearl oyster; (*nácar*) mother-of-pearl

madreselva f honeysuckle

madriga•do -da *adj* twice-married; (*toro*) that has sired; worldly-wise

madriguera f burrow, lair, den

madrile•ño -ña *adj* Madrid ‖ *mf* native or inhabitant of Madrid

madrina f godmother; patroness, protectress; prop, shore, brace; joke; leading mare; **madrina de boda** bridesmaid; **madrina de guerra** war mother

madrugada f early morning, dawn; early rising

madruga•dor -dora *adj* early-rising ‖ *mf* early riser

madrugar §44 *intr* to get up early; be out in front

madurar *tr* to ripen; mature; think out ‖ *intr* to ripen; mature

madurez f ripeness; maturity

madu•ro -ra ripe; mature

maestra f teacher; elementary girls' school; **maestra de escuela** schoolmistress

maestranza f arsenal, armory; navy yard; order of equestrian knights

maestría f mastery; mastership

maes•tro -tra *adj* master; masterly; chief, main; (*perro*) trained ‖ *m* master; teacher; (*en la música y la pintura*) maestro; **maestro de capilla** choirmaster; **maestro de ceremonias** master of ceremonies; **maestro de equitación** riding master; **maestro de escuela** elementary schoolteacher; **maestro de esgrima** fencing master; **maestro de obras** master builder ‖ f see **maestra**

Magallanes *m* Magellan

magancear *intr* (Col, Chile) to loaf around

magan•to -ta *adj* dull, spiritless

magia f magic

magiar *adj & mf* Magyar; Hungarian

mági•co -ca *adj* magic ‖ *mf* magician, wizard ‖ f magic

magín *m* fancy, imagination

magisterio *m* teaching; teachers

magistrado *m* magistrate

magistral *adj* masterly

magnáni•mo -ma *adj* magnanimous

magnesio *m* magnesium; (phot) flashlight

magnéti•co -ca *adj* magnetic

magnetismo *m* magnetism

magnetizar §60 *tr* magnetize

magneto *m & f* magneto

magnetófón *m* or **magnetófono** *m* tape recorder

magnetoscopia f video recorder

magnificar §73 *tr* to magnify; exalt

magnífi•co -ca *adj* magnificent

magnitud f magnitude

mag•no -na *adj* great, e.g., **Alejandro Magno** Alexander the Great

mago *m* magician; soothsayer; (fig) wizard, expert; **Magos de Oriente** Wise Men of the East

ma•gro -gra *adj* lean, thin ‖ *m* loin of pork ‖ f slice of ham

maguar §10 *ref* (Ven, W-I) to be disappointed

magüeta f heifer

magüeto *m* young bull

maguey *m* century plant

magullar *tr* to bruise ‖ *ref* to get bruised

magullón *m* bruise; contusion

mahometa•no -na *adj & mf* Mohammedan

mahometismo *m* Mohammedanism

mahones *mpl* (P-R, S-D) blue jeans

mahonesa f mayonnaise

maído *m* meow

maitines *mpl* matins

maíz *m* maize, Indian corn; **comer maíz** to accept bribes; **maíz en la mazorca** corn on the cob

maizal *m* cornfield

maja f flashy dame

majada f sheepfold; dung, manure

majaderear *tr* to bother, annoy

majadería f nonsensical remark; bother, nuisance

majade•ro -ra *adj* pestiferous, stupid ‖ *mf* bore, dunce ‖ *m* pestle

majar *tr* to crush, mash, grind, pound; annoy, bother

majestad f majesty

majestuo•so -sa *adj* majestic

ma•jo -ja *adj* sporty; handsome, dashing; pretty, nice; all dressed up ‖ *mf* sport ‖ *m* bully ‖ f see **maja**

mal *adj* apocopated form of **malo,** used only before nouns in masculine singular ‖ *adv* badly, poorly; wrong; hardly, scarcely; **mal de** short of; **mal que le pese** in spite of him ‖ *m* evil; damage, harm; wrong; sickness; misfortune; **mal de altura** mountain sickness; **mal de la tierra** homesickness; **mal de mar** seasickness; **mal de piedra** (pathol) stone; **mal de rayos** radiation sickness; **mal de vuelo** airsickness; **por mal de mis pecados** to my sorrow; **tener a mal** to object to; **¡mal haya . . . !** curses on . . . !

mala f mail; mailbag; mailboat

malabarista *mf* juggler; sneak thief

malacate *m* whim; (*hoisting machine*) (Mex, Hond) spindle

malaconseja•do -da *adj* ill-advised

malacrianza f var of **malcriadez**

malagradeci•do -da *adj* ungrateful

malandante *adj* unlucky, unfortunate

malandanza f bad luck, misfortune

malan•drín -drina *adj* evil, wicked ‖ *mf* scoundrel, rascal

malaria f malaria

malaventura f misfortune

mala•yo -ya *adj & mf* Malay

mala•zo -za *adj* perverse; evil; wicked

malbaratar *tr* to undersell; squander

malcasa•do -da *adj* mismated; undutiful

malcasar *tr* to mismate ‖ *intr & ref* to be mismated

malcaso *m* treachery

malconten•to -ta *adj & mf* malcontent

malcriadez f rudeness; bad manners

malcria•do -da *adj* ill-bred

malcriar §77 *tr* to spoil, pamper

maldad f evil, wickedness
maldecir §11 tr to curse ‖ intr to curse, damn; **maldecir de** to slander, vilify
maldición f malediction, curse; oath, curse
maldispues•to -ta adj ill, indisposed; unwilling, ill-disposed
maldi•to -ta adj damned, accursed; wicked; (Mex) coarse, crude, indecent; **no saber maldita la cosa de** to not know a single thing about ‖ **el Maldito** the Evil One ‖ f (coll) tongue; **soltar la maldita** to talk too much
maleante adj wicked, evil ‖ mf crook, hoodlum, rowdy
malear tr to spoil; corrupt ‖ ref to spoil, get spoiled; be corrupted
malecón m levee, dike, mole, jetty
maledicencia f calumny, slander
maleficiar tr to damage, harm; to curse, bewitch, cast a spell on
maleficio m curse, spell; witchcraft
maléfi•co -ca adj evil; harmful
malentender §51 tr to misunderstand
malentendido m misunderstanding, misapprehension
malestar m malaise, indisposition
maleta m bungler; ham bullfighter ‖ f valise; **hacer la maleta** to pack up
maletín m satchel
malevolencia f malice, malevolence
malévo•lo -la adj malevolent
maleza f thicket, underbrush; weeds
malfuncionamiento m malfunction
malgasta•do -da adj ill-spent
malgastar tr to waste, squander
malgenio•so -sa adj ill-tempered, irritable
malhabla•do -da adj foul-mouthed
malhada•do -da adj ill-starred
malhe•cho -cha adj deformed ‖ m misdeed
malhe•chor -chora mf malefactor ‖ f malefactress
malherir §68 tr to injure badly
malhumora•do -da adj ill-humored
malicia f (maldad) evil; (bellaquería, malevolencia) malice; insidiousness, trickiness; suspicion
malicio•so -sa adj evil; malicious; insidious, tricky
malignar tr to corrupt, vitiate; spoil
malignidad f malignity
malig•no -na adj (malévolo; pernicioso) malign; (malicioso; perjudicial) malignant; (pathol) malignant
malintenciona•do -da adj ill-disposed, evil-minded
malmaridada f faithless wife
malmeter tr to lead astray, misguide; alienate, estrange
ma•lo -la adj bad, poor, evil; (travieso) naughty, mischievous; (enfermo) sick, ill; (que no es como debiera ser) wrong; (inflamado, dolorido) sore; **a la mala** (Cuba, P-R) by force; (Mex) insincere; (Mex) mean; **estar de malas** to be out of luck; **lo malo es que** the trouble is that; **malo con** or **para con** mean to; **por malas o por buenas** willingly or unwillingly; **ser malo**

de engañar to be hard to trick ‖ **el Malo** the Evil One ‖ f see **mala**
malogra•do -da adj late, ill-fated
malograr tr to miss ‖ ref to fail; come to an untimely end
malogro m failure, disappointment
maloliente adj malodorous, foul-smelling
malón m mean trick; (SAm) Indian incursion; (Chile) surprise party
malpara•do -da adj hurt; **salir malparado (de)** to fail (in), come out worsted (in)
malparar tr to mistreat
malparir intr to miscarry, have a miscarriage
malparto m miscarriage
malquerencia f dislike
malquerer §55 tr to dislike
malquistar tr to alienate, estrange ‖ ref to become alienated
malquis•to -ta adj disliked, unpopular
malrotar tr to squander
malsa•no -na adj unhealthy
malsín m mischief-maker
malsonante adj obnoxious, odious
malsufri•do -da adj impatient
malta m malt ‖ f asphalt, tar; dark beer; (Chile) premium beer
maltraer §75 tr to abuse, ill-treat; call down, scold
maltratar tr to abuse, ill-treat, maltreat; damage, spoil
maltre•cho -cha adj battered, damaged
malu•co -ca or **malu•cho -cha** adj sickish, upset
malva f mallow; **malva arbórea** hollyhock, rose mallow; **ser como una malva** to be meek and mild
malva•do -da adj evil, wicked ‖ mf evildoer
malvarrosa f hollyhock, rose mallow
malvavisco m marsh mallow
malvender tr to sell at a loss
malversación f graft, embezzlement, misappropriation
malversar tr & intr to graft, embezzle
malvezar §60 tr to give bad habits to ‖ ref to acquire bad habits
malla f mesh, meshing; (de la armadura) mail; (traje) tights; bathing suit
mallete m mallet
Mallorca f Majorca
mallor•quín -quina adj & mf Majorcan
mama f mamma
ma•má f (pl -más) mamma
mamada f suck; sucking; cinch; advantageous deal; easy profit
mama•lón -lona adj (Ven, W-I) loafing ‖ mf (Cuba) sponger
mamama f (Hond) granny
mamamama f (Peru) granny
mamar tr to suck; learn as a child; swallow; wangle; **mamóla** he was taken in ‖ intr to suck ‖ ref to swallow; (obtener sin mérito) wangle; (SAm) to get drunk; **mamarse a uno** to get the best of someone; take someone in; (Col, Chile, Peru) to do away with someone
mamarracho m mess, sight; (hombre ridículo) milksop

ma
ma

mamelón *m* knoll, mound

mamífe•ro -ra *adj* mammalian ‖ *m* mammal, mammalian

mamola *f* chuck (*under the chin*); **hacer la mamola a** to chuck under the chin; take in, make a fool of

ma•món -mona *adj* sucking; fond of sucking ‖ *mf* suckling ‖ *m* shoot, sucker; (Guat, Hond) club; (Mex) soft cake ‖ *f* chuck (*under chin*)

mamonear *tr* (Guat, Hond) to beat, cudgel; (S-D) to put off, delay; (*el tiempo*) (S-D) to waste

mamotreto *m* memo book; batch of papers; hulk, bulk

mampara *f* screen; folding screen; (Peru) glass door

mamparo *m* bulkhead

mampostería *f* rubble, rubblework; masonry, stone masonry

ma•mut *m* (*pl* **-muts**) mammoth

manada *f* (*de ganado vacuno*) herd, drove; (*de ganado lanar*) flock; (*de lobos*) pack; (*de gente*) gang, troop; (*de hierba, trigo, etc.*) handful

manade•ro -ra *adj* flowing ‖ *m* spring, source; shepherd

manantial *adj* flowing, running ‖ *m* spring, source; (fig) source

manar *tr* to run with ‖ *intr* to pour forth, run; abound

manaza *f* big hand

mancar §73 *tr* to maim, cripple ‖ *intr* (*el viento*) (naut) to abate, subside

manca•rrón -rrona *adj* (*caballería*) skinny, worn-out; (Chile) tired out, exhausted ‖ *m* old nag; (Chile, Peru) dam, dike

manceba *f* mistress, concubine

mancebía *f* bawdyhouse, brothel; wild oats; youth

mance•bo -ba *adj* youthful ‖ *m* youngster; youth, young man; (*en una farmacia, barbería, etc.*) helper ‖ *f* see **manceba**

mancerina *f* saucer with hook to hold chocolate cup

mancilla *f* spot, blemish

mancillar *tr* to spot, blemish

man•co -ca *adj* armless, one-armed; one-handed; defective, faulty ‖ *mf* cripple ‖ *m* (Chile) old nag

mancomún — **de mancomún** jointly, in common

mancomunar *tr* to unite, combine; (*fuerzas, caudales, etc.*) pool ‖ *ref* to unite, combine

mancomunidad *f* association, union; (*asociación de provincias*) commonwealth

mancornar §61 *tr* (*un novillo*) to throw and hold on the ground; (*una res vacuna*) tie a horn and front leg of; (*dos reses*) tie together by the horns; (coll) to join, bring together

mancornas or **mancuernas** *fpl* (Mex) cuff links

mancuernillas *fpl* (Guat, Hond) cuff links

mancha *f* spot, stain; (*de vegetación*) patch; speckle; (fig) stain, blot; **mancha solar** sunspot

manchar *tr* to spot, stain; speckle; (fig) to stain, disgrace ‖ *intr* to spot; ¡**mancha!** wet paint!

manda *f* gift, offer; bequest, legacy

mandade•ro -ra *mf* messenger ‖ *m* errand boy

mandado *m* order, command; errand; **hacer un mandado** to run an errand

manda•más *m* (*pl* **-mases**) (slang) big shot; (*jefe político*) (slang) boss

mandamiento *m* order, command; (Bib) commandment; (law) writ; **los cinco mandamientos** the five fingers of the hand

mandar *tr* to order, command; (*legar*) bequeath; (*enviar*) send; **mandar a distancia** to operate by remote control; **mandar +** *inf* to have + *inf*, e.g., **la mandé leer en voz alta** I had her read aloud ‖ *intr* to be in command, be the boss; **mandar llamar** to send for; **mandar por** to send for; **mande Vd.** I beg your pardon ‖ *ref* (*un enfermo*) to manage to get around; (*dos piezas*) be communicating; **mandarse con** (*otra pieza*) to communicate with; be rude to

mandarina *f* tangerine

mandatario *m* agent, proxy; chief executive

mandato *m* mandate; term (*of office*)

mandíbula *f* jaw, jawbone; **reír a mandíbula batiente** to roar with laughter

mandil *m* apron

mando *m* command; control, drive; **alto mando** (mil) high command; **mando a distancia** remote control; **mando a punta de dedo** finger-tip control; **mando de las válvulas** timing gears; **mando por botón** push-button control; **tener el mando y el palo** to be the boss, rule the roost

mandolina *f* mandolin

man•dón -dona *adj* bossy ‖ *mf* domineering person ‖ *m* (*en las minas*) boss, foreman; (*en las carreras de caballos*) (Chile) starter

mandrágora *f* mandrake

mandril *m* (mach) chuck

mandrilar *tr* to bore

manea *f* hobble

manear *tr* to hobble

manecilla *f* (*de reloj*) hand; clasp, book clasp; (bot) tendril; (typ) fist, index

manejable *adj* manageable

manejar *tr* to manage; handle, wield; (*un automóvil*) drive ‖ *ref* to behave; get around, move about

manejo *m* management; handling; intrigue, scheming; horsemanship; driving; **manejo a distancia** remote control; **manejo doméstico** housekeeping

manera *f* manner, way; **a la manera de** in the manner of; like; **de manera que** so that; **en gran manera** to a great extent; extremely; **sobre manera** exceedingly

manga *f* (*parte del vestido*) sleeve; (*tubo de caucho*) hose; waterspout; (bridge) game; **en mangas de camisa** in shirt-sleeves; **ir de manga** to be in cahoots; **manga de**

agua waterspout; cloudburst; **manga de camisa** shirt-sleeve; **manga de riego** watering hose; **manga de viento** whirlwind; **manga marina** waterspout; **mangas** extras, profits

mangana f lasso

manganear tr to lasso; (Peru) to annoy, bother

manganeso m manganese

mango m handle; **mango de escoba** broomstick; (aer) stick, control stick

mangonear tr to plunder ‖ intr to loaf around; meddle; dabble

mangosta f mongoose

mangote m sleeve protector

manguera f hose; (tubo de ventilación) funnel

mangueta f fountain syringe; door jamb

manguitero m furrier

manguito m muff; sleeve guard; coffee cake; (mach) sleeve

ma•ní m (pl -níes or -nises) peanut

manía f mania; craze, whim; grudge; **tener manía a** to dislike

maniabier•to -ta adj open-handed

manía•co -ca adj maniac(al) ‖ mf maniac

maníaco-depresi•vo -va adj manic-depressive

maniatar tr to tie the hands of

maniáti•co -ca adj stubborn; queer, eccentric; (entusiasta) crazy ‖ mf crank, eccentric

manicero m peanut vendor

manicomio m madhouse, insane asylum

manicor•to -ta adj closefisted, tight

manicu•ro -ra mf manicure, manicurist ‖ f manicure, manicuring

mani•do -da adj shabby, worn; hackneyed; (culin) high ‖ f haunt, hangout

manifestación f manifestation; (reunión pública para dar a conocer un sentimiento u opinión) demonstration

manifestante mf demonstrator

manifestar §2 tr to manifest; (el Santísimo Sacramento) expose ‖ intr to demonstrate ‖ ref to become manifest

manifies•to -ta adj manifest ‖ m manifesto; (eccl) exposition of the Host; (naut) manifest

manigua f (Mex, W-I) thicket, jungle; **irse a la manigua** (W-I) to revolt

manija f handle; clamp; crank

manilar•go -ga adj ready-fisted; generous

manilla f bracelet; handcuff; manacle

manillar m handle bar

maniobra f handling; lever; maneuver; (naut) gear, tackle

maniobrar intr to work with the hands; maneuver; (rr) to shift

maniota f hobble

manipula•dor -dora mf manipulator ‖ m (telg) key

manipular tr to manipulate

mani•quí m (pl -quíes) manikin, mannequin; (para exponer prendas de ropa) dress form; (de pintores y escultores) lay figure; (fig) puppet; **ir hecho un maniquí** to be a fashion plate ‖ f (mujer joven que luce los trajes de última moda) mannequin, model

manirro•to -ta adj lavish, prodigal

manivací•o -a adj empty-handed

manivela f crank; **manivela de arranque** starting crank

manjar m dish, food, tidbit, delicacy; lift, recreation

mano m first to play, e.g., **soy mano** I'm first ‖ f hand; (de cuadrúpedo) forefoot; (de pintura) coat; (de papel) quire; (saetilla de reloj u otro instrumento) hand; (lance en un juego) round, hand; (del elefante) trunk, pestle, masher; **a la mano** at hand, on hand; within reach; understandable; **a mano airada** violently; **asidos de la mano** hand in hand; **bajo mano** underhandedly; **caer en manos de** to fall into the hands of; **¡dame esa mano!** put it here!; **dar la mano** to lend a hand; **darse las manos** to join hands; to shake hands; **de las manos** hand in hand; **de primera mano** at first hand; first-hand; **de segunda mano** second-hand; **echar mano de** to resort to; **echar una mano** to lend a hand; to play a game; **en buena mano está** after you, you drink first; **escribir a la mano** to take dictation; **escribir a manos de** to write in care of; **estrecharse la mano** to shake hands; **ganarle a uno por la mano** to steal a march on someone; **lavarse las manos de** to wash one's hands of; **llegar a las manos** to come to blows; **malas manos** awkwardness; **mano de gato** cat's-paw; master hand, master touch; **mano de obra** labor; **mano derecha** right-hand man; **mano de santo** sure cure; **¡manos a la obra!** let's get to work!; **manos libres** outside work; **manos limpias** extras, perquisites; clean hands; **manos puercas** graft; **probar la mano** to try one's hand; **tener mano con** to have a pull with; **tener mano izquierda** to be on one's toes; **untar la mano a** to grease the palm of; **venir a las manos** to come to blows; **vivir de la mano a la boca** to live from hand to mouth

manojo m bunch, bundle, handful; **a manojos** in abundance

manopla f gauntlet; postilion's whip; (Chile) knuckles, brass knuckles

manosear tr to finger, paw; muss, rumple; fiddle with; pet ‖ ref to spoon, neck

manotada f slap

manotear tr to slap, smack; (Arg, Mex) to steal, snitch; ‖ intr to gesticulate

manquedad f lack of one or both hands or arms; disability; deficiency

mansalva — **a mansalva** without risk; without warning; **a mansalva de** safe from

mansarda f mansard, mansard roof

mansedumbre f gentleness, mildness, meekness; tameness

mansión f stay, sojourn; abode, dwelling; **hacer mansión** to stop, stay

man•so -sa adj gentle, mild, meek; tame ‖ m bellwether; farm

ma
ma

manta _f_ blanket; heavy shawl; (coll) beating, thrashing; (Chile, Ecuad) poncho; (Col, Mex, Ven) coarse cotton cloth; **a manta de Dios** copiously; **dar una manta a** to toss in a blanket; **manta de coche** lap robe; **manta de viaje** steamer rug; **tirar de la manta** to let the cat out of the bag

mantear _tr_ to toss in a blanket; abuse, mistreat

manteca _f_ (_grasa de los animales, esp. la del cerdo_) lard; butter; pomade; (_dinero_) (slang) dough; **como manteca** smooth as butter; **manteca de puerco** lard; **manteca de vaca** butter

mantecado _m_ custard ice cream, French ice cream

mantecón _m_ mollycoddle, milksop

mantel _m_ tablecloth; altar cloth

mantelería _f_ table linen

mantelillo _m_ embroidered centerpiece

mantelito _m_ lunch cloth

mantener §71 _tr_ to maintain; keep; keep up; sustain, defend ‖ _ref_ to keep, remain, continue

mantenida _f_ kept woman

mantenido _m_ (_hombre que vive a expensas de su mujer_) (Guat, Mex, W-I) gigolo; (Guat, Mex, W-I) sponger

mantenimiento _m_ maintenance; food, support, living

manteo _m_ mantle, cloak

mantequera _f_ churn, butter churn; butter dish

mantequería _f_ creamery; delicatessen

mantequilla _f_ butter; **mantequilla azucarada** hard sauce; **mantequilla derretida** drawn butter

mantilla _f_ mantilla (_silk or lace head scarf_); **mantillas** swaddling clothes

mantillo _m_ humus, mold

manto _m_ mantle, cloak; (_de chimenea_) mantel; (_ropa talar de algunos religiosos, catedráticos, alumnos_) robe, gown; (fig) cloak

mantón _m_ shawl, kerchief

manuable _adj_ handy

manual _adj_ (_que se hace con las manos_) hand; (_fácil de manejar_) handy; easy; easy to understand; easy-going; manual ‖ _m_ manual, handbook; notebook

manubrio _m_ handle; crank, winch

manuela _f_ open hack (_in Madrid_)

manufactura _f_ (_fábrica_) factory; (_obra fabricada_) manufacture

manufacturar _tr_ to manufacture

manuscribir §83 _tr_ to write by hand

manuscri•to -ta _adj & m_ manuscript

manutención _f_ maintenance; care, upkeep; shelter, protection

manutener §71 _tr_ (law) to maintain, support

manzana _f_ apple; (_conjunto aislado de varias casas contiguas_) block, city block; (_remate en un mueble_) knob, finial; **manzana de Adán** (Chile) Adam's apple

manzanar _m_ apple orchard

manzanilla _f_ camomile; (_aceituna pequeña; vino blanco_) manzanilla (_small olive; white wine_); (_remate en un mueble_) knob, finial

manzano _m_ apple tree

maña _f_ skill, dexterity; cunning, craftiness; bad habit, vice; (_de lino, cáñamo, etc._) bunch; sister; **darse maña** to manage, contrive; **hacer maña** (Col) to fool around

mañana _adv_ tomorrow; ¡**hasta mañana!** see you tomorrow!; **pasado mañana** the day after tomorrow ‖ _m_ tomorrow; (_tiempo venidero_) morrow ‖ _f_ morning; **de mañana** in the morning; **muy de mañana** very early in the morning; **por la mañana** in the morning; **tomar la mañana** to get up early; have a shot of liquor before breakfast

mañanear _intr_ to be in the habit of getting up early

mañane•ro -ra _adj_ morning; early-rising

mañanica _f_ early morning, break of day

mañanita _f_ woman's bed jacket

mañear _tr_ to manage craftily ‖ _intr_ to act with cunning

mañerear _intr_ (Arg) to dawdle, dilly-dally

mañería _f_ sterility

mañe•ro -ra _adj_ clever, shrewd; simple, easy; skittish

ma•ño -ña _mf_ (coll) Aragonese ‖ _m_ brother ‖ _f_ see **maña**

maño•so -sa _adj_ skillful, clever; crafty, tricky; vicious

mañuela _f_ craftiness, trickiness

mañue•las _mf_ (_pl_ **-las**) tricky person

mapa _m_ map; **mapa itinerario** road map ‖ _f_ — **llevarse la mapa** to take the prize

mapache _m_ coon, raccoon

mapamundi _m_ map of the world; (coll) buttocks, behind

mapurite _m_ (CAm) skunk

maque _m_ lacquer

maquear _tr_ to lacquer; (Mex) to varnish

maqueta _f_ (_en tamaño reducido_) maquette; (_en tamaño natural_) mock-up; (_de un libro_) dummy

maquillador _m_ (theat) make-up man

maquillaje _m_ (theat) make-up

maquillar _tr & ref_ to make up

máquina _f_ machine; (_motor_) engine; locomotive; plan, project; (fig) machinery; (coll) heap, pile, lot; (Cuba) auto; (Chile) ganging up; **escribir a máquina** to typewrite; **máquina de afeitar** safety razor; **máquina de apostar** gambling machine; **máquina de componer** typesetter; **máquina de coser** sewing machine; **máquina de escribir** typewriter; **máquina de lavar** washing machine; **máquina de sumar** adding machine; **máquina de volar** flying machine; **máquina fotográfica** camera; **máquina sacaperras** slot machine

maquinación _f_ machination, scheming

máquina-herramienta _f_ (_pl_ **máquinas-herramientas**) machine tool

maquinal _adj_ mechanical

maquinar _tr_ to plot, scheme

maquinaria _f_ machinery; applied mechanics

maquinilla _f_ windlass, winch; clippers; **maquinilla cortapelos** clippers, hair clippers; **maquinilla de afeitar** safety razor; **maquinilla de rizar** curling iron

maquinista *mf* (*persona que fabrica máquinas*) machinist; (*persona que dirige una máquina o locomotora*) engineer; **segundo maquinista** (naut) machinist

mar *m & f* sea; tide, flood; **alta mar** high seas; **a mares** abundantly, copiously; **arrojarse a la mar** to plunge, take great risks; **baja mar** low tide; **correr los mares** to follow the sea; **hablar de la mar** to talk wildly, talk on and on; **hacerse a la mar** to put to sea; **la mar de** (fig) oceans of, large numbers of; **mar alta** rough sea; **mar ancha** high seas; **mar bonanza** calm sea; **mar Caribe** Caribbean Sea, Caribbean; **mar de las Antillas** Caribbean Sea; **mar de las Indias** Indian Ocean; **mar de nubes** cloud bank; **mar Latino** Mediterranean Sea; **mar llena** high tide; **meter la mar en un pozo** to attempt the impossible; **meterse mar adentro** (fig) to go beyond one's depth

maraña *f* undergrowth, thicket; silk waste; (*de hilo, pelo, etc.*) tangle; trick, scheme; puzzle

marañón *m* cashew

maraño•so -sa *adj* scheming ‖ *mf* schemer

maravilla *f* wonder, marvel; (bot) marigold, calendula; **a las maravillas** or **a las mil maravillas** magnificently; **a maravilla** wonderfully well; **por maravilla** rarely, occasionally

maravillar *tr* to astonish ‖ *ref* to wonder, marvel; **maravillarse con** or **de** to marvel at, wonder at

maravillo•so -sa *adj* wonderful, marvelous

marbete *m* label, tag; baggage check; edge, border; **marbete engomado** sticker

marca *f* mark; (*tipo de producto*) make, brand; (*de tamaño*) standard; score; record; height-measuring device; **de marca** outstanding; **marca de agua** watermark; **marca de fábrica** trademark; **marca de reconocimiento** (naut) landmark, seamark; **marca de taquilla** box-office record; **marca registrada** registered trademark

marca•do -da *adj* marked, pronounced

marcaje *m* (sport) scoring; (sport) interfering; (telp) dialing

marcapaso *m* or **marcapasos** *m* (heart) pacemaker

marcar §73 *tr* to mark; brand; embroider; (*p.ej., un pañuelo*) initial; (*la hora un reloj*) show; (*un tanto*) make, score; (*el número telefónico*) dial ‖ *ref* (*un buque*) to take bearings

marcear *tr* to shear ‖ *ref* to be Marchlike

marcial *adj* martial; gallant, noble

marcia•no -na *adj & mf* Martian

marco *m* frame; framework; (*de pesas y medidas*) standard

marcha *f* march; (*funcionamiento*) running, operation; (*p.ej., de los astros*) course, path; (*desenvolvimiento de un asunto*) course, march, progress; (*grado de velocidad*) rate of speed; (*de los engranajes*) (aut) speed; **cambiar de marcha** to shift gears; **en marcha** on the march; underway;

in motion; **marcha atrás** reverse; **marcha del hambre** hunger march; **marcha directa** high gear; **marcha forzada** (mil) forced march

marchamo *m* customhouse mark; (Arg, Bol) tax on slaughtered cattle

marchante *adj* commercial ‖ *m* dealer, merchant; customer

marchapié *m* running board

marchar *intr* to march; run, work, go; leave, go away; come along, proceed; **marchar en vacío** to idle ‖ *ref* to leave, go away

marchitar *tr* to wilt, wither ‖ *ref* to wilt, wither; languish

marchi•to -ta *adj* withered, faded; (fig) languid

marea *f* tide; tideland; gentle sea breeze; dew; drizzle; **marea alta** high tide; **marea baja** low tide; **marea creciente** or **entrante** flood tide; **marea menguante** ebb tide; **marea muerta** neap tide; **marea viva** spring tide; **rendir la marea** to stem the tide

marea•do -da *adj* nauseated, sick, light-headed; seasick

mareaje *m* navigation, seamanship; (*de un buque*) course

marear *tr* to sail; annoy, pester ‖ *intr* to be annoying ‖ *ref* to get sick, get giddy; get seasick; be damaged at sea; fade

marejada *f* heavy sea; (*de desorden*) stirring, undercurrent; **marejada de fondo** ground swell

maremagno *m* or **maremágnum** *m* big mess

mareo *m* nausea, dizziness, sickness; seasickness; annoyance

marfil *m* ivory

marfile•ño -ña *adj* ivory

mar•fuz -fuza *adj* (*pl* -**fuces** -**fuzas**) cast aside, rejected; deceptive

marga *f* marl

margar §44 *tr* to marl

margarita *f* pearl; (bot) daisy; **margarita de los prados** English daisy; **margarita** (*impresora*) (*ordenador*) daisy wheel

margen *m & f* margin; border, edge; marginal note; **al margen de** aloof from; outside of; independent of; aside from; **dar margen para** to give occasion for; **dejar al margen** to leave out; **quedar al margen** to be left out of

marginal *adj* marginal

mariache *m* Mexican band and singers

marica *m* sissy, milksop ‖ *f* magpie

maricón *m* sissy

maridable *adj* marital

maridaje *m* married life; (fig) union

maridar *tr* to combine, unit ‖ *intr* to get married; to live as man and wife

marido *m* husband

mariguana *f* marihuana

mariganza *f* (Chile) hocus-pocus; (Chile) pirouette; **mariguanzas** (Chile) clowning; (Chile) powwowing

marimacho *m* mannish woman

marimandona *f* queen bee, bossy woman

marimarica *m* sissy

ma
ma

marimorena f fight, row

marina f navy; (*conjunto de buques*) marine, fleet; (*cuadro o pintura*) seascape; shore, seaside; sailing, navigation; **marina de guerra** navy; **marina mercante** merchant marine

marinar tr to marinate, salt; (*un buque*) staff, man ‖ intr to be a sailor

marinera f sailor blouse; (*blusa de niño*) middy, middy blouse

marinería f sailoring; sailors

marine•ro -ra adj sea, marine; seaworthy; seafaring ‖ m mariner, seaman, sailor; **marinero de agua dulce** (*el que ha navegado poco*) landlubber (*person unacquainted with the sea*); **marinero matalote** (*hombre de mar, rudo y torpe*) landlubber (*awkward and unskilled seaman*) ‖ f see **marinera**

marines•co -ca adj sailor; sailorly

mari•no -na adj marine, sea ‖ m mariner, seaman, sailor ‖ f see **marina**

marioneta f marionette

mariposa f butterfly; butterfly valve; wing nut; rushlight; (Col) blindman's buff; **mariposa nocturna** moth

mariposear intr to flit about; be fickle

mariposón m (Cuba, Guat, Mex) fickle flirt

mariquita f sissy, milksop, popinjay ‖ f (ent) ladybird

marisabidilla f bluestocking

mariscal m blacksmith; (mil) marshal; **mariscal de campo** (mil) field marshal

marisco m shellfish; **mariscos** seafood

marisma f swamp, marsh, salt marsh

marisquería f seafood store, seafood restaurant

maríti•mo -ma adj maritime; marine, sea

maritor•nes f (pl **-nes**) mannish maidservant, wench

marmita f pot, boiler, kettle

marmitón m kitchen scullion

mármol m marble

marmóre•o -a adj marble

marmosete m vignette

marmota f marmot; sleepyhead; worsted cap; **marmota de Alemania** hamster; **marmota de América** ground hog, woodchuck

maroma f hemp rope, esparto rope; acrobatic stunt

maromear intr to perform acrobatic stunts, walk the tight rope; wobble, sway from side to side (*e.g., in politics*); hesitate

marome•ro -ra mf acrobat, tightrope walker; weaseler; opportunist

marqués m marquis; **los marqueses** the marquis and marchioness

marquesa f marchioness, marquise; (*sobre la puerta de un hotel*) marquee

marquesina f cover over field tent; (*sobre la puerta de un hotel*) marquee; locomotive cab

marquetería f cabinetwork, woodwork; (*taracea*) marquetry

marra•jo -ja adj sly, tricky; (*toro*) vicious

marrana f sow; slattern, slut

marranada f piggishness, filth

marranalla f rabble, riffraff

marra•no -na adj base, vile; dirty, sloppy ‖ mf hog ‖ m male hog, boar; filthy person, hog; cad, cur ‖ f see **marrana**

marrar intr to miss, fail; go astray

marras adv long ago; **hacer marras que** (Bol, Ecuad) to be a long time since

marro m game resembling quoits and played with a stone; (*juego de muchachos*) tag; (*ladeo*) dodge, duck; slip, miss

marrón adj invar maroon (*dark-red*); tan (*shoes*) ‖ m maroon; candied chestnut; stone (*used as a sort of quoit*)

marro•quí (pl **-quíes**) adj & mf Moroccan ‖ m morocco, morocco leather

marro•quín -quina adj & mf var of **marroquí**

marrubio m horehound

marrue•co -ca adj & mf Moroccan

Marruecos m Morocco

marrulle•ro -ra adj cajoling, wheedling ‖ mf cajoler, wheedler

Marsella f Marseille

marsopa f or **marsopla** f porpoise

mart. abbr **martes**

marta f pine marten; **marta cebellina** sable, Siberian sable; **marta del Canadá** fisher

Marte m Mars

mar•tes m (pl **-tes**) Tuesday; **martes de carnaval** or **carnestolendas** Shrove Tuesday

martillar tr to hammer; pester, worry ‖ intr to hammer

martillazo m blow with a hammer

martillear tr & intr var of **martillar**

martillero m (Chile) auctioneer

martillo m hammer; auction house; (*persona*) scourge; (mus) tuning hammer; (*de arma de fuego*) cock

martín m — **martín pescador** (pl **martín pescadores**) kingfisher

martinete m drop hammer; pile driver; (*del piano*) hammer

martinico m ghost, goblin

mártir mf martyr

martirio m martyrdom

márts. abbr **mártires**

marullo m surge, swell

marxista adj & mf Marxist or Marxian

marzo m March

mas conj but

más adv more; most; **a lo más** at most, at the most; **a más de** besides, in addition to; **como el que más** as the next one, as well as anybody; **cuando más** at the most; **de más** extra; too much, too many; **estar de más** to be in the way; be unnecessary; be superfluous; **los más de** most of, the majority of; **más bien** rather; **más de +** *número* more than; **más de lo que +** *verbo* more than; **más que** more than; better than; **no . . . más** no longer; **no . . . más nada** nothing more; **no . . . más que** only ‖ prep plus ‖ m more; (*signo de adición*) plus

masa f mass; (*pasta que se forma con agua y harina*) dough; (*masa aplastada*) mash;

nature, disposition; (Chile, Ecuad) puff paste; (*p.ej., de un automóvil*) (elec) ground; **las masas** the masses
masada *f* farm
masadero *m* farmer
masaje *m* massage; **masaje facial** facial
masajear *tr* to massage
masajista *m* masseur ‖ *f* masseuse
masar *tr* to knead; massage
mascar §73 *tr* to chew; mumble, mutter ‖ *ref* (*un cabo*) (naut) to gall
máscara *mf* (*persona*) mask, mummer ‖ *f* mask; (*traje, disfraz*) masquerade; **máscara antigás** gas mask
mascarada *f* masquerade
mascarilla *f* half mask; false face; death mask
mascarón *m* false face; (*persona fea*) fright; (archit) mask; **mascarón de proa** (naut) figurehead
mascota *f* mascot
mascujar *tr & intr* to chew with difficulty; mumble
masculi•no -na *adj* masculine; (*sexo*) male; (*traje*) men's ‖ *m* masculine
mascullar *tr & intr* to mumble, mutter; to chew with difficulty
masera *f* kneading trough
masilla *f* putty
masita *f* (mil) money withheld for clothing; (Arg, Bol) cake
masón *m* Mason
masonería *f* Masonry
masoquis•to -ta *adj* masochistic ‖ *mf* masochist
mastelero *m* (naut) topmast
masticar §73 *tr* to chew, masticate; meditate on; mumble
mástil *m* (*de una embarcación*) mast; (*de un violín o guitarra*) neck; stalk; (*de pluma*) shaft, stem; upright
mas•tín -tina *mf* mastiff; **mastín danés** Great Dane
mastodonte *m* mastodon
mastuerzo *m* (bot) cress; dolt
masturbación *f* masturbation
masturbar *tr & ref* to masturbate
mat. *abbr* **matemática**
mata *f* bush, shrub; blade, sprig; brush, underbrush; **mata de pelo** crop of hair, head of hair; **mata parda** chaparro (*oak*); **saltar de la mata** to come out of hiding
mataca•bras *m* (*pl* **-bras**) cold blast from the north
matacán *m* dog poison
matacande•las *m* (*pl* **-las**) candle snuffer
matadero *m* abattoir, slaughterhouse; drudgery
mata•dor -dora *mf* killer ‖ *m* matador; **matador de mujeres** lady-killer
matadura *f* sore, gall
matafue•gos *m* (*pl* **-gos**) fire extinguisher; (*oficial*) fireman
matalo•bos *m* (*pl* **-bos**) wolf's-bane
mata•lón -lona *mf* skinny old nag
matalotaje *m* (naut) ship stores; mess, hodgepodge

matamale•zas *m* (*pl* **-zas**) weed killer
matamari•dos *f* (*pl* **-dos**) many times a widow
matamo•ros *m* (*pl* **-ros**) bully
matamos•cas *m* (*pl* **-cas**) fly swatter; flypaper
matanza *f* slaughter, massacre; butchering; pork products; (CAm) butcher shop; (Ven) slaughterhouse
matape•rros *m* (*pl* **-rros**) harum-scarum, street urchin
matar *tr* to kill; butcher; (*el fuego, la luz*) put out; (*la cal*) slack; (*el metal*) mat; (*un color*) tone down; (*un naipe*) spot; play a card higher than; (*a un caballo*) gall; bore to death; (*el tiempo, el hambre, etc.*) (fig) to kill ‖ *intr* to kill ‖ *ref* to kill oneself; drudge, overwork; be disappointed; **matarse con** to quarrel with; **matarse por** to struggle for; struggle to
matarratas *m* rat poison; (*aguardiente de mala calidad*) rotgut
matarro•tos *m* (*pl* **-tos**) (Chile) pawnshop
matasa•nos *m* (*pl* **-nos**) quack doctor
matasellar *tr* to cancel, postmark
matase•llos *m* (*pl* **-llos**) postmark
matasie•te *m* (*pl* **-te**) bully, swashbuckler
matatí•as *m* (*pl* **-as**) moneylender, pawnbroker
matazar•zas *m* (*pl* **-zas**) weed killer
mate *adj* dull, flat ‖ *m* checkmate; (SAm) maté; (SAm) maté gourd; **dar mate a** to checkmate; make fun of; **dar mate ahogado a** to stalemate; **mate ahogado** stale-mate
matear *tr* to plant at regular intervals; make dull; (Chile) to checkmate ‖ *ref* (*el trigo*) to sprout; (*un perro de caza*) hunt through the bushes
matemáti•co -ca *adj* mathematical ‖ *mf* mathematician ‖ *f* mathematics; **matemáticas** mathematics
materia *f* matter; material, stuff; **materia colorante** dyestuff; **materia de guerra** matériel; **materia prima** or **primera materia** raw material
material *adj* material; (*grosero*) crude ‖ *m* material; (*conjunto de objetos necesario para un servicio*) matériel; (typ) matter, copy; **material de guerra** matériel; **material fijo** (rr) permanent way; **material móvil** or **rodante** (rr) rolling stock; **ser material** to be immaterial
materialismo *m* materialism
materialista *mf* materialist; (Mex) truck driver
materializar §60 *tr* (*beneficios*) to realize
maternal *adj* maternal, mother; (*afectos, cuidados, etc.*) motherly
maternidad *f* maternity; motherhood
mater•no -na *adj* maternal, mother
matinal *adj* morning
matinée *f* matinée; dressing gown, wrapper
ma•tiz *m* (*pl* **-tices**) shade, hue, nuance
matizar §60 *tr* (*diversos colores*) to blend; (*un color, un sonido*) shade; (*en cuanto al color*) match
matón *m* bully, browbeater

matorral *m* thicket, underbrush
matraca *f* rattle, noisemaker; taunting, bantering; bore, pest; **dar matraca a** to taunt, to tease
matraquear *intr* to make a racket; to taunt, tease
ma•traz *m* (*pl* **-traces**) flask
matre•ro -ra *adj* cunning, shrewd ‖ *m* (SAm) cheat, swindler
matriarca *f* matriarch
matricida *adj* matricidal ‖ *mf* matricide
matricidio *m* matricide
matrícula *f* register, roster, roll; license; registry
matricular *tr & ref* to matriculate
matrimonialmente *adv* as husband and wife
matrimoniar *intr* to marry, get married
matrimonio *m* marriage, matrimony; (*marido y mujer*) married couple; **matrimonio consensual** common-law marriage
ma•triz *adj* (*pl* **-trices**) main, first, mother ‖ *f* matrix; (*de libro talonario*) stub; screw nut; first draft
matrona *f* matron; matronly lady
matronal *adj* matronly
matun•go -ga *adj* skinny, full of sores ‖ *m* old nag
maturran•go -ga *adj* (SAm) poor, clumsy ‖ *m* (SAm) stranger; (SAm) old nag ‖ *f* trickery
Matusalén *m* Methuselah; **vivir más años que Matusalén** to be as old as Methuselah
matute *m* smuggling; smuggled goods; gambling den
matutear *intr* to smuggle
matute•ro -ra *mf* smuggler
matutinal or **matuti•no -na** *adj* morning
maula *mf* lazy loafer; poor pay; tricky person, cheat ‖ *f* junk, trash; remnant; trickery
maulería *f* remnant shop; trickiness
maullar §8 *intr* to meow
maullido *m* or **maúllo** *m* meow
mausoleo *m* mausoleum
máxima *f* maxim; principle
máxime *adv* chiefly, mainly, especially
máxi•mo -ma *adj* maximum; top; superlative ‖ *m* maximum ‖ *f* see **máxima**
may. *abbr* **mayúscula**
maya *f* May queen; English daisy
mayal *m* flail
mayear *intr* to be Maylike
mayestáti•co -ca *adj* royal
mayido *m* meow
mayo *m* May; Maypole
mayonesa *f* mayonnaise
mayor *adj* greater; larger; older, elder; greatest; largest; oldest, eldest; major; elderly; (*calle*) main; (*altar; misa*) high; **hacerse mayor de edad** to come of age; **ser mayor de edad** to be of age ‖ *m* chief, head, superior; **al por mayor** wholesale; **mayor de edad** (*persona de edad legal*) major; **mayores** elders; ancestors, forefathers; **mayor general** staff officer
mayoral *m* boss, foreman; head shepherd; stagecoach driver; (Arg) streetcar conductor

mayorazgo *m* primogeniture; entailed estate descending by primogeniture; first-born son
mayordoma *f* stewardess, housekeeper
mayordomo *m* steward, butler, majordomo
mayoreo *m* wholesale
mayoría *f* (*mayor edad; el mayor número, la mayor parte*) majority; superiority; **alcanzar su mayoría de edad** to come of age; **mayoría cómoda** solid majority; **mayoría de edad** majority
mayoridad *f* majority
mayorista *adj* (Arg, Chile) wholesale ‖ *mf* (Arg, Chile) wholesaler
mayorita•rio *adj* majority
mayormente *adv* chiefly, mainly, mostly
mayúscu•lo -la *adj* (*letra*) capital; awful, tremendous ‖ *f* capital, capital letter
maza *f* mace; heavy drumstick; bore, pedant; **la maza y la mona** constant companions; **maza de gimnasia** Indian club
mazacote *m* barilla; concrete, cement; botched job; tough, doughy food; (coll) bore
mazar §60 *tr* to churn
mazmorra *f* dungeon
mazo *m* mallet, maul; bunch; (*de la campana*) clapper; (*hombre fastidioso*) bore, pest
mazonería *f* stone masonry; (*obra de relieve*) relief; gold or silver embroidery
mazorca *f* ear of corn; cocoa bean; (*husada*) spindleful; (*de un balustre*) spindle; **comer maíz de** or **en la mazorca** to eat corn on the cob
mazorral *adj* coarse, crude
m/c *abbr* **mi cargo, mi cuenta, moneda corriente**
m/cta *abbr* **mi cuenta**
m/cte *abbr* **moneda corriente**
me (used as object of verb) *pron pers* me, to me ‖ *pron reflex* myself; to myself
meada *f* urination, water; urine stain
meadero *m* urinal
meados *mpl* urine
meaja *f* crumb; **meaja de huevo** tread
meandro *m* meander; wandering speech, wandering writing
mear *tr* to urinate on ‖ *intr & ref* to urinate
Meca, La Mecca
¡mecachis! *interj* wow!, geez!
mecáni•co -ca *adj* mechanical; low, mean ‖ *m* (*obrero perito en el arreglo de las máquinas*) mechanic; (*obrero que fabrica y compone máquinas*) machinist; workman, repairman; driver, chauffeur; **mecánicos** (CAm, Cuba, S-D) blue jeans ‖ *f* mechanics; (*aparato que da movimiento a un artefacto*) machinery, works; meanness; **mecánicas** household chores
mecánico-dentista *m* dental technician
mecanismo *m* mechanism, machinery
mecanizar §60 *tr* to mechanize; motorize
mecanógrafa *f* typist
mecanografía *f* typewriting; **mecanografía al tacto** touch typewriting
mecanografiar §77 *tr & intr* to typewrite

mecanógra•fo -fa *mf* typist, typewriter

mecapale•ro -ra *m* (Mex) messenger, porter

mece•dor -dora *adj* swinging, rocking ‖ *m* stirrer; (*columpio*) swing ‖ *f* rocker, rocking chair

mecer §46 *tr* (*un líquido*) to stir; (*la cuna*) rock ‖ *ref* to rock, swing

mecha *f* (*de vela o bujía*) wick; (*tubo de pólvora*) fuse; lock of hair; (*para mechar carne*) slice of bacon; bundle of thread; (Col, Ecuad, Ven) joke

mechar *tr* (*la carne*) to lard, interlard

mechera *f* shoplifter

mechero *m* (*p.ej., de cigarrillos*) lighter, pocket lighter; (*de aparato de alumbrado*) burner; (*de candelero*) socket; shoplifter; **mechero encendedor** pilot, pilot light

mechón *m* cowlick; (Guat) torch

medalla *f* medal; medallion

medallón *m* medallion; (*joya en que se colocan retratos, etc.*) locket

médano *m* dune, sandbank

media *f* stocking; (math) mean; **media corta** (Arg) sock; **media media** (Arg, Ecuad, Ven) sock; **y media** half past, e.g., **las dos y media** half past two

mediación *f* mediation

media•do -da *adj* half over; half-full; **a mediados de** about the middle of; **mediada la tarde** in the middle of the afternoon

media•dor -dora *mf* mediator

mediana *f* long billiard cue

medianería *f* party wall; party fence

mediane•ro -ra *adj* middle; mediating ‖ *mf* mediator; partner; owner of a row house

medianía *f* average; (*persona que carece de dotes relevantes*) mediocrity

media•no •-na *adj* middling, medium; average, fair; mediocre ‖ *f* see **mediana**

medianoche *f* midnight; small meat pie

mediante *adj* interceding ‖ *prep* by means of, by virtue of

mediar *intr* to be half over; be in the middle; intercede, mediate; elapse; take place

mediatinta *f* half-tone

medible *adj* measurable

medical *adj* medical

medicamento *m* medicine

medicamento•so -sa *adj* medicinal

medicastro *m* quack

medicina *f* medicine; **medicina general** general medicine

medicinar *tr* to treat ‖ *ref* to take medicine

medición *f* measurement; metering

médi•co -ca *adj* medical ‖ *mf* doctor, physician; **médico de cabecera** family physician; **médico de urgencia** emergency doctor; **médico general** general practitioner

medida *f* measurement; measure; caution, moderation; **a medida de** in proportion to; according to; **a medida que** in proportion as; **en la medida que** to the extent that; **hecho a la medida** custom-made; **medida para áridos** dry measure; **medida para líquidos** liquid measure; **tomarle a uno las medidas** to take someone's measure, size up someone

medidamente *adv* with moderation

medidor *m* measurer; (Mex, SAm) meter

medie•ro -ra *mf* hosier; partner

medieval *adj* medieval

medievalista *mf* medievalist

medievo *m* Middle Ages

me•dio -dia *adj* middle; medium; medieval; half; a half, e.g., **media libra** a half pound; half a, e.g., **media naranja** half an orange; average, mean; mid, in the middle of, e.g., **a media tarde** in mid afternoon, in the middle of the afternoon; **a medias** half; half-and-half; **ir a medias** (**con**) to go halves (with), go fifty-fifty (with) ‖ *m* middle; medium, environment; step, measure; means; (*en el espiritismo*) medium; (baseball) shortstop; (arith) half; (*del ruedo*) (taur) center; **a medio** half; **en medio de** in the middle of; in the midst of; **justo medio** happy medium, golden mean; **medio ambiente** environment; situation; **medio centro** (*deporte*) center half; **medios de comunicación** mass media; **por medio de** by means of; **quitarse de en medio** to get out of the way ‖ *f* see **media** ‖ **medio** *adv* half

mediocre *adj* mediocre

mediocridad *f* mediocrity

mediodía *m* noon, midday; south; **en pleno mediodía** at high noon; **hacer mediodía** to stop for the noon meal

mediquillo *m* quack

medir §50 *tr* to measure ‖ *intr* to measure ‖ *ref* to act with moderation

meditabun•do -da *adj* meditative

meditar *tr* to meditate; plan, contemplate ‖ *intr* to meditate

mediterráne•o -a *adj* inland ‖ **Mediterráne•o -na** *adj & m* Mediterranean

mé•dium *m* (*pl* **-dium** or **diums**) medium

medra *f* growth, prosperity

medrana *f* fear

medrar *intr* to thrive, prosper, improve

medro *m* growth, prosperity; **medros** progress

medro•so -sa *adj* fearful, scared; frightful, terrible

médula *f* or **medula** *f* marrow, medulla; (bot) pith; (fig) pith, gist, essence; **médula espinal** spinal cord

medular *adj* pithy

medusa *f* jellyfish

mefistoféli•co -ca *adj* Mephistophelian

megaciclo *m* megacycle

megáfono *m* megaphone

me•go -ga *adj* meek, gentle, mild

megohmio *m* megohm

Méj. *abbr* **Méjico**

mejica•no -na *adj & mf* Mexican

Méjico *m* Mexico; **Nuevo Méjico** New Mexico

meji•do -da *adj* beaten with sugar and milk

mejilla *f* cheek

mejor *adj* better; best; (*licitador*) highest; **a lo mejor** unexpectedly; worse luck; perhaps, maybe; **el mejor día** some fine day ‖ *adv* better; best; **mejor dicho** rather

ma
me

mejora *f* growth, improvement; higher bid; alteration

mejoramiento *m* improvement

mejorana *f* sweet marjoram

mejorar *tr* to improve; (*los licitadores el precio de una cosa*) raise; **mejorando lo presente** present company excepted ‖ *intr* & *ref* to improve, get better, recover; make progress; (*el tiempo*) to clear up; **¡que se mejore!** get well!

mejoría *f* improvement; (*en una enfermedad*) betterment, recovery

mejunje *m* brew, potion, mixture

mela•do -da *adj* honey-colored ‖ *m* thick cane syrup

melancolía *f* (*tristeza vaga*) melancholy; (*depresión moral*) melancholia

melancóli•co -ca *adj* melancholy

melaza *f* molasses

melcocha *f* taffy, molasses candy

melchor *m* German silver

melena *f* hair falling over the eyes; long hair, loose hair; (*del león*) mane; (*del caballo*) forelock; **andar a la melena** to pull each other's hair; to get into a fight; **estar en melena** (coll) to have one's hair down

melga *f* ridge made by plow; (Col, Chile) plot of ground to be sown; (Hond) small piece of work to be finished

melindre *m* honey fritter; (*dulce de pasta de mazapán*) ladyfinger; narrow ribbon; prudery, finickiness

melindrear *intr* to be prudish, be finicky

melindro•so -sa *adj* prudish, finicky

melocotón *m* peach tree; peach

melocotonero *m* peach tree

melodía *f* melody

melodio•so -sa *adj* melodious

melodramáti•co -ca *adj* melodramatic

melón *m* melon; (*Cucumis melo*) muskmelon; blockhead; bald head; **melón de agua** watermelon

melo•so -sa *adj* sweet, honeyed; gentle, mild, mellow

mella *f* dent, nick, notch; gap, hollow; harm, injury; **hacer mella a** to have an effect on; **hacer mella en** to harm

mellar *tr* to dent, nick, notch; harm

melli•zo -za *adj* & *mf* twin

membrana *f* membrane; (*del teléfono, micrófono*) diaphragm

membrete *m* note, memo; letterhead; heading; written invitation

membrillero *m* quince tree

membrillo *m* quince; quince tree

membru•do -da *adj* brawny, burly

memeches — a memeches (CAm) on horseback

memela *f* (CAm, Mex) cornmeal pancake

me•mo -ma *adj* foolish, simple ‖ *mf* fool, simpleton

memorán•dum *m* (*pl* -dum) memorandum book, notebook; (*sección en los periódicos*) professional services; (*papel con membrete*) letterhead

memorar *tr* & *ref* to remember

memoria *f* memory; (*exposición de ciertos hechos*) memoir; account, record; (*ordenador*) data storage, memory; **de memoria** by heart; **encomendar a la memoria** to commit to memory; **hablar de memoria** (coll) to say the first thing that comes to one's mind; **hacer memoria de** to bring up; **memorias** memoirs; regards

memorial *m* memorandum book; memorial, petition; (law) brief

memorizar §60 *tr* to memorize

mena *f* ore

menaje *m* household furniture; school supplies

mención *f* mention

mencionar *tr* to mention

men•daz *adj* (*pl* -daces) mendacious ‖ *mf* liar

mendicante *adj* & *mf* mendicant

mendigante *adj* begging, mendicant ‖ *mf* beggar, mendicant

mendigar §44 *tr* to beg for ‖ *intr* to beg, go begging

mendi•go -ga *mf* beggar

mendiguez *f* begging

mendo•so -sa *adj* false, wrong

mendrugo *m* crumb, crust

menear *tr* to stir, shake; wiggle; (*la cola*) wag; (*un negocio*) manage; **peor es meneallo** (i.e., **menearlo**) better keep hands off ‖ *ref* to shake; wiggle; wag; hustle, bestir oneself

meneo *m* stirring, shaking; wagging; hustling; drubbing, thrashing

menester *m* need; want, lack; job, occupation; **haber menester** to be necessary, to be need for; **menesteres** bodily needs; property; implements, tools; **ser menester** to be necessary

menestero•so -sa *adj* needy ‖ *mf* needy person

menestra *f* vegetable soup

menes•tral -trala *mf* mechanic

meng. *abbr* **menguante**

mengua *f* want, lack; poverty; decline; decrease, diminution; **en mengua de** to the discredit of

mengua•do -da *adj* timid, cowardly; simple, silly; mean, stingy; wretched, miserable; poor, needy; fatal

menguante *adj* decreasing; declining; waning ‖ *f* decrease; decline; low water; ebb tide; **menguante de la luna** wane, waning of the moon

menguar §10 *tr* to diminish, lessen; discredit ‖ *intr* to diminish, lessen; decline; decrease; (*la luna*) wane; (*la marea*) fall

mengue *m* (coll) devil

menina *f* young lady in waiting

menino *m* noble page of the royal family

menor *adj* less, lesser; smaller; younger; least; smallest; youngest; slightest; minor ‖ *m* minor; **al por menor** retail; **menor de edad** minor; **por menor** retail; in detail, minutely ‖ *f* minor premise

Menorca *f* Minorca

menoría *f* inferiority, subordination; (*tiempo de menor edad*) minority

menorista *adj* (Arg, Chile) retail ‖ *mf* (Arg, Chile) retailer

menor•quín -quina *adj* & *mf* Minorcan

menos *adv* less; fewer; least; fewest; **al menos** at least; **a lo menos** at least; **a menos que** unless; **echar de menos** to miss; **¡menos mal!** lucky break!; **menos mal que** it is a good thing that; **no poder menos de** + *inf* to not be able to help + *ger*; **por lo menos** at least; **tener en menos** to think little of; **venir a menos** to decline; become poor ‖ *prep* less, minus; (*al decir la hora*) of, to, e.g., **las tres menos diez** ten minutes of (or to) three ‖ *m* less; (*signo de resta o sustracción*) minus, minus sign

menoscabar *tr* to lessen, diminish, reduce; damage; discredit

menoscabo *m* lessening, reduction; damage; discredit; **con menoscabo de** to the detriment of

menoscuenta *f* part payment

menospreciable *adj* despicable, contemptible

menospreciar *tr* to underestimate, underrate; scorn, despise

menosprecio *m* underestimation; scorn

mensaje *m* message

mensajería *f* public conveyance; **mensajerías** transportation company; shipping line

mensaje•ro -ra *mf* messenger ‖ *m* harbinger

men•so -sa *adj* (Mex) foolish, stupid

menstruar §21 *intr* to menstruate

menstruo *m* menses

mensual *adj* monthly

mensualidad *f* monthly pay, monthly installment

ménsula *f* bracket; elbow rest

mensurar *tr* to measure

menta *f* mint; **menta piperita** peppermint; **menta romana** or **verde** spearmint

menta•do -da *adj* famous, renowned

mentar §2 *tr* to mention

mente *f* mind

mentecatería or **mentecatez** *f* simpleness, folly

menteca•to -ta *adj* simple, foolish ‖ *mf* simpleton, fool

mentidero *m* hangout; gossip column

mentir §68 *tr* to disappoint ‖ *intr* to lie; be misleading; (*un color*) clash; **¡miento!** my mistake!

mentira *f* lie; error, mistake; **mentira inocente** or **oficiosa** white lie; **parece mentira** it's hard to believe

mentirilla *f* fib, white lie; **de mentirillas** for fun

mentirón *m* whopper

mentiro•so -sa *adj* lying; false, deceptive; full of errors ‖ *mf* liar

men•tís *m* (*pl* -**tís**) insulting contradiction; **dar un mentís a** to give the lie to

mentón *m* chin

me•nú *m* (*pl* -**nús**) menu

menudamente *adv* in detail; at retail

menudear *tr* to make frequently; tell in detail; (Col) to sell at retail ‖ *intr* to happen frequently, be frequent; go into detail; (Arg) to grow, increase

menudencia *f* smallness; trifle; meticulousness; **menudencias** pork products; (Col, Mex) giblets

menudeo *m* constant repetition; detailed accounting; **al menudeo** at retail

menudillos *mpl* giblets

menu•do -da *adj* small, slight, minute; futile, worthless; meticulous; common, vulgar; petty ‖ *m* innards (*of fowl and other animals*); rice coal; **al menudo** at retail; **a menudo** often; **menudos** small change; **por menudo** in detail; at retail

meñique *adj* little, tiny; (*dedo*) little ‖ *m* little finger

meollo *m* marrow; pith; (*seso*) brain; brains, intelligence; gist, marrow, essence

me•ón -ona *adj* (*niño*) piddling; (*niebla*) dripping

mequetrefe *m* whippersnapper

mercachifle *m* peddler; small dealer

mercadear *intr* to deal, trade

merca•der -dera *mf* merchant; **mercader de grueso** wholesale merchant

mercadería *f* merchandise, commodity; **mercaderías** goods, merchandise

mercado *m* market; **lanzar al mercado** to put on the market; **mercado de valores** stock market; **mercado negro** black market

mercaduría *f* commodity

mercancía *f* trade, commerce; merchandise; piece of merchandise; **mercancías** goods, merchandise ‖ **mercancías** *msg* (*pl* -**as**) freight train

mercante *adj* & *m* merchant

mercantil *adj* mercantile

mercar §73 *tr* to buy ‖ *intr* to trade

merced *f* pay, wages; favor, grace; **a merced de** at the mercy of; **merced a** thanks to; **merced de agua** distribution of irrigating water; **vuestra merced** your grace

mercena•rio -ria *adj* mercenary ‖ *m* mercenary; day laborer, hireling

mercería *f* haberdashery, notions store; dry-goods store; hardware store

mercología *f* marketing

mercurio *m* mercury

merecer §22 *tr* to deserve, merit; (*lo que se desea*) attain; (*alabanza*) win; (*cierta suma*) be worth; **merecer la pena** to be worthwhile ‖ *intr* to be deserving; **merecer bien de** to deserve the gratitude of

mereci•do -da *adj* deserved ‖ *m* just deserts; **llevar su merecido** to get what's coming to one

mereciente *adj* deserving

merecimiento *m* desert, merit

merendar §2 *tr* to lunch on, have for lunch; keep an eye on, peep at ‖ *intr* to lunch ‖ *ref* to manage to get; (*en el juego*) (Chile) to clean out

merendero *m* lunchroom; picnic grounds

merendona *f* fine spread

merengar §44 *tr* to whip (*cream*)

merengue *m* meringue

mere•triz f (pl **-trices**) harlot

meridiana f lounge, couch; afternoon nap; meridian line; **a la meridiana** at noon

meridia•no -na adj meridian; bright, dazzling || m meridian || f see **meridiana**

meridional adj southern || mf southerner

merienda f lunch, snack; hunchback

meri•no -na adj merino; (cabello) thick and curly || mf merino || m merino shepherd; merino wool

mérito m merit, desert; value, worth; **hacer mérito de** to make mention of; **hacer méritos** to try to please, put one's best foot forward

merito•rio -ria adj meritorious || m volunteer worker; unpaid learner, apprentice

merluza f (pez) hake; drunk, spree

merma f decrease, reduction; leakage, shrinkage

mermar tr to decrease, reduce || intr to decrease, shrink, dwindle

mermelada f marmalade

me•ro -ra adj mere, pure; (Col, Ven) alone || m grouper, jewfish || **mero** adv (CAm) almost, soon

merodea•dor -dora adj marauding || m marauder

merodear intr to maraud

mes m month; monthly pay; menses; **caer en el mes del obispo** to come at the right time

mesa f table; (mostrador) counter; (escritorio) desk; (de arma blanca o herramienta) flat side; (de escalera) landing; (comida) fare, food; (conjunto de dirigentes) board; **alzar la mesa** to clear the table; **hacer mesa limpia** to clean up (in gambling); **levantar la mesa** to clear the table; **mesa de batalla** sorting table; **mesa de extensión** extension table; **mesa de juego** gambling table; **mesa de milanos** scanty fare; **mesa de trucos** pool table; **mesa perezosa** drop table; **poner la mesa** to set or lay the table; **tener a mesa y mantel** to feed, support; **tener mesa** to keep open house

mesana f (naut) mizzen

mesar tr (los cabellos) to tear, pull out || ref — **mesarse los cabellos** to pull out one's hair; pull out each other's hair

mescolanza f jumble, hodgepodge, medley

meseguería f harvest watch

mesera f waitress

mesero m journeyman on monthly pay; waiter

meseta f plateau, tableland; (de escalera) landing

Mesías m Messiah

mesilla f mantel, mantelpiece; (de escalera) landing; window sill

mesita f stand, small table; **mesita portateléfono** telephone table

mesnada f armed retinue; band, company

mesón m inn, tavern; (Chile) bar; (Chile) counter

mesone•ro -ra adj inn, tavern || mf innkeeper, tavern keeper

mester m (archaic) craft, trade; (archaic) literary genre; **mester de clerecía** clerical verse of the Middle Ages; **mester de ju-**

glaría popular minstrelsy of the Middle Ages

mesti•zo -za adj & mf half-breed; (perro) mongrel

mesura f dignity, gravity; calm, restraint; courtesy, civility

mesura•do -da adj dignified, sedate; calm, restrained; polite; moderate, temperate

mesurar tr to temper, moderate || ref to act with restraint

meta f goal

metafonía f umlaut

metáfora f metaphor

metafóri•co -ca adj metaphorical

metal m metal; money; (de la voz) timbre; condition, quality; (mus) brass; **el vil metal** filthy lucre; **metal blanco** nickel silver; **metal de imprenta** type metal

metale•ro -ra adj (Bol, Chile, Peru) metal || m (Bol, Chile, Peru) metalworker

metáli•co -ca adj metallic || m metalworker; cash, coin

metalistería f metalwork

metalizar §60 tr to make metallic; put a metal coating on; turn into cash || ref to become mercenary

metaloide m nonmetal

metalurgia f metallurgy

metamorfo•sis f (pl **-sis**) metamorphosis

metano m methane

metástasis f metastasis

metate m (CAm, Mex) flat stone on which corn is ground

metáte•sis f (pl **-sis**) metathesis

mete•dor -dora mf smuggler

metedura f disgrace, shame

meteduría f smuggling

metemuer•tos m (pl **-tos**) stagehand; busybody, meddler

meteo f weather bureau, weather report

meteóri•co -ca adj meteoric

meteoro m or **metéoro** m meteor; atmospheric phenomenon

meteorología f meteorology

meter tr to put, place; insert; (un ruido) make; (miedo) cause; (mentiras) tell; (chismes, enredos) start; (dinero en el juego) stake; to smuggle; (un golpe) strike || ref to project; meddle, butt in; **meterse a** to set oneself up as; take it upon oneself to; **meterse con** to pick a quarrel with; **meterse en** to get into; to plunge into; empty into

meticulo•so -sa adj meticulous; shy, timid

meti•do -da adj close, tight; rich, abundant; meddlesome; **muy metido con** on close terms with; **muy metido en** deeply involved in || m push; punch; strong lye; loose leaf; (tela) seam

metódi•co -ca adj methodic(al)

metodista adj & mf Methodist

método m method

metraje m distance or length in meters; (cine) **de corto metraje** short; (cine) **de largo metraje** full-length

metralla f scrap iron; grapeshot; shrapnel

métri•co -ca adj metric(al) || f prosody

metro *m* meter; ruler; tape measure; subway; **metro plegadizo** folding rule

metrónomo *m* metronome

metrópoli *f* metropolis; mother country

metropolita•no -na *adj* metropolitan ‖ *m* subway; (eccl) metropolitan

Méx. *abbr* **México**

mexcal *m* agave liquor

mexica•no -na *adj & mf* Mexican

México *m* Mexico; **Nuevo México** New Mexico

mezcal *m* var of **mexcal**

mezcla *f* mixture; (*argamasa*) mortar; (*tejido*) tweed

mezclar *tr* to mix; blend ‖ *ref* to mix; (*introducirse uno entre otros*) mingle; intermarry; meddle

mezclilla *f* light tweed

mezcolanza *f* jumble, hodgepodge, medley

mezquinar *tr* to be stingy with ‖ *intr* to be stingy

mezquindad *f* meanness, stinginess; need, poverty; smallness, tininess; wretchedness

mezqui•no -na *adj* mean, stingy; needy, poor; small, tiny; wretched

mezquita *f* mosque

mi *adj poss* my

mí (used as object of a preposition) *pron pers* me ‖ *pron reflex* myself

miar §77 *intr* to meow

miau *m* meow

mica *f* mica; (Guat) flirt; **ponerse una mica** (CAm) to go on a jag

mico *m* long-tailed monkey; libertine; hoodlum; **dar mico** to not keep a date

microbio *m* microbe

microbiología *f* microbiology

microbús *m* (Chile) jitney

microfaradio *m* microfarad

microficha *f* microcard

micro•film *m* (*pl* **-films** or **-filmes**) microfilm

microfilmar *tr* to microfilm

micrófono *m* microphone

microonda *f* microwave

microordenador *m* microcomputer

micropelícula *f* microfilm

microprocesador *m* chip, microprocessor

microscópi•co -ca *adj* microscopic

microscopio *m* microscope

microsurco *adj invar* microgroove ‖ *m* microgroove

microteléfono *m* handset, French telephone

mi•cho -cha *mf* pussy cat

miedo *m* fear, dread; **miedo cerval** great fear; **por miedo de** for fear of; **por miedo (de) que** for fear that; **tener miedo (a)** to be afraid (of); **tener miedo de** to be in fear of, be afraid of; be afraid to

miedo•so -sa *adj* fearful, afraid

miel *f* honey; (*jarabe saturado*) molasses; **dejar con la miel en los labios** to spoil the fun for; **hacerse de miel** to be peaches and cream

mielga *f* lucerne

miembro *m* member; (*extremidad del hombre y los animales*) member, limb

mientes *fpl* mind, thought; wish, desire; **caer en las mientes** or **en mientes** to come to mind; **parar** or **poner mientes en** to reflect on; **venírsele a uno a las mientes** to come to one's mind

mientras *conj* while; whereas; **mientras que** while; whereas; **mientras tanto** meanwhile

miérco•les *m* (*pl* **-les**) Wednesday; **miércoles de ceniza** Ash Wednesday

mies *f* cereal, grain; harvest time; **mieses** grain fields

miga *f* (*porción pequeña*) bit; (*parte más blanda del pan*) crumb; (fig) substance; **hacer buenas migas con** to get along well with; **migas** fried crumbs

migaja *f* bit, piece; (*de inteligencia*) smattering; **migajas** crumbs; leavings

migajón *m* crumb; substance

migar §44 *tr* (*el pan*) to crumb; (*p.ej., la leche*) put crumbs in

migrato•rio -ria *adj* migratory

miguelear *tr* (CAm) to make love to

miguele•ño -ña *adj* (Hond) impolite, discourteous

mijo *m* millet

mil *adj & m* thousand, a thousand, one thousand; **a las mil quinientas** at an unearthly hour

milagre•ro -ra *adj* superstitious; miracle-working

milagro *m* (*hecho sobrenatural*) miracle; (*cosa rara*) wonder; votive offering; **colgar el milagro a** to put the blame on; **vivir de milagro** to have a hard time getting along; have had a narrow escape

milagrón *m* fuss, excitement

milagro•so -sa *adj* miraculous; marvelous; wonderful

milano *m* burr, down; (orn) kite

mil•deu *m* (*pl* **-deus**) mildew

milena•rio -ria *adj* millennial ‖ *m* millennium

milenio *m* millennium

milenrama *f* yarrow

milési•mo -ma *adj & m* thousandth

miliamperio *m* milliampere

milicia *f* militia; soldiery; warfare; military service

milicia•no -na *adj* military ‖ *m* militiaman

miligramo *m* milligram

milímetro *m* millimeter

militante *adj* militant

militar *adj* military; army ‖ *m* soldier, military man ‖ *intr* to fight, go to war; struggle; serve in the army; (*surtir efecto*) militate

militarismo *m* militarism

militarista *adj & mf* militarist

militarizar §60 *tr* to militarize

mílite *m* soldier

milpa *f* (CAm, Mex) cornfield

milla *f* mile

millar *m* thousand

millarada *f* about a thousand; **echar millaradas** to boast about one's wealth

millo *m* millet

millón *m* million

millona•rio -ria *adj* of a million or more inhabitants ‖ *mf* millionaire

mimar *tr* to fondle, pet; pamper, indulge, spoil

mimbre *m & f* (bot) osier; wicker, withe

mimbrear *intr & ref* to sway

mimbre•ño -ña *adj* willowy

mimbrera *f* (bot) osier, osier willow

mimbro•so -sa *adj* osier; (*hecho de mimbre*) wicker

mimeografiar §77 *tr* to mimeograph

mimeógrafo *m* mimeograph

mímica *f* mimicry; sign language

mimo *m* (*entre los griegos y romanos*) mime; fondling, petting; pampering

mimo•so -sa *adj* delicate, tender; finicky, fussy

mina *f* mine; (*de lápiz*) lead; (fig) mine, gold mine, storehouse; underground passage; (SAm) moll; **beneficiar una mina** to work a mine; **mina de carbón** or **mina hullera** coal mine; **voló la mina** the truth is out

minado *m* mine work; (nav) mining

mina•dor -dora *adj* (nav) mine-laying ‖ *m* (mil) miner; (nav) mine layer

minar *tr* to mine; undermine; consume; plug away at ‖ *intr* to mine

minarete *m* minaret

mineraje *m* mining; **mineraje a tajo abierto** strip mining

mineral *adj & m* mineral

mineralogía *f* mineralogy

minería *f* mining; mine operators

mine•ro -ra *adj* mining ‖ *m* miner; mine operator; (fig) source, origin

mingitorio *m* street urinal

min•gón -gona *adj* (Ven) spoiled, pampered

miniar *tr* to paint in miniature; (*un manuscrito*) illuminate

miniatura *f* miniature

miniaturización *f* miniaturization

minifalda *f* miniskirt

míni•mo -ma *adj* minimum; tiny, small, minute; least, smallest ‖ *m* minimum ‖ *f* tiny bit

mini•no -na *mf* kitty, pussy

miniordenador *m* minicomputer

ministerial *adj* ministerial

ministerio *m* ministry, cabinet, government; **formar ministerio** to form a government; **ministerio de Hacienda** Treasury Department (U.S.A.); Treasury (Brit); **ministerio de la Gobernación** Department of the Interior (U.S.A.); Home Office (Brit); **ministerio del Ejército** Department of the Army (U.S.A.); War Office (Brit); **ministerio de Marina** Department of the Navy (U.S.A.); Board of Admiralty (Brit); **Ministerio de Relaciones Exteriores** State Department; Foreign Ministry; **ministerio radiofónico** (theol) radio ministry

ministrar *tr* to administer; furnish

ministro *m* minister; bailiff, constable; **ministro de asuntos exteriores** foreign minister; **ministro de Gobernación** Home Secretary (Brit); **ministro de Hacienda** Secretary of the Treasury (U.S.A.); Chan-

cellor of the Exchequer (Brit); **ministro de Justicia** Attorney General (U.S.A.); **primer ministro** prime minister, premier

minorar *tr* to diminish, reduce; weaken

minorati•vo -va *adj & m* laxative

minoría *f* minority

minoridad *f* minority

minorista *m* retailer

minorita•rio -ria *adj* minority

minucia *f* trifle; **minucias** minutiae

minucio•so -sa *adj* minute, meticulous

minué *m* or **minuete** *m* minuet

minúscu•lo -la *adj* (*letra*) small; small, tiny ‖ *f* small letter

minusvalía *f* (physical) handicap

minuta *f* first draft, rough draft; memorandum; menu, bill of fare; roll, list

minutero *m* minute hand

minu•to -ta *adj* minute ‖ *m* minute ‖ *f* see **minuta**

mí•o -a *adj poss* mine; of mine, e.g., **un amigo mío** a friend of mine ‖ *pron poss* mine

miope *adj* near-sighted ‖ *mf* near-sighted person

miopía *f* near-sightedness

mira *f* (*de arma de fuego, telescopio, etc.*) sight; aim, object, purpose; target; watchtower; **estar a la mira** to be on the lookout; **poner la mira en** to have designs on

mirada *f* glance, look; **apuñalar con la mirada** to look daggers at; **mirada de soslayo** side glance

miradero *m* (*lugar desde donde se mira*) lookout; (*persona o cosa que es objeto de la atención pública*) cynosure

mira•do -da *adj* cautious, circumspect; **bien mirado** highly regarded ‖ *f* see **mirada**

mirador *m* belvedere; bay window, oriel

miramiento *m* considerateness, courtesy, regard; look; **miramientos** fuss, bother

miranda *f* eminence, vantage point

mirar *tr* to look at, watch; consider, contemplate; **mirar bien** to look with favor on; **mirar por encima** to glance at ‖ *intr* to look, glance; **¡mira!** look out!; **mirar a** to look at, glance at; face, overlook; aim at; aim to; **mirar por** to look after ‖ *ref* to look at oneself; look at each other; **mirarse en ello** to watch one's step; **mirarse en una persona** to be all wrapped up in a person

mirasol *m* sunflower

miríada *f* myriad

mirilla *f* peephole; (*para dirigir visuales*) target; (phot) finder

miriñaque *m* hoop skirt, crinoline; bauble, trinket; (Arg) cowcatcher

mirística *f* nutmeg tree

mirlar *ref* to try to look important

mirlo *m* blackbird; solemn look; **mirlo blanco** rare bird; **soltar el mirlo** to start to jabber

mirmidón *m* tiny fellow, nincompoop

mi•rón -rona *adj* onlooking; nosy ‖ *mf* onlooker; (*de una partida de juego*) kibitzer; busybody

mirra *f* myrrh
mirto *m* myrtle
misa *f* mass; **cantar misa** to say mass; **como en misa** in dead silence; **misa cantada** High Mass; **misa de prima** early mass; **misa mayor** High Mass; **misa rezada** Low Mass
misal *m* missal
misantropía *f* misanthropy
misántropo *m* misanthrope
misar *intr* to say mass; to hear mass
misario *m* acolyte
misceláne•o -a *adj* miscellaneous ‖ *f* miscellany
miserable *adj* miserable, wretched; mean, stingy; despicable, vile ‖ *mf* cur, cad; wretch; miser
miseran•do -da *adj* pitiful
miserear *intr* to be stingy
miseria *f* misery, wretchedness; poverty; stinginess; trifle, pittance; **comerse de miseria** to live in great poverty
misericordia *f* compassion, mercy, pity
misericordio•so -sa *adj* merciful
míse•ro -ra *adj* miserable, wretched ‖ *mf* wretch
mísil *m* missile; **mísil crucero** cruise missile; **mísil dirigible** guided missile
misión *f* mission; ration for harvesters; **ir a misiones** to go away as a missionary
misional *adj* missionary
misionario *m* missionary; envoy, messenger
misionero *m* missionary
misi•vo -va *adj & f* missive
mismísi•mo -ma *adj* very same, self-same
mis•mo -ma *adj & pron indef* same; own, very; -self, e.g., **ella misma** herself; myself, e.g., **yo mismo** I myself; yourself, himself, herself, itself; **así mismo** likewise, also; **casi lo mismo** much the same; **lo mismo** just the same; **lo mismo me da** it's all the same to me; **mismo . . . que** same . . . as; **por lo mismo** for that very reason ‖ **mismo** *adv* right, e.g., **ahora mismo** right now; **aquí mismo** right here
mistela *f* flavored brandy; needled must, spiked must
misterio *m* mystery; **hablar de misterio** to talk mysteriously
misterio•so -sa *adj* mysterious
misticismo *m* mysticism
místi•co -ca *adj* mystic(al) ‖ *mf* mystic
mistificación *f* hoax, mystification
mistificar §73 *tr* to hoax, mystify
mistifori *m* hodgepodge
misturera *f* (Peru) flower girl
mita *f* mite, cheese mite; (SAm) Indian slave labor; (*turno en el trabajo*) (Arg, Chile) shift, turn
mitad *f* half; middle; **a (la) mitad de** halfway through; **cara mitad** better half; **en la mitad de** in the middle of; **la mitad de** half the; **mitad y mitad** half-and-half; **por la mitad** in half, in the middle
míti•co -ca *adj* mythical
mitigar §44 *tr* to mitigate, appease, allay
mitin *m* (*pl* **mitins** or **mítines**) meeting, rally

mito *m* myth
mitología *f* mythology
mitológi•co -ca *adj* mythological
mitón *m* mitten
mitra *f* chimney pot; (eccl) miter
mixtificación *f* hoax, mystification
mixtificar §73 *tr* to hoax, mystify
mixtifori *m* hodgepodge
mixtión *f* mixture
mix•to -ta *adj* mixed ‖ *m* compound number; sulphur match; explosive compound
mixtura *f* mixture
mixturar *tr* to mix
mixturera *f* (Peru) flower girl
miz *interj* here, pussy!, here, kitty!
mízcalo *m* edible milk mushroom
m/l *abbr* **mi letra**
m/n *abbr* **moneda nacional**
mobilia•rio -ria *adj* personal (*property*) ‖ *m* furniture, suite of furniture
moblaje *m* furniture, suite of furniture
moblar §61 *tr* to furnish
moca *m* Mocha coffee ‖ *f* (Ecuad) mudhole; (Mex) wineglass
mocador *m* handkerchief
mocar §73 *tr* to blow the nose of ‖ *ref* to blow one's nose
mocarro *m* snot
mocasín *m* moccasin
mocear *intr* to act young; sow one's wild oats
mocedad *f* youth; wild oats
mocerío *m* young people
mocero *adj masc* woman-crazy
mocetón *m* strapping young fellow
mocetona *f* buxom young woman
mocil *adj* youthful
moción *f* motion, movement; (*en junta deliberante*) motion; **hacer** or **presentar una moción** to make a motion
mocionante *mf* mover
mocionar *tr & intr* to move
moci•to -ta *adj* young ‖ *mf* youngster
moco *m* (*humor segregado por una membrana mucosa*) mucus; (*mocarro*) snot; (*extremo del pabilo de una vela*) snuff; **a moco de candil** by candle light; **llorar a moco tendido** to cry like a baby; **moco de pavo** crest of a turkey; trifle; (bot) cockscomb
moco•so -sa *adj* snotty, snively; rude, illbred; flip, saucy; mean, worthless ‖ *mf* brat
mochar *tr* to butt; chop off; (Arg) to rob; (Col) to fire
mochil *m* errand boy for farmers in the field
mochila *f* knapsack, haversack; tool bag; (mil) ration
mochín *m* (slang) executioner
mo•cho -cha *adj* blunt, stub, flat; (*árbol*) topped; stub-horned; mutilated; (Mex) reactionary ‖ *m* butt end
mochuelo *m* (orn) little owl; (*de una o más palabras*) omission; **cargar con el mochuelo** or **tocarle a** (*uno*) **el mochuelo** to get the worst of a deal
moda *f* fashion, mode, style; **a la moda de** after the fashion of, in the style of; **alta**

mi
mo

moda haute couture; **de moda** in fashion; **fuera de moda** out of fashion; **pasar de moda** to go out of fashion
modales *mpl* manners
modalidad *f* manner, way, nature, kind
modelar *tr* to model; to form, shape; to mold ‖ *ref* to model; **modelarse sobre** to pattern oneself after
modelo *adj invar* model, e.g., **ciudad modelo** model city ‖ *mf* model, mannequin, fashion model ‖ *m* model, pattern; form, blank; equal, peer; style; **modelo estrella** (aut) crest-line model
modera•do -da *adj* moderate
moderador *m* regulator; (*para retardar el efecto de los neutrones*) moderator
moderar *tr* to moderate, control, restrain ‖ *ref* to moderate, control oneself, restrain oneself
modernizar §60 *tr* to modernize
moder•no -na *adj* modern
modestia *f* modesty
modes•to -ta *adj* modest
modicidad *f* moderateness, reasonableness
módi•co -ca *adj* moderate, reasonable
modificante *adj* modifying ‖ *m* (gram) modifier
modificar §73 *tr* to modify
modismo *m* idiom
modista *f* dressmaker; **modista de sombreros** milliner
modistería *f* dressmaking; ladies' dress shop
modistilla *f* dressmaker's helper; unskilled dressmaker
modisto *m* ladies' tailor
modo *m* manner, mode, way; (gram) mood, mode; **al** or **a modo de** like, on the order of; **de buen modo** politely; **de ese modo** at that rate; **de tal modo que** with the result that; **de modo que** so that; and so; **de ningún modo** by no means; **de todos modos** anyhow, at any rate; **en cierto modo** after a fashion; **modo de empleo** usage; instructions for use; **modo de ser** nature, disposition; **por modo de** as, by way of; **sobre modo** extremely; **uno a modo de** a sort of, a kind of
modorra *f* drowsiness, heaviness
modorrar *tr* to make drowsy ‖ *ref* to get drowsy, fall asleep; (*la fruta*) get squashy
modo•rro -rra *adj* drowsy, heavy; dull, stupid; (*fruta*) squashy ‖ *f* see **modorra**
modo•so -sa *adj* quiet, well-behaved
modrego *m* boor, awkward fellow
modulación *f* modulation; **modulación de altura** or **de amplitud** amplitude modulation; **modulación de frecuencia** frequency modulation
modular *tr & intr* to modulate
módulo *m* module; **módulo lunar** lunar lander, lunar module
modulo•so -sa *adj* harmonious
mofa *f* jeering, scoffing, mockery
mofeta *f* skunk; (*gas pernicioso que se desprende de las minas*) blackdamp, firedamp
moflete *m* fat cheek, jowl
mofletu•do -da *adj* fat-cheeked

mo•gol -gola *adj & mf* Mongol, Mongolian
mogollón *m* — **comer de mogollón** (coll) to sponge
mo•gón -gona *adj* one-horned, broken-horned
mogote *m* knoll, hillock; stack of sheaves; budding antler
mohatra *f* fake sale; cheating
mohien•to -ta *adj* moldy, musty; (*hierro*) rusty
mohín *m* face, grimace
mohina *f* annoyance, displeasure
mohi•no -na *adj* sad, melancholy, moody; (*caballo, buey, vaca*) black, black-nosed ‖ *mf* hinny ‖ *m* blue magpie ‖ *f* see **mohina**
moho *m* mold, must; (*del hierro*) rust; laziness; **no dejar criar moho** to keep in constant use, to use up quickly
moho•so -sa *adj* moldy, rusty; (*hierro*) rusty; (*chiste*) stale
Moisés *m* Moses
moja•do -da *adj* wet; (*p.ej., por la lluvia*) drenched, soaked; (*húmedo*) moist; (*phonet*) liquid ‖ *m* (Mex) wetback
mojar *tr* to wet; (*la lluvia a una persona*) drench, soak; (*humedecer*) dampen, moisten; (*ensopar*) dunk; stab ‖ *intr* — **mojar en** to get mixed up in ‖ *ref* to get wet; get drenched, get soaked
mojarrilla *mf* jolly person
moje *m* or **mojete** *m* sauce, gravy
mojicón *m* muffin, bun; slap in the face
mojiganga *f* masquerade, mummery; clowning
mojigatería or **mojigatez** *f* hypocrisy; prudery, sanctimoniousness
mojiga•to -ta *adj* hypocritical; prudish, sanctimonious ‖ *mf* hypocrite; prude, sanctimonious person
mojinete *m* (*de un muro*) coping; (*de un tejado*) ridge; (Arg) gable; (Chile) gable end
mojón *m* boundary stone, landmark; (*montón sin orden*) pile, heap; (*guía en desplobado*) road mark; (*porción de excremento humano*) turd
moldar *tr* to mold; put molding on
molde *m* mold; pattern; cast, stamp, matrix; (*persona*) model, ideal; (*letra*) **de molde** printed; **venir de molde** to be just right
moldear *tr* to mold; (*vaciar*) cast; put molding on
moldura *f* molding
moldurar *tr* to put molding on
mole *adj* soft ‖ *m* (Mex) stew seasoned with chili sauce ‖ *f* bulk, mass
molécula *f* molecule
molende•ro -ra *mf* miller, grinder ‖ *m* chocolate grinder; (CAm) grinding table
moler §47 *tr* (*granos*) to grind, mill; annoy, harass, weary; tire out, fatigue; chew; **moler a palos** to beat up
molesquina *f* moleskin
molestar *tr* to disturb, molest; bother, annoy; tire, weary ‖ *ref* to bother; be annoyed; **molestarse en** to take the trouble to

molestia f disturbance, discomfort; annoyance, bother, nuisance

moles•to -ta adj bothersome, troublesome; boring, tedious; bored, tired

molesto•so -sa adj bothersome

moleteado m knurl

moletear tr to knurl

molibdeno m molybdenum

molicie f softness; effeminacy; voluptuous living

moli•do -da adj ground; exhausted, worn out

molienda f grinding, milling; (cantidad que se muele de una vez) grist; (molino) mill; bore, annoyance; fatigue, weariness

molimiento m grinding; weariness

moline•ro -ra adj mill ‖ m miller ‖ f miller's wife

molinete m little mill; ventilating fan; (juguete de papel) windmill; (movimiento que se hace con el bastón) twirl; (con la espada) flourish; (naut) windlass; (rueda de cohetes) (Mex) pinwheel

molinillo m hand mill; **molinillo de café** coffee grinder

molino m mill; **luchar con los molinos de viento** to tilt at windmills; **molino de sangre** animal-driven mill; **molino de viento** windmill; **molino harinero** gristmill, flour mill

moloc m (Ecuad) mashed potatoes

molondrón m lazy bum; (Ven) large inheritance, much money

molusco m mollusk

mollar adj soft, tender; mushy, squashy; (carne) lean; profitable; gullible, easily taken in

mollear intr to give, yield; bend

molleja f gizzard; **criar molleja** to get lazy; **mollejas** sweetbread

mollejón m grindstone; big fat loafer; good-natured fellow

mollera f crown (of the head); brains, sense; **cerrado de mollera** stupid; **duro de mollera** stubborn

mollete m muffin

molli•no -na adj drizzly ‖ f drizzle

mollizna f drizzle

momentáne•o -a adj momentary

momento m moment; **a cada momento** constantly, all the time; **al momento** at once; **de un momento a otro** at any moment

momería f clowning

mome•ro -ra adj clowning ‖ mf clown

momia f mummy

momificar §73 tr to mummify

mo•mio -mia adj lean, skinny ‖ m extra; (ganga) bargain; sinecure ‖ f see **momia**

momo m face, grimace; (coll) caress

mona f female monkey; Barbary ape; ape, copycat; drunkenness; (persona) drunk; (taur) guard for right leg; **dormir la mona** to sleep off a drunk; **pillar una mona** to go on a jag; **pintar la mona** to put on airs

monacal adj monachal

monacato m monkhood

monacillo m altar boy, acolyte

monada f monkeyshine; (gesto) face, grimace, monkey face; darling; cuteness; flattery; folly, childishness

monaguillo m altar boy, acolyte

monaquismo m monasticism

monarca m monarch

monarquía f monarchy

monárqui•co -ca adj monarchic(al) ‖ mf monarchist

monasterio m monastery

monásti•co -ca adj monastic

monda f pruning, trimming; parings, peelings; beating, whipping

mondadien•tes m (pl -tes) toothpick

mondadura f pruning, trimming; **mondaduras** peelings

mondar tr to clean; prune, trim; peel, pare, hull, husk; (quitar con engaño los bienes a) fleece; beat, whip

mon•do -da adj clean; pure; **mondo y lirondo** pure, unadulterated ‖ f see **monda**

mondonga f kitchen wench

mondongo m intestines, insides; (del hombre) guts

monear intr to act like a monkey; boast ‖ ref (Hond) to plug away; (Hond) to punch each other

moneda f coin; money; **la Moneda** the government of Chile; **moneda corriente** currency; common knowledge; **moneda falsa** counterfeit; **moneda menuda** change; **moneda metálica** or **sonante** specie; **moneda suelta** change; **pagar en la misma moneda** to pay back in one's own coin

monedar tr to coin, mint

monedero m moneybag; **monedero falso** counterfeiter

monería f monkeyshine; cuteness; childishness

mones•co -ca adj apish

moneta•rio -ria adj monetary

mon•gol -gola adj & mf Mongol, Mongolian

monigote m lay brother; rag figure, stuffed form; botched painting, botched statue; sap, boob

monipodio m collusion, deal, plot

monís m trinket; **monises** money, dough

mónita f cunning, smoothness, slickness

monitor m monitor

monja f nun; **monjas** lingering sparks in burning paper

monje m monk

monjía f monkhood

monjil adj nunnish ‖ m nun's dress

mono -na adj cute, nice; blond; (cabello) red ‖ m monkey, ape; (traje de faena) coveralls; whippersnapper, squirt; (drogas) withdrawal symptom; (coll) clown; (taur) attendant of picador; (Chile) pyramid of fruit or vegetables; **estar de monos** to be on the outs; **mono de Gibraltar** Barbary ape ‖ f see **mona**

monóculo m monocle

monogamia f monogamy

monografía f monograph

monograma m monogram

monolíti•co -ca adj monolithic

mo
mo

monologar §44 *intr* to soliloquize
monólogo *m* monologue
monomanía *f* monomania
monomio *m* monomial
mono•no -na *adj* cute, sweet
monopatín *m* scooter
monoplano *m* monoplane
monopolio *m* monopoly
monopolizar §60 *tr* to monopolize
monorriel *m* monorail
monosabio *m* (taur) attendant of picador
monosílabo *m* monosyllable
monoteísta *adj* monotheistic ‖ *mf* monotheist
monotipia *f* or **monotipo** *m* monotype
monotonía *f* monotony
monóto•no -na *adj* monotonous
monóxido *m* monoxide
monseñor *m* monseigneur; (eccl) monsignor
monserga *f* gibberish
monstruo *m* monster
monstruosidad *f* monstrosity
monstruo•so -sa *adj* monstrous
monta *f* sum, total; **de poca monta** of little account
montacar•gas *m* (*pl* **-gas**) hoist, freight elevator
montadero *m* horse block
montadura *f* mounting; (*de una caballería de silla*) harness; (*engaste*) setting, mount
montaje *m* montage; setting up; (mach) assembly; (rad) hookup
montanero *m* forest ranger
montante *m* post, upright; (*suma*) amount; (*hueco cuadrilongo sobre una puerta*) transom; (*espadón*) broadsword ‖ *f* flood tide
montaña *f* mountain; mountain country; **la Montaña** the Province of Santander, Spain; **montaña de hielo** iceberg; **montaña rusa** roller coaster
monta•nés -ñesa *adj* mountain ‖ *mf* mountaineer, highlander
montaño•so -sa *adj* mountainous
montapla•tos *m* (*pl* **-tos**) dumbwaiter
montar *tr* to mount, get on; (*un caballo, una bicicleta, los hombros de una persona*) ride; (*un servicio*) set up, establish; (*un fusil*) cock; (*una piedra preciosa*) set, mount; (*el caballo a la yegua*) cover; (*un reloj*) wind; (elec) to hook up; (mach) to assemble, to mount; (*la guardia*) (mil) to mount; (*un cabo*) (naut) to round; (*un buque*) (naut) to command; (*importar*) amount to ‖ *intr* to mount; get on top; weigh, be important; **tanto monta** it's all the same ‖ *ref* to mount; get on top; **montarse en cólera** to fly into a rage
monta•raz *adj* (*pl* **-races**) backwoods; wild, untamed ‖ *m* forester, warden
monte *m* mountain, mount; woods, woodland; obstruction, interference; backwoods, wilds; bank, kitty; dirty head of hair; **andar al monte** to take to the woods; **monte alto** forest; **monte bajo** thicket, brushwood; **monte de piedad** pawnshop; **monte pío** pension fund for widows and orphans; mutual benefit society; **monte tallar** tree farm

montear *tr* to hunt, track down; make a working drawing of; arch, vault
montecillo *m* mound, hillock
montepío *m* pension fund for widows and orphans; mutual benefit society
montera *f* cloth cap; glass roof; wife of hunter; bullfighter's black bicorne; (Hond) drunk, jag
montería *f* hunting, big-game hunting; hunting party; (Bol, Ecuad) canoe to shoot the rapids; (Mex) lumberman's camp
monterilla *f* (naut) moonsail
montero *m* hunter, huntsman; (Mex) sawmill
montés or **montesi•no -na** *adj* wild (*e.g., goat*)
montículo *m* mound, hillock
montilla *f* montilla (*a pale dry sherry*)
monto *m* sum, total
montón *m* pile, heap; (*de gente*) crowd; lot, great deal, great many; **a, de,** or **en montón** taken together; **a montones** in abundance; **ser del montón** to be quite ordinary
montonera *f* heap, pile; band of mounted rebels
montonero *m* guerrilla
montu•no -na *adj* wooded; wild, untamed, rustic
montuo•so -sa *adj* wooded, woody; rugged, hilly
montura *f* (*cabalgadura*) mount; (*de una cabalgadura*) harness; seat, saddle; (*de una piedra preciosa, de un instrumento astronómico*) mounting; (*de gafas*) frame
monumento *m* monument
monzón *m* monsoon
moña *f* doll; mannequin; ribbon, hair ribbon; drunk, jag
moño *m* topknot; crest, top; (Col) caprice, whim; (*de caballo*) (Chile) forelock; **moños** frippery
moquear *intr* to snivel
moqueo *m* snivel, sniveling
moquero *m* handkerchief
moquete *m* punch in the nose
moquillo *m* runny nose; (vet) distemper
moquita *f* mucus, snivel
mor *m* — **por mor de** for love of; because of
mora *f* black mulberry; blackberry; brambleberry; white mulberry
morada *f* dwelling; stay, sojourn
mora•do -da *adj* purple, mulberry ‖ *f* see **morada**
moral *adj* moral ‖ *m* black mulberry tree ‖ *f* (*ciencia de la conducta; conducta*) morals; (*espíritu, confianza*) morale; (*p.ej., de una fábula*) moral
moraleja *f* moral
moralidad *f* morality; (*de una fábula*) moral
morar *intr* to live, dwell
moratoria *f* moratorium
mórbi•do -da *adj* (*perteneciente a la enfermedad*) morbid; soft, delicate, mellow
morbo *m* sickness, illness; **morbo gálico** syphilis; **morbo regio** jaundice
morbo•so -sa *adj* morbid, diseased

morcilla *f* blood pudding, black pudding; (*añadidura que mete un actor en su papel*) gag

mor•daz *adj* (*pl* **-daces**) mordant, mordacious, sharp, caustic

mordaza *f* (*pañuelo o instrumento que se pone en la boca para impedir el hablar*) gag; (*aparato que sirve para apretar*) clamp, jaw; pipe vise; **poner la mordaza a** to gag

mordedura *f* bite

morder §47 *tr* to bite; nibble at; wear away; gossip about, ridicule; (Mex, Ven, W-I) to cheat ‖ *intr* to bite; take hold

mordicar §73 *tr & intr* to bite, sting

mordida *f* bite; (*para eludir una multa*) (Mex) payoff

mordiente *m* mordant

mordiscar §73 *tr* to nibble at ‖ *intr* to nibble, gnaw away; champ

mordisco *m* nibble, bite; champ

more•no -na *adj* brown, dark-brown; dark, dark-complexioned; (*de la raza negra*) black; mulato ‖ *mf* black person; mulato ‖ *m* brunet ‖ *f* brunette; loaf of brown bread; rick of new-mown hay

morería *f* Moorish quarter; Moorish land

moretón *m* black-and-blue mark

morfina *f* morphine

morfinomanía *f* morphine habit, drug habit

morfinóma•no -na *adj* addicted to morphine, addicted to drugs ‖ *mf* morphine addict, drug addict

morfología *f* morphology

moribun•do -da *adj* moribund, dying ‖ *mf* dying person

morillo *m* andiron, firedog

morir §30 & §83 *intr* to die; (*el fuego, la luz, etc.*) die away; **morir ahogado** to drown; **morir de risa** to die laughing; **morir de viejo** to die of old age; **morir helado** to freeze to death; **morir quemado** to burn to death; **morir vestido** to die a violent death ‖ *ref* to die; be dying; die away, die out; (*una pierna, un brazo*) go to sleep; **morirse por** to be crazy about; be dying to

moris•co -ca *adj* Morisco, Moorish ‖ *mf* Moor converted to Christianity (*after the Reconquest*); (*descendiente de mulato y española o de mulata y español*) (Mex) Morisco

mo•ro -ra *adj* Moorish; (*vino*) unwatered ‖ *mf* Moor; **hay moros en la costa** there's trouble brewing; **moro de paz** man of peace ‖ *f* see **mora**

moro•cho -cha *adj* strong, robust; (SAm) dark

morón *m* mound, knoll; moron

moron•do -da *adj* bare, stripped

moronga *f* (CAm, Mex) sausage

moro•so -sa *adj* slow, tardy; (*retrasado en el pago de deudas*) delinquent

morra *f* (*de la cabeza*) top, crown; (*de gato*) purr; **andar a la morra** to come to blows

morrada *f* slap, punch; (*golpe dado con la cabeza*) butt

morral *m* nose bag; (*saco de cazador*) game bag; (*de soldado, viandante, etc.*) knapsack; boor, lout

morralla *f* small fish; (*gente de escaso valor*) rabble, trash; (*mezcla de cosas inútiles*) junk, trash; (Mex) change, small change

morriña *f* blues, melancholy; **morriña de la tierra** homesickness

morriño•so -sa *adj* sickly; (coll) blue, melancholy

morrión *m* helmet; (mil) bearskin

morro *m* (*cosa redonda*) knob; (*monte redondo*) knoll; (*guijarro*) pebble; (*saliente que forman los labios*) snout; **beber a morro** (slang) to drink out of the bottle; **estar de morro** or **de morros** to be on the outs; **poner morro** to make a snout; **por el morro** just like that, simply so

morrocotu•do -da *adj* strong, thick, heavy; (*asunto, negocio*) weighty; big, enormous; (Col) rich, wealthy; (Chile) graceless, monotonous

morsa *f* walrus

mortaja *f* shroud, winding sheet; cigarette paper; (carp) mortise

mortal *adj* mortal; deadly; mortally ill; deathly pale; sure, conclusive ‖ *m* mortal

mortalidad *f* mortality; death rate

mortandad *f* massacre, mortality, butchery

morteci•no -na *adj* dead; dying; failing, weak; **hacer la mortecina** to play dead, to play possum

mortero *m* (*vaso que sirve para machacar; argamasa*) mortar; (*en los molinos de aceite*) nether stone; (arti) mortar

mortífe•ro -ra *adj* deadly

mortificar §73 *tr* to vex, annoy, bother; mortify ‖ *ref* (Mex) to be mortified, be embarrassed

mortual *m* (CAm, Mex) inheritance

mortuo•rio -ria *adj* mortuary, funeral; (*casa*) of the deceased ‖ *m* (archaic) funeral

morueco *m* ram

moru•no -na *adj* Moorish

mosai•co -ca *adj* Mosaic ‖ *m* tile, paving tile; mosaic; **mosaico de madera** marquetry

mosca *f* fly; (*barba*) imperial; cash, dough; disappointment; bore, nuisance; **aflojar la mosca** to shell out, to fork out; **mosca borriquera** horsefly; **mosca de las frutas** fruit fly; **mosca del vinagre** fruit fly; **mosca muerta** hypocrite; **moscas** sparks; **moscas volantes** spots before the eyes; **papar moscas** to gape, gawk

moscareta *f* (orn) flycatcher

moscona *f* hussy, brazen woman

Moscú Moscow

mosquear *tr* (*moscas*) to shoo; beat, whip; answer sharply ‖ *intr* (Mex) to sneak a ride ‖ *ref* to shake off annoyances; take offense

mosquero *m* flytrap; fly swatter

mosquete *m* musket

mosquetear *intr* (Arg, Bol) to snoop

mosquete•ro -ra *adj* idle ‖ *mf* (Arg, Bol) bystander, snooper ‖ *m* musketeer ‖ *f* wallflower

mosquetón *m* snap hook

mosquitera *f* or **mosquitero** *m* mosquito net; fly net

mosquito *m* (*Culex pungens*) mosquito; (*insecto parecido al anterior*) gnat; (coll) tippler

mostacera *f* mustard jar

mostacho *m* mustache; spot on the face

mostachón *m* macaroon

mostaza *f* mustard; (*semilla; munición*) mustard seed; **subírsele a** (*uno*) **la mostaza a las narices** to fly into a rage

mosto *m* must; **mosto de cerveza** wort

mostrador *m* (*en las tiendas*) counter; (*en las tabernas*) bar; (*de reloj*) dial

mostrar §61 *tr* to show ‖ *ref* to show; show oneself to be

mostrear *tr* to spot, splash

mostren•co -ca *adj* ownerless, unclaimed; (*que no tiene casa ni hogar*) homeless; (*animal*) stray; slow, dull; fat, heavy ‖ *mf* dolt, dullard

mota *f* mote, speck; (*en el paño*) burl, knot; hill, rise; defect, fault; (Mex, W-I) powder puff

mote *m* device, emblem, riddle; (*apodo*) nickname; (Chile) mistake; (SAm) stewed corn

motear *tr* to speck, speckle; dapple, mottle ‖ *intr* (Peru) to eat stewed corn

motejar *tr* to call names; scoff at, make fun of; **motejar de** to brand as

motín *m* mutiny, riot

motinista *m* (Peru) rioter

motivar *tr* to explain, account for; rationalize

moti•vo -va *adj* motive ‖ *m* motive, reason; (mus) motif; **con motivo de** because of; on the occasion of; **de su motivo propio** on his own accord; **motivo conductor** (mus) leitmotif; **motivos** grounds, reasons; (Chile) finickiness, prudery

moto *m* guidepost, landmark ‖ *f* motorcycle

motobomba *f* fire truck, fire engine

motocarro *m* three-wheel delivery truck

motocicleta *f* motorcycle

motocine *m* drive-in theater

motogrúa *f* truck crane

motoli•to -ta *adj* simple, stupid; **vivir de motolito** to be a sponger, live on other people ‖ *f* (orn) wagtail; (Ven) decent woman

motón *m* (naut) block, pulley

motonáuti•co -ca *adj* motorboat ‖ *f* motorboating

motonautismo *m* (sport) motorboating

motonave *f* motor launch; motor ship

motoneta *f* motor scooter; moped; light three-wheel delivery truck

mo•tor -tora *adj* motor, motive ‖ *m* motor, engine; **motor a chorro** jet engine; **motor de arranque** (aut) starter, starting motor; **motor de cuatro tiempos** four-cycle engine; **motor de dos tiempos** two-cycle engine; **motor de explosión** internal-combustion engine; **motor de reacción** jet engine; **motor fuera de borda** outboard motor; **motor térmico** heat engine ‖ *f* small motor boat

motorista *mf* motorist; motorcyclist; motorcycle racer ‖ *m* motorcycle policeman; motorman

motorización *f* motorization

motorizar §60 *tr* to motorize

motosegadora *f* power mower

motovelero *m* (naut) motor sailer

motriz *adj fem* (*fuerza*) motive

movedi•zo -za *adj* shaky, unsteady; fickle, inconstant; (*arena*) quick, shifting

mover §47 *tr* to move; (*la cola el perro*) wag; (*discordia*) stir up ‖ *intr* to move; abort, miscarry; bud, sprout ‖ *ref* to move; be moved

movible *adj* movable; fickle, inconstant, changeable

móvil *adj* movable, mobile; fickle, changeable; moving ‖ *m* moving body; cause, motive

movilizar §60 *tr* to mobilize

movimiento *m* movement, motion; **movimiento feminista** women's liberation (movement)

moza *f* girl, lass; mistress, concubine; maid, kitchen maid; (*en algunos juegos de naipes*) last hand; wash bat; **buena moza** or **real moza** good-looking woman; **moza de fortuna** or **del partido** prostitute; **moza de taberna** barmaid

mozalbete *m* lad, young fellow

mozárabe *adj* Mozarabic ‖ *mf* Mozarab

mo•zo -za *adj* young, youthful; single, unmarried ‖ *m* youth, lad; (*camarero*) waiter; (*criado*) servant; porter; (*cuelgacapas*) cloak hanger; **buen mozo** or **real mozo** handsome fellow; **mozo de caballerías** hostler, stable boy; **mozo de café** waiter; **mozo de cámara** (naut) cabin boy; **mozo de ciego** blind man's guide; **mozo de cordel** street porter, public errand boy; **mozo de cuadra** stable boy; **mozo de cuerda** public errand boy; **mozo de espuelas** groom who walks in front of master's horse; **mozo de esquina** street porter, public errand boy; **mozo de estación** station porter; **mozo de estoques** (taur) sword handler; **mozo de hotel** porter, bellhop; **mozo de paja y cebada** hostler (*at an inn*); **mozo de restaurante** waiter ‖ *f* see **moza**

mozue•lo -la *mf* youngster ‖ *m* lad, young fellow ‖ *f* lass, young woman

m/p *abbr* **mi pagaré**

m/r *abbr* **mi remesa**

Mro. *abbr* **Maestro**

M.S. *abbr* **manuscrito**

mtd. *abbr* **mitad**

mu *m* moo ‖ *f* bye-bye; **ir a la mu** to go bye-bye

muaré *adj invar* & *m* moiré

muca•mo -ma *mf* (Arg, Urug) house servant ‖ *f* (Arg, Chile, Urug) servant girl

muceta *f* (*de los doctores en los actos universitarios*) hood; (eccl) mozzetta

muco•so -sa *adj* mucous ‖ *f* mucous membrane

múcura *f* (Bol, Col, Ven, W-I) water pitcher; (Col) thickhead

muchacha f girl; young woman; servant girl

muchachada f youthful prank

muchachez f boyishness, girlishness

mucha·cho -cha adj young, youthful ‖ mf youth, young person; servant ‖ m boy ‖ f see muchacha

muchedumbre f crowd, multitude, flock

mu·cho -cha adj much, a lot of, a great deal of; (tiempo) a long ‖ pron much, a lot, a great deal ‖ **mu·chos -chas** adj & pron many ‖ **mucho** adv much; (más de lo regular) hard; often; a long time; **con mucho** by far; **ni con mucho** or **ni mucho menos** not by a long shot; **por mucho que** however much; **sentir mucho** to be very sorry; **tener mucho de** to take after

muda f change; change of voice, change of clothes; (cambio de plumas o de piel) molt, molting; molting season; **estar de muda** to be changing one's voice; **estar en muda** (coll) to keep too quiet; **hacer la muda** to molt; **muda de ropa** change of clothing

mudable adj fickle, inconstant

mudada f change of clothing; move, change of residence

mudadi·zo -za adj fickle, inconstant

mudanza f change; (cambio de domicilio) moving; fickleness, inconstancy; (en el baile) figure

mudar tr to change ‖ intr to change; **mudar de** to change ‖ ref to change; change clothing; move; move away; have a bowel movement; **mudarse de** to change

mudez f muteness, dumbness; continued silence

mu·do -da adj dumb, mute; (phonet) voiceless, surd ‖ mf mute ‖ f see muda

mueblaje m furniture, suite of furniture

mueble adj movable ‖ m piece of furniture; (p.ej., de un aparato de radio) cabinet; **muebles** furniture

mueblería f furniture shop

mueblista mf furniture dealer

mueca f face, grimace

muela f grindstone; knoll, mound; back tooth, grinder; **muela cordal** wisdom tooth; **muela de esmeril** emery wheel; **muela del juicio** wisdom tooth; **muela de molino** millstone

muellaje m dockage, wharfage

muelle adj soft; voluptuous ‖ m (pieza elástica de metal) spring; (obra en la orilla del mar o de un río) dock, wharf, pier; (rr) freight platform; **muelle real** mainspring

muérdago m mistletoe

muérgano m (Col, Ven) piece of junk, drug on the market; (Col, Ecuad, Ven) boor, nobody

muermo m (vet) glanders

muerte f death; **cada muerte de obispo** once in a blue moon; **dar la muerte a** to put to death; **de mala muerte** crummy, not much of a; **estar a la muerte** to be at death's door; **muerte chiquita** nervous shudder

muer·to -ta adj dead; (apagado, marchito) flat, dull; (cal, yeso) slaked; **muerto de** dying of; **muerto por** crazy about ‖ mf

corpse, dead person ‖ m (en los naipes) dummy; **hacerse el muerto** to play possum; play deaf; **tocar a muerto** to toll

muesca f nick, notch; (carp) mortise

muestra f (porción de un producto que sirve para conocer su calidad) sample; model, specimen; (rótulo sobre una tienda u hotel) sign; show, exhibition, indication; (esfera de reloj) dial, face; (parada del perro para levantar la caza) set; (ademán, porte) bearing; **dar muestras de** to show signs of

mugido m moo, low; bellow, roar

mugir §27 intr (la res vacuna) to moo, low; (con ira) bellow; (el viento, el mar) roar

mugre f dirt, filth, grime

mugrien·to -ta adj dirty, filthy, grimy

muguete m lily of the valley

mujer f woman; (esposa) wife; **mujer de gobierno** housekeeper; **mujer de su casa** good manager; **mujer fatal** vamp; **ser mujer** to be a grown woman

mujeren·go -ga adj (Arg, Urug, CAm) effeminate

mujerie·go -ga adj feminine, womanly; effeminate, womanish; fond of women; **a mujeriegas** sidesaddle ‖ m flock of women

mujeril adj womanly; womanish

mújol m mullet, striped mullet

mula f mule, she-mule; junk, trash; (Arg) ingrate, traitor; (Arg) hoax; (C-R) jag, drunk; (Guat, Hond) anger, rage; (Mex) drug on the market; (Ven) flask; **devolver la mula** (CAm) to pay back in one's own coin; **echar la mula a** (Mex) to rake over the coals; **en mula de San Francisco** on shank's mare

mulada f drove of mules

muladar m dungheap, dunghill; dump, trash heap; filth

mula·to -ta adj & mf mulatto

muleta f (palo para apoyarse al andar) crutch; muleta (cloth attached to a stick, used by matador); support, prop; snack

muletilla f cross-handle cane; pet word, pet phrase; (taur) muleta

mulo m mule

multa f fine

multar tr to fine

multicopista m copying machine

multigrafiar §77 tr to multigraph

multígrafo m multigraph

multilateral adj multilateral

multiláte·ro -ra adj multilateral

multinacionales mpl multinational corporations

múltiple adj multiple, manifold ‖ m manifold; **múltiple de admisión** intake manifold; **múltiple de escape** exhaust manifold; **múltiple de uso** multipurpose

multiplicar §73 tr, intr & ref to multiply

multiplicidad f multiplicity

múlti·plo -pla adj multiple, manifold ‖ m (math) multiple

multitud f multitude

mulli·do -da adj soft, fluffy ‖ m stuffing (for cushions, pillows, etc.) ‖ f bedding, litter (for animals)

mo
mu

mullir §13 *tr* to soften, fluff up; (*la cama*) beat up, shake up; (*la tierra*) loosen around a stalk ‖ *ref* to get fluffy
munda•no -na *adj* mundane, worldly; (*mujer*) loose
mundial *adj* world-wide, world
mundillo *m* arched clotheshorse; cushion for making lace; warming pan; guelder-rose, cranberry tree; world (*of artists, scholars, etc.*)
mundo *m* world; **así va el mundo** so it goes; **desde que el mundo es mundo** since the world began; **echar al mundo** to bring into the world; to bring forth; **el otro mundo** the other world; **gran mundo** high society; **medio mundo** (*mucha gente*) half the world; **nada del otro mundo** nothing special, no great thing; **tener mucho mundo** to know one's way around; **todo el mundo** everybody; **ver mundo** to see the world, to travel
mundonuevo *m* peep show
munición *f* munition, ammunition; **de munición** (mil) government issue; (coll) done hurriedly
municionar *tr* to supply with munition
municipal *adj* municipal ‖ *m* policeman
munícipe *m* citizen
municipio *m* municipality; town council
munidad *f* susceptibility to infection
munífi•co -ca *adj* munificent
muñeca *f* (*figurilla infantil con que juegan las niñas*) doll; (*parte del cuerpo humano en donde se articula la mano con el brazo*) wrist; manikin, dress form; tea bag; (*mujer linda; mozuela frívola*) doll; **muñeca de trapo** rag doll, rag baby; **muñeca parlante** talking doll
muñeco *m* doll (*representing a male child or animal*); dummy, manikin; fop, effeminate fellow; (fig) puppet; (coll) lad, little fellow
muñequera *f* strap for wrist watch
muñequilla *f* (mach) chuck; (Arg, Chile) young ear of corn
muñidor *m* heeler, henchman
muñir §12 *tr* to convoke, summon; (pol) to fix, rig
muñón *m* (*p.ej., de un brazo cortado*) stump; (mach) journal, gudgeon; **muñón de cola** dock
mural *adj* mural
muralla *f* wall, rampart
murar *tr* to surround with a wall
murciélago *m* bat
murga *f* tin-pan band; trouble, bother; torment
muriente *adj* dying, faint
murmujear *tr & intr* to mumble
murmullar *intr* to murmur
murmullo *m* murmur; whisper; (*de aguas corrientes*) ripple; (*del viento*) rustle

murmurar *tr* to murmur, mutter; murmur at ‖ *intr* to murmur, mutter; whisper; (*las aguas corrientes*) ripple, purl; (*el viento*) rustle; gossip
muro *m* wall; **muro del sonido** sound barrier
murria *f* (coll) blues, dejection
musa *f* muse; **las Musas** the Muses; **soplarle a uno la musa** to be inspired to write poetry; be lucky at games of chance
musaraña *f* shrew, shrewmouse; bug, worm; **mirar a las musarañas** to stare vacantly
músculo *m* muscle
musculo•so -sa *adj* muscular
muselina *f* muslin
museo *m* museum; **museo de cera** waxworks
muserola *f* noseband
mus•go -ga *adj* dark-brown ‖ *m* moss
musgo•so -sa *adj* mossy, moss-covered
música *f* music; (*músicos que tocan juntos*) band; noise, racket; **con la música a otra parte** don't bother me, get out; **música celestial** nonsense; **música de fondo** background music; **poner en música** to set to music
musical *adj* musical
musicalidad *f* musicianship
music-hall *s* vaudeville theater, burlesque show
músi•co -ca *adj* musical ‖ *mf* musician; **músico mayor** bandmaster ‖ *f* see **música**
musicología *f* musicology
musicólo•go -ga *mf* musicologist
musiquero *m* music cabinet
musitar *tr & intr* to mutter, mumble
muslime *adj & mf* Muslim
muslo *m* thigh; (*de ave cocida*) leg, drumstick
mustiar *ref* to wither
mus•tio -tia *adj* sad, gloomy; (*marchito*) withered; (Mex) hypocritical; (Mex) standoffish
musul•mán -mana *adj & mf* Muslim
mutación *f* mutation; unsettled weather, change of weather; (biol) mutation, sport; (theat) change of scene
mutila•do -da *adj* crippled ‖ *mf* cripple
mutilar *tr* to mutilate; cripple
múti•lo -la *adj* mutilated; crippled
mutis *m* (theat) exit; **hacer mutis** (theat) to exit; keep quiet
mutual *adj* mutual
mutualidad *f* mutuality; mutual benefit; mutual benefit association
mutualista *mf* member of a mutual benefit association
mu•tuo -tua *adj* mutual, reciprocal
muy *adv* very; very much; too, e.g., **es muy tarde para dar un paseo tan largo** it is too late to take such a long walk; **muy de noche** late at night; **Muy señor mío** Dear Sir

N

N, n (ene) *f* sixteenth letter of the Spanish alphabet

n/ *abbr* **nuestro**

N. *abbr* **Norte**

nabo *m* turnip; (naut) mast

Nabucodonosor *m* Nebuchadnezzar

nácar *m* mother-of-pearl

nacara•do -da *adj* mother-of-pearl

nacatamal *m* (CAm, Mex) meat-filled tamale

nacela *f* nacelle

nacencia *f* birth; growth, tumor

nacer §22 *intr* to be born; bud, take rise, originate, appear; dawn ‖ *ref* bud, shoot, sprout; (*abrirse la ropa por las costuras*) split

naci•do -da *adj* natural, innate; apt, proper, fit; **nacida** née or nee ‖ *m* human being; growth, boil

naciente *adj* incipient; resurgent; (*sol*) rising ‖ *m* east

nacimiento *m* birth; origin, beginning, fountainhead; descent, lineage; (*de agua*) spring, fountainhead; crèche

nación *f* nation

nacional *adj* national; domestic ‖ *mf* national ‖ *m* militiaman

nacionalidad *f* nationality

nacionalismo *m* nationalism

nacionalista *adj* & *mf* nationalist

nacionalizar §60 *tr* to nationalize ‖ *ref* to be naturalized; become a citizen

nacista *adj* & *mf* Nazi

naco *m* (Arg, Bol, Urug) black rolled leaf of chewing tobacco; (Arg) fear, scare; (Col) stewed corn; (Col) mashed potatoes

nada *pron indef* nothing, not . . . anything; **de nada** don't mention it, you're welcome ‖ *adv* not at all

nadaderas *fpl* water wings

nada•dor -dora *adj* swimming, floating ‖ *mf* swimmer ‖ *m* (Chile) fishnet float

nadar *intr* to swim; float; fit loosely or too loosely; **nadar en** (*riqueza*) to be rolling in; (*suspiros*) be full of; (*sangre*) be bathed in

nadear *tr* to destroy, wipe out

nadería *f* trifle

nadie *pron indef* nobody, not . . . anybody; **nadie más** nobody else; **nadie más que** nobody but ‖ *m* nobody; **un don nadie** a nonentity

nado — **a nado** swimming, floating; **echarse a nado** to dive in; **pasar a nado** to swim across

nafta *f* naphtha

nagual *m* (Guat, Hond) (*dícese de un animal*) inseparable companion; (Mex) sorcerer, wizard; (Mex) lie

nagualear *intr* (Mex) to lie; (Mex) to be out looking for trouble all night

naguas *fpl* petticoat

naipe *m* playing card; deck of cards; **naipe de figura** face card; **tener buen naipe** to be lucky

naire *m* mahout

nalgada *f* shoulder, ham; blow on or with the buttocks

nalgas *fpl* buttocks, rump

nana *f* grandma; lullaby, cradlesong; (CAm, Mex, W-I) child's nurse; (Arg, Chile, Urug) child's complaint

nao *f* ship, vessel

napoleóni•co -ca *adj* Napoleonic

Nápoles *f* Naples

napolita•no -na *adj* & *mf* Neapolitan

naranja *f* orange; **media naranja** (coll) sidekick, better half; **naranja cajel** Seville orange, sour orange; **¡naranjas!** nonsense!

naranjada *f* orangeade; orange juice; orange marmalade

naranjal *m* orange grove

naranjo *m* orange tree; boob, simpleton

narciso *m* narcissus; fop, dandy; **narciso trompón** daffodil ‖ **Narciso** *m* Narcissus

narcóti•co -ca *adj* & *m* narcotic

narcotizar §60 *tr* to dope, drug

narcotraficante *mf* drug dealer

narguile *m* hookah

narigada *f* (SAm) pinch of snuff

nari•gón -gona *adj* big-nosed ‖ *m* big nose

narigu•do -da *adj* big-nosed; nose-shaped

nariguera *f* nose ring

na•riz *f* (*pl* -**rices**) nose; nostril; sense of smell; (*del vino*) bouquet; **nariz de pico de loro** hooknose; **sonarse las narices** to blow one's nose; **tabicarse las narices** to hold one's nose; **tener agarrado por las narices** to lead by the nose

narración *f* narration

narra•dor -dora *adj* narrating ‖ *mf* narrator

narrar *tr* to narrate

narrati•vo -va *adj* narrative ‖ *f* (*relato; habilidad en narrar*) narrative

narria *f* sled, sledge, drag

nasal *adj* & *f* nasal

nasalizar §60 *tr* to nasalize

nata *f* cream; whipped cream; élite, choice; skim, scum

natación *f* swimming

natal *adj* natal; native ‖ *m* birth; birthday

natali•cio -cia *adj* birth ‖ *m* birthday

natalidad *f* birth rate

naterón *m* cottage cheese

natillas *fpl* custard

natividad *f* birth; Christmas; (*día; festividad; pintura*) Nativity

nati•vo -va *adj* native; natural; natural-born; innate

na•to -ta *adj* born, e.g., **criminal nato** born criminal ‖ *f* see **nata**

natural *adj* natural; native; (mus) natural ‖ *mf* native ‖ *m* temper, disposition, nature; **al natural** au naturel; rough, unfinished; live; **del natural** from life, from nature

naturaleza *f* nature; disposition, temperament; nationality; **naturaleza muerta** still life

naturalidad *f* naturalness; nationality

naturalismo *m* naturalism

naturalista *mf* naturalist

mu
na

naturalización f naturalization
naturalizar §60 tr to naturalize; acclimatize || ref to become·naturalized; go native
naturalmente adv naturally; easily, readily
naturismo m nudism
naufragar §44 intr to be shipwrecked; fail
naufragio m shipwreck; failure, ruin
náufra·go -ga adj shipwrecked || mf shipwrecked person || m shark
náusea f nausea; **dar náuseas a** to nauseate; sicken, disgust; **tener náuseas** to be nauseated, be sick at one's stomach
nauseabun·do -da adj nauseating, nauseous, loathsome, sickening
nauta m mariner, sailor
náuti·co -ca adj nautical || f sailing, navigation
nava f hollow plain between mountains
navaja f folding knife; razor; penknife; tusk of wild boar; razor clam; evil tongue; **navaja barbera** straight razor
navajada f or **navajazo** m slash, gash
navajero m razor case; razor cloth
naval adj naval; nautical; **naval militar** naval
nava·rro -rra adj & mf Navarrese || **Navarra** f Navarre
navazo m garden in sandy marshland
nave f ship, vessel; (de un taller, fábrica, tienda, iglesia, etc.) aisle; commercial ground floor; hall, shed, bay, building; **nave central** or **principal** (archit) nave; **nave lateral** (archit) aisle
navegable adj navigable
navegación f navigation; sailing; sea voyage; **navegación a vela** sailing
navega·dor -dora or **navegante** adj navigating || mf navigator
navegar §44 tr to sail || intr to navigate, sail; move around; (Mex) to suffer, bear
navel f (pl -vels) navel orange
Navidad f Christmas; Christmas time; ¡**Felices Navidades!** Merry Christmas!; **contar** or **tener muchas Navidades** to be pretty old
navidal m Christmas card
navide·ño -ña adj Christmas
navie·ro -ra adj ship, shipping || m shipowner; outfitter
navío m ship, vessel; **navío de guerra** warship
náyade f naiad
nazare·no -na adj & mf Nazarene || m penitent in Passion Week procession || **nazarenas** fpl (SAm) large gaucho spurs
nazi adj & mf Nazi
N.B. abbr **nota bene** (Lat) note well
nébeda f catnip
neblina f fog, mist
neblino·so -sa adj foggy, misty
nebulo·so -sa adj nebulous, cloudy, misty, hazy, vague; gloomy, sullen || f nebula
necedad f foolishness, stupidity, nonsense
necesa·rio -ria adj necessary || f water closet, privy
neceser m toilet case; sewing kit; **neceser de belleza** vanity case; **neceser de costura** workbasket

necesidad f necessity; need, want; starvation; **de necesidad** from weakness; of necessity; **necesidad mayor** bowel movement; **necesidad menor** urination
necesita·do -da adj necessitous, poor, needy; **estar necesitado de** to be in need of || mf needy person
necesitar tr to necessitate; need; **necesitar + inf** to have to, need to + inf || intr to be in need; **necesitar de** to be in need of, need || ref to be needed, be necessary
ne·cio -cia adj foolish, stupid; imprudent; stubborn; touchy || mf fool
necrología f necrology
necromancia f necromancy
néctar m nectar
neerlan·dés -desa adj Netherlandish, Dutch || mf Netherlander || m Dutchman; (idioma) Netherlandish or Dutch || f Dutchwoman
nefalista mf teetotaler
nefan·do -da adj base, infamous
nefas·to -ta adj ominous, fatal, tragic
negable adj deniable
negación f negation; denial; refusal
nega·do -da adj unfit, incompetent; dull, indifferent
negar §66 tr to deny; refuse; prohibit; disown; conceal || intr to deny || ref to avoid; refuse; deny oneself to callers; **negarse a** to refuse; **negarse a + inf** to refuse to + inf
negati·vo -va adj negative || f negative; denial; refusal
negligencia f negligence
negligente adj negligent
negociable adj negotiable
negociación f negotiation; deal, matter
negociado m department, bureau; affair, business; (SAm) illegal dealing; (Chile) store
negociante m dealer, trader
negociar tr to negotiate || intr to negotiate, deal, trade
negocio m business; affair, deal, transaction; profit; (SAm) store
negocio·so -sa adj businesslike
negrear intr to turn black; look black
negre·ro -ra adj slave-trading; (fig) slave-driving || mf slave trader; (fig)·slave driver
negrilla f (typ) boldface
ne·gro -gra adj black, dark; gloomy; fatal; wicked; (coll) broke || mf black (person); dear, darling || m black; **negro de humo** lampblack
negror m or **negrura** f blackness
negruz·co -ca adj blackish
néme·sis f (pl -sis) (justo castigo; castigador) nemesis || **Némesis** Nemesis
nemoro·so -sa adj (poet) woody, sylvan
ne·ne -na mf baby; dear, darling || m rascal, villain
nenúfar m white water lily
neo m neon
neocelan·dés -desa adj New Zealand || mf New Zealander
neoesco·cés -cesa adj & mf Nova Scotian
neófi·to -ta mf neophyte

neologismo *m* neologism
neomejica•no -na *adj & mf* New Mexican
neomicina *f* neomycin
neón *m* neon
neoyorki•no -na *adj* New York || *mf* New Yorker
Nepal, el Nepal
nepa•lés -lesa *adj & mf* Nepalese
nepente *m* nepenthe
nepóte *m* relative and favorite of the Pope || **Nepote** Nepos
neptunio *m* neptunium
Neptuno *m* Neptune
nereida *f* Nereid
Nerón *m* Nero
nervio *m* nerve; (*del ala del insecto*) rib; strength, vigor
nerviosidad *f* nervousness
nervio•so -sa *adj* nervous; energetic, vigorous, sinewy; (*célula; centro; tónico*) nerve; (*sistema; enfermedad; postración, colapso*) nervous
nervosidad *f* nervosity; ductility, flexibility; (*de un argumento*) force, cogency
nervo•so -sa *adj* var of **nervioso**
nervu•do -da *adj* vigorous, sinewy
nervura *f* backbone (*of book*)
nesga *f* gore
nesgar §44 *tr* to gore
ne•to -ta *adj* net
neumáti•co -ca *adj* pneumatic; air || *m* tire
neumonía *f* pneumonia
neuralgia *f* neuralgia
neurología *f* neurology
neurona *f* neuron
neuro•sis *f* (*pl* **-sis**) neurosis; **neurosis de guerra** shell shock
neuróti•co -ca *adj & mf* neurotic
neutral *adj & mf* neutral
neutralidad *f* neutrality
neutralismo *m* neutralism
neutralista *adj & mf* neutralist
neutralizar §60 *tr* to neutralize
neu•tro -tra *adj* neuter; (*que no es de un color ni de otro*) neutral; (bot, chem, elec, phonet, zool) neutral; (*verbo*) intransitive
neutrón *m* neutron
neva•do -da *adj* snow-covered; snow-white || *f* snowfall
nevar §2 *tr* to make snow-white || *intr* to snow
nevasca *f* snowfall; snowstorm, blizzard
nevazón *f* (SAm) snowfall
nevera *f* icebox, refrigerator; icehouse; (P-R) jail
nevería *f* ice-cream parlor
neve•ro -ra *mf* ice-cream dealer || *m* place of perpetual snow; perpetual snow || *f* see **nevera**
nevisca *f* snow flurry
neviscar §73 *intr* to snow lightly
nevo *m* mole; **nevo materno** birth mark
nevo•so -sa *adj* snowy
ni *conj* neither, nor; **ni . . . ni** neither . . . nor; **ni . . . siquiera** not even
niacina *f* niacin

nicaragüense or **nicaragüe•ño -ña** *adj & mf* Nicaraguan
Nicolás *m* Nicholas
nicotina *f* nicotine
nicho *m* niche
nidada *f* (*huevos en el nido*) nestful of eggs; (*pajarillos en el nido*) nest, brood, hatch
nidal *m* (*donde la gallina pone sus huevos*) nest; nest egg; haunt; source; basis, foundation
nido *m* nest; haunt; home; source; (*de ladrones*) nest, den
niebla *f* fog, mist, haze; mildew; fog, confusion; **hay niebla** it is foggy; **niebla artificial** smoke screen
nie•to -ta *mf* grandchild || *m* grandson; **nietos** grandchildren || *f* granddaughter
nieve *f* snow; water ice
nigromancia *f* necromancy
nihilismo *m* nihilism
nihilista *mf* nihilist
Nilo *m* Nile; **Nilo Azul** Blue Nile
nilón *m* nylon
nimbo *m* nimbus; halo
nimiedad *f* excess; fussiness, fastidiousness; timidity
ni•mio -mia *adj* excessive; fussy, fastidious; tiny
ninfa *f* nymph; **ninfa marina** mermaid
ninfea *f* white water lily
ningún *adj indef* apocopated form of **ninguno,** used only before masculine singular nouns and adjectives
ningu•no -na *adj indef* no, not any || *pron indef* none, not any; neither, neither one; **ninguno de los dos** neither one || **ninguno** *pron indef* nobody, no one
niña *f* child, girl; (*del ojo*) pupil; **niña del ojo** apple of one's eye; **niña exploradora** girl scout
niñada *f* childishness
niñera *f* nursemaid
niñería *f* childishness; trifle
niñero -ra *adj* fond of children || *f* see **niñera**
niñez *f* childhood; childishness; (fig) infancy
ni•ño -ña *adj* childlike, childish; young, inexperienced || *mf* child; (*persona joven e inexperta*) babe; **desde niño** from childhood; **niño expósito** foundling; **niño travieso** imp || *m* child, boy; **niño bonito** playboy; **niño de coro** choirboy; **niño de la bola** child Jesus; lucky fellow; **niño explorador** boy scout; **niño gótico** playboy || *f* see **niña**
niño-probeta *m* test-tube baby
ni•pón -pona *adj & mf* Nipponese
níquel *m* nickel
niquelar *tr* to nickel-plate
nirvana, el nirvana
níspero *m* medlar (*tree and fruit*)
níspola *f* medlar (*fruit*)
nitidez *f* brightness, clearness; sharpness
níti•do -da *adj* bright, clear; sharp
nitrato *m* nitrate
nítri•co -ca *adj* nitric
nitro *m* niter; **nitro de Chile** saltpeter
nitrógeno *m* nitrogen

na
ni

nitroglicerina *f* nitroglycerine
nitro•so -sa *adj* nitrous
nitruro *m* nitride
nivel *m* level; **nivel de burbuja** spirit level; **nivel de vida** standard of living; **nivel sonoro** noise level
nivelar *tr* to level; even, make even, grade; survey
no *adv* not; no; **¿cómo no?** why not?; of course, certainly; **creer que no** to think not, believe not; **¿no?** is it not so?; **no bien** no sooner; **no más que** not more than; only; **no sea que** lest; **no . . . sino** only; **ya no** no longer
nobabia *f* (aer) dope
noble *adj* noble || *m* noble, nobleman
nobleza *f* nobility
noción *f* notion, idea; rudiment
nocividad *f* harmfulness
noci•vo -va *adj* noxious, harmful
noctur•no -na *adj* nocturnal; lonely, sad, melancholy; night, nighttime
noche *f* night, nighttime; darkness; **buenas noches** good evening; good night; **de la noche a la mañana** overnight; unexpectedly, suddenly; **de noche** at night, in the nighttime; **esta noche** tonight; **hacer noche en** to spend the night in; **hacerse de noche** to grow dark; **muy de noche** late at night; **por la noche** at night, in the nighttime; **noche buena** Christmas Eve; **noche de estreno** (theat) first night; **noche de uvas** New Year's Eve; **noche vieja** New Year's Eve; watch night
nochebuena *f* Christmas Eve
nochebueno *f* Christmas cake; Yule log
nochero *m* sleepwalker
nodo *m* (astr, med, phys) node
No-Do *m* (acronym for **Noticiario y Documentales**) newsreel; newsreel theater
nodriza *f* wet nurse; vacuum tank
Noé *m* Noah
nogal *m* walnut; **nogal de la brujería** witch hazel
nómada or **nómade** *adj & mf* nomad
nomádi•co -ca *adj* nomadic
nombradía *f* fame, renown, reputation
nombra•do -da *adj* famous
nombramiento *m* naming; appointment
nombrar *tr* to name; appoint
nombre *m* name; fame, reputation; nickname; watchword; noun; **del mismo nombre** (elec) like; **de nombres contrarios** (elec) unlike; **nombre comercial** firm name; **nombre de lugar** place name; **nombre de pila** first name, Christian name; **nombre de soltera** maiden name; **nombre substantivo** noun; **nombre supuesto** alias
nomeolvi•des *f* (*pl* -des) forget-me-not
nómina *f* list, roll; payroll
nominal *adj* nominal; noun
nominar *tr* to name; appoint
nominati•vo -va *adj & m* nominative
non *adj* odd, uneven || *m* odd number
nonada *f* trifle, nothing

no•no -na *adj & m* ninth
nopal *m* prickly pear
norcorea•no -na *adj & mf* North Korean
nordestada *f* or **nordeste** *m* (*viento*) northeaster (*wind*)
noria *f* chain pump; (*pozo*) draw well; Ferris wheel; treadmill, drudgery
norma *f* norm, standard; rule, method; (carp) square
normal *adj* normal; standard; perpendicular
Normandía *f* Normandy
norman•do -da *adj & mf* Norman || *m* Norseman
norte *m* north; north wind; (*guía*) (fig) polestar, lodestar
Norteamérica *f* North America; America, the United States
norteamerica•no -na *adj & mf* North American; (*estadunidense*) American
norte•ño -ña *adj* northern
norue•go -ga *adj & mf* Norwegian || **Noruega** *f* Norway
nos (used as object of verb) *pron pers* us; to us || *pron reflex* ourselves, to ourselves; each other, to each other
noso•tros -tras *pron pers* we; us; ourselves
nostalgia *f* nostalgia
nota *f* note; (*en la escuela*) mark, grade; (*en el restaurante*) check; (mus) note; **nota de adorno** grace note; **nota tónica** keynote
notables *mpl* notables; prominent persons; (coll) VIPs
notar *tr* to note; dictate; annotate; criticize; discredit
notario *m* notary, notary public
noticia *f* news; notice, information; notion, rudiment; knowledge; **noticias de actualidad** news of the day; **noticias de última hora** late news; **una noticia** a piece of news, a news item
noticiar *tr* to notify; give notice of
noticia•rio -ria *adj* news || *m* up-to-the-minute news; newsreel; newscast; **noticiario gráfico** picture page; **noticiario teatral** theater page
noticie•ro -ra *adj* news || *m* newsman, reporter; late news
noticio•so -sa *adj* informed; learned; well-informed; newsy || *m* news item
notificar §73 *tr* to notify; report on
no•to -ta *adj* known, well-known || *m* south wind || *f* see **nota**
notoriedad *f* general knowledge; fame
noto•rio -ria *adj* manifest, well-known
nov. *abbr* noviembre
novatada *f* hazing; beginner's blunder
nova•to -ta *adj* beginning || *mf* beginner; freshman
novecien•tos -tas *adj & pron* nine hundred || **novecientos** *m* nine hundred
novedad *f* newness, novelty; news; fashion; happening; change; failing health; **sin novedad** as usual; safe; well; without anything happening
novel *adj* new, inexperienced, beginning || *m* beginner

novela f novel; story, lie; **novela caballista** novel of western life; **novela policíaca** or **policial** detective story; **novela por entregas** serial
novele•ro -ra adj fond of novelty; fond of fiction; gossipy; fickle
noveles•co -ca adj novelistic, fictional; romantic, fantastic
novelista mf novelist
novelísti•co -ca adj fictional ‖ f fiction
novelizar §60 tr to fictionalize
nove•no -na adj & m ninth
noventa adj, pron & m ninety
noventa•vo -va adj & m ninetieth
novia f fiancée; bride; **novia de guerra** war bride
noviazgo m engagement, courtship
novi•cio -cia adj & mf novice
noviembre m November
novilunio m new moon
novilla f heifer
novillada f drove of young bulls; (taur) fight with young bulls by aspiring bullfighters
novillero m herdsman of young cattle; (taur) aspiring fighter, untrained fighter; truant
novillo m young bull; (coll) cuckold; (Mex, P-R) fiancé; **hacer novillos** to play truant
novio m suitor; fiancé; bridegroom; **novios** engaged couple; bride and groom, newlyweds
novocaína f novocaine
nro. abbr **nuestro**
N.S. abbr **Nuestro Señor**
ntro. abbr **nuestro**
nubada f local shower; abundance
nubarrón m storm cloud
nube f cloud; **andar** (los precios) **por las nubes** to be sky-high; **bajar de las nubes** to come back to or down to earth; **poner en** or **sobre las nubes** to praise to the skies
nube-hongo f mushroom cloud
nubla•do -da adj cloudy ‖ m storm cloud; impending danger; abundance; **aguantar el nublado** to suffer resignedly
nublar tr to cloud, cloud over ‖ ref to become cloudy
nu•blo -bla adj cloudy ‖ m storm cloud
nublo•so -sa adj cloudy; adverse, unfortunate
nubosidad f clouding, clouds
nubo•so -sa adj cloudy
nuca f nape
nuclear adj nuclear
núcleo m nucleus; core; (de nuez) kernel; (de la fruta) stone; (de un electroimán) core
nudillo m knuckle; stocking stitch; plug (in wall)
nudo m knot; bond, tie, union; crux; tangle; plot; difficulty; (en el drama) crisis; center, juncture; (bot) node; (naut) knot; **cortar el**

nudo gordiano to cut the Gordian knot; **hacérsele a** (uno) **un nudo en la garganta** to get a lump in one's throat
nudo•so -sa adj knotted, knotty
nuera f daughter-in-law
nues•tro -tra adj poss our ‖ pron poss ours
nueva f news; piece of news; **nuevas** fpl news
Nueva York m & f New York; **el Gran Nueva York** Greater New York
Nueva Zelandia New Zealand
nueve adj & pron nine; **las nueve** nine o'clock ‖ m nine; (en las fechas) ninth
nue•vo -va adj new; **de nuevo** again, anew; **nuevo flamante** brand-new; **¿qué hay de nuevo?** what's new? ‖ mf novice; freshman ‖ f see **nueva**
nuevomejica•no -na adj & mf New Mexican
Nuevo Méjico m New Mexico
nuez f (pl **nueces**) nut; walnut; Adam's apple; **nuez dura** (árbol) hickory; hickory nut; **nuez moscada** nutmeg
nulidad f nullity; incapacity; nobody
nu•lo -la adj null, void, worthless
núm. abbr **número**
numen m deity; inspiration
numeral adj numeral
numerar tr to number; count; numerate
numerario m cash, coin, specie
numéri•co -ca adj numerical
número m number; (de un periódico) copy, issue; (de zapatos) size; lottery ticket; **cargar** or **cobrar al número llamado** (telp) to reverse the charges; **de número** (dícese de los individuos de una sociedad) regular; **mirar por el número uno** to look out for number one; **número de serie** series number; **número equivocado** (telp) wrong number
numero•so -sa adj numerous
nunca adv never; **no . . . nunca** not . . . ever, never; **nunca jamás** nevermore
nupcial adj nuptial
nupcialidad f marriage rate
nupcias fpl nuptials, marriage; **casarse en segundas nupcias** to marry the second time
nutria f otter
nutrición f nutrition
nutri•do -da adj great, intense, robust, vigorous, steady; full, abounding, rich, heavy; (carácter, letra) thick; (cañoneo) heavy, sustained
nutrimento m or **nutrimiento** m nourishment, nutriment
nutrir tr to nourish, feed; supply, stock; support, back up; fill to overflowing
nu•triz f (pl **-trices**) wet nurse

ni
nu

Ñ

Ñ, ñ (eñe) *f* seventeenth letter of the Spanish alphabet

ñadi *m* (Chile) broad, shallow swamp

ñajú *m* okra, gumbo

ñámbar *m* Jamaica rosewood

ñame *m* yam; (W-I) blockhead, dunce

ñan•dú *m* (*pl* **-dúes**) nandu, American ostrich

ñaño -ña *adj* close, intimate; spoiled, overindulged ‖ *m* elder brother ‖ *f* elder sister; nursemaid; dear

ñapa *f* something thrown in, lagniappe; **de ñapa** in the bargain

ñaque *m* junk, pile of junk

ña•to -ta *adj* pug-nosed; (Arg) ugly, deformed

ñeque *adj* (Am) strong, vigorous; (*dícese de los ojos*) drooping ‖ *m* slap, blow; pep

ñiqueñaque *m* (coll) trash

ñisca *f* bit, fragment; excrement

ñoclo *m* macaroon

ñolombre *m* old peasant; **¡viene ñolombre!** here comes the bogeyman

ñon•go -ga *adj* slow, lazy; foolish, stupid; tricky; suspicious

ñoñería *f* or **ñoñez** *f* timidity; inanity; dotage

ño•ño -ña *adj* timid; inane; doting

O

O, o (o) eighteenth letter of the Spanish alphabet

o *conj* or; **o . . . o** either . . . or

oa•sis *m* (*pl* **-sis**) oasis

ob. *abbr* **obispo**

obduración *f* obduracy

obedecer §22 *tr* (with personal **a**) to obey ‖ *intr* to obey; **obedecer a** to yield to, be due to, be in keeping with, arise from

obediencia *f* obedience

obediente *adj* obedient

obelisco *m* obelisk; (typ) dagger

obertura *f* (mus) overture

obesidad *f* obesity

obe•so -sa *adj* obese

obispo *m* bishop

óbito *m* decease, demise

obituario *m* obituary

objeción *f* objection

objetable *adj* objectionable (*open to objection*)

objetar *tr* to object; (*dudas*) raise; (*una razón contraria*) set up, offer, present; object to

objeti•vo -va *adj* & *m* objective

objeto *m* object; subject matter; **objetos de cotillión** favors; **objeto volante no identificado** (**ovni**) unidentified flying object (UFO)

oblea *f* wafer; pill, tablet; **hecho una oblea** nothing but skin and bones

obli•cuo -cua *adj* oblique

obligación *f* obligation, duty; bond, debenture; **obligaciones** family responsibilities

obligacionista *mf* bondholder

obliga•do -da *adj* obliged, grateful; submissive; (mus) obbligato ‖ *m* (mus) obbligato

obligar §44 *tr* to obligate; oblige

obliterar *tr* to cancel

oblon•go -ga *adj* oblong

oboe *m* oboe; oboist

oboísta *mf* oboist

óbolo *m* mite

obra *f* work; **obra de** a matter of; **obra de consulta** reference work; **obra maestra** masterpiece; **obra pía** charity; useful effort; **obra prima** shoemaking; **obras** construction, repairs, alterations; **obra segunda** shoe repairing; **poner por obra** to undertake, set to work on

obra•dor -dora *mf* worker ‖ *m* workman; shop, workshop ‖ *f* workingwoman

obraje *m* manufacture; processing

obrajero *m* foreman; (Arg) lumberman; (Bol) artisan

obrar *tr* to build; perform; work ‖ *intr* to work; act, operate, proceed; have a movement of the bowels; **obra en mi poder** I have at hand, I have in my possession

obrera *f* workingwoman

obrerismo *m* labor; labor movement

obre•ro -ra *adj* working; labor ‖ *m* workman; **los obreros** labor ‖ *f* see **obrera**

obrero-patronal *adj* labor management

obscenidad *f* obscenity

obsce•no -na *adj* obscene

obscurecer §22 *tr* to darken; dim; discredit; cloud, confuse ‖ *intr* to grow dark ‖ *ref* to cloud over; become dimmed; fade away

obscuridad *f* obscurity; darkness

obscu•ro -ra *adj* obscure; dark; gloomy; uncertain, dangerous; **a obscuras** in the dark ‖ *m* dark; (paint) shading

obsequia•do -da *mf* recipient; guest of honor

obsequiar *tr* to fawn over, flatter; present, give; court, woo

obsequio *m* flattery; gift; attention, courtesy; **en obsequio de** in honor of

obsequio•so -sa *adj* obsequious; obliging, courteous

observación *f* observation

observa•dor -dora *adj* observant ‖ *mf* observer

observancia *f* observance; deference, respectfulness

observar *tr* to observe

observatorio *m* observatory

obsesión *f* obsession

obsesionar *tr* to obsess

obsole•to -ta *adj* obsolete
obstaculizar §60 *tr* to prevent; obstruct
obstáculo *m* obstacle
obstante *adj* standing in the way; **no obstante** however, nevertheless; in spite of
obstar *intr* to stand in the way; **obstar a** or **para** to hinder, check, oppose
obstetricia *f* obstetrics
obstétri•co -ca *adj* obstetrical ‖ *mf* obstetrician
obstinación *f* obstinacy
obstina•do -da *adj* obstinate
obstinar *ref* to be obstinate
obstrucción *f* obstruction
obstruccionar *tr* to hinder, obstruct
obstruir §20 *tr* to obstruct; block; stop up
obtención *f* obtaining
obtener §71 *tr* to obtain; keep
obtenible *adj* obtainable
obturación *f* plugging up, sealing off
obturador *m* stopper, plug; (aut) choke; (aut) throttle; (phot) shutter; **obturador de guillotina** drop shutter
obtu•so -sa *adj* obtuse
obús *m* howitzer; shell; (*de válvula de neumático*) plunger
obvención *f* extra, bonus, incidental
obvencional *adj* incidental
obviar §77 & regular *tr* to obviate, prevent ‖ *intr* to stand in the way
ob•vio -via *adj* obvious; unnecessary
oca *f* goose
ocasión *f* occasion; opportunity, chance; danger, risk; **aprovechar la ocasión** to improve the occasion; **aprovechar la ocasión de** to avail oneself of the opportunity to; **asir la ocasión por la melena** to take time by the forelock; **de ocasión** secondhand
ocasiona•do -da *adj* dangerous, risky; exposed, subject, liable; annoying
ocasionar *tr* to occasion, cause; stir up; endanger
ocasional *adj* occasional; causal; causing; (*causa*) responsible; accidental
ocaso *m* west; (*de un cuerpo celeste*) setting; sunset; decline; end, death
occidental *adj* western; occidental
occidente *m* occident
oceáni•co -ca *adj* oceanic
océano *m* ocean
ocio *m* idleness, leisure; distraction, pastime; spare time
ocio•so -sa *adj* idle; useless, needless
oclusión *f* occlusion
oclusi•vo -va *adj & f* occlusive
ocote *m* (Mex) torch pine
octava *f* octave
octavilla *f* handbill; eight-syllable verse
octavín *m* piccolo
octa•vo -va *adj* eighth ‖ *mf* octoroon ‖ *m* eighth ‖ *f* see **octava**
oct.ᵉ *abbr* **octubre**
octogési•mo -ma *adj & m* eightieth
octubre *m* October
ocular *adj* ocular, eye ‖ *m* eyepiece, eyeglass, ocular
oculista *mf* oculist; fawner, flatterer

ocultar *tr & ref* to hide
ocul•to -ta *adj* hidden, concealed; (*misterioso, sobrenatural*) occult
ocupación *f* occupation; occupancy; employment
ocupa•do -da *adj* busy; occupied; **ocupada** pregnant
ocupante *adj* occupying ‖ *mf* occupant ‖ **ocupantes** *mpl* occupying forces
ocupar *tr* to occupy; busy, keep busy; employ; bother, annoy; attract the attention of ‖ *ref* to be occupied; be busy; be preoccupied; bother
ocurrencia *f* occurrence; witticism; bright idea
ocurrente *adj* witty
ocurrir *intr* to occur, happen; come; (*venir a la mente*) occur
ocha•vo -va *adj* eighth; octagonal ‖ *m* eighth; octagon
ochenta *adj, pron & m* eighty
ochenta•vo -va *adj & m* eightieth
ocho *adj & pron* eight; **las ocho** eight o'clock ‖ *m* eight; (*en las fechas*) eighth
ochocien•tos -tas *adj & pron* eight hundred ‖ **ochocientos** *m* eight hundred
oda *f* ode
odiar *tr* to hate
odio *m* hate, hatred
odio-amor *m* love-hate
odio•so -sa *adj* odious, hateful
Odisea *f* Odyssey
Odiseo *m* Odysseus
odontología *f* odontology, dentistry
odontólo•go -ga *mf* odontologist, dentist
odre *m* goatskin wine bag; (coll) toper
OEA *f* OAS
oeste *m* west; west wind
ofender *tr & intr* to offend ‖ *ref* to take offense
ofensa *f* offense
ofensi•vo -va *adj & f* offensive
ofen•sor -sora *adj* offending ‖ *mf* offender
oferta *f* offer; gift, present; **oferta y demanda** supply and demand
oficial *adj* official ‖ *m* official, officer; skilled workman; clerk, office worker; journeyman; commissioned officer; **oficial de derrota** navigator
oficiar *tr* to announce officially in writing; (*la misa*) celebrate; officiate at ‖ *intr* to officiate; **oficiar de** to act as
oficina *f* office; shop; pharmacist's laboratory; **oficina de objetos perdidos** lost-and-found department
oficines•co -ca *adj* office, clerical; bureaucratic
oficinista *mf* clerk, office worker
oficio *m* office, occupation; function, rôle; craft, trade; memo, official note; (eccl) office, service; **de oficio** officially; professionally; **hacer oficios de** to function as; **tomar por oficio** to take to, keep at
oficio•so -sa *adj* diligent; obliging; officious, meddlesome; profitable; unofficial
ofrecer *tr & intr* to offer; (*una recepción*) give ‖ *ref* to offer; offer oneself; happen

ñ
of

ofrecimiento *m* offer, offering; **ofrecimiento de presentación** introductory offer
ofrenda *f* offering; gift
ofrendar *tr* to make offerings of; contribute
oftalmología *f* ophthalmology
oftalmólo·go -ga *mf* ophthalmologist
ofuscación *f* obfuscation; (mental) derangement
ofuscar §73 *tr* to obfuscate; dazzle
ogro *m* ogre
Oh *interj* O!, Oh!
ohmio *m* ohm
oíble *adj* audible
oída *f* hearing; **de** or **por oídas** by hearsay
oído *m* hearing; ear; **abrir tanto oído** to be all ears; **al oído** by listening; confidentially; **decir al oído** to whisper; **hacer** or **tener oídos de mercader** to turn a deaf ear
oír §48 *tr* to hear; listen to; (*una conferencia*) attend; **oír + inf** to hear + *inf*, e.g., **oí entrar a mi hermano** I heard my brother come in; hear + *ger*, e.g., **oí cantar a la muchacha** I heard the girl singing; hear + *pp*, e.g., **oí tocar la campana** I heard the bell rung; **oír decir que** to hear that; **oír hablar de** to hear about ‖ *intr* to hear; listen; **¡oíga!** say!, listen!; the idea!, the very idea!
ojada *f* (Col) skylight
ojal *m* buttonhole; eyelet; grommet
ojalá *interj* God grant . . . !, would to God . . . !; **¡ojalá que** would that . . . !, I hope that . . . !
ojeada *f* glimpse, glance; **buena ojeada** eyeful
ojear *tr* to eye, stare at; cast the evil eye on; (*la caza*) start, rouse; frighten, startle
ojera *f* eyecup, eyeglass; **ojeras** (*bajo los párpados inferiores*) rings, circles
ojeriza *f* grudge, ill will
ojero·so -sa *adj* with rings or circles under the eyes
ojete *m* eyelet, eyehole
ojienju·to -ta *adj* dry-eyed, tearless
ojituer·to -ta *adj* cross-eyed
ojiva *f* ogive, pointed arch
ojo *m* eye; (*de la escalera*) opening, well; (*del puente*) bay, span; (*de agua*) spring; **a ojos vistas** visibly, openly; **costar un ojo de la cara** to cost a mint, cost a fortune; **dar los ojos de la cara por** to give one's eyeteeth for; **hasta los ojos** up to one's ears; **mirar con ojos de carnero degollado** to make sheep's eyes at; **no pegar el ojo** to not sleep a wink; **ojo de buey** (archit, meteor, naut) bull's-eye; (bot) oxeye; **ojo de la cerradura** keyhole; **poner los ojos en blanco** to roll one's eyes; **saltar a los ojos** to be self-evident; **valer un ojo de la cara** to be worth a mint ‖ *interj* beware!; look out!; attention!; **¡mucho ojo!** be careful!, watch out!; **¡ojo con . . . !** look out for . . . !; **¡ojo, mancha!** fresh paint!
ojota *f* (SAm) sandal; (SAm) tanned llama hide
ola *f* wave; (*de gente apiñada*) surge

ole *m* or **olé** *m* bravo ‖ *interj* bravo!
oleada *f* big wave; (*de gente apiñada*) surge, swell
oleaje *m* surge, rush of waves
óleo *m* oil; holy oil; oil painting; **los santos óleos** extreme unction
oleoducto *m* pipe line
oler §49 *tr* to smell; pry into; sniff out ‖ *intr* to smell, smell fragrant, smell bad; **no oler bien** to look suspicious; **oler a** to smell of, smell like; smack of
olfatear *tr* to smell, scent, sniff; (*p.ej., un buen negocio*) scent, sniff out
olfato *m* smell, sense of smell; scent; keen insight
olíbano *m* frankincense
oliente *adj* smelling, odorous
oligarquía *f* oligarchy
Olimpíada *f* Olympiad
olímpi·co -ca *adj* Olympian; Olympic; haughty
oliscar §73 *tr* to smell, scent, sniff; investigate ‖ *intr* to smell bad
oliva *f* olive; olive tree; barn owl; olive branch, peace
olivar *m* olive grove
olivillo *m* mock privet
olivo *m* olive tree; **tomar el olivo** (taur) to duck behind the barrier; beat it
olmeda *f* or **olmedo** *m* elm grove
olmo *m* elm tree
olor *m* odor; promise, hope; trace, suspicion; **olores** (Chile, Mex) spice, condiment
oloro·so -sa *adj* odorous, fragrant
olote *m* (CAm & Mex) cob, corncob
olvidadi·zo -za *adj* forgetful; ungrateful
olvida·do -da *adj* forgetful; ungrateful
olvidar *tr & intr* to forget; **olvidar + inf** to forget to + *inf* ‖ *ref* to forget oneself; **olvidarse de** to forget; **olvidarse de + inf** to forget to + *inf*; **olvidársele a uno** to forget, e.g., **se me olvidó mi pasaporte** I forgot my passport; **olvidársele a uno + inf** to forget to + *inf*, e.g., **se me olvidó cerrar la ventana** I forgot to close the window
olvido *m* forgetfulness; oblivion
olla *f* pot, kettle; stew; eddy, whirlpool; **olla a** or **de presión** pressure cooker
ollería *f* potter's shop
ollero *m* potter
ombligo *m* navel; (*centro, punto medio*) (fig) navel
omino·so -sa *adj* ominous
omisión *f* omission; oversight, neglect
omi·so -sa *adj* neglectful, remiss
omitir *tr* to omit; overlook, neglect
ómni·bus *adj* (*tren*) accommodation ‖ *m* (*pl* -bus) bus, omnibus; **ómnibus de dos pisos** double-decker
omnímo·do -da *adj* all-inclusive
omnipotente *adj* omnipotent
omnisciente or **omnis·cio -cia** *adj* omniscient
omnívo·ro -ra *adj* omnivorous
omóplato *m* shoulder blade

once *adj* & *pron* eleven; **las once** eleven o'clock ‖ *m* eleven; (*en las fechas*) eleventh

oncea•vo -va *adj* & *m* eleventh

once•no -na *adj* & *mf* eleventh

oncología *f* oncology

onda *f* wave; flicker; (*en el pelo*) wave; **onda portadora** (rad) carrier wave; **ondas entretenidas** (rad) continuous waves

ondear *tr* (*en el pelo*) to wave ‖ *intr* to wave; ripple; flow; flicker; be wavy ‖ *ref* to wave, sway, swing

ondo•so -sa *adj* wavy

ondulación *f* undulation; wave; wave motion

ondula•do -da *adj* wavy, ripply; rolling; corrugated ‖ *m* (*en el pelo*) wave

ondular *tr* (*el pelo*) to wave ‖ *intr* to undulate; (*una bandera*) wave, flutter; (*las ondas del mar*) billow; (*una culebra*) wriggle

onero•so -sa *adj* onerous, burdensome

ónice *m* or **ónique** *m* or **ónix** *m* onyx

onomásti•co -ca *adj* of proper names ‖ *m* name day ‖ *f* study of proper names

onomatopéyi•co -ca *adj* onomatopoeic

ONU *f* UN

onza *f* ounce; (zool) snow leopard

onza•vo -va *adj* & *m* eleventh

opa•co -ca *adj* opaque; sad, gloomy

ópalo *m* opal

opción *f* option, choice; **opción nula** or **opción cero** zero option

ópera *f* opera; **ópera semiseria** light opera; **ópera seria** grand opera

operación *f* operation; transaction; **operaciones** (*ordenador*) software

operar *tr* to operate on ‖ *intr* to operate; work ‖ *ref* to occur, come about; be operated on

opera•rio -ria *mf* worker ‖ *m* workman ‖ *f* working woman

opereta *f* operetta

operista *mf* opera singer

operísti•co -ca *adj* operatic

opia•to -ta *adj m* & *f* opiate

opinable *adj* moot

opinar *intr* to opine; think; pass judgment

opinión *f* opinion, view; reputation, public image

opio *m* opium

opípa•ro -ra *adj* sumptuous, lavish

oponer §54 *tr* to oppose; (*resistencia*) to offer, put up ‖ *ref* to oppose each other; face each other; **oponerse a** to oppose, be opposed to; be against, resist; compete for

oporto *m* port, port wine

oportunidad *f* opportunity; opportuneness; **oportunidades** *fpl* witticisms

oportunista *adj* opportunistic ‖ *mf* opportunist

oportu•no -na *adj* opportune, timely; proper; witty

oposición *f* opposition; competitive examination

oposi•tor -tora *adj* rivaling, competing ‖ *mf* opponent; competitor

opresión *f* oppression

opresi•vo -va *adj* oppressive

opre•sor -sora *adj* oppressive ‖ *mf* oppressor

oprimir *tr* to oppress; squeeze, press

oprobiar *tr* to defame, revile

oprobio *m* opprobrium

oprobio•so -sa *adj* opprobrious

optar *tr* to enter; assume ‖ *intr* — **optar entre** to choose between; **optar por** to choose to

ópti•co -ca *adj* optical ‖ *mf* optician ‖ *f* optics

óptimamente *adv* to perfection

óptimismo *m* optimism

optimista *adj* optimistic ‖ *mf* optimist

ópti•mo -ma *adj* fine, excellent

optometrista *mf* optometrist

opues•to -ta *adj* opposite, contrary

opugnar *tr* to attack; lay siege to; contradict

opulen•to -ta *adj* opulent

opúsculo *m* short work, opuscule

oquedad *f* hollow; hollowness

ora *conj* — **ora . . . ora** now . . . now, now . . . then

oración *f* oration, speech; prayer; sentence; **oración dominical** Lord's prayer; **ponerse en oración** to get down on one's knees

oráculo *m* oracle

ora•dor -dora *mf* orator, speaker; **orador de plazuela** soapbox orator; **orador de sobremesa** after-dinner speaker

oraje *m* rough weather, storm

oral *adj* oral

orangután *m* orang-outang

orar *intr* to pray; make a speech

orato•rio -ria *adj* oratorical ‖ *m* oratorio; (*capilla privada*) oratory ‖ *f* (*arte de la elocuencia*) oratory

orbe *m* orb; world

órbita *f* orbit

orca *f* killer whale

Órcadas *fpl* Orkney Islands

órdago — **de órdago** (coll) swell, real

orden *m* & *f* order; **hasta nueva orden** until further notice; **orden** *f* **de allanamiento** search warrant; **orden** *m* **de colocación** word order; **orden de pago** money order

ordenador *m* computer; **ordenador de viaje** on-board computer

ordenancista *adj* strict, severe ‖ *mf* taskmaster, disciplinarian, martinet

ordenanza *m* errand boy; (mil) orderly ‖ *f* ordinance; order, system; command; **ser de ordenanza** to be the rule

ordenar *tr* to order; put in order; ordain ‖ *ref* to be ordained, take orders

ordeñadero *m* milk pail

ordeñar *tr* to milk

ordeño *m* milking

ordinal *adj* orderly; ordinal ‖ *m* ordinal

ordinariez *f* coarseness, crudeness

ordina•rio -ria *adj* ordinary ‖ *m* daily household expenses; delivery man

orear *tr* to air ‖ *ref* to be aired; dry in the air; take an airing

orégano *m* pot or wild marjoram, winter sweet

of
or

oreja _f_ ear; (_de zapato_) flap; (_de martillo_) claw; lug, flange, **aguzar las orejas** to prick up one's ears; **con las orejas caídas** crestfallen; **con las orejas tan largas** all ears; **descubrir** or **enseñar las orejas** to give oneself away

oreja•no -na _adj_ (_res_) unbranded; (_animal_) skittish; shy; cautious

orejera _f_ earflap, earmuff

orejeta _f_ lug

ore•jón -jona _adj_ coarse, uncouth; (Mex) skinny ‖ _m_ strip of dried peach; pull on the ear; (_de la hoja de un libro_) dog's-ear

oreju•do -da _adj_ big-eared

oreo _m_ breeze

orfanato _m_ orphanage

orfandad _f_ orphanage, orphanhood

orfebre _m_ goldsmith; silversmith

orfelinato _m_ (SAm) orphanage

Orfeo _m_ Orpheus

orfeón _m_ glee club, choral society

organ•dí _m_ (_pl_ **-díes**) organdy

orgáni•co -ca _adj_ organic

organillero -ra _mf_ organ-grinder

organillo _m_ barrel organ, hand organ, hurdy-gurdy

organismo _m_ organism; organization

organista _mf_ organist

organización _f_ organization; **Organización de las Naciones Unidas** (**ONU**) United Nations (UN); **Organización de los Estados Americanos** (**OEA**) Organization of American States (OAS); **Organización del Tratado del Sudeste Asiático** (**O.T.A.S.E.**) Southwest Asia Treaty Organization (SEATO); **Organización para el Tratado del Atlántico Norte** (**O.T.A.N.**) North Atlantic Treaty Organization (NATO)

organizar §60 _tr_ to organize

órgano _m_ organ; (_de una máquina_) part; (_medio, conducto_) organ; (mus) organ

orgasmo _m_ orgasm

orgía _f_ orgy

orgiásti•co -ca _adj_ orgiastic

orgullo _m_ haughtiness; pride

orgullo•so -sa _adj_ haughty; proud

oriental _adj_ eastern; oriental

orientar _tr_ to orient; guide, direct; (_una vela_) trim ‖ _ref_ to orient oneself; find one's bearings

oriente _m_ east; source, origin; east wind; youth ‖ **Oriente** _m_ Orient; **el Cercano Oriente** the Near East; **el Extremo Oriente** the Far East; **el Lejano Oriente** the Far East; **el Oriente Medio** the Middle East; **el Próximo Oriente** the Near East; **gran oriente** (_logia masónica central_) grand lodge

orificar §73 _tr_ to fill with gold

orífice _m_ goldsmith

orificio _m_ orifice, aperture, hole

origen _m_ origin; source

original _adj_ original; strange, odd, quaint ‖ _m_ original; character; **de buen original** on good authority; **original de imprenta** copy

originar _tr_ & _ref_ to originate, start

orilla _f_ border, edge; margin; bank, shore; sidewalk; breeze; **orillas** (Arg, Mex) outskirts; **salir a la orilla** to manage to get through

orillar _tr_ to put a border or edge on; trim ‖ _intr_ to come up to the shore

orillo _m_ selvage, list

orín _m_ rust; **orines** urine; **tomarse de orines** to get rusty

orina _f_ urine

orinal _m_ chamber pot

orinar _tr_ to pass, urinate ‖ _intr_ & _ref_ to urinate

oriun•do -da _adj_ & _mf_ native; **ser oriundo de** to come from, hail from

orla _f_ border, edge; trimming, fringe

orlar _tr_ to border, put an edge on; trim, trim with a fringe

orn. _abbr_ **orden**

ornamentar _tr_ to ornament, adorn

ornamento _m_ ornament, adornment

ornar _tr_ to adorn

ornato _m_ adornment, show

oro _m_ gold; playing card (_representing a gold coin_) equivalent to diamond; **de oro y azul** all dressed up; **oro batido** gold leaf; **oro de ley** standard gold; **poner de oro y azul** to rake over the coals; **ponerle colores al oro** to gild the lily

oron•do -da _adj_ big-bellied; hollow, spongy, puffed up; pompous, self-satisfied

oropel _m_ tinsel; **gastar mucho oropel** to put up a big front

oropéndola _f_ golden oriole

orozuz _m_ licorice

orquesta _f_ orchestra; **orquesta típica** regional orchestra

orquestar _tr_ to orchestrate

órquide _f_ or **orquídea** _f_ orchid

ortiga _f_ nettle; **ser como unas ortigas** to be a grouch

orto _m_ rise (_of sun or star_)

ortodoncia _f_ orthodontics; **aparato de ortodoncia** orthodontic appliance, braces

ortodo•xo -xa _adj_ orthodox

ortografía _f_ orthography; spelling

ortografiar §77 _tr_ & _intr_ to spell

oruga _f_ caterpillar

orujo _m_ bagasse of grapes or olives

orzuelo _m_ sty

os _pron pers_ & _reflex_ (used as object of verb and corresponding to **vos** and **vosotros**) you, to you; yourself, to yourself; yourselves, to yourselves; each other, to each other

osa _f_ she-bear; **Osa mayor** Great Bear; **Osa menor** Little Bear

osadía _f_ boldness, daring

osa•do -da _adj_ bold, daring

osamenta _f_ skeleton; bones

osar _intr_ to dare

osario _m_ ossuary, charnel house

oscilar _intr_ to oscillate; fluctuate; waver, hesitate

ósculo _m_ kiss

oscurecer §22 _tr_, _intr_ & _ref_ var of **obscurecer**

oscuridad *f* var of **obscuridad**
oscu•ro -ra *adj* & *m* var of **obscuro**
osera *f* bear's den
osificar §73 *tr* & *ref* to ossify
oso *m* bear; **hacer el oso** to make a fool of oneself; to make love in the open; **oso blanco** polar bear; **oso hormiguero** ant bear; anteater; **oso lavador** raccoon
ostensorio *m* (eccl) monstrance
ostentar *tr* to show; make a show of ‖ *ref* to show off; boast
ostentati•vo -va *adj* ostentatious
ostento *m* portent, prodigy
ostento•so -sa *adj* magnificent, showy
osteópata *mf* osteopath
osteopatía *f* osteopathy
ostión *m* large oyster
ostra *f* oyster; **ostras en su concha** oyster cocktail, oysters on the half shell
ostracismo *m* ostracism
ostral *m* oyster bed, oyster farm
ostrería *f* oysterhouse
ostre•ro -ra *adj* oyster ‖ *m* oysterman; oyster bed, oyster farm
osu•do -da *adj* bony
osu•no -na *adj* bearish, bearlike
O.T.A.N., la NATO
O.T.A.S.E., la SEATO
otate *m* Mexican giant grass (*Guadua amplexifolia*); otate stick
otero *m* hillock, knoll
otomán *m* ottoman
otoma•no -na *adj* & *mf* Ottoman ‖ *f* ottoman
otoñal *adj* autumnal
otoño *m* autumn, fall
otorgar §44 *tr* to agree to; grant, confer; (law) to execute

o•tro -tra *adj indef* other, another ‖ *pron indef* other one, another one; **como dijo el otro** as someone said
ovación *f* ovation
ovacionar *tr* to give an ovation to
oval *adj* oval
óvalo *m* oval
ovante *adj* victorious, triumphant
ovario *m* ovary
oveja *f* ewe, female sheep; **oveja negra** (fig) black sheep; **oveja perdida** (fig) lost sheep
oveje•ro -ra *adj* sheep ‖ *mf* sheep raiser
oveju•no -na *adj* sheep, of sheep
ove•ro -ra *adj* blossom-colored; egg-colored
overol *m* overall
Ovidio *m* Ovid
ovillar *tr* to wind up; sum up ‖ *intr* to form into a ball ‖ *ref* to curl up into a ball
ovillo *m* ball of yarn; ball, heap; tangled ball; **hacerse un ovillo** to cower, recoil; (*hablando*) get all tangled up
ovni *m* UFO
óvulo *m* ovule; ovum
oxear *tr* & *intr* to shoo
oxiacanta *f* hawthorn
oxidación *f* oxidation
oxidar *tr* to oxidize ‖ *ref* to oxidize; get rusty
óxido *m* oxide; **óxido de carbono** carbon monoxide; **óxido de mercurio** mercuric oxide
oxígeno *m* oxygen
oxíto•no -na *adj* oxytone
oxte *interj* get out!, beat it!, **sin decir oxte ni moxte** without opening one's mouth
oyente *mf* hearer; (*a la radio*) listener; (*en la escuela*) auditor
ozono *m* ozone

P

P, p (pe) *f* nineteenth letter of the Spanish alphabet
P. *abbr* **Padre, Papa, Pregunta**
pabellón *m* pavilion; bell tent; flag, banner; (*de fusiles*) stack; canopy; summerhouse; (*de instrumento de viento*) bell
pabilo or **pábilo** *m* wick
Pablo *m* Paul
pábulo *m* food; support, encouragement, fuel
pacana *f* pecan
paca•to -ta *adj* mild, gentle
pacer §22 *tr* to pasture, graze; gnaw, eat away ‖ *intr* to pasture, graze
paciencia *f* patience
paciente *adj* & *mf* patient
pacienzu•do -da *adj* long-suffering
pacificar §73 *tr* to pacify ‖ *intr* to sue for peace ‖ *ref* to calm down
pacífi•co -ca *adj* pacific
pacifismo *m* pacifism
pacifista *adj* & *mf* pacifist

pa•co -ca *adj* (Chile) bay, reddish ‖ *m* paco, alpaca; Moorish sniper; sniper ‖ **Paco** *m* Frank
pacotilla *f* trash, junk; (Chile) rabble, mob; **hacer su pacotilla** to make a cleanup; **ser de pacotilla** to be shoddy, be poorly made
pacotille•ro -ra *mf* (Chile, Ven) peddler
pactar *tr* to agree upon ‖ *intr* to come to an agreement
pacto *m* pact, covenant
pacha•cho -cha *adj* (Chile) short-legged; (Chile) lax, lazy; (Chile) chubby
pa•chón -chona *adj* (CAm) shaggy, hairy, wooly ‖ *m* (*perro*) pointer; (*hombre flemático*) sluggard
pachorra *f* sluggishness, indolence
pachotada *f* silliness
padecer §22 *tr* to suffer; be victim of ‖ *intr* to suffer
padrastro *m* stepfather; hangnail

or
pa

padre *adj* huge; (Peru) terrific ‖ *m* father; stallion, sire; **padres** parents; ancestors; **tener el padre alcalde** to have pull, have a friend at court

padrina *f* godmother

padrinazgo *m* godfathership; sponsorship, patronage

padrino *m* godfather; sponsor; (*en un desafío*) second; **padrino de boda** best man; **padrinos** godparents

padrón *m* poll, census; pattern, model; memorial column; indulgent father; stallion; (Col) stock bull

padrote *m* stock animal; (Mex) pimp, procurer

paella *f* saffron-flavored stew of chicken, seafood, and rice with vegetables

paf *interj* bang!

pág. *abbr* **página**

paga *f* pay, payment; wages; fine; **como paga y señal** on account; as down payment

paga-alquiler *f* rent, rent money

pagadero -ra *adj* payable

paga·do -da *adj* pleased, cheerful; **estamos pagados** we are quits; **pagado de sí mismo** self-satisfied, conceited

paga·dor -dora *adj* paying ‖ *mf* payer ‖ *m* paymaster

paganismo *m* paganism

paga·no -na *adj & mf* pagan ‖ *m* easy mark

pagar §44 *tr* to pay; pay for; (*una bondad, una visita*) return ‖ *intr* to pay ‖ *ref* to become fond; be flattered; boast; be satisfied

pagaré *m* promissory note, I.O.U.

página *f* page

paginar *tr* to page

pago *m* payment; (*de viñas u olivares*) district, region

pagote *m* easy mark

paila *f* large pan

pairar *intr* (naut) to lie to

país *m* country, land; landscape; **el país de Gales** Wales; **los Países Bajos** (*Bélgica, Holanda y Luxemburgo*) the Low Countries; (*Holanda*) The Netherlands; **países no alineados** nonaligned nations; Third World countries

paisaje *m* landscape

paisajista *mf* landscape painter

paisa·no -na *adj* of the same country ‖ *mf* peasant; civilian; (Mex) Spaniard ‖ *m* fellow countryman; **de paisano** in civies

paja *f* straw; chaff; trash, rubbish; **no dormirse en las pajas** to not let the grass grow under one's feet; **no levantar paja del suelo** to not lift a hand, not do a stroke of work

pájara *f* paper kite; paper rooster; bird; crafty female

pajarera *f* aviary; large bird cage

pajarería *f* flock of birds; bird store; pet shop

pajare·ro -ra *adj* bright, cheerful; bright-colored; gaudy ‖ *m* bird dealer; bird fancier ‖ *f* see **pajarera**

pajarita *f* paper kite; bow tie; wing collar; piccadilly

pájaro *m* bird; crafty fellow; expert; **pájaro bobo** penguin; motmot; **pájaro carpintero** woodpecker; **pájaro de cuenta** big shot; **pájaro mosca** hummingbird

pajarota *f* or **pajarotada** *f* hoax, canard

paje *m* page; valet; dressing table; (naut) cabin boy

pajilla *f* cornhusk cigarette; **pajilla de madera** excelsior

paji·zo -za *adj* straw; straw-colored; straw-thatched

pajuela *f* short straw; sulfur match or fuse; toothpick; (Bol) match

Pakistán, el var of **Paquistán**

pakista·ní (*pl* **-níes**) *adj & mf* var of **paquistaní**

pala *f* shovel; (*de remo, de la azada, etc.*) blade; (*del panadero*) peel; scoop; racket; (*del calzado*) upper; (*de excavadora*) bucket; shoulder strap; (coll) cunning, craftiness

palabra *f* word; speech; (*de una canción*) words; (*derecho para hablar en asambleas*) floor; **palabras mayores** words, angry words; **remojar la palabra** to wet one's whistle; **usar de la palabra** to speak, make a speech

palabre·ro -ra *adj* wordy, windy ‖ *mf* windbag

palabrota *f* vulgarity, obscenity

palabru·do -da *adj* talkative; chattering

palacie·go -ga *adj* palace, court ‖ *m* courtier

palacio *m* palace; mansion; **palacio municipal** city hall

palada *f* shovelful; (*de remo*) stroke

paladar *m* palate; taste; gourmet

paladear *tr* to taste, relish

paladín *m* champion, hero

palafrén *m* palfrey

palanca *f* lever; pole; crowbar; **palanca de mando** (aer) control stick; **palanca de mayúsculas** shift key

palancada *f* leverage

palangana *f* washbowl, basin

palanganear *intr* to brag, give oneself airs

palanganero *m* washstand

palangre *m* trawl, trawl line

palanqueta *f* jimmy; **palanquetas** (Arg) dumbbell

palatal *adj & f* palatal

palco *m* (theat) box

palear *tr* to beat, pound; shovel

palenque *m* paling, palisade; (SAm) hitching post; (C-R) Indian ranch; (Chile) pandemonium

paleta *f* palette; small shovel; trowel; (*de una rueda*) paddle; blade, bucket, vane; shoulder blade; (*dulce con un palito que sirve de mango*) lollipop

paletilla *f* shoulder blade

paleto *m* fallow deer; rustic, yokel

palia *f* altar cloth; (eccl) pall

paliacate *m* (Mex) bandanna

paliar §77 & regular *tr* to palliate

palidecer §22 *intr* to pale, to turn pale

palidez *f* paleness, pallor

páli·do -da *adj* pale, pallid

palillo *m* toothpick; drumstick; bobbin; **palillos** chopsticks; castanets; rudiments; trifles

palinodia *f* backdown; **cantar la palinodia** to eat crow, eat humble pie

palique *m* chit-chat, small talk

paliquear *intr* to chat, to gossip

paliza *f* beating, thrashing

palizada *f* fenced-in enclosure; stockade; embankment

palma *f* (*de la mano*) palm; (*árbol y hoja*) palm; **batir palmas** to clap, to applaud; **llevarse la palma** to carry off the palm

palmada *f* slap; hand, applause, clapping; **dar palmadas** to clap hands

palma•rio -ria *adj* clear, evident

palmatoria *f* candlestick

palmera *f* date palm

palmito *m* palmetto; woman's face; slender figure

palmo *m* span, palm; **dejar con un palmo de narices** to disappoint

palmotear *tr* to pat; clap, applaud ‖ *intr* to clap, applaud

palo *m* stick; pole; staff; handle; tree; (*golpe*) whack; (*madera*) wood; (*grupo de naipes de la baraja*) suit; (*naut*) mast; **dar palos de ciego** to lay about, swing wildly; **de tal palo tal astilla** like father like son; **palo de escoba** broomstick; **palo en alto** (fig) big stick; **palo mayor** (naut) mainmast; **servir del palo** to follow suit

paloma *f* pigeon, dove; prostitute; (fig) dove, meek person; **paloma mensajera** carrier pigeon; **palomas** whitecaps

palomar *m* pigeon house, dovecot

palomilla *f* doveling; small butterfly; white horse; (*del caballo*) back; pillow block, journal bearing; (CAm, Mex) rabble, scum; **palomillas** whitecaps

palomita *f* doveling; (baseball) fly; **palomitas** popcorn

palpable *adj* palpable

palpar *tr* to touch, feel; grope through ‖ *intr* to grope

palpitante *adj* throbbing; thrilling; (*cuestión*) burning

palpitar *intr* to palpitate, throb; (*un afecto*) flash, break forth

pálpito *m* (SAm) hunch

palta *f* (SAm) alligator pear, avocado (*fruit*)

palto *m* (SAm) alligator pear, avocado (*tree*)

palúdi•co -ca *adj* marshy; malarial

paludismo *m* malaria

palur•do -da *adj* rustic, boorish ‖ *mf* rustic, boor

pallador *m* (SAm) Gaucho minstrel

pampa *f* pampa; **La Pampa** the Pampas

pámpana *f* vine leaf

pámpano *m* tendril; vine leaf

pan *m* bread; loaf; loaf of bread; wheat; food; livelihood; pie dough; (*de jabón, cera, etc.*) cake; gold foil or leaf; silver foil or leaf; **como el pan bendito** as easy as pie; **de pan llevar** arable, tillable; **llamar al pan pan y al vino vino** to call a spade a spade; **panes** grain, breadstuff; **venderse**

como pan bendito to sell like hot cakes ‖ **Pan** *m* Pan

pana *f* corduroy; (aut) breakdown

panacea *f* panacea

panadería *f* bakery; baking business

panade•ro -ra *mf* baker; (Chile) flatterer

panadizo *m* felon; sickly person

panal *m* honeycomb

pana•má *m* (*pl* **-maes**) Panama hat

paname•ño -ña *adj & mf* Panamanian

panamerica•no -na *adj* Pan-American

pancarta *f* placard, poster

pancista *adj* weaseling ‖ *mf* weaseler

páncre•as *m* (*pl* **-as**) pancreas

pancho *m* paunch, belly

pandear *intr & ref* to warp, bulge, buckle, sag, bend

pandereta *f* tambourine

pandilla *f* party, faction; gang, band; picnic, excursion

pan•do -da *adj* bulging; slow-moving; slow, deliberate

pandorga *f* kite; fat, lazy woman

panecillo *m* roll, crescent

panfleto *m* pamphlet

paniaguado *m* servant, minion; protégé, favorite

páni•co -ca *adj* panic, panicky ‖ *m* panic

panizo *m* Italian millet; (Chile) gangue; (Chile) abundance

panocha *f* ear of grain; ear of corn; pancake made of corn and cheese; (Mex) panocha (*brown sugar*)

panoja *f* ear of grain; ear of corn

panorama *m* panorama

pano•so -sa *adj* mealy

panqué *m* or **panqueque** *m* pancake

pantalán *m* pier, wooden pier

pantalón *m* trousers; **calzarse los pantalones** to wear the pants; **pantalones** trousers, pants; **pantalones azules** (CAm) blue jeans; **pantalones de mezclilla** (C-R, Mex) blue jeans

pantalla *f* lamp shade; fire screen; motion-picture screen; television screen; (*persona que encubre a otra*) blind; (*cine, arte del cine*) screen; fan; **llevar a la pantalla** to put on the screen; **pantalla acústica** loudspeaker; **pantalla de plata** silver screen; **pequeña pantalla** television screen; **servir de pantalla a** to be a blind for

pantano *m* bog, marsh, swamp; dam, reservoir; trouble, obstacle

pantano•so -sa *adj* marshy, swampy; muddy; knotty, difficult

panteísmo *m* pantheism

panteón *m* pantheon; cemetery

pantera *f* panther

pantomima *f* pantomime

pantoque *m* (naut) bilge

pantorrilla *f* calf (*of leg*)

pantufla *f* or **pantuflo** *m* house slipper

panty *m* panty hose

panza *f* paunch, belly

panzu•do -da *adj* paunchy, big-bellied

pañal *m* diaper; shirttail; **pañales** swaddling clothes; infancy; early stages

pañe•ro -ra *adj* dry-goods, cloth ‖ *mf* dry-goods dealer, clothier

paño *m* cloth; rag; (*de agujas*) paper; (*ancho de la tela*) breadth; (*mancha en el rostro*) spot; (*en, p.ej., un espejo*) blur; sailcloth, canvas; **al paño** off-stage; **conocer el paño** to know one's business, to know the ropes; **paño de adorno** doily; **paño de cocina** washrag, dishcloth; **paño de lágrimas** helping hand, stand-by; **paño de mesa** tablecloth; **paño de tumba** crape; **paño mortuorio** pall; **paños menores** under-clothing; **paños tibios** appeasement attempts

pañuelo *m* handkerchief; shawl; **pañuelo de hierbas** bandanna

papa *m* pope ‖ *f* potato; fake, hoax; food, grub; snap, cinch; **ni papa** nothing

pa•pá *m* (*pl* **-pás**) papa, daddy

papada *f* double chin; (*de animal*) dewlap; (Guat) stupidity

papado *m* papacy

papagayo *m* parrot

papalina *f* sunbonnet; drunk

papana•tas *m* (*pl* **-tas**) simpleton, gawk

paparrucha *f* hoax; trifle

papel *m* paper; piece of paper; rôle, part; character, figure; **desempeñar** or **hacer un papel** to play a rôle; **papel alquitranado** tar paper; **papel cebolla** onionskin; **papel de empapelar** wallpaper; **papel de esmeril** emery paper; **papel de estaño** tin foil; **papel de excusado** toilet paper; **papel de fumar** cigarette paper; **papel de lija** sandpaper; **papel de oficio** foolscap; **papel de seda** tissue paper; **papel de segundón** (fig) second fiddle; **papel de tornasol** litmus paper; **papel filtrante** filter paper; **papel higiénico** toilet paper; **papel moneda** paper money; **papel pintado** wallpaper; **papel secante** blotting paper; **papel viejo** waste paper; **papel volante** handbill, printed leaflet

papelada *f* farce; ridiculous act

papeleo *m* red tape

papelera *f* paper case; writing desk; waste-basket; paper factory

papelería *f* stationery store; mess of papers, litter

papelerío *m* paper work

papele•ro -ra *adj* paper; boastful, showy ‖ *mf* stationer; paper manufacturer; (Mex) paperboy ‖ *f* see **papelera**

papeleta *f* slip of paper; card, file card; ticket; **papeleta de empeño** pawn ticket

papelista *m* paper maker, paper manufacturer; stationer; paper hanger

pape•lón -lona *adj* bluffing, four-flushing ‖ *mf* bluffer, four-flusher ‖ *m* thin cardboard

papelonear *intr* to bluff, to four-flush

papelote *m* worthless piece of paper; paper kite

papel-prensa *m* newsprint

papera *f* goiter; mumps

papilla *f* pap; guile, deceit

papiro *m* papyrus

papirote *m* fillip, flick; nincompoop

paq. *abbr* **paquete**

paquear *tr* to snipe at ‖ *intr* to snipe

paque•te -ta *adj* self-important, pompous; (Arg) chic, dolled-up ‖ *m* package, parcel, bundle, bale; sport, dandy; **darse paquete** (Guat, Mex) to put on airs; **en paquete aparte** under separate cover, in a separate package; **paquetes postales** parcel post

Paquistán, el Pakistan

paquista•ní (*pl* **-níes**) or **paquistano -na** *adj* & *mf* Pakistani

Paquita *f* Fanny

par *adj* like, similar, equal; (math) even ‖ *m* pair, couple; peer; (elec, mech) couple; (math) even number; **a pares** in twos; **de par en par** wide-open; completely; overtly; **¿pares o nones?** odd or even? ‖ *f* par; **a la par** equally; jointly; at the same time; at par; **bajo la par** below par, under par; **sobre la par** above par

para *prep* to, for; towards; compared to; (*antes de*) by; **para + *inf*** in order to + *inf*; **para con** towards; **para que** in order that, so that

parabién *m* congratulation

parábola *f* parable

parabri•sa *m* or **parabri•sas** *m* (*pl* **-sas**) windshield

paracaí•das *m* (*pl* **-das**) parachute; **lanzarse en paracaídas** to parachute; **salvarse en paracaídas** to parachute to safety

paracaidismo *m* parachute jumping; (sport) sky diving

paracaidista *mf* parachutist ‖ *m* paratrooper

parachis•pas *m* (*pl* **-pas**) spark arrester

paracho•ques *m* (*pl* **-ques**) bumper

parachutar *intr* to parachute

parada *f* stop; end; stay; shutdown; (*en el juego*) stake; dam; (*para el ganado*) stall; stud farm; (*en la esgrima*) parry; (*tiro de caballerías de reemplazo*) relay; (mil) parade, dress parade, review; **parada de taxi** taxi stand

paradero *m* end; whereabouts; stopping place; wayside station

para•do -da *adj* slow, spiritless, witless; idle, unemployed; closed; proud, stiff; **quedar bien parado** to be lucky; **quedar mal parado** to be unlucky ‖ *f* see **parada**

paradoja *f* paradox

paradóji•co -ca *adj* paradoxical

parador *m* inn, wayside inn; motel; **parador de carretera** drive-in restaurant

parafina *f* paraffin

paragol•pes *m* (*pl* **-pes**) buffer, bumper

para•guas *m* (*pl* **-guas**) umbrella

Paraguay, el Paraguay

paraguayo -na or **paragua•yo -ya** *adj* & *mf* Paraguayan

paragüero *m* umbrella man; umbrella stand

paraíso *m* paradise

paraje *m* place, spot; state, condition

paralela *f* parallel, parallel line; **paralelas** parallel bars

paralelizar §60 *tr* to parallel, compare

parale•lo -la *adj* parallel ‖ *m* (geog) parallel ‖ *f* see **paralela**

paráli•sis *f* (*pl* **-sis**) paralysis
paralíti•co -ca *adj* & *mf* paralytic
paralizar §60 *tr* to paralyze ‖ *ref* to become
  · paralyzed
parámetro *m* parameter; established boundary
páramo *m* high barren plain; bleak windy
  spot; (Bol, Col, Ecuad) cold drizzle
paranie•ves *m* (*pl* **-ves**) snow fence
paraninfo *m* assembly hall, auditorium
paranoi•co -ca *adj* & *mf* paranoiac
parapeto *m* parapet
paraplegia *f* paraplegia
parar *tr* to stop; check; change; prepare; put
  up, stake; parry; order; get, acquire; (*la
  atención*) fix; (*la caza*) point; (typ) to set ‖
  intr to stop; (*en un hotel*) put up; **parar en**
  to become; run to, run as far as ‖ *ref* to
  stop; stop work; stand; turn, become; (*el
  perro de muestra*) point; (*el pelo*) stand on
  end; **pararse en** to pay attention to
pararra•yo *m* or **pararra•yos** *m* (*pl* **-yos**)
  (*barra metálica que sirve para preservar
  los edificios del rayo*) lightning rod; (*dispositivo que sirve para preservar una instalación eléctrica de la electricidad atmosférica o de las chispas que produce*) lightning
  arrester
parasíti•co -ca *adj* parasitic
parási•to -ta *adj* parasitic; (elec) stray ‖ *m*
  parasite; **parásitos atmosféricos** atmospherics, static
parasol *m* parasol
parato•pes *m* (*pl* **-pes**) bumper
Parcas *fpl* Fates
parcela *f* particle; plot of ground
parcelar *tr* to parcel, divide into lots
parcial *adj* partial; partisan ‖ *mf* partisan
par•co -ca *adj* frugal, sparing; moderate
parcómetro *m* parking meter
parchar *tr* to mend, patch
parche *m* plaster, sticking plaster; patch;
  drum; drumhead; daub, botch, splotch;
  parche poroso porous plaster
pardal *m* linnet; sly fellow
pardiez *interj* by Jove!
pardillo *m* linnet
par•do -da *adj* brown, drab; dark; cloudy;
  (*voz*) dull, flat; (*cerveza*) dark; mulatto ‖
  mf mulatto ‖ *m* brown, drab; leopard
pardus•co -ca *adj* dark-brown, drabbish
parea•do -da *adj* rhymed ‖ *m* couplet
parear *tr* to pair; match ‖ *ref* to pair off
parecer *m* opinion; look, mien, countenance
  ‖ *v* §22 *intr* to appear; show up; look,
  seem; **me parece que. . . .** I think
  that. . . . ‖ *ref* to look alike, resemble each
  other; **parecerse a** to look like
pareci•do -da *adj* like, similar; **bien parecido** good-looking; **parecido a** like, e.g.,
  esta casa es parecida a la otra this house
  is like the other one; **parecidos** alike, e.g.,
  estas casas son parecidas these houses are
  alike ‖ *m* similarity, resemblance, likeness;
  tener un gran parecido to be a good
  likeness

pared *f* wall; **dejar pegado a la pared** to
  nonplus; **paredes** house
pareja *f* pair, couple; dancing partner; **correr
  parejas** or **a las parejas** to be abreast,
  arrive together; go together, match, be
  equal; **correr parejas con** to keep up with,
  keep abreast of; **parejas** (*de naipes*) pair
pareje•ro -ra *adj* even, equal; servile, fawning; forward, overfamiliar ‖ *m* race horse
pare•jo -ja *adj* equal, like; even, smooth ‖ *m*
  (CAm) dancing partner ‖ *f* see **pareja**
parentela *f* kinsfolk, relations
parentesco *m* relationship; bond, tie
parénte•sis *m* (*pl* **-sis**) parenthesis; break,
  interval
parhilera *f* ridgepole
paria *mf* pariah, outcast
paridad *f* par, parity; comparison
parien•te -ta *adj* related ‖ *mf* relative; (coll)
  spouse
parihuela *f* handbarrow; (*camilla*) stretcher
parir *tr* to bear, give birth to, bring forth ‖
  intr to give birth; come forth, come to
  light; talk well
parisiense *adj* & *mf* Parisian
parking *m* parking (space)
parlamentar *intr* to talk, chat; parley
parlamento *m* parliament; parley; speech;
  (theat) speech
parlan•chín -china *adj* jabbering ‖ *mf* chatterbox
parlante *m* loudspeaker
parlar *intr* to speak with facility; chatter, talk
  too much; (*el loro*) talk
parle•ro -ra *adj* loquacious, garrulous; gossipy; (*ave*) singing, song; (*ojos*) expressive; (*arroyo, fuente*) babbling
parlotear *intr* to prattle, jabber, chin
parloteo *m* jabber, prattle
parnaso *m* (*colección de poesías*) Parnassus;
  el Parnaso Parnassus, Mount Parnassus
paro *m* shutdown, work stoppage; lockout;
  titmouse; (*de dados*) (SAm) throw; **paro
  forzoso** layoff
parodia *f* parody, travesty
parodiar *tr* to parody, travesty, burlesque
parón *m* stop; delay
paroxíto•no -na *adj* & *m* paroxytone
parpadear *intr* to blink, wink; flicker
parpadeo *m* blinking, winking; flicker
párpado *m* eyelid
parque *m* park; parking; parking lot; **parque
  de atracciones** amusement park
parqué *m* floor, inlaid floor
parqueadero *m* (Col) parking lot
parquear *tr* to park
parquímetro *m* parking meter
parra *f* grapevine; earthen jug
párrafo *m* paragraph; chat
parral *m* grape arbor
parranda *f* spree, party; (Col) large number;
  andar de parranda to go out on a spree,
  go out to celebrate
parricida *mf* patricide, parricide
parricidio *m* patricide, parricide

parrilla *f* grill, gridiron, broiler; grate, grating; grillroom, grill; **asar a la parrilla** to broil

párroco *m* parish priest

parroquia *f* parish; parish church; customers, clientele

parroquial *adj* parochial

parroquia•no -na *mf* parishioner; customer

parte *m* dispatch, communiqué; **parte meteorológico** weather report ‖ *f* part; share; party; side; direction; (*papel de un actor*) role; (law) party; **de un mes a esta parte** for about a month past; **en ninguna otra parte** nowhere else; **en ninguna parte** nowhere; **ir a la parte** to go shares; **la mayor parte** most, the majority; **parte del león** lion's share; **parte de por medio** (theat) bit part, walk-on; **partes** parts, gifts, talent; faction; parts; genitals; **por otra parte** in another direction; elsewhere; on the other hand; **por todas partes** everywhere; **salva sea la parte** excuse me for not mentioning where

partea•guas *m* (*pl* **-guas**) divide, ridge

partear *tr* to deliver

parte•luz *m* (*pl* **-luces**) mullion, sash bar

Partenón *m* Parthenon

partera *f* midwife

partición *f* partition, division

participar *tr* to notify, inform; give notice of ‖ *intr* to participate; partake

participio *m* participle

partícula *f* particle

particular *adj* particular; peculiar; private, personal ‖ *m* particular; matter, subject; individual; **particular a particular** (telp) person-to-person

particularizar §60 *tr* to itemize ‖ *ref* to stand out; specialize

partida *f* departure; entry, item; certificate; party, group, band; band of guerrillas; game; (*de cartas*) hand; (*de tenis*) set; lot, shipment; behavior; **mala partida** mean trick; **partida de campo** picnic; **partida doble** (com) double entry; **partida sencilla** (com) single entry

partida•rio -ria or **partidista** *adj & mf* partisan

parti•do -da *adj* generous, open-handed ‖ *m* (pol) party; decision; profit; advantage; step, measure; deal, agreement; protection, support; (*casamiento que elegir*) match; district, county; (sport) team; (sport) game; match; **partido de desempate** play-off; **tomar partido** to take a stand, take sides ‖ *f* see **partida**

partir *tr* to divide; distribute; share; split, split open; break, crack; upset, disconcert ‖ *intr* to start, depart, leave, set out; **a partir de** beginning with ‖ *ref* to become divided; crack, split

partisa•no -na *mf* (mil) partisan

partitura *f* (mus) score

parto *m* childbirth, confinement; newborn child; offspring; **estar de parto** to be in labor, be confined; **parto del ingenio** brain child

parva *f* light breakfast (*on fast days*); heap of unthreshed grain; heap, pile

parvulario *m* nursery school; kindergarten

parvulista *mf* kindergarten teacher

párvu•lo -la *adj* small, tiny; simple, innocent; humble ‖ *mf* child, tot; (*niño*) kindergartner

pasa *f* raisin; (*del pelo de los negros*) kink; **pasa de Corinto** currant

pasada *f* passage; passing; **de pasada** in passing, hastily; **mala pasada** mean trick

pasade•ro -ra *adj* passable ‖ *f* stepping stone; walkway, catwalk

pasadizo *m* passage, corridor, hallway, alley; catwalk

pasa•do -da *adj* past; gone by; overripe, spoiled; overdone; stale; burned out; antiquated; faded ‖ *m* past; **pasados** ancestors ‖ *f* see **pasada**

pasa•dor -dora *mf* smuggler ‖ *m* door bolt; bolt, pin; hatpin; brooch; stickpin; safety pin; strainer

pasaje *m* passage; fare; fares; passengers; **cobrar el pasaje** to collect fares

pasaje•ro -ra *adj* passing, fleeting; (*camino, calle*) common, traveled ‖ *mf* passenger; hotel guest; **pasajero colgado** straphanger; **pasajero no presentado** no-show

pasamano *m* lace trimming; (*baranda*) handrail; (naut) gangway

pasamonta•ña *m* or **pasamonta•ñas** *m* (*pl* **-ñas**) ski mask, storm hood

pasaporte *m* passport

pasapuré *m* potato masher

pasar *m* livelihood ‖ *tr* to pass; cross; take across; send, transfer, transmit; (*contrabando*) slip in; spend; swallow; excel; overlook, stand for; undergo, suffer; (*un libro*) go through; (*una película*) show; dry in the sun; tutor; study with or under; **pasarlo** to get along; live; (*dícese de la salud*) be; **pasar por alto** to disregard; omit, leave out, skip ‖ *intr* to pass; go; pass away; pass over; happen; last; spread; get along; yield; come in, e.g., **pase Vd.** come in; **pasar de** to go beyond, exceed; to go above; be more than; **pasar por** to pass by, down, through, over, etc.; pass as, pass for; stop or call at; **pasar sin** to do without ‖ *ref* to pass; go; excel; pass over; get along; pass away; take an examination; leak; go too far; become overripe, become overcooked; rot; melt; burn out; (*una llave, un tornillo*) not fit, be loose; forget; **pasarse por** to stop or call at; **pasarse sin** to do without

pasarela *f* footbridge; catwalk, gangplank

pasatiempo *m* pastime

pascua *f* Passover; Easter; Twelfth-night; Pentecost; Christmas; **dar las pascuas** to wish a Happy New Year; **estar como una pascua** or **unas pascuas** (coll) to be bubbling over with joy; **¡Felices Pascuas!** Merry Christmas!; **Pascua de flores** Easter; **Pascua del Espíritu Santo** Pentecost; **Pascua de Navidad** Christmas; **Pascua de Resurrección** or **Pascua florida** Easter; **Pascuas navideñas** Christmas

pase *m* (*permiso; billete gratuito; movimiento de las manos del mesmerista, el torero*) pass; (*en la esgrima*) feint; **pase de cortesía** complimentary ticket

paseante *adj* strolling ‖ *mf* stroller

pasear *tr* to walk; promenade; show off ‖ *intr* to take a walk; go for a ride ‖ *ref* to take a walk; go for a ride; wander, ramble; take it easy

paseíllo *m* processional entrance of bullfighters

paseo *m* walk, stroll, promenade; ride; drive; avenue; **dar un paseo** to take a walk; take a ride; **enviar a paseo** to send on his way, dismiss without ceremony; **paseo de caballos** bridle path; **paseo de la cuadrilla** processional entrance of the bullfighters

pasillo *m* short step; passage, corridor; (theat) short piece, sketch

pasión *f* passion

pasi•vo -va *adj* passive; (*pensión*) retirement ‖ *m* liabilities; debit side

pasmar *tr* to chill; frostbite; stun, benumb; dumbfound, astound ‖ *ref* to chill; become frostbitten; be astounded; get lockjaw; (*los colores*) become dull or flat

pasmo *m* cold; lockjaw, tetanus; astonishment; wonder, prodigy

pasmo•so -sa *adj* astounding; awesome

paso *m* step; pace; (*de la escalera*) step; gait; walk; passing; passage; step, measure, démarche; pass, permit; strait; footstep, footprint; incident, happening; (*de hélice, tornillo*) pitch; (elec) pitch; (rad) stage; (theat) short piece, sketch, skit; **al paso** in passing, on the way; **al paso que** at the rate that; (*a la vez que, mientras*) while, whereas; **ceder el paso** to make way; to keep clear; **de paso** in passing; at the same time; **paso a nivel** grade crossing; **paso de ganado** cattle crossing; **paso de ganso** goose step

paspa *f* (SAm) crack in the lips

pasquín *m* lampoon

pasquinar *tr* to lampoon

pasta *f* paste, dough, pie crust, soup paste; mash; (*para hacer papel*) pulp; cardboard; board binding; (*de un diente*) filling; (*dinero*) (coll) dough; **pasta dentrífica** toothpaste; **pasta española** marbled leather binding, tree calf; **pastas** noodles, macaroni, spaghetti, etc.; **pasta seca** cookie

pastar *tr & intr* to graze

pastel *m* pie; pastry roll; pastel; settlement, pacification; cheat, trick; (typ) pi; (typ) smear; (coll) plot, deal; **pastel de cumpleaños** birthday cake

pastelería *f* pastry; pastry shop

pastele•ro -ra *mf* pastry cook

pastelillo *m* tart, cake; (*de mantequilla*) pat

pasterizar §60 *tr* to pasteurize

pastilla *f* tablet, lozenge, drop; (*pequeña masa pastosa*) dab; (*de jabón, chocolate, etc.*) cake

pasto *m* pasture; grass; food, nourishment; **a pasto** to excess; in abundance; **a todo pasto** freely, without restriction; **de pasto** ordinary, everyday

pastor *m* shepherd; pastor

pastora *f* shepherdess

pastoral *adj & f* pastoral

pastorear *tr* (*a las ovejas o los fieles*) to shepherd; lie in ambush for; spoil, pamper; (Arg, Urug) to court

pasto•so -sa *adj* pasty, doughy; (*voz*) mellow; (Arg, Chile) grassy

pastura *f* pasture; fodder

pasu•do -da *adj* kinky

pata *f* paw, foot, leg; (*de un mueble*) leg; duck; **a cuatro patas** on all fours; **estirar la pata** to kick the bucket; **meter la pata** to butt in, to put one's foot in it; **pata de gallo** crow's-foot; blunder; piece of nonsense; **pata de palo** peg leg, wooden leg; **pata galana** game leg; lame person; **patas arriba** on one's back, upside down; topsyturvy

patada *f* kick; stamp, stamping; step; footstep, track; **en dos patadas** in a jiffy

patalear *intr* to kick; stamp the feet

pataleta *f* fit; feigned fit or convulsion; (dial) tantrum

patán *m* churl, boor, lout; peasant

pataplún *interj* kerplunk!

patata *f* potato

patear *tr* to kick; trample on ‖ *intr* to stamp one's foot; bustle around; kick

patentar *tr* to patent

patente *adj* patent, clear, evident ‖ *f* grant, privilege, warrant; patent; **de patente** (Chile) excellent, first-class; **patente de circulación** owner's license; **patente de invención** patent; **patente de sanidad** bill of health

paternal *adj* paternal, fatherly

paternidad *f* paternity, fatherhood; **paternidad literaria** authorship

pater•no -na *adj* paternal

pateta *m* (coll) the devil; cripple

patéti•co -ca *adj* pathetic

patetismo *m* pathos

patibula•rio -ria *adj* hair-raising

patíbulo *m* scaffold

patiesteva•do -da *adj* bowlegged

patilla *f* small paw or foot; pocket flap; watermelon; (naut) compass; **patillas** sideburns, side whiskers

patín *m* small patio; skate; skid, slide, runner; (*ave marina*) petrel; **patín de cuchilla** or **de hielo** ice skate; **patín de ruedas** roller skate

patinada *f* (SAm) (aut) skidding

patinadero *m* skating rink

patina•dor -dora *mf* skater

patinaje *m* skating; skidding; **patinaje artístico** figure skating; **patinaje de fantasía** fancy skating; **patinaje de figura** figure skating

patinar *intr* to skate; skid; slip

patinazo *m* skid; slip; slip, blunder

patinete *m* scooter

patio *m* patio, court, yard; campus; (rr) yard, switchyard; **patio de recreo** playground

patituer•to -ta *adj* crooked-legged; crooked, lopsided

patizam•bo -ba *adj* knock-kneed

pato *m* duck, drake; **pagar el pato** to be the goat; **pato de flojel** eider duck

patochada *f* blunder, stupidity

patojo *m* (CAm) street urchin

patología *f* pathology

patota *f* (Arg, Urug) teen-age gang

patraña *f* fake, humbug, hoax

patria *f* country; mother country, fatherland, native land; birthplace; (*p.ej., de las artes*) home; **patria chica** native heath

patriarca *m* patriarch

patri•cio -cia *adj* & *mf* patrician

patrimonio *m* patrimony

pa•trio -tria *adj* native, home; paternal ‖ *f* see **patria**

patriota *mf* patriot

patrióti•co -ca *adj* patriotic

patriotismo *m* patriotism

patrocinar *tr* to sponsor, patronize

patrocinio *m* sponsorship

patrón *m* sponsor, protector; patron saint; patron; landlord; owner, master; boss, foreman; host; (*de un barco*) skipper; pattern; standard; **patrón oro** gold standard; **patrón picado** stencil

patrona *f* patroness; landlady; owner, mistress; hostess

patronal *adj* management, employers

patronato *m* employers' association; foundation; board of trustees; patronage

patronear *tr* to skipper

patro•no -na *mf* sponsor, protector; employer ‖ *m* patron; landlord; boss, foreman; lord of the manor; **los patronos** the management ‖ *f* see **patrona**

patrulla *f* patrol; gang, band

patrullar *tr* & *intr* to patrol

paulati•no -na *adj* slow, gradual

pausa *f* pause; slowness, delay; (mus) rest

pausa•do -da *adj* slow, calm, deliberate ‖ **pausado** *adv* slowly, calmly

pausar *tr* & *intr* to slow down

pauta *f* ruler; guide lines; guideline, rule, guide, standard, model

pava *f* turkey hen; **pelar la pava** to make love at a window

pavesa *f* ember, cinder, spark

pavimentar *tr* to pave

pavimento *m* pavement

pa•vo -va *adj* (coll) silly, stupid ‖ *m* turkey; turkey cock; **comer pavo** to be a wallflower; **pavo real** peacock

pavón *m* bluing; peacock

pavonar *tr* to blue

pavonear *intr* & *ref* to strut, swagger

pavor *m* fear, terror, dread

pavoro•so -sa *adj* frightful, dreadful

payador *m* (SAm) gaucho minstrel

payasada *f* clownishness, clownish remark

payaso *m* clown; laughingstock

paz *f* (*pl* **paces**) peace; peacefulness; **dejar en paz** to leave alone, stop pestering; **estar en paz** to be even; to be quits; **hacer las paces con** to make peace with, to come to terms with; **salir en paz** to break even

pazgua•to -ta *adj* simple, doltish ‖ *mf* simpleton, dolt

pazpuerca *f* slut, slattern

P.D. *abbr* **posdata**

peaje *m* toll

peatón *m* pedestrian; rural postman

pebete *m* punk, joss stick; fuse; (*cosa hedionda*) (coll) stinker

peca *f* freckle

pecado *m* sin

peca•dor -dora *adj* sinning, sinful ‖ *mf* sinner

pecamino•so -sa *adj* sinful

pecar §73 *intr* to sin; **pecar de** to be too, e.g., **pecar de confiado** to be too trusting

pecera *f* fish globe, fish bowl

pecino•so -sa *adj* slimy

pecio *m* flotsam

pecíolo *m* leafstalk

pécora *f* head of sheep; **buena pécora** or **mala pécora** schemer, scheming woman

peco•so -sa *adj* freckly, freckle-faced

peculado *m* embezzlement, peculation

peculiar *adj* peculiar

pecunia•rio -ria *adj* pecuniary

pechada *f* bump or push with the chest; tossing an animal (*with a bump of horse's chest*); bumping contest between two horsemen

pechar *tr* to pay as a tax; fulfill; take on; drive one's horse against; bump with the chest; strike for a loan ‖ *ref* (*dos jinetes*) to vie in a bumping contest

pechera *f* shirt front, shirt bosom; chest protector; (*del delantal*) bib; breast strap; (coll) bosom; **pechera postiza** dickey

pecho *m* chest; breast, bosom; heart, courage; **dar el pecho** to nurse, suckle; face it out; **de dos pechos** double-breasted; **de un solo pecho** single-breasted; **echar el pecho al agua** to put one's shoulder to the wheel; (coll) to speak out; **en pechos de camisa** in shirt sleeves; **tomar a pecho** to take to heart; **¡pecho al agua!** take heart!, put your shoulder to the wheel!

pechuga *f* (*del ave*) breast; slope, hill; brass, cheek; treachery, perfidy; (coll) bosom, breast

pechu•gón -gona *adj* big-chested; brazen ‖ *mf* sponger ‖ *m* slap or blow on the chest; fall on the chest

pedagogía *f* pedagogy

pedal *mf* pedal, treadle

pedalear *intr* to pedal

pedante *adj* pedantic ‖ *mf* pedant

pedantería *f* pedantry

pedantes•co -ca *adj* pedantic

pedantismo *m* pedantry

pedazo *m* piece; **hacer pedazos** to break to pieces; **hacerse pedazos** (coll) to fall to pieces; to strain, to wear oneself out; **pedazo de alcornoque, de animal** or **de bruto** dolt, imbecile, good-for-nothing; **pedazo del alma, de las entrañas** or **del corazón** (*niño*) darling, apple of one's eye; **pedazo de pan** (*pequeña cantidad*) crumb; (*precio bajo*) song

pederastia *f* pederasty

pedernal *m* flint; flintiness; flint-hearted person

pedestal *m* pedestal

pedestre *adj* pedestrian

pedestrismo *m* pedestrianism; walking; foot racing; cross-country racing

pediatra *mf* pediatrician

pediatría *f* pediatrics

pedido *m* request; (*encargo de mercancías*) order

pedigüe•ño -ña *adj* insistent, demanding, bothersome

pedir §50 *tr* to ask, ask for; request; demand, require; need; ask for the hand of; (*mercancías*) order; (gram) to govern; **pedir prestado a** to borrow from ‖ *intr* to ask; beg; bring suit; **a pedir de boca** opportunely; as desired

pedorre•ro -ra *adj* flatulent ‖ *f* flatulence; (orn) tody; **pedorreras** tights

pedrada *f* stoning; hit or blow with a stone; hint, taunt

pedregal *m* rocky ground; pile of rocks

pedrego•so -sa *adj* stony, rocky; suffering from gallstones ‖ *mf* sufferer from gallstones

pedrejón *m* boulder

pedrera *f* quarry, stone quarry

pedrería *f* precious stones, jewelry

pedrusco *m* boulder

pedúnculo *m* stem, stalk

peer §43 *intr & ref* to break wind

pega *f* sticking; pitch varnish; drubbing; (*en un examen*) catch question; trick, joke; (W-I) work, jobs; **de pega** (coll) fake

pegadi•zo -za *adj* sticky; catching, contagious; sponging; fake, imitation

pegajo•so -sa *adj* sticky; contagious; tempting; soft, gentle; mushy

pegapega *f* glue

pegar §44 *tr* to stick, paste; fasten, attach, tie; (*carteles*) post; (*fuego*) set; (*una enfermedad*) transmit; (*un botón*) sew on; (*un grito*) let out; (*un salto*) take; (*un golpe, una bofetada*) let go; beat; **no pegar el ojo** to not sleep a wink ‖ *intr* to stick, catch; take root, take hold; cling; fit, match; be fitting; pass, be accepted; beat; knock ‖ *ref* to stick, catch; take root, take hold; hang on, stick around; (*una enfermedad*) be catching; **pegársela a uno** to make a fool of someone

pegatina *f* sticker (or tag)

pegotear *intr* to hang around, sponge

peina•do -da *adj* groomed; effeminate ‖ *m* hairdo, coiffure; (*manera de componer el pelo*) hairstyle; (*policía, soldados*) search; **peinado al agua** finger wave

peina•dor -dora *mf* hairdresser ‖ *m* wrapper, dressing gown; dressing table

peinar *tr* to comb; (*policía, soldados*) search ‖ *ref* to comb oneself, comb one's hair

peine *m* comb; sly fellow

peineta *f* back comb

pelada *f* pelt, sheepskin

peladero *m* wasteland

peladilla *f* sugar almond; small pebble

peladillo *m* clingstone peach

pela•do -da *adj* bare; bald; barren; penniless; (*decena, centena, etc.*) even ‖ *m* raggedy fellow; (W-I) haircut ‖ *f* see **pelada**

pelafus•tán -tana *mf* derelict, good-for-nothing

pelaga•tos *m* (*pl* **-tos**) wretch, ragamuffin

pelaje *m* coat, fur; (*especie, calidad*) sort, stripe

pelar *tr* (*pelo*) to cut; (*pelo, plumas*) pluck, pull out; peel, skin, husk, hull, shell; (*los dientes*) show; (*en el juego*) clean out; beat, thrash ‖ *ref* to peel off; lose one's hair; get a haircut; clear out, make a getaway; **pelárselas por** to crave; crave to

pelazón *f* poverty; misery

peldaño *m* step

pelea *f* fight; quarrel; struggle; **pelea de gallos** cockfight

pelear *intr* to fight; quarrel; struggle ‖ *ref* to fight, fight each other

pele•ón -ona *adj* pugnacious, quarrelsome; (*vino*) cheap, ordinary ‖ *mf* quarrelsome person ‖ *m* cheap wine ‖ *f* row, scuffle, fracas

peletería *f* furriery; fur shop; (Cuba) shoe store

pelete•ro -ra *mf* furrier; (Cuba) shoe dealer

peliagu•do -da *adj* furry, long-haired; arduous, ticklish

película *f* film; motion picture; **película de dibujos** animated cartoon; **película del Oeste** western; **película de terror** or **película horripilante** horror movie; **película sonora** sound film

pelicule•ro -ra *adj* moving-picture ‖ *mf* scenario writer ‖ *m* movie actor ‖ *f* movie actress

peligrar *intr* to be in danger

peligro *m* danger, peril, risk; **ponerse en peligro de paz** to be alerted for war

peligro•so -sa *adj* dangerous

pelillo *m* trifle; **echar pelillos a la mar** to bury the hatchet; **no pararse en pelillos** to not bother about trifles, pay no attention to small matters; **no tener pelillos en la lengua** to speak right out

pelirro•jo -ja *adj* red-haired, redheaded ‖ *mf* redhead

pelo *m* hair; (*en las frutas y el cuerpo humano*) down; (*del paño*) nap; (*de la madera*) grain; (*de un animal*) coat; (*en las piedras preciosas*) flaw; (*del caballo*) color; (*en el billar*) kiss; (*del reloj*) hairspring; hair trigger; fiber, filament; raw silk; **al pelo** with the hair, with the nap; perfectly, to the point; **con todos sus pelos y señales** chapter and verse; **en pelo** bareback; **escapar por un pelo** to escape by a hairbreadth, have a narrow escape; **no tener pelos en la lengua** to be outspoken, not mince words; **ponerle a uno los pelos de punta** to make one's hair stand on end; **tomar el pelo a** to make fun of, make a fool of; **venir a pelo** to come in handy

pe•lón -lona *adj* bald, hairless; dull, stupid; penniless

Pélope *m* Pelops

peloponense *adj* & *mf* Peloponnesian

Peloponeso *m* Peloponnesus

pelo•so -sa *adj* hairy

pelota *f* ball; ball game; handball; **en pelota** stripped; stark-naked; **pelota acuática** water polo; **pelota rodada** (baseball) grounder; **pelota vasca** pelota, jai alai

pelotari *mf* pelota player

pelotear *intr* to knock a ball around; wrangle, argue

pelotera *f* row, brawl

pelotón *m* large ball; gang, crowd; platoon; **pelotón de fusilamiento** firing squad; **pelotón de los torpes** awkward squad

peltre *m* pewter

peluca *f* wig

peluche *m* plush, pile

pelu•do -da *adj* hairy, furry; bushy

peluquear *tr* (Col, Ven) to cut the hair of ‖ *intr* (Col, Ven) to get a haircut

peluquería *f* hairdresser's, barbershop

peluque•ro -ra *mf* hairdresser; barber; wigmaker

peluquín *m* hairpiece; toupee

pelusa *f* down; lint, fuzz; nap; jealousy, envy

pellejo *m* skin; pelt, rawhide; peel, rind; wineskin; (*la vida de uno*) (coll) hide, skin; (coll) sot, drunkard; **dar, dejar** or **perder el pellejo** to die

pellizcar §73 to pinch; nip; take a pinch of ‖ *ref* to long, pine

pellizco *m* pinch; nip; bit, pinch

pena *f* punishment; penalty; pain, hardship, toil; sorrow, grief; effort, trouble; **a duras penas** hardly, with great difficulty; **de pena** of a broken heart; **pena privativa de libertad** imprisonment; **¡qué pena!** what a pity!; **so pena de** on pain of, under penalty of; **valer la pena** to be worthwhile (to)

penacho *m* crest; tuft, plume; arrogance; (bot) tassel

pena•do -da *adj* afflicted, grieved; difficult ‖ *mf* convict

penalidad *f* trouble, hardship; (law) penalty

penalizar §60 *tr* to punish; penalize

penar *tr* to penalize; punish ‖ *intr* to suffer; linger; **penar por** to pine for, long for ‖ *ref* to grieve

penca *f* pulpy leaf; cowhide; **coger una penca** to get a jag on

penco *m* nag, jade; boor

pendejo *m* pubes; pubic hair; (coll) coward

pendencia *f* dispute, quarrel, fight; pending litigation

pendencie•ro -ra *adj* quarrelsome ‖ *mf* wrangler

pender *intr* to hang, dangle; depend; be pending

pendiente *adj* pendent, hanging, dangling; pending; under way; expecting; **estar pendiente de** (*las palabras de una persona*) to hang on; depend on; be in the process of ‖ *m* earring, pendant; watch chain ‖ *f* slope, grade; dip, pitch

péndola *f* feather; pendulum; clock; pen, quill; queen post

pendolón *m* king post

pendón *m* banner, standard, pennon

péndulo *m* pendulum; clock

pene *m* penis

penetrar *tr* to penetrate; pierce; grasp, fathom ‖ *intr* to penetrate ‖ *ref* to grasp, fathom; realize; become convinced

penicilina *f* penicillin

península *f* peninsula

peninsular *adj* & *mf* peninsular; (*ibero*) Peninsular

penique *m* penny

penitencia *f* penitence; penance; **hacer penitencia** to do penance; eat sparingly; take potluck

penitente *adj* & *mf* penitent

penol *m* (naut) yardarm

peno•so -sa *adj* arduous, difficult; suffering; conceited; shy

pensa•dor -dora *adj* thinking ‖ *mf* thinker

pensamiento *m* thought; (*planta y flor*) pansy

pensar §2 *tr* to think; think over; (*un naipe, un número, etc.*) think of; intend to; **pensar de** to think of, e.g., **¿qué piensa Vd. de este libro?** what do you think of this book? ‖ *intr* to think; **pensar en** (*dirigir sus pensamientos a*) to think of (*to turn one's thoughts to*)

pensati•vo -va *adj* pensive, thoughtful

pensión *f* pension; annuity; allowance; boardinghouse; (*para ampliar estudios*) fellowship; **pensión completa** board and lodging

pensionar *tr* to pension

pensionista *mf* pensioner; boarder; boarding-school pupil; **medio pensionista** day boarder

pentagrama *m* staff, musical staff

Pentecostés, el Pentecost

penúlti•mo -ma *adj* penultimate; next to last ‖ *f* penult

penumbra *f* penumbra; semidarkness, half-light

penuria *f* shortage

peña *f* rock, boulder; cliff; club, group, circle

peñasco *m* pinnacle; crag

peñasco•so -sa *adj* rocky, craggy

peñón *m* rock, spire; **peñón de Gibraltar** rock of Gibraltar

peón *m* laborer; pedestrian; foot soldier; farm hand; (*en el ajedrez*) pawn; (*en las damas*) man; top, peg top; spindle, axle; (taur) attendant; **peón de albañil** or **de mano** hod carrier

peor *adj* & *adv* worse; worst

pepa *f* (*de la manzana*) (Col) seed; (*del durazno*) (Arg) stone; (*canica*) (Arg) marble; (Col) lie, cheat, trick

pepe *mf* foundling ‖ *m* bib; **Pepe** *m* Joe

pepinillo *m* gherkin

pepino *m* cucumber; **me importa un pepino** I couldn't care less

pepita *f* seed, pip; nugget; (vet) pip

peque *m* tot

pequén *m* (Chile) burrowing owl

peque•ñez *f* (*pl* **-ñeces**) smallness; infancy; trifle

peque•ño -ña *adj* little, small; young; low, humble

pequeño-burgués *adj* petit bourgeois

Pequín *m* Peking

pequi•nés -nesa *adj* & *mf* Pekinese

pera *f* pear; goatee; cinch, sinecure; pear-shaped bulb; pear-shaped switch

peral *m* pear tree

perca *f* (ichth) perch

percance *m* mischance, misfortune; **percances** perquisites

percatar *ref* — **percatarse de** to be aware of; beware of, guard against

percebe *m* barnacle; fool, sap

percepción *f* perception; collection

percibir *tr* to perceive; collect

percudir *tr* to tarnish, dull; spread through

percha *f* perch, pole, roost; clothes tree; coat hanger; coat hook; barber pole

perchero *m* rack, clothes rack, clothes hanger

perde•dor -dora *adj* losing ‖ *mf* loser

perder §51 *tr* to lose; waste, squander; (*un tren, una ocasión*) miss; (*una asignatura*) flunk; ruin; spoil ‖ *intr* to lose; fade ‖ *ref* to get lost; miscarry; sink; become ruined; spoil; go to the dogs

perdición *f* perdition; loss; outrage; ruination

pérdida *f* loss; waste; ruination; **no tener pérdida** to be easy to find; **pérdida de reclamable** tax loss

perdi•do -da *adj* (*bala*) stray, wild; (*manga*) wide, loose; fruitless; (*horas*) off, spare, idle; distracted; inveterate; madly in love ‖ *m* profligate, rake

perdido•so -sa *adj* unlucky; easily lost

perdigón *m* young partridge; profligate; heavy loser; (*alumno*) failure; **perdigones** (*granos de plomo*) shot; **perdigón zorrero** buckshot

per•diz *f* (*pl* **-dices**) partridge

perdón *m* pardon, forgiveness; **con perdón** by your leave

perdonable *adj* pardonable

perdonar *tr* to pardon, forgive, excuse; **no perdonar** to not miss, not omit

perdula•rio -ria *adj* careless, sloppy; incorrigible, vicious ‖ *mf* good-for-nothing, profligate

perdurable *adj* long-lasting; everlasting

perdurar *intr* to last, last a long time, survive

perecede•ro -ra *adj* perishable; mortal ‖ *m* extreme want

perecer §22 *intr* to perish; suffer; be in great want ‖ *ref* to pine; **perecerse por** to be dying for; (*una mujer*) be mad about

peregrinación *f* peregrination; pilgrimage

peregri•no -na *adj* wandering, traveling; foreign; rare, strange; beautiful; mortal; (*ave*) migratory ‖ *mf* pilgrim

perejil *m* parsley; (coll) frippery

perenne *adj* perennial

pereza *f* laziness; slowness

perezo•so -sa *adj* lazy; slow, dull, heavy ‖ *mf* lazybones; sleepyhead ‖ *m* (zool) sloth

perfección *f* perfection

perfeccionar *tr* to perfect, improve

perfec•to -ta *adj* & *m* perfect

perfidia *f* perfidy

pérfi•do -da *adj* perfidious

perfil *m* profile; side view; cross section; thin stroke; outline, sketch; **perfil aerodinámico** streamlining; **perfiles** finishing touches; courtesies

perfila•do -da *adj* (*cara*) long and thin; (*nariz*) well-formed; (*facciones*) delicate; streamlined

perfilar *tr* to profile, outline; perfect, polish, finish ‖ *ref* to be outlined; show one's profile, stand sidewise; stand out; dress up

perforación *f* perforation; drilling; puncture; keypunching

perfora•dor -dora *adj* perforating; drilling ‖ *f* pneumatic drill, rock drill

perforar *tr* to perforate; drill, bore; puncture; (*una tarjeta*) punch

perforista *mf* keypuncher

perfumar *tr* to perfume

perfume *m* perfume

pergamino *m* parchment

pergenio *m* rascal

pericia *f* skill, expertness

periclitar *intr* to be in jeopardy, be shaky

perico *m* (*pelo postizo*) periwig; parakeet; (slang) chamber pot; (CAm) compliment; **perico entre ellas** lady's man

periferia *f* periphery; surroundings

perifollos *mpl* finery, frippery, chiffons

perilla *f* pear-shaped ornament; goatee; knob, doorknob; (*del arzón*) pommel; (*de la oreja*) lobe; **de perilla** apropos, to the point

periodísti•co -ca *adj* newspaper, journalistic

periódi•co -ca *adj* periodic ‖ *m* newspaper; periodical

periodismo *m* journalism

periodista *mf* journalist ‖ *m* newspaperman ‖ *f* newspaperwoman

período *m* period; compound sentence; (phys) cycle; **período lectivo** (*en la escuela*) term

peripues•to -ta *adj* dudish, all spruced up, sporty

periquete *m* jiffy; **en un periquete** in a jiffy

periquito *m* parakeet; **periquito de Australia** budgerigar

periscopio *m* periscope

peri•to -ta *adj* skilled, skillful; expert ‖ *m* expert

perjudicar §73 *tr* to damage, impair, hurt, prejudice

perjudicial *adj* harmful, injurious, detrimental, prejudicial

perjuicio *m* harm, injury, damage, prejudice; **en perjuicio de** to the detriment of

perjurar *intr* to commit perjury; swear, be profane ‖ *ref* to commit perjury; perjure oneself

perjurio *m* perjury

perla *f* pearl; **de perlas** perfectly

perlesía *f* palsy

permanecer §22 *intr* to stay, remain

permanencia *f* permanence; stay, sojourn

permanente *adj* permanent ‖ *f* permanent wave

permiso *m* permission; permit; time off; (*en el monedaje*) tolerance; leave; **con permiso** excuse me; **permiso de circulación** owner's license; **permiso de conducir** driver's license

permitir *tr* to permit, allow ‖ *ref* to be permitted; **no se permite fumar** no smoking

permutar *tr* to interchange; barter; to permute

pernear *intr* to kick; hustle; fuss, fret

pernera *f* trouser leg

pernicio•so -sa *adj* pernicious

pernil *m* trouser leg; (*anca y muslo*) ham

perno *m* bolt; **perno con anillo** ringbolt; **perno roscado** screw bolt

pernoctar *intr* to spend the night

pero *conj* but, yet ‖ *m* but; fault, defect; **poner pero a** to find fault with

perogrullada *f* platitude, inanity

peroración *f* peroration; harangue

perorar *intr* to perorate; orate

peróxido *m* peroxide; **peróxido de hidrógeno** hydrogen peroxide

perpendicular *adj & f* perpendicular

perpetrar *tr* to perpetrate

perpetuar §21 *tr* to perpetuate

perpe•tuo -tua *adj* perpetual; life

perplejidad *f* perplexity; worry, anxiety

perple•jo -ja *adj* perplexed; worried, anxious; baffling, perplexing

perra *f* bitch; tantrum; drunkenness

perrada *f* pack of dogs; dirty trick

perrera *f* kennel, doghouse; tantrum; toil, drudgery

perro *m* dog; **el perro del hortelano** dog in the manger; **perro caliente** (slang) hot dog; **perro cobrador** retriever; **perro de aguas** spaniel; **perro de lanas** poodle; **perro de muestra** pointer; **perro faldero** lap dog; **perro marino** dogfish, shark; **perro raposero** foxhound; **perro viejo** (coll) wise old owl

perro-lazarillo *m* (*pl* **perros-lazarillos**) Seeing Eye dog

persa *adj & mf* Persian

persecución *f* persecution; pursuit; annoyance, harassment

perseguir §67 *tr* to persecute; pursue; annoy, harass

perseverar *intr* to persevere

persiana *f* slatted shutter; flowered silk; louver; Venetian blind; **persiana del radiador** (aut) louver

persistir *intr* to persist

persona *f* person; personage; **persona desplazada** displaced person; **personas** people; **por persona** per capita

personaje *m* personage; (theat) character; person of importance

personal *adj* personal ‖ *m* personnel, staff, force

personalidad *f* personality

personificar §73 *tr* to personify

perspectiva *f* perspective; outlook, prospect; appearance

perspi•caz *adj* (*pl* **-caces**) perspicacious, discerning; keen-sighted

persuadir *tr* to persuade

persuasión *f* persuasion

pertenecer §22 *intr* to belong; pertain ‖ *ref* to be independent, be free

perteneciente *adj* pertaining

pértiga *f* pole, rod, staff

perti•naz *adj* (*pl* **-naces**) pertinacious; (*dolor de cabeza*) persistent

pertinente *adj* pertinent, relevant

pertrechos *mpl* supplies, provisions, equipment; tools; **pertrechos de guerra** ordnance

perturbar *tr* to perturb; disturb; upset, disconcert; confuse, interrupt

Perú, el Peru

perua•no -na *adj & mf* Peruvian

perversidad *f* perversity

perversión *f* perversion

perver•so -sa *adj* perverse; wicked, depraved ‖ *mf* profligate

perverti•do -da *mf* pervert

pervertir §68 *tr* to pervert ‖ *ref* to become perverted; go to the bad

pesa *f* weight; (CAm, Col, Ven) butcher shop

pesacar•tas *m* (*pl* **-tas**) letter scales

pesadez *f* heaviness; slowness; tiresomeness; harshness; (phys) gravity

pesadilla *f* nightmare

pesa•do -da *adj* heavy; slow; tiresome; harsh; boring

pesadumbre *f* sorrow, grief; trouble; weight, heaviness

pesaje *m* weighing; (sport) weigh-in

pésame *m* condolence; **dar el pésame a** to extend one's sympathy to

pesantez *f* (phys) gravity

pesar *m* sorrow, regret; **a pesar de** in spite of ‖ *tr* to weigh; make sorry ‖ *intr* to weigh; be heavy; cause regret, cause sorrow

pesaro•so -sa *adj* sorrowful, regretful

pesca *f* fishing; catch; **ir de pesca** to go fishing; **pesca de bajura** off-shore fishing; **pesca de gran altura** deep-sea fishing

pescadería *f* fish market; fish store; fish stand

pescade•ro -ra *mf* fish dealer, fishmonger

pescado *m* fish (*that has been caught*)

pesca•dor -dora *adj* fishing ‖ *m* fisherman ‖ *f* fisherwoman, fishwife

pescante *m* coach box; (*de una grúa*) jib; (aut) front seat; (naut) davit; (theat) trap door

pescar §73 *tr* to fish; fish for; fish out; (*peces*) catch; (coll) to manage to get ‖ *intr* to fish

pescozón *m* slap on the neck or head

pescuezo *m* neck

pesebre *m* crib, rack, manger; crèche

pesero *m* (CAm, Col, Ven) butcher; (Mex) shared taxi

pesimismo *m* pessimism

pesimista *adj* pessimistic ‖ *mf* pessimist

pési•mo -ma *adj* very bad, abominable

peso *m* weight; scale, balance; burden, load; judgment, good sense; (*unidad monetaria*) peso; **caerse de su peso** to be self-evident; **llevar el peso de la batalla** to bear the brunt of the battle; **peso atómico** atomic weight; **peso molecular** molecular weight

pespuntar *tr & intr* to backstitch

pespunte *m* backstitch

pesquera *f* fishery; fishing grounds; (*presa para detener los peces*) weir

pesquería *f* fishing; fishery

pesque·ro -ra *adj* fishing ‖ *m* fishing boat ‖ *f* see **pesquera**

pesquis *m* acumen, keenness

pesquisa *m* (Arg) detective ‖ *f* inquiry, investigation

pesquisar *tr* to investigate, inquire into

pestaña *f* eyelash; flange; fringe, edging; index tab

pestañear *intr* to wink, blink; **sin pestañear** without batting an eye

peste *f* pest, plague; epidemic; stink, stench; abundance; (Col, Peru) head cold; (Chile) smallpox; **pestes** insults

pesticida *m* pesticide

pestífe·ro -ra *adj* pestiferous; stinking

pestilencia *f* pestilence

pestillo *m* bolt; doorlatch

petaca *f* cigar case; cigarette case; tobacco pouch; leather-covered hamper

pétalo *m* petal

petardear *tr* to swindle ‖ *intr* (aut) to backfire

petardeo *m* swindling; (aut) backfire

petardo *m* petard; bomb; swindle, cheat

petate *m* sleeping bag; bedding; luggage; cheat; poor soul; **liar el petate** to pack up and get out; to kick the bucket

petición *f* petition; request; plea; (law) claim, bill; **a petición de** at the request of; **petición de mano** formal betrothal

petimetre *m* dude, sport, dandy

petirrojo *m* redbreast, robin

Petrarca *m* Petrarch

petrificar §73 *tr & ref* to petrify

petróleo *m* petroleum; **petróleo combustible** fuel oil

petrole·ro -ra *adj* oil, petroleum ‖ *mf* oil dealer ‖ *m* oil tanker

petroquími·co -ca *adj* petrochemical

petulancia *f* flippancy, pertness

petulante *adj* flippant, pert

pez *m* (*pl* **peces**) fish; reward, just desert; **como un pez en el agua** snug as a bug in a rug; **pez de plata** (ent) silverfish; **salga pez o salga rana** blindly, hit or miss ‖ *f* pitch, tar

pezón *m* stem; nipple, teat

pezonera *f* linchpin

pezuña *f* hoof

piado·so -sa *adj* merciful; pitiful; pious

piafar *intr* (*el caballo*) to paw, to stamp

piano *m* piano; **piano de cola** grand piano; **piano de media cola** baby grand

piar §77 *intr* to peep, chirp

pica *f* pike; pikeman; picador's goad; (Col) pique, resentment

picada *f* peck; bite; (Bol) knock at the door; (Arg, Bol, Urug) narrow ford; (SAm) path, trail

picadillo *m* (*carne, verduras, ajos, etc. reducidos a pequeños trozos*) hash; (*carne picada*) mincemeat

pica·do -da *adj* perforated; pitted; (*tabaco*) cut; (*hielo*) cracked; (*mar*) choppy; piqued ‖ *m* mincemeat; (aer) dive; **picado con motor** (aer) power dive ‖ *f* see **picada**

picador *m* horsebreaker; (*torero de a caballo*) picador (*mounted bullfighter*); chopping block; meat grinder

picadura *f* bite, prick, sting; nick; puncture; cut tobacco; (*en un diente*) cavity

picaflor *m* hummingbird

picahie·los *m* (*pl* **-los**) ice pick

picamade·ros *m* (*pl* **-ros**) green woodpecker

picante *adj* biting, pricking, stinging; piquant, juicy, racy; (SAm) highly seasoned ‖ *m* mordancy; piquancy

pícap *m* (Bol, Chile, Col) var of **pick-up**

picapedrero *m* stonecutter

picaplei·tos *m* (*pl* **-tos**) troublemaker; shyster, pettifogger

picaporte *m* latch; latchkey; door knocker

picar §73 *tr* to prick, pierce, puncture; sting; bite; burn; peck; nibble; pit, pock; mince, chop up, cut up; stick, poke; spur; goad; perforate; (*hielo*) crack; harass, pursue; tame; pique, annoy ‖ *intr* to itch; (*el sol*) burn; nibble; have a smattering; be catching; (*los negocios*) pick up; (aer) to dive; (*caer en el lazo*) (coll) to bite; **picar en** to nibble at; dabble in; **picar muy alto** aim high, expect too much ‖ *ref* to rot; (*la ropa*) be moth-eaten; (*el vino*) turn sour; (*un diente*) be decayed; (*el mar*) get rough; be offended; get drunk; (*drogas*) get a fix, shoot up; **picarse de** to boast of being

picardía *f* roguishness, knavery; crudeness, coarseness; mischief

picares·co -ca *adj* roguish, rascally; picaresque; rough, coarse, crude; witty, humorous

píca·ro -ra *adj* roguish; scheming, tricky; low, vile; mischievous ‖ *mf* rogue; schemer

picaza *f* magpie

picazón *f* itch, itching; annoyance

pícea *f* spruce tree

pick-up *m* pickup; phonograph

pico *m* beak, bill; (*de jarra*) spout; (*del yunque*) beak; (*del pañuelo*) corner; nib, tip; (*de la pluma de escribir*) point; peak; (*herramienta*) pick; (*de dinero*) pile, lot; talkativeness; (elec) peak; (naut) bow, prow; **callar el pico** to shut up; **darse el pico** (*las palomas*) to bill; **pico de oro** silver-tongue; **tener mucho pico** to talk too much; **y pico** odd, e.g., **trescientos y pico** three hundred odd; a little after, e.g., **a las tres y pico** a little after three o'clock

picor *m* (*del paladar*) smarting; itch, itching, burning

pico·so -sa *adj* pock-marked

picota *f* pillory; peak, point, spire

picotazo *m* peck

picotear *tr* to peck ‖ *intr* (*el caballo*) to toss the head; chatter, jabber, gab; (*las mujeres*) wrangle

pichel *m* pewter tankard

pichón -chona *mf* darling ‖ *m* young pigeon; **pichón de barro** clay pigeon

pie *m* foot; footing; foothold; base, stand; (*de copa*) stem; (*de la cama*) footboard; cause, origin, reason; (*de la página*) foot, bottom; (theat) cue; (Chile) down payment; **a cuatro pies** on all fours; **al pie de fábrica** at the factory; **al pie de la letra** literally; **al pie de la obra** (com) delivered; **a pie** on foot, walking; **buscar cinco** (or **tres**) **pies al gato** to be looking for trouble; **de pie** standing; up and about; firm, steady; firmly, steadily; **en pie de guerra** on a war footing; **ir a pie** to go on foot, to walk; **morir al pie del cañón** to die in the harness, to die with one's boots on; **nacer de pie** or **de pies** to be born with a silver spoon in one's mouth; **pie de atleta** athlete's foot; **pie de cabra** crowbar; **pie de imprenta** imprint, printer's mark; **pie derecho** upright, stanchion; **pie marino** sea legs; **pie plano** flatfoot; **pie quebrado** (*de verso*) short line; **vestirse por los pies** to be a man

piedad *f* (*devoción a las cosas santas*) piety; (*misericordia*) pity, mercy

piedra *f* stone; rock; (*pedernal*) flint; heavy hailstone; (pathol) stone; **piedra angular** cornerstone; (fig) cornerstone, keystone; **piedra arenisca** sandstone; **piedra azul** (chem) bluestone; **piedra de albardilla** copestone; **piedra de amolar** grindstone; **piedra de chispa** flint; **piedra de pipas** meerschaum; **piedra imán** loadstone; **piedra miliar** or **miliaria** milestone; **piedra movediza** rolling stone; **piedra pómez** pumice, pumice stone

piel *f* skin; hide, pelt; fur; leather; (*de las frutas*) peel, skin; **piel de cabra** goatskin; **piel de foca** sealskin; **piel de gallina** goose flesh ‖ *m* — **piel roja** (*pl* **pieles rojas**) (*indio norteamericano*) redskin

pienso *m* feed, feeding; **ni por pienso** by no means, don't think of it

pierna *f* leg; post, upright; **dormir a pierna suelta** or **tendida** to sleep like a log; **estirar la pierna** to lie down on the job; kick the bucket; **estirar** or **extender las piernas** to stretch one's legs, go for a walk; **ser buena pierna** (Arg, Urug) to be a good-natured fellow

pieza *f* (*órgano de una máquina o artefacto; obra dramática; composición suelta de música; cañón; figura que sirve para jugar a las damas, al ajedrez, etc.; moneda*) piece; (*objeto; mueble; porción de tela*) piece or article; (*habitación, cuarto*) room; **buena pieza** hussy; sly fox; **pieza de recambio** or **de repuesto** spare part; **quedarse en una pieza** or **hecho una pieza** to be dumbfounded, stand motionless

pífano *m* fife; fifer

pifia *f* (billiards) miscue; (coll) miscue, slip

pifiar *intr* to miscue

pigmentar *tr* & *ref* to pigment

pigmento *m* pigment

pigme•o -a *adj* & *mf* pygmy

pijama *f* pajamas

pila *f* basin; trough; sink; font; pile, heap; (elec) battery, cell; (elec & phys) pile; **pila de linterna** flashlight battery

pilar *m* (*de una fuente*) basin, bowl; pillar; stone post, milestone; (*persona*) (fig) pillar ‖ *tr* (*el grano*) to crush, pound

Pilatos *m* Pilate

píldora *f* pill; bad news; **píldora para dormir** sleeping pill

pileta *f* sink; basin, bowl; font; swimming pool

pilón *m* pylon; drinking trough; loaf of sugar; counterpoise; drop hammer; (Mex, Ven) tip, gratuity; **de pilón** in addition, on top of it

pilotar *tr* to pilot

pilote *m* pile

piloto *m* pilot; first mate; (Chile) hail fellow well met

pillar *tr* to pillage, plunder; catch

pi•llo -lla *adj* roguish, rascally; sly, crafty ‖ *m* rogue, rascal; crafty fellow

pilluelo *m* scamp, little scamp

pimentero *m* pepper, black pepper; pepper-box

pimentón *m* cayenne pepper, red pepper; (*condimento preparado moliendo pimientos encarnados secos*) paprika

pimienta *f* pepper, black pepper; allspice, pimento; allspice tree

pimiento *m* (*planta*) pepper, black pepper; Guinea pepper

pimpante *adj* smart, spruce

pimpollo *m* sucker, shoot, sprout; rosebud; (*árbol nuevo*) sapling; handsome child; handsome young person

pina *f* fellow

pinacoteca *f* picture gallery

pináculo *m* pinnacle

pincel *m* brush; painter; painting; (*de luz*) pencil, beam

pincelada *f* brush stroke; touch, finish, flourish

pincelar *tr* to paint; picture; (med) to pencil

pincia•no -na *adj* Valladolid ‖ *mf* native or inhabitant of Valladolid

pincha *f* kitchenmaid

pinchar *tr* to prick, jab, pierce, puncture; stir up, prod, provoke ‖ *intr* to have a puncture; **no pinchar ni cortar** to have no say ‖ *ref* (*drogas*) to get a fix, shoot up

pinchazo *m* prick, jab, puncture; provocation; **a prueba de pinchazos** puncture-proof

pinche *m* scullion, kitchen boy; helper

pincho *m* thorn, prick; snack; spike

Píndaro *m* Pindar

pingajo *m* rag, tatter

pingo *m* rag, tatter; ragamuffin; horse; **andar** or **ir de pingo** (*una mujer*) to gad about

pingüe *adj* oily, greasy, fat; abundant, rich; fertile; profitable

pingüino *m* penguin

pinito *m* first step, little step; **hacer pinitos** to begin to walk; (fig) to take the first steps

pino *m* pine tree; first step; **hacer pinos** to begin to walk; (fig) to take the first steps

pinocha *f* pine needle

pinta *m* scoundrel ‖ *f* spot, mark, sign; dot; pint

pintacilgo *m* goldfinch

pintada *f* Guinea hen

pinta•do -da *adj* spotted, mottled; tipsy; accented; **el más pintado** the aptest one; the shrewdest one; the best one; **venir como pintado** to be just the thing ‖ *m* (*acto de pintar*) painting ‖ *f* see **pintada**

pintar *tr* to paint; (*una letra, un acento, etc.*) draw; picture, depict; put an accent mark on; **pintarla** to put it on, put on airs ‖ *intr* to paint; begin to turn red, begin to ripen; show, turn out ‖ *ref* to paint, put on make-up; begin to turn red, begin to ripen

pintarrajear *tr* to daub, smear

pin•to -ta *adj* speckled, spotted ‖ *f* see **pinta**

pin•tor -tora *mf* painter; **pintor de brocha gorda** painter, house painter; dauber

pintores•co -ca *adj* picturesque

pintura *f* (*color preparado para pintar*) paint; (*arte; obra pintada*) painting; **hacer pinturas** to prance; **no poder ver ni en pintura** to not be able to stand the sight of

pinture•ro -ra *adj* showy, conceited ‖ *mf* show-off

pinza *f* clothespin; (*de langosta, cangrejo, etc.*) claw; **pinzas** pliers; pincers; tweezers; forceps

pinzón *m* pump handle; (orn) finch

piña *f* fir cone, pine cone; knob; plug; cluster, knot; pineapple

piñonear *intr* (*un arma de fuego*) to click; reach the age of puberty; (coll) to be an old goat

piñoneo *m* click (*of a firearm*)

pí•o -a *adj* pious; merciful, compassionate; (*caballo*) pied, dappled ‖ *m* peeping, chirping; keen desire

piocha *f* jeweled head adornment; artificial flower made of feathers; pick

piojo *m* louse

piojo•so -sa *adj* lousy; mean, stingy

piola *f* string, cord

pione•ro -ra *adj* & *mf* pioneer

pipa *f* (*para fumar tabaco*) pipe; (*medida para vinos*) butt; wine cask; (*simiente*) pip; (mus) pipe, reed; (coll) handgun; **pipa de espuma de mar** meerschaum pipe; **pipa de riego** watering cart; **pipa de tierra** clay pipe

pipí *m* (coll) pee, urine; **hacer pipí** to pee, urinate

pipiolo *m* (CAm, Mex) child

pique *m* pique, resentment; eagerness; (*insecto*) chigger; (*naipe*) spade; **a pique** steep; **a pique de** in danger of; on the verge of; **echar a pique** to sink; ruin; **irse a pique** to sink; go to ruin, be ruined

piquera *f* bung, bunghole; (Mex) dive, joint

piquete *m* sharp jab; small hole; stake, picket; (*de soldados, de huelguistas*) picket; **piquete de ejecución** firing squad; **piquete de salvas** firing squad

pira *f* pyre

piragua *f* pirogue; (sport) single shell

piragüismo *m* canoeing

piragüista *m* (sport) crewman

pirámide *f* pyramid

pirata *m* pirate; **pirata aéreo** hijacker

piratear *intr* to pirate, be a pirate

piratería *f* piracy; **piratería aérea** hijacking, skyjacking, air piracy

pirca *f* (SAm) dry stone wall

pirco *m* (Chile) succotash

Pireo, el Piraeus

pirine•o -a *adj* Pyrenean ‖ **Pirineos** *mpl* Pyrenees

pirita *f* pyrites

pirófa•go -ga *adj* fire-eating ‖ *mf* fire-eater

piropear *tr* to flatter, flirt with

piropo *m* garnet, carbuncle; flattery, compliment, flirtatious remark

piróscafo *m* steamship

pirotecnia *f* pyrotechnics

pirotécni•co -ca *adj* pyrotechnical ‖ *m* powder maker, fireworks manufacturer

pirueta *f* pirouette; somersault; caper

piruetear *intr* to pirouette

pisada *f* tread; footstep; footprint; trampling

pisapape•les *m* (*pl* **-les**) paperweight

pisar *tr* to trample, tread on, step on; tamp, pack down; (*p.ej., uvas*) tread; cover part of; ram; (*una tecla*) strike; (mus) to pluck; (coll) to abuse, tread all over; **pisar algo a alguien** to snitch something from someone ‖ *intr* to be right above; step ‖ *ref* (Arg) to guess wrong, come out wrong

pisaverde *m* fop, dandy

piscina *f* swimming pool; fishpond

Piscis *m* (astr) Pisces

pisco *m* Peruvian brandy

pisicorre *f* (W-I) station wagon

piso *m* tread; floor; flooring; (*de una carretera*) surface; flat, apartment; **buscar piso** to be looking for a place to live; **piso alto** top floor; **piso bajo** street floor, ground floor; **piso principal** main floor, second floor

pisón *m* ram, tamper

pisotear *tr* to trample, tread on, tread under foot; abuse, tread all over

pisotón *m* stamp, tread

pista *f* track; trace, trail; clew; race track; (*de bolera*) alley; (*de cabaret*) floor; (aer) runway; **pista de esquí** ski run; **pista de patinar** skating rink

pisto *m* (*para los enfermos*) chicken broth; vegetable cutlet; jumbled speech or writing; mess; (CAm, Mex) money

pistola *f* pistol; sprayer; rock drill; **pistola de arzón** horse pistol; **pistola engrasadora** grease gun

pistolera *f* holster

pistolerismo *m* gangsterism

pistolero *m* gangster, gunman

pistón *m* piston

pistonear *intr* to knock
pistoneo *m* knock
pistonu•do -da *adj* stunning, swank
pita *f* century plant; hiss, hissing; glass marble; string, thread
pitar *tr* to pay, pay off; (*a un torero*) whistle disapproval of ‖ *intr* to blow a whistle, whistle; blow the horn, honk; talk nonsense; **no pitar** to not be popular; **salir pitando** to run away, dash away
pitazo *m* blast, toot, honk, whistle (sound)
pitear *intr* to whistle
pitillera *f* cigarette maker; cigarette case
pitillo *m* cigarette
pito *m* whistle; horn; fife; fifer; cigarette; jackstone; (*insecto*) tick; woodpecker; (coll) continental, straw, tinker's damn
pitón *m* lump, sprig; tenderling; (*del cuerno*) tip; nozzle, spout; python
pitonisa *f* witch, siren; pythoness
pitu•so -sa *adj* tiny, cute ‖ *mf* tot
piular *intr* to peep, chirp
pivotar *intr* to pivot
pivote *m* pivot; **pivote de dirección** (aut) kingpin
píxide *f* pyx
pizarra *f* slate; blackboard
pizarrero *m* roofer, slater
pizarrín *m* slate pencil
pizca *f* mite, whit, jot
placa *f* plaque, tablet; badge; plate; slab, sheet; scab; (anat, elec, electron, phot, zool) plate; **placa de matrícula** license plate; **placa giratoria** (*de ferrocarril; de gramófono*) turntable
placaminero *m* persimmon
placebo *m* placebo
pláceme *m* congratulation
placente•ro -ra *adj* pleasant, agreeable
placer *m* pleasure; sandbank, reef; **a placer** at one's convenience ‖ *v* §52 *tr* to please
place•ro -ra *adj* public ‖ *mf* market vendor; loafer, town gossip
pláci•do -da *adj* placid; pleasing
plaga *f* plague; pest; scourge; abundance; sore; clime, region
plagar §44 *tr* to plague, infest; (*de minas*) sow
plagiar *tr* to plagiarize
plagio *m* plagiarism; abduction, kidnaping
plan *m* plan; level, height; **plan de estudios** or **plan escolar** curriculum
plana *f* plain, flat country; trowel; cooper's plane; page
plancha *f* plate, sheet; iron, flatiron; gangplank; (coll) blunder; **a la plancha** grilled; (*huevo*) fried; **plancha de blindaje** armor plate
planchado *m* ironing; pressing
planchar *tr* (*la ropa interior blanca*) to iron; (*un traje de hombre*) to press ‖ *intr* to be a wallflower
planchear *tr* to plate
planear *tr* to plan, outline; (*una tabla*) plane ‖ *intr* to hover; (aer) to volplane, glide
planeta *m* planet
planicie *f* plain

planificar §73 *tr* to plan
planilla *f* list, roll, schedule; (*de candidatos para un puesto público*) (Mex) panel; (Mex) ballot; (Mex) commutation ticket
pla•no -na *adj* plane; level, smooth, even; flat ‖ *m* plan; map; (*superficie*) plane; (aer) plane; **de plano** clearly, plainly, flatly; flat; **levantar un plano** to make a survey; **primer plano** foreground ‖ *f* see **plana**
planta *f* (*del pie*) sole; foot; plan; project; floor plan; (*del personal de una oficina*) roster; plant, factory; (bot) plant; (sport) stance; **de planta** from the ground up; **echar plantas** to swagger, bully; **planta baja** ground floor; **planta del sortilegio** (bot) witch hazel; **tener buena planta** to make a fine appearance
plantar *tr* to plant; establish, found; (*un golpe*) plant; jilt; (*en la calle, en la cárcel*) throw ‖ *ref* to take a stand; gang together; (*un animal*) balk; land, arrive
plantear *tr* to plan, outline; establish, execute, carry out; state, set up, expound, pose
plantel *m* nursery garden; educational establishment
plantificar §73 *tr* to plan, outline; (*un golpe*) plant; (*en la calle, la cárcel*) throw ‖ *ref* to land, arrive
plantilla *f* plantlet, young plant; insole; reinforced sole; model, pattern, template; (*de empleados*) staff; (*del personal de una oficina*) roster; plan, design; (*bizcocho*) ladyfinger
plantío *m* planting; garden patch; tree nursery
plantón *m* (*que ha de ser transplantado*) shoot; graft; guard, watchman; waiting, standing around
plañide•ro -ra *adj* mournful, plaintive ‖ *f* hired mourner
plañir §12 *tr* to lament, grieve over ‖ *intr* to lament, grieve, bewail
plasma *m* plasma
plasmar *tr* to mold, shape
plasta *f* paste, soft mass; flattened object; poor job, bungle
plástica *f* (*arte de plasmar*) plastic; plastic arts
plásti•co -ca *adj* plastic ‖ *m* (*substancia*) plastic ‖ *f* see **plástica**
plata *f* silver; (*moneda o monedas*) silver; wealth; money; **en plata** briefly, to the point; plainly; **plata de ley** sterling silver
plataforma *f* platform; platform car; (*del ferrocarril*) roadbed; (*programa político*) platform; (*de lanzamiento de cohete*) pad; **plataforma giratoria** (rr) turntable
platal *m* piles of money, fortune
platanal *m* or **platanar** *m* banana plantation
plátano *m* banana; banana tree; plane tree; **plátano de occidente** buttonwood tree
platea *f* (theat) orchestra, parquet
platea•do -da *adj* silvered; silver-plated; (coll) well-to-do
platear *tr* to silver, coat or plate with silver
platero *m* silversmith; jeweler

plática *f* talk, chat; talk, informal lecture; sermon

platicar §73 *tr* to talk over, discuss ‖ *intr* to talk, chat; discuss; preach

platillo *m* plate; saucer; (*de la balanza*) pan; (mus) cymbal; **platillo volador** or **volante** flying saucer

platino *m* platinum

plato *m* dish; plate; (*de una comida*) course; daily fare; **plato fuerte** main course; **plato giratorio** (*del gramófono*) turntable

pla•tó *m* (*pl* **-tós**) (mov) set

Platón *m* Plato

platu•do -da *adj* rich

plausible *adj* praiseworthy; acceptable

playa *f* beach, shore, strand; **playa infantil** sand pile

playera *f* fishwoman; beach shoe

plaza *f* plaza, square; market place; town, city; fortified town; space, room; yard; office, employment; character, reputation; seat; **sentar plaza** to enlist; **plaza de armas** parade ground; public square; **plaza de gallos** cockpit; **plaza de toros** bullring; **plaza mayor** main square

plazo *m* term; time; time limit; date of payment; instalment; **a plazo** on credit, on time; **en plazos** in installments

pleamar *f* high tide, high water

plebe *f* common people

plebe•yo -ya *adj & mf* plebeian

plegadi•zo -za *adj* folding; pliable

plegar §66 *tr* to fold; crease; pleat ‖ *ref* to yield, give in

plegaria *f* prayer; noon call to prayer

pleito *m* litigation, lawsuit; dispute, quarrel; fight; **pleito de acreedores** bankruptcy proceedings; **pleito homenaje** (feud) homage; **pleito viciado** mistrial

plenilunio *m* full moon

plenitud *f* fullness, abundance

ple•no -na *adj* full; **en plena marcha** in full swing; **en pleno rostro** right in the face

pleuresía *f* pleurisy

pliego *m* (*de papel*) sheet; folder; cover, envelope; bid, specification; sealed letter; printer's proof

pliegue *m* fold, crease, pleat; **pliegue de tabla** box pleat

plisar *tr* to pleat

plomada *f* carpenter's lead pencil; plummet; plumb bob; sinker, sinkers; scourge tipped with lead balls

plomar *tr* to seal with lead

plomazo *m* (Guat, Mex, W-I) gunshot

plomería *f* lead roofing; leadwork, plumbing

plomero *m* lead worker; plumber

plomi•zo -za *adj* lead, leaden

plomo *m* lead; (*pedazo de plomo; bala*) lead; (elec) fuse; (coll) bore; **a plomo** plumb, perpendicularly; straight down; just right

pluma *f* feather; quill; plume; pen; faucet; (CAm) hoax; (Chile) crane, derrick; **pluma esferográfica** ball-point pen; **pluma estilográfica** or **pluma fuente** fountain pen

plumaje *m* plumage

plúmbe•o -a *adj* lead

plumero *m* (*caja o vaso para las plumas*) penholder; feather duster

plumífe•ro -ra *adj* (*escritor*) hack, second-rate; (poet) feathered ‖ *m* padded or quilted jacket, ski jacket; hack writer; newshound

plumilla *f* small feather; (*de la pluma fuente*) point, tip; (Ven) ball-point pen

plumón *m* down; feather bed; (Mex) felt-tipped pen

plumo•so -sa *adj* downy, feathery

plural *adj & m* plural

pluriempleo *m* moonlighting

plus *m* extra, bonus

plusmarca *f* (sport) record

plusmarquista *mf* (sport) record breaker

plusvalía *f* appreciation (*in value*)

Plutarco *m* Plutarch

plutonio *m* plutonium

población *f* population; village, town, city

poblada *f* (SAm) riot, mob

pobla•do -da *adj* thick, bushy ‖ *m* town, community ‖ *f* see **poblada**

poblar §61 *tr* to people, populate; found, settle, colonize; (*un estanque, una colmena*) stock; (*con árboles*) plant ‖ *intr* to settle, colonize; multiply, be prolific ‖ *ref* to become full, covered, or crowded

pobre *adj* poor ‖ *mf* pauper; beggar

pobreza *f* poverty, want; poorness

pocilga *f* pigpen

poción *f* potion, dose

po•co -ca *adj & pron* (*comp & super* **menos**) little; few, e.g., **poca gente** few people; **pocos** few; **unos pocos** a few ‖ **poco** *adv* little; **a poco** shortly afterwards; **a poco de** shortly after; **dentro de poco** shortly; **por poco** almost, nearly; **tener en poco** to hold in low esteem, think little of; **un poco (de)** a little

po•cho -cha *adj* faded, discolored; overripe; rotten; (Chile) chubby

podar *tr* to prune, to trim

podenco *m* hound

poder *m* power; power of attorney, proxy; **el cuarto poder** the fourth estate; **obra en mi poder** I have at hand, I have in my possession; **poder adquisitivo** purchasing power ‖ *v* §53 *intr* to be possible; be able, have power or strength; **a más no poder** as hard as possible; **no poder con** to not be able to stand, not be able to manage; **no poder más** to be exhausted, be all in; **no poder menos de** to not be able to keep from, not be able to help ‖ *v aux* to be able to, may, can, might, could; **no poder ver** to not be able to stand

poderhabiente *mf* attorney, proxy

poderío *m* power, might; wealth, riches; sway, dominion

podero•so -sa *adj* powerful, mighty; wealthy, rich

podio *m* podium

podre *f* pus

podredumbre *f* corruption, putrefaction; pus; deep grief

poema *m* poem

poesía f poetry; poem; **bella poesía** (fig) fairy tale

poeta m poet

poéti·co -ca adj poetic(al) ‖ f poetics

poetisa f poetess

pola·co -ca adj Polish ‖ mf Pole ‖ m (idioma) Polish

polaina f legging

polar adj pole; polar ‖ f polestar

polarizar §60 tr to polarize

polea f pulley

poleame m (naut) tackle

polen m pollen

policía m policeman ‖ f police; policing; politeness; cleanliness; neatness; **policía urbana** street cleaning

policía·co -ca or policial adj police; (novela) detective

polifacéti·co -ca adj many-sided

políga·mo -ma adj polygamous ‖ mf polygamist

poliglo·to -ta adj polyglot ‖ mf polyglot, linguist

polígono m polygon

polígrafo m prolific writer; copying machine; ball-point pen; lie detector

polilla f moth

Polimnia f Polyhymnia

polinizar §60 tr to pollinate

polinomio m polynomial

polio f (path) polio

pólipo m polyp

polisón m bustle

polista mf poloist, polo player

politeísta adj polytheistic ‖ mf polytheist

política f politics; policy; manners, politeness, courtesy; **política de café** parlor politics; **política del buen vecino** Good Neighbor Policy

políti·co -ca adj political; politic, tactful; polite, courteous; -in-law; e.g., **padre político** father-in-law ‖ mf politician ‖ f see **política**

polivalente adj manifold; (chem, bact) polyvalent

póliza f policy, contract; draft, check; customhouse permit; **póliza de seguro** insurance policy

polizón m bum, tramp; stowaway

polizonte m cop, policeman

polo m pole; popsicle; (juego) polo; **polo de agua** water polo; **polo de atracción popular** drawing card

pololear tr to bother, annoy; (Chile) to flirt with

polo·lo -la adj (Chile) youngster ‖ m (Chile) flirt; side job

Polonia f Poland

pol·trón -trona adj idle, lazy, comfort-loving ‖ f easy chair

polución f (del ambiente) pollution

polvareda f cloud of dust; rumpus

polvera f compact, powder case

polvo m dust; powder; pinch of snuff; **polvo dentífrico** tooth powder; **polvos** dust; powder; **polvos de la madre Celestina**

hocus-pocus; **polvos de talco** talcum powder

pólvora f powder, gunpowder; fireworks; (persona avispada) live wire; **correr como pólvera en reguero** to spread like wildfire

polvorear tr to dust, sprinkle with dust or powder

polvorien·to -ta adj dusty; powdery

polvorín m powder magazine; powder flask; (insecto) tick; (Chile) spitfire

polvoro·so -sa adj dusty; **poner pies en polvorosa** to take to one's heels

polla f pullet; (puesta en juegos de naipes) stake, kitty; (coll) lassie

pollera f poultry woman; chicken coop; poultry yard; go-cart; (Arg, Chile) skirt

pollero m poulterer; poultry yard

polli·no -na mf donkey, ass

polli·to -ta mf chick; (persona joven) chick, chicken

pollo m chicken; (persona joven) chicken

pomada f pomade

pómez f pumice stone

pomo m pome; (de la guarnición de la espada) pommel; (bola aromática) pomander; (frasco para perfume) flacon; **pomo de puerta** doorknob

pompa f pomp; soap bubble; swell, bulge; (de la ropa) billowing, ballooning; (de las alas del pavo real) spread; (naut) pump; **pompa fúnebre** funeral

pompis m behind, butt, rear end

pompo·so -sa adj pompous; high-flown, highfalutin

pómulo m cheekbone

ponche m (bebida) punch; **ponche de huevo** eggnog

ponchera f punch bowl

pon·cho -cha adj lazy, careless, easy-going; (Col) chubby ‖ m poncho; greatcoat

ponderar tr to weigh; ponder, ponder over; exaggerate; praise to the skies; balance; weight

ponencia f paper, report

poner §54 tr to put, place, lay, set; arrange, dispose; (una observación) put in; (una pieza dramática) put on; (la mesa) set; assume, suppose; (una ley, un impuesto) impose; wager, stake; (huevos) lay; (por escrito) set down, put down; (tiempo) take; (p.ej., miedo) cause; make, turn; (la luz, la radio) turn on; (marcha directa) (aut) to go in; **poner en acción** to set in motion; **poner en limpio** to make a clean copy of; **poner por encima** to prefer, put ahead ‖ ref to put or place oneself; become, get, turn; (el sol, los astros) set; (sombrero, saco, etc.) put on; dress, dress up; get spotted; get, reach, arrive; **ponerse a** to set out to, begin to; **ponerse tan alto** to take offense, become hoity-toity

poniente m west; west wind

ponqué m poundcake

pontífice m pontiff

pontón m pontoon; pontoon bridge; (buque viejo) hulk

ponzoña f poison

ponzoño•so -sa *adj* poisonous

popa *f* poop, stern

popote *m* (Mex) straw for brooms; (*para tomar refrescos*) (Mex) straw

populache•ro -ra *adj* popular; cheap, vulgar; rabble-rousing ‖ *mf* rabble-rouser

populacho *m* populace, mob, rabble

popular *adj* popular

popularizar §60 *tr* to popularize

populo•so -sa *adj* populous

popu•rrí *m* (*pl* **-rríes**) medley

poquedad *f* paucity, scantiness; scarcity; timidity; trifle

poqui•to -ta *adj* very little; timid, shy, backward

por *prep* by; through, over; via, by way of; in, e.g., **por la mañana** in the morning; for; because of; for the sake of; on account of; in exchange for; in order to; as; about, e.g., **por Navidad** about Christmastime; out of, e.g., **por ignorancia** out of ignorance; times, e.g., **tres por cuatro** four times three; **estar por** to be on the point of, be ready to; be still to be, e.g., **la carta está por escribir** the letter is still to be written; **ir por** to go for, to go after; to follow; **por ciento** per cent; **por entre** among, between; **por que** because; in order that; **por qué** why; **por** + *adj* or *adv* + **que** however

porcelana *f* porcelain, chinaware; (*usado por los plateros*) enamel; (Mex) washbowl

porcentaje *m* percentage

porción *f* portion

porche *m* porch, portico

pordiosear *intr* to beg, go begging

pordiose•ro -ra *mf* beggar

porfía *f* persistence, stubbornness, obstinacy; **a porfía** in emulation; insistently

porfia•do -da *adj* persistent, stubborn, obstinate; opinionated

porfiar §77 *intr* to persist; argue stubbornly

pórfido *m* porphyry

pormenor *m* detail, particular

pormenorizar §60 *tr* to detail, tell in detail; to itemize

poro *m* pore

poro•so -sa *adj* porous

poroto *m* (SAm) bean, string bean; (Chile) little runt

porque *conj* because; in order that

porqué *m* why; quantity, share; wherewithal, money

porquería *f* dirt, filth; trifle; crudity; (*alimento dañoso a la salud*) junk

porra *f* club, bludgeon; bore, nuisance; boasting; (*pelos enredados*) (Arg, Bol) knot, tangle; (Mex) claque

porrazo *m* clubbing; blow, bump, thump

porro *m* (*mariguana*) joint

porta *f* porthole

portaavio•nes *m* (*pl* **-nes**) aircraft carrier, flattop

portacandado *m* hasp

portada *f* front, façade; portal; title page; (*de una revista*) cover; **falsa portada** half title

portadis•cos *m* (*pl* **-cos**) turntable

porta•dor -dora *adj* (*onda*) (rad) carrier ‖ *mf* bearer; carrier ‖ *m* waiter's tray

portaequipaje *m* (aut) trunk

portaequipa•jes *m* (*pl* **-jes**) baggage rack

portaguan•tes *m* (*pl* **-tes**) (aut) glove compartment

portal *m* vestibule, entrance hall; porch, portico; arcade; city gate; (*de un túnel*) portal *m*; crèche

portalámpa•ras *m* (*pl* **-ras**) (elec) socket

portalón *m* gate, portal; (*en el costado del buque*) gangway

portamira *m* (surv) rodman

portamone•das *m* (*pl* **-das**) pocketbook

portanue•vas *mf* (*pl* **-vas**) newsmonger

portañuela *f* (*de los pantalones*) fly; (Col, Mex) carriage door

portapape•les *m* (*pl* **-les**) brief case

portaplu•mas *m* (*pl* **-mas**) penholder

portar *tr* to carry, bear; (hunt) to retrieve ‖ *ref* to behave, conduct oneself

portase•nos *m* (*pl* **-nos**) brassiere

portátil *adj* portable

portatinte•ro *m* inkstand

portavian•das *m* (*pl* **-das**) dinner pail

porta•voz *m* (*pl* **-voces**) megaphone; mouthpiece, spokesperson

portazgo *m* toll, road toll

portazo *m* bang, slam

porte *m* portage; carrying charge, freight; postage; behavior, conduct; dress, bearing; size, capacity; (Chile) birthday present; **porte concertado** mailing permit; **porte pagado** postage prepaid, freight prepaid

portear *tr* to carry, transport ‖ *intr* to slam ‖ *ref* (*las aves*) to migrate

portento *m* prodigy, wonder

portento•so -sa *adj* portentous, extraordinary

porte•ño -ña *adj* Buenos Aires; Valparaiso; pertaining to any large South American city with a port ‖ *mf* native or inhabitant of Buenos Aires, Valparaiso or any large South American city with a port

porte•ro -ra *mf* doorkeeper; gatekeeper; (sport) goalkeeper ‖ *m* porter, janitor; doorman; **portero electrónico** automatic door opener ‖ *f* portress, janitress

portezuela *f* small door; (*de un coche o automóvil*) door; pocket flap

pórtico *m* portico, porch; little gate

portilla *f* porthole; private cart road, private cattle pass

portillo *m* gap, opening; nick, notch; (*puerta chica en otra mayor*) wicket; gate; narrow pass; side entrance

portorrique•ño -ña *adj* & *mf* Puerto Rican

portua•rio -ria *adj* port, harbor, dock ‖ *m* dock hand, dock worker

Portugal *m* Portugal

portu•gués -guesa *adj* & *mf* Portuguese

porvenir *m* future

pos — **en pos de** after, behind; in pursuit of

posa *f* knell, toll

posada *f* inn, wayside inn; lodging; boardinghouse; home, dwelling; camp; **posadas** (Mex) pre-Christmas celebration

po
po

posade•ro -ra *mf* innkeeper; **posaderas** buttocks
posar *tr* to put down ‖ *intr* to put up, lodge; alight, perch; pose ‖ *ref* to alight, perch; settle; rest
posbéli•co -ca *adj* postwar
posdata *f* postscript
pose *f* pose; (phot) exposure
poseer §43 *tr* to own, possess, hold; have a mastery of ‖ *ref* to control oneself
posesión *f* possession; **tomar posesión** (*un cargo*) to take up
posesionar *tr* to give possession to ‖ *ref* to take possession
posesor *m* owner
poseta *f* (Ven) toilet, washroom
posfecha *f* postdate
posguerra *f* postwar period
posible *adj* possible; **hacer todo lo posible** to do one's best ‖ **posibles** *mpl* means, income, property
posición *f* position; standing
positi•vo -va *adj* positive ‖ *f* (phot) print, positive
poso *m* sediment, dregs; grounds; rest, quiet; **poso del café** coffee grounds
posponer §54 *tr* to subordinate; think less of
posta *f* (*de caballos*) relay; posthouse; stage; stake, wager; slice; **a posta** on purpose; **por la posta** posthaste; **postas** buckshot
postal *adj* postal ‖ *f* post card; **postal ilustrada** picture post card
poste *m* post, pillar, pole; **poste de alumbrado** or **de farol** lamppost; **poste de telégrafo** telegraph pole; (*persona muy alta y delgada*) beanpole; **poste indicador** road sign
póster *m* poster
postergar §44 *tr* to delay, postpone; pass over
posteridad *f* posterity; posthumous fame
posterior *adj* back, rear; later, subsequent
postigo *m* (*puerta chica en otra mayor*) wicket; (*puertecilla en una ventana*) peep window; (*puerta excusada*) postern; shutter
posti•zo -za *adj* false, artificial; (*cuello*) detachable ‖ *m* switch, false hair, rat
postóni•co -ca *adj* posttonic
postor *m* bidder; **el mejor postor** the highest bidder
postración *f* prostration
postrar *tr* to prostrate; weaken, exhaust ‖ *ref* to collapse, be prostrated; prostrate oneself
postre *adj* last, final; **a la postre** at last; afterwards ‖ *m* dessert; **postres** dessert
postulación *f* postulation; nomination
postulante *mf* applicant, candidate
póstu•mo -ma *adj* posthumous
postura *f* posture; attitude, stand; stake, wager; agreement, pact; egg, eggs; (*de huevos*) laying; **postura del sol** sunset
potabilizar §60 *tr* to make drinkable
potable *adj* drinkable
potaje *m* pottage; jumble; (*bebida*) mixture; scheme; **potajes** vegetables
potasa *f* potash
potasio *m* potassium

pote *m* pot, jug; flowerpot; **a pote** in abundance
potencia *f* potency; power; **potencia de choque** striking power
potenciación *f* (math) involution
potencial *adj* & *m* potential
potenciar *tr* (*las aguas de un río; el entusiasmo de una persona*) to harness; (*elevar a una potencia*) (math) to raise
potentado *m* potentate
potente *adj* powerful; big, huge
potestad *f* power
potista *mf* toper, soak
potosí *m* great wealth, gold mine
potra *f* filly; hernia, rupture
potranca *f* young mare
potro *m* colt; pest, annoyance
pozal *m* bucket, pail
pozo *m* well; pit; whirlpool; (min) shaft; (naut) hold; (Chile, Col) pool, puddle; (Ecuad) spring, fountain; **pozo de ciencia** fountain of knowledge; **pozo de lanzamiento** launching silo; **pozo de lobo** (mil) foxhole; **pozo negro** cesspool
P.P. *abbr* **porte pagado, por poder**
p.p.^{do} *abbr* **próximo pasado**
práctica *f* practice; method; skill; **prácticas** studies, training
prácticamente *adv* through practice, by experience
practicar §73 *tr* to practice; bring about; (*un agujero*) make, cut
prácti•co -ca *adj* practical; skillful, practiced; practicing ‖ *m* medical practitioner; (naut) pilot ‖ *f* see **práctica**
pradera *f* meadowland; prairie
prado *m* meadow, pasture; promenade
Praga *f* Prague
pral. *abbr* **principal**
pralte. *abbr* **principalmente**
prángana — **estar en la prángana** (Mex, W-I) to be broke; (P-R) to be naked
preámbulo *m* preamble; evasion; **no andarse en preámbulos** to come to the point
prebéli•co -ca *adj* prewar
prebenda *f* prebend; sinecure
preca•rio -ria *adj* precarious
precaución *f* precaution
precaver *tr* to stave off, head off ‖ *intr* & *ref* to be on one's guard; **precaverse contra** or **de** to guard against
precavido -da *adj* cautious
precedente *adj* preceding ‖ *m* precedent
preceder *tr* & *intr* to precede
precepto *m* precept; order, injunction; **los preceptos** the Ten Commandments
preces *fpl* devotions; supplications
precia•do -da *adj* esteemed, valued; precious, valuable; boastful, proud
preciar *tr* to appraise, estimate ‖ *ref* to boast
precintar *tr* to bind, strap; seal
precio *m* price; value, worth; esteem, credit; **a precio de quemazón** at a giveaway price; **precios de cierre** closing prices; **precio tope** ceiling price
preciosidad *f* preciousness; beauty, gem, jewel

precio•so -sa *adj* precious; valuable; witty; beautiful

preciosura *f* beauty; pretty woman

precipicio *m* precipice; destruction

precipitación *f* precipitation; **precipitación acuosa** rainfall; **precipitación radiactiva** fallout

precipitar *tr* to precipitate; rush, hurl, throw headlong ‖ *ref* to rush, throw oneself headlong

precipito•so -sa *adj* precipitous, rash, reckless; risky,·dangerous

precisar *tr* to state precisely, specify; fix; need; oblige, force; determine ‖ *intr* to be necessary; be important; be urgent; **precisar de** to need

precisión *f* precision; necessity, obligation; (Chile) haste; **precisiones** data

preci•so -sa *adj* necessary; precise; (Ven) haughty

precita•do -da *adj* above-mentioned

precla•ro -ra *adj* illustrious, famous

preconizar §60 *tr* to proclaim, commend publicly

pre•coz *adj* (*pl* -coces) precocious

predato•rio -ria *adj* predatory

predecir §24 *tr* to predict, foretell

prédica *f* Protestant sermon; harangue

predicar §73 *tr* to preach; praise to the skies; scold, preach to

predicción *f* prediction; **predicción del tiempo** weather forecasting

predilec•to -ta *adj* favorite, preferred

predio *m* property, estate

predisponer §54 *tr* to predispose

predominante *adj* predominant

preeminente *adj* preëminent

preestreno *m* (mov) preview

prefabricar §73 *tr* to prefabricate

prefacio *m* preface

preferencia *f* preference; **de preferencia** preferably

preferente *adj* preferable; favored; (*acciones*) preferred

preferible *adj* preferable

preferir §68 *tr* to prefer

prefigurar *tr* to foreshadow

prefijar *tr* to prefix; prearrange

prefijo *m* prefix

pregón *m* proclamation, public announcement (*by town crier*)

pregonar *tr* to proclaim, announce publicly; hawk; reveal; outlaw; praise openly

pregonero *m* auctioneer; town crier

preguerra *f* prewar period

pregunta *f* question; **hacer una pregunta** to ask a question

preguntar *tr* to ask; to question ‖ *intr* to ask, inquire; **preguntar por** to ask after or for ‖ *ref* to ask oneself; wonder

pregun•tón -tona *adj* inquisitive ‖ *mf* inquisitive person

prejudicio *m* or **prejuicio** *m* prejudgment; prejudice

prelado *m* prelate

preliminar *adj* & *m* preliminary; **preliminares** (*de un libro*) front matter

preludio *m* prelude

premeditar *tr* to premeditate

premiar *tr* to reward; give an award to

premio *m* reward, prize; premium; **a premio** at a premium; **premio de enganche** (mil) bounty; **premio gordo** first prize

premio•so -sa *adj* tight, close; bothersome; strict, rigid; slow, dull

premisa *f* premise; mark, token, clue

premura *f* pressure, haste, urgency

premuro•so -sa *adj* pressing, urgent

prenda *f* pledge; security; pawn; jewel, household article; garment, article of clothing; gift, talent; darling, loved one; **en prenda** in pawn; **en prenda de** as a pledge of; **prenda perdida** forfeit; **prendas** (*juego*) forfeits; **prendas interiores** underwear

prendar *tr* to pawn; pledge; charm, captivate ‖ *ref* — **prendarse de** to take a liking for, fall in love with

prendedero *m* or **prendedor** *m* fillet, brooch; stickpin

prender *tr* to seize, grasp; catch; imprison; dress up; pin; fasten ‖ *intr* to catch; catch fire; take root; turn out well ‖ *ref* to dress up; be fastened; catch hold

prendería *f* second-hand shop

prende•ro -ra *mf* second-hand dealer

prenombra•do -da *adj* above-mentioned; foregoing

prensa *f* press; printing press; vise; press, newspapers; press, frame; **entrar en prensa** to go to press; **meter en prensa** to put the squeeze on; **prensa amarilla** yellow press; **prensa taladradora** drill press

prensado *m* pressing; (*lustre de los tejidos prensados*) sheen

prensador *m* (CAm) paper clip

prensar *tr* to press; squeeze

preña•do -da *adj* pregnant; sagging, bulging; full, charged

preñez *f* pregnancy; fullness; impending danger; inherent confusion

preocupación *f* (*posesión anticipada; cuidado, desvelo*) preoccupation; (*posesión anticipada*) preoccupancy; bias, prejudice

preocupar *tr* to preoccupy, worry ‖ *ref* to become preoccupied, be worried

preparación *f* preparation

prepara•do -da *adj* ready, prepared ‖ *m* (pharm) preparation

preparar *tr* to prepare ‖ *ref* to prepare, get ready

preparati•vo -va *adj* preparatory ‖ *m* preparation, readiness

preponderante *adj* preponderant

preposición *f* preposition

prepóste•ro -ra *adj* reversed, upset, out of order, inopportune

prerrogativa *f* prerogative

presa *f* capture, seizure; catch, prey; booty; spoils; dam; trench, ditch, flume; bit, morsel; fang, tusk, claw; fishweir; (sport) hold; **hacer presa** to seize; **ser presa de** to be a victim of; be prey to

presagiar *tr* to presage, forebode

po
pr

presagio *m* presage, omen, token
présbita or **présbite** *adj* far-sighted ‖ *mf* far-sighted person
presbiteria•no -na *adj & mf* Presbyterian
prescindir *intr* — **prescindir de** to leave aside, leave out, disregard; do without, dispense with; avoid
prescribir §83 *tr & intr* to prescribe
presencia *f* presence; show, display; **presencia de ánimo** presence of mind
presenciar *tr* to witness, be present at
presentación *f* presentation; (*de una persona en el trato de otra u otras*) introduction; (*de un nuevo automóvil, libro, etc.*) appearance
presentador *m* or **presentadora** *f* (telv) moderator
presentar *tr* to present; introduce ‖ *ref* to present oneself; appear, show up; introduce oneself
presente *adj* present; **hacer presente** to notify of, remind of; **tener presente** to bear or keep in mind ‖ *interj* here!, present! ‖ *m* present, gift; person present
presentimiento *m* presentiment, premonition
presentir §68 *tr* to have a presentiment of
preservar *tr* to preserve, protect
preservati•vo -va *adj & m* preventive; preservative
presidencia *f* presidency; chairmanship
presidente *m* president; chairman; presiding judge
presidiario *m* convict
presidio *m* garrison; fortress; citadel; penitentiary; imprisonment; hard labor; aid, help
presidir *tr* to preside over; dominate ‖ *intr* to preside
presilla *f* loop, fastener; clip; paper clip; shoulder strap
presión *f* pressure; (*cerveza*) **a presión** on draught; **presión de inflado** tire pressure
presionar *tr* to press; put pressure on ‖ *intr* to press; **presionar sobre** to put pressure on
pre•so -sa *adj* seized; imprisoned ‖ *mf* prisoner; convict; **preso preventivo** pretrial prisoner; *f* see **presa**
presta•do -da *adj* lent, loaned; **dar prestado** to lend; **pedir** or **tomar prestado** to borrow
prestamista *mf* moneylender; pawnbroker
préstamo *m* loan; **préstamo lingüístico** loan word, borrowing
prestar *tr* to lend, loan; (*oído; ayuda; noticias*) give; (*atención*) pay; (*un favor*) do; (*un servicio*) render; (*juramento*) take; (*silencio*) keep; (*paciencia*) show ‖ *intr* (*un paño, la ropa*) give, yield; be useful ‖ *ref* to lend oneself, lend itself
prestata•rio -ria *mf* borrower
presteza *f* speed, promptness, readiness
prestidigitación *f* sleight of hand
prestidigita•dor -dora *adj* captivating ‖ *mf* magician; faker, impostor
prestigio *m* prestige; good standing; spell; illusion
prestigio•so -sa *adj* captivating, spellbinding; famous, renowned; illusory

pres•to -ta *adj* quick, prompt, ready; nimble ‖ **presto** *adv* right away
presumi•do -da *adj* conceited, vain ‖ *mf* would-be
presumir *tr* to presume ‖ *intr* to boast, be conceited
presunción *f* presumption; conceit
presuntuo•so -sa *adj* conceited, vain
presuponer §54 *tr* to presuppose; budget
presupuestar *tr* to budget; (*el coste de una obra*) estimate
presupuesto *m* budget; reason, motive; supposition; estimate
presuro•so -sa *adj* speedy, quick, hasty; zealous, persistent
pretencio•so -sa *adj* pretentious, showy; conceited, vain
pretender *tr* to claim, pretend to; try for, try to do; be a suitor for ‖ *intr* to insist; **pretender + *inf*** to try to + *inf*
pretendiente *mf* pretender, claimant; office seeker ‖ *m* suitor
pretensión *f* pretension; claim; pretense; presumption; effort, pursuit
pretéri•to -ta *adj & m* past
pretil *m* parapet, railing; walk along a parapet
pretina *f* girdle, belt; waistband
pretóni•co -ca *adj* pretonic
prevalecer §22 *intr* to prevail; take root; thrive
prevaler §76 *ref* — **prevalerse de** to avail oneself of, take advantage of
prevaricar §73 *intr* to collude, connive; play false; transgress; rave, be delirious
prevención *f* preparation; prevention; foresight; warning; prejudice; stock, supply; jail, lockup; guardhouse; **a** or **de prevención** spare, emergency
preveni•do -da *adj* prepared, ready; foresighted, forewarned; stocked, full
prevenir §79 *tr* to prepare, make ready; forestall, prevent, anticipate; overcome; warn; prejudice ‖ *intr* (*una tempestad*) to come up ‖ *ref* to get ready; come to mind
prever §80 *tr* to foresee
pre•vio -via *adj* previous; preliminary; after, with previous, subject to, e.g., **previo acuerdo** subject to agreement; **cita previa** by appointment
previsión *f* prevision, foresight; foresightedness; forecast; **previsión del tiempo** weather forecasting
prie•to -ta *adj* dark, blackish; stingy, mean; tight, compact; dark-complexioned ‖ *mf* (W-I) darling
prima *f* early morning; bonus, bounty; (ins) premium; (mil) first quarter of the night; (*cuerda*) (mus) treble
pri•mal -mala *adj & mf* yearling
prima•rio -ria *adj* primary ‖ *m* (elec) primary
primavera *f* spring, springtime; cowslip, primrose; robin
primer *adj* apocopated form of **primero,** used only before masculine singular nouns and adjectives

prime•ro -ra *adj* first; former; early; primary; prime; (*materia*) raw ‖ *m* first; **a primeros de** around the beginning of ‖ **primero** *adv* first

primicia *f* first fruits

primige•nio -nia *adj* original, primitive

primiti•vo -va *adj* primitive

pri•mo -ma *adj* first; prime, excellent; skillful; (*materia*) raw ‖ *mf* cousin; sucker, dupe; **primo carnal** or **primo hermano** first cousin, cousin-german ‖ *f* see **prima** ‖ **primo** *adv* in the first place

primogéni•to -ta *adj & mf* first-born

primor *m* care, skill, elegance; beauty

primoro•so -sa *adj* careful, skillful, elegant; fine, exquisite

princesa *f* princess; **princesa viuda** dowager princess

principal *adj* principal, main, chief; first, foremost; essential, important; famous, illustrious; (*piso*) second ‖ *m* principal, head, chief

príncipe *m* prince; **portarse como un príncipe** to live like a prince; **príncipe de Asturias** heir apparent of the King of Spain; **príncipe de Gales** prince of Wales; **príncipes** prince and princess

principiante *adj* beginning ‖ *mf* beginner, apprentice, novice

principiar *tr, intr & ref* to begin

principio *m* start, beginning; principle; origin, source; (culin) entree; **a principios de** around the beginning of; **en un principio** at the beginning; **principio de admiración** inverted exclamation point; **principio de interrogación** inverted question mark

pringar §44 *tr* to dip or soak in grease or fat; spot or stain with grease; make bleed; slander, run down; splash ‖ *intr* to meddle; (CAm, Mex) to drizzle ‖ *ref* to peculate

pringo•so -sa *adj* greasy, fatty

prioridad *f* priority; **de máxima prioridad** of the highest priority

prisa *f* hurry, haste; urgency; crush, crowd; **darse prisa** to hurry, make haste; **estar de prisa** or **tener prisa** to be in a hurry

prisión *f* seizure, capture; imprisonment; prison; **prisión celular** cell house; **prisiones** shackles, fetters

prisione•ro -ra *mf* prisoner; (*cautivo de una pasión o afecto*) captive ‖ *m* setscrew; studbolt

prisma *m* prism

prismáticos *mpl* binoculars

priva•do -da *adj* private ‖ *m* (*de un alto personaje*) favorite ‖ *f* cesspool

privar *tr* to deprive; forbid, prohibit ‖ *intr* to be in vogue; prevail; be in favor ‖ *ref* to deprive oneself; **privarse de** to give up

privilegiar *tr* to grant a privilege to

privilegio *m* privilege

pro *m & f* profit, advantage; **¡buena pro!** good appetite!; **de pro** of note, of worth; **el pro y el contra** the pros and the cons; **en pro de** on behalf of

proa *f* (aer) nose; (naut) prow

probable *adj* probable, likely

probador *m* fitting room

probar §61 *tr* to prove; test; try; (*clothing*) try on; try out; sample; fit; suit; (*vino*) touch ‖ *intr* to taste; **probar de** to take a taste of ‖ *ref* to try on

probidad *f* probity, integrity, honesty

problema *m* problem

pro•caz *adj* (*pl* **-caces**) impudent, insolent, bold

procedencia *f* origin, source; point of departure

procedente *adj* coming, originating; proper

proceder *m* conduct, behavior ‖ *intr* to proceed; originate; behave; be proper

procedimiento *m* procedure; proceeding; process

procelo•so -sa *adj* tempestuous, stormy

prócer *adj* high, lofty ‖ *m* hero, leader

procesamiento *m* (data) processing

procesar *tr* to sue, prosecute; indict; try; (*ordenador*) to process, data-process

procesión *f* procession; origin, emergence

proceso *m* process; progress; suit, lawsuit; **proceso verbal** minutes

proclama *f* proclamation; marriage banns

proclamar *tr* to proclaim; acclaim

proclíti•co -ca *adj & m* proclitic

procurador *m* attorney, solicitor; proxy

procurar *tr* to strive for; manage as attorney; yield, produce; try to

prodigar §44 *tr* to lavish; squander; waste ‖ *ref* to be a show-off

prodigio *m* prodigy

prodigio•so -sa *adj* prodigious, marvelous; fine, excellent

pródigo -ga *adj* prodigal; lavish ‖ *mf* prodigal

producción *f* production; crop, yield, produce; **producción en masa** or **en serie** mass production

producir §19 *tr* to produce; yield, bear; cause, bring about ‖ *ref* to explain oneself; come about; take place

producto *m* product; produce; proceeds

proeza *f* prowess; feat, stunt

prof. *abbr* **profeta**

profanar *tr* to profane

profa•no -na *adj* profane; indecent, immodest; worldly; lay ‖ *mf* profane; worldly person; layman

profecía *f* prophecy ‖ **las Profecías** (Bib) the Prophets

proferir §68 *tr* to utter

profesar *tr & intr* to profess

profesión *f* profession; **profesión de fe** confession of faith

profe•sor -sora *mf* teacher; professor

profeta *m* prophet

profetisa *f* prophetess

profetizar §60 *tr* to prophesy

profilácti•co -ca *adj & m* prophylactic; preventive ‖ *f* hygiene

prófu•go -ga *adj & mf* fugitive ‖ *m* slacker, draft dodger

profundidad *f* profundity; depth

profundizar §60 *tr* to deepen; fathom, get to the bottom of

pr
pr

profun•do -da *adj* profound; deep
progenie *f* descent, lineage, parentage
progno•sis *f* (*pl* **-sis**) prognosis; (*del tiempo*) forecast
programa *m* program; **programa continuo** (mov) continuous showing; **programa de estudios** curriculum; **programa (para ordenador)** program(me), software
programación *f* (*ordenador*) program(m)ing; (telv) scheduling
programador *m* or **programadora** *f* (*ordenador*) program(m)er
programar *tr* to program; (*ordenador*) program(me)
progresar *intr* to progress
progresista *adj & mf* (pol) progressive
progreso *m* progress; **hacer progresos** to make progress
prohibir *tr* to prohibit, forbid ‖ *ref* **se prohibe fijar carteles** post no bills
prohijar *tr* to adopt
prohombre *m* (*en los gremios de los artesanos*) master; leader, head; (coll) big shot
prójimo *m* fellow man, fellow creature, neighbor; fellow
pról. *abbr* **prólogo**
prole *f* progeny, offspring
proletariado *m* proletariat
proleta•rio -ria *adj & m* proletarian
proliferar *intr* to proliferate
prolífi•co -ca *adj* prolific
proli•jo -ja *adj* tedious, too long; fussy, fastidious; long-winded; tiresome
prologar §44 *tr* to preface, write a preface for
prólogo *m* prologue; preface
prolongar §44 *tr* to prolong, extend; (geom) to produce
promediar *tr* to divide into two equal parts; average ‖ *intr* to mediate; be half over
promedio *m* average, mean; middle
promesa *f* promise
promete•dor -dora *adj* promising
prometer *tr & intr* to promise ‖ *ref* to become engaged
prometi•do -da *adj* engaged, betrothed ‖ *m* promise; fiancé ‖ *f* fiancée
prominente *adj* prominent
promiso•rio -ria *adj* promissory
promoción *f* promotion; advancement; (*conjunto de individuos que obtienen un grado en un mismo año*) class, year, crop
promontorio *m* promontory, headland; unwieldy thing
promover §47 *tr* to promote; advance, further
promulgar §44 *tr* to promulgate
pronombre *m* pronoun
pronosticar §73 *tr* to prognosticate, foretell
pronóstico *m* prognostic, forecast; almanac; (med) prognosis
pron•to -ta *adj* quick, speedy; prompt; ready ‖ *m* jerk; sudden impulse, fit of anger ‖ **pronto** *adv* right away, soon; early; promptly; **lo más pronto posible** as soon as possible; **tan pronto como** as soon as
pronunciación *f* pronunciation

pronuncia•do -da *adj* marked; (*curva*) sharp; (*pendiente*) steep; bulky
pronunciamiento *m* insurrection, uprising; (*golpe de estado militar*) pronunciamento; (law) decree
pronunciar *tr* to pronounce; utter; (*un discurso*) make, deliver; decide on ‖ *ref* to rebel; declare oneself
propaganda *f* propaganda; advertising
propagar §44 *tr* to propagate; spread; broadcast
propalar *tr* to divulge, spread
proparoxíto•no -na *adj & m* proparoxytone
propasar *ref* to go too far, take undue liberty
propender *intr* to tend, incline, be inclined
propensión *f* propensity; predisposition
propen•so -sa *adj* inclined, disposed, prone
propiciar *tr* to propitiate; support, favor, sponsor
propi•cio -cia *adj* propitious, favorable
propiedad *f* property; ownership; naturalness, likeness; **es propiedad** copyrighted; **propiedad horizontal** one-floor ownership in an apartment house; **propiedad literaria** copyright
propieta•rio -ria *mf* owner ‖ *m* proprietor ‖ *f* proprietress
propina *f* tip, fee, gratuity
propinar *tr* (*algo a beber*) to offer; (*medicamentos*) prescribe or administer; (*palos, golpes, etc.*) give ‖ *ref* (*una bebida*) to treat oneself to
propin•cuo -cua *adj* near, close at hand
pro•pio -pia *adj* proper, suitable; peculiar, characteristic; natural; same; himself, herself, etc.; own ‖ *m* messenger; native; **propios** public lands
proponer §54 *tr* to propose; propound; (*a una persona para un empleo*) name, present ‖ *ref* to plan; propose
proporción *f* proportion; opportunity
proporciona•do -da *adj* proportionate; fit, suitable
proporcionar *tr* to furnish, provide, supply; give; proportion; adapt, adjust
proposición *f* proposition; **proposición dominante** main clause
propósito *m* aim, purpose, intention; subject matter; **a propósito** by the way; apropos, fitting; in place; **a propósito de** apropos of; **de propósito** on purpose; **fuera de propósito** irrelevant, beside the point
propuesta *f* proposal, proposition
propulsar *tr* to propel, drive
propulsión *f* propulsion; **propulsión a chorro** jet propulsion; **propulsión a cohete** rocket propulsion
pror. *abbr* **procurador**
prorratear *tr* to prorate
prórroga *f* extension, renewal
prorrogar §44 *tr* to defer, postpone; extend
prorrumpir *intr* to spurt, shoot forth; break forth, burst out
prosa *f* prose; chatter, idle talk
prosai•co -ca *adj* prose; prosaic, dull
proscribir §83 *tr* to outlaw, proscribe
proscrip•to -ta *mf* exile, outlaw

prosecución *f* continuation, prosecution; pursuit

proseguir §67 *tr* to continue, carry on ‖ *intr* to continue

prosélito *m* proselyte

prosista *mf* prose writer; chatterbox

prosódi•co -ca *adj (acento)* stress

prospectar *tr & intr* to prospect

prosperar *tr* to make prosper ‖ *intr* to prosper, thrive

prosperidad prosperity

próspe•ro -ra *adj* prosperous, thriving, successful

prosternar *ref* to prostrate oneself

prostituir §20 *tr* to prostitute ‖ *ref* to prostitute oneself; become a prostitute

prostituta *f* prostitute

prosu•do -da *adj* (Chile, Ecuad, Peru) pompous, solemn

protagonista *mf* protagonist

protagonizar §60 *tr* to play the leading rôle of

protección *f* protection; **protección aduanera** protective tariff; **protección a la infancia** child welfare

proteger §17 *tr* to protect

protegida *f* protégée

protegido *m* protégé

proteína *f* protein

proter•vo -va *adj* perverse

protesta *f* protest; pledge, promise

protestante *adj & mf* protestant; Protestant

protestar *tr* to protest, asseverate; *(la fe)* profess ‖ *intr* to protest; **protestar de** *(aseverar con ahinco)* to protest *(to state positively)*; **protestar contra** *(negar la validez de)* to protest *(to deny forcibly)*

protocolo *m* protocol

protoplasma *m* protoplasm

prototipo *m* prototype

protozoario *m* or **protozoo** *m* protozoön

provec•to -ta *adj* old, ripe

provecho *m* advantage, benefit; profit, gain; advance, progress; **¡buen provecho!** good luck!; good appetite!; **de provecho** useful; **provechos** perquisites

provecho•so -sa *adj* advantageous, beneficial; profitable; useful

proveedor -dora *mf* supplier, provider, purveyor; steward

proveer §43 & §83 *tr* to provide, furnish; supply; resolve, settle ‖ *intr* to provide; **proveer a** to provide for ‖ *ref* to supply oneself; have a bowel movement

provenir §79 *intr* to come, arise

Provenza, la Provence

provenzal *adj & mf* Provençal

proverbio *m* proverb

providencia *f* providence, foresight; step, measure

providencial *adj* providential

provincia *f* province

provisión *f* provision; supply, stock; **provisiones de boca** foodstuffs

proviso•rio -ria *adj* provisory, provisional

provocar §73 *tr* to provoke; promote, bring about; incite, tempt, move ‖ *intr* to provoke; vomit

proxeneta *mf* go-between

proximidad *f* proximity; **proximidades** neighborhood

próxi•mo -ma *adj* next; near; neighboring, close; early; **próximo pasado** last

proyección *f* projection; influence

proyectar *tr* to project; cast; design ‖ *ref* to project, stick out; *(una sombra)* be projected, fall

proyectil *m* projectile; **proyectil buscador del blanco** homing missile; **proyectil dirigido** or **teleguiado** guided missile

proyecto *m* project; **proyecto de ley** bill

proyector *m* projector, searchlight; projection machine

prudencia *f* prudence

prudente *adj* prudent

prueba *f* proof; trial, test; examination; *(de un traje)* fitting; *(de un alimento o una bebida)* sample, sampling; evidence; acrobatics; sleight of hand; (sport) event; **a prueba** on approval, on trial; **a prueba de** proof against, -proof, e.g., **a prueba de escaladores** burglarproof; **a prueba de incendio** fireproof; **prueba de alcohol** alcohol-level test; **pruebas de planas** page proof; **pruebas de primeras** first proof *(for proofreader)*; **pruebas de segundas** galley proof *(for author)*

pruebista *mf* acrobat

prurito *m* itching; eagerness, itch

psicoanálisis *m* psychoanalysis

psicoanalizar §60 *tr* to psychoanalyze

psicodéli•co -ca *adj* psychedelic

psicología *f* psychology

psicológi•co -ca *adj* psychologic(al)

psicólo•go -ga *mf* psychologist

psicópata *mf* psychopath

psico•sis *f (pl -sis)* psychosis; **psicosis de guerra** war psychosis, war scare

psicoterapia *f* psychotherapy; **psicoterapia de grupo** group therapy

psicóti•co -ca *adj & mf* psychotic

psique *f* cheval glass ‖ **Psique** *f* Psyche

psiquiatra *mf* psychiatrist

psiquiatría *f* psychiatry

psíqui•co -ca *adj* psychic

P.S.M. *abbr* **por su mandato**

pte. *abbr* **parte, presente**

púa *f* point; prick, barb; tine, prong; *(del fonógrafo)* needle; *(del peine)* tooth; thorn; *(del puerco espín)* spine, quill; sting; graft; plectrum; tricky person

pubertad *f* puberty

publicación *f* publication

publicar §73 *tr* to publish; publicize

publicidad *f* publicity; advertising; **publicidad de lanzamiento** advance publicity

publicita•rio -ria *adj* publicity; advertising

públi•co -ca *adj & m* public

pucha *f* (W-I) small bouquet; (Mex) crescent roll

púcher *m (drogas)* pusher

pr
pu

puchero _m_ pot, kettle; stew; daily bread; pouting; **hacer pucheros** to pout, screw up one's face

pucho _m_ fag end, remnant; (_de cigarro_) stump; trifle, trinket; (_el hijo menor_) baby

puden•do -da _adj_ ugly, shameful; obscene; (_partes_) private

pudiente _adj_ powerful; well-off, well-to-do

pudín _m_ pudding

pudor _m_ modesty, shyness; chastity

pudoro•so -sa _adj_ modest, shy; chaste

pudrición _f_ rot, rotting

pudrir §83 _tr_ to rot; worry ‖ _intr_ to be dead and buried ‖ _ref_ to rot; be worried; (_en la cárcel_) languish

pueblo _m_ people; common people; town, village; **puebla de Dios** or **de Israel** children of Israel

puente _m_ bridge; (dent, mus) bridge; (aut) axle, rear axle; **hacer puente** to take the intervening day off; **puente aéreo** airlift, air bridge; **puente colgante** suspension bridge; **puente de engrase** grease lift; **puente levadizo** drawbridge, lift bridge

puer•co -ca _adj_ piggish, hoggish; dirty, filthy; slovenly; coarse, mean; lewd ‖ _m_ hog; **puerco espín** or **espino** porcupine ‖ _f_ sow; slattern, slut

puericia _f_ childhood

puericultura _f_ child rearing, infant care

pueril _adj_ puerile, childish

puerilidad _f_ puerility, childishness

puerro _m_ leek; (_mariguana, hachich_) joint

puerta _f_ door, doorway; gate, gateway; **a puerta cerrada** or **a puertas cerradas** behind closed doors

puerto _m_ harbor, port; haven; mountain pass; **puerto aéreo** airport; **puerto brigantino** Corunna; **puerto de arribada** port of call; **puerto de mar** seaport; **puerto franco** free port; **puerto marítimo** dock, port; **puerto seco** frontier customhouse

puertorrique•ño -ña _adj & mf_ Puerto Rican

pues _adv_ then; well; yes, certainly; why; anyhow; **pues bien** well then; **pues que** since ‖ _conj_ for, since, because, inasmuch as ‖ _interj_ well!, then!

puesta _f_ setting; laying; putting; (_dinero apostado_) stake; **a puesta del sol** or **a puestas del sol** at sunset; **puesta a punto** adjustment; carrying out, completion; **puesta a tierra** (elec) grounding; **puesta de largo** coming out, social debut

pues•to -ta _adj_ dressed; **puesto que** since, inasmuch as ‖ _m_ place; booth, stand; office; station; barracks; (_para cazadores_) blind; **puesto a punto** (aut) tuning; **puesto de socorros** first-aid station ‖ _f_ see **puesta**

púgil _m_ pugilist

pugilato _m_ boxing; fist fight

pugilismo _m_ pugilism

pugna _f_ fight, battle; struggle, conflict; **en pugna con** at issue; **en pugna con** at odds with

pugnar _intr_ to fight, struggle; strive, persist

pug•naz _adj_ (_pl_ **-naces**) pugnacious

pujante _adj_ powerful, mighty, vigorous

pujar _tr_ (_un proyecto_) to push; (_un precio_) raise, bid up ‖ _intr_ to struggle, strain; falter; (_por decir una cosa_) grope; snivel; **pujar para adentro** (CAm, W-I) to keep silent, say nothing

pul•cro -cra _adj_ neat, tidy, trim; circumspect

pulga _f_ flea; **de malas pulgas** peppery, hot-tempered; **hacer de una pulga un camello** or **un elefante** to make a mountain out of a molehill; **no aguantar pulgas** to stand for no nonsense

pulgada _f_ inch

pulgar _m_ thumb

puli•do -da _adj_ pretty; neat; polished; clean, spotless

pulimentar _tr_ to polish

pulimento _m_ polish

pulir _tr_ to polish; finish; give a polish to

pulmón _m_ lung; **pulmón de acero** or **de hierro** iron lung

pulmonía _f_ pneumonia

púlpito _m_ pulpit

pulpo _m_ octopus

pulque _m_ (Mex) agave brandy

pulsación _f_ pulsation, throb, beat; strike, striking; (_del pianista, el mecanógrafo_) touch

pulsar _tr_ (_un botón_) to push; (_un piano, arpa, guitarra_) play; (_una tecla_) strike; feel or take the pulse of; sound out, examine ‖ _intr_ to pulsate, throb, beat

pulsear _intr_ to hand-wrestle

pulsera _f_ bracelet; wristlet; watch strap; **pulsera de pedida** engagement bracelet

pulso _m_ pulse; steadiness, steady hand; tact, care, caution; bracelet; wrist watch; **a pulso** with hand and wrist; by main strength; (_dibujo_) freehand; **sacar a pulso** to carry out against odds; **tomar el pulso a** to take the pulse of

pulular _intr_ to swarm; bud, sprout

pulverizar §60 _tr_ to pulverize; atomize; spray

pulla _f_ dig, cutting remark; filthy remark; witticism

pum _interj_ bang!

puma _m_ cougar

puna _f_ (SAm) bleak tableland in the Andes; (SAm) mountain sickness

pundonor _m_ point of honor; face

pundonoro•so sa _adj_ punctilious, scrupulous; haughty, dignified

pungir §27 _tr_ to prick; sting

punta _f_ (_extremo agudo_) point; tip, end; (_del cigarro_) butt; nail; point, cape, headland; (_del toro_) horn; (_del asta del ciervo_) tine, prong; style, graver; touch, tinge, trace; (_del vino_) souring; (elec) point; **de punta** on end; on tiptoe; **de punta en blanco** in full armor; in full regalia; **estar de punta (con)** to be at odds (with); **punta de combate** (_del torpedo_) warhead; **punta de lanza** spearhead; **punta de París** wire nail; **sacar punta a** to put a point on, to sharpen; **tener en la punta de la lengua** to have on the tip of one's tongue

puntabola _f_ (Bol) ball-point pen

puntada f hint; (sew) stitch; (*dolor agudo*) stitch, sharp pain
puntal m prop, support; stay, stanchion; backing, support; bite, snack; (naut) depth of hold
puntapié m kick; **echar a puntapiés** to kick out
puntear tr to dot, mark with dots; (*guitarra*) pluck; stipple; stitch ‖ intr (naut) to tack
puntera f toe, toe patch; leather tip; (coll) kick
puntería f aim, aiming; marksmanship
puntero m pointer; (*del reloj*) hand; stonecutter's chisel; punch; leading animal
puntiagu•do -da adj sharp-pointed
puntilla f brad; narrow lace edging; (*de la pluma fuente*) point; (carp) tracing point; dagger; **de puntillas** on tiptoe; **puntilla francesa** finishing nail
puntillero m bullfighter who delivers coup de grace with dagger
puntillo•so -sa adj punctilious
punto m (*señal de dimensiones poco perceptibles*) point, dot; stitch, loop; mesh; (*rotura en un tejido de punto*) break; jot; cabstand, hackstand; (gram) period; (math, typ, sport, fig) point; **a buen punto** opportunely; **al punto** at once; **a punto de** on the point of; **a punto fijo** for certain; **de punto** knitted; **dos puntos** (gram) colon; **en punto** sharp, on the dot; **poner punto final a** to wind up, to bring to an end; **punto de admiración** exclamation mark or point; **punto de aguja** knitting; **punto de Hungría** herringbone; **punto de media** knitwork; **punto de mira** aim; center of attraction; **¡punto en boca!** mum's the word!; **punto interrogante** question mark; **punto menos** almost; **punto muerto** dead center; (aut) neuter; **puntos y rayas** dots and dashes; **punto y coma** msg semicolon
puntuación f punctuation; mark, grade; scoring
puntual adj punctual; certain, sure; exact, accurate
puntualizar §60 tr to fix in the memory; give a detailed account of; finish; draw up
puntuar §21 tr & intr to punctuate; score
puntura f puncture, prick
punzada f prick; shooting pain; (*del remordimiento*) pang
punzante adj sharp, pricking; barbed, biting, caustic

punzar §60 tr to prick, puncture, punch; to sting; to grieve ‖ intr to sting
punzón m punch; pick; burin, graver; budding horn, tenderling; **punzón de marcar** center punch
puñada f punch
puñado m handful, bunch
puñal m dagger, poniard
puñalada f stab; blow, sudden sorrow; **puñalada de misericordia** coup de grâce; **puñalada trapera** stab in the back
puñetazo m punch; bang with the fist
puño m fist; cuff; wristband; grasp; fistful, handful; hilt; (*p.ej., del paraguas*) handle; (*del bastón*) head; punch; **como un puño** whopping big; tiny, microscopic; close-fisted; **de su propio puño** or **de su puño y letra** in his own hand, in his own writing; **puño de herro** brass knuckles
pupa f pimple; fever blister
pupila f (*del ojo*) pupil
pupi•lo -la mf boarder; orphan, ward; pupil ‖ f see **pupila**
pupitre m writing desk
puquio m (SAm) spring or pool of fresh, clear water
puré m purée; **puré de patatas** mashed potatoes; **puré de tomates** stewed tomatoes
purera f cigar case
pureza f purity
purga f purge; purgative; drain valve
purgante adj & m purgative
purgar §44 tr to purge; physic; drain; purify, refine; expiate; (*pasiones*) control, check; (*sospechas*) clear away ‖ ref to take a physic; unburden oneself
puridad f purity
purificar §73 tr to purify
purita•no -na adj & mf puritan; Puritan
pu•ro -ra adj pure; sheer; (*cielo*) clear; out-and-out, outright; **de puro** completely, totally; because of being ‖ m cigar
púrpura f purple
purpura•do -da adj purple ‖ m (eccl) cardinal
purpúre•o -a adj purple
pusilánime adj pusillanimous
pústula f pustule
puta f whore
putañear or **putear** intr to whore around, chase after lewd women
putati•vo -va adj spurious
putrefac•to -ta adj rotten, putrid
pútri•do -da adj putrid, rotten
puya f steel point; (*del gallo*) spur

Q

Q, q (cu) f twentieth letter of the Spanish alphabet
q.b.s.m. abbr **que besa su mano**
q.e.p.d. abbr **que en paz descanse**
q.e.s.m. abbr **que estrecha su mano**
quántum m (pl **quanta**) quantum

que pron rel that, which; who, whom; **el que** he who; which, the one which; who, the one who ‖ adv than ‖ conj that; for, because; let, e.g., **que entre** let him come in; **a que** I'll bet that
qué adj & pron interr what, which; **¿qué tal?**

how?; hello, how's everything? || *interj*, what!; what a!; how!

quebrada *f* gorge, ravine, gap; brook; failure, bankruptcy

quebradi•zo -za *adj* brittle, fragile; frail

quebra•do -da *adj* weakened; bankrupt; ruptured; rough; winding || *m* (math) fraction || *f* see **quebrada**

quebrantable *adj* breakable

quebrantar *tr* to break; break open; break out of; grind, crush; soften, mollify; (*un contrato; la ley; un hábito; un testamento; el corazón de una persona*) break || *ref* to break; become broken

quebrantaterro•nes *m* (*pl* **-nes**) clodhopper

quebranto *m* break, breaking; heavy loss; great sorrow; discouragement

quebrar §2 *tr* to break; bend, twist; crush; overcome; temper, soften || *intr* to break; fail; weaken, give in || *ref* to break; weaken; become ruptured

queda *f* curfew

quedar *intr* to remain; stay; be left; be left over; stop, leave off; turn out; be; be found, be located; **quedar en** to agree on; agree to; **quedar por** + *inf* or **sin** + *inf* to remain to be + *pp* || *ref* to remain; stay; stop; be; be left; put up; **quedarse con** to keep, to take; **quedarse tan fresco** to show no offense

que•do -da *adj* quiet, still; gentle || *f* see **queda** || **quedo** *adv* softly, in a low voice; gropingly

quehacer *m* work, task, chore

queja *f* complaint, lament; whine, moan

quejar *ref* to complain, lament; whine, moan

quejido *m* complaint, whine, moan

quejumbre *f* complaining, whine, moan

quejumbro•so -sa *adj* complaining; whining, whiny

quema *f* fire; burning; **a quema ropa** point-blank; **de quema** distilled; **hacer quema** (Arg, Bol) to hit the mark

quemada *f* burnt brush; (Mex) fire

quemadero *m* incinerator; (*poste destinado para quemar a los condenados a la pena de fuego*) stake

quema•do -da *adj* burned; burnt out; angry || *m* burnt brush; **oler a quemado** to smell of fire; **saber a quemado** to taste burned || *f* see **quemada**

quema•dor -dora *adj* burning; incendiary || *m* burner

quemadura *f* burn; (agr) smut

quemar *tr* to burn; scald; set on fire; scorch; frostbite; sell too cheap; (CAm, Mex) to betray, inform against || *intr* to burn, be hot || *ref* to burn; be burning up; fret; (*estar cercano a lo que se busca*) be warm, be hot; **quemarse las cejas** to burn the midnight oil

quemarropa — **a quemarropa** point-blank

quemazón *f* burn; burning; intense heat; (*de un fusible*) blowout; itch; cutting remark; pique, anger; (hum) bargain sale; (Arg, Bol, Chile) mirage on the pampas

que•pis *m* (*pl* **-pis**) kepi

queque *m* cake

querella *f* complaint; dispute, quarrel

querellar *ref* to complain; whine

querencia *f* liking, affection; attraction; love of home; (*de animales*) haunt; favorite spot

querencio•so -sa *adj* homing; (*sitio*) favorite

querer *m* love, affection; liking, fondness || *v* §55 *tr* to wish, want, desire; like; love; **como quiera** anyhow; anyway; **como quiera que** whereas; inasmuch as; no matter how; **cuando quiera** any time; **donde quiera** anywhere; **querer bien** to love; **sin querer** unwillingly; unintentionally || *v aux* to wish to, want to, desire to; will; be about to, be trying to, e.g., **quiere llover** it is trying to rain; **querer decir** to mean; **querer más** to prefer to, would rather

queri•do -da *adj* dear || *mf* lover; paramour; dearie || *f* mistress

quermés *f* or **quermese** *f* bazaar; village or country fair

queroseno *m* var of **keroseno**

querubín *m* cherub

quesadilla *f* cheesecake; sweet pastry

quese•ro -ra *adj* cheesy || *mf* cheesemonger; cheesemaker || *f* cheese board; cheese mold; cheese dish

queso *m* cheese; **queso de cerdo** headcheese; **queso helado** brick ice cream; **queso para extender** cheese spread

quevedos *mpl* nose glasses

quiá *interj* oh, no!

quicio *m* pivot hole (*of hinge*); **fuera de quicio** out of order; **sacar de quicio** to put out of order; unhinge

quiebra *f* crack; damage, loss; bankruptcy

quien *pron rel* who, whom; he who, she who; someone who, anyone who

quién *pron interr* who, whom

quienquiera *pron indef* anyone, anybody; **quienquiera que** whoever; **a quienquiera que** whomever

quie•to -ta *adj* quiet, calm; virtuous

quietud *f* quiet, calm, stillness

quijada *f* jaw, jawbone

quijotes•co -ca *adj* quixotic

quilate *m* carat

quilo *m* kilogram; **sudar el quilo** to slave, be a drudge

quilla *f* keel; (*de ave*) breastbone; **dar de quilla** (naut) to keel over

quimera *f* chimera; dispute, quarrel

química *f* chemistry

quími•co -ca *adj* chemical || *mf* chemist || *f* see **química**

quimicultura *f* tank farming

quimono *m* kimono

quimioterapia *f* chemotherapy

quina *f* cinchona, Peruvian bark

quincalla *f* hardware

quincallería *f* hardware store; hardware business; hardware factory

quincalle•ro -ra *mf* hardware merchant

quince *adj & pron* fifteen || *m* fifteen; (*en las fechas*) fifteenth

quincea•vo -va *adj & m* fifteenth

quince•no -na *adj & m* fifteenth || *f* fortnight, two weeks; two weeks' pay
quincuagési•mo -ma *adj & m* fiftieth
quiniela *f* pelota game of five; soccer lottery; daily double; (Arg, Urug) numbers game
quinien•tos -tas *adj & pron* five hundred || **quinientos** *m* five hundred
quinina *f* quinine
quinqué *m* student lamp, oil lamp
quinquenal *adj* five-year
quinta *f* villa, country house; draft, induction; **ir a quintas** to be drafted; **redimirse de las quintas** to be exempted from the draft
quintacolumnista *mf* fifth columnist
quintal *m* quintal, hundredweight
quintar *tr* to draft
quinteto *m* quintet
quintilla *f* five-line stanza of eight syllables and two rhymes; any five-line stanza with two rhymes
quintilli•zo -za *mf* quint, quintuplet
Quintín — **armar la de San Quintín** to raise a rumpus, raise a row
quin•to -ta *adj* fifth || *m* fifth; lot; pasture; draftee || *f* see **quinta**
quinza•vo -va *adj & m* fifteenth
quiosco *m* kiosk, summerhouse; stand; **quiosco de música** bandstand; **quiosco de necesidad** comfort station; **quiosco de periódicos** newsstand
quiquiri•quí *m* (*pl* **-quíes**) cock-a-doodle-doo; cock of the walk
quirófano *m* operating room
quiromancia *f* or **quiromancía** *f* palmistry
quiropodista *mf* chiropodist
quiroprácti•co -ca *adj* chiropractic || *mf* chiropractor
quirúrgi•co -ca *adj* surgical
quirurgo *m* surgeon
quiscal *m* grackle

quisicosa *f* puzzler
quisqui•do -da *adj* (Arg) constipated
quisquilla *f* trifle, triviality; **pararse en quisquillas** to bicker, make a fuss over trifles; **quisquillas** hairsplitting, quibbling
quisquillo•so -sa *adj* trifling; touchy; fastidious; hairsplitting
quiste *m* cyst
quis•to -ta *adj* — **bien quisto** well-liked, welcome; **mal quisto** disliked, unwelcome
quitaesmalte *m* nail-polish remover
quitaman•chas *mf* (*pl* **-chas**) (*persona*) clothes cleaner, spot remover || *m* (*substancia*) clothes cleaner, spot remover
quitamo•tas *mf* (*pl* **-tas**) bootlicker, apple polisher
quitanie•ve *m* or **quitanie•ves** *m* (*pl* **-ves**) snowplow
quitapie•dras *m* (*pl* **-dras**) cowcatcher
quitapintura *m* paint remover
quitapón *m* pompon for draft mules; **de quitapón** detachable, removable
quitar *tr* to remove; take away; (*la mesa*) clear; (*esfuerzo, trabajo*) save; (*tiempo*) take; free; parry; **quitar algo a algo** to take something off something, remove something from something; **quitar algo a uno** to remove something from someone; take something away from someone || *intr* — **de quita y pon** detachable, removable || *ref* (*el sombrero, una prenda de vestir*) to take off; (*el sombrero en señal de cortesía*) tip; (*una mancha*) come out, come off; (*un vicio*) give up; withdraw
quitasol *m* parasol
quite *m* removal; hindrance; dodge; (*en la esgrima*) parry; (taur) passes made with the cape to draw the bull away from the man in danger
quizá or **quizás** *adv* maybe, perhaps
quó•rum *m* (*pl* **-rum**) quorum

R

R, r (ere) *f* twenty-first letter of the Spanish alphabet
R. *abbr* **respuesta, Reverencia, Reverendo**
rabada *f* hind quarter, rump
rabadilla *f* base of the spine
rábano *m* radish; **rábano picante** or **rusticano** horseradish; **tomar el rábano por las hojas** to be on the wrong track
ra•bí *m* (*pl* **-bíes**) rabbi
rabia *f* anger, rage; (*hidrofobia*) rabies; **tener rabia a** to have a grudge against
rabiar *intr* to rage, rave; get mad; go mad, have rabies; **que rabia** like the deuce; **rabiar por** to be dying for; be dying to
rabieta *f* tantrum
rabillo *m* leafstalk; flower stalk; (*en los cereales*) mildew spot; (*del ojo*) corner

rabio•so -sa *adj* mad, rabid
rabo *m* tail; (*del ojo*) corner; (fig) tail, train; **rabo verde** (CAm) old rake
ra•bón -bona *adj* bobtail; (Chile) bare, naked; (Mex) mean, wretched || *f* camp follower; **hacer rabona** to play hooky
rabotada *f* swish of the tail; coarse remark
rabu•do -da *adj* long-tailed
racial *adj* racial
racimar *ref* to cluster, gather together
racimo *m* bunch; cluster; (*de perlas*) string
raciocinio *m* reasoning
ración *f* ration; allowance; **ración de hambre** starvation wages
racional *adj* rational
racionar *tr* to ration
racismo *m* racism

racista *adj & mf* racist

racha *f* split, crack; chip; squall, gust of wind; streak of luck

rada *f* (naut) road, roadstead

radar *m* radar

radiación *f* radiation

radiacti·vo -va *adj* radioactive

radia·dor -dora *adj* radiating ‖ *m* radiator

radiante *adj* radiant; (*alegre, sonriente*) radiant

radiar *tr* to radiate; radio; broadcast; cross out, erase ‖ *intr* to radiate

radicación *f* taking root; (math) evolution

radical *adj & m* radical

radicar §73 *intr* to take root; be located ‖ *ref* to take root; settle; (*un negocio*) be based

radio *m* edge, outskirts; (*de una rueda*) spoke, rung; (*de acción*) radius; (chem) radium; (math) radius ‖ *m & f* radio

radioaficiona·do -da *mf* radio amateur, radio fan

radiodifundir *tr & intr* to broadcast

radiodifusión *f* broadcasting

radioemisora *f* broadcasting station

radioescucha *mf* radio listener; radio monitor

radiofrecuencia *f* radio frequency

radiografiar §77 *tr* to X-ray; radio

radiograma *m* X-ray (*photograph*)

radiola *f* record player

radioperturbación *f* jamming

radioteléfono *m* radio(tele)phone

radioterapia *f* radiotherapy

radioyente *mf* radio listener

raer §56 *tr* to scrape, scrape off; smooth, level; wipe ‖ *ref* to become frayed, wear away

ráfaga *f* gust, puff; gust of wind; flash of light; (*de ametralladora*) burst; **ráfaga violenta** (aer) wind shear

raí·do -da *adj* threadbare; barefaced

ra·íz *f* (*pl* **-íces**) root; **a raíz de** close to the root of; even with; right after, hard upon; **de raíz** by the root; completely; **echar raíces** to take root

raja *f* crack, split; splinter, chip; slice

rajar *tr* to crack, split; splinter, chip; slice ‖ *intr* to boast; chatter ‖ *ref* to crack, split; splinter, chip; (Mex, CAm, W-I) to back down, break one's promise

rajatabla — **a rajatabla** desperately, ruthlessly

ralea *f* kind, quality; breed, ilk

ralear *intr* to thin out; be true to form

ralentí *m* slow motion

ra·lo -la *adj* sparse, thin

rallador *m* grater

rallar *tr* to grate; grate on, annoy

rallo *m* grater; scraper; rasp; (*de la regadera*) spout, nozzle; unglazed porous jug (*for cooling water by evaporation*)

rama *f* branch, bough; **andarse por las ramas** to beat about the bush; **en rama** raw; unbound, in sheets; in the grain

ramaje *m* branches, foliage

ramal *m* (*de una cuerda*) strand; halter; branch; (rr) branch line

ramalazo *m* lash; (*señal en el cutis por un golpe o enfermedad*) spot, pock; sharp pain; blow, sudden sorrow

rambla *f* dry ravine; avenue, boulevard

ramera *f* whore, harlot

ramificar §73 *tr & ref* to ramify

ramillete *m* bouquet; centerpiece, epergne; (bot) cluster

ramo *m* branch, limb; bouquet, cluster; (*de géneros, negocios, etc.*) line; (*p.ej., de una ciencia*) branch; (*de una enfermedad*) touch, slight attack

ramojo *m* brushwood, dead wood

ramonear *intr* to trim twigs; browse

rampa *f* ramp; cramp; (aer) apron; (Bol) litter, stretcher; **rampa de lanzamiento** launching pad

ram·plón -plona *adj* (*zapato*) heavy, coarse; common, vulgar

ramplonería *f* coarseness, vulgarity

rana *f* frog; **no ser rana** to be a past master; **rana toro** bullfrog

ran·cio -cia *adj* rank, rancid, stale; (*vino*) old; old, ancient; old, old-fashioned

ranchar *ref* (Col, Ven) to balk

ranchear *tr* to sack, pillage ‖ *intr & ref* to build huts, form a settlement

ranchera *f* (Ven) station wagon

ranchero *m* messman; rancher, ranchman

rancho *m* mess; meeting, gathering; camp; thatched hut; ranch; (naut) stock of provisions; (Arg) straw hat; **hacer rancho** to make room; **hacer rancho aparte** to be a lone wolf, go one's own way

randa *m* pickpocket ‖ *f* lace trimming

rango *m* rank; class, nature; pomp, splendor; (*elevada condición social*) status, standing

ranura *f* groove; slot

rapagón *m* stripling

rapar *tr* to shave; crop; scrape; snatch, filch ‖ *ref* to shave; (*una vida regalada*) lead

ra·paz (*pl* **-paces**) *adj* thievish; rapacious ‖ *m* young boy, lad

rapaza *f* young woman, lass

rapé *m* snuff

rápi·do -da *adj* rapid ‖ *m* (rr) express; **rápidos** (*de un río*) rapids

raposa *f* fox; female fox; (*persona*) (coll) fox

raposo *m* male fox; foxy fellow; slipshod fellow

raptar *tr* to abduct; kidnap

rapto *m* abduction; kidnaping; rapture; faint, swoon

raque *m* beachcombing; **andar al raque** to go beachcombing

raquear *intr* to beachcomb

raquero *m* priate; beachcomber

raqueta *f* racket; battledore; badminton; snowshoe; **raqueta y volante** battledore and shuttlecock

raquíti·co -ca *adj* (*que padece raquitis*) rickety; flimsy, weak, miserable

raquitis *f* rickets

raramente *adv* rarely, seldom; oddly

rareza *f* rareness; rarity; oddness, strangeness; peculiarity

ra•ro -ra *adj* rare; odd, strange; thin, sparse
ras *m* evenness; **a ras** close, even, flush; **a ras de** even with, flush with; **ras con ras** flush, at the same level; grazing
rasar *tr* to graze, skim ‖ *ref* to clear up
rascacie•los *m* (*pl* **-los**) skyscraper
rascamoño *m* fancy hairpin; (bot) zinnia
rascar §73 *tr* to scrape; scuff; scratch; scrape clean ‖ *ref* (*una cicatriz, un grano*) to pick; get drunk
rasete *m* satinet
rasga•do -da *adj* (*boca; ventana*) wide-open; (*ojos*) large; outspoken; (Col) generous ‖ *m* tear, rip, rent
rasgar §44 *tr* to tear, rip ‖ *ref* to become torn
rasgo *m* (*de una pluma de escribir*) flourish, stroke; trait, characteristic; feat, deed; flash of wit, bright remark; **a grandes rasgos** in bold strokes; **rasgos** (*de la cara*) features
rasguear *tr* to thrum on ‖ *intr* to make a flourish
rasgón *m* tear, rip, rent
rasguñar *tr* to scratch; sketch, outline
rasguño *m* scratch; sketch, outline
ra•so -sa *adj* smooth, flat, level, even; common, plain; clear, cloudless; (coll) brazen, shameless ‖ *m* flat country; satin; **al raso** in the open
raspa *f* stalk, stem; (*de mazorca de maíz*) beard; (*de pez*) spine, backbone; shell, rind; (CAm, Mex) dirty trick, nasty joke
raspadura *f* scraping; erasure; pan sugar
raspar *tr* to scrape, scrape off; scratch, scratch out; graze; (*el vino*) bite; take, steal; (W-I) to dismiss, fire; (W-I) to scold ‖ *intr* (Ven) to go away; (Ven) to die
raspear *tr* (SAm) to scold ‖ *intr* (*una pluma*) to scratch
rastra *f* rake; harrow; drag; track, trail; (*p.ej., de cebollas*) string; (naut) drag; **pescar a la rastra** to trawl
rastracuero *m* show-off; upstart; sharper, adventurer
rastreador *m* dredge; (nav) mine sweeper
rastrear *tr* to trail, track, trace; drag; dredge; check into ‖ *intr* to rake; skim the ground, fly low
rastre•ro -ra *adj* dragging, trailing; creeping; low-flying, groveling, cringing; low, vile
rastrillar *tr* to rake; (*cáñamo, lino*) hatchel, comb; (Arg, Col) to shoot, to fire; (*un fósforo*) (Arg, Col) to strike (*a match*)
rastrillo *m* rake; hackle, hatchel, flax comb; (*de cerradura o llave*) ward; grating, iron grate; (rr) cowcatcher
rastro *m* rake; harrow; track, trail; scent; trace, vestige; slaughterhouse; wholesale meat market; rag fair; **rastro de condensación** (aer) contrail
rastrojo *m* stubble
rasura *f* shaving; scraping
rasurar *tr & ref* to shave
rata *f* rat; female rat; **rata del trigo** hamster
ratear *tr* to apportion; snitch
ratería *f* baseness, meanness, vileness; petty thievery; petty theft

rate•ro -ra *adj* thievish; trailing, dragging; base, vile ‖ *mf* sneak thief
raticida *f* rat poison
ratificar §73 *tr* to ratify
rato *m* time, while, little while; **a ratos** from time to time; **a ratos perdidos** in spare time, in one's leisure hours; **buen rato** pleasant time; large amount; **pasar el rato** to waste one's time; **un rato** awhile
ratón *m* mouse; (Ven) hangover; **ratón de biblioteca** bookworm
ratonera *f* (*trampa*) mousetrap; (*agujero*) mousehole; nest of mice; hut, shop
raudal *m* stream, torrent; abundance
rau•do -da *adj* rapid, swift, impetuous
raya *f* stripe; (*línea fina; pez*) ray; (*en la imprenta, la escritura y la telegrafía*) dash; (*de los pantalones*) crease; (*en los cabellos*) part; boundary line, limit; (*para impedir la comunicación del incendio en los campos*) firebreak; (*del espectro*) (phys) line; (Mex) pay, wages; **a rayas** striped; **hacerse la raya** to part one's hair; **pasar de la raya** to go too far; **tener a raya** to keep within bounds
raya•no -na *adj* bordering; borderline
rayar *tr* (*papel*) to rule, line; stripe; scratch, score, mark; cross out; underscore ‖ *intr* to border; stand out; (*el alba, el día, la luz, el sol*) begin, arise, come forth; **rayar en** to verge on, border on ‖ *ref* (Col) to get rich
rayo *m* (*de luz*) ray; (*de rueda*) spoke; lightning, flash of lightning, stroke of lightning, thunderbolt; (*persona*) (fig) live wire; **echar rayos** to blow up, hit the ceiling; **rayo mortífero** death ray; **rayos X** X rays
rayón *m* rayon
raza *f* race; breed, stock; crack, slit; quality; ray of light (*coming through a crack*)
razón *f* reason; right, justice; account, story; (*cantidad o grado medidos por otra cosa tomada como unidad*) rate; (math) ratio; **a razón de** at the rate of; **con razón o sin ella** right or wrong; **hacer la razón** to return a toast; join at table; **meterse en razón** to listen to reason; **no tener razón** to be wrong; **razón social** firm name, trade name; **tener razón** to be right; be in the right
razonable *adj* reasonable
razonar *tr* to reason, reason out; itemize ‖ *intr* to reason
reabrir §83 *tr & ref* to reopen
reacción *f* reaction; **reacción en cadena** chain reaction
reaccionar *intr* to react
reacciona•rio -ria *adj & mf* reactionary
rea•cio -cia *adj* stubborn, obstinate
reactivo *m* reagent
real *adj* real; royal; fine, splendid ‖ *m* army camp; fairground; real (*old Spanish coin; Spanish money of account equal to a quarter of a peseta*)
realce *m* embossment, raised work; enhancement, lustre; emphasis; **bordar de realce** to embroider in relief; (fig) to embroider, to exaggerate

ra
re

realeza f royalty
realidad f reality; truth; **hecho realidad** come true, e.g., **un sueño hecho realidad** a dream come true
realismo m realism
realista mf (persona que tiende a ver las cosas como son) realist; (partidario de la monarquía) royalist
realización f realization, fulfillment; achievement; sale; **realización de beneficios** profit taking
realizar §60 tr to fulfill; carry out; turn into cash || ref to become fulfilled; be carried out
realquilar tr to sublet
realzar §60 tr to raise, elevate; emboss; enhance, set off; emphasize
reanimar tr to revive, restore; cheer, encourage || ref to revive, recover one's spirits
reanudar tr to renew, resume
reaparecer §22 intr to reappear
reata f rope to keep animals in single file; single file; **de reata** in single file; in blind submission; next, following
rebaba f burr, fin
rebaja f rebate; diminution
rebajar tr to lower; diminish, reduce; rebate; (precios) mark down; (a una persona) deflate; (carp) to rabbet || ref to stoop; humble oneself
rebajo m rabbet, groove; offset, recess
rebalsar tr to dam || ref to become dammed up; be checked; pile up, accumulate
rebanada f slice
rebanar tr to slice; cut through
rebañadera f grapnel
rebaño m flock
rebarbati•vo -va adj crabbed, surly
rebasar tr to exceed; overflow; sail past
rebatiña f grabbing, scramble; **andar a la rebatiña** to scramble
rebatir tr to repel, drive back; check; resist; strengthen; rebut, refute; deduct, rebate; beat hard
rebato m alarm, call to arms; alarm, excitement; (mil) surprise attack
rebeca f cardigan
rebelar ref to revolt, rebel; resist; break away
rebelde adj rebellious; stubborn || mf rebel
rebeldía f rebelliousness; defiance, stubbornness
rebelión f rebellion, revolt
rebe•lón -lona adj balky, restive
rebobinar tr to rewind; unwind
reborde m flange, rim, collar
rebosar tr to cause overflow || intr to overflow, run over; be in abundance; **rebosar de** or **en** to overflow with, burst with; be rich in; have an abundance of || ref to overflow, run over
rebotar tr to bend back; repel; annoy, worry || intr to bounce; bounce back, rebound || ref to become annoyed, become worried
rebote m bounce; rebound
rebozar §60 tr (la cara) to muffle up; cover with batter || ref to muffle up, muffle oneself up

rebozo m muffling; muffler; shawl; **de rebozo** secretly; **sin rebozo** frankly, openly
rebulta•do -da adj bulky, massive
rebullicio m hubbub, loud uproar
rebullir §13 intr to stir, begin to move; give signs of life || ref to stir, begin to move
rebusca f seeking, searching; gleaning; leavings, refuse
rebusca•do -da adj affected, unnatural, recherché
rebuscar §73 tr to seek after; search into; to glean
rebuznar intr to bray; talk nonsense
rebuzno m braying; nonsense
recade•ro -ra mf messenger || m errand boy
recado m errand; message; gift, present; daily marketing; compliments, regards; safety, security; equipment, outfit; **mandar recado** to send word; **recado de escribir** writing materials
recaer §15 intr to fall again; fall back; relapse; backslide; **recaer en** to fall to; **recaer sobre** to fall upon, devolve upon
recaída f relapse; backsliding
recalar tr to soak, saturate || intr to sight land
recalcar §73 tr to press, squeeze; cram, pack, stuff; (sus palabras) stress || intr (naut) to list, heel; **recalcar en** to lay stress on || ref to harp on the same string; sprawl; (p.ej., la muñeca) sprain
recalentar §2 tr to overheat; (la comida) to warm over
recalmón m (naut) lull
recamado m embroidery
recamar tr to embroider
recámara f dressing room; (de un arma de fuego) breech, chamber; reserve, caution; (Mex) bedroom
recamarera f (Mex) chambermaid
recambio m spare part; (parte, rueda, etc.) **de recambio** spare
recapacitar tr to run over in one's mind || intr to refresh one's memory; reflect
recargable adj rechargeable
recargar §44 tr to reload; overload; recharge; overcharge; overadorn; (una cuota de impuesto) increase; (elec) to recharge || ref to become more feverish
recargo m new burden; extra charge; new charge; (que paga el contribuyente moroso) penalty; (pathol) rise in temperature; **recargo de tarifa** extra fare
recata•do -da adj cautious, circumspect; modest; shy
recatar tr to hide, conceal || ref to hide; be afraid to take a stand
recato m caution, reserve; modesty
recauchutaje m recapping, retreading
recauchutar tr to recap, retread
recaudar tr (impuestos, tributos) to gather, collect; guard, watch over
recaudo m tax collecting; care, precaution; bail, surety; **a buen recaudo** under guard, in safety
recelar tr to fear, distrust || intr & ref to fear, be afraid
recelo m fear, distrust

recelo•so -sa *adj* fearful, distrustful
recensión *f* review, book review
recepción *f* reception; reception desk
recepcionista *m* room clerk ‖ *f* receptionist
receptáculo *m* receptacle; shelter, refuge
receptador *m* (coll) fence, holder of stolen goods
receptar *tr* to receive, welcome; (*delincuentes*) hide, conceal; (*cosas robadas*) receive
recepti•vo -va *adj* receptive; susceptible
receptor *m* receiver; **receptor de cabeza** headpiece; **receptor telefónico** receiver
receta *f* recipe; (pharm) prescription
recetar *tr* (*un medicamento*) to prescribe; request
recibí *m* receipt; received payment
recibida *f* reception; admission
recibi•dor -dora *mf* receiver; receiving teller; ticket collector ‖ *m* reception room
recibimiento *m* reception; welcome; reception room; (*visita en que una persona recibe a sus amistades*) at-home
recibir *tr* to receive; (*visitas*) entertain ‖ *intr* to receive; entertain ‖ *ref* to be received, be admitted; **recibirse de** to be admitted to practice as; be graduated as
recibo *m* reception; receipt; hall; parlor; athome; **acusar recibo de** to acknowledge receipt of; **estar de recibo** to be at home; **ser de recibo** to be acceptable
reciclable *adj* recyclable
reciclado *m* or **reciclaje** *m* recycling
reciclar *tr* to recycle
recién *adv* (used before past participles) recently, just, newly, e.g., **recién llegado** newly arrived; just now, recently
reciente *adv* recently
recinto *m* area, inclosure, place
re•cio -cia *adj* strong; thick, coarse, heavy; harsh; hard, bitter, arduous; (*tiempo*) severe; swift, impetuous ‖ **recio** *adv* strongly; swiftly; hard; loud
reciprocidad *f* reciprocity
recípro•co -ca *adj* reciprocal
recital *m* (*de música o poesía*) recital
recitar *tr* to recite; (*un discurso*) deliver
reclamación *f* claim, demand; objection; protest, complaint
reclamar *tr* to claim, demand; (*un ave*) decoy, lure ‖ *intr* to cry out, protest, complain
réclame *m & f* advertising
reclamo *m* bird call; decoy bird; (*para aves*) lure; allurement, attraction; advertisement; blurb, puff; reference; (typ) catchword; (SAm) complaint
reclinar *tr* (*p.ej., la cabeza*) to lean, bend ‖ *ref* to recline
reclinatorio *m* prie-dieu; couch, lounge
recluir §20 *tr* to seclude, shut in; imprison ‖ *ref* to go into seclusion
reclusión *f* seclusion; imprisonment
reclu•so -sa *adj* secluded; imprisoned ‖ *mf* prisoner; inmate
recluta *m* recruit ‖ *f* recruiting; (*del ganado disperso*) (Arg) roundup

reclutar *tr* to recruit; (Arg) to round up
recobrar *tr* to recover ‖ *ref* to recover; come to
recobro *m* recovery; (*de un motor*) pickup
recodar *intr* to lean; bend, twist, turn, wind
recodo *m* bend, twist, turn
recoger §17 *tr* to pick up; gather, collect; harvest; shorten, draw in; keep; welcome; lock up ‖ *ref* to take shelter, take refuge; withdraw; (*echarse en la cama*) retire; go home; cut down expenses
recogida *f* collection; withdrawal; suspension; **recogida de basuras** garbage collection
recogimiento *m* gathering, collecting; harvesting, seclusion, retreat; concentration; self-communion
recolectar *tr* to gather, gather in; (*el algodón*) pick
recombina•do -da *adj* (*genética*) recombinant
recomendable *adj* commendable
recomendar §2 *tr* to recommend; commend
recompensa *f* recompense, reward
recompensar *tr* to recompense, reward
recompostura *f* repair
recomprar *tr* to buy back, repurchase
reconcentrar *tr* to bring together; (*un sentimiento o afecto*) conceal, disguise ‖ *ref* to come together; be absorbed in thought
reconciliar *tr* to reconcile ‖ *ref* to become reconciled
recóndi•to -ta *adj* hidden, concealed
reconfortar *tr* to comfort, cheer
reconocer §22 *tr* to recognize; admit, acknowledge; examine; (mil) to reconnoiter ‖ *intr* (mil) to reconnoiter ‖ *ref* to be clear
reconoci•do -da *adj* grateful
reconocimiento *m* recognition; admission, acknowledgment; gratitude; reconnaissance; **reconocimiento médico** inquest
reconquista *f* reconquest
reconsiderar *tr* to reconsider
reconstruir §20 *tr* to reconstruct, rebuild, recast
recontar §61 *tr* (*volver a contar; narrar*) to recount (*to count again; narrate*)
reconvenir §79 *tr* to expostulate with, to remonstrate with
reconversión *f* reconversion
recopilar *tr* to compile
record *m* (*pl* **records**) (sport) record; **batir un record** to break a record; **establecer un récord** to make a record
recordar §61 *tr* to remember; remind ‖ *intr* to remember; get awake; come to; **si mal no recuerdo** if I remember correctly
recordati•vo -va *adj* reminding, reminiscent ‖ *m* reminder
recordatorio *m* reminder; memento
record•man (*pl* **-men**) record holder
recorrer *tr* to go over, go through; look over, look through; (*un libro*) run through; overhaul
recorrido *m* trip, run, route; (*del émbolo*) stroke; repair
recortado *m* cutout

recortar *tr* to trim, cut off; (*figuras en una tela, en un papel*) cut out; outline ‖ *ref* to stand out

recorte *m* cutting; (*de un periódico*) clipping; dodge, duck; **recortes** cuttings, trimmings

recostar §61 *tr* to lean ‖ *ref* to lean, lean back, sit back

recova *f* poultry business; poultry stand; (Arg) portico; (SAm) food market

recoveco *m* bend, turn, twist; subterfuge, trick

recreación *f* recreation

recreo *m* recreation; place of amusement

recrudecer §22 *intr* & *ref* to flare up, get worse

rectángu•lo -la *adj* right-angled ‖ *m* rectangle

rectificar §73 *tr* to rectify; (*un cilindro de motor*) rebore

rec•to -ta *adj* straight; (*ángulo*) right; right, just, righteous ‖ *m* rectum

rec•tor -tora *adj* governing, managing ‖ *mf* principal, superior ‖ *m* rector; (*de una universidad*) rector, president

recua *f* drove; (*de personas o cosas*) string, line

recuadro *m* panel, square; (*sección de un impreso encerrada dentro de un marco*) box

recubrir §83 *tr* to cover, cap, coat

recuento *m* count; recount; inventory

recuerdo *m* memory, remembrance; keepsake, souvenir

recuero *m* muleteer

recular *intr* to back up; (*un arma de fuego*) recoil; back down

reculón *m* backing; **a reculones** backing away, recoiling

recuperar *tr* & *ref* to recuperate, recover

recurrir *intr* to resort, have recourse; revert

recurso *m* recourse; resource; resort; appeal, petition

recusar *tr* to refuse, reject; (law) to challenge

rechazar §60 *tr* to refuse, reject; repel, drive back

rechazo *m* rejection; rebound, recoil

rechifla *f* catcall

rechiflar *tr* & *intr* to catcall, hiss ‖ *ref* to make fun

rechinar *intr* to creak, grate, squeak; act with bad grace; (Mex) to rage

rechistar *intr* to stir, say a word; **sin rechistar** without protest

rechon•cho -cha *adj* chubby, tubby, plump

rechupete — **de rechupete** fine, wonderful

red *f* net; netting; network, system; baggage netting; (fig) net, snare, trap; **a red barredera** with a clean sweep; **red barredera** dragnet

redacción *f* writing; editing; editorial staff; newspaper office, city room

redactar *tr* to write up; edit

redac•tor -tora *mf* writer; editor, newspaper editor; **redactor publicitario** copy writer

redada *f* (*de peces*) catch, netful; (*p.ej., de criminales*) haul, roundup

redecilla *f* hair net

rededor *m* surroundings; **al rededor (de)** around

redención *f* redemption; help, recourse

reden•tor -tora *mf* redeemer

redición *f* constant repetition

redi•cho -cha *adj* overprecise

redil *m* sheepfold

redimir *tr* to redeem; ransom; buy back

rédito *m* income, revenue, yield

redituar §21 *tr* to yield, produce

redobla•do -da *adj* stocky, heavy-built; heavy, strong; (mil) double-quick

redoblar *tr* to double; clinch; repeat ‖ *intr* (*un tambor*) to roll

redoble *m* doubling; clinching; repeating; roll of a drum

redoma *f* phial, flask

redoma•do -da *adj* sly, crafty

redonda *f* district, neighborhood; (mus) semibreve; **a la redonda** around, roundabout

redondear *tr* to round, make round; round off; round out ‖ *ref* to be well-off; be out of debt

redondel *m* circle; round cloak; (*espacio destinado a la lidia*) (taur) ring

redondilla *f* eight-syllable quatrain with rhyme abba or abab

redon•do -da *adj* round; straightforward; (*terreno*) pasture; honest; stupid ‖ *m* ring, circle; cash ‖ *f* see **redonda**

redopelo *m* row, scuffle; **al redopelo** against the grain, the wrong way; roughly, violently

reducir §19 *tr* & *ref* to reduce; **reducirse a** to come to, amount to; be obliged to

reducto *m* (fort) redoubt

redundante *adj* redundant

redundar *intr* to redound; overflow; **redundar en** to redound to

reduplicación *f* doubling

reelección *f* reëlection

reembarcar §73 *tr*, *intr* & *ref* to reship, reëmbark

reembarco *m* reshipment (*of persons*), reëmbarkation

reembarque *m* reshipment (*of goods*)

reembolsar *tr* to reimburse; refund ‖ *ref* to collect a debt, be reimbursed

reembolso *m* reimbursement; refund; **contra reembolso** collect on delivery; cash on delivery

reemplazar §60 *tr* to replace

reemplazo *m* replacement; (mil) replacements; (*hombre que sirve en lugar de otro*) (mil) replacement

reencuadernar *tr* (bb) to rebind

reencuentro *m* collision; (*de tropas*) clash

reenganchar *tr* & *ref* to reënlist

reentrada *f* reëntry

reestrenar *tr* (theat) to revive

reestreno *m* (theat) revival

reexamen *m* or **reexaminación** *f* reëxamination

reexpedición *f* forwarding, reshipment

reexpedir §50 *tr* to forward, reship

refacción *f* refreshment; allowance; repair, repairs; extra, bonus; spare part

refaccionar *tr* to finance; (SAm) to repair, renovate
refajo *m* underskirt, slip
referencia *f* reference; account, report
referi•do -da *adj* above-mentioned
referir §68 *tr* to refer; tell, report ‖ *ref* to refer
refinamiento *m* refinement
refinar *tr* to refine; polish, perfect
refinería *f* refinery
reflejar *tr* to reflect; reflect on; show, reveal ‖ *intr* to reflect
reflejo *m* glare; reflection; reflex; **reflejo acondicionado** conditioned reflex; **reflejo patelar** or **rotuliano** knee jerk
reflexión *f* reflection
reflexionar *tr* to reflect on or upon ‖ *intr* to reflect
reflugo *m* ebb
refocilar *tr* to cheer; strengthen ‖ *intr* (Arg, Urug) to lighten ‖ *ref* to be cheered; take it easy
reforma *f* reform; reformation; alteration, renovation ‖ **la Reforma** the Reformation
reformación *f* reformation
reformar *tr* to reform; mend, repair; alter, renovate; revise; reorganize ‖ *ref* to reform; hold oneself in check
reforzar §35 *tr* to reinforce; strengthen; encourage
refracción *f* refraction
refracta•rio -ria *adj* rebellious, unruly, stubborn
refrán *m* proverb, saying
refregar §66 *tr* to rub; upbraid
refrenar *tr* to curb, rein; check, restrain
refrendar *tr* to countersign; authenticate; visé; repeat
refrescar §73 *tr* to refresh; cool, refrigerate ‖ *intr* & *ref* to refresh; refresh oneself; cool off; go out for fresh air; (el viento) (naut) to blow up
refresco *m* refreshment; cold drink, soft drink
refriega *f* fray, scuffle
refrigerador *m* refrigerator; ice bucket
refrigerio *m* coolness; relief; pick-me-up, light lunch
refuerzo *m* reinforcement
refugia•do -da *mf* refugee
refugiar *tr* to shelter ‖ *ref* to take refuge
refugio *m* refuge; hospice; shelter; haunt; (para peatones en medio de la calle) safety zone; **refugio antiaéreo** air-raid shelter; **refugio antiatómico** fallout shelter
refundición *f* recast; revision; (de una pieza dramática) adaptation
refundir *tr* to recast; revise; (una pieza dramática) adapt ‖ *intr* to redound
refunfuñar *intr* to grumble, growl
refutar *tr* to refute
regadera *f* watering can; street sprinkler
regadí•o -a or **regadi•zo -za** *adj* irrigable ‖ *m* irrigated land
regala *f* gunwale
regala•do -da *adj* dainty, delicate; pleasing, pleasant; (vida) of ease

regalar *tr* to give; regale, entertain; treat; caress, fondle; indulge
regalía *f* privilege, perquisite; bonus; royalty; (Arg, Chile) muff
regaliz *m* licorice
regalo *m* gift, present; treat; joy, pleasure; **regalos de fiesta** favors
rega•lón -lona *adj* comfort-loving, pampered; (vida) soft, easy
regañar *tr* to scold ‖ *intr* to growl, snarl; grumble; quarrel; scold
regaño *m* scolding; growl, snarl; grumble
regar §66 *tr* to water, sprinkle; irrigate; spread, sprinkle, strew
regate *m* dodge, duck; (fig) dodge, subterfuge
regatear *tr* to haggle over; sell at retail; avoid, shun ‖ *intr* to haggle, bargain; duck, dodge; (naut) to race
regazo *m* lap
regenerar *tr* & *ref* to regenerate
regente *m* director, manager; registered pharmacist; (typ) foreman
regicida *mf* regicide
regicidio *m* regicide
regi•dor -dora *adj* ruling, governing ‖ *m* alderman, councilman
régimen *m* (pl **regímenes**) regime; diet; rate; management; (gram) government; **régimen de hambre** starvation diet; **régimen de justicia** rule of law
regimental *adj* regimental
regimentar §2 *tr* to regiment
regimiento *m* regiment; rule, government; city council
re•gio -gia *adj* regal, royal; magnificent
región *f* region
regir §57 *tr* to rule, govern; control, manage; guide, steer; (gram) to govern ‖ *intr* to prevail, be in force
registra•dor -dora *adj* registering; recording ‖ *m* registrar, recorder; inspector ‖ *f* cash register
registrar *tr* to register; record; examine, inspect ‖ *ref* to register; be recorded; take place
registro *m* registration, registry; recording; examination, inspection; entry, record; bookmark; manhole; (de chimenea) damper; (de reloj) regulator; (de órgano) (mus) stop; (de piano) (mus) pedal
regla *f* rule; (para trazar líneas) ruler; measure, moderation; order; menstruation; **regla de cálculo** slide rule; **reglas** monthlies, menses
reglamenta•rio -ria *adj* prescribed, statutory
reglamento *m* rules, regulations
reglar *tr* to regulate; (papel) rule ‖ *ref* to guide oneself, be guided
regleta *f* (typ) lead
regletear *tr* (typ) to lead, space
regocijar *tr* to cheer, delight ‖ *ref* to rejoice
regocijo *m* cheer, delight, rejoicing
regoldar §3 *intr* to belch
regolfar *intr* & *ref* to surge back, flow back, back up
regorde•te -ta *adj* dumpy, plump

re
re

regresar *intr* to return
regreso *m* return; **estar de regreso** to be back
regüeldo *m* belch, belching
reguero *m* drip, trickle; (*señal que deja una cosa que se va vertiendo*) track; irrigating ditch; **ser un reguero de pólvora** to spread like wildfire
regulador *m* regulator; (*de locomotora*) throttle; (mach) governor
regular *adj* regular; fair, moderate, medium; **por lo regular** as a rule ‖ *tr* to regulate; put in order; throttle
rehabilitación *f* rehabilitation
rehacer §39 *tr* to remake, make over, do over; mend, repair, renovate ‖ *ref* to recover, rally
rehén *m* hostage; **llevarse en rehenes** to carry off as a hostage; **toma de rehenes** hostage taking
rehilandera *f* pinwheel
rehilar *intr* to quiver; whiz by
rehilete *m* shuttlecock; (*que se lanza por diversión*) dart; dig, cutting remark; (taur) banderilla
rehuir §20 *tr* to avoid, shun; shrink from; refuse; dislike ‖ *intr & ref* to flee
rehusar *tr* to refuse, turn down
reimpresión *f* reprint
reimprimir §83 *tr* to reprint
reina *f* queen; **reina Margarita** aster, China aster; **reina viuda** queen dowager
reinado *m* reign
reinar *intr* to reign; prevail
reincidir *intr* to backslide; repeat an offense
reingreso *m* reëntry
reino *m* kingdom; **Reino Unido** United Kingdom
reinstalar *tr* to reinstate, reinstall
reintegrar *tr* to refund, pay back
reintegro *m* refund, payment
reír §58 *tr* to laugh at ‖ *intr & ref* to laugh; **reír de** or **reírse de** to laugh at
reja *f* grate, grating, grille; plowshare, colter; **entre rejas** behind bars
rejilla *f* screen; grating; lattice, latticework; cane, cane upholstery; foot brasier; fire grate; (electron) grid; (*de acumulador*) (elec) grid; (rr) baggage rack
rejón *m* spear; dagger; (taur) lance
rejonear *tr* (*el jinete al toro*) (taur) to jab with a lance made to break off in the bull's neck
rejuvenecimiento *m* rejuvenation
relación *f* relation; account, list; (*en un drama*) speech; **relación de ciego** blind man's ballad; **relaciones** betrothal, engagement; **relaciones públicas** public relations
relacionar *tr* to relate ‖ *ref* to be related
relai *m* or **relais** *m* (elec) relay
relajación *f* or **relajamiento** *m* relaxation; slackening; laxity; rupture, hernia
relajar *tr* to relax; slacken; debauch ‖ *intr* to relax ‖ *ref* to relax, become relaxed; become debauched; be ruptured
relamer *ref* to lick one's lips; gloat; to relish; boast; slick oneself up
relami•do -da *adj* prim, overnice

relámpago *m* flash of lightning; flash of wit; **relámpago fotogénico** flash bulb, flashlight; **relámpagos** lightning
relampaguear *intr* to lighten; flash
relatar *tr* to relate, report
relati•vo -va *adj* relative
relato *m* story; statement, report
relé *m* (elec) relay; **relé de televisión** television relay system
releer §43 *tr* to reread
relegar §44 *tr* to relegate; banish, exile; shelve, lay aside
relente *m* night dew, light drizzle
relevador *m* (elec) relay
relevancia *f* relevance; significance
relevante *adj* outstanding
relevar *tr* to emboss; make stand out; relieve; release; absolve; replace ‖ *intr* to stand out in relief
relevo *m* (elec) relay; (mil) relief; **relevos** (sport) relay race
relicario *m* shrine; (*medallón*) locket
relieve *m* relief; merit, distinction; **en relieve** in relief; **poner de relieve** to point out; to make stand out; **relieves** scraps, leftovers
religión *f* religion
religio•so -sa *adj* religious
relinchar *intr* to neigh
relincho *m* neigh, neighing; cry of joy
reliquia *f* relic; trace, vestige; **reliquia de familia** heirloom
reloj *m* watch; clock; meter; **como un reloj** like clockwork; **conocer el reloj** to know how to tell time; **reloj de caja** grandfather's clock; **reloj de carillón** chime clock; **reloj de cuarzo** quartz watch; **reloj de cuclillo** cuckoo clock; **reloj de ocho días cuerda** eight-day clock; **reloj de pulsera** wrist watch; **reloj de sol** sundial; **reloj despertador** alarm clock; **reloj registrador** time clock; **reloj registrador de tarjetas** punch clock
relojera *f* watch case; watch pocket
relojería *f* watchmaking, clockmaking; watchmaker's shop
reloje•ro -ra *mf* watchmaker, clockmaker ‖ *f* see **relojera**
reluciente *adj* shining, brilliant, flashing
relucir §45 *intr* to shine
relumbrar *intr* to shine, dazzle, glare
relumbre *m* beam, sparkle; flash; dazzle, glare
relumbrón *m* flash, glare; tinsel; **de relumbrón** showy, tawdry
rellano *m* (*en la pendiente de un terreno*) level stretch; (*de escalera*) landing
rellenar *tr* to refill; fill up; stuff; pad; fill out; cram, stuff ‖ *ref* to fill up; cram, stuff oneself
relle•no -na *adj* full, packed; stuffed ‖ *m* refill; filling, stuffing; padding, wadding; (*en un escrito*) filler
remachar *tr* (*un clavo ya clavado*) to clinch; (*un roblón*) rivet; stress, emphasize ‖ *ref* (Col) to maintain strict silence
remache *m* clinching; riveting; rivet
remanso *m* dead water, backwater

remar *intr* to row; toil, struggle
remata•do -da *adj* hopeless; **loco rematado** raving mad
rematador *m* auctioneer
rematar *tr* to finish, put an end to; finish off, kill off; (*en una subasta*) knock down ‖ *intr* to end ‖ *ref* to come to ruin
remate *m* end; crest, top, finial; closing; highest bid; (*en una subasta*) sale; **de remate** hopelessly
rembolsar *tr* to reimburse; repay; redeem
rembolso *m* reimbursement; **contra rembolso** C.O.D. (cash on delivery)
remecer §46 *tr & ref* to shake, swing, rock
remedar *tr* to copy, imitate; ape, mimic; mock
remediar *tr* to remedy; help; prevent; (*del peligro*) free, save
remediava•gos *m* (*pl* **-gos**) short cut
remedio *m* remedy; help; recourse; **no hay remedio** or **no hay más remedio** it can't be helped; **no tener remedio** to be unavoidable
remedión *m* (theat) substitute performance
remedo *m* copy, imitation; poor imitation
remendar §2 *tr* to patch, mend, repair; darn; emend, correct; touch up
remen•dón -dona *mf* mender, repairer; shoe mender; tailor (*who does mending*)
reme•ro -ra *mf* rower ‖ *m* oarsman
remesa *f* remittance; shipment
remesar *tr* to remit; ship
remezón *m* hard shake; tremor
remiendo *m* patch; mending, repair; retouching; emendation, correction; job printing, job work; **a remiendos** piecemeal
remilga•do -da *adj* prim and finicky; affected, smirking
remilgar §44 *intr* to be prim and finicky; smirk
remilgo *m* primness, affectation
remira•do -da *adj* circumspect, discreet
remisión *f* remission; reference
remitente *mf* sender, shipper
remitido *m* (*noticia de un particular a un periódico*) personal; letter to the editor
remitir *tr* to remit; forward, send, ship; refer; defer, postpone; pardon, forgive ‖ *intr* to remit, let up; refer ‖ *ref* to remit, let up; defer, yield
remo *m* oar; leg, arm, wing; toil, labor; (sport) rowing; **aguantar los remos** to lie or rest on one's oars
remoción *f* discharge, dismissal; removal
remodelación *f* remodeling
remodelar *tr* to remodel
remojar *tr* to soak, steep, dip; celebrate with a drink; **remojar la palabra** to wet one's whistle
remojo *m* soaking, steeping; **poner en remojo** to put off to a more suitable time
remolacha *f* beet; **remolacha azucarera** sugar beet
remolcador *m* tug, tugboat; towboat; tow car
remolcar §73 *tr* to tow; take in tow
remoler §47 *tr* to grind up; bore
remolinear *tr, intr & ref* to eddy, whirl about

remolino *m* eddy, whirlpool; swirl, whirl; disturbance, commotion; throng, crowd; cowlick
remo•lón -lona *adj* lazy, indolent ‖ *mf* shirker, quitter
remolonear *intr* to refuse to budge
remolque *m* tow; towing; trailer; **a remolque** in tow
remontar *tr* to mend, repair; frighten away; elevate, raise up; (*p.ej., un río*) go up ‖ *intr* (*en el tiempo*) go back ‖ *ref* to rise, rise up; soar; (*en el tiempo*) go back
remontuar *m* stem-winder
remoquete *m* punch; nickname; sarcasm; flirting
rémora *f* hindrance, obstacle
remordimiento *m* remorse
remo•to -ta *adj* remote; unlikely; **estar remoto** to be rusty
remover §47 *tr* to remove; shake; stir; disturb, upset; dismiss, discharge ‖ *ref* to move away
remozar §60 *tr* to rejuvenate ‖ *ref* to become rejuvenated
rempujar *tr* to push, jostle
rempujón *m* push, jostle
remuda *f* change, replacement; change of clothes
remudar *tr* to change, replace; move around
remuneración *f* remuneration; **remuneración por rendimiento** piece wage
renacer §22 *intr* to be reborn, be born again; recover
renacimiento *m* rebirth; renaissance
renacuajo *m* tadpole; (coll) shrimp, little squirt
Renania *f* Rhineland
ren•co -ca *adj* lame
rencor *m* rancor; **guardar rencor** to bear malice
rendición *f* surrender; submission; fatigue, exhaustion; yield
rendi•do -da *adj* tired, worn-out; submissive
rendija *f* crack, split, slit
rendimiento *m* submission; exhaustion; yield; output; (mech) efficiency
rendir §50 *tr* to conquer; subdue; surrender; exhaust, wear out; return, give back; yield, produce; (*gracias, obsequios, homenaje*) render ‖ *intr* to yield ‖ *ref* to surrender; yield, give in; be exhausted, be worn out
renegar §66 *tr* to deny vigorously; abhor, detest ‖ *intr* to curse; be insulting; **renegar de** to deny; curse; abhor, detest
renegociación *f* renegotiation
Renfe, la acronym for **la Red Nacional de los Ferrocarriles Españoles** the Spanish National Railroad System
renglón *m* line; **a renglón sequido** right below; **leer entre renglones** to read between the lines
reniego *m* curse
reno *m* reindeer
renombra•do -da *adj* renowned, famous
renombre *m* renown, fame
renovar §61 *tr* to renew; renovate; transform, restore; remodel

re
re

renquear *intr* to limp

renta *f* income; private income; annuity; public debt; rent; **renta nacional** gross national product

rentar *tr* to produce, yield

rentista *mf* bondholder; financier; person of independent means

renuente *adj* reluctant, unwilling

renuevo *m* sprout, shoot; renewal

renuncia *f* renunciation; resignation; (law) waiver

renunciar *tr* to renounce; resign ‖ *intr* to renounce; (*no servir al palo que se juega*) renege; **renunciar a** to give up, renounce, waive

renuncio *m* slip, mistake; (*en juegos de naipes*) renege; lie

reñi•do -da *adj* on bad terms; bitter, hardfought

reñir §72 *tr* (*regañar*) to scold; (*una batalla, un desafío*) fight ‖ *intr* to fight; be at odds, fall out

re•o -a *adj* guilty, criminal ‖ **reo** *mf* offender, criminal; (law) defendant

reojo — **de reojo** askance, out of the corner of one's eye; hostilely

reorganizar §60 *tr & ref* to reorganize

reorientación *f* reorientation

reóstato *m* rheostat

repanchigar or **repantigar** §44 *ref* to sprawl, loll

reparar *tr* to repair, mend; make amends for; notice, observe; (*un golpe*) parry ‖ *intr* to stop; **reparar en** to notice, pay attention to ‖ *ref* to stop; refrain

reparo *m* repairing, repairs; notice, observation; doubt, objection; shelter; bashfulness

repa•rón -rona *adj* faultfinding ‖ *mf* faultfinder

repartida *f* distribution; issuing

repartir *tr* to distribute; (*naipes*) deal

reparto *m* distribution; (*de naipes*) deal; (theat) cast; **reparto de acciones gratis** stock dividend

repasar *tr* to repass; retrace; review; revise; (*la ropa*) mend

repasata *f* scolding, reprimand

repaso *m* revision; (*de una lección*) review; mending; reprimand

repatriar §77 *tr* to repatriate; send home ‖ *intr & ref* to be repatriated; go or come home

repeler *tr* to repel, repulse

repente *m* start, sudden movement; **de repente** suddenly

repenti•no -na *adj* sudden, unexpected

repentista *mf* (mus) improviser; (mus) sight reader

repentizar §60 *intr* to improvise; (mus) to sight-read, perform at sight

repercutir *intr* to rebound; reëcho, reverberate

repertorio *m* repertory

repetición *f* repetition; (mus) repeat

repetir §50 *tr & intr* to repeat

repicar §73 *tr* to mince, chop up; ring, sound; sting again ‖ *intr* peal, ring out, resound ‖ *ref* to boast, be conceited

repique *m* chopping, mincing; peal, ringing; squabble, quarrel

repiqueteo *m* pealing, ringing; beating, rapping

repisa *f* shelf, ledge; bracket; **repisa de chimenea** mantelpiece; **repisa de ventana** window sill

replantear *tr* to lay out again; reaffirm, reimplement

replegar §66 *tr* to fold over and over ‖ *ref* to fold, fold up; (mil) to fall back

reple•to -ta *adj* replete, full, loaded; fat, chubby

réplica *f* answer, retort; replica

replicar §73 *tr* to argue against ‖ *intr* to answer back, retort

repli•cón -cona *adj* saucy, flip

repliegue *m* fold, crease; (mil) falling back

repollo *m* cabbage; (*p.ej., de lechuga, col*) head

reponer §54 *tr* to replace, put back; restore; (*una pieza dramática*) revive; **repuso** he replied ‖ *ref* to recover; calm down

reportaje *m* reporting; news coverage; report

reportar *tr* to check, restrain; get, obtain; bring, carry; report ‖ *ref* to restrain or control oneself

reporte *m* report, news report; gossip

repórter *m* reporter

reporte•ro -ra *mf* reporter

reposa cabezas *f* (aut) head rest

reposar *intr & ref* to rest, repose; take a nap; (*en la sepultura*) lie, be at rest; (*poso, sedimento*) settle

reposición *f* replacement; (*de la salud*) recovery; (theat) revival

reposo *m* rest, repose

repostar *tr, intr & ref* to stock up; refuel

repostería *f* pastry shop, confectionery; pantry

reposte•ro -ra *mf* pastry cook, confectioner

repregunta *f* (law) cross-examination

repreguntar *tr* (law) to cross-examine

reprender *tr* to reprehend, scold

represa *f* dam; damming, repression, check; (*de un buque*) recapture

represalia *f* reprisal; retaliation

represar *tr* to dam; repress, check; (*de un buque*) to recapture

representación *f* representation; dignity, standing; performance; **en representación de** representing; **representación exclusiva** sole dealership

representante *adj* representing ‖ *mf* representative; actor, player; (com) agent, representative

representar *tr* to represent; show, express; state, declare; act, perform, play; (*determinada edad*) appear to be ‖ *ref* to imagine

representati•vo -va *adj* representative

reprimenda *f* reprimand

reprimir *tr* to repress

reprobación *f* reproof; flunk, failure

reprobar §61 *tr* to reprove; flunk, fail

reprochar *tr* to reproach

reproche *m* reproach
reproducción *f* reproduction; breeding
reproducir §19 *tr & ref* to reproduce
repro•pio -pia *adj* balky
reptar *intr* to crawl; to cringe
reptil *m* reptile
república *f* republic
republica•no -na *adj & mf* republican ‖ *m* patriot
repudiar *tr* to repudiate, disown, disavow
repues•to -ta *adj* secluded; spare, extra ‖ *m* stock, supply; serving table; pantry; **de repuesto** spare, extra
repugnante *adj* repugnant, disgusting
repugnar *tr* to conflict with; contradict; object to, avoid; revolt, be repugnant to ‖ *intr* to be repugnant
repujar *tr* to emboss
repulgar §44 *tr* to hem, border
repulgo *m* hem, border
repuli•do -da *adj* highly polished; all dolled up
repulsar *tr* to reject, refuse
repulsi•vo -va *adj* repulsive
repuntar *tr* (*animales dispersos*) (Arg, Chile, Urug) to round up ‖ *intr* to begin to appear; (naut) to begin to rise; (naut) to begin to ebb ‖ *ref* to begin to turn sour; fall out
repuso see **reponer**
reputación *f* reputation, repute
reputar *tr* to repute; esteem
requebra•dor -dora *adj* flirtatious ‖ *mf* flirt
requebrar §2 *tr* to break into smaller pieces; flatter, flirt with
requemar *tr* to burn again; parch; overcook; inflame; bite, sting ‖ *ref* to become tanned or sunburned; smolder, burn within
requerir §68 *tr* to notify; summon; request; urge; check, examine; require; seek, look for; reach for; court, make love to
requesón *m* cottage cheese
requiebro *m* fine crushing; flattery, flattering remarks, flirtation
requisi•to -ta *adj* requisite ‖ *m* requisite, requirement; accomplishment; **requisito previo** prerequisite
res *f* head of cattle; beast; **reses** cattle
resabio *m* unpleasant aftertaste; bad habit, vice
resabio•so -sa *adj* sly, crafty; (*caballo*) vicious
resaca *f* surge, surf; undertow; (com) redraft; (slang) hangover
resalir §65 *intr* to jut out, project
resaltar *tr* to emphasize ‖ *intr* to bounce, rebound; jut out, project; stand out
resanar *tr* to retouch, patch, repair
resarcir §36 *tr* to indemnify, make amends to; (*un daño, un agravio*) repay; (*una pérdida*) make good; to mend, repair ‖ *ref* — **resarcirse de** to make up for
resbaladi•zo -za *adj* slippery; skiddy; risky; (*memoria*) shaky
resbalar *intr* to slide; skid; slip ‖ *ref* to slide; slip; (fig) to slip, to misstep

rescatar *tr* to ransom, redeem; rescue; (*el tiempo perdido*) make up for; relieve; atone for; (Mex) to resell
rescate *m* ransom, redemption; rescue; salvage; ransom money
rescindir *tr* to rescind
rescoldera *f* heartburn
rescoldo *m* embers; smoldering; doubt, scruple; **arder en rescoldo** to smolder
resenti•do -da *adj* resentful
resentimiento *m* resentment; sorrow, disappointment
resentir §68 *ref* to be resentful; **resentirse de** to feel the bad effects of; resent; suffer from
reseña *f* outline; book review; newspaper account; (mil) review
reseñador *m* reviewer; critic
reseñar *tr* to outline; (*un libro*) review; (mil) to review
reserva *f* reserve; reservation; **con** or **bajo la mayor reserva** in strictest confidence; **reserva de caza** game preserve
reservar *tr* to reserve; put aside; postpone; exempt; keep secret ‖ *ref* to save oneself, bide one's time; beware, be distrustful
resfriado *m* cold
resfriar §77 *tr* to cool, chill ‖ *intr* to turn cold ‖ *ref* to catch cold; cool off, grow cold
resguardar *tr* to defend; protect, shield ‖ *ref* to take shelter; protect oneself
resguardo *m* defense; protection; check, voucher; collateral; (naut) wide berth, sea room
residencia *f* residence; impeachment; **residencia de ancianos** nursing home; home for the aged
residenciar *tr* to call to account; impeach
residir *intr* to reside
residuo *m* residue, remains; remainder; **residuos radiactivos** radioactive waste
resignación *f* resignation
resignar *tr* to resign ‖ *ref* to resign, become resigned; **resignarse con** (*p.ej., su suerte*) to be resigned to
resina *f* resin
resistencia *f* resistance; strength; **resistencia de rejilla** (electron) grid leak
resistente *adj* resistant; strong; (hort) hardy; **resistente al rayado** scratch-resistant
resistir *tr* to bear, stand; (*la tentación*) resist ‖ *intr* to resist; hold out; **resistir a** (*la violencia; la risa*) resist; refuse to ‖ *ref* to resist; struggle; **resistirse a** to refuse to
resma *f* ream
resobrina *f* grandniece, greatniece
resobrino *m* grandnephew, greatnephew
resolución *f* resolution; **en resolución** in brief, in a word
resolver §47 & §83 *tr* to resolve; solve; decide on; dissolve ‖ *ref* to resolve; make up one's mind
resollar §61 *intr* to breathe; breathe hard, pant; stop for a rest
resonar §61 *intr* to resound, echo
resoplar *intr* to puff; snort
resoplido *m* puffing; snort

re
re

resorte *m* spring; springiness; means; province, scope; rubber band; **resorte espiral** coil spring; **tocar resortes** to pull wires, pull strings

respailar *intr* — **ir respailando** to scurry along

respaldar *m* back; ‖ *tr* to back; indorse ‖ *ref* to lean back; sprawl

respaldo *m* back; backing; indorsement

respectar *tr* (with personal **a**) to concern; **por lo que respecta a . . .** as far as . . . is concerned

respecti•vo -va *adj* respective

respecto *m* respect, reference, relation; **al respecto** in the matter; **respecto a** or **de** with respect to, in or with regard to

respetable *adj* respectable

respetar *tr* to respect

respeto *m* respect; consideration; **campar por sus respetos** to be inconsiderate, go one's (his, her, etc.) own way; **de respeto** spare, extra

respetuo•so -sa *adj* respectful; awesome, impressive; humble, obedient

respigón *m* hangnail

respingar §44 *intr* to balk, shy; (*elevarse el borde, p.ej., de la falda*) curl up; give in unwillingly

respin•gón -gona *adj* (*nariz*) snubby, upturned; surly, churlish

respirar *tr* to breathe ‖ *intr* to breathe; breathe freely; breathe a sigh of relief; catch one's breath, stop for a rest; **no respirar** to not breathe a word; **sin respirar** without respite, without letup

respiro *m* breathing; respite, breather, breathing spell; (*para el pago de una deuda*) extension of time

resplandecer §22 *intr* to shine; flash, glitter

resplandeciente *adj* brilliant; resplendent

resplandor *m* brilliance, radiance; resplendence; glare

responder *tr* to answer ‖ *intr* to answer, respond; correspond; answer back; **responder de** (*una cosa*) to answer for; **responder por** (*una persona*) to answer for

respon•dón -dona *adj* (coll) saucy

responsable *adj* responsible; **responsable de** responsible for

responsabilizar *tr* to put in charge; hold responsible ‖ *ref* to assume responsibility

respuesta *f* answer, response

resquebrajar *tr* & *ref* to crack, split

resquemar *tr* & *intr* to bite, sting ‖ *ref* to be parched; (*resentirse sin manifestarlo*) smolder

resquemo *m* bite, sting

resquicio *m* crack, chink; chance, opportunity

restablecer §22 *tr* to reëstablish, restore ‖ *ref* to recover

restañar *tr* to retin; (*sangre*) stanch, stop the flow of

restar *tr* to deduct; reduce; take away; (*una pelota*) return; subtract ‖ *intr* to remain, be left

restaurante *m* restaurant; **restaurante automático** automat

restaurar *tr* to restore; to recover

restitución *f* restitution, return

restituir §20 *tr* to return, give back; restore ‖ *ref* to return, come back

resto *m* rest, remainder, residue; (*en juegos de naipes*) stakes; (*de una pelota*) return; **a resto abierto** without limit; **echar el resto** to stake all, shoot the works; **restos** remains, mortal remains; **restos de serie** remnants

restregar §66 *tr* to rub hard; scrub hard

restringir §27 *tr* to restrict; constrict, to contract

resucitar *tr* & *intr* to resuscitate; resurrect; revive,

resuel•to -ta *adj* resolute, resolved, determined; prompt, quick

resuello *m* breathing; hard breathing, panting

resulta *f* result; outcome; vacancy; **de resultas de** as a result of

resultado *m* result

resultar *intr* to result; prove to be, turn out to be; be, become

resumen *m* summary, résumé; **en resumen** in brief, in a word

resumir *tr* to summarize, sum up ‖ *ref* to be reduced, be transformed

resurrección *f* resurrection

retaguardia *f* rearguard

retal *m* piece, remnant

retama *f* Spanish broom; **retama de escoba** furze

retar *tr* to challenge, dare; blame, find fault with

retardación *f* retardation

retardar *tr* to retard, slow down

retardo *m* retard, delay

retazo *m* piece, remnant; scrap, fragment

retén *m* store, stock, reserve; catch, pawl; (mil) reserve

retener §71 *tr* to retain, keep, withhold; detain, arrest; (*el pago de un haber*) stop

retentiva *f* memory; recall

reticente *adj* deceptive, misleading; noncommittal

retintín *m* jingle, tinkling; (*en el oído*) ringing; tone of reproach, sarcasm, mockery

retiñir §12 *intr* to jingle, tinkle (*los oídos*) ring

retirada *f* retirement, withdrawal; place of refuge; (mil) retreat, retirement; (*toque*) (mil) retreat; **batirse en retirada** to beat a retreat

retirar *tr* to retire, withdraw; take away; pull back ‖ *ref* to retire, withdraw; (mil) to retire

reto *m* challenge, dare; threat

retocar §73 *tr* to retouch; touch up; (*un disco de fonógrafo*) play back

retoño *m* sprout, shoot, sucker

retorcer §74 *tr* to twist; twist together; (*las manos*) wring; (fig) to twist, misconstrue ‖ *ref* to twist; writhe

retóri•co -ca *adj* rhetorical ‖ *f* rhetoric

retornar *tr* to return, give back; back, back up ‖ *intr & ref* to return, go back

retorno *m* return; barter, exchange; reward, requital; **retorno terrestre** (elec) ground

retorta *f* (chem) retort

retozar §60 *intr* to frolic, gambol, romp

retozo *m* frolic, gambol, romping; **retozo de la risa** giggle, titter

reto•zón -zona *adj* frolicsome, frisky

retracción *f* retraction; (pathol) atrophy

retractar *tr & ref* to retract

retráctil *adj* retractable

retraer §75 *tr* to bring again, bring back; dissuade ‖ *ref* to withdraw, retire; take refuge

retraí•do -da *adj* solitary; reserved, shy

retransmisión *f* rebroadcasting

retransmitir *tr* to rebroadcast

retrasa•do -da *adj* (mentally) retarded

retrasar *tr* to delay, retard; put off; (*un reloj*) set or turn back ‖ *intr* to be too slow; (*en los estudios*) be or fall behind ‖ *ref* to delay, be late, be slow, be behind time; (*un reloj*) go or be slow

retraso *m* delay; **tener retraso** to be late

retratar *tr* to portray; photograph; imitate ‖ *ref* to sit for a portrait; have one's picture taken

retrato *m* portrait; photograph; copy, imitation; description; **el vivo retrato de** the living image of

retrepar *ref* to lean back, lean back in the chair

retreta *f* (mil) retreat, tattoo; outdoor band concert

retrete *m* toilet, lavatory

retribuir §20 *tr* to repay, pay back

retroacti•vo -va *adj* retroactive

retroalimentación *f* feedback

retroceder *intr* to retrogress; back away; back down, back out

retroceso *m* retrogression; (*de un arma de fuego*) recoil; (*de una enfermedad*) flare-up; (mach, mov) rewind(ing)

retrocohete *m* retrorocket

retrodisparo *m* retrofiring

retropropulsión *f* (aer) jet propulsion

retrospecti•vo -va *adj* retrospective ‖ *f* (mov) flashback

retrovisor *m* rear-view mirror

retrucar §73 *intr* to answer, reply; (billiards) kiss

retruco *m* (billiards) kiss

retruécano *m* pun

retumbar *intr* to resound, rumble

retumbo *m* resounding, rumble, echo

reumáti•co -ca *adj & mf* rheumatic

reumatismo *m* rheumatism

reunificación *f* reunification

reunión *f* reunion, gathering, meeting; assemblage

reunir §59 *tr* to join, unite; assemble, gather together, bring together; reunite; (*dinero*) raise ‖ *ref* to unite; assemble, gather together, come together, meet; reunite

reválida *f* final examination (*for a higher degree*)

revalorar *tr* to revaluate

revalorizar §60 *tr* to revaluate

revejecer §22 *intr & ref* to grow old before one's time

revelación *f* revelation

revelado *m* (phot) development

revelador *m* (phot) developer

revelar *tr* to reveal; (phot) to develop

revender *tr* to resell; retail

reventa *f* resale

reventar §2 *tr* to smash, crush; burst, blow out, explode; ruin; annoy, bore; (*a una persona*) work to death; (*a un caballo*) run to death ‖ *intr* to burst, blow out, explode; (*las olas*) break; (*morir*) croak; (*de ira*) blow up, hit the ceiling; **reventar por** to be dying to ‖ *ref* to burst, blow out, explode; be worked to death; (*un caballo*) be run to death

reventón *m* burst; (aut) blowout

rever §80 *tr* to revise, review; (*un caso legal*) retry

reverberar *intr* to reverberate

reverbero *m* reflector; street lamp; chafing dish

reverencia *f* reverence; bow, curtsy

reverenciar *tr* to revere, reverence ‖ *intr* to bow, curtsy

reveren•do -da *adj & m* reverend

reverso *m* back; wrong side; reverse

revertir §68 *intr* to revert

revés *m* back, reverse; wrong side; backhand; (*desgracia, contratiempo*) reverse, setback; **al revés** wrong side out; inside out; upside down; backwards

revestir §50 *tr* to put on, don; cover, coat, face, line, surface; assume, take on; disguise; (*un cuento*) adorn; invest ‖ *ref* to put on vestments; be haughty; gird oneself

revirar *tr* to turn, twist; turn over

revisada *f* examination; revision

revisar *tr* to revise, review, check; audit

revisión *f* revision, review, check

revisionismo *m* revisionism

revisionista *adj & mf* revisionist

revisor *m* inspector, examiner; (rr) conductor, ticket collector

revista *f* review; (mil) review; (theat) review, revue; (law) new trial

revistar *tr* (mil) to review

revivir *tr & intr* to revive

revocar §73 *tr* to revoke; dissuade; drive back, drive away; plaster, stucco

revocatoria *f* (SAm) recall; repeal; cancellation

revolar §61 *intr & ref* to flutter, flutter around

revolcar §81 *tr* to knock down; (*a un adversario*) floor; (*a un alumno en un examen*) flunk, fail ‖ *ref* to wallow, roll around; be stubborn

revolotear *tr* to fling up ‖ *intr* to flutter, flutter around, flit

revoltijo *m* or **revoltillo** *m* mess, jumble; stew

re
re

revolto•so -sa *adj* rebellious, riotous; (*niño*) unruly, mischievous; complicated; winding ‖ *mf* troublemaker, rioter

revolución *f* revolution

revoluciona•rio -ria *adj & mf* revolutionary

revolver §47 & §83 *tr* to shake; stir; turn around; turn upside down; wrap up; mess up; disturb; (*sus pasos*) retrace; alienate, estrange ‖ *intr* to retrace one's steps ‖ *ref* to retrace one's steps; turn around; toss and turn; (*un astro en su órbita*) revolve; (*el mar*) get rough

revólver *m* revolver

revuelco *m* upset, tumble; wallowing

revuelo *m* whirl, flying around; stir, commotion

revuelta *f* revolution, revolt; disturbance; turning point; fight, row

rey *m* king; swineherd; **los Reyes Católicos** Ferdinand and Isabella; **los Reyes Magos** the Three Wise Men; **ni rey ni roque** nobody; **rey de zarza** wren; **reyes** king and queen; **Reyes** Twelfth-night

reyerta *f* quarrel, wrangle

reyezuelo *m* (orn) kinglet; **reyezuelo mo•ñudo** goldcrest

rezaga•do -da *mf* straggler, laggard

rezagar §44 *tr* to outstrip, leave behind; postpone ‖ *ref* to fall behind

rezar §60 *tr* (*una oración*) to pray; (*una oración; la misa*) say; (coll) to say, to read; (*anunciar*) (coll) to call for ‖ *intr* to pray; grumble; (coll) to say, to read; **rezar con** to concern

rezo *m* prayer; devotions

rezón *m* grapnel

rezongar §44 *tr* (CAm) to scold ‖ *intr* to grumble, growl

rezumar *intr* to ooze, seep ‖ *ref* to ooze, seep; to leak; (*una especie*) leak out

ría *f* estuary, fiord

riachuelo *m* rivulet, streamlet

riada *f* flood, freshet

ribazo *m* slope, embarkment

ribera *f* bank, shore; riverside

ribere•ño -ña *adj* riverside

ribero *m* levee, dike

ribete *m* edge, trimming, border; (*a un cuento*) embellishment

ribetear *tr* to edge, trim, border, bind

ri•co -ca *adj* rich; dear, darling

ridiculizar §60 *tr* to ridicule

ridícu•lo -la *adj* ridiculous; touchy ‖ *m* ridiculous situation; **poner en ridículo** to ridicule, expose to ridicule

riego *m* irrigation; watering

riel *m* ingot; curtain rod; rail

rielar *intr* to shimmer, gleam; (poet) to twinkle

rienda *f* rein; **a rienda suelta** swiftly, violently; with free rein

riente *adj* laughing; bright, cheerful

riesgo *m* risk, danger; **correr riesgo** to run or take a risk

riesgo•so -sa *adj* risky; dangerous

rifa *f* raffle; fight, quarrel

rifar *tr* to raffle, raffle off ‖ *intr* to raffle; fight, quarrel

rígi•do -da *adj* rigid, stiff; strict, severe

riguro•so -sa *adj* rigorous; severe

rima *f* rhyme; **rimas** poems, poetry

rimar *tr & ref* to rhyme

rimbombante *adj* resounding; flashy

rímel *m* mascara

rimero *m* heap, pile

Rin *m* Rhine

rincón *m* corner; nook; piece of land; (coll) home

rinconera *f* corner piece of furniture; corner table; corner cupboard

ringla *f*, **ringle** *m* or **ringlera** *f* row, tier

ringorrango *m* curlicue; frill, frippery

rinoceronte *m* rhinoceros

riña *f* fight, scuffle

riñón *m* kidney; (fig) heart, center, interior; **tener bien cubierto el riñón** to be wellheeled

río *m* river; **pescar en río revuelto** to fish in troubled waters

riostra *f* brace, stay; guy wire

riostrar *tr* to brace, stay

ripia *f* shingle

ripio *m* debris; rubble; (*palabras inútiles empleadas para completar el verso*) padding; **no perder ripio** to not miss a trick

riqueza *f* riches, wealth; richness; **riquezas del subsuelo** mineral resources

risa *f* laugh, laughter

risco *m* cliff, crag; honey fritter

risible *adj* laughable

risotada *f* guffaw, horse laugh

ristra *f* string of onions, string of garlic; (coll) string, row, file

ristre *m* lance rest

risue•ño -ña *adj* smiling

rítmi•co -ca *adj* rhythmic(al)

ritmo *m* rhythm; **a gran ritmo** at great speed

rito *m* rite

rival *mf* rival

rivalidad *f* rivalry; enmity

rivalizar §60 *intr* to vie, compete; **rivalizar con** to rival

riza•do -da *adj* curly; ripply ‖ *m* curl, curling; rippling

rizador *m* curling iron, hair curler

rizar §60 *tr & ref* to curl; (*la superficie del agua*) ripple

ri•zo -za *adj* curly ‖ *m* curl, ringlet; ripple; (aer) loop; **rizar el rizo** (aer) to loop the loop

ro *interj* — **¡ro ro!** hushaby!, bye-bye!

roba•dor -dora *mf* robber, thief

róbalo or **robalo** *m* (*Labrax lupus*) bass; (*Centropomus undecimalis*) snook

robar *tr* to rob, steal; (*un naipe o ficha de dominó*) draw ‖ *intr & ref* to steal

robinete *m* faucet, spigot, cock

roblar *tr* to clinch, rivet

roble *m* oak; (*Quercus robur*) British oak tree; husky fellow

roblón *m* rivet

robo *m* robbery, theft; (*naipe tomado del monte*) draw; **robo con escalamiento** burglary

ro•bot *m* (*pl* **-bots**) robot

robótica *f* robotics

robotización *f* use of robots; robotization

robus•to -ta *adj* robust

roca *f* rock

rocalla *f* pebbles; stone chips; large glass bead

rocallo•so -sa *adj* stony, pebbly

roce *m* rubbing; close contact

rociada *f* sprinkling; dew; (*de balas, piedras, etc.*) shower; (*de invectivas*) volley

rociadera *f* sprinkling can

rociar §77 *tr* to sprinkle; spray; bedew; scatter ‖ *intr* to drizzle; **rocía** there is dew

rocín *m* hack, nag; work horse, draft horse; riding horse; rough guy

rocío *m* dew; drizzle; sprinkling

rocke•ro -ra *mf* rock singer

roco•so -sa *adj* rocky

rodada *f* rut, track

roda•do -da *adj* (*fácil, flúido*) rounded, fluent; (*tránsito*) vehicular ‖ *f* see **rodada**

rodadura *f* rolling; rut; (*de neumático*) tread

rodaja *f* disk, caster; round slice

rodaje *m* wheels; (*de una película cinematográfica*) shooting, filming; **en rodaje** (aut) being run in; (mov) being filmed

rodamiento *m* bearing; (*de un neumático*) tread; **rodamientos** running gear

Ródano *m* Rhone

rodante *adj* rolling; on wheels; (Chile) wandering

rodapié *m* baseboard, washboard

rodar §61 *tr* to roll; (*una película cinematográfica*) shoot, film, take; screen, project; drag along; (*una llave*) turn; (*la escalera*) roll down; (*un nuevo coche*) run in; (*válvulas de un motor*) grind ‖ *intr* to roll, roll along; roll down; rotate, revolve; tumble; roam, wander about; (*por medio de ruedas*) run; prowl

Rodas *f* Rhodes

rodear *tr* to surround; round up ‖ *intr* to go around; go by a roundabout way; beat about the bush ‖ *ref* to turn, twist, toss about

rodela *f* buckler, target; padded ring

rodeo *m* detour, roundabout way; dodge, duck; rodeo, roundup; **andar con rodeos** to beat about the bush; **dar un rodeo** to go a roundabout way

rodilla *f* knee; floor rag, mop; padded ring; **de rodillas** kneeling, on one's knees

rodillera *f* kneepad; baggy knee; (*de prenda de vestir*) knee; (*del órgano*) (mus) knee swell

rodillo *m* roller; rolling pin; road roller; inking roller; (*de la máquina de escribir*) platen

rodrigar §44 *tr* to prop, prop up, stake

rodrigón *m* prop, stake

roer §62 *tr* to gnaw, gnaw away at; (*un hueso*) pick; wear down

rogar §63 *tr & intr* to beg; pray; **hacerse de rogar** to like to be coaxed

roí•do -da *adj* miserly, stingy

ro•jo -ja *adj* red; ruddy; red-haired; Red ‖ *mf* (*comunista*) Red ‖ *m* red; **al rojo** to a red heat

rollar *tr* to roll, roll up

rolli•zo -za *adj* round, cylindrical; plump, stocky ‖ *m* round log

rollo *m* roll, coil; roller, rolling pin; round log; yoke pad; rôle; (*de tela*) bolt

romadizo *m* cold in the head

romance *adj* (*neolatino*) Romance ‖ *m* Romance language; Spanish language; romance of chivalry; octosyllabic verse with alternate lines in assonance; narrative poem in octosyllabic verse; ballad; **romance heroico** hendecasyllabic verse with alternate lines in assonance

romancero *m* collection of Old Spanish romances

romancillo *m* verse of less than eight syllables with alternate lines in assonance

románi•co -ca *adj* (*neolatino*) Romance, Romanic; (*arquitectura*) Romanesque ‖ *m* Romanesque

roma•no -na *adj & mf* Roman

romanticismo *m* romanticism

románti•co -ca *adj* romantic

romanza *f* (mus) romance, romanza

romería *f* pilgrimage; crowd, gathering

rome•ro -ra *mf* pilgrim ‖ *m* rosemary

ro•mo -ma *adj* blunt, dull; flat-nosed

rompeáto•mos *m* (*pl* **-mos**) atom smasher

rompecabe•zas *m* (*pl* **-zas**) riddle, puzzle; (*figura que ha sido cortada en trozos menudos y que hay que recomponer*) jigsaw puzzle

rompehie•los *m* (*pl* **-los**) iceboat, icebreaker

rompehuel•gas *m* (*pl* **-gas**) strikebreaker

rompeo•las *m* (*pl* **-las**) mole, breakwater

romper §83 *tr* to break; break through; break up; tear ‖ *intr* to break; (*las flores*) break open, burst open; break down; **romper a** to start to, burst out

rompiente *m* reef, shoal; (*oleaje que choca contra las rocas*) breaker

rompope *m* eggnog

ron *m* rum; **ron de laurel** or **de malagueta** bay rum

ronca *f* (*época del celo*) rut; cry of buck in rutting season; bullying

roncar §73 *intr* to snore; (*el viento, el mar*) roar; cry in rutting season; bully

ronce•ro -ra *adj* slow, poky; grouchy

ron•co -ca *adj* hoarse; harsh ‖ *f* see **ronca**

roncha *f* weal, welt; black-and-blue mark

ronchar *tr* to crunch

ronda *f* (*de un policía; de visitas; de cigarros o bebidas*) round; (*juego del corro*) (Chile) ring-around-a-rosy; **ronda negociadora** round of negotiations

rondar *tr* to go around; fly around; patrol; hang around; court ‖ *intr* to patrol by night; gad about at nighttime; go serenading; prowl; (mil) to make the rounds

ronquedad *f* hoarseness; harshness

re
ro

ronquera *f* hoarseness
ronquido *m* snore; rasping sound
ronronear *intr* to purr
ronroneo *m* purr, purring
ronzal *m* halter
ronzar §60 *tr* to crunch, munch
roña *f* scab, mange; sticky dirt; pine bark; stinginess; spite, ill will; (Col) malingering; **jugar a roña** (Peru) to play for fun
roño•so -sa *adj* scabby, mangy; dirty, filthy; stingy; spiteful
ropa *f* clothing, clothes; dry goods; **a quema ropa** point-blank; **ropa blanca** linen; **ropa de cama** bed linen; bed-clothes; **ropa dominguera** Sunday best; **ropa hecha** ready-made clothes; **ropa interior** underwear; **ropa sucia** laundry
ropaje *m* clothes, clothing; gown, robe; drapery
ropaveje•ro -ra *mf* old-clothes dealer
rope•ro -ra *mf* ready-made clothier; wardrobe keeper ‖ *m* wardrobe, clothes closet
roque *m* rook, castle
roque•ño -ña *adj* rocky; hard, flinty
rorro *m* baby; (Mex) doll
rosa *f* rose; **rosa de los vientos** or **rosa náutica** (naut) compass card; **rosas** popcorn; **verlo todo de color de rosa** to see everything through rose-colored glasses
rosa•do -da *adj* rose-colored, rosy; pink; flushed ‖ *f* frost
rosaleda or **rosalera** *f* rose garden
rosario *m* rosary; (de sucesos) string; chain pump
ros•bif *m* (pl **-bifs**) roast beef
rosca *f* coil, spiral; (de una espiral) turn; twisted roll; (de un tornillo) thread; (Chile) padded ring
roscar §73 *tr* to thread
roseta *f* sprinkling spout or nozzle; red spot on cheek; **rosetas** popcorn
rosetón *m* rose window
rosita *f* little rose; (Chile) earring; **rositas** popcorn
rosquilla *f* coffeecake, doughnut, cruller
rostro *m* face; snout; beak; (retrato) **de rostro entero** full-faced
rostropáli•do -da *mf* paleface
rota *f* rout, defeat; (naut) route, course
rotisería *f* fast-food restaurant; delicatessen
rotograbado *m* rotogravure
rótula *f* lozenge; kneecap; knuckle
rotulador *m* felt pen
rotular *tr* to label, title, letter
rótulo *m* label, title; poster, show bill
rotun•do -da *adj* round; rotund, sonorous, full; peremptory
rotura *f* break, breaking; breach, opening; tear, tearing
roturación *f* (agr) reclamation
roya *f* (agr) blight, rust
rozamiento *m* rubbing; friction; (desavenencia) (fig) friction
rozar §60 *tr* to graze; scrape; border on; grub, stub; (las tierras) clear; (la hierba) nibble; (leña menuda) cut and gather ‖ *intr*

to graze by ‖ *ref* to be on close terms, rub elbows, hobnob; falter, stammer; be alike
roznar *tr* to crunch ‖ *intr* to bray
roznido *m* crunch, crunching noise; bray, braying
Rte. *abbr* **Remite**
ru•bí *m* (pl **-bíes**) ruby; (de un reloj) ruby, jewel
rubia *f* blonde; station wagon; peseta; **rubia oxigenada** peroxide blonde; **rubia platino** platinum blonde
rubia•les *mf* (pl **-les**) goldilocks
ru•bio -bia *adj* blond, fair; golden ‖ *m* blond ‖ *f* see **rubia**
rublo *m* ruble
rubor *m* bright red; blush, flush; bashfulness
ruborizar §60 *tr* to make blush ‖ *ref* to blush
rúbrica *f* title, heading; (rasgo después de la firma de uno) flourish
rubricación *f* listing; itemization
ru•bro -bra *adj* red ‖ *m* title, heading; (Chile) (com) entry
rudimento *m* rudiment
ru•do -da *adj* coarse, rough; rude, crude; dull, stupid; hard, severe
rueca *f* distaff
rueda *f* wheel; caster, roller; (de gente) ring, circle; round slice; pinwheel; (de la cola del pavo) spread; sunfish; **hacer la rueda** (el pavo) to spread its tail; **hacer la rueda a** to play up to; **rueda de andar** treadmill; **rueda de cadena** sprocket, sprocket wheel; **rueda de escape** escapement wheel; **rueda de fuego** pinwheel; **rueda dentada** gearwheel; **rueda de paletas** paddle wheel; **rueda de prensa** press conference; **rueda de presos** line-up; **rueda de recambio** spare wheel; **rueda de tornillo sin fin** worm wheel; **rueda motriz** drive wheel
ruedo *m* turn, rotation; round mat; selvage; hemline; (taur) ring; **a todo ruedo** at all events
ruego *m* request, entreaty; prayer
ru•fián -fiana *mf* bawd, go-between ‖ *m* cur, cad
ru•fo -fa *adj* sandy, sandy-haired; curly-haired
rugido *m* roar; (de las tripas) rumble
rugir §27 *intr* to roar; rumble
rugo•so -sa *adj* rugged, wrinkled
ruibarbo *m* rhubarb
ruido *m* noise; rumor; row, rumpus
ruido•so -sa *adj* noisy; loud; sensational
ruin *adj* base, mean, vile; stingy; (animal) vicious
ruina *f* ruin
ruindad *f* baseness, meanness, vileness; stinginess; viciousness
ruino•so -sa *adj* tottery, run-down
ruiseñor *m* nightingale
ruleta *f* roulette; (CAm, Arg) tape measure
ruletero *m* (Mex) cruising taxi driver (in search of fares)
rulo *m* roll; rolling pin; (hair) curler
ruma•no -na *adj* & *mf* Rumanian

rumbo *m* bearing, course, direction; pomp, show; generosity; (CAm) noisy celebration; **por aquellos rumbos** in those parts; **rumbo a** bound for

rumbo•so -sa *adj* pompous, magnificent; generous

rumiar *tr & intr* to ruminate

rumor *m* rumor; (*de voces*) murmur, buzz; rumble

rumorear *tr* to rumor, circulate by a rumor ‖ *intr* to murmur, buzz, rumble ‖ *ref* to be rumored; **se rumorea que** it is rumored that

rumoro•so -sa *adj* noisy, loud, rumbling

runfla *f* or **runflada** *f* string, row; (*en los naipes*) sequence

ruptor *m* (elec) contact breaker

ruptura *f* rupture, break; crack, split; (*cesación de relaciones*) rupture

Rusia *f* Russia; **la Rusia Soviética** Soviet Russia

ru•so -sa *adj & mf* Russian

rúst. *abbr* **rústica**

rústi•co -ca *adj* rustic; coarse, crude, clumsy; (*latín*) Vulgar; **en rústica** paper-bound ‖ *m* rustic, peasant

ruta *f* route; **ruta aérea** air lane

rutilante *adj* shining, sparkling

rutina *f* routine

rutina•rio -ria *adj* routine

S

S, s (ese) *f* twenty-second letter of the Spanish alphabet

S. *abbr* **San, Santo, sobresaliente, sur**

sábado *m* (*de los cristianos*) Saturday; (*de los judíos*) Sabbath

sábalo *m* shad

sabana *f* savanna, pampa; **ponerse en la sabana** (Ven) to get rich overnight

sábana *f* sheet; altar cloth

sabandija *f* insect, bug, worm; (*persona*) vermin; **sabandijas** (*animales o personas*) vermin

sabanilla *f* kerchief; altar cloth

sabañón *m* chilblain

sabe•dor -dora *adj* aware, informed

sabelotodo *m* (*pl* **sabelotodo**) know-it-all, wise guy

saber *m* knowledge, learning ‖ *v* §64 *tr & intr* to know; to find out; to taste; **a saber** namely, to wit; **me sabe mal** I'm sorry, I regret; **no saber dónde meterse** to not know which way to turn; **que yo sepa** as far as I know; **saber a** to taste of; smack of; **saber a poco** to be just a taste, taste like more; **saber de** to be aware of; hear from ‖ *ref* to know; be or become known

sabidi•llo -lla *adj & mf* know-it-all

sabi•do -da *adj* well-informed; learned; **de sabido** certainly, surely

sabiduría *f* wisdom; knowledge, learning

sabiendas — **a sabiendas** knowingly, consciously; **a sabiendas de que** knowing that, aware that

sabihon•do -da *adj & mf* know-it-all

sa•bio -bia *adj* wise; learned; (*animal*) trained ‖ *mf* wise person, scholar, scientist ‖ *m* wise man, sage

sablazo *m* stroke with a saber, wound made by a saber; sponging; **dar un sablazo a** to hit for a loan

sable *m* saber, cutlass; (coll) sponging

sablear *tr* to hit for a loan, sponge on ‖ *intr* to go around sponging

sablista *mf* sponger

sabor *m* taste, flavor

saborcillo *m* slight taste, touch

saborear *tr* to flavor; taste; savor; entice; ‖ *ref* to smack one's lips; **saborearse de** to taste; to savor

sabotaje *m* sabotage

sabotear *tr & intr* to sabotage

sabro•so -sa *adj* tasty, savory, delicious

sabueso *m* bloodhound; sleuth

saburro•so -sa *adj* (*boca*) foul; (*lengua*) coated

sacaboca•do *m* or **sacaboca•dos** *m* (*pl* **-dos**) ticket punch; sure thing

sacabotas *m* (*pl* **-tas**) bootjack

sacacor•chos *m* (*pl* **-chos**) corkscrew

sacaman•chas *mf* (*pl* **-chas**) clothes cleaner, spot remover; dry cleaner; dyer

sacamue•las *m* (*pl* **-las**) tooth puller; quack, cheat

sacamuer•tos *m* (*pl* **-tos**) stagehand

sacapintura *m* paint remover

sacapun•tas *m* (*pl* **-tas**) pencil sharpener

sacar §73 *tr* (*un clavo, una espada, agua, una conclusión*) to draw; pull out; pull up; take out; extract, remove; show; bring out; publish; find out, solve; (*un secreto*) elicit, draw out; copy; (*una fotografía*) take; except, exclude; get, obtain; produce, invent, imitate; (*un premio*) win; (*una pelota*) serve; (*el pecho*) stick out; **sacar a bailar** to drag in; **sacar a relucir** to bring up unexpectedly; **sacar en claro** or **en limpio** to recopy clearly; deduce, clear up ‖ *ref* (Mex) to make off

sacarina *f* saccharin

sacasi•llas *m* (*pl* **-llas**) stagehand

sacerdocio *m* priesthood

sacerdote *m* priest

saciar *tr* to satiate

ro
sa

saco *m* bag, sack; coat, jacket; sack, plunder, pillage; (*de mentiras*) pack; **saco de dormir** sleeping bag; **saco de noche** overnight bag

sacramento *m* sacrament

sacrificar §73 *tr* to sacrifice; slaughter ‖ *intr* to sacrifice ‖ *ref* to sacrifice; sacrifice oneself

sacrificio *m* sacrifice; **sacrificio del altar** Sacrifice of the Mass

sacrilegio *m* sacrilege

sacríle·go -ga *adj* sacrilegious

sacristán *m* sacristan; sexton; **sacristán de amén** yes man

sacristía *f* sacristy, vestry

sa·cro -cra *adj* sacred

sacudida *f* shake, jar, jolt, jerk, bump; (elec) shock

sacudi·do -da *adj* intractable; determined ‖ *f* see **sacudida**

sacudir *tr* to shake; beat; jar, jolt; rock; shake off ‖ *ref* to shake, to shake oneself; rock; **sacudirse bien** to wangle one's way out

sádi·co -ca *adj* sadistic ‖ *mf* sadist

saeta *f* arrow, dart; (*del reloj*) hand; magnetic needle

saetilla *f* small arrow; (*del reloj*) hand; magnetic needle; (bot) arrowhead

saetín *m* flume, millrace

sa·gaz *adj* (*pl* **-gaces**) sagacious; keen-scented

Sagitario *m* (astr) Sagittarius

sagra·do -da *adj* sacred ‖ *m* asylum, haven, sanctuary; **acogerse a sagrado** to take sanctuary

sagrario *m* sanctuary, shrine; ciborium

sahariana *f* tight-fitting military jacket

sahornar *ref* to skin oneself

sahumar *tr* to perfume with smoke or incense; (Chile) to gold-plate, silver-plate

sainete *m* one-act farce; flavor, relish, spice, zest; sauce, seasoning; tidbit

sa·jón -jona *adj* & *mf* Saxon

sal *f* salt; grace, charm; wit; (CAm) misfortune; **sal de sosa** washing soda; **sales aromáticas** smelling salts; **sal gema** rock salt

sala *f* hall; drawing room, living room, sitting room; **sala de batalla** sorting room; **sala de calderas** boiler room; **sala de enfermos** infirmary; **sala de espera** waiting room; **sala de estar** living room, sitting room; **sala de fiestas** night club; **sala del cine** moving-picture house; **sala de máquinas** engine room

saladillo *m* salted peanut

Salamina *f* Salamis

salar *tr* to salt; spoil, ruin; bring bad luck to

salario *m* wages, pay; **salario de hambre** starvation wages

salcochar *tr* to boil in salt water

salcocho *m* food boiled in salt water

salchicha *f* sausage

salchiche·ro -ra *mf* pork butcher

saldar *tr* to settle, liquidate; sell out

saldo *m* settlement; balance; remnant; bargain; **saldo de mercancías** job lot; **saldo deudor** debit balance

salero *m* saltshaker, saltcellar; salt lick; grace, charm, wit

salero·so -sa *adj* charming, winsome, lively; salty, witty

salgar §44 *tr* (*el ganado*) to salt

salida *f* start; departure; exit; outcome, result; subterfuge; pretext; outlay, expenditure; projection; outlying fields; (elec) output; (sport) start; (mil) sally, sortie; (coll) witticism, sally; **salida de baño** bathrobe; **salida del sol** sunrise; **salida de teatro** evening wrap; **salida de teatros** after-theater party; **salida de tono** irrelevancy, impropriety; **salida lanzada** (sport) running start; **tener salida** to sell well; (*una muchacha*) to be popular with the boys

saliente *adj* projecting; (*p.ej., tren*) outbound; (*sol*) rising ‖ *m* east ‖ *f* projection; (*de la carretera*) shoulder

salir §65 *intr* to go out, come out; leave, go away, depart; sail; run out, come to an end; appear, show up; (*una mancha*) come out, come off; (*p.ej., el sol*) rise; shoot, spring, come up; project, stick out; make the first move; result, turn out; be elected; **salga lo que saliere** come what may; **salir a** to amount to; open into; resemble, look like; **salir al, encuentro a** to go to meet; take a stand against; get ahead of; **salir bien en un examen** to pass an examination; **salir con bien** to be successful; **salir de** to depart from; cease being; get rid of; (*p.ej., su juicio, sentido*) lose; **salir disparado** to start like a shot; **salir pitando** to start off on a mad run; blow up, hit the ceiling; **salir reprobado** (*en un examen*) to fail ‖ *ref* to slip out, escape; slip off, run off; leak; boil over; **salirse con la suya** to have one's own way; carry one's point

salitre *m* saltpeter

saliva *f* saliva; **gastar saliva** to rattle along; to waste one's breath

salmo *m* psalm

salmón *m* salmon

salmuera *f* brine, pickle; salty food or drink

salobre *adj* brackish, saltish

salón *m* salon, drawing room; (*de un buque*) saloon; meeting room; **salón de actos** auditorium; **salón de baile** ballroom; **salón de belleza** beauty parlor; **salón del automóvil** automobile show; **salón de refrescos** ice-cream parlor; **salón de tertulia** or **salón social** lounge

saloncillo *m* (*p.ej., de un teatro*) rest room

salpicadero *m* control panel; (aut) dashboard

salpicar §73 *tr* to splash; sprinkle

salpimentar §2 *tr* to salt and pepper, season with salt and pepper; (fig) to sweeten

salpullido *m* rash, eruption

salpullir §13 *tr* to cause a rash on; splotch ‖ *ref* to break out

salsa *f* sauce, dressing, gravy; **salsa de ají** chili sauce; **salsa de tomate** catsup, ketchup; **salsa inglesa** Worcestershire sauce

salsera *f* gravy dish; small saucer (*to mix paints*)

saltaban•co *m* or **saltaban•cos** *m* (*pl* -cos) quack, mountebank; prestidigitator; nuisance

saltamon•tes *m* (*pl* -tes) grasshopper

saltar *tr* to jump, jump over; skip, skip over ‖ *intr* to jump, leap, hop, skip; bounce; shoot up, spurt; come loose, come off; crack, break, burst; chip; project, stick out; **saltar a la vista** or **los ojos** to be self-evident; **saltar por** to jump over, jump out of ‖ *ref* to skip; come off

saltatum•bas *m* (*pl* -bas) burying parson

salteador *m* highwayman, holdup man

saltear *tr* to attack, hold up, waylay; take by surprise

saltimbanco *m* var of **saltabanco**

salto *m* jump, leap, bound; skip; dive; fall, waterfall; leapfrog; **salto de altura** high jump; **salto de ángel** swan dive; **salto de cama** morning wrap, dressing gown; **salto de carpa** jackknife; **salto de esquí** ski jump; **salto de viento** (naut) sudden shift in the wind; **salto mortal** somersault; **salto ornamental** fancy dive

salubre *adj* healthful, salubrious

salud *f* health; welfare; salvation; greeting; **gastar, vender** or **verter salud** to radiate health ‖ *interj* greetings!; **¡salud y pesetas!** health and wealth!

saludar *tr* to greet, salute, hail, bow to; give regards to ‖ *intr* to salute; bow

saludo *m* greeting, salute, bow; salutation; **saludo final** conclusion

salutación *f* salutation, greeting, bow

salva *f* greeting, welcome; salvo; oath; tray; (*de aplausos; de una batería de artillería*) round

salvado *m* bran

salva•dor -dora *mf* savior, saver, rescuer ‖ **el Salvador** the Saviour; (*país de la América Central*) El Salvador

salvadore•ño -ña *adj* & *mf* Salvadoran

salvaguardar *tr* to safeguard

salvaguardia *m* bodyguard, escort ‖ *f* safeguard, safe-conduct; protection, shelter

salvaje *adj* wild, uncultivated; savage; stupid ‖ *mf* savage; dolt

salvaji•no -na *adj* wild; (*de la carne de los animales monteses*) gamy ‖ *f* wild animal; wild animals

salvamante•les *m* (*pl* -les) coaster

salvamento *m* salvation; lifesaving; rescue; salvage; place of safety

salvar *tr* to save, rescue; to salvage; (*una dificultad*) avoid, overcome; (*un obstáculo*) clear, get around; (*una distancia*) cover, get over; rise above; jump over; make an exception of; **salvar apariencias** to save face ‖ *ref* to save oneself, escape danger; be saved; **sálvese el que pueda** every man for himself

salvavi•das *m* (*pl* -das) life preserver; lifeboat; (*empleado de una estación de salvamento*) lifeguard

salvedad *f* reservation, exception

salvia *f* (bot) sage

sal•vo -va *adj* safe; omitted; **a salvo** safe, out

of danger; **a salvo de** safe from ‖ **salvo** *prep* save, except for; **salvo error u omisión (s.e.u.o.)** barring error or omission; **salvo que** unless ‖ *f* see **salva**

salvoconducto *m* safe-conduct

sámara *f* (bot) key, key fruit

san *adj* apocopated and unstressed form of **santo**

sanaloto•do *m* (*pl* -do) cure-all

sanar *tr* to cure, heal ‖ *intr* to heal; recover

sanción *f* (*aprobación*) sanction; (*castigo, pena*) penalty

sancionar *tr* (*aprobar*) to sanction; (*imponer pena a*) penalize

sancochar *tr* to parboil

sandalia *f* sandal

sándalo *m* (yellow) sandalwood

san•dez *f* (*pl* -deces) folly, nonsense; piece of folly

sandía *f* watermelon

san•dio -dia *adj* foolish, nonsensical

saneamiento *m* sanitation, drainage; guarantee

sanear *tr* to guarantee; indemnify; make sanitary, drain, dry up

sangrar *tr* to bleed; drain; tap; (typ) to indent; (coll) to rob ‖ *intr* to bleed; **estar sangrando** to be new or recent; be plain or obvious ‖ *ref* to have oneself bled; (*los colores*) run

sangre *f* blood; **a sangre** by horsepower; **a sangre fría** in cold blood; **pura sangre** *m* thoroughbred; **sangre torera** bullfighting in the blood

sangría *f* bleeding; outlet, draining; ditch, trench; (*bebida*) sangaree; tap; tapping; (typ) indentation

sangrien•to -ta *adj* bloody; bleeding; cruel, sanguinary

sangrigor•do -da *adj* unpleasant

sangrilige•ro -ra *adj* nice, pleasant

sangripesa•do -da *adj* unpleasant

sangüesa *f* raspberry

sangüeso *m* raspberry bush

sanguijuela *f* leech

sanguina•rio -ria *adj* sanguinary, bloodthirsty

sanidad *f* healthiness; healthfulness; health; sanitation; **sanidad pública** health department

sanita•rio -ria *adj* sanitary

sa•no -na *adj* hale, healthy; healthful; sound; sane; earnest, sincere; safe, sure; whole, untouched, unharmed; **sano y salvo** safe and sound

santiague•ro -ra *adj* Santiago de Cuba ‖ *mf* native or inhabitant of Santiago de Cuba

santia•gués -guesa *adj* Santiago de Compostela ‖ *mf* native or inhabitant of Santiago de Compostela

santigui•no -na *adj* Santiago de Chile ‖ *mf* native or inhabitant of Santiago de Chile

santiamén *m* jiffy; **en un santiamén** in the twinkling of an eye

santidad *f* holiness, sanctity, saintliness; **su Santidad** his Holiness

sa
sa

santificar §73 *tr* to sanctify, hallow, conse-crate; (*las fiestas*) keep; excuse, justify
santiguar §10 *tr* to bless, make the sign of the cross over; punish, slap, abuse ‖ *ref* to cross oneself, make the sign of the cross
san·to -ta *adj* holy, saintly, blessed; (*día*) live-long; artless, simple; santo y bueno well and good ‖ *mf* saint ‖ *m* name day; image of a saint; a santo de because of, on; desnudar a un santo para vestir a otro to rob Peter to pay Paul; írsele a uno el santo al cielo to forget what one was up to; santo y seña password, watchword
Santo Domingo Hispaniola
santuario *m* sanctuary, shrine; (Col) buried treasure; (Col, Ven) Indian idol
santu·rrón -rrona *adj* sanctimonious ‖ *mf* sanctimonious person
saña *f* fury, rage; cruelty
sañu·do -da *adj* furious, enraged; cruel
sapiente *adj* wise, intelligent
sapo *m* toad; (coll) stuffed shirt; (Chile) little runt
saque *m* (*en el tenis*) serve, service; server; service line; (Col) distillery; tener buen saque to be a heavy eater and drinker
saquear *tr* to sack, plunder, pillage, loot
sarampión *m* measles
sarao *m* soirée, evening party
sarape *m* (Guat, Mex) bright-colored woolen poncho
sarcasmo *m* sarcasm
sarcásti·co -ca *adj* sarcastic
sardina *f* sardine; como sardinas en banasta or en lata packed in like sardines
sar·do -da *adj & mf* Sardinian
sarga *f* serge
sargento *m* sergeant
sarmiento *m* vine shoot, running stem
sarna *f* itch, mange
sarno·so -sa *adj* itchy, mangy
sarrace·no -na *adj & mf* Saracen
sarracina *f* scuffle, free fight; bloody brawl
sarro *m* crust; (*p.ej., en la lengua*) fur; (*en los dientes*) tartar
sarta *f* string; line, fine, series
sartén *f* frying pan; saltar de la sartén y dar en las brasas to jump from the frying pan into the fire
sastre *m* tailor
satélite *m* satellite; satélite de comunica-ciones communications satellite; satélite espía spy satellite
satelizar §60 *tr* to put into orbit; (pol) to make a satellite of ‖ *ref* to go into orbit
satén *m* sateen
satíri·co -ca *adj* satiric(al) ‖ *mf* satirist
satirizar §60 *tr & intr* to satirize
satisfacción *f* satisfaction
satisfacer §39 *tr & intr* to satisfy ‖ *ref* to satisfy oneself, be satisfied, take satisfac-tion
satisfacto·rio -ria *adj* satisfactory
saturar *tr* to saturate; satiate
sauce *m* willow tree; sauce de Babilonia or sauce llorón weeping willow
saúco *m* elder, elderberry

savia *f* sap
saxofón *m* or saxófono *m* saxophone
saya *f* skirt; petticoat
sayo *m* smock frock, tunic; garment
sazón *f* ripeness; season; time, occasion; taste, seasoning; a la sazón at that time; en sazón in season, ripe; on time, opportunely
sazonar *tr* to ripen; season ‖ *ref* to ripen, mature
s/c *abbr* su cuenta
S.E. *abbr* Su Excelencia
se *pron reflex* himself, to himself; herself, to herself; itself, to itself; themselves, to themselves; yourself, to yourself; your-selves, to yourselves; oneself, to oneself; each other, to each other ‖ *pron pers* (used before the pronouns lo, la, le, etc.) to him, to her, to it, to them, to you
sebo *m* tallow; fat, suet
seca *f* drought; dry season
secador *m* drier, hair drier
secadora *f* clothes drier
secafir·mas *m* (*pl* -mas) blotter
secano *m* dry land, unwatered land
secansa *f* sequence
secante *m* blotting paper
secar §73 *tr* to dry, wipe dry; annoy, bore ‖ *ref* to dry, get dry; dry oneself; wither; be dry, be thirsty; (*un pozo*) run dry
secarropa *f* clothes dryer; secarropa de tra-vesaños clotheshorse
sección *f* section; cross section; sección de fondo editorial section
secesión *f* secession
se·co -ca *adj* dry; dried up, withered; lank, lean; harsh, sharp; (*bebida*) straight, indif-ferent; plain, unadorned ‖ *f* see seca
secreta·rio -ria *adj* confidential, trusted ‖ *mf* secretary
secreter *m* secretary (*writing desk*)
secre·to -ta *adj* secret ‖ *m* secret; secrecy; hiding place, secret drawer; (*mecanismo oculto para abrir una cerradura*) key; en el secreto de las cosas on the inside
secta *f* sect
secta·rio -ria *adj & mf* sectarian
sector *m* sector; sector de distribución house current, power line
se·cuaz *adj* (*pl* -cuaces) partisan ‖ *mf* parti-san, follower
secuela *f* sequel, result
secuencia *f* sequence
secuestrar *tr* to kidnap; (*un avión*) to hijack; (law) to sequester
secular *adj* secular
secundar *tr* to second, back
secunda·rio -ria *adj* secondary ‖ *m* (elec) secondary
sed *f* thirst; drought; tener sed to be thirsty
seda *f* silk; como una seda smooth as silk; easy as pie; sweet-natured; seda encerada dental floss
sedal *m* fish line
sedán *m* sedan; sedán de reparto delivery truck
sede *f* (*p.ej., del gobierno*) seat; (eccl) see; Santa Sede Holy See

sedenta·rio -ria *adj* sedentary
sede·ño -ña *adj* silk, silken
sedición *f* sedition
sedicio·so -sa *adj* seditious
sedien·to -ta *adj* thirsty; (*terreno*) dry; anxious, eager
sedimento *m* sediment
sedo·so -sa *adj* silky
seducción *f* seduction; charm, captivation
seducir §19 *tr* to seduce; tempt, lead astray; charm, captivate
seducti·vo -va *adj* seductive; tempting; charming, captivating
seduc·tor -tora *adj* seductive; tempting; charming || *mf* seducer; tempter; charmer
sefar·dí (*pl* **-díes**) *adj* Sephardic || *mf* Sephardi
sega·dor -dora *adj* harvesting || *m* harvestman || *f* harvester; mowing machine; **segadora de césped** lawn mower; **segadora trilladora** combine
segar §66 *tr* to reap, harvest, mow; mow down || *intr* to reap, harvest, mow
segazón *f* harvest; harvest time
seglar *adj* secular, lay || *m* layman || *f* laywoman
segmento *m* segment; **segmento de émbolo** piston ring
segregacionista *mf* segregationist
segregar §44 *tr* to segregate
seguida *f* series, succession; **de seguida** without interruption, continuously; at once; in a row; **en seguida** at once, immediately
seguidilla *f* Spanish stanza made up of a quatrain and a tercet; **seguidillas** seguidilla (*Spanish dance and music*)
segui·do -da *adj* continued, successive; straight, direct; running, in a row; **todo seguido** straight ahead || *f* see **seguida**
seguimiento *m* chase, hunt, pursuit; continuation; (*de vehículos espaciales*) tracking
seguir §67 *tr* to follow; pursue; continue; dog, hound || *intr* to go on, continue; still be, be now; keep + *ger* || *ref* to follow, ensue; issue, spring
según *prep* according to, as per; **según que** according as || *conj* as, according as
segunda *f* double meaning; (aut & mus) second
segundero *m* second hand; **segundero central** sweep-second, center-second
segun·do -da *adj* second || *m* second; **ser sin segundo** to be second to none || *f* see **segunda**
segur *f* axe; sickle
segurador *s* security, bondsman
seguridad *f* security; safety; surety; certainty; assurance; confidence
segu·ro -ra *adj* sure, certain; secure, safe; reliable; constant; steady, unfailing || *m* assurance, certainty; safety; confidence; insurance; **a buen seguro** surely, truly; **seguro contra accidentes** accident insurance; **seguro de desempleo** or **desocupación** unemployment insurance; **seguro de enfermedad** health insurance; **seguro de incendios** fire insurance; **seguro**

sobre la vida life insurance; **sobre seguro** without risk || **seguro** *adv* surely
seis *adj* & *pron* six; **las seis** six o'clock || *m* six; (*en las fechas*) sixth
seiscien·tos -tas *adj* & *pron* six hundred || **seiscientos** *m* six hundred
selección *f* selection
seleccionar *tr* to select, choose
selec·to -ta *adj* select, choice
selva *f* forest, woods; jungle
selváti·co -ca *adj* woodsy; rustic, wild
sellar *tr* to seal; stamp; close; finish up
sello *m* seal; stamp; signet; wafer; **sello aéreo** air-mail stamp; **sello de correo** postage stamp; **sello de urgencia** special-delivery stamp; **sello fiscal** revenue stamp
semáforo *m* semaphore; traffic light
semana *f* week; week's pay; **semana inglesa** working week of five and a half days
semanal *adj* weekly
semanalmente *adv* weekly
semana·rio -ria *adj* & *m* weekly
semánti·co -ca *adj* semantic || *f* semantics
semblante *m* face, mien, countenance; appearance, expression, look
semblanza *f* biographical sketch, portrait
sembrado *m* sown ground, grain field
sembrar §2 *tr* to seed, sow; scatter, spread; sprinkle
semejante *adj* like, similar; such; **semejante a** like; **semejantes** alike, e.g., **estas sillas son semejantes** these chairs are alike || *m* resemblance, likeness; fellow, fellow man
semejanza *f* similarity, resemblance; simile; **a semejanza de** like
semejar *tr* to resemble, be like || *intr* & *ref* to be alike; **semejar a** or **semejarse a** to resemble, be like
semen *m* semen
semental *adj* (*animal*) stud, breeding || *m* sire; stallion; stock bull
semestral *adj* semester
semestre *m* semester
semibola *f* little slam
semibreve *f* (mus) whole note
semiconductor *m* semiconductor
semiconsciente *adj* semiconscious
semicul·to -ta *adj* semilearned
semidifun·to -ta *adj* half-dead
semidormi·do -da *adj* half-asleep
semifinal *adj* & *f* (sport) semifinal
semilla *f* seed; **semilla de césped** grass seed
semillero *m* seedbed
seminario *m* seminary; seminar; nursery
semi-remolque *m* semitrailer
semita *mf* Semite || *m* (*idioma*) Semitic
semíti·co -ca *adj* Semitic
semivi·vo -va *adj* half-alive
semovientes *mpl* stock, livestock
sempiter·no -na *adj* everlasting
Sena *m* Seine
senado *m* senate
senador *m* senator
senaduría *f* senatorship
sencillez *f* simplicity, plainness, candor
senci·llo -lla *adj* simple, plain, candid; single || *m* change, loose change

sa
se

senda *f* path, footpath

sendero *m* path, footpath, byway

sen·dos -das *adj pl* one each, one to each, e.g., **les dio sendos libros** he gave one book to each of them, he gave each of them a book

senectud *f* age, old age

senil *adj* senile

senilidad *f* senility

senilismo *m* (pathol) senility

seno *m* bosom, breast; lap; heart; womb; bay, gulf; cavity, hollow, recess; asylum, refuge

sensación *f* sensation

sensatez *f* good sense

sensa·to -ta *adj* sensible

sensibilizar §60 *tr* to sensitize

sensible *adj* appreciable, perceptible, noticeable, sensible; considerable; sensitive; deplorable, regrettable

sensiblería *f* mawkishness

sensible·ro -ra *adj* mawkish

sensiti·vo -va *adj* (*de los sentidos*) sense, sensitive; sentient; stimulating

senso·rio -ria *adj* sensory

sensual *adj* sensual, sensuous

sentada *f* sitting; **de una sentada** at one sitting

senta·do -da *adj* seated; settled; stable, permanent; sedate; **dar por sentado** to take for granted ‖ *f* see **sentada**

sentar §2 *tr* to seat; settle; fit, suit; agree with ‖ *ref* to sit, sit down; settle, settle down

sentencia *f* maxim; (law) sentence

sentenciar *tr* to sentence; (*una cuestión*) to decide; (*p.ej., un libro a la hoguera*) to consign

senti·do -da *adj* felt; deep-felt; sensitive; eloquent; **darse por sentido** to take offense ‖ *m* sense, meaning; direction; consciousness; **sentido común** common sense

sentimiento *m* sentiment; feeling; sorrow, regret

sentir *m* feeling; opinion; judgment ‖ §68 *tr* to feel; hear; be or feel sorry for; sense ‖ *intr* to feel; be sorry, feel sorry ‖ *ref* to feel; feel oneself to be; be resentful; crack, be cracked; **sentirse de** to feel; have a pain in; resent

seña *f* sign, mark, token; password, watchword; **por las señas** to all appearances; **por más señas** or **por señas** as a greater proof; **seña de tráfico** traffic sign; **señas** address, description

señal *f* sign, mark, token; landmark; bookmark; trace, vestige; scar; signal; traffic light; representation; reminder; pledge; brand; down payment; **señal de ocupado** (telp) busy signal; **señal de tramo** (rr) block signal; **señal de vídeo** video signal; **señal digital** fingerprint; **señal para marcar** (telp) dial tone

señala *f* (Chile) earmark (*on livestock*)

señala·do -da *adj* noted, distinguished

señalar *tr* to mark; show, indicate; point at, point out; signal; brand; determine, fix;

appoint; sign and seal; scar; threaten ‖ *ref* to distinguish oneself, excel

señalizar §60 *tr* to signal

señor *m* sir, mister; lord, master, owner; **muy señor mío** Dear Sir; **señores** Mr. and Mrs.; ladies and gentlemen

señora *f* madam, missus; mistress, owner; wife; **muy señora mía** Dear Madam; **Nuestra Señora** our Lady; **señora de compañía** chaperon

señorear *tr* to dominate, rule; master, control; seize, take control of; tower over; excel ‖ *intr* to strut, swagger ‖ *ref* to strut, swagger; control oneself; **señorearse de** to seize, take control of

señoría *f* lordship; ladyship; rule, sway

señoril *adj* lordly; haughty; majestic

señorío *m* dominion, sway, rule; mastery; arrogance, lordliness, majesty; gentry, nobility

señorita *f* young lady; miss

señorito *m* master; young gentleman; playboy

señuelo *m* decoy, lure; bait; enticement

separación *f* separation; **separación de poderes** (pol) separation of powers

separa·do -da *adj* separate; separated; apart; **por separado** separately; under separate cover

separar *tr* to separate; dismiss, discharge ‖ *ref* to separate; resign

separata *f* reprint, offprint

sept.ᵉ *abbr* **septiembre**

septeto *m* septet

sépti·co -ca *adj* septic

septiembre *m* September

sépti·mo -ma *adj & m* seventh

sepulcro *m* sepulcher, tomb, grave; **santo sepulcro** Holy Sepulcher

sepultar *tr* to bury; hide away

sepultura *f* burial; grave; **estar con un pie en la sepultura** to have one foot in the grave

sepulturero *m* gravedigger

sequedad *f* dryness, drought; gruffness, surliness

sequía *f* drought

séquito *m* retinue, suite; following, popularity

ser *m* being; essence; life ‖ *v* §69 *v aux* (to form passive voice) to be, e.g., **el discurso fue aplaudido por todos** the speech was applauded by everybody ‖ *intr* to be; **a no ser por** if it were not for; **a no ser que** unless; **érase que se era** once upon a time there was; **es decir** that is to say; **sea lo que fuere** be that as it may; **ser de** to belong to; become of; be, e.g., **el reloj es de oro** the watch is gold; **ser de ver** to be worth seeing; **soy yo** it is me, it is I

serafín *m* seraph; great beauty (*person*)

serena *f* night love song; night dew, night air

serenar *tr* to calm; pacify; cool; settle

serenata *f* serenade

serenidad *f* serenity; **serenidad del espíritu** peace of mind

sere•no -na *adj* serene, calm; clear, cloudless ‖ *m* night watchman; night dew, night air ‖ *f* see **serena**

serial *adj* serial ‖ *m* (telv) serial; **serial lacrimógeno** soap opera; **serial radiado** (rad) serial

serie *f* series; **de serie** serial; stock, e.g., **coche de serie** stock car; **en serie** mass; **fuera de serie** custom-built, special; outsize

seriedad *f* seriousness; reliability; sternness, severity; solemnity

se•rio -ria *adj* serious; reliable; stern; solemn

sermón *m* sermon

sermonear *tr & intr* to sermonize

serpear or **serpentear** *intr* to wind, meander; wriggle, squirm

serpentín *m* coil

serpiente *f* serpent, snake; **serpiente de cascabel** rattlesnake

serranía *f* range of mountains, mountainous country

serra•no -na *adj* highland, mountain ‖ *mf* highlander, mountaineer

serrar §2 *tr* to saw

serrería *f* sawmill

serrín *m* sawdust

serrucho *m* handsaw

Servia *f* Serbia

servicial *adj* accommodating, obliging

servicio *m* service; (tennis) service, serve; (Am) toilet; **en acto de servicio** in the line of duty; **fuera de servicio** out of service; inoperative; (coll) down; **libre servicio** self-service; **servicio de grúa** (aut) towing service; **servicio postventa** customer service; **servicio telegráfico y telefónico** wire service

servi•dor -dora *mf* servant; humble servant; (tennis) server; **servidor de Vd.** your servant, at your service ‖ *m* waiter; suitor ‖ *f* waitress

servidumbre *f* servitude; servants, help; compulsion; (law) easement; **servidumbre de la gleba** serfdom; **servidumbre de paso** (law) right of way; **servidumbre de vía** (rr) right of way

servil *adj* servile

servilleta *f* napkin

servilletero *m* napkin ring

ser•vio -via *adj & mf* Serbian ‖ *f* see **Servia**

servir §50 *tr* to serve; help, wait on; (*un pedido*) fill; (tennis) serve; **para servir a Vd.** at your service ‖ *intr* to serve; (*en los naipes*) follow suit; **servir de** to serve as; be used as; **servir para** to be good for, be used for ‖ *ref* to help oneself, serve oneself; have the kindness to, deign to; **servirse de** to use, make use of; **sírvase** please

serv.° *abbr* **servicio**

servocroata *adj & mf* Serbo-Croatian

servodirección *f* (aut) power steering

servoembrague *m* (aut) automatic clutch

servofreno *m* power brake

sésamo *m* sesame; **sésamo ábrete** open sesame

sesenta *adj, pron & m* sixty

sesenta•vo -va *adj & m* sixtieth

sesgar §44 *tr* (*el paño*) to cut on the bias; bevel, slant, slope

ses•go -ga *adj* beveled, slanting, sloped; oblique; stern; calm ‖ *m* bevel; bias; slant, slope; turn; compromise; **al sesgo** obliquely; on the bias

sesión *f* session; sitting; meeting; (*cada representación de un drama o película*) show; **sesión continua** (mov) continuous showing; **sesión de espiritistas** séance, spiritualistic séance

sesionar *intr* to be in session

seso *m* brain; brains, intelligence; **calentarse** or **devanarse los sesos** to rack one's brain

sestear *intr* to take a siesta; (*el ganado*) rest in the shade

sesu•do -da *adj* brainy; (Chile) stubborn

seta *f* bristle; toadstool

setecien•tos -tas *adj & m* seven hundred ‖ **setecientos** *m* seven hundred

setenta *adj, pron & m* seventy

setenta•vo -va *adj & m* seventieth

seto *m* fence; **seto vivo** hedge, quickset

seudónimo *m* pseudonym, pen name

s.e.u.o. *abbr* **salvo error u omisión**

seve•ro -ra *adj* severe; stern; strict

sevicia *f* ferocity, cruelty

sexo *m* sex; **el bello sexo** the fair sex; **el sexo feo** the sterner sex

sextante *m* sextant

sex•to -ta *adj & m* sixth

sexual *adj* sexual, sex

si *conj* if; whether; I wonder if; **por si acaso** just in case; **si acaso** if by chance; **si no** otherwise

sí *adv* yes; indeed; (gives emphasis to verb and is often equivalent to English auxiliary verb) **él sí habla español** he does speak Spanish ‖ *pron reflex* himself, herself, itself, themselves; yourself, yourselves; oneself; each other ‖ *m* (*pl* -síes) yes; **dar el sí** to say yes

sia•més -mesa *adj & mf* Siamese

siberia•no -na *adj & mf* Siberian

sibila *f* sibyl

sicalipsis *f* spiciness, suggestiveness

sicalípti•co -ca *adj* spicy, suggestive, sexy

Sicilia *f* Sicily

sicilia•no -na *adj & mf* Sicilian

sico. . . var of **psico. . .**

sicofanta *m* or **sicofante** *m* informer, spy; slanderer

sico•sis *f* (*pl* -sis) psychosis; (*afección de la piel*) sycosis

SIDA *abbr* **síndrome de inmunidad deficiente adquirida**

sideral or **sidére•o -a** *adj* sidereal

siderurgia *f* iron and steel industry

sidra *f* cider; **sidra achampañada** hard cider

siega *f* reaping, mowing; harvest; crop

siembra *f* sowing; seeding; seedtime; sown field

se
si

siempre adv always; **de siempre** usual; **para siempre** or **por siempre** forever; **por siempre jamás** forever and ever; **siempre que** whenever; provided

siempreviva f everlasting flower

sien f temple (of head)

sierpe f serpent, snake

sierra f saw; sierra, mountain range; **sierra circular** buzz saw; **sierra continua** band saw; **sierra de armero** hacksaw; **sierra de bastidor** bucksaw; **sierra de hilar** ripsaw; **sierra de vaivén** jig saw; **sierra sin fin** band saw

sier•vo -va mf slave; servant; **siervo de la gleba** serf

sieso m anus

siesta f siesta; hot time of day; **siesta del carnero** nap before lunch

siete adj & pron seven; **las siete** seven o'clock ‖ m seven; (en las fechas) seventh; (coll) V-shaped tear or rip

sífilis f syphilis

sifón m siphon; siphon bottle; (tubo doblemente acodado) trap

sig.ᵉ abbr **siguiente**

sigilar tr to seal, stamp; conceal, keep silent

sigilo m seal; concealment, reserve; **sigilo sacramental** inviolable secrecy of the confessional

sigilo•so -sa adj tight-lipped; reserved

sigla f initial; abbreviation, symbol

siglo m (cien años) century; (comercio de los hombres) world; (largo tiempo) age; **siglo de la ilustración** or **de las luces** Age of Enlightenment

signar tr to mark; sign; make the sign of the cross over

signatura f library number; (mus & typ) signature

significado m meaning

significar §73 tr to signify, mean; point out, make known ‖ intr to be important

signo m sign; mark; sign of the cross; fate, destiny; **signo de admiración** exclamation mark; **signo de interrogación** question mark; **signo externo** status symbol

siguiente adj following; next

sílaba f syllable; **última sílaba** ultima

silbar tr (p.ej., una canción) to whistle; (un silbato) blow; (a un actor) hiss ‖ intr to whistle; (ir zumbando por el aire) whiz, whiz by

silbato m whistle

silbido m whistle, whistling, hiss; (rad) howling, squealing; **silbido de oídos** ringing in the ears

silbo m whistle, hiss

silenciador m silencer; (aut) muffler

silencio m silence; (toque que manda que cada cual se acueste) (mil) taps; (mus) rest

silencio•so -sa adj silent, noiseless; quiet, still ‖ m (aut) muffler

sílfide f sylph

silo m silo; cave, dark place

silogismo m syllogism

silueta f silhouette

silva f (materias escritas sin orden) miscellany; verse of iambic hendecasyllables intermingled with seven-syllable lines

silvestre adj wild; rustic, uncultivated

silvicultura f forestry

silla f chair; **silla alta** high chair; **silla de balanza** rocking chair; **silla de cubierta** deck chair; **silla de junco** rush-bottomed chair; **silla de manos** sedan chair; **silla de montar** saddle, riding saddle; **silla de ruedas** wheel chair; **silla de tijera** folding chair; **silla giratoria** swivel chair; **silla hamaca** (Arg) rocking chair; **silla plegadiza** folding chair; **silla poltrona** armchair, easy chair; **sillas apilables** chairs that can be stacked or nested

sillar m ashlar

silleta f bedpan

sillico m chamber pot, commode

sillín m saddle (of bicycle)

sillón m armchair, easy chair; **sillón de orejas** wing chair

sima f chasm, abyss

simbióti•co -ca adj symbiotic

simbóli•co -ca adj symbolic(al)

simbolizar §60 tr to symbolize

símbolo m symbol; **Símbolo de la fe** or **de los Apóstoles** Apostles' Creed

simetría f symmetry

simétri•co -ca adj symmetric(al)

simiente f seed, sperm

símil adj like, similar ‖ m similarity; (rhet) simile

similar adj similar

similgrabado m (typ) half-tone

similor m ormolu, similor; **de similor** fake, sham

simio m monkey

simpatía f affection, attachment, liking; friendliness; congeniality; **tomar simpatía a** to take a liking for

simpáti•co -ca adj agreeable, pleasant, likeable, congenial

simpatizar §60 intr to be congenial, get on well together; **simpatizar con** to get on well with

simple adj simple; single ‖ mf simpleton ‖ m (planta medicinal) simple

simpleza f simpleness; stupidity

simplificar §73 tr to simplify

simulacro m phantom, vision; idol, image; semblance, show; pretense; sham battle; **simulacro de ataque aéreo** air-raid drill; **simulacro de combate** sham battle

simula•do -da adj fake; (com) pro forma

simular tr to simulate, feign, fake ‖ intr to malinger; pretend

simultanear tr to do simultaneously ‖ intr to work simultaneously

simultáne•o -a adj simultaneous

sin prep without; **sin embargo** nevertheless, however; **sin que** + subj without + ger

sinagoga f synagogue

sinapismo m mustard plaster; bore, nuisance

sincerar tr to vindicate, justify

sinceridad f sincerity

since•ro -ra adj sincere

síncopa *f* (phonet) syncope
síncope *m* fainting spell
sincróni•co -ca *adj* synchronous
sincronizar §60 *tr* & *intr* to synchronize
sindicar §73 *tr* & *ref* to syndicate
sindicato *m* syndicate; labor union
síndico *m* trustee; (*en una quiebra*) receiver
sin•diós (*pl* **-diós**) *adj* godless ‖ *mf* atheist
síndrome *m* syndrome; **síndrome de choque tóxico** toxic-shock syndrome; **síndrome de inmunidad deficiente adquirida (SIDA)** acquired immune-deficiency syndrome (AIDS)
sinecura *f* sinecure
sinfín *m* endless amount, number
sinfonía *f* symphony
sinfóni•co -ca *adj* symphonic
singladura *f* (naut) day's run
singular *adj* singular; special; single ‖ *m* singular; **en singular** in particular
singularizar §60 *tr* to distinguish, single out ‖ *ref* to distinguish oneself, stand out
sinhueso *f* (coll) tongue
sinies•tro -tra *adj* evil, perverse; calamitous, disastrous ‖ *m* calamity, disaster ‖ *f* left hand, left-hand side
sinnúmero *m* great amount, great number
sino *conj* but, except; **no . . . sino** only; **no . . . sino que** only; **no solo . . . sino que** not only . . . but also ‖ *m* fate, destiny
sinóni•mo -ma *adj* synonymous ‖ *m* synonym
sinop•sis *f* (*pl* **-sis**) synopsis
sinrazón *f* wrong, injustice
sinsabor *m* displeasure; anxiety, trouble, worry
sinsonte *m* mockingbird
sinsostenismo *m* (coll) bra-less fashion
sintaxis *f* syntax
sínte•sis *f* (*pl* **-sis**) synthesis
sintéti•co -ca *adj* synthetic(al)
sintetizar §60 *tr* to synthesize
síntoma *m* symptom; sign; **síntoma de abstinencia** withdrawal symptom
sintonía *f* (rad) tuning; (rad) theme song
sintonizar §60 *tr* (*el aparato receptor*) to tune; (*la estación emisora*) tune in
sinuo•so -sa *adj* sinuous, winding; wavy; evasive
sinvergüenza *adj* brazen, shameless ‖ *mf* scoundrel, rascal
sionismo *m* Zionism
siqui. . . var of **psiqui. . .**
siquiera *adv* even; at least ‖ *conj* although, even though
sirena *f* siren; mermaid; **sirena de la playa** bathing beauty; **sirena de niebla** foghorn
sirga *f* towrope, towline
sirgar §44 *tr* to tow
Siria *f* Syria
si•rio -ria *adj* & *mf* Syrian ‖ **Sirio** *m* (astr) Sirius ‖ *f* see **Siria**
sirvienta *f* maid, servant girl
sirviente *m* servant; waiter
sisa *f* petty theft; (*para fijar los panes de oro*) sizing
sisal *m* sisal, sisal hemp

sisar *tr* to filch, snitch; (*lo que se ha de dorar*) size
sisear *tr* to hiss ‖ *intr* to hiss; sizzle
siseo *m* hiss, hissing; sizzle, sizzling
Sísifo *m* Sisyphus
sismógrafo *m* seismograph
sismología *f* seismology
sistema *m* system; **el Sistema** the Establishment, established order
sistematizar §60 *tr* to systematize
sístole *f* systole
sitial *m* place of honor
sitiar *tr* to surround, hem in; siege, besiege
sitio *m* place, spot, room; location, site; country place; seat; cattle ranch; taxi stand; (mil) siege
si•to -ta *adj* situated, located
situación *f* situation, position; **pedir situación** (aer) to ask for bearings
situar §21 *tr* to situate, locate, place; (*dinero*) place, invest; (*un pedido*) place ‖ *ref* to take a position; settle; take place; (aer) to get one's bearings
s.l. *abbr* **sin lugar**
S.M. *abbr* **Su majestad**
smo•king *m* (*pl* **-kings**) tuxedo, dinner coat
so *prep* under, e.g., **so pena de** under penalty of ‖ *interj* whoa!; you. . . !, e.g., **¡so animal!** you beast!
sobaco *m* armpit
sobajar *tr* to crush, to rumple; to humiliate
sobaquera *f* (*en el vestido*) armhole; (*para resguardar el sudor la parte del vestido correspondiente al sobaco*) shield
sobaquina *f* underarm odor
sobar *tr* to knead; massage; beat, slap; paw, pet, feel; annoy, be fresh to; flatter; (*un hueso dislocado*) (CAm) to set; (*la cabalgadura*) (Arg) to tire out; (Col) to flay, skin; (P-R) to bribe
soberanía *f* sovereignty
sobera•no -na *adj* sovereign; superb ‖ *mf* sovereign ‖ *m* (*moneda*) sovereign
sober•bio -bia *adj* proud, haughty; arrogant; magnificent, superb ‖ *f* pride, haughtiness; arrogance; magnificence
so•bón -bona *adj* malingering; fresh, mushy, spoony
soborna•do -da *adj* twisted; out of shape
sobornar *tr* to bribe
soborno *m* bribery; (SAm) extra load; **de soborno** (Bol) in addition; **soborno de testigo** (law) subornation of perjury
sobra *f* extra, surplus; **sobras** leftovers, leavings; trash
sobradillo *m* penthouse
sobra•do -da *adj* excessive, superfluous; bold, daring; rich, wealthy ‖ *m* attic, garret ‖ **sobrado** *adv* too
sobrante *adj* remaining, leftover, surplus ‖ *m* leftover, surplus
sobrar *tr* to exceed, surpass ‖ *intr* to be more than enough; be in the way; be left, remain
sobre *prep* on, upon; over; above; about; near; after; in addition to; out of, e.g., **en nueve casos sobre diez** in nine out of ten

cases ‖ *m* envelope; **sobre de ventanilla** window envelope

sobrealimentar *tr* to overfeed; supercharge

sobrecama *f* bedspread

sobrecarga *f* overload, extra load; overcharge; surcharge

sobrecargar §44 *tr* to overload, overburden; overcharge; surcharge; (aer) to pressurize

sobrecargo *m* (naut) supercargo; purser ‖ *f* flight attendant, stewardess

sobrecejo *m* frown

sobreceño *m* frown

sobrecoger §17 *tr* to surprise, catch; scare, terrify ‖ *ref* to be surprised; be scared; **sobrecogerse de** to be seized with

sobrecubierta *f* extra cover; (*de un libro*) jacket, dust jacket

sobredi·cho -cha *adj* above-mentioned

sobredosis *f* overdose

sobreestimar *tr* to overestimate

sobreexcitar *tr* to overexcite ‖ *ref* to become overexcited

sobreexponer §54 *tr* to overexpose

sobreexposición *f* overexposure

sobregirar *tr* & *intr* to overdraw

sobregiro *m* overdraft

sobreherido *adj* slightly wounded

sobrehombre *m* superman

sobrehuma·no -na *adj* superhuman

sobrellevar *tr* to bear, carry; (*la carga de otra persona*) ease; (*los trabajos o molestias de la vida*) share; (*molestias*) suffer with patience

sobremanera *adv* exceedingly, beyond measure

sobremesa *f* tablecloth, table cover; **de sobremesa** desk, e.g., **reloj de sobremesa** desk clock; after-dinner, e.g., **discurso de sobremesa** after-dinner speech

sobremodo *adv* var of **sobremanera**

sobrenadar *intr* to float

sobrenatural *adj* supernatural

sobrenombrar *tr* to surname; nickname

sobrenombre *m* surname; nickname

sobrentender §51 *tr* to understand ‖ *ref* to be understood, be implied

sobrepasar *tr* to excel, surpass, outdo; exceed; overtake ‖ *ref* to outdo each other; go too far

sobrepeine *adv* slightly, briefly ‖ *m* hair trimming

sobrepe·lliz *f* (*pl* **-llices**) surplice

sobreponer §54 *tr* to superpose, put on top; superimpose ‖ *ref* to control oneself; triumph over adversity; **sobreponerse a** to overcome

sobreprecio *m* extra charge, surcharge

sobreproducción *f* overproduction

sobrepujar *tr* to excel, surpass

sobresaliente *adj* projecting; conspicuous, outstanding; (*en un examen*) distinguished ‖ *mf* substitute; understudy

sobresalir §65 *intr* to project, jut out; stand out, excel

sobresaltar *tr* to assail, rush upon; startle, frighten ‖ *intr* to stand out clearly ‖ *ref* to be startled, be frightened; start, wince

sobresalto *m* fright, scare; start, shock, wince; **de sobresalto** suddenly, unexpectedly

sobrescribir §83 *tr* to address

sobrescrito *m* address

sobrestante *m* boss, foreman

sobresueldo *m* extra wages, extra pay

sobretiro *m* offprint

sobretodo *adv* especially ‖ *m* overcoat, topcoat

sobrevenir §79 *intr* to happen, take place; supervene, set in; **sobrevenir a** to overtake

sobrevidriera *f* window screen; window grill; storm window

sobrevivencia *f* (Ecuad) survival

sobreviviente *adj* surviving ‖ *mf* survivor

sobrevivir *intr* to survive; **sobrevivir a** to survive, outlive

sobrevolar §61 *tr* to overfly

sobriedad *f* sobriety, moderation

sobrina *f* niece

sobrino *m* nephew

so·brio -bria *adj* sober, moderate, temperate

socaire *m* (naut) lee; **al socaire de** (naut) under the lee of; (coll) under the shelter of; **estar al socaire** to shirk

socapa *f* subterfuge; **a socapa** clandestinely

socarrén *m* eaves

socarrar *tr* to singe, scorch

soca·rrón -rrona *adj* crafty, cunning, sly; sneering; roguish

socavar *tr* to undermine, dig under

socavón *m* cave-in; cave; (min) gallery

sociable *adj* sociable

social *adj* social; company, e.g., **edificio social** company building

socialismo *m* socialism

socialista *mf* socialist

sociedad *f* society; company, firm; **buena sociedad** (*mundo elegante*) society; **sociedad anónima** stock company; **sociedad de control** holding company; **Sociedad de las Naciones** League of Nations; **sociedad distribuidora** (wholesale) distributor

so·cio -cia *mf* partner; companion; member ‖ *m* fellow; (scornful) guy

sociología *f* sociology

socorrer *tr* to aid, help, succor

socorri·do -da *adj* ready; handy, useful; hackneyed, trite, worn; well stocked

socorrismo *m* first aid

socorro *m* aid, help, succor

socoyote *m* (Mex) baby, youngest son

soda *f* soda; soda water

sodio *m* sodium

so·ez *adj* (*pl* **-eces**) base, mean, vile

so·fá *m* (*pl* **-fás**) sofa; **sofá cama** day bed

soflama *f* glow, flicker; blush; deceit, cheating

soflamar *tr* to flimflam; make blush ‖ *ref* to become scorched

sofocar §73 *tr* to choke, suffocate, stifle, smother; quench, extinguish; make blush; bother, harass ‖ *ref* to choke, suffocate; blush; get excited; get out of breath

sofoco *m* blush, embarrassment

sofrenar *tr* (*un caballo*) to check suddenly; (*una pasión*) control; chide, reprimand

soga *m* sly fellow ‖ *f* rope, cord; **dar soga a** to make fun of; **hacer soga** to lag behind

soja *f* soy, soy bean

sojuzgar §44 *tr* to subjugate, subdue

sol *m* sun; sunlight; sunny side; **de sol a sol** from sunrise to sunset; **hacer sol** to be sunny; **soles** (poet) eyes

solamente *adv* only

solana *f* sunny spot; sun porch

solanera *f* sunburn; sunny spot

solapa *f* lapel; pretext, pretense; flap

solapa•do -da *adj* overlapping; cunning, underhanded, sneaky

solapar *tr* to put lapels on; overlap; conceal, cover up ‖ *intr* to overlap

solapo *m* lapel; flap; chuck under chin

solar *adj* solar; ancestral ‖ *m* ground, plot; backyard; manor house, ancestral mansion; noble lineage; (Cuba) tenement ‖ *v* §61 *tr* to pave, floor; (*zapatos*) sole

solarie•go -ga *adj* ancestral; manorial

solario *m* sun porch

so•laz *m* (*pl* **-laces**) solace, consolation; recreation; **a solaz** with pleasure

soldada *f* wages, pay

soldadera *f* (Mex) camp follower

soldadesca *f* soldiery; undisciplined troops

soldado *m* soldier; **soldado de a pie** foot soldier; **soldado de juguete** toy soldier; **soldado de marina** marine; **soldado de plomo** tin soldier; **soldado de primera** private first class; **soldado raso** buck private

soldadura *f* solder; soldering; weld; welding; **soldadura al arco** arc welding; **soldadura autógena** welding; **soldadura a tope** butt welding; **soldadura por puntos** spot welding

soldar §61 *tr* to solder; (*sin materia extraña*) weld ‖ *ref* (*los huesos*) to knit

solear *tr* to sun ‖ *ref* to sun, sun oneself

soledad *f* solitude, loneliness; longing, grieving; lonely spot

soledo•so -sa *adj* solitary, lonely; longing, grieving

solemne *adj* solemn; (*error, mentira, etc.*) downright

soler §47 *intr* to be accustomed to

solera *f* crossbeam; lumber, timber; mother liquor, mother of the wine; blend of sherry; old vintage sherry; tradition, standing; (Chile) curb; (Mex) brick, tile, stone; **de solera** or **de rancia solera** of the good old school, of the good old times

solevantar *tr* to raise up; rouse, stir up, incite ‖ *ref* to rise up; revolt

solevar *tr* to raise up; incite to rebellion ‖ *ref* to rise up; revolt

solicitante *mf* petitioner; applicant

solicitar *tr* to solicit, ask for; apply for; woo, court; drive, pull; (*la atención*) attract; (phys) to attract

solíci•to -ta *adj* solicitous; careful, diligent; obliging; fond, affectionate

solicitud *f* solicitude; petition, request; application

solidar *tr* to harden; establish, prove

solida•rio -ria *adj* jointly liable; jointly binding; **solidario con** or **de** integral with

solidarizar §60 *ref* to declare one's solidarity (with); identify (with)

solidez *f* solidity; strength, soundness; constancy

sóli•do -da *adj* solid; strong, sound ‖ *m* solid

soliloquio *m* soliloquy

solista *adj* (*p.ej., instrumento*) (mus) solo ‖ *mf* (mus) soloist

solita•rio -ria *adj* solitary; lonely ‖ *mf* hermit, recluse, solitary ‖ **en solitario** alone, solo ‖ *m* (*juego y diamante*) solitaire ‖ *f* tapeworm

sóli•to -ta *adj* accustomed, customary

soliviantar *tr* to rouse, stir up, incite

soliviar *tr* to lift, lift up

so•lo -la *adj* only, sole; alone; lonely; (*p.ej., whisky*) straight; (*café*) black; **a mis solas** alone, all by myself; **a solas** alone, unaided ‖ *pron* only one ‖ *m* (mus) solo

sólo *adv* only, solely

solomillo *m* sirloin

solomo *m* sirloin; loin of pork

solsticio *m* solstice

soltador *m* release; **soltador del margen** margin release

soltar §61 *tr* to untie, unfasten, loosen; let go; let go of; (*una observación*) drop, let slip; (*el agua*) turn on ‖ *ref* to get loose or free; come loose, come off; loosen up; burst out; thaw out, let oneself go

solte•ro -ra *adj* single, unmarried ‖ *m* bachelor ‖ *f* unmarried woman

solterona *f* older unmarried woman

soltura *f* looseness; agility, ease, freedom; fluency; dissoluteness; release

solución *f* solution

solucionar *tr* to solve, resolve

solventar *tr* (*lo que uno debe*) to settle, pay up; (*una dificultad*) solve

solvente *adj* solvent; (*fuente*) believable; reliable ‖ *m* solvent

sollastre *m* scullion

sollozar §60 *intr* to sob

sollozo *m* sob

sombra *f* (*falta de luz brillante*) shade; (*imagen obscura que proyecta un cuerpo opaco*) shadow; shady side; darkness; parasol; ignorance; ghost, spirit; grace, charm, wit; favor, protection; luck; **a la sombra** in the shade; in jail; **a sombra de tejado** stealthily, sneakingly; **ni por sombra** by no means; without any notice; **no ser su sombra** to be but a shadow of one's former self; **sombra (de ojos)** eye shadow; **tener buena sombra** to be likeable; to bring good luck

sombrear *tr* to shade; (*un dibujo*) hatch

sombrerera *f* bandbox, hatbox

sombrerería *f* hat store, hat factory; millinery shop

sombrere•ro -ra *mf* hatter, hat maker ‖ *f* see **sombrerera**

SO
SO

sombrero *m* hat; **sombrero de copa** high hat, top hat; **sombrero de muelles** opera hat; **sombrero de paja** straw hat; **sombrero de pelo** high hat; **sombrero de tres picos** three-cornered hat; **sombrero gacho** slouch hat; **sombrero hongo** derby; **sombrero jarano** sombrero

sombrilla *f* parasol, sunshade; **sombrilla de playa** beach umbrella; **sombrilla protectora** (mil) umbrella

sombrí•o -a *adj* shady; somber; gloomy

sombro•so -sa *adj* shadowy, full of shadows; shady

some•ro -ra *adj* brief, summary; slight; superficial, shallow

someter *tr* to subdue, subject; (*razones, reflexiones; un negocio*) submit ‖ *ref* to yield, submit, surrender

someti•do -da *adj* humble, submissive

sometimiento *m* subjection

somier *m* bedspring, spring mattress

somnolencia *f* sleepiness, drowsiness

somorgujar *tr* to plunge, submerge ‖ *intr* to dive, ‖ *ref* to plunge

son *m* sound; news, rumor; pretext, motive; manner, mode; **en son de** in the manner of, by way of; as

sona•do -da *adj* talked-about; famous, noted

sonaja *f* jingle

sonajero *m* rattle, child's rattle

sonámbu•lo -la *mf* sleepwalker, somnambulist

sonar §61 *tr* to sound, ring; (*un instrumento de viento, un silbato*) blow; (*un instrumento de viento*) play ‖ *intr* to sound, ring; (*un reloj*) strike; seem; sound familiar; **sonar a** to sound like, have the appearance of ‖ *ref* to be rumored; (*las narices*) blow

sonda *f* sounding; plummet, lead; drill; (surg) probe, sound

sondar or **sondear** *tr & intr* to sound, probe

sonetizar §60 *intr* to sonneteer

soneto *m* sonnet

sóni•co -ca *adj* sonic

sonido *m* sound; report, rumor

sonido silencioso ultrasound

sonoridad *f* sonority

sonorizar §60 *intr* (*una película cinematográfica*) to record sound effects on; (*una consonante sorda*) voice ‖ *ref* to voice

sono•ro -ra *adj* sound; clear, loud, resounding

sonreír §58 *intr & ref* to smile

sonriente *adj* smiling

sonrisa *f* smile

sonrojar or **sonrojear** *tr* to make one blush ‖ *ref* to blush

sonrojo *m* blush; word that causes blushing

sonrosar or **sonrosear** *tr* to rose-color; make blush ‖ *ref* to become rose-colored; blush

sonsacar §73 *tr* to pilfer; entice away; elicit, draw out

son•so -sa *adj* stupid

sonsonete *m* rhythmical tapping; sing-song

soña•dor -dora *adj* dreamy ‖ *mf* dreamer

soñar §61 *tr* to dream; **ni soñarlo** not even in a dream, by no means ‖ *intr* to dream;

soñar con to dream of; **soñar despierto** to daydream

soñolien•to -ta *adj* sleepy, dozy, drowsy, somnolent; lazy

sopa *f* (*pan u otra cosa empapada en un líquido*) sop; soup; **hecho una sopa** soaked to the skin, sopping wet; **sopa de pastas** noodle soup

sopapo *m* chuck under the chin; blow; slap

sopetear *tr* to dip, dunk; abuse

sopetón *m* slap, box; **de sopetón** suddenly

sopista *mf* beggar

soplar *tr* to blow; blow away; blow up, inflate; snitch, swipe; inspire; prompt; tip off; (*la dama a un rival*) cut out; squeal on ‖ *intr* to blow; squeal ‖ *ref* to be puffed up, be conceited; swill, gulp, gobble

soplete *m* blowpipe

soplillo *m* blower, fan; chiffon, silk gauze; light sponge cake

soplo *m* blowing, blast; breath; gust of wind; instant, moment; (*informe dado en secreto*) tip; squealing; squealer

so•plón -plona *adj* tattletale ‖ *mf* tattletale, squealer

sopor *m* sleepiness, drowsiness; stupor

soporífico *m* soporific; nightcap

soportal *m* porch, portico, arcade

soportar *tr* to support, hold up, bear; endure, suffer

soporte *m* support, bearing, rest, standard; base, stand

soprano *mf* (*persona*) soprano ‖ *m* (*voz*) soprano

sor *f* (used before names of nuns) Sister

sorber *tr* to sip; absorb, soak up

sorbete *m* sherbet, water ice

sorbetera *f* ice-cream freezer; high hat

sorbo *m* sip; gulp

sordera or **sordez** *f* deafness

sórdi•do -da *adj* sordid

sordina *f* silencer; (mus) mute; (mus) damper; **a la sordina** silently, on the quiet

sor•do -da *adj* deaf; silent, mute; muffled, dull; (*dolor, ruido*) dull ‖ *mf* deaf person; **hacerse el sordo** to pretend to be deaf; turn a deaf ear

sordomu•do -da *adj* deaf and dumb ‖ *mf* deaf-mute

sorgo *m* sorghum, broomcorn

sorna *f* slowness; sluggishness; cunning

sorochar *ref* to blush; (SAm) to become mountain-sick

soroche *m* flush, blush; (SAm) mountain sickness; (Bol, Chile) silver-bearing galena

sorprendente *adj* surprising

sorprender *tr* to surprise; catch; (*un secreto*) discover ‖ *ref* to be surprised

sorpresa *f* surprise; surprise package

sorpresi•vo -va *adj* surprising

sortear *tr* to draw or cast lots for; choose by lot; dodge; duck through ‖ *intr* to draw or cast lots

sorteo *m* drawing, casting of lots; choosing by lot; dodging; (taur) workout, performance

sortija *f* ring; curl; hoop; **sortija de sello** signet ring

sortilegio *m* sorcery, witchery

sortíle•go -ga *mf* fortuneteller ‖ *m* sorcerer ‖ *f* sorceress

sosa *f* soda

sosega•do -da *adj* calm, quiet, peaceful

sosegar §66 *tr* to calm, quiet, allay ‖ *intr* to become calm, rest ‖ *ref* to calm down, quiet down

sosiega *f* nightcap

sosiego *m* calm, quiet, serenity

sosla•yo -ya *adj* slanting, oblique; **al soslayo** or **de soslayo** slantingly; askance

so•so -sa *adj* insipid; tasteless; dull, inane ‖ *f* see **sosa**

sospecha *f* suspicion

sospechar *tr* to suspect

sospecho•so -sa *adj* suspicious; suspect ‖ *m* suspect

sostén *m* support; (*de un buque*) steadiness; brassiere

sostener §71 *tr* to support, hold up; sustain; maintain; bear, stand ‖ *ref* to remain

sosteni•do -da *adj & m* (mus) sharp

sota *m* (Chile) boss, foreman ‖ *f* (*en los naipes*) jack; jade, hussy

sotana *f* soutane, cassock

sótano *m* basement, cellar

sotavento *m* (naut) leeward

soterrar §2 *tr* to bury; hide away

soto *m* grove; brush, thicket, copse

so•viet *m* (*pl* -**viets**) soviet

soviéti•co -ca *adj* soviet, sovietic

sovoz — a sovoz sotto voce, in a low tone

soya *f* soybean

Sr. *abbr* **Señor**

Sra. *abbr* **Señora**

Srta. *abbr* **Señorita**

S.S.S. *abbr* **su seguro servidor**

ss.ss. *abbr* **seguros servidores**

stock *m* stock; inventory; **tener en stock** to carry; have in stock

su *adj poss* his, her, its, their, your, one's

suave *adj* suave, smooth, soft; gentle, mild, meek

suavizador *m* razor strop

suavizar §60 *tr* to smooth, ease, sweeten, soften, mollify; (*una navaja de afeitar*) strop

subalter•no -na *adj & mf* subaltern, subordinate

subasta *f* auction, auction sale; **sacar a pública subasta** to sell at auction

subastar *tr* to auction, sell at auction

subcampe•ón -ona *mf* (sport) runner-up

subcentral *f* (elec) substation

subconsciencia *f* subconscious, subconsciousness

subconsciente *adj* subconscious

subdesarrolla•do -da *adj* underdeveloped

súbdi•to -ta *adj & mf* subject

subentender §51 *tr* to understand ‖ *ref* to be understood, be implied

subestimar *tr* to underestimate

subfusil *m* submachine gun

subi•do -da *adj* high, fine, superior; strong, intense; (*color*) bright; high, high-priced ‖ *f* rise; ascent; (*p.ej.*, *al trono*) accession

subir *tr* to raise; lift; carry up; (*p.ej.*, *una escalera*) go up; (mus) to raise the pitch of ‖ *intr* to go up, come up; rise; get worse; spread; **subir a** to climb; climb on; get in or into; get on, mount ‖ *ref* to rise

súbi•to -ta *adj* sudden, unexpected; hurried; hasty, impetuous ‖ **súbito** *adv* suddenly

subjeti•vo -va *adj* subjective

subjunti•vo -va *adj & m* subjunctive

sublevación *f* uprising, revolt

sublevado *m* rebel, insurrectionist

sublevar *tr* to incite to rebellion ‖ *ref* to revolt

submarinista *mf* (sport) scuba diver; skin diver ‖ *m* (nav) submariner

submari•no -na *adj* underwater, submarine ‖ *m* submarine

subnormal *adj* (mentally) retarded

suboficial *m* sergeant major; noncommissioned officer

subordina•do -da *adj & mf* subordinate

subordinar *tr* to subordinate

subproducto *m* by-product

subrayar *tr* to underline; emphasize

subrepti•cio -cia *adj* surreptitious

subsanar *tr* to excuse, overlook; correct, repair

subscribir §83 *tr* to subscribe; subscribe to; endorse; subscribe to or for; sign; sign up ‖ *ref* to subscribe

subseguir §67 *intr & ref* to follow next

subsidiar *tr* to subsidize

subsidiarias *fpl* feeder industries

subsidiario *m* subsidiary

subsidio *m* subsidy; aid, help

subsiguiente *adj* subsequent

subsistencia *f* subsistence, sustenance

subsistir *intr* to subsist

subsóni•co -ca *adj* subsonic

substancia *f* substance

substanciar *tr* to abstract, abridge

substanti•vo -va *adj & m* substantive

substitución *f* replacement; (chem, law, math) substitution

substitui•dor -dora *adj & mf* substitute

substituir §20 *tr* to replace; substitute for, take the place of ‖ *intr* to take someone's place ‖ *ref* to be replaced; relieve each other

substituti•vo -va *adj & m* substitute

substitu•to -ta *mf* substitute

substraer §75 *tr* to remove; deduct; rob, steal; subtract ‖ *ref* to withdraw; **substraerse a** to evade, avoid, slip away from

subte *m* (Arg, Urug) subway

subteniente *m* second lieutenant

subterráne•o -a *adj* subterranean, underground ‖ *m* subterranean; (Arg) subway

subtitular *tr* to subtitle

subtítulo *m* subtitle, subheading

suburbio *m* suburb; outlying slum

subvención *f* subvention, subsidy

subvencionar *tr* to subvention, subsidize

so

su

subvenir §79 *intr* to provide; **subvenir a** to provide for; (*gastos*) defray

subvertir §68 *tr* to subvert

subyugar §44 *tr* to subjugate, subdue

sucedáne·o -a *adj & m* substitute

suceder *tr* to succeed, follow ‖ *intr* to happen; **suceder a** (*p.ej., el trono*) to succeed to ‖ *ref* to follow one another

sucesi·vo -va *adj* successive; **en lo sucesivo** in the future

suceso *m* event, happening; issue, outcome; **sucesos de actualidad** current events

suciedad *f* dirt, filth; dirtiness, filthiness

su·cio -cia *adj* dirty, filthy; base, low; tainted; blurred; (sport) foul ‖ **sucio** *adv* (sport) foully, unfairly

sucumbir *intr* to succumb

sucursal *f* branch, branch office

Sudamérica *f* South America

sudamerica·no -na *adj & mf* South American

sudar *tr* to sweat; cough up ‖ *intr* to sweat; (*trabajar mucho*) sweat

sudario *m* shroud, winding sheet

sudcorea·no -na *adj & mf* South Korean

sudor *m* sweat; (fig) sweat, toil; **chorrear de sudor** to swelter

sudoro·so -sa *adj* sweaty

Suecia *f* Sweden

sue·co -ca *adj* Swedish ‖ *mf* Swede ‖ *m* (*idioma*) Swedish

suegra *f* mother-in-law

suegro *m* father-in-law

suela *f* sole; sole leather; (*fish*) sole

sueldacostilla *f* grape hyacinth

sueldo *m* salary, pay; **a sueldo** (*gángster*) on a contract, hired (to kill)

suelo *m* ground, soil, land; floor, flooring; pavement; (*p.ej., de una botella*) bottom; **no pisar en el suelo** to walk on air; **suelo franco** loam; **suelo natal** home country

suel·to -ta *adj* loose; free; easy; swift, agile, nimble; fluent; bold, daring; (*ejemplar*) single; (*verso*) blank; odd, separate; spare; bulk; **suelto de lengua** loose-tongued ‖ *m* small change; news item

sueñecillo *m* nap; **descabezar un sueñecillo** to take a nap

sueño *m* sleep; dream; (*cosa de gran belleza*) (fig) dream; **conciliar el sueño** to manage to go to sleep; **ni por sueños** by no means; **no dormir sueño** to not sleep a wink; **tener sueño** to be sleepy; **último sueño** (*muerte*) last sleep; **sueño hecho realidad** dream come true; **sueños dorados** daydreams

suero *m* serum

suerte *f* fortune, luck; piece of luck; fate, lot; kind, sort; way, manner; feat, trick; (taur) play, suerte; (Peru) lottery ticket; **de esta suerte** in this way; **de suerte que** so that, with the result that; **la suerte está echada** the die is cast; **suerte de capa** (taur) capework

suerte·ro -ra *adj* fortunate, lucky ‖ *m* (coll) lucky dog

sué·ter *m* (*pl* -ters) sweater

suficiente *adj* sufficient; adequate; fit, competent

sufijo *m* suffix

sufragar §44 *tr* to help, support, favor; defray ‖ *intr* (SAm) to vote

sufragio *m* help, succor; benefit; (*voto*) suffrage

sufragismo *m* woman suffrage

sufragista *mf* woman-suffragist ‖ *f* suffragette

sufri·do -da *adj* long-suffering; (*color*) serviceable; (*marido*) complaisant

sufrir *tr* to suffer; undergo, experience; support, hold up; tolerate; (*un examen*) take ‖ *intr* to suffer

sugerencia *f* suggestion

sugerir §68 *tr* to suggest

sugestión suggestion

sugestionar *tr* to influence by suggestion

sugesti·vo -va *adj* suggestive; stimulating, striking, conspicuous

suicida *adj* suicidal ‖ *mf* suicide

suicidar *ref* to commit suicide

suicidio *m* suicide

Suiza *f* Switzerland

sui·zo -za *adj & mf* Swiss ‖ *f* see **Suiza**

sujeción *f* subjection; surrender; fastening; fastener

sujetador *m* bra(ssiere)

sujetahilo *m* (elec) binding post

sujetapape·les *m* (*pl* -les) paper clip

sujetar *tr* to subject; subdue; fasten, tighten ‖ *ref* to subject oneself, submit; stick, adhere

suje·to -ta *adj* subject, liable; able, capable ‖ *m* subject; fellow, individual; **buen sujeto** good egg

sulfato *m* sulfate

sulfito *m* sulfite

sulfúri·co -ca *adj* sulfuric

sulfuro *m* sulfide; **sulfuro de hidrógeno** hydrogen sulfide

sulfuro·so -sa *adj* sulfurous

sultán *m* sultan; (*galanteador*) sheik

suma *f* sum, addition; summary; sum and substance; **en suma** in short, in a word

sumadora *f* adding machine

sumamente *adv* extremely, exceedingly

sumar *tr* to add; sum up; amount to ‖ *intr* to add; amount; **suma y sigue** add and carry ‖ *ref* to add up; adhere

suma·rio -ria *adj & m* summary

sumergir §27 *tr* to submerge ‖ *ref* to submerge; (*un submarino*) dive

sumersión *f* submersion; (*de un submarino*) dive

sumidad *f* top, apex, summit

sumidero *m* drain, sewer; sink

suministrar *tr* to provide, supply

suministro *m* provision, supply; **suministros** supplies

sumir *tr* to sink; press down; overwhelm ‖ *ref* to sink; (*p.ej., los carrillos, el pecho*) be sunken; shrink, shrivel; cower; (*p.ej., el sombrero*) pull down

sumisión *f* submission (*sometimiento*) subjection

sumi·so -sa *adj* submissive

su•mo -ma *adj* high, great, extreme; supreme; **a lo sumo** at most, at the most ‖ *f* see **suma**

suncho *m* hoop

suntuo•so -sa *adj* sumptuous

supeditar *tr* to hold down, oppress

superar *tr* to surpass, excel; conquer

superávit *m* (com) surplus

supercarburante *m* high-test fuel

superchería *f* fraud, deceit

superficial *adj* superficial; surface

superficie *f* surface; exterior, outside; area; **superficie de sustentación** (aer) airfoil

super•fluo -flua *adj* superfluous

superhombre *m* superman

superintendente *mf* superintendent, supervisor; **superintendente de patio** (rr) yardmaster

superior *adj* superior; upper; higher; **superior a** superior to; higher than; more than; larger than ‖ *m* superior

superiora *f* mother superior

superiordad *f* superiority; authorities

superlati•vo -va *adj & m* superlative

supermercado *m* supermarket

super•no -na *adj* highest, supreme

supérpetrolero *m* supertanker

superpoblar §61 *tr* to overpopulate

superponer §54 *tr* to superpose

superproduction *f* overproduction

supersóni•co -ca *adj* supersonic ‖ *f* supersonics

superstición *f* superstition

supersticio•so -sa *adj* superstitious

supertanquero *m* (SAm) supertanker

supervisar *tr* to supervise

supervivencia *f* survival; (law) survivorship

súpi•to -ta *adj* sudden; impatient; (Col) dumbfounded

suplantar *tr* to supplant by treachery; (*un documento*) to alter fraudulently

suplefal•tas *mf* (*pl* **-tas**) substitute, fill-in

suplemento *m* supplement; excess fare; **suplemento dominical** (*periódico*) Sunday supplement

súplica *f* entreaty, supplication; request

suplicante *adj & mf* suppliant

suplicar §73 *tr & intr* to entreat, implore; (law) to petition

suplicio *m* torture; punishment, execution; anguish

suplir *tr* to supplement, make up for; replace, take the place of; (*un defecto de otra persona*) cover up; (gram) to understand

suponer §54 *tr* to suppose; presuppose, imply; entail ‖ *intr* to have weight, have authority

suposición *f* supposition; distinction; falsehood, imposture

supositorio *m* suppository

supradi•cho -cha *adj* above-mentioned

supre•mo -ma *adj* supreme

supresión *f* suppression, elimination, omission; cancellation; deletion

suprimir *tr* to suppress, eliminate, do away with; cancel; delete

supues•to -ta *adj* supposed, assumed, hypothetical; **supuesto que** since, inasmuch as ‖ *m* assumption, hypothesis; **dar por supuesto** to take for granted; **por supuesto** of course, naturally

supurar *intr* suppurate, discharge pus

sur *m* south; south wind

Suramérica *f* South America

surcar §73 *tr* to furrow; plough; cut through; streak through

surco *m* furrow; wrinkle, rut, cut; (*del disco gramofónico*) groove; **echarse en el surco** to lie down on the job

surcorea•no -na *adj & mf* South Korean

sure•ño -ña *adj* southern ‖ *mf* southerner

surestada *f* (Arg) southeaster

surgir §27 *intr* to spout, spurt; come forth, spring up; arise, appear

suripanta *f* (hum) chorus girl; (scornful) slut, jade

surti•do -da *adj* assorted ‖ *m* assortment; supply, stock

surtidor *m* jet, spout, fountain; **surtidor de gasolina** gasoline pump

surtir *tr* to furnish, provide, supply ‖ *intr* to spout, spurt, shoot up

susceptible *adj* susceptible; touchy

suscitar *tr* to stir up, provoke; (*dudas, una cuestión*) to raise

susodi•cho -cha *adj* above-mentioned

suspender *tr* to hang; suspend; astonish; postpone; fail, flunk ‖ *ref* to be suspended

suspensión *f* suspension; astonishment; **suspensión de fuegos** cease fire

suspen•so -sa *adj* suspended, hanging; baffled, bewildered; (theat) closed ‖ *m* flunk, condition

suspensores *mpl* suspenders

suspensorio *m* jockstrap, supporter

suspi•caz *adj* (*pl* **-caces**) suspicious, distrustful

suspirar *intr* to sigh

suspiro *m* sigh; ladyfinger; (mus) quarter rest

sustentación *f* support, prop; (aer) lift

sustentar *tr* to sustain, support, feed; maintain; (*una tesis*) defend

sustento *m* sustenance, support, food; maintenance

susto *m* scare, fright

susurrar *tr* to whisper ‖ *intr* to whisper; murmur, rustle, purl, hum; be bruited about ‖ *ref* to be bruited about

susurro *m* whisper; murmur, rustle, purling, hum

susu•rrón -rrona *adj* whispering ‖ *mf* whisperer

sutil *adj* subtle; keen, observant; thin, delicate

su•yo -ya *adj poss* of his, of hers, of yours, of theirs, e.g., **un amigo suyo** a friend of his; *pron poss* his, hers, yours, theirs, its, one's; **hacer de las suyas** to be up to one's old tricks; **salirse con la suya** to have one's way; to carry one's point

T

T, t (te) *f* twenty-third letter of the Spanish alphabet

t. *abbr* **tarde**

taba *f* anklebone; (*del carnero*) knucklebone; (*juego*) knucklebones

tabaco *m* tobacco; cigar; snuff; (Cuba, CAm, Mex) punch; **tabaco en rama** leaf tobacco; **tabaco sin humo** smokeless tobacco

tabalada *f* bump, thump, heavy fall; slap

tabalear *tr* to rock, sway ‖ *intr* to drum with the fingers

tabanazo *m* slap; slap in the face

tabanco *m* stand, stall, booth

tábano *m* horsefly, gadfly

tabanque *m* treadle wheel

tabaola *f* noise, hubbub

tabaquera *f* snuffbox; (*de la pipa de fumar*) bowl; (Arg, Chile) tobacco pouch

tabaquería *f* tobacco store, cigar store

tabaque•ro -ra *adj* tobacco ‖ *mf* tobacconist; cigar maker ‖ *m* (Bol) pocket handkerchief ‖ *f* see **tabaquera**

tabardete *m* or **tabardillo** *m* sunstroke; harum-scarum

tabarra *f* bore, tiresome talk

taberna *f* tavern, saloon, barroom, pub

tabernáculo *m* tabernacle

tabernera *f* barmaid

tabernero *m* tavern keeper; bartender

tabica *f* (*para cubrir un hueco*) board; (*del frente de un escalón*) riser

tabicar §73 *tr* to close up, shut up; wall up

tabique *m* thin wall; partition wall, partition

tabla *f* (*de madera*) board; (*de metal*) sheet; (*de piedra*) slab; (*de tierra*) strip; (*cuadro pintado en una tabla*) panel; (*lista, catálogo; índice de materias*) table; **escapar** or **salvarse en una tabla** to have a narrow escape; **tabla de lavar** washboard; **tabla de planchar** ironing board; **tabla de salvación** lifesaver, helping hand; **tablas** draw, tie; (*escenario del teatro*) stage; (*de la plaza de toros*) barrier; **tener tablas** to have stage presence

tablado *m* flooring; scaffold; (*escenario del teatro*) stage

tablear *tr* to cut into boards; divide into plots or patches; level, grade

tablero *m* boarding; timber; table top; gambling table; cutting board; checkerboard, chessboard; counter; blackboard; **poner al tablero** to risk; **tablero de instrumentos** (aer) control panel; (aut) dashboard

tableta *f* small board; (*taco de papel; comprimido, pastilla*) tablet

tabletear *intr* to rattle

tabilla *f* tablet; splint; bulletin board

tablón *m* plank; beam

tabloncillo *m* (taur) seat in last row

ta•bú *m* (*pl* **-búes**) taboo

tabuco *m* hovel

tabulador *m* tabulator

tabular *tr* to tabulate

taburete *m* stool

tac *m* tick

tacada *f* stroke (*of a billiard cue*)

taca•ño -ña *adj* stingy

táci•to -ta *adj* tacit; silent

taciturn•no -na *adj* taciturn; melancholy

taco *m* bung, plug; wad, wadding; billiard cue; pad, tablet; drumstick; snack, bite; drink; oath, curse; heel; muddle, mess; (Mex) rolled-up tortilla with fillings, taco

tacón *m* heel

taconear *tr* (Chile) to fill, stuff ‖ *intr* to click the heels; strut

taconeo *m* click, clicking (*of heels*)

tácti•co -ca *adj* tactical ‖ *m* tactician ‖ *f* tactics

tacto *m* (sense of) touch; (*del dactiló-grafo, el pianista, el instrumento*) touch; skill; tact

tacha *f* defect, fault, flaw

tachar *tr* to erase; strike out; blame, find fault with

tacho *m* tin sheet; (Arg) garbage can; (Arg) watch; (Arg, Chile) boiler; (Cuba) sugar pan

tachón *m* scratch, erasure; ornamental tack or nail; trimming

tachonar *tr* to adorn with ornamental tacks; trim with ribbon; spangle, stud

tachuela *f* tack; hobnail; (Chile, Mex) runt, half pint; (SAm) drinking cup

Tadeo *m* Thaddeus

tafetán *m* taffeta; **tafetanes** flags, colors; finery; **tafetán inglés** court plaster

tafilete *m* morocco leather; sweatband

tagarote *m* sparrow hawk; scrivener; lout; gentleman sponger

tagua *f* (Chile) mud hen; (*arbusto*) (SAm) ivory palm; (*fruto*) (SAm) ivory nut

taha•lí *m* (*pl* **-líes**) baldric

tahona *f* horse-driven flour mill; bakery

ta•hur -hura *adj* gambling; cheating ‖ *mf* gambler; cheat; cardsharp

tailan•dés -desa *adj & mf* Thai

Tailandia *f* Thailand

taima•do -da *adj* sly, crafty; (Arg, Ecuad) lazy; (Chile) gruff, sullen

tajada *f* cut; slice; hoarseness; drunk

tajadero *m* chopping block

tajalá•piz *m* (*pl* **-pices**) pencil sharpener

tajamar *m* cutwater; dike, dam

tajar *tr* to cut; slice; (*un lápiz*) sharpen

tajo *m* cut; cutting edge; chopping block; execution block; steep cliff ‖ **Tajo** *m* Tagus

tal *adj indef* such; such a ‖ *pron indef* so-and-so; such a thing; someone ‖ *adv* so; in such a way; **con tal (de) que** provided (that); **¿qué tal?** how?; hello!, how's everything?

talabarte *m* sword belt

talabartero *m* saddler, harness maker

talache *m* or **talacho** *m* (Mex) mattock

taladrar *tr* to bore, drill, pierce, perforate; (*un billete*) punch; (*un problema*) get to the bottom of

taladro *m* drill; auger; drill hole; drill press

tálamo *m* bridal bed

talán *m* ding-dong
talante *m* countenance, mien; desire, will, pleasure; way, manner
talar *adj* (*traje, vestidura*) long ‖ *tr* (*árboles*) to fell; destroy, lay waste
talco *m* tinsel; talc; **talco en polvo** talcum powder
talega *f* bag, sack; **talegas** money, wealth
talego *m* big bag, sack; slob; **tener talego** to have money tucked away
taleguilla *f* small bag; bullfighter's breeches
talento *m* talent
talento·so -sa *adj* talented
Tales *m* Thales
Talía *f* Thalia
talismán *m* talisman
talón *m* heel; (aut) lug, flange; check, voucher, coupon; (*de un cheque*) stub
talona·rio -ria *adj* stub ‖ *m* stub book, checkbook
talonear *intr* to dash along
talud *m* slope
talla *f* cut; carving; height, stature; size; ransom; reward; (*diamante*) cut, polish; (Arg) chatting, prattle; (CAm) fraud, lie; (Col) beating, thrashing
tallar *tr* to carve; (*una piedra preciosa*) cut; (*naipes*) deal; appraise; engrave; grind; size up; (Col) beat, thrash ‖ *intr* (Arg) to chat, converse; (Chile) to make love
tallarín *m* noodle
talle *m* shape, figure, stature; waist; fit; appearance, outline; bodice
taller *m* shop, workshop; factory, mill; atelier, studio; laboratory; **taller agremiado** closed shop; **taller carrocero** (aut) body shop; **taller franco** open shop; **taller penitenciario** workhouse
tallo *m* stem, stalk; shoot, sprout; (Col) cabbage
tamal *m* (CAm, Mex) tamale; (Chile) bundle; (coll) intrigue
tamañi·to -ta *adj* so small; very small; confused, disconcerted
tama·ño -ña *adj* so big; such a big; very big, very large; so small; **abrir tamaños ojos** to open one's eyes wide ‖ *m* size
tambaleante *adj* staggering
tambalear *intr* & *ref* to stagger, reel, totter
también *adv* also, too
tambo *m* (Arg, Chile) brothel; (SAm) roadside inn; (Arg, Urug) dairy
tambor *m* drum; (*persona que toca el tambor*) drummer; sieve, screen; eardrum, coffee roaster; **a tambor batiente** with drums beating; in triumph; **tambor mayor** drum major
tamborilear *tr* to praise to the skies ‖ *intr* to drum
Támesis *m* Thames
ta·miz *m* (*pl* **-mices**) sieve
tamizar §60 *tr* to sift, sieve
tamo *m* fuzz, fluff
tampoco *adv* neither, not either; **ni yo tampoco** nor I either
tampón *m* stamp pad
tan *adv* so; **tan . . . como** or **cuan** as . . . as;

tan siquiera at least; **un tan** + *adj* such a + *adj* ‖ *m* boom (*of a drum*)
tanatología *f* thanatology
tanda *f* turn; shift, relay; task; coat, layer; game, match; flock, lot, pack; show; habit, bad habit
tangente *adj* & *f* tangent; **escaparse, irse** or **salir por la tangente** to evade the issue
Tánger *f* Tangier
tanguista *f* hostess (*in a night club*)
ta·no -na *adj* & *mf* (Arg) Neapolitan, Italian
tanque *m* tank; (dial) dipper, drinking cup
tantán *m* tom-tom; clanging; boom
tantear *tr* to compare; size up; probe, test, feel out; sketch, outline; keep the score of ‖ *intr* to keep score; to grope; **¡tantee Vd.!** just imagine!, fancy that!
tanteo *m* comparison; careful consideration; test, probe, trial; trial and error; score
tan·to -ta *adj* & *pron indef* so much; as much; **tanto . . . como** as much . . . as; both . . . and; **tan·tos -tas** so many; as many; **tantos . . . como** as many . . . as; **y tantos** odd, or more, e.g., **veinte y tantos** twenty odd, twenty or more ‖ *m* copy; counter, chip; point; portion, part; **apuntar los tantos** to keep score; **entre tanto** in the meantime; **estar al tanto de** to be aware of, to be or keep informed about; **poner al tanto de** to make aware of, to keep informed of; **por lo tanto** or **por tanto** therefore ‖ *tanto adv* so much; so hard; so often; so long; as much
tañer §70 *tr* (*un instrumento músico*) to play; (*una campana*) to ring ‖ *intr* to drum with the fingers
tañido *m* sound, tone; twang; ring, tang
tapa *f* lid, cover, top, cap; (*de un cilindro, un barril*) head; (*de una compuerta*) gate; (*de un libro*) board cover; shirt front; (aut) valve cap; **levantarse** or **saltarse la tapa de los sesos** to blow one's brains out; **tapas** appetizer, free lunch
tapabalazo *m* fly (*of trousers*)
tapabarro *m* (Chile) mudguard
tapaboca *f* slap in the mouth; muffler; squelch, squelcher
tapacu·bo *m* or **tapacu·bos** *m* (*pl* **-bos**) (aut) hubcap
tapadera *f* lid, cover, cap
tapagote·ras *m* (*pl* **-ras**) (Arg) roofing cement; (Col) roofer
tapaguje·ros *m* (*pl* **-ros**) (coll) bungling mason; substitute, replacement
tapar *tr* to cover; cover up, hide; plug, stop, stop up; conceal; obstruct; wrap up; (*un diente*) (Chile) to fill
tapara *f* (Ven) gourd; **vaciarse como una tapara** (Ven) to spill all one knows
taparrabo *m* loincloth; bathing trunks
tapera *f* (SAm) ruins; (SAm) shack
tapete *m* rug; runner; table scarf; **estar sobre el tapete** to be on the carpet, be under discussion; **tapete verde** card table, gambling table
tapia *f* mud wall, adobe wall
tapiar *tr* to wall up, wall in; close up

t
ta

tapicería *f* tapestries; upholstery; tapestry shop; upholstery shop

tapicero *m* tapestry maker; upholsterer; carpet maker; carpet layer

ta·piz *m* (*pl* **-pices**) tapestry

tapizar §60 *tr* to tapestry; upholster; carpet; cover

tapon *m* stopper, cork; cap; bottle cap; bung, plug; (elec) fuse; (surg) tampon; **tapón de algodón** (surg) swab; **tapón de cubo** (aut) hubcap; **tapón de desagüe** drain plug; **tapón de tráfico** traffic jam; **tapón de vaciado** (aut) drain plug

taponar *tr* to plug, stop up; (surg) to tampon

taponazo *m* pop

taque *m* click; knock, rap

taqué *m* (aut) tappet

taquigrafía *f* shorthand, stenography

taquigrafiar §77 *tr* to take down in shorthand ‖ *intr* to take shorthand

taquígra·fo -fa *mf* stenographer

taquilla *f* ticket rack; ticket window; ticket office; box office; gate, take; file; (C-R) inn, tavern

taquille·ro -ra *adj* box-office ‖ *mf* ticket agent

taquimeca *mf* shorthand-typist

taquimecanógra·fo -fa *mf* shorthand-typist

tarabilla *f* millclapper; catch; turnbuckle; (*de la hebilla de la correa*) tongue; chatterbox; jabber; **soltar la tarabilla** to talk a blue streak

tarabita *f* (*clavillo de la hebilla*) tongue; (SAm) rope of rope bridge

taracea *f* marquetry, inlaid work

tarambana *adj* & *mf* (coll) crackpot

tararear *tr* & *intr* to hum

tarasca *f* dragon (*in Corpus Christi procession*); (*mujer fea*) hag

tarascada *f* bite; tart reply

tardanza *f* slowness, delay, tardiness

tardar *intr* to be long, be slow; be late; **a más tardar** at the latest; **tardar en** + *inf* to be late in + *ger* ‖ *ref* to be long, be slow; be late

tarde *adv* late; too late; **hacerse tarde** to grow late; **tarde o temprano** sooner or later ‖ *f* afternoon; evening; **de la tarde a la mañana** overnight; suddenly, in no time; unexpectedly

tardecer §22 *intr* to grow dark, grow late

tardí·do -a *adj* late, delayed; dilatory, tardy; slow

tar·do -da *adj* slow; late; slow, dull, dense

tar·dón -dona *mf* poke, slow poke

tarea *f* task, job; care, worry

tarifa *f* tariff; price list; rate; fare; (telp) toll; **tarifa recargada** extra fare

tarima *f* platform; stand; stool; low bench; (*entablado para dormir*) bunk

tarjeta *f* card; **tarjeta de buen deseo** or **de felicitación** greeting card; **tarjeta de crédito** credit card; **tarjeta de visita** calling card, visiting card; **tarjeta navideña** Christmas card; **tarjeta perforada** punch card; **tarjeta postal** post card, postal card

tarjetero *m* card case; card index

tarquín *m* mire, slime, mud

tarro *m* jar; milk pail; horn; (SAm) top hat

tarta *f* tart, cake; pan

tartajear *intr* to stutter

tartalear *intr* to stagger, sway; be speechless

tartamudear *intr* to stutter, stammer

tartamudeo *m* stuttering, stammering

tartamu·do -da *mf* stutterer, stammerer

tartán *m* Scotch plaid

tarugo *m* wooden plug; wooden paving block; (Guat, Mex) dolt, blockhead

tasa *f* appraisal; measure, standard; rate; ceiling price

tasación *f* appraisal; regulation

tasajo *m* jerked beef

tasar *tr* to appraise; regulate; hold down, keep within bounds; grudge

tasca *f* dive, joint; tavern; (Peru) surf, breakers

tata *m* daddy ‖ *f* nursemaid; little sister

tate *m* hashish; hashish user

tato *m* little brother

tatuaje *m* tattoo, tattooing

tatuar §21 *tr* & *ref* to tattoo

tauri·no -na *adj* bullfighting

Tauro *m* (astr) Taurus

taurófi·lo -la *mf* bullfight fan

tauromaquia *f* bullfighting

taxear *intr* (aer) to taxi

taxi *m* taxi, taxicab ‖ *f* taxi dancer

taxista *mf* taxi driver

taza *f* cup; (*de la fuente*) basin; (*del inodoro*) bowl

te *pron pers* & *reflex* thee, to thee; you, to you; thyself, to thyself; yourself, to yourself

té *m* tea; **té bailable** tea dance

tea *f* torch, firebrand

teatral *adj* theatrical

teatre·ro -ra *mf* theater-goer

teatro *m* theater; **dar teatro a** to bally-hoo; **teatro de estreno** first-run house; **teatro de repetorio** stock company

teatrólo·go -ga *mf* theater critic ‖ *m* actor ‖ *f* actress

Tebas *f* Thebes

tebe·o -a *adj* & *mf* Theban ‖ *m* comic book, funny paper

teca *f* teak

tecla *f* (*de piano, máquina de escribir, etc.*) key; touchy subject; **dar en la tecla** to get the knack of it; **tecla de cambio** shift key; **tecla de escape** margin release; **tecla de espacios** space bar; **tecla de retroceso** backspacer

teclado *m* keyboard; **teclado manual** (mus) manual

teclear *tr* to feel out ‖ *intr* to run over the keys; drum, thrum; (Chile) to be at death's door; (*un jugador*) (Chile) to be losing one's last cent

tecleo *m* fingering; touch; (*de la máquina de escribir*) click

técni·co -ca *adj* technical ‖ *m* technician; expert ‖ *f* technique; technics

tecolote *m* eagle owl (*of Central America*); (Mex) night policeman

techado *m* roof; **bajo techado** indoors

techar *tr* to roof

techo *m* ceiling; roof; (*sombrero*) hat; **techo de paja** thatched roof

techumbre *f* ceiling; roof

tedio *m* ennui, boredom

tedio•so -sa *adj* tedious, boresome

teja *f* roofing tile; shovel hat; yew tree; linden tree; **a toca teja** (coll) for cash; **teja de madera** shingle

tejadillo *m* cover, top; (*de coche*) roof

tejado *m* tile roof; roof; **tejado de vidrio** (fig) glass house

tejama•ní *m* (*pl* **-níes**) shake (*long shingle*)

tejar *m* tile works || *tr* to tile, roof with tiles

teja•roz *m* (*pl* **-roces**) eaves

teje•dor -dora *adj* weaving; scheming || *mf* weaver; schemer

tejer *tr & intr* to weave

tejido *m* weave, texture; web; fabric, textile; tissue; (biol & fig) tissue; **tejido adhesivo** friction tape; **tejido conjunctivo** (anat) connective tissue; **tejido de saco** (Mex) burlap; **tejido de punto** knitted fabric, jersey

tejo *m* disk; quoit; yew tree

tejón *m* badger

tela *f* cloth, fabric; (*de cebolla*) skin; (*del insecto*) web; film; (bb) cloth; (paint) canvas; (*dinero*) (slang) dough; **poner en tela de juicio** to question, doubt; **tela de alambre** wire screen; **tela de araña** spider web, cobweb; **tela emplástica** court plaster; **tela metálica** chicken wire; wire screen

telar *m* loom; frame; embroidery frame; (bb) sewing press

telaraña *f* spider web, cobweb

telecomedia serial *f* sitcom

telecontrol *m* remote control

telediario *m* daytime television news

teledifundir *tr & intr* to telecast

teledifusión *f* telecasting; telecast

telefonar *tr & intr* to telephone

telefonazo *m* telephone call

telefonear *tr & intr* to telephone

telefonema *m* telephone message

telefonista *mf* telephone operator

teléfono *m* telephone; **teléfono automático** dial telephone; **teléfono público** pay phone

teleg. *abbr* **telégrafo, telegrama**

telegrafiar §77 *tr & intr* to telegraph

telegrafista *mf* telegrapher

telégrafo *m* telegraph; **telégrafo de banderas** wigwagging; **telégrafo de máquinas** (naut) engine-room telegraph; **telégrafo sin hilos** wireless telegraph

telegrama *m* telegram

teleimpresor *m* teletype, teleprinter

Telémaco *m* Telemachus

telemando *m* remote control

telemetrar *tr* to telemeter

telemetría *f* telemetry

telémetro *m* telemeter; (mil) range finder

telen•do -da *adj* sprightly, lively

telerreceptor *m* television set

telescopar *tr & ref* to telescope

telescopio *m* telescope

telesilla *f* chair lift

telespecta•dor -dora *mf* viewer, televiewer; **telespectadores** television audience

telesquí *m* ski lift, ski tow

teleta *f* blotter, blotting paper

teletipo *m* teletype

teletubo *m* (telv) picture tube

televidente *mf* viewer, televiewer

televisar *tr* to televise

televisión *f* television; **televisión en circuito cerrado** closed-circuit television; **televisión en colores** color television; **televisión por cable** cable television

televi•sor -sora *adj* televising; television || *m* television set || *f* television transmitter

telón *m* drop curtain; **telón de acero** (fig) iron curtain; **telón de boca** (theat) front curtain; **telón de fondo** or **foro** (theat) backdrop

tema *m* theme, subject; exercise; (gram) stem; (mus) theme || *f* fixed idea; persistence; grudge; **a tema** in emulation

temario *m* agenda

temblar §2 *intr* to tremble, shake, quiver, shiver; **estar temblando** to teeter

tem•blón -blona *adj* shaking, tremulous || *m* aspen tree

temblor *m* temor, shaking, trembling; **temblor de tierra** earthquake

tembloro•so -sa *adj* trembling, shaking, tremulous

tem•bo -ba *adj* (Col) silly, stupid

temer *tr & intr* to fear

temera•rio -ria *adj* rash, reckless, foolhardy

temeridad *f* rashness, recklessness, foolhardiness, temerity

temero•so -sa *adj* frightful, dread; timid; fearful

temible *adj* dreadful, terrible, fearful

temor *m* fear, dread

témpano *m* small drum; drumhead; (*de barril*) head; (*de tocino*) flitch; (*de hielo*) iceberg, floe; (archit) tympan; (mus) kettledrum

temperamental *adj* temperamental

temperamento *m* temperament; conciliation, compromise; weather

temperar *tr* to temper, soften, moderate, calm; tune || *intr* to go to a warmer climate

temperatura *f* temperature; weather

temperie *f* weather, state of the weather

tempestad *f* storm, tempest; **tempestad de arena** sandstorm; **tempestades de risas** gales of laughter

tempesti•vo -va *adj* opportune, timely

tempestuo•so -sa *adj* stormy, tempestuous

templa•do -da *adj* temperate; moderate; lukewarm, medium; brave, courageous; drunk, tipsy; (SAm) in love; (CAm, Mex) clever

templanza *f* temperence; mildness

templar *tr* to temper; soften; ease, dilute; (*colores*) blend; (*velas*) trim || *intr* (*el tiempo*) to warm up || *ref* to temper; moderate; fall in love; die

ta
te

temple *m* weather, state of the weather; temper, disposition; humor; average; dash, boldness; (*del acero, el vidrio, etc.*) temper

templo *m* temple

témpora *f* Ember days

temporada *f* season; period; (*p.ej., de buen tiempo*) spell; **de temporada** temporarily; vacationing

temporal *adj* temporal; temporary ‖ *m* weather; storm, tempest; spell of rainy weather

temporáne•o -a or **tempora•rio -ria** *adj* temporary

temporizar §60 *intr* to temporize; putter around

temprane•ro -ra *adj* early

tempra•no -na *adj* early ‖ **temprano** *adv* early

tenacidad *f* tenacity; persistence

tenacillas *fpl* sugar tongs; hair curler; tweezers; snuffers

te•naz *adj* (*pl* **-naces**) tenacious; persistent

tenazas *fpl* pincers, pliers; tongs

tenazón — a or **de tenazón** without taking aim; offhand

tenazuelas *fpl* tweezers

tendedera *f* clothesline; litter

tendedero *m* drier, frame for drying clothes; drying ground

tendencia *f* tendency

tender §51 *tr* to spread; stretch out; extend; reach out; offer, tender; (*la ropa*) hang out; (*con una capa de cal o yeso*) coat; (*un puente*) throw, build; (*una trampa*) set; (*conductores eléctricos, vías de ferrocarril, cañerías*) lay; (*la cama*) make; (*un cadáver*) lay out ‖ *intr* to tend ‖ *ref* to stretch out; throw one's cards on the table; run at full gallop

ténder *m* tender

tenderete *m* stand, booth

tende•ro -ra *mf* shopkeeper, storekeeper ‖ *m* tent maker

tendido *m* (*p.ej., de un cable*) laying; (*de una cortina de humo*) spreading; (*de alambres*) hanging, stretching; wires; (*trecho de ferrocarril*) stretch; (*ropa que tiende la lavandera*) wash; (*de cal o yeso*) coat; (*del tejado*) slope; (*de panes*) batch; (*taur*) uncovered stand; (Col) bedclothes

tendón *m* tendon

tenducha *f* or **tenducho** *m* miserable old store

tenebro•so -sa *adj* dark, gloomy; (*negocio*) dark, shady; (*estilo*) obscure

tenedor *m* holder, bearer; fork, table fork; **tenedor de acciones** stockholder; **tenedor de bonos** bondholder; **tenedor de libros** bookkeeper

teneduría *f* bookkeeping

tenencia *f* tenure, tenancy; (mil & nav) lieutenancy

tener §71 *tr* to have; hold; keep; own, possess; consider; (*recibir*) get; esteem; stop; **no tenerlas todas consigo** to be alarmed, dismayed; **no tener nada que ver con** to have nothing to do with; **no tener sobre qué caerse muerto** to not have a cent to one's name; **tener que** to have to; for expressions like **tener hambre** to be hungry, see the noun ‖ *ref* to stop; catch oneself, keep from falling; consider oneself; fit, go

tenería *f* tannery

tenida *f* meeting, session

teniente *adj* holding, owning; unripe; mean, miserly; (mech) hard of hearing ‖ *m* lieutenant; **teniente coronel** lieutenant colonel; **teniente de navío** (nav) lieutenant

tenis *m* tennis

tenista *mf* tennis player

tenor *m* tenor, character, import, drift; (mus) tenor; **a tenor de** in accordance with

tenorio *m* lady-killer

tensión *f* tension, stress; (elec) tension, voltage; (mech) stress; **tensión arterial** or **sanguínea** blood pressure

ten•so -sa *adj* tense, tight, taut

tentación *f* temptation

tentáculo *m* tentacle, feeler

tenta•dor -dora *adj* tempting ‖ *m* tempter

tentar §2 *tr* to touch; (*el camino*) feel; try, attempt; examine; try out, test; tempt; probe

tentati•vo -va *adj* tentative ‖ *f* attempt; trial, feeler

tentempié *m* snack, bite, pick-me-up; (*juguete*) tumbler

tenue *adj* tenuous; light, soft; faint, subdued; (*estilo*) simple

teñir §72 *tr* to dye; stain; tinge, shade, color

teología *f* theology; **no meterse en teologías** to keep out of deep water; **teología liberacionista** liberation theology

teorema *m* theorem

teoría *f* theory; **teoría ondulatoria** wave theory

tepe *m* turf, sod

tequila *m* (Mex) tequila (*distilled liquor*)

terapéuti•co -ca *adj* therapeutic(al) ‖ *f* therapeutics

terapia *f* therapy; **terapia vocacional** occupational therapy

tercena *f* government tobacco warehouse; (Ecuad) butcher shop

tercermundista *adj* Third World

terce•ro -ra *adj* third ‖ *mf* third; mediator; go-between ‖ *m* procurer, bawd; referee, umpire

Tercero Mundo *m* Third World; nonaligned nations

terceto *m* tercet; trio

terciar *tr* to place diagonally; divide into three parts; (*p.ej., la capa, el fusil*) to swing over one's shoulder; (*licor*) water ‖ *intr* to intercede, mediate ‖ *ref* to happen; be opportune

tercia•rio -ria *adj* tertiary

ter•cio -cia *adj* third ‖ *m* third; (mil) corps; **hacer buen tercio a** to do a good turn

terciopelo *m* velvet

ter•co -ca *adj* stubborn; hard, resistant

Teresa *f* Theresa

tergiversar *tr* to slant, twist, distort
terliz *m* ticking
termal *adj* thermal; steam
termas *fpl* hot baths
térmi•co -ca *adj* temperature; steam; steam-generated
terminación *f* termination
terminal *adj* terminal || *m* (elec) terminal
terminante *adj* final, definitive, peremptory
terminar *tr* to end, terminate; finish || *intr* to end, terminate
término *m* end, limit; boundary; bearing; manner; term; **medio término** subterfuge, evasion; compromise; **primer término** foreground; (mov) close-up; **segundo término** middle distance; **término medio** average; **último término** background
termistor *m* (elec) thermistor
termite *m* termite
termoaislante *adj* heat-insulated
termodinámi•co -ca *adj* thermodynamic || *f* thermodynamics
termómetro *m* thermometer; **termómetro clínico** clinical thermometer
termonuclear *adj* thermonuclear
termopar *m* (elec) thermocouple
Termópilas, las Thermopylae
ter•mos *m* (*pl* **-mos**) thermos bottle; hot-water heater; **termos de acumulación** (elec) off-peak heater
termosifón *m* hot-water boiler
termóstato *m* thermostat
terna *f* trio
terne•jo -ja *adj* (Ecuad, Peru) peppy, energetic
ternera *f* calf; (*carne*) veal
terneza *f* tenderness; fondness; love; **ternezas** flirting, flirtation
ternilla *f* gristle
terno *m* suit of clothes; oath, curse; trio; piece of luck; (Col) cup and saucer; (W-I) set of jewelry
ternura *f* tenderness; fondness, love
terquedad *f* stubbornness; hardness, resistance
terraja *f* diestock
terral *adj* (*viento*) land || *m* land breeze
Terranova *m* (*perro*) Newfoundland (*dog*) || *f* (*isla y provincia*) Newfoundland (*island and province*)
terraplén *m* fill; embankment; terrace, platform; earthwork, rampart
terrateniente *mf* landholder, landowner
terraza *f* terrace; veranda; flat roof; (*de jardín*) border; edge; sidewalk cafe; glazed jar with two handles
terremoto *m* earthquake
terrenal *adj* earthly, mundane, worldly
terre•no -na *adj* terrestrial; mundane, worldly || *m* land, ground, terrain; lot, plot; (sport) field; (fig) field, sphere; **sobre el terreno** on the spot; with data in hand; **terreno echadizo** refuse dump
terre•ro -ra *adj* earthly; of earth; humble || *m* pile, heap; mark, target; terrace; public square; (min) dump
terrestre *adj* terrestrial; ground, land

terrible *adj* terrible; gruff, surly, ill-tempered
territorio *m* territory
terromontero *m* hill, butte
terrón *m* clod; lump, cake
terror *m* terror
terrorismo *m* terrorism, frightfulness
terrorista *adj & mf* terrorist
terro•so -sa *adj* earthly, dirty
terruño *m* piece of ground; soil; country, native soil
ter•so -sa *adj* smooth, glossy, polished; smooth, limpid, flowing
tertulia *f* party, social gathering; literary gathering; game room; **estar de tertulia** to sit around and talk
tertulia•no -na *mf* party-goer; regular member
Tesalia, la Thessaly
te•sis *f* (*pl* **-sis**) thesis
te•so -sa *adj* taut, tight, tense || *m* top of hill; (*en superficie lisa*) rough spot
tesón *m* grit, pluck, tenacity
tesone•ro -ra *adj* obstinate, stubborn, tenacious
tesorería *f* treasury
tesore•ro -ra *mf* treasurer
tesoro *m* treasure; treasury; treasure house; thesaurus
Tespis *m* Thespis
testa *f* head; front; head, brains; **testa coronada** crowned head
testaferro *m* dummy, figurehead, straw man
testamento *m* testament, will; **Antiguo Testamento** Old Testament; **Nuevo Testamento** New Testament; **Viejo Testamento** Old Testament
testar *tr* (Ecuad) to cross out || *intr* to make a will
testaru•do -da *adj* stubborn, pig-headed
testera *f* front; (*de animal*) forehead; (*de coche*) back seat
testículo *m* testicle
testificar §73 *tr & intr* to testify
testigo *mf* witness; **testigo de vista, testigo ocular,** or **testigo presencial** eyewitness || *m* (*evidencia*) witness; (*en un experimento*) control
testimoniar *tr* to attest, testify to, bear witness to
testimonio *m* testimony; affidavit; false witness
tes•tuz *m* (*pl* **-tuces**) (*p.ej., de caballo*) face; nape
teta *f* teat; breast
tetera *f* teapot; teakettle
tetilla *f* nipple
tétri•co -ca *adj* dark gloomy; sad, sullen, gloomy
textil *adj & m* textile
texto *m* text; **fuera de texto** tipped-in
textura *f* texture
tez *f* complexion
ti *pron pers* thee; you
tía *f* aunt; old lady, old woman; bawd; **no hay tu tía** there's no chance; **tía abuela** grandaunt
tiara *f* tiara

tibante *adj* (Col) haughty, proud
tibia *f* shinbone; pipe, flute
ti•bio -bia *adj* tepid, lukewarm; (SAm) angry ‖ *f* see **tibia**
tibor *m* large porcelain vase; chamber pot
tiburón *m* shark
Ticiano, El Titian
tictac *m* tick-tock
tiempo *m* time; weather; (gram) tense; (*de un motor de combustión interna*) cycle; (*de una sinfonía*) (mus) movement; (mus) tempo; **darse buen tiempo** to have a good time; **de cuatro tiempos** (mach) four-cycle; **de dos tiempos** (mach) two-cycle; **de un tiempo a esta parte** for some time now; **el Tiempo** Father Time; **fuera de tiempo** untimely, at the wrong time; **hacer buen tiempo** to be clear; **mucho tiempo** a long time; **tomarse tiempo** to bide one's time
tienda *f* store, shop; tent; **ir de tiendas** to go shopping; **tienda de campaña** army tent; camping tent; **tienda de modas** ladies' dress shop; **tienda de objetos de regalo** gift shop; **tienda de raya** (Mex) company store
tienta *f* cleverness; probe; (taur) testing the mettle of a young bull; **andar a tientas** to grope in the dark; feel one's way
tiento *m* touch; blind man's stick; rope-walker's pole; steady hand; care, caution; mahlstick; blow, hit; swig; **andarse con tiento** to watch one's step; **perder el tiento** to lose one's touch
tier•no -na *adj* tender; loving; tearful; soft
tierra *f* earth; ground; land; dirt; (elec) ground; **dar en tierra con** to upset, overthrow, ruin; **echar tierra a** to hush up; **en tierra, mar y aire** on land, on sea, and in the air; **irse a tierra** to topple, to collapse; **la tierra de nadie** (mil) no man's island; **tierra adentro** inland; **tierra de pan llevar** wheat land, cereal-growing land; **tierra firme** mainland; land, terra firma; **Tierra Firme** Spanish Main; **Tierra Santa** Holy Land; **tierra y escombros** landfill; **tomar tierra** to land; to fine one's way around; **venir** or **venirse a tierra** to topple, to collapse; **ver tierras** to see the world, to go traveling
tierral *m* cloud of dust
tie•so -sa *adj* stiff; tight, taut, tense; stubborn; bold, enterprising; strong, well; stiff, stuck-up; **tenérselas tiesas a** or **con** to stand up to ‖ **tieso** *adv* hard
ties•to -ta *adj* stiff; tight, taut, tense; stubborn ‖ *m* flowerpot; (*pedazo roto*) potsherd ‖ **tiesto** *adv* hard
tiesura *f* stiffness
ti•fo -fa *adj* full, satiated ‖ *m* typhus; **tifo de América** yellow fever; **tifo de Oriente** bubonic plague
tifón *m* waterspout; typhoon
tigra *f* tigress; (female) jaguar
tigre *m* tiger; (male) jaguar
tijera *f* scissors, shears; sawbuck; **buena tijera** good cutter; good eater; gossip; **tijeras** scissors, shears

tijeretear *tr* to snip, clip, cut; meddle with ‖ *intr* to gossip
tila *f* linden tree; linden-blossom tea
tildar *tr* to put a tilde or dash over; erase, strike out; **tildar de** to brand as
tilde *m & f* tilde; accent mark; superior dash; blemish, flaw; censure ‖ *f* jot, tittle
tiliche *m* (CAm, Mex) trinket
tiliche•ro -ra *mf* (CAm) peddler
tilín *m* ting-a-ling
tilo *m* linden tree; linden-blossom tea
tilo•so -sa *adj* (CAm) dirty, filthy
timar *tr* to snitch; swindle ‖ *ref* to make eyes at each other
timba *f* game of chance; gambling den; (CAm, Mex) belly
timbal *m* kettledrum; (*pastel relleno*) casserole
timbrar *tr* to stamp
timbre *m* stamp, seal; tax stamp; stamp tax; deed of glory; (phonet & phys) timbre; **timbre nasal** twang; **timbres** glockenspiel
tími•do -da *adj* timid, bashful
timo *m* theft, swindle; lie; catch phrase
timón *m* (*del arado*) beam; rudder; (fig) helm; **timón de dirección** (aer) vertical rudder; **timón de profundidad** (aer) elevator
timonel *m* helmsman, steersman
timonera *f* (naut) pilot house, wheelhouse
timora•to -ta *adj* God-fearing; chicken-hearted
tímpano *m* eardrum; kettledrum
tina *f* large earthen jar; wooden vat; bathtub
tinaja *f* large earthen jar
tincazo *m* (Arg, Ecuad) fillip
tinglado *m* shed; intrigue, trick; (zool) leatherback
tinieblas *fpl* darkness
tino *m* feel (*for things*); good aim; knack; insight, wisdom; **coger el tino** to get the knack of it
tinta *f* ink; tint, hue; dyeing; **de buena tinta** on good authority; **tinta china** India ink; **tinta simpática** invisible ink
tinte *m* dye; dyeing; dyer's shop; (fig) coloring, false appearance
tinterillo *m* clerk, lawyer's clerk; pettifogger
tintero *m* inkstand, inkwell
tintín *m* clink; jingle
tintinear *intr* to clink; jingle
tin•to -ta *adj* red ‖ *m* red table wine ‖ *f* see **tinta**
tintorería *f* dyeing; dyeing establishment; dry-cleaning establishment
tintore•ro -ra *mf* dyer; dry cleaner
tintura *f* dye; dyeing; rouge; tincture; (fig) smattering; **tintura de tornasol** litmus, litmus solution; **tintura de yodo** iodine
tiña *f* ringworm; stinginess
tiño•so -sa *adj* scabby, mangy; stingy
tío *m* uncle; old man; guy, fellow; **tío abuelo** granduncle; **tíos** uncle and aunt
tiovivo *m* merry-go-round, carrousel
tipiadora *f* (*máquina*) typewriter; (*mujer*) typist
tipiar *tr & intr* to type, typewrite

tipicista *adj* regional, local
tipi·co -ca *adj* typical; regional; quaint
tipismo *m* quaintness
tipista *mf* typist, typewriter
tiple *mf* soprano (*person*); treble-guitar player ‖ *m* soprano (*voice*); treble guitar
tipo *m* type; (*de descuento, de interés, de cambio*) rate; shape, figure, build; fellow, guy, specimen; **tener buen tipo** to have a good figure; **tipo de ensayo** or **prueba** eye-test chart; **tipo de impuesto** tax rate; **tipo de letra** typeface; **tipo menudo** small print
tipografía *f* typography
típula *f* (ent) daddy-longlegs
tira *m* (Arg, Chile, Col) detective ‖ *f* strip; **hecho tiras** (Chile) in rags; **tira emplástica** (Arg) court plaster; **tira proyectable** film strip; **tiras cómicas** comics, funnies
tirabala *f* popgun
tirabuzón *m* corkscrew; corkscrew curl
tirada *f* throw; distance, stretch; time, period; printing; edition, issue; shooting party, hunting party; tirade; **de** or **en una tirada** at one stroke; **tirada aparte** reprint
tira·do -da *adj* dirt-cheap; (*letra*) cursive ‖ *f* see **tirada**
tira·dor -dora *mf* shot, good shot ‖ *m* knob; doorknob; pull chain; **tirador certero** sharpshooter; **tirador emboscado** sniper
tirafondo *m* wood screw
tiraje *m* draft; printing, edition
tiramira *f* long, narrow mountain range; (*de personas o cosas*) string; distance, stretch
tiranía *f* tyranny
tiráni·co -ca *adj* tyrannic(al)
tira·no -na *adj* tyrannous ‖ *mf* tyrant
tirante *adj* tense, taut, tight; (fig) tense, strained ‖ *m* (*de los arreos de una caballería*) trace; **tirantes** suspenders
tirantez *f* tenseness, tautness, tightness; strain
tirar *tr* to throw, cast, fling; throw away; shoot, fire; (*alambre*) draw, pull, stretch; (*una línea*) draw; (*una coz, un pellizco*) give; print; attract; tear down, knock down; (phot) to print ‖ *intr* to pull; last; appeal, have an appeal; (*una chimenea*) draw; (*a la derecha, a la izquierda*) bear, turn; **ir tirando** to get along; **tirar a** to shoot at; (*la espada*) handle; shade into; tend to; aspire to; **tirar de** to pull, pull on; (*una espada*) draw; attract; boast of being; **tira y afloja** give and take; hot and cold ‖ *ref* to rush, throw oneself; give oneself over; lie down; serve time (in prison)
tirilla *f* neckband; **tirilla de bota** bootstrap; **tirilla de camisa** collarband
tiritar *intr* to shiver
tiro *m* throw; shot; charge, load; (*estampido*) report; rifle range; (*p.ej., de chimenea*) draft; (*de caballos*) team; (*de escalera*) flight; (*de las guarniciones*) trace; (*de un paño*) length; pull cord, pull chain; reach; hurt, damage; trick; theft; (min) shaft; (sport) drive, shot; (*alusión desfavorable*) shot; (fig) shot, marksman; **a tiro de fusil** within gunshot; **a tiro de piedra** within a

stone's throw; **matar a tiros** to shoot to death; **ni a tiros** not for love nor money; **poner el tiro muy alto** to hitch one's wagon to a star; **tiro al blanco** target practice; **tiro al vuelo** trapshooting; **tiro de la pesa** (sport) shot-put
tirón *m* tyro, novice; jerk; tug, pull; **de un tirón** all at once; at a stretch
tirotear *tr* to snipe at, blaze away at ‖ *ref* to fire at each other; bicker
tirria *f* dislike, grudge; **tener tirria a** to have it in for
tisana *f* tea, infusion
tísi·co -ca *adj* tubercular ‖ *mf* tubercular person, tubercular
tisis *f* consumption, tuberculosis
titanio *m* titanium
tít. *abbr* título
títere *m* marionette, puppet; fixed idea; whipper-snapper, nincompoop; **no dejar títere con cabeza** or **cara** to upset the applecart; **títeres** puppet show
titilar *tr* to titillate ‖ *intr* to flutter, quiver; twinkle
titubear *intr* to stagger, totter; stammer, stutter; waver, hesitate
titular *m* bearer, holder; incumbent; headline ‖ *f* capital letter ‖ *tr* to title, entitle ‖ *intr* to receive a title ‖ *ref* to be called; call oneself
titulillo *m* running head
título *m* title; titled person; regulation; bond; certificate; degree; diploma; headline; **a título de** as a, by way of, on the score of; **títulos** credentials
tiza *f* chalk
tiznar *tr* to soil with soot; spot, stain; to defame ‖ *ref* to become soiled; get spotted or stained; (Arg, Chile, CAm) to get drunk
tizne *m & f* soot ‖ *m* firebrand
tiznón *m* smudge, spot of soot
tizón *m* brand, firebrand; wheat smut; brand, dishonor
tizonear *intr* to stir up the fire
tlapalería *f* (Mex) paint store
toalla *f* towel; **toalla rusa** Turkish towel; **toalla sin fin** roller towel
toallero *m* towel rack
toar *tr* (naut) to tow
tobar *tr* (Col) to tow
tobillera *f* anklet; (sport) ankle support; (coll) subdeb; (coll) flapper
tobillo *m* ankle
tobo *m* (Ven) bucket
tobogán *m* toboggan; chute, slide
toca *f* toque; headdress
tocadis·cos *m* (*pl* -cos) record player; **tocadiscos automático** record changer
toca·do -da *adj* (*echado a perder; medio loco*) touched; **tocado de la cabeza** touched in the head ‖ *m* hairdo, coiffure; headdress
toca·dor -dora *mf* performer; player ‖ *m* boudoir; dressing table; dressing case, toilet case
tocante *adj* touching; **tocante a** concerning, with reference to

ti
to

tocar §73 *tr* to touch; touch on; feel; ring; toll; strike; come to know, suffer, feel; (*el cabello*) do; (*un tambor*) beat; (mus) to play; (paint) to touch up ‖ *intr* to touch; **tocar a** to knock at; pertain to, concern; fall to the lot of; be the turn of; (*el fin*) approach; **tocar en** (*un puerto*) to touch at; (*tierra*) touch; touch on; approach, border on ‖ *ref* to put one's hat on, cover one's head; touch each other; be related; make one's toilet; become mentally unbalanced; (*el sombrero*) tip; **tocárselas** to beat it

toca•yo -ya *mf* namesake

tocino *m* bacon; salt pork

tocón *m* stump

tocuyo *m* (SAm) coarse cotton cloth

tochimbo *m* (Peru) smelting furnace

to•cho -cha *adj* rough, coarse, crude

todavía *adv* still, yet; **todavía no** not yet

to•do -da *adj* all, whole, every; any ‖ *m* whole; everything; **con todo** still, however; **del todo** wholly, entirely; **jugar el todo por el todo** to stake everything, shoot the works; **sobre todo** above all, especially; **todo el que** everybody who; **todo lo que** all that; **todos** all, everybody; **todos cuantos** all those who

todopodero•so -sa *adj* all-powerful, almighty

toga *f* (academic) gown

toldilla *f* poop, poop deck

toldería *f* (SAm) Indian camp, Indian village

toldo *m* awning; pride, haughtiness; (SAm) Indian hut

tole *m* hubbub, uproar; **tole tole** gossip, talk; **tomar el tole** to run away

tolerancia *f* tolerance; **por tolerancia** on sufferance

tolerar *tr* to tolerate

tolete *m* club, cudgel; raft; (Cuba) dunce

toletole *m* (Col) persistence, obstinacy; (Ven) merry life of a wanderer

tolon•dro -dra *adj* scatterbrained ‖ *mf* scatterbrain ‖ *m* bump, lump

tolva *f* hopper; chute

tolvanera *f* dust storm

tolla *f* quagmire; (Cuba) watering trough

tom. *abbr* **tomo**

toma *f* taking; seizure, capture; tap; intake; inlet; (elec) tap, outlet; (elec) plug; (elec) terminal; (*de rapé*) pinch; **toma de posesión** installation, induction; inauguration; **toma de tierra** (aer) landing; (rad) ground connection; **toma directa** high gear

toma-corrien•te *m* or **toma-corrien•tes** *m* (*pl -tes*) (elec) current collector; (elec) tap, outlet; (elec) plug

tomadero *m* handle; intake, inlet

toma•dor -dora *mf* (com) drawee; thief; drinker, toper

tomar *tr* to take; get; seize; take on; (*un resfriado*) catch; (*p.ej., el desayuno*) have, eat; (*el café, un trago*) take, drink; **tomar a bien** to take in the right spirit; **tomar a mal** to take offense at; **tomarla con** to pick a quarrel with; have a grudge against; **tomar prestado** to borrow; **tomar sobre sí** to take upon oneself ‖ *intr* to take, turn ‖

ref to take; (*p.ej., el desayuno*) have, eat; (*el café*) take, drink; get rusty

tomate *m* tomato; (*en medias, calcetines, etc.*) tear, run

tomavis•tas *m* (*pl -tas*) movie camera; cameraman

tómbola *f* raffle, charity raffle

tomillo *m* thyme

tomo *m* volume; bulk, importance, consequence; **de tomo y lomo** of consequence; bulky and heavy

ton. *abbr* **tonelada**

ton — *sin* **ton ni son** without rhyme or reason

tonada *f* air, melody, song; singsong; (Cuba) hoax; (*pronunciación particular*) (Arg, Chile) accent

tonel *m* cask, barrel

tonelada *f* (*unidad de peso; unidad de volumen; unidad de desplazamiento*) ton; (*medida de capacidad para el vino*) tun

tonelaje *m* tonnage

tonele•ro -ra *mf* barrelmaker, cooper

tonga *f* coat, layer; (Arg, Col) task; (Col) sleep; (Cuba) heap, pile

tongonear *ref* to strut, swagger

tóni•co -ca *adj & m* tonic ‖ *f* (mus) keynote

tonillo *m* singsong; (*pronunciación particular*) accent

tono *m* tone; tune; (mus) pitch; (mus) key; (*de un instrumento de bronce*) (mus) slide; **dar el tono** to set the standard; **darse tono** to put on airs; **de buen tono** stylish, elegant; **estar a tono** to be in style; **poner a tono** (*un motor de automóvil*) to tune up; **tono mayor** (mus) major key; **tono menor** (mus) minor key

tonsila *f* tonsil

tonsilitis *f* tonsilitis

tonsurar *tr* to shear, clip

tontear *intr* to talk nonsense, act foolishly

tontería *f* foolishness, nonsense

ton•to -ta *adj* foolish, stupid, silly; **a tontas y a locas** wildly, recklessly; in disorder, haphazardly ‖ *mf* fool, dolt; **tonto de capirote** blatant fool

tonu•do -da *adj* (Arg) magnificent, showy, conceited

topacio *m* topaz

topar *tr* to butt; bump; run into, encounter ‖ *intr* to butt; succeed; lie, be found; **topar con** or **en** to run into, encounter

tope *adj* (*precio*) top; (*fecha*) last ‖ *m* butt; bumper; bump, collision; rub, difficulty; scuffle; masthead; **al tope** or **a tope** end to end; flush; **estar hasta el tope** or **los topes** to be loaded to the gunwales; be fed up; **tope de puerta** doorstop

topera *f* molehill

topetada *f* butt

topetar *tr* to butt ‖ *intr* to butt; **topetar con** to bump, bump into; to run across

topetón *m* butt; bump, collision

tópi•co -ca *adj* local ‖ *m* topic; (med) external application

topinera *f* molehill; **beber como una topinera** to drink like a fish

topo *m* mole; blunderer; stumbler, awkward person

topografía *f* topography

toque *m* touch; (*de una campana*) ringing; (*del tambor*) beat; sound; knock; stroke; check, test; (*punto esencial*) gist; (paint) touch; (coll) blow; **dar un toque a** to put to the test; feel out, sound out; **toque a muerto** knell, toll; **toque de diana** reveille; **toque de queda** curfew; **toque de retreta** (mil) tattoo; **toque de tambor** drumbeat

torada *f* drove of bulls

tó•rax *m* (*pl* -**rax**) thorax

torbellino *m* whirlwind; (*persona bulliciosa*) harum-scarum

torcecuello *m* (orn) wryneck

torcedura *f* twist; sprain; dislocation

torcer §74 *tr* to twist; bend; turn; sprain; (*la cara*) screw up; (*el tobillo*) wrench; turn; (*interpretar mal*) distort, misconstrue ‖ *intr* to turn ‖ *ref* to twist; bend; sprain, dislocate; turn sour; go crooked; fail

torci•do -da *adj* twisted; crooked; bent; (*ojos*) cross; (*persona o conducta*) crooked; (Guat) unlucky ‖ *f* wick, lampwick; curlpaper

tor•do -da *adj* dapple-gray ‖ *mf* dapple-gray horse ‖ *m* thrush; starling

torear *tr* (*toros*) to fight; banter, tease, string along ‖ *intr* to fight bulls, be a bullfighter

toreo *m* bullfighting; (taur) performance

tore•ro -ra *adj* bullfighting ‖ *mf* bullfighter

toril *m* (taur) bull pen

tormenta *f* storm; adversity, misfortune

tormento *m* torment, torture; anguish

tormento•so -sa *adj* stormy; (*barco*) storm-ridden

torna *f* return; dam; tap; **se han vuelto las tornas** the luck has changed; **volver las tornas** to give tit for tat

tornar *tr* to return, give back; turn, make ‖ *intr* to return; turn; **tornar a** + *inf* verb + again, e.g., **tornó a abrir la puerta** he opened the door again ‖ *ref* to turn, become

tornasol *m* sunflower; litmus; iridescence

tornasola•do -da *adj* changeable, iridescent

tornavía *m* (rr) turntable

torna•voz *m* (*pl* -**voces**) sounding board; **hacer tornavoz** to cup one's hands to one's mouth

tornear *tr* to turn, turn up ‖ *intr* to go around; tourney; muse, meditate

torneo *m* tourney; match, tournament; **torneo radiofónico** quiz program

tornillo *m* (*cilindro que entra en la tuerca*) screw; (*clavo con resalto helicoidal*) bolt; (*instrumento con dos mandíbulas*) vise; (mil) desertion; (CAm, Ven) screw tree; **apretar los tornillos a** to put the screws on; **tener flojos los tornillos** to have a screw loose; **tornillo de mariposa** or **de orejas** thumbscrew; **tornillo de presión** setscrew; **tornillo para metales** machine screw

torniquete *m* (*para contener hemorragias*) tourniquet; (*torno para cerrar un paso*) turnstile; **dar torniquete a** to twist the meaning of

torno *m* turn, revolution; (*máquina simple que consiste en un cilindro que gira sobre su eje*) winch, windlass; (*de alfarero*) potter's wheel; (*instrumento con dos mandíbulas*) vise; (*máquina herramienta que sirve para labrar metal o madera*) lathe; (*de coche*) brake; (*de un río*) bend, turn; revolving server; **en torno a** or **de** around; **torno de alfarero** potter's wheel; **torno de banco** bench vise; **torno de hilar** spinning wheel

toro *m* bull; **toro corrido** smart fellow; **toros** bullfight

torón *m* strand

toronja *f* grapefruit

toronjo *m* grapefruit (*tree*)

torpe *adj* slow, heavy; clumsy, awkward; stupid; lewd; crude, ugly

torpedear *tr* to torpedo

torpedo *m* torpedo; touring car

torpeza *f* torpidity, slowness; clumsiness, awkwardness; stupidity; lewdness; turpitude; crudeness, ugliness

torrar *tr* to toast

torre *f* tower; watchtower; (*en el ajedrez*) castle, rook; **torre del homenaje** donjon, keep; **torre de lanzamiento** launching tower; **torre de marfil** (fig) ivory tower; **torre de vigía** (naut) crow's-nest; **torre maestra** donjon, keep; **torre reloj** clock tower

torreja *f* (dial, Am) French toast

torrentada *f* flash flood

torrente *m* torrent

torreón *m* (archit) turret

torreta *f* (nav) turret

tórri•do -da *adj* torrid

torrija *f* French toast

torta *f* cake; (typ) font; slap; **ser tortas y pan pintado** to be a cinch; **torta a la plancha** hot cake, griddle cake

torticolis *m* or **tortícolis** *m* wryneck, stiff neck

tortilla *f* omelet; (CAm, Mex) tortilla (*cornmeal cake*); **tortilla a la española** potato omelet; **tortilla a la francesa** plain omelet; **tortilla de tomate** Spanish omelet

tórtola *f* turtledove

tortuga *f* tortoise, turtle

tortuo•so -sa *adj* winding; (fig) devious

tortura *f* torture

torturar *tr* to torture

tor•vo -va *adj* grim, stern

tos *f* cough; **tos ferina** whooping cough

tosca•no -na *adj* Tuscan ‖ **la Toscana** Tuscany

tos•co -ca *adj* coarse, rough; uncouth

toser *intr* to cough

tósigo *m* poison; sorrow

tosiguero *m* poison ivy

tosquedad *f* coarseness, roughness; uncouthness

tostada *f* piece of toast; toast; **dar** or **pegar la tostada** or **una tostada a** to cheat, trick; **tostadas** toast

tosta•do -da *adj* brown; tan, sunburned ‖ *m* toasting; roasting ‖ *f* see **tostada**

tostador *m* toaster, roaster

tostar §61 *tr* & *ref* to toast; roast; tan, burn

tostón *m* roasted chickpea; toast dipped in olive oil; roast pig; scorched food

total *adj* & *m* total ‖ *adv* in a word

totalidad *f* totality; entirety; **en su totalidad** in its entirety

tóxi•co -ca *adj* & *m* toxic

toxicomanía *f* drug addiction

toxicóma•no -na *adj* drug-addicted ‖ *mf* drug addict

tozu•do -da *adj* stubborn

tpo. *abbr* **tiempo**

traba *f* bond, tie; clasp, lock; hobble, clog; obstacle, hindrance

traba•do -da *adj* tied, fastened; joined, connected; robust, sinewy; (*sílaba*) checked; tongue-tied; (*ojos*) (Col) cross

trabaja•do -da *adj* overworked, worn-out; strained, forced, labored; busy

trabaja•dor -dora *adj* working; industrious, hard-working ‖ *mf* worker, toiler ‖ *m* workman, workingman ‖ *f* workingwoman

trabajar *tr* to work; till; bother, disturb; (*a una persona*) work, drive ‖ *intr* to work; strain; warp; **trabajar en** or **por** to strive to ‖ *ref* to strive, exert oneself

trabajo *m* work; trouble; (*en contraposición de capital*) labor; **costar trabajo** + *inf* to be hard to + *inf*; **trabajo a destajo** piecework; **trabajo a domicilio** homework; **trabajo a jornal** timework; **trabajo de menores** child labor; **trabajo de oficina** clerical work; **trabajo de taller** shopwork; **trabajos** hardships, tribulations; **trabajos forzados** or **forzosos** hard labor, penal labor

trabajo•so -sa *adj* arduous, laborious; (*maganto*) wan, languid; (*falto de espontaneidad*) labored; unpleasant, annoying

trabalen•guas *m* (*pl* **-guas**) tongue twister, jawbreaker

trabar *tr* to join, unite; catch, seize; fasten; fetter; lock; begin; (*una batalla*) join; (*una conversación, amistad*) strike up ‖ *intr* to take hold ‖ *ref* to become entangled; jam; to foul; **trabársele a uno la lengua** to become tongue-tied

trabe *f* beam

trabilla *f* gaiter strap; belt loop; end stitch, loose stitch

trabuco *m* blunderbuss; popgun

trac *m* stage fright

tracale•ro -ra *adj* (CAm, Mex, W-I) cheating, tricky ‖ *mf* (CAm, Mex, W-I) cheat, trickster

tracción *f* traction; **tracción delantera** front drive; **tracción trasera** rear drive

tractor *m* tractor; **tractor de oruga** caterpillar tractor

tradición *f* tradition

tradicionista *mf* folklorist

traducción *f* translation; **traducción automática** machine translation

traducir §19 *tr* to translate; change

traduc•tor -tora *mf* translator

traer §75 *tr* to bring; bring on; draw, pull; make, keep; wear; have, carry; **traer a mal traer** to abuse, mistreat ‖ *intr* — **traer y llevar** to gossip ‖ *ref* to dress; behave; **traérselas** to get worse and worse, cause a lot of trouble

tráfago *m* traffic, trade; toil, drudgery

trafa•gón -gona *adj* hustling, lively; slick, tricky ‖ *mf* hustler, live wire

traficante *mf* dealer, merchant

traficar §73 *intr* to deal, trade, traffic; travel about

tráfico *m* trade; traffic

tragaderas *fpl* gullibility; tolerance; **tener buenas tragaderas** to be too gullible

tragalda•bas *mf* (*pl* **-bas**) glutton; easy mark

tragale•guas *mf* (*pl* **-guas**) (coll) great walker

traga•luz *m* (*pl* **-luces**) skylight, bull's-eye; cellar window

tragamone•das *m* (*pl* **-das**) or **tragape•rras** *m* (*pl* **-rras**) slot machine

tragar §44 *tr* to swallow; swallow up; gulp down; (*creer fácilmente*) swallow; overlook; **no poder tragar** to not be able to stomach ‖ *intr* & *ref* to swallow

tragasable *m* sword swallower

tragavenado *f* (SAm) anaconda

tragaviro•tes *m* (*pl* **-tes**) stuffed shirt

tragedia *f* tragedy

trági•co -ca *adj* tragic(al) ‖ *m* tragedian

trago *m* swallow; swig; misfortune; **a tragos** slowly

tra•gón -gona *adj* gluttonous ‖ *mf* glutton

traición *f* treachery, betrayal; (*delito contra la patria*) treason; treacherous act; **alta traición** high treason; **a traición** treacherously; **hacer traición a** to betray

traicionar *tr* to betray

traicione•ro -ra *adj* treacherous; treasonable ‖ *mf* traitor

traída *f* conveyance, transfer; (Guat) sweetheart; **traída de aguas** water supply

traí•do -da *adj* worn, threadbare ‖ *f* see **traída**

trai•dor -dora *adj* treacherous; treasonable ‖ *mf* traitor; betrayer ‖ *m* villain ‖ *f* traitoress

traílla *f* leash; road scraper

traje *m* suit; clothes; dress; gown; **cortar un traje a** to gossip about; **traje a la medida** suit made to order; **traje de baño** bathing suit; **traje de calle** street clothes; **traje de ceremonia** or **de etiqueta** dress suit; full dress; evening clothes; **traje de faena** (mil) fatigue clothes; **traje de luces** bullfighter's costume; **traje de malla** tights; **traje de montar** riding habit; **traje de paisano** civilian clothes; **traje hecho** ready-made suit; **traje sastre** lady's tailor-made suit; **traje serio** formal dress; **vestir su primer traje largo** to come out, make one's debut

trajear *tr* to dress, clothe

trajín *m* carrying, transfer, conveyance; going and coming; bustle, commotion

trajinar *tr* to carry, convey; (Arg, Chile) to poke into; (Arg, Chile) to deceive; (Pan) to annoy ‖ *intr* to bustle around

tralla *f* lash, whiplash, whipcord

trama *f* weft, woof; plot, scheme, machination; (*de un drama o novela*) plot

tramar *tr* to weave; plot, scheme; (*un enredo*) hatch (*a plot*)

trambucar §73 *intr* (Col, Ven) to be shipwrecked; (Col, Ven) to go out of one's mind

tramitación *f* transaction, negotiation; procedure, steps; **tramitación automática de datos** data processing

tramitar *tr* to transact, negotiate

trámite *m* step, procedure; proceeding; transaction

tramo *m* tract; stretch; (*de una escalera*) flight; (*de un puente*) span; (*de un canal entre dos esclusas*) level

tramontana *f* north; north wind; pride, haughtiness

tramoya *f* stage machinery; scheme

tramoyista *adj* scheming, tricky ‖ *mf* schemer, impostor ‖ *m* stagehand

trampa *f* trap; trap door; (*de un mostrador*) flap; (*de los pantalones*) fly; **armar una trampa a** to lay a trap for; **trampa explosiva** (mil) booby trap

trampear *tr* to trick, swindle ‖ *intr* to cheat; manage to get along

trampilla *f* peephole in the floor; (*de los pantalones*) fly; (*de un secreter*) top, lid; (*de una mesa*) leaf, hinged leaf

trampolín *m* diving board; springboard; ski jump

trampo•so -sa *adj* tricky, crooked ‖ *mf* cheat, swindler

tranca *f* beam, pole; crossbar; (Arg, Chile) drunk, spree; (P-R) dollar; **a trancas y barrancas** through fire and water

trancar §73 *tr* to bar ‖ *intr* to stride along

trance *m* crisis; peril; trance; **a todo trance** at any cost; **último trance** (*de la vida*) last stage, end

tranco *m* long stride; threshold

tranquera *f* palisade, fence

tranquilidad *f* tranquillity

tranquilizante *m* tranquilizer

tranquilizar §60 *tr, intr & ref* to tranquilize, calm down

tranqui•lo -la *adj* tranquil, calm

tranquilla *f* feeler

tranquillo *m* knack

transacción *f* settlement, compromise; transaction

transaéreo *m* airliner

transar *tr* to settle ‖ *intr* to yield, give in, compromise

transatlánti•co -ca *adj & m* transatlantic

transbordador *m* ferry; **transbordador espacial** space shuttle

transbordar *tr* to transship; transfer ‖ *intr* to transfer, change trains

transbordo *m* transshipment; transfer

transcribir §83 *tr* to transcribe

transcripción *f* transcription

transcurrir *intr* to pass, elapse

transcurso *m* course (*of time*)

transepto *m* transept

transeúnte *adj* transient ‖ *mf* transient; passer-by

transferencia *f* transfer

transferir §68 *tr* to transfer; postpone

transformador *m* transformer

transformar *tr* to transform ‖ *ref* to transform, be transformed

tránsfuga *mf* turncoat; fugitive

transfusión *f* transfusion; **transfusión de sangre** transfusion, blood transfusion

transgredir §1 *tr* to transgress

transgresión *f* transgression

transi•do -da *adj* overcome, paralyzed; mean, cheap, stingy

transigencia *f* compromise; compromising

transigente *adj* compromising

transigir §27 *tr* to settle, compromise ‖ *intr* to settle, compromise; agree

transistor *m* transistor

transistorizar §60 *tr* transistorize

transitable *adj* passable, practicable

transitar *intr* to go, walk; to travel

transiti•vo -va *adj* transitive

tránsito *m* transit; traffic; stop; passage; transfer

transito•rio -ria *adj* transitory

translúci•do -da *adj* translucent

transmisión *f* transmission; **transmisión del pensamiento** thought transference

transmisor *m* transmitter; **transmisor de órdenes** (naut) engine-room telegraph

transmitir *tr & intr* to transmit

transmudar *tr* to transfer; persuade, convince

transmutar *tr, intr & ref* to transmute

transparecer §22 *intr* to show through

transparencia *f* transparency; slide

transparentar *ref* to show through

transparente *adj* transparent ‖ *m* curtain, window curtain; **transparente de resorte** window blind or shade

transpirar *intr* to transpire; (*dejarse conocer una cosa secreta*) transpire

transplantar *tr* to transplant

transponer §54 *tr* to transpose; disappear behind ‖ *ref* (*ocultarse detrás del horizonte*) to set; get sleepy

transportar *tr* to transport; (mus) to transpose

transporte *m* transport; transportation; (aer & naut) transport; **transporte colectivo** public transportation

transportista *mf* transport worker

transvesti•do -da *adj & mf* transvestite

tranvestismo *m* transvestism

tranvía *m* trolley, trolley car, streetcar; **tranvía de sangre** horsecar

tranzar §60 *tr* to cut off, rip off; plait, braid

trapacear *tr* to chear, swindle

trapacería *f* cheating, swindling

trapace•ro -ra *adj* cheating, swindling ‖ *mf* cheat, swindler

trapajo *m* rag, tatter

to
tr

trápala *adj* chattering; cheating ‖ *mf* chatterbox; cheat ‖ *m* loquacity ‖ *f* noise, uproar; (*del trote de un caballo*) clatter; cheating

trapear *tr* to mop

trapecio *m* (geom) trapezoid; (sport) trapeze

trapecista *mf* trapeze performer

trape•ro -ra *mf* ragpicker; junk dealer

trapiche *m* sugar mill; olive press; ore crusher

trapien•to -ta *adj* raggedy, in rags

trapío *m* flipness, pertness; (*del toro de lidia*) spirit

trapisonda *f* brawl, row; scheming

trapisondista *mf* schemer

trapo *m* rag; (naut) canvas, sails; bullfighter's bright-colored cape; (*de la muleta*) cloth; **a todo trapo** full sail; **poner como un trapo** to rake over the coals; **sacar los trapos a la colada, a relucir** or **al sol** to wash one's dirty linen in public; **soltar el trapo** to burst out crying, to burst out laughing; **trapos** rags, duds; **trapos de cristianar** Sunday best

trapo•so -sa *adj* raggedy, in rags

tráquea *f* trachea, windpipe

traquea•do -da *adj* (*sendero*) (Arg) beaten

traquear *tr* to shake, rattle; fool with ‖ *intr* to crackle; rattle, chatter

traqueo *m* shake, rattle, chatter

traquetear *tr & intr* to rattle, jerk

tras *prep* after; behind; **tras de** behind; in addition to

trasatlánti•co -ca *adj & m* var of **transatlántico**

trasbordador *m* var of **transbordador**

trasbordar *tr & intr* var of **trasbordar**

trasbordo *m* var of **transbordo**

trascendencia *f* penetration, keenness; importance

trascendente *adj* penetrating; important

trascender §51 *tr* to go into, dig up ‖ *intr* to smell; come to be known, leak out

trascendi•do -da *adj* keen, perspicacious

trascocina *f* scullery

trascorral *m* back yard; backside

trascribir §83 *tr* var of **transcribir**

trascripción *f* var of **transcripción**

trascuarto *m* back room

trascurrir *intr* var of **transcurrir**

trascurso *m* var of **transcurso**

trasegar §66 *tr* to upset, turn topsy-turvy; decant, draw off

trase•ro -ra *adj* back, rear ‖ *m* buttock, rump

trasferir §68 *tr* var of **transferir**

trasformador *m* var of **transformador**

trasformar *tr & intr* var of **transformar**

trásfuga *mf* var of **tránsfuga**

trasfusión *f* var of **transfusión**

trasgo *m* goblin, hobgoblin; imp

trashojar *tr* to leaf through

trashumante *adj* nomadic, migrating

trasiego *m* upset, disorder; decantation

trasladar *tr* to transfer; postpone; copy, transcribe; transmit; move ‖ *intr* to go; move

traslado *m* transfer; copy, transcript; moving

traslapar *tr, intr & ref* to overlap

traslapo *m* lap, overlap

traslúci•do -da *adj* var of **translúcido**

traslucir §45 *tr* to guess ‖ *intr* to leak out ‖ *ref* to be translucent; leak out

traslumbrar *tr* to dazzle ‖ *ref* to be dazzled; vanish

trasluz *m* diffused light; glint, gleam; **al trasluz** against the light

trasmisión *f* var of **transmisión**

trasmisor *m* var of **transmisor**

trasmitir *tr & intr* var of **transmitir**

trasmóvil *m* (Col) mobile unit, radio pickup

trasmudar *tr* var of **transmudar**

trasmundo *m* afterlife, future life

trasmutar *tr, intr & ref* var of **transmutar**

trasnocha•do -da *adj* stale; haggard, run-down; hackneyed ‖ *f* last night; sleepless night; (mil) night attack

trasnocha•dor -dora *mf* night owl

trasnochar *tr* (*un problema*) to sleep over ‖ *intr* to spend the night; spend a sleepless night; stay up late

trasoír §48 *tr* to hear wrong

traspapelar *tr* to mislay ‖ *ref* to become mislaid

trasparecer §22 *intr* var of **transparecer**

trasparencia *f* var of **transparencia**

trasparente *adj & m* var of **transparente**

traspasar *tr* to cross, cross over; send; transfer; move; pierce, transfix; pain, grieve ‖ *ref* to go too far

traspié *m* slip, stumble; trip

traspirar *intr* var of **transpirar**

trasplantar *tr* var of **transplantar**

trasponer §54 *tr & ref* var of **transponer**

trasportar *tr* var of **transportar**

trasporte *m* var of **transporte**

trasportista *mf* var of **transportista**

traspunte *m* (theat) callboy

traspuntín *m* flap seat, folding seat, jump seat

trasquilar *tr* to crop, lop; (*las ovejas*) shear; curtail

trastazo *m* whack, blow

traste *m* fret; **dar al traste con** to throw away, ruin, spoil

trastera *f* attic, junk room

trastienda *f* back room

trasto *m* piece of furniture; piece of junk; good-for-nothing; **trastos** tools, implements, utensils; arms, weapons; junk; muleta and sword

trastornar *tr* to upset; overturn; disturb; perplex; daze, make dizzy; persuade

trastorno *m* upset; disturbance

trastrocar §81 *tr* to turn around, reverse, change

trasudor *m* cold sweat

trasueño *m* blurred dream, vague recollection

trasuntar *tr* to copy; abstract, sum up

trasunto *m* copy; record; likeness

trasverter §51 *intr* to run over, overflow

trasvolar §61 *tr* to fly over

trata *f* traffic, trade, slave trade; **trata de blancas** white slavery; **trata de esclavos** slave trade

tratado *m* (*escrito, libro*) treatise; (*convenio entre gobiernos*) treaty; agreement

tratamiento *m* treatment; title; **apear el tratamiento** to leave off the title

tratante *mf* dealer, retailer

tratar *tr* to handle; deal with; treat; **tratar a uno de** to address someone as; charge someone with being ‖ *intr* to deal; treat; try; **tratar de** to deal with; treat of; come in contact with; try to ‖ *ref* to deal; behave; (*bien o mal*) live; **tratarse de** to deal with; be a question of

trate•ro -ra *mf* (Chile) pieceworker

trato *m* treatment; deal, agreement; manner; business; title; friendly relations; **tener buen trato** to be very nice, be very pleasant; **trato colectivo** collective bargaining; **trato doble** double-dealing; **¡trato hecho!** it's a deal!

través *m* bend, bias, turn; reverse, misfortune; (naut) beam; **al** or **a través de** through, across; **dar al través con** to do away with; **mirar de través** to squint; look at out of the corner of one's eye

travesaño *m* crosspiece; (*de cama*) bolster; (*p.ej., de una sila*) rung

travesear *intr* to romp, carry on; sparkle, be witty; lead a wild life

travesía *f* crossing, voyage; crossroad; distance, passage; cross wind; (Arg, Bol) wasteland; (Chile) west wind

travesura *f* prank, antic, caper; mischief; sparkle, wit; slick trick

traviesa *f* crossing, voyage; rafter; side bet; (rr) tie

travie•so -sa *adj* cross; keen, shrewd; restless, fidgety; naughty, mischievous; debauched ‖ *f* see **traviesa**

trayecto *m* journey, passage, course; stretch, run

trayectoria *f* trajectory; path

traza *f* plan, design; scheme; means; appearance; mark, trace; footprint; streak, trait; **tener trazas de** to show signs of; look like

trazar §60 *tr* to plan, design; outline; trace; (*una línea*) draw; lay out, plot

trazo *m* line, stroke; trace; outline

trebejo *m* implement; chessman

trébol *m* clover; (*naipe que corresponde al basto*) club

trece *adj & pron* thirteen ‖ *m* thirteen; (*en las fechas*) thirteenth; **estarse, mantenerse** or **seguir en sus trece** to stand firm

trecea•vo -va *adj & m* thirteenth

trecho *m* stretch; while; **a trechos** at intervals

tregua *f* truce; respite, letup

treinta *adj & pron* thirty ‖ *m* thirty; (*en las fechas*) thirtieth

treinta•vo -va *adj & m* thirtieth

tremar *intr* to tremble, shake

tremen•do -da *adj* frightful, terrible, tremendous; (*muy grande*) tremendous

trementina *f* turpentine

tremer *intr* to tremble, shake

tremolar *tr & intr* to wave

tren *m* (*de coches o vagones; de ondas*) train; outfit; equipment; following; retinue; show, pomp; (*de la vida*) way; **tren aerodinámico de lujo** (rr) streamliner; **tren**

ascendente (rr) up train; **tren correo** (rr) mail train; **tren de aterrizaje** (aer) landing gear; **tren de laminadores** rolling mill; **tren de lavado** laundry; **tren de mercancías** freight train; **tren de mudadas** moving company; **tren descendente** (rr) down train; **tren de viajeros** passenger train; **tren ómnibus** (rr) accomodation train; **tren rápido** (rr) flyer

treno *m* dirge

trenza *f* braid, plait; tress; (*p.ej., de ajos*) string; **en trenzas** with her hair down

trenzar §60 *tr* to braid, plait ‖ *intr* to caper; prance

trepa•dor -dora *adj* climbing ‖ *mf* climber ‖ *f* (bot) climber

trepar *tr* to climb; drill, bore ‖ *intr* to climb; **trepar por** to climb up ‖ *ref* to lean back

trepidar *intr* to shake, vibrate; (Chile) to hesitate, waver

tres *adj & pron* three; **las tres** three o'clock ‖ *m* three; (*en las fechas*) third

trescien•tos -tas *adj & pron* three hundred ‖ **trescientos** *m* three hundred

tresillo *m* ombre; three-piece living-room suite; (mus) triplet

tresnal *m* (agr) shock

treta *f* trick, scheme; (*del esgrimidor*) feint

treza•vo -va *adj & m* thirteenth

triángulo *m* triangle

triar §77 *tr* to sort

tribu *f* tribe

tribuna *f* tribune, rostrum, platform; grandstand; (*en la iglesia*) gallery; **tribuna de la prensa** press box; **tribuna del órgano** (mus) organ loft; **tribuna de los acusados** (law) dock

tribunal *m* tribunal, court; **tribunal de apelación** appellate court; **tribunal tutelar de menores** juvenile court

tributar *tr* (*contribuciones, impuestos, etc.*) to pay; (*admiración, gratitud, etc.*) render

tributario -ria *adj* tributary; tax; **ser tributario de** to be indebted to ‖ *m* tributary

tributo *m* tribute; tax

tricornio *m* tricorn, three-cornered hat

trifocal *adj* trifocal

trifulca *f* wrangle, squabble

trigési•mo -ma *adj & m* thirtieth

trigo *m* wheat; (slang) dough, money; **trigo entero** whole wheat; **trigo sarraceno** buckwheat

trigonometría *f* trigonometry

trigue•ño -ña *adj* swarthy, olive-skinned

trilogía *f* trilogy

trilla *f* threshing

trilla•do -da *adj* (*sendero*) beaten; trite, commonplace

trilladora *f* threshing machine

trillar *tr* to thresh; mistreat; frequent

trilli•zo -za *mf* triplet

trillón *m* British trillion; quintillion (*in U.S.A.*)

trimestral *adj* quarterly

trimestre *m* quarter

trinado *m* trill, warble

.tr
tr

trinar *intr* to trill, warble, quaver; get angry
trinca *f* trinity
trincar §73 *tr* to bind, lash, tie fast; crush; (slang) to kill ‖ *intr* to take a drink
trinchar *tr* to carve, slice
trinchera *f* cut; trench; trench coat
trímeo *m* sleigh, sled
Trinidad *f* Trinity
trino *m* trill
trinquete *m* pawl, ratchet; (naut) foresail
trin•quis *m* (*pl* **-quis**) drink, swig
trío *m* sorting; trio; (mus) trio
tripa *f* gut, intestine; belly; (*del cigarro*) filler; **hacer de tripas corazón** to pluck up courage
triple *adj* & *m* triple
triplica•do -da *adj* & *m* triplicate; **por triplicado** in triplicate
triplicar §73 *tr* to triplicate ‖ *intr* to treble
trípode *m* tripod
tríptico *m* triptych
tripu•do -da *adj* big-bellied, potbellied
tripulación *f* crew
tripulante *m* crew member
tripular *tr* to man; fit out, equip
trique *m* crack, swish; **a cada trique** at every turn; **triques** (Mex) tools, implements
triquiñuela *f* chicanery, subterfuge
triquitraque *m* clatter; firecracker.
tris *m* crackle; shave, inch; trice
trisar *tr* (Chile) to crack, chip ‖ *intr* to chirp
triscar §73 *tr* to mix; (*una sierra*) set ‖ *intr* to stamp the feet; romp, frisk around; (Col) to gossip
trismo *m* lockjaw
triste *adj* sad; dismal, gloomy; (*despreciable, ridículo*) sorry
tristeza *f* sadness; gloominess
tris•tón -tona *adj* wistful, melancholy
tritón *m* eft, newt, triton; (*hombre experto en la natación*) merman
trituradora *f* crushing machine
triturar *tr* to grind, crush; abuse
triunfal *adj* triumphal
triunfante *adj* triumphant
triunfar *intr* to triumph; trump; **triunfar de** to triumph over; trump
triunfo *m* triumph; trump; **sin triunfo** no trump
trivial *adj* trivial; trite, commonplace; (*sendero*) beaten
trivialidad *f* triviality; triteness
triza *f* shred; **hacer trizas** to tear to pieces
trizar §60 *tr* to tear to pieces
trocar §81 *tr* to exchange, swap; barter; confuse, twist, distort ‖ *intr* to swap ‖ *ref* to change; change seats
trocha *f* trail, narrow path; gauge
trofeo *m* trophy; victory
troj *f* or **troje** *f* granary; olive bin
trole *m* trolley pole
trolebús *m* trolley bus, trackless trolley
tromba *f* (*de polvo, agua, etc.*) whirl, column; **tromba marina** waterspout; **tromba terrestre** tornado
trombón *m* trombone
trompa *f* (*del elefante*) trunk; waterspout;

top; nozzle; (anat) duct, tube; (mus) horn; (Col, Chile) cowcatcher; **trompa de armonía** French horn; **trompa de Eustaquio** Eustachian tube
trompada *f* bump, collision; punch
trompar *intr* to spin a top
trompeta *f* trumpet; bugle, clarion; good-for-nothing; drunkenness   –
trompetear *intr* to trumpet, sound the trumpet
trompetilla *f* ear trumpet; Bronx cheer
trompicar §44 *tr* to trip, make stumble ‖ *intr* to stumble
trompicón *m* stumble
trompiza *f* fist fight
trompo *m* (*juguete*) top; (*en el ajedrez*) man; (*buque malo y pesado*) tub
tronada *f* thunderstorm
tronar §61 *tr* (Mex) to shoot ‖ *intr* to thunder; fail, collapse; **por lo que pueda tronar** just in case
troncar §44 *tr* to cut off the head of; (*un escrito*) cut, shorten
tronco *m* (*del cuerpo, del árbol, de una familia, del ferrocarril*) trunk; (*leño*) log; (*de caballerías*) team; sap, fathead; **estar hecho un tronco** to be knocked out; be sound asleep
troncha *f* slice; cinch
tronchar *tr* to smash, split; chop off
tronera *m* madcap, roisterer ‖ *f* embrasure, loophole; louver; (*de la mesa de billar*) pocket
tronido *m* thunderclap
trono *m* throne
tronquista *m* driver, teamster
tronzar §60 *tr* to shatter, break to pieces; pleat; wear out
tropa *f* troop; herd, drove; **en tropa** straggling, without formation; **tropas de asalto** shock troops, storm troops
tropel *m* crowd, throng; rush, hurry; jumble; **de** or **en tropel** in a mad rush
tropelía *f* mad rush; outrage
tropero *m* (Arg) cowboy
tropezar §18 *tr* to strike ‖ *intr* to stumble; slip, blunder; **tropezar con** or **en** to stumble over, trip over; run into; come upon
trope•zón -zona *adj* stumbly ‖ *m* stumble; stumbling place; **a tropezones** by fits and starts; falteringly; **dar un tropezón** to stumble, trip
tropical *adj* tropic(al)
trópico *m* tropic
tropiezo *m* stumble; stumbling block; slip, blunder, fault; obstacle; quarrel
tropilla *f* (Arg, Urug) drove of horses following a leading mare
troposfera *f* troposphere
troquel *m* die
trotaconven•tos *f* (*pl* **-tos**) procuress, bawd
trotamun•dos *m* (*pl* **-dos**) globetrotter
trotar *intr* to trot; to hustle
trote *m* trot; chore; **al trote** right away; **para todo trote** for everyday wear; **trote de perro** jog trot
trotona *f* chaperone

trovador *m* troubadour
trovadores•co -ca *adj* troubadour
trovero *m* trouvère
Troya *f* Troy; **ahí fué Troya** it's a shambles; **¡arda Troya!** come what may!
troya•no -na *adj & mf* Trojan
troza *f* log
trozar §60 *tr* to break to pieces; (*un tronco*) cut into logs
trozo *m* piece, fragment; block; excerpt, selection
truco *m* contrivance, device; trick; pocketing of ball; **truco de naipes** card trick; **trucos** pool
truculen•to -ta *adj* truculent
trucha *f* trout
trueno *m* thunder, thunderclap; shot, report; rake, roué; **trueno gordo** finale (*of fireworks*); big scandal; **truenos** (Ven) heavy shoes
trueque *m* barter; exchange, swap; trade-in; **a trueque de** in exchange for; **trueques** (Col) change
trufa *f* truffle; fib, lie
tru•hán -hana *adj* crooked; clownish ‖ *mf* crook; clown
trujal *m* wine press; oil press
trulla *f* noise, bustle; crowd; trowel
truncar §73 *tr* to cut off the head of; (*palabras o frases*) cut, slash; cut off, interrupt
trusas *fpl* trunk hose; trunks
tu *adj poss* thy, your
tú *pron pers* thou, you
tubérculo *m* (*rizoma engrosado, p.ej., de la patata*) tuber; (*protuberancia*) tubercle
tuberculosis *f* tuberculosis
tubería *f* tubing; piping
tubo *m* tube; pipe; **tubo de desagüe** drainpipe; **tubo de ensayo** test tube; **tubo de humo** flue; **tubo de imagen** picture tube; **tubo de vacío** vacuum tube; **tubo digestivo** alimentary canal; **tubo sonoro** chime
tuerca *f* nut; **tuerca de aletas** wing nut
tuer•to -ta *adj* crooked, bent; one-eyed; **a tuertas** upside down; crosswise; **a tuertas o a derechas** rightly or wrongly; thoughtlessly ‖ *mf* one-eyed person ‖ *m* wrong, harm, injustice; **tuertos** afterpains
tuétano *m* marrow; pith; **hasta los tuétanos** through and through; head over heels
tufi•llas *mf* (*pl* -llas) touchy person
tufillo *m* whiff, smell
tufo *m* fume, vapor; sidelock; foul odor, foul breath; **tufos** airs, conceit
tugurio *m* shepherd's hut; hovel
tuición *f* protection, custody
tulipán *m* tulip
tullecer §22 *tr* to abuse, mistreat ‖ *intr* to be crippled
tulli•do -da *adj* paralyzed, crippled ‖ *mf* paralytic, cripple
tullir §13 *tr* to cripple, paralyze; abuse, mistreat ‖ *ref* to become crippled or paralyzed
tumba *f* grave, tomb; tombstone; arched top; felling of trees

tumbacuarti•llos *mf* (*pl* -llos) old toper, rounder
tumbar *tr* to knock down; catch, trick; stun ‖ *intr* to tumble; capsize ‖ *ref* to lie down
tumbo *m* fall, tumble; boom, rumble; crisis; rise and fall of sea; rough surf
tumbona *f* hammock
tumor *m* tumor
túmulo *m* catafalque
tumulto *m* tumult
tuna *f* loafing, bumming; (bot) prickly pear
tunante *adj* bumming, loafing; crooked, tricky ‖ *mf* bum, loafer; crook
tundidora *f* lawn mower
tuneci•no -na *adj & mf* Tunisian
túnel *m* tunnel; **túnel de lavado** automatic car wash
tunes *mpl* (Col) little steps, first steps
Túnez (*ciudad*) Tunis; (*país*) Tunisia
tungsteno *m* tungsten
túnica *f* tunic
tu•no -na *adj* crooked, tricky ‖ *mf* crook ‖ *f* see **tuna**
tupé *m* toupee; nerve, cheek, brass
tupi•do -da *adj* thick, dense, compact; dull, stupid; clogged up
tupir *tr* to pack tight ‖ *ref* to stuff, stuff oneself
turba *f* crowd, mob; peat
turbamulta *f* job, rabble
turbar *tr* to disturb, trouble; stir up ‖ *ref* to be confused
turbiedad *f* muddiness; confusion
turbina *f* turbine
tur•bio -bia *adj* turbid, muddy, cloudy; confused; obscure
turbión *m* squall, thunderstorm; (*p.ej., de balas*) (fig) hail
turbocompresor *m* turbocompressor
turbohélice *m* turboprop
turbopropulsor *m* turboprop (*engine*)
turborreactor *m* turbojet (*engine*)
turbosupercargador *m* turbosupercharger
turbulen•to -ta *adj* turbulent
tur•co -ca *adj* Turkish ‖ *mf* Turk ‖ *m* (*idioma*) Turkish ‖ *f* (coll) binge; boozing; **coger una turca** to get drunk
turfista *adj* horsy ‖ *m* turfman
turismo *m* touring; touring car
turista *mf* tourist
turísti•co -ca *adj* tourist; touring
turnar *intr* to alternate, take turns
tur•nio -nia *adj* (*ojos*) cross; cross-eyed; (*que mira con ceño*) cross-looking
turno *m* turn, shift; **aguardar turno** to wait one's turn; **por turno** in turn; **turno diurno** day shift
turón *m* polecat
turquesa *s* turquoise
Turquía *s* Turkey
turrón *m* nougat; plum
tusa *f* corncob; corn silk; (Chile) mane; (Col) pockmark; (CAm, W-I) trollop
tusar *tr* to shear, clip, cut
tutear *tr* to thou, address familiarly ‖ *ref* to thou each other, address each other familiarly

tr
tu

tutela *f* guardianship; protection
tutelar *adj* guardian; protecting ‖ *tr* to protect, shelter, guide
tu•tor -tora or **-triz** *mf* (*pl* **-trices**) guardian, tutor

tu•yo -ya *adj poss* of thee ‖ *pron poss* thine, yours
tuza *f* gopher

U

U, u (u) *f* twenty-fourth letter of the Spanish alphabet
u *conj* (used before words beginning with *o* or *ho*) or
U. *abbr* **usted**
ubicar §73 *tr* to locate, place ‖ *intr & ref* to be situated
ubi•cuo -cua *adj* ubiquitous
ubre *f* udder
Ucrania *f* Ukraine
ucrania•no -na *adj & mf* Ukrainian
ucra•nio -nia *adj & mf* Ukrainian ‖ *f* see **Ucrania**
Ud. *abbr* **usted**
Uds. *abbr* **ustedes**
ufanar *ref* — **ufanarse con** or **de** to boast of, be proud of
ufanía *f* pride, conceit; cheer, satisfaction; ease, smoothness
ufa•no -na *adj* proud, conceited; cheerful, satisfied; easy, smooth
ujier *m* doorman, usher
úlcera *f* ulcer, fester, sore; **úlcera de decú-bito** bedsore
ulcerar *tr & ref* to ulcerate, fester
ulterior *adj* ulterior; subsequent
ulteriormente *adv* subsequently, later
últimamente *adv* finally; lately, recently
ultimar *tr* to finish, end, conclude, wind up; kill, finish off
ultimátum *m* (*pl* **-tums**) ultimatum; definite decision
últi•mo -ma *adj* last, latest; final; excellent, superior; (*precio*) lowest, final; most remote; (*piso*) top; (*hora*) late; **a la última** in the latest fashion; **a última hora** at the eleventh hour; **a últimos de** toward the end of, in the latter part of; **de última hora** last-minute; **estar a lo último** or **en las últimas** to be up to date, be well-informed; be on one's last-legs; **por último** at last, finally; **último suplicio** capital punishment
ultraatmosféri•co -ca *adj* outer (*space*)
ultraeleva•do -da *adj* (rad) ultrahigh
ultrajar *tr* to outrage, offend
ultraje *m* outrage, offense
ultrajo•so -sa *adj* outrageous, offensive
ultramar *m* country overseas
ultramari•no -na *adj* overseas ‖ **ultrama-rinos** *mpl* groceries, delicatessen
ultranza — **a ultranza** to the death; unflinchingly
ultrarro•jo -ja *adj & m* infrared
ultratumba *adv* beyond the grave

ultraviola•do -da or **ultravioleta** *adj & m* ultraviolet
ululación *f* howl; whoop; (*del buho*) hoot; (*del disco del fonógrafo*) wow
ulular *intr* to howl; whoop; (*el buho*) hoot
ululato *m* howl; (*del buho*) hoot
umbilical *adj* umbilical
umbral *m* threshold, doorsill; (*madero que sostiene el muro encima de un vano*) lintel; (physiol, psychol & fig) threshold; **atrave-sar** or **pisar los umbrales** to cross the threshold; **estar en los umbrales de** to be on the threshold of
umbralada *f* (Col) threshold
umbrí•o -a *adj* shady ‖ *f* shady side
umbro•so -sa *adj* shady
un, una (the apocopated form **un** is used before masculine singular nouns and adjectives and before feminine singular nouns beginning with stressed *a* or *ha*) *art indef* a ‖ *adj* one
unánime *adj* unanimous
unanimidad *f* unanimity
unción *f* unction
uncir §36 *tr* (*bueyes*) to yoke, hitch
undéci•mo -ma *adj & m* eleventh
undo•so -sa *adj* wavy
ungir §27 *tr* to smear with ointment or with oil; anoint
ungüento *m* unguent, ointment, salve
únicamente *adv* only, solely
úni•co -ca *adj* only, sole; (*sin otro de su especie*) unique; one, e.g., **precio único** one price
unicornio *m* unicorn
unidad *f* (*concepto de una sola cosa o persona; cantidad que se toma como me-dida común de todas las demás de su clase; el número entero más pequeño*) unit; (*división; armonía de conjunto; el nú-mero uno*) unity
uni•do -da *adj* united; smooth, even; close-knit
unifamiliar *adj casa* one-family
unificar §73 *tr* to unify
uniformar *tr* to make uniform; provide with a uniform
uniforme *adj* uniform ‖ *m* uniform; **uni-forme de gala** (mil) full dress
uniformidad *f* uniformity
unilateral *adj* unilateral
unión *f* union; double ring; **Unión Soviética** Soviet Union
unir *tr & ref* to unite

unisonancia f (mus) unison; (de un orador) monotony

unísono — **al unísono** in unison; unanimously; **al unísono de** in unison with

unita·rio -ria adj unit

universal adj universal; all-purpose; (teclado de máquina de escribir) standard

universidad f university

universita·rio -ria adj university ‖ mf university student, college student ‖ m university professor

universo m universe

u·no -na pron one, someone; **a una** of one accord; **la una** one o'clock; **somos uno** we are one; **uno a otro, unos a otros** each other, one another; **uno que otro** one or more, a few; **u·nos -nas** some; pair of, e.g., **unas gafas** a pair of glasses; **unas tijeras** a pair of scissors; **unos cuantos** some; **uno y otro** both ‖ pron indef one, e.g., **uno no sabe qué hacer aquí** one does not know what to do here ‖ m (unidad y signo que la representa) one

untar tr to smear, grease; anoint; bribe ‖ ref to get smeared; grease oneself; embezzle

unto m grease; (gordura del cuerpo del animal) fat; (Chile) shoe polish; **unto de Méjico** or **de rana** bribe money

untuo·so -sa adj unctuous, greasy, sticky

uña f nail, fingernail, toenail; (pezuña) hoof; (del ancla) fluke, bill; (mach) claw, gripper; **enseñar** or **mostrar las uñas** to show one's teeth; **ser largo de uñas** to have long fingers; **ser uña y carne** to be hand in glove; **tener en la uña** to have on the tip of one's fingers

uñada f scratch, nail scratch; (impulso dado con la uña) flip

uñero m ingrowing nail; (inflamación del dedo en la raíz de la uña) whitlow

ural adj Ural ‖ **Urales** mpl Urals

uranio m uranium

urbanidad f urbanity

urbanismo m city planning

urbanista mf city planner

urbanísti·co -ca adj city-planning ‖ f city planning

urbanizar §60 tr (convertir en poblado) to urbanize; refine; polish

urba·no -na adj urban, city; (atento, cortés) urbane ‖ m policeman

urbe f metropolis

urdema·las mf (pl -las) schemer

urdimbre f warp; scheme, scheming; **estar en la urdimbre** (Chile) to be thin, be emaciated

urdir tr (los hilos) to beam; (una conspiración) hatch

urente adj burning, smarting

uretra f urethra

urgencia f urgency; **de urgencia** special-delivery

urgente adj urgent; (correo) special-delivery

urgir §27 intr to be urgent

urina·rio -ria adj urinary ‖ m urinal

urna f glass case; ballot box; (para guardar las cenizas de los cadáveres) urn; **acudir** or **ir a las urnas** to go to the polls

urología f urology

urraca f magpie

U.R.S.S. abbr **Unión de Repúblicas Socialistas Soviéticas**

urticaria f hives

Uruguay, el Uruguay

urugua·yo -ya adj & mf Uruguayan

usa·do -da adj (empleado; gastado por el uso; acostumbrado) used; skilled, experienced; (vocablo) **poco usado** rare

usanza f use, usage, custom

usar tr to use, make use of; (un cargo, un oficio) follow ‖ intr — **usar + inf** to be accustomed to + inf; **usar de** to use, have recourse to; **usar de la palabra** to speak, make a speech ‖ ref to be the custom

usina f factory, plant; powerhouse; (estación de tranvía) (Arg) carbarn

uso m use; custom, usage; wear, wear and tear; habit, practice; **al uso** according to custom; **en buen uso** in good condition; **hacer uso de la palabra** to speak, make a speech

usted pron pers you

usual adj (de uso común) usual; (que se usa con facilidad) usable; sociable

usualmente adv usually

usua·rio -ria adj user

usufructo m use, enjoyment

usufructuar §21 tr to enjoy the use of

usura f usury; profit; **pagar con usura** to pay back a thousandfold

usurero m loan shark; profiteer

usurpar tr to usurp

utensilio m utensil

útero m uterus, womb

útil adj useful ‖ **útiles** mpl utensils, tools, equipment

utilería f (Arg) properties, stage equipment

utilero m (Arg) property man

utilidad f utility, usefulness; profit, earnings

utilita·rio -ra adj utilitarian

utilizable adj usable

utilizar §60 tr to utilize, use ‖ ref — **utilizarse con, de** or **en** to make use of; **utilizarse para** to be good for

utopía f utopia

utopista adj & mf utopian

UU. abbr **ustedes**

uva f grape; wart on eyelid; (baya) berry; **estar hecho una uva** to have a load on; **uva crespa** gooseberry; **uva de Corinto** currant; **uva de raposa** nightshade; **uva espín** or **espina** gooseberry; **uva pasa** raisin; **uvas verdes** (de la fábula de Esopo) sour grapes

uve f (letra del alfabeto) V

uxoricida m uxoricide (husband)

uxoricidio m uxoricide (act)

uxo·rio -ria adj uxorious

V

V, v (ve *or* uve) *f* twenty-fifth letter of the Spanish alphabet

V. *abbr* **usted, vease, venerable**

V.A. *abbr* **Vuestra Alteza**

vaca *f* cow; (*cuero*) cowhide; (*carne de vaca o de buey*) beef; gambling pool; **hacer vaca** (Peru) to play truant; **vaca de la boda** (coll) goat, laughingstock; friend in need; **vaca de leche** milch cow; **vaca de San Antón** (ent) ladybird

vacación *f* (*cargo que está sin proveer*) vacancy; **de vacaciones** on vacation; **vacaciones** vacation; **vacaiones retribuídas** vacation with pay

vacacionista *mf* vacationist

vacancia *f* vacancy

vacante *adj* vacant ‖ *f* vacancy

vacar §73 *intr* (*un empleo, un cargo*) to be vacant, be unfilled; take off, take a vacation; **vacar a** to attend to; **vacar de** to lack, be devoid of

vacia•do -da *adj* hollow-ground ‖ *m* cast, casting; plaster cast

vaciante *f* ebb tide

vaciar §77 **& regular** *tr* to empty, drain; cast, mold; (*formar un hueco en*) hollow out; sharpen on a grindstone; copy, transcribe; explain in detail ‖ *intr* to empty; flow; (*el agua en el río*) fall, go down ‖ *ref* to blab

vacilación *f* vacillation; flickering; hesitancy, hesitation

vacilada *f* (Mex) spree, high time; (Mex) drunk

vacilante *adj* vacillating; (*luz*) flickering; (*irresoluto*) hesitant

vacilar *intr* to vacillate; (*la luz*) flicker; shake, wobble; (*estar irresoluto*) hesitate, waver

vací•o -a *adj* empty; (*hueco*) hollow; idle; useless, unsuccessful; (*vaca*) barren; presumptuous ‖ *m* emptiness; (*laguna, abertura; vacante*) vacancy; (*espacio que no contiene ninguna materia*) void; (*espacio de que se ha extraído el aire*) vacuum; (*ijada*) side, flank; **de vacío** light, unloaded; **hacer el vacío a** to isolate

vacuidad *f* vacuity, emptiness

vacuna *f* (*enfermedad de las vacas*) cowpox; (*virus cuya inoculación preserva de una enfermedad determinada*) vaccine

vacunación *f* vaccination

vacunar *tr* to vaccinate

vacu•no -na *adj* bovine; cowhide ‖ *f* see **vacuna**

va•cuo -cua *adj* vacant ‖ *m* cavity, hollow

vadear *tr* (*un río*) to ford; wade through; overcome; sound out ‖ *ref* to behave; manage

vado *m* ford; expedient, resource; **al vado o a la puente** one way or another; **no hallar vado** to see no way out; **tentar el vado** to feel one's way

vagabundaje *m* vagrancy

vagabundear *intr* to wander, roam; loaf around

vagabun•do -da *adj* vagabond ‖ *mf* vagabond, tramp; wanderer

vagancia *f* loafing, vagrancy

vagar *m* leisure; **con vagar** slowly; **estar de vagar** to have nothing to do ‖ §44 *intr* to wander, roam; be idle; have plenty of leisure; (*una cosa*) lie around; (*p.ej., una sonrisa por los labios*) play

vagido *m* cry of a newborn baby

vagina *f* vagina

vagneria•no -na *adj* & *mf* Wagnerian

va•go -ga *adj* wandering, roaming; idle, loafing; lax, loose; hesitating, wavering; (*indefinido, indeciso*) vague; (*mirada*) blank ‖ *m* vagabond; idler, loafer; **en vago** shakily; in vain; in the air; **poner en vago** to tilt

vagón *m* car, railroad car; **vagón cama** sleeping car; **vagón carbonero** coal car; **vagón cerrado** boxcar; **vagón cisterna** tank car; **vagón de carga** freight car; **vagón de cola** caboose; **vagón de mercancías** freight car; **vagón de plataforma** flatcar; **vagón frigorífico** refrigerator car; **vagón salón** chair car; **vagón tolva** hopper-bottom car; **vagón volquete** dump car

vagoneta *f* tip car; station wagon

vaguear *intr* to wander around

vaguedad *f* vagueness; vague remark

vaguido *m* faintness, fainting spell

vaharada *f* breath, exhalation

vahear *intr* to emit odors, give forth an aroma

vahido *f* faintness, fainting spell

vaho *m* odor, aroma, vapor, fume

vaina *f* sheath; scabbard; knife case; (*de ciertas semillas*) pod, husk; annoyance, bother; (Col) luck, stroke of luck

vainica *f* hemstitch

vainilla *f* vanilla

vainita *f* (Ven) string bean

vaivén *m* swing, seesaw, backward and forward motion; unsteadiness, inconstancy; risk, chance

vajilla *f* dishes, set of dishes; **lavar la vajilla** to wash the dishes; **vajilla de oro** gold plate; **vajilla de plata** silver plate, silverware; **vajilla de porcelana** chinaware

vale *m* promissory note; voucher; farewell; (Ven) chum, pal; **vale respuesta** reply coupon

valede•ro -ra *adj* valid, effective

vale•dor -dora *mf* defender, protector; (Mex) friend, companion

valedura *f* (Mex) favor, protection

valencia *f* (chem) valence

valentía *f* bravery, valor; feat, exploit; dash, boldness; boast; **pisar de valentía** to strut, swagger

valen•tón -tona *adj* arrogant, boastful ‖ *mf* braggart, boaster ‖ *f* bragging

valer *m* worth, merit, value ‖ §76 *tr* to defend, protect; favor, patronize; avail; yield; be worth, be valued at; be equal to; suit; **valer la pena** to be worthwhile (to);

valerle a uno + *inf* to help someone to + *inf*, to get someone to + *inf*; **valor lo que pesa** to be worth its (his, her, etc.) weight in gold; **valga lo que valiere** come what may; **¡válgame Dios!** bless my soul!, so help me God! ‖ *intr* to have worth; be worthy; be valuable; be valid; prevail; hold, count; have influence; **hacer valer** (*sus derechos*) to assert; make felt; make good; turn to account; **más vale** it is better (to); **vale O.K.; valer para** to be useful for; **valer por** to be equal to ‖ *ref* to help oneself, defend oneself; **valerse de** to make use of, avail oneself of

valero•so -sa *adj* valorous, brave; strong, active, effective

va•let *m* (*pl* **-lets**) (cards) jack

valía *f* value, worth; favor, influence; **mayor valía** or **plus valía** appreciation, increased value; unearned increment

validación *f* validation

validar *tr* to validate

validez *f* validity; strength, vigor

vali•do -da *adj* highly esteemed, influential ‖ *m* court favorite; prime minister

váli•do -da *adj* valid; strong, robust

valiente *adj* valiant; strong, robust; fine, excellent; (*grande y excesivo*) terrific ‖ *m* brave fellow; bully

valija *f* satchel, brief case; mailbag, mailpouch; mail; **valija diplomática** diplomatic pouch

valimiento *m* favor, protection; favor at court, favoritism

valio•so -sa *adj* valuable; influential; wealthy

va•lón -lona *adj & mf* Walloon

valor *m* value, worth; valor, courage; meaning, import; efficacy; equivalence; (*rédito*) income, return; effrontery; (*persona, cosa o cualidad dignas de ser poseídas*) (fig) asset; **¿cómo va ese valor?** how are you?; **valor de rescate** (ins) surrender value; **valores** securities

valoración *f* valuation, appraisal

valorar or **valorear** *tr* (*poner precio a*) to value, appraise; enhance the value of

valorizar §60 *tr* to value; enhance the value of; sell of (*for quick realization*)

vals *m* waltz

valsar *intr* to waltz

valuación *f* valuation, appraisal

valuar §21 *tr* to estimate

válvula *f* valve; **válvula corrediza** slide valve; **válvula de admisión** intake valve; **válvula de escape** exhaust valve; **válvula de escape libre** cutout; **válvula de seguridad** safety valve; **válvula en cabeza** valve in the head, overhead valve

valla *f* fence, railing; barricade; hindrance, obstacle; (sport) hurdle; (W-I) cockpit; **valla paranieves** snow fence

vallado *m* barricade, stockade

valle *m* valley; river bed; valley dwellings; **valle de lágrimas** vale of tears

vampiresa *f* vampire

vampíri•co -ca *adj* vampire; ghoulish

vampiro *m* vampire; (*persona que se deleita con cosas horribles*) ghoul

vànadio *m* vanadium

vanagloriar §77 **& regular** *ref* to boast

vanaglorio•so -sa *adj* vainglorious, conceited, boastful

vanamente *adv* vainly

vandalismo *m* vandalism

vánda•lo -la *adj & mf* Vandal; (fig) vandal

vanguardia *f* (mil & fig) vanguard, van; **a vanguardia** in the vanguard

vanguardismo *m* avant-garde

vanguardista *adj* avant-garde ‖ *mf* avant-gardist

vanidad *f* vanity; (*fausto*) pomp, show; **ajar la vanidad de** to take down a peg; **hacer vanidad de** to boast of

vanido•so -sa *adj* vain, conceited

va•no -na *adj* vain; hollow, empty; **en vano** in vain ‖ *m* opening in a wall

vapor *m* steam; (*el visible: exhalación, vaho, niebla, etc.*) vapor; steamer, steamboat; **al vapor** at full speed; **vapores** gas (*belched*); blues; **vapor volandero** tramp steamer

vaporar *tr & ref* to evaporate

vaporizador *m* atomizer, sprayer

vaporizar §60 *tr* to vaporize; spray ‖ *ref* to vaporize

vaporo•so -sa *adj* vaporous

vapular or **vapulear** *tr* whip, flog

vaquería *f* drove of cattle; dairy; (Mex) party

vaqueri•zo -za *adj* cattle ‖ *f* winter stable for cattle

vaque•ro -ra *adj* cattle ‖ *mf* cattle tender; (Peru) truant ‖ *m* cow hand; cowboy; **vaqueros** blue jeans

vaqueta *f* leather; (P-R) strop; **zurrarle a uno la vaqueta** to tan someone's hide

vaquillona *f* (Arg, Chile) heifer

vara *f* pole, rod, staff; (*de carruaje*) shaft; (*bastón de mando*) wand; measuring stick; (taur) thrust with goad; **tener vara alta** to have the upper hand; **vara alcándara** shaft; **vara alta** upper hand; **vara buscadora** divining rod (*ostensibly to discover water or metals*); **vara de adivinar** divining rod; **vara de oro** goldenrod; **vara de pescar** fishing rod; **vara de San José** goldenrod

vara-alta *m* boss

varada *f* beaching; running aground

varadero *m* repair dock

varapalo *m* long pole; setback, disappointment, reverse

varar *tr* (*una embarcación*) to beach ‖ *intr* to run aground; (*un negocio*) come to a standstill

varear *tr* (*los frutos de los árboles*) to beat down, knock down; beat, strike; (taur) to goad; (*los caballos de carreras*) (SAm) to exercise, train ‖ *ref* to lose weight, get thin

varec *m* (bot) wrack

varenga *f* (naut) floor, floor timber

vareta *f* twig, stick; lime twig for catching birds; colored stripe; cutting remark; hint; **irse de vareta** to have diarrhea

variable *adj & f* variable

variación *f* variation

v
va

varia·do -da *adj* varied; variegated

variante *adj & f* variant

variar §77 to vary, change ‖ *intr* to vary, change; be different; **variar de** or **en opinión** to change one's mind

varice *f* or **várice** *f* varicose veins

varicela *f* chicken pox

varico·so -sa *adj* varicose

variedad *f* variety; **variedades** variety show, vaudeville

varilla *f* rod, stem, twig; (*bastón de mando*) wand; (*de paraguas, abanico, etc.*) rib; (*del corsé*) stay; (*de rueda*) wire spoke; jawbone; (Mex) peddler's wares; **varilla de nivel** dipstick; **varilla de virtudes** wand, magician's wand

varillaje *m* ribs, ribbing; (*de máquina de escribir*) type bars

varille·ro -ra *adj* (*caballo*) (Ven) race ‖ *m* (Mex) peddler

va·rio -ria *adj* (*de diversos colores; que tiene variedad*) various, varied; fickle, inconstant; **varios** various; several

varón *adj* male, e.g., **hijo varón** male child ‖ *m* man, male; grown man, adult male; man of standing; **santo varón** plain artless fellow

varonía *f* male issue

varonil *adj* manly, virile; courageous

Varsovia *f* Warsaw

vasa·llo -lla *adj & mf* vassal

vas·co -ca *adj & mf* Basque (*of Spain and France*) ‖ *m* Basque (*language*)

vas·cón -cona *adj & mf* Basque (*of old Spain*)

vasconga·do -da *adj & mf* Basque (*of Spain*) ‖ *m* Basque (*language*) ‖ **las Vascongadas** the Basque Provinces

vascuence *adj & m* Basque (*language*) ‖ *m* gibberish

vaselina *f* Vaseline

vasera *f* kitchen shelf; bottle rack, tumbler rack

vasija *f* container, vessel

vaso *m* tumbler, glass; vase, flower jar; (anat) duct, vessel; **vaso de engrase** (mach) grease cup; **vaso de noche** pot, chamber pot; **vaso graduado** measuring glass; **vaso sanguíneo** blood vessel

vástago *m* shoot, sapling; scion, offspring; rod, stem; **vástago de émbolo** piston rod; **vástago de válvula** valve stem

vastedad *f* vastness

vas·to -ta *adj* vast

vate *m* bard, seer, poet

váter *m* toilet, water closet

vataije *m* wattage

vaticinar *tr* to prophesy, predict

vaticinio *m* prophecy, prediction

vatídi·co -ca *adj* prophetical ‖ *mf* prophet

vatímetro *m* wattmeter

vatio *m* watt

vatio-hora *m* (*pl* **vatios-hora**) watt-hour

vaya *f* jest, jeer

Vd. *abbr* **usted**

Vds. *abbr* **ustedes**

V.E. *abbr* **Vuestra Excelencia**

vece·ro -ra *adj* alternating; yielding in alternate years ‖ *mf* person waiting his turn

vecinamente *adv* nearby

vecindad *f* neighborhood, vicinity; residency; residents; **hacer mala vecindad** to be a bad neighbor

vecindario *m* neighborhood, community; people, population

veci·no -na *adj* neighboring; like, similar ‖ *mf* neighbor; resident, citizen

veda *f* prohibition; (*de la caza y la pesca*) closed season

vedado *m* game preserve

vedar *tr* to forbid, prohibit; hinder, stop; veto

vedija *f* fleece, tuft of wool; mat of hair; matted hair

vee·dor -dora *adj* curious, spying ‖ *mf* busybody ‖ *m* supervisor, overseer

vega *f* fertile plain; (Cuba) tobacco plantation

vegetación *f* vegetation; **vegetaciones adenoideas** adenoids

vegetal *adj & m* vegetable

vegetaria·no -na *adj & mf* vegetarian

vego·so -sa *adj* (Chile) damp, wet

vehemencia *f* vehemence

vehemente *adj* vehement

vehículo *m* vehicle; **vehículo espacial** space vehicle

veinta·vo -va *adj & m* twentieth

veinte *adj & pron* twenty; **a las veinte** late, untimely ‖ *m* twenty; (*en las fechas*) twentieth

vientena *f* score, twenty

veintiún *adj* this apocopated form of **veintiuno** is used before masculine singular nouns and adjectives

veintiu·no -na *adj & pron* twenty-one ‖ *m* twenty-one; (*en las fechas*) twenty-first ‖ *f* (*juego de naipes*) twenty-one

vejación *f* vexation, annoyance

vejamen *m* vexation, annoyance; bantering, taunting

vejar *tr* to vex, annoy; taunt

vejestorio *m* old dodo

vejete *m* little old fellow

vejez *f* old age; oldness; dotage; platitude, old story; **a la vejez, viruelas** there's no fool like an old fool

vejiga *f* (*órgano que recibe la orina de los riñones*) bladder; (*ampolla*) blister; (*saco hecho de piel, goma, etc.*) bag, pouch, bladder; **vejiga de la bilis** or **de la hiel** gall bladder

vela *f* wakefulness; pilgrimage; evening; work in the evening; sail; sailboat; (*cilindro con una torcida que sirve para alumbrar*) candle; vigil (*before Eucharist*) awning; (Mex) scolding; **a toda vela** full sail; **a la vela** under sail; **a vela llena** under full sail; **en vela** awake; **estar entre dos velas** to be half-seas over, have a sheet in the wind; **hacerse a la vela** to set sail; **vela latina** lateen sail; **vela mayor** mainsail; **vela romana** Roman candle

velada *f* evening party, soirée; vigil, watch

vela·do -da *adj* veiled, hidden; (phot) lightstruck ‖ *f* see **velada**

velador *m* pedestal table, gueridon; wooden candlestick; watchman; (SAm) night table; (Mex) lamp globe

velaje *m* or **velamen** *m* (naut) canvas, sails

velar *adj & f* velar ‖ *tr* to watch over; guard; (*la guardia*) keep; hold a wake over; (*cubrir con un velo*) veil; (phot) to fog; (fig) to veil, hide, conceal ‖ *intr* to stay awake; stay awake working; keep vigil; (*el viento*) keep up all night; (*un escollo, un peñasco*) stick up out of the water; **velar por** or **sobre** to watch over ‖ *ref* (phot) to fog, be light-struck

velatorio *m* wake

veleidad *f* whim, caprice; fickleness, flightiness

veleido•so -sa *adj* whimsical, capricious; fickle, flighty

vele•ro -ra *adj* swift-sailing ‖ *m* sailboat

veleta *mf* (*persona inconstante*) weathercock ‖ *f* vane, weathervane, weathercock; (*de un molino*) rudder vane; (*de la caña de pescar*) bob; streamer, pennant; **veleta de manga** (aer) air sleeve, air sock

velís *m* (Mex) valise

velita *f* little candle

velo *m* veil; taking the veil; confusion, perplexity; (*disfraz*) veil; (*de lágrimas*) mist; (phot) fog; **correr el velo** to pull aside the curtain, to dispel the mystery; **tomar el velo** to take the veil; **velo del paladar** soft palate

velocidad *f* (*rapidez*) speed, velocity; (mech) velocity; **en gran velocidad** (rr) by express; **en pequeña velocidad** (rr) by freight; **primera velocidad** (aut) low gear; **segunda velocidad** (aut) second; **tercera velocidad** (aut) high gear; **velocidad con respecto al suelo** (aer) ground speed; **velocidad de crucero** cruising speed; **velocidad permitida** speed limit

velocímetro *m* speedometer

velón *m* brass olive-oil lamp

velorio *m* evening party or bee; wake; wake for a dead child; dull party; come-on

ve•loz *adj* (*pl* **-loces**) swift, speedy; agile, quick

vello *m* down, fuzz

vellocino *m* fleece; **vellocino de oro** Golden Fleece

vellón *m* fleece; unsheared sheepskin; lock of wool; copper coin; copper-silver alloy

vello•so -sa *adj* downy, hairy, fuzzy

velludillo *m* velveteen

vellu•do -da *adj* shaggy, hairy, fuzzy ‖ *m* (*felpa*) plush; (*terciopelo*) velvet

vena *f* vein; (*en piedras*) grain; (fig) poetical inspiration; **estar en vena** to be all set, be inspired; sparkle with wit; **vena de loco** fickle disposition

venablo *m* dart, javelin; **echar venablos** to burst forth in anger

venado *m* deer, stag; **pintar el venado** (Mex) to play hooky

venáti•co -ca *adj* fickle, unsteady; daffy, nutty

vence•dor -dora *adj* conquering, victorious ‖ *mf* conqueror, victor

vencejo *m* band, string; (orn) European swift, black martin

vencer §78 *tr* to vanquish, conquer; excel, outdo; overcome, surmount ‖ *intr* to conquer, be victorious; (*un plazo*) be up; (*un contrato*) expire; (*una letra*) mature, fall due ‖ *ref* to control oneself; (*un camino*) bend, turn; (Chile) to wear out, become useless

vencetósigo *m* milkweed, tame poison

venci•do -da *adj* conquered; (com) due, mature, payable

vencimiento *m* (*acción de vencer*) victory; (*hecho de ser vencido*) defeat; (com) expiration, maturity

venda *f* (*para ligar un miembro herido*) bandage; (*para tapar los ojos*) blindfold

vendaje *m* bandage, dressing; **vendaje enyesado** plaster cast

vendar *tr* (*un miembro, una herida*) to bandage; (*los ojos*) blindfold; (*cegar*) (fig) to blind; (*engañar*) (fig) to hoodwink

vendaval *m* strong southeasterly wind from the sea; strong wind, gale

vendedera *f* saleswoman, saleslady

vende•dor -dora *adj* selling ‖ *m* salesman ‖ *f* saleslady, sales girl

vendehu•mos *mf* (*pl* **-mos**) influence peddler

vendeja *f* public sale

vender *tr* to sell; betray, sell out; **vender salud** to be the picture of health ‖ *intr* to sell; **¡vendo, vendo, vendí!** going, going, gone! ‖ *ref* to sell oneself; sell, be for sale; betray oneself, give oneself away; **venderse caro** to be hard to see; be quite a stranger; **venderse en** (*p.ej., cien pesetas*) to sell for; **venderse por** to pass oneself off as

ven•dí *m* (*pl* **-díes**) certificate of sale

vendible *adj* salable, marketable

vendimia *f* vintage; (fig) big profit

vendimia•dor -dora *mf* vintager

vendimiar *tr* (*la uva*) to gather, harvest; (*las viñas*) gather the grapes of; make off with; kill

venduta *f* public sale; (W-I) greengrocery

Venecia *f* (*ciudad*) Venice; (*provincia*) Venetia

venecia•no -na *adj & mf* Venetian

veneno *m* poison, venom

veneno•so -sa *adj* poisonous, venomous

venera *f* scallop shell; (*manantial de agua*) spring; **empeñar la venera** to go all out, spare no expense

venerable *adj* venerable

venerar *tr* to venerate, revere; worship

venére•o -a *adj* venereal ‖ *m* venereal disease

venero *m* (*de agua*) spring; (*filón de mineral*) lode, vein; (fig) source

venezola•no -na *adj & mf* Venezuelan

Venezuela *f* Venezuela

venga•dor -dora *adj* avenging ‖ *mf* avenger

venganza *f* vengeance, revenge

vengar §44 *tr* to avenge ‖ *ref* to take revenge; **vengarse de** to take revenge on

va
ve

vengati•vo -va adj vengeful, vindictive

venia f forgiveness, pardon; leave, permission; bow, greeting

venida f coming; return; flood, freshet

venide•ro -ra adj coming, future ‖ **venideros** mpl successors, posterity

venir §79 intr to come; **que viene** coming, next; **venga lo que viniere** come what may; **venir** + ger to be + ger; **venir a** + inf to come to + inf; to amount to + ger; to happen to + inf; to finally + inf, e.g., **después de una larga enfermedad, vino a morir** after a long illness he finally died; **venir a ser** to turn out to be ‖ ref to ferment; **venirse abajo** to collapse

veno•so -sa adj venous

venta f sale; roadside inn; (Chile) refreshment stand; (S-D) grocery store; **de venta** or **en venta** on sale, for sale; **ser una venta** to be an expensive place; **venta al descubierto** short sale

ventaja f advantage; (en juegos o apuestas) odds; extra pay

ventajo•so -sa adj advantageous

ventalla f valve

ventana f window; (de la nariz) nostril; **echar la casa por la ventana** to go to a lot of expense; **ventana batiente** casement; **ventana de guillotina** sash window; **ventana salediza** bay window

ventanal m church window; picture window

ventanear intr to be at the window all the time

ventanilla f (de coche, de banco, de sobre) window; ticket window; (de la nariz) nostril

ventanillo m (postigo de puerta o ventana) wicket; (mirilla) peephole

ventar §2 tr to sniff ‖ impers — **vienta** it is windy

ventarrón m gale, windstorm

ventear tr to sniff; dry in the wind; snoop into ‖ intr to snoop, pry around ‖ impers — **ventea** it is windy ‖ ref (henderse) to split; break wind; spend a lot of time in the open

vente•ro -ra mf innkeeper

ventilador m ventilator; fan; (naut) funnel; **ventilador aspirador** exhaust fan

ventilar tr to ventilate; (fig) to air, ventilate

ventisca f drift, snowdrift; (borrasca) blizzard

ventiscar §73 intr to snow and blow; (la nieve) drift

ventisquero m snowdrift; blizzard; snow-capped mountain; glacier

ventolera f blast of wind; (molinete) pinwheel; vanity, pride; wild idea; (Mex) wind

ventosa f vent, air hole; **pegar una ventosa a** to swindle

ventosear intr to break wind

vento•so -sa adj windy ‖ f see **ventosa**

ventregada f brood, litter; outpouring, abundance

ventrículo m ventricle

ventrílo•cuo -cua mf ventriloquist

ventriloquia f or **ventriloquismo** m ventriloquism

ventura f happiness; luck, chance; danger, risk; **a la ventura** at random; at a risk; **por ventura** perhaps, perchance; **probar ventura** to try one's luck

venture•ro -ra adj adventurous; fortunate, lucky ‖ mf adventurer

ventu•ro -ra adj future, coming ‖ f see **ventura**

venturón m stroke of luck

venturo•so -sa adj fortunate, lucky

Venus m (astr) Venus ‖ f (myth) Venus; (mujer de belleza) Venus

venus•to -ta adj beautiful, graceful

venza f goldbeater's skin

ver m (vista) sight; (apariencia) appearance; opinion; **a mi ver** in my opinion ‖ §80 tr to see; look at; (law) to hear, try; **no poder ver** to not be able to bear; **no tener nada que ver con** to have nothing to do with; **ver** + inf to see + inf, e.g., **ví entrar a mi hermano** I saw my brother come in; to see + ger, e.g., **ví bailar a la muchacha** I saw the girl dancing; to see + pp. e.g., **ví ahorcar al criminal** I saw the criminal hanged; **ver venir a uno** to see what someone is up to ‖ intr to see; **a más ver** so long; **a ver** let's see; **hasta más ver** good-bye, so long; **ver de** to try to; **ver y creer** seeing is believing ‖ ref to be seen; be obvious; see oneself; see each other; meet; (encontrarse) be, find oneself; **verse con** to see, have a talk with; **ya se ve** of course, certainly

vera f edge, border; **a la vera de** near, beside; **de veras** in truth; **jugar de veras** to play for keeps; **veras** truth, reality; earnestness

veracidad f veracity, truthfulness

veranda f verandah; bay window, closed porch

veraneante mf summer vacationist, summer resident

veranear intr to summer

veranie•go -ga adj summer; unimportant, insignificant

veranillo m Indian summer; **veranillo de San Martín** Indian summer

ve•raz adj (pl **-races**) veracious, truthful

verbena f fair, country fair, night festival; (bot) verbena

verbigracia adv for example

verbo m verb ‖ **Verbo** m (theol) Word

verbo•so -sa adj verbose, wordy

verdacho m green earth

verdad f truth; **a la verdad** in truth, as a matter of fact; **de verdad** really; **la verdad desnuda** the plain truth; **¿no es verdad?** or **¿verdad?** isn't that so? La traducción al inglés de esta pregunta depende generalmente de la aseveración que la precede. Si la aseveración es afirmativa, la pregunta es negativa, p.ej., **Vd. vivió aquí. ¿No es verdad?** You lived here. Did you not?; Si la aseveración es negativa, la pregunta es afirmativa, p.ej., **Vd. no vivió aquí. ¿No**

es verdad? You did not live here? Did you? Si el sujeto de la aseveración es un nombre sustantivo, va representado en la pregunta con un pronombre personal, p.ej., **Juan no estuvo aquí anoche. ¿No es verdad?** John was not here last evening. Was he?; **ser verdad** to be true; **verdad trillada** truism

verdade•ro -ra *adj* true; real; (*que dice siempre la verdad*) truthful

verde *adj* green; young, youthful; (*viuda*) merry; (*cuento*) shady, off-color; **están verdes** they're hard to reach ‖ *m* green; foliage, verdure

verdear *intr* to turn green, look green

verdecer §22 *intr* to turn green, grow green again

verdecillo *m* (orn) greenfinch

verdemar *m* sea green

verdete *m* verdigris

verdín *m* fresh green; (*capa verde de aguas estancadas*) mold, pond scum; (*cardenillo*) verdigris

verdise•co -ca *adj* half-dry

verdor *m* verdure; youth

verdo•so -sa *adj* greenish

verdugado *m* hoop skirt

verdugo *m* shoot, sucker; (*estoque*) rapier; (*azote*) scourge; (*roncha*) welt; executioner, hangman; torment; butcher bird, shrike

verdugón *m* wale, weal

verdulería *f* greengrocery

verdule•ro -ra *mf* greengrocer ‖ *f* fishwife

verdura *f* greenness; (*color verde de las plantas*) verdure; (*obscenidad*) smuttiness; **verduras** vegetables, greens

verecundia *f* bashfulness, shyness

verecun•do -da *adj* bashful, shy

vereda *f* path, lane; sidewalk

veredicto *m* verdict

verga *f* (naut) yard

vergel *m* flower and fruit garden

vergonzo•so -sa *adj* (*que causa vergüenza*) shameful; (*que tiene vergüenza*) ashamed; (*que se avergüenza con facilidad*) bashful, shy; (*que causa humillación*) embarrassing; shabby, wretched ‖ *mf* bashful person ‖ *m* armadillo

vergüenza *f* (*arrepentimiento*) shame; (*oprobio*) shamefulness; (*pudor, timidez*) bashfulness, shyness; (*desconcierto, humillación*) embarrassment; (*pundonor*) dignity, face; public punishment; **¡qué vergüenza!** shame on you!; **tener vergüenza** to be ashamed; **vergüenzas** privates, genitals

vericueto *m* rough, rocky ground

verídi•co -ca *adj* truthful

verificación *f* verification; checking, testing, inspection; **verificación a la ventura** spot check

verifica•dor -dora *adj* verifying ‖ *m* meter inspector

verificar §73 *tr* to verify, check; (*llevar a cabo*) carry out; (*los contadores de agua, gas y electricidad*) inspect ‖ *ref* to prove true; take place

verja *f* iron gate, iron fence, grating

ver•mú *m* (*pl* **-mús**) vermouth; matinée

vernácu•lo -la *adj* vernacular

verónica *f* (bot) veronica; (taur) veronica (*graceful pass in which the bullfighter waits for the bull with open cape*)

veroniquear *intr* (taur) to perform veronicas

verosímil *adj* likely, probable

verraco *m* male hog, boar

verraquear *intr* to grunt, grumble; cry hard

verruga *f* wart; bore, nuisance

verrugo *m* miser

versal *adj* & *f* capital

versalilla or **versalita** *f* small capital

Versalles Versailles

versar *intr* — **versar acerca de** or **sobre** to deal with, treat of ‖ *ref* — **versarse en** to be or become versed in

versátil *adj* fickle; versatile; (*arma*) multipurpose

versículo *m* verse (*in the Bible*)

versificación *f* versification

versificar §73 *tr* & *intr* to versify

versión *f* version; translation

verso *m* verse; (typ) verso; **versos pareados** rhymed couplet

vertebra•do -da *adj* & *m* vertebrate

vertedero *m* dump; weir, spillway

verter §51 *tr* (*un líquido, un polvo*) to pour; (*un recipiente*) empty; (*lágrimas; luz; sangre*) shed; (*descargar*) dump; translate ‖ *intr* to flow ‖ *ref* to run, empty

vertical *adj* & *f* vertical

vértice *m* vertex

vertiente *m* & *f* (*declive*) slope; (*colina por donde corre el agua*) shed ‖ *f* (Arg, Col, Chile) spring, fountain

vertigino•so -sa *adj* dizzy

vértigo *m* vertigo, dizziness; fit of insanity

vesícula *f* vesicle; **vesícula biliar** gall bladder

veso *m* polecat

Véspero *m* Vesper

vesperti•no -na *adj* evening ‖ *m* evening sermon

vestíbulo *m* vestibule; (theat) foyer, lobby

vestido *m* clothing, dress; (*de mujer*) gown, dress; (*de hombre*) suit; costume; **vestido de ceremonia** dress suit; **vestido de etiqueta** evening clothes; **vestido de etiqueta de mujer** or **vestido de noche** evening gown; **vestido de gala** (mil) full dress; **vestido de serio** evening clothes; **vestido de tarde-noche** cocktail dress

vestidura *f* clothing; (*del sacerdote*) vestment

vestigio *m* vestige, trace; track, footprint

vestir §50 *tr* to dress, clothe; adorn; cover up; disguise; (*tal o cual vestido*) wear; put on; **vestir el cargo** to look the part ‖ *intr* to dress; (*una prenda o la materia*) be dressy; **vestir de** (*p.ej., blanco*) to dress in; **vestir de etiqueta** to dress in evening clothes; **vestir de paisano** to dress in civilian clothes ‖ *ref* to dress, get dressed; dress oneself; (*de una enfermedad*) be up, be about; **vestirse de** (*nubes, flores, hierba, etc.*) to be covered with; (*importancia, humildad, etc.*) assume

vestuario *m* (*las prendas de uno*) wardrobe;

dressing room; bathhouse; checkroom, cloakroom; (mil) uniform; (theat) dressing room
Vesubio, el Vesuvius
veta f vein; streak, stripe; **descubrir la veta de** to be on to
vetar tr to veto
vetea•do -da adj veined, striped ‖ m graining ‖ f (Ecuad) whipping
vetear tr to grain, stripe; (Eucad) to whip, flog
veteranía f experience, know-how
vetera•no -na adj & mf veteran
veterina•rio -ria adj veterinary ‖ mf veterinarian ‖ f veterinary medicine
vetus•to -ta adj old, ancient
vez f (pl **veces**) time; (tiempo de hacer una cosa por turno) turn; **a la vez** at the same time; **a la vez que** while; **alguna vez** sometimes; ever; **a su vez** in turn; on his part; **a veces** at times, sometimes; **cada vez** every time; **cada vez más** more and more; **cuántas veces** how often; **de una vez** at one time; once and for all; **de vez en cuando** once in a while; **dos veces** twice; **en vez de** instead of; **esperar vez** to wait one's turn; **hacer las veces de** to take the place of; **las más veces** most of the time; **muchas veces** often; **otra vez** again; **raras veces** or **rara vez** seldom, rarely; **repetidas veces** over and over again; **tal vez** perhaps; **tomar la vez a** to get ahead of; **una que otra vez** once in a while; **una vez** once
veza f vetch, spring vetch
v.g. or **v.gr.** abbr **verbigracia**
vía f road, route, way; (par de rieles y el suelo en que se asientan) (rr) track; (el mismo carril) (rr) rail, track; (anat) passage, tract; (fig) way; **por la vía de** via; **por vía aérea** by air; **por vía bucal** by mouth; **vía aérea** airway; **vía ancha** (rr) broad gauge; **vía de agua** waterway; (naut) leak; **vía estrecha** (rr) narrow gauge; **vía férrea** railway; **vía fluvial** waterway; **Vía Láctea** Milky Way; **vía muerta** (rr) siding; **vía normal** (rr) standard gauge; **vía pública** thoroughfare; **vías de hecho** (law) assault and battery ‖ prep via
viable adj feasible
viaducto m viaduct
viajante adj traveling ‖ mf traveler ‖ m drummer, traveling salesman
viajar tr to sell on the road; (ciertas comarcas) cover as salesman ‖ intr to travel, journey
viaje m trip, journey; travel book; water supply; (drogas) trip; **¡buen viaje!** bon voyage!; **viaje de ida y vuelta** or **viaje redondo** round trip; **viaje de pruebas** shakedown cruise, trial cruise
viaje•ro -ra adj traveling ‖ mf traveler; passenger
vial adj road, highway ‖ m tree-lined road
vianda f food, viand; meal
viandante mf traveler; itinerant
vitático m travel allowance; (eccl) viaticum

víbora f viper
vibración f vibration
vibrar tr to vibrate; (la voz; la r) roll; (una lanza) hurl ‖ intr to vibrate ‖ ref to be thrilled
vicaría f vicarage
vicario m vicar
vice•almirante m vice-admiral
vicepresiden•te -ta mf vice-president
viceversa adv vice versa
viciar tr to vitiate; (una proposición) to slant ‖ ref to become vitiated; give oneself up to vice; become addicted; (una tabla) warp
vicio m vice; pampering, spoiling; luxuriance, overgrowth; **hablar de vicio** to talk all the time, talk too much; **quejarse de vicio** to be a chronic complainer
vicio•so -sa adj vicious; faulty, defective; strong, robust; luxuriant, overgrown; dissolute; (niño) spoiled
víctima f victim, **víctima propiciatoria** scapegoat
victimar tr to kill, murder
victoria f victory
victorio•so -sa adj victorious
vid f vine, grapevine
vida f life; living, livelihood; **darse buena vida** to live high; live in comfort; **de por vida** for life; **en mi vida** never; **escapar con vida** to have a narrow escape; **ganar** or **ganarse la vida** to earn one's livelihood, make a living; **hacer por la vida** to get a bite to eat; **mudar de vida** to mend one's ways; **¡por vida mía!** upon my soul!; **vida airada** licentious living; **vida ancha** loose living; **vida de familia** or **de hogar** home life; **vida mía** my darling
vidalita f (Arg, Chile, Urug) mournful love song
vidente mf clairvoyant ‖ m prophet, see ‖ f seeress
videocasete m video cassette
videodisco m video disk
videograbación f video-tape recording
video-juego m video game
videoseñal f picture signal
videotocadiscos m video-disk player
vidria•do -da adj glazed; brittle ‖ m glaze, glazing; glazed pottery; dishes
vidriar §77 & regular tr to glaze ‖ ref (los ojos) to become glassy
vidriera f glass window, glass door; shop-window, store window; **vidriera de colores** or **vidriera pintada** stained-glass window
vidriería f glassworks; glass store
vidriero m glass blower, glassworker; glazier; glass dealer
vidrio m glass; piece of glass; windowpane; **pagar los vidrios rotos** to take the blame, to be the goat; **vidrio cilindrado** plate glass; **vidrio de aumento** magnifying glass; **vidrio de color** stained glass; **vidrio deslustrado** ground glass; **vidrio tallado** cut glass
vidrio•so -sa adj glassy, vitreous; (quebradizo) brittle; (resbaladizo) slippery; (que se

resiente fácilmente) touchy; (*mirada, ojos*) (fig) glassy

vie·jo -ja *adj* old ‖ *m* old man; **viejo verde** old goat, old rake ‖ *f* old woman

vie·nés -nesa *adj & mf* Viennese

viento *m* wind; course, direction; (*cuerda que mantiene una cosa derecha*) guy; (*gases intestinales*) wind; **ceñir el viento** (naut) to sail close to the wind; **viento de cola** (aer) tail wind; **viento en popa** (naut) tail wind; **vientos alisios** trade winds

vientre *m* belly; (*parte de la ondulación entre dos nodos*) (phys) loop; **evacuar** or **exonerar el vientre** to have a bowel movement; **vientre flojo** loose bowels

vier·nes *m* (*pl* **-nes**) Friday; **Viernes santo** Good Friday

viertea·guas *m* (*pl* **-guas**) *m* flashing

vietna·més -mesa *adj & mf* Vietnamese

viga *f* beam, girder, rafter; **estar contando las vigas** to gaze blankly at the ceiling; **viga de celosía** lattice girder

vigencia *f* force, operation; (*de una póliza de seguro*) life; **en vigencia** in force, in effect

vigente *adj* effective, in force

vigési·mo -ma *adj & m* twentieth

vigía *m* lookout, watch; **vigía de incendios** firewarden ‖ *f* watch; watchtower; (naut) rock, reef

vigiar §77 *tr* to watch over

vigilancia *f* vigilance, watchfulness; **bajo vigilancia médica** under the care of a physician

vigilante *adj* vigilant, watchful ‖ *m* guard, watchman; **vigilante nocturno** night watchman

vigilar *tr* to watch over; look out for ‖ *intr* to watch, keep guard

vigilia *f* vigil; wakefulness; night work, night study; (*víspera*) eve; (mil) guard, watch; **comer de vigilia** to fast, abstain from meat

vigor *m* vigor; **en vigor** in force; into effect

vigoriza·dor -dora *adj* invigorating ‖ *m* tonic; **vigorizador del cabello** hair tonic

vigorizante *adj* invigorating

vigorizar §60 *tr* to invigorate; encourage

vigoro·so -sa *adj* vigorous

vigueta *f* small beam, small girder

vihuela *f* Spanish lute

vil *adj* vile, base, mean ‖ *mf* scoundrel

vilano *m* bur, down

vileza *f* vileness, baseness

vilipendiar *tr* to scorn, despise

vilipendio·so -sa *adj* contemptible

vilo — **en vilo** in the air; (fig) up in the air

vilorta *f* reed hoop; (*arandela*) washer

villa *f* town; (*casa de recreo en el campo*) villa; **la Villa** the city (*Madrid*)

villancico *m* carol, Christmas carol

villanes·co -ca *adj* boorish, crude, rustic

villanía *f* humbleness, humble birth; vileness, meanness; foul remark

villa·no -na *adj* base, vile; rude, impolite ‖ *mf* peasant; knave, scoundrel

villorrio *m* small country town

vinagre *m* vinegar; (*persona de genio áspero*) grouch

vinagrera *f* vinaigrette; (bot) sorrel; (SAm) heartburn; **vinagreras** cruet stand

vinagreta *f* French dressing, vinaigrette sauce

vinagro·so -sa *adj* vinegary

vinariego *m* vineyardist

vinatería *f* wine business; wine shop

vinate·ro -ra *adj* wine ‖ *m* wine dealer, vintner

vincular *tr* to bind, tie, unite; continue, perpetuate; (*esperanzas*) found, base; (law) entail

vínculo *m* bond, tie; (law) entail

vindicar §73 *tr* (*vengar*) to avenge; (*exculpar*) vindicate

vindicta *f* revenge

vinicul·tor -tora *mf* winegrower

vinicultura *f* winegrowing

vinilo *m* vinyl

vino *m* wine; sherry reception, wine party; **tener mal vino** to be a quarrelsome drunk; **vino cubierto** dark-red wine; **vino de Jerez** sherry; **vino del terruño** local wine; **vino de mesa** table wine; **vino de Oporto** port wine; **vino de pasto** table wine; **vino de postre** after-dinner wine; **vino de segunda** second-run wine; **vino de solera** solera sherry; **vino tinto** red table wine

vinolen·to -ta *adj* too fond of wine

viña *f* vineyard; **ser una viña** to be a mine; **tener una viña** to have a sinecure

viña·dor -dora *mf* vineyardist, vinedresser ‖ *m* guard of a vineyard

viñedo *m* vineyard

viñeta *f* vignette, headpiece

viola·do -da *adj & m* violet (*color*)

violar *m* bed of violets ‖ *tr* to violate; ravish, rape; profane, desecrate; tamper with

violencia *f* violence

violentar *tr* to do violence to; (*p.ej., una casa*) break into ‖ *ref* to force oneself

violen·to -ta *adj* violent

violeta *m* (*color; colorante*) violet ‖ *f* (bot) violet

violín *m* violin; (billiards) bridge, cue rest; **embolsar el violín** (Arg, Ven) to cower, to slink away

violinista *mf* violinist

violón *m* (mus) bass viol; **tocar el violón** to talk nonsense

violoncelista *mf* cellist, violoncellist

violoncelo *m* (mus) cello, violoncello

violonchelista *mf* cellist, violoncellist

violonchelo *m* (mus) cello, violoncello

vira *f* welt; (*saetilla*) dart

virada *f* turn, change of direction; (naut) tack

virago *f* mannish woman

viraje *m* turn, swerve; (phot) toning

virar *tr* (naut) to wind; (naut) to tack, veer; (phot) to tone ‖ *intr* to turn, swerve; (naut) to tack, veer

virgen *adj* virgin ‖ *f* virgin, maiden

virginidad *f* virginity

Virgo *m* (astr) Virgo

vírgula *f* rod; thin line, light dash

virgulilla *f* fine line; diacritic mark

virilidad *f* virility

virin·go -ga *adj* (Col) naked

virolen•to -ta *adj* pock-marked; having smallpox
virología *f* virology
virote *m* (*saeta*) bolt; sporty young fellow; (coll) stuffed shirt
virrey *m* viceroy
virtual *adj* virtual
virtud *f* virtue
virtuosismo *m* virtuosity
virtuo•so -sa *adj* virtuous || *m* virtuoso
viruela *f* smallpox; pock mark; **viruelas locas** chicken pox
virulencia *f* virulence
virulen•to -ta *adj* virulent
vi•rus *m* (*pl* **-rus**) virus
viruta *f* shaving
virutilla *f* thin shaving; **virutillas de acero** steel wool
visado *m* visa
visaje *m* face, grimace
visar *tr* to visa; to O.K.; (arti & surv) to sight
vísceras *fpl* viscera
visco *m* birdlime
viscosa *f* viscose
viscosilla *f* rayon thread
visco•so -sa *adj* viscous || *f* see **viscosa**
visera *f* (*del yelmo, de las gôrras, del parabrisas del automóvil, etc.*) visor; (*pequeña pantalla que se pone en la frente para resguardar la vista*) eyeshade; (W-I) blinder, blinker
visible *adj* visible; (*manifiesto*) evident; (*que llama la antención*) conspicuous
visigo•do -da *adj* Visigothic || *mf* Visigoth
visillo *m* window curtain, window shade
visión *f* vision; view; (*persona fea y ridícula*) sight, scarecrow; **ver visiones** to be seeing things; **visión negra** (*del aviador*) blackout
visionar *tr* to contemplate, look at
visiona•rio -ria *adj* & *mf* visionary
visir *m* vizier; **gran visir** grand vizier
visita *f* visit; visitor, caller; inspection; **ir de visitas** to go calling; **pagar la visita a** to return the call of; **tener visita** to have callers; **visita de cumplido** formal call; **visita de médico** short call
visita•dor -dora *mf* frequent caller || *m* inspector || *f* (Hond, Ven) enema
visitante *adj* visiting || *mf* visitor
visitar *tr* to visit; inspect
visite•ro -ra *adj* visiting; (*médico*) fond of making calls || *mf* visitor
vislumbrar *tr* to descry, glimpse; surmise, suspect || *ref* (*verse confusamente por la distancia*) glimmer; (*aparecer en la distancia*) loom
vislumbre *f* glimpse, glimmer; **vislumbres** inkling, notion
viso *m* sheen, gleam; (*de ciertas telas*) luster; streak, strain; appearance, thin veneer; elevation, height; colored material worn under transparent outer garment; **a dos visos** with a double purpose; **de viso** conspicuous; **hacer visos** to be iridescent
visón *m* mink
visor *m* (aer) bombsight; (phot) finder
víspera *f* eve, day before; **en vísperas de** on

the eve of; **víspera de año nuevo** New Year's Eve; **víspera de Navidad** Christmas Eve; **vísperas** (eccl) vespers, evensong
vista *m* custom-house inspector || *f* (*sentido del ver*) vision, sight; (*paisaje que se ve desde un punto; estampa que representa un lugar*) view; (*panorama, perspectiva*) vista; comparison; purpose, design; (*ojeada*) glance, look; interview; eye; eyes; (law) hearing, trial; **a la vista** (com) at sight; **a vista de** in view of; compared with; **con vistas a** with a view to; **de vista** by sight; **doble vista** second sight; **hacer la vista gorda ante** to shut one's eyes to; **hasta la vista** good-bye, so long; **medir con la vista** to size up; **saltar a la vista** to be self-evident; **tener a la vista** to keep one's eyes on; (*p.ej., una carta*) to have at hand; **torcer la vista** to squint; **vista a ojo de pájaro** bird's-eye view; **vistas** (*aberturas de un edificio*) lights, openings; view, outlook; visible parts, parts that show
vistazo *m* look, glance
vistillas *fpl* eminence, height; **irse a las vistillas** to try to get a look at one's opponent's cards
vis•to -ta *adj* evident, obvious; in view of; **bien visto** looked upon with approval; **mal visto** looked upon with disapproval; **no visto** or **nunca visto** unheard-of; **por lo visto** apparently, judging from the facts; **visto bueno** approved, O.K.; **visto que** whereas, inasmuch as || *m* whereas || *f* see **vista**
visto•so -sa *adj* showy, flashy, loud
visual *adj* visual || *f* line of sight
vital *adj* vital
vitali•cio -cia *adj* life. lifetime || *m* life-insurance policy; life annuity
vitalidad *f* vitality
vitalizar §60 *tr* to vitalize
vitamina *f* vitamin
vitan•do -da *adj* hateful, odious; being shunned
vitela *f* vellum
viticul•tor -tora *mf* grape grower, vineyardist
viticultura *f* grape growing
vitola *f* cigar size; mien, appearance; (Cuba) cigar band
vítor *interj* hurray! || *m* panegyric tablet; triumphal pageant
vitorear *tr* to cheer, acclaim
vitral *m* stained-glass window
vítre•o -a *adj* vitreous, glassy
vitrina *f* showcase, glass cabinet; shopwindow
vitrióli•co -ca *adj* (chem) vitriolic
vitrola *f* record player
vituallas *fpl* victuals
vituperable *adj* vituperable
vituperar *tr* to vituperate
viuda *f* widow; **viuda de marido vivo** or **viuda de paja** grass widow
viudedad *f* widowhood; dower; widow's pension

viudez *f* (*estado de viuda*) widowhood; (*estado de viudo*) widowerhood

viu•do -da *adj* left a widow; left a widower ‖ *m* widower ‖ *f* see **viuda**

viva *interj* viva!, long live! ‖ *m* viva

vivacidad *f* longevity; vivacity, liveliness; brightness, brilliance

vivande•ro -ra *mf* (mil) sutler, camp follower

vivaque *m* bivouac; guardhouse; police headquarters; **estar al vivaque** to bivouac

vivaquear *intr* to bivouac

vivar *m* warren, burrow; aquarium ‖ *tr* to cheer, acclaim

vivara•cho -cha *adj* vivacious, lively

vi•vaz *adj* (*pl* **-vaces**) long-lived; vivacious, lively; keen, perceptive; (bot) perennial

víveres *mpl* food, provisions, victuals

vivero *m* tree nursery; fishpond; (*origen de cosas perjudiciales*) (fig) hotbed

viveza *f* agility, briskness; ardor, vehemence; sharpness, keenness; perception; brightness, brilliance; witticism; (*de los ojos*) sparkle; (*acción o palabra poco consideradas*) thoughtlessness

vivide•ro -ra *adj* livable

vívi•do -da *adj* quick, perceptive; lively

vivienda *f* dwelling; life, way of life; **vivienda unifamiliar** one-family house

viviente *adj* living, alive

vivificar §73 *tr* to vivify, enliven

vivir *m* life, living ‖ *tr* (*una experiencia o ventura*) to live; (*toda la vida; la vejez*) live out; (*habitar*) live in ‖ *intr* to live; **¿quién vive?** (mil) who goes there?; **vivir de** (*p.ej., carne*) to live on; **vivir para ver** to live and learn; **vivir y dejar vivir** to live and let live

vivisección *f* vivisection

vi•vo -va *adj* living, alive, live; (*lleno de vida; intenso*) live; (*sutil, agudo*) sharp, keen; (*dolor*) acute; (*carne*) raw; active, effective; (*luz*) bright, intense; (*pronto y ágil*) quick; (*idioma*) living, modern; **de viva voz** viva voce, by word of mouth; **herir en lo vivo** to cut or to sting to the quick ‖ *mf* living person; **los vivos y los muertos** the quick and the dead ‖ *m* edging, border; (vet) mange

Vizcaya *f* Biscay; **llevar hierro a Vizcaya** to carry coals to Newcastle

vizconde *m* viscount

vizcondesa *f* viscountess

V.M. *abbr* **Vuestra Majestad**

V.°B.° *abbr* **visto bueno**

vocablista *mf* punster

vocablo *m* word; **jugar del vocablo** to pun

vocabulario *m* vocabulary

vocación *f* vocation, calling

vocal *adj* vocal ‖ *mf* director ‖ *f* vowel

vocalista *mf* singer, vocalist

vocativo *m* vocative

voceador *m* town crier; (Col, Ecuad) paper boy

vocear *tr* to cry, shout; cheer, acclaim; call, page; boast about publicly ‖ *intr* to shout

vocería *f* shouting, outcry; spokesmanship

vocerío *m* shouting, outcry

vocero *m* spokesman, mouthpiece

vociferar *tr* (*injurias*) to shout; boast loudly about ‖ *intr* to vociferate, shout

vocingle•ro -ra *adj* loudmouthed; loud, talkative

vo•dú *m* (*pl* **-dúes**) voodoo

voduísta *adj & mf* voodoo

vol. *abbr* **volumen, voluntad**

volada *f* short flight; (*del jugador de billar*) (Arg) stroke; (Col, Ecuad) trick; (*noticia inventada*) (Mex) hoax

voladi•zo -za *adj* projecting ‖ *m* projection

vola•do -da *adj* (typ) superior ‖ *f* see **volada**

vola•dor -dora *adj* flying; hanging, dangling; swift, fast ‖ *m* rocket; flying fish

voladura *f* blast, explosion

volandas — en volandas in the air; fast

volante *adj* flying; unsettled ‖ *m* shuttlecock; battledore and shuttlecock; (*rueda que regula el movimiento de una máquina*) flywheel; (*rueda de mano para la dirección del automóvil*) steering wheel; (*pieza del reloj movida por el espiral*) balance wheel; flunkey, lackey; (*criado que iba a pie delante del coche o caballo*) outrunner; (*de papel*) slip, leaflet; (sew) flounce, ruffle; **un buen volante** a good driver

volan•tín -tina *adj* unsettled ‖ *m* fish line; kite

volantista *m* driver, man at the wheel

volan•tón -tona *mf* fledgling ‖ *f* (Ven) loose woman

volapié *m* (taur) stroke in which the matador moves in for the kill; a **volapié** half running, half flying; half walking, half swimming

volar §61 *tr* (*llevar en un aparato de aviación*) to fly; blow up, explode; irritate; (*una letra, tipo o signo*) (typ) to raise ‖ *intr* to fly; fly away; disappear; jut out, project; (*una especie*) spread rapidly; (*p.ej., una torre*) rise in the air; **volar sin motor** (aer) to glide ‖ *ref* to fly away; fly off the handle

volatería *f* fowling with decoys; **de volatería** offhand

volátil *adj* volatile

volatilizar *tr & ref* to volatilize

volatín *m* ropewalker, acrobat, tumbler

volatine•ro -ra *mf* ropewalker, acrobat, tumbler

volcán *m* volcano

volcar §81 *tr* to upset, overturn, dump; tip, tilt; (*a una persona un olor fuerte*) to make dizzy; change the mind of; irritate, tease ‖ *intr* to upset ‖ *ref* to turn upside down

volear *tr* (tennis) to volley

voleo *m* (tennis) volley; reeling punch; **del primer voleo** or **de un voleo** with a smash, all at once; **sembrar al voleo** to sow, broadcast

volframio *m* wolfram

volibol *m* volleyball

volquete *m* dumpcart, dump truck

voltai•co -ca *adj* voltaic

voltaje *m* voltage

volta•rio -ria *adj* fickle, inconstant; (Chile) willful; (Chile) sporty

vi
vo

voltea•do -da *mf* (Col) turncoat, deserter

voltear *tr* to upset, turn over; turn around; move, transform ‖ *intr* to roll over, tumble

volteo *m* upset, overturning; tumbling; (P-R) scolding

voltereta *f* tumble; turning up card to determine trump

voltímetro *m* voltmeter

voltio *m* volt

volti•zo -za *adj* curled, twisted; fickle

voluble *adj* easily turned; fickle, inconstant

volumen *m* volume; **volumen sonoro** volume; (geom) volume

volumino•so -sa *adj* voluminous

voluntad *f* will; (*amor, cariño*) fondness, love; **a voluntad** at will; **buena voluntad** willingness; **de buena voluntad** willingly; **de mala voluntad** unwillingly; **de su propia voluntad** of one's own volition; **última voluntad** last will and testament; last wish; **voluntad de hierro** iron will

voluntariedad *f* willfulness

volunta•rio -ra *adj* (*que se hace por espontánea voluntad*) voluntary; (*que tiene voluntad obstinada*) willful; (*que se presta voluntariamente a hacer algo*) volunteer ‖ *mfr* volunteer

voluntario•so -sa *adj* willful

voluptuo•so -sa *adj* (*que inspira complacencia en los placeres sensuales*) voluptuous; (*dado a los placeres sensuales*) voluptuary ‖ *mf* voluptuary

voluta *f* (archit) scroll, volute; (*p.ej., de humo*) ring

volvedor *m* screwdriver; (Col) extra, something thrown in; **volvedor de machos** tap wrench

volver §47 & §83 *tr* to turn; turn upside down; turn inside out; return, send back, give back; (*una puerta*) push to, pull to; translate; vomit ‖ *intr* to turn; return, come back; **volver a** + *inf* verb + again, e.g., **volvió a abrir la puerta** he opened the door again; **volver en sí** to come to; **volver por** to defend, stand up for ‖ *ref* to become; turn around; return, come back; change one's mind; turn, turn sour; **volverse atrás** to back out; **volverse contra** to turn on

vomitar *tr* to vomit, throw up; (*fuego los cañones*) belch forth; (*maldiciones*) utter; (*un secreto*) let out; (*lo que uno retiene indebidamente*) cough up ‖ *intr* to vomit, throw up; come across, disgorge

vómito *m* vomit, vomiting; **provocar a vómito** to nauseate; **vómitos del embarazo** morning sickness

voracidad *f* voracity

vorágine *f* whirlpool, vortex

vo•raz *adj* (*pl* **-races**) voracious

vormela *f* polecat

vórtice *m* vortex

vos *pron pers* (subject of verb and object of preposition; takes plural form of verb but is singular in meaning; used in addressing the Deity, the Virgin, etc., and distinguished

persons; in Spanish America is much used instead of **tú**) you

voso•tros -tras *pron pers* (plural of **tú**) you

votación *f* vote, voting; **votación de desempate** runoff election

votante *adj* voting ‖ *mf* voter

votar *tr* to vote for; (*sí, no*) vote; (*p.ej., un cirio a la Virgen*) vow ‖ *intr* to vote; vow; swear, curse

voti•vo -va *adj* votive

voto *m* (*sufragio; derecho de votar; persona que da su voto*) vote; (*promesa solemne*) vow; (*exvoto*) votive offering; (*blasfemia*) oath, curse; wish, desire; **echar votos** to swear, to curse; **regular los votos** to tally the votes; **voto de amén** vote of a yes man; yes man; **voto de calidad** casting vote; **voto informativo** straw vote; **votos** good wishes; **¡voto va!** come now!

voz *f* (*pl* **voces**) voice; (*vocablo*) word; **aclarar la voz** to clear one's throat; **a una voz** with one voice; **a voces** shouting; **a voz en cuello** or **en grito** at the top of one's voice; **correr la voz que** to be rumored that; **dar voces** to shout, cry out; **de viva voz** viva voce, by word of mouth; **en alta voz** aloud, in a loud voice; **en voz baja** in a low voice; **llevar la voz cantante** to have the say, be the boss; **voces** outcry

voz-guía *f* (*diccionario*) entry word

vro. *abbr* **vuestro**

V.S. *abbr* **Vueseñoría**

vuelco *m* upset, overturn; **darle a uno un vuelco el corazón** to have a presentiment

vuelo *m* flight; flying; (*de una falda*) flare, fullness; projection; lace cuff trimming; **al vuelo** at once; on the wing; scattered at random; (chess) en passant; **alzar el vuelo** to take flight; to dash away; **echar a vuelo las campanas** to ring a full peal; **tirar al vuelo** to shoot on the wing; **tocar a vuelo las campanas** to ring a full peal; **vuelo a ciegas** (aer) blind flying; **vuelo de distancia** (aer) long-distance flight; **vuelo de enlace** connecting flight; **vuelo de ensayo** or **de prueba** (aer) test flight; **vuelo espacial tripulado** manned space flight; **vuelo planeado** (aer) volplane; **vuelo rasante** (aer) hedgehopping; **vuelo sin escala** (aer) nonstop flight; **vuelo sin motor** (aer) glide, gliding

vuelta *f* turn; (*regreso; devolución*) return; (*dinero sobrante de un pago*) change; (*de un camino*) bend, turn; (*del pantalón*) cuff; cuff trimming; (*paseo corto*) stroll; (*revés*) other side; (*paliza*) beating, whipping; (*en un cabo*) loop; (*en la media*) clock; (*mudanza*) change; **a la vuelta** on returning; please turn the page; **a la vuelta de** at the end of; at the turn of; (*la esquina*) around; **a vuelta de** about; **a vuelta de correo** by return mail; **dar cien vueltas a** to run rings around, be way ahead of; **dar la vuelta de campana** to turn somersault; **darse una vuelta a la redonda** to tend to one's own business; **dar una vuelta** to take a stroll, take a walk; take a look; change one's ways; **dar vuelta** to turn around; (*el vino*) turn sour; **dar vuelta a** to reverse, turn around; **estar de vuelta** to be back; **quedarse con la vuelta** to keep the change; **vuelta de campana** somersault; **vuelta del mundo** trip around the world

vuelto *m* change

vues•tro -tra (corresponds to **vos** and **vosotros**) *adj poss* your ‖ *pron poss* yours

vulcanizar §60 *tr* to vulcanize

vulgacho *m* populace, mob

vulgar *adj* vulgar, popular, common, vernacular

vulgarismo *m* popular expression; (philol) popular word, popular form

vulgarizar §60 *tr* to popularize; translate into the vernacular ‖ *ref* to associate with the people

Vulgata *f* Vulgate

vulgo *adv* commonly ‖ *m* common people; (*personas que en una materia sólo conocen la parte superficial*) laity

vulnerable *adj* vulnerable

vulnerar *tr* to hurt, injure; (*la reputación de una persona*) damage; (*una ley, un precepto*) break

vulpeja *f* she-fox, vixen

V.V. or **VV** *abbr* **ustedes**

X

X, x (equis) *f* twenty-sixth letter of the Spanish alphabet

xenia *f* xenia

xenofobia *f* xenophobia

xenófo•bo -ba *mf* xenophobe

xenón *m* xenon

xerografía *f* xerography

xerografiar §77 *tr* to xerograph ‖ *intr* to make xerograph copies

xilófono *m* (mus) xylophone

xilografía *f* (*arte*) xylography; (*grabado*) xylograph

xpiano *abbr* **cristiano**

Xpo *abbr* **Cristo**

xptiano *abbr* **cristiano**

Xpto *abbr* **Cristo**

xunde *m* (Mex) reed basket, palm basket

Y

Y, y (ye) *f* twenty-seventh letter of the Spanish alphabet

y *conj* and

ya *adv* already; right away; now; **no ya** not only; **ya no** no longer; **ya que** since, inasmuch as

yac *m* (*bandera de proa*) (naut) jack; (*bóvido del Tibet*) yak

yacer §82 *intr* to lie

yacija *f* bed, couch; (*sepultura*) grave

yacimiento *m* bed, field, deposit; **yacimiento de petróleo** oil field

yámbi•co -ca *adj* iambic

yambo *m* iamb, iambus

yanqui *adj & mf* Yankee

Yanquilandia *f* Yankeedom

yapa *f* bonus, extra, allowance; **de yapa** in the bargain, extra

yarda *f* yard, yardstick

yate *m* yacht

yedra *f* ivy

yegua *f* mare; (CAm) cigar butt

yeguada *f* stud

yelmo *m* helmet

yema *f* (*de huevo*) yolk; candied yolk; (*del invierno*) dead; (*renuevo*) bud; (fig) cream; **dar en la yema** to put one's finger on the

spot; **yema del dedo** finger tip; **yema mejida** eggnog

yente — **yentes y vinientes** *mpl* habitués, frequenters

yerba *f* var of **hierba**

yer•mo -ma *adj* deserted, uninhabited; (*suelo*) unsown; (*mujer*) not pregnant ‖ *m* desert, wilderness

yerno *m* son-in-law

yerro *m* error, mistake; **yerro de cuenta** miscalculation; **yerro de imprenta** printer's error

yer•to -ta *adj* stiff, rigid

yesca *f* punk, tinder; (*cosa que excita una pasión*) fuel; **echar una yesca** to strike a light

yeso *m* gypsum; plaster cast

yo *pron pers* **I; soy yo** it's me, it is I

yodhídri•co -ca *adj* hydriodic

yodo *m* iodine

yoduro *m* iodide

yoga *f* yoga

yogui *m* yogi

yogurt *m* yogurt

yola *f* shell (*boat*)

yonquí *m* (*drogas*) junkie, drug addict

yugo *m* yoke; **sacudir el yugo** to throw off the yoke

Yugoeslavia *f* Yugoslavia
yugoesla•vo -va *adj & mf* Yugoslav
yugular *adj & f* jugular ‖ *tr* to cut off, nip in the bud
yunque *m* anvil; drudge, work horse

yunta *f* yoke, team
yute *m* jute
yuxtaponer §54 *tr* to juxtapose
yuyo *m* (Arg, Chile) weed; **yuyos** (Col, Ecuad, Peru) greens

Z

Z, z (zeda or zeta) *f* twenty-eighth letter of the Spanish alphabet
zabordar *intr* (naut) to run aground
zabullir §13 *tr* (*p.ej., a un perro*) to duck, give a ducking to; throw, hurl ‖ *ref* (*meterse debajo del agua con ímpetu*) to dive; (*esconderse rápidamente*) duck
zacapela *f* or **zacapella** *f* row, rumpus
zacate *m* (CAm, Mex) hay, fodder; **zacate de empaque** excelsior
zacateca *m* (Cuba) undertaker, gravedigger
zacatín *m* old-clothes market
zacear *tr* (*al perro*) to chase away ‖ *intr* to lisp
zafaduría *f* (Arg) brazenness, effrontery
zafar *tr* to adorn, bedeck; loosen, untie; clear, free; (*un buque*) lighten ‖ *ref* to slip away; slip off, come off; **zafarse de** to get out of
zafarrancho *m* (naut) clearing the decks; (coll) havoc, ravage; (coll) scuffle, row; **zafarrancho de combate** (naut) clearing the deck for action
za•fio -fia *adj* rough, uncouth, boorish
zafiro *m* sapphire
za•fo -fa *adj* unhurt, intact; (naut) free, clear ‖ **zafo** *prep* (Col) except
zafra *f* olive-oil can; drip jar; sugar crop; sugar making; sugar-making season; (min) rubbish, muck
zaga *f* rear; load carried in the rear; (mil) rearguard; **a la zaga, a zaga** or **en zaga** behind, in the rear; **no ir en zaga a** to not be behind, be as good as
zagal *m* young fellow; strapping young fellow; shepherd boy; footboy
zagala *f* lass, maiden; young shepherdess
zaguán *m* vestibule, hall, entry
zague•ro -ra *adj* back, rear ‖ *m* (sport) back, backstop
zaherir §68 *tr* to upbraid, reproach; scold shamefully
zahones *mpl* chaps, hunting breeches
zaho•rí *m* (*pl* **-ríes**) keen observer; seer, clairvoyant
zahurda *f* pigpen
zai•no -na *adj* treacherous, false; (*caballo*) vicious; (*caballo*) dark-chestnut; **mirar a lo zaino** or **de zaino** to look askance at
za•lá *f* (*pl* **-laes**) Muslim prayer; **hacer la zalá a** to fawn on

zalagarda *f* ambush; skirmish; (*trampa para cazar animales*) trap; trick; row, rumpus; mock fight
zalamería *f* flattery, cajolery
zalame•ro -ra *adj* flattering, fawning ‖ *mf* flatterer, fawner
zalea *f* unsheared sheepskin
zalear *tr* to drag around, shake; (*al perro*) chase away
zalema *f* salaam
zamacuco *m* blockhead; sullen fellow; drunkenness
zamacueca *f* cueca (*Chilean courtship dance*)
zamarra *f* undressed sheepskin; sheepskin jacket
zam•bo -ba *adj* knock-kneed
zambra *f* merrymaking, celebration; Moorish boat
zambucar §73 *tr* to slip away, hide away
zambullida *f* dive, plunge; (fencing) thrust to the breast
zambulli•dor -dora *adj* diving, plunging ‖ *mf* diver, plunger ‖ *m* (orn) diver, loon
zambullir §13 *tr* (*p.ej., a un perro*) to duck, give a ducking to; throw, hurl ‖ *ref* (*meterse debajo del agua con ímpetu*) to dive; (*esconderse rápidamente*) duck
zampa *f* pile, bearing pile
zampacuarti•llos *mf* (*pl* **-llos**) toper, soak
zampalimos•nas *mf* (*pl* **-nas**) bum, ordinary bum
zampar *tr* to slip away, hide away; gobble down ‖ *ref* to slip away, hide away
zampator•tas *mf* (*pl* **-tas**) glutton; boor
zampear *tr* (*el terreno*) to strengthen with piles and rubble
zampoña *f* shepherd's pipe, rustic flute; nonsense, folly
zampuzar §60 *tr* to duck, give a ducking to; slip away, hide away
zanahoria *f* carrot
zanca *f* long leg; (*de la escalera*) horse
zancada *f* long stride; **en dos zancadas** in a flash, in a jiffy
zancadilla *f* booby trap; **echar la zancadilla a** to stick out one's foot and trip
zancajo *m* heel; **no llegar a los zancajos a** to not come up to, not be equal to
zancajo•so -sa *adj* duck-toed; down-at-the-heel
zancarrón *m* dirty old fellow
zanco *m* stilt; **en zancos** from a vantage point

zancu•do -da *adj* long-legged; (orn) wading ‖ *m* mosquito ‖ *f* wading bird

zanfonía *f* hurdy-gurdy

zangala *f* buckram

zangamanga *f* trick

zanganada *f* impertinence, impudence

zanganear *intr* to loaf around

zángano *m* (ent) drone; (fig) drone, loafer; (CAm) scoundrel

zangarrear *intr* to thrum a guitar

zangolotear *tr* to jiggle ‖ *intr* to fuss around ‖ *ref* to jiggle, flop around, rattle

zangoloteo *m* jiggle, jiggling, rattle; fuss, bother

zanguanga *f* malingering; flattery; **hacer la zanguanga** to malinger

zanguan•go -ga *adj* slow, lazy ‖ *mf* loafer ‖ *f* see **zanguanga**

zanja *f* ditch, trench; (SAm) gully; **abrir las zanjas** to lay the foundations

zanquear *intr* to waddle; to rush around

zanquilar•go -ga *adj* leggy, long-legged

zanquituer•to -ta *adj* bandy-legged

zapa *f* spade; sharkskin, (mil) sap

zapapico *m* mattock, pickax

zapar *tr* (mil) to sap, mine, excavate

zaparrastrar *intr* — **ir zaparrastrando** to go along trailing one's clothes on the ground

zapateado *m* clog dance, tap dance

zapatear *tr* to hit with the shoe; tap with the feet; abuse, ill-treat ‖ *intr* to tap-dance; (*las velas*) flap ‖ *ref* — **zapatearse con** to hold out against

zapatería *f* shoemaking; shoemaker's shop; (*tienda*) shoe store

zapate•ro -ra *adj* poorly cooked ‖ *mf* shoemaker; shoe dealer; **quedarse zapatero** to not take a trick; **¡zapatero, a tus zapatos!** stick to your last!; **zapatero de viejo** or **zapatero remendón** cobbler, shoemaker

zapatilla *f* slipper; (*escarpín*) pump; (*del grifo*) washer; (*del florete*) leather tip or button; cloven hoof

zapato *m* shoe, low shoe; **andar con zapatos de fieltro** to gumshoe; **como tres en un zapato** hard up; like sardines; **zapato de goma** overshoe; **zapato inglés** low shoe

zapatón *m* (Guat, SAm) overshoe

zapear *tr* (*al gato*) to scare away, chase away

zaque *m* wineskin; tippler, drunk

zaquiza•mí *m* (*pl* -míes) attic, garret; hovel, pigpen

zar *m* czar

zarabanda *f* (mus) saraband; noise, confusion, uproar; (Mex) beating, thrashing

zaragata *f* scuffle, row; **zaragatas** (W-I) flattery

Zaragoza *f* Saragossa

zaranda *f* sieve, screen; colander; (Ven) horn; (Ven) top

zarandajas *fpl* odds and ends, trinkets

zarandar *tr* to sift, screen; winnow, pick out, select; jiggle ‖ *ref* to jiggle; swagger, strut

zaraza *f* chintz, printed cotton

zarcillo *m* eardrop; (bot) tendril

zarigüeya *f* opossum

zarina *f* czarina

zarpa *f* claw, paw; (naut) weighing anchor

zarpar *tr* (*el ancla*) (naut) to weigh (*anchor*) ‖ *intr* (naut) to weigh anchor, set sail

zarpo•so -sa *adj* mud-splashed

zarracatería *f* cajolery, insincere flattery

zarracatín *m* sharp trader

zarramplín *m* botcher, bungler

zarrien•to -ta *adj* mud-splashed

zarza *f* blackberry, bramble (*bush*)

zarzamora *f* blackberry (*fruit*)

zarzaparrilla *f* sarsaparilla

zarzo *m* hurdle, wattle

zarzo•so -sa *adj* brambly

zarzuela *f* small bramble; (theat) zarzuela (*Spanish musical comedy*); **zarzuela grande** three-act zarzuela

zas *interj* bang!; **¡zas, zas!** bing, bang!

zascandilear *intr* to meddle, scheme

zepelín *m* zeppelin

Zeus *m* Zeus

zigzag *m* zigzag

zigzaguear *intr* to zigzag

zinc *m* (*pl* **zinces**) zinc

zipizape *m* scuffle, row, rumpus

ziszás *m* zigzag

zoca *f* public square

zócalo *m* (archit) socle; (*de una pared*) dado; (rad) socket; (Mex) public square, center square

zoca•to -ta *adj* (*fruto*) corky, pithy; left; left-handed ‖ *mf* left-handed pèrson

zoclo *m* clog, wooden shoe

zo•co -ca *adj* left; left-handed ‖ *mf* left-handed person ‖ *m* clog, wooden shoe; Moroccan market place; (archit) socle; **andar de zocos en colodros** to jump from the frying pan into the fire ‖ *f* see **zoca**

zodíaco *m* zodiac

zofra *f* Moorish carpet, Moorish rug

zolo•cho -cha *adj* stupid, simple ‖ *mf* simpleton

zollipar *intr* to sob

zollipo *m* sob

zona *m* (pathol) shingles ‖ *f* zone; (*banda, faja*) belt, girdle; **zona a batir** target area; **zona desmilitarizada** demilitarized zone; **zona siniestrada** disaster area

zon•zo -za *adj* tasteless, insipid; dull, inane ‖ *mf* dolt, dimwit

zoófito *m* zoöphyte

zoología *f* zoölogy

zoológi•co -ca *adj* zoölogic(al)

zoólo•go -ga *mf* zoölogist

zopen•co -ca *adj* dull, stupid ‖ *mf* dullard, blockhead

zopilote *m* (Mex, CAm) turkey buzzard, turkey vulture

zo•po -pa *adj* crippled; awkward, gauche ‖ *mf* cripple

zoquete *m* (*de madera*) block, chunk, end; (*de pan*) bit, crust; chump, lout

zoquetu•do -da *adj* coarse, crude

zorra *f* fox; female fox; cunning person; prostitute; drunkenness; dray, truck; **pillar una zorra** to get drunk

zorrera *f* (*cueva de zorros*) foxhole; smoke-filled room; worry, confusion

zorrería *f* foxiness, craftiness

zorre•ro -ra *adj* sly, foxy; slow, heavy, tardy ‖ *f* see **zorrera**

zorrillo *m* skunk

zorro *m* male fox; (*piel*) fox; (*hombre taimado*) fox; **estar hecho un zorro** to be overwhelmed with sleep; be dull and sullen; **zorros** duster

zorral *m* (orn) fieldfare; sly fellow; (Chile) simpleton

zozobra *f* capsizing, sinking; anxiety

zozobrar *tr* (*un buque*) to sink; (*un negocio*) wreck ‖ *intr* to capsize, sink; (*la embarcación en la tempestad*) wallow; (*un negocio*) be in great danger; be greatly worried ‖ *ref* to capsize, sink

zueco *m* clog, wooden shoe, sabot

zulacar §73 *tr* to waterproof

zulaque *m* waterproofing

zulú *adj* & *mf* (*pl* **-lús** o **-lúes**) Zulu

zullar *ref* to have a bowel movement; break wind

zullen•co -ca *adj* windy, flatulent

zumaque *m* sumach; wine

zumaya *f* (*autillo*) tawny owl; (*chotacabras*) goatsucker

zumba *f* bell worn by leading mule; (Mex) drunkenness; **hacer zumba a** to make fun of; **sin zumba** (Mex) in a rush, in a hurry

zumbador *m* buzzer; (Mex) pauraque; (Mex, CAm, W-I) hummingbird

zumbar *tr* to make fun of; (*un golpe, una bofetada*) let have ‖ *intr* to buzz; zoom; (*los oídos*) ring; **zumbar a** (*frisar con*) to be close to, border on ‖ *ref* (Cuba) to go too far, forget oneself; (P-R) to rush ahead; **zumbarse de** to make fun of

zumbido *m* buzz; zoom; blow, smack; **zumbido de ocupación** (telp) busy signal; **zumbido de oídos** ringing in the ears

zum•bón -bona *adj* waggish, playful ‖ *mf* wag, jester

zumien•to -ta *adj* juicy

zumo *m* juice; advantage, profit; **zumo de cepas** or **de parras** fruit of the vine

zumo•so -sa *adj* juicy

zunchar *tr* to band, hoop

zuncho *m* band, hoop

zupia *f* (*del vino*) dregs; slop, wine full of dregs; (fig) junk, trash

zurcido *m* darning; darn; invisible mending

zurcir §36 *tr* to darn; (*una mentira*) hatch, concoct; (*unas mentiras*) weave (*a tissue of lies*)

zurdazo *m* (box) left, blow with the left

zur•do -da *adj* left; left-handed; **a zurdas** with the left hand; the wrong way ‖ *mf* left-handed person

zurear *intr* to coo

zuro *m* stripped corncob

zurra *f* dressing, currying; scuffle, quarrel; drubbing, thrashing; (*trabajo o estudio continuados*) grind

zurrapa *f* thread, filament; trash, rubbish; **con zurrapas** in a sloppy manner

zurrar *tr* (*el cuero*) to dress, curry; get the best of; (*censurar con dureza*) dress down; (*castigar con azotes*) drub, thrash ‖ *ref* (*hacer sus necesidades involuntariamente*) to have an accident; be scared to death; (Arg) to break wind noiselessly

zurriagar §44 *tr* to whip, horsewhip

zurriago *m* whip, lash

zurribanda *f* rain of blows; rumpus, scuffle

zurrir *intr* to buzz, grate

zurrón *m* shepherd's leather bag; leather bag; (*cáscara*) husk

zurrona *f* loose, evil woman

zurullo *m* soft roll; turd

zurupeto *m* unregistered broker; shyster notary

zuta•no -na *mf* so-and-so

Spanish Irregular Verbs

All simple tenses are shown in these tables if they contain one irregular form or more, except the conditional (which can always be derived from the stem of the future indicative) and the imperfect and future subjunctive (which can always be derived from the third plural preterit indicative minus the last syllable -ron).

The numbers are those that accompany the respective verbs and verbs of identical patterns where they are listed in their alphabetical places in this Dictionary. The letters (a) to (h) identify the tenses as follows:

(a) gerund
(b) past participle
(c) imperative
(d) present indicative

(e) present subjunctive
(f) imperfect indicative
(g) future indicative
(h) preterit indicative

§1 **abolir:** defective verb used only in forms whose endings contain the vowel **i**

§2 **acertar**
   (c) **acierta,** acertad
   (d) **acierto, aciertas, acierta,** acertamos, acertáis, **aciertan**
   (e) **acierte, aciertes, acierte,** acertemos, acertéis, **acierten**

§3 **agorar:** like §61 but with diaeresis on the **u** of **ue**
   (c) **agüera,** agorad
   (d) **agüero, agüeras, agüera,** agoramos, agoráis, **agüeran**
   (e) **agüere, agüeres, agüere,** agoremos, agoréis, **agüeren**

§4 **airar**
   (c) **aíra,** airad
   (d) **aíro, aíras, aíra,** airamos, airáis, **aíran**
   (e) **aíre, aíres, aíre,** airemos, airéis, **aíren**

§5 **andar**
   (h) **anduve, anduviste, anduvo, anduvimos, anduvisteis, anduvieron**

§6 **argüir:** like §20 but with diaeresis on **u** in forms with accented **i** in the ending
   (a) **arguyendo**
   (b) **argüído**
   (c) **arguye,** argüid
   (d) **arguyo, arguyes, arguye,** argüimos, argüís, **arguyen**
   (e) **arguya, arguyas, arguya, arguyamos, arguyáis, arguyan**
   (h) **argüí, argüiste, arguyó,** argüimos, argüisteis, **arguyeron**

§7 **asir**
   (d) **asgo,** ases, ase, asimos, asís, asen
   (e) **asga, asgas, asga, asgamos, asgáis, asgan**

§8 **aunar**
   (c) **aúna,** aunad
   (d) **aúno, aúnas, aúna,** aunamos, aunáis, **aúnan**
   (e) **aúne, aúnes, aúne,** aunemos, aunéis, **aúnen**

§9 **avergonzar:** combination of §3 and §60
   (c) **avergüenza,** avergonzad
   (d) **avergüenzo, avergüenzas, avergüenza,** avergonzamos, avergonzáis, **avergüenzan**
   (e) **avergüence, avergüences, avergüence,** avergoncemos, avergoncéis, **avergüencen**
   (h) **avergoncé,** avergonzaste, avergonzó, avergonzamos, avergonzasteis, avergonzaron

§10 **averiguar**
   (e) **averigüe, averigües, averigüe, averigüemos, averigüéis, averigüen**
   (h) **averigüé,** averiguaste, averiguó, averiguamos, averiguasteis, averiguaron

§11 **bendecir**
   (a) **bendiciendo**
   (c) **bendice,** bendecid
   (d) **bendigo, bendices, bendice,** bendecimos, bendecís, **bendicen**
   (e) **bendiga, bendigas, bendiga, bendigamos, bendigáis, bendigan**
   (h) **bendije, bendijiste, bendijo, bendijimos, bendijisteis, bendijeron**

§12 **bruñir**
   (a) **bruñendo**
   (h) **bruñí, bruñiste, bruñó,** bruñimos, bruñisteis, **bruñeron**

§13 **bullir**
   (a) **bullendo**
   (h) **bullí, bulliste, bulló,** bullimos, bullisteis, **bulleron**

§14 **caber**
   (d) **quepo,** cabes, cabe, cabemos, cabéis, caben
   (e) **quepa, quepas, quepa, quepamos, quepáis, quepan**
   (g) **cabré, cabrás, cabrá, cabremos, cabréis, cabrán**
   (h) **cupe, cupiste, cupo, cupimos, cupisteis, cupieron**

§15 **caer**
   (a) **cayendo**
   (b) **caído**
   (d) **caigo,** caes, cae, caemos, caéis, caen
   (e) **caiga, caigas, caiga, caigamos, caigáis, caigan**
   (h) caí, **caíste, cayó, caímos, caísteis, cayeron**

§16 **cocer:** combination of §47 and §78
   (c) **cuece,** coced
   (d) **cuezo, cueces, cuece,** cocemos, cocéis, **cuecen**
   (e) **cueza, cuezas, cueza, cozamos, cozáis, cuezan**

§17 **coger**
   (d) **cojo,** coges, coge, cogemos, cogéis, cogen
   (e) **coja, cojas, coja, cojamos, cojáis, cojan**

§18 **comenzar:** combination of §2 and §60
   (c) **comienza,** comenzad
   (d) **comienzo, comienzas, comienza,** comenzamos, comenzáis, **comienzan**
   (e) **comience, comiences, comience, comencemos, comencéis, comiencen**
   (h) **comencé,** comenzaste, comenzó, comenzamos, comenzasteis, comenzaron

§19 **conducir**
   (d) **conduzco,** conduces, conduce, conducimos, conducís, conducen
   (e) **conduzca, conduzcas, conduzca, conduzcamos, conduzcáis, conduzcan**
   (h) **conduje, condujiste, condujo, condujimos, condujisteis, condujeron**

§20 **construir**
   (a) **construyendo**
   (b) **construído**
   (c) **construye,** construid
   (d) **construyo, construyes, construye,** construimos, construís, **construyen**
   (e) **construya, construyas, construya, construyamos, construyáis, constru-yan**
   (h) construí, construiste, **construyó,** construimos, construisteis, **construyeron**

§21 **continuar**
   (c) **continúa,** continuad
   (d) **continúo, continúas, continúa,** continuamos, continuáis, **continúan**
   (e) **continúe, continúes, continúe,** continuemos, continuéis, **continúen**

§22 **crecer**
   (d) **crezco,** creces, crece, crecemos, crecéis, crecen
   (e) **crezca, crezcas, crezca, crezcamos, crezcáis, crezcan**

§23 dar
    (d) **doy,** das, da, damos, dais, dan
    (e) **dé,** des, **dé,** demos, deis, den
    (h) **dí, diste, dio, dimos, disteis, dieron**

§24 decir
    (a) **diciendo**
    (b) **dicho**
    (c) **di,** decid
    (d) **digo, dices, dice,** decimos, decís, **dicen**
    (e) **diga, digas, diga, digamos, digáis, digan**
    (g) **diré, dirás, dirá, diremos, diréis, dirán**
    (h) **dije, dijiste, dijo, dijimos, dijisteis, dijeron**

§25 delinquir
    (d) **delinco,** delinques, delinque, delinquimos, delinquís, delinquen
    (e) **delinca, delincas, delinca, delincamos, delincáis, delincan**

§26 desosar: like §61 but with **h** before **ue**
    (c) **deshuesa,** desosad
    (d) **deshueso, deshuesas, deshuesa,** desosamos, desosáis, **deshuesan**
    (e) **deshuese, deshueses, deshuese,** desosemos, desoséis, **deshuesen**

§27 dirigir
    (d) **dirijo,** diriges, dirige, dirigimos, dirigís, dirigen
    (e) **dirija, dirijas, dirija, dirijamos, dirijáis, dirijan**

§28 discernir
    (c) **discierne,** discernid
    (d) **discierno, disciernes, discierne,** discernimos, discernís, **disciernen**
    (e) **discierna, disciernas, discierna,** discernamos, discernáis, **disciernan**

§29 distinguir
    (d) **distingo,** distingues, distingue, distinguimos, distinguís, distinguen
    (e) **distinga, distingas, distinga, distingamos, distingáis, distingan**

§30 dormir
    (a) **durmiendo**
    (c) **duerme,** dormid
    (d) **duermo, duermes, duerme,** dormimos, dormís, **duermen**
    (e) **duerma, duermas, duerma, durmamos, durmáis, duerman**
    (h) dormí, dormiste, **durmió,** dormimos, dormisteis, **durmieron**

§31 empeller
    (a) **empellendo**
    (h) empellí, empelliste, **empelló,** empellimos, empellisteis, **empelleron**

§32 enraizar: combination of §4 and §60
    (c) **enraíza,** enraizad
    (d) **enraízo, enraízas, enraíza,** enraizamos, enraizáis, **enraízan**
    (e) **enraíce, enraíces, enraíce, enraicemos, enraicéis, enraícen**
    (h) **enraicé,** enraizaste, enraizó, enraizamos, enraizasteis, enraizaron

§33 erguir: combination of §29 and §50 or §68
    (a) **irguiendo**
    (c) **irgue** or **yergue,** erguid
    (d) **irgo, irgues, irgue,** ⎫ erguimos, erguís, ⎧ **irguen**
           yergo, yergues, yergue, ⎭   ⎩ **yerguen**
    (e) **irga, irgas, irga,** ⎫   ⎧ **irgan**
           yerga, yergas, yerga, ⎭ **irgamos, irgáis,** ⎩ **yergan**
    (h) erguí, erguiste, **irguió,** erguimos, erguisteis, **irguieron**

§34 errar: like §2 but with initial **ye** for **ie**
    (c) **yerra,** errad
    (d) **yerro, yerras, yerra,** erramos, erráis, **yerran**
    (e) **yerre, yerres, yerre,** erremos, erréis, **yerren**

§35 esforzar: combination of **§60** and **§61**
  (c) **esfuerza,** esforzad
  (d) **esfuerzo, esfuerzas, esfuerza,** esforzamos, esforzáis, **esfuerzan**
  (e) **esfuerce, esfuerces, esfuerce, esforcemos, esforcéis, esfuercen**
  (h) **esforcé,** esforzaste, esforzó, esforzamos, esforzasteis, esforzaron

§36 esparcir
  (d) **esparzo,** esparces, esparce, esparcimos, esparcís, esparcen
  (e) **esparza, esparzas, esparza, esparzamos, esparzáis, esparzan**

§37 estar
  (c) **está,** estad
  (d) **estoy, estás, está,** estamos, estáis, **están**
  (e) **esté, estés, esté,** estemos, estéis, **estén**
  (h) **estuve, estuviste, estuvo, estuvimos, estuvisteis, estuvieron**

§38 haber
  (c) **hé,** habed
  (d) **he, has, ha, hemos,** habéis, **han** (*v impers*) **hay**
  (e) **haya, hayas, haya, hayamos, hayáis, hayan**
  (g) **habré, habrás, habrá, habremos, habréis, habrán**
  (h) **hube, hubiste, hubo, hubimos, hubisteis, hubieron**

§39 hacer
  (b) **hecho**
  (c) **haz,** haced
  (d) **hago,** haces, hace, hacemos, hacéis, hacen
  (e) **haga, hagas, haga, hagamos, hagáis, hagan**
  (g) **haré, harás, hará, haremos, haréis, harán**
  (h) **hice, hiciste, hizo, hicimos, hicisteis, hicieron**

§40 inquirir
  (c) **inquiere,** inquirid
  (d) **inquiero, inquieres, inquiere,** inquirimos, inquirís, **inquieren**
  (e) **inquiera, inquieras, inquiera,** inquiramos, inquiráis, **inquieran**

§41 ir
  (a) **yendo**
  (c) **vé, vamos,** id
  (d) **voy, vas, va, vamos, vais, van**
  (e) **vaya, vayas, vaya, vayamos, vayáis, vayan**
  (f) **iba, ibas, iba, íbamos, ibais, iban**
  (h) **fui, fuiste, fue, fuimos, fuisteis, fueron**

§42 jugar: like **§63** but with radical **u**
  (c) **juega,** jugad
  (d) **juego, juegas, juega,** jugamos, jugáis, **juegan**
  (e) **juegue, juegues, juegue, juguemos, juguéis, jueguen**
  (h) **jugué,** jugaste, jugó, jugamos, jugasteis, jugaron

§43 leer
  (a) **leyendo**
  (b) **leído**
  (h) **leí,** leíste, **leyó, leímos, leísteis, leyeron**

§44 ligar
  (e) **ligue, ligues, ligue, liguemos, liguéis, liguen**
  (h) **ligué,** ligaste, ligó, ligamos, ligasteis, ligaron

§45 lucir
  (d) **luzco,** luces, luce, lucimos, lucís, lucen
  (e) **luzca, luzcas, luzca, luzcamos, luzcáis, luzcan**

§46 mecer
  (d) **mezo,** meces, mece, mecemos, mecéis, mecen
  (e) **meza, mezas, meza, mezamos, mezáis, mezan**

§47 **mover**
    (c) **mueve,** moved
    (d) **muevo, mueves, mueve,** movemos. movéis. **mueven**
    (e) **mueva, muevas, mueva,** movamos. mováis, **muevan**

§48 **oír**
    (a) **oyendo**
    (b) **oído**
    (c) **oye, oíd**
    (d) **oigo, oyes, oye, oímos,** oís. **oyen**
    (e) **oiga, oigas, oiga, oigamos, oigáis, oigan**
    (h) oí. **oíste, oyó, oímos, oísteis, oyeron**

§49 **oler:** like §47 but with **h** before **ue**
    (c) **huele,** oled
    (d) **huelo, hueles, huele,** olemos. oléis. **huelen**
    (e) **huela, huelas, huela,** olamos. oláis, **huelan**

§50 **pedir**
    (a) **pidiendo**
    (c) **pide,** pedid
    (d) **pido, pides, pide,** pedimos. pedís. **piden**
    (e) **pida, pidas, pida, pidamos, pidáis, pidan**
    (h) pedí. pediste. **pidió,** pedimos. pedisteis. **pidieron**

§51 **perder**
    (c) **pierde,** perded
    (d) **pierdo, pierdes, pierde,** perdemos. perdéis. **pierden**
    (e) **pierda, pierdas, pierda,** perdamos. perdáis. **pierdan**

§52 **placer**
    (d) **plazco,** places. place. placemos. placéis. placen
    (e) **plazca, plazcas, plazca, plazcamos, plazcáis, plazcan**
    (h) plací. placiste. plació (or **plugo).** placimos. placisteis. placieron

§53 **poder**
    (a) **pudiendo**
    (c) (**puede,** poded)
    (d) **puedo, puedes, puede,** podemos. podéis. **pueden**
    (e) **pueda, puedas, pueda,** podamos. podáis. **puedan**
    (g) **podré, podrás, podrá, podremos, podréis, podrán**
    (h) **pude, pudiste, pudo, pudimos, pudisteis, pudieron**

§54 **poner**
    (b) **puesto**
    (c) **pon,** poned
    (d) **pongo,** pones. pone. ponemos. ponéis. **ponen**
    (e) **ponga, pongas, ponga, pongamos, pongáis, pongan**
    (g) **pondré, pondrás, pondrá, pondremos, pondréis, pondrán**
    (h) **puse, pusiste, puso, pusimos, pusisteis, pusieron**

§55 **querer**
    (c) **quiere,** quered
    (d) **quiero, quieres, quiere,** queremos. queréis. **quieren**
    (e) **quiera, quieras, quiera,** queramos. queráis. **quieran**
    (g) **querré, querrás, querrá, querremos, querréis, querrán**
    (h) **quise, quisiste, quiso, quisimos, quisisteis, quisieron**

§56 **raer**
    (a) **rayendo**
    (b) **raído**
    (d) **raigo** (or **rayo).** raes. rae. raemos. raéis. raen
    (e) **raiga** (or **raya). raigas, raiga, raigamos, raigáis, raigan**
    (h) **raí, raíste, rayó, raímos, raísteis, rayeron**

§57 **regir:** combination of §27 and §50
    (a) **rigiendo**
    (c) **rige,** regid
    (d) **rijo, riges, rige,** regimos, regís, **rigen**
    (e) **rija, rijas, rija, rijamos, rijáis, rijan**
    (h) regí, registe, **rigió,** regimos, registeis, **rigieron**

§58 **reír**
    (a) **riendo**
    (b) **reído**
    (c) **ríe, reíd**
    (d) **río, ríes, ríe, reímos,** reís, **ríen**
    (e) **ría, rías, ría, riamos, riáis, rían**
    (h) reí, **reíste, rió, reímos, reísteis, rieron**

§59 **reunir**
    (c) **reúne,** reunid
    (d) **reúno, reúnes, reúne,** reunimos, reunís, **reúnen**
    (e) **reúna, reúnas, reúna,** reunamos, reunáis, **reúnan**

§60 **rezar**
    (e) **rece, reces, rece, recemos, recéis, recen**
    (h) **recé,** rezaste, rezó, rezamos, rezasteis, rezaron

§61 **rodar**
    (c) **rueda,** rodad
    (d) **ruedo, ruedas, rueda,** rodamos, rodáis, **ruedan**
    (e) **ruede, ruedes, ruede,** rodemos, rodéis, **rueden**

§62 **roer**
    (a) **royendo**
    (b) **roído**
    (d) **roo (roigo,** or **royo),** roes, roe, roemos, roéis, roen
    (e) **roa (roiga,** or **roya),** roas, roa, roamos, roáis, roan
    (h) roí, **roíste, royó, roímos, roísteis, royeron**

§63 **rogar:** combination of §44 and §61
    (c) **ruega,** rogad
    (d) **ruego, ruegas, ruega,** rogamos, rogáis, **ruegan**
    (e) **ruegue, ruegues, ruegue, roguemos, roguéis, rueguen**
    (h) **rogué,** rogaste, rogó, rogamos, rogasteis, rogaron

§64 **saber**
    (d) **sé,** sabes, sabe, sabemos, sabéis, saben
    (e) **sepa, sepas, sepa, sepamos, sepáis, sepan**
    (g) **sabré, sabrás, sabrá, sabremos, sabréis, sabrán**
    (h) **supe, supiste, supo, supimos, supisteis, supieron**

§65 **salir**
    (c) **sal,** salid
    (d) **salgo,** sales, sale, salimos, salís, salen
    (e) **salga, salgas, salga, salgamos, salgáis, salgan**
    (g) **saldré, saldrás, saldrá, saldremos, saldréis, saldrán**

§66 **segar:** combination of §2 and §44
    (c) **siega,** segad
    (d) **siego, siegas, siega,** segamos, segáis, **siegan**
    (e) **siegue, siegues, siegue, seguemos, seguéis, sieguen**
    (h) **segué,** segaste, segó, segamos, segasteis, segaron

§67 **seguir:** combination of §29 and §50
    (a) **siguiendo**
    (c) **sigue,** seguid
    (d) **sigo, siegues, sigue,** seguimos, seguís, **siguen**
    (e) **siga, sigas, siga, sigamos, sigáis, sigan**
    (h) seguí, seguiste, **siguió,** seguimos, seguisteis, **siguieron**

§68 sentir
(a) **sintiendo**
(c) **siente**, šentid
(d) **siento, sientes, siente**, sentimos, sentís, **sienten**
(e) **sienta, sientas, sienta, sintamos, sintáis, sientan**
(h) sentí, sentiste, **sintió**, sentimos, sentisteis, **sintieron**

§69 ser
(c) **sé**, sed
(d) **soy, eres, es, somos, sois, son**
(e) **sea, seas, sea, seamos, seáis, sean**
(f) **era, eras, era, éramos, erais, eran**
(h) **fui, fuiste, fue, fuimos, fuisteis, fueron**

§70 tañer
(a) **tañendo**
(h) tañí, tañiste, **tañó**, tañimos, tañisteis, **tañeron**

§71 tener
(c) **ten**, tened
(d) **tengo, tienes, tiene**, tenemos, tenéis, **tienen**
(e) **tenga, tengas, tenga, tengamos, tengáis, tengan**
(g) **tendré, tendrás, tendrá, tendremos, tendréis, tendrán**
(h) **tuve, tuviste, tuvo, tuvimos, tuvisteis, tuvieron**

§72 teñir: combination of §12 and §50
(a) **tiñendo**
(c) **tiñe**, teñid
(d) **tiño, tiñes, tiñe**, teñimos, teñis, **tiñen**
(e) **tiña, tiñas, tiña, tiñamos, tiñáis, tiñan**
(h) teñi, teñiste, **tiñó**, teñimos, teñisteis, **tiñeron**

§73 tocar
(e) **toque, toques, toque, toquemos, toquéis, toquen**
(h) **toqué**, tocaste, tocó, tocamos, tocasteis, tocaron

§74 torcer: combination of §47 and §78
(c) **tuerce**, torced
(d) **tuerzo, tuerces, tuerce**, torcemos, torcéis, **tuercen**
(e) **tuerza, tuerzas, tuerza, torzamos, torzáis, tuerzan**

§75 traer
(a) **trayendo**
(b) **traído**
(d) **traigo**, traes, trae, traemos, traéis, traen
(e) **traiga, traigas, traiga, traigamos, traigáis, traigan**
(h) **traje, trajiste, trajo, trajimos, trajisteis, trajeron**

§76 valer
(d) **valgo**, vales, vale, valemos, valéis, valen
(e) **valga, valgas, valga, valgamos, valgáis, valgan**
(g) **valdré, valdrás, valdrá, valdremos, valdréis, valdrán**

§77 variar
(c) **varía**, variad
(d) **varío, varías, varía**, variamos, variáis, **varían**
(e) **varíe, varíes, varíe**, variemos, variéis, **varíen**

§78 vencer
(d) **venzo**, vences, vence, vencemos, vencéis, vencen
(e) **venza, venzas, venza, venzamos, venzáis, venzan**

§79 venir
(a) **viniendo**
(c) **ven**, venid
(d) **vengo, vienes, viene**, venimos, venís, **vienen**
(e) **venga, vengas, venga, vengamos, vengáis, vengan**

(g) **vendré, vendrás, vendrá, vendremos, vendréis, vendrán**
(h) **vine, viniste, vino, vinimos, vinisteis, vinieron**

§80 **ver**
(b) **visto**
(d) **veo,** ves. ve, vemos, veis. ven
(e) **vea, veas, vea, veamos, veáis, vean**
(f) **veía, veías, veía, veíamos, veíais, veían**

§81 **volcar:** combination of **§61** and **§73**
(c) **vuelca,** volcad
(d) **vuelco, vuelcas, vuelca,** volcamos. volcáis. **vuelcan**
(e) **vuelque, vuelques, vuelque, volquemos, volquéis, vuelquen**
(h) **volqué,** volcaste. volcó, volcamos. volcasteis. volcaron

§82 **yacer**
(c) **yaz** (or yace), yaced
(d) **yazco (yazgo,** or **yago).** yaces. yace. yacemos. yacéis, yacen
(e) **yazca (yazga,** or **yaga). yazcas, yazca, yazcamos, yazcáis, yazcan**

§83 The following verbs. some of which are included in the foregoing table. and their compounds have irregular past participles:

abrir	hacer	escrito	poner	ver	podrido
cubrir	imprimir	frito	proveer	volver	roto
decir	abierto	hecho	pudrir	muerto	suelto
escribir	cubierto	impreso	romper	puesto	visto
freír	dicho	morir	solver	provisto	vuelto

English-Spanish
Inglés-Español

A, a [e] primera letra del alfabeto inglés

a [e] *art indef* un

aback [ə'bæk] *adv* atrás; **to be taken aback** quedar desconcertado; **to take aback** desconcertar

abaft [ə'bæft] *adv* a popa, en popa; *prep* detrás de

abandon [ə'bændən] *s* abandono ‖ *tr* abandonar

abandonment [ə'bændənmənt] *s* abandono, abandonamiento; desembarazo

abase [ə'bes] *tr* degradar, humillar

abash [ə'bæʃ] *tr* avergonzar

abashed [ə'bæʃt] *adj* avergonzado; humillado

abate [ə'bet] *tr* disminuir, reducir; deducir ‖ *intr* disminuir, moderarse

aba·tis ['æbətɪs] *s* (*pl* **-tis**) abatida

abattoir ['æbə,twar] *s* matadero

abba·cy ['æbəsi] *s* (*pl* **-cies**) abadía

abbess ['æbɪs] *s* abadesa

abbey ['æbi] *s* abadía

abbot ['æbət] *s* abad *m*

abbreviate [ə'brivi,et] *tr* abreviar

abbreviation [ə,brivi'eʃən] *s* (*shortening*) abreviación; (*shortened form*) abreviatura

A B C [,e,bi'si] *s* abecé *m*; **A B C's** abecedario

abdicate ['æbdɪ,ket] *tr* & *intr* abdicar

abdomen ['æbdəmən] o [æb'domən] *s* abdomen *m*

abduct [æb'dʌkt] *tr* raptar, secuestrar

abduction [æb'dʌkʃən] *s* rapto; secuestro

abed [ə'bɛd] *adv* en cama, acostado

aberration [,æbɛ'reʃən] *s* aberración; (*mind*) extravío

abet [ə'bɛt] *v* (*pret* & *pp* **abetted**; *ger* **abetting**) *tr* incitar (*a una persona, esp. al mal*); fomentar (*el crimen*)

abeyance [ə'be·əns] *s* suspensión; **in abeyance** en suspenso

ab·hor [æb'hɔr] *v* (*pret* & *pp* **-horred**; *ger* **-horring**) *tr* aborrecer, detestar

abhorrence [əb'hɔrəns] *s* aversión; aborrecimiento

abhorrent [æb'hɔrənt] *adj* aborrecible, detestable

abide [ə'baɪd] *v* (*pret* & *pp* **abode** o **abided**) *tr* esperar; tolerar ‖ *intr* permanecer; **to abide by** cumplir con; atenerse a

abili·ty [ə'bɪlɪti] *s* (*pl* **-ties**) habilidad, capacidad; talento

abject [æb'dʒɛkt] *adj* abyecto, servil

abjure [æb'dʒur] *tr* abjurar

ablative ['æblətɪv] *s* ablativo

ablaut ['æblaut] *s* apofonía

ablaze [ə'blez] *adj* brillante; ardiente; encolerizado ‖ *adv* en llamas, ardiendo

able ['ebəl] *adj* hábil, capaz; **to be able to** poder

able-bodied ['ebəl'bɑdid] *adj* sano; fornido; experto

abloom [ə'blum] *adj* floreciente ‖ *adv* en flor

abnormal [æb'nɔrməl] *adj* anormal

aboard [ə'bord] *adv* a bordo; al bordo; **all aboard!** ¡señores viajeros al tren!; **to go aboard** ir a bordo; **to take aboard** embarcar ‖ *prep* a bordo de; (*a train*) en

abode [ə'bod] *s* domicilio, residencia

abolish [ə'bɑlɪʃ] *tr* eliminar, suprimir

abolition [,æbə'lɪʃən] *s* abolición

A-bomb ['e,bɑm] *s* bomba atómica

abominable [ə'bɑmɪnəbəl] *adj* abominable

abomination [ə,bɑmɪ'neʃən] *s* abominación

aborigines [,æbə'rɪdʒɪ,niz] *spl* aborígenes *mf*

abort [ə'bɔrt] *tr* & *intr* abortar

abortion [ə'bɔrʃən] *s* aborto

abortionist [ə'bɔrʃənɪst] *s* abortista *mf*

abound [ə'baund] *intr* abundar

about [ə'baut] *adv* casi; aquí; **to be about to** estar a punto de, estar para ‖ *prep* acerca de; con respecto a; cerca de; hacia, a eso de; **to be about** tratar de

above [ə'bʌv] *adj* antedicho ‖ *adv* arriba, encima ‖ *prep* sobre, encima de, más alto que; superior a; **above all** sobre todo

above-mentioned [ə'bʌv'mɛnʃənd] *adj* sobredicho, antedicho, susodicho, prenombrado

abrasive [ə'bresɪv] o [ə'brezɪv] *adj* & *s* abrasivo

abreast [ə'brɛst] *adj* & *adv* de frente; **to be abreast of** correr parejas con; estar al corriente de

abridge [ə'brɪdʒ] *tr* abreviar; disminuir; condensar, resumir

abroad [ə'brɔd] *adv* al extranjero; en el extranjero; fuera de casa

abrupt [ə'brʌpt] *adj* brusco; repentino; áspero; abrupto, escarpado

abscess ['æbsɛs] *s* absceso

abscond [æb'skɑnd] *intr* irse a hurtadillas; **to abscond with** alzarse con

absence ['æbsəns] *s* ausencia

absent ['æbsənt] *adj* ausente ‖ [æb'sɛnt] *tr*— **to absent oneself** ausentarse

absentee [,æbsən`ti] s ausente *mf*

absent-minded [`æbsənt`maındıd] *adj* distraído, absorto

absinth [`æbsınθ] s (*plant*) absintio, ajenjo; (*drink*) absenta, ajenjo

absolute [`æbsə,lut] *adj* & s absoluto

absolutely `æbsə,lutli] *adv* absolutamente ‖ [,æbsə`lutli] *adv* (coll) positivamente

absolution [`æbsə`luʃən] s absolución

absolve [æb`salv] *tr* absolver

absorb [æb`sɔrb] *tr* absorber; **to be** or **become absorbed** ensimismarse

absorbent [æb`sɔrbənt] *adj* absorbente; (*cotton*) hidrófilo

absorbing [æb`sɔrbıŋ] *adj* absorbente

absorption [æb`sɔrpʃən] s abstracción; embebecimiento; absorción

abstain [æb`sten] *intr* abstenerse

abstemious [æb`stimı•əs] *adj* abstemio, sobrio

abstinent [`æbstınənt] *adj* abstinente

abstract [`æbstrækt] *adj* abstracto ‖ s resumen *m*, sumario, extracto ‖ *tr* resumir, compendiar, extractar ‖ [æb`strækt] *tr* abstraer; quitar

abstruse [æb`strus] *adj* abstruso

absurd [æb`sʌrd] o [æb`zʌrd] *adj* absurdo

absurdi•ty [æb`sʌrdıti] o [æb`zʌrdıti] s (*pl* **-ties**) absurdidad, absurdo

abundance [ə`bʌndəns] s abundancia, copia; (CAm) bastedad

abundant [ə`bʌndənt] *adj* abundante

abuse [ə`bjus] s maltrato; injuria, insulto; (*bad practice; injustice*) abuso ‖ [ə`bjuz] *tr* maltratar; injuriar, insultar; (*to misapply, take unfair advantage of*) abusar de

abusive [ə`bjusıv] *adj* injurioso, insultante; abusivo

abut [ə`bʌt] *v* (*pret* & *pp* **abutted;** *ger* **abutting**) *intr*—**to abut on** confinar con, terminar en

abutment [ə`bʌtmənt] s confinamiento; estribo, contrafuerte *m*

abyss [ə`bıs] s abismo

academic [,ækə`dɛmık] *adj* académico

academic costume s toga, traje *m* de catedrático

academic freedom s libertad de cátedra, libertad de enseñanza

academician [ə,kædə`mıʃən] s académico

academic subjects *spl* materias no profesionales

academic year s año escolar

acade•my [ə`kædəmi] s (*pl* **-mies**) academia

accede [æk`sid] *intr* acceder; **to accede to** acceder a, condescender a; (*e.g., the throne*) ascender a, subir a

accelerate [æk`sɛlə,ret] *tr* acelerar ‖ *intr* acelerarse

accelerator [æk`sɛlə,retər] s acelerador *m*

accent [`æksɛnt] s acento ‖ [`æksɛnt] o [æk`sɛnt] *tr* acentuar

accent mark s acento ortográfico

accentuate [æk`sɛntʃʊ,et] *tr* acentuar

accept [æk`sɛpt] *tr* aceptar

acceptable [æk`sɛptəbəl] *adj* aceptable

acceptance [æk`sɛptəns] s aceptación

access [`æksɛs] s acceso

accessible [æk`sɛsıbəl] *adj* accesible

accession [æk`sɛʃən] s accesión; (*to a dignity*) ascenso; (*of books in a library*) adquisición

accesso•ry [æk`sɛsəri] *adj* accesorio ‖ s (*pl* **-ries**) accesorio; (*to a crime*) cómplice *mf*

accident [`æksıdənt] s accidente *m*; **by accident** por casualidad

accidental [,æksı`dɛntəl] *adj* accidental

acclaim [ə`klem] s aclamación ‖ *tr* & *intr* aclamar

acclimate [`æklı,met] *tr* aclimatar ‖ *intr* aclimatarse

accolade [,ækə`led] s acolada; elogio, premio

accommodate [ə`kamə,det] *tr* acomodar; alojar

accommodating [ə`kamə,detıŋ] *adj* acomodadizo, servicial

accommodation [ə,kamə`deʃən] s acomodación; **accommodations** facilidades, comodidades; (*in a train*) localidad; (*in a hotel*) alojamiento

accommodation train s tren *m* omnibus

accompaniment [ə`kʌmpənımənt] s acompañamiento

accompanist [ə`kʌmpənıst] s acompañante *m*

accompa•ny [ə`kʌmpəni] *v* (*pret* & *pp* **-nied**) *tr* acompañar

accomplice [ə`kamplıs] s cómplice *mf*, codelincuente *mf*

accomplish [ə`kamplıʃ] *tr* realizar, llevar a cabo

accomplished [ə`kamplıʃt] *adj* realizado; culto, talentoso; (*fact*) consumado

accomplishment [ə`kamplıʃmənt] s realización; **accomplishments** prendas, talentos

accord [ə`kɔrd] s acuerdo; **in accord with** de acuerdo con: **of one's own accord** de buen grado, voluntariamente; **with one accord** de común acuerdo ‖ *tr* conceder, otorgar ‖ *intr* concordar, avenirse

accordance [ə`kɔrdəns] s conformidad; **in accordance with** de acuerdo con

according [ə`kɔrdıŋ] *adj* — **according as** según que; **according to** según

accordingly [ə`kɔrdıŋli] *adv* en conformidad; por consiguiente

accordion [ə`kɔrdı•ən] s acordeón *m*; filarmónica (Mex)

accost [ə`kɔst] o [ə`kast] *tr* abordar, acercarse a

accouchement [ə`kuʃmənt] s alumbramiento, parto

accoucheur [,æku`ʃʌr] s comadrón *m*

accoucheuse [,æku`ʃuz] s comadrona

account [ə`kaunt] s informe *m*, relato; cuenta; estado de cuenta; importancia; **by all accounts** según el decir general; **of no account** de poca importancia; **on account** como paga y señal; **on account of** a causa de; **to bring to account** pedir cuentas a; **to buy on account** comprar a plazos; **to turn to account** sacar provecho de, hacer valer

|| *intr*—**to account for** explicar; responder de

accountable [əˈkaʊntəbəl] *adj* responsable; explicable

accountant [əˈkaʊntənt] *s* contador *m*, contable *m*

accounting [əˈkaʊntɪŋ] *s* arreglo de cuentas; contabilidad

accouterments [əˈkutərmənts] *spl* equipo, avíos

accredit [əˈkrɛdɪt] *tr* acreditar

accrue [əˈkru] *intr* acumularse; resultar

acct. *abbr* **account**

accumulate [əˈkjumjə,let] *tr* acumular || *intr* acumularse

accuracy [ˈækjərəsi] *s* exactitud, precisión

accurate [ˈækjərɪt] *adj* exacto

accusation [,ækjəˈzeʃən] *s* acusación

accusative [əˈkjuzətɪv] *adj & s* acusativo

accuse [əˈkjuz] *tr* acusar

accustom [əˈkʌstəm] *tr* acostumbrar

ace [es] *s* as *m*; **to be within an ace of** estar a dos dedos de

acetate [ˈæsɪ,tet] *s* acetato

acetic acid [əˈsitɪk] *s* ácido acético

aceti•fy [əˈsɛtɪ,faɪ] *v* (*pret & pp* **-fied**) *tr* acetificar || *intr* acetificarse

acetone [ˈæsɪ,ton] *s* acetona

acetylene [əˈsɛtɪ,lin] *s* acetileno

acetylene torch *s* soplete oxiacetilénico

ache [ek] *s* achaque *m*, dolor *m* || *int* doler

achieve [əˈtʃiv] *tr* llevar a cabo; alcanzar, ganar, lograr

achievement [əˈtʃivmənt] *s* realización; (*feat*) hazaña

Achilles' heel [əˈkɪliz] *s* talón *m* de Aquiles

acid [ˈæsɪd] *adj* ácido; agrio, mordaz || *s* ácido

acidi•fy [əˈsɪdɪ,faɪ] *v* (*pret & pp* **-fied**) *tr* acidificar || *intr* acidificarse

acidi•ty [əˈsɪdɪti] *s* (*pl* **-ties**) acidez *f*

acid rain *s* lluvia ácida

acid test *s* prueba decisiva

ack•ack [ˈækˈæk] *s* (slang) artillería antiaérea; (slang) fuego antiaéreo

acknowledge [ækˈnɑlɪdʒ] *tr* reconocer; acusar (*recibo de una carta*); agradecer (*p.ej.*, *un favor*)

acknowledgment [ækˈnɑlɪdʒmənt] *s* reconocimiento; (*of receipt of a letter*) acuse *m*; (*of a favor*) agradecimiento

acme [ˈækmi] *s* auge *m*, colmo

acne [ˈækni] *s* acne *f*

acolyte [ˈækə,laɪt] *s* acólito

acorn [ˈekɔrn] o [ˈekərn] *s* bellota

acoustic [əˈkustɪk] *adj* acústico || **acoustics** *ssg* acústica

acquaint [əˈkwent] *tr* informar, poner al corriente; **to be acquainted** conocerse; **to be acquainted with** conocer; estar al corriente de

acquaintance [əˈkwentəns] *s* conocimiento; (*person*) conocido

acquiesce [,ækwiˈɛs] *intr* consentir, condescender, asentir

acquiescence [,ækwiˈɛsəns] *s* consentimiento, condescendencia, aquiescencia

acquire [əˈkwaɪr] *tr* adquirir

acquired im•mune'-de•fi'cien•cy syndrome (AIDS) *s* síndrome *m* de inmunidad deficiente adquirida (SIDA)

acquired taste *s* gusto adquirido

acquisition [,ækwɪˈzɪʃən] *s* adquisición

acquit [əˈkwɪt] *v* (*pret & pp* **acquitted;** *ger* **acquitting**) *tr* absolver, exculpar; **to acquit oneself** conducirse, portarse

acquittal [əˈkwɪtəl] *s* absolución, exculpación

acrid [ˈækrɪd] *adj* acre, acrimonioso

acrobat [ˈækrə,bæt] *s* acróbata *mf*

acrobatic [,ækrəˈbætɪk] *adj* acrobático || **acrobatics** *ssg* (*profession*) acrobatismo; *spl* (*stunts*) acrobacia

acronym [ˈækrənɪm] *s* acrónimo

acropolis [əˈkrɑpəlɪs] *s* acrópolis *f*

across [əˈkrɔs] o [əˈkrɑs] *prep* al través de; al otro lado de; **to come across** encontrarse con; **to go across** atravesar

across'-the-board' *adj* comprensivo, general

acrostic [əˈkrɔstɪk] o [əˈkrɑstɪk] *s* acróstico

act [ækt] *s* acto; (law) decreto; **in the act** en flagrante || *tr* representar; desempeñar (*un papel*); **to act the fool** hacer el bufón; **to act the part of** hacer o desempeñar el papel de || *intr* actuar; funcionar, obrar; conducirse; **to act as if** hacer como que; **to act for** representar; **to act up** travesear; **to act up to** hacer fiestas a

acting [ˈæktɪŋ] *adj* interino || *s* actuación

action [ˈækʃən] *s* acción; **to take action** tomar medidas

activate [ˈæktɪ,vet] *tr* activar

active [ˈæktɪv] *adj* activo

activi•ty [ækˈtɪvɪti] *s* (*pl* **-ties**) actividad

act of God *s* fuerza mayor

actor [ˈæktər] *s* actor *m*

actress [ˈæktrɪs] *s* actriz *f*

actual [ˈæktʃʊ•əl] *adj* real, efectivo

actually [ˈæktʃʊ•əli] *adv* en realidad

actuar•y [ˈæktʃʊ,ɛri] *s* (*pl* **-ies**) actuario (de seguros)

actuate [ˈæktʃʊ,et] *tr* actuar; estimular, mover

acuity [əˈkju•ɪti] *s* agudeza

acumen [əˈkjumən] *s* cacumen *m*, perspicacia

acupuncture [ˈækjə,pʌŋktʃər] *s* acupuntura

acute [əˈkjut] *adj* agudo

A.D. *abbr* **anno Domini** (Lat) **in the year of our Lord**

ad [æd] *s* (coll) anuncio

adage [ˈædɪdʒ] *s* adagio, refrán *m*

Adam [ˈædəm] *s* Adán *m*; **the old Adam** la inclinación al pecado

adamant [ˈædəmənt] *adj* firme, inexorable

Adam's apple *s* nuez *f*

adapt [əˈdæpt] *tr* adaptar; refundir (*un drama*)

adaptation [,ædæpˈteʃən] *s* adaptación; (*of a play*) refundición

add [æd] *tr* agregar, añadir; sumar || *intr* sumar; **to add up to** subir a; (coll) querer decir

added line *s* (mus) línea suplementaria

adder [ˈædər] s víbora; serpiente f
addict [ˈædɪkt] s enviciado; adicto, partidario ‖ [əˈdɪkt] tr enviciar; entregar; **to addict oneself to** enviciarse con o en; entregarse a
addiction [əˈdɪkʃən] s enviciamiento; adhesividad
adding machine s sumadora, máquina de sumar
addition [əˈdɪʃən] s adición; **in addition** de pilón; **in addition to** además de
additive [ˈædɪtɪv] adj & s aditivo
address [əˈdrɛs] o [ˈædrɛs] s dirección; consignación ‖ [əˈdrɛs] s alocución, discurso; **to deliver an address** hacer uso de la palabra ‖ tr dirigirse a; dirigir (p.ej., una alocución, una carta); consignar
addressee [ˌædrɛˈsi] s destinatario; (com) consignatario
addressing machine s máquina para dirigir sobres
adduce [əˈdjus] o [əˈdus] tr aducir
adenoids [ˈædəˌnɔɪdz] spl vegetaciones adenoides
adept [əˈdɛpt] adj & s experto, perito
adequate [ˈædɪkwɪt] adj suficiente
adhere [ædˈhɪr] intr adherir, adherirse; conformarse
adherence [ædˈhɪrəns] s adhesión
adherent [ædˈhɪrənt] adj & s adherente m
adhesion [ædˈhiʒən] s (sticking) adherencia; (support, loyalty) adhesión; (pathol) adherencia; (phys) adherencia o adhesión
adhesive [ædˈhisɪv] adj adhesivo
adhesive tape s tafetán adhesivo
adieu [əˈdju] o [əˈdu] interj ¡adiós! ‖ s (pl **adieus** o **adieux**) adiós m; **to bid adieu to** desperdirse de
adjacent [əˈdʒesənt] adj adyacente
adjective [ˈædʒɪktɪv] adj & s adjetivo
adjoin [əˈdʒɔɪn] tr lindar con ‖ intr colindar
adjoining [əˈdʒɔɪnɪŋ] adj colindante, contiguo
adjourn [əˈdʒʌrn] tr prorrogar, suspender ‖ intr prorrogarse, suspenderse; (coll) ir
adjournment [əˈdʒʌrnmənt] s prorrogación, suspensión
adjust [əˈdʒʌst] tr ajustar, arreglar; corregir, verificar; (ins) liquidar
adjustable [əˈdʒʌstəbəl] adj ajustable, arreglable
adjustment [əˈdʒʌstmənt] s ajuste m, arreglo; (ins) liquidación de la avería
adjutant [ˈædʒətənt] s ayudante m
ad-lib [ˌædˈlɪb] v (pret & pp **-libbed**; ger **-libbing**) tr & intr improvisar
Adm. abbr **Admiral**
administer [ædˈmɪnɪstər] tr administrar; **to administer an oath** tomar juramento ‖ intr — **to administer to** cuidar de
administrator [ædˈmɪnɪsˌtretər] s administrador m
admiral [ˈædmɪrəl] s almirante m; buque m almirante
admiral·ty [ˈædmɪrəlti] s (pl **-ties**) almirantazgo
admire [ædˈmaɪr] tr admirar

admirer [ædˈmaɪrər] s admirador m; enamorado
admissible [ædˈmɪsɪbəl] adj admisible
admission [ædˈmɪʃən] s admisión; (in a school) ingreso; (reception) recibida; precio de entrada; **to gain admission** lograr entrar
ad·mit [ædˈmɪt] v (pret & pp **-mitted**; ger **-mitting**) tr admitir ‖ intr dar entrada; **to admit of** admitir, permitir
admittance [ædˈmɪtəns] s admisión; derecho de entrar; **no admittance** acceso prohibido, se prohibe la entrada
admonish [ædˈmɑnɪʃ] tr amonestar
ado [əˈdu] s bulla, excitación
adobe [əˈdobi] s adobe m; casa de adobe
adolescence [ˌædəˈlɛsəns] s adolescencia
adolescent [ˌædəˈlɛsənt] adj & s adolescente mf
adopt [əˈdɑpt] tr adoptar
adoption [əˈdɑpʃən] s adopción
adorable [əˈdorəbəl] adj adorable
adore [əˈdor] tr adorar
adorn [əˈdorn] tr adornar
adornment [əˈdornmənt] s adorno
adrenal gland [ædˈrinəl] s glándula suprarrenal
Adriatic [ˌedrɪˈætɪk] adj & s Adriático
adrift [əˈdrɪft] adj & adv al garete, a la deriva
adroit [əˈdrɔɪt] adj diestro
adult [əˈdʌlt] o [ˈædʌlt] adj & s adulto
adulterate [əˈdʌltəˌret] tr adulterar
adulterer [əˈdʌltərər] s adúltero
adulteress [əˈdʌltərɪs] s adúltera
adulter·y [əˈdʌltəri] s (pl **-ies**) adulterio
adulthood [əˈdʌltˌhud] s adultez f
advance [ædˈvæns] adj adelantado; anticipado ‖ s adelanto, avance m; aumento, subida; **advances** propuestas; requerimiento amoroso; propuesta indecente; préstamo; **in advance** de antemano, por anticipado ‖ tr adelantar ‖ intr adelantar; adelantarse
advanced [ædˈvænst] adj avanzado; **advanced in years** avanzado de edad, entrado en años
advanced standing s traspaso de matrículas, traspaso de crédito académico
advanced studies spl altos estudios
advancement [ædˈvænsmənt] s adelanto, avance m; subida; promoción
advance publicity s publicidad de lanzamiento
advantage [ædˈvæntɪdʒ] s ventaja; lasca; **to take advantage of** aprovecharse de; abusar de, engañar
advantageous [ˌædvənˈtedʒəs] adj ventajoso
advent [ˈædvɛnt] s advenimiento ‖ **Advent** s (eccl) Adviento
adventure [ædˈvɛntʃər] s aventura ‖ tr aventurar ‖ intr aventurarse
adventurer [ædˈvɛntʃərər] s aventurero
adventuresome [ædˈvɛntʃərsəm] adj aventurero
adventuress [ædˈvɛntʃərɪs] s aventurera
adventurous [ædˈvɛntʃərəs] adj aventurero

adverb [ˈædvʌrb] *s* adverbio

adversar·y [ˈædvər,sɛri] *s* (*pl* **-ies**) adversario

adversi·ty [ædˈvʌrsiti] *s* (*pl* **-ties**) adversidad

advertise [ˈædvər,taiz] *tr & intr* anunciar

advertisement [,ædvərˈtaizmənt] o [ædˈvʌrtizmənt] *s* anuncio

advertiser [ˈædvər,taizər] *s* anunciante *mf*

advertising [ˈædvər,taiziŋ] *s* propaganda, publicidad, anuncios; reclame *m & f*

advertising agency *s* empresa anunciadora

advertising campaign *s* campaña de publicidad

advertising man *s* empresario de publicidad

advertising manager *s* gerente *m* de publicidad

advice [ædˈvais] *s* consejo; aviso, noticia; **a piece of advice** un consejo

advisable [ædˈvaizəbəl] *adj* aconsejable

advise [ædˈvaiz] *tr* aconsejar, asesorar; advertir, avisar

advisement [ædˈvaizmənt] *s* consideración; **to take under advisement** someter a consideración

advisory [ædˈvaizəri] *adj* consultivo

advocate [ˈædvə,ket] *s* defensor *m*; abogado ‖ *tr* abogar por

Aegean Sea [iˈdʒiən] *s* Archipiélago; (*of the ancients*) mar Egeo

aegis [ˈidʒis] *s* égida

aerate [ˈɛret] o [ˈeə,ret] *tr* airear

aerial [ˈɛriəl] *adj* aéreo ‖ *s* antena

aerialist [ˈɛri·əlist] *s* volatinero

aerial photograph *s* fotografía aérea

aerodrome [ˈɛrə,drom] *s* aeródromo

aerodynamic [,ɛrodaiˈnæmik] *adj* aerodinámico ‖ **aerodynamics** *ssg* aerodinámica

aeronaut [ˈɛrə,nɔt] *s* aeronauta *mf*

aeronautic [,ɛrəˈnɔtik] *adj* aeronáutico ‖ **aeronautics** *ssg* aeronáutica

aerosol [ˈɛrə,sol] *s* aerosol *m*

aerospace [ˈɛro,spes] *adj* aeroespacial

aesthete [ˈɛsθit] *s* esteta *mf*

aesthetic [ɛsˈθɛtik] *adj* estético ‖ **aesthetics** *ssg* estética

afar [əˈfar] *adv* lejos

affable [ˈæfəbəl] *adj* afable

affair [əˈfɛr] *s* asunto, negocio; lance *m*; amorío; encuentro, combate *m*; **affairs** negocios

affect [əˈfɛkt] *tr* influir en; impresionar, enternecer; (*to assume; to pretend*) afectar; aficionarse a

affectation [,æfɛkˈteʃən] *s* afectación

affected [əˈfɛktid] *adj* afectado

affection [əˈfɛkʃən] *s* afecto, cariño, afección; (pathol) afección

affectionate [əˈfɛkʃənit] *adj* afectuoso, cariñoso

affidavit [,æfiˈdevit] *s* declaración jurada, acta notarial

affiliate [əˈfili,et] *adj* afiliado ‖ *s* afiliado; filial *f* ‖ *tr* afiliar ‖ *intr* afiliarse

affini·ty [əˈfiniti] *s* (*pl* **-ties**) afinidad

affirm [əˈfʌrm] *tr & intr* afirmar

affirmative [əˈfʌrmətiv] *adj* afirmativo ‖ *s* afirmativa

affix [ˈæfiks] *s* añadidura; (gram) afijo ‖ [əˈfiks] *tr* añadir; atribuir (*p.ej.*, *culpa*); poner (*una firma, sello, etc.*)

afflict [əˈflikt] *tr* afligir; **to be afflicted with** sufrir de, adolecer de

affliction [əˈflikʃən] *s* aflicción, desgracia; achaque *m*

affluence [ˈæflu·əns] *s* (*abundance*) afluencia; (*wealth*) opulencia

afford [əˈford] *tr* proporcionar; **to be able to afford (to)** poder darse el lujo de, poder permitirse

affray [əˈfre] *s* pendencia, riña

affront [əˈfrʌnt] *s* afrenta ‖ *tr* afrentar

Afghan [ˈæfgæn] *adj & s* afgano

Afghanistan [æfˈgæni,stæn] *s* el Afganistán

afire [əˈfair] *adj & adv* ardiendo

aflame [əˈflem] *adj & adv* en llamas

afloat [əˈflot] *adj & adv* a flote; a bordo; inundado; sin rumbo; (*rumor*) en circulación

afoot [əˈfut] *adj & adv* a pie; en marcha

afoul [əˈfaul] *adj & adv* enredado; en colisión; **to run afoul of** enredarse con

afraid [əˈfred] *adj* asustado; **to be afraid** tener miedo

Africa [ˈæfrikə] *s* Africa

African [ˈæfrikən] *adj & s* africano

aft [æft] *adj & adv* en popa

after [ˈæftər] *adj* siguiente ‖ *adv* después ‖ *prep* después de; según; **after all** al fin y al cabo ‖ *conj* después de que

af·ter-din·ner speaker *s* orador *m* de sobremesa

after-dinner speech *s* discurso de sobremesa

af·ter-hours· *adv* después del trabajo

af·ter-life· *s* vida venidera; resto de la vida

aftermath [ˈæftər,mæθ] *s* segunda siega; consecuencias, consecuencias desastrosas

af·ter·noon· *s* tarde *f*

af·ter-shave· lotion *s* loción facial

af·ter-taste· *s* dejo, gustillo, resabio

af·ter-thought· *s* idea tardía, expediente tardío

afterward [ˈæftəwərd] *adv* después, luego

af·ter-while· *adv* dentro de poco

again [əˈgɛn] *adv* otra vez, de nuevo; además; **to + inf + again** volver a + *inf*, p.ej., **he will come again** volverá a venir

against [əˈgɛnst] *prep* contra; cerca de; en contraste con; por; para

agape [əˈgep] *adj* abierto de par en par ‖ *adv* con la boca abierta

agave [əˈgavi] *s* agave *f*

agave brandy *s* pulque *m* (Mex)

agave liquor *s* mexcal *m*, mezcal *m*

age [edʒ] *s* edad; (*old age*) vejez *f*; (*one hundred years; a long time*) siglo; edad mental; **of age** mayor de edad; **to come of age** alcanzar su mayoría de edad, llegar a mayor edad; **under age** menor de edad ‖ *tr* envejecer ‖ *intr* envejecer, envejecerse

age bracket *s* grupo de personas de la misma edad

aged [edʒd] *adj* de la edad de ‖ [ˈedʒid] *adj* anciano, viejo

ageism [ˈedʒɪzəm] s discriminación contra los ancianos

ageless [ˈedʒlɪs] adj eternamente joven

agen•cy [ˈedʒənsi] s (pl -cies) agencia; mediación

agenda [əˈdʒɛndə] s agenda, temario

agent [ˈədʒənt] s agente m

Age of Enlightenment s siglo de las luces

agglomeration [ə,glɑməˈreʃən] s aglomeración

aggrandizement [əˈgrændɪzmənt] s engrandecimiento

aggravate [ˈægrə,vet] tr agravar; (coll) exasperar, irritar

aggregate [ˈægrɪ,get] adj & s agregado ‖ tr agregar, juntar; ascender a

aggression [əˈgrɛʃən] s agresión

aggressive [əˈgrɛsɪv] adj agresivo

aggressor [əˈgrɛsər] s agresor m

aghast [əˈgæst] adj horrorizado

agile [ˈædʒɪl] adj ágil

agitate [ˈædʒɪ,tet] tr & intr agitar

aglow [əˈglo] adj & adv fulgurante

agnostic [ægˈnɑstɪk] adj & s agnóstico

ago [əˈgo] adv hace, p.ej., **two days ago** hace dos días

ago•ny [ˈægəni] s (pl -nies) angustia, congoja; (anguish; death struggle) agonía

agrarian [əˈgrɛri•ən] adj agrario ‖ s agrariense mf

agree [əˈgri] intr estar de acuerdo, ponerse de acuerdo; sentar bien; (gram) concordar

agreeable [əˈgri•əbəl] adj (to one's liking) agradable; (willing to consent) acorde, conforme

agreement [əˈgrimənt] s acuerdo, convenio; concordancia; **in agreement** de acuerdo

agric. abbr **agriculture**

agriculture [ˈægrɪ,kʌltʃər] s agricultura

agronomy [əˈgrɑnəmi] s agronomía

aground [əˈgraʊnd] adv encallado, varado; **to run aground** encallar, varar

agt. abbr **agent**

ague [ˈegju] s escalofrío; fiebre f intermitente

ahead [əˈhɛd] adj & adv delante, al frente; **ahead of** antes de; delante de; al frente de; **to get ahead (of)** adelantarse (a)

ahoy [əˈhɔɪ] interj — **ship ahoy!** ¡ah del barco!

aid [ed] s ayuda, auxilio; (mil) ayudante m ‖ tr ayudar, auxiliar; **to aid and abet** auxiliar e incitar, ser cómplice de ‖ intr ayudar

aide [ed] s ayudante m; (mil) edecán m

aide-de-camp [ˈeddəˈkæmp] s (pl **aides-de-camp**) ayudante m de campo, edecán m

AIDS [edz] abbr **acquired immune-deficiency syndrome**

ail [el] tr inquietar; **what ails you?** ¿qué tiene Vd.? ‖ intr sufrir, estar enfermo

aileron [ˈelə,rɑn] s alerón m

ailing [ˈelɪŋ] adj enfermo, achacoso

ailment [ˈelmənt] s enfermedad, achaque m

aim [em] s puntería; intento; punto de mira ‖ tr apuntar, encarar; dirigir (p.ej., una observación) ‖ intr apuntar

air [ɛr] s aire m; **by air** por vía aérea; **in the open air** al aire libre; **on the air** en antena, en la radio; **to let the air out of** desinflar; **to put on airs** darse aires; **to put on the air** llevar a las antenas; **to walk on air** no pisar en el suelo ‖ tr airear, ventilar; radiodifundir; (fig) ventilar

air'-a•tom'ic adj aeroatómico

air bag s (aut) globo de aire, bolsa de aire

air'borne' adj aerotransportado

air brake s freno de aire comprimido

air castle s castillo en el aire

air'-condi'tion tr climatizar

air conditioner s acondicionador m de aire

air conditioning s acondicionamiento del aire, clima m artificial, climatización

air corps s cuerpo de aviación

air'craft' ssg máquina de volar; spl máquinas de volar

aircraft carrier s portaaviones m

airdrome [ˈɛr,drom] s aeródromo

air'drop' s lanzamiento ‖ tr lanzar

air field s campo de aviación

air'foil' s superficie f de sustentación

air force s fuerza aérea, ejército del aire

air gap s (phys) entrehierro

air'-ground' adj aeroterrestre

air hostess s aeromoza, azafata

air humidifier s humidificador m

air lane s ruta aérea

air'lift' s puente aéreo

air liner s transaéreo, avión m de travesía

air mail s correo aéreo, aeroposta

air'-mail' letter s carta aérea, carta por avión

air-mail pilot s aviador m postal

air-mail stamp s sello aéreo

air•man [ˈɛrmən] s (pl -men [mən]) aviador m

air'plane' s avión m, aparato

airplane carrier s portaaviones m

air pocket s bache aéreo

air pollution s contaminación atmosférica

air'port' s aeropuerto

air raid s ataque aéreo

air'-raid' drill s simulacro de ataque aéreo

air-raid shelter s abrigo antiaéreo

air-raid warning s alarma aérea

air rifle s escopeta de viento, escopeta de aire comprimido

air'ship' s aeronave f

air'sick' adj mareado en el aire

air'sick'ness s mal m de vuelo

air sleeve o **sock** s veleta de manga

air'strip' s pista de despegue, pista de aterrizaje

air taxi s aerotaxi m

air'tight' adj herméticamente cerrado, estanco al aire

air'-traff'ic controller s controlador aéreo

air'waves' spl ondas de radio

air'way' s aerovía, vía aérea

airway lighting s balizaje m

air•y [ˈɛri] adj (comp -ier; super -iest) airoso; aireado; alegre; impertinente; (coll) afectado

aisle [aɪl] s (in theater, movie, etc.) pasillo; (in a store, factory, etc.) nave f; (archit) nave f lateral; (any of the long passageways of a church) (archit) nave f

ajar [ə'dʒɑr] *adj* entreabierto, entornado

akimbo [ə'kɪmbo] *adj & adv* — **with arms akimbo** en jarras

akin [ə'kɪn] *adj* emparentado; semejante

alabaster ['ælə,bæstər] *s* alabastro

alarm [ə'lɑrm] *s* alarma ‖ *tr* alarmar

alarm clock *s* reloj *m* despertador

alarmist [ə'lɑrmɪst] *s* alarmista *mf*

alas [ə'læs] o [ə'lɑs] *interj* ¡ay!, ¡ay de mí!

Albanian [æl'beni•ən] *adj & s* albanés *m*

albatross ['ælbə,trɔs] o ['ælbə,trɑs] *s* albatros *m*

album ['ælbəm] *s* álbum *m*

albumen [æl'bjumən] *s* albumen *m*; albúmina

alchemy ['ælkɪmi] *s* alquimia

alcohol ['ælkə,hɔl] o ['ælkə,hɑl] *s* alcohol *m*

alcoholic [,ælkə'hɔlɪk] o [,ælkə'hɑlɪk] *adj & s* alcohólico

al'co•hol-lev'el test *s* prueba de alcohol

alcove ['ælkov] *s* gabinete *m*, rincón *m*; (*in a bedroom*) trasalcoba; (*in a garden*) cenador *m*

alder ['ɔldər] *s* aliso

alder•man ['ɔldərmən] *s* (*pl* **-men** [mən]) concejal *m*

ale [el] *s* ale *f* (*cerveza inglesa, obscura, espesa y amarga*)

alembic [ə'lɛmbɪk] *s* alambique *m*

alert [ə'lʌrt] *adj* listo, vivo; vigilante ‖ *s* (aer) alarma; (mil) alerta *m*; **to be on the alert** estar sobre aviso, estar alerta ‖ *tr* alertar

Aleutian Islands [ə'luʃən] *spl* islas Aleutas, islas Aleutianas

Alexandrine [,ælɪg'zændrɪn] *adj & s* alejandrino

alg. *abbr* **algebra**

algae ['ældʒi] *spl* algas

algebra ['ældʒɪbrə] *s* álgebra

algebraic [,ældʒɪ'bre•ɪk] *adj* algebraico

Algeria [æl'dʒɪri•ə] *s* Argelia

Algerian [æl'dʒɪri•ən] *adj & s* argelino

Algiers [æl'dʒɪrz] *s* Argel *f*

alias ['eli•əs] *adv* alias ‖ *s* alias *m*, nombre supuesto

ali•bi ['ælɪ,baɪ] *s* (*pl* **-bis**) coartada; (coll) excusa

alien ['eli•ən] *adj & s* extranjero

alienate ['eljə,net] o ['eli•ə,net] *tr* enajenar, alienar; desenamorar

alight [ə'laɪt] *v* (*pret & pp* **alighted** o **alit** [ə'lɪt]) *intr* bajar, apearse; posarse (*un ave*)

align [ə'laɪn] *tr* alinear ‖ *intr* alinearse

alike [ə'laɪk] *adj* semejantes; **to look alike** parecerse ‖ *adv* igualmente

alimentary canal [,ælɪ'mɛntəri] *s* canal alimenticio, tubo digestivo

alimony ['ælɪ,moni] *s* alimentos

alive [ə'laɪv] *adj* vivo, viviente; animado; **alive to** despierto para, sensible a; **alive with** hormigueante en

alka•li ['ælkə,laɪ] *s* (*pl* **-lis** o **-lies**) álcali *m*

alkaline ['ælkə,laɪn] *adj* alcalino

all [ɔl] *adj indef* todo, todos; todo el, todos los ‖ *pron indef* todo; todos, todo el mundo; **after all** sin embargo; **all of** todo el, todos

los; **all that** todo lo que, todos los que; **for all I know** que yo sepa; a lo mejor; **not at all** nada; no hay de qué ‖ *adv* enteramente; **all along** desde el principio; a lo largo de; **all at once** de golpe; **all right** bueno, corriente; **all too** excesivamente

Allah ['ælə] *s* Alá *m*

allay [ə'le] *tr* aliviar, calmar

all-clear ['ɔl'klɪr] *s* cese *m* de alarma

allege [ə'lɛdʒ] *tr* alegar

allegiance [ə'lidʒəns] *s* fidelidad, lealtad; homenaje *m*; **to swear allegiance to** jurar fidelidad a; rendir homenaje a

allegoric(al) [,ælɪ'gɑrɪk(əl)] o [,ælɪ'gɔrɪk(əl)] *adj* alegórico

allego•ry ['ælɪ,gori] *s* (*pl* **-ries**) alegoría

aller•gy ['ælərdʒi] *s* (*pl* **-gies**) alergia

alleviate [ə'livi,et] *tr* aliviar

alleviation [ə,livi'eʃən] *s* aligeramiento

alley ['æli] *s* callejuela; paseo arbolado, paseo de jardín; (bowling) pista; (tennis) espacio lateral

All Fools' Day *s* var of **April Fools' Day**

Allhallows [,ɔl'hæloz] *s* día *m* de todos los santos

alliance [ə'laɪ•əns] *s* alianza

alligator ['ælɪ,getər] *s* caimán *m*

alligator pear *s* aguacate *m*

alligator wrench *s* llave *f* de mandíbulas dentadas

alliteration [ə,lɪtə'reʃən] *s* aliteración

all-knowing ['ɔl'no•ɪŋ] *adj* omnisciente

allocate ['ælə,ket] *tr* asignar, distribuir

allot [ə'lɑt] *v* (*pret & pp* **allotted;** *ger* **allotting**) *tr* asignar, distribuir

all'-out' *adj* acérrimo

allow [ə'laʊ] *tr* dejar, permitir; admitir; conceder ‖ *intr* — **to allow for** tener en cuenta; **to allow of** permitir; admitir

allowance [ə'laʊ•əns] *s* permiso; concesión; ración; descuento, rebaja; tolerancia; **to make allowance for** tener en cuenta

alloy ['ælɔɪ] o [ə'lɔɪ] *s* aleación, liga ‖ [ə'lɔɪ] *tr* alear, ligar

all'-pow'er•ful *adj* todopoderoso

all'-pur'pose *adj* universal, para todo uso

All Saints' Day *s* día *m* de todos los santos

All Souls' Day *s* día *m* de los difuntos

allspice ['ɔl,spaɪs] *s* pimienta inglesa

all'-star' game *s* (sport) juego de estrellas

allude [ə'lud] *intr* aludir

allure [ə'lʊr] *s* tentación, encanto, fascinación ‖ *tr* tentar, encantar

alluring [ə'lʊrɪŋ] *adj* tentador, encantador, fascinante

allusion [ə'luʒən] *s* alusión

all'-weath'er *adj* para todo tiempo

al•ly ['ælaɪ] o [ə'laɪ] *s* (*pl* **-lies**) aliado ‖ [ə'laɪ] *v* (*pret & pp* **-lied**) *tr* aliar ‖ *intr* aliarse

almanac ['ɔlmə,næk] *s* almanaque *m*

almighty [ɔl'maɪti] *adj* todopoderoso, omnipotente

almond ['ɑmənd] o ['æmənd] *s* almendra

almond brittle *s* crocante *m*

almond tree *s* almendro

almost ['ɔlmost] o [ɔl'most] *adv* casi

alms [amz] *s* limosna
alms'house' *s* casa de beneficencia
aloe [ˈælo] *s* áloe *m*
aloft [əˈlɔft] o [əˈlɑft] *adv* arriba; (aer) en vuelo; (naut) en la arboladura
alone [əˈlon] *adj* solo; **let alone** sin mencionar; y mucho menos; **to let alone** no molestar; no mezclarse en || *adv* solamente
along [əˈlɔŋ] o [əˈlɑŋ] *adv* conmigo, consigo, etc.; **all along** desde el principio; **along with** junto con || *prep* a lo largo de
along'side' *adv* a lo largo; (naut) al costado; **to bring alongside** acostar || *prep* a lo largo de; (naut) al costado de
aloof [əˈluf] *adj* apartado; reservado || *adv* lejos, a distancia
aloud [əˈlaud] *adv* alto, en voz alta
alphabet [ˈælfəˌbɛt] *s* alfabeto
alpine [ˈælpaɪn] *adj* alpestre, alpino
Alps [ælps] *spl* Alpes *mpl*
already [ɔlˈrɛdi] *adv* ya
Alsace [ælˈses] o [ˈælsæs] *s* Alsacia
Alsatian [ælˈseʃən] *adj* & *s* alsaciano
also [ˈɔlso] *adv* también
alt. *abbr* **alternate, altitude**
altar [ˈɔltər] *s* altar *m*; **to lead to the altar** conducir al altar
altar boy *s* acólito, monaguillo
altar cloth *s* sabanilla, palia
al'tar-piece' *s* retablo
altar rail *s* comulgatorio
alter [ˈɔltər] *tr* alterar || *intr* alterarse
alteration [ˌɔltəˈreʃən] *s* alteración; (*in a building*) reforma; (*in clothing*) arreglo
alternate [ˈɔltərnɪt] o [ˈæltərnɪt] *adj* alterno || [ˈɔltərˌnet] o [ˈæltərˌnet] *tr* & *intr* alternar
alternating current *s* corriente alterna o alternativa
although [ɔlˈðo] *conj* aunque
altimetry [ælˈtɪmɪtri] *s* altimetría
altitude [ˈæltɪˌtjud] *s* altitud, altura
al·to [ˈælto] *s* (*pl* **-tos**) contralto
altogether [ˌɔltəˈgɛðər] *adv* enteramente; en conjunto
altruist [ˈæltruˌɪst] *s* altruista *mf*
altruistic [ˌæltruˈɪstɪk] *adj* altruista
alum [ˈæləm] *s* alumbre *m*
aluminum [əˈlumɪnəm] *s* aluminio
alum·na [əˈlʌmnə] *s* (*pl* **-nae** [ni]) graduada
alum·nus [əˈlʌmnəs] *s* (*pl* **-ni** [naɪ]) graduado
alveo·lus [ælˈviˌələs] *s* (*pl* **-li** [ˌlaɪ]) **alvéolo**
always [ˈɔlwɪz] o [ˈɔlwez] *adv* siempre
A.M. *abbr* **ante meridiem**, i.e., **before noon; amplitude modulation**
Am. *abbr* **America, American**
amalgam [əˈmælgəm] *s* amalgama *f*
amalgamate [əˈmælgəˌmet] *tr* amalgamar || *intr* amalgamarse
amass [əˈmæs] *tr* amontonar; amasar (*dinero*)
amateur [ˈæmətʃər] *adj* & *s* chapucero, principiante *mf*; aficionado
amateur performance *s* función de aficionados
amaze [əˈmez] *tr* asombrar, maravillar

amazing [əˈmezɪŋ] *adj* asombroso, maravilloso
Amazon [ˈæməˌzɑn] *s* Amazonas *m*
ambassador [æmˈbæsədər] *s* embajador *m*
ambassadress [æmˈbæsədrɪs] *s* embajadora
amber [ˈæmbər] *adj* ambarino || *s* ámbar *m*
ambigui·ty [ˌæmbɪˈgjuˌɪti] *s* (*pl* **-ties**) ambigüedad
ambiguous [æmˈbɪgjuˌəs] *adj* ambiguo
ambition [æmˈbɪʃən] *s* ambición
ambitious [æmˈbɪʃəs] *adj* ambicioso
amble [ˈæmbəl] *s* ambladura || *intr* amblar
ambulance [ˈæmbjələns] *s* ambulancia
ambush [ˈæmbuʃ] *s* emboscada; **to lie in ambush** estar emboscado || *tr* (*to station in ambush*) emboscar; (*to lie in wait for and attack*) insidiar || *intr* emboscarse
ame·ba [əˈmibə] *s* (*pl* **-bas** o **-bae** [bi]) amiba
amelioration [əˌmiljəˈreʃən] *s* mejoramiento
amen [ˈeˈmɛn] o [ˈɑˈmɛn] *interj* ¡amén! || *s* amén *m*
amenable [əˈminəbəl] o [əˈmɛnəbəl] *adj* dócil; responsable
amend [əˈmɛnd] *tr* enmendar || *intr* enmendarse || **amends** *spl* enmienda; **to make amends for** enmendar
amendment [əˈmɛndmənt] *s* enmienda
ameni·ty [əˈmɪnɪti] o [əˈmɛnɪti] *s* (*pl* **-ties**) amenidad
America [əˈmɛrɪkə] *s* América
American [əˈmɛrɪkən] *adj* & *s* americano; norteamericano, estadounidense
Americanize [əˈmɛrɪkəˌnaɪz] *tr* americanizar
amethyst [ˈæmɪθɪst] *s* amatista
amiable [ˈemɪˌəbəl] *adj* amable, bonachón
amicable [ˈæmɪkəbəl] *adj* amigable
amid [əˈmɪd] *prep* en medio de
amidship [əˈmɪdˌʃɪp] *adv* en medio del navío
amiss [əˈmɪs] *adj* inoportuno; malo || *adv* inoportunamente; mal; **to take amiss** llevar a mal, tomar en mala parte
ami·ty [ˈæmɪti] *s* (*pl* **-ties**) amistad
ammeter [ˈæmˌmitər] *s* anmetro, amperímetro
ammonia [əˈmonɪˌə] *s* amoníaco; agua amoniacal
ammunition [ˌæmjəˈnɪʃən] *s* munición
amnes·ty [ˈæmnɪsti] *s* (*pl* **-ties**) amnistía || *v* (*pret* & *pp* **-tied**) *tr* amnistiar
amniocentesis [ˌæmnɪˈosenˈtisɪs] *s* amniocentesis *f*
amoeba [əˈmibə] *s* var of **ameba**
among [əˈmʌŋ] *prep* entre, en medio de, en el número de
amorous [ˈæmərəs] *adj* amoroso; erótico, sensual, voluptuoso
amortize [ˈæmərˌtaɪz] *tr* amortizar
amount [əˈmaunt] *s* cantidad, importe *m* || *intr* — **to amount to** ascender a; significar
amp. *abbr* **ampere, amperage**
ampere [ˈæmpɪr] *s* amperio
am'pere-hour' *s* amperio-hora *m*
amphibious [æmˈfɪbɪˌəs] *adj* anfibio
amphitheater [ˈæmfɪˌθiˌətər] *s* anfiteatro
ample [ˈæmpəl] *adj* amplio; bastante, suficiente; abundante
amplifier [ˈæmplɪˌfaɪˌər] *s* amplificador *m*

ampli·fy [`æmplɪ,faɪ] v (pret & pp **-fied**) tr amplificar ‖ intr espaciarse

amplitude [`æmplɪ,tjud] s amplitud

amplitude modulation s modulación de amplitud

ampule [`æmpjul] s inyectable m

amputate [`æmpjə,tet] tr amputar

amt. abbr **amount**

amuck [ə`mʌk] adv frenéticamente; **to run amuck** atacar a ciegas

amulet [`æmjəlɪt] s amuleto

amuse [ə`mjuz] tr divertir, entretener

amusement [ə`mjuzmənt] s diversión, entretenimiento; pasatiempo, recreación; (in a park or circus) atracción

amusement park s parque m de atracciones

amusing [ə`mjuzɪŋ] adj divertido, gracioso

an [æn] o [ən] art indef (antes de sonido vocal) un

anachronism [ə`nækrə,nɪzəm] s anacronismo

anachronistic [ə,nækrə`nɪstɪk] adj anacrónico

anaemia [ə`nimɪ·ə] s anemia

anaemic [ə`nimɪk] adj anémico

anaesthesia [,ænɪs`θiʒə] s anestesia

anaesthetic [,ænɪs`θɛtɪk] adj & s anestésico

anaesthetize [æ`nɛsθɪ,taɪz] tr anestesiar

analogous [ə`næləgəs] adj análogo

analo·gy [ə`nælədʒi] s (pl **-gies**) analogía

analyse [`ænə,laɪz] tr analizar

analy·sis [ə`nælɪsɪs] s (pl **-ses** [,siz]) análisis m & f

analyst [`ænəlɪst] s analista mf

analytic(al) [,ænə`lɪtɪk(əl)] adj analítico

analyze [`ænə,laɪz] tr analizar

anarchist [`ænərkɪst] s anarquista mf

anarchy [`ænərki] s anarquía

anathema [ə`næθɪmə] s anatema m & f

anatomic(al) [,ænə`tɑmɪk(əl)] adj anatómico

anato·my [ə`nætəmi] s (pl **-mies**) anatomía

ancestor [`ænsɛstər] s antecesor m, antepasado

ances·try [`ænsɛstri] s (pl **-tries**) abolengo, alcurnia

anchor [`æŋkər] s ancla, áncora; (fig) áncora; **to cast anchor** echar anclas; **to weigh anchor** levar anclas ‖ tr sujetar con el ancla ‖ intr anclar, ancorar

ancho·vy [`ænt/ovi] s (pl **-vies**) anchoa

ancient [`enʃənt] adj antiguo

and [ænd] o [ənd] conj y; **and so forth** y así sucesivamente

Andalusia [,ændə`luʒə] s Andalucía

Andalusian [,ændə`luʒən] adj & s andaluz m

Andean [æn`di·ən] adj & s andino

Andes [`ændiz] spl Andes mpl

andirons [`ænd,aɪ·ərnz] spl morillos

anecdote [`ænɪk,dot] s anécdota

anemia [ə`nimɪ·ə] s anemia

anemic [ə`nimɪk] adj anémico

aneroid barometer [`ænə,rɔɪd] s barómetro aneroide

anesthesia [,ænɪs`θiʒə] s anestesia

anesthetic [,ænɪs`θɛtɪk] adj & s anestésico

anesthetize [æ`nɛsθɪ,taɪz] tr anestesiar

aneurysm [`ænjə,rɪzəm] s aneurisma m

anew [ə`nju] o [ə`nu] adv de nuevo, nuevamente

angel [`endʒəl] s ángel m; (financial backer) caballo blanco

angelic(al) [æn`dʒɛlɪk(əl)] adj angélico, angelical

anger [`æŋgər] s cólera, ira ‖ tr encolerizar, airar

angina pectoris [æn`dʒainə `pɛktərɪs] s angina de pecho

angle [`æŋgəl] s ángulo; punto de vista ‖ intr pescar con caña; intrigar

angle iron s ángulo de hierro, hierro angular

angler [`æŋglər] s pescador m de caña; intrigante mf

Anglo-Saxon [,æŋglo`sæksən] adj & s anglosajón m

an·gry [`æŋgri] adj (comp **-grier**; super **-griest**) encolerizado, airado; (pathol) inflamado, irritado; **to become angry at** enojarse de; **to become angry with** enojarse con o contra

anguish [`æŋgwɪʃ] s angustia, congoja

angular [`æŋgjələr] adj angular; (features) anguloso

anhydrous [æn`haidrəs] adj anhidro

aniline dyes [`ænɪlɪn] o [`ænɪ,lain] s colores mpl de anilina

animal [`ænɪməl] adj & s animal m

animal spirits spl ardor m, vigor m, vivacidad

animated cartoon [`ænɪ,metɪd] s película de dibujos, dibujo animado

animation [,ænɪ`meʃən] s animación

animosi·ty [,ænɪ`mɑsɪti] s (pl **-ties**) animosidad

anion [`æn,aɪ·ən] s anión m

anise [`ænɪs] s anís m

aniseed [`ænɪ,sid] s grano de anís

anisette [,ænɪ`zɛt] s anisete m

ankle [`æŋkəl] s tobillo

an´kle·bone´ s hueso del tobillo

ankle support s tobillera

anklet [`æŋklɪt] s ajorca; (sock) tobillera

annals [`ænəlz] spl anales mpl

anneal [ə`nil] tr recocer

annex [`ænɛks] s anexo; (of a building) pabellón m ‖ [ə`nɛks] tr anexar

annihilate [ə`nai·ɪ,let] tr aniquilar

anniversa·ry [,ænɪ`vʌrsəri] adj aniversario ‖ s (pl **-ries**) aniversario

annotate [`ænə,tet] tr anotar

announce [ə`nauns] tr anunciar

announcement [ə`naunsmənt] s anuncio

announcer [ə`naunsər] s anunciador m; (rad) locutor m

annoy [ə`nɔɪ] tr fastidiar, molestar; majaderear; pololear; (Cuba, Mex) ciscar

annoyance [ə`nɔɪ·əns] s fastidio, molestia

annoying [ə`nɔɪ·ɪŋ] adj fastidioso, molesto

annual [`ænju·əl] adj anual ‖ s publicación anual; planta anual

annui·ty [ə`nju·ɪti] o [ə`nu·ɪti] s (pl **-ties**) anualidad; renta vitalicia

an·nul [ə`nʌl] v (pret & pp **-nulled**; ger **-nulling**) tr anular, invalidar

anode [`ænod] s ánodo

anoint [ə'nɔɪnt] *tr* ungir, untar
anomalous [ə'namələs] *adj* anómalo
anoma•ly [ə'naməli] *s* (*pl* **-lies**) anomalía
anon. *abbr* **anonymous**
anonymity [,ænə'nɪmɪti] *s* anónimo; **to preserve one's anonymity** guardar o conservar el anónimo
anonymous [ə'nanɪməs] *adj* anónimo
another [ə'nʌðər] *adj & pron indef* otro
ans. *abbr* **answer**
answer ['ænsər] *s* contestación, respuesta; solución ‖ *tr* contestar, resolver (*un problema o un enigma*) ‖ *intr* contestar, responder; **to answer for** responder de (*una cosa*); responder por (*una persona*)
ant [ænt] *s* hormiga
antagonism [æn'tægə,nɪzəm] *s* antagonismo
antagonize [æn'tægə,naɪz] *tr* oponerse a; enemistar, enajenar
antarctic [æn'ɑrktɪk] *adj* antártico ‖ **the Antarctic** las Tierras Antárticas
antecedent [,æntɪ'sidənt] *adj* antecedente ‖ *s* antecedente *m*; **antecedents** antecedentes *mpl*; antepasados
antechamber ['æntɪ,tʃembər] *s* antecámara
antedate ['æntɪ,det] *tr* antedatar; preceder
antelope ['æntɪ,lop] *s* antílope *m*
anten•na [æn'tɛnə] *s* (*pl* **-nae** [ni]) (ent) antena ‖ *s* (*pl* **-nas**) (rad) antena
autepenult [,æntɪ'pinʌlt] *s* antepenúltima
anteroom ['æntɪ,rum] *s* antecámara
anthem ['ænθəm] *s* himno; antífona
ant'hill' *s* hormiguero
antholo•gy [æn'θalədʒi] *s* (*pl* **-gies**) antología
anthracite ['ænθrə,saɪt] *s* antracita
anthrax ['ænθræks] *s* ántrax *m*
anthropology [,ænθrə'palədʒi] *s* antropología
anti-aircraft [,æntɪ'ɛr,kræft] *adj* antiaéreo
antibiotic [,æntɪbaɪ'atɪk] *adj & s* antibiótico
antibod•y ['æntɪ,badi] *s* (*pl* **-ies**) anticuerpo
anticipate [æn'tɪsɪ,pet] *tr* esperar, prever; anticipar; (*to get ahead of*) anticiparse a; impedir; prometerse (*p.ej., un placer*); temerse (*algo desagradable*)
antics ['æntɪks] *spl* cabriolas, gracias, travesuras
antidote ['æntɪ,dot] *s* antídoto
antifreeze [,æntɪ'friz] *s* anticongelante *m*
antiglare [,æntɪ'glɛr] *adj* antideslumbrante
antiknock [,æntɪ'nak] *adj & s* antidetonante *m*
antilabor [,æntɪ'lebər] *adj* antiobrero
Antilles [æn'tɪliz] *spl* Antillas
antimatter ['æntɪ,mætər] *s* antimateria
antimissile [,æntɪ'mɪsɪl] *adj* antiproyectil
antimony ['æntɪ,moni] *s* antimonio
antipas•to [,antɪ'pasto] *s* (*pl* **-tos**) aperitivo, entremés *m*
antipa•thy [æn'tɪpəθi] *s* (*pl* **-thies**) antipatía
antipollution movement [,æntɪpə'luʃən] *s* lucha antipolución
antiquar•y ['æntɪ,kwɛri] *s* (*pl* **-ies**) anticuario
antiquated ['æntɪ,kwetɪd] *adj* anticuado
antique [æn'tik] *adj* antiguo ‖ *s* antigüedad
antique dealer *s* anticuario

antique store *s* tienda de antigüedades
antiqui•ty [æn'tɪkwɪti] *s* (*pl* **-ties**) antigüedad
anti-Semitic [,æntɪsɪ'mɪtɪk] *adj* antisemítico
antiseptic [,æntɪ'sɛptɪk] *adj & s* antiséptico
antislavery [,æntɪ'slevəri] *adj* antiesclavista
anti-Soviet [,æntɪ'sovɪ,ɛt] *adj* antisoviético
antitank [,æntɪ'tæŋk] *adj* antitanque
antiterrorist [,æntɪ'tɛrərɪst] *adj & s* antiterrorista *mf*
antithe•sis [æn'tɪθɪsɪs] *s* (*pl* **-ses** [,siz]) antítesis *f*
antitoxin [,æntɪ'taksɪn] *s* antitoxina
antitrust [,æntɪ'trʌst] *adj* anticartel
antiwar [,æntɪ'wɔr] *adj* antibélico
antler ['æntlər] *s* cuerna
antonym ['æntənɪm] *s* antónimo
Antwerp ['æntwərp] *s* Amberes *f*
anvil ['ænvɪl] *s* yunque *m*
anxie•ty [æŋ'zaɪ•əti] *s* (*pl* **-ties**) ansiedad, inquietud; ansia, anhelo
anxious ['æŋk/əs] *adj* ansioso, inquieto; anhelante; **to be anxious to** tener ganas de
any ['ɛni] *adj indef* algún, cualquier; todo; **any place** dondequiera; **any time** cuando quiera; alguna vez ‖ *pron indef* alguno, cualquiera ‖ *adv* algo
an'y•bod'y *pron indef* alguno, alguien, cualquiera, quienquiera; todo el mundo; **not anybody** nadie
an'y•how' *adv* de cualquier modo; de todos modos; sin embargo
an'y•one' *pron indef* alguno, alguien, cualquiera
an'y•thing' *pron indef* algo, alguna cosa; cualquier cosa; todo cuanto; **anything at all** cualquier cosa que sea; **anything else** cualquier otra cosa; **anything else?** ¿algo más?; **not anything** nada
an'y•way' *adv* de cualquier modo; de todos modos; sin embargo; sin esmero, sin orden ni concierto
an'y•where' *adv* dondequiera; adondequiera; **not anywhere** en ninguna parte
apace [ə'pes] *adv* aprisa
apart [ə'pɑrt] *adv* aparte; en pedazos; **to fall apart** caerse a pedazos; desunirse; ir al desastre; **to live apart** vivir separados; vivir aislado; **to stand apart** mantenerse apartado; **to take apart** descomponer, desarmar, desmontar; **to tell apart** distinguir
apartment [ə'pɑrtmənt] *s* apartamento
apartment house *s* casa de pisos
apathetic [,æpə'θɛtɪk] *adj* apático
apa•thy ['æpəθi] *s* (*pl* **-ties**) apatía; lerdera
ape [ep] *s* mono ‖ *tr* imitar, remedar
aperture ['æpərtʃər] *s* abertura, orificio
apex ['epɛks] *s* (*pl* **apexes** o **apices** ['æpɪ,siz]) ápex *m*, ápice *m*
aphorism ['æfə,rɪzəm] *s* aforismo
aphrodisiac [,æfrə'dɪzɪ,æk] *adj & s* afrodisíaco
apiar•y ['epɪ,ɛri] *s* (*pl* **-ies**) abejar *m*, colmenar *m*
apiece [ə'pis] *adv* cada uno; por persona
apish ['epɪʃ] *adj* monesco; tonto
aplomb [ə'plam] *s* aplomo, sangre fría
apogee ['æpə,dʒi] *s* apogeo

apologetic [ə,pɑlə'dʒɛtɪk] *adj* lleno de excusas

apologist [ə'pɑlədʒɪst] *s* defensor *m*; exponente *m*

apologize [ə'pɑlə,dʒaɪz] *intr* excusarse, disculparse; **to apologize for** disculparse de; **to apologize to** disculparse con

apology [ə'pɑlədʒi] *s* (*pl* **-gies**) excusa; (*makeshift*) expediente *m*

apoplectic [,æpə'plɛktɪk] *adj & s* apoplético

apoplexy [´æpə,plɛksi] *s* apoplejía

apostle [ə'pɑsəl] *s* apóstol *m*

apostrophe [ə'pɑstrəfi] *s* (*written sign*) apóstrofo; (*words addressed to absent person*) apóstrofe *m & f*

apothecar•y [ə'pɑθɪ,kɛri] *s* (*pl* **-ies**) boticario

apothecary's jar *s* bote *m* de porcelana

apothecary's shop *s* botica

appall [ə'pɔl] *tr* espantar, pasmar

appalling [ə'pɔlɪŋ] *adj* aterrador, espantoso, pasmoso

appara•tus [,æpə'retəs] o [,æpə'rætəs] *s* (*pl* **-tus** o **-tuses**) aparato

apparel [ə'pærəl] *s* indumentaria, vestido

apparent [ə'pærənt] *adj* aparente

apparition [,æpə'rɪʃən] *s* aparición

appeal [ə'pil] *s* súplica, instancia, solicitud; atracción, interés *m*; (law) apelación || *intr* ser atrayente; **to appeal to** (*to make an entreaty to*) suplicar; (*to be attractive to*) atraer, interesar; (law) apelar a

appear [ə'pɪr] *intr* (*to come into sight; to be in sight; to be published*) aparecer; (*to come into sight; to be in sight; to look; to seem*) parecer; (*to come before the public*) presentarse; (*to come before a court*) comparecer

appearance [ə'pɪrəns] *s* (*act of appearing*) aparición; (*outward look*) apariencia, aspecto; (law) comparecencia

appease [ə'piz] *tr* apaciguar

appeasement [ə'pizmənt] *s* apaciguamiento

appeasement attempts *spl* (coll) paños tibios *mpl*

appellate [ə'pɛlɪt] *adj* apelante

appellate court *s* tribunal *m* de apelación

appellate judge *s* juez *m* de alzadas

appendage [ə'pɛndɪdʒ] *s* apéndice *m*

appendicitis [ə,pɛndɪ'saɪtɪs] *s* apendicitis *f*

appen•dix [ə'pɛndɪks] *s* (*pl* **-dixes** o **-dices** [dɪ,siz]) apéndice *m*

appertain [,æpər'ten] *intr* relacionarse

appetite [´æpɪ,taɪt] *s* apetito

appetizer [´æpɪ,taɪzər] *s* aperitivo, apetite *m*

appetizing [´æpɪ,taɪzɪŋ] *adj* apetitoso

applaud [ə'plɔd] *tr & intr* aplaudir

applause [ə'plɔz] *s* aplauso, aplausos

apple [´æpəl] *s* manzana

ap´ple-jack´ *s* aguardiente *m* de manzana

apple of the eye *s* niña del ojo

apple pie *s* pastel *m* de manzana

apple polisher *s* (slang) quitamotas *mf*

ap´ple-sauce´ *s* compota de manzanas; (slang) música celestial

apple tree *s* manzano

appliance [ə'plaɪ•əns] *s* artificio, dispositivo, aparato; aplicación

applicant [´æplɪkənt] *s* aspirante *mf*, pretendiente *mf*, solicitante *mf*

ap•ply [ə'plaɪ] *v* (*pret & pp* **-plied**) *tr* aplicar || *intr* aplicarse; dirigirse; **to apply for** pedir, solicitar

appoint [ə'pɔɪnt] *tr* designar, nombrar; señalar; amueblar

appointment [ə'pɔɪntmənt] *s* designación, nombramiento; empleo, puesto; cita; **appointments** instalación, accesorios, adornos; **by appointment** cita previa

apportion [ə'pɔrʃən] *tr* prorratear

appraisal [ə'prezəl] *s* tasación, valoración, apreciación

appraise [ə'prez] *tr* tasar, valorar, apreciar

appreciable [ə'priʃɪ•əbəl] *adj* apreciable; sensible

appreciate [ə'priʃɪ,et] *tr* apreciar; aprobar; comprender; estar agradecido por || *intr* subir de valor

appreciation [ə,priʃɪ'eʃən] *s* aprecio; agradecimiento; plusvalía, aumento de valor

appreciative [ə'priʃɪ,etɪv] *adj* apreciador; agradecido

apprehend [,æprɪ'hɛnd] *tr* aprehender, prender; comprender; temer

apprehension [,æprɪ'hɛnʃən] *s* aprehensión; (*fear, worry*) aprensión; comprensión

apprehensive [,æprɪ'hɛnsɪv] *adj* (*fearful, worried*) aprehensivo, aprensivo

apprentice [ə'prɛntɪs] *s* aprendiz *m*, meritorio; chumero, chumera (CAm) || *tr* poner de aprendiz

apprenticeship [ə'prɛntɪs,ʃɪp] *s* aprendizaje *m*

apprise o **apprize** [ə'praɪz] *tr* informar; apreciar, tasar

approach [ə'protʃ] *s* acercamiento; vía de entrada; proposición; (*to a problem*) enfoque *m* || *tr* abordar, acercarse a; (*to bring closer*) acercar || *intr* acercarse, aproximarse

approbation [,æprə'beʃən] *s* aprobación

appropriate [ə'proprɪ•ɪt] *adj* apropiado, a propósito [ə'proprɪ,et] *tr* apropiarse; asignar, destinar (*el parlamento determinada suma a un determinado fin*)

approval [ə'pruvəl] *s* aprobación; **on approval** a prueba

approve [ə'pruv] *tr & intr* aprobar

approximate [ə'prɑksɪmɪt] *adj* aproximado || [ə'prɑksɪ,met] *tr* aproximar || *intr* aproximarse

apricot [´eprɪ,kɑt] o [´æprɪ,kɑt] *s* albaricoque *m*

apricot tree *s* albaricoquero

April [´eprɪl] *s* abril *m*

April fool *s* — **to make an April fool of** coger por inocente

April Fools' Day *s* día *m* de engañabobos, primer día de abril, en que se coge por inocente a la gente

apron [´eprən] *s* delantal *m*; (*of a workman*) mandil *m*; **tied to the apron strings of** cosido a las faldas de

apropos [,æprə`po] *adj* oportuno ‖ *adv* a propósito; **apropos of** a propósito de

apse [æps] *s* ábside *m*

apt [æpt] *adj* apto; a propósito; dispuesto, inclinado

aptitude [`æptɪ,tjud] *s* aptitud

aquamarine [,ækwəmə`rin] *s* aguamarina

aquaplane [`ækwə,plen] *s* acuaplano ‖ *intr* correr en acuaplano

aquari•um [ə`kwɛrɪ•əm] *s* (*pl* -ums o -a [ə]) acuario

Aquarius [ə`kwɛrɪ•əs] *s* (astr) Acuario

aquatic [ə`kwætɪk] o [ə`kwɑtɪk] *adj* acuático ‖ **aquatics** *spl* deportes acuáticos

aqueduct [`ækwə,dʌkt] *s* acueducto

aquiline nose [`ækwɪ,laɪn] *s* nariz aguileña

Arab [`ærəb] *adj* árabe ‖ *s* árabe *mf*; caballo árabe

Arabia [ə`rebɪ•ə] *s* la Arabia

Arabian [ə`rebɪ•ən] *adj* árabe; arábigo ‖ *s* árabe *mf*

Arabic [`ærəbɪk] *adj* arábigo ‖ *s* árabe *m*, arábigo

Aragon [`ærə,gɑn] *s* Aragón *m*

Arago•nese [,ærəgə`niz] *adj* aragonés ‖ *s* (*pl* -nese) aragonés *m*

arbiter [`ɑrbɪtər] *s* árbitro

arbitrary [`ɑrbɪ,trɛri] *adj* arbitrario

arbitrate [`ɑrbɪ,tret] *tr* & *intr* arbitrar

arbitration [,ɑrbɪ`treʃən] *s* arbitraje *m*

arbor [`ɑrbər] *s* emparrado, glorieta

arbore•tum [,ɑrbə`ritəm] *s* (*pl* -tums o -ta [tə]) jardín botánico de árboles

arbor vitae [`ɑrbər `vaɪti] *s* árbol *m* de la vida

arbutus [ɑr`bjutəs] *s* madroño

arc [ɑrk] *s* arco

arcade [ɑr`ked] *s* arcada, galería

arch. *abbr* **archaic, archaism, archipelago, architect**

arch [ɑrtʃ] *adj* astuto; travieso; principal ‖ *s* arco ‖ *tr* arquear, enarcar; atravesar

archaeology [,ɑrkɪ`ɑlədʒi] *s* arqueología

archaic [ɑr`ke•ɪk] *adj* arcaico

archaism [`ɑrke,ɪzəm] *s* arcaísmo

archangel [`ɑrk,endʒəl] *s* arcángel *m*

archbishop [`ɑrtʃ `bɪʃəp] *s* arzobispo

archduke [`ɑrtʃ `djuk] *s* archiduque *m*

archene•my [`ɑrtʃ,ɛnimi] *s* (*pl* -mies) archienemigo

archeology [,ɑrkɪ`ɑlədʒi] *s* arqueología

archer [`ɑrtʃər] *s* arquero, flechero

archery [`ɑrtʃəri] *s* tiro de flechas

archipela•go [,ɑrkɪ`pɛləgo] *s* (*pl* -gos o -goes) archipiélago

architect [`ɑrkɪ,tɛkt] *s* arquitecto

architectural [,ɑrkɪ`tɛktʃərəl] *adj* arquitectónico, arquitectural

architecture [`ɑrkɪ,tɛktʃər] *s* arquitectura

archives [`ɑrkaɪvz] *spl* archivo

arch'way' *s* arcada

arc lamp *s* lámpara de arco

arctic [`ɑrktɪk] *adj* ártico ‖ **the Arctic** las Tierras Articas

arc welding *s* soldadura de arco

ardent [`ɑrdənt] *adj* ardiente

ardor [`ɑrdər] *s* ardor *m*

arduous [`ɑrdju•əs] *adj* arduo, difícil; enérgico; (*steep*) escarpado

area [`ɛrɪ•ə] *s* área, superficie *f*; comarca, región; zona; patio

ar'ea•way' *s* entrada baja de un sótano

Argentina [,ɑrdʒən`tinə] *s* la Argentina

Argentine [`ɑrdʒən,tin] o [`ɑrdʒən,taɪn] *adj* & *s* argentino ‖ **the Argentine** la Argentina

Argentinean [,ɑrdʒən`tɪnɪ•ən] *adj* & *s* argentino

Argonaut [`ɑrgə,nɔt] *s* argonauta *m*

argue [`ɑrgju] *tr* argüir; **to argue into** persuadir a + *inf*; **to argue out of** disuadir de + *inf* ‖ *intr* argüir

argument [`ɑrgjəmənt] *s* argumento; disputa

argumentative [,ɑrgjə`mɛntətɪv] *adj* argumentador; ergotista *masc*

argumentativeness [,ɑrgjə`mɛntətɪvnɪs] *s* ergotismo

aria [`ɑrɪ•ə] o [`ɛrɪ•ə] *s* (mus) aria

arid [`ærɪd] *adj* árido

aridity [ə`rɪdɪti] *s* aridez *f*

Aries [`ɛriz] *s* (astr) Aries *m*

aright [ə`raɪt] *adv* acertadamente; **to set aright** rectificar

arise [ə`raɪz] *v* (*pret* **arose** [ə`roz]; *pp* **arisen** [ə`rɪzən]) *intr* levantarse; subir; aparecer; **to arise from** provenir de

aristocra•cy [,ærɪs`tɑkrəsi] *s* (*pl* -cies) aristocracia

aristocrat [ə`rɪstə,kræt] *s* aristócrata *mf*

aristocratic [ə,rɪstə`krætɪk] *adj* aristocrático

Aristotelian [,ærɪstə`tilɪ•ən] *adj* & *s* aristotélico

Aristotle [`ærɪs,tɑtəl] *s* Aristóteles *m*

arith. *abbr* **arithmetic**

arithmetic [ə`rɪθmətɪk] *s* aritmética

arithmetical [,ærɪθ`mɛtɪkəl] *adj* aritmético

arithmetician [ə,rɪθmə`tɪʃən] *s* aritmético

ark [ɑrk] *s* arca de Noé

ark of the covenant *s* arca de la alianza

arm [ɑrm] *s* brazo; (*weapon*) arma; **arm in arm** de bracero, asidos del brazo; **in arms** de pecho, de teta; **the three arms of the service** los tres ejércitos; **to be up in arms** estar en armas; **to keep at arm's length** mantener a distancia; mantenerse a distancia; **to lay down one's arms** rendir las armas; **to rise up in arms** alzarse en armas; **under arms** sobre las armas ‖ *tr* armar ‖ *intr* armarse

armament [`ɑrməmənt] *s* armamento

armature [`ɑrmə,tʃər] *s* armadura; (*of a dynamo or motor*) (elec) inducido

arm'chair' *adj* de gabinete ‖ *s* butaca, sillón *m*, silla de brazos

Armenian [ɑr`minɪ•ən] *adj* & *s* armenio

armful [`ɑrm,ful] *s* brazado

arm'hole' *s* (*in clothing*) sobaquera

armistice [`ɑrmɪstɪs] *s* armisticio

armor [`ɑrmər] *s* armadura; coraza, blindaje *m* ‖ *tr* acorazar, blindar

armored car *s* carro blindado

armorial bearings [ɑr`morɪ•əl] *spl* blasón *m*, escudo de armas

armor plate *s* plancha de blindaje

ar′mor-plate′ *tr* acorazar, blindar

armor·y [′ɑrməri] *s (pl* **-ies**) arsenal *m; (arms factory)* armería

arm′pit′ *s* sobaco, hueco de la axila

arm′rest′ *s* apoyabrazos *m*

arms race *s* carrera armanentista

arms reduction *s* desarmamiento

ar·my [′ɑrmi] *adj* militar, castrense ‖ *s (pl* **-mies**) ejército

army corps *s* cuerpo de ejército

aroma [ə′romə] *s* aroma *m*, fragancia

aromatic [,ærə′mætɪk] *adj* aromático

around [ə′raund] *adv* alrededor, a la redonda; en la dirección opuesta ‖ *prep* alrededor de, en torno a o de; cerca de; *(the corner)* a la vuelta de

arouse [ə′rauz] *tr* despertar; excitar, incitar

arpeg·gio [ɑr′pɛdʒo] *s (pl* **-gios**) arpegio

arraign [ə′ren] *tr* acusar; presentar al tribunal

arrange [ə′rendʒ] *tr* arreglar, disponer; (mus) adaptar, refundir

array [ə′re] *s* orden *m;* orden *m* de batalla; adorno, atavío ‖ *tr* poner en orden; poner en orden de batalla; adornar, ataviar

arrears [ə′rɪrz] *spl* atrasos; **in arrears** atrasado en pagos

arrest [ə′rɛst] *s* arresto, prisión; detención; **under arrest** bajo arresto ‖ *tr* arrestar; detener; atraer *(la atención)*

arresting [ə′rɛstɪŋ] *adj* impresionante

arrhythmia [ə′rɪθmi·ə] *s* arritmia

arrival [ə′raɪvəl] *s* llegada; *(person)* llegado

arrive [ə′raɪv] *intr* llegar; tener éxito

arrogance [′ærəgəns] *s* arrogancia

arrogant [′ærəgənt] *adj* arrogante

arrogate [′ærə,get] *tr* — **to arrogate to oneself** arrogarse

arrow [′æro] *s* flecha

ar′row-head′ *s* punta de flecha; (bot) saetilla

arsenal [′ɑrsənəl] *s* arsenal *m*

arsenic [′ɑrsɪnɪk] *s* arsénico

arson [′ɑrsən] *s* incendio premeditado, delito de incendio

art [ɑrt] *s* arte *m & f*

arter·y [′ɑrtəri] *s (pl* **-ies**) arteria

artful [′ɑrtfəl] *adj* astuto, mañoso; diestro, ingenioso

arthritic [ɑr′θrɪtɪk] *adj & s* artrítico

arthritis [ɑr′θraɪtɪs] *s* artritis *f*

artichoke [′ɑrtɪ,tʃok] *s* alcachofa

article [′ɑrtɪkəl] *s* artículo; **an article of clothing** una prenda de vestir

articulate [ɑr′tɪkjəlɪt] *adj* claro, distinto; capaz de hablar ‖ [ɑr′tɪkjə,let] *tr* articular

artifact [′ɑrtɪ,fækt] *s* artefacto

artifice [′ɑrtɪfɪs] *s* artificio

artificial [,ɑrtɪ′fɪʃəl] *adj* artificial

artillery [ɑr′tɪləri] *s* artillería

artillery·man [ɑr′tɪlərimən] *s (pl* **-men** [mən]) artillero

artisan [′ɑrtɪzən] *s* artesano

artist [′ɑrtɪst] *s* artista *mf*

artistic [ɑr′tɪstɪk] *adj* artístico

artistry [′ɑrtɪstri] *s* habilidad artística

artless [′ɑrtlɪs] *adj* sencillo, natural; ingenuo, inocente; *(crude, clumsy)* chabacano

arts and crafts *spl* artes y oficios

art·y [′ɑrti] *adj (comp* **-ier**; *super.* **-iest**) (coll) ostentosamente artístico

Aryan [′ɛrɪ·ən] o [′ɑrjən] *adj & s* ario

as [æz] o [əz] *pron rel* que; **the same as** el mismo que ‖ *adv* tan; **as . . . as** tan . . . como; **as for** en cuanto a; **as long as** mientras que; ya que; **as many as** tantos como; **as much as** tanto como; **as regards** en cuanto a; **as soon as** tan pronto como; **as soon as possible** cuanto antes, los más pronto posible; **as though** como si; **as to** en cuanto a; **as well** también; **as yet** hasta ahora ‖ *conf* como; que; ya que; a medida que; **as it seems** por lo visto, según parece ‖ *prep* por, como; **as a rule** por regla general

asbestos [æs′bɛstəs] *s* asbesto, amianto

ascend [ə′sɛnd] *tr* subir a *(p.ej., el trono)* ‖ *intr* ascender

ascendancy [ə′sɛndənsi] *s* ascendiente *m*

ascension [ə′sɛnʃən] *s* ascensión

Ascension Day *s* fiesta de la Ascensión

ascent [ə′sɛnt] *s* ascensión, subida; ascenso, promoción

ascertain [,æsər′ten] *tr* averiguar

ascertainable [,æsər′tenəbəl] *adj* averiguable

ascetic [ə′sɛtɪk] *adj* ascético ‖ *s* asceta *mf*

ascorbic acid [ə′skɔrbɪk] *s* ácido ascórbico

ascribe [ə′skraɪb] *tr* atribuir

aseptic [ə′sɛptɪk] o [e′sɛptɪk] *adj* aséptico

ash [æʃ] *s* ceniza; *(tree; wood)* fresno; **ashes** ceniza, cenizas; *(mortal remains)* cenizas

ashamed [ə′ʃemd] *adj* avergonzado; **to be ashamed** tener vergüenza

ashlar [′æʃlər] *s* sillar *m*

ashore [ə′ʃor] *adv* en tierra, a tierra

ash tray *s* cenicero

Ash Wednesday *s* miércoles *m* de ceniza

Asia [′eʒə] o [′eʃə] *s* Asia

Asia Minor *s* el Asia Menor

Asian [′eʒən] o [′eʃən] o **Asiatic** [,eʒɪ′ætɪk] o [,eʃɪ′ætɪk] *adj & s* asiático

aside [ə′saɪd] *adv* aparte; **aside from** además de; **to step aside** hacerse a un lado ‖ *s* (theat) aparte *m*

asinine [′æsɪ,naɪn] *adj* tonto, necio

ask [æsk] o [ɑsk] *tr (to request)* pedir; *(to inquire of)* preguntar; hacer *(una pregunta)*; invitar; **to ask in** invitar a entrar ‖ *intr*—**to ask about, after, or for**; preguntar por; **to ask for** pedir

askance [ə′skæns] *adv* al sesgo, de soslayo; con desdén, sospechosamente

asleep [ə′slip] *adj* dormido; **to fall asleep** dormirse

asp [æsp] *s* áspid *m*

asparagus [ə′spærəgəs] *s* espárrago

aspect [′æspɛkt] *s* aspecto

aspen [′æspən] *s* tiemblo, álamo temblón

aspersion [ə′spʌrʒən] o [ə′spʌrʃən] *s* calumnia, difamación

asphalt [′æsfɔlt] *s* asfalto ‖ *tr* asfaltar

asphyxiate [æs′fɪksɪ,et] *tr* asfixiar

aspirant [ə′spaɪrənt] o [′æspɪrənt] *s* pretendiente *mf*, candidato

aspire [ə′spaɪr] *intr* aspirar

aspirin [′æspɪrɪn] *s* aspirina

**ap
as**

ass [æs] *s* asno
assail [ə'sel] *tr* asaltar. acometer
assassin [e'sæsɪn] *s* asesino
assassinate [ə'sæsɪ,net] *tr* asesinar
assassination [ə,sæsɪ'neʃən] *s* asesinato
assault [ə'sɔlt] *s* asalto ‖ *tr* asaltar
assault and battery *s* vías de hecho, violencias
assay [ə'se] o ['æse] *s* ensaye *m;* muestra de ensaye ‖ [ə'se] *tr* ensayar; apreciar
assemble [ə'sɛmbəl] *tr* reunir; (mach) armar, montar ‖ *intr* reunirse
assem•bly [ə'sɛmblɪ] *s* (*pl* -**blies**) asamblea; reunión; (mach) armadura, montaje *m*
assembly hall *s* aula magna, paraninfo; salón *m* de sesiones
assembly line *s* línea de montaje
assembly plant *s* fábrica de montaje
assembly room *s* sala de reunión; (mach) taller *m* de montaje
assent [ə'sɛnt] *s* asentimiento, asenso ‖ *intr* asentir
assert [ə'sʌrt] *tr* afirmar, aseverar, declarar; **to assert oneself** imponerse, hacer valer sus derechos
assertion [ə'sʌrʃən] *s* aserción, aseveración
assess [ə'sɛs] *tr* amillarar, gravar; fijar (*daños y perjuicios*); apreciar, estimar
assessment [ə'sɛsmənt] *s* amillaramiento, gravamen *m;* fijación; apreciación, estimación
asset ['æsɛt] *s* posesión, ventaja; (*person, thing, or quality worth having*) (fig) valor *m;* **assets** (com) activo
assiduous [ə'sɪdju•əs] *adj* asiduo
assign [ə'saɪn] *tr* asignar
assignment [ə'saɪnmənt] *s* asignación, cometido; lección
assimilate [ə'sɪmɪ,let] *tr* asimilarse (*los alimentos, el conocimiento*) ‖ *intr* asimilarse
assist [ə'sɪst] *tr* ayudar, asistir, auxiliar
assistant [ə'sɪstənt] *adj & s* auxiliar *mf,* ayudante *mf*
assistantship [ə'sɪstənt,ʃɪp] *s* ayudantía
assn. *abbr* **association**
associate [ə'soʃɪ•ɪt] *adj* asociado ‖ *s* asociado, socio ‖ [ə'soʃɪ,et] *tr* asociar ‖ *intr* asociarse
association [ə,soʃɪ'eʃən] *s* asociación
assort [ə'sɔrt] *tr* clasificar, ordenar
assortment [ə'sɔrtmənt] *s* surtido; clase *f,* grupo
asst. *abbr* **assistant**
assume [ə'sum] o [ə'sjum] *tr* asumir (*p.ej., responsabilidades*); arrogarse; suponer, dar por sentado
assumption [ə'sʌmpʃən] *s* asunción; suposición
assurance [ə'ʃurəns] *s* aseguramiento; seguridad, confianza; (com) seguro
assure [ə'ʃur] *tr* asegurar; (com) asegurar
Assyria [ə'sɪrɪ•ə] *s* Asiria
Assyrian [ə'sɪrɪ•ən] *adj & s* asirio
astatine ['æstə,tin] *s* ástato
aster ['æstər] *s* (bot) aster *m;* (*China aster*) reina Margarita
asterisk ['æstə,rɪsk] *s* asterisco

astern [ə'stʌrn] *adv* por la popa
asthma ['æzmə] o ['æsmə] *s* asma *f*
astonish [ə'stanɪʃ] *tr* asombrar
astonishing [ə'stanɪʃɪŋ] *adj* asombroso
astound [ə'staund] *tr* pasmar
astounding [ə'staundɪŋ] *adj* pasmoso
astraddle [ə'strædəl] *adv* a horcajadas
astray [ə'stre] *adv* por mal camino; **to go astray** extraviarse; **gone astray** desviado; **to lead astray** extraviar
astride [ə'straɪd] *adv* a horcajadas ‖ *prep* a horcajadas de
astrology [ə'stralədʒɪ] *s* astrología
astronaut ['æstrə,nɔt] *s* astronauta *m*
astronautic [,æstrə'nɔtɪk] *adj* astronáutico ‖ **astronautics** *s* astronáutica
astronavigation [,æstro,nævɪ'geʃən] *s* astronavigación
astronomer [ə'stranəmər] *s* astrónomo
astronomic(al) [,æstrə'namɪk(əl)] *adj* astronómico
astronomy [ə'stranəmɪ] *s* astronomía
astrophysics [,æstro'fɪzɪks] *s* astrofísica
Asturian [ə'sturɪ•ən] *adj & s* asturiano
astute [ə'stjut] *adj* astuto, sagaz
asunder [ə'sʌndər] *adv* a pedazos, en dos
asylum [ə'saɪləm] *s* asilo
asymmetry [ə'sɪmɪtri] *s* asimetría
at [æt] o [ət] *prep* en, p.ej., **I saw her at the library** la vi en la biblioteca; a, p.ej., **at five o'clock** a las cinco; de, p.ej., **to be surprised at** estar sorprendido de; **to laugh at** reírse de; en casa de, p.ej., **at John's** en casa de Juan
atavistic [,ætə'vɪstɪk] *adj* atávico
atheism ['eθi,ɪzəm] *s* ateísmo
atheist ['eθi•ɪst] *s* ateísta *mf,* ateo
Athenian [ə'θini•ən] *adj & s* ateniense *mf*
Athens ['æθɪnz] *s* Atenas *f*
athirst [ə'θʌrst] *adj* sediento
athlete ['æθlit] *s* atleta *mf*
athlete's foot *s* pie *m* de atleta
athletic [æθ'lɛtɪk] *adj* atlético ‖ **athletics** *s* atletismo
Atlantic [æt'læntɪk] *adj & s* Atlántico
atlas ['ætləs] *s* atlas *m*
atmosphere ['ætməs,fɪr] *s* atmósfera
atmospheric [,ætməs'fɛrɪk] *adj* atmosférico ‖ **atmospherics** *spl* parásitos atmosféricos
atom ['ætəm] *s* átomo
atom bomb *s* bomba atómica
atomic [ə'tamɪk] *adj* atómico
atomic bomb *s* bomba atómica
atomic weight *s* peso atómico
atomize ['ætə,maɪz] *tr* atomizar
atomizer ['ætə,maɪzər] *s* pulverizador *m,* vaporizador *m*
atom smasher *s* rompeátomos *m*
atone [ə'ton] *intr* dar reparación; **to atone for** dar reparación por, expiar
atonement [ə'tonmənt] *s* reparación, expiación
atop [ə'tap] *adv* encima ‖ *prep* encima de
atrocious [ə'troʃəs] *adj* atroz; (coll) abominable, muy malo
atroci•ty [ə'trasɪti] *s* (*pl* -**ties**) atrocidad

atro•phy [`ætrəfi] s (pathol) atrofia, retracción ‖ v (pret & pp **-phied**) tr atrofiar ‖ intr atrofiarse

attach [ə`tætʃ] tr atar, ligar; atribuir (p.ej., importancia); (law) embargar; **to be attached to** aficionarse a; (to be officially associated with) depender de

attaché [,ætə`ʃe] s agregado

attachment [ə`tætʃmənt] s atadura, enlace m; atribución; apego, cariño; accesorio; (law) embargo

attack [ə`tæk] s ataque m ‖ tr & intr atacar

attain [ə`ten] tr alcanzar, lograr

attainment [ə`tenmənt] s consecución, logro; **attainments** dotes fpl, prendas

attempt [ə`tɛmpt] s tentativa; (assault) atentado, conato ‖ tr procurar, intentar; (e.g., the life of a person) atentar a o contra

attend [ə`tɛnd] tr atender, asistir; asistir a (p.ej., la escuela); auxiliar (a un moribundo) ‖ intr atender; **to attend to** atender a

attendance [ə`tɛndəns] s asistencia, concurrencia; **to dance attendance** hacer antesala

attendant [ə`tɛndənt] adj & s asistente mf; concomitante m

attention [ə`tɛnʃən] s atención; **to attract attention** llamar la atención; **to call attention to** hacer presente; **to pay attention to** hacer caso de

attentive [ə`tɛntɪv] adj atento

attenuate [ə`tɛnjuˌet] tr adelgazar; debilitar ‖ intr debilitarse; desaparecer

attest [ə`tɛst] tr atestiguar; juramentar ‖ intr dar fe; **to attest to** dar fe de

attic [`ætɪk] s buharda, guardilla, desván m

attire [ə`taɪr] s atavío, traje m ‖ tr ataviar, vestir

attitude [`ætɪˌtjud] o [`ætɪˌtud] s actitud, ademán m

attorney [ə`tʌrni] s abogado; procurador m

attract [ə`trækt] tr atraer; llamar (la atención)

attraction [ə`trækʃən] s atracción; (personal charm) atractivo

attractive [ə`træktɪv] adj atractivo; (agreeable, interesting) atrayente

attribute [`ætrɪˌbjut] s atributo ‖ [ə`trɪbjut] tr atribuir

atty. abbr **attorney**

auburn [`ɔbərn] adj & s castaño rojizo

auction [`ɔkʃən] s almoneda, remate m, subasta ‖ tr rematar, subastar

auctioneer [,ɔkʃən`ɪr] s subastador m, rematador m ‖ tr & intr rematar, subastar

auction house s martillo

audacious [ɔ`deʃəs] adj audaz

audaci•ty [ɔ`dæsɪti] s (pl **-ties**) audacia

audience [`ɔdɪəns] s (hearing; formal interview) audiencia; público, auditorio

audio frenquency [`ɔdɪ,o] s audiofrecuencia

audiometer [,ɔdɪ`amɪtər] s audiómetro

audit [`ɔdɪt] s intervención ‖ tr intervenir

audition [ɔ`dɪʃən] s audición ‖ tr dar audición a

auditor [`ɔdɪtər] s oyente mf; (com) interventor m

auditorium [,ɔdɪ`torɪəm] s auditorio, anfiteatro, paraninfo

auger [`ɔgər] s barrena

augment [ɔg`mɛnt] tr & intr aumentar

augur [`ɔgər] s augur m ‖ tr & intr augurar; **to augur well** ser de buen agüero

augu•ry [`ɔgəri] s (pl **-ries**) augurio

august [ɔ`gʌst] adj augusto ‖ **August** [`ɔgəst] s agosto

aunt [ænt] o [ɑnt] s tía

aurora [e`rorə] s aurora

auspice [`ɔspɪs] s auspicio; **under the auspices of** bajo los auspicios de

austere [ɔs`tɪr] adj austero

Australia [ɔ`streljə] s Australia

Australian [ɔ`streljən] adj & s australiano

Austria [`ɔstrɪə] s Austria

Austrian [`ɔstrɪən] adj & s austríaco

authentic [ɔ`θɛntɪk] adj auténtico

authenticate [ɔ`θɛntɪˌket] tr autenticar

author [`ɔθər] s autor m

authoress [`ɔθərɪs] s autora

authoritarian [ɔ,θɔrɪ`tɛrɪən] adj & s autoritario

authoritative [ɔ`θɔrɪˌtetɪv] adj autorizado; (dictatorial) autoritario

authori•ty [ɔ`θɔrɪti] s (pl **-ties**) autoridad; **on good authority** de buena tinta, de fuente fidedigna

authorize [`ɔθəˌraɪz] tr autorizar

authorship [`ɔθərˌʃɪp] s paternidad literaria

autistic [ɔ`tɪstɪk] s autístico

au•to [`ɔto] s (pl **-tos**) (coll) auto, coche m

autobiogra•phy [,ɔtobaɪ`agrəfi] s (pl **-phies**) autobiografía

autobus [`ɔtoˌbʌs] s autobús m

autocratic(al) [,ɔtə`krætɪk(əl)] adj autocrático

autograph [`ɔtəˌgræf] adj & s autógrafo ‖ tr autografiar

autograph seeker s cazaautógrafos m

automat [`ɔtəˌmæt] s restaurante automático

automatic [,ɔtə`mætɪk] adj automático

automatic car wash s túnel m de lavado

automatic clutch s servoembrague m

automation [,ɔtə`meʃən] s automación, automatización

automa•ton [ɔ`tamətan] s (pl **-tons** o **-ta** [tə]) autómata

automobile [,ɔtəmo`bil] u [,ɔtə`mobil] s automóvil m

automobile show s salón m del automóvil

autonomous [ɔ`tanəməs] adj autónomo

autonomy [ɔ`tanəmi] s autonomía

autop•sy [`ɔtapsi] s (pl **-sies**) autopsia

autumn [`ɔtəm] s otoño

autumnal [ɔ`tʌmnəl] adj otoñal

auxilia•ry [ɔg`zɪljəri] adj auxiliar ‖ s (pl **-ries**) auxiliar mf; **auxiliaries** tropas auxiliares

av. abbr **avenue, average, avoirdupois**

avail [ə`vel] s provecho, utilidad ‖ tr beneficiar; **to avail oneself of** aprovecharse de, valerse de ‖ intr aprovechar

available [ə`veləbəl] adj disponible; **to make available to** poner a la disposición de

avalanche [`ævəˌlæntʃ] s alud m, avalancha

avant-garde [ə,vɑnt'gɑrd] *adj* vanguardista ‖ *s* vanguardismo

avant-guardist [ə,vɑnt'gɑrdist] *s* vanguardista *mf*

avarice ['ævərıs] *s* avaricia

avaricious [,ævə'rıʃəs] *adj* avaricioso, avariento

Ave. *abbr* **Avenue**

avenge [ə'vɛndʒ] *tr* vengar; **to avenge oneself on** vengarse en

avenue ['ævə,nju] o ['ævə,nu] *s* avenida

aver [ə'vʌr] *v* (*pret & pp* **averred;** *ger* **averring**) *tr* afirmar, declarar

average ['ævərıdʒ] *adj* común, mediano, ordinario ‖ *s* promedio, término medio; (naut) avería ‖ *tr* calcular el término medio de; prorratear; ser de un promedio de

averse [ə'vʌrs] *adj* renuente, contrario

aversion [ə'vʌrʒen] *s* aversión, antipatía; cosa aborrecida

avert [ə'vʌrt] *tr* apartar, desviar; impedir

aviar·y ['evı,ɛri] *s* (*pl* **-ies**) avería, pajarera

aviation [,evı'eʃən] *s* aviación

aviation medicine *s* aeromedicina

aviator ['evı,etər] *s* aviador *m*

avid ['ævıd] *adj* ávido

avidity [ə'vıdıti] *s* avidez *f*

avocado [,ævə'kɑdo] *s* aguacate *m*

avocation [,ævə'keʃən] *s* distracción, diversión

avoid [ə'vɔid] *tr* evitar

avoidable [ə'vɔidəbəl] *adj* evitable

avoidance [ə'vɔidəns] *s* evitación

avow [ə'vau] *tr* admitir, confesar

avowal [ə'vau·əl] *s* admisión, confesión

await [ə'wet] *tr* aguardar, esperar

awake [ə'wek] *adj* despierto ‖ *v* (*pret & pp* **awoke** [ə'wok] o **awaked**) *tr & intr* despertar

awaken [ə'wekən] *tr & intr* despertar

awakening [ə'wekəniŋ] *s* despertamiento; desilusión

award [ə'wɔrd] *s* premio; condecoración; adjudicación ‖ *tr* conceder; adjudicar

aware [ə'wɛr] *adj* enterado; **to become aware of** enterarse de, darse cuenta de

awareness [ə'wɛrnıs] *s* conciencia

away [ə'we] *adj* ausente; distante ‖ *adv* lejos; a lo lejos; **away from** lejos de; **to do away with** deshacerse de; **to get away** escapar; **to go away** irse; **to make away with** robar, hurtar; **to run away** fugarse; **to send away** enviar; despedir; **to take away** llevarse; quitar

awe [ɔ] *s* temor *m* reverencial ‖ *tr* infundir temor reverencial a

awesome ['ɔsəm] *adj* imponente

awestruck ['ɔ,strʌk] *adj* espantado

awful ['ɔfəl] *adj* atroz, horrible; impresionante; (coll) muy malo, muy feo, enorme

awfully ['ɔfəli] *adv* atrozmente, horriblemente; (coll) muy, excesivamente

awfulness ['ɔfəlnıs] *s* espantosidad (SAm)

awhile [ə'hwail] *adv* un rato, algún tiempo

awkward ['ɔkwərd] *adj* desmañado, torpe, lerdo; embarazoso, delicado

awkward squad *s* pelotón *m* de los torpes

awl [ɔl] *s* alesna, lezna

awning ['ɔniŋ] *s* toldo

ax [æks] *s* hacha

axiom ['æksı·əm] *s* axioma *m*

axiomatic [,æksı·ə'mætık] *adj* axiomático

axis ['æksıs] *s* (*pl* **axes** ['æksiz]) *s* eje *m*

axle ['æksəl] *s* eje *m*, árbol *m*

axle load *s* carga por eje

ax'le·tree' *s* eje *m* de carretón

ay [ai] *adv & s* sí ‖ [e] *adv* siempre; **for ay** por siempre ‖ [e] *interj* ¡ay!

aye [ai] *adv & s* sí ‖ [e] *adv* siempre; **for aye** por siempre

azimuth ['æzıməθ] *s* acimut *m*

Azores [ə'zorz] o ['ezorz] *spl* Azores *fpl*

Aztec ['æztɛk] *adj & s* azteca *mf*

azure ['æʒər] o ['eʒər] *adj & s* azul *m*

B

B, b [bi] segunda letra del alfabeto inglés

b. *abbr* **bass, bay, born, brother**

baa [bɑ] *s* be *m*, balido ‖ *intr* balar

babble ['bæbəl] *s* barboteo; charla; (*of a brook*) murmullo ‖ *tr* barbotar; decir indiscretamente ‖ *intr* barbotar; murmurar (*un arroyo*)

babe [beb] *s* rorro, criatura; (*innocent, gullible person*) niño; (slang) chica, chica hermosa

baboon [bæ'bun] *s* babuíno

ba·by ['bebi] *s* (*pl* **-bies**) rorro, criatura, bebé *m*; (*the youngest child*) benjamín *m* ‖ *v* (*pret & pp* **-bied**) *tr* mimar; tratar como niño

baby carriage *s* cochecillo para niños

baby grand *s* piano de media cola

babyhood ['bebi,hud] *s* primera infancia, niñez *f*

babyish ['bebi,ıʃ] *adj* aniñado, infantil

Babylon ['bæbılən] o ['bæbı,lɑn] *s* Babilonia (*ciudad*)

Babylonia [,bæbı'loni·ə] *s* Babilonia (*imperio*)

Babylonian [,bæbı'loni·ən] *adj & s* babilonio

baby sitter *s* niñera tomada por horas

baccalaureate [,bækə'lɔri·ıt] *s* bachillerato

bachelor ['bætʃələr] *s* (*unmarried man*) soltero; (*holder of bachelor's degree*) bachiller *mf*; (*apprentice knight*) doncel *m*

bachelorhood ['bætʃələr,hud] *s* celibato, soltería (*del hombre*)

bacil·lus [bə'sɪləs] s (pl -li [laɪ]) bacilo
back [bæk] adj trasero, posterior; atrasado ‖ adv atrás, detrás; de vuelta; (ago) hace; **back of** detrás de; **to go back to** remontarse a; **to send back** devolver ‖ s espalda; dorso; (of a coin) reverso; (of a chair) espaldar m, respaldo; (of an animal, of a book) lomo; (of a hall, a room) fondo; (of a writing, a book) final m; **behind one's back** a espaldas de uno; **on one's back** postrado, en cama; a cuestas ‖ tr mover hacia atrás; apoyar, respaldar ‖ intr moverse hacia atrás; **to back down** u **out** volverse atrás, echarse atrás; **to back up** retroceder; regolfar (el agua)
back'ache' s dolor m de espalda
back'bone' s espinazo; (of a book) nervura; firmeza, resistencia
back'break'ing adj deslomador
back'down' s palinodia, retractación
back'drop' s telón m de fondo o de foro
backer ['bækər] s sostenedor m, defensor m; (of a business venture) impulsador m
back'fire' s (aut) petardeo ‖ intr (aut) petardear
back'ground' s fondo; antecedentes mpl; conocimientos, educación; (of a painting) lontananza
background music s música de fondo
backing ['bækɪŋ] s apoyo, sostén m; garantía, respaldo; financiamiento; (bb) lomera
back'lash' s (mach) contragolpe m; (mach) juego; (fig) reacción violenta
back'log' s (com) reserva de pedidos pendientes; (e.g., of work) acumulación
back number s número atrasado; (coll) persona anticuada
back pay s sueldo retrasado
back seat s puesto secundario; **to take a back seat** perder influencia
back'side' s espalda; trasero
back'slide' v (pret & pp -slid [,slɪd]) intr reincidir
backspacer ['bæk,spesər] s tecla de retroceso
back'stage' adv detrás del telón; entre bastidores
back'stairs' adj indirecto, secreto
back stairs spl escalera trasera; medios indirectos
back'stitch' s pespunte m ‖ tr & intr pespuntar
back'stop' s reja o red f para detener la pelota
back'swept' wing s (aer) ala en flecha
back talk s respuesta insolente
backward ['bækwərd] adj atrasado, tardío; tímido ‖ adv de atrás; de espaldas; al revés; cada vez peor; para atrás, hacia atrás
back'wa'ter s remanso; (fig) atraso, yermo
back'woods' spl monte m, región alejada de los centros de población
back yard s patio trasero, corral trasero
bacon ['bekən] s tocino
bacteria [bæk'tɪrɪ·ə] pl de **bacterium**
bacterial [bæk'tɪrɪ·əl] adj bacteriano
bacteriologist [bæk,tɪrɪ'ɑlədʒɪst] s bacteriólogo

bacteriology [bæk,tɪrɪ'ɑlədʒi] s bacteriología
bacteri·um [bæk'tɪrɪ·əm] s (pl -a [ə]) bacteria
bad [bæd] adj (comp **worse** [wʌrs]; super **worst** [wʌrst]) malo; (money) falso; (debt) incobrable; **from bad to worse** de mal en peor; **to be in bad** (coll) caer en desgracia; **to be too bad** ser lástima; **to go to the bad** (coll) ir por mal camino; (coll) arruinarse; **to look bad** tener mala cara
bad breath s mal aliento
badge [bædʒ] s divisa, insignia
badger ['bædʒər] s tejón m
badly ['bædli] adv mal; con urgencia; gravemente
badly off adj malparado; muy enfermo
badminton ['bædmɪntən] s juego del volante
baffle ['bæfəl] s deflector m; (rad) pantalla acústica ‖ tr confundir; burlar, frustrar
baffling ['bæflɪŋ] adj perplejo, desconcertador
bag [bæg] s saco; saquito de mano; (in clothing) bolsa; (purse) bolso; (take of game) caza; **to be in the bag** (slang) ser cosa segura ‖ v (pret & pp **bagged**; ger **bagging**) tr ensacar; coger, cazar ‖ intr hacer bolsa (un vestido)
baggage ['bægɪdʒ] s equipaje m; (mil) bagaje m
baggage car s furgón m de equipajes
baggage check s contraseña de equipajes
baggage rack s red f de equipajes
baggage room s sala de equipajes
bag'pipe' s gaita, cornamusa
bag'pi'per s gaitero
bail [bel] s caución, fianza; **to go bail for** salir fiador por ‖ tr caucionar, afianzar; achicar (la embarcación; el agua); **to bail out** salir fiador por; achicar ‖ intr achicar; **to bail out** lanzarse en paracaídas
bailiff ['belɪf] s alguacil m, corchete m
bailiwick ['belɪwɪk] s alguacilazgo; **to be in the bailiwick of** ser de la pertenencia de
bait [bet] s carnada, cebo; señuelo; **to swallow the bait** tragar el anzuelo ‖ tr cebar, encarnar (el anzuelo); tentar, seducir; (to pester) hostigar
baize [bez] s bayeta
bake [bek] tr cocer al horno; cocer (loza, gres, etc.)
bakelite ['bekə,laɪt] s baquelita
baker ['bekər] s panadero, hornero
baker's dozen s docena del fraile
baker·y ['bekəri] s (pl -ies) panadería
baking powder ['bekɪŋ] s levadura en polvo
baking soda s bicarbonato de sosa
bal. abbr **balance**
balance ['bæləns] s (instrument for weighing) balanza; (state of equilibrium) equilibrio; (amount left over) resto; (amount still owed) saldo; (statement of debits and credits) balance m; **to lose one's balance** perder el equilibrio; **to strike a balance** hacer o pasar balance ‖ tr balancear; equilibrar; equilibrar, nivelar (el presupuesto) ‖ intr equilibrarse; (to waver) balancear

av
ba

balanced ['bælənst] *adj* equilibrado
balance of payments *s* balanza de pagos
balance of power *s* equilibrio político
balance sheet *s* balance *m*, avanzo
balco•ny ['bælkəni] *s* (*pl* **-nies**) balcón *m*; (*in a theater*) galería, paraíso
bald [bɔld] *adj* calvo; franco, directo
baldness ['bɔldnɪs] *s* calvicie *f*
baldric ['bɔldrɪk] *s* tahalí *m*
bale [bel] *s* bala || *tr* embalar
Balearic [,bælɪ'ærɪk] *adj* balear
Balearic Islands *spl* islas Baleares
baleful ['belfəl] *adj* funesto, maligno
balk [bɔk] *tr* burlar, frustrar || *intr* emperrarse, resistirse
Balkan ['bɔlkən] *adj* balcánico || **the Balkans** los Balcanes
balk•y ['bɔki] *adj* (*comp* **-ier**; *super* **-iest**) rebelón, repropio
ball [bɔl] *s* bola, pelota; esfera, globo; (*of wool, yarn*) ovillo; (*of finger*) yema; (*projectile*) bala; (*dance*) baile *m*
ballad ['bæləd] *s* balada
ballade [bə'lad] *s* (mus) balada
ballast ['bæləst] *s* (aer, naut) lastre *m*; (rr) balasto || *tr* lastrar; balastar
ball bearing *s* cojinete *m* de bolas
ballerina [,bælə'rinə] *s* bailarina
ballet ['bæle] *s* ballet *m*, baile *m*
ballistic [bə'lɪstɪk] *adj* balístico
balloon [bə'lun] *s* globo
ballot ['bælət] *s* balota; sufragio || *intr* balotar
ballot box *s* urna electoral
ball′play′er *s* pelotari *m*; beisbolero
ball′-point′ pen *s* bolígrafo, pluma estilográfica; biro (Arg); birome *f* (Arg, Urug); puntabola, punto bola (Bol); lapicero (CAm, Col); lápiz *m* de pasta (Chile); esferográfica, esfero (Col); estenógrafo (Cuba); lápiz *n*: de bolilla (Peru); plumilla (Ven)
ball′room′ *s* salón *m* de baile
ballyhoo ['bælɪ,hu] *s* alharaca, bombo || *tr* dar teatro a, dar bombo a
balm [bɑm] *s* bálsamo
balm•y ['bɑmi] *adj* (*comp* **-ier**; *super* **-iest**) bonancible, suave
baloney [bə'loni] *interj* (coll) ¡aprieta!
balsam ['bɔlsəm] *s* bálsamo
Baltic ['bɔltɪk] *adj* báltico
Baltimore oriole ['bɔltɪ,mor] *s* cacique veranero
baluster ['bæləstər] *s* balaustre *m*
bamboo [bæm'bu] *s* bambú *m*
bamboozle [bæm'buzəl] *tr* (coll) embaucar, engañar
bamboozler [bæm'buzlər] *s* (coll) embaucador *m*, engañabobos *mf*
ban [bæn] *s* prohibición; excomunión, entredicho; (*of marriage*) amonestación || *v* (*pret* & *pp* **banned**; *ger* **banning**) *tr* prohibir; excomulgar
banana [bə'nænə] *s* banana, plátano; (*tree*) banano, bananero, plátano
banana oil *s* esencia de pera

band [bænd] *s* banda; (*of people*) cuadrilla; (*of a hat*) cintillo; (*of a cigar*) anillo; liga de goma; (mus) banda, música, charanga || *intr* abanderizarse
bandage ['bændɪdʒ] *s* venda || *tr* vendar
bandanna [bæn'dænə] *s* pañuelo de hierbas
band′box′ *s* sombrerera
bandit ['bændɪt] *s* bandido
band′mas′ter *s* músico mayor
bandoleer [,bændə'lɪr] *s* bandolera
band saw *s* sierra continua, sierra sin fin
band′stand′ *s* quiosco de música
baneful ['benfəl] *adj* nocivo, venenoso; (*e.g., influence*) funesto
bang [bæŋ] *adv* de golpe || *interj* ¡pum! || *s* golpazo; (*of a door*) portazo; **bangs** flequillo || *tr* golpear con ruido; cerrar (*p.ej., una puerta*) de golpe || *intr* hacer estrépito
banish ['bænɪʃ] *tr* desterrar; despedir (*p.ej., miedo*)
banishment ['bænɪʃmənt] *s* destierro
banister ['bænɪstər] *s* balaustre *m*
bank [bæŋk] *s* banco; (*in certain games*) banca; (*small container for coins*) alcancía; (*of a river*) ribera, orilla; (*of earth, snow, clouds*) montón *m* || *tr* depositar o guardar (*dinero*) en un banco; amontonar; cubrir (*un fuego*) con cenizas || *intr* depositar dinero; **to bank on** (coll) contar con
bank account *s* cuenta de banco
bank′book′ *s* libreta de banco
banker ['bæŋkər] *s* banquero
banking ['bæŋkɪŋ] *adj* bancario || *s* banca
bank note *s* billete *m* de banco
bank roll *s* lío de papel moneda
bankrupt ['bæŋkrʌpt] *adj* & *s* bancarrotero; **to go bankrupt** hacer bancarrota || *tr* hacer quebrar; arruinar
bankrupt•cy ['bæŋkrʌptsi] *s* (*pl* **-cies**) bancarrota
banner ['bænər] *s* bandera, estandarte *m*
banner cry *s* grito de combate
banquet ['bæŋkwɪt] *s* banquete *m* || *tr* & *intr* banquetear
bantamweight ['bæntəm,wet] *s* (box) gallo
banter ['bæntər] *s* burla, chanza || *intr* burlar, chancear
baptism ['bæptɪzəm] *s* bautismo, bautizo; (fig) bautismo
Baptist ['bæptɪst] *adj* & *s* baptista *mf*, bautista *mf*
baptister•y ['bæptɪstəri] *s* (*pl* **-ies**) baptisterio, bautisterio
baptize ['bæptaɪz] *tr* bautizar
bar. *abbr* **barometer, barrel, barrister**
bar [bɑr] *s* barra; (*of door or window*) tranca; (*of jail*) reja; barrera; (*legal profession*) abogacía; (*members of legal profession*) curia; (*of public opinion*) tribunal *m*; (mus) barra; (*unit between two bars*) (mus) compás *m*; **behind bars** entre rejas || *prep* salvo; **bar none** sin excepción || *v* (*pret* & *pp* **barred**; *ger* **barring**) *tr* barrear, atrancar; impedir; prohibir; excluir
bar association *s* colegio de abogados
barb [bɑrb] *s* púa, lengüeta; (*of a pen*) barbilla

Barbados [bar'bedɔz] *s* la Barbada
barbarian [bar'bɛrɪ·ən] *s* bárbaro
barbaric [bar'bærɪk] *adj* bárbaro
barbarism ['barbə,rɪzəm] *s* barbaridad *f; (gram)* barbarismo
barbari·ty [bar'bærɪti] *s (pl -ties)* barbarie *f*
barbarous ['barbərəs] *adj* bárbaro
Barbary ape ['barbəri] *s* mono de Gibraltar
barbed [barbd] *adj* armado de púas; mordaz, punzante
barbed wire *s* alambre *m* de espino, alambre de púas
barber ['barbər] *adj* barberil || *s* barbero, peluquero
barber pole *s* percha de barbero
bar'ber·shop' *s* barbería, peluquería
bard [bard] *s* bardo; *(horse armor)* barda || *tr* bardar
bare [bɛr] *adj* desnudo; *(head)* descubierto; *(unfurnished)* desamueblado; *(wire)* sin aislar; mero, sencillo, puro || *tr* desnudar; descubrir
bare'back' *adj & adv* en pelo, sin silla
barefaced ['bɛr,fest] *adj* desvergonzado
bare'foot' *adj* descalzo || *adv* con los pies desnudos
bareheaded ['bɛr,hɛdɪd] *adj* descubierto || *adv* con la cabeza descubierta
barelegged ['bɛr,lɛgɪd] o ['bɛr,lɛgd] *adj* con las piernas desnudas
barely ['bɛrli] *adv* aspenas; escasamente
bargain ['bargɪn] *s (deal)* convenio, trato; *(cheap purchase)* ganga; **in the bargain** de añadidura || *tr* — **to bargain away** vender regalado || *intr* negociar; *(to haggle)* regatear
bargain counter *s* baratillo
bargain sale *s* venta de saldos
barge [bardʒ] *s* gabarra, lanchón *m;* bongo (SAm) || *intr* moverse pesadamente; **to barge in** entrar sin pedir permiso, entrar sin llamar a la puerta
barium ['bɛrɪ·əm] *s* bario
bark [bark] *s (of tree)* corteza; *(of dog)* ladrido; *(boat)* barca || *tr* ladrar *(p.ej., injurias)* || *intr* ladrar
barley ['barli] *s* cebada
barley water *s* hordiate *m*
bar magnet *s* barra imantada
bar'maid' *s* moza de taberna
barn [barn] *s* granero, troje *m;* caballeriza; establo; cochera
barnacle ['barnəkəl] *s* cirrópodo
barn owl *s* lechuza, oliva
barn'yard' *s* corral *m*
barnyard fowl *spl* aves *fpl* de corral
barometer [bə'ramɪtər] *s* barómetro
baron ['bærən] *s* barón *m*
baroness ['bærənɪs] *s* baronesa
baroque [bə'rok] *adj & s* barroco
barracks ['bærəks] *spl* cuartel *m*
barrage [bə'raʒ] *s (dam)* presa; (mil) barrera de fuego
barrel ['bærəl] *s* barril *m*, tonel *m; (of a gun, pen, etc.)* cañón *m*
barrel organ *s* organillo
barren ['bærən] *adj* árido, estéril

barricade [,bærɪ'ked] *s* barrera || *tr* barrear
barrier ['bærɪ·ər] *s* barrera
barrier reef *s* barrera de arrecifes
barrister ['bærɪstər] *s* (Brit) abogado
bar'room' *s* bar *m*, cantina
bar'tend'er *s* cantinero, tabernero, barman *m*
barter ['bartər] *s* trueque *m* || *tr* trocar
base [bes] *adj* bajo, humilde; infame, vil; *(metal)* bajo de ley || *s* base *f; (of electric light or vacuum tube; of projectile)* culote *m;* (mus) bajo || *tr* basar
base'ball' *s* beisbol *m;* pelota de beisbol
baseball player *s* beisbolero, beisbolista *m*
base'board' *s* rodapié *m*
Basel ['bazəl] *s* Basilea
baseless ['beslɪs] *adj* infundado
basement ['besmənt] *s* sótano
bashful ['bæʃfəl] *adj* encogido, tímido
basic ['besɪk] *adj* básico
basic commodities *spl* artículos de primera necesidad
basilica [bə'sɪlɪkə] *s* basílica
basin ['besɪn] *s* jofaina, palangana; *(of a fountain)* tazón *m; (of a river)* cuenca; *(of a harbor)* dársena
ba·sis ['besɪs] *s (pl -ses* [siz]) base *f;* **on the basis of** a base de
bask [bæsk] o [bask] *intr* asolearse, calentarse
basket ['bæskɪt] *s* cesta; *(large basket)* cesto; *(with two handles)* canasta; *(with lid)* excusabaraja; *(sport)* cesto, red *f*
bas'ket·ball' *s* baloncesto, basquetbol *m*
Basle [bal] *s* Basilea
Basque [bæsk] *adj & s (of Spain)* vascongado; *(of Spain and France)* vasco; *(of old Spain)* vascón *m*
bas-relief [,barɪ'lif] *s* bajo relieve
bass [bes] *adj & s* (mus) bajo || [bæs] *s* (ichth) róbalo; (ichth) micróptero
bass drum *s* bombo
bass horn *s* tuba
bas·so ['bæso] *s (pl -sos* o *-si* [si]) (mus) bajo
bassoon [bə'sun] *s* bajón *m*
bass viol ['vaɪ·əl] *s* violón *m*, contrabajo
bastard ['bæstərd] *adj & s* bastardo
bastard title *s* anteportada
baste [best] *tr (to sew slightly)* hilvanar; *(to moisten with drippings while roasting)* enlardar; *(to thrash)* azotar; *(to scold)* regañar
bat. *abbr* **battalion, battery**
bat [bæt] *s* palo; (coll) golpe *m;* (zool) murciélago *|| v (pret & pp* **batted;** *ger* **batting)** *tr* golpear; batear *(una pelota)*; **without batting an eye** sin inmutarse, sin pestañear || *intr* golpear
batch [bætʃ] *s (of bread)* hornada; *(of papers)* lío
bath [bæθ] *s* baño
bathe [beð] *tr* bañar || *intr* bañarse; **to go bathing** ir a bañarse
bather ['beðər] *s* bañista *mf*
bath'house' *s* casa de baños; caseta de baños
bathing beach *s* playa de baños
bathing beauty *s* sirena de la playa
bathing resort *s* estación balnearia
bathing suit *s* traje *m* de baño, bañador *m*

bathing trunks *spl* taparrabo
bath'robe' *s* albornoz *m*, bata de baño; bata, peinador *m*
bath'room' *s* baño, cuarto de baño
bathroom fixtures *spl* aparatos sanitarios
bath'tub' *s* bañera, baño
bathyscaphe ['bæθə,skæf] *s* batiscafo
baton [bæ'tɑn] *s* bastón *m*; (mus) batuta
battalion [bə'tæljən] *s* batallón *m*
batter ['bætər] *s* pasta, batido; (baseball) bateador *m* ‖ *tr* magullar, estropear
battering ram *s* ariete *m*
batter•y ['bætəri] *s* (pl -ies) batería; (primary) (elec) pila; (secondary) (elec) acumulador *m*; (law) violencia
battle ['bætəl] *s* batalla; **to do battle** librar batalla ‖ *tr* batallar
battle array *s* orden *m* de batalla
battle cry *s* grito de combate
battledore ['bætəl,dor] *s* raqueta; **battledore and shuttlecock** raqueta y volante
bat'tlefield' *s* campo de batalla
battle front *s* frente *m* de combate
battlement ['bætəlmənt] *s* almenaje *m*
battle piece *s* (paint) batalla
bat'tle•ship' *s* acorazado
battue [bæ'tu] o [bæ'tju] *s* batida
bauble ['bɔbəl] *s* chuchería; cetro de bufón
Bavaria [bə'vɛrɪ•ə] *s* Baviera
Bavarian [bə'vɛrɪ•ən] *adj* & *mf* bávaro
bawd [bɔd] *s* alcahuete *m*, alcahueta
bawd•y ['bɔdi] *adj* (comp -ier; super -iest) indecente, obsceno
bawd'y•house' *s* mancebía, lupanar *m*
bawl [bɔl] *s* voces *fpl*, gritos ‖ *tr* — **to bawl out** (slang) regañar ‖ *intr* vocear, gritar; llorar ruidosamente
bay [be] *adj* bayo ‖ *s* bahía; aullido, ladrido; caballo bayo; (bot) laurel *m*; **to keep at bay** tener a raya ‖ *intr* aullar, ladrar
Bay of Biscay *s* golfo de Vizcaya
bayonet ['be•ənɪt] *s* bayoneta ‖ *tr* herir o matar con bayoneta
bay rum *s* ron *m* de laurel, ron de malagueta
bay window *s* ventana salediza, mirador *m*
bazooka [bə'zukə] *s* bazuca
bbl. *abbr* barrel, barrels
B.C. *abbr* before Christ
bd. *abbr* board
be [bi] *v* (pres am [æm], is [ɪz] are [ɑr]; pret was [wɑz] o [wʌz], were [wʌr]; pp been [bɪn]) *intr* estar; ser; tener, p.ej., **to be cold** tener frío; **to be wrong** no tener razón: tener la culpa; **here is** o **here are** aquí tiene Vd.; **there is** o **there are** hay ‖ *v aux* estar, p.ej., **he is studying** está estudiando; ser, p.ej., **she was hit by a car** fué atropellada por un coche; deber, p.ej., **what am I to do?** ¿qué debo hacer? ‖ *v impers* ser, p.ej., **it is necessary to get up early** es necesario levantarse temprano; haber, p.ej., **it is sunny** hay sol; hacer, p.ej., **it is cold** hace frío
beach [bitʃ] *s* playa
beach'comb' *intr* raquear; **to go beachcombing** andar al raque
beach'comb'er *s* raquero; vago de playa

beach'head' *s* cabeza de playa
beach robe *s* albornoz *m*
beach shoe *s* playera
beach umbrella *s* sombrilla de playa
beach wagon *s* rubia, coche *m* rural
beacon ['bikən] *s* señal luminosa; (lighthouse) faro; (hill overlooking sea) hacho; radiofaro; (guide) faro ‖ *tr* iluminar, guiar ‖ *intr* brillar
bead [bid] *s* cuenta; (of glass) abalorio; (of sweat) gota; (moulding on corner of wall) guardavivo; **to say** o **tell one's beads** rezar el rosario
beadle ['bidəl] *s* bedel *m*
beagle ['bigəl] *s* sabueso
beak [bik] *s* pico; cabo, promontorio
beam [bim] *s* (of wood) viga; (of light, heat, etc.) rayo; (naut) bao; (direction perpendicular to the keel) (naut) través *m*; (of hope) (fig) rayo; **on the beam** siguiendo el haz del radiofaro; (coll) siguiendo el buen camino ‖ *tr* emitir (luz, ondas) ‖ *intr* brillar; sonreír alegremente
bean [bin] *s* haba (Vicia faba); alubia, judía (Phaseolus vulgaris); (of coffee, cocoa) haba; (slang) cabeza
bean'pole' *s* rodrigón *m* para frijoles; (tall, skinny person) (coll) poste *m* de telégrafo
bear [bɛr] *s* oso; (in stock market) bajista *mf* ‖ *v* (pret **bore** [bor]; pp **borne** [born]) *tr* cargar; traer; llevar (armas); apoyar; aguantar; sentir, experimentar; producir, rendir (frutos; interés); (to give birth to) parir; tener (amor, odio); **to bear out** confirmar ‖ *intr* dirigirse, volver; **to bear on** referirse a; **to bear up** no perder la esperanza; **to bear with** ser indulgente para con
beard [bɪrd] *s* barba; (of wheat) arista
beardless ['bɪrdlɪs] *adj* imberbe
bearer ['bɛrər] *s* portador *m*
bearing ['bɛrɪŋ] *s* porte *m*, presencia; referencia, relación; (mach) cojinete *m*; **bearings** orientación; **to lose one's bearings** desorientarse
bearish ['bɛrɪʃ] *adj* bajista
bear'skin' *s* piel *f* de oso; (military cap) morrión *m*
beast [bist] *s* bestia
beast•ly ['bistli] *adj* (comp -lier; super -liest) bestial; (coll) muy malo ‖ *adv* (coll) muy mal
beast of burden *s* bestia de carga, acémila
beat [bit] *s* golpe *m*; (of heart) latido; (of rhythm) compás *m*; marca del compás; (mus) tiempo; (phys) batimiento; (rad) batido; (of a policeman) ronda; (sponger) (slang) embestidor *m* ‖ *v* (pret **beat**; pp **beat** o **beaten**) *tr* azotar, pegar; batir; sacudir (una alfombra); aventajar; llevar (el compás); tocar (un tambor); (a una persona en una contienda) ganar; **to beat it** (slang) largarse; **to beat up** batir (p.ej., huevos); (slang) aporrear ‖ *intr* batir; latir (el corazón); **to beat against** azotar
beaten path ['bitən] *s* camino trillado
beater ['bitər] *s* batidor *m*; (mixer) batidora

beati·fy [bɪ'ætɪ,faɪ] v (pret & pp **-fied**) tr beatificar

beating ['bitɪŋ] s golpeo; (of wings) aleteo; (with a whip) paliza; (defeat) derrota

beau [bo] s (pl **beaus** o **beaux** [boz]) galán m, cortejo; novio; elegante m

beautician [bju'tɪʃən] s embellecedora, esteta mf, esteticista mf

beautiful ['bjutɪfəl] adj bello, hermoso

beauti·fy ['bjutɪ,faɪ] v (pret & pp **-fied**) tr hermosear, embellecer

beau·ty ['bjuti] s (pl **-ties**) beldad f, belleza; (person) preciosura

beauty contest s concurso de belleza

beauty parlor s salón m de belleza

beauty queen s reina de la belleza

beauty sleep s primer sueño (antes de medianoche)

beauty spot s lunar postizo; sitio pintoresco

beaver ['bivər] s castor m; piel f de castor

becalm [bɪ'kɑm] tr calmar, serenar

because [bɪ'kɔz] conj porque; **because of** por, por causa de

beck [bɛk] s seña (con la cabeza o la mano); **at the beck and call of** a la disposición de

beckon ['bɛkən] s seña (con la cabeza o la mano) || tr llamar por señas; atraer, tentar || intr hacer señas

be·come [bɪ'kʌm] v (pret **-came**; pp **-come**) tr convenir, sentar bien || intr hacerse; llegar a ser; ponerse, volverse; convertirse en; **to become of** ser de, p.ej., **what will become of the soldier?** ¿qué será del soldado? hacerse, p.ej., **what became of his pencil?** ¿qué se ha hecho su lápiz?

becoming [bɪ'kʌmɪŋ] adj conveniente, decente; que sienta bien

bed [bɛd] s cama; (of a river) cauce m; (of flower garden) macizo; **to go to bed** acostarse; **to take to bed** encamarse

bed and board s pensión completa, casa y comida

bed'bug' s chinche f

bed'cham'ber s alcoba, cuarto de dormir

bed'clothes' spl ropa de cama

bed'cov'er s cubrecama, cobertor m

bedding ['bɛdɪŋ] s ropa de cama; (for animals) cama

bedev·il [bɪ'dɛvəl] v (pret & pp **-iled** o **-illed**; ger **-iling** o **-illing**) tr atormentar, confundir

bed'fast' adj postrado en cama

bed'fel'low s compañero o compañera de cama

bedlam ['bɛdləm] s confusión, desorden m, tumulto

bed linen s ropa de cama

bed'pan' s silleta

bed'post' s pilar m de cama

bedridden ['bɛd,rɪdən] adj postrado en cama

bed'room' s alcoba, cuarto de dormir

bed'side' s cabecera

bed'sore' s úlcera de decúbito; **to get bedsores** decentarse

bed'spread' s sobrecama, cobertor m

bed'spring' s colchón m de muelles, somier m

bed'stead' s cuja

bed'straw' s paja de jergón

bed'tick' s cutí m

bed'time' s hora de acostarse

bed warmer s calientacamas m

bee [bi] s abeja

beech [bitʃ] s haya

beech'nut' s hayuco

beef [bif] s carne f de vaca; ganado vacuno de engorde; (coll) fuerza muscular; (slang) queja || tr — **to beef up** (coll) reforzar || intr (slang) quejarse; (slang) soplar

beef cattle s ganado vacuno de engorde

beef'steak' s biftec m

bee'hive' s colmena

bee'line' s — **to make a beeline for** ir en línea recta hacia, ir derecho a

beer [bɪr] s cerveza; **dark beer** cerveza parda, cerveza negra; **light beer** cerveza clara

beeswax ['biz,wæks] s cera de abejas || tr encerar

beet [bit] s remolacha

beetle ['bitəl] s escarabajo

beetle-browed ['bitəl,braʊd] adj cejijunto; (sullen) ceñudo

beet sugar s azúcar m de remolacha

be·fall [bɪ'fɔl] v (pret **-fell** ['fɛl]; pp **-fallen** ['fɔlən]) tr acontecer a || intr acontecer

befitting [bɪ'fɪtɪŋ] adj conveniente; decoroso

before [bɪ'for] adv antes; delante, enfrente || prep (in time) antes de; (in place) delante de; (in the presence of) ante || conj antes (de) que

before'hand' adv de antemano, con anticipación

befriend [bɪ'frɛnd] tr ofrecer amistad a, amparar, proteger

befuddle [bɪ'fʌdəl] tr aturdir, confundir

beg [bɛg] v (pret & pp **begged**; ger **begging**) tr pedir, rogar, solicitar; mendigar; huesar || intr mendigar; **to beg off** excusarse

be·get [bɪ'gɛt] v (pret **-got** ['gɑt]; pp **-gotten** o **-got**; ger **-getting**) tr engendrar

beggar ['bɛgər] s mendigo; pobre mf; pícaro, bribón m; sujeto, tipo

be·gin [bɪ'gɪn] v (pret **-gan** ['gæn]; pp **-gun** ['gʌn]; ger **-ginning**) tr & intr comenzar, empezar; **beginning with** a partir de

beginner [bɪ'gɪnər] s principiante mf; iniciador m

beginning [bɪ'gɪnɪŋ] s comienzo, principio

begrudge [bɪ'grʌdʒ] tr dar de mala gana; envidiar

beguile [bɪ'gaɪl] tr engañar; divertir, entretener; engañar (el tiempo)

behalf [bɪ'hæf] s — **on behalf of** en nombre de; a favor de

behave [bɪ'hev] intr conducirse, comportarse; portarse bien; funcionar

behavior [bɪ'hevjər] s conducta, comportamiento; funcionamiento

behaviorism [bɪ'hevjə,rɪzəm] s comportamentismo

behead [bɪ'hɛd] tr decapitar, descabezar

behind [bɪ'haɪnd] adv detrás; hacia atrás; con retraso; **to stay behind** quedarse atrás ||

prep detrás de; **behind the back of** a espaldas de; **behind the times** atrasado de noticias; **behind time** tarde ǁ *s* (slang) trasero, pompis *m*

behold [bɪ'hold] *v* (*pret* & *pp* **-held** ['hɛld]) *tr* contemplar ǁ *interj* ¡he aquí!

behoove [bɪ'huv] *tr* convenir, tocar

being ['biɪŋ] *adj* existente; **for the time being** por ahora, por el momento ǁ *s* ser, ente *m*

belch [bɛltʃ] *s* eructo, regüeldo ǁ *tr* vomitar (*p.ej., llamas, injurias*) ǁ *intr* eructar, regoldar

beleaguer [bɪ'ligər] *tr* sitiar, cercar

bel·fry ['bɛlfri] *s* (*pl* **-fries**) campanario

Belgian ['bɛldʒən] *adj* & *s* belga *mf*

Belgium ['bɛldʒəm] *s* Bélgica

be·lie [bɪ'laɪ] *v* (*pret* & *pp* **-lied** ['laɪd]; *ger* **-lying** ['laɪ·ɪŋ]) *tr* desmentir

belief [bɪ'lif] *s* creencia

believable [bɪ'livəbəl] *adj* creíble; (*source*) solvente

believe [bɪ'liv] *tr* & *intr* creer

believer [bɪ'livər] *s* creyente *mf*

belittle [bɪ'lɪtəl] *tr* empequeñecer, despreciar

bell [bɛl] *s* campana; (*electric bell*) timbre *m*, campanilla; (*ring of bell*) campanada ǁ *intr* bramar, berrear

bell'boy' *s* botones *m*

belle [bɛl] *s* beldad *f*, belleza

belles-lettres [,bɛl'lɛtrə] *spl* bellas letras

bell gable *s* espadaña

bell glass *s* fanal *m*

bell'hop' *s* (slang) botones *m*

bellicose ['bɛlɪ,kos] *adj* belicoso

belligerent [bə'lɪdʒərənt] *adj* & *s* beligerante *mf*

bellow ['bɛlo] *s* bramido; **bellows** fuelle *m*, barquín *m* ǁ *tr* gritar ǁ *intr* bramar

bell ringer *s* campanero

bellwether ['bɛl,wɛðər] *s* manso

bel·ly ['bɛli] *s* (*pl* **-lies**) barriga, vientre *m*; estómago ǁ *v* (*pret* & *pp* **-lied**) *intr* hacer barriga; hacer bolso (*las velas*)

bel'ly·ache' *s* (slang) dolor *m* de barriga ǁ *intr* (slang) quejarse

belly button *s* (coll) ombligo

belly dance *s* (coll) danza del vientre

bellyful ['bɛlɪ,fʊl] *s* (slang) panzada

bel'ly-land' *intr* (aer) aterrizar de panza

belong [bɪ'lɔŋ] *intr* pertenecer; deber estar

belongings [bɪ'lɔŋɪŋz] *spl* pertenencias, efectos; corotos

beloved [bɪ'lʌvɪd] o [bɪ'lʌvd] *adj* & *s* querido, amado

below [bɪ'lo] *adv* abajo; (*in a text*) más abajo; bajo cero, p.ej., **ten below** diez grados bajo cero ǁ *prep* debajo de; inferior a

belt [bɛlt] *s* cinturón *m*; (aer, mach) correa; (geog) faja, zona; **to tighten one's belt** ceñirse

bemoan [bɪ'mon] *tr* deplorar, lamentar

bench [bɛntʃ] *s* banco; (law) tribunal *m*

bend [bɛnd] *s* curva; (*in a road, river, etc.*) recodo, vuelta ǁ *v* (*pret* & *pp* **bent** [bɛnt]) *tr* encorvar; doblar (*un tubo; la rodilla*);

inclinar (*la cabeza*); dirigir (*sus esfuerzos*) ǁ *intr* encorvarse; doblarse; inclinarse

beneath [bɪ'niθ] *adv* abajo ǁ *prep* debajo de; inferior a

benediction [,bɛnɪ'dɪkʃən] *s* bendición *f*

benefaction [,bɛnɪ'fækʃən] *s* beneficio

benefactor ['bɛnɪ,fæktər] o [,bɛnɪ'fæktər] *s* bienhechor *m*

benefactress ['bɛnɪ,fæktrɪs] o [,bɛnɪ'fæktrɪs] *s* bienhechora

beneficence [bɪ'nɛfɪsəns] *s* beneficencia

beneficent [bɪ'nɛfɪsənt] *adj* bienhechor

beneficial [,bɛnɪ'fɪʃəl] *adj* beneficioso

beneficiar·y [,bɛnɪ'fɪʃɪ,ɛri] *s* (*pl* **-ies**) beneficiario

benefit ['bɛnɪfɪt] *s* beneficio; lasca; **for the benefit of** a beneficio de ǁ *tr* beneficiar

benefit performance *s* beneficio

benevolence [bɪ'nɛvələns] *s* benevolencia

benevolent [bɪ'nɛvələnt] *adj* benévolo; (*e.g., institution*) benéfico

benign [bɪ'naɪn] *adj* benigno

benigni·ty [bɪ'nɪgnɪti] *s* (*pl* **-ties**) benignidad

bent [bɛnt] *adj* encorvado, doblado, torcido; **bent on** resuelto a, empeñado en; **bent over** cargado de espaldas ǁ *s* encorvadura; inclinación *f*, propensión *f*

benzedrine ['bɛnzə,drin] *s* bencedrina

benzine [bɛn'zin] *s* bencina

bequeath [bɪ'kwið] o [bɪ'kwiθ] *tr* legar

bequest [bɪ'kwɛst] *s* manda, legado

berate [bɪ'ret] *tr* regañar, reñir

be·reave [bɪ'riv] *v* (*pret* & *pp* **-reaved** o **-reft** ['rɛft]) *tr* despojar, privar; desconsolar

bereavement [bɪ'rivmənt] *s* despojo, privación *f*; desconsuelo

berkelium [bər'kilɪ·əm] *s* berkelio

Berliner [bər'lɪnər] *s* berlinés *m*

ber·ry ['bɛri] *s* (*pl* **-ries**) baya; (*of coffee plant*) grano, haba

berserk ['bʌrsʌrk] *adj* frenético ǁ *adv* frenéticamente

berth [bʌrθ] *s* (*bed*) litera; (*room*) camarote *m*; (*for a ship*) amarradero; (coll) empleo, puesto

beryllium [bə'rɪlɪ·əm] *s* berilio

be·seech [bɪ'sitʃ] *v* (*pret* & *pp* **-sought** ['sɔt] o **-seeched**) *tr* suplicar

be·set [bɪ'sɛt] *v* (*pret* & *pp* **-set;** *ger* **-setting**) *tr* acometer, acosar; cercar, asaltar

beside [bɪ'saɪd] *adv* además, también ǁ *prep* cerca de, junto a; en comparación de; excepto; **beside oneself** fuera de sí; **beside the point** incongruente

besiege [bɪ'sidʒ] *tr* asediar, sitiar

besmirch [bɪ'smʌrtʃ] *tr* ensuciar, manchar

bespatter [bɪ'spætər] *tr* salpicar

be·speak [bɪ'spik] *v* (*pret* **-spoke** ['spok]; *pp* **-spoken**) *tr* apalabrar, pedir de antemano

best [bɛst] *adj* *super* mejor; óptimo ǁ *adv* *super* mejor; **had best** debería ǁ *s* (lo) mejor; (lo) más; **at best** a lo más; **to do one's best** hacer lo mejor posible; **to get the best of** aventajar, sobresalir; **to make the best of** sacar el mejor partido de

best girl *s* (coll) amiga preferida, novia

be•stir [bɪ'stʌr] v (pret & pp **-stirred;** ger **-stirring**) tr excitar, incitar; **to bestir one-self** esforzarse, afanarse

best man s padrino de boda

bestow [bɪ'sto] tr otorgar, conferir; dedicar

best seller s éxito de venta, campeón m de venta; éxito de librería

bet. abbr **between**

bet [bɛt] s apuesta ‖ v (pret & pp **bet** o **betted;** ger **betting**) tr & intr apostar; **I bet a que,** apuesto a que; **to bet on** apostar por; **you bet** (slang) ya lo creo

be•take [bɪ'tek] v (pret **-took** ['tʊk]; pp **-taken**) tr — **to betake oneself** dirigirse; darse, entregarse

be•think [bɪ'θɪŋk] v (pret & pp **-thought** ['θɔt]) tr — **to bethink oneself of** considerar, acordarse de

Bethlehem ['bɛθlɪ,hɛm] s Belén m

betide [bɪ'taɪd] tr presagiar; acontecer a ‖ intr acontecer

betoken [bɪ'tokən] tr anunciar, indicar, presagiar

betray [bɪ'tre] tr traicionar; descubrir, revelar

betrayal [bɪ'tre•əl] s traición; descubrimiento, revelación

betroth [bɪ'troð] o [bɪ'trɔθ] tr prometer en matrimonio; **to become betrothed** desposarse

betrothal [bɪ'troðəl] o [bɪ'trɔθəl] s desposorios, esponsales mpl

betrothed [bɪ'troð] o [bɪ'trɔθ] s prometido, novio

better ['bɛtər] adj comp mejor; **it is better to** más vale; **to grow better** mejorarse; **to make better** mejorar ‖ adv comp mejor; más; **had better** debería; **to like better** preferir ‖ s superior; ventaja; **to get the better of** llevar la ventaja a ‖ tr aventajar; mejorar; **to better oneself** mejorar su posición

better half s (coll) cara mitad

betterment ['bɛtərmənt] s mejoramiento; (in an illness) mejoría

between [bɪ'twin] adv en medio, entremedias ‖ prep entre; **between you and me** entre Vd. y yo; acá para los dos

be•tween'-decks' s entrecubiertas, entrepuentes mpl

between decks adv entrecubiertas

bev•el ['bɛvəl] adj biselado ‖ s (instrument) cartabón m; (sloping part) bisel m ‖ v (pret & pp **-eled** o **-elled;** ger **-eling** o **-elling**) tr biselar

beverage ['bɛvərɪdʒ] s bebida

bev•y ['bɛvi] s (pl **-ies**) (of birds) bandada; (of girls) grupo

bewail [bɪ'wel] tr & intr lamentar

beware [bɪ'wɛr] tr guardarse de ‖ intr tener cuidado; **beware of . . . !** ¡ojo con . . . !, ¡cuidado con . . . !; **to beware of** guardarse de

bewilder [bɪ'wɪldər] tr aturdir, dejar perplejo, desatinar

bewilderment [bɪ'wɪldərmənt] s aturdimiento, perplejidad

beyond [bɪ'jɑnd] adv más allá, más lejos ‖ prep más allá de; además de; no capaz de; **beyond a doubt** fuera de duda; **beyond the reach of** fuera del alcance de ‖ s — **the great beyond** el más allá, el otro mundo

bg. abbr **bag**

bias ['baɪ•əs] s sesgo, diagonal f; prejuicio; (electron) polarización de rejilla ‖ tr predisponer, prevenir

Bib. abbr **Bible, Biblical**

bib [bɪb] s babero; pepe m; (of apron) pechera

Bible ['baɪbəl] s Biblia

Biblical ['bɪblɪkəl] adj bíblico

bibliographer [,bɪblɪ'ɑgrəfər] s bibliógrafo

bibliogra•phy [,bɪblɪ'ɑgrəfi] s (pl **-phies**) bibliografía

bibliophile ['bɪblɪ•ə,faɪl] s bibliófilo

bicameral [baɪ'kæmərəl] adj bicameral

bicarbonate [baɪ'kɑrbə,net] s bicarbonato

bicker ['bɪkər] s discusión ociosa ‖ intr discutir ociosamente

bicycle ['baɪsɪkəl] s bicicleta

bid [bɪd] s oferta, postura; (in bridge) declaración ‖ v (pret **bade** [bæd] o **bid;** ger **bidden** ['bɪdən]) tr & intr ofrecer, pujar, licitar; (in bridge) declarar

bidder ['bɪdər] s postor m; (in bridge) declarante mf; **the highest bidder** el mejor postor

bidding ['bɪdɪŋ] s mandato, orden f; postura; (in bridge) declaración

bide [baɪd] tr — **to bide one's time** esperar la hora propicia

biennial [baɪ'ɛnɪ•əl] adj bienal

bier [bɪr] s féretro, andas

bifocal [baɪ'fokəl] adj bifocal ‖ **bifocals** spl anteojos bifocales

big [bɪg] adj (comp **bigger;** super **biggest**) grande; (considerable) importante; (grown-up) adulto; **big with child** preñada ‖ adv (coll) con jactancia; **to talk big** (coll) hablar gordo

bigamist ['bɪgəmɪst] s bígamo

bigamous ['bɪgəməs] adj bígamo

bigamy ['bɪgəmi] s bigamia

big-bellied ['bɪg,bɛlɪd] adj panzudo

Big Dipper s Carro mayor

big game s caza mayor

big-hearted ['bɪg,hɑrtɪd] adj magnánimo, generoso

bigot ['bɪgət] s intolerante mf, fanático

bigoted ['bɪgətɪd] adj intolerante, fanático

bigot•ry ['bɪgətri] s (pl **-ries**) intolerancia, fanatismo

big shot s (slang) pájaro de cuenta, señorón m, capitoste m

big stick s palo en alto

big toe s dedo gordo o grande (del pie)

bikini [bɪ'kini] s bikini m

bile [baɪl] s bilis f

bilge [bɪldʒ] s pantoque m ‖ tr desfondar

bilge pump s bomba de sentina

bilge water s agua de pantoque

bilge ways spl anguilas

bilingual [baɪ'lɪŋgwəl] adj bilingüe

bilious ['bɪljəs] *adj* bilioso
bilk [bɪlk] *tr* estafar, trampear
bill [bɪl] *s* (*statement of charges for goods or service*) cuenta, factura; (*paper money*) billete *m*; (*poster*) cartel *m*, aviso; cartel de teatro; (*draft of law*) proyecto de ley; (*handbill*) hoja suelta; (*of bird*) pico; (*com*) giro, letra de cambio ‖ *tr* facturar; cargar en cuenta a; anunciar por carteles ‖ *intr* darse el pico (*las palomas*); acariciarse (*los enamorados*); **to bill and coo** acariciarse y arrullarse
bill'board' *s* cartelera
billet ['bɪlɪt] *s* (mil) boleta; (mil) alojamiento ‖ *tr* (mil) alojar
billet-doux ['bɪle'du] *s* (*pl* **billets-doux** ['bɪle'duz]) esquela amorosa
bill'fold' *s* cartera de bolsillo, billetero
bill'head' *s* encabezamiento de factura
billiards ['bɪljərdz] *s* billar *m*
billion ['bɪljən] *s* (U.S.A.) mil millones; (Brit) billón *m*
bill of exchange *s* letra de cambio
bill of fare *s* lista de comidas, menú *m*
bill of lading ['ledɪŋ] *s* conocimiento de embarque
bill of sale *s* escritura de venta
billow ['bɪlo] *s* oleada, ondulación ‖ *intr* ondular, hincharse
bill'post'er *s* fijacarteles *m*, fijador *m* de carteles
bil·ly ['bɪli] *s* (*pl* **-lies**) cachiporra
billy goat *s* macho cabrío
bin [bɪn] *s* arcón *m*, hucha
bind [baɪnd] *v* (*pret & pp* **bound** [baʊnd]) *tr* ligar, atar; juntar, unir; (*with a garland*) enguirlandar; ribetear (*la orilla del vestido*); agavillar (*las mieses*); vendar (*una herida*); encuadernar (*un libro*); estreñir (*el vientre*)
binder·y ['baɪndəri] *s* (*pl* **-ies**) taller *m* de encuadernación
binding ['baɪndɪŋ] *s* atadura; (*of a book*) encuadernación
binding post *s* borne *m*, sujetahilo
binge [bɪndʒ] *s* (slang) borrachera; turca; **to go on a binge** (slang) pegarse una mona, coger una turca
binnacle ['bɪnəkəl] *s* bitácora
binoculars [bɪ'nɑkjələrz] o [baɪ'nɑkjələrz] *spl* gemelos, prismáticos
biochemical [,baɪə'kɛmɪkəl] *adj* bioquímico
biochemist [,baɪə'kɛmɪst] *s* bioquímico
biochemistry [,baɪə'kɛmɪstri] *s* bioquímica
biodegradable [,baɪə'dɪ'gredəbəl] *adj* biodegradable
biog. *abbr* **biographical, biography**
biographer [baɪ'ɑgrəfər] *s* biógrafo
biographic(al) [,baɪə'græfɪk(əl)] *adj* biográfico
biogra·phy [baɪ'ɑgrəfi] *s* (*pl* **-phies**) biografía
biologist [baɪ'ɑlədʒɪst] *s* biólogo
biology [baɪ'ɑlədʒi] *s* biología
biophysical [,baɪə'fɪzɪkəl] *adj* biofísico
biophysics [,baɪə'fɪzɪks] *s* biofísica
bioplasm ['baɪə,plæzəm] *s* bioplasma

biopsy ['baɪ·ɑpsi] *s* biopsia
biped ['baɪpɛd] *adj & s* bípedo
birch [bʌrtʃ] *s* abedul *m* ‖ *tr* azotar, varear
bird [bʌrd] *s* ave *f*, pájaro
bird cage *s* jaula
bird call *s* reclamo
bird'lime' *s* liga
bird of passage *s* ave *f* de paso
bird of prey *s* ave *f* de rapiña
bird'seed' *s* alpiste *m*, cañamones *mpl*
bird's'-eye' view *s* vista a ojo de pájaro
bird shot *s* perdigones *mpl*
birth [bʌrθ] *s* nacimiento; (*childbirth*) parto; origen *m*
birth certificate *s* partida de nacimiento
birth control *s* limitación de la natalidad, control de la natalidad, control de los nacimientos
birth'day' *s* cumpleaños *m*, natal *m*; (*of any event*) aniversario; **to have a birthday** cumplir años
birthday cake *s* pastel *m* de cumpleaños
birthday present *s* regalo de cumpleaños
birth'mark' *s* antojo, nevo materno
birth'place' *s* suelo natal, patria, lugar *m* de nacimiento
birth rate *s* natalidad
birth'right' *s* derechos de nacimiento; primogenitura
Biscay ['bɪske] *s* Vizcaya
biscuit ['bɪskɪt] *s* panecillo redondo; bizcocho
bisect [baɪ'sɛkt] *tr* bisecar ‖ *intr* empalmar (*dos caminos*)
bishop ['bɪʃəp] *s* obispo; (*in chess*) alfil *m*
bismuth ['bɪzməθ] *s* bismuto
bison ['baɪsən] *s* bisonte *m*
bit [bɪt] *s* poquito, pedacito; (*of food*) bocado; (*of time*) ratito; (*part of bridle*) bocado, freno; (*for drilling*) barrena; **a good bit** una buena cantidad
bitch [bɪtʃ] *s* (*dog*) perra; (*fox*) zorra; (*wolf*) loba; (vulg) mujer *f* de mal genio
bite [baɪt] *s* mordedura; (*of bird or insect*) picadura; (*burning sensation on tongue*) resquemo; (*of food*) bocado; (*snack*) (coll) tentempié *m*, refrigerio ‖ *v* (*pret* **bit** [bɪt]; *pp* **bit** o **bitten** ['bɪtən]) *tr* morder; picar (*los peces, los insectos*); resquemar (*la lengua los alimentos*); comerse (*las uñas*) ‖ *intr* morder; picar; resquemar; (*to be caught by a trick*) (slang) picar
biting ['baɪtɪŋ] *adj* penetrante; mordaz, picante
bitter ['bɪtər] *adj* amargo; (*e.g., struggle*) encarnizado; **to the bitter end** hasta el extremo; hasta la muerte
bitter almond *s* almendra amarga
bitterness ['bɪtərnɪs] *s* amargura
bitumen [bɪ'tjumən] *s* betún *m*
bivou·ac ['bɪvu,æk] *s* vivaque *m* ‖ *v* (*pret & pp* **-acked**; *ger* **-acking**) *intr* vivaquear
bizarre [bɪ'zɑr] *adj* original, raro
bk. *abbr* **bank, block, book**
bkg. *abbr* **banking**
bl. *abbr* **barrel**
b.l. *abbr* **bill of lading**

blabber ['blæbər] *tr* & *intr* barbullar
black [blæk] *adj* negro ‖ *s* negro; luto; **to wear black** ir de luto
black'-and-blue' *adj* encardenalado, amoratado
black'-and-white' *adj* en blanco y negro
black'ber'ry *s* (*pl* **-ries**) (*bush*) zarza; (*fruit*) zarzamora
black'bird' *s* mirlo
black'board' *s* encerado, pizarra
black box *s* registrador *m* de vuelo
black'damp' *s* mofeta
blacken ['blækən] *tr* ennegrecer; (*to defame*) desacreditar, denigrar
blackguard ['blægard] *s* bribón *m*, canalla *m* ‖ *tr* injuriar, vilipendiar
black'head' *s* espinilla, comedón *m*
black hole *s* (astr) agujero negro
blackish ['blækɪʃ] *adj* negruzco
black'jack' *s* (*club*) cachiporra; (*flag*) bandera negra (*de pirata*) ‖ *tr* aporrear
black'mail' *s* chantaje *m* ‖ *tr* amenazar con chantaje
blackmailer ['blæk,melər] *s* chantajista *mf*
Black Maria [mə'raɪ•ə] *s* (coll) coche *m* celular
black market *s* estraperlo, mercado negro
blackness ['blæknɪs] *s* negror *m*, negrura
black'out' *s* (*in wartime*) apagón *m*; (*in theater*) apagamiento de luces; (*of aviators*) visión negra; pérdida de la memoria; ceguera
black sheep *s* (fig) oveja negra, garbanzo negro
black'smith' *s* (*man who works with iron*) herrero; (*man who shoes horses*) herrador *m*
black'thorn' *s* espino negro, endrino
black tie corbata de smoking; smoking *m*
bladder ['blædər] *s* vejiga
blade [bled] *s* (*of a knife, sword*) hoja; (*of a propeller*) aleta; (*of a fan*) paleta; (*of an oar*) pala; (*of an electric switch*) cuchilla; (*sword*) espada; tallo de hierba; (coll) gallardo joven
blame [blem] *s* culpa ‖ *tr* culpar
blameless ['blemlɪs] *adj* inculpable, irreprochable
blanch [blænʧ] *tr* blanquear ‖ *intr* palidecer
bland [blænd] *adj* apacible; suave; (*character; weather*) blando
blandish ['blændɪʃ] *tr* engatusar, lisonjear
blank [blæŋk] *adj* en blanco; blanco, vacío; (*stare, look*) vago ‖ *s* blanco; papel blanco; formulario
blank check *s* firma en blanco; (fig) carta blanca
blanket ['blæŋkɪt] *adj* general, comprensivo ‖ *s* manta, frazada; (fig) capa, manto ‖ *tr* cubrir con manta; cubrir, obscurecer
blasé [bla'ze] *adj* hastiado
blaspheme [blæs'fim] *tr* blasfemar contra ‖ *intr* blasfemar
blasphemous ['blæsfɪməs] *adj* blasfemo
blasphe•my ['blæsfɪmi] *s* (*pl* **-mies**) blasfemia

blast [blæst] *s* (*of wind*) ráfaga; (*of air, sand, water*) chorro; (*of bellows*) soplo; (*of a horn*) toque *m*; carga de pólvora; voladura, explosión; **full blast** en plena marcha ‖ *tr* (*to blow up*) volar; arruinar; infamar, maldecir
blast furnace *s* alto horno
blast'off' *s* lanzamiento de cohete
blatant ['bletənt] *adj* ruidoso; vociglero; intruso; chillón, cursi
blaze [blez] *s* llamarada; (*fire*) incendio; (*bonfire*) hoguera; luz *f* brillante ‖ *tr* encender, inflamar; **to blaze a trail** abrir una senda ‖ *intr* encenderse; resplandecer
bldg. *abbr* **building**
bleach [bliʧ] *s* blanqueo ‖ *tr* blanquear; colar (*la ropa*)
bleachers ['bliʧərz] *spl* gradas al aire libre
bleak [blik] *adj* desierto, yermo, frío, triste
bleat [blit] *s* balido ‖ *intr* balar
bleed [blid] *v* (*pret* & *pep* **bled** [blɛd]) *tr* & *intr* sangrar
blemish ['blɛmɪʃ] *s* mancha ‖ *tr* manchar
blend [blɛnd] *s* mezcla; armonía ‖ *v* (*pret* & *pp* **blended** o **blent** [blɛnt]) *tr* mezclar; armonizar; fusionar ‖ *intr* mezclarse; armonizar; fusionarse
bless [blɛs] *tr* bendecir; **to be blessed with** estar dotado de
blessed ['blɛsɪd] *adj* bendito, santo
blessedness ['blɛsɪdnɪs] *s* bienaventuranza
blessing ['blɛsɪŋ] *s* bendición
blight [blaɪt] *s* niebla, roya; ruina ‖ *tr* anublar; arruinar
blimp [blɪmp] *s* dirigible pequeño
blind [blaɪnd] *adj* ciego ‖ *s* (*window shade*) estor *m*, transparente *m* de resorte; (*Venetian blind*) persiana; pretexto, subterfugio ‖ *tr* cegar; (*to dazzle*) deslumbrar; (*to deceive*) cegar, vendar
blind alley *s* callejón *m* sin salida
blind date *s* cita a ciegas
blinder ['blaɪndər] *s* anteojera
blind flying *s* (aer) vuelo a ciegas
blind'fold' *adj* vendado de ojos ‖ *s* venda ‖ *tr* vendar los ojos a
blind landing *s* aterrizaje *m* a ciegas
blind man *s* ciego
blind'man's' buff *s* gallina ciega
blindness ['blaɪndnɪs] *s* ceguedad
blink [blɪŋk] *s* guiñada, parpadeo ‖ *tr* guiñar (*el ojo*) ‖ *intr* guiñar, parpadear, pestañear; oscilar (*la luz*)
blip [blɪp] *s* bache *m*
bliss [blɪs] *s* bienaventuranza, felicidad
blissful ['blɪsfəl] *adj* bienaventurado, feliz
blister ['blɪstər] *s* ampolla, vejiga ‖ *tr* ampollar ‖ *intr* ampollarse
blithe [blaɪð] *adj* alegre, animado
blitzkrieg ['blɪts,krig] *s* guerra relámpago
blizzard ['blɪzərd] *s* ventisca, chubasco de nieve
bloat [blot] *tr* hinchar ‖ *intr* hincharse, abotagarse
block [blak] *s* bloque *m*; (*of hatter*) horma; (*of houses*) manzana; (*for chopping meat*)

bi
bl

tajo; estorbo, obstáculo || *tr* cerrar, obstruir; conformar (*un sombrero*)

blockade [blɑ'ked] *s* bloqueo || *tr* bloquear

blockade runner *s* forzador *m* de bloqueo

block and tackle *s* aparejo de poleas

block'bust'er *s* (coll) bomba rompedora

block'head' *s* tonto, zoquete *m*

block signal *s* (rr) señal *f* de tramo

blond [blɑnd] *adj* rubio, blondo || *s* rubio (*hombre rubio*)

blonde [blɑnd] *s* rubia (*mujer rubia*)

blood [blʌd] *s* sangre *f;* **in cold blood** a sangre fría

bloodcurdling ['blʌd,kʌrdlɪŋ] *adj* horripilante

blood'hound' *s* sabueso

blood poisoning *s* envenenamiento de la sangre

blood pressure *s* presión arterial

blood pudding *s* morcilla

blood relation *s* pariente consanguíneo

blood'shed' *s* efusión de sangre

blood'shot' *adj* inyectado en sangre, encarnizado

blood'stream' *s* corriente *f* sanguínea

blood test *s* análisis *m* de sangre

blood'thirst'y *adj* sanguinario

blood transfusion *s* transfusión de sangre

blood vessel *s* vaso sanguíneo

blood·y ['blʌdi] *adj* (*comp* **-ier;** *super* **-iest**) sangriento || *v* (*pret & pp* **-ied**) *tr* ensangrentar

bloom [blum] *s* florecimiento; flor *f* || *intr* florecer

blossom ['blɑsəm] *s* brote *m,* flor *f;* **in blossom** en cierne || *intr* cerner, florecer

blot [blɑt] *s* borrón *m* || *v* (*pret & pp* **blotted;** *ger* **blotting**) *tr* (*to smear*) borrar; secar con papel secante; **to blot out** borrar || *intr* borrarse; echar borrones (*una pluma*)

blotch [blɑtʃ] *s* manchón *m; (in the skin)* erupción

blotter ['blɑtər] *s* teleta, secafirmas *m*

blotting paper *s* papel *m* secante

blouse [blaʊs] *s* blusa

blow [blo] *s* (*hit, stroke*) golpe; (*blast of air*) soplo, soplido; (*blast of wind*) ventarrón *m;* (*of horn*) toque *m,* trompetazo; (*sudden sorrow*) estocada, ramalazo; (*boaster*) (slang) fanfarrón *m;* **to come to blows** venir a las manos || *v* (*pret* **blew** [blu]; *pp* **blown**) || *tr* soplar; sonar, tocar (*un instrumento de viento*); silbar (*un silbato*); sonarse (*las narices*); quemar (*un fusible*); (slang) malgastar (*dinero*); **to blow out** apagar soplando; quemar (*un fusible*); **to blow up** (*with air*) inflar; (*e.g., with dynamite*) volar, hacer saltar; ampliar (*una foto*) || *intr* soplar; (*to pant*) jadear, resoplar; fundirse (*un fusible*); (slang) fanfarronear; **to blow out** apagarse con el aire; quemarse, fundirse (*un fusible*); reventar (*un neumático*); **to blow up** volarse; (*to fail*) fracasar; (*with anger*) (slang) estallar, reventar

blow'out' *s* (aut) reventón *m; (of a fuse)* quemazón *f;* (slang) tertulia concurrida, festín *m*

blowout patch *s* parche *m* para neumático

blow'pipe' *s* (*torch*) soplete *m; (peashooter)* cerbatana

blow'torch' *s* antorcha a soplete, lámpara de soldar

blubber ['blʌbər] *s* grasa de ballena; lloro ruidoso || *intr* llorar ruidosamente

bludgeon ['blʌdʒən] *s* cachiporra || *tr* aporrear; intimidar

blue [blu] *adj* azul; abatido, triste || *s* azul *m;* **the blues** la murria, la morriña || *tr* azular; añilar (*la ropa blanca*) || *intr* azularse

blue'ber'ry *s* (*pl* **-ries**) mirtilo

blue chip *s* valor *m* de primera fila

blue'jay' *s* cianocita

blue jeans *spl* blujins *mpl,* vaqueros; pantalones de mezclilla (C-R, Mex); mecánicos (CAm, Cuba, S-D); pantalones azules (CAm); azulones (El Salv); mahones (P-R, S-D)

blue moon *s* cosa muy rara; **once in a blue moon** cada muerte de obispo, de Pascuas a Ramos

Blue Nile *s* Nilo Azul

blue'-pen'cil *tr* marcar o corregir con lápiz azul

blue'print' *s* cianotipo || *tr* copiar a la cianotipia

blue'stock'ing *s* (coll) marisabidilla

blue streak *s* (coll) rayo; **to talk a blue streak** (coll) soltar la tarabilla

bluff [blʌf] *adj* escarpado; *s* risco, peñasco escarpado; (*deception*) farol *m,* blof *m;* **to call someone's bluff** cogerle la palabra a uno || *intr* farolear, papelonear

blunder ['blʌndər] *s* disparate *m,* desatino || *intr* disparatar, desatinar

blunt [blʌnt] *adj* despuntado, embotado; brusco, franco, directo || *tr* despuntar, embotar

bluntness ['blʌntnɪs] *s* embotadura; brusquedad, franqueza

blur [blʌr] *s* borrón *m,* mancha || *v* (*pret & pp* **blurred;** *ger* **blurring**) *tr* empañar; obscurecer (*la vista*) || *intr* empañarse

blurb [blʌrb] *s* anuncio efusivo

blurt [blʌrt] *tr* — **to blurt out** soltar abrupta e impulsivamente

blush [blʌʃ] *s* rubor *m,* sonrojo || *intr* ruborizarse, sonrojarse

bluster ['blʌstər] *s* tumulto, gritos; jactancia || *intr* soplar con furia (*el viento*); bravear, fanfarronear

blustery ['blʌstəri] *adj* tempestuoso; (*wind*) violento; (*swaggering*) fanfarrón

blvd. *abbr* **boulevard**

boar [bor] *s* (*male swine*) verraco; (*wild hog*) jabalí *m*

board [bord] *s* tabla; (*to post announcements*) tablillo; (*table with meal*) mesa; (*daily meals*) pensión; (*organized group*) junta, consejo; (naut) bordo; **in boards** (bb) en cartoné; **on board** en el tren; (naut) a bordo || *tr* entablar; subir a (*un tren*);

embarcarse en (*un buque*) ‖ *intr* hospedarse; estar de pupilo

board and lodging *s* mesa y habitación, pensión completa

boarder ['bordər] *s* pensionista *mf*, pupilo

boarding house *s* pensión, casa de huéspedes

boarding school *s* escuela de internos

board of health *s* junta de sanidad

board of trade *s* junta de comercio

board of trustees *s* consejo de administración

board'walk' *s* paseo entablado a la orilla del mar

boast [bost] *s* jactancia, baladronada ‖ *intr* jactarse, baladronear, bravatear

boastful ['bostfəl] *adj* jactancioso

boat [bot] *s* barco, buque *m*, nave *f*; (*small boat*) bote *m*; **to be in the same boat** correr el mismo riesgo

boat hook *s* bichero

boat'house' *s* casilla para botes

boating ['botɪŋ] *s* paseo en barco

boat•man ['botmən] *s* (*pl* **-men** [mən]) barquero, lanchero

boat race *s* regata

boatswain *s* ['bosən] *s* contramaestre *m*

boatswain's chair *s* guindola

boatswain's mate *s* segundo contramaestre

bob [bɑb] *s* (*of pendulum of clock*) lenteja; (*of plumb line*) plomo; (*of a fishing line*) corcho; (*of a horse*) cola cortada; (*of a girl*) pelo cortado corto; (*jerky motion*) sacudida ‖ *v* (*pret & pp* **bobbed;** *ger* **bobbing**) *tr* cortar corto ‖ *intr* agitarse, menearse; **to bob up and down** subir y bajar con sacudidas cortas

bobbin ['babɪn] *s* broca, canilla, bobina

bobby pin ['babi] *s* horquillita para el pelo

bob'by•socks' *spl* (coll) tobilleras (*de jovencita*)

bobbysoxer ['babɪ,saksər] *s* (coll) tobillera

bobolink ['babə,lɪŋk] *s* chambergo

bob'sled' *s* doble trineo articulado

bob'tail' *s* animal *m* rabón; cola corta; cola cortada

bob'white' *s* colín *m* de Virginia

bock beer [bɑk] *s* cerveza de marzo

bode [bod] *tr & intr* anunciar, presagiar; **to bode ill** ser un mal presagio; **to bode well** ser un buen presagio

bodice ['badɪs] *s* jubón *m*, corpiño

bodily ['badɪli] *adj* corporal, corpóreo ‖ *adv* en persona; en conjunto

bodkin ['badkɪn] *s* (*needle*) aguja roma; (*for lady's hair*) espadilla; (*to make holes in cloth*) punzón *m*

bod•y ['badi] *s* (*pl* **-ies**) cuerpo; (*of a carriage or auto*) caja, carrocería

bod'y•guard' *s* (mil) guardia de corps; guardaespaldas *m*

body shop *s* taller *m* carrocero

Boer [bor] o [bʊr] *s* bóer *mf*

Boer War *s* guerra del Transvaal

bog [bɑg] *s* pantano ‖ *v* (*pret & pp* **bogged;** *ger* **bogging**) *intr* — **to bog down** atascarse, hundirse

bogey ['bogi] *s* duende *m*, coco

bo'gey•man' *s* (*pl* **-men** [,mɛn]) duende *m*, espantajo

bogus ['bogəs] *adj* (coll) fingido, falso

bo•gy ['bogi] *s* (*pl* **-gies**) duende *m*, demonio, coco

Bohemian [bo'himɪ•ən] *adj & s* bohemio

boil [bɔɪl] *s* hervor *m*, ebullición; (pathol) divieso, furúnculo ‖ *tr* hacer hervir, herventar ‖ *intr* hervir, bullir; **to boil over** salirse (*un líquido*) al hervir

boiler ['bɔɪlər] *s* caldera; (*for cooking*) marmita, olla

boil'er•mak'er *s* calderero

boiler room *s* sala de calderas

boiling ['bɔɪlɪŋ] *adj* hirviente, hirviendo ‖ *s* hervor *m*, ebullición

boiling point *s* punto de ebullición

boisterous ['bɔɪstərəs] *adj* bullicioso, ruidoso, estrepitoso

bold [bold] *adj* audaz, arrojado, osado; descarado, impudente; temerario

bold'face' *s* negrilla

boldness ['boldnɪs] *s* audacia, arrojo, osadía; descaro, impudencia; temeridad

Bolivia [bo'lɪvɪ•ə] *s* Bolivia

Bolivian [bo'lɪvɪ•ən] *adj & s* boliviano

boll weevil [bol] *s* gorgojo del algodón

Bologna [bə'lonjə] *s* Bolonia

Bolshevik ['balʃəvɪk] o ['bolʃəvɪk] *adj & s* bolchevique *mf*

Bolshevism ['balʃə,vɪzəm] o ['bolʃə,vɪzəm] *s* bolchevismo

bolster ['bolstər] *s* (*of bed*) larguero, travesaño; refuerzo, soporte *m* ‖ *tr* apoyar, sostener; animar, alentar

bolt [bolt] *s* perno; (*to fasten a door*) cerrojo, pasador *m*; (*arrow*) cuadrillo; (*of lightning*) rayo; (*of cloth or paper*) rollo ‖ *tr* empernar; acerrojar; deglutir de una vez; cribar, tamizar; disidir de (*un partido político*) ‖ *intr* salir de repente; disidir; desbocarse (*un caballo*)

bolter ['boltər] *s* disidente *mf*; (*sieve*) criba, tamiz *m*

bolt from the blue *s* rayo en cielo sin nubes; suceso inesperado

bomb [bam] *s* bomba ‖ *tr* bombear, bombardear

bombard [bam'bard] *tr* bombardear; (*e.g., with questions*) asediar

bombardment [bam'bardmənt] *s* bombardeo

bombast ['bambæst] *s* ampulosidad

bombastic [bam'bæstɪk] *adj* ampuloso

bomb crater *s* (mil) embudo de bomba

bomber ['bamər] *s* bombardero

bomb'proof' *adj* a prueba de bombas

bomb release *s* lanzabombas *m*

bomb'shell' *s* bomba; **to fall like a bombshell** caer como una bomba

bomb shelter *s* refugio antiaéreo

bomb'sight' *s* mira de bombardeo, visor *m*

bona fide ['bonə,faɪdə] *adj & adv* de buena fe

bonbon ['ban,ban] *s* bombón *m*, confite *m*

bond [band] *s* (*tie, union*) enlace *m*, vínculo, lazo de unión; (*interest-bearing certificate*) bono. obligación; (*surety*) fianza; (mas) aparejo; **bonds** cadenas, grillos; **in bond** en depósito bajo fianza

bondage ['bɑndɪdʒ] *s* cautiverio, servidumbre

bonded warehouse *s* depósito comercial

bond'hold'er *s* obligacionista *mf*, tenedor *m* de bonos

bonds•man ['bɑndzmən] *s* (*pl* **-men** [mən]) fiador *m*

bone [bon] *s* hueso; (*of fish*) espina; **bones** esqueleto; (*mortal remains*) huesos; castañuelas; (*dice*) (coll) dados; **to have a bone to pick with** tener una queja con; **to make no bones about** no andarse con rodeos en ‖ *tr* desosar; quitar la espina a; emballenar (*un corsé*) ‖ *intr* — **to bone up on** (coll) empollar, estudiar con ahinco

bone'head' *s* (coll) mentecato, zopenco

boneless ['bonlɪs] *adj* mollar, desosado; (*fish*) sin espinas

boner ['bonər] *s* (coll) patochada, plancha, gazapo

bonfire ['bɑn,faɪr] *s* hoguera

bonnet ['bɑnɪt] *s* gorra; (*sunbonnet*) papalina; (*of auto*) cubierta, capó *m*

bonus ['bonəs] *s* prima, plus *m*; dividendo extraordinario

bon•y ['boni] *adj* (*comp* **-ier;** *super* **-iest**) osudo; descarnado; (*fish*) espinoso

boo [bu] *s* rechifla; **not to say boo** no decir ni chus ni mus ‖ *tr & intr* abuchear, rechiflar

boo•by ['bubi] *s* (*pl* **-bies**) bobalicón *m*, zopenco; el peor jugador

booby prize *s* premio al peor jugador

booby trap *s* (*mine*) trampa explosiva; (*trick*) zancadilla

boogie-woogie ['bugi'wugi] *s* bugui-bugui *m*

book [buk] *s* libro; (*bankbook*) libreta; (*book containing records of business transactions*) libro-registro; (*of cigaret paper, stamps, etc.*) librillo; **to keep books** llevar libros ‖ *tr* reservar (*un pasaje*); escriturar (*a un actor*)

bookbinder ['buk,baɪndər] *s* encuadernador *m*

book'bind'er•y *s* (*pl* **-ies**) encuadernación (*taller*)

book'bind'ing *s* encuadernación (*acción, arte*)

book'case' *s* armario para libros, estante *m* para libros

book end *s* apoyalibros *m*

bookie ['buki] *s* (coll) corredor *m* de apuestas

booking ['bukɪŋ] *s* (*of passage*) reservación; (*of an actor*) escritura

booking clerk *s* taquillero (*que despacha pasajes o localidades*)

bookish ['bukɪʃ] *adj* libresco

book'keep'er *s* tenedor *m* de libros

book'keep'ing *s* teneduría de libros, contabilidad

book'mak'er *s* corredor *m* de apuestas

book'mark' *s* registro

book'plate' *s* ex libris *m*

book review *s* reseña

book'sell'er *s* librero

book'shelf' *s* (*pl* **-shelves** [,ʃɛlvz] estante *m* para libros

book'stand' *s* (*rack*) atril *m*; mostrador *m* para libros; puesto de venta para libros

book'store' *s* librería

book'worm' *s* polilla que roe los libros; (fig) ratón *m* de biblioteca

boom [bum] *s* (*sudden prosperity*) auge *m*, boom *m*; (*noise*) estampido, trueno; (*of a crane*) aguilón *m*; (naut) botalón *m* ‖ *intr* hacer estampido, tronar; estar en auge

boomerang ['bumə,ræŋ] *s* bumerán *m*

boom town *s* pueblo en bonanza

boon [bun] *s* bendición, dicha

boon companion *s* buen compañero

boor [bur] *s* patán *m*, rústico

boorish ['burɪʃ] *adj* rústico, zafio

boost [bust] *s* empujón *m* hacia arriba; (*in price*) alza; alabanza; ayuda ‖ *tr* empujar hacia arriba; alzar (*el precio*); alabar; ayudar

booster ['bustər] *s* cohete *m* lanzador; primera etapa de un cohete lanzador; (*enthusiastic backer*) bombista *mf*

booster shot *s* inyección secundaria

boot [but] *s* bota; **to boot** de añadidura, además; **to die with one's boots on** morir al pie del cañón ‖ *tr* dar un puntapié a; **to boot out** (slang) poner en la calle

boot'black' *s* limpiabotas *m*

booth [buθ] *s* casilla, quiosco; (*to telephone, to vote, etc.*) cabina; (*at a fair or market*) puesto

boot'jack' *s* sacabotas *m*

boot'leg' *adj* contrabandista; de contrabando ‖ *s* contrabando de licores ‖ *v* (*pret & pp* **-legged;** *ger* **-legging**) *tr* pasar de contrabando ‖ *intr* contrabandear en bebidas alcohólicas

bootlegger ['but,lɛgər] *s* destilador *m* clandestino, contrabandista *m*

boot'leg'ging *s* contrabando en bebidas alcohólicas

bootlicker ['but,lɪkər] *s* (slang) quitamotas *mf*, lavacaras *mf*

boot'strap' *s* tirilla de bota

boo•ty ['buti] *s* (*pl* **-ties**) botín *m*, presa

booze [buz] *s* (coll) bebida alcohólica ‖ *intr* borrachear

bor. *abbr* **borough**

borax ['boræks] *s* bórax *m*

Bordeaux [bɔr'do] *s* Burdeos

border ['bɔrdər] *adj* frontero, fronterizo ‖ *s* borde *m*, margen *m & f*; frontera; **borders** bambalinas ‖ *tr* bordear; deslindar ‖ *intr* confinar

border clash *s* encuentro fronterizo

bor'der•line' *adj* incierto, indefinido ‖ *s* frontera

bore [bor] *s* (*drill hole*) barreno; (*size of hole*) calibre *m*; (*of firearm*) alma, ánima; (*of cylinder*) alesaje *m*; (*wearisome person*) latoso, machaca *mf*; fastidio ‖ *tr* aburrir, fastidiar; barrenar, hacer (*un agujero*)

boredom ['bordəm] *s* aburrimiento, fastidio

boring ['borɪŋ] *adj* aburrido, pesado; **that's terribly boring** es una lata

born [bɔrn] *adj* nacido; (*natural, by birth*) nato, innato; **to be born** nacer

borough [ˈbʌro] *s* (*town*) villa; distrito electoral de municipio

borrow [ˈbaro] o [ˈbɔro] *tr* pedir o tomar prestado; apropiarse (*p.ej., una idea*); incorporar (*un elemento lingüístico extranjero*); **to borrow trouble** tomarse una molestia sin motivo alguno

borrower [ˈbaro•ər] o [ˈbɔro•ər] *s* prestatario

borrowing [ˈbaro•ɪŋ] o [ˈbɔro•ɪŋ] *s* préstamo; préstamo lingüístico, extranjerismo

bosom [ˈbuzəm] *s* seno; (*of shirt*) pechera; corazón *m*, pecho

bosom friend *s* amigo de la mayor confianza

Bosporus [ˈbaspərəs] *s* Bósforo

boss [bɔs] o [bas] *s* (*coll*) amo, capataz *m*, mandamás *m*, jefe *m*; (*in politics*) (*coll*) cacique *m*; protuberancia ‖ *tr* (*coll*) mandar, dominar

bossism [ˈbɔsɪzəm] *s* caciquismo

boss•y [ˈbɔsi] *adj* (*comp* **-ier**; *super* **-iest**) mandón

botanical [bəˈtænɪkəl] *adj* botánico

botanist [ˈbatənɪst] *s* botánico

botany [ˈbatəni] *s* botánica

botch [batʃ] *s* remiendo chapucero ‖ *tr* remendar chapuceramente

both [boθ] *adj & pron* ambos ‖ *adv* igualmente ‖ *conj* a la vez; **both . . . and** tanto . . . como, así . . . como

bother [ˈbaðər] *s* incomodidad, molestia, majadería, murga ‖ *tr* incomodar, molestar, majaderear, pololear ‖ *intr* molestarse

bothersome [ˈbaðərsəm] *adj* incómodo, molesto, fastidioso

bottle [ˈbatəl] *s* botella, frasco ‖ *tr* embotellar; **to bottle up** (nav) embotellar

bot′tle•neck′ *s* gollete *m*; (*in traffic*) embotellado

bottle opener [ˈopənər] *s* abrebotellas *m*

bottom [ˈbatəm] *adj* (*price*) (el) más bajo; (*e.g., dollar*) último; (*of a chair*) asiento; (*of jar*) culo; (*coll*) trasero; **at bottom** en el fondo; **to go to the bottom** irse a pique

bottomless [ˈbatəmlɪs] *adj* sin fondo, insondable

boudoir [buˈdwar] *s* tocador *m*

bough [baʊ] *s* rama

bouillon [ˈbuljan] *s* caldo

boulder [ˈboldər] *s* pedrejón *m*

boulevard [ˈbulə,vard] *s* bulevar *m*

bounce [baʊns] *s* rebote *m* ‖ *tr* hacer botar; (*slang*) despedir ‖ *intr* botar, rebotar; saltar; **to bounce along** dar saltos al andar

bouncer [ˈbaʊnsər] *s* cosa grande; (*slang*) apagabroncas *m*

bouncing [ˈbaʊnsɪŋ] *adj* frescachón, vigoroso; (*baby*) gordinflón

bound [baʊnd] *adj* atado, ligado; (*book*) encuadernado; dispuesto, propenso; puesto en aprendizaje; **bound for** con destino a, con rumbo a; **bound in boards** (bb) encartonado, en cartoné; **bound up in** entregado

a, muy adicto a; absorto en ‖ *s* salto; (*of a ball*) bote *m*; límite *m*, confín *m*; **bounds** región, comarca; **out of bounds** fuera de los límites; **within bounds** a raya

bounda•ry [ˈbaʊndəri] *s* (*pl* **-ries**) límite *m*, frontera; (*established*) parámetro

boundary mark *s* (*annotation*) acotamiento

boundary stone *s* mojón *m*

bounder [ˈbaʊndər] *s* persona vulgar y malcriada

boundless [ˈbaʊndlɪs] *adj* ilimitado, inmenso, infinito

bountiful [ˈbaʊntɪfəl] *adj* generoso, liberal; abundante

boun•ty [ˈbaʊnti] *s* (*pl* **-ties**) generosidad, liberalidad; don *m*, favor *m*; galardón *m*, premio; (*bonus*) prima; (*mil*) premio de enganche

bouquet [buˈke] *s* ramillete *m*; (*aroma of a wine*) nariz *f*

bourgeois [ˈbʊrʒwa] *adj & s* burgués *m*

bourgeoisie [,bʊrʒwaˈzi] *s* burguesía

bout [baʊt] *s* encuentro; rato; (*of an illness*) ataque *m*

bow [baʊ] *s* inclinación, reverencia; (*of a ship*) proa ‖ *tr* inclinar (*la cabeza*) ‖ *intr* inclinarse; **to bow and scrape** hacer reverencias obsequiosas; **to bow to** saludar, inclinarse delante ‖ [bo] *s* (*for shooting an arrow*) arco; lazo, nudo; (*mus*) arco; (*stroke of bow*) (mus) arqueada ‖ *tr* (mus) tocar con arco ‖ *intr* arquearse

bowdlerize [ˈbaʊdlə,raɪz] *tr* expurgar

bowel [ˈbaʊ•əl] *s* intestino; **bowels** intestinos; (*inner part*) entrañas

bowel movement *s* evacuación del vientre; **to have a bowel movement** evacuar el vientre

bower [ˈbaʊ•ər] *s* emparrado, glorieta

bower•y [ˈbaʊ•əri] *adj* frondoso, sombreado ‖ *s* (*pl* **-ies**) finca, granja

bowknot [ˈbo,nat] *s* lazada

bowl [bol] *s* (*for soup or broth*) escudilla, cuenco; (*for washing hands*) jofaina, palangana; (*of toilet*) cubeta, taza; (*of fountain*) tazón *m*; (*of spoon*) paleta; (*of pipe*) hornillo; (*hollow place*) concavidad, cuenco ‖ *tr* — **to bowl over** tumbar ‖ *intr* jugar a los bolos; **to bowl along** rodar

bowlegged [ˈbo,lɛgd] o [ˈbo,lɛgɪd] *adj* patiestevado

bowler [ˈbolər] *s* jugador *m* de bolos; (Brit) sombrero hongo

bowling [ˈbolɪŋ] *s* juego de bolos, boliche *m*

bowling alley *s* bolera, boliche *m*

bowling green *s* bolera encespada

bowshot [ˈbo,ʃat] *s* tiro de flecha

bowsprit [ˈbaʊsprit] o [ˈbosprɪt] *s* bauprés *m*

bow tie [bo] *s* corbata de mariposa, pajarita

bowwow [ˈbaʊ,waʊ] *interj* ¡guau! ‖ *s* guau guau *m*

box [baks] *s* caja; (*slap*) bofetada; (*plant*) boj *m*; (*in newspaper*) recuadro; (theat) palco ‖ *tr* encajonar; (*to slap*) abofetear; (naut) cuartear (*la aguja*) ‖ *intr* boxear

box′car′ *s* vagón *m* de carga cerrado

boxer ['bɑksər] *s* embalador *m;* (sport) boxeador *m*
boxing ['bɑksɪŋ] *s* embalaje *m;* (sport) boxeo
boxing gloves *spl* guantes *mpl* de boxeo
box office *s* taquilla, despacho de localidades; boletería
box'-of'fice hit *s* éxito de taquilla
box-office record *s* marca de taquilla
box-office sale *s* venta de localidades en taquilla
box pleat *s* pliegue *m* de tabla
box seat *s* asiento de palco
box'wood' *s* boj *m*
boy [bɔɪ] *s* muchacho; (servant) mozo; (coll) compadre *m*
boycott ['bɔɪkɑt] *s* boicoteo ‖ *tr* boicotear
boyhood ['bɔɪhʊd] *s* muchachez *f;* muchachería
boyish ['bɔɪ•ɪʃ] *adj* amuchachado, muchachil
boy scout *s* niño explorador
Bp. *abbr* **bishop**
b.p. *abbr* **bills payable, boiling point**
br. *abbr* **brand, brother**
b.r. *abbr* **bills receivable**
bra [brɑ] *s* (coll) portasenos *m*, sostén *m*, sujetador *m*
brace [bres] *s* riostra; berbiquí *m;* **braces** (Brit) tirantes *mpl;* (on teeth) aparato de ortodoncia ‖ *tr* arriostrar; asegurar, vigorizar; **to brace oneself** (coll) cobrar ánimo ‖ *intr* — **to brace up** (coll) cobrar ánimo
brace and bit *s* berbiquí y barrena
bracelet ['breslɪt] *s* brazalete *m*, pulsera
bracer ['bresər] *s* (coll) trago de licor
bracing ['bresɪŋ] *adj* fortificante, tónico
bracket ['brækɪt] *s* puntal *m*, soporte *m;* ménsula, repisa; (mark used in printing) corchete *m;* clase *f*, categoría ‖ *tr* acorchetar; agrupar
brackish ['brækɪʃ] *adj* salobre
brad [bræd] *s* clavito, estaquilla
brag [bræg] *s* jactancia ‖ *v* (pret & pp **bragged;** ger **bragging**) *intr* jactarse, bravatear, palanganear
braggart ['brægərt] *s* fanfarrón *m*
braid [bred] *s* (flat strip of cotton, silk, etc.) cinta, galón *m;* (something braided) trenza ‖ *tr* encintar, galonear; trenzar
brain [bren] *s* cerebro; **brains** cerebro, inteligencia; **to rack one's brains** devanarse los sesos ‖ *tr* descerebrar
brain child *s* parto del ingenio
brain drain *s* (coll) éxodo de técnicos
brainless ['brenlɪs] *adj* tonto, sin seso
brain power *s* capacidad mental
brain'storm' *s* acceso de locura; confusión mental; buena idea, hallazgo
brain trust *s* grupo de peritos
brain'wash'ing *s* lavado cerebral
brain wave *s* onda encefálica; (coll) buena idea, hallazgo
brain'work' *s* trabajo intelectual
brain•y ['breni] *adj* (comp -**ier;** super -**iest**) (coll) inteligente, sesudo
braise [brez] *tr* soasar y cocer (la carne) a fuego lento en vasija bien tapada

brake [brek] *s* freno; breque *m;* (for dressing flax) agramadera; (thicket) matorral *m;* (fern) helecho común ‖ *tr* frenar; brequear; agramar (el lino o el cañamo)
brake band *s* cinta de freno
brake drum *s* tambor *m* de freno
brake lining *s* forro o cinta de freno
brake•man ['brekmən] *s* (pl -**men** [mən]) guardafrenos *m*
brake shoe *s* zapata de freno
bramble ['bræmbəl] *s* frambueso, zarza
bram•bly ['bræmbli] *adj* (comp -**blier;** super -**bliest**) zarzoso
bran [bræn] *s* afrecho, salvado
branch [bræntʃ] *s* (of tree) rama; (smaller branch; branch cut from tree; of a science, etc.) ramo; (of vine) sarmiento; (of road, railroad) ramal *m;* (of candlestick, river, etc.) brazo; (of a store, bank) sucursal *f* ‖ *intr* ramificarse; **to branch out** extender sus actividades
branch line *s* ramal *m*, línea de empalme
branch office *s* sucursal *f*
brand [brænd] *s* (kind, make) marca; (trademark) marca de fábrica; (branding iron) hierro de marcar; (mark stamped with hot iron) hierro; (dishonor) tizón *m* ‖ *tr* poner marca de fábrica en; herrar con hierro candente; tiznar (la reputación de una persona); **to brand as** tildar de
brandied ['brændid] *adj* macerado en aguardiente
branding iron *s* hierro de marcar; fierro
brandish ['brændɪʃ] *tr* blandear
brand'-new' *adj* nuevecito, flamante
bran•dy ['brændi] *s* (pl -**dies**) aguardiente *m*
brash [bræʃ] *adj* atrevido, impetuoso; descarado, respondón ‖ *s* acceso, ataque *m*
brass [bræs] *s* latón *m;* (in army and navy) (slang) los mandamases; (coll) descaro; **brasses** (mus) cobres *mpl*
brass band *s* banda, charanga
brass hat *s* (slang) espadón *m*, mandamás *m*
brassiere [brə'zɪr] *s* portasenos *m*, sostén *m*, sujetador *m*
brass knuckles *spl* llave inglesa, bóxer *m*
brass tack *s* clavito dorado de tapicería; **to get down to brass tacks** (coll) entrar en materia
brass winds *spl* (mus) cobres *mpl*, instrumentos músicos de metal
brass•y ['bræsi] *adj* (comp -**ier;** super -**iest**) hecho de latón; metálico; descarado
brat [bræt] *s* rapaz *m*, mocoso, braguillas *m*
brava•do [brə'vado] *s* (pl -**does** o -**dos**) bravata
brave [brev] *adj* bravo, valiente ‖ *s* valiente *m;* guerrero indio norteamericano ‖ *tr* hacer frente a, arrostrar; desafiar, retar
bravery ['brevəri] *s* bravura, valor *m*
bra•vo ['bravo] *interj* ¡bravo! ‖ *s* (pl -**vos**) bravo
brawl [brɔl] *s* pendencia, reyerta; alboroto ‖ *intr* armar pendencia; alborotar
brawler ['brɔlər] *s* pendenciero; alborotador *m*
brawn [brɔn] *s* fuerza musculosa

brawn•y [ˈbrɔni] *adj* (*comp* **-ier;** *super* **-iest**) fornido, musculoso

bray [bre] *s* rebuzno ‖ *intr* rebuznar

braze [brez] *s* soldadura de latón ‖ *tr* soldar con latón; cubrir de latón; adornar con latón

brazen [ˈbrezən] *adj* de latón; descarado ‖ *tr* — **to brazen through** llevar a cabo descaradamente

brazier [ˈbreʒər] *s* brasero

Brazil [brəˈzɪl] *s* el Brasil

Brazilian [brəˈzɪljən] *adj & s* brasileño

Brazil nut *s* castaña de Pará

breach [britʃ] *s* (*opening*) abertura; (*in a wall*) brecha; abuso, violación ‖ *tr* abrir brecha en

breach of faith *s* falta de fidelidad

breach of peace *s* perturbación del orden público

breach of promise *s* incumplimiento de la palabra de matrimonio

breach of trust *s* abuso de confianza

bread [brɛd] *s* pan *m* ‖ *tr* empanar

bread and butter *s* pan *m* con mantequilla; (coll) pan de cada día

bread crumbs *spl* pan rallado

breaded [ˈbrɛdɪd] *adj* empanado

bread line *s* cola del pan

breadth [brɛdθ] *s* anchura; alcance *m*, extensión; (*e.g., of judgment*) amplitud *f*

bread'win'ner *s* sostén *m* de la familia

break [brek] *s* rompimiento; interrupción; intervalo, pausa; (*split*) hendidura, grieta; (*in prices*) baja; (*in clouds*) claro; (*from jail*) evasión, huída; (*among friends*) ruptura; (*luck, good or bad*) suerte *f*; (slang) disparate *m*; **to give someone a break** abrirle a uno la puerta ‖ *v* (*pret* **broke** [brok]; *pp* **broken**) *tr* romper, quebrar; cambiar (*un billete*); comunicar (*una mala noticia*); suspender (*relaciones*); faltar a (*la palabra*); batir (*un récord*); cortar (*un circuito*); quebrantar (*un testamento; un hábito*); romper (*una ley*); levantar (*el campo*); (mil) degradar; **to break in** forzar (*una puerta*); **to break open** abrir por la fuerza ‖ *intr* romperse, quebrarse; reventar; aclarar (*el tiempo*); bajar (*los precios*); quebrantarse (*la salud*); **to break down** perder la salud; prorrumpir en llanto; **to break even** salir sin ganar ni perder; **to break in** entrar por fuerza; irrumpir en; **to break loose** desprenderse; escaparse; desbocarse (*un caballo*); desencadenarse (*una tempestad*); **to break out** estallar, declararse; (*in laughter, weeping*) romper; (*on the skin*) brotar granos; **to break through** abrirse paso; abrir paso por entre; **to break up** desmenuzarse; levantarse (*una reunión*); **to break with** romper con

breakable [ˈbrekəbəl] *adj* rompible

breakage [ˈbrekɪdʒ] *s* estropicio; indemnización por objetos rotos

break'down' *s* mal éxito; avería, pana; (*in health*) colapso; (*in negotiations*) ruptura; análisis *m*

breaker [ˈbrekər] *s* cachón *m*, rompiente *m*

breakfast [ˈbrɛkfəst] *s* desayuno ‖ *intr* desayunar

breakfast food *s* cereal *m* para el desayuno

break'neck' *adj* vertiginoso; **at breakneck speed** a mata caballo

break of day *s* alba, amanecer *m*

break'through' *s* (mil) brecha, ruptura; (fig) descubrimiento sensacional

break'up' *s* disolución, dispersión; desplome *m;* (*in health*) postración

break'wa'ter *s* rompeolas *m*, escollera

breast [brɛst] *s* pecho, seno; (*of fowl*) pechuga; (*of garment*) pechera; **to make a clean breast of it** confesarlo todo

breast'bone' *s* esternón *m;* (*of fowl*) quilla

breast drill *s* berbiquí *m* de pecho

breast'pin' *s* alfiler *m* de pecho

breast stroke *s* brazada de pecho

breath [brɛθ] *s* aliento, respiración; **out of breath** sin aliento; **short of breath** corto de resuello; **to gasp for breath** respirar anhelosamente; **under one's breath** por lo bajo, en voz baja

breathe [brið] *tr* respirar; **to breathe one's last** dar el último suspiro ‖ *intr* respirar; **to breathe freely** cobrar aliento; **to breathe in** aspirar; **to breathe out** espirar

breathing spell *s* respiro, rato de descanso

breathless [ˈbrɛθlɪs] *adj* falto de aliento, jadeante; intenso, vivo; sin aliento

breath'tak'ing *adj* conmovedor, imponente

breech [britʃ] *s* culata, recámara; **breeches** [ˈbrɪtʃɪz] calzones *mpl;* (coll) pantalones *mpl;* **to wear the breeches** (coll) calzarse los pantalones

breed [brid] *s* casta, raza; clase *f*, especie *f* ‖ *v* (*pret & pp* **bred** [brɛd]) *tr* criar ‖ *intr* criar; criarse

breeder [ˈbridər] *s* (*of animals*) criador *m;* (*animal*) reproductor *m*

breeding [ˈbridɪŋ] *s* cría; crianza, modales *mpl;* **bad breeding** mala crianza; **good breeding** buena crianza

breeze [briz] *s* brisa

breez•y [ˈbrizi] *adj* (*comp* **-ier;** *super* **-iest**) airoso; animado, vivo; (coll) desenvuelto, vivaracho

brevi•ty [ˈbrɛvɪti] *s* (*pl* **-ties**) brevedad

brew [bru] *s* calderada de cerveza; mezcla ‖ *tr* fabricar (*cerveza*); preparar (*té*); (fig) tramar, urdir ‖ *intr* amenazar (*una tormenta*)

brewer [ˈbruər] *s* cervecero

brewer's yeast *s* levadura de cerveza

brewer•y [ˈbruəri] *s* (*pl* **-ies**) cervecería, fábrica de cerveza

bribe [braɪb] *s* soborno; **to take bribes** comer maíz ‖ *tr* sobornar

briber•y [ˈbraɪbəri] *s* (*pl* **-ies**) soborno

bric-a-brac [ˈbrɪkə,bræk] *s* chucherías, curiosidades *fpl*

brick [brɪk] *s* ladrillo; (coll) buen sujeto ‖ *tr* enladrillar

brick'bat' *s* pedazo de ladrillo; (coll) palabra hiriente

bo
br

brick ice cream *s* queso helado, helado al corte

brickkiln ['brɪk,kɪln] *s* horno de ladrillero

bricklayer ['brɪk,le•ər] *s* ladrillador *m*

brick'yard' *s* ladrillal *m*

bridal ['braɪdəl] *adj* nupcial; de novia

bridal wreath *s* corona nupcial

bride [braɪd] *s* desposada, novia

bride'groom' *s* desposado, novio

bridesmaid ['braɪdz,med] *s* madrina de boda

bridge [brɪdʒ] *s* puente *m;* (*of nose*) caballete *m;* (*card game*) bridge *m* ‖ *tr* tender un puente sobre; salvar (*un obstáculo*); colmar, llenar (*un vacío*)

bridge'head' *s* (mil) cabeza de puente

bridle ['braɪdəl] *s* brida ‖ *tr* embridar ‖ *intr* engallarse, erguirse

bridle path *s* camino de herradura

brief [brif] *adj* breve, corto, conciso ‖ *s* resumen *m;* (law) escrito; **in brief** en resumen ‖ *tr* resumir; dar consejos anticipados a; dar informes a

brief case *s* cartera

briefing ['brifɪŋ] *s* órdenes *fpl;* (*of the press*) informe *m*

brier ['braɪ•ər] *s* zarza; brezo blanco

brig [brɪg] *s* (naut) bergantín *m;* prisión en buque de guerra

brigade [brɪ'ged] *s* brigada

brigadier [,brɪgə'dɪr] *s* general *m* de brigada

brigand ['brɪgənd] *s* bandolero

brigantine ['brɪgən,tin] *s* (naut) bergantín *m* goleta

bright [braɪt] *adj* brillante; (*e.g., day*) claro; (*color*) subido; listo, inteligente, despierto; (*idea, thought*) luminoso; (*disposition*) alegre, vivo

brighten ['braɪtən] *tr* abrillantar; alegrar, avivar ‖ *intr* avivarse; alegrarse; despejarse (*el cielo*)

bright lights *spl* luces *fpl* brillantes; (aut) faros o luces de carretera

brilliance ['brɪljəns] o **brilliancy** ['brɪljənsi] *s* brillantez *f*, brillo

brilliant ['brɪljənt] *adj* brillante

brillantine ['brɪljəntin] *s* brillantina

brim [brɪm] *s* borde *m;* (*of hat*) ala

brim'stone' *s* azufre *m*

brine [braɪn] *s* salmuera, agua salobre

bring [brɪŋ] *v* (*pret & pp* **brought** [brɔt]) *tr* traer; llevar; **to bring about** efectuar; **to bring back** devolver; **to bring down** abatir; **to bring forth** sacar a luz; **to bring in** traer a colación; servir (*una comida*); introducir, presentar; **to bring into play** poner en juego; **to bring on** causar, producir; **to bring out** sacar; presentar al público; **to bring suit** poner pleito; **to bring to** sacar de un desmayo; **to bring together** reunir; confrontar; reconciliar; **to bring to pass** efectuar, llevar a cabo; **to bring up** arrimar (*p.ej., una silla*); educar, criar; traer a colación; **to bring upon oneself** atraerse (*un infortunio*)

bringing-up ['brɪŋɪŋ'ʌp] *s* educación, crianza

brink [brɪŋk] *s* borde *m*, margen *m;* **on the brink of** al borde de

brisk [brɪsk] *adj* animado, vivo, vivaz

bristle ['brɪsəl] *s* cerda ‖ *intr* erizarse, encresparse; (*to be visibly annoyed*) encresparse

bris•tly ['brɪsli] *adj* (*comp* **-tlier;** *super* **-tliest**) cerdoso, erizado

Britannic [brɪ'tænɪk] *adj* británico

British ['brɪtɪʃ] *adj* británico ‖ **the British** los britanos

Britisher ['brɪtɪʃər] *s* britano

Briton ['brɪtən] *s* britano

Brittany ['brɪtəni] *s* Bretaña

brittle ['brɪtəl] *adj* quebradizo, frágil

bro. *abbr* **brother**

broach [brotʃ] *s* (*skewer*) asador *m*, espetón *m;* (*ornamental pin*) broche *m*, prendedero ‖ *tr* sacar a colación

broad [brɔd] *adj* ancho; liberal, tolerante; (*day, noon, etc.*) pleno

broad'cast' *s* radiodifusión; audición, programa radiotelefónico ‖ *v* (*pret & pp* **-cast**) *tr* difundir, esparcir ‖ (*pret & pp* **-cast** o **-casted**) *tr* radiodifundir, radiar, emitir

broadcasting station *s* emisora, estación de radiodifusión

broad'cloth' *s* paño fino

broaden ['brɔdən] *tr* ensanchar ‖ *intr* ensancharse

broad'loom' *adj* tejido en telar ancho y en color sólido

broad-minded ['brɔd'maɪndɪd] *adj* tolerante, de amplias miras

broad-shouldered ['brɔd'ʃoldərd] *adj* ancho de espaldas

broad'side' *s* (naut) costado; (naut) andanada; (coll) torrente *m* de injurias

broad'sword' *s* espada ancha

brocade [bro'ked] *s* brocado

broccoli ['brɑkəli] *s* brécol *m*, brécoles *mpl*

brochure [bro'ʃur] *s* folleto

brogue [brog] *s* acento irlandés

broil [brɔɪl] *tr* asar a la parrilla ‖ *intr* asarse

broiler ['brɔɪlər] *s* parrilla; pollo para asar a la parrilla

broken ['brokən] *adj* roto, quebrado; agotado; amansado; (*accent*) chapurrado; suelto

bro'ken-down' *adj* abatido; descompuesto; destartalado

broken-hearted ['brokən'hartɪd] *adj* abrumado por el dolor

broker ['brokər] *s* corredor *m*

brokerage ['brokərɪdʒ] *s* corretaje *m*

bromide ['bromaɪd] *s* bromuro; (slang) trivialidad

bromine ['bromin] *s* bromo

bronchitis [brɑŋ'kaɪtɪs] *s* bronquitis *f*

bron•co ['brɑŋko] *s* (*pl* **-cos**) potro cerril

bron'co•bust'er *s* domador *m* de potros; vaquero

bronze [brɑnz] *adj* bronceado ‖ *s* bronce *m* ‖ *tr* broncear ‖ *intr* broncearse

brooch [brotʃ] o [brutʃ] *s* alfiler *m* de pecho, prendedero, pasador *m*

brood [brud] *s* cría; nidada; casta, raza ‖ *tr* empollar ‖ *intr* enclocar; **to brood on** meditar con preocupación

brook [brʊk] *s* arroyo ‖ *tr* — **to brook no** no tolerar, no aguantar

broom [brum] o [brʊm] *s* escoba; (bot) hiniesta

broom'corn' *s* sorgo

broom'stick' *s* palo de escoba

bros. *abbr* **brothers**

broth [brɔθ] o [braθ] *s* caldo

brothel [ˈbraθəl] o [ˈbraðəl] *s* burdel *m*; (Mex) congal *m*

brother [ˈbrʌðər] *s* hermano

brotherhood [ˈbrʌðər͵hʊd] *s* hermandad

broth'er-in-law' *s* (*pl* **brothers-in-law**) cuñado, hermano político; (*husband of one's wife's or husband's sister*) concuñado

brotherly [ˈbrʌðərli] *adj* fraternal

brow [braʊ] *s* (*forehead*) frente *f*; (*eyebrow*) ceja; **to knit one's brow** fruncir las cejas

brow'beat' *v* (*pret* **-beat;** *pp* **beaten**) *tr* intimidar con mirada ceñuda

brown [braʊn] *adj* pardo, castaño, moreno; (*race*) cobrizo; tostado del sol ‖ *s* castaño, moreno ‖ *tr* poner moreno; tostar, quemar, broncear; (culin) dorar

brownish [ˈbraʊnɪʃ] *adj* que tira a moreno

brown study *s* absorción, pensamiento profundo, ensimismamiento

brown sugar *s* azúcar terciado

browse [braʊz] *intr* (*to nibble at twigs*) ramonear; (*to graze*) pacer; hojear un libro ociosamente; **to browse about** o **around** curiosear

bruise [bruz] *s* contusión, magulladura, magullón *m* ‖ *tr* contundir, magullar ‖ *intr* contundirse, magullarse

brunet [bruˈnɛt] *adj* moreno ‖ *s* moreno (*hombre moreno*)

brunette [bruˈnɛt] *s* morena (*mujer morena*)

brunt [brʌnt] *s* fuerza, choque *m*, empuje *m*; (*e.g., of a battle*) peso, (lo) más reñido

brush [brʌʃ] *s* brocha, cepillo, escobilla; (*stroke*) brochada; (*light touch*) roce *m*; (*brief encounter*) encuentro, escaramuza; (*growth of bushes*) maleza; (elec) escobilla ‖ *tr* acepillar; (*to graze*) rozar; **to brush aside** echar a un lado ‖ *intr* pasar ligeramente; **to brush up on** repasar

brush'-off' *s* (slang) desaire *m*; **to give the brush-off to** (slang) despedir noramala

brush'wood' *s* broza, ramojo

brusque [brʌsk] *adj* brusco, rudo

brusqueness [ˈbrʌsknɪs] *s* brusquedad

Brussels [ˈbrʌsəlz] *s* Bruselas

Brussels sprouts *spl* bretones *mpl*, col *f* de Bruselas

brutal [ˈbrutəl] *adj* brutal, bestial

brutali•ty [bruˈtælɪti] *s* (*pl* **-ties**) brutalidad, crueldad

brutalization [͵brutələˈzeʃən] *s* embrutecimiento

brute [brut] *adj* bruto; (*force*) inconsciente, ciego ‖ *s* bruto

brutish [ˈbrutɪʃ] *adj* abrutado, estúpido

bu. *abbr* **bushel**

bubble [ˈbʌbəl] *s* burbuja; ampolla; ilusión, quimera ‖ *intr* burbujear; **to bubble over** desbordar, rebosar

buck [bʌk] *s* (*goat*) cabrón *m*; (*deer*) gamo; (*rabbit*) conejo; (*of a horse*) corveta, encorvada; (*youth*) pisaverde *m*; (slang) dólar *m*; **to pass the buck** (coll) echar la carga a otro ‖ *tr* hacer frente a, resistir a; (*to butt*) acornear, topetar; colar (*la ropa*); **to buck up** (coll) alentar, animar ‖ *intr* botarse, encorvarse; **to buck against** embestir contra

bucket [ˈbʌkɪt] *s* balde *m*, cubo; (*of a well*) pozal *m*; **to kick the bucket** (slang) estirar la pata, liar el petate

bucket seat *s* baquet *m*

buckle [ˈbʌkəl] *s* hebilla; (*bend, bulge*) alabeo, pandeo ‖ *tr* abrochar con hebilla ‖ *intr* (*to bend, bulge*) alabearse, pandear; **to buckle down to** (coll) dedicarse con empeño a

buck private *s* (slang) soldado raso

buckram [ˈbʌkrəm] *s* zangala; (bb) bocací *m*, bucarán *m*

buck'saw' *s* sierra de bastidor

buck'shot' *s* postas

buck'tooth' *s* (*pl* **-teeth**) diente *m* saliente

buck'wheat' *s* alforfón *m*, trigo sarraceno

bud [bʌd] *s* botón *m*, brote *m*; **to nip in the bud** cortar de raíz ‖ *v* (*pret* & *pp* **budded;** *ger* **budding**) *intr* abotonar, brotar

bud-dy [ˈbʌdi] *s* (*pl* **-dies**) (coll) camarada *m*, cumpa *m* (coll) muchachito

budge [bʌdʒ] *tr* mover ‖ *intr* moverse

budget [ˈbʌdʒɪt] *s* presupuesto ‖ *tr* presuponer, presupuestar

budgetary [ˈbʌdʒɪ͵tɛri] *adj* presupuestario

buff [bʌf] *adj* de ante ‖ *s* (*leather*) ante *m*; color *m* de ante; chaqueta de ante; rueda pulidora; (coll) piel desnuda; aficionado ‖ *tr* dar color de ante a; pulimentar

buffa•lo [ˈbʌfə͵lo] *s* (*pl* **-loes** o **-los**) búfalo ‖ *tr* (slang) intimidar

buffer [ˈbʌfər] *s* amortiguador *m* de choques; tope *m*, paragolpes *m*; pulidor *m*

buffer state *s* estado tapón

buffet [buˈfe] *s* (*piece of furniture*) aparador *m*; restaurante *m* de estación ‖ [ˈbʌfɪt] *tr* abofetear, golpear, pegar

buffet car *s* coche *m* bar

buffet lunch *s* servicio de bufet

buffet supper *s* ambigú *m*, bufet *m*

buffoon [bəˈfun] *s* bufón *m*, payaso

buffooner•y [bəˈfunəri] *s* (*pl* **-ies**) bufonada, chocarrería

bug [bʌg] *s* insecto, bicho, sabandija; microbio; (*bedbug*) (Brit) chinche *f*; (coll) defecto; (slang) micrófono escondido; (slang) loco; (slang) entusiasta *mf* ‖ *v* (*pret* & *pp* **bugged;** *ger* **bugging**) *tr* (slang) esconder un micrófono en

bug'bear' *s* espantajo; aversión

bug-gy [ˈbʌgi] *adj* (*comp* **-gier;** *super* **-giest**) infestado de bichos; (slang) loco ‖ *s* (*pl* **-gies**) calesa

bug'house' *adj* (slang) loco ‖ *s* (slang) manicomio, casa de locos

bugle [ˈbjugəl] s corneta
bugle call s toque m de corneta
bugler [ˈbjuglər] s corneta m
build [bɪld] s forma, hechura, figura; (of human being) talle m ‖ v (pret & pp **built** [bɪlt]) tr construir, edificar; componer; establecer, fundar; crearse (p.ej., una clientela)
builder [ˈbɪldər] s constructor m; aparejador m, maestro de obras
building [ˈbɪldɪŋ] s construcción; edificio; (one of several in a group) pabellón m
building and loan association s sociedad f de crédito para la construcción
building lot s solar m
building site s terreno para construir
building trades spl oficios de edificación
build´-up´ s acumulación, formación; (coll) propaganda anticipada
built´in´ adj integrante, incorporado, empotrado
built´-up´ adj armado, montado; (land) aglomerado
bulb [bʌlb] s (of plant) bulbo; (of thermometer) bola, cubeta; (of syringe) pera; (of electric light) ampolla, bombilla
Bulgaria [bʌlˈgɛrɪ•ə] s Bulgaria
Bulgarian [bʌlˈgɛrɪ•ən] adj & s búlgaro
bulge [bʌldʒ] s protuberancia, bulto, bombeo; **to get the bulge on** (coll) llevar la ventaja a ‖ intr hacer bulto, bombearse
bulimia [bjuˈlimi•ə] s bulimia
bulk [bʌlk] s bulto, volumen m; (main mass) grueso; **in bulk** a granel ‖ intr abultar, hacer bulto; tener importancia
bulk´head´ s mamparo; tabique hermético
bulk•y [ˈbʌlki] adj (comp **-ier**; super **-iest**) abultado, voluminoso, grueso
bull [bʊl] s toro; (in stockmarket) alcista m; (papal document) bula; disparate m; **to take the bull by the horns** asir al toro por las astas ‖ tr — **to bull the market** jugar al alza
bull´dog´ s dogo
bulldoze [ˈbʊl,doz] tr coaccionar, intimidar con amenazas
bulldozer [ˈbʊl,dozər] s explanadora de empuje, empujatierra
bullet [ˈbʊlɪt] s bala
bulletin [ˈbʊlətɪn] s boletín m; comunicado; (of a school) anuario
bulletin board s tablilla
bul´let•proof´ adj a prueba de balas, blindado
bull´fight´ s corrida de toros
bull´fight´er s torero
bull´fight´ing adj torero ‖ s toreo
bull´finch´ s (orn) camachuelo
bull´frog´ s rana toro
bull-headed [ˈbʊl,hɛdɪd] adj obstinado, terco
bullion [ˈbʊljən] s oro en barras, plata en barras; (twisted fringe) entorchado
bullish [ˈbʊlɪʃ] adj obstinado; (market) en alza; (speculator) alcista; optimista
bullock [ˈbʊlək] s buey m
bull´pen´ s (taur) toril m; (jail) (coll) prevención

bull´ring´ s plaza de toros
bull's-eye [ˈbʊlz,aɪ] s (of a target) diana; (archit, meteor, naut) ojo de buey; **to hit the bull's-eye** hacer diana
bul•ly [ˈbʊli] adj (coll) excelente, magnífico ‖ s (pl **-lies**) matón m, valentón m ‖ v (pret & pp **-lied**) tr intimidar, maltratar
bulrush [ˈbʊl,rʌʃ] s junco; junco de laguna; (Typha) anea, espadaña; (Bib) papiro
bulwark [ˈbʊlwərk] s baluarte m ‖ tr abaluartar; defender, proteger
bum [bʌm] s (slang) holgazán m; (slang) vagabundo; (slang) mendigo ‖ v (pret & pp **bummed**; ger **bumming**) tr (slang) mendigar ‖ intr (slang) holgazanear; (slang) vagabundear; (slang) mendigar
bumblebee [ˈbʌmbəl,bi] s abejorro
bump [bʌmp] s (collision) topetón m; (shake) sacudida; (on falling) batacazo; (of plane in rough air) rebote m; (swelling) hinchazón f, chichón m; protuberancia ‖ tr dar contra, topar; (to bruise) abollar ‖ intr chocar; dar sacudidas; **to bump into** tropezar con; encontrarse con
bumper [ˈbʌmpər] adj (coll) abundante, grande ‖ s tope m, paratopes m; (aut) amortiguador m, parachoques m; vaso lleno
bumpkin [ˈbʌmpkɪn] s patán m, palurdo
bumptious [ˈbʌmpʃəs] adj engreído, presuntuoso
bump•y [ˈbʌmpi] adj (comp **-ier**; super **-iest**) (ground) desigual, áspero; (air) agitado
bun [bʌn] s buñuelo, bollo; (of hair) castaña
bunch [bʌntʃ] s manojo, puñado; (of grapes, bananas, etc.) racimo; (of flowers) ramillete m; (of people) grupo ‖ tr agrupar, juntar ‖ intr agruparse; arracimarse
bundle [ˈbʌndəl] s atado, bulto, lío, paquete m; (of papers) legajo; (of wood) haz m ‖ tr atar, liar, empaquetar, envolver; **to bundle off** despedir precipitadamente; **to bundle up** arropar ‖ intr — **to bundle up** arroparse
bung [bʌŋ] s bitoque m, tapón m
bungalow [ˈbʌŋgə,lo] s bungalow m, casa de una sola planta
bung´hole´ s piquera, boca de tonel
bungle [ˈbʌŋgəl] s chapucería ‖ tr & intr chapucear
bungler [ˈbʌŋglər] s chapucero
bungling [ˈbʌŋglɪŋ] adj chapucero ‖ s chapucería
bunion [ˈbʌnjən] s juanete m
bunk [bʌŋk] s tarima; (slang) palabrería vana, música celestial
bunker [ˈbʌŋkər] s carbonera; (mil) fortín m
bun•ny [ˈbʌni] s (pl **-nies**) conejito
bunting [ˈbʌntɪŋ] s banderas colgadas como adorno; (of a ship) empavesado; (orn) gorrión triguero
buoy [bɔɪ] o [ˈbu•i] s boya; boya salvavidas, guindola ‖ tr — **to buoy up** mantener a flote; animar, alentar
buoyancy [ˈbɔɪ•ənsi] o [ˈbujənsi] s flotación; alegría, animación
buoyant [ˈbɔɪ•ənt] o [ˈbujənt] adj boyante, alegre, animado

bur [bʌr] s erizo, vilano
burble ['bʌrbəl] s burbujeo ‖ intr burbujear
burden ['bʌrdən] s carga; (of a speech) tema m; (of a poem) estribillo ‖ tr cargar; agobiar, gravar
burden of proof s peso de la prueba
burdensome ['bʌrdənsəm] adj gravoso, oneroso
burdock ['bʌrdak] s bardana, cadillo
bureau ['bjʊro] s cómoda; despacho, oficina; departamento, negociado
bureaucra·cy [bjʊ'rakrəsi] s (pl -cies) burocracia; funcionariado
bureaucrat ['bjʊrə,kræt] s burócrata mf
bureaucratic [,bjʊrə'krætɪk] adj burocrático
burgess ['bʌrdʒɪs] s burgués m, ciudadano; alcalde m de un pueblo o villa
burglar ['bʌrglər] s escalador m
burglar alarm s alarma de ladrones
bur'glar·proof' adj a prueba de escaladores; antirrobo
burglar·y ['bʌrgləri] s (pl -ies) robo con escalamiento
Burgundian [bər'gʌndi·ən] adj & s borgoñón m
Burgundy ['bʌrgəndi] s la Borgoña; (wine) borgoña m
burial ['bɛrɪ·əl] s entierro
burial ground s cementerio
burlap ['bʌrlæp] s arpillera
burlesque [bər'lɛsk] adj burlesco, festivo ‖ s parodia ‖ tr parodiar
burlesque show s espectáculo de bailes y cantos groseros, music-hall m; bataclán m (SAm)
bur·ly ['bʌrli] adj (comp -lier; super -liest) fornido, corpulento, membrudo
Burma ['bʌrmə] s Birmania
Bur·mese [bər'miz] adj birmano ‖ s (pl -mese) birmano
burn [bʌrn] s quemadura, quemazón f ‖ v (pret & pp burned o burnt [bʌrnt]) tr quemar ‖ intr quemar, quemarse; estar encendido (p.ej., un faro); **to burn out** quemarse (un fusible); fundirse (una bombilla); **to burn within** requemarse
burner ['bʌrnər] s (of furnace) quemador m; (of gas fixture or lamp) mechero
burning ['bʌrnɪŋ] adj ardiente ‖ s quema, incendio
burning question s cuestión palpitante
burnish ['bʌrnɪʃ] s bruñido ‖ tr bruñir ‖ intr bruñirse
burnoose [bər'nus] s albornoz m
burnt almond [bʌrnt] s almendra tostada
burr [bʌr] s (of plant) erizo; (of cut in metal) rebaba
burrow ['bʌro] s madriguera, conejera ‖ tr hacer madrigueras en; socavar ‖ intr amadrigarse; esconderse
bursar ['bʌrsər] s tesorero universitario
burst [bʌrst] s explosión, reventón m, estallido; (of machine gun) ráfaga; salida brusca ‖ v (pret & pp burst) tr reventar ‖ intr reventar, reventarse; partirse (el corazón); **to burst into** irrumpir en (un cuarto); desatarse en (amenazas); prorrumpir en

(lágrimas); **to burst out crying** deshacerse en lágrimas; **to burst with laughter** reventar de risa
bur·y ['bɛri] v (pret & pp -ied) tr enterrar; **to be buried in thought** estar absorto en meditación; **to bury the hatchet** hacer la paz, echar pelillos a la mar
burying ground s cementerio
bus. abbr **business**
bus [bʌs] s (pl **busses** o **buses**) autobús m ‖ tr llevar en un autobús
bus boy s ayudante m de camarero
bus·by ['bʌzbi] s (pl -bies) morrión m de húsar, colbac m
bush [bʊʃ] s arbusto; (scrubby growth) matorral m, monte m; **to beat about the bush** andar con rodeos
bushel ['bʊʃəl] s medida para áridos (35,23 litros en E.U.A. y 36,35 litros en Inglaterra)
bushing ['bʊʃɪŋ] s buje m, forro
bush·y ['bʊʃi] adj (comp -ier; super -iest) arbustivo; peludo, lanudo; espeso
business ['bɪznɪs] adj comercial, de negocios ‖ s negocio, comercio; (company, concern) empresa; (job, employment) empleo, oficio; (matter) asunto, cuestión; (duty) obligación; (right) derecho; **on business** por negocios; **to have no business to** no tener derecho a; **to make it one's business to** proponerse; **to mean business** (coll) obrar en serio, hablar en serio; **to mind one's own business** no meterse en lo que no le importa a uno; **to send about one's business** mandar a paseo
business district s barrio comercial
businesslike ['bɪznɪs,laɪk] adj práctico, sistemático, serio
business·man ['bɪznɪs,mæn] s (pl -men [,mɛn]) comerciante m, hombre m de negocios
business suit s traje m de calle
bus·man ['bʌsmən] s (pl -men [mən]) conductor m de autobús
buss [bʌs] s (coll) beso sonado ‖ tr dar besos sonados a ‖ intr dar besos sonados; darse besos sonados
bust [bʌst] s busto; (of woman) pecho; (slang) fracaso, borrachera ‖ tr (slang) reventar, romper; (slang) arruinar; (slang) golpear, pegar ‖ intr (slang) reventar, fracasar
buster ['bʌstər] s muchachito
bustle ['bʌsəl] s (of woman's dress) polisón m; alboroto, bullicio ‖ intr ajetrearse, menearse
bus·y ['bɪzi] adj (comp -ier; super -iest) ocupado; (e.g., street) concurrido; (meddling) intruso, entremetido ‖ v (pret & pp -ied) tr ocupar; **to busy oneself with** ocuparse de
busybod·y ['bɪzi,badi] s (pl -ies) entremetido, fisgón m
busy signal s (telp) señal f de ocupado
but [bʌt] adv sólo, solamente, no . . . más que; **but for** a no ser por; **but little** muy poco ‖ prep excepto, salvo; **all but** casi ‖

conj pero; sino, p.ej., **nobody came but John** no vino sino Juan

butcher [ˈbʊtʃər] *s* carnicero; pesero (CAm, Col, Ven) ‖ *tr* matar (*reses para el consumo*); dar muerte a; (*to bungle*) chapucear

butcher knife *s* cuchilla de carnicero

butcher shop *s* carnicería; pesa (CAm, Col, Ven)

butcher·y [ˈbʊtʃəri] *s* (*pl* **-ies**) (*slaughterhouse*) matadero; (*wanton slaughter*) matanza, carnicería

butler [ˈbʌtlər] *s* despensero, mayordomo

butt [bʌt] *s* (*of gun*) culata; (*of cigaret*) colilla, punta; (*of horned animal*) cabezada, topetada, topetón *m*; (*target*) blanco; hazmerreír *m*; (*large cask*) pipa; (*rear end*) pompis *m* ‖ *tr* topar, topetar; acornear ‖ *intr* dar cabezadas; **to butt against** confinar con; **to butt in** (slang) entremeterse

butter [ˈbʌtər] *s* mantequilla ‖ *tr* untar con mantequilla; **to butter up** (coll) adular, lisonjear

but′ter·cup′ *s* botón *m* de oro

butter dish *s* mantequillera

but′ter·fly′ *s* (*pl* **-flies**) mariposa

butter knife *s* cuchillo mantequillero

but′ter·milk′ *s* leche *f* de manteca

butter sauce *s* mantequilla fundida

but′ter·scotch′ *s* bombón *m* escocés, bombón hecho con azúcar terciado y mantequilla

buttocks [ˈbʌtəks] *spl* nalgas; fundillo (Cuba, Mex)

button [ˈbʌtən] *s* botón *m* ‖ *tr* abotonar, abrocharse

but′ton·hole′ *s* ojal *m* ‖ *tr* detener con conversación

but′ton·hook′ *s* abotonador *m*

but′ton·wood′ **tree** *s* plátano de occidente

buttress [ˈbʌtrɪs] *s* contrafuerte *m*; (fig) apoyo, sostén *m* ‖ *tr* estribar; (fig) apoyar, sostener

butt weld *s* soldadura a tope

buxom [ˈbʌksəm] *adj* rolliza, frescachona

buy [baɪ] *s* (coll) compra; (*bargain*) (coll) ganga ‖ *v* (*pret* & *pp* **bought** [bɔt]) *tr* comprar; **to buy back** recomprar; **to buy off** comprar, sobornar; **to buy out** comprar la parte de (*un socio*); **to buy up** acaparar

buyer [ˈbaɪər] *s* comprador *m*

buzz [bʌz] *s* zumbido ‖ *intr* zumbar; **to buzz about** ajetrearse, cazcalear

buzzard [ˈbʌzərd] *s* alfaneque *m*

buzz bomb *s* bomba volante

buzzer [ˈbʌzər] *s* zumbador *m*

buzz saw *s* sierra circular

bx. *abbr* **box**

by [baɪ] *adv* cerca; a un lado; **by and by** luego ‖ *prep* por; cerca de, al lado de; (*not later than*) para; **by far** con mucho; **by the way** de paso; a propósito

by-and-by [ˈbaɪ·ənd·baɪ] *s* porvenir *m*

bye-bye [ˈbaɪ·baɪ] *s* mu *f*; **to go bye-bye** ir a la mu ‖ *interj* (coll) ¡adiosito!; (*to a child*) ¡ro ro!

bygone [ˈbaɪˌgɔn] o [ˈbaɪˌgɑn] *adj* pasado ‖ *s* pasado; **let bygones be bygones** olvidemos lo pasado

bylaw [ˈbaɪˌlɔ] *s* reglamento, estatuto

bypass [ˈbaɪˌpæs] *s* desviación; tubo de paso ‖ *tr* desviar; eludir

by′-prod′uct *s* subproducto, derivado

bystander [ˈbaɪˌstændər] *s* asistente *mf*, circunstante *mf*

byway [ˈbaɪˌwe] *s* camino apartado

byword [ˈbaɪˌwʌrd] *s* objeto de oprobio; refrán *m*, muletilla; apodo

Byzantine [ˈbɪzənˌtin] o [bɪˈzæntin] *adj* & *s* bizantino

Byzantium [bɪˈzænʃiˌəm] o [bɪˈzæntiˌəm] *s* Bizancio

C

C, c [si] tercera letra del alfabeto inglés

c. *abbr* **cent, center, centimeter**

C. *abbr* **centigrade, Congress, Court**

cab [kæb] *s* coche *m* de plaza o de punto; taxi *m*; (*of a truck*) casilla

cabaret [ˌkæbəˈre] *s* cabaret *m*

cabbage [ˈkæbɪdʒ] *s* col *f*, berza

cab driver *s* cochero de plaza; taxista *mf*

cabin [ˈkæbɪn] *s* (*hut, cottage*) cabaña; (aer) cabina; (naut) camarote *m*

cabin boy *s* mozo de cámara

cabinet [ˈkæbɪnɪt] *s* (*piece of furniture for displaying objects*) escaparate *m*, vitrina; (*for a radio*) caja, mueble *m*; (*closet*) armario; (*private room; ministry of a government*) gabinete *m*

cab′inet·ma′ker *s* ebanista *m*

cab′inet·ma′king *s* ebanistería

cable [ˈkebəl] *adj* cablegráfico ‖ *s* cable *m*; cablegrama *m* ‖ *tr* & *intr* cablegrafiar

cable address *s* dirección cablegráfica

cable car *s* tranvía *m* de tracción por cable

cablegram [ˈkebəlˌgræm] *s* cablegrama *m*

cable television *s* televisión por cable

caboose [kəˈbus] *s* (rr) furgón de cola

cab′stand′ *s* punto de coches, punto de taxis

cache [kæʃ] *s* escondrijo; víveres escondidos ‖ *tr* depositar en un escondrijo; ocultar

cachet [kæˈʃe] *s* sello

cackle [ˈkækəl] *s* (*of a hen*) cacareo; (*idle talk*) charla ‖ *intr* cacarear; charlar

cac·tus [ˈkæktəs] *s* (*pl* **-tuses** o **-ti** [taɪ]) cacto

cad [kæd] *s* sinvergüenza *mf*; **to behave like a cad** tener mala leche

cadaver [kə'dævər] *s* cadáver *m*

cadaverous [kə'dævərəs] *adj* cadavérico

caddie ['kædi] *s* caddie *m* (*muchacho que lleva los utensilios en el juego de golf*) || *intr* servir de caddie

cadence ['kedəns] *s* cadencia

cadet [kə'dɛt] *s* hermano menor, hijo menor; (*student at military school*) cadete *m*

cadmium ['kædmɪ·əm] *s* cadmio

cadre ['kædri] *s* (mil) cuadro

Caesar ['sizər] *s* César *m*

café [kæ'fe] *s* bar *m*, cabaret *m*; restaurante *m*

café society *s* gente *f* del mundo elegante que frecuenta los cabarets de moda

cafeteria [,kæfə'tɪrɪ·ə] *s* cafetería

cage [kedʒ] *s* jaula || *tr* enjaular

cageling ['kedʒlɪŋ] *s* pájaro enjaulado

ca·gey ['kedʒi] *adj* (*comp* **-gier**; *super* **-giest**) (coll) astuto

cahoots [kə'huts] *s* — **to be in cahoots** (slang) confabularse (*dos o más personas*); **to go cahoots** (slang) entrar por partes iguales

Cain [ken] *s* Caín *m*; **to raise Cain** (slang) armar camorra

Cairo ['kaɪro] *s* El Cairo

caisson ['kesən] *s* cajón *m* de aire comprimido, esclusa de aire

cajole [kə'dʒol] *tr* adular, lisonjear, halagar

cajoler·y [kə'dʒoləri] *s* (*pl* **-ies**) adulación, lisonja, halago

cake [kek] *s* pastel *m*, bollo, queque *m*; (*small cake*) pastelillo; (*sponge cake*) bizcocho; (*of fish*) fritada; (*of earth*) terrón *m*; (*of soap*) pan *m*, pastilla; (*of ice*) témpano; **to take the cake** (coll) ser el colmo || *intr* apelmazarse, aterronarse

calabash ['kælə,bæʃ] *s* calabacera; jícaro; (*fruit*) calabaza

calamitous [kə'læmɪtəs] *adj* calamitoso

calami·ty [kə'læmɪti] *s* (*pl* **-ties**) calamidad

calci·fy ['kælsɪ,faɪ] *v* (*pret & pp* **-fied**) calcificar || *intr* calcificarse

calcium ['kælsɪ·əm] *s* calcio

calculate ['kælkjə,let] *tr* calcular; (*to reckon*) (coll) calcular || *intr* calcular; **to calculate on** contar con

calculating ['kælkjə,letɪŋ] *adj* de calcular; astuto, intrigante

calculating machine *s* calculadora, máquina de calcular

calcu·lus ['kælkjələs] *s* (*pl* **-luses** o **-li** [,laɪ]) (math, pathol) cálculo

caldron ['kɔldrən] *s* calderón *m*

calendar ['kæləndər] *s* calendario, almanaque *m*

calf [kæf] o [kɑf] *s* (*pl* **calves** [kævz] o [kɑvz]) ternero; (*of the leg*) pantorrilla

calf'skin' *s* becerro, becerrillo

caliber ['kælɪbər] *s* calibre *m*

calibrate ['kælɪ,bret] *tr* calibrar

cali·co ['kælɪ,ko] *s* (*pl* **-coes** o **-cos**) calicó *m*, indiana

California [,kælɪ'fɔrnɪ·ə] *s* California

calipers ['kælɪpərz] *spl* calibrador *m*, compás *m* de calibres

caliph ['kelɪf] o ['kælɪf] *s* califa *m*

caliphate ['kælɪ,fet] *s* califato

calisthenic [,kælɪs'θɛnɪk] *adj* calisténico || **calisthenics** *spl* calistenia

calk [kɔk] *tr* calafatear

calking ['kɔkɪŋ] *s* calafateo

call [kɔl] *s* llamada; visita; (*of a boat or airplane*) escala; vocación; **within call** al alcance de la voz || *tr* llamar; convocar (*p.ej., una huelga*); **to call back** mandar volver; **to call down** (coll) reprender, regañar; **to call in** hacer entrar; (*from circulation*) retirar; **to call off** aplazar, suspender; desconvocar; **to call out** llamar (*a uno*) que salga; **to call together** convocar, reunir; **to call up** llamar por teléfono; evocar, recordar || *intr* llamar, gritar; hacer una visita; (naut) hacer escala; **to call on** acudir a; visitar; **to call out** gritar; **to go calling** ir de visitas

calla lily ['kælə] *s* cala, lirio de agua

call bell *s* timbre *m* de llamada

call'boy' *s* (*in a hotel*) botones *m*; (theat) traspunte *m*

caller ['kɔlər] *s* visitante *mf*

call girl *s* chica de cita

calling ['kɔlɪŋ] *s* profesión, vocación

calling card *s* tarjeta de visita

calliope [kə'laɪ·əpi] o ['kælɪ·op] *s* (mus) órgano de vapor || **Calliope** [kə'laɪ·əpi] *s* Calíope *f*

call number *s* número de teléfono; (*of a book*) número de clasificación

callous ['kæləs] *adj* calloso; (fig) duro, insensible

call to arms *s* — **to sound the call to arms** (mil) batir o tocar a llamada

call to the colors *s* (mil) llamada a filas

callus ['kæləs] *s* callo

calm [kɑm] *adj* tranquilo, quieto; (*sea*) bonancible || *s* tranquilidad, calma || *tr* tranquilizar, calmar || *intr* — **to calm down** tranquilizarse, calmarse; abonanzar, calmar (*el viento, el tiempo*)

calmness ['kɑmnɪs] *s* tranquilidad, calma

calorie ['kæləri] *s* caloría

calum·ny ['kæləmni] *s* (*pl* **-nies**) calumnia

calva·ry ['kælvəri] *s* (*pl* **-ries**) (*at the entrance to a town*) humilladero || **Calvary** *s* Calvario

calyp·so [kə'lɪpso] *s* (*pl* **-sos**) calipso || **Calypso** *s* Calipso *f*

cam [kæm] *s* leva

cambric ['kembrɪk] *s* batista

camel ['kæməl] *s* camello

came·o ['kæmɪ·o] *s* (*pl* **-os**) camafeo

camera ['kæmərə] *s* cámara fotográfica, máquina fotográfica

camera·man ['kæmərə,mæn] *s* (*pl* **-men** [,mɛn]) camarógrafo, tomavistas *m*

camomile ['kæmə,maɪl] *s* manzanilla

camouflage ['kæmə,flɑʒ] *s* camuflaje *m* || *tr* camuflar

camp [kæmp] *s* campamento || *intr* acampar

campaign [kæm'pen] *s* campaña || *intr* hacer campaña

campaigner [kæm'penər] *s* propagandista *mf*; veterano

camp'fire' *s* hoguera de campamento
camphor ['kæmfər] *s* alcanfor *m*
camp'stool' *s* silla de tijera, catrecillo
campus ['kæmpəs] *s* terrenos, recinto (*de la universidad*)
cam'shaft' *s* árbol *m* de levas
can [kæn] *s* bote *m*, envase *m*, lata || *v* (*pret & pp* **canned;** *ger* **canning**) *tr* envasar, enlatar || *v* (*pret & cond* **could**) *v aux* **he can come tomorrow** puede venir mañana; **can you swim?** ¿sabe Vd. nadar?
Canada ['kænədə] *s* el Canadá
Canadian [kə'nedɪ-ən] *adj & s* canadiense
canal [kə'næl] *s* canal *m*
canar•y [kə'nɛri] *s* (*pl* **-ies**) canario || **Canaries** *spl* Canarias
can•cel ['kænsəl] *v* (*pret & pp* **-celed** o **-celled;** *ger* **-celing** o **-celling**) *tr* cancelar, eliminar, suprimir; matasellar, obliterar (*sellos de correo*)
canceler ['kænsələr] *s* matasellos *m*
cancellation [,kænsə'leʃən] *s* cancelación, eliminación, supresión; revocatoria; (*of stamps*) obliteración
cancer ['kænsər] *s* cáncer *m;* **Cancer** *s* (astr) Cáncer *m*
cancerous ['kænsərəs] *adj* canceroso
candela•brum [,kændə'lebrəm] *s* (*pl* **-bra** [brə] o **-brums**) candelabro
candid ['kændɪd] *adj* franco, sincero; imparcial
candida•cy ['kændɪdəsi] *s* (*pl* **-cies**) candidatura
candidate ['kændɪ,det] *s* candidato; (*for a degree*) graduando
candid camera *s* cámara indiscreta
candle ['kændəl] *s* bujía, candela, vela
can'dle•hold'er *s* candelero
can'dle•light' *s* luz *f* de vela; crepúsculo
candle power *s* bujía
can'dle•stick' *s* palmatoria
candor ['kændər] *s* franqueza, sinceridad; imparcialidad
can•dy ['kændi] *s* (*pl* **-dies**) bombón *m*, confite *m*, dulce *m;* dulces *mpl* || *v* (*pret & pp* **-died**) *tr* almibarar, confitar, garapiñar || *intr* almibararse
candy box *s* bombonera, confitera
candy store *s* confitería, dulcería
cane [ken] *s* (*plant; stem*) caña; (*walking stick*) bastón *m;* (*for chair seats*) junco, mimbre *m*, rejilla
cane seat *s* asiento de rejilla
cane sugar *s* azúcar *m* de caña
canine ['kenaɪn] *adj* canino || *s* (*tooth*) canino; perro
canned goods *spl* conservas alimenticias
canner•y ['kænəri] *s* (*pl* **-ies**) conservera, fábrica de conservas
cannibal ['kænɪbəl] *adj & s* caníbal *mf*
canning ['kænɪŋ] *adj* conservero || *s* conservería
cannon ['kænən] *s* cañón *m;* cañones
cannonade [,kænə'ned] *s* cañoneo || *tr* cañonear
cannon ball *s* bala de cañón
· cannon fodder *s* carne *f* de cañón

can•ny ['kæni] *adj* (*comp* **-nier;** *super* **-niest**) cauteloso, cuerdo; astuto
canoe [kə'nu] *s* canoa; bongo (SAm)
canoeing [kə'nu•ɪŋ] *s* piraguismo
canoeist [kə'nu•ɪst] *s* canoero
canon ['kænən] *s* canon *m;* (*priest*) canónigo
canonical [kə'nɑnɪkəl] *adj* canónico; aceptado, auténtico, establecido || **canonicals** *spl* vestiduras sacerdotales
canonize ['kænə,naɪz] *tr* canonizar
canon law *s* cánones *mpl*, derecho canónico
canon•ry ['kænənri] *s* (*pl* **-ries**) canonjía
can opener ['opənər] *s* abrelatas *m*
cano•py ['kænəpi] *s* (*pl* **-pies**) dosel *m*, pabellón *m;* (*over an entrance*) marquesina; (*for electrical fixtures*) campana
canopy of heaven *s* bóveda celeste
cant [kænt] *s* hipocresía; jerga, jerigonza
cantaloupe ['kæntə,lop] *s* cantalupo
cantankerous [kæn'tæŋkərəs] *adj* de mal genio, pendenciero
canteen [kæn'tin] *s* (*shop*) cantina; (*water flask*) cantimplora; (mil) centro de recreo
canter ['kæntər] *s* medio galope || *intr* ir a medio galope
canticle ['kæntɪkəl] *s* cántico
cantilever ['kæntɪ,livər] *adj* voladizo || *s* viga voladiza
cantle ['kæntəl] *s* arzón trasero
canton [kæn'tɑn] *tr* acantonar
cantonment [kæn'tɑnmənt] *s* acantonamiento
cantor ['kæntər] *s* chantre *m;* (*in a synagogue*) cantor *m* principal
canvas ['kænvəs] *s* cañamazo, lona; (naut) vela, lona; (*painting*) lienzo; **under canvas** (mil) en tiendas; (naut) con las velas izadas
canvass ['kænvəs] *s* pesquisa, escrutinio; (*of votes*) solicitación || *tr* escrutar, solicitar; discutir detenidamente
canyon ['kænjən] *s* cañón *m*
cap. *abbr* **capital, capitalize**
cap [kæp] *s* gorra, gorra de visera; (*of academic costume*) birrete *m;* (*of bottle*) cápsula; (*e.g., of a fountain pen*) capuchón *m* || *v* (*pret & pp* **capped;** *ger* **capping**) *tr* cubrir con gorra; capsular (*una botella*); **to cap the climax** ser el colmo
capabili•ty [,kepə'bɪlɪti] *s* (*pl* **-ties**) habilidad, capacidad
capable ['kepəbəl] *adj* hábil, capaz
capacious [kə'peʃəs] *adj* espacioso, capaz
capaci•ty [kə'pæsɪti] *s* (*pl* **-ties**) (*room, space; ability, aptitude*) capacidad; (*status, function*) calidad; **in the capacity of** en calidad de
cap and bells *spl* caperuza de bufón; cetro de la locura
cap and gown *s* birrete y toga
caparison [kə'pærɪsən] *s* caparazón *m* || *tr* engualdrapar
cape [kep] *s* cabo, promontorio; (*garment*) capa, esclavina
Cape Colony *s* la Colonia del Cabo
Cape Horn *s* el Cabo de Hornos
Cape of Good Hope *s* Cabo de Buena Esperanza

caper [ˈkepər] s (*gay jump*) cabriola; (*prank*) travesura; **to cut capers** dar cabriolas; hacer travesuras ‖ *intr* cabriolear; retozar

Cape'town' o **Cape Town** s El Cabo, la Ciudad del Cabo

cape'work' s (taur) suerte f de capa, lance m

capital [ˈkæpɪtəl] *adj* capital ‖ s (*money*) capital m; (*city*) capital f; (*top of a column*) capitel m; **to make capital out of** sacar beneficio de

capital flight s fuga de capitales

capitalism [[ˈkæpɪtəˌlɪzəm] s capitalismo

capitalize [ˈkæpɪtəˌlaɪz] *tr* escribir con mayúscula; capitalizar ‖ *intr* — **to capitalize on** aprovecharse de

capital letter s letra mayúscula

capital punishment s pena capital, último suplicio

capitol [ˈkæpɪtəl] s capitolio

capitulate [kəˈpɪtʃəˌlet] *intr* capitular

capon [ˈkepɑn] s capón m

caprice [kəˈpris] s capricho, antojo; veleidad

capricious [kəˈprɪʃəs] *adj* caprichoso, antojadizo

Capricorn [ˈkæprɪˌkɔrn] s (astr) Capricornio

capsize [ˈkæpsaɪz] *tr* volcar ‖ *intr* volcar; tumbar, zozobrar (*un barco*)

capstan [ˈkæpstən] s cabrestante m

cap'stone' s coronamiento

capsule [ˈkæpsəl] s cápsula

Capt. *abbr* **Captain**

captain [ˈkæptən] s capitán m ‖ *tr* capitanear

captain•cy [ˈkæptənsi] s (*pl* **-cies**) capitanía

caption [ˈkæpʃən] s título; (*in a movie*) subtítulo

captivate [ˈkæptɪˌvet] *tr* cautivar, encantar

captive [ˈkæptɪv] *adj* & s cautivo

captivi•ty [kæpˈtɪvɪti] s (*pl* **-ties**) cautividad, cautiverio

captor [ˈkæptər] s aprenhensor m

capture [ˈkæptʃər] s apresamiento, captura; (*of a stronghold*) toma ‖ *tr* apresar, capturar; tomar (*una plaza*); captar (*p.ej., la atención de una persona*)

Capuchin nun [ˈkæpjutʃɪn] o [ˈkæpjuʃɪn] s capuchina

car [kɑr] s coche m; (*of an elevator*) caja, carro

carafe [kəˈræf] s garrafa

caramel [ˈkærəməl] o [ˈkɑrməl] s (*burnt sugar*) caramelo; bombón m de caramelo

carat [ˈkærət] s quilate m

caravan [ˈkærəˌvæn] s caravana

caravansa•ry [ˌkærəˈvænsəri] s (*pl* **-ries**) caravanera

caraway [ˈkærəˌwe] s alcaravea

car'barn' s cochera de tranvías

carbide [ˈkɑrbaɪd] s carburo

carbine [ˈkɑrbaɪn] s carabina

carbolic acid [kɑrˈbɑlɪk] s ácido carbólico

car bomb s coche bomba

carbon [ˈkɑrbən] s (*chemical element*) carbono; (*pole of arc light or battery*) carbón m; papel m carbón; (*in auto cylinders*) carbonilla

carbon copy s copia al carbón

carbon dioxide s dióxido de carbono

carbon monoxide s óxido de carbono, monóxido de carbono

carbon paper s papel m carbón

car'boy' s bombona, garrafón m

carbuncle [ˈkɑrbʌŋkəl] s (*stone*) carbunclo, carbúnculo; (pathol) carbunclo, carbunco

carburetor [ˈkɑrbəˌretər] s carburador m

car caller s avisacoches m

carcass [ˈkɑrkəs] s res muerta, cadáver m

carcinogen [kɑrˈsɪnəjən] s carcinógeno

carcinoma [ˌkɑrsəˈnomə] s carcinoma

card [kɑrd] s tarjeta; (*for playing games*) naipe m, carta; (*for filing*) ficha; (*person*) (coll) sujeto, tipo

card'board' s cartón m

cardboard binding s encuadernación en pasta

card case s tarjetero

card catalogue s catálogo de fichas

cardiac [ˈkɑrdɪˌæk] *adj* cardíaco ‖ s (*medicine; sufferer*) cardíaco

cardigan [ˈkɑrdɪgən] s albornoz m, rebeca

cardinal [ˈkɑrdɪnəl] *adj* cardinal; purpurado ‖ s (*prelate; bird*) cardenal m; número cardinal

card index s fichero, tarjetero

card party s tertulia de baraja

card'sharp' s fullero, tahur m

card trick s truco de naipes

care [kɛr] s (*worry*) inquietud, ansiedad; (*watchful attention*) esmero; (*charge*) cargo, custodia; **care of** suplicada en casa de; **to take care of oneself** cuidarse ‖ *intr* inquietarse, preocuparse; **to care for** cuidar de; amar, querer; **to care to** tener ganas de; **I couldn't care less** me importe un pepino

careen [kəˈrin] *intr* inclinarse; mecerse precipitadamente

career [kəˈrɪr] *adj* de carrera ‖ s carrera

care'free' *adj* despreocupado, libre de cuidados

careful [ˈkɛrfəl] *adj* (*acting with care*) cuidadoso; (*done with care*) esmerado; **to be careful to** cuidarse de

careless [ˈkɛrlɪs] *adj* descuidado, negligente

carelessness [ˈkɛrlɪsnɪs] s descuido, negligencia

car enthusiast s devoto del volante

caress [kəˈrɛs] s caricia ‖ *tr* acariciar ‖ *intr* acariciarse

caretaker [ˈkɛrˌtekər] s curador m, guardián m, custodio

care'worn' *adj* fatigado, rendido

car'fare' s pasaje m de tranvía o autobús

car•go [ˈkɑrgo] s (*pl* **-goes** o **-gos**) carga, cargamento

cargo boat s barco de carga

Caribbean [ˌkærɪˈbiən] o [kəˈrɪbiən] *adj* caribe ‖ s mar m Caribe

caricature [ˈkærɪkətʃər] s caricatura ‖ *tr* caricaturizar

caricaturist [ˈkærɪkətʃərɪst] s caricaturista mf

carillon [ˈkærɪˌlɑn] o [kəˈrɪljən] s carillón m

car'load' s furgonada, vagonada

ca
ca

carnage [ˈkɑrnɪdʒ] s carnicería, matanza
carnation [kɑrˈneʃən] adj encarnado ‖ s clavel m, clavel reventón
carnival [ˈkɑrnɪvəl] adj carnavalesco ‖ s (period before Lent) carnaval m; verbena, espectáculo de atracciones
car·ol [ˈkærəl] s canción alegre, villancico ‖ v (pret & pp -oled o -olled; ger -oling o -olling); tr celebrar con villancicos ‖ intr cantar con alegría
carom [ˈkærəm] s carambola ‖ intr carambolear
carousal [kəˈrauzəl] s juerga, borrachera, jarana
carouse [kəˈrauz] intr emborracharse, jaranear
carp [kɑrp] s (pez) carpa ‖ intr quejarse
carpenter [ˈkɑrpəntər] s carpintero
carpentry [ˈkɑrpəntri] s carpintería
carpet [ˈkɑrpɪt] s alfombra; **to be on the carpet** estar sobre el tapete ‖ tr alfombrar
carpet sweeper s barredora de alfombras
car′-rent′al service s alquiler m de coches
carriage [ˈkærɪdʒ] s carruaje m; (cost of carrying) porte m, transporte m; (bearing) porte m, continente m; (mach) carro
carrier [ˈkærɪ·ər] s portador m, transportador m; portador de gérmenes; empresa de transportes; (mailman) cartero; vendedor m de periódicos; portaaviones m; (rad) onda portadora
carrier pigeon s paloma mensajera
carrier wave s (rad) onda portadora
carrion [ˈkærɪ·ən] adj carroño; inmundo ‖ s carroña; inmundicia
carrot [ˈkærət] s zanahoria
carrousel [ˌkærəˈzɛl] s caballitos, tiovivo
car·ry [ˈkæri] v (pret & pp -ried) tr llevar, portar, traer; transportar; sostener (una carga); **to carry away** llevarse; encantar, entusiasmar; **to carry into effect** llevar a cabo; **to carry one's point** salirse con la suya; **to carry out** llevar a cabo; **to carry the day** quedar victorioso, ganar la palma; **to carry weight** ser de peso ‖ intr tener alcance; **to carry on** continuar, perseverar; (coll) travesear; (coll) comportarse de un modo escandaloso; (coll) hacer locuras
cart [kɑrt] s carreta, carro ‖ tr carretear
carte blanche [ˈkɑrtˈblɑnʃ] s carta blanca
cartel [kɑrˈtɛl] s cartel m
Carthage [ˈkɑrθɪdʒ] s Cartago
Carthaginian [ˌkɑrθəˈdʒɪnɪ·ən] adj & s cartaginés m
cart horse s caballo de tiro
cartilage [ˈkɑrtɪlɪdʒ] s cartílago
cartoon [kɑrˈtun] s caricatura; (comic strip) tira cómica; (film) película de dibujos ‖ tr caricaturizar
cartoonist [kɑrˈtunɪst] s caricaturista mf
cartridge [ˈkɑrtrɪdʒ] s cartucho
cartridge belt s canana
carve [kɑrv] tr trinchar (carne); esculpir, tallar
carving knife [ˈkɑrvɪŋ] s cuchillo de trinchar
car washer s lavacoches m
caryatid [ˌkærɪˈætɪd] s cariátide f

cascade [kæsˈked] s cascada
case [kes] s (instance; form of a word) caso; (box) caja; (small container) estuche m; (for cigarettes) pitillera; (sheath) vaina, funda; (law) causa, pleito; **in case** caso que; **in no case** de ninguna manera ‖ tr encajonar, enfundar
casement [ˈkesmənt] s ventana batiente; bastidor m (de la ventana)
cash [kæʃ] s dinero contante; **cash on delivery** contra reembolso, pago contra entrega; **to pay cash** pagar al contado ‖ tr cobrar (un cheque el portador); abonar, pagar (un cheque el banco) ‖ intr — **to cash in on** (coll) sacar provecho de
cash and carry s pago al contado con transporte a cargo del comprador
cash′box′ s caja
cashew [ˈkæʃu] s anacardo, marañón m
cashew nut s anacardo, nuez f de marañón
cashier [kæˈʃɪr] s cajero ‖ tr destruir; (in the army) degradar
cashier's check s cheque m de caja
cashier's desk s caja
cashmere [ˈkæʃmɪr] s casimir m, cachemir m
cash on hand s efectivo en caja
cash payment s pago al contado
cash purchase s compra al contado
cash register s caja registradora
casing [ˈkesɪŋ] s caja, cubierta, envoltura; (of door or window) marco, cerco; (of tire) cubierta; (sew) jareta
cask [kæsk] o [kɑsk] s casco, pipa, tonel m
casket [ˈkæskɪt] s (box for valuables) cajita, joyero; (coffin) caja, ataúd m
cassava [kəˈsɑvə] s cazabe m, casabe m
casserole [ˈkæsəˌrol] s cacerola; (dish cooked in a casserole) timbal m
cassette [kæˈsɛt] s casete m
cassette player s grabador-reproductor m
cassock [ˈkæsək] s balandrán m, sotana
cast [kæst] s echada, tiro; forma, molde m; aire m, semblante m; matiz m, tinte m; (of actors) reparto ‖ v (pret & pp cast) tr echar, tirar; volver (los ojos); proyectar (una sombra); colar, fundir (metales); depositar (votos); echar (suertes); (theat) repartir (papeles); **to cast aside** desechar; **to cast loose** soltar; **to cast out** arrojar, echar fuera; despedir, desterrar ‖ intr echar los dados; arrojar el sedal o el anzuelo; **to cast about** revolver proyectos; **to cast off** (naut) soltar las amarras
castanet [ˌkæstəˈnɛt] s castañuela, castañeta
cast′a·way′ adj & s proscrito, réprobo; náufrago
caste [kæst] s casta; **to lose caste** desprestigiarse
caster [ˈkæstər] s ruedecilla de mueble; (cruet stand) angarillas, vinagreras; frasco
Castile [kæsˈtil] s Castilla
Castile soap s jabón m de Castilla
Castilian [kæsˈtɪljən] adj & s castellano
casting [ˈkæstɪŋ] s fundición, pieza fundida; (theat) reparto
casting vote s voto de calidad

cast iron *s* hierro colado, hierro fundido

cast'-i'ron *adj* de hierro colado; fuerte, endurecido; duro, inflexible

castle ['kæsəl] *s* castillo; (chess) roque *m*, torre *f* ‖ *tr & intr* (chess) enrocar

castle in Spain o **castle in the air** *s* castillo en el aire

cast'off' *adj* abandonado, desechado; (*clothing*) de desecho ‖ *s* desecho

castor oil ['kæstər] *s* aceite *m* de ricino

castrate ['kæstret] *tr* capar, castrar

casual ['kæʒʊ·əl] *adj* casual, fortuito; descuidado, indiferente

casual·ty ['kæʒu·əlti] *s* (*pl* **-ties**) desgracia, accidente *m*; accidentado, víctima; (*in war*) baja

casualty list *s* lista de bajas

cat. *abbr* **catalogue, catechism**

cat [kæt] *s* gato; mujer maligna; **to bell the cat** ponerle cascabel al gato; **to let the cat out of the bag** revelar el secreto

catacomb ['kætə,kom] *s* catacumba

Catalan ['kætə,læn] *adj & s* catalán *m*

catalogue ['kætə,lɔg] o ['kætə,lag] *s* catálogo ‖ *tr* catalogar

Catalonia [,kætə'loni·ə] *s* Cataluña

Catalonian [,kætə'loni·ən] *adj & s* catalán *m*

catapult ['kætə,pʌlt] *s* catapulta ‖ *tr* catapultar

cataract ['kætə,rækt] *s* catarata; (pathol) catarata

catarrh [kə'tar] *s* catarro

catastrophe [kə'tæstrəfi] *s* catástrofe *f*

cat'call' *s* rechifla ‖ *tr & intr* rechiflar

catch [kætʃ] *s* (*of a ball*) cogida; (*of fish*) pesca; (*of a lock*) cerradera, pestillo; (*booty*) botín *m*, presa; (*fastener*) broche *m*; (*good match*) buen partido ‖ *v* (*pret & pp* **caught** [kɔt]) *tr* asir, coger, atrapar; llegar a oír; coger (*un resfriado*); (*to come upon suddenly*) sorprender; comprender; capturar (*al delincuente*); **to catch fire** encenderse; **to catch hold of** agarrar, coger; apoderarse de; **to catch it** (coll) merecerse un regaño; **to catch oneself** contenerse; recobrar el equilibrio; **to catch sight of** alcanzar a ver; **to catch up** arrebatar; coger al vuelo; (*in a mistake*) cazar ‖ *intr* pegarse (*una enfermedad*); enredarse; encenderse; **to catch at** agarrarse a, tratar de asir; **to catch on** prender en (*p.ej., un gancho*); comprender, coger el tino; **to catch up** salir del atraso; (*in one's debts*) ponerse al día; **to catch up with** emparejar con

catcher ['kætʃər] *s* (baseball) receptor, parador *m*

catching ['kætʃɪŋ] *adj* pegajoso, contagioso; atrayente, cautivador

catch question *s* pega

catchup ['kætʃəp] *s* salsa de tomate condimentada

catch'word' *s* lema *m*, palabra de efecto; (*actor's cue*) pie *m*; (typ) reclamo

catch·y ['kætʃi] *adj* (*comp* **-ier**; *super* **-iest**) (*tune*) animado, vivo; (*title of a book*) impresionante, llamativo; (*question*) intrincado; (*breathing*) espasmódico

catechism ['kæti,kɪzəm] *s* catecismo

catego·ry ['kæti,gori] *s* (*pl* **-ries**) categoría; (*sports*) division

cater ['ketər] *tr & intr* abastecer, proveer; **to cater to** proveer a

cater-cornered ['kætər,kɔrnərd] *adj* diagonal ‖ *adv* diagonalmente

caterer ['ketərər] *s* abastecedor *m*, proveedor *m* de alimentos (*esp. para fiestas caseras*)

caterpillar ['kætər,pɪlər] *s* oruga

caterpillar tractor *s* tractor *m* de oruga

cat'fish' *s* bagre *m*

cat'gut' *s* (mus) cuerda de tripa; (surg) catgut *m*

Cath. *abbr* **Catholic**

cathartic [kə'θartɪk] *adj & s* catártico

cathedral [kə'θidrəl] *s* catedral *f*

catheter ['kæθɪtər] *s* catéter *m*

catheterize ['kæθɪtə,raɪz] *tr* cateterizar

cathode ['kæθod] *s* cátodo

catholic ['kæθəlɪk] *adj* católico ‖ **Catholic** *adj & s* católico

catkin ['kætkɪn] *s* candelilla, amento

cat nap *s* sueñecito

catnip ['kætnɪp] *s* hierba gatera, nébeda

cat-o'-nine-tails [,kætə'naɪn,telz] *s* azote *m* con nueve ramales

cat's cradle *s* juego de la cuna

cat's-paw o **catspaw** ['kæts,pɔ] *s* mano *f* de gato, instrumento

catsup ['kætsəp] o [ketʃəp] *s* salsa de tomate condimentada

cat'tail' *s* anea, espadaña; amento

cattle ['kætəl] *s* ganado vacuno

cattle crossing *s* paso de ganado

cattle·man ['kætəlmən] *s* (*pl* **-men** [mən]) *s* ganadero

cattle raising *s* ganadería

cattle ranch *s* hacienda de ganado

cat·ty ['kæti] *adj* (*comp* **-tier**; *super* **-tiest**) (*like a cat*) felino, gatuno; (*spiteful*) malicioso; (*gossipy*) chismoso

cat'walk' *s* pasadero, pasarela

Caucasian [kɔ'keʒən] *adj & s* caucasiano, caucásico

Caucasus ['kɔkəsəs] *s* Cáucaso

caucus ['kɔkəs] *s* junta de políticos

cauliflower ['kɔli,flaʊ·ər] *s* coliflor *f*

cause [kɔz] *s* causa; (*person*) causante *mf* ‖ *tr* causar

cause'way' *s* (*highway*) calzada; calzada elevada

caustic ['kɔstɪk] *adj* cáustico

cauterize ['kɔtə,raɪz] *tr* cauterizar

caution ['kɔʃən] *s* (*carefulness*) cautela; (*warning*) advertencia, amonestación ‖ *tr* advertir, amonestar

cautious ['kɔʃəs] *adj* cauteloso, cauto

Cav. *abbr* **Cavalry**

cavalcade [,kævəl'ked] o ['kævəl,ked] *s* cabalgata

cavalier [,kævə'lɪr] *adj* (*haughty*) altivo, desdeñoso; (*offhand*) alegre, desenvuelto, inceremonioso ‖ *s* (*horseman*) caballero; (*lady's escort*) galán *m*

caval·ry ['kævəlri] *s* (*pl* **-ries**) caballería

cavalry·man [ˈkævəlrimən] s (pl -men [mən]) soldado de caballería
cave [kev] s cueva, caverna ‖ intr — **to cave in** hundirse; (to give in, yield) (coll) ceder, rendirse
cave'-in' s hundimiento, derrumbe m, socavón m
cave man s hombre grosero
cavern [ˈkævərn] s caverna
cav·il [ˈkævɪl] v (pret & pp -iled o -illed; ger -iling o -illing) intr buscar quisquillas
cavi·ty [ˈkævɪti] s (pl -ties) cavidad; (in a tooth) picadura
cavort [kəˈgɔrt] intr (coll) cabriolar
caw [kɔ] s graznido ‖ intr graznar
CB abbr **citizens band**
cc. abbr **cubic centimeter**
CD abbr **compact disk**
cease [sis] tr parar, suspender ‖ intr cesar; cesar de, dejar de + inf
cease'fire' s cese m de fuego ‖ intr suspender hostilidades
ceaseless [ˈsislɪs] adj incesante, continuo
cedar [ˈsidər] s cedro
cede [sid] tr ceder, traspasar
ceiling [ˈsilɪŋ] s techo, cielo raso; (aer) techo, cielo máximo
ceiling price s precio tope
celebrant [ˈsɛlɪbrənt] s celebrante m
celebrate [ˈsɛlɪˌbret] tr celebrar ‖ intr (to say mass) celebrar; divertirse, festejarse; farrear
celebrated [ˈsɛlɪˌbretɪd] adj célebre, renombrado
celebration [ˌsɛlɪˈbreʃən] s celebración; diversión, festividad
celebri·ty [sɪˈlɛbrɪti] s (pl -ties) (fame; famous person) celebridad
celery [ˈsɛləri] s apio
celestial [sɪˈlɛstʃəl] adj celeste, celestial
celiba·cy [ˈsɛlɪbəsi] s (pl -cies) celibato
celibate [ˈsɛlɪbɪt] adj & s célibe mf
cell [sɛl] s (of convent or jail) celda; (of honeycomb) celdilla; (of electric battery) elemento; (of plant or animal; of photoelectric device; of political group) célula
cellar [ˈsɛlər] s sótano; (for wine) bodega
cellaret [ˌsɛləˈrɛt] s licorera
cell house s prisión celular
cellist o **'cellist** [ˈtʃɛlɪst] s violoncelista mf
cel·lo o **'cel·lo** [ˈtʃɛlo] s (pl -los) violoncelo
cellophane [ˈsɛləˌfen] s celofán m
celluloid [ˈsɛljəˌlɔɪd] s celuloide m
Celt [sɛlt] o [kɛlt] s celta mf
Celtic [ˈsɛltɪk] o [ˈkɛltɪk] adj céltico ‖ s (language) celta m
cement [sɪˈmɛnt] s cemento ‖ tr revestir con cemento; (la amistad) consolidar
cemeter·y [ˈsɛmɪˌtɛri] s (pl -ies) cementerio
cen. abbr **central**
censer [ˈsɛnsər] s incensario
censor [ˈsɛnsər] s censor m ‖ tr censurar
censure [ˈsɛnʃər] s censura ‖ tr censurar
census [ˈsɛnsəs] s censo; **to take the census** levantar el censo
cent. abbr **centigrade, central, century**
cent [sɛnt] s centavo

centaur [ˈsɛntɔr] s centauro
centennial [sɛnˈtɛnɪ·əl] adj & s centenario
center [ˈsɛntər] adj centrista ‖ s centro ‖ tr centrar
center half s (ball games) medio centro
cen'ter·piece' s centro de mesa
center punch s granete m, punzón m de marcar
centigrade [ˈsɛntɪˌgred] adj centígrado
centimeter [ˈsɛntɪˌmitər] s centímetro
centipede [ˈsɛntɪˌpid] s ciempiés m
central [ˈsɛntrəl] adj central ‖ s (telp) central f, central de teléfonos; (operator) telefonista mf
Central America s Centro América, la América Central
Central American adj & mf centroamericano
centralize [ˈsɛntrəˌlaɪz] tr centralizar ‖ intr centralizarse
centrifuge [ˈsɛntrəfjudʒ] s centrifugadora
centu·ry [ˈsɛntʃəri] s (pl -ries) siglo
century plant s pita, maguey m
ceramic [sɪˈræmɪk] adj cerámico
cereal [ˈsɪrɪ·əl] adj & s cereal m
ceremonious [ˌsɛrɪˈmoni·əs] adj ceremonioso, etiquetero
ceremo·ny [ˈsɛrɪˌmoni] s (pl -nies) ceremonia; **to stand on ceremony** hacer ceremonias, ser etiquetero
certain [ˈsʌrtən] adj cierto; **a certain** cierto; **for certain** por cierto
certainly [ˈsɛrtənli] adj ciertamente; (gladly) con mucho gusto
certain·ty [ˈsʌrtənti] s (pl -ties) certeza; **with certainty** a ciencia cierta
certificate [sərˈtɪfɪkɪt] s certificación, certificado; (of birth, death, etc.) partida, fe f; (document representing financial assets) título ‖ [sərˈtɪfɪˌket] tr certificar
certified public accountant [ˈsʌrtɪˌfaɪd] s contador público, censor jurado de cuentas
certi·fy [ˈsʌrtɪˌfaɪ] v (pret & pp -fied) tr certificar
cervix [ˈsʌrvɪks] s (pl cervices [sərˈvaɪsɪz]) cerviz f
cessation [sɛˈseʃən] s cesación
cessation of hostilities s suspensión de hostilidades
cesspool [ˈsɛsˌpul] s pozo negro; (fig) sitio inmundo
Ceylon [sɪˈlɑn] s Ceilán
Ceylo·nese [ˌsiləˈniz] adj ceilanés ‖ s (pl -nese) ceilanés m
cf. abbr **confer, i.e., compare**
C.F.I., c.f.i. abbr **cost, freight, and insurance**
cg. abbr **centigram**
ch. abbr **chapter, church**
chafe [tʃef] s fricción, roce m; desgaste m; irritación ‖ tr (to rub) frotar; (to rub and make sore) escocer; (to wear) desgastar; irritar ‖ intr escocerse; desgastarse; irritarse
chaff [tʃæf] s barcia; paja menuda; broza, desperdicio
chafing dish [ˈtʃefɪŋ] s cocinilla, infernillo

chagrin [ʃəˈgrɪn] s desazón f, disgusto ‖ tr desazonar, disgustar

chain [tʃen] s cadena ‖ tr encadenar

chain gang s cadena de presidiarios, collera, cuerda de presos

chain reaction s reacción en cadena

chain'smoke' intr fumar un pitillo tras otro

chain store s empresa con una cadena de tiendas; tienda de una cadena de tiendas

chair [tʃɛr] s silla; (de catedrático) cátedra; presidencia; **to take the chair** presidir la reunión; abrir la sesión ‖ tr presidir (una reunión)

chair lift s telesilla

chair·man [ˈtʃɛrmən] s (pl -men [mən]) presidente m

chairmanship [ˈtʃɛrmən,ʃɪp] s presidencia

chair rail s guardasilla

chalice [ˈtʃælɪs] s cáliz m

chalk [tʃɔk] s (soft white limestone) creta; (piece used for writing) tiza ‖ tr marcar o escribir con tiza; **to chalk up** apuntar; marcar (un tanto)

challenge [ˈtʃælɪndʒ] s desafío; (law) recusación ‖ tr desafiar; (law) recusar

chamber [ˈtʃembər] s cámara; (of a gun) recámara; dormitorio; **chambers** oficina de juez

chamberlain [ˈtʃembərlɪn] s chambelán m

cham'ber·maid' s camarera

chamber pot s orinal m

chameleon [kəˈmiliˑən] s camaleón m

chamfer [ˈtʃæmfər] s chaflán m ‖ tr chaflanar

cham·ois [ˈʃæmi] s (pl -ois) gamuza

champ [tʃæmp] s mordisco; (slang) campeón m ‖ tr & intr mordiscar; (el freno) morder

champagne [ʃæmˈpen] s champaña m

champion [ˈtʃæmpɪˑən] s campeón m ‖ tr defender

championess [ˈtʃæmpiˑənɪs] s campeona

championship [ˈtʃæmpiˑən,ʃɪp] s campeonato

chance [tʃæns] o [tʃɑns] adj casual, imprevisto ‖ s oportunidad, ocasión; casualidad, suerte f; probabilidad; peligro, riesgo; chance m (SAm); **by chance** por casualidad; **to not stand a chance** no tener probabilidad de éxito; **to take a chance** probar fortuna; comprar un billete de lotería; **to take chances** probar fortuna; **to wait for, a chance** esperar la oportunidad ‖ intr acontecer; **to chance on** o **upon** tropezar con; **to chance to** acertar a

chancel [ˈtʃænsəl] o [ˈtʃɑnsəl] s entrecoro

chanceller·y [ˈtʃænsələri] o [ˈtʃɑnsələri] s (pl -ies) cancillería

chancellor [ˈtʃænsələr] s canciller m

chandelier [,ʃændəˈlɪr] s araña de luces

change [tʃendʒ] s cambio, mudanza; suelto, moneda suelta; (surplus money returned with a purchase) vuelta; (of clothing) muda; **for a change** por variedad; **to keep the change** quedarse con la vuelta; ‖ tr cambiar, mudar; cambiar de, mudar de; reemplazar; **to change clothes** cambiar de ropa; **to change gears** cambiar de velocidades; **to change hands** cambiar de dueño;

to change money cambiar moneda; **to change one's mind** cambiar de parecer; **to change trains** cambiar de tren, transbordar ‖ intr cambiar, mudar; corregirse

changeable [ˈtʃendʒəbəl] adj cambiable; inconstante, cambiante, mudable

change of clothing s muda de ropa

change of heart s arrepentimiento, conversión

change of life s cesación natural de las reglas

change of voice s muda

chan·nel [ˈtʃænəl] s (body of water joining two others) canal m; (bed of river) álveo, cauce m; (means of communication) vía; (passage) conducto; (groove) ranura, surco; (telv) canal m; **the Channel** el Canal de la Mancha ‖ v (pret & pp -neled o -nelled; ger -neling o -nelling) tr acanalar; canalizar (esfuerzos, dinero, etc.)

chant [tʃænt] s (song) canción; (song sung in a monotone) canto ‖ tr & intr cantar

chanter [ˈtʃæntər] s cantor m; (priest) chantre m

chanticleer [ˈtʃæntɪ,klɪr] s el gallo

chaos [ˈkeˑɑs] s caos m

chaotic [keˈɑtɪk] adj caótico

chap. abbr **chaplain, chapter**

chap [tʃæp] s (jaw) mandíbula; (cheek) mejilla; (crack in the skin) grieta; chico, tipo; **chaps** zahones mpl ‖ v (pret & pp chapped; ger chapping) tr agrietar, rajar ‖ intr agrietarse, rajarse

chapel [ˈtʃæpəl] s capilla

chaperon o **chaperone** [ˈʃæpə,ron] s carabina, señora de compañía ‖ tr acompañar (una señora a una o más señoritas)

chaplain [ˈtʃæplɪn] s capellán m

chaplet [ˈtʃæplɪt] s (wreath for head) guirnalda; rosario

chapter [ˈtʃæptər] s capítulo; (of the Scriptures) capítula; (of a cathedral) cabildo

chapter and verse adv con todos sus pelos y señales

char [tʃɑr] v (pret & pp charred; ger charring) tr carbonizar; (to scorch) socarrar

character [ˈkærɪktər] s carácter m; (conspicuous person; person in a play or novel) personaje m; (part or role in a play) papel m; (fellow) (coll) tipo, sujeto

character assassination s asesinato de carácter

characteristic [,kærɪktəˈrɪstɪk] adj característico ‖ s característica

characterize [ˈkærɪktə,raɪz] tr caracterizar

char'coal' s carbón m de leña; (for sketching) carboncillo; (sketch) dibujo al carbón

charcoal burner s (person) carbonero; horno para hacer carbón de leña

charge [tʃɑrdʒ] s (of an explosive, of electricity, of soldiers against the enemy; responsibility) carga; (accusation; amount owed; recording of amount owed) cargo; encargamiento; (heral) blasón m; (attack) embestida; **in charge of** a cargo de; **to put in charge** responsabilizar; **to reverse the charges** (telp) cargar al número llamado; **to take charge of** hacerse cargo de ‖ tr cargar; cobrar (*cierto precio*); (*to order*) encargar, mandar; cargar (*un acumulador; al enemigo*); **to charge to the account of someone** cargarle a uno en cuenta; **to charge with** cargar de || *intr* embestir

charge account *s* cuenta corriente

chargé d'affaires [ʃɑrˈʒe dəˈfɛr] *s* (*pl* **chargés d'affaires**) encargado de negocios

charger [ˈtʃɑrdʒər] *s* caballo de guerra; (*of a battery*) cargador *m*

chariot [ˈtʃærɪət] *s* carro romano

charioteer [ˌtʃærɪəˈtɪr] *s* carretero, auriga *m*

charisma [kəˈrɪzmə] *s* carisma

charismatic [ˌkɑrɪzˈmætɪk] *adj* carismático

charitable [ˈtʃærɪtəbəl] *adj* caritativo

chari·ty [ˈtʃærɪti] *s* (*pl* **-ties**) caridad; asociación de beneficencia, obra *pía*; **charity begins at home** la caridad bien ordenada empieza por uno mismo

charity performance *s* función benéfica

charlatan [ˈʃɑrlətən] *s* charlatán *m*

charlatanism [ˈʃɑrlətənˌɪzəm] *s* charlatanismo

Charlemagne [ˈʃɑrləˌmen] *s* Carlomagno

Charles [tʃɑrlz] *s* Carlos *m*

charlotte [ˈʃɑrlət] *s* carlota || **Charlotte** *s* Carlota

charlotte russe [ˈʃɑrlət ˈrus] *s* carlota rusa

charm [tʃɑrm] *s* encanto, hechizo; (*trinket*) amuleto, dije *m* || *tr* encantar, hechizar

charming [ˈtʃɑrmɪŋ] *adj* encantador

charnel [ˈtʃɑrnəl] *adj* cadavérico, horrible || *s* carnero, osario

charnel house *s* carnero, osario

chart [tʃɑrt] *s* mapa geográfico; (naut) carta de marear; cuadro, diagrama *m* || *tr* bosquejar; **to chart a course** trazar una ruta

charter [ˈtʃɑrtər] *s* carta (de privilegio) || *tr* alquilar (*un autobús*); fletar (*un barco*)

charter member *s* socio fundador

char·woman [ˈtʃɑrˌwʊmən] *s* (*pl* **-women** [ˌwɪmɪn]) alquilona, asistenta

Charybdis [kəˈrɪbdɪs] *s* Caribdis *f*

chase [tʃes] *s* caza, persecución || *tr* cazar, perseguir; **to chase away** ahuyentar

chasm [ˈkæzəm] *s* abismo

chas·sis [ˈtʃæsi] *s* (*pl* **-sis** [siz]) chasis *m*

chaste [tʃest] *adj* casto; (*style*) castizo

chasten [ˈtʃesən] *tr* castigar, corregir

chastise [tʃæsˈtaɪz] *tr* castigar

chastity [ˈtʃæstɪti] *s* castidad

chasuble [ˈtʃæzjəbəl] *s* casulla

chat [tʃæt] *s* charla, plática || *v* (*pret & pp* **chatted;** *ger* **chatting**) *intr* charlar, platicar

chatelaine [ˈʃætəˌlen] *s* castellana

chattels [ˈtʃætəlz] *spl* bienes *mpl* muebles, enseres *mpl*

chatter [ˈtʃætər] *s* (*talk*) cháchara; (*rattling*) traqueo; (*of teeth*) castañeteo; (*of birds*) chirrido || *intr* chacharear; traquear; castañetear, dentellar (*los dientes*)

chat·ter·box *s* charlador *m*, tarabilla

chattering [ˈtʃætərɪŋ] *adj* palabrudo

chauffeur [ˈʃofər] *o* [ʃoˈfʌr] *s* chófer *m*

chauvinism [ˈʃovɪnɪzəm] *s* chauvinismo

cheap [tʃip] *adj* barato; (*charging low prices*) no carero, baratero; (*flashy*) cursi; baladí;

to feel cheap sentirse avergonzado || *adv* barato

cheapen [ˈtʃipən] *tr* abaratar

cheapness [ˈtʃipnɪs] *s* baratura; baratía; (*flashiness*) cursilería

cheat [tʃit] *s* trampa, fraude *m;* (*person*) trampista *mf,* defraudador *m* || *tr* trampear, defraudar

check [tʃɛk] *s* (*of bank*) cheque *m;* (*for baggage*) talón *m,* contraseña; (*in a restaurant*) cuenta; (*in theater or movie*) contraseña, billete *m* de salida; (*restraint*) freno; (*to hold a door*) amortiguador *m;* (*in chess*) jaque *m;* inspección; comprobación, verificación; (*cloth*) paño a cuadros; **in check** en jaque; **to hold in check** contener, refrenar || *interj* ¡jaque! || *tr* parar súbitamente; contener, refrenar; amortiguar; facturar (*equipajes*); inspeccionar; comprobar, verificar; marcar, señalar; chequear; (*in chess*) jaquear, dar jaque a; **to check up** comprobar, verificar || *intr* pararse súbitamente; corresponder punto por punto; **to check in** (*at a hotel*) llegar e inscribirse; **to check out** pagar la cuenta y despedirse; (slang) morir

check'book' *s* talonario (de cheques), chequera

checker [ˈtʃɛkər] *s* inspector *m;* cuadro; dibujo a cuadros; (*in game of checkers*) ficha, pieza; **checkers** damas, juego de damas || *tr* marcar con cuadros; diversificar, variar

check'er·board' *s* damero, tablero

check girl *s* moza de guardarropa

checking account *s* cuenta corriente

check'mate' *s* mate *m,* jaque *m* mate || *tr* dar mate a, dar jaque mate a; (fig) derrotar completamente

check'out' *s* (*from a hotel*) salida; hora de salida; (*in a self-service retail store*) revisión y pago

checkout counter *s* mostrador *m* de revisión

check'point' *s* punto de inspección

check'rein' *s* engallador *m*

check'room' *s* guardarropa *m;* (rr) consigna, depósito de equipajes

check'up' *s* verificación rigurosa; chequeo; (*of an automobile*) revisión; (med) reconocimiento general

cheek [tʃik] *s* mejilla, carrillo; (coll) descaro, frescura

cheek'bone' *s* pómulo

cheek by jowl *adv* cara a cara, en estrecha intimidad

cheek·y [ˈtʃiki] *adj* (*comp* **-ier;** *super* **-iest**) (coll) descarado, fresco

cheer [tʃir] *s* alegría, regocijo; (*shout*) viva *m,* aplauso; **what cheer?** ¿qué tal? || *tr* alegrar, animar; aplaudir, vitorear; dar la bienvenida a, con vivas y aplausos || *intr* alegrarse, animarse; **cheer up!** ¡ánimo!

cheerful [ˈtʃɪrfəl] *adj* alegre

cheerio [ˈtʃɪrɪˌo] *interj* (coll) ¡hola! ¡qué tal!; (coll) ¡adiós! ¡hasta la vista!

cheerless [ˈtʃɪrlɪs] *adj* sombrío, triste

cheese [tʃiz] *s* queso

cheese'cloth' s estopilla
cheese spread s queso para extender
cheetah ['tʃitə] s gatopardo; leopardo indio
chef [ʃɛf] s primer cocinero, jefe m de cocina
chem. abbr **chemical, chemist, chemistry**
chemical ['kɛmɪkəl] adj químico ‖ s producto químico, substancia química
chemise [ʃə'miz] s camisa (de mujer)
chemist ['kɛmɪst] s químico
chemistry ['kɛmɪstri] s química
chemotherapy [,kimo'θɛrəpi] s quimioterapia
cherish ['tʃɛrɪʃ] tr acariciar; (a hope) abrigar, acariciar
cher•ry ['tʃɛri] s (pl **-ries**) (fruit; color) cereza; (tree) cerezo
cher•ub ['tʃɛrəb] s (pl **-ubim** [əbɪm]) querubín m ‖ s (pl **-ubs**) niño angelical
chess [tʃɛs] s ajedrez m
chess'board' s tablero de ajedrez
chess•man ['tʃɛs,mæn] s (pl **-men** [,mɛn]) pieza de ajedrez, trebejo
chess player s ajedrecista mf
chess set s ajedrez m
chest [tʃɛst] s (part of body) pecho; (receptacle) cajón m, cofre m; (piece of furniture) cómoda
chestnut ['tʃɛsnət] s (tree, wood, color) castaño; (fruit) castaña
chest of drawers s cómoda
cheval glass [ʃə'væl] s psique f
chevalier [, ʃɛvə'lɪr] s caballero
chevron ['ʃɛvrən] s galón m en forma de V invertida
chew [tʃu] s mascadura ‖ tr mascar; **to chew gum** chiclear; **to chew the rag** (slang) dar la lengua ‖ intr mascar
chewing gum s goma de mascar, chicle m
chg. abbr **charge**
chic [ʃik] adj & s chic m
chicaner•y [ʃɪ'kɛnəri] s (pl **-ies**) triquiñuela
chick [tʃɪk] s pollito; (slang) polla
chicken ['tʃɪkən] s pollo; (young person) pollo; (young girl) polla
chicken coop s pollera
chicken feed s (coll) calderilla
chickenhearted ['tʃɪkən,hɑrtɪd, varicela] adj gallina
chicken pox s viruelas locas, varicela
chicken wire s alambrada, tela metálica
chick'pea' s garbanzo
chico•ry ['tʃɪkəri] s (pl **-ries**) achicoria
chide [tʃaɪd] v (pret **chided** o **chid** [tʃɪd]; pp **chided, chid** o **chidden** ['tʃɪdən]) tr reprender, regañar
chief [tʃif] adj principal ‖ s jefe m; (of American Indians) cacique m
chief executive s jefe m del gobierno
chief justice s presidente m de sala; presidente del tribunal supremo
chiefly ['tʃifli] adv principalmente, mayormente
chief of staff s jefe m de estado mayor
chief of state s jefe m del estado
chieftain ['tʃiftən] s (of a clan or tribe) jefe m; adalid m, caudillo

chiffon [ʃɪ'fɑn] s gasa, soplillo; **chiffons** atavíos, perifollos
chiffonier [, ʃɪfə'nɪr] s cómoda alta
chignon ['ʃɪnjɑn] s castaña, moño
chilblain ['tʃɪl,blen] s sabañón m
child [tʃaɪld] s (pl **children** ['tʃɪldrən]) s (infant, youngster) niño; pipiolo (CAm, Mex); (one's offspring) hijo; descendiente mf; **with child** encinta, embarazada
child'birth' s alumbramiento, parto
childhood ['tʃaɪldhʊd] s niñez f, puericia; **from childhood** desde niño
childish ['tʃaɪldɪʃ] adj aniñado, pueril
childishness ['tʃaɪldɪnɪs] s puerilidad
child labor s trabajo de menores
childless ['tʃaɪldlɪs] adj sin hijos
child'like' adj aniñado
child'-rear'ing s puericultura
child's play s juego de niños
child welfare s protección a la infancia
Chile ['tʃɪli] s Chile m
Chilean ['tʃɪlɪ•ən] adj & s chileno
chili sauce ['tʃɪli] s ají m, salsa de ají
chill [tʃɪl] adj frío ‖ s frío desapacible; (sensation of cold) escalofrío; (lack of cordiality) frialdad ‖ tr enfriar ‖ intr calofriarse
chill•y ['tʃɪli] adj (comp **-ier;** super **-iest**) (causing shivering) frío; (sensitive to cold) escalofriado, friolero; (indifferent) (fig) frío
chime [tʃaɪm] s campaneo, repique m; tubo sonoro; **chimes** juego de campanas ‖ tr & intr campanear, repicar
chime clock s reloj m de carillón
chimera [kaɪ'mɪrə] o [kɪ'mɪrə] s quimera
chimney ['tʃɪmni] s chimenea; (for a lamp) tubo
chimney cap s caperuza
chimney flue s cañón m de chimenea
chimney pot s mitra, guardavientos m
chimney sweep s limpiachimeneas m, deshollinador m
chimpanzee [tʃɪm'pænzi] o [,tʃɪmpæn'zi] s chimpancé m
chin [tʃɪn] s barba, mentón m; **to keep one's chin up** (coll) no desanimarse ‖ v (pret & pp **chinned;** ger **chinning**) intr (coll) charlar
china ['tʃaɪnə] s china, porcelana ‖ **China** s China
china closet s chinero
China•man ['tʃaɪnəmən] s (pl **-men** [mən]) (offensive) chino
chi'na•ware' s porcelana, vajilla de porcelana
Chi•nese [tʃaɪ'niz] adj chino ‖ s (pl **-nese**) chino
Chinese gong s batintín m
Chinese lantern s farolillo veneciano
Chinese puzzle s problema embrollado
chink [tʃɪŋk] s grieta, hendidura; sonido metálico
chin strap s barboquejo, carrillera
chintz [tʃɪnts] s zaraza
chip [tʃɪp] s astilla, brizna; (in china) desconchado; (in poker) ficha; **chip off the old block** hijo de su padre ‖ v (pret & pp **chipped;** ger **chipping**) tr astillar (la ma-

dera); desconchar (*la porcelana*); **to chip in** contribuir con su cuota ‖ *intr* astillarse; desconcharse

chipmunk [ˈtʃɪpˌmʌŋk] *s* ardilla listada

chipper [ˈtʃɪpər] *adj* (coll) alegre, jovial, vivo

chiropodist [kaɪˈrɑpədɪst] o [kɪˈrɑpədɪst] *s* quiropodista *mf*

chiropractor [ˈkaɪrəˌpræktər] *s* quiropráctico

chirp [tʃʌrp] *s* chirrido, gorjeo ‖ *intr* chirriar, gorjear; hablar alegremente

chis·el [ˈtʃɪzəl] *s* (*for wood*) escoplo, formón *m*; (*for stone and metal*) cincel *m* ‖ *v* (*pret & pp* **-eled** o **-elled**; *ger* **-eling** o **-elling**) *tr* escoplear; cincelar; (slang) estafar

chit-chat [ˈtʃɪtˌtʃæt] *s* charla, palique *m*; hablilla, chismes *mpl*

chivalric [ˈʃɪvəlrɪk] o [ʃɪˈvælrɪk] *adj* caballeresco

chivalrous [ˈʃɪvəlrəs] *adj* caballeroso

chivalry [ˈʃɪvəlri] *s* (*knighthood*) caballería; (*gallantry, gentlemanliness*) caballerosidad

chloride [ˈkloraɪd] *s* cloruro

chlorine [ˈklorin] *s* cloro

chloroform [ˈklorəˌfɔrm] *s* cloroformo ‖ *tr* cloroformizar

chlorophyll [ˈklorəfɪl] *s* clorofila

chock-full [ˈtʃɑkˈful] *adj* de bote en bote, colmado

chocolate [ˈtʃɑkəlɪt] *s* chocolate *m*

choice [tʃɔɪs] *adj* escogido, selecto, superior ‖ *s* elección, selección; lo más escogido; **to have no choice** no tener alternativa

choir [kwaɪr] *s* coro

choir' boy' *s* niño de coro, infante *m* de coro

choir desk *s* facistol *m*

choir loft *s* coro

choir' mas' ter *s* jefe *m* de coro, maestro de capilla

choke [tʃok] *s* estrangulación; (*of carburetor*) cierre *m*, obturador *m*; (elec) choque *m* ‖ *tr* ahogar, sofocar, estrangular; obstruir, tapar; (aut) obturar; **to choke down** atragantar ‖ *intr* sofocarse; atragantarse; **to choke on** atragantarse con

choke coil *s* (elec) bobina de reacción, choque *m*

cholera [ˈkɑlərə] *s* cólera *m*

choleric [ˈkɑlərɪk] *adj* colérico

cholesterol [kəˈlɛstəˌrol] *s* colesterol *m*

choose [tʃuz] *v* (*pret* **chose** [tʃoz]; *pp* **chosen** [ˈtʃozən]) *tr* escoger, elegir ‖ *intr* — **to choose between** optar entre; **to choose to** optar por

chop [tʃɑp] *s* golpe *m* cortante; (*of meat*) chuleta; **chops** boca, labios ‖ *v* (*pret & pp* **chopped**; *ger* **chopping**) *tr* cortar, tajar; picar (*la carne*); **to chop off** tronchar; **to chop up** desmenuzar

chop' house' *s* restaurante *m*, figón *m*, colmado

chopper [ˈtʃɑpər] *s* (*person*) tajador *m*; (*tool*) hacha; (*of butcher*) cortante *m*; (slang) helicóptero

chopping block *s* tajo

chop·py [ˈtʃɑpi] *adj* (*comp* **-pier**; *super* **-piest**) (*sea*) agitado, picado; (*wind*) variable; (*style*) cortado, inciso

chop' sticks' *spl* palillos

choral [ˈkorəl] *adj* coral

chorale [koˈral] *s* coral *m*

choral society *s* orfeón *m*

chord [kɔrd] *s* (*harmonious combination of tones*) (mus) acorde *m*; (aer, anat, geom) cuerda

chore [tʃor] *s* tarea, quehacer *m*

choreography [ˌkɔrɪˈɑgrəfi] *s* coreografía

chorine [koˈrin] *s* (slang) corista, suripanta

chorus [ˈkorəs] *s* coro; (*refrain of a song*) estribillo

chorus girl *s* corista, conjuntista

chorus man *s* corista *m*, conjuntista *m*

chowder [ˈtʃaudər] *s* estofado de almejas o pescado

Chr. *abbr* **Christian**

Christ [kraɪst] *s* Cristo

christen [ˈkrɪsən] *tr* bautizar

Christendom [ˈkrɪsəndəm] *s* cristiandad

christening [ˈkrɪsənɪŋ] *s* bautismo, bautizo

Christian [ˈkrɪstʃən] *adj & s* cristiano

Christianity [ˌkrɪstʃɪˈænɪti] *s* cristianismo

Christianize [ˈkrɪstʃəˌnaɪz] *tr* cristianizar

Christian name *s* nombre *m* de pila

Christmas [ˈkrɪsməs] *adj* navideño ‖ *s* Navidad, Pascua de Navidad

Christmas card *s* aleluya navideña

Christmas carol *s* villancico

Christmas Eve *s* nochebuena

Christmas gift *s* aguinaldo, regalo de Navidad

Christmas tree *s* árbol *m* de Navidad

Christopher [ˈkrɪstəfər] *s* Cristóbal *m*

chrome [krom] *adj* cromado ‖ *s* cromo ‖ *tr* cromar

chromium [ˈkromɪ•əm] *s* cromo

chro·mo [ˈkromo] *s* (*pl* **-mos**) (*colored picture*) cromo; (*piece of junk*) (slang) trasto

chromosome [ˈkroməˌsom] *s* cromosoma *m*

chron. *abbr* **chronological, chronology**

chronic [ˈkrɑnɪk] *adj* crónico

chronicle [ˈkrɑnɪkəl] *s* crónica ‖ *tr* narrar en una crónica; narrar, contar

chronicler [ˈkrɑnɪklər] *s* cronista *mf*

chronolo·gy [krəˈnɑlədʒi] *s* (*pl* **-gies**) cronología

chronometer [krəˈnɑmɪtər] *s* cronómetro

chrysanthemum [krɪˈsænθɪməm] *s* crisantemo

chub·by [ˈtʃʌbi] *adj* (*comp* **-bier**; *super* **-biest**) rechoncho, regordete

chuck [tʃʌk] *s* (*throw*) echada, tirada; (*under the chin*) mamola; (*of a lathe*) mandril *m* ‖ *tr* arrojar; **to chuck under the chin** hacer la mamola a

chuckle [ˈtʃʌkəl] *s* risa ahogada ‖ *intr* reírse con risa ahogada

chug [tʃʌg] *s* ruido explosivo sordo; (*of a locomotive*) resoplido ‖ *v* (*pret & pp* **chugged**; *ger* **chugging**) *intr* hacer ruidos explosivos sordos, moverse con ruidos explosivos sordos

chum [tʃʌm] *s* (coll) compinche *mf;* compañero de cuarto ‖ *v* (*pret* & *pp* **chummed; ger chumming**) *intr* (coll) ser compinche, ser compinches; (coll) compartir un cuarto

chum·my [ˈtʃʌmi] *adj* (*comp* **-mier;** *super* **-miest**) muy amigable, íntimo

chump [tʃʌmp] *s* tarugo, zoquete *m;* (coll) estúpido, tonto

chunk [tʃʌnk] *s* trozo, pedazo grueso

church [tʃʌrt] *s* iglesia

churchgoer [ˈtʃʌrtʃˌgoˑər] *s* persona que frecuenta la iglesia

church·man [ˈtʃʌrtʃmən] *s* (*pl* **-men** [mən]) sacerdote *m,* eclesiástico; feligrés *m*

church member *s* feligrés *m*

Church of England *s* Iglesia Anglicana

church'ward'en *s* capiller *m*

church'yard' *s* patio de iglesia; cementerio

churl [tʃʌrl] *s* palurdo, patán *m*

churlish [ˈtʃʌrlɪʃ] *adj* palurdo, insolente

churn [tʃʌrn] *s* mantequera ‖ *tr* mazar (*leche*); hacer (*mantequilla*) en una mantequera; agitar, revolver ‖ *intr* revolverse

chute [ʃut] *s* cascada, salto de agua; rápidos; conducto inclinado; (*e.g., into a swimming pool*) tobogán *m;* (*e.g., for grain*) tolva; paracaídas *m*

** cibori·um** [sɪˈboriˑəm] *s* (*pl* **-a** [ə]) (*canopy*) ciborio, baldaquín *m;* (*cup*) copón *m*

Cicero [ˈsɪsəˌro] *s* Cicerón *m*

cider [ˈsaɪdər] *s* sidra

C.I.F., c.i.f. *abbr* **cost, insurance, and freight**

cigar [sɪˈgɑr] *s* cigarro, puro

cigar band *s* anillo de cigarro

cigar case *s* cigarrera, petaca

cigar cutter *s* cortacigarros *m*

cigaret o **cigarette** [ˌsɪgəˈrɛt] *s* cigarrillo, pitillo

cigarette case *s* pitillera

cigarette holder *s* boquilla

cigarette lighter *s* mechero, encendedor *m* de bolsillo

cigarette paper *s* papel *m* de fumar

cigar holder *s* boquilla

cigar store *s* estanco, tabaquería

cinch [sɪntʃ] *s* (*of saddle*) cincha; (*sure grip*) (coll) agarro; (*something easy*) (slang) breva ‖ *tr* cinchar; (coll) agarrar

cinder [ˈsɪndər] *s* ceniza; (*coal burning without flame*) pavesa

cinder bank *s* escorial *m*

Cinderella [ˌsɪndəˈrɛlə] *s* la Cenicienta

cinder track *s* pista de cenizas

cinema [ˈsɪnəmə] *s* cine *m*

cinematograph [ˌsɪnəˈmætəˌgræf] o [ˌsɪnəˈmætəˌgrɑf] *s* cinematógrafo ‖ *tr* & *intr* cinematografiar

cinnabar [ˈsɪnəˌbɑr] *s* cinabrio

cinnamon [ˈsɪnəmən] *s* canela

cipher [ˈsaɪfər] *s* cifra; cero; (*nonentity*) cero a la izquierda; (*key to a cipher*) clave *f* ‖ *tr* cifrar; calcular

circle [ˈsʌrkəl] *s* círculo ‖ *tr* circundar; dar la vuelta a; girar alrededor de

circuit [ˈsʌrkɪt] *s* circuito

circuit breaker *s* disyuntor *m*

circuitous [sərˈkjuˑɪtəs] *adj* indirecto, tortuoso

circular [ˈsʌrkjələr] *adj* tortuoso ‖ *s* circular *f,* carta circular

circularize [ˈsʌrkjələˌraɪz] *tr* anunciar por circular; enviar circulares a

circulate [ˈsʌrkjəˌlet] *tr* & *intr* circular

circumcise [ˈsʌrkəmˌsaɪz] *tr* circuncidar

circumference [sərˈkʌmfərəns] *s* circunferencia

circumflex [ˈsʌrkəmˌflɛks] *adj* circunflejo

circumlocution [ˌsʌrkəmloˈkjuʃən] *s* circunlocución, circunloquio

circumnavigate [ˌsʌrkəmˈnævɪˌget] *tr* circunnavegar

circumnavigation [ˌsʌrkəmˌnævɪˈgeʃən] *s* circunnavegación

circumscribe [ˌsʌrkəmˈskraɪb] *tr* circunscribir

circumspect [ˈsʌrkəmˌspɛkt] *adj* circunspecto

circumstance [ˈsʌrkəmˌstæns] *s* circunstancia; ceremonia, ostentación; **in easy circumstances** acomodado; **under no circumstances** de ninguna manera, ni a bala

circumstantial [ˌsʌrkəmˈstænʃəl] *adj* (*derived from circumstances*) circunstancial; (*detailed*) circunstanciado

circumstantial evidence *s* (law) indicios vehementes

circumstantiate [ˌsʌrkəmˈstænʃɪˌet] *tr* apoyar con pruebas y detalles; (*to describe in detail*) circunstanciar

circumvent [ˌsʌrkəmˈvɛnt] *tr* (*to catch by a trick*) entrampar, embaucar; (*to outwit*) burlar; (*to keep away from, get around*) evitar

circus [ˈsʌrkəs] *s* circo

cistern [ˈsɪstərn] *s* cisterna, aljibe *m*

citadel [ˈsɪtədəl] *s* ciudadela

citation [saɪˈteʃən] *s* (*of a text*) cita; (*before a court of law*) citación; (*for gallantry*) mención

cite [saɪt] *tr* (*to quote; to summon*) citar; (*for gallantry*) mencionar

citizen [ˈsɪtɪzən] *s* ciudadano; (*civilian*) paisano

citizen·ry [ˈsɪtɪzənri] *s* (*pl* **-ries**) conjunto de ciudadanos

citizens band *s* banda ciudadana

citizenship [ˈsɪtɪzən, ʃɪp] *s* ciudadanía

citron [ˈsɪtrən] *s* (*fruit*) cidra; (*tree*) cidro; (*candied rind*) cidrada

citronella [ˌsɪtrəˈnɛlə] *s* limoncillo (*Andropogon nardus*); aceite *m* de limoncillo

citrus fruit [ˈsɪtrəs] *s* agrios, frutas cítricas

cit·y [ˈsɪti] *s* (*pl* **-ies**) ciudad

city clerk *s* archivero

city council *s* ayuntamiento

city editor *s* redactor de periódico encargado de noticias locales

city fathers *spl* concejales *mpl*

city hall *s* casa consistorial

city plan *s* plano de la ciudad

city planner *s* urbanista *mf*

city planning *s* urbanismo

city room *s* redacción

cit′y-state′ s ciudad-estado f

civic [ˈsɪvɪk] adj cívico ‖ **civics** s estudio de los deberes y derechos del ciudadano

civic-mindedness [ˈmaɪndɪdnɪs] s civismo

civies [ˈsɪviz] spl (coll) traje m de paisano; **in civies** (coll) de paisano

civil [ˈsɪvɪl] adj civil

civilian [sɪˈvɪljən] adj civil ‖ s civil mf, paisano

civilian clothes spl traje m de paisano

civili‧ty [sɪˈvɪlɪti] s (pl **-ties**) civilidad

civilization [ˌsɪvɪlɪˈzeʃən] s civilización

civilize [ˈsɪvɪˌlaɪz] tr civilizar

civil servant s funcionario del estado

claim [klem] s demanda, pretensión, reclamación ‖ tr demandar, pretender, reclamar; afirmar, declarar; **to claim to** + inf pretender + inf

claim check s comprobante m

clairvoyance [klɛrˈvɔɪəns] s clarividencia

clairvoyant [klɛrˈvɔɪ‧ənt] adj & s clarividente mf

clam [klæm] s almeja; (tight-lipped person) (coll) chiticalla m ‖ intr — **to clam up** (coll) callarse la boca

clamber [ˈklæmər] intr — **to clamber up** subir gateando

clamor [ˈklæmər] s clamor m, clamoreo ‖ intr clamorear

clamorous [ˈklæmərəs] adj clamoroso

clamp [klæmp] s abrazadera, grapa; (vise-like device) mordaza ‖ tr agrapar, afianzar con abrazadera; sujetar en una mordaza ‖ intr — **to clamp down on** (coll) apretar los tornillos a

clan [klæn] s clan m

clandestine [klænˈdɛstɪn] adj clandestino

clang [klæŋ] s tantán m, sonido metálico resonante ‖ tr hacer sonar fuertemente ‖ intr sonar fuertemente

clank [klæŋk] s sonido metálico seco ‖ tr hacer sonar secamente ‖ intr sonar secamente

clannish [ˈklænɪʃ] adj exclusivista

clap [klæp] s golpe seco; (of the hands) palmada; (of thunder) estampido ‖ v (pret & pp **clapped**; ger **clapping**) tr batir (palmas); palmotear, aplaudir; **to clap shut** cerrar de golpe ‖ intr palmotear, dar palmadas

clap of thunder s estampido de trueno

clapper [ˈklæpər] s palmoteador m; (of a bell) badajo; (to cause grain to slide) tarabilla

clap′trap′ s faramalla; (of an actor) latiguillo

claque [klæk] s (paid clappers) claque f; (crush hat) clac m

claret [ˈklærɪt] s clarete m

clari‧fy [ˈklærɪˌfaɪ] v (pret & pp **-fied**) tr clarificar; encolar (el vino)

clarinet [ˈklærɪˈnet] s clarinete m

clarion [ˈklærɪ‧ən] adj claro, brillante ‖ s clarín m

clarity [ˈklærɪti] s claridad

clash [klæʃ] s choque m, encontrón m; estruendo, ruido ‖ intr chocar, entrechocarse

clasp [klæsp] s (fastener) abrazadera, cierre m; (for, e.g., a necktie) broche m; (buckle) hebilla; (embrace) abrazo; (grip) agarro ‖ tr abrochar; abrazar; agarrar, apretar (la mano); apretarse (la mano)

class. abbr **classical**

class [klæs] s clase f; ó (slang) elegancia, buen tono; (sports) división ‖ tr clasificar ‖ intr clasificarse

class consciousness s sentimiento de clase

classic [ˈklæsɪk] adj & s clásico; **the classics** las obras clásicas

classical [ˈklæsɪkəl] adj clásico

classical scholar s erudito en las lenguas clásicas

classicist [ˈklæsɪsɪst] s clasicista mf

classified [ˈklæsɪˌfaɪd] adj clasificado; clasificado como secreto

classified ads spl anuncios clasificados en secciones

classi‧fy [ˈklæsɪˌfaɪ] v (pret & pp **-fied**) tr clasificar

class′mate′ s compañero de clase

class′room′ s aula, sala de clase

class struggle s lucha de clases

class‧y [ˈklæsi] adj (comp **-ier**; super **-iest**) (slang) elegante

clatter [ˈklætər] s estruendo confuso; algazara, gresca; (of hoofs) trápala ‖ intr caer o moverse con estruendo confuso; hablar rápida y ruidosamente; **to clatter down the stairs** bajar la escalera ruidosamente

clause [klɔz] s (article in a legal document) cláusula; (gram) oración dependiente

clavichord [ˈklævɪˌkɔrd] s clavicordio

clavicle [ˈklævɪkəl] s clavícula

clavier [ˈklævɪ‧ər] o [kləˈvɪr] s teclado ‖ [kləˈvɪr] s instrumento musical con teclado

claw [klɔ] s garra, uña; (of lobster, crab, etc.) pinza; (of hammer, wrench, etc.) oreja; (coll) dedos, mano f ‖ tr (to clutch) agarrar; (to scratch) arañar; (to tear) desgarrar

clay [kle] adj arcilloso ‖ s arcilla

clay pigeon s pichón m de barro

clay pipe s pipa de tierra

clean [klin] adj limpio; distinto, neto, nítido; completo ‖ adv completamente; **to come clean** (slang) confesarlo todo ‖ tr limpiar; (to tidy up) asear; **to be cleaned out** (of money) (slang) quedar limpio; **to clean out** limpiar; (slang) dejar limpio ‖ intr limpiarse; asearse; **to clean up** limpiarse; (coll) llevárselo todo; (in gambling) (slang) hacer mesa limpia; **to clean up after someone** limpiar lo que alguno ha ensuciado

clean bill of health s patente limpia de sanidad

cleaner [ˈklinər] s limpiador m; (dry cleaner) tintorero; (preparation) quitamanchas m; **to send to the cleaners** (slang) dejar limpio.

cleaning [ˈklinɪŋ] s limpieza

cleaning fluid s quitamanchas m

cleaning woman s criada que hace la limpieza, alquilona

cleanliness ['klɛnlɪnɪs] *s* limpieza

clean·ly ['klɛnli] *adj* (*comp* **-lier;** *super* **-liest**) limpio (*que tiene el hábito del aseo*)

cleanse [klɛnz] *tr* limpiar, lavar, depurar

clean-shaven ['klin'ʃevən] *adj* lisamente afeitado

clean′up′ *s* limpieza general; **to make a cleanup** (slang) hacer su pacotilla

clear [klɪr] *adj* claro; (*cloudless*) despejado; (*of debts, etc.*) libre ‖ *adv* claro, claramente; **clear through** de parte a parte ‖ *tr* despejar (*un bosque*); clarificar (*lo que estaba turbio*); (*to make less dark*) aclarar; saltar por encima de; (*to prove the innocence of*) absolver; sacar (*una ganancia neta*); abonar, acreditar; liquidar (*una cuenta*); (*in the customhouse*) despachar; salvar (*un obstáculo*); levantar (*la mesa*); desmontar (*un terreno*); **to clear the way** abrir camino ‖ *intr* clarificarse; aclararse; **to clear away** irse, desaparecer; **to clear up** abonanzarse (*el tiempo*); despejarse (*el cielo, el tiempo*)

clearance ['klɪrəns] *s* aclaración; abono, acreditación; espacio libre; (*in a cylinder*) espacio muerto; (com) compensación

clearance sale *s* venta de liquidación

clearing ['klɪrɪŋ] *s* (*in a woods*) claro; (com) compensación

clearing house *s* cámara de compensación

clear-sighted ['klɪr'saɪtɪd] *adj* clarividente, perspicaz

clear′sto′ry *s* (*pl* **-ries**) var of **clerestory**

cleat [klit] *s* abrazadera, listón *m*

cleavage ['klivɪdʒ] *s* división, hendidura; (fig) desunión

cleave [kliv] *v* (*pret & pp* **cleft** [klɛft] o **cleaved**) *tr* rajar, partir; hender (*las aguas un buque, los aires una flecha*) ‖ *intr* adherirse, pegarse; apegarse, ser fiel

cleaver ['klivər] *s* cortante *m*, cuchilla de carnicero

clef [klɛf] *s* (mus) clave *f*

cleft palate [klɛft] *s* fisura del paladar

clematis ['klɛmətɪs] *s* clemátide *f*

clemen·cy ['klɛmənsi] *s* (*pl* **-cies**) clemencia; (*of the weather*) benignidad

clement ['klɛmənt] *adj* clemente; (*weather*) benigno

clench [klɛntʃ] *s* agarro ‖ *tr* agarrar; apretar, cerrar (*el puño, los dientes*)

cleresto·ry ['klɪr,stori] *s* (*pl* **-ries**) claraboya

cler·gy ['klɜrdʒi] *s* (*pl* **-gies**) clerecía, clero

clergy·man ['klɜrdʒimən] *s* (*pl* **-men** [mən]) clérigo, pastor *m*

cleric ['klɛrɪk] *s* clérigo

clerical ['klɛrɪkəl] *adj* (*of clergy*) clerical; (*of office work*) oficinesco ‖ *s* clérigo, eclesiástico; (*supporter of power of clergy*) clerical *m*; **clericals** (coll) hábitos clericales

clerical error *s* error *m* de pluma

clerical work *s* trabajo de oficina

clerk [klɜrk] *s* (*in a store*) dependiente *mf*; (*in an office*) oficinista *mf*; (*in a city hall*) archivero; (*in a church*) lego, seglar *m*; (*in law office, in court*) escribano

clever ['klɛvər] *adj* hábil, diestro, mañoso; inteligente

cleverness ['klɛvərnɪs] *s* habilidad, destreza, maña; inteligencia

clew [klu] *s* indicio, pista

cliché [kli'ʃe] *s* (*printing plate*) clisé *m*; (*trite expression*) cliché *m*

click [klɪk] *s* golpecito; (*of typewriter*) tecleo; (*of firearm*) piñoneo; (*of heels*) taconeo; (*of tongue*) claqueo, chasquido ‖ *tr* hacer sonar con un golpecito seco; chascar (*la lengua*); **to click the heels** taconear; cuadrarse (*un soldado*) ‖ *intr* sonar con un golpecito seco; piñonear (*el gatillo de un arma de fuego*); claquear (*la lengua*)

client ['klaɪ·ənt] *s* cliente *mf*; cliente de abogado

clientele [,klaɪ·ən'tɛl] *s* clientela

cliff [klɪf] *s* acantilado, escarpa, risco

climate ['klaɪmɪt] *s* clima *m*

climax ['klaɪmæks] *s* colmo; orgasmo; **to cap the climax** ser el colmo

climb [klaɪm] *s* subida, trepa ‖ *tr & intr* escalar, subir, trepar

climber ['klaɪmər] *s* trepador *m*; ambicioso de figurar; (bot) enredadera, trepadora

clinch [klɪntʃ] *s* agarro, abrazo; (*of a nail*) remache *m* ‖ *tr* afianzar, sujetar; agarrar, abrazar; apretar (*el puño*); remachar (*un clavo ya clavado*); resolver decisivamente

cling [klɪŋ] *v* (*pret & pp* **clung** [klʌŋ]) *intr* adherirse, pegarse; **to cling to** agarrarse a, asirse de

cling′stone′ peach *s* albérchigo, peladillo

clinic ['klɪnɪk] *s* clínica

clinical ['klɪnɪkəl] *adj* clínico

clinical chart *s* hoja clínica

clinician [klɪ'nɪʃən] *s* clínico

clink [klɪŋk] *s* tintín *m* ‖ *tr* hacer tintinear; chocar (*vasos, copas*) ‖ *intr* tintinear

clinker ['klɪŋkər] *s* escoria de hulla

clip [klɪp] *s* tijereteo, esquileo; grapa, pinza; (*to fasten papers*) sujetapapeles *m*, presilla de alambre; **at a good clip** a buen paso ‖ *v* (*pret & pp* **clipped;** *ger* **clipping**) *tr* tijeretear, esquilar; (*to fasten with a clip*) afianzar, sujetar; recortar (*p.ej., un cupón*) ‖ *intr* moverse con rapidez

clipper ['klɪpər] *s* tijera, cizalla; **clippers** maquinilla cortapelos; tijeras podadoras

clipping ['klɪpɪŋ] *s* tijereteo, esquileo; (*from a newspaper*) recorte *m*

clique [klik] *s* pandilla, corrillo ‖ *intr* — **to clique together** apandillarse

cliquish ['klikɪʃ] *adj* exclusivista

clk. *abbr* **clerk, clock**

cloak [klok] *s* capote *m*; (*disguise, excuse*) capa ‖ *tr* encapotar; disimular, encubrir

cloak-and-dagger ['klokən'dægər] *adj* de capa y espada (*dícese de duelos, espionaje, etc.*)

cloak-and-sword ['klokən'sord] *adj* de capa y espada (*dícese, p.ej., de las costumbres caballerescas*)

cloak hanger *s* cuelgacapas *m*

cloak′room′ *s* guardarropa *m*; (Brit) excusado

clock [klɑk] *s* reloj *m* (de pared o de mesa); (*in a stocking*) cuadrado ‖ *tr* registrar; (*sport*) cronometrar

clock'mak'er *s* relojero

clock tower *s* torre *f* reloj

clock'wise' *adj & adv* en el sentido de las agujas del reloj

clock'work' *s* mecanismo de relojería; **like clockwork** como un reloj

clod [klɑd] *s* terrón *m*

clod'hop'per *s* destripaterrones *m*, quebrantaterrones *m*; **clodhoppers** zapatos fuertes de trabajo

clog [klɑg] *s* estorbo, obstáculo; (*wooden shoe*) zueco; (*dance*) zapateado; (*hobble on animal*) traba ‖ *v* (*pret & pp* **clogged**; *ger* **clogging**) *tr* atascar ‖ *intr* atascarse; bailar el zapateado

clog dance *s* zapateado

cloister ['klɔɪstər] *s* claustro ‖ *tr* enclaustrar

cloistral ['klɔɪstrəl] *adj* claustral

close [klos] *adj* cercano, próximo; casi igual; (*translation*) fiel, exacto; (*fabric*) compacto; (*weather, atmosphere*) pesado, sofocante; (*stingy*) tacaño; (*battle, race, election*) reñido; (*friend*) íntimo; (*shut in, enclosed*) cerrado; (*narrow*) estrecho ‖ *adv* cerca; **close to** cerca de ‖ [kloz] *s* fin *m*, terminación; (*of business, of stock market*) cierre *m*; **at the close of day** a la caída de la tarde; **to bring to a close** poner término a; **to come to a close** tocar a su fin ‖ *tr* cerrar; (*to cover*) tapar; (*to finish*) concluir; saldar (*una cuenta*); cerrar (*un trato*); **to close in** cerrar, encerrar; **to close ranks** cerrar las filas ‖ *intr* cerrar, cerrarse; **to close in on** cerrar con (*el enemigo*)

close call [klos] *s* (coll) escape *m* por un pelo

closed car [klozd] *s* coche cerrado, conducción interior

closed chapter *s* asunto concluido

closed season *s* veda

closed shop *s* taller agremiado

closefisted ['klos'fɪstɪd] *adj* cicatero, tacaño, manicorto

close-fitting ['klos'fɪtɪŋ] *adj* ajustado, ceñido al cuerpo

close-lipped ['klos'lɪpt] *adj* callado, reservado

closely ['klosli] *adv* de cerca; estrechamente; fielmente; atentamente

close quarters [klos] *spl* lugar muy estrecho, lugares estrechos

close shave [klos] *s* afeitado a ras; (coll) escape *m* por un pelo

closet ['klɑzɪt] *s* (*wall*) alacena, closet *m*; (*wardrobe*) armario; (*small private room*) aposento, gabinete *m*; (*for keeping clothing*) guardarropa *m*; (*toilet*) retrete *m* ‖ *tr* — **to be closeted with** encerrarse con

close-up ['klos,ʌp] *s* (*moving picture*) vista de cerca; fotografía de cerca

closing ['klozɪŋ] *s* cerradura, cierre *m*

closing prices *spl* precios de cierre

closing time *s* hora de cierre

clot [klɑt] *s* grumo, coágulo ‖ *v* (*pret & pp* **clotted**; *ger* **clotting**) *intr* engrumecerse, coagularse

cloth [klɔθ] o [klɑθ] *s* paño, tela; ropa clerical; (*canvas, sails*) lona, trapo, vela; (*for binding books*) tela; **the cloth** la clerecía

clothe [kloð] *v* (*pret & pp* **clothed** o **clad** [klæd]) *tr* trajear, vestir; cubrir; (*e.g., with authority*) investir

clothes [kloz] o [kloðz] *spl* ropa, vestidos; ropa de cama

clothes'bas'ket *s* cesto de la ropa, cesto de la colada

clothes'brush' *s* cepillo de ropa

clothes closet *s* ropero

clothes dryer *s* secadora de ropa, secarropa

clothes hanger *s* colgador *m*, perchero

clothes'horse' *s* enjugador *m*, secarropa de travesaños

clothes'line' *s* cordel *m* para tender la ropa, tendedera

clothes'pin' *s* pinza, alfiler *m* de madera

clothes tree *s* percha

clothes wringer *s* exprimidor *m* de ropa

clothier ['kloðjər] *s* (*person who sells ready-made clothes*) ropero; (*dealer in cloth*) pañero

clothing ['kloðɪŋ] *s* ropa, vestidos, ropaje *m*

cloud [klaud] *s* nube *f* ‖ *tr* anublar ‖ *intr* — **to cloud over** anublarse

cloud bank *s* mar *m* de nubes

cloud'burst' *s* aguacero, chaparrón *m*

cloud-capped ['klaud,kæpt] *adj* coronado de nubes

cloudless ['klaudlɪs] *adj* despejado, sin nubes

cloud of dust *s* polvareda, nube *f* de polvo

cloud·y ['klaudi] *adj* (*comp* **-ier**; *super* **-iest**) nuboso, nublado; (*muddy, turbid*) turbio; confuso, obscuro; melancólico, sombrío

clove [klov] *s* (*flower*) clavo de especia; (*spice*) clavo

clover ['klovər] *s* trébol *m*; **to be in clover** vivir en el lujo

clo'ver·leaf' *s* (*pl* **-leaves** [,livz]) *s* cruce *m* en trébol

clove tree *s* clavero

clown [klaun] *s* bufón *m*, payaso; (*rustic*) patán *m* ‖ *intr* hacer el payaso

clownish ['klaunɪʃ] *adj* bufonesco; rústico

cloy [klɔɪ] *tr* hastiar, empalagar

club [klʌb] *s* porra, clava; (*playing card*) basto, trébol *m*; club *m*, casino ‖ *v* (*pret & pp* **clubbed**; *ger* **clubbing**) *tr* aporrear ‖ *intr* — **to club together** unirse; formar club

club car *s* coche *m* club, coche bar

club'house' *s* casino, club *m*

club·man ['klʌbmən] *s* (*pl* **-men** [mən]) clubista *m*

club·woman ['klʌb,wumən] *s* (*pl* **-women** [,wɪmɪn]) clubista *f*

cluck [klʌk] *s* cloqueo, clo clo ‖ *intr* cloquear, hacer clo clo

clue [klu] *s* indicio, pista

clump [klʌmp] *s* (*of earth*) terrón *m*; (*of trees or shrubs*) grupo; pisada fuerte ‖ *intr* — **to clump along** andar pesadamente

clum·sy ['klʌmzi] *adj* (*comp* **-sier;** *super* **-siest**) (*worker*) chapucero, desmañado, torpe; (*work*) chapucero, tosco, grosero

cluster ['klʌstər] *s* grupo; (*of grapes or other things growing or joined together*) racimo ‖ *intr* arracimarse; **to cluster around** reunirse en torno a; **to cluster together** agruparse

clutch [klʌtʃ] *s* (*grasp, grip*) agarro, apretón *m* fuerte; (aut) embrague *m*; (aut) pedal *m* de embrague; **to fall into the clutches of** caer en las garras de; **to throw the clutch in** embragar; **to throw the clutch out** desembragar ‖ *tr* agarrar, empuñar

clutter ['klʌtər] *tr* — **to clutter up** cubrir o llenar desordenadamente

cm. *abbr* **centimeter**

cml. *abbr* **commercial**

Co. *abbr* **Company, County**

coach [kotʃ] *s* coche *m*, diligencia; (aut) coche cerrado; (rr) coche de viajeros, coche ordinario *m*; (sport) entrenador *m* ‖ *tr* aleccionar; (sport) entrenar ‖ *intr* entrenarse

coach house *s* cochera

coaching ['kotʃɪŋ] *s* lecciones *fpl* particulares; (sport) entrenamiento

coach·man ['kotʃmən] *s* (*pl* **-men** [mən]) *s* cochero

coagulate [ko'ægjə,let] *tr* coagular ‖ *intr* coagularse

coal [kol] *s* carbón *m*, hulla ‖ *tr* proveer de carbón ‖ *intr* proveerse de carbón

coal'bin' *s* carbonera

coal bunker *s* carbonera

coal car *s* vagón carbonero

coal'deal'er *s* carbonero

coaling ['kolɪŋ] *adj* carbonero ‖ *s* toma de carbón

coalition [,ko·ə'lɪʃən] *s* unión; (*alliance between states or factions*) coalición

coal mine *s* mina de carbón

coal oil *s* aceite *m* mineral

coal scuttle *s* cubo para carbón

coal tar *s* alquitrán *m* de hulla

coal'yard' *s* carbonería

coarse [kors] *adj* (*of inferior quality*) basto, burdo; (*composed of large particles*) grueso; (*crude in manners*) grosero, rudo, vulgar

coarseness ['korsnɪs] *s* bastedad

coast [kost] *s* costa; **the coast is clear** ya no hay peligro ‖ *tr* costear ‖ *intr* deslizarse cuesta abajo; **to coast along** avanzar sin esfuerzo

coastal ['kostəl] *adj* costero

coaster ['kostər] *s* salvamanteles *m*

coaster brake *s* freno de contrapedal

coast guard *s* guardacostas *mpl*; guardia *m* de los guardacostas

coast guard cutter *s* escampavía de los guardacostas

coasting trade *s* cabotaje *m*

coast'land' *s* litoral *m*

coast'line' *s* línea de la costa

coast'wise' *adj* costanero ‖ *adv* a lo largo de la costa

coat [kot] *s* (*jacket*) americana, saco; (*topcoat*) abrigo, sobretodo; (*of an animal*) lana, pelo; (*of paint*) capa, mano *f* ‖ *tr* cubrir, revestir; dar una capa de pintura a

coated ['kotɪd] *adj* revestido; (*tongue*) saburroso

coat hanger *s* colgador *m*

coating ['kotɪŋ] *s* revestimiento; (*of paint*) capa; (*of plaster*) enlucido

coat of arms *s* escudo de armas

coat'room' *s* guardarropa *m*

coat'tail' *s* faldón *m*

coax [koks] *tr* engatusar

cob [kɑb] *s* zuro; **to eat corn on the cob** comer maíz en la mazorca

cobalt ['kobɔlt] *s* cobalto

cobbler ['kɑblər] *s* remendón *m*, zapatero de viejo

cob'ble·stone' *s* guijarro

cob'web' *s* telaraña

cocaine [ko'ken] *s* cocaína; (slang) coca

cock [kɑk] *s* (*rooster*) gallo; (*faucet, valve*) espita, grifo; (*of firearm*) martillo; (*weathervane*) veleta; caudillo, jefe *m* ‖ *tr* amartillar (*un arma de fuego*); ladear (*la cabeza*); enderezar, levantar

cockade [[ka'ked] *s* cucarda, escarapela

cock-a-doodle-doo ['kakə,dudəl'du] *s* quiquiriquí *m*

cock-and-bull story ['kakənd'bul] *s* cuento absurdo, cuento increíble

cocked hat [kakt] *s* sombrero de candil, sombrero de tres picos; **to knock into a cocked hat** (slang) apabullar

cockeyed ['kak,aɪd] *adj* bisojo, bizco; (coll) encorvado, torcido; (slang) disparatado, extravagante

cock'fight' *s* pelea de gallos

cockney ['kakni] *s* londinense *mf* de la clase pobre que habla un dialecto característico; dialecto de la clase pobre de Londres

cock of the walk *s* quiquiriquí *m*, gallito del lugar

cock'pit' *s* gallera; (aer) carlinga

cock'roach' *s* cucaracha

cockscomb ['kaks,kom] *s* cresta de gallo; gorro de bufón; (bot) cresta de gallo, moco de pavo

cock'sure' *adj* muy seguro de sí mismo

cock'tail' *s* coctel *m*; (*of fruit, oysters, etc.*) aperitivo

cocktail party *s* coctel *m*

cocktail shaker ['ʃekər] *s* coctelera

cock·y ['kaki] *adj* (*comp* **-ier;** *super* **-iest**) (coll) arrogante, hinchado; **to be cocky** (coll) tener mucho gallo

cocoa ['koko] *s* cacao; (*drink*) chocolate *m*

cocoanut o **coconut** ['kokə,nʌt] *s* coco

cocoanut palm o **tree** *s* cocotero

cocoon [kə'kun] *s* capullo

C.O.D., c.o.d. *abbr* **collect on delivery;** (Brit) **cash on delivery**

cod [kad] *s* abadejo, bacalao

coddle ['kadəl] *tr* consentir, mimar

code [kod] *s* (*of laws; of manners; of signals*) código; (*of telegraphy*) alfabeto; (*secret system of writing*) cifra, clave *f*; (com) cifrario; **in code** en cifra ‖ *tr* (*to put in code*) cifrar

code word *s* clave telegráfica

codex [ˈkɔdɛks] *s* (*pl* **codices** [ˈkodɪ,siz] o [ˈkadɪ,siz]) *s* códice *m*

cod'fish' *s* abadejo, bacalao

codger [ˈkadʒər] *s* — **old codger** (coll) anciano, tío

codicil [ˈkadɪsɪl] *s* codicilo; apéndice *m*

codi•fy [ˈkadɪ,faɪ] o [ˈkodɪ,faɪ] *v* (*pret & pp* **-fied**) *tr* codificar

cod'-liv'er oil *s* aceite *m* de hígado de bacalao

coed o **co-ed** [ˈko,ɛd] *s* alumna de una escuela coeducativa

coeducation [,ko,ɛdʒəˈkeʃən] *s* coeducación

coefficient [,ko•ɪˈfɪʃənt] *adj & s* coeficiente *m*

coerce [koˈʌrs] *tr* forzar, coactar

coercion [koˈʌrʃən] *s* compulsión, coacción

coeval [koˈivəl] *adj & s* coetáneo

coexist [,ko•ɪgˈzɪst] *intr* coexistir

coexistence [,ko•ɪgˈzɪstəns] *s* coexistencia

coffee [ˈkɔfɪ] o [ˈkafɪ] *s* café *m*; (*plant*) cafeto; **black coffee** café solo; **to drink coffee** cafetear

coffee bean *s* grano de café

cof'fee•cake' *s* rosquilla (que se come con el café)

coffee dealer *s* cafetalero

coffee grinder *s* molinillo de café

coffee grounds *spl* poso del café

coffee mill *s* molinillo de café

coffee plantation *s* cafetal *m*

coffee planter *s* cafetalero

coffee pot *s* cafetera

coffee tree *s* cafeto

coffer [ˈkɔfər] o [ˈkafər] *s* arca, cofre *m*; **coffers** tesoro, fondos

cof'fer•dam' *s* ataguía, encajonado

coffin [ˈkɔfɪn] o [ˈkafɪn] *s* ataúd *m*

C. of S. *abbr* **Chief of Staff**

cog [kag] *s* diente *m* (*de rueda dentada*); rueda dentada; **to slip a cog** equivocarse

cogency [ˈkodʒənsi] *s* fuerza (*de un argumento*)

cogent [ˈkodʒənt] *adj* fuerte, convincente

cogitate [ˈkadʒɪ,tet] *tr & intr* cogitar, meditar

cognac [ˈkanjæk] *s* coñac *m*

cognizance [ˈkagnɪzəns] o [ˈkanɪzəns] *s* conocimiento; **to take cognizance of** enterarse de

cognizant [ˈkagnɪzənt] o [ˈkanɪzənt] *adj* sabedor, enterado

cog'wheel' *s* rueda dentada

cohabit [koˈhæbɪt] *intr* cohabitar

coheir [koˈɛr] *s* coheredero

cohere [koˈhɪr] *intr* adherirse, pegarse; conformarse, corresponder

coherent [koˈhɪrənt] *adj* coherente

cohesion [koˈhiʒən] *s* cohesión

coiffeur [kwaˈfʌr] *s* peluquero

coiffure [kwaˈfjur] *s* peinado, tocado

coil [kɔɪl] *s* (*something wound in a spiral*) rollo; (*single turn of spiral*) vuelta; (*of a still*) serpentín *m*; (*of hair*) rizo; (*of a spring*) espiral *f*; (elec) carrete *m* ‖ *tr*

arrollar, enrollar; (naut) adujar ‖ *intr* arrollarse, enrollarse; (*like a snake*) serpentear

coil spring *s* resorte *m* espiral

coin [kɔɪn] *s* moneda; (*wedge*) cuña; **to pay back in one's own coin** pagar en la misma moneda; **to toss a coin** echar a cara o cruz ‖ *tr* acuñar; forjar, inventar (*palabras o frases*); **to coin money** (coll) ganar mucho dinero

coincide [,ko•ɪnˈsaɪd] *intr* coincidir

coincidence [koˈɪnsɪdəns] *s* coincidencia

coition [koˈɪʃən] o **coitus** [ˈko•ɪtəs] *s* coito

coke [kok] *s* coque *m*, cok *m*

col. *abbr* **colored, colony, column**

colander [ˈkʌləndər] o [ˈkaləndər] *s* colador *m*, escurridor *m*

cold [kold] *adj* frío; **to be cold** (*said of a person*) tener frío; (*said of the weather*) hacer frío ‖ *s* frío; (*indisposition*) resfriado; **to catch cold** resfriarse, coger un resfriado

cold blood *s* — **in cold blood** a sangre fría

cold chisel *s* cortafrío

cold comfort *s* poca consolación

cold cream *s* colcrén *m*

cold cuts *spl* fiambres *mpl*

cold feet *spl* (coll) desánimo, miedo

cold'heart'ed *adj* duro, insensible

cold meat *s* carne *f* fiambre

coldness [ˈkoldnɪs] *s* frialdad

cold shoulder *s* — **to turn a cold shoulder on** (coll) tratar con suma frialdad

cold snap *s* corto rato de frío agudo

cold storage *s* conservación en cámara frigorífica

cold war *s* guerra fría

coleslaw [ˈkol,slɔ] *s* ensalada de col

colic [ˈkalɪk] *adj & s* cólico

coliseum [,kalɪˈsi•əm] *s* coliseo

colitis [kəˈlaɪtɪs] *s* colitis *f*

coll. *abbr* **colleague, collection, college, colloquial**

collaborate [kəˈlæbə,ret] *intr* colaborar

collaborationist [kə,læbəˈreʃənɪst] *s* colaboracionista *mf*

collaborator [kəˈlæbə,retər] *s* colaborador *m*

collapse [kəˈlæps] *s* desplome *m*; (*in business*) fracaso; (pathol) colapso ‖ *intr* desplomarse; fracasar; postrarse, sufrir colapso

collapsible [kəˈlæpsɪbəl] *adj* abatible, plegable, desmontable

collar [ˈkalər] *s* cuello; (*of dog, horse*) collar *m*; (mach) collar

col'lar•band' *s* tirilla de camisa

col'lar•bone' *s* clavícula

collate [kəˈlet] o [ˈkalet] *tr* colacionar, cotejar

collateral [kəˈlætərəl] *adj* colateral ‖ *s* (*relative*) colateral *mf*; (com) colateral *m*

collation [kəˈleʃən] *s* (*act of comparing; light meal*) colación

colleague [ˈkalig] *s* colega *mf*; homólogo

collect [ˈkalɛkt] *s* (eccl) colecta ‖ [kəˈlɛkt] *tr* acumular, reunir; colectar, recaudar (*impuestos*); coleccionar (*sellos de correo, antiguallas*); recolectar (*cosechas*); cobrar (*pasajes*); recoger (*billetes; el correo*); **to**

collect oneself reponerse ǁ *intr* acumularse; **collect on delivery** contra reembolso, cobro contra entrega

collect call *s* llamada por cobrar

collected [kə'lɛktɪd] *adj* sosegado, dueño de sí mismo

collection [kə'lɛkʃən] *s* colección; (*of taxes*) recaudación; (*of mail*) recogida

collection agency *s* agencia de cobros de cuentas

collective [kə'lɛktɪv] *adj* colectivo

collector [kə'lɛktər] *s* (*of stamps, antiques*) coleccionista *mf; (of taxes)* recaudador *m; (of tickets)* cobrador *m*

college ['kalɪdʒ] *s* colegio universitario; (*of cardinals, electors, etc.*) colegio

collide [kə'laɪd] *intr* chocar; **to collide with** chocar con

collie ['kali] *s* perro pastoril escocés

collier ['kaljər] *s* barco carbonero; minero de carbón

collier•y ['kaljəri] *s* (*pl* -ies) mina de carbón

collision [kə'lɪʒən] *s* colisión

colloid ['kalɔɪd] *adj & s* coloide *m*

colloquial [kə'lokwɪ•əl] *adj* coloquial, familiar

colloquialism [kə'lokwɪ•ə‚lɪzəm] *s* coloquialismo

collo•quy ['kaləkwi] *s* (*pl* -quies) coloquio

collusion [kə'luʒən] *s* colusión, confabulación; **to be in collusion with** estar en inteligencia con

cologne [kə'lon] *s* agua de colonia, colonia ǁ **Cologne** *s* Colonia

colon ['kolən] *s* (anat) colon *m;* (gram) dos puntos

colonel ['kʌrnəl] *s* coronel *m*

colonel•cy ['kʌrnəlsi] *s* (*pl* -cies) coronelía

colonial [kə'lonɪ•əl] *adj* colonial ǁ *s* colono

colonize ['kalə‚naɪz] *tr & intr* colonizar

colonnade [‚kalə'ned] *s* columnata

colo•ny ['kaləni] *s* (*pl* -nies) colonia

colophon ['kalə‚fan] *s* colofón *m*

color ['kʌlər] *s* color; **the colors** los colores, la bandera; **to call to the colors** llamar a filas; **to give or lend color to** dar visos de probabilidad a; **under color of** so color de, bajo pretexto de; **with flying colors** con banderas desplegadas ǁ *tr* colorar, colorear; (*to excuse, palliate*) colorear; (*to dye*) teñir ǁ *intr* sonrojarse, ponerse colorado, demudarse

col′or-blind′ *adj* ciego para los colores

colored ['kʌlərd] *adj* de color; (*specious*) colorado

colorful ['kʌlərfəl] *adj* colorido; pintoresco

coloring ['kʌlərɪŋ] *adj & s* colorante *m*

colorless ['kʌlərlɪs] *adj* incoloro; (fig) insulso

color photography *s* fotografía en colores

color salute *s* (mil) saludo con la bandera

color sergeant *s* sargento abanderado

color screen *s* (phot) pantalla de color

color television *s* televisión en colores

colossal [kə'lasəl] *adj* colosal

colossus [kə'lasəs] *s* coloso

colt [kolt] *s* potro

Columbus [kə'lʌmbəs] *s* Colón *m*

Columbus Day *s* día *m* de la raza, fiesta de la hispanidad

column ['kaləm] *s* columna

columnist ['kaləmɪst] *s* columnista *mf*

com. *abbr* **comedy, commerce, common**

Com. *abbr* **Commander, Commissioner, Committee**

coma ['komə] *s* (pathol) coma *m*

comb [kom] *s* peine *m; (currycomb)* almohaza; (*of rooster*) cresta; cresta de ola ǁ *tr* peinar; explorar con minuciosidad

com·bat ['kambæt] *s* combate *m* ǁ ['kambæt] o [kəm'bæt] *v* (*pret & pp* **-bated** o **-batted**; *ger* **-bating** o **-batting**) *tr & intr* combatir

combatant ['kambətənt] *adj & s* combatiente *m*

combat duty *s* servicio de frente

combination [‚kambɪ'neʃən] *s* combinación

combine ['kambaɪn] *s* monopolio; segadora trilladora; (coll) combinación ǁ [kəm'baɪn] *tr* combinar ǁ *intr* combinarse

combining form *s* (gram) elemento de compuestos

combustible [kəm'bʌstɪbəl] *adj* combustible; (fig) ardiente, impetuoso ǁ *s* combustible *m*

combustion [kəm'bʌstʃən] *s* combustión

combustion chamber *s* cámara de combustión

come [kʌm] *v* (*pret* **came** [kem]; *pp* **come**) *intr* venir; **to come about** suceder; **to come across** encontrarse con; **to come after** venir detrás de; venir después de; venir por, venir en busca de; **to come again** volver; **to come apart** desunirse, desprenderse; **to come around** restablecerse; volver en sí; rendirse; ponerse de acuerdo; cambiar de dirección; **to come at** alcanzar; **to come back** volver; rehabilitarse; **to come before** anteponerse; **to come between** interponerse; desunir, separar; **to come by** conseguir; **to come down** bajar; (*in social position, etc.*) descender; (*from one person to another*) ser transmitido; **to come downstairs** bajar (*de un piso a otro*); **to come down with** enfermarse de; **to come for** venir por, venir en busca de; **to come forth** salir; aparecer; **to come forward** avanzar; presentarse; **to come from** venir de; provenir de; **to come in** entrar; entrar en; empezar; ponerse en uso; **to come in for** conseguir, recibir; **to come into one's own** ser reconocido; **to come off** desprenderse; acontecer; **to come out** salir; salir a luz; ponerse de largo (*una joven*); divulgarse (*una noticia*); **to come out for** anunciar su apoyo de; **to come out with** descolgarse con; **to come over** dejarse persuadir; pasar, p.ej., **what's come over him?** ¿qué le ha pasado?; **to come through** salir bien, tener éxito; ganar; **to come to** volver en sí; **to come together** juntarse, reunirse; **to come true** hacerse realidad; **to come up** subir; presentarse; **to come upstairs** subir (*de un piso a otro*); **to come up to** acercarse a;

subir a; estar a la altura de; **to come up with** proponer

come'back' *s* rehabilitación; (slang) respuesta aguda; **to stage a comeback** rehabilitarse

comedian [kə'mɪdɪ•ən] *s* cómico, comediante *m*; autor *m* de comedias

comedienne [kə,mɪdɪ'ɛn] *s* cómica, comedianta

come'down' *s* humillación, revés *m*

come•dy ['kamədi] *s* (*pl* **-dies**) comedia cómica; (*comicalness*) comicidad

come•ly ['kʌmli] *adj* (*comp* **-lier**; *super* **-liest**) (*attractive*) donairoso, gracioso; (*decorous*) conveniente, decente

comet ['kamɪt] *s* cometa *m*

comfort ['kʌmfərt] *s* comodidad, confort *m*; (*encouragement, consolation*) confortación; (*person*) confortador *m*; (*bed cover*) colcha, cobertor *m* ‖ *tr* confortar

comfortable ['kʌmfərtəbəl] *adj* cómodo, confortable; (*fairly well off*) holgado; (*salary*) (coll) suficiente ‖ *s* colcha, cobertor *m*

comforter ['kʌmfərtər] *s* confortador *m*, consolador *m*; colcha, cobertor *m*; bufanda de lana

comforting ['kʌmfərtɪŋ] *adj* confortante

comfort station *s* quiosco de necesidad

comfrey ['kʌmfri] *s* consuelda

comic ['kamɪk] *adj* cómico ‖ *s* cómico; periódico cómico; **comics** tiras cómicas

comical ['kamɪkəl] *adj* cómico

comic book *s* tebeo

comic opera *s* ópera cómica

comic strip *s* tira cómica

coming ['kʌmɪŋ] *adj* que viene, venidero; prometedor ‖ *s* venida

coming out *s* (*of stocks, bonds, etc.*) emisión; (*of a young girl*) puesta de largo, entrada en sociedad

comma ['kamə] *s* coma

command [kə'mænd] *s* (*commanding*) dominio, mando; (*order, direction*) mandato, orden *f*; (*e.g., of a foreign language*) dominio; (mil) comando; **to be in command of** estar al mando de; **to take command** tomar el mando ‖ *tr* mandar, ordenar; dominar (*un idioma extranjero*); merecer (*p.ej., respeto*); (mil) comandar ‖ *intr* mandar

commandant [,kamən'dænt] o [,kamən'dant] *s* comandante *m*

commandeer [,kamən'dɪr] *tr* reclutar forzosamente; expropiar; (coll) apoderarse de

commander [kə'mændər] *s* comandante *m*; (*of a military order*) comendador *m*

commandment [,kə'mændmənt] *s* (Bib) mandamiento

commemorate [kə'mɛmə,ret] *tr* conmemorar

commence [kə'mɛns] *tr* & *intr* comenzar, empezar

commencement [kə'mɛnsmənt] *s* comienzo, principio; día *m* de graduación; ceremonia de graduación

commend [kə'mɛnd] *tr* (*to entrust*) encargar, encomendar; (*to recommend*) recomendar; (*to praise*) alabar, elogiar

commendable [kə'mɛndəbəl] *adj* recomendable

commendation [,kamən'deʃən] *s* encargo, encomienda; recomendación; alabanza, elogio

comment ['kamɛnt] *s* comentario, comento ‖ *intr* comentar; **to comment on** comentar

commentar•y ['kamən,tɛri] *s* (*pl* **-ies**) comentario

commentator ['kamən,tetər] *s* comentarista *mf*

commerce ['kamərs] *s* comercio

commercial [kə'mʌrʃəl] *adj* comercial ‖ *s* anuncio publicitario radiofónico o televisivo; (rad & telv) programa publicitario

commercial traveler *s* agente viajero

commiserate [kə'mɪzə,ret] *intr* — **to commiserate with** condolerse de

commiseration [kə,mɪzə'reʃən] *s* conmiseración

commissar [,kamɪ'sar] *s* comisario (*en Rusia*)

commissar•y ['kamɪ,sɛri] *s* (*pl* **-ies**) (*deputy*) comisario; (*store*) economato

commission [kə'mɪʃən] *s* comisión; (mil) nombramiento; **to put in commission** poner en uso; poner (*un buque*) en servicio activo; **to put out of commission** inutilizar, descomponer; retirar (*un buque*) del servicio activo ‖ *tr* comisionar; poner en uso; poner (*un buque*) en servicio activo; (mil) nombrar

commissioned officer *s* oficial *m*

commissioner [kə'mɪʃənər] *s* comisario; (*person authorized by a commission*) comisionado

com•mit [kə'mɪt] *v* (*pret* & *pp* **-mitted**; *ger* **-mitting**) *tr* cometer (*un crimen, una falta*; *un negocio a una persona*); (*to hand over*) confiar, entregar; dar, empeñar (*la palabra*); (*to bind, pledge*) comprometer; internar (*a un demente*); (*to memory*) encomendar; **to commit oneself** comprometerse, empeñarse; **to commit to writing** poner por escrito

commitment [kə'mɪtmənt] *s* (*act of committing*) comisión; (*to an asylum*) internación; (*written, order*) auto de prisión; compromiso, cometido, empeño

committee [kə'mɪti] *s* comité *m*, comisión

commode [kə'mod] *s* (*chest of drawers*) cómoda; (*washstand*) lavabo; (*chamber pot*) sillico

commodious [kə'modɪ•əs] *adj* espacioso, holgado

commodi•ty [kə'madɪti] *s* (*pl* **-ties**) artículo de consumo, mercancía

commodity exchange *s* lonja, bolsa mercantil

common ['kamən] *adj* común ‖ *s* campo común, ejido; **commons** estado llano; (*of a school*) refectorio; **the Commons** (Brit) los Comunes

common carrier *s* empresa de transportes públicos

commoner ['kamənər] *s* plebeyo; (Brit) miembro de la Cámara de los Comunes

common law *s* derecho consuetudinario

com'mon-law' marriage *s* matrimonio consensual

com'mon•place' *adj* común, trivial, ordinario ‖ *s* lugar *m* común, trivialidad

common sense *s* sentido común

com'mon-sense' *adj* cuerdo, razonable

common stock *s* acción ordinaria; acciones ordinarias

commonweal ['kamən,wil] *s* bien público

com'mon•wealth' *s* estado, nación; república; (*state of U.S.A.*) estado; (*self-governing associated country*) estado libre asociado; (*association of states*) mancomunidad

commotion [kə'moʃən] *s* conmoción

commune [kə'mjun] *intr* conversar; (eccl) comulgar

communicant [kə'mjunɪkənt] *s* comunicante *mf*; (eccl) comulgante *mf*

communicate [kə'mjunɪ,ket] *tr* comunicar ‖ *intr* comunicarse

communicating [kə'mjunɪ,ketɪŋ] *adj* comunicador

communication [kə,mjunə'keʃən] *s* comunicación

communications satellite *s* satélite *m* de comunicaciones

communicative [kə'mjunɪ,ketɪv] *adj* comunicativo

communion [kə'mjunjən] *s* comunión; **to take communion** comulgar

communion rail *s* comulgatorio

communiqué [kə,mjunɪ'ke] o [kə'mjunɪ,ke] *s* comunicado, parte *m*

communism ['kamjə,nɪzəm] *s* comunismo

communist ['kamjənɪst] *s* comunista *mf*

communi•ty [kə'mjunɪti] *s* (*pl* **-ties**) vecindario; (*group of people living together*) comunidad

communize ['kamjə,naɪz] *tr* comunizar

commutation ticket [,kamjə'teʃən] *s* billete *m* de abono

commutator ['kamjə,tetər] *s* (elec) colector *m*

commute [kə'mjut] *tr* conmutar ‖ *intr* viajar con billete de abono

commuter [kə'mjutər] *s* abonado al ferrocarril

comp. *abbr* **compare, comparative, composer, composition, compound**

compact [kəm'pækt] *adj* compacto; breve, preciso ‖ ['kampækt] *s* convenio, pacto; estuche *m* de afeites

compact disk *s* disco compacto

companion [kəm'pænjən] *s* compañero

companionable [kəm'pænjənəbəl] *adj* afable, sociable, simpático

companionship [kəm'pænjən,ʃɪp] *s* compañerismo

companionway [kəm'pænjən,we] *s* (naut) escalera de cámara

compa•ny ['kʌmpəni] *s* (*pl* **-nies**) compañía; visita, visitas, invitado, invitados; (naut) tripulación; **to be good company** ser compañero alegre; **to keep company** ir juntos (*un hombre y una mujer*); **to keep some-**

one company hacerle compañía a una persona; **to part company** separarse; enemistarse

company building *s* edificio social

company office *s* domicilio social

comparative [kəm'pærətɪv] *adj* & *s* comparativo

compare [kəm'pɛr] *s* — **beyond compare** sin comparación, sin par ‖ *tr* comparar

comparison [kəm'pærɪsən] *s* comparación

compartment [kəm'partmənt] *s* compartimiento; (rr) departamento

compass ['kʌmpəs] *s* brújula, compás *m*; ámbito, recinto; alcance *m*, extensión; **compass** o **compasses** (*for drawing circles*) compás *m*

compass card *s* (naut) rosa náutica, rosa de los vientos

compassion [kəm'pæʃən] *s* compasión

compassionate [kəm'pæʃənɪt] *adj* compasivo

com•pel [kəm'pɛl] *v* (*pret* & *pp* **-pelled;** *ger* **-pelling**) *tr* forzar, obligar, compeler; imponer (*respeto, silencio*)

compendious [kəm'pɛndɪ•əs] *adj* compendioso

compendi•um [kəm'pɛndɪ•əm] *s* (*pl* **-ums** o **-a** [ə]) compendio

compensate ['kampən,set] *tr* & *intr* compensar; **to compensate for** compensar

compensation [,kampən'seʃən] *s* compensación

compete [kəm'pit] *intr* competir

competence ['kampɪtəns] o **competency** ['kampɪtənsi] *s* (*aptitude; legal capacity*) competencia; (*sufficient means to live comfortably*) buen pasar *m*

competent ['kampɪtənt] *adj* competente

competition [,kampɪ'tɪʃən] *s* (*rivalry*) competencia; (*in a match, examination, etc.*) certamen *m*, concurso; (*in business*) concurrencia

competitive [kəm'pɛtɪtɪv] *adj* — **to be competitive** poder competir

competitive examination *s* oposición

competitiveness [kəm'pɛtɪtɪvnɪs] *s* capacidad competiva

competitive prices *spl* precios de competencia

competitor [kəm'pɛtɪtər] *s* competidor *m*

compilation [,kampɪ'leʃən] *s* compilación, recopilación

compile [kəm'paɪl] *tr* compilar, recopilar

complacence [kəm'plesəns] o **complacency** [kəm'plesənsi] *s* (*quiet satisfaction*) complacencia; satisfacción de sí mismo

complacent [kəm'plesənt] *adj* (*willing to please*) complaciente; satisfecho de sí mismo

complain [kəm'plen] *intr* quejarse

complainant [kəm'plenənt] *s* (law) demandante *mf*

complaint [kəm'plent] *s* queja; reclamo; (*grievance*) agravio; (*illness*) enfermedad, mal *m*; (law) demanda, querella

complaisance [kəm'plezəns] o ['kamplɪ,zæns] *s* amabilidad, cortesía

complaisant [kəm'plezənt] o ['kamplɪ,zænt] *adj* amable, cortés

complement ['kɑmplɪmənt] *s* complemento; (nav) dotación ‖ *tr* complementar

complete [kəm'plit] *adj* completo ‖ *tr* completar, terminar, realizar

completion [kəm'pliʃən] *s* terminación, realización

complex [kəm'plɛks] o ['kɑmplɛks] *adj* (*not simple*) complexo; (*composite*) complejo; (*intricate*) complicado ‖ ['kɑmplɛks] *s* complejo; (psychol) complejo; (coll) obsesión

complexion [kəm'plɛkʃən] *s* (*constitution*) complexión; (*texture of skin, esp. of face*) tez *f*; aspecto general, índole *f*

compliance [kəm'plaɪ•əns] *s* condescendencia; sumisión, rendimiento; **in compliance with** de acuerdo con, en conformidad con

complicate ['kɑmplɪ,ket] *tr* complicar

complicated ['kɑmplɪ,ketɪd] *adj* complicado

complication ['kɑmplɪ,keʃən] *s* complicación

complici•ty [kəm'plɪsɪti] *s* (*pl* **-ties**) complicidad, codelincuencia

compliment ['kɑmplɪmənt] *s* (*show of courtesy*) cumplimiento; (*praise*) alabanza, halago; perico (CAm); **compliments** saludos, recuerdos ‖ ['kɑmplɪ,mɛnt] *tr* cumplimentar; alabar, halagar

complimentary copy [,kɑmplɪ'mɛntəri] *s* ejemplar *m* de cortesía

complimentary ticket *s* billete *m* de regalo, pase *m* de cortesía

com•ply [kəm'plaɪ] *v* (*pret & pp* **-plied**) *intr* conformarse; **to comply with** conformarse con, obrar de acuerdo con

component [kəm'ponənt] *adj* componente ‖ *m* componente *m*

compose [kəm'poz] *tr* componer; **to be composed of** estar compuesto de

composed [kəm'pozd] *adj* sosegado, tranquilo

composer [kəm'pozer] *s* componedor *m*; (mus) compositor *m*; autor *m*

composing stick *s* componedor *m*

composite [kəm'pɑzɪt] *adj & s* compuesto

composition [,kɑmpə'zɪʃən] *s* composición

compositor [kəm'pɑzɪtər] *s* cajista *mf*, componedor *m*

composure [kəm'poʒər] *s* serenidad, sosiego

compote ['kɑmpot] *s* (*stewed fruit*) compota; (*dish*) compotera

compound ['kɑmpaund] *adj* compuesto ‖ *s* compuesto; (gram) vocablo compuesto ‖ [kɑm'paund] *tr* componer, combinar; (*interest*) capitalizar

comprehend [,kɑmprɪ'hɛnd] *tr* comprender

comprehensible [,kɑmprɪ'hɛnsɪbəl] *adj* comprensible

comprehension [,kɑmprɪ'hɛnʃən] *s* comprensión

comprehensive [,kɑmprɪ'hɛnsɪv] *adj* comprensivo, inclusivo, completo

compress ['kɑmprɛs] *s* (med) compresa, bilma ‖ [kəm'prɛs] *tr* comprimir

compression [kəm'prɛʃən] *s* compresión

comprise o **comprize** [kəm'praɪz] *tr* abarcar, comprender, incluir

compromise ['kɑmprə,maɪz] *s* (*adjustment*) componenda, transigencia, transacción; (*endangering*) comprometimiento ‖ *tr* (*by mutual concessions*) componer, transigir; (*to endanger*) comprometer, exponer ‖ *intr* transigir, avenirse

comptroller [kən'trolər] *s* contralor *m*, interventor *m*

compulsory [kəm'pʌlsəri] *adj* obligatorio

computable [kəm'pjutəbəl] *adj* calculable

computation [,kɑmpju'teʃən] *s* cálculo, cómputo

compute [kəm'pjut] *tr & intr* computar, calcular

computer [kəm'pjutər] *s* ordenador *m*, computador *m*; (*person*) computador *m*, calculador *m*

computer dating *s* citas computerizadas

computer science *s* informática

comrade ['kɑmræd] o ['kɑmrɪd] *s* camarada *m*; cumpa *m* (SAm)

con. *abbr* **conclusion, consolidated, contra**

con [kɑn] *s* (*opposite opinion*) contra *m*; (*slang*) engaño ‖ *v* (*pret & pp* **conned;** *ger* **conning**) *tr* leer con atención, aprender de memoria; (*slang*) engañar

concave ['kɑnkev] o [kɑn'kev] *adj* cóncavo

conceal [kən'sil] *tr* encubrir, ocultar

concealment [kən'silmənt] *s* encubrimiento, ocultación; (*place*) escondite *m*

concede [kən'sid] *tr* conceder

conceit [kən'sit] *s* (*vanity*) orgullo, engreimiento; (*witty expression*) concepto, dicho ingenioso

conceited [kən'sitɪd] *adj* orgulloso, engreído

conceivable [kən'sivəbəl] *adj* concebible

conceive [kən'siv] *tr & intr* concebir

concentrate ['kɑnsən,tret] *tr* concentrar ‖ *intr* concentrarse; **to concentrate on** o **upon** reconcentrarse en

concentric [kən'sɛntrɪk] *adj* concéntrico

concept ['kɑnsɛpt] *s* concepto

conception [kən'sɛpʃən] *s* concepción

concern [kən'sʌrn] *s* (*business establishment*) empresa, casa comercial, razón *f* social; (*worry*) inquietud, preocupación; (*relation, reference*) concernencia; (*matter*) asunto, negocio ‖ *tr* atañer, concernir; interesar; **as concerns** respecto de; **to whom it may concern** a quien pueda interesar, a quien corresponda

concerning [kən'sʌrnɪŋ] *prep* respecto de, tocante a

concert ['kɑnsərt] *s* concierto ‖ [kən'sʌrt] *tr & intr* concertar

con'cert•mas'ter *s* concertino

concer•to [kən'tʃɛrto] *s* (*pl* **-tos** o **-ti** [ti]) concierto

concession [kən'sɛʃən] *s* concesión

concessive [kən'sɛsɪv] *adj* concesivo

concierge [,kɑnsɪ'ʌrʒ] *s* conserje *m*

conciliate [kən'sɪlɪ,et] *tr* conciliar; conciliarse (*el respeto, la estima*)

conciliatory [kən'sɪlɪ•ə,tori] *adj* conciliador

concise [kən'saɪs] *adj* conciso

conclude [kən'klud] *tr & intr* concluir

concluding [kən'kludɪŋ] *adj* final

conclusion [kən'kluʒən] *s* conclusión; (*of a letter*) despedida

conclusive [kən'klusɪv] *adj* concluyente

concoct [kən'kakt] *tr* confeccionar; (*a story*) forjar, inventar

concomitant [kən'kamɪtənt] *adj & s* concomitante *m*

concord ['kaŋkɔrd] *s* concordia; (gram, mus) concordancia

concordance [kən'kɔrdəns] *s* concordancia

concourse ['kaŋkors] *s* (*of people*) concurso; (*of streams*) confluencia; bulevar *m*, gran vía; (*of railroad station*) gran salón *m*

concrete ['kankrit] o [kan'krit] *adj* concreto; de hormigón ‖ *s* hormigón *m*

concrete block *s* bloque *m* de hormigón

concrete mixer *s* hormigonera, mezcladora de hormigón

concubine ['kaŋkjə,baɪn] *s* concubina

con•cur [kən'kʌr] *v* (*pret & pp* -**curred**; *ger* -**curring**) *intr* concurrir

concurrence [kən'kʌrəns] *s* (*happening together*) concurrencia; (*agreement*) acuerdo

concussion [kən'kʌʃən] *s* concusión

condemn [kən'dɛm] *tr* condenar

condemnation [,kandɛm'neʃən] *s* condenación

condense [kən'dɛns] *tr* condensar ‖ *intr* condensarse

condescend [,kandɪ'sɛnd] *intr* dignarse

condescending [,kandɪ'sɛndɪŋ] *adj* condescendiente con inferiores

condescension [,kandɪ'sɛnʃən] *s* dignación, aire *m* protector

condiment ['kandɪmənt] *s* condimento

condition [kən'dɪʃən] *s* condición; **on condition that** a condición (de) que ‖ *tr* acondicionar

conditional [kən'dɪʃənəl] *adj* condicional

conditioned reflex [kən'dɪʃənd] *s* reflejo acondicionado

condole [kən'dol] *intr* condolerse

condolence [kən'doləns] *s* condolencia

condominium [,kandə'mɪni•əm] *s* condominio

condone [kən'don] *tr* condonar; (*legally*) despenalizar

condor ['kandər] *s* cóndor *m*

conduce [kən'djus] *intr* conducir

conducive [kən'djusɪv] *adj* conducente, contribuyente

conduct ['kandʌkt] *s* conducta ‖ [kən'dʌkt] *tr* conducir; **to conduct oneself** conducirse, comportarse

conductor [kən'dʌktər] *s* conductor *m*, guía *mf*; (elec & phys) conductor *m*, conductora *f*; (rr) revisor *m*; (*on trolley or bus*) cobrador *m*

conduit ['kandɪt] o ['kandu•ɪt] *s* canal *f* para alambres o cables

cone [kon] *s* cono; (*of pastry*) barquillo; (*of paper*) cucurucho

confectioner•y [kən'fɛkʃə,nɛri] *s* (*pl* -**ies**) (*shop*) confitería; (*sweetmeats*) dulces *mpl*, confites *mpl*, confituras

confedera•cy [kən'fɛdərəsi] *s* (*pl* -**cies**) confederación; (*for unlawful purpose*) conjuración

confederate [kən'fɛdərɪt] *s* confederado; cómplice *mf* ‖ [kən'fɛdə,ret] *tr* confederar ‖ *intr* confederarse

con•fer [kən'fʌr] *v* (*pret & pp* -**ferred**; *ger* -**ferring**) *tr* conferir ‖ *intr* conferenciar, consultar

conference ['kanfərəns] *s* conferencia, coloquio

confess [kən'fɛs] *tr* confesar ‖ *intr* confesar, confesarse

confession [kən'fɛʃən] *s* confesión

confessional [kən'fɛʃənəl] *s* confesonario

confession of faith *s* profesión de fe

confessor [kən'fɛsər] *s* (*person who confesses*) confesante *mf*; (*Christian, esp. in spite of persecution; priest*) confesor *m*

confide [kən'faɪd] *tr* confiar ‖ *intr* confiar, confiarse; **to confide in** confiarse en

confidence ['kanfɪdəns] *s* confianza; (*secret*) confidencia; **in strictest confidence** bajo la mayor reserva

confident ['kanfɪdənt] *adj* seguro ‖ *s* confidente *m*, confidenta

confidential [,kanfɪ'dɛnʃəl] *adj* confidencial

confine ['kanfaɪn] *s* confín *m;* **the confines** los confines ‖ [kən'faɪn] *tr* (*to keep within limits*) limitar, restringir; (*to keep shut in*) encerrar; **to be confined** estar de parto; **to be confined to bed** tener que guardar cama

confinement [kən'faɪnmənt] *s* limitación; encierro; parto, sobreparto

confirm [kən'fʌrm] *tr* confirmar

confirmed [kən'fʌrmd] *adj* confirmado; empedernido, inveterado

confiscate ['kanfɪs,ket] *tr* confiscar

conflagration [,kanflə'greʃən] *s* conflagración

conflict ['kanflɪkt] *s* conflicto; (*of interests, class hours, etc.*) incompatibilidad ‖ [kən'flɪkt] *intr* chocar, desavenirse

conflicting [kən'flɪktɪŋ] *adj* contradictorio; (*events, appointments, class hours, etc.*) incompatible, conflictivo

confluence ['kanflu•əns] *s* confluencia

conform [kən'fɔrm] *intr* conformar, conformarse

conformance [kən'fɔrməns] *s* conformidad

conformi•ty [kən'fɔrmɪti] *s* (*pl* -**ties**) conformidad

confound [kan'faund] *tr* confundir ‖ ['kan'faund] *tr* maldecir; **confound it!** ¡maldito sea!

confounded [kan'faundɪd] *adj* confundido; aborrecible; maldito

confrere ['kanfrɛr] *s* colega *m*

confront [kən'frʌnt] *tr* (*to face boldly*) confrontarse con, hacer frente a; (*to meet face to face*) encontrar cara a cara; (*to bring face to face; to compare*) confrontar

confrontation [,kanfrʌn'teʃən] *s* enfrentamiento

confuse [kən'fjuz] *tr* confundir

confusedness [kən'fjuzɪdnɪs] *s* desorientación

CO
CO

confusion [kən'fjuʒən] s confusión
confute [kən'fjut] tr confutar
Cong. abbr **Congregation, Congressional**
congeal [kən'dʒil] tr congelar ‖ intr congelarse
congenial [kən'dʒinjəl] adj simpático; agradable; compatible; (having the same nature) congenial
congenital [kən'dʒɛnɪtəl] adj congénito
conger eel ['kaŋgər] s congrio
congest [kən'dʒɛst] tr congestionar ‖ intr congestionarse
congestion [kən'dʒɛstʃən] s congestión
congratulate [kən'grætʃə‚let] tr congratular, felicitar
congratulation [kən‚grætʃə'leʃən] s congratulación, felicitación
congregate ['kaŋgrɪ‚get] intr congregarse
congregation [‚kaŋgrɪ'geʃən] s congregación; feligresía, fieles mf (de una iglesia)
congress ['kaŋgrɪs] s congreso
congress•man ['kaŋgrɪsmən] s (pl -men [mən]) congresista m
conical ['kanɪkəl] adj cónico
conj. abbr **conjugation, conjunction**
conjecture [kən'dʒɛktʃər] s conjetura ‖ tr & intr conjeturar
conjugal ['kandʒəgəl] adj conyugal
conjugate ['kandʒə‚get] tr conjugar
conjugation [‚kandʒə'geʃən] s conjugación
conjunction [kən'dʒʌŋkʃən] s conjunción
conjuration [‚kandʒə'reʃən] s (superstitious invocation) conjuro; (magic spell) hechizo
conjure [kən'dʒʊr] tr (to appeal to solemnly) conjurar ‖ ['kʌndʒər] o ['kandʒər] tr (to exorcise, drive away) conjurar; **to conjure away** conjurar; **to conjure up** evocar; crear, suscitar (dificultades)
con man [kan] s (coll) embaucador m, embaucadora
connect [kə'nɛkt] tr conectar; asociar, relacionar ‖ intr enlazarse; asociarse, relacionarse; empalmar, enlazar (dos trenes)
connecting flight s vuelo de enlace
connecting rod s biela
connection [kə'nɛkʃən] s conexión; (relative) pariente mf; (of trains) combinación, enlace m, empalme m; (in subway) correspondencia; **in connection with** con respecto a; juntamente con
connective tissue [kə'nɛktɪv] s (anat) tejido conjuntivo
conning tower ['kanɪŋ] s torreta de mando
conniption [kə'nɪpʃən] s pataleta, berrinche m
connive [kə'naɪv] intr confabularse, estar en connivencia
conquer ['kaŋkər] tr vencer; (by force of arms) conquistar ‖ intr triunfar
conqueror ['kaŋkərər] s conquistador m, vencedor m
conquest ['kaŋkwɛst] s conquista
conscience ['kanʃəns] s conciencia; **in all conscience** en conciencia
conscientious [‚kanʃɪ'ɛnʃəs] adj concienzudo
conscientious objector [ab'dʒɛktər] s objetante m de conciencia

conscious ['kanʃəs] adj (aware of one's own existence) consciente; (deliberate) intencional; (self-conscious) encogido, tímido; **to become conscious** volver en sí
consciousness ['kanʃəsnɪs] s conciencia, conocimiento
consciousness raising s concienciación
conscript ['kanskrɪpt] s conscripto, quinto ‖ [kən'skrɪpt] tr reclutar
conscription [kən'skrɪpʃən] s conscripción, quinta
consecrate ['kansɪ‚kret] tr consagrar
consecutive [kən'sɛkjətɪv] adj (successive) consecutivo; (continuous) consecuente
consensus [kən'sɛnsəs] s consenso; **the consensus of opinion** la opinión general
consent [kən'sɛnt] s consentimiento; **by common consent** de común acuerdo ‖ intr consentir; **to consent to** consentir en
consequence ['kansɪ‚kwɛns] s consecuencia; aires mpl de importancia
consequential [‚kansɪ'kwɛnʃəl] adj consiguiente; importante; altivo, pomposo
consequently ['kansɪ‚kwɛntli] adv por consiguiente
conservation [‚kansər'veʃən] s conservación
conservatism [kən'sʌrvə‚tɪzəm] s conservadurismo
conservative [kən'sʌrvətɪv] adj (preservative) conservativo; (disposed to maintain existing views and institutions) conservador; cauteloso, moderado ‖ s preservativo; conservador m
conservato•ry [kən'sʌrvə‚tori] s (pl -ries) (school of music) conservatorio; (greenhouse) invernadero
consider [kən'sɪdər] tr considerar
considerable [kən'sɪdərəbəl] adj considerable
considerate [kən'sɪdərɪt] adj considerado
consideration [kən‚sɪdə'reʃən] s consideración; **for a consideration** por un precio; **in consideration of** en consideración de; en cambio de; **on no consideration** bajo ningún concepto; **out of consideration for** por respeto a; **without due consideration** sin reflexión
considering [kən'sɪdərɪŋ] adv (coll) teniendo en cuenta las circunstancias ‖ prep en vista de, en razón de ‖ conj en vista de que
consign [kən'saɪn] tr consignar
consignee [‚kansaɪ'ni] s consignatario
consignment [kən'saɪnmənt] s consignación
consist [kən'sɪst] intr — **to consist in** consistir en; **to consist of** consistir en, constar de
consisten•cy [kən'sɪstənsi] s (pl -cies) (firmness, amount of firmness) consistencia; (logical connection) consecuencia
consistent [kən'sɪstənt] adj (holding firmly together) consistente; (agreeing with itself or oneself) consecuente; **consistent with** (in accord with) compatible con
consisto•ry [kən'sɪstəri] s (pl -ries) consistorio
consolation [‚kansə'leʃən] s consolación, consuelo

console ['kɑnsol] *s* consola; mesa de consola ‖ [kən'sol] *tr* consolar

consommé [,kɑnsə'me] *s* consumado, consommé *m*

consonant ['kɑnsənənt] *adj & s* consonante *f*

consort ['kɑnsɔrt] *s* consorte *mf;* embarcación que acompaña a otra ‖ [kən'sɔrt] *tr* asociar ‖ *intr* asociarse; armonizar, concordar

consorti·um [kən'sɔrʃɪ·əm] *s* (*pl* **-a** [ə]) consorcio

conspicuous [kən'spɪkju·əs] *adj* manifiesto, claro, evidente; llamativo, vistoso, sugestivo; conspicuo, notable

conspira·cy [kən'spɪrəsɪ] *s* (*pl* **-cies**) conspiración, conjuración

conspire [kən'spaɪr] *intr* conspirar, conjurar

constable ['kɑnstəbəl] o ['kʌnstəbəl] *s* policía *m*, guardia *m*, alguacil *m*

constancy ['kɑnstənsɪ] *s* constancia; fidelidad

constant ['kɑnstənt] *adj* constante; incesante; fiel ‖ *s* constante *f*

constellation [,kɑnstə'leʃən] *s* constelación

constipate ['kɑnstɪ,pet] *tr* estreñir

constipation [,kɑnstɪ'peʃən] *s* estreñimiento, estitiquez *f*

constituen·cy [kən'stɪtʃu·ənsɪ] *s* (*pl* **-cies**) votantes *mpl;* clientela; comitentes *mpl;* distrito electoral

constituent [kən'stɪtʃu·ənt] *adj* constitutivo, componente; (*having power to create or revise a constitution*) constituyente ‖ *s* constitutivo, componente *m;* (*person who appoints another to act for him*) comitente *m*

constitute ['kɑnstɪ,tjut] *tr* constituir

constitution [,kɑnstɪ'tjuʃən] *s* constitución

constrain [kən'stren] *tr* constreñir; detener, encerrar; restringir

construct [kən'strʌkt] *tr* construir

construction [kən'strʌkʃən] *s* construcción; interpretación

construe [kən'stru] *tr* interpretar; deducir, inferir; traducir; (*to combine syntactically*) construir; (*to explain the syntax of*) analizar

consul ['kɑnsəl] *s* cónsul *m*

consular ['kɑnsələr] *adj* consular

consulate ['kɑnsəlɪt] *s* consulado

consulship ['kɑnsəl,ʃɪp] *s* consulado

consult [kən'sʌlt] *tr & intr* consultar

consultant [kən'sʌltənt] *s* consultor *m*

consultation [,kɑnsəl'teʃən] *s* (*consulting*) consulta; (*meeting*) consulta, consultación

consume [kən'sum] o [kən'sjum] *tr* consumir; (*to absorb the interest of*) preocupar; ‖ *intr* consumirse

consumer [kən'sumər] *s* consumidor *m;* (*of gas, electricity, etc.*) abonado

consumer credit *s* crédito consuntivo

consumer goods *spl* bienes *mpl* de consumo

consumerism [kən'sumə,rɪzəm] *s* consumerismo

consummate [kən'sʌmɪt] *adj* consumado ‖ ['kɑnsə,met] *tr* consumar

consumption [kən'sʌmpʃən] *s* consunción, consumo; (*pathol*) consunción, tisis *f*

consumptive [kən'sʌmptɪv] *adj* consuntivo; (*path*) tísico ‖ *s* tísico

cont. *abbr* **contents, continental, continued**

contact ['kɑntækt] *s* contacto; (elec) contacto; (elec) toma de corriente ‖ *tr* (coll) ponerse en contacto con ‖ *intr* contactar

contact breaker *s* (elec) ruptor *m*

contact lens *s* lente *m* de contacto, lente invisible, lentilla

contagion [kən'tedʒən] *s* contagio

contagious [kən'tedʒəs] *adj* contagioso

contain !kən'ten] *tr* contener; **to contain oneself** contenerse, refrenarse

container [kən'tenər] *s* continente *m*, recipiente *m*, vaso, caja, envase *m*, contenedor *m*

containment [kən'tenmənt] *s* contención, refrenamiento

contaminate [kən'tæmɪ,net] *tr* contaminar

contamination [kən,tæmɪ'neʃən] *s* contaminación

contd. *abbr* **continued**

contemplate ['kɑntəm,plet] *tr & intr* contemplar; pensar, proyectar

contemplation [,kɑntəm'pleʃən] *s* contemplación; intención, propósito

contemporaneous [kən,tɛmpə'renɪ·əs] *adj* contemporáneo

contemporar·y [kən'tɛmpə,rɛrɪ] *adj* contemporáneo, coetáneo ‖ *s* (*pl* **-ies**) contemporáneo, coetáneo

contempt [kən'tɛmpt] *s* desprecio; (law) contumacia

contemptible [kən'tɛmptɪbəl] *adj* despreciable

contemptuous [kən'tɛmptʃu·əs] *adj* despreciativo, desdeñoso

contend [kən'tɛnd] *tr* sostener, mantener ‖ *intr* contender

contender [kən'tɛndər] *s* contendiente *mf,* concurrente *mf*

content [kən'tɛnt] *adj & s* contento ‖ ['kɑntɛnt] *s* contenido; **contents** contenido ‖ [kən'tɛnt] *tr* contentar

contented [kən'tɛntɪd] *adj* contento, satisfecho

contentedness [kən'tɛndɪdnɪs] *s* contentamiento, satisfacción

contention [kən'tɛnʃən] *s* (*strife; dispute*) contención; (*point argued for*) argumento

contentious [kən'tɛnʃəs] *adj* contencioso

contentment [kən'tɛntmənt] *s* contentamiento, contento

contest ['kɑntɛst] *s* (*struggle, fight*) contienda; (*competition*) competencia, concurso ‖ [kən'tɛst] *tr* disputar; tratar de conseguir ‖ *intr* contender

contestant [kən'tɛstənt] *s* contendiente *mf*

context ['kɑntɛkst] *s* contexto

contiguous [kən'tɪgju·əs] *adj* contiguo

continence ['kɑntɪnəns] *s* continencia

continent ['kɑntɪnənt] *adj & s* continente *m;* **the Continent** la Europa continental

continental [,kɑntɪ'nɛntəl] *adj* continental ‖ **Continental** *s* habitante *mf* del continente europeo

CO
CO

contingen•cy [kən'tɪndʒənsi] s (pl **-cies**) contingencia

contingent [kən'tɪndʒənt] adj & s contingente m

continual [kən'tɪnjʊ•əl] adj continuo

continue [kən'tɪnjʊ] tr & intr continuar; **to be continued** continuará

continui•ty [,kɑntɪ'nju•ɪti] o [,kɑntɪ'nu•ɪti] s (pl **-ties**) continuidad; (mov, rad, telv) guión m; (rad, telv) comentarios o anuncios entre las partes de un programa

continuous [kən'tɪnjʊ•əs] adj continuo

continuous showing s (mov) sesión continua

continuous waves spl (rad) ondas entretenidas

contortion [kən'tɔrʃən] s contorsión

contour ['kɑntʊr] s contorno

contr. abbr **contracted, contraction**

contraband ['kɑntrə,bænd] adj contrabandista ‖ s contrabando

contrabass ['kɑntrə,bes] s contrabajo

contraceptive [,kɑntrə'sɛptɪv] adj & s anticonceptivo, contraceptivo

contract ['kɑntrækt] s contrato; **on a contract (to kill)** a sueldo ‖ ['kɑntrækt] o [kən'trækt] tr contraer (p.ej., matrimonio ‖ intr (to shrink) contraerse; (to enter into an agreement) comprometerse; **to contract for** contratar

contraction [kən'trækʃən] s contracción

contractor [kən'træktər] s contratista mf

contradict [,kɑntrə'dɪkt] tr contradecir

contradiction [,kɑntrə'dɪkʃən] s contradicción

contradictory [,kɑntrə'dɪktəri] adj (involving contradiction) contradictorio; (inclined to contradict) contradictor

contrail ['kɑn,trel] s (aer) estela de vapor, rastro de condensación

contral•to [kən'trælto] s (pl **-tos**) (person) contralto mf; (voice) contralto m

contraption [kən'træpʃən] s (coll) artilugio, dispositivo

contra•ry ['kɑntreri] adv contrariamente ‖ adj contrario ‖ [kən'treri] adj obstinado, terco ‖ ['kɑntreri] s (pl **-ries**) contrario; **on the contrary** al contrario

contrast ['kɑntræst] s contraste m ‖ [kən'træst] tr comparar; poner en contraste ‖ intr contrastar

contravene [,kɑntrə'vin] tr contradecir; contravenir a (una ley)

contribute [kən'trɪbjut] tr contribuir ‖ intr contribuir; (to a newspaper, conference, etc.) colaborar

contribution [,kɑntrɪ'bjuʃən] s contribución; (to a newspaper, conference, etc.) colaboración

contributor [kən'trɪbjutər] s contribuidor m, contribuyente mf; colaborador m

contrite [kən'traɪt] adj contrito

contrition [kən'trɪʃən] s contrición

contrivance [kən'traɪvəns] s aparato, dispositivio; idea, plan m, designio

contrive [kən'traɪv] tr (to devise) idear, inventar; (to scheme up) maquinar, tramar;

(to bring about) efectuar; **to contrive to** + inf ingeniarse a + inf ‖ intr maquinar

con•trol [kən'trol] s gobierno, mando; chequeo; (of a scientific experiment) contrarregistro, control m; **controls** mandos; **to get under control** conseguir dominar (un incendio) ‖ v (pret & pp **-trolled**; ger **-trolling**) tr gobernar, mandar; comprobar, controlar; **to control oneself** dominarse

controlling interest s (el) mayor porcentaje de acciones

control panel s (aer) tablero de instrumentos

control stick s (aer) mango de escoba, palanca de mando

controversial [,kɑntrə'vʌrʃəl] adj controvertible, disputable; disputador

controver•sy ['kɑntrə,vʌrsi] s (pl **-sies**) controversia, polémica

controvert ['kɑntrə,vʌrt] o [,kɑntrə'vʌrt] tr (to argue against) contradecir; (to argue about) controvertir

contumacious [,kɑntju'meʃəs] adj contumaz

contuma•cy ['kɑntjuməsi] s (pl **-cies**) contumacia

contume•ly ['kɑntjumɪli] s (pl **-lies**) contumelia

contusion [kən'tjuʒən] s contusión; magullón m

conundrum [kə'nʌndrəm] s acertijo, adivinanza; problema complicado

convalesce [,kɑnvə'lɛs] intr convalecer

convalescence [,kɑnvə'lɛsəns] s convalecencia

convalescent [,kɑnvə'lɛsənt] adj & s convaleciente mf

convalescent home s clínica de reposo

convene [kən'vin] tr convocar ‖ intr convenir, reunirse

convenience [kən'vinjəns] s comodidad, conveniencia; **at your earliest convenience** a la primera oportunidad que Vd. tenga

convenient [kən'vinjənt] adj cómodo, conveniente; próximo

convent ['kɑnvɛnt] s convento; convento de religiosas

convention [kən'vɛnʃən] s (agreement) convención, conveniencia; (accepted usage) costumbre f, conveniencia social, convención; (meeting) congreso, convención

conventional [kən'vɛnʃənəl] adj convencional

conventionali•ty [kən,vɛnʃə'nælɪti] s (pl **-ties**) precedente m convencional

converge [kən'vʌrdʒ] intr convergir

conversant [kən'vʌrsənt] adj familiarizado, versado

conversation [,kɑnvər'seʃən] s conversación

conversational [,kɑnvər'seʃənəl] adj conversacional

converse ['kɑnvʌrs] adj & s contrario ‖ [kən'vʌrs] intr conversar

conversion [kən'vʌrʒən] s conversión; (unlawful appropriation) malversación

convert ['kɑnvʌrt] s convertido, converso ‖ [kən'vʌrt] tr convertir ‖ intr convertirse

convertible [kən'vʌrtɪbəl] adj convertible ‖ s (aut) convertible m, descapotable m

convex [ˈkɑnvɛks] o [kɑnˈvɛks] *adj* convexo

convey [kənˈve] *tr* llevar, transportar; comunicar, participar (*informes*); transferir, traspasar (*bienes de una persona a otra*)

conveyance [kənˈve•əns] *s* transporte *m;* comunicación, participación; vehículo; (*transfer of property*) traspaso; escritura de traspaso

convict [ˈkɑnvɪkt] *s* reo convicto, presidiario ‖ [kənˈvɪkt] *tr* probar la culpabilidad de; declarar convicto (*a un acusado*)

conviction [kənˈvɪkʃən] *s* convencimiento; condena, fallo de culpabilidad

convince [kənˈvɪns] *tr* convencer

convincing [kənˈvɪnsɪŋ] *adj* convincente

convivial [kənˈvɪvɪ•əl] *adj* jovial

convocation [ˌkɑnvəˈkeʃən] *s* asamblea

convoke [kənˈvok] *tr* convocar

convoy [ˈkɑnvɔɪ] *s* convoy *m,* conserva ‖ *tr* convoyar

convulse [kənˈvʌls] *tr* convulsionar; agitar; **to convulse with laughter** mover a risas convulsivas

coo [ku] *intr* arrullar

cook [kʊk] *s* cocinero ‖ *tr* cocer, cocinar, guisar; **to cook up** (coll) falsificar; (coll) maquinar, tramar ‖ *intr* cocer, cocinar

cook′book′ *s* libro de cocina

cookie [ˈkʊki] *s* var de **cooky**

cooking [ˈkʊkɪŋ] *s* cocina, arte *m* de cocinar

cook′stove′ *s* cocina económica

cook•y [ˈkʊki] *s* (*pl* -ies) pasta seca, pastelito dulce

cool [kul] *adj* fresco; frío, indiferente ‖ *s* fresco ‖ *tr* refrescar; moderar ‖ *intr* refrescarse; moderarse; **to cool off** refrescarse; serenarse

cooler [ˈkulər] *s* heladera, refrigerador *m;* refrigerante *m;* cárcel *f*

cool′-head′ed *adj* sereno, tranquilo, juicioso

coolie [ˈkuli] *s* culí *m*

coolish [ˈkulɪʃ] *adj* fresquito

coolness [ˈkulnɪs] *s* fresco, frescura; (fig) frialdad

coon [kun] *s* mapache *m,* oso lavandero

coop [kup] *s* gallinero; (*for fattening capons*) caponera; jaula, redil *m;* (*jail*) (slang) caponera; **to fly the coop** (slang) escabullirse ‖ *tr* encerrar en un gallinero; enjaular; **to coop up** emparedar

coöp. *abbr* **cooperative**

cooper [ˈkupər] *s* barrilero, tonelero

coöperate [koˈɑpə‚ret] *intr* cooperar

coöperation [ko‚ɑpəˈreʃən] *s* cooperación

coöperative [koˈɑpə‚retɪv] *adj* cooperativo

coöpt [koˈɑpt] *tr* cooptar

coördinate [koˈɔrdɪnɪt] *adj* coordenado; (gram) coordinante ‖ *s* (math) coordenada ‖ [koˈɔrdɪ‚net] *tr & intr* coordinar

cootie [ˈkuti] *s* (slang) piojo

cop [kɑp] *s* (slang) polizonte *m* ‖ *v* (*pret & pp* **copped;** *ger* **copping**) *tr* (slang) hurtar

copartner [koˈpɑrtnər] *s* consocio, copartícipe *mf*

cope [kop] *intr* — **to cope with** hacer frente a, enfrentarse con

cope′stone′ *s* piedra de albardilla

copier [ˈkɑpɪ•ər] *s* (*person who copies*) copiante *mf,* copista *mf,* imitador *m;* (*apparatus*) copiador *m,* copiadora

copilot [ˈko‚paɪlət] *s* copiloto

coping [ˈkopɪŋ] *s* albardilla

copious [ˈkopɪ•əs] *adj* copioso

copper [ˈkɑpər] *adj* cobreño; (*in color*) cobrizo ‖ *s* cobre *m;* (*coin*) calderilla, vellón *m;* (slang) polizonte *m*

cop′per•head′ *s* víbora de cabeza de cobre

cop′per•smith′ *s* cobrero

coppery [ˈkɑpəri] *adj* cobreño; (*in color*) cobrizo

coppice [ˈkɑpɪs] o **copse** [kɑps] *s* soto, monte bajo

copulate [ˈkɑpjə‚let] *intr* copularse

cop•y [ˈkɑpi] *s* (*pl* -ies) copia; (*of a book*) ejemplar *m;* (*of a magazine*) número; (*document to be reproduced in print*) original *m,* manuscrito ‖ *v* (*pret & pp* -ied) *tr* copiar

cop′y•book′ *s* cuaderno de escritura

copyist [ˈkɑpɪ•ɪst] *s* copiante *mf,* copista *mf;* imitador *m*

cop′y•right′ *s* (derechos de) propiedad literaria ‖ *tr* registrar en el registro de la propiedad literaria

copy writer *s* escritor publicitario

co•quet [koˈkɛt] *v* (*pret & pp* -quetted; *ger* -quetting) *intr* coquetear; burlarse

coquet•ry [ˈkokətri] o [koˈkɛtri] *s* (*pl* -ries) coquetería; burla

coquette [koˈkɛt] *s* coqueta

coquettish [koˈkɛtɪʃ] *adj* coqueta

cor. *abbr* **corner, coroner, correction, corresponding**

coral [ˈkɑrəl] o [ˈkɔrəl] *adj* coralino ‖ *s* coral *m*

coral reef *s* arrecife *m* de coral

cord [kɔrd] *s* cordón *m;* piola ‖ *tr* acordonar

cordial [ˈkɔrdʒəl] *adj* cordial ‖ *s* licor tónico; (*medicine*) cordial *m*

cordiali•ty [kɔrˈdʒælɪti] *s* (*pl* -ties) cordialidad

corduroy [ˈkɔrdə‚rɔɪ] *s* pana; **corduroys** pantalones *mpl* de pana

core [kor] *s* corazón *m;* (*of an electromagnet*) núcleo

corespondent [‚korɪsˈpɑndənt] *s* cómplice *mf* del demandado en juicio de divorcio

Corinth [ˈkɔrɪnθ] *s* Corinto *f*

cork [kɔrk] *s* corcho; corcho, tapón *m* de corcho; tapón (*de cualquier materia*) ‖ *tr* encorchar, tapar con corcho

corking [ˈkɔrkɪŋ] *adj* (slang) brutal, extraordinario

cork oak *s* alcornoque *m*

cork′screw′ *s* sacacorchos *m,* tirabuzón *m*

cormorant [ˈkɔrmərənt] *s* cormorán *m,* cuervo marino

corn [kɔrn] *s* (*in U.S.A.*) maíz *m;* (*in England*) trigo; (*in Scotland*) avena; grano (*de maíz, trigo*); (*on the foot*) callo; (coll) aguardiente *m;* (slang) trivialidad

corn bread *s* pan *m* de maíz

corn′cake′ *s* tortilla de maíz

corn′cob′ *s* mazorca de maíz, carozo

CO
CO

corncob pipe *s* pipa de fumar hecha de una mazorca de maíz
corn′crib′ *s* granero para maíz
corn cure *adj* callicida *m*
cornea [′kɔrnɪə] *s* córnea
corner [′kɔrnər] *s* ángulo; (*esp. where two streets meet*) esquina; (*inside angle formed by two or more surfaces; secluded place; region, quarter*) rincón *m*; (*of eye*) comisura, rabillo; (*of lips*) comisura, (*awkward position*) apuro, aprieto; monopolio; **around the corner** a la vuelta de la esquina; **to turn the corner** doblar la esquina; pasar el punto más peligroso ‖ *tr* arrinconar; monopolizar
corner cupboard *s* rinconera
corner room *s* habitación de esquina
cor′ner•stone′ *s* piedra angular; (*of a new building*) primera piedra
cornet [kɔr′nɛt] *s* corneta
corn exchange *s* bolsa de granos
corn′field′ *s* (*in U.S.A.*) maizal *m*; (*in England*) trigal *m*; (*in Scotland*) avenal *m*
corn flour *s* harina de maíz
corn′flow′er *s* cabezuela
corn′husk′ *s* perfolla
cornice [′kɔrnɪs] *s* cornisa
Cornish [′kɔrnɪʃ] *adj & s* córnico
corn liquor *s* chicha
corn meal *s* harina de maíz
corn on the cob *s* maíz *m* en la mazorca
corn plaster *s* emplasto para los callos
corn silk *s* cabellos, barbas del maíz
corn′stalk′ *s* tallo de maíz
corn′starch′ *s* almidón *m* de maíz
cornucopia [,kɔrnə′kopɪə] *s* cornucopia
Cornwall [′kɔrn,wɔl] *s* Cornualles
corn•y [′kɔrnɪ] *adj* (*comp* **-ier**; *super* **-iest**) de maíz; (coll) gastado, trivial, pesado
corollar•y [′karə,lɛrɪ] o [′kɔrə,lɛrɪ] *s* (*pl* **-ies**) corolario
coronation [,karə′neʃən] o [,kɔrə′neʃən] *s* coronación
coroner [′karənər] o [′kɔrənər] *s* juez *m* de guardia
coroner's inquest *s* pesquisa dirigida por el juez de guardia
coronet [′karə,nɛt] o [′kɔrə,nɛt] *s* (*worn by members of nobility*) corona; (*ornamental band of jewels worn on head*) diadema *f*
Corp. *abbr* **Corporation**
corporal [′kɔrpərəl] *adj* corporal ‖ *s* (mil) cabo
corporation [,kɔrpə′reʃən] *s* (*provincial, municipal, or service entity*) corporación; sociedad anónima por acciones
corps [kor] *s* (*pl* **corps** [korz]) cuerpo; (mil) cuerpo
corps de ballet [kor də bæ′lɛ] *s* cuerpo de baile
corpse [kɔrps] *s* cadáver *m*
corpulent [′kɔrpjələnt] *adj* corpulento
corpuscle [′kɔrpəsəl] *s* corpúsculo, partícula; (physiol) glóbulo
corr. *abbr* **correspondence, corresponding**
cor•ral [kə′ræl] *s* corral *m* ‖ *v* (*pret & pp* **-ralled**; *ger* **-ralling**) *tr* acorralar

correct [kə′rɛkt] *adj* correcto; (*proper*) cumplido ‖ *tr* corregir
correction [kə′rɛkʃən] *s* corrección
corrective [kə′rɛktɪv] *adj & s* correctivo
correctness [kə′rɛktnɪs] *s* corrección; cumplimiento, cumplido
correlate [′kɔrə,let] *tr* correlacionar ‖ *intr* correlacionarse
correlation [,kɔrə′leʃən] *s* correlación
correlative [kə′rɛlətɪv] *adj & s* correlativo
correspond [,karɪ′spand] o [,kɔrɪ′spand] *intr* corresponder; (*to communicate by writing*) corresponderse
correspondence [,karɪ′spandəns] o [,kɔrɪ′spandəns] *s* correspondencia
correspondence school *s* escuela por correspondencia
correspondent [,karɪ′spandənt] o [,kɔrɪ′spandənt] *adj* correspondiente ‖ *s* correspondiente *mf*; (*for a newspaper*) corresponsal *mf*
corresponding [,karɪ′spandɪŋ] o [,kɔrɪ′spandɪŋ] *adj* correspondiente
corridor [′karɪdər] o [′kɔrɪdər] *s* corredor *m*, pasillo
corroborate [kə′rabə,ret] *tr* corroborar
corrode [kə′rod] *tr* corroer ‖ *intr* corroerse
corrosion [kə′roʒən] *s* corrosión
corrosive [kə′rosɪv] *adj & s* corrosivo
corrugated [′karə,getɪd] o [′kɔrə,getɪd] *adj* acanalado, ondulado
corrupt [kə′rʌpt] *adj* corrompido ‖ *tr* corromper ‖ *intr* corromperse
corruption [kə′rʌpʃən] *s* corrupción
corsage [kɔr′saʒ] *s* (*bodice*) corpiño, jubón *m*; (*bouquet*) ramillete *m* que se lleva en el pecho o la cintura
corsair [′kɔr,sɛr] *s* corsario
corset [′kɔrsɪt] *s* corsé *m*
corset cover *s* cubrecorsé *m*
Corsica [′kɔrsɪkə] *s* Córcega
Corsican [′kɔrsɪkən] *adj & s* corso
cortege [kɔr′teʒ] *s* procesión; (*retinue*) cortejo, séquito
cor•tex [′kɔr,tɛks] *s* (*pl* **-tices** [tɪ,siz]) corteza; corteza cerebral
cortisone [′kɔrtɪ,son] *s* cortisona
corvette [kɔr′vɛt] *s* corbeta
cosmetic [kaz′mɛtɪk] *adj & s* cosmético
cosmic [′kazmɪk] *adj* cósmico
cosmonaut [′kazmə,nɔt] *s* cosmonauta *mf*
cosmopolitan [,kazmə′palɪtən] *adj & s* cosmopolita *mf*
cosmos [′kazməs] *s* cosmos *m*; (bot) cosmos
Cossack [′ka,sæk] *adj & s* cosaco
cost [kɔst] o [kast] *s* coste *m*, costo; **at cost** a coste y costas; **at all costs** a toda costa; **costs** (law) costas ‖ *v* (*pret & pp* **cost**) *intr* costar; **cost what it may** cueste lo que cueste
cost accounting *s* escandallo
Costa Rican [′kastə ′rikən] o [′kɔste ′rikən] *adj & s* costarricense *mf*, costarriqueño
cost′-ben′e•fit analysis *s* análisis costebeneficio
cost exemption *s* gratuidad

cost, insurance, and freight costo, seguro y flete

cost•ly [ˈkɔstli] o [ˈkɑstli] *adj* (*comp* **-lier;** *super* **-liest**) costoso, dispendioso; (*lavish*) pródigo; (*magnificent*) suntuoso

cost of living *s* costo de la vida, carestía de la vida

costume [ˈkɑstjum] *s* traje *m;* (*garb worn on stage, at balls, etc.*) disfraz *m*, traje de época

costume ball *s* baile *m* de trajes

costume jewelry *s* joyas de fantasía, bisutería

cot [kɑt] *s* catre *m*

coterie [ˈkotəri] *s* círculo, grupo; (*clique*) corrillo

cottage [ˈkɑtɪdʒ] *s* cabaña; casita de campo

cottage cheese *s* naterón *m*, requesón *m*

cotter pin [ˈkɑtər] *s* chaveta

cotton [ˈkɑtən] *s* algodón *m* ‖ *intr* — **to cotton up to** (coll) aficionarse a

cotton field *s* algodonal *m*

cotton gin *s* desmotadera de algodón

cotton picker [ˈpɪkər] *s* recogedor *m* de algodón; máquina para recolectar el algodón

cot′ton•seed′ *s* semilla de algodón

cottonseed oil *s* aceite *m* de algodón

cotton waste *s* hilacha de algodón, estopa de algodón

cot′ton•wood′ *s* chopo del Canadá, chopo de Virginia

cottony [ˈkɑtəni] *adj* algodonoso

couch [kautʃ] *s* canapé *m*, sofá *m* ‖ *tr* expresar

cougar [ˈkugər] *s* puma *m*

cough [kɔf] o [kɑf] *s* tos *f* ‖ *tr* — **to cough up** arrojar por la boca; (slang) sudar, entregar ‖ *intr* toser; (*artificially, to attract attention*) destososerse

cough drop *s* pastilla para la tos

cough syrup *s* jarabe *m* para la tos

could [kud] *v aux* pude, podía; podría

council [ˈkaunsəl] *s* (*deliberative or legislative assembly*) consejo; (*of a municipality*) concejo; (eccl) concilio

council•man [ˈkaunsəlmən] *s* (*pl* **-men** [mən]) concejal *m*

councilor [ˈkaunsələr] *s* consejero

coun•sel [ˈkaunsəl] *s* consejo; (*advisor*) consejero; (*consultant*) consultor *m;* (*lawyer*) abogado consultor; **to keep one's own counsel** no revelar sus intenciones ‖ *v* (*pret & pp* **-seled** o **-selled;** *ger* **-seling** o **-selling**) *tr* aconsejar ‖ *intr* aconsejarse

counselor [ˈkaunsələr] *s* consejero; abogado

count [kaunt] *s* (*act of counting*) cuenta, recuento; (*result of counting*) suma, total *m;* (*nobleman*) conde *m;* (*charge*) (law) cargo; **to take the count** (box) dejarse contar diez ‖ *tr* contar; **to count off** separar contando; **to count out** no incluir; (sport) declarar vencido ‖ *intr* contar; (*to be worth consideration*) valer; **to count for** valer; **to count on** contar con

countable [ˈkauntəbəl] *adj* contable

count′-down′ *s* cuenta a cero, cuenta atrás

countenance [ˈkauntɪnəns] *s* cara, rostro, semblante *m;* (*composure*) compostura, serenidad; **to keep one's countenance** contenerse; **to lose countenance** conturbarse; **to put out of countenance** avergonzar, confundir ‖ *tr* aprobar, apoyar, favorecer

counter [ˈkauntər] *adj* contrario ‖ *adv* en el sentido opuesto; **counter to** a contrapelo de ‖ *s* contador *m;* (*piece of wood or metal for keeping score*) ficha; (*board in shop over which business is transacted*) mostrador *m;* (box) contragolpe *m* ‖ *tr* oponerse a; contradecir ‖ *intr* (box) dar un contragolpe; **to counter with** replicar con

coun′ter•act′ *tr* contrarrestar, contrariar

coun′ter•attack′ *s* contraataque *m* ‖ **coun′ter•attack′** *tr & intr* contraatacar

coun′ter•bal′ance *s* contrabalanza, contrapeso ‖ **coun′ter•bal′ance** *tr* contrabalancear, contrapesar

coun′ter•clock′wise′ *adj & adv* en el sentido contrario al de las agujas del reloj

coun′ter•cul′ture *s* contracultura

coun′ter•es′pionage *s* contraespionaje *m*

counterfeit [ˈkauntərfɪt] *adj* contrahecho, falsificado ‖ *s* contrahechura, falsificación; moneda falsa ‖ *tr* contrahacer, falsificar

counterfeiter [ˈkauntərˌfɪtər] *s* contrahacedor *m*, falsificador *m;* monedero falso

counterfeit money *s* moneda falsa

countermand [ˈkauntərˌmænd] o [ˈkauntər,-mænd] *s* contramandato ‖ *tr* contramandar; hacer volver

coun′ter•march′ *s* contramarcha ‖ *intr* contramarchar

coun′ter•offen′sive *s* contraofensiva

coun′ter•pane′ *s* cubrecama

coun′ter•part′ *s* contraparte *f;* copia, duplicado

coun′ter•plot′ *s* contratreta ‖ *v* (*pret & pp* **-plotted;** *ger* **-plotting**) *tr* complotar contra (*la treta de otro u otros*)

coun′ter•point′ *s* contrapunto

Counter Reformation *s* Contrarreforma

coun′ter•rev′olu′tion *s* contrarrevolución

coun′ter•sign′ *s* contraseña ‖ *tr* refrendar

coun′ter•sink′ *v* (*pret & pp* **-sunk**) *tr* avellanar

coun′ter•spy′ *s* (*pl* **-spies**) contraespía *mf*

coun′ter•stroke′ *s* contragolpe *m*

coun′ter•weight′ *s* contrapeso

countess [ˈkauntɪs] *s* condesa

countless [ˈkauntlɪs] *adj* incontable, innumerable

countrified [ˈkʌntrɪˌfaɪd] *adj* campesino, rústico

coun•try [ˈkʌntri] *s* (*pl* **-tries**) (*territory of a nation*) país *m;* (*land of one's birth*) patria; (*not the city*) campo

country club *s* club *m* campestre

country cousin *s* isidro

country estate *s* heredad, hacienda de campo

coun'try·folk' s gente f del campo, campesinos

country gentleman s propietario acomodado de finca rural

country house s casa de campo, quinta

country jake [dʒek] s (coll) patán m

country life s vida rural

country·man ['kʌntrimən] s (pl **-men** [mən]) compatriota m; campesino

country people s gente f del campo, gente de capa parda

coun'try·side' s campiña

coun'try·wide' adj nacional

country·woman ['kʌntrɪ,wumən] s (pl **-women** [,wɪmɪn]) compatriota f; campesina

coun·ty ['kaunti] s (pl **-ties**) (small political unit) partido; (domain of a count) condado

county seat s cabeza de partido

coup [ku] s golpe m

coup de grâce [ku də 'grɑs] s puñalada de misericordia, golpe m de gracia

coup d'état [ku de'tɑ] s golpe m de estado

coupé [ku'pe] s cupé m

couple ['kʌpəl] s (man and wife) matrimonio; (two people dancing together) pareja; (elec, mech) par m; (two more or less) (coll) par m ‖ tr acoplar, juntar, unir ‖ intr juntarse, unirse

coupler ['kʌplər] s (rr) enganche m

couplet ['kʌplɪt] s copla, pareado

coupon [ku'pɑn] o [kju'pɑn] s (of a bond) cupón m; (piece detached from larger piece) talón m

courage ['kʌrɪdʒ] s valor m, ánimo; firmeza, resolución; **to have the courage of one's convictions** ajustarse abiertamente con su conciencia; **to pluck up courage** hacer de tripas corazón

courageous [kə'redʒəs] adj valiente, animoso

courier ['kʌrɪ·ər] o ['kurɪ·ər] s estafeta, mensajero; guía m

course [kors] s (onward movement) curso; (of a ship) derrota, rumbo; (of time) transcurso; (of events) marcha; (in school) asignatura, curso; (of a meal) plato; campo de golf; (mas) hilada; **in the course of** en el decurso de; **of course** por supuesto, naturalmente

court [kort] s (of justice) tribunal m; (of a king) corte f; (open space enclosed by a building) atrio, patio; (for tennis) cancha, pista; **to pay court to** hacer la corte a ‖ tr cortejar; buscar, solicitar

courteous ['kʌrtɪ·əs] adj cortés

courtesan ['kʌrtɪzən] o ['kortɪzən] s cortesana

courte·sy ['kʌrtɪsi] s (pl **-sies**) cortesía

court'house' s palacio de justicia

courtier ['kortɪ·ər] s cortesano, palaciego

court jester s bufón m

court·ly ['kortli] adj (comp **-lier**; super **-liest**) cortés, cortesano; (pertaining to the court) cortesano

court'-mar'tial s (pl **courts-martial**) consejo de guerra ‖ v (pret & pp **-tialed** o

-tialled; ger **-tialing** o **-tialling**) tr someter a consejo de guerra

court plaster s tafetán m inglés

court'room' s sala de justicia, tribunal m

courtship ['kortʃɪp] s cortejo, galanteo; noviazgo

court'yard' s atrio, patio

cousin ['kʌzɪn] s primo

cove [kov] s cala, ensenada

covenant ['kʌvənənt] s convenio, pacto; contrato; (Bib) alianza ‖ tr & intr pactar

cover ['kʌvər] s cubierta; (of a magazine) portada; (place for one person at table) cubierto; (for a bed) cobertor m; **to take cover** ocultarse; **under cover** bajo cubierto, bajo techado; oculto; disfrazado; **under cover of** (e.g., the night) a cubierto de; so capa de; **under separate cover** bajo cubierta separada, por separado ‖ tr cubrir; (to line, to coat) recubrir, revestir; recorrer (cierta distancia); cubrirse (la cabeza); tapar (una olla) ‖ intr cubrirse

coverage ['kʌvərɪdʒ] s (amount or space covered) alcance m; (of news) reportaje m; (funds to meet liabilities) cobertura

coveralls ['kʌvər,ɔlz] s mono

cover charge s precio del cubierto

covered ['kʌvərd] adj cubierto; (wire) forrado; (bridge) cubierto

covered wagon s carromato

cover girl s (coll) muchacha hermosa en la portada de una revista

covering ['kʌvərɪŋ] s cubierta, envoltura

covert ['kʌvərt] adj disimulado, secreto

cov'er·up' s efugio, subterfugio

covet ['kʌvɪt] tr codiciar

covetous ['kʌvɪtəs] adj codicioso

covetousness ['kʌvɪtəsnɪs] s codicia

covey ['kʌvi] s (brood) nidada; (in flight) bandada; corro, grupo

cow [kau] s vaca ‖ tr acobardar, intimidar

coward ['kau·ərd] s cobarde mf

cowardice ['kau·ərdɪs] s cobardía; llamada (Mex)

cowardly ['kau·ərdli] adj cobarde; correlón (Col, Mex); llamón (Mex) ‖ adv cobardemente

cow'bell' s cencerro

cow'boy' s vaquero; gaucho (Arg)

cowcatcher ['kau,kætʃər] s quitapiedras m, rastrillo; trompa (Col, Chile)

cower ['kau·ər] intr agacharse

cow'herd' s vaquero, pastor m de ganado vacuno

cow'hide' s cuero; (whip) zurriago ‖ tr zurriagar

cowl [kaul] s capucha, cogulla; (aer) cubierta del motor; (aut) cubretablero, bóveda

cow'lick' s mechón m, remolino (pelos que se levantan sobre la frente)

cowpox ['kau,pɑks] s vacuna

coxcomb ['kɑks,kom] s petimetre m, mequetrefe m

coxswain ['kɑksən] o ['kɑk,swen] s timonel m; contramaestre m

coy [kɔɪ] adj recatado, modesto; coquetón

co•zy [ˈkozi] *adj* (*comp* **-zier;** *super* **-ziest)** cómodo ‖ *s* (*pl* **-zies)** cubretetera

cp. *abbr* **compare**

c.p. *abbr* **candle power**

C.P.A. *abbr* **certified public accountant**

cpd. *abbr* **compound**

cr. *abbr* **credit, creditor**

crab [kræb] *s* cangrejo; (*grouch*) cascarrabias *mf*

crab apple *s* manzana silvestre

crabbed [ˈkræbɪd] *adj* avinagrado, ceñudo

crab grass *s* garranchuelo

crab louse *s* ladilla

crack [kræk] *adj* (coll) de primera clase; (*shot*) (coll) certero ‖ *s* grieta, hendidura; (*noise*) crujido, estallido; (coll) instante *m*, momento; (*joke*) (slang) chiste *m*; **at the crack of dawn** al romper el alba ‖ *tr* agrietar, hender; chasquear (*un látigo*); abrir (*una caja fuerte*) por la fuerza; cascar (*nueces*); descifrar (*un código*); (slang) decir (*un chiste*); (slang) descubrir (*un secreto*); **to crack a smile** (slang) sonreír; **to crack up** (coll) alabar, elogiar ‖ *intr* agrietarse; crujir; cascarse (*la voz de una persona*); enloquecerse; ceder, someterse; **to crack up** fracasar; perder la salud; estrellarse (*un avión*)

cracked [krækt] *adj* agrietado; (*ice*) picado; (coll) mentecato, loco

cracker [ˈkrækər] *s* galleta

crack'le•ware' *s* grietado

crack'pot' *adj* & *s* (slang) excéntrico, tarambana *mf*

crack'up' *s* fracaso; colisión; derrota; (aer) aterrizaje violento; (coll) colapso

cradle [ˈkredəl] *s* cuna; (*of handset*) horquilla ‖ *tr* acunar

cra'dle•song' *s* canción de cuna, arrullo

craft [kræft] *o* [krɑft] *s* arte *m*, arte manual; astucia, maña; nave *f* ‖ *spl* naves

craftiness [ˈkræftɪnɪs] *s* astucia

crafts•man [ˈkræftsmən] *s* (*pl* **-men** [mən]) artesano; artista *m*

craftsmanship [ˈkræftsmən, ʃɪp] *s* artesanía

craft•y [ˈkræfti] *o* [ˈkrɑfti] *adj* (*comp* **-ier;** *super* **-iest)** astuto, mañoso

crag [kræg] *s* peñasco, despeñadero

cram [kræm] *v* (*pret* & *pp* **crammed;** *ger* **cramming)** *tr* atascar, atracar, embutir; (coll) aprender apresuradamente ‖ *intr* atracarse; (*to study hard*) (coll) empollar

cramp [kræmp] *s* (*metal bar*) grapa, laña; (*clamp*) abrazadera; (*painful contraction of muscle*) calambre *m*; **cramps** retortijón *m* de tripas ‖ *tr* engrapar, lañar; apretar; dar calambre a

cranber•ry [ˈkræn,bɛri] *s* (*pl* **-ries)** arándano agrio

crane [kren] *s* (*bird*) grulla; (*derrick*) grúa, guinche *m*, güinche *m* ‖ *tr* estirar (*el cuello*) ‖ *intr* estirar el cuello

crani•um [ˈkreni•əm] *s* (*pl* **-a** [ə]) cráneo

crank [kræŋk] *s* manivela, manubrio; (coll) estrafalario ‖ *tr* hacer girar (*el motor*) con la manivela

crank'case' *s* caja de cigüeñal, cárter *m* del cigüeñal

crank'shaft' *s* cigüeñal *m*

crank•y [ˈkræŋki] *adj* (*comp* **-ier;** *super* **-iest)** malhumorado; (*queer*) estrafalario

cran•ny [ˈkræni] *s* (*pl* **-nies)** hendidura, grieta, rendija

crape [krep] *s* crespón *m*; crespón fúnebre, crespón negro

crape'hang'er *s* (slang) aguafiestas *mf*

craps [kræps] *s* juego de dados; **to shoot craps** jugar a los dados

crash [kræʃ] *s* caída, desplome *m*; colisión, choque *m*; estallido, estrépito; fracaso; crac financiero; lienzo grueso; (aer) aterrizaje violento ‖ *tr* romper con estrépito, estrellar; **to crash a party** (slang) asistir a una fiesta sin invitación; **to crash the gate** (slang) colarse de gorra ‖ *intr* caer, desplomarse; romperse con estrépito, estallar; (*in business*) quebrar; aterrizar violentamente, estrellarse (*un avión*); **to crash into** chocar con

crash dive *s* sumersión instantánea (*de submarino*)

crash landing *s* aterrizaje violento

crash program *s* programa intensivo

crash test *s* (aut) ensayo de choque

crass [kræs] *adj* espeso, tosco; (*ignorance, mistake*) craso

crate [kret] *s* (*box made of slats*) jaula; (*basket*) banasta, cuévano ‖ *tr* embalar en jaula, embalar con listones

crater [ˈkretər] *s* cráter *m*

cravat [krəˈvæt] *s* corbata

crave [krev] *tr* anhelar, ansiar; pedir (*indulgencia*) ‖ *intr* — **to crave for** anhelar, ansiar; pedir con insistencia

craven [ˈkrevən] *adj* & *s* cobarde *mf*

craving [ˈkrevɪŋ] *s* anhelo, ansia, deseo ardiente

craw [krɔ] *s* buche *m*

crawl [krɔl] *s* arrastre *m*; gateado ‖ *intr* reptar, arrastrarse, gatear; (*to have a feeling of insects on skin*) hormiguear; **to crawl along** andar paso a paso; **to crawl up** trepar

crayon [ˈkre•ən] *s* creyón *m*

craze [krez] *s* boga, moda; locura, manía ‖ *tr* enloquecer

cra•zy [ˈkrezi] *adj* (*comp* **-zier;** *super* **-ziest)** loco; (*rickety*) desvencijado; achacoso, débil; **crazy as a bedbug** (slang) loco de atar; **to be crazy about** (coll) estar loco por; **to drive crazy** volver loco

crazy bone *s* hueso de la alegría

creak [krik] *s* crujido, rechinamiento ‖ *intr* crujir, rechinar

creak•y [ˈkriki] *adj* (*comp* **-ier;** *super* **-iest)** crujidero, rechinador

cream [krim] *s* crema; (*e.g., of society*) crema, nata y flor ‖ *tr* desnatar (*la leche*)

creamer•y [ˈkriməri] *s* (*pl* **-ies)** mantequería, quesería, lechería

cream puff *s* bollo de crema

cream separator *s* desnatadora

co
cr

cream·y [ˈkrimɪ] *adj* (*comp* **-ier;** *super* **-iest**) cremoso
crease [kris] *s* arruga, pliegue *m;* (*in trousers*) raya ‖ *tr* arrugar, plegar
create [kriˈet] *tr* crear
creation [kriˈeʃən] *s* creación
creative [kriˈetɪv] *adj* creativo
creator [kriˈetər] *s* creador *m*
creature [ˈkritʃər] *s* criatura; (*being, strange being*) ente *m;* animal *m*
credence [ˈkridəns] *s* creencia; **to give credence to** dar fe a
credentials [krɪˈdɛnʃəlz] *spl* credenciales *fpl*
credible [ˈkrɛdɪbəl] *adj* creíble
credit [ˈkrɛdɪt] *s* crédito; **to take credit for** atribuirse el mérito de ‖ *tr* acreditar; **to credit a person with** atribuirle a una persona el mérito de
creditable [ˈkrɛdɪtəbəl] *adj* honorable, estimable
credit card *s* tarjeta de crédito
creditor [ˈkrɛdɪtər] *s* acreedor *m*
cre·do [ˈkrido] o [ˈkredo] *s* (*pl* **-dos**) credo
credulous [ˈkrɛdʒələs] *adj* crédulo; creído
creed [krid] *s* credo
creek [krik] *s* arroyo, riachuelo
creep [krip] *v* (*pret & pp* **crept** [krɛpt]) *intr* arrastrarse; (*on all fours*) gatear; (*to climb*) trepar; (*with a sensation of insects*) hormiguear; **to creep up on** acercarse insensiblemente a
creeper [ˈkripər] *s* planta rastrera, planta trepadora
creeping [ˈkripɪŋ] *adj* lento, progresivo; (*plant*) rastrero ‖ *s* arrastramiento
cremate [ˈkrimet] *tr* incinerar
cremation [krɪˈmeʃən] *s* cremación; incineración
cremato·ry [ˈkrimə‚tori] *adj* crematorio ‖ *s* (*pl* **-ries**) crematorio
crème de menthe [krɛm də ˈmãt] *s* crema de menta
Creole [ˈkriol] *adj & s* criollo
crescent [ˈkrɛsənt] *s* (*moon in first or last quarter*) creciente *f* de la luna; (*shape of moon in either of these phases*) media luna; panecillo (*en forma de media luna*)
cress [krɛs] *s* mastuerzo
crest [krɛst] *s* cresta
crestfallen [ˈkrɛst‚fɔlən] *adj* cabizbajo
crest'-line' model *s* (aut) modelo estrella
Cretan [ˈkritən] *adj & s* cretense *mf*
Crete [krit] *s* Creta
cretonne [krɪˈtan] *s* cretona
crevice [ˈkrɛvɪs] *s* grieta
crew [kru] *s* equipo; (*of a ship*) dotación, tripulación; (*group, esp. of armed men*) banda, cuadrilla
crew cut *s* corte *m* de pelo a cepillo
crib [krɪb] *s* pesebre *m;* camita de niño; (coll) plagio; (*student's pony*) (coll) chuleta ‖ *v* (*pret & pp* **cribbed;** *ger* **cribbing**) *tr & intr* (coll) hurtar
cricket [ˈkrɪkɪt] *s* (ent) grillo; (sport) cricquet *m;* (coll) juego limpio
crier [ˈkraɪ·ər] *s* pregonero
crime [kraɪm] *s* crimen *m,* delito

criminal [ˈkrɪmɪnəl] *adj & s* criminal *mf;* delictivo
criminal code *s* código penal
criminal law *s* derecho penal
criminal negligence *s* imprudencia temeraria
criminology [‚krɪməˈnalədʒi] *s* criminología
crimp [krɪmp] *s* rizado, rizo; **to put a crimp in** (coll) estorbar, impedir ‖ *tr* rizar
crimple [ˈkrɪmpəl] *tr* arrugar, rizar ‖ *intr* arrugarse, rizarse
crimson [ˈkrɪmzən] *adj & s* carmesí *m* ‖ *intr* enrojecerse
cringe [krɪndʒ] *intr* arrastrarse, reptar, encogerse
crinkle [ˈkrɪŋkəl] *s* arruga, pliegue *m;* (*in the water*) rizo u onda ‖ *tr* arrugar, plegar ‖ *intr* arrugarse
cripple [ˈkrɪpəl] *s* zopo, lisiado ‖ *tr* lisiar, estropear; dañar, perjudicar
cri·sis [ˈkraɪsɪs] *s* (*pl* **-ses**) [siz] crisis *f*
crisp [krɪsp] *adj* frágil, quebradizo; (*air, weather*) refrescante; decisivo
criteri·on [kraɪˈtɪrɪ·ən] *s* (*pl* **-a** [ə]) u **-ons**) criterio
critic [ˈkrɪtɪk] *s* crítico; (*reviewer*) reseñador; (*faultfinder*) criticón *m*
critical [ˈkrɪtɪkəl] *adj* crítico; (*faultfinding*) criticón
criticism [ˈkrɪtɪ‚sɪzəm] *s* crítica
criticize [ˈkrɪtɪ‚saɪz] *tr & intr* criticar
critique [krɪˈtik] *s* (*art of criticism*) crítica; ensayo crítico
croak [krok] *s* (*of raven*) graznido; canto de ranas ‖ *intr* graznar (*el cuervo*); croar (*la rana*); (*morir*) (slang) reventar
Croat [ˈkro·æt] *s* (*native or inhabitant*) croata *mf;* (*language*) croata *m*
Croatian [kroˈeʃən] *adj & mf* croata *mf*
cro·chet [kroˈʃe] *s* croché *m* ‖ *v* (*pret & pp* **-cheted** [ˈʃed]; *ger* **-cheting** [ˈʃe·ɪŋ]) *tr* trabajar con aguja de gancho ‖ *intr* hacer croché
crocheting [kroˈʃə·ɪŋ] *s* labor *f* de ganchillo
crochet needle *s* aguja de gancho
crock [krak] *s* cacharro, vasija de barro cocido
crockery [ˈkrakəri] *s* loza
crocodile [ˈkrakə‚daɪl] *s* cocodrilo
crocodile tears *spl* lágrimas de cocodrilo
crocus [ˈkrokəs] *s* azafrán *m,* croco
crone [kron] *s* vieja acartonada, vieja arrugada
cro·ny [ˈkroni] *s* (*pl* **-nies**) compinche *mf*
crook [krʊk] *s* gancho, garfio; curva; (*of shepherd*) cayado; (coll) fullero, ladrón *m;* chalecón *m* (Mex) ‖ *tr* encorvar; (slang) empinar (*el codo*) ‖ *intr* encorvarse
crooked [ˈkrʊkɪd] *adj* encorvado, torcido; (*person or his conduct*) torcido; **to go crooked** (coll) torcerse
croon [krun] *intr* cantar con voz suave, cantar con melancolía exagerada
crooner [ˈkrunər] *s* cantor de voz suave, cantor melancólico
crop [krap] *s* cosecha; (*head of hair*) cabellera; cabello corto; (*of a bird*) buche *m;* (*whip*) látigo; (*of appointments, promo-*

tions, heroes, etc.) hornada ‖ *v* (*pret & pp*
cropped; *ger* **cropping**) *tr* desmochar (*un árbol*); desorejar (*a un animal*); esquilar, trasquilar ‖ *intr* — **to crop out** o **up** aflorar; asomar, dejarse ver, manifestarse inesperadamente
crop dusting *s* aerofumigación, fumigación aérea
croquet [kroˈke] *s* crocquet *m*
croquette [kroˈket] *s* croqueta
crosier [ˈkroʒər] *s* báculo pastoral, cayado
cross [krɑs] o [krɔs] *adj* transversal, travieso; (*breed*) cruzado; malhumorado, enfadado ‖ *s* cruz *f*; (*of races; of two roads*) cruce *m*; **to take the cross** (*to join a crusade*) cruzarse ‖ *tr* cruzar; (*to oppose*) contrariar, frustrar; **to cross off** u **out** borrar; **to cross oneself** hacerse la señal de la cruz; **to cross one's mind** ocurrírsele a uno; **to cross one's t's** poner travesaño a las tes, poner el palo a las tes ‖ *intr* cruzar; cruzarse; **to cross over** atravesar de un lado a otro
cross'bones' *spl* huesos cruzados (*símbolo de la muerte*)
cross'bow' *s* ballesta
cross'breed' *v* (*pret & pp* **-bred** [ˌbrɛd]) *tr* cruzar (*animales o plantas*)
cross'coun'try *adj* a campo traviesa; a través del país
cross'cur'rent contracorriente *f*; (fig) tendencia encontrada
cross'-exam'i·na'tion *s* interrogatorio riguroso; (law) repregunta
cross'ex·am'ine *tr* interrogar rigurosamente; (law) repreguntar
cross-eyed [ˈkrɑsˌaɪd] *adj* bisojo, bizco, ojituerto
crossing [ˈkrɑsɪŋ] *s* (*of lines, streets, etc.*) cruce *m*; (*of the ocean*) travesía; (*of a river*) vado; (rr) crucero, paso a nivel
crossing gate *s* barrera, barrera de paso a nivel
crossing point *s* punto de cruce
cross'patch' *s* (coll) gruñón *m*
cross'piece' *s* travesaño
cross reference *s* contrarreferencia, remisión
cross'road' *s* vía transversal; **crossroads** encrucijada, cruce *m*; **at the crossroads** en el momento crítico
cross section *s* corte *m* transversal; (fig) sección representativa
cross street *s* calle traviesa, calle de travesía
cross'word' puzzle *s* crucigrama *m*
crotch [krɑtʃ] *s* (*forked piece*) horcajadura, bifurcación; (*between legs*) entrepierna, bragadura, horcajadura
crotchety [ˈkrɑtʃɪti] *adj* caprichoso, estrambótico, de mal genio
crouch [kraʊtʃ] *s* posición agachada ‖ *intr* agacharse, acuclillarse
croup [krup] *s* garrotillo, crup *m*; (*of horse*) anca, grupa
croupier [ˈkrupɪ·ər] *s* crupié *m*
crouton [ˈkrutɑn] *s* corteza de pan
crow [kro] *s* corneja, grajo, chova; (*cry of the cock*) quiquiriquí *m*; (*crowbar*) alzaprima; **as the crow flies** a vuelo de pájaro; **to eat**

crow (coll) cantar la palinodia; **to have a crow to pick with** (coll) tener que habérselas con ‖ *intr* cantar (*el gallo*); jactarse; **to crow over** jactarse de
crow'bar' *s* alzaprima, pie *m* de cabra
crowd [kraʊd] *s* gentío, multitud; (*flock of people*) caterva, tropel *m*; (*mob, common people*) populacho, vulgo; (*clique, set*) corrillo, grupo ‖ *tr* apiñar, apretar, atestar; (*to push*) empujar ‖ *intr* apiñarse, apretarse, atestarse; (*to mill around*) arremolinarse
crowded [ˈkraʊdɪd] *adj* atestado, concurrido
crown [kraʊn] *s* corona; (*of hat*) copa ‖ *tr* coronar; (checkers) coronar; (slang) golpear en la cabeza
crowned head *s* testa coronada
crown prince *s* príncipe heredero
crown princess *s* princesa heredera
crow's'-foot' *s* (*pl* **-feet'**) pata de gallo
crow's'-nest' *s* (naut) cofa de vigía, torre *f* de vigía
crucial [ˈkruʃəl] *adj* crucial; difícil, penoso
crucible [ˈkrusɪbəl] *s* crisol *m*
crucifix [ˈkrusɪfɪks] *s* crucifijo
crucifixion [ˌkrusɪˈfɪkʃən] *s* crucifixión
cruci·fy [ˈkrusɪˌfaɪ] *v* (*pret & pp* **-fied**) *tr* crucificar
crude [krud] *adj* (*raw, unrefined*) crudo; (*lacking culture*) grosero, tosco; (*unfinished*) basto, sin labrar
crudi·ty [ˈkrudɪti] *s* (*pl* **-ties**) crudeza, grosería, tosquedad; bastedad
cruel [ˈkru·əl] *adj* cruel
cruel·ty [ˈkru·əlti] *s* (*pl* **-ties**) crueldad
cruet [ˈkru·ɪt] *s* ampolleta
cruet stand *s* angarillas, vinagreras
cruise [kruz] *s* viaje *m* por mar; (aer, naut) crucero ‖ *tr* (naut) cruzar ‖ *intr* cruzar; (coll) andar de un lado a otro
cruise missile *s* misil *m* crucero
cruiser [ˈkruzər] *s* (nav) crucero
cruising [ˈkruzɪŋ] *adj* de crucero ‖ *s* (aer, naut) crucero
cruising radius *s* autonomía
cruising speed *s* velocidad de crucero
cruller [ˈkrʌlər] *s* buñuelo
crumb [krʌm] *s* migaja; (*soft part of bread*) miga; (*given to a beggar*) mendrugo ‖ *tr* desmigar (*el pan*); (culin) empanar, cubrir con pan rallado; limpiar (*la mesa*) de migajas ‖ *intr* desmigarse, desmenuzarse
crumble [ˈkrʌmbəl] *tr* desmenuzar ‖ *intr* desmenuzarse; (*to fall to pieces gradually*) desmoronarse
crum·my [ˈkrʌmi] *adj* (*comp* **-mier**; *super* **-miest**) (slang) desaseado, sucio; (slang) de mal gusto, de mala muerte
crumple [ˈkrʌmpəl] *tr* arrugar, ajar, chafar ‖ *intr* arrugarse, ajarse
crunch [krʌntʃ] *tr* ronchar, ronzar ‖ *intr* crujir
crusade [kruˈsed] *s* cruzada ‖ *intr* hacer una cruzada
crusader [kruˈsedər] *s* cruzado
crush [krʌʃ] *s* aplastamiento; (*of people*) aglomeración, bullaje *m*; **to have a crush on**

cr
cr

(slang) estar perdido por ‖ *tr* aplastar, machacar, magullar; (*to grind*) moler; bocartear (*el mineral*); (*to oppress, grieve*) abrumar

crush hat *s* clac *m*

crust [krʌst] *s* corteza; corteza de pan; (*scab*) costra

crustacean [krʌs'teʃən] *s* crustáceo

crustaceous [krʌs'teʃəs] *adj* crustáceo

crust·y ['krʌsti] *adj* (*comp* **-ier;** *super* **-iest**) (*scabby*) costroso; áspero, grosero, rudo

crutch [krʌtʃ] *s* muleta

crux [krʌks] *s* punto capital; enigma *m*

cry [kraɪ] *s* (*pl* **cries**) grito; (*weeping*) lloro, llorera; (*of peddler*) pregón *m;* (*of wolf*) aullido; (*of bull*) bramido; **in full cry** en plena persecución; **to have a good cry** desahogarse en lágrimas abundantes ‖ *v* (*pret* & *pp* **cried**) *tr* decir a gritos; (*to announce publicly*) pregonar; **to cry one's eyes** o **heart out** llorar amargamente; **to cry out** decir a gritos; pregonar ‖ *intr* gritar; (*to weep*) llorar; aullar (*el lobo*); bramar (*el toro*); **to cry for** clamar por; **to cry for joy** llorar de alegría; **to cry out** clamar; **to cry out against** clamar contra; **to cry out for** clamar, clamar por

cry'ba'by *s* (*pl* **-bies**) llorón *m*, llorona, lloraduelos *mf*

crypt [krɪpt] *s* cripta

cryptic(al) ['krɪptɪk(əl)] *adj* enigmático, misterioso

crystal ['krɪstəl] *s* cristal *m*

crystal ball *s* bola de cristal

crystalline ['krɪstəlɪn] o ['krɪstə,laɪn] *adj* cristalino

crystallize ['krɪstə,laɪz] *tr* cristalizar ‖ *intr* cristalizarse

C.S. *abbr* **Christian Science, Civil Service**

ct. *abbr* **cent**

cu. *abbr* **cubic**

cub [kʌb] *s* cachorro

Cuban ['kjubən] *adj* & *s* cubano

cubbyhole ['kʌbɪ,hol] *s* chiribitil *m*

cube [kjub] *adj* (*root*) cúbico ‖ *s* cubo; (*of ice*) cubito ‖ *tr* cubicar

cubic ['kjubɪk] *adj* cúbico

cub reporter *s* (coll) reportero novato

cuckold ['kʌkəld] *adj* & *s* cornudo ‖ *tr* encornudar

cuckoo ['kuku] *adj* (slang) mentecato, loco ‖ *s* cuclillo, cuco; (*call of cuckoo*) cucú *m*

cuckoo clock *s* reloj *m* de cuclillo

cucumber ['kjukʌmbər] *s* pepino

cud [kʌd] *s* bolo alimenticio; **to chew the cud** rumiar

cuddle ['kʌdəl] *s* abrazo cariñoso ‖ *tr* abrazar con cariño ‖ *intr* estar abrazados, arrimarse cariñosamente

cudg·el ['kʌdʒəl] *s* garrote *m*, porra; **to take up the cudgels for** salir a la defensa de ‖ *v* (*pret* & *pp* **-eled** o **-elled;** *ger* **-eling** o **-elling**) *tr* apalear, aporrear

cue [kju] *s* señal *f*, indicación; (*hint*) indirecta; (*rôle*) papel *m;* (*rod used in billiards*) taco; (*of hair*) coleta; (*of people in line*) cola; (theat) apunte *m*

cuff [kʌf] *s* (*of shirt*) puño; (*of trousers*) doblez *f*, vuelta; (*blow*) bofetada ‖ *tr* abofetear

cuff links *spl* gemelos

cuirass [kwɪ'ræs] *s* coraza

cuisine [kwɪ'zin] *s* cocina (*arte culinario*)

culinary ['kjulɪ,nɛri] *adj* culinario

cull [kʌl] *tr* (*to choose, pick*) entresacar, escoger; (*to gather, pluck*) coger, recoger

culm [kʌlm] *s* (*coal dust*) cisco; (*stalk of grasses*) caña, tallo

culminate ['kʌlmɪ,net] *intr* culminar; **to culminate in** conducir a, terminar en

culpable ['kʌlpəbəl] *adj* culpable

culprit ['kʌlprɪt] *s* acusado; reo

cult [kʌlt] *s* culto; secta

cultivate ['kʌltɪ,vet] *tr* cultivar

cultivated ['kʌltɪ,vetɪd] *adj* culto, cultivado

cultivation [,kʌltɪ've∫ən] *s* (*of the land, the arts, one's memory, etc.*) cultivo; (*refinement*) cultura

culture ['kʌltʃər] *s* cultura

cultured ['kʌltʃərd] *adj* culto

culvert ['kʌlvərt] *s* alcantarilla

cumbersome ['kʌmbərsəm] *adj* incómodo, molesto; (*clumsy*) pesado, inmanejable

cunning ['kʌnɪŋ] *adj* (*sly*) astuto; (*clever*) hábil; (*attractive*) gracioso, mono ‖ *s* astucia; habilidad, destreza

cup [kʌp] *s* taza; (*of thermometer*) cubeta; (mach) vaso de engrase; (sport) copa; (*of sorrow*) (fig) copa; **in one's cups** borracho ‖ *v* (*pret* & *pp* **cupped;** *ger* **cupping**) *tr* ahuecar dando forma de taza o copa a; poner ventosa a

cupboard ['kʌbərd] *s* alacena, aparador *m*, armario

cupidity [kju'pɪdɪti] *s* codicia

cupola ['kjupələ] *s* cúpula

cur [kʌr] *s* perro mestizo, perro de mala raza; (*despicable fellow*) canalla *m*

curate ['kjʊrɪt] *s* cura *m*

curative ['kjʊrətɪv] *adj* curativo ‖ *s* curativa

curator [kju'retər] *s* conservador *m*

curb [kʌrb] *s* (*of sidewalk*) encintado; (*of well*) brocal *m;* (*of bit*) barbada; (*market*) bolsín *m;* (*check, restraint*) freno; (vet) corva ‖ *tr* contener, refrenar

curb'stone' *s* piedra de encintado; brocal *m* de pozo

curd [kʌrd] *s* cuajada ‖ *tr* cuajar ‖ *intr* cuajarse

curdle ['kʌrdəl] *tr* cuajar; **to curdle the blood** horrorizar ‖ *intr* cuajar

cure [kjʊr] *s* cura, curación ‖ *tr* curar ‖ *intr* curar; curarse

cure'-all' *s* sanalotodo

curfew ['kʌrfju] *s* queda, cubrefuego; toque *m* de queda; hora de cierre

curi·o ['kjʊri,o] *s* (*pl* **-os**) curiosidad

curios·i·ty [,kjʊri'ɑsiti] *s* (*pl* **-ties**) curiosidad

curious ['kjʊri·əs] *adj* curioso

curl [kʌrl] *s* bucle *m*, rizo; (*spiral-shaped curl*) tirabuzón *m;* (*of smoke*) espiral *f;* (*curling*) rizado ‖ *tr* encrespar, ensortijar, rizar; (*to coil, to roll up*) arrollar; fruncir (*los labios*) ‖ *intr* encresparse, ensortijarse, rizarse; arrollarse; **to curl up** arrollarse; (*in bed*) encogerse; (*to break up, collapse*) (coll) desplomarse

curler ['kʌrlər] *s* (*hair*) rulo, bigudí *m*

curlicue ['kʌrlɪ,kju] *s* ringorrango

curling iron *s* rizador *m*, maquinilla de rizar

curl'pa'per *s* torcida, papelito para rizar el pelo

curl·y ['kʌrli] *adj* (*comp* -**ier**; *super* -**lest**) crespo, rizo

curmudgeon [kər'mʌdʒən] *s* cicatero, tacaño, erizo

currant ['kʌrənt] *s* pasa de Corinto; (*Ribes alpinum*) calderilla

curren·cy ['kʌrənsi] *s* (*pl* -**cies**) moneda corriente, dinero en circulación; uso corriente

current ['kʌrənt] *adj* corriente ‖ *s* corriente *f;* (elec) corriente *f*

current account *s* cuenta corriente

current events *spl* actualidades, sucesos de actualidad

curricu·lum [kə'rɪkjələm] *s* (*pl* -**lums** o -**la** [lə]) plan *m* de estudios

cur·ry ['kʌri] *s* (*pl* -**ries**) cari *m* ‖ *v* (*pret & pp* -**ried**) *tr* curtir (*las pieles*); almohazar (*el caballo*); **to curry favor** procurar complacer

cur'ry·comb' *s* almohaza ‖ *tr* almohazar

curse [kʌrs] *s* maldición; (*profane oath*) reniego, voto; (*evil, misfortune*) calamidad ‖ *tr* maldecir ‖ *intr* jurar, echar votos; echar carnes (Mex)

cursed ['kʌrsɪd] o [kʌrst] *adj* maldito; aborrecible

cursive ['kʌrsɪv] *adj* cursivo ‖ *s* cursiva

cursory ['kʌrsəri] *adj* apresurado, rápido, superficial, de paso

curt [kʌrt] *adj* áspero, brusco; corto, conciso

curtail [kər'tel] *tr* acortar, abreviar, cercenar

curtain ['kʌrtən] *s* cortina; (theat) telón *m;* **to draw the curtain** correr la cortina; **to drop the curtain** (theat) bajar el telón ‖ *tr* encortinar; separar con cortina; cubrir, ocultar

curtain call *s* llamada a la escena para recibir aplausos

curtain raiser ['rezər] *s* (theat) pieza preliminar

curtain ring *s* anilla

curtain rod *s* riel *m*

curt·sy ['kʌrtsi] *s* (*pl* -**sies**) cortesía, reverencia ‖ *v* (*pret & pp* -**sied**) *intr* hacer una cortesía

curve [kʌrv] *s* curva ‖ *tr* encorvar ‖ *intr* encorvarse; volver, virar

curved [kʌrvd] *adj* curvo, encorvado; (*crooked*) combo

cushion ['kʊʃən] *s* cojín *m*, almohada; (*of billiard table*) baranda ‖ *tr* amortiguar

cusp [kʌsp] *s* cúspide *f*

cuspidor ['kʌspɪ,dɔr] *s* escupidera

custard ['kʌstərd] *s* flan *m*, natillas

custodian [kəs'todɪ·ən] *s* custodio; (*of a house or building*) casero

custo·dy ['kʌstədi] *s* (*pl* -**dies**) custodia; **in custody** en prisión; **to take into custody** prender

custom ['kʌstəm] *s* costumbre; (*customers*) parroquia, clientela; **customs** aduana; derechos de aduana

customary ['kʌstə,mɛri] *adj* acostumbrado, de costumbre

cus'tom-built' *adj* hecho por encargo, fuera de serie

customer ['kʌstəmər] *s* parroquiano, cliente *mf;* (*of a café or restaurant*) consumidor *m;* (coll) individuo, sujeto, tipo

customer service *s* servicio postventa

cus'tom-house' *adj* aduanero ‖ *s* aduana

cus'tom-made' *adj* hecho a la medida

customs clearance *s* despacho de aduana

customs officer *s* aduanero

custom tailor *s* sastre *m* a la medida

custom work *s* trabajo hecho a la medida

cut [kʌt] *s* corte *m;* (*piece cut off*) tajada; (*wound*) cuchillada; (*for a canal, highway, etc.*) desmonte *m;* (*shortest way*) atajo; (*in prices, wages, etc.*) reducción; (*of a garment*) corte *m*, hechura; (*in winnings, earnings, etc.*) parte *f;* (*diamond*) talla; (typ) estampa, grabado; (tennis) golpe *m* cortante; (*absence from school*) (coll) falta de asistencia; (*snub*) (coll) desaire *m;* (coll) palabra hiriente ‖ *v* (*pret & pp* **cut**; *ger* **cutting**) *tr* cortar; practicar (*un agujero*); reducir (*gastos*); capar, castrar; desleír, diluir; (coll) ausentarse de, faltar a (*la clase*); (coll) desairar; (coll) herir; **to cut down** cortar; derribar cortando; castigar (*gastos*); **to cut off** cortar; desheredar; amputar (*una pierna*); (elec) cortar (*la corriente, la ignición*); cerrar (*el carburador*); **to cut open** abrir cortando; **to cut out** cortar; sacar cortando; labrar; suprimir, omitir; (*to take the place of*) desbancar; soplar (*la dama a un rival*); (slang) dejarse de (*disparates*); **to cut short** terminar de repente; interrumpir, chafar; **to cut teeth** endentecer; **to cut up** desmenuzar, despedazar; criticar severamente; (coll) afligir ‖ *intr* cortar; cortarse; salir (*los dientes*); (coll) fumarse la clase; **to cut in** entrar de repente; interrumpir; (*in a dance*) cortar o separar la pareja; **to cut under** vender a menor precio que; **to cut up** (slang) travesear, hacer travesuras; (slang) jaranear

cut-and-dried ['kʌtən'draɪd] *adj* dispuesto de antemano; monótono, poco interesante

cutaway coat ['kʌtə,we] *s* chaqué *m*

cut'back' *s* reducción; discontinuación, incumplimiento; (mov) retorno a una época anterior

cute [kjut] *adj* (coll) mono, monono; (coll) astuto, listo

cut glass *s* cristal tallado

cuticle ['kjutɪkəl] *s* cutícula

cutlass ['kʌtləs] *s* alfanje *m*

cutler ['kʌtlər] *s* cuchillero

cutlery ['kʌtləri] *s* cuchillería; (*knives, forks, and spoons*) cubierto

cutlet ['kʌtlɪt] *s* chuleta; croqueta

cut'out' *s* (*design to be cut out*) recortado; (aut) escape *m* libre, válvula de escape libre

cut′-rate′ *adj* de precio reducido

cutter [ˈkʌtər] *s* cortador *m;* (*machine*) cortadora; (naut) escampavía

cut′throat′ *adj* asesino; implacable ‖ *s* asesino

cutting [ˈkʌtɪŋ] *adj* cortante; hiriente, mordaz ‖ *s* corte *m;* (*from a newspaper*) recorte *m;* (hort) esqueje *m*

cutting edge *s* canto de corte

cuttlefish [ˈkʌtəl,fɪʃ] *s* jibia

cut′wa′ter *s* espolón *m,* tajamar *m*

cwt. *abbr* **hundredweight**

cyanamide [saɪˈænə,maɪd] *s* cianamida; cianamida de calcio

cyanide [ˈsaɪ•ə,naɪd] *s* cianuro

cybernetics [,saɪbərˈnɛtɪks] *s* cibernética

cycle [ˈsaɪkəl] *s* ciclo; bicicleta; (*of an internal-combustion engine*) tiempo; (phys) periódo ‖ *intr* montar en bicicleta

cyclic(al) [ˈsaɪklɪk(əl)] o [ˈsɪklɪk(əl)] *adj* cíclico

cyclone [ˈsaɪklon] *s* ciclón *m*

cyl. *abbr* **cylinder, cylindrical**

cylinder [ˈsɪlɪndər] *s* cilindro

cylinder block *s* bloque *m* de cilindros

cylinder bore *s* alesaje *m*

cylinder head *s* (*of steam engine*) tapa del cilindro; (*of gas engine*) culata del cilindro

cylindric(al) [sɪˈlɪndrɪk(əl)] *adj* cilíndrico

cymbal [ˈsɪmbəl] *s* címbalo, platillo

cynic [ˈsɪnɪk] *adj* & *s* cínico

cynical [ˈsɪnɪkəl] *adj* cínico

cynicism [ˈsɪnɪ,sɪzəm] *s* cinismo

cynosure [ˈsaɪnə,ʃʊr] o [ˈsɪnə,ʃʊr] *s* blanco de las miradas; guía, norte *m*

cypress [ˈsaɪprəs] *s* ciprés *m*

Cyprus [ˈsaɪprəs] *s* Chipre *f*

Cyrillic [sɪˈrɪlɪk] *adj* cirílico

Cyrus [ˈsaɪrəs] *s* Ciro

cyst [sɪst] *s* quiste *m*

czar [zɑr] *s* zar *m;* (fig) autócrata *m*

czarina [zɑˈrinə] *s* zarina

Czech [tʃɛk] *adj* & *s* checo

Czecho-Slovak [ˈtʃɛkoˈslovæk] *adj* & *s* checoeslovaco o checoslovaco

Czecho-Slovakia [,tʃɛkosloˈvækɪ•ə] *s* Checoeslovaquia o Checoslovaquia

D

D, d [di] cuarta letra del alfabeto inglés

d. *abbr* **date, day, dead, degree, delete, diameter, died, dollar, denarius (penny)**

D. *abbr* **December, Democrat, Duchess, Duke, Dutch**

D.A. *abbr* **District Attorney**

dab [dæb] *s* toque ligero; masa pastosa ‖ *v* (*pret* & *pp* **dabbed;** *ger* **dabbing**) *tr* tocar ligeramente, frotar suavemente

dabble [ˈdæbəl] *tr* salpicar ‖ *intr* chapotear; **to dabble in** meterse en; jugar a (*la Bolsa*); especular en (*granos*)

dad [dæd] *s* (coll) papá *m*

dad•dy [ˈdædi] *s* (*pl* **-dies**) (coll) papá *m*

daffodil [ˈdæfədɪl] *s* narciso trompón

daff•y [ˈdæfi] *adj* (*comp* **-ier;** *super* **-iest**) (coll) chiflado

dagger [ˈdægər] *s* daga, puñal *m;* (typ) cruz *f,* obelisco; **to look daggers at** apuñalar con la mirada

dahlia [ˈdæljə] *s* dalia

dai•ly [ˈdeli] *adj* cotidiano, diario ‖ *adv* diariamente ‖ *s* (*pl* **-lies**) diario

dain•ty [ˈdenti] *adj* (*comp* **-tier;** *super* **-tiest**) delicado ‖ *s* (*pl* **-ties**) golosina

dair•y [ˈdɛri] *s* (*pl* **-ies**) lechería, vaquería

dais [ˈde•ɪs] *s* estrado

dai•sy [ˈdezi] *s* (*pl* **-sies**) margarita

daisy wheel *s* (*computer*) margarita (*impresora*)

dal•ly [ˈdæli] *v* (*pret* & *pp* **-lied**) *intr* juguetear, retozar; tardar, malgastai el tiempo

dam [dæm] *s* represa, embalse *m;* (*female quadruped*) madre *f;* (dent) dique *m* ‖ *v* (*pret* & *pp* **dammed;** *ger* **damming**) *tr*

represar, embalsar; cerrar, tapar, obstruir

damage [ˈdæmɪdʒ] *s* daño, perjuicio; (*to one's reputation*) desdoro; (com) avería; **damages** daños y perjuicios ‖ *tr* dañar, perjudicar; averiar

damascene [ˈdæmə,sin] o [,dæməˈsin] *adj* damasquino ‖ *s* ataujía, damasquinado ‖ *tr* ataujiar, damasquinar

dame [dem] *s* dama, señora; (coll) mujer *f*

damn [dæm] *s* terno; **I don't give a damn** (slang) maldito lo que me importa; **that's not worth a damn** (slang) eso no vale un pito ‖ *tr* condenar (a pena eterna); condenar; maldecir ‖ *intr* maldecir, echar ternos

damnation [dæmˈneʃən] *s* damnación; (theol) condenación

damned [dæmd] *adj* condenado (a pena eterna); abominable, detestable ‖ **the damned** los malditos, los condenados (a pena eterna)

damp [dæmp] *adj* húmedo, mojado ‖ *s* humedad; (*firedamp*) grisú *m* ‖ *tr* humedecer, mojar; (*to deaden, muffle*) amortecer, amortiguar; (*to discourage*) abatir, desalentar; (elec) amortiguar (*ondas electromagnéticas*)

dampen [ˈdæmpən] *tr* humedecer, mojar; amortecer, amortiguar; abatir, desalentar

damper [ˈdæmpər] *s* (*of chimney*) registro; (*of piano*) apagador *m,* sordina

damsel [ˈdæmzəl] *s* señorita, muchacha

dance [dæns] *s* baile *m,* danza ‖ *tr* & *intr* bailar, danzar

dance band *s* orquesta de jazz

dance floor s pista de baile
dance hall s salón m de baile
dancer ['dænsər] s bailador m, danzador m; (*professional*) bailarín m
dancing partner s pareja (de baile)
dandelion ['dændɪ,laɪ•ən] s diente m de león
dandruff ['dændrəf] s caspa
dan•dy ['dændi] adj (*comp* **-dier;** *super* **-diest**) (coll) excelente, magnífico ‖ s (*pl* **-dies**) currutaco, petimetre m; lagarto (Mex)
Dane [den] s danés m, dinamarqués m
danger ['dendʒər] s peligro
dangerous ['dendʒərəs] adj peligroso; riesgoso
dangle ['dæŋgəl] tr & intr colgar flojamente, colgar en el aire
Danish ['denɪʃ] adj & s danés m, dinamarqués m
dank [dæŋk] adj húmedo, liento
Danube ['dænjub] s Danubio
dapper ['dæpər] adj aseado, apuesto
dapple ['dæpəl] adj habado, rodado ‖ tr motear
dare [dɛr] s desafío, reto ‖ tr retar; **to dare to** (*to challenge to*) desafiar a ‖ intr osar, atreverse; **I dare say** talvez; **to dare to** (*to have the courage to*) atreverse a
dare'dev'il s calavera m, temerario
daring ['dɛrɪŋ] adj atrevido, osado ‖ s atrevimiento, osadía
dark [dɑrk] adj obscuro; (*in complexion*) moreno; secreto, oculto; (*gloomy*) lóbrego; (*beer*) pardo ‖ s obscuridad, tinieblas; noche f; **in the dark** a obscuras
Dark Ages spl edad media; principios de la edad media
dark-complexioned ['dɑrkkəm'plɛkʃənd] adj moreno
darken ['dɑrkən] tr obscurecer; entristecer; cegar ‖ intr obscurecerse
dark horse s caballo desconocido; candidato nombrado inesperadamente
darkly ['dɑrkli] adv obscuramente; secretamente, misteriosamente
dark meat s carne f del ave que no es la pechuga
darkness ['dɑrknɪs] s obscuridad
dark'room' s (phot) cuarto obscuro
darling ['dɑrlɪŋ] adj & s querido, amado; predilecto; (*as address*) chata (Mex)
darn [dɑrn] tr & intr zurcir; (coll) maldecir
darnel ['dɑrnəl] s cizaña
darning ['dɑrnɪŋ] s zurcido
darning needle s aguja de zurcir
dart [dɑrt] s dardo; (*small missile used in a game*) rehilete m ‖ intr lanzarse, precipitarse; volar como dardo
Darwinian [dɑr'wɪnɪ•ən] adj darviniano
Darwinism ['dɑrwə,nɪzəm] s darvinismo
Darwinist ['dɑrwənɪst] s darviniano
dash [dæʃ] s arranque m; (*splash*) rociada; carrera corta; (*spirit*) brío; pequeña cantidad; (*in printing, writing, telegraphy*) raya ‖ tr lanzar; estrellar, romper; frustrar (*las esperanzas de uno*); rociar, salpicar; **to dash off** escribir de prisa; **to dash to**

pieces hacer añicos ‖ intr estrellarse (*las olas del mar*); lanzarse, precipitarse; **to dash by** pasar corriendo; **to dash in** entrar como un rayo
dash'board' s tablero de instrumentos; cuadro de mando; (aut) guardabarros m, salpicadero
dashing' ['dæʃɪŋ] adj brioso; ostentoso, vistoso ‖ s (*of waves*) embate m
dastard ['dæstərd] adj & s vil mf, miserable mf, cobarde mf
data bank ['detə] s banco de datos, almacenamiento
da'ta-proc'ess tr & intr procesar
data processing s procesamiento; tramitación automática de datos
data storage s memoria, almacenamiento
date [det] s (*time*) fecha, data; (*palm*) datilera; (*fruit*) dátil m; (*appointment*) (coll) cita; **out of date** anticuado, fuera de moda; **to date** hasta la fecha; **under date of** con fecha de ‖ tr fechar, datar; (coll) tener cita con ‖ intr **—to date from** datar de
date line s línea de cambio de fecha
date palm s palmera (datilera)
dative ['detɪv] adj & s dativo
datum ['detəm] o ['dætəm] s (*pl* **data** ['detə] o ['dætə]) dato
dau. abbr **daughter**
daub [dɔb] s embadurnamiento ‖ tr embadurnar
daughter ['dɔtər] s hija
daughter-in-law ['dɔtərɪn,lɔ] s (*pl* **daughters-in-law**) nuera, hija política
daunt [dɔnt] tr asustar, espantar; desanimar, acobardar
dauntless ['dɔntlɪs] adj atrevido, intrépido, impávido
dauphin ['dɔfɪn] s delfín m
davenport ['dævən,port] s sofá m cama
davit ['dævɪt] s (naut) pescante m, grúa de bote
daw [dɔ] s corneja
dawdle ['dɔdəl] intr malgastar el tiempo, haronear
dawn [dɔn] s amanecer m, alba ‖ intr amanecer; despuntar (*el día, la mañana*); empezar a mostrarse; **to dawn on** empezar a hacerse patente a
day [de] adj diurno ‖ s día m; (*of travel, work, worry, etc.*) jornada; (*from noon to noon*) (naut) singladura; **any day now** de un día para otro; **by day** de día; **the day after** el día siguiente; **the day after tomorrow** pasado mañana; **the day before** la víspera; la víspera de; **the day before yesterday** anteayer; **to call it a day** (coll) dejar de trabajar; **to win the day** ganar la jornada
day bed s sofá m cama, diván m cama
day'break' s amanecer m
day coach s (rr) coche m de viajeros
day'dream' s ensueño ‖ intr soñar despierto
day laborer s jornalero
day'light' s luz f del día; amanecer m; **in broad daylight** en pleno día; **to see daylight** comprender; ver el fin de una tarea difícil

cu
da

day′light′-sav′ing time *s* hora de verano
day nursery *s* guardería infantil
day off *s* asueto
day of reckoning *s* día *m* de ajustar cuentas
day shift *s* turno diurno
day′time′ *adj* diurno ‖ día *m*
daze [dez] *s* aturdimiento; **in a daze** aturdido ‖ *tr* aturdir
dazzle [′dæzəl] *s* deslumbramiento ‖ *tr* deslumbrar
dazzling [′dæzlɪŋ] *adj* deslumbrante
deacon [′dikən] *s* diácono
deaconess [′dikənɪs] *s* diaconisa
dead [dɛd] *adj* muerto; (coll) cansado ‖ *adv* (coll) completamente, muy ‖ *s* — **in the dead of night** en plena noche; **the dead** los muertos; **the dead of winter** lo más frío del invierno
dead beat *s* (slang) gorrón *m*; (slang) holgazán *m*
dead bolt *s* cerrojo dormido
dead calm *s* calma chicha, calmazo
dead center *s* punto muerto
dead′drunk′ *adj* difunto de taberna
deaden [′dɛdən] *tr* amortiguar, amortecer
dead end *s* callejón *m* sin salida
dead′latch′ *s* aldaba dormida
dead′-let′ter office *s* departamento de cartas no reclamadas
dead′line′ *s* línea vedada; fin *m* del plazo
dead′lock′ *s* cerradura dormida; desacuerdo insuperable ‖ *tr* estancar
dead·ly [′dɛdli] *adj* (comp **-lier**; super **-liest**) mortal; (sin) capital; abrumador
dead pan *s* (slang) semblante *m* sin expresión
dead reckoning *s* (naut) estima
dead ringer [′rɪŋər] *s* segunda edición
dead′wood′ *s* leña seca; cosa inútil, gente *f* inútil
deaf [dɛf] *adj* sordo; **to turn a deaf ear** hacerse el sordo, hacer oídos de mercader
deaf and dumb *adj* sordomudo
deafen [′dɛfən] *tr* asordar, ensordecer
deafening [′dɛfənɪŋ] *adj* ensordecedor
deaf′-mute′ *s* sordomudo
deafness [′dɛfnɪs] *s* sordera
deal [dil] *s* negocio, trato; (of cards) mano *f*; turno de dar; (share) parte *f*, porción; (coll) convenio secreto; **a good deal (of)** o **a great deal (of)** mucho; **to make a great deal of** hacer fiestas a ‖ *v* (pret & pp **dealt** [dɛlt]) *tr* asestar (un golpe); repartir (la baraja) ‖ *intr* negociar, comerciar; intervenir; (in card games) ser mano; **to deal with** entender en; tratar de; tratar con
dealer [′dilər] *s* comerciante *mf*, concesionario; (of cards) repartidor *m*
dean [din] *s* decano; (eccl) deán *m*
deanship [′dinʃɪp] *s* decanato, deanato, deanazgo
dear [dɪr] *adj* (beloved) caro; (expensive) caro; (charging high prices) carero; **dear me!** ¡Dios mío! ‖ *s* queriao
dearie [′dɪri] *s* (coll) queridito
dearth [dʌrθ] *s* carestía
death [dɛθ] *s* muerte *f*; **to bleed to death** morir desangrado; **to bore to death** matar de aburrimiento; **to burn to death** morir quemado; **to choke to death** morir atragantado; **to die a violent death** morir vestido; **to freeze to death** morir helado; **to put to death** dar la muerte a; **to shoot to death** matar a tiros; **to stab to death** escabechar; **to starve to death** matar de hambre; morir de hambre
death′bed′ *s* lecho de muerte
death′blow′ *s* golpe *m* mortal
death certificate *s* fe *f* de óbito, partida de defunción
death house *s* capilla (de los reos de muerte)
deathless [′dɛθlɪs] *adj* inmortal, eterno
deathly [′dɛθli] *adj* mortal, de muerte ‖ *adv* mortalmente; excesivamente
death penalty *s* pena de muerte
death rate *s* mortalidad
death rattle *s* estertor agónico
death ray *s* rayo mortífero
death warrant *s* sentencia de muerte; fin *m* de toda esperanza
death′watch′ *s* vela de un difunto; guardia de un reo de muerte
debacle [de′bakəl] *s* desastre *m*, ruina, derrota; (in a river) deshielo
de·bar [dɪ′bar] *v* (pret & pp **-barred;** ger **-barring**) *tr* excluir; prohibir
debark [dɪ′bark] *tr* & *intr* desembarcar
debarkation [‚dibar′keʃən] *s* (of passengers) desembarco; (of freight) desembarque *m*
debase [dɪ′bes] *tr* degradar; falsificar
debatable [dɪ′betəbəl] *adj* disputable
debate [dɪ′bet] *s* debate *m* ‖ *tr* debatir ‖ *intr* debatir; deliberar
debauchee [‚dɛbɔ′ʃi] o [‚dɛbɔ′tʃi] *s* libertino, disoluto
debaucher·y [dɪ′bɔtʃəri] *s* (pl **-ies**) libertinaje *m*, crápula
debenture [dɪ′bɛntʃər] *s* (bond) obligación; (voucher) vale *m*
debilitate [dɪ′bɪlɪ‚tet] *tr* debilitar
debili·ty [dɪ′bɪlɪti] *s* (pl **-ties**) debilidad
debit [′dɛbɪt] *s* debe *m*; (entry on debit side) cargo ‖ *tr* adeudar, cargar
debit balance *s* saldo deudor
debonair [‚dɛbə′nɛr] *adj* alegre; cortés
debris [de′bri] *s* despojos, ruinas
debt [dɛt] *s* deuda; **to run into debt** endeudarse, entramparse
debtor [′dɛtər] *s* deudor *m*
debut [de′bju] o [′debju] *s* estreno, debut *m*, **to make one's debut** estrenarse, debutar; ponerse de largo, entrar en sociedad (una joven)
debutante [‚dɛbju′tant] o [′dɛbjə‚tænt] *s* joven *f* que se pone de largo; debutante *f*
dec. abbr **deceased**
decade [′dɛked] *s* decenio, década
decadence [dɪ′kedəns] *s* decadencia
decadent [dɪ′kedənt] *adj* & *s* decadente *mf*
decanter [dɪ′kæntər] *s* garrafa
decapitate [dɪ′kæpɪ‚tet] *tr* decapitar
decay [dɪ′ke] *s* (decline) decaimiento, descaecimiento; (rotting) podredumbre; (of teeth) caries *f* ‖ *tr* pudrir ‖ *intr* pudrirse; decaer; cariarse (los dientes)

decease [dɪˈsis] *s* fallecimiento ‖ *intr* fallecer
deceased [dɪˈsist] *adj & s* difunto
deceit [dɪˈsit] *s* engaño, fraude *m*
deceitful [dɪˈsitfəl] *adj* engañoso, fraudulento
deceive [dɪˈsiv] *tr & intr* engañar
decelerate [dɪˈsɛləˌret] *tr* desacelerar ‖ *intr* desacelerarse
December [dɪˈsɛmbər] *s* diciembre *m*
decen•cy [ˈdisənsi] *s* (*pl* **-cies**) decencia, honestidad; (*propriety*) conveniencia
decent [ˈdisənt] *adj* decente, honesto; (*proper*) conveniente
decentralize [dɪˈsɛntrəˌlaɪz] *tr* descentralizar
deception [dɪˈsɛpʃən] *s* engaño
deceptive [dɪˈsɛptɪv] *adj* engañoso
decide [dɪˈsaɪd] *tr & intr* decidir
decimal [ˈdɛsɪməl] *adj & s* decimal *m*
decimal point *s* (*in Spanish the comma is used to separate the decimal fraction from the integer*) coma
decimate [ˈdɛsɪˌmet] *tr* diezmar
decipher [dɪˈsaɪfər] *tr* descifrar
deciphering [dɪˈsaɪfərɪŋ] *s* desciframiento
decision [dɪˈsɪʒən] *s* decisión
decisive [dɪˈsaɪsɪv] *adj* decisivo; determinado, resuelto
deck [dɛk] *s* (*of cards*) baraja; (*of ship*) cubierta; **between decks** (naut) entre cubiertas ‖ *tr* — **to deck out** adornar, engalanar
deck chair *s* silla de cubierta
deck hand *s* marinero de cubierta
deck′-land′ *intr* apontizar
deck′-land′ing *s* apontizaje *m*
deckle edge [ˈdɛkəl] *s* barba
declaim [dɪˈklem] *tr & intr* declamar
declaration [ˌdɛkləˈreʃən] *s* declaración
declarative [dɪˈklærətɪv] *adj* declarativo; (*gram*) enunciativo
declare [dɪˈklɛr] *tr & intr* declarar
declension [dɪˈklɛnʃən] *s* declinación
declination [ˌdɛklɪˈneʃən] *s* declinación
decline [dɪˈklaɪn] *s* bajada, declinación; (*in prices*) baja; (*in health, wealth, etc.*) bajón *m*; (*of sun*) ocaso ‖ *tr & intr* declinar; rehusar
declivi•ty [dɪˈklɪvɪti] *s* (*pl* **-ties**) declividad, declive *m*
decode [diˈkod] *tr* descifrar
decoder [diˈkodər] *s* (telv) decodificador *m*
decoding [diˈkodɪŋ] *s* desciframiento
décolleté [ˌdekɑlˈte] *adj* escotado
decompose [ˌdikəmˈpoz] *tr* descomponer ‖ *intr* descomponerse
decomposition [ˌdikɑmpəˈzɪʃən] *s* descomposición
decompression [ˌdikəmˈprɛʃən] *s* descompresión
decongest [ˌdikənˈdʒɛst] *tr* descongestionar
decongestion [ˌdikənˈdʒɛstʃən] *s* descongestión
decontamination [ˌdikəmˌtæmɪˈneʃən] *s* descontaminación; **radioactive decontamination** descontaminación de radiactividad
decon•trol [ˌdikənˈtrol] *v* (*pret & pp* **-trolled**; *ger* **-trolling**) descontrolar

décor [deˈkɔr] *s* decoración; (theat) decorado
decorate [ˈdɛkəˌret] *tr* decorar; (*with medal, badge*) condecorar
decoration [ˌdɛkəˈreʃən] *s* decoración; (*medal, badge*) condecoración
decorator [ˈdɛkəˌretər] *s* decorador *m;* (*of interiors*) adornista *mf*
decorous [ˈdɛkərəs] o [dɪˈkorəs] *adj* decoroso
decorum [dɪˈkorəm] *s* decoro
decoy [dɪˈkɔɪ] o [ˈdɪkɔɪ] *s* añagaza, señuelo; (*person*) entruchón *m* ‖ [dɪˈkɔɪ] *tr* atraer con señuelo; entruchar
decoy pigeon *s* cimbel *m*
decrease [ˈdikris] o [ˈdikris] *tr* disminuir ‖ *intr* disminuir, disminuirse
decree [dɪˈkri] *s* decreto ‖ *tr* decretar
decrepit [dɪˈkrɛpɪt] *adj* decrépito
de•cry [dɪˈkraɪ] *v* (*pret & pp* **-cried**) *tr* censurar, denigrar
dedicate [ˈdɛdɪˌket] *tr* dedicar
dedication [ˌdɛdɪˈkeʃən] *s* dedicación; (*inscription in a book*) dedicatoria
deduce [dɪˈdjus] *tr* deducir (*inferir, concluir; derivar*)
deduct [dɪˈdʌkt] *tr* deducir (*rebajar, substraer*)
deduction [dɪˈdʌkʃən] *s* deducción
deed [did] *s* acto, hecho; (*feat, exploit*) hazaña; (*law*) escritura ‖ *tr* traspasar por escritura
deem [dim] *tr & intr* creer, juzgar
deep [dip] *adj* profundo; (*sound*) grave; (*color*) subido; de hondo, p.ej., **two meters deep** dos metros de hondo; **deep in debt** cargado de deudas; **deep in thought** absorto en la meditación ‖ *adv* hondo; **deep into the night** muy entrada la noche
deepen [ˈdipən] *tr* profundizar ‖ *intr* profundizarse
deep-laid [ˈdipˌled] *adj* concebido con astucia
deep mourning *s* luto riguroso
deep-rooted [ˈdipˌrutɪd] *adj* profundamente arraigado
deep′-sea′ fishing *s* pesca de gran altura
deep-seated [ˈdipˌsitɪd] *adj* profundamente arraigado
deer [dɪr] *s* ciervo, venado
deer′skin′ *s* piel *f* de ciervo
def. *abbr* **defendant, deferred, definite**
deface [dɪˈfes] *tr* desfigurar
de facto [diˈfækto] *adv* de hecho
defamation [ˌdɛfəˈmeʃən] o [ˌdifəˈmeʃən] *s* difamación
defame [dɪˈfem] *tr* difamar
default [dɪˈfɔlt] *s* falta, incumplimiento; **by default** (sport) por no presentarse; **in default of** por falta de ‖ *tr* dejar de cumplir; no pagar ‖ *intr* faltar; (sport) perder por no presentarse
defeat [dɪˈfit] *s* derrota ‖ *tr* derrotar, vencer
defeatism [dɪˈfitɪzəm] *s* derrotismo
defeatist [dɪˈfitɪst] *adj & s* derrotista *mf*
defecate [ˈdɛfɪˌket] *intr* defecar
defect [ˈdifɛkt] o [dɪˈfɛkt] *s* defecto, imperfección ‖ [dɪˈfɛkt] *intr* desertar

da de

defection [dɪ'fɛkʃən] s defección; (*lack, failure*) falta

defective [dɪ'fɛktɪv] *adj* defectivo, defectuoso

defend [dɪ'fɛnd] *tr* defender

defendant [dɪ'fɛndənt] s (law) demandado, acusado

defender [dɪ'fɛndər] s defensor *m*

defense [dɪ'fɛns] s defensa

defenseless [dɪ'fɛnslɪs] *adj* indefenso

defensive [dɪ'fɛnsɪv] *adj* defensivo ‖ s defensiva

de•fer [dɪ'fʌr] *v* (*pret* & *pp* **-ferred**; *ger* **-ferring**) *tr* aplazar, diferir ‖ *intr* deferir

deference ['dɛfərəns] s deferencia

deferential [,dɛfə'rɛnʃəl] *adj* deferente

deferment [dɪ'fʌrmənt] s aplazamiento, dilación

defiance [dɪ'faɪ•əns] s oposición; desafío, provocación; **in defiance of** sin mirar a, a despecho de

defiant [dɪ'faɪ•ənt] *adj* provocante, hostil

deficien•cy [dɪ'fɪʃənsi] s (*pl* **-cies**) carencia, deficiencia; (com) descubierto

deficient [dɪ'fɪʃənt] *adj* deficiente, defectuoso

deficit ['dɛfɪsɪt] *adj* deficitario ‖ s déficit *m*

defile [dɪ'faɪl] o ['difaɪl] s desfiladero ‖ [dɪ'faɪl] *tr* corromper, manchar ‖ *intr* desfilar

define [dɪ'faɪn] *tr* definir

definite ['dɛfɪnɪt] *adj* definido

definition [,dɛfɪ'nɪʃən] s definición

definitive [dɪ'fɪnɪtɪv] *adj* definitivo

deflate [dɪ'flet] *tr* desinflar

deflation [dɪ'fleʃən] s desinflación; (*of prices*) deflación

deflect [dɪ'flɛkt] *tr* desviar ‖ *intr* desviarse

deflower [di'flaʊ•ər] *tr* desflorar

deforest [di'fɑrɛst] o [di'fɔrɛst] *tr* desforestar, despoblar

deform [dɪ'fɔrm] *tr* deformar

deformed [dɪ'fɔrmd] *adj* deforme

deformi•ty [dɪ'fɔrmɪti] s (*pl* **-ties**) deformidad

defraud [dɪ'frɔd] *tr* defraudar

defray [di'fre] *tr* sufragar, subvenir a

defrost [di'frɔst] *tr* descongelar, deshelar

defroster [di'frɔstər] s descongelador *m*

deft [dɛft] *adj* diestro, hábil

defunct [dɪ'fʌŋkt] *adj* difunto

de•fy [dɪ'faɪ] *v* (*pret* & *pp* **-fied**) *tr* desafiar, provocar

deg. *abbr* **degree**

degeneracy [dɪ'dʒɛnərəsi] s degeneración

degenerate [dɪ'dʒɛnərɪt] *adj* & s degenerado ‖ [dɪ'dʒɛnə,ret] *intr* degenerar

degrade [dɪ'gred] *tr* degradar

degrading [dɪ'gredɪŋ] *adj* degradante

degree [dɪ'gri] s grado; **by degrees** de grado en grado; **to take a degree** graduarse, recibir un grado o título

dehumidifier [,dihju'mɪdɪ,faɪ•ər] s deshumedecedor *m*

dehydrate [di'haɪdret] *tr* deshidratar

deice [di'aɪs] *tr* deshelar

dei•fy ['di•ɪ,faɪ] *v* (*pret* & *pp* **-fied**) *tr* deificar

deign [den] *intr* dignarse

dei•ty ['di•ɪti] s (*pl* **-ties**) deidad; **the Deity** Dios *m*

dejected [dɪ'dʒɛktɪd] *adj* abatido

dejection [dɪ'dʒɛkʃən] s abatimiento

del. *abbr* **delegate, delete**

delay [dɪ'le] s retraso, tardanza; parón ‖ *tr* retrasar ‖ *intr* demorarse

delectable [dɪ'lɛktəbəl] *adj* deleitable

delegate ['dɛlɪgɪt] s diputado, delegado; (*to a convention*) congresista *mf* ‖ ['dɛlɪ,get] *tr* delegar

delete [dɪ'lit] *tr* borrar, suprimir

deletion [dɪ'liʃən] s supresión

deliberate [dɪ'lɪbərɪt] *adj* pensado, reflexionado; (*slow in deciding*) cauto, circunspecto; (*slow in moving*) espacioso, lento ‖ [dɪ'lɪbə,ret] *tr* & *intr* deliberar

delica•cy ['dɛlɪkəsi] s (*pl* **-cies**) delicadeza; (*choice food*) golosina

delicatessen [,dɛlɪkə'tɛsən] s colmado, tienda de ultramarinos ‖ *spl* ultramarinos

delicious [dɪ'lɪʃəs] *adj* delicioso, sabroso

delight [dɪ'laɪt] s deleite *m*, delicia ‖ *tr* deleitar ‖ *intr* deleitarse

delightful [dɪ'laɪtfəl] *adj* deleitoso, ameno, exquisito

delinquen•cy [dɪ'lɪŋkwənsi] s (*pl* **-cies**) culpa; (*in payment of debt*) morosidad; (*debt in arrears*) atrasos

delinquent [dɪ'lɪŋkwənt] *adj* culpado; (*in payment*) moroso, atrasado; no pagado ‖ s culpado; deudor moroso

delirious [dɪ'lɪrɪ•əs] *adj* delirante

deliri•um [dɪ'lɪrɪ•əm] s (*pl* **-ums** o **-a** [ə]) delirio

deliver [dɪ'lɪvər] *tr* entregar; asestar (*un golpe*); pronunciar, recitar (*un discurso*); transmitir, rendir (*energía*); partear (*a la mujer que está de parto*)

deliver•y [dɪ'lɪvəri] s (*pl* **-ies**) entrega; (*of mail*) distribución, reparto; (*of a speech*) declamación; (*childbirth*) alumbramiento, parto

delivery•man [dɪ'lɪvərɪmən] s (*pl* **-men** [mən]) mozo de reparto

delivery room s sala de alumbramiento

delivery service s servicio a domicilio

delivery truck s sedán *m* de reparto

dell [dɛl] s vallecito

delouse [di'laʊs] *tr* despiojar

delphinium [dɛl'fɪnɪ•əm] s (*Delphinium ajacis*) espuela de caballero; (*Delphinium consolida*) consuelda real

delude [dɪ'lud] *tr* deludir, engañar

deluge ['dɛljudʒ] s diluvio ‖ *tr* inundar

delusion [dɪ'luʒən] s engaño, decepción

de luxe [dɪ'lʌks] *adj* & *adv* s de lujo

delve [dɛlv] *intr* cavar; **to delve into** cavar en

demagnetize [di'mægnɪ,taɪz] *tr* desimantar

demagogue ['dɛmə,gɑg] s demagogo

demand [dɪ'mænd] o [dɪ'mɑnd] s demanda; **to be in demand** tener demanda ‖ *tr* demandar perentoriamente

demanding [dɪ'mændɪŋ] *adj* exigente

demarcate [dɪ'mɑrket] o ['dimɑr,ket] *tr* demarcar

démarche [de`marʃ] *s* diligencia, gestión, paso

demeanor [dɪ`minər] *s* conducta, porte *m*

demented [dɪ`mɛntɪd] *adj* demente, dementado

demigod [`dɛmɪ,gad] *s* semidiós *m*

demijohn [`dɛmɪ,dʒɑn] *s* damajuana

demilitarize [di`mɪlɪtə,raɪz] *tr* desmilitarizar

demilitarized zone *s* zona desmilitarizada

demimonde [`dɛmɪ,mand] *s* mujeres de vida alegre

demise [dɪ`maɪz] *s* fallecimiento

demisemiquaver [,dɛmɪ`sɛmɪ,kwevər] *s* (mus) fusa

demitasse [`dɛmɪ,tæs] o [`dɛmɪ,tas] *s* taza pequeña

demobilize [di`mobɪ,laɪz] *tr* desmovilizar

democra•cy [dɪ`markrəsi] *s* (*pl* **-cies**) democracia

democrat [`dɛmə,kræt] *s* demócrata *mf*

democratic [,dɛmə`krætɪk] *adj* democrático

demodulate [di`madjə,let] *tr* desmodular

demolish [dɪ`malɪʃ] *tr* demoler

demolition [,dɛmə`lɪʃən] o [,dimə`lɪʃən] *s* demolición

demon [`dimən] *s* demonio

demoniacal [,dimə`naɪ•əkəl] *adj* demoníaco

demonstrate [`dɛmən,stret] *tr* demostrar ‖ *intr* demostrar; (*to show feelings in public gatherings*) manifestar

demonstration [,dɛmən`streʃən] *s* demostración; (*public show of feeling*) manifestación

demonstrative [dɪ`manstrətɪv] *adj* demostrativo; (*giving open exhibition of emotion*) extremoso

demonstrator [`dɛmən,stretər] *s* demostrador *m;* manifestante *mf*

demoralize [dɪ`mɔrə,laɪz] *tr* desmoralizar

demote [dɪ`mot] *tr* degradar

demotion [dɪ`moʃən] *s* degradación

de•mur [dɪ`mʌr] *v* (*pret & pp* **-murred;** *ger* **-murring**) *intr* poner reparos

demure [dɪ`mjʊr] *adj* modesto, recatado; grave, serio

demurrage [dɪ`mʌrɪdʒ] *s* (com) estadía

den [dɛn] *s* (*of animals, thieves*) madriguera; (*dirty little room*) cuchitril *m;* lugar *m* de retiro; cuarto de estudio; (*of lions*) (Bib) fosa

denaturalize [di`nætjərə,laɪz] *tr* desnaturalizar

denatured alcohol [di`netʃərd] *s* alcohol desnaturalizado

denial [dɪ`naɪ•əl] *s* denegación; negación, desmentida

denim [`dɛnɪm] *s* dril *m* de algodón

denizen [`dɛnɪzən] *s* habitante *mf*, vecino

Denmark [`dɛnmark] *s* Dinamarca

denomination [dɪ,namɪ`neʃən] *s* denominación; categoría, clase *f;* secta, confesión, comunión

denote [dɪ`not] *tr* denotar

dénoument [denu`mã] *s* desenlace *m*

denounce [dɪ`naʊns] *tr* denunciar

dense [dɛns] *adj* denso; estúpido

densi•ty [`dɛnsɪti] *s* (*pl* **-ties**) densidad

dent [dɛnt] *s* abolladura, mella ‖ *tr* abollar, mellar ‖ *intr* abollarse, mellarse

dental [`dɛntəl] *adj & s* dental *f*

dental floss *s* hilo dental, seda encerada

dental technician *s* mecánico-dentista *m*

dentrifrice [`dɛntɪfrɪs] *s* dentífrico

dentist [`dɛntɪst] *s* dentista *mf*

dentistry [`dɛntɪstri] *s* odontología

denture [`dɛntʃər] *s* dentadura artificial

denunciation [dɪ,nʌnsɪ`eʃən] o [dɪ,nʌnʃɪ`eʃən] *s* denuncia

de•ny [dɪ`naɪ] *v* (*pret & pp* **-nied**) *tr* (*to declare not to be true*) negar; (*to refuse*) denegar; **to deny oneself to callers** negarse ‖ *intr* negar; denegar

deodorant [di`odərənt] *adj & s* desodorante *m*

deodorize [di`odə,raɪz] *tr* desodorizar

deoxidize [di`aksɪ,daɪz] *tr* desoxidar

dep. *abbr* **department, departs, deputy**

depart [dɪ`part] *intr* partir, salir, irse; desviarse

department [dɪ`partmənt] *s* departamento; (*of government*) ministerio

department store *s* grandes almacenes *mpl*

departure [dɪ`partʃər] *s* partida, salida; desviación

depend [dɪ`pɛnd] *intr* depender; **to depend on** depender de

dependable [dɪ`pɛndəbəl] *adj* confiable, fidedigno

dependence [dɪ`pɛndəns] *s* dependencia

dependen•cy [dɪ`pɛndənsi] *s* (*pl* **-cies**) dependencia; (*country, territory*) posesión

dependent [dɪ`pɛndənt] *adj* dependiente ‖ *s* carga de familia, familiar *m* dependiente

depict [dɪ`pɪkt] *tr* describir, representar, pintar

deplete [dɪ`plit] *tr* agotar, depauperar

deplorable [dɪ`plorəbəl] *adj* deplorable

deplore [dɪ`plor] *tr* deplorar

deploy [dɪ`plɔɪ] *tr* (mil) desplegar ‖ *intr* (mil) desplegarse

deployment [dɪ`plɔɪmənt] *s* (mil) despliegue *m*

depolarize [di`polə,raɪz] *tr* despolarizar

depopulate [di`papjə,let] *tr* despoblar

deport [dɪ`port] *tr* deportar; **to deport oneself** conducirse, portarse

deportation [,dipor`teʃən] *s* deportación

deportee [,dipor`ti] *s* deportado

deportment [dɪ`portmənt] *s* conducta, comportamiento

depose [dɪ`poz] *tr & intr* deponer

deposit [dɪ`pazɪt] *s* depósito; (*down payment*) señal *f*, pago anticipado; (min) yacimiento ‖ *tr* depositar ‖ *intr* depositarse

deposit account *s* cuenta corriente

depositor [dɪ`pazɪtər] *s* cuentacorrentista *mf*, imponente *mf*

depot [`dipo] o [`dɛpo] *s* almacén *m*, depósito; (mil) depósito; (rr) estación

depraved [dɪ`prevd] *adj* depravado

depravi•ty [dɪ`prævɪti] *s* (*pl* **-ties**) depravación

deprecate [`dɛprɪ,ket] *tr* desaprobar

de
de

depreciate [dɪ'priʃɪ,et] *tr* (*to lower value or price of*) depreciar; (*to disparage*) desapreciar ‖ *intr* depreciarse

depreciation [dɪ,priʃɪ'eʃən] *s* (*drop in value*) depreciación; (*disparagement*) desaprecio

depress [dɪ'prɛs] *tr* deprimir; desanimar, desalentar; bajar (*los precios*)

depression [dɪ'prɛʃən] *s* depresión; desaliento; (*slump*) crisis *f*

deprive [dɪ'praɪv] *tr* privar

deprived [dɪ'praɪvd] *adj* desventajado

dept. *abbr* **department**

depth [dɛpθ] *s* profundidad; (*of a house, of a room*) fondo; **in the depth of night** en mitad de la noche; **in the depth of winter** en pleno invierno; **to go beyond one's depth** meterse en agua demasiado profunda; (fig) meterse en honduras

depth of hold *s* (naut) puntal *m*

depu•ty ['dɛpjəti] *s* (*pl* **-ties**) diputado

derail [dɪ'rel] *tr* hacer descarrilar ‖ *intr* descarrilar

derailment [dɪ'relmənt] *s* descarrilamiento

derange [dɪ'rendʒ] *tr* desarreglar, descomponer; trastornar el juicio a

derangement [dɪ'rendʒmənt] *s* desarreglo, descompostura; locura; obfuscación

der•by ['dʌrbi] *s* (*pl* **-bies**) sombrero hongo

deregulate [di'rɛgjə,let] *tr* descontrolar

derelict ['dɛrɪlɪkt] *adj* abandonado; negligente ‖ *s* pelafustán *m;* (naut) derrelicto

deride [dɪ'raɪd] *tr* burlarse de, ridiculizar

derision [dɪ'rɪʒən] *s* burla, irrisión

derive [dɪ'raɪv] *tr & intr* derivar

dermatitis [,dʌrmə'taɪtɪs] *s* dermatitis *f*

derogatory [dɪ'rɑgə,tori] *adj* despreciativo

derrick ['dɛrɪk] *s* grúa; (min) castillete *m*

dervish ['dʌrvɪʃ] *s* derviche *m*

desalinization [dɪ,selɪnɪ'zeʃən] *s* desalinización

desalt [di'sɔlt] *tr* desalar

descend [dɪ'sɛnd] *tr* bajar, descender (*la escalera*) ‖ *intr* bajar, descender; **to descend on** caer sobre, invadir

descendant [dɪ'sɛndənt] *adj* descendente ‖ *s* descendiente *mf*

descendent [dɪ'sɛndənt] *adj* descendente

descent [dɪ'sɛnt] *s* (*passing from higher to lower state*) descenso; (*extraction; lineage*) descendencia; cuesta, bajada; invasión

describe [dɪ'skraɪb] *tr* describir

description [dɪ'skrɪpʃən] *s* descripción

descriptive [dɪ'skrɪptɪv] *adj* descriptivo

de•scry [dɪ'skraɪ] *v* (*pret & pp* **-scried**) *tr* avistar, divisar; descubrir

desecrate ['dɛsɪ,kret] *tr* profanar

desegregation [di,sɛgrɪ'geʃən] *s* desegregación

desert ['dɛzərt] *adj & s* desierto, yermo ‖ [dɪ'zʌrt] *s* mérito; **he received his just deserts** llevó su merecido ‖ *tr* desertar de ‖ *intr* desertar

deserter [dɪ'zʌrtər] *s* desertor *m*

desertion [dɪ'zʌrʃən] *s* deserción; abandono de cónyuge

deserve [dɪ'zʌrv] *tr & intr* merecer

deservedly [dɪ'zʌrvɪdli] *adv* merecidamente

design [dɪ'zaɪn] *s* diseño; (*combination of details; art of designing*) dibujo; (*plan, scheme*) designio; **to have designs on** poner la mira en ‖ *tr* deseñar, dibjuar; idear, proyectar ‖ *intr* diseñar, dibujar

designate ['dɛzɪg,net] *tr* designar

designing [dɪ'zaɪnɪŋ] *adj* intrigante, maquinador

desirable [dɪ'zaɪrəbəl] *adj* deseable

desire [dɪ'zaɪr] *s* deseo ‖ *tr* desear

desirous [dɪ'zaɪrəs] *adj* deseoso

desist [dɪ'zɪst] *intr* desistir

desk [dɛsk] *s* bufete *m*, escritorio; (*lectern*) atril *m;* (*clerk's counter in a hotel*) caja

desk clerk *s* cajero, recepcionista *m*

desk set *s* juego de escritorio

desolate ['dɛsəlɪt] *adj* (*hopeless*) desolado; despoblado, yermo, desierto; solitario; (*dismal*) lúgubre ‖ ['dɛsə,let] *tr* desconsolar; (*to lay waste*) desolar, devastar; despoblar

desolation [,dɛsə'leʃən] *s* (*devastation; great affliction*) desolación; (*dreariness*) lobreguez *f*

despair [dɪ'spɛr] *s* desesperación ‖ *intr* desesperar, desesperarse

despairing [dɪ'spɛrɪŋ] *adj* desesperado

despera•do [,dɛspə'redo] o [,dɛspə'rɑdo] *s* (*pl* **-does** o **-dos**) criminal dispuesto a todo

desperate ['dɛspərɪt] *adj* dispuesto a todo; (*bitter, excessive*) encarnizado; (*hopeless*) desesperado; (*remedy*) heroico

despicable ['dɛspɪkəbəl] *adj* despreciable, ruin

despise [dɪ'spaɪz] *tr* despreciar, desdeñar

despite [dɪ'spaɪt] *prep* a despecho de

desponden•cy [dɪ'spɑndənsi] *s* (*pl* **-cies**) abatimiento, desaliento

despondent [dɪ'spɑndənt] *adj* abatido, desalentado

despot ['dɛspət] *s* déspota *m*

despotic [dɛs'pɑtɪk] *adj* despótico

despotism ['dɛspə,tɪzəm] *s* despotismo

dessert [dɪ'zʌrt] *s* postre *m*

destination [,dɛstɪ'neʃən] *s* (*end of a journey or shipment*) destino; (*purpose*) destinación

destine ['dɛstɪn] *tr* destinar

desti•ny ['dɛstɪni] *s* (*pl* **-nies**) destino

destitute ['dɛstɪ,tjut] *adj* (*being in complete poverty*) indigente; (*lacking, deprived*) desprovisto

destitution [,dɛstɪ'tjuʃən] *s* indigencia

destroy [dɪ'strɔɪ] *tr* destruir

destroyer [dɪ'strɔɪ•ər] *s* (nav) destructor *m*

destruction [dɪ'strʌkʃən] *s* destrucción

destructive [dɪ'strʌktɪv] *adj* destructivo

desultory ['dɛsəl,tori] *adj* deshilvanado, descosido

detach [dɪ'tætʃ] *tr* desprender, separar; (mil) destacar

detachable [dɪ'tætʃəbəl] *adj* desprendible, separable; (*collar*) postizo

detached [dɪ'tætʃt] *adj* separado, suelto; imparcial, desinteresado

detachment [dɪ'tætʃmənt] *s* desprendimiento, separación; imparcialidad, desinterés *m;* (mil) destacamento

detail [dɪ'tel] o ['ditel] s detalle m, pormenor m; (mil) destacamento ‖ [dɪ'tel] tr detallar; (mil) destacar

detain [dɪ'ten] tr detener; tener preso

detect [dɪ'tɛkt] tr detectar

detection [dɪ'tɛkʃən] s detección

detective [dɪ'tɛktɪv] s detective m

detective story s novela policíaca o policial

detector [dɪ'tɛktər] s detector m

detention [dɪ'tɛnʃən] s detención

de·ter [dɪ'tʌr] v (pret & pp **-terred;** ger **-terring**) tr impedir, refrenar

detergent [dɪ'tərdʒənt] adj & s detergente m

deteriorate [dɪ'tɪrɪ·ə'ret] tr deteriorar ‖ intr deteriorarse

determination [dɪ,tʌrmə'neʃən] s resolución; empecinamiento

determine [dɪ'tʌrmɪn] tr determinar

deterrent [dɪ'tʌrənt] s impedimento, refrenamiento

detest [dɪ'tɛst] tr detestar, aborrecer

dethrone [dɪ'θron] tr destronar

detonate ['dɛtə,net] o ['ditə,net] tr hacer estallar ‖ intr detonar

detour ['ditur] o [dɪ'tur] s desvío; rodeo, vuelta; manera indirecta ‖ tr desviar (el tráfico) ‖ intr desviarse

detoxification [di,taksəfə'keʃən] s desintoxicación

detoxi·fy [di'taksə,faɪ] v (pret & pp **-fied**) tr desintoxicar

detract [dɪ'trækt] tr detraer ‖ intr — **to detract from** disminuir, rebajar

detriment ['dɛtrɪmənt] s perjuicio, detrimento; **to the detriment of** en perjuicio de

detrimental [,dɛtrɪ'mɛntəl] adj perjudicial

deuce [djus] o [dus] s (in cards) dos m; **the deuce!** ¡demonio!

devaluation [di,vælju'eʃən] s desvalorización, devaluación

devastate ['dɛvəs,tet] tr devastar

devastation [,dɛvəs'teʃən] s devastación

develop [dɪ'vɛləp] tr desarrollar, desenvolver; (phot) revelar; explotar (una mina) ‖ intr desarrollarse, desenvolverse; evolucionar, manifestarse

developer [dɪ'vɛləpər] s fomentador m; (phot) revelador m

development [dɪ'vɛləpmənt] s desarrollo, desenvolvimiento; (phot) revelado; (of a mine) explotación; acontecimiento nuevo

developmental aid [dɪ,vɛləp'mɛntəl] s ayuda al desarrollo

deviate ['divɪ,et] tr desviar ‖ intr desviarse

deviation [,divɪ'eʃən] s desviación

deviationism [,divɪ'e·ə,nɪzəm] s desviacionismo

deviationist [,divɪ'e·ənɪst] s desviacionista mf

device [dɪ'vaɪs] s dispositivo, aparato; (trick) ardid m, treta; (motto) lema m, divisa; **to leave someone to his own devices** dejarle a uno que haga lo que se le antoje

dev·il ['dɛvəl] s diablo; **between the devil and the deep blue sea** entre la espada y la pared; **to raise the devil** (slang) armar un

alboroto ‖ v (pret & pp **iled** o **-illed;** ger **-iling** o **illing**) tr condimentar con picantes; (coll) acosar, molestar

devilish ['dɛvəlɪʃ] adj diabólico

devilment ['dɛvəlmənt] s (mischief) diablura; (evil) maldad

devil·try ['dɛvəltri] s (pl **-tries**) maldad, crueldad; (mischief) diablura

devious ['divɪ·əs] adj (straying) desviado, extraviado; (roundabout; shifty) tortuoso

devise [dɪ'vaɪz] tr idear, inventar; (law) legar

devoid [dɪ'vɔɪd] adj desprovisto

devote [dɪ'vot] tr dedicar

devoted [dɪ'votɪd] adj (zealous, ardent) devoto; dedicado

devotee [,dɛvə'ti] s devoto

devotion [dɪ'voʃən] s devoción; (to study, work, etc.) dedicación; **devotions** oraciones, preces fpl

devour [dɪ'vaur] tr devorar

devout [dɪ'vaut] adj devoto; cordial, sincero

dew [dju] o [du] s rocío

dew'drop' s gota de rocío

dew'lap' s papada

dew·y ['dju·i] o ['du·i] adj rociado

dexterity [dɛks'tɛrɪti] s destreza

D.F. abbr **Defender of the Faith**

diabetes [,daɪ·ə'bitɪs] s diabetes f

diabetic [,daɪ·ə'bɛtɪk] adj & s diabético

diabolic(al) [,daɪ·ə'balɪk(əl)] adj diabólico

diacritical [,daɪ·ə'krɪtɪkəl] adj diacrítico

diadem ['daɪ·ə,dɛm] s diadema f

diaere·sis [daɪ'ɛrɪsɪs] s (pl **-ses** [,siz]) diéresis f

diagnose [,daɪ·əg'nos] tr diagnosticar

diagno·sis [,daɪ·əg'nosɪs] s (pl **-ses** [siz]) diagnosis f, diagnóstico

diagonal [daɪ'ægənəl] adj & s diagonal f

diagram ['daɪ·ə,græm] s diagrama m

dial. abbr **dialect**

dial ['daɪ·əl] s (of radio) cuadrante m; (of watch) cuadrante m, esfera, muestra; (of telephone) disco selector ‖ tr sintonizar (el radiorreceptor); marcar (el número telefónico); llamar (a una persona) por teléfono automático ‖ intr (telp) marcar

dialect ['daɪ·ə,lɛkt] s dialecto

dialing ['daɪ·əlɪŋ] s (telp) marcaje m

dialogue ['daɪ·ə,lɔg] s diálogo

dial telephone s teléfono automático

dial tone s (telp) señal f para marcar

diam. abbr **diameter**

diameter [daɪ'æmɪtər] s diámetro

diametric(al) [,daɪ·ə'mɛtrɪk(əl)] adj diamétrico

diamond ['daɪmənd] s diamante m; (figure of a rhombus) losange m; (playing card) carró m, diamante m; (baseball) losange m

diaper ['daɪpər] s pañal m

diaphanous [daɪ'æfənəs] adj diáfano

diaphragm ['daɪ·ə,fræm] s diafragma m

diarrhea [,daɪ·ə'ri·ə] s diarrea; **to have diarrhea** cursear

dia·ry ['daɪ·əri] s (pl **-ries**) diario

diastole [daɪ'æstəli] s diástole f

diathermy ['daɪ·ə,θʌrmi] s diatermia

de
di

dice [daɪs] *spl* dados; (*small cubes*) cubitos; **to load the dice** cargar los dados ‖ *tr* cortar en cubos

dice'box' *s* cubilete *m*

dichloride [daɪˈkloraɪd] *s* dicloruro

dichoto·my [daɪˈkɑtəmi] *s* (*pl* **-mies**) dicotomía

dickey [ˈdɪki] *s* camisolín *m*, pechera postiza; babero de niño

dict. *abbr* **dictionary**

dictaphone [ˈdɪktə,fon] *s* dictáfono

dictate [ˈdɪktet] *s* mandato ‖ [ˈdɪktet] o [dɪkˈtet] *tr* dictar; mandar

dictation [dɪkˈteʃən] *s* dictado; (*orders; giving orders*) mandato; **to take dictation** escribir al dictado

dictator [ˈdɪktetər] o [dɪkˈtetər] *s* dictador *m*

dictatorship [dɪkˈtetərʃɪp] *s* dictadura

diction [ˈdɪkʃən] *s* dicción

dictionar·y [ˈdɪkʃən,ɛri] *s* (*pl* **-ies**) diccionario

dic·tum [ˈdɪktəm] *s* (*pl* **-ta** [tə]) dictamen *m*; aforismo, sentencia

didactic(al) [daɪˈdæktɪk(əl)] o [dɪˈdæktɪk(əl)] *adj* didáctico

die [daɪ] *s* (*pl* **-dice** [daɪs]) dado; **the die is cast** la suerte está echada ‖ *s* (*pl* **dies**) (*for stamping coins, medals, etc.*) troquel *m*; (*for cutting threads*) hembra de terraja ‖ *v* (*pret & pp* **died;** *ger* **dying**) *intr* morir; **to be dying** estar agonizando; **to die laughing** morir de risa

die'hard' *adj & s* intransigente *mf*

die'sel-elec'tric [ˈdizəl] *adj* dieseléctrico

diesel engine *s* diesel *m*

diesel oil *s* gas-oil *m*

die'stock' *s* terraja

diet [ˈdaɪ·ət] *s* dieta, régimen alimenticio ‖ *intr* estar a dieta

dietitian [,daɪ·əˈtɪʃən] *s* dietista *mf*

diff. *abbr* **difference, different**

differ [ˈdɪfər] *intr* (*to be different*) diferir, diferenciarse; (*to dissent*) diferenciar; **to differ with** desavenirse con

difference [ˈdɪfərəns] *s* diferencia; **to make no difference** no importar; **to split the difference** partir la diferencia

different [ˈdɪfərənt] *adj* diferente

differentiate [,dɪfəˈrɛnʃi,et] *tr* diferenciar ‖ *intr* diferenciarse

difficult [ˈdɪfɪ,kʌlt] *adj* difícil

difficul·ty [ˈdɪfɪ,kʌlti] *s* (*pl* **-ties**) dificultad

diffident [ˈdɪfɪdənt] *adj* apocado, tímido

diffuse [dɪˈfjus] *adj* difuso ‖ [dɪˈfjuz] *tr* difundir ‖ *intr* difundirse

dig [dɪg] *s* (*poke*) empuje *m*; (*jibe*) pulla, palabra hiriente ‖ *v* (*pret & pp* **dug** [dʌg] o **digged;** *ger* **digging**) *tr* cavar, excavar; **to dig up** desenterrar ‖ *intr* cavar, excavar; **to dig in** (coll) poner manos a la obra; (mil) atrincherarse; **to dig under** socavar

digest [ˈdaɪdʒɛst] *s* compendio, resumen *m*; (law) digesto ‖ [dɪˈdʒɛst] o [daɪˈdʒɛst] *tr & intr* digerir

digestible [dɪˈdʒɛstɪbəl] o [daɪˈdʒɛstɪbəl] *adj* digerible, digestible

digestion [dɪˈdʒɛstʃən] o [daɪˈdʒɛstʃən] *s* digestión

digestive [dɪˈdʒɛstɪv] o [daɪˈdʒɛstɪv] *adj & s* digestivo

digit [ˈdɪdʒɪt] *s* dígito

digital telephone [ˈdɪdʒətəl] *s* teléfono digital

dignified [ˈdɪgnɪ,faɪd] *adj* digno, grave, decoroso

digni·fy [ˈdɪgnɪ,faɪ] *v* (*pret & pp* **-fied**) *tr* dignificar; engrandecer el mérito de

dignitar·y [ˈdɪgnɪ,tɛri] *s* (*pl* **-ies**) dignatario

digni·ty [ˈdɪgnɪti] *s* (*pl* **-ties**) dignidad; **to stand upon one's dignity** ponerse tan alto

digress [dɪˈgrɛs] o [daɪˈgrɛs] *intr* divagar

digression [dɪˈgrɛʃən] o [daɪˈgrɛʃən] *s* digresión, divagación

dike [daɪk] *s* dique *m*; (*bank of earth thrown up in digging*) montón *m*; (*causeway*) arrecife *m*, malecón *m*

dilapidated [dɪˈlæpɪ,detɪd] *adj* destartalado, desvencijado

dilate [daɪˈlet] *tr* dilatar ‖ *intr* dilatarse

dilatory [ˈdɪlə,tori] *adj* tardío

dilemma [dɪˈlɛmə] *s* dilema *m*, disyuntiva; encerrona

dilettan·te [,dɪləˈtænti] *adj* diletante ‖ *s* (*pl* **-tes** o **-ti** [ti]) diletante *mf*

diligence [ˈdɪlɪdʒəns] *s* diligencia; dedicación

diligent [ˈdɪlɪdʒənt] *adj* diligente

dill [dɪl] *s* eneldo

dillydal·ly [ˈdɪlɪ,dæli] *v* (*pret & pp* **-lied**) *intr* malgastar el tiempo, haraganear

dilute [dɪˈlut] o [daɪˈlut] *adj* diluído ‖ [dɪˈlut] *tr* diluir ‖ *intr* diluirse

dilution [dɪˈluʃən] *s* dilución

dim [dɪm] *adj* (*comp* **dimmer;** *super* **dimmest**) débil, indistinto, confuso; obscuro, poco claro; (*chance*) escaso; (*not clearly understanding*) torpe, lerdo; **to take a dim view of** mirar escépticamente ‖ *v* (*pret & pp* **dimmed;** *ger* **dimming**) *tr* amortiguar (*la luz*); poner (*un faro*) a media luz; disminuir ‖ *intr* obscurecerse

dime [daɪm] *s* moneda de diez centavos

dimension [dɪˈmɛnʃən] *s* dimensión

diminish [dɪˈmɪnɪʃ] *tr* disminuir ‖ *intr* disminuir, disminuirse

diminution [,dɪmɪˈnuʃən] *s* disminución

diminutive [dɪˈmɪnjətɪv] *adj* (*tiny*) diminuto; (gram) diminutivo ‖ *s* diminutivo

dimi·ty [ˈdɪmɪti] *s* (*pl* **-ties**) cotonía

dimly [ˈdɪmli] *adv* indistintamente

dimmer [ˈdɪmər] *s* amortiguador *m* de luz; (aut) lámpara de cruce, luz *f* de cruce

dimple [ˈdɪmpəl] *s* hoyuelo

dimwit [ˈdɪm,wɪt] *s* (slang) mentecato, bobo

dim-witted [ˈdɪm,wɪtɪd] *adj* (slang) mentecato, bobo

din [dɪn] *s* estruendo, ruido ensordecedor ‖ *v* (*pret & pp* **dinned;** *ger* **dinning**) *tr* ensordecer con mucho ruido; repetir insistentemente; impresionar con repetición ruidosa ‖ *intr* sonar estrepitosamente

dine [daɪn] *tr* dar de comer a; obsequiar con una cena o comida ‖ *intr* cenar, comer; **to dine out** cenar fuera de casa

diner [ˈdaɪnər] *s* invitado a una cena, convidado a una comida; coche-comedor *m*

ding-dong [ˈdɪŋˌdɔŋ] *s* dindán *m*

din·gy [ˈdɪndʒi] *adj* (*comp* **-gier;** *super* **-giest**) deslustrado, sucio

dining car *s* coche-comedor *m*

dining room *s* comedor *m*

din'ing-room' suite *s* juego de comedor

dinner [ˈdɪnər] *s* cena, comida; (*formal meal*) banquete *m*

dinner coat o **jacket** *s* smoking *m*

dinner pail *s* fiambrera, portaviandas *m*

dinner set *s* vajilla

dinner time *s* hora de la cena o comida

dint [dɪnt] *s* abolladura; **by dint of** a fuerza de ‖ *tr* abollar

diocese [ˈdaɪ·ə·sis] o [ˈdaɪ·əsis] *s* diócesi *f* o diócesis *f*

diode [ˈdaɪ·od] *s* diodo

dioxide [daɪˈɑksaɪd] *s* dióxido

dip [dɪ] *s* zambullida, inmersión; baño corto; (*in a road*) depresión; (*of magnetic needle*) inclinación ‖ *v* (*pret & pp* **dipped;** *ger* **dipping**) *tr* sumergir; sacar con cuchara; (*bread*) sopetear; **to dip the colors** saludar con la bandera ‖ *intr* sumergirse; inclinarse hacia abajo; desaparecer súbitamente; **to dip into** hojear (*un libro*); meterse en (*un comercio*); **to dip into one's purse** gastar dinero

diphtheria [dɪfˈθɪri·ə] *s* difteria

diphthong [ˈdɪfθɔŋ] *s* diptongo

diphthongize [ˈdɪfθɔŋˌgaɪz] *tr* diptongar ‖ *intr* diptongarse

diploma [dɪˈplomə] *s* diploma *m*

diploma·cy [dɪˈploməsi] *s* (*pl* **-cies**) diplomacia

diplomat [ˈdɪpləˌmæt] *s* diplomático

diplomatic [ˌdɪpləˈmætɪk] *adj* diplomático

diplomatic pouch *s* valija diplomática

dipper [ˈdɪpər] *s* cazo, cucharón *m*

dip'stick' *s* varilla de nivel

dire [daɪr] *adj* horrendo, espantoso

direct [dɪˈrɛkt] o [daɪˈrɛkt] *adj* directo; franco, sincero ‖ *tr* dirigir; mandar, ordenar

direct current *s* corriente continua

direct discourse *s* (gram) estilo directo

direct hit *s* blanco directo, impacto directo

direction [dɪˈrɛkʃən] o [daɪˈrɛkʃən] *s* dirección; instrucción; **directions** (*for use*) modo de empleo

direction light *s* (aut) intermitente *m*

direct object *s* (gram) complemento directo

director [dɪˈrɛktər] o [daɪˈrɛktər] *s* director *m*, administrador *m*; (*member of a governing body*) vocal *m*

directorship [dɪˈrɛktərˌʃɪp] o [daɪˈrɛktərˌʃɪp] *s* dirección, directorio

direc·to·ry [dɪˈrɛktəri] o [daɪˈrɛktəri] *s* (*pl* **-ries**) (*list of names and addresses; board of directors*) directorio; anuario telefónico, guía telefónica

dirge [dʌrdʒ] *s* endecha, canto fúnebre, treno; (eccl) misa de réquiem

dirigible [ˈdɪrɪdʒɪbəl] *adj & s* dirigible *m*

dirt [dʌrt] *s* (*soil*) tierra, suelo; (*dust*) polvo; (*mud*) barro, lodo; excremento; (*accumulation of dirt*) suciedad; (*moral filth*) suciedad, porquería, obscenidad; (*gossip*) chismes *mpl*

dirt'cheap' *adj* tirado, muy barato

dirt road *s* camino de tierra

dirt·y [ˈdʌrti] *adj* (*comp* **-ier;** *super* **-iest**) puerco, sucio; berroso, enlodado; polvoriento; (*obscene*) hediondo; bajo, vil ‖ *v* (*pret & pp* **-tied**) *tr* ensuciar

dirty linen *s* ropa sucia; **to air one's dirty linen in public** sacar los trapos sucios a relucir

dirty trick *s* (slang) perrada, mala partida

disabili·ty [ˌdɪsəˈbɪlɪti] *s* (*pl* **-ties**) incapacidad, inhabilidad; disminución (*física*)

disable [dɪsˈebəl] *tr* incapacitar, inhabilitar, lisiar; (law) descalificar

disabled veteran *s* lisiado de guerra

disabuse [ˌdɪsəˈbjuz] *tr* desengañar

disadvantage [ˌdɪsədˈvæntɪdʒ] o [ˌdɪsədˈvɑntɪdʒ] *s* desventaja

disadvantaged [ˌdɪsədˈvæntɪdʒd] *adj & s* desventajado

disadvantageous [dɪsˌædvənˈteʒəs] *adj* desventajoso

disagree [ˌdɪsəˈgri] *intr* desavenirse, desconvenirse; (*to quarrel*) altercar, contender; **to disagree with** no estar de acuerdo con; no sentar bien

disagreeable [ˌdɪsəˈgri·əbəl] *adj* desagradable

disagreement [ˌdɪsəˈgrimənt] *s* desavenencia, desacuerdo; disensión; inconformidad

disappear [ˌdɪsəˈpɪr] *intr* desaparecer, desaparecerse

disappearance [ˌdɪsəˈpɪrəns] *s* desaparecimiento, desaparición

disappoint [ˌdɪsəˈpɔɪnt] *tr* decepcionar, desilusionar, chasquear; **to be disappointed** chasquearse, llevarse chasco

disappointment [ˌdɪsəˈpɔɪntmənt] *s* decepción, desilusión, chasco

disapproval [ˌdɪsəˈpruvəl] *s* desaprobación

disapprove [ˌdɪsəˈpruv] *tr & intr* desaprobar

disarm [dɪsˈɑrm] *tr* desarmar ‖ *intr* desarmar, desarmarse

disarmament [dɪsˈɑrməmənt] *s* desarme *m*, desarmamiento

disarming [dɪsˈɑrmɪŋ] *adj* congraciador, simpático

disarray [ˌdɪsəˈre] *s* desorden *m;* (*in apparel*) desatavío ‖ *tr* desordenar; desataviar

disaster [dɪˈzæstər] *s* desastre *m*, siniestro

disaster area *s* zona siniestrada

disastrous [dɪˈzæstrəs] *adj* desastroso, desastrado

disavow [ˌdɪsəˈvau] *tr* desconocer, negar, repudiar

disband [dɪsˈbænd] *tr* disolver (*una asamblea*); licenciar (*tropas*) ‖ *intr* desbandarse

dis·bar [dɪsˈbɑr] *v* (*pret & pp* **-barred;** *ger* **-barring**) *tr* (law) expulsar del foro

di
di

disbelief [ˈdɪsbɪˈlif] *s* incredulidad
disbelieve [ˈdɪsbɪˈlig] *tr & intr* descreer
disburse [dɪsˈbʌrs] *tr* desembolsar
disbursement [dɪsˈbʌrsmənt] *s* desembolso
disc. *abbr* **discount, discoverer**
disc [dɪsk] *s* disco
discard [dɪsˈkɑrd] *s* descarte *m;* **to put into the discard** desechar ‖ *tr* descartar; desechar
discern [dɪˈzʌrn] o [dɪˈsʌrn] *tr* discernir, percibir
discerning [dɪˈzʌrnɪŋ] o [dɪˈsʌrnɪŋ] *adj* discerniente, perspicaz
discharge [dɪsˈtʃɑrdʒ] *s* (*of a gun, of a battery*) descarga; (*of a prisoner*) liberación; (*of a duty*) desempeño; (*of a debt, of an obligation*) descargo; (*from a job*) despedida, remoción; (mil) certificado de licencia; (pathol) derrame *m* ‖ *tr* descargar; desempeñar (*un deber*); libertar (*a un preso*); despedir, remover (*a un empleado*); (*from the hospital*) dar de alta; (mil) licenciar ‖ *intr* descargar (*un tubo, río, etc.*); descargarse (*un arma de fuego*)
disciple [dɪˈsaɪpəl] *s* discípulo
disciplinarian [ˌdɪsɪplɪˈnɛriˑən] *s* ordenancista *mf*
discipline [ˈdɪsɪplɪn] *s* disciplina; castigo ‖ *tr* disciplinar; castigar
disclaim [dɪsˈklem] *tr* desconocer, negar
disclose [dɪsˈkloz] *tr* divulgar, revelar; descubrir
disclosure [dɪsˈkloʒər] *s* divulgación, revelación; descubrimiento
disco [ˈdɪsko] *abbr* **discotheque**
discolor [dɪsˈkʌlər] *tr* descolorar ‖ *intr* descolorarse
discomfiture [dɪsˈkʌmfɪtʃər] *s* desconcierto; frustración
discomfort [dɪsˈkʌmfərt] *s* incomodidad ‖ *tr* incomodar
disconcert [ˌdɪskənˈsʌrt] *tr* desconcertar, confundir
disconnect [ˌdɪskəˈnɛkt] *tr* desunir, separar; desconectar
disconsolate [dɪsˈkɑnsəlɪt] *adj* desconsolado, desolado
discontent [ˌdɪskənˈtɛnt] *adj & s* descontento ‖ *tr* descontentar
discontented [ˌdɪskənˈtɛntɪd] *adj* descontento
discontinue [ˌdɪskənˈtɪnju] *tr* descontinuar
discord [ˈdɪskɔrd] *s* desacuerdo, discordia; discordancia
discordance [dɪsˈkɔrdəns] *s* discordancia
discotheque [ˌdɪskoˈtɛk] *s* discoteca
discount [ˈdɪskaʊnt] *s* descuento ‖ [ˈdɪskaʊnt] o [dɪsˈkaʊnt] *tr* descontar; descontar por exagerado
discount rate *s* tipo de descuento; tipo de redescuento
discourage [dɪsˈkʌrɪdʒ] *tr* desalentar, desanimar; desaprobar; disuadir
discouragement [dɪsˈkʌrɪdʒmənt] *s* desaliento; desaprobación; disuasión
discourse [ˈdɪskors] o [dɪsˈkors] *s* discurso ‖ [dɪsˈkors] *intr* discurrir
discourteous [dɪsˈkʌrtiˑəs] *adj* descortés

discourtesy [dɪsˈkʌrtəsi] *s* (*pl* **-sies**) descortesía
discover [dɪsˈkʌvər] *tr* descubrir
discovery [dɪsˈkʌvəri] *s* (*pl* **-ies**) descubrimiento
discredit [dɪsˈkrɛdɪt] *s* descrédito ‖ *tr* desacreditar
discreditable [dɪsˈkrɛdɪtəbəl] *adj* deshonroso
discreet [dɪsˈkrit] *adj* discreto
discrepancy [dɪsˈkrɛpənsi] *s* (*pl* **-cies**) discrepancia
discrete [dɪsˈkrit] *adj* discreto
discretion [dɪsˈkrɛʃən] *s* discreción; **at discretion** a discreción
discriminate [dɪsˈkrɪmɪˌnet] *intr* discriminar; **to discriminate against** discriminar
discrimination [dɪsˌkrɪmɪˈneʃən] *s* discriminación
discriminatory [dɪsˈkrɪmɪnəˌtori] *adj* discriminatorio
discus [ˈdɪskəs] *s* (sport) disco
discuss [dɪsˈkʌs] *tr & intr* discutir
discussion [dɪsˈkʌʃən] *s* discusión
discus thrower [ˈθroˑər] *s* discóbolo
disdain [dɪsˈden] *s* desdén *m* ‖ *tr* desdeñar
disdainful [dɪsˈdenfəl] *adj* desdeñoso
disease [dɪˈziz] *s* enfermedad
diseased [dɪˈzizd] *adj* morboso
disembark [ˌdɪsɛmˈbɑrk] *tr & intr* desembarcar
disembarkation [dɪsˌɛmbɑrˈkeʃən] *s* (*of passengers*) desembarco; (*of freight*) desembarque *m*
disembowel [ˌdɪsɛmˈbauˑəl] *tr* desentrañar
disenchant [ˌdɪsɛnˈtʃænt] *tr* desencantar
disenchantment [ˌdɪsɛnˈtʃæntmənt] *s* desencanto
disengage [ˌdɪsɛnˈgedʒ] *tr* (*from a pledge*) desempeñar; (*to disconnect*) desenganchar; desembragar (*el motor*)
disengagement [ˌdɪsɛnˈgedʒmənt] *s* desempeño; desenganche *m;* desembrague *m*
disentangle [ˌdɪsɛnˈtæŋgəl] *tr* desenredar
disentanglement [ˌdɪsɛnˈtæŋgəlmənt] *s* desenredo
disestablish [ˌdɪsɛsˈtæblɪʃ] *tr* separar (*la Iglesia*) del Estado
disfavor [dɪsˈfevər] *s* disfavor *m*
disfigure [dɪsˈfɪgjər] *tr* desfigurar
disfranchise [dɪsˈfræntʃaɪz] *tr* privar de los derechos de ciudadanía
disgorge [dɪsˈgɔrdʒ] *tr & intr* vomitar
disgrace [dɪsˈgres] *s* deshonra, vergüenza; disfavor *m;* metedura ‖ *tr* deshonrar, avergonzar; despedir con ignominia
disgraceful [dɪsˈgresfəl] *adj* deshonroso, vergonzoso
disgruntle [dɪsˈgrʌntəl] *tr* disgustar, enfadar
disguise [dɪsˈgaɪz] *s* disfraz *m* ‖ *tr* disfrazar
disgust [dɪsˈgʌst] *s* asco, repugnancia ‖ *tr* dar asco a, repugnar
disgusting [dɪsˈgʌstɪŋ] *adj* asqueroso, repugnante; bofe (CAm)
dish [dɪʃ] *s* (*any container used at table*) vasija; (*shallow, circular dish; its contents*) plato; **to wash the dishes** lavar la vajilla ‖ *tr* servir en un plato; (slang) arruinar

dish'cloth' s albero
dishearten [dɪs'hɑrtən] tr descorazonar, desalentar, desanimar
dishev•el [dɪ'ʃɛvəl] v (pret & pp -eled o -elled; ger -eling o -elling) desgreñar, desmelenar
dishonest [dɪs'ɑnɪst] adj no honrado, ímprobo
dishones•ty [dɪs'ɑnɪsti] s (pl -ties) falta de honradez, improbidad
dishonor [dɪs'ɑnər] s deshonra, deshonor m ‖ tr deshonrar, deshonorar; (com) no aceptar, no pagar
dishonorable [dɪs'ɑnərəbəl] adj ignominioso, deshonroso
dish'pan' s paila de lavar la vajilla
dish rack s escurreplatos m
dish'rag' s albero
dish'tow'el s paño para secar platos
dish'wash'er s (person) fregona; (machine) lavaplatos m, lavavajillas m
dish'wa'ter s agua de lavar platos, agua sucia
disillusion [,dɪsɪ'luʒən] s desilusión ‖ tr desilusionar
disillusionment [,dɪsɪ'luʒənmənt] s desilusión
disinclination [dɪs,ɪnklɪ'neʃən] s aversión, desafición
disinclined [,dɪsɪn'klaɪnd] adj desinclinado
disinfect [,dɪsɪn'fɛkt] tr desinfectar, desinficionar
disinfectant [,dɪsɪn'fɛktant] adj & s desinfectante m
disingenuous [,dɪsɪn'dʒɛnju•əs] adj insincero, poco ingenuo
disinherit [,dɪsɪn'hɛrɪt] tr desheredar
disintegrate [dɪs'ɪntɪ,gret] tr desagregar, desintegrar ‖ intr desagregarse, desintegrarse
disintegration [dɪs,ɪntɪ'greʃən] s desagregación, desintegración
disin•ter [,dɪsɪn'tʌr] v (pret & pp -terred; ger -terring) tr desenterrar
disinterested [dɪs'ɪntə,rɛstɪd] o [dɪs'ɪntrɪstɪd] adj desinteresado
disinterestedness [dɪs'ɪntə,rɛstɪdnɛs] o [dɪs'ɪntrɪstɪdnɪs] s desinterés m
disjunctive [dɪs'dʒʌŋktɪv] adj disyuntivo
disk [dɪsk] s disco
disk brake s freno de disco
disk jockey s (rad) locutor m de un programa de discos
dislike [dɪs'laɪk] s aversión, antipatía; **to take a dislike for** cobrar aversión a ‖ tr desamar
dislocate ['dɪslo,ket] tr dislocar, dislocarse (un hueso)
dislodge [dɪs'lɑdʒ] tr desalojar
disloyal [dɪs'lɔɪ•əl] adj desleal
disloyal•ty [dɪs'lɔɪ•əlti] s (pl -ties) deslealtad
dismal ['dɪzməl] adj lúgubre, tenebroso; terrible, espantoso
dismantle [dɪs'mæntəl] tr desarmar, desmontar
dismay [dɪs'me] s consternación ‖ tr consternar
dismember [dɪs'mɛmbər] tr desmembrar

dismiss [dɪs'mɪs] tr despedir, destituir; desechar; alejar del pensamiento, echar en olvido
dismissal [dɪs'mɪsəl] s despedida, destitución
dismount [dɪs'maunt] tr desmontar ‖ intr desmontarse
disobedience [,dɪsə'bidɪ•əns] s desobediencia
disobedient [,dɪsə'bidɪ•ənt] adj desobediente
disobey [,dɪsə'be] tr & intr desobedecer
disorder [dɪs'ɔrdər] s desorden m ‖ tr desordenar
disorderly [dɪs'ɔrdərli] adj desordenado; alborotador, revoltoso
disorderly conduct s conducta contra el orden público
disorderly house s burdel m, lupanar m
disorganize [dɪs'ɔrgə,naɪz] tr desorganizar
disorientation [dɪs,ɔriɛn'teʃən] s desorientación
disown [dɪs'on] tr desconocer, repudiar
disparage [dɪs'pærɪdʒ] tr desacreditar, desdorar
disparagement [dɪs'pærɪdʒmənt] s descrédito, desdoro
disparate ['dɪspərɪt] adj disparejo
dispari•ty [dɪs'pærɪti] s (pl -ties) disparidad
dispassionate [dɪs'pæʃənɪt] adj desapasionado
dispatch [dɪs'pætʃ] s despacho ‖ tr despachar; (coll) despabilar (una comida)
dis•pel [dɪs'pɛl] v (pret & pp -pelled; ger -pelling) tr desvanecer, disipar
dispensa•ry [dɪs'pɛnsəri] s (pl -ries) dispensario
dispense [dɪs'pɛns] tr dispensar (medicamentos); administrar (justicia); expender (p.ej., gasolina); (to exempt) eximir ‖ intr — **to dispense with** deshacerse de; pasar sin, prescindir de
disperse [dɪs'pʌrs] tr dispersar ‖ intr dispersarse
displace [dɪs'ples] tr remover, trasladar; despedir, deponer; reemplazar; desplazar (un volumen de agua)
displaced person s persona desplazada
display [dɪs'ple] s despliegue m; exhibición, exposición; ostentación ‖ tr (to unfold; to reveal) desplegar; (to exhibit, show) exhibir, exponer; (to show ostentatiously) ostentar
display cabinet s vitrina, escaparate m
display window s escaparate m de tienda
displease [dɪs'pliz] tr desagradar, disgustar, desplacer
displeasing [dɪs'plizɪŋ] adj desagradable
displeasure [dɪs'plɛʒər] s desagrado, disgusto, desplacer m
disposable [dɪs'pozəbəl] adj (available for any use) disponible; (made to be thrown away after serving its purpose) desechable, descartable
disposal [dɪs'pozəl] s disposición; donación, liquidación, venta; **at the disposal of** a la disposición de; **to have at one's disposal** disponer de

di
di

dispose [dɪs'poz] *tr* disponer; inducir, mover ‖ *intr* disponer; **to dispose of** disponer de; deshacerse de; dar, vender; acabar con

disposition [,dɪspə'zɪʃən] *s* disposición; índole *f*, genio, natural *m*; ajuste *m*, arreglo; venta

dispossess [,dɪspə'zɛs] *tr* desposeer; (*to evict, oust*) desahuciar

disproof [dɪs'pruf] *s* confutación, refutación

disproportionate [,dɪsprə'pərʃənɪt] *adj* desproporcionado

disprove [dɪs'pruv] *tr* confutar, refutar

dispute [dɪs'pjut] *s* disputa; **beyond dispute** sin disputa; **in dispute** disputado ‖ *tr* & *intr* disputar

disquali•fy [dɪs'kwɑlɪ,faɪ] *v* (*pret* & *pp* -**fied**) *tr* descalificar, desclasificar

disquiet [dɪs'kwaɪ•ət] *s* desasosiego, inquietud ‖ *tr* desasosegar, inquietar

disregard [,dɪsrɪ'gɑrd] *s* desatención, desaire *m* ‖ *tr* desatender, desairar, pasar por alto

disrepair [,dɪsrɪ'pɛr] *s* desconcierto, descompostura

disreputable [dɪs'rɛpjətəbəl] *adj* desacreditado, de mala fama; raído, usado, desaliñado

disrepute [,dɪsrɪ'pjut] *s* descrédito, mala fama; **to bring into disrepute** desacreditar, dar mala fama a

disrespect [,dɪsrɪ'spɛkt] *s* desacato ‖ *tr* desacatar

disrespectful [,dɪsrɪ'spɛktfəl] *adj* irrespetuoso

disrobe [dɪs'rob] *tr* desnudar ‖ *intr* desnudarse, despelotarse

disrupt [dɪs'rʌpt] *tr* romper; (*to throw into disorder*) desbaratar

dissatisfaction [,dɪssætɪs'fækʃən] *s* desagrado, descontento, insatisfacción

dissatisfied [dɪs'sætɪs,faɪd] *adj* descontento

dissatis•fy [dɪs'sætɪs,faɪ] *v* (*pret* & *pp* -**fied**) *tr* descontentar

dissect [dɪ'sɛkt] *tr* disecar

dissemble [dɪ'sɛmbəl] *tr* disimular ‖ *intr* disimular; obrar hipócritamente

disseminate [dɪ'sɛmɪ,net] *tr* diseminar, difundir

dissension [dɪ'sɛnʃən] *s* disensión

dissent [dɪ'sɛnt] *s* disensión; (*nonconformity*) disidencia ‖ *intr* disentir; (*from doctrine or authority*) disidir

dissenter [dɪ'sɛntər] *s* disidente *mf*

disservice [dɪ'sʌrvɪs] *s* deservicio

dissidence ['dɪsɪdəns] *s* disidencia

dissident ['dɪsɪdənt] *adj* & *s* disidente *mf*

dissimilar [dɪ'sɪmɪlər] *adj* disímil, desemejante

dissimilate [dɪ'sɪmɪ,let] *tr* disimilar ‖ *intr* disimilarse

dissimulate [dɪ'sɪmjə,let] *tr* & *intr* disimular

dissipate ['dɪsɪ,pet] *tr* disipar ‖ *intr* disiparse; entregarse a la disipación

dissipated ['dɪsɪ,petɪd] *adj* disipado, disoluto

dissipation [,dɪsɪ'peʃən] *s* disipación

dissociate [dɪ'soʃɪ,et] *tr* disociar

dissolute ['dɪsə,lut] *adj* disoluto

dissolution [,dɪsə'luʃən] *s* disolución

dissolve [dɪ'zɑlv] *tr* disolver ‖ *intr* (*to have the power of dissolving*) disolver; (*to pass into a liquid*) disolverse

dissonance ['dɪsənəns] *s* disonancia

dissuade [dɪ'swed] *tr* disuadir

dissyllabic [,dɪssɪ'læbɪk] *adj* disílabo, disilábico

dissyllable [dɪ'sɪləbəl] *s* disílabo

dist. *abbr* **distance, distinguish, district**

distaff ['dɪstæf] o ['dɪstɑf] *s* rueca

distaff side *s* rama femenina de la familia

distance ['dɪstəns] *s* distancia; **at a distance** a distancia; **in the distance** a lo lejos; **to keep at a distance** no permitir familiaridades; **to keep one's distance** mantenerse a distancia

distant ['dɪstənt] *adj* distante; (*relative*) lejano; (*not familiar*) frío, indiferente

distaste [dɪs'test] *s* aversión, repugnancia

distasteful [dɪs'testfəl] *adj* desagradable, repugnante

distemper [dɪs'tɛmpər] *s* enfermedad; (*of dogs*) moquillo

distend [dɪs'tɛnd] *tr* ensanchar, distender ‖ *intr* ensancharse, distender

distension [dɪs'tɛnʃən] *s* ensanche *m*, distensión

distill [dɪs'tɪl] *tr* destilar

distillation [,dɪstɪ'leʃən] *s* destilación

distiller•y [dɪs'tɪləri] *s* (*pl* -**ies**) destilería, destilatorio

distinct [dɪs'tɪŋkt] *adj* distinto; cierto, indudable; (*not blurred*) nítido, bien definido

distinction [dɪs'tɪŋkʃən] *s* distinción; (*distinguishing characteristic*) distintivo

distinctive [dɪs'tɪŋktɪv] *adj* distintivo

distinguish [dɪs'tɪŋgwɪʃ] *tr* distinguir

distinguished [dɪs'tɪŋgwɪʃt] *adj* distinguido

distort [dɪs'tɔrt] *tr* deformar, torcer; distorsionar; (*the truth*) falsear

distortion [dɪs'tɔrʃən] *s* deformación, torcimiento; (*of the truth*) falseamiento; (rad) deformación, distorsión

distract [dɪs'trækt] *tr* distraer

distraction [dɪs'trækʃən] *s* distracción

distraught [dɪs'trɔt] *adj* trastornado, perplejo, aturdido

distress [dɪs'trɛs] *s* pena, aflicción, angustia; infortunio, peligro ‖ *tr* apenar, afligir, angustiar

distressing [dɪs'trɛsɪŋ] *adj* penoso, angustioso

distress signal *s* señal *f* de socorro

distribute [dɪs'trɪbjut] *tr* distribuir, repartir

distribution [,dɪstrɪ'bjuʃən] *s* distribución, repartimiento, repartida

distributor [dɪs'trɪbjətər] *s* distribuidor *m*; (aut) distribuidor

district ['dɪstrɪkt] *s* comarca, región; (*of a city*) barrio; (*administrative division*) distrito ‖ *tr* dividir en distritos

district attorney *s* fiscal *m*

distrust [dɪs'trʌst] *s* desconfianza ‖ *tr* desconfiar de

distrustful [dɪs'trʌstfəl] *adj* desconfiado

disturb [dɪs'tʌrb] *tr* disturbar, incomodar, molestar; desordenar, revolver; inquietar,

dejar perplejo; perturbar (*el orden público*)
disturbance [dɪs'tʌrbəns] *s* disturbio, molestia; desorden *m;* inquietud; tumulto, trastorno
disuse [dɪs'jus] *s* desuso
ditch [dɪtʃ] *s* zanja ‖ *tr* zanjar; echar en una zanja; (slang) deshacerse de ‖ *intr* amarar forzosamente
ditch reed *s* carrizo
dither ['dɪðər] *s* agitación, temblor; **to be in a dither** (coll) estar muy agitado
dit•to ['dɪto] *s* (*pl* -**tos**) ídem *m; (ditto symbol)* íd.; copia, duplicado ‖ *tr* copiar, duplicar
ditto mark *s* la sigla " (*es decir:* íd.)
dit•ty ['dɪti] *s* (*pl* -**ties**) cancioneta
diuretic [,daɪə'rɛtɪk] *adj* & *s* diurético
div. *abbr* **dividend, division**
diva ['divə] *s* (mus) diva
divan ['daɪvæn] o [dɪ'væn] *s* diván *m*
dive [daɪv] *s* zambullida; (*of a submarine*) sumersión; (aer) picado; (coll) leonera, tasca ‖ *v* (*pret & pp* **dived** o **dove** [dov]) *intr* zambullirse; (*to work as a diver*) bucear; sumergirse (*un submarino*); (aer) picar
dive′-bomb′ *tr* & *intr* bombardear en picado
dive bombing *s* bombardeo en picado
diver ['daɪvər] *s* zambullidor *m;* buceador; (*person who works under water*) escafandrista *mf*, buzo; (orn) zambullidor *m*
diverge [dɪ'vʌrdʒ] o [daɪ'vʌrdʒ] *intr* divergir
divers ['daɪvərz] *adj* diversos, varios
diverse [dɪ'vʌrs] o [daɪ'vʌrs] *adj* (*different*) diverso; (*of various kinds*) variado
diversification [dɪ'vʌrsɪfɪ'keʃən] o [daɪ,vʌrsɪfɪ'keʃən] *s* diversificación
diversi•fy [dɪ'vʌrsɪ,faɪ] o [daɪ'vʌrsɪ,faɪ] *v* (*pret & pp* -**fied**) *tr* diversificar ‖ *intr* diversificarse
diversion [dɪ'vʌrʒən] o [daɪ'vʌrʒən] *s* diversión
diversi•ty [dɪ'vʌrsɪti] o [daɪ'vʌrsɪti] *s* (*pl* -**ties**) diversidad
divert [dɪ'vʌrt] o [daɪ'vʌrt] *tr* apartar, divertir; (*to entertain*) divertir, entretener; (mil) divertir
diverting [dɪ'vʌrtɪŋ] o [daɪ'vʌrtɪŋ] *adj* divertido
divest [dɪ'vɛst] o [daɪ'vɛst] *tr* desnudar; despojar, desposeer; **to divest oneself of** desposeerse de
divide [dɪ'vaɪd] *s* (geog) divisoria ‖ *tr* dividir ‖ *intr* dividirse
dividend ['dɪvɪ,dɛnd] *s* dividendo
dividers [dɪ'vaɪdərz] *spl* compás *m* de división
divination [,dɪvɪ'neʃən] *s* adivinación
divine [dɪ'vaɪn] *adj* divino ‖ *s* sacerdote *m*, clérigo ‖ *tr* adivinar
diving ['daɪvɪŋ] *s* zambullida; buceo
diving bell *s* campana de buzo
diving board *s* trampolín *m*
diving suit *s* escafandra
divining rod [dɪ'vaɪnɪŋ] *s* vara de adivinar; (*ostensibly to discover water or metals*) vara buscadora

divini•ty [dɪ'vɪnɪti] *s* (*pl* -**ties**) divinidad; teología; **the Divinity** Dios *m*
division [dɪ'vɪʒən] *s* división
divisor [dɪ'vaɪzər] *s* (math) divisor *m*
divorce [dɪ'vors] *s* divorcio; **to get a divorce** divorciarse ‖ *tr* divorciar (*los cónyuges*); divorciarse de (*la mujer o el marido*) ‖ *intr* divorciarse
divorcee [dɪvor'si] *s* persona divorciada; mujer divorciada
divulge [dɪ'vʌldʒ] *tr* divulgar, revelar
dizziness ['dɪzɪnɪs] *s* vértigo; confusión, perplejidad
diz•zy ['dɪzi] *adj* (*comp* -**zier;** *super* -**ziest**) (*suffering or causing dizziness*) vertiginoso; confuso, perplejo; aturdido, incauto; (coll) tonto
do. *abbr* **ditto**
do [du] *v* (*tercera persona* **does** [dʌz]; *pret* **did** [dɪd]; *pp* **done** [dʌn]) *tr* hacer; resolver (*un problema*); recorrer (*cierta distancia*); cumplir con (*un deber*); aprender (*una lección*); componer (*la cama*); tocar (*el cabello*); rendir (*homenaje*); **to do one's best** hacer todo lo posible; **to do over** volver a hacer; repetir; renovar; **to do right by** tratar bien; **to do someone out of something** (coll) defraudar algo a alguien; **to do to death** despachar, matar; **to do up** empaquetar; poner en orden; almidonar y planchar (*una camisa*) ‖ *intr* actuar, obrar; conducirse; servir, ser suficiente; estar, hallarse; **how do you do?** ¿cómo está Vd.?; **that will do** eso sirve, eso es bastante; no digas más; **to have done** haber terminado; **to have done with** no tener más que ver con; **to have nothing to do with** no tener nada que ver con; **to have to do with** tratar de; **to do away with** suprimir; matar; **to do for** servir para; **to do well** salir bien; **to do without** pasar sin ‖ *v aux* úsase 1) en oraciones interrogativas: **Do you speak Spanish?** ¿Habla Vd. español?; 2) en oraciones negativas; **I do not speak Spanish** No hablo español; 3) para substituir a otro verbo en oraciones elípticas; **Did you go to church this morning? Yes, I did** ¿Fué Vd. a la iglesia esta mañana? Sí, fuí; 4) para dar más energía a la oración; **I do believe what you told me** Yo sí creo lo que me dijo Vd.; 5) en inversiones después de ciertos adverbios; **Seldom does he come to see me** él rara vez viene a verme; 6) en tono suplicante con el imperativo; **Do come in** pase Vd., por favor
docile ['dɑsɪl] *adj* dócil
dock [dɑk] *s* (*wharf*) muelle *m;* (*waterway between two piers*) dársena; (*area including piers and waterways*) puerto de mar; muñón *m* de cola; (law) tribuna de los acusados ‖ *tr* (naut) atracar en el muelle; derrabar, descolar (*a un animal*); reducir o suprimir (*el salario*) ‖ *intr* (naut) atracar
dockage ['dɑkɪdʒ] *s* entrada en un puerto; (*charges*) muellaje *m*

di
do

docket ['dɑkɪt] *s* actas, orden *m* del día; lista de causas pendientes; **on the docket** (coll) pendiente, entre manos

dock hand *s* portuario

dock'yard' *s* arsenal *m*, astillero

doctor ['dɑktər] *s* doctor *m;* (*physician*) médico ‖ *tr* medicinar; (coll) componer, reparar ‖ *intr* (coll) ejercer la medicina; (coll) tomar medicinas

doctorate ['dɑktərɪt] *s* doctorado

doctrine ['dɑktrɪn] *s* doctrina

document ['dɑkjəmənt] *s* documento ‖ ['dɑkjə,mɛnt] *tr* documentar

documenta·ry [,dɑkjə'mɛntəri] *adj* documental ‖ *s* (*pl* -ries) documental *m*

documentation [,dɑkəmɛn'teʃən] *s* documentación

doddering ['dɑdərɪŋ] *adj* chocho, temblón

dodge [dɑdʒ] *s* esguince *m*, regate *m;* (fig) regate ‖ *tr* evitar (*un golpe*); (fig) evitar mañosamente ‖ *intr* regatear, hurtar el cuerpo; **to dodge around the corner** voltear la esquina

do-do ['dodo] *s* (*pl* -dos o -does) (coll) inocente *m* de ideas anticuadas

doe [do] *s* cierva, gama, coneja

doeskin ['do,skɪn] *s* ante *m*, piel *f* de ante; tejido fino de lana

doff [dɑf] o [dɔf] *tr* quitarse (*el sombrero, la ropa*)

dog [dɔg] o [dɑg] *s* perro; **to go to the dogs** darse al abandono; **lucky dog** (coll) lechero, suertero; **to put on the dog** (coll) darse ínfulas ‖ *v* (*pret & pp* **dogged;** *ger* **dogging**) *tr* acosar, perseguir

dog'catch'er *s* lacero

dog days *spl* canícula, canicularse *mpl*

doge [dodʒ] *s* dux *m*

dogged ['dɔgɪd] *adj* tenaz, terco

doggerel ['dɔgərəl] *s* coplas de ciego

dog·gy ['dɔgi] *adj* (*comp* -gier; *super* -giest) emperejilado ‖ *s* (*pl* -gies) perrito

dog'house' *s* perrera

dog in the manger *s* el perro del hortelano

dog Latin *s* latinajo, latín *m* de cocina

dogmatic [dɑg'mætɪk] *adj* dogmático; ergotista

dog racing *s* carreras de galgos

dog's-ear ['dɔgzɛɪr] *s* orejón *m*

dog show *s* exposición canina

dog's life *s* vida miserable

Dog Star *s* Canícula

dog'-tired' *adj* cansadísimo

dog'tooth' *s* (*pl* -teeth [,tiθ]) colmillo

dog track *s* galgódromo

dog'watch' *s* (naut) guardia de cuartillo

dog'wood' *s* cornejo

doi·ly ['dɔɪli] *s* (*pl* -lies) pañito de adorno

doings ['duɪŋz] *spl* acciones, obras, actividad

doldrums ['dɑldrəmz] *spl* (naut) calmas ecuatoriales; desanimación, inactividad

dole [dol] *s* limosna; subsidio a los desocupados ‖ *tr* — **to dole out** distribuir en pequeñas porciones

doleful ['dolfəl] *adj* triste, lúgubre

doll [dɑl] *s* muñeca ‖ *intr* — **to doll up** (slang) emperejilarse

dollar ['dɑlər] *s* dólar *m*

dollar mark *s* signo del dólar

dol·ly ['dɑli] *s* (*pl* -lies) muñequita; (*low, wheeled frame for moving heavy loads*) gato rodante

dolphin ['dɑlfɪn] *s* delfín *m*

dolt [dolt] *s* bobalicón *m*

doltish ['doltʃ] *adj* bobalicón

dom. *abbr* **domestic, dominion**

domain [do'men] *s* dominio, heredad, propiedad; (*of learning*) campo

dome [dom] *s* cúpula, domo

dome light *s* (aut) lámpara de techo

domestic [də'mɛstɪk] *adj & s* doméstico

domesticate [də'mɛstɪ,ket] *tr* domesticar

domicile ['dɑmɪsɪl] o ['dɑmɪ,saɪl] *s* domicilio ‖ *tr* domiciliar

dominance ['dɑmɪnəns] *s* dominación

dominant ['dɑmɪnənt] *adj & s* dominante *f*

dominate ['dɑmɪ,net] *tr & intr* dominar

domination [,dɑmɪ'neʃən] *s* dominación

domineer [,dɑmɪ'nɪr] *intr* dominar

domineering [,dɑmɪ'nɪrɪŋ] *adj* dominante, mandón

Dominican [də'mɪnɪkən] *adj & s* dominicano

dominion [də'mɪnjən] *s* dominio

domi·no ['dɑmɪ,no] *s* (*pl* -noes o -nos) (*costume*) dominó *m*; antifaz *m*; persona que lleva dominó; ficha (*del juego de dominó*); **dominoes** *ssg* dominó (*juego*)

don [dɑn] *s* caballero, señor *m*, personaje *m* de alta categoría; (coll) preceptor *m*, socio de uno de los colegios de las Universidades de Oxford y Cambridge ‖ *v* (*pret & pp* **donned;** *ger* **donning**) *tr* ponerse (*el sombrero, la ropa*)

donate ['donet] *tr* dar, donar

donation [do'neʃən] *s* donación

done [dʌn] *adj* hecho, terminado; cansado, rendido; bien asado

done for *adj* (coll) cansado, rendido, agotado; (coll) arruinado, destruído; (coll) fuera de combate; (coll) muerto

donjon ['dʌndʒən] *s* torre *f* del homenaje

donkey ['dɑŋki] *s* asno, burro

donnish ['dɑnɪʃ] *adj* magistral, pedantesco

donor ['donər] *s* donador *m*

doodle ['dudəl] *tr & intr* borrajear

doom [dum] *s* ruina, perdición, muerte *f;* condena, juicio; juicio final; hado, destino ‖ *tr* condenar; sentenciar a muerte; predestinar a la ruina, a la muerte

doomsday ['dumz,de] *s* día *m* del juicio final; día del juicio

door [dor] *s* puerta; (*of a carriage or automobile*) portezuela; (*one part of a double door*) hoja, batiente *m;* **behind closed doors** a puertas cerradas; **to see to the door** acompañar a la puerta

door'bell' *s* campanilla de puerta, timbre *m* de puerta

door check *s* amortiguador *m*, cierre *m* de puerta

door′frame′ s bastidor m de puerta, marco de puerta

door′head′ s dintel m

door′jamb′ s jamba de puerta

door′knob′ s botón m de puerta, pomo de puerta

door knocker s aldaba

door latch s pestillo

door•man ['dormən] s (pl -men [mən]) portero; (one who helps people in and out of cars) abrecoches m

door′mat′ s felpudo de puerta

door′nail′ s clavo de adorno para puertas; **dead as a doornail** (coll) muerto sin duda alguna

door′post′ s jamba de puerta

door scraper s limpiabarros m

door′sill′ s umbral m

door′step′ s escalón m delante de la puerta; escalera exterior

door′stop′ s tope m de puerta

door′way′ s puerta, portal m

dope [dop] s grasa lubricante; (aer) barniz m, nobabia; (slang) bobo, tonto; (slang) informes mpl; (slang) narcótico ‖ tr (slang) narcotizar, drogar; **to dope out** (slang) descifrar

dope fiend s (slang) toxicómano

dope sheet s (slang) hoja confidencial sobre los caballos de carreras

dormant ['dɔrmənt] adj durmiente, latente

dormer window ['dɔrmər] s buharda, buhardilla

dormito•ry ['dɔrmɪ,tori] s (pl -ries) dormitorio común

dor•mouse ['dɔr,maʊs] s (pl -mice [,maɪs]) lirón m

dosage ['dosɪdʒ] s dosificación

dose [dos] s dosis f; (coll) mal trago ‖ tr medicinar; dosificar (un medicamento)

dossier ['dɑsɪ,e] s expediente m

dot [dɑt] s punto; **on the dot** (coll) en punto ‖ v (pret & pp **dotted**; ger **dotting**) tr (to make with dots) puntear; poner punto a; **to dot one's i's** poner los puntos sobre las íes

dotage ['dotɪdʒ] s chochera, chochez f; **to be in one's dotage** chochear

dotard ['dotərd] s viejo chocho

dote [dot] intr chochear; **to dote on** estar chocho por

doting ['dotɪŋ] adj chocho

dots and dashes spl (telg) puntos y rayas

dotted line ['dɑtɪd] s línea de puntos; **to sign on the dotted line** firmar ciegamente

double ['dʌbəl] adj doble ‖ adv doble; dos juntos ‖ s doble m, duplo m; (mov, theat) doble mf; **doubles** (tennis juego de dobles ‖ tr doblar; ser el doble de; (bridge) doblar ‖ intr doblarse; (mov, theat, bridge) doblar; **to double up** doblarse en dos; ocupar una misma habitación, dormir en una misma cama (dos personas)

double-barreled ['dʌbəl'bærəld] adj de dos cañones; (fig) para dos fines

double bass [bes] s contrabajo

double bassoon s contrabajón m

double bed s cama de matrimonio

double-breasted ['dʌbəl'brɛstɪd] adj cruzado, de dos pechos

double chin s papada

dou′ble-cross′ tr traicionar (a un cómplice)

double date s cita de dos parejas

doub′le-deal′er s persona doble

double-edged ['dʌbəl'ɛdʒd] adj de dos filos

double entry s (com) partida doble

double feature s (mov) programa m doble, programa de dos películas de largo metraje

doubleheader ['dʌbəl'hɛdər] s tren m con dos locomotoras; (baseball) dos partidos jugados sucesivamente

double-jointed ['dʌbəl'dʒɔɪntɪd] adj de articulaciones dobles

dou′ble-park′ tr & intr aparcar en doble fila

dou′ble-quick′ adj & adv a paso ligero ‖ s paso ligero ‖ intr marchar a paso ligero

doublet ['dʌblɪt] s (close-fitting jacket) jubón m; (counterfeit stone; each of two words having the same origin) doblete m

double talk s (coll) galimatías m; (coll) habla ambigua para engañar

double time s pago doble por horas extraordinarias de trabajo; (mil) paso redoblado

doubleton ['dʌbəltən] s doblete m

double track s doble vía

doubling ['dʌblɪŋ] s reduplicación

doubt [daʊt] s duda; **beyond doubt** sin duda; **if in doubt** en caso de duda; **no doubt** sin duda ‖ tr dudar, dudar de ‖ intr dudar

doubter ['daʊtər] s incrédulo

doubtful ['daʊtfəl] adj dudoso

doubtless ['daʊtlɪs] adj indudable ‖ adv sin duda; probablemente

douche [duʃ] s ducha; (instrument) jeringa ‖ tr duchar ‖ intr ducharse

dough [do] s masa, pasta; (money) (slang) pasta

dough′boy′ s (coll) soldado norteamericano de infantería

dough′nut′ s rosquilla, buñuelo

dough•ty ['daʊti] adj (comp -tier; super -tiest) (hum) fuerte, valiente

dough•y ['do•i] adj (comp -ier; super -iest) pastoso

dour [daʊr] o [dʊr] adj triste, melancólico, austero

douse [daʊs] tr empapar, mojar, salpicar; (slang) apagar (la luz)

dove [dʌv] s paloma

dovecote ['dʌv,kot] s palomar m

dove′tail′ s cola de milano, cola de pato ‖ tr ensamblar a cola de milano, ensamblar a cola de pato; (to make fit) encajar ‖ intr (to fit) encajar; concordar, corresponder

dowager ['daʊ•ədʒər] s viuda con título o bienes que proceden del marido, p.ej., **dowager duchess** duquesa viuda; (coll) matrona, señora anciana respetable

dow•dy ['daʊdi] adj (comp -dier; super -diest) desaliñado

dow•el ['daʊ•əl] s clavija ‖ v (pret & pp -eled o -elled; ger -eling o -elling) tr enclavijar

dower ['daʊ•ər] s (widow's portion) viudedad; (marriage portion) dote m & f; (natu-

ral gift) prenda ‖ *tr* señalar viudedad a; dotar

down [daʊn] *adj* descendente; abatido, triste; enfermo, malo; acostado, echado; (*money, payment*) anticipado; (*storage battery*) agotado; (mach) (coll) fuera de servicio ‖ *adv* abajo; hacia abajo; en tierra; al sur; por escrito; al contado; **down and out** arruinado; sin blanca; **down from** desde; **down on one's knees** de rodillas; **down to** hasta; **down under** entre los antípodas; **down with . . . !** ¡abajo . . . !; **to get down to work** aplicarse resueltamente al trabajo; **to go down** bajar; **to lie down** acostarse; **to sit down** sentarse ‖ *prep* bajando; **down the river** río abajo; **down the street** calle abajo ‖ *s* (*of fruit and human body*) vello; (*of birds*) plumón *m;* descenso, revés *m* de fortuna; (*sand hill*) duna ‖ *tr* derribar; (coll) tragar

down'cast' *adj* cariacontecido

down'fall' *s* caída, ruina; chaparrón *m;* nevazo

down'grade' *adj* (coll) pendiente, en declive ‖ *adv* (coll) cuesta abajo ‖ *s* bajada, declive *m;* **to be on the downgrade** decaer, declinar ‖ *tr* disminuir la categoría de

downhearted ['daʊn,hɑrtɪd] *adj* abatido, desanimado

down'hill' *adj* pendiente ‖ *adv* cuesta abajo; **to go downhill** ir cabeza abajo

down'pour' *s* aguacero, chaparrón *m*

down'right' *adj* absoluto, categórico; franco; claro ‖ *adv* absolutamente

down'stairs' *adj* de abajo ‖ *adv* abajo ‖ *s* piso inferior, pisos inferiores; (*the help*) la servidumbre

down'stream' *adv* aguas abajo, río abajo

down'stroke' *s* carrera descendente

down'town' *adj* céntrico ‖ *adv* al centro de la ciudad, en el centro de la ciudad ‖ *s* barrios céntricos, calles céntricas

down train *s* tren *m* descendente

down'trend' *s* tendencia a la baja

downtrodden ['daʊn,trɑdən] *adj* pisoteado, oprimido

downward ['daʊnwərd] *adj* descendente ‖ *adv* hacia abajo; hacia una época posterior

down•y ['daʊni] *adj* (*comp* **-ier;** *super* **-iest**) plumoso, felpudo, velloso; suave, blando

dow•ry ['daʊri] *s* (*pl* **-ries**) dote *m & f*

doz. *abbr* **dozen**

doze [doz] *s* duermevela, sueño ligero ‖ *intr* dormitar

dozen ['dʌzən] *s* docena

dozy ['dozi] *adj* soñoliento

D.P. *abbr* **displaced person**

dpt. *abbr* **department**

dr. *abbr* **debtor, drawer, dram**

Dr. *abbr* **debtor, Doctor**

drab [dræb] *adj* (*comp* **drabber;** *super* **drabbest**) gris amarillento; monótono ‖ *s* gris amarillento; ramera; mujer desaliñada

drach•ma ['drækmə] *s* (*pl* **-mas** o **-mae** [mi]) dracma

draft [dræft] *s* corriente *f* de aire; (*pulling; current of air in a chimney*) tiro; (*sketch,*

outline) bosquejo; (*first form of a writing*) borrador *m;* (*drink*) bebida, trago; (com) giro, letra de cambio, libranza; aire inspirado; (naut) calado; (mil) conscripción, quinta; **drafts** damas, juego de damas; **on draft** a presión; **to be exempted from the draft** redimirse de las quintas ‖ *tr* dibujar; bosquejar; hacer un borrador de; redactar (*un documento*); (mil) quintar; **to be drafted** (mil) ir a quintas

draft age *s* edad *f* de quintas

draft beer *s* cerveza a presión

draft board *s* (mil) junta de reclutamiento

draft call *s* llamada a quintas

draft dodger ['dɑdʒər] *s* emboscado

draftee [,dræf'ti] *s* conscripto, quinto

draft horse *s* caballo de tiro

drafting room *s* sala de dibujo

drafts•man ['dræftsmən] *s* (*pl* **-men** [mən]) dibujante *m;* (*man who draws up documents*) redactor *m;* (*in checkers*) peón *m*

draft treaty *s* proyecto de convenio

draft•y ['dræfti] *adj* (*comp* **-ier;** *super* **-iest**) airoso, con corrientes de aire

drag [dræg] *s* (*sledge for conveying heavy bodies*) narria; (*on a cigarette*) chupada; fumada; (naut) rastra; (aer) resistencia al avance; (fig) estorbo, impedimento; **to have a drag** (slang) tener buenas aldabas, tener enchufe ‖ *v* (*pret & pp* **dragged;** *ger* **dragging**) *tr* arrastrar; (naut) rastrear ‖ *intr* arrastrarse por el suelo; avanzar muy lentamente; decaer (*el interés*); **to drag on** ser interminable, prolongarse interminablemente

drag'net' *s* red barredera

dragon ['drægən] *s* dragón *m*

drag'on-fly' *s* (*pl* **-flies**) caballito del diablo, libélula

dragoon [drə'gun] *s* (*soldier*) dragón *m* ‖ *tr* tiranizar; forzar, constreñir

drain [dren] *s* dren *m,* desaguadero, desagüe *m;* (surg) dren *m;* (*source of continual expense*) (fig) desaguadero ‖ *tr* drenar, desaguar; avenar (*terrenos húmedos*); escurrir (*una vasija; un líquido*) ‖ *intr* desaguarse; escurrirse

drainage ['drenɪdʒ] *s* drenaje *m,* desagüe *m*

drain'board' *s* escurridero

drain cock *s* llave *f* de purga

drain'pipe' *s* tubo de desagüe, escurridero

drain plug *s* tapón *m* de desagüe; (aut) tapón de vaciado

drake [drek] *s* pato

dram [dræm] *s* dracma; trago de aguardiente

drama ['drɑmə] o ['dræmə] *s* drama *m;* (*art and genre*) dramática

dramatic [drə'mætɪk] *adj* dramático ‖ **dramatics** *ssg* representación de aficionados; *spl* obras representadas por aficionados

dramatist ['dræmətɪst] *s* dramático

dramatize ['dræmə,taɪz] *tr* dramatizar

dram'shop' *s* bar *m,* taberna

drape [drep] *s* cortina, colgadura; (*hang of a curtain, skirt, etc.*) caída ‖ *tr* cubrir con colgaduras; adornar con colgaduras; disponer los pliegues de (*una colgadura, una prenda de vestir*)

draper·y ['drepəri] *s* (*pl* **-ies**) colgaduras, ropaje *m*

drastic ['dræstɪk] *adj* drástico

draught [dræft] *s & tr* var de **draft**

draught beer *s* cerveza a presión

draw [drɔ] *s* (*in a game or other contest*) empate *m;* (*in chess or checkers*) tablas; (*in a lottery*) sorteo; (*card drawn from the bank*) robo; (*of a drawbridge*) compuerta; (*of a chimney*) tiro ‖ *v* (*pret* **drew** [dru]; *pp* **drawn** [drɔn]) *tr* tirar (*una línea; alambre*); (*to attract*) tirar; (*to pull*) tirar de; derretir (*la mantequilla*); sacar (*un clavo, una espada, agua, una conclusión*); atraerse (*aplausos*); atraer (*a la gente*); aspirar (*el aire*); llamar (*la atención*); dar (*un suspiro*); correr (*una cortina*); cobrar (*un salario*); sacarse (*un premio*); empatar (*una partida*); robar (*fichas, naipes*); levantar (*un puente levadizo*); calar (*un buque cierta profundidad*); hacer (*una comparación*); consumir (*amperios*); (*to sketch in lines*) dibujar; (*to sketch in words*) redactar; (*com*) girar, librar; (*com*) devengar (*interés*); **to draw forth** hacer salir; **to draw off** sacar, extraer; trasegar (*un líquido*); **to draw on** ocasionar, provocar; ponerse (*p.ej., los zapatos*); (*com*) girar a cargo de; **to draw oneself up** enderezarse con dignidad; **to draw out** (*to persuade to talk*) sonsacar, tirar de la lengua a; **to draw up** redactar (*un documento*); (*mil*) ordenar para el combate ‖ *intr* tirar, tirar bien (*una chimenea*); empatar; echar suertes; atraer mucha gente; dibujar; **to draw aside** apartarse; **to draw back** retroceder, retirarse; **to draw near** acercarse; acercarse a; **to draw to a close** estar para terminar; **to draw together** juntarse, unirse

draw'back' *s* desventaja, inconveniente *m*

draw'bridge' *s* puente levadizo

drawee [,drɔ'i] *s* girado, librado

drawer ['drɔ·ər] *s* dibujante *mf;* (*com*) girador *m*, librador *m* ‖ [drɔr] *s* cajón *m*, gaveta; **drawers** calzoncillos

drawing ['drɔ·ɪŋ] *s* dibujo; (*in a lottery*) sorteo

drawing board *s* tablero de dibujo

drawing card *s* polo de atracción popular

drawing room *s* sala, salón *m*

draw'knife' *s* (*pl* **-knives** [,naɪvz]) cuchilla de dos mangos

drawl [drɔl] *s* habla lenta y prolongada ‖ *tr* decir lenta y prolongadamente ‖ *intr* hablar lenta y prolongadamente

drawn butter [drɔn] *s* mantequilla derretida

drawn work *s* calado, deshilado

dray [dre] *s* carro fuerte, camión *m;* (*sledge*) narria

drayage ['dre·ɪdʒ] *s* acarreo

dread [drɛd] *adj* espantoso, terrible ‖ *s* pavor *m*, terror *m* ‖ *tr & intr* temer

dreadful ['drɛdfəl] *adj* espantoso, terrible; (*coll*) feo, desagradable

dread'naught' *s* (*nav*) gran buque acorazado

dream [drim] *s* sueño, ensueño; (*thing of great beauty*) sueño; (*fancy, illusion*) ensueño; **dream come true** sueño hecho realidad ‖ *v* (*pret & pp* **dreamed** o **dreamt** [drɛmt]) *tr* soñar; **to dream up** (*coll*) imaginar, inventar; ‖ *intr* soñar; **to dream of** soñar con

dreamer ['drimər] *s* soñador *m*

dream'land' *s* reino del ensueño

dream'world' *s* tierra de la fantasía

dream·y ['drimi] *adj* (*comp* **-ier;** *super* **-iest**) soñador; visionario; vago

drear·y ['drɪri] *adj* (*comp* **-ier;** *super* **-iest**) sombrío, triste; monótono, pesado

dredge [drɛdʒ] *s* draga ‖ *tr* dragar, rastrear; (*culin*) enharinar

dredger ['drɛdʒər] *s* draga (*barco*)

dredging ['drɛdʒɪŋ] *s* dragado

dregs [drɛgz] *spl* heces *fpl;* (*of society*) hez *f*

drench [drɛntʃ] *tr* mojar, empapar

dress [drɛs] *s* ropa, vestidos; vestido de mujer; (*skirt*) falda; traje *m* de etiqueta; (*of a bird*) plumaje *m* ‖ *tr* vestir; (*to provide with clothing*) trajear; peinar (*el pelo*); curar (*una herida*); zurrar (*el cuero*); empavesar (*un barco*); adornar, ataviar; aderezar, aliñar (*los manjares*); **to dress down** (*coll*) reprender; **to get dressed** vestirse ‖ *intr* (*to put one's clothing on*) vestirse; (*to wear clothes*) vestir; (*mil*) alinearse; **to dress up** vestirse de etiqueta; ponerse de veinticinco alfileres; disfrazarse

dress ball *s* baile *m* de etiqueta

dress coat *s* frac *m*

dresser ['drɛsər] *s* tocador *m;* cómoda con espejo; (*sideboard*) aparador *m;* **to be a good dresser** vestir con elegancia

dress form *s* maniquí *m*

dress goods *spl* géneros para vestidos

dressing ['drɛsɪŋ] *s* adorno; (*for food*) aliño, salsa; (*stuffing for fowl*) relleno; (*fertilizer*) abono; (*for a wound*) vendaje *m*

dress'ing-down' *s* (*coll*) repasata, regaño

dressing gown *s* bata, peinador *m*

dressing room *s* cuarto de vestir; (*theat*) camarín *m*

dressing station *s* (*mil*) puesto de socorro

dressing table *s* tocador *m;* peinador *m*

dress'mak'er *s* costurera, modista

dress'mak'ing *s* costura, modistería

dress rehearsal *s* ensayo general

dress shirt *s* camisa de pechera almidonada, camisa de pechera de encaje

dress shop *s* casa de modas

dress suit *s* traje *m* de etiqueta

dress tie *s* corbata de smoking, corbata de frac

dress·y ['drɛsi] *adj* (*comp* **-ier;** *super* **-iest**) (*coll*) elegante; (*showy*) acicalado, vistoso, peripuesto

dribble ['drɪbəl] *s* goteo; (*coll*) llovizna ‖ *tr* (*sport*) driblar ‖ *intr* gotear; (*at the mouth*) babear; (*sport*) driblar

driblet ['drɪblɪt] *s* gotita; pedacito

dried beef [draɪd] *s* cecina

dried fig *s* higo paso

dried peach *s* orejón *m*

do
dr

drier [ˈdraɪ•ər] s enjugador m; (for hair) secador m; (for clothes) secadora; (rack for drying clothes) tendedero (de ropa)

drift [drɪft] s movimiento; (of sand, snow) montón m; (movement of snow) ventisca; tendencia, dirección; intención, sentido; (aer, naut) deriva; (rad, telv) desviación || intr flotar a la deriva; amontonarse (la nieve); ventiscar; (aer, naut) derivar, ir a la deriva; (fig) vivir sin rumbo

drift ice s hielo flotante

drift′wood′ s madera flotante; madera llevada por el agua; madera arrojada a la playa por el agua; (people) vagos

drill [drɪl] s taladro; instrucción; (fabric) dril m; (mil) ejercicio || tr taladrar; instruir; (mil) enseñar el ejercicio a || intr adiestrarse; (mil) hacer el ejercicio

drill′mas′ter s amaestrador m; (mil) instructor m

drill press s prensa taladradora

drink [drɪŋk] s bebida; **the drinks are on the house!** ¡convida la casa! || v (pret **drank** [dræŋk]; pp **drunk** [drʌŋk]) tr beber; beberse (su sueldo); **to drink down** beber de una vez; **to drink in** beber (las palabras de una persona); beberse (un libro); aspirar (el aire) || intr beber; **to drink out of** beber de o en; **to drink to the health of** beber a o por la salud de

drinkable [ˈdrɪŋkəbəl] adj bebedizo, potable

drinker [ˈdrɪŋkər] s bebedor m

drinking [ˈdrɪŋkɪŋ] s (el) beber

drinking cup s taza para beber

drinking fountain s fuente f para beber

drinking song s canción báquica, canción de taberna

drinking spree s bebezón m; bimba (Mex)

drinking trough s abrevadero

drinking water s agua para beber

drip [drɪp] s goteo; gotas || v (pret & pp **dripped**; ger **dripping**) intr caer gota a gota, gotear

drip coffee s café m de maquinilla

drip′-dry′ adj de lava y pon

drip pan s colector m de aceite

drive [draɪv] s paseo en coche; calzada; fuerza, vigor m; urgencia; campaña vigorosa; venta a bajo precio; (aut) tracción (delantera o trasera); (mach) transmisión, mando || v (pret **drove** [drov]; pp **driven** [ˈdrɪvən]) tr conducir, guiar, manejar (un automóvil); clavar, hincar (un clavo); arrear (a las bestias); (in a carriage or auto) llevar (a una persona); empujar, impeler; estimular; forzar, compeler; obligar a trabajar mucho; (sport) golpear con gran fuerza; **to drive away** ahuyentar; **to drive away** ahuyentar; **to drive back** rechazar; **to drive mad** volver loco || intr ir en coche; **to drive at** aspirar a; querer decir; **to drive hard** trabajar mucho; **to drive in** entrar en coche; entrar en (un sitio) en coche; **to drive on the right** circular por la derecha; **to drive out** salir en coche; **to drive up** llegar en coche

drive-in restaurant [ˈdraɪv،ɪn] s parador m de carretera

drive-in theater s auto-teatro, motocine m; autocine m (Chile, Cuba); autocínema f (Mex)

driv•el [ˈdrɪvəl] s (slobber) baba; (nonsense) bobería || v (pret **-eled** o **-elled**; ger **eling** o **-elling**) intr babear; (to talk nonsense) bobear

driver [ˈdraɪvər] s conductor m; (of a carriage) cochero; (of a locomotive) maquinista m; (of pack animals) arriero

driver's license s carnet m de chófer, permiso de conducir

drive shaft s árbol m de mando, eje m motor

drive′way′ s calzada; camino de entrada para coches

drive wheel s rueda motriz

drive′-your•self′ service s alquiler m sin chófer

driving school s auto-escuela

drizzle [ˈdrɪzəl] s llovizna || intr lloviznar, garnar

droll [drol] adj chusco, gracioso

dromedar•y [ˈdrɑmə،dɛri] s (pl **-ies**) dromedario

drone [dron] s zángano; (buzz, hum) zumbido; (of bagpipe) bordón m, roncón m; avión radiodirigido || tr decir monótonamente || intr hablar monótonamente; (to live in idleness) zanganear; (to buzz, hum) zumbar

drool [drul] s (slobber) baba; (slang) bobería || intr babear; (slang) bobear

droop [drup] s inclinación || intr caer, colgar; inclinarse; marchitarse; abatirse; encamarse (el grano)

drooping [ˈdrupɪŋ] adj (eyelid, shoulder) caído

drop [drɑp] s gota; (slope) pendiente f; (earring) pendiente m; (in temperature) descenso; (of supplies from an airplane) lanzamiento; (trap door) escotillón m; (gallows) horca; (lozenge) pastilla; (small amount) chispa; (slit for letters) buzón m; (curtain) telón m; **a drop in the bucket** una gota en el mar || v (pret & pp **dropped**; ger **dropping**) tr dejar caer; echar (una carta) al buzón; bajar (una cortina); soltar (una indirecta); escribir (una esquela); omitir, suprimir; abandonar, dejar; echar (el ancla); borrar de la lista (a un alumno); lanzar (bombas o suministros de un avión) || intr caer; bajar; cesar, terminar; **to drop dead** caer muerto; **to drop in** entrar al pasar, visitar de paso; **to drop off** desaparecer; quedarse dormido; morir de repente; **to drop out** desaparecer; retirarse; darse de baja

drop curtain s telón m

drop hammer s martinete m

drop′-leaf′ table s mesa de hoja plegadiza

drop′light′ s lámpara colgante

drop′out′ s fracasado, desertor m escolar; **to become a dropout** ahorcar los libros

dropper [ˈdrɑpər] s cuentagotas m

drop shutter s obturador m de guillotina

dropsical [ˈdrɑpsɪkəl] *adj* hidrópico

dropsy [ˈdrɑpsɪ] *s* hidropesía

drop table *s* mesa perezosa

dross [drɔs] o [drɑs] *s* (*of metals*) escoria; (fig) escoria, hez *f*

drought [draʊt] *s* (*long period of dry weather*) sequía; (*dryness*) sequedad

drove [drov] *s* manada, rebaño, hato; gentío, multitud

drover [ˈdrovər] *s* ganadero

drown [draʊn] *tr* anegar, ahogar || *intr* anegarse, ahogarse

drowse [draʊz] *intr* adormecerse, amodorrarse

drow·sy [ˈdraʊzi] *adj* (*comp* **-sier;** *super* **-siest**) soñoliento, modorro

drub [drʌb] *v* (*pret & pp* **drubbed;** *ger* **drubbing**) *tr* apalear, pegar, tundir; derrotar completamente

drudge [drʌdʒ] *s* yunque *m*, esclavo del trabajo || *intr* afanarse

drudger·y [ˈdrʌdʒəri] *s* (*pl* **-ies**) trabajo penoso

drug [drʌg] *s* droga, medicamento; narcótico; **drug on the market** macana, artículo invendible || *v* (*pret & pp* **drugged;** *ger* **drugging**) *tr* narcotizar; mezclar con drogas

drug addict *s* toxicómano, drogadicto; (coll) yonquí *m*

drug´-ad·dict´ed *adj* drogadicto

drug addiction *s* toxicomanía

drug dealer *s* narcotraficante *mf*

druggist [ˈdrʌgɪst] *s* boticario, farmacéutico; (*dealer in drugs, chemicals, dyes, etc.*) droguero

drug habit *s* vicio de los narcóticos

drug store *s* farmacia, botica, droguería

drug traffic *s* contrabando de narcóticos

druid [ˈdruˑɪd] *s* druida *m*

drum [drʌm] *s* (*cylinder; instrument of percussion*) tambor *m*; (*container for oil, gasoline, etc.*) bidón *m* || *v* (*pret & pp* **drummed;** *ger* **drumming**) *tr* reunir a toque de tambor; **to drum up trade** fomentar ventas || *intr* tocar el tambor; (*with the fingers*) teclear

drum´beat´ *s* toque *m* de tambor

drum brake *s* freno de tambor

drum corps *s* banda de tambores

drum´fire´ *s* fuego graneado, fuego nutrido

drum´head´ *s* parche *m* de tambor

drum major *s* tambor *m* mayor

drummer [ˈdrʌmər] *s* tambor *m*, baterista *mf*, tamborilero; agente viajero

drum´stick´ *s* baqueta, palillo; (coll) muslo (*de ave cocida*)

drunk [drʌŋk] *adj* borracho; bolo (CAm, Mex); **to get drunk** emborracharse; coger una turca; embolarse (CAm, Mex) enchicharse (SAm) || *s* (coll) borracho; (*spree*) (coll) borrachera

drunkard [ˈdrʌŋkərd] *s* borrachín *m*

drunken [ˈdrʌŋkən] *adj* borracho

drunken driving *s* — **to be arrested for drunken driving** ser arrestado por conducir en estado de embriaguez

drunkenness [ˈdrʌŋkənnɪs] *s* embriaguez *f*; bimba (Mex)

dry [draɪ] *adj* (*comp* **drier;** *super* **driest**) seco; (*thirsty*) sediento; (*dull, boring*) árido || *s* (*pl* **drys**) (*prohibitionist*) (coll) seco || *v* (*pret & pp* **dried**) *tr* secar; (*to wipe dry*) enjugar || *intr* secarse; **to dry up** secarse completamente; (slang) callar, dejar de hablar

dry battery *s* pila seca; (*group of dry cells*) batería seca

dry cell *s* pila seca

dry´-clean´ *tr* lavar en seco, limpiar en seco

dry cleaner *s* tintorero

dry cleaning *s* lavado a seco, limpieza en seco

dry´-clean´ing establishment *s* tintorería

dry dock *s* dique seco

dryer [ˈdraɪˑər] *s* var de **drier**

dry´eyed´ —*adj* ojienjuto

dry farming *s* cultivo de secano

dry goods *spl* mercancías generales (*tejidos, lencería, pañería, sedería*)

dry ice *s* carbohielo, hielo seco

dry law *s* ley seca

dry measure *s* medida para áridos

dryness [ˈdraɪnɪs] *s* sequedad; (*e.g., of a speaker*) aridez *f*

dry nurse *s* ama seca

dry season *s* estación de la seca

dry wash *s* ropa lavada y secada pero no planchada

d.s. *abbr* **days after sight, daylight saving**

D.S.T. *abbr* **Daylight Saving Time**

dual [ˈdjuˑəl] o [ˈduˑəl] *adj & s* dual *m*

dual axle *s* eje tandem

duali·ty [djuˈælɪti] *s* (*pl* **-ties**) dualidad

dub [dʌb] *s* (slang) jugador *m* torpe || *v* (*pret & pp* **dubbed;** *ger* **dubbing**) *tr* apellidar; armar caballero; (mov) doblar

dubbing [ˈdʌbɪŋ] *s* doblado, doblaje *m*

dubious [ˈdubɪˑəs] *adj* dudoso

ducat [ˈdʌkət] *s* ducado

duchess [ˈdʌtʃɪs] *s* duquesa

duch·y [ˈdʌtʃi] *s* (*pl* **-ies**) ducado

duck [dʌk] *s* pato; (*female*) pata; agachada rápida; (*in the water*) zambullida; **ducks** (coll) pantalones *mpl* de dril || *tr* bajar rápidamente (*la cabeza*); (*in water*) chapuzar; (coll) esquivar, evitar (*un golpe*) || *intr* chapuzar; **to duck out** (coll) escabullirse

duck´-toed´ *adj* zancajoso

duct [dʌkt] *s* conducto, canal *m*

ductile [ˈdʌktɪl] *adj* dúctil

ductless gland [ˈdʌktlɪs] *s* glándula cerrada

duct´work´ *s* canalización

dud [dʌd] *s* (slang) bomba que no estalla; (slang) fracaso; **duds** (coll) trapos, prendas de vestir

dude [dud] *s* caballerete *m*

due [dju] o [du] *adj* debido; aguardado, esperado; pagadero; **due to** debido a; **to fall due** vencer; **when is the train due?** ¿a qué hora debe llegar el tren? || *adv* directamente, derecho ‖ *s* deuda; **dues** derechos; (*of a member*) cuota; **to get one's due** llevar su merecido; **to give the devil his due** ser justo hasta con el diablo

duel ['dju•əl] o ['du•əl] *s* duelo; **to fight a duel** batirse en duelo ‖ *v* (*pret & pp* **dueled** o **duelled;** *ger* **dueling** o **duelling**) *intr* batirse en duelo

duelist o **duellist** ['dju•əlɪst] o ['duəlɪst] *s* duelista *m*

dues-paying ['djuz,pe•ɪŋ] o ['duz,peɪŋ] *adj* cotizante

duet [dju'ɛt] o [du'ɛt] *s* dúo

duke [djuk] *s* duque *m*

dukedom ['djukdəm] *s* ducado

dull [dʌl] *adj* (*not sharp*) embotado, romo; (*color*) apagado; (*sound; pain*) sordo; (*stupid*) lerdo, torpe; (*business*) inactivo, muerto; (*boring*) aburrido, tedioso; (*flat*) deslucido, deslustrado ‖ *tr* embotar, enromar; deslucir, deslustrar; enfriar (*el entusiasmo*) ‖ *intr* embotarse, enromarse; deslucirse, deslustrarse

dullard ['dʌlərd] *s* estúpido

duly ['djuli] o ['duli] *adv* debidamente

dumb [dʌm] *adj* (*lacking the power to speak*) mudo; (coll) estúpido, torpe

dumb'bell' *s* halterio; (slang) estúpido, tonto

dumb creature *s* animal *m*, bruto

dumb show *s* pantomima

dumb'wait'er *s* montaplatos *m*

dumfound [,dʌm'faʊnd] *tr* pasmar, dejar sin habla

dum•my ['dʌmi] *adj* falso, fingido, simulado ‖ *s* (*pl* **-mies**) (*dress form*) maniquí *m;* cabeza para pelucas; (*in card games*) muerto; cartas del muerto; (*figurehead, straw man*) testaferro; (*skeleton copy of a book*) maqueta; imitación, copia; (slang) estúpido

dump [dʌmp] *s* basurero, vertedero; montón *m* de basuras; (mil) depósito de municiones; (min) terrero; **to be down in the dumps** (coll) tener murria ‖ *tr* descargar, verter; vaciar de golpe; vender en grandes cantidades y a precios inferiores a los corrientes

dumping ['dʌmpɪŋ] *s* descarga; venta en grandes cantidades y a precios inferiores a los corrientes

dumpling ['dʌmplɪŋ] *s* bola de pasta rellena de fruta o carne

dump truck *s* camión *m* volquete

dump•y ['dʌmpi] *adj* (*comp* **-ier;** *super* **-iest**) regordete, rollizo

dun [dʌn] *adj* bruno, pardo, castaño ‖ *s* acreedor importuno; (*demand for payment*) apremio ‖ *v* (*pret & pp* **dunner;** *ger* **dunning**) *tr* importunar para el pago, apremiar (*a un deudor*)

dunce [dʌns] *s* zopenco, bodoque *m*

dunce cap *s* capirote *m* que se le pone al alumno torpe

dune [djun] o [dun] *s* duna, médano

dung [dʌŋ] *s* estiércol *m* ‖ *tr* estercolar

dungarees [,dʌŋgə'riz] *spl* pantalones *mpl* de trabajo de tela basta de algodón

dungeon ['dʌndʒən] *s* calabozo, mazmorra; (*fortified tower of medieval castle*) torre *f* del homenaje

dung'hill' *s* estercolar *m;* lugar inmundo

dunk [dʌŋk] *tr* sopetear, ensopar

duo ['dju•o] o ['du•o] *s* dúo

duode•num [,du•ə'dinəm] *s* (*pl* **-na** [nə]) duodeno

dupe [djup] o [dup] *s* víctima, primo, inocentón *m* ‖ *tr* embaucar, engañar

duplex house ['dupleks] *s* casa para dos familias

duplicate ['duplɪkɪt] *adj & s* duplicado; **in duplicate** por duplicado ‖ ['duplɪ,ket] *tr* duplicar

duplici•ty [dju'plɪsɪti] *s* (*pl* **-ties**) duplicidad

durable ['djurəbəl] o ['durəbəl] *adj* durable, duradero

durable goods *spl* artículos duraderos

duration [dju're∫ən] o [du're∫ən] *s* duración

during ['djurɪŋ] *prep* durante

dusk [dʌsk] *s* crepúsculo

dust [dʌst] *s* polvo ‖ *tr* (*to free of dust*) desempolvar; (*to sprinkle with dust*) polvorear; **to dust off** desempolvar

dust bowl *s* cuenca de polvo

dust'cloth' *s* trapo para quitar el polvo

dust cloud *s* nube *f* de polvo, polvareda

duster ['dʌstər] *s* paño, plumero; (*light overgarment*) guardapolvo

dust jacket *s* sobrecubierta

dust'pan' *s* pala para recoger la basura

dust rag *s* trapo para quitar el polvo

dust storm *s* tolvanera

dust•y ['dʌsti] *adj* (*comp* **-ier;** *super* **-iest**) polvoriento; (*grayish*) grisáceo

Dutch [dʌt∫] *adj* holandés; (slang) alemán ‖ *s* (*language*) holandés *m;* (*language*) (slang) alemán *m;* **in Dutch** (slang) en la desgracia; (slang) en un apuro; **the Dutch** los holandeses; (slang) los alemanes; **to go Dutch** (coll) pagar a escote

Dutch•man ['dʌt∫mən] *s* (*pl* **-men** [mən]) holandés *m;* (slang) alemán *m*

Dutch treat *s* (coll) convite *m* a escote

dutiable ['djutɪ•əbəl] *adj* sujeto a derechos de aduana

dutiful ['djutɪfəl] *adj* obediente, sumiso, solícito

du•ty ['djuti] *s* (*pl* **-ties**) deber *m;* (*task*) faena, quehacer *m;* derechos de aduana; **in the line of duty** en acto de servicio; **off duty** libre; **on duty** de servicio, de guardia; **to do one's duty** cumplir con su deber; **to take up one's duties** entrar en funciones

du'ty-free' *adj* libre de derechos

D.V. *abbr* Deo volente, i.e., God willing

dwarf [dwɔrf] *adj & s* enano ‖ *tr* achicar, empequeñecer ‖ *intr* achicarse, empequeñecerse

dwarfish ['dwɔrfɪ∫] *adj* enano, diminuto

dwell [dwɛl] *v* (*pret & pp* **dwelled** o **dwelt** [dwɛlt]) *intr* vivir, morar; **to dwell on** o **upon** hacer hincapié en

dwelling ['dwɛlɪŋ] *s* morada, vivienda

dwelling house *s* casa, domicilio

dwindle [ˈdwɪndəl] *intr* disminuir; decaer, consumirse

dwt. *abbr* **pennyweight**

dye [daɪ] *s* tinte *m*, tintura, color *m* ‖ *v* (*pret* & *pp* **dyed;** *ger* **dyeing**) *tr* teñir

dyed-in-the-wool [ˈdaɪdɪnðəˌwul] *adj* intransigente

dyeing [ˈdaɪ•ɪŋ] *s* tinte *m*, tintura

dyer [ˈdaɪ•ər] *s* tintorero

dye'stuff *s* materia, colorante

dying [ˈdaɪ•ɪŋ] *adj* moribundo

dynamic [daɪˈnæmɪk] o [dɪˈnæmɪk] *adj* dinámico

dynamite [ˈdaɪnəˌmaɪt] *s* dinamita ‖ *tr* dinamitar

dyna•mo [ˈdaɪnəˌmo] *s* (*pl* **-mos**) dínamo *f*

dynast [ˈdaɪnæst] *s* dinasta *m*

dynas•ty [ˈdaɪnəsti] *s* (*pl* **-ties**) dinastía

dysentery [ˈdɪsənˌtɛri] *s* disentería

dysfunction [dɪsˈfʌŋʃən] *s* disfunción

dyspepsia [dɪsˈpɛpsɪ•ə] o [dɪsˈpɛp/ə] *s* dispepsia

dz. *abbr* **dozen**

E

E, e [i] quinta letra del alfabeto inglés

ea. *abbr* **each**

each [itʃ] *adj indef* cada ‖ *pron indef* cada uno; **each other** nos, se; uno a otro, unos a otros ‖ *adv* cada uno; por persona

eager [ˈigər] *adj* (*enthusiastic*) ardiente, celoso; **eager for** muy deseoso de; **eager to** + *inf* muy deseoso de + *inf*

eagerness [ˈigərnɪs] *s* ardor *m*, celo; deseo ardiente, empeño

eagle [ˈigəl] *s* águila

eagle owl *s* buho

ear [ɪr] *s* (*organ and sense of hearing*) oído; (*external part*) oreja; (*of corn*) mazorca; (*of wheat*) espiga; **all ears** con las orejas tan largas; **to be all ears** ser todo oídos, abrir tanto oído; **box on the ear** guantón *m;* **to prick up one's ears** aguzar las orejas; **to turn a deaf ear** hacer o tener oídos de mercader

ear'ache *s* dolor *m* de oído

ear'drop *s* arete *m*

ear'drum *s* tímpano

ear'flap *s* orejera

earl [ʌrl] *s* conde *m*

earldom [ˈʌrldəm] *s* condado

ear•ly [ˈʌrli] (*comp* **-lier;** *super* **-liest**) *adj* (*occurring before customary time*) temprano; (*first in a series*) primero; (*far back in time*) primero, remoto, antiguo; (*occurring in near future*) cercano, próximo ‖ *adv* temprano; al principio; en los primeros tiempos; **as early as** (*a certain time of day*) ya a; (*a certain time or date*) ya en; **as early as possible** lo más pronto posible; **early in** (*e.g., the month of December*) ya en; **early in the morning** muy de mañana; **early in the year** a principios del año; **to rise early** madrugar

early bird *s* (coll) madrugador *m*

early mass *s* misa de prima

early riser *s* madrugador *m*

ear'mark *s* señal *f*, distintivo ‖ *tr* destinar, poner aparte (*para un fin determinado*)

ear'muff *s* orejera

earn [ʌrn] *tr* ganar, ganarse; (*to get as one's due*) merecerse; (com) devengar (*intereses*) ‖ *intr* ganar; rendir

earnest [ˈʌrnɪst] *adj* serio, grave; **in earnest** en serio, de buena fe ‖ *s* arras

earnest money *s* arras

earnings [ˈʌrnɪŋz] *s* ganancia; salario

ear of corn *s* ilote *m;* chilote (ˈCAm); **green ear of corn** jilote (Mex)

ear'phone *s* audífono

ear'piece *s* auricular *m*

ear'ring *s* arete *m*

ear'shot *s* alcance *m* del oído; **within earshot** al alcance del oído

ear'split'ting *adj* ensordecedor

earth [ʌrθ] *s* tierra; **to come back to** o **down to earth** bajar de las nubes

earthen [ˈʌrθən] *adj* de tierra; de barro

ear'then•ware *s* loza, vasijas de barro

earthly [ˈʌrθli] *adj* terrenal; concebible, posible; **to be of no earthly use** no servir para nada

earth'quake *s* terremoto, temblor *m* de tierra

earth'work *s* terraplén *m*

earth'worm *s* lombriz *f* de tierra

earth•y [ˈʌrθi] *adj* (*comp* **-ier;** *super* **-iest**) terroso; (*worldly*) mundanal; (*unrefined*) grosero; franco, sincero

ear trumpet *s* trompetilla

ear'wax *s* cera de los oídos

ease [iz] *s* facilidad; (*readiness, naturalness*) desenvoltura, soltura; (*comfort, wellbeing*) comodidad, bienestar *m;* **with ease** con facilidad ‖ *tr* facilitar; aligerar (*un peso*); (*to let up on*) aflojar, soltar; aliviar, mitigar ‖ *intr* aliviarse, mitigarse, disminuir; moderar la marcha

easel [ˈizəl] *s* caballete *m*

easement [ˈizmənt] *s* alivio; (law) servidumbre

easily [ˈizɪli] *adv* fácilmente; suavemente; sin duda; probablemente

easiness [ˈizɪnɪs] *s* facilidad; desenvoltura, soltura; (*e.g., of motion of a machine*) suavidad; indiferencia

east [ist] *adj* oriental, del este ‖ *adv* al este, hacia el este ‖ *s* este *m*

du
ea

Easter ['istər] s Pascua de flores, Pascua de Resurrección, Pascua florida

Easter egg s huevo duro decorado o huevo de imitación que se da como regalo en el día de Pascua de Resurrección

Easter Monday s lunes m de Pascua de Resurrección

eastern ['istərn] adj oriental

East'er·tide' s alelúya m, tiempo de Pascua

eastward ['istwərd] adv hacia el este

eas·y ['izi] adj (comp -ier; super -iest) fácil; (conducive to ease) cómodo; (not tight) holgado; (amenable) manejable; (not forced or hurried) lento, pausado, moderado; **to have an easy job** (o **life**) estar echado (CAm, Mex, P-R) ‖ adv fácilmente; (coll) despacio; **to take it easy** (coll) descansar, holgar; (coll) ir despacio

easy chair s poltrona, silla poltrona

eas'y·go'ing adj despacioso, comodón

easy mark s (coll) víctima, inocentón m

easy money s dinero ganado sin pena; (com) dinero abundante

easy payments spl facilidades de pago

eat [it] v (pret **ate** [et]; pp **eaten** ['itən]) tr comer; **to eat away** corroer; **to eat up** comerse ‖ intr comer

eatable ['itəbəl] adj comestible ‖ **eatables** spl comestibles mpl

eaves [ivz] spl alero, socarrén m, tejaroz m

eaves'drop' v (pret & pp **-dropped**; ger **-dropping**) intr escuchar a escondidas, estar de escucha

ebb [εb] s reflujo; decadencia ‖ intr bajar (la marea); decaer

ebb and flow s flujo y reflujo

ebb tide s marea menguante

ebon·y ['εbəni] s (pl **-ies**) ébano

ebullient [ɪ'bʌljənt] adj hirviente; entusiasta

eccentric [εk'sεntrɪk] adj excéntrico ‖ m (odd person) excéntrico; (device) excéntrica

eccentrici·ty [,εksεn'trɪsɪti] s (pl **-ties**) excentricidad

ecclesiastic [ɪ,klizɪ'æstɪk] adj & s eclesiástico

echelon ['εʃə,lɑn] s escalón m; (mil) escalón ‖ tr (mil) escalonar

ech·o ['εko] s (pl **-oes**) eco ‖ tr repetir (un sonido); imitar ‖ intr hacer eco

éclair [e'klεr] s bollo de crema

eclectic [εk'lεktɪk] adj & s ecléctico

eclipse [ɪ'klɪps] s eclipse m ‖ tr eclipsar

eclogue ['εklɔg] o ['εklɑg] s égloga

ecologic(al) [,ikə'lɑdʒɪk(əl)] adj ecológico

ecologist [i'kɑlədʒɪst] s ecologista mf, ecólogo

ecology [i'kɑlədʒi] s ecología

economic [,ikə'nɑmɪk] adj económico (perteneciente a la economía)

economical [,ikə'nɑmɪkəl] adj económico (ahorrador; poco costoso)

economics [,ikə'nɑmɪks] s economía política

economist [ɪ'kɑnəmɪst] s economista mf

economize [ɪ'kɑnə,maɪz] tr & intr economizar

econo·my [ɪ'kɑnəmi] s (pl **-mies**) economía

ecsta·sy ['εkstəsi] s (pl **-sies**) éxtasis m

ecstatic [εk'stætɪk] adj extático

Ecuador ['εkwə,dɔr] s el Ecuador

Ecuadoran [,εkwə'dorən] o; **Ecuadorian** [,εkwə'doriən] adj & s ecuatoriano

ecumenic(al) [,εkjə'mεnɪk(əl)] adj ecuménico

eczema ['εksɪmə] o [εg'zimə] s eczema m & f, eccema m & f

ed. abbr **edited, edition, editor**

ed·dy ['εdi] s (pl **-dies**) remolino ‖ v (pret & pp **-died**) tr & intr remolinear

edelweiss ['edəl,vaɪs] s estrella de los Alpes

edema [ɪ'dimə] s edema

edge [εdʒ] s (of a knife, sword, etc.) filo, corte m; (of a cup, glass, piece of paper, piece of cloth, an abyss, etc.) borde m; (of a piece of cloth; of a body of water) orilla; (of a table) canto; (of a book) corte m; (of clothing) ribete m; (slang) ventaja; **on edge** de canto; (fig) nervioso; **to have the edge on** (coll) llevar ventaja a; **to set the teeth on edge** dar dentera ‖ tr afilar, aguzar; bordear; ribetear (un vestido) ‖ intr avanzar de lado; **to edge in** lograr entrar

edgeways ['εdʒ,wez] adv de filo, de canto; **to not let a person get a word in edgeways** no dejarle a una persona decir ni una palabra

edging ['εdʒɪŋ] s orla, pestaña

edgy ['εdʒi] adj agudo, angular; nervioso, irritable

edible ['εdɪbəl] adj & s comestible m

edict ['idɪkt] s edicto

edification [,εdɪfɪ'keʃən] s edificación

edifice ['εdɪfɪs] s edificio

edi·fy ['εdɪ,faɪ] v (pret & pp **-fied**) tr edificar

edifying ['εdɪ,faɪ·ɪŋ] adj edificante

edit. abbr **edited, edition, editor**

edit ['εdɪt] tr preparar para la publicación; dirigir, redactar (un periódico)

edition [ɪ'dɪʃən] s edición

editor ['εdɪtər] s (of a newspaper or magazine) director m, redactor m; (of a manuscript) revisor m; (of an editorial) cronista mf

editorial [,εdɪ'torɪ·əl] adj editorial ‖ s editorial m, artículo de fondo

editorial staff s redacción, cuerpo de redacción

editor in chief s jefe m de redacción

educate ['εdʒʊ,ket] tr educar, instruir

education [,εdʒʊ'keʃən] s educación, instrucción

educational [,εdʒʊ'keʃənəl] adj educativo, educacional

educational institution s centro docente

educator ['εdʒʊ,ketər] s educador m

eel [il] s anguila; **to be as slippery as an eel** escurrirse como una anguila

ee·rie o **ee·ry** ['iri] adj (comp **-rier**; super **-riest**) espectral, misterioso

efface [ɪ'fes] tr destruir; borrar; **to efface oneself** retirarse, no dejarse ver

effect [ɪ'fεkt] s efecto; **in effect** vigente; en efecto, en realidad; **to feel the effects of** resentirse de; **to go into effect** o **to take**

effect hacerse vigente, entrar en vigor; **to put into effect** poner en vigor ‖ *tr* efectuar

effective [ɪˈfɛktɪv] *adj* eficaz; *(actually in effect)* efectivo; *(striking)* impresionante; **to become effective** hacerse efectivo, entrar en vigencia

effectual [ɪˈfɛktʃʊ•əl] *adj* eficaz

effectuate [ɪˈfɛktʃʊ,et] *tr* efectuar

effeminacy [ɪˈfɛmɪnəsi] *s* afeminación

effeminate [ɪˈfɛmɪnɪt] *adj* afeminado

effervesce [ˌɛfərˈvɛs] *intr* estar en efervescencia

effervescence [ˌɛfərˈvɛsəns] *s* efervescencia

effervescent [ˌɛfərˈvɛsənt] *adj* efervescente

effete [ɪˈfit] *adj* estéril, infructuoso

efficacious [ˌɛfɪˈkeʃəs] *adj* eficaz

effica•cy [ˈɛfɪkəsi] *s* (*pl* **-cies**) eficacia

efficien•cy [ɪˈfɪʃənsi] *s* (*pl* **-cies**) eficiencia; (mech) rendimiento, efecto útil

efficient [ɪˈfɪʃənt] *adj* eficiente, eficaz; *(person)* competente; *(mech)* de buen rendimiento

effi•gy [ˈɛfɪdʒi] *s* (*pl* **-gies**) efigie *f*

effort [ˈɛfərt] *s* esfuerzo, empeño

effronter•y [ɪˈfrʌntəri] *s* (*pl* **-ies**) desfachatez *f*, descaro

effusion [ɪˈfjuʒən] *s* efusión

effusive [ɪˈfjusɪv] *adj* efusivo, expansivo

e.g. *abbr* **exempli gratia**, i.e., **for example**

egg [ɛg] *s* huevo; (slang) buen sujeto ‖ *tr* — **to egg on** incitar, instigar

egg beat′er *s* batidor *m* de huevos

egg′cup′ *s* huevera

egg′head′ *s* intelectual *mf*, erudito

eggnog [ˈɛg,nɑg] *s* caldo de la reina, yema mejida

egg′plant′ *s* berenjena

egg′shell′ *s* cascarón *m*, cáscara de huevo

egoism [ˈɛgo,ɪzəm] o [ˈigo,ɪzəm] *s* egoísmo

egoist [ˈɛgo•ɪst] o [ˈigo•ɪst] *s* egoísta *mf*

egotism [ˈɛgo,tɪzəm] o [ˈigo,tɪzəm] *s* egotismo

egotist [ˈɛgotɪst] o [ˈigotɪst] *s* egotista *mf*

egregious [ɪˈgridʒəs] *adj* enorme, escandaloso

egress [ˈgrɛs] *s* salida

Egypt [ˈedʒɪpt] *s* Egipto

Egyptian [ɪˈdʒɪpʃən] *adj & s* egipcio

eider [ˈaɪdər] *s* pato de flojel

eid′erdown′ *s* edredón *m*

eight [et] *adj & pron* ocho ‖ *s* ocho; **eight o'clock** las ocho

eight′-day′ clock *s* reloj *m* de ocho días cuerda

eighteen [ˈetˈtin] *adj, pron & s* dieciocho, diez y ocho

eighteenth [ˈetˈtinθ] *adj & s* (*in a series*) decimoctavo; (*part*) dieciochavo ‖ *s* (*in dates*) dieciocho, diez y ocho

eighth [etθ] *adj & s* octavo, ochavo ‖ *s* (*in dates*) ocho

eight hundred *adj & pron* ochocientos ‖ *s* ochocientos *m*

eightieth [ˈetɪ•θ] *adj & s* (*in a series*) octogésimo; (*part*) ochentavo

eigh•ty [ˈeti] *adj & pron* ochenta ‖ *s* (*pl* **-ties**) ochenta *m*

either [ˈiðər] o [ˈaɪðər] *adj* uno u otro, cada . . . (de los dos), cualquier . . . de los dos; ambos ‖ *pron* uno u otro, cualquiera de los dos ‖ *adv* — **not either** tampoco, no . . . tampoco ‖ *conj* — **either . . . or** o . . . o

ejaculate [ɪˈdʒækjə,let] *tr & intr* exclamar; (physiol) eyacular

eject [ɪˈdʒɛkt] *tr* arrojar, expulsar, echar; (*to evict*) desahuciar

ejection [ɪˈdʒɛkʃən] *s* expulsión; (*of a tenant*) desahucio

ejection seat *s* (aer) asiento lanzable

eke [ik] *tr* — **to eke out** ganarse (*la vida*) con dificultad

elaborate [ɪˈlæbərɪt] *adj* (*done with great care*) elaborado; (*detailed, ornate*) primoroso, recargado ‖ [ɪˈlæbə,ret] *tr* elaborar ‖ *intr* — **to elaborate on** o **upon** explicar con más detalles

elapse [ɪˈlæps] *intr* pasar, transcurrir

elastic [ɪˈlæstɪk] *adj & s* elástico

elasticity [ˌilæsˈtɪsɪti] *s* elasticidad

elated [ɪˈletɪd] *adj* alborozado, regocijado

elation [ɪˈleʃən] *s* alborozo, regocijo

elbow [ˈɛlbo] *s* codo; (*in a river*) recodo; (*of a chair*) brazo; **at one's elbow** a la mano; **out at the elbows** andrajoso, enseñando los codos; **to crook the elbow** empinar el codo; **to rub elbows** codearse, rozarse; **up to the elbows** hasta los codos ‖ *tr* — **to elbow one's way** abrirse paso a codazos ‖ *intr* codear

elbow grease *s* (coll) muñeca, jugo de muñeca

elbow patch *s* codera

elbow rest *s* ménsula

el′bow•room′ *s* espacio suficiente; libertad de acción

elder [ˈɛldər] *adj* mayor, más antiguo ‖ *s* mayor, señor *m* mayor; (eccl) anciano; (*plant*) saúco

el′der•ber′ry *s* (*pl* **-ries**) saúco; baya del saúco

elderly [ˈɛldərli] *adj* viejo, anciano

elder statesman *s* veterano de la política

eldest [ˈɛldɪst] *adj* (el) mayor, (el) más antiguo

elec. *abbr* **electrical, electricity**

elect [ɪˈlɛkt] *adj* (*chosen*) escogido; (*selected but not yet installed*) electo ‖ *s* elegido; **the elect** los elegidos ‖ *tr* elegir

election [ɪˈlɛkʃən] *s* elección

electioneer [ɪ,lɛkʃəˈnɪr] *intr* solicitar votos

elective [ɪˈlɛktɪv] *adj* electivo ‖ *s* asignatura electiva

electorate [ɪˈlɛktərɪt] *s* electorado

electric(al) [ɪˈlɛktrɪk(əl)] *adj* eléctrico

electric appliance *s* electrodoméstico

electric fan *s* ventilador eléctrico

electrician [ˌɛlɛkˈtrɪʃən] *s* electricista *mf*

electricity [ˌɛlɛkˈtrɪsɪti] *s* electricidad

electric percolator *s* cafetera eléctrica

electric shaver *s* electrofeitadora

electric tape *s* cinta aislante

electri•fy [ɪˈlɛktrɪ,faɪ] *v* (*pret & pp* **-fied**) *tr* (*to provide with electric power*) electrifi-

car; (*to communicate electricity to; to thrill*) electrizar
electrocute [ɪ'lɛktrə,kjut] *tr* electrocutar
electrode [ɪ'lɛktrod] *s* electrodo
electrolysis [,ɛlɛk'trɑlɪsɪs] *s* electrólisis *f*
electrolyte [ɪ'lɛktrə,laɪt] *s* electrólito
electromagnet [ɪ,lɛktrə'mægnɪt] *s* electro, electroimán *m*
electromagnetic [ɪ,lɛktrəmæg'nɛtɪk] *adj* electromagnético
electromotive [ɪ,lɛktrə'motɪv] *adj* electromotor
electron [ɪ'lɛktrɑn] *s* electrón *m*
electronic [,ɛlɛk'trɑnɪk] *adj* electrónico ‖ **electronics** *s* electrónica
electroplating [ɪ'lɛktrə,pletɪŋ] *s* galvanoplastia
electrostatic [ɪ,lɛktrə'stætɪk] *adj* electrostático
electrotype [ɪ'lɛktrə,taɪp] *s* electrotipo ‖ *tr* electrotipar.
eleemosynary [,ɛlɪ'mɑsɪ,nɛri] *adj* limosnero
elegance ['ɛlɪgəns] *s* elegancia
elegant ['ɛlɪgənt] *adj* elegante, elegantoso
elegiac [,ɛlɪ'dʒaɪæk] o [ɪ'lidʒɪ,æk] *adj* elegíaco
ele·gy ['ɛlɪdʒi] *s* (*pl* **-gies**) elegía
element ['ɛlɪmənt] *s* elemento; **to be in one's element** estar en su elemento
elementary [,ɛlɪ'mɛntəri] *adj* elemental
elephant ['ɛlɪfənt] *s* elefante *m*
elevate ['ɛlɪ,vet] *tr* elevar
elevated ['ɛlɪ,vetɪd] *adj* elevado ‖ *s* (coll) ferrocarril aéreo o elevado
elevation [,ɛlɪ'veʃən] *s* elevación
elevator ['ɛlɪ,vetər] *s* ascensor *m*; elevador *m* (Am); (*for freight*) montacargas *m*; (*for hoisting grain*) elevador de granos; (*warehouse for storing grain*) depósito de cereales; (aer) timón *m* de profundidad
eleven [ɪ'lɛvən] *adj* & *pron* once ‖ *s* once *m*; **eleven o'clock** las once
eleventh [ɪ'lɛvənθ] *adj* & *s* (*in a series*) undécimo, onceno; (*part*) onzavo ‖ *s* (*in dates*) once *m*
eleventh hour *s* último momento
elf [ɛlf] *s* (*pl* **elves** [ɛlvz]) elfo, trasgo; enano
elicit [ɪ'lɪsɪt] *tr* sacar, sonsacar
elide [ɪ'laɪd] *tr* elidir
eligible ['ɛlɪdʒɪbəl] *adj* elegible; deseable, aceptable
eliminate [ɪ'lɪmɪ,net] *tr* eliminar
elision [ɪ'lɪʒən] *s* elisión
elite [e'lit] *adj* selecto ‖ *s* — **the elite** la élite
elitist [e'litɪst] *adj* & *s* elitista *mf*
elk [ɛlk] *s* alce *m*
ellipse [ɪ'lɪps] *s* (geom) elipse *f*
ellip·sis [ɪ'lɪpsɪs] *s* (*pl* **-ses** [siz]) (gram) elipsis *f*
elliptic(al) [ɪ'lɪptɪk(əl)] *adj* (geom & gram) elíptico
elm tree [ɛlm] *s* olmo
elope [ɪ'lop] *intr* fugarse con un amante
elopement [ɪ'lopmənt] *s* fuga con un amante
eloquence ['ɛləkwəns] *s* elocuencia
eloquent ['ɛləkwənt] *adj* elocuente

else [ɛls] *adj* — **nobody else** ningún otro, nadie más; **nothing else** nada más; **somebody else** algún otro, otra persona; **something else** otra cosa; **what else** qué más, qué otra cosa; **who else** quién más; **whose else** de qué otra persona ‖ *adv* de otro modo; **how else** de qué otro modo; **or else** si no, o bien; **when else** en qué otro tiempo; a qué otra hora; **where else** en qué otra parte
else'where' *adv* en otra parte, a otra parte
elucidate [ɪ'lusɪ,det] *tr* elucidar
elude [ɪ'lud] *tr* eludir
elusive [ɪ'lusɪv] *adj* fugaz, efímero; evasivo; elusivo; (*baffling*) deslumbrador
emaciated [ɪ'meʃɪ,etɪd] *adj* enflaquecido, macilento
emancipate [ɪ'mænsɪ,pet] *tr* emancipar
embalm [ɛm'bɑm] *tr* embalsamar
embankment [ɛm'bæŋkmənt] *s* terraplén *m*
embar·go [ɛm'bɑrgo] *s* (*pl* **-goes**) embargo ‖ *tr* embargar
embark [ɛm'bɑrk] *intr* embarcarse
embarkation [,ɛmbɑr'keʃən] *s* (*of passengers*) embarco; (*of freight*) embarque *m*
embarrass [ɛm'bærəs] *tr* (*to make feel self-conscious*) avergonzar; (*to put obstacles in the way of*) embarazar; poner en apuros de dinero
embarrassing [ɛm'bærəsɪŋ] *adj* desconcertante, vergonzoso; embarazoso
embarrassment [ɛm'bærəsmənt] *s* desconcierto, vergüenza; (*interference; perplexity*) embarazo; (*financial difficulties*) apuros
embas·sy ['ɛmbəsi] *s* (*pl* **-sies**) embajada
em·bed [ɛm'bɛd] *v* (*pret* & *pp* **-bedded;** *ger* **-bedding**) *tr* empotrar, encajar
embellish [ɛm'bɛlɪʃ] *tr* embellecer
embellishment [ɛm'bɛlɪʃmənt] *s* embellecimiento
ember ['ɛmbər] *s* ascua, pavesa; **embers** rescoldo
Ember days *spl* témpora
embezzle [ɛm'bɛzəl] *tr* & *intr* desfalcar, malversar
embezzlement [ɛm'bɛzəlmənt] *s* desfalco, malversación
embezzler [ɛm'bɛzlər] *s* malversador *m*
embitter [ɛm'bɪtər] *tr* blasonar; (fig) blasonar
emblem ['ɛmbləm] *s* emblema *m*
emblematic(al) [,ɛmblə'mætɪk(əl)] *adj* emblemático
embodiment [ɛm'bɑdɪmənt] *s* incorporación; personificación, encarnación
embod·y [ɛm'bɑdi] *v* (*pret* & *pp* **-ied**) *tr* incorporar; personificar, encarnar
embolden [ɛm'boldən] *tr* envalentonar
embolism ['ɛmbə,lɪzəm] *s* embolia
emboss [ɛm'bɔs] o [ɛm'bɑs] *tr* (*to raise in relief*) realzar; abollonar (*metal*); repujar (*cuero*)
embrace [ɛm'bres] *s* abrazo ‖ *tr* abrazar ‖ *intr* abrazarse
embrasure [ɛm'breʒər] *s* alféizar *m*
embroider [ɛm'brɔɪdər] *tr* bordar, recamar

embroider•y [ɛm'brɔɪdəri] *s* (*pl* **-ies**) bordado, recamado

embroil [ɛm'brɔɪl] *tr* embrollar; (*to involve in contention*) envolver

embroilment [ɛm'brɔɪlmənt] *s* embrollo; (*in contention*) envolvimiento

embry•o ['ɛmbrɪ,o] *s* (*pl* **-os**) embrión *m*

embryology [,ɛmbrɪ'ɑlədʒɪ] *s* embriología

emend [ɪ'mɛnd] *tr* enmendar

emendation [,imɛn'deʃən] *s* enmienda

emerald ['ɛmərəld] *s* esmeralda

emerge [ɪ'mʌrdʒ] *intr* emerger

emergence [ɪ'mʌrdʒəns] *s* emergencia (*acción de emerger*)

emergen•cy [ɪ'mʌrdʒənsi] *s* (*pl* **-cies**) emergencia (*caso urgente*)

emergency exit *s* salida de auxilio

emergency landing *s* aterrizaje forzoso

emergency landing field *s* aeródromo de urgencia

emergency physician *s* médico de urgencia

emersion [ɪ'mʌrʒən] o [ɪ'mʌrʃən] *s* emersión

emery ['ɛməri] *s* esmeril *m*

emery cloth *s* tela de esmeril

emery wheel *s* esmeriladora, rueda de esmeril, muela de esmeril

emetic [ɪ'mɛtɪk] *adj* & *s* emético

emigrant ['ɛmɪgrənt] *adj* & *s* emigrante *mf*

emigrate ['ɛmɪ,gret] *intr* emigrar

émigré [émi'gre] o ['ɛmɪ,gre] *s* emigrado

eminence ['ɛmɪnəns] *s* eminencia

eminent ['ɛmɪnənt] *adj* eminente

emissar•y ['ɛmɪ,sɛri] *s* (*pl* **-ies**) emisario

emission [ɪ'mɪʃən] *s* emisión

emit [ɪ'mɪt] *v* (*pret* & *pp* **emitted;** *ger* **emitting**) *tr* emitir

emotion [ɪ'moʃən] *s* emoción

emotional [ɪ'moʃənəl] *adj* emocional, emotivo

emperor ['ɛmpərər] *s* emperador *m*

empathy ['ɛmpəθi] *s* empatía

empha•sis ['ɛmfəsɪs] *s* (*pl* **-ses** [,siz]) énfasis *m*

emphasize ['ɛmfə,saɪz] *tr* acentuar, hacer hincapié en

emphatic [ɛm'fætɪk] *adj* enfático

emphysema [,ɛmfɪ'simə] *s* enfisema *m*

empire ['ɛmpaɪr] *s* imperio

empiric(al) [ɛm'pɪrɪk(əl)] *adj* empírico

empiricist [ɛm'pɪrɪsɪst] *s* empírico

emplacement [ɛm'plesmənt] *s* emplazamiento

employ [ɛm'plɔɪ] *s* empleo ‖ *tr* emplear

employee [ɛm'plɔɪ•i] o [,ɛmplɔɪ'i] *s* empleado

employer [ɛm'plɔɪ•ər] *s* patrono

employment [ɛm'plɔɪmənt] *s* empleo, colocación

employment agency *s* agencia de colocaciones

empower [ɛm'pau•ər] *tr* autorizar, facultar; habilitar, permitir

empress ['ɛmprɪs] *s* emperatriz *f*

emptiness ['ɛmptɪnɪs] *s* vaciedad, vacuidad

emp•ty ['ɛmpti] *adj* (*comp* **-tier;** *super* **-tiest**) vacío; (coll) hambriento ‖ *v* (*pret* & *pp* **-tied**) *tr* & *intr* vaciar

empty-handed ['ɛmpti'hændɪd] *adj* manivacío

empty-headed ['ɛmpti'hɛdɪd] *adj* tonto, ignorante

empye•ma [,ɛmpɪ'imə] *s* (*pl* **-mata** [mətə]) empiema *m*

empyrean [,ɛmpɪ'ri•ən] *adj* & *s* empíreo

emulate ['ɛmjə,let] *tr* & *intr* emular

emulator ['ɛmjə,letər] *s* émulo

emulous ['ɛmjələs] *adj* émulo

emulsi•fy [ɪ'mʌlsɪ,faɪ] *v* (*pret* & *pp* **-fied**) *tr* emulsionar

emulsion [ɪ'mʌlʃən] *s* emulsión

enable [ɛn'ebəl] *tr* habilitar, facilitar

enact [ɛn'ækt] *tr* decretar, promulgar; hacer el papel de

enactment [ɛn'æktmənt] *s* ley *f*; (*of a law*) promulgación; (*of a play*) representación

enam•el [ɛn'æməl] *s* esmalte *m* ‖ *v* (*pret* & *pp* **-eled** o **-elled;** *ger* **-eling** o **-elling**) *tr* esmaltar

enam'el•ware' *s* utensilios de cocina de hierro esmaltado

enamor [ɛn'æmər] *tr* enamorar

encamp [ɛn'kæmp] *tr* acampar ‖ *intr* acampar, acamparse

encampment [ɛn'kæmpmənt] *s* acampamiento

enchant [ɛn'tʃænt] *tr* encantar

enchanting [ɛn'tʃæntɪŋ] *adj* encantador

enchantment [ɛn'tʃæntmənt] *s* encanto

enchantress [ɛn'tʃæntrɪs] *s* encantadora

enchase [ɛn'tʃes] *tr* engastar

encircle [ɛn'sʌrkəl] *tr* encerrar, rodear; (mil) envolver

enclitic [ɛn'klɪtɪk] *adj* & *s* enclítico

enclose [ɛn'kloz] *tr* encerrar; (*in a letter*) adjuntar, incluir; **to enclose herewith** remitir adjunto

enclosure [ɛn'kloʒər] *s* recinto; cosa inclusa, carta inclusa

encomi•um [ɛn'komɪ•əm] *s* (*pl* **-ums** o **-a** [ə]) encomio

encompass [ɛn'kʌmpəs] *tr* encuadrar, abarcar

encore ['ɑnkor] *s* bis *m* ‖ *interj* ¡bis!, ¡que se repita! ‖ *tr* pedir la repetición de (*p.ej., de una pieza o canción*); pedir la repetición a (*un actor*)

encounter [ɛn'kauntər] *s* encuentro ‖ *tr* encontrar, encontrarse con ‖ *intr* batirse, combatirse

encourage [ɛn'kʌrɪdʒ] *tr* animar, alentar; (*to foster*) fomentar

encouragement [ɛn'kʌrɪdʒmənt] *s* ánimo, aliento; fomento

encroach [ɛn'krotʃ] *intr* — **to encroach on** o **upon** pasar los límites de; abusar de; invadir, entremeterse en

encumber [ɛn'kʌmbər] *tr* embarazar, estorbar, impedir; (*to load with debts, etc.*) gravar

encumbrance [ɛn'kʌmbrəns] *s* embarazo; estorbo; gravamen *m*

ency. o **encyc.** *abbr* encyclopedia

encyclical [ɛn'sɪklɪkəl] o [ɛn'saɪklɪkəl] *s* encíclica

el
en

encyclopedia [ɛn,saɪklə'pidɪ•ə] s enciclopedia

encyclopedic [ɛn,saɪklə'pidɪk] adj enciclopédico

end [ɛnd] s (in time) fin m; (in space) extremo, remate m; (e.g., of the month) fines mpl; (small piece) cabo, pieza, fragmento; (purpose) intento, objeto, fin, mira; **at the end of** al cabo de; a fines de; **in the end** al fin; **no end of** (coll) un sin fin de; **to make both ends meet** pasar con lo que se tiene; **to no end** sin efecto; **to stand on end** poner de punta; ponerse de punta; erizarse, encresparse (el pelo); **to the end that** a fin de que ‖ tr acabar, terminar ‖ intr acabar, terminar; desembocar (p.ej., una calle); **to end up** acabar, morir; **to end up as** acabar siendo, parar en (p.ej., ladrón)

endanger [ɛn'dendʒər] tr poner en peligro

endear [ɛn'dɪr] tr hacer querer; **to endear oneself to** hacerse querer por

endearment [ɛn'dɪrmənt] s encariñamento

endeavor [ɛn'dɛvər] s esfuerzo, empeño ‖ intr esforzarse, empeñarse

endemic [ɛn'dɛmɪk] adj endémico ‖ s endemia

ending ['ɛndɪŋ] s fin m, terminación; (gram) desinencia, terminación

endive ['ɛndaɪv] s escarola

endless ['ɛndlɪs] adj interminable; (chain, screw, etc.) sin fin

end'most' adj último, extremo

endorse [ɛn'dɔrs] tr endosar; (fig) apoyar, aprobar

endorsee [,ɛndɔr'si] s endosatario

endorsement [ɛn'dɔrsmənt] s endoso; (fig) apoyo, aprobación

endorser [ɛn'dɔrsər] s endosante mf

endow [ɛn'dau] tr dotar

endowment [ɛn'daumənt] adj dotal ‖ s (of an institution) dotación; (gift, talent) dote f, prenda

end paper s hoja de encuadernador

endurance [ɛn'djurəns] o [ɛn'durəns] s aguante m, paciencia; (ability to hold out) resistencia, fortaleza; (lasting time) duración

endure [ɛn'djur] o [ɛn'dur] tr aguantar, tolerar, sufrir ‖ intr durar; sufrir con paciencia

enduring [ɛn'djurɪŋ] o [ɛn'durɪŋ] adj duradero, permanente, resistente

enema ['ɛnəmə] s enema, ayuda; (liquid and apparatus) lavativa

ene•my ['ɛnəmi] adj enemigo ‖ s (pl -mies) enemigo

enemy alien s extranjero enemigo

energetic [,ɛnər'dʒɛtɪk] adj enérgico, vigoroso

ener•gy ['ɛnərdʒi] s (pl -gies) energía; **alternate energy sources** energías alternas

energy crisis s crisis energética

enervate ['ɛnər,vet] tr enervar

enfeeble [ɛn'fibəl] tr debilitar

enfold [ɛnfold] tr arrollar, envolver

enforce [ɛn'fors] tr hacer cumplir, poner en vigor; obtener por fuerza; (e.g., obedience) imponer; (an argument) hacer valer

enforcement [ɛn'forsmənt] s compulsión; (e.g., of a law) ejecución

enfranchise [ɛn'fræntʃaɪz] tr franquear, libertar; conceder el derecho de sufragio a

eng. abbr **engineer, engraving**

engage [ɛn'gedʒ] tr ocupar, emplear; alquilar, reservar; atraer (p.ej., la atención de una persona); engranar con; trabar batalla con; **to be engaged, to be engaged to be married** estar prometido, estar comprometido para casarse; **to engage someone in conversation** entablar conversación con una persona ‖ intr empeñarse, comprometerse; empotrar, encajar; engranar; **to engage in** ocuparse en

engaged [ɛn'gedʒd] adj comprometido, prometido; (column) embebido, entregado

engagement [ɛn'gedʒmənt] s ajuste m, contrato, empeño; esponsales mpl, palabra de casamiento; (duration of betrothal) noviazgo; (appointment) cita; (mil) acción, batalla

engagement ring s anillo de compromiso, anillo de pedida

engaging [ɛn'gedʒɪŋ] adj agraciado, simpático

engender [ɛn'dʒɛndər] tr engendrar

engine ['ɛndʒɪn] s máquina; (of automobile) motor m; (rr) máquina, locomotora

engine driver s maquinista m

engineer [,ɛndʒə'nɪr] s ingeniero; (engine driver) maquinista m ‖ tr dirigir o construir como ingeniero; llevar a cabo con acierto

engineering [,ɛndʒə'nɪrɪŋ] s ingeniería

engine house s cuartel m de bomberos

engine•man ['ɛndʒɪnmən] s (pl -men [mən]) maquinista m, conductor m de locomotora

engine room s sala de máquinas; (naut) cámara de las máquinas

en'gine-room' telegraph s (naut) transmisor m de órdenes, telégrafo de máquinas

England ['ɪŋglənd] s Inglaterra

Englander ['ɪŋgləndər] s natural m inglés

English ['ɪŋglɪʃ] adj inglés ‖ s inglés m; (in billiards) efecto; **the English** los ingleses

English Channel s Canal m de la Mancha

English daisy s margarita de los prados

English horn s (mus) corno inglés, cuerno inglés

English•man ['ɪŋglɪʃmən] s (pl -men [mən]) inglés m

Eng'lish-speak'ing adj de habla inglesa, angloparlante

Eng'lish•wom'an s (pl -wom'en) inglesa

engraft [ɛn'græft] tr (hort & surg) injertar; (fig) implantar

engrave [ɛn'grev] tr grabar; (in the memory) grabar

engraver [ɛn'grevər] s grabador m

engraving [ɛn'grevɪŋ] s grabado

engross [ɛn'gros] tr absorber; poner en limpio; copiar califgáficamente

engrossing [ɛn'grosɪŋ] adj acaparador, absorbente

engulf [ɛn'gʌlf] *tr* hundir, inundar
enhance [ɛn'hæns] *tr* realzar
enhancement [ɛn'hænsmənt] *s* realce *m*
enigma [ɪ'nɪgmə] *s* enigma *m*
enigmatic(al) [,ɪnɪg'mætɪk(əl)] *adj* enigmático
enjambment [ɛn'dʒæmmənt] o [ɛn'dʒæmbmənt] *s* encabalgamiento
enjoin [ɛn'dʒɔɪn] *tr* encargar, ordenar
enjoy [ɛn'dʒɔɪ] *tr* gozar; **to enjoy** + *ger* gozarse en + *inf;* **to enjoy oneself** divertirse
enjoyable [ɛn'dʒɔɪ•əbəl] *adj* agradable, deleitable
enjoyment [ɛn'dʒɔɪmənt] *s* (*pleasure*) placer *m; (pleasurable use)* goce *m*
enkindle [ɛn'kɪndəl] *tr* encender
enlarge [ɛn'lardʒ] *tr* agrandar, aumentar; (phot) ampliar ‖ *intr* agrandarse, aumentar; *(to talk at length)* explayarse; exagerar; **to enlarge on** o **upon** tratar con más extensión; exagerar
enlargement [ɛn'lardʒmənt] *s* agrandamiento, aumento; (phot) ampliación
enlighten [ɛn'laɪtən] *tr* ilustrar, instruir
enlightenment [ɛn'laɪtənmənt] *s* ilustración, instrucción; dilucidación
enlist [ɛn'lɪst] *tr* alistar; ganar (*a una persona; el favor, los servicios de una persona*) ‖ *intr* alistarse; **to enlist in** (*a cause*) poner empeño en
enliven [ɛn'laɪvən] *tr* avivar, animar
enmesh [ɛn'mɛʃ] *tr* enredar
enmi•ty ['ɛnmɪti] *s* (*pl* **-ties**) enemistad
ennoble [ɛn'nobəl] *tr* ennoblecer
ennui ['anwi] *s* aburrimiento, tedio
enormous [ɪ'nɔrməs] *adj* enorme
enough [ɪ'nʌf] *adj, adv* & *s* bastante *m* ‖ *interj* ¡basta!, ¡no más!
enounce [ɪ'nauns] *tr* enunciar; pronunciar
en passant [,an pæ'sant] *adv* (chess) al vuelo
enrage [ɛn'redʒ] *tr* enrabiar, encolerizar
enrapture [ɛn'ræptʃər] *tr* embelesar, transportar, arrebatar
enrich [ɛn'rɪtʃ] *tr* enriquecer
enroll [ɛn'rol] *tr* alistar, inscribir; (*to wrap up*) envolver, enrollar ‖ *intr* alistarse, inscribirse
en route [an 'rut] *adv* en camino; **en route to** camino de, rumbo a
ensconce [ɛn'skans] *tr* esconder, abrigar; **to ensconce oneself** instalarse cómodamente
ensemble [an'sambəl] *s* conjunto; grupo de músicos que tocan o cantan juntos; traje armonioso
ensign ['ɛnsaɪn] *s* (*standard*) enseña, bandera; (*badge*) divisa, insignia ‖ ['ɛnsən] o ['ɛnsaɪn] *s* (nav) alférez *m* de fragata
enslave [ɛn'slev] *tr* esclavizar
enslavement [ɛn'slevmənt] *s* esclavización
ensnare [ɛn'snɛr] *tr* entrampar
ensue [ɛn'su] *intr* seguirse; resultar
ensuing [ɛn'su•ɪŋ] *adj* siguiente; resultante
ensure [ɛn'ʃur] *tr* asegurar, garantizar
entail [ɛn'tel] *s* (law) vínculo ‖ *tr* acarrear, ocasionar; (law) vincular
entangle [ɛn'tæŋgəl] *tr* enmarañar, enredar

entanglement [ɛn'tæŋgəlmənt]*s* enmarañamiento, enredo
enter ['ɛntər] *tr* entrar en (*una habitación*); entrar por (*una puerta*); (*in the customhouse*) declarar; (*to make a record of*) registrar, asentar; matricular (*a un alumno*); matricularse en; hacer miembro a; hacerse miembro de; (*to undertake*) emprender; asentar (*un pedido*); **to enter one's head** metérsele a uno en la cabeza ‖ *intr* entrar; (theat) entrar en escena, salir; **to enter into** entrar en; celebrar (*p.ej., un contrato*); **to enter on** o **upon** emprender
enterprise ['ɛntər,praɪz] *s* (*undertaking*) empresa; (*spirit, push*) empuje *m*
enterprising ['ɛntər,praɪzɪŋ] *adj* emprendedor
entertain [,ɛntər'ten] *tr* entretener, divertir; (*to show hospitality to*) recibir; considerar, abrigar (*esperanzas, ideas, etc.*) ‖ *intr* recibir
entertainer [,ɛntər'tenər] *s* (*host*) anfitrión *m;* (*in public*) actor *m*, bailador *m*, músico, vocalista *mf* (*esp. en un café cantante*)
entertaining [,ɛntər'tenɪŋ] *adj* entretenido
entertainment [,ɛntər'tenmənt] *s* entretenimiento, diversión; atracción, espectáculo; buen recibimiento; (*of hopes, ideas, etc.*) consideración, abrigo
enthrall [ɛn'θrɔl] *tr* cautivar, encantar; esclavizar, sojuzgar
enthrone [ɛn'θron] *tr* entronizar
enthuse [ɛn'θuz] o [ɛn'θjuz] *tr* (coll) entusiasmar ‖ *intr* (coll) entusiasmarse
enthusiasm [ɛn'θuzɪ,æzəm] *s* entusiasmo
enthusiast [ɛn'θuzɪ,æst] *s* entusiasta *mf;* devoto
enthusiastic [ɛn,θuzɪ'æstɪk] *adj* entusiástico
entice [ɛn'taɪs] *tr* atraer, tentar; inducir al mal, extraviar
enticement [ɛn'taɪsmənt] *s* atracción, tentación; extravío
entire [ɛn'taɪr] *adj* entero
entirely [ɛn'taɪrli] *adv* enteramente; (*exclusively*) solamente
entire•ty [ɛtaɪrti] *s* (*pl* **-ties**) entereza; conjunto, totalidad
entitle [ɛn'taɪtəl] *tr* dar derecho a; (*to give a name to; to honor with a title*) intitular
enti•ty ['ɛntɪti] *s* (*pl* **-ties**) entidad
entomb [ɛn'tum] *tr* sepultar
entombment [ɛn'tummənt] *s* sepultura
entomology [,ɛntə'malədʒi] *s* entomología
entourage [,antu'raʒ] *s* cortejo, séquito
entrails ['ɛntrelz] *spl* entrañas
entrain [ɛn'tren] *tr* despachar en el tren ‖ *intr* embarcar, salir en el tren
entrance ['ɛntrəns] *s* entrada, ingreso; (theat) entrada en escena ‖ [ɛn'træns] *tr* arrebatar, encantar
entrance examination *s* examen *m* de ingreso; **to take entrance examinations** examinarse de ingreso
entrancing [ɛn'trænsɪŋ] *adj* arrebatador, encantador
entrant ['ɛntrənt] *s* entrante *mf;* (sport) concurrente *mf*

en·trap [ɛn'træp] v (pret & pp **-trapped;** ger **-trapping**) tr entrampar

entreat [ɛn'trit] tr rogar, suplicar

entreat·y [ɛn'triti] s (pl **-ies**) ruego, súplica

entree ['ɑntre] s entrada, ingreso; (culin) entrada, principio

entrench [ɛn'trɛntʃ] tr atrincherar ‖ intr — **to entrench on** o **upon** infringir, violar

entrust [ɛn'trʌst] tr confiar

en·try ['ɛntri] s (pl **-tries**) entrada; (item) partida, entrada; (in a dictionary) artículo; (sport) concurrente mf

entry word s (in dictionary) voz-guía f

entwine [ɛn'twaɪn] tr entretejer, entrelazar

enumerate [ɪ'numə,ret] tr enumerar

enunciate [ɪ'nʌnsɪ,et] o [ɪ'nʌnʃɪ,et] tr enunciar; pronunciar

envelop [ɛn'vɛləp] tr envolver

envelope ['ɛnvə,lop] o ['ɑnvə,lop] s (for a letter) sobre m; (wrapper) envoltura

envenom [ɛn'vɛnəm] tr envenenar

enviable ['ɛnvɪ·əbəl] adj envidiable

envious ['ɛnvɪ·əs] adj envidioso

environment [ɛn'vaɪrənmənt] s medio ambiente; entorno; (surroundings) inmediaciones

environmental [ɛn,vaɪrən'mɛntəl] adj ambiental

environmental pollution s contaminación ambiental

environs [ɛn'vaɪrəns] spl inmediaciones, alrededores mpl

envisage [ɛn'vɪzɪdʒ] tr (to look in the face of) encarar; considerar, representarse

envoi ['ɛnvɔɪ] s despedida (copla al fin de una composición poética)

envoy ['ɛnvɔɪ] s (diplomatic agent) enviado; (short concluding stanza) despedida

en·vy ['ɛnvi] s (pl **-vies**) envidia ‖ v (pret & pp **-vied**) tr envidiar

enzyme ['ɛnzaɪm] s enzima f

epaulet o **epaulette** ['ɛpə,lɛt] s charretera

epenthe·sis [ɛ'pɛnθɪsɪs] s (pl **-ses** [,siz]) epéntesis f

epergne [ɪ'pʌrn] o [e'pɛrn] s ramillete m, centro de mesa

ephemeral [ɪ'fɛmərəl] adj efímero

epic ['ɛpɪk] adj épico ‖ s epopeya

epicure ['ɛpɪ,kjur] s epicúreo

epicurean [,ɛpɪkjʊ'ri·ən] adj & s epicúreo

epidemic [,ɛpɪ'dɛmɪk] adj epidémico ‖ s epidemia

epidemiology [,ɛpɪ,dimɪ'ɑlədʒi] s epidemiología

epidermis [,ɛpɪ'dʌrmɪs] s epidermis f

epigram ['ɛpɪ,græm] s epigrama m

epilepsy ['ɛpɪ,lɛpsi] s epilepsia

epileptic [,ɛpɪ'lɛptɪk] adj & s epiléptico

Epiphany [ɪ'pɪfəni] s Epifanía

Episcopalian [ɪ,pɪskə'peli·ən] adj & s episcopalista mf

episode ['ɛpɪ,sod] s episodio

epistemology [ɪ,pɪstɪ'mɑlədʒi] s epistemología

epistle [ɪ'pɪsəl] s epístola

epitaph ['ɛpɪ,tæf] s epitafio

epithet ['ɛpɪ,θɛt] s epíteto

epitome [ɪ'pɪtəmi] s epítome m; (fig) esencia, personificación

epitomize [ɪ'pɪtə,maɪz] tr epitomar; (fig) encarnar, personificar

epoch ['ɛpək] o ['ipɑk] s época

epochal ['ɛpəkəl] adj memorable, trascendental

ep'och-mak'ing adj que hace época

equable ['ɛkwəbəl] o ['ikwəbəl] adj constante, uniforme; sereno

equal ['ikwəl] adj igual; **equal to** a la altura de ‖ s igual mf ‖ v (pret & pp **equaled** o **equalled;** ger **equaling** o **equalling**) tr (to be equal to) igualarse a o con; (to make equal) igualar

equali·ty [ɪ'kwɑlɪti] s (pl **-ties**) igualdad

equalize ['ikwə,laɪz] tr igualar; (to make uniform) equilibrar

equally ['ikwəli] adv igualmente

equal opportunity s igualdad de oportunidades

equanimity [,ikwə'nɪmɪti] s ecuanimidad, igualdad de ánimo

equate [i'kwet] tr poner en ecuación; considerar equivalente(s)

equation [i'kweʃən] s ecuación

equator [i'kwetər] s ecuador m

equer·ry ['ɛkwəri] o [ɪ'kwɛri] s (pl **-ries**) caballerizo

equestrian [ɪ'kwɛstrɪ·ən] adj ecuestre ‖ m jinete m, caballista m

equestrian sport s hípica

equilateral [,ikwɪ'lætərəl] adj equilátero

equilibrium [,ikwɪ'lɪbrɪ·əm] s equilibrio

equinoctial [,ikwɪ'nɑkʃəl] adj equinoccial

equinox ['ikwɪ,nɑks] s equinoccio

equip [ɪ'kwɪp] v (pret & pp **equipped;** ger **equipping**) tr equipar

equipment [ɪ'kwɪpmənt] s equipo, avíos, pertrechos; aptitud, capacidad

equipoise ['ikwɪ,pɔɪz] o ['ɛkwɪ,pɔɪz] s equilibrio; contrapeso ‖ tr equilibrar; equipesar

equitable ['ɛkwɪtəbəl] adj equitativo

equi·ty ['ɛkwɪti] s (pl **-ties**) (fairness) equidad; valor líquido

equivalent [ɪ'kwɪvələnt] adj & s equivalente m

equivocal [ɪ'kwɪvəkəl] adj equívoco

equivocate [ɪ'kwɪvə,ket] intr usar de equívocos para engañar, mentir

equivocation [ɪ,kwɪvə'keʃən] s equívoco

era ['ɪrə] o ['irə] s era

eradicate [ɪ'rædɪ,ket] tr erradicar

erase [ɪ'res] tr borrar

eraser [ɪ'resər] s goma de borrar; (for blackboard) cepillo

erasure [ɪ'reʃər] o [ɪ'reʒər] s borradura, tachón m

ere [ɛr] prep antes de ‖ conj antes de que; más bien que

erect [ɪ'rɛkt] adj derecho, enhiesto, erguido; (hair) erizado ‖ tr (to set in upright position) erguir, enhestar; erigir (un edificio); armar, montar (una máquina)

erection [ɪ'rɛkʃən] s erección

erg [ʌrg] s ergio

ermine [ˈʌrmɪn] s armiño; (fig) toga, judicatura

erode [ɪˈrod] tr erosionar ‖ intr erosionarse

erosion [ɪˈroʒən] s erosión

err [ʌr] intr errar, equivocarse, marrar; pecar, marrar

errand [ˈɛrənd] s mandado, recado, comisión; **to run an errand** hacer un mandado

errand boy s recadero, mandadero

erratic [ɪˈrætɪk] adj irregular, inconstante, variable; excéntrico

erra·tum [ɪˈretəm] o [ɪˈratəm] s (pl **-ta** [tə]) errata

erroneous [ɪˈronɪ·əs] adj erróneo

error [ˈɛrər] s error m; **human error** fallo humano

erudite [ˈɛrʊˌdaɪt] adj erudito

erudition [ˌɛrʊˈdɪʃən] s erudición

erupt [ɪˈrʌpt] intr hacer erupción (la piel, los dientes de un niño); erumpir (un volcán)

eruption [ɪˈrʌpʃən] s erupción

escalate [ˈɛskəˌlet] intr escalarse

escalation [ˌɛskəˈleʃən] s escalada, escalación

escalator [ˈɛskəˌletər] s escalera mecánica, móvil o rodante

escallop [ɛsˈkæləp] s concha de peregrino; (on edge of cloth) festón m ‖ tr hornear a la crema y con migajas de pan; cocer (p.ej., ostras) en su concha; festonear

escapade [ɛskəˈped] s calaverada, aventura atolondrada; (flight) escapada

escape [ɛsˈkep] s (getaway) escape m, escapatoria; (from responsibilities, duties, etc.) escapatoria ‖ tr evitar, eludir; **to escape someone** escapársele a uno; olvidársele a uno ‖ intr escapar, escaparse; **to escape from** escaparse a (una persona); escaparse de (la cárcel)

escapee [ɛskəˈpi] s evadido

escape literature s literatura de escape o de evasión

escapement [ɛsˈkepmənt] s escape m

escapement wheel s rueda de escape

escarpment [ɛsˈkarpmənt] s escarpa

eschew [ɛsˈtʃu] tr evitar, rehuir

escort [ˈɛskɔrt] s escolta; (man or boy who accompanies a woman or girl in public) acompañante m, caballero, galán m ‖ [ɛsˈkɔrt] tr escoltar

escutcheon [ɛsˈkʌtʃən] s escudo de armas; (plate in front of lock on door) escudo, escudete m

Eski·mo [ˈɛskɪˌmo] adj esquimal ‖ s (pl **-mos** o **-mo**) esquimal mf

esopha·gus [iˈsafəgəs] s (pl **-gi** [ˌdʒaɪ]) esófago

esp. abbr **especially**

espalier [ɛsˈpæljər] s espaldar m, espalera

especial [ɛsˈpɛʃəl] adj especial

espionage [ˈɛspɪ·ənɪdʒ] o [ˌɛspɪ·əˈnaʒ] s espionaje m

esplanade [ˌɛspləˈned] s explanada

espousal [ɛsˈpauzəl] s desposorios; (of a cause) adhesión

espouse [ɛsˈpauz] tr casarse con; (to advocate, adopt) abogar por, adherirse a

Esq. abbr **Esquire**

esquire [ɛsˈkwair] o [ˈɛskwair] s escudero ‖ **Esquire** s título de cortesía que se escribe después del apellido y que se usa en vez de **Mr.**

essay [ˈɛse] s ensayo

essayist [ˈɛse·ɪst] s ensayista mf

essence [ˈɛsəns] s esencia

essential [eˈsɛnʃəl] adj & s esencial m

est. abbr **established, estate, estimated**

establish [ɛsˈtæblɪʃ] tr establecer

establishment [ɛsˈtæblɪʃmənt] s establecimiento; **the Establishment** (established order) el Sistema

estate [ɛsˈtet] s estado; situación social; (landed property) finca, hacienda, heredad; (a person's possessions) bienes mpl, propiedad; (left by a decedent) herencia, bienes relictos

esteem [ɛsˈtim] s estima ‖ tr estimar

esthete [ˈɛsθit] s esteta mf

esthetic [ɛsˈθɛtɪk] adj estético ‖ **esthetics** ssg estética

estimable [ˈɛstɪməbəl] adj estimable

estimate [ˈɛstɪmɪt] s (calculation of value, judgment of worth) estimación; (statement of cost of work to be done) presupuesto ‖ [ˈɛstɪˌmet] tr (to judge, deem) estimar; presupuestar (el coste de una obra)

estimation [ˌɛstɪˈmeʃən] s estimación

estrangement [ɛsˈtrendʒmənt] s extrañeza

estuar·y [ˈɛstʃʊˌɛri] s (pl **-ies**) estero

etc. abbr **et cetera**

etch [ɛtʃ] tr & intr grabar al agua fuerte

etcher [ˈɛtʃər] s aguafortista mf

etching [ˈɛtʃɪŋ] s aguafuerte f

eternal [ɪˈtʌrnəl] adj eterno

eterni·ty [ɪˈtʌrnɪti] s (pl **-ties**) eternidad

ether [ˈiθər] s éter m

ethereal [ɪˈθɪrɪ·əl] adj etéreo

ethical [ˈɛθɪkəl] adj ético

ethics [ˈɛθɪks] ssg ética

Ethiopian [ˌiθɪˈopɪ·ən] adj & s etíope mf

Ethiopic [ˌiθɪˈopɪk] adj & s etiópico

ethnic(al) [ˈɛθnɪk(əl)] adj étnico

ethnography [ɛθˈnagrəfi] s etnografía

ethnology [ɛθˈnalədʒi] s etnología

ethyl [ˈɛθɪl] s etilo

ethylene [ˈɛθɪˌlin] s etileno

etiquette [ˈɛtɪˌkɛt] s etiqueta

et seq. abbr **et sequens, et sequentes, et sequentia** (Lat) **and the following**

étude [eˈtjud] s (mus) estudio

etymology [ˌɛtɪˈmalədʒi] s etimología

ety·mon [ˈɛtɪˌman] s (pl **-mons** o **-ma** [mə]) étimo

eucalyp·tus [ˌjukəˈlɪptəs] s (pl **-tuses** o **-ti** [taɪ]) eucalipto

Eucharist [ˈjukərɪst] s Eucaristía

euchre [ˈjukər] s juego de naipes ‖ tr (coll) ser más listo que

eugenics [juˈdʒɛnɪks] s eugenesia

eulogistic [ˌjuləˈdʒɪstɪk] adj elogiador

eulogize [ˈjuləˌdʒaɪz] tr elogiar

eulo·gy [ˈjulədʒi] s (pl **-gies**) elogio

eunuch [ˈjunək] s eunuco

euphemism [ˈjufɪˌmɪzəm] s eufemismo

euphemistic [,jufɪˈmɪstɪk] *adj* eufemístico
euphonic [juˈfɑnɪk] *adj* eufónico
eupho‧ny [ˈjufəni] *s* (*pl* **-nies**) eufonía
euphoria [juˈforɪ‧ə] *s* euforia
euphuism [ˈjufju,ɪzəm] *s* eufuísmo
euphuistic [,jufjuˈɪstɪk] *adj* eufuístico
Europe [ˈjurəp] *s* Europa
European [,jurəˈpi‧ən] *adj* & *s* europeo
euthanasia [,juθəˈneʒə] *s* eutanasia
evacuate [ɪˈvækju,et] *tr* & *intr* evacuar
evacuation [ɪ,vækjuˈeʃən] *s* evacuación
evade [ɪˈved] *tr* evadir ‖ *intr* evadirse
evaluate [ɪˈvælju,et] *tr* evaluar
Evangel [ɪˈvændʒəl] *s* Evangelio
evangelic(al) [,ivænˈdʒɛlɪk(əl)] o [,ɛvənˈdʒɛlɪk(əl)] *adj* evangélico
Evangelist [ɪˈvændʒəlɪst] *s* Evangelista *m*
evaporate [ɪˈvæpə,ret] *tr* evaporar ‖ *intr* evaporarse
evasion [ɪˈveʒən] *s* evasión, evasiva
evasive [ɪˈvesɪv] *adj* evasivo; elusivo
eve [iv] *s* víspera; **on the eve of** en vísperas de
even [ˈivən] *adj* (*smooth*) parejo, llano, liso; (*number*) par; constante, uniforme, invariable; (*temperament*) apacible, sereno; exacto, igual; **even with** al nivel de; **to be even** estar en paz; no deber nada a nadie; **to get even** desquitarse ‖ *adv* aun, hasta; sin embargo; también; exactamente, igualmente; **even as** así como; **even if** aunque, aun cuando; **even so** aun así; **even though** aunque, aun cuando; **even when** aun cuando; **not even** ni . . . siquiera; **to break even** salir sin ganar ni perder; (*in gambling*) salir en paz ‖ *tr* allanar, igualar
evening [ˈivnɪŋ] *adj* vespertino ‖ *s* tarde *f*
evening clothes *spl* traje *m* de etiqueta
evening gown *s* vestido de noche (*de mujer*)
evening primrose *s* hierba del asno
evening star *s* estrella vespertina, lucero de la tarde
evening wrap *s* salida de teatro
e‧ven‧song *s* canción de la tarde; (*eccl*) vísperas
event [ɪˈvɛnt] *s* acontecimiento, suceso; (*outcome*) resultado; (*public function*) acto; (*sport*) prueba; **at all events** o **in any event** en todo caso; **in the event that** en caso que
e‧ven-tem‧pered *adj* equilibrado
eventful [ɪˈvɛntfəl] *adj* lleno de acontecimientos; importante, memorable
eventual [ɪˈvɛntʃu‧əl] *adj* final
eventuali‧ty [ɪˈvɛntʃuˈælɪti] *s* (*pl*-**ties**) eventualidad
eventually [ɪˈvɛntʃu‧əli] *adv* finalmente, con el tiempo
eventuate [ɪˈvɛntʃu,et] *intr* concluir, resultar
ever [ˈɛvər] *adv* (*at all times*) siempre; (*at any time*) jamás, nunca, alguna vez; **as ever** como siempre; **as much as ever** tanto como antes; **ever since** (*since that time*) desde entonces; después de que; **ever so** muy; **ever so much** muchísimo; **hardly ever** o **scarcely ever** casi nunca; **not . . . ever** no . . . nunca

ev‧er‧glade *s* tierra pantanosa cubierta de hierbas altas
ev‧er‧green *adj* siempre verde ‖ *s* planta siempre verde; **evergreens** ramas colgadas como adorno
ev‧er‧last‧ing *adj* sempiterno; (*lasting indefinitely*) duradero; (*wearisome*) aburrido, cansado ‖ *s* eternidad; (bot) siempreviva
ev‧er‧more *adv* eternamente; **for evermore** para siempre jamás
every [ˈɛvri] *adj* todos los; (*each*) cada, todo; (*being each in a series*) cada, p.ej., **every three days** cada tres días; **every bit** (coll) todo, p.ej., **every bit a man** todo un hombre; **every now and then** de vez en cuando; **every once in a while** una que otra vez; **every other day** cada dos días, un día sí y otro no; **every which way** (coll) por todas partes; (coll) en desarreglo
ev‧ery‧bod‧y *pron indef* todo el mundo
ev‧ery‧day *adj* de todos los días; cotidiano, diario; común, ordinario
every man Jack o **every mother's son** *s* cada hijo de vecino
ev‧ery‧one o **every one** *pron indef* cada uno, todos, todo el mundo
ev‧ery‧thing *pron indef* todo
ev‧ery‧where *adv* en o por todas partes; a todas partes
evict [ɪˈvɪkt] *tr* desahuciar
eviction [ɪˈvɪkʃən] *s* desahucio
evidence [ˈɛvɪdəns] *s* evidencia; (law) prueba
evident [ˈɛvɪdənt] *adj* evidente
evil [ˈivəl] *adj* malo, malvado, malazo, maléfico ‖ *s* mal *m*, maldad
e‧vil‧do‧er *s* malhechor *m*, malvado
e‧vil‧do‧ing *s* malhecho, maldad
evil eye *s* mal *m* de ojo
evil-minded [ˈivəlˈmaɪndɪd] *adj* mal pensado, malintencionado
Evil One, the el enemigo malo
evince [ɪˈvɪns] *tr* manifestar, mostrar
evoke [ɪˈvok] *tr* evocar
evolution [,ɛvəˈluʃən] *s* evolución; (math) extracción de raíces, radicación
evolutionary [,ɛvəˈluʃə,nɛri] o **evolutionist** [,ɛgəˈluʃənɪst] *s* evolucionista *mf*
evolve [ɪˈvɑlv] *tr* desarrollar; desprender (*olores, gases, calor*) ‖ *intr* evolucionar
ewe [ju] *s* oveja
ewer [ˈju‧ər] *s* aguamanil *m*
ex. *abbr* **examination, example, except, exchange, executive**
ex [ɛks] *prep* sin incluir, sin participación en
exact [ɛgˈzækt] *adj* exacto ‖ *tr* exigir
exacting [ɛgˈzæktɪŋ] *adj* exigente
exaction [ɛgˈzækʃən] *s* exacción
exactly [ɛgˈzæktli] *adv* exactamente; (*sharp, on the dot*) en punto
exactness [ɛg,zæktnɪs] *s* exactitud
exaggerate [ɛgˈzædʒə,ret] *tr* exagerar
exalt [ɛgˈzɔlt] *tr* exaltar, ensalzar
exam [ɛgˈzæm] *s* (coll) examen *m*
examination [ɛg,zæmɪˈneʃən] *s* examen *m*; **to take an examination** sufrir un examen, examinarse
examine [ɛgˈzæmɪn] *tr* examinar

example 453 **exhaust pipe**

example [ɛg'zæmpəl] o [ɛg'zɑmpəl] s ejemplo; (case serving as a warning to others) ejemplar m; (of mathematics) problema m; **for example** por ejemplo

exasperate [ɛg'zæspə,ret] tr exasperar

excavate ['ɛkskə,vet] tr excavar

exceed [ɛk'sid] tr exceder; sobrepasar (p.ej., el límite de velocidad)

exceedingly [ɛk'sidɪŋli] adv sumamente, sobremanera

ex•cel [ɛk'sɛl] v (pret & pp **-celled;** ger **-celling**) tr aventajar ‖ intr sobresalir

excellence ['ɛksələns] s excelencia

excellen•cy ['ɛksələnsi] s (pl **-cies**) excelencia; **Your Excellency** Su Excelencia

excelsior [ɛk'sɛlsɪ•ər] s pajilla de madera, virutas de madera

except [ɛk'sɛpt] prep excepto; **except for** sin; **except that** a menos que ‖ tr exceptuar

exception [ɛk'sɛpʃən] s excepción; **to take exception** poner reparos, objetar; ofenderse; **with the exception of** a excepción de

exceptional [ɛk'sɛpʃənəl] adj excepcional

excerpt ['ɛksʌrpt] s excerta, selección ‖ [ɛk'sʌrpt] tr escoger

excess ['ɛksɛs] o [ɛk'sɛs] adj excedente, sobrante ‖ [ɛk'sɛs] s (amount or degree by which one thing exceeds another) exceso, excedente m; (excessive amount; immoderate indulgence, unlawful conduct) exceso; **in excess of** más que, superior a

excess baggage s exceso de equipaje

excess fare s suplemento

excessive [ɛk'sɛsɪv] adj excesivo

ex′cess-prof′its tax s impuesto sobre beneficios extraordinarios

excess weight s exceso de peso

exchange [ɛks'tʃendʒ] s (of greetings, compliments, blows, etc.) cambio; (of prisoners, merchandise, newspapers, credentials, etc.) canje m; periódico de canje; (place for buying and selling) bolsa, lonja; estación telefónica, central f de teléfonos; **in exchange for** en cambio de, a trueque de ‖ tr cambiar; canjear (prisioneros, mercancías, etc.); darse, hacerse (cortesías); **to exchange greetings** saludarse; **to exchange shots** cambiar disparos

exchequer [ɛks'tʃɛkər] o ['ɛkstʃɛkər] s tesorería; fondos nacionales

excise tax [ɛk'saɪz] o ['ɛksaɪz] m impuesto sobre ciertas mercancías de comercio interior

excitable [ɛk'saɪtəbəl] adj excitable

excite [ɛk'saɪt] tr excitar

excitement [ɛk'saɪtmənt] s excitación

exciting [ɛk'saɪtɪŋ] adj emocionante, conmovedor; (stimulating) excitante

exclaim [ɛks'klem] tr & intr exclamar

exclamation [,ɛkskləˈmeʃən] s exclamación

exclamation mark o **point** s punto de admiración

exclude [ɛks'klud] tr excluir

exclusion [ɛks'kluʒən] s exclusión; **to the exclusion of** con exclusión de

exclusive [ɛks'klusɪv] adj exclusivo; (clannish) exclusivista; (expensive) (coll) carero; (fashionable) (coll) muy de moda; **exclusive of** con exclusión de

excommunicate [,ɛkskəˈmjunɪ,ket] tr excomulgar

excommunication [,ɛkskə,mjunɪˈkeʃən] s excomunión

excoriate [ɛks'kori,et] tr (fig) desollar, vituperar

excrement ['ɛkskrəmənt] s excremento

excruciating [ɛks'kruʃɪ,etɪŋ] adj atroz, agudísimo, vivísimo

exculpate ['ɛkskʌl,pet] o [ɛks'kʌlpet] tr exculpar

excursion [ɛks'kʌrʒən] s excursión

excursionist [ɛks'kʌrʒənɪst] s excursionista mf

excusable [ɛks'kjusəbəl] adj excusable

excuse [ɛks'kjus] s excusa ‖ [ɛks'kjuz] tr excusar, disculpar; dispensar, perdonar

execute ['ɛksɪ'kjut] tr ejecutar; (law) celebrar, finalizar (una escritura)

execution [,ɛksɪˈkjuʃən] s ejecución

executioner [,ɛksɪˈkjuʃənər] s ejecutor m de la justicia, verdugo

executive [ɛg'zɛkjətɪv] adj ejecutivo ‖ m poder ejecutivo; (of a school, business, etc.) dirigente mf

Executive Mansion s (U.S.A.) palacio presidencial

executor [ɛg'zɛkjətər] s albacea m, ejecutor testamentario

executrix [ɛg'zɛkjətrɪks] s albacea f, ejecutora testamentaria

exemplary [ɛg'zɛmpləri] o ['ɛgzəm,plɛri] adj ejemplar

exempli•fy [ɛg'zɛmplɪ,faɪ] v (pret & pp **-fied**) tr ejemplificar

exempt [ɛg'zɛmpt] adj exento ‖ tr eximir, exentar

exemption [ɛg'zɛmpʃən] s exención

exercise ['ɛksər,saɪz] s ejercicio; ceremonia; **to take exercise** hacer ejercicio ‖ tr ejercer (p.ej., caridad, influencia); ejercitar (un arte, profesión, etc.; adiestrar con el ejercicio); inquietar, preocupar; poner (cuidado) ‖ ref ejercitarse

exert [ɛg'zʌrt] tr ejercer (una fuerza); **to exert oneself** esforzarse

exertion [ɛg'zʌrʃən] s esfuerzo, empeño; (active use) ejercicio

exhalation [,ɛks•hə'leʃən] s (of gas, vapors, etc.) exhalación; (of air from lungs) espiración

exhale [ɛks'hel] o [ɛg'zel] tr exhalar (gases, vapores); espirar (el aire aspirado) ‖ intr exhalarse; espirar

exhaust [ɛg'zɔst] s escape m; tubo de escape ‖ tr (to wear out, fatigue; to use up) agotar; hacer el vacío en; apurar (todos los medios)

exhaust fan s ventilador m aspirador

exhaustion [ɛg'zɔstʃən] s agotamiento

exhaustive [ɛg'zɔstɪv] adj exhaustivo; comprensivo

exhaust manifold s múltiple m de escape

exhaust pipe s tubo de escape

eu
ex

exhaust valve s válvula de escape

exhibit [ɛg'zɪbɪt] s exhibición; (law) documento de prueba ‖ tr exhibir

exhibition [,ɛksɪ'bɪʃən] s exhibición

exhibitor [ɛg'zɪbɪtər] s expositor m

exhilarating [ɛg'zɪlə,retɪŋ] adj alegrador, regocijador, alborozador

exhort [ɛg'zɔrt] tr exhortar

exhume [ɛks'hjum] tr exhumar

exigen·cy ['ɛksɪdʒənsi] s (pl -cies) exigencia

exigent ['ɛksɪdʒənt] adj exigente

exile ['ɛgzaɪl] o ['ɛksaɪl] s destierro; (person) desterrado ‖ tr desterrar

exist [ɛg'zɪst] intr existir

existence [ɛg'zɪstəns] s existencia

existing [ɛg'zɪstɪŋ] adj existente

exit ['ɛgzɪt] o ['ɛksɪt] s salida ‖ intr salir

exobiology [,ɛksobaɪ'alədʒi] s exobiología

exodus ['ɛksədəs] s éxodo

exonerate [ɛg'zɑnə,ret] tr (to free from blame) exculpar; (to free from an obligation) exonerar

exorbitant [ɛg'zɔrbɪtənt] adj exorbitante

exorcise ['ɛksɔr,saɪz] tr exorcizar

exotic [ɛg'zɑtɪk] adj exótico

exp. abbr **expenses, expired, export, express**

expand [ɛks,pænd] tr dilatar (un gas, el metal); (to enlarge, develop) ampliar, ensanchar; (to unfold, stretch out) desplegar, extender; (math) desarrollar (una ecuación) ‖ intr dilatarse; ampliarse, ensancharse; desplegarse, extenderse

expanse [ɛks'pæns] s extensión

expansion [ɛks'pænʃən] s expansión

expansive [ɛks'pænsɪv] adj expansivo

expatiate [ɛks'peʃɪ,et] intr espaciarse, explayarse

expatriate [ɛks'petrɪ·ɪt] adj & s expatriado

expect [ɛks'pɛkt] tr esperar; (coll) creer, suponer

expectan·cy [ɛks'pɛktənsi] s (pl -cies) expectación

expectant mother [ɛks'pɛktənt] s futura madre

expectation [,ɛks'pɛkteʃən] s expectativa

expectorate [ɛks'pɛktə,ret] tr & intr expectorar

expedien·cy [ɛks'pidɪ·ənsi] s (pl -cies) conveniencia, oportunidad; ventaja personal

expedient [ɛks'pidɪ·ənt] adj conveniente, oportuno; egoísta, ventajoso; (acting with self-interest) ventajista ‖ s expediente m

expedite ['ɛkspɪ,daɪt] tr apresurar, despachar; expediar; dar curso a (un documento)

expedition [,ɛkspɪ'dɪʃən] s expedición

expeditious [,ɛkspɪ'dɪʃəs] adj expeditivo

expeditiously [,ɛkspɪ'dɪʃəsli] adv ejecutivamente

ex·pel [ɛks'pɛl] v (pret & pp -pelled; ger -pelling) tr expeler, expulsar

expend [ɛks'pɛnd] tr gastar, consumir

expendable [ɛks'pɛndəbəl] adj gastable; (to be thrown away after use) desechable; (soldier) sacrificable

expenditure [ɛks'pɛndɪtʃər] s gasto, consumo

expense [ɛks'pɛns] s gasto; **expenses** gastos, expensas; **to go to the expense of** meterse en gastos con; **to meet expenses** hacer frente a los gastos

expense account s cuenta de gastos

expensive [ɛks'pɛnsɪv] adj caro, costoso, dispendioso; (charging high prices) carero

experience [ɛks'pɪrɪ·əns] s experiencia ‖ tr experimentar

experienced [ɛksɪ'ənst] adj experimentado

experiment [ɛks'pɛrɪmənt] s experiencia, experimento ‖ [ɛks'pɛrɪ,mɛnt] intr experimentar

expert ['ɛkspərt] adj & s experto

expiate ['ɛkspɪ,et] tr expiar

expiation [,ɛkspɪ'eʃən] s expiación

expire [ɛks'paɪr] tr expeler (el aire de los pulmones) ‖ intr expirar (expeler el aire de los pulmones; acabarse, p.ej., un plazo; fallecer)

explain [ɛks'plen] tr explicar; **to explain away** descartar con explicaciones; (to make excuse for) explicar ‖ intr explicar, explicarse

explanation [,ɛksplə'neʃən] s explicación; dilucidación

explanatory [ɛks'plænə,tori] adj explicativo

explicit [ɛks'plɪsɪt] adj explícito

explode [ɛks'plod] tr volar, hacer saltar; desacreditar (una teoría) ‖ intr explotar, estallar, reventar

exploit ['ɛksplɔɪt] s hazaña, proeza ‖ [ɛks'plɔɪt] tr explotar

exploitation [,ɛksplɔɪ'teʃən] s explotación

exploration [,ɛksplə'reʃən] s exploración

explore [ɛks'plor] tr explorar

explorer [ɛks'plorər] s explorador m

explosion [ɛks'ploʒən] s explosión; (of a theory) refutación

explosive [ɛks'plosɪv] adj explosivo ‖ s explosivo; (phonet) explosiva

exponent [ɛks'ponənt] s exponente m, expositor m; (math) exponente m

export ['ɛksport] adj de exportación ‖ s exportación; **exports** (articles exported) exportación ‖ [ɛks'port] o ['ɛksport] tr & intr exportar

exportation [,ɛkspor'teʃən] s exportación

exporter [ɛks'portər] s exportador m

expose [ɛks'poz] tr exponer; (to unmask) desenmascarar; (the Host) manifestar, exponer; (phot) impresionar

exposé [,ɛkspo'ze] s desenmascaramiento

exposition [,ɛkspə'zɪʃən] s exposición; (rhet) exposición

expostulate [ɛks'pastʃə,let] intr protestar; **to expostulate with** reconvenir

exposure [ɛks'poʒər] s (to a danger; position with respect to points of compass) exposición; (unmasking) desenmascaramiento; (phot) exposición

expound [ɛks'paʊnd] tr exponer

express [ɛks'prɛs] adj expreso ‖ adv (for a special purpose) expresamente; por expreso ‖ s expreso; **by express** (rr) en gran velocidad ‖ tr expresar; (to squeeze out) exprimir; enviar por expreso; **to express oneself** expresarse

express company *s* compañía de transportes rápidos

expression [ɛks'prɛʃən] *s* expresión

expressive [ɛks'prɛsɪv] *adj* expresivo

expressly [ɛks'prɛsli] *adv* expresamente

express•man [ɛks'prɛsmən] *s* (*pl* -men [mən]) (U.S.A.) empleado del servicio de transportes rápidos

express train *s* tren expreso

express'way *s* carretera de vía libre

expropriate [ɛks'propri,et] *tr* expropiar

expulsion [ɛks'pʌlʃən] *s* expulsión

expunge [ɛks'pʌndʒ] *tr* borrar, cancelar, arrasar

expurgate ['ɛkspər,get] *tr* expurgar

exquisite ['ɛkskwɪzɪt] o [ɛks'kwɪzɪt] *adj* exquisito; agudo, vivo; sensible

ex-service•man [,ɛks'sʌrvɪs,mæn] *s* (*pl* -men [,mɛn]) ex militar *m*, ex combatiente *m*

extant ['ɛkstənt] o [ɛks'tænt] *adj* existente

extemporaneous [ɛks,tɛmpə'reni•əs] *adj* sin preparación; (*made for the occasion*) provisional

extempore [ɛks'tɛmpəri] *adj* improvisado ‖ *adv* improvisadamente

extemporize [ɛks'tɛmpə,raɪz] *tr & intr* improvisar

extend [ɛks'tɛnd] *tr* extender; dar, ofrecer; hacer extensivos (*p.ej., vivos deseos*); prorrogar (*un plazo*) ‖ *intr* extenderse

extended [ɛks'tɛndɪd] *adj* extenso; prolongado

extension [ɛks'tɛnʃən] *s* extensión; prolongación

extension ladder *s* escalera extensible

extension table *s* mesa de extensión

extensive [ɛks'tɛnsɪv] *adj* (*having great extent*) extenso; (*characterized by extension*) extensivo

extent [ɛks'tɛnt] *s* extensión; **to a certain extent** hasta cierto punto; **to a great extent** en sumo grado; **to the full extent** en toda su extensión

extenuate [ɛks'tɛnju,et] *tr* (*to make seem less serious*) atenuar; (*to underrate*) menospreciar, no dar importancia a

exterior [ɛks'tɪri•ər] *adj & s* exterior *m*

exterminate [ɛks'tʌrmɪ,net] *tr* exterminar; (*insects*) desinsectar

external [ɛks'tʌrnəl] *adj* externo ‖ **externals** *spl* exterioridad

extinct [ɛks'tɪŋkt] *adj* desaparecido; (*volcano*) extinto

extinguish [ɛkstɪŋgwɪʃ] *tr* extinguir

extinguisher [ɛks'tɪŋgwɪʃər] *s* apagador *m*, extintor *m*

extirpate ['ɛkstər,pet] o [ɛks'tʌrpet] *tr* extirpar

ex•tol [ɛks'tol] o [ɛks'tɑl] *v* (*pret & pp* -tolled; *ger* -tolling) *tr* ensalzar

extort [ɛks'tɔrt] *tr* obtener por amenazas, fuerza o engaño

extortion [ɛks'tɔrʃən] *s* extorción

extra ['ɛkstrə] *adj* extra; (*spare*) de repuesto ‖ *adv* extraordinariamente ‖ *s* (*of a newspaper*) extra *m;* pieza de repuesto; (*something additional*) extra *m;* (theat) extra *mf*

extract ['ɛkstrækt] *s* selección; (pharm) extracto ‖ [ɛks'trækt] *tr* (*to pull out, remove*) extraer; seleccionar (*pasajes de un libro*); (math) extraer

extraction [ɛks'trækʃən] *s* extracción

extracurricular [,ɛkstrəkə'rɪkjələr] *adj* extracurricular

extradition [,ɛkstrə'dɪʃən] *s* extradición

extra fare *s* recargo de tarifa, tarifa recargada

ex'tra-flat' *adj* extraplano

extragalactic [,ɛkstrəgə'læktɪk] *adj* extragaláctico

extramural [,ɛkstrə'mjurəl] *adj* extramural

extraneous [ɛks'treni•əs] *adj* ajeno, extraño

extraordinary [,ɛkstrə'ɔrdɪ,nɛri] o [ɛks'trɔrdɪ,nɛri] *adj* extraordinario

extrapolate [ɛks'træpə,let] *tr & intr* extrapolar

extrasensory [,ɛkstrə'sɛnsəri] *adj* extrasensorio

extraterrestrial [,ɛkstrətə'rɛstri•əl] *adj* extraterrestre

extravagance [ɛks'trævəgəns] *s* derroche *m*, prodigalidad, gasto excesivo; (*wildness, folly*) extravagancia

extravagant [ɛks'trævəgənt] *adj* derrochador, pródigo, gastador; (*wild, foolish*) extravagante

extreme [ɛks'trim] *adj & s* extremo; **in the extreme** en sumo grado; **to go to extremes** excederse, propasarse

extremely [ɛks'trimli] *adv* extremadamente, sumamente

extreme unction *s* extremaunción

extremism [ɛks'trimɪzəm] *s* extremismo

extremi•ty [ɛks'trɛmɪti] *s* (*pl* -ties) extremidad; (*great want*) extrema necesidad; **extremities** medidas extremas; (*hands and feet*) extremidades

extricate ['ɛskstrɪ,ket] *tr* desembarazar, desenredar

extrinsic [ɛks'trɪnsɪk] *adj* extrínseco

extroversion [,ɛkstrə'vʌrʒən] *s* extroversión

extrovert ['ɛkstrə,vʌrt] *s* extrovertido

extrude [ɛks'trud] *intr* resaltar, sobresalir

exuberant [ɛg'zubərənt] *adj* exuberante

exude [ɛg'zud] o [ɛk'sud] *tr & intr* exudar

exult [ɛg'zʌlt] *intr* exultar, gloriarse

exultant [ɛg'zʌltənt] *adj* exultante

eye [aɪ] *s* ojo; (*of hook and eye*) hembra, corcheta; **to catch one's eye** llamar la atención a uno; **to feast one's eyes on** deleitar la vista en; **to lay eyes on** alcanzar a ver; **to make eyes at** hacer guiños a; **to roll one's eyes** poner los ojos en blanco; **to see eye to eye** estar completamente de acuerdo; **to shut one's eyes to** hacer la vista gorda ante; **without batting an eye** sin pestañear, sin inmutarse ‖ *v* (*pret & pp* **eyed;** *ger* **eying** o **eyeing**) *tr* ojear; **to eye up and down** mirar de hito en hito

eye'ball' *s* globo del ojo

eye'bolt' *s* armella, cáncamo

eye'brow' *s* ceja; **to raise one's eyebrows** arquear las cejas

ex
ey

eye′cup′ *s* ojera, lavaojos *m*
eyeful [′aɪfʊl] *s* (coll) buena ojeada
eye′glass′ *s* (*of optical instrument*) ocular *m;* (*eyecup*) ojera, lavaojos *m;* **eyeglasses** gafas, anteojos
eye′lash′ *s* pestaña
eyelet [′aɪlɪt] *s* ojete *m*, ojal *m;* (*hole to look through*) mirilla
eye′lid′ *s* párpado
eye of the morning *s* sol *m*
eye opener [′opənər] *s* noticia asombrosa o inesperada; (coll) trago de licor
eye′piece′ *s* ocular *m*
eye′shade′ *s* visera
eye shadow *s* crema para los párpados; sombra (de ojos)

eye′shot′ *s* alcance *m* de la vista
eye′sight′ *s* vista; (*range*) alcance *m* de la vista
eye socket *s* cuenca del ojo
eye′sore′ *s* cosa que ofende la vista
eye′strain′ *s* vista fatigada
eye′-test′ chart *s* escala tipográfica oftalmométrica, tipo de ensayo, tipo de prueba
eye′tooth′ *s* (*pl* teeth′) colmillo, diente canino; **to cut one's eyeteeth** (coll) tener el colmillo retorcido; **to give one's eyeteeth for** (coll) dar los ojos de la cara por
eye′wash′ *s* colirio; (slang) halago para engañar
eye′wit′ness *s* testigo ocular, testigo presencial
ey·rie o ey·ry [′ɛri] *s* (*pl* -ries) nido de águilas, nido de aves de rapiña; (fig) altura, morada elevada

F

F, f [ɛf] sexta letra del alfabeto inglés
f. *abbr* **feminine, folio**
F. *abbr* **Fahrenheit, Friday**
fable [′febəl] *s* fábula
fabric [′fæbrɪk] *s* tejido; textura; (*structure*) fábrica
fabricate [′fæbrɪ, ket] *tr* fabricar
fabrication [,fæbrɪ′keʃən] *s* fabricación; mentira
fabulous [′fæbjələs] *adj* fabuloso
façade [fə′sɑd] *s* fachada
face [fes] *s* cara, rostro; (*of cloth*) haz *f;* (*of earth*) faz *f;* (*grimace*) mueca; (*of watch*) esfera, muestra; (*impudence*) descaro; **in the face of** en presencia de; **to keep a straight face** contener la risa; **to lose face** desprestigiarse; **to save face** salvar las apariencias; **to show one's face** dejarse ver ‖ *tr* volver la cara hacia; arrostrar; revestir (*un muro*); forrar (*un vestido*); **facing** cara a ‖ *intr* — **to face about** volver la mirada; dar media vuelta; cambiar de opinión; **to face on** dar a o sobre; **to face up to** encararse con
face card *s* figura, naipe *m* de figura
face lifting *s* cirugía estética
face powder *s* polvos de tocador
facet [′fæsɪt] *s* faceta
facial [′feʃəl] *adj* facial ‖ *s* masaje *m* facial
facilitate [fə′sɪlɪ,tet] *tr* facilitar
facil·ity [fə′sɪlɪti] *s* (*pl* -ties) facilidad
facing [′fesɪŋ] *s* revestimiento, paramento
facsimile [fæk′sɪmɪli] *s* facsímile *m* ‖ *tr* facsimilar
fact [fækt] *s* hecho; **in fact** en realidad; **the fact is that** ello es que
faction [′fækʃən] *s* facción; discordia
factional [′fækʃənəl] *adj* faccionario
factionalism [′fækʃənə,lɪzəm] *s* parcialidad, partidismo

factor [′fæktər] *s* factor *m* ‖ *tr* descomponer en factores
facto·ry [′fæktəri] *s* (*pl* -ries) fábrica
factual [′fæktʃʊ·əl] *adj* verdadero, objetivo
facul·ty [′fækəlti] *s* (*pl* -ties) facultad
fad [fæd] *s* afición pasajera, moda pasajera
fade [fed] *tr* desteñir ‖ *intr* desteñir, desteñirse; apagarse (*un sonido*); (rad) desvanecerse
fade′out′ *s* desaparición gradual; (rad) desvanecimiento
fag [fæg] *s* (*drudge*) yunque *m;* (coll) cigarrillo ‖ *tr*—**to fag out** cansar
fagot [′fægət] *s* haz *m* de leña
fail [fel] *s*—**without fail** sin falta ‖ *tr* faltar a; reprobar, suspender (a un alumno); salir mal en (un examen) ‖ *intr* malograrse, fracasar; salir mal (un alumno); fallar (un motor); (com) quebrar, hacer bancarrota; **to fail to** dejar de
failure [′feljər] *s* malogro, fracaso, mal éxito; (*student*) perdigón *m;* (com) quiebra
faint [fent] *adj* débil; **to feel faint** sentirse desfallecido ‖ *s* desmayo ‖ *intr* desmayarse
faint-hearted [′fent′hɑrtɪd] *adj* cobarde, tímido, apocado
fair [fer] *adj* justo, imparcial; regular, ordinario; favorable, propicio; (*hair*) rubio; (*complexion*) blanco; (*sky*) despejado; (*weather*) bueno, bonancible ‖ *adv* imparcialmente; **to play fair** jugar limpio ‖ *s* (*exhibition*) feria; (*carnival*) quermese *m*, verbena
fair′ground′ *s* real *m*, campo de una feria
fairly [′ferli] *adv* justamente; bastante
fair-minded [′fer′maɪndɪd] *adj* justo, imparcial
fairness [′fɛrnɪs] *s* justicia, imparcialidad; (*of weather*) serenidad; (*of complexion*) blancura
fair play *s* juego limpio, limpieza

fair sex *s* bello sexo
fair to middling *adj* bastante bueno, mediano
fair'weath'er *adj*—**a fair-weather friend** amigo del buen viento
fair·y ['fɛri] *adj* feérico ‖ *s* (*pl* -ies) hada
fairy godmother *s* hada madrina
fair'y·land' *s* tierra de las hadas
fairy ring *s* corro de brujas
fairy tale *s* cuento de hadas; (*fig*) bella poesía
faith [feθ] *s* fe *f;* **to break faith with** faltar a la palabra dada a; **to keep faith with** cumplir la palabra dada a; **to pin one's faith on** tener puesta su esperanza en; **upon my faith!** ¡a fe mía!
faithful ['feθfəl] *adj* fiel, leal ‖ **the faithful** los fieles
faithless ['feθlɪs] *adj* infiel, desleal
fake [fek] *adj* (*coll*) falso, fingido ‖ *s* impostura, patraña; (*person*) farsante *mf* ‖ *tr & intr* falsificar, fingir
faker ['fekər] *s* (*coll*) impostor *m*, patrañero; (*peddler*) (*coll*) buhonero
falcon ['fɔkən] o ['fɔlkən] *s* halcón *m*
falconer ['fɔkənər] o ['fɔlkənər] *s* cetrero, halconero
falconry ['fɔkənri] o ['fɔlkənri] *s* cetrería, halconería
fall [fɔl] *adj* otoñal ‖ *s* caída; (*of water*) catarata, salto de agua; (*of prices*) baja; (*autumn*) otoño; **falls** catarata, caída de agua ‖ *v* (*pret* **fell** [fɛl]; *pp* **fallen** ['fɔlən]) *intr* caer, caerse; **to fall apart** caerse a pedazos; **to fall back** (*mil*) replegarse; **to fall behind** quedarse atrás; **to fall down** caerse; **to fall due** vencer (*una letra*); **to fall flat** caer tendido; no tener éxito; **to fall for** (*slang*) ser engañado por; (*slang*) enamorarse de; **to fall in** desplomarse (*un techo*); ponerse de acuerdo; **to fall in with** trabar amistades con; ponerse de acuerdo con; **to fall off** caer de; disminuir; **to fall out** desavenirse; **to fall out of** caerse de; **to fall out with** esquinarse con; **to fall over** caerse; (*coll*) adular, halagar; **to fall through** fracasar, malograrse; **to fall to** recaer (*la herencia, la elección*) en; **to fall under** estar comprendido en
fallacious [fə'leʃəs] *adj* erróneo, engañoso
falla·cy ['fæləsi] *s* (*pl* -cies) error *m*, equivocación
fall guy *s* (*slang*) cabeza de turco
fallible ['fælɪbəl] *adj* falible
falling star *s* estrella fugaz
fall'out' *s* caída radiactiva, precipitación radiactiva
fallout shelter *s* refugio antiatómico
fallow ['fælo] *adj* barbechado; **to lie fallow** estar en barbecho (*tierra labrantía*); (*fig*) quedar sin emplear, quedar sin ejecutar (*una cosa provechosa*) ‖ *s* barbecho ‖ *tr* barbechar
false [fɔls] *adj* falso; (*hair, teeth, etc.*) postizo ‖ *adv* falsamente; **to play false** traicionar
false colors *spl* pretextos falsos

false face *s* mascarilla; (*ugly false face*) carantamaula
false-hearted ['fɔls'hɑrtɪd] *adj* pérfido
falsehood ['fɔls·hud] *s* falsedad
false pretenses *spl* impostura, falsas apariencias
false return *s* declaración falsa
falset·to [fɔl'sɛto] *s* (*pl* -tos) (*voice*) falsete *m;* (*person*) falsetista *m*
falsi·fy ['fɔlsɪ,faɪ] *v* (*pret & pp* -fied) *tr* falsificar; (*to disprove*) refutar ‖ *intr* falsificar; mentir
falsi·ty ['fɔlsɪti] *s* (*pl* -ties) falsedad
falter ['fɔltər] *s* vacilación; (*in speech*) balbuceo ‖ *intr* vacilar; balbucear
fame [fem] *s* fama
famed [femd] *adj* afamado
familiar [fə'mɪljər] *adj* familiar; conocido, común; **familiar with** familiarizado con
familiari·ty [fə,mɪlɪ'ærɪti] *s* (*pl* -ties) familiaridad; conocimiento
familiarize [fə'mɪljə,raɪz] *tr* familiarizar
fami·ly ['fæmɪli] *adj* familiar; **in the family way** (*coll*) en estado de buena esperanza ‖ *s* (*pl* -lies) familia
family man *s* padre *m* de familia; hombre casero
family name *s* apellido
family physician *s* médico de cabecera
family tree *s* árbol genealógico
famish ['fæmɪʃ] *tr & intr* hambrear
famished ['fæmɪʃt] *adj* famélico
famous ['feməs] *adj* famoso; (*notable, excellent*) (*coll*) famoso
fan [fæn] *s* abanico; ventilador *m;* (*slang*) hincha *mf*, aficionado ‖ *v* (*pret & pp* **fanned;** *ger* **fanning**) *tr* abanicar; (*to winnow*) aventar; ahuyentar con abanico; avivar (*el fuego*); excitar (*las pasiones*); (*slang*) azotar ‖ *intr* abanicarse; **to fan out** salir (*un camino*) en todas direcciones
fanatic [fə'nætɪk] *adj & s* fanático
fanatical [fə'nætɪkəl] *adj* fanático
fanaticism [fə'nætɪ,sɪzəm] *s* fanatismo
fancied ['fænsid] *adj* imaginario
fancier ['fænsɪ·ər] *s* aficionado; visionario; (*of animals*) criador aficionado
fanciful ['fænsɪfəl] *adj* fantástico, extravagante; imaginativo
fan·cy ['fænsi] *adj* (*comp* -cier; *super* -ciest) de fantasía, de imitación; fino, de lujo, precioso; ornamental; primoroso; fantástico, extravagante ‖ *s* (*pl* -cies) fantasía; afición, gusto; **to take a fancy to** aficionarse a, prendarse de ‖ *v* (*pret & pp* -cied) *tr* imaginar
fancy ball *s* baile *m* de trajes
fancy dive *s* salto ornamental
fancy dress *s* traje *m* de fantasía
fancy foods *spl* comestibles *mpl* de lujo
fan'cy-free' *adj* libre del poder del amor
fancy jewelry *s* joyas de fantasía
fancy skating *s* patinaje *m* de fantasía
fan'cy·work' *s* (*sew*) labor *f*
fanfare ['fænfɛr] *s* fanfarria
fang [fæŋ] *s* colmillo; (*of reptile*) diente *m*
fan'light' *s* abanico

ey
fa

fantastic(al) [fæn`tæstɪk(əl)] *adj* fantástico
fanta·sy [`fæntəsi] *s* (*pl* **-sies**) fantasía
far [fɑr] *adj* lejano; **on the far side of** del otro lado de ‖ *adv* lejos; **as far as** hasta; en cuanto; **as far as I am concerned** por lo que a mí me toca; **as far as I know** que yo sepa; **by far** con mucho; **far and near** por todas partes; **far away** muy lejos; **far be it from me** no lo permita Dios; **far better** mucho mejor; **far different** muy diferente; **far from** lejos de; **far from it** ni con mucho; **far into** hasta muy adentro de; hasta muy tarde de; **far more** mucho más; **far off** a gran distancia; **how far** cuán lejos; **how far is it?** ¿cuánto hay de aquí?; **in so far as** en cuanto; **thus far** hasta ahora; **thus far this year** en lo que va del año; **to go far towards** contribuir mucho a
faraway [`fɑrə,we] *adj* lejano, distante; abstraído, preocupado
farce [fɑrs] *s* farsa; (*ridiculous act*) papelada
farcical [`fɑrsɪkəl] *adj* ridículo
fare [fer] *s* pasaje *m;* pasajero; alimento; comida; **to collect fares** cobrar el pasaje ‖ *intr* pasarlo, p.ej., **how did you fare?** ¿cómo lo pasó Vd.?
Far East *s* Extremo Oriente, Lejano Oriente
fare´well´ *s* despedida; **to bid farewell to** o **to take farewell of** despedirse de ‖ *interj* ¡adiós!
far·fetched [`fɑr`fɛtʃt] *adj* traído por los pelos
far-flung [`fɑr`flʌŋ] *adj* de gran alcance, vasto
farm [fɑrm] *adj* agrícola; agropecuario ‖ *s* granja; terreno agrícola ‖ *tr* cultivar, labrar (*la tierra*) ‖ *intr* cultivar la tierra y criar animales
farmer [`fɑrmər] *s* granjero; agricultor *m,* labrador *m*
farm hand *s* peón *m,* mozo de granja
farm´house´ *s* alquería, cortijo
farming [`fɑrmɪŋ] *s* agricultura, labranza
farm´yard´ *s* corral *m* de granja
far´-off´ *adj* lejano, distante
far-reaching [`fɑr`ritʃɪŋ] *adj* de mucho alcance
far-sighted [`fɑr`saɪtɪd] *adj* longividente; precavido; présbita
farther [`fɑrðər] *adj* más lejano; adicional ‖ *adv* más lejos, más allá; además, también; **farther on** más adelante
farthest [`fɑrðɪst] *adj* (el) más lejano; último ‖ *adv* más lejos; más
farthing [`fɑrðɪŋ] *s* (Brit) cuarto de penique
Far West *s* (U.S.A.) Lejano Oeste
fascinate [`fæsɪ,net] *tr* fascinar
fascinating [`fæsɪ,netɪŋ] *adj* fascinante, cautivador
fascism [`fæʃɪzəm] *s* fascismo
fascist [`fæʃɪst] *adj* & *s* fascista *mf*
fashion [`fæʃən] *s* moda, boga; estilo, manera; alta sociedad; **after a fashion** en cierto modo; **in fashion** de moda; **out of fashion** fuera de moda; **to go out of fashion** pasar de moda ‖ *tr* labrar, forjar
fashion designing *s* alta costura

fashion plate *s* figurín *m;* (*person*) (coll) figurín *m,* elegante *mf;* **to be a fashion plate** (coll) ir o hecho un maniquí
fashion show *s* desfile *m* de modas
fast [fæst] *adj* rápido, veloz; (*clock*) adelantado; fijado; disipado; (*friend*) fiel ‖ *adv* aprisa, rápidamente; firmemente; (*asleep*) profundamente; **to hold fast** mantenerse firme; **to live fast** vivir de una manera disipada ‖ *s* ayuno; **to break one's fast** romper el ayuno ‖ *intr* ayunar
fast day *s* día *m* de ayuno
fasten [`fæsən] *tr* fijar; atar; abrochar; cerrar con llave; (*one's belt*) ajustarse; (*blame*) aplicar ‖ *intr* fijarse
fastener [`fæsənər] *s* asilla; (*snap, clasp*) cierre *m;* (*for papers*) sujetapapeles *m*
fast´-food´ restaurant *s* rotisería
fast forward *s* (mach, mov) avance rápido
fastidious [fæs`tɪdɪ·əs] *adj* esquilmoso, quisquilloso, descontentadizo
fasting [`fæstɪŋ] *s* ayuno
fat [fæt] *adj* (*comp* **fatter;** *super* **fattest**) gordo; poderoso; opulento; (*profitable*) pingüe; (*spark*) caliente; **to get fat** engordar ‖ *s* grasa; (*suet*) gordo, sebo
fatal [`fetəl] *adj* fatal
fatalism [`fetə,lɪzəm] *s* fatalismo
fatalist [`fetəlɪst] *s* fatalista *mf*
fatali·ty [fə`tælɪti] *s* (*pl* **-ties**) fatalidad; (*in accidents, war, etc.*) muerte *f*
fate [fet] *s* sino, hado; **the Fates** las Parcas ‖ *tr* condenar, predestinar
fated [`fetɪd] *adj* hadado, predestinado
fateful [`fetfəl] *adj* fatídico; fatal
fat´head´ *s* (coll) tronco, estúpido
father [`fɑðər] *s* padre *m;* (*an elderly man*) (coll) tío ‖ *tr* servir de padre a; engendrar; inventar
fatherhood [`fɑðər,hud] *s* paternidad
fa´ther-in-law´ *s* (*pl* **fathers-in-law**) suegro
fa´ther·land´ *s* patria
fatherless [`fɑðərlɪs] *adj* huérfano de padre, sin padre
fatherly [`fɑðərli] *adj* paternal
Father's Day *s* día *m* del padre
Father Time *s* el Tiempo
fathom [`fæðəm] *s* braza ‖ *tr* sondear; profundizar
fathomless [`fæðəmlɪs] *adj* insondable
fatigue [fə`tig] *s* fatiga; (mil) faena ‖ *tr* fatigar, cansar
fatigue clothes *spl* (mil) traje *m* de faena
fatigue duty *s* faena
fatten [`fætən] *tr* & *intr* engordar
fat·ty [`fæti] *adj* (*comp* **-tier;** *super* **-tiest**) graso; (pathol) grasoso; (*chubby*) (coll) gordiflón ‖ *s* (*pl* **-ties**) (coll) gordiflón *m*
fatuous [`fætʃu·əs] *adj* fatuo; irreal, ilusivo
faucet [`fɔsɪt] *s* grifo
fault [fɔlt] *s* (*misdeed, blame*) culpa; (*defect*) falta; (geol) falla; (sport) falta; **it's your fault Vd.** tiene la culpa; **to a fault** excesivamente; **to find fault with** culpar, echar la culpa a; hallar defecto en
fault´find´er *s* criticón *m,* reparón *m*

fault'find'ing *adj* criticón, reparón || *s* manía de criticar

faultless ['fɔltlɪs] *adj* perfecto, impecable

fault·y ['fɔlti] *adj* (*comp* **-ier;** *super* **-iest**) defectuoso, imperfecto

faun [fɔn] *s* fauno

fauna ['fɔnə] *s* fauna

favor ['fevər] *s* favor *m*; (*letter*) atenta, grata; **do me the favor to** hágame Vd. el favor de; **by your favor** con permiso de Vd.; **favors** regalos de fiesta, objetos de cotillón; **to be in favor with** disfrutar del favor de; **to be out of favor** caer en desgracia || *tr* favorecer; (coll) parecerse a

favorable ['fevərəbəl] *adj* favorable

favorite ['fevərɪt] *adj* & *s* favorito

favoritism ['fevərɪ,tɪzəm] *s* favoritismo

fawn [fɔn] *s* cervato || *intr* — **to fawn on** adular servilmente; hacer fiestas a

faze [fez] *tr* (coll) molestar, desanimar

FBI [,ɛf,bi'aɪ] *s* (letterword) **Federal Bureau of Investigation**

fear [fɪr] *s* miedo; **for fear of** por miedo de, por temor de; **for fear that** por miedo (de) que; **no fear** no hay peligro; **to be in fear of** tener miedo de || *tr* & *intr* temer

fearful ['fɪrfəl] *adj* medroso; (coll) enorme, muy malo

fearless ['fɪrlɪs] *adj* arrojado, intrépido

feasible ['fɪsɪbəl] *adj* factible, viable

feast [fist] *s* fiesta; (*sumptuous meal*) festín *m*, banquete *m* || *tr* & *intr* banquetear; **to feast on** regalarse con

feat [fit] *s* hazaña, proeza

feather ['fɛðər] *s* pluma; (*plume; arrogance*) penacho; clase *f*, género; **in fine feather** de buen humor; en buena salud || *tr* emplumar; (carp) machihembrar; **to feather one's nest** hacer todo para enriquecerse

feather bed *s* colchón *m* de plumas; (*comfortable situation*) lecho de plumas

feath'er·bed'ding *s* empleo de más obreros de lo necesario (*exigido por los sindicatos*)

feath'er·brain' *s* cascabelero

feath'er·edge' *s* (*of board*) bisel *m*; (*of sharpened tool*) filván *m*

feathery ['fɛðəri] *adj* plumoso

feature ['fitʃər] *s* facción; característica, rasgo distintivo; película principal; artículo principal; **features** facciones || *tr* delinear; ofrecer como cosa principal; (coll) destacar, hacer resaltar

feature writer *s* articulista *mf*

February ['fɛbru,ɛri] *s* febrero

feces ['fisiz] *spl* heces *fpl*, excremento

feckless ['fɛklɪs] *adj* abatido, sin valor; débil

federal ['fɛdərəl] *adj* & *s* federal *mf*

federate ['fɛdə,ret] *adj* federado || *tr* federar || *intr* federarse

federation [,fɛdə'reʃən] *s* federación

fedora [fɪ'dorə] *s* sombrero de fieltro suave con ala vuelta

fed up [fɛd] *adj* harto; **to get fed up with** desenamorarse de

fee [fi] *s* honorarios; (*for admission, tuition, etc.*) cuota, precio; (*tip*) propina || *tr* pagar; dar propina a

feeble ['fibəl] *adj* débil; caedizo

feeble-minded ['fibəl'maɪndɪd] *adj* imbécil; irresoluto, vacilante

feed [fid] *s* alimento, comida; (mach) dispositivo de alimentación || *v* (*pret* & *pp* **fed** [fɛd]) *tr* alimentar || *intr* alimentarse

feed'back' *s* regeneración, realimentación, retroalimentación; comentarios *fpl*; informaciones *fpl*; comentario privado y confidencial

feed bag *s* cebadera, morral *m*

feeder industries *spl* subsidiarias *fpl*

feed pump *s* bomba de alimentación

feed trough *s* comedero

feed wire *s* (elec) conductor *m* de alimentación

feel [fil] *s* sensación; (*sense of what is right*) tino || *v* (*pret* & *pp* **felt** [fɛlt]) *tr* sentir; (*e.g., with the hands*) palpar, tentar; tomar (*el pulso*); tantear (*el camino*) || *intr* (*sick, tired, etc.*) sentirse; palpar; **to feel bad** sentirse mal; condolerse; **to feel cheap** avergonzarse; **to feel comfortable** sentirse a gusto; **to feel for** buscar tentando; condolerse de; **to feel like** tener ganas de; **to feel safe** sentirse a salvo; **to feel sorry** sentir; arrepentirse; **to feel sorry for** compadecer; arrepentirse de

feeler ['filər] *s* (*something said to draw someone out*) buscapié *m*, tranquilla; **feelers** (*of insect*) anténulas, palpos; (*of mollusk*) tentáculos

feeling ['filɪŋ] *s* (*with senses*) sensación; (*impression, emotion*) sentimiento; presentimiento; parecer *m*

feign [fen] *tr* aparentar, fingir || *intr* fingir; **to feign to be** fingirse

feint [fent] *s* (*threat*) finta; (*of fencer*) pase *m*, treta || *intr* hacer una finta

feldspar ['fɛld,spar] *s* feldespato

felicitate [fə'lɪsɪ,tet] *tr* felicitar

felicitous [fə'lɪsɪtəs] *adj* (*opportune*) feliz; elocuente

fell [fɛl] *adj* cruel, feroz, mortal || *tr* talar (*árboles*)

felloe ['fɛlo] *s* aro de la rueda; (*part of this*) pina

fellow ['fɛlo] *s* (coll) mozo, tipo, sujeto; (coll) pretendiente *m*; prójimo; (*of a society*) socio, miembro; (*holder of fellowship*) pensionista *mf*

fellow being *s* prójimo

fellow citizen *s* conciudadano

fellow countryman *s* compatriota *mf*

fellow man *s* prójimo

fellow member *s* consocio

fellowship ['fɛlo,ʃɪp] *s* compañerismo; (*for study*) pensión

fellow traveler *s* compañero de viaje

felon ['fɛlən] *s* delincuente *mf* de mayor cuantía; (pathol) panadizo

felo·ny ['fɛləni] *s* (*pl* **-nies**) delito de mayor cuantía; **to compound a felony** aceptar dinero para no procesar

felt [fɛlt] *s* fieltro

felt'-tipped' pen *s* rotulador *m*; plumón *m* (Mex)

female [ˈfimel] *adj* (*sex*) femenino; (*animal, plant, piece of a device*) hembra || *s* hembra
feminine [ˈfɛmɪnɪn] *adj & s* femenino
feminism [ˈfɛmɪˌnɪzəm] *s* feminismo
fen [fɛn] *s* pantano
fence [fɛns] *s* cerca, cercado; (*for stolen goods*) alcahuete *m; receptador*; (*of a saw*) guía; **on the fence** (coll) indeciso || *tr* cercar || *intr* esgrimir
fencing [ˈfɛnsɪŋ] *s* (*art*) esgrima; (*act*) esgrimidura
fencing academy *s* escuela de esgrima
fend [fɛnd] *tr* — **to fend off** apartar, resguardarse de || *intr* — **to fend for oneself** (coll) tirar por su lado
fender [ˈfɛndər] *s* (*mudguard*) guardafango, guardabarros *m;* (*of locomotive*) quitapiedras *m;* (*of trolley car*) salvavidas *m;* (*of fireplace*) guardafuego
fennel [ˈfɛnəl] *s* hinojo
ferment [ˈfɛrmɛnt] *s* fermento; fermentación || [fərˈmɛnt] *tr & intr* fermentar
fern [fʌrn] *s* helecho
ferocious [fəˈroʃəs] *adj* feroz
feroci·ty [fəˈrɑsɪti] *s* (*pl* **-ties**) ferocidad
ferret [ˈfɛrɪt] *s* hurón *m* || *tr* — **to ferret out** huronear || *intr* huronear
Ferris wheel [ˈfɛrɪs] *s* rueda de feria, noria
fer·ry [ˈfɛri] *s* (*pl* **-ries**) bote *m* de paso, ferry-boat *m* || *v* (*pret & pp* **-ried**) *tr* pasar (*viajeros, mercancías*) a través del río || *intr* cruzar el río en barco
fer′ry·boat′ *s* bote *m* de paso, ferry-boat *m*
fertile [ˈfʌrtɪl] *adj* fértil
fertilize [ˈfʌrtɪˌlaɪz] *tr* abonar, fertilizar; (*to impregnate*) fecundar
fervid [ˈfʌrvɪd] *adj* férvido, vehemente
fervor [ˈfʌrvər] *s* fervor *m*
fervent [ˈfʌrvənt] *adj* ferviente, fervoroso
fester [ˈfɛstər] *s* úlcera || *tr* enconar || *intr* enconarse (*una herida; el ánimo de uno*)
festival [ˈfɛstɪvəl] *adj* festivo || *s* fiesta; (*of music*) festival *m*
festive [ˈfɛstɪv] *adj* festivo
festivi·ty [fɛsˈtɪvɪti] *s* (*pl* **-ties**) festividad
festoon [fɛsˈtun] *s* festón *m* || *tr* festonear
fetch [fɛtʃ] *tr* ir por, hacer venir, traer; venderse a, venderse por
fetching [ˈfɛtʃɪŋ] *adj* (coll) encantador, atractivo
fete [fet] *s* fiesta || *tr* festejar
fetid [ˈfɛtɪd] *o* [ˈfitɪd] *adj* fétido
fetish [ˈfitɪʃ] *o* [ˈfɛtɪʃ] *s* fetiche *m*
fetlock [ˈfɛtlɑk] *s* espolón *m;* (*tuft of hair*) cerneja
fetter [ˈfɛtər] *s* grillete *m*, grillo || *tr* engrillar; impedir
fettle [ˈfɛtəl] *s* estado, condición; **in fine fettle** en buena condición
fetus [ˈfitəs] *s* feto
feud [fjud] *s* odio hereditario, enemistad de larga duración
feudal [ˈfjudəl] *adj* feudal
feudalism [ˈfjudəˌlɪzəm] *s* feudalismo
fever [ˈfivər] *s* fiebre *f*, calentura

fever blister *s* escupidura, fuegos en los labios
feverish [ˈfivərɪʃ] *adj* febril, calenturiento
few [fju] *adj & pron* pocos, no muchos; **a few** unos pocos, unos cuantos; **quite a few** muchos
fiancé [ˌfiˑɑnˈse] *s* novio, prometido; novillo (Mex, P-R)
fiancée [ˌfiˑɑnˈse] *s* novia, prometida
fias·co [fiˈæsko] *s* (*pl* **-cos** *o* **-coes**) fiasco
fib [fɪb] *s* mentirilla || *v* (*pret & pp* **fibbed; ger fibbing**) *intr* decir mentirillas, macanear
fiber [ˈfaɪbər] *s* fibra; carácter *m*, índole *f*
fibrous [ˈfaɪbrəs] *adj* fibroso
fickle [ˈfɪkəl] *adj* inconstante, veleidoso
fiction [ˈfɪkʃən] *s* (*invention*) ficción; (*branch of literature*) novelística; **pure fiction!** ¡puro cuento!
fictional [ˈfɪkʃənəl] *adj* novelesco
fictionalize [ˈfɪkʃənəˌlaɪz] *tr* novelizar
fictitious [fɪkˈtɪʃəs] *adj* ficticio
fiddle [ˈfɪdəl] *s* violín *m* || *tr* tocar (*un aire*) con el violín; **to fiddle away** (coll) malgastar || *intr* tocar el violín; **to fiddle with** manosear
fiddler [ˈfɪdlər] *s* (coll) violinista *mf*
fiddling [ˈfɪdlɪŋ] *adj* (coll) despreciable, insignificante
fideli·ty [fɪˈdɛlɪti] *s* (*pl* **-ties**) fidelidad
fidget [ˈfɪdʒɪt] *intr* agitarse, menearse; **to fidget with** manosear
fidgety [ˈfɪdʒɪti] *adj* inquieto, nervioso
fiduciar·y [fɪˈdjuʃɪˌɛri] *adj* fiduciario || *s* (*pl* **-ies**) fiduciario
fie [faɪ] *interj* ¡qué vergüenza!
fief [fif] *s* feudo
field [fild] *adj* (mil) de campaña || *s* campo; (*sown with grain*) sembrado; (baseball) jardín *m;* (elec) campo magnético; (*of motor or dynamo*) (elec) inductor *m*
fielder [ˈfildər] *s* (baseball) jardinero
field glasses *spl* gemelos de campo
field hockey *s* hockey *m* sobre hierba
field magnet *s* imán *m* inductor
field marshal *s* (mil) mariscal *m* de campo
field′piece′ *s* cañón *m* de campaña
fiend [find] *s* diablo; (*person*) fiera; **to be a fiend for** ser una fiera para
fiendish [ˈfindɪʃ] *adj* diabólico
fierce [fɪrs] *adj* feroz, fiero; (*wind*) furioso; (coll) muy malo
fierceness [ˈfɪrsnɪs] *s* ferocidad, fiereza; furia
fier·y [ˈfaɪri] *adj* (*comp* **-ier;** *super* **-iest**) ardiente, caliente; brioso
fife [faɪf] *s* pífano
fifteen [ˈfɪfˈtin] *adj, pron & s* quince *m*
fifteenth [ˈfɪfˈtinθ] *adj & s* (*in a series*) decimoquinto; (*part*) quinzavo || *s* (*in dates*) quince *m*
fifth [fɪfθ] *adj & s* quinto || *s* (*in dates*) cinco *m*
fifth column *s* quinta columna
fifth columnist *s* quintacolumnista *mf*
fiftieth [ˈfɪftɪˑɪθ] *adj & s* (*in a series*) quincuagésimo; (*part*) cincuentavo
fif·ty [ˈfɪfti] *adj & pron* cincuenta || *s* (*pl* **-ties**) cincuenta *m*

fif′ty-fif′ty *adv*—**to go fifty-fifty** (coll) ir a medias

fig. *abbr* **figure, figuratively**

fig [fɪg] *s* higo, breva; (*tree*) higuera; (*merest trifle*) bledo

fight [faɪt] *s* lucha, pelea; ánimo, brío; **to pick a fight with** meterse con, buscar la lengua a ‖ *tr* luchar con; dar (*batalla*); lidiar (*al toro*) ‖ *intr* luchar, pelear; **to fight shy of** tratar de evitar

fighter [′faɪtər] *s* luchador *m*, peleador *m*; (*warrior*) combatiente *m*; (*game person*) porfiador *m*; (aer) avión *m* de combate, caza *m*

fig leaf *s* hoja de higuera; (*on statues*) hoja de parra

figment [′fɪgmənt] *s* ficción, invención

figurative [′fɪgjərətɪv] *adj* figurado; (*representing by a likeness*) figurativo

figure [′fɪgjər] *s* figura; (*bodily form*) talle *m*; precio; **to be good at figures** ser listo en aritmética; **to cut a figure** hacer figura; **to have a good figure** tener buen tipo; **to keep one's figure** conservar la línea ‖ *tr* adornar con figuras; figurarse, imaginar; suponer, calcular; **to figure out** descifrar ‖ *intr* figurar; **to figure on** contar con

fig′ure•head′ *s* (naut) figurón *m* de proa, mascarón *m* de proa; (*straw man*) testaferro

figure of speech *s* figura retórica

figure skating *s* patinaje artístico

figurine [‚fɪgjə′rin] *s* figurilla, figurina

filament [′fɪləmənt] *s* filamento

filch [fɪltʃ] *tr* birlar, ratear

file [faɪl] *s* fila, hilera; (*tool*) lima; (*collection of papers*) archivo; (*cabinet*) archivador *m*, fichero ‖ *tr* poner en fila; limar; archivar, clasificar; anotar ‖ *intr* desfilar; **to file for** solicitar

file case *s* fichero

file clerk *s* fichador *m*

filet [fɪ′le] o [′fɪle] *s* filete *m* ‖ *tr* cortar en filetes

filial [′fɪlɪ•əl] o [′fɪljəl] *adj* filial

filiation [‚fɪlɪ′eʃən] *s* filiación

filibuster [′fɪlɪ‚bʌstər] *s* obstrucción (*de la aprobación de una ley*); obstruccionista *mf*; (*buccaneer*) filibustero ‖ *tr* obstruir (*la aprobación de una ley*)

filigree [′fɪlɪ‚gri] *adj* afiligranado ‖ *s* filigrana ‖ *tr* afiligranar

filing [′faɪlɪŋ] *s* (*of documents*) clasificación; limadura; **filings** limadura, limalla

filing cabinet *s* archivador *m*, clasificador *m*

filing card *s* ficha

Filipi•no [‚fɪlɪ′pino] *adj* filipino ‖ *s* (*pl* **-nos**) filipino

fill [fɪl] *s* (*sufficiency*) hartazgo; (*place filled with earth*) terraplén *m*; **to have o get one's fill of** darse un hartazgo de ‖ *tr* llenar; rellenar; despachar (*un pedido*); tapar (*un agujero*); empastar (*un diente*); inflar (*un neumático*); llenar, ocupar (*un puesto*); colmar (*lagunas*); **to fill out** llenar (*un formulario*) ‖ *intr* llenarse; rellenarse; **to fill in** hacer de suplente; **to fill up** ahogarse de emoción

filler [′fɪlər] *s* relleno; (*of cigar*) tripa; *sizing* aparejo; (*in a writing*) relleno

fillet [′fɪlɪt] *s* cinta, tira; (*for hair*) prendedero; (archit, bb) filete *m* ‖ *tr* filetear ‖ [′fɪle] o [′fɪlɪt] *s* (*of meat or fish*) filete *m* ‖ *tr* cortar en filetes

filling [′fɪlɪŋ] *s* (*of a tooth*) empaste *m*; (*e.g., of a turkey*) relleno; (*of cigar*) tripa

filling station *s* estación gasolinera

fillip [′fɪlɪp] *s* aguijón *m*, estímulo; (*with finger*) capirotazo

fil•ly [′fɪli] *s* (*pl* **-lies**) potra; (coll) muchacha retozona

film [fɪlm] *s* película; (mov) película, film *m*; (phot) película ‖ *tr* filmar

film library *s* cinemateca

film star *s* estrella de la pantalla

film strip *s* tira proyectable

film•y [′fɪlmi] *adj* (*comp* **-ier**; *super* **-iest**) delgadísimo, diáfano, sutil

filter [′fɪltər] *s* filtro ‖ *tr* filtrar ‖ *intr* filtrarse

filtering [′fɪltərɪŋ] *s* filtración

filter paper *s* papel *m* filtrante

filter tip *s* embocadura de filtro

filth [fɪlθ] *s* suciedad, porquería

filth•y [′fɪlθi] *adj* (*comp* **-ier**; *super* **-iest**) sucio, puerco

filthy lucre [′lukər] *s* (coll) el vil metal (*dinero, raíz de muchos males*)

filtrate [′fɪltret] *s* filtrado ‖ *tr* filtrar ‖ *intr* filtrarse

fin. *abbr* **finance**

fin [fɪn] *s* aleta

final [′faɪnəl] *adj* final; (*last in a series*) último; decisivo, terminante ‖ *s* examen *m* final; **finals** (sport) final *f*

finale [fɪ′nɑli] *s* (mus) final *m*

finalist [′faɪnəlɪst] *s* finalista *mf*

finally [′faɪnəli] *adv* finalmente, por último

finance [′faɪnæns] *s* financiación; **finances** finanzas ‖ *tr* financiar

financial [faɪ′nænʃəl] *adj* financiero

financier [‚faɪnən′sɪr] *s* financiero

financing [′faɪnænsɪŋ] *s* financiación, financiamiento

finch [fɪntʃ] *s* pinzón *m*

find [faɪnd] *s* hallazgo ‖ *v* (*pret & pp* **found** [faʊnd]) *tr* hallar, encontrar; **to find out** averiguar, darse cuenta de ‖ *intr* (*law*) pronunciar fallo; **to find out about** informarse de

finder [′faɪndər] *s* (*of camera*) visor *m*; (*of microscope*) portaobjeto cuadriculado

finding [′faɪndɪŋ] *s* descubrimiento; (law) laudo, fallo

fine [faɪn] *adj* fino; (*weather*) bueno; divertido ‖ *adv* (coll) muy bien; **to feel fine** (coll) sentirse muy bien de salud ‖ *s* multa ‖ *tr* multar

fine arts *spl* bellas artes

fineness *s* fineza; (*of metal*) ley *f*

fine print *s* letra menuda, tipo menudo

finer•y [′faɪnəri] *s* (*pl* **-ies**) adorno, galas, atavíos

fine-spun [′faɪn‚spʌn] *adj* estirado en hilo finísimo; (fig) alambicado

finesse [fɪ'nɛs] s sutileza; (*in bridge*) impás *m* ‖ *tr* hacer el impás con ‖ *intr* hacer un impás

fine-toothed comb ['faɪn,tuθt] s lendrera, peine *m* de púas finas; **to go over with a fine-toothed comb** escudriñar minuciosamente

finger ['fɪŋgər] s dedo; **to burn one's fingers** cogerse los dedos; **to put one's finger on the spot** poner el dedo en la llaga; **to slip between the fingers** irse de entre los dedos; **to snap one's fingers at** tratar con desprecio; **to twist around one's little finger** manejar a su gusto ‖ *tr* manosear; (slang) acechar, espiar; (slang) identificar

finger board s (*of guitar*) diapasón *m;* (*of piano*) teclado

finger bowl s lavadedos *m,* lavafrutas *m*

finger dexterity s (mus) dedeo

fingering ['fɪŋgərɪŋ] s manoseo; (mus) digitación

fin'ger•nail' s uña

fingernail polish s esmalte *m* para las uñas

fin'ger•print' s huella digital, dactilograma *m* ‖ *tr* tomar las huellas digitales de

finger tip s punta del dedo; **to have at one's finger tips** tener en la punta de los dedos, saber al dedillo

finial ['fɪnɪ•əl] s florón *m*

finical ['fɪnɪkəl] o **finicky** ['fɪnɪki] *adj* delicado, melindroso

finish ['fɪnɪʃ] s acabado; fin *m,* conclusión ‖ *tr* acabar; **to be finished** estar listo ‖ *intr* acabar; **to finish** + *ger* acabar de + *inf;* **to finish by** + *ger* acabar por + *inf*

finishing nail s puntilla francesa

finishing school s escuela particular de educación social para señoritas

finishing touch s toque *m* final, última mano

finite ['faɪnaɪt] *adj* finito

finite verb s forma verbal flexional

Finland ['fɪnlənd] s Finlandia

Finlander ['fɪnləndər] s finlandés *m*

Finn [fɪn] s (*member of a Finnish-speaking group of people*) finés *m;* (*native or inhabitant of Finland*) finlandés *m*

Finnish ['fɪnɪʃ] *adj* finlandés ‖ s (*language*) finlandés *m*

fir [fʌr] s abeto

fire [faɪr] s fuego; (*destructive burning*) incendio; **through fire and water** a trancos y barrancos; **to be on fire** estar ardiendo; **to be under enemy fire** estar expuesto al fuego del enemigo; **to catch fire** encenderse; **to hang fire** estar en suspensión; **to open fire** abrir fuego, romper el fuego; **to set on fire, to set fire to** pegar fuego a; **under fire** bajo el fuego del enemigo; acusado, inculpado ‖ *interj* (mil) ¡fuego! ‖ *tr* encender; calentar (*el horno*); cocer (*ladrillos*); disparar (*un arma de fuego*); pegar (*un tiro*); excitar (*la imaginación*); (coll) despedir (*a un empleado*) ‖ *intr* encenderse; **to fire on** hacer fuego sobre; **to fire up** cargar el horno; calentar el horno

fire alarm s alarma de incendios, avisador *m* de incendios; **to sound the fire alarm** tocar a fuego

fire'arm' s arma de fuego

fire'ball' s bola de fuego; (*lightning*) rayo en bola

fire'bird' s cacique veranero

fire'boat' s buque *m* con mangueras para incendios

fire'box' s caja de fuego, fogón *m*

fire'brand' s tizón *m;* (*hothead*) botafuego

fire'break' s raya

fire'brick' s ladrillo refractario

fire brigade s cuerpo de bomberos

fire'bug' s (coll) incendiario

fire company s cuerpo de bomberos; compañía de seguros

fire'crack'er s triquitraque *m*

fire'damp' s grisú *m,* mofeta

fire department s servicio de bomberos

fire'dog' s morillo

fire drill s ejercicio para caso de incendio

fire engine s coche *m* bomba, bomba de incendios, motobomba

fire escape s escalera de salvamento

fire extinguisher s extintor *m,* apagafuegos *m,* extinguidor *m*

fire'fly' s (*pl* -**flies**) luciérnaga

fire'guard' s guardafuego

fire hose s manguera para incendios

fire'house' s cuartel *m* de bomberos, estación de incendios

fire hydrant s boca de incendio

fire insurance s seguro contra incendios

fire irons *spl* badil *m* y tenazas

fireless cooker ['faɪrlɪs] s cocinilla sin fuego

fire•man ['faɪrmən] s (*pl* -**men** [mən]) (*man who stokes fires*) fogonero; (*man who extinguishes fires*) bombero

fire'place' s chimenea, chimenea francesa

fire plug s boca de agua

fire power s (mil) potencia de fuego

fire'proof' *adj* incombustible; **a prueba de incendio** ‖ *tr* hacer incombustible

fire sale s venta de mercancías averiadas en un incendio

fire screen s pantalla de chimenea

fire ship s brulote *m*

fire shovel s badil *m*

fire'side' s hogar *m*

fire'trap' s edificio sin medios adecuados de escape en caso de incendio

fire wall s cortafuego

fire'ward'en s vigía *m* de incendios

fire'wa'ter s aguardiente *m*

fire'wood' s leña

fire'works' *spl* fuegos artificiales

firing ['faɪrɪŋ] s encendimiento; (*of bricks*) cocción; (*of a gun*) disparo; (*of soldiers*) tiroteo; (*of an internal-combustion engine*) encendido; (*of an employee*) (coll) despedida

firing line s línea de fuego, frente *m* de batalla

firing order s (aut) orden *m* del encendido

firing squad s (*for saluting at a burial*) piquete *m* de salvas; (*for executing*) pelotón *m* de fusilamiento, piquete *m* de ejecución

firm [fʌrm] *adj* firme ‖ *s* empresa, casa comercial

firmament [ˈfʌrməmənt] *s* firmamento

firm name *s* razón *f* social

firmness [ˈfʌrmnɪs] *s* firmeza

first [fʌrst] *adj* primero ‖ *adv* primero; **first of all** ante todo ‖ *s* primero; (aut) primera (velocidad); (mus) voz *f* principal; **at first** al principio; en primer lugar; **from the first** desde el principio

first aid *s* cura de urgencia, primeros auxilios

first′-aid′kit *s* botiquín *m*, equipo de urgencia

first-aid station *s* puesto de socorro, puesto de primera intención

first′-born′ *adj & s* primogénito

first′-class′ *adj* de primera, de primera clase ‖ *adv* en primera clase

first cousin *s* primo hermano

first draft *s* borrador *m*

first finger *s* dedo índice, dedo mostrador

first floor *s* piso bajo

first fruits *spl* primicia

first lieutenant *s* teniente

firstly [ˈfʌrstli] *adv* en primer lugar

first mate *s* (naut) piloto

first name *s* nombre *m* de pila

first night *s* (theat) noche *f* de estreno

first′-night′er *s* (theat) estrenista *mf*

first officer *s* (naut) piloto

first quarter *s* cuarto creciente (*de la luna*)

first′-rate′ *adj* de primer orden; (coll) excelente ‖ *adv* (coll) muy bien

first′-run′ house *s* teatro de estreno

fiscal [ˈfɪskəl] *adj* (*pertaining to public treasury*) fiscal; económico ‖ *s* (*public prosecutor*) fiscal *m*

fiscal year *s* año económico, ejercicio

fish [fɪʃ] *s* pez *m*; (*that has been caught, that is ready to eat*) pescado; **to be like a fish out of water** estar como gallina en corral ajeno; **to be neither fish nor fowl** no ser carne ni pescado; **to drink like a fish** beber como una topinera, beber como una esponja ‖ *tr* pescar ‖ *intr* pescar; **to fish for compliments** buscar alabanzas; **to go fishing** ir de pesca; **to take fishing** llevar de pesca

fish′bone′ *s* espina de pez

fish bowl *s* pecera

fisher [ˈfɪʃər] *s* pescador *m*; embarcación de pesca; (zool) marta del Canadá

fisher·man [ˈfɪʃərmən] *s* (*pl* **-men** [mən]) pescador *m*; barco pesquero

fisher·y [ˈfɪʃəri] *s* (*pl* **-ies**) (*activity*) pesca; (*business*) pesquería; (*grounds*) pesquera

fish glue *s* cola de pescado

fish hawk *s* halieto

fish′hook′ *s* anzuelo

fishing [ˈfɪʃɪŋ] *adj* pesquero ‖ *s* pesca

fishing ground *s* pesquería, pesquera

fishing reel *s* carrete *m*

fishing rod *s* caña de pescar

fishing tackle *s* aparejo de pescar, avíos de pesca

fishing torch *s* candelero

fish line *s* sedal *m*

fish market *s* pescadería

fish′plate′ (rr) eclisa

fish′pool′ *s* piscina

fish spear *s* fisga

fish story *s* (coll) andaluzada, patraña; **to tell fish stories** (coll) mentir por la barba

fish′tail′ *s* (aer) coleadura ‖ *intr* (aer) colear

fish′wife′ *s* (*pl* **-wives** [ˌwaɪvz]) pescadera; (*foul-mouthed woman*) verdulera

fish′worm′ *s* lombriz *f* de tierra (*cebo para pescar*)

fish·y [ˈfɪʃi] *adj* (*comp* **-ier**; *super* **-iest**) que huele o sabe a pescado; (coll) dudoso, inverosímil

fission [ˈfɪʃən] *s* (biol) escisión; (phys) fisión

fissionable [ˈfɪʃənəbəl] *adj* fisionable; físil

fissure [ˈfɪʃər] *s* hendidura, grieta; (anat, min) fisura

fist [fɪst] *s* puño; (typ) manecilla; **to shake one's fist at** amenazar con el puño

fist fight *s* pelea con los puños

fisticuff [ˈfɪstɪˌkʌf] *s* puñetazo; **fisticuffs** pelea a puñetazos

fit [fɪt] *adj* (*comp* **-fitter**; *super* **-fittest**) apropiado, conveniente; apto; sano; **fit to be tied** (coll) impaciente, encolerizado; **fit to eat** bueno de comer; **to feel fit** gozar de buena salud; **to see fit** juzgar conveniente ‖ *s* ajuste *m*, talle *m*; (*of one piece with another*) encaje *m*; (*of coughing*) acceso, ataque *m*; (*of anger*) arranque *m*, chivo; **by fits and starts** intermitentemente ‖ *v* (*pret & pp* **-fitted**; *ger* **fitting**) *tr* ajustar, entallar; cuadrar, sentar; encajar; cuadrar con (*p.ej., las señas de una persona*); equipar, preparar; servir para; estar de acuerdo con (*p.ej., los hechos*); **to fit out** o **up** pertrechar ‖ *intr* ajustar; encajar; sentar; **to fit in** caber en; encajar en

fitful [ˈfɪtfəl] *adj* caprichoso; intermitente, vacilante

fitness [ˈfɪtnɪs] *s* conveniencia; aptitud; tempestividad; buena salud

fitter [ˈfɪtər] *s* ajustador *m*; (*of machinery*) montador *m*; (*of clothing*) probador *m*

fitting [ˈfɪtɪŋ] *adj* apropiado, conveniente, justo ‖ *s* ajuste *m*; encaje *m*; (*of a garment*) prueba; tubo de ajuste; **fittings** accesorios, avíos; (*iron trimmings*) herraje *m*

fitting room *s* probador *m*

five [faɪv] *adj & pron* cinco ‖ *s* cinco; **five o'clock** las cinco

five hundred *adj & pron* quinientos ‖ *s* quinientos *m*

five′-year′ plan *s* plan *m* quinquenal

fix [fɪks] *s*—**in a tight fix** (coll) en calzas prietas; **to be in a fix** (coll) hallarse en un aprieto; **to get a fix** (*drugs*) picarse, pincharse ‖ *tr* arreglar, componer, reparar; fijar (*una fecha; los cabellos; una imagen fotográfica; los precios; la atención; una hora, una cita*); calar (*la bayoneta*); (coll) desquitarse con; (pol) muñir ‖ *intr* fijarse; **to fix on** decidir, escoger

fixed [fɪkst] *adj* fijo

fixing [ˈfɪksɪŋ] *adj* fijador ‖ *s* (*fastening*) fijación; (phot) fijado
fixing bath *s* fijador *m*
fixture [ˈfɪkstʃər] *s* accesorio, artefacto; (*of a lamp*) guarnición; **fixtures** (*e.g., of a store*) instalaciones
fizz [fɪz] *s* ruido sibilante; bebida gaseosa; (Brit) champaña ‖ *intr* hacer un ruido sibilante
fizzle [ˈfɪzəl] *s* (coll) fracaso ‖ *intr* chisporrotear débilmente; (coll) fracasar
fl. *abbr* **flourished, fluid**
flabbergast [ˈflæbər,gæst] *tr* (coll) dejar sin habla, dejar estupefacto
flab•by [ˈflæbi] *adj* (*comp* **-bier**; *super* **-biest**) flojo, lacio
flag [flæg] *s* bandera ‖ *v* (*pret & pp* **flagged**; *ger* **flagging**) *tr* hacer señal a (*una persona*) con una bandera; hacer señal de parada a (*un tren*) ‖ *intr* aflojar, flaquear
flag captain *s* (nav) capitán *m* de bandera
flageolet [,flædʒəˈlɛt] *s* chirimía, dulzaina
flag•man [ˈflægmən] *s* (*pl* **-men** [mən]) (rr) guardafrenos *m*; (rr) guardavía *m*
flag of truce *s* bandera de parlamento
flag'pole' *s* asta de bandera; (surv) jalón *m*
flagrant [ˈflegrənt] *adj* enorme, escandaloso
flag'ship' *s* (nav) capitana
flag'staff' *s* asta de bandera
flag'stone' *s* losa
flag stop *s* (rr) apeadero
flail [flel] *s* mayal *m* ‖ *tr* golpear con mayal; golpear, azotar
flair [flɛr] *s* instinto, perspicacia
flak [flæk] *s* fuego antiaéreo
flake [flek] *s* (*thin piece*) hojuela; (*of snow*) copo ‖ *intr* desprenderse en hojuelas; caer en copos pequeños
flak•y [ˈfleki] *adj* (*comp* **-ier**; *super* **-iest**) escamoso, laminoso
flamboyant [flæmˈbɔɪ•ənt] *adj* flameante; llamativo; rimbombante; (archit) flameante, flamígero
flame [flem] *s* llama ‖ *tr* (*to sterilize with a flame*) llamear ‖ *intr* flamear
flame thrower [ˈθro•ər] *s* lanzallamas *m*
flaming [ˈflemɪŋ] *adj* llameante; flamante, resplandeciente; apasionado
flamin•go [fləˈmɪŋgo] *s* (*pl* **-gos** o **-goes**) flamenco
flammable [ˈflæməbəl] *adj* inflamable
Flanders [ˈflændərz] *s* Flandes *f*
flange [flændʒ] *s* pestaña
flank [flæŋk] *s* flanco; *tr* flanquear
flannel [ˈflænəl] *s* franela
flap [flæp] *s* (*fold in clothing; of a hat*) falda; (*of a pocket*) cartera; (*of a table*) hoja plegadiza; (*of shoe*) oreja; (*of an envelope*) tapa; (*of wings*) aletazo; (*of the counter in a store*) trampa ‖ *v* (*pret & pp* **flapped**; *ger* **flapping**) *tr* golpear con ruido seco; batir, sacudir (*las alas*) ‖ *intr* aletear; flamear con ruido
flare [flɛr] *s* llamarada, destello; cohete *m* de señales; (aer) bengala; (*outward curvature*) abocinamiento; (*of a dress*) vuelo ‖ *tr* abocinar ‖ *intr* arder con gran llamarada, destellar; (*to spread outward*) abocinarse; **to flare up** inflamarse; recrudecer (*una enfermedad*); encolerizarse
flare star *s* (astr) estrella fulgurante
flare'-up' *s* llamarada; (*of an illness*) retroceso; (coll) llamarada, arrebato de cólera
flash [flæʃ] *s* (*of light*) relumbrón *m*, ráfaga; (*of lightning*) relámpago; (*of hope*) rayo; (*of joy*) acceso; (*of insight*) rasgo; mensaje *m* urgente ‖ *tr* quemar (*pólvora*); enviar (*un mensaje*) como un rayo ‖ *intr* destellar, centellear; relampaguear (*los ojos*); **to flash by** pasar como un rayo
flash'back' *s* (mov) retrospectiva, flashback *m*
flash bulb *s* luz *f* de magnesio; bombilla de destello
flash flood *s* torrentada, avenida repentina
flashing [ˈflæʃɪŋ] *s* despidiente *m* de agua, vierteaguas *m*
flash'light' *s* linterna eléctrica, lámpara eléctrica de bolsillo; (*of a lighthouse*) luz *f* intermitente, fanal *m* de destellos; (*for taking photographs*) flash *m*, relámpago
flashlight battery *s* pila de linterna
flashlight bulb *s* bombilla de linterna
flashlight photography *s* fotografía instantánea de relámpago
flash sign *s* anuncio intermitente
flash•y [ˈflæʃi] *adj* (*comp* **-ier**; *super* **-iest**) chillón, llamativo
flask [flæsk] *s* frasco; frasco de bolsillo; (*for laboratory use*) matraz *m*, redoma
flat [flæt] *adj* (*comp* **flatter**; *super* **flattest**) plano; (*nose; boat*) chato; (*surface*) mate, deslustrado; (*beer*) muerto; (*tire*) desinflado; (*e.g., denial*) terminante; (mus) bemol ‖ *adv* — **to fall flat** caer de plano; (fig) no surtir efecto, no tener éxito ‖ *s* banco, bajío; (*apartment*) piso; (mus) bemol *m*; (coll) neumático desinflado
flat'boat' *s* chalana
flat'car' *s* vagón *m* de plataforma
flat'foot' *s* pie plano
flat-footed [ˈflæt,futɪd] *adj* de pies planos; (coll) inflexible
flat'head' *s* (*of a bolt*) cabeza chata; clavo, tornillo o perno de cabeza chata; (coll) tonto, mentecato
flat'i'ron *s* plancha
flatten [ˈflætən] *tr* allanar, aplanar; chafar, aplastar; achatar ‖ *intr* allanarse, aplanarse; aplastarse; achatarse; **to flatten out** ponerse horizontal, enderezarse
flatter [ˈflætər] *tr* lisonjear; cepillar (*to make more attractive than is*) favorecer ‖ *intr* lisonjear
flatterer [ˈflætərər] *s* lisonjero; (coll) limpiabotas *m*
flattering [ˈflætərɪŋ] *adj* lisonjero
flatter•y [ˈflætəri] *s* (*pl* **-ies**) lisonja
flat'top' *s* portaaviones *m*
flatulence [ˈflætʃələns] *s* flatulencia
flat'ware' *s* vajilla de plata; vajilla de porcelana
flaunt [flɔnt] *tr* ostentar, hacer gala de
flautist [ˈflɔtɪst] *s* flautista *mf*

flavor [`fleνǝr] s sabor m, gusto; condimento, sazón f; (of ice cream) clase f ‖ tr saborear; condimentar, sazonar; aromatizar, perfumar

flavoring [`fleνǝrɪŋ] s condimento, sainete m

flaw [flɔ] s defecto, imperfección; (crack) grieta

flawless [`flɔlɪs] adj perfecto, entero

flax [flæks] s lino

flaxen [`flæksǝn] adj blondo, rubio

flax′seed′ s linaza

flay [fle] tr desollar

flea [fli] s pulga

flea′bite′ s picadura de pulga; molestia insignificante

fleck [flɛk] s pinta, punto; partícula, pizca ‖ tr puntear

fledgling [`flɛdʒlɪŋ] s pajarito, volantón m; (fig) novato, novel m

flee [fli] v (pret & pp fled [flɛd]) tr & intr huir

fleece [flis] s (coat of wool) lana; (wool shorn at one time; tuft of wool or hair) vellón m ‖ tr esquilar; (to strip of money) desplumar

fleec•y [`flisi] adj (comp -ier; super -iest) lanudo; (clouds) aborregado

fleet [flit] adj veloz ‖ s armada; (of merchant vessels, airplanes, automobiles) flota

fleeting [`flitɪŋ] adj fugaz, efímero; transitorio

Fleming [`flɛmɪŋ] s flamenco

Flemish [`flɛmɪʃ] adj & s flamenco

flesh [flɛʃ] s carne f; in the flesh en persona; to lose flesh perder carnes; to put on flesh cobrar carnes

flesh and blood s (relatives) carne y sangre; el cuerpo humano

fleshiness [`flɛʃɪnɪs] s carnosidad

fleshless [`flɛʃlɪs] adj descarnado

flesh′pot′ s olla, marmita; fleshpots vida regalona; suntuosos nidos de vicios

flesh wound s herida superficial

flesh•y [`flɛʃi] adj (comp -ier; super -iest) carnoso

flex [flɛks] tr doblar ‖ intr doblarse

flexible [`flɛksɪbǝl] adj flexible

flexible cord s (elec) flexible m

flick [flɪk] s (with finger) papirote m; (with whip) latigazo; ruido seco ‖ tr golpear rápida y ligeramente

flicker [`flɪkǝr] s llama trémula; (of eyelids) parpadeo; (of emotion) temblor momentáneo ‖ intr flamear con llama trémula; aletear

flier [`flaɪ•ǝr] s aviador m; tren rápido; (coll) negocio arriesgado; (coll) hoja volante

flight [flaɪt] s fuga, huída; (of an airplane) vuelo; (of birds) bandada; (of stairs) tramo; (of fancy) arranque m; to put to flight poner en fuga; to take flight darse a la fuga

flight attendant s sobrecargo, sobrecarga

flight deck s (nav) cubierta de vuelo

flight•y [`flaɪti] adj (comp -ier; super -iest) veleidoso; casquivano

flim•flam [`flɪm,flæm] s (coll) engaño, trampa; (coll) tontería ‖ v (pret & pp -flammed; ger -flamming) tr (coll) engañar, trampear

flim•sy [`flɪmzi] adj (comp -sier; super -siest) débil, endeble, flojo

flinch [flɪntʃ] intr encogerse de miedo

fling [flɪŋ] s echada, tiro; baile escocés muy vivo; to go on a fling echar una cana al aire; to have a fling at ensayar, probar; to have one's fling correrla, mocear ‖ v (pret & pp flung [flʌŋ]) tr arrojar; (e.g., on the floor, out the window, in jail) echar; to fling open abrir de golpe; to fling shut cerrar de golpe

flint [flɪnt] s pedernal m

flint′lock′ s llave f de chispa; trabuco de chispa

flint•y [`flɪnti] adj (comp -ier; super -iest) pedernalino; (fig) empedernido

flip [flɪp] adj (comp flipper; super flippest) (coll) petulante ‖ s capirotazo ‖ v (pret & pp flipped; ger flipping) tr echar de un capirotazo, mover de un tirón; to flip a coin echar a cara o cruz; to flip one's lid (coll) deschavetar; to flip shut cerrar de golpe (p. ej., un abanico)

flippancy [`flɪpǝnsi] s petulancia

flippant [`flɪpǝnt] adj petulante

flip side s contraportada (del disco)

flirt [flʌrt] s (woman) coqueta; (man) galanteador m ‖ intr coquetear (una mujer); galantear (un hombre); to flirt with flirtear con; pololear (Chile); acariciar (una idea); jugar con (la muerte)

flit [flɪt] v (pret & pp flitted; ger flitting) intr revolotear, volar; pasar rápidamente

flitch [flɪtʃ] s hoja de tocino

float [flot] s (raft) balsa; (of fishing line) flotador m; (of mason) llana; carroza alegórica, carro alegórico ‖ tr poner a flote; lanzar (una empresa); emitir (acciones, bonos, etc.) ‖ intr flotar

floating [`flotɪŋ] adj flotante

flock [flak] s (of birds) bandada; (of sheep) grey f, rebaño, manada; (of people) muchedumbre; (e.g., of nonsense) hatajo; (of faithful) grey f, rebaño ‖ intr congregarse, reunirse; llegar en tropel

floe [flo] s banquisa, témpano

flog [flag] v (pret & pp flogged; ger flogging) tr azotar, fustigar

flood [flʌd] s inundación; (caused by heavy rain) diluvio; (sudden rise of river) crecida; (of tide) pleamar f; (of words, etc.) diluvio, torrente m ‖ tr inundar; (to overwhelm) abrumar ‖ intr desbordar, rebosar; entrar a raudales

flood′gate′ s (of a dam) compuerta; (of a canal) esclusa

flood′light′ s faro de inundación ‖ tr iluminar con faro de inundación

flood tide s pleamar f, marea montante

floor [flor] s (inside bottom surface of room) piso, suelo; (story of a building) piso, alto; (of the sea, a swimming pool, etc.) fondo; (of an assembly hall) hemiciclo; (naut) varenga; to ask for the floor pedir la palabra; to have the floor tener la palabra; to take the floor tomar la palabra ‖ tr entarimar; derribar, echar al suelo; (coll)

confundir, envolver, revolcar (*al adversario en controversia*); (*coll*) vencer
floor lamp *s* lámpara de pie
floor mop *s* fregasuelos *m*, estropajo
floor plan *s* planta
floor show *s* espectáculo de cabaret
floor timber *s* (naut) varenga
floor'walk'er *s* jefe *m* de sección
floor wax *s* cera de pisos
flop [flɑp] *s* fracaso, caída; (*person*) berzas *m*, berzotas *m;* **to take a flop** caerse ‖ *v* (*pret & pp* **flopped;** *ger* **flopping**) *intr* agitarse; caerse; venirse abajo; fracasar; **to flop over** volcarse; cambiar de partido
flora [ˈflorə] *s* flora
floral [ˈflorəl] *adj* floral
Florentine [ˈflorən,tin] *adj & s* florentino
florescence [floˈrɛsəns] *s* florescencia
florid [ˈflorɪd] *adj* (*complexion*) encarnado; (*showy, ornate*) florido
Florida Keys [ˈflorɪdə] *s* Cayos de la Florida
florist [ˈflorɪst] *s* florero, florista *mf*
floss [flɑs] *s* cadarzo; (*of corn*) cabellos
floss silk *s* seda floja sin torcer
floss•y [ˈflɑsi] *adj* (*comp* **-ier;** *super* **-iest**) ligero, velloso; (slang) cursi, vistoso
flotsam [ˈflɑtsəm] *s* pecio
flotsam and jetsam *s* pecios, despojos; (*trifles*) baratijas; gente *f* trashumante, gente perdida
flounce [flɑuns] *s* faralá *m*, volante *m* ‖ *tr* adornar con faralaes o volantes ‖ *intr* moverse airadamente
flounder [ˈflɑundər] *s* platija ‖ *intr* forcejear, obrar torpemente, andar tropezando
flour [flɑur] *adj* harinero ‖ *s* harina
flourish [ˈflʌrɪʃ] *s* (*with the sword*) molinete *m;* (*with the pen*) plumada, rasgo; (*as part of signature*) rúbrica; (mus) floreo ‖ *tr* blandir (*la espada*) ‖ *intr* florecer, prosperar
flourishing [ˈflʌrɪʃɪŋ] *adj* floreciente, próspero
flour mill *s* molino de harina
floury [ˈflɑuri] *adj* harinoso
flout [flɑut] *tr* mofarse de, burlarse de ‖ *intr* mofarse, burlarse
flow [flo] *s* flujo ‖ *intr* fluir; subir (*la marea*); ondear (*el pelo en el aire*); **to flow into** desaguar en, desembocar en; **to flow over** rebosar; **to flow with** nadar en, abundar en
flower [ˈflɑuˌər] *s* flor *f* ‖ *tr* florear ‖ *intr* florecer
flower bed *s* macizo, parterre *m*
flower garden *s* jardín *m*
flower girl *s* florera; (*at a wedding*) damita de honor
flower piece *s* ramillete *m;* (*painting*) florero
flow'er•pot' *s* tiesto, maceta
flower shop *s* floristería
flower show *s* exposición de flores
flower stand *s* florero
flowery [ˈflɑuˌəri] *adj* florido, cubierto de flores
flu [flu] *s* (coll) gripe *f*, influenza
fluctuate [ˈflʌktʃu,et] *intr* fluctuar

flue [flu] *s* cañón *m* de chimenea; tubo de humo
fluency [ˈfluˌənsi] *s* afluencia, facundia
fluent [ˈfluˌənt] *adj* (*flowing*) fluente; afluente, facundo, flúido
fluently [ˈfluˌəntli] *adv* corrientemente
fluff [flʌf] *s* pelusa, tamo; vello, pelusilla; (*of an actor*) gazapo ‖ *tr* esponjar, mullir ‖ *intr* esponjarse
fluff•y [ˈflʌfi] *adj* (*comp* **-ier;** *super* **-iest**) fofo, esponjoso, mullido; velloso
fluid [ˈfluˌɪd] *adj & s* flúido
fluidity [fluˈɪdɪti] *s* fluidez *f*
fluke [fluk] *s* (*of anchor*) uña; (*in billiards*) chiripa
flume [flum] *s* caz *m*, saetín *m*
flunk [flʌŋk] *s* (coll) reprobación ‖ *tr* (coll) reprobar, dar calabazas a; perder (*un examen o asignatura*) ‖ *intr* (coll) fracasar, salir mal; **to flunk out** (coll) tener que abandonar los estudios por no poder aprobar
flunk•y [ˈflʌŋki] *s* (*pl* **-ies**) lacayo; adulador *m*
fluor [ˈfluˌor] *s* fluorita
fluorescence [,fluˌəˈrɛsəns] *s* fluorescencia
fluorescent [,fluˌəˈrɛsənt] *adj* fluorescente
fluoridate [ˈfluˌərɪ,det] *tr* fluorizar
fluoridation [ˈfluˌərɪˈdeʃən] *s* fluorización
fluoride [ˈfluˌə,raɪd] *s* fluoruro
fluorine [ˈfluˌə,rin] *s* flúor *m*
fluorite [ˈfluˌə,raɪt] *s* fluorita
fluoroscope [ˈfluˌərə,skop] *s* fluoroscopio
fluor spar *s* espato flúor
flur•ry [ˈflʌri] *s* (*pl* **-ries**) agitación; (*of wind*) racha, ráfaga; (*of rain*) chaparrón *m;* (*of snow*) nevisca ‖ *v* (*pret & pp* **-ried**) *tr* agitar
flush [flʌʃ] *adj* rasante, nivelado; (*set in, in order to be flush*) embutido; abundante; robusto, vigoroso; próspero, bien provisto; coloradote; (*in printing*) justificado; **flush with** a ras de ‖ *adv* ras con ras, al mismo nivel ‖ *s* (*of water*) flujo repentino; (*in the cheeks*) rubor *m;* sonrojo; (*in the springtime*) floración repentina; (*of joy*) acceso; (*of youth*) vigor *m;* chorro del inodoro; (*in poker*) flux *m* ‖ *tr* (*to cause to blush*) abochornar; limpiar con un chorro de agua; hacer saltar (*una liebre*) ‖ *intr* abochornarse, estar encendido (*el rostro*); (*to gush*) brotar
flush outlet *s* (elec) caja de enchufe embutida
flush switch *s* (elec) llave embutida
flush tank *s* depósito de limpia
flush toilet *s* inodoro con chorro de agua
fluster [ˈflʌstər] *s* confusión, aturdimiento ‖ *tr* confundir, aturdir
flute [flut] *s* (*of a column*) estría; (mus) flauta ‖ *tr* estriar, acanalar
flutist [ˈflutɪst] *s* flautista *mf*
flutter [ˈflʌtər] *s* aleteo, revoloteo; confusión, turbación ‖ *intr* aletear, revolotear; flamear, ondear; agitarse; alterarse (*el pulso*); palpitar (*el corazón*)
flux [flʌks] *s* (*flow; flowing of tide*) flujo; (*for fusing metals*) flujo, fundente *m*

fly [flaɪ] s (pl **flies**) mosca; (of trousers) portañuela, bragueta; (for fishing) mosca artificial; **flies** (theat) bambalinas; **to die like flies** morir como chinches ‖ v (pret **flew** [flu]; pp **flown** [flon]) tr hacer volar (una cometa); dirigir (un avión); (to carry in an airship) volar; atravesar en avión; desplegar, llevar (una bandera) ‖ intr volar; huir; ondear (una bandera); **to fly off** salir volando; desprenderse; **to fly open** abrirse de repente; **to fly over** trasvolar; **to fly shut** cerrarse de repente
fly ball s (baseball) palomita
fly'blow' s cresa
fly'-by-night' adj indigno de confianza
fly'catch'er s moscareta, papamoscas m
fly chaser s espantamoscas m
flyer ['flaɪ•ər] s var de **flier**
fly'-fish' tr & intr pescar con moscas artificiales
flying ['flaɪ•ɪŋ] adj volante; rápido, veloz ‖ s aviación
flying boat s hidroavión m
flying buttress s arbotante m
flying colors spl gran éxito
flying field s campo de aviación
flying saucer s platillo volante
flying sickness s mal m de altura
flying time s horas de vuelo
fly in the ointment s mosca muerta que malea el perfume
fly'leaf' s (pl **-leaves'**) guarda, hoja de guarda
fly net s (for a bed) mosquitero; (for a horse) espantamoscas m
fly'pa'per s papel m matamoscas
fly'speck' s mancha de mosca
fly'swatter ['swɑtər] s matamoscas m
fly'trap' s atrapamoscas m
fly'wheel' s volante m
fm. abbr **fathom**
F.M. abbr **frequency modulation**
foal [fol] s potro ‖ intr parir (la yegua)
foam [fom] s espuma ‖ intr espumar
foam extinguisher s lanzaespumas m, extintor m de espuma
foam rubber s caucho esponjoso, espuma de caucho
foam•y ['fomi] adj (comp **-ier**; super **-iest**) espumoso, espumajoso
fob [fɑb] s faltriquera de reloj; (chain) leopoldina; (ornament) dije m
F.O.B. abbr **free on board**
focal ['fokəl] adj focal
fo•cus ['fokəs] s (pl **-cuses** o **-ci** [saɪ]) foco; **in focus** enfocado; **out of focus** desenfocado ‖ v (pret & pp **-cused** o **-cussed**; ger **-cusing** o **-cussing**) tr enfocar; fijar (la atención) ‖ intr enfocarse
fodder ['fɑdər] s forraje m
foe [fo] s enemigo
fog [fɑg] o [fɔg] s niebla; (phot) velo ‖ v (pret & pp **fogged**; ger **fogging**) tr envolver en niebla; (to blur) empañar; (phot) velar ‖ intr empañarse; (phot) velarse
fog bank s banco de nieblas
fog bell s campana de nieblas

fog'bound' adj atascado en la niebla, envuelto en la niebla
fog•gy ['fɑgi] o ['fɔgi] adj (comp **-gier**; super **-giest**) neblinoso, brumoso; confuso; (phot) velado; **it is foggy** hay neblina
fog'horn' s sirena de niebla
foible ['fɔɪbəl] s flaqueza, lado flaco
foil [fɔɪl] s (thin sheet of metal) hojuela, laminilla; (of mirror) azogado, plateado; contraste m, realce m; (sword) florete m ‖ tr frustrar; azogar, platear (un espejo)
foist [fɔɪst] tr — **to foist something on someone** encajar una cosa a uno
fol. abbr **folio, following**
fold [fold] s pliegue m, doblez m; arruga; (for sheep) aprisco, redil m; (of the faithful) rebaño ‖ tr plegar, doblar; cruzar (los brazos); **to fold up** doblar (p.ej., un mapa) ‖ intr plegarse, doblarse
folder ['foldər] s (covers for holding papers) carpeta; (pamphlet) folleto
folderol ['fɑldə,rɑl] s tontería, necedad; bagatela
folding ['foldɪŋ] adj plegadizo, plegable; plegador
folding camera s cámara de fuelle
folding chair s silla de tijera, silla plegadiza; (of canvas) catrecillo
folding cot s catre m de tijera
folding door s puerta plegadiza
folding rule s metro plegadizo
foliage ['foli•ɪdʒ] s follaje m
foli•o ['foli•o] adj en folio ‖ s (pl **-os**) (sheet) folio; infolio, libro en folio ‖ tr foliar
folk [fok] adj popular, tradicional, del pueblo ‖ s (pl **folk** o **folks**) gente f; **folks** (coll) gente (familia)
folk etymology s etimología popular
folk'lore' s folkore m
folk music s música folklórica
folk song s canción típica, canción tradicional
folk•sy ['foksi] adj (comp **-sier**; super **-siest**) (coll) sociable, tratable; (like common people) (coll) plebeyo
folk'way' s costumbre tradicional
follicle ['fɑlɪkəl] s folículo
follow ['fɑlo] tr seguir; seguir el hilo de; interesarse en (las noticias del día) ‖ intr seguir; resultar; **as follows** como sigue; **it follows** síguese
follower ['fɑlo•ər] s seguidor m; secuaz mf, partidario; imitador m; discípulo
following ['fɑlo•ɪŋ] adj siguiente ‖ s séquito; partidarios
fol'low-up' adj consecutivo; recordativo ‖ s carta recordativa, circular recordativa
fol•ly ['fɑli] s (pl **-lies**) desatino, locura; empresa temeraria; **follies** revista teatral
foment [fo'ment] tr fomentar
fond [fɑnd] adj afectuoso, cariñoso; **to become fond of** encariñarse con, aficionarse a o de
fondle ['fɑndəl] tr acariciar, mimar
fondness ['fɑndnɪs] s afición, cariño
font [fɑnt] s (source; source of water) fuente f; (for holy water) pila; (of type) fundición

food [fud] *adj* alimenticio ‖ *s* comida, alimento; **food for thought** cosa en qué pensar
food store *s* tienda de comestibles, colmado
food'stuffs' *spl* comestibles *mpl*, víveres *mpl*
fool [ful] *s* tonto, necio; (*jester*) bufón *m;* (*person imposed on*) inocente *mf*, víctima; **to make a fool of** poner en ridículo; **to play the fool** hacer el tonto ‖ *tr* embaucar, engañar; **to fool away** malgastar (*tiempo, dinero*) ‖ *intr* tontear; **to fool around** (coll) malgastar el tiempo; **to fool with** (coll) ajar, manosear
fooler•y [ˈfuləri] *s* (*pl* **-ies**) locura, tontería, babosada
fool'har'dy *adj* (*comp* **-dier;** *super* **-diest**) temerario
fooling [ˈfulɪŋ] *s* broma; engaño; **no fooling** hablando en serio
foolish [ˈfulɪʃ] *adj* tonto; ridículo; gilí
fool'proof' *adj* (coll) a prueba de mal trato; (coll) infalible
fools'cap' *s* gorro de bufón; papel *m* de oficio
fool's errand *s* caza de grillos
fool's scepter *s* cetro de locura
foot [fut] *s* (*pl* **feet** [fit]) pie *m;* **to drag one's feet** ir a paso de caracol; **to have one foot in the grave** estar con un pie en la sepultura; **to put one's best foot forward** (coll) hacer méritos; **to put one's foot in it** (coll) meter la pata; (coll) tirarse una plancha; **to stand on one's own feet** volar con sus propias alas; **to tread under foot** hollar ‖ *tr* pagar (*la cuenta*); **to foot it** andar a pie; bailar
footage [ˈfutɪdʒ] *s* distancia o largura en pies
foot'ball' *s* (*game*) balompié *m*, fútbol *m;* (*ball*) balón *m*
foot'board' *s* (*support for foot*) estribo; (*of bed*) pie *m*
foot'bridge' *s* pasarela, puente *m* para peatones
foot'fall' *s* paso
foot'hill' *s* colina al pie de una montaña
foot'hold' *s* arraigo, pie *m;* **to gain a foothold** ganar pie
footing [ˈfutɪŋ] *s* pie *m*, p.ej., **he lost his footing** perdió el pie; **on a friendly footing** en relaciones amistosas; **on an equal footing** en pie de igualdad; **on a war footing** en pie de guerra
foot'lights' *spl* candilejas, batería; (fig) tablas, escena
foot'loose' *adj* libre, no comprometido
foot•man [ˈfutmən] *s* (*pl* **-men** [mən]) lacayo, criado de librea
foot'mark' *s* huella
foot'note' *s* nota al pie de la página
foot'path' *s* senda para peatones
foot'print' *s* huella
foot race *s* carrera a pie
foot'rest' *s* apoyapié *m*, descansapié *m*
foot rule *s* regla de un pie
foot soldier *s* soldado de a pie
foot'sore' *adj* despeado
foot'step' *s* paso; **to follow in the footsteps of** seguir los pasos de

foot'stone' *s* lápida al pie de una sepultura
foot'stool' *s* escabel *m*, escañuelo
foot warmer *s* calientapiés *m*
foot'wear' *s* calzado
foot'work' *s* juego de piernas
foot'worn' *adj* (*road*) trillado; (*person*) despeado
foozle [ˈfuzəl] *s* chambonada; (coll) chambón *m*, torpe *m* ‖ *tr* chafallar; errar (*un golpe*) de manera torpe ‖ *intr* chambonear
fop [fɑp] *s* currutaco, petimetre *m;* lagarto (Mex)
for [fər] *prep* para; por; como, p.ej., **he uses his living room for an office** usa la sala como oficina; de, p.ej., **time for bed** hora de acostarse; desde hace, p.ej., **he has been here for a week** está aquí desde hace una semana; en honor de; a pesar de ‖ *conj* pues, porque
for. *abbr* **foreign**
forage [ˈfɔrɪdʒ] *adj* forrajero ‖ *s* forraje *m* ‖ *tr* & *intr* forrajear; saquear
foray [ˈfɑre] o [ˈfɔre] *s* correría; saqueo ‖ *intr* hacer correrías
for•bear [fɔrˈbɛr] *v* (*pret* **-bore** [ˈbor]; *pp* **-borne** [ˈborn]) *tr* abstenerse de ‖ *intr* contenerse
forbearance [fɔrˈbɛrəns] *s* abstención; paciencia
for•bid [fɔrˈbɪd] *v* (*pret* **-bade** [ˈbæd] o **-bad** [ˈbæd]; *pp* **-bidden** [ˈbɪdən]; *ger* **-bidding**) *tr* prohibir
forbidding [fɔrˈbɪdɪŋ] *adj* repugnante, repulsivo
force [fors] *s* fuerza; (*staff of workers*) personal *m;* (*of soldiers, police, etc.*) cuerpo; (phys) fuerza; **by force** a la mala (Cuba, P-R); **by force of** a fuerza de; **by main force** con todas sus fuerzas; **in force** vigente, en gran número; **to join forces** juntar diestra con diestra ‖ *tr* forzar; obligar; **to force back** hacer retroceder; **to force open** abrir por fuerza; **to force through** llevar a cabo por fuerza
forced [forst] *adj* forzado
forced air *s* aire *m* a presión
forced landing *s* aterrizaje forzado o forzoso
forced march *s* marcha forzada
forceful [ˈforsfəl] *adj* enérgico, eficaz
for•ceps [ˈforsəps] *s* (*pl* **-ceps** o **-cipes** [sɪ,piz]) (dent, surg) pinzas; (obstet) fórceps *m*
force pump *s* bomba impelente
forcible [ˈforsɪbəl] *adj* eficaz, convincente; forzado
ford [ford] *s* vado ‖ *tr* vadear
fore [for] *adj* anterior; (naut) de proa ‖ *adv* antes, anteriormente; delante; (naut) avante ‖ *interj* ¡ojo!, ¡cuidado! ‖ *s* delantera; **to the fore** destacado; a mano; vivo
fore and aft *adv* de popa a proa
fore'arm' *s* antebrazo ‖ **fore•arm'** *tr* armar de antemano; prevenir
fore'bear' *s* antepasado
forebode [forˈbod] *tr* (*to portend*) presagiar; (*to have a presentiment of*) presentir, prever

foreboding [for'bodɪŋ] s presagio; presentimiento

fore'cast' s pronóstico ‖ v (pret & pp -cast o -casted) tr pronosticar

forecastle ['foksəl], ['for,kæsəl], o ['for,kasəl] s castillo de proa

fore•close' tr excluir; extinguir el derecho de redimir (una hipoteca); privar del derecho de redimir una hipoteca

fore•doom' tr condenar de antemano, predestinar al fracaso

fore edge s canal f

fore'fa'ther s antepasado

fore'fin'ger s dedo índice, dedo mostrador

fore'front' s puesto delantero; sitio de actividad más intensa; **in the forefront** a vanguardia

fore•go' v (pret -went'; pp -gone') tr & intr preceder

foregoing ['for,go•ɪŋ] o [for'go•ɪŋ] adj anterior, precedente, prenombrado

fore'gone' conclusion s resultado inevitable; decisión adoptada de antemano

fore'ground' s primer plano, primer término

forehanded ['for,hændɪd] adj (thrifty) ahorrado; hecho de antemano

forehead ['fɑrɪd] o ['fɔrɪd] s frente f

foreign ['fɑrɪn] adj extranjero, exterior; **foreign to** (not belonging to or connected with) ajeno a

foreign affairs spl asuntos exteriores

for'eign-born' adj nacido en el extranjero

foreigner ['fɑrɪnər] s extranjero

foreign exchange s cambio extranjero; (currency) divisa

foreign minister s ministro de asuntos exteriores

foreign ministry s ministerio de relaciones exteriores

foreign office s ministerio de asuntos exteriores

foreign service s servicio diplomático y consular; servicio militar extranjero

foreign trade s comercio extranjero

fore'leg' s brazo, pata delantera

fore'lock' s mechón m de pelo sobre la frente; (of a horse) copete m; **to take time by the forelock** asir la ocasión por la melena

fore•man ['formən] s (pl -men [mən]) capataz m, mayoral m, sobrestante m; (in a machine shop) contramaestre m; presidente m de jurado

foremast ['forməst], ['for,mæst], o ['for,mast] s palo de trinquete

foremost ['for,most] adj primero, principal, más eminente

fore'noon' adj matinal ‖ s mañana

fore'part' s parte delantera; primera parte

fore'paw' s pata delantera

fore'quar'ter s cuarto delantero

fore'run'ner s precursor m; predecesor m; antepasado; anuncio, presagio

fore•sail ['forsəl] o ['for,sel] s trinquete m

fore•see' v (pret -saw'; pp -seen') tr prever

foreseeable [for'si•əbəl] adj previsible

fore•shad'ow tr presagiar, prefigurar

fore•short'en tr escorzar

fore•short'ening s escorzo

fore'sight' s previsión, presciencia

fore'sight'ed adj previsor, presciente

fore'skin' s prepucio

forest ['fɑrɪst] o ['fɔrɪst] adj forestal ‖ s bosque m

fore•stall' tr impedir, prevenir; anticipar; acaparar

forest ranger ['rendʒər] s guarda m forestal, montanero

forestry ['fɑrɪstri] o ['fɔrɪstri] s silvicultura, ciencia forestal

fore'taste' s goce anticipado, conocimiento anticipado

fore•tell' v (pret & pp -told') tr predecir; presagiar

fore'thought' s premeditación; providencia, previsión

forever [fɔr'ɛvər] adv por siempre; siempre

fore•warn' tr prevenir, poner sobre aviso

fore'word' s advertencia, prefacio

forfeit ['fɔrfɪt] adj perdido ‖ s multa, pena; prenda perdida; **forfeits** (game) prendas ‖ tr perder el derecho a

forfeiture ['fɔrfɪtʃər] s multa, pena; prenda perdida

forgather [fɔr'gæðər] intr reunirse; encontrarse; **to forgather with** asociarse con

forge [fordʒ] s fragua; (blacksmith shop) herrería ‖ tr fraguar, forjar; falsificar (la firma de otra persona); fraguar, forjar (mentiras) ‖ intr fraguar, forjar; **to forge ahead** avanzar despacio y con esfuerzo

forger•y ['fordʒəri] s (pl -ies) falsificación

for•get [fɔr'gɛt] v (pret -got [gɑt], pp -got o -gotten; ger -getting) tr olvidar, olvidarse de, olvidársele a uno, p.ej., **he forgot his overcoat** se le olvidó su abrigo; **forget it!** ¡no se preocupe!; **to forget oneself** no pensar en sí mismo; ser distraído; propasarse

forgetful [fɔr'gɛtfəl] adj olvidado, olvidadizo; descuidado

forgetfulness [fɔr'gɛtfəlnɪs] s olvido; descuido

for•get'-me-not' s nomeolvides m

forgivable [fɔr'gɪvəbəl] adj perdonable

for•give [fɔr'gɪv] v (pret -gave'; pp -giv'en) tr perdonar

forgiveness [fɔr'gɪvnɪs] s perdón m; misericordia

forgiving [fɔr'gɪvɪŋ] adj perdonador, misericordioso, clemente

for•go [fɔr'go] v (pret -went'; pp -gone') tr privarse de

fork [fɔrk] s horca; (of a gardener; of bicycle) horquilla; (of two rivers) horcajo; (of railroad) ramal m; (of a tree) horqueta; (for eating) tenedor m ‖ tr ahorquillar; cargar con horquilla; (in chess) amenazar (dos piezas); **to fork out** (slang) entregar, sudar ‖ intr bifurcarse

forked [fɔrkt] adj ahorquillado

forked lightning s relámpago en zigzag

fork'lift' truck s carretilla elevadora de horquilla

forlorn [fɔr'lɔrn] *adj* desamparado; desesperado; miserable

forlorn hope *s* empresa desesperada

form [fɔrm] *s* forma; (*paper to be filled out*) formulario; (*construction to give shape to cement*) encofrado; (*type in a frame*) molde *m* ‖ *tr* formar ‖ *intr* formarse

formal ['fɔrməl] *adj* formal, ceremonioso; etiquetero

formal attire *s* vestido de etiqueta

formal call *s* visita de cumplido

formali•ty [fɔr'mælɪti] *s* (*pl* **-ties**) (*standard procedure*) formalidad; ceremonia, etiqueta

formal party *s* reunión de etiqueta

formal speech *s* discurso de aparato

format ['fɔrmæt] *s* formato

formation [fɔr'meʃən] *s* formación

former ['fɔrmər] *adj* (*preceding*) anterior; (*long past*) antiguo; primero (*de dos*); **the former** aquél

formerly ['fɔrmərli] *adv* antes, en tiempos pasados

form'-fit'ting *adj* ceñido al cuerpo

formidable ['fɔrmɪdəbəl] *adj* formidable

formless ['fɔrmlɪs] *adj* informe

form letter *s* carta general

formu•la ['fɔrmjələ] *s* (*pl* **-las** o **-lae** [,li] fórmula

formulate ['fɔrmjə,let] *tr* formular

fornicate ['fɔrnə,ket] *intr* fornicar

fornication [,fɔrnə'keʃən] *s* fornicación

for•sake [fɔr'sek] *v* (*pret* **-sook** ['suk]; *pp* **-saken** ['sekən]) *tr* abandonar, desamparar; dejar

fort [fort] *s* fuerte *m*, fortaleza

forte [fort] *s* (*strong point*) fuerte *m*, caballo de batalla ‖ ['forte] *adj* (mus) fuerte

forth [forθ] *adv* adelante; **and so forth** y así sucesivamente; **from this day forth** de hoy en adelante; **to go forth** salir

forth'com'ing *adj* próximo, venidero

forth'right' *adj* directo, franco, sincero ‖ *adv* derecho; sinceramente, francamente; en seguida

forth'with' *adv* inmediatamente

fortieth ['fɔrtɪ•ɪθ] *adj* & *s* (*in a series*) cuadragésimo; (*part*) cuarentavo

fortification [,fɔrtɪfɪ'keʃən] *s* fortificación

forti•fy ['fɔrtɪ,faɪ] *v* (*pret* & *pp* **-fied**) *tr* fortificar; encabezar (*vinos*)

fortitude ['fɔrtɪ,tjud] *s* fortaleza, firmeza

fortnight ['fɔrtnaɪt] *s* quincena, dos semanas

fortress ['fɔrtrɪs] *s* fortaleza

fortuitous [fɔr'tju•ɪtəs] *adj* fortuito

fortunate ['fɔrtʃənɪt] *adj* afortunado

fortune ['fɔrtʃən] *s* fortuna; (*money*) platal *m*; **to make a fortune** enriquecerse; **to tell someone his fortune** decirle a uno la buenaventura

fortune hunter *s* cazador *m* de dotes

for'tune•tel'ler *s* adivino, agorero

for•ty ['fɔrti] *adj* & *pron* cuarenta ‖ *s* (*pl* **-ties**) cuarenta *m*

fo•rum ['forəm] *s* (*pl* **-rums** o **-ra** [rə]) foro; (*e.g., of public opinion*) tribunal *m*

forward ['fɔrwərd] *adj* delantero; precoz; atrevido, impertinente ‖ *adv* hacia ade-

lante; **to bring forward** pasar a cuenta nueva; **to come forward** adelantarse; **to look forward to** esperar con placer anticipado ‖ *tr* cursar, hacer seguir, reexpedir; fomentar, patrocinar

fossil ['fɑsɪl] *adj* & *s* fósil *m*

foster ['fɑstər] o ['fɔstər] *adj* adoptivo, de leche, de crianza ‖ *tr* fomentar

foster brother *s* hermano de leche

foster home *s* hogar *m* de adopción

foster mother *s* madre adoptiva; (*nurse*) ama de leche

foster sister *s* hermana de leche

foul [faul] *adj* sucio, puerco; (*air*) viciado; (*wind*) contrario; (*weather*) malo; obsceno; pérfido; (*breath*) fétido; (*baseball*) fuera del cuadro

foul-mouthed ['faul'mauðd] o ['faul'mauθt] *adj* deslenguado

foul play *s* mal encuentro; (sport) juego sucio

foul'spo'ken *adj* malhablado

found [faund] *tr* fundar; (*to melt, to cast*) fundir

foundation [faun'deʃən] *s* fundación; (*endowment*) dotación; (*basis*) fundamento; (*masonry support*) cimiento

founder ['faundər] *s* fundador *m*; (*of metals*) fundidor *m* ‖ *intr* despearse (*un caballo*); hundirse, irse a pique (*un buque*); (*to fail*) fracasar

foundling ['faundlɪŋ] *s* niño expósito; pepe *mf*

foundling hospital *s* casa de expósitos

found•ry ['faundri] *s* (*pl* **-ries**) fundición

foundry•man ['faundrɪmən] *s* (*pl* **-men** [mən]) fundidor *m*

fount [faunt] *s* fuente *f*

fountain ['fauntən] *s* fuente *f*, manantial *m*

foun'tain•head' *s* nacimiento

fountain pen *s* pluma estilográfica, pluma fuente

fountain syringe *s* mangueta

four [for] *adj* & *pron* cuatro ‖ *s* cuatro; **four o'clock** las cuatro; **on all fours** a gatas

four'-cy'cle *adj* (mach) de cuatro tiempos

four'-cyl'inder *adj* (mach) de cuatro cilindros

four'-flush' *intr* (coll) bravear, papelonear

four•flusher ['for,flʌʃər] *s* bravucón *m*

four-footed ['for'futɪd] *adj* cuadrúpedo

four hundred *adj* & *pron* cuatrocientos ‖ *s* cuatrocientos *m*; **the four hundred** la alta sociedad

four'-in-hand' *s* corbata de nudo corredizo; coche tirado por cuatro caballos

four'-lane' *adj* cuadriviario

four'-leaf' *adj* cuadrifoliado

four-legged ['for'lɛgɪd] o ['for'lɛgd] *adj* de cuatro patas; (*schooner*) de cuatro mástiles

four'-let'ter word *s* palabra impúdica de cuatro letras

four'-mo'tor plane *s* cuadrimotor *m*

four'-o'clock' *s* dondiego

four'post'er *s* cama imperial

four'score' *adj* cuatro veintenas de

foursome ['forsəm] *s* cuatrinca; cuatro jugadores; juego de cuatro

fourteen [ˈforˈtin] *adj, pron & s* catorce *m*
fourteenth [ˈforˈtinθ] *adj & s* (*in a series*) decimocuarto; (*part*) catorzavo ‖ *s* (*in dates*) catorce *m*
fourth [forθ] *adj & s* cuarto ‖ *s* (*in dates*) cuatro
fourth estate *s* cuarto poder
four'-way' *adj* de cuatro direcciones; (elec) de cuatro terminales
fowl [faul] *s* ave *f;* aves; gallina; gallo; carne *f* de ave
fowling piece *s* escopeta de caza
fox [faks] *s* zorra; (*fur*) zorro; (*cunning person*) (fig) zorro ‖ *tr* (coll) engañar con astucia
fox'glove' *s* dedalera
fox'hole' *s* zorrera; (mil) pozo de lobo
fox'hound' *s* perro raposero, perro zorrero
fox hunt *s* caza de zorras
fox terrier *s* fox-terrier *m* (*casta de perro de talla pequeña*)
fox trot *s* trote corto (*de caballo*); fox-trot *m* (*baile de compás cuaternario*)
fox•y [ˈfaksi] *adj* (*comp* **-ier;** *super* **-iest**) (coll) hermosa y erótica; zorrero, astuto, taimado
foyer [ˈfɔɪ•ər] *s* (*of a private house*) vestíbulo; (theat) salón *m* de entrada, vestíbulo
fr. *abbr* **fragment, franc, from**
Fr. *abbr* **Father, French, Friday**
Fra [fra] *s* fray *m*
fracas [ˈfrekəs] *s* alboroto, riña
fraction [ˈfrækʃən] *s* fracción; porción muy pequeña
fractional [ˈfrækʃənəl] *adj* fraccionario; insignificante
fractious [ˈfrækʃəs] *adj* reacio, rebelón; quisquilloso, regañón
fracture [ˈfræktʃər] *s* fractura ‖ *tr* fracturar; (*e.g., an arm*) fracturarse; *intr* fracturarse
fragile [ˈfrædʒɪl] *adj* frágil
fragment [ˈfrægmənt] *s* fragmento
fragrance [ˈfregrəns] *s* fragancia
fragrant [ˈfregrənt] *adj* fragante
frail [frel] *adj* (*not robust*) débil; (*easily broken; morally weak*) frágil ‖ *s* cesto de junco
frail•ty [ˈfrelti] *s* (*pl* **-ties**) debilidad; (*moral weakness*) fragilidad
frame [frem] *s* (*of a picture, mirror*) marco, (*of glasses*) montura, armadura; (*structure*) armazón *f*, esqueleto; (*for embroidering*) bastidor *m;* (*of government*) sistema *m;* (mov, telv) encuadre *m;* (naut) cuaderna ‖ *tr* (*to put in a frame*) enmarcar; formar, forjar; construir; redactar, formular; (slang) incriminar (*a un inocente*)
frame house *s* casa de madera
frame of mind *s* manera de pensar
frame'-up' *s* (slang) treta, trama para incriminar a un inocente
frame'work' *s* armazón *f*, esqueleto, entramado
franc [fræŋk] *s* franco
France [fræns] *o* [frɑns] *s* Francia
franchise [ˈfræntʃaɪz] *s* franquicia, privilegio; (*right to vote*) sufragio

Franciscan [frænˈsɪskən] *adj & s* franciscano
frank [fræŋk] *adj* franco, sincero ‖ *s* carta franca, envío franco; franquicia postal; sello de franquicia ‖ *tr* franquear ‖ **Frank** *s* (*member of a Frankish tribe*) franco; (*masculine name*) Paco
frankfurter [ˈfræŋkfərtər] *s* salchicha de carne de vaca y de cerdo
frankincense [ˈfræŋkɪn,sɛns] *s* olíbano
Frankish [ˈfræŋkɪʃ] *adj & s* franco
frankness [ˈfræŋknɪs] *s* franqueza, abertura, sinceridad
frantic [ˈfræntɪk] *adj* frenético
frappé [fræˈpe] *adj* helado ‖ *s* refresco helado de zumo de frutas
frat [fræt] *s* (slang) club *m* de estudiantes
fraternal [frəˈtʌrnəl] *adj* fraternal
fraterni•ty [frəˈtʌrnɪti] *s* (*pl* **-ties**) (*brotherliness*) fraternidad; cofradía; asociación secreta; (U.S.A.) club *m* de estudiantes
fraternize [ˈfrætər,naɪz] *intr* fraternizar
fraud [frɔd] *s* fraude *m;* embelequería (Col, Mex, W-I); (*person*) (coll) impostor *m*
fraudulent [ˈfrɔdjələnt] *adj* fraudulento
fraught [frɔt] *adj*—**fraught with** cargado de, lleno de
fray [fre] *s* combate *m*, riña, batalla ‖ *intr* deshilacharse, raerse
freak [frik] *s* (*sudden fancy*) capricho, antojo; (*person, animal*) fenómeno, esperpento
freakish [ˈfrikɪʃ] *adj* caprichoso, antojadizo; raro, fantástico
freckle [ˈfrɛkəl] *s* peca
freckle-faced [ˈfrɛkəl,fest] *adj* pecoso
freckly [ˈfrɛkli] *adj* pecoso
free [fri] *adj* (*comp* **freer** [ˈfri•ər]; *super* **freest** [ˈfri•ɪst]) libre; gratis, franco; liberal, generoso; **to be free with** dar abundantemente; **to set free** libertar ‖ *adv* libremente; en libertad; de balde, gratis ‖ *v* (*pret & pp* **freed** [frid]; *ger* **freeing** [ˈfri•ɪŋ]) *tr* libertar, poner en libertad; soltar; exentar, eximir
free and easy *adj* despreocupado
freebooter [ˈfri,butər] *s* forbante *m*, filibustero, pirata *m*
free'born' *adj* nacido libre; propio de un pueblo libre
freedom [ˈfridəm] *s* libertad
freedom of speech *s* libertad de palabra
freedom of the press *s* libertad de imprenta
freedom of the seas *s* libertad de los mares
freedom of worship *s* libertad de cultos
free enterprise *s* libertad de empresa
free fight *s* sarracina, riña tumultuaria
free'-for-all' *s* concurso abierto a todo el mundo; sarracina, riña tumultuaria
free hand *s* plena libertad, carta blanca
free'hand' drawing *s* dibujo a pulso
freehanded [ˈfri,hændɪd] *adj* dadivoso, generoso
free'hold' *s* (law) feudo franco
free lance *s* soldado mercenario; periodista *mf* sin empleo fijo; (*writer not on regular salary*) destajista *mf*

fo
fr

free lunch s tapas, enjutos
free•man ['frimən] s (pl **-men** [mən]) hombre m libre; ciudadano
Free'ma'son s francmasón m
Free'ma'sonry s francmasonería
free of charge adj gratis, de balde
free on board adj franco a bordo
free port s puerto franco
free ride s llevada gratuita
free service s servicio post-venta
free'-spo'ken adj franco, sin reserva
free'stone' adj & s abridero
free'think'er s librepensador m
free thought s librepensamiento
free trade s librecambio
free'trad'er s librecambista mf
free'way' s autopista
free will s libre albedrío
freeze [friz] s helada || v (pret **froze** [froz]; pp **frozen**) tr helar; congelar (créditos, fondos, etc.) || intr helarse; congelarse; helársele a uno la sangre (p.ej., de miedo)
freeze'-dry' v (pret & pp **-dried**) tr liofilizar
freeze drying s liofilización
freezer ['frizər] s heladora, sorbetera
freezing ['friziŋ] s glaciación
freight [fret] s carga; (naut) flete m; **by freight** como carga; (rr) en pequeña velocidad || tr enviar por carga
freight car s vagón m de carga, vagón de mercancías
freighter ['fretər] s buque m de carga, carguero
freight platform s (rr) muelle m
freight station s (rr) estación de carga
freight train s mercancías msg, tren m de mercancías
freight yard s (rr) patio de carga
French [frɛntʃ] adj & s francés m; **the French** los franceses
French chalk s jaboncillo de sastre
French doors spl puertas vidrieras dobles
French dressing s salsa francesa, vinagreta
French fried potatoes spl patatas fritas en trocitos
French horn s (mus) trompa de armonía
French horsepower s caballo de fuerza, caballo de vapor
French leave s despedida a la francesa; **to take French leave** despedirse a la francesa
French•man ['frɛntʃmən] s (pl **-men** [mən]) francés m
French telephone s microteléfono
French toast s torrija
French window s puerta ventana
French'wom'an s (pl **-wom'en**) francesa
frenzied ['frɛnzid] adj frenético
fren•zy ['frɛnzi] (pl **-zies**) frenesí m
frequen•cy ['frikwənsi] s (pl **-cies**) frecuencia
frequency list s lista de frecuencia
frequency modulation s modulación de frecuencia
frequent ['frikwənt] adj frecuente || ['frikwɛnt] o ['frikwənt] tr frecuentar
frequently ['frikwəntli] adv con frecuencia, frecuentemente

fres•co ['frɛsko] s (pl **-coes** o **-cos**) fresco || tr pintar al fresco
fresh [frɛʃ] adj fresco; (water) dulce; (wind) fresquito; novicio, inexperto; (cheeky) (slang) fresco; (toward women) (slang) atrevido; **fresh paint!** ¡ojo mancha! || adv recientemente, recién; **fresh in** (coll) recién llegado, acabado de llegar; **fresh out** (coll) recién agotado
freshen ['frɛʃən] tr refrescar || intr refrescarse
freshet ['frɛʃɪt] s avenida, crecida
fresh•man ['frɛʃmən] s (pl **-men** [mən]) novato; estudiante mf de primer año
freshness ['frɛʃnɪs] s frescura; (cheek) (slang) frescura
fresh'-wa'ter adj de agua dulce; no acostumbrado a navegar; de poca monta
fret [frɛt] s (interlaced design) calado; (mus) ceja, traste m; queja || v (pret & pp **fretted**; ger **fretting**) tr adornar con calados || intr irritarse, quejarse, agitarse
fretful ['frɛtfəl] adj irritable, enojadizo, displicente
fret'work' s calado
Freudianism ['frɔɪdɪ•ə,nɪzəm] s freudismo
friar ['fraɪ•ər] s fraile m **friar•y** ['fraɪ•əri] s (pl **-ies**) convento de frailes
fricassee [,frikə'si] s fricasé m
friction ['frikʃən] s fricción, rozamiento; (fig) desavenencia, rozamiento
friction tape s cinta aislante
Friday ['fraɪdi] s viernes m
fried [fraɪd] adj frito
fried egg s huevo a la plancha, huevo frito o estrellado
friend [frɛnd] s amigo; (in answer to "Who is there?") gente f de paz; **to be friends with** ser amigo de; **to make friends** trabar amistades; **to make friends with** hacerse amigo de
friend•ly ['frɛndli] adj (comp **-lier**; super **-liest**) amigo, amistoso, amigable
friendship ['frɛndʃɪp] s amistad
frieze [friz] s (archit) friso
frigate ['frigit] s fragata
fright [fraɪt] s susto, espanto; (grotesque or ridiculous person) (coll) espantajo; **to take fright** at asustarse de
frighten ['fraɪtən] tr asustar, espantar; **to frighten away** espantar, ahuyentar || intr asustarse
frightful ['fraɪtfəl] adj espantoso, horroroso; (coll) feúcho, repugnante; (coll) enorme, tremendo
frightfulness ['fraɪtfəlnɪs] s espanto, horror m; terrorismo; espantosidad (SAm)
frigid ['frɪdʒɪd] adj frío; (fig) frío; (zone) glacial
frigidity [fri'dʒɪdɪti] s frialdad; (pathol) frialdad; (fig) frialdad, frigidez f
frill [frɪl] s lechuga; (of birds and other animals) collarín m; (frippery) (coll) ringorrango; (in dress, speech etc.) (coll) afectación
fringe [frɪndʒ] s franja, orla; (opt) franja || tr franjar, orlar

fringe benefits *spl* beneficios accesorios; beneficios sociales

fripper·y [ˈfrɪpəri] *s* (*pl* **-ies**) (*flashiness*) cursilería; (*flashy clothes*) perejil *m*, perifollos

frisk [frɪsk] *tr* (slang) cachear; (slang) registrar y robar ‖ *intr* retozar

frisk·y [ˈfrɪski] *adj* (*comp* **-ier;** *super* **-iest**) juguetón, retozón; (*horse*) fogoso

fritter [ˈfrɪtər] *s* fruta de sartén; fragmento ‖ *tr* **—to fritter away** desperdiciar, malgastar poco a poco

frivolous [ˈfrɪvələs] *adj* frívolo

friz [frɪz] *s* (*pl* **frizzes**) rizo, pelo rizado apretadamente ‖ *v* (*pret & pp* **frizzed;** *ger* **frizzing**) *tr* rizar, rizar apretadamente

frizzle [ˈfrɪzəl] *s* rizo apretado; chirrido, siseo ‖ *tr* rizar apretadamente; asar o freír en parrilla ‖ *intr* chirriar, sisear

friz·zly [ˈfrɪzli] *adj* (*comp* **-zlier;** *super* **-zliest**) muy ensortijado

fro [fro] *adv* **— to and fro** de acá para allá; **to go to and fro** ir y venir

frock [frɑk] *s* vestido; bata, blusa; (*of priest*) vestido talar

frock coat *s* levita

frog [frɑg] o [frɔg] *s* rana; (*button and loop on a garment*) alamar *m;* (*in throat*) ronquera, gallo

frog'man *s* (*pl* **-men'**) hombre-rana *m*

frol·ic [ˈfrɑlɪk] *s* juego alegre, travesura; fiesta, holgorio ‖ *v* (*pret & pp* **-icked;** *ger* **-icking**) *intr* juguetear, travesear, jaranear

frolicsome [ˈfrɑlɪksəm] *adj* juguetón, travieso

from [frʌm], [frɑm] o [frəm] *prep* de; desde; de parte de; según; a, p.ej., **to take something away from someone** quitarle algo a alguien

front [frʌnt] *adj* delantero; anterior ‖ *s* frente *m & f;* (*of a shirt*) pechera; (*of a book*) principio; apariencia falsa (*p.ej., de riqueza*); ademán estudiado; (mil) frente *m;* **in front of** delante de, frente a, en frente de; **to put on a front** (coll) gastar mucho oropel; **to put up a bold front** (coll) hacer de tripas corazón ‖ *tr* (*to face*) dar a; (*to confront*) afrontar, arrostrar; (*to supply with a front*) poner frente o fachada a ‖ *intr* **— to front on** dar a; **to front towards** mirar hacia

frontage [ˈfrʌntɪdʒ] *s* fachada, frontera; terreno frontero

front door *s* puerta de entrada

front drive *s* (aut) tracción delantera

frontier [frʌnˈtɪr] *adj* fronterizo ‖ *s* frontera

frontiers·man [frʌnˈtɪrzmən] *s* (*pl* **-men** [mən]) hombre *m* de la frontera, explorador *m*

frontispiece [ˈfrʌntɪs,pis] *s* (*of book*) portada; (archit) frontispicio

front matter *s* preliminares *mpl* (*de un libro*)

front page *s* primera plana

front porch *s* soportal *m*

front room *s* cuarto que da a la calle

front row *s* primera fila

front seat *s* asiento delantero

front steps *spl* escalones *mpl* de acceso a la puerta de entrada

front view *s* vista de frente

frost [frɔst] o [frɑst] *s* (*freezing*) helada; (*frozen dew*) escarcha; (slang) fracaso ‖ *tr* cubrir de escarcha; escarchar (*confituras*); helar (*el frío las plantas*); deslustrar (*el vidrio*)

frost'bit'ten *adj* dañado por la helada; quemado por la helada o la escarcha

frosted glass *s* vidrio deslustrado

frosting [ˈfrɔstɪŋ] o [ˈfrɑstɪŋ] *s* garapiña; (*of glass*) deslustre *m*

frost·y [ˈfrɔsti] o [ˈfrɑsti] *adj* (*comp* **-ier;** *super* **-iest**) cubierto de escarcha; escarchado; frío, poco amistoso; canoso, gris

froth [frɔθ] o [frɑθ] *s* espuma; frivolidad, vanidad ‖ *intr* espumar, echar espuma; (*at the mouth*) espumajear

froth·y [ˈfrɔθi] o [ˈfrɑθi] *adj* (*comp* **-ier;** *super* **-iest**) espumoso; frívolo, vano

froward [ˈfrowərd] *adj* díscolo, indócil

frown [fraʊn] *s* ceño, entrecejo ‖ *intr* fruncir el entrecejo; **to frown at** *u* **on** mirar con ceño, desaprobar

frows·y o **frowz·y** [ˈfraʊzi] *adj* (*comp* **-ier;** *super* **-iest**) desaseado, desaliñado; maloliente; mal peinado

frozen foods [ˈfrozən] *spl* viandas congeladas

frt. *abbr* **freight**

frugal [ˈfrugəl] *adj* (*moderate in the use of things*) parco; (*not very abundant*) frugal

fruit [frut] *adj* (*tree*) frutal; (*boat, dish*) frutero ‖ *s* (*such as apple, pear, strawberry*) fruta; frutas, p.ej., **I like fruit** me gustan las frutas; (*part containing seed*) fruto; (*effect, result*) (fig) fruto

fruit cake *s* torta de frutas

fruit cup *s* compota de frutas picadas

fruit fly *s* mosca del vinagre; mosca de las frutas

fruitful [ˈfrutfəl] *adj* fructuoso

fruition [fruˈɪʃən] *s* buen resultado, cumplimiento; **to come to fruition** lograrse cumplidamente

fruit jar *s* tarro para frutas

fruit juice *s* jugo de frutas

fruitless [ˈfrutlɪs] *adj* infructuoso

fruit of the vine *s* zumo de cepas o de parras

fruit salad *s* ensalada de frutas, macedonia de frutas

fruit stand *s* puesto de frutas

fruit store *s* frutería

frumpish [ˈfrʌmpɪʃ] *adj* basto, desgarbado, desaliñado

frustrate [ˈfrʌstret] *tr* frustrar

fry [fraɪ] *s* (*pl* **fries**) fritada ‖ *v* (*pret & pp* **fried**) *tr & intr* freír

frying pan [ˈfraɪ·ɪŋ] *s* sartén *f;* **to jump from the frying pan into the fire** saltar de la sartén y dar en las brasas

ft. *abbr* **foot, feet**

fudge [fʌdʒ] *s* dulce *m* de chocolate

fuel [ˈfju·əl] *s* combustible *m;* (fig) pábulo; **alternate fuel** combustible alternativo ‖ *v* (*pret & pp* **fueled** o **fuelled;** *ger* **fueling** o

fr
fu

fuelling) *tr* aprovisionar de combustible ‖ *intr* aprovisionarse de combustible

fuel cell *s* cámara de combustible, célula electrógena

fuel oil *s* aceite *m* combustible

fuel tank *s* depósito de combustible

fugitive ['fjudʒɪtɪv] *adj* & *s* fugitivo

fugue [fjug] *s* (mus) fuga

ful·crum ['fʌlkrəm] *s* (*pl* **-crums** o **-cra** [krə]) fulcro

fulfill [fʊl'fɪl] *tr* (*to carry out*) cumplir, realizar; cumplir con (*una obligación*); llenar (*una condición*)

fulfillment [fʊl'fɪlmənt] *s* cumplimiento, realización

full [fʊl] *adj* lleno; (*dress, garment*) amplio, holgado; (*formal dress*) de etiqueta; (*voice*) sonoro, fuerte; (*of food*) harto; **full of aches and pains** lleno de goteras; **full of fun** muy divertido, muy chistoso; **full of play** muy juguetón; **full to overflowing** lleno a rebosar ‖ *adv* completamente; **full many (a)** muchísimos; **full well** muy bien, perfectamente ‖ *s* colmo; **in full** por completo; sin abreviar; **to the full** completamente ‖ *tr* abatanar

full-blooded ['fʊl'blʌdɪd] *adj* vigoroso; completo, pletórico; de raza

full-blown ['fʊl'blon] *adj* (*flower, blossom*) abierto; desarrollado, maduro

full-bodied ['fʊl'badɪd] *adj* fuerte, espeso, consistente; aromático

full dress *s* traje *m* de etiqueta; (mil) uniforme *m* de gala

full'-dress' coat *s* frac *m*

full-faced ['fʊl'fest] *adj* carilleno; (*view*) de cuadrado; (*portrait*) de rostro entero

full-fledged ['fʊl'flɛdʒd] *adj* hecho y derecho, nada menos que

full-grown ['fʊl'gron] *adj* crecido, completamente desarrollado

full house *s* lleno, entrada llena; (poker) fulján *m*

full'-length' mirror *s* espejo de cuerpo entero, espejo de vestir

full-length movie *s* largometraje *m*, cinta de largo metraje

full load *s* plena carga; (aer) peso total

full moon *s* luna llena, plenilunio

full name *s* nombre *m* y apellidos

full'-page' *adj* a página entera

full powers *spl* plenos poderes, amplias facultades

full sail *adv* a todo trapo

fulll'-scale' *adj* de tamaño natural; total, completo; pleno

full-sized ['fʊl'saɪzd] *adj* de tamaño natural

full speed *adv* a toda velocidad

full stop *s* parada completa; (gram) punto

full swing *s* plena actividad

full tilt *adv* a toda velocidad

full'-time' *adj* a tiempo completo

full'-view' *adj* de vista completa

full volume *s* (rad) máximo de volumen

fully ['fʊli] o ['fʊlli] *adv* completamente; cabalmente; por lo menos

fulsome ['fʊlsəm] *adj* bajo, craso, de mal gusto

fumble ['fʌmbəl] *tr* no coger (*la pelota*), dejar caer (*la pelota*) desmañadamente; manosear desmañadamente ‖ *intr* revolver papeles; titubear; andar a tientas; (*in one's pockets*) buscar con las manos

fume [fjum] *s* humo, vapor *m*, gas *m*, vaho ‖ *tr* (*to treat with fumes*) ahumar ‖ *intr* (*to give off fumes*) humear; (*to show anger*) echar pestes; **to fume at** echar pestes contra

fumigate ['fjumɪˌget] *tr* fumigar

fumigation [ˌfjumɪ'geʃən] *s* fumigación

fun [fʌn] *s* divertimiento; broma, chacota; **to be fun** ser divertido; **to have fun** divertirse; **to make fun of** reírse de, burlarse de

function ['fʌŋkʃən] *s* función ‖ *intr* funcionar

functional ['fʌŋkʃənəl] *adj* funcional

functionar·y ['fʌŋkʃəˌnɛri] *s* (*pl* **-ies**) funcionario

fund [fʌnd] *s* fondo; **funds** fondos ‖ *tr* consolidar (*una deuda*)

fundamental [ˌfʌndə'mɛntəl] *adj* fundamental ‖ *s* fundamento

funeral ['fjunərəl] *adj* funeral; (*march, procession*) fúnebre; (*expense*) funerario ‖ *s* funeral *m*, funerales *mpl*, pompa fúnebre (*de cuerpo presente*); **it's not my funeral** (slang) no corre a mi cuidado

funeral director *s* empresario de pompas fúnebres

funeral home o **parlor** *s* funeraria

funeral service *s* oficio de difuntos, misa de cuerpo presente

funereal [fju'nɪriəl] *adj* fúnebre

fungous ['fʌŋgəs] *adj* fungoso

fungus ['fʌŋgəs] *s* (*pl* **funguses** o **fungi** ['fʌndʒaɪ]) hongo; (pathol) fungo

funicular [fju'nɪkjələr] *adj* & *s* funicular *m*

funk [fʌŋk] *s* (coll) miedo, cobardía; cobarde *mf*; **in a funk** asustado

fun·nel ['fʌnəl] *s* embudo; (*smokestack*) chimenea; (*tube for ventilation*) manguera, ventilador *m* ‖ *v* (*pret* & *pp* **-neled** o **-nelled**; *ger* **-neling** o **-nelling**) *tr* verter por medio de un embudo

funnies ['fʌniz] *spl* páginas cómicas, tiras cómicas, tebeo

fun·ny ['fʌni] *adj* (*comp* **-nier**; *super* **-niest**) cómico; divertido, chistoso; (coll) extraño, raro; **to strike someone as funny** hacerle a uno gracia

funny bone *s* hueso de la alegría

funny paper *s* páginas cómicas

fur. *abbr* **furlong, furnished**

fur [fʌr] *s* piel *f*; abrigo de pieles; (*on the tongue*) sarro

furbelow ['fʌrbəˌlo] *s* (*ruffle*) faralá *m*; (*frippery*) ringorrango

furbish ['fʌrbɪʃ] *tr* acicalar, limpiar; **to furbish up** renovar

furious ['fjurɪəs] *adj* furioso

furl [fʌrl] *tr* enrollar; (naut) aferrar

fur-lined ['fʌrˌlaɪnd] *adj* forrado con pieles

furlong ['fʌrlɔŋ] o ['fʌrlɑŋ] *s* estadio

furlough [ˈfʌrlo] s licencia ‖ tr dar licencia a
furnace [ˈfʌrnɪs] s horno; (to heat a house) calorífero
furnish [ˈfʌrnɪʃ] tr amueblar; proporcionar, suministrar
furnishings [ˈfʌrnɪʃɪŋz] spl muebles mpl; (things to wear) artículos
furniture [ˈfʌrnɪtʃər] s muebles mpl, móbiliario; (naut) aparejo; **a piece of furniture** un mueble
furniture dealer s mueblista mf
furniture store s mueblería
furrier [ˈfʌrɪ•ər] s peletero
furrier•y [ˈfʌrɪ•əri] s (pl -ies) peletería
furrow [ˈfʌro] s surco ‖ tr surcar
further [ˈfʌrðər] adj adicional; nuevo; más lejano ‖ adv además; más lejos ‖ tr adelantar, promover, fomentar
furtherance [ˈfʌrðərəns] s adelantamiento, promoción, fomento
furthermore [ˈfʌrðər,mor] adv además
furthest [ˈfʌrðɪst] adj (el) más lejano ‖ adv más lejos
furtive [ˈfʌrtɪv] adj furtivo
fu•ry [ˈfjuri] s (pl -ries) furia
furze [fʌrz] s aulaga; retama de escoba
fuse [fjuz] s (tube or wick filled with explosive material) mecha; (device for detonating an explosive charge) espoleta; (elec) fusible m, cortacircuitos m, tapón m; **to burn out a fuse** quemar un fusible ‖ tr fundir; (to unite) fusionar ‖ intr fundirse; fusionarse
fuse box s caja de fusibles
fuselage [ˈfjuzəlɪdʒ] s fuselaje m
fusible [ˈfjuzɪbəl] adj fundible, fusible

fusillade [,fjuzɪˈled] s fusilería; (e.g., of questions) andanada ‖ tr atacar o matar con una descarga de fusilería, fusilar
fusion [ˈfjuʒən] s fusión
fuss [fʌs] s alharaca, hazañería; (coll) disputa por ligero motivo; **to make a fuss** hacer alharacas; **to make a fuss over** hacer fiestas a; disputar sobre ‖ tr atolondrar, inquietar, confundir ‖ intr hacer alharacas, inquietarse por bagatelas
fuss•y [ˈfʌsi] adj (comp -ier; super -iest)] alharaquiento, alborotado; descontentadizo, quisquilloso, melindroso; funcionero, hazañero; muy adornado
fustian [ˈfʌstʃən] s (coarse cloth) fustán m; (sort of velveteen) pana; (bombast) cultedad, follaje m
fust•y [ˈfʌsti] adj (comp -ier; super -iest) mohoso, rancio; que huele a cerrado; pasado de moda
futile [ˈfjutɪl] adj (unproductive) estéril; (unimportant) fútil
futili•ty [fjuˈtɪlɪti] s (pl -ties) esterilidad; futilidad
future [ˈfjutʃər] adj futuro ‖ s futuro, porvenir m; (gram) futuro; **futures** (com) futuros; **in the future** en el futuro; **in the near future** en un futuro próximo
fuze [fjuz] s (tube or wick filled with explosive material) mecha; (device for detonating an explosive charge) espoleta; (elec) fusible m ‖ tr poner la espoleta a
fuzz [fʌz] s (as on a peach) pelusa, vello; (in pockets and corners) borra, tamo; **the fuzz** (slang) policía m, guardia m urbano
fuzz•y [ˈfʌzi] adj (comp -ier; super -iest) cubierto de pelusa, velloso; polvoriento; (indistinct) borroso

fu
ga

G

G, g [dʒi] s séptima letra del alfabeto inglés
G. abbr **German, Gulf**
g. abbr **gender, genitive, gram**
gab [gæb] s (coll) cotorreo ‖ (pret & pp **gabbed;** ger **gabbing**) intr (coll) cotorrear
gabardine [ˈgæbər,din] s gabardina
gabble [ˈgæbəl] s cotorreo, parloteo ‖ intr cotorrear, parlotear
gable (ˈgebəl] s (of roof) aguilón m; (over a door or window) gablete m, frontón m
gable end s hastial m
gable roof s tejado de dos aguas
gad [gæd] v (pret & pp **gadded;** ger **gadding**) intr callejear, andar de acá para allá; **to gad about** pindonguear (una mujer)
gad'a•bout adj callejero ‖ s cirigallo; (woman) pindonga
gad'fly' s (pl -flies) tábano
gadget [ˈgædʒɪt] s adminículo, chisme m, artilugio
Gael [gel] s gaélico
Gaelic [ˈgelɪk] adj & s gaélico

gaff [gæf] s garfio, arpón m; **to stand the gaff** (slang) tener aguante
gag [gæg] s mordaza; (interpolation by an actor) morcilla; (joke) chiste m, payasada ‖ v (pret & pp **gagged;** ger **gagging**) tr amordazar; dar bascas a ‖ intr sentir bascas, arquear
gage [gedʒ] s (pledge) prenda; (challenge) desafío
gaie•ty [ˈge•ɪti] s (pl -ties) alegría, algazara, diversión; (of colors) viveza
gaily [ˈgeli] adv alegremente
gain [gen] s ganancia; (increase) aumento ‖ tr ganar; (to reach) alcanzar ‖ intr ganar terreno; mejorar (un enfermo); adelantarse (un reloj); **to gain on** ir alcanzando
gainful [ˈgenfəl] adj ganancioso, provechoso
gain'say' v (pret & pp **-said** [ˈsed] o [ˈsɛd]) tr negar; contradecir; prohibir
gait [get] s paso, manera de andar
gaiter [ˈgetər] s polaina corta
gal. abbr **gallon**

gala ['gelə] *adj* de gala ‖ *s* fiesta

galax•y ['gæləksi] *s* (*pl* **-ies**) galaxia

gale [gel] *s* ventarrón *m;* **gales of laughter** tempestades de risas; **to weather the gale** correr el temporal; (fig) ir tirando

Galician [gə'lɪ/ən] *adj* & *s* gallego

gall [gɔl] *s* bilis *f*, hiel *f;* vejiga de la bilis; (*something bitter*) (fig) hiel *f;* rencor *m*, odio; (*gallnut*) agalla; (*audacity*) (coll) descaro ‖ *tr* lastimar rozando; irritar ‖ *intr* raerse; (naut) mascarse (*un cabo*)

gallant ['gælənt] *adj* (*attentive to women*) galante; (*pertaining to love*) amoroso ‖ ['gælənt] *adj* (*stately, grand*) gallardo; (*spirited, daring*) hazañoso; (*showy, gay*) vistoso, festivo ‖ *s* hombre *m* valiente; (*man attentive to women*) galán *m*

gallant•ry ['gæləntri] *s* (*pl* **-ries**) galantería; gallardía

gall bladder *s* vejiga de la bilis, vesícula biliar

gall duct *s* conducto biliar

galleon ['gælɪ•ən] *s* (naut) galeón *m*

galler•y ['gæləri] *s* (*pl* **-ies**) galería; (*in church, theater, etc.*) tribuna; (*cheapest seats in theater*) gallinero; **to play to the gallery** (coll) hablar para la galería

galley ['gæli] *s* (naut & typ) galera; (naut) cocina

galley proof *s* (typ) galerada, pruebas de segundas

galley slave *s* galeote *m;* (*drudge*) esclavo del trabajo

Gallic ['gælɪk] *adj* gálico

galling ['gɔlɪŋ] *adj* irritante, ofensivo

gallivant ['gælɪ,vænt] *intr* andar a placer

gall'nut' *s* agalla

gallon ['gælən] *s* galón *m* (*medida*)

galloon [gə'lun] *s* galón *m* (*cinta*)

gallop ['gæləp] *s* galope *m;* **at a gallop** a galope ‖ *tr* hacer galopar ‖ *intr* galopar; **to gallop through** (fig) hacer muy aprisa

gal•lows ['gæloz] *s* (*pl* **-lows** o **-lowses**) horca

gallows bird *s* (coll) carne *f* de horca

gall'stone' *s* cálculo biliar

galore [gə'lor] *adv* en abundancia

galosh [gə'lɑ/] *s* chanclo alto

galvanize ['gælvə,naɪz] *tr* galvanizar

galvanized iron *s* hierro galvanizado

gambit ['gæmbɪt] *s* gambito

gamble ['gæmbəl] *s* (coll) empresa arriesgada ‖ *tr* aventurar en el juego; **to gamble away** perder en el juego ‖ *intr* jugar; (*in the stock market*) especular, aventurarse

gambler ['gæmblər] *s* jugador *m;* especulador *m*

gambling ['gæmblɪŋ] *s* juego

gambling den *s* garito

gambling house *s* casa de juego, juego público

gambling table *s* mesa de juego

gam•bol ['gæmbəl] *s* cabriola, retozo, salto ‖ *v* (*pret* & *pp* **-boled** o **-bolled;** *gen* **-boling** o **-bolling**) *intr* cabriolar, retozar, saltar

gambrel ['gæmbrəl] *s* corvejón *m*

gambrel roof *s* techo a la holandesa

game [gem] *adj* bravo, peleón; dispuesto, resuelto; (*leg*) cojo; de caza ‖ *s* (*form of play*) juego; (*single contest*) partida; (*score*) tantos; (*in bridge*) manga; (*any sport*) deporte *m;* (*animal or bird hunted for sport or food*) caza; (*any pursuit*) actividad; (*pursuit of diplomacy*) juego; **the game is up** estamos frescos; **to make game of** burlarse de; **to play the game** jugar limpio

game bag *s* morral *m*

game bird *s* ave *f* de caza

game'cock' *s* gallo de pelea

game'keep'er *s* guardabosque *m*

game of chance *s* juego de azar

game preserve *s* vedado

game warden *s* guardabosque *m*

gamut ['gæmət] *s* (mus & fig) gama

gam•y ['gemi] *adj* (*comp* **-ier;** *super* **-iest**) (*having flavor of uncooked game*) salvajino; bravo, peleón

gander ['gændər] *s* ganso

gang [gæŋ] *adj* múltiple ‖ *s* (*of workmen*) brigada, cuadrilla; (*of thugs*) pandilla ‖ *intr* — **to gang up** acuadrillarse; **to gang up against** u **on** atacar juntos; conspirar contra

gangling ['gæŋglɪŋ] *adj* larguirucho

gangli•on ['gæŋglɪ•ən] *s* (*pl* **-ons** o **-a** [ə]) ganglio

gang'plank' *s* plancha, pasarela

gangrene ['gæŋgrin] *s* gangrena ‖ *tr* gangrenar ‖ *intr* gangrenarse

gangster ['gæŋstər] *adj* gangsteril ‖ *s* gángster *m*, pistolero

gangsterism ['gæŋstə,rɪzəm] *s* gangsterismo; acciones de los gangsters

gang'way' *s* (*passageway*) pasillo; (*gangplank*) plancha, pasarela; (*in ship's side*) portalón *m* ‖ *interj* ¡abran paso!, ¡paso libre!

gantlet ['gɔntlɪt] *s* (rr) vía traslapada

gan•try ['gæntri] *s* (*pl* **-tries**) caballete *m*, poíno; (rr) puente *m* transversal de señales

gantry crane *s* grúa de caballete

gap [gæp] *s* (*break, open space*) laguna; (*in a wall*) boquete *m;* (*between mountains*) garganta, quebrada; (*between two points of view*) sima

gape [gep] o [gæp] *s* abertura, brecha; (*yawn*) bostezo; mirada de asombro; **the gapes** ganas de bostezar ‖ *intr* estar abierto de par en par; bostezar; embobarse; **to gape at** mirar embobado; **to stand gaping** embobarse

G.A.R. *abbr* **Grand Army of the Republic**

garage [gə'rɑz] *s* garage *m*

garb [gɑrb] *s* vestidura ‖ *tr* vestir

garbage ['gɑrbɪdʒ] *s* basuras, desperdicios, bazofia

garbage can *s* cubo para bazofia, latón *m* de la basura

garbage collection *s* recogida de basuras

garbage disposal *s* evacuación de basuras

garbage heap *s* basural *m* (CAm)

garble ['gɑrbəl] *tr* mutilar (*un texto*)

garden ['gɑrdən] *s* (*of vegetables*) huerto; (*of flowers*) jardín *m*

gardener ['gɑrdənər] s (of vegetables) hortelano; (of flowers) jardinero

gardenia [gɑr'dini•ə] s gardenia, jazmín m de la India

gardening ['gɑrdənɪŋ] s horticultura; jardinería

garden party s fiesta que se da en un jardín o parque

gargle ['gɑrgəl] s gargarismo ‖ intr gargarizar

gargoyle ['gɑrgɔɪl] s gárgola

garish ['gɛrɪʃ] adj charro, chillón, cursi

garland ['gɑrlənd] s guirnalda

garlic ['gɑrlɪk] s ajo

garment ['gɑrmənt] s prenda de vestir

garner ['gɑrnər] tr (to gather, collect) acopiar; adquirir; (cereales) entrojar

garnet ['gɑrnɪt] adj & s granate m

garnish ['gɑrnɪʃ] s adorno; (culin) aderezo, condimento de adorno ‖ tr adornar; (culin) aderezar; (law) embargar

garret ['gærɪt] s buhardilla, desván m

garrison ['gærɪsən] s plaza fuerte; (troops) guarnición ‖ tr guarnecer, guarnicionar (una plaza fuerte); guarnecer una plaza fuerte de (tropas)

garrote [gə'rɑt] o [gə'rot] s estrangulación para robar; (method of execution; iron collar used for such execution) garrote m ‖ tr estrangular; estrangular para robar; agarrotar, dar garrote a

garrulous ['gærələs] adj gárrulo, locuaz

garter ['gɑrtər] s liga, jarretera

garth [gɑrθ] s patio de claustro

gas [gæs] s gas m; gasolina; (coll) palabrería ‖ v (pret & pp **gassed;** ger **gassing**) tr abastecer de gas; (to attack, asphyxiate, or poison with gas) gasear; abastecer de gasolina ‖ intr despedir gas; (slang) charlar

gas'bag' s (aer) cámara de gas; (slang) charlatán m

gas burner s mechero de gas

Gascony ['gæskəni] s Gascuña

gas engine s motor m a gas

gaseous ['gæsɪ•əs] adj gaseoso

gas fitter s gasista m

gas generator s gasógeno

gash [gæʃ] s cuchillada, chirlo ‖ tr acuchillar

gas heat s calefacción por gas

gas'hold'er s gasómetro

gasi•fy ['gæsɪ,faɪ] v (pret & pp **-fied**) tr gasificar ‖ intr gasificarse

gas jet s mechero de gas; llama de gas

gasket ['gæskɪt] s empaquetadura

gas'light' s luz f de gas

gas main s cañería de gas

gas mask s careta antigás

gas meter s contador m de gas

gasohol ['gæsə,hɔl] s alconafta

gasoline ['gæsə,lin] o [,gæsə'lin] s gasolina

gasoline pump s poste m distribuidor m de gasolina, surtidor m de gasolina

gasp [gæsp] s respiración entrecortada; (of death) boqueada ‖ tr decir con voz entrecortada ‖ intr boquear

gas producer s gasógeno

gas range s cocina a gas

gas station s estación gasolinera

gas stove s cocina a gas

gas tank s gasómetro; (aut) **depósito** de gasolina

gastric ['gæstrɪk] adj gástrico

gastronomy [gæs'trɑnəmi] s gastronomía

gas'works' s fábrica de gas

gate [get] s puerta; (in fence or wall; of bird cage) portillo; (of sluice or lock) compuerta; (number of people paying admission; amount they pay) entrada, taquilla; (rr) barrera; (fig) entrada, camino; **to crash the gate** (coll) colarse de gorra

gate'keep'er s portero; (rr) guardabarrera mf

gate'post' s poste m de una puerta de cercado

gate'way' s entrada, paso, camino

gather ['gæðər] tr recoger, reunir; recolectar (la cosecha); coger (leña, flores, etc.); cubrirse de (polvo); recoger (una persona sus pensamientos); (bb) alzar; (sew) fruncir; (to deduce) (fig) calcular, deducir; **to gather oneself together** componerse ‖ intr reunirse; amontonarse; saltar (lágrimas)

gathering ['gæðərɪŋ] s reunión; recolección; (bb) alzado; (sew) frunce m

gaud•y ['gɔdi] adj (comp **-ier;** super **-iest**) cursi, chillón, llamativo

gauge [gedʒ] s medida, norma; calibre m; (of liquid in a container) nivel m; (of carpenter) gramil m; (of gasoline) medidor m; (rr) ancho de vía, entrevía ‖ tr medir; calibrar; graduar; aforar (la cantidad de agua de una corriente); arquear (una nave)

gauge glass s tubo indicador, vidrio de nivel

Gaul [gɔl] s la Galia; (native) galo

Gaulish ['gɔlɪʃ] adj & s galo

gaunt [gɔnt] o [gɑnt] adj desvaído, macilento; hosco, tétrico

gauntlet ['gɔntlɪt] o ['gɑntlɪt] s guantelete m; guante con puño abocinado; carrera de baquetas; (rr) vía traslapada; **to run the gauntlet** correr baquetas, pasar por baquetas; **to take up the gauntlet** recoger el guante; **to throw down the gauntlet** arrojar el guante

gauze [gɔz] s gasa, cendal m

gavel ['gævəl] s mazo, martillo

gavotte [gə'vɑt] s gavota

gawk [gɔk] s (coll) palurdo, papanatas m ‖ intr (coll) mirar de modo impertinente; papar moscas, mirar embobado

gawk•y ['gɔki] adj (comp **-ier;** super **-iest**) desgarbado, torpe, bobo

gay [ge] adj homosexual; alegre, festivo; (brilliant) vistoso; amigo de los placeres

gaye•ty ['ge•ɪti] s var de **gaiety**

gaze [gez] s mirada fija ‖ intr mirar fijamente

gazelle [gə'zɛl] s gacela

gazette [gə'zɛt] s periódico; anuncio oficial

gazetteer [,gæzə'tɪr] s diccionario geográfico

gear [gɪr] s pertrechos, utensilios; (of transmission, steering, etc.) mecanismo, aparato; rueda dentada; (two or more toothed wheels meshed together) engranaje m; **out of gear** desengranado; (fig) descompuesto; **to throw into gear** engranar; **to throw out**

ga
ge

of gear desengranar; (fig) descomponer ‖ *tr & intr* engranar

gear'box' *s* caja de engranajes; (aut) caja de velocidades

gear case *s* caja de engranajes

gear'shift' *s* cambio de marchas, cambio de velocidades

gearshift lever *s* palanca de cambio de marchas

gear'wheel' *s* rueda dentada

gee [dʒi] *interj* ¡caramba!; **gee up!** (*get up!*, *said to a horse*) ¡arre!; **geez!** ¡mecachis!

Gehenna [gɪ'hɛnə] *s* gehena *m*

Geiger counter ['gaɪgər] *s* contador *m* de Geiger

gel [dʒɛl] *s* gel *m* ‖ *v* (*pret & pp* **gelled;** *ger* **gelling**) *intr* cuajarse en forma de gel

gelatine ['dʒɛlətɪn] *s* gelatina

geld [gɛld] *v* (*pret & pp* **gelded** o **gelt** [gɛlt]) *tr* castrar

gem [dʒɛm] *s* gema, piedra preciosa; (fig) joya, preciosidad

Gemini ['dʒɛmɪ,naɪ] *s* (*constellation*) Géminis *m* o Gemelos; (*sign of zodiac*) Géminis *m*

gen. *abbr* **gender, general, genitive, genus**

gender ['dʒɛndər] *s* (gram) género; (coll) sexo

genealo•gy [,dʒɛnɪ'ælədʒi] *s* (*pl* **-gies**) genealogía

general ['dʒɛnərəl] *adj & s* general *m;* **general of the army** capitán general de ejército; **in general** en general o por lo general

general delivery *s* lista de correos

generalissi•mo [,dʒɛnərə'lɪsɪmo] *s* (*pl* **-mos**) generalísimo

generali•ty [,dʒɛnə'rælɪti] *s* (*pl* **-ties**) generalidad

generalize ['dʒɛnərə'laɪz] *tr & intr* generalizar

generally ['dʒɛnərəli] *adv* por lo general

general medicine *s* medicina general

general practitioner *s* médico general

generalship ['dʒɛnərəl,ʃɪp] *s* generalato; don *m* de mando

general staff *s* estado mayor general

general strike *s* huelga general

generate ['dʒɛnə,ret] *tr* (*to beget*) engendrar; generar (*electricidad*); (geom) engendrar

generating station *s* central *f*

generation ['dʒɛnə'reʃən] *s* generación

generator ['dʒɛnə,retər] *s* generador *m*

generic [dʒɪ'nɛrɪk] *adj* genérico

generous ['dʒɛnərəs] *adj* generoso; abundante, grande

gene•sis ['dʒɛnɪsɪs] *s* (*pl* **-ses** [,siz]) génesis *f* ‖ **Genesis** *s* (Bib) el Génesis

genetic [dʒɪ'nɛtɪk] *adj* genético

genetic engineering *s* ingeniería genética

genetics [dʒɪ'nɛtɪks] *s* genética

Geneva [dʒɪ'nivə] *s* Ginebra

Genevan [dʒɪ'nivən] *adj & s* ginebrino

genial ['dʒiniəl] *adj* afable, complaciente

genie ['dʒini] *s* genio

genital ['dʒɛnɪtəl] *adj* genital ‖ **genitals** *spl* genitales *mpl*, órganos genitales

genitive ['dʒɛnɪtɪv] *adj & s* genitivo

genitourinary [,dʒɛnəto'jurɪ,nɛrɪ] *adj* genitourinario

genius ['dʒinjəs] o ['dʒini•əs] *s* (*pl* **geniuses**) (*great inventive gift; person possessing it*) genio ‖ *s* (*pl* **genii** ['dʒini,aɪ]) (*guardian spirit; pagan deity*) genio

Genoa ['dʒɛno•ə] *s* Génova

genocidal [,dʒɛnə'saɪdəl] *adj* genocida

genocide ['dʒɛnə'saɪd] *s* (*act*) genocidio; (*person*) genocida *mf*

Geno•ese [,dʒɛno'iz] *adj* genovés ‖ *s* (*pl* **-ese**) genovés *m*

genre ['ʒanrə] *adj* de género

gent. o **Gent.** *abbr* **gentleman, gentlemen**

genteel [dʒɛn'til] *adj* gentil, elegante; cortés, urbano

gentian ['dʒɛnʃən] *s* genciana

gentile ['dʒɛntɪl] o ['dʒɛntaɪl] *adj* gentilicio; (gram) gentilicio ‖ ['dʒɛntaɪl] *adj & s* no judío; cristiano; (*pagan*) gentil *mf*

gentili•ty [dʒɛn'tɪlɪti] *s* (*pl* **-ties**) gentileza

gentle ['dʒɛntəl] *adj* apacible, benévolo; dulce, manso, suave; cortés, fino; (*e.g., tap on the shoulder*) ligero

gen'tle•folk' *s* gente bien nacida

gentle•man ['dʒɛntəlmən] *s* (*pl* **-men** [mən]) *s* caballero; (*attendant to a person of high rank*) gentilhombre *m*

gentleman in waiting *s* gentilhombre *m* de cámara

gentlemanly ['dʒɛntəlmənli] *adj* caballeroso

gentleman of leisure *s* señor *m* que vive sin trabajar, caballero de vida holgada

gentleman of the road *s* salteador *m* de caminos

gentleman's agreement *s* acuerdo verbal

gentle sex *s* bello sexo, sexo débil

gentry ['dʒɛntri] *s* gente bien nacida

genuine ['dʒɛnju•ɪn] *adj* genuino; sincero, franco

genus ['dʒinəs] *s* (*pl* **genera** ['dʒɛnərə] o **genuses**) (biol, log) género

geog. *abbr* **geography**

geographer [dʒɪ'agrəfər] *s* geógrafo

geographic(al) [,dʒi•ə'græfɪk(əl)] *adj* geográfico

geogra•phy [dʒɪ'agrəfi] *s* (*pl* **-phies**) geografía

geol. *abbr* **geology**

geologic(al) [,dʒi•ə'ladʒɪk(əl)] *adj* geológico

geologist [dʒɪ'alədʒɪst] *s* geólogo

geology [dʒɪ'alədʒi] *s* (*pl* **-gies**) geología

geom. *abbr* **geometry**

geometric(al) [,dʒi•ə'mɛtrɪk(əl)] *adj* geométrico

geometrician [dʒɪ,ami'trɪʃən] *s* geómetra *mf*

geome•try [dʒɪ'amɪtri] *s* (*pl* **-tries**) geometría

geophysics [,dʒi•ə'fɪzɪks] *s* geofísica

geopolitics [,dʒi•ə'palɪtɪks] *s* geopolítica

George [dʒɔrdʒ] *s* Jorge *m*

geranium [dʒɪ'reni•əm] *s* geranio

geriatrical [,dʒɛri'ætrɪkəl] *adj* geriátrico

geriatrician [,dʒɛri•ə'trɪʃən] *s* geriatra *mf*

geriatrics [,dʒɛri'ætrɪks] *s* geriatría

germ [dʒʌrm] *s* germen *m*

German ['dʒʌrmən] *adj & s* alemán *m*

germane [dʒərˈmen] *adj* pertinente, relacionado

Germanize [ˈdʒʌrməˌnaɪz] *tr* germanizar

German measles *s* rubéola

German silver *s* melchor *m*, alpaca

Germany [ˈdʒʌrməni] *s* Alemania

germ carrier *s* portador *m* de gérmenes

germ cell *s* célula germen

germicidal [ˌdʒʌrmɪˈsaɪdəl] *adj* germicida

germicide [ˈdʒʌrmɪˌsaɪd] *s* germicida *m*

germinate [ˈdʒʌrmɪˌnet] *intr* germinar

germ plasm *s* germen *m* plasma

germ theory *s* teoría germinal

germ warfare *s* guerra bacteriana, guerra bacteriológica

gerontology [ˌdʒɛrənˈtalədʒi] *s* gerontología

gerund [ˈdʒɛrənd] *s* gerundio

gerundive [dʒɪˈrʌndɪv] *s* gerundio adjetivo

gestation [dʒɛsˈteʃən] *s* gestación

gesticulate [dʒɛsˈtɪkjəˌlet] *intr* accionar, manotear

gesticulation [dʒɛsˌtɪkjəˈleʃən] *s* ademán *m*, manoteo

gesture [ˈdʒɛstʃər] *s* ademán *m*, gesto; demostración, muestra ‖ *intr* hacer ademanes, hacer gestos

get [gɛt] *v* (*pret* **got** [gat]; *pp* **got** o **gotten** [ˈgatən]; *ger* **getting**) *tr* conseguir, obtener; recibir; ir por, buscar; tomar (*p.ej., un billete*); alcanzar; encontrar, hallar; hacer (*p.ej., la comida*); resolver (*un problema*); aprender de memoria; captar (*una estación emisora*); **to get across** hacer aceptar; hacer comprender; **to get back** recobrar; **to get down** descolgar; (*to swallow*) tragar; **to get off** quitar (*p.ej., una mancha*); **to get someone** + *inf* lograr que alguien + *subj;* **to get** + *pp* hacer + *inf;* **to have got** (coll) tener; **to have got to** + *inf* (coll) tener que + *inf* ‖ *intr* (*to become*) hacerse, ponerse, volverse; (*to arrive*) llegar; **get up!** (*to an animal*) ¡arre!; **to get about** estar levantado (*un convaleciente*); **to get along** seguir andando; irse; ir tirando; tener éxito; llevarse bien; **to get along in years** ponerse viejo; **to get along with** congeniar con; **to get angry** enfadarse; **to get around** divulgarse; salir mucho, ir a todas partes; eludir; manejar (*a una persona*); **to get away** conseguir marcharse; evadirse; **to get away with** llevarse, escaparse con; (coll) hacer impunemente; **to get back** volver, regresar; **to get back at** (coll) desquitarse con; **to get behind** quedarse atrás; apoyar, abogar por; **to get by** lograr pasar; (*to manage to shift*) (coll) arreglárselas; **to get going** ponerse en marcha; **to get in** entrar; volver a casa; llegar (*un tren*); **to get in with** llegar a ser amigo de; **to get married** casarse; **to get off** apearse; marcharse; **to get old** envejecer; **to get on** subir; llevarse bien; **to get out** salir, marcharse, divulgarse; **to get out of** bajar de (*un coche*); librarse de; perder (*la paciencia*); **to get out of the way** quitarse de en medio; **to get run over** ser atropellado; **to get through** pasar por entre; terminar; **to get to be** llegar a ser; **to get under way** ponerse en camino; **to get up** levantarse; **to not get over it** (coll) no volver de su asombro

get'a·way' *s* escapatoria, escape *m;* (*of an automobile*) arranque *m*

get'-to·geth'er *s* reunión, tertulia

get'-up' *s* (coll) disposición, presentación; (coll) atavío, traje *m*

gewgaw [ˈgjugɔ] *adj* cursi, charro, chillón ‖ *s* fruslería, chuchería; adorno, charro

geyser [ˈgaɪzər] *s* géiser *m* ‖ [ˈgizər] *s* (Brit) calentador *m* de agua

ghast·ly [ˈgæstli] *adj* (*comp* **-lier;** *super* **-liest**) cadavérico, espectral; espantoso, horrible

Ghent [gɛnt] *s* Gante

gherkin [ˈgʌrkɪn] *s* pepinillo

ghet·to [ˈgɛto] *s* (*pl* **-tos**) ghetto

ghost [gost] *s* espectro, fantasma *m;* (telv) fantasma *m;* **not a ghost of a** ni sombra de; **to give up the ghost** entregar el alma, rendir el alma

ghost·ly [ˈgostli] *adj* (*comp* **-lier;** *super* **-liest**) espectral

ghost story *s* cuento de fantasmas

ghost writer *s* colaborador anónimo, escritor anónimo de obras firmadas por otra persona

ghoul [gul] *s* demonio que se alimenta de cadáveres; ladrón *m* de tumbas; (*person who revels in horrible things*) vampiro

ghoulish [ˈgulɪʃ] *adj* vampírico, horrible

G.H.Q. *abbr* **General Headquarters**

GI [ˈdʒiˈaɪ] *s* (*pl* **GI's**) (coll) soldado raso (*del ejército norteamericano*)

giant [ˈdʒaɪ·ənt] *adj & s* gigante *m*

giantess [ˈdʒaɪ·əntɪs] *s* giganta

gibberish [ˈdʒɪbərɪʃ] o [ˈgɪbərɪʃ] *s* guirigay *m*

gibbet [ˈdʒɪbɪt] *s* horca ‖ *tr* ahorcar; poner a la vergüenza

gibe [dʒaɪb] *s* remoque *m*, mofa ‖ *intr* mofarse; **to gibe at** mofarse de

giblets [ˈdʒɪblɪts] *spl* menudillos

giddiness [ˈgɪdɪnɪs] *s* vértigo, vahido; falta de juicio

gid·dy [ˈgɪdi] *adj* (*comp* **-dier;** *super* **-diest**) vertiginoso; mareado; casquivano, ligero de cascos

Gideon [ˈgɪdɪ·ən] *s* (Bib) Gedeón *m*

gift [gɪft] *s* regalo; (*natural ability*) don *m*, dote *f*, prenda

gifted [ˈgɪftɪd] *adj* talentoso; muy inteligente

gift horse *s* —**never look a gift horse in the mouth** a caballo regalado no se le mira el diente

gift of gab *s* (coll) facundia, labia

gift shop *s* comercio de objetos de regalo, tienda de regalos

gift'wrap' *v* (*pret & pp* **-wrapped;** *ger* **-wrapping**) *tr* envolver en paquete regalo

gigantic [dʒaɪˈgæntɪk] *adj* gigantesco

giggle [ˈgɪgəl] *s* risita, risa ahogada, retozo de la risa ‖ *intr* reírse bobamente

ge
gi

gigo·lo [ˈdʒɪgə ˌlo] s (pl **-los**) acompañante m profesional de mujeres; (man supported by a woman) mantenido

gild [gɪld] v (pret & pp **gilded** o **gilt** [gɪlt]) tr dorar

gilding [ˈgɪldɪŋ] s dorado

gill [gɪl] s (of fish) agalla; (of cock) barba ‖ [dʒɪl] s cuarta parte de una pinta

gillyflower [ˈdʒɪlɪˌflauˌər] s alhelí m

gilt [gɪlt] adj & s dorado

gilt-edged [ˈgɪltˌɛdʒd] adj de toda confianza, de lo mejor que hay

gilt′head′ s dorada

gimcrack [ˈdʒɪmˌkræk] adj de oropel ‖ s chuchería

gimlet [ˈgɪmlɪt] s barrena de mano

gimmick [ˈgɪmɪk] s (slang) adminículo; (slang) adminículo mágico

gin [dʒɪn] s (alcoholic liquor) ginebra; desmotadera de algodón; trampa; (fish trap) garlito; torno de izar ‖ v (pret & pp **ginned**; ger **ginning**) tr desmotar

gin fizz s ginebra con gaseosa

ginger [ˈdʒɪndʒər] s jenjibre m; (coll) energía, viveza

ginger ale s cerveza de jengibre gaseosa

gin′ger·bread′ s pan m de jengibre; adorno charro

gingerly [ˈdʒɪndʒərli] adj cauteloso, cuidadoso ‖ adv cautelosamente

gin′ger·snap′ s galletita de jengibre

gingham [ˈgɪŋəm] s guinga

giraffe [dʒɪˈræf] s jirafa

girandole [ˈdʒɪrənˌdol] s girándula

gird [gʌrd] v (pret & pp **girt** [gʌrt] o **girded**) tr ceñir; (to equip) dotar; (to prepare) aprestar; (to surround, hem in) rodear, encerrar

girder [ˈgʌrdər] s viga, trabe f

girdle [ˈgʌrdəl] s faja; corsé pequeño ‖ tr ceñir; circundar, rodear

girl [gʌrl] s muchacha, niña, chica; (servant) moza

girl friend s (coll) amiguita

girlhood [ˈgʌrlhʊd] s muchachez f; juventud femenina

girlish [gʌrlɪʃ] adj de muchacha; juvenil

girl scout s niña exploradora

girth [gʌrθ] s (band) cincha; (waistband) pretina; circunferencia

gist [dʒɪst] s esencia

give [gɪv] s elasticidad ‖ v (pret **gave** [gev]; pp **given** [ˈgɪvən]) tr dar; ocasionar (molestia, trabajo, etc.); representar (una obra dramática); (lessons) impartir; pronunciar (un discurso); **to give away** dar de balde; revelar; llevar (a la novia); (coll) traicionar; **to give back** devolver; **to give forth** despedir (p.ej. olores); **to give oneself up** entregarse; **to give up** abandonar, dejar (un empleo); renunciar ‖ intr dar; dar de sí; romperse (p.ej., una cuerda); **to give in** ceder, rendirse; **to give out** agotarse; no poder más; **to give up** darse por vencido

give′-and-take′ s concesiones mutuas; conversación sazonada de burlas

give′a·way′ s (coll) revelación involuntaria; (coll) traición; (e.g., in checkers) (coll) ganapierde m & f

given [ˈgɪvən] adj dado; (math) conocido; **given that** dado que, suponiendo que

given name s nombre m de pila

giver [ˈgɪvər] s dador m, donador m

gizzard [ˈgɪzərd] s molleja

glacial [ˈgleʃəl] adj glacial

glacier [ˈgleʃər] s glaciar m, helero

glad [glæd] adj (comp **gladder;** super **gladdest**) alegre, contento; **to be glad (to)** alegrarse (de)

gladden [ˈglædən] tr alegrar

glade [gled] s claro, claro herboso (en un bosque)

glad hand s (coll) acogida efusiva

gladiola [ˌglædɪˈolə] s estoque m

gladly [ˈglædli] adv alegremente; de buena gana, con mucho gusto

gladness [ˈglædnɪs] s alegría, regocijo

glad rags spl (slang) trapitos de cristianar; (slang) vestido de etiqueta

glamorous [ˈglæmərəs] adj fascinador, elegante

glamour [ˈglæmər] s fascinación, elegancia, hechizo

glamour girl s belleza exótica

glance [glæns] s ojeada, vistazo, golpe m de vista; **at a glance** de un vistazo; **at first glance** a primera vista ‖ intr lanzar una mirada; **to glance at** lanzar una mirada a; examinar de paso; **to glance off** desviarse de soslayo; desviarse de, al chocar; **to glance over** mirar por encima

gland [glænd] s glándula

glanders [ˈglændərz] spl muermo

glandulous [ˈglændʒələs] adj glanduloso

glare [glɛr] s fulgor m deslumbrante, luz intensa; mirada feroz, mirada de indignación ‖ intr relumbrar; lanzar miradas feroces; **to glare at** echar una mirada feroz a

glaring [ˈglɛrɪŋ] adj deslumbrante, relumbrante; (look) feroz, penetrante; manifiesto, que salta a la vista

glass [glæs] s vidrio, cristal m; (tumbler) vaso, copa; (mirror) espejo; (glassware) vajilla de cristal; **glasses** anteojos

glass blower [ˈbloˌər] s soplador m de vidrio, vidriero

glass case s vitrina

glass cutter s cortavidrios m

glass door s puerta vidriera

glassful [ˈglæsful] s vaso

glass′house′ s invernadero; (fig) tejado de vidrio

glassine [glæˈsin] s papel m cristal

glass′ware′ s cristalía, vajilla de vidrio

glass wool s cristal hilado

glass′works′ s cristalería vidriería

glass′work′er s vidriero

glass·y [ˈglæsi] adj (comp **-ier;** super **-iest**) vidrioso

glaze [glez] s vidriado, esmalte m; (of ice) capa resbaladiza ‖ tr vidriar, esmaltar; garapiñar (golosinas)

glazier [ˈgleʒər] s vidriero

gleam [glim] s destello, rayo de luz; luz f tenue; (of hope) rayo ‖ intr destellar; brillar con luz tenue

glean [glin] tr espigar; (to gather bit by bit, e.g., out of books) espigar

glee [gli] s alegría, regocijo

glee club s orfeón m

glib [glɪb] adj (comp **glibber**; super **glibbest**) locuaz; (tongue) suelto; fácil e insincero

glide [glaɪd] s deslizamiento; (aer) vuelo sin motor, planeo; (mus) ligadura ‖ intr deslizarse; (aer) volar sin motor, planear; **to glide along** pasar suavemente

glider ['glaɪdər] s (aer) planeador m, deslizador m

glimmer ['glɪmər] s luz f tenue; (faint perception) vislumbre f ‖ intr brillar con luz tenue; (to appear faintly) vislumbrarse

glimmering ['glɪmərɪŋ] adj tenue, trémulo ‖ s luz f tenue; vislumbre f

glimpse [glɪmps] s vislumbre f; **to catch a glimpse of** entrever, vislumbrar ‖ tr vislumbrar

glint [glɪnt] s destello, rayo ‖ intr destellar

glisten ['glɪsən] s centelleo ‖ intr centellear

glitter ['glɪtər] s resplandor m, brillo ‖ intr resplandecer, brillar

gloaming ['glomɪŋ] s crepúsculo vespertino

gloat [glot] intr relamerse; **to gloat over** mirar con satisfacción maligna

globe [glob] s globo

globetrotter ['glob,tratər] s trotamundos m

globule ['glabjul] s glóbulo

glockenspiel ['glɑkən,spil] s juego de timbres, órgano de campanas

gloom [glum] s lobreguez f tinieblas, obscuridad; abatimiento, tristeza; aspecto abatido

gloom•y ['glumi] adj (comp **-ier**; super **-iest**) (dark; sad) lóbrego; pesimista

glori•fy ['glorɪ,faɪ] v (pret & pp **-fied**) tr glorificar; (to enhance) realzar

glorious ['glorɪ•əs] adj glorioso; espléndido, magnífico; (coll) alegre

glo•ry ['glori] s (pl **-ries**) gloria; **to go to glory** ganar la gloria; (slang) fracasar ‖ v (pret & pp **-ried**) intr gloriarse

gloss [glas] s brillo, lustre m; (note, commentary) glosa; glosario ‖ tr (to annotate) glosar; lustrar, satinar; **to gloss over** disculpar, paliar

glossa•ry ['glasəri] s (pl **-ries**) glosario

gloss•y ['glasi] adj (comp **-ier**; super **-iest**) brillante, lustroso; (silk) joyante

glottal ['glatəl] adj glótico

glove [glʌv] s guante m

glove compartment s portaguantes m

glove stretcher s ensanchador m, juanas

glow [glo] s (light of incandescence) resplandor m; (e.g., of sunset) brillo, esplendor m; sensación de calor; color m en las mejillas ‖ intr brillar sin llama; estar encendido (el rostro, el cielo); estar muy animado

glower ['glau•ər] s ceño, mirada ceñuda ‖ intr mirar con ceño

glowing ['glo•ɪŋ] adj ardiente, encendido; radiante; entusiasta, elogioso

glow'worm' s gusano de luz, luciérnaga

glucose ['glukos] s glucosa

glue [glu] s cola; pegapega ‖ tr encolar; pegar fuertemente

glue pot s cazo de cola

gluey ['glu•i] adj (comp **gluier**; super **gluiest**) pegajoso; (smeared with glue) encolado

glug [glʌg] s gluglú m ‖ v (pret & pp **glugged**; ger **glugging**) intr hacer gluglú (el agua)

glum [glʌm] adj (comp **glummer**; super **glummest**) hosco

glut [glʌt] s abundancia, gran acopio; exceso; **to be a glut on the market** abarrotarse ‖ v (pret & pp **glutted**; ger **glutting**) tr hartar, saciar; inundar (el mercado); obstruir

glutton ['glʌtən] adj & s glotón m

gluttonous ['glʌtənəs] adj glotón

glutton•y ['glʌtəni] s (pl **-ies**) glotonería, gula

glycerine ['glɪsərɪn] s glicerina

G.M. abbr **general manager, Grand Master**

G-man ['dʒi,mæn] s (pl **-men** [,mɛn]) (coll) agente m de la policía federal

G.M.T. abbr **Greenwich mean time**

gnarl [nɑrl] s nudo ‖ tr torcer ‖ intr gruñir

gnarled [nɑrld] adj nudoso, retorcido

gnash [næʃ] tr hacer rechinar (los dientes) ‖ intr hacer rechinar los dientes

gnat [næt] s jején m

gnaw [nɔ] tr roer; practicar (un agujero) royendo

gnome [nom] s gnomo

go [go] s (pl **goes**) ida; (coll) energía, ímpetu m; (coll) boga; (coll) ensayo; (for traffic) paso libre; **it's a go** (coll) es un trato hecho; **it's all the go** (coll) hace furor; **it's no go** (coll) es imposible; **on the go** (coll) en continuo movimiento; **to make a go of** (coll) lograr éxito en ‖ v (pret **went** [wɛnt]; pp **gone** [gɔn] o [gɑn]) tr (coll) soportar, tolerar; **to go it alone** obrar sin ayuda ‖ intr ir; (to work, operate) funcionar, marchar; andar (p.ej., desnudo); volverse (p.ej., loco); **going, going, gone!** ¡vendo, vendo, vendí!; **so it goes** así va el mundo; **to be going to** + inf ir a + inf; **to be gone** haber ido; haberse agotado; haber dejado de ser; **to go against** ir en contra de; **to go ahead** seguir adelante; **to go away** irse, marcharse; **to go back** volver; **to go by** pasar por; guiarse por; atenerse a; **to go down** bajar; hundirse (un buque); **to go fishing** ir de pesca; **to go for** ir por; **to go get** ir por, ir a buscar; **to go house hunting** ir a buscar casa; **to go hunting** ir de caza; **to go in** entrar; entrar en; (to fit in) caber en; **to go in for** dedicarse a, interesarse por; **to go into** entrar en; investigar; (aut) poner (p.ej., primera); **to go in with** asociarse con; **to go off** irse, marcharse; llevarse a cabo; estallar (p.ej., una bomba); dispararse (un fusil); **to go on** seguir adelante; ir tirando; **to go on** + ger seguir + ger; **to go on with** continuar; **to**

go out salir; pasar de moda; apagarse (*un fuego, una luz*); declararse en huelga; (*for entertainment, etc.*) salir; **to go over** tener éxito; releer; examinar, revisar; pasar por encima de; **to go over to** pasarse a las filas de; **to go through** pasar por; llegar al fin de; agotar (*una fortuna*); **to go with** ir con, acompañar; salir con (*una muchacha*); hacer juego con; **to go without** andarse sin, pasarse sin

goad [god] *s* aguijada, aguijón *m* ‖ *tr* aguijonear; (SAm) espuelar

go'-a•head' *adj* (coll) emprendedor ‖ *s* (coll) señal *f* para seguir adelante, luz *f* verde

goal [gol] *s* meta; (*in football*) gol *m*

goal'keep'er *s* guardameta *m*, portero

goal line *s* raya de la meta

goal post *s* poste *m* de la meta

goat [got] *s* cabra; (*male goat*) macho cabrío; (coll) víctima inocente; **to be the goat** (slang) pagar el pato; **to get the goat of** (slang) tomar el pelo a; **to ride the goat** (coll) ser iniciado en una sociedad secreta

goatee (go'ti) *s* perilla

goat'herd' *s* cabrero

goat'skin' *s* piel *f* de cabra

goat'suck'er *s* chotacabras *m*

gob [gab] *s* (coll) masa informe y pequeña; (coll) marinero de guerra

gobble ['gabəl] *s* gluglú *m* ‖ *tr* engullir; **to gobble up** engullirse ávidamente; (coll) asir de repente, apoderarse ávidamente de ‖ *intr* engullir; gluglutear, gorgonear (*el pavo*)

gobbledegook ['gabəldɪ,guk] *s* (coll) lenguaje obscuro e incomprensible, galimatías *m*

go'-be•tween' *s* (*intermediary*) medianero; (*in promoting marriages*) casamentero; (*in shady love affairs*) alcahuete *m*, alcahueta

goblet ['gablɪt] *s* copa

goblin ['gablɪn] *s* duende *m*, trasgo

go'-by' *s* (coll) desaire *m*; **to give someone the go-by** (coll) negarse al trato de alguien

go'cart' *s* andaderas; cochecito para niños; carruaje ligero

god [gad] *s* dios *m*; **God forbid** no lo quiera Dios; **God grant** permita Dios; **God willing** Dios mediante

god'child' *s* (*pl* **chil'dren**) ahijado, ahijada

god'daugh'ter *s* ahijada

goddess ['gadɪs] *s* diosa

god'fa'ther *s* padrino

God'-fear'ing *adj* timorato; devoto, pío

God'for•sak'en *adj* dejado de la mano de Dios; (coll) desolado, desierto

god'head' *s* divinidad ‖ **Godhead** *s* Dios *m*

godless ['gadlɪs] *adj* infiel, impío; desalmado, malvado

god•ly ['gadlɪ] *adj* (*comp* **-lier;** *super* **-liest**) devoto, pío

god'moth'er *s* madrina

God's acre *s* campo santo

god'send' *s* cosa llovida del cielo, bendición

god'son' *s* ahijado

God'speed' *s* bienandanza, buena suerte, buen viaje *m*

go'-get'ter *s* (slang) buscavidas *mf*, persona emprendedora

goggle ['gagəl] *intr* volver los ojos; abrir los ojos desmesuradamente

goggle-eyed ['gagəl,aɪd] *adj* de ojos saltones

goggles ['gagəlz] *spl* anteojos de camino, gafas contra el polvo

going ['go•ɪŋ] *adj* en marcha, funcionando; **going on** casi, p.ej., **it is going on nine o'clock** son casi las nueve ‖ *s* ida, partida

going concern *s* empresa que marcha

goings on *spl* actividades; bulla, jarana

goiter ['gɔɪtər] *s* bocio

gold [gold] *adj* áureo, de oro; dorado ‖ *s* oro

gold'beat'er *s* batidor *m* de oro, batihoja *m*

goldbeater's skin *s* venza

gold brick *s* — **to sell a gold brick** (coll) vender gato por liebre

gold'crest' *s* reyezuelo moñudo

gold digger ['dɪgər] *s* (slang) extractora de oro

golden ['goldən] *adj* áureo, de oro; (*gilt*) dorado; (*hair*) rubio; excelente, favorable, floreciente

golden age *s* edad de oro, siglo de oro

golden calf *s* becerro de oro

Golden Fleece *s* vellocino de oro

golden mean *s* justo medio

golden plover *s* chorlito

gold'en•rod' *s* vara de oro, vara de San José

golden rule *s* regla de la caridad cristiana

golden wedding *s* bodas de oro

gold-filled ['gold,fɪld] *adj* empastado en oro

gold'finch' *s* jilguero, pintacilgo

gold'fish' *s* carpa dorada, pez *m* de color

goldilocks ['goldɪ,laks] *s* rubiales *mf*

gold leaf *s* pan *m* de oro

gold mine *s* mina de oro; **to strike a gold mine** (fig) encontrar una mina

gold plate *s* vajilla de oro

gold'-plate' *tr* dorar

gold'smith' *s* orfebre *m*

gold standard *s* patrón *m* oro

golf [galf] *s* golf *m* ‖ *intr* jugar al golf

golf club *s* palo de golf; asociación de jugadores de golf

golfer ['galfər] *s* golfista *mf*

golf links *spl* campo de golf

Golgotha ['galgəθə] *s* el Gólgota

gondola ['gandələ] *s* góndola

gondolier [,gandə'lɪr] *s* gondolero

gone [gɔn] o [gan] *adj* agotado; arruinado; desaparecido; muerto; **gone on** (coll) enamorado de

gong [gɔŋ] o [gaŋ] *s* batintín *m*

gonorrhea [,ganə'ri•ə] *s* gonorrea

goo [gu] *s* (slang) substancia pegajosa

good [gʊd] *adj* (*comp* **better;** *super* **best**) bueno; **good and . . .** (coll) muy, p.ej., **good and cheap** muy barato; **good for** bueno para; capaz de hacer; capaz de pagar; capaz de vivir (*cierto tiempo*); **to be good at** tener talento para; **to be no good** (coll) no servir para nada; (coll) ser un perdido; **to make good** tener éxito; cumplir (*sus promesas*); pagar (*una deuda*); responder de (*los daños*) ‖ *s* bien *m*, provecho, utilidad; **for good** para siempre; **for good and all** de una vez para siempre; **goods** efectos; géneros, mercancías; **the good** lo bueno; los buenos; **to catch with the goods** (slang) coger en flagrante; **to deliver the goods** (slang) cumplir lo prometido; **to do good** hacer el bien; dar salud o fuerzas a; **to the good** de sobra, en el haber; **what is the good of . . . ?** ¿para qué sirve . . . ?

good afternoon s buenas tardes

good′by′ o **good′bye′**s adiós m ‖ interj ¡adiós!

good day s buenos días

good evening s buenas noches, buenas tardes

good fellow s (coll) buen chico, buen sujeto

good fellowship s compañerismo

good′-for-noth′ing adj inútil, sin valor ‖ s pelafustán m perdido

Good Friday s Viernes santo

good graces spl favor m, estimación

good-hearted [′gʊd′hɑrtɪd] adj de buen corazón

good-humored [′gʊd′jumərd] adj de buen humor; afable

good-looking [′gʊd′lʊkɪŋ] adj guapo, bien parecido

good looks spl hermosura, guapeza

good•ly [′gʊdli] adj (comp **-lier;** super **-liest**) considerable; bien parecido, hermoso; bueno, excelente

good morning s buenos días

good-natured [′gʊd′netʃərd] adj bonachón, afable

Good Neighbor Policy s política del buen vecino

goodness [′gʊdnɪs] s bondad; **for goodness' sake!** ¡por Dios!; **goodness knows!** ¡quién sabe! ‖ interj ¡válgame Dios!

good night s buenas noches

good sense s buen sentido, sensatez f

good-sized [′gʊd′saɪzd] adj bastante grande, de buen tamaño

good speed s adiós m y buena suerte

good-tempered [′gʊd′tɛmpərd] adj de natural apacible

good time s rato agradable; **to have a good time** divertirse; **to make good time** ir a buen paso; llegar en poco tiempo

good turn s favor m, servicio

good way s buen trecho

good will s buena voluntad; (com) buen nombre m, clientela

good•y [′gʊdi] adj (coll) beatuco, santurrón ‖ s (pl **-ies**) (coll) golosina ‖ interj (coll) ¡qué bien!, ¡qué alegría!

gooey [′gu•i] adj (comp **gooier;** super **gooiest**) (slang) pegajoso, fangoso

goof [guf] s (slang) tonto ‖ tr & intr (slang) chapucear ‖ intr — **to goof off** farrear

goof•y [′gufi] adj (comp **-ier;** super **-iest**) (slang) tonto, mentecato

goon (gun) s (roughneck) (coll) gamberro, canalla m; (coll) terrorista m de alquiler; (slang) estúpido

goose [gus] s (pl **geese** [gis] ánsar m, ganso, oca; **the goose hangs high** todo va a pedir de boca; **to cook one's goose** malbaratarle a uno los planes; **to kill the goose that lays the golden eggs** matar la gallina de los huevos de oro ‖ s (pl **gooses**) plancha de sastre

goose′ber′ry s (pl **-ries**) (plant) grosellero silvestre; (fruit) grosella silvestre

goose egg s huevo de ɔca; (slang) cero

goose flesh s carne f de gallina

goose′neck′ s cuello de cisne; (naut) gancho de botalones

goose pimples spl carne f de gallina

goose step s (mil) paso de ganso

G.O.P. abbr **Grand Old Party**

gopher [′gofər] s ardilla de tierra, ardillón m; (Geomys) tuza

Gordian knot [′gɔrdɪ•ən] s nudo gordiano; **to cut the Gordian knot** cortar el nudo gordiano

gore [gor] s sangre derramada, sangre cuajada; (insert in a piece of cloth) cuchillo, nesga ‖ tr (to pierce with a horn) acornar; poner cuchillo o nesga a; nesgar

gorge [gɔrdʒ] s garganta, desfiladero; (in a river) atasco de hielo ‖ tr atiborrar ‖ intr atiborrarse

gorgeous [′gɔrdʒəs] adj primoroso, brillante, magnífico, suntuoso

gorilla [gə′rɪlə] s gorila

gorse [gɔrs] s aulaga

gor•y [′gori] adj (comp **-ier;** super **-iest**) ensangrentado, sangriento

gosh [gɑʃ] interj ¡caramba!

goshawk [′gɑs,hɔk] s azor m

gospel [′gɑspəl] s evangelio ‖ **Gospel** s Evangelio

gospel truth s evangelio, pura verdad

gossamer [′gɑsəmər] s telaraña flotante; gasa sutilísima; tela impermeable muy delgada; impermeable m de tela muy delgada

gossip [′gɑsɪp] s chismes m; (person) chismoso, bocaza; **piece of gossip** chisme m ‖ intr chismear

gossip column s mentidero

gossip columnist s gacetillero, cronista mf social

gossipy [′gɑsɪpi] adj chismoso

Goth [gɑθ] s godo; (fig) bárbaro

Gothic [′gɑθɪk] adj & s gótico

gouge [gaʊdʒ] s gubia; (cut made with a gouge) muesca; (coll) estafa ‖ tr excavar con gubia; (coll) estafar

goulash [′gulɑʃ] s puchero húngaro

gourd [gord] o [gʊrd] s calabaza

gourmand [′gʊrmənd] s gastrónomo; glotón m, goloso

gourmet [′gʊrme] s gastrónomo delicado

gout [gaʊt] s gota

gout•y [′gaʊti] adj (comp **-ier;** super **-iest**) gotoso

gov. abbr **governor, government**

govern [′gʌvərn] tr gobernar; (gram) regir ‖ intr gobernar

governess [′gʌvərnɪs] s aya, institutriz f

government [′gʌvərnmənt] s gobierno; (gram) régimen m

go
go

governmental [,gʌvərn'mɛntəl] *adj* gubernamental, gubernativo
government in exile *s* gobierno exilado
governor ['gʌvərnər] *s* gobernador *m; (of a
jail, castle, etc.)* alcaide *m;* (mach) regulador *m*
governorship ['gʌvərnərʃɪp] *s* gobierno
govt. *abbr* **government**
gown [gaun] *s (of a woman)* vestido; *(of a
professor, judge, etc.)* toga; *(of a priest)*
traje *m* talar; *(dressing gown)* bata, peinador *m; (nightgown)* camisa de dormir
G.P.O. *abbr* **General Post Office, Government Printing Office**
gr. *abbr* **gram, grams, grain, grains, gross**
grab [græb] *s* asimiento, presa; (coll) robo ‖
v (pret & pp **grabbed;** *ger* **grabbing)** *tr*
asir, agarrar; arrebatar ‖ *intr* — **to grab at**
tratar de asir
grace [gres] *s (charm; favor; pardon)* gracia;
(prayer at table) benedícite *m; (extension
of time)* demora; **to be in the good graces
of** gozar del favor de; **to say grace** rezar el
benedícite; **with good grace** de buen talante ‖ *tr* adornar, engalanar; favorecer
graceful ['gresfəl] *adj* agraciado, gracioso
grace note *s* apoyatura, nota de adorno
gracious ['greʃəs] *adj* graciable, gracioso;
misericordioso ‖ *interj* ¡válgame Dios!
grackle ['grækəl] *s (myna)* estornino de los
pastores; *(purple grackle)* quiscal *m*
grad. *abbr* **graduate**
gradation [gre'deʃən] *s (gradual change)*
paso gradual; *(arrangement in grades)* graduación; *(step in a series)* paso, grado
grade [gred] *s* grado; *(slope)* pendiente *f;
(mark for work in class)* calificación, nota;
to make the grade lograr subir la cuesta;
vencer los obstáculos ‖ *tr* graduar, calificar; dar nota a *(un alumno)*; explanar,
nivelar
grade crossing *s* (rr) paso a nivel, cruce *m* a
nivel
grade school *s* escuela elemental
gradient ['gredɪ•ənt] *adj* pendiente ‖ *s* pendiente *f;* (phys) gradiente *m*
gradual ['grædʒu•əl] *adj* paulatino
gradually [grædʒu•əli] *adv* paulatinamente,
gradualmente, poco a poco
graduate ['grædʒu•ɪt] *adj* graduado ‖ *s* graduado; *(candidate for a degree)* graduando;
vasija graduada ‖ ['grædʒu,et] *tr* graduar ‖
intr graduarse
graduate school *s* facultad de altos estudios
graduate student *s* estudiante graduado
graduate work *s* altos estudios
graduation [,grædʒu'eʃən] *s* graduación, ceremonia de graduación
graft [græft] *s* (hort & surg) injerto; (coll)
soborno político, ganancia ilegal ‖ *tr &
intr* (hort & surg) injertar; (coll) malversar
graham bread ['gre•əm] *s* pan *m* integral
graham flour *s* harina de trigo sin cerner
grain [gren] *s (small seed; tiny particle of
sand, etc.; small unit of weight)* grano;
(cereal seeds) granos; *(in stone)* vena; *(in
wood)* fibra; **against the grain** a contrapelo

‖ *tr* granear *(la pólvora; una piedra litográfica)*; crispir, vetear *(la madera)*; granular *(una piel)*
grain elevator *s* elevador *m* de granos; *(tall
building where grain is stored)* depósito de
cereales
grain'field' *s* sembrado
graining ['grenɪŋ] *s* veteado
gram [græm] *s* gramo
grammar ['græmər] *s* gramática
grammarian [grə'mɛrɪ•ən] *s* gramático
grammar school *s* escuela pública elemental
grammatical [grə'mætɪkəl] *adj* gramático
gramophone ['græmə,fon] *s* (trademark) gramófono
grana•ry ['grænəri] *s (pl* **-ries)** granero
grand [grænd] *adj* espléndido, grandioso,
importante, principal
grand'aunt' *s* tía abuela
grand'child' *s (pl* **chil'dren)** nieto, nieta
grand'daugh'ter *s* nieta
grand duchess *s* gran duquesa
grand duchy *s* gran ducado
grand duke *s* gran duque *m*
grandee [græn'di] *s* grande *m* de España
grandeur ['grændʒər] *o* ['grændʒur] *s* grandeza, magnificencia
grand'fa'ther *s* abuelo; *(forefather)* antepasado
grandfather's clock *s* reloj *m* de caja
grandiose ['grændɪ,os] *adj* grandioso; hinchado, pomposo
grand jury *s* jurado de acusación
grand larceny *s* hurto mayor
grand lodge *s* gran oriente *m*
grandma ['grænd,ma], ['græm,ma], *o*
['græmə] *s* (coll) abuela, abuelita
grand'moth'er *s* abuela
grand'neph'ew *s* resobrino
grand'niece *s* resobrina
grand opera *s* ópera seria
grandpa ['grænd,pa], ['græn,pa], *o*
['græmpə] *s* (coll) abuelo, abuelito
grand'par'ent *s* abuelo, abuela
grand piano *s* piano de cola
grand slam *s* (bridge) bola
grand'son' *s* nieto
grand'stand' *s* gradería cubierta, tribuna
grand strategy *s* alta estrategia
grand total *s* gran total *m*, suma de totales
grand'un'cle *s* tío abuelo
grand vizier *s* gran visir *m*
grange [grendʒ] *s (farm with barns, etc.)*
granja; *(organization of farmers)* cámara
agrícola
granite ['grænɪt] *s* granito
grant [grænt] *o* [grant] *s* concesión; donación, subvención; traspaso de propiedad ‖
tr conceder; dar *(permiso, perdón)*; transferir *(bienes inmuebles)*; **to take for
granted** dar por sentado; tratar con indiferencia
grantee [græn'ti] *o* [gran'ti] *s* cesionario
grant'-in-aid' *s (pl* **grants-in-aid)** subvención concedida por el gobierno para obras
de utilidad pública; pensión para estimular

conocimientos científicos, literarios, artísticos

grantor ['græn'tɔr] or [grɑn'tɔr] s cesionista *mf*, otorgante *mf*

grant winner s bequista *mf* (CAm, Cuba)

granular ['grænjələr] *adj* granular

granulate ['grænjə,let] *tr* granular ‖ *intr* granularse

granule ['grænjul] s gránulo

grape [grep] s (*fruit*) uva; (*vine*) vid *f*

grape arbor s parral

grape'fruit' s (*fruit*) toronja; (*tree*) toronjo

grape hyacinth s sueldacostilla

grape juice s zumo de uva

grape'shot' s metralla

grape'vine' s vid *f*, parra; **by the grapevine** por vías secretas, por vías misteriosas

graph [græf] s (*diagram*) gráfica; (*gram*) grafía

graphic(al) ['græfɪk(əl)] *adj* gráfico

graphite ['græfaɪt] s grafito

graph paper s papel cuadriculado

grapnel ['græpnəl] s rebañadera; (*anchor*) rezón *m*

grapple ['græpəl] s asimiento, presa; lucha cuerpo a cuerpo ‖ *tr* asir, agarrar ‖ *intr* agarrarse; luchar a brazo partido; **to grapple with** luchar a brazo partido con; tratar de resolver

grappling iron s arpeo

grasp [græsp] s asimiento; (*power, reach*) poder *m*, alcance *m*; (fig) comprensión; **to have a good grasp of** saber a fondo; **within the grasp of** al alcance de ‖ *tr* (*with hand*) empuñar; (*to get control of*) apoderarse de; (fig) comprender ‖ *intr* — **to grasp at** tratar de asir; aceptar con avidez

grasping ['græspɪŋ] *adj* avaro, codicioso

grass ['græs] s hierba; (*pasture land*) pasto; (*lawn*) césped *m*; **to go to grass** ir a pacer; disfrutar de una temporada de descanso; gastarse, arruinarse; morir; **to not let the grass grow under one's feet** no dormirse en las pajas

grass court s cancha de césped

grass'hop'per s saltamontes *m*

grass pea s almorta, guija

grass'-roots' *adj* de la gente común

grass seed s semilla de césped

grass widow s viuda de paja, viuda de marido vivo

grass•y ['græsi] *adj* (*comp* **-ier;** *super* **-iest**) herboso

grate [gret] s (*at a window*) reja; (*for cooking*) parrilla ‖ *tr* (*to put a grate on*) enrejar; rallar (*p.ej., queso*) ‖ *intr* crujir, rechinar; **to grate on** (fig) rallar

grateful ['gretfəl] *adj* agradecido; (*pleasing*) agradable

grater ['gretər] s rallador *m*

grati•fy ['grætɪ,faɪ] *v* (*pret & pp* **-fied**) *tr* complacer, gratificar

gratifying ['grætɪ,faɪ•ɪŋ] *adj* grato, satisfactorio

grating ['gretɪŋ] *adj* áspero, irritante; (*sound*) chirriante ‖ s enrejado

gratis ['gretɪs] o ['grætɪs] *adj* gracioso, gratuito ‖ *adv* gratis, de balde

gratitude ['grætɪ,tjud] s gratitud, reconocimiento

gratuitous [grə'tju•ɪtəs] o [grə'tu•ɪtəs] *adj* gratuito

gratui•ty [grə'tju•ɪti] s (*pl* **-ties**) propina; feria (CAm, Mex)

grave [grev] *adj* (*serious, dangerous; important*) grave; solemne; (*sound; accent*) grave ‖ s sepulcro, sepultura; **to have one foot in the grave** estar con un pie en la sepultura

gravedigger ['grev,dɪgər] s enterrador *m*, sepulturero, entierramuertos *m*

gravel ['grævəl] s grava, cascajo

graven image ['grevən] s ídolo

grave'stone' s lápida sepulcral

grave'yard' s camposanto

gravitate ['grævɪ,tet] *intr* gravitar; ser atraído

gravitation [,grævɪ'teʃən] s gravitación

gravi•ty ['grævɪti] s (*pl* **-ties**) gravedad

gravure [grə'vjur] s fotograbado

gra•vy ['grevi] s (*pl* **-vies**) (*juice from cooking meat*) jugo; (*sauce made with this juice*) salsa; (slang) ganga, breva

gravy dish s salsera

gray [gre] *adj* gris; (*gray-haired*) cano, canoso ‖ s gris *m*; traje *m* gris ‖ *intr* encanecer

gray'beard' s anciano, viejo

gray-haired ['gre,herd] *adj* canoso

gray'hound' s galgo

grayish ['gre•ɪʃ] *adj* grisáceo; (*person; hair*) entrecano

gray matter s substancia gris; (*intelligence*) (coll) materia gris

graze [grez] *tr* (*to touch lightly*) rozar; (*to scratch lightly in passing*) raspar; pacer (*la hierba*); apacentar (*el ganado*); (*to lead to the pasture*) pastar ‖ *intr* pacer, pastar

grease [gris] s grasa ‖ [gris] o [griz] *tr* engrasar; (slang) sobornar

grease cup [gris] s vaso de engrase

grease gun [gris] s engrasador *m* de pistón, jeringa de engrase, bomba de engrase

grease lift [gris] s puente *m* de engrase

grease paint [gris] s maquillaje *m*

grease pit [gris] s fosa de engrase

grease spot [gris] s lámpara, mancha de grasa

greas•y ['grisi] o ['grizi] *adj* (*comp* **-ier;** *super* **-iest**) grasiento, pringoso

great [gret] *adj* grande; (coll) excelente ‖ **the great** los grandes

great'-aunt' s tía abuela

Great Bear s Osa Mayor

Great Britain ['brɪtən] s la Gran Bretaña

great'coat' s gabán *m* de mucho abrigo

Great Dane s mastín *m* danés

Greater London s el Gran Londres

Greater New York s el Gran Nueva York

great'-grand'child' s (*pl* **-chil'dren**) bisnieto, bisnieta

great'-grand'daugh'ter s bisnieta

great'-grand'fa'ther s bisabuelo

great'-grand'moth'er s bisabuela

great'-grand'par'ent s bisabuelo, bisabuela

go
gr

great'-grand'son' *s* bisnieto
greatly ['gretli] *adj* grandemente
great'-neph'ew *s* resobrino
greatness ['gretnɪs] *s* grandeza
great'-niece' *s* resobrina
great'-un'cle *s* tío abuelo
Great War *s* Gran guerra
Grecian ['griʃən] *adj & s* griego
Greece [gris] *s* Grecia
greed [grid] *s* codicia, avaricia; (*in eating and drinking*) glotonería
greed•y ['gridi] *adj* (*comp* -ier; *super* -iest) codicioso, avaro; glotón
Greek [grik] *adj & s* griego
green [grin] *adj* verde; inexperto ‖ *s* verde *m;* (*lawn*) césped *m;* **greens** verduras
green'back' *s* (U.S.A.) billete *m* de banco (*de dorso verde*)
green corn *s* maíz tierno
green earth *s* verdacho
greener•y ['grinəri] *s* (*pl* -ies) (*foliage*) verdura; (*hothouse*) invernáculo
green-eyed ['grin,aɪd] *adj* de ojos verdes; celoso
green'gage' *s* ciruela claudia
green grasshopper *s* langostón *m*
green'gro'cer *s* verdulero
green'gro'cer•y *s* (*pl* -ies) verdulería
green'horn' *s* novato; (*dupe*) primo, inocentón *m;* papanatas *m,* isidro; colegial *mf* (Mex)
green'house' *s* invernáculo
greenish ['grinɪʃ] *adj* verdoso
Greenland ['grinlənd] *s* Groenlandia
greenness ['grinnɪs] *s* verdura, verdor *m;* falta de experiencia
green'room' *s* saloncillo; chismería de teatro
greensward ['grin,swɔrd] *s* césped *m*
green thumb *s* pulgares *mpl* verdes (*don de criar plantas*)
green vegetables *spl* verduras
green'wood' *s* bosque *m* verde, bosque frondoso
greet [grit] *tr* saludar; acoger, recibir; presentarse a (*los ojos u los oídos de uno*)
greeting ['gritɪŋ] *s* saludo; acogida, recibimiento ‖ **greetings** *interj* ¡salud!
greeting card *s* tarjeta de buen deseo
gregarious [grɪ'gɛri•əs] *adj* (*living in the midst of others*) gregario; (*fond of the company of others*) sociable
Gregorian [grɪ'gori•ən] *adj* gregoriano
grenade [grɪ'ned] *s* granada; (*to put out fires*) granada extintora
grenadier [,grɛnə'dɪr] *s* granadero
grenadine [,grɛnə'din] *s* granadina
grey [gre] *adj. s & intr* var de **gray**
grid [grɪd] *s* parrilla, rejilla; (*electron*) rejilla; (*of a storage battery*) (elec) rejilla
griddle ['grɪdəl] *s* plancha
grid'dle•cake' *s* tortada (de harina) a la plancha
grid'i'ron *s* parrilla; campo de fútbol
grid leak *s* (electron) resistencia de rejilla, escape *m* de rejilla

grief [grif] *s* aflicción, pesar *m;* (coll) desgracia, disgusto; **to come to grief** fracasar, arruinarse
grievance ['grivəns] *s* agravio, injusticia; despecho, disgusto; motivo de queja
grieve [griv] *tr* afligir, penar ‖ *intr* afligirse, apenarse; **to grieve over** añorar
grievous ['grivəs] *adj* doloroso, penoso; atroz, cruel; (*deplorable*) lastimoso
griffin ['grɪfɪn] *s* (myth) grifo
grill [grɪl] *s* parrilla ‖ *tr* emparrillar; someter (*a un acusado*) a un interrogatorio muy apremiante
grille [grɪl] *s* reja, verja; (*of an automobile*) parrilla, rejilla
grill'room' *s* parrilla
grim [grɪm] *adj* (*comp* **grimmer;** *super* **grimmest**) (*fierce*) cruel, feroz; (*repellent*) horrible, siniestro; (*unyielding*) formidable, implacable; (*stern-looking*) ceñudo
grimace ['grɪməs] *o* [grɪ'mes] *s* mueca, gesto ‖ *intr* hacer muecas, gestear
grime [graɪm] *s* mugre *f;* (*soot*) tizne *m & f*
grim•y ['graɪmi] *adj* (*comp* -ier; *super* -iest) mugriento; tiznado
grin [grɪn] *s* sonrisa bonachona; mueca (*mostrando los dientes*) ‖ *v* (*pret & pp* **grinned;** *ger* **grinning**) *intr* sonreírse bonachonamente; hacer una mueca (*mostrando los dientes*)
grind [graɪnd] *s* molienda; (*long hard work or study*) (coll) zurra; (*student*) (coll) empollón *m* ‖ *v* (*pret & pp* **ground** [graʊnd]) *tr* moler; (*to sharpen*) afilar, amolar; tallar (*lentes*); pulverizar; picar (*carne*); rodar (*las válvulas de un motor*); dar vueltas a (*un manubrio*) ‖ *intr* hacer molienda; molerse; rechinar; (coll) echar los bofes
grinder ['graɪndər] *s* (*to sharpen tools*) muela, esmoladera; (*to grind coffee, pepper, etc.*) molinillo; (*back tooth*) muela
grind'stone' *s* esmoladera, piedra de amolar; **to keep one's nose to the grindstone** trabajar con ahinco
grin•go ['grɪŋgo] *s* (*pl* -gos) (disparaging) gringo
grip [grɪp] *s* (*grasp*) asimiento; (*withhand*) apretón *m;* (*handle*) asidero; saco de mano; **to come to grips (with)** luchar cuerpo a cuerpo (con); arrostrarse (con) ‖ *v* (*pret & pp* **gripped;** *ger* **gripping**) *tr* asir, agarrar; tener asido; absorber (*la atención*); absorber la atención a (*una persona*)
gripe [graɪp] *s* (coll) queja; **gripes** retortijón *m* de tripas ‖ *intr* (coll) quejarse, refunfuñar
grippe [grɪp] *s* gripe *f*
gripping ['grɪpɪŋ] *adj* conmovedor, impresionante
gris•ly ['grɪzli] *adj* (*comp* -lier; *super* -liest) espantoso, espeluznante
grist [grɪst] *s* (*batch of grain for one grinding*) molienda; (*grain that has been ground*) harina; (coll) acopio, acervo; **to be grist to one's mill** (coll) serle a uno de mucho provecho

gristle ['grɪsəl] *adj* (*comp* **-tlier;** *super* **-tliest**) cartilaginoso, ternilloso

grist'mill' *s* molino harinero

grit [grɪt] *s* arena, guijo fino; (fig) ánimo, valentía; **grits** farro, sémola ‖ *v* (*pret & pp* **gritted;** *ger* **gritting**) *tr* hacer rechinar (*los dientes*); cerrar fuertemente (*los dientes*)

grit·ty ['grɪti] *adj* (*comp* **-tier;** *super* **-tiest**) arenoso; (fig) valiente, resuelto

griz·zly ['grɪzli] *adj* (*comp* **-zlier;** *super* **-zliest**) grisáceo; canoso ‖ *s* (*pl* **-zlies**) oso gris

grizzly bear *s* oso gris

groan [gron] *s* gemido, quejido ‖ *intr* gemir, quejarse; estar muy cargado, crujir por exceso de peso

grocer ['grosər] *s* abacero, tendero de ultramarinos

grocer·y ['grosəri] *s* (*pl* **-ies**) abacería, tienda de ultramarinos, colmado; **groceries** víveres *mpl*, ultramarinos

grocery store *s* abacería, tienda de ultramarinos, colmado

grog [grɑg] *s* grog *m*

grog·gy ['grɑgi] *adj* (*comp* **-gier;** *super* **-giest**) (coll) inseguro, vacilante; (*shaky, e.g., from a blow*) (coll) atontado; (coll) borracho

groin [grɔɪn] *s* (anat) ingle *f;* (archit) arista de encuentro

groom [grum] *s* (*bridegroom*) novio; mozo de caballos ‖ *tr* asear, acicalar; almohazar (*caballos*); enseñar (*a un político*) para presentarse como candidato

grooms·man ['grumzmən] *s* (*pl* **-men** [mən]) padrino de boda

groove [gruv] *s* ranura; (*of a pulley*) garganta; (*of a phonograph record*) surco; (*mark left by a wheel*) rodada; (coll) rutina, hábito arraigado ‖ *tr* ranurar, acanalar

grope [grop] *intr* andar a tientas; (*for words*) pujar; **to grope for** buscar a tientas, buscar tentando; **to grope through** palpar (*p.ej., la obscuridad*)

gropingly ['gropɪŋli] *adv* a tientas

grosbeak ['gros ,bik] *s* pico duro

gross [gros] *adj* (*dense, thick*) denso, espeso; (*coarse; vulgar*) grosero; (*fat, burly*) grueso; (*with no deductions*) bruto ‖ *s* conjunto, totalidad; (*twelve dozen*) gruesa; **in gross** en grueso ‖ *tr* obtener un ingreso bruto de

grossly ['grosli] *adv* aproximadamente

gross national product *s* renta nacional

grotesque [gro'tɛsk] *adj* (*ridiculous, extravagant*) grotesco; (fa) grutesco ‖ *s* (fa) grutesco

grot·to ['grɑto] *s* (*pl* **-toes** o **-tos**) gruta

grouch [grautʃ] *s* (coll) mal humor *m;* (*person*) (coll) cascarrabias *mf*, vinagre *m* ‖ *intr* (coll) refunfuñar

grouch·y ['grautʃi] *adj* (*comp* **-ier;** *super* **-iest**) (coll) gruñón, malhumorado

ground [graund] *adj* molido ‖ *s* (*earth, soil, land*) tierra; (*piece of land*) terreno; (*basis foundation*) causa, fundamento; motivo, razón *f;* (elec) tierra; (*body of auto-*

mobile corresponding to ground) (elec) masa; (elec) borne *m* de tierra; **ground for complaint** motivo de queja; **grounds** terreno; jardines *mpl;* causa, fundamento; (*of coffee*) posos; **on the ground of** con motivo de; **to break ground** empezar la excavación; **to fall to the ground** fracasar, abandonarse; **to gain ground** ganar terreno; **to give ground** ceder terreno; **to lose ground** perder terreno; **to stand one's ground** mantenerse firme; **to yield ground** ceder terreno ‖ *tr* establecer, fundar; (elec) poner a tierra; **to be grounded** estar sin volar (*un avión*); **to be well grounded** ser muy versado ‖ *intr* (naut) encallar, varar

ground connection *s* (rad) toma de tierra

ground crew *s* (aer) personal *m* de tierra

grounder ['graundər] *s* (baseball) pelota rodada

ground floor *s* piso bajo

ground glass *s* vidrio deslustrado

ground hog *s* marmota de América

ground lead [lid] *s* (elec) conductor *m* a tierra

groundless ['graundlɪs] *adj* infundado; inmotivado

ground plan *s* primer proyecto; (*of a building*) planta

ground speed *s* (aer) velocidad con respecto al suelo

ground swell *s* marejada de fondo

ground troops *spl* (mil) tropas terrestres

ground wire *s* (rad) alambre *m* de tierra; (aut) hilo de masa

ground'work' *s* infraestructura

group [grup] *adj* grupal; colectivo ‖ *s* grupo ‖ *tr* agrupar ‖ *intr* agruparse

group therapy *s* psicoterapia de grupo

grouse [graus] *s* perdiz blanca, bonasa americana, gallo de bosque; (slang) refunfuño ‖ *intr* (slang) refunfuñar

grout [graut] *s* lechada ‖ *tr* enlechar

grove [grov] *s* arboleda, bosquecillo

grov·el ['grʌvəl] o ['grɑvəl] *v* (*pret & pp* **-eled** o **-elled;** *ger* **-eling** o **-elling**) *intr* arrastrarse servilmente; rebajarse servilmente; deleitarse en vilezas

grow [gro] *v* (*pret* **grew** [gru]; *pp* **grown** [gron]) *tr* cultivar (*plantas*); criar (*animales*); dejarse (*la barba*) ‖ *intr* crecer; cultivarse; criarse; brotar, nacer; (*to become*) hacerse, ponerse, volverse; **to grow angry** enfadarse; **to grow old** envejecerse; **to grow out of** tener su origen en; perder (*p.ej., la costumbre*); **to grow together** adherirse el uno al otro; **to grow up** crecer, desarrollar

growing child ['groɪŋ] *s* muchacho de creces

growl [graul] *s* gruñido; refunfuño ‖ *intr* gruñir (*el perro*); refunfuñar

grown'up' *adj* adulto; juicioso ‖ *s* (*pl* **grown-ups**) adulto; **grown-ups** personas mayores

growth [groθ] *s* crecimiento; desarrollo; aumento; (*of trees, grass, etc.*) cobertura; (pathol) tumor *m*

growth stock *s* acción crecedera

gr
gr

grub [grʌb] s (*drudge*) esclavo del trabajo; (*larva*) gorgojo; (coll) comida, alimento ‖ v (*pret & pp* **grubbed;** *ger* **grubbing**) *tr* arrancar (*tocones*); desmalezar (*un terreno*) ‖ *intr* cavar; trabajar como esclavo

grub·by [ˈgrʌbi] *adj* (*comp* **-bier;** *super* **-biest**) gorgojoso; sucio, roñoso

grudge [grʌdʒ] s rencor *m*, inquina; **to have a grudge against** guardar rencor a, tener inquina a ‖ *tr* dar de mala gana; envidiar

grudgingly [ˈgrʌdʒɪŋli] *adv* de mala gana

gru·el [ˈgruəl] s avenate *m* ‖ v (*pret & pp* **-eled** o **-elled;** *ger* **-elling** o **-elling**) *tr* agotar, castigar cruelmente

gruesome [ˈgrusəm] *adj* espantoso, horripilante

gruff [grʌf] *adj* áspero, brusco, rudo; (*voice, tone*) ronco

grumble [ˈgrʌmbəl] s gruñido, refunfuño; ruido sordo y prolongado ‖ *intr* gruñir, refunfuñar; retumbar

grump·y [ˈgrʌmpi] *adj* (*comp* **-ier;** *super* **-iest**) gruñón, malhumorado

grunt [grʌnt] s gruñido ‖ *intr* gruñir

G-string [ˈdʒiˌstrɪŋ] s (*loincloth*) taparrabo; (*worn by women entertainers*) cubresexo

gt. *abbr* **great; gutta** (Lat) **drop**

g.u. *abbr* **genitourinary**

Guadeloupe [ˌgwɑdəˈlup] s Guadalupe *f*

guarantee [ˌgærənˈti] s garantía; (*guarantor*) garante *mf*; persona de quien otra sale fiadora ‖ *tr* garantizar

guarantor [ˈgærənˌtɔr] s garante *mf*

guaran·ty [ˈgærənti] s (*pl* **-ties**) garantía ‖ v (*pret & pp* **-tied**) *tr* garantizar

guard [gɑrd] s (*act of guarding; part of handle of sword*) guarda; (*person who guards or takes care of something*) guarda *mf*; (*group of armed men; posture in fencing*) guardia; (*member of group of armed men*) guardia *m*; (*in front of trolley car*) salvavidas *m*; (sport) coraza; (rr) guardabarrera *mf*; (rr) guardafrenos *m*; **off guard** desprevenido; **on guard** alerta, prevenido; de centinela; **to mount guard** montar la guardia; **under guard** a buen recaudo ‖ *tr* guardar ‖ *intr* estar de centinela; **to guard against** guardarse de, precaverse contra o de

guard'house' s cuartel *m* de la guardia; prisión militar

guardian [ˈgɑrdɪən] *adj* tutelar ‖ s guardián *m*; (law) curador *m*, tutor *m*

guardian angel s ángel *m* custodio, ángel de la guarda

guardianship [ˈgɑrdɪənˌʃɪp] s amparo, protección; (law) curaduría, tutela

guard'rail' s baranda; (naut) barandilla; (rr) contracarril *m*

guard'room' s cuarto de guardia; cárcel *f* militar

guards·man [ˈgɑrdzmən] s (*pl* **-men** [mən]) guardia *m*, soldado de guardia

Guatemalan [ˌgwɑtɪˈmɑlən] *adj & s* guatemalteco

guerrilla [gəˈrɪlə] s guerrillero; montonero

guerrilla warfare s guerra de guerrillas

guess [gɛs] s conjetura, suposición; adivinación ‖ *tr & intr* conjeturar, suponer; (*to judge correctly*) acertar, adivinar; (coll) creer, suponer; **I guess so** (coll) creo que sí, me parece que sí

guess'work' s conjetura; **by guesswork** por conjeturas

guest [gɛst] s convidado; (*lodger*) huésped *m*; (*of a boarding house*) pensionista *mf*; (*of a hotel*) cliente *mf*; (*caller*) vista

guest book s libro de oro

guest room s cuarto de reserva

guffaw [gəˈfɔ] s risotada, carcajada ‖ *intr* risotear, reír a carcajadas

guidance [ˈgaɪdəns] s guía, gobierno, dirección; **for your guidance** para su gobierno

guide [gaɪd] s (*person*) guía *mf*; (*book*) guía; (*guidance*) guía; dirección; poste *m* indicador; (mach) guía, guiadera; (mil) guía *m* ‖ *tr* guiar

guide'board' s señal *f* de carretera

guide'book' s guia *m*, guía del viajero

guided missile [ˈgaɪdɪd] s proyectil dirigido o teleguiado; misil *m* dirigible

guide dog s perro-lazarillo

guide'line' s cuerda de guía; norma, pauta, directorio

guide'post' s poste *m* indicador

guidon [ˈgaɪdən] s (mil) guión *m*; (mil) portaguión *m*

guild [gɪld] s (*medieval association of craftsmen*) gremio; asociación benéfica

guild'hall' s casa consistorial

guile [gaɪl] s astucia, dolo, maña

guileful [ˈgaɪlfəl] *adj* astuto, doloso, mañoso

guileless [ˈgaɪllɪs] *adj* cándido, inocente, sencillo

guillotine [ˈgɪləˌtin] s guillotina ‖ [ˌgɪləˈtin] *tr* guillotinar

guilt [gɪlt] s culpa

guiltless [ˈgɪltlɪs] *adj* inocente, libre de culpa

guilt·y [ˈgɪlti] *adj* (*comp* **-ier;** *super* **-iest**) culpable; (*charged with guilt*) culpado; (*found guilty*) reo

guimpe [gɪmp] o [gæmp] s canesú *m*

guinea [ˈgɪni] s (*monetary unit*) guinea; gallina de Guinea

guinea fowl s pintada, gallina de Guinea

guinea hen s pintada, gallina de Guinea (*hembra*)

guinea pig s conejillo de Indias; (fig) cobayo

guise [gaɪz] s traje *m*; aspecto, semejanza; **under the guise of** so capa de

guitar [gɪˈtɑr] s guitarra

guitarist [gɪˈtɑrɪst] s guitarrista *mf*

gulch [gʌltʃ] s barranco, quebrada

gulf [gʌlf] s golfo

Gulf of Mexico s golfo de Méjico

Gulf Stream s Corriente *f* del Golfo

gull [gʌl] s gaviota; (coll) bobo ‖ *tr* estafar, engañar

gullet [ˈgʌlɪt] s gaznate *m*, garguero; esófago

gullible [ˈgʌlɪbəl] *adj* crédulo; creído; **to be too gullible** tener buenas tragaderas

gul·ly [ˈgʌli] s (*pl* **-lies**) barranca, arroyada; (*channel made by rain water*) badén *m*

gulp [gʌlp] *s* trago ‖ *tr* — **to gulp down** engullir; reprimir (*p.ej.*, *sollozos*) ‖ *intr* respirar entrecortadamente

gum [gʌm] *s* goma; chanclo de goma; (*firm flesh around base of teeth*) encía; (*mucous on edge of eyelid*) legaña ‖ *v* (*pret & pp* **gummed;** *ger* **gumming**) *tr* engomar ‖ *intr* exudar goma

gum arabic *s* goma arábiga

gum'boil' *s* flemón *m*

gum boot *s* bota de agua

gum'drop' *s* frutilla

gum•my ['gʌmi] *adj* (*comp* **-mier;** *super* **-miest**) gomoso; (*eyelid*) legañoso

gumption ['gʌmpʃən] *s* ánimo, iniciativa, empuje *m*, fuerza; juicio, seso

gum'shoe' *s* chanclo de goma; (coll) detective *m* ‖ *v* (*pret & pp* **-shoed;** *ger* **-shoeing**) *intr* (slang) andar con zapatos de fieltro

gun [gʌn] *s* escopeta, fusil *m;* cañón *m;* (*for injections*) jeringa; (coll) revólver *m;* **to stick to one's guns** mantenerse en sus trece ‖ *v* (*pret & pp* **gunned;** *ger* **gunning**) *tr* hacer fuego sobre; (slang) acelerar rápidamente (*un motor, un avión*) ‖ *intr* andar a caza; disparar; **to gun for** ir en busca de; buscar para matar

gun'boat' *s* cañonero

gun carriage *s* cureña, encabalgamiento

gun'cot'ton *s* fulmicotón *m*, algodón *m* pólvora

gun'fire' *s* fuego (*de armas de fuego*); cañoneo

gun•man ['gʌnmən] *s* (*pl* **-men** [mən]) bandido armado, pistolero; gángster *m*

gun metal *s* bronce *m* de cañón; metal pavonado

gunnel ['gʌnəl] *s* (naut) borda, regala

gunner ['gʌnər] *s* artillero; cazador *m*

gunnery ['gʌnəri] *s* artillería

gunny sack ['gʌni] *s* saco de yute

gun'pow'der *s* pólvora

gun'run'ner *s* contrabandista *m* de armas de fuego

gun'run'ning *s* contrabando de armas de fuego

gun'shot' *s* escopetazo, tiro de fusil; alcance *m* de un fusil; **within gunshot** a tiro de fusil

gunshot wound *s* escopetazo

gun'smith' *s* armero

gun'stock' *s* caja de fusil

gunwale ['gʌnəl] *s* (naut) borda, regala

gup•py ['gʌpi] *s* (*pl* **-pies**) lebistes *m*

gurgle ['gʌrgəl] *s* gorgoteo, gluglú *m;* (*of a child*) gorjeo ‖ *intr* gorgotear, hacer gluglú; gorjearse (*el niño*)

gush [gʌʃ] *s* borbollón *m*, chorro ‖ *intr* surgir, salir a borbollones; (coll) hacer extremos, ser extremoso

gusher ['gʌʃər] *s* pozo de chorro de petróleo; (coll) personal extremosa

gushing ['gʌʃɪŋ] *adj* surgente; (coll) extremoso ‖ *s* borbollón *m*, chorro; (coll) efusión, extremos

gush•y ['gʌʃi] *adj* (*comp* **-ier;** *super* **-iest**) (coll) efusivo, extremoso

gusset ['gʌsɪt] *s* escudete *m*

gust [gʌst] *s* (*of wind*) ráfaga; (*of rain*) aguacero; (*of smoke*) bocanada; (*of noise*) explosión; (*of anger or enthusiasm*) arrebato

gusto ['gʌsto] *s* deleite *m*, entusiasmo; **with gusto** con sumo placer

gust•y ['gʌsti] *adj* (*comp* **-ier;** *super* **-iest**) tempestuoso, borrascoso

gut [gʌt] *s* tripa; cuerda de tripa; **guts** tripas; (slang) agallas ‖ *v* (*pret & pp* **gutted;** *ger* **gutting**) *tr* destripar; destruir lo interior de

gutta-percha ['gʌtə'pʌrtʃə] *s* gutapercha

gutter ['gʌtər] *s* (*on side of road*) cuneta; (*in street*) arroyo; (*of roof*) canal *f;* (*ditch formed by rain water*) badén *m;* **barrios bajos**

gut'ter-snipe' *s* pilluelo, hijo de la miseria; gamberro

guttural ['gʌtərəl] *adj* gutural ‖ *s* sonido gutural

guy [gaɪ] *s* viento, cable *m* de retén; (coll) tipo, tío, sujeto ‖ *tr* (coll) burlarse de

Guyana [gaɪ'ænə] *s* Guayana

guy wire *s* cable *m* de retén

guzzle ['gʌzəl] *tr & intr* beber con exceso

guzzler ['gʌzlər] *s* borrachín *m*

gym [dʒɪm] *s* (coll) gimnasio

gymnasi•um [dʒɪm'nezɪəm] *s* (*pl* **-ums** o **-a** [ə]) gimnasio

gymnast ['dʒɪmnæst] *s* gimnasta *mf*

gymnastic [dʒɪm'næstɪk] *adj* gimnástico ‖ **gymnastics** *spl* gimnasia, gimnástica

gym suit *s* chandal *m*, chándal *m*

gynecologic(al) [,gaɪnəko'lɑdʒɪk(əl)] or [,dʒaɪnəko'lɑdʒɪk(əl)] *adj* ginecológico

gynecologist [,gaɪnə'kɑlədʒɪst] or [,dʒaɪnə-'kɑlədʒɪst] *s* ginecólogo

gynecology [,gaɪnə'kɑlədʒi] or [,dʒaɪnə-'kɑlədʒi] *s* ginecología

gyp [dʒɪp] *s* (slang) estafa, timo; (*person*) (slang) estafador *m*, timador *m* ‖ *v* (*pret & pp* **gypped;** *ger* **gypping**) *tr* (slang) estafar, timar

gypsum ['dʒɪpsəm] *s* yeso, aljez *m*

gyp•sy ['dʒɪpsi] *adj* gitano ‖ *s* (*pl* **-sies**) gitano ‖ **Gypsy** *s* gitano (*idioma*)

gypsyish ['dʒɪpsi•ɪʃ] *adj* gitanesco

gypsy moth *s* lagarta

gyrate ['dʒaɪret] *intr* girar

gyroscope ['dʒaɪrə,skop] *s* giroscopio

gr
gy

H

H, h [etʃ] octava letra del alfabeto inglés
h. *abbr* **harbor, high, hour, husband**
haberdasher [ˈhæbər ˌdæʃər] *s* camisero;
(*dealer in notions*) mercero
haberdasher•y [ˈhæbər ˌdæʃəri] *s* (*pl* **-ies**)
camisería, tienda de artículos para hom-
bres; artículos para hombres
habit [ˈhæbɪt] *s* costumbre *f*, hábito; (*costume*) traje *m*; **to be in the habit of**
acostumbrar
habitat [ˈhæbɪˌtæt] *s* habitación
habitation [ˌhæbɪˈteʃən] *s* habitación
habit-forming [ˈhæbɪt ˌfɔrmɪŋ] *adj* envicia-
dor
habitual [həˈbɪtʃʊ•əl] *adj* habitual
habitué [həˌbɪtʃʊˈe] *s* habituado
hack [hæk] *s* (*cut*) corte *m*; (*notch*) mella;
(*cough*) tos seca; coche *m* de alquiler;
caballo de alquiler; caballo de silla; (*old
nag*) rocín *m*; escritor *m* a sueldo ‖ *tr*
cortar, machetear
hack•man [ˈhækmən] *s* (*pl* **-men** [mən]) cochero de punto
hackney [ˈhækni] *s* caballo de silla; coche *m*
de alquiler; esclavo del trabajo
hackneyed [ˈhæknid] *adj* trillado, gastado
hack′saw′ *s* sierra de armero, sierra de cortar
metales
haddock [ˈhædək] *s* eglefino
haem ... [hɛm] o [him] = **hemo ...**
haft [hæft] o [hɑft] *s* mango, puño
hag [hæg] *s* (*ugly old woman*) tarasca; (*witch*)
bruja
haggard [ˈhægərd] *adj* ojeroso, macilento,
trasnochado
haggle [ˈhægəl] *intr* regatear
Hague, The [heg] La Haya
hail [hel] *s* (*frozen rain*) granizo; (*greeting*)
saludo; **within hail** al alcance de la voz ‖
interj ¡salud!, ¡salve! ‖ *tr* saludar; dar vivas
a, acoger con vivas; aclamar; granizar
(*p.ej., golpes*) ‖ *intr* granizar; **to hail from**
venir de, ser oriundo de
hail′-fel′low well met *s* compañero muy afable y simpático
Hail Mary *s* avemaría
hail′stone′ *s* piedra de granizo
hail′storm′ *s* granizada
hair [hɛr] *s* pelo, cabellos; **to a hair** con la
mayor exactitud; **to cut the hair of** peluquear; **to get in one's hair** (slang) enojarle
a uno; **to have one's hair down** estar en
melena; **to let one's hair down** (slang)
hablar con mucha desenvoltura; **to make
one's hair stand on end** ponerle a uno los
pelos de punta; **to not turn a hair** no
inmutarse; **to split hairs** pararse en quisquillas
hair′breadth′ *s* (el) grueso de un pelo, casi
nada; **to escape by a hairbreadth** escapar
por un pelo
hair′brush′ *s* cepillo de cabeza
hair′cloth′ *s* tela de crin; (*worn as a penance*) cilicio

hair curler [ˈkʌrlər] *s* rizador *m*, tenacillas,
bigudí *m*, rulo
hair′cut′ *s* corte *m* de pelo; **to get a haircut**
cortarse el pelo, peluquear
hair′do′ *s* (*pl* **-dos**) peinado, tocado
hair′dress′er *s* peinador *m*, peluquero
hair dryer *s* secador *m*
hair dye *s* tinte *m* para el pelo
hairless [ˈhɛrlɪs] *adj* pelón
hair net *s* redecilla
hair piece *s* peluquín *m*
hair′pin′ *s* horquilla
hair-raising [ˈhɛrˌrezɪŋ] *adj* (coll) espeluznante, horripilante
hair restorer [rɪˈstorər] *s* crecepelo
hair ribbon *s* cinta para el cabello
hair set *s* fijapeinados *m*
hair shirt *s* calicio
hairsplitting [ˈhɛrˌsplɪtɪŋ] *adj* quisquilloso
‖ *s* quisquillas
hair spray *s* laca
hair′spring′ *s* espiral *f*
hair′style′ *s* peinado
hair tonic *s* vigorizador *m* del cabello
hair•y [ˈhɛri] *adj* (*comp* **-ier**; *super* **-iest**)
peludo, cabelludo
hake [hek] *s* merluza; (genus: *Urophycis*) fice
m
halberd [ˈhælbərd] *s* alabarda
halberdier [ˌhælbərˈdɪr] *s* alabardero
halcyon days [ˈhælsɪ•ən] *s* días tranquilos,
época de paz
hale [hel] *adj* sano, robusto; **hale and hearty**
sano y fuerte ‖ *tr* llevar a la fuerza
half [hæf] *adj* medio; **a half** o **half a** medio;
half the la mitad de ‖ *adv* medio, p.ej.,
half asleep medio dormido; a medio, p.ej.,
half finished a medio acabar; a medias,
p.ej., **half owner** dueño a medias; **half
past** y media, p.ej., **half past three** las
tres y media; **half . . . half** medio . . .
medio ‖ *s* (*pl* **halves** [hævz]) mitad; (arith)
medio; **in half** por la mitad; **to go halves** ir
a medias
half′-and-half′ *adj* mitad y mitad; indeterminado ‖ *adv* a medias, en partes iguales ‖ *s*
mezcla de leche y crema; mezcla de dos
cervezas inglesas
half′back′ *s* (football) medio
half-baked [ˈhæfˌbekt] *adj* a medio cocer;
incompleto; poco juicioso, inexperto
half binding *s* (bb) encuadernación a la holandesa, media pasta
half′-blood′ *s* mestizo; medio hermano
half boot *s* bota de media caña
half′-bound′ *adj* (bb) a la holandesa
half′-breed′ *s* mestizo
half′ brother *s* medio hermano
half-cocked [ˈhæfˈkɑkt] *adv* (coll) con precipitación; **to go off half-cocked** obrar precipitadamente y antes del momento propio
half fare *s* medio billete
half′-full′ *adj* mediado
half-hearted [ˈhæfˌhɑrtɪd] *adj* indiferente,
frío

half holiday *s* mañana o tarde *f* de asueto
half hose *spl* calcetines *mpl*
half'-hour *s* media hora; **on the half-hour** a la media en punto, cada media hora
half leather *s* (bb) encuadernación a la holandesa, media pasta
half'-length' *adj* de medio cuerpo
half'-mast' *s* — **at half mast** a media asta
half moon *s* media luna
half mourning *s* medio luto
half note *s* (mus) nota blanca
half pay *s* media paga; medio sueldo
halfpen·ny ['hepǝni] o ['hepni] *s* (*pl* **-nies**) medio penique
half pint *s* media pinta; (*little runt*) (slang) gorgojo, mirmidón *m*
half'-seas' over *adj* — **to be half-seas over** (slang) estar entre dos velas, estar entre dos luces
half shell *s* (*either half of a bivalve*) concha; (*oysters*) **on the half shell** en su concha
half sister *s* media hermana
half sole *s* media suela
half'-sole' *tr* poner media suela a
half'-staff' *s* — **at half-staff** a media asta
half through *prep* a la mitad de
half-timbered ['hæf,tɪmbǝrd] *adj* entramado
half title *s* anteportada, falsa portada
half'tone' *s* (phot & paint) mediatinta; (typ) similigrabado
half'-track' *s* media oruga, semitractor *m*
half'-truth' *s* verdad a medias
half'way' *adj* a medio camino; incompleto, hecho a medias ‖ *adv* a medio camino; **halfway through** a la mitad de; **to meet halfway** partir el camino con; partir la diferencia con; hacer concesiones mutuas (*dos personas*)
half-witted ['hæf ,wɪtɪd] *adj* imbécil; necio, tonto
halibut ['hælɪbǝt] *s* halibut *m*
halide ['hælaɪd] o ['helaɪd] *s* (chem) haluro
halitosis [,hælɪ'tosɪs] *s* halitosis *f*, aliento fétido
hall [hɔl] (*passageway*) corredor *m;* (*entranceway*) vestíbulo, zaguán *m;* (*large meeting room*) sala, salón *m;* (*assembly room of a university*) paraninfo; (*building, e.g., of a university*) edificio
halleluiah o **hallelujah** [,hælɪ'lujǝ] *s* aleluya *m & f* ‖ *interj* ¡aleluya!
hall'mark' *s* marca de constraste; (*distinguishing feature*) (fig) sello
hal·lo [hǝ'lo] *s* (*pl* **-los**) grito ‖ *interj* ¡hola!; (*to incite dogs in hunting*) ¡sus! ‖ *intr* gritar
hallow ['hælo] *tr* santificar
hallowed ['hælod] *adj* santo, sagrado
Halloween o **Hallowe'en** [,hælo'in] *s* víspera de Todos los Santos
hallucination [hǝ,lusɪ'nefǝn] *s* alucinación
hallucinogenic [hǝ,lusino'dʒɛnɪk] *adj* alucinante
hall'way' *s* corredor *m;* vestíbulo, zaguán *m*
ha·lo ['helo] *s* (*pl* **-los** o **-loes**) halo
halogen ['hælǝdʒǝn] *s* halógeno
halt [hɔlt] *adj* cojo, renco ‖ *s* alto, parada; **to call a halt** mandar hacer alto; **to come to a**

halt pararse, detenerse, interrumpirse ‖ *tr* parar, detener ‖ *intr* hacer alto
halter ['hɔltǝr] *s* (*for leading or fastening horse*) cabestro, ronzal *m*, dogal *m;* (*noose*) dogal *m*, cuerda de ahorcar; muerte *f* en la horca
halting ['hɔltɪŋ] *adj* cojo, renco; vacilante
halve [hæv] *tr* partir en dos, partir por la mitad
halyard ['hæljǝrd] *s* (naut) driza
ham [hæm] *s* (*part of leg behind knee*) corva; (*thigh and buttock*) pernil *m;* (*cured meat from hog's hind leg*) jamón *m;* (slang) comicastro; (slang) aficionado (*a la radio*); **hams** nalgas
ham and eggs *spl* huevos con jamón
hamburger ['hæm,bʌrgǝr] *s* hamburguesa
hamlet ['hæmlɪt] *s* aldehuela, caserío
hammer ['hæmǝr] *s* martillo; (*of piano*) macillo, martinete *m;* **to go under the hammer** venderse en pública subasta ‖ *tr* martillar; **to hammer out** formar a martillazos; sacar en limpio a fuerza de mucho esfuerzo‖ *intr* martillar; **to hammer away** trabajar asiduamente
hammock ['hæmǝk] *s* hamaca
hamper ['hæmpǝr] *s* canasto, cesto grande con tapa ‖ *tr* estorbar, impedir
hamster ['hæmstǝr] *s* marmota de Alemania, rata del trigo
ham·string ['hæm,strɪŋ] *v* (*pret & pp* **-strung**) *tr* desjarretar; (fig) estropear, incapacitar
hand [hænd] *adj* (*done or operated with the hands*) manual ‖ *s* mano *f;* (*workman*) obrero, peón *m;* (*way of writing*) escritura, puño y letra; (*signature*) firma; (*clapping of hands*) salva de aplausos; (*of clock or watch*) mano *f;* manecilla; (*all the cards in one's hand*) juego; (*a round of play*) mano *f;* (*player*) jugador *m;* (*source, origin*) fuente *f;* (*skill*) destreza; **all hands** (naut) toda la tripulación; (coll) todas; **at first hand** de primera mano; directamente, de buena tinta; **at hand** disponible; **hand in glove** uña y carne; **hand in hand** asidos de la mano; juntos; **hands up!** ¡arriba las manos! **hand to hand** cuerpo a cuerpo; **in hand** entre manos; **in his own hand** de su propio puño; **on hand** entre manos; disponible; **on hands and knees** (*crawling*) a gatas; (*beseeching*) de rodillas; **on the one hand** por una parte; **on the other hand** por otra parte; **out of hand** luego, en seguida; desmandado; **to be at hand** obrar en mi (nuestro) poder (*una carta*); **to change hands** mudar de manos; **to clap hands** batir palmas; **to eat out of one's hand** aceptar dócilmente la autoridad de uno; **to fall into the hands of** caer en manos de; **to have a hand in** tomar parte en; **to have one's hands full** estar ocupadísimo; **to hold hands** tomarse de las manos; **to hold up one's hands** (*as a sign of surrender*) alzar las manos; **to join hands** darse las manos; casarse; **to keep one's hands off** no tocar, no meterse en; **to lend a hand**

echar una mano; **to live from hand to mouth** vivir al día, vivir de la mano a la boca; **to not lift a hand** no levantar paja del suelo; **to play into the hands of** hacer el caldo gordo a; **to raise one's hand** (*in taking an oath*) alzar el dedo; **to shake hands** estrecharse la mano; **to show one's hand** descubrir su juego; **to take in hand** hacerse cargo de; tratar, estudiar (*una cuestión*); **to throw up one's hands** darse por vencido; **to try one's hand** probar la mano; **to turn one's hand to** dedicarse a, ocuparse en; **to wash one's hands of** lavarse las manos de; **under my hand** con mi firma, bajo mi firma, de mi puño y letra; **under the hand and seal of** firmado y sellado por ‖ *tr* dar, entregar; **to hand in** entregar; **to hand on** transmitir; **to hand out** repartir

hand′bag′ *s* saco de noche; bolso de señora
hand baggage *s* equipaje *m* de mano
hand′ball′ *s* pelota; juego de pelota a mano
hand′bill′ *s* hoja volante
hand′book′ manual *m; guía de turistas; registro para apuestas
hand′breadth′ *s* palmo menor
hand′car′ *s* (rr) carrito de mano
hand′cart′ *s* carretilla de mano
hand control *s* mando a mano
hand′cuff′ *s* manilla; **handcuffs** manillas, esposas ‖ *tr* poner esposas a
handful ['hænd,ful] *s* puñado, manojo
hand glass *s* espejo de mano; lupa
hand grenade *s* granada de mano
hand gun *s* (coll) pipa
hand′-held′ calculator *s* calculador a mano
handi-cap ['hændɪ,kæp] *s* desventaja, obstáculo; (sport) handicap *m;* (med) disminución, minusvalía ‖ *v* (*pret & pp* **-capped;** *ger* **-capping**) *tr* poner trabas a; (sport) handicapar
handicraft ['hændɪ,kræft] *s* destreza manual; arte mecánica
handiwork ['hændɪ,wʌrk] *s* hechura, trabajo, obra manual
handkerchief ['hæŋkərtʃɪf] *s* pañuelo
handle ['hændəl] *s* (*of a basket, crock, pitcher*) asa; (*of a shovel, rake, etc.*) mango; (*of an umbrella, sword*) puño; (*of a door, drawer*) tirador *m;* (*of a hand organ*) manubrio; (*of a water pump*) guimbalete *m;* (*opportunity, pretext*) asidero; **to fly off the handle** (slang) salirse de sus casillas ‖ *tr* manosear, manipular; dirigir, manejar, gobernar; comerciar en ‖ *intr* manejarse
handle bar *s* manillar *m,* guía
handler ['hændlər] *s* (sport) entrenador *m*
hand′made′ *adj* hecho a mano
hand′maid′ o **hand′maid′en** *s* criada, sirvienta
hand′-me-down′ *s* (coll) prenda de vestir de segunda mano
hand organ *s* organillo
hand′out′ *s* comida que se da de limosna; comunicado de prensa

hand-picked ['hænd,pɪkt] *adj* escogido a mano; escogido escrupulosamente; escogido con motivos ocultos
hand′rail′ *s* barandilla, pasamano
hand′saw′ *s* serrucho, sierra de mano
hand′set′ *s* microteléfono
hand′shake′ *s* apretón *m* de manos
handsome ['hænsəm[*adj* hermoso, elegante, guapo; considerable
hand′spring′ *s* voltereta sobre las manos
hand′-to-hand′ *adj* cuerpo a cuerpo
hand′-to-mouth′ *adj* inseguro, precario; impróvido
hand′work′ *s* trabajo a mano
hand′-wres′tle *intr* pulsear
hand′-writ′ing *s* escritura; (*writing by hand which characterizes a particular person*) letra
hand•y ['hændɪ] *adj* (*comp* **-ier;** *super* **-iest**) (*easy to handle*) manuable; (*within easy reach*) próximo, a la mano; (*skillful*) diestro, hábil; **to come in handy** venir a pelo
handy man *s* dije *m,* factótum *m*
hang [hæŋ] *s* (*of a dress, curtain, etc.*) caída; (*skill; insight*) tino; **I don't care a hang** (coll) no me importa un bledo; **to get the hang of it** (coll) coger el tino ‖ *v* (*pret & pp* **hung** [hʌŋ]) *tr* colgar; tender (*la ropa mojada*); pegar (*el papel pintado*); fijar (*un cartel, un letrero*); enquiciar (*una puerta, una ventana*); bajar (*la cabeza*); **hang it!** (coll) ¡caramba!; **to hang up** colgar (*el sombrero*); impedir los progresos de ‖ *intr* colgar, pender; estar agarrado; vacilar; **to hang around** esperar sin hacer nada; haraganear; rondar; **to hang on** colgar de; depender de; estar pendiente de (*las palabras de una persona*); estar sin acabar de morir; agarrarse; **to hang out** asomarse; (slang) recogerse, alojarse; **to hang over** (*to threaten*) cernerse sobre; **to hang together** mantenerse unidos; **to hang up** (telp) colgar ‖ *v* (*pret* **hanged** o **hung**) *tr* ahorcar ‖ *intr* ahorcarse
hangar ['hæŋər] o ['hæŋgɑr] *s* cobertizo; (aer) hangar *m*
hang′bird′ *s* pájaro de nido colgante; (*Baltimore oriole*) cacique veranero
hanger ['hæŋər] *s* colgador *m,* suspensión; (*hook*) colgadero
hang′er•on′ *s* (*pl* **hangers-on**) secuaz *mf;* parásito; (*sponger*) pegote *m*
hanging ['hæŋɪŋ] *adj* colgante, pendiente ‖ *s* ahorcadura, muerte *f* en la horca; **hangings** colgaduras
hang•man ['hæŋmən] *s* (*pl* **-men** [mən]) verdugo
hang′nail′ *s* padrastro, respigón *m*
hang′out′ *s* guarida, querencia; (*place to loaf and gossip*) mentidero
hang′o′ver *s* (slang) resaca
hank [hæŋk] *s* madeja
hanker ['hæŋkər] *intr* sentir anhelo
Hannibal ['hænɪbəl] *s* Aníbal *m*
haphazard [,hæp'hæzərd] *adj* casual, fortuito, impensado ‖ *adv* al acaso, a la ventura

hapless [ˈhæplɪs] *adj* desgraciado, desventurado

happen [ˈhæpən] *intr* acontecer, suceder; (*to turn out*) resultar; (*to be the case by chance*) dar la casualidad; **to happen in** entrar por casualidad; **to happen on** encontrarse con; **to happen to** hacerse de; **to happen to** + *inf* por casualidad + *ind*, p.ej., **I happened to see her at the theater** por casualidad la ví en el teatro

happening [ˈhæpənɪŋ] *s* acontecimiento, suceso

happily [ˈhæpɪli] *adv* felizmente

happiness [ˈhæpɪnɪs] *s* felicidad

hap·py [ˈhæpi] *adj* (*comp* **-pier**; *super* **-piest**) feliz; (*pleased*) contento; **to be happy to** alegrarse de, tener gusto en

hap'py-go-luck'y *adj* irresponsable, impróvido ‖ *adv* a la buenaventura

happy medium *s* justo medio

Happy New Year *interj* ¡Feliz Año Nuevo!

harangue [həˈræŋ] *s* arenga ‖ *tr. & intr* arengar

harass [ˈhærəs] o [həˈræs] *tr* acosar, hostigar; molestar, vejar

harbinger [ˈhɑrbɪndʒər] *s* precursor *m*; anuncio, presagio ‖ *tr* anunciar, presagiar

harbor [ˈhɑrbər] *adj* portuario ‖ *s* puerto ‖ *tr* albergar; alcahuetar, encubrir (*delincuentes u objetos robados*); guardar (*sentimientos de odio*)

harbor master *s* capitán *m* de puerto

hard [hɑrd] *adj* duro; (*difficult*) difícil; (*water*) crudo, duro; (*solder*) fuerte; (*work*) asiduo; (*drinker*) empedernido; espiritoso, fuertemente alcohólico; **to be hard on** (*to treat severely*) ser muy duro con; (*to wear out fast*) gastar, echar a perder ‖ *adv* duro; fuerte; mucho; **hard upon** a raíz de; **to drink hard** beber de firme; **to rain hard** llover de firme

hard and fast *adj* inflexible, riguroso ‖ *adv* firmemente

hard-bitten [ˈhɑrdˈbɪtən] *adj* terco, tenaz, inflexible

hard-boiled [ˈhɑrdˈbɔɪld] *adj* (*egg*) duro, muy cocido; duro, inflexible

hard candy *s* caramelos

hard cash *s* dinero contante y sonante

hard cider *s* sidra muy fermentada

hard coal *s* antracita

hard-earned [ˈhɑrdˈʌrnd] *adj* ganado a pulso

harden [ˈhɑrdən] *tr* endurecer ‖ *intr* endurecerse

hardening [ˈhɑrdənɪŋ] *s* endurecimiento

hard facts *spl* realidades

hard-fought [ˈhɑrdˈfɔt] *adj* reñido

hard-headed [ˈhɑrdˈhɛdɪd] *adj* astuto, sagaz; terco, tozudo

hard-hearted [ˈhɑrdˈhɑrtɪd] *adj* duro de corazón

hardihood [ˈhɑrdɪˌhʊd] *s* audacia, resolución; descaro, insolencia

hardiness [ˈhɑrdɪnɪs] *s* fuerza, robustez; audacia, resolución

hard labor *s* trabajos forzados

hard luck *s* mala suerte

hard'-luck' story *s* (coll) cuento de penas; **to tell a hard-luck story** (coll) contar lástimas

hardly [ˈhɑrdli] *adv* apenas; escasamente; casi no; (*with great difficulty*) a duras penas; (*grievously*) penosamente; **hardly ever** casi nunca

hardness [ˈhɑrdnɪs] *s* dureza; (*of water*) crudeza

hard of hearing *adj* duro de oído, teniente

hard-pressed [ˈhɑrdˈprɛst] *adj* acosado; (*for money*) apurado, alcanzado

hard rubber *s* vulcanita

hard sauce *s* mantequilla azucarada

hard'-shell' clam *s* almeja redonda

hard'-shell' crab *s* cangrejo de cáscara dura

hardship [ˈhɑrdʃɪp] *s* penalidad, infortunio, apuro

hard'tack' *s* galleta, sequete *m*

hard times *spl* período de miseria, apuros

hard to please *adj* difícil de contentar

hard up *adj* (coll) apurado, alcanzado

hard'ware' *s* ferretería, quincalla; (*metal trimmings*) herraje *m*; (*computer*) ordenador *m*

hardware·man [ˈhɑrdˌwɛrmən] *s* (*pl* **-men** [mən]) ferretero, quincallero

hardware store *s* ferretería, quincallería

hard-won [ˈhɑrdˌwʌn] *adj* ganado a pulso

hard'wood' *s* madera dura; árbol *m* de madera dura

hardwood floor *s* entarimado

har·dy [ˈhɑrdi] *adj* (*comp* **-dier**; *super* **-diest**) fuerte, robusto; audaz, resuelto; (*rash*) temerario; (hort) resistente

hare [hɛr] *s* liebre *f*

harebrained [ˈhɛrˌbrend] *adj* atolondrado

hare'lip' *s* labio leporino

harelipped [ˈhɛrˌlɪpt] *adj* labiohendido

harem [ˈhɛrəm] *s* harén *m*

hark [hɑrk] *intr* escuchar; **to hark back** volver (*la jauría*) sobre la pista; **to hark back to** volver a, recordar

harken [ˈhɑrkən] *intr* escuchar, atender

harlequin [ˈhɑrləkwɪn] *s* arlequín *m*

harlot [ˈhɑrlət] *s* meretriz *f*

harm [hɑrm] *s* daño, perjuicio ‖ *tr* dañar, perjudicar, hacer daño a

harmful [ˈhɑrmfəl] *adj* dañoso, perjudicial; maléfico; (*e.g., pests*) dañino

harmfulness [ˈhɑrmfəlnɪs] *s* nocividad

harmless [ˈhɑrmlɪs] *adj* innocuo, inofensivo

harmlessness [ˈhɑrmlɪsnɪs] *s* innocuidad

harmonic [hɑrˈmɑnɪk] *adj & s* armónico

harmonica [hɑrˈmɑnɪkə] *s* armónica

harmonious [hɑrˈmoni·əs] *adj* armonioso

harmonize [ˈhɑrməˌnaɪz] *tr & intr* armonizar

harmo·ny [ˈhɑrməni] *s* (*pl* **-nies**) armonía

harness [ˈhɑrnɪs] *s* arreos, guarniciones; **to get back in the harness** volver a la rutina; **to die in the harness** morir al pie del cañón ‖ *tr* enjaezar, poner las guarniciones a; enganchar; captar (*las aguas de un río*)

harness maker *s* guarnicionero

harness race *s* carrera con sulky

harp [hɑrp] *s* arpa ‖ *intr* — **to harp on** repetir porfiadamente

harpist ['harpɪst] *s* arpista *mf*
harpoon [har'pun] *s* arpón *m* ‖ *tr & intr* arponear
harpsichord ['harpsɪ,kɔrd] *s* clave *m*
har·py ['harpi] *s* (*pl* **-pies**) arpía
harrow ['hæro] *s* (agr) grada ‖ *tr* (agr) gradar; atormentar
harrowing ['hæro·ɪŋ] *adj* horripilante, espantoso
har·ry ['hæri] *v* (*pret & pp* **-ried**) *tr* acosar, hostilizar, hostigar; atormentar, molestar
harsh [harʃ] *adj* (*to touch, taste, eyes, hearing*) áspero; duro, cruel
harshness ['harʃnɪs] *s* aspereza; dureza, crueldad
hart [hart] *s* ciervo
harum-scarum ['hɛrəm'skɛrəm] *adj* atolondrado ‖ *adv* atolondradamente ‖ *s* mataperros *m*
harvest ['harvɪst] *s* cosecha; corte *m* ‖ *tr & intr* cosechar
harvester ['harvɪstər] *s* cosechero; (*helper*) agostero; (*machine*) segadora
harvest home *s* entrada de los frutos; fiesta de segadores; canción de segadores
harvest moon *s* luna de la cosecha
has-been ['hæz,bɪn] *s* (coll) antigualla
hash [hæʃ] *s* picadillo ‖ *tr* picar
hash house *s* bodegón *m*
hashish ['hæʃɪʃ] *s* hachich *m;* (coll) tate *m*
hashish user *s* (coll) tate *m*
hasp [hæsp] o [hɑsp] *s* portacandado; (*of book covers*) broche *m*
hassle ['hæsəl] *s* (coll) riña, disputa
hassock ['hæsək] *s* cojín *m* (*para los pies o las rodillas*)
haste [hest] *s* prisa; **in haste** de prisa; **to make haste** darse prisa
hasten ['hesən] *tr* apresurar; apretar (*el paso*) ‖ *intr* apresurarse
hast·y ['hesti] *adj* (*comp* **-ier;** *super* **-iest**) apresurado, inconsiderado, impulsivo, colérico
hat [hæt] *s* sombrero; **to keep under one's hat** (coll) callar, no divulgar; **to throw one's hat in the ring** (coll) decidirse a bajar a la arena
hat'band' *s* cintillo; (*worn to show mourning*) gasa
hat block *s* horma, conformador *m*
hat'box' *s* sombrerera
hatch [hætʃ] *s* (*brood*) cría, nidada; (*trap door*) escotillón *m;* (*lower half of door*) media puerta; (*opening in ship's deck*) escotilla; (*lid for opening in ship's deck*) cuartel *m* ‖ *tr* empollar (*huevos*); sombrear (*un dibujo*); maquinar, tramar ‖ *intr* empollarse; salir del huevo
hat'-check' girl *s* guardarropa
hatchet ['hætʃɪt] *s* destral *m*, hacha pequeña; **to bury the hatchet** envainar la espada
hatch'way' *s* (*trap door*) escotillón *m;* (*opening in ship's deck*) escotilla
hate [het] *s* odio, aborrecimiento ‖ *tr & intr* odiar, aborrecer, detestar
hateful ['hetfəl] *adj* odioso, aborrecible
hat'pin' *s* aguja de sombrero, pasador *m*

hat'rack' *s* percha
hatred ['hetrɪd] *s* odio, aborrecimiento
hat shop *s* bonetería
hatter ['hætər] *s* sombrerero
haughtiness ['hɔtɪnɪs] *s* altanería, altivez *f*
haugh·ty ['hɔti] *adj* (*comp* **-tier;** *super* **-iest**) altanero, altivo
haul [hɔl] *s* (*pull, tug*) tirón *m;* (*amount caught*) redada; (*distance transported*) trayecto, recorrido; (*roundup, e.g., of thieves*) redada ‖ *tr* acarrear, transportar; (naut) halar
haunch [hɔntʃ] o [hɑntʃ] *s* (*hip*) cadera; (*hind quarter of an animal*) anca; (*leg of animal used for food*) pierna
haunt [hɔnt] o [hɑnt] *s* guarida, nidal *m*, querencia ‖ *tr* andar por, vagar por; frecuentar; inquietar, molestar; perseguir (*las memorias a una persona*)
haunted house *s·*casa de fantasmas
haute couture [ot ku'tyr] *s* alta moda
Havana [hə'vænə] *s* La Habana
have [hæv] *v* (*pret & pp* had [hæd]) *tr* tener; (*to get, to take*) tomar; **to have and to hold** (úsase sólo en el infinitivo) para ser poseído en propiedad; **to have got** (coll) tener, poseer; **to have got to** + *inf* (coll) tener que + *inf;* **to have it in for** (coll) tener tirria a; **to have it out with** (coll) habérselas con, emprenderla con; **to have on** llevar puesto; **to have** (*something*) **to do with** tener que ver con; **to have what it takes to** tener madera de; **to have** + *inf* hacer, mandar + *inf*, p.ej., **I had him go out that door** le hice salir por esa puerta; **to have** + *pp* hacer, mandar + *inf*, p.ej., **I had my watch repaired** hice componer mi reloj ‖ *intr* — **to have at** atacar, embestir; **to have to** + *inf* tener que + *inf;* **to have to do with** (*to be concerned with*) tratar de; (*to have connections with*) tener relaciones con ‖ *v aux* haber, p.ej., **he has studied his lesson** ha estudiado su lección
havelock ['hævlɑk] *s* cogotera
haven ['hevən] *s* puerto; abrigo, asilo, buen puerto
have-not ['hæv,nɑt] *s* — **the haves and the have-nots** (coll) los ricos y los desposeídos
haversack ['hævər,sæk] *s* barjuleta; (*of soldier*) mochila
havoc ['hævək] *s* estrago, estragos; **to play havoc with** hacer grandes estragos en
haw [hɔ] *s* (*of hawthorn*) baya, simiente *f;* (*in speech*) vacilación ‖ *interj* ¡a la izquierda! ‖ *tr & intr* volver a la izquierda
haw'-haw' *s* carcajada
hawk [hɔk] *s* halcón *m*, gavilán *m;* (*mortarboard*) esparavel *m;* (*sharper*) (coll) fullero ‖ *tr* pregonar; **to hawk up** arrojar tosiendo ‖ *intr* carraspear, gargajear
hawker ['hɔkər] *s* buhonero
hawksbill turtle ['hɔks,bɪl] *s* carey *m*
hawse [hɔz] *s* (naut) muz *m;* (*hole*) (naut) escobén *m;* (naut) longitud de cadenas
hawse'hole' *s* (naut) escobén *m*
hawser ['hɔzər] *s* (naut) guindaleza
haw'thorn' *s* espino, oxiacanta

hay [he] *s* heno; **to hit the hay** (slang) acostarse; **to make hay while the sun shines** hacer su agosto

hay fever *s* fiebre *f* del heno

hay'field' *s* henar *m*

hay'fork' *s* horca; (*machine*) elevador *m* de heno

hay'loft' *s* henil *m*, henal *m*

hay'mak'er *s* (box) golpe *m* que pone fuera de combate

haymow [ˈheˌmaʊ] *s* henil *m;* acopio de heno

hay'rack' *s* pesebre *m*

hayrick [ˈheˌrɪk] *s* almiar *m*

hay ride *s* paseo de placer en carro de heno

hay'seed' *s* simiente *f* de heno; (coll) patán *m*, campesino

hay'stack' *s* almiar *m*

hay'wire' *adj* (slang) descompuesto; (slang) destornillado, loco ‖ *s* alambre *m* para embalar el heno

hazard [ˈhæzərd] *s* peligro, riesgo; (*chance*) acaso, azar *m;* (golf) obstáculo; **at all hazards** por grande que sea el riesgo ‖ *tr* arriesgar; aventurar (*una opinión*)

hazardous [ˈhæzərdəs] *adj* peligroso, arriesgado

haze [hez] *s* calina, bruma; (fig) confusión, vaguedad ‖ *tr* dar novatada a

hazel [ˈhezəl] *adj* castaño claro ‖ *s* avellano

ha'zel·nut *s* avellana

hazing [ˈhezɪŋ] *s* novatada

ha·zy [ˈhezi] *adj* (*comp* **-zier;** *super* **-ziest**) calinoso, brumoso; confuso, vago

H-bomb [ˈetʃˌbɑm] *s* bomba de hidrógeno

H.C. *abbr* **House of Commons**

hd. *abbr* **head**

hdqrs. *abbr* **headquarters**

H.E. *abbr* **His Eminence, His Excellency**

he [hi] *pron pers* (*pl* **they**) él ‖ *s* (*pl* **hes**) macho, varón *m*

head [hɛd] *s* cabeza; (*of a bed*) cabecera; (*caption*) encabezamiento; (*of a boil*) centro; (*on a glass of beer*) espuma; (*of a drum*) parche *m;* (*of a cane*) puño; (*of a barrel, cylinder, etc.*) fondo, tapa; (*of cylinder of automobile engine*) culata; crisis *f*, punto decisivo; **at the head of** al frente de; **from head to foot** de pies a cabeza; **head over heels** en un salto mortal; hasta los tuétanos; precipitadamente; **heads** (*of a coin*) cara; **heads or tails?** ¿cara o cruz?; ¿águila o sol? (Mex); **over one's head** fuera del alcance de uno; (*going to a higher authority*) por encima de uno; **to be out of one's head** (coll) delirar; **to come into one's head** pasarle a uno por la cabeza; **to go to one's head** subírsele a uno a la cabeza; **to keep one's head** no perder la cabeza; **to keep one's head above water** no dejarse vencer; **to put heads together** consultarse entre sí; **to not make head or tail of** no ver pies ni cabeza a ‖ *tr* acaudillar, dirigir, mandar; estar a la cabeza de (*p.ej., la clase*); venir primero en (*una lista*) ‖ *intr* — **to head towards** dirigirse hacia

head'ache' *s* dolor *m* de cabeza

head'band' *s* cinta para la cabeza; (*of a book*) cabezada

head'board' *s* cabecera de cama

head'cheese' *s* queso de cerdo

head'dress' *s* (*style of hair*) tocado; prenda para la cabeza

header [ˈhɛdər] *s* — **to take a header** (coll) caerse de cabeza

head'first' *adv* de cabeza; precipitadamente

head'gear' *s* sombrero; (*for protection*) casco

head'hunt'er *s* cazador *m* de cabezas

heading [ˈhɛdɪŋ] *s* encabezamiento; (*of a letter*) membrete *m;* (*of a chapter of a book*) cabecera

headland [ˈhɛdlənd] *s* promontorio

headless [ˈhɛdlɪs] *adj* sin cabeza; sin jefe; estúpido

head'light' *s* (aut) faro; (naut) farol *m* de tope; (rr) farol *m*

head'line' *s* (*of newspaper*) cabecera; (*of a page of a book*) titulillo, título de página ‖ *tr* poner cabecera a; (slang) destacar, dar cartel a (*un actor*)

head'lin'er *s* (slang) atracción principal

head'long' *adj* de cabeza; precipitado ‖ *adv* de cabeza; precipitadamente

head·man [ˈhɛdˌmæn] *s* (*pl* **-men** [ˌmɛn]) caudillo, jefe *m*

head'mas'ter *s* director *m* de un colegio

head'most' *adj* delantero, primero

head office *s* oficina central

head of hair *s* cabellera

head'-on' *adj & adv* de frente; **head-on collision** colisión de frente

head'phone' *s* auricular *m* de casco, receptor *m* de cabeza

head'piece' *s* (*any covering for head*) casco, yelmo, morrión *m;* (*brains, judgment*) cabeza, juicio; cabecera de cama; (*headset*) auricular *m* de casco, receptor *m* de cabeza; (typ) cabecera, viñeta

head'quar'ters *s* centro de dirección; (*of police*) jefatura; (mil) cuartel *m* general

head'rest' *s* apoyo para la cabeza; (aut) reposa cabezas

head'set' *s* auricular *m* de casco, receptor *m* de cabeza

head'ship' *s* jefatura, dirección

head'stone' *s* (*cornerstone*) piedra angular; (*on a grave*) lápida sepulcral

head'stream' *s* afluente *m* principal

head'strong' *adj* cabezudo, terco

head'wait'er *s* jefe *m* de camareros, encargado de comedor

head'wa'ters *spl* cabecera

head'way' *s* avance *m*, progreso; espacio libre; **to make headway** avanzar, progresar

head'wear' *s* prendas de cabeza

head wind *s* viento de frente, viento por la proa

head'work' *s* trabajo intelectual

head·y [ˈhɛdi] *adj* (*comp* **-ier;** *super* **-iest**) excitante, emocionante; impetuoso, violento; (*intoxicating*) cabezudo; (*clever*) sesudo

heal [hil] *tr* curar, sanar; cicatrizar; remediar (*un daño*) ‖ *intr* curar, sanar; cicatrizarse; remediarse

healer [ˈhilər] *s* curador *m*, sanador *m*

health [hɛlθ] *s* salud *f;* **to be in good health** estar bien de salud; **to be in poor health** estar mal de salud; **to drink to the health of** beber a la salud de; **to radiate health** verter salud; **to your health!** ¡a su salud!

healthful [ˈhɛlθfəl] *adj* saludable; sano

health insurance *s* seguro de enfermedad

health•y [ˈhɛlθi] *adj* (*comp* **-ier;** *super* **-iest**) sano; saludable

heap [hip] *s* montón *m* ‖ *tr* amontonar, apilar; (*to supply with, e.g., favors*) colmar; (*to bestow in great quantity*) dar generosamente ‖ *intr* amontonarse, apilarse

hear [hɪr] *v* (*pret & pp* **heard** [hʌrd]) *tr* oír; **to hear it said** oírlo decir ‖ *intr* oír; **hear! hear!** ¡bravo!; **to hear about;** oír hablar de; **to hear from** tener noticias de; **to hear of** oír hablar de; **to hear tell of** oír hablar de; **to hear that** oír decir que

hearer [ˈhɪrər] *s* (*sense*) oyente *mf*

hearing [ˈhɪrɪŋ] *s* (*sense*) oído; (*act*) oída; audiencia; **in the hearing of** en presencia de; **within hearing** al alcance del oído

hearing aid *s* aparato auditivo

hear′say′ *s* rumor *m;* **by hearsay** de o por oídas

hearse [hʌrs] *s* coche *m* fúnebre, carroza fúnebre

heart [hɑrt] *s* corazón *m;* (*e.g., of lettuce*) cogollo; **after one's heart** enteramente del gusto de uno; **by heart** de memoria; **heart and soul** de todo corazón; **to break the heart of** partir el corazón de; **to die of a broken heart** morir de pena; **to eat one's heart out** sufrir en silencio; **to get to the heart of** llegar al fondo de; **to have one's heart in one's work** trabajar con entusiasmo; **to have one's heart in the right place** tener buenas intenciones; **to lose heart** descorazonarse; **to open one's heart to** descubrirse con; **to take heart** cobrar aliento; **to take to heart** tomar a pecho; **to wear one's heart on one's sleeve** llevar el corazón en la mano; **with all one's heart** con toda el alma de uno; **with one's heart in one's mouth** con el credo en la boca

heart′ache′ *s* angustia, congoja

heart attack *s* ataque *m* de corazón, ataque cardíaco

heart′beat′ *s* latido del corazón

heart′break′ *s* angustia, dolor *m* abrumador

heart′break′er *s* ladrón *m* de corazones

heartbroken [ˈhɑrtˌbrokən] *adj* transido de dolor, muerto de pena

heart′burn′ *s* acedía, rescoldera; (*jealousy*) celos

heart disease *s* enfermedad del corazón

hearten [ˈhɑrtən] *tr* alentar, animar

heart failure *s* debilidad coronaria; (*death*) paro del corazón; (*faintness*) desfallecimiento, desmayo

heartfelt [ˈhɑrtˌfɛlt] *adj* cordial, sentido, sincero

hearth [hɑrθ] *s* hogar *m*

hearth′stone′ *s* solera del hogar; (*home*) hogar *m*

heartily [ˈhɑrtɪli] *adv* cordialmente; con buen apetito; de buena gana; bien, mucho

heartless [ˈhɑrtlɪs] *adj* cruel, inhumano

heart pacemaker *s* marcapaso, marcapasos *m*

heart-rending [ˈhɑrtˌrɛndɪŋ] *adj* angustioso, que parte el corazón

heart′seed′ *s* farolillo

heart′sick′ *adj* afligido, desconsolado

heart′strings′ *spl* fibras del corazón, entretelas

heart′-to-heart′ *adj* franco, sincero

heart trouble *s* — **to have heart trouble** enfermar del corazón

heart′wood′ *s* madera de corazón

heart•y [ˈhɑrti] *adj* (*comp* **-ier;** *super* **-iest**) cordial, sincero; sano, fuerte; (*meal*) abundante; (*laugh*) bueno; (*eater*) grande

heat [hit] *adj* térmico ‖ *s* calor *m;* (*warming of a room, house, etc.*) calefacción; (*rut of animals*) celo; (*in horse racing*) carrera de prueba; (*fig*) ardor *m*, ímpetu *m;* **in heat** encelo ‖ *tr* calentar; calefaccionar (*p.ej., una casa*); (*fig*) acalorar, excitar ‖ *intr* calentarse; (*fig*) acalorarse, excitarse

heated [ˈhitɪd] *adj* acalorado

heater [ˈhitər] *s* calentador *m;* (*for central heating*) calorífero; (*electron*) calefactor *m*

heater man *s* calefactor *m*

heath [hiθ] *s* (*shrub*) brezo; (*tract of land*) brezal *m*

hea•then [ˈhiðən] *adj* gentil, pagano; irreligioso ‖ *s* (*pl* **-then** o **-thens**) gentil *mf*, pagano

heathendom [ˈhiðəndəm] *s* gentilidad

heather [ˈhɛðər] *s* brezo

heating [ˈhitɪŋ] *adj* calentador ‖ *s* calefacción

heat′-in′su·lat·ed *adj* termoaislante

heat lightning *s* fucilazo, relámpago de calor

heat shield *s* blindaje térmico, escudo térmico

heat′stroke′ *s* insolación; golpe *m* de calor

heat wave *s* (*phys*) onda calorífica; (*coll*) ola de calor

heave [hiv] *s* esfuerzo para levantar; esfuerzo para levantarse; **heaves** (*vet*) huélfago ‖ *v* (*pret & pp* **heaved** o **hov** [hov]) *tr* alzar, levantar; arrojar, lanzar; exhalar (*un suspiro*) ‖ *intr* levantarse y bajar alternativamente; palpitar (*el pecho*); elevarse; hacer esfuerzos por vomitar

heaven [ˈhɛvən] *s* cielo; **for heaven's sake!** o **good heavens!** ¡válgame Dios!; **heavens** (*firmament*) cielo ‖ **Heaven** *s* cielo (*mansión de los bienaventurados*)

heavenly [ˈhɛvənli] *adj* (*body*) celeste; (*life, home*) celestial; (*fig*) celestial

heavenly body *s* astro, cuerpo celeste

heav•y [ˈhɛvi] *adj* (*comp* **-ier;** *super* **-iest**) (*of great weight*) pesado; (*liquid*) espeso, denso; (*cloth, paper, sea, line*) grueso, (*traffic*) denso; (*crop, harvest*) abundante, copioso; (*expense*) fuerte; (*rain*) recio; (*features*) basto; (*eyes*) agravado; (*gunfire*) fragoroso; (*heart*) abatido, triste; (*drinker*) grande; (*stock market*) postrado; (*clothing*) de mucho abrigo ‖ *adv* pesadamente; **to hang heavy;** pasar (*el tiempo*) con gran lentitud

heav′y‧du′ty *adj* extrafuerte

heavy-hearted [′hɛvi′hɑrtɪd] *adj* afligido, acongojado

heav′y‧set′ *adj* costilludo, espaldudo

heav′y‧weight′ *s* (box) peso pesado

Hebrew [′hibru] *adj & s* hebreo

hecatomb [′hɛkə,tom] *s* hecatombe *f*

heckle [′hɛkəl] *tr* interrumpir (*a un orador*) con preguntas impertinentes

hectic [′hɛktɪk] *adj* (coll) agitado, turbulento

hedge [hɛdʒ] *s* cercado, vallado; (*of bushes*) seto vivo; apuesta compensatoria; (*in stock market*) operación compensatoria ‖ *tr* cercar con vallado; cercar con seto vivo; **to hedge in** encerrar, rodear ‖ *intr* no querer comprometerse; hacer apuestas compensatorias; hacer operaciones compensatorias

hedge′hog′ *s* erizo; (*porcupine*) puerco espín *m*

hedge′hop′ *v* (*pret & pp* **-hopped;** *ger* **-hopping**) *intr* (aer) volar rasando el suelo

hedgehopping [′hɛdʒ,hɑpɪŋ] *s* (aer) vuelo rasante

hedge′row′ *s* cercado de arbustos, seto vivo

heed [hid] *s* atención, cuidado; **to take heed** ir con cuidado ‖ *tr* atender a, hacer caso de ‖ *intr* atender, hacer caso

heedless [′hidlɪs] *adj* desatento, descuidado

heehaw [′hi,hɔ] *s* (*of donkey*) rebuzno; risotada ‖ *intr* rebuznar; reír groseramente

heel [hil] *s* (*of foot*) calcañar *m*, talón *m*; (*of stocking or shoe*) talón *m*; (*raised part of shoe below heel*) tacón *m*; (slang) sinvergüenza *mf*; **down at the heel** desaliñado, mal vestido; **to cool one's heels** (coll) hacer antesala; **to kick up one's heels** (slang) mostrarse alegre; **to show a clean pair of heels** o **to take to one's heels** poner pies en polvorosa

heeler [′hilər] *s* (slang) muñidor *m*

heft‧y [′hɛfti] *adj* (*comp* **-ier;** *super* **-iest**) (*heavy*) pesado; (*strong*) fuerte, fornido

hegemo‧ny [hɪ′dʒɛməni] o [′hɛdʒɪ‑,moni] *s* (*pl* **-nies**) hegemonía

hegira [hɪ′dʒɛɪrə] o [′hɛdʒɪrə] *s* fuga, huída

heifer [′hɛfər] *s* novilla, vaquilla

height [hɑɪt] *s* altura; (*e.g., of folly*) colmo

heighten [′hɑɪtən] *tr* hacer más alto; (*to increase the amount of*) aumentar; (*to set off, bring out*) realzar ‖ *intr* aumentarse

heinous [′henəs] *adj* atroz, nefando

heir [ɛr] *s* heredero

heir apparent *s* (*pl* **heirs apparent**) heredero forzoso

heirdom [′ɛrdəm] *s* herencia

heiress [′ɛrɪs] *s* heredera

heirloom [′ɛr,lum] *s* joya de familia, reliquia de familia

helicopter [′hɛlɪ,kaptər] *s* helicóptero

heliotrope [′hili‧ə,trop] *s* heliotropo

heliport [′hɛlɪ,port] *s* helipuerto

helium [′hili‧əm] *s* helio

helix [′hilɪks] *s* (*pl* **helixes** o **helices** [′hɛlɪ,siz]) hélice *f*

hell [hɛl] *s* infierno

hell-bent [′hɛl′bɛnt] *adj* (slang) muy resuelto; **hell-bent on** (slang) empeñado en

hell′cat′ *s* (*bad-tempered woman*) arpía, mujer perversa; (*witch*) bruja

hellebore [′hɛlɪ,bor] *s* eléboro

Hellene [′hɛlin] *s* heleno

Hellenic [hɛ′lɛnɪk] *adj* helénico

hell′fire′ *s* fuego del infierno

hellish [′hɛlɪʃ] *adj* infernal

hel‧lo [hɛ′lo] *s* saludo ‖ *interj* ¡qué tal!; (*on telephone*) ¡diga!

hello girl *s* (coll) chica telefonista

helm [hɛlm] *s* barra del timón; rueda del timón; (fig) timón *m* ‖ *tr* dirigir, gobernar

helmet [′hɛlmɪt] *s* casco; (*of ancient armor*) yelmo

helms‧man [′hɛlmzmən] *s* (*pl* **-men** [mən]) timonel *m*

help [hɛlp] *s* ayuda, socorro; (*of food*) ración; (*relief*) remedio, p.ej., **there's no help for it** no hay remedio; criados; empleados; obreros; **to come to the help of** acudir en socorro de ‖ *interj* ¡socorro! ‖ *tr* ayudar, socorrer; aliviar, mitigar; (*to wait on*) servir; **it can't be helped** no hay remedio; **so help me God!** ¡así Dios me salve!; **to help down** ayudar a bajar; **to help a person with his coat** ayudarle a una persona a ponerse el abrigo; **to help oneself** valerse por sí mismo; servirse; **to help up** ayudar a subir; ayudar a levantarse; **to not be able to help** + *ger* no poder menos de + *inf*, p.ej., **he can't help laughing** no puede menos de reír ‖ *intr* ayudar

helper [′hɛlpər] *s* ayudante *mf*; (*in a drug store, barbershop, etc.*) mancebo

helpful [′hɛlpfəl] *adj* útil, provechoso; servicial

helping [[′hɛlpɪŋ] *s* ración (*de alimento*)

helpless [′hɛlplɪs] *adj* (*weak*) débil; (*powerless*) impotente; (*penniless*) desvalido; (*confused*) perplejo; (*situation*) irremediable

help′meet′ *s* compañero; (*wife*) compañera

helter-skelter [′hɛltər′skɛltər] *adj, adv & s* cochite hervite *m*

hem [hɛm] *s* tos fingida; (*of a garment*) bastilla, dobladillo ‖ *interj* ¡ejem! ‖ *v* (*pret & pp* **hemmed;** *ger* **hemming**) *tr* bastillar, dobladillar; **to hem in** encerrar, rodear ‖ *intr* destoserse; vacilar; **to hem and haw** vacilar al hablar; ser evasivo

hemisphere [′hɛmɪ,sfɪr] *s* hemisferio

hemistich [′hɛmɪ,stɪk] *s* hemistiquio

hem′line′ *s* ruedo de la falda, borde *m* de la falda

hem′lock′ *s* (*Tsuga canadensis*) abeto del Canadá; (*herb and poison*) cicuta

hemoglobin [,hɛmə′globɪn] o [,himə′globɪn] *s* hemoglobina

he
he

hemophilia [,hɛmə'fɪlɪ•ə] o [,himə'fɪlɪ•ə] *s* hemofilia

hemorrhage ['hɛmərɪdʒ] *s* hemorragia

hemorrhoids ['hɛmə,rɔɪdz] *spl* hemorroides *fpl*

hemostat ['hɛmə,stæt] o ['himə,stæt] *s* hemóstato

hemp [hɛmp] *s* cáñamo

hemstitch ['hɛm,stɪtʃ] *s* vainica ‖ *tr* hacer vainica en ‖ *intr* hacer vainica

hen [hɛn] *s* gallina

hence [hɛns] *adv* de aquí; desde ahora; por lo tanto, por consiguiente; de aquí a, p.ej., **three weeks hence** de aquí a tres semanas

hence'forth' *adv* de aquí en adelante

hench•man ['hɛntʃmən] *s* (*pl* **-men** [mən]) secuaz *m*, servidor *m*; (*political schemer*) muñidor *m*

hen'coop' *s* gallinero

hen'house' *s* gallinero

henna ['hɛnə] *s* alcana, alheña; (*dye*) henna *f* ‖ *tr* alheñarse (*el pelo*)

hen'peck' *tr* dominar (*la mujer al marido*)

henpecked husband *s* calzonazos *m*, gurrumino

hep [hɛp] *adj* (slang) enterado; **to be hep to** (slang) estar al corriente de

her [hʌr] *adj poss* su; el . . . de ella ‖ *pron pers* la; ella; **to her** le; a ella

herald ['hɛrəld] *s* heraldo; anunciador *m* ‖ *tr* anunciar; ser precursor de

heraldic [hɛ'rældɪk] *adj* heráldico

herald•ry ['hɛrəldri] *s* (*pl* **-ries**) (*office or duty of herald*) heraldía; (*science of armorial bearings*) blasón *m*, heráldica; (*heraldic device; coat of arms*) blasón; pompa heráldica

herb [ʌrb] o [hʌrb] *s* hierba; hierba aromática; hierba medicinal

herbaceous [hʌr'beʃəs] *adj* herbáceo

herbage ['ʌrbɪdʒ] o ['hʌrbɪdʒ] *s* herbaje *m*

herbal ['ʌrbəl] o ['hʌrbəl] *adj & s* herbario

herbalist ['hʌrbəlɪst] o ['ʌrbəlɪst] *s* herbolario

herbari•um [hʌr'bɛrɪ•əm] *s* (*pl* **-ums** o **-a** [ə]) herbario

herb doctor *s* herbolario

herculean [hʌr'kuli•ən] *adj* (*hard to perform*) penoso, laborioso; (*strong, big*) hercúleo

herd [hʌrd] *s* manada, rebaño, hato; (*of people*) chusma, multitud ‖ *tr* reunir en manada; reunir ‖ *intr* reunirse en manada; reunirse, ir juntos

herds•man ['hʌrdzmən] *s* (*pl* **-men** [mən]) manadero; (*of sheep*) pastor *m*; (*of cattle*) vaquero

here [hɪr] *adj* presente ‖ *adv* aquí; **here and there** acá y allá; **here is** o **here are** aquí tiene Vd.; **that's neither here nor there** eso no viene al caso ‖ *s* — **the here and the hereafter** esta vida y la futura ‖ *interj* ¡presente!

hereabouts ['hɪrə,baʊts] *adv* por aquí, cerca de aquí

here•af'ter *adv* de aquí en adelante; en lo sucesivo; en la vida futura ‖ **the hereafter** la otra vida, el más allá

here•by' *adv* por esto; por la presente

hereditary [hɪ'rɛdɪ,tɛri] *adj* hereditario

heredi•ty [hɪ'rɛdɪti] *s* (*pl* **-ties**) herencia

here•in' *adv* aquí dentro; en este asunto

here•of' *adv* de esto

here•on' *adv* en esto, sobre esto

here•sy ['hɛrəsi] *s* (*pl* **-sies**) herejía

heretic ['hɛrətɪk] *adj* herético ‖ *s* hereje *mf*

heretical [hɪ'rɛtɪkəl] *adj* herético

heretofore [,hɪtru'for] *adv* antes, hasta ahora

here'u•pon' *adv* en esto, sobre esto; en seguida

here•with' *adv* adjunto, con la presente; de este modo

heritage ['hɛrɪtɪdʒ] *s* herencia

hermetic(al) [hʌr'mɛtɪk(əl)] *adj* hermético

hermit ['hʌrmɪt] *s* eremita *m*, ermitaño

hermitage ['hʌrmɪtɪdʒ] *s* ermita

herni•a ['hʌrnɪ•ə] *s* (*pl* **-as** o **-ae** [,i]) hernia

he•ro ['hɪro] *s* (*pl* **-roes**) héroe *m*

heroic [hɪ'ro•ɪk] *adj* heroico ‖ **heroics** *spl* verso heroico; lenguaje rimbombante

heroin ['hɛro•ɪn] *s* heroína (*polvo cristalino*); (slang) caballo

heroin addict *s* heroinómano

heroine ['hɛro•ɪn] *s* heroína (*mujer*)

heroism ['hɛro,ɪzəm] *s* heroísmo

heron ['hɛrən] *s* garza; (*Ardea cinerea*) airón *m*, garza real

herring ['hɛrɪŋ] *s* arenque *m*

her'ring•bone' *s* (*in fabrics*) espina de pescado; (*in hardwood floors*) espinapez *m*, punto de Hungría

hers [hʌrz] *pron poss* el suyo, el de ella; suyo

herself [hʌr'sɛlf] *pron pers* ella misma; sí, sí misma; se, p.ej., **she enjoyed herself** se divirtió; **with herself** consigo

hesitan•cy ['hɛzɪtənsi] *s* (*pl* **-cies**) vacilación

hesitant ['hɛzɪtənt] *adj* vacilante

hesitate ['hɛzɪ,tet] *intr* vacilar, titubear; (*to stutter*) titubear

hesitation [,hɛzɪ'teʃən] *s* vacilación

heterodox ['hɛtərə,dɑks] *adj* heterodoxo

heterodyne ['hɛtərə,daɪn] *adj* heterodino ‖ *tr* heterodinar

heterogenei•ty [,hɛtərədʒɪ'ni•ɪti] *s* (*pl* **-ties**) heterogeneidad

heterogeneous [,hɛtərə'dʒini•əs] *adj* heterogéneo

hew [hju] *v* (*pret* **hewed**; *pp* **hewed** o **hewn**) *tr* cortar, tajar; (*with an ax*) hachear; labrar (*madera*); picar (*piedra*); **to hew down** derribar a hachazos ‖ *intr* — **to hew close to the line** (coll) hilar delgado

hex [hɛks] *s* (coll) bruja; (coll) hechizo ‖ *tr* (coll) embrujar

hexameter [hɛks'æmɪtər] *s* hexámetro

hey [he] *interj* ¡oye!, ¡oiga!

hey'day' *s* época de mayor prosperidad

hf. *abbr* half

H.H. *abbr* His Highness, Her Highness; His Holiness

hia•tus [haɪ'etəs] *s* (*pl* **-tuses** o **-tus**) (*gap*) abertura, laguna; (*in a text; in verse*) hiato

hibernate [ˈhaɪbər‚net] *intr* invernar; estar inactivo

hibiscus [hɪˈbɪskəs] o [haɪˈbɪskəs] *s* hibisco

hiccough o **hiccup** [ˈhɪkəp] *s* hipo ‖ *intr* hipar

hick [hɪk] *adj & s* (coll) campesino, palurdo

hicko•ry [ˈhɪkəri] *s* (*pl* **-ries**) nuez encarcelada, nuez dura (*árbol*)

hickory nut *s* nuez encarcelada, nuez dura (*fruto*)

hidden [ˈhɪdən] *adj* escondido, oculto; obscuro

hide [haɪd] *s* cuero, piel *f;* **hides** corambre *f;* **neither hide nor hair** ni un vestigio; **to tan someone's hide** (coll) zurrarle a uno la badana ‖ *v* (*pret* **hid** [hɪd]; *pp* **hid** o **hidden** [ˈhɪdən]) *tr* esconder, ocultar ‖ *intr* esconderse, ocultarse; **to hide out** (coll) recatarse

hide′-and-seek′ *s* escondite *m;* **to play hide-and-seek** jugar al escondite

hide′bound′ *adj* fanático, obstinado, dogmático

hideous [ˈhɪdɪ•əs] *adj* (*very ugly*) feote; (*heinous*) atroz, nefando; (*distressingly large*) brutal, enorme

hide′-out′ *s* (coll) guarida, refugio, escondrijo

hiding [ˈhaɪdɪŋ] *s* ocultación; (*place of concealment*) escondite *m*, escondrijo; **in hiding** escondido, oculto; (*in ambush*) emboscado

hiding place *s* escondite *m*, escondrijo

hie [haɪ] *v* (*pret & pp* **hied**; *ger* **hieing** o **hying**) *tr* — **hie thee home** apresúrate a volver a casa ‖ *intr* apresurarse, ir volando

hierar•chy [ˈhaɪ•ə‚rɑrki] *s* (*pl* **-chies**) jerarquía

hieroglyphic [‚haɪ•ərəˈglɪfɪk] *adj & s* jeroglífico

hi-fi [ˈhaɪˈfaɪ] *adj* de alta fidelidad ‖ *s* alta fidelidad

hi-fi fan *s* aficionado a la alta fidelidad

hi-fi set *s* equipo de alta fidelidad

higgledy-piggledy [ˈhɪgəldiˈpɪgəldi] *adj* confuso, revuelto ‖ *adv* confusamente, revueltamente

high [haɪ] *adj* alto; (*river*) crecido; (*sound*) agudo; (*wind*) fuerte; (coll) borracho; (*intoxicated*) embriagado; (*drugs*) emporrado; (culin) manido; **high and dry** abandonado, desamparado; **high and mighty** (coll) muy arrogante ‖ *adv* en sumo grado; a gran precio; **to aim high** poner el tiro muy alto; **to come high** venderse caro ‖ *s* (aut) marcha directa; **on high** en el cielo

high altar *s* altar *m* mayor

high′ball′ *s* highball *m*

high blood pressure *s* hipertensión arterial

high′born′ *adj* linajudo, de ilustre cuna

high′boy′ *s* cómoda alta con patas altas

high′brow′ *adj & s* (slang) erudito

high chair *s* silla alta

high command *s* alto mando

high cost of living *s* carestía de la vida

higher education *s* enseñanza superior

higher-up [‚haɪ•ərˈʌp] *s* (coll) superior jerárquico

high explosive *s* explosivo rompedor

highfalutin [‚haɪfəˈlutən] *adj* (coll) pomposo, presuntuoso

high fidelity *s* alta fidelidad

high′ ′fre′quency *adj* de alta frecuencia

high gear *s* marcha directa, toma directa

high′-grade′ *adj* de calidad superior

high-handed [ˈhaɪˈhændɪd] *adj* arbitrario

high hat *s* sombrero de copa

high′-hat′ *adj* (coll) copetudo, esnob; **to be high-hat** tener mucho copete ‖ **high′-hat′** *v* (*pret & pp* **-hatted;** *ger* **-hatting**) *tr* desairar

high-heeled shoe [ˈhaɪ‚hild] *s* zapato de tacón alto

high horse *s* ademán *m* arrogante

high′jack′ *tr* var de **hijack**

high jinks [dʒɪŋks] *spl* (slang) jarana, payasada

high jump *s* salto de altura

highland [ˈhaɪlənd] *s* región montañosa; **highlands** montañas, tierras altas

high life *s* alta sociedad, gran mundo

high′light′ *s* elemento sobresaliente ‖ *tr* destacar

highly [ˈhaɪli] *adv* altamente; en sumo grado; a gran precio; con aplauso general; **to speak highly of** decir mil bienes de

High Mass *s* misa cantada, misa mayor

high-minded [ˈhaɪˈmaɪndɪd] *adj* noble, magnánimo

highness [ˈhaɪnɪs] *s* altura ‖ **Highness** *s* Alteza

high noon *s* pleno mediodía

high-pitched [ˈhaɪˈpɪtʃt] *adj* agudo; tenso, impresionable

high-powered [ˈhaɪˈpau•ərd] *adj* de alta potencia

high′-pres′sure *adj* de alta presión; (fig) emprendedor, enérgico ‖ *tr* (coll) apremiar

high-priced [ˈhaɪˈpraɪst] *adj* de precio elevado

high priest *s* sumo sacerdote

high rise *s* edificio de muchos pisos

high′road′ *s* camino real

high school *s* escuela de segunda enseñanza

high sea *s* mar gruesa; **high seas** alta mar

high society *s* alta sociedad, gran mundo

high′-speed′ *adj* de alta velocidad

high-spirited [ˈhaɪˈspɪrɪtɪd] *adj* animoso; vivaz; (*horse*) fogoso

high spirits *spl* alegría, buen humor *m*, animación

high-strung [ˈhaɪˈstrʌŋ] *adj* tenso, impresionable

high′-test′ fuel *s* supercarburante *m*

high tide *s* pleamar *f*, marea alta; (fig) punto culminante

high time *s* hora, p.ej., **it is high time for you to go** ya es hora de que Vd. se marche; (slang) jarana, parranda

high treason *s* alta traición

high water *s* aguas altas; pleamar *f*, marea alta

high′way′ *s* carretera

highway·man [ˈhaɪˌwemən] *s* (*pl* **-men** [mən]) salteador *m* de caminos

hijack [ˈhaɪˌdʒæk] *tr* (coll) robar (*a un contrabandista de licores*); (coll) robar (*el licor a un contrabandista*)

hijacker [ˈhaɪˌdʒækər] *s* pirata aéreo

hijacking [ˈhaɪˌdʒækɪŋ] *s* piratería aérea

hike [haɪk] *s* caminata, marcha; (*increase, rise*) aumento ‖ *tr* elevar de un tirón; aumentar ‖ *intr* dar una caminata

hiker [ˈhaɪkər] *s* caminador *m*, aficionado a las caminatas

hilarious [hɪˈlɛrɪ·əs] o [haɪˈlɛrɪ·əs] *adj* jubiloso, regocijado

hill [hɪl] *s* colina, collado ‖ *tr* aporcar (*las hortalizas*)

hillbil·ly [ˈhɪlˌbɪli] *s* (*pl* **-lies**) (coll) rústico montañés (*del sur de los EE.UU.*)

hillock [ˈhɪlək] *s* altozano, montecillo

hill′side′ *s* ladera

hill′top′ *s* cumbre *f*, cima

hill·y [ˈhɪli] *adj* (*comp* **-ier;** *super* **-iest**) colinoso; (*steep*) empinado

hilt [hɪlt] *s* empuñadura, puño; **up to the hilt** completamente

him [hɪm] *pron pers* le, lo; él; **to him** le; a él

himself [hɪmˈsɛlf] *pron pers* él mismo; sí, sí mismo; se, p.ej., **he enjoyed himself** se divirtió; **with himself** consigo

hind [haɪnd] *adj* posterior, trasero ‖ *s* cierva

hinder [ˈhɪndər] *tr* estorbar, impedir; obstruccionar

hindmost [ˈhaɪndˌmost] *adj* postrero, último

Hindoo [ˈhɪndu] *adj & s* hindú *m*

hind′quar′ter *s* cuarto trasero

hindrance [ˈhɪndrəns] *s* estorbo, impedimento, obstáculo

hind′sight′ *s* (*of a firearm*) mira posterior; percepción tardía, sabiduría tardía

Hindu [ˈhɪndu] *adj & s* hindú *m*

hinge [hɪndʒ] *s* (*of a door*) charnela, gozne *m*, bisagra; (*of a mollusk*) charnela; (bb) cartivana; punto capital ‖ *tr* engoznar ‖ *intr* — **to hinge on** depender de

hin·ny [ˈhɪni] *s* (*pl* **-nies**) burdégano, mohino

hint [hɪnt] *s* indirecta, insinuación; **to take the hint** darse por aludido ‖ *tr & intr* insinuar; indicar; **to hint at** aludir indirectamente a

hinterland [ˈhɪntərˌlænd] *s* región interior

hip [hɪp] *s* cadera; (*of a roof*) caballete *m*, lima

hip′bone′ *s* cía, hueso de la cadera

hipped [hɪpt] *adj* (*livestock*) renco; (*roof*) a cuatro aguas; **hipped on** (coll) obsesionado por

hippety-hop [ˈhɪpɪtɪˈhɑp] *adv* (coll) a coxcojita

hip·po [ˈhɪpo] *s* (*pl* **-pos**) (coll) hipopótamo

hippodrome [ˈhɪpəˌdrom] *s* hipódromo

hippopota·mus [ˌhɪpəˈpɑtəməs] *s* (*pl* **-muses** o **-mi** [ˌmaɪ]) hipopótamo

hip roof *s* tejado a cuatro aguas

hire [haɪr] *s* alquiler *m*; precio; salario; **for hire** de alquiler ‖ *tr* alquilar (*p.ej., un coche*); ajustar (*p.ej., a un criado*) ‖ *intr* —**to hire out** ajustarse

hired girl *s* criada

hired man *s* (coll) mozo de campo

hireling [ˈhaɪrlɪŋ] *adj & s* alquiladizo

his [hɪz] *adj poss* su; el . . . de él ‖ *pron poss* el suyo, el de él; suyo

Hispanic [hɪsˈpænɪk] *adj & s* hispánico

Hispaniola [ˌhɪspənˈjolə] *s* Santo Domingo

hispanist [ˈhɪspənɪst] *s* hispanista *mf*

hispanophilia [hɪsˌpænoˈfɪlɪ·ə] *s* españolería

hiss [hɪs] *s* siseo, silbido ‖ *tr* sisear, silbar (*p.ej., una escena, a un actor por malo*) ‖ *intr* sisear, silbar

hist. *abbr* **historian, history**

histology [hɪsˈtɑlədʒi] *s* histología

historian [hɪsˈtorɪ·ən] *s* historiador *m*

historic(al) [hɪsˈtorɪk(əl)] *adj* histórico

histo·ry [ˈhɪstəri] *s* (*pl* **-ries**) historia

histrionic [ˌhɪstrɪˈɑnɪk] *adj* histriónico; teatral ‖ **histrionics** *s* actitud teatral, modales *mpl* teatrales

hit [hɪt] *s* golpe *m*; (*of a bullet*) impacto; (*blow that hits its mark*) tiro certero; (*sarcastic remark*) censura acerba; (baseball) batazo; (coll) éxito; **to make a′ hit** (coll) dar golpe; **to make a hit with** caer en la gracia de (*una persona*) ‖ *v* (*pret & pp* **hit;** *ger* **hitting**) *tr* golpear, pegar; dar con, dar contra, chocar con; dar en (*p.ej., el blanco*); censurar acerbamente; (*to run over in a car*) atropellar; afectar mucho (*un acontecimiento a una persona*) ‖ *intr* chocar; **to hit against** dar contra; **to hit on** dar con (*lo que se busca*)

hit′-and-run′ *adj* que atropella y se da a la huída

hitch [hɪtʃ] *s* (*jerk*) tirón *m*; dificultad; obstáculo; **without a hitch** a pedir de boca, sin tropiezo ‖ *tr* (*to tie*) atar, sujetar; enganchar (*un caballo*); uncir (*bueyes*); (slang) casar

hitch′hike′ *intr* (coll) hacer autostop, viajar en autostop

hitch′hik′er *s* autostopista *mf*

hitching post *s* poste *m* para atar a las cabalgaduras

hither [ˈhɪðər] *adv* acá, hacia acá; **hither and thither** acá y allá

hith′er·to′ *adv* hasta ahora, hasta aquí

hit′-or-miss′ *adj* descuidado, casual

hit parade *s* (rad) canciones que gozan de más popularidad en la actualidad

hit record *s* (coll) disco de mucho éxito

hit′-run′ *adj* que atropella y se da a la huída

hive [haɪv] *s* (*box for bees*) colmena; (*swarm*) enjambre *m*; **hives** urticaria ‖ *tr* encorchar (*abejas*)

H.M. *abbr* **Her Majesty, His Majesty**

H.M.S. *abbr* **Her Majesty's Ship, His Majesty's Ship**

hoard [hord] *s* (*of money, provisions, etc.*) cúmulo; tesoro escondido ‖ *tr* acumular secretamente; atesorar (*dinero*) ‖ *intr* guardar víveres, atesorar dinero

hoarding [ˈhordɪŋ] *s* acumulación secreta; atesoramiento

hoar′frost′ *s* helada blanca, escarcha

hoarse [hors] *adj* ronco

hoarseness ['horsnɪs] s ronquedad; (*from a cold*) ronquera

hoar·y ['hori] adj (*comp* **-ier;** *super* **-iest**) cano, canoso; (*old*) vetusto

hoax [hoks] s pajarota, mistificación ‖ tr mistificar

hob [hab] s repisa interior del hogar; **to play hob with** (coll) trastornar

hobble ['habəl] s (*limp*) cojera; (*rope used to tie legs of animal*) manea, traba ‖ tr dejar cojo; manear, trabar; dificultar ‖ intr cojear; tambalear

hobble skirt s falda de medio paso

hob·by ['habɪ] s (*pl* **-bies**) comidilla, afición favorita, trabajo preferido; **to ride a hobby** entregarse demasiado al tema favorito

hob'by·horse' s (*stick with horse's head*) caballito; (*rocking horse*) caballo mecedor

hob'gob'lin s duende m, trasgo; (*bogy*) bu m, coco

hob'nail' s tachuela ‖ tr clavetear con tachuelas; (fig) atropellar

hob·nob ['hab,nab] v (*pret & pp* **-nobbed;** *ger* **-nobbing**) intr codearse, rozarse; beber juntos

ho·bo ['hobo] s (*pl* **-bos** o **-boes**) vagabundo

Hobson's choice ['habsənz] s alternativa entre la cosa ofrecida o ninguna

hock [hak] s jarrete m, corvejón m ‖ tr (*to hamstring*) desjarretar; (coll) empeñar

hockey ['hakɪ] s hockey m, chueca

hock'shop' s (slang) casa de empeños, monte m de piedad

hocus-pocus ['hokəs'pokəs] s (*meaningless formula*) abracadabra m; burla, engaño; juego de manos

hod [had] s capacho, cuezo; cubo para carbón

hod carrier s peón m de albañil, peón de mano

hodgepodge ['hadʒ,padʒ] s baturrillo

hoe [ho] s azada, azadón m ‖ tr & intr azadonar

hog [hag] o [hɔg] s cerdo, puerco ‖ v (*pret & pp* **hogged;** *ger* **hogging**) tr (slang) tragarse lo mejor de

hog'back' s cuchilla

hoggish ['hagɪʃ] o ['hɔgɪʃ] adj comilón; glotón; egoísta

hog Latin s latín m de cocina

hogs'head' s pipa de 63 galones o más; medida de capacidad de 63 galones

hog'wash' s bazofia

hoist [hɔɪst] s (*apparatus for lifting*) montacargas m, torno izador, grúa; empujón m hacia arriba ‖ tr alzar, levantar; enarbolar (*p.ej., una bandera*); (naut) izar

hoity-toity ['hɔɪtɪ'tɔɪtɪ] adj frívolo, veleidoso; arrogante, altanero; **to be hoity-toity** ponerse tan alto

hokum ['hokəm] s (coll) música celestial, tonterías

hold [hold] s (*grip*) agarro; (*handle*) asa, mango; autoridad, dominio; (*in wrestling*) presa; (aer) cabina de carga; (mus) calderón m; (naut) bodega; **to take hold of** agarrar, coger; apoderarse de ‖ v (*pret & pp* **held** [hɛld]) tr tener, retener; (*to hold*

up, support*) apoyar, sostener; (*e.g., with a pin*) sujetar; contener, tener cabida para; ocupar (*un cargo, puesto, etc.*); celebrar (*una reunión*); sostener (*una opinión*); (mus) sostener (*una nota*); **to hold back** detener; retener; contener; **to hold in** refrenar; **to hold one's own** mantenerse firme, no perder terreno; **to hold over** aplazar, diferir; **to hold up** apoyar, sostener; (*to rob*) (coll) atracar ‖ intr ser valedero, seguir vigente; pegarse; **hold on!** ¡un momento!; **to hold back** refrenarse; **to hold forth** poner cátedra; **to hold off** esperar; mantenerse a distancia; **to hold on** agarrarse bien; **to hold on to** asirse de; **to hold out** no cejar; ir tirando; **to hold out for** insistir en

holder ['holdər] s tenedor m, posesor m; (*for a cigar or cigaret*) boquilla; (*to hold, e.g., a hot plate*) cojinillo; (*e.g., of a passport*) titular m; asa, mango

holding ['holdɪŋ] s tenencia, posesión; **holdings** valores habidos

holding company s sociedad de control, compañía tenedora

hold'up' s (*stop, delay*) detención; atraco, asalto; precio excesivo

holdup man s atracador m, salteador m

hole [hol] s agujero; (*in cheese, bread, etc.*) ojo; (*in a road*) bache m; (*den of animals; den of vice*) guarida; (*dirty, disorderly dwelling*) cochitril m; **in the hole** adeudado, perdidoso; **to burn a hole in one's pocket** írsele a uno (*el dinero*) de entre las manos; **to pick holes in** (coll) poner reparos a ‖ intr — **to hole up** encovarse; buscar un rincón cómodo

holiday ['halɪ,de] s día festivo; vacación

holiday attire s trapos de cristianar

holiness ['holɪnɪs] s santidad; **his Holiness** su Santidad

Holland ['halənd] s Holanda

Hollander ['haləndər] s holandés m

hollow ['halo] adj hueco; (*voice*) ahuecado, sepulcral; (*eyes, cheeks*) hundido; falso, engañoso ‖ adv — **to beat all hollow** (coll) derrotar completamente ‖ s hueco, cavidad; (*small valley*) vallecito ‖ tr ahuecar, excavar

hol·ly ['halɪ] s (*pl* **-lies**) acebo

hol'ly·hock' s malva arbórea

holm oak [hom] s encina

holocaust ['halə,kɔst] s holocausto

holster ['holstər] s pistolera

ho·ly ['holi] adj (*comp* **-lier;** *super* **-liest**) santo; (*e.g., writing*) sagrado; (*e.g., water*) bendito

Holy Ghost s Espíritu Santo

holy orders spl órdenes sagradas; **to take holy orders** recibir las órdenes sagradas, ordenarse

holy rood [rud] s crucifijo ‖ **Holy Rood** s Santa Cruz

Holy Scripture s Sagrada Escritura

Holy See s Santa Sede

Holy Sepulcher s santo sepulcro

hi
ho

holy water *s* agua bendita
Holy Writ *s* Sagrada Escritura
homage [ˈhɑmɪdʒ] o [ˈɑmɪdʒ] *s* homenaje *m;* (feud) homenaje, pleito homenaje
home [hom] *adj* casero, doméstico; nacional ‖ *s* casa, domicilio, hogar *m; (native heath)* patria chica; *(of the arts, etc.)* patria; *(for the sick, poor, etc.)* asilo; (sport) meta; **at home** en casa; en su propio país; *(ready to receive callers)* de recibo; *(at ease, comfortable)* a gusto; (sport) en campo propio; **away from home** fuera de casa; **make yourself at home** está Vd. en su casa ‖ *adv* en casa; a casa; **to see home** acompañar a casa; **to strike home** dar en lo vivo
home'bod'y *s* (*pl* **-ies**) hogareño
homebred [ˈhomˌbrɛd] *adj* doméstico; sencillo, inculto, tosco
home'brew' *s* cerveza o vino caseros
homecoming [ˈhomˌkʌmɪŋ] *s* regreso al hogar
home country *s* suelo natal
home delivery *s* distribución a domicilio
home front *s* frente doméstico
home'land' *s* tierra natal, patria
homeless [ˈhomlɪs] *adj* sin casa, sin hogar
home life *s* vida de familia
home-loving [ˈhomˌlʌvɪŋ] *adj* casero, hogareño
home•ly [ˈhomli] *adj* (*comp* **-lier;** *super* **-liest**) *(not attractive or good-looking)* feo; *(plain, not elegant)* sencillo, llano
homemade [ˈhomˈmed] *adj* casero, hecho en casa
homemaker [ˈhomˌmekər] *s* ama de casa
home office *s* domicilio social, oficina central ‖ **Home Office** *s* (Brit) ministerio de la Gobernación
homeopath [ˈhomɪ•əˌpæθ] o [ˈhɑmɪ•əˌpæθ] *s* homeópata *mf*
homeopathy [ˌhomɪˈɑpəθi] o [ˌhɑmɪˈɑpəθi] *s* homeopatía
home plate *s* (baseball) puesto meta
home port *s* puerto de origen
home rule *s* autonomía, gobierno autónomo
home run *s* (baseball) jonrón *m,* cuadrangular *m*
home'sick' *adj* nostálgico; **to be homesick (for)** sentir nostalgia (de)
home'sick'ness *s* nostalgia, mal *m* de la tierra
homespun [ˈhomˌspʌn] *adj* hilado en casa; sencillo, llano
home'stead' *s* casa y terrenos, heredad
home stretch *s* esfuerzo final, último trecho
home town *s* ciudad natal
homeward [ˈhomwərd] *adj* de regreso ‖ *adv* hacia casa; hacia su país
home'work' *s* trabajo a domicilio; *(of a student)* deber *m,* trabajo escolar
homey [ˈhomi] *adj* (*comp* **homier;** *super* **homiest**) (coll) íntimo, cómodo
homicidal [ˌhɑmɪˈsaɪdəl] *adj* homicida
homicide [ˈhɑmɪˌsaɪd] *s* (*act*) homicidio; *(person)* homicida *mf*
homi•ly [ˈhɑmɪli] *s* (*pl* **-lies**) homilía

homing [ˈhomɪŋ] *adj (animal)* querencioso; *(weapon)* buscador del blanco
homing pigeon *s* paloma mensajera
hominy [ˈhɑmɪni] *s* maíz molido
homogenei•ty [ˌhɑmədʒɪˈni•ɪti] *s* (*pl* **-ties**) homogeneidad
homogeneous [ˌhɑməˈdʒini•əs] *adj* homogéneo
homogenize [həˈmɑdʒəˌnaɪz] *tr* homogeneizar
homonym [ˈhɑmənɪm] *s* homónimo
homonymous [həˈmɑnɪməs] *adj* homónimo
homosexual [ˌhɑməˈsɛkʃʊ•əl] *adj & s* homosexual *mf*
hon. *abbr* honorary
Hon. *abbr* **Honorable**
Honduran [hɑnˈdʊrən] *adj & s* hondureño
hone [hon] *s* piedra de afilar ‖ *tr* afilar, amolar, asentar
honest [ˈɑnɪst] *adj* honrado, probo, recto; *(money)* bien adquirido; sincero; genuino
honesty [ˈɑnɪsti] *s* honradez *f,* probidad, rectitud; (bot) hierba de la plata
hon•ey [ˈhʌni] *adj* meloso, dulce; (coll) querido ‖ *s* miel *f;* (coll) vida mía; **it's a honey** (slang) es una preciosidad ‖ *v* (*pret & pp* **-eyed** o **-ied**) *tr* enmelar, endulzar con miel; adular, lisonjear
hon'ey•bee' *s* abeja doméstica, abeja de miel
hon'ey•comb' *s* panal *m* ‖ *tr* (*to riddle*) acribillar; llenar, penetrar
hon'ey•dew' melon *s* melón muy dulce, blanco y terso
honeyed [ˈhʌnid] *adj* dulce, enmelado; melodioso; adulador
honey locust *s* acacia de tres espinas
hon'ey•moon' *s* luna de miel; viaje *m* de bodas ‖ *intr* pasar la luna de miel
honeysuckle [ˈhʌniˌsʌkəl] *s* madreselva
honk [hɑŋk] *s (of wild goose)* graznido; *(of automobile horn)* bocinazo ‖ *tr* tocar *(la bocina)* ‖ *intr* graznar *(el ganso silvestre);* tocar la bocina
honkytonk [ˈhɑŋkiˌtɑŋk] *s* (slang) sala de fiestas de mala muerte
honor [ˈɑnər] *s (distinction; award for distinction; integrity)* honor *m; (good reputation; chastity)* honor, honra ‖ *tr* honrar; hacer honor a *(su firma);* aceptar y pagar *(una letra)*
honorable [ˈɑnərəbəl] *adj (behaving with honor; performed with honor)* honrado; *(bringing honor; associated with honor)* honroso; *(worthy, of honor)* honorable
honorary [ˈɑnəˌrɛri] *adj* honorario
honorific [ˌɑnəˈrɪfɪk] *adj* honorífico ‖ *s* antenombre *m*
honor system *s* acatamiento voluntario del reglamento
hood [hʊd] *s* capilla; *(one with a point)* caperuza; *(one which covers the face)* capirote *m; (worn with academic gown)* muceta, capirote *m; (of a chimney)* sombrerete *m;* (aut) capó *m,* cubierta; (slang) gamberro ‖ *tr* encapirotar; ocultar
hoodlum [ˈhudləm] *s* (coll) gamberro, maleante *m*

hoodoo [`hudu] s (*body of primitive rites*) vudú m; (coll) mala suerte ‖ tr traer mala suerte a

hood'wink' tr burlar, engañar, vendar

hooey [`hu•i] s (slang) música celestial

hoof [huf] o [huf] s casco, pezuña; **on the hoof** (*cattle*) vivo, en pie ‖ tr & intr (coll) caminar; **to hoof it** (coll) caminar, ir a pie; (coll) bailar

hoof'beat' s pisada, ruido de la pisada (*de animal ungulado*)

hook [huk] s gancho; (*for fishing*) anzuelo; (*to join two things*) enganche m; (*bend, curve*) ángulo, recodo; (box) crochet m, golpe m de gancho; (*of hook and eye*) corchete m, macho; **by hook or by crook** por fas o por nefas; **to swallow the hook;** tragar el anzuelo ‖ tr enganchar; (*to bend*) encorvar, doblar; coger, pescar (*un pez*); (*to wound with the horns*) acornar ‖ intr engancharse; encorvarse, doblarse

hookah [`hukə] s narguile m

hook and eye s broche m, corchete m (*macho y hembra*)

hook and ladder s carro de escaleras de incendio

hooked rug s tapete m de crochet

hook'nose' s nariz f de pico de loro

hook'up' s montaje m

hook'worm' s anquilostoma m

hooky [`huki] s — **to play hooky** hacer novillos

hooligan [`huligən] s gamberro

hooliganism [`huligən,izəm] s gamberrismo

hoop [hup] o [hup] s aro ‖ tr herrar, enarcar, enzunchar

hoop skirt s miriñaque m

hoot [hut] s resoplido, ululato; grito ‖ tr reprobar a gritos; echar a gritos (*p.ej., a un cómico*) ‖ intr resoplar, ulular; **to hoot at** dar grita a

hoot owl s autillo, cárabo

hop [hap] s saltito; (coll) vuelo en avión; (coll) sarao; (coll) baile m; lúpulo, hombrecillo; **hops** (*dried flowers of hop vine*) lúpulo ‖ v (*pret & pp* **hopped;** *ger* **hopping**) tr cruzar de un salto; (coll) atravesar (*p.ej., el mar*) en avión; (coll) subir a (*un tren, taxi, etc.*) ‖ intr saltar, brincar; (*on one foot*) saltar a la pata coja

hope [hop] s esperanza ‖ tr & intr esperar; **to hope for** esperar

hope chest s ajuar m de novia

hopeful [`hopfəl] adj (*feeling hope*) esperanzado; (*giving hope*) esperanzador

hopeless [`hoplis] adj desesperanzado, (*situation*) desesperado

hopper [`hapər] s (*funnel-shaped container*) tolva; (*of blast furnace*) tragante m

hopper car s (rr) vagón m tolva

hop'scotch' s infernáculo

horde [hord] s horda

horehound [`hor,haund] s marrubio; extracto de marrubio

horizon [hə`raizən] s horizonte m

horizontal [,hari`zantəl] o [,hɔri`zantəl] adj & s horizontal f

hormone [`hɔrmon] s hormón m u hormona

horn [hɔrn] s (*bony projection on head of certain animals*) cuerno; (*of bull*) asta, cuerno; (*of moon, anvil, etc.*) cuerno; (*of automobile*) bocina; (mus) cuerno; (*French horn*) (mus) trompa de armonía; **to blow one's own horn** cantar sus propias alabanzas; **to pull in one's horns** contenerse, volverse atrás ‖ intr — **to horn in** (slang) entrometerse (en)

hornet [`hɔrnit] s crabrón m, avispón m

hornet's nest s panal m del avispón; **to stir up a hornet's nest** (coll) armar camorra, armar cisco

horn of plenty s cuerno de la abundancia

horn'pipe' s chirimía

horn-rimmed glasses [`hɔrn`rimd] spl anteojos de concha

horn•y [`hɔrni] adj (*comp* **-ier;** *super* **-iest**) córneo; (*callous*) calloso; (*having hornlike projections*) cornudo

horoscope [`harə,skop] o [`hɔrə,skop] s horóscopo; **to cast a horoscope** sacar un horóscopo

horrible [`haribəl] o [`hɔribəl] adj horrible; (coll) muy desagradable

horrid [`harid] o [`hɔrid] adj horroroso; (coll) muy desagradable

horri•fy [`hari,fai] o [`hɔri,fai] v (*pret & pp* **-fied**) tr horrorizar

horror [`harər] o [`hɔrər] s horror m; **to have a horror of** tener horror a

horror movie s película de terror, película horripilante

hors d'oeuvre [ɔr `dʌrv] s (*pl* **hors d'oeuvres** [ɔr `dʌrvz]) entremés m

horse [hɔrs] s caballo; (*of carpenter*) caballete m; **hold your horses** (coll) pare Vd. el carro; **to back the wrong horse** (coll) jugar a la carta mala; **to be a horse of another color** (coll) ser harina de otro costal

horse'back' s — **on horseback** a caballo ‖ adv — **to ride horseback** montar a caballo

horseback riding s hípica

horse blanket s manta para caballo

horse block s montadero

horse'break'er s domador m de caballos

horse'car' s tranvía m de sangre

horse chestnut s (*tree*) castaño de Indias; (*nut*) castaña de Indias

horse collar s collera

horse dealer s chalán m

horse doctor s veterinario

horse'fly' s (*pl* **-flies**) mosca borriquera, tábano

horse'hair' s crines fpl de caballo; (*fabric*) tela de crin

horse'hide' s cuero de caballo

horse laugh s risotada

horse•man [`hɔrsmən] s (*pl* **-men** [mən]) jinete m, caballista m

horsemanship [`hɔrsmən,ʃip] s equitación, manejo

horse meat s carne f de caballo

horse opera s (U.S.A.) melodrama m del Oeste

ho
ho

horse pistol s pistola de arzón
horse′play′ s chanza pesada, payasada
horse′pow′er s caballo de vapor inglés
horse race s carrera de caballos
horse′rad′ish s (*plant*) rábano picante o rusticano; (*condiment*) mostaza de los alemanes
horse sense s (coll) sentido común
horse′shoe′ s herradura
horseshoe magnet s imán m de herradura
horseshoe nail s clavo de herrar
horse show s concurso hípico
horse′tail′ s cola de caballo
horse thief s abigeo, cuatrero
horse′-trade′ intr chalanear
horse trading s chalanería
horse′-trad′ing adj chalanesco
horse′whip′ s látigo ‖ v (*pret & pp* -whipped; *ger* -whipping) tr dar latigazos a
horse•woman [′hɔrs,wumən] s (*pl* -women [,wImIn]) amazona, caballista f
hors•y [′hɔrsi] adj (*comp* -ier; *super* -iest) caballar, hípico; (*interested in Horses and horse racing*) carrerista, turfista; (coll) desmañado
horticultural [,hɔrtI′kʌltʃərəl] adj hortícola
horticulture [′hɔrtI,kʌltʃər] s horticultura
horticulturist [,hɔrtI′kʌltʃərIst] s horticultor m
hose [hoz] s (*stocking*) media; (*sock*) calcetín m; (*flexible tube*) manguera ‖ **hose** spl calzas
hosier [′hoʒər] s mediero, calcetero
hosiery [′hoʒəri] s calcetas; calcetería
hospice [′hɑspIs] s hospicio
hospitable [′hɑspItəbəl] o [hɑs′pItəbəl] adj hospitalario
hospital [′hɑspItəl] s hospital m
hospitali•ty [,hɑspI′tælIti] s (*pl* -ties) hospitalidad
hospitalize [′hɑspItə,laIz] tr hospitalizar
host [host] s anfitrión m; (*at an inn*) huésped m, mesonero; (*army*) hueste f; multitud, sinnúmero ‖ **Host** s (eccl) hostia
hostage [′hɑstIdʒ] s rehén m; **to be held a hostage** quedar en rehenes
hostage taking s toma de rehenes
hostel•ry [′hɑstəlri] s (*pl* -ries) parador m, hostería
hostess [′hostIs] s anfitriona; dueña, patrona; (*in a night club*) tanguista; (aer) azafata, aeromoza; (*e.g., on a bus*) jefa de ruta
hostile [′hɑstIl] adj hostil
hostili•ty [hɑs′tIlIti] s (*pl* -ties) hostilidad
hostler [′hɑslər] o [′ɑslər] s mozo de cuadra, mozo de paja y cebada
hot [hɑt] adj (*comp* **hotter**; *super* **hottest**) (*water, air, coffee, etc.*) caliente; (*climate, country; taste*) cálido; (*fiery, excitable*) caluroso; (*pursuit*) enérgico; (*in rut*) caliente; (coll) muy radiactivo; **to be hot** (*said of a person*) tener calor; (*said of the weather*) hacer calor; **to make it hot for** (coll) hostilizar
hot air s (slang) palabrería, música celestial
hot′-air′ furnace s calorífero de aire

hot and cold running water s circulación de agua fría y caliente
hot baths spl caldas, termas
hot′bed′ s (hort) almájara; (*e.g., of vice*) sementera, semillero
hot-blooded [′hɑt′blʌdId] adj apasionado; temerario, irreflexivo
hot cake s torta a la plancha; **to sell like hot cakes** (coll) venderse como pan bendito
hot dog s (slang) perro caliente
hotel [ho′tɛl] adj hotelero ‖ s hotel m
ho•tel′-keep′er s hotelero
hot′head′ s botafuego
hot-headed [′hɑt′hɛdId] adj caliente de cascos
hot′house′ s estufa, invernáculo
hot plate s hornillo, calientaplatos m
hot springs spl fuentes fpl termales
hot-tempered [′hɑt′tɛmpərd] adj irascible
hot water s — **to be in hot water** (coll) estar en calzas prietas
hot′-wa′ter boiler s termosifón m
hot-water bottle s bolsa de agua caliente
hot-water heater s calentador m de acumulación
hot-water heating s calefacción por agua caliente
hot-water tank s depósito de agua caliente
hound [haund] s podenco, perro de caza; **to follow the hounds** o **to ride the hounds** cazar a caballo con jauría ‖ tr acosar, hostigar
hour [aur] s hora; **by the hour** por horas; **in an evil hour** en hora mala; **on the hour** a la hora en punto cada hora; **to keep late hours** acostarse tarde; **to work long hours** trabajar muchas horas cada día
hour′glass′ s reloj m de arena
hour hand s horario, horero
hourly [′aurli] adj de cada hora; por hora ‖ adv cada hora; muy a menudo
house [haus] s (*pl* **houses** [′hauzIz]) casa; (*legislative body*) cámara; teatro; (*size of audience*) entrada, p.ej., **a good house** mucha entrada; **to keep house** tener casa puesta; hacer los quehaceres domésticos; **to put one's house in order** arreglar sus asuntos ‖ [hauz] tr domiciliar, alojar, hospedar
house arrest s arresto domiciliario
house′boat′ s barco vivienda
house′break′er s escalador m
housebreaking [′haus,brekIŋ] s escalo, allanamiento de morada
housebroken [′haus,brokən] adj (*perro o gato*) enseñado (*a hábitos de limpieza*)
house cleaning s limpieza de la casa
house coat s bata
house current s sector m de distribución, canalización de consumo
house′fly′ s (*pl* -flies) mosca doméstica
houseful [′haus,ful] s casa llena
house′fur′nishings spl menaje m, enseres domésticos
house′hold′ adj casero, doméstico ‖ s casa, familia

house′hold′er s dueño de la casa; jefe m de familia

house′-hunt′ intr — **to go house-hunting** ir a buscar casa

house′keep′er s ama de llaves, mujer f de gobierno

house′keep′ing s manejo doméstico, gobierno doméstico; **to set up housekeeping** poner casa

housekeeping apartment s apartamento con cocina

house′maid′ s criada de casa

house meter s contador m de abonado

house′moth′er s mujer encargada de una residencia de estudiantes

house of cards s castillo de naipes

house of ill fame s lupanar m, casa de prostitución

house painter s pintor m de brocha gorda

house physician s médico residente

house′top′ s tejado; **to shout from the housetops** pregonar a los cuatro vientos

housewarming [′haʊs,wɔrmɪŋ] s fiesta para celebrar el estreno de una casa; **to have a housewarming** estrenar la casa

house′wife′ s (pl **-wives**) ama de casa, madre f de familia

house′work′ s quehaceres domésticos

housing [′haʊzɪŋ] s (of a horse) gualdrapa; (aut) cárter m; (mach) caja, bastidor m

housing shortage s crisis f de viviendas

hovel [′hʌvəl] s casucha, choza; (shed for cattle, tools, etc.) cobertizo

hover [′hʌvər] intr cernerse (un ave); (to hesitate; to be in danger) fluctuar; asomar (p.ej., una sonrisa en los labios de uno)

how [haʊ] adv cómo; (at what price) a cómo; **how early** cuándo, a qué hora; **how else** de qué otra manera; **how far** hasta dónde; cuánto, p.ej., **how far is it to the airport?** ¿cuánto hay de aquí al aeropuerto?; **how long** cuánto tiempo; **how many** cuántos; **how much** cuánto; **how the** que; **how often** cuántas veces; **how old are you?** ¿cuántas años tiene Vd.?; **how soon** cuándo, a qué hora; **how + adj** qué + adj, p.ej., **how beautiful she is!** ¡qué hermosa es!; lo + adj, p.ej., **you know how intelligent he is** Vd. sabe lo inteligente que es; **to know how to + inf** saber + inf

howdah [′haʊdə] s castillo

how•ev′er adv no obstante, sin embargo; por muy . . . que, por mucho . . . que

howitzer [′haʊɪtsər] s cañón m obús

howl [haʊl] s aullido; chillido; risa muy aguda; (of wind) bramido ‖ tr decir a gritos; **to howl down** imponerse a gritos a (una persona) ‖ intr aullar; chillar; reír a más no poder; bramar (el viento)

howler [′haʊlər] s aullador m; (coll) plancha, desacierto

hoyden [′hɔɪdən] s muchacha traviesa, tunantuela

H.P. abbr **horsepower**

hr. abbr **hour**

H.R.H. abbr **Her** (o **His**) **Royal Highness**

ht. abbr **height**

hub [hʌb] s cubo; (fig) centro, eje m

hubbub [′hʌbəb] s gritería, alboroto

hub′cap′ s tapacubo, embellecedor m

huck′ster [′hʌkstər] s (peddler) buhonero; vendedor m ambulante de hortalizas; vil traficante m, sujeto ruin

huddle [′hʌdəl] s (coll) reunión secreta; **to go into a huddle** (coll) conferenciar en secreto ‖ intr acurrucarse, arrimarse

hue [hju] s matiz m; gritería; **hue and cry** vocería de indignación

huff [hʌf] s arrebato de cólera; **in a huff** encolerizado, ofendido

hug [hʌg] s abrazo ‖ v (pret & pp **hugged**; ger **hugging**) tr abrazar; apretar con los brazos; ahogar entre los •brazos; navegar muy cerca de (la costa); ceñirse a (p.ej., un muro) ‖ intr abrazarse

huge [hjudʒ] adj enorme, descomunal

huh [hʌ] interj ¡eh!

hulk [hʌlk] s (body of an old ship) casco; (clumsy old ship) carcamán m, carraca; (old ship tied up at a wharf and used as a warehouse, prison, etc.) pontón m; (shell of an old building, piece of furniture, machine, etc.; heavy, unwieldy person) armatoste m

hulking [′hʌlkɪŋ] adj grueso, pesado

hull [hʌl] s (of ship or hydroplane) casco; (of a dirigible) armazón f; (of certain vegetables) hollejo, vaina ‖ tr deshollejar, desvainar; mondar, pelar

hullabaloo [′hʌləbə,lu] o [,hʌləbə′lu] s alboroto, gritería, tumulto

hum [hʌm] s canturreo, tararareo; (of a bee, machine, etc.) zumbido ‖ interj ¡ejem! ‖ v (pret & pp **hummed**; ger **humming**) tr canturrear, tararear ‖ intr canturrear, tararear; (to buzz) zumbar; (coll) estar muy activo

human [′hjumən] adj humano (perteneciente al hombre)

human being s ser humano

humane [hju′men] adj humano (compasivo)

humanist [′hjumənɪst] adj & s humanista mf

humanitarian [hju,mænɪ′tɛrɪ•ən] adj & s humanitario

humani•ty [hju′mænɪti] s (pl **-ties**) humanidad

hu′man•kind′ s género humano

humble [′hʌmbəl] adj humilde ‖ tr humillar

humble pie s — **to eat humble pie** cantar la palinodia

hum′bug′ s patraña; (person) patrañero ‖ v (pret & pp **-bugged**; ger **-bugging**) tr embaucar, engañar

hum′drum′ adj monótono, tedioso

humer•us [′hjumərəs] s (pl **-i** [,aɪ]) húmero

humid [′hjumɪd] adj húmedo

humidifier [hju′mɪdɪ,faɪ•ər] s humectador m

humidi•fy [hju′mɪdɪ,faɪ] v (pret & pp **-fied**) tr humedecer

humidity [hju′mɪdɪti] s humedad

humiliate [hju′mɪlɪ,et] tr humillar

humiliating [hju′mɪlɪ,etɪŋ] adj humillante

humili•ty [hju′mɪlɪti] s (pl **-ties**) humildad

ho
hu

hummingbird [ˈhʌmɪŋˌbʌrd] s colibrí m, pájaro mosca

humongous [hjuˈmʌŋəs] adj (coll) descomunal

humor [ˈhjumər] o [ˈjumər] s humor m; **out of humor** de mal humor; **to be in the humor for** estar de humor para || tr seguir el humor a; manejar con delicadeza

humorist [ˈhjumərɪst] s humorista mf

humorous [ˈhjumərəs] adj humorístico

hump [hʌmp] s corcova, joroba; (in the ground) montecillo

hump′back′ s corcova, joroba; (person) corcovado, jorobado

humus [ˈhjuməs] s mantillo

hunch [hʌntʃ] s corcova, joroba; (premonition) (coll) corazonada || tr encorvar || intr encorvarse

hunch′back′ s corcova, joroba; (person) corcovado, jorobado

hundred [ˈhʌndrəd] adj cien || s ciento, cien; **a hundred** u **one hundred** ciento; cien; **by the hundreds** a centenares

hundredth [ˈhʌndredθ] adj & s centésimo

hun′dred•weight′ s quintal m

Hundred Years' War s guerra de los Cien Años

Hungarian [hʌŋˈgɛrɪ•ən] adj & s húngaro

Hungary [ˈhʌŋgəri] s Hungría

hunger [ˈhʌŋgər] s hambre f || intr hambrear; **to hunger for** tener hambre de

hunger march s marcha del hambre

hunger strike s huelga de hambre

hun•gry [ˈhʌŋgri] adj (comp **-grier**; super **-griest**) hambriento; **to be hungry** tener hambre; galguear (Arg, CAm, Mex); **to go hungry** pasar hambre

hunk [hʌŋk] s (coll) buen pedazo, pedazo grande

hunt [hʌnt] s (act of hunting) caza; (hunting party) cacería; (a search) busca; **on the hunt for** a caza de || tr cazar; (to seek, look for) buscar || intr cazar; buscar; **to go hunting** ir de caza; **to hunt for** buscar; **to take hunting** llevar de caza

hunter [ˈhʌntər] s cazador m; perro de caza

hunting [ˈhʌntɪŋ] adj de caza || s (act) caza; (art) cacería, montería

hunting dog s perro de caza

hunting ground s cazadero

hunt′ing•horn′ s cuerno de caza

hunting jacket s cazadora

hunting lodge s casa de montería

hunting season s época de caza

huntress [ˈhʌntrɪs] s cazadora

hunts•man [ˈhʌntsmən] s (pl **-men** [mən]) cazador m, montero

hurdle [ˈhʌrdəl] s (hedge over which horses must jump) zarzo; (wooden frame over which runners and horses must jump) valla; (fig) obstáculo; **hurdles** carrera de vallas || tr saltar por encima de

hurdle race s carrera de vallas

hurdy-gur•dy [ˈhʌrdiˌgʌrdi] s (pl **-dies**) organillo

hurl [hʌrl] s lanzamiento || tr lanzar

hurrah [huˈrɑ] o **hurray** [huˈre] s viva m || interj ¡viva!; **hurrah for. . . !** ¡viva. . . ! || tr aplaudir, vitorear || intr dar vivas

hurricane [ˈhʌrɪˌken] s huracán m

hurried [ˈhʌrid] adj apresurado; hecho de prisa

hur•ry [ˈhʌri] s (pl **-ries**) prisa; **to be in a hurry** tener prisa, estar de prisa || v (pret & pp **-ried**) tr apresurar, dar prisa a || intr apresurarse, darse prisa; **to hurry after** correr en pos de; **to hurry away** marcharse de prisa; **to hurry back** volver de prisa; **to hurry up** darse prisa

hurt [hʌrt] adj (injured) lastimado, herido; (offended) resentido, herido || s (harm) daño; (injury) herida; (pain) dolor m || v (pret & pp **hurt**) tr (to harm) dañar, perjudicar; (to injure) lastimar, herir; (to offend) ofender, herir; (to pain) doler || intr doler

hurtle [ˈhʌrtəl] intr lanzarse con violencia, pasar con gran estruendo

husband [ˈhʌzbənd] s marido, esposo || tr manejar con economía

husband•man [ˈhʌzbəndmən] s (pl **-men** [mən]) agricultor m, granjero

husbandry [ˈhʌzbəndri] s agricultura, labranza; buena dirección, buen gobierno (de la hacienda de uno)

hush [hʌʃ] s silencio || interj ¡chito! || tr callar; **to hush up** echar tierra a (un escándalo) || intr callarse

hushaby [ˈhʌʃəˌbaɪ] interj ¡ro ro!

hush′-hush′ adj muy secreto

hush money s precio del silencio

husk [hʌsk] s cáscara, hollejo, vaina; (of corn) perfolla || tr descascarar, deshollejar, desvainar; espinochar (el maíz)

husk•y [ˈhʌski] adj (comp **-ier**; super **-iest**) fortachón, fornido; (voice) ronco

hus•sy [ˈhʌzi] o [ˈhʌsi] s (pl **-sies**) buena pieza, moza descarada; mujer desvergonzada

hustle [ˈhʌsəl] s (coll) energía, vigor m || tr apresurar; echar a empellones || intr apresurarse; (coll) menearse, trabajar con gran ahinco

hustler [ˈhʌslər] s trafagón m, buscavidas mf

hut [hʌt] s casucha, choza

hyacinth [ˈhaɪ•əsɪnθ] s jacinto

hybrid [ˈhaɪbrɪd] adj & s híbrido

hybridization [ˌhaɪbrɪdɪˈzefən] s hibridación

hybridize [ˈhaɪbrɪˌdaɪz] tr & intr hibridar

hy•dra [ˈhaɪdrə] s (pl **-dras** o **-drae** [dri]) hidra

hydrant [ˈhaɪdrənt] s boca de agua, boca de riego; (water faucet) grifo

hydrate [ˈhaɪdret] s hidrato || tr hidratar || intr hidratarse

hydraulic [haɪˈdrɔlɪk] adj hidráulico || **hydraulics** s hidráulica

hydraulic ram s ariete hidráulico

hydriodic [ˌhaɪdrɪˈɑdɪk] adj yodhídrico

hydrobromic [ˌhaɪdrəˈbromɪk] adj bromhídrico

hydrocarbon [ˌhaɪdrəˈkɑrbən] s hidrocarburo

hydrochloric [ˌhaɪdrəˈklorɪk] adj clorhídrico

hydroelectric [,haɪdro•ɪˈlɛktrɪk] *adj* hidroeléctrico

hydrofluoric [,haɪdrəfluˈɔrɪk] *adj* fluorhídrico

hydrofoil [ˈhaɪdrə,fɔɪl] *s* superficie hidrodinámica; (*wing designed to lift vessel*) hidroaleta; (*vessel*) hidroala *m*

hydrogen [ˈhaɪdrədʒən] *s* hidrógeno

hydrogen bomb *s* bomba de hidrógeno

hydrogen peroxide *s* peróxido de hidrógeno

hydrogen sulfide *s* sulfuro de hidrógeno

hydrometer [haɪˈdrɑmɪtər] *s* areómetro

hydrophobia [,haɪdrəˈfobɪ•ə] *s* hidrofobia

hydroplane [ˈhaɪdrə,plen] *s* hidroavión *m*

hydroxide [haɪˈdrɑksaɪd] *s* hidróxido

hyena [haɪˈinə] *s* hiena

hygiene [ˈhaɪdʒin] *s* higiene *f*

hygienic [,haɪdʒɪˈɛnɪk] *adj* higiénico

hymn [hɪm] *s* himno

hymnal [ˈhɪmnəl] *s* himnario

hyp. *abbr* **hypotenuse, hypothesis**

hyperacidity [,haɪpərəˈsɪdɪti] *s* hiperacidez *f*

hyperbola [haɪˈpʌrbələ] *s* (geom) hipérbola

hyperbole [haɪˈpʌrbəli] *s* (rhet) hipérbole *f*

hyperbolic [,haɪpərˈbɑlɪk] *adj* (geom & rhet) hiperbólico

hypersensitive [,haɪpərˈsɛnsɪtɪv] *adj* extremadamente sensible; (*allergic*) hipersensible

hypertension [,haɪpərˈtɛnʃən] *s* hipertensión

hyphen [ˈhaɪfən] *s* guión *m*

hyphenate [ˈhaɪfə,net] *tr* unir con guión; escribir con guión

hypno•sis [hɪpˈnosɪs] *s* (*pl* -**ses** [siz]) hipnosis *f*

hypnotic [hɪpˈnɑtɪk] *adj* hipnótico ‖ *s* (*person; sedative*) hipnótico

hypnotism [ˈhɪpnə,tizəm] *s* hipnotismo

hypnotist [ˈhɪpnətɪst] *s* hipnotista *mf*

hypnotize [ˈhɪpnə,taɪz] *tr* hipnotizar

hypochondriac [,haɪpəˈkɑndrɪ,æk] *s* hipocondríaco

hypocri•sy [hɪˈpɑkrəsi] *s* (*pl* -**sies**) hipocresía

hypocrite [ˈhɪpəkrɪt] *s* hipócrita *mf*

hypocritical [,hɪpəˈkrɪtɪkəl] *adj* hipócrita

hypodermic [,haɪpəˈdʌrmɪk] *adj* hipodérmico

hyposulfite [,haɪpəˈsʌlfaɪt] *m* hiposulfito

hypotenuse [haɪˈpɑtɪ,nus] *s* hipotenusa

hypothe•sis [haɪˈpɑθɪsɪs] *s* (*pl* -**ses** [,siz] hipótesis *f*

hypothetic(al) [,haɪpəˈθɛtɪk(əl)] *adj* hipotético

hyssop [ˈhɪsəp] *s* (bot) hisopo

hysteria [hɪsˈtɪrɪ•ə] *s* histerismo, histeria

hysteric [hɪsˈtɛrɪk] *adj* histérico ‖ **hysterics** *s* paroxismo histérico

hysterical [hɪsˈtɛrɪkəl] *adj* histérico

hu
ic

I

I, i [aɪ] novena letre del alfabeto inglés

I. *abbr* **Island**

I [aɪ] *pron pers* (*pl* **we** [wi]) yo; **it is I** soy yo

iambic [aɪˈæmbɪk] *adj* yámbico

iam•bus [aɪˈæmbəs] *s* (*pl* -**bi** [bar]) yambo

ib. *abbr* **ibidem**

Iberian [aɪbˈɪrɪ•ən] *adj* ibérico ‖ *s* ibero

ibex [ˈaɪbɛks] *s* (*pl* **ibexes** o **ibices** [ˈɪbɪ,siz]) íbice *m*, cabra montés

ibid. *abbr* **ibidem**

ice [aɪs] *s* hielo; **to break the ice** (*to overcome reserve*) romper el hielo; **to cut no ice** (coll) no importar nada; **to skate on thin ice** (coll) buscar el peligro ‖ *tr* helar; enfriar con hielo; (*to cover with icing*) garapiñar ‖ *intr* helarse

ice age *s* época glacial

ice bag *s* bolsa para hielo

iceberg [ˈaɪs,bʌrg] *s* banquisa, iceberg *m*

ice'boat' *s* cortahielos *m*, rompehielos *m*; trineo con vela para deslizarse sobre el hielo

ice'bound' *adj* rodeado de hielo; detenido por el hielo

ice'box' *s* nevera, fresquera

ice'break'er *s* cortahielos *m*, rompehielos *m*

ice'cap' *s* bolsa para hielo; manto de hielo

ice cream *s* helado

ice'-cream' cone *s* cucurucho de helado, barquillo de helado

ice-cream freezer *s* heladora, garapiñera

ice-cream parlor *s* salón *m* de refrescos, tienda de helados

ice-cream soda *s* agua gaseosa con helado

ice cube *s* cubito de hielo

ice hockey *s* hockey *m* sobre patines

Iceland [ˈaɪslənd] *s* Islandia

Icelander [ˈaɪs,lændər] *s* islandés *m*

Icelandic [aɪsˈlændɪk] *adj* islandés ‖ *s* islandés *m* (*idioma*)

ice•man [ˈaɪs,mæn] *s* (*pl* -**men** [,mɛn]) vendedor *m* de hielo, repartidor *m* de hielo

ice pack *s* hielo flotante; bolsa de hielo

ice pail *s* enfriadera

ice pick *s* picahielos *m*

ice skate *s* patín *m* de cuchilla, patín de hielo

ice skating *s* patinaje *m* sobre hielo

ice tray *s* bandejita de hielo

ice water *s* agua helada

ichthyology [,ɪkθɪˈalədʒi] *s* ictiología

icicle [ˈaɪsɪkəl] *s* carámbano

icing [ˈaɪsɪŋ] *s* garapiña, capa de azúcar; (aer) formación de hielo

iconoclasm [aɪˈkanə,klæzəm] *s* iconoclasia, iconoclasmo

iconoclast [aɪˈkanə,klæst] *s* iconoclasta *mf*

icy [`aɪsi] adj (comp **icier**; super **iciest**) cubierto de hielo; (slippery) resbaladizo; (fig) frío

id. abbr **idem**

id [ɪd] s (psychoanalysis) ello

I.D. abbr **identity card**

idea [aɪ`di·ə] s idea

ideal [aɪ`di·əl] adj & s ideal m

idealist [aɪ`di·əlɪst] adj & s idealista mf

idealize [aɪ`di·ə,laɪz] tr idealizar

identic(al) [aɪ`dɛntɪk(əl)] adj idéntico

identification [aɪ,dɛntɪfɪ`keʃən] s identificación

identification tag s disco de identificación

identify [aɪ`dɛntɪ,faɪ] v (pret & pp **-fied**) tr identificar ǁ intr — **to identify with** solidarizar con

identi·ty [aɪ`dɛntɪti] s (pl **-ties**) identidad

identity card s carta de identificación

ideolo·gy [,aɪdɪ`ɑlədʒi] o [,ɪdɪ`ɑlədʒi] s (pl **-gies**) ideología

ides [aɪdz] spl idus mpl

idio·cy [`ɪdɪ·əsi] s (pl **-cies**) idiotez f

idiom [`ɪdɪ·əm] s (expression that is contrary to the usual patterns of the language) modismo; (style of language) idioma m, lenguaje m; (style of an author) estilo; (character of a language) índole f

idiomatic [,ɪdɪ·ə`mætɪk] adj idiomático

idiosyncra·sy [,ɪdɪ·ə`sɪnkrəsi] s (pl **-sies**) idiosincrasia

idiot [`ɪdɪ·ət] s idiota mf

idiotic [,ɪdɪ·`ɑtɪk] adj idiota

idle [`aɪdəl] adj desocupado, ocioso; **at idle moments** a ratos perdidos; **to run idle** marchar en ralentí ǁ tr — **to idle away** gastar ociosamente (el tiempo) ǁ intr estar ocioso, holgar; marchar (un motor) en ralentí

idleness [`aɪdəlnɪs] s desocupación, ociosidad

idler [`aɪdlər] s haragán m, ocioso

idol [`aɪdəl] s ídolo

idola·try [aɪ`dɑlətri] s (pl **-tries**) idolatría

idolize [`aɪdə,laɪz] tr idolatrar

idyll [`aɪdəl] s idilio

idyllic [aɪ`dɪlɪk] adj idílico

if [ɪf] conj si; **as if** como si; **even if** aunque; **if so** si es así; **if true** si es cierto

ignis fatuus [`ɪgnɪs`fætʃu·əs] s (pl **ignes fatui** [`ɪgniz`fætʃu,aɪ]) fuego fatuo

ignite [ɪg`naɪt] tr encender ǁ intr encenderse

ignition [ɪg`nɪʃən] s inflamación; (aut) encendido

ignition switch s (aut) interruptor m de encendido

ignoble [ɪg`nobəl] adj innoble

ignominious [,ɪgnə`mɪnɪ·əs] adj ignominioso

ignoramus [,ɪgnə`reməs] s ignorante mf

ignorance [`ɪgnərəns] s ignorancia

ignorant [`ɪgnərənt] adj ignorante

ignore [ɪg`nor] tr no hacer caso de, pasar por alto

ilk [ɪlk] s especie f, jaez m

ill. abbr **illustrated, illustration**

ill [ɪl] adj (comp **worse** [wʌrs]; super **worst** [wʌrst]) enfermo, malo ǁ adv mal; **to take ill** tomar a mal; caer enfermo

ill-advised [`ɪləd`vaɪzd] adj desaconsejado, malaconsejado, desavisado

ill at ease adj inquieto, incómodo

ill-bred [`ɪl`brɛd] adj malcriado

ill-considered [`ɪlkən`sɪdərd] adj desconsiderado, mal considerado

ill-disposed [`ɪldɪs`pozd] adj malintencionado, maldispuesto

illegal [ɪ`ligəl] adj ilegal

illegible [ɪ`lɛdʒɪbəl] adj ilegible

illegitimate [,ɪlɪ`dʒɪtɪmɪt] adj ilegítimo

ill fame s mala fama, reputación de inmoral

ill-fated [`ɪl`fetɪd] adj aciago, funesto

ill-gotten [`ɪl`gɑtən] adj mal ganado

ill health s mala salud

ill-humored [`ɪl`hjumərd] adj malhumorado

illicit [ɪ`lɪsɪt] adj ilícito

illitera·cy [ɪ`lɪtərəsi] s (pl **-cies**) ignorancia; analfabetismo

illiterate [ɪ`lɪtərɪt] adj (uneducated) iliterato; (unable to read or write) analfabeto ǁ s analfabeto

ill-mannered [`ɪl`mænərd] adj de malos modales

illness [`ɪlnɪs] s enfermedad

illogical [ɪ`lɑdʒɪkəl] adj ilógico

ill-spent [`ɪl`spɛnt] adj malgastado

ill-starred [`ɪl`stɑrd] adj malhadado

ill-tempered [`ɪl`tɛmpərd] adj de mal genio

ill-timed [`ɪl`taɪmd] adj inoportuno, intempestivo

ill'-treat' tr maltratar

illuminate [ɪ`lumɪ,net] tr alumbrar, iluminar; miniar (un manuscrito)

illuminating gas s gas m de alumbrado

illumination [ɪ,lumɪ`neʃən] s iluminación

illusion [ɪ`luʒən] s ilusión

illusive [ɪ`lusɪv] adj ilusivo

illusory [ɪ`lusəri] adj ilusorio

illustrate [`ɪləs,tret] o [ɪ`lʌstret] tr ilustrar

illustration [,ɪləs`treʃən] s ilustración

illustrious [ɪ`lʌstrɪ·əs] adj ilustre

ill will s mala voluntad

image [`ɪmɪdʒ] s imagen f; **the very image of** la propia estampa de

image·ry [`ɪmɪdʒri] s (pl **-ries**) (formation of mental images; product of the imagination) fantasía; (images collectively) imágenes fpl

imaginary [ɪ`mædʒɪ,nɛri] adj imaginario

imagination [ɪ,mædʒɪ`neʃən] s imaginación

imagine [ɪ`mædʒɪn] tr & intr imaginar; (to conjecture) imaginarse

imbecile [`ɪmbɪsɪl] adj & s imbécil mf

imbecili·ty [,ɪmbɪ`sɪlɪti] s (pl **-ties**) imbecilidad

imbibe [ɪm`baɪb] tr (to drink) beber; (to absorb) embeber; (to become absorbed in) embeberse de o en ǁ intr beber, empinar el codo

imbue [ɪm`bju] tr imbuir

imitate [`ɪmɪ,tet] tr imitar

imitation [,ɪmɪ`teʃən] adj (e.g., jewelry) imitado, imitación, de imitación ǁ s imitación; **in imitation of** a imitación de

immaculate [ɪ'mækjəlɪt] *adj* inmaculado
immaterial [,ɪmə'tɪrɪ•əl] *adj* inmaterial; poco importante
immature [,ɪmə'tjʊr] *adj* inmaturo
immeasurable [ɪ'mɛʒərəbəl] *adj* inmensurable
immediacy [ɪ'midɪ•əsi] *s* inmediación
immediate [ɪ'midɪ•ɪt] *adj* inmediato
immediately [ɪ'midɪ•ɪtli] *adv* inmediatamente, en seguida
immemorial [,ɪmɪ'morɪ•əl] *adj* inmemorial
immense [ɪ'mɛns] *adj* inmenso; (coll) excelente
immerge [ɪ'mʌrdʒ] *intr* sumergirse
immerse [ɪ'mʌrs] *tr* sumergir, inmergir
immersion [ɪ'mʌrʃən] o [ɪ'mʌrʒən] *s* sumersión, inmersión
immigrant ['ɪmɪgrənt] *adj & s* inmigrante *mf*
immigrate ['ɪmɪ,gret] *intr* inmigrar
immigration [,ɪmɪ'greʃən] *s* inmigración
imminent ['ɪmɪnənt] *adj* inminente
immobile [ɪ'mobɪl] *adj* inmoble, inmóvil
immobilize [ɪ'mobɪ,laɪz] *tr* inmovilizar
immoderate [ɪ'madərɪt] *adj* inmoderado
immodest [ɪ'madɪst] *adj* inmodesto
immoral [ɪ'mɔrəl] *adj* inmoral
immortal [ɪ'mɔrtəl] *adj & s* inmortal *mf*
immortalize [ɪ'mɔrtə,laɪz] *tr* inmortalizar
immune [ɪ'mjun] *adj* inmune
immunize ['ɪmjə,naɪz] *tr* inmunizar
imp [ɪmp] *s* diablillo; (child) niño travieso
impact ['ɪmpækt] *s* impacto
impair [ɪm'pɛr] *tr* empeorar, deteriorar
impan•el [ɪm'pænəl] *v* (*pret & pp* **-eled** o **-elled**; *ger* **-eling** o **-elling**) *tr* inscribir en la lista de los jurados; elegir (*un jurado*)
impart [ɪm'part] *tr* (*to make known*) dar a conocer, hacer saber; (*to transmit, communicate*) imprimir
impartial [ɪm'parʃəl] *adj* imparcial
impassable [ɪm'pæsəbəl] *adj* intransitable, impracticable
impasse [ɪm'pæs] o ['ɪmpæs] *s* callejón *m* sin salida
impassible [ɪm'pæsɪbəl] *adj* impasible
impassioned [ɪm'pæʃənd] *adj* ardiente, vehemente
impassive [ɪm'pæsɪv] *adj* impasible
impatience [ɪm'peʃəns] *s* impaciencia
impatient [ɪm'peʃənt] *adj* impaciente
impeach [ɪm'pitʃ] *tr* residenciar
impeachment [ɪm'pitʃmənt] *s* residencia
impeccable [ɪm'pɛkəbəl] *adj* impecable
impecunious [,ɪmpɪ'kjunɪ•əs] *adj* inope
impedance [ɪm'pidəns] *s* impedancia
impede [ɪm'pid] *tr* estorbar, dificultar
impediment [ɪm'pɛdɪmənt] *s* impedimento; (*e.g., in speech*) defecto
im•pel [ɪm'pɛl] *v* (*pret & pp* **-pelled**; *ger*-**pelling**) *tr* impeler, impulsar
impending [ɪm'pɛndɪŋ] *adj* inminente
impenetrable [ɪm'pɛnətrəbəl] *adj* impenetrable
impenitent [ɪm'pɛnɪtənt] *adj & s* impenitente *mf*

imperative [ɪm'pɛrɪtɪv] *adj* (*commanding*) imperativo; (*urgent, absolutely necessary*) imperioso ‖ *s* imperativo
imperceptible [,ɪmpər'sɛptɪbəl] *adj* imperceptible, inapreciable
imperfect [ɪm'pʌrfɪkt] *adj & s* imperfecto
imperfection [,ɪmpər'fɛkʃən] *s* imperfección
imperial [ɪm'pɪrɪ•əl] *adj* imperial; majestuoso ‖ *s* (*goatee*) perilla; (*top of coach*) imperial *f*
imperialist [ɪm'pɪrɪ•əlɪst] *adj & s* imperialista *mf*
imper•il [ɪm'pɛrɪl] *v* (*pret & pp* **-iled** o **-illed**; *ger* **-iling** o **-illing**) *tr* poner en peligro
imperious [ɪm'pɪrɪ•əs] *adj* imperioso
imperishable [ɪm'pɛrɪʃəbəl] *adj* imperecedero
impersonal [ɪm'pʌrsənəl] *adj* impersonal
impersonate [ɪm'pʌrsə,net] *tr* personificar; hacer el papel de
impertinence [ɪm'pʌrtɪnəns] *s* impertinencia
impertinent [ɪm'pʌrtɪnənt] *adj & s* impertinente *mf*
impetuous [ɪm'pɛtʃʊ•əs] *adj* impetuoso
impetus ['ɪmpɪtəs] *s* ímpetu *m*
impie•ty [ɪm'paɪ•əti] *s* (*pl* **-ties**) impiedad
impinge [ɪm'pɪndʒ] *intr* — **to impinge on** o **upon** incidir eno sobre, herir; infringir, violar
impious ['ɪmpɪ•əs] *adj* impío
impish ['ɪmpɪʃ] *adj* endiablado, travieso
implant [ɪm'plænt] *tr* implantar
implement ['ɪmplɪmənt] *s* instrumento, utensilio, herramienta; **implements** implementos *mpl* ‖ ['ɪmplɪ,mɛnt] *tr* poner por obra, llevar a cabo; (*to provide with implements*) pertrechar
implicate ['ɪmplɪ,ket] *tr* implicar, comprometer, enredar
implicit [ɪm'plɪsɪt] *adj* implícito; (*unquestioning*) absoluto, ciego
implied [ɪm'plaɪd] *adj* implícito, sobrentendido
implore [ɪm'plor] *tr* implorar, suplicar
im•ply [ɪm'plaɪ] *v* (*pret & pp* **-plied**) *tr* dar a entender; implicar, incluir en esencia
impolite [,ɪmpə'laɪt] *s* descortés; desacomodido (SAm)
import ['ɪmport] *s* importación; artículo importado; importancia, significación ‖ *tr* importar; significar ‖ *intr* importar
importance [ɪm'portəns] *s* importancia
important [ɪm'portənt] *adj* importante
importation [,ɪmpor'teʃən] *s* importación
importer [ɪm'portər] *s* importador *m*
importunate [ɪm'portʃənɪt] *adj* importuno
importune [,ɪmpor'tjun] *tr* importunar
impose [ɪm'poz] *tr* imponer ‖ *intr* — **to impose on** o **upon** abusar de
imposing [ɪm'pozɪŋ] *adj* imponente
imposition [,ɪmpə'zɪʃən] *s* (*of someone's will*) imposición; abuso, engaño
impossible [ɪm'pasɪbəl] *adj* imposible
impostor [ɪm'pastər] *s* impostor *m*; embaucador *m*
imposture [ɪm'pastʃər] *s* impostura
impotence ['ɪmpətəns] *s* impotencia

ic
im

impotent [ˈɪmpətənt] *adj* impotente
impound [ɪmˈpaʊnd] *tr* acorralar, encerrar; rebalsar (*agua*); (law) embargar, secuestrar
impoverish [ɪmˈpavərɪʃ] *tr* empobrecer
impracticable [ɪmˈpræktɪkəbəl] *adj* impracticable; (*intractable*) intratable
impractical [ɪmˈpræktkəl] *adj* impracticable; soñador, utópico
impregnable [ɪmˈprɛgnəbəl] *adj* inexpugnable
impregnate [ɪmˈprɛgnet] *tr* (*to make pregnant*) empreñar; (*to soak*) empapar; (*to fill the interstices of*) impregnar; (*to infuse, infect*) imbuir
impresari•o [ˌɪmprɪˈsɑrɪˌo] *s* (*pl* **-os**) empresario, empresario de teatro
impress [ɪmˈprɛs] *tr* (*to have an effect on the mind or emotions of*) impresionar; (*to mark by using pressure*) imprimir; (*on the memory*) grabar; (mil) enganchar
impression [ɪmˈprɛʃən] *s* impresión
impressionable [ɪmˈprɛʃənəbəl] *adj* impresionable
impressive [ɪmˈprɛsɪv] *adj* impresionante
imprint [ˈɪmprɪnt] *s* impresión; (typ) pie *m* de imprenta ‖ [ɪmˈprɪnt] *tr* imprimir
imprison [ɪmˈprɪzən] *tr* encarcelar
imprisonment [ɪmˈprɪzənmənt] *s* encarcelamiento; pena privativa de libertad
improbable [ɪmˈprɑbəbəl] *adj* improbable
impromptu [ɪmˈprɑmptju] o [ɪmˈprɑmptu] *adj* improvisado ‖ *adv* de improviso ‖ *s* improvisación; (mus) impromptu *m*
improper [ɪmˈprɑpər] *adj* impropio; (*contrary to good taste or decency*) indecoroso
improve [ɪmˈpruv] *tr* perfeccionar, mejorar; aprovechar (*la oportunidad*) ‖ *intr* perfeccionarse, mejorar; **to improve on** o **upon** mejorar
improvement [ɪmˈpruvmənt] *s* perfeccionamiento, mejoramiento; (*e.g., in health*) mejoría; (*useful employment, e.g., of time*) aprovechamiento
improvident [ɪmˈprɑvɪdənt] *adj* imprevisor
improvise [ˈɪmprəˌvaɪz] *tr & intr* improvisar
imprudent [ɪmˈprudənt] *adj* imprudente
impudence [ˈɪmpjədəns] *s* insolencia, descaro, impertinencia
impudent [ˈɪmpjədənt] *adj* insolente, descarado, impertinente
impugn [ɪmˈpjun] *tr* poner en tela de juicio
impulse [ˈɪmpʌls] *s* impulso
impulsive [ɪmˈpʌlsɪv] *adj* impulsivo
impunity [ɪmˈpjunɪti] *s* impunidad
impure [ɪmˈpjʊr] *adj* impuro
impuri•ty [ɪmˈpjʊrɪti] *s* (*pl* **-ties**) impureza, impuridad
impute [ɪmˈpjut] *tr* imputar
in [ɪn] *adj* interior ‖ *adv* dentro; en casa, en la oficina; **in here** aquí dentro; **in there** allí dentro; **to be in** estar en casa; **to be in for** estar expuesto a; **to be in with** gozar del favor de ‖ *prep* en; (*within*) dentro de; (*over, through*) por; (*a period of the day*) en o por; **dressed in . . .** vestido de . . . ; **in so far as** en tanto que; **in that** en que,

por cuanto ‖ *s* — **ins and outs** recovecos, pormenores minuciosos
inability [ˌɪnəˈbɪlɪti] *s* inhabilidad, incapacidad
inaccessible [ˌɪnækˈsɛsɪbəl] *adj* inaccesible
inaccura•cy [ɪnˈækjərəsi] *s* (*pl* **-cies**) inexactitud, incorrección
inaccurate [ɪnˈækjərɪt] *adj* inexacto, incorrecto
inaction [ɪnˈækʃən] *s* inacción
inactive [ɪnˈæktɪv] *adj* inactivo
inactivity [ˌɪnækˈtɪvɪti] *s* inactividad
inadequate [ɪnˈædɪkwɪt] *adj* insuficiente, inadecuado
inadvertent [ˌɪnədˈvʌrtənt] *adj* inadvertido
inadvisable [ˌɪnədˈvaɪzəbəl] *adj* poco aconsejable, imprudente
inane [ɪnˈen] *adj* inane
inanimate [ɪnˈænɪmɪt] *adj* inanimado
inappreciable [ˌɪnəˈpriʃɪˌəbəl] *adj* inapreciable
inappropriate [ˌɪnəˈproprɪˌɪt] *adj* no apropiado, no a propósito
inarticulate [ˌɪnɑrˈtɪkjəlɪt] *adj* (*sounds, words*) inarticulado; (*person*) incapaz de expresarse
inartistic [ˌɪnɑrˈtɪstɪk] *adj* antiartístico, inartístico
inasmuch as [ˌɪnəzˈmʌtʃˌæz] *conj* ya que, puesto que; en cuanto, hasta donde
inattentive [ˌɪnəˈtɛntɪv] *adj* desatento
inaugural [ɪnˈɔgjərəl] *adj* inaugural ‖ *s* discurso inaugural
inaugurate [ɪnˈɔgjəˌret] *tr* inaugurar
inauguration [ɪnˌɔgjəˈreʃən] *s* (*formal initiation or opening*) inauguración; (*investiture of a head of government*) toma de posesión
inborn [ˈɪnˈbɔrn] *adj* innato, ingénito
inbreeding [ˈɪnˌbridɪŋ] *s* intracruzamiento
inc. *abbr* **inclosure, included, including, incorporated, increase**
Inca [ˈɪŋkə] *adj* incaico ‖ *s* inca *mf*
incandescent [ˌɪnkənˈdɛsənt] *adj* incandescente
incapable [ɪnˈkepəbəl] *adj* incapaz
incapacitate [ˌɪnkəˈpæsɪˌtet] *tr* incapacitar, inhabilitar
incapaci•ty [ˌɪnkəˈpæsɪti] *s* (*pl* **-ties**) incapacidad
incarcerate [ɪnˈkɑrsəˌret] *tr* encarcelar
incarnate [ɪnˈkɑrnɪt] *adj* encarnado ‖ [ɪnˈkɑrnet] *tr* encarnar
incarnation [ˌɪnkɑrˈneʃən] *s* encarnación
incendiarism [ɪnˈsɛndɪˌəˌrɪzəm] *s* incendio intencionado; incitación al desorden
incendiar•y [ɪnˈsɛndɪˌɛri] *adj* incendiario ‖ *s* (*pl* **-ies**) incendiario
incense [ˈɪnsɛns] *s* incienso ‖ *tr* (*to burn incense before*) incensar ‖ [ɪnˈsɛns] *tr* exasperar, encolerizar
incense burner *s* incensario
incentive [ɪnˈsɛntɪv] *adj & s* incentivo
inception [ɪnˈsɛpʃən] *s* principio, comienzo
incertitude [ɪnˈsʌrtɪˌtjud] *s* incertidumbre
incessant [ɪnˈsɛsənt] *adj* incesante
incest [ˈɪnsɛst] *s* incesto
incestuous [ɪnˈsɛstʃʊˌəs] *adj* incestuoso

inch [ɪntʃ] *s* pulgada; **to be within an inch of** estar a dos dedos de ‖ *intr* — **to inch ahead** avanzar poco a poco

incidence ['ɪnsɪdəns] *s* incidencia; (*range of occurrence*) extensión

incident ['ɪnsɪdənt] *adj* & *s* incidente *m*

incidental [,ɪnsɪ'dɛntəl] *adj* incidente; (*incurred in addition to the regular amount*) obvencional ‖ *s* elemento incidental; **incidentals** gastos menudos

incidentally [,ɪnsɪ'dɛntəli] *adv* incidentemente; a propósito

incipient [ɪn'sɪpɪ•ənt] *adj* incipiente

incision [ɪn'sɪʒən] *s* incisión

incisive [ɪn'saɪsɪv] *adj* incisivo

incite [ɪn'saɪt] *tr* incitar

incl. *abbr* **inclosure, inclusive**

inclemen•cy [ɪn'klɛmənsi] *s* (*pl* -cies) inclemencia

inclement [ɪn'klɛmənt] *adj* inclemente

inclination [,ɪnklɪ'neʃən] *s* inclinación

incline ['ɪnklaɪn] o [ɪn'klaɪn] *s* declive *m*, pendiente *f* ‖ [ɪn'klaɪn] *tr* inclinar ‖ *intr* inclinarse

inclose [ɪn'kloz] *tr* encerrar; (*in a letter*) adjuntar, incluir; **to inclose herewith** remitir adjunto

inclosure [ɪn'kloʒər] *s* recinto; cosa inclusa, carta inclusa

include [ɪn'klud] *tr* incluir, comprender

including [ɪn'kludɪŋ] *prep* incluso, inclusive; imbíbito (Guat, Mex)

inclusive [ɪn'klusɪv] *adj* inclusivo; **inclusive of** comprensivo de ‖ *adv* inclusive

incogni•to [ɪn'kagnɪ,to] *adj* incógnito ‖ *adv* de incógnito ‖ *s* (*pl* -tos) incógnito

incoherent [,ɪnko'hɪrənt] *adj* incoherente

incombustible [,ɪnkəm'bʌstɪbəl] *adj* incombustible

income ['ɪnkʌm] *s* renta, ingreso, utilidad

income tax *s* impuesto sobre rentas

in'come-tax' return *s* declaración de impuesto sobre rentas

in'com'ing *adj* de entrada, entrante; (*tide*) ascendente ‖ *s* entrada

incommunicado [,ɪnkə,mjunə'kado] *adj* incomunicado

incomparable [ɪn'kampərəbəl] *adj* incomparable; inigualable

incompatible [,ɪnkəm'pætɪbəl] *adj* incompatible

incompetent[ɪn'kampɪtənt] *adj* incompetente

incomplete [,ɪnkəm'plit] *adj* incompleto

incomprehensible [,ɪnkamprɪ'hɛnsɪbəl] *adj* incomprehensible

incomprehension [ɪn,kamprɪ'hɛnʃən] *s* incomprensión

inconceivable [,ɪnkən'sivəbəl] *adj* inconcebible

inconclusive [,ɪnkən'klusɪv] *adj* inconcluyente

incongruous [ɪn'kaŋgru•əs] *adj* incongruo

inconsequential [ɪn,kansɪ'kwɛnʃəl] *adj* (*lacking proper sequence of thought or speech*) inconsecuente; (*trivial*) de poca importancia

inconsiderate [,ɪnkən'sɪdərɪt] *adj* desconsiderado, inconsiderado

inconsisten•cy [,ɪnkən'sɪstənsi] *s* (*pl* -cies) (*lack of coherence*) inconsistencia; (*lack of logical connection or uniformity*) inconsecuencia

inconsistent [,ɪnkən'sɪstənt] *adj* (*lacking coherence of parts*) inconsistente; (*not agreeing with itself or oneself*) inconsecuente

inconsolable [,ɪnkən'soləbəl] *adj* inconsolable

inconspicuous [,ɪnkən'spɪkju•əs] *adj* poco impresionante, poco aparente

inconstant [ɪn'kanstənt] *adj* inconstante

incontinent [ɪn'kantɪnənt] *adj* incontinente

incontrovertible [,ɪnkantrə'vʌrtɪbəl] *adj* incontrovertible

inconvenience [,ɪnkən'vini•əns] *s* incomodidad, inconveniencia, molestia ‖ *tr* incomodar, molestar

inconvenient [,ɪnkən'vzini•ənt] *adj* incómodo, inconveniente, molesto

incorporate [ɪn'kɔrpə,ret] *tr* incorporar; constituir en sociedad anónima ‖ *intr* incorporarse; constituirse en sociedad anónima

incorporation [ɪn'kɔrpə'reʃən] *s* incorporación; constitución en sociedad anónima

incorrect [,ɪnkə'rɛkt] *adj* incorrecto

increase ['ɪnkris] *s* aumento; ganancia, interés *m*; **to be on the increase** ir en aumento ‖ [ɪn'kris] *tr* aumentar; (*by propagation*) multiplicar ‖ *intr* aumentar; multiplicarse

increasingly [ɪn'krisɪŋli] *adv* cada vez más

incredible [ɪn'krɛdɪbəl] *adj* increíble

incredulous [ɪn'krɛdʒələs] *adj* incrédulo

increment ['ɪnkrɪmənt] *s* incremento

incriminate [ɪn'krɪmɪ,net] *tr* acriminar, incriminar

incrust [ɪn'krʌst] *tr* incrustar

incubate ['ɪnkjə,bet] *tr* & *intr* incubar

incubator ['ɪnkjə,betər] *s* incubadora

inculcate [ɪn'kʌlket] o ['ɪnkʌl,ket] *tr* inculcar

incumben•cy [ɪn'kʌmbənsi] *s* (*pl* -cies) incumbencia

incumbent [ɪn'kʌmbənt] *adj* — **to be incumbent on** incumbir a ‖ *s* titular *m*

incunabula [,ɪnkju'næbjələ] *spl* (*beginnings*) orígenes *mpl*; (*early printed books*) incunables *mpl*

in•cur [ɪn'kʌr] *v* (*pret* & *pp* -curred; *ger* -curring) *tr* incurrir en; (*a debt*) contraer

incurable [ɪn'kjurəbəl] *adj* & *s* incurable *mf*

incursion [ɪn'kʌrʒən] *s* incursión, correría

ind. *abbr* **independent, industrial**

indebted [ɪn'dɛtɪd] *adj* adeudado; obligado

indebtedness [ɪn'dɛtɪdnɪs] *s* endeudamiento

indecen•cy [ɪn'disənsi] *s* (*pl* -cies) indecencia, deshonestidad

indecent [ɪn'disənt] *adj* indecente, deshonesto; lépero (CAm, Mex)

indecisive [,ɪndɪ'saɪsɪv] *adj* indeciso

indeclinable [,ɪndɪ'klaɪnəbəl] *adj* (gram) indeclinable

indeed [ɪn'did] *adv* verdaderamente, claro ‖ *interj* ¡de veras!

indefatigable [,ɪndɪ'fætɪgəbəl] *adj* incansable, infatigable

im
in

indefensible [,ɪndɪ'fɛnsɪbəl] *adj* indefendible
indefinable [,ɪndɪ'faɪnəbəl] *adj* indefinible
indefinite [ɪn'dɛfɪnɪt] *adj* indefinido
indelible [ɪn'dɛlɪbəl] *adj* indeleble
indelicate [ɪn'dɛlɪkɪt] *adj* indelicado
indemnification [ɪn,dɛmnɪfɪ'keʃən] *s* indemnización
indemni•fy [ɪn'dɛmnɪ,faɪ] *v* (*pret & pp* **-fied**) *tr* indemnizar
indemni•ty [ɪn'dɛmnɪti] *s* (*pl* **-ties**) (*security against loss*) indemnidad; (*compensation*) indemnización
indent [ɪn'dɛnt] *tr* dentar, mellar; (typ) sangrar
indentation [,ɪndɛn'teʃən] *s* mella, muesca; (typ) sangría
indenture [ɪn'dɛntʃər] *s* escritura, contrato; contrato de aprendizaje || *tr* obligar por contrato
independence [,ɪndɪ'pɛndəns] *s* independencia
independen•cy [,ɪndɪ'pɛndənsi] *s* (*pl* **-cies**) independencia; país *m* independiente
independent [,ɪndɪ'pɛndənt] *adj & s* independiente *mf*
indescribable [,ɪndɪ'skraɪbəbəl] *adj* indescriptible
indestructible [,ɪndɪ'strʌktɪbəl] *adj* indestructible
indeterminate [,ɪndɪ'tʌrmɪnɪt] *adj* indeterminado
index ['ɪndɛks] *s* (*pl* **indexes** o **indices** ['ɪndɪ,siz] *s* índice *m*; (typ) manecilla || *tr* poner índice a; poner en un índice || **Index** *s* *Índice de los libros prohibidos*
index card *s* ficha catalográfica
index finger *s* dedo índice
index tab *s* pestaña
India ['ɪndɪ•ə] *s* la India
India ink *s* tinta china
Indian ['ɪndɪ•ən] *adj & s* indio
Indian club *s* maza de gimnasia
Indian corn *s* maíz *m*, panizo
Indian file *s* fila india || *adv* en fila india
Indian Ocean *s* mar *m* de las Indias, océano Índico
Indian summer *s* veranillo de San Martín
India paper *s* papel *m* de China
India rubber *s* caucho
indicate ['ɪndɪ,ket] *tr* indicar
indication [,ɪndɪ'keʃən] *s* indicación
indicative [ɪn'dɪkətɪv] *adj & s* indicativo
indicator ['ɪndɪ,ketər] *s* indicador *m*
indict [ɪn'daɪt] *tr* (law) acusar, procesar
indictment [ɪn'daɪtmənt] *s* acusación, procesamiento; auto de acusación formulado por el gran jurado
indifferent [ɪn'dɪfərənt] *adj* indiferente; (*not particularly good*) pasadero, mediano
indigenous [ɪn'dɪdʒɪnəs] *adj* indígena
indigent ['ɪndɪdʒənt] *adj* indigente
indigestible [,ɪndɪ'dʒɛstɪbəl] *adj* indigestible
indigestion [,ɪndɪ'dʒɛstʃən] *s* indigestión
indignant [ɪn'dɪgnənt] *adj* indignado
indignation [,ɪndɪg'neʃən] *s* indignación
indigni•ty [ɪn'dɪgnɪti] *s* (*pl* **-ties**) indignidad

indi•go ['ɪndɪgo] *adj* azul de añil || *s* (*pl* **-gos** o **-goes**) índigo
indirect [,ɪndɪ'rɛkt] *adj* indirecto
indirect discourse *s* estilo indirecto
indiscernible [,ɪndɪ'zʌrnɪbəl] o [,ɪndɪ'sʌrnɪbəl] *adj* indiscernible
indiscreet [,ɪndɪs'krit] *adj* indiscreto
indiscriminate [,ɪndɪs'krɪmɪnɪt] *adj* indiscriminado
indispensable ['ɪndɪs'pɛnsəbəl] *adj* indispensable, imprescindible
indispose [,ɪndɪs'poz] *tr* indisponer
indisposed [,ɪndɪs'pozd] *adj* (*disinclined*) maldispuesto; (*somewhat ill*) indispuesto
indissoluble [,ɪndɪ'saljəbəl] *adj* indisoluble
indistinct [,ɪndɪ'stɪŋkt] *adj* indistinto
indite [ɪn'daɪt] *tr* redactar, poner por escrito
individual [,ɪndɪ'vɪdʒʊ•əl] *adj* individual || *s* individuo
individuali•ty [,ɪndɪ,vɪdʒʊ,'ælɪti] *s* (*pl* **-ties**) individualidad; (*person of distinctive character*) personaje *m*
Indochina ['ɪndo'tʃaɪnə] *s* la Indochina
Indo-Chi•nese ['ɪndotʃaɪ'niz] *adj* indochino || *s* (*pl* **-nese**) indochino
indoctrinate [ɪn'daktrɪ,net] *tr* adoctrinar
Indo-European ['ɪndo,jʊrə'pi•ən] *adj & s* indoeuropeo
indolent ['ɪndələnt] *adj* indolente
Indonesia [,ɪndo'niʃə] o [,ɪndo'niʒə] *s* la Indonesia
Indonesian [,ɪndo'niʃən] o [,ɪndo'niʒən] *adj & s* indonesio
indoor ['ɪn,dor] *adj* interior, de puertas adentro; (*inclined to stay in the house*) casero
indoors ['ɪn'dorz] *adv* dentro, en casa, bajo techado, bajo cubierto
indorse [ɪn'dors] *tr* endosar; (fig) apoyar, aprobar
indorsee [,ɪndor'si] *s* endosatario
indorsement [ɪn'dorsmənt] *s* endoso; (fig) apoyo, aprobación
indorser [ɪn'dorsər] *s* endosante *mf*
induce [ɪn'djus] *tr* inducir; causar, ocasionar
inducement [ɪn'djusmənt] *s* aliciente *m*, estímulo, incentivo
induct [ɪn'dʌkt] *tr* instalar; introducir, iniciar; (mil) quintar
induction [ɪn'dʌkʃən] *s* instalación; introducción; (elec & log) inducción; (mil) quinta
indulge [ɪn'dʌldʒ] *tr* gratificar (*p.ej., los deseos de uno*); mimar (*a un niño*) || *intr* abandonar; **to indulge in** entregarse a, permitirse el placer de
indulgence [ɪn'dʌldʒəns] *s* gusto, inclinación; intemperancia, desenfreno; (*leniency*) indulgencia
indulgent [ɪn'dʌldʒənt] *adj* indulgente
industrial [ɪn'dʌstrɪ•əl] *adj* industrial
industrialist [ɪn'dʌstrɪ•əlɪst] *s* industrial *m*
industrialize [ɪn'dʌstrɪ•ə,laɪz] *tr* industrializar
industrious [ɪn'dʌstrɪ•əs] *adj* industrioso, aplicado
indus•try ['ɪndəstri] *s* (*pl* **-tries**) industria
inebriation [ɪn,ibrɪ'eʃən] *s* embriaguez *f*
inedible [ɪn'ɛdɪbəl] *adj* incomible

ineffable [ɪnˈɛfəbəl] *adj* inefable
ineffective [ˌɪnɪˈfɛktɪv] *adj* ineficaz; *(person)* incapaz
ineffectual [ˌɪnɪˈfɛktʃʊ•əl] *adj* ineficaz, fútil
inefficacy [ɪnˈɛfɪkəsɪ] *s* ineficacia
inefficient [ˌɪnɪˈfɪʃənt] *adj* de mal rendimiento
ineligible [ɪnˈɛlɪdʒɪbəl] *adj* inelegible
inequali•ty [ˌɪnɪˈkwɑlɪtɪ] *s* (*pl* **-ties**) desigualdad
inequi•ty [ɪnˈɛkwɪtɪ] *s* (*pl* **-ties**) inequidad
ineradicable [ˌɪnɪˈrædɪkəbəl] *adj* inextirpable
inertia [ɪnˈʌrʃə] *s* inercia
inescapable [ˌɪnesˈkepəbəl] *adj* ineludible
inevitable [ɪnˈɛvɪtəbəl] *adj* inevitable
inexact [ˌɪnɛgˈzækt] *adj* inexacto
inexcusable [ˌɪnɛksˈkjuzəbəl] *adj* indisculpable, inexcusable
inexhaustible [ˌɪnɛgˈzɔstɪbəl] *adj* inagotable
inexorable [ɪnˈɛksərəbəl] *adj* inexorable
inexpedient [ˌɪnɛkˈspidɪ•ənt] *adj* malaconsejado, inoportuno
inexpensive [ˌɪnɛkˈspɛnsɪv] *adj* barato, poco costoso
inexperience [ˌɪnɛkˈspɪrɪ•əns] *s* inexperiencia
inexplicable [ɪnˈɛksplɪkəbəl] *adj* inexplicable
inexpressible [ˌɪnɛkˈsprɛsɪbəl] *adj* inexpresable
Inf. *abbr* **Infantry**
infallible [ɪnˈfælɪbəl] *adj* infalible
infamous [ˈɪnfəməs] *adj* infame
infa•my [ˈɪnfəmɪ] *s* (*pl* **-mies**) infamia
infan•cy [ˈɪnfənsɪ] *s* (*pl* **-cies**) infancia
infant [ˈɪnfənt] *adj* infantil;•(*in the earliest stage*) (fig) naciente ‖ *s* criatura, nene *m*
infant care *s* puericultura
infantile [ˈɪnfənˌtaɪl] o [ˈɪnfəntɪl] *adj* infantil; *(childish)* aniñado
infan•try [ˈɪnfəntrɪ] *s* (*pl* **-tries**) infantería
infantry•man [ˈɪnfəntrɪmən] *s* (*pl* **-men** [mən]) infante *m*, soldado de infantería
infarct [ɪnˈfɑrkt] *s* infarto
infatuated [ɪnˈfætʃʊˌetɪd] *adj* apasionado, locamente enamorado
infect [ɪnˈfɛkt] *tr* inficionar, infectar; influir sobre
infection [ɪnˈfɛkʃən] *s* infección
infectious [ɪnˈfɛkʃəs] *adj* infeccioso
in•fer [ɪnˈfʌr] *v* (*pret & pp* **-ferred;** *ger* **-ferring**) *tr* inferir; (coll) conjeturar, suponer
inferior [ɪnˈfɪrɪ•ər] *adj & s* inferior *m*
inferiority [ɪnˌfɪrɪˈɑrɪtɪ] *s* inferioridad
inferiority complex *s* complejo de inferioridad
infernal [ɪnˈfʌrnəl] *adj* infernal
infest [ɪnˈfɛst] *tr* infestar
infidel [ˈɪnfɪdəl] *adj & s* infiel *mf*
infideli•ty [ˌɪnfɪˈdɛlɪtɪ] *s* (*pl* **-ties**) infidelidad
in'field' *s* (baseball) cuadro interior
infiltrate [ˈɪnfɪlˌtret] *tr* infiltrar; infiltrarse en ‖ *intr* infiltrarse
infinite [ˈɪnfɪnɪt] *adj & s* infinito
infinitive [ɪnˈfɪnɪtɪv] *adj & s* infinitivo

infini•ty [ɪnˈfɪnɪtɪ] *s* (*pl* **-ties**) infinidad; (math) infinito
infirm [ɪnˈfʌrm] *adj* infirme, achacoso; *(unsteady)* inestable, inseguro; poco firme, poco sólido
infirma•ry [ɪnˈfʌrmərɪ] *s* (*pl* **-ries**) enfermería
infirmi•ty [ɪnˈfʌrmɪtɪ] *s* (*pl* **-ties**) achaque *m;* inestabilidad
in'fix *s* (gram) infijo
inflame [ɪnˈflem] *tr* inflamar
inflammable [ɪnˈflæməbəl] *adj* inflamable
inflammation [ˌɪnfləˈmeʃən] *s* inflamación
inflate [ɪnˈflet] *tr* inflar ‖ *intr* inflarse
inflation [ɪnˈfleʃən] *s* inflación; *(of a tire)* inflado
inflationary [ɪnˈfleʃənˌɛrɪ] *adj* inflacionario
inflect [ɪnˈflɛkt] *tr* doblar, torcer; modular (*la voz*); (gram) modificar por inflexión
inflection [ɪnˈflɛkʃən] *s* inflexión
inflexible [ɪnˈflɛksɪbəl] *adj* inflexible
inflict [ɪnˈflɪkt] *tr* infligir
influence [ˈɪnflu•əns] *s* influencia ‖ *tr* influir sobre, influenciar
influential [ˌɪnfluˈɛnʃəl] *adj* influyente
influenza [ˌɪnfluˈɛnzə] *s* influenza
inform [ɪnˈfɔrm] *tr* informar, avisar, enterar ‖ *intr* informar
informal [ɪnˈfɔrməl] *adj* (*not according to established rules*) informal; *(unceremonious; colloquial)* familiar
information [ˌɪnfərˈmeʃən] *s* información, informes *mpl*
informational [ˌɪnfərˈmeʃənəl] *adj* informativo
informed sources *spl* los entendidos
infraction [ɪnˈfrækʃən] *s* infracción
infrared [ˌɪnfrəˈrɛd] *adj & s* infrarrojo
infrequent [ɪnˈfrikwənt] *adj* infrecuente
infringe [ɪnˈfrɪndʒ] *tr* infringir ‖ *intr*—**to infringe on** o **upon** invadir, abusar de
infringement [ɪnˈfrɪndʒmənt] *s* infración
infuriate [ɪnˈfjʊrɪˌet] *tr* enfurecer
infuse [ɪnˈfjuz] *tr* infundir
infusion [ɪnˈfjuʒən] *s* infusión
ingenious [ɪnˈdʒinjəs] *adj* ingenioso
ingenui•ty [ˌɪndʒɪˈnju•ɪtɪ] o [ˌɪndʒɪˈnu•ɪtɪ] *s* (*pl* **-ties**) ingeniosidad
ingenuous [ɪnˈdʒɛnjʊ•əs] *adj* ingenuo
ingenuousness [ɪnˈdʒɛnjʊ•əsnɪs] *s* ingenuidad
ingest [ɪnˈdʒɛst] *tr* injerir
in'go'ing *adj* entrante
ingot [ˈɪŋgət] *s* lingote *m*
ingraft [ɪnˈgræft] *tr* (hort & surg) injertar; (fig) implantar
ingrate [ˈɪngret] *s* ingrato
ingratiate [ɪnˈgreʃɪˌet] *tr*—**to ingratiate oneself with** congraciarse con
ingratiating [ɪnˈgreʃɪˌetɪŋ] *adj* atrayente, obsequioso
ingratitude [ɪnˈgrætɪˌtjud] *s* ingratitud, desagradecimiento
ingredient [ɪnˈgridɪ•ənt] *s* ingrediente *m*
in'grow'ing nail *s* uñero
ingulf [ɪnˈgʌlf] *tr* hundir, inundar
inhabit [ɪnˈhæbɪt] *tr* habitar, poblar

in
in

inhabitant [ɪnˈhæbɪtənt] *s* habitante *mf*
inhale [ɪnˈhel] *tr* aspirar, inspirar ‖ *intr* aspirar, inspirar; tragar el humo
inherent [ɪnˈhɪrənt] *adj* inherente
inherit [ɪnˈhɛrɪt] *tr & intr* heredar
inheritance [ɪnˈhɛrɪtəns] *s* herencia; mortual *m* (CAm, Mex)
inheritor [ɪnˈhɛrɪtər] *s* heredero
inhibit [ɪnˈhɪbɪt] *tr* inhibir, prohibir
inhospitable [ɪnˈhɑspɪtəbəl] o [ˌɪnhɑsˈpɪtəbəl] *adj* inhospitalario; (*affording no shelter or protection*) inhóspito
inhuman [ɪnˈhjumən] *adj* inhumano
inhumane [ˌɪnhjuˈmen] *adj* inhumano
inhumani•ty [ˌɪnhjuˈmænɪti] *s* (*pl* -ties) inhumanidad
inimical [ɪˈnɪmɪkəl] *adj* enemigo
iniqui•ty [ɪˈnɪkwɪti] *s* (*pl* -ties) iniquidad
ini•tial [ɪˈnɪʃəl] *adj & s* inicial *f* ‖ *v* (*pret* -tialed o -tialled; *ger* -tialing o -tialling) *tr* firmar con sus iniciales; marcar (*p.ej., un pañuelo*)
initiate [ɪˈnɪʃɪˌet] *tr* iniciar
initiation [ɪˌnɪʃɪˈeʃən] *s* iniciación
initiative [ɪˈnɪʃɪˌetɪv] o [ɪˈnɪʃətɪv] *s* iniciativa
inject [ɪnˈdʒɛkt] *tr* inyectar; introducir (*una especie, una advertencia*)
injection [ɪnˈdʒɛkʃən] *s* inyección
injudicious [ˌɪndʒuˈdɪʃəs] *adj* imprudente
injunction [ɪnˈdʒʌŋkʃən] *s* admonición, mandato; (law) entredicho
injure [ˈɪndʒər] *tr* (*to harm*) dañar, hacer daño a; (*to wound*) herir, lisiar, lastimar; (*to offend*) agraviar
injurious [ɪnˈdʒʊrɪ•əs] *adj* dañoso, perjudicial; (*offensive*) agravioso
inju•ry [ˈɪndʒəri] *s* (*pl* -ries) (*harm*) daño; (*wound*) herida, lesión; (*offense*) agravio
injustice [ɪnˈdʒʌstɪs] *s* injusticia
ink [ɪŋk] *s* tinta ‖ *tr* entintar
inkling [ˈɪŋklɪŋ] *s* sospecha, indicio, noción vaga, vislumbre *f*
ink′stand′ *s* (*cuplike container*) tintero; (*stand for ink, pens, etc.*) portatintero
ink′well′ *s* tintero
ink•y [ˈɪŋki] *adj* (*comp* -ier; *super* -iest) entintado; negro
inlaid [ˈɪn,led] o [ˌɪnˈled] *adj* embutido, taraceado
inland [ˈɪnlənd] *adj & s* interior *m* ‖ *adv* tierra adentro
in′-law′ *s* (coll) pariente político
in•lay [ˈɪn,le] *s* embutido ‖ [ɪnˈle] o [ˈɪn,le] *v* (*pret & pp* -laid) *tr* embutir, taracear
in′let *s* ensenada, cala, caleta
in′mate′ *s* (*in a hospital or home*) asilado, recluso, acogido; (*in a jail*) presidiario, preso
inn [ɪn] *s* mesón *m*, posada
innate [ɪˈnet] o [ˈɪnet] *adj* ingénito, innato
inner [ˈɪnər] *adj* interior; secreto
in′ner•spring′ mattress *s* colchón *m* de muelles interiores
inner tube *s* cámara (de neumático)
inning [ˈɪnɪŋ] *s* mano *f*, entrada, turno
inn′keep′er *s* mesonero, posadero
innocence [ˈɪnəsəns] *s* inocencia

innocent [ˈɪnəsənt] *adj & s* inocente *mf*
innovate [ˈɪnə,vet] *tr* innovar
innovation [ˌɪnəˈveʃən] *s* innovación
innuen•do [ˌɪnjuˈɛndo] *s* (*pl* -does) indirecta, insinuación
innumerable [ɪˈnumərəbəl] *adj* innumerable, incontable
inoculate [ɪnˈakjə,let] *tr* inocular; (fig) imbuir
inoculation [ɪn,akjəˈleʃən] *s* inoculación
inoffensive [ˌɪnəˈfɛnsɪv] *adj* inofensivo
inoperative [ɪnˈapərətɪv] *adj* fuera de servicio
inopportune [ɪn,apərˈtjun] *adj* inoportuno
inordinate [ɪnˈɔrdɪnɪt] *adj* excesivo; (*unrestrained*) desenfrenado
inorganic [ˌɪnɔrˈgænɪk] *adj* inorgánico
in′put′ *s* gasto, consumo; (elec) entrada; (mech) potencia consumida
inquest [ˈɪnkwɛst] *s* encuesta; (*of coroner*) pesquisa judicial, levantamiento del cadáver
inquire [ɪnˈkwaɪr] *tr* averiguar, inquirir ‖ *intr* preguntar; **to inquire about, after** o **for** preguntar por; **to inquire into** averiguar, inquirir
inquir•y [ɪnˈkwaɪri] o [ˈɪnkwɪri] *s* (*pl* -ies) averiguación, encuesta; pregunta
inquisition [ˌɪnkwɪˈzɪʃən] *s* inquisición
inquisitive [ɪnˈkwɪzɪtɪv] *adj* curioso, preguntón
in′road′ *s* incursión
ins. *abbr* **insulated, insurance**
insane [ɪnˈsen] *adj* loco, insano, dementado
insane asylum *s* manicomio, casa de locos
insani•ty [ɪnˈsænɪti] *s* (*pl* -ties) demencia, locura, insania, loquera
insatiable [ɪnˈseʃəbəl] *adj* insaciable
inscribe [ɪnˈskraɪb] *tr* inscribir; dedicar (*una obra literaria*)
inscription [ɪnˈskrɪpʃən] *s* inscripción; (*of a book*) dedicatoria
inscrutable [ɪnˈskrutəbəl] *adj* inescrutable
insect [ˈɪnsɛkt] *s* insecto
insect control *s* desinsectación
insecticide [ɪnˈsɛktɪ,saɪd] *adj & s* insecticida *m*
insecure [ˌɪnsɪˈkjur] *adj* inseguro
inseparable [ɪnˈsɛpərəbəl] *adj* inseparable
insert [ˈɪnsʌrt] *s* inserción ‖ [ɪnˈsʌrt] *tr* insertar
insertion [ɪnˈsʌrʃən] *s* inserción; (*strip of lace*) entredós *m*
in•set [ˈɪn,sɛt] *s* intercalación ‖ [ɪnˈsɛt] o [ˈɪn,sɛt] *v* (*pret & pp* -set; *ger* -setting) *tr* intercalar, encastrar
in′shore′ *adj* cercano a la orilla ‖ *adv* cerca de la orilla; hacia la orilla
in′side′ *adj* interior; interno; secreto ‖ *adv* dentro, adentro; **inside of** dentro de; **to turn inside out** volver al revés; volverse al revés ‖ *prep* dentro de ‖ *s* interior *m*; **insides** (coll) entrañas; **on the inside** (coll) en el secreto de las cosas
inside information *s* informes *mpl* confidenciales
insider [ˌɪnˈsaɪdər] *s* persona enterada

insidious [ɪnˈsɪdɪ•əs] *adj* insidioso
in'sight' *s* penetración
insigni•a [ɪnˈsɪgnɪ•ə] *s* (*pl* **-a** o **-as**) insignia
insignificant [ˌɪnsɪgˈnɪfɪkənt] *adj* insignificante
insincere [ˌɪnsɪnˈsɪr] *adj* insincero; malo (Mex)
insinuate [ɪnˈsɪnjuˌet] *tr* insinuar
insipid [ɪnˈsɪpɪd] *adj* insípido
insist [ɪnˈsɪst] *intr* insistir
insofar as [ˌɪnsoˈfɑrˌæz] *conj* en cuanto
insolence [ˈɪnsələns] *s* insolencia
insolent [ˈɪnsələnt] *adj* insolente
insoluble [ɪnˈsɑljəbəl] *adj* insoluble
insolven•cy [ɪnˈsɑlvənsi] *s* (*pl* **-cies**) insolvencia
insomnia [ɪnˈsɑmnɪ•ə] *s* insomnio
insomuch [ˌɪnsoˈmʌtʃ] *adv* hasta tal punto; **insomuch as** ya que, puesto que; **insomuch that** hasta el punto que
inspect [ɪnˈspɛkt] *tr* inspeccionar
inspection [ɪnˈspɛkʃən] *s* inspección
inspiration [ˌɪnspɪˈreʃən] *s* inspiración
inspire [ɪnˈspaɪr] *tr & intr* inspirar
inspiring [ɪnˈspaɪrɪŋ] *adj* inspirante
inst. *abbr* **instant** (*i.e.,* **present month**)
Inst. *abbr* **Institute, Institution**
install [ɪnˈstɔl] *tr* instalar
installment [ɪnˈstɔlmənt] *s* instalación; entrega; **in installments** por entregas; a plazos
installment buying *s* compra a plazos
installment plan *s* pago a plazos, compra a plazos; **on the installment plan** con facilidades de pago
instance [ˈɪnstəns] *s* caso, ejemplo; **for instance** por ejemplo
instant [ˈɪnstənt] *adj* instantáneo ‖ *s* instante *m*, momento; mes *m* corriente
instantaneous [ˌɪnstənˈtenɪ•əs] *adj* instantáneo
instantly [ˈɪnstəntli] *adv* al instante
instead [ɪnˈstɛd] *adv* preferiblemente; en su lugar; **instead of** en vez de, en lugar de
in'step' *s* empeine *m*
instigate [ˈɪnstɪˌget] *tr* instigar
in•still' *tr* instilar
instinct [ˈɪnstɪŋkt] *s* instinto
instinctive [ɪnˈstɪŋktɪv] *adj* instintivo
institute [ˈɪnstɪˌtjut] *s* instituto ‖ *tr* instituir
institution [ˌɪnstɪˈtjuʃən] *s* institución
instruct [ɪnˈstrʌkt] *tr* instruir
instruction [ɪnˈstrʌkʃən] *s* instrucción
instructions for use *spl* modo de empleo
instructive [ɪnˈstrʌktɪv] *adj* instructivo
instructor [ɪnˈstrʌktər] *s* instructor *m*
instrument [ˈɪnstrəmənt] *s* instrumento ‖ [ˈɪnstrəˌmɛnt] *tr* instrumentar
instrumentalist [ˌɪnstrəˈmɛntəlɪst] *s* instrumentista *m*
instrumentali•ty [ˌɪnstrəmənˈtælɪti] *s* (*pl* **-ties**) agencia, mediación
instrument panel *s* cuadro de mando; salpicadero
insubordinate [ˌɪnsəˈbɔrdɪnɪt] *adj* insubordinado
insufferable [ɪnˈsʌfərəbəl] *adj* insufrible

insufficient [ˌɪnsəˈfɪʃənt] *adj* insuficiente
insular [ˈɪnsələr] o [ˈɪnsjulər] *adj* insular; (fig) de miras estrechas
insulate [ˈɪnsəˌlet] *tr* aislar
insulation [ˌɪnsəˈleʃən] *s* aislación
insulator [ˈɪnsəˌlətər] *s* aislador *m*
insulin [ˈɪnsəlɪn] *s* insulina
insult [ˈɪnsʌlt] *s* insulto, insultada, escopetazo ‖ [ɪnˈsʌlt] *tr* insultar
insurable [ɪnˈʃurəbəl] *adj* asegurable
insurance [ɪnˈʃurəns] *s* seguro
insure [ɪnˈʃur] *tr* asegurar
insurer [ɪnˈʃurər] *s* asegurador *m*
insurgent [ɪnˈsʌrdʒənt] *adj & s* insurgente *mf*
insurmountable [ˌɪnsərˈmauntəbəl] *adj* insuperable
insurrection [ˌɪnsəˈrɛkʃən] *s* insurrección
insusceptible [ˌɪnsəˈsɛptɪbəl] *adj* insusceptible
int. *abbr* **interest, interior, internal, international**
intact [ɪnˈtækt] *adj* intacto, ileso
in'take' *s* (*place of taking in*) entrada; (*act or amount*) toma; (mach) admisión
intake manifold *s* múltiple *m* de admisión, colector *m* de admisión
intake valve *s* válvula de admisión
intangible [ɪnˈtændʒɪbəl] *adj* intangible; vago, indefinido
integer [ˈɪntɪdʒər] *s* (arith) entero
integral [ˈɪntɪgrəl] *adj* íntegro; **integral with** solidario de ‖ *s* conjunto
integration [ˌɪntɪˈgreʃən] *s* integración
integrity [ɪŋˈtɛgrɪti] *s* integridad
intellect [ˈɪntəˌlɛkt] *s* intelecto; (*person*) intelectual *mf*
intellectual [ˌɪntəˈlɛktʃu•əl] *adj & s* intelectual *mf*
intellectuali•ty [ˌɪntəˌlɛktʃuˈælɪti] *s* (*pl* **-ties**) intelectualidad
intelligence [ɪnˈtɛlɪdʒəns] *s* inteligencia; información
intelligence bureau *s* departamento de inteligencia
intelligence quotient *s* cociente *m* intelectual
intelligent [ɪnˈtɛlɪdʒənt] *adj* inteligente; espabilado
intelligentsia [ɪnˌtɛlɪˈdʒəntsɪ•ə] o [ɪnˌtɛlɪˈgɛntsɪ•ə] *s* intelectualidad (*conjunto de los intelectuales de un país o región*)
intelligible [ɪnˈtɛlɪdʒɪbəl] *adj* inteligible
intemperance [ɪnˈtɛmpərəns] *s* intemperancia
intemperate [ɪnˈtɛmpərɪt] *adj* intemperante; (*climate*) riguroso
intend [ɪnˈtɛnd] *tr* pensar, proponerse, intentar; (*to mean for a particular purpose*) destinar; (*to signify*) querer decir
intendance [ɪnˈtɛndəns] *s* intendencia
intendant [ɪnˈtɛndənt] *s* intendente *m*
intended [ɪnˈtɛndɪd] *adj & s* (coll) prometido, prometida
intense [ɪnˈtɛns] *adj* intenso

in
in

intensi•fy [ɪnˈtɛnsɪ,faɪ] v (pret & pp **-fied**) tr intensificar, intensar; (phot) reforzar ‖ intr intensificarse, intensarse

intensi•ty [ɪnˈtɛnsɪti] s (pl **-ties**) intensidad

intensive [ɪnˈtɛnsɪv] adj intensivo

intent [ɪnˈtɛnt] adj atento; resuelto; intenso; **intent on** resuelto a ‖ s (purpose) intento; (meaning) acepción, sentido; **to all intents and purposes** en realidad de verdad

intention [ɪnˈtɛnʃən] s intención

intentional [ɪnˈtɛnʃənəl] adj intencional, deliberado

in•ter [ɪnˈtʌr] v (pret & pp **-terred;** ger **-terring**) tr enterrar

interact [ˈɪntər,ækt] s (theat) entreacto ‖ [,ɪntərˈækt] intr obrar recíprocamente

interaction [,ɪntərˈækʃən] s interacción

inter-American [,ɪntərəˈmɛrɪkən] adj interamericano

inter•breed [,ɪntərˈbrid] v (pret & pp **-bred** [ˈbrɛd]) tr entrecruzar ‖ intr entrecruzarse

intercalate [ɪnˈtʌrkə,let] tr intercalar

intercede [,ɪntərˈsid] intr interceder

intercept [,ɪntərˈsɛpt] tr interceptar

interceptor [,ɪntərˈsɛptər] s interceptor m

interchange [ˈɪntərˌtʃendʒ] s intercambio; (on a highway) correspondencia ‖ [,ɪntərˈtʃendʒ] tr intercambiar ‖ intr intercambiarse

intercollegiate [,ɪntərkəˈlidʒɪ•ɪt] adj interescolar

intercom [ˈɪntərˌkɑm] s interfono

intercourse [ˈɪntərˌkors] s comunicación, trato; (interchange of products, ideas, etc.) intercambio; (copulation) cópula, comercio; **to have intercourse** juntarse

intercross [,ɪntərˈkrɔs] o [,ɪntərˈkrɑs] tr entrecruzar ‖ intr entrecruzarse

interdict [ˈɪntərˌdɪkt] s entredicho ‖ [,ɪntərˈdɪkt] tr interdecir

interest [ˈɪntərɪst] s interés m; **the interests** las grandes empresas, el grupo influyente; **to put out at interest** poner a interés ‖ tr interesar

interested [ˈɪntə,rɛstɪd] adj interesado

interesting [ˈɪntə,rɛstɪŋ] adj interesante

interface [ˈɪntərˌfes] s (computer) entrecara

interfere [,ɪntərˈfɪr] intr inmiscuirse, injerirse, interferir; (sport) parar una jugada; **to interfere with** dificultar, impedir, interferir

interference [,ɪntərˈfɪrəns] s injerencia, interferencia

interim [ˈɪntərɪm] adj interino ‖ s intermedio, intervalo; **in the interim** entretanto

interior [ɪnˈtɪrɪ•ər] adj & s interior m

interject [,ɪntərˈdʒɛkt] tr interponer ‖ intr interponerse

interjection [,ɪntərˈdʒɛkʃən] s interposición; exclamación; (gram) interjección

interlard [,ɪntərˈlɑrd] tr interpolar; mechar (la carne)

interline [,ɪntərˈlaɪn] tr interlinear; entretelar (una prenda de vestir)

interlining [ˈɪntərˌlaɪnɪŋ] s (of a garment) entretela

interlink [,ɪntərˈlɪŋk] tr eslabonar

interlock [,ɪntərˈlɑk] tr trabar ‖ intr trabarse

interlope [,ɪntərˈlop] intr entremeterse; traficar sin derecho

interloper [,ɪntərˈlopər] s intruso

interlude [ˈɪntərˌlud] s intervalo; (mus) interludio; (theat) intermedio

intermarriage [,ɪntərˈmærɪdʒ] s casamiento entre parientes; casamiento entre personas de distintas razas, castas, etc.

intermediar•y [,ɪntərˈmidɪ,ɛri] adj intermediario ‖ s (pl **-ies**) intermediario

intermediate [,ɪntərˈmidɪ•ɪt] adj intermedio

in•ter•me′di•ate-range′ missile s cohete m de alcance medio

interment [ɪnˈtʌrmənt] s entierro

intermez•zo [,ɪntərˈmɛtso] o [,ɪntərmɛdzo] s (pl **-zos** o **-zi** [tsi] o [dzi]) (mus) intermedio, intermezzo

intermingle [,ɪntərˈmɪŋgəl] tr entremezclar ‖ intr entremezclarse

intermittent [,ɪntərˈmɪtənt] adj intermitente

intermix [,ɪntərˈmɪks] tr entremezclar ‖ intr entremezclarse

intern [ˈɪntʌrn] s interno de hospital ‖ [ɪnˈtʌrn] tr internar, recluir

internal [ɪnˈtʌrnəl] adj interno

inter′nal-combus′tion engine s motor m de explosión

internal revenue s rentas internas

international [,ɪntərˈnæʃənəl] adj internacional

international date line s línea internacional de cambio de fecha

internationalize [,ɪntərˈnæʃənə,laɪz] tr internacionalizar

internecine [,ɪntərˈnisɪn] adj sanguinario

internee [,ɪntʌrˈni] s (mil) internado

internist [ɪnˈtʌrnɪst] s internista mf

internment [ɪnˈtʌrnmənt] s internamiento

internship [ˈɪntʌrn,ʃɪp] s residencia de un médico en un hospital

interpellate [,ɪntərˈpɛlet] o [ɪnˈtʌrpɪ,let] tr interpelar

interplay [ˈɪntərˌple] s interacción

interpolate [ɪnˈtʌrpə,let] tr interpolar

interpose [,ɪntərˈpoz] tr interponer

interpret [ɪnˈtʌrprɪt] tr interpretar

interpreter [ɪnˈtʌrprɪtər] s intérprete mf; (fig) exponente mf

interrogate [ɪnˈtɛrə,get] tr & intr interrogar

interrogation [ɪn,tɛrəˈgeʃən] s interrogación

interrogation mark o **point** s signo de interrogación

interrupt [,ɪntəˈrʌpt] tr interrumpir

interscholastic [,ɪntərskəˈlæstɪk] adj interescolar

intersection [,ɪntərˈsɛkʃən] s (of streets, roads, etc.) cruce m, bocacalle f; cruza (SAm); (geom) intersección

intersperse [,ɪntərˈspʌrs] tr entremezclar, esparcir

interstice [ɪnˈtʌrstɪs] s intersticio

intertwine [,ɪntərˈtwaɪn] tr entrelazar ‖ intr entrelazarse

interval [ˈɪntərvəl] s intervalo; **at intervals** (now and then) de vez en cuando; (here and there) de trecho en trecho

intervene [,ɪntər'vin] *intr* intervenir
intervening [,ɪntər'vinɪŋ] *adj* intermedio
intervention [,ɪntər'vɛnʃən] *s* intervención
interview ['ɪntər,vju] *s* entrevista, interview *m* ‖ *tr* entrevistarse con
inter•weave [,ɪntər'wiv] *v* (*pret* **-wove** ['wov] o **-weaved**; *pp* **-wove, woven** o **weaved**) *tr* entretejer
intestate [ɪn'tɛstet] *adj* & *s* intestado
intestine [ɪn'tɛstɪn] *s* intestino
inthrall [ɪn'θrɔl] *tr* cautivar, encantar; esclavizar, sojuzgar
inthrone [ɪn'θron] *tr* entronizar
intima•cy ['ɪntɪməsi] *s* (*pl* **-cies**) intimidad
intimate ['ɪntɪmɪt] *adj* íntimo ‖ *s* amigo íntimo ‖ ['ɪntɪ,met] *tr* insinuar, intimar
intimation [,ɪntɪ'meʃən] *s* insinuación
intimidate [ɪn'tɪmɪ,det] *tr* intimidar
intitle [ɪn'taɪtəl] *tr* dar derecho a; (*to give a name to; to honor with a title*) intitular
into ['ɪntu] o ['ɪntʊ] *prep* en; hacia; hacia el interior de
intolerant [ɪn'talərənt] *adj* & *s* intolerante *mf*
intomb [ɪn'tum] *tr* sepultar
intombment [ɪn'tummənt] *s* sepultura
intonation [,ɪnto'neʃən] *s* entonación
intone [ɪn'ton] *tr* entonar
intoxicant [ɪn'taksɪkənt] *s* bebida alcohólica
intoxicate [ɪn'taksɪ,ket] *tr* embriagar, emborrachar; (*to exhilarate*) alegrar, excitar; (*to poison*) envenenar, intoxicar
intoxication [ɪn,taksɪ'keʃən] *s* embriaguez *f*; alegría, excitación; (*poisoning*) envenenamiento, intoxicación
intractable [ɪn'træktəbəl] *adj* intratable
intransigent [ɪn'trænsɪdʒənt] *adj* & *s* intransigente *mf*
intransitive [ɪn'trænsɪtɪv] *adj* intransitivo
intrench [ɪn'trɛntʃ] *tr* atrincherar ‖ *intr*—**to intrench on** o **upon** infringir, violar
intrepid [ɪn'trɛpɪd] *adj* intrépido
intrepidity [,ɪntrɪ'pɪdɪti] *s* intrepidez *f*
intricate ['ɪntrɪkɪt] *adj* intrincado
intrigue [ɪn'trig] *s* intriga; intriga amorosa, enredo amoroso ‖ *tr* (*to arouse the curiosity of*) intrigar ‖ *intr* intrigar; tener intrigas amorosas
intrinsic(al) [ɪn'trɪnsɪk(əl)] *adj* intrínseco
introd. *abbr* **introduction**
introduce [,ɪntrə'djus] *tr* introducir; (*to make acquainted*) presentar
introduction [,ɪntrə'dʌkʃən] *s* introducción; (*of one person to another or others*) presentación
introductory offer [,ɪntrə'dʌktəri] *s* ofrecimiento de presentación, oferta preliminar
introit ['ɪntro•ɪt] *s* (eccl) introito
introspective [,ɪntrə'spɛktɪv] *adj* introspectivo
introvert ['ɪntrə,vʌrt] *s* introvertido
intrude [ɪn'trud] *intr* injerirse, entremeterse
intruder [ɪn'trudər] *s* intruso, entremetido
intrusive [ɪn'trusɪv] *adj* intruso
intrust [ɪn'trʌst] *tr* confiar
intuition [,ɪntju'ɪʃən] *s* intuición
inundate ['ɪnən,det] *tr* inundar
inundation [,ɪnən'deʃən] *s* inundación

inure [ɪn'jʊr] *tr* acostumbrar, endurecer, aguerrir ‖ *intr* ponerse en efecto; **to inure to** redundar en
inv. *abbr* **inventor, invoice**
invade [ɪn'ved] *tr* invadir
invader [ɪn'vedər] *s* invasor *m*
invalid [ɪn'vælɪd] *adj* inválido (*nulo, de ningún valor*) ‖ ['ɪnvəlɪd] *adj* inválido (*por viejo o por enfermo*) ‖ ['ɪnvəlɪd] *s* inválido
invalidate [ɪn'vælɪ,det] *tr* invalidar
invalidity [,ɪnvə'lɪdɪti] *s* invalidez *f*
invaluable [ɪn'vælju•əbəl] *adj* inestimable, inapreciable
invariable [ɪn'vɛri•əbəl] *adj* invariable
invasion [ɪn'veʒən] *s* invasión
invective [ɪn'vɛktɪv] *s* invectiva
inveigh [ɪn've] *intr*—**to inveigh against** lanzar invectivas contra
inveigle [ɪn'vegəl] o [ɪn'vigəl] *tr* engatusar
invent [ɪn'vɛnt] *tr* inventar
invention [ɪn'vɛnʃən] *s* invención, invento
inventive [ɪn'vɛntɪv] *adj* inventivo
inventiveness [ɪn'vɛntɪvnɪs] *s* inventiva
inventor [ɪn'vɛntər] *s* inventor *m*
invento•ry ['ɪnvən,tori] *s* (*pl* **-ries**) inventario; stock *m* ‖ *v* (*pret* & *pp* **-ried**) *tr* inventariar
inverse [ɪn'vʌrs] *adj* inverso
inversion [ɪn'vʌrʒən] o [ɪn'vʌrʃən] *s* inversión
invert ['ɪnvʌrt] *s* invertido ‖ [ɪn'vʌrt] *tr* invertir
invertebrate [ɪn'vʌrtɪ,bret] o [ɪn'vʌrtɪbrɪt] *adj* & *s* invertebrado
inverted exclamation point *s* principio de admiración
inverted question mark *s* principio de interrogación
invest [ɪn'vɛst] *tr* (*to vest, to install*) investir; invertir (*dinero*); (*to besiege*) cercar, sitiar; (*to surround, envelop*) cubrir, envolver
investigate [ɪn'vɛstɪ,get] *tr* investigar
investigation [ɪn,vɛstɪ•geʃən] *s* investigación
investment [ɪn'vɛstmənt] *s* (*of money*) inversión; (*with an office or dignity*) investidura; (*siege*) cerco, sitio
investment capital *s* capital *m* de inversión
investor [ɪn'vɛstər] *s* inversionista *mf*; inversor *m*
inveterate [ɪn'vɛtərɪt] *adj* inveterado, empedernido
invidious [ɪn'vɪdi•əs] *adj* irritante, odioso, injusto
invigorate [ɪn'vɪgə,ret] *tr* vigorizar
invigorating [ɪn'vɪgə,retɪŋ] *adj* vigorizador, vigorizante
invincible [ɪn'vɪnsɪbəl] *adj* invencible
invisible [ɪn'vɪzɪbəl] *adj* invisible
invisible ink *s* tinta simpática
invitation [,ɪnvɪ'teʃən] *s* invitación, convite *m*
invite [ɪn'vaɪt] *tr* invitar, convidar
inviting [ɪn'vaɪtɪŋ] *adj* atractivo, seductor; (*e.g., food*) apetitoso
invoice ['ɪnvɔɪs] *s* factura; **as per invoice** según factura ‖ *tr* facturar

in
in

invoke [ɪn'vok] *tr* invocar; evocar, conjurar (*p.ej., los demonios*)

involuntary [ɪn'vɑlən,tɛri] *adj* involuntario

involution [,ɪnvə'luʃən] *s* (math) elevación a potencias, potenciación

involve [ɪn'vɑlv] *tr* envolver, comprometer

invulnerable [ɪn'vʌlnərəbəl] *adj* invulnerable

inward ['ɪnwərd] *adj* interior || *adv* interiormente, hacia dentro

iodide ['aɪ•ə,daɪd] *s* yoduro

iodine ['aɪ•ə,dɪn] *s* yodo || ['aɪ•ə,daɪn] *s* tintura de yodo

ion ['aɪ•ən] o ['aɪ•ɑn] *s* ion *m*

ionize ['aɪ•ə,naɪz] *tr* ionizar

ionosphere [aɪ'ɑnə,sfɪr] *s* ionosfera

IOU ['aɪ,o'ju] *s* (letterword) pagaré *m*

I.Q. ['aɪ'kju] *abbr* & *s* (letterword) **intelligence quotient**

Iran [ɪ'rɑn] o [aɪ'ræn] *s* el Irán

Iranian [ɪ'reni•ən] o [aɪ'reni•ən] *adj* & *s* iranés *m* o iranio

Iraq [ɪ'rɑk] *s* el Irak

Ira•qi [ɪ'rɑki] *adj* iraqués o iraquiano || *s* (*pl* **-qis**) iraqués *m* o iraquiano

irate ['aɪret] o [aɪ'ret] *adj* airado

ire [aɪr] *s* ira, cólera

Ireland ['aɪrlənd] *s* Irlanda

iris ['aɪrɪs] *s* (*of the eye*) iris *m;* (*rainbow*) iris, arco iris; (bot) lirio

Irish ['aɪrɪʃ] *adj* irlandés || *s* (*language*) irlandés *m;* whisky *m* de Irlanda; **the Irish** los irlandeses

Irish•man ['aɪrɪʃmən] *s* (*pl* **-men** [mən]) irlandés *m*

Irish stew *s* guisado de carne con patatas y cebollas

I'rish•wom'an *s* (*pl* **-wom'en**) irlandesa

irk [ʌrk] *tr* fastidiar, molestar

irksome ['ʌrksəm] *adj* fastidioso, molesto

iron ['aɪ•ərn] *adj* férreo || *s* hierro; (*implement used to press or smooth clothes*) plancha; **irons** (*fetters*) hierros, grilletes *mpl;* **strike while the iron is hot** a hierro caliente batir de repente || *tr* planchar (*la ropa*); **to iron out** allanar (*una dificultad*)

i'ron-bound' *adj* zunchado con hierro; (*unyielding*) férreo, duro, inflexible; (*rockbound*) escabroso, rocoso

ironclad ['aɪ•ərn'klæd] *adj* acorazado, blindado; inflexible, exigente

iron curtain *s* (fig) telón *m* de hierro, cortina de hierro

iron digestion *s* estómago de avestruz

ironhanded ['aɪ•ərn,hændɪd] *adj* severo; rigoroso; de mano férrea

iron horse *s* (coll) locomotora

ironic(al) [aɪ'rɑnɪk(əl)] *adj* irónico

ironing ['aɪ•ərnɪŋ] *s* planchado; ropa planchada; ropa por planchar

ironing board *s* tabla de planchar

iron lung *s* pulmón *m* de acero o de hierro

i'ron•ware' *s* ferretería

iron will *s* voluntad de hierro

i'ron•work' *s* herraje *m;* **ironworks** ferrería, herrería

i'ron•work'er *s* herrero de grueso; (*metalworker*) cerrajero

iro•ny ['aɪrəni] *s* (*pl* **-nies**) ironía

irradiate [ɪ'redɪ,et] *tr* irradiar; (med) someter a radiación || *intr* irradiar

irrational ['ɪræʃənəl] *adj* irracional

irrecoverable [,ɪrɪ'kʌvərəbəl] *adj* incobrable, irrecuperable

irredeemable [,ɪrɪ'diməbəl] *adj* irredimible

irrefutable [,ɪrɪ'fjutəbəl] o [ɪ'rɛfjutəbəl] *adj* irrebatible

irregular [ɪ'rɛgələr] *adj* irregular || *s* (mil) irregular *m*

irrelevance [ɪ'rɛləvəns] *s* impertinencia, inaplicabilidad

irrelevant [ɪ'rɛləvənt] *adj* impertinente, inaplicable; irrelevante

irreligious [,ɪrɪ'lɪdʒəs] *adj* irreligioso

irremediable [,ɪrɪ'midi•əbəl] *adj* irremediable

irremovable [,ɪrɪ'muvəbəl] *adj* inamovible

irreparable [ɪ'rɛpərəbəl] *adj* irreparable

irreplaceable [,ɪrɪ'plesəbəl] *adj* insubstituíble, irreemplazable

irrepressible [,ɪrɪ'prɛsɪbəl] *adj* irreprimible, incontenible

irreproachable [,ɪrɪ'protʃəbəl] *adj* irreprochable

irresistible [,ɪrɪ'zɪstɪbəl] *adj* irresistible

irrespective [,ɪrɪ'spɛktɪv] *adj* — **irrespective of** sin hacer caso de, independiente de

irresponsible [,ɪrɪ'spɑnsɪbəl] *adj* irresponsable

irretrievable [,ɪrɪ'trivəbəl] *adj* irrecuperable

irreverent [ɪ'rɛvərənt] *adj* irreverente

irrevocable [ɪ'rɛvəkəbəl] *adj* irrevocable

irrigate ['ɪrɪ,get] *tr* irrigar

irrigation [,ɪrɪ'geʃən] *s* irrigación

irritant ['ɪrɪtənt] *adj* & *s* irritante *m*

irritate ['ɪrɪ,tet] *tr* irritar

irruption [ɪ'rʌpʃən] *s* irrupción

is. *abbr* **island**

isinglass ['aɪzɪŋ,glæs] o ['aɪzɪŋ,glɑs] *s* (*form of gelatine*) cola de pescado, colapez *f;* mica

isl. *abbr* **island**

Islam ['ɪsləm] o [ɪs'lɑm] *s* el Islam

island ['aɪlənd] *adj* isleño || *s* isla

islander ['aɪləndər] *s* isleño

isle [aɪl] *s* isleta

isolate ['aɪsə,let] *tr* aislar

isolated ['aɪsə,letɪd] *adj* aislado; insulado; alejado

isolation [,aɪsə'leʃən] *s* aislamiento

isolationist [,aɪsə'leʃənɪst] *s* aislacionista *mf*

isometric [,aɪsə'mɛtrɪk] *adj* isométrico

isometrics *s* isométrica

isosceles [aɪ'sɑsə,liz] *adj* isósceles

isotope ['aɪsə,top] *s* isótopo

Israe•li [ɪz'reli] *adj* israelí || *s* (*pl* **-lis** [liz]) israelí *mf*

Israelite ['ɪzrɪ•ə,laɪt] *adj* & *s* israelita *mf*

issuance ['ɪʃu•əns] *s* emisión, expedición

issue ['ɪʃu] *s* (*outgoing, outlet*) salida; (*result*) consecuencia, resultado; (*offspring*) descendencia, sucesión; (*of a magazine*) edición, impresión, tirada, número; (*e.g.,*

of a bond) emisión; (*yield, profit*) beneficios, producto; punto en disputa; (*distribution*) repartida; (pathol) flujo; **at issue** en
disputa; **to face the issue** afrontar la situación; **to force the issue** forzar la solución;
to take issue with llevar la contraria a ‖ *tr*
publicar, dar a luz (*un nuevo libro, una
revista, etc.*); emitir, expedir (*títulos, obligaciones, etc.*); distribuir (*ropa, alimento*)
‖ *intr* salir; **to issue from** provenir de
isthmus [ˈɪsməs] *s* istmo
it [ɪt] *pron pers* (aplícase a cosas inanimadas,
a niños de teta, a animales cuyo sexo no se
conoce; y muchas veces no se traduce) él,
ella; lo, la; **it is I** soy yo; **it is snowing**
nieva; **it is three o'clock** son las tres
ital. *abbr* **italics**
Ital. *abbr* **Italian, Italy**
Italian [ɪˈtæljən] *adj & s* italiano
italic [ɪˈtælɪk] *adj* (typ) itálico ‖ **italics** *s*
(typ) itálica, bastardilla ‖ **Italic** *adj* itálico
italicize [ɪˈtælɪˌsaɪz] *tr* imprimir en bastardilla; subrayar
Italy [ˈɪtəli] *s* Italia
itch [ɪtʃ] *s* comezón *f;* (pathol) sarna; (*eager-*

ness) (fig) comezón, prurito ‖ *tr* dar comezón a ‖ *intr* picar; **to itch to** tener prurito
por
itch·y [ˈɪtʃi] *adj* (*comp* **-ier;** *super* **-iest**)
picante, hormigoso; (pathol) sarnoso
item [ˈaɪtəm] *s* artículo; noticia, suelto; (*in an
account*) partida
itemization [ˌaɪtəmaɪˈzeʃən] *s* rubricación
itemize [ˈaɪtəˌmaɪz] *tr* particularizar, especificar, pormenorizar
itinerant [aɪˈtɪnərənt] o [ɪˈtɪnərənt] *adj* ambulante, errante ‖ *s* viandante *mf*
itinerar·y][aɪˈtɪnəˌrɛri] o [ɪˈtɪnəˌrɛri] *adj*
itinerario ‖ *s* (*pl* **-ies**) itinerario
its [ɪts] *adj poss* su ‖ *pron poss* el suyo; suyo
itself [ɪtˈsɛlf] *pron pers* mismo; sí, sí mismo;
se
ivied [ˈaɪvid] *adj* cubierto de hiedra
ivo·ry [ˈaɪvəri] *adj* marfileño ‖ *s* (*pl* **-ries**)
marfil *m;* **ivories** (slang) teclas del piano;
(slang) bolas de billar; (*dice*) (slang) dados;
(slang) dientes *mpl*
ivory tower *s* (fig) torre *f* de marfil; (fig)
inocencia
ivy [ˈaɪvi] *s* (*pl* **-ivies**) hiedra

J

J. j [dʒe] décima letra del alfabeto inglés
J. *abbr* **Judge, Justice**
jab [dʒæb] *s* hurgonazo; (*prick*) pinchazo;
(*with elbow*) codazo ‖ *v* (*pret & pp* **jabbed;**
ger **jabbing**) *tr* hurgonear; dar un codazo a
‖ *intr* hurgonear
jabber [ˈdʒæbər] *s* chapurreo ‖ *tr & intr*
chapurrear
jabot [dʒæˈbo] o [ˈdʒæbo] *s* chorrera
jack [dʒæk] *s* (*for lifting heavy objects*) gato,
cric *m;* (*fellow*) mozo, sujeto, (*jackass*)
asno, burro; (*in card games*) sota, valet *m;*
(*small ball for bowling*) boliche *m;* (*jackstone*) cantillo; (*device for turning a spit*)
torno de asador; (*figure which strikes a
clock bell*) jaquemar *m;* (*to remove a boot*)
sacabotas *m;* marinero; (*flag at the bow*)
(naut) yac *m;* (rad & telv) jack *m;* (elec)
caja de enchufe; (slang) dinero; **every man
Jack** cada hijo de vecino; **jacks** cantillos,
juego de los cantillos ‖ *tr* **— to jack up**
alzar con el gato; (coll) subir (*sueldos,
precios, etc.*); (coll) recordar su obligación
a
jackal [ˈdʒækəl] *s* chacal *m*
jackanapes [ˈdʒækəˌneps] *s* mequetrefe *m*
jack'ass' *s* asno, burro
jack'daw' *s* corneja
jacket [ˈdʒækɪt] *s* chaqueta; (*folded paper*)
cubierta, envoltura; (*paper cover of a book*)
sobrecubierta; (*metal casing*) camisa
jack'ham'mer *s* martillo perforador
jack'-in-the-box' *s* caja de sorpresa, jugete-

sorpresa *m,* muñeco en una caja de resorte
jack'knife' *s* (*pl* **-knives'**) navaja de bolsillo;
(*fancy dive*) salto de carpa
jack of all trades *s* hombre que hace toda
clase de oficios dije *m*
jack-o'-lantern [ˈdʒækəˌlæntərn] *s* fuego fatuo; linterna hecha con una calabaza cortado de modo que remede una cabeza
humana
jack pot *s*—**to hit the jack pot** (slang)
ponerse las botas
jack rabbit *s* liebre grande norteamericana
jack'screw' *s* cric *m* o gato de tornillo
jack'stone' *s* cantillo; **jackstones** cantillos,
juego de los cantillos
jack'-tar' *s* (coll) marinero
jade [dʒed] *adj* verdoso como el jade ‖ *s*
(*ornamental stone*) jade *m;* verde *m* de
jade; (*worn-out horse*) jamelgo; picarona,
mujerzuela ‖ *tr* cansar, ahitar, saciar
jaded [ˈdʒedɪd] *adj* ahito, saciado
jag [dʒæg] *s* diente *m,* púa; **to have a jag on**
(slang) estar borracho
jagged [ˈdʒægɪd] *adj* dentado, mellado; ras-
gado en sietes
jaguar [ˈdʒægwɑr] *s* jaguar *m*
jail [dʒel] *s* cárcel *f;* **to break jail** escaparse
de la cárcel ‖ *tr* encarcelar
jail'bird' *s* (coll) preso, encarcelado; (coll)
infractor *m* habitual
jail'break' *s* escapatoria de la cárcel
jail delivery *s* evasión de la cárcel
jailer [ˈdʒelər] *s* carcelero

jalop•y [dʒə'lɑpi] s (pl **-ies**) automóvil viejo y ruinoso

jam [dʒæm] s apiñadura, apretura; (e.g., in traffic) embotellamiento, bloqueo; (preserve) compota, conserva; (difficult situation) (coll) aprieto, apuros ‖ v (pret & pp **jammed;** ger **jamming**) tr apiñar, apretujar; machucarse (p.ej., un dedo); (rad) perturbar, sabotear; **to jam on the brakes** frenar de golpe

Jamaican [dʒə'mekən] adj & s jamaicano; jamaiquino (Am)

jamb [dʒæm] s jamba

jamboree [,dʒæmbə'ri] s (coll) francachela, holgorio; reunión de niños exploradores

jamming ['dʒæmɪŋ] s radioperturbación

jam nut s contratuerca

jam-packed ['dʒæm'pækt] adj (coll) apiñado, apretujado, atestado

jam session s reunión de músicos de jazz para tocar improvisaciones

jangle ['dʒæŋgəl] s cencerreo; altercado, riña ‖ tr hacer sonar con ruido discordante ‖ intr cencerrear; reñir

janitor ['dʒænɪtər] s portero, conserje m

janitress ['dʒænɪtrɪs] s portera

January ['dʒænjuˌɛri] s enero

Ja•pan [dʒə'pæn] s laca japonesa; obra japonesa laqueada; aceite m secante japonés ‖ v (pret & pp **-panned;** ger **-panning**) tr barnizar, charolar, laquear con laca japonesa ‖ **Japan** s el Japón

Japa•nese [,dʒæpə'niz] adj japonés ‖ s (pl **-nese**) japonés m

Japanese beetle s escarabajo japonés

Japanese lantern s farolillo veneciano

Japanese persimmon s caqui m

jar [dʒɑr] s tarro; (e.g., of olives) frasco; (of a storage battery) recipiente m; (jolt) sacudida; ruido desapacible; sorpresa desagradable; **on the jar** (said of a door) entreabierto, entornado ‖ v (pret & pp **jarred;** ger **jarring**) tr sacudir; chocar; (with a noise) traquetear ‖ intr sacudirse; traquetear; disputar; **to jar on** irritar

jardiniere [,dʒɑrdɪ'nɪr] s (stand) jardinera; (pot, bowl) florero

jargon ['dʒɑrgən] s jerga, jerigonza

jasmine ['dʒæsmɪn] s jazmín m

jasper ['dʒæspər] s jaspe m

jaundice ['dʒɔndɪs] o ['dʒɑndɪs] s ictericia; (fig) envidia, celos, negro humor

jaundiced ['dʒɔndɪst] o ['dʒɑndɪst] adj ictericiado; (fig) avinagrado

jaunt [dʒɔnt] o [dʒɑnt] s caminata, excursión, paseo

jaun•ty ['dʒɔnti] o ['dʒɑnti] adj (comp **-tier;** super **-tiest**) airoso, gallardo, vivo; elegante, de buen gusto

Java•nese [,dʒævə'niz] adj javanés ‖ s (pl **-nese**) javanés m

javelin ['dʒævlɪn] o ['dʒævəlɪn] s jabalina

jaw [dʒɔ] s mandíbula, quijada; **into the jaws of death** a las garras de la muerte; **jaws** boca, garganta ‖ tr (slang) regañar ‖ intr (slang) regañar; (slang) chacharear, chismear

jaw'bone' s mandíbula, quijada

jaw'break'er s (word) (coll) trabalenguas m; (candy) (coll) hinchabocas m; (mach) trituradora de quijadas

jay [dʒe] s (orn) arrendajo; (coll) tonto, necio

jay'walk' intr (coll) cruzar la calle descuidadamente

jay'walk'er s (coll) peatón descuidado

jazz [dʒæz] s (mus) jazz m; (coll) animación, viveza ‖ tr—**to jazz up** (coll) animar, dar viveza a

jazz band s orquesta de jazz

J.C. abbr **Jesus Christ, Julius Caesar**

jct. abbr **junction**

jealous ['dʒɛləs] adj celoso; envidioso; (watchful in keeping or guarding something) solícito, vigilante

jealous•y ['dʒɛləsi] s (pl **-ies**) celosía, celos; envidia; solicitud, vigilancia

jean [dʒin] s dril m; **jeans** pantalones mpl de dril

Jeanne d'Arc [,ʒɑn'dɑrk] s Juana de Arco

jeep [dʒip] s jip m, pequeño automóvil de propulsión total

jeer [dʒɪr] s befa, mofa, vaya ‖ tr befar ‖ intr mofarse; **to jeer at** befar, mofarse de

jelab [dʒə'lab] s chilaba

jell [dʒɛl] s jalea ‖ intr (to become jellylike) cuajarse; (to take hold, catch on) (fig) cuajar

jel•ly ['dʒɛli] s (pl **-lies**) jalea ‖ v (pret & pp) tr convertir en jalea ‖ intr convertirse en jalea

jel'ly•bean' s frutilla

jel'ly•fish' s aguamala, medusa; (weak person) (coll) calzonazos m

jeopardize ['dʒɛpərˌdaɪz] tr arriesgar, exponer, poner en peligro

jeopardy ['dʒɛpərdi] s riesgo, peligro

jeremiad [,dʒɛrɪ'maɪˌæd] s jeremiada

Jericho ['dʒɛrɪˌko] s Jericó

jerk [dʒʌrk] s arranque m, estirón m, tirón m; tic m, espasmo muscular; **by jerks** a sacudidas ‖ tr mover de un tirón; arrojar de un tirón; atasajar (carne) ‖ intr avanzar a tirones

jerked beef s tasajo

jerkin ['dʒʌrkɪn] s jubón m, justillo

jerk'wa'ter train s (coll) tren de ferrocarril económico

jerk•y ['dʒʌrki] adj (comp **-ier;** super **-iest**) (road; style) desigual; que va dando tumbos, que anda a tirones

jersey ['dʒʌrsi] s jersey m, chaqueta de punto

Jerusalem [dʒɪ'rusələm] s Jerusalén

jest [dʒɛst] s broma, chanza, chiste m; cosa de risa; **in jest** en broma ‖ intr bromear

jester ['dʒɛstər] s bromista mf, burlón m; (professional fool of medieval rulers) bufón m

Jesuit ['dʒɛʒʊ•ɪt] o ['dʒɛʒjˌɪt] adj & s jesuíta m

Jesuitic(al) [,dʒɛʒʊ'ɪtɪk(əl)] o [,dʒɛʒju'ɪtɪk(əl)] adj jesuítico

Jesus ['dʒizəs] s Jesús m

Jesus Christ s Jesucristo

jet [dʒɛt] *adj* de azabache; azabachado ‖ *s* (*of a fountain*) surtidor *m;* (*of gas*) mechero; (*stream shooting forth from nozzle, etc.*) chorro; avión *m* a reacción, avión de chorro; (*hard black mineral; lustrous black*) azabache *m* ‖ *v* (*pret & pp* **jetted;** *ger* **jetting**) *tr* arrojar en chorro ‖ *intr* chorrear, salir en chorro; volar en avión de chorro

jet age *s* era de los aviones de chorro

jet'-black' *adj* azabachado

jet bomber *s* bombardero de reacción a chorro

jet coal *s* carbón *m* de bujía, carbón de llama larga

jet engine *s* motor *m* a chorro, motor de reacción

jet fighter *s* caza *m* de reacción, cazarreactor *m*

jet'lin'er *s* avión *m* de travesía con propulsión a chorro

jet plane *s* avión *m* de chorro

jet propulsion *s* propulsión a chorro, propulsión de escape

jetsam ['dʒɛtsəm] *s* (naut) echazón *f;* cosas desechadas

jet set *s* gente acomodada que viajan mucho por avión

jet stream *s* escape *m* de un motor cohete; (meteor) chorros de viento (*que soplan de oeste a este a la altura de 10 kilómetros*)

jettison ['dʒɛtɪsən] *s* (naut) echazón *f* ‖ *tr* (naut) echar al mar; desechar, rechazar

jettison gear *s* (aer) lanzador *m*

jet'ty ['dʒɛti] *s* (*pl* **-ties**) (*structure projecting into sea to protect harbor*) excollera, malecón *m;* (*wharf*) muelle *m*, desembarcadero

Jew [dʒu] *s* judío

jewel ['dʒu•əl] *s* piedra preciosa; (*valuable personal ornament*) alhaja; joya; (*of a watch*) rubí *m;* (*article of costume jewelry*) joya de imitación; (*highly prized person or thing*) alhaja, joya

jewel case *s* guardajoyas *m*, estuche *m*, joyero

jeweler o **jeweller** ['dʒu•ələr] *s* joyero; relojero

jewelry ['dʒu•əlri] *s* joyería, joyas

jewelry shop *s* joyería; relojería

Jewess ['dʒu•ɪs] *s* judía

jew'fish' *s* mero

Jewish ['dʒu•ɪʃ] *adj* judío

Jew·ry ['dʒu•ri] *s* (*pl* **-ries**) judería

jews'-harp o **jew's-harp** ['dʒuz,harp] *s* birimbao

jib [dʒɪb] *s* (*of a crane*) aguilón *m*, pescante *m;* (naut) foque *m*

jib boom *s* (naut) botalón *m* de foque

jibe [dʒaɪb] *s* remoque *m*, mofa ‖ *intr* mofarse; (coll) concordar (*dos cosas*); **to jibe at** mofarse de

jif·fy ['dʒɪfi] *s* (*pl* **-fies**)—**in a jiffy** (coll) en un santiamén

jig [dʒɪg] *s* (*dance and music*) giga; **the jig is up** (slang) ya se acabó todo, estamos perdidos

jigger ['dʒɪgər] *s* (*for fishing*) anzuelo de cuchara; (*for separating ore*) criba de vaivén; (*flea*) nigua; (*gadget*) cosilla, chisme *m*, dispositivo; vasito para medir el licor de un coctel (*onza y media*)

jiggle ['dʒɪgəl] *s* zangoloteo ‖ *tr* zangolotear ‖ *intr* zangolotearse

jig saw *s* sierra de vaivén

jig'saw' puzzle *s* rompecabezas *m* (*figura que ha sido cortada caprichosamente en trozos menudos y que hay que recomponer*)

jilt [dʒɪlt] *tr* dar calabazas a (*un novio*)

jim·my ['dʒɪmi] *s* (*pl* **-mies**) palanqueta ‖ *v* (*pret & pp* **-mied**) *tr* forzar con palanqueta; **to jimmy open** abrir con palanqueta

jingle ['dʒɪŋgəl] *s* (*small bell*) cascabel *m;* (*of tambourine*) sonaja; (*sound*) cascabeleo; rima infantil; (rad) anuncio rimado y cantado ‖ *tr* hacer sonar ‖ *intr* cascabelear

jin·go ['dʒɪŋgo] *adj* jingoísta ‖ *s* (*pl* **-goes**) jingoísta *mf;* **by jingo!** (coll) ¡caramba!

jingoism ['dʒɪŋgo,ɪzəm] *s* jingoísmo

jinx [dʒɪŋks] *s* gafe *m* ‖ *tr* (coll) traer mala suerte a

jitters ['dʒɪtərz] *spl* (coll) inquietud, nerviosidad; **to give the jitters to** (coll) poner nervioso; **to have the jitters** (coll) ponerse nervioso

jittery ['dʒɪtəri] *adj* (coll) nervioso

Joan of Arc ['dʒon əv 'ark] *s* Juana de Arco

job [dʒab] *s* (*piece of work*) trabajo; (*task, chore*) quehacer *m*, tarea; (*work done by contract*) destajo; (*employment*) empleo, oficio; (coll) robo; **by the job** a destajo; **on the job** trabajando de aprendiz; (slang) vigilante, atento a sus obligaciones; **to be out of a job** estar desocupado, estar sin trabajo; **to lie down on the job** (slang) echarse en el surco, estirar la pierna

job analysis *s* análisis *m* ocupacional

jobber ['dʒabər] *s* comerciante medianero; (*pieceworker*) destajero; (*dishonest official*) agiotista *m*

job'hold'er *s* empleado; (*in the government*) burócrata *mf*

jobless ['dʒablɪs] *adj* desocupado, sin empleo

job lot *s* saldo de mercancías

job market *s* oportunidades *fpl* de empleo

job printer *s* impresor *m* de remiendos

job printing *s* remiendo

job security *s* garantía de empleo continuo

jock [dʒak] *s* (slang) atleta *m*

jockey ['dʒaki] *s* jockey *m* ‖ *tr* montar (*un caballo*) en la pista; maniobrar; embaucar

jockstrap ['dʒak,stræp] *s* suspensorio (*para sostener el escroto*)

jocose [dʒo'kos] *adj* jocoso

jocular ['dʒakjələr] *adj* jocoso, festivo

jodhpurs ['dʒadpərz] *spl* pantalones *mpl* de equitación

jog [dʒag] *s* golpecito; (*to the memory*) estímulo; trote corto ‖ *v* (*pret & pp* **jogged;** *ger* **jogging**) *tr* empujar levemente; estimular (*la memoria*) ‖ *intr*—**to jog along** avanzar al trote corto

jogging ['dʒagɪŋ] *s* trote *m* corto

jog trot *s* trote *m* de perro; (fig) rutina

ja
jo

john [dʒɑn] *s* (slang) retrete *m;* inodoro
John Bull *s* el inglés típico, el pueblo inglés
John Hancock [ˈhænkɑk] *s* (coll) la firma de uno
johnnycake [ˈdʒɑni,kek] *s* pan *m* de maíz
John′ny-come′-late′ly *s* recién llegado
John′ny-jump′-up *s* (*pansy*) pensamiento, trinitaria, violeta
John′ny-on-the-spot′ *s* (coll) el que está siempre presente y listo
John the Baptist *s* San Juan Bautista
join [dʒɔɪn] *tr* juntar, unir, ensamblar; asociarse a, unirse a; incorporarse a, ingresar en; abrazar (*un partido*); hacerse socio de (una asociación); alistarse en (*el ejército*); trabar (*batalla*); desaguar en (*el océano*) ‖ *intr* juntarse, unirse; confluir (*p.ej., dos ríos*)
joiner [ˈdʒɔɪnər] *s* carpintero; (coll) el que tiene la manía de incorporarse a muchas asociaciones
joint [dʒɔɪnt] *s* (*in a pipe*) empalme *m,* juntura, (*of bones*) articulación, juntura, coyuntura; (*backbone of book*) nervura; (*hinge of book*) cartivana; (*in woodwork*) emsambladura; (*of meat*) tajada; (*marijuana*) porro, puerro; (elec) empalme *m;* (*gambling den*) (slang) garito; (slang) restaurante *m* de mala muerte; **out of joint** desencajado, descoyuntado; (fig) en desorden, desbarajustado; **to throw out of joint** descoyuntarse (*p.ej., el brazo*)
joint account *s* cuenta en común
Joint Chiefs of Staff *spl* (U.S.A.) Estado mayor conjunto
jointly [ˈdʒɔɪntli] *adv* juntamente, en común
joint owner *s* condueño
joint session *s* sesión conjunta
joint′-stock′ company *s* sociedad anónima, compañía por acciones
jointure [ˈdʒɔɪntʃər] *s* bienes *mpl* parafernales
joist [dʒɔɪst] *s* viga
joke [dʒok] *s* broma, chiste *m;* (*trifling matter*) cosa de reír; (*person laughed at*) bufón *m,* hazmerreír *m;* **no joke** cosa seria; **to tell a joke** contar un chiste, **to play a joke on** gastar una broma a ‖ *tr*—**to joke one's way into** conseguir (*p.ej., un empleo*) burla burlando ‖ *intr* bromear, hablar en broma; **joking aside** o **no joking** burlas aparte
joke book *s* libro de chistes
joker [ˈdʒokər] *s* bromista *mf;* (*wise guy*) sábelotodo; (*playing card*) comodín *m;* (*hidden provision*) cláusula engañadora
jol•ly [ˈdʒɑli] *adj* (*comp* **-lier;** *super* **-liest**) alegre, festivo ‖ *adv* (coll) muy, harto ‖ *v* (*pret & pp* **-lied**) *tr* (coll) candonguear
jolt [dʒolt] *s* sacudida ‖ *tr* sacudir ‖ *intr* dar tumbos
Jonah [ˈdʒonə] *s* Jonás *m;* (fig) ave *f* de mal agüero
jongleur [ˈdʒɑŋglər] *s* juglar *m,* trovador *m*
jonquil [ˈdʒɑŋkwɪl] *s* junquillo
Jordan [ˈdʒɔrdən] *s* (*country*) Jordania; (*river*) Jordán *m*
Jordan almond *s* almendra de Málaga

Jordanian [dʒɔrˈdɛnɪ•ən] *adj & s* jordano
josh [dʒɑʃ] *tr* (coll) dar broma a ‖ *intr* dar broma
jostle [ˈdʒɑsəl] *s* empellón *m,* empujón *m* ‖ *tr* empellar, empujar ‖ *intr* chocar, encontrarse; avanzar a fuerza de empujones o codazos
jot [dʒɑt] *s*—**I don't care a jot for** no se me da un bledo de *s v* (*pret & pp* **jotted;** *ger* **jotting**) *tr*—**to jot down** apuntar, anotar
jounce [dʒɑuns] *s* sacudida ‖ *tr* sacudir ‖ *intr* dar tumbos
journal [ˈdʒʌrnəl] *s* (*newspaper*) periódico; (*magazine*) revista; (*daily record*) diario; (com) libro diario; (naut) cuaderno de bitácora; (mach) gorrón *m,* muñón *m*
journalese [,dʒʌrnəˈliz] *s* lenguaje periodístico
journalism [ˈdʒʌrnə,lɪzəm] *s* periodismo
journalist [ˈdʒʌrnəlɪst] *s* periodista *mf*
journalistic [,dʒʌrnəˈlɪstɪk] *adj* periodístico
journey [ˈdʒʌrni] *s* viaje *m* ‖ *intr* viajar
journey•man [ˈdʒʌrnimən] *s* (*pl* **-men** [mən]) oficial *m*
joust [dʒʌst] o [dʒust] o [dʒaust] *s* justa ‖ *intr* justar
jovial [ˈdʒovɪ•əl] *adj* jovial
joviality [,dʒovɪˈæliti] *s* jovialidad
jowl [dʒaul] *s* (*cheek*) moflete *m;* (*jawbone*) quijada; (*of cattle*) papada; (*of fowl*) barba
joy [dʒɔɪ] *s* alegría, regocijo; **to leap with joy** saltar de gozo
joyful [ˈdʒɔɪfəl] *adj* alegre; **joyful over** gozoso con o de
joyless [ˈdʒɔɪlɪs] *adj* triste, sin alegría
joyous [ˈdʒɔɪ•əs] *adj* alegre
joy ride *s* (coll) paseo de recreo en coche; (coll) paseo alocado en coche
J.P. *abbr* **Justice of the Peace**
Jr. *abbr* **junior**
jubilant [ˈdʒubɪlənt] *adj* jubiloso
jubilation [,dʒubɪˈleʃən] *s* júbilo, viva alegría
jubilee [ˈdʒubɪ,li] *s* (*jubilation*) júbilo; aniversario; quincuagésimo aniversario; (eccl) jubileo
Judaism [ˈdʒude,ɪzəm] *s* judaísmo
judge [dʒʌdʒ] *s* juez *m;* **to be a good judge of** tener buen juez de o en ‖ *tr & intr* juzgar; **judging by** a juzgar por
judge advocate *s* (*in the army*) auditor *m* de guerra; (*in the navy*) auditor de marina
judgeship [ˈdʒʌdʒʃɪp] *s* judicatura
judgment [ˈdʒʌdʒmənt] *s* juicio; (*legal decision*) sentencia, fallo
judgment day *s* día *m* del juicio
judgment seat *s* tribunal *m*
judicature [ˈdʒudɪkətʃər] *s* judicatura
judicial [dʒuˈdɪʃəl] *adj* judicial; (*becoming a judge*) crítico, juicioso
judiciar•y [dʒuˈdɪʃɪ,ɛri] *adj* judicial ‖ *s* (*pl* **-ies**) (*judges of a city, country, etc.*) judicatura; (*branch of government that administers justice*) poder *m* judicial
judicious [dʒuˈdɪʃəs] *adj* juicioso
jug [dʒʌg] *s* botija, jarra, cántaro; (*jail*) (slang) chirona

juggle [ˈdʒʌgəl] *s* juego de manos; (*trick, deception*) trampa ‖ *tr* hacer suertes con (*p.ej., bolas*); alterar fraudulentamente, falsear (*cuentas, documentos, etc.*); **to juggle away** escamotear ‖ *intr* hacer suertes; hacer trampas

juggler [ˈdʒʌglər] *s* malabarista *mf*; impostor *m*

juggling [ˈdʒʌglɪŋ] *s* juegos malabares

Jugoslav [ˈjugoˈslɑv] *adj & s* yugoeslavo

Jugoslavia [ˈjugoˈslɑvɪ•ə] *s* Yugoslavia

jugular [ˈdʒʌgjələr] *adj & s* yugular *f*

juice [dʒus] *s* jugo, zumo; (*natural fluid of an animal body*) jugo; (*slang*) electricidad; (*slang*) gasolina; **to stew in one's own juice** (coll) freír en su aceite

juic•y [ˈdʒusi] *adj* (*comp* **-ier;** *super* **-iest**) jugoso, zumoso; (*interesting, spicy*) picante

jukebox [ˈdʒuk,bɑks] *s* tocadiscos *m* tragamonedas

julep [ˈdʒulɪp] *s* julepe *m*

julienne [,dʒulɪˈɛn] *s* sopa juliana

July [dʒuˈlaɪ] *s* julio

jumble [ˈdʒʌmbəl] *s* revoltijo, masa confusa ‖ *tr* emburujar, revolver

jum•bo [ˈdʒʌmbo] *adj* (coll) enorme, colosal ‖ *s* (*pl* **-bos**) (*large clumsy person*) (coll) elefante *m*; (coll) objeto enorme

jump [dʒʌmp] *s* salto; (*in a parachute*) lanzamiento; (*of prices*) alza repentina; **to be always on the jump** (coll) andar siempre de aquí para allí; **to get** o **to have the jump on** (slang) ganar la ventaja a ‖ *tr* saltar; hacer saltar (*a un caballo*); (*in checkers*) comer; salir (*un tren*) fuera de (*el carril*) ‖. *intr* saltar; (*in a parachute from an airplane*) lanzarse; pasar del tope (*el carro de la máquina de escribir*); **to jump at** apresurarse a aceptar (*un convite*); apresurarse a aprovechar (*la oportunidad*); **to jump on** saltar a (*un tren*); (slang) regañar, criticar; **to jump over** saltar por, pasar de un salto; saltar (*la página de un libro*); **to jump to a conclusion** sacar una conclusión precipitadamente

jumper [ˈdʒʌmpər] *s* saltador *m*; blusa de obrero; **jumpers** traje holgado de juego para niños

jumping jack [ˈdʒʌmpɪŋ] *s* títere *m*

jump'ing-off' place *s* fin *m* del camino

jump seat *s* estrapontín *m*, traspuntín *m*

jump spark *s* (elec) chispa de enrehierro

jump suit *s* vestido unitario (*como de paracaidista*)

jump wire *s* (elec) alambre *m* de cierre

jump•y [ˈdʒʌmpi] *adj* (*comp* **-ier;** *super* **-iest**) saltón; asustadizo, nervioso

junc. *abbr* **junction**

junction [ˈdʒʌŋkʃən] *s* juntura, unión; (*of pieces of wood*) ensambladura; (*of two rivers*) confluencia; (*rail connection*) empalme *m*; (rr) estación de empalme

juncture [ˈdʒʌŋktʃər] *s* juntura, unión; (*time, occasion*) coyuntura; **at this juncture** a esta sazón, a estas alturas

June [dʒun] *s* junio

jungle [ˈdʒʌŋgəl] *s* jungla, selva; revoltijo, maraña

junior [ˈdʒunjər] *adj* menor, de menor edad; joven; del penúltimo año; hijo, p.ej., **John Jones, Junior** Juan Jones, hijo ‖ *s* menor *m*; socio menor; alumno del penúltimo año

junior college *s* escuela de estudios universitarios de primero y segundo años

junior high school *s* escuela intermedia entre la primaria y la secundaria

juniper [ˈdʒunɪpər] *s* enebro; (*red cedar*) cedro de Virginia

juniper berry *s* enebrina

junk [dʒʌŋk] *s* chatarra, hierro viejo; ropa vieja; (*useless stuff*) (coll) trastos viejos, baratijas viejas; (*old cable*) jarcia trozada; (*Chinese ship*) junco; (naut) carne salada ‖ *tr* (slang) echar a la basura; reducir a hierro viejo

junk dealer *s* chatarrero, chapucero

junket [ˈdʒʌŋkɪt] *s* manjar *m* de leche, cuajo y azúcar; (*outing*) viaje *m* de recreo; (*trip paid out of public funds*) jira ‖ *intr* hacer un viaje de recreo; ir de jira

junkie [ˈdʒʌŋki] *s* (slang) toxicómano, narcotómano, yonquí *m*

junk•man [ˈdʒʌŋk,mæn] *s* (*pl* **-men** [,mɛn]) chatarrero, chapucero; ropavejero; tripulante *m* de junco

junk room *s* leonera, trastera

junk shop o **junk store** *s* tienda de trastos viejos; baratío (CAm); barata (Col, Mex)

junk yard *s* chatarrería

juridical [dʒuˈrɪdɪkəl] *adj* jurídico

jurisdiction [,dʒurɪsˈdɪkʃən] *s* jurisdicción

jurisprudence [,dʒurɪsˈprudəns] *s* jurisprudencia

jurist [ˈdʒurɪst] *s* jurista *mf*

juror [ˈdʒurər] *s* (*individual*) jurado

ju•ry [ˈdʒuri] *s* (*pl* **-ries**) (*group*) jurado

jury box *s* tribuna del jurado

jury•man [ˈdʒurimən] *s* (*pl* **-men** [mən]) (*individual*) jurado

jury-rig [ˈdʒuri,rɪg] *v* (*pret & pp* **-rigged;** *ger* **-rigging**) *tr* (naut) aparejar temporariamente

Jus. P. *abbr* **justice of the peace**

just [dʒʌst] *adj* justo ‖ *adv* justamente, justo; hace poco, apenas; sólo; (coll) absolutamente; **just + pp** acabado de + *inf*, p.ej., **just received** acabado de recibir; recién + pp. p.ej., **just arrived** recién llegado; **just as** como; en el momento en que; tal como, lo mismo que; **just beyond** un poco más allá (de); **just now** hace poco; ahora mismo; **just out** acabado de aparecer, recién publicado; **to have just + pp** acabar de + *inf*. p.ej., **I have just arrived** acabo de llegar; **I had just arrived** acababa de llegar

justice [ˈdʒʌstɪs] *s* justicia; (*judge*) juez *m*; (*just deserts*) premio merecido; **to bring to justice** aprehender y condenar por justicia; **to do justice to** hacer justicia a; apreciar debidamente

justice of the peace *s* juez *m* de paz

justifiable [ˈdʒʌstɪ,faɪ•əbəl] *adj* justificable

jo
ju

justi·fy [ˈdʒʌstɪˌfaɪ] v (pret & pp **-fied**) tr justificar; (typ) justificar

justly [ˈdʒʌstli] adj justamente, debidamente

jut [dʒʌt] v (pre & pp **jutted**; ger **jutting**) intr—**to jut out** resaltar, proyectarse

jute [dʒut] s yute m ‖ **Jute** m juto

Jutland [ˈdʒʌtlənd] s Jutlandia

juvenile [ˈdʒuvənɪl] o [ˈdʒuvəˌnaɪl] adj juvenil; para jóvenes ‖ s joven mf, mocito; libro para niños; (theat) galán m, galancete m

juvenile court s tribunal m tutelar de menores

juvenile delinquency s delincuencia de menores

juvenile lead [lid] s (theat) papel m de galancete; (theat) galancete m

juvenilia [ˌdʒuvəˈnɪliˑə] spl obras de juventud

juxtapose [ˌdʒʌkstəˈpoz] tr yuxtaponer

K

K, k [ke] undécima letra del alfabeto inglés

k. abbr **karat, kilogram**

K. abbr **King, Knight**

kale [kel] s col f, berza; (slang) dinero, pasta

kaleidoscope [keˈlaɪdəˌskop] s calidoscopio

kangaroo [ˌkæŋgəˈru] s canguro

kapok [ˈkepɑk] s capoc m, lana de ceiba

kaput [kəˈput] adj (slang) roto; gastado; inútil

karate [kəˈrɑti] m karate m, karaté m

karate expert s karateka m

katydid [ˈketɪdɪd] s saltamontes m cuyo macho emite un sonido chillón

kayak [ˈkaɪæk] s kayak m

kc. abbr **kilocycle**

kedge [kɛdʒ] s (naut) anclote m

keel [kil] s quilla ‖ intr—**to keel over** (naut) dar de quilla; volcarse; (coll) desmayarse

keelson [ˈkɛlsən] o [ˈkilsən] s (naut) sobrequilla

keen [kin] adj (having a sharp edge) agudo, afilado; (sharp, cutting) mordaz, penetrante; (sharp-witted) sutil, astuto, perspicaz; (eager, much interested) entusiasta; intenso, vivo; (slang) maravilloso; **to be keen on** ser muy aficionado a

keep [kip] s manutención, subsistencia; (of medieval castle) torre f del homenaje; **for keeps** (coll) de veras; (coll) para siempre; **to earn one's keep** (coll) ganarse la vida ‖ v (pret & pp **kept** [kɛpt] tr guardar, conservar; (deciding to make a purchase) quedarse con; cumplir, guardar (su palabra, su promesa); llevar (cuentas); apuntar (los tantos); tener (criados, caballos, huéspedes); cultivar (una huerta); dirigir (un hotel, una escuela); celebrar (una fiesta); hacer tardar (a una persona); **to keep away** tener alejado; **to keep back** retener; beberse (las lágrimas); reservar, no divulgar; **to keep down** reprimir; reducir (los gastos) al mínimo; **to keep** (a person) **from** + ger no dejarle (a una persona) + inf; **to keep in** no dejar salir; **to keep off** tener a distancia; no dejar penetrar (p.ej., la lluvia); evitar (p.ej., el polvo); **to keep out** no dejar entrar; no dejar penetrar; **to keep someone informed**

(about) ponerle a uno al corriente (de); **to keep someone waiting** hacerle a uno esperar; **to keep up** mantener, conservar ‖ intr permanecer, quedarse; conservarse, no echarse a perder; **to keep** + ger seguir + ger; **to keep away** mantenerse a distancia; no dejarse ver; **to keep from** + ger abstenerse de + inf; **to keep informed (about)** ponerse al corriente (de); **to keep in with** (coll) congraciarse con, no perder el favor de; **to keep off** no acercarse a; no pisar (el césped); **to keep on** + ger seguir + ger; **to keep on with** continuar con; **to keep out** mantenerse fuera, no entrar; **to keep out of** no entrar en; no meterse en; evitar (el peligro); **to keep quiet** estarse quieto; **to keep to** seguir por, llevar (la derecha, la izquierda); **to keep to oneself** quedarse a solas; **to keep up** continuar; no rezagarse; **to keep up with** correr parejas con; llevar adelante, proseguir

keeper [ˈkipər] s guardián m, custodio; (of a game preserve) guardabosque m; (of a magnet) armadura, culata

keeping [ˈkipɪŋ] s custodia, cuidado; (of a holiday) celebración; **in keeping with** de acuerdo con, en armonía con; **in safe keeping** en lugar seguro, a buen recaudo; **out of keeping with** en desacuerdo con

keep·sake· s recuerdo

keg [kɛg] s cuñete m, cubeto

ken [kɛn] s alcance m de la vista, alcance del saber; **beyond the ken of** fuera del alcancé de

kennel [ˈkɛnəl] s perrera

kep·i [ˈkepi] o [ˈkɛpi] s (pl **-is**) quepis m

kept woman [kɛpt] s entretenida, manceba

kerchief [ˈkʌrtʃif] s pañuelo, mantón m

kerchoo [kərˈtʃu] interj ¡ah-chís!

kernel [ˈkʌrnəl] s (inner part of a nut or fruit stone) almendra núcleo; (of wheat or corn) grano; (fig) medula

kerosene [ˈkɛrəˌsin] o [ˌkɛrəˈsin] s keroseno

kerosene lamp s lámpara de petróleo

kerplunk [kərˈplʌŋk] interj ¡pataplún!

ketchup [ˈkɛtʃəp] s salsa de tomate condimentada

kettle ['kɛtəl] s caldera, marmita; (*teakettle*) tetera

ket'tle•drum' s timbal m, tímpano

key [ki] adj clave ‖ s (*of door, trunk, etc.*) llave f; (*of piano, typewriter, etc.*) tecla; (*wedge or cotter used to lock parts together*) clavija, cuña, chaveta; (*reef or low island*) cayo; (bot) sámara; (*tone of voice*) tono; (mus) clave f o llave f; (telg) manipulador m; (*to a puzzle, secret, translation, code*) (fig) clave o llave; (*place giving control to a region*) (fig) llave f; (fig) persona principal; **off key** desafinado; desafinadamente ‖ tr acuñar, enchavetar; **to key up** alentar, excitar

key'board' s teclado

key fruit s sámara

key'hole' s ojo de la cerradura; (*of a clock*) agujero de cuerda

key money s pago ilícito al casero

key'note' s (mus) tónica, nota tónica; (fig) idea fundamental

keynote speech s discurso de apertura (*en que se expone el programa de un partido político*)

key'punch'er s perforista mf

key ring s llavero

key'stone' s clave f, espinazo, (fig) piedra angular

Key West s Cayo Hueso

key word s palabra clave

kg. abbr **kilogram**

K.G. abbr **Knight of the Garter**

kha•ki ['kɑki] o ['kæki] adj caqui ‖ s (pl **-kis**) caqui m

khedive [kə'div] s jedive m

kibitz ['kɪbɪts] intr (coll) dar consejos molestos a los jugadores

kibitzer ['kɪbɪtsər] s (coll) mirón molesto (*de una partida de juego*); (coll) entremetido

kiblah ['kɪblɑ] s alquibla

kibosh ['kaɪbɑʃ] o [kɪ'bɑʃ] s (coll) música celestial; **to put the kibosh on** (coll) desbaratar, imposibilitar

kick [kɪk] s puntapié m; (*of an animal*) coz f; (*of a gun*) coz, culatazo; (*complaint*) (slang) queja, protesta; (*of liquor*) (slang) fuerza, estímulo; (*thrill*) gusto, placer intenso; **to get a kick out of** (slang) hallar mucho placer en ‖ tr acocear, dar de puntapiés a; sacudir (*los pies*); **to kick out** (coll) echar a puntapiés a la calle; (coll) echar, despedir; **to kick the bucket** (coll) morir; **to kick up a row** (slang) armar un bochinche ‖ intr cocear; dar culetazos (*un arma de fuego*); (coll) quejarse; **to kick about** (coll) quejarse de; **to kick against the pricks** dar coces contra el aguijón; **to kick off** (football) dar el golpe de salida

kick'back' s (coll) contragolpe m; (slang) devolución a un cómplice de una parte de lo robado

kick'off' s (football) golpe m de salida, puntapié m inicial

kid [kɪd] s (*young goat*) cabrito; (*leather*) cabritilla; (coll) chiquillo, chico; **kids** guantes mpl o zapatos de cabritilla ‖ v (pret

& pp **kidded**; ger **kidding**) tr (slang) embromar, tomar el pelo a; **to kid oneself** (slang) forjarse ilusiones ‖ intr (slang) decirlo en broma

kidder ['kɪdər] s (slang) bromista mf

kid gloves spl guantes mpl de cabritilla; **to handle with kid gloves** tratar con suma discreción o cautela

kid'nap' v (pret & pp **-naped** o **-napped**; ger **naping** o **-napping**) tr secuestrar

kidnaper o **kidnapper** ['kɪd,næpər] s secuestrador m, ladrón m de niños

kidney ['kɪdni] s riñon m; (coll) clase f, especie f; (coll) carácter m

kidney bean s judía

kidney stone s cálculo renal

kill [kɪl] s matanza; (*of a wild beast, an army, a pack of hounds*) ataque m final; (*creek*) arroyo, riachuelo; **for the kill** para el golpe final ‖ tr matar; ahogar (*un proyecto de ley*); quitar (*el sabor*); producir una impresión irresistible en

killer ['kɪlər] s matador m

killer whale s orca

killing ['kɪlɪŋ] adj matador; (*exhausting*) abrumador; (coll) muy divertido, de lo más ridículo ‖ s matanza; (*game killed on a hunt*) cacería, piezas; (coll) gran ganancia; **to make a killing** (coll) enriquecerse de golpe

kill'-joy' s aguafiestas mf

kiln [kɪl] o [kɪln] s horno

kil•o ['kɪlo] o ['kilo] s (pl **-os**) kilo, kilogramo; kilómetro

kilocycle ['kɪlə,saɪkəl] s kilociclo

kilogram ['kɪlə,græm] s kilogramo

kilometer ['kɪlə,mitər] s kilómetro (*distancia*); **kilometer** [kɪ'lɑmətər] s kilómetro (*instrumento*)

kilometric [,kɪlə'mɛtrɪk] adj kilométrico

kilowatt ['kɪlə,wɑt] s kilovatio

kilowatt-hour ['kɪlə,wɑt'aʊr] s (pl **kilowatt-hours**) kilovatio-hora

kilt [kɪlt] s enagüillas, falda corta

kilter ['kɪltər] s—**to be out of kilter** (coll) estar descompuesto

kimo•no [kɪ'monə] s (pl **-nos**) quimono

kin [kɪn] s (*family relationship*) parentesco; (*relatives*) deudos; **near of kin** muy allegado; **of kin** allegado; **the next of kin** el pariente más próximo, los parientes próximos

kind [kaɪnd] adj bueno, bondadoso; (*greeting*) afectuoso; **kind to** bueno para con ‖ s clase f, especie f, suerte f, género; **a kind of** uno a modo de; **all kinds of** (coll) gran cantidad de; **in kind** en especie; en la misma moneda; **kind of** (coll) algo, más bien; **of a kind** de una misma clase; (*poor, mediocre*) de poco valor, de mala muerte; **of the kind** por el estilo

kindergarten ['kɪndər,gɑrtən] s parvulario, escuela de párvulos, jardín m de la infancia

kindergartner ['kɪndər,gɑrtnər] s (*child*) párvulo; (*teacher*) parvulista mf

kind-hearted ['kaɪnd'hɑrtɪd] adj bondadoso, de buen corazón

kindle [ˈkɪndəl] *tr* encender ‖ *intr* encenderse
kindling [ˈkɪndlɪŋ] *s* encendajas
kindling wood *s* leña
kind·ly [ˈkaɪndli] *adj* (*comp* **-lier;** *super*
  -liest) (*kind-hearted*) bondadoso; apacible,
  benigno; favorable ‖ *adv* bondadosamente;
  cordialmente; con gusto; por favor; **to not
  take kindly to** no aceptar de buen grado
kindness [ˈkaɪndnɪs] *s* bondad; **have the
  kindness to** tenga Vd. la bondad de
kindred [ˈkɪndrɪd] *adj* emparentado; afín;
  semejante ‖ *s* parentela; semejanza, afinidad
Kinescope [ˈkɪnɪˌskop] *s* (*trademark*) cinescopio, kinescopio
kinetic [kɪˈnɛtɪk] *adj* cinético ‖ **kinetics** *s*
  cinética
kinetic energy *s* fuerza viva, energía cinética
kinfolk [ˈkɪnˌfok] *s* (*coll*) pariente(s)
king [kɪŋ] *s* rey *m;* (cards, chess, & fig) rey;
  (checkers) dama
king'bolt' *s* pivote *m* central
kingdom [ˈkɪŋdəm] *s* reino
king'fish'er *s* martín *m* pescador
king·ly [ˈkɪŋli] *adj* (*comp* **-lier;** *super* **-liest**)
  real, regio; (*stately*) majestuoso ‖ *adv* re-
  giamente
king'pin' *s* (bowling) bolo delantero; pivote
  m central; (aut) pivote de dirección; (coll)
  persona principal; (coll) jefe *m* de criminales
king post *s* pendolón *m*
king's evil *s* escrófula
kingship [ˈkɪŋʃɪp] *s* dignidad real
king'-size' *adj* de tamaño largo
king's ransom *s* riquezas de Creso
kink [kɪŋk] *s* (*twist, e.g., in a rope*) enroscadura, coca; (*e.g., in hair*) pasa; (*soreness
  in neck*) tortícolis *m;* (*flaw, difficulty*)
  estorbo, traba; (*mental twist*) chifladura,
  manía ‖ *tr* enroscar ‖ *intr* enroscarse
kink·y [ˈkɪŋki] *adj* (*comp* **-ier;** *super* **-iest**)
  encarrujado, ensortijado; (coll) perverso,
  raro
kinsfolk [ˈkɪnzˌfok] *s* parentela, familia, deudos
kinship [ˈkɪnʃɪp] *s* parentesco; semejanza,
  afinidad
kins·man [ˈkɪnzmən] *s* (*pl* **-men** [mən]) pariente *m*
kins·woman [ˈkɪnzˌwʊmən] *s* (*pl* **-women**
  [ˌwɪmɪn]) *s* parienta
kipper [ˈkɪpər] *s* arenque acecinado, salmón
  acecinado ‖ *tr* acecinar (*el arenque o el
  salmón*)
kiss [kɪs] *s* beso; (billiards) retruco; (*confection*) dulce *m,* merengue *m* ‖ *tr* besar; **to
  kiss away** borrar con besos (*las pensas de
  una persona*) ‖ *intr* besar; besarse; (billiards) retrucar
kit [kɪt] *s* cartera de herramientas; (*case and
  its contents for various purposes*) estuche
  m; (*of a soldier*) equipo, pertrechos; (*of a
  traveler*) equipaje *m;* (*pail, tub*) balde *m*
kitchen [ˈkɪtʃən] *s* cocina
kitchenette [ˌkɪtʃəˈnɛt] *s* cocinilla
kitchen garden *s* huerto

kitch'en·maid' *s* ayudanta de cocina, pincha
kitchen police *s* (mil) trabajo de cocina;
  soldados que están de cocina
kitchen range *s* cocina económica
kitchen sink *s* fregadero; **everything but the
  kitchen sink** sin faltar apenas nada; com-
  pletísimo
kitch'en·ware' *s* utensilios de cocina
kite [kaɪt] *s* cometa; (orn) milano; **to fly a
  kite** hacer volar una cometa
kith and kin [kɪθ] *spl* parientes *mpl;* parientes y amigos
kitten [ˈkɪtən] *s* gatito, minino
kittenish [ˈkɪtənɪʃ] *adj* juguetón, retozón;
  (*coy, flirtatious*) coquetón
kit·ty [ˈkɪti] *s* (*pl* **-ties**) gatito, minino; (*in
  card games*) polla, puesta ‖ *interj* ¡miz!
kleptomaniac [ˌklɛptəˈmɛnɪˌæk] *s* clep-
  tómano
km. *abbr* **kilometer**
knack [næk] *s* tino, tranquillo, maña
knapsack [ˈnæpˌsæk] *s* mochila
knave [nev] *s* bribón *m,* pícaro; (cards) sota
knaver·y [ˈnevəri] *s* (*pl* **-ies**) bribonería, picardía
knead [nid] *tr* amasar, sobar
knee [ni] *s* rodilla; (*of animal*) codillo; (*e.g.,
  of trousers*) rodillera; (mach) ángulo, codo;
  to bring (*someone*) **to his knees** rendir,
  vencer; **to go down on one's knees** hincarse de rodillas, caer de rodillas; **to go
  down on one's knees to** implorar de rodillas
knee breeches [ˈbrɪtʃɪz] *spl* pantalones cortos
knee'cap' *s* rótula; (*protective covering*) rodillera
knee'-deep' *adj* metido hasta las rodillas
knee'high' *adj* que llega hasta la rodilla
knee'-hole' *s* hueco para acomodar las rodillas
knee jerk *s* reflejo rotuliano
kneel [nil] *v* (*pret & pp* **knelt** [nɛlt] o
  kneeled) *intr* arrodillarse; estar de rodillas
knee'pad' *s* rodillera
knee'pan' *s* rótula
knee swell *s* (*of organ*) (mus) rodillera
knell [nɛl] *s* doble *m,* toque *m* de difuntos;
  mal agüero; **to toll the knell of** anunciar la
  muerte de, anunciar el fin de ‖ *intr* doblar,
  tocar a muerto; sonar tristemente
knickers [ˈnɪkərz] *spl* pantalones *mpl* de media pierna
knickknack [ˈnɪkˌnæk] *s* chuchería, bujería,
  baratija
knife [naɪf] *s* (*pl* **-knives** [naɪvz]) cuchillo; (*of
  a paper cutter or other instrument*) cu-
  chilla; **to go under the knife** (coll) hacerse
  operar ‖ *tr* acuchillar; (slang) traicionar
knife sharpener *s* afilador *m,* afilón *m*
knife switch *s* (elec) interruptor *m* de cuchilla
knight [naɪt] *s* caballero; (chess) caballo ‖ *tr*
  armar caballero
knight-errant [ˈnaɪtˈɛrənt] *s* (*pl* **knights-
  errant**) caballero andante
knight-errant·ry [ˈnaɪtˈɛrəntri] *s* (*pl* **-ries**)
  caballería andante; (*quixotic behavior*) qui-
  jotada

knighthood ['naɪt•hʊd] s caballería
knightly ['naɪtli] adj caballeroso, caballeresco
Knight of the Rueful Countenance s Caballero de la triste figura (*Don Quijote*)
knit [nɪt] v (*pret & pp* **knitted** o **knit**; *ger* **knitting**) *tr* tejer a punto de aguja; enlazar, unir; fruncir (*las cejas*) arrugar (*la frente*) ‖ *intr* hacer calceta, hacer malla; trabarse, unirse; soldarse (*un hueso*)
knit goods spl géneros de punto
knitting ['nɪtɪŋ] s punto de media, trabajo de punto
knitting machine s máquina de hacer tejidos de punto
knitting needle s aguja de hacer media
knit'wear' s géneros de punto
knob [nɑb] s (*lump*) bulto, protuberancia; (*of a door*) botón m, tirador m; (*of a radio set*) botón, perilla; (*ornament on furniture*) manzana; colina o montaña redondeada
knock [nɑk] s golpe m; (e.g., on a door) toque m, llamada; (*with a door knocker*) aldabazo; (*of an internal-combustion engine*) pistoneo; (slang) censura, crítica ‖ *tr* golpear; (*repeatedly*) golpetear; (slang) censurar, criticar; **to knock down** (*with a blow, punch, etc.*) derribar; (*to the highest bidder*) rematar; desarmar, desmontar (*un aparato o máquina*); **to knock off** hacer saltar con un golpe; suspender (*el trabajo*); poner fin a; (slang) matar; **to knock out** agotar; (box) poner fuera de combate ‖ *intr* tocar, llamar; golpear, pistonear (*el motor de combustión interna*); (slang) censurar, criticar; **to knock about** andar vagando; **to knock against** dar contra, tropezar con; **to knock at** tocar a, llamar a (*la puerta*); **to knock off** dejar de trabajar
knocker ['nɑkər] s (*on a door*) aldaba; (coll) criticón m
knock-kneed ['nɑk,nid] adj patizambo, zambo
knock'out' s golpe decisivo, puñetazo decisivo; (box) (el) fuera de combate; (elec) destapadero; real moza
knockout drops spl (slang) gotas narcóticas
knoll [nol] s loma, otero
knot [nɑt] s nudo; (*worn as ornament*) lazo; corrillo, grupo; (*difficult matter; bond or tie*) nudo; nudo o lazo de matrimonio; (*protuberance in a fabric*) envoltorio; (naut) nudo; **to tie the knot** (coll) casarse ‖ v (*pret & pp* **knotted**; *ger* **knotting**) *tr* anudar; fruncir (*las cejas*) ‖ *intr* anudarse
knot'hole' s agujero en la madera (*que deja un nudo al desprenderse*)
knot•ty ['nɑti] adj (*comp* **-tier;** *super* **-tiest**) nudoso; (fig) espinoso, difícil

know [no] s —**to be in the know** estar enterado, tener informes secretos ‖ v (*pret* **knew** [nju] o [nu]; *pp* **known**) *tr & intr* (*by reasoning or learning*) saber; (*by the senses or by perception; through acquaintance or recognition*) conocer; **as far as I know** que yo sepa; **to know about** saber de; **to know best** ser el mejor juez, saber lo que más conviene; **to know how to** + *inf* saber + *inf;* **to know it all** (coll) sabérselo todo; **to know what one is doing** obrar con conocimiento de causa; **to know what's what** (coll) saber cuántas son cinco; **you ought to know better** deberías tener vergüenza
knowable ['no•əbəl] adj conocible
know'-how' s conocimiento, destreza, habilidad
knowingly ['no•ɪŋli] adv a sabiendas, con conocimiento de causa; (*on purpose*) adrede
know'-it-all' adj & s (coll) sabidillo, sabelotodo mf
knowledge ['nɑlɪdʒ] s (*faculty*) ciencia, conocimientos, el saber; (*awareness, acquaintance, familiarity*) conocimiento; **to have a thorough knowledge of** conocer a fondo; **to my knowledge** que yo sepa; **to the best of my knowledge** según mi leal saber y entender; **with full knowledge** con conocimiento de causa; **without my knowledge** sin saberlo yo
knowledgeable ['nɑlɪdʒəbəl] adj (coll) conocedor, inteligente
know'-noth'ing s ignorante mf
knuckle ['nʌkəl] s nudillo; (*of a quadruped*) jarrete m; (*mach*) junta de charnela; **knuckles** bóxer m ‖ *intr*—**to knuckle down** someterse, darse por vencido; aplicarse con empeño al trabajo
knurl [nʌrl] s moleteado ‖ *tr* moletear, cerrillar (*p.ej., las piezas de moneda*)
k.o. *abbr* **knockout**
kook [kuk] s (coll) tipo raro; excéntrico
Koran [ko'rɑn] o [ko'ræn] s Corán m
Korea [ko'ri•ə] s Corea
Korean [ko'ri•ən] adj & s coreano
kosher ['koʃər] adj autorizado por la ley judía; (coll) genuino, auténtico
kowtow ['kaʊ,taʊ] o ['ko,taʊ] *intr* arrodillarse y tocar el suelo con la frente; doblegarse servilmente, mostrarse servilmente obsequioso
Kt. *abbr* **Knight**
kudos ['kjudɑs] o ['kudɑs] s (coll) gloria, renombre m, fama
kw. *abbr* **kilowatt**
K.W.H. *abbr* **kilowatt-hour**

ki
kw

L

L, l [ɛl] duodécima letra del alfabeto inglés
l. *abbr* **liter, line, league, length**
L. *abbr* **Latin, Low**
la·bel [`lebəl] *s* etiqueta, marbete *m*, rótulo; (*descriptive word*) calificación ‖ *v* (*pret & pp* **-beled** o **-belled;** *ger* **-beling** o **-belling**) *tr* poner etiqueta o marbete a, rotular; calificar
labial [`lebɪ·əl] *adj & s* labial *f*
labor [`lebər] *adj* obrero ‖ *s* trabajo, labor *f;* (*job, task*) tarea, faena; (*manual work involved in an undertaking; the wages for such work*) mano *f* de obra; (*wage-earning workers as contrasted with capital and management*) los obreros; (*childbirth*) parto; **labors** esfuerzos; **to be in labor** estar de parto ‖ *intr* trabajar; (*to exert oneself*) forcejar; estar de parto; moverse penosamente; cabecear y balancear (*un buque*); **to labor under** ser víctima de
labor and management *spl* los obreros y los patronos
laborato·ry [`læbərə,tori] *s* (*pl* **-ries**) laboratorio
labored [`lebərd] *adj* penoso, dificultoso; artificial, forzado
laborer [`lebərər] *s* trabajador *m*, obrero; (*unskilled worker*) bracero, jornalero, peón *m*
laborious [lə`borɪ·əs] *adj* laborioso
la'bor-man'agement *adj* obrero-patronal
labor union *s* gremio obrero, sindicato
Labourite [`lebə,raɪt] *s* laborista *mf*
Labrador [`læbrə,dɔr] *s* el Labrador
labyrinth [`læbɪrɪnθ] *s* laberinto
lace [les] *s* encaje *m;* (*string to tie shoe, corset, etc.*) cordón *m*, lazo; (*braid*) galón *m* de oro o plata ‖ *tr* adornar con encaje; atar (*los zapatos, el corsé*); (*coll*) dar una paliza a
lace trimming *s* randa
lace'work' *s* encaje *m*, obra de encaje
lachrymose [`lækrɪ,mos] *adj* lacrimoso
lacing [`lesɪŋ] *s* cordón *m;* lazo; galón *m;* (*coll*) paliza
lack [læk] *s* carencia, falta; (*complete lack*) defecto ‖ *tr* carecer de, necesitar ‖ *intr* (*to be lacking*) faltar
lackadaisical [,lækə`dezɪkəl] *adj* desaprovechado, indiferente
lackey [`læki] *s* lacayo; secuaz *m* servil
lacking [`lækɪŋ] *prep* sin, carente de
lack'lus'ter *adj* deslustrado, deslucido
laconic [lə`kɑnɪk] *adj* lacónico
lacquer [`lækər] *s* laca ‖ *tr* laquear
lacquer ware *s* lacas, objetos de laca
lacu·na [lə`kjunə] *s* (*pl* **-nas** o **-nae** [ni]) laguna
lac·y [`lesi] *adj* (*comp* **-ier;** *super* **-iest**) de encaje; (*fig*) diáfano
lad [læd] *s* muchacho, chico
ladder [`lædər] *s* escalera; (*stepladder*) escala, escalera de mano; (*two ladders fastened together at the top with hinges*) escalera de tijera; (*stepping stone*) (fig) escalón *m*
ladder truck *s* carro de escaleras de incendio
ladies' room *s* cuarto tocador
ladle [`ledəl] *s* cazo; (*for soup*) cucharón *m;* (*of tinsmith*) cucharilla ‖ *tr* servir con cucharón; sacar con cucharón
la·dy [`ledi] *s* (*pl* **-dies**) señora, dama
la'dy-bird' o **la'dy·bug'** *s* mariquita, vaca de San Antón
la'dy·fin'ger *s* melindre *m*
lady-in-waiting *s* camarera de la reina
la'dy-kil'ler *s* ladrón *m* de corazones
la'dy·like' *adj* elegante; **to be ladylike** ser muy dama
la'dy·love' *s* amada, amiga querida
lady of the house *s* ama de casa
ladyship [`ledi,ʃɪp] *s* señoría
lady's maid *s* doncella
lady's man *s* perico entre ellas
lag [læg] *s* retraso ‖ *v* (*pret & pp* **lagged;** *ger* **lagging**) *intr* retrasarse; **to lag behind** quedarse atrás, rezagarse
lager beer [`lɑgər] *s* cerveza reposada
laggard [`lægərd] *s* perezoso, rezagado
lagoon [lə`gun] *s* laguna
laid paper [led] *s* papel vergueteado
laid up *adj* almacenado, ahorrado; (naut) inactivo; (coll) encamado por estar enfermo
lair [lɛr] *s* cubil *m*
lai·ty [`le·ɪti] *s* legos
lake [lek] *adj* lacustre ‖ *s* lago
lamb [læm] *s* cordero; carne *f* de cordero; piel *f* de cordero; (*meek person*) (fig) cordero
lambaste [læm`best] *tr* (*to thrash*) (coll) dar una paliza a; (*to reprimand harshly*) (coll) dar una jabonadura a
lamb chop *s* chuleta de cordero
lambkin [`læmkɪn] *s* corderito; (fig) nenito
lamb'skin' *s* piel *f* de cordero, corderina; (*dressed with its wool*) corderillo
lame [lem] *adj* cojo; (*sore*) dolorido; (*e.g., excuse*) débil, pobre ‖ *tr* encojar
lament [lə`mɛnt] *s* lamento; (*dirge*) elegía ‖ *tr* lamentar ‖ *intr* lamentarse
lamentable [`læməntəbəl] *adj* lamentable
lamentation [,læmən`teʃən] *s* lamentación
laminate [`læmɪ,net] *tr* laminar
laminated glass *s* cristal laminado
lamp [læmp] *s* lámpara
lamp'black' *s* negro de humo
lamp chimney *s* tubo de lámpara
lamp'light' *s* luz *f* de lámpara
lamp'light'er *s* farolero
lampoon [læm`pun] *s* pasquín *m*, libelo ‖ *tr* pasquinar
lamp'post' *s* poste *m* de farol
lamp shade *s* pantalla de lámpara
lamp'wick' *s* mecha de lámpara, torcida
lance [læns] o [lɑns] *s* lanza; (surg) lanceta ‖ *tr* alancear; (surg) abrir con lanceta
lance rest *s* ristre *m*
lancet [`lænsɪt] *s* (surg) lanceta

land [lænd] *adj* terrestre; (*wind*) terral ‖ *s* tierra; **on land, on sea, and in the air** en tierra, mar y aire; **to make land** atracar a tierra; **to see how the land lies** medir el terreno, ver el cariz que van tomando las cosas ‖ *tr* desembarcar; conducir (*un avión*) a tierra; coger (*un pez*); (coll) conseguir ‖ *intr* desembarcar; (*to reach land*) arribar, aterrar; aterrizar (*un avión*); (*to arrive or come to rest*) ir a dar, ir a parar; **to land on one's feet** caer de pies; **to land on one's head** caer de cabeza

landau ['lændɔ] o ['lændau] *s* landó *m*

land breeze *s* terral *m*

landed ['lændɪd] *adj* (*owning land*) hacendado; (*real-estate*) inmobiliario; **landed property** bienes *mpl* raíces

land'fall' *s* (*sighting land*) aterrada; (*landing of ship or plane*) tierra vista desde el mar; (*landslide*) derrumbe *m*

land'fill' *s* tierra y escombros

land grant *s* donación de tierras

land'hold'er *s* terrateniente *mf*, hacendado

landing ['lændɪŋ] *s* (*of ship or plane*) aterraje *m*; (*of passengers*) desembarco; (*place where passengers and goods are landed*) desembarcadero; (*of stairway*) desembarco, descanso

landing beacon *s* (aer) radiofaro de aterrizaje

landing craft *s* (nav) lancha de desembarco

landing field *s* (aer) pista de aterrizaje

landing force *s* (nav) compañía de desembarco

landing gear *s* (aer) tren *m* de aterrizaje

landing stage *s* embarcadero flotante

landing strip *s* (aer) faja de aterrizaje

land'la'dy *s* (*pl* **-dies**) (*e.g., of an apartment*) casera, dueña; (*of a lodging house*) ama, patrona; (*of an inn*) mesonera, posadera

landlocked ['lænd,lɑkt] *adj* rodeado de tierra

land'lord' *s* (*e.g., of an apartment*) casero, dueño; (*of a lodging house*) amo, patrón *m*; (*of an inn*) mesonero, posadero

land'lub'ber *s* (*person unacquainted with the sea*) marinero de agua dulce; (*awkward and unskilled seaman*) marinero matalote

land'mark' *s* (*boundary stone*) mojón *m*; (*feature of landscape that marks a location*) guía; suceso que hace época; (naut) marca de reconocimiento

land office *s* oficina del catastro

land'-of'fice business *s* (coll) negocio de mucho movimiento

land'own'er *s* terrateniente *mf*, hacendado

landscape ['lænd,skep] *s* paisaje *m* ‖ *tr* ajardinar

landscape architect *s* arquitecto paisajista

landscape gardener *s* jardinero adornista, jardinista *mf*

landscape painter *s* paisajista *mf*

landscapist ['lænd,skepɪst] *s* paisajista *mf*

land'slide' *s* derrumbe *m*, derrumbamiento de tierra, corrimiento; (fig) mayoría de votos abrumadora; (fig) victoria arrolladora

landward ['lændwərd] *adv* hacia tierra, hacia la costa

land wind *s* terral *m*

lane [len] *s* (*narrow street or passage*) callejuela; (*path*) carril *m*; (*of an automobile highway*) faja; (*of an air or ocean route*) derrotero, vía

langsyne ['læŋ'saɪn] *adv* (Scotch) hace mucho tiempo ‖ *s* (Scotch) tiempo de antaño

language ['læŋgwɪdʒ] *s* idioma *m*, lengua; (*way of speaking or writing, style; figurative or poetic expression; communication of meaning said to be employed by flowers, birds, art, etc.*) lenguaje *m*; (*of a special group of people*) jerga

language laboratory *s* laboratorio de idiomas

languid ['læŋgwɪd] *adj* lánguido

languish ['læŋgwɪʃ] *intr* languidecer; afectar languidez

languor ['læŋgər] *s* languidez *f*

languorous ['læŋgərəs] *adj* lánguido; (*causing languor*) enervante

lank [læŋk] *adj* descarnado, larguirucho; (*hair*) lacio

lank•y ['læŋki] *adj* (*comp* **-ier**; *super* **-iest**) descarnado, larguirucho

lantern ['læntərn] *s* linterna

lantern slide *s* diapositiva, tira de vidrio

lanyard ['lænjərd] *s* (naut) acollador *m*

lap [læp] *s* (*of human body or clothing*) regazo; (*loose fold*) caída, doblez *f*; (*overlap of garment*) traslapo; (*with the tongue*) lametada; (*of the waves*) chapaleteo; (*in a race*) (sport) etapa, vuelta; **to live in the lap of luxury** llevar una vida regalada ‖ *v* (*pret & pp* **lapped**; *ger* **lapping**) *tr* beber con la lengua; lamer (*las olas la playa*); (*to overlap*) traslapar; juntar a traslapo; **to lap up** tragar a lengüetadas; (coll) aceptar con entusiasmo ‖ *intr* traslapar; traslaparse (*dos o más cosas*); **to lap against** lamer (*las olas la playa*); **to lap over** salir fuera, rebosar

lap'board' *s* tabla faldera

lap dog *s* perro de falda

lapel [lə'pɛl] *s* solapa

Lap'land' *s* Laponia

Laplander ['læp,lændər] *s* lapón *m* (*habitante*)

Lapp [læp] *s* lapón *m* (*habitante; idioma*)

lap robe *s* manta de coche

lapse [læps] *s* (*passing of time; slipping into guilt or error*) lapso; (*fall, decline*) caída, caída en desuso; (*e.g., of an insurance policy*) invalidación ‖ *intr* caer en culpa o error; decaer, pasar (*p.ej., el entusiasmo*); caducar (*p.ej., una póliza de seguro*)

lap'wing' *s* ave fría

larce•ny ['lɑrsəni] *s* (*pl* **-nies**) hurto, robo

larch [lɑrtʃ] *s* alerce *m*, lárice *m*

lard [lɑrd] *s* cochevira, manteca de puerco ‖ *tr* (culin) mechar

larder ['lɑrdər] *s* despensa

large ['lɑrdʒ] *adj* grande; **at large** en libertad

large intestine *s* intestino grueso

largely ['lɑrdʒli] *adj* por la mayor parte

largeness ['lɑrdʒnɪs] *s* grandeza

large'-scale' *adj* en grande escala, grande escala

I
la

lariat [´lærɪ·ət] s (*for catching animals*) lazo; (*for tying grazing animals*) cuerda, soga
lark [lɑrk] s alondra; (coll) parranda; **to go on a lark** (coll) andar de parranda, echar una cana al aire
lark´spur´ s (*rocket larkspur*) espuela de caballero; (*field larkspur*) consuelda real
lar·va [´lɑrvə] s (pl **-vae** [vi]) larva
laryngeal [lə´rɪndʒɪ·əl] adj laríngeo
laryngitis [,lærɪn´dʒaɪtɪs] s laringitis f
laryngoscope [lə´rɪŋgə,skop] s laringoscopio
larynx [´lærɪŋks] s (pl **larynxes** o **larynges** [lə´rɪndʒiz]) laringe f
lascivious [lə´sɪvɪ·əs] adj lascivo
lasciviousness [lə´sɪvɪ·əsnɪs] s lascivia
laser [´lezər] s láser m
lash [læʃ] s (*cord on end of whip*) tralla; (*blow with whip; scolding*) latigazo; (*e.g., of animal's tail*) coletazo; (*of waves*) embate m; (*eyelash*) pestaña || tr (*to beat, whip*) azotar; (*to bind, tie*) atar; (*to shake, to switch*) agitar, sacudir; (*to attack with words*) increpar, reñir || intr lanzarse, pasar rápidamente; **to lash out at** azotar; embestir; vituperar
lashing [´læʃɪŋ] s atadura; paliza, zurra; (*severe scolding*) latigazo
lass [læs] s muchacha, chica; amada
las·so [´læso] o [læ´su] s (pl **-sos** o **-soes**) lazo || tr lazar
last [læst] o [lɑst] adj (*after all others; the only remaining; utmost, extreme*) último; (*most recent*) pasado; **before last** antepasado; **every last one** todos sin excepción; **last but one** penúltimo || adv después de todos; por último; por última vez || s última persona; última cosa; fin m; (*for holding shoe*) horma; **at last** por fin; **at long last** al fin y al cabo; **stick to your last!** ¡zapatero, a tus zapatos!; **the last of the month** a fines del mes; **to breathe one's last** dar el último suspiro; **to see the last of** no volver a ver; **to the last** hasta el fin || intr durar; resistir; dar buen resultado (*p.ej., una prenda de vestir*); seguir así
lasting [´læstɪŋ] adj perdurable, duradero
lastly [´læstli] adv finalmente, por último
last´-min´ute news s noticias de última hora
last name s apellido
last night adv anoche
last quarter s cuarto menguante
last rites spl (theol) extremaunción
last sleep s último sueño
last straw s acabóse m, colmo
Last Supper, the la Cena
last will and testament s última disposición, última voluntad
last word s última palabra; (*latest style*) (coll) última palabra
lat. abbr **latitude**
Lat. abbr **Latin**
latch [lætʃ] s picaporte m || tr cerrar con picaporte
latch´key´ s llavín m
latch´string´ s cordón m de aldaba; **the latchstring is out** ya sabe Vd. que ésta es su casa

late [let] adj (*happening after the usual time*) tardío; (*person*) atrasado; (*hour of the night*) avanzado; (*news*) de última hora; (*party, meeting, etc.*) que termina tarde; (*coming toward the end of a period of time*) de fines de; (*incumbent of an office*) anterior; (*deceased*) difunto, fallecido; **of late** recientemente, últimamente; **to be late** ser tarde; tardar (*p.ej., el tren*); **to be late in** + ger tardar en + inf; **to grow late** hacerse tarde || adv tarde; **late in** (*the week, the month, etc.*) a fines de, hacia fines de; **late in life** a una edad avanzada
late-comer [´let,kʌmər] s recién llegado; (*one who arrives late*) rezagado
lateen sail [læ´tin] s vela latina
lateen yard s entena
lately [´letli] adv recientemente, últimamente
latent [´letənt] adj latente
lateral [´lætərəl] adj lateral
lath [læθ] o [lɑθ] s lata, listón; enlistonado || tr enlistonar
lathe [leð] s torno (*máquina que sirve para labrar madera, hierro, etc. con un movimiento circular*)
lather [´læðər] s espuma de jabón; espuma de sudor || tr enjabonar; (coll) tundir, zurrar || intr espumar
lathery [´læðəri] adj espumoso, jabonoso
lathing [´læθɪŋ] s enlistonado
Latin [´lætɪn] o [´lætən] adj latino || s (*language*) latín m; (*person*) latino
Latin America s Latinoamérica, América Latina
Latin American s latinoamericano
Lat´in-Amer´ican adj latinoamericano
latitude [´lætɪ,tjud] s latitud
latrine [lə´trin] s letrina
latter [´lætər] adj (*more recent*) posterior; segundo (*de dos*); **the latter** éste; **the latter part of** fines mpl de (*p.ej., el siglo*)
lattice [´lætɪs] s enrejado || tr enrejar
lattice girder s viga de celosía
lat´tice·work´ s enrejado
Latvia [´lætvɪ·ə] s Letonia, Latvia
laudable [´lɔdəbəl] adj laudable
laudanum [´lɔdənəm] o [´lɔdnəm] s láudano
laudatory [´lɔdə,tori] adj laudatorio
laugh [læf] s risa || tr—**to laugh away** ahogar en risas; **to laugh off** tomar a risa || intr reír, reírse
laughable [´læfəbəl] adj risible
laughing [´læfɪŋ] adj reidor; **to be no laughing matter** no ser cosa de risa || s risa, (el) reír
laughing gas s gas m hilarante
laugh´ing·stock´ s hazmerreír m
laughter [´læftər] s risa, risas
launch [lɔntʃ] s (*of a ship*) botadura; (*of a rocket*) lanzamiento; (*open motorboat*) lancha automóvil; (nav) lancha || tr botar, lanzar (*un buque*); (*to throw; to start, set going, send forth*) lanzar || intr lanzarse
launching [´lɔntʃɪŋ] s lanzamiento
launching pad s plataforma de lanzamiento
launching tower s torre f de lanzamiento

launder [ˈlɔndər] *tr* lavar y planchar ‖ *intr* resistir el lavado
launderer [ˈlɔndərər] *s* lavandero
laundress [ˈlɔndrɪs] *s* lavandera
laun·dry [ˈlɔndri] *s* (*pl* **-dries**) lavadero; lavado de la ropa; ropa lavada o para lavar
laundry·man [ˈlɔndrimən] *s* (*pl* **-men** [mən]) lavandero
laun'dry·wom'an *s* (*pl* **-wom'en**) lavandera
laureate [ˈlɔri·ɪt] *adj* laureado ‖ *s* laureado; poeta laureado
lau·rel [ˈlɔrəl] *s* laurel *m;* **laurels** laurel (*de la victoria*); **to rest** o **sleep on one's laurels** dormirse sobre sus laureles ‖ *v* (*pret & pp* **-reled** o **-relled**) *ger* **-reling** o **-relling**) *tr* laurear, coronar de laurel
lava [ˈlɑvə] o [ˈlævə] *s* lava
lavato·ry [ˈlævə,tori] *s* (*pl* **-ries**) (*room equipped for washing hands and face*) lavabo; (*bowl with running water*) lavamanos *m; (toilet)* excusado
lavender [ˈlævəndər] *s* alhucema, espliego, lavanda
lavender water *s* agua de alhucema, agua de lavanda
lavish [ˈlævɪʃ] *adj* pródigo ‖ *tr* prodigar
law [lɔ] *s* (*of man, of nature, of science*) ley *f; (branch of knowledge concerned with law; body of laws; study of law; profession of law*) derecho; **to enter the law** hacerse abogado; **to go to law** recurrir a la ley; **to lay down the law** dar órdenes terminantes; **to maintain law and order** mantener la paz; **to practice law** ejercer la profesión de abogado; **to read law** estudiar derecho
law-abiding [ˈlɔ·ə,baɪdɪŋ] *adj* observante de la ley
law'break'er *s* infractor *m* de la ley
law court *s* tribunal *m* de justicia
lawful [ˈlɔfəl] *adj* legal, legítimo
lawless [ˈlɔlɪs] *adj* ilegal; (*unbridled*) desenfrenado, licencioso
law'mak'er *s* legislador *m*
lawn [lɔn] *s* césped *m; (fabric)* linón *m*
lawn mower *s* cortacésped *m*, tundidora de césped
law office *s* bufete *m*, despacho de abogado
law of nations *s* derecho de gentes
law of the jungle *s* ley *f* de la selva
law student *s* estudiante *mf* de derecho
law'suit' *s* pleito, proceso, litigio
lawyer [ˈlɔjər] *s* abogado
lax [læks] *adj* (*in morals, discipline, etc.*) laxo, relajado; vago, indeterminado; (*loose, not tense*) laxo, flojo, suelto
laxative [ˈlæksətɪv] *adj & s* laxante *m*
lay [le] *adj* (*not belonging to clergy*) lego, seglar; (*not having special training*) lego, profano ‖ *s* situación, orientación ‖ *v* (*pret & pp* **laid** [led]) *tr* poner, colocar; dejar en el suelo; tender (*un cable*); echar (*los cimientos; la culpa*); situar (*la acción de un drama*); asentar (*el polvo*); poner (*huevos la gallina; la mesa una criada*); formar (*planes*); hacer (*una apuesta*); **to be laid in** ser (*la escena*) en; **to lay aside** echar a un

lado; ahorrar; **to lay down** afirmar, declarar; dar (*la vida*); deponer (*las armas*); **to lay low** abatir, derribar; obligar a guardar cama; matar; **to lay off** despedir (*a obreros*); (*to mark off the boundaries of*) marcar, trazar; **to lay open** descubrir, revelar; (*to a risk or danger*) exponer; **to lay out** extender, tender; marcar (*una tarea, un trabajo*); gastar (*dinero*); amortajar (*a un difunto*); **to lay up** obligar a guardar cama; ahorrar; (*naut*) desarmar ‖ *intr* poner (*las gallinas*); **to lay about** dar palos de ciego; **to lay for** acechar; **to lay off** (*coll*) dejar de trabajar; (*coll*) dejar de molestar; **to lay over** detenerse durante un viaje; **to lay to** (*naut*) capear
lay brother *s* donado, lego
lay day *s* (naut) día *m* de estadía
layer [ˈle·ər] *s* (*e.g., of paint*) capa; (*e.g., of bricks*) camada; (*e.g., of coal, rocks*) estrato, capa; (*hort*) codadura ‖ *tr* (hort) acodar
layer cake *s* bizcocho de varias camadas
layette [leˈɛt] *s* canastilla
lay figure *s* maniquí *m*
laying [ˈle·ɪŋ] *s* colocación; (*of eggs*) postura; (*of a cable*) tendido
lay·man [ˈlemən] *s* (*pl* **-men** [mən]) (*person who is not a clergyman*) lego, seglar *m; (person who has no special training*) lego, profano
lay'off' *s* (*dismissal of workmen*) despido; (*period of unemployment*) paro forzoso
lay of the land *s* cariz *m* que van tomando las cosas
lay'out' *s* plan *m; (of tools)* equipo; disposición, organización; (*coll*) banquete *m*, festín *m*
lay'o'ver *s* parada en un viaje
lay sister *s* donada
laziness [ˈlezɪnɪs] *s* pereza; lerdera; (*coll*) galbana
la·zy [ˈlezi] *adj* (*comp* **-zier;** *super* **-ziest**) perezoso; (*coll*) galbanoso
la'zy·bones' *s* (coll) perezoso
lb. *abbr* **pound**
l.c. *abbr* **lower case; loco citato (Lat) in the place cited**
Ld. *abbr* **Lord**
lea [li] *s* prado
lead [lɛd] *adj* plomizo ‖ *s* plomo; (*of lead pencil*) mina; (*for sounding depth*) (naut) escandallo; (*typ*) interlínea, regleta ‖ [lɛd] *v* (*pret & pp* **leaded**) *ger* **leading**) *tr* emplomar; (*typ*) interlinear, regletear ‖ *s* [lid] *s* (*foremost place*) primacía; (*guidance*) conducta, guía, dirección; indicación; ejemplo; (cards) salida; (*leash*) traílla; (*of a newspaper article*) primer párrafo; (*elec*) conductor *m;* (elec & mach) avance *m;* (min) filón *m;* (rad) alambre *m* de entrada; (theat) papel *m* principal; (theat) galán *m;* (theat) dama; **to take the lead** tomar la delantera ‖ [lid] *v* (*pret & pp* **led** [lɛd]) *tr* conducir, llevar; liderar; (*to command*) acaudillar, mandar; estar a la cabeza de; dirigir (*p.ej., una orquesta*); llevar

(*buena o mala vida*); salir con (*cierto naipe*); (elec & mach) avanzar; **to lead someone to** + *inf* llevar a alguien a + *inf* ‖ *intr* ir delante, enseñar el camino; ser el primero; tener el mando; (cards) salir, ser mano; (mus) llevar la batuta; **to lead up to** conducir a, llevar a; llevar la conversación a

leaded gasoline ['lɛdɪd] *s* gasolina con plomo

leaden ['lɛdən] *adj* (*of lead; like lead*) plomizo; (*heavy as lead*) plúmbeo; (*sluggish*) tardo, indolente; (*with sleep*) cargado; triste, lóbrego

leader ['lidər] *s* caudillo, jefe *m*, líder *m*; (*ringleader*) cabecilla *m*; (*of an orchestra*) director *m*; (*in a dance; among animals*) guión *m*; (*horse*) guía; (*in a newspaper*) artículo de fondo

leader dog *s* perro-lazarillo

leadership ['lidərʃɪp] *s* caudillaje *m*, jefatura; dotes *fpl* de mando

leading ['lidɪŋ] *adj* primero, principal; preeminente; delantero; líder

leading article *s* artículo de fondo

leading edge *s* (aer) borde *m* de ataque

leading lady *s* primera actriz, dama

leading man *s* primer actor *m*, primer galán *m*

leading question *s* pregunta tendenciosa

leading strings *spl* andadores *mpl*

lead-in wire ['lid,ɪn] *s* (rad) bajada de antena, alambre *m* de entrada

lead pencil [lɛd] *s* lápiz *m*

leaf [lif] *s* (*pl* **leaves** [livz]) hoja; (*of vine*) pámpano; (*hinged leaf of table*) trampilla; **to shake like a leaf** temblar como un azogado; **to turn over a new leaf** hacer libro nuevo ‖ *intr* echar hojas; **to leaf through** hojear, trashojar

leafless ['liflɪs] *adj* deshojado

leaflet ['liflɪt] *s* hoja suelta, hoja volante; (*blade of compound leaf*) hojuela

leaf′stalk′ *s* pecíolo

leaf·y ['lifi] *adj* (*comp* **-ier**; *super* **-iest**) hojoso, frondoso

league [lig] *s* (*unit of distance*) legua; (*association, alliance*) liga; (*sports*) división ‖ *tr* asociar ‖ *intr* asociarse, ligarse

League of Nations *s* Sociedad de las Naciones

leak [lik] *s* (*in a roof*) gotera; (*in a ship*) agua, vía de agua; (*of water, gas, electricity, steam*) escape *m*, fuga, salida; agujero, grieta, raja (*por donde se escapa el agua, etc.*); (*of money, news, etc.*) filtración; **to spring a leak** tener un escape; (naut) empezar a hacer agua ‖ *tr* dejar escapar, dejar salir (*el agua, gas, etc.*); dejar filtrar (*una noticia*) ‖ *intr* rezumarse (*un barril*); escaparse, salirse (*el agua, gas, etc.*); (naut) hacer agua; **to leak away** filtrarse (*el dinero*); **to leak out** rezumarse (*una especie*); trascender (*un hecho que estaba oculto*)

leakage ['likɪdʒ] *s* escape *m*, fuga, salida; (com) merma

leak·y ['liki] *adj* (*comp* **-ier**; *super* **-iest**) agujereado, roto; (*roof*) llovedizo; (naut) que hace agua; (coll) indiscreto

lean [lin] *adj* magro, mollar; (*thin*) flaco; (*gasoline mixture*) pobre; **lean years** años de carestía ‖ *v* (*pret & pp* **leaned** o **leant** [lɛnt] *tr* inclinar, ladear, arrimar ‖ *intr* inclinarse, ladearse, arrimarse; (fig) inclinarse, tender; **to lean against** arrimarse a, estar arrimado a; **to lean back** retreparse, recostarse; **to lean on** apoyarse en; (*with the elbows*) acodarse sobre; **to lean out (of)** asomarse (a); **to lean over backwards** (coll) extremar la imparcialidad; **to lean toward** (fig) inclinarse a, ladearse a

leaning ['linɪŋ] *adj* inclinado ‖ *s* inclinación; (fig) inclinación, tendencia

lean′-to′ *s* (*pl* **-tos**) colgadizo

leap [lip] *s* salto; **by leaps and bounds** a pasos agigantados; **leap in the dark** salto a ciegas, salto en vago ‖ *v* (*pret & pp* **leaped** o **leapt** [lɛpt]) *tr* saltar *s* ‖ *intr* saltar; dar un salto (*el corazón de uno*)

leap day *s* día *m* intercalar

leap′frog′ *s* fil derecho, juego del salto; **to play leapfrog** jugar a la una la mula

leap year *s* año bisiesto

learn [lʌrn] *v* (*pret & pp* **learned** o **learnt** [lʌrnt]) *tr* aprender; oír decir; saber (*una noticia*) ‖ *intr* aprender

learned ['lʌrnɪd] *adj* docto, erudito; (*e.g., word*) culto

learned journal *s* revista científica

learned society *s* sociedad de eruditos

learned word *s* cultismo, voz culta

learned world *s* mundo de la erudición

learner ['lʌrnər] *s* principiante *mf*, aprendiz *m*, estudiante *mf*

learning ['lʌrnɪŋ] *s* (*act and time devoted*) aprendizaje *m*; (*scholarship*) erudición

lease [lis] *s* arrendamiento, locación; **to give a new lease on life** renovar completamente; volver a hacer feliz ‖ *tr* arrendar ‖ *intr* arrendarse

lease′hold′ *adj* arrendado ‖ *s* arrendamiento; bienes raíces arrendados

leash [liʃ] *s* traílla; **to strain at the leash** sufrir la sujeción con impaciencia ‖ *tr* atraillar

least [list] *adj* (el) menor, mínimo, más pequeño ‖ *adv* menos ‖ *s* (el) menor; (lo) menos; **at least** o **at the least** al menos, a los menos, por lo menos; **not in the least** de ninguna manera

leather ['lɛðər] *s* cuero

leath′er·back′ turtle *s* laúd *m*

leath′er·neck′ *s* (slang) soldado de infantería de marina de los EE.UU.

leathery ['lɛðəri] *adj* correoso, coriáceo

leave [liv] *s* (*permission*) permiso; (*permission to be absent*) licencia; (*farewell*) despedida; **on leave** con licencia; **to give leave to** dar licencia a; **to take leave (of)** despedirse (de) ‖ *v* (*pret & pp* **left** [lɛft]) *tr* (*to let stay; to stop, give up; to disregard*) dejar; (*to go away from*) salir de; (*to bequeath*) legar; **leave it to me!** ¡déjemelo a mí!; **to be left** quedar p.ej., **the letter was left unanswered** la carta quedó sin contestar; **to leave alone** dejar en paz, dejar tranquilo; **to leave no stone unturned** no dejar piedra por mover; **to leave off** dejar; no ponerse (*una prenda de vestir*); **to leave out** omitir; **to leave things as they are** dejarlo como está ‖ *intr* irse, marcharse; eliminarse (Mex); salir (*un avión, un tren, un vapor*)

leaven [ˈlɛvən] *s* levadura; (fig) influencia ‖ *tr* leudar; (fig) transformar

leavening [ˈlɛvənɪŋ] *s* levadura

leave of absence *s* licencia

leave'-tak'ing *s* despedida

leavings [ˈlivɪŋz] *spl* desperdicios, sobras

Leba·nese [ˌlɛbəˈniz] *adj* libanés ‖ *s* (*pl* -nese) libanés *m*

Lebanon [ˈlɛbənən] *s* el Líbano

Lebanon Mountains *spl* cordillera del Líbano

lecher [ˈlɛtʃər] *s* libertino, lujurioso

lecherous [ˈlɛtʃərəs] *adj* lascivo, lujurioso

lechery [ˈlɛtʃəri] *s* lascivia, lujuria

lectern [ˈlɛktərn] *s* atril *m*

lecture [ˈlɛktʃər] *s* conferencia; (*tedious reprimand*) sermoneo ‖ *tr* instruir por medio de una conferencia; sermonear ‖ *intr* dar una conferencia, dar conferencias

lecturer [ˈlɛktʃərər] *s* conferenciante *mf*

ledge [lɛdʒ] *s* (*projection in a wall*) retallo; cama de roca; arrecife *m*

ledger [ˈlɛdʒər] *s* (com) libro mayor

ledger line *s* (mus) línea suplementaria

lee [li] *s* (*shelter*) (naut) socaire *m;* (*quarter sheltered from the wind*) sotavento; **lees** heces *fpl*

leech [litʃ] *s* sanguijuela; **to stick like a leech** pegarse como ladilla

leek [lik] *s* puerro

leer [lɪr] *s* mirada de soslayo, mirada lujuriosa ‖ *intr*—**to leer at** mirar de soslayo, mirar lujuriosamente

leery [ˈlɪri] *adj* (coll) receloso, suspicaz

leeward [ˈliwərd] o [ˈluˑərd] *adj* (naut) de sotavento ‖ *adv* (naut) a sotavento ‖ *s* (naut) sotavento

Leeward Islands [ˈliwərd] *spl* islas de Sotavento

lee'way' *s* (aer & naut) deriva; (coll) tiempo de sobra, espacio de sobra, dinero de sobra; (coll) libertad de acción

left [lɛft] *adj* izquierdo ‖ *adv* hacia la izquierda ‖ *s* (*left hand*) izquierda; (box) zurdazo; (pol) izquierda; **on the left** a la izquierda

left field *s* (baseball) jardín izquierdo

left'-hand' drive *s* conducción o dirección a la izquierda

left-handed [ˈlɛftˈhændɪd] *adj* (*individual*) zurdo; (*clumsy*) desmañado, torpe; insincero; contrario a las agujas del reloj

leftist [ˈlɛftɪʃ] *adj* izquierdizante

leftist [ˈlɛftɪst] *adj* & *s* izquierdista *mf*

left'o'ver *adj* & *s* sobrante *m;* **leftovers** *spl* sobras

left'-wing' *adj* izquierdista

left-winger [ˈlɛftˈwɪŋər] *s* (coll) izquierdista *mf*

leg. *abbr* **legal, legislature**

leg [lɛg] *s* (*of man or animal*) pierna; (*of animal, table, chair, etc.*) pata; (*of boot or stocking*) caña; (*of trousers*) pernera; (*of a cooked fowl*) muslo; (*of a journey*) etapa, trecho; **to be on one's last legs** estar sin recursos; estar en las últimas; **to not have a leg to stand on** (coll) no tener justificación alguna, no tener disculpa alguna; **to pull the leg of** (coll) tomar el pelo a; **to shake a leg** (coll) darse prisa; (*to dance*) (coll) bailar; **to stretch one's legs** estirar las piernas, dar un paseíto

lega·cy [ˈlɛgəsi] *s* (*pl* -cies) legado

legal [ˈligəl] *adj* legal

legali·ty [liˈgælti] *s* (*pl* -ties) legalidad

legalization [ˌligələˈzeʃən] *s* legalización despenalización

legalize [ˈligəˌlaɪz] *tr* legalizar; despenalizar

legal tender *s* curso legal

legate [ˈlɛgɪt] *s* legado

legatee [ˌlɛgəˈti] *s* legatario

legation [liˈgeʃən] *s* legación

legend [ˈlɛdʒənd] *s* leyenda

legendary [ˈlɛdʒənˌdɛri] *adj* legendario

legerdemain [ˌlɛdʒərdɪˈmen] *s* juego de manos, prestidigitación; (*cheating, trickery*) trapacería

legging [ˈlɛgɪŋ] *s* polaina

leg·gy [ˈlɛgi] *adj* (*comp* -gier; *super* -giest) zanquilargo; de piernas largas y elegantes

leg'horn' *s* sombrero de paja de Italia ‖ **Leghorn** *s* Liorna

legible [ˈlɛdʒɪbəl] *adj* legible

legion [ˈlidʒən] *s* legión

legislate [ˈlɛdʒɪsˌlet] *tr* imponer mediante legislación ‖ *intr* legislar

legislation [ˌlɛdʒɪsˈleʃən] *s* legislación

legislative [ˈlɛdʒɪsˌletɪv] *adj* legislativo

legislator [ˈlɛdʒɪsˌletər] *s* legislador *m*

legislature [ˈlɛdʒɪsˌletʃər] *s* asamblea legislativa, cuerpo legislativo

legitimacy [lɪˈdʒɪtɪməsi] *s* legitimidad

legitimate [lɪˈdʒɪtɪmɪt] *adj* legítimo ‖ [lɪˈdʒɪtɪˌmet] *tr* legitimar

legitimate drama *s* drama serio (*a distinción del cine o el melodrama*)

legitimize [lɪˈdʒɪtɪˌmaɪz] *tr* legitimar

leg'work' *s* (coll) el mucho caminar

leisure [ˈliʒər] o [ˈlɛʒər] *s* desocupación, ocio; **at leisure** desocupado, libre; **at one's leisure** a la comodidad de uno, cuando uno pueda

leisure activities *spl* recreos pasatiempos

leisure class *s* gente acomodada

leisure hours *spl* horas de ocio, ratos perdidos

leisurely [ˈliʒərli] o [ˈlɛʒərli] *adj* lento, pausado ‖ *adv* lentamente, despacio, sin prisa

leisure wear *s* ropa de recreo, traje *m* informal

lemon [ˈlɛmən] *s* limón *m;* (slang) artículo de fábrica defectuosa

lemonade [ˌlɛməˈned] *s* limonada

lemon squeezer *s* exprimidera de limón

le
le

lemon verbena *s* luisa
lend [lɛnd] *s* (*pret & pp* **lent** [lɛnt]) *tr* prestar
lending library *s* biblioteca de préstamo
length [lɛŋθ] *s* largura, largo; (*of time*) extensión; (naut) eslora; **at length** por fin; largamente; **to go to any length** hacer cuanto esté de su parte; **to keep at arm's length** mantener a distancia; mantenerse a distancia
lengthen [ˈlɛŋθən] *tr* alargar ‖ *intr* alargarse
length'wise' *adj* longitudinal ‖ *adv* longitudinalmente
length·y [ˈlɛŋθi] *adj* (*comp* **-ier;** *super* **-iest**) muy largo, prolongado
leniency [ˈliniˌənsi] *s* clemencia, indulgencia, lenidad
lenient [ˈliniˌənt] *adj* clemente, indulgente
lens [lɛnz] *s* lente *m & f;* (*of the eye*) cristalino
Lent [lɛnt] *s* cuaresma *f*
Lenten [ˈlɛntən] *adj* cuaresmal
lentil [ˈlɛntəl] *s* lenteja
Leo [ˈliˌo] *s* (astr) Leo
leopard [ˈlɛpərd] *s* leopardo
leotard [ˈliˌəˌtɑrd] *s* leotardo
leper [ˈlɛpər] *s* leproso
leper house *s* leprosería
leprosy [ˈlɛprəsi] *s* lepra
leprous [ˈlɛprəs] *adj* leproso; (*covered with scales*) escamoso
Lesbian [ˈlɛzbiˌən] *adj* lesbio ‖ *s* lesbio; (*female homosexual*) lesbia
lesbianism [ˈlɛzbiˌəˌnizəm] *s* lesbianismo
lese majesty [ˈlizˈmædʒisti] *s* delito de lesa majestad
lesion [ˈliʒən] *s* lesión
less [lɛs] *adj* menor ‖ *adv* menos; **less and less** cada vez menos; **less than** menos que; (*followed by numeral*) menos de; (*followed by verb*) menos de lo que ‖ *s* menos *m*
lessee [lɛsˈi] *s* arrendatario
lessen [ˈlɛsən] *tr* disminuir, reducir a menos; quitar importancia a ‖ *intr* disminuirse, reducirse; amainar (*el viento*)
lesser [ˈlɛsər] *adj* menor, más pequeño
lesson [ˈlɛsən] *s* lección
lessor [ˈlɛsər] *s* arrendador *m*
lest [lɛst] *conj* no sea que, de miedo que
let [lɛt] *v* (*pret & pp* **let;** *ger* **letting**) *tr* dejar, permitir; alquilar, arrendar; **let + inf** que **+** *subj*, p.ej., **let him come in** que entre; **let alone** y mucho menos; **let good enough alone** bueno está lo bueno; **let us + inf** vamos a + *inf*, p.ej., **let us eat** vamos a comer, comamos; **to let** se alquila; **to let alone** dejar en paz, dejar tranquilo; **to let be** no tocar; dejar en paz; **to let by** dejar pasar; **to let down** dejar bajar; desilusionar, traicionar; dejar plantado; **to let fly** disparar; (fig) disparar, soltar (*palabras injuriosas*); **to let go** soltar, desasirse de; vender; **to let in** dejar entrar, dejar entrar en; **to let it go at that** no hacer o decir nada más; **to let know** hacer saber; **to let loose** soltar; **to let on** (coll) dar a entender; **to let out** dejar salir; revelar, publicar; dar, soltar (*p.ej., más cuerda*); dar (*un grito*);

ensanchar (*un vestido que aprieta*); dar en arrendamiento; (coll) despedir; **to let through** dejar pasar, dejar pasar por; **to let up** dejar subir; dejar levantarse ‖ *intr* alquilarse, arrendarse; **to let down** (coll) ir más despacio; **to let go** desasirse; **to let go of** desasirse de; **to let on** (coll) fingir; **to let out** (coll) despedirse, cerrarse (*p.ej., la escuela*); **to let up** (coll) desistir; (coll) aflojar, amainar
let'down' *s* disminución; aflojamiento; desilusión, decepción; humillación
lethal [ˈliθəl] *adj* letal
lethargic [lɪˈθɑrdʒɪk] *adj* (*affected with lethargy*) letárgico; (*producing lethargy*) letargoso
lethar·gy [ˈlɛθərdʒi] *s* (*pl* **-gies**) letargo
Lett [lɛt] *s* letón *m*
letter [ˈlɛtər] *s* (*written message*) carta; (*of the alphabet*) letra; (*literal meaning*) (fig) letra; **letters** (*literature*) letras; **to the letter** al pie de la letra ‖ *tr* estampar o marcar con letras
letter box *s* buzón *m* (*caja*)
letter carrier *s* cartero
letter drop *s* buzón *m* (*agujero*)
letter file *s* guardacartas *m*
let'ter·head' *s* membrete *m;* (*paper with printed heading*) memorándum *m*
lettering [ˈlɛtərɪŋ] *s* inscripción; letras
letter of credit *s* carta de crédito
letter opener [ˈopənər] *s* abrecartas *m*
letter paper *s* papel *m* de cartas
let'ter·per'fect *adj* que tiene bien aprendido su papel; correcto, exacto
let'ter·press' *s* impresión tipográfica; texto (*a distinción de los grabados*)
letter scales *spl* pesacartas *m*
Lettish [ˈlɛtɪʃ] *adj* letón ‖ *s* letón *m*
lettuce [ˈlɛtɪs] *s* lechuga
let'up' *s* (coll) calma, interrupción; **without letup** (coll) sin cesar
leucorrhea [ˌlukəˈriˌə] *s* leucorrea
leukemia [luˈkimiˌə] *s* leucemia
Levant [lɪˈvænt] *s* Levante *m* (*países de la parte oriental del Mediterráneo*)
Levantine [ˈlɛvənˌtin] *o* [lɪˈvæntin] *adj & s* levantino
levee [ˈlɛvi] *s* (*embankment to hold back water*) ribero; (*reception at court*) besamanos *m*
lev·el [ˈlɛvəl] *adj* raso, llano; nivelado; (coll) sensato, juicioso; **level with** al nivel de, a flor de, a ras de ‖ *s* (*device for determining horizontal position; degree of elevation*) nivel *m;* (*flat and even area of land*) terreno llano, llanura; (*part of a canal between two locks*) tramo; **to be on the level** obrar sin engaño, decir la pura verdad; **to find one's level** hallar su propio nivel ‖ *v* (*pret & pp* **-eled** *o* **-elled;** *ger* **-eling** *o* **-elling**) *tr* nivelar; (*to smooth, flatten out*) arrasar, allanar; (*to bring down*) derribar, echar por tierra; apuntar (*un arma de fuego*); (fig) allanar (*dificultades*) ‖ *intr*—**to level off** (aer) enderezarse para aterrizar

level-headed ['lɛvəl'hɛdɪd] *adj* sensato, juicioso
leveling rod *s* (surv) jalón *m* de mira
lever ['livər] o [lɛvər] *s* palanca ‖ *tr* apalancar
leverage ['livərɪdʒ] o ['lɛvərɪdʒ] *s* palancada; poder *m* de una palanca; (fig) influencia, poder *m*
leviathan [lɪ'vaɪ•əθən] *s* (Bib & fig) leviatán *m;* buque *m* muy grande
levitation [,lɛvɪ'teʃən] *s* levitación
levi•ty ['lɛvɪti] *s* (*pl* **-ties**) frivolidad; (*fickleness*) ligereza
lev•y ['lɛvi] *s* (*pl* **-ies**) (*of taxes*) exacción, recaudación; dinero recaudado; (mil) leva, enganche *m*, recluta ‖ *v* (*pret & pp* **-ied**) *tr* exigir, recaudar (*impuestos*); (mil) enganchar, reclutar; hacer (*la guerra*)
lewd [lud] *adj* lascivo, lujurioso; obsceno
lewdness ['ludnɪs] *s* lascivia, lujuria; obscenidad
lexical ['lɛksɪkəl] *adj* léxico
lexicographer [,lɛksɪ'kɑgrəfər] *s* lexicógrafo
lexicographic(al) [,lɛksɪkə'græfɪk(əl)] lexicográfico
lexicography [,lɛksɪ'kɑgrəfi] *s* lexicografía
lexicology [,lɛksɪ'kalədʒi] *s* lexicología
lexicon ['lɛksɪkən] *s* léxico, lexicón *m*
liabili•ty [,laɪ•ə'bɪlɪti] *s* (*pl* **-ties**) (*e.g., to disease*) propensión; responsabilidad, obligación; desventaja; **liabilities** deudas; (*as detailed in balance sheet*) pasivo
liability insurance *s* seguro de responsabilidad civil
liable ['laɪ•əbəl] *adj* (*e.g., to disease*) propenso, expuesto; responsable; **to be liable to** + *inf* (coll) amenazar + *inf*
liaison ['li•ə,zɑn] o [li'ezən] *s* enlace *m*, unión; (*illicit relationship between a man and woman*) amancebamiento, enredo, lío; (mil, nav & phonet) enlace *m*
liaison officer *s* (mil) oficial *m* de enlace
liar ['laɪ•ər] *s* mentiroso
lib. *abbr* librarian, library
libation [laɪ'beʃən] *s* libación; (*drink*) libación
li•bel ['laɪbəl] *s* calumnia, difamación; levante (CAm, P-R); (*defamatory writing*) libelo ‖ *v* (*pret & pp* **-beled** o **-belled;** *ger* **-beling** o **-belling**) *tr* calumniar, difamar
libelous ['laɪbələs] *adj* calumniador
liberal ['lɪbərəl] *adj* (*generous; done or given generously*) liberal; (*open-minded*) tolerante, de amplias miras; (*translation*) libre; (pol) liberal ‖ *s* liberal *mf*
liberali•ty [,lɪbə'rælɪti] *s* (*pl* **-ties**) liberalidad
liberal-minded ['lɪbərəl'maɪndɪd] *adj* tolerante, de amplias miras
liberate ['lɪbə,ret] *tr* libertar; (*to disengage from a combination*) (chem) desprender
liberation [,lɪbə'reʃən] *s* liberación; (chem) desprendimiento
liberation theology *s* teología liberacionista
liberator ['lɪbə,retər] *s* libertador *m*
libertine ['lɪbər,tin] *adj & s* libertino
liber•ty ['lɪbərti] *s* (*pl* **-ties**) libertad; **to take the liberty to** tomarse la libertad de

liberty-loving ['lɪbərti'lʌvɪŋ] *adj* amante de la libertad
libidinous [lɪ'bɪdɪnəs] *adj* libidinoso
libido [lɪ'bido] o [lɪ'baɪdo] *s* libídine *f*, libido *f*
Libra ['librə] *s* (astr) Libra
librarian [laɪ'brɛri•ən] *s* bibliotecario
librar•y ['laɪ,brɛri] o ['laɪbrəri] *s* (*pl* **-ies**) biblioteca
library number *s* signatura
library school *s* escuela de bibliotecarios
library science *s* bibliotecnia; biblioteconomía
libret•to [lɪ'brɛto] *s* (*pl* **-tos**) (mus) libreto
license ['laɪsəns] *s* licencia ‖ *tr* licenciar
license number *s* número de matrícula
license plate o **tag** *s* chapa de circulación, placa de matrícula
licentious [laɪ'sɛnʃəs] *adj* licencioso, disoluto
lichen ['laɪkən] *s* liquen *m*
lick [lɪk] *s* lamedura; (*place where animals go to lick*) lamedero; (*blow*) (coll) bofetón *m*; (*speed*) (coll) velocidad; (*beating*) (coll) zurra; (*quick cleaning*) (coll) limpión *m*; **to give a lick and a promise to** (coll) hacer rápida y superficialmente ‖ *tr* lamer; lamerse (*p.ej., los dedos*); lamer (*las llamas un tejado*); (*to beat, thrash*) (coll) zurrar; (*to conquer*) (coll) vencer ‖ *intr* lengüetear
licorice ['lɪkərɪs] *s* regaliz *m*, orozuz *m;* dulce *m* de regaliz
lid [lɪd] *s* (*of a box, trunk, chest, etc.*) tapa, tapadera; (*of a dish, pot, etc.*) cobertera; (*eyelid*) párpado; (*hat*) (slang) techo
lie [laɪ] *s* mentira; **to catch in a lie** coger en una mentira; **to give the lie to** dar un mentís a ‖ *v* (*pret & pp* **lied;** *ger* **lying**) *tr*—**to lie oneself out of** o **to lie one's way out of** librarse de un aprieto mintiendo ‖ *intr* mentir ‖ *v* (*pret* **lay** [le]; *pp* **lain** [len]; *ger* **lying**) *intr* estar echado; hallarse, estar situado; (*e.g., in the grave*) yacer, estar enterrado; **to lie down** echarse, acostarse
lie detector *s* detector *m* de mentiras
lien [lin] o ['li•ən] *s* gravamen *m*, derecho de retención
lieu [lu] *s*—**in lieu of** en lugar de, en vez de
lieutenant [lu'tɛnənt] *s* lugarteniente *m;* (mil) teniente *m;* (nav) teniente de navío
lieutenant colonel *s* (mil) teniente coronel *m*
lieutenant commander *s* (nav) capitán *m* de corbeta
lieutenant governor *s* (U.S.A.) vicegobernador *m* (*de un Estado*)
lieutenant junior grade *s* (nav) alférez *m* de navío
life [laɪf] *adj* (*animate*) vital; (*lifelong*) perpetuo; (*annuity, income*) vitalicio; (*working from nature*) (fa) del natural ‖ *s* (*pl* **lives** [laɪvz]) vida; (*of an insurance policy*) vigencia; **for life** de por vida; **for the life of me** así me maten; **the life and soul of** (*e.g., a party*) la alegría de; **to come to life** volver a la vida; **to depart this life** partir de esta vida; **to run for one's life** salvarse por los pies

life annuity s renta vitalicia
life belt s cinturón m salvavidas
life'boat' s bote m de salvamento, bote salvavidas; (*for shore-based rescue services*) lancha de auxilio
life buoy s boya salvavidas, guindola
life expectancy s expectación de vida
life float s balsa salvavidas
life'guard' s salvavidas m, guardavida m
life imprisonment s cadena perpetua
life insurance s seguro sobre la vida
life jacket s chaleco salvavidas
lifeless ['laɪflɪs] adj muerto, sin vida; (*in a faint*) desmayado, exánime; (*dull, colorless*) deslucido
life'like' adj natural, vivo
life line s cuerda salvavidas; cuerda de buzo
life'long' adj perpetuo, de toda la vida
life of leisure s vida de ocio
life of Riley ['raɪli] s (slang) vida regalada
life of the party s (coll) alegría de la fiesta, alma de la fiesta
life preserver [prɪ'zʌrvər] s chaleco salvavidas
lifer ['laɪfər] s (slang) presidiario de por vida
life'sav'er s salvador m (*de vidas*); (*something that saves a person from a predicament*) (coll) tabla de salvación
lifesaving ['laɪf,sevɪŋ] adj de salvamento ‖ s salvamento (*de vidas*)
life sentence s condena a cadena perpetua
life'-size' adj de tamaño natural
life span s período de vida
life'time' adj vitalicio ‖ s vida, curso de la vida, jornada
life'work' s obra principal de la vida de uno
lift [lɪft] s elevación, levantamiento; ayuda (*para levantar una carga*); (aer) sustentación; **to give a lift to** invitar (*a un peatón*) a subir a un coche; llevar en un coche; (fig) reanimar ‖ tr elevar, levantar; quitarse (*el sombrero*); (naut) izar (*velas, vergas, etc.*); (fig) reanimar, exaltar; (coll) robar; (coll) plagiar ‖ intr elevarse, levantarse; disiparse (*las nubes, las nieblas, la obscuridad, etc.*)
lift bridge s puente levadizo
lift'-off' s despegue m vertical
lift truck s carretilla elevadora
ligament ['lɪgəmənt] s ligamento
ligature ['lɪgətʃər] s (mus & surg) ligadura; (mus & typ) ligado
light [laɪt] adj (*in weight*) ligero, leve, liviano; (*having illumination; whitish*) claro; (*hair*) blondo, rubio; (*complexion*) blanco; (*oil*) flúido; (*beer*) claro; (*reading*) poco serio; (*heart*) alegre, despreocupado; (*carrying a small cargo or none at all*) (naut) boyante; **light in the head** (*dizzy*) aturdido, mareado; (*simple, silly*) tonto, necio; **to make light of** no dar importancia a, no tomar en serio ‖ adv sin carga; sin equipaje ‖ s luz f; (*to light a cigarette*) lumbre f, fuego; (*to control traffic*) luz, señal f; (*window or other opening in a wall*) luz, claro, hueco; (*example, shining figure*) lumbrera; **according to one's lights** según Dios le da

a uno a entender; **against the light** al trasluz; **in this light** desde este punto de vista; **lights** noticias; (*of sheep, etc.*) bofes mpl; **to come to light** salir a luz, descubrirse; **to shed** o **throw light on** echar luz sobre; **to strike a light** echar una yesca; encender un fósforo ‖ v (*pret & pp* **lighted** o **lit** [lɪt] tr (*to furnish with illumination*) alumbrar, iluminar; (*to set afire, ignite*) encender; **to light up** iluminar ‖ intr alumbrarse; encenderse; posar (*un ave*); (*from an auto*) bajar; **to light into** (*to attack*) (slang) arremeter contra; (*to scold, berate*) (slang) poner de oro y azul; **to light out** (slang) poner pies en polvorosa; **to light upon** tropezar con, hallar por casualidad
light bulb s (elec) bombilla
light complexion s tez blanca
lighten ['laɪtən] tr (*to make lighter in weight*) aligerar; iluminar; (*to cheer up*) alegrar, regocijar ‖ intr (*to become less dark*) iluminarse; (*to give off flashes of lightning*) relampaguear; (fig) iluminarse (*los ojos, la cara de una persona*)
lighter ['laɪtər] s (*to light a cigarette*) encendedor m; (*flat-bottomed barge*) alijador m
light-fingered ['laɪt'fɪŋgərd] adj largo de uñas, listo de manos
light-footed ['laɪt'fʊtɪd] adj ligero de pies
light-headed ['laɪt'hɛdɪd] adj (*dizzy*) aturdido, mareado; (*simple, silly*) tonto, necio, ligero de cascos
light-hearted ['laɪt'hɑrtɪd] adj alegre, libre de cuidados
light'house' s faro
lighthouse keeper s farero
lighting ['laɪtɪŋ] s alumbrado, iluminación
lighting engineer s iluminador m
lighting fixtures spl artefactos de alumbrado
lightly ['laɪtli] adj ligeramente
light meter s exposímetro
lightness ['laɪtnɪs] s (*in weight*) ligereza; (*in illumination*) claridad
lightning ['laɪtnɪŋ] s relámpagos, relampagueo ‖ intr relampaguear
lightning arrester [ə'rɛstər] s pararrayos m
lightning bug s luciérnaga
lightning rod s pararrayos m
light opera s opereta
light'ship' s buque m fanal, buque faro
light•struck ['laɪt,strʌk] adj velado
light'weight' adj ligero; de entretiempo, p.ej., **lightweight coat** abrigo de entretiempo
light'-year' s año luz
lignite ['lɪgnaɪt] s lignito
lignum vitae ['lɪgnəm'vaɪti] s guayaco, palo santo
likable ['laɪkəbəl] adj simpático
like [laɪk] adj parecido, semejante; parecido a, semejante a, p.ej., **this hat is like mine** este sombrero es parecido al mío; (elec) del mismo nombre; **like father like son** de tal palo tal astilla; **to feel like** + *ger* tener ganas de + *inf*; **to look like** parecerse a; parecer que, p.ej., **it looks like rain** parece que va a llover ‖ adv como; **like enough**

(coll) probablemente; **nothing like** ni con mucho ‖ *prep* a semejanza de ‖ *conj* (coll) del mismo modo que; (coll) que, p.ej., **it seems like he is right** parece que tiene razón ‖ *s* (*liking*) gusto, preferencia; (*fellow, fellow man*) prójimo, semejante *m;* **and the like** y cosas por el estilo; **to give like for like** pagar en la misma moneda ‖ *tr* gustar de, p.ej., **I like music** gusto de la música; gustar p.ej., **Mary likes peaches** a María. le gustan los melocotones; **to like best** o **better** preferir; **to like it in** encontrarse a gusto en (*p.ej., el campo*); **to like to** + *inf* gustarle a uno + *inf*, p.ej., **I like to travel** me gusta viajar; gustarle a uno que + *subj*, p.ej., **I should like him to come to see me** me gustaría que él viniese a verme ‖ *intr* querer, p.ej., **as you like** como Vd. quiera; **if you like** si Vd. quiere

likelihood [ˈlaɪklɪˌhʊd] *s* probabilidad

like•ly [ˈlaɪkli] *adj* (*comp* **-lier;** *super* **-liest**) probable; a propósito; prometedor; **to be likely to** + *inf* ser probable que + *ind*, p.ej., **Mary is likely to come to see us tomorrow** es probable que María vendrá a vernos mañana ‖ *adv* probablemente

like-minded [ˈlaɪkˈmaɪndɪd] *adj* del mismo parecer; de natural semejante

liken [ˈlaɪkən] *tr* asemejar, comparar

likeness [ˈlaɪknɪs] *s* (*picture or image*) retrato; (*similarity*) semejanza, parecido; forma, aspecto, apariencia

like'wise' *adv* igualmente, asimismo; **to do likewise** hacer lo mismo

liking [ˈlaɪkɪŋ] *s* gusto, afición, simpatía; **to be to the liking of** ser del gusto de; **to have a liking for** aficionarse a

lilac [ˈlaɪlək] *adj* de color lila ‖ *s* lilac *m*, lila

Lilliputian [ˌlɪlɪˈpjuʃən] *adj & s* liliputiense *mf*

lilt [lɪlt] *s* paso airoso, movimiento airoso; canción cadenciosa, música alegre

lil•y [ˈlɪli] *s* (*pl* **-ies**) (*Lilium candidum*) azucena, lirio blanco; cala, lirio de agua; (*fleur-de-lis, the royal arms of France*) flor *f* de lis; **to gild the lily** ponerle colores al oro

lily of the valley *s* lirio de los valles, muguete *m*

lily pad *s* hoja de nenúfar

lima bean [ˈlaɪmə] *s* judía de la peladilla, frijol *m* de media luna

limb [lɪm] *s* (*arm or leg*) miembro; (*of a tree*) rama; (*of a cross; of the sea*) brazo; **to be out on a limb** (coll) estar en un aprieto

limber [ˈlɪmbər] *adj* ágil; flexible ‖ *intr*—**to limber up** agilitarse

lim•bo [ˈlɪmbo] *s* (*pl* **-bos**) lugar *m* de olvido; (theol) limbo

lime [laɪm] *s* (*calcium oxide*) cal *f*; (*Citrus aurantifolia*) limero agrio; (*its fruit*) lima agria; (*linden tree*) tila o tilo

lime'kiln' *s* calera, horno de cal

lime'light' *s* —**to be in the limelight** estar a la vista del público

limerick [ˈlɪmərɪk] *s* quintilla jocosa

lime'stone' *adj* calizo ‖ *s* caliza, piedra caliza

limit [ˈlɪmɪt] *s* límite *m;* **to be the limit** (slang) ser el colmo; **to go the limit** no dejar piedra por mover ‖ *tr* limitar

lim'ited-ac'cess high'way *s* carretera de vía libre

limited monarchy *s* monarquía constitucional

limitless [ˈlɪmɪtlɪs] *adj* ilimitado

limousine [ˈlɪməˌzin] o [ˌlɪməˈzin] *s* (aut) limusina

limp [lɪmp] *adj* flojo, débil, flexible ‖ *s* cojera ‖ *intr* cojear

limpid [ˈlɪmpɪd] *adj* diáfano, cristalino

linage [ˈlaɪnɪdʒ] *s* (typ) número de líneas

linchpin [ˈlɪntʃˌpɪn] *s* pezonera

linden [ˈlɪndən] *s* tila, tilo

line [laɪn] *s* línea; (*of people, houses, etc.*) hilera; (*rope, string*) cuerda, cordel *m;* (*wrinkle*) arruga; (*for fishing*) sedal *m;* (*written or printed line; line of goods*) renglón *m;* manera (*de pensar*); (*of the spectrum*) (phys) raya; **all along the line** por todas partes; desde cualquier punto de vista; **in line** alineado; dispuesto, preparado; **in line with** de acuerdo con; **out of line** desalineado; en desacuerdo; **to bring into line** poner de acuerdo; **to draw the line at** no ir más allá de; **to fall in line** conformarse; formar cola; alinearse; **to have a line on** (coll) estar enterado de; **to read between the lines** leer entre líneas; **to stand in line** hacer cola; **to toe the line** obrar como se debe; **to wait in line** hacer cola, esperar vez ‖ *tr* alinear, rayar; arrugar (*p.ej., la cara*); formar hilera a lo largo de (*la acera, la calle*); forrar (*un vestido*); guarnecer (*un freno*) ‖ *intr*—**to line up** ponerse en fila; hacer cola

lineage [ˈlɪnɪˌɪdʒ] *s* linaje *m*

lineaments [ˈlɪnɪ•əmənts] *spl* lineamentos

linear [ˈlɪnɪ•ər] *adj* lineal

line•man [ˈlaɪnmən] *s* (*pl* **-men** [mən]) (elec) celador *m*, recorredor *m* de la línea; (rr) guardavía *m;* (surv) cadenero

linen [ˈlɪnən] *adj* de lino ‖ *s* (*fabric*) lienzo, lino; (*yarn*) hilo de lino; ropa blanca, ropa de cama

linen closet *s* armario para la ropa blanca

line of battle *s* línea de batalla

line of fire *s* (mil) línea de tiro

line of least resistance *s* ley *f* del menor esfuerzo; **to follow the line of least resistance** seguir la corriente, no oponer resistencia

line of sight *s* visual *f;* (*of firearm*) línea de mira

liner [ˈlaɪnər] *s* vapor *m* de travesía; (baseball) pelota rasa, lineazo

line'-up' *s* agrupación, formación; (*of prisoners*) rueda

linger [ˈlɪŋgər] *intr* estarse, quedarse; (*to be tardy*) demorar, tardar; tardar en marcharse; tardar en morirse; pasearse con paso lento; **to linger over** contemplar, reflexionar

lingerie [,læn3ə`ri] *s* ropa interior de mujer
lingering [`lɪŋgərɪŋ] *adj* prolongado
lingual [`lɪŋgwəl] *adj & s* lingual *f*
linguist [`lɪŋgwɪst] *s* (*person skilled in several languages*) poligloto; (*specialist in linguistics*) lingüista *mf*
linguistic [lɪŋ`gwɪstɪk] *adj* lingüístico ‖ **linguistics** *s* lingüística
liniment [`lɪnɪmənt] *s* linimento
lining [`laɪnɪŋ] *s* (*of a coat*) forro, forrado; (*of auto brake*) guarnición; (*of a furnace*) camisa; (*of a wall*) revestimiento
link [lɪŋk] *s* eslabón *m*; **links** campo de golf ‖ *tr* eslabonar ‖ *intr* eslabonarse
linkup [`lɪŋk,ʌp] *s* conexión; (*in space*) acoplamiento
linnet [`lɪnɪt] *s* pardillo
linoleum [lɪ`nolɪ•əm] *s* linóleo
linotype [`laɪnə,taɪp] (*trademark*) *adj* linotípico ‖ *s* (*machine*) linotipia; (*matter produced by machine*) linotipo ‖ *tr* componer con linotipia
linotype operator *s* linotipista *mf*
linseed [`lɪn,sid] *s* linaza
linseed oil *s* aceite *m* de linaza
lint [lɪnt] *s* borra, pelusa, hilaza; (*used to dress wounds*) hilas
lintel [`lɪntəl] *s* dintel *m*, umbral *m*
lion [`laɪ•ən] *s* león *m*; (*man of strength and courage*) (fig) león; (fig) celebridad muy solicitada; **to beard the lion in his den** ir a desafiar la cólera de un jefe; **to put one's head in the lion's mouth** meterse en la boca del lobo
lioness [`laɪ•ənɪs] *s* leona
lion-hearted [`laɪ•ən,hɑrtɪd] *adj* valiente
lionize [`laɪ•ə,naɪz] *tr* agasajar
lions' den *s* (Bib) fosa de los leones
lion's share *s* (la) parte *f* del león
lip [lɪp] *s* labio; (slang) lenguaje *m* insolente; **to hang on the words of** estar pendiente de las palabras de; **to smack one's lips** chuparse los labios
lip'-read' *v* (*pret & pp* -read [,rɛd]) *tr & intr* leer en los labios
lip reading *s* labiolectura
lip service *s* homenaje *m* de boca, jarabe *m* de pico
lip'stick' *s* lápiz *m* de labios, lápiz labial
liq. *abbr* **liquid, liquor**
lique•fy [`lɪkwɪ,faɪ] *v* (*pret & pp* -**fied**) *tr* liquidar ‖ *intr* liquidarse
liqueur [lɪ`kʌr] *s* licor *m*
liquid [`lɪkwɪd] *adj* líquido ‖ *s* líquido; (phonet) líquida
liquidate [`lɪkwɪ,det] *tr & intr* liquidar
liquidity [lɪ`kwɪdɪti] *s* liquidez *f*
liquid measure *s* medida para líquidos
liquor [`lɪkər] *s* licor *m*
Lisbon [`lɪzbən] *s* Lisboa
lisle [laɪl] *s* hilo fino de algodón, muy retorcido, sedalina
lisp [lɪsp] *s* ceceo ‖ *intr* cecear
lissome [`lɪsəm] *adj* flexible, elástico; ágil, ligero
list [lɪst] *s* lista; (*strip*) lista, tira; (*border*) orilla; (*selvage*) orillo; (naut) ladeo; **lists**

liza; **to enter the lists** entrar en liza; **to have a list** (naut) irse a la banda ‖ *tr* alistar, listar; registrar ‖ *intr* (naut) irse a la banda
listen [`lɪsən] *intr* escuchar; obedecer; **to listen in** escuchar a hurtadillas; escuchar por radio; **to listen to** escuchar; obedecer; **to listen to reason** meterse en razón
listener [`lɪsənər] *s* oyente *mf*; radioescucha *mf*, radioyente *mf*
listening post [`lɪsənɪŋ] *s* puesto de escucha
listing [`lɪstɪŋ] *s* (*items*) rubricación
listless [`lɪstlɪs] *adj* distraído, desatento, indiferente
listlessness [`lɪstlɪsnɪs] *s* apatía; indiferencia
list price *s* precio de catálogo, precio de tarifa
lit. *abbr* **liter, literal, literature**
lita•ny [`lɪtəni] *s* (*pl* -**nies**) letanía; (*repeated series*) (fig) letanía
liter [`lɪtər] *s* litro
literacy [`lɪtərəsi] *s* capacidad de leer y escribir; instrucción
literal [`lɪtərəl] *adj* literal
literary [`lɪtə,rɛri] *adj* literario; (*individual*) literato
literate [`lɪtərɪt] *adj* que sabe leer y escribir; (*well-read*) literato, muy leído; (*educated*) instruído ‖ *s* persona que sabe leer y escribir; literato, erudito
literati [,lɪtə`rɑti] *spl* literatos
literature [`lɪtərət/ər] *s* literatura; impresos, escritos de publicidad
lithe [laɪθ] *adj* flexible, cimbreño
lithia [`lɪθɪ•ə] *s* (chem) litina
lithium [`lɪθɪ•əm] *s* (chem) litio
lithograph [`lɪθə,græf] *s* litografía ‖ *tr* litografiar
lithographer [lɪ`θɑgrəfər] *s* litógrafo
lithography [lɪ`θɑgrəfi] *s* litografía
litigant [`lɪtɪgənt] *adj & s* litigante *mf*
litigate [`lɪtɪ,get] *tr & intr* litigar
litigation [,lɪtɪ`gə/ən] *s* litigación; (*lawsuit*) litigio
litigious [lɪ`tɪdʒəs] *adj* litigioso
litmus [`lɪtməs] *s* tornasol *m*
litmus paper *s* papel *m* de tornasol
litter [`lɪtər] *s* desorden *m*; (*scattered rubbish*) basura, papelería; (*young brought forth at one birth*) camada, ventregada; (*bedding for animals*) cama, paja; (*vehicle carried by men or animals*) litera; (*stretcher*) camilla, parihuela ‖ *tr* esparcir papeles por; esparcir (*desechos, papeles, etc.*); cubrir (*el suelo*) con paja ‖ *intr* parir
lit'ter•bug' *s* persona que ensucia las calles tirando papeles rotos
littering [`lɪtərɪŋ] *s*—**no littering** se prohibe tirar papeles rotos
little [`lɪtəl] *adj* (*in size*) pequeño; (*in amount*) poco, p.ej., **little money** poco dinero; **a little** un poco de, p.ej., **a little money** un poco de dinero ‖ *adv* poco; **little by little** poco a poco ‖ *s* poco; **a little** un poco; (*somewhat*) algo; **to make little of** no dar importancia a, no tomar en serio; **to think little of** tener en poco; no vacilar en

Little Bear s Osa menor
Little Dipper s Carro menor
little finger s dedo auricular, dedo meñique; **to twist around one's little finger** manejar con suma facilidad
lit·tle·neck' s almeja redonda (*Venus mercenaria*)
little owl s mochuelo (*Athene noctua*)
little people spl hadas; gente menuda
Little Red Ridinghood ['raɪdɪŋ,hʊd] s Caperucita Roja
little slam s (bridge) semibola
liturgic(al) [lɪ'tʌrdʒɪk(əl)] adj litúrgico
litur·gy ['lɪtərdʒi] s (pl -gies) liturgia
livable ['lɪvəbəl] adj habitable, vividero; llevadero, tolerable
live [laɪv] adj (*living; full of life; intense*) vivo; (*coals; flame*) ardiente; de actualidad; (elec) cargado ‖ [lɪv] tr llevar (*tal o cual vida*); vivir (*una experiencia, una aventura; un actor sus personajes*); **to live down** borrar (*una falta*); **to live out** vivir (*toda la vida*); salir con vida de (*un desastre, una guerra*) ‖ intr vivir; **to live and learn** vivir para ver; **to live and let live** vivir y dejar vivir; **to live high** darse buena vida; **to live on** seguir viviendo; vivir de (*p.ej., carne*); vivir a expensas de; **to live up to** cumplir (*lo prometido*); gastar (*todas sus rentas*)
live coal s ascua
livelihood ['laɪvlɪ,hʊd] s vida; **to earn one's livelihood** ganarse la vida
livelong ['lɪv,lɔŋ] o ['lɪv,lɑŋ] adj—**all the livelong day** todo el santo día
live·ly ['laɪvli] adj (comp -lier; super -liest) animado, vivaz; alegre, festivo; (*active, keen*) vivo; (*resilient*) elástico
liven ['laɪvən] tr animar, regocijar ‖ intr animarse, regocijarse
liver ['lɪvər] s vividor m; habitante mf; (anat) hígado
liver·y ['lɪvəri] s (pl -ies) librea
livery·man ['lɪvərimən] s (pl -men [mən]) dueño de una cochera; mozo de cuadra
livery stable s cochera de carruajes de alquiler
live'stock' adj ganadero ‖ s ganadería
live wire s (elec) alambre cargado; (slang) trafagón m
livid ['lɪvɪd] adj lívido, amoratado; encolerizado; pálido
living ['lɪvɪŋ] adj vivo, viviente ‖ s vida; **to earn** o **to make a living** ganarse la vida
living quarters spl aposentos, habitaciones
living room s sala, sala de estar
living wage s jornal m suficiente para vivir
lizard ['lɪzərd] s lagarto; (slang) holgón m
load [lod] s carga; **loads** (coll) muchísimo; **loads of** (coll) gran cantidad de; **to get a load of** (slang) escuchar, oír; (slang) mirar; **to have a load on** (slang) estar borracho ‖ tr cargar ‖ intr cargar; cargarse
loaded ['lodɪd] adj cargado; (slang) muy borracho; (slang) muy rico
loaded dice spl dados cargados
load'stone' s piedra imán; (fig) imán m

loaf [lof] s (pl **loaves** [lovz]) pan m; (*of sugar*) pilón m ‖ intr haraganear
loafer ['lofər] s haragán m
loam [lom] s suelo franco; (*mixture used in making molds*) tierra de moldeo
loamy ['lomi] adj franco
loan [lon] s (*among individuals*) préstamo; (*between companies or governments*) empréstito; **to hit for a loan** (coll) dar un sablazo a ‖ tr prestar
loan shark s (coll) usurero
loan word s préstamo lingüístico
loath [loθ] adj poco dispuesto; **nothing loath** de buena gana
loathe [loð] tr abominar, detestar
loathing ['loðɪŋ] s abominación, detestación
loathsome ['loðsəm] adj abominable, asqueroso
lob [lɑb] v (pret & pp **lobbed**; ger **lobbing**) tr (tennis) volear desde muy alto
lob·by ['lɑbi] s (pl -bies) salón m de entrada, vestíbulo; cabilderos ‖ v (pret & pp -bied) intr cabildear
lobbying ['lɑbɪ·ɪŋ] s cabildeo
lobbyist ['lɑbɪ·ɪst] s cabildero
lobster ['lɑbstər] s (*spiny lobster*) langosta; (*Homarus*) bogavante m
lobster pot s langostera
local ['lokəl] adj local ‖ s tren suburbano; (*branch of a union*) junta local; noticia de interés local
locale [lo'kæl] s localidad
locali·ty [lo'kælɪti] s (pl -ties) localidad
localize ['lokə,laɪz] tr localizar
local option s derecho local de legislar sobre la venta de bebidas alcohólicas
locate [lo'ket] o ['loket] tr (*to discover the location of*) localizar; (*to place, to settle*) colocar, establecer; (*to ascribe a particular location to*) situar ‖ intr establecerse
location [lo'keʃən] s (*place, position*) localidad; (*act of placing*) colocación; (*act of finding*) localización; **on location** (mov) en exteriores
loc. cit. abbr **loco citato** (Lat) **in the place cited**
lock [lɑk] s cerradura; (*of a canal*) esclusa; (*of hair*) bucle m; (*of a firearm*) llave f; **lock, stock, and barrel** (coll) del todo, por completo; **under lock and key** bajo llave ‖ tr echar la llave a, cerrar con llave; (*to key*) acuñar; hacer pasar (*un buque*) por la esclusa; abrazar, enlazar; **to lock in** encerrar, poner debajo de llave; **to lock out** cerrar la puerta a, dejar en la calle; dejar sin trabajo (*a los obreros*); **to lock up** encerrar poner debajo de llave; encarcelar
locker ['lɑkər] s armario cerrado con llave
locket ['lɑkɪt] s guardapelo, medallón m
lock'jaw' s trismo, oclusión forzosa de la boca
lock nut s contratuerca
lock'out' s huelga patronal
lock'smith' s cerrajero
lock step s marcha en fila apretada
lock stitch s punto encadenado
lock tender s esclusero

li
lo

lock'up' *s* cárcel *f*

lock washer *s* arandela de seguridad

locomotive [,lokə'motɪv] *s* locomotora

lo•cus ['lokəs] *s* (*pl* **-ci** [saɪ]) sitio, lugar *m;* lugar (geométrico)

locust ['lokəst] *s* (ent) langosta (*Pachytylus*); (ent) cigarra (*Cicada*); (bot) acacia falsa

lode [lod] *s* filón *m,* venero, veta

lode'star' *s* (astr) estrella polar; estrella de guía; (*guide, direction*) guía, norte *m*

lodge [ladʒ] *s* casa de guarda; casa de campo; (*e.g., of Masons*) logia ‖ *tr* alojar, hospedar; depositar, colocar; presentar (*una queja*) ‖ alojarse, hospedarse; quedar colgado, ir a parar

lodger ['ladʒər] *s* inquilino (*en parte de una casa*)

lodging ['ladʒɪŋ] *s* alojamiento, hospedaje *m;* (*without meals*) cobijo

loft [lɔft] *s* (*attic*) desván *m,* sobrado; (*hayloft*) henal *m,* pajar *m;* (*in theater or church*) galería; (*in a store or office building*) piso alto

loft•y ['lɔfti] *adj* (*comp* **-ier;** *super* **-iest**) (*towering; sublime*) encumbrado; (*haughty*) altivo, orgulloso

log. *abbr* **logarithm**

log [lɔg] *s* leño, tronco; (*log chip*) (naut) barquilla; (*chip and line*) (naut) corredera; (aer) diario de vuelo; **to sleep like a log** dormir como un leño ‖ *v* (*pret & pp* **logged;** *ger* **logging**) *tr* registrar; recorrer (*cierta distancia*)

logarithm ['lɔgə,rɪðəm] *s* logaritmo

log'book' *s* (aer) libro de vuelo; (naut) cuaderno de bitácora

log cabin *s* cabaña de troncos

log chip *s* (naut) barquilla

log driver *s* ganchero, maderero

log driving *s* flotaje *m*

logger ['lɔgər] o ['lagər] *s* leñador *m,* maderero; grúa de troncos; tractor *m*

log'ger•head' *s* mentecato; **at loggerheads** reñidos

loggia ['lodʒə] *s* (archit) logia

logic ['ladʒɪk] *s* lógica

logical ['ladʒɪkəl] *adj* lógico

logician [lo'dʒɪʃən] *s* lógico

logistic(al) [lo'dʒɪstɪk(əl)] *adj* logístico

logistics [lo'dʒɪstɪks] *s* logística

log'jam' *s* atasco de rollizos; (fig) estancación

log line *s* (naut) corredera

log'roll' *intr* trocar favores políticos

log'wood' *s* campeche *m*

loin [lɔɪn] *s* lomo; **to gird up one's loins** apercibirse para la acción

loin'cloth' *s* taparrabo

loiter ['lɔɪtər] *tr* —**to loiter away** malgastar (*el tiempo*) ‖ *intr* holgazanear, rezagarse

loiterer ['lɔɪtərər] *s* holgazán *m,* rezagado

loll [lal] *intr* colgar flojamente; arrellanarse, repantigarse

lollipop ['lali,pap] *s* paleta (*dulce en el extremo de un palito*)

Lombard ['lambərd] *adj & s* lombardo

Lombardy ['lambərdi] *s* Lombardía

Lombardy poplar *s* álamo de Italia, chopo lombardo

lon. *abbr* **longitude**

London ['lʌndən] *adj* londinense ‖ *s* Londres *m*

Londoner ['lʌndənər] *s* londinense *mf*

lone [lon] *adj* solo, solitario; (*sole, single*) único

loneliness ['lonlɪnɪs] *s* soledad

lone•ly ['lonli] *adj* (*comp* **-lier;** *super* **-liest**) soledoso

lonesome ['lonsəm] *adj* soledoso; (*spot, atmosphere*) solitario

lone wolf *s* (fig) lobo solitario

long. *abbr* **longitude**

long [lɔŋ] o [laŋ] (*comp* **longer** ['lɔŋgər] o ['laŋgər];** *super* **longest** ['lɔŋgɪst] o ['laŋgɪst]) *adj* largo; de largo, p.ej., **two meters long** dos metros de largo ‖ *adv* mucho tiempo, largo tiempo; **as long as** mientras; (*provided*) con tal de que; (*inasmuch as*) puesto que; **before long** dentro de poco; **how long** cuánto tiempo; **long ago** hace mucho tiempo; **long before** mucho antes; **longer** más tiempo; **long since** desde hace mucho tiempo; **no longer** ya no; **so long!** (coll) ¡hasta luego!; **so long as** con tal de que ‖ *intr* anhelar, suspirar; **to long for** anhelar por, ansiar

long'boat' *s* (naut) lancha

long'-dis'tance call *s* (telp) llamada a larga distancia

long-distance flight *s* (aer) vuelo a distancia

long'-drawn'-out' *adj* prolongado, pesado

longeron ['landʒərən] *s* larguero

longevity [lan'dʒɛviti] *s* longevidad

long face *s* (coll) cara triste

long'hair' *adj & s* intelectual *mf;* aficionado a la música clásica

long'hand' *s* escritura a mano

longing ['lɔŋɪŋ] *adj* anhelante ‖ *s* anhelo, ansia

longitude ['landʒɪ,tjud] *s* longitud

long johns *spl* ropa interior que cubre brazos y piernas

long-lived ['lɔŋ'laɪvd] o (coll) ['lɔŋ'lɪvd] *adj* longevo, de larga vida

long-playing record ['lɔŋ'ple•ɪŋ] *s* disco de larga duración; elepé *m*

long primer ['prɪmər] *s* (typ) entredós *m*

long'-range' *adj* de largo alcance

longshore•man ['lɔŋ,ʃormən] *s* (*pl* **-men** [mən]) *s* estibador *m,* portuario

long'-stand'ing *adj* que existe desde hace mucho tiempo

long'-suf'fering *adj* longánimo, sufrido

long suit *s* (cards) palo fuerte; (fig) fuerte *m*

long'-term' *adj* a largo plazo

long'-wind'ed *adj* difuso, palabrero, discursisto

look [lʊk] *s* (*appearance*) aspecto, apariencia; (*glance*) mirada; (*search*) búsqueda; **looks** aspecto, apariencia; **to take a look at** echar una mirada a ‖ *tr* expresar con la mirada; representar (*la edad que uno tiene*); **to look daggers at** apuñalar con la mirada; **to look the part** vestir el cargo; **to look up**

(*e.g., in a dictionary*) buscar; ir a visitar, venir a ver ‖ *intr* mirar; buscar; parecer; **look out!** ¡cuidado!, ¡ojo!; **to look after** mirar por; ocuparse en; **to look at** mirar; **to look back** mirar hacia atrás; (fig) mirar el pasado; **to look down on** mirar por encima del hombro; **to look for** buscar; creer, p.ej., **I look for rain** creo que va á llover; **to look forward to** esperar con placer anticipado; **to look ill** tener mala cara; **to look in on** pasar por la casa o la oficina de; **to look into** averiguar, estudiar; **to look like** parecerse a; amenazar, p.ej., **it looks like rain** amenaza lluvia, parece que va a llover; **to look oneself** parecer el mismo; tener buena cara; **to look out** tener cuidado; mirar por (*p.ej., la ventana*); **to look out for** mirar por, cuidar de; guardarse de; **to look out on** dar a; **to look through** mirar por; hojear (*un libro*); **to look toward** dar a; **to look up to** admirar, mirar con respeto; **to look well** tener buena cara
lookalike ['lukə,laɪk] *adj & s* doble; parecido
looker-on [,lukər'an] *s* (*pl* **lookers-on**) mirón *m*, espectador *m*
looking glass ['lukɪŋ] *s* espejo
look'out' *s* vigilancia; (*tower*) atalaya; (*person keeping watch*) vigilante *mf*; (*man watching from lookout tower*) atalaya *m*; (*care, concern*) (coll) cuidado; **to be on the lookout for** estar a la mira de
loom
[lum] *s* telar *m* ‖ *intr* (*to appear indistinctly*) vislumbrarse; amenazar, parecer inevitable
loon [lun] *s* tonto, bobo; (orn) zambullidor *m*
loon·y ['luni] *adj* (*comp* -ier; *super* -iest) (slang) loco ‖ *s* (*pl* -ies) (slang) loco
loop [lup] *s* lazo; (*in a cable or rope*) vuelta; (*of a river*) meandro; (*of a road*) recoveco; (*for fastening a button*) presilla; (aer) rizo; (elec) circuito cerrado; (*part of vibrating body between two nodes*) vientre *m*; **to loop the loop** (aer) rizar el rizo ‖ *tr* hacer lazos en; enlazar ‖ *intr* formar lazo; (aer) hacer el rizo
loop'hole' *s* (*narrow opening in wall*) lucerna; (*means of evasion*) efugio, escapatoria
loose [lus] *adj* (*dress, tooth, screw, bowels*) flojo; (*fitting, thread, wire, rivet, tongue, bowels*) suelto; (*sleeve*) perdido; (*earth, soil*) desmenuzado; (*unpackaged*) a granel, sin envase; (*unbound papers*) sin encuadernar; (*pulley*) loco; (*translation*) libre; (*life, morals*) relajado; (*woman*) fácil, frágil; **to become loose** desatarse, aflojarse; **to break loose** ponerse en libertad; **to turn loose** soltar ‖ *s*—**to be on the loose** ser libre, estar sin trabas; estar de juerga ‖ *tr* soltar; desatar, desencadenar
loose end *s* cabo suelto; **at loose ends** desarreglado, indeciso
loose'-leaf' notebook *s* cuaderno de hojas cambiables, cuaderno de hojas sueltas
loosen ['lusən] *tr* desatar, aflojar, desapretar; aflojar, laxar (*el vientre*) ‖ *intr* desatarse, aflojarse, desapretarse

looseness ['lusnɪs] *s* flojedad, soltura; (*in morals*) relajamiento
loose'strife' *s* lisimaquia; salicaria
loose-tongued ['lus'tʌŋd] *adj* largo de lengua, ligero de lengua
loot [lut] *s* botín *m*, presa ‖ *tr* saquear, pillar
lop [lap] *v* (*pret & pp* **lopped;** *ger* **lopping**) *tr* dejar caer (*p.ej., los brazos*); **to lop off** cortar; podar (*un árbol, una vid*) ‖ *intr* colgar
lopsided ['lap'saɪdɪd] *adj* ladeado, sesgado; desproporcionado, asimétrico, patituerto
loquacious [lo'kweʃəs] *adj* locuaz
loran ['lɔræn] *s* (naut) lorán *m*
lord [lɔrd] *s* señor *m*; (Brit) lord *m*; (hum & poet) marido ‖ *tr*—**to lord it over** dominar despóticamente, imponerse a
lord·ly ['lɔrdli] *adj* (*comp* -lier; *super* -liest) señoril; magnífico; despótico, imperioso; altivo, arrogante
Lord's Day, the el domingo
lordship ['lɔrdʃɪp] *s* señoría, excelencia
Lord's Prayer *s* oración dominical, padrenuestro
Lord's Supper *s* sagrada comunión; Cena del Señor
lore [lor] *s* ciencia, saber *m*; ciencia popular, saber *m* popular
lorgnette [lɔrn'jɛt] *s* (*eyeglasses*) impertinentes *mpl*; (*opera glasses*) gemelos de teatro con manija
lor·ry ['lɑri] o ['lɔri] *s* (*pl* -ries) carro de plataforma; (Brit) autocamión *m*; (Brit) vagoneta
lose [luz] *v* (*pret & pp* **lost** [lɔst] o [last]) *tr* perder; no lograr salvar (*el médico al enfermo*); **to lose heart** desalentarse; **to lose oneself** perderse, errar el camino; ensimismarse ‖ *intr* perder; quedar vencido; retrasarse (*el reloj*)
loser ['luzər] *s* perdedor *m*
losing ['luzɪŋ] *adj* perdedor ‖ **losings** *spl* pérdidas, dinero perdido
loss [lɔs] o [las] *s* pérdida; **to be at a loss** estar perplejo, no saber qué hacer; **to be at a loss** o + *inf* no saber como + *inf*; **to sell at a loss** vender con pérdida
loss leader *s* artículo vendido a gran descuento
loss of face *s* pérdida de prestigio, desprestigio
lost [lɔst] o [last] *adj* perdido; (fig) desviado; **lost in thought** ensimismado, abismado; **lost** o **perdido para;** insensible a
lost'-and-found' department *s* oficina de objetos perdidos
lost sheep *s* oveja perdida
lot [lat] *s* (*for building*) solar *m*, parcela; (*fate, destiny*) suerte *f*; (*portion, parcel*) lote *m*; (*of people*) grupo; (coll) gran cantidad, gran número; (coll) sujeto, tipo; **a lot (of)** o **lots of** (coll) mucho, muchos; **to cast** o **to throw in one's lot with** compartir la suerte de; **to draw** o **to cast lots** echar suertes
lotion ['loʃən] *s* loción
lotter·y ['latəri] *s* (*pl* -ies) lotería

lo
lo

lotto ['lɑto] s lotería
lotus ['lotəs] s loto
loud [laud] adj alto; (*noisy*) ruidoso; (*voice*) fuerte; (*garish*) chillón, llamativo; (*conspicuously vulgar*) charro, cursi; (*foul-smelling*) apestoso, maloliente ‖ adv alto, en voz alta; ruidosamente
loud'mouth' s bocaza, bocona, bocón m
loudmouthed ['laud,mauθt] o ['laud-,mauðd] adj vocinglero
loud'speak'er s altavoz m, parlante m, pantalla acústica
lounge [laundʒ] s diván m, sofá m cama; salón m de descanso, salón social ‖ intr repantigarse a su sabor, recostarse cómodamente; **to lounge around** estar arrimado a la pared, pasearse perezosamente
lounge lizard s (slang) holgón m
louse [laus] s (pl **lice** [lais]) piojo
lous•y ['lauzi] adj (comp **-ier;** super **-iest**) piojoso; (*mean*) vil, ruin; (*filthy*) asqueroso, sucio; (*bungling*) chapucero; **lousy with** (slang) colmado de (*p.ej., dinero*)
lout [laut] s patán m
louver ['luvər] s (*opening to let in air and light*) lumbrera, tablilla de persiana; (aut) persiana del radiador
lovable ['lʌvəbəl] adj amable
love [lʌv] s amor m; (*tennis*) cero, nada; **not for love nor money** ni a tiros; **to be in love (with)** estar enamorado (de); **to fall in love (with)** enamorarse (de); **to make love to** cortejar, galantear ‖ tr amar, querer; gustar de, tener afición a
love affair s amores mpl, amorío
love'bird' s inseparable m; **lovebirds** recién casados muy enamorados
love child s hijo del amor
love feast s ágape m
love'-hate' s odio-amor m
loveless ['lʌvlɪs] adj abandonado, sin amor; (*feeling no love*) desamado
lovelorn ['lʌv,lɔrn] adj abandonado por su amor, herido de amor
love•ly ['lʌvli] adj (comp **-lier;** super **-liest**) bello, hermoso; adorable, precioso; (coll) encantador, gracioso
love match s matrimonio de amor
love potion s filtro, filtro de amor
lover ['lʌvər] s amante mf; (*e.g., of hunting, sports*) aficionado; (*e.g., of work*) amigo
love seat s confidente m
love'sick' adj enfermo de amor
love'sick'ness s mal m de amor
love song s canción de amor
loving ['lʌvɪŋ] adj amoroso, afectuoso
lov'ing-kind'ness s bondad infinita, misericordia
low [lo] adj bajo; (*diet; visibility; opinion*) malo; (*dress, waist*) escotado; (*depressed*) abatido; gravemente enfermo; (*fire*) lento; **to lay low** dejar tendido, derribar; matar; **to lie low** no dejarse ver ‖ adv bajo ‖ s punto bajo; precio más bajo, precio mínimo; (*moo of cow*) mugido; (aut) primera marcha, primera velocidad; (meteor) depresión ‖ intr mugir (*la vaca*)

low'born' adj de humilde cuna
low'boy' s cómoda baja con patas cortas
low'brow' adj & s (slang) ignorante mf
low'-cost' housing s casas baratas
Low Countries, the los Países Bajos
low'-down' adj (coll) bajo, vil, ruin ‖ **low'-down'** s (slang) informes mf confidenciales, hechos verdaderos
lower ['lo•ər] adj bajo, inferior ‖ tr & intr bajar ‖ ['lau•ər] intr poner mala cara, fruncir el entrecejo; encapotarse (*el cielo*)
lower berth ['lo•ər] s litera baja, cama baja
Lower California ['lo•ər] s la Baja California
lower case ['lo•ər] s (typ) caja baja
lower middle class ['lo•ər] s pequeña burguesía
lowermost ['lo•ər,most] adj (el) más bajo
low'-fre'quency adj de baja frecuencia
low gear s primera marcha, primera velocidad
low'-key' adj modesto; moderado
lowland ['lolənd] s tierra baja ‖ **Lowlands** spl Tierra Baja (*de Escocia*)
low life s gentuza
low•ly ['loli] adj (comp **-lier;** super **-liest**) humilde; (*in growth or position*) bajo
Low Mass s misa rezada
low-minded ['lo'maindid] adj vil, ruin
low neck s escote m, escotado
low-necked ['lo'nɛkt] adj escotado
low-pitched ['lo'pitʃt] adj (*sound*) grave; (*roof*) de poco declive
low'-pres'sure adj de baja presión
low-priced ['lo'praist] adj barato, de precio bajo
low shoe s zapato inglés
low'-speed' adj de baja velocidad
low-spirited ['lo'spiritid] adj abatido
low spirits spl abatimiento
low tide s bajamar f, marea baja; (fig) punto más bajo
low visibility s (aer) poca visibilidad
low water s (*of a river*) nivel mínimo; (*because of drought*) estiaje m; bajamar f, marea baja
loyal ['lɔɪəl] adj leal
loyalist ['lɔɪ•əlɪst] s leal m
loyal•ty ['lɔɪ•əlti] s (pl **-ties**) lealtad
lozenge ['lɑzɪndʒ] s losange m; (*candy cough drop*) pastilla, tableta
LP ['ɛl'pi] s (letterword) (trademark) disco de larga duración; elepé m
Ltd. abbr **limited**
lubricant ['lubrɪkənt] adj & s lubricante m
lubricate ['lubrɪ,ket] tr lubricar
lubricous ['lubrɪkəs] adj (*slippery; lewd*) lúbrico (*resbaladizo; lascivo*); incierto, inconstante
lucerne [lu'sʌrn] s mielga
lucid ['lusɪd] adj claro, inteligible; (*rational, sane*) lúcido; (*bright, shining*) luciente; (*clear, transparent*) cristalino
Lucifer ['lusɪfər] s Lucifer m
luck [lʌk] s (*good or bad*) suerte f; (*good*) suerte, buena suerte; **down on one's luck** de mala suerte, de malas; **in luck** de buena

suerte, de buenas; **out of luck** de mala suerte, de malas; **to bring luck** traer buena suerte; **to try one's luck** probar fortuna; **worse luck** desgraciadamente

luckily ['lʌkɪli] *adj* afortunadamente
luckless ['lʌklɪs] *adj* desgraciado
luck·y ['lʌki] *adj* (*comp* **-ier**; *super* **-iest**) afortunado; derecho (CAm); (*supposed to bring luck*) de buen agüero; **to be lucky** tener suerte; quedar bien parado
lucky hit *s* (coll) golpe *m* de fortuna
lucrative ['lukrətɪv] *adj* lucrativo
ludicrous ['ludɪkrəs] *adj* absurdo, ridículo
lug [lʌg] *s* orejeta; (*pull, tug*) estirón *m*, esfuerzo ǁ *v* (*pret & pp* **lugged;** *ger* **lugging**) *tr* tirar con fuerza de; (*to bring up irrelevantly*) (coll) traer a colación
luggage ['lʌgɪdʒ] *s* equipaje *m*
lugubrious [lu'gubrɪ·əs] o [lu'gjubrɪ·əs] *adj* lúgubre
lukewarm ['luk,wɔrm] *adj* tibio, templado
lull [lʌl] *s* momento de calma, momento de silencio; (naut) recalmón *m* ǁ *tr* adormecer; calmar, aquietar; apaciguar
lulla·by ['lʌlə,baɪ] *s* (*pl* **-bies**) arrullo, canción de cuna
lumbago [lʌm'bego] *s* lumbago
lumber ['lʌmbər] *s* madera aserrada, madera aserradiza, madera de sierra; trastos viejos ǁ *intr* andar pesadamente
lum'ber·jack' *s* leñador *m*, hachero
lumber·man ['lʌmbərmən] *s* (*pl* **-men** [mən]) (*dealer*) maderero; (*man who cuts down lumber*) leñador *m*, hachero
lumber room *s* leonera, trastera
lum'ber·yard' *s* maderería, depósito de maderas
luminar·y ['lumɪ,nɛri] *s* (*pl* **-ies**) luminar *m*, lumbrera
luminescent [,lumɪ'nɛsənt] *adj* luminiscente
luminous ['lumɪnəs] *adj* luminoso
lummox ['lʌməks] *s* (coll) jergón *m*
lump [lʌmp] *s* terrón *m;* (*swelling*) chichón *m*, bulto, hinchazón *m;* (*stupid person*) (coll) bodoque *m;* **in the lump** en grueso, por junto; **to get a lump in one's throat** hacérsele a (*uno*) un nudo en la garganta ǁ *tr* juntar, mezclar; (*to make into lumps*) aterronar; (coll) aguantar, tragar (cosa repulsiva)
lumpish ['lʌmpɪʃ] *adj* hobachón, torpe, pesado
lump sum *s* suma global, suma total
lump·y ['lʌmpi] *adj* (*comp* **-ier**; *super* **-iest**) aterronado, borujoso; torpe, pesado; (*sea*) agitado
luna·cy ['lunəsi] *s* (*pl* **-cies**) demencia, locura
lunar ['lunər] *adj* lunar
lunar lander o **lunar module** *s* módulo lunar
lunar landing *s* alunizaje *m*
lunatic ['lunətɪk] *adj* & *s* lunático, loco
lunatic asylum *s* manicomio
lunatic fringe *s* minoría fanática
lunch [lʌnʃ] *s* (*regular midday meal*) almuerzo; (*light meal*) colación, merienda ǁ *intr* almorzar; merendar, tomar una colación

lunch basket *s* fiambrera
lunch cloth *s* mantelito
luncheon ['lʌnʃən] *s* almuerzo; almuerzo de ceremonia
lunch'room' *s* cantina, merendero
lung [lʌŋ] *s* pulmón *m*
lung cancer *s* cáncer *m* pulmonar
lunge [lʌndʒ] *s* arremetida, embestida; (*with a sword*) estocada ǁ *intr* arremeter, lanzarse; **to lunge at** arremeter contra
lurch [lʌrtʃ] *s* sacudida, tumbo; (naut) bandazo; **to leave in the lurch** dejar en la estacada, dejar colgado ǁ *intr* dar una sacudida, dar un tumbo; (naut) dar un bandazo
lure [lur] *s* (*decoy*) cebo, señuelo; (fig) aliciente *m*, señuelo ǁ *tr* atraer con cebo, atraer con señuelo; (fig) atraer, tentar, seducir; **to lure away** llevarse con señuelo; (*from one's obligations*) desviar
lurid ['lurɪd] *adj* sensacional; (*gruesome*) espeluznante; (*fiery*) ardiente, encendido
lurk [lʌrk] *intr* acechar, andar furtivamente
luscious ['lʌʃəs] *adj* delicioso; lujoso; voluptuoso
lush [lʌʃ] *adj* jugoso, lozano; lujuriante; lujoso
Lusitanian [,lusɪ'tenɪ·ən] *adj* & *s* lusitano
lust [lʌst] *s* deseo vehemente; (*greed*) codicia; (*strong sexual appetite*) lujuria; entusiasmo ǁ *intr* lujuriar; **to lust after** o **for** codiciar; desear con lujuria
luster ['lʌstər] *s* (*gloss*) lustre *m;* (*of certain fabrics*) viso; (*fame, glory*) (fig) lustre
lus'ter·ware' *s* loza con visos metálicos
lustful ['lʌstfəl] *adj* lujurioso
lustrous ['lʌstrəs] *adj* lustroso
lust·y ['lʌsti] *adj* (*comp* **-ier**; *super* **-iest**) fuerte, robusto, lozano
lute [lut] *s* (mus) laúd *m;* (*substance used to close or seal a joint*) (chem) lodo
Lutheran ['luθərən] *adj* & *s* luterano
luxuriance [lʌg'ʒurɪ·əns] *s* lozanía
luxuriant [lʌg'ʒurɪ·ənt] *adj* lozano, lujuriante; (*overornamented*) recargado
luxuriate [lʌg'ʒurɪ,et] o [lʌk'ʃurɪ,et] *intr* crecer con lozanía; entregarse al lujo; (*to find keen pleasure*) lozanearse
luxurious [lʌg'ʒurɪ·əs] o [lʌk'ʃurɪ·əs] *adj* lujoso
luxu·ry ['lʌkʃəri] o ['lʌgʒəri] *s* (*pl* **-ries**) lujo
lye [laɪ] *s* lejía
lying ['laɪ·ɪŋ] *adj* mentiroso ǁ *s* el mentir
ly'ing-in' hospital *s* casa de maternidad, clínica de parturientas
lymph [lɪmf] *s* linfa
lymphatic [lɪm'fætɪk] *adj* linfático
lynch [lɪntʃ] *tr* linchar
lynching ['lɪntʃɪŋ] *s* linchamiento
lynch law *s* justicia de la soga
lynx [lɪŋks] *s* lince *m*
lynx-eyed ['lɪŋks,aɪd] *adj* de ojos linces
lyonnaise [,laɪ·ə'nez] *adj* (culin) a la lionesa
lyre [laɪr] *s* (mus) lira
lyric ['lɪrɪk] *adj* lírico ǁ *s* poema lírico; (*words of a song*) (coll) letra
lyrical ['lɪrɪkəl] *adj* lírico
lyricism ['lɪrɪ,sɪzəm] *s* lirismo
lyricist ['lɪrɪsɪst] *s* (*writer of words for songs*) letrista *mf;* (*poet*) poeta lírico

lo
ly

M

M, m [ɛm] decimotercera letra del alfabeto inglés

m. *abbr* **married, masculine, meter, midnight, mile, minute, month**

ma'am [mæm] o [mɑm] *s* (coll) señora

macadam [mə'kædəm] *s* macadán *m*

macadamize [mə'kædə,maɪz] *tr* macadamizar

macaro•ni [,mækə'roni] *s* (*pl* **-nis** o **-nies**) macarrones *mpl*

macaroon [,mækə'run] *s* mostachón *m*, almendrado

macaw [mə'kɔ] *s* aracanga, guacamayo

mace [mes] *s* maza; (*spice*) macis *m*

mace'bear'er *s* macero

machination [,mækɪ'neʃən] *s* maquinación

machine [mə'ʃin] *s* máquina; automóvil *m*, coche *m*; (*of a political party*) camarilla ‖ *tr* trabajar a máquina

machine gun *s* ametralladora

ma•chine'-gun' *tr* ametrallar

ma•chine'-made' *adj* hecho a máquina

machiner•y [mə'ʃinəri] *s* (*pl* **-ies**) maquinaria

machine screw *s* tornillo para metales

machine shop *s* taller mecánico

machine stenography *s* estenotipia

machine tool *s* máquina-herramienta

machine translation *s* traducción automática

machinist [mə'ʃinɪst] *s* (*person who makes machines*) maquinista *mf*; (*person who operates machines*) mecánico; (naut) segundo maquinista; (theat) maquinista *mf*, tramoyista *mf*

mackerel ['mækərəl] *s* caballa, escombro

mackerel sky *s* cielo aborregado

mackintosh ['mækɪn,tɑʃ] *s* impermeable *m*

mad [mæd] *adj* (*comp* **madder**; *super* **maddest**) (*angry*) enojado, furioso; (*crazy*) loco; (*foolish*) tonto, necio; (*rabid*) rabioso; **to be mad about** (coll) estar loco por; **to drive mad** volver loco; **to go mad** volverse loco; rabiar (*un perro*)

madam ['mædəm] *s* señora

mad'cap' *s* alocado, tarambana *mf*

madden ['mædən] *tr* (to make angry) enojar, enfurecer; (*to make insane*) enloquecer

made-to-order ['medtə'ɔrdər] *adj* hecho de encargo; (*clothing*) hecho a la medida

made'-up' *adj* inventado, ficticio; (*artificial*) postizo; (*face*) pintado

mad'house' *s* casa de locos, manicomio

madman ['mæd,mæn] *s* (*pl* **-men** [,mɛn]) loco

madness ['mædnɪs] *s* furia, rabia; locura; (*of a dog*) rabia

Madonna lily [mə'dɑnə] *s* azucena

maelstrom ['melstrəm] *s* remolino

mag. *abbr* **magazine**

magazine ['mægə,zin] o [,mægə'zin] *s* (*periodical*) revista, magazine *m*; (*warehouse*) almacén *m*; (*for cartridges*) cámara; (*for powder*) polvorín *m*; (naut) santabárbara; (phot) almacén *m*

Magellan [mə'dʒɛlən] *s* Magallanes *m*

maggot ['mægət] *s* cresa

Magi ['medʒaɪ] *spl* magos de Oriente, Reyes Magos

magic ['mædʒɪk] *adj* mágico ‖ *s* magia; ilusionismo, prestidigitación; **as if by magic** como por encanto

magician [mə'dʒɪʃən] *s* (*entertainer with sleight of hand*) ilusionista *mf*, prestidigitador *m*; (*sorcerer*) mágico

magistrate ['mædʒɪs,tret] *s* magistrado

magnanimous [mæg'nænɪməs] *adj* magnánimo

magnesium [mæg'niʃɪ•əm] o [mæg'niʒɪ•əm] *s* magnesio

magnet ['mægnɪt] *s* imán *m*

magnetic [mæg'nɛtɪk] *adj* magnético; (fig) atrayente, cautivador

magnetic curves *spl* fantasma magnético

magnetic field *s* campo magnético

magnetism ['mægnɪ,tɪzəm] *s* magnetismo

magnetize ['mægnɪ,taɪz] *tr* magnetizar, imanar

magne•to [mæg'nito] *s* (*pl* **-tos**) magneto *m* & *f*

magnificent [mæg'nɪfɪsənt] *adj* magnífico

magni•fy ['mægnɪ,faɪ] *v* (*pret* & *pp* **-fied**) *tr* magnificar; exagerar

magnifying glass *s* lupa, vidrio de aumento

magnitude ['mægnɪ,tjud] *s* magnitud

magpie ['mæg,paɪ] *s* picaza, urraca

Magyar ['mægjɑr] *adj* & *s* magiar *mf*

mahlstick ['mɑl,stɪk] o ['mɔl,stɪk] *s* tiento

mahoga•ny [me'hɑgəni] *s* (*pl* **-nies**) caoba

Mahomet [mə'hɑmɪt] *s* Mahoma *m*

mahout [mə'haʊt] *s* naire *m*, cornaca *m*

maid [med] *s* (*female servant*) criada, moza; (*young girl; housemaid*) doncella; gata (Mex); (*spinster*) soltera

maiden ['medən] *s* doncella

maid'en•hair' *s* (bot) cabello de Venus

maid'en•head' *s* himen *m*

maidenhood ['medən,hʊd] *s* doncellez *f*

maiden lady *s* soltera

maiden name *s* apellido de soltera

maiden voyage *s* primera travesía

maid'-in-wait'ing *s* (*pl* **maids-in-waiting**) dama

maid of honor *s* (*at a wedding*) primera madrina de boda; (*attendant on a princess*) doncella de honor; (*attendant on a queen*) dama de honor

maid'serv'ant *s* criada, doméstica

mail [mel] *s* correspondencia, correo; (*of armor*) malla; **by return mail** a vuelta de correo ‖ *tr* echar al correo

mail'bag' *s* valija

mail'boat' *s* vapor *m* correo

mail'box' *s* buzón *m*

mail car *s* carro correo, coche-correo, ambulancia de correos

mail carrier *s* cartero

mailing list *s* lista de envío

mailing permit *s* porte concertado

mail•man ['mel,mæn] *s* (*pl* **-men** [,mɛn]) cartero

mail order *s* pedido postal

mail'-or'der house *s* casa de ventas por correo

mail'plane' *s* avión-correo

mail train *s* tren *m* correo

maim [mem] *tr* estropear, mutilar

main [men] *adj* principal, primero, maestro, mayor ‖ *s* cañería maestra; **in the main** mayormente

main clause *s* proposición dominante

main course *s* plato principal, plato fuerte

main deck *s* cubierta principal

mainland [`men,lænd] o [`menlənd] *s* continente *m*, tierra firme

main line *s* (rr) tronco, línea principal

mainly [`menli] *adv* principalmente, en su mayor parte

mainmast [`menməst], o [`men,mæst] o [`men,mɑst] *s* palo mayor

mainsail [`mensəl] o [`men,sel] *s* vela mayor

main'spring' *s* (*of watch*) muelle *m* real; (fig) móvil *m*, origen *m*

main'stay' *s* (naut) estay *m* mayor; (fig) soporte *m* principal

main'stream' *s* vía principal

main street *s* calle *f* mayor

maintain [men`ten] *tr* mantener; (*to support*) (law) manutener

maintenance [`mentɪnəns] *s* mantenimiento; (*upkeep*) conservación; gastos de conservación

maître d'hôtel [,metər do`tɛl] *s* (*butler*) mayordomo; (*headwaiter*) jefe *m* de comedor

maize [mez] *s* maíz *m*

majestic [mə`dʒɛstɪk] *adj* majestuoso

majes•ty [`mædʒɪsti] *s* (*pl* -**ties**) majestad

major [`medʒər] *adj* (*greater*) mayor; (*elder*) mayor de edad; (mus) mayor ‖ *s* (educ) especialización; (mil) comandante *m* ‖ *intr* (educ) especializarse

Majorca [mə`dʒɔrkə] *s* Mallorca

Majorcan [mə`dʒɔrkən] *adj & s* mallorquín *m*

major•do•mo [,medʒər`domo] *s* (*pl* -**mos**) mayordomo

major general *s* general *m* de división

majori•ty [mə`dʒɔrɪti] *adj* mayoritario ‖ *s* (*pl* -**ties**) (*being of full age; larger number or part*) mayoría; (*full age*) mayoridad; (mil) comandancia

make [mek] *s* (*brand*) marca; (*form, build*) hechura; carácter *m*, natural *m*; **on the make** (slang) buscando provecho ‖ *v* (*pret & pp* **made** [med]) *tr* hacer; cometer (*un error*); efectuar (*un pago*); ganar (*dinero; una baza*); coger (*un tren*); dar (*dinero una empresa*); pronunciar (*un discurso*); cerrar (*un circuito*); poner (*a uno, p.ej., nervioso*); ser, p.ej., **she will make a good wife** será una buena esposa; **to make** + *inf* hacer + *inf*, p.ej., **she made him study** le hizo estudiar; **to make into** convertir en; **to make known** declarar; dar a conocer; **to make of** pensar de; **to make oneself known** darse a conocer; **to make out** distinguir, vislumbrar; descifrar; escribir (*una receta*); llenar (*un cheque*); **to make over** convertir; rehacer (*un traje*); (com) transfe-

rir; **to make up** preparar, confeccionar; inventar (*un cuento*); recobrar (*el tiempo perdido*); (theat) maquillar ‖ *intr* estar (*p.ej., seguro*); **to make away with** llevarse; deshacerse de; matar; **to make believe** fingir, p.ej., **he made believe he knew me** fingió conocerme; **to make for** ir hacia; embestir contra; contribuir a (*p.ej., mejores relaciones*); **to make much of** (coll) hacer fiestas a, mostrar cariño a; **to make off** largarse; **to make off with** llevarse, hacerse con; **to make out** arreglárselas; **to make toward** encaminarse a; **to make up** maquillarse, pintarse; componerse, hacer las paces; **to make up for** suplir; compensar por (*una pérdida*); **to make up to** (coll) tratar de congraciarse con

make'-be•lieve' *adj* simulado ‖ *s* pretexto, simulación, fantasía

maker [`mekər] *s* constructor *m*, fabricante *mf*

make'shift' *adj* de fortuna, provisional ‖ *s* expediente *m;* (*person*) tapagujeros *m*

make'-up' *s* composición, constitución; afeite *m*, maquillaje *m;* (typ) imposición

make-up man *s* (theat) maquillador *m*

make'weight' *s* contrapeso; suplente *mf*

making [`mekɪŋ] *s* fabricación; material necesario; causa del éxito; **makings** elementos, materiales *mpl;* (*personal qualities necessary for some purpose*) madera

malachite [`mælə,kaɪt] *s* malaquita

maladjustment [,mælə`dʒʌstmənt] *s* desadaptación

mala•dy [`mælədi] *s* (*pl* -**dies**) dolencia, enfermedad

malaise [mæ`lez] *s* indisposición, malestar *m*

malapropism [,mælæ`prɑp,ɪzəm] *s* despropósito

malapropos [,mælæprə`po] *adj* impropio ‖ *adv* fuera de propósito

malaria [mə`lɛrɪ•ə] *s* malaria, paludismo

Malay [`mele] o [mə`le] *adj & s* malayo

malcontent [`mælkən,tɛnt] *adj & s* malcontento

male [mel] *adj* (*sex*) masculino; (*animal, plant, piece of a device*) macho; (*human being*) varón, p.ej., **male child** hijo varón ‖ *s* macho; varón *m*

male chauvinism *s* machismo

male chauvinist *s* machista *m*

malediction [,mælɪ`dɪkʃən] *s* maldición

malefactor [`mælɪ,fæktər] *s* malhechor *m*

male nurse *s* enfermero

malevolent [mə`lɛvələnt] *adj* malévolo

malfunction [,mæl`fʌŋkʃən] *s* malfuncionamiento *s intr* ir de través; estropearse

malice [`mælɪs] *s* malicia, malevolencia; **to bear malice** guardar rencor; **with malice prepense** [prɪ`pɛns] (law) con malicia y premeditación

malicious [mə`lɪʃəs] *adj* malicioso, malévolo

malign [mə`laɪn] *adj* maligno ‖ *tr* calumniar

malignant [mə`lɪgnənt] *adj* maligno

maligni•ty [mə`lɪgnɪti] *s* (*pl* -**ties**) malignidad

m
ma

malinger [mə'lɪŋgər] *intr* hacer la zanguanga, fingirse enfermo

mall [mɔl] o [mæl] *s* alameda, paseo de árboles

mallet [ˈmælɪt] *s (wooden hammer)* mazo; *(for croquet and polo)* mallete *m*

mallow [ˈmælo] *s* malva

malnutrition [ˌmælnjuˈtrɪʃən] *s* desnutrición

malodorous [mælˈodərəs] *adj* maloliente

malt [mɔlt] *s* malta *m;* (coll) cerveza

maltreat [mælˈtrit] *tr* maltratar

mamma [ˈmɑmə] o [məˈmɑ] *s* mama o mamá *f*

mammal [ˈmæməl] *s* mamífero

mammalian [mæˈmelɪ•ən] *adj & s* mamífero

mammoth [ˈmæməθ] *adj* gigantesco, enorme ‖ *s* mamut *m*

man [mæn] *s (pl* **-men** [mɛən]) *s* hombre *m;* (*in chess*) pieza; (*in checkers*) pieza, peón *m;* **a man** uno, p.ej., **a man can't get work in this town** uno no puede obtener empleo en este pueblo; **as one man** unánimamente; **man alive!** ¡hombre!; **man and wife** marido y mujer; **to be one's own man** no depender de nadie ‖ *v (pret & pp* **manned;** *ger* **manning)** *tr* dotar, tripular (*un buque*); guarnecer (*una fortaleza*); servir (*los cañones*)

man about town *s* bulevardero, hombre *m* de mucho mundo

manacle [ˈmænəkəl] *s* manilla; **manacles** esposas ‖ *tr* poner esposas a

manage [ˈmænɪdʒ] *tr* manejar ‖ *intr* arreglárselas; **to manage to** ingeniarse a o para; **to manage to get along** ingeniarse para ir viviendo

manageable [ˈmænɪdʒəbəl] *adj* manejable

management [ˈmænɪdʒmənt] *s* manejo, dirección, gerencia; (*group who manage a business*) la empresa, la parte patronal, los patronos

manager [ˈmænədʒər] *s* director *m*, administrador *m*, gerente *mf;* empresario; (sport) manager *m*

managerial [ˌmænəˈdʒɪrɪ•əl] *adj* empresarial

mandate [ˈmændet] *s* mandato ‖ *tr* asignar por mandato

mandolin [ˈmændəlɪn] *s* mandolina

mandrake [ˈmændrek] *s* mandrágora

mane [men] *s (of horse)* crines *fpl;* (*of lion, of person*) melena

maneuver [məˈnuvər] *s* maniobra ‖ *tr* hacer maniobrar ‖ *intr* maniobrar

manful [ˈmænfəl] *adj* varonil, resuelto

manganese [ˈmæŋgə,nis] o [ˈmæŋgə,niz] *s* manganeso

mange [mendʒ] *s* sarna

manger [ˈmendʒər] *s* pesebre *m*

mangle [ˈmæŋgəl] *tr* lacerar, aplastar

man•gy [ˈmendʒi] *adj (comp* **-gier;** *super* **-giest)** sarnoso; (*dirty, squalid*) roñoso

man'han'dle *tr* maltratar

man'hole' *s* caja de registro, pozo de inspección

manhood [ˈmænhʊd] *s* virilidad; hombres *mpl*

man hunt *s* caza al hombre

mania [ˈmenɪ•ə] *s* manía

maniac [ˈmenɪ,æk] *adj & s* maníaco

manic-depressive [ˈmænɪkdɪˈprɛsɪv] *adj & s* maníaco-depresivo

manicure [ˈmænɪ,kjʊr] *s (care of hands)* manicura; (*person*) manicuro, manicura ‖ *tr* hacer la manicura a (*una persona*); hacer (*las manos y las uñas*)

manicurist [ˈmænɪ,kjʊrɪst] *s* manicuro, manicura

manifest [ˈmænɪ,fɛst] *adj* manifiesto ‖ *s* (naut) manifiesto ‖ *tr* manifestar

manifes•to [ˌmænɪˈfɛsto] *s (pl* **-toes)** manifiesto

manifold [ˈmænɪ,fold] *adj* múltiple, vario; polivalente ‖ *s* copia, ejemplar *m;* (*pipe with outlets or inlets*) colector *m*, múltiple *m*

manikin [ˈmænɪkɪn] *s* maniquí *m;* (*dwarf*) enano

man in the moon *s* cara o cuerpo de hombre imaginarios en la luna llena

manioc [ˈmænɪak] *s* cazabe *m*, casabe *m*

manipulate [məˈnɪpjə,let] *tr* manipular

man'kind' *s* el género humano ‖ **man'kind'** *s* el sexo masculino, los hombres

manliness [ˈmænlɪnɪs] *s* masculinidad, virilidad

man•ly [ˈmænli] *adj (comp* **-lier;** *super* **-liest)** masculino, varonil

manned spaceship [mænd] *s* astronave tripulada

mannequin [ˈmænɪkɪn] *s* maniquí *m;* (*young woman employed to exhibit clothing*) maniquí *f*

manner [ˈmænər] *s* manera; **bad manners** malcriadez *f*, malacrianza; **by all manner of means** de todos modos; **in a manner of speaking** como si dijéramos; **in the manner of** a la manera de; **manners** modales *mpl*, crianza; **to the manner born** avezado desde la cuna

mannish [ˈmænɪʃ] *adj* hombruno

man of letters *s* hombre *m* de letras

man of means *s* hombre *m* de dinero

man of parts *s* hombre *m* de buenas prendas

man of straw *s* hombre *m* de suposición

man of the world *s* hombre *m* de mundo

man-of-war [ˌmænəvˈwɔr] *s (pl* **men-of-war** [ˌmɛnəvˈwɔr]) *s* buque *m* de guerra

manor [ˈmænər] *s* señorío

manor house *s* casa solariega

man overboard *interj* ¡hombre al agua!

man'pow'er *s* número de hombres; personal *m* competente; (mil) fuerzas nacionales

mansard [ˈmænsard] *s* mansarda; piso de mansarda

man'serv'ant *s (pl* **men'serv'ants)** criado

mansion [ˈmænʃən] *s* hotel *m*, palacio; (*manor house*) casa solariega

man'slaugh'ter *s* (law) homicidio sin premeditación

mantel [ˈmæntəl] *s* manto (*de chimenea*); (*shelf above it*) mesilla, repisa de chimenea

man'tel•piece' *s* mesilla, repisa de chimenea

mantle [ˈmæntəl] s capa, manto ‖ tr vestir con manto; cubrir, tapar; ocultar ‖ intr encenderse (el rostro)

manual [ˈmænjʊ•əl] adj manual ‖ s (book) manual m; (mil) ejercicio; (mus) teclado manual

manual training s enseñanza de los artes y oficios

manufacture [ˌmænjəˈfæktjər] s fabricación; obraje m; (thing manufactured) manufactura ‖ tr fabricar, manufacturar

manufacturer [ˌmænjəˈfæktjərər] s fabricante mf

manure [məˈnjʊr] o [məˈnʊr] s estiércol m ‖ tr estercolar

manuscript [ˈmænjəˌskrɪpt] adj & s manuscrito

many [ˈmɛni] adj & pron muchos; **a good many** o **a great many** un buen número; **as many as** tantos como; hasta, p.ej., **as many as twenty** hasta veinte; **how many** cuántos; **many a** muchos, p.ej., **many a person** muchas personas; **many another** muchos otros; **many more** muchos más; **so many** tantos; **too many** demasiados; **twice as many as** dos veces más que

many-sided [ˈmɛniˌsaɪdɪd] adj multilátero; (having many interests or capabilities) polifacético

map [mæp] s mapa m; (of a city) plano ‖ v (pret & pp **mapped**; ger **mapping**) tr trazar el mapa de; indicar en el mapa; **to map out** trazar el plan de

maple [ˈmepəl] s arce m

maquette [maˈkɛt] s maqueta

Mar. abbr **March**

mar [mɑr] v (pret & pp **marred**; ger **marring**) tr desfigurar, estropear; frustrar

maraud [məˈrɔd] tr saquear ‖ intr merodear

marauder [məˈrɔdər] s merodeador m

marble [ˈmɑrbəl] adj marmóreo ‖ s mármol m; (little ball of glass, etc.) canica; **marbles** (game) canica ‖ tr crispir, jaspear

march [mɑrtʃ] s marcha; (frontier, territory) marca; **to steal a march on someone** ganarle a uno por la mano ‖ tr hacer marchar ‖ intr marchar ‖ **March** s marzo

marchioness [ˈmɑrʃənɪs] s marquesa

mare [mɛr] s (female horse) yegua; (female donkey) asna

margarine [ˈmɑrdʒərɪn] s margarina

margin [ˈmɑrdʒɪn] s margen m & f; (collateral deposited with a broker) doble m

marginal [ˈmɑrdʒɪnəl] adj marginal

margin release s tecla de escape

margin stop s fijamárgenes m, cierrarrenglón m, cortarrenglón m

marigold [ˈmærɪˌgold] s clavelón m; (Calendula) maravilla, flamenquilla

marihuana o **marijuana** [ˌmɑrɪˈhwɑnə] s mariguana; grifa, grifo (Mex)

marina [məˈrinə] s dársena

marinate [ˈmærɪˌnet] tr escabechar, marinar

marine [məˈrin] adj marino, marítimo ‖ s marina; soldado de infantería de marina; **marines** infantería de marina; **tell that to the marines** (coll) cuénteselo a su abuela, a otro perro con ese hueso

mariner [ˈmærɪnər] s marino

marionette [ˌmærɪ•əˈnɛt] s marioneta, títere m

marital status [ˈmærɪtəl] s estado civil

maritime [ˈmærɪˌtaɪm] adj marítimo

marjoram [ˈmɑrdʒərəm] s orégano; mejorana

mark [mɑrk] s marca, señal f; (label) marbete m; (of punctuation) punto; (in an examination) calificación, nota; (used instead of signature by an illiterate person) cruz f, signo; (spot, stain) mancha; (coin) marco; (starting point in a race) raya; (target to shoot at) blanco; **to be beside the mark** no venir al caso; **to hit the mark** dar en el blanco; **to leave one's mark** dejar memoria de sí; **to make one's mark** llegar a ser célebre; **to miss the mark** errar el tiro; **to toe the mark** ponerse en la raya; obedecer rigurosamente ‖ tr marcar, señalar; dar nota a (un alumno); calificar (un examen); advertir, notar; **to mark down** poner por escrito; rebajar el precio de

mark'down' s reducción de precio

market [ˈmɑrkɪt] s mercado; **to bear the market** jugar a la baja; **to bull the market** jugar al alza; **to play the market** jugar a la bolsa; **to put on the market** lanzar al mercado ‖ tr llevar al mercado; vender

marketable [ˈmɑrkɪtəbəl] adj comerciable, vendible

market basket s cesta para compras

marketing [ˈmɑrkɪtɪŋ] s mercología, mercadotecnia

market place s plaza del mercado

market price s precio corriente

market research s investigación mercológica

marking gauge [ˈmɑrkɪŋ] s gramil m

marks•man [ˈmɑrksmən] s (pl **-men** [mən]) tirador m; **a good marksman** un buen tiro

marksmanship [ˈmɑrksmən,ʃɪp] s puntería

mark'up' s aumento de precio

marl [mɑrl] s marga ‖ tr margar

marmalade [ˈmɑrmə,led] s mermelada

marmot [ˈmɑrmət] s marmota

maroon [məˈrun] adj & s marrón m, castaño obscuro ‖ tr dejar abandonado (en una isla desierta)

marquee [mɑʃˈki] s marquesina

marquess [ˈmɑrkwɪs] s marqués m

marque•try [ˈmɑrkətri] s (pl **-tries**) marquetería (taracea)

marquis [ˈmɑrkwɪs] s marqués m

marquise [mɑrˈkiz] s marquesa; (over the entrance to a hotel) marquesina

marriage [ˈmærɪdʒ] s casamiento, matrimonio; (married life; intimate union) maridaje m

marriageable [ˈmærɪdʒəbəl] adj casadero

marriage portion s dote m & f

marriage rate s nupcialidad

married life [ˈmærɪd] s vida conyugal

marrow [ˈmæro] s médula, tuétano

mar•ry [ˈmæri] v (pret & pp **-ried**) tr casar (el sacerdote o el juez a un hombre y una *mujer*); (*to take in marriage*) casar con, casarse con; (*to unite intimately*) maridar; **to get married to** casar con, casarse con ‖ *intr* casar, casarse; **to marry into** emparentar con (*p.ej., una familia rica*); **to marry the second time** casarse en segundas nupcias

Mars [mɑrz] *s* Marte *m*

Marseille [mɑrˈsɛːj] *s* Marsella

marsh [mɑrʃ] *s* ciénaga, pantano

mar·shal [ˈmɑrʃəl] *s* cursor *m* de procesiones, maestro de ceremonias; (mil) mariscal *m;* (U.S.A.) oficial *m* de justicia ‖ *v* (*pret & pp* **-shaled** o **-shalled;** *ger* **-shaling** o **-shalling**) *tr* conducir con ceremonia; ordenar, reunir (*los hechos de una argumentación*)

marsh mallow *s* (bot) malvavisco

marsh'mal'low *s* bombón *m* de merengue y gelatina; bombón de malvavisco

marsh·y [ˈmɑrʃi] *adj* (*comp* **-ier;** *super* **-iest**) pantanoso, palúdico

marten [ˈmɑrtən] *s* (*pine marten*) marta; (*beech marten*) garduña

martial [ˈmɑrʃəl] *adj* marcial

martial law *s* ley *f* marcial; **to be under martial law** estar en estado de guerra

Martian [ˈmɑrʃən] *adj & s* marciano

martin [ˈmɑrtɪn] *s* (orn) avión *m*

martinet [ˌmɑrtɪˈnɛt] o [ˈmɑrtɪˌnɛt] *s* ordenancista *mf*

martyr [ˈmɑrtər] *s* mártir *mf*

martyrdom [ˈmɑrtərdəm] *s* martirio

mar·vel [ˈmɑrvəl] *s* maravilla ‖ *v* (*pret & pp* **-veled** o **-velled;** *ger* **-veling** o **-velling**) *intr* maravillarse; **to marvel at** maravillarse con o de

marvelous [ˈmɑrvələs] *adj* maravilloso

Marxist [ˈmɑrksɪst] *adj & s* marxista *mf*

masc. *abbr* **masculine**

mascara [mæsˈkærə] *s* tinte *m* para las pestañas; rímel *m*

mascot [ˈmæskət] *s* mascota

masculine [ˈmæskjəlɪn] *adj & s* masculino

mash [mæʃ] *s* (*crushed mass*) masa; (*to form wort*) masa de cebada ‖ *tr* machacar, majar

mashed potatoes [mæʃt] *spl* puré *m* de patatas

masher [ˈmæʃər] *s* (*device*) mano *f;* (slang) galanteador atrevido

mask [mæsk] o [mɑsk] *s* máscara; (*of beekeeper*) carilla; (*made from a corpse*) mascarilla; (*person*) máscara *mf;* (phot) desvanecedor *m* ‖ *tr* enmascarar; (phot) desvanecer ‖ *intr* enmascararse

masked ball [mæskt] *s* baile *m* de máscaras

masochism [ˈmæsəˌkɪzəm] *s* masoquismo

masochist [ˈmæsəkɪst] *s* masoquista *mf*

masochistic [ˌmæsəˈkɪstɪk] *adj* masoquista

mason [ˈmesən] *s* albañil *m* ‖ **Mason** *s* masón *m*

mason·ry [ˈmesənri] *s* (*pl* **-ries**) albañilería ‖ **Masonry** *s* masonería

masquerade [ˌmæskəˈred] o [ˌmɑskəˈred] *s* mascarada; (*costume, disguise*) máscara; (*false show*) farsa ‖ *intr* enmascararse; **to masquerade as** disfrazarse de

masquerade ball *s* baile *m* de máscaras

mass [mæs] *s* masa; gran cantidad; (*bulk, heap*) mole *f;* (*something glimpsed, e.g., in the fog*) bulto informe; (*big splotch in a painting*) gran mancha; (*celebration of the Eucharist*) misa; **the masses** las masas ‖ *tr* juntar, reunir; enmasar (*tropas*) ‖ *intr* juntarse, reunirse

massacre [ˈmæsəkər] *s* carnicería, matanza ‖ *tr* degollar, matar

massage [məˈsɑʒ] *s* masaje *m* ‖ *tr* masar, masajear

masseur [mæˈsœr] *s* masajista *m*

masseuse [mæˈsœz] *s* masajista *f*

massive [ˈmæsɪv] *adj* macizo; sólido, imponente

mass media *spl* medios *spl* de comunicación

mass meeting *s* mitin *m* popular

mass production *s* fabricación en serie

mast [mæst] o [mɑst] *s* (*for a flag*) palo; (*of a ship*) palo, mástil *m;* (*food for swine*) bellotas, hayucos; **before the mast** como simple marinero

master [ˈmæstər] o [ˈmɑstər] *s* (*employer*) dueño, patrón *m;* (*male head of household*) amo; (*man who possesses some special skill; teacher*) maestro; (*commander of merchant vessel*) capitán *m;* (*title of respect for a boy*) señorito ‖ *tr* dominar

master bedroom *s* alcoba de respeto

master blade *s* hoja maestra (*de una ballesta*)

master builder *s* maestro de obras

masterful [ˈmæstərfəl] o [ˈmɑstərfəl] *adj* hábil, experto; dominante, imperioso

master key *s* llave maestra

masterly [ˈmæstərli] o [ˈmɑstərli] *adj* magistral ‖ *adv* magistralmente

master mechanic *s* maestro mecánico

mas'ter·mind' *s* mente directora ‖ *tr* dirigir con gran acierto

master of ceremonies *s* maestro de ceremonias; (*in a night club, radio, etc.*) animador *m*

mas'ter·piece' *s* obra maestra

master stroke *s* golpe maestro

mas'ter·work' *s* obra maestra

master·y [ˈmæstəri] o [ˈmɑstəri] *s* (*pl* **-ies**) (*command, as of a subject*) dominio; ventaja, superioridad; (*skill*) maestría

mast'head' *s* (*of a newspaper*) cabecera editorial; (naut) tope *m*

masticate [ˈmæstɪˌket] *tr* masticar

mastiff [ˈmæstɪf] o [ˈmɑstɪf] *s* mastín *m*

masturbate [ˈmæstərˌbet] *tr* masturbar ‖ *intr* masturbarse

masturbation [ˌmæstərˈbeʃən] *s* masturbación

mat [mæt] *s* (*for floor*) estera; (*for a cup, vase, etc.*) esterilla, ruedo; (*before a door*) felpudo; (*around a picture*) borde *m* de cartón ‖ *v* (*pret & pp* **matted;** *ger* **matting**) *tr* (*to cover with matting*) esterar; enmarañar ‖ *intr* enmarañarse

match [mætʃ] *s* fósforo; (*wick*) mecha; (*counterpart*) compañero; (*suitable partner in marriage*) partido; (*suitably associated* *pair*) pareja; (*game, contest*) match *m,* partido; **to be a match for** poder con, poder vencer; **to meet one's match** hallar la horma de su zapato ‖ *tr* igualar; aparear, emparejar; hacer juego con; **to match someone for the drinks** jugarle a uno las bebidas ‖ *intr* hacer juego, correr parejas; **to match** a juego, p.ej., **a chair to match** una silla a juego

match'box' *s* fosforera; (*of wax matches*) cerillera

matchless ['mætʃlɪs] *adj* incomparable, sin par

matchmaker ['mætʃ,mekər] *s* casamentero

mate [met] *s* compañero; (*e.g., of a shoe*) compañero, hermano; (*husband or wife*) cónyuge *mf;* (*to a female*) macho; (*to a male*) hembra; (*in chess*) mate *m;* (*naut*) piloto ‖ *tr* aparear, casar; (*in chess*) dar jaque mate a; **to be well mated** hacer una buena pareja ‖ *intr* aparearse, casarse

material [mə'tɪrɪ•əl] *adj* material; importante ‖ *s* material *m;* (*what a thing is made of*) materia; (*cloth, fabric*) tela, género

materialism [mə'tɪrɪ•ə,lɪzəm] *s* materialismo

materialist [mə'tɪrɪ•əlɪst] *s* materialista *mf*

materialize [mə'tɪrɪ•ə,laɪz] *intr* realizarse

matériel [mə,tɪrɪ'ɛl] *s* material *m;* material de guerra

maternal [mə'tʌrnəl] *adj* materno; (*motherly*) maternal

maternity [mə'tʌrnɪti] *s* maternidad

maternity hospital *s* casa de maternidad

math. *abbr* **mathematics**

mathematical [,mæθɪ'mætɪkəl] *adj* matemático

mathematician [,mæθɪmə'tɪʃən] *s* matemático

mathematics [,mæθɪ'mætɪks] *s* matemática, matemáticas

matinée [,mætɪ'ne] *s* matinée *f,* función de tarde

mating season *s* época de celo

matins ['mætɪnz] *spl* maitines *mpl*

matriarch ['metrɪ•ɑrk] *s* matriarca

matricidal [,metrɪ'saɪdəl] *adj* matricida

matricide ['metrɪ,saɪd] *s* (*act*) matricidio; (*person*) matricida *mf*

matriculate [mə'trɪkjə,let] *tr* matricular ‖ *intr* matricularse

matrimo•ny ['mætrɪ,moni] *s* (*pl* **-nies**) matrimonio

matron ['metrən] *s* matrona

matronly ['metrənli] *adj* matronal

matter ['mætər] *s* (*physical substance; pus*) materia; (*subject talked or written about*) asunto; (*reason, ground*) motivo; (*copy for printer*) material *m;* (*printed material*) impresos; **a matter of** cosa de, obra de; **for that matter** en cuanto a eso; **in the matter** al respecto; **no matter** no importa; **no matter when** cuando quiera; **no matter where** dondequiera; **what is the matter?** ¿qué hay?; **what is the matter with you?** ¿qué tiene Vd.? ‖ *intr* importar

matter of course *s* cosa de cajón; **as a matter of course** por rutina

matter of fact *s*—**as a matter of fact** en realidad, en honor a la verdad

matter-of-fact ['mætərəv,fækt] *adj* prosaico, práctico, de poca imaginación

mattock ['mætək] *s* zapapico

mattress ['mætrɪs] *s* colchón *m*

mature [mə'tʃʊr] o [mə'tʊr] *adj* maduro; (*due*) pagadero, vencido ‖ *tr* madurar ‖ *intr* madurar; (*to become due*) (com) vencer

maturity [mə'tʃʊrɪti] o [mə'tʊrɪti] *s* madurez *f;* (com) vencimiento

maudlin ['mɔdlɪn] *adj* lacrimoso, sensiblero; chispo y lloroso

maul [mɔl] *tr* aporrear, maltratar

maulstick ['mɔl,stɪk] *s* tiento

maundy ['mɔndi] *s* lavatorio

Maundy Thursday *s* Jueves Santo

mausole•um [,mɔsə'li•əm] *s* (*pl* **-ums** o **-a** [ə]) mausoleo

maw [mɔ] *s* (*of fowl*) buche *m;* (*of fish*) vejiga de aire

mawkish ['mɔkɪʃ] *adj* (*sickening*) empalagoso; (*sentimental*) sensiblero

max. *abbr* **maximum**

maxim ['mæksɪm] *s* máxima

maximum ['mæksɪməm] *adj & s* máximo

may *v aux* **it may be** puede ser; **may I come in?** ¿puedo entrar? **may you be happy!** ¡que seas feliz! ‖ **May** *s* mayo

maybe ['mebi] o ['mebɪ] *adv* acaso, quizá, tal vez

May Day *s* primero de mayo; fiesta del primero de mayo

Mayday ['me,de] *interj* (*ships, airplanes*) ¡socorro!

mayhem ['mehɛm] o ['me•əm] *s* (law) mutilación criminal

mayonnaise [,me•ə'nez] *s* mayonesa

mayor ['me•ər] o [mɛr] *s* alcalde *m*

mayoress ['me•ərɪs] o ['mɛrɪs] *s* alcaldesa

May'pole' *s* mayo

Maypole dance *s* danza de cintas

May queen *s* maya

maze [mez] *s* laberinto

M.C. *abbr* **Master of Ceremonies, Member of Congress**

mdse. *abbr* **merchandise**

me [mi] *pron pers* me; mí; **to me** me; a mí; **with me** conmigo

meadow ['mɛdo] *s* prado, vega

mead'ow-land' *s* pradera

meager ['migər] *adj* escaso, pobre; flaco, magro

meal [mil] *s* (*regular repast*) comida; (*edible grain coarsely ground*) harina

meal'time' *s* hora de comer

mean [min] *adj* (*intermediate*) medio; (*low in station or rank*) humilde, obscuro; (*shabby*) andrajoso, raído; (*stingy*) mezquino, tacaño; (*of poor quality*) inferior, pobre; (*small-minded*) vil, ruin, innoble; insignificante; (*vicious, as a horse*) arisco, mal intencionado; (coll) indisupuesto; (coll) avergonzado; (coll) de mal genio; **no mean** famoso, excelente ‖ *s* promedio, término medio; **by all means** sí, por cierto, sin falta; **by means of** por medio de; **by no means** de ningún modo, en ningún caso; **means** bienes *mpl* de fortuna; *(agency)* medio, medios; **means to an end** paso para lograr un fin; **to live on one's means** vivar de sus rentas ‖ *v (pret & pp* **meant** [mɛnt]) *tr* significar, querer decir; **to mean to** pensar ‖ *intr*—**to mean well** tener buenas intenciones

meander [mɪˈændər] *s* meandro ‖ *intr* serpentear; vagar

meaning [ˈminɪŋ] *s* sentido, significado

meaningful [ˈminɪŋfəl] *adj* significativo

meaningless [ˈminɪŋlɪs] *adj* sin sentido

meanness [ˈminnɪs] *s* bajeza, vileza, ruindad; *(stinginess)* mezquindad; *(lowliness)* humildad, pobreza

mean′time′ *adv* entretanto, mientras tanto ‖ *s* medio tiempo; **in the meantime** entretanto, mientras tanto

mean′while′ *adv & s* var de **meantime**

measles [ˈmizəlz] *s* sarampión *m; (German measles)* rubéola

mea•sly [ˈmizli] *adj (comp* **-slier;** *super* **-sliest)** sarampioso; (slang) despreciable, mezquino

measurable [ˈmɛʒərəbəl] *adj* medible

measure [ˈmɛʒər] *s* medida; *(step, procedure)* paso, gestión; *(legislative bill)* proyecto de ley; *(of verse)* pie *m;* (mus) compás *m;* **beyond measure** con exceso; **in a measure** hasta cierto punto; **in great measure** en gran parte; *(suit)* **to measure** hecho a la medida; **to take measures** tomar las medidas necesarias; **to take someone's measure** tomarle a uno las medidas ‖ *tr* medir; recorrer *(cierta distancia);* **to measure out** medir; distribuir ‖ *intr* medir

measurement [ˈmɛʒərmənt] *s (act of measuring)* medición; *(measuring; dimension)* medida

measuring glass *s* vaso graduado

meat [mit] *s* carne *f; (food in general)* manjar *m,* vianda; *(substance, gist)* meollo

meat ball *s* albóndiga

meat grinder *s* picador *m*

meat′hook′ *s* garabato de carnicero

meat market *s* carnicería

meat•y [ˈmiti] *adj (comp* **-ier;** *super* **-iest)** carnoso; (fig) jugoso, substancioso

Mecca [ˈmɛkə] *s* La Meca

mechanic [mɪˈkænɪk] *s* mecánico

mechanical [mɪˈkænɪkəl] *adj* mecánico, maquinal; *(machinelike)* (fig) maquinal

mechanical toy *s* juguete *m* de movimiento

mechanics [mɪˈkænɪks] *ssg* mecánica

mechanism [ˈmɛkəˌnɪzəm] *s* mecanismo

mechanize [ˈmɛkəˌnaɪz] *tr* mecanizar

med. *abbr* **medicine, medieval**

medal [ˈmɛdəl] *s* medalla

medallion [mɪˈdæljən] *s* medallón *m*

meddle [ˈmɛdəl] *intr* meterse, entremeterse

meddler [ˈmɛdlər] *s* entremetido

meddlesome [ˈmɛdəlsəm] *adj* entremetido

media [ˈmidɪə] *abbr* **mass media**

median [ˈmidɪ•ən] *adj* intermedio, medio ‖ *s* punto medio, número medio

median strip *s* faja central o divisoria

mediate [ˈmidɪˌet] *tr* dirimir *(una controversia);* reconciliar ‖ *intr (to be in the middle)* mediar; *(to intervene to settle a dispute)* intervenir

mediation [ˌmidɪˈeʃən] *s* mediación

mediator [ˈmidɪˌetər] *s* mediador *m*

medical [ˈmɛdɪkəl] *adj* médico

medical student *s* estudiante *mf* de medicina

medicine [ˈmɛdɪsɪn] *s (science and art)* medicina; *(remedy, treatment)* medicina, medicamento

medicine cabinet *s* armario botiquín

medicine kit *s* botiquín *m*

medicine man *s* curandero, hechicero *(entre los pieles rojas)*

medieval [ˌmidɪˈivəl] o [ˌmɛdɪˈivəl] *adj* medieval

medievalist [ˌmidɪˈivəlɪst] o [ˌmɛdɪˈivəlɪst] *s* medievalista *mf*

mediocre [ˈmidɪˌokər] o [ˌmidɪˈokər] *adj* mediocre

mediocri•ty [ˌmidɪˈɑkrɪti] *s (pl* **-ties)** mediocridad

meditate [ˈmɛdɪˌtet] *tr & intr* meditar

Mediterranean [ˌmɛdɪtəˈrenɪ•ən] *adj & s* Mediterráneo

medi•um [ˈmidɪ•əm] *adj* intermedio; a medio asar ‖ *s (pl* **-ums** o **-a** [ə]) medio; *(in spiritualism)* medio, médium *m; (publication)* órgano; **through the medium of** por medio de

me′dium-range′ *adj* de alcance medio

medlar [ˈmɛdlər] *s (tree and fruit)* níspero; *(fruit)* níspola

medley [ˈmɛdli] *s* mescolanza; (mus) popurrí *m*

medul•la [mɪˈdʌlə] *s (pl* **-lae** [li]) médula

meek [mik] *adj* dócil, manso

meekness [ˈmiknɪs] *s* docilidad, mansedumbre

meerschaum [ˈmɪrʃəm] *s* [ˈmɪrʃɔm] *s* espuma de mar; pipa de espuma de mar

meet [mit] *adj* conveniente, a propósito ‖ *s* concurso deportivo ‖ *v (pret & pp* **met** [mɛt]) *tr* encontrar, encontrarse con; *(to make the acquaintance of)* conocer; empalmar con *(otro tren o autobús);* ir a esperar; honrar, pagar *(una letra);* hacer frente a *(gastos);* cumplir *(sus obligaciones);* batirse con; hallar *(la muerte);* tener *(mala suerte);* aparecer a *(la vista)* ‖ *intr* encontrarse; reunirse; conocerse; **till we meet again** hasta la vista; **to meet with** encontrarse con; reunirse con; empalmar *(un tren)* con *(otro tren);* tener *(un accidente)*

meeting [ˈmitɪŋ] *s* junta, sesión; reunión; encuentro; *(of two rivers or roads)* confluencia; desafío, duelo

meeting of the minds *s* concierto de voluntades

meeting place *s* lugar *m* de reunión

megabucks [ˈmɛgəˌbʌks] *s* (slang) vastas cantidades de dinero

megacycle [ˈmɛgəˌsaɪkəl] *s* megaciclo

megaphone [ˈmɛgəˌfon] *s* megáfono

megohm [ˈmɛgˌom] *s* megohmio

melancholia [,mɛlən'koli·ə] s melancolía
melanchol·y ['mɛlən,kɑli] adj melancólico ‖ s (pl -ies) melancolía
melee ['mele] o ['mɛle] s refriega, reyerta
mellow ['mɛlo] adj maduro, jugoso; suave, meloso; melodioso ‖ tr suavizar ‖ intr suavizarse
melodious [mɪ'lodɪ·əs] adj melodioso
melodramatic [,mɛlədrə'mætɪk] adj melodramático
melo·dy ['mɛlədi] s (pl -dies) melodía
melon ['mɛlən] s melón m
melt [mɛlt] tr derretir; fundir (metales); ablandar, aplacar ‖ intr derretirse; fundirse; ablandarse, aplacarse; **to melt away** desvanecerse; **to melt into** convertirse gradualmente en; deshacerse en (lágrimas)
melt'down' s fusión; (atomic reactor) fusión del combustible por fisión no controlada
melting pot s crisol m; (fig) caldero de razas
member ['mɛmbər] s miembro
membership ['mɛmbər,ʃɪp] s asociación; (e.g., of a club) personal m; número de miembros
membrane ['mɛmbren] s membrana
memen·to [mɪ'mɛnto] s (pl -tos o -toes) recordatorio, prenda de recuerdo
mem·o ['mɛmo] s (pl -os) (coll) apunte m, membrete m
memoir ['mɛmwɑr] s memoria; biografía; **memoirs** memorias
memoran·dum [,mɛmə'rændəm] s (pl -dums o -da [də]) apunte m, membrete m
memorial [mɪ'morɪ·əl] adj conmemorativo ‖ s monumento conmemorativo; (petition) memorial m
memorial arch s arco triunfal
Memorial Day s día m de los caídos
memorialize [mɪ'morɪ·ə,laɪz] tr conmemorar
memorize ['mɛmə,raɪz] tr aprender de memoria
memo·ry ['mɛməri] s (pl -ries) memoria; (recall) retentiva; (computer) memoria, almacenaje m o almacenamiento (de datos); **to commit to memory** encomendar a la memoria
menace ['mɛnɪs] s amenaza ‖ tr & intr amenazar
ménage [me'naʒ] s casa, hogar m; economía doméstica
menagerie [mə'næʒəri] o [mə'nædʒəri] s casa de fieras; colección de fieras
mend [mɛnd] s remiendo; **to be on the mend** ir mejorando ‖ tr (to repair) componer, reparar; (to patch) remendar; (to improve) reformar, mejorar ‖ intr mejorar
mendacious [mɛn'deʃəs] adj mendaz
mendicant ['mɛndɪkənt] adj & s mendicante mf
mending ['mɛndɪŋ] s remiendo, zurcido
menfolk ['mɛn,fok] spl hombres mpl
menial ['minɪ·əl] adj bajo, servil ‖ s criado, doméstico
menses ['mɛnsiz] spl menstruo
men's furnishings spl artículos para caballeros
men's room s lavabo para caballeros

menstruate ['mɛnstru,et] intr menstruar
mental case s (coll) paciente mf mental; estrafalario
mental giant s (coll) genio
mental hygiene s higiene f mental
mental illness ['mɛntəl] s enfermedad mental
mental reservation s reserva mental
mental test s prueba de inteligencia
mention ['mɛnʃən] s mención ‖ tr mencionar; **don't mention it** no hay de qué; **not to mention** sin contar
menu ['mɛnju] o ['menju] s menú m, lista de comidas; comida
meow [mɪ'au] s maullido ‖ intr maullar
Mephistophelian [,mɛfɪstə'filɪ·ən] adj mefistofélico
mercantile ['mʌrkən,til] o ['mʌrkən,taɪl] adj mercantil
mercenar·y ['mʌrsə,nɛri] adj mercenario ‖ s (pl -ies) mercenario
merchandise ['mʌrtʃən,daɪz] s mercancías, mercaderías
merchant ['mʌrtʃənt] adj mercante ‖ s mercante m, mercader m
merchant·man ['mʌrtʃəntmən] s (pl -men [mən]) buque m mercante
merchant marine s marina mercante
merchant vessel s buque m mercante
merciful ['mʌrsɪfəl] adj misericordioso
merciless ['mʌrsɪlɪs] adj despiadado, cruel, implacable
mercu·ry ['mʌrkjəri] s (pl -ries) mercurio, azogue m; columna de mercurio
mer·cy ['mʌrsi] s (pl -cies) misericordia; (discretionary power) merced f; **at the mercy of** a merced de
mere [mir] adj mero, puro; nada más que
meretricious [,mɛrɪ'trɪʃəs] adj postizo, de oropel; cursi, llamativo
merge [mʌrdʒ] tr enchufar, fusionar ‖ intr enchufarse, fusionarse; convergir (p.ej., dos caminos); **to merge into** convertirse gradualmente en
merger ['mʌrdʒər] s fusión de empresas
meridian [mə'rɪdɪ·ən] adj meridiano; (el) más elevado ‖ s meridiano; (fig) auge m, apogeo
meringue [mə'ræŋ] s merengue m
meri·no [mə'rino] adj merino ‖ s (pl -nos) merino
merit ['mɛrɪt] s mérito ‖ tr merecer
merlon ['mʌrlən] s almena, merlón m
mermaid ['mʌr,med] s sirena; (girl who swims well) ninfa marina
mer·man ['mʌr,mæn] s (pl -men [,mɛn]) tritón m; (good swimmer) tritón
merriment ['mɛrɪmənt] s alegría, regocijo
mer·ry ['mɛri] adj (comp -rier; super -riest) alegre, regocijado; **to make merry** divertirse
Merry Christmas interj ¡Felices Pascuas!, ¡Felices Navidades!
mer'ry-go-round' s tiovivo, caballito; serie ininterrumpida (de fiestas, tertulias, etc.)
mer'ry-mak'er s fiestero, jaranero
mesh [mɛʃ] s (net, network) red f; (each open space of net) malla; (engagement of gears)

engrane *m;* **meshes** celada, red *f* ‖ *tr* enredar; (mach) engranar ‖ *intr* enredarse; (mach) engranar

mess [mɛs] *s* (*dirty condition*) cochinería; fregado, lío, embrollo; (*meal for a group of people; such a group*) rancho; (*refuse*) bazofia; **to get into a mess** meterse en un lío; **to make a mess of** ensuciar, echar a perder ‖ *tr* ensuciar; desarreglar; estropear, echar a perder ‖ *intr* comer; **to mess around** (coll) ocuparse en fruslerías

message [ˈmɛsɪdʒ] *s* mensaje *m;* recado

messenger [ˈmɛsəndʒər] *s* mensajero; (*one who goes on errands*) mandadero; precursor *m*

mess hall *s* sala de rancho; comedor *m* de militares

Messiah [məˈsaɪ·ə] *s* Mesías *m*

mess kit *s* utensilios de rancho

mess′mate′ *s* comensal *mf,* compañero de rancho

mess of pottage [ˈpɑtɪdʒ] *s* (Bib) plato de lentejas; cosa de ningún valor

Messrs. [ˈmɛsərz] *pl* de **Mr.**

mess·y [ˈmɛsi] *adj* (*comp* **-ier;** *super* **-iest**) desaliñado, desarreglado; sucio

met. *abbr* **metropolitan**

metal [ˈmɛtəl] *adj* metálico ‖ *s* metal *m;* (fig) brío, ánimo

metallic [mɪˈtælɪk] *adj* metálico

metallurgy [ˈmɛtə,lʌrdʒi] *s* metalurgia

metal polish *s* limpiametales *m*

met′al·work′ *s* metalistería

metamorpho·sis [,mɛtəˈmɔrfəsɪs] *s* (*pl* **-ses** [,siz]) metamorfosis *f*

metaphor [ˈmɛtə,fɔr] *s* metáfora

metaphorical [,mɛtəˈfɑrɪkəl] o [,mɛtəˈfɔrɪkəl] *adj* metafórico

metastasis [məˈtæstəsɪs] *s* metástasis *f*

metathe·sis [mɪˈtæθɪsɪs] *s* (*pl* **-ses** [,siz]) metátesis *f*

mete [mit] *tr*—**to mete out** repartir

meteor [ˈmitɪ·ər] *s* estrella fugaz; (*atmospheric phenomenon*) meteoro

meteorology [,mitɪ·əˈrɑlədʒi] *s* meteorología

meter [ˈmitər] *s* (*unit of measurement; verse*) metro; (*instrument for measuring gas, electricity, water*) contador *m;* (mus) compás *m,* tiempo ‖ *tr* medir (con contador)

metering [ˈmitərɪŋ] *s* medición

meter reader *s* lector *m* (del contador)

methane [ˈmɛθen] *s* metano

method [ˈmɛθəd] *s* método

methodic(al) [mɪˈθɑdɪk(əl)] *adj* metódico

Methodist [ˈmɛθədɪst] *adj* & *s* metodista *mf*

Methuselah [mɪˈθuzələ] *s* Matusalén *m;* **to be as old as Methuselah** vivir más años que Matusalén

meticulous [mɪˈtɪkjələs] *adj* meticuloso, minucioso

metric(al) [ˈmɛtrɪk(əl)] *adj* métrico

metronome [ˈmɛtrə,nom] *s* metrónomo

metropolis [mɪˈtrɑpəlɪs] *s* metrópoli *f*

metropolitan [,mɛtrəˈpɑlɪtən] *adj* metropolitano ‖ *s* (eccl) metropolitano

mettle [ˈmɛtəl] *s* ánimo, brío; **on one's mettle** dispuesto a hacer todo el esfuerzo posible

mettlesome [ˈmɛtəlsəm] *adj* animoso, brioso

mew [mju] *s* maullido; (orn) gaviota; **mews** (Brit) caballerizas alrededor de un corral

Mexican [ˈmɛksɪkən] *adj* & *s* mejicano

Mexico [ˈmɛksɪ,ko] *s* Méjico

mezzanine [ˈmɛzə,nin] *s* entresuelo

mfr. *abbr* **manufacturer**

mi. *abbr* **mile**

mica [ˈmaɪkə] *s* mica

microbe [ˈmaɪkrob] *s* microbio

microbiology [,maɪkrəbaɪˈɑlədʒi] *s* microbiología

microcard [ˈmaɪkrə,kɑrd] *s* microficha

microcomputer [ˈmaɪkrəkəm,pjutər] *s* microordenador *m*

microfarad [,maɪkrəˈfæræd] *s* microfaradio

microfilm [ˈmaɪkrə,fɪlm] *s* microfilm *m,* micropelícula ‖ *tr* microfilmar

microgroove [ˈmaɪkrə,gruv] *adj* microsurco ‖ *s* microsurco; disco microsurco

microphone [ˈmaɪkrə,fon] *s* micrófono

microprocessor [ˈmaɪkrə,prasɛsər] *s* microprocesador *m*

microscope [ˈmaɪkrə,skop] *s* microscopio

microscopic [,maɪkrəˈskɑpɪk] *adj* microscópico

microwave [ˈmaɪkrə,wev] *s* microonda

mid [mɪd] *adj* medio, p.ej., **in mid course** a medio camino

mid′day′ *adj* del mediodía ‖ *s* mediodia *m*

middle [ˈmɪdəl] *adj* medio ‖ *s* centro, medio; (*of the human body*) cintura; **about the middle of** a mediados de; **in the middle of** en medio de

middle age *s* mediana edad ‖ **Middle Ages** *spl* Edad Media

middle class *s* burguesía, clase media

Middle East *s* Oriente Medio

Middle English *s* el inglés medio

middle finger *s* dedo cordial, de en medio o del corazón

mid′dle·man′ *s* (*pl* **-men** [,mɛn]) intermediario

middling [ˈmɪdlɪŋ] *adj* mediano, regular, pasadero ‖ *adv* (coll) medianamente; (coll) así, así ‖ *s* (*coarsely ground wheat*) cabezuela; **middlings** artículos de calidad o precio medianos

mid·dy [ˈmɪdi] *s* (*pl* **-dies**) (coll) aspirante *m* de marina; (*child's blouse*) marinera

middy blouse *s* marinera

midget [ˈmɪdʒɪt] *s* enano, liliputiense *mf*

midland [ˈmɪdlənd] *adj* de tierra adentro ‖ *s* región central

mid′night′ *adj* de medianoche; **to burn the midnight oil** quemarse las cejas ‖ *s* medianoche *f*

midriff [ˈmɪdrɪf] *s* (anat) diafragma *m;* talle *m*

midship·man [ˈmɪd,ʃɪpmən] *s* (*pl* **-men** [mən]) guardia marina *m,* aspirante *m* de marina

midst [mɪdst] *s* centro; **in the midst of** en medio de; en lo más recio de

mid'stream' s—in midstream en pleno río
mid'sum'mer s pleno verano
mid'way' adj situado a mitad del camino ‖ adv a mitad del camino ‖ s mitad del camino; (of a fair or exposition) avenida central
mid'week' s mediados de la semana
mid'wife' s (pl -wives) partera, comadrona
mid'win'ter s pleno invierno
mid'year' adj de mediados del año ‖ s mediados del año; midyears (coll) examen m de mediados del año escolar
mien [min] s aspecto, semblante m, porte m
miff [mɪf] s (coll) desavenencia ‖ tr (coll) ofender
might [maɪt] s fuerza, poder m; with might and main con todas sus fuerzas, a más no poder ‖ v aux se emplea para formar el modo potencial, p.ej., she might not come es posible que no venga
might•y [ˈmaɪti] adj (comp -ier; super -iest) potente, poderoso; (of great size) grandísimo ‖ adv (coll) muy
migrant worker [ˈmaɪgrənt] s bracero migratorio
migrate [ˈmaɪgret] intr emigrar
migratory [ˈmaɪgrə,tori] adj migratorio
mil abbr military, militia
milch [mɪltʃ] adj lechero
mild [maɪld] adj blando, suave; dócil, manso; leve, ligero; (climate) templado
mildew [ˈmɪl,dju] s (mold) moho; (plant disease) mildeu m
mile [maɪl] s milla inglesa
mileage [ˈmaɪlɪdʒ] s recorrido en millas
mileage ticket s billete contado por millas, semejante al billete kilométrico
mile'post' s poste miliario
mile'stone' s piedra miliaria; to be a milestone hacer época
milieu [mɪlˈju] s ambiente m, medio
militancy [ˈmɪlɪtənsi] s belicosidad
militant [ˈmɪlɪtənt] adj militante, belicoso
militarism [ˈmɪlɪtə,rɪzəm] s militarismo
militarist [ˈmɪlɪtərɪst] adj & s militarista mf
militarize [ˈmɪlɪtə,raɪz] tr militarizar
military [ˈmɪlɪ,tɛri] adj militar ‖ s (los) militares
Military Academy s (U.S.A.) Academia General Militar
military police s policía militar
militate [ˈmɪlɪ,tet] intr militar
militia [mɪˈlɪʃə] s milicia
militia•man [mɪˈlɪʃəmən] s (pl -men [mən]) miliciano
milk [mɪlk] adj lechero, de leche ‖ s leche f ‖ tr ordeñar; chupar (los bienes de uno); abusar de, explotar ‖ intr dar leche
milk can s lechera
milk diet s régimen lácteo
milking [ˈmɪlkɪŋ] s ordeño
milk'maid' s lechera
milk•man [ˈmɪlk,mæn] s (pl -men [,mɛn]) lechero
milk of human kindness s compasión, humanidad
milk pail s ordeñadero

milk shake s batido de leche
milk'sop' s calzonazos m, marica m
milk'weed' s algodoncillo, vencetósigo
milk•y [ˈmɪlki] adj (comp -ier; super -iest) lechoso, lácteo
Milky Way s Vía Láctea
mill [mɪl] s (for grinding grain) molino; (for making fabrics) hilandería; (for cutting wood) aserradero; (for refining sugar) ingenio; (for producing steel) fábrica; (to grind coffee) molinillo; (part of a dollar) milésima; to put through the mill (coll) poner a prueba, someter a un entrenamiento riguroso ‖ tr moler (granos); acordonar, cerrillar (monedas); laminar (el acero); triturar (mena); (with a milling cutter) fresar; batir (chocolate) ‖ intr—to mill about o around arremolinarse
mill end s retal m de hilandería
millennial [mɪˈlɛni•əl] adj milenario
millenni•um [mɪˈlɛni•əm] s (pl -ums o -a [ə]) milenario, milenio
miller [ˈmɪlər] s molinero; (ent) polilla blanca
millet [ˈmɪlɪt] s mijo, millo
milliampere [,mɪlɪˈæmpɪr] s miliamperio
milligram [ˈmɪlɪ,græm] s miligramo
millimeter [ˈmɪlɪ,mitər] s milímetro
milliner [ˈmɪlɪnər] s modista mf de sombreros
millinery [ˈmɪlɪ,nɛri] o [ˈmɪlɪnəri] s artículos para sombreros de señora; confección de sombreros de señora; venta de sombreros de señora
millinery shop s sombrerería
milling [ˈmɪlɪŋ] s (of grain) molienda; (of coins) acordonamiento, cordoncillo; fresado
milling machine s fresadora
million [ˈmɪljən] adj millón de, millones de ‖ s millón m
millionaire [,mɪljənˈɛr] s millonario
millionth [ˈmɪljənθ] adj & s millonésimo
millivolt [ˈmɪlɪ,volt] s vmilivoltio
mill'pond' s represa de molino
mill'race' s caz m
mill'stone' s muela de molino; (fig) carga pesada
mill wheel s rueda de molino
mill'work' s carpintería de taller
mime [maɪm] s mimo ‖ tr remedar
Mimeograph [ˈmɪm•ə,græf] o [ˈmɪmɪ•ə,graf] s (trademark) mimeógrafo ‖ tr mimeografiar
mim•ic [ˈmɪmɪk] s imitador m, remedador m ‖ v (pret & pp -icked; ger -icking) tr imitar, remedar
mimic•ry [ˈmɪmɪkri] s (pl -ries) mímica, remedo
min. abbr minimum, minute
minaret [,mɪnəˈrɛt] o [ˈmɪnə,rɛt] s alminar m, minarete m
mince [mɪns] tr desmenuzar; picar (carne) ‖ intr andar remilgadamente; hablar remilgadamente
mince'meat' s cuajado, picadillo
mince pie s pastel relleno de carne picada con frutas

mind [maind] *s* mente *f*, espíritu *m;* **to bear in mind** tener presente; **to be not in one's right mind** no estar en sus cabales; **to be of one mind** estar de acuerdo; **to be out of one's mind** estar fuera de juicio; **to change one's mind** mudar de parecer; **to go out of one's mind** volverse loco; **to have a mind to** tener ganas de; **to have in mind to** pensar en; **to have on one's mind** preocuparse con; **to lose one's mind** perder el juicio; **to make up one's mind** resolverse; **to my mind** a mi parecer; **to say whatever comes into one's mind** decir lo que se le viene a la boca; **to set one's mind on** resolverse a; **to slip one's mind** escaparse de la memoria; **to speak one's mind** decir su parecer; **with one mind** unánimamente || *tr* (*to take care of*) cuidar, estar al cuidado de; obedecer; fijarse en; sentir molestia por; **do you mind the smoke?** ¿le molesta el humo?; **mind your own business** no se meta Vd. en lo que no le toca || *intr* tener inconveniente; tener. cuidado; **never mind** no se preocupe, no se moleste
mind'-bend'ing *adj* (coll) alucinante
mind'-blow'ing *adj* (coll) alucinante en exceso
mind'-bog'gling *adj* deslumbrante; abrumador
mindful ['maindfəl] *adj* atento; **mindful of** atento a, cuidadoso de
mind reader *s* adivinador *m* del pensamiento ajeno, lector *m* mental
mind reading *s* adivinación del pensamiento ajeno, lectura de la mente
mine [main] *pron poss* el mío; mío || *s* mina; **to work a mine** beneficiar una mina || *tr* minar; beneficiar (*un terreno*); extraer (*mineral, carbón, etc.*) || *intr* minar; abrir minas
mine field *s* campo de minas
mine layer *s* buque *m* portaminas, lanzaminas *m*
miner ['mainər] *s* minero; (mil, nav) minador *m*
mineral ['minərəl] *adj & s* mineral *m*
mineralogy [,minə'rælədʒi] *s* mineralogía
mineral resources *spl* riquezas del subsuelo
mineral wool *s* lana de escorias
mine sweeper *s* dragaminas *m*
mingle ['mingəl] *tr* mezclar, confundir || *intr* mezclarse, confundirse; asociarse
miniature ['mini•ət/ər] o ['minit/ər] *s* miniatura; **to paint in miniature** miniar, pintar de miniatura
miniaturization [,mini•ət/əri'zeʃən] o [,min-it/əri'zeʃən] *s* miniaturización
minicomputer ['minikəm,pjutər] *s* miniordenador *m*
minimal ['miniməl] *adj* mínimo
minimize ['mini,maiz] *tr* empequeñecer
minimum ['miniməm] *adj & s* mínimo
minimum wage *s* jornal mínimo
mining ['mainin] *adj* minero || *s* mineraje *m*, minería; (nav) minado
minion ['minjən] *s* paniaguado

minion of the law *s* esbirro, polizonte *m*
miniskirt ['mini,skʌrt] *s* minifalda
minister ['ministər] *s* ministro; pastor *m* protestante || *tr & intr* ministrar
ministerial ['minis'tiri•əl] *adj* ministerial
minis•try ['ministri] *s* (*pl* -tries) ministerio
mink [mink] *s* visón *m*
minnow ['mino] *s* pececillo; (ichth) foxino
minor ['mainər] *adj* (*smaller*) menor; de menor importancia; (*younger*) menor de edad; (mus) menor || *s* menor *m* de edad; (educ) asignatura secundaria
Minorca [mi'nɔrkə] *s* Menorca
Minorcan [mi'nɔrkən] *adj & s* menorquín *m*
minori•ty [mai'nɔriti] *adj* minoritario || *s* (*pl* -ties) (*being under age; smaller number or part*) minoría; (*less than full age*) minoridad
minstrel ['minstrəl] *s* (*retainer who sang and played for his lord*) ministril *m;* (*medieval musician and poet*) juglar *m*, trovador *m;* (U.S.A.) cantor cómico disfrazado de negro
minstrel•sy ['minstrəlsi] *s* (*pl* -sies) juglaría; compañía de juglares; poesía trovadoresca
mint [mint] *s* casa de moneda; (plant) menta, hierbabuena; montón *m* de dinero; fuente *f* inagotable || *tr* acuñar; (fig) inventar
minuet [,minju'et] *s* minué *m*, minuete *m*
minus ['mainəs] *adj* menos || *prep* menos; falto de, sin || *s* menos *m*
minute [mai'njut] o [mai'nut] *adj* diminuto, menudo || ['minit] *s* minuto; (*short space of time*) momento; **minutes** acta; **to write up the minutes** levantar acta; **up to the minute** al corriente; de última hora
minute hand ['minit] *s* minutero
minutiae [mi'nju/i,i] o [mi'nu/i,i] *spl* minucias
minx [minks] *s* moza descarada
miracle ['mirəkəl] *s* milagro
miracle play *s* auto
miraculous [mi'rækjələs] *adj* milagroso
mirage [mi'raʒ] *s* espejismo
mire [mair] *s* fango, lodo
mirror ['mirər] *s* espejo; (aut) retrovisor *m* || *tr* reflejar
mirth [mʌrθ] *s* alegría, regocijo
mir•y ['mairi] *adj* (*comp* -ier; *super* -iest) fangoso, lodoso; sucio
misadventure [,misəd'vent/ər] *s* desgracia, contratiempo
misanthrope ['misən,θrop] *s* misántropo
misanthropy [mis'ænθrəpi] *s* misantropía
misapprehension [,misæpri'hen/ən] *s* malentendido
misappropriation [,misə,propri'e/ən] *s* malversación
misbehave [,misbi'hev] *intr* conducirse mal, portarse mal
misbehavior [,misbi'hevi•ər] *s* mala conducta, mal comportamiento
misc. *abbr* **miscellaneous, miscellany**
miscalculation [,miskælkjə'le/ən] *s* mal cálculo
miscarriage [mis'kæridʒ] *s* aborto, malparto; fracaso, malogro; (*of a letter*) extravío

miscar·ry [mɪsˈkæri] v (*pret & pp* **-ried**) *intr* abortar, malparir; malograrse; extraviarse (*una carta*)

miscellaneous [ˌmɪsəˈleniˑəs] *adj* misceláneo

miscella·ny [ˈmɪsəˌleni] s (*pl* **-nies**) miscelánea

mischief [ˈmɪstʃɪf] s (*harm*) daño, mal *m*; (*disposition to annoy*) malicia; (*prankishness*) travesura

mis'chief-mak'er s malsín *m*, cizañero

mischievous [ˈmɪstʃɪvəs] *adj* dañoso, malo; malicioso; travieso

misconception [ˌmɪskənˈsɛpʃən] s concepto erróneo, mala interpretación

misconduct [mɪsˈkɑndəkt] s mala conducta

misconstrue [ˌmɪskənˈstru] o [mɪsˈkɑnstru] *tr* interpretar mal

miscount [mɪsˈkaʊnt] s cuenta errónea ‖ *tr & intr* contar mal

miscue [mɪsˈkju] s (*in billiards*) pifia; (*slip*) pifia ‖ *intr* pifiar; (*theat*) equivocarse de apunte

misdate [mɪsˈdet] *tr* fechar erróneamente

mis·deal [ˈmɪsˌdil] s repartición errónea ‖ [mɪsˈdil] v (*pret & pp* **-dealt** [ˈdɛlt]) *tr & intr* repartir mal

misdeed [mɪsˈdid] o [ˈmɪsˌdid] s malhecho, fechoría

misdemeanor [ˌmɪsdɪˈminər] s mala conducta; (*law*) delito de menor cuantía

misdirect [ˌmɪsdɪˈrɛkt] o [ˌmɪsdaɪˈrɛkt] *tr* dirigir erradamente; hacer perder el camino

misdoing [mɪsˈduˑɪŋ] s mala acción

miser [ˈmaɪzər] s avaro, verrugo; codo (Guat, Mex)

miserable [ˈmɪzərəbəl] *adj* miserable; (coll) achacoso, indispuesto

miserly [ˈmaɪzərli] *adj* avariento, mezquino

miser·y [ˈmɪzəri] s (*pl* **-ies**) miseria; pelazón *f*

misfeasance [mɪsˈfizəns] s (law) fraude *m*

misfire [mɪsˈfaɪr] s falla de tiro; (*of internal-combustion engine*) falla de encendido ‖ *intr* fallar (*un arma de fuego, el encendido de un motor*)

mis·fit [ˈmɪsˌfɪt] s vestido mal cortado; cosa que no encaja bien; persona mal adaptada a su ambiente ‖ [mɪsˈfɪt] v (*pret & pp* -fitted; *ger* -fitting) *tr & intr* encajar mal, sentar mal

misfortune [mɪsˈfɔrtʃən] s desgracia

misgiving [mɪsˈgɪvɪŋ] s mal presentimiento, rescoldo

misgovern [mɪsˈgʌvərn] *tr* desgobernar

misguidance [mɪsˈgaɪdəns] s error *m*, extravío

misguided [mɪsˈgaɪdɪd] *adj* descarriado, malaconsejado

mishap [ˈmɪshæp] o [mɪsˈhæp] s accidente *m*, percance *m*

mishmash [ˈmɪʃˌmæʃ] s baturrillo; mezcolanza

misinform [ˌmɪsɪnˈfɔrm] *tr* dar informes erróneos a

misinterpret [ˌmɪsɪnˈtɛrprɪt] *tr* interpretar mal

misjudge [mɪsˈdʒʌdʒ] *tr & intr* juzgar mal

mis·lay [mɪsˈle] v (*pret & pp* **-laid** [ˌled]) *tr* extraviar, perder; (*among one's papers*) traspapelar

mis·lead [mɪsˈlid] v (*pret & pp* **-led** [ˌlɛd]) *tr* (*to lead astray*) extraviar, descaminar; (*to lead into wrongdoing*) seducir, inducir al mal; (*to deceive*) engañar

misleading [mɪsˈlidɪŋ] *adj* engañoso

mismanagement [mɪsˈmænɪdʒmənt] s mala administración, desgobierno

misnomer [mɪsˈnomər] s nombre improprio, mal nombre

misplace [mɪsˈples] *tr* colocar fuera de su lugar; colocar mal; (*to mislay*) (coll) extraviar, perder

misprint [ˈmɪsˌprɪnt] s errata de imprenta ‖ [mɪsˈprɪnt] *tr* imprimir con erratas

mispronounce [ˌmɪsprəˈnaʊns] *tr* pronunciar mal

mispronunciation [ˌmɪsprəˌnʌnsɪˈeʃən] o [ˌmɪsprəˌnʌnʃɪˈeʃən] s pronunciación incorrecta

misquote [mɪsˈkwot] *tr* citar equivocadamente

misrepresent [ˌmɪsrɛprɪˈzɛnt] *tr* tergiversar

miss [mɪs] s falta, error *m*; fracaso, malogro; tiro errado; jovencita, muchacha ‖ *tr* echar de menos; perder (*el tren, la función, la oportunidad*); errar (*el blanco; la vocación*); no entender, no comprender; omitir; no ver; no dar con, no encontrar; librarse de (*p.ej., la muerte*); escapársele a uno, p.ej., **I missed what you said** se me escapó lo que dijo Vd.; por poco, p.ej., **the car missed hitting me** el coche por poco me atropella ‖ *intr* fallar; errar el blanco; malograrse ‖ **Miss** s señorita

missal [ˈmɪsəl] s misal *m*

misshapen [mɪsˈʃepən] *adj* deforme, contrahecho

missile [ˈmɪsɪl] *adj* arrojadizo ‖ s arma arrojadiza; proyectil *m*; proyectil dirigido, misil *m*

missile gap s desigualdad de armas proyectiles poseídas por dos potencias

missil(e)ry [ˈmɪsəlri] s cohetería; ciencia de las armas proyectiles

missing [ˈmɪsɪŋ] *adj* extraviado, perdido; desaparecido; ausente; **to be missing** hacer falta; haber desaparecido

missing link s hombre *m* mono

missing persons spl desaparecidos

mission [ˈmɪʃən] s misión; casa de misión

missionar·y [ˈmɪʃənˌɛri] *adj* misional ‖ s (*pl* -ies) (*one sent to work to propagate his faith*) misionario, misionero; (*on a political or diplomatic mission*) misionario

missive [ˈmɪsɪv] *adj* misivo ‖ s misiva

mis·spell [mɪsˈspɛl] v (*pret & pp* -spelled o -spelt [ˈspɛlt]) *tr & intr* deletrear mal, escribir mal

misspelling [mɪsˈspɛlɪŋ] s falta de ortografía

misspent [mɪsˈspɛnt] *adj* malgastado

misstatement [mɪsˈstetmənt] s relación equivocada, relación falsa

misstep [mɪsˈstɛp] s paso falso; (*slip in conduct*) resbalón *m*

miss•y [ˈmɪsɪ] s (pl **-ies**) (coll) señorita
mist [mɪst] s neblina; (of tears) velo; (fine spray) vapor m
mis•take [mɪsˈtek] s error m, equivocación; **and no mistake** sin duda alguna; **by mistake** por descuido; **to make a mistake** equivocarse ‖ v (pret **-took** [ˈtuk]; pp **-taken**) tr tomar (por otro; por lo que no es); entender mal; **to be mistaken for** equivocarse con
mistaken [mɪsˈtekən] adj (person) equivocado; (idea) erróneo; (act) desacertado
mistakenly [mɪsˈtekənlɪ] adv equivocadamente, por error
mistletoe [ˈmɪsəl,to] s (Viscum album) muérdago; (Phoradendron flavescens, used in Christmas decorations in the U.S.A.) cabellera
mistreat [mɪsˈtrit] tr maltratar
mistreatment [mɪsˈtritmənt] s maltratamiento
mistress [ˈmɪstrɪs] s (of a household) ama, dueña; moza, querida, manceba; (Brit) maestra de escuela
mistrial [mɪsˈtraɪ•əl] s pleito viciado de nulidad
mistrust [mɪsˈtrʌst] s desconfianza ‖ tr desconfiar de ‖ intr desconfiar
mistrustful [mɪsˈtrʌstfəl] adj desconfiado
mist•y [ˈmɪstɪ] adj (comp **-ier**; super **-iest**) brumoso, neblinoso; indistinto
misunder•stand [,mɪsʌndərˈstænd] v (pret & pp **-stood** [ˈstud]) tr no comprender, entender mal
misunderstanding [,mɪsʌndərˈstændɪŋ] s malentendido; (disagreement) desavenencia
misuse [mɪsˈjus] s abuso, mal uso; (of funds) malversación ‖ [mɪsˈjuz] tr abusar de, emplear mal; malversar (fondos)
misword [mɪsˈwʌrd] tr redactar mal
mite [maɪt] s (small contribution) óbolo; (small amount) pizca; (ent) ácaro
miter [ˈmaɪtər] s mitra; (carp) inglete m ‖ tr cortar ingletes en; juntar con junta a inglete
miter box s caja de ingletes
mitigate [ˈmɪtɪ,get] tr mitigar, atenuar, paliar
mitten [ˈmɪtən] s confortante m, mitón m
mix [mɪks] tr mezclar; amasar (una torta); aderezar (ensalada); **to mix up** equivocar, confundir ‖ intr mezclarse; asociarse
mixed [mɪkst] adj mixto, mezclado; (e.g., candy) variados; (coll) confundido
mixed company s reunión de personas de ambos sexos
mixed drink s bebida mezclada
mixed feelings s concepto vacilante
mixer [ˈmɪksər] s (of concrete) mezcladora, hormigonera; **to be a good mixer** (coll) tener don de gentes
mixture [ˈmɪkstʃər] s mezcla, mixtura
mix′-up′ s confusión; enredo, lío; (of people) equivocación
mizzen [ˈmɪzən] s mesana
mo. abbr **month**
M.O. abbr **money order**
moan [mon] s gemido ‖ intr gemir

moat [mot] s foso
mob [mɑb] s chusma, populacho; (crowd bent on violence) muchedumbre airada ‖ v (pret & pp **mobbed**; ger **mobbing**) tr asaltar, atropellar
mobile [ˈmobɪl] o [ˈmobil] adj móvil
mobility [moˈbɪlɪtɪ] s movilidad
mobilization [,mobɪlɪˈzeʃən] s movilización
mobilize [ˈmobɪ,laɪz] tr movilizar ‖ intr movilizar, movilizarse
mob rule s gobierno del populacho
mobster [ˈmɑbstər] s (slang) gamberro, pandillero, gángster
mobsterism [ˈmɑbstə,rɪzəm] s gangsterismo; acciones de los gangsters
moccasin [ˈmɑkəsɪn] s mocasín m
Mocha coffee [ˈmokə] s moca m, café m de moca
mock [mɑk] adj simulado, fingido ‖ s burla, mofa ‖ tr burlarse de, mofarse de; despreciar; engañar ‖ intr mofarse; **to mock at** mofarse de
mocker•y [ˈmɑkərɪ] s (pl **-ies**) burla, mofa, escarnio; (subject of derision) hazmerreír m; (poor imitation) mal remedo; (e.g., of justice) negación
mock′ing•bird′ s burlón m, sinsonte m
mock orange s jeringuilla, celinda
mock privet s olivillo
mock turtle soup s sopa de cabeza de ternera
mock′-up′ s maqueta
mode [mod] s modo, manera; (fashion) moda; (gram) modo
mod•el [ˈmɑdəl] adj modelo, p.ej., **model city** ciudad modelo ‖ s modelo ‖ v (pret & pp **-eled** o **-elled**; ger **-eling** o **-elling**) tr (to fashion in clay, wax, etc.) modelar ‖ intr modelarse; servir de modelo
model airplane s aeromodelo
mod′el-air′plane builder s aeromodelista mf
model-airplane building s aeromodelismo
model sailing s navegación de modelos a vela
moderate [ˈmɑdərɪt] adj moderado; (tiempo) templado; (precio) módico ‖ [ˈmɑdə,ret] tr moderar; presidir (una asamblea) ‖ intr moderarse
moderator [ˈmɑdə,retər] s (over an assembly) presidente m; (mediator) árbitro; (telv) presentador m, presentadora; (for slowing down neutrons) moderador m
modern [ˈmɑdərn] adj moderno
modernize [ˈmɑdər,naɪz] tr modernizar
modest [ˈmɑdɪst] adj modesto
modes•ty [ˈmɑdɪstɪ] s (pl **-ties**) modestia
modicum [ˈmɑdɪkəm] s pequeña cantidad
modifier [ˈmɑdɪ,faɪ•ər] s (gram) modificante m
modi•fy [ˈmɑdɪ,faɪ] v (pret & pp **-fied**) tr modificar
modish [ˈmodɪʃ] adj de moda, elegante
modulate [ˈmɑdʒə,let] tr & intr modular
modulation [,mɑdʒəˈleʃən] s modulación
mohair [ˈmo,hɛr] s mohair m (pelo de cabra de Angora)
Mohammedan [moˈhæmɪdən] adj & s mahometano

Mohammedanism [mo'hæmɪdə,nɪzəm] *s* mahometismo

moist [mɔɪst] *adj* húmedo, mojado; (*weather*) lluvioso; (*eyes*) lagrimoso

moisten ['mɔɪsən] *tr* humedecer ‖ *intr* humedecerse

moisture ['mɔɪstʃər] *s* humedad

molar ['molər] *s* diente *m* molar

molasses [mə'læsɪz] *s* melaza

molasses candy *s* melcocha

mold [mold] *s* molde *m;* cosa moldeada; (*shape*) forma; (*fungus*) moho; (*humus*) mantillo; (*fig*) carácter *m*, índole *f* ‖ *tr* amoldar, moldear; (*to make moldy*) enmohecer ‖ *intr* enmohecerse

molder ['moldər] *s* moldeador *m* ‖ *intr* convertirse en polvo, consumirse

molding ['moldɪŋ] *s* moldeado; (*cornice, shaped strip of wood, etc.*) moldura

mold·y ['moldi] *adj* (*comp* -ier; *super* -iest) (*overgrown with mold*) mohoso; (*stale*) rancio, pasado

mole [mol] *s* (*breakwater*) rompeolas *m;* (*inner harbor*) dársena; (*spot on skin*) lunar *m;* (*small mammal*) topo

molecular physics [mə'lɛkjələr] *s* física molecular

molecular weight *s* peso molecular

molecule ['malɪ,kjul] *s* molécula

mole'hill' *s* topinera

mole'skin' *s* piel *f* de topo, molesquina

molest [mə'lɛst] *tr* molestar; faltar al respeto a (*una mujer*)

moll [mal] *s* (slang) mujer *f* del hampa; (slang) ramera

molli·fy ['malɪ,faɪ] *v* (*pret & pp* -fied) *tr* apaciguar, aplacar

mollusk ['maləsk] *s* molusco

mollycoddle ['malɪ,kadəl] *s* mantecón *m*, marica *m* ‖ *tr* consentir, mimar

molt [molt] *s* muda ‖ *intr* hacer la muda

molten ['moltən] *adj* fundido, derretido; fundido, vaciado

molybdenum [mə'lɪbdɪnəm] o [,malɪb'dɪnəm] *s* molibdeno

moment ['momənt] *s* momento; **at any moment** de un momento a otro

momentary ['momən,tɛri] *adj* momentáneo

momentous [mo'mɛntəs] *adj* importante, grave

momen·tum [mo'mɛntəm] *s* (*pl* -tums o -ta [te]) ímpetu *m;* (*mech*) cantidad de movimiento

monarch ['manərk] *s* monarca *m*

monarchic(al) [mə'narkɪk(əl)] *adj* monárquico

monarchist ['manərkɪst] *adj & s* monárquico, monarquista *mf*

monar·chy ['manərki] *s* (*pl* -chies) monarquía

monaster·y ['manəs,tɛri] *s* (*pl* -ies) monasterio

monastic [mə'næstɪk] *adj* monástico

monasticism [mə'næstɪ,sɪzəm] *s* monaquismo

Monday ['mʌndi] *s* lunes *m*

monetary ['manɪ,tɛri] *adj* monetario; pecuniario

money ['mʌni] *s* dinero; **to make money** ganar dinero; dar dinero (*una empresa*)

mon'ey·bag' *s* monedero, talega; **money-bags** (*wealth*) (coll) talegas; (*wealthy person*) (coll) ricacho

moneychanger ['mʌni,tʃendʒər] *s* cambista *mf*

moneyed ['mʌnid] *adj* adinerado

moneylender ['mʌni,lɛndər] *s* prestamista *mf*

mon'ey·mak'er *s* acaudalador *m;* (fig) manantial *m* de beneficios

money order *s* giro postal, orden *m* de pago

Mongol ['maŋgəl] *adj & s* mogol *mf*

Mongolian [maŋ'golɪən] *adj & s* mogol *mf*

mon·goose ['maŋgus] *s* (*pl* -gooses) mangosta

mongrel ['mʌŋgrəl] *adj & s* mestizo

monitor ['manɪtər] *s* monitor *m* ‖ *tr* controlar (*la señal*); escuchar (*radio-transmisiones*); superentender

monk [mʌŋk] *s* monje *m*

monkey ['mʌŋki] *s* mono; simio; **to make a monkey of** tomar el pelo a ‖ *intr* — **to monkey around** haraganear; **to monkey with** ajar, manosear

mon'key·shine' *s* (slang) monería, monada, payasada

monkey wrench *s* llave inglesa

monkhood ['mʌŋkhud] *s* monacato; los monjes

monkshood ['mʌŋks·hud] *s* cogulla de fraile

monocle ['manəkəl] *s* monóculo

monogamy [mə'nagəmi] *s* monogamia

monogram ['manə,græm] *s* monograma *m*

monograph ['manə,græf] *s* monografía

monolithic [,manə'lɪθɪk] *adj* monolítico

monologue ['manə,lɔg] *s* monólogo

monomania [,manə'menɪ·ə] *s* monomanía

monomial [mə'nomɪ·əl] *s* monomio

monopolize [mə'napə,laɪz] *tr* monopolizar; acaparar (*p.ej., la conversación*)

monopo·ly [mə'napəli] *s* (*pl* -lies) monopolio

monorail ['manə,rel] *s* monorriel *m*

monosyllable ['manə,sɪləbəl] *s* monosílabo

monotheist ['manə,θi·ɪst] *adj & s* monoteísta *mf*

monotonous [me'natənəs] *adj* monótono

monotony [me'natəni] *s* monotonía

monotype ['manə,taɪp] *s* (*machine; method*) monotipia; (*machine*) monotipo

monotype operator *s* monotipista *mf*

monoxide [mə'naksaɪd] *s* monóxido

monseigneur [,mansen'jər] *s* monseñor *m*

monsignor [man'sinjər] *s* (*pl* **monsignors** o **monsignori** [,mɔnsi'njori]) (eccl) monseñor *m*

monsoon [man'sun] *s* monsón *m*

monster ['manstər] *adj* monstruoso ‖ *s* monstruo

monstrance ['manstrəns] *s* custodia, ostensorio

monstrosi·ty [man'strasiti] *s* (*pl* -ties) monstruosidad; esperpento

monstrous ['manstrəs] *adj* monstruoso

mi
mo

month [mʌnθ] s mes *m*

month•ly [`mʌnθli] *adj* mensual ‖ *adv* mensualmente ‖ *s* (*pl* **-lies**) revista mensual; **monthlies** (coll) reglas

monument [`mɑnjəmənt] *s* monumento

moo [mu] *s* mugido ‖ *intr* mugir

mood [mud] *s* humor *m*, genio; (gram) modo; **moods** accesos de mal humor

mood•y [`mudi] *adj* (*comp* **-ier;** *super* **-iest**) triste, hosco, melancólico; caprichoso, veleidoso

moon [mun] *s* luna

moon′beam′ *s* rayo lunar

moon′light′ *s* claror *m* de luna, luz *f* de la luna

moon′light′ing *s* multiempleo, pluriempleo

moon′sail′ *s* (naut) monterilla

moon′shine′ *s* luz *f* de la luna; (*idle talk*) cháchara, música celestial; (coll) whisky destilado ilegalmente

moon shot *s* lanzamiento a la Luna

moor [mʊr] *s* brezal *m*, páramo ‖ *tr* (naut) amarrar ‖ *intr* (naut) echar las amarras ‖ **Moor** *s* moro

Moorish [`mʊrɪʃ] *adj* moro

moor′land′ *s* brezal *m*

moose [mus] *s* (*pl* **moose**) alce *m* de América

moot [mut] *adj* discutible, dudoso

mop [mɑp] *s* aljofifa, fregasuelos *m*, estropajo; (*of hair*) espesura ‖ *v* (*pret & pp* **mopped;** *ger* **mopping**) *tr* aljofifar; enjugarse (*la frente con un pañuelo*); **to mop up** limpiar de enemigos

mope [mop] *intr* andar abatido, entregarse a la melancolía

moped [`mopɛd] *s* motoneta

mopish [`mopɪʃ] *adj* abatido, melancólico

moral [`mɑrəl] o [`mɔrəl] *adj* moral ‖ *s* (*of a fable*) moraleja, moral *f*; **morals** (*ethics; conduct*) moral *f*

moral certainty *s* evidencia moral

morale [mə`ræl] o [mə`rɑl] *s* moral *f* (*estado de ánimo, confianza en sí mismo*)

morali•ty [mə`ræliti] *s* (*pl* **-ties**) moralidad

morals charge *s* acusación por delito sexual

morass [mə`ræs] *s* pantano

moratori•um [,mɔrə`tori•əm] o [,mɑrə`tori•əm] *s* (*pl* **-ums** o **-a** [əl]) *s* moratoria

morbid [`mɔrbɪd] *adj* (*feelings, curiosity*) malsano; (*gruesome*) horripilante; (*pertaining to disease; pathologic*) morboso

mordacious [mɔr`deʃəs] *adj* mordaz

mordant [`mɔrdənt] *adj* mordaz ‖ *s* mordiente *m*

more [mor] *adj & adv* más; **more and more** cada vez más; **more than** más que; (*followed by numeral*) más de; (*followed by verb*) más de lo que ‖ *s* más *m*

more•o′ver *adv* además, por otra parte

Moresque [mo`rɛsk] *adj* moro; (archit) árabe ‖ *s* estilo árabe

morgue [mɔrg] *s* depósito de cadáveres

moribund [`mɔri,bʌnd] o [`mɑri,bʌnd] *adj* moribundo

Moris•co [mə`risko] *adj* morisco, moro ‖ *s* (*pl* **-cos** o **-coes**) moro; moro de España;

(*offspring of mulatto and Spaniard, in Mexico*) morisco

morning [`mɔrnɪŋ] *adj* matinal ‖ *s* mañana; (*time between midnight and dawn*) madrugada; **in the morning** de mañana, por la mañana

morning coat *s* chaqué *m*

morn′ing•glo′ry *s* (*pl* **-ries**) dondiego de día

morning sickness *s* vómitos del embarazo

morning star *s* lucero del alba

Moroccan [mə`rɑkən] *adj & s* marroquí *mf* o marroquín *m*

morocco [mə`rɑko] *s* (*leather*) marroquí *m* o marroquín *m* ‖ **Morocco** *s* Marruecos *m*

moron [`mɑrɑn] *s* (*person of arrested intelligence*) morón *m*; (coll) imbécil *mf*

morose [mə`ros] *adj* adusto, hosco, malhumorado

morphine [`mɔrfin] *s* morfina

morphology [mɔr`fɑlədʒi] *s* morfología

Morris chair [`mɑrɪs] o [`mɔrɪs] *s* poltrona extensible

morrow [`mɑro] o [`mɔro] *s* (*future time*) mañana *m*; (*time following some event*) día *m* siguiente; **on the morrow** en el día de mañana; el día siguiente

morsel [`mɔrsəl] *s* bocadito; pedacito

mortal [`mɔrtəl] *adj & s* mortal *m*

mortality [mɔr`tæliti] *s* mortalidad; (*death or destruction on a large scale*) mortandad

mortar [`mɔrtər] *s* (*bowl used for crushing; mixture of lime, etc.*) mortero; (arti) mortero

mor′tar•board′ *s* esparavel *m*; gorro académico cuadrado

mortgage [`mɔrgɪdʒ] *s* hipoteca ‖ *tr* hipotecar

mortgagee [,mɔrgɪ`dʒi] *s* acreedor hipotecario

mortgagor [`mɔrgɪdʒər] *s* deudor hipotecario

mortician [mɔr`tɪʃən] *s* empresario de pompas fúnebres

morti•fy [`mɔrti,faɪ] *v* (*pret & pp* **-fied**) *tr* humillar; mortificar (*el cuerpo, las pasiones*); **to be mortified** avergonzarse

mortise [`mɔrtɪs] *s* mortaja, muesca ‖ *tr* amortajar, enmuescar

mortise lock *s* cerradura embutida

mortuar•y [`mɔrtʃʊ,ɛri] *adj* mortuorio ‖ *s* (*pl* **-ies**) depósito de cadáveres; funeraria

mosaic [mo`ze•ɪk] *m* mosaico

Moscow [`mɑskaʊ] o [`mɑsko] *s* Moscú

Moses [`mozɪz] o [`mozɪs] *s* Moisés *m*

Mos•lem [`mɑzləm] o [`mɑsləm] *adj & s* var of **Muslim**, musulmán *m*

mosque [mɑsk] *s* mezquita

mosqui•to [məs`kito] *s* (*pl* **-toes** o **-tos**) mosquito

mosquito net *s* mosquitero

moss [mɔs] o [mɑs] *s* musgo

moss′back′ *s* (coll) reaccionario; (*old-fashioned person*) (coll) fósil *m*

moss•y [`mɔsi] o [`mɑsi] *adj* (*comp* **-ier;** *super* **-iest**) musgoso

most [most] *adj* más; la mayor parte de, los más de ‖ *adv* más; muy, sumamente; (coll) casi ‖ *s* la mayor parte, el mayor número, los más; **most of** la mayor parte de, el mayor número de; **to make the most of** sacar el mejor partido de

mostly ['mostli] *adv* por la mayor parte, mayormente; casi

moth [mɔθ] o [maθ] *s* mariposa nocturna; (*clothes moth*) polilla

moth ball *s* bola de alcanfor, bola de naftalina

moth'-ball' fleet *s* (nav) flota en conserva

moth'-eat'en *adj* apolillado; (fig) anticuado

mother ['mʌðər] *adj* (*love*) maternal; (*tongue*) materno; (*country*) madre; (*church*) metropolitano || *s* madre *f*; (*an elderly woman*) (coll) tía || *tr* servir de madre a

mother country *s* madre patria

Mother Goose *s* supuesta autora o narradora de una colección de cuentos infantiles (in Spain: *Cuentos de Calleja*)

motherhood ['mʌðər,hud] *s* maternidad

moth'er-in-law' *s* (*pl* **mothers-in-law**) suegra

moth'er·land' *s* patria

motherless ['mʌðərlɪs] *adj* huérfano de madre, sin madre

motherly ['mʌðərli] *adj* maternal

mother-of-pearl ['mʌðərəv'pʌrl] *adj* nacarado || *s* nácar *m*

Mother's Day *s* día *m* de la madre

mother superior *s* superiora

mother tongue *s* (*language naturally acquired by reason of nationality*) lengua materna; (*language from which another language is derived*) lengua madre, lengua matriz

mother wit *s* gracia natural, chispa

moth hole *s* apolilladura

moth·y ['mɔθi] o ['maθi] *adj* (*comp* **-ier**; *super* **-iest**) apolillado

motif [mo'tif] *s* motivo

motion ['moʃən] *s* movimiento; (*signal, gesture*) seña, indicación; (*in a deliberating assembly*) moción; **to set in motion** poner en acción || *intr* hacer señas con la mano o la cabeza

motionless ['moʃənlɪs] *adj* inmoble, inmóvil

motion picture *s* película cinematográfica

mo'tion-pic'ture *adj* cinematográfico

motivate ['motɪ,vet] *tr* animar, incitar, mover

motive ['motɪv] *adj* (*promoting action*) motivo; (*producing motion*) motor || *s* motivo

motive power *s* fuerza motriz, potencia motora o motriz; (rr) conjunto de locomotoras de un ferrocarril

motley ['matli] *adj* abigarrado; mezclado, variado

motor ['motər] *adj* motor || *s* motor *m*; motor eléctrico; automóvil *m* || *intr* viajar en automóvil

mo'tor·boat' *s* gasolinera, canoa automóvil

mo'tor·bus' *s* autobús *m*

motorcade ['motər,ked] *s* caravana de automóviles

mo'tor·car' *s* automóvil *m*

mo'tor·cy'cle *s* motocicleta

motorist ['motərɪst] *s* motorista *mf*, automovilista *mf*

motorize ['motə,raɪz] *tr* motorizar

motor launch *s* lancha automóvil

motor·man ['motərmən] *s* (*pl* **-men** [mən]) conductor *m* de tranvía, conductor de locomotora eléctrica

motor sailer ['selər] *s* motovelero

motor scooter *s* motoneta

motor ship *s* motonave *f*

motor truck *s* autocamión *m*

motor vehicle *s* vehículo motor, autovehículo

mottle ['matəl] *tr* abigarrar, jaspear, motear

mot·to ['mato] *s* (*pl* **-toes** o **-tos**) lema *m*, divisa

mould [mold] *s, tr, & intr* var de **mold**

moulder ['moldər] *s & intr* var de **molder**

moulding ['moldɪŋ] *s* var de **molding**

mouldy ['moldi] *adj* var de **moldy**

mound [maund] *s* montón *m* de tierra; montecillo

mount [maunt] *s* (*hill, mountain*) monte *m*; (*horse for riding*) montura; (*setting for a jewel*) montadura; soporte *m*; cartón *m*, tela (*en que está pegada una fotografía*); (mach) montaje *m* || *tr* subir (*una escalera, una cuesta*); subir a (*una plataforma*); escalar (*una muralla*); montar (*un servicio; una piedra preciosa*); poner a caballo; pegar (*vistas, pruebas*); (mil) montar (*la guardia*) || *intr* montar, montarse; aumentar, subir (*los precios*)

mountain ['mauntən] *s* montaña; **to make a mountain out of a molehill** hacer de una pulga un camello

mountain climbing *s* alpinismo, montañismo

mountaineer [,mauntə'nɪr] *s* montañés *m*

mountainous ['mauntənəs] *adj* montañoso

mountain railroad *s* ferrocarril *m* de cremallera

mountain range *s* cordillera, sierra

mountain sickness *s* mal *m* de las montañas

mountebank ['maunti,bæŋk] *s* saltabanco

mounting ['mauntɪŋ] *s* (*of a precious stone, of an astronomical instrument*) montura; papel *m* de soporte; papel o tela (*en que está pegada una fotografía*); (mach) montaje *m*

mourn [morn] *tr* llorar (*p.ej., la muerte de una persona*); lamentar (*una desgracia*) || *intr* lamentarse; vestir de luto

mourner ['mornər] *s* doliente *mf*; (*person who makes a public profession of penitence*) penitente *mf*; (*person hired to attend a funeral*) plañidera; **mourners** duelo

mourners' bench *s* banco de los penitentes

mournful ['mornfəl] *adj* (*sorrowful*) doloroso; (*gloomy*) lúgubre

mourning ['mornɪŋ] *s* luto; **to be in mourning** estar de luto

mourning band *s* crespón *m* fúnebre, brazal *m* de luto

mouse [maus] *s* (*pl* **mice** [maɪs]) ratón *m*

mouse'hole' *s* ratonera

mouser ['mauzər] *s* desmurador *m*

mouse'trap' *s* ratonera

mo
mo

moustache [məs'tæʃ] o [məs'tɑʃ] *s* bigote *m*, mostacho

mouth [mauθ] *s* (*pl* **mouths** [mauðz]) boca; (*of a river*) desembocadura, embocadura; **by mouth** por vía bucal; **to be born with a silver spoon in one's mouth** nacer de pie; **to make one's mouth water** hacérsele a uno la boca agua; **to not open one's mouth** no decir esta boca es mía

mouthful ['mauθ,ful] *s* bocado

mouth organ *s* armónica de boca

mouth'piece' *s* (*of wind instrument*) boquilla; (*of bridle*) embocadura; (*spokesman*) portavoz *m*

mouth'wash' *s* enjuague *m*, enjuagadientes *m*

movable ['muvəbəl] *adj* movible, móvil

move [muv] *s* movimiento; (*démarche*) acción, gestión, paso; (*from one house to another*) mudanza; **on the move** en marcha, en movimiento; **to get a move on** (slang) menearse, darse prisa; **to make a move** dar un paso; hacer una jugada ‖ *tr* mover; evacuar (*el vientre*); (*to stir, excite the feelings of*) conmover, enternecer; **to move up** adelantar (*una fecha*) ‖ *intr* moverse; desplazarse (*un viajante; un planeta*); mudarse, mudar de casa; (*e.g., to another store, to another city*) trasladarse; hacer una jugada; hacer una moción; venderse, tener salida (*una mercancía*); evacuarse, moverse (*el vientre*); **to move away** apartarse; marcharse; mudarse de casa; **to move in** instalarse; alternar con, frecuentar (*la buena sociedad*); **to move off** alejarse

movement ['muvmənt] *s* movimiento; aparato de relojería; (*of the bowels*) evacuación; (*e.g., of a symphony*) tiempo

movie ['muvi] *s* película, cinta

movie camera *s* filmadora, cámara cinematográfica

movie•goer ['movi,go•ər] *s* aficionado al cine

movie house *s* cineteatro

mov'ie•land' *s* (coll) cinelandia

movie star *s* cineasta *m*

moving ['muvɪŋ] *adj* conmovedor, impresionante ‖ *s* movimiento; (*from one house to another*) mudanza

moving picture *s* película cinematográfica

moving spirit *s* alma (*de una empresa*)

moving stairway *s* escalera mecánica, móvil o rodante

mow [mo] *v* (*pret* **mowed**; *pp* **mowed** o **mown**) *tr* segar; **to mow down** matar (*soldados*) con fuego graneado ‖ *intr* segar

mower ['mo•ər] *s* segador *m*; segadora mecánica

mowing machine *s* segadora mecánica

Mozarab [mo'zærəb] *s* mozárabe *mf*

Mozarabic [mo'zærəbɪk] *adj* mozárabe

M.P. *abbr* **Member of Parliament, Military Police**

m.p.h. *abbr* **miles per hour**

Mr. ['mɪstər] *s* (*pl* **Messrs.** ['mɛsərz]) señor *m* (*tratamiento*)

Mrs. ['mɪsɪz] *s* señora (*tratamiento*)

MS. o **ms.** *abbr* **manuscript**

Mt. *abbr* **Mount**

much [mʌtʃ] *adj* & *pron* mucho; **too much** demasiado ‖ *adv* mucho; **however much** por mucho que; **how much** cuánto; **too much** demasiado; **very much** muchísimo

mucilage ['mjusɪlɪdʒ] *s* goma para pegar; (*gummy secretion in plants*) mucílago

muck [mʌk] *s* estiércol húmedo; suciedad, porquería; (min) zafra

muck'rake' *intr* (coll) exponer ruindades

mucous ['mjukəs] *adj* mucoso

mucus ['mjukəs] *s* moco

mud [mʌd] *s* barro, fango, lodo; **to sling mud at** llenar de fango

muddle ['mʌdəl] *s* confusión, embrollo ‖ *tr* confundir, embrollar; atontar, aturdir ‖ *intr* obrar torpemente; **to muddle through** salir del paso a pesar suyo

mud'dle•head' *s* farraguista *mf*, cajón *m* de sastre

mud•dy ['mʌdi] *adj* (*comp* **-dier**; *super* **-diest**) barroso, fangoso, lodoso; (*obscure*) turbio ‖ *v* (*pret* & *pp* **-died**) *tr* embarrar, enturbiar

mud'guard' *s* guardabarros *m*

mud'hole' *s* atolladero, ciénaga

mudslinger ['mʌd,slɪŋər] *s* (fig) lanzador *m* de lodo

muezzin [mju'ɛzɪn] *s* almuecín *m*, almuédano

muff [mʌf] *s* manguito ‖ *tr* & *intr* chapucear

muffin ['mʌfɪn] *s* mollete *m*

muffle ['mʌfəl] *tr* arropar; (*about the face*) embozar; amortiguar (*un ruido*); enfundar (*un tambor*)

muffler ['mʌflər] *s* bufanda, tapaboca; (aut) silenciador *m*, silencioso

mufti ['mʌfti] *s* traje *m* de paisano

mug [mʌg] *s* pichel *m*; (slang) jeta, hocico ‖ *v* (*pret* & *pp* **mugged**; *ger* **mugging**) *tr* (slang) fotografiar; (slang) atacar ‖ *intr* (slang) hacer muecas

mugger ['mʌgər] *s* ladrón *m* asaltador

mug•gy ['mʌgi] *adj* (*comp* **-gier**; *super* **-giest**) bochornoso, sofocante

mulat•to [mju'læto] o [mə'læto] *s* (*pl* **-toes**) mulato

mulber•ry ['mʌl,bɛri] *s* (*pl* **-ries**) (*tree*) moral *m*; (*fruit*) mora

mulct [mʌlkt] *tr* defraudar

mule [mjul] *s* mulo, macho; (*slipper*) babucha

mule chair *s* artolas, jamugas

muleteer [,mjulə'tɪr] *s* mulatero

mulish ['mjulɪʃ] *adj* terco, obstinado

mull [mʌl] *tr* calentar (*vino*) con especias ‖ *intr*—**to mull over** reflexionar sobre

mullion ['mʌljən] *s* parteluz *m*

Multigraph ['mʌltɪ,græf] o ['mʌltɪ,grɑf] *s* (trademark) multígrafo ‖ *tr* multigrafiar

multilateral [,mʌltɪ'lætərəl] *adj* (*having many sides*) multilátero; (*participated in by more than two nations*) multilateral

multinational corporations *spl* multinacionales *mpl*

multiple ['mʌltɪpəl] *adj* múltiple, múltiplo ‖ *s* (math) múltiplo

multiple sclerosis *s* esclerosis *f* múltiple
multiplex [ˈmʌltɪˌplɛks] *adj* múltiple
multiplici·ty [ˌmʌltɪˈplɪsɪti] *s* (*pl* **-ties**) multiplicidad
multi·ply [ˈmʌltɪˌplaɪ] *v* (*pret & pp* **-plied**) *tr* multiplicar || *intr* multiplicar, multiplicarse
multipurpose [ˌmʌltɪˈpʌrpəs] *adj* múltiple de uso; versátil
multitude [ˈmʌltɪˌtjud] o [ˈmʌltɪˌtud] *s* multitud
mum [mʌm] *adj* callado; **mum's the word!** ¡punto en boca!; **to keep mum about** callar || *interj* ¡chitón!
mumble [ˈmʌmbəl] *tr & intr* mascullar, mascujar
mummer·y [ˈmʌməri] *s* (*pl* **-ies**) mojiganga
mum·my [ˈmʌmi] *s* (*pl* **-mies**) momia
mumps [mʌmps] *s* papera
munch [mʌnʧ] *tr* ronzar
mundane [ˈmʌnden] *adj* mundano
municipal [mjuˈnɪsɪpəl] *adj* municipal
municipali·ty [mjuˌnɪsɪˈpælɪti] *s* (*pl* **-ties**) municipio
munificent [mjuˈnɪfɪsənt] *adj* munífico
munition [mjuˈnɪʃən] *s* munición || *tr* municionar
munition dump *s* depósito de municiones
mural [ˈmjʊrəl] *adj* mural || *s* pintura mural; decoración mural
murder [ˈmʌrdər] *s* asesinato, homicidio || *tr* asesinar; (*to spoil, mar*) (coll) estropear
murderer [ˈmʌrdərər] *s* asesino
murderess [ˈmʌrdərɪs] *s* asesina
murderous [ˈmʌrdərəs] *adj* asesino; cruel, sanguinario
murk·y [ˈmʌrki] *adj* (*comp* **-ier**; *super* **-iest**) (*hazy*) calinoso; (*gloomy*) lóbrego
murmur [ˈmʌrmər] *s* murmullo || *tr & intr* murmurar
mus. *abbr* **museum, music**
muscle [ˈmʌsəl] *s* músculo; (fig) fuerza muscular
muscular [ˈmʌskjələr] *adj* musculoso
muse [mjuz] *s* musa; **the Muses** las Musas || *intr* meditar, reflexionar; **to muse on** contemplar
museum [mjuˈzi·əm] *s* museo
mush [mʌʃ] *s* gachas; (coll) sentimentalismo exagerado, sensiblería
mush'room' *s* hongo, seta || *intr* aparecer de la noche a la mañana; **to mushroom into** convertirse rápidamente en
mushroom cloud *s* nube-hongo *f*
mush·y [ˈmʌʃi] *adj* (*comp* **-ier**; *super* **-iest**) mollar, pulposo; (coll) sensiblero, sobón; (*with women*) (coll) baboso; **to be mushy** (coll) hacerse unas gachas
music [ˈmjuzɪk] *s* música; **to face the music** (coll) afrontar las consecuencias; **to set to music** poner en música
musical [ˈmjuzɪkəl] *adj* musical, músico
musical comedy *s* comedia musical
musicale [ˌmjuzɪˈkæl] *s* velada musical, concierto casero
music box *s* caja de música
music cabinet *s* musiquero

music hall *s* salón *m* de conciertos; (Brit) teatro de variedades
musician [mjuˈzɪʃən] *s* músico
musicianship [mjuˈzɪʃənˌʃɪp] *s* musicalidad
musicologist [ˌmjuzɪˈkalədʒɪst] *s* musicólogo
musicology [ˌmjuzɪˈkalədʒi] *s* musicología
music rack o **music stand** *s* atril *m*
musk [mʌsk] *s* almizcle *m*; olor *m* de almizcle
musk deer *s* almizclero
musket [ˈmʌskɪt] *s* mosquete *m*
musketeer [ˌmʌskɪˈtɪr] *s* mosquetero
musk'mel'on *s* melón *m*
musk'rat' *s* almizclera
Muslim [ˈmʌzləm] o [ˈmʌsləm] *adj* muslime, islámico, mahometano || *s* muslime *mf*, musulmán *m*
muslin [ˈmʌzlɪn] *s* muselina
muss [mʌs] *tr* (*the hair*) (coll) descabellar, desarreglar; (*clothing*) (coll) chafar, arrugar
muss·y [ˈmʌsi] *adj* (*comp* **-ier**; *super* **-iest**) desaliñado, desgreñado
must [mʌst] *s* mosto; (*mold*) moho; cosa que debe hacerse || *v aux* **I must study my lesson** debo estudiar mi lección; **he must work tomorrow** tiene que trabajar mañana; **she must be ill** estará enferma
mustache [məsˈtæʃ], [məsˈtɑʃ], o [ˈmʌstæʃ] *s* bigote *m*, mostacho
mustard [ˈmʌstərd] *s* mostaza
mustard gas *s* gas *m* mostaza
mustard plaster *s* sinapismo, cataplasma *f*
muster [ˈmʌstər] *s* asamblea; matrícula de revista; **to pass muster** pasar revista; ser aceptable || *tr* llamar a asamblea; reunir para pasar revista; reunir, acumular; **to muster in** alistar; **to muster out** dar de baja a; **to muster up courage** cobrar ánimo
muster roll *s* lista de revista
mus·ty [ˈmʌsti] *adj* (*comp* **-tier**; *super* **-tiest**) (*moldy*) mohoso; (*stale*) trasnochado; anticuado, pasado de moda
mutation [mjuˈteʃən] *s* mutación
mute [mjut] *adj & s* mudo || *tr* poner sordina a
mutilate [ˈmjutɪˌlet] *tr* mutilar
mutilated *adj* mútilo, mutilado, mocho
mutineer [ˌmjutɪˈnɪr] *s* amotinado
mutinous [ˈmjutɪnəs] *adj* amotinado
muti·ny [ˈmjutɪni] *s* (*pl* **-nies**) motín *m* || *v* (*pret & pp* **-nied**) *intr* amotinarse
mutt [mʌt] *s* (slang) perro cruzado; (slang) bobo, tonto
mutter [ˈmʌtər] *tr & intr* murmurar
mutton [ˈmʌtən] *s* carnero, carne *f* de carnero
mutton chop *s* chuleta de carnero
mutual [ˈmuʧu·əl] *adj* mutual, mutuo
mutual aid *s* apoyo mutuo
mutual benefit association *s* mutualidad
mutual fund *s* sociedad inversionista mutualista
muzzle [ˈmʌzəl] *s* (*projecting part of head of animal*) hocico; (*device to keep animal from biting*) bozal *m*; (*of firearm*) boca || *tr*

mo
mu

abozalar; (*to keep from speaking*) amordazar
my [maɪ] *adj poss* mi
myriad [ˈmɪrɪ•əd] *s* miríada
myrrh [mʌr] *s* mirra
myrtle [ˈmʌrtəl] *s* arrayán *m*, mirto
myself [maɪˈsɛlf] *pron pers* yo mismo; mí, mí mismo; me, p.ej., **I enjoyed myself** me divertí; **with myself** conmigo
mysterious [mɪsˈtɪrɪ•əs] *adj* misterioso
myster•y [ˈmɪstəri] *s* (*pl* **-ies**) misterio
mystic [ˈmɪstɪk] *adj* & *s* místico
mystical [ˈmɪstɪkəl] *adj* místico

mysticism [ˈmɪstɪˌsɪzəm] *s* misticismo
mystification [ˌmɪstɪfɪˈkeʃən] *s* confusión, mistificación
mysti•fy [ˈmɪstɪˌfaɪ] *v* (*pret* & *pp* **-fied**) *tr* rodear de misterio; (*to hoax*) confundir, mistificar
myth [mɪθ] *s* mito
mythical [ˈmɪθɪkəl] *adj* mítico
mythological [ˌmɪθəˈlɑdʒɪkəl] *adj* mitológico
mytholo•gy [mɪˈθɑlədʒi] *s* (*pl* **-gies**) mitología

N

N, n [ɛn] decimocuarta letra del alfabeto inglés
n. *abbr* **neuter, nominative, noon, north, noun, number**
N. *abbr* **Nationalist, Navy, Noon, North, November**
N.A. *abbr* **National Academy, National Army, North America**
nab [næb] *v* (*pret* & *pp* **nabbed**; *ger* **nabbing**) *tr* (slang) agarrar, coger; (slang) poner preso, prender
nag [næg] *s* caballejo, jaco; pequeño caballo de silla ‖ *v* (*pret* & *pp* **nagged**; *ger* **nagging**) *tr* importunar regañando ‖ *intr* regañar
naiad [ˈne•æd] o [ˈnaɪ•æd] *s* náyade *f*; (fig) nadadora
nail [nel] *s* (*of finger*) uña; (*to fasten wood, etc.*) clavo; **to hit the nail on the head** dar en el clavo ‖ *tr* clavar
nail brush *s* cepillo de uñas
nail clippers *spl* cortauñas *m*
nail file *s* lima para las uñas
nail polish *s* esmalte *m* para las uñas, laca de uñas
nailset [ˈnel,sɛt] *s* contrapunzón *m*
naïve [nɑˈiv] *adj* cándido, ingenuo
naked [ˈnekɪd] *adj* desnudo; **to go naked** ir desnudo, andar a la cordobana; **to strip naked** desnudar; desnudarse; **with the naked eye** a simple vista
name [nem] *s* nombre *m*; (*first name*) nombre de pila; (*last name*) apellido; fama, reputación, renombre *m*; linaje, *m*, raza; **to call someone names** maltratar a uno de palabra; **to go by the name of** ser conocido por el nombre de; **to make a name for oneself** darse a conocer, hacerse un nombre; **what is your name?** ¿cómo se llama Vd.? ‖ *tr* nombrar; fijar (*un precio*)
name day *s* santo
nameless [ˈnemlɪs] *adj* sin nombre, anónimo
namely [ˈnemli] *adv* a saber, es decir
namesake [ˈnem,sek] *s* homónimo, tocayo
nanny goat [ˈnæni] *s* (coll) cabra

nap [næp] *s* lanilla, flojel *m*; sueñecillo; **to take a nap** descabezar un sueñecillo ‖ *v* (*pret* & *pp* **napped**; *ger* **napping**) *intr* echar un sueñecillo; estar desprevenido; **to catch napping** coger desprevenido
napalm [ˈnepɑm] *s* (mil) gelatina incendiaria
nape [nep] *s* cogote *m*, nuca
naphtha [ˈnæfθə] *s* nafta
napkin [ˈnæpkɪn] *s* servilleta; (*of a baby*) (Brit) pañal *m*
napkin ring *s* servilletero
Naples [ˈnepəlz] *s* Nápoles
Napoleonic [nə,polɪˈɑnɪk] *adj* napoleónico
narc [nɑrk] *s* (slang) agente *m* de policía antidroga
narcissus [nɑrˈsɪsəs] *s* (bot) narciso ‖ **Narcissus** *s* Narciso
narcotic [nɑrˈkɑtɪk] *adj* & *s* narcótico
narrate [næˈret] *tr* narrar
narration [næˈreʃən] *s* narración
narrative [ˈnærətɪv] *adj* narrativo ‖ *s* (*story, tale; art of telling stories*) narrativa
narrator [næˈretər] *s* narrador *m*
narrow [ˈnæro] *adj* angosto, estrecho; intolerante; minucioso; (*sense of a word*) estricto ‖ **narrows** *spl* angostura, paso estrecho ‖ *tr* enangostar, estrechar; reducir, limitar ‖ *intr* enangostarse, estrecharse; reducirse, limitarse
narrow escape *s* trance *m* difícil; **to have a narrow escape** escapar por un pelo, salvarse en una tabla
narrow gauge *s* trocha angosta, vía estrecha
narrow-minded [ˈnæroˈmaɪndɪd] *adj* intolerante, de miras estrechas, poco liberal
nasal [ˈnezəl] *adj* & *s* nasal *f*
nasalize [ˈnezə,laɪz] *tr* nasalizar ‖ *intr* ganguear
nasturtium [nəˈstʌrʃəm] *s* capuchina, espuela de galán
nas•ty [ˈnæsti] *adj* (*comp* **-tier**; *super* **-tiest**) asqueroso, sucio; desagradable; desvergonzado; amenazador; horrible
natatorium [ˌnetəˈtorɪ•əm] *s* piscina de natación
nation [ˈneʃən] *s* nación

national [ˈnæʃənəl] *adj & s* nacional *mf*
national anthem *s* himno nacional
national hero *s* benemérito de la patria
national holiday *s* fiesta nacional
nationalism [ˈnæʃənəˌlɪzəm] *s* nacionalismo
nationalist [ˈnæ‚ʃənəlɪst] *adj & s* nacionalista *mf*
nationali·ty [ˈnæ‚ʃənˌælɪti] *s* (*pl* **-ties**) nacionalidad, naturalidad
nationalize [ˈnæʃənəˌlaɪz] *tr* nacionalizar
na'tion-wide *adj* de toda la nación
native [ˈnetɪv] *adj* nativo, natural; indígena; (*language*) materno; **to go native** vivir como los indígenas ǁ *s* natural *mf;* indígena *mf*
native land *s* patria
nativi·ty [nəˈtɪvɪti] *s* (*pl* **-ties**) nacimiento ǁ **Nativity** *s* (*day; festival; painting*) natividad
NATO [ˈneto] *s* (acronym) la O.T.A.N.
nat·ty [ˈnæti] *adj.* (*comp* **-tier;** *super* **-tier;** *super* **-tiest**) elegante, garboso
natural [ˈnætʃərəl] *adj* natural; (*mus*) natural ǁ *s* imbécil *mf;* (mus) tono natural, nota natural; (*sign*) (mus) becuadro; (mus) tecla blanca; (coll) cosa de éxito certero
naturalism [ˈnætʃərəˌlɪzəm] *s* naturalismo
naturalist [ˈnætʃərəlɪst] *s* naturalista *mf*
naturalization [ˌnætʃərəlɪˈzəʃən] *s* naturalización
naturalization papers *spl* carta de naturaleza
naturalize [ˈnætʃərəˌlaɪz] *tr* naturalizar
naturally [ˈnætʃərəli] *adv* naturalmente; claro, desde luego, por supuesto
nature [ˈnetʃər] *s* naturaleza; **from nature** del natural
naught [nɔt] *s* nada; cero; **to bring to naught** anular, invalidar, destruir; **to come to naught** reducirse a nada, frustrarse
naugh·ty [ˈnɔti] *adj* (*comp* **-tier;** *super* **-tiest**) desobediente, pícaro; desvergonzado; (*story, tale*) verde
nausea [ˈnɔʃɪ·ə] o [ˈnɔsɪ·ə] *s* náusea
nauseate [ˈnɔʃɪˌet] o [ˈnɔsɪˌet] *tr* dar náuseas a ǁ *intr* nausear, marearse
nauseating [ˈnɔʃɪˌetɪŋ] o [ˈnɔsɪˌetɪŋ] *adj* nauseabundo, asqueroso
nauseous [ˈnɔʃɪ·əs] o [ˈnɔsɪ·əs] *adj* nauseabundo
nautical [ˈnɔtɪkəl] *adj* náutico, marino, naval
nav. *abbr* **naval, navigation**
naval [ˈnevəl] *adj* naval, naval militar
Naval Academy *s* (U.S.A.) Escuela Naval Militar
naval officer *s* oficial *m* de marina
naval station *s* apostadero
nave [nev] *s* (*of a church*) nave *f* central, nave principal; (*of a wheel*) cubo
navel [ˈnevəl] *s* ombligo; (*center point, middle*) (fig) ombligo
navel orange *s* navel *f,* naranja de ombligo
navigability [ˌnævɪgəˈbɪlɪti] *s* (*of a river*) navegabilidad; (*of a ship*) buen gobierno
navigable [ˈnævɪgəbəl] *adj* (*river, canal, etc.*) navegable; (*ship*) marinero, de buen gobierno
navigate [ˈnævɪˌget] *tr & intr* navegar

navigation [ˈnævɪˌgeʃən] *s* navegación
navigator [ˈnævɪˌgetər] *s* navegador *m,* navegante *m;* (*he who is in charge of course of ship or plane*) oficial *m* de derrota; (Brit) peón *m*
nav·vy [ˈnævi] *s* (*pl* **-vies**) (Brit) bracero, peón *m*
na·vy [ˈnevi] *adj* azul oscuro ǁ *s* (*pl* **-vies**) marina de guerra; (*personnel*) marina; azul oscuro
navy bean *s* frijol blanco común
navy blue *s* azul marino, azul oscuro
navy yard *s* arsenal *m* de puerto
Nazarene [ˌnæzəˈrin] *adj & s* nazareno
Nazi [ˈnɑtsi] o [ˈnætsi] *adj & s* nazi *mf,* nacista *mf*
n.b. *abbr* **nota bene** (Lat) **note well**
N-bomb [ˈenˌbɑm] *s* bomba de neutrones
Neapolitan [ˌni·əˈpɑlitən] *adj & s* napolitano
neap tide [nip] *s* marea muerta
near [nɪr] *adj* cercano, próximo; íntimo; imitado ǁ *adv* cerca; íntimamente ǁ *prep* cerca de; hacia, por ǁ *tr* acercarse a ǁ *intr* acercarse
nearby [ˈnɪrˌbaɪ] *adj* cercano, próximo ǁ *adv* cerca
Near East *s* Cercano Oriente, Próximo Oriente
nearly [ˈnɪrli] *adv* casi; de cerca; íntimamente; por poco, p.ej., **he nearly fell** por poco se cae
near-sighted [ˈnɪrˌsaɪtɪd] *adj* miope
near-sightedness *s* miopía
neat [nit] *adj* aseado, pulcro; pulido; diestro, primoroso; puro, sin mezcla ǁ *ssg* res vacuna ǁ *spl* ganado vacuno
neat's'-foot oil *s* aceite *m* de pie de buey
Nebuchadnezzar [ˌnɛbjəkədˈnɛzər] *s* Nabucodonosor *m*
nebu·la [ˈnɛbjələ] *s* (*pl* **-lae** [ˌli] o **-las**) nebulosa
nebular [ˈnɛbjələr] *adj* nebular
nebulous [ˈnɛbjələs] *adj* nebuloso
necessary [ˈnɛsɪˌsɛri] *adj* necesario
necessitate [nɪˈsɛsɪˌtet] *tr* necesitar, exigir
necessitous [nɪˈsɛsɪtəs] *adj* necesitado
necessi·ty [nɪˈsɛsɪti] *s* (*pl* **-ties**) necesidad
neck [nɛk] *s* cuello; (*of a bottle*) gollete *m;* (*of violin or guitar*) mástil *m;* istmo, península; estrecho; **neck and neck** parejos; **to break one's neck** (coll) matarse trabajando; **to stick one's neck out** (coll) descubrir el cuerpo ǁ *intr* (slang) acariciarse (*dos enamorados*)
neck'band' *s* tirilla de camisa
necklace [ˈnɛklɪs] *s* gargantilla, collar *m*
necktie [ˈnɛkˌtaɪ] *s* corbata
necktie pin *s* alfiler *m* de corbata
necrology [nɛˈkrɑlədʒi] *s* necrología
necromancy [ˈnɛkrəˌmænsi] *s* necromancia, nigromancia
nectarine [ˌnɛktəˈrin] *s* griñón *m*
née o **nee** [ne] *adj* nacida o de soltera, p.ej., **Mary Wilson, née Miller** Maria Wilson, nacida Miller o María Wilson, de soltera Miller

need [nid] *s* necesidad; pobreza; **in need** necesitado || *tr* necesitar || *intr* estar necesitado; ser necesario || *v aux*—**if need be** si fuere necesario; **to need** + *inf* deber, tener que + *inf*

needful ['nidfəl] *adj* necesario || **the needful** lo necesario; (slang) el dinero

needle ['nidəl] *s* aguja; **to look for a needle in a haystack** buscar una aguja en un pajar || *tr* coser con aguja; (coll) aguijonear, incitar; (coll) añadir alcohol a (*la cerveza o el vino*)

needle bath *s* ducha en alfileres

needle′case′ *s* alfiletero

needle point *s* bordado al pasado; encaje *m* de mano

needless ['nidlɪs] *adj* innecesario, inútil

needle′work′ *s* costura, labor *f*

needs [nidz] *adv* necesariamente, forzosamente

need∙y ['nidi] *adj* (*comp* **-ier;** *super* **-iest**) necesitado, indigente || **the needy** los necesitados

ne′er-do-well ['nɛrdu,wɛl] *adj & s* holgazán, perdido

negation [nɪ'geʃən] *s* negación

negative ['nɛgətɪv] *adj* negativo || *s* negativa; electricidad negativa, borne negativo; (gram) negación; (math) término negativo; (phot) prueba negativa || *tr* desaprobar; anular

neglect [nɪ'glɛkt] *s* negligencia, descuido || *tr* descuidar; **to neglect to** dejar de, olvidarse de

neglectful [nɪ'glɛktfəl] *adj* negligente, descuidado

négligée o **negligee** [,nɛglɪ'ʒe] *s* bata de mujer, traje *m* de casa

negligence ['nɛglɪdʒəns] *s* negligencia, descuido

negligent ['nɛglɪdʒənt] *adj* negligente, descuidado

negligible ['nɛglɪdʒɪbəl] *adj* insignificante, imperceptible

negotiable [nɪ'goʃɪ•əbəl] *adj* negociable; transitable

negotiate [nɪ'goʃɪ,et] *tr* negociar; (coll) salvar, vencer || *intr* negociar

negotiation [nɪ,goʃɪ'eʃən] *s* negociación; trámite *m;* **round of negotiations** ronda negociadora

Ne∙gro ['nigro] *adj* (*usually offensive*) negro || *s* (*pl* **-groes**) (*usually offensive*) negro

neigh [ne] *s* relincho || *intr* relinchar

neighbor ['nebər] *adj* vecino || *s* vecino; (*fellow man*) prójimo || *tr* ser vecino de; ser amigo de || *intr* estar cercano; tener relaciones amistosas

neighborhood ['nebər,hʊd] *s* vecindad, vecindario, cercanías; **in the neighborhood of** en las inmediaciones de; (coll) cerca de, aproximadamente

neighboring ['nebərɪŋ] *adj* vecino, colindante

neighborly ['nebərli] *adj* buen vecino, amable, sociable

neither ['niðər] o ['naɪðər] *adj indef* ninguno . . . (de los dos); **neither one** ninguno de los dos || *pron indef* ninguno (de los dos); ni uno ni otro, ni lo uno ni lo otro || *conj* ni; tampoco, ni . . . tampoco, p.ej., **neither do I** yo tampoco, ni yo tampoco; **neither . . . nor** ni . . . ni

neme∙sis ['nɛmɪsɪs] *s* (*pl* **-ses** [,siz]) (*someone or something that punishes*) némesis *f* || **Nemesis** *s* Némesis *f*

neologism [ni'ɑlə,dʒɪzəm] *s* neologismo

neomycin [,ni•ə'maɪsɪn] *s* neomicina

neon ['ni•ɑn] *s* neo, neón *m*

neophyte ['ni•ə,faɪt] *s* neófito

Nepal [nɪ'pɔl] *s* el Nepal

Nepa∙lese [,nɛpə'liz] *adj* nepalés || *s* (*pl* **-lese**) nepalés *m*

nepenthe [nɪ'pɛnθi] *s* nepente *m*

nephew ['nɛfju] o ['nɛvju] *s* sobrino

Nepos ['nipɑs] o ['nipəs] *s* Nepote *m*

Neptune ['nɛptʃun] o ['nɛptjun] *s* Neptuno

neptunium [nɛp'tʃuni•əm] o [nɛp'tjuni•əm] *s* neptunio

nerd [nʌrd] *s* (slang) tipo insípido; sujeto estúpido

Nereid ['nɪri•ɪd] *s* nereida

Nero ['niro] *s* Nerón *m*

nerve [nʌrv] *adj* (*center; system; tonic; disease; prostration; breakdown*) nervioso || *s* nervio; ánimo, valor *m;* audacia; (coll) descaro; **nerves** excitabilidad nerviosa; **to get on one's nerves** irritar los nervios a uno; **to strain every nerve** esforzarse al máximo

nerve-racking ['nʌrv,rækɪŋ] *adj* irritante, exasperante

nervous ['nʌrvəs] *adj* nervioso

nervous breakdown *s* colapso nervioso

nervousness ['nʌrvəsnɪs] *s* nerviosidad

nervous shudder *s* muerte chiquita

nerv∙y ['nʌrvi] *adj* (*comp* **-ier;** *super* **-iest**) (*strong, vigorous*) nervioso; atrevido, audaz; (coll) descarado

nest [nɛst] *s* nido; (*where hen lays eggs*) nidal *m;* (*birds in a nest*) nidada; (*set of things fitting within each other*) juego; (*of, e.g., thieves*) nido; **to feather one's nest** hacer todo para enriquecerse || *tr* colocar en un nido || *intr* anidar

nest egg *s* (*eggs left in a nest to induce hen to lay more*) nidal *m;* ahorros, hucha

nestle ['nɛsəl] *tr* poner en un nido; arrimar afectuosamente || *intr* anidar; arrimarse cómodamente; **to nestle up to** arrimarse a

net [nɛt] *adj* neto, líquido || *s* red *f;* precio neto, peso neto, ganancia líquida || *v* (*pret & pp* **netted;** *super* **netting**) *tr* enredar, tejer; coger con red; producir (*cierta ganancia líquida*)

nether ['nɛðər] *adj* inferior, más bajo

Netherlander ['nɛðər,lændər] o ['nɛðərləndər] *s* neerlandés *m*

Netherlandish ['nɛðər,lændɪʃ] o ['nɛðərləndɪʃ] *adj* neerlandés || *s* neerlandés *m*

Netherlands, The ['nɛðərləndz] los Países Bajos (*Holanda*)

netting ['nɛtɪŋ] s red f
nettle ['nɛtəl] s ortiga ‖ tr irritar, provocar
net'work' s red f; (rad & telv) cadena
neuralgia [njuˈrældʒə] s neuralgia
neurology [njuˈralədʒi] s neurología
neuron ['njurɑn] o ['nurɑn] s neurona
neuro•sis [njuˈrosɪs] s (pl -ses [siz]) neurosis f
neurotic [njuˈrɑtɪk] adj & s neurótico
neut. abbr **neuter**
neuter ['ˈnjutər] adj neutro ‖ s género neutro; (aut) punto muerto
neutral ['njutrəl] adj (on neither side in a quarrel or war) neutral; (having little or no color) neutro; (bot, chem, elec, phonet, zool) neutro ‖ s neutral mf; (aut) punto neutral, punto muerto
neutralism ['njutrə,lɪzəm] s neutralismo
neutralist ['njutrəlɪst] adj & s neutralista mf
neutrality [njuˈtrælɪti] s neutralidad
neutralize ['njutrə,laɪz] tr neutralizar
neutron ['njutrɑn] s neutrón m
neutron bomb s bomba de neutrones, bomba neutrónica
never ['nɛvər] adv nunca; en mi vida; de ningún modo; **never fear** no hay cuidado; **never mind** no importa
nev'er•more' adv nunca más
nevertheless [,nɛvərðəˈlɛs] adv no obstante, sin embargo
new [nju] o [nu] adj nuevo; **what's new?** ¿qué hay de nuevo?
new arrival s recién llegado; recién nacido
new'born' adj recién nacido; renacido
New Castile s Castilla la Nueva
New'cas'tle s—**to carry coals to Newcastle** echar agua al mar, llevar hierro a Vizcaya, llevar leña al monte
newcomer ['nju,kʌmər] s recién llegado, recién venido
New England s la Nueva Inglaterra
newfangled ['nju,fæŋgəld] adj de última moda, recién inventado
Newfoundland ['njufənd,lænd] s (island and province) Terranova ‖ [njuˈfaʊndlənd] s (dog) Terranova m
newly ['njuli] adv nuevamente; **newly** + pp recién + pp
new'ly•wed' s recién casado
New Mexican adj & s neomejicano, nuevo-mejicano
New Mexico s Nuevo Méjico
new moon s luna nueva, novilunio
news [njuz] o [nuz] s noticias; periódico; **a news item** una noticia; **a piece of news** una noticia
news agency s agencia de noticias
news beat s exclusiva, anticipación de una noticia por un periódico
news'boy' s vendedor m de periódicos
news'cast' s noticiario radiofónico ‖ tr radiodifundir (noticias) ‖ intr radiodifundir noticias
news'cast'er s cronista mf de radio
news conference s var de **press conference**
news coverage s reportaje m
news'let'ter s circular f noticiera

news•man ['njuzmən] s (pl -men [mən]) noticiero
New South Wales s la Nueva Gales del Sur
news'pa'per adj periodístico ‖ s periódico
newspaper•man ['njuz,pepər,mæn] s (pl -men [,mɛn]) periodista m
news'print' s papel-prensa m
news'reel' s actualidades, noticiario cinematográfico
news'stand' s quiosco de periódicos, puesto de periódicos
news'week'ly s (pl -lies) semanario de noticias
news'wor'thy adj de gran actualidad, de interés periodístico
news•y ['njuzi] adj (comp -ier; super -iest) (coll) informativo
new'-world' adj del Nuevo Mundo
New Year's card s tarjeta de felicitación de Año Nuevo
New Year's Day s el Día de Año Nuevo
New Year's Eve s la noche vieja, la víspera de año nuevo
New York [jɔrk] adj neoyorkino ‖ s Nueva York
New Yorker ['jɔrkər] s neoyorkino
New Zealand ['zilənd] adj neocelandés ‖ s Nueva Zelanda
New Zealander ['ziləndər] s neocelandés m
next [nɛkst] adj próximo, siguiente; de al lado; venidero, que viene ‖ adv luego, después; la próxima vez; **next to** junto a; después de; **next to nothing** casi nada; **the next best** lo mejor después de eso; **to come next** venir después, ser el que sigue
next door s la casa de al lado; **next door to** en la casa siguiente de; (coll) casi
next'door' adj siguiente, de al lado
next of kin s (pl **next of kin**) pariente más cercano
niacin ['naɪ•əsɪn] s niacina
Niagara Falls [naɪˈægərə] spl las Cataratas del Niágara
nibble ['nɪbəl] s mordisco ‖ tr & intr mordiscar; picar (un pez); **to nibble at** picar de o en
Nicaraguan [,nɪkəˈrɑgwən] adj & s nicaragüense, nicaragüeño
nice [naɪs] adj delicado, fino, sutil; primoroso, pulido, refinado; dengoso, melindroso; atento, cortés, culto; escrupuloso, esmerado; agradable, simpático; decoroso, conveniente; complaciente; preciso; satisfactorio; (weather) bueno; (attractive) bonito; **nice and . . .** (coll) muy, mucho; **not nice** (coll) feo
nice-looking ['naɪsˈlukɪŋ] adj hermoso, guapo, bien parecido
nicely ['naɪsli] adv con precisión; escrupulosamente; satisfactoriamente; (coll) muy bien
nice•ty ['naɪsəti] s (pl -ties) precisión; sutileza; finura; **to a nicety** con la mayor precisión
niche [nɪtʃ] s hornacina, nicho; colocación conveniente
Nicholas ['nɪkələs] s Nicolás m

ne
ni

nick [nɪk] s mella, muesca; **in the nick of time** en el momento crítico ‖ tr mellar, hacer muescas en; cortar

nickel [ˈnɪkəl] s níquel m; (U.S.A.) moneda de cinco centavos ‖ tr niquelar

nick´el-plate´ tr niquelar

nicknack [ˈnɪkˌnæk] s chuchería, friolera

nick´name´ s apodo, mote m ‖ tr apodar

nicotine [ˈnɪkəˌtin] s nicotina

niece [nis] s sobrina

nif•ty [ˈnɪfti] adj (comp **-tier;** super **-tiest**) (slang) elegante; (slang) excelente

niggard [ˈnɪgərd] adj & s tacaño

night [naɪt] adj nocturno ‖ s noche f; **at** o **by night** de noche o por la noche; **night before last** anteanoche; **to make a night of it** (coll) divertirse hasta muy entrada la noche

night´cap´ s gorro de dormir; trago antes de acostarse, sosiega

night club s cabaret m, café m cantante, sala de fiestas

night driving s conducción de noche

night´fall´ s anochecer m, caída de la noche

night´gown´ s camisa de dormir

nightingale [ˈnaɪtənˌgel] s ruiseñor m

night latch s cerradura de resorte

night letter s carta telegráfica nocturna

night´long´ adj de toda la noche ‖ adv durante toda la noche

nightly [ˈnaɪtli] adj nocturno; de cada noche ‖ adv de noche, por la noche; cada noche

night´mare´ s pesadilla

nightmarish [ˈnaɪtˌmɛrɪʃ] adj espeluznante, horroroso

night owl s buho nocturno; (coll) anochecedor m, trasnochador m

night´shirt´ s camisa de dormir

night´time´ adj nocturno ‖ s noche f

night´walk´er s vagabundo nocturno; ladrón nocturno; ramera callejera nocturna; sonámbulo

night watch s guardia de noche, ronda de noche; sereno; (mil) vigilia

night watchman s vigilante nocturno

nihilism [ˈnaɪ•ɪˌlɪzəm] s nihilismo

nihilist [ˈnaɪ•ɪlɪst] s nihilista mf

nil [nɪl] s nada

Nile [naɪl] s Nilo

nimble [ˈnɪmbəl] adj ágil, ligero; listo, vivo

nim•bus [ˈnɪmbəs] s (pl **-buses** o **-bi** [baɪ]) nimbo

Nimrod [ˈnɪmrɑd] s Nemrod m

nincompoop [ˈnɪnkəmˌpup] s badulaque m, papirote m

nine [naɪn] adj & pron nueve ‖ s nueve m; equipo de béisbol; **nine o'clock** las nueve; **the Nine** las nueve musas

nine hundred adj & pron novecientos ‖ s novecientos m

nineteen [ˈnaɪnˈtin] adj, pron & s diecinueve m, diez y nueve m

nineteenth [ˈnaɪnˈtinθ] adj & s (in a series) decimonono; (part) diecinueveavo ‖ s (in dates) diecinueve m

ninetieth [ˈnaɪntɪ•ɪθ] adj & s (in a series) nonagésimo; (part) noventavo

nine•ty [ˈnaɪnti] adj & pron noventa ‖ s (pl **-ties**) noventa m

ninth [naɪnθ] adj & s nono, noveno ‖ s (in dates) nueve m

nip [nɪp] s mordisco, pellizco; helada, escarcha; traguito; **nip and tuck** a quién ganará ‖ v (pret & pp **nipped;** ger **nipping**) tr mordiscar, pellizcar; helar, escarchar; (slang) asir, coger; **to nip in the bud** atajar en el principio ‖ intr beborrotear

nipple [ˈnɪpəl] s (of female) pezón m; (of male; of nursing bottle) tetilla; (mach) tubo roscado de unión, entrerrosca

Nippon [nɪˈpɑn] s el Japón

Nippon•ese [ˌnɪpəˈniz] adj nipón ‖ s (pl **-ese**) nipón m

nip•py [ˈnɪpi] adj (comp **-pier;** super **-piest**) mordaz, picante; frío, helado; (Brit) ágil, ligero

nirvana [nɪrˈvɑnə] s el nirvana

nit [nɪt] s piojito; (egg of insect) liendre f

niter [ˈnaɪtər] s nitro; (agr) nitro de Chile

nitrate [ˈnaɪtret] s nitrato; (agr) nitrato de potasio, nitrato de sodio

nitric acid [ˈnaɪtrɪk] s ácido nítrico

nitride [ˈnaɪtraɪd] s nitruro

nitrogen [ˈnaɪtrədʒən] s nitrógeno

nitroglycerin [ˌnaɪtrəˈglɪsərɪn] s nitroglicerina

nitrous oxide [ˈnaɪtrəs] s óxido nitroso

nitwit [ˈnɪtˌwɪt] s (slang) bobalicón m

no [no] adj indef ninguno; **no admittance** no se permite la entrada; **no matter** no importa; **no parking** se prohibe estacionarse; **no smoking** se prohibe fumar; **no thoroughfare** prohibido el paso; **no use** inútil; **with no** sin ‖ adv no; **no good** de ningún valor; ruin, vil; **no longer** ya no; **no sooner** no bien

Noah [ˈno•ə] s Noé m

nob•by [ˈnɑbi] adj (comp **-bier;** super **-biest**) (slang) elegante; (slang) excelente

nobili•ty [noˈbɪlɪti] s (pl **-ties**) nobleza; (of sentiments, character, etc.) nobleza, ennoblecimiento

noble [ˈnobəl] adj & s noble m

noble•man [ˈnobəlmən] s (pl **-men** [mən]) noble m, hidalgo

nobod•y [ˈnoˌbɑdi] o [ˈnobədi] pron indef nadie, ninguno; **nobody but** nadie más que; **nobody else** nadie más, ningún otro ‖ s (pl **-ies**) nadie m, don nadie

nocturnal [nɑkˈtʌrnəl] adj nocturno

nod [nɑd] s inclinación de cabeza; seña con la cabeza; (of a person going to sleep) cabezada ‖ v (pret & pp **nodded;** ger **nodding**) tr inclinar (la cabeza); indicar con una inclinación de cabeza ‖ intr inclinar la cabeza; (in going to sleep) cabecear

node [nod] s bulto, protuberancia; nudo, enredo; (astr, med & phys) nodo; (bot) nudo

no´-fault´ adj (divorce, insurance) libre de culpa

nohow [ˈnoˌhau] adv (coll) de ninguna manera

noise [nɔɪz] s ruido ‖ tr divulgar

noiseless [ˈnɔɪzlɪs] adj silencioso, sin ruido

noise level *s* nivel sonoro

nois•y [ˈnɔɪzi] *adj* (*comp* **-ier;** *super* **-iest**) ruidoso; bullero; (*boisterous*) estrepitoso

nom. *abbr* **nominative**

nomad [ˈnoˈmæd] *adj* & *s* nómada *mf*

nomadic [noˈmædɪk] *adj* nomádico

no man's land *s* terreno sin reclamar; (mil) la tierra de nadie

nominal [ˈnamɪnəl] *adj* nominal; (*price*) módico

nominate [ˈnamɪˌnet] *tr* postular como candidato; (*to appoint*) nombrar, designar

nomination [ˌnamɪˈneʃən] *s* postulación

nominative [ˈnamɪnətɪv] *adj* & *s* nominativo

nominee [ˌnamɪˈni] *s* propuesto, candidato

nonaligned nations [ˌnanəˈlaɪnd] *spl* países no alineados; países no comprometidos

nonbelligerent [ˌnanbəˈlɪdʒərənt] *adj* & *s* no beligerante *m*

nonbreakable [nanˈbrekəbəl] *adj* irrompible

nonchalance [ˈnanʃələns] *s* indiferencia, desenvoltura

nonchalant [ˈnanʃələnt] *adj* indiferente, desenvuelto

noncom [ˈnanˌkam] *s* (coll) clase, suboficial *m*

noncombatant [nanˈkambətənt] *adj* & *s* no combatiente *m*

noncommissioned officer [ˌnankəˈmɪʃənd] *s* clase, suboficial *m*

noncommittal [ˌnankəˈmɪtəl] *adj* evasivo, reticente

noncommitted [ˌnankəˈmɪtɪd] *adj* no empeñado

non compos mentis [ˈnanˈkampəsˈmɛntɪs] *adj* falto de juicio, loco

nonconformist [ˌnankənˈfɔrmɪst] *s* disidente *mf;* inconformista *mf*

nonconformity [ˌnankənˈfɔrmɪti] *s* inconformidad

nondelivery [ˌnandɪˈlɪvəri] *s* falta de entrega

nondescript [ˈnandɪˌskrɪpt] *adj* inclasificable, indefinido

nondiscriminating [ˌnandɪsˈkrɪmɪˌnetɪŋ] *adj* indiscriminado

none [nʌn] *pron indef* nadie, ninguno, ningunos; **none of** ninguno de; nada de; **none other** ningún otro ‖ *adv* nada, de ninguna manera; **none the less** sin embargo, no obstante

nonenti•ty [nanˈɛntɪti] *s* (*pl* **-ties**) cosa inexistente; (*person*) nulidad

nonessential [ˌnanɛˈsɛnʃəl] *adj* intrascendente

nonexistence [ˌnanɛgˈzɪstəns] *s* inexistencia

nonfiction [nanˈfɪkʃən] *s* literatura no novelesca

nonfulfillment [ˌnanfʊlˈfɪlmənt] *s* incumplimiento

nonintervention [ˌnanɪntərˈvɛnʃən] *s* no intervención

nonmetal [ˈnanˌmɛtəl] *s* metaloide *m*

nonpartisan [nanˈpartɪzən] *adj* imparcial

nonpayment [nanˈpemənt] *s* falta de pago

non•plus [ˈnanplʌs] o [nanˈplʌs] *s* estupefacción ‖ *v* (*pret* & *pp* **-plused** o **-plussed;** *ger* **-plusing** o **-plussing**) *tr* dejar estupefacto, dejar pegado a la pared

nonprofit [nanˈprafɪt] *adj* sin fin lucrativo

nonrefillable [ˌnanrɪˈfɪləbəl] *adj* irrellenable

nonresident [nanˈrɛzɪdənt] *s* transeúnte *mf*

nonresidential [nanˌrɛzɪˈdɛnʃəl] *adj* comercial

nonscientific [nanˌsaɪənˈtɪfɪk] *adj* anticientífico

nonsectarian [ˌnansɛkˈtɛrɪˈən] *adj* no sectario

nonsense [ˈnansɛns] *s* disparate *m*, tontería; esperpento; **to talk nonsense** hablar en gringo

nonsensical [nanˈsɛnsɪkəl] *adj* disparatado, tonto

nonskid [ˈnanˈskɪd] *adj* antideslizante

nonstop [ˈnanˈstap] *adj* & *adv* sin parar, sin escala

nonsupport [ˌnansəˈport] *s* falta de manutención

noodle [ˈnudəl] *s* tallarín *m;* (slang) mentecato, tonto; (slang) cabeza

noodle soup *s* sopa de pastas, sopa de fideos

nook [nʊk] *s* rinconcito

noon [nun] *s* mediodía *m;* **at high noon** en pleno mediodía

no one o **no-one** [ˈnoˌwʌn] *pron indef* nadie, ninguno; **no one else** nadie más, ningún otro

noontime [ˈnunˌtaɪm] *s* mediodía *m*

noose [nus] *s* lazo corredizo; (*to hang a criminal*) dogal *m;* trampa ‖ *tr* lazar; hacer un lazo corredizo en

nor [nɔr] *conj* ni

Nordic [ˈnɔrdɪk] *adj* & *s* nórdico

norm [nɔrm] *s* norma

normal [ˈnɔrməl] *adj* normal

Norman [ˈnɔrmən] *adj* & *s* normando

Normandy [ˈnɔrməndi] *s* Normandía

Norse [nɔrs] *adj* nórdico; noruego ‖ *s* (*ancient Scandinavian language*) nórdico; (*language of Norway*) noruego; **the Norse** los nórdicos; los noruegos

Norse•man [ˈnɔrsmən] *s* (*pl* **-men** [mən]) normando

north [nɔrθ] *adj* septentrional, del norte ‖ *adv* al norte, hacia el norte ‖ *s* norte *m*

North America *s* Norteamérica, la América del Norte

North American *adj* & *s* norteamericano

north'east'er *s* (*wind*) nordestada, nordeste *m* (*viento*)

northern [ˈnɔrðərn] *adj* septentrional; (*Hemisphere*) boreal

North Korea *s* la Corea del Norte

North Korean *adj* & *s* norcoreano

northward [ˈnɔrθwərd] *adv* hacia el norte

north wind *s* norte *m*, aquilón *m*

Norway [ˈnɔrwe] *s* Noruega

Norwegian [nɔrˈwidʒən] *adj* & *s* noruego

nos. *abbr* **numbers**

nose [noz] *s* nariz *f;* (aer) proa; **to blow one's nose** sonarse las narices; **to count noses** averiguar cuántas personas hay; **to follow one's nose** seguir todo derecho; avanzar guiándose por el instinto; **to hold one's**

nose tabicarse las narices; **to lead by the nose** llevar por la barba, tener agarrado por las narices; **to look down one's nose at** mirar por encima del hombro; **to pay through the nose** pagar un precio escandaloso; **to pick one's nose** hurgarse las narices; **to poke one's nose into** meter las narices en; **to speak through the nose** ganguear; **to thumb one's nose at** señalar (*a una persona*) poniendo el pulgar sobre la nariz en son de burla; tratar con sumo desprecio; **to turn up one's nose at** mirar con desprecio; **under the nose of** en las narices de, en las barbas de ‖ *tr* olfatear ‖ *intr* ventear; **to nose about** curiosear; **to nose over** capotar (*un avión*); **to nose up** encabritarse (*un buque, un avión*)

nose bag *s* cebadera, morral *m*
nose'band' *s* muserola, sobarba
nose'bleed' *s* hemorragia nasal
nose cone *s* cono de proa
nose dive *s* (aer) descenso de picado; (fig) descenso precipitado
nose'-dive' *intr* (aer) picar; (fig) descender precipitadamente
nosegay ['noz,ge] *s* ramillete *m*
nose ring *s* nariguera
no'-show' *s* pasajero no presentado
nostalgia [na'stældʒə] *s* nostalgia
nostril ['nastrɪl] *s* nariz *f*, ventana
nos•y ['nozi] *adj* (*comp* **-ier**; *super* **-iest**) (coll) curioso, husmeador
not [nat] *adv* no; **not at all** nada, de ningún modo; **not yet** todavía no; **to think not** creer que no; **why not?** ¿cómo no?
notable ['notəbəl] *adj* & *s* notable *m*
notarize ['notə,raɪz] *tr* abonar con fe notarial
nota•ry ['notəri] *s* (*pl* **-ries**) notario
notch [natʃ] *s* muesca, mella, corte *m;* (U.S.A.) desfiladero, paso; (coll) grado ‖ *tr* hacer muescas en, mellar
note [not] *s* nota; apunte *m;* esquela, cartita; marca, señal *f;* (com) pagaré *m*, vale *m;* canto, melodía; acento, voz *f;* (mus) nota ‖ *tr* notar, apuntar; marcar, señalar
note'book' *s* cuaderno, libro de apuntes
noted ['notɪd] *adj* aramado, conocido
note paper *s* papel *m* de cartas
note'wor'thy *adj* notable, digno de notarse
nothing ['nʌθɪŋ] *pron indef* nada; **for nothing** inútilmente; de balde, gratis; **nothing doing** (slang) ni por pienso; **nothing else** nada más; **that's nothing to me** eso nada me importa; **to make nothing of** no hacer caso de; no aprovecharse de; no entender; despreciar; **to think nothing of** no hacer caso de; tener por fácil; despreciar ‖ *adv* nada, de ninguna manera; **nothing daunted** sin temor alguno ‖ *s* nada; nadería, friolera
notice ['notɪs] *s* atención, reparo, advertencia; aviso, noticia; letrero, mención, reseña; llamada; notificación; **on short notice** con poco tiempo de aviso; **to escape one's notice** pasarle inadvertido a uno; **to serve notice** dar noticia, hacer saber ‖ *tr* notar, observar, reparar, reparar en; mencionar

noticeable ['notɪsəbəl] *adj* sensible, perceptible; notable
noti•fy ['notɪ,faɪ] *v* (*pret* & *pp* **-fied**) *tr* notificar, avisar, hacer saber
notion ['noʃən] *s* noción; capricho; **notions** mercería, artículos menudos; **to have a notion to** + *inf* pensar + *inf*, tener ganas de + *inf*
notorie•ty [,notə'raɪəti] *s* (*pl* **-ties**) mala reputación; (*condition of being well known*) notoriedad; (*person*) notable *mf*
notorious [no'torɪ•əs] *adj* reputado, mal reputado; bien conocido
no'-trump' *adj* & *s* sin triunfo; **a no-trump hand** un sin triunfo
notwithstanding [,natwɪð'stændɪŋ] o [,natwɪθ'stændɪŋ] *adv* no obstante ‖ *prep* a pesar de ‖ *conj* a pesar de que
nougat ['nugət] *s* turrón *m*
noun [naun] *s* nombre, nombre sustantivo
nourish ['nʌrɪʃ] *tr* alimentar, nutrir; abrigar (*p.ej., esperanzas*)
nourishing ['nʌrɪʃɪŋ] *adj* alimenticio, nutritivo
nourishment ['nʌrɪʃmənt] *s* alimento, nutrimento
Nov. *abbr* **November**
Nova Scotia ['novə'skoʃə] *s* la Nueva Escocia
Nova Scotian ['novə'skoʃən] *adj* & *s* neoescocés *m*
novel ['navəl] *adj* nuevo; insólito, extraño, original ‖ *s* novela
novelist ['navəlɪst] *s* novelista *mf*
novel•ty ['navəlti] *s* (*pl* **-ties**) novedad, innovación; **novelties** bisutería, baratijas
November [no'vɛmbər] *s* noviembre *m*
novice ['navɪs] *s* novicio
novocaine ['novə,ken] *s* novocaína
now [nau] *adv* ahora; ya; entonces; **from now on** de ahora en adelante; **how now?** ¿cómo?; **just now** hace un momento; **now and again** o **now and then** de vez en cuando; **now . . . now** ora . . . ora, ya . . . ya; **now that** ya que; **now then** ahora bien ‖ *interj* ¡vamos! ‖ *s* actualidad
nowadays ['nau•ə,dez] *adv* hoy en día, hoy día
no'way' o **no'ways'** *adv* de ningún modo
no'where' *adv* en ninguna parte, a ninguna parte; **nowhere else** en ninguna otra parte
noxious ['nakʃəs] *adj* nocivo
nozzle ['nazəl] *s* (*of hoe*) lanza; (*of sprinkling can*) rallow, roseta; (*of candlestick*) cubo; (slang) nariz *f*
N.T. *abbr* **New Testament**
nth [ɛnθ] *adj* n^{mo} (*enésimo*); **to the nth degree** elevado a la potencia *n;* a más no poder
nuance [nju'ans] o ['nju•ans] *s* matiz *m*
nub [nʌb] *s* protuberancia; pedazo; (coll) meollo
nuclear ['nuklɪ•ər] *adj* nuclear
nu'cle•ar-pow'ered *adj* accionado por energía nuclear

nuclear test ban *s* proscripción de las pruebas nucleares

nuclear war *s* guerra nuclear

nucle•us [ˈnuklɪ•əs] *s* (*pl* **-i** [ˌaɪ] o **-uses**) núcleo

nude [njud] o [nud] *adj* desnudo ‖ *s* — **in the nude** desnudo; **the nude** el desnudo

nudism [ˈnjudɪzəm] o [ˈnudɪzəm] *s* (des)nudismo; naturismo

nudge [nʌdʒ] *s* codazo suave ‖ *tr* dar un codazo suave a, empujar suavemente

nugget [ˈnʌgɪt] *s* pedazo; (*of, e.g., gold*) pepita; preciosidad

nuisance [ˈnjusəns] o [ˈnusəns] *s* molestia, estorbo; majadería; persona o cosa fastidiosas; **to be a nuisance** ser un higado

nuke [njuk] o [nuk] *s* (slang) arma atómica ‖ *tr* (slang) atacar con arma atómica; aniquilar

null [nʌl] *adj* nulo; **null and void** nulo, írrito, nulo y sin valor

nulli•ty [ˈnʌlɪti] *v* (*pl* **-ties**) nulidad

nulli•fy [ˈnʌlɪfaɪ] *v* (*pret & pp* **-fied**) anular, invalidor

numb [nʌm] *adj* entumecido; **to get numb** envararse ‖ *tr* entumecer

number [ˈnʌmbər] *s* número; **a number of** varios ‖ *tr* numerar; ascender a (*cierto número*); **his days are numbered** tiene sus días contados o sus horas contadas; **to be numbered among** hallarse entre; **to number among** contar entre

numberless [ˈnʌmbərlɪs] *adj* innumerable

numeral [ˈnjumərəl] o [ˈnumərəl] *adj* numeral ‖ *s* número

numerical [njuˈmɛrɪkəl] o [nuˈmɛrɪkəl] *adj* numérico

numerous [ˈnjumərəs] o [ˈnumərəs] *adj* numeroso

numskull [ˈnʌmˌskʌl] *s* (coll) bodoque *m*, mentecato

nun [nʌn] *s* monja, religiosa

nuptial [ˈnʌpʃəl] *adj* nupcial ‖ **nuptials** *spl* nupcias, bodas

nurse [nʌrs] *s* enfermera; (*to suckle a child*) ama de cría, nodriza; (*to take care of a child*) niñera ‖ *tr* cuidar (*a una persona enferma*); amamantar; alimentar, criar; tratar de curarse de (*p.ej., un resfriado*); abrigar (*p.ej., odio*) ‖ *intr* ser enfermera

nurser•y [ˈnʌrsəri] *s* (*pl* **-ies**) cuarto de los niños; (*of plants*) criadero, plantel *m*, semillero; (fig) semillero

nursery•man [ˈnʌrsərɪmən] *s* (*pl* **-men** [mən]) cultivador *m* de semillero

nursery rhymes *spl* versos para niños

nursery tales *spl* cuentos para niños

nursing bottle *s* biberón *m*

nursing home *s* clínica de reposo; (*for the aged*) residencia de ancianos

nurture [ˈnʌrtʃər] *s* alimentación, nutrimento; crianza, educación ‖ *tr* alimentar, nutrir; criar, educar; acariciar (*p.ej., una esperanza*)

nut [nʌt] *s* nuez *f*; (*to screw on a bolt*) tuerca; (slang) estrafalario; **a hard nut to crack** (coll) hueso duro de roer

nut′crack′er *s* cascanueces *m*

nutmeg [ˈnʌtˌmɛg] *s* nuez moscada; (*tree*) mirística

nutriment [ˈnjutrɪmənt] *s* nutrimento

nutrition [njuˈtrɪʃən] *s* nutrición

nutritious [njuˈtrɪʃəs] *adj* nutricioso, nutritivo

nuts *adj* (slang) loco; estrafalario ‖ *interj* (slang) ¡no!, ¡niego!, ¡de ninguna manera!

nut′shell′ *s* cáscara de nuez; **in a nutshell** en pocas palabras

nut•ty [ˈnʌti] *adj* (*comp* **-tier**; *super* **-tiest**) abundante en nueces; que sabe a nueces; (slang) chiflado, loco; **nutty about** (slang) loco por

nuzzle [ˈnʌzəl] *tr* hocicar, hozar ‖ *intr* hocicar; arrimarse cómodamente; arroparse bien

nylon [ˈnaɪlɑn] *s* nilón *m*; **nylons** medias de nilón

nymph [nɪmf] *s* ninfa

no
ob

O

O, o [o] decimoquinta letra del alfabeto inglés

O *interj* ¡oh!; ¡ay!, p.ej., **how pretty she is!** ¡Ay qué linda!; **O that. . . !** ¡Ojalá que. . . !

oaf [of] *s* zoquete *m*, zamacuco; niño contrahecho

oak [ok] *s* roble *m*

oaken [ˈokən] *adj* hecho de roble

oakum [ˈokəm] *s* estopa, estopa de calafatear

oar [or] *s* remo; **to lie** o **rest on one's oars** aguantar los remos; aflojar en el trabajo ‖ *tr* conducir a remo ‖ *intr* remar, bogar

oars•man [ˈorzmən] *s* (*pl* **-men** [mən]) remero

OAS [ˈoˈeˈɛs] *s* (*letterword*) OEA *f*

oa•sis [oˈesɪs] *s* (*pl* **-ses** [siz]) oasis *m*

oat [ot] *s* avena; **oats** (*edible grain*) avena; **to feel one's oats** (slang) estar fogoso y brioso; (slang) estar muy pagado de sí mismo; **to sow one's wild oats** correrla, pasar las mocedades

oath [oθ] *s* juramento; **on oath** bajo juramento; **to take an oath** prestar juramento

oat′meal′ *s* harina de avena; gachas de avena

ob. *abbr* **obiit** (Lat) **died**

obbligato [ˌɑblɪˈgato] *adj & s* obligado

obduracy [ˈɑbdjərəsi] *s* obduración

obdurate [ˈabdjərɪt] *adj* obstinado, terco; empedernido

obedience [oˈbidɪ·əns] *s* obediencia

obedient [oˈbidɪ·ənt] *adj* obediente

obeisance [oˈbesəns] u [oˈbisəns] *s* saludo respetuoso; homenaje *m*, respeto

obelisk [ˈabəlɪsk] *s* obelisco

obese [oˈbis] *adj* obeso

obesity [oˈbisɪti] *s* obesidad

obey [oˈbe] *tr & intr* obedecer

obfuscate [abˈfʌsket] o [ˈabfəs,ket] *tr* ofuscar

obituar·y [oˈbɪtʃʊ,ɛri] *adj* necrológico ‖ *s* (*pl* **-ies**) necrología

obj. *abbr* **object, objection, objective**

object [ˈabdʒɪkt] *s* objeto ‖ [abˈdʒɛkt] *tr* objetar ‖ *intr* hacer objeciones

objection [abˈdʒɛkʃən] *s* reparo, objeción; **to have no objections to make** no tener nada que objetar

objectionable [abˈdʒɛkʃənəbəl] *adj* desagradable, reprensible; (*causing disapproval*) objetable

objective [abˈdʒɛktɪv] *adj & s* objetivo

obl. *abbr* **oblique, oblong**

obligate [ˈablɪ,get] *tr* obligar

obligation [,ablɪˈgeʃən] *s* obligación; encargamiento

oblige [əˈblaɪdʒ] *tr* obligar; complacer; **much obliged** muchas gracias

obliging [əˈblaɪdʒɪŋ] *adj* complaciente, condescendiente, servicial

oblique [əˈblik] *adj* oblicuo; indirecto, evasivo

obliterate [əˈblɪtə,ret] *tr* borrar; arrasar, destruir

oblivion [əˈblɪvɪ·ən] *s* olvido

oblivious [əˈblɪvɪ·əs] *adj* olvidadizo

oblong [ˈablɔŋ] o [ˈablaŋ] *adj* oblongo

obnoxious [abˈnakʃəs] *adj* detestable, ofensivo

oboe [ˈobo] *s* oboe *m*

oboist [ˈobo·ɪst] *s* oboísta *mf*

obs. *abbr* **obsolete**

obscene [abˈsin] *adj* obsceno

obsceni·ty [abˈsɛnɪti] o [abˈsinɪti] *s* (*pl* **-ties**) obscenidad

obscure [əbˈskjʊr] *adj* obscuro; (*vowel*) relajado, neutro

obscuri·ty [əbˈskjʊrɪti] *s* (*pl* **-ties**) obscuridad

obsequies [ˈabsɪkwiz] *spl* exequias

obsequious [əbˈsikwɪ·əs] *adj* obsequioso, servil, rastrero

observance [əbˈzʌrvəns] *s* observancia; ceremonia, rito

observant [əbˈzʌrvənt] *adj* observador

observation [,abzərˈveʃən] *s* observación; observancia

observato·ry [əbˈzʌrvə,tori] *s* (*pl* **-ries**) observatorio

observe [əbˈzʌrv] *tr* observar; (*a holiday; silence*) guardar

observer [əbˈzʌrvər] *s* observador *m*

obsess [əbˈsɛs] *tr* obsesionar

obsession [əbˈsɛʃən] *s* obsesión

obsolescent [,absəˈlɛsənt] *adj* arcaizante

obsolete [ˈabsə,lit] *adj* desusado, caído en desuso; obsoleto

obstacle [ˈabstəkəl] *s* obstáculo

obstetrical [abˈstɛtrɪkəl] *adj* obstétrico

obstetrics [abˈstɛtrɪks] *ssg* obstetricia

obstina·cy [ˈabstɪnəsi] *s* (*pl* **-cies**) obstinación

obstinate [ˈabstɪnɪt] *adj* obstinado

obstruct [abˈstrʌkt] *tr* obstruir; obstruccionar

obstruction [əbˈstrʌkʃən] *s* obstrucción

obtain [əbˈten] *tr* obtener ‖ *intr* existir, prevalecer

obtrusive [əbˈtrusɪv] *adj* entremetido, intruso

obtuse [əbˈtjus] o [əbˈtus] *adj* obtuso

obviate [ˈabvɪ,et] *tr* obviar

obvious [ˈabvɪ·əs] *adj* obvio

occasion [əˈkeθən] *s* ocasión; **to improve the occasion** aprovechar la ocasión

occasional [əˈkeʒənəl] *adj* raro, poco frecuente; alguno que otro; de circunstancia

occasionally [əˈkeʒənəli] *adv* ocasionalmente, de vez en cuando

occident [ˈaksɪdənt] *s* occidente *m*

occidental [,aksɪˈdɛntəl] *adj* occidental

occlusive [əˈklusɪv] *adj* oclusivo ‖ *s* oclusiva

occult [əˈkʌlt] o [ˈakʌlt] *adj* oculto

occupancy [ˈakjepənsi] *s* ocupación

occupant [ˈakjepənt] *s* ocupante *mf*; inquilino

occupation [,akjəˈpeʃən] *s* ocupación

occupational therapy *s* terapia vocacional

occu·py [ˈakjə,paɪ] *v* (*pret & pp* **-pied**) *tr* ocupar; habitar

oc·cur [əˈkʌr] *v* (*pret & pp* **-curred**; *ger* **-curring**) *intr* ocurrir, acontecer, suceder; encontrarse; (*to come to mind*) ocurrir

occurrence [əˈkʌrəns] *s* acontecimiento; caso, aparición

ocean [ˈoʃən] *s* océano

o'cean-go'ing *adj* transoceánico

oceanic [,oʃɪˈænɪk] *adj* oceánico

ocean liner *s* buque transoceánico

o'clock [əˈklak] *adv* por el reloj; **it is one o'clock** es la una; **it is two o'clock** son las dos; **what o'clock is it?** ¿qué hora es?

Oct. *abbr* **October**

octave [ˈaktɪv] o [ˈaktev] *s* octava

October [akˈtobər] *s* octubre *m*

octo·pus [ˈaktəpəs] *s* (*pl* **-puses** o **-pi** [,paɪ]) pulpo

octoroon [,aktəˈrun] *s* octavo

ocular [ˈakjələr] *adj & s* ocular *m*

oculist [ˈakjəlɪst] *s* oculista *mf*

O.D. *abbr* **officer of the day, olive drab, overdose**

odd [ad] *adj* suelto; (*number*) impr; (*that doesn't match*) dispar; libre, de ocio; sobrante; extraño, raro, singular; y pico, y tantos, p.ej., **two hundred odd** doscientos y pico ‖ **odds** *ssg* o *spl* (*in betting*) ventaja; apuesta desigual; puntos de ventaja; **at odds** de monos, riñendo; **by all odds** muy probablemente, sin duda alguna; **it makes no odds** lo mismo da; **the odds are** lo probable es; la ventaja es de; **to be at odds** estar de punta, estar encontrados; **to set at odds** enemistar, malquistar

odd'ball' *adj & s* excéntrico; disente

oddi•ty ['ɑdɪti] *s* (*pl* **-ties**) rareza, cosa rara

odd jobs *spl* pequeñas tareas

odd lot *s* lote *m* inferior al centenar

odds and ends *spl* pedacitos varios, cajón *m* de sastre

ode [od] *s* oda

odious ['odɪ•əs] *adj* odioso, abominable

odor ['odər] *s* olor *m;* **to be in bad odor** tener mala fama

odorless ['odərlɪs] *adj* inodoro

odorous ['odərəs] *adj* oloroso

Odysseus [o'dɪsjus] u [o'dɪsɪ•əs] *s* Odiseo

Odyssey ['adɪsi] *s* Odisea

Oedipus ['ɛdɪpəs] o ['idɪpəs] *s* Edipo

oenology [i'nalədʒi] *s* enotecnia

of [ɑv] o [əv] *prep* de, p.ej., **the top of the mountain** la cima de la montaña; a: **to smell of** oler a; con: **to dream of** soñar con; en: **to think of** pensar en; menos: **a quarter of two** las dos menos un cuarto

off. *abbr* **office, officer, official**

off [ɔf] o [ɑf] *adj* malo, p.ej., **off day** día, malo; (*account, sum*) errado; más distante; libre; sin trabajo; quitado; apagado; (*electric current*) cortado; de descuento, de rebaja; de la parte del mar; (*season*) muerto ‖ *adv* fuera, a distancia, lejos; allá; off of (coll) de; (coll) a expensas de; **to be off** ponerse en marcha ‖ *prep* de, desde, al lado de, a nivel de; fuera de; libre de; (*naut*) a la altura de ‖ *tr* (slang) matar, asesinar

offal ['afəl] u ['ɔfəl] *s* (*of butchered meat*) carniza; basura, desperdicios

off and on *adv* unas veces sí y otras no

off'beat' *adj* (slang) insólito, chocante, original

off'chance' *s* posibilidad poco probable

off'-col'or *adj* descolorido; indispuesto; (*indecent, risqué*) colorado, subido de color

offend [ə'fɛnd] *tr & intr* ofender

offender [ə'fɛndər] *s* ofensor *m*

offense [ə'fɛns] *s* ofensa; **to take offense (at)** ofenderse (de)

offensive [ə'fɛnsɪv] *adj* ofensivo ‖ *f* ofensiva

offer ['ɔfər] o ['afər] *s* ofrecimiento, oferta ‖ *tr* ofrecer; rezar (*oraciones*); oponer (*resistencia*)

offering ['ɔfərɪŋ] o ['afərɪŋ] *s* ofrecimiento; (*gift, present*) oferta; (*presentation in worship*) ofrenda

off'hand' *adj* hecho de improviso; brusco, desenvuelto ‖ *adv* de improviso, súbitamente; bruscamente

office ['ɔfɪs] o ['afɪs] *s* oficina, despacho; función, oficio; cargo, ministerio; (*of a lawyer*) bufete *m;* (*of a doctor*) consultorio

office boy *s* mandadero

office desk *s* escritorio ministro

of'fice•hold'er *s* funcionario, burócrata *m*

office hours *spl* horas de oficina; (*of a doctor*) horas de consulta

officer ['ɔfɪsər] o ['afɪsər] *s* jefe *m,* director *m;* (*of army, an order, a society, etc.*) oficial *m;* agente *m* de policía

office seeker ['sikər] *s* aspirante *m,* pretendiente *m*

office supplies *spl* suministros para oficinas

official [ə'fɪʃəl] *adj* oficial ‖ *s* jefe *m,* director *m;* (*of a society*) dignatario

officiate [ə'fɪʃɪ,et] *intr* oficiar

officious [ə'fɪʃəs] *adj* oficioso

off'-peak' *adj* (*hours, stop, etc.*) de valle; de menor tránsito

off-peak heater *s* (elec) termos *m* de acumulación

off-peak load *s* (elec) carga de las horas de valle

off'print' *s* sobretiro

off'set' *s* compensación; (typ) offset *m* ‖ **off'set'** *v* (*pret & pp* **-set;** *ger* **-setting**) *tr* compensar; imprimir por offset

off'shoot' *s* (*of plant*) retoño, renuevo; (*of a family or race*) descendiente *mf;* (*branch*) ramal *m;* consecuencia

off'shore' *adj* (*wind*) terral; (*fishing*) de bajura; (*said of islands*) costero; **offshore drilling rig** barca perforador ‖ *adv* a lo largo

off'spring' *s* descendencia, sucesión; hijo, hijos

off'-stage' *adj* de entre bastidores

off'-the-rec'ord *adj* extraoficial, confidencial

often ['ɔfən] o (ɑfən] *adv* a menudo, muchas veces; **how often?** ¿cuántas veces?; **not often** pocas veces

ogive ['odʒaɪv] u [o'dʒaɪv] *s* ojiva

ogle ['ogəl] *tr & intr* ojear; mirar amorosamente

ogre ['ogər] *s* ogro

ohm [om] *s* ohmio

oil [ɔɪl] *adj* (*burner; field; well*) de petróleo; (*pump; stove*) de aceite; (*company, tanker*) petrolero; (*land*) petrolífero ‖ *s* aceite *m;* (*consecrated oil; painting*) óleo; **to burn the midnight oil** quemarse las cejas; **to pour oil on troubled waters** mojar la pólvora; **to strike oil** encontrar una capa de petróleo; (fig) enriquecerse de súbito ‖ *tr* aceitar; lubricar; lisonjear; (*to bribe*) untar ‖ *intr* proveerse de petróleo (*un buque*)

oil'can' *s* aceitera

oil'cloth' *s* encerado, hule *m*

oil field *s* yacamiento de petróleo

oil gauge *s* indicador *m* del nivel de aceite

oil pan *s* colector *m* de aceite

oil shortage *s* carestía (*or* escasez *f*) de petróleo

oil tanker *s* petrolero

oil•y ['ɔɪli] *adj* (*comp* **-ier;** *super* **-iest**) aceitoso; liso, resbaladizo; zalamero

ointment ['ɔɪntmənt] *s* ungüento

O.K. ['o'ke] *adj* (coll) aprobado, conforme ‖ *adv* (coll) muy bien, está bien ‖ *s* (coll) aprobación ‖ *v* (*pret & pp* **O.K.'d;** *ger* **O.K.'ing**) *tr* (coll) aprobar

okra ['okrə] *s* quingombó *m*

old [old] *adj* viejo; antiguo; (*wine*) añejo; **how old is . . . ?** ¿cuántos años tiene . . . ?; **of old** de antaño, antiguamente; **to be . . . years old** tener . . . años

ob
ol

old age *s* ancianidad, vejez *f;* **to die of old age** morir de viejo

old boy *s* viejo; graduado; **the Old Boy** (slang) el diablo

Old Castile *s* Castilla la Vieja

old-clothes•man ['old'kloðz,mæn] *s* (*pl* **-men** [mɛn]) ropavejero

old country *s* madre patria

old-fashioned ['old'fæʃənd] *adj* chapado a la antigua; anticuado, fuera de moda

old fo•gey u **old fo•gy** ['fogi] *s* (*pl* **-gies**) persona un poco ridícula por sus ideas o costumbres atrasadas

Old Glory *s* la bandera de los Estados Unidos

Old Guard *s* (U.S.A.) bando conservador del partido republicano

old hand *s* práctico *m*, veterano

old maid *s* solterona

old master *s* (paint) gran maestro; obra de un gran maestro

old moon *s* luna menguante

old salt *s* lobo de mar

old school *s* gente chapada a la antigua

old'-time' *adj* del tiempo viejo

old-timer ['old'taɪmər] *s* (coll) antiguo residente, veterano; (coll) persona chapada a la antigua

old wives' tale *s* cuento de viejas

old'-world' *adj* del Viejo Mundo

oleander [,olɪ'ændər] *s* adelfa

oligar•chy ['alɪ,garki] *s* (*pl* **-chies**) oligarquía

olive ['alɪv] *adj* aceitunado ‖ *s* aceituna

olive branch *s* ramo de olivo; (*peace*) oliva; hijo, vástago

olive grove *s* olivar *m*

olive oil *s* aceite *m*, aceite de oliva

olive tree *s* aceituno, olivo

Olympiad [o'lɪmpɪ,æd] *s* Olimpíada

Olympian [o'lɪmpɪ•ən] *adj* olímpico ‖ *s* dios griego

Olympic [o'lɪmpɪk] *adj* olímpico

omelet u **omelette** ['aməlɪt] o ['amlɪt] *s* tortilla (de huevos)

omen ['omən] *s* agüero

ominous ['amɪnəs] *adj* ominoso

omission [o'mɪʃən] *s* omisión

omit [o'mɪt] *v* (*pret & pp* **omitted**; *ger* **omitting**) *tr* omitir

omnibus ['amnɪ,bʌs] o ['amnɪbəs] *adj* general; (*volume*) colecticio ‖ *s* ómnibus *m*

omnipotent [am'nɪpətənt] *adj* omnipotente

omniscient [am'nɪʃənt] *adj* omnisciente

omnivorous [am'nɪvərəs] *adj* omnívoro

on [an] u [ɔn] *adj* puesto, p.ej., **with his hat on** con el sombrero puesto; principiando; en funcionamiento; encendido; conectado; **the deal is on** ya está concertado el trato; **the game is on** ya están jugando; **the race is on** allá van los corredores; **what is on at the theater this evening?** ¿qué representan esta noche? ‖ *adv* adelante; encima; **and so on** y así sucesivamente; **come on!** ¡anda, anda!; **farther on** más allá, más adelante; **later on** más tarde, después; **to be on to a person** (coll) conocerle a uno el juego; **to have on** tener puesto; **to . . . on** sequir + *ger*, **he played on** siguió to-

cando ‖ *prep* en, sobre, encima de; a, p.ej., **on foot** a pie; **on my arrival** a mi llegada; bajo, p.ej., **on my responsibility** bajo mi responsabilidad; contra, p.ej., **an attack on liberty** un ataque contra la libertad; de, p.ej., **on good authority** de buena tinta; **on a journey** de viaje; hacia, p.ej., **to march on the capital** marchar hacia la capital; por, p.ej., **on all sides** por todos lados; tras, p.ej., **defeat on defeat** derrota tras derrota; **on** + *ger* al + *inf*, p.ej., **on arriving** al llegar

on and on *adv* continuamente, sin cesar, sin parar

on'-board' computer *s* ordenador de viaje

once [wʌns] *adv* una vez; antes, p.ej., **once so happy** antes tan feliz; alguna vez, p.ej., **if this once becomes known** si esto llega a saberse alguna vez; **all at once** de súbito, de repente; **at once** en seguida; a la vez en el mismo momento; **for once** una vez por lo menos; **once and again** repetidas veces; **once in a blue moon** cada muerte de obispo; **once in a while** de vez en cuando; luego; **once more** otra vez más; **once upon a time there was** érase una vez, érase que se era ‖ *conj* una vez que ‖ *s* una vez; vez, p.ej., **this once** esta vez

once'-o'ver *s* (slang) examen rápido; **to give a thing the once-over** (coll) examinar una cosa superficialmente

oncology [aŋ'kalədʒi] *s* oncología

one [wʌn] *adj* un, uno; un tal, p.ej., **one Smith** un tal Smith; único, p.ej., **one price** precio único ‖ *pron* uno, p.ej., **one does not know what to do here** uno no sabe qué hacer aquí; se, p.ej., **how does one go to the station?** ¿cómo se va a la estación?; **I for one** yo por lo menos; **it's all one and the same to me** me es igual; **my little one** mi chiquito; **of one another** el uno del otro, los unos de los otros, p.ej., **we took leave of one another** nos despedimos el uno del otro; **one and all** todos; **one another** se, p.ej., **they greeted one another** se saludaron; uno a otro, unos a otros, p.ej., **they looked at one another** se miraron uno a otro; **one by one** uno a uno; **one o'clock** la una; **one or two** unos pocos; **one's** su, el . . . de uno; **the blue book and the red one** el libro azul y el rojo; **the one and only** el único; **the one that** el que, la que; **this one** éste; **that one** ése, aquél; **to make one** unir; casar ‖ *s* uno

one'-fam'i•ly house *s* vivienda unifamiliar

one'-horse' *adj* de un solo caballo, tirado por un solo caballo; (coll) insignificante, de poca monta

onerous ['anərəs] *adj* oneroso

one'self' *pron* uno mismo; sí, sí mismo; se; **to be oneself** tener dominio de sí mismo; conducirse con naturalidad

one-sided ['wʌn'saɪdɪd] *adj* de un solo lado; injusto, parcial; desigual; unilateral

one'-track' *adj* de carril único; (coll) con un solo interés

one'-way' *adj* de una solo dirección, de dirección única; (*ticket*) sencillo, de ida

onion [ˈʌnjən] *s* cebolla

on'ion·skin' *s* papel *m* de seda, papel cebolla

on'look'er *s* mirón *m*, espectador *m*

only [ˈonlɪ] *adj* solo, único || *adv* solamente, sólo, únicamente; no . . . más que; **not only . . . but also** no sólo . . . sino también || *conj* sólo que, pero

onomatopoeic [ˌɑnəˌmætəˈpiˑɪk] *adj* onomatopéyico

on'set' *s* arremetida, embestida; (*of an illness*) principio

onward [ˈɑnwərd] u **onwards** [ˈɑnwərdz] *adv* adelante, hacia adelante

onyx [ˈɑnɪks] *s* ónice *m* u ónix *m*

ooze [uz] *s* chorro suave; cieno; limo, lama || *tr* rezumar || *intr* rezumar, rezumarse; manar suavemente (*p.ej., la sangre de una herida*); agotarse poco a poco

op. *abbr* **opera, operation, opus, opposite**

opal [ˈopəl] *s* ópalo

opaque [oˈpek] *adj* opaco; (*writer's style*) obscuro; estúpido

open [ˈopən] *adj* abierto; descubierto, destapado; sin tejado; vacante; (*hour*) libre; discutible, pendiente; (*hand*) liberal; (*hunting season*) legal; **to break** o **to crack open** abrir con violencia, abrir por la fuerza; **to throw open** abrir de par en par || *s* abertura; (*in the woods*) claro; **in the open** al aire libre; a campo raso; en alta mar; abiertamente || *tr* abrir; desbullar (*una ostra*) || *intr* abrir; abrirse; estrenarse (*un drama*); **to open into** desembocar en; **to open on** dar a; **to open up** descubrirse; descubrir el pecho

o'pen-air' *adj* al aire libre, a cielo abierto

open-eyed [ˈopənˌaɪd] *adj* alerta, vigilante; con ojos asombrados; hecho con los ojos abiertos

open-handed [ˈopənˈhændɪd] *adj* maniabierto, liberal

open-hearted (opənˈhɑrtɪd) *adj* franco, sincero

open house *s* coliche *m*; **to keep open house** recibir a todos, gustar de tener siempre convidados en casa

opening [ˈopənɪŋ] *s* abertura; (*of, e.g., school*) apertura; (*in the woods*) claro; (*vacancy*) hueco, vacante *f*; (*chance to say something*) ocasión

opening night *s* noche *f* de estreno

opening number *s* primer número

opening price *s* primer curso, precio de apertura

open-minded [ˈopənˈmaɪndɪd] *adj* receptivo, razonable, imparcial

open secret *s* secreto a voces

open shop *s* taller franco

o'pen·work' *s* calado

opera [ˈɑpərə] *s* ópera

opera glasses *spl* gemelos de teatro

opera hat *s* clac *m*, sombrero de muelles

opera house *s* teatro de la ópera

operate [ˈɑpəˌret] *tr* hacer funcionar; dirigir, manejar; explotar || *intr* funcionar; operar;

to operate on operar (*p.ej., una hernia; a un niño*)

operatic [ˌɑpəˈrætɪk] *adj* operístico

operating expenses *spl* gastos de explotación

operating room *s* quirófano

operating table *s* mesa operatoria

operation [ˌɑpəˌreˈtʃən] *s* operación; funcionamiento; explotación

operator [ˈɑpəˌretər] *s* operador *m*, maquinista *m*; (com) empresario; (coll) corredor *m* de bolsa; (surg, telp) operador *m*

operetta [ˌɑpəˈretə] *s* opereta

opiate [ˈopiˑɪt] u [ˈopˌet] *adj & s* opiato

opinion [əˈpɪnjən] *s* opinión; **in my opinion** a mi parecer; **to have a high opinion of** tener buen concepto de

opinionated [əˈpɪnjəˌnetɪd] *adj* porfiado en su parecer, dogmático

opinion poll *s* encuesta demoscópica

opium [ˈopiˑəm] *s* opio

opium den *s* fumadero de opio

opossum [əˈpɑsəm] *s* zarigüeya

opponent [əˈponənt] *s* contrario

opportune [ˌɑpərˈtjun] *adj* oportuno

opportunist [ˌɑpərˈtjunɪst] *s* oportunista *mf*; maromero

opportuni·ty [ˌɑpərˈtjunɪti] *s* (*pl* **-ties**) oportunidad, ocasión

oppose [əˈpoz] *tr* oponerse a

opposite [ˈɑpəsɪt] *adj* opuesto; de enfrente, p.ej., **the house opposite** la casa de enfrente || *prep* enfrente de || *s* contrario

opposite number *s* igual *mf*, doble *mf*

opposition [ˌɑpəˈzɪʃən] *s* oposición

oppress [əˈpres] *tr* oprimir

oppression [əˈprɛʃən] *s* opresión

oppressive [əˈprɛsɪv] *adj* opresivo; sofocante, bochornoso

opprobrious [əˈprobriˑəs] *adj* oprobioso

opprobrium [əˈprobriˑəm] *s* oprobio

optic [ˈɑptɪk] *adj* óptico || *s* (coll) ojo; **optics** *ssg* óptica

optical [ˈɑptɪkəl] *adj* óptico

optician [ɑpˈtɪʃən] *s* óptico

optimism [ˈɑptɪˌmɪzəm] *s* optimismo

optimist [ˈɑptɪmɪst] *s* optimista *mf*

optimistic [ˌɑptɪˈmɪstɪk] *adj* optimístico

optimize [ˈɑptəˌmaɪz] *tr* mejorar en todo lo posible

option [ˈɑpʃən] *s* opción

optional [ˈɑpʃənəl] *adj* facultativo, potestativo

optometrist [ɑpˈtɑmɪtrɪst] *s* optometrista *mf*

opulent [ˈɑpjələnt] *adj* opulento

or [ɔr] *conj* o, u

oracle [ˈɑrəkəl] u [ˈɔrəkəl] *s* oráculo

oracular [oˈrækjələr] *adj* sentencioso; ambiguo, misterioso; fatídico; sabio

oral [ˈorəl] *adj* oral

orange [ˈɑrɪndʒ] u [ˈɔrɪndʒ] *adj* anaranjado || *s* naranja

orangeade [ˌɑrɪndʒˈed] u [ˌɔrɪndʒˈed] *s* naranjada

orange blossom *s* azahar *m*

orange grove *s* naranjal *m*

orange juice *s* zumo de naranja

orange squeezer *s* exprimidera de naranjas

ol
or

orange tree *s* naranjo
orang-outang [o'ræŋu,tæŋ] *s* orangután *m*
oration [o're/ən] *s* oración, discurso
orator ['arətər] u ['ɔrətər] *s* orador *m*
oratorical [,ɔrə'tɔrıkəl] *adj* oratorio
oratori•o [,ɔrə'tɔri,o] *s* (*pl* **-os**) oratorio
orato•ry ['ɔrə,tori] *s* (*pl* **-ries**) (*art of public speaking*) oratoria; (*small chapel*) oratorio
orb [ɔrb] *s* orbe *m*
orbit ['ɔrbıt] *s* órbita; **to go into orbit** entrar en órbita || *tr* poner en órbita; moverse en órbita alrededor de || *intr* moverse enorbita
orbiter ['ɔrbıtər] *s* satélite *m* (artificial)
orchard ['ɔrt/ərd] *s* huerto
orchestra ['ɔkıstrə] *s* orquesta; (*parquet*) platea
orchestrate ['ɔrkıs,tret] *tr* orquestar
orchid ['ɔrkıd] *s* orquídea
ordain [ɔr'den] *tr* (eccl) ordenar; destinar; mandar
ordeal [ɔr'dil] u [ɔr'di•əl] *s* prueba rigurosa o penosa; (hist) juicio de Dios
order ['ɔrdər] *s* (*way one thing follows another; formal or methodical arrangement; peace, quiet; class, category*) orden *m*; (*command; honor society; monastic brotherhood; fraternal organization*) orden *f*; tarea, p.ej., **a big order** una tarea peliaguda; (com) pedido; (com) giro, libranza; (*formation*) (mil) orden 1m; (*command*) (mil) orden *f*; **in order that** para que, a fin de que; **in order to** + *inf* para + *inf*, a fin de + *inf*; **to get out of order** descomponerse; **to give an order** dar una orden; (com) hacer un pedido || *tr* ordenar; mandar; encargar, pedir; mandar hacer; **to order around** ser muy mandón con; **to order someone away** mandar a uno que se marche
order blank *s* hoja de pedidos
order•ly ['ɔrdərli] *adj* ordenado, gobernoso; tranquilo, obediente || *s* (*pl* **-lies**) asistente *m* en un hospital; (mil) ordenanza *m*
ordinal ['ɔrdınəl] *adj* & *s* ordinal *m*
ordinance ['ɔrdınəns] *s* ordenanza
ordinary ['ɔrdı,nɛri] *adj* ordinario
ordnance ['ɔrdnəns] *s* artillería, cañones *mpl*; pertrechos de guerra
ore [or] *s* mena, mineral metalífero
organ ['ɔrgən] *s* órgano
organ•dy ['ɔrgəndi] *s* (*pl* **-dies**) organdí *m*
or'gan-grind'er *s* organillero
organic [ɔr'gænık] *adj* orgánico
organism ['ɔrgə,nızəm] *s* organismo
organist ['ɔrgənıst] *s* organista *mf*
organize ['ɔrgə,naız] *tr* organizar
organ loft *s* tribuna del órgano
orgasm ['ɔrgæzəm] *s* orgasmo
orgiastic [,ɔrdʒi'æstık] *adj* orgiástico
or•gy ['ɔrdʒi] *s* (*pl* **-gies**) orgía
orient ['ɔri•ənt] *s* oriente *m* || **Orient** *s* oriente || **orient** ['ɔri,ɛnt] *tr* orientar
oriental [,ɔri'ɛntəl] *adj* oriental
orifice ['ɔrıfıs] *s* orificio
origin ['ɔrıdʒın] *s* origen *m*
original [ə'rıdʒınəl] *adj* & *s* original *m*

originate [ə'rıdʒı,net] *tr* originar || *intr* originarse
oriole ['ori,ol] *s* oropéndola
Orkney Islands ['ɔrkni] *spl* Órcadas
ormolu ['ɔrmə,lu] *s* (*gold powder used in gilding*) oro molido; (*alloy of zinc and copper*) similor *m*; bronce dorado
ornament ['ɔrnəmənt] *s* ornamento || ['ɔrnə,mɛnt] *tr* ornamentar
ornate [ɔr'net] u ['ɔrnet] *adj* muy ornado; (*style*) florido
orphan ['ɔrfən] *adj* & *s* huérfano || *tr* dejar huérfano
orphanage [.'ɔrfənıdʒ] *s* (*institution*) orfanato; órfelinato (SAm); (*state, condition*) orfandad
orphan asylum *s* asilo de huérfanos
Orpheus ['ɔrfjus] u ['ɔrfi•əs] *s* Orfeo
orthodontic appliance [,ɔrθə'dantık] *s* aparato de ortodoncia
orthodontics [,ɔrθə'dantıks] *s* ortodoncia
orthodox ['ɔrθə,daks] *adj* ortodoxo
orthogra•phy [ɔr'θagrəfi] *s* (*pl* **-phies**) ortografía
oscillate ['ɑsı,let] *intr* oscilar
osier ['oʒər] *s* mimbre *m* & *f*; sauce mimbrero
ossi•fy ['ɑsı,faı] *v* (*pret* & *pp* **-fied**) *tr* osificar || *intr* osificarse
ostensible [ɑs'tɛnsıbəl] *adj* aparente, pretendido, supuesto
ostentatious [,ɑstɛn'te/əs] *adj* (*pretentious*) ostentativo; (*showy*) ostentoso
osteopath ['ɑstı•ə,pæθ] *s* osteópata *mf*
osteopathy [,ɑstı'ɑpəθi] *s* osteopatía
ostracism ['ɑstrə,sızəm] *s* ostracismo
ostrich ['ɑstrı/] *s* avestruz *m*
O.T. *abbr* **Old Testament**
other ['ʌðər] *adj* & *pron indef* otro || *adv*— **other than** de otra manera que
otherwise ['ʌðər,waız] *adv* otramente, de otra manera; en otras circunstancias; fuera de eso; si no, de otro modo
otherworldly ['ʌðər,wʌrldli] *adj* extraterrestre
otter ['ɑtər] *s* nutria
ottoman ['ɑtəmən] *s* (*corded fabric*) otomán *m*; (*sofa*) otomana; escañuelo con cojín || **Ottoman** *adj* & *s* otomano
ouch [aʊt/] *interj* ¡ax!
ought [ɔt] *s* alguna cosa; cero; **for ought I know** por lo que yo sepa || *v aux* se emplea para formar el modo potencial, p.ej., **he ought to go at once** debiera salir en seguida
ounce [aʊns] *s* onza
our [aʊr] *adj poss* nuestro
ours [aʊrz] *pron poss* el nuestro; nuestro
ourselves [aʊr'sɛlvz] *pron pers* nosotros mismos; nos, p.ej., **we enjoyed ourselves** nos divertimos
oust [aʊst] *tr* echar fuera, desposeer; desahuciar (*al inquilino*)
out [aʊt] *adj* ausente; apagado; exterior; divulgado; publicado; (*size*) poco común || *adv* afuera, fuera; al aire libre; hasta el fin; **out for** buscando; **out of** de; entre; de

entre; fuera de; más allá de; (*kindness, fear, etc.*) por; (*money*) sin; (*a suit of cards*) fallo a; sobre, p.ej., **in nine out of ten cases** en nueve casos sobre diez; **out to** + *inf* esforzándose por + *inf* ‖ *prep* por; allá en ‖ *interj* ¡fuera de aquí! ‖ *s* cesante *mf*; **to be at outs** u **on the outs** estar de monos

out and away *adv* con mucho

out'-and-out' *adj* perfecto, verdadero, rematado ‖ *adv* completamente

out'-and-out'er *s* intransigente *mf*; extremista *mf*

out•bid' *v* (*pret* **-bid**; *pp* **-bid** o **-bidden**; *ger* **-bidding**) *tr* pujar más que (*otra persona*); (*bridge*) sobrepasar

out'board' motor *s* motor *m* fuera de borda, fuera-bordo *m*

out'break' *s* tumulto, motín *m*; (*of anger*) arranque *m*; (*of war*) estallido; (*of an epidemic*) brote *m*

out'build'ing *s* dependencia, edificio accesorio

out'burst' *s* explosión, arranque *m*; **outburst of laughter** carcajada

out'cast' *s* proscripto, paria *mf*; vagabundo

out'come' *s* resultado

out'cry' *s* (*pl* **-cries**) grito; gritería, clamoreo

out•dat'ed *adj* fuera de moda, anticuado

out•do' *v* (**-did**; *pp* **-done**) *tr* exceder; **to outdo oneself** excederse a sí mismo

out'door' *adj* al aire libre

out'doors' *adv* al aire libre, fuera de casa ‖ *s* aire *m* libre, campo raso

outer space [`aʊtər] *s* espacio exterior

out'field' *s* (baseball) jardín *m*

out'field'er *s* (baseball) jardinero

out'fit *s* equipo; traje *m*; juego de herramientas; (*of soldiers*) cuerpo; (*of a bride*) ajuar *m*; (com) compañía ‖ *v* (*pret & pp* **-fitted**; *ger* **-fitting**) *tr* equipar

out'go'ing *adj* de salida; cesante; (*tide*) descendente; (*nature, character*) exteriorista ‖ *s* salida

out•grow' *v* (*pret* **-grew**; *pp* **-grown**) *tr* crecer más que; ser ya grande para; ser ya viejo para; ser ya más apto que; dejar (*las cosas de los niños; a los amigos de la niñez, etc.*) ‖ *intr* extenderse

out'growth' *s* excrecencia, bulto; (*of leaves in springtime*) nacimiento; consecuencia, resultado

outing [`aʊtɪŋ] *s* jira, excursión al campo

outlandish [aʊt`lændɪʃ] *adj* estrafalario; de aspecto extranjero; de acento extranjero

out•last' *tr* durar más que; sobrevivir a

out'law' *s* forajido, bandido; prófugo, proscrito ‖ *tr* proscribir; declarar ilegal

out'lay' *s* desembolso ‖ **out•lay'** *v* (*pret & pp* **-laid**) *tr* desembolsar

out'let *s* salida; desaguadero; orificio de salida; (elec) caja de enchufe; (*tap*) (elec) toma de corriente *m*

out'line' *s* contorno; trazado; esquema *m*; esbozo, bosquejo; compendio ‖ *tr* contornar; trazar; trazar el esquema de; esbozar, bosquejar; compendiar

out•live' *tr* sobrevivir a; durar más que

out'look' *s* perspectiva; expectativa; concepto de la vida, punto de vista; atalaya

out'ly'ing *adj* remoto, circundante, de las afueras

out•mod'ed *adj* fuera de moda

out•num'ber *tr* exceder en número, ser más numeroso que

out'-of-date' *adj* fuera de moda, anticuado

out'-of-door' *adj* al aire libre

out'-of-doors' *adj* al aire libre ‖ *adv* al aire libre, fuera de casa ‖ *s* aire *m* libre, campo raso

out'-of-print' *adj* agotado

out'-of-the-way' *adj* apartado, remoto; poco usual, poco común

out of tune *adj* desafinado ‖ *adv* desafinadamente

out of work *adj* desempleado, sin trabajo

out'pa'tient *s* paciente *mf* de consulta externa

out'post' *s* avanzada

out'put' *s* rendimiento; (elec) salida; (mech) rendimiento de trabajo, efecto útil

out'rage' *s* atrocidad; ultraje *m* ‖ *tr* maltratar; ultrajar; escandalizar

outrageous [aʊt`redʒəs] *adj* (*grossly offensive*) ultrajoso; (*shocking, fierce*) atroz; (*extreme*) extravagante

out•rank' *tr* exceder en rango o grado

out'rid'er *s* carrerista *m*; (Brit) viajante *m* de comercio

out'right' *adj* cabal, completo; franco, sincero ‖ *adv* enteramente; de una vez; sin rodeos; en seguida

out'run'ner *s* volante *m* (*criado*)

out'set' *s* principio

out'side' *adj* exterior; superficial; ajeno; (*price*) (el) máximo ‖ *adv* fuera, afuera; **outside of** fuera de ‖ *prep* fuera de; más allá de; (coll) a excepción de ‖ *s* exterior *m*; superficie *f*; apariencia

outsider [,aʊt`saɪdər] *s* forastero; intruso

out'skirts' *spl* afueras

out'spo'ken *adj* boquifresco, franco

out•stand'ing *adj* sobresaliente; prominente; sin pagar, sin cobrar

outward [`aʊtwərd] *adj* exterior; superficial ‖ *adv* exteriormente, hacia fuera

out•weigh' *tr* pesar más que; contrapesar, compensar

out•wit' *v* (*pret & pp* **-witted**; *ger* **-witting**) *tr* burlar, ser más listo que; despistar (*al perseguidor*)

oval [`ovəl] *adj* oval ‖ *s* óvalo

ova•ry [`ovəri] *s* (*pl* **-ries**) ovario

ovation [o`veʃən] *s* ovación

oven [`ʌvən] *s* horno

over [`ovər] *adj* acabado, concluído; superior; adicional; excesivo ‖ *adv* encima; al otro lado, a la otra orilla; hacia abajo; al revés; patas arriba; otra vez, de nuevo; de añadidura; (*at the bottom of a page*) a la vuelta; acá, p.ej., **hand over the money** déme acá el dinero; **over again** una vez más; **over against** enfrente de; a distinción de; en contraste con; **over and over** repetidas veces; **over here** acá; **over in** allá en; **over there** allá ‖ *prep* sobre, encima de, por encima de; por; de un extremo a otro de; al otro lado de; más allá de; desde; (*a certain number*) más de; acerca de; por causa de; durante; **over and above** además de, en exceso de

o′ver•all′ *adj* cabal, completo; extremo, total ‖ **overalls** *spl* pantalones *mf* de trabajo; overol *m*

o′ver•bear′ing *adj* altanero, imperioso

o′ver•board′ *adv* al agua; **man overboard!** ¡hombre al agua!; **to throw overboard** arrojar, echar o tirar por la borda

o′ver•cast′ *adj* encapotado, nublado ‖ *s* cielo encapotado ‖ *v* (*pret & pp* **-cast**) *tr* nublar

o′ver•charge′ *s* cargo excesivo; recargo de precio; sobrecarga; (elec) carga excesiva ‖ o′ver•charge′ *tr* hacer pagar más del valor, cobrar demasiado a; cargar (*p.ej.*, *50 pesetas*) de más; (elec) poner una carga excesiva a

o′ver•coat′ *s* abrigo, gabán *m*, sobretodo

o′ver•come′ *v* (*pret* **-came;** *pp* **-come**) *tr* vencer; rendir; superar (*dificultades*)

o′ver•crowd′ *tr* atestar, apiñar; poblar con exceso

o′ver•do *v* (*pret* **-did;** *pp* **-done**) *tr* exagerar; agobiar; asurar, requemar ‖ *intr* cansarse mucho, excederse en el trabajo

o′ver•dose′ *s* sobredosis *f*, dosis excesiva ‖ *intr* tomar una dosis excesiva

o′ver•draft′ *s* sobregiro, giro en descubierto

o′ver•draw′ *v* (*pret* **-drew;** *pp* **-drawn**) *tr & intr* sobregirar

o′ver•due′ *adj* atrasado; vencido y no pagado

o′ver•eat′ *v* (*pret* **-ate;** *pp* **-eaten**) *tr & intr* comer con exceso

o′ver•es′ti•mate *tr* sobreestimar

o′ver•exer′tion *s* esfuerzo excesivo

o′ver•ex′ploi•ta′tion *s* (*of resources*) explotación abusiva

o′ver•expose′ *tr* sobreexponer

o′ver•expo′sure *s* sobreexposición

o′ver•flow′ *s* desbordamiento, rebosamiento, derrame *m*; caño de reboso ‖ o′ver•flow′ *intr* desbordar, rebosar

o′ver•fly′ *v* (*pret* **-flew;** *pp* **-flown**) *tr* sobrevolar

o′ver•grown′ *adj* demasiado grande para su edad; denso, frondoso

o′ver•hang′ *v* (*pret & pp* **-hung**) *tr* sobresalir por encima de, estar pendiente o colgando sobre; salir fuera del nivel de; amenazar ‖ *intr* estar pendiente, estar colgando

o′ver•haul′ *tr* examinar, registrar, revisar; ir alcanzando, alcanzar; componer, rehabilitar, reacondicionar

o′ver•head′ *adj* de arriba; aéreo, elevado; general, de conjunto ‖ o′ver•head′ *adv* por encima de la cabeza; arriba, en lo alto ‖ o′ver•head′ *s* gastos generales

o′ver•hear′ *v* (*pret & pp* **-heard**) *tr* oír por casualidad; acertar a oír, alcanzar a oír

o′ver•heat′ *tr* recalentar ‖ *intr* recalentarse

overjoyed [‚over′dʒɔɪd] *adj* lleno de alegría; **to be overjoyed** no caber de contento

o′ver•kill′ *s* exceso de potencia; exceso de eficacia ‖ *intr* exceder lo necesario

overland [′ovər‚lænd] u [′ovərlənd] *adj & adv* por tierra, por vía terrestre

o′ver•lap′ *v* (*pret & pp* **-lapped;** *ger* **-lapping**) *tr* solapar, traslapar ‖ *intr* solapar, traslapar; traslaparse (*dos o más cosas*); suceder (*dos hechos*) en parte al mismo tiempo

o′ver•load′ *s* sobrecarga ‖ o′ver•load′ *tr* sobrecargar

o′ver•look′ *tr* dominar con la vista; pasar por alto, no hacer caso de; perdonar, tolerar; espiar, vigilar; cuidar de, dirigir; dar a, p.ej., **the window overlooks the garden** la ventana da al jardín

o′ver•lord′ *s* jefe supremo ‖ o′ver•lord′ *tr* dominar despóticamente, imponerse a

overly [′ovərli] *adv* (coll) excesivamente, demasiado

o′ver•night′ *adv* toda la noche; de la tarde a la mañana; **to stay overnight** pasar la noche

overnight bag *s* saco de noche

o′ver•pass′ *s* viaducto

o′ver•pop′u•late′ *tr* superpoblar

o′ver•pow′er *tr* dominar, supeditar, subyugar; colmar, dejar estupefacto

overpowering *adj* abrumador, arrollador, irresistible

o′ver•produc′tion *s* superproducción, sobreproducción

o′ver•rate′ *tr* exagerar el valor de

o′ver•run′ *v* (*pret* **-ran;** *pp* **-run;** *ger* **-running**) *tr* cubrir enteramente; infestar; exceder; **to overrun one's time** quedarse más de lo justo; hablar más de lo justo

o′ver•sea′ u o′ver•seas′ *adj* de ultramar ‖ o′ver•sea′ u o′ver•seas′ *adv* allende los mares, en ultramar

o′ver•seer′ *s* director *m*, superintendente *mf*

o′ver•shad′ow *tr* sombrear; (fig) eclipsar

o′ver•shoe′ *s* chanclo, zapato de goma

o′ver•shoot′ *v* (*pret & pp* **-shot**) *tr* tirar por encima de o más allá de; **to overshoot oneself** pasarse de listo, excederse

o′ver•sight′ *s* inadvertencia, descuido

o′ver•sleep′ *v* (*pret & pp* **-slept**) *intr* dormir demasiado tarde

o′ver•step′ *v* (*pret & pp* **-stepped;** *ger* **-stepping**) *tr* exceder, traspasar

o′ver•stock′ *tr* abarrotar

o′ver•sup•ply′ *s* (*pl* **-plies**) provisión excesiva ‖ o′ver•sup•ply′ *v* (*pret* **-plied**) *tr* proveer en exceso

overt [′ovərt] u [o′vʌrt] *adj* abierto, manifiesto; premeditado

o′ver•take′ *v* (*pret* **-took;** *pp* **-taken**) *tr* alcanzar; sobrepasar; sorprender; sobrevenir a

o′ver•the-count′er *adj* vendido directamente al comprador; vendido en tienda al por mayor

o′ver•throw′ *s* derrocamiento; trastorno ‖ o′ver•throw′ *v* (*pret* **-threw;** *pp* **-thrown**) *tr* derrocar; trastornar o'ver•time' *adj & adv* en exceso de las horas regulares ‖ *s* horas extraordinarias de trabajo, horas extra

o'ver•trump *s* contrafallo ‖

o'ver•trump' *tr & intr* contrafallar

overture ['ovərtʃər] *s* insinuación, proposición; (mus) obertura

o'ver•turn' *s* vuelco; movimiento de mercancías ‖ o'ver•turn' *tr* volcar; trastornar; derrocar ‖ *intr* volcar; trastornarse

overweening [,ovər'winɪŋ] *adj* arrogante, presuntuoso

o'ver•weight' *adj* excesivamente gordo o grueso ‖ *s* sobrepeso; exceso de peso; peso de añadidura

overwhelm [,ovər'hwɛlm] *tr* abrumar; inundar; anonadar; (*with favors, gifts, etc.*) colmar

o'ver•work' *s* trabajo excesivo, exceso de trabajo; trabajo fuera de las horas regulares ‖ o'ver•work' *tr* hacer trabajar demasiado; oprimir con el trabajo ‖ *intr* trabajar demasiado

Ovid ['avɪd] *s* Ovidio

ovum ['ovəm] *s* óvulo

ow [au] *interj* ¡ax!

owe [o] *tr* deber, adeudar ‖ *intr* tener deudas

owing ['o•ɪŋ] *adj* adeudado; debido, pagadero; owing to debido a, por causa de

owl [aul] *s* buho, lechuza, mochuelo

own [on] *adj* propio, p.ej., my own brother mi propio hermano ‖ *s* suyo, lo suyo; on one's own (coll) por su propia cuenta; (*without taking advice from anyone*) por su cabeza; (*without help from anyone*) de su cabeza; to come into one's own entrar en posesión de lo suyo; tener el éxito merecido, recibir el honor merecido; to hold one's own no aflojar, no cejar, mantenerse firme ‖ *tr* poseer; reconocer ‖ *intr* confesar; to own up to (coll) confesar de plano (*una culpa, un delito, etc.*)

owner ['onər] *s* amo, dueño, poseedor *m*, posesor *m*, proprietario

ownership ['onər,ʃɪp] *s* posesión, propiedad

owner's license *s* permiso de circulación, patente *f* de circulación

ox [aks] *s* (*pl* oxen) ['aksən] buey *m*

ox'cart' *s* carreta de bueyes

oxide ['aksaɪd] *s* óxido

oxidize ['aksɪ,daɪz] *tr* oxidar ‖ *intr* oxidarse

oxygen ['aksɪdʒən] *s* oxígeno

oxygen tent *s* cámara o tienda de oxígeno

oxytone ['aksɪ,ton] *adj & s* oxítono

oyster ['ɔɪstər] *adj* ostrero ‖ *s* ostra

oyster bed *s* ostrero

oyster cocktail *s* ostras en su concha

oyster fork *s* desbullador *m*

oys'ter•house' *s* ostrería

oys'ter•knife' *s* abreostras *m*

oyster•man ['ɔɪstərmən] *s* (*pl* -men [mən]) ostrero

oyster opener ['opənər] *s* desbullador *m*

oyster shell *s* desbulla, concha de ostra

oyster stew *s* sopa de ostras

oz. *abbr* ounce, ounces

ozone ['ozon] *s* ozono; (coll) aire fresco

ozone layer *s* capa de ozono

ozs. *abbr* ounces

ov
pa

P

P, p [pi] decimosexta letra del alfabeto inglés

p. *abbr* page, participle

P.A. *abbr* Passenger Agent, power of attorney, Purchasing Agent

pace [pes] *s* paso; to keep pace with ir, andar o avanzar al mismo paso que; to put through one's paces poner (*a uno*) a prueba; dar a (*uno*) ocasión de lucirse; to set the pace establecer el paso; dar el ejemplo ‖ *tr* establecer el paso para; medir a pasos; recorrer a pasos; to pace the floor pasearse desesperadamente por la habitación ‖ *intr* andar a pasos regulares

pace'mak'er *s* (med) marcapaso, marcapasos *m*

pacific [pə'sɪfɪk] *adj* pacífico ‖ Pacific *adj & s* Pacífico

pacifier ['pæsɪ,faɪ•ər] *s* pacificador *m*, chupón *m*; (*teething ring*) chupador *m*

pacifism [ˈpæsɪ,fɪzəm] *s* pacifismo

pacifist ['pæsɪfɪst] *adj & s* pacifista *mf*

paci•fy ['pæsɪ,faɪ] *v* (*pret & pp* -fied) *tr* pacificar

pack [pæk] *s* lío, fardo; paquete *m*; (*of hounds*) jauría; (*of cattle*) manada; (*of evildoers*) pandilla; (*of lies*) sarta, montón *m*; (*of playing cards*) baraja; (*of cigarettes*) cajetilla; (*of floating ice*) témpano (med) compresa ‖ *tr* empaquetar; embaular; encajonar; hacer (*el baúl, la maleta*); conservar en latas; apretar, atestar; cargar (*una acémila*); escoger de modo fraudulento (*un jurado*); to be packed in (coll) estar como sardinas en banasta ‖ *intr* empaquetarse; hacer el baúl, hacer la maleta; consolidarse, formar masa compacta

package ['pækɪdʒ] *s* paquete *m* ‖ *tr* empaquetar

pack animal *s* acémila, animal *m* de carga

packing box o case *s* caja de embalaje

packing house *s* frigorífico

packing slip *s* hoja de embalaje

pack'sad'dle *s* albarda

pack'thread' *s* bramante *m*

pack train *s* recua

pact [pækt] *s* pacto

pad [pæd] *s* conjincillo, almohadilla; (*of writing paper*) bloc *m;* (*for inking*) tampón *m;* (*of an aquatic plant*) hoja; (*for launching a rocket*) plataforma *f;* (*sound of footsteps*) pisada ‖ *v* (*pret & pp* **padded;** *ger* **padding**) *tr* acolchar, rellenar; meter mucho ripio en (*un escrito*) ‖ *intr* andar, caminar; caminar despacio y pesadamente

paddle [ˈpædəl] *s* (*of a canoe*) canalete *m;* (*of a wheel*) pala, paleta; (*for spanking*) palo ‖ *tr* impulsar con canalete; (*to spank*) apalear ‖ *intr* remar con canalete; remar suavemente; (*to splash*) chapotear

paddle wheel *s* rueda de paletas

paddock [ˈpædək] *s* dehesa; (*at a racecourse*) paddock *m*

paddy wagon [ˈpædi] *s* (coll) camión *m* de policía

pad'lock' *s* candado ‖ *tr* cerrar con candado; (*to lock up officially*) condenar (*una habitación, un teatro*)

pagan [ˈpegən] *adj & s* pagano

paganism [ˈpegə͵nɪzəm] *s* paganismo

page [pedʒ] *s* (*of a book*) página; (*boy attendant*) paje *m;* (*in a hotel or club*) botones *m* ‖ *tr* paginar; buscar llamando

pageant [ˈpædʒənt] *s* espectáculo público

pageant•ry [ˈpædʒəntri] *s* (*pl* -**ries**) pompa, fausto; (*empty display*) bambolla

pail [pel] *s* balde *m,* cubo

pain [pen] *s* dolor *m;* **on pain of** so pena de; **pains** esmero, trabajo; dolores de parto; **to take pains** esmerarse ‖ *tr & intr* doler

painful [ˈpenfəl] *adj* doloroso; penoso

pain'kill'er *s* analgésico; calmante *m* del dolor

painless [ˈpenlɪs] *adj* sin dolor, indoloro; fácil, sin trabajo

pains'tak'ing *adj* esmerado

paint [pent] *s* pintura‖ *tr* pintar ‖ *intr* pintar; pintarse, repintarse

paint'box' *s* caja de colores

paint'brush' *s* brocha, pincel *m*

painter [ˈpentər] *s* pintor *m*

painting [ˈpentɪŋ] *s* pintura

paint remover [rɪˈmuvər] *s* sacapintura *m,* quitapintura *m*

pair [pɛr] *s* par *m;* (*of people*) pareja; (*of cards*) parejas ‖ *tr* aparear ‖ *intr* aparearse

pair of scissors *s* tijeras

pair of trousers *s* pantalones *mpl*

pajamas [peˈdʒɑməz] o [peˈdʒæməz] *spl* pijama

Pakistan [͵pɑkɪˈstɑn] *s* el Paquistán

Pakistani [͵pɑkɪˈstɑni] *adj & s* paquistano, paquistaní *mf*

pal [pæl] *s* (coll) compañero; cumpa *m* (SAm) ‖ *v* (*pret & pp* **palled;** *ger* **palling**) *intr* (coll) ser compañeros

palace [ˈpælɪs] *s* palacio

palatable [ˈpælətəbəl] *adj* sabroso, apetitoso

palatal [ˈpælətəl] *adj & s* palatal *f*

palate [ˈpælɪt] *s* paladar *m*

pale [pel] *adj* pálido; (*color*) claro ‖ *s* estaca; palizada; límite *m,* término ‖ *intr* palidecer

pale'face' *s* rostropálido

palette [ˈpælɪt] *s* paleta

palfrey [ˈpɔlfri] *s* palafrén *m*

palisade [͵pælɪˈsed] *s* estaca; estacada; (*line of cliffs*) acantilado

pall [pɔl] *s* paño de ataúd, paño mortuorio; (eccl) palia ‖ *tr* hartar, saciar; quitar el sabor a ‖ *intr* perder el sabor; **to pall on** hartar, saciar

pall'bear'er *s* acompañante *m* de un cadáver; portador *m* del féretro

palliate [ˈpælɪ͵et] *tr* paliar

pallid [ˈpælɪd] *adj* pálido

pallor [ˈpælər] *s* palidez *f,* palor *m*

palm [pɑm] *s* (*of the hand*) palma; (*measure*) palmo; (*tree and leaf*) palma; **to carry off the palm** llevarse la palma; **to grease the palm of** (slang) untar la mano a; **to yield the palm to** reconocer por vencedor ‖ *tr* esconder en la mano; escamotear (*una carta*); **to palm off something on someone** encajarle una cosa a uno

palmet•to [pælˈmɛto] *s* (*pl* -**tos** o -**toes**) palmito

palmist [ˈpɑmɪst] *s* quiromántico

palmistry [ˈpɑmɪstri] *s* quiromancia

palm leaf *s* palma, hoja de la palmera

palm oil *s* aceite *m* de palma; (slang) propina; (slang) soborno

Palm Sunday *s* domingo de ramos

palpable [ˈpælpəbəl] *adj* palpable

palpitate [ˈpælpɪ͵tet] *intr* palpitar

pal•sy [ˈpɔlzi] *s* (*pl* -**sies**) perlesía ‖ *v* (*pret & pp* -**sied**) *tr* paralizar

pal•try [ˈpɔltri] *adj* (*comp* -**trier;** *super* -**triest**) vil, ruin, mezquino

pamper [ˈpæmpər] *tr* mimar, consentir

pamphlet [ˈpæmflɪt] *s* folleto, panfleto

pan [pæn] *s* cacerola, cazuela, sartén *f;* caldera, perol *m* ‖ *v* (*pret & pp* **panned;** *ger* **panning**) *tr* cocer, freír; separar (*el oro*) en la gamella; (coll) criticar ásperamente ‖ *intr* separar el oro en la gamella; dar oro; **to pan out well** (coll) tener éxito, dar buen resultado

Pan *s* Pan

panacea [͵pænəˈsi•ə] *s* panacea

Panama Canal [ˈpænə͵mɑ] *s* canal *m* de Panamá

Panama Canal Zone *s* Zona del Canal

Panama hat *s* panamá *m*

Panamanian [͵pænəˈmeni•ən] *adj & s* panameño

Pan-American [͵pænəˈmɛrɪkən] *adj* panamericano

pan'cake' *s* hojuela, panqueque *m* ‖ *intr* (aer) desplomarse

pancake landing *s* aterrizaje aplastado, aterrizaje en desplome

pancreas [ˈpænkrɪ•əs] *s* páncreas *m*

panda [ˈpændə] *s* panda *mf*

pander [ˈpændər] *s* alcahuete *m* ‖ *intr* alcahuetear; **to pander to** gratificar

pane [pen] *s* cristal *m,* vidrio, hoja de vidrio

pan•el [ˈpænəl] *s* panel *m,* entrepaño, cuarterón *m;* grupo de personas en discusión cara al público; (aut, elec) tablero, panel *m;* (law) lista de personas que pueden servir como jurados ‖ *v* (*pret & pp* **peled** o -**elled;**

ger **-elling** o **-elling**) *tr* adornar con cuarterones, labrar en cuarterones; artesonar (*un techo o bóveda*)

panel discussion *s* coloquio cara al público

panelist ['pænəlɪst] *s* coloquiante *mf* cara al público

panel lights *spl* luces *fpl* del tablero

pang [pæŋ] *s* dolor agudo; (*of remorse*) punzada; (*of death*) agonía

pan'han'dle *s* mango de sartén ‖ *intr* (slang) mendigar, pedir limosna

pan•ic ['pænɪk] *adj & s* pánico ‖ *v* (*pret & pp* **-icked;** *ger* **-icking**) *tr* sobrecoger de pánico ‖ *intr* sobrecogerse de pánico

pan'ic-strick'en *adj* muerto de miedo, sobrecogido de terror

pano•ply ['pænəpli] *s* (*pl* **-plies**) panoplia, traje *m* ceremonial

panorama [,pænə'ræmə] o [,pænə'rɑmə] *s* panorama *m*

pan•sy ['pænzi] *s* (*pl* **-sies**) pensamiento

pant [pænt] *s* jadeo; palpitación; **pants** pantalones *mpl*; **to wear the pants** (coll) calzarse los pantalones ‖ *intr* jadear; palpitar

pantheism ['pænθɪ,ɪzəm] *s* panteísmo

pantheon ['pænθɪ,ɑn] *s* panteón *m*

panther ['pænθər] *s* pantera; puma

panties ['pæntiz] *spl* pantaloncillos de mujer

pantomime ['pæntə,maɪm] *s* pantomima

pan•try ['pæntri] *s* (*pl* **-tries**) despensa

panty hose *s* panty *m*

pap [pæp] *s* papilla, papas

papa•cy ['pepəsi] *s* (*pl* **-cies**) papado

paper ['pepər] *s* papel *m;* (*newspaper*) periódico; (*of needles*) paño ‖ *tr* empapelar

pa'per•back' *s* libro en rústica

pa'per•boy' *s* vendedor *m* de periódicos

paper clip *s* clip *m,* sujetapapeles *m;* presilla; prensador (CAm); gancho de papel (Col)

paper cone *s* cucurucho

paper cutter *s* cortapapeles *m,* guillotina

paper doll *s* muñeca de papel

paper hanger *s* empapelador *m,* papelista *mf*

paper knife *s* cortapapeles *m*

paper mill *s* fábrica de papel

paper money *s* papel *m* moneda

paper profits *spl* ganancias no realizadas sobre valores no vendidos

paper tape *s* cinta perforada

pa'per•weight' *s* pisapapeles *m*

paper work *s* preparación o comprobación de escritos; papelerío

paprika [pæ'prikə] o ['pæprɪkə] *s* pimentón *m*

papy•rus [pe'paɪrəs] *s* (*pl* **-ri** [raɪ]) papiro

par. *abbr* **paragraph, parallel, parenthesis, parish**

par [pɑr] *adj* a la par; nominal; normal ‖ *s* paridad; valor *m* nominal; **above par** sobre la par; con beneficio; con premio; **below par** o **under par** bajo la par; con pérdida; (coll) indispuesto; **to be on a par with** correr parejas con

parable ['pærəbəl] *s* parábola

parachute ['pærə,ʃut] *s* paracaídas *m* ‖ *intr* parachutar, lanzarse en paracaídas; **to parachute to safety** salvarse en paracaídas

parachute jump *s* salto en paracaídas

parachutist ['pærə,ʃutɪst] *s* paracaidista *mf*

parade [pə'red] *s* desfile *m;* paseo; ostentación ‖ *tr* ostentar, pasear ‖ *intr* desfilar, pasar por las calles; (mil) formar en parada

paradise ['pærə,daɪs] *s* paraíso

paradox ['pærə,dɑks] *s* paradoja; persona o cosa incomprensibles

paradoxical [,pærə'dɑksɪkəl] *adj* paradójico

paraffin ['pærəfɪn] *s* parafina

paragon ['pærə,gɑn] *s* dechado

paragraph ['pærə,græf] *s* párrafo

Paraguay *s* el Paraguay

Paraguayan [,pærə'gwaɪ•ən] *adj & s* paraguayano, paraguayo

parakeet ['pærə,kit] *s* perico, periquito

paral•lel ['pærə,lɛl] *adj* paralelo ‖ *s* (línea) paralela; (plano) paralelo; (geog) paralelo; **parallels** (typ) doble raya vertical ‖ *v* (*pret & pp* **-leled** o **-lelled;** *ger* **-leling** o **-lelling**) *tr* ser paralelo a; poner en dirección paralela; correr parejas con; (*to compare*) paralelizar

parallel bars *spl* paralelas, barras paralelas

paraly•sis [pə'rælɪsɪs] *s* (*pl* **-ses** [,siz]) parálisis *f*

paralytic [,pærə'lɪtɪk] *adj & s* paralítico

paralyze ['pærə,laɪz] *tr* paralizar

parameter [pə'ræmətər] *s* parámetro

paramount ['pærə,maunt] *adj* capital, supremo, principalísimo

paranoiac [,pærə'nɔɪ•æk] o **paranoid** [pærə,nɔɪd] *adj & s* paranoico

parapet [,pærə,pɛt] *s* parapeto

paraphernalia [,pærəfər'neli•ə] *spl* trastos, atavíos

paraplegia [,pærə'plidʒə] *s* paraplegia

parasite ['pærə,saɪt] *s* parásito

parasitic(al) [,pærə'sɪtɪk(el)] *adj* parasítico, parasitario

parasol ['pærə,sɔl] *s* quitasol *m,* parasol *m*

pa'ra•troop'er *s* paracaidista *m*

pa'ra•troops' *spl* tropas paracaidistas

parboil ['pɑr,bɔɪl] *tr* sancochar; calentar con exceso

par•cel [pɑrsəl] *s* paquete *m,* atado, bulto ‖ *v* (*pret & pp* **-celed** o **-celled;** *ger* **-celing** o **-celling**) *tr* empaquetar; parcelar (*el terreno*); **to parcel out** repartir

parcel post *s* paquetes *mpl* postales

parch [pɑrtʃ] *tr* abrasar, tostar; **to be parched** tener mucha sed

parchment ['pɑrtʃmənt] *s* pergamino

pardon ['pɑrdən] *s* perdón *m;* (*remission of penalty by the state*) indulto; **I beg your pardon** dispense Vd. ‖ *tr* perdonar, dispensar; indultar

pardonable ['pɑrdənəbəl] *adj* perdonable

pardon board *s* junta de perdones

pare [pɛr] *tr* mondar (*fruta*); pelar (*patatas*); cortar (*callos, uñas*); despalmar (*la palma córnea de los animales*); adelgazar; reducir (*gastos*)

parent ['pɛrənt] *adj* madre, matriz, principal ‖ *s* padre o madre; autor *m,* fuente *f,* origen *m;* **parents** padres *mpl*

pa
pa

parentage [ˈpɛrəntɪdʒ] *s* paternidad o maternidad; abolengo, linaje *m*

parent company compañía matriz.

parenthe·sis [pəˈrɛnθɪsɪs] *s* (*pl* **-ses** [ˌsiz]) paréntesis *m*

parenthood [ˈpɛrənt,hʊd] *s* paternidad o maternidad

pariah [pəˈraɪ·ə] o [ˈparɪ·ə] *s* paria *mf*

paring knife [ˈpɛrɪŋ] *s* cuchillo para mondar

parish [ˈpærɪʃ] *s* parroquia, feligresía

parishioner [pəˈrɪʃənər] *s* parroquiano, feligrés *m*

Parisian [pəˈrɪʒən] *adj & s* parisiense *mf*

parity [ˈpærɪti] *s* paridad

park [park] *s* parque *m* ‖ *tr* estacionar, parquear; (coll) colocar, dejar ‖ *intr* estacionar, parquear

parking [ˈparkɪŋ] *s* aparcamiento, estacionamiento; (*space*) parking *m*; **no parking** se prohibe estacionarse

parking lights *spl* (aut) faros de situación

parking lot *s* parque *m* de estacionamiento

parking meter *s* reloj *m* de estacionamiento, parquímetro, parcómetro

parking ticket *s* aviso de multa

park'way *s* gran vía adornado con árboles

parley [ˈparli] *s* parlamento ‖ *intr* parlamentar

parliament [ˈparlɪmənt] *s* parlamento

parlor [ˈparlər] *s* sala; parlatorio, locutorio

parlor car *s* coche-salón *m*

parlor politics *spl* política de café

Parnassus [parˈnæsəs] *s* (*collection of poems*) parnaso; el Parnaso; **to try to climb Parnassus** hacer pinos en poesía

parochial [pəˈrokɪ·əl] *adj* parroquial; estrecho, limitado

paro·dy [ˈpærədi] *s* (*pl* **-dies**) parodia ‖ *v* (*pret & pp* **-died**) *tr* parodiar

parole [pəˈrol] *s* palabra de honor; libertad bajo palabra ‖ *tr* dejar libre bajo palabra

paroxytone [pærˈaksɪ,ton] *adj & s* paroxítono

par·quet [parˈke] *s* entarimado; (theat) platea ‖ *v* (*pret & pp* **-queted** [ˈked]); *ger* **-queting** [ˈke·ɪŋ] *tr* entarimar

parricide [ˈpærɪ,saɪd] *s* (*act*) parricidio; (*person*) parricida *mf*

parrot [ˈpærət] *s* papagayo, loro; (fig) papagayo ‖ *tr* repetir o imitar como loro

par·ry [ˈpæri] *s* (*pl* **-ries**) parada, quite *m* ‖ *v* (*pret & pp* **-ried**) *tr* parar; defenderse de

parse [pars] *tr* analizar (*una oración*) gramaticalmente; describir (*una palabra*) gramaticalmente

parsley [ˈparsli] *s* perejil *m*

parsnip [ˈparsnɪp] *s* chirivía

parson [ˈparsən] *s* cura *m*, párroco; clérigo; pastor *m* protestante

part [part] *s* parte *f*; (*of a machine*) pieza; (*of the hair*) raya; (theat) parte *f*, papel *m*; **part and parcel** parte esencial, parte inseparable, elemento esencial; **parts** partes *fpl*; prendas, dotes *fpl*; **to do one's part** cumplir con su obligación; **to look the part** vestir el cargo; **to take the part of** tomar el partido de, defender; desempeñar

el papel de ‖ *tr* dividir, partir, separar; **to part the hair** hacerse la raya ‖ *intr* separarse; **to part with** deshacerse de, abandonar; despedirse de

par·take [parˈtek] *v* (*pret* **-took** [ˈtʊk]; *pp* **-taken**) *tr* compartir; comer; beber ‖ *intr* participar

Parthenon [ˈparθɪ,nan] *s* Partenón *m*

partial [ˈparʃəl] *adj* parcial; aficionado

participate [parˈtɪsɪ,pet] *intr* participar

participle [ˈpartɪ,sɪpəl] *s* participio

particle [ˈpartɪkəl] *s* partícula, corpúsculo

particle physics *s* física de las partículas

particular [pərˈtɪkjələr] *adj* particular; difícil, exigente, quisquilloso; esmerado; minucioso; **a particular . . .** cierto . . . ‖ *s* particular *m*

partisan [ˈpartɪzən] *adj & s* partidario, partidista *mf*; (mil) partisano

partition [parˈtɪʃən] *s* partición, distribución; división; proción; tabique *m* ‖ *tr* repartir; dividir en cuartos, aposentos; tabicar

partner [ˈpartnər] *s* compañero; (*wife or husband*) cónyuge *mf*; (*in a dance*) pareja *f*; (*in business*) socio

partnership [ˈpartnər,ʃɪp] *s* asociación; consorcio, vida en común; (com) sociedad, asociación comercial

partridge [ˈpartrɪdʒ] *s* perdiz *f*

part'-time *adj* por horas, parcial

par·ty [ˈparti] *adj* de partido; de gala ‖ *s* (*pl* **-ties**) convite *m*, reunión, fiesta, tertulia, recepción; (*for fishing, hunting, etc.; of armed men*) partida; cómplice *mf*, interesado; (pol) partido; (coll) persona, individuo

party girl *s* chica de vida alegre

party-goer [ˈparti,go·ər] *s* tertuliano; fiestero

party line *s* (*between two properties*) linde *m*, lindero; (*of communist party*) línea del partido; (telp) línea compartida

party politics *s* política de partido

pass. *abbr* passenger, passive

pass [pæs] o [pas] *s* paso; (*permit; free ticket; movement of hands of mesmerist, of bullfighter*) pase *m*; (*in an examination*) aprobación; nota de aprobación ‖ *tr* pasar; pasar de largo (*una luz roja*); aprobar (*un proyecto de ley; un examen; a un alumno*); ser aprobado en (*un examen*); dejar atrás; cruzarse con; expresar (*una opinión*); pronunciar (*una sentencia*), dar (*la palabra*); dejar sin protestar; no pagar (*un dividendo*); **to pass off** colar, pasar, hacer aceptar (*una moneda falsa*); disimular (*p.ej., una ofensa con una risa*); **to pass over** omitir, pasar por alto; excusar; desdeñar; dejar sin protestar; postergar (*a un empleado*) ‖ *intr* pasar; pasarse (*introducirse*); aprobar; **to bring to pass** llevar a cabo; **to come to pass** suceder; **to pass as** pasar por; **to pass away** pasar, pasar a mejor vida; **to pass off** pasar (*una enfermedad, una tempestad, etc.*); tener lugar; **to pass out** salir; (slang) desmayarse; **to pass over to** pasarse a (p.ej., el enemigo)

passable ['pæsəbəl] o ['pɑsəbəl] *adj* pasadero; (*law*) promulgable

passage ['pæsɪdʒ] *s* pasaje *m;* paso; pasillo; (*of time*) transcurso; (*of bowels*) evacuación

pass'book' *s* cartilla, libreta de banco

passenger ['pæsəndʒer] *adj* de viajeros ‖ *s* pasajero, viajero

passer-by ['pæsər'baɪ] o ['pɑsər'baɪ] *s* (*pl* **passers-by**) transeúnte *mf*

passing ['pæsɪŋ] o ['pɑsɪŋ] *adj* pasajero; corriente; de aprobado ‖ *s* (*act of passing; death*) paso; (*in an examination*) aprobación

passion ['pæʃən] *s* pasión

passionate ['pæʃənɪt] *adj* apasionado

passive ['pæsɪv] *adj* pasivo ‖ *s* voz pasiva, verbo pasivo

pass'key' *s* llave *f* de paso

Pass'o'ver *s* pascua (*de los hebreos*)

pass'port' *s* pasaporte *m*

pass'word' *s* santo y seña

past [pæst] o [pɑst] *adj* pasado; último; que fué, p.ej., **past president** presidente que fué; acabado, concluído ‖ *adv* más allá; por delante ‖ *prep* más allá de; más de; por delante de; fuera de; después de, p.ej., **past two o'clock** después de las dos; **past belief** increíble; **past cure** incurable; **past hope** sin esperanza ‖ *s* pasado

paste [pest] *s* (*dough; spaghetti, etc.*) pasta; (*for sticking things together*) engrudo ‖ *tr* engrudar, pegar con engrudo

paste'board' *s* cartón *m*

pasteurize ['pæstə,raɪz] *tr* pasterizar

pastime ['pæs,taɪm] *s* pasatiempo

pastor ['pæstər] *s* pastor *m*, clérigo, cura *m*

pastoral ['pæstərəl] *adj* & *s* pastoral *f*

pas•try ['pestri] *s* (*pl* **-tries**) pastelería

pastry cook *s* pastelero, repostero

pastry shop *s* pastelería, repostería

pasture ['pæstər] *s* pasto, pastura, dehesa ‖ *tr* apacentar, pacer ‖ *intr* apacentarse, pacer

past•y ['pesti] *adj* (*comp* **-ier;** *super* **-iest**) pastoso; flojo, fofo, pálido

pat [pæt] *s* golpecito, palmadita; ruido de pasos ligeros; (*of butter*) pastelillo ‖ *v* (*pret* & *pp* **patted;** *ger* **patting**) *tr* dar golpecitos a, golpear ligeramente; palmotear, acariciar con la mano; **to pat on the back** elogiar, cumplimentar

patch [pætʃ] *s* remiendo, parche *m;* terreno, pedazo de terreno; mancha; lunar postizo ‖ *tr* remendar; **to patch up** componer (*una desavenencia*); componer lo mejor posible (*una cosa descompuesta*); hacer aprisa y mal

patent ['petənt] *adj* patente; abierto ‖ ['pætənt] *adj* de patentes ‖ *s* patente *f*, patente de invención; propiedad industrial; **patent applied for** se ha solicitado patente ‖ *tr* patentar

patent leather ['pætənt] *s* charol *m*

patent medicine ['pætənt] *s* medicamento de patente

patent rights ['pætənt] *spl* derechos de patente

paternal [pə'tʌrnəl] *adj* paterno; (*affection*) paternal

paternity [pe'tʌrnɪti] *s* paternidad

path [pæθ] *s* senda, sendero; trayectoria

pathetic [pə'θɛtɪk] *adj* patético

path'find'er baquiano; explorador *m*

patholo•gy [pə'θɑlədʒi] *s* patología

pathos ['peθɑs] *s* patetismo

path'way' *s* senda, sendero

patience ['peʃəns] *s* paciencia

patient ['peʃənt] *adj* paciente ‖ *s* paciente *mf*, enfermo

patriarch ['petrɪ,ɑrk] *s* patriarca *m*

patrician [pə'trɪʃən] *adj* & *s* patricio

patricide ['pætrɪ,saɪd] *s* (*act*) parricidio; (*person*) parricida *mf*

Patrick ['pætrɪk] *s* Patricio

patrimo•ny ['pætrɪ,moni] *s* (*pl* **-nies**) patrimonio

patriot ['petrɪ•ət] *s* patriota *mf*

patriotic [,petrɪ'ɑtɪk] *adj* patriótico

patriotism ['petrɪ•ə,tɪzəm] *s* patriotismo

pa•trol [pə'trol] *s* patrulla ‖ *v* (*pret* & *pp* **-troled** o **-trolled;** *ger* **-troling** o **-trolling**) *tr* & *intr* patrullar

patrol•man [pə'trolmən] *s* (*pl* **-men** [mən]) guardia *m* municipal, vigilante *m* de policía

patrol wagon *s* camion *m* de policía; carro-patrulla *m* (SAm)

patron ['petrən] *adj* tutelar ‖ *s* parroquiano; patrocinador *m*

patronize ['petrə,naɪz] *tr* ser parroquiano de (*un tendero*); comprar de costumbre en; patrocinar; tratar con aire protector

patron saint *s* patrón *m*, santo titular

patter ['pætər] *s* golpeteo; (*of rain*) chapaleteo; charla, parloteo ‖ *intr* golpetear; charlar, parlotear

pattern ['pætərn] *s* patrón *m;* modelo

P.A.U. *abbr* **Pan American Union**

paucity ['pɔsɪti] *s* corto número; falta, escasez *f*, insuficiencia

Paul [pɔl] *s* Pablo; (*name of popes*) Paulo

paunch [pɔntʃ] *s* panza

paunchy ['pɔntʃi] *adj* panzudo

pauper ['pɔpər] *s* pobre *mf*, indigente *mf*

pause [pɔz] *s* pausa; (*mus*) calderón *m;* **to give pause (to)** dar que pensar (a) ‖ *intr* hacer pausa, detenerse brevemente; vacilar

pave [pev] *tr* pavimentar; (*with flagstones*) enlosar; (*with bricks*) enladrillar; (*with pebbles*) enchinar; **to pave the way (for)** preparar el terreno (para), abrir el camino (a)

pavement ['pevmənt] *s* pavimento; (*of brick*) enladrillado; (*of flagstone*) enlosado; (*sidewalk*) acera

pavilion [pə'vɪljən] *s* pabellón *m*

paw [pɔ] *s* pata; garra, zarpa; (coll) mano *f* ‖ *tr* dar zarpazos a, restregar con las uñas; golpear, patear (*el. suelo los caballos*); (coll) manosear; (*to handle overfamiliarly*) (coll) sobar ‖ *intr* piafar (*el caballo*)

pawn [pɔn] *s* (*in chess*) peón *m;* (*security, pledge*) prenda; (*tool of another person*) instrumento; víctima ‖ *tr* empeñar, dar en prenda

pawn'bro'ker s prestamista *mf*

pawn'shop' s casa de empeños, monte *m* de piedad

pawn ticket s papeleta de empeño

pay [pe] s paga; recompensa; castigo merecido ‖ *v* (*pret* & *pp* **paid** [ped]) *tr* pagar; prestar o poner (*atención*); dar (*cumplidos*); dar (*dinero una actividad comercial*); dar dinero a, ser provechoso a; pagar en la misma moneda; pagar con creces; sufrir (*el castigo de una ofensa*); hacer (*una visita*); cubrir (*los gastos*); **to pay back** devolver; pagar en la misma moneda; **to pay off** pagar y despedir (*a un empleado*); pagar todo lo adeudado a; vengarse de; redimir (*una hipoteca*) ‖ *intr* pagar; ser provechoso, valer la pena; **pay as you enter** pague a la entrada; **pay as you go** pagar el impuesto de utilidades con descuentos anticipados; **pay as you leave** pague a la salida

payable ['pe•əbəl] *adj* pagadero

pay boost s aumento de salario

pay'check' s cheque *m* en pago del sueldo; sueldo

pay'day' s día *m* de pago

payee [pe'i] s portador *m* o tenedor *m* (*de un giro*)

pay envelope s sobre *m* con el jornal; jornal *m*, salario

payer ['pe•ər] s pagador *m*

pay load s carga útil

pay'mas'ter s pagador *m*

payment ['pemənt] s pago; castigo

pay roll s nómina, hoja de paga

pay station s teléfono público

pd. *abbr* **paid**

p.d. *abbr* **per diem, potential difference**

pea [pi] s guisante *m*, chícharo

peace [pis] s paz *f;* **to make peace with** hacer las paces con

peaceable ['pisəbəl] *adj* pacífico

Peace Corps s Cuerpo de Paz

peaceful ['pisfəl] *adj* tranquilo, pacífico, sosegado

peace'mak'er s iris *m* de paz

peace of mind s serenidad del espíritu

peace pipe s pipa ceremonial (*de los pieles rojas*)

peach [pitʃ] s melocotón *m;* (slang) persona o cosa admirables

peach tree s melocotonero

peach•y ['pitʃi] *adj* (*comp* **-ier;** *super* **-iest**) (slang) estupendo, magnífico

pea'cock' s pavo real, pavón *m;* (fig) pinturero

peak [pik] s pico, cima, cumbre *f;* punta, extremo; máximo; (*of a cap*) visera; (*of a curve*) cresta; (elec) pico

peak hour s hora punta

peak load s (elec) carga de punta; demanda máxima

peal [pil] s fragor *m;* estruendo; (*of bells*) repique *m;* juego de campanas ‖ *intr* repicar; resonar

peal of laughter s carcajada

peal of thunder s trueno

pea'nut' s cacahuete *m*, aráquida; **to work for peanuts** recibir poco sueldo

peanut vendor s manicero

pear [pɛr] s pera

pearl [pʌrl] s margarita, perla; (*of running water*) murmullo ‖ *tr* alijofarar

pearl oyster s madreperla

pear tree s peral *m*

peasant ['pɛzənt] *adj* & s campesino, rústico

pea'shoot'er s cerbatana, bodoquera

pea soup s sopa de guisantes; (coll) neblina espesa y amarillenta

peat [pit] s turba

pebble ['pɛbəl] s china, guija ‖ *tr* agranelar (*el cuero*)

peck [pɛk] s medida de áridos (*nueve litros*); montón *m;* picotazo; beso dado de mala gana ‖ *tr* picotear ‖ *intr* picotear; (coll) comer melindrosamente; **to peck at** querer picar; regañar constantemente; (coll) comer melindrosamente

peculate ['pɛkjə,let] *tr* & *intr* malversar

peculíar [pɪ'kjuljər] *adj* peculiar; singular, raro; excéntrico

pedagogue ['pɛdə,gɑg] s pedagogo; dómine *m*, pedante *m*

pedagogy ['pɛdə,godʒi] o ['pɛdə,gɑdʒi] s pedagogía

ped•al ['pɛdəl] s pedal *m* ‖ *v* (*pret* & *pp* **-aled** o **-alled;** *ger* **-aling** o **-alling**) *tr* impulsar pedaleando ‖ *intr* pedalear

pedant ['pɛdənt] s pedante *mf*

pedantic [pɪ'dæntɪk] *adj* pedantesco

pedant•ry ['pɛdəntri] s (*pl* **-ries**) pedantería

peddle ['pɛdəl] *tr* ir vendiendo de puerta en puerta; traer y llevar (*chismes*); vender (*favores*) ‖ *intr* ser buhonero

peddler ['pɛdlər] s buhonero

pederasty ['pɛdə,ræsti] s pederastia

pedestal ['pɛdɪstəl] s pedestal *m*

pedestrian [pɪ'dɛstrɪ•ən] *adj* pedestre ‖ s peatón *m*

pediatrician [,pidɪ•ə'trɪʃən] s pediatra *mf*

pediatrics [,pidɪ'ætrɪks] *ssg* pediatría

pedigree ['pɛdɪ,gri] s árbol genealógico; ascendencia; fuente *f,* origen *m*

pediment ['pɛdɪmənt] s frontón *m*

pee [pi] s (coll) pipí *m* ‖ *intr* (coll) hacer pipí

peek [pik] s mirada rápida y furtiva ‖ *intr* mirar a hurtadillas

peel [pil] s cáscara, pellejo ‖ *tr* pelar ‖ *intr* pelarse

peep [pip] s mirada a hurtadillas; (*of chickens*) pío ‖ *intr* mirar a hurtadillas; piar (*los pollos*)

peep'hole' s atisbadero; (*in a door*) mirilla, ventanillo

peep show s mundonuevo; (slang) vistas sicalípticas

peer [pir] s par *m* ‖ *intr* mirar fijando la vista de cerca; **to peer at** mirar con ojos de miope; **to peer into** mirar hacia lo interior de, escudriñar

peerless ['pɪrlɪs] *adj* sin par

peeve [piv] s (coll) cojijo ‖ *tr* (coll) enojar, irritar

peevish ['pivɪʃ] *adj* cojijoso, displicente

peg [pɛg] s clavija, claveta, estaquilla; **to take down a peg** (coll) bajar los humos a ‖ v (pret & pp **pegged;** ger **pegging**) tr enclavijar; señalar con clavijas; fijar (precios) ‖ intr trabajar con ahinco; **to peg away at** afanarse en

peg leg s pata de palo

peg top s peonza; **peg tops** pantalones anchos de caderas y perniles ajustados

Peking ['pi'kɪŋ] s Pequín

Peking·ese [,pikɪ'niz] adj pequinés ‖ s (pl -ese) pequinés m

pelf [pɛlf] s dinero mal ganado

pell-mell ['pɛl'mɛl] adj tumultuoso ‖ adv atropelladamente

Peloponnesian [,pɛləpə'niʃən] adj & s peloponense mf

Peloponnesus [,pɛləpə'nisəs] s Peloponeso

Pelops ['pilɑps] s Pélope m

pelota [pɛ'lotə] s pelota vasca

pelt [pɛlt] s pellejo; golpe violento; (of a person) (hum) pellejo ‖ tr golpear violentamente; apedrear ‖ intr golpear violentamente; caer con fuerza (el granizo, la lluvia, etc.); apresurarse

pen. abbr **peninsula**

pen [pɛn] s pluma; corral m, redil m; **the pen and the sword** las letras y las armas ‖ v (pret & pp **penned;** ger **penning**) tr escribir (con pluma); redactar ‖ v (pret & pp **penned** o **pent** [pɛnt]) tr acorralar, encerrar

penalize ['pinə,laɪz] tr penar; penalizar; (sport) sancionar

penal·ty ['pɛnəlti] s (pl -ties) pena; (for late payment) recargo; (sport) sanción; **under penalty of** so pena de

penance ['pɛnəns] s penitencia; **to do penance** hacer penitencia

penchant ['pɛnʃənt] s afición, inclinación, tendencia

pen·cil ['pɛnsəl] s lápiz m; (of light) pincel m, haz m ‖ v (pret & pp -ciled o -cilled; ger -ciling o -cilling) tr marcar con lápiz; (med) pincelar

pencil sharpener s afilalápices m, cortalápices m

pendent ['pɛndənt] adj pendiente; sobresaliente ‖ s medallón m; (earring) pendiente m

pending ['pɛndɪŋ] adj pendiente ‖ prep hasta; durante

pendulum ['pɛndʒələm] s péndulo; (of a clock) péndola

pendulum bob s lenteja

penetrate ['pɛnɪ,tret] tr & intr penetrar

penguin ['pɛŋgwɪn] s pingüino, pájaro bobo

pen'hold'er s (handle) portaplumas m; (box) plumero

penicillin [,pɛnɪ'sɪlɪn] s penicilina

peninsula [pə'nɪnsələ] s península

peninsular [pə'nɪnsələr] adj & s peninsular mf ‖ **Peninsular** adj & s (Iberian) peninsular mf

penis ['pinəs] s pene m, falo

penitence ['pɛnɪtəns] s penitencia

penitent ['pɛnɪtənt] adj & s penitente mf

pen'knife' s (pl -knives) navaja, cortaplumas m

penmanship ['pɛnmən,ʃɪp] s caligrafía; (hand of a person) letra

pen name s seudónimo

pennant ['pɛnənt] s gallardete m

penniless ['pɛnɪlɪs] adj pelón, sin dinero

pennon ['pɛnən] s pendón m

pen·ny ['pɛni] s (pl -nies) (U.S.A.) centavo ‖ s (pl **pence** [pɛns]) (Brit) penique m

pen'ny·weight' s peso de 24 granos

pen pal s (coll) amigo por correspondencia

pen point s punta de la pluma; puntilla de la pluma fuente

pension ['pɛnʃən] s pensión, jubilación ‖ tr pensionar, jubilar

pensioner ['pɛnʃənər] s pensionista mf; **pensioners** clases pasivas

pensive ['pɛnsɪv] adj pensativo; melancólico

Pentecost ['pɛntɪ,kɔst] s el Pentecostés

penthouse ['pɛnt,haʊs] s el alpende m, colgadizo; casa de azotea

pent-up ['pɛnt,ʌp] adj contenido, reprimido

penult ['pinʌlt] s penúltima

penum·bra [pɪ'nʌmbrə] s (pl -brae [bri] o -bras) penumbra

penurious [pɪ'nʊri·əs] adj (stingy) tacaño, mezquino; (poor) pobre, indigente

penury ['pɛnjəri] s tacañería, mezquindad; pobreza, miseria

pen'wip'er s limpiaplumas m

people ['pipəl] spl gente f; personas; gente del pueblo; se, p.ej., **people say** se dice ‖ ssg (pl **peoples**) pueblo, nación ‖ tr poblar

pep [pɛp] s (slang) ánimo, brío, vigor m ‖ v (pret & pp **pepped;** ger **pepping**) tr—**to pep up** (slang) animar, dar vigor a

pepper ['pɛpər] s (spice) pimienta; (plant and fruit) pimiento ‖ tr sazonar con pimienta; (with bullets) acribillar; salpicar

pep'per·box' s pimentero

pep'per·mint' s (plant) menta piperita; esencia de menta; pastilla de menta

pep talk s palabras alentadoras

per [pʌr] prep por; **as per** según

perambulator [pər'æmbjə,letər] s cochecillo de niño

per capita [pər 'kæpɪtə] por cabeza, por persona

perceive [pər'siv] tr percibir

per cent o **percent** [pər'sɛnt] por ciento

percentage [pər'sɛntɪdʒ] s porcentaje; (slang) provecho, ventaja

perception [pər'sɛpʃən] s percepción; comprensión, penetración

perch [pʌrtʃ] s percha, rama, varilla; sitio o posición elevada; (fish) perca ‖ tr colocar en un sitio algo elevado intr sentarse en un sitio algo elevado; posar (un ave)

percolator ['pʌrkə,letər] s cafetera filtradora

per diem [pər'daɪ·əm] por día

perdition [pər'dɪʃən] s perdición

perennial [pə'rɛni·əl] adj perenne; (bot) vivaz ‖ s planta vivaz

perfect ['pʌrfɛkt] adj & s perfecto ‖ [pər'fɛkt] tr perfeccionar

perfidious [pər'fɪdi·əs] adj pérfido

pa
pe

perfi·dy ['pʌrfɪdi] s (pl -dies) perfidia
perforate ['pʌrfə,ret] tr perforar
perforce [pər'fors] adv por fuerza, necesariamente
perform [pər'fɔrm] tr ejecutar; (theat) representar ‖ intr ejecutar; funcionar (p.ej., una máquina)
performance [pər'fɔrməns] s ejecución; representación; funcionamiento; (theat) función
performer [pər'fɔrmər] s ejecutante mf; actor m; acróbata mf
perfume ['pʌrfjum] s perfume m ‖ [pər'fjum] tr perfumar
perfunctory [pər'fʌŋktəri] adj hecho sin cuidado, hecho a la ligera; indiferente, negligente
perhaps [pər'hæps] adv acaso, tal vez, quizá
per·il ['pɛrəl] s peligro ‖ v (pret & pp -iled o -illed; ger -iling o -illing) tr poner en peligro
perilous ['pɛrɪləs] adj peligroso
period ['pɪrɪ·əd] s período; (in school) hora; (gram) punto; (sport) division
period costume s traje m de época·
periodic [,pɪrɪ'adɪk] adj periódico
periodical [,pɪrɪ'adɪkəl] adj periódico ‖ s periódico, revista periódica
peripher·y [pə'rɪfəri] s (pl -ies) periferia
periscope ['pɛrɪ,skop] s periscopio
perish ['pɛrɪʃ] intr perecer
perishable ['pɛrɪʃəbəl] adj perecedero; (merchandise) corruptible
periwig ['pɛrɪ,wɪg] s perico
perjure ['pʌrdʒər] tr hacer (a una persona) quebrantar el juramento; **to perjure oneself** perjurarse
perju·ry ['pʌrdʒəri] s (pl -ries) perjurio
perk [pʌrk] tr alzar (la cabeza); aguzar (las orejas) ‖ intr pavonearse; engalanarse; **to perk up** reanimarse, sentirse mejor
permanence ['pʌrmənəns] s permanencia
permanency ['pʌrmənənsi] s (pl -cies) permanencia; persona, cosa o posición peremanentes
permanent ['pʌrmənənt] adj permanente ‖ s permanente f, ondulación permanente
permanent tenure s inamovilidadperversión
permanent way s (rr) material fijo
permeate ['pʌrmɪ,et] tr & intr penetrar
permission [pər'mɪʃən] s permisión
per·mit ['pʌrmɪt] s permiso; cédula de aduana ‖ [pər'mɪt] v (pret & pp -mitted; ger -mitting) tr permitir
permute [per'mjut] tr permutar
pernicious [pər'nɪʃəs] adj pernicioso
pernickety [per'nɪkɪti] adj (coll) descontentadizo, quisquilloso
perorate ['pɛrə,ret] intr perorar
peroration [,pɛrə'reʃən] s peroración
peroxide [pər'aksaɪd] s peróxido; peróxido de hidrógeno
peroxide blonde s rubia oxigenada
perpendicular [,pʌrpən'dɪkjələr] adj & s perpendicular f
perpetrate ['pʌrpɪ,tret] tr perpetrar
perpetual [pər'pɛtʃu·əl] adj perpetuo

perpetuate [pər'pɛtʃu,et] tr perpetuar
perplex [pər'plɛks] tr dejar perplejo
perplexed [pər'plɛkst] adj perplejo
perplexi·ty [pər'plɛksɪti] s (pl -ties) perplejidad; problema m
per se [per 'si] por sí mismo, en sí mismo, esencialmente
persecute ['pʌrsɪ,kjut] tr perseguir
persecution [,pʌrsɪ'kjuʃən] s persecución
persevere [,pʌrsɪ'vɪr] intr perseverar
Persian ['pʌrʒən] adj & s persa mf
persimmon [pər'sɪmən] s placaminero
persist [pər'sɪst] o [pər'zɪst] intr persistir; empecinarse
persistent [pər'sɪstənt] o [pər'zɪstənt] adj persistente; (insistent) porfiado; (e.g., headache) pertinaz
person ['pʌrsən] s persona; **no person** nadie
personage ['pʌrsənɪdʒ] s personaje m; persona
personal ['pʌrsənəl] adj personal; de uso personal ‖ s nota de sociedad; (in a newspaper) remitido
personali·ty [,pʌrsə'nælɪti] s (pl -ties) personalidad
personality cult s culto a la personalidad
personal property s bienes mpl muebles
personi·fy [pər'sɑnɪ,faɪ] v (pret pp -fied) tr personificar
personnel [,pʌrsə'nɛl] s personal m
per·son-to-per·son adv (telp) particular a particular
perspective [pər'spɛktɪv] s perspectiva
perspicacious [,pʌrspɪ'keʃəs] adj perspicaz
perspire [pər'spaɪr] intr sudar, transpirar
persuade [pər'swed] tr persuadir
persuasion [pər'sweʒən] s persuasión; creencia religiosa; creencia fuerte
pert [pʌrt] adj atrevido, descarado; (coll) animado, vivo
pertain [pər'ten] intr pertenecer; **pertaining to** perteneciente a
pertinacious [,pʌrtɪ'neʃəs] adj pertinaz
pertinent ['pʌrtɪnənt] adj pertinente
perturb [pər'tʌrb] tr perturbar
Peru [pə'ru] s el Perú
perusal [pə'ruzəl] s lectura cuidadosa
peruse [pə'ruz] tr leer con atención
Peruvian [pəruvi·ən] adj & s peruano
pervade [pər'ved] tr penetrar, esparcirse por, extenderse por
perverse [pər'vʌrs] adj perverso; avieso, díscolo; contumaz; malazo
perversion [pər'vʌrʒən] s perversión
perversi·ty [pər'vʌrsɪti] s (pl -ties) perversidad; indocilidad; contumacia
pervert ['pʌrvərt] s renegado, apóstata; pervertido ‖ [pər'vʌrt] tr pervertir; emplear mal (p.ej., los talentos que uno tiene)
pes·ky ['pɛski] adj (comp -kier; super -kiest) (coll) cargante, molesto
pessimism ['pɛsɪ,mɪzəm] s pesimismo
pessimist ['pɛsɪmɪst] s pesimista mf
pessimistic [,pɛsɪ'mɪstɪk] adj pesimista
pest [pɛst] s peste f; insecto nocivo; (misfortune) plaga; (annoying person, bore) machaca mf
pester ['pɛstər] tr molestar, importunar

pest'house' s lazareto, hospital m de contagiosos

pesticide ['pɛstɪ,saɪd] s pesticida m

pestiferous [pɛs'tɪfərəs] adj pestífero; (coll) engorroso, molesto

pestilence ['pɛstɪləns] s pestilencia

pestle ['pɛsəl] s mano f de almirez

pet [pɛt] s animal mimado, animal casero; niño mimado; favorito; enojo pasajero ‖ v (pret & pp **petted;** ger **petting**) tr acariciar, mimar ‖ intr (slang) besuquearse

petal [pɛtəl] s pétalo

petard [pɪ'tɑrd] s petardo

pet'cock' s llave f de desagüe, llave de purga

Peter ['pitər] s Pedro; **to rob Peter to pay Paul** desnudar a un santo para vestir a otro

petit-bourgeois [pə'ti'bʊrʒwɑ] adj pequeño-burgués

petition [pɪ'tɪʃən] s petición; (formal request signed by a number of people) memorial m, instancia, solicitud ‖ tr suplicar; dirigir una instancia a, solicitar

pet name s nombre m de cariño

Petrarch ['pitrɑrk] s Petrarca m

petri·fy ['pɛtrɪ,faɪ] v (pret & pp **-fied**) tr petrificar ‖ intr petrificarse

petrochemical [,pɛtro'kɛmɪkəl] adj petroquímico

petrol ['pɛtrəl] s (Brit) gasolina

petroleum [pɪ'trolɪ·əm] s petróleo

pet shop s pajarería

petticoat ['pɛtɪ,kot] s enaguas; (woman, girl) (slang) falda

pet·ty ['pɛti] adj (comp **-tier;** super **-tiest**) insignificante, pequeño; mezquino; intolerante

petty cash s caja de menores, efectivo para gastos menores

petty larceny s ratería, hurto

petty officer s (naut) suboficial m

petulant ['pɛtjələnt] adj malhumorado, enojadizo

pew [pju] s banco de iglesia

pewter ['pjutər] s peltre m; vajilla de peltre

Phaëthon ['fe·ɪθən] s Faetón m

phalanx ['felæŋks] s falange f

phallic ['fælɪk] adj fálico

phallus ['fæləs] s falo

phantasm ['fæntæzəm] s fantasma m

phantom ['fæntəm] s fantasma m

Pharaoh ['fɛro] s Faraón m

pharisee ['færɪ,si] s fariseo ‖ **Pharisee** s fariseo

pharmaceutical [,fɑrmə'sutɪkəl] adj farmacéutico

pharmacist ['fɑrməsɪst] s farmacéutico

pharma·cy ['fɑrməsi] s (pl **-cies**) farmacia

pharynx ['færɪŋks] s faringe f

phase [fez] s fase f ‖ tr poner en fase; llevar a cabo a etapas uniformes; (coll) inquietar, molestar; **to phase out** deshacer paulatinamente

pheasant ['fɛzənt] s faisán m

phenobarbital [,fino'bɑrbɪ,tæl] s fenobarbital m

phenomenal [fɪ'nɑmɪ,nɑn] s (pl **-na** [nə]) fenómenal

phial ['faɪ·əl] s frasco pequeño; inyectable m

Phidias ['fɪdɪ·əs] s Fidias m

philanderer [fɪ'lændərər] s galanteador m, tenorio

philanthropist [fɪ'lænθrəpɪst] s filántropo

philanthro·py [fɪ'lænθrəpi] s (pl **-pies**) filantropía

philatelist [fɪ'lætəlɪst] s filatelista mf

philately [fɪ'lætəli] s filatelia

Philip ['fɪlɪp] s Felipe m; (of Macedon) Filipo

Philippine ['fɪlɪ,pin] adj filipino ‖ **Philippines** spl Islas Filipinas

Philistine [fɪ'lɪstɪn] o ['fɪlɪ,stin] o ['fɪlɪ,staɪn] adj & s filisteo

philologist [fɪ'lɑlədʒɪst] s filólogo

philology [fɪ'lɑlədʒi] s filología

philosopher [fɪ'lɑsəfər] s filósofo

philosophic(al) [,fɪləsɑfɪk(əl)] adj filosófico

philoso·phy [fɪ'lɑsəfi] s (pl **-phies**) filosofía

philter ['fɪltər] s filtro

phlebitis [flɪ'baɪtɪs] s flebitis f

phlegm [flɛm] s flema f, gargajo; **to cough up phlegm** gargajear

phlegmatic(al) [flɛg'mætɪk(əl)] adj flemático; (coll) galbanoso

Phoebe ['fibi] s Febe f

Phoebus ['fibəs] s Febo

Phoenicia [fɪ'nɪʃə] o [fɪ'niʃə] s Fenicia

Phoenician [fɪ'nɪʃən] o [fɪ'niʃən] adj & s fenicio

phoenix ['finɪks] s fénix m

phone [fon] s (coll) teléfono; **to come** o **to go to the phone** acudir al teléfono, ponerse al aparato ‖ tr & intr (coll) telefonear

phone call s llamada telefónica

phoneme ['fonim] s fonema m

phonetic [fo'nɛtɪk] adj fonético

phonics ['fanɪks] s fónica

phonograph ['fonə,græf] s fonógrafo

phonology [fə'nɑlədʒi] s fonología

pho·ny ['foni] adj (comp **-nier;** super **-niest**) falso, contrahecho ‖ s (pl **-nies**) (slang) farsa; (coll) farsante mf

phosphate ['fɑsfet] s fosfato

phosphorescent [,fɑsfə'rɛsənt] adj fosforescente

phospho·rus ['fɑsfərəs] s (pl **-ri** [,raɪ]) fósforo

pho·to ['foto] s (pl **-tos**) foto f

photocopier ['foto,kɑpɪ·ər] s fotocopiador m; fotóstato m

pho'to·cop'y s fotocopia ‖ v (pret & pp **-ied**) tr fotocopiar

photoengraving [,foto·ɛn'grevɪŋ] s fotograbado

photo finish s (sport) llegada a la meta, determinada mediante el fotofija

pho'to·fin'ish camera s fotofija m

photogenic [,foto'dʒɛnɪk] adj fotogénico

photograph ['fotə,græf] s fotografía ‖ tr & intr fotografiar

photographer [fə'tɑgrəfər] s fotógrafo

photography [fə'tɑgrəfi] s fotografía

pe
ph

photojournalism [,fotə'dʒʌrnə,lɪzəm] s fotoperiodismo

pho'to•play' s fotodrama m

photostat ['fotə,stæt] s fotóstato || tr & intr fotostatar

phototube ['fotə,tjub] fototubo

phrase [frez] s frase f || tr frasear

phrenology [frɪ'nɑlədʒi] s frenología

phys. abbr **physical, physician, physics, physiology**

phys•ic ['fɪzɪk] s medicamento; purgante m || v (pret & pp **-icked**; ger **-icking**) tr curar; purgar

physical ['fɪzɪkəl] adj físico

physician [fɪ'zɪʃən] s médico

physicist ['fɪzɪsɪst] s físico

physics ['fɪzɪks] s física

physiognomy [,fɪzɪ'ɑgnəmi] o [,fɪzɪ'ɑnəmi] s fisonomía

physiological [,fɪzɪ•ə'lɑdʒɪkəl] adj fisiológico

physiology [,fɪzɪ'ɑlədʒi] s fisiología

physique [fɪ'zik] s físico, talle m, exterior m

pi [paɪ] s (math) pi f; (typ) pastel m || v (pret & pp **pied**; ger **piing**) tr (typ) empastelar

pian•o [pɪ'æno] s (pl **-os**) piano

picaresque [,pɪkə'rɛsk] adj picaresco

picayune [,pɪkə'jun] adj de poca monta, mezquino

piccadil•ly [,pɪkə'dɪli] s (pl **-lies**) cuello de pajarita

picco•lo ['pɪkə,lo] s (pl **-los**) flautín m

pick [pɪk] s (tool) pico; (choice) selección; (choicest) flor f || tr escoger; recoger (p.ej., flores); recolectar (p.ej., algodón); romper (el hielo) con un picahielos; escarbarse (los dientes); descañonar, desplumar (un ave); hurgarse (la nariz); rascarse (una cicatriz, un grano); roer (un hueso); mondar (las frutas); falsear, forzar (una cerradura); armar (una pendencia); herir (las cuerdas de un instrumento); buscar (defectos); hurtar de (los bolsillos); **to pick out** entresacar; **to pick someone to pieces** (coll) no dejarle a uno un hueso sano; **to pick up** recoger; recobrar (ánimo; velocidad); descolgar (el receptor); hallar por casualidad; aprender con la práctica; aprender de oidas; invitar a subir a un coche; entablar conservación con (sin presentación previa); captar (una señal de radio) || intr comer melindrosamente; escoger esmeradamente; **to pick at** comer melindrosamente; tomarla con, regañar; **to pick on** escoger; (coll) regañar; (coll) molestar; **to pick over** ir revolviendo y examinando; **to pick up** (coll) ir mejor, sentirse mejor; recobrar velocidad

pick'ax' s zapapico

picket ['pɪkɪt] s (stake, pale) piquete m; (of strikers; of soldiers) piquete m || tr poner un cordón de piquetes a || intr servir de piquete

picket fence s cerca de estacas

picket line s línea de piquetes

pickle ['pɪkəl] s encurtido; escabeche m, salmuera; (coll) apuro, aprieto || tr encurtir; escabechar

pick-me-up ['pɪkmi,ʌp] s (coll) tentempié m; (coll) trago fortificante

pick'pock'et s carterista m, ratero; bolsero (Mex)

pick'up' s recolección; (of a motor) recobro; (of an automobile) aceleración; (elec) pick-up, fonocaptor m

pic•nic ['pɪknɪk] s jira, partida de campo || v (pret & pp **-nicked**; ger **-nicking**) intr hacer una jira al campo, merendar en el campo

pictorial [pɪk'torɪ•əl] adj gráfico; ilustrado || s revista ilustrada

picture ['pɪktʃər] s cuadro; retrato; imagen f; lámina, grabado; fotografía; película; pintura || tr dibujar; pintar; describir; **to picture to oneself** representarse

picture book s libro en imágenes

picture gallery s galería de pinturas

picture post card s postal ilustrada

picture show s exhibición de pinturas; cine m

picture signal s videoseñal f

picturesque [,pɪktʃə'rɛsk] adj pintoresco

picture tube s tubo de imagen, tubo de televisión

picture window s ventana panorámica

piddling ['pɪdlɪŋ] adj de poca monta, insignificante

pie [paɪ] s pastel m; (bird) picaza; (typ) pastel m || v (pret & pp **pied**; ger **pieing**) tr (typ) empastelar

piece [pis] s (fragment; section of cloth) pedazo; (part of a machine; drama; single composition of music; coin; figure or block used in checkers, chess, etc.) pieza; (of land) lote m, parcela; **a piece of advice** un consejo; **a piece of baggage** un bulto; **a piece of furniture** un mueble; **to break to pieces** despedazar, hacer pedazos; despedazarse; **to fall to pieces** desbaratarse, caer en ruina; **to give someone a piece of one's mind** decirle a uno su parecer con toda franqueza; **to go to pieces** desvencijarse; darse a la desesperación; ir al desastre (un negocio); sufrir un ataque de nervios; perder por completo la salud; **to pick someone to pieces** (coll) no dejarle a uno un hueso sano || tr formar juntando piezas; remendar || intr (coll) comer a deshora

piece goods spl géneros de pieza

piece'work' s destajo, trabajo a destajo

piece'work'er s destajero, destajista mf

pier [pɪr] s muelle m; (of a bridge) estribo, sostén m; (of a harbor) rompeolas m; (wall between two openings) (archit) entrepaño

pierce [pɪrs] tr agujerear, horadar, taladrar; atravesar, traspasar; picar; pinchar, punzar; (fig) traspasar (de dolor) || intr penetrar, entrar a la fuerza

piercing ['pɪrsɪŋ] adj agudo, penetrante, desgarrador; (pain) lancinante

pier glass s espejo de cuerpo entero

pie•ty ['paɪ•əti] s (pl **-ties**) piedad, devoción

piffle ['pɪfəl] s (coll) disparates mpl, música celestial

pig [pɪg] s cerdo; (young hog) lechón m; (domestic hog) puerco, cochino; carne f de puerco; (metal) lingote *m*; (*person who acts like a pig*) (coll) marrano, cochino

pigeon [ˈpɪdʒən] *s* paloma

pi'geon•hole' *s* hornilla, casilla de paloma; casilla ‖ *tr* encasillar

pigeon house *s* palomar *m*

piggish [ˈpɪgɪʃ] *adj* glotón, voraz

pig'gy•back' *adv* a cuestas, en hombros

pig'-head'ed *adj* terco, cabezudo

pig iron *s* arrabio, hierro en lingotes

pigment [ˈpɪgmənt] *s* pigmento ‖ *tr* pigmentar ‖ *intr* pigmentarse

pig'pen' *s* pocilga; (fig) pocilga, corral *m* de vacas

pig'skin' *s* piel *f* de cerdo; (coll) balón *m* (*con que se juega al fútbol*)

pig'sty' *s* (*pl* **-sties**) pocilga

pig'tail' *s* coleta, trenza; (*of tobacco*) andullo

pike [paɪk] *s* pica; (*of an arrow*) punta; carretera; camino de barrera; (*fish*) lucio

piker [ˈpaɪkər] *s* (slang) persona de poco fuste

Pilate [ˈpaɪlət] *s* Pilatos *m*

pile [paɪl] *s* pila, montón *m*; (*stake*) pilote *m*; lanilla, pelusa; pira; (elec, phys) pila; (coll) caudal *m*; **piles** almorranas ‖ *tr* apilar, amontonar ‖ *intr* apilarse, amontonarse; **to pile in** o **into** entrar atropelladamente en; entrar todos en; subir todos a (*p.ej., un coche*)

pile driver *s* martinete *m*

pileup [ˈpaɪlˌʌp] *s* (*collision*) choque en cadena

pilfer [ˈpɪlfər] *tr & intr* ratear

pilgrim [ˈpɪlgrɪm] *s* peregrino, romero

pilgrimage [ˈpɪlgrɪmɪdʒ] *s* peregrinación, romería

pill [pɪl] *s* píldora; mal trago, sinsabor *m*; (coll) persona molesta

pillage [ˈpɪlɪdʒ] *s* pillaje *m*, saqueo ‖ *tr & intr* pillar, saquear

pillar [ˈpɪlər] *s* pilar *m*; **from pillar to post** de acá para allá sin objeto determinado

pillo•ry [ˈpɪləri] *s* (*pl* **-ries**) picota ‖ *v* (*pret & pp* **-ried**) *tr* empicotar; (fig) motejar, poner en ridículo

pillow [ˈpɪlo] *s* almohada

pil'low•case' o **pil'low•slip'** *s* funda de almohada

pilot [ˈpaɪlət] *s* piloto; (*of a harbor*) práctico; (*of a gas range*) mechero encendedor; (rr) trompa, delantera ‖ *tr* pilotar; conducir

pilot run o **pilot test** *s* experimento piloto

pimp [pɪmp] *s* alcahuete *m*

pimple [ˈpɪmpəl] *s* barro, grano

pim•ply [ˈpɪmpli] *adj* (*comp* **-plier**; *super* **-pliest**) granujoso

pin [pɪn] *s* alfiler *m*; (*e.g., for a necktie*) prendedero; (*peg*) clavija; (*e.g., to hold scissors together*) clavillo, clavito; (bowling) bolo; **to be on pins and needles** estar en espinas ‖ *v* (*pret & pp* **pinned**; *ger* **pinning**) *tr* alfilerar, clavar, fijar, sujetar; **to pin something on someone** (coll) acusarle a uno de una cosa; **to pin up** recoger y apuntar con alfileres; fijar en la pred con alfileres

pinafore [ˈpɪnəˌfor] *s* delantal *m* de niño

pin'ball' *s* billar romano, bagatela

pince-nez [ˈpæns.ne] *s* lentes *mpl* de nariz, lentes de pinzas

pincers [ˈpɪnsərz] *ssg* o *spl* pinzas

pinch [pɪntʃ] *s* pellizco; (*of hunger*) tormento; (slang) arresto; (slang) hurto, robo; **in a pinch** en un aprieto; en caso necesario ‖ *tr* pellizcar!, cogerse (*los dedos, p.ej., en una puerta*); apretar (*p.ej., el zapato a una persona*); contraer (*el frío la cara de uno*); limitar los gastos de; (slang) arrestar, prender; (slang) hurtar, robar ‖ *intr* apretar; economizar, privarse de lo necesario

pinchers [ˈpɪntʃərz] *ssg* o *spl* var of **pincers**

pin'cush'ion *s* acerico

Pindar [ˈpɪndər] *s* Píndaro

pine [paɪn] *s* pino ‖ *intr* languidecer; **to pine away** consumirse; **to pine for** penar por

pine'ap'ple *s* ananás *m*, piña

pine cone *s* piña

pine needle *s* pinocha

ping [pɪŋ] *s* silbido de bala ‖ *intr* silbar (*una bala*); silbar como una bala

pin'head' *s* cabecilla de alfiler; cosa muy pequeña o insignificante; (coll) bobalicón *m*

pink [pɪŋk] *adj* rosado, sonrosado ‖ *s* estado perfecto; comunistoide *mf*; (bot) clavel *m*, clavellina

pin money *s* alfileres *mpl*

pinnacle [ˈpɪnəkəl] *s* pináculo

pin'point' *adj* exacto, preciso ‖ *s* punta de alfiler ‖ *tr & intr* señalar con precisión

pin'prick' *s* alfilerazo

pinup girl [ˈpɪn.ʌp] *s* guapa

pin'wheel' *s* rueda de fuego, rueda giratoria de fuegos artificiales; molinete *m* (Mex); (*child's toy*) rehilandera, ventolera

pioneer [ˌpaɪə'nɪr] *s* pionero; (mil) zapador *m* ‖ *intr* abrir nuevos caminos, explorar

pious [ˈpaɪ•əs] *adj* pío, piadoso; mojigato; respetuoso

pip [pɪp] *s* (*seed*) pepita; (*on a card, dice, etc.*) punto; (vet) pepita

pipe [paɪp] *s* caño, conducto, tubo; (*to smoke tobacco*) pipa; (mus) pipa, caramillo, zampoña; (*of an organ*) cañón *m* ‖ *tr* conducir por medio de tubos o cañerías; proveer de tuberías o cañerías ‖ *intr* tocar el caramillo; **to pipe down** (slang) callarse

pipe cleaner *s* limpiapipas *m*

pipe dream *s* esperanza imposible, castillo en el aire

pipe line *s* cañería; tubería; oleoducto; fuente *f* de informes confidenciales

pipe organ *s* (mus) órgano

piper [ˈpaɪpər] *s* flautista *m*; gaitero; **to pay the piper** pagar los vidrios rotos

pipe wrench *s* llave *f* para tubos

pippin [ˈpɪpɪn] *s* (*apple*) camuesa; (*tree*) camueso; (slang) real moza

piquancy [ˈpikənsi] *s* picante *m*

piquant [ˈpikənt] *adj* picante

pique [pik] *s* pique *m*, resentimiento ‖ *tr* picar, enojar; despertar, excitar

piracy [ˈpaɪrəsi] *s* piratería

ph
pi

Piraeus [paɪ'ri·əs] s el Pireo
pirate ['paɪrɪt] s pirata m ‖ tr pillar, robar; publicar fraudulentamente ‖ intr piratear
pirouette [,pɪru'ɛt] s pirueta ‖ intr piruetear
Pisces ['paɪsiz] s (astr) Piscis m
pistol ['pɪstəl] s pistola
piston ['pɪstən] s (mach) émbolo, pistón m; (mus) pistón m
piston displacement s cilindrada
piston ring s anillo de émbolo, aro de émbolo, segmento de émbolo
piston rod s vástago de émbolo
piston stroke s carrera de émbolo
pit [pɪt] s hoyo; (in the skin) cacaraña; (of certain fruit) hueso; (for cockfights, etc.) cancha, reñidero; (of the stomach) boca; abismo, infierno; (min) pozo; (theat) foso ‖ v (pret & pp **pitted**; ger **pitting**) tr marcar con hoyos; dejar hoyoso (el rostro); deshuesar (p.ej., una ciruela)
pitch [pɪtʃ] s (black sticky substance) pez f; echada, lanzamiento; cosa lanzada; pelota lanzada; (of a boat) arfada, cabezada; (of a roof) pendiente f; (of, e.g., a screw) paso; (of a winding) (elec) paso; (mus) tono, altura; (fig) grado, extremo; (coll) bombo, elogio ‖ tr echar, lanzar; elevar (el heno) con la horquilla; armar o plantar (una tienda de campaña); embrear; (mus) graduar el tono de ‖ intr caerse, caer de cabeza; bajar en declive, inclinarse; arfar, cabecear (un buque); **to pitch in** (coll) poner manos a la obra; (coll) comenzar a comer
pitch accent s acento de altura
pitcher ['pɪtʃər] s jarro; (in baseball) lanzador m
pitch'fork' s horca, horquilla; **to rain pitchforks** (coll) llover a cántaros
pitch pipe s (mus) diapasón m
pit'fall' s callejo, trampa; (danger for the unwary) escollo, atascadero
pith [pɪθ] s médula; (essential part) (fig) médula; (fig) fuerza, vigor m
pith·y ['pɪθi] adj (comp -ier; super -iest) medular; enérgico, expresivo
pitiful ['pɪtɪfəl] adj lastimoso; compasivo; despreciable
pitiless ['pɪtɪlɪs] adj despiadado, empedernido, incompasivo
pit·y ['pɪti] s (pl -ies) piedad, compasión, lástima; **for pity's sake!** ¡por piedad!; **to have o to take pity on** tener piedad de, apiadarse de; **what a pity!** ¡qué lástima!, ¡qué pena! ‖ v (pret & pp -ied) tr apiadarse de, compadecer
pivot ['pɪvət] s pivote m, gorrón m, eje m de rotación; (fig) eje m ‖ intr pivotar; **to pivot on** girar sobre; depender de
placard ['plækɑrd] s cartel m ‖ tr fijar carteles en; fijar (un anuncio) en sitio público; publicar por medio de carteles
place [ples] s sitio, lugar m; (of business) local m; (job) puesto; grado, rango; **in no place** en ninguna parte; **in place of** en lugar de; **out of place** fuera de su lugar; fuera de propósito; **to be looking for a**

place to live buscar piso; **to take place** tener lugar; situar ‖ tr poner, colocar; acordarse bien de; dar empleo a; prestar (dinero) a interés ‖ intr colocarse (un caballo en las carreras)
place·bo [plə'sibo] s (pl -bos o -boes) placebo
place card s tarjetita con el nombre (que indica la colocación de uno en la mesa)
placement ['plesmənt] s colocación
place name s nombre m de lugar, topónimo
placid ['plæsɪd] adj plácido, tranquilo
plagiarism ['pledʒə,rɪzəm] s plagio
plagiarize ['pledʒə,raɪz] tr plagiar
plague [pleg] s peste f, plaga; (great public calamity) plaga ‖ tr apestar, plagar; atormentar, molestar
plaid [plæd] s (cloth) tartán m; cuadros a la escocesa
plain [plen] adj llano, claro, evidente; abierto, franco; ordinario; feo; humilde; solo, natural; **in plain English** sin rodeos; **in plain sight o view** en plena vista ‖ s llano, llanura
plain clothes spl traje m de calle, traje de paisano
plainclothesman ['plen'kloðz,mæn] s (pl -men [,mɛn]) policía m que lleva traje de paisano
plain omelet s tortilla a la francesa
plains·man ['plenzmən] s (pl -men [mən]) llanero
plaintiff ['plentɪf] s (law) demandante mf
plaintive ['plentɪv] adj quejumbroso
plan [plæn] s plan m, intento, proyecto; (drawing, diagram) plan m, plano; **to change one's plans** cambiar de proyecto ‖ v (pret & pp **planned**; ger **planning**) tr planear, planificar; **to plan to** proponerse ‖ intr hacer proyectos
plane [plen] adj plano ‖ s (surface) plano; aeroplano, avión m; (of an airplane) plano; (carp) cepillo; (tree) plátano ‖ tr cepillar ‖ intr viajar en aeroplano
plane sickness s mareo del aire, mal m de vuelo
planet ['plænɪt] s planeta m
plane tree s plátano
planing mill ['plenɪŋ] s taller m de cepillado
plank [plæŋk] s tabla gruesa, tablón m; artículo de un programa político ‖ tr entablar, entarimar
plant [plænt] s fábrica, taller m; (of an automobile) grupo motor; (educational establishment) plantel m; (bot) planta ‖ tr plantar; sembrar (semillas); inculcar (doctrinas); (slang) ocultar (géneros robados)
plantation [plæn'teʃən] s plantación, campo de plantas; (estate cultivated by workers living on it) hacienda
planter ['plæntər] s plantador m, cultivador m
plasma ['plæzmə] s plasma m
plaster ['plæstər] s (gypsum) yeso; (mixture of lime, sand, water, etc.) argamasa; (coating) enlucido; (poultice) emplasto ‖ tr en-

yesar; argamasar; enlucir; emplastar; embadurnar; pegar (*anuncios*)

plas′ter·board′ *s* cartón *m* de yeso y fieltro

plaster cast *s* (surg) vendaje enyesado; (sculp) yeso

plaster of Paris *s* estuco de París

plastic [′plæstɪk] *adj* plástico ‖ *s* (*substance*) plástico; (*art of modeling*) plástica

plate [plet] *s* (*dish*) plato; (*sheet of metal, etc.*) chapa, placa; vajilla de oro, vajilla de plata; dentadura postiza, base *f* de la dentadura postiza; (baseball) puesto meta, puesto del batter; (anat, elec, electron, phot, zool) placa; (typ) clisé *m* ‖ *tr* chapear, planchear; blindar; platear, dorar; niquelar (*por la galvanoplastia*); (typ) clisar

plateau [plæ′to] *s* meseta

plate glass *s* vidrio o cristal cilindrado

platen [′plætən] *s* rodillo

platform [′plæt,fɔrm] *s* plataforma *f;* (*of passenger station*) andén *m;* (*of freight station*) cargadero; (*of a speaker*) tribuna; (*political program*) plataforma

platform car *s* plataforma *f*

platinum [′plætɪnəm] *s* platino

platinum blonde *s* rubia platino

platitude [′plætɪ,tjud] o [′plætɪ,tud] *s* perogrullada, trivialidad

Plato [′pleto] *s* Platón *m*

platoon [plə′tun] *s* pelotón *m*

platter [′plætər] *s* fuente *f;* (slang) disco de fonógrafo

plausible [′plɔzɪbəl] *adj* aparente, especioso; bien hablado; (coll) creíble

play [ple] *s* juego; (*act or move in a game*) jugada; (*drama*) pieza; (*of water, colors, lights*) juego; (mach) huelgo, juego; **to give full play to** dar rienda suelta a ‖ *tr* jugar (*p.ej., un naipe, una partida de juego*); jugar a (*p.ej., los naipes*); jugar con (*un contrario*); dar (*un chasco*); gastar (*una broma*); hacer (*una mala jugada*); dirigir (*agua, una manguera*); desempeñar (*un papel*); desempeñar el papel de; representar (*una obra dramática, un film*); apostar por (*un caballo*); tocar (*un instrumento, una pieza, un disco de fonógrafo*) ‖ *intr* jugar; desempeñar un papel, representar; correr (*una fuente*); rielar (*la luz en la superficie del agua*); vagar (*p.ej., una sonrisa por los labios*); **to play out** rendirse; agotarse; acabarse; **to play safe** tomar sus precauciones; **to play sick** hacerse el enfermo; **to play up to** hacer la rueda a

play′back′ *s* lectura; aparato de lectura

play′bill′ *s* (*poster*) cartel *m;* (*of a play*) programa *m*

player piano [′ple•ər] *s* autopiano

playful [′plefəl] *adj* juguetón, retozón; dicho en broma

playgoer [′ple,go•ər] *s* aficionado al teatro

play′ground′ *s* campo de juego; patio de recreo

play′house′ *s* casita de muñecas; teatro

playing card [′ple•ɪŋ] *s* naipe *m*

playing field *s* campo de deportes

play′mate′ *s* compañero de juego

play′-off′ *s* partido de desempate

play′pen′ *s* parque *m*, corral *m* (*para bebés*)

play′thing′ *s* juguete *m*

play′time′ *s* hora de recreo, hora de juego

playwright [′ple,raɪt] *s* dramaturgo, autor dramático; comediógrafo

play′writ′ing *s* dramaturgia, dramática

plea [pli] *s* ruego, súplica; disculpa, excusa; (law) contestación a la demanda

plead [plid] *v* (*pret & pp* **pleaded** o **pled** [pled]) *tr* defender (*una causa*) ‖ *intr* suplicar; abogar; **to plead guilty** confesarse culpable; **to plead not guilty** negar la acusación, declararse inocente

pleasant [′plezənt] *adj* agradable; simpático; sangriligero

pleasant·ry [′plezəntri] *s* (*pl* **-ries**) broma, chiste *m*, dicho gracioso

please [pliz] *tr & intr* gustar; **as you please** como Vd. quiera; **if you please** si me hace el favor; **please** + *inf* hágame Vd. el favor de + *inf;* **to be pleased to** alegrarse de, complacerse en; **to be pleased with** estar satisfecho de o con

pleasing [′plizɪŋ] *adj* agradable, grato

pleasure [′pleʒər] *s* placer *m*, gusto; **what is your pleasure?** ¿en′ qué puedo servirle?, ¿qué es lo que Vd. desea?; **with pleasure** con mucho gusto

pleasure seeker [′sikər] *s* amigo de los placeres

pleat [plit] *s* pliegue *m*, plisado ‖ *tr* plegar, plisar

plebeian [plɪ′bi•ən] *adj & s* plebeyo

pledge [pledʒ] *s* empeño, prenda; (*vow*) voto, promesa; (*toast*) brindis *m;* **as a pledge of** en prenda de; **to take the pledge** comprometerse a no tomar bebidas alcohólicas ‖ *tr* empeñar, prendar; dar (*la palabra*); brindar por

plentiful [′plentɪfəl] *adj* abundante, copioso

plenty [′plenti] *adv* (coll) completamente ‖ *s* abundancia, copia; suficiencia

pleurisy [′plʊrɪsi] *s* pleuresía

pliable [′plaɪ•əbəl] *adj* flexible, plegable; dócil

pliers [′plaɪ•ərz] *ssg* o *spl* alicates *mpl*

plight [plaɪt] *s* estado, situación; apuro, aprieto; compromiso solemne ‖ *tr* dar o empeñar (*su palabra*); **to plight one's troth** prometer fidelidad; dar palabra de casamiento

plod [plad] *v* (*pret & pp* **plodded;** *ger* **plodding**) *tr* recorrer (*un camino*) pausada y pesadamente ‖ *intr* caminar pausada y pesadamente; trabajar laboriosamente

plot [plat] *s* complot *m*, conspiración; (*of a play or novel*) argumento, trama, parcela; solar *m;* cuadro de flores; cuadro de hortalizas; plano, mapa *m* ‖ *v* (*pret & pp* **plotted;** *ger* **plotting**) *tr* fraguar, tramar, urdir, maquinar; dividir en parcelas o solares; trazar el plano de; trazar, tirar (*líneas*) ‖ *intr* conspirar

plough [plau] *s, tr & intr* var de **plow**

plover [′plʌvər] o [′plovər] *s* chorlito

pi
pl

plow [plau] *s* arado; quitanieve *m* ‖ *tr* arar; surcar; quitar o barrer (*la nieve*); **to plow back** reinvertir (*ganancias*) ‖ *intr* arar; avanzar como un arado

plow·man [ˈplaumən] *s* (*pl* **-men** [mən]) arador *m*, yuguero

plow′share′ *s* reja de arado

pluck [plʌk] *s* ánimo, coraje *m*, valor *m*; tirón *m* ‖ *tr* arrancar; coger (*flores*); desplumar (*un ave*); puntear (*p.ej., una guitarra*) ‖ *intr* dar un tirón; **to pluck up** recobrar ánimo

pluck·y [ˈplʌki] *adj* (*comp* **-ier**; *super* **-iest**) animoso, valiente

plug [plʌg] *s* taco, tarugo; boca de agua; tableta de tabaco; (*hat*) (slang) chistera; (elec) clavija, toma, ficha; (aut) bujía; (coll) rocín; (slang) elogio incidental ‖ *v* (*pret & pp* **plugged**; *ger* **plugging**) *tr* atarugar; calar (*un melón*); **to plug in** (elec) enchufar ‖ *intr* (coll) trabajar con ahinco

plum [plʌm] *s* (*tree*) ciruelo; (*fruit*) ciruela; (slang) turrón *m*, pingüe destino

plumage [ˈplumɪdʒ] *s* plumaje *m*

plumb [plʌm] *adj* vertical; (coll) completo ‖ *adv* a plomo; (coll) verticalmente; (coll) directamente ‖ *tr* aplomar; sondear

plumb bob *s* plomada

plumber [ˈplʌmər] *s* fontanero; (*worker in lead*) plomero

plumbing [ˈplʌmɪŋ] *s* instalación sanitaria; conjunto de cañerías; (*working in lead*) plomería; sondeo

plumbing fixtures *spl* artefactos sanitarios

plumb line *s* cuerda de plomada

plum cake *s* pastel aderezado con pasas de Corinto y ron

plume [plum] *s* (*of a bird*) pluma; (*tuft of feathers worn as ornament*) penacho ‖ *tr* emplumar; componerse (*las plumas*); **to plume oneself on** enorgullecerse de

plummet [ˈplʌmɪt] *s* plomada ‖ *intr* caer a plomo, precipitarse

plump [plʌmp] *adj* rechoncho, regordete; brusco, franco ‖ *adv* de golpe; francamente ‖ *s* (coll) caída pesada; (coll) ruido sordo ‖ *intr* caer a plomo

plum pudding *s* pudín *m* inglés con pasas de Corinto, corteza de limón, huevos y ron

plum tree *s* ciruelo

plunder [ˈplʌndər] *s* pillaje *m*; botín *m* ‖ *tr* pillar, saquear

plunge [plʌndʒ] *s* zambullida; caída a plomo; sacudida violenta; salto; baño de agua fría; (*of a boat*) cabeceo ‖ *tr* zambullir; sumergir; hundir (*p.ej., un puñal*) ‖ *intr* zambullirse; sumergirse; hundirse (*p.ej., en la tristeza*); caer a plomo; arrojarse, precipitarse; cabecear (*un buque*); (slang) entregarse al juego, entregarse a las especulaciones

plunger [ˈplʌndʒər] *s* zambullidor *m*; émbolo buzo; (*of a tire valve*) obús *m*; (slang) jugador o especulador desenfrenado

plunk [plʌŋk] *adv* (coll) con un golpe seco, con un ruido de golpe seco ‖ *tr* (coll) arrojar, empujar o dejar caer pesadamente ‖ *intr* sonar o caer con un ruido de golpe seco

plural [ˈplurəl] *adj & s* plural *m*

plus [plʌs] *adj* más; y pico; **to be plus** (coll) tener por añadidura ‖ *prep* más ‖ *s* (*sign*) más *m*; añadidura

plush [plʌʃ] *adj* afelpado; (coll) lujoso, suntuoso ‖ *s* felpa; peluche *m*

Plutarch [ˈplutɑrk] *s* Plutarco

plutonium [pluˈtonɪəm] *s* plutonio

ply [plaɪ] *s* (*pl* **plies**) (*e.g., of a cloth*) capa, doblez *m*; (*of a cable*) cordón *m* ‖ *v* (*pret & pp* **plied**) *tr* manejar (*la aguja, etc.*); ejercer (*un oficio*); batir (*el agua con los remos*); importunar; navegar por (*p.ej., un río*) ‖ *intr* avanzar; **to ply between** hacer (*un barco*) el servicio entre

ply′wood′ *s* chapeado, madera laminada

P.M. *abbr* **Postmaster, post meridiem** (Lat) **afternoon**

pneumatic [njuˈmætɪk] o [nuˈmætɪk] *adj* neumático

pneumatic drill *s* perforadora de aire comprimido

pneumonia [njuˈmonɪ·ə] o [nuˈmonɪ·ə] *s* neumonía o pulmonía

P.O. *abbr* **post office**

poach [potʃ] *tr* escalfar (*huevos*) ‖ *intr* cazar o pescar en vedado

poacher [ˈpotʃər] *s* cazador furtivo, pescador furtivo

pock [pɑk] *s* cacaraña, hoyuelo

pocket [ˈpɑkɪt] *s* bolsillo, faltriquera; (*in billiards*) tronera; (aer) bolsa de aire; (mil) bolsón *m* ‖ *tr* embolsar; entronerar (*una bola de billar*); tragarse (*injurias*)

pock′et·book′ *s* portamonedas *m*; (*of a woman*) bolsa

pocket calculator *s* bolsicalculadora, calculadora de bolsillo

pocket handkerchief *s* pañuelo de bolsillo o de mano

pock′et·knife′ *s* (*pl* **-knives**) navaja, cortaplumas *m*

pocket money *s* alfileres *mpl*, dinero de bolsillo

pock′mark′ *s* cacaraña, hoyuelo

pod [pɑd] *s* vaina

podium [ˈpodɪ·əm] *s* podio

poem [ˈpo·ɪm] *s* poema *m*, poesía

poet [ˈpo·ɪt] *s* poeta *m*

poetess [ˈpo·ɪtɪs] *s* poetisa

poetic [poˈɛtɪk] *adj* poético ‖ **poetics** *ssg* poética

poetry [ˈpo·ɪtri] *s* poesía

pogrom [ˈpogrəm] *s* levantamiento contra los judíos

poignancy [ˈpɔɪnyənsi] *s* picante *m*, viveza, intensidad

poignant [ˈpɔɪnyənt] *adj* picante, vivo, intenso

point [pɔɪnt] *s* (*of a sword, pencil; of land*) punta; (*of pen*) pico; (*of fountain pen*) puntilla; (*mark of imperceptible dimensions*) punto; (*of a joke*) gracia; (elec) punta; (math, typ, sport, fig) punto; (coll) indirecta, insinuación; **beside the point**

fuera de propósito; **on the point of** a punto de; **to carry one's point** salirse con la suya; **to come to the point** venir al caso o al grano; **to get to the point** caer en la cuenta ‖ *tr* aguzar, sacar punta a; apuntar (*p.ej.*, *un arma de fuego*); resanar (*una pared*); **to point one's finger at** señalar con el dedo; **to point out** señalar, indicar, hacer notar ‖ *intr* apuntar; pararse (*el perro de muestra*); **to point at** señalar con el dedo

point'blank' *adj & adv* a quemarropa

pointed ['pɔɪntɪd] *adj* puntiagudo; picante; acentuado, directo

pointer ['pɔɪntər] *s* puntero; indicador *m*; (*of a clock*) manecilla; perro de muestra; (*mas*) fijador *m*; (coll) indicación, dirección

poise [pɔɪz] *s* aplomo, equilibrio ‖ *tr* equilibrar; considerar ‖ *intr* equilibrarse; estar suspendido

poison ['pɔɪzən] *s* veneno, ponzoña ‖ *tr* envenenar

poison ivy *s* tosiguero

poisonous ['pɔɪzənəs] *adj* venenoso

poi'son-pen' letter *s* carta calumniosa

poke [pok] *s* (*push*) empuje *m*, empujón *m*; (*thrust*) hurgonazo; (*with elbow*) codazo; (*slow person*) tardón *m* ‖ *tr* empujar; hacer (*un agujero*) a empujones; abrirse (*paso*) a empujones; atizar, hurgar (*el fuego*); **to poke fun at** burlarse de; **to poke one's nose into** entremeterse en ‖ *intr* fisgar, husmear; andar perezosamente

poker ['pokər] *s* hurgón *m*; (*card game*) póker *m*, pócar *m*

poker face *s* cara de jugador de póker; **to keep a poker face** disfrazar la expresión del rostro, mantener una expresión imperturbable

pok•y ['poki] *adj* (*comp* -ier; *super* -iest) (coll) tardo, roncero

Poland ['polənd] *s* Polonia

polar bear ['polər] *s* oso blanco

polarize ['polə,raɪz] *tr* polarizar

pole [pol] *s* (*long rod or staff*) pértiga; (*of a flag*) asta; (*upright support*) poste *m*; (*to push a boat*) botador *m*; (astr, biol, elec, geog, math) polo ‖ *tr* impeler (*un barco*) con botador ‖ **Pole** *s* polaco

pole'cat' *s* turón *m*, veso

pole'star' *s* estrella polar; (*guide*) norte *m*; (*center of interest*) miradero

pole vault *s* salto con garrocha o con pértiga

police [pə'lis] *s* policía ‖ *tr* poner o mantener servicio de policía en; (mil) limpiar

police car *s* carro-patrulla *m*

police•man [pə'lismən] *s* (*pl* -men [mən]) policía *m*, guardia urbano

police record *s* ficha

police state *s* estado-policía *m*

police station *s* cuartel *m* o estación de policía

poli•cy ['palɪsi] *s* (*pl* -cies) política; (ins) póliza

polio ['polɪ•o] *s* (coll) polio *f*

polish ['palɪʃ] *s* pulimento; cera de lustrar; (*for shoes*) bola, betún *m*, lustre *m*; (*dia-*

mond) talla; elegancia; cultura, urbanidad ‖ *tr* pulimentar, pulir; embolar, dar betún a (*los zapatos*); **to polish off** (coll) terminar de prisa; (slang) engullir (*la comida*, *un trago*) ‖ **Polish** ['polɪʃ] *adj & s* polaco

polisher ['palɪʃər] *s* pulidor *m*; (*machine*) pulidora; (*for floors*, *tables*, *etc.*) enceradora

polite [pə'laɪt] *adj* cortés, fino, urbano; culto

politeness [pə'laɪtnɪs] *s* cortesía, fineza, urbanidad; cultura

politic ['palɪtɪk] *adj* prudente, sagaz; astuto; juicioso

political [pə'lɪtɪkəl] *adj* político

politician [,palɪ'tɪʃən] *s* político; (*politician seeking personal or partisan gain*) politiquero

politics ['palɪtɪks] *ssg o spl* política

poll [pol] *s* (*questionnaire to determine opinion*) encuesta; votación; lista electoral; cabeza; **polls** urnas electorales; **to go to the polls** acudir a las urnas; **to take a poll** hacer una encuesta ‖ *tr* dar (*un voto*); recibir (*votos*)

pollen ['palən] *s* polen *m*

pollinate ['palɪ,net] *tr* polinizar

polling booth ['polɪŋ] *s* cabina o caseta de votar

polliwog ['palɪ,wag] *s* renacuajo; (slang) persona que atraviesa el ecuador en un barco por primera vez

pollster ['polstʌr] *s* encuestador *m*

poll tax *s* capitación, impuesto por cabeza

pollutant [pə'lutənt] *s* contaminante *m*

pollute [pə'lut] *tr* contaminar, corromper, ensuciar

pollution [pə'luʃən] *s* contaminación; (*of the environment*) polución; (fig) corrupción

polo ['polo] *s* polo

polo player *s* polista *mf*, jugador *m* de polo

polygamist [pə'lɪgəmɪst] *s* polígamo

polygamous [pə'lɪgəməs] *adj* polígamo

polyglot ['palɪ,glat] *adj & s* poligloto

polygon ['palɪ,gan] *s* polígono

Polyhymnia [,palɪ'hɪmnɪ•ə] *s* Polimnia

polynomial [,palɪ'nomɪ•əl] *s* polinomio

polyp ['palɪp] *s* pólipo

polytheist ['palɪ,θi•ɪst] *s* politeísta *mf*

polytheistic [,palɪθi'ɪstɪk] *adj* politeísta

polyvalent [,pali'velənt] *adj* (chem, bact) polivalente

pomade [pə'med] *s* pomada

pomegranate ['pam,grænɪt] *s* (*shrub*) granado; (*fruit*) granada

pom•mel ['pʌməl] o ['paməl] *s* (*on hilt of sword*) pomo; (*on saddle*) perilla ‖ *v* (*pret & pp* -meled o -melled; *ger* -meling o -melling*) *tr* apuñear, aporrear

pomp [pamp] *s* pompa, fausto

pompadour ['pampə,dur] *s* copete *m*

pompous ['pampəs] *adj* pomposo, faustoso

pon•cho ['pantʃo] *s* (*pl* -chos) capote *m* de monte, poncho

pond [pand] *s* estanque *m*, charca

ponder ['pandər] *tr* ponderar ‖ *intr* meditar; **to ponder over** ponderar, considerar con cuidado

pl
po

ponderous [ˈpɑndərəs] *adj* pesado, inmanejable; tedioso, fastidioso

pond scum *s* lama, verdín *m*

poniard [ˈpɑnjərd] *s* puñal *m*

pontiff [ˈpɑntɪf] *s* pontífice *m*

pontoon [pɑnˈtun] *s* pontón *m*

po•ny [ˈponi] *s* (*pl* **-nies**) jaca, caballito; (*for drinking liquor*) (coll) pequeño vaso; (*translation used dishonestly in school*) (coll) chuleta

poodle [ˈpudəl] *s* perro de lanas

pool [pul] *s* (*small puddle*) charco; (*for swimming*) piscina; (*game*) trucos; (*in certain games*) polla, puesta; combinación de intereses; caudales unidos para un fin ‖ *tr* mancomunar

pool′room′ *s* sala de trucos

pool table *s* mesa de trucos

poop [pup] *s* popa; (*deck*) toldilla

poor [pʊr] *adj* (*having few possessions; arousing pity*) pobre; (*not good, inferior*) malo

poor box *s* cepillo, caja de limosnas

poor′house′ *s* asilo de pobres, casa de caridad

poorly [ˈpʊrli] *adv* mal

poor white *s* pobre *mf* de la raza blanca (*en el sur de los EE.UU.*)

pop. *abbr* **popular, population**

pop [pɑp] *s* estallido, taponazo; bebida gaseosa ‖ *v* (*pret & pp* **popped**; *ger* **popping**) *tr* hacer estallar; **to pop the question** (coll) hacer una declaración de amor ‖ *intr* estallar

pop′corn′ *s* rosetas, palomitas (de maíz)

pope [pop] *s* papa *m*

popeyed [ˈpɑpˌaɪd] *adj* de ojos saltones; (*with fear, surprise, etc.*) desorbitado

pop′gun′ *s* tirabala

poplar [ˈpɑplər] *s* álamo, chopo

pop•py [ˈpɑpi] *s* (*pl* **-pies**) amapola

pop′py•cock′ *s* (coll) necedad, tontería

popsicle [ˈpɑpsɪkəl] *s* polo

populace [ˈpɑpjəlɪs] *s* populacho; chamuchina

popular [ˈpɑpjələr] *adj* popular

popularize [ˈpɑpjələˌraɪz] *tr* popularizar, vulgarizar

populous [ˈpɑpjələs] *adj* populoso

porcelain [ˈpɔrsəlɪn] *s* porcelana

porch [pɔrtʃ] *s* porche *m*, pórtico

porcupine [ˈpɔrkjəˌpaɪn] *s* puerco espín

pore [por] *s* poro ‖ *intr*—**to pore over** estudiar larga y detenidamente

pork [pork] *s* carne *f* de cerdo

pork chop *s* chuleta de cerdo

pornography [pɔrˈnɑgrəfi] *s* pornografía

pornographic [ˌpɔrnəˈgræfɪk] *adj* pornográfico

porno queen [ˈpɔrno] *s* (slang) actriz *f* de películas pornográficas

porous [ˈporəs] *adj* poroso

porous plaster *s* parche poroso

porphy•ry [ˈpɔrfɪri] *s* (*pl* **-ries**) pórfido

porpoise [ˈpɔrpəs] *s* marsopa, puerco de mar; (*dolphin*) delfín *m*

porridge [ˈpɔrɪdʒ] *s* gachas

port [port] *adj* portuario ‖ *s* puerto; (*opening in ship′s side*) portilla; (*left side of ship or airplane*) babor *m;* oporto, vino de Oporto; (mach) lumbrera

portable [ˈportəbəl] *adj* portátil

portal [ˈportəl] *s* portal *m*

portend [porˈtɛnd] *tr* anunciar de antemano, presagiar

portent [ˈportent] *s* augurio, presagio

portentous [porˈtɛntəs] *adj* portentoso, extraordinario; amenazante, ominoso

porter [ˈportər] *s* (*doorkeeper*) portero, conserje *m;* (*in hotels and trains*) mozo de servicio; pórter *m* (*cerveza de Inglaterra de color obscuro*)

portfoli•o [portˈfoli,o] *s* (*pl* **-os**) cartera

port′hole′ *s* porta, portilla

porti•co [ˈportɪˌko] *s* (*pl* **-coes o -cos**) pórtico

portion [ˈporʃən] *s* porción; (*dowry*) dote *m & f*

port•ly [ˈportli] *adj* (*comp* **-lier;** *super* **-liest**) corpulento; grave, majestuoso

port of call *s* escala

portrait [ˈportret] *o* [ˈportrɪt] *s* retrato; **to sit for a portrait** retratarse

portray [porˈtre] *tr* retratar

portrayal [porˈtre•əl] *s* representación gráfica; retrato, descripción acertada

Portugal [ˈportʃəgəl] *s* Portugal *m*

Portu•guese [ˈportʃəˌgiz] *adj* portugués ‖ *s* (*pl* **-guese**) portugués *m*

port wine *s* vino de Oporto

pose [poz] *s* pose *f* ‖ *tr* plantear (*una pregunta, cuestión, etc.*) ‖ *intr* posar (*para retratarse; como modelo*); tomar una postura afectada; **to pose as** hacerse pasar por

posh [pɑʃ] *adj* (slang) elegante; (slang) lujoso, suntuoso

position [pəˈzɪʃən] *s* posición; empleo, puesto; opinión; **to be in a position to** estar en condiciones de

positive [ˈpɑzɪtɪv] *adj* positivo ‖ *s* positiva

possess [pəˈzɛs] *tr* poseer

possession [pəˈzɛʃən] *s* posesión

possible [ˈpɑsɪbəl] *adj* posible

possum [ˈpɑsəm] *s* zarigüeya; **to play possum** hacer la mortecina

post [post] *s* (*piece of wood, metal, etc. set upright*) poste *m;* (*position*) puesto; (*job*) puesto, cargo; casa de correos ‖ *tr* fijar (*carteles*); echar al correo; apostar, situar; tener al corriente; **post no bills** se prohíbe fijar carteles

postage [ˈpostɪdʒ] *s* porte *m*, franqueo; **postage will be paid by addressee** a franquear en destino

postage meter *s* franqueadora

postage stamp *s* sello de correo; estampilla, timbre *m* (Am)

postal [ˈpostəl] *adj* postal ‖ *s* postal *f*

postal card *s* tarjeta postal

postal permit *s* franqueo concertado

postal savings bank *s* caja postal de ahorros

post card *s* tarjeta postal

post′date′ *s* posfecha ‖ **post′date′** *tr* posfechar

poster [´postər] s cartel m, cartelón m, letrero; póster m

posterity [pɑs´tɛrɪti] s posteridad

postern [´postərn] s postigo, portillo

post'haste' adv por la posta, a toda prisa

posthumous [´pɑstʃuməs] adj póstumo

post•man [´postmən] s (pl -men [mən]) cartero

post'mark' s matasellos m, timbre m de correos ‖ tr matasellar, timbrar

post'mas'ter s administrador m de correos

post-mortem [,post´mɔrtəm] adj posterior a la muerte ‖ s examen m de un cadáver

post office s casa de correos

post'-of'fice box s apartado de correos, casilla postal

postpaid [´post,ped] adj con porte pagado, franco de porte

postpone [post´pon] tr aplazar

postscript [´post,skrɪpt] s posdata

posttonic [post´tɑnɪk] adj postónico

posture [´pɑstʃər] s postura ‖ intr adoptar una postura

post'war' adj de la posguerra

po•sy [´pozi] s (pl -sies) flor f, ramillete m

pot [pɑt] s pote m; (for flowers) tiesto; (for the kitchen) caldera, olla, puchero; vaso de noche, orinal m; (in gambling) puesta; (slang) mariguana

potash [´pɑt,æʃ] s potasa

potassium [pə´tæsɪ•əm] s potasio

pota•to [pə´teto] s (pl -toes) patata, papa; (sweet potato) batata, buniato

potato masher s pasapuré m

potato omelet s tortilla a la española

potbellied [´pɑt´bɛlid] adj barrigón, panzudo

poten•cy [´potənsi] s (pl -cies) potencia

potent [´potənt] adj potente

potentate [´potən,tet] s potentado

potential [pə´tɛnʃəl] adj & s potencial m

pot'hang'er s llares fpl

pot'hook' s garabato

potion [´poʃən] s poción

pot'luck' s lo que hay de comer; **to take potluck** hacer penitencia

pot shot s tiro a corta distancia

potter [´pɑtər] s alfarero; ollero ‖ intr ocuparse en fruslerías

potter's clay s arcilla figulina

potter's field s cementerio de los pobres, hoyanca

potter's shop s ollería

potter's wheel s torno de alfarero

potter•y [´pɑtəri] s (pl -ies) alfarería; cacharros (de alfarería)

pouch [pautʃ] s bolsa, saquillo; (of kangaroo) bolsa; (for tobacco) petaca; valija

poulterer [´poltərər] s pollero

poultice [´poltɪs] s cataplasma f

poultry [´poltri] s aves fpl de corral

pounce [pauns] intr—**to pounce on** saltar sobre, precipitarse sobre

pound [paund] s (weight) libra; (for stray animals) corral m de concejo ‖ tr golpear; machacar, moler; encerrar en el corral de concejo; bombardear incesantemente; (to keep walking over) desempedrar ‖ intr golpear

pound'cake' s pastel m en que entra una libra de cada ingrediente; ponqué m (Am)

pound sterling s libra esterlina

pour [por] tr vaciar, verter, derramar; echar, servir (p.ej., té); escanciar (vino) ‖ intr fluir rápidamente; llover a torrentes; **to pour out of** salir a montones de (p.ej., el teatro)

pout [paut] s mala cara, puchero ‖ intr poner mala cara, hacer pucheros

poverty [´pɑvərti] s pobreza; pelazón f

POW abbr **prisoner of war**

powder [´paudər] s polvo; (for face) polvos; (explosive) pólvora ‖ tr pulverizar; (to sprinkle with powder) empolvar, polvorear

powder puff s borla para empolvarse

powder room s cuarto tocador, cuarto de aseo

powdery [´paudəri] adj (like powder) polvoriento; (sprinkled with powder) empolvado; (crumbly) quebradizo

power [´pau•ər] s (ability to act or do something; possession) poder m; (control, influence; wealth) poderío; (influential nation; energy, force, strength) potencia; **the powers that be** las autoridades, los que mandan ‖ tr accionar, impulsar

power brake s servofreno

power dive s (aer) picado con motor

power failure s interrupción de fuerza

powerful [´pau•ərfəl] adj poderoso

pow'er•house' s central eléctrica

powerless [´pau•ərlɪs] adj impotente

power line s (elec) sector m de distribución

power mower s motosegadora

power of attorney s poder m

power plant s (aer) grupo motopropulsor; (aut) grupo motor; (elec) central eléctrica, estación generadora

power steering s (aut) servodirección

power tool s herramienta motriz

pp. abbr **pages**

p.p. abbr **parcel post, postpaid**

pr. abbr **pair, present, price**

P.R. abbr **public relations**

practical [´præktɪkəl] adj práctico

practically [´præktɪkəli] adv poco más o menos

practice [´præktɪs] s práctica; uso, costumbre; ensayo; (of a profession) ejercicio; (of a doctor) clientela ‖ tr practicar; ejercitar (p.ej., la caridad); ejercer (una profesión); estudiar (p.ej., el piano); tener por costumbre ‖ intr ejercitarse; practicar la medicina; ensayarse; entrenarse, adiestrarse; **to practice as** ejercer de (p.ej., abogado)

practitioner [præk´tɪʃənər] s (medical doctor) práctico

Prague [prɑg] o [preg] s Praga

prairie [´prɛri] s pradera, llanura, pampa

prairie dog s ardilla ladradora

prairie wolf s coyote m

praise [prez] s alabanza, elogío ‖ tr alabar, elogiar

praise'wor'thy adj laudable, plausible

po

pr

pram [præm] *s* cochecillo de niño
prance [præns] o [prɑns] *s* cabriola, trenzado ‖ *intr* cabriolar, trenzar
prank [præŋk] *s* travesura
prate [pret] *intr* charlar, parlotear
prattle [`prætəl] *s* charla, parloteo ‖ *intr* charlar, parlotear, balbucear (*un niño*)
pray [pre] *tr* implorar, rogar, suplicar; rezar (*una oración*) ‖ *intr* orar, rezar; **pray tell me** sírvase decirme
prayer [prɛr] *s* ruego, súplica; oración, rezo
prayer book *s* devocionario
preach [pritʃ] *tr* predicar; aconsejar (*p.ej., la paciencia*) ‖ *intr* predicar
preacher [`pritʃər] *s* predicador *m*
preamble [`pri,æmbəl] *s* preámbulo
prebend [`prɛbənd] *s* prebenda
precarious [pri`kɛri•əs] *adj* precario
precaution [pri`kɔʃən] *s* precaución
precede [pri`sid] *tr & intr* preceder
precedent [`prɛsɪdənt] *s* precedente *m*
precept [`prisɛpt] *s* precepto
precinct [`prisɪŋkt] *s* barriada; distrito electoral
precious [`prɛʃəs] *adj* precioso; caro, amado; (coll) considerable ‖ *adv* (coll) muy, p.ej., **precious little** muy poco
precipice [`prɛsɪpɪs] *s* precipicio
precipitate [pri`sɪpɪ,tet] *adj & s* precipitado ‖ *tr* precipitar ‖ *intr* precipitarse
precipitous [pri`sɪpɪtəs] *adj* empinado, escarpado; (*hurried, reckless*) precipitoso
precise [pri`sais] *adj* preciso; meticuloso
precision [pri`sɪʒən] *s* precisión
preclude [pri`klud] *tr* excluir, imposibilitar
precocious [pri`koʃəs] *adj* precoz
predatory [`prɛdə,tori] *adj* predatorio
predicament [pri`dɪkəmənt] *s* apuro, situación difícil
predict [pri`dɪkt] *tr* predecir
prediction [pri`dɪkʃən] *s* predicción
predispose [,pridɪs`poz] *tr* predisponer
predominant [pri`dɑmɪnənt] *adj* predominante
preëminent [pri`ɛmɪnənt] *adj* preeminente
preëmpt [pri`ɛmpt] *tr* apropiarse o apropiarse de
preen [prin] *tr* arreglarse (*las plumas*) con el pico; **to preen oneself** componerse, vestirse cuidadosamente
pref. *abbr* **preface, preferred, prefix**
prefabricate [pri`fæbri,ket] *tr* prefabricar
preface [`prɛfɪs] *s* prefacio, advertencia ‖ *tr* introducir, empezar
pre•fer [pri`fʌr] *v* (*pret & pp* **-ferred**; *ger* **-ferring**) *tr* preferir; presentar; promover
preferable [`prɛfərəbəl] *adj* preferible
preference [`prɛfərəns] *s* preferencia
prefix [`prifɪks] *s* prefijo ‖ *tr* prefijar
pregnan•cy [`prɛgnənsi] *s* (*pl* **-cies**) preñez *f*, embarazo
pregnant [`prɛgnənt] *adj* preñado; encinta; **to make pregnant** dejar encinta
prejudice [`prɛdʒədɪs] *s* prejuicio; (*detriment*) perjuicio; **to the prejudice of** con perjuicio de; **without prejudice** (law) sin detrimento de sus propios derechos ‖ *tr*

predisponer, prevenir; (*to harm*) perjudicar
prejudicial [,prɛdʒə`dɪʃəl] *adj* perjudicial
prelate [`prɛlɪt] *s* prelado
pre-Lenten [pri`lɛntən] *adj* carnavalesco
prelim [pri`lɪm] *s* (coll) examen *m* preliminar
preliminar•y [pri`lɪmɪ,nɛri] *adj* preliminar ‖ *s* (*pl* **-ies**) preliminar *m*
prelude [`prɛljud] o [`prilud] *s* preludio ‖ *tr* preludiar
premeditate [pri`mɛdɪ,tet] *tr* premeditar
premier [pri`mɪr] o [`pri`mɪr] *s* primer ministro, presidente *m* del consejo
première [pre`mjɛr] o [`primi•ər] *s* estreno; actriz *f* principal
premise [`prɛmɪs] *s* premisa; **on the premises** en el local mismo; **premises** predio, local *m*
premium [`primi•əm] *s* premio; (ins) prima
premonition [,primə`nɪʃən] *s* presagio; presentimiento
preoccupancy [pri`akjəpənsi] *s* preocupación
preoccupation [pri`akjə`peʃən] *s* preocupación
preoccu•py [pri`akjə,pai] *v* (*pret & pp* **-pied**) *tr* preocupar
prepaid [pri`ped] *adj* pagado por adelantado; con porte pagado
preparation [,prɛpə`reʃən] *s* preparación; (*e.g., for a trip*) preparativo; (pharm) preparado
preparatory [pri`pærə,tori] *adj* preparativo, preparatorio
prepare [pri`pɛr] *tr* preparar ‖ *intr* prepararse
preparedness [pri`pɛrɪdnɪs] o [pri`pɛrdnɪs] *s* preparación; preparación militar
pre•pay [pri`pe] *v* (*pret & pp* **-paid**) *tr* pagar por adelantado
preponderant [pri`pandərənt] *adj* preponderante
preposition [,prɛpə`zɪʃən] *s* preposición
prepossessing [,pripə`zɛsɪŋ] *adj* atractivo, simpático
preposterous [pri`pastərəs] *adj* absurdo, ridículo
prep school [prɛp] *s* (coll) escuela preparatoria
prerecorded [,prirɪ`kɔrdɪd] *adj* (rad & telv) grabado de antemano
prerequisite [,pri`rɛkwɪzɪt] *s* requisito previo
prerogative [pri`ragətɪv] *s* prerrogativa
Pres. *abbr* **Presbyterian, President**
presage [`prɛsɪdʒ] *s* presagio ‖ [pri`sedʒ] *tr* presagiar
Presbyterian [,prɛzbɪ`tiri•ən] *adj & s* presbiteriano
prescribe [pri`skraib] *tr & intr* prescribir
prescription [pri`skrɪpʃən] *s* prescripción; (pharm) receta
presence [`prɛzəns] *s* presencia
present [`prɛzənt] *adj* presente ‖ *s* presente *m*, regalo ‖ [pri`zɛnt] *tr* presentar, obsequiar
presentable [pri`zɛntəbəl] *adj* bien apersonado
presentation [,prɛzən`teʃən] o [,prizən`teʃən] *s* presentación

presentation copy *s* ejemplar *m* de cortesía con dedicatoria del autor

presentiment [prɪ'zɛntɪmənt] *s* presentimiento

presently ['prɛzəntli] *adv* luego, dentro de poco

preserve [prɪ'zʌrv] *s* conserva, compota; (*for game*) vedado ‖ *tr* conservar; preservar, proteger

preserved fruit *s* dulce *m* de almíbar

preside [prɪ'zaɪd] *intr* presidir; **to preside over** presidir

presiden·cy ['prɛzɪdənsi] *s* (*pl* **-cies**) presidencia

president ['prɛzɪdənt] *s* presidente *m;* (*of a university*) rector *m*

pres′i·dent-e·lect′ *s* presidente *m* electo (*todavía sin gobierno*)

press [prɛs] *s* apretón *m,* empujón *m;* (*e.g., of business*) urgencia; muchedumbre; (*machine for printing, for making wine; newspapers and newspapermen*) prensa; (*printing*) imprenta; (*closet*) armario; **to go to press** entrar en prensa ‖ *tr* apretar (*p.ej., un botón*); (*in a press*) prensar; planchar (*la ropa*); imprimir (*discos de fonógrafo*); oprimir (*una tecla*); apresurar; abrumar; apremiar, instar; insistir en

press agent *s* agente *m* de publicidad

press conference *s* conferencia de prensa, rueda de prensa

pressing ['prɛsɪŋ] *adj* apremiante, urgente ‖ *s* planchado

press release *s* comunicado de prensa

pressure ['prɛʃər] *s* presión; premura, urgencia

pressure cooker ['kʊkər] *s* olla de presión, cocina de presión

pressurize ['prɛʃə,raɪz] *tr* (aer) sobrecargar

prestige [prɛs'tiʒ] o ['prɛstɪdʒ] *s* prestigio

presumably [prɪ'zuməbli] *adv* probablemente, verosímilmente

presume [prɪ'zjum] *tr* presumir; suponer; **to presume** tomar la libertad de ‖ *intr* suponer; **to presume on** o **upon** abusar de

presumption [prɪ'zʌmpʃən] *s* presunción; pretensión

presumptuous [prɪ'zʌmptʃʊ·əs] *adj* confianzudo, desenvuelto

presuppose [,prisə'poz] *tr* presuponer

pretend [prɪ'tɛnd] *tr* aparentar, fingir ‖ *intr* fingir; **to pretend to** pretender (*p.ej., el trono*)

pretender [prɪ'tɛndər] *s* pretendiente *mf*

pretense [prɪ'tɛns] o ['pritɛns] *s* pretensión; fingimiento; **under false pretenses** con apariencias fingidas; **under pretense of** so pretexto de

pretentious [prɪ'tɛnʃəs] *adj* pretencioso, aparatoso; ambicioso, vasto

pretonic [prɪ'tɑnɪk] *adj* pretónico

pretrial prisoner *s* preso preventivo

pret·ty ['prɪti] *adj* (*comp* **-tier;** *super* **-tiest**) bonito, lindo; (coll) bastante, considerable ‖ *adv* algo; bastante; muy

prevail [prɪ'vel] *intr* prevalecer, reinar; **to prevail on** o **upon** persuadir

prevailing [prɪ'velɪŋ] *adj* prevaleciente, reinante; común, corriente

prevalent ['prɛvələnt] *adj* común, corriente, en boga

prevaricate [prɪ'værɪ,ket] *intr* mentir

prevent [prɪ'vɛnt] *tr* impedir ‖ *intr* obstar

prevention [prɪ'vɛnʃən] *s* (el) impedir; medidas de precaución

preventive [prɪ'vɛntɪv] *adj* & *s* preservativo

preview ['pri,vju] *s* vista anticipada; (*private showing*) (mov) preestreno; (*showing of brief scenes for advertising*) (mov) avance *m*

previous ['privi·əs] *adj* previo, anterior ‖ *adv* previamente; **previous to** con anterioridad a, antes de

prewar ['pri,wɔr] *adj* prebélico, de preguerra

prey [pre] *s* presa; víctima; **to be prey to** ser presa de ‖ *intr* cazar; **to prey on** o **upon** apresar y devorar; pillar, robar; tener preocupado

price [praɪs] *s* precio ‖ *tr* apreciar, estimar; fijar el precio de, poner precio a; pedir el precio de

price control *s* intervención de precios

price cutting *s* reducción de precios

price fixing *s* fijación de precios

price freezing *s* congelación de precios

priceless ['praɪslɪs] *adj* inapreciable, sin precio; (coll) absurdo, divertido

price war *s* guerra de precios

prick [prɪk] *s* (*pointed weapon or instrument*) espiche *m;* (*sharp point*) púa; (*small hole made with sharp point*) agujerillo; (*spur*) aguijón *m;* (*jab; sharp pain*) pinchazo, punzada; **to kick against the pricks** dar coces contra el aguijón ‖ *tr* pinchar; marcar con agujerillos; dar una punzada a; (*to sting*) punzar; **to prick up** aguzar (*las orejas*)

prick·ly ['prɪkli] *adj* (*comp* **-lier;** *super* **-liest**) espinoso, puado, punzante

prickly heat *s* salpullido causado por el calor

prickly pear *s* (*plant*) chumbera; (*fruit*) higo chumbo

pride [praɪd] *s* orgullo; arrogancia; **the pride of** la flor y nata de ‖ *tr*—**to pride oneself on** o **upon** enorgullecerse de

priest [prist] *s* sacerdote *m*

priesthood ['prist·hʊd] *s* sacerdocio

priest·ly ['pristli] *adj* (*comp* **-lier;** *super* **-liest**) sacerdotal

prig [prɪg] *s* gazmoño, pedante *mf*

prim [prɪm] *adj* (*comp* **primmer;** *super* **primmest**) estirado, relamido

primary ['praɪ,mɛri] o ['praɪməri] *adj* primario ‖ *s* (*pl* **-ries**) elección preliminar; (elec) primario

prime [praɪm] *adj* primero, principal; (*of the best quality*) primo ‖ *s* flor *f,* juventud, primavera; alba, aurora; (la) flor y nata; (*of a degree*) (phys) minuto; (typ) virgulilla; **prime of life** edad viril, flor *f* de edad ‖ *tr* informar de antemano; cebar (*un arma de fuego, una bomba, un carburador*); (*for painting*) imprimar; poner la primera capa o la primera mano a; poner virgulilla a

pr
pr

prime minister *s* primer ministro

primer [`prɪmər] *s* cartilla ‖ [`praɪmər] *s (for paint)* aprestado *m;* (mach) cebador *m*

primitive [`prɪmɪtɪv] *adj* primitivo

primp [prɪmp] *tr* acicalar, engalanar ‖ *intr* acicalarse, engalanarse

prim′rose′ *s* primavera

primrose path *s* vida dada a los placeres de los sentidos

prin. *abbr* **principal**

prince [prɪns] *s* príncipe *m;* **to live like a prince** portarse como un príncipe

Prince of Wales *s* príncipe *m* de Gales

princess [`prɪnsɪs] *s* princesa

principal [`prɪnsɪpəl] *adj* principal ‖ *s* principal *m,* jefe *m; (of a school)* director *m;* criminal *mf; (main sum, not interest)* capital *m*

principle [`prɪnsɪpəl] *s* principio

print [prɪnt] *s* marca, impresión; *(printed cloth)* estampado; *(design in printed cloth)* diseño; grabado, lámina; letras de molde; *(act of printing)* impresión; edición; tirada; (phot) impreso, publicado; **in print** impreso, publicado; **out of print** agotado ‖ *tr* imprimir; estampar; hacer imprimir; publicar; escribir en caracteres de imprenta; (phot) tirar, imprimir; (fig) imprimir o grabar *(en la memoria)*

printed matter *s* impresos

printer [`prɪntər] *s* impresor *m*

printer's devil *s* aprendiz *m* de imprenta

printer's ink *s* tinta de imprenta

printer's mark *s* pie *m* de imprenta

printing [`prɪntɪŋ] *s* impresión; caracteres impresos; edición; tirada; letras de mano imitación de las impresas; (phot) tiraje *m*

printout [`prɪnt,aʊt] *s (computer)* impreso derivado

prior [`praɪər] *adj* anterior ‖ *adv* anteriormente; **prior to** antes de

priori•ty [praɪ`ɔrɪti] *s (pl* **-ties)** prioridad; **of the highest priority** de máxima prioridad

prism [`prɪzəm] *s* prisma *m*

prison [`prɪzən] *s* cárcel *f,* prisión ‖ *tr* encarcelar

prisoner [`prɪzənər] o [`prɪznər] *s* preso; (mil) prisionero

prison van *s* coche *m* celular

pris•sy [`prɪsi] *adj (comp* **-sier;** *super* **-siest)** (coll) remilgado, melindroso

priva•cy [`praɪvəsi] *s (pl* **-cies)** aislamiento, retiro; secreto, reserva

private [`praɪvɪt] *adj* particular, privado; confidencial; ‖ *s* soldado raso; **in private** privadamente; en secreto; **privates** partes pudendas

private first class *s* soldado de primera, aspirante *m* a cabo

private hospital *s* clínica, casa de salud

private property *s* bienes *mpl* particulares

private view *s* día *m* de inauguración

privet [`prɪvɪt] *s* aligustre *m*

privilege [`prɪvɪlɪdʒ] *s* privilegio

priv•y [`prɪvi] *adj* privado; **privy to** enterado secretamente de ‖ *s (pl* **-ies)** letrina

prize [praɪz] *s* premio; *(something captured)* presa ‖ *tr* apreciar, estimar

prize fight *s* partido de boxeo profesional

prize fighter *s* boxeador *m* profesional

prize ring *s* cuadrilátero de boxeo

pro [pro] *prep* en pro de ‖ *s (pl* **pros)** voto afirmativo; (coll) deportista *mf* profesional; **the pros and the cons** el pro y el contra

probabili•ty [,prabə`bɪlɪti] *s (pl* **-ties)** probabilidad; acontecimiento probable; tiempo probable

probable [`prabəbəl] *adj* probable

probation [pro`beʃən] *s* libertad vigilada; período de prueba

probe [prob] *s* encuesta, indagación; *(instrument)* sonda ‖ *tr* indagar; sondar

problem [`prabləm] *s* problema *m*

procedure [pro`sidʒər] *s* procedimiento

proceed [pro`sid] *intr* proceder ‖ **proceeds** [`prosidz] *spl* producto, ganancia

proceeding [pro`sidɪŋ] *s* procedimiento; **proceedings** actas; diligencias

process [`prasɛs] *s* procedimiento; proceso, progreso; **in the process of time** con el tiempo ‖ *tr* elaborar; *(electronic data)* procesar

processing [`prasɛsɪŋ] *s (electronic data)* procesamiento

process server [`sʌrvər] *s* entregador *m* de la citación

proclaim [pro`klem] *tr* proclamar

proclitic [pro`klɪtɪk] *adj & s* proclítico

procommunist [pro`kamjənɪst] *adj & s* filocomunista *mf*

procrastinate [pro`kræstɪ,net] *tr* diferir de un día para otro ‖ *intr* tardar, no decidirse

procure [pro`kjʊr] *tr* conseguir, obtener ‖ *intr* alcahuetear

prod [prad] *s* aguijada; empuje *m* ‖ *v (pret & pp* **prodded;** *ger* **prodding)** *tr* aguijar, pinchar; aguijonear, estimular

prodigal [`pradɪgəl] *adj & s* pródigo

prodigious [pro`dɪdʒəs] *adj & s* prodigioso, maravilloso; enorme, inmenso

prodi•gy [`pradɪdʒi] *s (pl* **-gies)** prodigio

produce [`prodjus] o [`produs] *s* producto; productos agrícolas ‖ [pro`djus] o [pro`dus] *tr* producir; presentar *(p.ej., un drama)* al público; (geom) prolongar

product [`pradəkt] *s* producto

production [pro`dʌkʃən] *s* producción

profane [pro`fen] *adj* profano; *(language)* injurioso, blasfemo ‖ *s* profano ‖ *tr* profanar

profani•ty [pro`fænɪti] *s (pl* **-ties)** blasfemia

profess [pro`fɛs] *tr & intr* profesar

profession [pro`fɛʃən] *s* profesión

professor [pro`fɛsər] *s* profesor *m,* catedrático; (coll) profesor, maestro

proffer [`prafər] *s* oferta, propuesta ‖ *tr* ofrecer, proponer

proficient [pro`fɪʃənt] *adj* perito, diestro, hábil

profile [`profaɪl] *s* perfil *m* ‖ *tr* perfilar

profit [`prafɪt] *s* provecho, beneficio, utilidad, ganancia; **at a profit** con ganancia ‖ *tr* servir, ser de utilidad a ‖ *intr* sacar

provecho, ganar; adelantar, mejorar; **to profit by** aprovechar, sacar provecho de
profitable [ˈprɑfɪtəbəl] *adj* provechoso
profit and loss *s* ganancias y pérdidas
profiteer [ˌprɑfɪˈtɪr] *s* logrero, explotador *m* ‖ *intr* logrear, explotar
profit margin *s* excedente *m* de ganancia
profit taking *s* realización de beneficios
profligate [ˈprɑflɪgɪt] *adj & s* libertino; pródigo
pro forma invoice [pro ˈfɔrmə] *s* factura simulada
profound [proˈfaʊnd] *adj* profundo
profuse [proˈfjus] *adj* (*extravagant*) pródigo; (*abundant*) profuso
proge·ny [ˈprɑdʒeni] *s* (*pl* **-nies**) prole *f*
progno·sis [prɑgˈnosɪs] *s* (*pl* **-ses** [siz]) pronóstico
progno·sis [prɑgˈnɑstɪk] *s* pronóstico
program [ˈprogræm] *s* programa *m;* (*computer*) **program(me)** programa (para ordenador) ‖ *tr* programar; (*computer*) **program(me)** programar
program(m)er [ˈprogræmər] *s* (*computer*) programador *m*, programadora
program(m)ing [ˈprogræmɪŋ] *s* (*computer*) programación (de ordenadores)
progress [ˈprɑgrɛs] *s* progreso; progresos; **to make progress** hacer progresos ‖ [prəˈgrɛs] *intr* progresar
progressive [prəˈgrɛsɪv] *adj* progresivo; (pol) progresista ‖ *s* (pol) progresista *mf*
prohibit [proˈhɪbɪt] *tr* prohibir
project [ˈprɑdʒɛkt] *s* proyecto ‖ [prəˈdʒɛkt] *tr* proyectar ‖ *intr* proyectarse
projectile [prəˈdʒɛktɪl] *s* proyectil *m*
projection [prəˈdʒɛkʃən] *s* proyección
projector [prəˈdʒɛktər] *s* proyector *m*
proletarian [ˌprolɪˈtɛrɪən] *adj & s* proletario
proletariat [ˌprolɪˈtɛrɪət] *s* proletariado
proliferate [prəˈlɪfəˌret] *intr* proliferar
prolific [prəˈlɪfɪk] *adj* prolífico
prolix [ˈprolɪks] o [proˈlɪks] *adj* difuso, verboso
prologue [ˈprolɔg] *s* prólogo
prolong [proˈlɔŋ] *tr* prolongar
promenade [ˌprɑmɪˈned] *s* paseo; garbeo; baile *m* de gala ‖ *intr* pasear o pasearse
promenade deck *s* (naut) cubierta de paseo
prominent [ˈprɑmɪnənt] *adj* prominente
promise [ˈprɑmɪs] *s* promesa ‖ *tr & intr* prometer
promising young man *s* joven *m* de esperanzas
promissory [ˈprɑmɪˌsori] *adj* promisorio
promissory note *s* pagaré *m*
promonto·ry [ˈprɑmənˌtori] *s* (*pl* **-ries**) promontorio
promote [prəˈmot] *tr* promover; fomentar
promotion [prəˈmoʃən] *s* promoción; fomento
prompt [prɑmpt] *adj* pronto, puntual; listo, dispuesto ‖ *tr* incitar, mover; inspirar, sugerir; (theat) apuntar
prompter [ˈprɑmptər] *s* (theat) apuntador *m*
prompter's box *s* (theat) concha

promulgate [ˈprɑməlˌget] o [proˈmʌlget] *tr* promulgar
prone [pron] *adj* postrado boca abajo; extendido sobre el suelo; dispuesto, propenso
prong [prɔŋ] o [praŋ] *s* punta (*de un tenedor, horquilla, etc.*)
pronoun [ˈpronaʊn] *s* pronombre *m*
pronounce [prəˈnaʊns] *tr* pronunciar
pronouncement [prəˈnaʊnsmənt] *s* declaración; decisión, opinión
pronunciamen·to [prəˌnʌnsɪ·əˈmɛnto] *s* (*pl* **-tos**) pronunciamiento
pronunciation [prəˌnʌnsɪˈeʃən] o [prəˌnʌnʃɪˈeʃən] *s* pronunciación
proof [pruf] *adj* de prueba; **proof against** a prueba de ‖ *s* prueba
proof·read·er *s* corrector *m* de pruebas
prop [prɑp] *s* apoyo, puntal *m;* (*to hold up a plant*) rodrigón *m;* **props** (theat) accesorios ‖ *v* (*pret & pp* **propped**; *ger* **propping**) *tr* apoyar, apuntalar; poner un rodrigón a
propaganda [ˌprɑpəˈgændə] *s* propaganda
propagate [ˈprɑpəˌget] *tr* propagar
proparoxytone [ˌprɑpærˈɑksɪˌton] *adj & s* proparoxítono
pro·pel [prəˈpɛl] *v* (*pret & pp* **-pelled;** *ger* **-pelling**) *tr* propulsar, impeler
propeller [prəˈpɛlər] *s* hélice *f*
propensi·ty [prəˈpɛnsiti] *s* (*pl* **-ties**) propensión
proper [ˈprɑpər] *adj* propio, conveniente; decente, decoroso; exacto, justo
proper·ty [ˈprɑpərti] *s* (*pl* **-ties**) propiedad; **properties** (theat) accesorios
property owner *s* propietario de bienes raíces
prophe·cy [ˈprɑfɪsi] *s* (*pl* **-cies**) profecía
prophe·sy [ˈprɑfɪˌsaɪ] *v* (*pret & pp* **-sied**) *tr* profetizar
prophet [ˈprɑfɪt] *s* profeta *m*
prophetess [ˈprɑfɪtɪs] *s* profetisa
prophylactic [ˌprɑfɪˈlæktɪk] *adj & s* profiláctico
propitiate [prəˈpɪʃɪˌet] *tr* propiciar
propitious [prəˈpɪʃəs] *adj* propicio
prop·jet *s* turbohélice *m*
proportion [prəˈporʃən] *s* proporción; **in proportion as** a medida que; **out of proportion** desproporcionado ‖ *tr* proporcionar
proportionate [prəˈporʃənɪt] *adj* proporcionado
proposal [prəˈpozəl] *s* propuesta; oferta de matrimonio
propose [prəˈpoz] *tr* proponer ‖ *intr* proponer matrimonio; **to propose to** pedir la mano a; proponerse a + *inf*
proposition [ˌprɑpəˈzɪʃən] *s* proposición, propuesta
propound [prəˈpaʊnd] *tr* proponer
proprietor [prəˈpraɪ·ətər] *s* propietario
proprietress [prəˈpraɪ·ətrɪs] *s* propietaria
proprie·ty [prəˈpraɪ·əti] *s* (*pl* **-ties**) corrección, conducta decorosa, conveniencia; **proprieties** cánones *mpl* sociales, convenciones
propulsion [prəˈpʌlʃən] *s* propulsión
prorate [proˈret] *tr* prorratear

pr
pr

prosaic [pro'ze•ɪk] *adj* prosaico
proscribe [pro'skraɪb] *tr* proscribir
prose [proz] *adj* prosaico ‖ *s* prosa
prosecute ['prɑsɪ,kjut] *tr* llevar a cabo; (*law*) procesar
prosecutor ['prɑsɪ,kjutər] *s* acusador *m*, demandante *mf;* (*lawyer*) fiscal *m*
proselyte ['prɑsɪ,laɪt] *s* prosélito
prose writer *s* prosista *mf*
prosody ['prɑsədi] *s* métrica
prospect ['prɑspɛkt] *s* vista; esperanza; probabilidad de éxito; cliente *mf* o comprador *m* probable ‖ *tr* & *intr* prospectar; **to prospect for** buscar (*p.ej., oro, petróleo*)
prosper ['prɑspər] *tr* & *intr* prosperar
prosperi•ty [prɑs'pɛrɪti] *s* (*pl* **-ties**) prosperidad
prosperous ['prɑspərəs] *adj* próspero
prostitute ['prɑstɪ,tjut] *s* prostituta; güila (Mex) ‖ *tr* prostituir
prostrate ['prɑstret] *adj* postrado, prosternado ‖ *tr* postrar
prostration [prɑs'treʃən] *s* postración
Prot. *abbr* **Protestant**
protagonist [pro'tægənɪst] *s* protagonista *mf*
protect [prə'tɛkt] *tr* proteger
protection [prə'tɛkʃən] *s* protección
protégé ['protə,ʒe] *s* protegido
protégée ['protə,ʒe] *s* protegida
protein ['proti•ɪn] o ['protin] *s* proteína
pro-tempore [pro'tɛmpəri] *adj* interino
protest ['protɛst] *s* protesta ‖ [pro'tɛst] *tr* & *intr* protestar
protestant ['prɑtɪstənt] *adj* & *s* protestante *mf* ‖ **Protestant** *adj* & *s* protestante *mf*
prothonotar•y [pro'θɑnə,tɛri] *s* (*pl* **-ies**) escribano principal (*de un tribunal*)
protocol ['protə,kɑl] *s* protocolo
protoplasm ['protə,plæzəm] *s* protoplasma *m*
prototype ['protə,taɪp] *s* prototipo
protozoön [,protə'zo•ɑn] *s* protozoo
protract [pro'trækt] *tr* prolongar
protrude [pro'trud] *intr* resaltar
proud [praud] *adj* orgulloso; soberbio; glorioso
proud flesh *s* carnosidad, bezo
prov. *abbr* **provincialism**
prove [pruv] *v* (*pret* **proved;** *pp* **proved** o **proven**) *tr* probar ‖ *intr* resultar; **to prove to be** venir a ser, resultar
proverb ['prɑvərb] *s* proverbio
provide [prə'vaɪd] *tr* proporcionar, suministrar ‖ *intr*—**to provide for** proveer a; asegurarse (*el porvenir*)
provided [prə'vaɪdɪd] *conj* a condición (de) que, con tal (de) que
providence ['prɑvɪdəns] *s* providencia
providential [,prɑvɪ'dɛnʃəl] *adj* providencial
providing [prə'vaɪdɪŋ] *conj* var de **provided**
province ['prɑvɪns] *s* provincia; (*sphere of activity or knowledge*) competencia
proving ground ['pruvɪŋ] *s* campo de ensayos
provision [prə'vɪʒən] *s* provisión; condición, estipulación
provi•so [prə'vaɪzo] *s* (*pl* **-sos** o **-soes**) condición, estipulación, salvedad

provoke [prə'vok] *tr* provocar
provoking [prə'vokɪŋ] *adj* provocador, irritante
prow [prau] *s* proa
prowess ['prau•ɪs] *s* proeza; destreza
prowl [praul] *intr* cazar al acecho, rodar, vagabundear
prowler ['praulər] *s* rondador *m;* ladrón *m*
proximity [prɑk'sɪmɪti] *s* proximidad
prox•y ['prɑksi] *s* (*pl* **-ies**) poder *m*, poderhabiente *mf*
prude [prud] *s* mojigato, gazmoño
prudence ['prudəns] *s* prudencia
prudent ['prudənt] *adj* prudente
pruder•y ['prudəri] *s* (*pl* **-ies**) mojigatería, gazmoñería
prudish ['prudɪʃ] *adj* mojigato, gazmoño
prune [prun] *s* ciruela pasa ‖ *tr* podar, escamondar
pry [praɪ] *v* (*pret* & *pp* **pried**) *tr*—**to pry open** forzar con la alzaprima o palanca; **to pry out of** arrancar (*p.ej., un secreto*) a (*una persona*) ‖ *intr* entremeterse; **to pry into** entremeterse en
P.S. *abbr* **postscript, Privy Seal**
psalm [sɑm] *s* salmo
Psalter ['sɔltər] *s* Salterio
pseudo ['sudo] o ['sjudo] *adj* supuesto, falso, fingido
pseudonym ['sudənɪm] o ['sjudənɪm] *s* seudónimo
Psyche ['saɪki] *s* Psique *f*
psychedelic [,saɪkə'dɛlɪk] *adj* psicodélico
psychiatrist [saɪ'kaɪ•ətrɪst] *s* psiquiatra *mf*
psychiatry [saɪ'kaɪ•ətri] *s* psiquiatría
psychic ['saɪkɪk] *adj* psíquico; mediúmnico ‖ *s* médium *m*
psychoanalysis [,saɪko•ə'nælɪsɪs] *s* psicoanálisis *m*
psychoanalyze [,saɪko'ænə,laɪz] *tr* psicoanalizar
psychologic(al) [,saɪkə'lɑdʒɪk(əl)] *adj* psicológico
psychologist [saɪ'kɑlədʒɪst] *s* psicólogo
psychology [saɪ'kɑlədʒi] *s* psicología
psychopath ['saɪkə,pæθ] *s* psicópata *mf*
psycho•sis [saɪ'kosɪs] *s* (*pl* **-ses** [siz]) psicosis *f;* estado mental
psychotherapy [,saɪkə'θɛrəpi] *s* psicoterapia
psychotic [saɪ'kɑtɪk] *adj* & *s* psicótico
pt. *abbr* **part, pint, point**
pub [pʌb] *s* (Brit) taberna
puberty ['pjubərti] *s* pubertad
public ['pʌblɪk] *adj* & *s* público
publication [,pʌblɪ'keʃən] *s* publicación
public conveyance *s* vehículo de servicio público
publicity [pʌb'lɪsɪti] *s* publicidad
publicize ['pʌblɪ,saɪz] *tr* publicar
public library *s* biblioteca municipal
public relations *spl* relaciones publicas
public school *s* (U.S.A.) escuela pública; (Brit) internado privado con dote
public speaking *s* elocución, oratoria

public spirit *s* celo patriótico del buen ciudadano

public toilet *s* quiosco de necesidad

public transportation *s* transporte colectivo

public utility *s* empresa de servicio público; **public utilities** acciones emitidas por empresas de servicio público

publish [`pʌblɪʃ] *tr* publicar

publisher [`pʌblɪʃər] *s* editor *m*

publishing house *s* casa editorial

pucker [`pʌkər] *s* (*small fold*) frunce *m*; pliego mal hecho || *tr* fruncir (*una tela; la frente*); plegar mal || *intr* plegarse mal

pudding [`pʊdɪŋ] *s* budín *m*, pudín *m*

puddle [`pʌdəl] *s* aguazal *m*, charco

pudg•y [`pʌdʒi] *adj* (*comp* **-ier;** *super* **-iest**) gordinflón, rechoncho

puerile [`pjuˑərɪl] *adj* pueril

puerili•ty [ˌpjuˑəˈrɪlɪti] *s* (*pl* **-ties**) puerilidad

Puerto Rican [`pwɛrto `rikən] *adj & s* puertorriqueño

puff [pʌf] *s* soplo vivo; (*of smoke*) bocanada; (*in clothing*) bullón *m;* borla de polvos; pastelillo de crema o jalea; alabanza exagerada; ráfaga, ventolera || *tr* soplar; hinchar; alabar exageradamente || *intr* soplar; hincharse; enorgullecerse exageradamente

puff paste *s* hojaldre *m & f*

pugilism [`pjudʒɪˌlɪzəm] *s* pugilismo

pugilist [`pjudʒɪlɪst] *s* pugilista *m*

pug-nosed [`pʌgˌnozd] *adj* braco

puke [pjuk] *s* (*slang*) vómito || *tr & intr* (*slang*) vomitar

pull [pʊl] *s* estirón *m*, tirón *m; (on a cigar)* chupada; (*of a door*) tirador *m*, (slang) enchufe *m*, buenas aldabas || *tr* tirar de; torcer (*un ligamento*); (typ) sacar (*una impresión a prueba*); **to pull down** demoler, derribar; bajar (*p.ej., la cortinilla*); abatir, degradar; **to pull oneself together** componerse, recobrar la calma || *intr* tirar; moverse despacio, moverse con esfuerzo; **to pull at** tirar de (*p.ej., la corbata*); chupar (*p.ej., un cigarro*); **to pull for** (slang) abogar por, ayudar; **to pull for oneself** tirar por su lado; **to pull in** llegar (*un tren*) a la estación; **to pull out** partir (*un tren*) de la estación; **to pull strings** usar enchufe; **to pull through** salir a flote; recobrar la salud

pullet [`pʊlɪt] *s* polla

pulley [`pʊli] *s* polea

pulp [pʌlp] *s* pulpa; (*to make paper*) pasta; (*of tooth*) bulbo

pulpit [`pʊlpɪt] *s* púlpito

pulsate [`pʌlset] *intr* pulsar; vibrar

pulsation [pʌl`seʃən] *s* pulsación; vibracion

pulse [pʌls] *s* pulso; **to feel o take the pulse of** tomar el pulso a

pulverize [`pʌlvəˌraɪz] *tr* pulverizar

pumice stone [`pʌmɪs] *s* pómez *f*, piedra pómez

pum•mel [`pʌməl] *v* (*pret & pp* **-meled** o **-melled;** *ger* **-meling** o **-melling**) *tr* apuñear, aporrear

pump [pʌmp] *s* bomba; (*slipperlike shoe*) escarpín *m*, zapatilla || *tr* elevar o sacar (*agua*) por medio de una bomba; (coll)

tirar de la lengua a (*una persona*); **to pump up** hinchar, inflar (*un neumático*)

pump handle *s* guimbalete *m*

pumpkin [`pʌmpkɪn] o [`pʌŋkɪn] *s* calabaza común; **some pumpkins** persona de muchas campanillas

pump-priming [`pʌmp,praɪmɪŋ] *s* inyección económica (*por parte del gobierno*)

pun [pʌn] *s* equívoco, retruécano || *v* (*pret & pp* **punned;** *ger* **punning**) *intr* decir equívocos, jugar del vocablo

punch [pʌntʃ] *s* puñetazo; (*tool*) punzón *m;* (*for tickets*) sacabocado; (*drink*) ponche *m* || *tr* dar un puñetazo a; taladrar, perforar (*un billete, una tarjeta*)

punch bowl *s* ponchera

punch card *s* tarjeta perforada, ficha perforada

punch clock *s* reloj *m* registrador de tarjetas

punch'-drunk' *adj* atontado (*p.ej., por una tunda de golpes*); completamente aturdido

punched tape *s* cinta perforada

punching bag *s* punching *m*, boxibalón *m*

punch line *s* broche *m* de oro, colofón *m* del artículo

punctilious [pʌŋk`tɪliˑəs] *adj* puntilloso, pundonoroso

punctual [`pʌŋktʃuˑəl] *adj* puntual

punctuate [`pʌŋktʃuˌet] *tr* puntuar; acentuar, destacar; interrumpir || *intr* puntuar

punctuation [ˌpʌŋktʃuˈeʃən] *s* puntuación

punctuation mark *s* signo de puntuación

puncture [`pʌŋktʃər] *s* puntura; (*of a tire*) picadura, pinchazo || *tr* pinchar, picar, perforar

punc'ture-proof' *adj* a prueba de pinchazos

pundit [`pʌndɪt] *s* erudito, sabio

pungent [`pʌndʒənt] *adj* picante; estimulante

punish [`pʌnɪʃ] *tr* castigar; penalizar; (coll) maltratar

punishable [`pʌnɪʃəbəl] *adj* delictivo

punishment [`pʌnɪʃmənt] *s* castigo; (coll) maltrato

punk [pʌŋk] *adj* (slang) malo, de mala calidad || *s* yesca, pebete *m;* (*decayed wood*) hupe *m;* (slang) pillo, gamberro

punster [`pʌnstər] *s* equivoquista *mf*, vocablista *mf*

pu•ny [`pjuni] *adj* (*comp* **-nier;** *super* **-niest**) encanijado, débil; insignificante, mezquino

pup [pʌp] *s* cachorro

pupil [`pjupəl] *s* alumno; (*of the eye*) pupila

puppet [`pʌpɪt] *s* títere *m; (doll)* muñeca; (*person controlled by another*) maniquí *m*

puppet government *s* gobierno de monigotes

puppet show *s* función de títeres

puppy love [`pʌpi] *s* (coll) primeros amores

purchase [`pʌrtʃəs] *s* compra; agarre *m* firme || *tr* comprar

purchasing power *s* poder adquisitivo

pure [pjʊr] *adj* puro

purgative [`pʌrgətɪv] *adj & s* purgante *m*

purge [pʌrdʒ] *s* purga || *tr* purgar

puri•fy [`pjʊrɪˌfaɪ] *v* (*pret & pp* **-fied**) *tr* purificar

puritan [`pjʊrɪtən] *adj & s* puritano || **Puritan** *adj & s* puritano

pr
pu

purity [ˈpjurɪti] s pureza

purloin [pərˈlɔɪn] tr & intr robar, hurtar

purple [ˈpʌrpəl] adj purpurado, rojo morado ‖ m púrpura, rojo morado

purport [ˈpʌrport] s significado, idea principal ‖ [pərˈport] tr significar, querer decir

purpose [ˈpʌrpəs] s intención, propósito; fin m, objeto; **for the purpose** al efecto; **for what purpose?** ¿con qué fin?; **on purpose** adrede, de propósito; **to good purpose** con buenos resultados; **to no purpose** sin resultado; **to serve one's purpose** servir para el caso

purposely [ˈpʌrpəsli] adv adrede, de propósito

purr [pʌr] s ronroneo ‖ intr ronronear

purse [pʌrs] s bolsa; (money collected for charity) colecta ‖ tr fruncir

purser [ˈpʌrsər] s contador m de navío, comisario de a bordo

purse snatcher [ˈsnætʃər] s carterista mf

purse strings spl cordones mpl de la bolsa; **to hold the purse strings** tener las llaves de la caja

pursue [pərˈsu] o [pərˈsju] tr perseguir (al que huye); proseguir (lo empezado); seguir (una carrera); dedicarse a

pursuit [pərˈsut] o [pərˈsjut] s persecución; prosecución; (e.g., of happiness) busca o búsqueda; empleo

pursuit plane s caza m, avión m de caza

purvey [pərˈve] tr proveer, suministrar

pus [pʌs] s pus m

push [puʃ] s empuje m, empujón m ‖ tr empujar; pulsar (un botón); extender (p.ej., conquistas); **to push around** (coll) tratar a empujones; **to push aside** hacer a un lado; **to push through** forzar (p.ej., una resolución) ‖ intr empujar; **to push off** (coll) irse, salir; (naut) desatracarse

push button s botón m de llamada, botón interruptor

push'-but'ton control s mando por botón

push'cart' s carretilla de mano

pusher [ˈpuʃər] s (drugs) púcher m

pushing [ˈpuʃɪŋ] adj emprendedor; entremetido, agresivo

pushy [ˈpuʃi] adj (coll) agresivo; presumido

pusillanimous [ˌpjusɪˈlænɪməs] adj pusilánime

puss [pus] interj ¡miz! ‖ s micho; chica, muchacha; (slang) cara, boca

puss in the corner s las cuatro esquinas

puss•y [ˈpusi] s (pl -ies) michito

pussy willow s sauce norteamericano de amentos muy sedosos

pustule [ˈpʌstʃul] s pústula

put [put] v (pret & pp **put;** ger **putting**) tr poner, colocar; arrojar, echar, lanzar; hacer (una pregunta); **to put across** llevar a cabo; hacer aceptar; **to put aside** poner aparte; rechazar; ahorrar (dinero); **to put down** anotar, apuntar; sofocar (una insurrección); rebajar (los precios); **to put off** posponer; deshacerse de; **to put on** ponerse (la ropa); poner en escena; llevar (p.ej., un drama a la pantalla); accionar (un freno); cargar (impuestos); fingir; atribuir; **to put oneself out** incomodarse, molestarse; afanarse, desvivirse; **to put out** extender (la mano); apagar (el fuego, la luz); poner en la calle; dar a luz, publicar; decepcionar; (sport) sacar fuera de la partida; **to put over** o **through** (coll) llevar a cabo; **to put up** construir, edificar; abrir (un paraguas); conservar (fruta, legumbres); (coll) incitar ‖ intr dirigirse; **to put on** fingir; **to put up** parar, hospedarse; **to put up with** aguantar, tolerar

put'-out' adj contrariado, enojado

putrid [ˈpjutrɪd] adj pútrido; corrompido, perverso

putsch [putʃ] s intentona de sublevación; sublevación; cuartelazo

putter [ˈpʌtər] intr trabajar sin orden ni sistema; **to putter around** ocuparse en fruslerías, temporizar

put•ty [ˈpʌti] s (pl -ties) masilla ‖ v (pret & pp -tied) tr enmasillar

putty knife s cuchillo de vidriero, espátula

put'-up' adj (coll) premeditado con malicia

puzzle [ˈpʌzəl] s enigma m; acertijo, rompecabezas m ‖ tr confundir, poner perplejo; **to puzzle out** descifrar ‖ intr estar perplejo; **to puzzle over** tratar de descifrar

puzzler [ˈpʌzlər] s quisicosa

PW abbr **prisoner of war**

pyg•my [ˈpɪgmi] adj pigmeo ‖ s (pl -mies) pigmeo

pylon [ˈpaɪlan] s pilón m

pyramid [ˈpɪrəmɪd] s pirámide f ‖ tr aumentar (su dinero) comprando o vendiendo al crédito y empleando las ganancias para comprar o vender más

pyre [paɪr] s pira

Pyrenean [ˌpɪrɪˈniˑən] adj pirineo

Pyrenees [ˈpɪrɪˌniz] spl Pirineos

pyrites [paɪˈraɪtiz] o [ˈpaɪraɪts] s pirita

pyrotechnical [ˌpaɪrəˈtɛknɪkəl] adj pirotécnico

pyrotechnics [ˌpaɪrəˈtɛknɪks] spl pirotecnia

python [ˈpaɪθən] s pitón m

pythoness [ˈpaɪθənɪs] s pitonisa

pyx [pɪks] s píxide f, copón m

Q

Q, q [kju] decimoséptima letra del alfabeto inglés

Q. abbr **quarto, queen, question, quire**

Q.M. abbr **quartermaster**

qr. abbr **quarter, quire**

qt. abbr **quantity, quart**

qu. *abbr* **quart, quarter, quarterly, queen, query, question**

quack [kwæk] *adj* falso ‖ *s* graznido del pato; charlatán *m;* medicastro, curandero ‖ *intr* parpar (*el pato*)

quacker·y [ˈkwækəri] *s* (*pl* **-ies**) charlatanismo

quadrangle [ˈkwɑd,ræŋgəl] *s* cuadrángulo; patio cuadrangular

quadrant [ˈkwɑdrənt] *s* cuadrante *m*

quadroon [kwɑdˈrun] *s* cuarterón *m*

quadruped [ˈkwɑdru,pɛd] *adj* & *s* cuadrúpedo

quadruple [ˈkwɑdrupəl] o [kwɑdˈrupəl] *adj* & *s* cuádruple *m* ‖ *tr* cuadruplicar ‖ *intr* cuadruplicarse

quadruplet [ˈkwɑdru,plɛt] o [kwɑdˈruplɛt] *s* cuatrillizo

quaff [kwɑf] o [kwæf] *s* trago grande ‖ *tr* & *intr* beber en gran cantidad

quail [kwel] *s* codorniz *f* ‖ *intr* acobardarse

quaint [kwent] *adj* curioso, raro; afectado, rebuscado; fantástico, singular

quake [kwek] *s* temblor *m*, terremoto ‖ *intr* temblar

Quaker [ˈkwekər] *adj* & *s* cuáquero

Quaker meeting *s* reunión de cuáqueros; reunión en que hay poca conversación

quali·fy [ˈkwɑlɪ,faɪ] *v* (*pret* & *pp* **-fied**) *tr* calificar; capacitar, habilitar ‖ *intr* capacitarse, habilitarse

quali·ty [ˈkwɑlɪti] *s* (*pl* **-ties**) (*characteristic; virtue*) calidad; (*property, attribute*) cualidad; (*of a sound*) timbre *m*

quality of life *s* calidad de vida

qualm [kwɑm] *s* escrúpulo de conciencia; duda, inquietud; (*nausea*) basca

quanda·ry [ˈkwɑndəri] *s* (*pl* **-ries**) incertidumbre, perplejidad

quanti·ty [ˈkwɑntɪti] *s* (*pl* **-ties**) cantidad

quan·tum [ˈkwɑntəm] *adj* cuántico ‖ *s* (*pl* **-ta** [tə]) cuanto, quántum *m*

quantum theory *s* teoría cuántica

quarantine [ˈkwɑrən,tin] o [ˈkwɔrən,tin] *s* cuarentena; estación de cuarentena ‖ *tr* poner en cuarentena

quar·rel [ˈkwɑrəl] o [ˈkwɔrəl] *s* disputa, riña, pelea; **to have no quarrel with** no estar en desacuerdo con; **to pick a quarrel with** tomarse con ‖ *v* (*pret* & *pp* **-reled** o **-relled**; *ger* **-reling** o **-relling**) *intr* disputar, reñir, pelear

quarrelsome [ˈkwɑrəlsəm] o [ˈkwɔrəlsəm] *adj* pendenciero

quar·ry [ˈkwɑri] o [ˈkwɔri] *s* (*pl* **-ries**) cantera, pedrera; caza, presa ‖ *v* (*pret* & *pp* **-ried**) *tr* sacar de una cantera; extraer, sacar

quart [kwɔrt] *s* cuarto de galón

quarter [ˈkwɔrtər] *adj* cuarto ‖ *s* cuarto, cuarta parte; (*three months*) trimestre *m*; moneda de 25 centavos; cuarto de luna; barrio; región, lugar *m;* (*clemency*) (mil) cuartel *m;* **quarters** morada, vivienda; local *m;* (mil) cuarteles *mpl;* **to take up quarters** alojarse ‖ *tr* descuartizar

quar'ter·deck' *s* alcázar *m*

quar'ter-hour' *s* cuarto de hora; **on the quarter-hour** al cuarto en punto cada cuarto de hora

quarter·ly [ˈkwɔrtərli] *adj* trimestral ‖ *adv* trimestralmente ‖ *s* (*pl* **-lies**) publicación o revista trimestral

quar'ter·mas'ter *s* (mil) comisario; (nav) cabo de brigadas

quartet [kwɔrˈtɛt] *s* cuarteto

quartz [kwɔrts] *s* cuarzo

quartz watch *s* reloj de cuarzo

quasar [ˈkwesɑr] *s* (astr) objeto del espacio, fuente *f* cuasiestelar de radio

quash [kwɑʃ] *tr* sofocar, reprimir; anular, invalidar

quaver [ˈkwevər] *s* temblor *m*, estremecimiento; (mus) trémolo ‖ *intr* temblar, estremecerse

quay [ki] *s* muelle *m*, desembarcadero

queen [kwin] *s* reina; (*in chess*) dama o reina; (*in cards*) dama (*que corresponde al caballo*); abeja reina

queen bee *s* abeja reina, abeja maestra; (slang) marimandona, la que lleva la voz cantante

queen dowager *s* reina viuda

queen·ly [ˈkwinli] *adj* (*comp* **-lier**; *super* **-liest**) de reina; como reina; regio

queen mother *s* reina madre

queen olive *s* aceituna de la reina, aceituna gordal

queen post *s* péndola

queen's English *s* inglés castizo

queer [kwɪr] *adj* curioso, raro; estrambótico, estrafalario; aturdido, indispuesto; (coll) sospechoso, misterioso ‖ *tr* (slang) echar a perder; (slang) comprometer

quell [kwɛl] *tr* sofocar, reprimir; mitigar (*una pena o dolor*)

quench [kwɛntʃ] *tr* apagar (*el fuego; la sed*); sofocar, reprimir; (electron) amortiguar

que·ry [ˈkwɪri] *s* (*pl* **-ries**) pregunta; signo de interrogación; duda ‖ *v* (*pret* & *pp* **-ried**) *tr* interrogar; marcar con signo de interrogación; dudar

ques. *abbr* **question**

quest [kwɛst] *s* búsqueda; (*of the Holy Grail*) demanda; **in quest of** en busca de

question [ˈkwɛstʃən] *s* pregunta; (*problem for discussion*) cuestión; asunto, proposición; **beside the question** que no viene al caso; **beyond question** fuera de duda; **out of the question** imposible, indiscutible; **to ask a question** hacer una pregunta; **to be a question of** tratarse de, ser cuestión de; **to call in question** poner en duda; **without question** sin duda ‖ *tr* interrogar; cuestionar (*poner en tela de juicio*)

questionable [ˈkwɛstʃənəbəl] *adj* cuestionable

question mark *s* punto interrogante, signo de interrogación

questionnaire [,kwɛstʃənˈɛr] *s* cuestionario

queue [kju] *s* (*of hair*) coleta; (*of people*) cola ‖ *intr* hacer cola

quibble [ˈkwɪbəl] *intr* sutilizar

pu
qu

quick [kwɪk] *adj* rápido, veloz; ágil, vivo; despierto, listo; **the quick and the dead** los vivos y los muertos; **to cut** o **to sting to the quick** herir en lo vivo, tocar en la herida

quicken [ˈkwɪkən] *tr* acelerar, avivar; animar ‖ *intr* acelerarse; animarse

quick′lime′ *s* cal viva

quick lunch *s* servicio de la barra, servicio rápido

quick′sand′ *s* arena movediza

quick′sil′ver *s* azogue *m*

quiet [ˈkwaɪ•et] *adj* (still) quieto; silencioso; (*market*) (com) encalmado; **to keep quiet** callarse ‖ *s* quietud; silencio; **on the quiet** a las calladas ‖ *tr* aquietar; acallar ‖ *intr* aquietarse; callarse; **to quiet down** calmarse ‖ *interj* ¡silencio!

quill [kwɪl] *s* pluma de ave; cañón *m* de pluma; (*of hedgehog, porcupine*) púa

quilt [kwɪlt] *s* edredón *m*, colcha ‖ *tr* acolchar

quince [kwɪns] *s* membrillo

quinine [ˈkwaɪnaɪn] *s* quinina

quinsy [ˈkwɪnzɪ] *s* cinanquia, esquinencia

quintessence [kwɪnˈtɛsəns] *s* quintaesencia

quintet [kwɪnˈtɛt] *s* quinteto

quintuplet [kwɪnˈtjuplɛt] o [kwɪnˈtuplɛt] *s* quintillizo

quip [kwɪp] *s* chufleta, pulla ‖ *v* (*pret & pp* **quipped;** *ger* **quipping**) *tr* decir en son de burla ‖ *intr* echar pullas

quire [kwaɪr] *s* mano *f* de papel; (bb) alzado

quirk [kwʌrk] *s* excentricidad, rareza; sutileza; vuelta repentina

quit [kwɪt] *adj* libre, descargado; **to be quits** estar desquitados; **to call it quits** no seguir;

descontinuar; **to cry quits** pedir treguas ‖ *v* (*pret & pp* **quit** o **quitted;** *ger* **quitting**) *tr* dejar ‖ *intr* irse; (coll) dejar de trabajar

quite [kwaɪt] *adv* enteramente; verdaderamente; (coll) bastante, muy

quitter [ˈkwɪtər] *s* remolón *m;* (*of a cause*) desertor *m*

quiver [ˈkwɪvər] *s* temblor *m;* (*to hold arrows*) aljaba, carcaj *m* ‖ *intr* temblar

quixotic [kwɪksˈɑtɪk] *adj* quijotesco

quiz [kwɪz] *s* (*pl* **quizzes**) examen *m;* interrogatorio ‖ *v* (*pret & pp* **quizzed;** *ger* **quizzing**) *tr* examinar; interrogar

quiz game *s* torneo de preguntas y respuestas

quiz program *s* programa *m* de preguntas y respuetas, torneo radiofónico

quiz section *s* grupo de práctica

quizzical [ˈkwɪzɪkəl] *adj* curioso; cómico; burlón

quoin [kɔɪn] o [kwɔɪn] *s* esquina; piedra angular; (*wedge*) cuña ‖ *tr* (typ) acuñar

quoit [kwɔɪt] o [kɔɪt] *s* herrón *m*, tejo; **quoits** *ssg* hito

quondam [ˈkwɑndæm] *adj* antiguo, de otro tiempo

quorum [ˈkworəm] *s* quórum *m*

quota [ˈkwotə] *s* cuota

quotation [kwoˈteʃən] *s* (*from a book*) cita; (*of prices*) cotización

quotation marks *spl* comillas

quote [kwot] *s* (coll) cita; (coll) cotización; **close quote** fin de la cita; **quotes** (coll) comillas ‖ *tr & intr* citar; cotizar; **quote cito**

quotient [ˈkwoʃənt] *s* cociente *m*

q.v. *abbr* **quod vide** (Lat) **which see**

R

R, r [ɑr] decimoctava letra del alfabeto inglés

r. *abbr* **railroad, railway, road, rod, ruble, rupee**

R. *abbr* **railroad, railway, Regina** (Lat) **Queen; Republican, response, Rex** (Lat) **King; River, Royal**

rabbet [ˈræbɪt] *s* barbilla, rebajo ‖ *tr* embarbillar, rebajar

rab•bi [ˈræbaɪ] *s* (*pl* **-bis** o **-bies**) rabino

rabbit [ˈræbɪt] *s* conejo

rabbit ears *spl* (telv, rad) antena de conejo

rabble [ˈræbəl] *s* canalla, gentuza, palomilla, chamuchina

rabble rouser [ˈrauzər] *s* populachero, alborotapueblos *mf*

rabies [ˈrebiz] o [ˈrebɪ,iz] *s* rabia

raccoon [ræˈkun] *s* mapache *m*, oso lavador

race [res] *s* (*people of same stock*) raza; (*contest in speed, etc.*) carrera; (*channel to lead water*) caz *m* ‖ *tr* competir con, en una carrera; hacer correr de prisa; hacer

funcionar (*un motor*) a velocidad excesiva ‖ *intr* correr de prisa; correr en una carrera; competir en una carrera; embalarse (*un motor*); (naut) regatear

race horse *s* caballo de carreras

race riot *s* disturbio racista

race track *s* pista de carreras

racial [ˈreʃəl] *adj* racial

racing car *s* coche *m* de carreras

racism [ˈresɪzəm] *s* racismo

racist [ˈresist] *adj & s* racista

rack [ræk] *s* (*sort of shelf*) estante *m;* (*to hang clothes*) percha; (*for fodder for cattle*) pesebre *m;* (*for baggage*) red *f* de equipaje; (*for guns*) armero; (*bar made to gear with a pinion*) cremallera; **to go to rack and ruin** desvencijarse; ir al desastre ‖ *tr* estirar, forzar; atormentar; despedazar; oprimir, agobiar; **to rack off** trasegar (*el vino*); **to rack one's brains** calentarse la cabeza, devanarse los sesos

racket [ˈrækɪt] *s* raqueta; (*noise*) baraúnda, alboroto; (slang) trapisonda, trapacería; **to raise a racket** armar un alboroto

racketeer [ˌrækəˈtir] *s* trapisondista *mf*, trapacista *mf* ‖ *intr* trapacear

rack railway *s* ferrocarril *m* de cremallera

rac•y [ˈresɪ] *adj* (*comp* **-ier;** *super* **-iest**) espiritoso, chispeante; perfumado; (*somewhat indecent*) picante

radar [ˈredɑr] *s* radar *m*

radar scanner *s* explorador *m* de radar

radiant [ˈredɪ•ənt] *adj* radiante, resplandeciente; (*cheerful, smiling*) radiante

radiate [ˈredɪ,et] *tr* radiar; difundir (*p.ej., felicidad*) ‖ *intr* radiar, irradiar

radiation [ˌredɪˈeʃən] *s* radiación

radiation sickness *s* enfermedad de radiación, mal *m* de rayos

radiator [ˈredɪ,etər] *s* radiador *m*

radiator cap *s* tapón *m* de radiador

radical [ˈrædɪkəl] *adj & s* radical *m*

radi•o [ˈredɪ,o] *s* (*pl* **-os**) radio *f*; radiograma *m* ‖ *tr* radiodifundir

radioactive [ˌredɪ•oˈæktɪv] *adj* radiactivo

radioactive waste *s* residuos radiactivos

radio amateur *s* radioaficionado

radio announcer *s* locutor *m* de radio

ra•dio•broad•cast•ing *s* radiodifusión

radio frequency *s* radiofrecuencia

radio listener *s* radioescucha *mf*, radioyente *mf*

radiology [ˌredɪˈɑlədʒɪ] *s* radiología

radio ministry *s* (theol) ministerio radiofónco

radio network *s* red *f* de emisoras

radio newscaster *s* cronista *mf* de radio

radio receiver *s* radiorreceptor *m*

radio set *s* aparato de radio

ra•dio•(tel'e)phone *s* radioteléfono

ra•di•o•ther•apy *s* radioterapia

radish [ˈrædɪ] *s* rábano

radium [redɪ•əm] *s* radio

radi•us [ˈredɪ•əs] *s* (*pl* **-i** [ˌɑɪ] o **-uses**) radio; (*range of operation*) radio; **within a radius of en . . .** a la redonda

raffle [ˈræfəl] ‖ *tr & intr* rifar

raft [ræft] *s* armadía, balsa; (coll) gran número

rafter [ˈræftər] *s* cabrio, contrapar *m*, traviesa

rag [ræg] *s* trapo; **to chew the rag** (slang) dar la lengua; **in rags** hilachento

ragamuffin [ˈrægə,mʌfɪn] *s* pelagatos *m*; golfo, chiquillo haraposo

rag baby o **rag doll** *s* muñeca de trapo

rage [redʒ] *s* rabia; **to be all the rage** estar en boga, hacer furor; **to fly into a rage** montar en cólera

ragged [ˈrægɪd] *adj* andrajoso; (*edge*) cortado en dientes

ragpicker [ˈræg,pɪkər] *s* andrajero, trapero

rag'weed' *s* ambrosía

raid [red] *s* incursión, invasión; ataque de sorpresa; ataque aéreo ‖ *tr* invadir; atacar inesperadamente; capturar (*p.ej., la policía un garito*)

rail [rel] *s* carril *m*, riel *m*; (*railing*) barandilla; (*of a bridge*) guardalado; (*at a bar*) apoyo para los pies; palo; **by rail** por ferocarril; **rails** títulos o valores de ferrocarril ‖ *tr* poner barandilla a ‖ *intr* quejarse amargamente; **to rail at** injuriar, ultrajar

rail fence *s* cerca hecha de palos horizontales

rail'head' *s* (rr) cabeza de línea

railing [ˈrelɪŋ] *s* barandilla, pasamano

rail'road' *adj* ferroviario ‖ *s* ferrocarril *m* ‖ *tr* (coll) llevar a cabo con demasiada precipitación; (slang) encarcelar falsamente ‖ *intr* trabajar en el ferrocarril

railroad crossing *s* paso a nivel

rail'way' *adj* ferroviario ‖ *s* ferrocarril *m*

raiment [ˈremənt] *s* prendas de vestir, indumentaria

rain [ren] *s* lluvia; **rain or shine** llueva o no, con buen o mal tiempo ‖ *tr & intr* llover

rain'bow' *s* arco iris

rain'coat' *s* impermeable *m*

rain'fall' *s* lluvia repentina; precipitación acuosa

rain•y [ˈreni] *adj* (*comp* **-ier;** *super* **-iest**) lluvioso

rainy day *s* día lluvioso; tiempo futuro de posible necesidad

raise [rez] *s* aumento ‖ *tr* levantar; aumentar; criar (*a niños, animales*); cultivar (*plantas*); reunir (*dinero*); suscitar (*una duda*); resucitar (*a los muertos*); dejarse (*barba, bigote*); poner (*una objeción*); plantear (*una pregunta*); levantar (*tropas; un sitio*); (math) elevar; (*to come in sight of*) (naut) avistar

raisin [ˈrezən] *s* pasa, uva seca

rake [rek] *s* rastro, rastrillo; (*person*) calavera *m*, libertino ‖ *tr* rastrillar; **to rake together** acumular (*dinero*)

rake'-off' *s* (slang) dinero obtenido ilícitamente

rakish [ˈrekɪʃ] *adj* airoso, gallardo; listo, vivo; libertino

ral•ly [ˈræli] *s* (*pl* **-lies**) reunión popular, reunión política; recuperación, recobro ‖ *v* (*pret & pp* **-lied**) *tr* reunir; reanimar; recobrar (*la fuerza, la salud, el ánimo*) ‖ *intr* reunirse; recobrarse (*p.ej., los precios en la Bolsa*); recobrar la fuerza, la salud, el ánimo; **to rally to the side of** acudir a, ir en socorro de

ram [ræm] *s* (*male sheep*) morueco, carnero padre; (*device for battering, crushing, etc.*) pisón *m* ‖ *v* (*pret & pp* **rammed;** *ger* **ramming**) *tr* dar contra, chocar en; atestar, rellenar ‖ *intr* chocar; **to ram into** chocar en

ramble [ˈræmbəl] *s* paseo ‖ *intr* pasear; serpentear (*p.ej., un río*); extenderse serpenteando (*las enredaderas*); (*to wander aimlessly; to talk in an aimless way*) divagar

rami•fy [ˈræmɪ,faɪ] *v* (*pret & pp* **-fied**) *tr* ramificar ‖ *intr* ramificarse

ram'jet'(engine) *s* motor *m* autorreactor; estatorreactor *m*

ramp [ræmp] *s* rampa

qu
ra

rampage ['ræmpedʒ] *s* alboroto; **to go on a rampage** alborotar, comportarse como un loco

rampart ['ræmpɑrt] *s* muralla, terraplén *m;* amparo, defensa

ram'rod' *s* atacador *m*, baqueta

ram'shack'le *adj* desvencijado, destartalado

ranch [ræntʃ] *s* granja, hacienda

rancid ['rænsɪd] *adj* rancio

rancor ['ræŋkər] *s* rencor *m*

random ['rændəm] *adj* casual, fortuito; **at random** al azar, a la ventura

range [rendʒ] *s* (*row, line*) fila, hilera; (*scope, reach*) alcance *m;* (*of speeds, prices, etc.*) escala; campo de tiro; terreno de pasto; (*of a boat or airplane*) autonomía; (*of the voice*) extensión; (*of colors*) gama, serie *f;* (*stove*) cocina económica; **within range of** al alcance de ‖ *tr* alinear; recorrer (*un terreno*); ir a lo largo de (*la costa*); arreglar, ordenar ‖ *intr* fluctuar, variar (*entre ciertos límites*); extenderse; divagar, errar; **to range over** recorrer

range finder *s* telémetro

rank [ræŋk] *adj* exuberante, lozano; denso; espeso; grosero; maloliente; excesivo; incorregible, rematado; indecente, vulgar ‖ *s* categoría, rango; condición, posición; distinción; (*line of soldiers standing abreast*) fila; (*mil*) empleo, grado ‖ *tr* alinear; ordenar; tener grado o posición más alta que ‖ *intr* ocupar el último grado; **to rank high** ocupar alta posición; ser tenido en alta estima; sobresalir; **to rank low** ocupar baja posición; **to rank with** estar al nivel de; tener el mismo grado que

rank and file *s* soldados de fila; pueblo, gente *f* común

rankle ['ræŋkəl] *tr* enconar, irritar ‖ *intr* enconarse

ransack ['rænsæk] *tr* registrar, escudriñar; robar, saquear

ransom ['rænsəm] *s* rescate *m* ‖ *tr* rescatar

rant [rænt] *intr* desvariar, despotricar

rap [ræp] *s* golpe corto y seco; (*noise*) taque *m;* (coll) ardite *m*, bledo; (slang) crítica mordaz; **to take the rap** (slang) pagar la multa; sufrir las consecuencias ‖ *v* (*pret & pp* **rapped;** *ger* **rapping**) *tr* golpear con golpe corto y seco; decir vivamente; (slang) criticar mordazmente ‖ *intr* golpear con golpe corto y seco; **to rap at the door** tocar a la puerta

rapacious [rə'peʃəs] *adj* rapaz

rape [rep] *s* rapto; (*of a woman*) estupro, violación ‖ *tr* raptar; estuprar, violar

rapid ['ræpɪd] *adj* rápido ‖ **rapids** *spl* (*of a river*) rápidos

rap'id-fire' *adj* de tiro rápido; hecho vivamente

rapier ['repɪər] *s* estoque *m*, espadín *m*

rapt [ræpt] *adj* arrebatado, extático, transportado; absorto

rapture ['ræptʃər] *s* embeleso, éxtasis *f*, rapto

rare [rɛr] *adj* raro; (*word*) poco usado; (*meat*) poco asado; (*gem*) precioso

rare bird *s* mirlo blanco

rare•fy ['rɛrɪ,faɪ] *v* (*pret & pp* **-fied**) *tr* enrarecer ‖ *intr* enrarecerse

rarely ['rɛrli] *adv* rara vez

rascal ['ræskəl] *s* bellaco, bribón *m*, pícaro, pergenio

rash [ræʃ] *adj* temerario ‖ *s* brote *m*, salpullido, erupción

rasp [ræsp] o [rɑsp] *s* escofina; (*sound of a rasp*) sonido áspero ‖ *tr* escofinar; irritar, molestar; decir con voz ronca ‖ *intr* hacer sonido áspero

raspber•ry ['ræz,bɛri] o ['rɑz,bɛri] *s* (*pl* **-ries**) frambuesa, sangüesa

raspberry bush *s* frambueso, sangüeso

rat [ræt] *s* rata; (*false hair*) (coll) postizo; **to smell a rat** (coll) olerse una trama, sospechar una intriga

ratchet ['rætʃɪt] *s* trinquete *m*

rate [ret] *s* (*amount or degree measured in proportion to something else*) razón *f;* (*of interest*) tipo; velocidad; precio; **at any rate** de todos modos; **at the rate of** a razón de ‖ *tr* valuar; estimar, juzgar; clasificar ‖ *intr* ser considerado, ser tenido; estar clasificado

rate of exchange *s* tipo de cambio

rate table *s* baremo

rather ['ræðər] o ['rɑðər] *adv* algo, un poco; bastante; antes, más bien; mejor dicho; por el contrario; muy, mucho; **rather than** antes que, más bien que ‖ *interj* ¡ya lo creo!

rati•fy ['rætɪ,faɪ] *v* (*pret & pp* **-fied**) *tr* ratificar

ra•tio ['reʃo] o ['reʃɪ,o] *s* (*pl* **-tios**) (math) razón *f;* (math) cociente *m*

ration ['reʃən] o ['ræʃən] *s* ración ‖ *tr* racionar

ration book *s* cartilla de racionamiento

ration coupon *s* cupón *m* de racionamiento

rational ['ræʃənəl] *adj* racional

rat poison *s* matarratas *m;* raticida

rat race *s* (coll) lucha diaria por ganarse el pan

rattle ['rætəl] *s* (*number of short, sharp sounds*) traqueteo; (*noise-making device*) carraca, matraca; (*child's toy*) sonajero; baraúnda; (*in the throat*) estertor *m* ‖ *tr* tabletear, traquetear; (*to confuse*) (coll) atortolar, desconcertar; **to rattle off** decir rápidamente ‖ *intr* tabletear, traquetear

rat'tle•snake' *s* serpiente *f* de cascabel

rat'trap' *s* ratonera; trance apurado, atolladero

raucous ['rɔkəs] *adj* ronco

ravage ['rævɪdʒ] *s* destrucción, estrago, ruina ‖ *tr* destruir, estragar, arruinar

rave [rev] *intr* desvariar, delirar; bramar, enfurecerse; **to rave about** hacerse lenguas de, deshacerse en elogios de

raven ['revən] *s* cuervo

ravenous ['rævənəs] *adj* famélico, hambriento, voraz; rapaz

ravine [rə'vin] *s* cañón *m*, hondonada

ravish ['rævɪʃ] *tr* encantar, entusiasmar; raptar; violar (*a una mujer*)

ravishing ['rævɪʃɪŋ] *adj* encantador

raw [rɔ] *adj* crudo; (*cotton, silk*) en rama; inexperto, principiante; ulceroso; (*weather, day*) crudo

raw deal *s* (slang) mala pasada

raw'hide' *s* cuero en verde; látigo hecho de cuero en verde

raw material *s* primera materia, materia prima

ray [re] *s* (*of light*) rayo; (*fine line; fish*) raya

rayon [ˈreˑɑn] *s* rayón *m*

raze [rez] *tr* arrasar, asolar

razor [ˈrezər] *s* navaja de afeitar

razor blade *s* hoja u hojita de afeitar

razor strop *s* asentador *m*, suavizador *m*

razz [ræz] *s* (slang) irrisión ‖ *tr* (slang) mofarse de

R.C. *abbr* **Red Cross, Reserve Corps, Roman Catholic**

R.D. *abbr* **Rural Delivery**

reach [ritʃ] *s* alcance *m;* extensión; **out of reach (of)** fuera del alcance (de); **within reach of** al alcance de ‖ *tr* alcanzar; extender; entregar con la mano; llegar a; ponerse en contacto con; influenciar; cumplir (*cierto número de años*) ‖ *intr* alcanzar; extender la mano o el brazo; **to reach after** o **for** esforzarse por coger

react [rɪˈækt] *intr* reaccionar

reaction [rɪˈækʃən] *s* reacción

reactionar·y [rɪˈækʃən,ɛri] *adj* reaccionario; mocho (Mex) ‖ *s* (*pl* **-ies**) reaccionario

read [rid] *v* (*pret & pp* **read** [rɛd]) *tr* ler; recitar (*poesía*); estudiar (*derecho*); leer en; adivinar (*el pensamiento ajeno*); **to read over** recorrer, repasar ‖ *intr* leer; rezar, p.ej., **this page reads thus** esta página reza así; leerse, p.ej., **this book reads easily** este libro se lee con facilidad; **to read on** seguir leyendo

reader [ˈridər] *s* lector *m;* libro de lectura

readily [ˈrɛdɪli] *adv* de buena gana; fácilmente

reading [ˈridɪŋ] *s* lectura; recitación

reading desk *s* atril *m*

reading glass *s* lente *f* para leer, vidrio de aumento; **reading glasses** anteojos para la lectura

reading lamp *s* lámpara de sobremesa

reading room *s* gabinete *m* de lectura; sala de lectura

read·y [ˈrɛdi] *adj* (*comp* **-ier**; *super* **-iest**) listo, preparado, pronto; ágil, diestro; vivo; disponible; **to make ready** preparar; prepararse ‖ *v* (*pret & pp* **-ied**) *tr* preparar ‖ *intr* prepararse

ready cash *s* dinero a la mano, dinero contante y sonante

read'y-made' clothing *s* ropa hecha

ready-made suit *s* traje hecho

reagent [rɪˈedʒənt] *s* reactivo

real [ˈriˑəl] *adj* real, verdadero

real estate *s* bienes *mpl* raíces, bienes inmuebles

re'al-es·tate' *adj* inmobiliario

realism [ˈriˑə,lɪzəm] *s* realismo

realist [ˈriˑəlɪst] *s* realista *mf*

reali·ty [rɪˈælɪti] *s* (*pl* **-ties**) realidad

realize [ˈriˑə,laɪz] *tr* darse cuenta de; realizar, llevar a cabo; adquirir (*ganancias*); reportar (*ganancias*) ‖ *intr* (*to sell property for ready money*) realizar

realm [rɛlm] *s* reino

Realtor [ˈriˑəl,tɔr] o [ˈriˑəltər] *s* corredor *m* de bienes raíces

realty [ˈriˑəlti] *s* bienes *mpl* raíces, bienes inmuebles

ream [rim] *s* resma; **reams** (coll) montones *mpl* ‖ *tr* escariar

reap [rip] *tr & intr* (*to cut*) segar; (*to gather*), cosechar

reaper [ˈripər] *s* (*person*) segador *m;* máquina segadora

reappear [,riˑəˈpɪr] *intr* reaparecer

reapportionment [,riˑəˈpɔrʃənmənt] *s* nuevo prorrateo

rear [rɪr] *adj* posterior, trasero; de atrás ‖ *s* espalda; (*of a room*) fondo; (*of a row; of an automobile*) cola; retaguardia; (slang) culo, trasero ‖ *tr* levantar; edificar; criar, educar ‖ *intr* encabritarse (*un caballo*)

rear admiral *s* contraalmirante *m*

rear drive *s* tracción trasera

rear end *s* (*buttocks*) nalgas, pompis *m*

rearmament [riˈɑrməmənt] *s* rearme *m*

rear'-view' mirror *s* retrovisor *m*, espejo de retrovisión

rear window *s* (aut) luneta, luneta posterior

reason [ˈrizən] *s* razón *f;* **by reason of** con motivo de, a causa de; **to listen to reason** meterse en razón; **to stand to reason** ser razonable ‖ *tr & intr* razonar

reasonable [ˈrizənəbəl] *adj* razonable

reassessment [,riˑəˈsɛsmənt] *s* nuevo amillaramiento; nueva estimación

reassure [,riˑəˈʃur] *tr* volver a asegurar; tranquilizar

reawaken [,riˑəˈwekən] *tr* volver a despertar ‖ *intr* volver a despertarse

rebate [ˈribet] o [rɪˈbet] *s* rebaja ‖ *tr* rebajar

rebel [ˈrɛbəl] *adj & s* rebelde *mf* ‖ **re·bel** [rɪˈbɛl] *v* (*pret & pp* **-belled;** *ger* **-belling**) *intr* rebelarse

rebellion [rɪˈbɛljən] *s* rebelión

rebellious [rɪˈbɛljəs] *adj* rebelde

re·bind [riˈbaɪnd] *v* (*pret & pp* **-bound** [ˈbaund]) reatar; (*to edge, to border*) ribetear; (bb) reencuadernar

rebirth [ˈribʌrθ] o [rɪˈbʌrθ] *s* renacimiento

rebore [riˈbor] *tr* rectificar

rebound [ˈri,baund] o [rɪˈbaund] *s* rebote *m* ‖ [rɪˈbaund] *intr* rebotar

rebroad·cast [riˈbrɔd,kæst] *s* retransmisión ‖ *v* (*pret & pp* **-cast** o **-casted**) *tr* retransmitir

rebuff [rɪˈbʌf] *s* desaire *m*, rechazo ‖ *tr* desairar, rechazar

re·build [riˈbɪld] *v* (*pret & pp* **-built** [ˈbɪlt]) *tr* reconstruir, reedificar

rebuke [rɪˈbjuk] *s* reprensión ‖ *tr* reprender

re·but [rɪˈbʌt] *v* (*pret & pp* **-butted;** *ger* **-butting**) *tr* rebatir, refutar

rebuttal [rɪˈbʌtəl] *s* rebatimiento, refutación

rec. *abbr* **receipt, recipe, record, recorder**

recall [rɪˈkɔl] o [ˈrikɔl] *s* llamada; (*memory*) recordación, retentiva; (*repeal*) revocación,

ra
re

revocatoria; (*of a diplomat*) retirada ‖ [rɪˈkɔl] *tr* hacer volver, mandar volver; recordar; revocar; retirar (*a un diplomático*)

recant [rɪˈkænt] *tr* retractar ‖ *intr* retractarse

re•cap [ˈriˌkæp] o [riˈkæp] *v* (*pret & pp* **-capped;** *ger* **-capping**) *tr* recauchutar

recapitalization [riˌkæpɪtəlɪˈzeʃən] *s* recapitalización

recapitulation [ˌrikəˌpɪtʃəˈleʃən] *s* recapitulación

re•cast [ˈriˌkæst] *s* refundición; (*of a sentence*) reconstrucción ‖ [riˈkæst] *v* (*pret & pp* **-cast**) *tr* refundir; reconstruir (*p.ej., una frase*)

recd. o **rec'd.** *abbr* **received**

recede [rɪˈsid] *intr* (*to move back*) retroceder; (*to move away*) alejarse, retirarse; deprimirse (*p.ej., la frente de una persona*)

receipt [rɪˈsit] *s* recepción; (*acknowledgment*) recibo; (*acknowledgment of payment*) recibí *m*; (*recipe*) receta; **receipt in full** finiquito; **receipts** entradas, ingresos ‖ *tr* poner el recibí a

receive [rɪˈsiv] *tr* recibir; receptar (*cosas que son materia de delito*); **received payment** recibí ‖ *intr* recibir

receiver [rɪˈsivər] *s* receptor *m*; (*in bankruptcy*) contador *m*, síndico; receptor telefónico

receivership [rɪˈsivərˌʃɪp] *s* (law) sindicatura

receiving set *s* aparato receptor

receiving teller *s* recibidor *m* (*de un banco*)

recent [ˈrisənt] *adj* reciente

recently [ˈrisəntli] *adv* recientemente; endenantes; recién, p.ej., **recently arrived** recién llegado

receptacle [rɪˈsɛptəkəl] *s* receptáculo

reception [rɪˈsɛpʃən] *s* recepción; recibida (*welcome*) recibimiento

reception desk *s* recepción

receptionist [rɪˈsɛpʃənɪst] *s* recepcionista *f*

receptive [rɪˈsɛptɪv] *adj* receptivo

recess [rɪˈsɛs] o [ˈrisɛs] *s* intermisión; descanso; hora de recreo; (*in a surface*) depresión; (*in a wall*) hueco, nicho; escondrijo ‖ [rɪˈsɛs] *tr* ahuecar; empotrar; deprimir ‖ *intr* prorrogarse, suspenderse

recession [rɪˈsɛʃən] *s* retroceso, retirada; (*e.g., in a wall*) depresión; procesión de vuelta; contracción económica

rechargeable [rɪˈtʃɑrdʒəbəl] *adj* recargable

recipe [ˈrɛsɪˌpi] *s* receta (*de cocina*)

reciprocal [rɪˈsɪprəkəl] *adj* recíproco

reciprocity [ˌrɛsɪˈprɑsɪti] *s* reciprocidad

recital [rɪˈsaɪtəl] *s* narración; (*of music or poetry*) recital *m*

recite [rɪˈsaɪt] *tr* narrar; (*formally*) recitar

reckless [ˈrɛklɪs] *adj* atolondrado, temerario

reckon [ˈrɛkən] *tr* calcular; considerar; (coll) calcular, conjeturar ‖ *intr* calcular; **to reckon on** contar con; **to reckon with** tener en cuenta

reclaim [rɪˈklem] *tr* hacer utilizable; hacer labrantío (*un terreno*); ganar (*terreno*) a la mar; recuperar (*materiales usados*); conducir, guiar (*a los que hacen mala vida*)

reclamation [ˌrɛkləˈmeʃən] *s* (agr) roturación

recline [rɪˈklaɪn] *intr* reclinarse

recluse [rɪˈklus] o [ˈrɛklus] *s* solitario, ermitaño

recognize [ˈrɛkəgˌnaɪz] *tr* reconocer

recoil [rɪˈkɔɪl] *s* reculada; (*of a firearm*) reculada, culetazo ‖ *intr* recular, apartarse; recular (*un arma de fuego*)

recollect [ˌrɛkəˈlɛkt] *tr & intr* recordar

recombinant [rɪˈkɑmbɪnənt] *adj* (*genetics*) recombinado

recommend [ˌrɛkəˈmɛnd] *tr* recomendar

recompense [ˈrɛkəmˌpɛns] *s* recompensa ‖ *tr* recompensar

reconcile [ˈrɛkənˌsaɪl] *tr* reconciliar; **to reconcile oneself** resignarse

reconnaissance [rɪˈkɑnɪsəns] *s* reconocimiento

reconnoiter [ˌrɛkəˈnɔɪtər] o [ˌrikəˈnɔɪtər] *tr & intr* reconocer

reconquest [riˈkɑŋkwɛst] *s* reconquista

reconsider [ˌrikənˈsɪdər] *tr* reconsiderar

reconstruct [ˌrikənˈstrʌkt] *tr* reconstruir

reconversion [ˌrikənˈvʌrʒən] *s* reconversión

record [ˈrɛkərd] *s* anotación; ficha, historial *m*, historia personal; (*of a notary*) protocolo; (*of a phonograph*) disco; (educ) expediente académico; (sport) record *m*, plusmarca; **off the record** confidencialmente; **records** anales *mpl*, memorias; archivo; **to break a record** batir un record; **to have no (criminal) record** (coll) estar limpio; **to make a record** establecer un record; grabar un disco ‖ [rɪˈkɔrd] *tr* asentar; registrar; inscribir; grabar (*un sonido, una canción, un disco fonográfico, etc.*)

record breaker *s* plusmarquista *mf*

record changer [ˈtʃendʒər] *s* cambiadiscos *m*, tocadiscos automático

record holder *s* (sport) recordman *m*

recording [rɪˈkɔrdɪŋ] *adj* registrador; (wire or tape) magnetofónico ‖ *s* registro; (*of phonograph records*) grabación o grabado

recording secretary *s* secretario escribiente, secretario de actas

record player *s* tocadiscos *m*, pícap *m*, fonógrafo, vitrola, radiola

record store *s* disquería

recount [ˈriˌkaʊnt] *tr* (*to count again*) recontar ‖ [rɪˈkaʊnt] *tr* (*to narrate*) recontar

recourse [rɪˈkors] o [ˈrikors] *s* recurso; (*helping hand*) paño de lágrimas; **to have recourse to** recurrir a

recover [rɪˈkʌvər] *tr* recobrar; rescatar; **to recover consciousness** recobrar el conocimiento, volver en sí ‖ *intr* recobrarse; recobrar la salud; ganar un pleito

recover•y [rɪˈkʌvəri] *s* (*pl* **-ies**) recobro, recuperación; **past recovery** sin remedio

recreant [ˈrɛkrɪənt] *adj & s* cobarde *mf*, traidor *m*

recreation [ˌrɛkriˈeʃən] *s* recreación

recruit [rɪˈkrut] *s* recluta *m* ‖ *tr* reclutar ‖ *intr* alistar reclutas; ganar reclutas; restablecerse, reponerse

rect. *abbr* **receipt, rector, rectory**

rectangle [ˈrɛkˌtæŋgəl] *s* rectángulo

recti·fy ['rɛktɪ,faɪ] v (pret & pp **-fied**) tr rectificar

rec·tum ['rɛktəm] s (pl **-ta** [tə]) recto

recumbent [rɪ'kʌmbənt] adj reclinado, recostado

recuperate [rɪ'kjupə,ret] tr recuperar; restablecer, reponer ‖ intr recuperarse, recobrarse

re·cur [rɪ'kʌr] v (pret & pp **-curred;** ger **-curring**) intr volver a ocurrir; volver a presentarse (a la memoria); volver (a un asunto)

recurrent [rɪ'kʌrənt] adj repetido; periódico; (illness) recurrente

recyclable [rɪ'saɪkləbəl] adj reciclable

recycling [rɪ'saɪklɪŋ] s reciclado, reciclaje m

red [rɛd] adj (comp **redder;** super **reddest**) rojo, colorado; (wine) tinto; enrojecido, inflamado ‖ s rojo; **in the red** (coll) endeudado; **to see red** (coll) enfurecerse ‖ **Red** adj & s (communist) rojo

red'bait' tr motejar (a uno) de rojo o comunista

red'bird' s cardenal m; piranga

red-blooded ['rɛd,blʌdɪd] adj fuerte, valiente, vigoroso

red'breast' s petirrojo

red'bud' s ciclamor m del Canadá

red'cap' s (Brit) policía militar; (U.S.A.) mozo de estación

red cell s glóbulo rojo, hematíe m

red'coat' s (hist) soldado inglés

redden ['rɛdən] tr enrojecer ‖ intr enrojecerse

redeem [rɪ'dim] tr redimir; cumplir (una promesa)

redeemer [rɪ'dimər] s redentor m

redemption [rɪ'dɛmpʃən] s redención

red-haired ['rɛd,hɛrd] adj pelirrojo

red'head' s pelirrojo

red herring s artificio para distraer la atención del asunto de que se trata

red'-hot' adj candente, calentado al rojo; ardiente, entusiasta; fresco, nuevo

rediscount rate [rɪ'dɪskaʊnt] s tipo de redescuento

rediscover [,rɪdɪs'kʌvər] tr redescubrir

red'-let'ter day s día m memorable

red'-light' district s barrio de los lupanares, barrio de mala vida

red man s piel roja m

re·do ['ri'du] v (pret **-did**, ['dɪd]; pp **-done** ['dʌn]) tr rehacer, repetir; refundir; reformar

redolent ['rɛdələnt] adj fragante, perfumado; **redolent of** que huele a

redoubt [rɪ'daʊt] s (fort) reducto

redound [rɪ'daʊnd] intr redundar; **to redound to** redundar en

red pepper s pimentón m

redress [rɪ'drɛs] o ['ridrɛs] s reparación; remedio ‖ [rɪ'drɛs] tr repara; remediar

Red Ridinghood ['raɪdɪŋ,hʊd] s Caperucita Roja

red'skin' s piel roja m

red tape s expedienteo, papeleo

reduce [rɪ'djus] o [rɪ'dus] tr reducir; (mil) degradar ‖ intr reducirse; reducir peso

reducing exercises spl ejercicios físicos para reducir peso

redundant [rɪ'dʌndənt] adj redundante

red'wood' s secoya

reed [rid] adj (organ, musical instrument) de lengüeta ‖ s (stalk) caña; (plant) carrizo, caña; (mus) instrumento de lengüeta; (of instrument) lengüeta

reëdit [ri'ɛdɪt] tr refundir

reef [rif] s arrecife m, escollo; (min) filón m, veta ‖ tr (naut) arrizar

reefer ['rifər] s chaquetón m; (slang) pitillo de mariguana

reek [rik] intr vahear, humear; estar bañado en sudor; estar mojado con sangre; **to reek of** o **with** oler a

reel [ril] s (spool) carrete m; (of a shuttle) broca; (of motion pictures) cinta; (sway, staggering) tambaleo; **off the reel** (coll) fácil y prestamente ‖ tr aspar, devanar; **to reel off** (coll) narrar fácil y prestamente ‖ intr tambalear; cejar (p.ej., el enemigo)

reëlection [,ri·ɪ'lɛkʃən] s reelección

reënlist [,ri·ɛn'lɪst] tr reenganchar ‖ intr reengancharse

reën·try [ri'ɛntri] s (pl **-tries**) reingreso, nueva entrada; (return to earth's atmosphere) reentrada

reëxamination [,ri·ɛg,zæmɪ'neʃən] s reexaminación

ref. abbr referee, reference, reformation

re·fer [rɪ'fʌr] v (pret & pp **-ferred;** ger **-ferring**) tr referir ‖ intr referirse

referee [,rɛfə'ri] s árbitro ‖ tr & intr arbitrar

reference ['rɛfərəns] adj (library, book, work) de consulta ‖ s referencia

referen·dum [,rɛfə'rɛndəm] s (pl **-da** [də]) s referéndum m

refill ['rifɪl] s relleno ‖ [ri'fɪl] tr rellenar

refine [rɪ'faɪn] tr refinar

refinement [rɪ'faɪnmənt] s refinamiento; buena crianza, cultura

refiner·y [rɪ'faɪnəri] s (pl **-ies**) refinería

reflect [rɪ'flɛkt] tr reflejar; (to meditate) reflexionar; **to reflect on** o **upon** reflexionar en o sobre; perjudicar

reflection [rɪ'flɛkʃən] s (thinking) reflexión; (reflected light; image) reflejo

reflex ['riflɛks] s reflejo

reforestation [,rifɑrɪs'teʃən] o [,rifɑrɪs'teʃən] s reforestación

reform [rɪ'fɔrm] s reforma ‖ tr reformar ‖ intr reformarse

reformation [,rɛfər'meʃən] s reformación ‖ **the reformation** la Reforma

reformato·ry [rɪ'fɔrmə,tori] s (pl **-ies**) reformatorio

reform school s casa de corrección

refraction [rɪ'frækʃən] s refracción

refrain [rɪ'fren] s estribillo ‖ intr abstenerse

refresh [rɪ'frɛʃ] tr refrescar ‖ intr refrescarse

refreshing [rɪ'frɛʃɪŋ] adj confortante, restaurante

refreshment [rɪ'frɛʃmənt] s refresco

refrigerator [rɪ'frɪdʒəretər] *s* heladera, nevera, refrigerador *m*

refrigerator car *s* carro o vagón frigorífico

refuel [ri'fjul] *tr & intr* repostar

refuge ['refjudʒ] *s* refugio; expediente *m*, subterfugio; **to take refuge (in)** refugiarse (en)

refugee [,refju'dʒi] *s* refugiado

refund ['rifʌnd] *s* reembolso ‖ [rɪ'fʌnd] *tr* reembolsar ‖ [rɪ'fʌnd] *tr* consolidar

refurnish [ri'fʌrnɪʃ] *tr* amueblar de nuevo

refusal [rɪ'fjuzəl] *s* negativa

refuse ['refjus] *s* basura, desecho, desperdicios ‖ [rɪ'fjuz] *tr* rehusar; rechazar, no querer aceptar; **to refuse to** negarse a

refute [rɪ'fjut] *tr* refutar

reg. *abbr* **register, registrar, registry, regular**

regain [rɪ'gen] *tr* recobrar, recuperar; volver a alcanzar; **to regain consciousness** recobrar el conocimiento, volver en sí

regal ['rigəl] *adj* regio

regale [rɪ'gel] *tr* regalar, agasajar

regalia [rɪ'geli•ə] *spl (of an office or order)* distinctivos; galas, trajes *mpl* de lujo

regard [rɪ'gɑrd] *s* consideración, miramiento; *(esteem)* respeto; *(particular matter)* respecto; *(look)* mirada; **in regard to** respecto a o de; **regards** recuerdos; **without regard to** sin hacer caso de; **with regard to** respecto a o de ‖ *tr* considerar; mirar; tocar a, referirse a; **as regards** en cuanto a

regarding [rɪ'gɑrdɪŋ] *prep* tocante a, respecto a o de

regardless [rɪ'gɑrdlɪs] *adj* desatento, indiferente ‖ *adj* (coll) pese a quien pese, cueste lo que cueste; **regardless of** sin hacer caso de; a pesar de

regenerate [rɪ'dʒɛnə,ret] *tr* regenerar ‖ *intr* regenerarse

regent [,ridʒənt] *s* regente *mf*

regicide ['redʒɪ,saɪd] *s (act)* regicidio; *(person)* regicida *mf*

regime o **régime** [re'ʒim] *s* régimen *m*

regiment ['redʒɪmənt] *s* regimiento ‖ ['redʒɪ-,ment] *tr* regimentar

regimental [,redʒɪ,mɛntəl] *adj* regimental ‖ **regimentals** *spl* uniforme *m* militar

region ['ridʒən] *s* región, comarca

register ['redʒɪstər] *s (record; book for keeping such a record)* registro; reja regulable de calefacción; *(of the voice or an instrument)* extensión ‖ *tr (to indicate by a record; to show, as on a scale)* registrar; empadronar *(los vecinos en el padrón)*; manifestar, dar a conocer; certificar *(envíos por correo)*; inscribir ‖ *intr* registrarse; empadronarse; inscribirse

registered letter *s* carta certificada

registrar ['redʒɪs,trɑr] *s* registrador *m*, archivero

registration fee [,redʒɪs'treʃən] *s* derechos de matrícula

re•gret [rɪ'grɛt] *s* pesar *m*, sentimiento; pesadumbre, remordimiento; **regrets** excusas ‖ *v (pret & pp* -**gretted;** *ger* -**gretting)** *tr* sentir, lamentar; lamentar la pérdida de; arrepentirse de; **I regret** *(apology)* lo siento; me sabe mal; **to regret to** sentir

regrettable [rɪ'grɛtəbəl] *adj* lamentable

regular ['rɛgjələr] *adj* regular; (coll) cabal, completo, verdadero ‖ *s* obrero permanente; parroquiano regular; **regulars** tropas regulares

regulate ['rɛgjə,let] *tr* regular

rehabilitate [,rihə'bɪlɪ,tet] *tr* rehabilitar

rehabilitation [,rihə,bɪlɪ'teʃən] *s* rehabilitación

rehearsal [rɪ'hʌrsəl] *s* ensayo

rehearse [rɪ'hʌrs] *tr* ensayar ‖ *intr* ensayarse

reign [ren] *s* reinado ‖ *intr* reinar

reimburse [,ri•ɪm'bʌrs] *tr* reembolsar, rembolsar

rein [ren] *s* rienda; **to give free rein to** dar rienda suelta a ‖ *tr* dirigir por medio de riendas; contener, refrenar, gobernar

reincarnation [,ri•ɪnkɑr'neʃən] *s* reencarnación

reindeer ['ren,dɪr] *s* reno

reinforce [,ri•ɪn'fors] *tr* reforzar; armar *(el hormigón)*

reinforcement [,ri•ɪn'forsmənt] *s* refuerzo

reinstate [,ri•ɪn'stet] *tr* reinstalar

reiterate [ri'ɪtə,ret] *tr* reiterar

reject [rɪ'dʒɛkt] *tr* rechazar

rejection [rɪ'dʒɛkʃən] *s* rechazamiento

rejoice [rɪ'dʒɔɪs] *intr* regocijarse

rejoinder [rɪ'dʒɔɪndər] *s* contestación; (law) contrarréplica

rejuvenation [rɪ,dʒuvɪ'neʃən] *s* rejuvenecimiento

rel. *abbr* **relating, relative, religion, religious**

relapse [rɪ'læps] *s* recaída ‖ *intr* recaer

relate [rɪ'let] *tr (to establish relationship between)* relacionar; *(to narrate)* contar, relatar

relation [rɪ'leʃən] *s (connection; narration)* relación; *(narration)* relato; *(relative)* pariente *mf*; *(kinship)* parentesco; **in relation to** o **with** tocante a, respecto a o de

relationship [rɪ'leʃən,ʃɪp] *s (connection)* relación; *(kinship)* parentesco

relative ['rɛlətɪv] *adj* relativo ‖ *s* deudo, pariente *mf*

relax [rɪ'læks] *tr & intr* relajar

relaxation [,rilæks'eʃən] *s* relajación; despreocupación

relaxation of tension *s* disminución de tensión; disminución de la tirantez internacional

relaxing [rɪ'læksɪŋ] *adj* relajador; despreocupante, tranquilizador

relay ['rile] o [rɪ'le] *s* (elec) relais *m*, relevador *m*, relevo; (mil & sport) relevo; (sport) carrera de relevos ‖ *v (pret & pp* -**layed)** transmitir relevándose; transmitir con un relais; retransmitir *(una emisión)*; reexpedir *(un radiotelegrama)* ‖ [rɪ'le] *v (pret & pp* -**laid)** *tr* volver a colocar, volver a tender

relay race *s* carrera de relevos

release [rɪ'lis] *s* liberación; *(from jail)* excarcelación; alivio; permiso de publicación, venta, etc.; obra o pieza lista para la publicación, venta, etc.; (aer) lanzamiento; (mach) escape *m*, disparador *m* ‖ *tr* soltar; libertar; excarcelar (*a un preso*); permitir la publicación, venta, etc. de; (aer) lanzar (*una bomba*)

relent [rɪ'lɛnt] *intr* ablandarse, aplacarse

relentless [rɪ'lɛntlɪs] *adj* implacable

relevance ['rɛlɪvəns] *s* relevancia

relevant ['rɛlɪvənt] *adj* pertinente

reliable [rɪ'laɪ•əbəl] *adj* confiable, fidedigno; (*source*) solvente

reliance [rɪ'laɪ•əns] *s* confianza

relic ['rɛlɪk] *s* reliquia

relief [rɪ'lif] *s* alivio; caridad; (*projection of figures; elevation*) relieve *m*; (mil) relevo; **in relief** en relieve; **on relief** viviendo de socorro, recibiendo auxilio social

relieve [rɪ'liv] *tr* (*to release from a post*) relevar; aliviar; auxiliar (*a los necesitados*); (mil) relevar

religion [rɪ'lɪdʒən] *s* religión

religious [rɪ'lɪdʒəs] *adj* religioso

relinquish [rɪ'lɪŋkwɪʃ] *tr* abandonar, dejar

relish ['rɛlɪʃ] *s* buen sabor, gusto; condimento, sazón *f*; entremés *m*; buen apetito ‖ *tr* gustar de; comer o beber con placer

relocate [ri'loket] *tr* trasladar ‖ *intr* trasladarse

relocation [,rilo'keʃən] *s* traslado

reluctance [rɪ'lʌktəns] *s* renuencia, aversión

reluctant [rɪ'lʌktənt] *adj* renuente, maldispuesto

re•ly [rɪ'laɪ] *v* (*pret & pp* **-lied**) *intr* depender, confiar; **to rely on** depender de, confiar en

remain [rɪ'men] *intr* permanecer, quedarse ‖ **remains** *spl* desechos, restos; restos mortales; obra póstuma

remainder [rɪ'mendər] *s* resto, residuo; libro casi invendible ‖ *tr* saldar (*libros que ya no se venden*)

re•make [ri'mek] *v* (*pret & pp* **-made** ['med]) *tr* rehacer

remark [rɪ'mɑrk] *s* observación ‖ *tr & intr* observar; **to remark on** aludir a, comentar

remarkable [rɪ'mɑrkəbəl] *adj* notable, extraordinario

remar•ry [rɪ'mæri] *v* (*pret & pp* **-ried**) *intr* volver a casarse

reme•dy ['rɛmɪdi] *s* (*pl* **-dies**) remedio ‖ *v* (*pret & pp* **-died**) *tr* remediar

remember [rɪ'mɛmbər] *tr* acordarse de, recordar; dar recuerdos de parte de, p.ej., **remember me to your brother** déle Vd. a su hermano recuerdos de mi parte ‖ *intr* acordarse, recordar; **if I remember correctly** si mal no me acuerdo

remembrance [rɪ'mɛmbrəns] *s* recuerdo

remind [rɪ'maɪnd] *tr* recordar

reminder [rɪ'maɪndər] *s* recordatorio, recordativo

reminisce [,rɛmɪ'nɪs] *intr* entregarse a los recuerdos, contar sus recuerdos

remiss [rɪ'mɪs] *adj* descuidado, negligente

re•mit [rɪ'mɪt] *v* (*pret & pp* **-mitted;** *ger* **-mitting**) *tr* (*to send, to ship; to pardon*) remitir

remittance [rɪ'mɪtəns] *s* remesa

remnant ['rɛmnənt] *s* (*something left over*) remanente *m*; (*of cloth*) retal *m*, retazo; (*piece of cloth to be sold at reduced price*) saldo; vestigio

remod•el [ri'mɑdəl] *v* (*pret & pp* **-eled** o **-elled;** *ger* **-eling** o **-elling**) *tr* modelar de nuevo; rehacer, reconstruir; convertir, transformar; remodelar

remodeling [ri'mɑdəlɪŋ] *s* remodelación

remonstrate [rɪ'mɑnstret] *intr* protestar; **to remonstrate with** reconvenir

remorse [rɪ'mɔrs] *s* remordimiento

remorseful [rɪ'mɔrsfəl] *adj* compungido, arrepentido

remote [rɪ'mot] *adj* remoto

remote control *s* comando a distancia, telecontrol *m*, control remoto; **to operate by remote control** (co)mandar a distancia

removable [rɪ'muvəbəl] *adj* amovible

removal [rɪ'muvəl] *s* remoción; mudanza, traslado; (*dismissal*) deposición

remove [rɪ'muv] *tr* remover; quitar de en medio, apartar matando ‖ *intr* removerse

remuneration [rɪ,mjunər'eʃən] *s* remuneración

renaissance [,rɛnə'sɑns] o [rɪ'nesəns] *s* renacimiento

rend [rɛnd] *v* (*pret & pp* **rent** [rɛnt]) *tr* (*to tear*) desgarrar; (*to split*) hender, rajar; estremecer (*un ruido el aire*)

render ['rɛndər] *tr* rendir (*gracias, obsequios, homenaje*); prestar, suministrar (*ayuda*); pagar (*tributo*); desempeñar (*un papel*); traducir (*sentimientos*); (*from one language to another*) verter; hacer (*justicia*); ejecutar (*una pieza de música*); derretir (*cera, manteca*); extraer la grasa o el sebo de; poner, volver

rendezvous ['rɑndə,vu] *s* (*pl* **-vous** [,vuz]) cita; (*in space*) encuentro, reunión ‖ *v* (*pret & pp* **-voused** [,vud];* ger* **-vousing** [,vu•ɪŋ]) *intr* reunirse en una cita

rendition [rɛn'dɪʃən] *s* rendición; traducción; (mus) ejecución

renege [rɪ'nɪg] *s* renuncio ‖ *intr* renunciar; (coll) volverse atrás

renegotiation [,rinɪ,goʃɪ'eʃən] *s* renegociación

renew [rɪ'nju] o [rɪ'nu] *tr* renovar ‖ *intr* renovarse

renewable [rɪ'nju•əbəl] o [rɪ'nu•əbəl] *adj* renovable

renewal [rɪ'nju•əl] o [rɪ'nu•əl] *s* renovación

renounce [rɪ'nauns] *tr* renunciar; renunciar a (*p.ej., el mundo*) ‖ *intr* renunciar

renovate ['rɛnə,vet] *tr* renovar; refaccionar; reformar (*p.ej., una tienda, una casa*)

renown [rɪ'naun] *s* renombre *m*

renowned [rɪ'naund] *adj* renombrado

rent [rɛnt] *adj* desgarrado ‖ *s* alquiler *m*, arriendo; (*tear, slit*) desgarro ‖ *tr* alquilar, arrendar ‖ *intr* alquilarse, arrendarse

rental ['rɛntəl] *s* alquiler *m*, arriendo

renunciation [rɪ,nʌnsɪ'eʃən] o [rɪ,nʌnʃɪ'eʃən] *s* renunciación

reopen [ri'opən] *tr* reabrir ‖ *intr* reabrirse

re
re

reorganize [ri`ɔrgə,naɪz] *tr* reorganizar ‖ *intr* reorganizarse
reorientation [ri,orɪ•ən`tefən] *s* reorientación
rep. *abbr* **report, reporter, representative, republic**
repair [rɪ`pɛr] *s* reparación; recompostura; **in repair** en buen estado ‖ *tr* reparar; refaccionar ‖ *intr* dirigirse; volver
repaper [ri`pepər] *tr* empapelar de nuevo
reparation [,rɛpə`refən] *s* reparación
repartee [,rɛpɑr`ti] *s* respuesta viva; agudeza y gracia en responder
repast [rɪ`pæst] o [rɪ`pɑst] *s* comida, comilona
repatriate [ri`petrɪ,et] *tr* repatriar
re•pay [rɪ`pe] *v* (*pret & pp* **-paid** [`ped]) *tr* reembolsar, rembolsar; resarcir (*un daño, una injuria*); compensar
repayment [rɪ`pemənt] *s* reembolso; resarcimiento; compensación
repeal [rɪ`pil] *s* abrogación, revocación; revocatoria ‖ *tr* abrogar, revocar
repeat [rɪ`pit] *s* repetición ‖ *tr & intr* repetir
re•pel [rɪ`pɛl] *v* (*pret & pp* **-pelled;** *ger* **-pelling**) *tr* rechazar, repeler; repugnar
repent [rɪ`pɛnt] *tr* arrepentirse de ‖ *intr* arrepentirse
repentance [rɪ`pɛntəns] *s* arrepentimiento
repentant [rɪ`pɛntənt] *adj* arrepentido
repertory theater [`rɛpər,tori] *s* teatro de repertorio
repetition [,rɛpɪ`tɪfən] *s* repetición
repine [rɪ`paɪn] *intr* afligirse, quejarse
replace [rɪ`ples] *tr* (*to put back*) reponer; (*to take the place of*) reemplazar
replacement [rɪ`plesmənt] *s* reposición; reemplazo; pieza de repuesto; soldado reemplazante
replenish [rɪ`plɛnɪf] *tr* rellenar; reaprovisionar
replete [rɪ`plit] *adj* repleto
replica [`rɛplɪkə] *s* réplica
re•ply [rɪ`plaɪ] *s* (*pl* **-plies**) contestación, respuesta; contesto (Mex) ‖ *v* (*pret & pp* **-plied**) *tr & intr* contestar, responder
reply coupon *s* vale *m* respuesta
report [rɪ`port] *s* relato, informe *m;* voz *f,* rumor *m;* (*e.g., of a firearm*) detonación, tiro; denuncia ‖ *tr* relatar, informar acerca de; denunciar ‖ *intr* hacer un relato; redactar un informe; ser repórter; presentarse; **to report on** dar cuenta de, notificar
report card *s* certificado escolar
reportedly [rɪ`portɪdli] *adv* según se informa
reporter [rɪ`portər] *s* repórter *m*
reporting [rɪ`portɪŋ] *s* reportaje *m*
repose [rɪ`poz] *s* descanso ‖ *tr* descansar; poner (*confianza*) ‖ *intr* descansar
reprehend [,rɛprɪ`hɛnd] *tr* reprender
represent [,rɛprɪ`zɛnt] *tr* representar
representative [,rɛprɪ`zɛntətɪv] *adj* representativo ‖ *s* representante *mf*
repress [rɪ`prɛs] *tr* reprimir
reprieve [rɪ`priv] *s* suspensión temporal de un castigo, suspensión temporal de la pena de muerte; respiro, alivio temporal ‖ *tr* suspender temporalmente el castigo de o la

pena de muerte de; aliviar temporalmente
reprimand [`rɛprɪ,mænd] *s* reprimenda ‖ *tr* reconvenir, reprender
reprint [`ri,prɪnt] *s* reimpresión; tirada aparte ‖ [ri`prɪnt] *tr* reimprimir
reprisal [rɪ`praɪzəl] *s* represalia
reproach [rɪ`protf] *s* reproche *m;* oprobio ‖ *tr* reprochar; oprobiar
reproduce [,riprə`djus] *tr* reproducir ‖ *intr* reproducirse
reproduction [,riprə`dʌkfən] *s* reproducción
reproof [rɪ`pruf] *s* reprobación
reprove [rɪ`pruv] *tr* reprobar
reptile [`rɛptɪl] *s* reptil *m*
republic [rɪ`pʌblɪk] *s* república
republican [rɪ`pʌblɪkən] *adj & s* republicano
repudiate [rɪ`pjudɪ,et] *tr* repudiar; no reconocer (*p.ej., una deuda*)
repugnant [rɪ`pʌgnənt] *adj* repugnante
repulse [rɪ`pʌls] *s* repulsión, rechazo ‖ *tr* repeler, rechazar
repulsive [rɪ`pʌlsɪv] *adj* repulsivo
reputation [,rɛpjə`tefən] *s* reputación; buena reputación
repute [rɪ`pjut] *s* reputación; buena reputación ‖ *tr* reputar
reputedly [rɪ`pjutɪdli] *adv* según la opinión común
request [rɪ`kwɛst] *s* petición, solicitud; **at the request of** a petición de ‖ *tr* pedir
require [rɪ`kwaɪr] *tr* exigir, requerir
requirement [rɪ`kwaɪrmənt] *s* requisito; necesidad
requisite [`rɛkwɪzɪt] *adj & s* requisito
requital [rɪ`kwaɪtəl] *s* compensación, retorno
requite [rɪ`kwaɪt] *tr* corresponder a (*los beneficios, el amor, etc.*); corresponder con (*el bienhechor*)
re•read [ri`rid] *v* (*pret & pp* **-read** [`rɛd]) *tr* releer
rerun [`ri,rʌn] *s* (*film, play, etc.*) exhibición repetida, programa *m* repetido
resale [`ri,sel] o [ri`sel] *s* reventa
rescind [rɪ`sɪnd] *tr* rescindir
rescue [`rɛskju] *s* salvación, rescate *m,* liberación; **to go to the rescue of** acudir al socorro de ‖ *tr* salvar, rescatar, libertar
rescue party *s* pelotón *m* de salvamento
research [rɪ`sʌrtf] o [`risʌrtf] *s* investigación ‖ *intr* investigar
re•sell [ri`sɛl] *v* (*pret & pp* **-sold** [`sold]) *tr* revender; rescatar (Mex)
resemblance [rɪ`zɛmbləns] *s* parecido, semejanza
resemble [rɪ`zɛmbəl] *tr* parecerse a, asemejarse a
resent [rɪ`zɛnt] *tr* resentirse de o por
resentful [rɪ`zɛntfəl] *adj* resentido
resentment [rɪ`zɛntmənt] *s* resentimiento
reservation [,rɛzər`vefən] *s* reserva
reserve [rɪ`zʌrv] *s* reserva ‖ *tr* reservar
reservoir [`rɛzər,vwɑr] *s* depósito; (*where water is dammed back*) embalse *m,* pantano; (*of wisdom*) fuente *f*
re•ship [ri`fɪp] *v* (*pret & pp* **-shipped;** *ger* **-shipping**) *tr* reenviar, reexpedir; (*on a ship*) reembarcar ‖ *intr* reembarcarse

reshipment [riˈʃɪpmənt] s reenvío, reexpedición; (of persons) reembarco; (of goods) reembarque m

reside [rɪˈzaɪd] intr residir

residence [ˈrɛzɪdəns] s residencia

resident [ˈrɛzɪdənt] adj & s residente mf, vecino

residue [ˈrɛzɪˌdju] s residuo

resign [rɪˈzaɪn] tr dimitir, resignar, renunciar ‖ intr dimitir; (to yield, submit) resignarse; **to resign to** resignarse con (p.ej., su suerte)

resignation [ˌrɛzɪgˈneʃən] s (from a job, etc.) dimisión; (state of being submissive) resignación

resin [ˈrɛzɪn] s resina

resist [rɪˈzɪst] tr resistir (la tentación); resistir a (la violencia; la risa) ‖ intr resistirse

resistance [rɪˈzɪstəns] s resistencia; **without resistance** sin rechistar

resole [riˈsol] tr sobresolar

resolute [ˈrɛzəˌlut] adj resuelto

resolution [ˌrɛzəˈluʃən] s resolución; **good resolutions** buenos propósitos

resolve [rɪˈzɔlv] s resolución ‖ tr resolver ‖ intr resolverse

resort [rɪˈzɔrt] s lugar muy frecuentado; (e.g., for vacations) estación; (for help or support) recurso; **as a last resort** como último recurso ‖ intr recurrir

resound [rɪˈzaʊnd] intr resonar

resource [rɪˈsors] o [ˈrisors] s recurso

resourceful [rɪˈsorsfəl] adj ingenioso

respect [rɪˈspɛkt] s (deference, esteem) respeto; (reference, relation; detail) respecto; **respects** recuerdos, saludos; **to pay one's respects (to)** ofrecer sus respetos (a); **with respect to** respecto a o de ‖ tr respetar

respectable [rɪˈspɛktəbəl] adj respetable; decente, presentable

respectful [rɪˈspɛktfəl] adj respetuoso

respectfully [rɪˈspɛktfəli] adj respetuosamente; **respectfully yours** de Vd. atento y seguro servidor

respecting [rɪˈspɛktɪŋ] prep con respecto a, respecto de

respective [rɪˈspɛktɪv] adj respectivo

respire [rɪˈspaɪr] tr & intr respirar

respite [ˈrɛspɪt] s (temporary relief) respiro; (postponement, especially of death sentence) suspensión; **without respite** sin respirar

resplendent [rɪˈsplɛndənt] adj resplandeciente

respond [rɪˈspɑnd] intr responder

response [rɪˈspɑns] s respuesta

responsibility [rɪˌspɑnsɪˈbɪlɪti] s responsabilidad; **to assume responsibility** responsabilizarse

responsible [rɪˈspɑnsɪbəl] adj responsable; (job, position) de confianza; **to hold responsible** responsabilizar; **responsible for** responsable de

rest [rɛst] s (after exertion or work; sleep) descanso; (lack of motion) reposo; (of the dead) paz f; (what remains) resto; (mus) pausa; **at rest** (not moving) en reposo;

tranquilo; dormido; (dead) muerto; **the rest** lo demás; los demás; **to come to rest** venir a parar; **to lay to rest** enterrar ‖ tr descansar; parar; poner (p.ej., confianza) ‖ intr descansar; estar, hallarse; **to rest assured (that)** estar seguro, tener la seguridad (de que); **to rest on** descansar en o sobre, estribar en

restaurant [ˈrɛstərənt] s restaurante m

rest cure s cura de reposo

restful [ˈrɛstfəl] adj descansado, tranquilo, reposado

rest home s casa de reposo

resting place s lugar m de descanso; (of a staircase) descansadero; (of the dead) última morada

restitution [ˌrɛstɪˈtjuʃən] s restitución

restless [ˈrɛstlɪs] adj intranquilo; (sleepless) insomne

restock [riˈstɑk] tr reaprovisionar; repoblar (p.ej., un acuario)

restore [rɪˈstor] tr restaurar; (to give back) devolver

restrain [rɪˈstren] tr contener, refrenar; aprisionar

restraint [rɪˈstrent] s restricción; comedimiento, moderación

restrict [rɪˈstrɪkt] tr restringir

rest room s sala de descanso; excusado, retrete m; (of a theater) saloncillo

result [rɪˈzʌlt] s resultado; **as a result of** de resultas de ‖ intr resultar; **to result in** dar por resultado, parar en

resume [rɪˈzum] o [rɪˈzjum] tr reasumir; reanudar (el vuelo, etc.); volver a tomar (su asiento) ‖ intr continuar; recomenzar; reanudar el hilo del discurso

résumé [ˌrɛzuˈme] s resumen m

resurface [riˈsʌrfɪs] tr dar nueva superficie a ‖ intr volver a emerger (un submarino)

resurrect [ˌrɛzəˈrɛkt] tr & intr resucitar

resurrection [ˌrɛzəˈrɛkʃən] s resurrección

resuscitate [rɪˈsʌsɪˌtet] tr & intr resucitar

retail [ˈritel] adj & adv al por menor ‖ s venta al por menor ‖ tr detallar, vendor al por menor ‖ intr vender al por menor; venderse al por menor

retailer [ˈritelər] s detallista mf, minorista m, comerciante mf al por menor

retain [rɪˈten] tr retener; contratar (a un abogado)

retaliate [rɪˈtælɪˌet] intr desquitarse, vengarse

retaliation [rɪˌtælɪˈeʃən] s desquite m, venganza

retard [rɪˈtɑrd] s retardo ‖ tr retardar

retardation [ˌritɑrˈdeʃən] s retardación

retarded [rɪˈtɑrdɪd] adj subnormal, atrasado, retrasado

retch [rɛtʃ] tr vomitar ‖ intr arquear, esforzarse por vomitar

retching [ˈrɛtʃɪŋ] s arcadas

ret'd. abbr **returned**

reticence [ˈrɛtɪsəns] s reserva, circunspección, sigilo

reticent [ˈrɛtɪsənt] adj reservado, circunspecto

retinue [ˈrɛtɪˌnju] s comitiva, séquito

retire [rɪ'taɪr] *tr* retirar; jubilar (*a un empleado*) ‖ *intr* retirarse; jubilarse; (*to go to bed*) recogerse; (mil) retirarse

retirement [rɪ'taɪrmənt] *s* retiro; (*of an employee with pension*) jubilación; (mil) retirada

retirement annuity *s* jubilación

retort [rɪ'tɔrt] *s* respuesta pronta y aguda, réplica; (chem) retorta ‖ *intr* replicar

retouch [rɪ'tʌtʃ] *tr* retocar

retrace [rɪ'tres] *tr* repasar; **to retrace one's steps** volver sobre sus pasos

retract [rɪ'trækt] *tr* retractarse de, desdecirse de (*lo que se ha dicho*) ‖ *intr* retractarse, desdecirse

retractable [rɪ'træktəbəl] *adj* retráctil

retraction [rɪ'trækʃən] *s* retracción

re•tread ['ri,trɛd] *s* neumático recauchutado; neumático ranurado ‖ [rɪ'trɛd] *v* (*pret & pp* -treaded) *tr* recauchutar; volver a ranurar ‖ *v* (*pret* -trod ['trɑd]; *pp* -trod o -trodden) *tr* desandar ‖ *intr* volverse atrás

retreat [rɪ'trit] *s* (*act of withdrawing; place of seclusion*) retiro; (eccl) retiro; (mil) retreta, retirada; (*signal*) (mil) retreta; **to beat a retreat** retirarse; (mil) batirse en retirada ‖ *intr* retirarse

retrench [rɪ'trɛntʃ] *tr* cercenar ‖ *intr* recogerse

retribution [,rɛtrɪ'bjuʃən] *s* justo castigo; (theol) juicio final

retrieve [rɪ'triv] *tr* cobrar; reparar (*p.ej., un daño*); desquitarse de (*una pérdida, una derrota*); (hunt) cobrar, portar ‖ *intr* (hunt) cobrar, portar

retriever [rɪ'trivər] *s* perro cobrador, perro traedor

retroactive [,rɛtro'æktɪv] *adj* retroactivo

retrofiring [,rɛtro'faɪrɪŋ] *s* retrodisparo

retrogress ['rɛtrə,grɛs] *intr* retroceder; empeorar

retrorocket [,rɛtro'rɑkɪt] *s* retrocohete *m*

retrospect ['rɛtrə,spɛkt] *s* retrospección; **in retrospect** retrospectivamente

retrospective [,rɛtrə,spɛktɪv] *adj* retrospectivo

re•try [rɪ'traɪ] *v* (*pret & pp* -tried) *tr* reensayar; rever (*un caso legal*); procesar de nuevo (*a una persona*)

return [rɪ'tʌrn] *adj* repetido; de vuelta; **by return mail** a vuelta de correo ‖ *s* vuelta; devolución; recompensa; respuesta; informe *m*, noticia; ganancia, beneficio, rédito; (*of an election*) resultado; (*of income tax*) declaración; **in return (for)** en cambio (de); **many happy returns of the day!** ¡que cumpla muchos más! ‖ *tr* devolver; dar en cambio; corresponder a (*un favor*); dar (*una respuesta, las gracias*) ‖ *intr* volver; responder

return address *s* dirección del remitente

return bout o **engagement** *s* (box) combate *m* revancha

return game *s* desquite *m*

return ticket *s* billete *m* de vuelta; billete de ida y vuelta

return trip *s* viaje *m* de vuelta

reunification [ri,junɪfɪ'keʃən] *s* reunificación

reunion [rɪ'junjən] *s* reunión

reunite [,riju'naɪt] *tr* reunir ‖ *intr* reunirse

rev. *abbr* **revenue, reverse, review, revised, revision, revolution**

Rev. *abbr* **Revelation, Reverend**

rev [rɛv] *s* revolución ‖ *v* (*pret & pp* **revved; ger revving**) *tr* cambiar la velocidad de; **to rev up** acelerar ‖ *intr* acelerarse

revaluate [rɪ'vælju,et] *tr* revalorar, revalorizar, revaluar

revamp [rɪ'væmp] *tr* componer, renovar, remendar

reveal [rɪ'vil] *tr* revelar

reveille [rɛvəli] *s* diana, toque *m* de diana

rev•el ['rɛvəl] *s* jarana, regocijo tumultuoso ‖ *v* (*pret & pp* -eled o -elled; *ger* -eling o -elling) *intr* jaranear; deleitarse

revelation [,rɛvə'leʃən] *s* revelación

revel•ry ['rɛvəlri] *s* (*pl* -ries) jarana, diversión tumultuosa

revenge [rɪ'vɛndʒ] *s* venganza ‖ *tr* vengar

revengeful [rɪ'vɛndʒfəl] *adj* vengativo

revenue ['rɛvə,nju] *s* renta, rédito; rentas públicas

revenue cutter *s* escampavía

revenue stamp *s* sello fiscal, timbre *m* del estado

reverberate [rɪ'vʌrbə,ret] *intr* reverberar

revere [rɪ'vɪr] *tr* reverenciar, venerar

reverence ['rɛvərəns] *s* reverencia ‖ *tr* reverenciar

reverend ['rɛvərənd] *adj & s* reverendo

reverie ['rɛvəri] *s* ensueño

reversal [rɪ'vʌrsəl] *s* inversión (*e.g., of opinion*) cambio

reverse [rɪ'vʌrs] *adj* invertido; contrario; de marcha atrás ‖ *s* (*opposite or rear*) revés *m*; contrario; contramarcha, marcha atrás; (*check, defeat*) revés *m*, contratiempo ‖ *tr* invertir; dar vuelta a; poner en marcha atrás; **to reverse oneself** cambiar de opinión; **to reverse the charges** cobrar al destinatario; (telp) cobrar al número llamado ‖ *intr* invertirse

reverse lever *s* palanca de marcha atrás

revert [rɪ'vʌrt] *intr* revertir; saltar atrás; **to revert to one's old tricks** volver a las andadas

review [rɪ'vju] *s* (*reëxamination; survey; magazine; musical show*) revista; (*of a book*) reseña, revista; (*of a lesson*) repaso; (mil) reseña, revista ‖ *tr* rever, revisar; reseñar (*un libro*); repasar (*una lección*); (mil) revistar

reviewer [rɪ'vju•ər] *s* (*critic*) reseñador *m*

revile [rɪ'vaɪl] *tr* ultrajar, vilipendiar

revise [rɪ'vaɪz] *s* revisión; refundición; (typ) segunda prueba ‖ *tr* rever, revisar; refundir (*un libro*); enmendar

revision [rɪ'vɪʒən] *s* revisión; revisada; (*of a book*) refundición; enmienda

revisionism [rɪ'vɪʒə,nɪzəm] *s* revisionismo

revisionist [rɪ'vɪʒənɪst] *adj & s* revisionista

revival [rɪ'vaɪvəl] *s* resucitación; reanimación; (*e.g., of learning*) renacimiento; despertamiento religioso; (theat) reestreno, reposición

revive [rɪ'vaɪv] tr revivir; (theat) reestrenar, reponer ‖ intr revivir; volver en sí, recordar

revoke [rɪ'vok] tr revocar

revolt [rɪ'volt] s rebelión, sublevación ‖ tr dar asco a, repugnar ‖ intr rebelarse, sublevarse

revolting [rɪ'voltɪŋ] adj asqueroso, repugnante; rebelde

revolution [,rɛvə'luʃən] s revolución

revolutionar•y [,rɛvə'luʃə,nɛri] adj revolucionario ‖ s (pl -ies) revolucionario

revolve [rɪ'vɑlv] tr hacer girar; (in one's mind) revolver ‖ intr girar; revolverse (un astro en su órbita)

revolver [rɪ'vɑlvər] s revólver m

revolving bookcase s giratoria

revolving door s puerta giratoria

revolving fund s fondo rotativo

revue [rɪ'vju] s (theat) revista

revulsion [rɪ'vʌlʃən] s aversión, repugnancia; reacción fuerte

reward [rɪ'wɔrd] s premio, recompensa; (money used to recapture or recover) rescate m; hallazgo, p.ej., **five dollars reward** cinco dólares de hallazgo ‖ tr premiar, recompensar

rewarding [rɪ'wɔrdɪŋ] adj remunerador, provechoso, agradecido

re•wind ['ri,waɪnd] s (mach, mov) retroceso ‖ [ri'waɪnd] v (pret & pp **-wound** [waʊnd] tr (mach, mov) rebobinar

re•write [ri'raɪt] v (pret **-wrote** ['rot]; pp **-written** ['rɪtən] tr escribir de nuevo; refundir (un escrito); redactar (un escrito de otra persona)

R.F. abbr **radio frequency**

R.F.D. abbr **Rural Free Delivery**

R.H. abbr **Royal Highness**

rhapso•dy ['ræpsədi] s (pl -dies) rapsodia

rheostat ['ri•ə,stæt] s reóstato

rhesus ['risəs] s macaco de la India

rhetoric ['rɛtərɪk] s retórica

rhetorical [rɪ'tɔrɪkəl] adj retórico

rheumatic [ru'mætɪk] adj & s reumático

rheumatism ['rumə,tɪzəm] s reumatismo

Rhine [raɪn] s Rin m

Rhineland ['raɪn,lænd] s Renania

rhine'stone' s diamante de imitación hecho de vidrio

rhinoceros [raɪ'nɑsərəs] s rinoceronte m

Rhodes [rodz] s Rodas f

Rhone [ron] s Ródano

rhubarb ['rubɑrb] s ruibarbo

rhyme [raɪm] s rima; **without rhyme or reason** sin ton ni son ‖ tr & intr rimar

rhythm ['rɪðəm] s ritmo

rhythmic(al) ['rɪðmɪk(əl)] adj rítmico

rial•to [rɪ'ælto] s (pl -tos) mercado ‖ **the Rialto** el puente del Rialto; el centro teatral de Nueva York

rib [rɪb] s costilla; (of a fan or umbrella) varilla; (of a tire) cuerda; (in cloth) canilla; (of the wing of an insect) nervio ‖ v (pret & pp **ribbed**; ger **ribbing**) tr proveer de

costillas; hacer canillas en; (slang) tomar el pelo a

ribald ['rɪbəld] adj grosero y obsceno

ribbon ['rɪbən] s cinta

rice [raɪs] s arroz m

rich [rɪtʃ] adj rico; (coll) platudo; (color) vivo; (voice) sonoro; (wine) generoso; azucarado, condimentado; (coll) divertido; (coll) ridículo; **to strike it rich** descubrir un buen filón ‖ **riches** spl riquezas; **the rich** los ricos

rickets ['rɪkɪts] s raquitis f

rickety ['rɪkɪti] adj (object) destartalado, desvenciado; (person) tambaleante, vacilante; (suffering from rickets) raquítico

rid [rɪd] v (pret & pp **rid**; ger **ridding**) tr desembarazar; **to get rid of** desembarazarse de, deshacerse de; matar

riddance ['rɪdəns] s supresión, libramiento; **good riddance!** ¡adiós, gracias!, ¡de buena me he librado!

riddle ['rɪdəl] s acertijo, adivinanza; (person or thing hard to understand) enigma m; criba gruesa ‖ tr acribillar; destruir (un argumento; la reputación de una persona); **to riddle with bullets** acribillar a balazos; **to riddle with questions** acribillar a preguntas

ride [raɪd] s paseo ‖ v (pret **rode** [rod]; pp **ridden** ['rɪdən]) tr montar (un caballo); montar sobre (los hombros de una persona); recorrer a caballo; flotar sobre (las olas); dominar, tiranizar; (coll) burlarse de; **to ride down** atropellar; vencer; **to ride out** luchar felizmente con (una tempestad); aguantar con buen éxito (una desgracia) ‖ intr montar; pasear en coche o carruaje; **to let ride** (slang) dejar correr; **to take riding** llevar de paseo

rider ['raɪdər] s jinete m; pasajero

ridge [rɪdʒ] s (of a roof; of earth between two furrows) caballete m; (of a fabric) cordoncillo; (of mountains) cordillera; (of two plane surfaces) arista

ridge'pole' s parhilera

ridicule ['rɪdɪ,kjul] s irrisión; **to expose to ridicule** poner en ridículo ‖ tr ridiculizar

ridiculous [rɪ'dɪkjələs] adj ridículo

riding academy s escuela de equitación

riding boot s bota de montar

riding habit s amazona; traje m de montar

rife [raɪf] adj común, corriente, general; abundante, lleno; **rife with** abundante en, lleno de

riffraff ['rɪf,ræf] s bahorrina, canalla

rifle ['raɪfəl] s rifle m, fusil m ‖ tr hurtar, robar; escudriñar y robar; desnudar, despojar

rifle range s tiro de rifle

rift [rɪft] s abertura, raja; desacuerdo, desavenencia

rig [rɪg] s equipaje m; carruaje m con caballo o caballos; traje extraño; (naut) aparejo ‖ v (pret & pp **rigged**; ger **rigging**) tr equipar, aprestar, disponer; improvisar; vestir de una manera extraña; arreglar de una manera fraudulenta; (naut) aparejar

re
ri

rigging [ˈrɪgɪŋ] s avíos, instrumentos, equipo; (naut) aparejo, cordaje m
right [raɪt] adj derecho; verdadero; exacto; conveniente; favorable; sano, normal; bien, correcto; señalado; correspondiente; que se busca, p.ej., **this is the right house** ésta es la casa que se busca; que se necesita, p.ej., **this is the right train** éste es el tren que se necesita; que debe, p.ej., **he is going the right way** sigue el camino que debe; **right or wrong** con razón o sin ella, bueno o malo; **to be all right** estar bien; estar bien de salud; **to be right** tener razón ‖ adv derechamente; directamente; correctamente; exactamente; favorablemente; en orden, en buen estado; hacia la derecha; completamente; (coll) muy; mismo, p.ej., **right here** aquí mismo; **all right** muy bien ‖ interj ¡bien! ‖ s (justice, reason) derecho; (right hand) derecha; (box) derechazo; (com) derecho; (pol) derecha; **by right** según derecho; **on the right** a la derecha; **to be in the right** tener razón ‖ tr enderezar; corregir, rectificar; hacer justicia a; deshacer (un entuerto) ‖ intr enderezarse
righteous [ˈraɪtʃəs] adj recto, justo; virtuoso
right field s (baseball) jardín derecho
rightful [ˈraɪtfəl] adj justo; legítimo
right'-hand' drive s conducción o dirección a la derecha
right-hand man s mano derecha, brazo derecho
rightist [ˈraɪtɪst] adj & s derechista mf
rightly [ˈraɪtli] adv derechamente; correctamente; con razón; convenientemente; **rightly or wrongly** con razón o sin ella; **rightly so** a justo título
right mind s entero juicio
right of way s derecho de tránsito o de paso; (law) servidumbre de paso; (rr) servidumbre de vía; **to yield the right of way** ceder el paso
rights of man spl derechos del hombre
right'-wing' adj derechista
right-winger [ˈraɪtˈwɪŋər] s (coll) derechista mf
rigid [ˈrɪdʒɪd] adj rígido
rigmarole [ˈrɪgməˌrol] s galimatías m
rigorous [ˈrɪgərəs] adj riguroso
rile [raɪl] tr (coll) exasperar
rill [rɪl] s arroyuelo
rim [rɪm] s canto, borde m; (of a wheel) llanta; (of a tire) aro
rime [raɪm] s (in verse) rima; (frost) escarcha; **without rime or reason** sin ton ni son ‖ tr & intr rimar
rind [raɪnd] s cáscara, corteza
ring [rɪŋ] s (circular band, line, or mark) anillo; (for the finger) sortija; (for curtains; for gymnastics) anilla; (for nose of animal) argolla; (for fruit jars) círculo de goma; (for some sport or exhibition) circo; (for boxing) cuadrilátero, ruedo; (for bullfight) redondel m, ruedo; boxeo; (of a group of people) corro; (of evildoers) pandilla; (under the eyes) ojera; (of the anchor) arga-

neo; (sound of a bell, of a clock) campanada; (of a small bell; of the glass of glassware) tintineo; (to summon a person) llamada; (character, nature, spirit) tono; **to be in the ring (for)** ser candidato (a); **to run rings around** dar cien vueltas a ‖ v (pret & pp ringed) tr cercar, rodear; (to put a ring on) anillar ‖ intr formar círculo o corro ‖ v (pret rang [ræŋ]; pp rung [rʌŋ]) tr tañer, tocar; (to peal, ring out) repicar; llamar al timbre; dar (las horas la campana del reloj); llamar por teléfono; **to ring up** llamar por teléfono; marcar (una compra) con el timbre ‖ intr sonar (una campana, un timbre, el teléfono); tintinear (el choque de copas, una campanilla); resonar, retumbar; llamar; zumbar (los oídos); **to ring for** llamar, llamar al timbre; **to ring off** terminar una llamada por teléfono; **to ring up** llamar por teléfono
ring-around-a-rosy [ˈrɪŋəˌraʊŋdəˈrozi] s juego del corro
ringing [ˈrɪŋɪŋ] adj resonante, retumbante ‖ s anillamiento; campaneo, repique m; (of the glass of glassware) tintineo; (in the ears) retintín m, silbido
ring'lead'er s cabecilla m
ring'mas'ter s hombre encargado de los ejercicios ecuestres y acrobáticos de un circo
ring'side' s lugar junto al cuadrilátero; lugar desde el cual se puede ver de cerca
ring'worm' s tiña
rink [rɪŋk] s patinadero
rinse [rɪns] s aclaración, enjuague m ‖ tr aclarar, enjuagar
riot [ˈraɪət] s alboroto, tumulto; regocijos ruidosos; (of colors) exhibición brillante; **to run riot** desenfrenarse; crecer lozanamente (las plantas) ‖ intr alborotarse, amotinarse
rioter [ˈraɪətər] s alborotador m, amotinado
riot squad s pelotón m de asalto
rip [rɪp] s rasgón m, siete m; (open seam) descosido ‖ v (pret & pp ripped; ger ripping) tr desgarrar, rasgar; descoser (lo que estaba cosido) ‖ intr desgarrarse, rasgarse; (coll) adelantar o moverse de prisa o con violencia; **to rip out with** (coll) decir con violencia
ripe [raɪp] adj maduro; acabado, hecho; dispuesto, preparado; (boil, tumor) madurado; (olive) negro
ripen [ˈraɪpən] tr & intr madurar
ripoff [ˈrɪpˌɔf] s (slang) estafa; timo
ripple [ˈrɪpəl] s temblor m, rizo; (sound) murmullo, susurro ‖ tr rizar ‖ intr rizarse; murmurar, susurrar
rise [raɪz] s (of temperature, prices, a road) subida; (of ground, of the voice) elevación; (of a heavenly body) salida; (of a step) altura; (in one's employment) ascenso; (of water) crecida; (of a source of water) nacimiento; (of a valve) levantamiento; **to get a rise out of** (slang) sacar una réplica mordaz a; **to give rise to** dar origen a ‖ v (pret rose [roz]; pp risen [ˈrɪzən]) intr subir; levantarse; salir (un astro); asomar (un

peligro); brotar (*un manantial, una planta*);
(*in someone's esteem*) ganar; resucitar; **to
rise above** alzarse por encima de; mostrarse superior a; **to rise early** madrugar;
to rise to ponerse a la altura de

riser [ˈraɪzər] *s* contraescalón *m*, contrahuella; **early riser** madrugador *m*; **late
riser** dormilón *m*

risk [rɪsk] *s* riesgo; **to run** o **take a risk**
correr riesgo, correr peligro ‖ *tr* arriesgar;
arriesgarse en (*una empresa dudosa*)

risk•y [ˈrɪskɪ] *adj* (*comp* -**ier**; *super* -**iest**)
arriesgado; riesgoso; escabroso

risqué [rɪsˈke] *adj* escabroso

rite [raɪt] *s* rito; **last rites** honras fúnebres

ritual [ˈrɪtʃʊəl] *adj* & *s* ritual *m*

riv. *abbr* **river**

ri•val [ˈraɪvəl] *s* rival *mf* ‖ *v* (*pret* & *pp*
-**valed** o -**valled**; *ger* -**valing** o -**valling**) *tr*
rivalizar con

rival•ry [ˈraɪvəlrɪ] *s* (*pl* -**ries**) rivalidad

river [ˈrɪvər] *s* río; **down the river** río abajo;
up the river río arriba

river basin *s* cuenca de río

river bed *s* cauce *m*

river front *s* orilla del río

riv'er•side' *adj* ribereño ‖ *s* ribera

rivet [ˈrɪvɪt] *s* roblón *m*, remache *m*; (*e.g., to
hold scissors together*) clavillo ‖ *tr* remachar; clavar (*p.ej., los ojos en una persona*)

rm. *abbr* **ream, room**

R.N. *abbr* **registered nurse, Royal Navy**

roach [rotʃ] *s* cucaracha

road [rod] *adj* itinerario, caminero ‖ *s* camino; (*naut*) rada; **to be in the road** estorbar el paso; incomodar; **to get out of the
road** quitarse de en medio

road'bed' *s* (*of a highway*) firme *m*; (rr)
infraestructura

road'block' *s* (mil) barricada; (fig) obstáculo

road'house' *s* posada en el camino

road laborer *s* peón caminero

road map *s* mapa itinerario

road service *s* auxilio en carretera

road'side' *s* borde *m* del camino, borde de la
carretera

roadside inn *s* posada en el camino

road sign *s* señal *f* de carretera, poste *m*
indicador

road'stead' *s* rada

road'way' *s* camino, vía

roam [rom] *s* vagabundeo ‖ *tr* vagar por,
recorrer a la ventura ‖ *intr* vagar, andar
errante

roar [ror] *s* bramido, rugido ‖ *intr* bramar,
rugir; reírse a carcajadas

roast [rost] *s* asado; café tostado ‖ *tr* asar;
tostar (*café*); (coll) despellejar ‖ *intr* asarse;
tostarse

roast beef *s* rosbif *m*

roast of beef *s* carne de vaca asada o para
asar

roast pork *s* carne de cerdo asada

rob [rɑb] *v* (*pret* & *pp* **robbed**; *ger* **robbing**)
tr & *intr* robar

robber [ˈrɑbər] *s* robador *m*, ladrón *m*

robber•y [ˈrɑbərɪ] *s* (*pl* -**ies**) robo

robe [rob] *s* manto; abrigo; (*of a woman*)
traje *m*, vestido; (*of a professor, judge,
etc.*) toga, túnica; (*of a priest*) traje *m* talar;
(*dressing gown*) bata; (*for lap in a carriage*) manta ‖ *tr* vestir ‖ *intr* vestirse

robin [ˈrɑbɪn] *s* (*in Europe*) petirrojo; (*in
North America*) primavera

robot [ˈrobɑt] *s* robot *m*

robotics [roˈbɑtɪks] *s* robótica

robust [roˈbʌst] *adj* robusto; vigoroso

rock [rɑk] *s* roca; (*sticking out of water*)
escollo; (*one that is thrown*) piedra; (slang)
diamante *m*, piedra preciosa; **on the rocks**
arruinado, en pobreza extrema; (*said of
hard liquor*) (coll) sobre hielo ‖ *tr* acunar,
mecer; (*to sleep*) arrullar; sacudir; **to rock
to sleep** adormecer meciendo ‖ *intr* mecerse; sacudirse ‖ *abbr* —**rock-'n'-roll**

rock'-bot'tom *adj* (el) mínimo, (el) más bajo

rock candy *s* azúcar *m* cande

rock crystal *s* cristal *m* de roca

rocker [ˈrɑkər] *s* (*chair*) mecedora; (*curved
piece at bottom of rocking chair or cradle*)
arco; (mach) balancín *m*; (mach) eje *m* de
balancín

rocket [ˈrɑkɪt] *s* cohete *m* ‖ *intr* subir como
un cohete

rocket bomb *s* bomba cohete

rocket launcher [ˈlɔntʃər] *s* lanzacohetes *m*

rocket ship *s* aeronave *f* cohete

rock garden *s* jardín *m* entre rocas

rocking chair *s* mecedora, sillón *m* de hamaca

rocking horse *s* caballo mecedor

rock-'n'-roll [ˈrɑkənˈrol] *s* rock *m*

Rock of Gibraltar [dʒɪˈbrɔltər] *s* peñón *m*
de Gibraltar

rock salt *s* sal *f* de compás, sal gema

rock singer *s* rockero, rockera

rock wool *s* lana mineral

rock•y [ˈrɑkɪ] *adj* (*comp* -**ier**; *super* -**iest**)
rocoso, roqueño; (slange) débil, poco firme

rod [rɑd] *s* vara; varilla; barra; (*authority*)
vara alta; opresión, tiranía; (*of the retina*)
bastoncillo; (*elongated microörganism*)
bastoncito; (mach) vástago; (surv) jalón *m*;
(Bib) linaje *m*, raza, vástago; (slang) revólver *m*, pistola; **to spare the rod** excusar
la vara

rodent [ˈrodənt] *adj* & *s* roedor *m*

rod•man [ˈrɑdmən] *s* (*pl* -**men** [mən]) jalonero, portamira *m*

roe [ro] *s* (*deer*) corzo; (*of fish*) hueva

rogue [rog] *s* bribón *m*, pícaro

rogues' gallery *s* colección de retratos de
malhechores para uso de la policía

roguish [ˈrogɪʃ] *adj* bribón, pícaro; travieso,
retozón

rôle o **role** [rol] *s* papel *m*; **to play a rôle**
desempeñar un papel

roll [rol] *s* (*of cloth, film, paper, fat, etc.*)
rollo; (*roller*) rodillo; (*cake of bread*) panecillo; (*of dice*) echada; (*of a boat*) balance
m; (*of a drum*) redoble *m*; (*of thunder*)
retumbo; bamboleo; ondulación; rol *m*;
lista; (*of paper money*) fajo; **to call the roll**

pasar lista ‖ *tr* hacer rodar; empujar hacia adelante; cilindrar, laminar; (*to wrap up with rolling motion*) arrollar; alisar con rodillo; liar (*un cigarrillo*); mover de un lado a otro; poner (*los ojos*) en blanco; tocar redobles con (*el tambor*); vibrar (*la voz; la r*); **to roll one's own** liárselos; **to roll up** arremangar (*p.ej., las mangas*); amontonar (*p.ej., una fortuna*) ‖ *intr* rodar; bambolear; balancear (*un barco*); girar; retumbar (*el trueno*); redoblar (*un tambor*); **to roll around** revolcarse

roll call *s* lista, (el) pasar lista

roller [`rolər] *s* rodillo; (*of a piece of furniture*) ruedecilla; (*of a skate*) rueda; ola larga y creciente

roller bearing *s* cojinete *m* de rodillos

roller coaster *s* montaña rusa

roller skate *s* patín *m* de ruedas

roller towel *s* toalla sin fin

rolling mill [`rolıŋ] *s* taller *m* de laminación; tren *m* de laminadores

rolling pin *s* rodillo, hataca, rulo

rolling stock *s* (rr) material *m* móvil, material rodante

rolling stone *s* piedra movediza

roll'-top' desk *s* escritorio norteamericano, escritorio de cortina corrediza

roly-poly [`roli'poli] *adj* regordete, rechoncho

Rom. *abbr* **Roman, Romance**

roman [`romən] *adj* (typ) redondo ‖ *s* (typ) letra redonda ‖ **Roman** *adj & s* romano

Roman candle *s* vela romana

Roman Catholic *adj & s* católico romano

romance [ro`mæns] o [`romæns] *s* (*tale of chivalry*) roman *m;* cuento de aventuras; cuento de amor; intriga amorosa; novela sentimental; (mus) romanza ‖ [ro`mæns] *intr* contar o escribir romances, cuentos de aventuras o cuentos de amor; pensar o hablar de un modo romántico; exagerar, mentir ‖ **Romance** [`romæns] o [ro`mæns] *adj* (*Neo-Latin*) romance o románico

romance languages *spl* lenguas romances *or* románicas

romance of chivalry *s* libro de caballerías

Roman Empire *s* Imperio romano

Romanesque [,romən`ɛsk] *adj & s* románico

Roman nose *s* nariz aguileña

romantic [ro`mæntık] *adj* romántico; (*spot, place*) encantador

romanticism [ro`mæntı,sızəm] *s* romanticismo

romp [ramp] *intr* corretear, triscar

rompers [`rampərz] *spl* traje holgado de juego

roof [ruf] o [rʊf] *s* (*top outer covering of a house*) tejado; (*of a car or bus*) imperial *f*, tejadillo; (*of the mouth*) paladar *m;* (*of heaven*) bóveda; (*home, dwelling*) (fig) techo; **to raise the roof** (slang) poner el grito en el cielo ‖ *tr* techar

roofer [`rufər] o [`rʊfər] *s* techador *m*, pizarrero

roof garden *s* (*garden on the roof*) pérgola, azotea de baile y diversión

rook [rʊk] *s* (*bird*) grajo; (*in chess*) roque *m* ‖ *tr* trampear

rookie [`rʊki] *s* (slang) bisoño, novato

room [rum] o [rʊm] *s* aposento, cuarto, habitación, pieza; espacio, sitio, lugar *m;* ocasión; **to make room** abrir paso, hacer lugar ‖ *intr* alojarse

room and board *s* pensión completa

room clerk *s* empleado en la recepción, encargado de las reservas

roomer [`rumər] *s* inquilino

rooming house *s* casa donde se alquilan cuartos

room'mate' *s* compañero de cuarto

room•y [`rumi] *adj* (*comp* **-ier;** *super* **-iest**) amplio, espacioso

roost [rust] *s* percha de gallinero; gallinero; lugar *m* de descanso; **to rule the roost** ser el amo del cotarro, tener el mando y el palo ‖ *intr* descansar (*las aves*) en la percha; estar alojado; pasar la noche

rooster [`rustər] *s* gallo

root [rut] o [rʊt] *s* raíz *f;* **to get to the root of** profundizar; **to take root** echar raíces ‖ *tr* hocicar, hozar ‖ *intr* arraigar; **to root for** (slang) gritar alentando

rooter [`rutər] o [`rʊtər] *s* (slang) hincha *mf*

rope [rop] *s* cuerda; (*of a hangman*) dogal *m;* (*to catch an animal*) lazo; **to jump rope** saltar a la comba; **to know the ropes** (slang) saber todas las tretas; espabilarse ‖ *tr* atar con una cuerda; coger con lazo; **to rope in** (slang) embaucar, engañar

rope'walk'er *sl* funámbulo, volatinero

rosa•ry [`rozəri] *s* (*pl* **-ries**) rosario

rose [roz] *adj* de color de rosa ‖ *s* rosa

rose'bud' *s* pimpollo, capullo de rosa

rose'bush' *s* rosal *m*

rose'-col'ored *adj* rosado; **to see everything through rose-colored glasses** verlo todo de color de rosa

rose garden *s* rosaleda, rosalera

rose hip *s* (bot) cinarrodón *m;* eterio

rosemar•y [`roz,mɛri] *s* (*pl* **-ies**) romero

rose of Sharon [`ʃɛrən] *s* granado blanco, rosa de Siria

rose window *s* rosetón *m*

rose'wood' *s* palisandro

rosin [`razın] *s* colofonia, brea seca

roster [`rastər] *s* catálogo, lista; horario escolar, horas de clase

rostrum [`rastrəm] *s* tribuna

ros•y [`rozi] *adj* (*comp* **-ier;** *super* **-iest**) rosado, sonrosado; alegre

rot [rat] *s* podredumbre; (slang) tontería ‖ *v* (*pret & pp* **rotted;** *ger* **rotting**) *tr* pudrir ‖ *intr* pudrirse

rotate [`rotet] o [ro`tet] *tr* hacer girar; alternar ‖ *intr* girar; alternar

rote [rot] *s* rutina, repetición maquinal; **by rote** de memoria, maquinalmente

rot'gut' *s* (slang) matarratas *m*

rotogravure [,rotəgrə`vjur] o [,rotə`grevjur] *s* rotograbado

rotten [`ratən] *adj* putrefacto, pútrido; corrompido

rotund [ro'tʌnd] *adj* redondo de cuerpo; (*language*) redondo

rouge [ruʒ] *s* arrebol *m*, colorete *m* ‖ *tr* arrebolar, pintar ‖ *intr* arrebolarse, pintarse

rough [rʌf] *adj* áspero; (*sea*) agitado, picado; (*crude, unwrought*) tosco, grosero; aproximado ‖ *tr* —**to rough it** vivir sin comodidades, hacer vida campestre

rough'cast' *s* modelo tosco; mezcla gruesa ‖ *v* (*pret & pp* -**cast**) *tr* (*to prepare in rough form*) bosquejar; dar a (*la pared*) una capa de mezcla gruesa

rough copy *s* borrador *m*

roughly ['rʌfli] *adv* asperamente; brutalmente; aproximadamente

roulette [ru'lɛt] *s* ruleta

round [raund] *adj* redondo ‖ *adv* redondamente; alrededor; de boca en boca; por todas partes ‖ *prep* alrededor de; (*e.g., the corner*) a la vuelta de; cerca de; acá y allá en ‖ *s* camino, circuito; (*of a policeman; of visits; of drinks or cigars*) ronda; (*of applause; discharge of guns*) salva; (*discharge of a single gun*) disparo, tiro; (*of people*) corro, círculo; (*of golf*) partido; rutina, serie *f*, sucesión; redondez *f*; revolución; (*box*) asalto; **to go the rounds** ir de boca en boca; ir de mano en mano ‖ *tr* (*to make round*) redondear; cercar, rodear; doblar (*una esquina, un promontorio*); **to round off** u **out** redondear; acabar, completar, perfeccionar; **to round up** juntar, recoger; rodear (*el ganado*)

roundabout ['raundə,baut] *adj* indirecto ‖ *s* curso indirecto; (Brit) tío vivo; (Brit) glorieta de tráfico

rounder ['raundər] *s* (coll) pródigo; (coll) catavinos *m*, borrachín habitual

round'house' *s* cocherón *m*, casa de máquinas, depósito de locomotoras

round-shouldered ['raund,ʃoldərd] *adj* cargado de espaldas

Round Table *s* Tabla Redonda

round'-trip' ticket *s* billete *m* de ida y vuelta

round'up' *s* (*of cattle*) rodeo; (*of criminals*) redada; (*of old friends*) reunión

rouse [rauz] *tr* despertar; excitar, provocar; levantar (*la caza*) ‖ *intr* despertarse, despabilarse

rout [raut] *s* derrota; fuga desordenada ‖ *tr* derrotar; poner en fuga desordenada; arrancar hozando ‖ *intr* hozar

route [rut] o [raut] *s* ruta; itinerario ‖ *tr* encaminar

routine [ru'tin] *adj* rutinario ‖ *s* rutina

rove [rov] *intr* andar errante, vagar

row [rau] *s* (coll) camorra, pendencia, riña; (coll) alboroto, bullicio; (coll) balumba; **to raise a row** (coll) armar camorra ‖ [ro] *s* fila, hilera; (*of houses*) crujía; **in a row** seguidos, p.ej., **five hours in a row** cinco horas seguidas ‖ *intr* remar

rowboat ['ro,bot] *s* bote *m*, bote de remos

row•dy ['raudi] *adj* (*comp* -**dier**; *super* -**diest**) gamberro ‖ *s* (*pl* -**dies**) gamberro

rower ['ro•ər] *s* remero

royal ['rɔɪ•əl] *adj* real; (*magnificent, splendid*) regio

royalist ['rɔɪ•əlɪst] *s* realista *mf*

royal•ty ['rɔɪ•əlti] *s* (*pl* -**ties**) realeza; personaje *m* real, personajes reales; derechos de autor; derechos de inventor

r.p.m. *abbr* **revolutions per minute**

R.R. *abbr* **railroad, Right Reverend**

rub [rʌb] *s* frotación, roce *m;* **there's the rub** ahí está el busilis ‖ *v* (*pret & pp* **rubbed**; *ger* **rubbing**) *tr* (*to rub elbows with* rozarse mucho con; **to rub out** borrar; (slang) asesinar ‖ *intr* frotar; **to rub off** quitarse frotando; borrarse

rubber ['rʌbər] *s* caucho, goma; goma de borrar; chanclo, zapato de goma; (*in bridge*) robre *m* ‖ *intr* (slang) estirar el cuello o volver la cabeza para ver

rubber band *s* liga de goma

rubber plant *s* árbol *m* del caucho

rubber plantation *s* cauchal *m*

rubber stamp *s* cajetín *m*, sello de goma; (*with a person's signature*) estampilla; (coll) persona que aprueba sin reflexionar

rub'ber-stamp' *tr* estampar con un sello de goma; (*with a person's signature*) estampillar; (coll) aprobar sin reflexionar

rubbish ['rʌbɪʃ] *s* basura, desecho, desperdicios; (coll) disparate *m*, tontería

rubble ['rʌbəl] *s* (*broken stone*) ripio; (*masonry*) mampostería

rub'down' *s* masaje *m*, fricción

rube [rub] *s* (slang) isidro, rústico

ruble ['rubəl] *s* rublo

ru•by ['rubi] *s* (*pl* -**bies**) rubí *m*

rudder ['rʌdər] *s* timón *m*, gobernalle *m*

rud•dy ['rʌdi] *adj* (*comp* -**dier**; *super* -**diest**) coloradote, rubicundo;

rude [rud] *adj* rudo; desacomodido (SAm)

rudiment ['rudɪmənt] *s* rudimento

rudeness ['rudnɪs] *s* malcriadez *f*, malacrianza

rue [ru] *tr* lamentar, arrepentirse de

rueful ['rufəl] *adj* lamentable; triste

ruffian ['rʌfɪ•ən] *s* hombre grosero y brutal

ruffle ['rʌfəl] *s* arruga; (*of drum*) redoble *m;* (sew) volante *m* ‖ *tr* arrugar; agitar, descomponer; enojar, molestar; confundir; redoblar (*el tambor*); (sew) fruncir un volante en, adornar o guarnecer con volante

rug [rʌg] *s* alfombra; alfombrilla; (*lap robe*) manta

rugged ['rʌgɪd] *adj* áspero, rugoso; recio, vigoroso; tempestuoso

ruin ['ru•ɪn] *s* ruina ‖ *tr* arruinar; estropear; echar a perder

rule [rul] *s* regla; autoridad, mando; regla de imprenta; (*reign*) reinado; (*of a court of law*) decisión, fallo; **as a rule** por regla general; **to be the rule** ser lo que se hace ‖ *tr* gobernar, regir; dirigir, guiar; contener; reprimir; (*to mark with lines*) reglar; (law) decidir, determinar; **to rule out** excluir, rechazar ‖ *intr* gobernar, regir; prevalecer; **to rule over** gobernar, regir

rule of law *s* régimen *m* de justicia

ruler ['rulər] *s* gobernante *mf;* soberano; *(for ruling lines)* regla

ruling ['rulɪŋ] *adj* gobernante, dirigente, imperante ‖ *s (of a court or judge)* decisión, fallo; *(of paper)* rayado

rum [rʌm] *s* ron *m; (any alcoholic drink)* (U.S.A.) aguardiente *m*

Rumanian [ru'menɪ•ən] *adj & s* rumano

rumble ['rʌmbəl] *s* retumbo; *(of the intestines)* rugido; (slang) riña entre pandillas ‖ *intr* retumbar; avanzar retumbando

ruminate ['rumɪ,net] *tr & intr* rumiar

rummage ['rʌmɪdʒ] *tr & intr* buscar revolviéndolo todo

rummage sale *s* venta de prendas usadas

rumor ['rumər] *s* rumor *m;* (coll) díceres *mpl;* bolado (CAm) ‖ *tr* rumorear; **it is rumored that** se rumorea que

rump [rʌmp] *s* anca, nalga; *(cut of beef)* cuarto trasero

rumple ['rʌmpəl] *s* arruga ‖ *tr* arrugar, ajar, chafar ‖ *intr* arrugarse

rumpus ['rʌmpəs] *s* (coll) batahola, alboroto; **to raise a rumpus** (coll) armar la de San Quintín

run [rʌn] *s* carrera; clase *f,* tipo; arroyo; *(e.g., in a stocking)* carrera; *(on a bank by depositors)* asedio; *(of consecutive performances of a play)* serie *f;* (baseball & mus) carrera; **in the long run** a la larga; **on the run** a escape; en fuga desordenada; **the common run of people** el común de las gentes; **the general run of** la generalidad de; **to have a long run** permanecer en cartel durante mucho tiempo; **to have the run of** hallar el secreto de; tener libertad de ir y venir por ‖ *v (pret* **ran** [ræn]; *pp* **run;** *ger* **running)** *tr* hacer funcionar; dirigir, manejar; trazar, tirar *(una línea);* exhibir *(un cine);* hacer *(mandados);* tener como candidato; burlar, violar *(un bloqueo);* tener *(calentura);* correr *(un caballo; un riesgo);* **to run down** cazar y matar; derribar; atropellar *(a un peatón);* (coll) denigrar, desacreditar; **to run in** rodar *(un nuevo coche);* **to run off** tocar *(una pieza de música);* tirar, imprimir; **to run up** (coll) aumentar *(gastos)* ‖ *intr* correr; *(on wheels)* rodar; darse prisa; trepar *(la vid);* ir y venir *(un vapor);* supurar *(una llaga);* colar *(un líquido);* correrse *(un color o tinte);* presentar su candidatura; andar, funcionar, marchar; deshilarse *(las medias);* migrar *(los peces);* estar en fuerza; *(to be worded or written)* rezar; **to run across** dar con, tropezar con; **to run away** correr, huir; desbocarse *(un caballo);* **to run down** escurrir, gotear *(un líquido);* descargarse *(un acumulador);* distenderse *(el muelle de un reloj);* acabarse la cuerda, p.ej., **the watch ran down** se acabó la cuerda; **to run for** presentar su candidatura a; **to run in the family** venir de familia; **to run into** tropezar con; chocar con, topar con; **to run off the track** descarrilar *(un tren);* **to run out** salir; expirar, terminar; acabarse; agotarse; **to run out of** acabársele a uno, e.g.,

I have run out of money se me ha acabado el dinero; **to run over** atropellar *(a un peatón);* registrar a la ligera; pasar por encima; leer rápidamente; rebosar *(un líquido);* **to run through** disipar rápidamente *(una fortuna);* registrar a la ligera; estar difundido en

run'a•way' *adj* fugitivo; *(horse)* desbocado ‖ *s* fugitivo; caballo desbocado; fuga

run'-down' *adj* desmedrado; desmantelado; inculto; *(clock spring)* sin cuerda, distendido; *(storage battery)* descargado

rung [rʌŋ] *s (of ladder or chair)* travesaño; *(of wheel)* radio, rayo

runner ['rʌnər] *s* corredor *m;* caballo de carreras; mensajero; *(of an ice skate)* cuchilla; *(of a sleigh)* patín *m; (long narrow rug)* pasacaminos *m; (strip of cloth for table top)* tapete *m; (in stockings)* carrera

run'ner-up' *s (pl* **runners-up)** subcampeón *m*

running ['rʌnɪŋ] *adj* corredor; *(expenses; water)* corriente; *(knot)* corredizo; *(sore)* supurante; *(writing)* cursivo; continuo; consecutivo; en marcha; *(start) (sport)* lanzado ‖ *s* carrera, corrida; administración, dirección; marcha, funcionamiento; **to be in the running** tener esperanzas o posibilidades de ganar

running board *s* estribo

running head *s* titulillo

running start *s* (sport) salida lanzada

run'off' e•lec'tion *s* votación de desempate

run-of-mine coal ['rʌnəv'maɪn] *s* carbón *m* tal como sale

run'-of-the-mill' *adj* (coll) ordinario; mediocre

run'proof' *adj* indesmallable

runt [rʌnt] *s* enano, hombrecillo; *(little child)* redrojo; animal achaparrado

run'way' *s (of a stream)* cauce *m;* senda trillada; (aer) pista de aterrizaje

rupture ['rʌptʃər] *s* ruptura; *(pathol)* quebradura; *(break in relations)* ruptura ‖ *tr* romper; causar una hernia en ‖ *intr* romperse; padecer hernia

rural free delivery ['rurəl] *s* distribución gratuita del correo en el campo

rural police *s* guardia civil

rural policeman *s* guardia civil *m*

ruse [ruz] *s* astucia, artimaña

rush [rʌʃ] *adj* urgente ‖ *s* prisa grande, precipitación; agolpamiento de gente; (bot) junco; **in a rush** de prisa ‖ *tr* empujar con violencia o prisa; despachar con prontitud; (slang) cortejar insistentemente *(a una mujer);* **to rush through** ejecutar de prisa, despachar rápidamente; expedir ‖ *intr* lanzarse, precipitarse; venir de prisa, ir de prisa; actuar con prontitud; **to rush through** lanzarse a través de, lanzarse por entre

rush-bottomed chair ['rʌʃ'bɑtəmd] *s* silla de junco

rush hour *s* hora de aglomeración, horas de punta, horas de afluencia

rush'light' *s* mariposa, lamparilla

rush order *s* pedido urgente
russet ['rʌsɪt] *adj* canelo
Russia ['rʌʃə] *s* Rusia
Russian ['rʌʃən] *adj & s* ruso
rust [rʌst] *s* orín *m*, moho, herrumbre; (agr) roña, roya; color rojizo o anaranjado ‖ *tr* aherrumbrar ‖ *intr* aherrumbrarse
rustic ['rʌstɪk] *adj* rústico; sencillo, sin artificio ‖ *s* rústico
rustle ['rʌsəl] *s* susurro, crujido ‖ *tr* hacer susurrar, hacer crujir; hurtar (*ganado*) ‖

intr susurrar, crujir; (slang) trabajar con ahinco
rusty ['rʌsti] *adj* (*comp* **-ier;** *super* **-iest**) herrumbroso, mohoso; rojizo; (*out of practice*) empolvado, desusado, remoto
rut [rʌt] *s* (*track, groove in road*) rodada, bache *m;* hábito arraigado; (*sexual excitement in animals*) celo; (*period of this excitement*) brama
ruthless ['ruθlɪs] *adj* despiadado, cruel
Ry. *abbr* **railway**
rye [raɪ] *s* centeno; whisky de centeno

S

S, s [ɛs] decimonona letra del alfabeto inglés
s *abbr* **second, shilling, singular**
Sabbath ['sæbəθ] *s* (*of Jews*) sábado; (*of Christians*) domínica; **to keep the Sabbath** observar el descanso dominical, guardar el domingo
saber ['sebər] *s* sable *m*
sable ['sebəl] *adj* negro ‖ *s* marta cebellina; **sables** vestidos de luto
sabotage ['sæbə,tɑʒ] *s* sabotaje *m* ‖ *tr & intr* sabotear
saccharin ['sækərɪn] *s* sacarina
sachet ['sæʃe] o [sæ'ʃe] *s* polvo oloroso; saquito de perfumes
sack [sæk] *s* saco; vino blanco generoso; (mil) saqueo, saco; (*of an employee*) (slang) despedida ‖ *tr* ensacar; saquear, pillar; (slang) despedir (*a un empleado*)
sack'cloth' *s* harpillera; (*worn for penitence*) cilicio
sacrament ['sækrəmənt] *s* sacramento
sacred ['sekrəd] *adj* sagrado
sacrifice ['sækrɪ,faɪs] *s* sacrificio; **at a sacrifice** con pérdida ‖ *tr* sacrificar; (*to sell at a loss*) malvender ‖ *intr* sacrificar; sacrificarse
Sacrifice of the Mass *s* sacrificio del altar
sacrilege ['sækrɪlɪdʒ] *s* sacrilegio
sacrilegious [,sækrɪ'lɪdʒəs] o [,sækrɪ'lidʒəs] *adj* sacrílego
sacristan ['sækrɪstən] *s* sacristán *m*
sacris•ty ['sækrɪsti] *s* (*pl* **-ties**) sacristía
sad [sæd] *adj* (*comp* **sadder;** *super* **saddest**) triste; (slang) malo
sadden ['sædən] *tr* entristecer ‖ *intr* entristecerse
saddle ['sædəl] *s* silla de montar; (*of a bicycle*) sillín *m* ‖ *tr* ensillar; **to saddle with** echar a cuestas a
sad'dle•bags' *spl* alforjas
sad'dle•bow' [,bo] *s* arzón delantero
sad'dle•tree' *s* arzón *m*
sadist ['sædɪst] *s* sádico
sadistic [sæ'dɪstɪk] *adj* sádico
sadness ['sædnɪs] *s* tristeza

safe [sef] *adj* seguro, ileso, salvo; cierto, digno de confianza; sin peligro, a salvo; **safe and sound** sano y salvo; **safe from** a salvo de ‖ *s* caja fuerte, caja de caudales
safe'-con'duct *s* salvoconducto
safe'-crack'er *s* ladrón *m* de cajas de caudales
safe'-depos'it box *s* caja de seguridad
safe'guard' *s* salvaguardia, medida de seguridad ‖ *tr* salvaguardar
safe•ty ['sefti] *adj* de seguridad ‖ *s* (*pl* **-ties**) seguridad; **to parachute to safety** lanzarse en paracaídas; **to reach safety** ponerse a salvo, llegar a lugar seguro
safety belt *s* (aer, aut) correa de seguridad, cinturón *m* de seguridad; (naut) cinturón *m* salvavidas; **retractable safety belt** cinturón *m* retráctil
safety match *s* fósforo de seguridad
safety pin *s* imperdible *m*, alfiler *m* de seguridad, gacilla
safety rail *s* guardarriel *m*
safety razor *s* maquinilla de seguridad
safety valve *s* válvula de seguridad
safety zone *s* (*for pedestrians*) isla de peatones *or* de seguridad
saffron ['sæfrən] *adj* azafranado ‖ *s* azafrán *m* ‖ *tr* azafranar
sag [sæg] *s* comba, combadura; (*e.g., of a cable*) flecha ‖ *v* (*pret & pp* **sagged;** *ger* **sagging**) *intr* combarse; (*to slacken, yield*) aflojar, ceder, doblegarse; bajar (*los precios*)
sagacious [sə'geʃəs] *adj* sagaz
sage ['sedʒ] *adj* sabio, cuerdo ‖ *s* sabio; (bot) salvia; (bot) artemisa
sage'brush' *s* (bot) artemisa
Sagittarius [,sædʒə'tɛri•əs] *s* (astr) Sagitario
sail [sel] *s* vela; barco de vela; paseo en barco de vela; **to set sail** hacerse a la vela; **under full sail** a vela llena ‖ *tr* gobernar (*un barco de vela*); navegar (*un mar, río, etc.*) ‖ *intr* navegar, navegar a la vela; salir, salir de viaje; deslizarse, flotar, volar; **to sail into** (slang) atacar, regañar, reñir

ru
sa

sail′boat′ s barco de vela, buque m de vela, velero

sail′cloth′ s lona, paño

sailing ['seliŋ] adj de salida ‖ s paseo en barco de vela; navegación; salida

sailing vessel s buque velero

sailor ['selər] s (one who makes a living sailing) marinero; (an enlisted man in the navy) marino

saint [sent] adj & s santo ‖ tr (coll) canonizar

saintliness ['sentlinɪs] s santidad

Saint Vitus's dance ['vaɪtəsəs] s (pathol) baile m de San Vito

sake [sek] s respeto, bien, amor m; **for his sake** por su bien; **for the sake of** por, por motivo de, por amor a; **for your own sake** por su propio bien

salaam [sə'lam] s zalema ‖ tr saludar con zalemas, hacer zalemas a

salable ['seləbəl] adj vendible

salad ['sæləd] s ensalada

salad bowl s ensaladera

salad oil s aceite m de comer

Salamis ['sæləmɪs] s Salamina

sala•ry ['sæləri] s (pl -ries) sueldo

sale [sel] s venta; (auction) almoneda, subasta; **for sale** de venta; se vende(n)

sales′clerk′ s dependiente mf de tienda

sales exhibit s exhibición-venta, exposición-venta

sales′la′dy s (pl -dies) venedora

sales•man ['selzmən] s (pl -men [mən]) vendedor m, dependiente m de tienda

sales manager s gerente m de ventas

sales′man•ship′ s arte de vender

sales′room′ s salón m de ventas; salón de exhibición

sales talk s argumento para inducir a comprar

sales tax s impuesto sobre ventas

saliva [sə'laɪvə] s saliva

sallow ['sælo] adj cetrino

sal•ly ['sæli] s (pl -lies) paseo, viaje m; ímpetu m, arranque m; salida, ocurrencia; (mil) salida, surtida ‖ v, (pret & pp -lied) intr salir, hacer una salida; ir de paseo; **to sally forth** salir, avanzar con denuedo

salmon ['sæmən] s salmón m

salon [sæ'lɑn] s salón m

saloon [sə'lun] s cantina, taberna; (on a steamer) salón m

saloon′keep′er s tabernero

salt [sɔlt] s sal f; **to be not worth one's salt** no valer (uno) el pan que come ‖ tr salar; (to preserve with salt) salpresar; marinar (el pescado); salgar (al ganado); **to salt away** (slang) ahorrar, guardar para uso futuro

salt′cel′lar s salero

salted peanuts spl saladillos

saltine [sɔl'tin] s galletita salada

saltish ['sɔltɪʃ] adj salobre

salt lick s salero, lamedero

salt of the earth, the lo mejor del mundo

salt′pe′ter s (potassium nitrate) salitre m; (sodium nitrate) nitro de Chile

salt′sha′ker s salero

salt•y ['sɔlti] adj (comp -ier; super -iest) salado

salubrious [sə'lubri•əs] adj salubre

salutation [,sæljə'teʃən] s salutación

salute [sə'lut] s saludo ‖ tr saludar

Salvadoran [,sælvə'dorən] o **Salvadorian** [,sælvə'dori•ən] adj & s salvadoreño

salvage ['sælvɪdʒ] s salvamento ‖ tr salvar; recobrar

Salvation Army [sæl'veʃən] s ejército de Salvación

salve [sæv] o [sɑv] s ungüento ‖ tr curar con ungüento; preservar; aliviar

sal•vo ['sælvo] s (pl -vos o -voes) salva

Samaritan [sə'mærɪtən] adj & s samaritano

same [sem] adj & pron indef mismo; **it's all the same to me** lo mismo me da; **just the same** lo mismo, sin embargo; **same . . . as** mismo . . . que

samite ['sæmɪt] o ['semaɪt] s jamete m

sample ['sæmpəl] s muestra ‖ tr catar, probar

sample copy s ejemplar m muestra

sancti•fy ['sæŋktɪ,faɪ] v (pret & pp -fied) tr santificar

sanctimonious [,sæŋktɪ'moni•əs] adj santurrón

sanction ['sæŋkʃən] s sanción ‖ tr sancionar

sanctuar•y ['sæŋktʃu,ɛri] s (pl -ies) santuario; asilo, refugio; **to take sanctuary** acogerse a sagrado

sand [sænd] s arena ‖ tr enarenar; lijar con papel de lija

sandal ['sændəl] s sandalia; cacle m (Mex)

san′dal•wood′ s (bot) sándalo

sand′bag′ s saco de arena

sand′bank′ s banco de arena

sand bar s barra de arena

sand′blast′ s chorro de arena ‖ tr limpiar con chorro de arena

sand′box′ s (rr) arenero

sand dune s duna, médano

sand′glass′ s reloj m de arena, ampolleta

sand′ pa′per s papel m de lija ‖ tr lijar

sand′stone′ s piedra arenisca

sand′storm′ s tempestad de arena

sandwich ['sændwɪtʃ] s emparedado, sandwich m ‖ tr intercalar

sandwich man s hombre-anuncio

sand•y ['sændi] adj (comp -ier; super -iest) arenoso; (hair) rufo; cambiante, movible

sane [sen] adj cuerdo, sensato; (principles) sano

sanguinary ['sæŋgwɪn,ɛri] adj sanguinario

sanguine ['sæŋgwɪn] adj confiado, esperanzado; (countenance) coloradote

sanitary ['sænɪ,tɛri] adj sanitario

sanitary napkin s compresa higiénica

sanitation [,sænɪ'teʃən] s (sanitary measures) sanidad; (drainage) saneamiento

sanity ['sænɪti] s cordura, sensatez f

Santa Claus ['sæntə,klɔz] s el Papá Noel, San Nicolás

sap [sæp] s savia; (mil) zapa; (coll) necio, tonto ‖ v (pret & pp sapped; ger sapping) tr agotar, debilitar; zapar, socavar

sap′head′ s (coll) cabeza de chorlito

sapling [ˈsæplɪŋ] s árbol m muy joven, pimpollo; jovenzuelo, mozuelo

sapphire [ˈsæfaɪr] s zafiro

saraband [ˈsærəˌbænd] s zarabanda

Saracen [ˈsærəsən] adj & s sarraceno

Saragossa [ˌsærəˈɡɑsə] s Zaragoza

sarcasm [ˈsɑrkæzəm] s sarcásmo; escopetazo (SAm)

sarcastic [sɑrˈkæstɪk] adj sarcástico

sardine [sɑrˈdin] s sardina; **packed in like sardines** como sardinas en banasta o en lata

Sardinia [sɑrˈdɪnɪ·ə] s Cerdeña

Sardinian [sɑrˈdɪnɪ·ən] adj & s sardo

sarsaparilla [ˌsɑrsəpəˈrɪlə] s zarzaparrilla

sash [sæʃ] s banda, faja; (of a window) marco

sash window s ventana de guillotina

satchel [ˈsætʃəl] s maletín m; (of a schoolboy) cartapacio

sateen [sæˈtin] s satén m

satellite [ˈsætəˌlaɪt] s satélite m

satellite country s país m satélite

satiate [ˈseʃɪˌet] adj ahito, harto ‖ tr saciar

satin [ˈsætən] s raso

satinet [ˌsætɪˈnɛt] s rasete m

satiric(al) [səˈtɪrɪk(əl)] adj satírico

satirist [ˈsætɪrɪst] s satírico

satirize [ˈsætɪˌraɪz] tr & intr satirizar

satisfaction [ˌsætɪsˈfækʃən] s satisfacción

satisfactory [ˌsætɪsˈfæktəri] adj satisfactorio

satis·fy [ˈsætɪsˌfaɪ] v (pret & pp -ified) tr & intr satisfacer

saturate [ˈsætʃəˌret] tr saturar

Saturday [ˈsætərdi] s sábado

sauce [sɔs] s salsa; moje f, mojete m; (of fruit) compota; (of chocolate) crema; gracia, viveza; (coll) insolencia, lenguaje descomedido ‖ tr condimentar ‖ [sɔs] o [sæs] tr (coll) ser respondón con

sauce'pan' s cacerola

saucer [ˈsɔsər] s platillo

sau·cy [ˈsɔsi] adj (comp -cier; super -ciest) descarado, insolente; gracioso, vivo

sauerkraut [ˈsaʊrˌkraʊt] s chucruta

saunter [ˈsɔntər] s paseo tranquilo y alegre ‖ intr dar un paseo tranquilo y alegre; pasear tranquila y alegremente

sausage [ˈsɔsɪdʒ] s salchicha, embutido; moronga (Mex)

savage [ˈsævɪdʒ] adj & s salvaje, mf

savant [ˈsævənt] s sabio, erudito

save [sev] prep salvo, excepto, menos ‖ tr salvar (p.ej., una vida, un alma); ahorrar (dinero); conservar, guardar, horrar; proteger, amparar; **God save the Queen!** ¡Dios guarde a la Reina!; **to save face** salvar las apariencias

saving [ˈsevɪŋ] prep, salvo, excepto; con el debido respeto a ‖ adj económico ‖ **savings** spl ahorros, economías

savings account s cuenta de ahorros

savings bank s banco de ahorros, caja de ahorros

savior [ˈsevjər] s salvador m

Saviour [ˈsevjər] s Salvador m

savor [ˈsevər] s sabor m ‖ tr saborear ‖ intr oler; **to savor of** oler a, saber a

savor·y [ˈsevəri] adj (comp -ier; super -iest) sabroso; picante; fragante ‖ s (pl -ies) (bot) ajedrea

saw [sɔ] s (tool) sierra; proverbio, refrán m ‖ tr aserrar, serrar

saw'buck' s cabrilla, caballete m

saw'dust' s aserrín m, serrín m

saw'horse' s cabrilla, ćaballete m

saw'mill' s aserradero, serrería; montero (Mex)

Saxon [ˈsæksən] adj & s sajón m

saxophone [ˈsæksəˌfon] s saxofón m

say [se] s decir m; **to have one's say** decir su parecer ‖ v (pret & pp said [sɛd] tr decir; **I should say so!** ¡ya lo creo!; **it is said** se dice; **no sooner said than done** dicho y hecho; **that is to say** es decir, esto es; **to go without saying** caerse de su peso

saying [ˈse·ɪŋ] s dicho; proverbio, refrán m; **sayings** (rumor) díceres mpl

sc. abbr **scene, science, scruple, scilicet** (Lat) **namely**

scab [skæb] s costra; (strikebreaker) esquirol m; (slang) bribón m, golfo

scabbard [ˈskæbərd] s funda, vaina

scab·by [ˈskæbi] adj (comp -bier; super -biest) costroso; (coll) ruin, vil

scabrous [ˈskæbrəs] adj escabroso

scads [skædz] spl (slang) montones mpl

scaffold [ˈskæfəld] s andamio; (to execute a criminal) cadalso, patíbulo

scaffolding [ˈskæfəldɪŋ]s andamiaje m

scald [skɔld] tr escaldar

scale [skel] s escama; balanza; platillo de balanza; (e.g., of a map) escala; (mus) escala; **on a scale of** en escala de; **on a large scale** en grande escala; **scales** balanza ‖ tr escamer; descortezar, descostrar; escalar, subir, trepar; graduar ‖ intr descamarse; descortezarse, descostrarse; subir, trepar

scallop [ˈskɑləp] o [ˈskæləp] s concha de peregrino; (shell or dish for serving fish) concha; (thin slice of meat) escalope m; (on edge of cloth) festón ‖ tr cocer (p.ej., ostras) en su concha; festonear

scalp [skælp] s cuero cabelludo ‖ tr escalpar; comprar y revender (billetes de teatro) a precios extraoficiales

scalpel [ˈskælpəl] s escalpelo

scal·y [ˈskeli] adj (comp -ier; super -iest) escamoso

scamp [skæmp] s bribón m, golfo

scamper [ˈskæmpər] intr escaparse precipitadamente; **to scamper away** escaparse precipitadamente

scan [skæn] v (pret & pp scanned; ger scanning) tr escudriñar; escandir (versos); (telv) explorar; (coll) dar un vistazo a

scandal [ˈskændəl] s escándalo

scandalize [ˈskændəˌlaɪz] tr escandalizar

scandalous [ˈskændələs] adj escandaloso

Scandinavian [ˌskændɪˈnevɪ·ən] adj & s escandinavo

scanning [ˈskænɪŋ] s (telv) escansión, exploración

scansion [ˈskænʃən] s escansión

sa
sc

scant [skænt] *adj* escaso, insuficiente; solo, apenas suficiente ‖ *tr* escatimar

scant·y ['skænti] *adj* (*comp* **-ier;** *super* **-iest**) escaso, insuficiente, poco suficiente; (*clothing*) ligero

scape'goat' *s* cabeza de turco, víctima propiciatoria

scar [skɑr] *s* cicatriz *f*, señal *f*, lacra ‖ *v* (*pret* & *pp* **scarred;** *ger* **scarring**) *tr* señalar, marcar ‖ *intr* cicatrizarse

scarce [skɛrs] *adj* escaso, raro; **to make oneself scarce** (coll) no dejarse ver

scarcely ['skɛrsli] *adv* apenas; probablemente no; ciertamente no; **scarcely ever** raramente

scarci·ty ['skɛrsɪti] *s* (*pl* **-ties**) escasez *f*, carestía

scare [skɛr] *s* susto, alarma ‖ *tr* asustar, espantar; **to scare away** espantar, ahuyentar; **to scare up** (coll) juntar, recoger (*dinero*)

scare'crow' *s* espantajo, espantapájaros *m*

scarf [skɑrf] *s* (*pl* **scarfs** o **scarves** [skɑrvz]) bufanda; pañuelo para el cuello; (*cover for a table, bureau, etc.*) tapete *m*; corbata

scarf'pin' *s* alfiler *m* de corbata

scarlet ['skɑrlɪt] *adj* escarlata

scarlet fever *s* escarlata

scar·y ['skɛri] *adj* (*comp* **-ier;** *super* **-iest**) (*easily frightened*) (coll) asustadizo, espantadizo; (*causing fright*) (coll) espantoso

scathing ['skeðɪŋ] *adj* acerbo, duro

scatter ['skætər] *tr* esparcir, dispersar ‖ *intr* esparcirse, dispersarse

scatterbrain ['skætər,bren] *s* (coll) farraquista *m*

scatterbrained *adj* (coll) alegre de cascos, casquivano

scattered showers *spl* lluvias aisladas

scenari·o [sɪ'nɛri,o] o [sɪ'nɑri,o] *s* (*pls* **-os**) guión *m*, escenario

scenarist [sɪ'nɛrɪst] o [sɪ'nɑrɪst] *s* guionista *mf*, escenarista *mf*

scene [sin] *s* (*view*) paisaje *m*; (*in literature, art, the theater, the movie*) escena; escándalo, demostración de pasión; **behind the scenes** entre bastidores; **to make a scene** causar escándalo

scener·y ['sinəri] *s* (*pl* **-ies**) paisaje *m*; (theat) decoraciones *f*

scene shifter ['ʃɪftər] *s* tramoyista *m*

scenic ['sinɪk] o ['sɛnɪk] *adj* pintoresco; (*representing an action graphically*) gráfico; (*pertaining to the stage*) escénico

scent [sɛnt] *s* olor *m*; perfume *m*; (*sense of smell*) olfato; (*trail*) rastro, pista ‖ *tr* oler; perfumar; olfatear, ventear; sospechar

scepter ['sɛptər] *s* cetro

sceptic ['skɛptɪk] *adj* & *s* escéptico

sceptical ['skɛptɪkəl] *adj* escéptico

schedule ['skɛdjʊl] *s* catálogo, cuadro, lista; plan *m*, programa *m*; (*of trains, planes, etc.*) horario ‖ *tr* catalogar; proyectar; fijar la hora de

scheme [skim] *s* esquema *m*; plan *m*, proyecto; (*trick*) ardid *m*, treta; (*plot*) intriga, trama ‖ *tr* & *intr* proyectar; tramar

schemer ['skimər] *s* proyectista *mf*; intrigante *mf*

scheming ['skimɪŋ] *adj* astuto, mañoso, intrigante ‖ *s* intriga

schism ['sɪzəm] *s* cisma *m*; facción cismática

schist [ʃɪst] *s* esquisto

scholar ['skɑlər] *s* (*pupil*) alumno; (*scholarship holder*) becario; (*learned person*) sabio, erudito

scholarly ['skɑkərli] *adj* sabio, erudito

scholarship ['skɑlər,ʃɪp] *s* erudición; (*grant to study*) beca

scholarship holder *s* bequista *mf* (CAm, Cuba)

school [skul] *s* escuela; (*of a university*) facultad; (*of fish*) banco, cardume *m* ‖ *tr* enseñar, instruir, disciplinar

school age *s* edad escolar

school attendance *s* escolaridad

school board *s* junta de instrucción pública

school'boy' *s* alumno de escuela

school day *s* día !ectivo

school'girl' *s* alumna de escuela

school'house' *s* escuela

schooling ['skulɪŋ] *s* instrucción, enseñanza; experiencia

school'mate' *s* compañero de escuela

school'room' *s* aula, sala de clase

school'teach'er *s* maestro de escuela

school year *s* año lectivo

schooner ['skunər] *s* goleta

sci. *abbr* **science, scientific**

science ['saɪəns] *s* ciencia

science fiction *s* ciencia-ficción; novela científica

scientific [,saɪən'tɪfɪk] *adj* científico

scientist ['saɪəntɪst] *s* científico, sabio, hombre *m* de ciencia

sci-fi ['saɪ'faɪ] *s* (slang) *abbr* **science fiction**

scil. *abbr* **scilicet** (Lat) **namely**

scimitar ['sɪmɪtər] *s* cimitarra

scintillate ['sɪntɪ,let] *intr* chispear, centellear

scion ['saɪən] *s* vástago

Scipio ['sɪpɪ,o] *s* Escipión *m*

scissors ['sɪzərz] *ssg* o *spl* tijeras

scoff [skɔf] o [skɑf] *s* burla, mofa ‖ *intr* burlarse, mofarse; **to scoff at** burlarse de, mofarse de

scold [skold] *s* regañón *m*, regañona ‖ *tr* & *intr* regañar

scoop [skup] *s* (*instrument like a spoon*) cuchara, cucharón *m*; (*tool like a shovel*) pala; (*kitchen utensil*) paleta; (*for water*) achicador *m*; cucharada, palada, paletada; (*hollow made by a scoop*) hueco; (*big haul*) (coll) buena ganancia ‖ *tr* sacar con cuchara, pala, paleta; achicar (*agua*); **to scoop out** ahuecar, vaciar

scoot [skut] *s* (coll) carrera precipitada ‖ *intr* (coll) correr precipitadamente

scooter ['skutər] *s* monopatín *m*, patinete *m*

scope [skop] *s* alcance *m*, extensión; campo, espacio; **to give free scope to** dar campo libre a

scorch [skɔrtʃ] *s* chamusco ‖ *tr* chamuscar; (*to dry, wither*) abrasar; criticar acerbamente ‖ *intr* chamuscarse; abrasarse

scorching ['skɔrtʃɪŋ] *adj* abrasador; acerbo, duro, mordaz

score [skor] *s* (*in a game*) cuenta, tantos; (*in an examination*) nota; entalladura, muesca; línea, raya; (*twenty*) veintena; (*mus*) partitura; **on the score of** a título de; **to keep score** apuntar los tantos ‖ *tr* anotar (*los tantos*); ganar, tantear (*tantos*); rayar, señalar; regañar acerbamente; (*mus*) instrumentar ‖ *intr* ganar tantos; marcar los tantos

score board *s* marcador *m*, cuadro indicador

scorn [skɔrn] *s* desdén *m*, desprecio ‖ *tr* & *intr* desdeñar, despreciar; **to scorn to** no dignarse

scornful ['skɔrnfəl] *adj* desdeñoso

Scorpio ['skɔrpɪ‧o] *s* (astr) Escorpión *m*

scorpion ['skɔrpɪ‧ən] *s* alacrán *m*, escorpión *m*

Scot [skɑt] *s* escocés *m*

Scotch [skɑtʃ] *adj* escocés ‖ *s* (*dialect*) escocés *m;* whiskey *m* escocés; **the Scotch** los escoceses

Scotch‧man ['skɑtʃmən] *s* (*pl* -**men** [mən]) escocés *m*

Scotland ['skɑtlənd] *s* Escocia

Scottish ['skɑtɪʃ] *adj* escocés ‖ *s* (*dialect*) escocés *m;* **the Scottish** los escoceses

scoundrel ['skaʊndrəl] *s* bribón *m*, pícaro

scour [skaʊr] *tr* fregar, estregar; recorrer, explorar detenidamente

scourge [skʌrdʒ] *s* azote *m* ‖ *tr* azotar

scout [skaʊt] *s* (mil) escucha, explorador *m;* niño explorador, niña exploradora; exploración, reconocimiento; (slang) individuo, sujeto, tipo ‖ *tr* explorar, reconocer (*un territorio*); observar (*al enemigo*); negarse a creer

scout‧mas‧ter *s* jefe *m* de tropa de niños exploradores

scowl [skaʊl] *s* ceño, semblante ceñudo ‖ *intr* mirar con ceño, poner mal gesto, poner mala cara

scramble ['skræmbəl] *s* arrebatiña ‖ *tr* arrebatar; recoger de prisa; revolver; hacer un revoltillo de (*huevos*); trepar ‖ *intr* luchar; trepar

scrambled eggs *spl* revoltillo, huevos revueltos

scrap [skræp] *s* fragmento, pedacito; desecho; chatarra; (slang) riña, contienda; **scraps** desperdicios, desechos; (*from the table*) sobras ‖ *v* (*pret* & *pp* **scrapped;** *ger* **scrapping**) *tr* desechar, descartar, echar a la basura; reducir a hierro viejo ‖ *intr* (slang) reñir, pelear

scrap‧book *s* álbum *m* de recortes, libro de recuerdos

scrape [skrep] *s* raspadura; (*place scratched*) raspaza; aprieto, enredo; ‖ *tr* raspar; (*to gather together with much difficulty*) arañar ‖ *intr* raspar; **to scrape along** ir tirando; **to scrape through** aprobar justo

scrap heap *s* montón *m* de cachivaches

scrap iron *s* chatarra, desecho de hierro

scrap paper *s* papel *m* para apuntes; papel de desecho

scratch [skrætʃ] *s* arañazo, rasguño; marca, raya, garrapato; (billiards) chiripa; (sport) línea de partida; **to start from scratch** empezar desde el principio, empezar de cero; **up to scratch** en buena condición ‖ *tr* arañar, rasguñar; borrar, rasgar (*lo escrito*); garrapatear; (sport) borrar (*a un corredor o caballo*) ‖ *intr* arañar, rasguñar; garrapatear; raspear (*una pluma*)

scratch pad *s* cuadernillo de apuntes

scratch paper *s* papel *m* para apuntes

scratch‧-re‧sist‧ant *adj* resistente al rayado

scrawl [skrɔl] *s* garrapatos ‖ *tr* & *intr* garrapatear

scraw‧ny ['skrɔni] *adj* (*comp* -**nier;** *super* -**niest**) huesudo, flaco

scream [skrim] *s* chillido, grito ‖ *tr* vociferar ‖ *intr* chillar, gritar; reírse a gritos

screech [skritʃ] *s* chillido ‖ *intr* chillar

screech owl *s* buharro; (*barn owl*) lechuza

screen [skrin] *s* mampara, biombo; (*in front of chimney*) pantalla; (*to keep flies out*) alambrera; (*to sift sand*) tamiz *m;* (mov, phys, telv) pantalla; **to put on the screen** llevar a la pantalla, llevar al celuloide ‖ *tr* defender, proteger; cubrir, ocultar; cinematografiar; rodar, proyectar (*una película*); adaptar para el cine; tamizar (*p.ej., arena*)

screen grid *s* (electron) rejilla blindada

screen‧play *s* cinedrama *m*

screw [skru] *s* tornillo; (*internal or female screw*) rosca, tuerca; (*of a boat*) hélice *f;* **to have a screw loose** (slang) tener flojos los tornillos; **to put the screws on** apretar los tornillos a ‖ *tr* atornillar; (*to twist, twist in*) enroscar; **to screw up** torcer (*el rostro*); ‖ *intr* atornillarse

screw‧ball *s* (slang) estrafalario, excéntrico

screw‧driv‧er *s* destornillador *m*, desatornillador *m*

screw eye *s* armella

screw jack *s* gato de tornillo

screw propeller *s* hélice *f*

scribal error ['skraɪbəl] *s* error *m* de escribiente

scribble ['skrɪbəl] *s* garrapatos ‖ *tr* & *intr* garrapatear

scribe [skraɪb] *s* (*teacher of Jewish law*) escriba *m;* escribiente *mf;* copista *mf;* autor *m*, escritor *m* ‖ *tr* arañar, rayar; trazar con punzón

scrimp [skrɪmp] *tr* & *intr* escatimar

script [skrɪpt] *s* escritura, letra cursiva; manuscrito, texto; (*of a play, movie, etc.*) palabras; (rad, telv) guión *m;* (typ) plumilla inglesa

scripture ['skrɪptʃər] *s* escrito sagrado ‖ **Scripture** *s* Escritura

script‧writ‧er *s* guionista *mf*, cinematurgo

scrofula ['skrɑfjələ] *s* escrófula

scroll [skrol] *s* rollo de papel, rollo de pergamino; (archit) voluta

scroll‧work *s* obra de volutas, adornos de voluta

scrub [skrʌb] *s* chaparral *m*, monte bajo; animal achaparrado; persona de poca monta; (*act of scrubbing*) fregado; (sport)

jugador *m* no oficial ‖ *v* (*pret* & *pp*
scrubbed; *ger* **scrubbing**) *tr* fregar, restregar
scrub oak *s* chaparro
scrub woman *s* fregona
scruff [skrʌf] *s* nuca; piel *f* que cubre la nuca;
capa, superficie *f;* espuma
scruple [ˈskrupəl] *s* escrúpulo
scrupulous [ˈskrupjələs] *adj* escrupuloso
scrutinize [ˈskrutɪˌnaɪz] *tr* escudriñar, escrutar
scruti·ny [ˈskrutɪni] *s* (*pl* **-nies**) escudriña-
miento, escrutinio
scubadiver [ˈskubəˌdɪvər] *s* submarinista *mf*
scuff [skʌf] *s* rascadura, desgaste *m* ‖ *tr*
rascar, desgastar
scuffle [ˈskʌfəl] *s* lucha, sarracina ‖ *intr*
forcejear, luchar
scull [skʌl] *s* espadilla‖ *tr* impulsar con espadilla ‖ *intr* remar con espadilla
sculler·y [ˈskʌləri] *s* (*pl* **-ies**) trascocina
scullery maid *s* fregona
scullion [ˈskʌljən] *s* pinche *m*
sculptor [ˈskʌlptər] *s* escultor *m*
sculptress [ˈskʌlptrɪs] *s* escultora
sculpture [ˈskʌlptʃər] *s* escultura ‖ *tr* & *intr*
esculpir
scum [skʌm] *s* espuma, nata; (*on metals*)
escoria; (fig) escoria, canalla, gente baja;
palomilla ‖ *v* (*pret* & *pp* **scummed;** *ger*
scumming) *tr* & *intr* espumar
scum·my [ˈskʌmi] *adj* (*comp* **-mier;** *super*
-miest) espumoso; (fig) vil, ruin
scurf [skʌrf] *s* (*shed by the skin*) caspa; (*shed
by any surface*) costra
scurrilous [ˈskʌrɪləs] *adj* chocarrero, grosero, insolente, difamatorio
scur·ry [ˈskʌri] *v* (*pret* & *pp* **-ried**) *intr* echar
a correr, escabullirse; **to scurry around**
menearse; **to scurry away** ir respailando
scur·vy [ˈskʌri] *adj* (*comp* **-vier;** *super*
-viest) despreciable, ruin, vil ‖ *s* escorbuto
scuttle [ˈskʌtəl] *s* (*bucket for coal*) cubo,
balde *m;* (*trap door*) escotillón *m;* fuga,
paso acelerado; (naut) escotilla ‖ *tr* barrenar, dar barreno a ‖ *intr* echar a correr
Scylla [ˈsɪlə] *s* Escila; **between Scylla and
Charybdis** entre Escila y Caribdis
scythe [saɪð] *s* dalle *m*, guadaña
sea [si] *s* mar *m* & *f;* **at sea** en el mar;
confuso, perplejo; **by the sea** a la orilla del
mar; **to follow the sea** correr los mares, ser
marinero; **to put to sea** hacerse a la mar
sea′board′ *adj* costanero, costero ‖ *s* costa
del mar, litoral *m*
sea breeze *s* brisa de mar
sea′coast′ *s* costa marítima, litoral *m*
sea dog *s* (*seal*) foca; (coll) marinero viejo,
lobo de mar
seafarer [ˈsiˌfɛrər] *s* marinero; viajero por
mar
sea′food′ *s* mariscos
seagoing [ˈsiˌgoʊɪŋ] *adj* de alta mar
sea gull *s* gaviota
seal [sil] *s* (*raised design; stamp; mark*) sello;
(*sea animal*) foca ‖ *tr* sellar; cerrar hermé-

ticamente; decidir irrevocablemente; (*with
sealing wax*) lacrar
sea legs *spl* pie marino
sea level *s* nivel *m* del mar
sealing wax *s* lacre *m*
seal′skin′ *s* piel *f* de foca
seam [sim] *s* costura; (*edges left after making
a seam*) metido; (*mark, line*) arruga; (*scar*)
costurón *m;* grieta, juntura; (min) filón *m*,
veta
sea·man [ˈsimən] *s* (*pl* **-men** [mən]) marinero; (nav) marino
sea mile *s* milla náutica
seamless [ˈsimlɪs] *adj* inconsútil, sin costura
seamstress [ˈsimstrɪs] *s* costurera; (*dressmaker's helper*) modistilla
seam·y [ˈsimi] *adj* (*comp* **-ier;** *super* **-iest**)
lleno de costuras; tosco, burdo; vil, soez;
miserable
séance [ˈseɑns] *s* sesión de espiritistas
sea′plane′ *s* hidroavión *m*, hidroplano
sea′port′ *s* puerto de mar
sea power *s* potencia naval
sear [sɪr] *adj* seco, marchito; gastado, raído ‖
s chamusco, socarra ‖ *tr* chamuscar, socarrar; quemar; marchitar; cauterizar
search [sʌrtʃ] *s* busca; pesquisa, indagación;
(*frisking a person*) cacheo; (*police, soldiers*) peinado; **in search of** en busca de ‖
tr averiguar, explorar; registrar ‖ *intr* buscar; (*police, soldiers*) peinar; **to search
for** buscar; **to search into** indagar, investigar
search′light′ *s* reflector *m*, proyector *m*
search warrant *s* auto de registro domiciliario, orden *f* de allanamiento
sea′scape′ *s* vista del mar; (*painting*) marina
sea shell *s* concha marina
sea′shore′ *s* costa, playa, ribera del mar
sea′sick′ *adj* mareado
sea′sick′ness *s* mareo
sea′side′ *s* orilla del mar, ribera del mar,
playa
season [ˈsizən] *s* (*one of four parts of year*)
estación; (*period of the year; period
marked by certain activities*) temporada;
(*opportune time; time of maturity, of rip-
ening*) sazón *f;* **in season** en sazón; **in
season and out of season** en tiempo y a
destiempo; **out of season** fuera de sazón ‖
tr condimentar, sazonar; curar (*la madera*); moderar, templar
seasonal [ˈsizənəl] *adj* estacional
seasoning [ˈsizənɪŋ] *s* aderezo, aliño, condimento; (*of wood*) cura; (fig) sal *f*, chiste *m*
season ticket *s* billete *m* de abono
seat [sit] *s* asiento; (*of trousers*) fondillos;
morada; sitio, lugar *m;* (*e.g., of government*) sede *f;* (*in parliament*) escaño; (*e.g.,
of a war*) teatro; (*e.g., of learning*) centro;
(*of a saddle*) batalla; (*of human body*)
nalgas; (theat) localidad; **reclining seat** (*as
in car*) asiento abatible; ‖ *tr* sentar; tener
asientos para; poner asiento a (*una silla*);
echar fondillos a (*pantalones*); arraigar,
establecer; **to be seated** estar. sentado; **to
seat oneself** sentarse

seat belt *s* cinturón *m* de asiento
seat cover *s* funda de asiento, cubreasiento
SEATO ['sito] *s* (acronym) la O.T.A.S.E.
sea wall *s* dique marítimo
sea'way' *s* ruta marítima; avance *m* de un buque por mar; vía de agua interior para buques de alta mar; mar gruesa
sea'weed' *s* alga marina; plantas marinas
sea wind *s* viento que sopla del mar
sea'wor'thy *adj* marinero, en condiciones de navegar
sec. *abbr* **secant, second, secondary, secretary, section, sector**
secede [sɪ'sid] *intr* separarse, retirarse
secession [sɪ'sɛʃən] *s* secesión
seclude [sɪ'klud] *tr* recluir
secluded [sɪ'kludɪd] *adj* aislado, apartado, solitario
seclusion [sɪ'kluʒən] *s* reclusión, soledad
second ['sɛkənd] *adj* segundo; **to be second to none** ser tan bueno como el que más, no tener segundo ‖ *adv* en segundo lugar ‖ *s* segundo; artículo de segunda calidad; (*in dates*) dos *m;* (*in a challenge*) padrino; (aut) segunda (velocidad); (mus) segunda ‖ *tr* secundar; apoyar (*una moción*)
secondar·y ['sɛkən,dɛri] *adj* secundario ‖ *s* (*pl* **-ies**) (elec) secundario
sec'ond-best' *adj* (el) mejor después del primero
sec'ond-class' *adj* de segunda clase
second hand *s* segundero
sec'ond-hand' *adj* de segunda mano, de ocasión
second-hand bookshop *s* librería de viejo
second lieutenant *s* alférez *m*, subteniente *m*
sec'ond•rate' *adj* de segundo orden; de calidad inferior
second sight *s* doble vista
second wind *s* nuevo aliento
secre•cy ['sikrəsi] *s* (*pl* **-cies**) secreto; **in secrecy** en secreto
secret ['sikrɪt] *adj & s* secreto; **in secret** en secreto
secretar·y ['sɛkrɪ,tɛri] *s* (*pl* **-ies**) secretario; (*desk*) secreter *m*, escritorio
secrete [sɪ'krit] *tr* encubrir, esconder; (physiol) secretar
secretive [sɪ'kritɪv] *adj* callado, reservado
sect [sɛkt] *s* secta, comunión
sectarian [sɛk'tɛri•ən] *adj & s* sectario
section ['sɛkʃən] *s* sección; (*of a country*) región; (*of a city*) barrio; (*of a law*) artículo; (*department, bureau*) negociado; (rr) tramo
secular ['sɛkjələr] *adj* secular, seglar ‖ *s* clérigo secular
secularism ['sɛkjələ,rɪzəm] *s* laicismo
secure [sɪ'kjur] *adj* seguro ‖ *tr* asegurar; conseguir, obtener
securi•ty [sɪ'kjurɪti] *s* (*pl* **-ties**) seguridad; (*person*) segurador *m*; **securities** valores *mpl*, obligaciones, títulos
secy. o **sec'y.** *abbr* **secretary**
sedan [sɪ'dæn] *s* silla de manos; (aut) sedán *m*
sedate [sɪ'det] *adj* sentado, sosegado

sedative ['sɛdətɪv] *adj & s* sedativo
sedentary ['sɛdən,tɛri] *adj* sedentario
sedge [sɛdʒ] *s* juncia
sediment ['sɛdɪmənt] *s* sedimento
sedition [sɪ'dɪʃən] *s* sedición
seditious [sɪ'dɪʃəs] *adj* sedicioso
seduce [sɪ'djus] *tr* seducir
seducer [sɪ'djusər] *s* seductor *m*
seduction [sɪ'dʌkʃən] *s* seducción
seductive [sɪ'dʌktɪv] *adj* seductivo
sedulous ['sɛdjələs] *adj* cuidadoso, diligente
see [si] *s* (eccl) sede *f* ‖ *v* (*pret* **saw** [sɔ; *pp* **seen** [sin] *tr* ver; **to see off** ir a despedir; **to see through** llevar a cabo; ayudar en un trance difícil ‖ *intr* ver; **see here!** ¡mire Vd.!; **to see into** o **to see through** conocer el juego de
seed [sid] *s* semilla, simiente *f;* **to go to seed** dar semilla; echarse a perder ‖ *tr* sembrar; (*to remove the seeds from*) despepitar ‖ *intr* sembrar; dejar caer semillas
seed'bed' *s* semillero
seedling ['sidlɪŋ] *s* planta de semilla; árbol *m* de pie
seed•y ['sidi] *adj* (*comp* **-ier;** *super* **-iest**) lleno de granos; (coll) andrajoso, raído
seeing ['si•ɪŋ] *adj* vidente ‖ *s* vista, visión ‖ *conj* visto que
Seeing Eye dog *s* perro-lazarillo
seek [sik] *v* (*pret & pp* **sought** [sɔt] *tr* buscar; recorrer buscando; dirigirse a ‖ *intr* buscar; **to seek after** tratar de obtener; **to seek to** esforzarse por
seem [sim] *intr* parecer
seemingly ['simɪŋli] *adv* aparentemente, al parecer
seem•ly ['simli] *adj* (*comp* **-lier;** *super* **-liest**) decente, decoroso, correcto; bien parecido
seep [sip] *intr* escurrirse, rezumarse
seer [sɪr] *s* profeta *m*, vidente *m*
see'saw' *s* balancín *m*, columpio de tabla; (*motion*) vaivén *m* ‖ *intr* columpiarse; alternar; vacilar
seethe [sið] *intr* hervir
segment ['sɛgmənt] *s* segmento
segregate ['sɛgrɪ,get] *tr* segregar
segregationist [,sɛgrɪ'geʃənɪst] *s* segregacionista *mf*
Seine [sen] *s* Sena *m*
seismograph ['saɪzmə,græf] *s* sismógrafo
seismology [saɪz'mɑlədʒi] *s* sismología
seize [siz] *tr* agarrar, asir, coger; atar, prender, sujetar; apoderarse de; comprender; (law) embargar, secuestrar; aprovecharse de (*una oportunidad*)
seizure ['siʒər] *s* prendimiento, prisión; captura, toma; (*of an illness*) ataque *m;* (law) embargo, secuestro
seldom ['sɛldəm] *adv* raramente, rara vez
select [sɪ'lɛkt] *adj* escogido, selecto ‖ *tr* seleccionar
selectee [sɪ,lɛk'ti] *s* (mil) quinto
selection [sɪ'lɛkʃən] *s* selección; trozo escogido; (*of goods for sale*) surtido
self [sɛlf] *adj* mismo ‖ *pron* sí mismo ‖ *s* (*pl* **selves** [sɛlvz]) uno mismo; ser *m;* yo; **all by one's self** sin ayuda de nadie

sc
se

self′-abuse′ *s* abuso de sí mismo; masturbación

self′-addressed′ envelope *s* sobre *m* con el nombre y dirección del remitente

self′-cen′tered *adj* egocéntrico

self′-con′scious *adj* cohibido, apocado, tímido

self′-con·trol′ *s* dominio de sí mismo; autodisciplina

self′-de·fense′ *s* autodefensa; **in self-defense** en defensa propia

self′-de·ni′al *s* abnegación

self′-de·ter′mi·na′tion *s* autodeterminación

self′-dis′cipline *s* autodisciplina

self′-ed′u·cat′ed *adj* autodidacto

self′-em·ployed′ *adj* que trabaja por su propia cuenta

self′-ev′i·dent *adj* patente, manifiesto

self′-ex·plan′a·tor′y *adj* que se explica por sí mismo

self′-glor′i·fi·ca′tion *s* egolatría

self′-gov′ernment *s* autogobierno, autonomía; dominio sobre sí mismo

self′-im·por′tant *adj* altivo, arrogante

self′-in·dul′gence *s* intemperancia, desenfreno

self′-in′terest *s* egoísmo, interés *m* personal

selfish [ˈsɛlfɪʃ] *adj* egoísta

selfishness [ˈsɛlfɪʃnɪs] *s* egoísmo

selfless [ˈsɛlflɪs] *adj* desinteresado

self′-liq′ui·dat′ing *adj* autoamortizable

self′-love′ *s* amor propio, egoísmo

self′-made′ man *s* hijo de sus propias obras

self′-por′trait *s* autorretrato

self′-pos·sessed′ *adj* dueño de sí mismo

self′-pres′er·va′tion *s* propia conservación

self′-re·li′ant *adj* confiado en sí mismo

self′-re·spect′ing *adj* lleno de dignidad, decoroso

self′-right′eous *adj* santurrón

self′-sac′ri·fice′ *s* sacrificio de sí mismo

self′-same′ *adj* mismísimo

self′-sat′is·fied′ *adj* pagado de sí mismo

self′-seal′ing *adj* autopegado

self′-seek′ing *adj* egoísta ‖ *s* egoísmo

self′-ser′vice restaurant *s* restaurante *m* de libre servicio, restaurante de autoservicio

self′-start′er *s* arranque automático

self′-sup·port′ *s* mantenimiento económico propio

self′-taught′ *adj* autodidacto

self′-willed′ *adj* obstinado, terco

self′-wind′ing clock *s* reloj *m* de cuerda automática, reloj de autocuerda

self′-wor′ship *s* egolatría

sell [sɛl] *v* (*pret & pp* **sold** [sold] *tr* vender; **to sell out** realizar, saldar; (*to betray*) vender ‖ *intr* venderse, estar de venta; **to sell for** venderse a o en (*p.ej., cien pesetas*); **to sell off** bajar (*el mercado de valores*); **to sell out** venderlo todo, realizar

seller [ˈsɛlər] *s* vendedor *m*

sell′out′ *s* (slang) realización, saldo; (slang) traición

Seltzer water [ˈsɛltsər] *s* agua de seltz

selvage [ˈsɛlvɪdʒ] *s* orillo, vendo

semantic [sɪˈmæntɪk] *adj* semántico ‖ **semantics** *s* semántica

semaphore [ˈsɛmə‚for] *s* semáforo; (rr) disco de señales

semblance [ˈsɛmbləns] *s* apariencia, imagen *f*, simulacro

semen [ˈsimɛn] *s* semen *m*

semester [sɪˈmɛstər] *adj* semestral ‖ *s* semestre *m*

semester hour *s* hora semestral

sem′ico′lon *s* punto y coma

sem′iconduc′tor *s* semiconductor *m*

sem′icon′scious *adj* semiconsciente

sem′ifi′nal *adj & s* (sport) semifinal *f*

sem′ilearn′ed *adj* semiculto

sem′imonth′ly *adj* quincenal ‖ *s* (*pl* **-lies**) periódico quincenal

seminar [ˈsɛmɪ‚nɑr] *s* seminario

seminar·y [ˈsɛmɪ‚nɛri] *s* (*pl* **-ies**) seminario

sem′ipre′cious *adj* semiprecioso, fino

Semite [ˈsɛmaɪt] o [ˈsimaɪt] *s* semita *mf*

Semitic [sɪˈmɪtɪk] *adj* semítico ‖ *s* semita *mf*; (*language*) semita *m*

sem′itrail′er *s* semi-remolque *m*

sem′iweek′ly *adj* bisemanal ‖ *s* (*pl* **-lies**) periódico bisemanal

sem′iyear′ly *adj* semestral

Sen. o **sen.** *abbr* **Senate, Senator, Senior**

senate [ˈsɛnɪt] *s* senado

senator [ˈsɛnətər] *s* senador *m*

senatorship [ˈsɛnətər‚ʃɪp] *s* senaduría

send [sɛnd] *v* (*pret & pp* **sent** [sɛnt]) *tr* enviar, mandar; expedir, remitir; lanzar (*una bola, flecha, etc.*); **to send back** devolver, reenviar; **to send packing** despedir con cajas destempladas ‖ *intr* (rad) transmitir; **to send for** enviar por, enviar a buscar

sender [ˈsɛndər] *s* remitente *mf*; (telg) transmisor *m*

send′-off′ *s* (coll) despedida afectuosa

senile [ˈsinaɪl] o [ˈsɪnɪl] *adj* senil

senility [sɪˈnɪlɪti] *s* senilidad; (pathol) senilismo

senior [ˈsinjər] *adj* mayor, de mayor edad; viejo; del último año; padre, p.ej., **John Jones, Senior** Juan Jones, padre ‖ *s* mayor *m*; socio más antiguo; alumno del último año

senior citizens *spl* gente *f* de edad

seniority [sinˈjɔrɪti] *s* antigüedad; precedencia, prioridad

sensation [sɛnˈseʃən] *s* sensación

sense [sɛns] *s* sentido; **to make sense out of** comprender, explicarse ‖ *tr* intuir, sentir, sospechar; comprender

senseless [ˈsɛnslɪs] *adj* falto de sentido; desmayado; insensato, necio

sense of guilt *s* cargo de conciencia

sense of humor *s* sentido de humor

sense organ *s* órgano sensorio

sensibili·ty [‚sɛnsɪˈbɪlɪti] *s* (*pl* **-ties**) sensibilidad; **sensibilities** sentimientos delicados

sensible [ˈsɛnsɪbəl] *adj* cuerdo, sensato; perceptible, sensible; equilibrado

sensitive [ˈsɛnsɪtɪv] *adj* sensible; (*of the senses*) sensorio, sensitivo sensitize ['sɛnsɪ,taɪz] tr sensibilizar

sensory ['sɛnsəri] adj sensorio

sensual ['sɛnʃu•əl] adj sensual, voluptuoso

sensuous ['sɛn/u•əs] adj sensual

sentence ['sɛntəns] s (gram) frase f, oración; (law) sentencia ‖ tr sentenciar, condenar

sentiment ['sɛntɪmənt] s sentimiento

sentimentali•ty [,sɛntɪmən'tælɪti] s (pl -ties) sentimentalismo

sentinel ['sɛntɪnəl] s centinela m or f; to stand sentinel estar de centinela, hacer centinela

sen•try ['sɛntri] s (pl -tries) centinela m or f

sentry box s garita de centinela

separate ['sɛpərɪt] adj separado; suelto ‖ ['sɛpə,ret] tr separar ‖ intr separarse

separation [,sɛpə'reʃən] s separación

separation of powers s (pol) separación de poderes

Sephardic [sɪ'fɑrdɪk] adj sefardí, sefardita

Sephardim [sɪ'fɑrdɪm] spl sefardíes mpl

September [sɛp'tɛmbər] s septiembre m

septet [sɛp'tɛt] s septeto

septic ['sɛptɪk] adj séptico

sepulcher ['sɛpəlkər] s sepulcro

seq. abbr sequentia (Lat) the following

sequel ['sikwəl] s resultado, secuela; continuación

sequence ['sikwəns] s serie f, sucesión; (cards) secansa, escalera, runfla; (gram, mov & mus) secuencia

sequester [sɪ'kwɛstər] tr apartar, separar; (law) secuestrar

sequin ['sikwɪn] s lentejuela

ser•aph ['sɛrəf] s (pl -aphs o -aphim [əfɪm]) serafín m

Serb [sʌrb] adj & s servio

Serbia ['sʌrbɪ•ə] s Servia

Serbian ['sʌrbɪ•ən] adj & s servio

Serbo-Croatian [,sʌrbokro'eʃən] adj & s servocroata mf

sere [sɪr] adj seco, marchito

serenade [,sɛrə'ned] s serenata ‖ tr dar serenata a ‖ intr dar serenatas

serene [sɪ'rin] adj sereno

serenity [sɪ'rɛnɪti] s serenidad

serf [sʌrf] s siervo de la gleba

serfdom ['sʌrfdəm] s servidumbre de la gleba

serge [sʌrdʒ] s sarga

sergeant ['sɑrdʒənt] s sargento

ser'geant•at•arms' s (pl sergeants-at-arms) oficial m de orden

sergeant major s (pl sergeant majors) sargento mayor

serial ['sɪrɪ•əl] adj serial; publicado por entregas ‖ s cuento o novela por entregas; (rad) serial m, serial radiado, emisión seriada

serially ['sɪrɪ•əli] adv en serie, por series; por entregas

serial number s número de serie

se•ries ['sɪriz] s (pl -ries) serie f

serious ['sɪrɪ•əs] adj (e.g., person, face, matter) serio; (e.g., condition, illness) grave

sermon ['sʌrmən] s sermón m

sermonize ['sʌrmə,naɪz] tr & intr sermonear

serpent ['sʌrpənt] s serpiente f

se•rum ['sɪrəm] s (pl -rums o -ra [rə]) suero

servant ['sʌrvənt] s criado, sirviente m

servant girl s criada, sirvienta

servant problem s crisis f del servicio doméstico

serve [sʌrv] s (in tennis) saque ,n, servicio ‖ tr servir; (to supply) abastecer, proporcionar; cumplir (una condena); (in tennis) servir; it serves me right bien me lo merezco ‖ intr servir; to serve as servir de

service ['sʌrvɪs] s servicio; at your service para servir a Vd.; out of service fuera de servicio; the services las fuerzas armadas ‖ tr instalar; mantener, reparar

serviceable ['sʌrvɪsəbəl] adj útil; duradero; cómodo

serviceman ['sʌrvɪs,mæn] s (pl -men [,mən]) reparador m, mecánico; militar m

service record s hoja de servicios

service station s estación de servicio, taller m de reparaciones

service stripe s galón m de servicio

servile ['sʌrvɪl] adj servil

servitude ['sʌrvɪ,tjud] s servidumbre; trabajos forzados

sesame ['sɛsəmi] s sésamo; open sesame sésamo ábrete

session ['sɛʃən] s sesión; to be in session sesionar

set [sɛt] adj determinado, resuelto; inflexible, obstinado; fijo, firme; estudiado, meditado ‖ s (of books, chairs, etc.) juego; (of gears) tren m; (of horses) pareja; (of diamonds) aderezo; (of tennis) partida; (of dishes) servicio; (of kitchen utensils) batería; clase f, grupo; equipo; porte m, postura; (of a garment) caída, ajuste m; (of glue) endurecimiento; (of cement) fraguado; (of artificial teeth) caja; (mov) plató m; (rad) aparato; (theat) decoración ‖ v (pret & pp set; ger setting) tr asentar; colocar, poner; establecer, instalar; arreglar, preparar; adornar; apostar; poner (un reloj) en hora; (in bridge) reenvidar; poner, meter, pegar (fuego); fijar (el precio); engastar, montar (una piedra preciosa); encasar (un hueso dislocado); disponer (los tipos); triscar (una sierra); armar, colocar (una trampa); fijar (el peinado); poner (la mesa); dar (un ejemplo); to set back parar; poner obstáculos a; hacer retroceder; atrasar, retrasar (el reloj); to set forth exponer, dar a conocer; to set one's heart on tener la esperanza puesta en; to set store by dar mucha importancia a; to set up shop poner tienda; to set up the drinks (coll) convidar a beber ‖ intr ponerse (el Sol, la Luna, etc.); cuajarse (un líquido); endurecerse (la cola); fraguar (el cemento, el yeso); empollar (una gallina); caer, sentar (una prenda de vestir); to set about ponerse a; to set out ponerse en camino; emprender un negocio; to set out to ponerse a; to set to work poner manos a la obra; to set upon acometer, atacar

set'back' s revés m, contrariedad

set'screw' s tornillo de presión

settee [sɛ'ti] s sofá m, canapé m
setting ['sɛtɪŋ] s (environment) ambiente m; (of a gem) engaste m, montadura; (of cement) fraguado; (e.g., of the sun) puesta, ocaso; (theat) escena; (theat) puesta en escena, decoración
set'ting-up' exercises spl ejercicios sin aparatos, gimnasia sueca
settle ['sɛtəl] tr asentar, colocar; asegurar, fijar; componer, conciliar; calmar, moderar; matar (el polvo); casar; poblar, colonizar; ajustar, arreglar (cuentas) ‖ intr asentarse (un líquido, un edificio); establecerse; componerse; calmarse, moderarse; solidificarse; **to settle down to work** ponerse seriamente a trabajar; **to settle on** escoger; fijar (p.ej., una fecha)
settlement ['sɛtəlmənt] s establecimiento; colonia, caserío; decisión; (of accounts) arreglo, ajuste m; traspaso; casa de beneficencia
settler ['sɛtlər] s fundador m; poblador m; colono; árbitro, conciliador m
set'up' s porte m, postura; (e.g., of the parts of a machine) disposición; (coll) organización; (slang) invitación a beber
seven ['sɛvən] adj & pron siete ‖ s siete m; **seven o'clock** las siete
seven hundred adj & pron setecientos ‖ s setecientos m
seventeen ['sɛvən'tin] adj, pron & s diecisiete m, diez y siete
seventeenth ['sɛvən'tinθ] adj & s (in a series) decimoséptimo; (part) diecisieteavo ‖ s (in dates) diecisiete m
seventh ['sɛvənθ] adj & s séptimo ‖ s (in dates) siete m
seventieth ['sɛvəntɪ·ɪθ] adj & s (in a series) septuagésimo; (part) setentavo
seven•ty ['sɛvəntɪ] adj & pron setenta ‖ s (pl -ties) setenta m
sever ['sɛvər] tr desunir, separar; romper (relaciones) ‖ intr desunirse, separarse
several ['sɛvərəl] adj diversos, varios; distintos, respectivos ‖ spl varios; algunos
severance pay ['sɛvərəns] s indemnización por despido
severe [sɪ'vɪr] adj severo; (weather) riguroso; recio, violento; (look) adusto; (pain) agudo; (illness) grave
sew [so] v (pret **sewed**; pp **sewed** o **sewn**) tr & intr coser
sewage ['su·ɪdʒ] o ['sju·ɪdʒ] s agua de albañal, aguas cloacales
sew'age-dis•pos'al plant s estación depuradora
sewer ['su·ər] o ['sju·ər] s albañal m, cloaca, alcantarilla ‖ tr alcantarillar
sewerage ['su·ərɪdʒ] o ['sju·ərɪdʒ] s desagüe m; (system) alcantarillado; aguas de albañal
sewing basket ['so·ɪŋ] s cesta de costura
sewing machine s máquina de coser
sex [sɛks] s sexo; **the fair sex** el bello sexo; **the sterner sex** el sexo feo
sex appeal s atracción sexual; encanto femenino
sexism ['sɛksɪzəm] s sexismo

sexist ['sɛksɪst] adj & s sexista
sextant ['sɛkstənt] s sextante m
sextet [sɛks'tɛt] s sexteto
sexton ['sɛkstən] s sacristán m
sexual ['sɛkʃu·əl] adj sexual
sex•y ['sɛksi] adj (comp **-ier**; super **-iest**) (slang) sicalíptico, erótico
shab•by ['ʃæbi] adj (comp **-bier**; super **-biest**) gastado, raído, usado; andrajoso, desaseado; ruin, vil
shack [ʃæk] s casucha, choza
shackle ['ʃækəl] s grillete m; (to tie an animal) maniota; (fig) impedimento, traba; **shackles** cadenas, esposas, grillos ‖ tr poner grilletes a; poner esposas a; encadenar; (fig) trabar
shad [ʃæd] s sábalo, alosa
shade [ʃed] s sombra; (of a lamp) pantalla; (of a window) cortina, estor m, visillo, cortina de resorte; (for the eyes) visera; (hue; slight difference) matiz m; **shades** (slang) gafas fpl de sol; **the shades** las tinieblas; (of the dead) las sombras ‖ tr sombrear; obscurecer; rebajar ligeramente (el precio)
shadow ['ʃædo] s sombra ‖ tr sombrear; simbolizar; acechar, espiar (a una persona); **to shadow forth** representar vagamente, representar de un modo profético
shadowy ['ʃædo·i] adj sombroso; ligero, vago; imaginario; simbólico
shad•y ['ʃedi] adj (comp **-ier**; super **-iest**) sombrío, umbroso; (coll) sospechoso; (coll) de mala fama; (story) (coll) verde; **to keep shady** (slang) no dejarse ver
shaft [ʃæft] s dardo, flecha, saeta; (of an arrow; of a feather) astil m; (of light) rayo; (of a wagon) vara alcándara, limonera; (of a mine; of an elevator) pozo; (of a column) fuste m, caña; (of a flag) asta; (of a motor) árbol m; (to make fun of someone) dardo
shag•gy ['ʃægi] adj (comp **-gier**; super **-giest**) hirsuto, peludo, veludo; lanudo; áspero
shake [ʃek] s sacudida; (coll) apretón m de manos; (slang) instante m, momento ‖ v (pret **shook** [ʃuk]; pp **shaken**) tr sacudir; agitar; apretar, estrechar (la mano a uno); inquietar, perturbar; (to get rid of) (slang) dar esquinazo a, zafarse de ‖ intr sacudirse; agitarse; temblar; inquietarse, perturbarse; (from cold) tiritar; **shake!** (coll) ¡choque Vd. esos cinco!, ¡vengan esos cinco!
shake'down' s (slang) exacción, concusión
shakedown cruise s viaje m de pruebas
shake'-up' s profunda conmoción; cambio de personal, reorganización completa
shak•y ['ʃeki] adj (comp **-ier**; super **-iest**) trémulo, vacilante, movedizo; indigno de confianza
shall [ʃæl] v (cond **should** [ʃud]) v aux empléase para formar (1) el fut de ind, p.ej., **I shall do it** lo haré; (2) el fut perf de ind, p.ej., **I shall have done it** lo habré hecho; (3) el modo potencial, p.ej., **what shall I do?** ¿qué he de hacer?, ¿qué debo hacer?

shallow [ˈʃælo] *adj* bajo, poco profundo; (fig) frívolo, superficial

sham [ʃæm] *adj* falso, fingido; postizo ‖ *s* fingimiento, falsificación, engaño; (*person*) (coll) farsante *mf;* ‖ *v* (*pret & pp* **shammed;** *ger* **shamming**) *tr & intr* fingir

sham battle *s* simulacro de combate

shambles [ˈʃæmbəlz] *s* destrucción, ruina; (*confusion, mess*) lío, revoltijo

shame [ʃem] *s* vergüenza; deshonra; (*disgrace*) metedura; **shame on you!** ¡qué vergüenza!; **what a shame!** ¡qué lástima! ‖ *tr* avergonzar; deshonrar

shameful [ˈʃemfəl] *adj* vergonzoso

shameless [ˈʃemlɪs] *adj* descarado, desvergonzado

shampoo [ʃæmˈpu] *s* champú *m* ‖ *tr* lavar (*la cabeza*); lavar la cabeza a

shamrock [ˈʃæmrak] *s* trébol *m* irlandés

shanghai [ˈʃæŋhaɪ] o [ʃæŋˈhaɪ] *tr* embarcar emborrachando, embarcar narcotizando; llevarse con violencia, llevarse con engaño

shank [ʃæŋk] *s* (*of the leg*) caña, canilla; (*of an animal*) pierna; (*of a bird*) zanca; (*of an anchor*) caña; (*of the sole of a shoe*) enfranque *m;* astil *m,* caña, fuste *m;* extremidad, remate *m;* **to go** o **to ride on shank's mare** caminar en coche de San Francisco

shan·ty [ˈʃænti] *s* (*pl* **-ties**) chabola, choza

shape [ʃep] *s* forma; **in bad shape** (coll) arruinado; (coll) muy enfermo; **out of shape** deformado; descompuesto; (*twisted*) sobornado ‖ *tr* formar, dar forma a; amoldar ‖ *intr* formarse; **to shape up** tomar forma; desarrollarse bien

shapeless [ˈʃeplɪs] *adj* informe

shape·ly [ˈʃepli] *adj* (*comp* **-lier:** *super* **-liest**) bien formado, esbelto

share [ʃɛr] *s* parte *f,* porción; (*of stock in a company*) acción; **to go shares** ir a la parte ‖ *tr* (*to enjoy jointly*) compartir; (*to apportion*) repartir ‖ *intr* participar, tener parte

share'hold'er *s* accionista *mf*

shark [ʃark] *s* tiburón *m; (swindler)* estafador *m;* (slang) experto, perito

sharp [ʃarp] *adj* afilado, agudo; anguloso; (*curve, slope, etc.*) fuerte, pronunciado; (*photograph*) nítido; (*hearing*) fino; (*step, gait*) rápido; atento, despierto; picante, mordaz; listo, vivo; (*mus*) sostenido; (slang) elegante ‖ **sharp features** facciones bien marcadas ‖ *adv* agudamente; en punto, p.ej., **at four o'clock sharp** a las cuatro en punto ‖ *s* (*mus*) sostenido

sharpen [ˈʃarpən] *tr* aguzar; sacar punta a (*un lápiz*) ‖ *intr* afilarse

sharper [ˈʃarpər] *s* fullero, jugador *m* de ventaja

sharp'shoot'er *s* tirador certero; (mil) tirador distinguido

shatter [ˈʃætər] *tr* hacer astillas, romper de un golpe; quebrantar (*la salud*); destruir, destrozar; agitar, perturbar ‖ *intr* hacerse pedazos, romperse

shat'ter·proof' *adj* inastillable

shave [ʃev] *s* afeitado; rebanada delgada; **to have a close shave** (coll) escapar en una tabla ‖ *tr* afeitar (*la cara*); raer, raspar; (*to graze; to cut close*) rozar; (*to slice thin*) rebanar; (carp) cepillar ‖ *intr* afeitarse

shaving [ˈʃevɪŋ] *adj* de afeitar, para afeitar, p.ej., **shaving soap** jabón *m* de o para afeitar ‖ *s* afeitado; **shavings** acepilladuras, virutas

shaving lotion *s* loción facial

shawl [ʃɔl] *s* chal *m,* mantón *m*

she [ʃi] *pron pers* (*pl* **they**) ella ‖ *s* (*pl* **shes**) hembra

sheaf [ʃif] *s* (*pl* **sheaves** [ʃivz]) gavilla; (*of paper*) atado

shear [ʃir] *s* hoja de la tijera; **shears** tijeras grandes); (*to cut metal*) cizallas ‖ *v* (*pret* **sheared;** *pp* **sheared** o **shorn** [ʃorn]) *tr* esquilar, trasquilar (*las ovejas*); cizallar; quitar cortando; tundir (*paño*)

sheath [ʃiθ] *s* (**sheaths** [ʃiðz]) envoltura, estuche *m,* funda; (*for a sword*) funda, vaina

sheathe [ʃið] *tr* enfundar, envainar

shed [ʃɛd] *s* cobertizo; (*line from which water flows in two directions*) vertiente *m & f* ‖ *v* (*pret & pp* **shed;** *ger* **shedding**) *tr* derramar, verter (*p.ej., sangre*); dar, echar, esparcir (*luz*); mudar (*la pluma, el pellejo*)

sheen [ʃin] *s* brillo, lustre *m;* (*of pressed cloth*) prensado

sheep [ʃip] *s* (*pl* **sheep**) carnero; (*female*) oveja; tonto; **to make sheep's eyes (at)** mirar con ojos de carnero degollado

sheep dog *s* perro ovejero, perro de pastor

sheep'fold' *s* aprisco, redil *m*

sheepish [ˈʃipɪʃ] *adj* avergonzado, corrido; tímido, tonto

sheep'skin' *s* (*undressed*) zalea; (*dressed*) badana; (coll) diploma *m*

sheer [ʃir] *adj* delgado, fino, ligero; casi transparente; escarpado; puro, sin mezcla; completo ‖ *intr* desviarse

sheet [ʃit] *s* (e.g., for the bed) sábana; (*of paper*) hoja; (*of metal*) hoja, lámina; (*of water*) extensión; hoja impresa; periódico; (naut) escota

sheet lightning *s* fucilazo

sheet metal *s* metal laminado

sheet music *s* música en hojas sueltas

sheik [ʃik] *s* jeque *m;* (*great lover*) (slang) sultán *m*

shelf [ʃɛlf] *s* (*pl* **shelves** [ʃɛlvz]) estante *m,* anaquel *m;* bajío, banco de arena; **on the shelf** arrinconado, desechado, olvidado

shell [ʃɛl] *s* (*of an egg, nut, etc.*) cáscara; (*of a crustacean*) caparazón *m,* concha; (*of a vegetable*) vaina; (*of a cartridge*) cápsula; (*of a boiler*) cuerpo; armazón *f,* esqueleto; bomba, proyectil *m;* (*long, narrow racing boat*) (sport) yola ‖ *tr* descascarar; desgranar, desvainar (*legumbres*); bombardear, cañonear; **to shell out** (coll) entregar (*dinero*)

shel·lac [ʃəˈlæk] *s* laca, goma laca ‖ *v* (*pret & pp* **-lacked;** *ger* **-lacking**) *tr* barnizar con goma laca; (slang) azotar, zurrar; (slang) derrotar

shell'fish' *s* marisco, mariscos

shell hole *s* (mil) embudo

se
sh

shell shock s neurosis f de guerra

shelter [ˈʃɛltər] s abrigo, asilo, amparo, refugio; **to take shelter** abrigarse, refugiarse ‖ tr abrigar, amparar, proteger

shelve [ʃɛlv] tr poner sobre un estante; proveer de estantes; arrinconar, dejar a un lado; diferir indefinidamente

shepherd [ˈʃɛpərd] s pastor m ‖ tr pastorear (a las ovejas o los fieles)

shepherd dog s perro ovejero, perro de pastor

shepherdess [ˈʃɛpərdɪs] s pastora

sherbet [ˈʃʌrbət] s sorbete m

shereef [ʃɛˈrif] s jerife m

sheriff [ˈʃɛrɪf] s alguacil m mayor

sher•ry [ˈʃɛri] s (pl -ries) jerez m, vino de Jerez

shield [ʃild] s escudo; (for armpit) sobaquera; (elec) blindaje m ‖ tr amparar, defender, escudar; (elec) blindar

shift [ʃɪft] s cambio; (order of work or other activity) turno; (group of workmen) tanda; maña, subterfugio ‖ tr cambiar; deshacerse de; echar (la culpa); (aut) cambiar de (marcha) ‖ intr cambiar, cambiar de puesto; mañear; (naut) correrse (el lastre); (rr) maniobrar; **to shift for oneself** ayudarse, ingeniarse

shift key s tecla de cambio, palanca de mayúsculas

shiftless [ˈʃɪftlɪs] adj desidioso, perezoso

shiftlessness [ˈʃɪftlɪsnɪs] s galbana

shift•y [ˈʃɪfti] adj (comp -ier; super -iest) ingenioso, mañoso; evasivo, tramoyista; (glance) huyente

shilling [ˈʃɪlɪŋ] s chelín m

shimmer [ˈʃɪmər] s luz trémula ‖ intr rielar

shin [ʃɪn] s espinilla ‖ v (pret & pp shinned; ger shinning) tr & intr trepar

shin'bone' s espinilla

shine [ʃaɪn] s brillo, luz f; bruñido, lustre m; buen tiempo; (on shoes) (coll) lustre m; **to take a shine to** (slang) tomar simpatía a ‖ v (pret & pp shined) tr pulir, lustrar; (coll) embolar, limpiar (el calzado) ‖ v (pret & pp shone [ʃon]) intr brillar, lucir, resplandecer; hacer sol, hacer buen tiempo; (to be distinguished, to stand out) (fig) brillar, lucir

shingle [ˈʃɪŋgəl] s ripia, teja de madera; tejamaní m (Am); pelo a la garçonne; (coll) letrero de oficina; **shingles** (pathol) zona; **to hang out one's shingle** (coll) abrir una oficina; (coll) abrir un consultorio médico ‖ tr cubrir con ripias; cortar (el pelo) a la garçonne

shining [ˈʃaɪnɪŋ] adj brillante, luciente

shin•y [ˈʃaɪni] adj (comp -ier; super -iest) brillante, lustroso; (paper) glaseado; (from much wear) brilloso

ship [ʃɪp] s nave f, buque m, barco, navío; (steamer) vapor m; aeronave f ‖ v (pret & pp shipped; ger shipping) tr embarcar; enviar, remitir, remesar; armar (los remos); embarcar (agua) ‖ intr embarcarse

ship'board' s bordo; **on shipboard** a bordo

ship'build'er s arquitecto naval, constructor m de buques

ship'build'ing s arquitectura naval, construcción de buques

ship'mate' s camarada m de a bordo

shipment [ˈʃɪpmənt] s embarque m (por agua); envío, expedición, remesa

shipper [ˈʃɪpər] s embarcador m; expedidor m, remitente mf

shipping memo [ˈʃɪpɪŋ] s nota de remisión

ship'shape' adj & adv en buen orden

ship'side' adj & adv al costado del buque ‖ s zona de embarque y desembarque; muelle m

ship's papers spl documentación del buque

ship's time s hora local del buque

ship'wreck' s naufragio; barco náufrago ‖ tr hacer naufragar ‖ intr naufragar

ship'yard' s astillero, varadero

shirk [ʃʌrk] tr evitar (el trabajo); faltar a (un deber) ‖ intr escurrir el hombro

shirred eggs [ʃʌrd] spl huevos al plato

shirt [ʃʌrt] s camisa; **to keep one's shirt on** (slang) quedarse sereno; **to lose one's shirt** (slang) perder hasta la camisa

shirt'band' s cuello de camisa

shirt front s pechera de camisa, cami solín m

shirt sleeve s manga de camisa; **in shirt sleeves** en mangas de camisa

shirt'tail' s faldón m, pañal m

shirt'waist' s blusa (de mujer)

shiver [ˈʃɪvər] s estremecimiento, tiritón m ‖ intr estremecerse, tiritar

shoal [ʃol] s bajío, banco de arena

shock [ʃak] s (sudden and violent blow or encounter) choque m; (sudden agitation of mind or emotions) sobresalto; temblor m de tierra; (of hair) greña; (agr) tresnal m; (elec) sacudida; (med) choque m; (profound depression) (pathol) choque m; (coll) parálisis f ‖ tr chocar; sobresaltar; dar una sacudida eléctrica a; chocar, escandalizar

shock absorber [æbˈsɔrbər] s amortiguador m

shocker [ˈʃakər] s (slang) novelucha; película horripilante

shocking [ˈʃakɪŋ] adj chocante, escandalizador

shock troops spl tropas de asalto

shod•dy [ˈʃadi] adj (comp -dier; super -diest) falso, de imitación

shoe [ʃu] s (which goes above the ankle) bota, botina; (which does not go above the ankle) zapato; (of a tire) cubierta; **to put on one's shoes** calzarse ‖ v (pret & pp shod [ʃad]) tr calzar; herrar (un caballo)

shoe'black' s limpiabotas m

shoe'horn' s calzador m

shoe'lace' s cordón m de zapato, lazo de zapato

shoe'mak'er s zapatero; zapatero remendón

shoe mender [ˈmɛndər] s zapatero remendón

shoe polish s betún m, bola

shoe'shine' s brillo, lustre m; limpiabotas m

shoe store s zapatería

shoe′string′ s cordón m de zapato, lazo de zapato; **on a shoestring** con muy poco dinero

shoe tree s horma

shoo [ʃu] tr & intr oxear

shoot [ʃut] s (sprout, twig) renuevo, vástago; conducto inclinado; (for grain, sand, etc.) tolva; tiro al blanco, cortamen m de tiradores; (hunting party) partida de caza ‖ v (pret & pp **shot** [ʃat]) tr tirar, disparar (un arma); herir o matar con arma; (to execute with a discharge of rifles) fusilar; fotografiar; (to take a moving picture of) rodar, filmar; echar (los dados); medir la altura de (p.ej., el Sol); **to shoot down** derribar (un avión); **to shoot up** (slang) destrozar echando balas a diestra y siniestra; (drugs) picarse, pincharse ‖ intr tirar; nacer, brotar; lanzarse, precipitarse, moverse rápidamente; punzar (un dolor, una llaga); **to shoot at** tirar a; (to strive for) (coll) poner el tiro en

shooting gallery s galería de tiro al blanco

shooting match s certamen m de tiro al blanco; (slang) conjunto, totalidad

shooting star s estrella fugaz, estrella filante

shoot′out′ s balaceo, balacera (SAm)

shop [ʃap] s (store) tienda; (workshop) taller m; **to talk shop** hablar de su oficio, hablar del propio trabajo (fuera de tiempo) ‖ v (pret & pp **shopped;** ger **shopping**) intr ir de compras, ir de tiendas; **to go shopping** ir de compras, ir de tiendas; **to send shopping** mandar a la compra; **to shop around** ir de tienda en tienda buscando gangas

shop′girl′ s muchacha de tienda

shop′keep′er s tendero, baratero

shoplifter [′ʃap,lɪftər] s mechera, ratero de tiendas

shopper [′ʃapər] s comprador m

shopping center s centro comercial (grupo de establecimientos minoristas, con aparcamiento)

shopping district s barrio comercial

shop′win′dow s escaparate m (de tienda); aparador m (Mex)

shop′work′ s trabajo de taller

shop′worn′ adj desgastado con el trajín de la tienda

shore [ʃor] s orilla, ribera; costa, playa; **shores** (poet) clima m, región ‖ tr acodalar, apuntalar

shore dinner s comida de pescado y mariscos

shore leave s (nav) permiso para ir a tierra

shore line s línea de la playa; línea de buques costeros

shore patrol s (nav) patrulla en tierra

short [ʃort] adj (in space, time, and quantity) corto; (in time) breve; (in stature) bajo; (fig) corto, sucinto; (fig) brusco, seco; **in a short time** dentro de poco; **in short** en fin; **on short notice** con poco tiempo de aviso; **to be short of** estar escaso de; **short of breath** corto de resuello ‖ adv brevemente; bruscamente; (without possessing the stock sold) al descubierto, p.ej., **to sell short** vender al descubierto; **to run short of**

acabársele a uno, p.ej., **I am running short of gasoline** se me acaba la gasolina; **to stop short** parar de repente ‖ s (elec) cortocircuito; (mov) cortometraje m; **shorts** calzones cortos, calzoncillos ‖ tr (elec) poner en cortocircuito ‖ intr (elec) ponerse en cortocircuito

shortage [′ʃortɪdʒ] s carestía, escasez f, falta; déficit m; (from pilfering) substracción

short′cake′ s torta de frutas; torta quebradiza

short′change′ tr (coll) no devolver la vuelta debida a

short circuit s (elec) cortocircuito

short′cir′cuit tr (elec) cortocircuitar ‖ intr (elec) cortocircuitarse

short′com′ing s falta, defecto, desperfecto

short cut s atajo; (method) remediavagos m

shorten [′ʃortən] tr acortar, abreviar ‖ intr acortarse, abreviarse

short′hand′ adj taquigráfico ‖ s taquigrafía; **to take shorthand** taquigrafiar

short-lived [′ʃort′laɪvd] o (coll) [′ʃort′lɪvd] adj de breve vida, de breve duración

shortly [′ʃortli] adv en breve, luego; descortésmente; **shortly after** poco tiempo después (de)

short′-range′ adj de poco alcance

short sale s (coll) venta al descubierto

short-sighted [′ʃort′saɪtɪd] adj miope; (fig) falto de perspicacia

short′stop′ s (baseball) medio; guardabosque m, torpedero (Am)

short story s cuento

short-tempered [′ʃort′tɛmpərd] adj de mal genio

short′-term′ adj a corto plazo

shot [ʃat] s tiro, disparo; (hit or wound made with a bullet) balazo; (distance) alcance m; (in certain games) jugada, tirada, golpe m; (of a rocket into space) lanzamiento; conjetura, tentativa; fotografía, instantánea; (small pellets of lead) perdigones mpl; munición; (marksman) tiro; (heavy metal ball) (sport) pesa; (hypodermic injection) (slang) jeringazo; (drink of liquor) (slang) trago; **not by a long shot** ni con mucho, ni por pienso; **to start like a shot** salir disparado

shot′gun′ s escopeta

shot′-put′ s (sport) tiro de la pesa

should [ʃud] v aux empléase para formar (1) el pres de cond, p.ej., **if I should wait for him, I should miss the train** si yo le esperase, perdería el tren; (2) el perf de cond, p.ej., **if I had waited for him, I should have missed the train** si yo le hubiese esperado, habría, perdido el tren; y (3) el modo potencial, p.ej., **he should go at once** debiera salir en seguida; **he should have gone at once** debiera haber salido en seguida

shoulder [′ʃoldər] s hombro; (of slaughtered animal) brazuelo; (of a garment) hombrera; **across the shoulder** en bandolera; **to put one's shoulders to the wheel** arrimar el hombro, echar el pecho al agua; **to turn a cold shoulder to** volver las espaldas a ‖ *tr* cargar sobre las espaldas; tomar sobre sí, hacerse responsable de; empujar con el hombro para abrirse paso

shoulder blade *s* escápula, omóplato

shoulder strap *s* (*of underwear*) presilla; (mil) charretera

shout [ʃaʊt] *s* grito, voz *f* ‖ *tr* gritar, vocear; **to shout down** hacer callar a gritos ‖ *intr* gritar, dar voces

shove [ʃʌv] *s* empujón *m* ‖ *tr* empujar ‖ *intr* dar empujones, avanzar a empujones; **to shove off** alejarse de la costa; (slang) ponerse en marcha, salir

shov·el [ˈʃʌvəl] *s* pala ‖ *v* (*pret & pp* **-eled** o **-elled;** *ger* **-eling** o **-elling**) *tr* traspalar; espalar (*p.ej., la nieve*) ‖ *intr* trabajar con pala

show [ʃo] *s* exhibición, exposición, muestra; espectáculo; (*in the theater*) función; (*each performance of a play or movie*) sesión; demostración, prueba; indicación, señal *f*, signo; apariencia; (*e.g., of confidence*) alarde *m;* (coll) ocasión, oportunidad; ostentación; espectáculo ridículo, hazmerreír *m;* **to make a show of** hacer gala de; **to steal the show from** robar la obra a (*otro actor*) ‖ *tr* mostrar, enseñar; demostrar, probar; poner, proyectar (*un film*); (*e.g., to the door*) acompañar; **to show up** (coll) desenmascarar ‖ *intr* mostrarse, aparecer, asomar; salir (*p.ej., las enaguas*); **to show off** fachendear; **to show through** clarearse, transparentarse; **to show up** (coll) presentarse, dejarse ver

show bill *s* cartel *m*

show business *s* comercio de los espectáculos

show′case′ *s* vitrina (de exposición)

show′down′ *s* cartas boca arriba; (coll) revelación forzosa, arreglo terminante

shower [ˈʃaʊ·ər] *s* (*sudden fall of rain*) aguacero, chaparrón *m;* (*shower bath*) ducha; (*e.g., of bullets*) rociada; despedida de soltera ‖ *tr* regar; **to shower with** colmar de ‖ *intr* llover

shower bath *s* ducha, baño de ducha

show girl *s* (theat) corista *f*, conjuntista *f*

show·man [ˈʃomən] *s* (*pl* **-men** [mən]) empresario de teatro, empresario de circo

show′-off′ *s* (coll) pinturero

show′piece′ *s* objeto de arte sobresaliente

show′place′ *s* sitio o edificio que se exhibe por su belleza o lujo

show′room′ *s* sala de muestras, sala de exhibición

show window *s* escaparate *m* (de tienda); aparador *m* (Mex)

show·y [ˈʃo·i] *adj* (*comp* **-ier;** *super* **-iest**) aparatoso, cursi, ostentoso

shrapnel [ˈʃræpnəl] *s* granada de metralla

shred [ʃrɛd] *s* jirón *m*, tira, triza; fragmento, pizca; **to tear to shreds** hacer trizas ‖ *v* (*pret & pp* **shredded** o **shred;** *ger* **shredding**) *tr* desmenuzar, hacer trizas; deshilar (*carne*)

shrew [ʃru] *s* (*nagging woman*) arpía, fierecilla; (*animal*) musaraña

shrewd [ʃrud] *adj* astuto; despierto; listo

shriek [ʃrik] *s* chillido, grito agudo; risotada chillona ‖ *intr* chillar

shrill [ʃrɪl] *adj* agudo, chillón

shrimp [ʃrɪmp] *s* camarón *m;* (*little insignificant person*) renacuajo

shrine [ʃraɪn] *s* relicario; sepulcro de santo; lugar sagrado

shrink [ʃrɪŋk] *v* (*pret* **shrank** [ʃræŋk] o **shrunk** [ʃrʌŋk]; *pp* **shrunk** o **shrunken**) *tr* contraer, encoger ‖ *intr* contraerse, encogerse; moverse hacia atrás; rehuirse, retirarse

shrinkage [ˈʃrɪŋkɪdʒ] *s* contracción, encogimiento; disminución, reducción; merma, pérdida

shriv·el [ˈʃrɪvəl] *v* (*pret & pp* **-eled** o **-elled;** *ger* **-eling** o **-elling**) *tr* arrugar, marchitar, fruncir ‖ *intr* arrugarse, marchitarse, fruncirse; **to shrivel up** avellanarse

shroud [ʃraʊd] *s* mortaja, sudario; cubierta, velo ‖ *tr* amortajar; cubrir, velar

Shrove Tuesday [ʃrov] *s* martes *m* de carnaval

shrub [ʃrʌb] *s* arbusto

shrubber·y [ˈʃrʌbəri] *s* (*pl* **-ies**) arbustos; plantío de arbustos

shrug [ʃrʌg] *s* encogimiento de hombros ‖ *v* (*pret & pp* **shrugged;** *ger* **shrugging**) *tr* contraer; **to shrug one's shoulders** encogerse de hombros ‖ *intr* encogerse de hombros

shudder [ˈʃʌdər] *s* estremecimiento ‖ *intr* estremecerse

shuffle [ˈʃʌfəl] *s* (*of cards*) barajadura; turno de barajar; (*of feet*) arrastramiento; evasiva; recomposición ‖ *tr* barajar (*naipes*); arrastrar (*los pies*); mezclar, revolver ‖ *intr* barajar; caminar arrastrando los pies; bailar arrastrando los pies; moverse rápidamente de un lado a otro; **to shuffle along** ir arrastrando los pies; ir tirando; **to shuffle off** irse arrastrando los pies

shuf′fle·board′ *s* juego de tejo

shun [ʃʌn] *v* (*pret & pp* **shunned;** *ger* **shunning**) *tr* esquivar, evitar, rehuir

shunt [ʃʌnt] *tr* apartar, desviar; (elec) poner en derivación; (rr) desviar

shut [ʃʌt] *adj* cerrado ‖ *v* (*pret & pp* **shut;** *ger* **shutting**) *tr* cerrar; **to shut in** encerrar; **to shut off** cortar (*electricidad, gas, etc.*); **to shut up** cerrar bien; aprisionar; (coll) hacer callar ‖ *intr* cerrarse; **to shut up** (coll) callarse la boca

shut′down′ *s* cierre *m*, paro

shutter [ˈʃʌtər] *s* celosía, persiana; (*outside a window*) contraventana; (*outside a show window*) cierre metálico; (phot) obturador *m*

shuttle [ˈʃʌtəl] *s* (*used in sewing*) lanzadera ‖ *intr* hacer viajes cortos de ida y vuelta

shuttle train *s* tren *m* lanzadera

shy [ʃaɪ] *adj* (*comp* **shyer** o **shier;** *super* **shyest** o **shiest**) arisco, recatado, tímido; (*fearful*) asustadizo; escaso, pobre; **I am shy a dollar** me falta un dólar ‖ *v* (*pret & pp* **shied**) *intr* esquivarse, hacerse a un lado; espantarse, respingar; **to shy away** alejarse asustado

shyster [ˈʃaɪstər] s (coll) abogado trampista

Sia·mese [ˌsaɪ·əˈmiz] adj siamés ‖ s (pl **-mese**) siamés m

Siamese twins spl hermanos siameses

Siberian [saɪˈbɪrɪ·ən] adj & s siberiano

sibilant [ˈsɪbɪlənt] adj & s sibilante f

sibling [ˈsɪblɪŋ] s hermano o hermana

sibyl [ˈsɪbɪl] s sibila

Sicilian [sɪˈsɪljən] adj & s siciliano

Sicily [ˈsɪsɪlɪ] s Sicilia

sick [sɪk] adj enfermo, malo; nauseado; (coll) mórbido, perverso; **sick and tired of** (coll) harto y cansado de; **sick at heart** afligido de corazón; **to be sick at one's stomach** tener náuseas; **to take sick** caer enfermo ‖ tr azuzar (a un perro)

sick'bed' s lecho de enfermo

sicken [ˈsɪkən] tr & intr enfermar

sickening [ˈsɪkənɪŋ] adj repelente, repugnante, nauseabundo

sick headache s jaqueca con náuseas

sickle [ˈsɪkəl] s hoz f

sick leave s licencia por enfermedad

sick·ly [ˈsɪklɪ] adj (comp **-lier**; super **-liest**) enfermizo

sickness [ˈsɪknɪs] s enfermedad; náusea

side [saɪd] adj lateral ‖ s lado; (of a solid; of a phonograph record) cara; (of a hill) falda; (of human body, of a ship) costado; facción, partido ‖ intr tomar partido; **to side with** tomar el partido de

side arms spl armas de cinto

side'board' s aparador m

side'burns' spl patillas

side dish s plato de entrada

side door s puerta lateral; puerta excusada

side effect s efecto secundario perjudicial (de ciertos medicamentos)

side glance s mirada de soslayo

side issue s cuestión secundaria

side'kick' s (slang) compañero regular

side line s negocio accesorio; **on the side lines** sin tomar parte

sidereal [saɪˈdɪrɪ·əl] adj sidéreo

side'sad'dle adv a asentadillas, a mujeriegas

side show s función secundaria, espectáculo de atracciones

side'split'ting adj desternillante

side'track' s apartadero, desviadero, vía muerta ‖ tr desviar (un tren); echar a un lado

side view s perfil m, vista de lado

side'walk' s acera; banqueta (Guat, Mex); vereda (Arg, Cuba, Peru)

sidewalk café s terraza, café m en la acera

sideward [ˈsaɪdwərd] adj oblicuo, sesgado ‖ adv de lado, hacia un lado

side'ways' adj oblicuo, sesgado ‖ adv de lado, hacia un lado; a través

side whiskers spl patillas

side'wise' s oblicuo, sesgado ‖ adv de lado, hacia un lado; a través

siding [ˈsaɪdɪŋ] s (rr) apartadero, desviadero, vía muerta

sidle [ˈsaɪdəl] intr ir de lado; **to sidle up to** acercarse de lado a (una persona) para no ser visto

siege [sidʒ] s sitio, cerco; **to lay siege to** poner sitio o cerco a; (fig) asediar (p.ej., el corazón de una mujer)

sieve [sɪv] s cedazo, tamiz m ‖ tr cerner, tamizar

sift [sɪft] tr cerner, cribar; escudriñar, examinar; (to screen, separate) entresacar; (to scatter with or as with a sieve) empolvar

sigh [saɪ] s suspiro; **to breathe a sigh of relief** respirar ‖ tr decir con suspiros ‖ intr suspirar; **to sigh for** suspirar por

sight [saɪt] s vista; cosa digna de verse; (of a firearm, telescope, etc.) (gun) cantidad, montón m; (coll) horror m, atrocidad; **at first sight** a primera vista; **at sight** a primera vista; (translation) a libro abierto; (com) a la vista; **out of sight** fuera del alcance de la vista; (prices) por las nubes; **to catch sight of** alcanzar a ver; **to know by sight** conocer de vista; **to not be able to stand the sight of** no poder ver ni en pintura; **to see the sights** visitar los puntos de interés ‖ tr avistar, alcanzar con la vista ‖ intr apuntar con una mira; (arti & surv) visar

sight draft s (com) giro a la vista, letra a la vista

sightless [ˈsaɪtlɪs] adj ciego

sight'-read' v (pret & pp **-read** [ˌrɛd]) tr leer a libro abierto; (mus) ejecutar a la primera lectura ‖ intr leer a libro abierto; (mus) repentizar

sight reader s lector m a libro abierto; (mus) repentista mf

sight'see'ing s turismo, visita de puntos de interés; **to go sightseeing** ir a ver los puntos de interés

sightseer [ˈsaɪtˌsi·ər] s turista mf, excursionista mf

sign [saɪn] s signo; señal f, marca; huella, vestigio; letrero, muestra; **to show signs of** dar muestras de, tener trazas de; **to make the sign of the cross** hacerse la señal de la cruz ‖ tr firmar; contratar; ceder, traspasar ‖ intr firmar; usar el alfabeto de los sordomudos; **to sign off** (rad) terminar la transmisión; **to sign up** (coll) firmar el contrato

sig·nal [ˈsɪgnəl] adj señalado, notable ‖ s señal f ‖ v (pret & pp **-naled** o **-nalled**; ger **-naling** o **-nalling**) tr señalar ‖ intr hacer señales

signal tower s (rr) garita de señales

signato·ry [ˈsɪgnɪˌtorɪ] s (pl **-ries**) firmante mf

signature [ˈsɪgnətʃər] s firma; (mus & typ) signatura

sign'board' s cartelón m, letrero

signer [ˈsaɪnər] s firmante mf

signet ring [ˈsɪgnɪt] s anillo sigilar, sortija de sello

significance [sɪgˈnɪfəkəns] s significado, significación; relevancia

signi·fy [ˈsɪgnɪˌfaɪ] v (pret & pp **-fied**) tr significar

sign'post' s hito, poste m de guía

sh
si

silence ['saɪləns] *s* silencio ‖ *tr* acallar; (mil) apagar el fuego de; (mil) apagar (*el fuego del enemigo*)

silent ['saɪlənt] *adj* silencioso

silent movie *s* cine mudo

silhouette [,sɪlu'ɛt] *s* silueta ‖ *tr* siluetear

silk [sɪlk] *adj* sedeño ‖ *s* seda; **to hit the silk** (slang) lanzarse en paracaídas

silken ['sɪlkən] *adj* sedeño

silk hat *s* sombrero de copa

silk'-stock'ing *adj* aristocrático ‖ *s* aristócrata *mf*

silk'worm' *s* gusano de seda

silk•y ['sɪlki] *adj* (*comp* **-ier**; *super* **-iest**) sedoso, asedado

sill [sɪl] *s* travesaño; (*of a door*) umbral *m*; (*of a window*) antepecho

silliness ['sɪlɪnɪs] tontería, simpleza, pachotada

sil•ly ['sɪli] *adj* (*comp* **-lier**; *super* **-liest**) necio, tonto; (coll) pavo

si•lo ['saɪlo] *s* (*pl* **-los**) silo ‖ *tr* asilar

silt [sɪlt] *s* cieno, sedimento

silver ['sɪlvər] *ad* de plata; (*voice*) argentino; elocuente ‖ *s* plata ‖ *tr* platear; azogar (*un espejo*)

sil'ver•fish' *s* (ent) pez *m* de plata

silver foil *s* hoja de plata

silver lining *s* aspecto agradable de una condición desgraciada o triste

silver plate *s* vajilla de plata

silver screen *s* pantalla de plata

sil'ver•smith' *s* platero, orfebre *m*

silver spoon *s* riqueza heredada; **to be born with a silver spoon in one's mouth** nacer de pie

sil'ver-tongue' *s* (coll) pico de oro

sil'ver•ware' *s* plata, vajilla de plata; plata; cubertería

similar ['sɪmɪlər] *adj* similar, semejante, análogo

simile ['sɪmɪli] *s* (rhet) símil *m*

simmer ['sɪmər] *tr* cocer a fuego lento ‖ *intr* cocer a fuego lento; (coll) estar a punto de estallar; **to simmer down** (coll) tranquilizarse lentamente

simoon [sɪ'mun] *s* simún *m*

simper ['sɪmpər] *s* sonrisa boba ‖ *intr* sonreír bobamente

simple ['sɪmpəl] *adj* simple, sencillo ‖ *s* (*medicinal plant*) simple *m*

simple-minded ['sɪmpəl'maɪndɪd] *adj* candoroso, ingenuo; idiota, mentecato; estúpido, ignorante

simple substance *s* (chem) cuerpo simple

simpleton ['sɪmpəltən] *s* simple *mf*, bobo, mentecato

simulate ['sɪmjə,let] *tr* simular

simultaneous [,saɪməl'tenɪ•əs] o [,sɪməl-'tenɪ•əs] *adj* simultáneo ‖ *adv*—**to do simultaneously** simultanear

sin [sɪn] *s* pecado ‖ *v* (*pret & pp* **sinned**; *ger* **sinning**) *intr* pecar

since [sɪns] *adv* desde entonces, después ‖ *prep* desde; después de ‖ *conj* desde que; después (de) que; ya que, puesto que

sincere [sɪn'sɪr] *adj* sincero

sincerity [sɪn'sɛrɪti] *s* sinceridad

sinecure ['saɪnɪ,kjur] *s* sinecura

sinew ['sɪnju] *s* tendón *m*; (fig) fibra, nervio, vigor *m*

sinful ['sɪnfəl] *adj* (*person*) pecador; (*act, intention, etc.*) pecaminoso

sing [sɪŋ] *v* (*pret* **sang** [sæŋ] o **sung** [sʌŋ]; *pp* **sung**) *tr* cantar; **to sing to sleep** arrullar ‖ *intr* cantar

singe [sɪndʒ] *v* (*ger* **singeing**) *tr* chamuscar, socarrar

singer ['sɪŋər] *s* cantante *mf*; (*in a night club*) vocalista *mf*

single ['sɪŋgəl] *adj* solo, único; simple, sencillo; particular; (*e.g., room in a hotel*) individual; (*copy*) suelto; (*unmarried*) soltero; solteril, de soltero ‖ *tr* escoger, elegir; **to single out** singularizar

single blessedness *s* el bendito celibato

single-breasted ['sɪŋgəl'brɛstɪd] *adj* sin cruzar, de un solo pecho

single entry *s* (com) partida simple

single file *s* fila india; **in single file** de reata

single-handed ['sɪŋgəl'hændɪd] *adj* solo, sin ayuda

single life *s* vida de soltero

sin'gle-track' *adj* de vía única; (coll) de cortos alcances

sing'song' *adj* monótono ‖ *s* sonsonete *m*

singular ['sɪŋgjələr] *adj & s* singular *m*

sinister ['sɪnɪstər] *adj* amenazante, ominoso, funesto

sink [sɪŋk] *s* fregadero, pila ‖ *v* (*pret* **sank** [sæŋk] o **sunk** [sʌŋk]; *pp* **sunk**) *tr* hundir, sumergir; echar a pique; abrir, cavar (*un pozo*); hincar (*los dientes*); invertir (*mucho dinero*) perdiéndolo todo; (*basketball*) encestar ‖ *intr* hundirse; irse a pique; hundirse (*p.ej., el Sol en el horizonte*); descender, desaparecer; decaer (*un enfermo; una llama*); (*e.g., in a chair*) dejarse caer

sinking fund *s* fondo de amortización

sinless ['sɪnlɪs] *adj* impecable

sinner ['sɪnər] *s* pecador *m*

sinuous ['sɪnju•əs] *adj* sinuoso

sinus ['saɪnəs] *s* seno

sip [sɪp] *s* sorbo, trago ‖ *v* (*pret & pp* **sipped**; *ger* **sipping**) *tr* sorber, beber a tragos

siphon ['saɪfən] *s* sifón *m* ‖ *tr* sacar con sifón, trasegar con sifón

siphon bottle *s* sifón *m*

sir [sʌr] *s* señor *m*; (*British title*) sir *m*; **Dear Sir** Muy señor mío, Estimado señor

sire [saɪr] *s* padre *m*, semental *m*; caballo padre ‖ *tr* engendrar

siren ['saɪrən] *s* sirena

Sirius ['sɪrɪ•əs] *s* (astr) Sirio

sirloin ['sʌrlɔɪn] *s* solomillo

sirup ['sɪrəp] o ['sʌrəp] *s* var de **syrup**

sissi•fy ['sɪsɪ,faɪ] *v* (*pret & pp* **-fied**) *tr* (coll) afeminar

sis•sy ['sɪsi] *s* (*pl* **-sies**) (coll) hermanita; (coll) maricón *m*, santito

sister ['sɪstər] *adj* (*ship*) gemelo; (*language*) hermano ‖ *s* hermana

sis′ter-in-law′ *s* (*pl* **sisters-in-law**) cuñada, hermana política; (*wife of one's husband's or wife's brother*) concuñada

Sisyphus [′sɪsɪfəs] *s* Sísifo

sit [sɪt] *v* (*pret* & *pp* **sat** [sæt]; *ger* **sitting**) *intr* estar sentado; sentarse; echarse (*un ave sobre los huevos*); reunirse, celebrar junta; descansar; **to sit down** sentarse; **to sit still** estarse quieto; **to sit up** incorporarse (*el que estaba echado*)

sitcom [′sɪt,kɑm] *s* (coll) telecomedia serial

sit′-down′ strike *s* hulega de sentados, huelga de brazos caídos

site [saɪt] *s* sitio, paraje *m*

sit′-in′ *s* manifestación pacífica a modo de bloqueo

sitting [′sɪtɪŋ] *s* (*period one remains seated*) sentada; (*before a painter*) estadía; (*of a court or legislature*) sesión; **at one sitting** de una sentada

sitting duck *s* pato sentado en el agua (*fácil de matar a tiro de escopeta*); (coll) blanco de fácil alcance

sitting room *s* sala de estar

situate [′sɪtʃu,et] *tr* situar

situation [,sɪtʃuefˈən] *s* situación; colocación; puesto; medio ambiente

sitz bath [sɪts] *s* baño de asiento

six [sɪks] *adj* & *pron* seis ‖ *s* seis *m*; **at sixes and sevens** en confusión, en desacuerdo; **six o'clock** las seis

six hundred *adj* & *pron* seiscientos ‖ *s* seiscientos *m*

sixteen [′sɪks′tin] *adj, pron* & *s* dieciséis *m*, diez y seis

sixteenth [′sɪks′tinθ] *adj* & *s* (*in a series*) decimosexto; (*part*) dieciseisavo ‖ *s* (*in dates*) dieciséis *m*

sixth [sɪksθ] *adj* & *s* sexto ‖ *s* (*in dates*) seis *m*

sixtieth [′sɪkstɪ·ɪθ] *adj* & *s* (*in a series*) sexagésimo; (*part*) sesentavo

six·ty [′sɪksti] *adj* & *pron* sesenta ‖ *s* (*pl* **-ties**) sesenta *m*

sizable [′saɪzəbəl] *adj* considerable, bastante grande

size [saɪz] *s* tamaño; (*of a person or garment*) talla; (*of a pipe, a wire*) diámetro; (*for gilding*) sisa, cola de retazo; (coll) verdadera situación ‖ *tr* clasificar según tamaño; sisar, encolar; **to size up** enfocar (*un problema*); medir con la vista

sizzle [′sɪzəl] *s* siseo ‖ *intr* sisear

S.J. *abbr* **Society of Jesus**

skate [sket] *s* patín *m*; (slang) adefesio, tipo ‖ *intr* patinar; **to skate on thin ice** buscar el peligro

skating rink *s* patinadero, pista de patinar

skein [sken] *s* madeja; enredo, maraña

skeleton [′skɛlɪtən] *adj* esquelético ‖ *s* esqueleto

skeleton key *s* llave maestra

skeptic [′skɛptɪk] *adj* & *s* escéptico

skeptical [′skɛptɪkəl] *adj* escéptico

sketch [skɛtʃ] *s* boceto, dibujo; bosquejo, esbozo; drama corto, pieza corta ‖ *tr* dibujar; bosquejar, esbozar

sketch′book′ *s* libro de bocetos; libro de esbozos literarios

skewer [′skju·ər] *s* broqueta ‖ *tr* espetar; traspasar con aguja

ski [ski] *s* (*pl* **skis** o **ski**) esquí *m* *intr* esquiar

skid [skɪd] *s* (*of an auto*) resbalón *m*; (*of a wheel*) patinaje *m*, patinazo; calzo ‖ *v* (*pret* & *pp* **skidded;** *ger* **skidding**) *tr* calzar ‖ *intr* resbalar (*un coche*); patinar (*una rueda*)

skid chain *s* cadena antirresbaladiza

skidding *s* (aut) patinada, derrapada, derrapaje *m*

skid row *s* barrio de mala vida

skier [′ski·ər] *s* esquiador *m*

skiff [skɪf] *s* esquife *m*

skiing [′ski·ɪŋ] *s* esquiismo

ski jacket *s* plumífero

skijoring [ski′dʒorɪŋ] *s* esquí remolcado

ski jump *s* salto de esquí; cancha de esquiar; trampolín *m*

ski lift *s* telesquí *m*

skill [skɪl] *s* destreza, habilidad, pericia

skilled [skɪld] *adj* hábil, experimentado, experto

skillet [′skɪlɪt] *s* cacerola de mango largo; sartén *f*

skillful [′skɪlfəl] *adj* diestro, hábil

skim [skɪm] *v* (*pret* & *pp* **skimmed;** *ger* **skimming**) *tr* desnatar (*la leche*); espumar (*el caldo, el almíbar*); (*to graze*) rasar, rozar; examinar ligeramente ‖ *intr* rozar; **to skim over** pasar rozando; examinar a la ligera

ski mask *s* pasamontaña

skimmer [′skɪmər] *s* (*utensil*) espumadera; (*straw hat*) canotié *m*

skim milk *s* leche desnatada

skimp [skɪmp] *tr* escatimar; chapucear ‖ *intr* economizar, apretarse; chapucear

skimp·y [′skɪmpi] *adj* (*comp* **-ier;** *super* **-iest**) escaso; tacaño, mezquino

skin [skɪn] *s* piel *f*; (*of an animal, of fruit*) pellejo; **to be nothing but skin and bones** estar hecho un costal de huesos, estar en los huesos; **to get soaked to the skin** calarse hasta los huesos; **to save one's skin** salvar el pellejo ‖ *v* (*pret* & *pp* **skinned;** *ger* **skinning**) *tr* pelar, desollar; escoriarse (*p.ej., el codo*); (coll) timar; **to skin alive** (coll) desollar vivo; (coll) vencer completamente

skin′-deep′ *adj* superficial

skin diver *s* submarinista *mf*

skin diving *s* submarinismo

skin′flint′ *s* escasero, avaro

skin game *s* (slang) fullería

skin·ny [′skɪni] *adj* (*comp* **-nier;** *super* **-niest**) flaco, enjuto, magro, seco, delgaducho

skin′-tight′ *adj* ajustado al cuerpo

skip [skɪp] *s* salto ‖ *v* (*pret* & *pp* **skipped;** *ger* **skipping**) *tr* saltar ‖ *intr* saltar; saltar espacios (*la máquina de escribir*); moverse saltando; irse precipitadamente

skip bombing *s* (aer) bombardeo de rebote

si
sk

ski pole *s* bastón *m* de esquiar

skipper ['skɪpər] *s* caudillo, jefe *m;* (*of a boat*) patrón *m;* gusano del queso ‖ *tr* patronear

skirmish ['skʌrmɪʃ] *s* escaramuza ‖ *intr* escaramuzar

skirt [skʌrt] *s* falda; borde *m*, orilla; (*woman*) (slang) falda ‖ *tr* seguir el borde de; moverse a lo largo de

ski run *s* pista de esquí

ski stick *s* bastón *m* de esquiar

skit [skɪt] *s* boceto burlesco, paso cómico

skittish ['skɪtɪʃ] *adj* caprichoso; asustadizo; tímido; (*bull*) abanto

skulduggery [skʌl'dʌgəri] *s* (coll) trampa, embuste *m*

skull [skʌl] *s* cráneo, calavera

skull'cap' *s* casquete *m*

skunk [skʌŋk] *s* mofeta; (*person*) (coll) canalla *m*

sky [skaɪ] *s* (*pl* **skies**) cielo; **to praise to the skies** poner por las nubes, poner en el cielo

sky'div'ing *s* paracaidismo con plomada suelta inicial

Skylab ['skaɪ,læb] *s* laboratorio espacial

sky'lark' *s* alondra ‖ *intr* jaranear

sky'light' *s* tragaluz *m*, claraboya

sky'line' *s* línea del horizonte, línea de los edificios contra el cielo

sky'rock'et *s* cohete *m* ‖ *intr* subir como un cohete

sky'scrap'er *s* rascacielos *m*

sky'writ'ing *s* escritura aérea

slab [slæb] *s* losa; plancha, tabla

slack [slæk] *adj* flojo; perezoso; negligente; inactivo ‖ *s* flojedad; inactividad; estación muerta, temporada inactiva; **slacks** pantalones flojos ‖ *tr* aflojar; apagar (*la cal*) ‖ *intr* atrasarse; descuidarse; **to slack up** aflojar el paso

slacker ['slækər] *s* perezoso; (mil) prófugo

slag [slæg] *s* escoria

slake [slek] *tr* aplacar, calmar; apagar (*la cal*)

slalom ['slaləm] *s* eslálom *m*

slam [slæm] *s* golpe *m;* (*of a door*) portazo; (coll) crítica acerba ‖ *v* (*pret & pp* **slammed;** *ger* **slamming**) *tr* cerrar de golpe; golpear o empujar estrepitosamente; (coll) criticar acerbamente ‖ *intr* cerrarse de golpe

slam'-bang' *adv* (coll) de golpe y porrazo

slander ['slændər] *s* calumnia, difamación; levante (CAm, P-R) ‖ *tr* calumniar, difamar

slanderous ['slændərəs] *adj* calumnioso, difamatorio

slang [slæŋ] *s* caló *m*, jerigonza

slant [slænt] *s* inclinación; parecer *m*, punto de vista ‖ *tr* inclinar, sesgar; deformar, tergiversar (*un informe*) ‖ *intr* inclinarse, sesgarse

slap [slæp] *s* manazo, palmada; (*in the face*) bofetada; (*in the back*) espaldarazo; desaire *m*, insulto ‖ *v* (*pret & pp* **slapped;** *ger* **slapping**) *tr* dar una palmada a; abofetear

slash [slæʃ] *s* cuchillada ‖ *tr* acuchillar; hacer fuerte rebaja de (*precios, sueldos, etc.*)

slat [slæt] *s* lámina, tablilla

slate [slet] *s* pizarra; candidatura, lista de candidatos ‖ *tr* empizarrar; designar, destinar; poner en la lista de candidatos

slate pencil *s* pizarrín *m*

slate roof *s* empizarrado

slattern ['slætərn] *s* mujer desaliñada, pazpuerca

slaughter ['slɔtər] *s* carnicería, matanza ‖ *tr* matar

slaughter house *s* matadero

Slav [slɑv] *o* [slæv] *adj & s* eslavo

slave [slev] *adj & s* esclavo ‖ *intr* trabajar como esclavo

slave driver *s* negrero; (fig) negrero

slave'hold'er *s* dueño de esclavos

slavery ['slevəri] *s* esclavitud

slave trade *s* trata de esclavos

slave trader *s* negrero

Slavic ['slɑvɪk] *o* ['slævɪk] *adj & s* eslavo

slay [sle] *v* (*pret* **slew** [slu]; *pp* **slain** [slen]) *tr* matar

slayer ['sle•ər] *s* matador *m*

sled [slɛd] *s* luge *m* ‖ *v* (*pret & pp* **sledded;** *ger* **sledding**) *intr* deslizarse en luge o trineo

sledge hammer [slɛdʒ] *s* acotillo

sleek [slik] *adj* liso y brillante ‖ *tr* alisar y pulir; suavizar

sleep [slip] *s* sueño; **to be overcome with sleep** caerse de sueño; **to go to sleep** dormirse; dormirse, morirse (*un miembro*); **to put to sleep** adormecer; matar por anestesia ‖ *v* (*pret & pp* **slept** [slɛpt]) *tr* pasar durmiendo; **to sleep it off** dormir la mona; **to sleep it over** consultar con la almohada; **to sleep off** dormir (*p.ej., una borrachera*) ‖ *intr* dormir

sleeper ['slipər] *s* (*person*) durmiente *mf;* (*girder*) durmiente *m*

sleeping bag *s* saco de dormir

Sleeping Beauty *s* la Bella Durmiente

sleeping car *s* coche-cama *m*

sleeping pill *s* píldora para dormir

sleepless ['sliplɪs] *adj* insomne, desvelado; pasado en vela

sleep'walk'er *s* sonámbulo; nochero

sleep•y ['slipi] *adj* (*comp* **-ier;** *super* **-iest**) soñoliento; **to be sleepy** tener sueño

sleep'y•head' *s* dormilón *m*

sleet [slit] *s* cellisca ‖ *intr* cellisquear

sleeve [sliv] *s* manga; (mach) manguito; **to laugh in** *o* **up one's sleeve** reírse para sí

sleigh [sle] *s* trineo ‖ *intr* pasearse en trineo

sleigh bell *s* cascabel *m*

sleigh ride *s* paseo en trineo

sleight of hand [slaɪt] *s* juego de manos, prestidigitación

slender ['slɛndər] *adj* esbelto, flaco, delgado; escaso, insuficiente

sleuth [sluθ] *s* sabueso

slew [slu] *s* (coll) montón *m*

slice [slaɪs] *s* rebanada, tajada; (*of an orange*) gajo ‖ *tr* rebanar, tajar; dividir; cortar

slick [slɪk] *adj* liso y brillante; meloso, suave; (coll) astuto, mañoso ‖ *s* lugar aceitoso y lustroso (*en el agua*)

slicker [ˈslɪkər] s impermeable m de hule; (coll) embaucador m

slide [slaɪd] s resbalón m; (slippery place) resbaladero; (slippery surface) desliz m; derrumbamiento de tierra; (image for projection) diapositiva, transparencia; (of a microscope) plaquilla de vidrio; (piece of a device that slides) cursor m; (of a trombone) corredera (tubular) || v (pret & pp slid [slɪd]) tr deslizar || intr deslizar, resbalar; **to let slide** dejar pasar, no hacer caso de

slide fastener s cierre m cremallera, cierre relámpago

slide rule s regla de cálculo

slide valve s corredera, válvula corrediza

sliding contact s cursor m

sliding door s puerta de corredera

sliding scale s regla de cálculo; (of salaries) escala móvil

slight [slaɪt] adj delgado; leve; pequeño; escaso; delgaducho || s desatención, descuido; desaire m, menosprecio || tr desatender, descuidar; desairar

slim [slɪm] adj (comp **slimmer**; super **slimmest**) delgado, esbelto; débil, leve, pequeño, escaso

slime [slaɪm] s légamo; (of snakes, fish, etc.) baba

slim·y [ˈslaɪmɪ] adj (comp **-ier**; super **-iest**) legamoso; baboso, viscoso; puerco, sucio

sling [slɪŋ] s (to shoot stones) honda; (to hold up a broken arm) cabestrillo || v (pret & pp slung [slʌŋ]) tr lanzar con una honda; lanzar, tirar; poner en cabestrillo; colgar flojamente

sling'shot' s honda

slink [slɪŋk] v (pret & pp slunk [slʌŋk]) intr andar furtivamente; **to slink away** escabullirse, salir con el rabo entre piernas

slip [slɪp] s resbalón m, desliz m; falta, error m, desliz m; lapso; embarcadero; (cover for a pillow, for furniture) funda; (piece of paper) papeleta; (cutting from a plant) sarmiento; (piece of underclothing) combinación; (of a dog) traílla; huída, evasión; mozuelo, mozuela; **to give the slip to** burlar la vigilancia de || v (pret & pp slipped; ger slipping) tr poner rápidamente; quitar rápidamente; pasar por alto; eludir, evadir; **to slip off** (coll) quitarse de prisa; **to slip on** (coll) ponerse de prisa; **to slip one's mind** olvidársele a uno || intr deslizarse; patinar (el embrague); errar, equivocarse; (coll) declinar, deteriorarse; **to let slip** dejar pasar; decir inadvertidamente; **to slip away** escurrirse; **to slip by** pasar inadvertido; pasar rápidamente (el tiempo); **to slip out of one's hands** escurrirse de entre las manos; **to slip up** (coll) errar, equivocarse

slip cover s funda

slip of the pen s error m de pluma

slip of the tongue s error m de lengua

slipper [ˈslɪpər] s zapatilla, babucha

slippery [ˈslɪpərɪ] adj deslizadizo, resbaladizo; astuto, zorro, evasivo

slip'-up' s (coll) error m, equivocación

slit [slɪt] s hendidura, raja; cortada, incisión || v (pret & pp slit; ger slitting) tr hender, rajar; cortar

slob [slɑb] s (slang) sujeto desaseado, puerco

slobber [ˈslɑbər] s baba; sensiblería || intr babear; hablar con sensiblería

sloe [slo] s (shrub) endrino; (fruit) endrina

slogan [ˈslogən] s lema m, mote m; grito de combate; (striking phrase used in advertising) eslogan m

sloop [slup] s balandra

slop [slɑp] s gacha, zupia, agua sucia || v (pret & pp slopped; ger slopping) tr salpicar, ensuciar || intr derramarse; chapotear

slope [slop] s cuesta, pendiente f; (of a continent or a roof) vertiente m & f || tr inclinar || intr inclinarse

slop·py [ˈslɑpɪ] adj (comp **-pier**; super **-piest**) mojado y sucio; (in one's dress) desgalichado; (in one's work) chapucero

slot [slɑt] s ranura; (for letters) buzón m

sloth [sloθ] o [slɔθ] s pereza; (zool) perezoso

slot machine s tragamonedas m, máquina sacaperras

slot meter s contador automático

slouch [slaʊtʃ] s postura relajada; persona torpe de movimientos || intr agacharse, andar caído de hombros; **to slouch in a chair** repanchigarse

slouch hat s sombrero gacho

slough [slaʊ] s cenagal m, fangal m; estado de abandono moral || [slʌf] s (of a snake) camisa; (pathol) escara || tr mudar, echar de sí || intr caerse, desprenderse

Slovak [ˈslovæk] o [sloˈvæk] adj & s eslovaco

sloven·ly [ˈslʌvənlɪ] adj (comp **-lier**; super **-liest**) desaseado, desaliñado

slow [slo] adj lento; (sluggish) cachazudo, despacioso; (clock, watch) atrasado; (in understanding) lerdo, tardo, torpe || adv despacio || tr retrasar; atrasar (un reloj) || intr retardarse, ir más despacio; atrasarse (un reloj)

slow'down' s huelga de brazos caídos

slow motion s (film) ralentí m; **in slow motion** al ralentí, a cámara lenta

slow'-mo'tion adj a cámara lenta

slowness [ˈslonɪs] s lentitud, lerdera

slow'poke' s tardón m

slug [slʌg] s (heavy piece of metal) lingote m; (metal disk used as a coin) ficha; (zool) limaza, babosa; (coll) porrazo, puñetazo || v (pret & pp slugged; ger slugging) tr (coll) aporrear, apuñear

sluggard [ˈslʌgərd] s pachón m, perezoso

sluggish [ˈslʌgɪʃ] adj inactivo, indolente, tardo; pachorrudo, perezoso

sluice [slus] s canal m; (floodgate) compuerta; (dam; flume) presa

sluice gate s compuerta de presa

slum [slʌm] s barrio bajo || v (pret & pp slummed; ger slumming) intr visitar los barrios bajos

slumber [ˈslʌmbər] s sueño ligero, sueño tranquilo || intr dormir; dormitar

sk
sl

slump [slʌmp] s depresión, crisis económica; (*in prices, stocks, etc.*) baja repentina ‖ *intr* hundirse, desplomarse; bajar repentinamente (*los precios, valores, etc.*)

slur [slʌr] s pronunciación indistinta; reparo crítico; (*mus*) ligado ‖ v (*pret & pp* **slurred;** *ger* **slurring**) *tr* comerse (*sonidos, sílabas*); despreciar, insultar; (*mus*) ligar

slush [slʌʃ] s fango muy blando, aguanieve fangosa, nieve f a medio derretir; sentimentalismo tonto

slut [slʌt] s perra; (*slovenly woman*) pazpuerca; ramera, mala mujer

sly [slaɪ] adj (*comp* **slyer** o **slier;** *super* **slyest** o **sliest**) furtivo, secreto; astuto, socarrón; travieso; **on the sly** a hurtadillas

smack [smæk] adv (coll) de golpe, de sopetón ‖ s dejo, gustillo; palmada, manotada; golpe m; beso sonado; (*of a whip*) chasquido ‖ tr dar una manotada a; golpear; hacer chasquidos con (*un látigo*); besar sonoramente; **to smack one's lips** chuparse los labios ‖ *intr*—**to smack of** saber a, oler a

small [smɔl] adj pequeño, chico; (*short in stature*) bajo; pobre, obscuro, humilde; (*typ*) minúsculo

small arms spl armas ligeras

small beer s cerveza floja; bagatela; persona de poca monta

small business s pequeña empresa

small capital s versalilla o versalita

small change s suelto, dinero menudo

small fry s gente menuda; gente de poca monta

small'-fry' adj de niños, para niños; de poca monta

small hours spl primeras horas (*de la mañana*)

small intestine s intestino delgado

small-minded ['smɔl'maɪndɪd] adj tacaño, mezquino; intolerante

smallpox ['smɔl,pɑks] s viruela

small print s tipo menudo

small talk s palique m, charlas frívolas

small'-time' adj de poca monta

small'-town' adj lugareño, apegado a cosas lugareñas

smart [smɑrt] adj listo, vivo, inteligente; agudo, penetrante; astuto; elegante, majo; picante, punzante; (coll) grande, considerable ‖ s escozor m; dolor vivo ‖ *intr* escocer, picar; padecer, sufrir

smart aleck ['ælɪk] s (coll) fatuo, sabihondo

smart money s (fig) inversionistas mpl/fpl astutos; gente f bien informada

smart set s gente f chic, gente de buen tono

smash [smæʃ] s rotura violenta; fracaso, ruina; quiebra, bancarrota; (coll) choque violento, tope violento ‖ tr romper con fuerza; arruinar, destrozar; aplastar ‖ *intr* romperse con fuerza; arruinarse, destrozarse; aplastarse; **to smash into** chocar con, topar con

smash hit s (coll) éxito rotundo

smash'-up' s colisión violenta; ruina, desastre m; quiebra, bancarrota

smattering ['smætərɪŋ] s barniz m, tintura, migaja

smear [smɪr] s embarradura; calumnia; (bact) frotis m ‖ tr embarrar; calumniar ‖ *intr* embarrarse

smear campaign s campaña de calumnias

smell [smɛl] s olor m; (*sense*) olfato; fragancia, perfume m ‖ v (*pret & pp* **smelled** o **smelt** [smɛlt]) tr oler, olfatear ‖ *intr* oler; heder, oler mal; **to smell of** oler a

smelling salts spl sales aromáticas

smell•y ['smɛli] adj (*comp* -ier; *super* -iest) hediondo, maloliente

smelt [smɛlt] s (*fish*) eperlano, esperinque m ‖ tr & *intr* fundir

smile [smaɪl] s sonrisa ‖ *intr* sonreír, sonreírse

smiling ['smaɪlɪŋ] adj risueño

smirk [smʌrk] s sonrisa fatua y afectada ‖ *intr* sonreír fatua y afectadamente

smite [smaɪt] v (*pret* **smote** [smot]; *pp* **smitten** ['smɪtən] o **smit** [smɪt]) tr golpear o herir súbitamente y con fuerza; caer con fuerza sobre; apenar, afligir; castigar

smith [smɪθ] s forjador m, herrero

smith•y ['smɪθi] s (*pl* -ies) herrería

smitten ['smɪtən] adj afligido; muy enamorado.

smock [smɑk] s bata

smock frock s blusa de obrero

smog [smɑg] s mezcla de humo y niebla

smoke [smok] s humo; **to go up in smoke** irse todo en humo ‖ tr (*to cure or treat with smoke*) ahumar; fumar (*tabaco*); **to smoke out** ahuyentar con humo, dar humazo a; descubrir ‖ *intr* humear; fumar; hacer humo (*una chimenea dentro de la habitación*)

smoked glasses spl gafas ahumadas

smoke evacuator s extractor de humos

smokeless powder ['smoklɪs] s pólvora sin humo

smokeless tobacco s tabaco sin humo

smoker ['smokər] s fumador m; (*room*) fumadero; (rr) coche-fumador m; reunión de fumadores

smoke rings spl anillos de humo; **to blow smoke rings** sacar humo formando anillos

smoke screen s cortina de humo

smoke'stack' s chimenea

smoking ['smokɪŋ] s el fumar; **no smoking** se prohíbe fumar

smoking car s coche-fumador m, vagón m de fumar

smoking jacket s batín m

smoking room s fumadero, saloncito para fumadores

smok•y ['smoki] adj (*comp* -ier; *super* -iest) humoso; (*emitting smoke*) humeante

smolder ['smoldər] s fuego lento sin llama y con mucho humo ‖ *intr* arder en rescoldo, arder sin llamas; (fig) estar latente; (*to burn within*) (fig) requemarse; (fig) expresar (*p.ej., los ojos*) una ira latente

smooth [smuð] adj liso, terso, suave; plano, llano; igual; acaramelado, afable, blando, meloso; (*water*) tranquilo; (*style*) fluido;

smooth as butter como manteca ‖ *tr* alisar, suavizar; allanar; facilitar; **to smooth away** quitar (*p.ej., obstáculos*) suavemente; **to smooth down** ablandar, calmar

smooth-faced [ˈsmuð‚fest] *adj* barbilampiño

smooth-spoken [ˈsmuθ‚spokən] *adj* meloso, lisonjero

smooth·y [ˈsmuði] *s* (*pl* **-ies**) galante *m;* elegante *m;* aludador *m*

smother [ˈsmʌðər] *tr* ahogar, sofocar; suprimir; reprimir

smudge [smʌdʒ] *s* tiznón *m;* mancha ‖ *tr* tiznar; manchar; ahumar, fumigar (*una huerta*)

smug [smʌg] *adj* (*comp* **smugger;** *super* **smuggest**) pagado de sí mismo; compuesto, pulcro; relamido

smuggle [ˈsmʌgəl] *tr* meter de contrabando ‖ *intr* contrabandear

smuggler [ˈsmʌglər] *s* contrabandista *mf*

smuggling [ˈsmʌglɪŋ] *s* contrabando

smut [smʌt] *s* tiznón *m;* obscenidad; (agr) carbón *m,* tizón *m*

smut·ty [ˈsmʌti] *adj* (*comp* **-tier;** *super* **-tiest**) tiznado, manchado; obsceno; (agr) atizonado

snack [snæk] *s* parte *f,* porción; bocadillo, tentempié *m*

snack bar *s* lonchería

snag [snæg] *s* (*of a tree*) tocón *m;* (*of a tooth*) raigón *m;* obstáculo, tropiezo; **to strike** o **to hit a snag** tropezar con un obstáculo

snail [snel] *s* caracol *m;* (*slow person*) pachón *m;* **at a snail's pace** a paso de caracol, a paso de tortuga

snake [snek] *s* culebra, serpiente *f*

snake in the grass *s* traidor *m,* amigo pérfido

snap [snæp] *s* (*crackling sound*) chasquido, estallido; (*of the fingers*) castañetazo; (*bite*) mordisco; (*cracker*) galletita; (*of cold weather*) corto período; (*catch or fastener*) broche *m* de presión; (phot) instantánea; (coll) brío, vigor *m;* (slang) breva, cosa fácil ‖ *v* (*pret* & *pp* **snapped;** *ger* **snapping**) *tr* asir, cerrar, etc. de golpe; castañetear (*los dedos*); chasquear (*el látigo*); fotografiar instantáneamente; tomar (*una instantánea*); **to snap one's fingers at** tratar con desprecio; **to snap up** aceptar con avidez, comprar con avidez; cortar la palabra a ‖ *intr* chasquear, estallar; (*to crack*) saltar; (*from fatigue*) estallar; **to snap at** querer morder; asir (*una oportunidad*); **to snap out of it** (slang) cambiarse repentinamente; **to snap shut** cerrarse de golpe

snap·drag·on *s* (bot) boca de dragón

snap fastener *s* corchete *m* de presión

snap judgment *s* decisión atolondrada

snap·py [ˈsnæpi] *adj* (*comp* **-pier;** *super* **-piest**) mordaz; (coll) elegante, garboso; (coll) enérgico, vivo; (*food*) acre, picante

snap·shot· *s* instantánea

snap switch *s* (elec) interruptor *m* de resorte

snare [sner] *s* lazo, trampa; (*of a drum*) bordón *m,* tirante *m*

snare drum *s* caja clara

snarl [snɑrl] *s* gruñido; regaño; maraña, enredo ‖ *tr* decir con un gruñido; enmarañar, enredar ‖ *intr* gruñir; regañar; enmarañarse, enredarse

snatch [snætʃ] *s* arrebatamiento; pedacito, trocito; ratito ‖ *tr* & *intr* arrebatar; **to snatch at** tratar de asir o agarrar; **to snatch from** arrebatar a

sneak [snik] *adj* furtivo ‖ *s* sujeto solapado ‖ *tr* mover a hurtadillas ‖ *intr* andar furtivamente, moverse a hurtadillas

sneaker [ˈsnikər] *s* sujeto solapado; (coll) zapato blando, zapato de lona

sneak thief *s* ratero, descuidero

sneak·y [ˈsniki] *adj* (*comp* **-ier;** *super* **-iest**) solapado, furtivo

sneer [snɪr] *s* expresión de desprecio ‖ *intr* hablar con desprecio, echar una mirada de desprecio; **to sneer at** mofarse de

sneeze [sniz] *s* estornudo ‖ *intr* estornudar; **not to be sneezed at** (coll) no ser despreciable

snicker [ˈsnɪkər] *s* risa tonta ‖ *intr* reírse tontamente

sniff [snɪf] *s* husmeo, venteo; sorbo por las narices ‖ *tr* husmear, ventear; sorber por las narices; (fig)ˈ husmear, averiguar; (fig) sospechar; (*heroin*) esnifar (*caballo*) ‖ *intr* ventear; **to sniff at** husmear; menospreciar

sniffle [ˈsnɪfəl] *s* resuello fuerte y repetido; **the sniffles** ataque *m* de resoplidos ‖ *intr* resollar fuerte y repetidamente

snip [snɪp] *s* tijeretada; recorte *m,* pedacito; (coll) persona pequeña e insignificante ‖ *v* (*pret* & *pp* **snipped;** *ger* **snipping**) *tr* tijeretear

snipe [snaɪp] *s* agachadiza, becacín *m* ‖ *intr* paquear, tirar desde un escondite

sniper [ˈsnaɪpər] *s* paco, tirador emboscado

snippet [ˈsnɪpɪt] *s* recorte *m;* (coll) persona pequeña e insignificante

snip·py [ˈsnɪpi] *adj* (*comp* **-pier;** *super* **-piest**) (coll) arrogante, desdeñoso; (coll) acre, brusco

snitch [snɪtʃ] *tr* & *intr* (slang) escamotear, ratear; manotear (Arg, Mex)

sniv·el [ˈsnɪvəl] *s* gimoteo, lloriqueo; moqueo ‖ *v* (*pret* & *pp* **-eled** o **-elled;** *ger* **-eling** o **-elling**) *intr* gimotear, lloriquear; (*to have a runny nose*) moquear

snob [snɑb] *s* esnob *mf*

snobbery [ˈsnɑbəri] *s* esnobismo

snobbish [ˈsnɑbɪʃ] *adj* esnob, esnobista

snoop [snup] *s* buscavidas *mf,* curioso ‖ *intr* curiosear, ventear

snoopy [ˈsnupi] *adj* curioso, entremetido

snoot [snut] *s* (slang) cara, narices *fpl*

snoot·y [ˈsnuti] *adj* (*comp* **-ier;** *super* **-iest**) (slang) esnob

snooze [snuz] *s* (coll) sueñecito ‖ *intr* echar un sueñecito

snore [snor] *s* ronquido ‖ *intr* roncar

snort [snɔrt] *s* bufido ‖ *intr* bufar

snot [snɑt] *s* (slang) mocarro

snot·ty [ˈsnɑti] *adj* (*comp* **-tier;** *super* **-tiest**) mocoso; asqueroso, sucio; (slang) engreído

snout [snaut] s hocico; (*something shaped like the snout of an animal*) morro; (*of a person*) (coll) hocico

snow [sno] s nieve *f* ‖ *intr* nevar

snow'ball' s bola de nieve ‖ *tr* lanzar bolas de nieve a ‖ *intr* aumentar rápidamente

snow'-blind' *adj* cegado por reflejos de la nieve

snow-capped ['sno,kæpt] *adj* coronado de nieve

snow'drift' s ventisquero, masa de nieve

snow'fall' s nevada

snow fence s valla paranieves

snow'flake' s copo de nieve, ampo

snow flurry s nevisca

snow job s (slang) decepción; engaño

snow line o **limit** s límite *m* de las nieves perpetuas

snow man s figura de nieve

snow'plow' s expulsanieves *m*, quitanieves *m*

snow'shoe' s raqueta de nieve

snow'storm' s nevasca, fuerte nevada

snow tire s llanta de invierno

snow'-white' *adj* blanco como la nieve

snow•y ['sno•i] *adj* (*comp* **-ier**; *super* **-iest**) nevoso

snowy owl s lechuza blanca

snub [snʌb] s desaire *m* ‖ *v* (*pret & pp* **snubbed**; *ger* **snubbing**) *tr* desairar

snub•by ['snʌbi] *adj* (*comp* **-bier**; *super -biest*) (*nose*) respingona

snuff [snʌf] s rapé; (*of a candlewick*) moco; **up to snuff** (slang) en buena condición; (slang) difícil de engañar ‖ *tr* husmear, olfatear; sorber por la nariz; despabilar (*una candela*); **to snuff out** apagar, extinguir

snuff'box' s tabaquera

snuffers ['snʌfərz] *spl* despabiladeras

snug [snʌg] *adj* (*comp* **snugger**; *super* **snuggest**) cómodo; (*garment*) ajustado, ceñido; (*well-off*) acomodado; (*in hiding*) escondido

snuggle ['snʌgəl] *intr* apretarse, arrimarse; dormir bien abrigado; **to snuggle up to** arrimarse a

so [so] *adv* así; tan + *adj* Q *adv*; por tanto; también; **and so** así pues; también, lo mismo; **and so on** y así sucesivamente; **or so** más o menos; **to think so** creer que sí; **so as to** + *inf* para + *inf*; **so far** hasta aquí; hasta ahora; **so long** hasta la vista; **so many** tantos; **so much** tanto; **so so** tal cual, así así; **so that** de modo que, de suerte que, así que; para que; con tal de que; **so to speak** por decirlo así ‖ *conj* as que ‖ *interj* ¡bien!; ¡verdad!

soak [sok] s mojada; (*toper*) (coll) potista *mf* ‖ *tr* empapar, remojar; embeber; (slang) aporrear; (slang) hacer pagar un precio exorbitante; **to soak up** absorber, embeber; (fig) entender; **soaked to the skin** calado hasta los huesos ‖ *intr* empaparse, remojarse

so'-and-so' s (*pl* **-sos**) fulano, fulano de tal, tal cosa

soap [sop] s jabón *m* ‖ *tr* jabonar

soap'box' s caja de jabón; tribuna callejera

soapbox orator m orador *m* de plazuela

soap bubble s burbuja de jabón, pompa de jabón

soap dish s jabonera

soap flakes *spl* copos de jabón

soap'mak'er s jabonero

soap opera s (coll) telenovela; serial lacrimógeno

soap powder s jabón *m* en polvo, polvo de jabón

soap'stone' s jaboncillo de sastre

soap'suds' *spl* jabonaduras

soap•y ['sopi] *adj* (*comp* **-ier**; *super* **-iest**) jabonoso

soar [sor] *intr* encumbrarse, subir muy alto, volar a gran altura; aspirar, pretender; (aer) planear

sob [sab] s sollozo ‖ *v* (*pret & pp* **sobbed**; *ger* **sobbing**) *tr* decir o expresar sollozando ‖ *intr* sollozar

sobbing s llorera

sober ['sobər] *adj* sobrio; no embriagado; grave, serio; cuerdo, sensato; sereno, tranquilo; (*color*) apagado ‖ *tr* poner sobrio; desembriagar; **to sober up** desintoxicar ‖ *intr* volverse sobrio; desemborracharse; **to sober down** calmarse, sosegarse; **to sober up** desemborracharse

sobriety [so'braɪ•əti] s sobriedad, moderación; gravedad, seriedad; cordura, sensatez; serenidad

sobriquet ['sobrɪ,ke] s apodo

sob sister s (slang) periodista llorona

sob story s (slang) historia de lagrimitas

soc. o **Soc.** *abbr* **society**

so'-called' *adj* llamado, así llamado; supuesto

soccer ['sakər] s fútbol *m* asociación

sociable ['soʃəbəl] *adj* sociable

social ['soʃəl] *adj* social ‖ s reunión social

social climber ['klaɪmər] s ambicioso de figurar

socialism ['soʃə,lɪzəm] s socialismo

socialist ['soʃəlɪst] s socialista *mf*

socialite ['soʃə,laɪt] s (coll) personaje *m* de la buena sociedad

social register s guía *m* social, registro de la buena sociedad

socie•ty [sə'saɪ•əti] s (*pl* **-ties**) sociedad; (*companionship or company*) compañía; buena sociedad, mundo elegante

society editor s cronista *mf* de la vida social

sociology [,sosɪ'aləʒi] o [,soʃɪ'aləʒi] s sociología

sock [sak] s calcetín *m*; (slang) golpe *m* fuerte ‖ *tr* (slang) golpear con fuerza

socket ['sakɪt] s (*of the eyes*) cuenca; (*of a tooth*) alvéolo; (*of a candlestick*) cañón *m*; (*of a socket wrench*) cubo; (elec) portalámparas; (rad) zócalo

socket wrench s llave *f* de caja, llave de cubo

sod [sad] s césped *m*; terrón *m* de césped ‖ *v* (*pret & pp* **sodded**; *ger* **sodding**) *tr* encespedar

soda ['sodə] s soda, sosa; (*drink*) soda

soda fountain s fuente *f* de sodas

soda water *s* agua gaseosa
sodium ['sodɪ•əm] *adj* sódico, de sodio ‖ *s* sodio
sofa ['sofə] *s* sofá *m*
soft [sɔft] o [saft] *adj* blando, muelle; (*skin*) suave; (*iron*) dulce; (*hat*) flexible; (*solder*) tierno; (coll) fácil
soft-boiled egg ['sɔft'bɔɪld] o ['saft'bɔɪld] *s* huevo pasado por agua
soft coal *s* hulla grasa
soft drink *s* bebida no alcohólica, refresco
soften ['sɔfən] o ['safən] *tr* ablandar; **to soften up** (*by bombardment*) ablandar ‖ *intr* ablandarse
soft'-ped'al *tr* (mus) disminuir la intensidad de, por medio del pedal suave; (slang) moderar ·
soft soap *tr* jabón blando o graso; (coll) adulación
soft'-soap' *s* (coll) enjabonar, dar jabón a
soft'ware' *s* (computer) programa *m* (para ordenador), operaciones *fpl*
sog•gy ['sagɪ] *adj* (*comp* **-gier;** *super* **-giest**) remojado, ensopado
soil [sɔɪl] *s* suelo; país *m*, región; (*spot, stain*) mancha; (fig) mancha, deshonra ‖ *tr* manchar, ensuciar; manchar, deshonrar; viciar, corromper ‖ *intr* mancharse, ensuciarse
soil pipe *s* tubo de desagüe sanitario
soiree o **soirée** [swa're] *s* sarao, velada
sojourn ['sodʒʌrn] *s* estancia, permanencia ‖ ['sodʒʌrn] o [so'dʒʌrn] *intr* estarse, permanecer
soil. *abbr* **soluble, solution**
solace ['salɪs] *s* solaz *m*, consuelo ‖ *tr* solazar, consolar
solar ['solər] *adj* solar
solar battery *s* fotopila
solder ['sadər] *s* soldadura ‖ *tr* soldar
soldering iron *s* cautín *m*, soldador *m*
soldier ['soldʒər] *s* (*enlisted man as distinguished from an officer*) soldado; (*man in military service*) militar *m* ‖ *intr* servir como soldado
soldier of fortune *s* aventurero militar
soldier•y ['soldʒəri] *s* (*pl* **-ies**) soldadesca
sold out [sold] *adj* agotado; **the theater is sold out** todas las localidades están vendidas; **we are sold out of those neckties** se nos han agotado esas corbatas
sole [sol] *adj* solo, único; exclusivo ‖ *s* (*of foot*) planta; (*of shoe*) suela; (*fish*) lenguado ‖ *tr* solar
solely ['solli] *adv* solamente, únicamente
solemn ['saləm] *adj* solemne
solicit [sə'lɪsɪt] *tr* solicitar; intentar seducir
solicitor [sə'lɪsɪtər] *s* solicitador *m*, agente *m;* (law) procurador *m*
solicitous [sə'lɪsɪtəs] *adj* solícito
solicitude [sə'lɪsɪtjud] o [sə'lɪsɪtud] *s* solicitud
solid ['salɪd] *adj* sólido; unánime; (*sound, good*) sólido, macizo; (*e.g., clouds*) denso; (*without pause or interruption*) entero; (*e.g., gold*) puro ‖ *s* sólido
solidarity [,salɪ'derɪtɪ] *s* solidaridad; **to declare one's solidarity with** solidarizar con

solid geometry *s* geometría del espacio
solidity [sə'lɪdɪtɪ] *s* (*pl* **-ties**) solidez *f*
solid majority *s* mayoría cómoda
sol'id-state' *adj* transistorizado
solid-state physics *s* física del estado sólido
solid tire *s* (aut) macizo
solilo•quy [sə'lɪləkwi] *s* (*pl* **-quies**) soliloquio
solitaire ['salɪ,tɛr] *s* (*game and diamond*) solitario; sortija solitario
solitar•y ['salɪ,tɛri] *adj* solitario; **in solitary confinement** incomunicado ‖ *s* (*pl* **-ies**) solitario
solitary confinement *s* incomunicación, aislamiento penal
solitude ['salɪ,tjud] o ['salɪ,tud] *s* soledad
so•lo ['solo] *adj* (*instrument*) solista; a solas, hecho a solas ‖ *s* (*pl* **-los**) (mus) solo
soloist ['solo•ɪst] *s* solista *mf*
solstice ['salstɪs] *s* solsticio
solution [sə'luʃən] *s* solución
solve [salv] *tr* resolver, solucionar; adivinar (*un enigma*)
solvent ['salvənt] *adj & s* solvente *m*
somber ['sambər] *adj* sombrío
some [sʌm] *adj indef* algún; un poco de; unos; (coll) grande, bueno, famoso ‖ *pron indef pl* algunos, unos
some'bod'y *pron indef* alguien; **somebody else** algún otro, otra persona ‖ *s* (*pl* **-ies**) (coll) personaje *m*
some'day' *adv* algún día
some'how' *adv* de algún modo, de alguna manera; **somehow or other** de un modo u otro
some'one' *pron indef* alguien; **someone else** algún otro, otra persona
somersault ['sʌmər,sɔlt] *s* salto mortal ‖ *intr* dar un salto mortal
something ['sʌmθɪŋ] *adv* algo, un poco; (coll) muy, excesivamente ‖ *pron indef* alguna cosa, algo; **something else** otra cosa
some'time' *adj* antiguo, de otro tiempo ‖ *adv* alguna vez; antiguamente
some'times' *adv* a veces, algunas veces
some'way' *adv* de algún modo
some'what' *adv* algo, un poco ‖ *s* alguna cosa, algo
some'where' *adv* en alguna parte, a alguna parte; en algún tiempo; **somewhere else** en otra parte, a otra parte
somnambulist [sam'næmbjəlɪst] *s* sonámbulo
somnolent ['samnələnt] *adj* soñoliento
son [sʌn] *s* hijo
song [sɔŋ] o [saŋ] *s* canción, canto; **for a song** muy barato; **to sing the same old song** volver a la misma canción
song'bird' *s* ave canora
Song of Songs *s* Cantar *m* de los Cantares
song writer *s* cantautor *m*
sonic ['sanɪk] *adj* sónico
sonic boom *s* (aer) estampido sónico
son'-in-law' *s* (*pl* **sons-in-law**) yerno, hijo político
sonnet ['sanɪt] *s* soneto

sonneteer [,sɑnɪ'tɪr] s sonetista mf; poetastro ‖ intr sonetizar

son•ny ['sʌni] s (pl **-nies**) hijito

sonori•ty [sə'nɔrɪti] s (pl **-ties**) sonoridad

soon [sun] adv pronto, en breve; temprano; de buena gana; **as soon as** así que, en cuanto, luego que, tan pronto como; **as soon as possible** cuanto antes, lo más pronto posible; **had sooner** preferiría; **how soon?** ¿cuándo?; **soon after** poco después, poco después de; **sooner or later** tarde o temprano

soot [sʊt] o [sut] s hollín m

soothe [suð] tr aliviar, calmar, sosegar

soothsayer ['suθ,se•ər] s adivino

soot•y ['sʊti] o ['suti] adj (comp **-ier**; super **-iest**) holliniento, tiznado

sop [sɑp] s (food soaked in milk, etc.) sopa; regalo (para acallar, apaciguar o sobornar) ‖ v (pret & pp **sopped**; ger **sopping**) tr empapar, ensopar; **to sop up** absorber

sophisticated [sə'fɪstɪ,ketɪd] adj mundano, falto de simplicidad, corrido

sophomore ['sɑfə,mor] s estudiante mf de segundo año

sopping ['sɑpɪŋ] adj empapado; **sopping wet** hecho una sopa

sopran•o [sə'præno] o [sə'prɑno] adj de soprano; para soprano ‖ s (pl **-os**) soprano mf

sorcerer ['sɔrsərər] s brujo, hechicero

sorceress ['sɔrsərɪs] s bruja, hechicera

sorcer•y ['sɔrsəri] s (pl **-ies**) brujería, hechicería, sortilegio

sordid ['sɔrdɪd] adj sórdido

sore [sor] adj enrojecido, inflamado; (coll) resentido, picado; **to be sore at** (coll) estar enojado con ‖ s llaga, úlcera; pena, dolor m, aflicción; **to open an old sore** renovar la herida

sorely ['sorli] adv penosamente; con urgencia

sore throat s dolor m de garganta

sorori•ty [sə'rɔrɪti] s (pl **-ties**) hermandad de estudiantas

sorrel ['sɔrəl] adj alazán

sorrow ['sɔro] s dolor m, pena pesar m; arrepentimiento ‖ intr dolerse, apenarse, sentir pena; arrepentirse; **to sorrow for** añorar

sorrowful ['sɔrəfəl] adj doloroso, pesaroso, acongojado

sor•ry ['sɑri] o ['sɔri] adj (comp **-rier**; super **-riest**) afligido, apenado, pesaroso; arrepentido; malo, pésimo; despreciable, ridículo; **to be** o **feel sorry** sentir; arrepentirse; **to be** o **feel sorry for** compadecer; arrepentirse de; **I am sorry** lo siento, me sabe mal

sort [sɔrt] s clase f, especie f; modo, manera; **a sort of** uno a modo de; **out of sorts** de mal humor; **sort of** (coll) algo, en cierta medida ‖ tr clasificar, separar; escoger, entresacar

so'-so' adj mediano, regular, talcualillo ‖ adv así así, tal cual

sot [sɑt] s borracho

sotto voce ['sɑto 'votʃə] adv a sovoz, en voz baja

soubrette [su'brɛt] s (theat) confidenta de comedia; (theat) doncella coquetona

soul [sol] s alma; **upon my soul!** ¡por vida mía!

sound [saʊnd] adj sano: sólido, firme; solvente; sonoro; (sleep) profundo, prudente; legal, válido ‖ adv profundamente ‖ s sonido; ruido; (passage of water) estrecho, brazo de mar; (surg) sonda, tienta; **within sound of** al alcance de ‖ tr sonar; tocar (p.ej., campanas); tantear, sondear; auscultar (p.ej., los pulmones); entonar (p.ej., alabanzas) ‖ intr sonar, resonar; sondar; parecer; **to sound like** sonar a, sonar como

sound'-ab•sorb'ent adj fonoabsorbente

sound barrier s muro del sonido, barrera de sonido, barrera sónica

sound'-dead'en•ing adj fonoabsorbente

sound film s película sonora

soundly ['saʊndli] adv sanamente; profundamente; a fondo, completamente

sound'proof' adj antisonoro; insonorizado ‖ tr insonorizar

soundproofing ['saʊnd,prufɪŋ] s insonorización

soup [sup] s sopa

soup kitchen s comedor m de beneficencia, dispensario de alimentos

soup spoon s cuchara de sopa

sour [saʊr] adj agrio ‖ tr agriar ‖ intr agriarse

source [sɔrs] s fuente f, manantial m

source material s fuentes fpl originales

sour cherry s (tree) guindo; (fruit) guinda

sour grapes interj ¡están verdes las uvas!

south [saʊθ] adj meridional, del sur ‖ adv al sur, hacia el sur ‖ s sur m, mediodía m

South America s Sudamérica, la América del Sur

South American adj & s sudamericano

southern ['sʌðərn] adj meridional

Southern Cross s Cruz f del Sur

southerner ['sʌðərnər] s meridional mf; sureño (Am)

South Korea s la Corea del Sur

South Korean adj & s surcoreano

south'paw' adj & s (slang in sport) zurdo

South Pole s polo sur, polo antártico

southward ['saʊθwərd] adv hacia el sur

south wind s austro, noto

souvenir [,suvə'nɪr] o ['suvə,nɪr] s recuerdo, memoria

sovereign ['sʌvrɪn] o ['sʌvrɪn] adj soberano ‖ s (king; coin) soberano; (queen) soberana

sovereign•ty ['sʌvrɪnti] o ['sʌvrɪnti] s (pl **-ties**) soberanía

soviet ['sovɪ,ɛt] o [,sovɪ'ɛt] adj soviético ‖ s soviet m

sovietize ['sovɪ•ɛ,taɪz] tr sovietizar

Soviet Russia s la Rusia Soviética

Soviet Union s Unión Soviética

sow [saʊ] s puerca ‖ [so] v (pret **sowed**; pp **sown** o **sowed**) tr sembrar; (with mines) plagar

soybean ['sɔɪ,bin] s soja; soya; semilla de soja

sp. abbr **special, species, specific, specimen, spelling**

spa [spɑ] *s* caldas, balneario

space [spes] *adj* espacial, del espacio ‖ *s* espacio; **in the space of** por espacio de ‖ *tr* espaciar

space bar *s* espaciador *m*, tecla de espacios

space'craft' *s* astronave *f*, cosmonave *f*

space flight *s* vuelo espacial

space key *s* llave *f* espacial

space•man ['spes,mæn] *s* (*pl* **-men** [,mɛn]) navegador *m* del espacio; astronauta *m*; visitante *m* a la Tierra del espacio exterior

space'ship' *s* nave *f* del espacio

space shuttle *s* transbordador *m* espacial

space station *s* apostadero espacial

space suit *s* escafandra espacial

space travel *s* cosmonavegación

space vehicle *s* vehículo espacial

spacious ['speʃəs] *adj* espacioso

spade [sped] *s* laya; (*playing card*) pique *m*; **to call a spade a spade** llamar al pan pan y al vino vino

spade'work' *s* trabajo preliminar

spaghetti [spə'gɛti] *s* espagueti *m*

Spain [spen] *s* España

span [spæn] *s* palmo, cuarta, llave *f* de la mano; espacio, lapso, trecho; (*of horses*) pareja; (*of a bridge*) ojo; (aer) envergadura ‖ *v* (*pret & pp* **spanned**; *ger* **spanning**) *tr* medir a palmos; atravesar, extenderse sobre

spangle ['spæŋgəl] *s* lentejuela ‖ *tr* adornar con lentejuelas; (*to stud with bright objects*) estrellar ‖ *intr* brillar

Spaniard ['spænjərd] *s* español *m*

spaniel ['spænjəl] *s* perro de aguas

Spanish ['spænɪʃ] *adj & s* español *m*; **the Spanish** los españoles

Spanish America *s* la América Española, Hispanoamérica

Spanish broom *s* retama

Spanish fly *s* abadejo, cantárida

Spanish Main *s* Costa Firme, Tierra Firme; mar *m* Caribe

Spanish moss *s* barba española

Spanish omelet *s* tortilla de tomate

Span'ish-speak'ing *adj* de habla española, hispanohablante, hispanoparlante

spank [spæŋk] *tr* azotar, zurrar

spanking ['spæŋkɪŋ] *adj* rápido; fuerte; (coll) muy grande, muy hermoso, extraordinario ‖ *s* azote *m*

spar *s* (mineral) espato; (naut) mástil *m*, palo, verga ‖ *v* (*pret & pp* **sparred**; *ger* **sparring**) *intr* pelear, reñir; boxear

spare [spɛr] *adj* sobrante; libre, disponible; de repuesto; delgado, enjuto, flaco; parco, sobrio ‖ *tr* pasar sin; perdonar; guardar, salvar; ahorrar; **to have . . . to spare** tener de sobra; **to spare oneself** ahorrarse esfuerzos

spare bed *s* cama de sobra

spare parts *spl* piezas de repuesto o de recambio

spare room *s* cuarto de reserva

sparing ['spɛrɪŋ] *adj* económico; (*scanty*) escaso

spark [spɑrk] *s* chispa; (*e.g., of truth*) centellita ‖ *tr* (coll) cortejar, galantear (*a una mujer*) ‖ *intr* chispear

spark coil *s* bobina de chispas, bobina de encendido

spark gap *s* (*of induction coil*) entrehierro; (*of spark plug*) espacio de chispa

sparkle ['spɑrkəl] *s* chispita, destello; (*wit*) travesura; alegría, viveza ‖ *intr* chispear; ser alegre; espumar, ser efervescente

sparkling ['spɑrklɪŋ] *adj* centelleante, chispeante; (*wine*) espumante, espumoso; (*water*) gaseoso

spark plug *s* bujía

sparrow ['spæro] *s* gorrión *m*

sparse [spɑrs] *adj* (*population*) poco denso; (*hair*) ralo

Spartan ['spɑrtən] *adj & s* espartano

spasm ['spæzəm] *s* espasmo; esfuerzo súbito y de breve duración

spasmodic ['spæz'mɑdɪk] *adj* espasmódico; intermitente; caprichoso

spastic ['spæstɪk] *adj* espástico

spat [spæt] *s* disputa, riña; botín *m*, polaina corta

spatial ['speʃəl] *adj* espacial

spatter ['spætər] *tr* salpicar; manchar ‖ *intr* chorrear; chapotear

spatula ['spætʃələ] *s* espátula

spavin ['spævɪn] *s* esparaván *m*

spawn [spɔn] *s* freza; prole *f*; producto, resultado ‖ *tr* engendrar ‖ *intr* desovar, frezar (*los peces*)

speak [spik] *v* (*pret* **spoke** [spok]; *pp* **spoken**) *tr* hablar (*un idioma*); decir (*la verdad*) ‖ *intr* hablar; **so to speak** por decirlo así; **speaking!** ¡al habla!; **to speak out** o **up** osar hablar, elevar la voz

speak'-eas'y *s* (*pl* **-ies**) (slang) taberna clandestina

speaker ['spikər] *s* hablante *mf*; orador *m*; (*of a legislative assembly*) presidente *m*; (rad) altavoz *m*

speaking ['spikɪŋ] *adj* hablante; **to be on speaking terms** hablarse ‖ *s* habla; elocuencia

speaking tube *s* tubo acústico

spear [spɪr] *s* lanza; (*for fishing*) arpón *m*; (*of grass*) hoja ‖ *tr* alancear, herir con lanza

spear'head' *s* punta de lanza ‖ *tr* dirigir, conducir; encabezar; dar impulso a

spear'mint' *s* menta verde, menta romana

spec. *abbr* **special**

special ['spɛʃəl] *adj* especial; **nothing special** (*no great thing*) nada del otro mundo ‖ *s* tren *m* especial

spe'cial-deliv'ery *adj* urgente, de urgencia

specialist ['spɛʃəlɪst] *s* especialista *mf*

speciali•ty [,spɛʃɪ'ælɪti] *s* (*pl* **-ties**) especialidad

specialize ['spɛʃə,laɪz] *tr* especializar ‖ *intr* especializar o especializarse

special•ty ['spɛʃəlti] *s* (*pl* **-ties**) especialidad

spe•cies ['spiʃiz] *s* (*pl* **-cies**) especie *f*

specific [spɪ'sɪfɪk] *adj & s* específico

speci•fy ['spɛsɪ,faɪ] *v* (*pret & pp* **-fied**) *tr* especificar

so
sp

specimen ['spɛsɪmən] s espécimen m; (coll) tipo, sujeto

specious ['spiʃəs] adj especioso, engañoso

speck [spɛk] s mota, manchita ‖ tr motear, manchar, salpicar de manchas

speckle ['spɛkəl] s mota, punto ‖ tr motear, puntear

spectacle ['spɛktəkəl] s espectáculo; **spectacles** anteojos, gafas

spectator ['spɛktetər] s espectador m

specter ['spɛktər] s espectro

spec·trum ['spɛktrəm] s (pl **-tra** [trə] o **-trums**) espectro

speculate ['spɛkjə,let] intr especular

speech [spitʃ] s habla; (of an actor) parlamento; (talk before an audience) conferencia, discurso

speech clinic s clínica de la palabra

speech correction s foniatría, logopedía

speech defect s defecto del habla

speechless ['spitʃlɪs] adj sin habla; estupefacto

speed [spid] s velocidad; (aut) marcha, velocidad; (slang) anfetaminas tomadas como alucinantes ‖ v (pret & pp **sped** [spɛd]) tr apresurar; despedir; ayudar ‖ intr apresurarse; adelantar, progresar; ir con exceso de velocidad

speeding ['spidɪŋ] s exceso de velocidad

speed king s as m del volante

speed limit s velocidad permitida

speedometer [spi'damɪtər] s (to indicate speed) velocímetro; velocímetro y cuentakilómetros unidos

speed record s marca de velocidad

speed·y ['spidi] adj (comp **-ier;** super **-iest**) rápido, veloz

spell [spɛl] s encanto, hechizo; tanda, turno, rato, poco tiempo; (e.g., of good weather) temporada; **to cast a spell on** encantar, hechizar ‖ v (pret & pp **spelled** o **spelt** [spɛlt]) tr deletrear; indicar, significar; **to spell out** (coll) explicar detalladamente ‖ intr deletrear ‖ v (pret & pp **spelled**) tr reemplazar, relevar

spell'bind'er s (coll) orador m fascinante, orador persuasivo

spelling ['spɛlɪŋ] adj ortográfico ‖ s (act) deletreo; (subject or study) ortografía; (way a word is spelled) grafía

spelunker [spɪ'lʌŋkər] s espeleólogo de afición

spend [spɛnd] v (pret & pp **spent** [spɛnt]) tr gastar; pasar (una hora, un día, etc.)

spender ['spɛndər] s gastador m

spending money s dinero para gastos menudos

spend'thrift' s derrochador m, pródigo

sperm [spʌrm] s esperma; (coll) leche f

sperm whale s cachalote m

spew [spju] tr & intr vomitar

sp. gr. abbr **specific gravity**

sphere [sfɪr] s esfera; astro, cuerpo celeste

spherical ['sfɛrɪkəl] adj esférico

sphinx [sfɪŋks] s (pl **sphinxes** o **sphinges** ['sfɪndʒiz]) esfinge f

spice [spaɪs] s especia; (zest, piquancy) sainete m; fragancia ‖ tr especiar; dar gusto o picante a

spice box s especiero

spick-and-span ['spɪkənd'spæn] adj flamante; limpio, pulcro

spic·y ['spaɪsi] adj (comp **-ier;** super **-iest**) especiado; picante; aromático; enchiloso (CAm, Mex); sicalíptico

spider ['spaɪdər] s araña

spider web s tela de araña, telaraña

spiff·y ['spɪfi] adj (comp **-ier;** super **-iest**) (slang) guapo, elegante

spigot ['spɪgət] s grifo; (plug to stop a vent) espiche m

spike [spaɪk] s (long, heavy nail) estaca, escarpia; (sharp projection or part) punta, pico, púa; (bot) espiga ‖ tr empernar; acabar, poner fin a

spill [spɪl] s derrame m; líquido derramado; (coll) caída, vuelco ‖ v (pret & pp **spilled** o **spilt** [spɪlt]) tr derramar, verter; (coll) hacer caer, volcar ‖ intr derramarse, verterse; (coll) caer, volcarse

spill'way' s bocacaz m, canal m de desagüe

spin [spɪn] s vuelta, giro muy rápido; (coll) paseo en coche, etc.; **to go into a spin** (aer) entrar en barrena ‖ v (pret & pp **spun** [spʌn]; ger **spinning**) tr hacer girar; hilar (p.ej., lino); bailar (un trompo); **to spin off** (derivative) rendir; **to spin out** extender, prolongar; **to spin yarns** contar cuentos increíbles ‖ intr dar vueltas, girar; hilar; bailar (un trompo); (aer) entrar en barrena

spinach ['spɪnɪtʃ] o ['spɪnɪdʒ] s espinaca; (leaves used as food) espinacas

spinal ['spaɪnəl] adj espinal

spinal column s espina dorsal, columna vertebral

spinal cord s médula espinal

spinal disk s disco vertebral

spindle ['spɪndəl] s (rounded rod tapering toward each end) huso; (small shaft, axle) eje m; (turned ornament in a baluster) mazorca

spine [spaɪn] s espina, púa; (rib, ridge) cordoncillo; loma, cerro; (anat) espina; (bb) lomo; (fig) ánimo, valor m

spineless ['spaɪnlɪs] adj sin espinas, sin espinazo; sin firmeza de carácter

spinet ['spɪnɪt] s espineta

spinner ['spɪnər] s hilandero; máquina de hilar

spinning ['spɪnɪŋ] adj hilador ‖ s (act) hila; (art) hilandería

spinning wheel s torno de hilar

spin'-off' s derivado; subproducto

spinster ['spɪnstər] s (obs or offensive) soltera, rona

spi·ral ['spaɪrəl] adj & s espiral f ‖ v (pret & pp **-raled** o **-ralled;** ger **-raling** o **-ralling**) intr dar vueltas como una espiral; (aer) volar en espiral

spiral staircase s escalera de caracol

spire [spaɪr] s cima, ápice m; (of a steeple) aguja, chapitel m; (e.g., of grass) tallo

spirit [ˈspɪrɪt] s espíritu m; humor m, temple m; personaje m; licur m ‖ tr—**to spirit away** llevarse misteriosamente
spirited [ˈspɪrɪtɪd] adj fogoso, espiritoso
spirit lamp s lámpara de alcohol
spiritless [ˈspɪrɪtlɪs] adj apocado, tímido, sin ánimo
spirit level s nivel m de burbuja
spiritual [ˈspɪrɪtʃʊ·əl] adj espiritual
spiritualism [ˈspɪrɪtʃʊə·lɪzəm] s espiritismo; (belief that all reality is spiritual) espiritualismo
spirituous liquors [ˈspɪrɪtʃʊ·əs] spl licores espirituosos
spit [spɪt] s esputo, saliva; (for roasting) asador m, espetón m; punta o lengua de tierra; **the spit and image of** la segunda edición de, el retrato de ‖ v (pret & pp **spat** [spæt] o **spit**; ger **spitting**) tr escupir ‖ intr escupir; lloviznar; neviscar; fufar (el gato)
spite [spaɪt] s despecho, rencor m, inquina; **in spite of** a pesar de, a despecho de; **out of spite** por despecho ‖ tr despechar, molestar, picar
spiteful [ˈspaɪtfəl] adj despechado, rencoroso
spit'fire' s fierabrás m; mujer f de mal genio
spittoon [spɪˈtun] s escupidera
splash [splæʃ] s rociada, salpicadura; (e.g., with the hands) chapaleo, chapoteo; **to make a splash** (coll) hacer impresión, llamar la atención, causar furor ‖ tr & intr salpicar; chapotear
splash'down' s acuatizaje m
spleen [splin] s mal humor m; (anat) bazo; **to vent one's spleen** descargar la bilis
splendid [ˈsplɛndɪd] adj espléndido; (coll) magnífico, maravilloso
splendor [ˈsplɛndər] s esplendor m
splice [splaɪs] s empalme m, junta ‖ tr empalmar, juntar
splint [splɪnt] s (splinter) astilla, tablilla; (surg) tablilla ‖ tr entablillar (un hueso roto)
splinter [ˈsplɪntər] s astilla; (of stone, glass, bone) esquirla ‖ tr astillar ‖ intr astillarse, hacerse astillas
splinter group s grupúsculo; grupo disidente
split [splɪt] adj hendido, partido; dividido ‖ s división, fractura; (slang) porción ‖ v (pret & pp **split**; ger **splitting**) tr dividir, partir; **to split one's sides with laughter** desternillarse de risa ‖ intr dividirse a lo largo; **to split away (from)** separarse (de)
split fee s dicotomía (entre médicos)
split personality s personalidad desdoblada
splitting [ˈsplɪtɪŋ] adj partidor; fuerte, violento; (headache) enloquecedor
splotch [splɑtʃ] s borrón m, mancha grande ‖ tr salpicar, manchar
splurge [splʌrdʒ] s (coll) fachenda, ostentación ‖ intr (coll) fachendear
splutter [ˈsplʌtər] s chisporroteo; (manner of speaking) farfulla ‖ tr farfullar ‖ intr chisporrotear; farfullar
spoil [spɔɪl] s botín m, presa; **spoils** (taken from an enemy) botín m, despojos; (of political victory) enchufes mpl ‖ v (pret & pp

spoiled o **spoilt** [spɔɪlt]) tr echar a perder, estropear; mimar (a un niño); amargar (una tertulia) ‖ intr echarse a perder
spoiled [spɔɪld] adj (child) consentido, mimado; (food) pasado, podrido
spoils·man [ˈspɔɪlzmən] s (pl -men [mən]) enchufista m
spoils system s enchufismo
spoke [spok] s (of a wheel) radio, rayo; (of a ladder) escalón m
spokes·man [ˈspoksmən] s (pl -men [mən]) o **spokesperson** s portavoz m, vocero
sponge [spʌndʒ] s esponja; **to throw in (o up) the sponge** (coll) tirar la esponja ‖ tr limpiar con esponja; borrar; absorber ‖ intr ser absorbente; **to sponge on** (coll) vivir a costa de
sponge cake s bizcocho muy ligero
sponger [ˈspʌndʒər] s esponja (gorrón, parásito); bolsero (SAm)
sponge rubber s caucho esponjoso
spon·gy [ˈspʌndʒi] adj (comp -gier; super -giest) esponjoso
sponsor [ˈspɑnsər] s patrocinador m; (godfather) padrino; (godmother) madrina ‖ tr patrocinar
sponsorship [ˈspɑnsər, ʃɪp] s patrocinio
spontaneous [spɑnˈtenɪ·əs] adj espontáneo
spoof [spuf] s (slang) mistificación, engaño; (slang) broma ‖ tr (slang) mistificar, engañar ‖ intr (slang) bromear, burlar; (slang) parodiar
spook [spuk] s aparecido, espectro
spook·y [ˈspuki] adj (comp -ier; super -iest) espectral, espeluznante; (horse) asustadizo
spool [spul] s carrete m, bobina
spoon [spun] s cuchara ‖ tr cucharear ‖ intr (slang) besuquearse (los enamorados)
spoonful [ˈspunˌful] s cucharada
spoon·y [ˈspuni] adj (comp -ier; super -iest) (coll) baboso, sobón
sporadic(al) [spəˈrædɪk(əl)] adj esporádico
spore [spor] s espora
sport [sport] adj deportivo, de deporte ‖ s deporte m; deportista mf; (person or thing controlled by some power or passion) juguete m; (laughingstock) hazmerreír m; (gambler) (coll) tahur m, jugador m; (in gambling or playing games) (coll) buen perdedor; (flashy fellow) (coll) guapo, majo; (biol) mutación; **to make sport of** burlarse de, reírse de ‖ tr (coll) lucir (p.ej., un traje nuevo) ‖ intr divertirse; estar de burla; juguetear
sport clothes spl trajes mpl de sport
sport fan s aficionado al deporte, deportista mf
sporting chance s riesgo de buen perdedor
sporting goods spl artículos de deporte
sporting house s casa de juego; casa de rameras
sports'cast'er s locutor deportivo
sports·man [ˈsportsmən] s (pl -men [mən]) deportista m; jugador honrado
sports news s noticiario deportivo
sports'wear' s trajes deportivos
sports writer s cronista deportivo

sp
sp

sport·y [ˈsporti] *adj* (*comp* **-ier;** *super* **-iest**) elegante, guapo; alegre, brillante; magnánimo; disipado, libertino

spot [spɑt] *s* mancha; sitio, lugar *m;* (coll) poquito; **on the spot** allí mismo; al punto; (slang) en dificultad; (slang) en peligro de muerte; **to hit the spot** tener razón; dar completa satisfacción ‖ *v* (*pret &* *pp* **spotted;** *ger* **spotting**) *tr* manchar; descubrir, reconocer ‖ *intr* mancharse, tener manchas

spot cash *s* dinero contante

spot check *s* verificación a la ventura

spotless [ˈspɑtlɪs] *adj* inmaculado, sin manchas

spot′light′ *s* proyector *m* orientable; luz concentrada; (aut) faro piloto, faro giratorio; (fig) atención del público

spot remover [rɪˈmuvər] *s* (*person*) quitamanchas *mf;* (*material*) quitamanchas *m*

spot welding *s* soldadura por puntos

spouse [spauz] o [spaus] *s* cónyuge *mf,* consorte *mf*

spout [spaut] *s* (*to carry off water from roof*) canalón *m;* (*of a jar, pitcher, etc.*) pico; (*of a sprinkling can*) rallo, roseta; (*jet*) chorro; **up the spout** (slang) acabado, arruinado ‖ *tr* echar en chorro; (coll) declamar ‖ *intr* chorrear; (coll) declamar

sprain [spren] *s* torcedura, esguince *m* ‖ *tr* torcer, torcerse

sprawl [sprɔl] *intr* arrellanarse

spray [spre] *s* rociada; (*of the sea*) espuma; (*device*) pulverizador *m;* (*twig*) ramita ‖ *tr & intr* rociar

sprayer [ˈspreər] *s* rociador *m*, pulverizador *m*, vaporizador *m*

spread [sprɛd] *s* extensión; amplitud, anchura; difusión; diferencia; cubrecama, sobrecama; mantel *m*, tapete *m;* (*of the wings of a bird; of the wings of an airplane*) envergadura; (coll) festín *m*, comilona ‖ *v* (*pret & pp* **spread**) *tr* extender; difundir, propagar; esparcir; escalonar; abrir, separar; poner (*la mesa*) ‖ *intr* extenderse; difundirse; esparcirse; abrirse, separarse

spree [spri] *s* juerga, parranda; borrachera; **to go on a spree** ir de juerga; pillar una mona

sprig [sprɪg] *s* ramita

spright·ly [ˈspraɪtli] *adj* (*comp* **-lier;** *super* **-liest**) alegre, animado, vivo

spring [sprɪŋ] *adj* primaveral; de manantial; de muelle, de resorte ‖ *s* (*season of the year*) primavera; (*issue of water from earth*) fuente *f*, manantial *m;* (*elastic device*) muelle *m*, resorte *m;* (*of an automobile or wagon*) ballesta; (*leap, jump*) brinco, salto; abertura, grieta; tensión, tirantez *f* ‖ *v* (*pret* **sprang** [spræŋ] o **sprung** [sprʌŋ]; *pp* **sprung**) *tr* soltar (*un muelle o resorte*); torcer, combar, encorvar; hacer saltar (*una trampa, una mina*) ‖ *intr* saltar; saltar de golpe; brotar, nacer, proceder; torcerse, combarse, encorvarse; **to spring at** abalanzarse sobre; **to spring forth** precipitarse; brotar; **to spring up** levantarse de un salto; brotar, nacer; presentarse a la vista

spring′board′ *s* trampolín *m*

spring chicken *s* polluelo; (*young person*) (coll) pollita

spring fever *s* (hum) ataque *m* primaveral, galbana

spring mattress *s* colchón *m* de muelles, somier *m*

spring′time′ *s* primavera

sprinkle [ˈsprɪŋkəl] *s* rociada; llovizna; pizca ‖ *tr* regar, rociar; salpicar, sembrar; espolvorear (*p.ej., azúcar*) ‖ *intr* rociar; lloviznar, gotear

sprinkling can *s* regadera, rociadera

sprint [sprɪnt] *s* (sport) embalaje *m* ‖ *intr* (sport) embalarse, lanzarse

sprite [spraɪt] *s* duende *m*, trasgo

sprocket [ˈsprɑkɪt] *s* diente *m* de rueda de cadena; rueda de cadena

sprout [spraut] *s* brote *m*, renuevo, retoño ‖ *intr* brotar, germinar, echar renuevos; crecer rápidamente

spruce [sprus] *adj* apuesto, elegante, garboso ‖ *s* abeto del Norte, abeto falso, pícea ‖ *tr* ataviar, componer ‖ *intr* ataviarse, componerse; **to spruce up** emperifollarse

spry [spraɪ] *adj* (*comp* **spryer** o **sprier;** *super* **spryest** o **spriest**) activo, ágil

spud [spʌd] *s* (*chisel*) escoplo; (agr) escoda; (coll) patata

spun glass [spʌn] *s* vidrio hilado, cristal hilado

spunk [spʌŋk] *s* (coll) ánimo, coraje *m*, corazón *m*, valor *m*

spun silk *s* seda cardada o hilada

spur [spʌr] *s* espuela; (*central point of an auger*) gusanillo; (*of a cock, mountain, warship*) espolón *m;* (rr) ramal corto; (*goad, stimulus*) (fig) espuela; **on the spur of the moment** impulsivamente, sin la reflexión debida ‖ *v* (*pret & pp* **spurred;** *ger* **spurring**) *tr* espolear; espuelar (SAm); **to spur on** espolear, aguijonear

spurious [ˈspjʊriəs] *adj* espurio

spurn [spʌrn] *s* desdén *m*, menosprecio ‖ *tr* desdeñar, menospreciar; rechazar con desdén

spurt [spʌrt] *s* chorro repentino; esfuerzo repentino; arranque *m* ‖ *intr* salir en chorro, salir a borbotones

sputnik [ˈspʌtnɪk] *s* sputnik *m;* satélite *m* artificial

sputter [ˈspʌtər] *s* (*manner of speaking*) farfulla; (*sizzling*) chisporroteo ‖ *tr* farfullar ‖ *intr* farfullar; chisporrotear

spy [spaɪ] *s* (*pl* **spies**) espía *mf* ‖ *v* (*pret & pp* **spied**) *tr* columbrar, divisar ‖ *intr* espiar; **to spy on** espiar

spy′glass′ *s* catalejo, anteojo

spy satellite *s* satélite *m* espía

sq. *abbr* square

squabble [ˈskwɑbəl] *s* reyerta, riña ‖ *intr* reñir, disputar

squad [skwɑd] *s* escuadra

squadron [ˈskwɑdrən] *s* (aer) escuadrilla; (*of cavalry*) (mil) escuadrón *m;* (nav) escuadra

squalid [ˈskwɑlɪd] *adj* escuálido

squall [skwɔl] *s* grupada, turbión *m;* (*quarrel*) (coll) riña; (*upset, commotion*) (coll) chubasco

squalor [ˈskwɑlər] *s* escualidez *f*

squander [ˈskwɑndər] *tr* despilfarrar, malgastar

square [skwɛr] *adj* cuadrado, p.ej., **eight square inches** ocho pulgadas cuadradas; en cuadro, de lado, p.ej., **eight inches square** ocho pulgadas en cuadro, ocho pulgadas de lado; rectangular; justo, recto; honrado, leal; saldado; fuerte, sólido; (coll) abundante, completo; **to get square with** (coll) hacérselas pagar a ǁ *adv* en cuadro; en ángulo recto; honradamente, lealmente ǁ *s* cuadrado; (*of checkerboard or chessboard*) casilla, escaque *m;* (*city block*) manzana; (*open area in town or city*) plaza; (*carpenter's tool*) escuadra; **to be on the square** (coll) obrar de buena fe ǁ *tr* cuadrar; dividir en cuadros; ajustar, nivelar, conformar; saldar (*una cuenta*); (carp) escuadrar ǁ *intr* cuadrarse; **to square off** (coll) colocarse en posición de defensa

square dance *s* danza de figuras

square deal *s* (coll) trato equitativo

square meal *s* (coll) comida abundante

square shooter [ˈʃutər] *s* (coll) persona leal y honrada

squash [skwɑʃ] *s* aplastamiento; (bot) calabaza; (sport) frontón *m* con raqueta; ǁ *tr* aplastar, despachurrar; confutar (*un argumento*); acallar con un argumento, respuesta, etc. ǁ *intr* aplastarse

squash•y [ˈskwɑʃi] *adj* (*comp* **-ier;** *super* **-iest**) mojado y blando; (*muddy*) lodoso; (*fruit*) modorro

squat [skwɑt] *adj* en cuclillas; rechoncho ǁ *v* (*pret & pp* **squatted;** *ger* **squatting**) *intr* acuclillarse, agacharse; sentarse en el suelo; establecerse en terreno ajeno sin derecho; establecerse en terreno público para crear un derecho

squatter [ˈskwɑtər] *s* advenedizo, intruso, colono usurpador

squaw [skwɔ] *s* india norteamericana; mujer, esposa, muchacha

squawk [skwɔk] *s* graznido; (slang) queja chillona ǁ *intr* graznar; (slang) quejarse chillando

squaw man *s* blanco casado con india

squeak [skwik] *s* chillido; chirrido ǁ *intr* dar chillidos; chirriar

squeal [skwil] *s* chillido ǁ *intr* dar chillidos; (slang) delatar, soplar; **to squeal on** (slang) delatar, soplar (*a una persona*)

squealer [ˈskwilər] *s* (coll) soplón *m*

squeamish [ˈskwimiʃ] *adj* escrupuloso, remilgado; excesivamente modesto; (*easily nauseated*) asqueroso

squeeze [skwiz] *s* apretón *m;* **to put the squeeze on someone** (coll) hacer a uno la forzosa, meter en prensa a uno ǁ *tr* apretar; agobiar, oprimir; exprimir ǁ *intr* apretar; **to squeeze through** abrirse paso a estrujones por entre; salir de un aprieto a duras penas

squeezer [ˈskwizər] *s* exprimidera

squelch [skwɛltʃ] *s* (coll) tapaboca ǁ *tr* apabullar, despachurrar

squid [skwɪd] *s* calamar *m*

squint [skwɪnt] *s* mirada bizca; mirada furtiva; (*strabismus*) bizquera ǁ *tr* achicar, entornar (*los ojos*) ǁ *intr* bizquear; torcer la vista; tener los ojos medio cerrados

squint-eyed [ˈskwɪnt‚aɪd] *adj* bisojo, bizco; malévolo, sospechoso

squire [skwaɪr] *s* acompañante *m* (*de una señora*); (Brit) terrateniente *m* de antigua heredad; (U.S.A.) juez *m* de paz, juez local ǁ *tr* acompañar (*a una señora*)

squirm [skwʌrm] *s* retorcimiento ǁ *intr* retorcerse; **to squirm out of** escaparse de (*p.ej., un aprieto*) haciendo mucho esfuerzo

squirrel [ˈskwʌrəl] *s* ardilla

squirt [skwʌrt] *s* chorro; jeringazo; (coll) mono, presuntuoso ǁ *tr* arrojar a chorros ǁ *intr* salir a chorros

Sr. *abbr* **senior, Sir**

S.S. *abbr* **Secretary of State, steamship, Sunday school**

St. *abbr* **Saint, Strait, Street**

stab [stæb] *s* puñalada; (coll) tentativa; **to make a stab at** (slang) esforzarse por hacer ǁ *v* (*pret & pp* **stabbed;** *ger* **stabbing**) *tr* apuñalar; traspasar ǁ *intr* apuñalar

stab in the back *s* puñalada trapera

stable [ˈstebəl] *adj* estable ǁ *s* establo, cuadra, caballeriza

stack [stæk] *s* montón *m*, pila; (*of rifles*) pabellón *m;* (*of books in a library*) estantería, depósito; (*of a chimney*) cañón *m;* (*of straw*) niara; (*of firewood*) hacina; (coll) montón *m*, gran número ǁ *tr* amontonar, apilar; florear (*el naipe*); hacinar (*leña*)

stadi•um [ˈstedɪ‚əm] *s* (*pl* **-ums** o **-a** [ə]) estadio

staff [stæf] *s* bastón *m*, apoyo, sostén *m;* personal *m;* (mil) estado mayor; (mus) pentagrama *m* ǁ *tr* dotar, proveer de personal, nombrar personal para

stag [stæg] *adj* exclusivo para hombres, de hombres solos ǁ *s* (*male deer*) ciervo; varón *m;* varón solo (*no acompañado de mujeres*)

stage [stedʒ] *s* escena; etapa, jornada; (*coach*) diligencia; (*scene of an event*) teatro; (*of a microscope*) portaobjeto; (rad) etapa; **by easy stages** a pequeñas etapas; lentamente; **to go on the stage** hacerse actor ǁ *tr* poner en escena, representar; preparar, organizar

stage′coach′ *s* diligencia

stage′craft′ *s* arte *f* teatral

stage door *s* (theat) entrada de los artistas

stage fright *s* trac *m*, miedo al público

stage′hand′ *s* tramoyista *m*, metemuertos *m*, metesillas *m*

stage manager *s* director *m* de escena

stage′-struck′ *adj* loco por el teatro

stage whisper *s* susurro en voz alta

stagger [ˈstægər] *tr* sorprender; asustar; escalonar (*las horas de trabajo*) ǁ *intr* tambalear, hacer eses al andar

staggering *adj* tambaleante; sorprendente

sp
st

stagnant [ˈstægnənt] *adj* estancado; (fig) estancado, inactivo, paralizado

staid [sted] *adj* grave, serio, formal

stain [sten] *s* mancha; tinte *m*, tintura; materia colorante ‖ *tr* manchar; teñir; colorar ‖ *intr* mancharse; hacer manchas

stained glass *s* vidrio de color

stained′glass′ window *s* vidriera de colores, vidriera pintada, vitral *m*

stainless [ˈstenlɪs] *adj* inmanchable; (*steel*) inoxidable; inmaculado

stair [stɛr] *s* escalera; (*step of a series*) escalón *m;* **stairs** escalera

stair′case′ *s* escalera

stair′way′ *s* escalera

stair well *s* hueco de escalera

stake [stek] *s* estaca; (*of a cart or truck*) telero; (*to hold up a plant*) rodrigón *m;* (*in gambling*) puesta; premio del vencedor; **at stake** en juego; en gran peligro; **to die at the stake** morir en la hoguera; **to pull up stakes** (coll) irse; (coll) mudarse de casa ‖ *tr* estacar; atar a una estaca; rodrigar (*plantas*); apostar; arriesgar, aventurar; **to stake all** jugarse el todo por el todo; **to stake off** o **to stake out** estacar, señalar con estacas

stale [stel] *adj* añejo, rancio, viejo; (*air*) viciado; (*joke*) mohoso; anticuado

stale′mate′ *s* mate ahogado; **to reach a stalemate** llegar a un punto muerto ‖ *tr* dar mate ahogado a; estancar, paralizar

stalk [stɔk] *s* tallo ‖ *tr* cazar al acecho; acechar, espiar ‖ *intr* cazar al acecho; andar con paso majestuoso; andar con paso altivo; **to stalk out** salir con paso airado

stall [stɔl] *s* cuadra, establo; pesebre *m;* (*booth in a market*) puesto; (*at a fair*) caseta; (Brit) butaca; (slang) pretexto ‖ *tr* encerrar en un establo; poner trabas a; parar (*un motor*); **to stall off** (coll) eludir, evitar ‖ *intr* atascarse, atollarse; pararse (*un motor*); (slang) eludir para engañar o demorar; **to stall for time** (slang) tardar para ganar tiempo

stallion [ˈstæljən] *s* caballo padre, caballo semental

stalwart [ˈstɔlwərt] *adj* fornido, forzudo; valiente; leal, constante ‖ *s* persona fornida; partidario leal

stamen [ˈstemən] *s* estambre *m*

stamina [ˈstæmɪnə] *s* fuerza, nervio, vigor *m*, resistencia

stammer [ˈstæmər] *s* balbuceo, tartamudeo ‖ *tr* balbucear (*p.ej., excusas*) ‖ *intr* balbucear, tartamudear

stamp [stæmp] *s* (*device used for making an impression; mark made with it; piece of paper or mark used to show payment of postage*) sello; (*tool used for crushing or marking*) pisón *m;* (*tool for stamping coins and medals*) cuño, troquel *m;* marca, impresión; clase *f*, tipo ‖ *tr* sellar; troquelar; estampar, imprimir; hollar, pisotear; indicar, señalar; poner el sello a; bocartear (*el mineral*); **to stamp out** apagar pateando;

extinguir por la fuerza; suprimir; **to stamp the feet** dar patadas ‖ *intr* patalear

stampede [stæmˈpid] *s* fuga precipitada; estampida (Am) ‖ *tr* hacer huir en desorden; provocar a pánico ‖ *intr* huir en tropel; obrar por común impulso

stamping grounds *spl* (slang) guarida (*sitio frecuentado por una persona*)

stamp pad *s* tampón *m*

stamp′-vend′ing machine *s* máquina expendedora de sellos

stance [stæns] *s* (sport) postura, planta

stanch [stɑntʃ] *adj* firme, fuerte; constante, leal; (*watertight*) estanco ‖ *tr* estancar; retañar (*la sangre de una herida*)

stand [stænd] *s* parada; alto para defenderse; postura, posición; resistencia; estrado, tribuna; sostén *m* soporte *m*, pie *m;* puesto, quiosco ‖ *v* (*pret & pp* **stood** [stʊd]) *tr* poner, colocar; poner derecho; soportar, tolerar, resistir; (coll) aguantar (*a una persona*); (coll) sufragar (*un gasto*); **to stand off** tener a raya; **to stand one's ground** mantenerse firme ‖ *intr* estar, estar situado; estar parado; estacionarse; estar de pie, estar derecho; ponerse de pie, levantarse; resultar; persistir; mantenerse; **to stand aloof, apart** o **aside** mantenerse apartado; **to stand back of** respaldar; **to stand for** significar, representar; apoyar, defender; apadrinar; mantener (*p.ej., una opinión*); presentarse como candidato de; navegar hacia; (coll) tolerar; **to stand in line** hacer cola; **to stand out** sobresalir; destacarse; resaltar; durar; **to stand up** ponerse de pie, levantarse; durar; **to stand up to** hacer; resueltamente frente a

standard [ˈstændərd] *adj* normal; (*typewriter keyboard*) universal; corriente, regular; legal; clásico ‖ *s* patrón *m;* norma, regla establecida; bandera, estandarte *m;* emblema *m*, símbolo; soporte *m*, pilar *m*

standardize [ˈstændərˌdaɪz] *tr* normalizar, estandardizar

standard of living *s* nivel *m* de vida

standard time *s* hora legal, hora oficial

standee [stænˈdi] *s* (coll) espectador *m* que asiste de pie; (coll) pasajero de pie

stand′-in′ *s* (theat & mov) doble *mf;* (coll) buenas aldabas

standing [ˈstændɪŋ] *adj* derecho, en pie; de pie; parado, inmóvil; (*water*) encharcado, estancado; (*army; committee*) permanente; vigente ‖ *s* condición, posición, reputación; parada; **in good standing** en posición acreditada; **of long standing** de mucho tiempo, de antigua fecha

standing army *s* ejército permanente

standing room *s* sitio para estar de pie

stand-offishness [ˌstænd′ɔfɪʃnɪs] *s* desarrimo

stand′point′ *s* punto de vista

stand′still′ *s* detención, parada; alto; descanso, inactividad; **to come to a standstill** cesar, pararse

stanza [ˈstænzə] *s* estancia, estrofa

staple [ˈstepəl] *adj* primero, principal; corriente, establecido ‖ *s* (*to fasten papers*) grapa; artículo o producto de primera necesidad; materia prima; fibra textil ‖ *tr* sujetar con grapas

stapler ['steplər] *s* engrapador *m*, cosepapeles *m*

star [stɑr] *s* (*heavenly body*) astro; (*heavenly body except sun and moon*) estrella; (*figure that represents a star*) estrella; (*mov & theat*) estrella; (*of football*) as *m*; (*typ*) estrella o asterisco; (*fate, destiny*) (fig) estrella; **to see stars** (coll) ver las estrellas; **to thank one's lucky stars** estar agradecido por su buena suerte ‖ *v* (*pret & pp* **starred;** *ger* **starring**) *tr* estrellar, adornar o señalar con estrellas; marcar con asterisco; presentar como estrella (*a un actor*) ‖ *intr* ser la estrella; lucirse; sobresalir

starboard ['stɑrbərd] o ['stɑr,bord] *adj* de estribor ‖ *adv* a estribor ‖ *s* estribor *m*

starch [stɑrʃ] *s* almidón *m*, fécula, arrogancia, entono; (slang) fuerza, vigor *m* ‖ *tr* almidonar

stare [stɛr] *s* mirada fija ‖ *intr* mirar fijamente; **to stare at** clavar la vista en mirar con fijeza

star′fish′ *s* estrella de mar, estrellamar *m*

star′gaze′ *intr* mirar las estrellas; ser distraído, soñar despierto

stark [stɑrk] *adj* cabal, completo, puro; rígido, tieso; duro, severo ‖ *adv* completamente, enteramente; rígidamente, severamente

stark′-na′ked *adj* en pelota, en cueros

star′light′ *s* luz *f* de las estrellas

starling ['stɑrlɪŋ] *s* estornino

Star′-Span′gled Banner *s* bandera estrellada (*bandera de los EE.UU.*)

start [stɑrt] *s* comienzo, principio; salida, partida; lugar *m* de partida; (*scare*) sobresalto; (*sudden start*) arranque *m*; (*advantage*) ventaja ‖ *tr* empezar, principiar; poner en marcha; hacer arrancar; dar la señal de partida a; entablar (*una conversación*); levantar (*la caza*) ‖ *intr* empezar, principiar; ponerse en marcha; arrancar; (*to be startled*) sobresaltar; nacer, provenir; **starting from** o **with** a partir de; **to start after** salir en busca de

starter ['stɑrtər] *s* iniciador *m*; (*of a series*) primero; (aut) arranque *m*, motor *m* de arranque; (sport) juez *m* de salida

starting ['stɑrtɪŋ] *adj* de salida; de arranque ‖ *s* puesta en marcha

starting crank *s* manivela de arranque

starting point *s* punto de partida, arrancadero

startle ['stɑrtəl] *tr* asustar, sorprender, sobrecoger ‖ *intr* asustarse, sorprenderse sobrecogerse

startling ['stɑrtlɪŋ] *adj* alarmante, asombroso

starvation [stɑr've∫ən] *s* hambre *f*, inanición

starvation diet *s* régimen *m* de hambre, cura de hambre

starvation wages *spl* salario de hambre

starve [stɑrv] *tr* hambrear; hacer morir de hambre; **to starve out** hacer rendirse por

hambre ‖ *intr* hambrear; morir de hambre; (coll) tener hambre

starving ['stɑrvɪŋ] *adj* hambriento, famélico

stat. *abbr* **statuary, statute, statue**

state [stet] *adj* de estado; del estado; estatal; público; de gala, de lujo ‖ *s* estado; fausto, ceremonia, pompa; **to lie in state** estar expuesto en capilla ardiente, estar de cuerpo presente; **to live in state** gastar mucho lujo; **to ride in state** pasear en carruaje de lujo ‖ *tr* afirmar, declarar; exponer, manifestar; plantear (*un problema*)

State Department *s* Ministerio de Relaciones Exteriores

state•ly ['stetli] *adj* (*comp* **-lier;** *super* **-liest**) imponente, majestuoso

statement ['stetmənt] *s* declaración; exposición, informe *m*, relación; (com) estado de cuentas

state of mind *s* estado de ánimo

state′room′ *s* camarote *m*; (rr) compartimiento particular

state′side′ *adv* (coll) en (*or* a) los Estados Unidos

states•man ['stetsmən] *s* (*pl* **-men** [mən]) estadista *m*, hombre *m* de estado

static ['stætɪk] *adj* estático; (rad) atmosférico ‖ *s* (rad) parásitos atmosféricos

station ['ste∫ən] *s* estación; condición, situación ‖ *tr* estacionar, apostar

station agent *s* jefe *m* de estación

stationary ['ste∫ən,ɛri] *adj* estacionario

station break *s* (rad) descanso, intermedio

stationer ['ste∫ənər] *s* papelero

stationery ['ste∫ən,ɛri] *s* efectos de escritorio; papel *m* para cartas

stationery store *s* papelería

station house *s* cuartelillo de policía

station identification *s* (rad & telv) indicativo de la emisora

sta′tion•mas′ter *s* jefe *m* de estación

station wagon *s* vagoneta, rubia, coche *m* rural; camioneta (Arg, CAm, Col. Pan, Peru, S-D); esteishon wagon *m* (Chile, Col, Cuba, P-R); guagüita (Cuba, P-R); camionetilla (Guat); carmelita (Hond); ranchera (Ven)

statistical [stə,tɪstɪkəl] *adj* estadístico

statistician [,stætɪs,tɪ∫ən] *s* estadístico

statistics [stə,tɪstɪks] *ssg* (*science*) estadística; *spl* (*data*) estadística o estadísticas

statue ['stæt∫u] *s* estatua

statuesque [,stæt∫u,ɛsk] *adj* escultural

stature [,stæt∫ər] *s* estatura, talla; carácter *m*, habilidad

status ['stetəs] *s* condición, estado; situación social, legal o profesional; (*prestige or superior rank*) categoría

status seeking *s* esfuerzo por adquirir categoría

status symbol *s* símbolo de categoría social

statute ['stæt∫ut] *s* estatuto, ley *f*

statutory ['stæt∫u,tori] *adj* estatutario, legal

staunch [stɔnt∫] o [stɑnt∫] *adj & tr* var de **stanch**

stave [stev] *s* (*of a barrel*) duela; (*of a ladder*) peldaño; (*mus*) pentagrama *m* ‖ *v* (*pret & pp* **staved** o **stove** [stov]) *tr* romper, destrozar; (*to break a hole in*) desfondar; (*to break a hole in*) desfondar; **to stave off** mantener a distancia; evitar, impedir, diferir

stay [ste] *s* morada, permanencia, estancia; suspensión; (*of a corset*) ballena, varilla; apoyo, sostén *m*; (*law*) espera; (*naut*) estay *m* ‖ *tr* aplazar, detener; poner freno a ‖ *intr* quedar, quedarse, permanecer; parar, hospedarse; habitar; **to stay up** no acostarse, velar

stay'-at-home' *adj & s* hogareño

stead [stɛd] *s* lugar *m*; **in his stead** en su lugar, en lugar de él; **to stand in good stead** ser de provecho, ser ventajoso

stead'fast' *adj* fijo; resuelto; constante

stead·y ['stɛdi] *adj* (*comp* **-ier**; *super* **-iest**) constante, firme, seguro; regular, uniforme; resuelto; asentado, serio ‖ *v* (*pret & pp* **-ied**) *tr* estabilizar, reforzar; calmar (*los nervios*) ‖ *intr* estabilizarse; calmarse

steak [stek] *s* lonja, tajada; biftec *m*

steal [stil] *s* (*coll*) hurto, robo ‖ *v* (*pret* **stole** [stol]; *pp* **stolen**) *tr* hurtar, robar; atraer, cautivar; manotear (Arg, Mex) ‖ *intr* hurtar, robar; **to steal away** escabullirse; **to steal into** meterse a hurtadillas en; **to steal upon** aproximarse sin ruido a

stealth [stɛlθ] *s* cautela, recato; **by stealth** a hurtadillas

steam [stim] *adj* de vapor ‖ *s* vapor *m*; vaho, humo; **to get up steam** dar presión; **to let off steam** descargar vapor; (*fig*) desahogarse ‖ *tr* cocer al vapor; saturar de vapor; empañar (*p.ej., las ventanas*) ‖ *intr* echar vapor, emitir vapor; evaporarse; funcionar o marchar a vapor; **to steam ahead** avanzar por medio del vapor; (*fig*) hacer grandes progresos

steam'boat' *s* buque *m* de vapor

steamer ['stimər] *s* vapor *m*

steamer rug *s* manta de viaje

steamer trunk *s* baúl *m* de camarote

steam heat *s* calefacción por vapor

steam roller *s* apisonadora movida a vapor; (*coll*) fuerza arrolladora

steam'ship' *s* vapor *m*, buque *m* de vapor

steam shovel *s* pala mecánica de vapor

steam table *s* plancha caliente

steed [stid] *s* caballo; (*high-spirited horse*) corcel *m*

steel [stil] *adj* acerado; (*business, industry*) siderúrgico; (*fig*) duro, frío ‖ *s* acero; (*for striking fire from flint; for sharpening knives*) eslabón *m* ‖ *tr* acerar; **to steel oneself** acerarse

steel wool *s* virutillas de acero, estopa de acero

steelyard ['stil,jɑrd] *s* romana

steep [stip] *adj* escarpado, empinado; (*price*) alto, excesivo ‖ *tr* empapar, remojar; **steeped in** absorbido en

steeple ['stipəl] *s* aguja, campanario

stee'ple·chase' *s* carrera de campanario, carrera de obstáculos

stee'ple·jack' *s* escalatorres *m*

steer [stɪr] *s* buey *m* ‖ *tr* conducir, gobernar, guiar ‖ *intr* conducirse; **to steer clear of** (*coll*) evitar, eludir

steerage ['stɪrɪdʒ] *s* dirección; (*naut*) proa, entrepuente *m*

steerage passenger *s* (*naut*) pasajero de entrepuente

steering column *s* columna de dirección

steering committee *s* comité *m* paneador

steering wheel *s* (*aut*) volante *m*; (*naut*) rueda del timón

stem [stɛm] *s* (*of a goblet*) pie *m*; (*of a pipe, of a feather*) cañón *m*; (*of a column*) fuste *m*; (*of a watch*) botón *m*; (*of a key*) espiga, tija; (*of a word*) tema *m*; (*bot*) tallo, vástago; **from stem to stern** de proa a popa ‖ *v* (*pret & pp* **stemmed**; *ger* **stemming**) *tr* (*to remove the stem from*) desgranar; (*to check*) detener, refrenar; (*to plug*) estancar; hacer frente a; rendir (*la marea*) ‖ *intr* nacer, provenir; **to stem from** originarse en, provenir de

stem'-wind'er *s* remontuar *m*

stench [stɛntʃ] *s* hedor *m*, hediondez *f*

sten·cil ['stɛnsəl] *s* cartón picado; (*work produced by it*) estarcido ‖ *v* (*pret & pp* **-ciled** o **-cilled**; *ger* **-ciling** o **-cilling**) *tr* estarcir

stenographer [stə'nɑgrəfər] *s* estenógrafo

stenography [stə'nɑgrəfi] *s* estenografía

step [stɛp] *s* paso; (*of staircase*) grada, peldaño; (*footprint*) huella, pisada; (*of carriage*) estribo; (*measure, démarche*) gestión, medida; (*mus*) intervalo; **step by step** paso a paso; **to watch one's step** proceder con cautela, andarse con tiento ‖ *v* (*pret & pp* **stepped**; *ger* **stepping**) *tr* escalonar; **to step off** medir a pasos ‖ *intr* dar un paso, dar pasos; caminar, ir; (*coll*) andar de prisa; **to step on it** (*coll*) acelerar la marcha, darse prisa; **to step on the starter** pisar el arranque

step'broth'er *s* medio hermano, hermanastro

step'child' *s* (*pl* **-children** [,tʃɪldrən]) hijastro

step'daugh'ter *s* hijastra

step'fa'ther *s* padrastro

step'lad'der *s* escala, escalera de tijera

step'moth'er *s* madrastra

steppe [stɛp] *s* estepa

stepping stone *s* estriberón *m*, pasadera; (*fig*) escalón *m*, escabel *m*

step'sis'ter *s* media hermana, hermanastra

step'son' *s* hijastro

stere·o ['stɛri,o] o ['stɪri,o] *adj* estereofónico; estereososcópico ‖ *s* (*pl* **-os**) música estereofónica, disco estereofónico; radiodifusión estereofónica; fotografía estereoscópica

stereo system *s* equipo de alta fidelidad

ster'e·o·type' *s* clisé *m*, estereotipo; concepción tradicional

stereotyped ['stɛri·ə,taɪpt] o ['stɪri·ə,taɪpt] *adj* estereotipado

sterile ['stɛrɪl] *adj* estéril

sterilization [,stɛrɪlɪ'zefən] *s* esterilización

sterilize ['stɛrɪ,laɪz] *tr* esterilizar

sterling ['stʌrlɪŋ] *adj* fino, de ley; verdadero, genuino, puro, excelente ‖ *s* libras esterlinas; plata de ley; vajilla de plata

stern [stʌrn] *adj* austero, severo; decidido, firme ‖ *s* popa

stethoscope ['stɛθə,skop] *s* estetoscopio

stevedore ['stivə,dor] *s* estibador *m*

stew [stju] o [stu] *s* guisado, estofado ‖ *tr* guisar, estofar ‖ *intr* abrasarse; (coll) estar apurado

steward ['stu·ərd] *s* mayordomo; administrador *m;* (*of ship or plane*) camarero

stewardess ['stu·ərdɪs] *s* mayordoma; (*of ship or plane*) camarera; (*of plane*) azafata, aeromoza

stewed fruit *s* compota de frutas

stewed tomatoes *spl* puré *m* de tomates

stick [stɪk] *s* palo, palillo; bastón *m*, vara; (*of dynamite*) barra; (naut) mástil *m*, verga; (typ) componedor *m* ‖ *v* (*pret & pp* **stuck** [stʌk]) *tr* picar, punzar; apuñalar; clavar, hincar; pegar; (coll) confundir; **to stick out** asomar (*la cabeza*); sacar (*la lengua*); **to stick up** (*in order to rob*) (slang) asaltar, atracar ‖ *intr* estar prendido, estar hincado; pegarse; agarrarse (*la pintura*); encastillarse (*p.ej., una ventana*); resaltar, sobresalir; continuar, persistir; permanecer; atascarse; **to stick out** salir (*p.ej., el pañuelo del bolsillo*); sobresalir, proyectarse; velar (*un escollo*); resultar evidente; **to stick together** (coll) quedarse unidos, no abandonarse (*p.ej., una ventana*); **to stick up** destacarse; estar de punta (*el pelo*); **to stick up for** (coll) defender

sticker ['stɪkər] *s* etiqueta engomada, marbete engomado; pegatina; punta, espina; (coll) problema arduo

sticking plaster *s* esparadrapo

stick'pin' *s* alfiler *m* de corbata

stick'-up' *s* (slang) asalto, atraco

stick·y ['stɪki] *adj* (*comp* **-ier;** *super* **-iest**) pegajoso; (coll) húmedo, mojado; (*weather*) bochornoso

stiff [stɪf] *adj* tieso; entorpecido, entumecido; arduo, difícil; (*price*) (coll) excesivo; **to get stiff** envararse ‖ *s* (slang) cadáver *m*

stiff collar *s* cuello almidonado

stiffen ['stɪfən] *tr* atiesar; endurecer; espesar ‖ *intr* atiesarse; endurecerse; espesarse; obstinarse

stiff neck *s* torticolis *m;* obstinación

stiff'-necked' ['stɪf,nɛkt] *adj* terco, obstinado

stiffness ['stɪfnɪs] *s* envaramiento

stiff shirt *s* camisola

stifle ['staɪfəl] *tr* ahogar, sofocar; apagar, suprimir

stig·ma ['stɪgmə] *s* (*pl* **-mas** o **-mata** [mətə]) estigma *m*

stigmatize ['stɪgmə,taɪz] *tr* estigmatizar

stilet·to [stɪ'lɛto] *s* (*pl* **-tos**) estilete *m*, puñal *m*

still [stɪl] *adj* inmóvil, quieto, tranquilo; callado, silencioso; (*wine*) no espumoso ‖ *adv* tranquilamente; silenciosamente; aún, todavía ‖ *conj* con todo, sin embargo ‖ *s* alambique *m*, destiladera; destilería; foto-

grafía de lo inmóvil; (poet) silencio ‖ *tr* acallar; amortiguar; calmar ‖ *intr* callar; calmarse

still'birth' *s* parto muerto

still'born' *adj* nacido muerto

still life *s* (*pl* **still lifes** o **still lives**) bodegón *m*, naturaleza muerta

stilt [stɪlt] *s* zanco; (*in the water*) pilote *m*

stilted ['stɪltɪd] *adj* elevado; hinchado, pomposo, tieso

stimulant ['stɪmjələnt] *adj & s* estimulante *m*, excitante *m*

stimulate ['stɪmjə,let] *tr* estimular

stimu·lus ['stɪmjələs] *s* (*pl* **-li** [,laɪ]) estímulo *m*

sting [stɪŋ] *s* picadura; aguijón *m*; lanceta ‖ *v* (*pret & pp* **stung** [stʌŋ]) *tr* picar; aguijonear ‖ *intr* picar

stin·gy ['stɪndʒi] *adj* (*comp* **-gier;** *super* **-giest**) mezquino, tacaño

stink [stɪŋk] *s* hedor *m*, mal olor *m* ‖ *v* (*pret* **stank** [stæŋk] o **stunk** [stʌŋk]; *pp* **stunk**) *tr* dar mal olor a ‖ *intr* heder, oler muy mal; **to stink of** heder a; (slang) poseer (*p.ej., dinero*) en un grado que da asco

stint [stɪnt] *s* faena, tarea ‖ *tr* limitar, restringir ‖ *intr* ser económico, ahorrar con mezquindad

stipend ['staɪpənd] *s* estipendio

stipulate ['stɪpjə,let] *tr* estipular

stir [stʌr] *s* agitación, meneo; alboroto, tumulto; **to create a stir** meter ruido, causar furor ‖ *v* (*pret & pp* **stirred;** *ger* **stirring**) *tr* agitar, mover; revolver; conmover, excitar; atizar, avivar (*el fuego*); remover (*un líquido*); **to stir up** revolver; despertar; conmover; fomentar (*discordias*) ‖ *intr* bullirse, moverse; (*say a word*) rechistar

stirring ['stʌrɪŋ] *adj* conmovedor, emocionante

stirrup ['stʌrəp] o ['stɪrəp] *s* estribo

stitch [stɪtʃ] *s* puntada, punto; pedazo de tela; punzada, dolor *m* punzante; (coll) poquito; **to be in stitches** (coll) desternillarse de risa ‖ *tr* coser, bastear, hilvanar ‖ *intr* coser

stock [stak] *adj* común, regular; banal, vulgar; bursátil; ganadero, del ganado; (theat) de repertorio ‖ *s* surtido; capital *f* comercial; acciones, valores *mpl;* (*inventory*) stock *m;* (*of meat*) caldo; (*of a tree*) tronco; (*of an anvil*) cepo; (*of a rifle*) caja, culata; (*of a tree; of a family*) cepa; mango, manija; palo, madero; leño; (*livestock*) ganado; (theat) programa *m*, repertorio; **to have in stock** tener en stock; **in stock** en existencia; **out of stock** agotado; **to take stock** hacer el inventario; **to take stock in** (coll) dar importancia a, confiar en ‖ *tr* abastecer, surtir; tener existencias de; acopiar, acumular; poblar (*un estanque, una colmena, etc.*)

stockade [sta'ked] *s* estacada, empalizada ‖ *tr* empalizar

stock'breed'er *s* criador *m* de ganado

stock'bro'ker *s* bolsista *mf*, corredor *m* de bolsa

stock car *s* (aut) coche *m* de serie; (rr) vagón *m* para el ganado

st
st

stock company s (com) sociedad anónima;
(theat) teatro de repertorio
stock dividend s acción liberada
stock exchange s bolsa
stock'hold'er s accionista *mf*, tenedor *m* de
acciones
stockholder of record s accionista *mf* que
como tal figura en el libro registro de la
compañía
Stockholm ['stakhom] s Estocolmo
stocking ['stakɪŋ] s media
stock market s bolsa, mercado de valores; **to
play the stock market** jugar a la bolsa
stock'pile' s reserva de materias primas ‖ *tr*
acumular (*materias primas*) ‖ *intr* acumular materias primas
stock raising s ganadería
stock'room' s almacén *m*; sala de exposición
stock split s reparto de acciones gratis
stock•y ['staki] s adj (*comp* **-ier;** *super* **-iest**)
bajo, grueso y fornido
stock'yard' s corral *m* de concentración de
ganado
stoic ['sto•ɪk] *adj & s* estoico
stoke [stok] *tr* atizar, avivar (*el fuego*); alimentar, cebar (*el horno*)
stoker ['stokər] s fogonero
stolid ['stɑlɪd] *adj* impasible, insensible
stomach ['stʌmək] s estómago; apetito; deseo, inclinación ‖ *tr* tragar; **to not be able
to stomach** (coll) no poder tragar
stomach pump s bomba estomacal
stone [ston] s piedra; (*of fruit*) hueso; (pathol)
mal *m* de piedra ‖ *tr* lapidar, apedrear;
deshuesar (*la fruta*)
stone'-broke' *adj* arrancado, sin blanca
stone'-deaf' *adj* sordo como una tapia
stone'ma'son s albañil *m*
stone quarry s cantera, pedrera
stone's throw s tiro de piedra; **within a
stone's throw** a tiro de piedra
ston•y ['stoni] *adj* (*comp* **-ier;** *super* **-iest**)
pedregoso; duro, empedernido
stool [stul] s escabel *m*, taburete *m*; sillico,
retrete *m*; (*bowel movement*) cámara, evacuación
stoop [stup] s encorvada, inclinación; escalinata de entrada ‖ *intr* doblarse, inclinarse,
encorvarse; andar encorvado; humillarse,
rebajarse
stoop•shouldered ['stup'ʃoldərd] *adj* cargado
de espaldas
stop [stɑp] s parada, alto; parón; estada,
estancia; cesación, fin *m*, suspensión; cerradura, tapadura; impedimento, obstáculo;
freno; tope *m*, retén *m*; (*in writing; in
telegrams*) punto; (*of a guitar*) llave *f*,
traste *m*; **to put a stop to** poner fin a ‖ *v*
(*pret & pp* **stopped;** *ger* **stopping**) *tr* parar, detener; acabar, terminar; estorbar,
obstruir; interceptar; suspender; cerrar, tapar; rechazar (*un golpe*); retener (*un sueldo
o parte de él*); **to stop up** cegar, obstruir,
tapar ‖ *intr* parar, pararse, detenerse; quedarse, permanecer; alojarse, hospedarse;
acabarse, terminarse; **to stop** + *ger* cesar
de + *inf*, dejar de + *inf*

stop'cock' s llave *f* de cierre, llave de paso
stop'gap' *adj* provisional ‖ s substituto provisional
stop light s luz *f* de parada
stop'o'ver s parada intermedia, escala; billete
m de parada intermedia
stoppage ['stɑpɪdʒ] s parada, detención; (*of
work*) paro; interrupción; suspensión; obstáculo; (*of wages*) retención; (pathol) obstrucción
stopper ['stɑpər] s tapón *m*; taco, tarugo
stop sign o **stop signal** s señal *f* de alto, señal
de parada
stop watch s reloj *m* de segundos muertos,
cronómetro
storage ['storɪdʒ] s almacenaje *m*; (*costs*)
derechos de almacenaje
storage battery s (elec) acumulador *m*
store [stor] s tienda, almacén *m*; **I know
what is in store for you** sé lo que le
espera; **to set store by** dar mucha importancia a ‖ *tr* abastecer; tener guardado,
almacenar; **to store away** acumular
store'house' s almacén *m*, depósito; (*e.g., of
wisdom*) (fig) mina
store'keep'er s tendero, almacenista *mf*
store'room' s cuarto de almacenar; (*for furniture*) guardamuebles *m*; (naut) despensa
store window s escaparate *m* (de tienda);
aparador *m* (Mex)
stork [stork] s cigüeña; **to have a visit from
the stork** recibir a la cigüeña
storm [storm] s borrasca, tempestad, tormenta; (mil) asalto; (naut) borrasca; (fig)
tempestad, tumulto; **to take by storm** tomar por asalto ‖ *tr* asaltar ‖ *intr* tem-
pestear; precipitarse
storm cloud s nubarrón *m*
storm door s contrapuerta, guardapuerta
storm sash s contravidriera
storm troops *spl* tropas de asalto
storm window s guardaventana, sobrevidriera
storm•y ['stormi] *adj* (*comp* **-ier;** *super* **-iest**)
borrascoso, tempestuoso; (*session, meet-
ing, etc.*) tumultuoso
sto•ry ['stori] s (*pl* **-ries**) historia, cuento,
anécdota; enredo, trama; (coll) mentira;
piso, alto ‖ *v* (*pret & pp* **-ried**) *tr* historiar
sto'ry•tel'ler s narrador *m*; (coll) mentiroso
stout [staut] *adj* corpulento, gordo, robusto;
animoso; leal; terco ‖ s cerveza obscura
fuerte
stove [stov] s (*for heating a house or room*)
estufa; (*for cooking*) hornillo, cocina de
gas, cocina eléctrica
stove'pipe' s tubo de estufa, tubo de hornillo;
(*hat*) (coll) chistera, chimenea
stow [sto] *tr* guardar, meter, esconder; (naut)
arrumar, estibar ‖ *intr*—**to stow away** embarcarse clandestinamente, esconderse en
un barco o avión
stowage ['sto•ɪdʒ] s arrumaje *m*, estiba
stow'a•way' s llovido, polizón *m*
str. *abbr* **strait, steamer**
straddle ['strædəl] s esparrancamiento ‖ *tr*
montar a horcajadas; (coll) tratar de favo-

recer a ambas partes en (*p.ej., un pleito*) ||
intr ponerse a horcajadas; (coll) tratar de
favorecer a ambas partes

strafe [strɑf] o [stref] *s* bombardeo violento ||
tr bombardear violentamente

straggle [ˈstrægəl] *intr* errar, vagar; andar
perdido, extraviarse; separarse; estar espar-
cido

straight [stret] *adj* derecho; recto; erguido;
(*hair*) lacio; continuo, seguido; honrado,
sincero; correcto; decidido, intransigente;
(*e.g., whiskey*) solo; **to set a person
straight** mostrar el camino a una persona;
dar consejo a una persona; mostrar a una
persona el modo de proceder || *adv* dere-
cho; sin interrupción; sinceramente; exactamente; en seguida; **straight ahead** todo
seguido, derecho; **to go straight** enmen-
darse

straighten [ˈstretən] *tr* enderezar; poner en
orden || *intr* enderezarse

straight face *s* cara seria

straight′for′ward *adj* franco, sincero; honrado

straight off *adv* luego, en seguida

straight razor *s* navaja barbera

straight′way′ *adv* luego, en seguida

strain [stren] *s* tensión, tirantez *f;* esfuerzo
muy grande; fatiga excesiva; agotamiento;
(*of a muscle*) torcedura; aire *m*, melodía;
(*of a family or lineage*) cepa; linaje *m*,
raza; rasgo racial; genio, vena; huella, ras-
tro || *tr* estirar; torcer o torcerse (*p.ej., la
muñeca*); forzar (*p.ej., los nervios, la vis-
ta*); apretar; deformar; colar, tamizar || *intr*
esforzarse; deformarse; colarse, tamizarse;
filtrarse; exprimirse (*un jugo*); resistirse; **to
strain at** hacer grandes esfuerzos por

strained [strend] *adj* (*smile*) forzado; (*friendship*) tirante

strainer [ˈstrenər] *s* colador *m*

strait [stret] *s* estrecho; **straits** estrecho; **to
be in dire straits** estar en el mayor apuro,
hallarse en gran estrechez

strait jacket *s* camisa de fuerza

strait-laced [ˈstret,lest] *adj* gazmoño

strand [strænd] *s* playa; filamento; (*of rope
or cable*) torón *m*, ramal *m;* (*of pearls*)
hilo; pelo || *tr* deshebrar; retorcer, trenzar
(*cuerda, cable, etc.*); dejar extraviado;
(naut) varar

stranded [ˈstrændɪd] *adj* desprovisto, desamparado; (*ship*) encallado; (*rope or cable*)
trenzado, retorcido

strange [strendʒ] *adj* extraño, singular;
nuevo, desconocido; novel, no acostumbrado

stranger [ˈstrendʒər] *s* forastero; visitador
m; intruso; desconocido; principiante *mf*

strangle [ˈstræŋgəl] *tr* estrangular; reprimir,
suprimir || *intr* estrangularse

strap [stræp] *s* (*of leather*) correa; (*of cloth,
metal, etc.*) banda, tira; (*to sharpen a
razor*) asentador *m* || *v* (*pret & pp*
strapped; *ger* **strapping**) *tr* atar o liar con
correa, banda o tira; azotar con una correa;
fajar, vendar; asentar (*una navaja*)

strap′hang′er *s* (coll) pasajero colgado

stratagem [ˈstrætədʒəm] *s* estratagema *f*

strategic(al) [strəˈtidʒɪk(əl)] *adj* estraté-
gico

strategist [ˈstrætɪdʒɪst] *s* estratega *m*

strate•gy [ˈstrætɪdʒi] *s* (*pl* **-gies**) estrategia

strati•fy [ˈstrætɪ,faɪ] *v* (*pret & pp* **-fied**) *tr*
estratificar || *intr* estratificarse

stratosphere [ˈstrætə,sfɪr] o [ˈstretə,sfɪr] *s*
estratosfera

stra•tum [ˈstretəm] o [ˈstrætəm] *s* (*pl* **-ta** [tə]
o **-tums**) estrato; (*e.g., of society*) clase *f*

straw [strɔ] *adj* pajizo; baladí, de poca im-
portancia; falso; ficticio || *s* paja; (*for
drinking*) pajita; **I don't care a straw** no se
me da un bledo; **to be the last straw** ser el
colmo, no faltar más

straw′ber′ry *s* (*pl* **-ries**) fresa

straw hat *s* sombrero de paja; chupalla *m;*
(*with low flat crown*) canotié *m*

straw man *s* figura de paja; (*figurehead*)
testaferro; testigo falso

straw vote *s* voto informativo

stray [stre] *adj* extraviado, perdido; aislado,
suelto || *s* animal extraviado o perdido ||
intr extraviarse, perderse

streak [strik] *s* lista, raya; vena, veta; rasgo,
traza; (*of light*) rayo; (*of good luck*) racha;
(coll) tiempo muy breve; **like a streak**
(coll) como un rayo || *tr* listar, rayar;
abigarrar || *intr* rayarse; (coll) andar o pasar
como un rayo

stream [strim] *s* (*current*) corriente *f;* arroyo,
río; chorro, flujo; (*of people*) torrente *m;*
(*e.g., of automobiles*) desfile *m* || *intr*
correr, manar (*un líquido*); chorrear; flotar,
ondear; salir a torrentes

streamer [ˈstrimər] *s* flámula, banderola;
cinta ondeante; rayo de luz

streamlined [ˈstrim,laɪnd] *adj* aerodinámico,
perfilado

stream′lin′er *s* tren aerodinámico de lujo

street [strit] *adj* callejero || *s* calle *f*

street′car′ *s* tranvía *m*

street cleaner *s* basurero; (*device*) barredera

street clothes *spl* traje *m* de calle

street floor *s* piso bajo

street lamp *s* farol *m* (de la calle)

street sprinkler [ˈsprɪŋklər] *s* carricuba,
carro de riego, regadera

street′walk′er *s* cantonera, carrerista

strength [strɛŋθ] *s* fuerza; intensidad; (*of
spirituous liquors*) graduación; (com) tendencia a la subida; (mil) número; **on the
strength of** fundándose en, confiando en

strengthen [ˈstrɛŋθən] *tr* fortificar, reforzar;
confirmar || *intr* fortificarse, reforzarse

strenuous [ˈstrɛnju•əs] *adj* estrenuo, enérgico, vigoroso; arduo, difícil

stress [strɛs] *s* tensión, fuerza; compulsión;
acento; (mech) tensión; **to lay stress on**
hacer hincapié en || *tr* someter a esfuerzo;
hacer hincapié en; acentuar

stress accent *s* acento prosódico

stretch [strɛtʃ] *s* estiramiento, estirón *m;*
(*distance in time or space*) trecho; (*section
of road*) tramo; extensión; (*of the imagina-*

tion) esfuerzo; (*confinement in jail*) (slang) condena; **at a stretch** de un tirón ‖ *tr* estirar; extender; tender; forzar, violentar; (fig) estirar (*el dinero*); **to stretch a point** hacer una concesión; **to stretch oneself** desperezarse ‖ *intr* estirarse; extenderse; tenderse; desperezarse; **to stretch out** (coll) echarse

stretcher ['stretʃər] *s* (*for gloves*) ensanchador *m*; (*for a painting*) bastidor *m*; (*to carry sick or wounded*) camilla

stretch′er-bear′er *s* camillero

strew [stru] *v* (*pret* **strewed;** *pp* **strewed** o **strewn**) *tr* derramar, esparcir; sembrar, salpicar; polvorear

stricken ['strɪkən] *adj* afligido; inhabilitado; herido; **stricken in years** debilitado por los años

strict [strɪkt] *adj* estricto, riguroso; (*exacting*) severo

stricture ['strɪktʃər] *s* crítica severa; (pathol) estrictura

stride [straɪd] *s* zancada, tranco; **to hit one's stride** alcanzar la actividad o velocidad acostumbrada; **to make great** (o **rapid**) **strides** avnzar a grandes pasos; **to take in one's stride** hacer sin esfuerzo ‖ *v* (*pret* **strode** [strod]; *pp* **stridden** ['strɪdən]) *tr* cruzar de un tranco; montar a horcajadas ‖ *intr* dar zancadas, caminar a paso largo; andar a trancos

strident ['straɪdənt] *adj* estridente

strife [straɪf] *s* contienda; rivalidad

strike [straɪk] *s* (*blow*) golpe *m*; (*stopping of work*) huelga; (*discovery of ore, oil, etc.*) descubrimiento repentino; golpe *m* de fortuna; **to go on strike** ir a la huelga ‖ *v* (*pret & pp* **struck** [strʌk]) *tr* golpear; pulsar (*una tecla*); herir, percutir; topar, dar con; acuñar (*monedas*); echar (*raíces*); frotar, rayar, encender (*un fósforo*); descubrir repentinamente (*mineral, aceite, etc.*); cerrar (*un trato*); arriar (*las velas*); dar (*la hora*); asumir, tomar (*una postura*); borrar, cancelar; impresionar; atraer (*la atención*); **to strike it rich** descubrir un buen filón, tener un golpe de fortuna ‖ *intr* dar, sonar (*una campana, un reloj*); declararse en huelga; (mil) dar el asalto; **to strike out** ponerse en marcha, echar camino adelante

strike′break′er *s* rompehuelgas *m*, esquirol *m*

strike pay *s* sueldo de huelguista

striker ['straɪkər] *s* golpeador *m*; huelguista *mf*

striking ['straɪkɪŋ] *adj* impresionante, llamativo, sorprendente; en huelga

striking power *s* potencia de choque

string [strɪŋ] *s* cuerdecilla; piola; pita; (*of pearls; of lies*) sarta; (*of beans*) hebra; (*of onions or garlic*) ristra; (row) hilera; (mus) cuerda; (*limitation, proviso*) (coll) condición; **strings** instrumentos de cuerda; **to pull strings** tocar resortes ‖ *v* (*pret & pp* **strung** [strʌŋ]) *tr* enhebrar, ensartar; atar con cuerdas; proveer de cuerdas; colgar de una cuerda; tender (*un cable, un alambre*);

encordar (*un violín, una raqueta*); colocar en fila; (slang) engañar, burlar; **to string along** (slang) traer al retortero; **to string up** (coll) ahorcar

string bean *s* habichuela verde, judía verde

stringed instrument [strɪŋd] *s* instrumento de cuerda

stringent ['strɪndʒənt] *adj* riguroso, severo, estricto; convincente

string quartet *s* cuarteto de cuerdas

strip [strɪp] *s* tira; (*of metal*) lámina; (*of land*) faja ‖ *v* (*pret & pp* **stripped;** *ger* **stripping**) *tr* desnudar; despojar; desforrar; deshacer (*la cama*); estropear (*el engranaje, un tornillo*); desvenar (*tabaco*); descortezar; **to strip of** despojar de ‖ *intr* desnudarse; despojarse; descortezarse

stripe [straɪp] *s* banda, lista, raya; gaya; cinta, franja; (mil & nav) galón *m*; índole *f*, tipo; **to win one's stripes** ganar los entorchados ‖ *tr* listar, rayar; gayar

strip mining *s* mineraje *m* a tajo abierto

strip′tease′ *s* espectáculo de desnudamiento sensual

strive [straɪv] *v* (*pret* **strove** [strov]; *pp* **striven** ['strɪvən]) *intr* esforzarse; luchar

stroke [strok] *s* golpe *m*; (*of bell or clock*) campanada; (*of pen*) plumada; (*of brush*) pincelada, brochada; (*of arms in swimming*) brazada; (*in a game*) jugada; (*caress with hand*) caricia; (*with a racket*) raquetazo; (*of a piston*) carrera, embolada; (*of a paddle*) palada; (*of an oar*) remada; (*of lightning*) rayo; (*line, mark*) raya; (*of good luck*) golpe *m*; (*of wit*) agudeza, chiste *m*; (*of genius*) rasgo; ataque *m* de parálisis; **at the stroke of** (*e.g., five*) al dar las (*p.ej., cinco*); **to not do a stroke of work** no dar golpe, no levantar paja del suelo ‖ *tr* frotar suavemente, acariciar con la mano

stroll [strol] *s* paseo; **to take a stroll** dar un paseo ‖ *intr* pasear, pasearse; callejear, errar, vagar

stroller ['strolər] *s* paseante *mf*; cochecito para niños

strong [strɔŋ] o [strɑŋ] *adj* fuerte, resistente; recio, robusto; intenso; (*stock market*) firme; enérgico; marcado; picante; rancio

strong′-arm′ man *s* (coll) gorila

strong′box′ *s* cofre *m* fuerte, caja de caudales

strong drink *s* bebida alcohólica, bebida fuerte

strong′hold′ *s* plaza fuerte

strong man *s* (*e.g., in a circus*) hércules *m*; (*leader, good planner*) alma, promotor *m*; (*dictator*) hombre *m* fuerte

strong-minded ['strɔŋ,maɪndɪd] o [strɑŋ-'maɪndɪd] *adj* independiente; de inteligencia vigorosa; (*e.g., woman*) hombruna

strontium ['strɑnʃɪ•əm] *s* estroncio

strop [strɑp] *s* suavizador *m* ‖ *v* (*pret & pp* **stropped;** *ger* **stropping**) *tr* suavizar, afilar

strophe ['strofi] *s* estrofa

structure ['strʌktʃər] *s* estructura; edificio

struggle ['strʌgəl] *s* lucha; esfuerzo, forcejeo ‖ *intr* luchar; esforzarse, forcejear

strum [strʌm] v (pret & pp **strummed;** ger **strumming**) tr arañar (un instrumento músico) sin arte ‖ intr cencerrear; **to strum on** rasguear

strumpet [ˈstrʌmpɪt] s ramera

strut [strʌt] s (brace, prop) riostra, tornapunta; contoneo, pavoneo ‖ v (pret & pp **strutted;** ger **strutting**) intr contonearse, pavonearse

strychnine [ˈstrɪknaɪn] o [ˈstrɪknɪn] s estricnina

stub [stʌb] s fragmento, trozo; (of a cigar) colilla; (of a tree) tocón m; (of a pencil) cabo; (of a check) talón m ‖ v (pret & pp **stubbed;** ger **stubbing**) tr —**to stub one's toe** dar un tropezón

stubble [ˈstʌbəl] s rastrojo; (of beard) cañón m

stubborn [ˈstʌbərn] adj terco, testarudo, obstinado; porfiado; intratable; **to be stubborn** ser obstinado, empecinarse

stubbornness [ˈstʌbərnɪs] obstinación, s empecinamiento

stuc•co [ˈstʌko] s (pl **-coes** o **-cos**) estuco ‖ tr estucar

stuck'-up' adj (coll) estirado, orgulloso

stud [stʌd] s tachón m; botón m de camisa; montante m, pie derecho; clavo de adorno; (bolt) espárrago; caballeriza; (of mares) yeguada ‖ v (pret & pp **studded;** ger **studding**) tr tachonar

stud bolt s espárrago

stud'book' s registro genealógico de caballos

student [ˈstjudənt] o [ˈstudənt] adj estudiantil ‖ s estudiante mf; (person who investigates), estudioso

student body s estudiantado, alumnado

stud'horse' s caballo padre, caballo semental

studied [ˈstʌdid] adj premeditado, hecho adrede; (affected) estudiado

studi•o [ˈstudɪ,o] s (pl **-os**) estudio, taller m; (mov & rad) estudio

studious [ˈstjudɪ•əs] o [ˈstudɪ•əs] adj estudioso; asiduo, solícito

stud•y [ˈstʌdi] s (pl **-ies**) estudio; solicitud; meditación profunda; (e.g., of a professor) gabinete m, estudio ‖ v (pret & pp **-ied**) tr & intr estudiar

stuff [stʌf] s materia; género, paño, tela; muebles mpl, baratijas; medicina; fruslerías; cosa, cosas ‖ tr rellenar; henchir, llenar; atascar, cerrar, tapar; embutir; (with food) atracar; meter sin orden, llenar sin orden; disecar (un animal muerto) ‖ intr atracarse, hartarse

stuffed shirt s (slang) tragavirotes m

stuffing [ˈstʌfɪŋ] s relleno

stuff•y [ˈstʌfi] adj (comp **-ier;** super **-iest**) sofocante, mal ventilado; aburrido, sin interés; (prim) (coll) relamido

stumble [ˈstʌmbəl] intr tropezar, dar un traspié; moverse a tropezones; hablar a tropezones; **to stumble on** o **upon** tropezar con

stumbling block s escollo, tropezadero

stump [stʌmp] s (of a tree, arm, etc.) tocón m; (of an arm) muñón m; (of a tooth) raigón m; (of a cigar) colilla; (of a tail)

rabo; paso pesado; fragmento, resto; tribuna pública; (for shading drawings) esfumino ‖ tr recorrer (el país) pronunciando discursos políticos; (coll) confundir, dejar sin habla; esfumar

stump speaker s orador callejero

stump speech s arenga electoral

stun [stʌn] v (pret & pp **stunned;** ger **stunning**) tr atolondrar, aturdir

stunning [ˈstʌnɪŋ] adj (coll) pasmoso, estupendo, pistonudo, elegante

stunt [stʌnt] s atrofia; (underdeveloped creature) engendro; (coll) suerte acrobática; (coll) faena, hazaña, proeza ‖ tr atrofiar ‖ intr (coll) hacer suertes acrobáticas

stunt flying s vuelo acrobático

stunt man s (mov) doble m que hace suertes peligrosas

stupe•fy [ˈstjupɪ,faɪ] v (pret & pp **-fied**) tr dejar estupefacto, pasmar; causar estupor a

stupendous [stuˈpɛndəs] adj estupendo; enorme

stupid [ˈstupɪd] adj estúpido; (coll) sonso, pavo, gilí

stupor [ˈstjupər] o [ˈstupər] s estupor m, modorra

stur•dy [ˈstʌrdi] adj (comp **-dier;** super **-diest**) fuerte, robusto, fornido; firme, tenaz

sturgeon [ˈstʌrdʒən] s esturión m

stutter [ˈstʌtər] s tartamudeo ‖ tr decir tartamudeando ‖ intr tartamudear

sty [staɪ] s (pl **sties**) pocilga, zahurda; (pathol) orzuelo

style [staɪl] s estilo; moda; elegancia; **to live in great style** vivir en gran lujo ‖ tr intitular, nombrar

stylish [ˈstaɪlɪʃ] adj de moda, elegante

styptic pencil [ˈstɪptɪk] s lápiz estíptico

Styx [stɪks] s Estigia

suave [swɑv] o [swev] adj suave; afable, fino, zalamero, pulido

sub. abbr **subscription, substitute, suburban**

subaltern [səbˈɔltərn] adj & s subalterno

subconscious [səbˈkɑnʃəs] adj subconsciente ‖ s subconsciencia

subconsciousness [səbˈkɑnʃəsnɪs] s subconsciencia

subdeb [ˈsʌb,dɛb] s tobillera

subdivide [ˈsʌbdɪ,vaɪd] o [,sʌbdɪˈvaɪd] tr subdividir ‖ intr subdividirse

subdue [səbˈdju] tr sojuzgar, subyugar; amansar, dominar; suavizar

subdued [səbˈdjud] adj sojuzgado; sumiso; (e.g., light) suave

subheading [ˈsʌb,hɛdɪŋ] s subtítulo

subject [ˈsʌbdʒɪkt] adj sujeto; súbdito ‖ s asunto, materia, tema m; (person in his relationship to a ruler or government) súbdito; (gram, med, philos) sujeto ‖ [səbˈdʒɛkt] tr sujetar, someter, sojuzgar

subject index s índice m de materias

subjection [səbˈdʒɛkʃən] s sumisión, sometimiento

subjective [səbˈdʒɛktɪv] adj subjetivo

subject matter s asunto, materia

subjugate [ˈsʌbdʒə,get] tr subyugar

subjunctive [səb'dʒʌŋktɪv] *adj* & *s* subjuntivo

sub·let [sʌb'lɛt] o ['sʌb,lɛt] *v* (*pret* & *pp* **-let;** *ger* **-letting**) *tr* realquilar, subarrendar

submachine gun [,sʌbmə'ʃin] *s* subfusil *m* ametrallador

submarine ['sʌbmə,rin] *adj* & *s* submarino ‖ *tr* (coll) atacar o hundir con un submarino

submarine chaser ['tʃesər] *s* cazasubmarinos *m*

submerge [səb'mʌrdʒ] *tr* sumergir ‖ *intr* sumergirse

submersion [səb'mʌrʒən] o [səb'mʌrʃən] *s* sumersión

submission [səb'mɪʃən] *s* sumisión

submissive [səb'mɪsɪv] *adj* sumiso

sub·mit [səb'mɪt] *v* (*pret* & *pp* **-mitted;** *ger* **-mitting**) *tr* someter; proponer, permitirse decir ‖ *intr* someterse

subordinate [səb'ɔrdɪnɪt] *adj* & *s* subordinado ‖ [səb'ɔrdɪ,net] *tr* subordinar

subornation of perjury [,sʌbər'neʃən] *s* (law) soborno de testigo

subplot ['sʌb,plɑt] *s* trama secundaria

subpoena o **subpena** [sʌb'pinə] o [sə'pinə] *s* comparendo ‖ *tr* mandar comparecer

sub rosa [sʌb'rozə] *adv* en secreto, en confianza

subscribe [səb'skraɪb] *tr* subscribir ‖ *intr* subscribir; subscribirse, abonarse; **to subscribe to** subscribirse a, abonarse a (*una publicación periódica*); subscribir (*una opinión*)

subscriber [səb'skraɪbər] *s* abonado

subsequent ['sʌbsɪkwənt] *adj* subsiguiente, posterior

subservient [səb'sʌrvɪ•ənt] *adj* servil; subordinado; útil

subside [səb'saɪd] *intr* calmarse; acabarse, cesar; bajar (*el nivel del agua*); amainar (*el viento*)

subsidiary [səb'sɪdɪ,ɛri] *adj* & *s* subsidiario

subsidize ['sʌbsɪ,daɪz] *tr* subsidiar, subvencionar; (*to bribe*) sobornar

subsi·dy ['sʌbsɪdi] *s* (*pl* **-dies**) subsidio, subvención

subsist [səb'sɪst] *intr* subsistir

subsistence [səb'sɪstəns] *s* subsistencia

subsonic [səb'sɑnɪk] *adj* subsónico

substance ['sʌbstəns] *s* substancia

substandard [sʌb'stændərd] *adj* inferior al nivel normal

substantial [səb'stænʃəl] *adj* considerable, importante; fuerte, sólido; acomodado, rico; esencial; (*food*) substancial

substantiate [səb'stænʃɪ,et] *tr* comprobar, establecer, verificar

substantive ['sʌbstəntɪv] *adj* & *s* substantivo

substation ['sʌb,steʃən] *s* (elec) subcentral *f*

substitute ['sʌbstɪ,tjut] o ['sʌbstɪ,tut] *adj* substitutivo ‖ *s* (*person*) substituto; (*thing, substance*) substitutivo; (mil) reemplazo ‖ *tr* poner (*a una persona o cosa*) en lugar de otra ‖ *intr* actuar de substituto; **to substitute for** substituir (with personal a)

substitution [,sʌbstɪ'tjuʃən] *s* empleo o uso (*de una persona o cosa en lugar de otra*);

(chem, law, math) substitución; imitación fraudulenta

subterranean [,sʌbtə'reni•ən] *adj* & *s* subterráneo

subtitle ['sʌb,taɪtəl] *s* substítulo ‖ *tr* subtitular

subtle ['sʌtəl] *adj* sutil; astuto; insidioso

subtle·ty ['sʌtəlti] *s* (*pl* **-ties**) sutileza; agudeza; distinción sutil

subtract [səb'trækt] *tr* substraer; (math) substraer, restar

suburb ['sʌbʌrb] *s* suburbio, arrabal *m*; **the suburbs** las afueras, los barrios externos

subvention [səb'vɛnʃən] *s* subvención ‖ *tr* subvencionar

subversive [səb'vʌrsɪv] *adj* subversivo ‖ *s* subversor *m*

subvert [səb'vʌrt] *tr* subvertir

subway ['sʌb,we] *s* galería subterránea; metro, ferrocarril subterráneo

succeed [sək'sid] *tr* suceder (*a una persona o cosa*) ‖ *intr* tener buen éxito

success [sək'sɛs] *s* buen éxito

successful [sək'sɛsfəl] *adj* feliz, próspero; acertado; logrado

succession [sək'sɛʃən] *s* sucesión; **in succession** seguidos, uno tras otro

successive [sək'sɛsɪv] *adj* sucesivo

succor ['sʌkər] *s* socorro ‖ *tr* socorrer

succotash ['sʌkə,tæʃ] *s* guiso de maíz tierno y habas

succumb [sə'kʌm] *intr* sucumbir

such [sʌtʃ] *adj* & *pron indef* tal, semejante; **such a** tal, semejante; **such a** + *adj* un tan + *adj*; **such as** quienes, los que

suck [sʌk] *s* chupada; mamada ‖ *tr* chupar; mamar; aspirar (*el aire*)

sucker ['sʌkər] *s* chupador *m*; mamón *m*; (bot & mach) chupón *m*; (coll) bobo, primo

suckle ['sʌkəl] *tr* lactar; criar, educar

suckling pig ['sʌklɪŋ] *s* lechón *m*, cerdo de leche

suction ['sʌkʃən] *adj* aspirante ‖ *s* succión

sudden ['sʌdən] *adj* súbito, repentino; **all of a sudden** de repente

suds [sʌdz] *spl* jabonadura; (coll) espuma, cerveza

sue [su] *tr* demandar; pedir; (law) procesar ‖ *intr* (law) poner pleito, entablar juicio; **to sue for damages** demandar por daños y perjuicios; **to sue for peace** pedir la paz

suede [swed] *s* gamuza, ante *m*

suet ['su•ɪt] o ['sju•ɪt] *s* sebo

suffer ['sʌfər] *tr* & *intr* sufrir, padecer

sufferance ['sʌfərəns] *s* tolerancia; paciencia; **on sufferance** por tolerancia

suffering ['sʌfərɪŋ] *adj* doliente ‖ *s* dolencia, sufrimiento

suffice [sə'faɪs] *intr* bastar, ser suficiente

sufficient [sə'fɪʃənt] *adj* suficiente

suffix ['sʌfɪks] *s* sufijo

suffocate ['sʌfə,ket] *tr* sofocar ‖ *intr* sofocarse

suffrage ['sʌfrɪdʒ] *s* sufragio; aprobación, voto favorable

suffragette [,sʌfrə'dʒɛt] *s* sufragista (*mujer*)

suffuse [sə'fjuz] *tr* saturar, bañar

sugar ['ʃʊgər] *adj* azucarero ‖ *s* azúcar *m* ‖ *tr* azucarar

sugar beet *s* remolacha azucarera

sugar bowl *s* azucarero

sugar cane *s* caña de azúcar

sug'ar-coat' *tr* azucarar; (fig) endulzar, dorar

suggest [səg'dʒɛst] *tr* sugerir

suggestion [səg'dʒɛstʃən] *s* sugestión, sugerencia; sombra, traza ligera

suggestive [səg'dʒɛstɪv] *adj* sugestivo; sicalíptico

suicidal [,suɪ'saɪdəl] o [,sjuɪ'saɪdəl] *adj* suicida

suicide ['suɪ,saɪd] *s* (*act*) suicidio; (*person*) suicida *mf;* **to commit suicide** suicidarse

suit [sut] o [sjut] *s* traje *m*, terno; (*of a lady*) traje *m* sastre; (*group forming a set*) juego; (*of cards*) palo; petición, súplica; cortejo, galanteo; (*law*) pleito, proceso; **to follow suit** servir del palo; seguir la corriente ‖ *tr* adaptar, ajustar; adaptarse a; sentar, ir o venir bien a; favorecer, satisfacer; **to suit oneself** hacer (*uno*) lo que le guste ‖ *intr* convenir, ser a propósito

suitable ['sutəbəl] *adj* apropiado, conveniente, adecuado

suit'case' *s* maleta, valija

suite [swit] *s* comitiva, séquito; (*group forming a set*) juego; serie *f;* (*of rooms*) crujía; habitación salón; (mus) suite *f*

suiting ['sutɪŋ] *s* corte *m* de traje

suit of clothes *s* traje completo (*de hombre*)

suitor ['sutər] o ['sjutər] *s* pretendiente *m;* (law) demandante *mf*

sulfa drugs ['sʌlfə] *spl* medicamentos sulfas

sulfate ['sʌlfet] *s* sulfato

sulfide ['sʌlfaɪd] *s* sulfuro

sulfite ['sʌlfaɪt] *s* sulfito

sulfur ['sʌlfər] *s* (chem) azufre *m;* véase **sulphur**

sulfuric [sʌl'fjʊrɪk] *adj* sulfúrico

sulfur mine *s* azufrera

sulfurous ['sʌlfərəs] *adj* sulfuroso ‖ *adj* (chem) sulfuroso

sulk [sʌlk] *s* murria ‖ *intr* amorrarse, enfurruñarse

sulk·y ['sʌlki] *adj* (*comp* **-ier;** *super* **-iest**) enfurruñado, murrio, resentido

sullen ['sʌlən] *adj* hosco, malhumorado, taciturno, triste

sul·ly ['sʌli] *v* (*pret & pp* **-lied**) *tr* empañar, manchar

sulphur ['sʌlfər] *adj* azufrado ‖ *s* azufre *m;* color de azufre ‖ *tr* azufrar

sultan ['sʌltən] *s* sultán *m*

sul·try ['sʌltri] *adj* (*comp* **-trier;** *super* **-triest**) bochornoso, sofocante

sum [sʌm] *s* suma; (coll) problema *m* de aritmética ‖ *v* (*pret & pp* **summed;** *ger* **summing**) *tr* sumar; **to sum up** sumar, resumir

sumac o **sumach** ['ʃumæk] o [sumæk] *s* zumaque *m*

summarize ['sʌmə,raɪz] *tr* resumir

summa·ry ['sʌməri] *adj* sumario ‖ *s* (*pl* **-ries**) sumario, resumen *m*

summer ['sʌmər] *adj* estival, veraniego ‖ *s* verano, estío ‖ *intr* veranear

summer resort *s* lugar *m* de veraneo

summersault ['sʌmər,sɔlt] *s* salto mortal ‖ *intr* dar un salto mortal

summer school *s* escuela de verano

summery ['sʌməri] *adj* estival, veraniego

summit ['sʌmɪt] *s* cima, cumbre *f*

summit conference o **summit meeting** *s* conferencia en la cumbre

summon ['sʌmən] *tr* convocar, llamar; evocar; (law) citar, emplazar

summons ['sʌmənz] *s* orden *f*, señal *f;* (law) citación, emplazamiento ‖ *tr* (coll) citar, emplazar

sumptuous ['sʌmptʃʊəs] *adj* suntuoso

sun [sʌn] *s* sol *m;* **to have a place in the sun** ocupar su puesto en el mundo ‖ *v* (*pret & pp* **sunned;** *ger* **sunning**) *tr* asolear ‖ *intr* asolearse

sun bath *s* baño de sol

sun'beam' *s* rayo de sol

sun'bon'net *s* papalina

sun'burn' *s* quemadura de sol ‖ *v* (*pret & pp* **-burned** o **burnt**) *tr* quemar al sol ‖ *intr* quemarse al sol

sundae ['sʌndi] *s* helado con frutas, jarabes o nueces

Sunday ['sʌndi] *adj* dominical; (*used or worn on Sunday*) dominguero ‖ *s* domingo

Sunday best *s* (coll) trapos de cristianar, ropa dominguera

Sunday's child *s* niño nacido de pies, niño mimado de la fortuna

Sunday school *s* escuela dominical, doctrina dominical

Sunday supplement *s* (*newspaper*) suplemento dominical

sunder ['sʌndər] *tr* separar; romper

sun'di'al *s* reloj *m* de sol, cuadrante *m* solar

sun'down' *s* puesta del sol

sundries ['sʌndriz] *spl* artículos diversos

sundry ['sʌndri] *adj* diversos, varios

sun'flow'er *s* girasol *m*, tornasol *m*

sun'glass'es *spl* gafas de sol, gafas para el sol

sunken ['sʌŋkən] *adj* hundido, sumido

sun lamp *s* lámpara de rayos ultravioletas

sun'light' *s* luz *f* del sol

sun'lit' *adj* iluminado por el sol

sun·ny ['sʌni] *adj* (*comp* **-nier;** *super* **-iest**) de sol; asoleado; brillante, resplandeciente; alegre, risueño; **to be sunny** hacer sol

sunny side *s* sol *m;* (fig) lado bueno, lado favorable

sun porch *s* solana

sun'rise' *s* salida del sol; **from sunrise to sunset** de sol a sol

sun'set' *s* puesta del sol

sun'shade' *s* quitasol *m*, sombrilla; toldo; visera contra el sol

sun'shine' *s* claridad del sol; alegría; **in the sunshine** al sol

sun'spot' *s* mancha solar

sun'stroke' *s* insolación

sun'tan' *s* bronceado

suntan lotion *s* bronceador *m*

su
su

sup. *abbr* **superior, supplement**

sup [sʌp] *v* (*pret & pp* **supped;** *ger* **supping**) *intr* cenar

superannuated [ˌsupərˈænju̇ˌetɪd] *adj* jubilado, inhabilitado por ancianidad o enfermedad; fuera de moda

superb [səˈpʌrb] *adj* soberbio, estupendo, magnífico

supercar·go [ˈsupərˌkɑrgo] *s* (*pl* **-goes** o **-gos**) (naut) sobrecargo

supercharge [ˌsupərˈtʃɑrdʒ] *tr* sobrealimentar

supercilious [ˌsupərˈsɪli·əs] *adj* arrogante, altanero, desdeñoso

superficial [ˌsupərˈfɪʃəl] *adj* superficial

superfluous [su̇ˈpʌrflu̇·əs] *adj* superfluo

superhuman [ˌsupərˈhjumən] *adj* sobrehumano

superimpose [ˌsupərɪmˈpoz] *tr* sobreponer

superintendent [ˌsupərɪnˈtɛndənt] *s* superintendente *mf*

superior [səˈpɪri·ər] *adj* superior; indiferente, sereno; arrogante; (typ) volado ‖ *s* superior *m*

superiority [səˌpɪriˈɑrɪti] *s* superioridad; indiferencia, serenidad; arrogancia

superlative [səˈpʌrlətɪv] *adj & s* superlativo

super·man [ˈsupərˌmæn] *s* (*pl* **-men** [ˌmɛn]) sobrehombre *m*, superhombre *m*

supermarket [ˈsupərˌmɑrkɪt] *s* supermercado

supernatural [ˌsupərˈnætʃərəl] *adj* sobrenatural

superpose [ˌsupərˈpoz] *tr* sobreponer, superponer

supersede [ˌsupərˈsid] *tr* reemplazar; desalojar

supersonic [ˌsupərˈsɑnɪk] *adj* supersónico ‖ **supersonics** *ssg* supersónica

superstitious [ˌsupərˈstɪʃəs] *adj* supersticioso

supertanker [ˈsupərˌtæŋkər] *s* superpetrolero, supertanquero

supervene [ˌsupərˈvin] *intr* sobrevenir

supervise [ˈsupərˌvaɪz] *tr* superintender, supervisar, dirigir

supervisor [ˈsupərˌvaɪzər] *s* superintendente *mf*, supervisor *m*, dirigente *mf*

supp. *abbr* **supplement**

supper [ˈsʌpər] *s* cena

supplant [səˈplænt] *tr* reemplazar

supple [ˈsʌpəl] *adj* flexible; dócil

supplement [ˈsʌpləmənt] *s* suplemento ‖ [ˈsʌpliˌmɛnt] *tr* suplir, completar

suppliant [ˈsʌpli·ənt] *adj & s* suplicante *mf*

supplication [ˌsʌpliˈkeʃən] *s* súplica

sup·ply [səˈplaɪ] *s* (*pl* **-plies**) suministro, provisión; surtido, repuesto; oferta, existencia; **supplies** pertrechos, provisiones, víveres *mf;* artículos, efectos ‖ *v* (*pret & pp* **-plied**) *tr* suministrar, aprovisionar; reemplazar

supply and demand *spl* oferta y demanda

support [səˈport] *s* apoyo, soporte *m*, sostén *m;* sustento ‖ *tr* apoyar, soportar, sostener; sustentar; aguantar

supporter [səˈportər] *s* partidario; (*jockstrap*) suspensorio; faja abdominal, faja medical

suppose [səˈpoz] *tr* suponer; creer; **to be supposed to** deber; **to suppose so** creer que sí

supposed [səˈpozd] *adj* supuesto

supposition [ˌsʌpəˈzɪʃən] *s* suposición

supposito·ry [səˈpɑzɪˌtori] *s* (*pl* **-ries**) supositorio

suppress [səˈprɛs] *tr* suprimir

suppression [səˈprɛʃən] *s* supresión

suppurate [ˈsʌpjəˌret] *intr* supurar

supreme [səˈprim] o [su̇ˈprim] *adj* supremo

supt. *abbr* **superintendent**

surcharge [ˈsʌrˌtʃɑrdʒ] *s* sobrecarga ‖ [ˌsʌrˈtʃɑrdʒ] o [ˈsʌrˌtʃɑrdʒ] *tr* sobrecargar

sure [ʃu̇r] *adj* seguro; **to be sure** seguramente, sin duda ‖ *adv* (coll) seguramente, claro; **sure enough** efectivamente

sure things *adv* (slang) seguramente ‖ *interj* ¡claro!, ¡seguro! ‖ *s* (slang) sacabocados *m*

sure·ty [ˈʃu̇rti] o [ˈʃu̇rɪti] *s* (*pl* **-ties**) seguridad, garantía, fianza

surf [sʌrf] *s* cachones *mpl*, olas que rompen en la playa

surface [ˈsʌrfɪs] *adj* superficial ‖ *s* superficie *f* ‖ *tr* alisar, allanar; recubrir ‖ *intr* emerger (*p.ej., un submarino*)

surface mail *s* correo por vía ordinaria

surf′board′ *s* patín *m* de mar

surfeit [ˈsʌrfɪt] *s* exceso; hartura, hastío; empacho, indigestión ‖ *tr* atracar, hastiar; encebadar (*las bestias*) ‖ *intr* atracarse, hastiarse; encebadarse

surf′-rid′ing *s* patinaje *m* sobre las olas

surge [sʌrdʒ] *s* oleada; (elec) sobretensión ‖ *intr* agitarse, ondular

surgeon [ˈsʌrdʒən] *s* cirujano

surger·y [ˈsʌrdʒəri] *s* (*pl* **-ies**) cirugía; sala de operaciones

surgical [ˈsʌrdʒɪkəl] *adj* quirúrgico

sur·ly [ˈsʌrli] *adj* (*comp* **-lier;** *super* **-liest**) áspero, rudo, hosco, insolente

surmise [sərˈmaɪz] o [ˈsʌrmaɪz] *s* conjetura, suposición ‖ [sərˈmaɪz] *tr & intr* conjeturar, suponer

surmount [sərˈmaʊnt] *tr* levantarse sobre; aventajar, sobrepujar; superar; coronar

surname [ˈsʌrˌnem] *s* apellido: (*added name*) sobrenombre *m* ‖ *tr* apellidar; sobrenombrar

surpass [sərˈpæs] o [sərˈpɑs] *tr* aventajar, sobrepasar

surplice [ˈsʌrplɪs] *s* sobrepelliz *f*

surplus [ˈsʌrplʌs] *adj* sobrante, excedente ‖ *s* sobrante *m*, exceso; (com) superávit *m*

surprise [sərˈpraɪz] *adj* inesperado, improviso ‖ *s* sorpresa; **to take by surprise** coger por sorpresa ‖ *tr* sorprender

surprise package *s* sorpresa

surprise party *s* reunión improvisada para felicitar por sorpresa a una persona

surprising [sərˈpraɪzɪŋ] *adj* sorprendente, sorpresivo

surrender [səˈrɛndər] *s* rendición ‖ *tr* rendir ‖ *intr* rendirse

surrender value *s* (ins) valor *m* de rescate

surreptitious [ˌsʌrɛpˈtɪʃəs] *adj* subrepticio

surround [sə'raʊnd] *tr* cercar, rodear, circundar; (mil) sitiar

surrounding [sə'raʊndɪŋ] *adj* circundante, circunstante ‖ **surroundings** *spl* alrededores *mpl*, contornos; ambiente *m*, medio

surtax ['sʌr,tæks] *s* impuesto complementario

surveillance [sər'veləns] o [sər'veljəns] *s* vigilancia

survey ['sʌrve] *s* estudio, examen *m*, inspección, reconocimiento; agrimensura, medición, plano; levantamiento de planos; (*of opinion*) encuesta; (*of literature*) bosquejo ‖ [sʌr've] o ['sʌrve] *tr* estudiar, examinar, inspeccionar, reconocer; medir; levantar el plano de ‖ *intr* levantar el plano

surveyor [sər've•ər] *s* inspector *m;* agrimensor *m*

survival [sər'vaɪvəl] *s* supervivencia

survive [sər'vaɪv] *tr* sobrevivir a (*otra persona; algún acontecimiento*) ‖ *intr* sobrevivir

surviving [sər'vaɪvɪŋ] *adj* sobreviviente

survivor [sər'vaɪvər] *s* sobreviviente *mf*

survivorship [sər'vaɪvər,ʃɪp] *s* (law) sobrevivencia

susceptible [sə'sɛptɪbəl] *adj* susceptible; (*to love*) enamoradizo

suspect ['sʌspɛkt] o [səs'pɛkt] *adj & s* sospechoso ‖ [səs'pɛkt] *tr* sospechar

suspend [səs'pɛnd] *tr* suspender ‖ *intr* dejar de obrar; suspender pagos

suspenders [səs'pɛndərz] *spl* tirantes *mpl*

suspense [səs'pɛns] *s* suspenso, suspensión; duda, incertidumbre; indecisión, irresolución; ansiedad

suspension bridge [səs'pɛnʃən] *s* puente *m* colgante

suspicion [səs'pɪʃən] *s* sospecha, suspicacia; sombra, traza ligera

suspicious [səs'pɪʃəs] *adj* (*inclined to suspect*) suspicaz; (*subject to suspicion*) sospechoso

sustain [səs'ten] *tr* sostener, sustentar; apoyar, defender; confirmar, probar; sufrir (*p.ej., un daño, una pérdida*)

sustenance ['sʌstɪnəns] *s* sustento, alimentos; sostenimiento

sutler ['sʌtlər] *s* (mil) vivandero

swab [swɑb] *s* escobón *m*, estropajo; (naut) lampazo; (surg) tapón *m* de algodón ‖ *v* (*pret & pp* **swabbed;** *ger* **swabbing**) *tr* fregar, limpiar; (naut) lampacear; (surg) limpiar con algodón

swaddle ['swɑdəl] *tr* empañar, fajar

swaddling clothes *spl* pañales *mpl*

swagger ['swægər] *adj* (coll) muy elegante ‖ *s* fanfarronada; contoneo, paso jactancioso ‖ *intr* fanfarronear; contonear

swain [swen] *s* (*lad*) zagal; galán *m*, amante *m*

swallow ['swɑlo] *s* trago; (orn) golondrina ‖ *tr* tragar, deglutir; (fig) tragar, tragarse ‖ *intr* tragar, deglutir

swallow-tailed coat ['swɑlo,teld] *s* frac *m*

swal′low•wort′ *s* vencetósigo

swamp [swɑmp] *s* pantano, marisma ‖ *tr* encharcar, inundar; (*e.g., with work*) abrumar

swamp•y ['swɑmpi] *adj* (*comp* -**ier;** *super* -**iest**) pantanoso

swan [swɑn] *s* cisne *m*

swan dive *s* salto de ángel

swank [swæŋk] *adj* (slang) elegante, vistoso ‖ *s* (slang) elegancia vistosa

swan knight *s* caballero del cisne

swan's-down ['swɑnz,daʊn] *s* plumón *m* de cisne; moletón *m*, paño de vicuña

swan song *s* canto del cisne

swap [swɑp] *s* (coll) truque *m*, cambalache *m* ‖ *v* (*pret & pp* **swapped;** *ger* **swapping**) *tr & intr* trocar, cambalachear

swarm [swɔrm] *s* enjambre *m* ‖ *intr* enjambrar; volar en enjambres; hormiguear (*una multitud de gente o animales*)

swarth•y ['swɔrði] o ['swɔrθi] *adj* (*comp* -**ier;** *super* -**iest**) atezado, carinegro, moreno

swashbuckler ['swɑʃ,bʌklər] *s* espada chín *m*, matasiete *m*, valentón *m*

swat [swɑt] *s* (coll) golpe violento ‖ *v* (*pret & pp* **swatted;** *ger* **swatting**) *tr* (coll) golpear con fuerza; (coll) aporrear, aplastar (*una mosca*)

sway [swe] *s* oscilación, vaivén *m;* dominio, imperio ‖ *tr* hacer oscilar; conmover; disuadir; gobernar, dominar ‖ *intr* oscilar; desviarse; tambalear, flaquear

swear [swɛr] *v* (*pret* **swore** [swor]; *pp* **sworn** [sworn]) *tr* jurar; juramentar; prestar (*juramento*); **to swear in** tomar juramento a; **to swear off** jurar renunciar a; **to swear out** obtener mediante juramento ‖ *intr* jurar; **to swear at** maldecir; **to swear by** jurar por; poner toda su confianza en; **to swear to** prestar juramento a; declarar bajo juramento; jurar + *inf*

sweat [swɛt] *s* sudor *m* ‖ *v* (*pret & pp* **sweat** o **sweated**) *tr* sudar (*agua por los poros; la ropa*); (slang) hacer sudar; **to sweat it out** (slang) aguantarlo hasta el fin ‖ *intr* sudar

sweater ['swɛtər] *s* suéter *m*

sweat shirt *s* pulóver *m* de mangas largas

sweat′shop′ *s* taller *m* de trabajo afanoso y de poco sueldo

sweat•y ['swɛti] *adj* (*comp* -**ier;** *super* -**iest**) sudoroso

Swede [swid] *s* sueco

Sweden ['swidən] *s* Suecia

Swedish ['swidɪʃ] *adj & s* sueco

sweep [swip] *s* barrido; alcance *m*, extensión; (*of wind*) soplo; (*of a well*) cigoñal *m* ‖ *v* (*pret & pp* **swept** [swɛpt]) *tr* barrer; arrastrar; rozar, tocar; recorrer con la mirada, los dedos, etc. ‖ *intr* barrer; pasar rápidamente; extenderse; precipitarse; andar con paso majestuoso

sweeper ['swipər] *s* (*person*) barrendero; (*machine for sweeping streets*) barredera; barredera de alfombra; (nav) dragaminas *m*

sweeping ['swipɪŋ] *adj* arrebatador; comprensivo, extenso, vasto ‖ **sweepings** *spl* barreduras

SU
SW

sweep′sec′ond *s* segundero central

sweep′stakes′ *ssg* o *spl* lotería en la cual una persona gana todas las apuestas; carrera que decide todas las apuestas; premio en las carreras de caballos

sweet [swit] *adj* dulce; oloroso; melodioso, grato al oído; fresco; bonito, lindo; amable; querido; **to be sweet on** (coll) estar enamorado de ‖ *adv* dulcemente; **to smell sweet** tener buen olor ‖ **sweets** *spl* dulces *mpl*, golosinas

sweet′bread′ *s* lechecillas, mollejas

sweet′bri′er *s* eglantina

sweeten [′switən] *tr* azucarar, endulzar; suavizar; purificar ‖ *intr* azucararse, endulzarse; suavizarse

sweetener [′switənər] *s* eculcorante

sweet′heart′ *s* enamorado o enamorada; amiga querida; galán *m*, cortejo

sweetish [′switʃ] *adj* dulzoso

sweet marjoram *s* mejorana

sweet′meats′ *spl* dulces *mpl*, confites *mpl*, confitura

sweet pea *s* guisante *m* de olor

sweet potato *s* batata, camote *m*

sweet-scented [′swit,sɛntɪd] *adj* oloroso, perfumado

sweet tooth *s* gusto por los dulces

sweet-toothed [′swit,tuθt] *adj* dulcero, goloso

sweet william *s* clavel *m* de ramillete, minutisa

swell [swɛl] *adj* (coll) muy elegante; (slang) de órdago, magnífico ‖ *s* hinchazón *f;* bulto; marejada; oleaje *m; (of a crowd of people)* oleada; (coll) petimetre *m*, pisaverde *m* ‖ *v* (*pret* **swelled;** *pp* **swelled** o **swollen** [′swolən]) *tr* hinchar, inflar; abultar, aumentar; elevar, levantar; (fig) hinchar, engreír ‖ *intr* hincharse; abultarse, aumentar, crecer; elevarse, levantarse; embravecerse (*el mar*); (fig) hincharse, engreírse

swelled head *s* entono; **to have a swelled head** estar muy pagado de sí mismo, creerse gran cosa

swelter [′swɛltər] *intr* sofocarse de sudor

swept′back′ wing *s* (aer) ala en flecha

swerve [swʌrv] *s* viraje *m*, desvío brusco ‖ *tr* desviar ‖ *intr* desviarse, torcer

swift [swɪft] *adj* rápido, veloz; pronto; repentino; correlón (SAm) ‖ *adv* rápidamente, velozmente ‖ *s* vencejo

swig [swɪg] *s* chisguete *m*, tragantada ‖ *v* (*pret* & *pp* **swigged;** *ger* **swigging**) *tr* & *intr* beber a grandes tragos

swill [swɪl] *s* basura, inmundicia; tragantada ‖ *tr* beber a grandes tragos; emborrachar ‖ *intr* beber a grandes tragos; emborracharse

swim [swɪm] *s* natación; **the swim** (*in affairs, society, etc.*) (coll) la corriente ‖ *v* (*pret* **swam** [swæm]; *pp* **swum** [swʌm]; *ger* **swimming**) *tr* pasar a nado ‖ *intr* nadar; deslizarse, escurrirse; padecer vahidos; dar vueltas (*la cabeza*); **to swim across** atravesar a nado

swimmer [′swɪmər] *s* nadador *m*

swimming pool *s* piscina

swimming suit *s* traje *m* de baño

swindle [′swɪndəl] *s* estafa, timo; leva (CAm, Col); embelequería (Col, Mex, P-R) ‖ *tr* & *intr* estafar, timar

swindler [′swɪndlər] *s* estafador *m*, estafadora; lana *m* (CAm)

swine [swaɪn] *s* cerdo, puerco; *spl* ganado porcino

swing [swɪŋ] *s* balance *m*, oscilación, vaivén *m; (device used for recreation)* columpio; hamaca; turno, período; fuerza, ímpetu *m; (trip)* jira; (box) golpe *m* de lado; (mus) ritmo constantemente repetido; **in full swing** en plena marcha ‖ *v* (*pret* & *pp* **swung** [swʌŋ]) *tr* blandir (*p.ej., un arma*); menear (*los brazos*); hacer oscilar; columpiar; manejar con éxito ‖ *intr* oscilar; balancearse; columpiar; estar colgado; dar una vuelta; **to swing open** abrirse de pronto (*una puerta*)

swinging door [′swɪŋɪŋ] *s* batiente *m* oscilante, puerta de vaivén

swinish [′swaɪnɪʃ] *adj* porcuno; (fig) cochino, puerco

swipe [swaɪp] *s* (coll) golpe *m* fuerte ‖ *tr* (coll) dar un golpe fuerte a; (slang) hurtar, robar

swirl [swʌrl] *s* remolino, torbellino ‖ *tr* hacer girar ‖ *intr* arremolinarse, remolinar; girar

swish [swɪʃ] *s* (*e.g., of a whip*) chasquido; (*of a dress*) crujido ‖ *tr* chasquear (*el látigo*) ‖ *intr* chasquear; crujir (*un vestido*)

Swiss [swɪs] *adj* & *s* suizo

Swiss chard [tʃɑrd] *s* acelga

Swiss cheese *s* Gruyère *m*, queso suizo

Swiss Guards *spl* guardia suiza

switch [swɪtʃ] *s* bastoncillo, latiguillo; latigazo; coletazo; (*false hair*) trenza postiza, moño postizo; (elec) llave *f*, interruptor *m*, conmutador *m;* (rr) agujas ‖ *tr* azotar, fustigar; (elec) conmutar; (rr) desviar; **to switch off** (elec) cortar, desconectar; **to switch on** (elec) cerrar (*el circuito*); (elec) encender, poner (*la luz, etc.*) ‖ *intr* cambiarse, moverse; desviarse

switch′back′ *s* vía en zigzag

switch′board′ *s* cuadro de distribución

switching engine *s* locomotora de maniobras

switch•man [′swɪtʃmən] *s* (*pl* **-men** [mən]) agujetero, guardagujas *m*

switch′yard′ *s* patio de maniobras

Switzerland [′swɪtsərlənd] *s* Suiza

swiv•el [′swɪvəl] *s* eslabón giratorio ‖ *v* (*pret* & *pp* **-eled** o **-elled;** *ger* **-eling** o **-elling**) *intr* girar sobre un eje

swivel chair *s* silla giratoria

swoon [swun] *s* desmayo ‖ *intr* desmayarse

swoop [swup] *s* descenso súbito; (*of a bird of prey*) calada ‖ *intr* bajar rápidamente, precipitarse; abatirse (*p.ej., el ave de rapiña*)

sword [sord] *s* espada; **at swords′ points** enemistados a sangre y fuego; **to put to the sword** pasar al filo de la espada, pasar a cuchillo

sword belt *s* cinturón *m*

sword′fish′ *s* pez *m* espada

sword handler s (taur) mozo de estoques
sword rattling s fanfarronería
swords•man ['sordzmən] s (pl -men [mən]) espada m; esgrimidor m
sword swallower ['swɑlo•ər] s tragasable m
sword thrust s estocada, golpe m de espada
sworn [sworn] adj (enemy) jurado
sycophant ['sɪkəfənt] s adulador m; parásito
syll. abbr **syllable**
syllable ['sɪləbəl] s sílaba
syllogism ['sɪlə,dʒɪzəm] s silogismo
sylph [sɪlf] s sílfide f
sym. abbr **symbol, symmetrical, symphony, symptom**
symbiosis [,sɪmbaɪ'osɪs] o [,sɪmbi'osɪs] s simbiosis
symbiotic [,sɪmbaɪ'ɑtɪk] o [,sɪmbi'ɑtɪk] adj simbiótico
symbol ['sɪmbəl] s símbolo
symbolic(al) [sɪm'bɑlɪk(əl]] adj simbólico
symbolize ['sɪmbə,laɪz] tr simbolizar
symmetric(al) [sɪ'mɛtrɪk(əl)] adj simétrico
symme•try ['sɪmɪtri] s (pl -tries) simetría
sympathetic [,sɪmpə'θɛtɪk] adj compasivo; favorablemente dispuesto
sympathize ['sɪmpə,θaɪz] intr compadecerse; **to sympathize with** compadecerse de; comprender
sympa•thy ['sɪmpəθi] s (pl -thies) compasión, conmiseración; **to be in sympathy with** estar de acuerdo con, ser partidario de; **to extend one's sympathy to** dar el pésame a
sympathy strike s huelga por solidaridad
symphonic [sɪm'fɑnɪk] adj sinfónico
sympho•ny ['sɪmfəni] s (pl -nies) sinfonía

symposi•um [sɪm'pozɪ•əm] s (pl -a [ə]) coloquio
symptom ['sɪmptəm] s síntoma m
syn. abbr **synonym, synonymous**
synagogue ['sɪnə,gɔg] s sinagoga
synchronize ['sɪŋkrə,naɪz] tr & intr sincronizar
synchronous ['sɪŋkrənəs] adj sincrónico
syncope ['sɪŋkə,pi] s (phonet) síncopa
syndicate ['sɪndɪkɪt] s sindicato || ['sɪndɪ,ket] tr sindicar || intr sindicarse
syndrome ['sɪndrom] s síndrome m
synonym ['sɪnənɪm] s sinónimo
synonymous [sɪ'nɑnɪməs] adj sinónimo
synop•sis [sɪ'nɑpsɪs] s (pl -ses [siz]) sinopsis f
syntax ['sɪntæks] s sintaxis f
synthe•sis ['sɪnθɪsɪs] s (pl -ses [,siz]) síntesis f
synthesize ['sɪnθɪ,saɪz] tr sintetizar
synthesizer s sintetizador m
synthetic(al) [sɪn'θɛtɪk(əl]] adj sintético
syphillis ['sɪfɪlɪs] s sífilis f
Syria ['sɪrɪ•ə] s Siria
Syrian ['sɪrɪ•ən] adj & s sirio
syringe [sɪ'rɪndʒ] o ['sɪrɪndʒ] s jeringa; (fountain syringe) mangueta; (syringe fitted with needle for hypodermic injections) jeringuilla || tr jeringar
syrup ['sɪrəp] s almíbar m; (with fruit juices or medicinal substances) jarabe m
system ['sɪstəm] s sistema m
systematic(al) [,sɪstə'mætɪk(əl)] adj sistemático
systematize ['sɪstəmə,taɪz] tr sistematizar
systems analysis s análisis m & f de sistemas
systole ['sɪstəli] s sístole f

T

T, t [ti] vigésima letra del alfabeto inglés
t. abbr **teaspoon, temperature, tenor, tense, territory, town**
T. abbr **Territory, Testament**
tab [tæb] s apéndice m, proyección; marbete m; **to keep tab on** (coll) tener a la vista; **to pick up the tab** (coll) pagar la cuenta
tab•by ['tæbi] s (pl -bies) gato atigrado; gata; solterona; chismosa
tabernacle ['tæbər,nækəl] s tabernáculo
table ['tebəl] s mesa; (list, catalogue; index of a book) tabla; **to set the table** poner la mesa; **to turn the tables** volver las tornas; **under the table** completamente emborrachado || tr aplazar la discusión de
tab•leau ['tæblo] s (pl -leaus o -leaux [loz]) cuadro vivo
ta′ble•cloth′ s mantel m
table d'hôte ['tɑbəl'dot] s mesa redonda; comida a precio fijo
ta′ble•land′ s meseta

table linen s mantelería
table manners spl modales mpl que uno tiene en la mesa
table of contents s índice m de materias, tabla de materias
ta′ble•spoon′ s cuchara de sopa
tablespoonful ['tebəl,spun,ful] s cucharada
tablet ['tæblɪt] s (writing pad) bloc m; (slab) lápida, placa; (lozenge, pastille) comprimido, tableta
table talk s conversación de sobremesa
table tennis s tenis de mesa
ta′ble•ware′ s servicio de mesa, artículos para la mesa
tabloid ['tæblɔɪd] s periódico sensacional
taboo [tə'bu] adj prohibido || s tabú m || tr prohibir
tabulate ['tæbjə,let] tr tabular
tabulator ['tæbjə,letər] s tabulador m
tacit ['tæsɪt] adj tácito
taciturn ['tæsɪ,tʌrn] adj taciturno

sw
ta

tack [tæk] *s* tachuela; nuevo plan de acción; (naut) virada; (sew) hilván *m* ‖ *tr* clavar con tachuelas; añadir; unir; (naut) virar; (sew) hilvanar ‖ *intr* cambiar de plan; (naut) virar

tackle ['tækəl] *s* avíos, enseres *mpl;* (naut) poleame *m* ‖ *tr* atacar, embestir; emprender

tack·y ['tæki] *adj* (*comp* **-ier;** *super* **-iest**) pegajoso; (coll) desaliñado

tact [tækt] *s* tacto, juicio, tino

tactful ['tæktfəl] *adj* discreto, político

tactical ['tæktɪkəl] *adj* táctico

tactician [tæk'tɪʃən] *s* táctico

tactics ['tæktɪks] *ssg* (mil) táctica ‖ *spl* táctica

tactless ['tæktlɪs] *adj* indiscreto

tad'pole' *s* renacuajo

taffeta ['tæfɪtə] *s* tafetán *m*

taffy ['tæfi] *s* arropía, melcocha; (coll) lisonja, zalamería

tag [tæg] *s* etiqueta, marbete *m;* herrete *m;* pingajo; mechón *m;* vedija; (*curlicue in writing*) ringorrango; **to play tag** jugar al tócame tú ‖ *v* (*pret & pp* **tagged;** *ger* **tagging**) *tr* pegar un marbete a; marcar con marbete ‖ *intr* (coll) seguir de cerca

tag end *s* cabo flojo; retal *m*, retazo

Tagus ['tegəs] *s* Tajo

tail [tel] *adj* de cola ‖ *s* cola; **tails** (*of a coin*) cruz *f;* (coll) frac *m;* **to turn tail** mostrar los talones ‖ *tr* atar, juntar ‖ *intr* formar cola; **to tail after** pisar los talones a

tail assembly *s* (aer) empenaje *m*, planos de cola

tail end *s* cola, extremo; conclusión; **at the tail end** al final

tail'gate' *tr & intr* (aut) seguir demasiado de cerca

tail'light' *s* faro trasero; (rr) disco de cola

tailor ['telər] *s* sastre *m* ‖ *tr* entallar (*un traje*) ‖ *intr* ser sastre

tailoring ['telərɪŋ] *s* sastrería, costura

tai'lor-made' suit *s* traje *m* de sastre, traje hecho a la medida

tail'piece' *s* apéndice *m*, cabo; (*of stringed instrument*) (mus) cordal *m;* (typ) florón *m*

tail'race' *s* cauce *m* de salida; (min) canal *m* de desechos

tail spin *s* (aer) barrena picada

tail wind *s* (aer) viento de cola; (naut) viento en popa

taint [tent] *s* mancha; corrupción, infección ‖ *tr* manchar; corromper, inficionar

take [tek] *s* toma; presa, redada; (mov) toma; (slang) entradas, ingresos ‖ *v* (*pret* **took** [tʊk]; *pp* **taken**) *tr* tomar; (*to carry off with one*) llevarse; (*to remove*) quitar; quedarse con (*p.ej., una compra en una tienda*); comer (*una pieza, en el juego de ajedrez y en el de damas*); dar (*un paso, un salto, un paseo*); hacer (*un viaje; ejercicio*); sacar (*una consejo; una asignatura*); sacar (*una fotografía*); calzar, usar (*cierto tamaño de zapatos o guantes*); estudiar (*p.ej., historia, francés, matemáticas*); echar (*una siesta*); tomar (*un tren, autobús, tranvía*); aguantar, tolerar; soportar; **to take amiss**

llevar a mal; **to take apart** descomponer, desarmar, desmontar; **to take down** bajar; descolgar; poner por escrito, tomar nota de; desmontar; (*to humble*) quitar los humos a; **to take for** tomar por, p.ej., **I took you for someone else** le tomé por otra persona; **to take from** quitar a; **to take in** acoger, admitir; (*to welcome into one's home, one's company*) recibir; (*to encompass*) abarcar, comprender; ganar (*dinero*); visitar (*los puntos de interés*); (*to win over by flattery or deceit*) cazar; meter (*p.ej., las costuras de una prenda de vestir*); **to take it that** suponer que; **to take off** quitarse (*p.ej., el sombrero*); descontar; (coll) imitar, parodiar; **to take on** tomar, contratar; empezar; cargar con, tomar sobre sí; desafiar; **to take out** sacar; pasear (*p.ej., a un niño, un caballo*); omitir; extraer, separar; **to take place** tener lugar; **to take up** subir; levantar; apretar; coger; recoger; emprender, comenzar; tomar posesión de (*un cargo, un puesto*); tomar, estudiar; ocupar, llenar (*un espacio*) ‖ *intr* arraigar, prender; cuajar; actuar, obrar; salir, resultar; adherirse; pegar; (coll) tener éxito; **to take after** parecerse a; **to take off** levantarse; salir; (aer) despegar; **to take up with** (coll) estrechar amistad con; (coll) vivir con; **to take well** (coll) sacar buen retrato

take'-home' pay *s* salario neto

take'-off' *s* (aer) despegue *m;* (coll) imitación burlesca, parodia

talcum powder ['tælkəm] *s* polvos de talco; talco en polvo

tale [tel] *s* cuento, relato; embuste *m*, mentira

tale'bear'er *s* chismoso, cuentista *mf*

talent ['tælənt] *s* talento; gente *f* de talento

talented ['tæləntɪd] *adj* talentoso

talent scout *s* buscador *m* de nuevas figuras

talk [tɔk] *s* charla, plática; (*gossip*) fábula, comidilla; (*lecture*) conferencia; **to cause talk** dar que hablar ‖ *tr* hablar; convencer hablando; **to talk up** ensalzar ‖ *intr* hablar; parlar (*el loro*); **to talk on** discutir (*un asunto*); hablar sin para; continuar hablando; **to talk up** elevar la voz, osar hablar

talkative ['tɔkətɪv] *adj* hablador, locuaz, palabrudo

talker ['tɔkər] *s* hablador *m;* orador *m;* charlatán *m*, parlón *m;* discursista *mf*

talkie ['tɔki] *s* (coll) cine hablado

talking doll ['tɔkɪŋ] *s* muñeca parlante

talking film *s* película hablada

talking machine *s* máquina parlante

talking picture *s* cine hablado, cine parlante

talk show *s* (telv, rad) programa *m* de conversación e interviú

tall [tɔl] *adj* alto; (coll) exagerado

tallow ['tælo] *s* sebo

tal·ly ['tæli] *s* (*pl* **-lies**) cuenta ‖ *v* (*pret & pp* **-lied**) *tr* echar la cuenta de ‖ *intr* echar la cuenta; concordar, corresponder, conformarse

tally sheet *s* hoja en que se anota una cuenta

talon ['tælən] s garra

tambourine [,tæmbə'rin] s pandereta

tame [tem] adj manso, domesticado; dócil, sumiso; insípido ‖ tr amansar, domesticar; domar (a un animal salvaje); someter; captar (una caída de agua)

tamp [tæmp] tr atacar (un barreno); apisonar

tamper ['tæmpər] s (person) apisonador m; (ram) pisón m ‖ intr entremeterse; **to tamper with** manosear, tocar ajando; tratar de forzar (una cerradura); falsificar (un documento); corromper (p.ej., a un testigo)

tampon ['tæmpɑn] s (surg) tapón m ‖ tr (surg) taponar

tan [tæn] adj requemado, tostado; de color de canela; marrón; café (Am) ‖ v (pret & pp **tanned**; ger **tanning**) tr adobar, curtir, zurrar; quemar, tostar; (coll) zurrar, dar una paliza a

tang [tæŋ] s sabor m u olor m fuerte y picante; dejo, gustillo (ringing sound) tañido

tangent ['tændʒənt] adj tangente ‖ s tangente f; **to fly off at a tangent** tomar subitamente nuevo rumbo, cambiar de repente

tangerine [,tændʒə'rin] s mandarina

tangible ['tændʒɪbəl] adj palpable, tangible

Tangier [tæn'dʒɪr] s Tánger f

tangle ['tæŋgəl] s enredo, maraña, lío ‖ tr enredar, enmarañar ‖ intr enredarse, enmarañarse

tank [tæŋk] s tanque m, depósito; (mil) tanque, carro de combate; (rr) ténder m; (heavy drinker) (slang) bodega

tank car s (rr) carro cuba, vagón m tanque

tanker ['tæŋkər] s barco tanque, buque m cisterna, barco cisternas; avión-nodriza m

tanker fleet s flota petrolera

tank farming s quimicultura, cultivo hidropónico

tank truck s camión m tanque

tanner ['tænər] s curtidor m

tanner•y ['tænəri] s (pl -ies) curtiduría, tenería

tantalize ['tæntə,laɪz] tr atormentar con falsas promesas

tantamount ['tæntə,maunt] adj equivalente

tantrum ['tæntrəm] s berrinche m, rabieta

tap [tæp] s golpecito, palmadita; canilla, espita; grifo; (elec) toma; (mach) macho de terraja; **on tap** sacado del barril, servido al grifo; listo, a mano; **taps** (signal to put out lights) (mil) silencio ‖ v (pret & pp **tapped**; ger **tapping**) tr dar golpecitos o un golpecito a o en; espitar, poner la espita a; sacar o tomar (quitando la espita); sangrar (un árbol); intervenir (un teléfono); derivar (electricidad); aterrajar (tuercas) ‖ intr dar golpecitos

tap dance s zapateado

tap'-dance' intr zapatear

tape [tep] s cinta ‖ tr proveer de cinta; medir con cinta; (coll) grabar en cinta magnetofónica

tape measure s cinta de medir

taper ['tepər] s cerilla, velita larga y delgada

‖ tr ahusar ‖ intr ahusarse; ir disminuyendo

tape'-re•cord' tr grabar sobre cinta

tape recorder [rɪ'kɔrdər] s magnetófono, grabadora de cinta

tapes•try ['tæpɪstri] s (pl -tries) tapiz m ‖ v (pret & pp -tried) tr tapizar

tape'worm' s solitaria, lombriz solitaria

tappet ['tæpɪt] s (aut) alzaválvulas m, taqué m

tap'room' s bodegón m, taberna

taps [tæps] s toque m de silencio; (slang) fin m, muerte f

tap water s agua de grifo

tap wrench s volvedor m de machos

tar [tɑr] s alquitrán m; (coll) marinero ‖ v (pret & pp **tarred**; ger **tarring**) tr alquitranar; **to tar and feather** embrear y emplumar

tar•dy ['tɑrdi] adj (comp -dier; super -diest) tardío

target ['tɑrgɪt] s blanco

target area s zona a batir

target practice s tiro al blanco

tariff ['tærɪf] adj arancelario ‖ (duties) arancel m; (rates in general) tarifa

tarnish ['tɑrnɪʃ] s deslustre m ‖ tr deslustrar ‖ intr deslustrarse

tar paper s papel alquitranado

tarpaulin [tɑr'pɔlɪn] s alquitranado, encerado, empegado

tar•ry ['tɑri] adj alquitranado, embreado ‖ ['tæri] v (pret & pp -ried) intr detenerse, quedarse; tardar

tart [tɑrt] adj acre, agrio; (fig) áspero, mordaz ‖ s tarta; (coll) puta

task [tæsk] s tarea; **to bring** o **take to task** llamar a capítulo

task'mas'ter s amo, superintendente mf; ordenancista mf, tirano

tassel ['tæsəl] s borla; (bot) penacho

taste [test] s gusto, sabor m; sorbo, trago; muestra; gusto, buen gusto; **in bad taste** de mal gusto; **in good taste** de buen gusto; **to acquire a taste for** tomar gusto a ‖ tr gustar; (to sample) probar ‖ intr saber; **to taste of** saber a

tasteless ['testlɪs] adj desabrido, insípido; de mal gusto

tast•y ['testi] adj (comp -ier; super -iest) sabroso; de buen gusto

tatter ['tætər] s andrajo, harapo, guiñapo ‖ tr hacer andrajos

tattered ['tætərd] adj andrajoso, haraposo, hilachento

tattle ['tætəl] s charla; habladuría ‖ intr charlar; chismear, murmurar

tat'tle•tale' adj revelador ‖ s cuentista mf, chismoso

tatto [tæ'tu] s tatuaje m; (mil) retreta ‖ tr tatuar o tatuarse

taunt [tɔnt] o [tɑnt] s mofa, pulla ‖ tr provocar con insultos

Taurus ['tɔrəs] s (astr) Tauro

taut [tɔt] adj tieso, tirante

tavern ['tævərn] s taberna; mesón m, posada; bayun(c)a (CAm); borrachería (Mex)

ta
ta

taw•dry ['tɔdri] *adj* (*comp* **-drier;** *super* **-driest**) cursi, charro, vistoso

taw•ny ['tɔni] *adj* (*comp* **-nier;** *super* **-niest**) leonado

tax [tæks] *s* contribución, impuesto ‖ *tr* poner impuestos a (*una persona*); poner impuestos sobre (*la propiedad*); abrumar, cargar; agotar (*la paciencia de uno*)

taxable ['tæksəbəl] *adj* imponible

taxation [tæk'seʃən] *s* imposición de contribuciones; contribuciones, impuestos

tax collector *s* recaudador *m* de impuestos

tax cut *s* reducción de impuestos

tax deduction *s* exclusión de contribución

tax evader [ɪ'vedər] *s* burlador *m* de impuestos

tax evasion *s* fraude *m* fiscal

tax'-ex•empt' *adj* exento de impuesto

tax haven *s* asilo de los impuestos

tax•i ['tæksi] *s* (*pl* **-is**) taxi *m* ‖ *v* (*pret & pp* **-ied;** *ger* **-iing** o **-ying**) *tr* (aer) carretear ‖ *intr* ir en taxi; (aer) carretear, taxear

tax'i•cab' *s* taxi *m*

taxi dancer *s* taxi *f*

taxi driver *s* taista *mf*

tax'i•plane' *s* avioneta de alquiler

taxi stand *s* parada de taxis

tax loss *s* pérdida de reclamable

tax'pay'er *s* contribuyente *mf*

tax rate *s* tipo impositivo

tax relief *s* aligeramiento de impuestos

tax return *s* declaración de renta

t.b. *abbr* **tuberculosis**

tbs. o **tbsp.** *abbr* **tablespoon, tablespoons**

tea [ti] *s* té *m;* (*medicinal infusion*) tisana; caldo de carne

tea bag *s* muñeca

tea ball *s* huevo del té

tea'cart' *s* mesita de té (*con ruedas*)

teach [titʃ] *v* (*pret & pp* **taught** [tɔt]) *tr & intr* enseñar

teacher ['titʃər] *s* maestro, instructor *m;* (*such as adversity*) (fig) maestra

teacher's pet *s* alumno mimado

teaching ['titʃɪŋ] *adj* docente ‖ *s* enseñanza; doctrina

teaching aids *spl* material *m* auxiliar de instrucción

teaching staff *s* personal *m* docente

tea'cup' *s* taza para té

tea dance *s* té *m* bailable

teak [tik] *s* teca

tea'ket'tle *s* tetera

team [tim] *s* (*e.g., of horses*) tiro, tronco; (*of oxen*) yunta; (sport) equipo ‖ *tr* enganchar, uncir, enyugar ‖ *intr*—**to team up** asociarse, unirse; formar un equipo

team'mate' *s* compañero de equipo, equipier *m*

teamster ['timstər] *s* (*of horses*) tronquista *m;* (*of a truck*) camionista *m*

team'work' *s* espíritu de equipo; trabajo de equipo

tea'pot' *s* tetera

tear [tɪr] *s* lágrima; **to burst into tears** romper a llorar; **to fill with tears** arrasarse (*los ojos*) de o en lágrimas; **to hold back one's tears** beberse las lágrimas; **to laugh away one's tears** convertir las lágrimas en risas ‖ [tɛr] *s* desgarro, rasgón *m* ‖ [tɛr] *v* (*pret* **tore** [tor]; *pp* **torn** [torn]) *tr* desgarrar, rasgar; acongojar, afligir; mesarse (*los cabellos*); **to tear apart** romper en dos; **to tear down** derribar (*un edificio*); desarmar (*una máquina*); **to tear off** desgajar; **to tear up** romper (*p.ej., un papel*) ‖ *intr* desgarrarse, rasgarse; **to tear along** correr a toda velocidad

tear bomb [tɪr] *s* bomba lacrimógena

tearful ['tɪrfəl] *adj* lacrimoso

tear gas [tɪr] *s* gas lacrimógeno

tear-jerker ['tɪr,dʒʌrkər] *s* (slang) drama *m* o cine *m* que arrancan lágrimas

tear-off ['tɛr,ɔf] *adj* exfoliador

tea'room' *s* salón *m* de té

tear sheet [tɛr] *s* hoja del anunciante

tease [tiz] *tr* embromar, azuzar

tea'spoon' *s* cucharilla, cucharita

teaspoonful ['ti,spun,fʊl] *s* cucharadita

teat [tit] *s* teta, pezón *m*

tea time *s* hora del té

technical ['tɛknɪkəl] *adj* técnico

technicali•ty [,tɛknɪ'kælɪti] *s* (*pl* **-ties**) detalle técnico

technician [tɛk'nɪʃən] *s* técnico

technics ['tɛknɪks] *ssg* técnica

technique [tɛk'nik] *s* técnica

Teddy bear ['tɛdi] *s* oso de juguete, oso de trapo

tedious ['tidɪ•əs] o ['tidʒəs] *adj* tedioso, enfadoso

teem [tim] *intr* hormiguear; llover a cántaros; **to teem with** hervir de

teeming ['timɪŋ] *adj* hormigueante; (*rain*) torrencial

teen age [tin] *s* edad de 13 a 19 años

teen-ager ['tin,edʒər] *s* joven *mf* de 13 a 19 años de edad

teens [tinz] *spl* números ingleses que terminan en **-teen** (de 13 a 19); edad de 13 a 19 años; **to be in one's teens** tener de 13 a 19 años

tee•ny ['tini] *adj* (*comp* **-nier;** *super* **-niest**) (coll) diminuto, pequeñito

teeter ['titər] *s* vaivén *m*, balanceo ‖ *intr* balancear, oscilar

teethe [tið] *intr* endentecer

teething ['tiðɪŋ] *s* dentición

teething ring *s* chupador *m*

teetotaler [ti'totələr] *s* teetotalista *mf*, nefalista *mf*, abstemio

tel. *abbr* **telegram, telegraph, telephone**

tele•cast ['tɛlɪ,kæst] *s* teledifusión ‖ *v* (*pret & pp* **-cast** o **-casted**) *tr & intr* teledifundir

telegram ['tɛlɪ,græm] *s* telegrama *m*

telegraph ['tɛlɪ,græf] *s* telégrafo ‖ *tr & intr* telegrafiar

telegrapher [tɪ,lɛgrəfər] *s* telegrafista *mf*

telegraph pole *s* poste *m* de telégrafo

Telemachus [tɪ'lɛməkəs] *s* Telémaco

telemeter [tɪ'lɛmɪtər] *s* telémetro ‖ *tr* telemetrar

telemetry [tɪ'lɛmɪtri] *s* telemetría

telephone [ˈtɛlɪˌfon] *s* teléfono ‖ *tr & intr* telefonear

telephone booth *s* locutorio, cabina telefónica

telephone call *s* llamada telefónica

telephone directory *s* anuario telefónico, guía telefónica

telephone exchange *s* estación telefónica, central *f* de teléfonos; conmutador *m* (SAm)

telephone operator *s* telefonista *mf*, centralista *mf*

telephone receiver *s* receptor telefónico

telephone table *s* mesita portateléfono

tele(photo)lens [ˈtɛlɪ(ˌfotə)lɛnz] *s* lente telefotográfica

teleprinter [ˈtɛlɪˌprɪntər] *s* teleimpresor *m*

telescope [ˈtɛlɪˌskop] *s* telescopio ‖ *tr* telescopar ‖ *intr* telescoparse

teletype [ˈtɛlɪˌtaɪp] *s* teletipo ‖ *tr & intr* transmitir por teletipo

teleview [ˈtɛlɪˌvju] *tr & intr* ver por televisión

televiewer [ˈtɛlɪˌvjuˑər] *s* televidente *mf*, telespectador *m*

televise [ˈtɛlɪˌvaɪz] *tr* televisar

television [ˈtɛlɪˌvɪʃən] *adj* televisor ‖ *s* televisión

television audience *s* telespectadores

television screen *s* pantalla televisora, pequeña pantalla

television set *s* televisor *m*, telerreceptor *m*

telex [ˈtɛlɛks] *s* servicio comerical de teletipo

tell [tɛl] *v* (*pret & pp* told [told]) *tr* decir; (*to narrate; to count*) contar; determinar; conocer, distinguir; **I told you so!** ¡por algo se lo dije!; **to tell someone to** + *inf* decircle a uno que + *subj* ‖ *intr* hablar; surtir efecto; **to tell on** dejarse ver en (*p.ej., la salud de uno*); (coll) denunciar

teller [ˈtɛlər] *s* narrador *m*; (*of a bank*) cajero; (*of votes*) escrutador *m*

temper [ˈtɛmpər] *s* temple *m*, natural *m*, genio; cólera; mal genio; (*of steel, glass, etc.*) temple *m*; **to keep one's temper** dominar su mal genio; **to lose one's temper** encolerizarse, perder la paciencia ‖ *tr* templar *intr* templarse

temperament [ˈtɛmpərəmənt] *s* disposición; temperamento sensible o excitable

temperamental [ˌtɛmpərəˈmɛntəl] *adj* temperamental

temperance [ˈtɛmpərəns] *s* templanza

temperate [ˈtɛmpərɪt] *adj* templado

temperature [ˌtɛmpərəˈtʃər] *s* temperatura

tempest [ˈtɛmpɪst] *s* tempestad

tempestuous [tɛmˈpɛstʃuˑəs] *adj* tempestuoso

temple [ˈtɛmpəl] *s* (*place of worship*) templo; (*side of forehead*) sien *f*; (*sidepiece of spectacles*) gafa

tem•po [ˈtɛmpo] *s* (*pl* **-pos** o **-pi** [pi]) (mus) tiempo; (fig) ritmo (*p.ej., de la vida*)

temporal [ˈtɛmpərəl] *adj* temporal

temporary [ˈtɛmpəˌrɛri] *adj* temporáneo, temporario, provisional, interino

temporize [ˈtɛmpəˌraɪz] *intr* contemporizar, temporizar

tempt [tɛmpt] *tr* tentar

temptation [tɛmptˈteʃən] *s* tentación

tempter [ˈtɛmptər] *s* tentador *m*

tempting [ˈtɛmptɪŋ] *adj* tentador

ten [tɛn] *adj & pron* diez ‖ *s* diez *m;* **ten o'clock** las diez

tenable [ˈtɛnəbəl] *adj* defendible

tenacious [tɪˈneʃəs] *adj* tenaz

tenacity [tɪˈnæsɪti] *s* tenacidad

tenant [ˈtɛnənt] *s* arrendatario, inquilino; morador *m*, residente *mf*

tend [tɛnd] *tr* cuidar, vigilar; servir ‖ *intr* tender, dirigirse; **to tend to** atender a; **to tend to** + *inf* tender a + *inf*

tenden•cy [ˈtɛndənsi] *s* (*pl* **-cies**) tendencia

tender [ˈtɛndər] *adj* tierno; (*painfully sensitive*) dolorido ‖ *n* oferta; (naut) alijador *m*, falúa; (rr) ténder *m* ‖ *tr* ofrecer, tender

tender-hearted [ˈtɛndərˌhɑrtɪd] *adj* compasivo, tierno de corazón

ten'der•loin' *s* filete *m* ‖ **Tenderloin** *s* barrio de mala vida

tenderness [ˈtɛndərnɪs] *s* ternura, terneza; sensibilidad

tendon [ˈtɛndən] *s* tendón *m*

tendril [ˈtɛndrɪl] *s* zarcillo

tenement [ˈtɛnɪmənt] *s* habitación, vivienda; casa de vecindad

tenement house *s* casa de vecindad

tenet [ˈtɛnɪt] *s* dogma *m*, credo, principio

tennis [ˈtɛnɪs] *s* tenis *m*

tennis court *s* campo de tenis

tennis player *s* tenista *mf*

tenor [ˈtɛnər] *s* tenor *m*, carácter *m*, curso, tendencia; (mus) tenor

tense [tɛns] *adj* tenso, tieso; (*person; situation*) (fig) tenso; (*relations*) tirante ‖ *s* (gram) tiempo

tension [ˈtɛnʃən] *s* tensión; ansia, congoja, esfuerzo mental; (*in personal or diplomatic relations*) tirantez *f*

tent [tɛnt] *s* tienda; tienda de campaña

tentacle [ˈtɛntəkəl] *s* tentáculo

tentative [ˈtɛntətɪv] *adj* tentativo

tenth [tɛnθ] *adj & s* décimo ‖ *s* (*in dates*) diez *m*

tenuous [ˈtɛnjuˑəs] *adj* tenue; (*thin in consistency*) raro

tenure [ˈtɛnjər] *s* (*of property*) tenencia; (*of an office*) ejercicio; (*protection from dismissal*) inamovilidad

tepid [ˈtɛpɪd] *adj* tibio

tercet [ˈtɑrsɪt] *s* terceto

term [tɑrm] *s* término; (*of imprisonment*) condena; semestre *m*, período escolar; (*of the presidency of the U.S.A.*) mandato, período; **terms** condiciones ‖ *tr* llamar, nombrar

termagant [ˈtɑrməgənt] *s* mujer regañona, mujer de mal genio

terminal [ˈtɑrmɪnəl] *adj* terminal ‖ *s* término, fin *m*; (elec) terminal *m*; (rr) estación de fin de línea

terminate [ˈtɑrmɪˌnet] *tr & intr* terminar

termination [ˌtɑrmɪˈneʃən] *s* terminación

terminus [ˈtɑrmɪnəs] *s* término; (rr) estación de cabeza, estación extrema

termite [ˈtɑrmaɪt] *s* termite *m*, comején *m*

terrace [ˈtɛrəs] *s* terraza; (*flat roof of a house*) azotea

terra firma [ˈtɛrə ˈfʌrmə] *s* tierra firme; **on terra firma** sobre suelo firme

terrain [tɛˈren] *s* terreno

terrestrial [təˈrɛstrɪəl] *adj* terrestre

terrible [ˈtɛrɪbəl] *adj* terrible; muy desagradable

terrific [təˈrɪfɪk] *adj* terrífico; (coll) enorme, intenso, brutal

terri•fy [ˈtɛrɪˌfaɪ] *v* (*pret & pp* **-fied**) *tr* aterrorizar, atemorizar

territo•ry [ˈtɛrɪˌtori] *s* (*pl* **-ries**) territorio

terror [ˈtɛrər] *s* terror *m*

terrorize [ˈtɛrəˌraɪz] *tr* aterrorizar; imponerse a, mediante el terror

terry cloth [ˈtɛri] *s* albornoz *m*

terse [tʌrs] *adj* breve, sucinto

tertiary [ˈtʌrʃɪˌɛri] o [ˈtʌrʃəri] *adj* terciario

Test. *abbr* **Testament**

test [tɛst] *s* prueba, ensayo; examen *m* ‖ *tr* probar, poner a prueba; examinar

testament [ˈtɛstəmənt] *s* testamento

test flight *s* vuelo de ensayo

testicle [ˈtɛstɪkəl] *s* testículo

testi•fy [ˈtɛstɪˌfaɪ] *v* (*pret & pp* **-fied**) *tr & intr* testificar

testimonial [ˌtɛstɪˈmonɪ•əl] *s* recomendación, certificado; (*expression of esteem, gratitude, etc.*) homenaje *m*

testimo•ny [ˈtɛstɪˌmoni] *s* (*pl* **-nies**) testimonio

testing grounds [ˈtɛstɪŋ] *spl* campo de pruebas

test pilot *s* (aer) piloto de pruebas

test tube *s* probeta, tubo de ensayo

test′-tube′ baby *s* niño-probeta *m*

tether [ˈtɛðər] *s* atadura, traba; **at the end of one's tether** al límite de las posibilidades o la paciencia de uno ‖ *tr* apersogar

tetter [ˈtɛtər] *s* empeine *m*

text [tɛkst] *s* texto; tema *m*, lema *m*

text′book′ *s* libro de texto

textile [ˈtɛkstɪl] o [ˈtɛkstaɪl] *adj & s* textil *m*

texture [ˈtɛkstʃər] *s* textura

Thai [ˈtɑ•i] o [ˈtaɪ] *adj & s* tailandés *m*

Thailand [ˈtaɪlənd] *s* Tailandia

Thales [ˈθeliz] *s* Tales *m*

Thalia [θəˈlaɪ•ə] *s* Talía

Thames [tɛmz] *s* Támesis *m*

than [ðæn] *conj* que, p.ej., **he is richer than I** es más rico que yo; (*before a numeral*) de, p.ej., **more than twenty** más de veinte; (*before a verb*) de lo que, p.ej., **the crop is larger than was expected** la cosecha es mayor de lo que se esperaba; (*before a verb with direct object understood*) del (de la, de los, de las) que, p.ej., **they sent us more coffee than we ordered** nos enviaron más café del que pedimos

thanatology [ˌθænəˈtɑlədʒi] *s* tanatología

thank [θæŋk] *tr* agradecer, dar las gracias a; **to thank someone for something** agradecerle a uno una cosa ‖ **thanks** *spl* gracias; **thanks to** gracias a, merced a ‖ **thanks** *interj* ¡gracias!

thankful [ˈθæŋkfəl] *adj* agradecido

thankless [ˈθæŋklɪs] *adj* ingrato

thanksgiving [ˌθæŋksˈgɪvɪŋ] *s* acción de gracias

Thanksgiving Day *s* (U.S.A.) día *m* de acción de gracias

that [ðæt] *adj dem* (*pl* **those**) ese; aquel; **that one** ése; aquél ‖ *pron dem* (*pl* **those**) ése; aquél; eso; aquello ‖ *pron rel* que, quien, el cual, el que ‖ *adv* tan; **that far** tan lejos; hasta allí; **that many** tantos; **that much** tanto ‖ *conj* que; para que

thatch [θætʃ] *s* barda, paja; techo de paja ‖ *tr* cubrir de paja, techar con paja, bardar

thaw [θɔ] *s* deshielo, derretimiento; descongelación ‖ *tr* deshelar, derretir ‖ *intr* deshelarse, derretirse

the [ðə], [ðɪ], o [ði] *art def* el ‖ *adv* cuanto, p.ej., **the more the merrier** cuanto más mejor; **the more . . . the more** cuanto más . . . tanto más

theater [ˈθi•ətər] *s* teatro

the′ater-go′er *s* teatrero

theater news *s* actualidad escénica

theater page *s* noticiario teatral

theatrical [θɪˈætrɪkəl] *adj* teatral

Thebes [θibz] *s* Tebas *f*

thee [ði] *pron pers* (archaic, poet, Bib) te; ti; **with thee** contigo

theft [θɛft] *s* hurto, robo

theft′-proof′ *adj* antirroba

their [ðɛr] *adj poss* su; el . . . de ellos

theirs [ðɛrz] *pron poss* el suyo, el de ellos

them [ðɛm] *pron pers* los; ellos; **to them** les; a ellos

theme [θim] *s* tema *m;* (mus) tema *m*

theme song *s* (mus) tema *m* central; (rad) sintonía

them•selves′ *pron pers* ellos mismos; sí, sí mismos; se, p.ej., **they enjoyed themselves** se divirtieron; **with themselves** consigo

then [ðɛn] *adv* entonces; después, luego, en seguida; además, también; **by then** para entonces; **from then on** desde entonces, de allí en adelante; **then and there** ahí mismo

thence [ðɛns] *adv* desde allí; desde entonces; por eso

thence′forth′ *adv* de allí en adelante; desde entonces

theolo•gy [θiˈɑlədʒi] *s* (*pl* **-gies**) teología

theorem [ˈθi•ərəm] *s* teorema *m*

theo•ry [ˈθi•əri] *s* (*pl* **-ries**) teoría

therapeutic [ˌθɛrəˈpjutɪk] *adj* terapéutico ‖ **therapeutics** *ssg* terapéutica

thera•py [ˈθɛrəpi] *s* (*pl* **-pies**) terapia

there [ðɛr] *adv* allí, allá; **there is** o **there are** hay; aquí tiene Vd.

there′a-bouts′ *adv* por allí; cerca, aproximadamente

there•af′ter *adv* de allí en adelante, después de eso

there•by′ *adv* con eso; así, de tal modo; por allí cerca

therefore [ˈðɛrfor] *adv* por lo tanto, por consiguiente

there•in′ *adv* en esto, en eso; en ese respecto

there•of′ *adv* de ello, de eso

Theresa [tə`risə] o [tə`rɛsə] s Teresa

there'u•pon' adv sobre eso, encima de eso; por consiguiente; en seguida

thermistor [θər`mɪstər] s (elec) termistor m

thermocouple [`θʌrmo,kʌpəl] s (elec) termopar m

thermodynamic [,θʌrmodaɪ`næmɪk] adj termodinámico ‖ **thermodynamics** ssg termodinámica

thermometer [θər`mɑmɪtər] s termómetro

thermonuclear [,θʌrmo`nuklɪ•ər] adj termonuclear

Thermopylae [θər`mɑpɪ,li] s las Termópilas

Thermos bottle [`θʌrməs] s termos m, botella termos, bolsa isotérmica

thermostat [`θʌrmə,stæt] s termóstato

thesau•rus [θɪ`sɔrəs] s (pl **-ri** [raɪ]) **tesoro**; (dictionary or the like) tesauro, tesoro

these [ðiz] pl de **this**

the•sis [`θisɪs] s (pl **-ses** [siz]) tesis f

Thespis [`θɛspɪs] s Tespis m

Thessaly [`θɛsəli] s la Tesalia

they [ðe] pron pers ellos, ellas

thick [θɪk] adj espeso; grueso; denso; (coll) estúpido; (coll) íntimo ‖ s espesor m; **the thick of** (e.g., a crowd) lo más denso de; (e.g., a battle) lo más reñido de; **through thick and thin** contra viento y marea

thicken [`θɪkən] tr espesar ‖ intr espesarse; complicarse (el enredo)

thicket [`θɪkɪt] s espesura, matorral m, soto

thick-headed [`θɪk`hɛdɪd] adj (coll) torpe, estúpido

thick'-set' adj grueso, rechoncho

thief [θif] s (pl **thieves** [θivz]) ladrón m

thieve [θiv] intr hurtar, robar

thiever•y [`θivəri] s (pl **-ies**) latrocinio, hurto, robo

thigh [θaɪ] s muslo

thigh'bone' s hueso del muslo, fémur m

thimble [`θɪmbəl] s dedal m

thin [θɪn] adj (comp **thinner;** super **thinnest**) delgado, flaco, tenue; (cloth, paper, sole of shoe, etc.) fino; (hair) ralo; (broth) aguado; (excuse) débil; claro, ligero, escaso ‖ v (pret & pp **thinned;** ger **thinning**) tr adelgazar, enflaquecer; enrarecer; aclarar; aguar; desleír (los colores) ‖ intr adelgazarse, enflaquecerse; enrarecerse; **to thin out** ralear (el pelo)

thine [ðaɪn] adj poss (archaic & poet) tu ‖ pron poss (archaic & poet) tuyo; el tuyo

thing [θɪŋ] s cosa; **of all things!** ¡qué sorpresa!; **to be the thing** ser la última moda; **to be the thing to do** ser lo que debe hacerse; **to see things** ver visiones, padecer alucinaciones

think [θɪŋk] v (pret & pp **thought** [θɔt]) tr pensar; **to think it over** pensarlo; **to think nothing of** tener en poco; creer fácil; no dar importancia a; **to think of** pensar de, p.ej., what do you think of this book? ¿qué piensa Vd. de este libro?; **to think up** imaginar; inventar (p.ej., una excusa) ‖ intr pensar; **to think not** creer que no; **to think of** (to turn one's thoughts to) pensar en; pensar (un número, un naipe, etc.); **to**

think so creer que sí; **to think well of** tener buena opinión de

thinker [`θɪŋkər] s pensador m

third [θʌrd] adj tercero ‖ s (in a series) tercero; (one of three equal parts) tercio; (in dates) tres m

third degree s (coll) interrogatorio bajo tortura

third rail s (rr) tercer carril m, carril de toma

third'-rate' adj de tercer orden; (fig) inferior

Third World adj tercermundista ‖ s Terrcero Mundo

Third World countries spl países no alineados

thirst [θʌrst] s sed f ‖ intr tener sed; **to thirst for** tener sed de

thirst•y [`θʌrsti] adj (comp **-ier;** super **-iest**) sediento; **to be thirsty** tener sed

thirteen [`θʌr`tin] adj, pron & s trece m

thirteenth [`θʌr`tinθ] adj & s (in a series) decimotercero; (part) trezavo ‖ s (in dates) trece m

thirtieth [`θʌrtɪ•ɪθ] adj & s (in a series) trigésimo; (part) treintavo ‖ s (in dates) treinta m

thir•ty [`θʌrti] adj & pron treinta ‖ s (pl **-ties**) treinta m

this [ðɪs] adj dem (pl **these**) este; **this one** éste ‖ pron dem (pl **these**) éste; esto ‖ adv tan

thistle [`θɪsəl] s cardo

thither [`θɪðər] o [`ðɪðər] adv allá, hacia allá

Thomas [`tɑməs] s Tomás m

thong [θɔŋ] o [θɑŋ] s correa

tho•rax [`θoræks] s (pl **-roxes** o **-raxes** o **-races** [rə,siz]) tórax m

thorn [θɔrn] s espina

thorn•y [`θɔrni] adj (comp **-ier;** super **-iest**) espinoso; espinudo; (difficult) (fig) espinoso, espinudo

thorough [`θʌro] adj cabal, completo; concienzudo, cuidadoso

thor'ough•bred adj de pura sangre; bien nacido ‖ s pura sangre m; persona bien nacida

thor'ough•fare' s vía pública; **no thoroughfare** se prohibe el paso

thor'ough•go'ing adj cabal, completo, esmerado, perfecto

thoroughly [`θʌroli] adv a fondo

those [ðoz] pl de **that**

thou [ðaʊ] pron pers (archaic, poet & Bib) tú ‖ tr & intr tutear

though [ðo] adv sin embargo ‖ conj aunque, bien que; **as though** como sí

thought [θɔt] s pensamiento

thoughtful [`θɔtfəl] adj pensativo; atento, considerado

thoughtless [`θɔtlɪs] adj irreflexivo; descuidado; inconsiderado

thought transference s transmisión del pensamiento

thousand [`θaʊzənd] adj & s mil m; **a thousand** u **one thousand** mil m

thousandth [`θaʊzəndθ] adj & s milésimo

te
th

thralldom [ˈθrɔldəm] s esclavitud, servidumbre

thrash [θræʃ] tr (agr) trillar; azotar, zurrar; **to thrash out** decidir después de una discusión cabal ‖ intr trillar; agitarse, menearse

thread [θrɛd] s hilo; (mach) filete m, rosca; (of a speech, of life) hilo; **to lose the thread of** perder el hilo de ‖ tr enhebrar, enhilar; ensartar (p.ej., cuentas); (mach) aterrajar, filetear

thread'bare' adj raído; gastado, desgastado, usado, viejo

threat [θrɛt] s amenaza

threaten [ˈθrɛtən] tr & intr amenazar

threatening [ˈθrɛtənɪŋ] adj amenazante

three [θri] adj & pron tres ‖ s tres m; **three o'clock** las tres

three'-cor'nered adj triangular; (hat) de tres picos

three hundred adj & pron trescientos ‖ s trescientos m

threepence [ˈθrɛpəns] o [ˈθrɪpəns] s suma de tres peniques; moneda de tres peniques

three'-ply' adj de tres capas

three R's [ɑrz] spl lectura, escritura y aritmética, primeras letras

three'score' adj tres veintenas de

threno•dy [ˈθrɛnədi] s (pl -dies) treno

thresh [θrɛʃ] tr (agr) trillar; **to thresh out** decidir después de una discusión cabal ‖ intr trillar; agitarse, menearse

threshing machine s máquina trilladora

threshold [ˈθrɛʃold] s umbral m; (physiol, psychol & fig) umbral, limen m; **to be on the threshold of** estar en los umbrales de; **to cross the threshold** atravesar o pisar los embrales

thrice [θraɪs] adv tres veces; repetidamente, sumamente

thrift [θrɪft] s economía, parquedad

thrift•y [ˈθrɪfti] adj (comp -ier; super -iest) económico, parco; próspero

thrill [θrɪl] s emoción viva ‖ tr emocionar, conmover ‖ intr emocionarse, conmoverse

thriller [ˈθrɪlər] s cuento o pieza de teatro espeluznante

thrilling [ˈθrɪlɪŋ] adj emocionante; espeluznante

thrive [θraɪv] v (pret thrived o throve [θrov]; pp thrived o thriven [ˈθrɪvən]) intr medrar, prosperar

throat [θrot] s garganta; **to clear one's throat** aclarar la voz

throb [θrɑb] s latido, palpitación, pulsación ‖ v (pret & pp throbbed; ger throbbing) intr latir, palpitar, pulsar

throe [θro] s congoja, dolor m; **throes** angustia, agonía, esfuerzo penoso

throne [θron] s trono

throng [θrɔŋ] s gentío, tropel m, muchedumbre ‖ intr agolparse, apiñarse

throttle [ˈθrɑtəl] s válvula reguladora; (of a locomotive) regulador m; (of an automobile) acelerador m ‖ tr ahogar, sofocar; impedir, suprimir; (mach) regular; **to throttle down** reducir la velocidad de

through [θru] adj directo, sin paradas; acabado, terminado; **to be through with** haber terminado; no querer ocuparse más de ‖ adv a través, de un lado a otro; completamente ‖ prep por, a través de; por medio de; a causa de; todo lo largo de

through•out adv por todas partes; en todos respectos; desde el principio hasta el fin ‖ prep por todo . . .; durante todo . . .; a lo largo de

through'way' s carretera de peaje de acceso limitado

throw [θro] s echada, tirada, lance m; cobertor ligero ‖ v (pret threw [θru]; pp thrown) tr arrojar, echar, lanzar; tirar (los dados); lanzar (una mirada); desarzonar (a un jinete); proyectar (una sombra); tender (un puente); perder con premeditación (un juego, una carrera); **to throw away** tirar; malgastar; perder, no aprovechar; **to throw in** añadir, dar de más; **to throw out** arrojar, botar, desechar; echar a la calle; chispar; **to throw over** abandonar, dejar ‖ intr arrojar, echar, lanzar; **to throw up** vomitar

thrum [θrʌm] v (pret & pp thrummed; ger thrumming) intr teclear; zangarrear; **to thrum on** rasguear

thrush [θrʌʃ] s tordo

thrust [θrʌst] s empuje m; acometida; (with horns) cornada; (with dagger) puñalada; (with sword) estocada; (with knife) cuchillada ‖ v (pret & pp thrust) tr empujar; acometer; clavar, hincar, atravesar, traspasar

thud [θʌd] s baque m, ruido sordo ‖ v (pret & pp thudded; ger thudding) tr & intr golpear con ruido sordo

thug [θʌg] s ladrón m, asesino; (coll) gorila

thumb [θʌm] s pulgar m, dedo gordo; **all thumbs** desmañado, chapucero, torpe; **to twiddle one's thumbs** menear ociosamente los pulgares; no hacer nada; **under the thumb of** bajo la férula de ‖ tr manosear sin suidado; ensuciar con los dedos; hojear (un libro) con el pulgar; **to thumb a ride** pedir ser llevado en automóvil indicando la dirección con el pulgar; **to thumb one's nose at** señalar (a una persona) poniendo el pulgar sobre la nariz en son de burla; tratar con sumo desprecio

thumb index s escalerilla, índice m con pestañas

thumb'print' s impresión del pulgar ‖ tr marcar con impresión del pulgar

thumb'screw' s tornillo de mariposa, tornillo de orejas

thumb'tack' s chinche m

thump [θʌmp] s golpazo, porrazo ‖ tr golpear, aporrear ‖ intr caer con golpe pesado; andar con pasos pesados; latir (el corazón) con golpes pesados

thumping [ˈθʌmpɪŋ] adj (coll) enorme, pesado

thunder [ˈθʌndər] s trueno; (of applause) estruendo; amenaza ‖ tr fulminar (p.ej., censuras) ‖ intr tronar; **to thunder at** tronar contra

thun′der·bolt′ s rayo
thun′der·clap′ s tronido
thunderous [ˈθʌndərəs] adj atronador, tronitoso
thun′der·show′er s chubasco con truenos
thun′der·storm′ s tronada
thun′der·struck′ adj atónito, estupefacto, pasmado
Thursday [ˈθʌrsdi] s jueves m
thus [ðʌs] adv así; **thus far** hasta aquí, hasta ahora
thwack [θwæk] s golpe m, porrazo ‖ tr golpear, pegar
thwart [θwɔrt] adj transversal, oblicuo ‖ adv de través ‖ tr desbaratar, impedir, frustrar
thy [ðaɪ] adj poss (archaic & poet) tu
thyme [taɪm] s tomillo
thyroid gland [ˈθaɪrɔɪd] s glándula tiroides
thyself [ðaɪˈsɛlf] pron (archaic & poet) tú mismo; ti mismo; te; ti
tiara [taɪˈɑrə] o [taɪˈɛrə] s (papal miter) tiara; (female adornment) diadema f
tick [tɪk] s tictac m; funda (de almohada o colchón) (coll) crédito; (ent) garrapata; **on tick** (coll) al fiado ‖ intr hacer tictac; latir (el corazón)
ticker [ˈtɪkər] s teleimpresor m de cinta; (slang) reloj m; (slang) corazón m
ticker tape s cinta de teleimpresor
ticket [ˈtɪkɪt] s billete m; boleto (Am); (theat) entrada, localidad; (for wrong parking) (coll) aviso de multa; (of a political party) (U.S.A.) lista de candidatos; **that's the ticket** (coll) eso es, eso es lo que se necesita
ticket agent s taquillero
ticket collector s revisor m
ticket office s taquilla, despacho de billetes
ticket scalper [ˈskælpər] s revendedor m de billetes de teatro
ticket window s taquilla, ventanilla
ticking [ˈtɪkɪŋ] s cutí m, terliz m
tickle [ˈtɪkəl] s cosquillas ‖ tr cosquillear; gustar, satisfacer; divertir ‖ intr cosquillear
ticklish [ˈtɪklɪʃ] adj cosquilloso; difícil, delicado; inseguro
tick-tock [ˈtɪk,tɑk] s tictac m
tidal wave [ˈtaɪdəl] s aguaje m, ola de marea; (e.g., of popular indignation) ola de
tidbit [ˈtɪd,bɪt] s buen bocado, bocadito
tiddlywinks [ˈtɪdli,wɪŋks] s juego de la pulga
tide [taɪd] s marea; temporada; **to go against the tide** ir contra la corriente; **to stem the tide** rendir la marea ‖ tr llevar, hacer flotar; **to tide over** ayudar un poco; superar (una dificultad)
tide′wa′ter adj costanero ‖ s agua de marea; orilla del mar
tidings [ˈtaɪdɪŋz] spl noticias, informes mpl
ti·dy [ˈtaɪdi] adj (comp -dier; super -diest) aseado, limpio, pulcro, ordenado ‖ s (pl -dies) pañito bordado, cubierta de respaldar ‖ v (pret & pp -died) tr asear, limpiar, arreglar, poner en orden ‖ intr asearse
tie [taɪ] s atadura; lazo, nudo; (worn on neck) corbata; (in games and elections) empate m; (mus) ligado; (rr) traviesa ‖ v (pret &

pp tied; ger tying) tr atar, liar; enlazar; hacer (la corbata); confinar, limitar; empatar (p.ej., una elección); empatársela a (una persona); **to be tied up** estar ocupado; **to tie down** confinar, limitar; **to tie up** atar; envolver; obstruir (el tráfico) ‖ intr atar; empatar o empatarse (dos candidatos, dos equipos)
tie′pin′ s alfiler m de corbata
tier [tɪr] s fila, ringlera; (theat) fila de palcos
tiger [ˈtaɪgər] s tigre m
tiger lily s azucena atigrada
tight [taɪt] adj apretado, estrecho, ajustado; bien cerrado, hermético; compacto, denso; fijo, firme, sólido; (com) escaso; (sport) casi igual; (coll) agarrado, tacaño; (slang) borracho ‖ adv firmemente; **to hold tight** mantener fijo; agarrarse bien ‖ **tights** spl traje m de malla
tighten [ˈtaɪtən] tr apretar; atiesar, estirar ‖ intr apretarse; atiesarse, estirarse
tight-fisted [ˈtaɪtˈfɪstɪd] adj agarrado, tacaño
tight′-fit′ting adj ceñido, muy ajustado
tight′rope′ s cuerda tirante
tight squeeze s (coll) brete m, aprieto
tightwad [ˈtaɪt,wɑd] s avaro; codo (Guat, Mex)
tigress [ˈtaɪgrɪs] s tigresa
tile [taɪl] s azulejo; (for floors) baldosa; (for roofs) reja ‖ tr azulejar; embaldosar; tejar
tile roof s tejado (de tejas)
till [tɪl] prep hasta ‖ conj hasta que ‖ s cajón m o gaveta del dinero ‖ tr labrar, cultivar
tilt [tɪlt] s inclinación; justa, torneo; **full tilt** a toda velocidad ‖ tr inclinar; asestar (una lanza) ‖ intr inclinarse; justar, tornear; luchar; **to tilt at** luchar con, arremeter contra; protestar contra
timber [ˈtɪmbər] s madera de construcción; madero, viga; bosque m, árboles mpl de monte
tim′ber·land′ s bosque m maderable
timber line s límite m de la vegetación, límite del bosque maderable
timbre [ˈtɪmbər] s (phonet & phys) timbre m
time [taɪm] s tiempo; hora, p.ej., **time to eat** hora de comer; vez, p.ej., **five times** cinco veces; rato, p.ej., **a nice time** un buen rato; (period for payment) plazo; horas de trabajo; sueldo; tiempo de parir, término del embarazo; última hora; (phot) tiempo de exposición; **all the time** a cada momento; **for the time being** por ahora, por el momento; **on time** a tiempo, a la hora debida; (in installments) a plazos, **to bide one's time** esperar la hora propicia; **to do time** (coll) cumplir una condena; **to have a good time** pasar buen tiempo; **to have no time for** no poder tolerar; **to lose time** atrasarse (el reloj); **to make time** avanzar con rapidez; **to pass the time of day** saludarse (dos personas); **to serve time** (in prison) tirarse; **to take one's time** no darse prisa, ir despacio; **what time is it?** ¿qué hora es? ‖ tr calcular el tiempo de; medir el tiempo de; (sport) cronometrar
time bomb s bomba-reloj f

time′card′ s hoja de presencia, tarjeta registradora

time clock s reloj m registrador

time exposure s exposición de tiempo

time fuse s espoleta de tiempos

time′keep′er s alistador m de tiempo; reloj m; (sport) cronometrador m, juez m de tiempo

time•ly [′taɪmli] adj (comp **-lier;** super **-liest**) oportuno

time′piece′ s reloj m

time signal s señal horaria

time′ta′ble s horario, itinerario

time′work′ s trabajo ajornal

time′worn′ adj gastado por el tiempo

time zone s huso horario

timid [′tɪmɪd] adj tímido

timing gears [′taɪmɪŋ] spl engranaje m de distribución, mando de las válvulas

timorous [′tɪmərəs] adj tímido, miedoso

tin [tɪn] s (element) estaño; (tin plate) hojalata; (cup, box, etc.) lata ‖ v (pret & pp **tinned;** ger **tinning**) tr estañar; (to pack in cans) enlatar; recubrir de hojalata

tin can s lata, envase m de hojalata

tincture [′tɪŋktʃər] s tintura

tin cup s taza de hojalata

tinder [′tɪndər] s yesca

tin′der•box′ s lumbres fpl, yesquero; persona muy excitable; semillero de violencia

tin foil s hojuela de estaño, papel m de estaño

ting-a-ling [′tɪŋə‚lɪŋ] s tilín m

tinge [tɪndʒ] s matiz m, tinte m; dejo, gustillo ‖ v (ger **tingeing** o **tinging**) tr matizar, teñir; dar gusto o sabor a

tingle [′tɪŋɡəl] s comezón f, picazón f ‖ intr sentir comezón; zumbar (los oídos); (e.g., with enthusiasm) estremecerse

tin hat s (coll) yelmo de acero

tinker [′tɪŋkər] s calderero remendón; chapucero ‖ intr ocuparse vanamente

tinkle [′tɪŋkəl] s retintín m ‖ tr hacer retiñir m ‖ tr hacer retiñir ‖ intr retiñir

tin plate s hojalata

tin roof s tejdo de hojalata

tinsel [′tɪnsəl] s oropel m; (e.g., for a Christmas tree) lentejuelas de hojas de estaño

tin′smith′ s hojalatero

tin soldier s soldadito de plomo

tint [tɪnt] s tinte m, matiz m ‖ tr teñir, matizar, colorar ligeramente

tin′type′ s ferrotipo

tin′ware′ s objetos de hojalata

ti•ny [′taɪni] adj (comp **-nier;** super **-niest**) diminuto, menudo, pequeñito

tip [tɪp] s extremo, extremidad; (of shoestring) herrete m; (of arrow) casquillo; (of umbrella) regatón m; (of tongue) punta; (of shoe) puntera; (of cigarette) embocadura; inclinación; golpecito; soplo, aviso confidencial; (fee) propina, feria ‖ v (pret & pp **tipped;** ger **tipping**) tr herretear; inclinar, ladear; volcar; golpear ligeramente; dar propina a; informar por debajo de cuerda; tocarse (el sombrero en señal de cortesía); **to tip in** (typ) encañonar (un pliego) ‖ intr

dar una propina o propinas; inclinarse, ladearse; volcarse

tip′cart′ s volquete m

tip′-off′ s (coll) informe dado por debajo de cuerda

tipped′-in′ adj (bb) fuera de texto

tipple [′tɪpəl] intr beborrotear

tip′staff′ s vara de justicia; alguacil m de vara

tip•sy [′tɪpsi] adj (comp **-sier;** super **-siest**) achispado

tip′toe′ s punta del pie; **on tiptoe** de puntillas; alerta; furtivamente ‖ v (pret & pp **-toed;** ger **-toeing**) intr andar de puntillas

tirade [′taɪred] s diatriba, invectiva

tire [taɪr] s neumático, llanta de goma; (of metal) calce m, llanta ‖ tr cansar; aburrir, fastidiar ‖ intr (to be tiresome) cansar; (to get tired) cansarse; aburrirse, fastidiarse

tire chain s cadena de llanta, cadena antirresbaladiza

tired [taɪrd] adj cansado, rendido

tire gauge s indicador m de presión de inflado

tireless [′taɪrlɪs] adj incansable, infatigable

tire pressure s presión de inflado

tire pump s bomba para inflar neumáticos

tiresome [′taɪrsəm] adj cansado, fatigante, aburrido, pesado

tissue [′tɪʃu] s tejido fino; papel m de seda; (biol & fig) tejido

tissue paper s papel m de seda

titanium [taɪ′teni•əm] o [tɪ′teni•əm] s titanio

tithe [taɪð] s décimo, décima parte; (tax paid to church) diezmo ‖ tr dizmar

Titian [′tɪʃən] adj castaño rojizo ‖ s el Ticiano

title [′taɪtəl] s título; (sport) campeonato ‖ tr titular

title deed s título de propiedad

ti′tle•hold′er s titulado; (sport) campeón m

title page s portada, frontispicio

title rôle s (theat) papel m principal (el que corresponde al título de la obra)

titter [′tɪtər] s risita ahogada, risita disimulada ‖ intr reír a medias, reír con disimulo

titular [′tɪtʃələr] adj titular; nominal

tn. abbr ton

to [tu] o [tʊ] o [tə] adv hacia adelante; **to and fro** de una parte a otra, de aquí para allá; **to come to** volver en sí ‖ prep a, p.ej., **he is going to Madrid** va a Madrid; **they gave something to the beggar** dieron algo al pobre; **we are learning to dance** aprendemos a bailar; para, p.ej., **he is reading to himself** lee para sí; por, p.ej., **work to do** trabajo por hacer; hasta, p.ej., **to a certain extent** hasta cierto punto; en, p.ej., **from door to door** de puerta en puerta; con, p.ej., **kind to her** amable con ella; segun, p.ej., **to my way of thinking** según mi modo de pensar; menos, p.ej., **five minutes to ten** las diez menos cinco

toad [tod] s sapo

toad′stool′ s agárico, seta; seta venenosa

to-and-fro [′tu•ənd′fro] adj alternativo, de vaivén

toast [tost] *s* tostadas; (*drink*) brindis *m;* **a piece of toast** una tostada ‖ *tr* tostar; brindar a o por ‖ *intr* tostarse; brindar

toaster [ˈtostər] *s* (*of bread*) tostador *m;* brindador *m*

toast′mas′ter *s* el que presenta a los oradores en un banquete, maestro de ceremonias

tobac•co [təˈbæko] *s* (*pl* **-cos**) tabaco

tobacco pouch *s* petaca

toboggan [təˈbagən] *s* tobogán *m* ‖ *intr* deslizarse en tobogán

tocsin [ˈtaksɪn] *s* campana de alarma; campanada de alarma

today [tʊˈde] *adv* & *s* hoy

toddle [ˈtadəl] *s* pasitos vacilantes ‖ *intr* andar con pasitos vacilantes; hacer pinitos (*un niño o un enfermo*)

tod•dy [ˈtadi] *s* (*pl* **-dies**) ponche *m*

to-do [təˈdu] *s* (coll) alharaca, alboroto

toe [to] *s* dedo del pie; (*of stocking*) punta ‖ *v* (*pret & pp* **toed**; *ger* **toeing**) *tr*—**to toe the line** o **the mark** ponerse a la raya; obrar como se debe

toe′nail′ *s* uña del dedo del pie

tog [tag] *s* (coll) prenda de vestir

together [tʊˈgɛðər] *adv* juntamente; juntos; al mismo tiempo; sin interrupción; de acuerdo; **to bring together** reunir; confrontar; reconciliar; **to call together** convocar; **to go together** ir juntos; ser novios; hacerjuego; **to stick together** (coll) quedarse unidos, no abandonarse

toil [tɔɪl] *s* afán *m*, fatiga; faena, obra laboriosa; **toils** red *f*, lazo ‖ *intr* atrafagar; moverse con fatiga

toilet [ˈtɔɪlɪt] *s* (*dress or adornment*) tocado, atavío; (*dressing table*) tocador *m;* (*rest room*) retrete *m*, inodoro, excusado; wáter *m* (Bol, Col, Chile, Peru, Urug); servicio (Bol, CAm, Ecuad); taza (Bol, Col, Guat, Mex); poseta (Ven); **to make one's toilet** asearse, acicalarse

toilet articles *spl* artículos de tocador

toilet paper *s* papel higiénico

toilet powder *s* polvos de tocador

toilet soap *s* jabón *m* de olor, jabón de tocador

toilet tank *s* cisterna

toilet water *s* agua de tocador

token [ˈtokən] *s* señal *f*, prueba; prenda, recuerdo; (*used as money*) ficha, tanto; **by the same token** por el mismo motivo; **in token of** en señal de

tolerance [ˈtalərəns] *s* tolerancia

tolerate [ˈtalə,ret] *tr* tolerar

toll [tol] *s* (*of bells*) doble *m;* (*to pass along a road or over a bridge*) peaje *m;* (*to use a canal*) derechos de paso; (*to use a telephone*) tarifa; (*number of victims*) baja, mortalidad ‖ *tr* tocar a muerto (*una campana*); llamar con toque de difuntos ‖ *intr* doblar

toll bridge *s* puente *m* de peaje

toll call *s* (telp) llamada a larga distancia

toll′gate′ *s* barrera de peaje

toma•to [təˈmeto] o [təˈmato] *s* (*pl* **-toes**) (*plant*) tomatera o tomate *m;* (*fruit*) tomate

tomb [tum] *s* tumba, sepulcro

tomboy [ˈtam,bɔɪ] *s* moza retozona, muchacha traviesa

tomb′stone′ *s* piedra o lápida sepulcral

tomcat [ˈtam,kæt] *s* gato macho

tome [tom] *s* tomo; libro grueso

tomorrow [tʊˈmɔro] *adv* mañana ‖ *s* mañana *m;* **the day after tomorrow** pasado mañana

tom-tom [ˈtam,tam] *s* tantán *m*

ton [tʌn] *s* tonelada; **tons** (coll) montones *mpl*

tone [ton] *s* tono ‖ *tr* entonar ‖ *intr* armonizar; **to tone down** moderarse; **to tone up** reforzarse

tone poem *s* poema sinfónico

tongs [tɔŋz] o [taŋz] *spl* tenazas; (*e.g., for sugar*) tenacillas

tongue [tʌŋ] *s* (anat) lengua; (*of a wagon*) vara, lanza; (*of a belt buckle*) tarabilla; (*of shoe*) lengua, lengüeta; (*language*) lengua, idioma *m;* **to hold one's tongue** morderse la lengua

tongue twister [ˈtwɪstər] *s* trabalenguas *m*

tonic [ˈtanɪk] *adj* & *s* tónico

tonic accent *s* acento prosódico

tonight [tʊˈnaɪt] *adv* & *s* esta noche

tonnage [ˈtʌnɪdʒ] *s* tonelaje *m*

tonsil [ˈtansəl] *s* tonsila, amígdala

tonsillitis [,tansɪˈlaɪtɪs] *s* tonsilitis *f*, amigdalitis *f*

ton•y [ˈtoni] *adj* (*comp* **-ier;** *super* **-iest**) (slang) elegante, aristocrático

too [tu] *adv* (*also*) también; (*more than enough*) demasiado; **too bad!** ¡qué lástima!; **too many** demasiados; **too much** demasiado

tool [tul] *s* herramienta; (*person used for one's own ends*) instrumento; **tools** implementos *mpl* ‖ *tr* trabajar con herramienta; (bb) filetear, estampar

tool bag *s* bolsa de herramientas

toolmak′er *s* tallador *m* de herramientas, herrero de herramientas

toot [tut] *s* (*of horn*) toque *m;* (*of klaxon*) bocinazo; (*of locomotive*) pitazo; (coll) parranda ‖ *tr* sonar; **to toot one's own horn** cantar sus propias alabanzas ‖ *intr* sonar

tooth [tuθ] *s* (*pl* **teeth** [tiθ]) diente *m*

tooth′ache′ *s* dolor *m* de muelas

tooth′brush′ *s* cepillo de dientes

toothless [ˈtuθlɪs] *adj* desdentado

tooth′paste′ *s* pasta dentífrica, crema dental, crema dentífrica

tooth′pick′ *s* limpiadientes *m*, mondadientes *m*, palillo

tooth powder *s* polvo dentífrico

top [tap] *s* (*of a mountain, tree, etc.*) cima; (*of a mountain; high point*) cumbre *f;* (*of a tree*) copa; (*of a barrel, box, etc.*) tapa; (*of a page*) principio; (*of a table*) tablero; (*of a wall*) coronamiento; (*of a bathing suit*) camiseta; (*of a carriage or auto*) capota; (*toy*) peón *m*, peonza; (naut) cofa; **at the top of** en lo alto de; (*e.g., one's class*) a la cabeza de; **at the top of one's voice** a voz en grito; **from top to bottom** de arriba abajo; de alto a bajo; completamente; **on top of** en lo alto de; encima de; **the tops** (slang) la flor de la canela; **to sleep like a top** dormir como un leño ‖ *v* (*pret & pp* **topped**; *ger* **topping**) *tr* coronar, rematar; cubrir; aventajar, superar; descopar (*p.ej., un árbol*)

topaz [ˈtopæz] *s* topacio

top billing *s* cabecera de cartel

top′coat′ *s* sobretodo; abrigo de entretiempo

toper [ˈtopər] *s* borrachín *m*

top hat *s* chistera, sombrero de copa

top′-heav′y *adj* más pesado arriba que abajo

topic [ˈtapɪk] *s* asunto, materia, tema *m*

top′knot′ *s* moño

top′mast′ *s* (naut) mastelero

top′most *adj* (el) más alto

topogra·phy [təˈpɑgrəfi] *s* (*pl* **-phies**) topografía

topple [ˈtapəl] *tr* derribar, volcar ‖ *intr* derribarse, volcarse; caerse, venirse abajo

top priority *s* máxima prioridad

topsail [ˈtapsəl] o [ˈtap‚sel] *s* (naut) gavia

top secret *adj* de mayor confidencia

top′soil′ *s* capa superficial del suelo

topsy-turvy [ˈtapsiˈtʌrvi] *adj* desbarajustado ‖ *adv* en cuadro, patas arriba ‖ *s* desbarajuste *m*

torch [tɔrtʃ] *s* antorcha; lámpara de bolsillo: **to carry the torch for** (slang) amar desesperadamente

torch′bear′er *s* hachero; (fig) adicto, partidario

torch′light′ *s* luz *f* de antorcha

torch song *s* canción lenta y melancólica de amor no correspondido

torment [ˈtɔrmɛnt] *s* tormento; murga ‖ [tɔrˈmɛnt] *tr* atormentar

torna·do [tɔrˈnedo] *s* (*pl* **-does** p **-dos**) tornado, tromba terrestre

torpe·do [tɔrˈpido] *s* (*pl* **-does**) torpedo ‖ *tr* torpedear

torrent [ˈtɔrənt] *s* torrente *m*

torrid [ˈtɔrɪd] *adj* tórrido

tor·so [ˈtɔrso] *s* (*pl* **-sos**) torso

tortoise [ˈtɔrtəs] *s* tortuga

tortoise shell *s* carey *m*

torture [ˈtɔrtʃər] *s* tortura ‖ *tr* torturar, atormentar

toss [tas] *s* echada; alcance *m* de una echada ‖ *tr* arrojar, echar; lanzar al aire; agitar, menear; levantar airosamente (*la cabeza*); lanzar (*p.ej., un comentario*); echar a cara o cruz; **to toss off** hacer muy rápidamente; tragar de un golpe ‖ *intr* agitarse, menearse; **to toss and turn** (*in bed*) revolverse, dar vueltas

toss′-up′ *s* cara o cruz; probabilidad igual

tot [tat] *s* párvulo, peque *m*, chiquitín *m*

to·tal [ˈtotəl] *adj* total; (*e.g., loss*) completo ‖ *s* total *m* ‖ *v* (*pret & pp* **-taled** o **-talled**; *ger* **-taling** o **-talling**) *tr* ascender a, sumar

totter [ˈtatər] *s* tambaleo ‖ *intr* tambalear; estar para desplomarse

touch [tʌtʃ] *s* (*act*) toque *m*; (*sense*) tacto, tiento; (*of piano, pianist, typewriter, typist*) tacto; (*of an illness*) ramo, ataque

ligero; pizca, poquito; **to get in touch with** ponerse en comunicación o contacto con; **to lose one's touch** perder el tiento ‖ *tr* tocar; conmover, enternecer; probar (*vino, licor*); (*for a loan*) (slang) pedir prestado a, dar un sablazo a; **to touch up** retocar ‖ *intr* tocar; **to touch at** tocar en (*un puerto*)

touching [ˈtʌtʃɪŋ] *adj* conmovedor, enternecedor ‖ *prep* tocante a

touch typewriting *s* escritura al tacto

touch·y [ˈtʌtʃi] *adj* (*comp* **-ier**; *super* **-iest**) quisquilloso, enojadizo

tough [tʌf] *adj* correoso; tenaz; difícil; gamberro; (*e.g., luck*) malo ‖ *s* gamberro, guapetón *m*; (coll) gorila

toughen [ˈtʌfən] *tr* hacer correoso; hacer tenaz; dificultar ‖ *intr* ponerse correoso; hacerse tenaz; hacerse difícil

toupee [tuˈpe] *s* peluquín *m*

tour [tur] *s* jira, paseo, vuelta; viaje largo; **on tour** de jira, de viaje ‖ *tr* viajar por, recorrer ‖ *intr* viajar por distracción o diversión

touring car [ˈturɪŋ] *s* coche *m* de turismo

tourist [ˈturɪst] *adj* turístico ‖ *s* turista *mf*

tourist guide *s* guía turística

tournament [ˈturnəmənt] o [ˈtʌrnəmənt] *s* torneo

tourney [ˈturni] o [ˈtʌrni] *s* torneo ‖ *intr* tornear

tourniquet [ˈturnɪ‚kɛt] *s* torniquete *m*

tousle [ˈtauzəl] *tr* despeinar, enmarañar

tow [to] *s* remolque *m*; (*e.g., of hemp*) estopa; **to take in tow** dar remolque a; (fig) encargarse de ‖ *tr* remolcar

towage [ˈtoɪdʒ] *s* remolque *m*; derechos de remolque

toward(s) [tord(z)] o [təˈwɔrd(z)] *prep* (*in the direction of*) hacia; (*with regard to*) para con; (*a certain hour*) cerca de, a eso de

tow′boat′ *s* remolcador *m*

tow·el [ˈtauəl] *s* toalla ‖ *v* (*pret & pp* **-eled** o **-elled**; *ger* **-eling** o **-elling**) *tr* secar con toalla

towel rack *s* toallero

tower [ˈtauər] *s* torre *f* ‖ *intr* encumbrarse, empinarse

towering [ˈtauərɪŋ] *adj* encumbrado; sobresaliente; excesivo

towing service [ˈtoɪŋ] *s* servicio de grúa

tow′line′ *s* cable *m* de remolque, sirga

town [taun] *s* problación, pueblo, villa; **in town** a la ciudad, en la ciudad

town clerk *s* escribano municipal

town council *s* concejo municipal

town crier *s* pregonero público

town hall *s* ayuntamiento, casa de ayuntamiento

towns′ folk′ *spl* vecinos del pueblo

township [ˈtaunʃɪp] *s* sexmo; terreno público de seis millas en cuadro

towns·man [ˈtaunzmən] *s* (*pl* **-men** [mən]) ciudadano, vecino; conciudadano, paisano

towns′peo′ple *spl* vecinos del pueblo

town talk *s* comidilla o hablillas del pueblo

tow′path′ *s* camino de sirga

tow plane *s* avión *m* de remolque
tow'rope' *s* cuerda de remolque
tow truck *s* camión-grúa *m*
toxic ['taksık] *adj & s* tóxico
toxic shock syndrome *s* síndrome *m* de choque tóxico
toy [tɔɪ] *adj* de juguete ‖ *s* juguete *m; (trifle)* bagatela; *(trinket)* dije *m*, bujería ‖ *intr* jugar; divertirse; **to toy with** jugar con *(los sentimientos de una persona)*; acariciar *(una idea)*
toy bank *s* alcancía hucha
toy soldier *s* soldado de juguete
trace [tres] *s* huella, rastro; indicio, vestigio; *(of harness)* tirante *m;* pizca ‖ *tr* rastrear; trazar *(p.ej., una curva; los rasgos de una persona o cosa)*; averiguar el paradero de; remontar al origen de
trace element *s* elemento rastro
trache•a ['trekı•ə] *s (pl -ae* [,i]) tráquea
track [træk] *s (of foot)* huella; *(of a wheel)* rodada, carril *m; (of a boat)* estela; *(of railroad)* vía; *(of an airplane, a hurricane)* trayectoria; *(of a tractor)* llanta de oruga; camino, senda; *(course followed by a boat)* derrota; *(of ideas, events, etc.)* sucesión; (sport) pista; **to keep track of** no perder de vista; no olvidar; **to lose track of** perder de vista; olvidar; **to make tracks** dejar pisadas; irse muy de prisa; **off the track** *(also* fig) desviado ‖ *tr* rastrear; seguir la huella o la pista de; dejar pisadas en, manchar pisando; **to track down** seguir y capturar; averiguar el origen de
tracking ['trækıŋ] *s* seguimiento *(de vehículos espaciales)*
tracing station *s* estación de seguimiento
trackless trolley ['træklıs] *s* filobús *m*, trolebús *m*
track meet *s* concurso de carreras y saltos
track'walk'er *s* guardavía *m*
tract [trækt] *s* espacio, tracto; folleto; (anat) canal *m*, sistema *m*
traction ['trækʃən] *s* tracción
traction company *s* empresa de tranvías
tractor ['træktər] *s* tractor *m*
trade [tred] *s* comercio; negocio, trato; trueque *m*, canje *m; (calling, job)* oficio; clientela, parroquia; *(e.g., in slaves)* trata ‖ *tr* cambiar, trocar; **to trade in** dar como parte del pago; **to trade off** cambalachear; ‖ *intr* comerciar; comprar; **to trade in** comerciar en; **to trade on** aprovecharse de
trade'mark' *s* marca de fábrica, marca registrada
trade name *s* nombre *m* comercial, razón *f* social; nombre de fábrica
trader ['tredər] *s* traficante *mf*
trade school *s* escuela de artes y oficios
trades•man ['tredzmən] *s (pl -men* [mən]) tendero; comerciante *m;* (Brit) artesano
trades union o **trade union** *s* sindicato, gremio de obreros
trade unionist *s* sindicalista *mf*
trade winds *spl* vientos alisios
trading post ['tredıŋ] *s* factoría; *(in stock exchange)* puesto de compraventa

trading stamp *s* sello de premio, sello de descuento
tradition [trə'dıʃən] *s* tradición
traduce [trə'djus] *tr* calumniar
traf•fic ['træfık] *s* tráfico, comercio; tráfico, circulación; *(e.g., in slaves)* trata ‖ *v (pret & pp -ficked; ger -ficking) intr* traficar
traffic circle *s* glorieta de tráfico
traffic court *s* juzgado de tráfico
traffic jam *s* embotellamiento, tapón *m* de tráfico
traffic light *s* luz *f* de tráfico, semáforo
traffic sign o **signal** *s* señal *f* de tráfico, seña de tráfico
traffic ticket *s* aviso de multa
tragedian [trə'dʒıdı•ən] *s* trágico
trage•dy ['trædʒıdi] *s (pl -dies)* tragedia
tragic ['trædʒık] *adj* trágico
trail [trel] *s* rastro, huella, pista; *(path through rough country)* trocha, senda, vereda; *(of a gown)* cola; *(of smoke, a rocket, etc.)* estela ‖ *tr* arrastrar; seguir la pista de; andar detrás de; llevar *(p.ej., barro)* con los pies ‖ *intr* arrastrar; rezagarse; arrastrarse, trepar *(una planta)*; **to trail off** desaparecer poco a poco
trailer ['trelər] *s* remolque *m*, cochehabitación *m*, casa rodante; planta rastrera
trailing arbutus ['trelıŋ] *s* epigea rastrera
train [tren] *s (of railway cars; of waves)* tren *m; (of thought)* hilo ‖ *tr* adiestrar; guiar *(las plantas)*; (sport) entrenar ‖ *intr* adiestrarse; (sport) entrenarse
trained nurse *s* enfermera graduada
trainer ['trenər] *s* (sport) entrenador *m*
training ['trenıŋ] *s* adiestramiento; instrucción; (sport) entrenamiento
training school *s* escuela práctica; reformatorio
training ship *s* buque *m* escuela
trait [tret] *s* característica, rasgo
traitor ['tretər] *s* traidor *m*
traitress ['tretrıs] *s* traidora
trajecto•ry [trə'dʒɛktəri] *s (pl -ries)* trayectoria
tramp [træmp] *s* vagabundo; marcha pesada; ruido de pisadas ‖ *tr* pisar con fuerza; recorrer a pie ‖ *intr* andar a pie; vagabundear
trample ['træmpəl] *tr* pisotear ‖ *intr—***to trample on** o **upon** pisotear
tramp steamer *s* vapor *m* volandero
trance [træns] o [trɑns] *s* arrobamiento, rapto; estado hipnótico
tranquil ['træŋkwıl] *adj* tranquilo
tranquilize ['træŋkwı,laız] *tr & intr* tranquilizar
tranquilizer ['træŋkwı,laızər] *s* tranquilizante *m*
tranquillity [træŋkwılıti] *s* tranquilidad
transact [træn'zækt] o [træns'ækt] *tr* tramitar; llevar a cabo
transaction [træn'zækʃən] o [træns'ækʃən] *s* tramitación, tramitación
transatlantic [,trænsət'læntık] *adj & s* transatlántico

transcend [træn'sɛnd] *tr* exceder, superar ‖ *intr* sobresalir

transcribe [træn'skraɪb] *tr* transcribir

transcript ['trænskrɪpt] *s* trasunto, traslado; (educ) hoja de estudios, certificado de estudios

transcription [træn'skrɪpʃən] *s* transcripción

transept ['trænsɛpt] *s* crucero, transepto

trans·fer ['trænsfər] *s* traslado; transbordo; contraseña o billete *m* de transferencia ‖ [træns'fʌr] o ['trænsfər] *s* (*pret & pp* **-ferred**; *ger* **-ferring**) *tr* trasladar, transferir; transbordar ‖ *intr* cambiar de tren, tranvía, etc.

transfix [træns'fɪks] *tr* espetar, traspasar; dejar atónito

transform [træns'fɔrm] *tr* transformar ‖ *intr* transformarse

transformer [træns'fɔrmər] *s* transformador *m*

transfusion [træns'fjuʃən] *s* transfusión; (med) transfusión de la sangre

transgress [træns'grɛs] *tr* transgredir, violar; exceder, traspasar (*p.ej., los límites de la prudencia*) ‖ *intr* pecar, prevaricar

transgression [træns'grɛʃən] *s* transgresión; pecado, prevaricación

transient ['trænʃənt] *adj* pasajero, transitorio; de tránsito ‖ *s* transeúnte *mf*

transistor [træn'zɪstər] *s* transistor *m*

transistorize [træn'zɪstə,raɪz] *tr* transistorizar

transit ['trænsɪt] o ['trænzɪt] *s* tránsito

transitive ['trænsɪtɪv] *adj* transitivo ‖ *s* verbo transitivo

transitory ['trænsɪ,tori] *adj* transitorio

translate [træns'let] o ['trænslet] *tr* (*from one language to another*) traducir; (*from one place to another*) trasladar ‖ *intr* traducirse

translation [træns'leʃən] *s* traducción; traslación

translator [træns'letər] *s* traductor *m*

transliterate [træns'lɪtə,ret] *tr* transcribir

translucent [træns'lusənt] *adj* translúcido

transmission [træns'mɪʃən] *s* transmissión; (aut) cambio de marchas, cambio de velocidades

transmis′sion-gear′ box *s* caja de cambio de marchas, caja de velocidades

trans·mit [træns'mɪt] *v* (*pret & pp* **-mitted**; *ger* **-mitting**) *tr & intr* transmitir

transmitter [træns'mɪtər] *s* transmisor *m*

transmitting set *s* aparato transmisor

transmitting station *s* estacion transmisora, emisora

transmute [træns'mjut] *tr & intr* transmutar

transom [trænsəm] *s* (*crosspiece*) travesaño; (*window over door*) montante *m*; (*of ship*) yugo de popa

transparen·cy [træns'pɛrənsi] *s* (*pl* **-cies**) transparencia

transparent [træns'pɛrənt] *adj* transparente

transpire [træns'paɪr] *intr* transpirar; (*to become known, leak out*) transpirar; (coll) acontecer, tener lugar

transplant ['træns,plænt] *s* transplante; injerto ‖ *tr* transplantar ‖ *intr* transplantarse

transport ['trænsport] *s* transporte *m*; (aer & naut) transporte *m*; rapto, éxtasis *m*, transporte *m* ‖ [træns'port] *tr* transportar

transportation [,trænspor'teʃən] *s* transporte *m*; (U.S.A.) pasaje *m*, billete *m* de viaje

transport worker *s* transportista *mf*

transpose [træns'poz] *tr* transponer; (mus) transportar

trans·ship [træns'ʃɪp] *v* (*pret & pp* **-shipped**; *ger* **-shipping**) *tr* transbordar

transshipment [træns'ʃɪpmənt] *s* transbordo

transvestism [træns'vɛstɪzəm] *s* transvestismo

transvestite [træns'vɛstaɪt] *adj & s* transvestido

trap [træp] *s* trampa; (*double-curved pipe*) sifón *m*; coche ligero de dos ruedas; (sport) lanzaplatos *m* ‖ *v* (*pret & pp* **trapped**; *ger* **trapping**) *tr* entrampar; atrapar (*a un ladrón*)

trap door *s* escotillón *m*, trampa; (theat) escotillón *m*, pescante *m*

trapeze [trə'piz] *s* trapecio

trapezold ['træpɪ,zɔɪd] *s* trapecio

trapper ['træpər] *s* cazador *m* de alforja

trappings ['træpɪŋz] *spl* (*adornments*) adornos, altavíos; (*of a horse's harness*) jaeces *mpl*

trap′shoot′ing *s* tiro al vuelo

trash [træʃ] *s* broza, basura, desecho; (*junk*) cachivaches *mpl*; (*nonsense*) disparates *mpl*; (*worthless people*) gentuza

trash can *s* basurero

trash pile *s* basural *m* (SAm)

travail ['trævel] o [trə'vel] *s* afán *m*, labor *f*, pena; dolores *mpl* del parto

trav·el ['trævəl] *s* viaje *m*; el viajar; (mach) recorrido ‖ *v* (*pret & pp* **-eled** o **-elled**; *ger* **-eling** o **-elling**) *tr* viajar por; recorrer ‖ *intr* vaijar; andar, recorrer

travel bureau *s* oficina de turismo

traveler ['trævələr] *s* viajero; (*salesman*) viajante *m*

traveler's check *s* cheque *m* de viajeros

traveling expenses *spl* gastos de viaje

traveling salesman *s* viajante *m*, agente viajero

traverse ['trævərs] o [trə'vʌrs] *tr* atravesar; recorrer, pasar por

traves·ty ['trævɪsti] *s* (*pl* **-ties**) parodia ‖ *v* (*pret & pp* **-tied**) *tr* parodiar

trawl [trɔl] *s* red barredera, espinel *m*, palangre *m* ‖ *tr & intr* pescar a la rastra

tray [tre] *s* bandeja; (chem & phot) cubeta

treacherous ['trɛtʃərəs] *adj* traicionero, traidor; incierto, poco seguro

treacher·y ['trɛtʃəri] *s* (*pl* **-ies**) traición alevosía

tread [trɛd] *s* (*stepping*) pisada; (*of stairs*) grada, huella, peldaño; (*of stilts*) horquilla; (*of a tire*) banda de rodamiento; (*of shoe*) suela; (*of an egg*) meaje, galladura ‖ *v* (*pret* **trod** [trɑd]; *pp* **trodden** ['trɑdən] o **trod**) *tr* pisar, pisotear; abrumar, agobiar ‖ *intr* andar, caminar

treadle ['trɛdəl] *s* pedal *m*

treadless ['trɛdlɪs] *adj* (*tire*) desgastado

tread′mill′ s rueda de andar; (*futile drudgery*) noria

treas. *abbr* **treasurer, treasury**

treason [ˈtrizən] s traición

treasonable [ˈtrizənəbəl] *adj* traicionero, traidor

treasure [ˈtrɛʒər] s tesoro ‖ *tr* atesorar

treasurer [ˈtrɛʒərər] s tesorero

treasur·y [ˈtrɛʒəri] s (*pl* **-ies**) tesorería; tesoro

treat [trit] s convite *m;* (*to a drink*) convidada; (*something providing particular enjoyment*) regalo, deleite *m* ‖ *tr* tratar; convidar, regalar; curar (*a un enfermo*) ‖ *intr* tratar; convidar, regalar; **to treat of** tratar de

treatise [ˈtritɪs] s tratado

treatment [ˈtritmənt] s tratamiento

trea·ty [ˈtriti] s (*pl* **-ties**) tratado

treble [ˈtrɛbəl] *adj* (*threefold*) tresdoble, triple; sobreagudo; (mus) atiplado; (mus) de tiple ‖ s (*person*) tiple *mf;* (*voice*) tiple ‖ *tr* triplicar ‖ *intr* triplicarse

tree [tri] s árbol *m*

tree farm s monte *m* tallar

treeless [ˈtrilɪs] *adj* pelado, sin árboles

tree′top′ s copa, cima de árbol

trellis [ˈtrɛlɪs] s enrejado, espaldera; emparrado

tremble [ˈtrɛmbəl] s temblor *m*, estremecimiento ‖ *intr* temblar, estremecerse

tremendous [trɪˈmɛndəs] *adj* tremendo

tremor [ˈtrɛmər] o [ˈtrimər] s temblor *m*

trench [trɛntʃ] s foso, zanja; (*for irrigation*) acequia; (mil) trinchera

trenchant [ˈtrɛntʃənt] *adj* mordaz, punzante; enérgico, bien definido

trench coat s trinchera

trench mortar s (mil) lanzabombas *m*

trench′-plow′ *tr* (agr) desfondar

trend [trɛnd] s curso, dirección, tendencia ‖ *intr* dirigirse, tender

trendy [ˈtrɛndi] *adj* (coll) de (última) moda

trespass [ˈtrɛspəs] s entrada sin derecho; infracción, violación; culpa, pecado ‖*intr* entrar sin derecho; pecar; **no trespassing** prohibida la entrada; **to trespass against** pecar contra; **to trespass on** entrar sin derecho en; infringir, violar; abusar de (*p.ej., la paciencia de uno*)

tress [trɛs] s (*braid of hair*) trenza; (*curl*) bucle *m*, rizo

trestle [ˈtrɛsəl] s caballete *m;* puente *m* o viaducto de caballetes

trial [ˈtraɪəl] s ensayo, prueba; aflicción, desgracia; (law) juicio, proceso, vista; **on trial** a prueba; (law) en juicio; **to bring to trial** encausar

trial and error s método de tanteos

trial balloon s globo sonda; **to send up a trial balloon** (fig) lanzar un globo sonda

trial by jury s juicio por jurado

trial jury s jurado procesal

trial order s (com) pedido de ensayo

trial run s experimento piloto

triangle [ˈtraɪˌæŋgəl] s triángulo

tribe [traɪb] s tribu *f*

tribunal. [trɪˈbjunəl] o [traɪˈbjunəl] s tribunal *m*

tribune [ˈtrɪbjun] s tribuna

tributar·y [ˈtrɪbjəˌtɛri] *adj* tributario ‖ s (*pl* **-ies**) tributario

tribute [ˈtrɪbjut] s tributo

trice [traɪs] s momento, instante *m;* **in a trice** en un periquete

trick [trɪk] s ardid *m*, artimaña; leva (CAm, Col); (*knack*) maña; (*feat*) suerte *f;* (*prank*) travesura, burla, chasco; tanda, turno; ilusión; (*feat with cards*) truco; (*cards in one round*) baza; (coll) chiquita; **to be up to one′s old tricks** hacer de las suyas; **to play a dirty trick on** hacer una mala jugada a ‖ *tr* trampear; burlar, engañar; ataviar

tricker·y [ˈtrɪkəri] s (*pl* **-ies**) trampería, malas mañas

trickle [ˈtrɪkəl] s chorro delgado, goteo ‖ *intr* escurrir, gotear; pasar gradual e irregularmente

trickster [ˈtrɪkstər] s tramposo, embustero, embaucador *m*, embaucadora

trick·y [ˈtrɪki] *adj* (*comp* **-ier;** *super* **-iest**) tramposo, engañoso, difícil; (*animal*) vicioso; (*ticklish to deal with*) delicado

tricorn [ˈtraɪkɔrn] *adj* & s tricornio

tried [traɪd] *adj* fiel, probado, seguro

trifle [ˈtraɪfəl] s bagatela, friolera, fruslería, basurita, chiquitura; (*trinket*) bagatela, baratija ‖ *tr*—**to trifle away** malgastar ‖ *intr* estar ocioso, holgar; **to trifle with** manosear; jugar con, burlarse de

trifling [ˈtraɪflɪŋ] *adj* frívolo, fútil, ligero; insignificante, trivial

trifocal [traɪˈfokəl] *adj* trifocal ‖ s lente *f* trifocal; **trifocals** anteojos trifocales

trig. *abbr* **trigonometric, trigonometry**

trigger [ˈtrɪgər] s (*e.g., of a gun*) disparador *m*, gatillo; (*of any device*) disparador ‖ *tr* poner en movimiento, provocar

trigonometry [ˌtrɪgəˈnɑmɪtri] s trigonometría

trill [trɪl] s trinado, trino; (*made with voice, esp. of birds*) gorjeo; (phonet) vibración ‖ *tr* decir o cantar gorjeando; pronunciar con vibración ‖ *intr* trinar; gorjear

trillion [ˈtrɪljən] s (U.S.A.) billón *m;* (Brit) trillón *m*

trilo·gy [ˈtrɪlədʒi] s (*pl* **-gies**) trilogía

trim [trɪm] *adj* (*comp* **trimmer;** *super* **trimmest**) acicalado, compuesto, elegante ‖ s condición, estado; buena condición; adorno, atavío; traje *m*, vestido; (*of sails*) orientación ‖ *v* (*pret* & *pp* **trimmed;** *ger* **trimming**) *tr* ajustar, adaptar; arreglar, componer; adornar, decorar; decorar, enguirnaldar (*el árbol de Navidad*); recortar; cortar ligeramente (*el pelo*); despabilar (*una lámpara o vela*); mondar, podar (*árboles, plantas*); acepillar, desbastar; (naut) orientar (*las velas*); (coll) derrotar, vencer; (coll) regañar

trimming [ˈtrɪmɪŋ] s adorno, guarnición; franja, orla; (coll) paliza, zurra; (coll) derrota; **trimmings** accesorios, arrequives *mpl;* recortes *mpl*

tr
tr

trini•ty [ˈtrɪnɪti] s (pl **-ties**) (group of three) trinca ‖ **Trinity** s Trinidad

trinket [ˈtrɪŋkɪt] s (small ornament) dije m; (trivial object) baratija, bujería, chuchería

tri•o [ˈtriˑo] s (pl **-os**) (group of three) terna, trío; (mus) trío

trip [trɪp] s viaje m; jira, recorrido; (stumble) tropiezo; (act of causing a person to stumble) traspié m, zancadilla; (blunder) desliz m; (drugs) viaje ‖ v (pret & pp **tripped;** ger **tripping**) tr tropicar, echar la zancadilla a; detener, estorbar; inclinar; coger en falta; coger en una mentira ‖ intr ir con paso rápido y ligero; brincar, saltar, correr; tropezar; **to trip over** tropezar con, contra o en

tripe [traɪp] s callos, mondongo; (slang) disparate m, barbaridad

trip′ham′mer s martillo pilón

triphthong [ˈtrɪfθɔŋ] s triptongo

triple [ˈtrɪpəl] adj & s triple m ‖ tr triplicar ‖ intr triplicarse

triplet [ˈtrɪplɪt] s (offspring) trillizo; (stanza of three lines) terceto; (mus) terceto, tresillo

triplicate [ˈtrɪplɪkɪt] adj & s triplicado; **in triplicate** por triplicado ‖ [ˈtrɪplɪˌket] tr triplicar

tripod [ˈtraɪpɑd] m trípode m

triptych [ˈtrɪptɪk] s tríptico

trite [traɪt] adj gastado, trillado, trivial

triumph [ˈtraɪˑəmf] s triunfo ‖ intr triunfar; **to triumph over** triunfar de

triumphal arch [traɪˈʌmfəl] s arco triunfal

triumphant [traɪˈʌmfənt] adj triunfante

trivia [ˈtrɪviˑə] spl bagatelas, trivialidades

trivial [ˈtrɪviˑəl] adj trivial, insignificante

triviali•ty [ˌtrɪviˈælɪti] s (pl **-ties**) trivialidad

Trojan [ˈtrodʒən] adj & s troyano

Trojan horse s caballo de Troya

Trojan War s guerra de Troya

troll [trol] tr & intr pescar a la cacea

trolley [ˈtrali] s polea o arco de trole; tranvía m

trolley bus s trolebús m

trolley car s coche m de tranvía

trolley pole s trole m

trolling [ˈtrolɪŋ] s cacea, pesca a la cacea

trollop [ˈtraləp] s (slovenly woman) cochina; mujer f de mala vida

trombone [ˈtrambon] s trombón m

troop [trup] s tropa; (of actors) compañía; (of cavalry) escuadrón m ‖ intr agruparse; marcharse en tropel

trooper [ˈtrupər] s soldado de caballería; corcel m de guerra; policía m de a caballo; (ship) transporte m; **to swear like a trooper** jurar como un carretero

tro•phy [ˈtrofi] s (pl **-phies**) trofeo; (any memento) recuerdo

tropic [ˈtrapɪk] adj tropical ‖ s trópico

tropical [ˈtrapɪkəl] adj tropical

tropics o **Tropics** [ˈtrapɪks] spl zona tropical

troposphere [ˈtrapəˌsfɪr] s troposfera

trot [trat] s trote m ‖ v (pret & pp **trotted;** ger **trotting**) tr hacer trotar; **to trot out** (slang) sacar para mostrar ‖ intr trotar

troth [trɔθ] o [troθ] s fe f; verdad; esponsales mpl; **in troth** en verdad; **to plight one's troth** prometer fidelidad; dar palabra de casamiento

troubadour [ˈtrubəˌdor] o [ˈtrubəˌdur] adj trovadoresco ‖ s trovador m

trouble [ˈtrʌbəl] s apuro, dificultad; confusión, estorbo; conflicto; inquietud, preocupación; pena, molestia; mal m, enfermedad; murga; (of a mechanical nature) avería, falla, pana; **not to be worth the trouble** no valer la pena; **to pour out one's troubles** jeremiquear; **that's the trouble** ahí está el busilis; **the trouble is that . . .** lo malo es que . . .; **to be in trouble** estar en un aprieto; **to be looking for trouble** buscar tres pies al gato; **to get into trouble** enredarse, meterse en líos; **to take the trouble to** tomarse la molestia de ‖ tr apurar; confundir, estorbar; inquietar, preocupar; apenar, afligir; incomodar, molestar; dar que hacer a; **to be troubled with** padecer de; **to trouble oneself** molestarse ‖ intr apurarse; inquietarse, preocuparse; molestarse, darse molestia; **to trouble to** molestarse en

trouble lamp s lámpara de socorro

trou′ble•mak′er s perturbador m, alborotador m

troubleshooter [ˈtrʌbəlˌʃutər] s localizador m de averías; (in disputes) componedor m

troubleshooting [ˈtrʌbəlˌʃutɪŋ] s localización de averías; (of disputes) composición, arbitraje m

troublesome [ˈtrʌbəlsəm] adj molesto, pesado, gravoso; impertinente; perturbador

trouble spot s lugar m de conflicto

trough [trɔf] o [traf] s (e.g., to knead bread) artesa; (for water for animals) abrevadero; (for feeding animals) comedero; (under eaves) canal f; (between two waves) seno

troupe [trup] s compañía de actores o de circo

trousers [ˈtrauzərz] spl pantalones mpl

trous•seau [truˈso] o [ˈtruso] s (pl **-seaux** o **-seaus**) ajuar m de novia, equipo de novia

trout [traut] s trucha

trouvère [truˈvɛr] s trovero

trowel [ˈtrauˑəl] s paleta, llana

Troy [trɔɪ] s Troya

truant [ˈtruˑənt] s novillero; **to play truant** hacer novillos

truce [trus] s tregua

truck [trʌk] s carro; vegoneta; camión m; autocamión m; (to be moved by hand) carretilla; (of locomotive or car) carretón m; hortalizas para el mercado; (coll) desperdicios; (coll) negocio, relaciones ‖ tr acarrear

truck driver s camionista mf; materialista m (Mex)

truck garden s huerto de hortalizas (para el mercado)

truculent [ˈtrʌkjələnt] o [ˈtrukjələnt] adj truculento

trudge [trʌdʒ] intr caminar, ir a pie; **to trudge along** marchar con pena y trabajo

true [tru] *adj* verdadero; exacto; constante, uniforme; fiel, leal; alineado; a plomo, a nivel; **to come true** hacerse realidad; **true to life** conforme a la realidad

true copy *s* copia fiel

true-hearted ['tru,hɑrtɪd] *adj* fiel, leal, sincero

true'love' *s* fiel amante *mf;* (bot) hierba de París

truelove knot *s* lazo de amor

truffle ['trʌfəl] o ['trufəl] *s* trufa

truism ['tru•ɪzəm] *s* perogrullada, verdad trillada

truly ['truli] *adv* verdaderamente; efectivamente; fielmente; **truly yours** de Vd. atto. y S.S., su seguro servidor

trump [trʌmp] *s* triunfo; (coll) buen chico, buena chica; **no trump** sin triunfo ‖ *tr* matar con un triunfo; aventajar, sobrepujar; **to trump up** forjar, inventar (*para engañar*) ‖ *intr* triunfar

trumpet ['trʌmpɪt] *s* trompeta; trompeta acústica; **to blow one's own trumpet** cantar sus propias alabanzas ‖ *tr* pregonar a son de trompeta ‖ *intr* trompetear

truncheon ['trʌntʃən] *s* cachiporra; bastón *m* de mando

trunk [trʌŋk] *s* (*of living body, tree, family, railroad*) tronco; (*chest for clothes, etc.*) baúl *m;* (*of an automobile*) portaequipaje *m;* (*of elephant*) trompa; **trunks** taparrabo

trunk hose *spl* trusas

truss [trʌs] *s* (*framework*) armadura; haz *m*, paquete *m*, lío; (*for holding back a hernia*) braguero ‖ *tr* armar; empaquetar; espetar; apretar (*barriles*)

trust [trʌst] *s* confianza; esperanza; cargo, custodia; depósito; crédito; obligación; (econ) trust *m*, cartel *m;* (law) fideicomiso; **in trust** en confianza; en depósito; **on trust** a crédito, al fiado ‖ *tr* confiar; confiar en; vender a crédito a ‖ *intr* confiar, fiar; **to trust in** fiarse a o de

trust company *s* banco fideicomisario, banco de depósitos

trustee [trʌs'ti] *s* administrador *m*, comisario; regente (universitario); (*of an estate*) fideicomisario

trusteeship [trʌs'ti/ɪp] *s* cargo de administrador, fideicomisario; (*of the UN*) fideicomiso

trustful ['trʌstfəl] *adj* confiado

trust'wor'thy *adj* confiable, fidedigno

trust•y ['trʌsti] *adj* (comp -**ier**; *super* -**iest**) honrado, fidedigno ‖ *s* (*pl* -**ies**) presidiario fidedigno (*que se ha merecido ciertos privilegios*)

truth [truθ] *s* verdad; **in truth** a la verdad, en verdad

truthful ['truθfəl] *adj* verídico, veraz

try [traɪ] *s* (*pl* **tries**) ensayo, intento, prueba ‖ *v* (*pret & pp* **tried**) *tr* ensayar, intentar, probar; comprobar, verificar; cansar; exasperar, irritar; (law) procesar (*a una persona*); (law) ver (*un pleito*); **to try on** probarse (*una prenda de vestir*) ‖ *intr*

ensayar, probar; esforzarse; **to try to** tratar de, intentar

trying ['traɪ•ɪŋ] *adj* cansado, molesto, irritante; penoso

tryst [trɪst] o [traɪst] *s* cita; lugar *m* de cita

tub [tʌb] *s* cuba, tina; (coll) baño; (*clumsy boat*) (coll) carcamán *m*, trompo; (*fat person*) (coll) cuba

tube [tjub] o [tub] *s* tubo; túnel *m;* (*of a tire*) cámara; (coll) ferrocarril subterráneo

tuber ['tjubər] o ['tubər] *s* tubérculo

tubercle ['tubərkəl] *s* tubérculo

tubercular [tu'bʌrkjələr] *adj & s* tísico

tuberculosis [tu,bʌrkjə'losɪs] *s* tuberculosis *f*

tuck [tʌk] *s* alforza ‖ *tr* alforzar; **to tuck away** encubrir, ocultar; **to tuck in** arropar, enmantar; remeter (*p.ej., la ropa de cama*); **to tuck up** arremangar (*un vestido*); guarnecer (*la cama*)

tucker ['tʌkər] *s* escote *m* ‖ *tr* —**to tucker out** (coll) agotar, cansar

Tuesday ['tjuzdi] *s* martes *m*

tuft [tʌft] *s* (*of feathers, hair, etc.*) penacho, copete *m;* manojo, racimo, ramillete *m;* borla ‖ *tr* empenachar ‖ *intr* crecer formando mechones

tug [tʌg] *s* estirón *m*, tirón *m;* (*boat*) remolcador *m* ‖ *v* (*pret & pp* **tugged;** *ger* **tugging**) *tr* arrastrar, tirar con fuerza de; remolcar (*un barco*) ‖ *intr* tirar con fuerza; esforzarse, luchar

tug'boat' *s* remolcador *m*

tug of war *s* lucha de la cuerda

tuition [tju'ɪʃən] *s* enseñanza; precio de la enseñanza

tulip ['tulɪp] *s* tulipán *m*

tumble ['tʌmbəl] *s* caída, tumbo; (*somersault*) voltereta, tumba; confusión, desorden *m* ‖ *intr* caerse, rodar; voltear; derribarse, volcarse; brincar, dar saltos; (*into bed*) echarse; (*to catch on*) (slang) caer, comprender; **to tumble down** desplomarse, hundirse, venirse abajo

tum'ble-down' *adj* destartalado, desvencijado

tumbler ['tʌmblər] *s* (*for drinking*) vaso; (*person who performs bodily feats*) volatinero; (*self-righting toy*) dominguillo, tentemozo

tumor ['tjumər] o ['tumər] *s* tumor *m*

tumult ['tumʌlt] *s* tumulto

tun [tʌn] *s* barril *m*, tonel *m;* (*measure of capacity for wine*) tonelada

tuna ['tunə] *s* atún *m*

tune [tjun] o [tun] *s* tonada, aire *m;* (*manner of acting or speaking*) tono; **in tune** afinado; afinadamente; **out of tune** desafinado; desafinadamente; **to change one's tune** mudar de tono ‖ *tr* acordar, afinar; (rad) sintonizar; **to tune in** (rad) sintonizar; **to tune out** (rad) desintonizar; **to tune up** poner a punto; poner a tono (*un motor de automóvil*)

tungsten ['tʌŋstən] *s* tungsteno

tunic ['tjunɪk] o ['tunɪk] *s* túnica

tuning *s* (aut) puesto a punto

tuning coil *s* (rad) bobina de sintonía

tr

tu

tuning fork *s* diapasón *m*
Tunis ['tʌnɪs] *s* Túnez (*ciudad*)
Tunisia [tu'nɪʒə] *s* Túnez (*país*)
Tunisian [tu'nɪʒən] *adj & s* tunecino
tun•nel ['tʌnəl] *s* túnel *m*; (min) galería ‖ *v* (*pret & pp* **-neled** o **-nelled**; *ger* **-neling** o **-nelling**) *tr* construir un túnel a través de o debajo de
turban ['tʌrbən] *s* turbante *m*
turbid ['tʌrbɪd] *adj* turbio
turbine ['tʌrbɪn] o ['tʌrbaɪn] *s* turbina
turbocompressor [,tʌrbokəm'prɛsər] *s* turbocompresor *m*
turbofan ['tʌrbo,fæn] *s* turboventilador *m*
turbojet ['tʌrbo,dʒet] *s* turborreactor *m;* avión *m* de turborreacción
turboprop ['tʌrbo,prɑp] *s* turbopropulsor *m;* turbohelice *m* avión *m* de turbopropulsión
turbosupercharger [,tʌrbo'supər,tʃɑrdʒər] *s* turbosupercargador *m*
turbulent ['tʌrbjələnt] *adj* turbulento
tureen [tu'rin] o [tju'rin] *s* sopera
turf [tʌrf] *s* (*surface layer of grassland*) césped *m;* terrón *m* de césped; (*peat*) turba; **the turf** el hipódromo; las carreras de caballos
turf•man ['tʌrfmən] *s* (*pl* **-men** [mən]) turfista *m*
Turk [tʌrk] *s* turco
turkey ['tʌrki] *s* pavo ‖ **Turkey** *s* Turquía
turkey vulture *s* aura
Turkish ['tʌrkɪʃ] *adj & s* turco
Turkish towel *s* toalla rusa
turmoil ['tʌrmɔɪl] *s* alboroto, disturbio, tumulto
turn [tʌrn] *s* vuelta; (*time of action*) turno; (*change of direction*) virada; (*bend*) recodo; (*walk*) paseo corto; (*of a spiral, roll of wire, etc.*) espira; aspecto; inclinación; vahido, vértigo; giro, expresión; servicio; (coll) sacudida, susto; **at every turn** a cada paso; **in trun** por turno; **to be one's turn** tocarle a uno, p.ej., **it's your turn** le toca a Vd.; **to take turns** alternar, turnar; **to wait one's turn** aguardar turno, esperar vez ‖ *tr* volver; dar vuelta a (*p.ej., una llave*); torcer (*p.ej., el tobillo*); doblar (*la esquina*); dirigir (*p.ej., los ojos*); (*to make sour*) agriar; (*on a lathe*) tornear; tener (*p.ej., veinte años cumplidos*); **to turn against** predisponer en contra de; **to turn around** volver; voltear; torcer (*las palabras de una persona*); **to turn aside** desviar; **to turn away** desviar; despedir; **to turn back** devolver; hacer retroceder; retrasar (*el reloj*); **to turn down** doblar hacia abajo; invertir; rechazar, rehusar; bajar (*p.ej., el gas*); **to turn in** doblar hacia adentro; entregar; **to turn off** apagar (*la luz, la radio*); cortar (*el agua, gas, etc.*; cerrar (*la llave del agua, gas, etc.;* la *radio, la televisión*); interrumpir (*la corriente eléctrica*); **to turn on** encender (*la luz*); poner (*la luz, la radio, etc.*); abrir (*la llave del agua, gas, etc.*); establecer (*la corriente eléctrica*); **to turn out** despedir; echar al campo (*a los animales*); volver al

revés; apagar (*la luz*); hacer, fabricar; **to turn up** doblar hacia arriba; levantar; arremangar (*p.ej., las mangas*); volver (*un naipe*); poner más alto o más fuerte (*la radio*); abrir la llave de (*p.ej., el gas*) ‖ *intr* volver, p.ej., **the road turns to the right** el camino vuelve a la derecha; virar (*un automóvil, un avión, etc.*); (*to revolve*) girar; volverse (*p.ej., la conversación; la opinión; ciertos licores*); **to turn against** cobrar aversión a; rebelarse contra; **to turn around** dar vuelta; **to turn aside** o **away** desviarse; alejarse; **to turn back** volver, regresar; retroceder; **to turn down** doblarse hacia abajo; invertirse; **to turn in** doblarse hacia adentro; replegarse; recogerse, volver a casa; (coll) recogerse, acostarse; **to turn into** entrar en; convertirse en; **to turn on** volverse contra; depender de; versar sobre; ocuparse de; **to turn out badly** salir mal; **to turn out right** acabar bien; **to turn out to be** venir a ser; resultar, salir; **to turn over** volcar, derribarse (*un vehículo*); **to turn up** doblarse hacia arriba; levantarse; acontecer; aparecer
turn′coat′ *s* tránsfuga *mf*, apóstata *mf*, renegado; **to become a turncoat** volver la casaca, cambiarse la camisa
turn′down′ *adj* (*collar*) caído ‖ *s* rechazamiento
turning light *s* (aut) intermitente *m*
turning point *s* punto de transición; punto decisivo
turnip ['tʌrnɪp] *s* nabo; (*cheap watch*) (slang) calentador *m;* (slang) tipo
turn′key′ *s* carcelero, llavero de cárcel
turn of life *s* menopausia
turn of mind *s* natural *m*, inclinación
turn′out′ *s* (*gathering of people*) con currencia; (*number attending a show, etc.*) entrada; (*side track or passage*) apartadero; (*amount produced*) producción; (*array, outfit*) equipaje *m;* carruaje *m* de lujo
turn′o′ver *s* (*spill, upset*) vuelco; cambio de personal; movimiento de mercancías; ciclo de compra y venta
turn′pike′ *s* carretera de peaje
turnstile ['tʌrn,staɪl] *s* torniquete *m*
turn′ta′ble *s* (*of phonograph*) placa giratoria, plato giratorio; (rr) placa giratoria, plataforma giratoria
turpentine ['tʌrpən,taɪn] *s* trementina
turpitude ['tʌrpɪ,tjud] *s* torpeza, infamia, vileza
turquoise ['tʌrkɔɪz] o ['tʌrkwɔɪz] *s* turquesa
turret ['tʌrɪt] *s* torrecilla; (archit) torreón *m;* (nav) torreta
turtle ['tʌrtəl] *s* tortuga; **to turn turtle** derribarse patas arriba
tur′tle•dove′ *s* tórtola
Tuscan ['tʌskən] *adj & s* toscano
Tuscany ['tʌskəni] *s* la Toscana
tusk [tʌsk] *s* colmillo
tussle ['tʌsəl] *s* agarrada ‖ *intr* agarrarse, asirse, reñir

tutor [´tjutǝr] o [´tutǝr] s maestro particular; (*guardian*) tutor m ‖ tr dar enseñanza particular a ‖ intr dar enseñanza particular; (coll) tomar lecciones particulares

tuxe•do [tʌk´sido] s (*pl* **-dos**) esmoquin m, smoking m

TV abbr **television**

twaddle [´twɑdǝl] s charla, tonterías, música celestial ‖ intr charlar, decir tonterías

twang [twæŋ] s (*of musical instrument*) tañido; (*of voice*) timbre m nasal ‖ tr tocar con un tañido; decir con timbre nasal ‖ intr hablar por la nariz

twang•y [´twæŋi] adj (*comp* **-ier**; *super* **-iest**) (*device*) tañente; (*person, voice*) gangoso

tweed [twid] s mezcla de lana; traje m de mezcla de lana; **tweeds** ropa de mezcla de lana

tweet [twit] s pío ‖ intr piar

tweeter [´twitǝr] s altavoz m para audiofrecuencias elevadas

tweezers [´twizǝrz] spl bruselas, pinzas, tenacillas

twelfth [twɛlfθ] adj & s (*in a seris*) duodécimo; (*part*) dozavo ‖ s (*in dates*) doce m

Twelfth´-night´ s la víspera del día de Reyes; la noche del día de Reyes

twelve [twɛlv] adj & pron doce ‖ s doce m; **twelve o'clock** las doce

twentieth [´twɛnti•ɪθ] adj & s (*in a series*) vigésimo; (*part*) veintavo ‖ s (*in dates*) veinte m

twen•ty [´twɛnti] adj & pron veinte ‖ s (*pl* **-ties**) veinte m

twice [twaɪs] adv dos veces

twice´-told´ ádj dicho dos veces; trilládo, sabido

twiddle [´twɪdǝl] tr menear o revolver ociosamente

twig [twɪg] s ramito; **twigs** leña menuda

twilight [´twaɪ,laɪt] adj crepuscular ‖ s crepúsculo

twill [twɪl] s tela cruzada; (*pattern of weave*) cruzado ‖ tr cruzar

twin [twɪn] adj & s gemelo

twine [twaɪn] s guita, cuerda, bramante m ‖ tr enroscar, retorcer ‖ intr enroscarse, retorcerse

twinge [twɪndʒ] s·punzada, dolor agudo

twin´jet´ plane s avión m birreactor

twinkle [´twɪŋkǝl] s centelleo; (*of eye*) pestañeo; instante m ‖ intr centellear; pestañear; moverse rápidamente

twin´-screw´ adj (naut) de doble hélice

twirl [twʌrl] s vuelta, giro ‖ tr hacer girar; (*baseball*) lanzar (*la pelota*) ‖ intr dar vueltas, girar; piruetear

twist [twɪst] s torcedura; enroscadura; curva, recodo; giro, vuelta; propensión, prejuicio; (*of mind or disposition*) sesgo ‖ tr torcer; retorcer; enroscar; hacer girar; entrelazar; desviar; (*to give a different meaning to*) torcer ‖ intr torcerse; retorcerse; enroscarse; dar vueltas; entrelazarse; desviarse; serpentear; **to twist and turn** (*in bed*) dar vueltas

twisted [´twɪstɪd] adj sobornado

twit [twɪt] v (*pret & pp* **twitted; ger twitting**) tr reprender (*a uno*) recordando algo desagradable o poniéndole en ridículo

twitch [twɪtʃ] s crispatura; ligero temblor ‖ intr crisparse; temblar (*p.ej., los párpados*)

twitter [´twɪtǝr] s gorjeo; risita sofocada; inquietud ‖ intr gorjear; reír sofocadamente; temblar de inquietud

two [tu] adj & pron dos ‖ s dos m; **to put two and two together** atar cabos, sacar la conclusión evidente; **two o'clock** las dos

two´-cy´cle adj (mach) de dos tiempos

two´-cyl´inder adj (mach) de dos cilindros

two-edged [´tu,ɛdʒd] adj de dos filos

two hundred adj & pron doscientos ‖ s doscientos m

twosome [´tusǝm] s pareja; pareja de jugadores; juego de dos

two´-time´ tr (slang) engañar en amor, ser infiel a (*una persona del otro sexo*)

tycoon [taɪ´kun] s (coll) magnate m

type [taɪp] s tipo; (*piece*) (typ) tipo, letra; (*pieces collectively*) (typ) letra; letras impresas, letras escritas a máquina ‖ tr escribir a máquina, tipiar; representar, simbolizar ‖ intr escribir a máquina

type´face´ s tipo de letra

type´script´ s material escrito a máquina

typesetter [´taɪp,sɛtǝr] s (typ) cajista mf; (typ) máquina de componer

type´write´ v (*pret* **-wrote** [,rot]; *pp* **-written** [,rɪtǝn]) tr & intr escribir a máquina, tipiar

type´writ´er s máquina de escribir; tipista mf

typewriter ribbon s cinta para máquinas de escribir

type´writ´ing s mecanografía; trabajo hecho con máquina de escribir

typhoid fever [´taɪfɔɪd] s fiebre tifoidea

typhoon [taɪ´fun] s tifón m

typical [´tɪpɪkǝl] adj típico

typi•fy [´tɪpɪ,faɪ] v (*pret & pp* **-fied**) tr simbolizar; ser ejemplo o modelo de

typist [´taɪpɪst] s mecanógrafo, tipista mf, mecanógrafa

typographic(al) [,taɪpǝ´græfɪk(ǝl)] adj tipográfico

typographical error s error m de imprenta

typography [taɪ´pɑgrǝfi] s tipografía

tyrannic(al) [tɪ´rænɪk(ǝl)] o [taɪ´rænɪk(ǝl)] adj tiránico

tyrannous [´tɪrǝnǝs] adj tirano

tyran•ny [´tɪrǝni] s (*pl* **-nies**) tiranía

tyrant [´taɪrǝnt] s tirano

ty•ro [´taɪro] s (*pl* **-ros**) tirón m, novicio

tu
ty

U

U, u [ju] vigésima primera letra del alfabeto inglés

U. *abbr* **University**

ubiquitous [juˈbɪkwɪtəs] *adj* ubicuo

udder [ˈʌdər] *s* ubre *f*

UFO *abbr* **unidentified flying object**

ugliness [ˈʌglɪnɪs] *s* fealdad; (coll) malhumor *m*

ug•ly [ˈʌgli] *adj* (*comp* **-lier;** *super* **-liest**) feo; (coll) malhumorado

ugly mug *s* (slang) carantamaula

Ukraine [ˈjukren] o [juˈkren] *s* Ucrania

Ukrainian [juˈkrenɪ•ən] *adj & s* ucraniano, ucranio

ulcer [ˈʌlsər] *s* llaga, úlcera; (*corrupting influence*) (fig) llaga

ulcerate [ˈʌlsə,ret] *tr* ulcerar ‖ *intr* ulcerarse

ulterior [ʌlˈtɪrɪ•ər] *adj* ulterior; (*concealed*) escondido, oculto

ultimate [ˈʌltɪmɪt] *adj* último

ultima•tum [,ʌltɪˈmetəm] *s* (*pl* **-tums** o **-ta** [tə]) ultimátum *m*

ultimo [ˈʌltɪ,mo] *adv* de o en el mes próximo pasado

ultrahigh [,ʌltrəˈhaɪ] *adj* (electron) ultraelevado

ultrasound [ˈʌltrə,saund] *s* sonido silencioso

ultraviolet [,ʌltrəˈvaɪ•əlɪt] *adj & s* ultravioleta, ultraviolado

umbilical cord [ʌmˈbɪlɪkəl] *s* cordón *m* umbilical

umbrage [ˈʌmbrɪdʒ] *s*—**to take umbrage at** resentirse de o por

umbrella [ʌmˈbrɛlə] *s* paraguas *m;* (mil) sombrilla protectora

umbrella man *s* paragüero

umbrella stand *s* paragüero

umlaut [ˈumlaut] *s* inflexión vocálica, metafonía; (*mark*) diéresis *f* ‖ *tr* inflexionar; escribir con diéresis

umpire [ˈʌmpaɪr] *s* árbitro ‖ *tr & intr* arbitrar

UN [ˈjuˈɛn] *s* (letterword) ONU *f*

unable [ʌnˈebəl] *adj* incapaz, imposibilitado; **to be unable to** no poder

unabridged [,ʌnəˈbrɪdʒd] *adj* sin abreviar, íntegro

unaccented [ʌnˈæksɛntɪd] o [,ʌnækˈsɛntɪd] *adj* inacentuado

unaccountable [,ʌnəˈkauntəbəl] *adj* inexplicable; irresponsable

unaccounted-for [,ʌnəˈkauntɪd,fɔr] *adj* inexplicado; no hallado

unaccustomed [,ʌnəˈkʌstəmd] *adj* (*unusual*) desacostumbrado; inhabituado

unafraid [,ʌnəˈfred] *adj* sin miedo

unaligned [,ʌnəˈlaɪnd] *adj* no empeñado

unanimity [,junəˈnɪmɪti] *s* unanimidad

unanimous [juˈnænɪməs] *adj* unánime

unanswerable [ʌnˈænsərəbəl] *adj* incontestable; (*argument*) incontrastable

unappreciative [,ʌnəˈpriʃɪ,etɪv] *adj* ingrato, desagradecido

unapproachable [,ʌnəˈprotʃəbəl] *adj* inabordable; incomparable; único

unarmed [ʌnˈɑrmd] *adj* desarmado, inerme

unascertainable [ʌn,æsərˈtenəbəl] *adj* inaveriguable

unasked [ʌnˈæskt] *adj* no solicitado; no convidado

unassembled [,ʌnəˈsɛmbəld] *adj* desmontado, desarmado

unassuming [,ʌnəˈsumɪŋ] o [,ʌnəˈsjumɪŋ] *adj* modesto, sencillo

unattached [,ʌnəˈtætʃt] *adj* independiente; (*loose*) suelto; (*not engaged to be married*) no prometido; (law) no embargado; (mil & nav) de reemplazo

unattainable [,ʌnəˈtenəbəl] *adj* inasequible, inalcanzable

unattractive [,ʌnəˈtræktɪv] *adj* poco atrayente, desairado

unavailable [,ʌnəˈveləbəl] *adj* indisponible

unavailing [,ʌnəˈvelɪŋ] *adj* ineficaz, inútil, vano

unavoidable [,ʌnəˈvɔɪdəbəl] *adj* inevitable, ineluctable

unaware [,ʌnəˈwɛr] *adj*—**to be unaware of** no estar al corriente de ‖ *adv* de improviso; sin saberlo

unawares [,ʌnəˈwɛrz] *adv* (*unexpectedly*) de improviso; (*unknowingly*) sin saberlo

unbalanced [ʌnˈbælənst] *adj* desequilibrado

unbandage [ʌnˈbændɪdʒ] *tr* desvendar

un•bar [ʌnˈbɑr] *v* (*pret & pp* **-barred;** *ger* **-barring**) *tr* desatrancar

unbearable [ʌnˈbɛrəbəl] *adj* inaguantable

unbeatable [ʌnˈbitəbəl] *adj* imbatible

unbecoming [,ʌnbɪˈkʌmɪŋ] *adj* inconveniente, indecente; que sienta mal

unbelievable [,ʌnbɪˈlivəbəl] *adj* increíble

unbending [ʌnˈbɛndɪŋ] *adj* inflexible

unbiased o **unbiassed** [ʌnˈbaɪ•əst] *adj* imparcial

un•bind [ʌnˈbaɪnd] *v* (*pret & pp* **-bound** [ˈbaund]) *tr* desatar

unbleached [ʌnˈblitʃt] *adj* sin blanquear

unbolt [ʌnˈbolt] *tr* desatrancar (*p.ej., una puerta*); (*to remove the bolts from*) desempernar

unborn [ʌnˈbɔrn] *adj* no nacido, por nacer, futuro

unbosom [ʌnˈbuzəm] *tr* confesar, descubrir (*sus pensamientos, sus secretos*); **to unbosom oneself** abrir su pecho, desahogarse

unbound [ʌnˈbaund] *adj* (*book*) sin encuadernar

unbreakable [ʌnˈbrekəbəl] *adj* irrompible

unbuckle [ʌnˈbʌkəl] *tr* deshebillar

unburden [ʌnˈbʌrdən] *tr* descargar; **to unburden oneself of** desahogarse de

unburied [ʌnˈbɛrid] *adj* insepulto

unbutton [ʌnˈbʌtən] *tr* desabotonar

uncalled-for [ʌnˈkɔld,fɔr] *adj* innecesario, no justificado; insolente

uncanny [ʌnˈkæni] *adj* espectral, misterioso; extraordinario, maravilloso

uncared-for [ʌnˈkɛrd,fɔr] *adj* desamparado, descuidado, abandonado

unceasing [ʌnˈsisɪŋ] *adj* incesante

unceremonious [ˌʌnsɛriˈmoniˌəs] *adj* inceremonioso

uncertain [ʌnˈsʌrtən] *adj* incierto

uncertain·ty [ʌnˈsʌrtənti] *s* (*pl* **-ties**) incertidumbre

unchain [ʌnˈtʃen] *tr* desencadenar

unchangeable [ʌnˈtʃendʒəbəl] *adj* incambiable, inmutable

uncharted [ʌnˈtʃɑrtɪd] *adj* inexplorado

unchecked [ʌnˈtʃɛkt] *adj* no verificado; no refrenado; desenfrenado

uncivilized [ʌnˈsɪvɪˌlaɪzd] *adj* incivilizado

unclad [ʌnˈklæd] *adj* desvestido

unclaimed [ʌnˈklemd] *adj* sin reclamar; (*mail*) rechazado, sobrante

unclasp [ʌnˈklæsp] *tr* desabrochar

unclassified [ʌnˈklæsɪˌfaɪd] *adj* no clasificado; no clasificado como secreto

uncle [ˈʌŋkəl] *s* tío

unclean [ʌnˈklin] *adj* desaseado, sucio

un·clog [ʌnˈklɑg] *v* (*pret & pp* **-clogged;** *ger* **-clogging**) *tr* desatrancar

unclouded [ʌnˈklaʊdɪd] *adj* despejado

uncollectible [ˌʌnkəˈlɛktɪbəl] *adj* incobrable

uncomfortable [ʌnˈkʌmfərtəbəl] *adj* incomodo

uncommitted [ˌʌnkəˈmɪtɪd] *adj* no empeñado, no comprometido

uncommon [ʌnˈkɑmən] *adj* raro, poco común

uncompromising [ʌnˈkɑmprəˌmaɪzɪŋ] *adj* intransigente

unconcerned [ˌʌnkənˈsʌrnd] *adj* despreocupado, indiferente

unconditional [ˌʌnkənˈdɪʃənəl] *adj* incondicional

uncongenial [ˌʌnkənˈdʒiniˌəl] *adj* antipático; incompatible; desagradable

unconquerable [ʌnˈkɑŋkərəbəl] *adj* inconquistable

unconquered [ʌnˈkɑŋkərd] *adj* invicto

unconscionable [ʌnˈkɑnʃənəbəl] *adj* inescrupuloso; desrazonable, excesivo

unconscious [ʌnˈkɑnʃəs] *adj* inconsciente; (*temporarily deprived of consciousness*) desmayado; (*unintentional*) involuntario

unconsciousness [ʌnˈkɑnʃəsnɪs] *s* inconsciencia; desmayo

unconstitutional [ˌʌnkɑnstɪˈtjuʃənəl] *adj* inconstitucional

uncontrollable [ˌʌnkənˈtroləbəl] *adj* ingobernable; incontrolable; (*laughter*) inextinguible

unconventional [ˌʌnkənˈvɛnʃənəl] *adj* no convencional

uncork [ʌnˈkɔrk] *tr* destapar, descorchar

uncouth [ʌnˈkuθ] *adj* desgarbado, torpe, rústico

uncover [ʌnˈkʌvər] *tr* descubrir

unction [ˈʌŋkʃən] *s* (*anointing*) unción; suavidad hipócrita

unctuous [ˈʌŋktʃuˌəs] *adj* untuoso; zalamero

uncultivated [ʌnˈkʌltɪˌvetɪd] *adj* inculto (*que no está cultivado; rústico, grosero*)

uncultured [ʌnˈkʌltʃərd] *adj* inculto, rústico, grosero

uncut [ʌnˈkʌt] *adj* sin cortar; (*book or magazine*) intonso

undamaged [ʌnˈdæmɪdʒd] *adj* indemne, ileso

undaunted [ʌnˈdɔntɪd] *adj* impávido, denodado

undecided [ˌʌndɪˈsaɪdɪd] *adj* indeciso

undefeated [ˌʌndɪˈfitɪd] *adj* invicto

undefended [ˌʌndɪˈfɛndɪd] *adj* indefenso

undefiled [ˌʌndɪˈfaɪld] *adj* inmaculado, impoluto

undeniable [ˌʌndɪˈnaɪˌəbəl] *adj* innegable

under [ˈʌndər] *adj* inferior; (*clothing*) interior ‖ *adv* debajo; más abajo; **to go under** hundirse; (*to fail*) fracasar ‖ *prep* bajo, debajo de; inferior a; **under full sail** a vela llena; **under lock and key** bajo llave; **under oath** bajo juramento; **under penalty of death** so pena de muerte; **under sail** a vela; **under separate cover** por separado, bajo cubierta separada; **under steam** bajo presión; **under the hand and seal of** firmado y sellado por; **under the nose of** en las barbas de; **under the weather** algo indispuesto; **under way** en camino

un'der·age' *adj* menor de edad

un'der·bid' *v* (*pret & pp* **-bid;** *ger* **-bidding**) *tr* ofrecer menos que

un'der·brush' *s* maleza

un'der·car'riage *s* carro inferior; (aer) tren *m* de aterrizaje

un'der·clothes' *s* ropa interior

un'der·con·sump'tion *s* infraconsumo

un'der·cov'er *adj* secreto

underdeveloped [ˌʌndərdɪˈvɛləpt] *adj* subdesarrollado

un'der·dog' *s* víctima, perdidoso; **the underdogs** los de abajo

underdone [ˈʌndərˌdʌn] *adj* a medio asar, soasado

un'der·es'ti·mate' *tr* subestimar

un'der·gar'ment *s* prenda de vestir interior

un'der·go' *v* (*pret* **-went;** *pp* **-gone**) *tr* experimentar; sufrir, padecer

un'der·grad'uate *adj* no graduado; (*course*) para el bachillerato ‖ *s* alumno no graduado de universidad

un'der·ground' *adj* subterráneo; clandestino ‖ *adv* bajo tierra; ocultamente ‖ *s* ferrocarril subterráneo; movimiento de resistencia

un'der·growth' *s* maleza

underhanded [ˈʌndərˈhændɪd] *adj* clandestino, taimado, disimulado

un'der·line' o **un'der·line'** *tr* subrayar

underling [ˈʌndərlɪŋ] *s* subordinado, secuaz *m* servil

un'der·mine' *tr* socavar, minar

underneath [ˌʌndərˈniθ] *adj* inferior, más bajo ‖ *adv* debajo ‖ *prep* debajo de ‖ *s* parte baja, superficie *f* inferior

undernourished [ˌʌndərˈnʌrɪʃt] *adj* desnutrido

un'der·nour'ish·ment *s* desnutrición

un'der·pass' *s* paso inferior

un'der·pay' *s* pago insuficiente ‖ *v* (*pret & pp* **-paid**) *tr & intr* pagar insuficientemente

u
un

un'der·pin' v (pret & pp -pinned; ger -pinning) tr apuntalar, socalzar

underprivileged [,ʌndər'prɪvɪlɪdʒd] adj desheredado, desamparado

un'der·rate' tr menospreciar

un'der·score' tr subrayar

un'der·sea' adj submarino ‖ un'der·sea' adv debajo de la superficie del mar

un'der·sec're·tar'y s (pl -ies) subsecretario

un'der·sell' v (pret & pp -sold) tr vender a menor precio que; (for less than the actual value) malbaratar

un'der·shirt' s camiseta

undersigned ['ʌndər,saɪnd] adj infrascrito, subscrito

un'der·skirt' s enaguas, refajo

un'der·stand' v (pret & pp -stood) tr entender, comprender; sobrentender, subentender (una cosa que no está expresa) ‖ intr entender, comprender

understandable [,ʌndər'stændəbəl] adj comprensible

understanding [,ʌndər'stændɪŋ] adj entendedor; (tolerant, sympathetic) comprensivo ‖ s comprensión; (intellectual faculty, mind) entendimiento; (agreement) acuerdo; to come to an understanding llegar a un acuerdo

un'der·stud'y s (pl -ies) sobresaliente mf

un'der·take' v (pret -took; pp -taken) tr emprender; (to agree to perform) comprometerse a

undertaker [,ʌndər'tekər] o ['ʌndər,tekər] s empresario ‖ ('ʌndər,tekər) s empresario de pompas fúnebres, director m de funeraria

undertaking [,ʌndər'tekɪŋ] s (task) empresa; (pledge) empeño ‖ ['ʌndər,tekɪŋ] s (business of funeral director) funeraria

un'der·tak'ing establishment s funeraria, empresa de pompas fúnebres

un'der·tone' s voz baja; (background sound) fondo; color apagado

un'der·tow' s (countercurrent below surface) contracorriente f; (on the beach) resaca

un'der·wear' s ropa interior, prendas interiores

un'der·world' s (criminal world) inframundo, bajos fondos sociales; (the earth) mundo terrenal; (pagan world of the dead) averno, infierno; (world under the water) mundo submarino; (opposite side of earth) antípodas

un'der·write' v (pret -wrote; pp -written) tr subscribir; (to insure) asegurar

un'der·writ'er s subscritor m; asegurador m; compañía aseguradora

undeserved [,ʌndɪ'zʌrvd] adj inmerecido

undesirable [,ʌndɪ'zaɪrəbəl] adj & s indeseable mf

undetachable [,ʌndɪ'tætʃəbəl] adj inamovible

undignified [ʌn'dɪgnɪ,faɪd] adj poco digno, poco grave, indecoroso

undiscernible [,ʌndɪ'zʌrnɪbəl] o [,ʌndɪ-'sʌrnəbəl] adj imperceptible, invisible

un·do' v (pret -did; pp -done) tr deshacer; anular, borrar; arruinar

undoing [ʌn'du·ɪŋ] s destrucción, pérdida, ruina

undone [ʌn'dʌn] adj sin hacer, por hacer; to come undone deshacerse, desatarse; to leave nothing undone no dejar nada por hacer

undoubtedly [ʌn'daʊtɪdli] adv indudablemente, sin duda

undramatic [,ʌndrə'mætɪk] adj poco dramático

undress ['ʌn,drɛs] o [ʌn'drɛs] s traje m de casa; vestido de calle; (mil) traje de cuartel ‖ [ʌn'drɛs] tr desnudar; desvendar (una herida) ‖ desnudarse

undrinkable [ʌn'drɪŋkəbəl] adj impotable

undue [ʌn'dju] adj indebido

undulate ['ʌndjə,let] intr ondular

unduly [ʌn'djuli] adv indebidamente

undying [ʌn'daɪ·ɪŋ] adj imperecedero

unearned increment [ʌn'ʌrnd] s plusvalía

unearth [ʌn'ʌrθ] tr desenterrar

unearthly [ʌn'ʌrθli] adj sobrenatural; fantástico, espectral; extraordinario

uneasy [ʌn'izi] adj (worried) inquieto; (constrained) encogido, embarazado

uneatable [ʌn'itəbəl] adj incomible

uneconomic(al) [,ʌnikə'nɑmɪk(əl)] adj antieconómico

uneducated [ʌn'ɛdjə,ketɪd] adj ineducado, sin instrucción; chontal

unemployed [,ʌnɛm'plɔɪd] adj desocupado, desempleado; improductivo

unemployment [,ʌnɛm'plɔɪmənt] s desocupación, desempleo

unemployment insurance s seguro de desempleo o desocupación, seguro contra el paro obrero

unending [ʌn'ɛndɪŋ] adj interminable

unequal [ʌn'ikwəl] adj desigual; to be unequal to (a task) no estar a la altura de

unequaled o unequalled [ʌn'ikwəld] adj inigualado

unerring [ʌn'ʌrɪŋ] o [ʌn'ɛrɪŋ] adj infalible, seguro

unessential [,ʌnɛsɛn'ʃəl] adj no esencial

uneven [ʌn'ivən] adj desigual; (number) impar

unexceptionable [,ʌnɛk'sɛpʃənəbəl] adj intachable, irreprensible

unexpected [,ʌnɛk'spɛktɪd] adj inesperado

unexplained [,ʌnɛk'splend] adj inexplicado

unexplored [,ʌnɛk'splord] adj inexplorado

unexposed [,ʌnɛk'spozd] adj (phot) inexpuesto

unfading [ʌn'fedɪŋ] adj inmarcesible

unfailing [ʌn'felɪŋ] adj indefectible; (inexhaustible) inagotable

unfair [ʌn'fɛr] adj injusto; desleal, doble, falso; (sport) sucio

unfaithful [ʌn'feθfəl] adj infiel

unfamiliar [,ʌnfə'mɪljər] adj poco familiar; poco familiarizado

unfasten [ʌn'fæsən] tr desatacar, desatar, soltar

unfathomable [ʌn'fæðəməbəl] adj insondable

unfavorable [ʌn'fevərəbəl] adj desfavorable

unfeathered [ʌnˈfɛðərd] *adj* implume
unfeeling [ʌnˈfiliŋ] *adj* insensible
unfetter [ʌnˈfɛtər] *tr* desencadenar
unfilled [ʌnˈfɪld] *adj* no lleno; por complir, pendiente
unfinished [ʌnˈfɪnɪʃt] *adj* sin acabar; imperfecto, mal acabado; (*business*) pendiente
unfit [ʌnˈfɪt] *adj* impropio, incapaz, inhábil; inservible, inútil
unfold [ʌnˈfold] *tr* desplegar ‖ *intr* desplegarse
unforeseeable [ˌʌnforˈsi•əbəl] *adj* imprevisible
unforeseen [ˌʌnforˈsin] *adj* imprevisto
unforgettable [ˌʌnfərˈgɛtəbəl] *adj* inolvidable
unforgivable [ˌʌnfərˈgɪvəbəl] *adj* imperdonable
unfortunate [ʌnˈfɔrtjənɪt] *adj & s* desgraciado
unfounded [ʌnˈfaundɪd] *adj* infundado
unfreeze [ʌnˈfriz].*tr* deshelar; desbloquear (*el crédito*)
unfriendly [ʌnˈfrɛndli] *adj* inamistoso; desfavorable
unfruitful [ʌnˈfrutfəl] *adj* infructuoso
unfulfilled [ˌʌnfəlˈfɪld] *adj* incumplido
unfurl [ʌnˈfʌrl] *tr* desplegar, extender
unfurnished [ʌnˈfʌrnɪʃt] *adj* desamueblado
ungainly [ʌnˈgenli] *adj* desgarbado, desmañado
ungentlemanly [ʌnˈdʒɛntəlmənli] *adj* poco caballeroso, descortés
ungird [ʌnˈgʌrd] *tr* desceñir
ungodly [ʌnˈgɑdli] *adj* impío, irreligioso; (*dreadful*) (coll) atroz
ungracious [ʌnˈgreʃəs] *adj* descortés; desagradable
ungrammatical [ˌʌngrəˈmætɪkəl] *adj* ingramatical
ungrateful [ʌnˈgretfəl] *adj* ingrato, desagradecido
ungrudgingly [ʌnˈgrʌdʒɪŋli] *adj* de buena gana, sin quejarse
unguarded [ʌnˈgɑrdɪd] *adj* indefenso; descuidado; (*moment*) de inadvertencia
unguent [ˈʌŋgwənt] *s* ungüento
unhandy [ʌnˈhændi] *adj* inmanejable; (*awkward*) desmañado
unhappiness [ʌnˈhæpɪnɪs] *s* infelicidad
unhap•py [ʌnˈhæpi] *adj* (*comp* -pier; *super* -piest) infeliz; (*unlucky*) desgraciado; (*fateful*) aciago
unharmed [ʌnˈhɑrmd] *adj* indemne
unharmonious [ˌʌnhɑrˈmoni•əs] *adj* inarmónico
unharness [ʌnˈhɑrnɪs] *tr* desenjaezar, desguarnecer; desenganchar
unhealthy [ʌnˈhɛlθi] *adj* malsano
unheard-of [ʌnˈhɑrd,ɑv] *adj* inaudito
unhinge [ʌnˈhɪndʒ] *tr* desgonzar; (fig) desequilibrar, trastornar
unhitch [ʌnˈhɪtʃ] *tr* desenganchar
unho•ly [ʌnˈholi] *adj* (*comp* -lier; *super* -liest) impío, malo, profano
unhook [ʌnˈhʊk] *tr* desabrochar; desenganchar; (*to take down from a hook*) descolgar

unhoped-for [ʌnˈhopt,fɔr] *adj* inesperado, no esperado
unhorse [ʌnˈhɔrs] *tr* desarzonar
unhurt [ʌnˈhʌrt] *adj* incólume, ileso
unicorn [ˈjuni,kɔrn] *s* unicornio
unidentified flying object (UFO) *s* objeto volante no identificado (ovni)
unification [ˌjunɪfɪˈkeʃən] *s* unificación
uniform [ˈjuni,fɔrm] *adj & s* uniforme *m* ‖ *tr* uniformar
uniformi•ty [ˌjuniˈfɔrmɪti] *s* (*pl* -ties) uniformidad
uni•fy [ˈjuni,faɪ] *v* (*pret & pp* -fied) *tr* unificar
unilateral [ˌjuniˈlætərəl] *adj* unilateral
unimpeachable [ˌʌnɪmˈpitʃəbəl] *adj* irrecusable, intachable
unimportant [ˌʌnɪmˈpɔrtənt] *adj* poco importante; intrascendente
uninhabited [ˌʌnɪnˈhæbɪtɪd] *adj* inhabitado
uninspired [ˌʌnɪnˈspaɪrd] *adj* sin inspiración; aburrido, fastidioso
unintelligent [ˌʌnɪnˈtɛlɪdʒənt] *adj* ininteligente
unintelligible [ˌʌnɪnˈtɛlɪdʒɪbəl] *adj* ininteligible
uninterested [ʌnˈɪntrɪstɪd] o [ʌnˈɪntə,rɛstɪd] *adj* desinteresado
uninteresting [ʌnˈɪntə,rɛstɪŋ] *adj* poco interesante
uninterrupted [ˌʌnɪntəˈrʌptɪd] *adj* ininterrumpido
union [ˈjunjən] *s* unión; (*organization of workmen*) gremio obrero, sindicato; unión matrimonial
unionize [ˈjunjə,naɪz] *tr* agremiar ‖ *intr* agremiarse
union shop *s* taller *m* de obreros agremiados
union suit *s* traje *m* interior de una sola pieza
unique [juˈnik] *adj* único
unison [ˈjunisən] *s* unisonancia; in unison (with) al unísono (de)
unit [ˈjunɪt] *adj* unitario ‖ *s* unidad; (mach & elec) grupo
unite [juˈnaɪt] *tr* unir ‖ *intr* unirse
united [juˈnaɪtɪd] *adj* unido
United Kingdom *s* Reino Unido
United Nations *spl* Naciones Unidas
United States *adj* estadounidense ‖ the United States *s* los Estados Unidos *mpl*; Estados Unidos *msg*
uni•ty [ˈjunɪti] *s* (*pl* -ties) unidad
univ. *abbr* universal, university
universal [ˌjuniˈvʌrsəl] *adj* universal
universal joint *s* cardán *m*, junta universal
universal product code (UPC) *s* código universal de producto
universe [ˈjuni,vʌrs] *s* universo
universi•ty [ˌjuniˈvʌrsɪti] *adj* universitario ‖ *s* (*pl* -ties) universidad
unjust [ʌnˈdʒʌst] *adj* injusto
unjustified [ʌnˈdʒʌstɪ,faɪd] *adj* injustificado
unkempt [ʌnˈkɛmpt] *adj* despeinado
unkind [ʌnˈkaɪnd] *adj* poco amable; duro, despiadado
unknowable [ʌnˈno•əbəl] *adj* inconocible, insabible

un
un

unknowingly [ʌnˈnoˑɪŋli] *adv* desconocidamente, sin saberlo

unknown [ʌnˈnon] *adj* desconocido, ignoto, incógnito ‖ *s* desconocido; (math) incógnita

unknown quantity *s* (math & fig) incógnita

unknown soldier *s* soldado desconocido

unlace [ʌnˈles] *tr* desenlazar; desatar (*los cordones del zapato*)

unlatch [ʌnˈlætʃ] *tr* abrir levantando el picaporte

unlawful [ʌnˈlɔfəl] *adj* ilegal

unleaded gasoline [ʌnˈlɛdɪd] *s* gasolina sin plomo

unleash [ʌnˈliʃ] *tr* destraillar; soltar, desencadenar

unleavened [ʌnˈlɛvənd] *adj* ázimo

unless [ʌnˈlɛs] *conj* a menos que, a no ser que

unlettered [ʌnˈlɛtərd] *adj* iletrado, indocto; sin rotular; (*illiterate*) analfabeto

unlike [ʌnˈlaɪk] *adj* desemejante; desemejante de; (*poles of a magnet*) (elec) de nombres contrarios; (elec) de signo contrario ‖ *prep* a diferencia de

unlikely [ʌnˈlaɪkli] *adj* improbable

unlimber [ʌnˈlɪmbər] *tr* preparar para la acción ‖ *intr* prepararse para la acción

unlined [ʌnˈlaɪnd] *adj* (*coat*) sin forro; (*paper*) sin rayar; (*face*) sin arrugas

unload [ʌnˈlod] *tr* descargar; (coll) deshacerse de ‖ *intr* descargar

unloading [ʌnˈlodɪŋ] *s* descarga, descargue *m*

unlock [ʌnˈlɑk] *tr* abrir (*p.ej.*, *una puerta*); (typ) desapretar

unloose [ʌnˈlus] *tr* aflojar, soltar, desatar

unloved [ʌnˈlʌvd] *adj* desamado

unlovely [ʌnˈlʌvli] *adj* desgraciado

unluck•y [ʌnˈlʌki] *adj* (*comp* **-ier**; *super* **-iest**) desgraciado, desdichado; aciago, nefasto; de mala suerte; **to be unlucky** quedar mal parado

un•make [ʌnˈmek] *v* (*pret & pp* **-made** [ˈmed]) *tr* deshacer; destruir

unmanageable [ʌnˈmænɪdʒəbəl] *adj* inmanejable

unmanly [ʌnˈmænli] *adj* afeminado; bajo, cobarde

unmannerly [ʌnˈmænərli] *adj* descortés, malcriado

unmarketable [ʌnˈmɑrkɪtəbəl] *adj* incomerciable

unmarriageable [ʌnˈmærɪdʒəbəl] *adj* incasable

unmarried [ʌnˈmærid] *adj* soltero

unmask [ʌnˈmæsk] *tr* desenmascarar ‖ *intr* desenmascararse

unmatchable [ʌnˈmætʃəbəl] *adj* incomparable, sin igual; (*price*) incompetible

unmerciful [ʌnˈmʌrsɪfəl] *adj* despiadado, inclemente

unmesh [ʌnˈmɛʃ] *tr* desengranar ‖ *intr* desengranarse

unmindful [ʌnˈmaɪndfəl] *adj* desatento, descuidado; **to be unmindful of** olvidar, no pensar en

unmistakable [ˌʌnmɪsˈtekəbəl] *adj* inequívoco, inconfundible

unmixed [ʌnˈmɪkst] *adj* puro, sin mezcla

unmoor [ʌnˈmʊr] *tr* desamarrar (*un buque*); desaferrar (*las áncoras*)

unmotivated [ˌʌnˈmotɪˌvetɪd] *adj* inmotivado

unmoved [ʌnˈmuvd] *adj* fijo, inmoto; impasible

unmuzzle [ˌʌnˈmʌzəl] *tr* desbozalar

unnatural [ʌnˈnætʃərəl] *adj* innatural; (*artificial, forced*) afectado; anormal; inhumano

unnecessary [ʌnˈnɛsəˌsɛri] *adj* innecessario

unnerve [ʌnˈnʌrv] *tr* acobardar, trastornar

unnoticeable [ʌnˈnotɪsəbəl] *adj* imperceptible

unnoticed [ʌnˈnotɪst] *adj* inadvertido

unobliging [ˌʌnəˈblaɪdʒɪŋ] *adj* poco servicial, poco amable

unobserved [ˌʌnəbˈzʌrvd] *adj* inadvertido, sin ser visto

unobtainable [ˌʌnəbˈtenəbəl] *adj* inencontrable, inasequible

unobtrusive [ˌʌnəbˈtrusɪv] *adj* discreto, reservado

unoccupied [ʌnˈɑkjəˌpaɪd] *adj* libre, vacante; (*not busy*) desocupado

unofficial [ˌʌnəˈfɪʃəl] *adj* extraoficial, oficioso

unopened [ʌnˈopənd] *adj* sin abrir; (*book*) no cortado

unorthodox [ʌnˈɔrθəˌdɑks] *adj* inortodoxo

unpack [ʌnˈpæk] *tr* desembalar, desempaquetar

unpalatable [ʌnˈpælətəbəl] *adj* desabrido, ingustable

unparalleled [ʌnˈpærəˌlɛld] *adj* incomparable, sin par, sin igual

unpardonable [ʌnˈpɑrdənəbəl] *adj* imperdonable

unpatriotic [ˌʌnpetrɪˈɑtɪk] o [ˌʌnpætrɪˈɑtɪk] *adj* antipatriótico

unperceived [ˌʌnpərˈsivd] *adj* inadvertido

unperturbable [ˌʌnpərˈtʌrbəbəl] *adj* infracto, imperturbable

unpleasant [ʌnˈplɛzənt] *adj* antipático, desagradable; sangrigordo, sangripesado; bofe (CAm)

unpopular [ʌnˈpɑpjələr] *adj* impopular

unpopularity [ʌnˌpɑpjəˈlæriti] *s* impopularidad

unprecedented [ʌnˈprɛsɪˌdɛntɪd] *adj* sin precedente, inaudito

unprejudiced [ʌnˈprɛdʒədɪst] *adj* sin prejuicios, imparcial

unpremeditated [ˌʌnprɪˈmɛdɪˌtetɪd] *adj* impremeditado

unprepared [ˌʌnprɪˈpɛrd] *adj* desprevenido; falto de preparación

unprepossessing [ˌʌnpripəˈzɛsɪŋ] *adj* poco atrayente

unpresentable [ˌʌnprɪˈzɛntəbəl] *adj* impresentable

unpretentious [ˌʌnprɪˈtɛnʃəs] *adj* modesto, sencillo

unprincipled [ʌnˈprɪnsɪpəld] *adj* sin principios, sin conciencia

unproductive [‚ʌnprə'dʌktɪv] *adj* improductivo

unprofitable [ʌn'prɑfɪtəbəl] *adj* no provechoso, inútil

unpronounceable [‚ʌnprə'naʊnsəbəl] *adj* impronunciable

unpropitious [‚ʌnprə'pɪʃəs] *adj* impropicio

unpublished [ʌn'pʌblɪʃt] *adj* inédito

unpunished [ʌn'pʌnɪʃt] *adj* impune

unpurchasable [ʌn'pʌrtʃəsəbəl] *adj* incomprable

unquenchable [ʌn'kwɛntʃəbəl] *adj* inextinguible

unquestionable [ʌn'kwɛstʃənəbəl] *adj* incuestionable

unravel [ʌn'rævəl] *v* (*pret & pp* **-eled** o **-elled**; *ger* **-eling** o **-elling**) *tr* deshebrar; desenredar, desenmarañar ‖ *intr* desenredarse, desenmarañarse

unreachable [ʌn'ritʃəbəl] *adj* inalcanzable

unreal [ʌn'ri•əl] *adj* irreal

unreali•ty [‚ʌnri‚ælɪti] *s* (*pl* **-ties**) irrealidad

unreasonable [ʌn'rizənəbəl] *adj* irrazonable, desrazonable

unrecognizable [ʌn'rɛkəg‚naɪzəbəl] *adj* irreconocible

unreel [ʌn'ril] *tr* desenrollar ‖ *intr* desenrollarse

unrefined [‚ʌnrɪ‚faɪnd] *adj* no refinado, impuro; grosero, rudo, tosco

unrelenting [‚ʌnrɪ'lɛntɪŋ] *adj* inexorable, inflexible, implacable

unreliable [‚ʌnrɪ'laɪ•əbəl] *adj* indigno de confianza, informal

unremitting [‚ʌnrɪ'mɪtɪŋ] *adj* constante, incesante; infatigable

unrenewable [‚ʌnrɪ'nju•əbəl] o [‚ʌnrɪ'nu•əbəl] *adj* irrenovable; (com) improrrogable

unrented [ʌn'rɛntɪd] *adj* desalquilado

unrepentant [‚ʌnrɪ'pɛntənt] *adj* impenitente

unrequited love [‚ʌnrɪ'kwaɪtɪd] *s* amor no correspondido

unresponsive [‚ʌnrɪ'spɑnsɪv] *adj* insensible, frío, desinteresado

unrest [ʌn'rɛst] *s* intranquilidad, inquietud; alboroto, desorden *m*

un•rig [ʌn'rɪg] *v* (*pret & pp* **-rigged**; *ger* **-rigging**) *tr* (naut) desaparejar

unrighteous [ʌn'raɪtʃəs] *adj* injusto, malvado, vicioso

unripe [ʌn'raɪp] *adj* inmaturo, verde; prematuro, precoz

unrivaled o **unrivalled** [ʌn'raɪvəld] *adj* sin rival, sin par

unroll [ʌn'rol] *tr* desenrollar, desplegar

unromantic [‚ʌnro'mæntɪk] *adj* poco romántico

unruffled [ʌn'rʌfəld] *adj* tranquilo, sereno

unruly [ʌn'ruli] *adj* ingobernable, indómito, revoltoso

unsaddle [ʌn'sædəl] *tr* desensillar (*un caballo*); desarzonar (*al jinete*)

unsafe [ʌn'sef] *adj* inseguro, peligroso

unsaid [ʌn'sɛd] *adj* callado, no dicho

unsalable [ʌn'seləbəl] *adj* invendible

unsanitary [ʌn'sænɪ‚tɛri] *adj* antihigiénico, insalubre

unsatisfactory [ʌn‚sætɪs'fæktəri] *adj* insatisfactorio, poco satisfactorio

unsatisfied [ʌn'sætɪs‚faɪd] *adj* insatisfecho

unsavory [ʌn'sevəri] *adj* desabrido; (fig) infame, deshonroso

unscathed [ʌn'skeðd] *adj* ileso, sano y salvo

unscientific [‚ʌnsaɪ•ən'tɪfɪk] *adj* anticientífico

unscrew [ʌn'skru] *tr* destornillar ‖ *intr* destornillarse

unscrupulous [ʌn'skrupjələs] *adj* inescrupuloso

unseal [ʌn'sil] *tr* desellar; (fig) abrir

unseasonable [ʌn'sizənəbəl] *adj* intempestivo, inoportuno

unseaworthy [ʌn'si‚wʌrði] *adj* innavegable

unseemly [ʌn'simli] *adj* impropio, indecoroso, indigno

unseen [ʌn'sin] *adj* invisible, oculto

unselfish [ʌn'sɛlfɪʃ] *adj* desinteresado, generoso, altruísta

unsettled [ʌn'sɛtəld] *adj* inhabitado, despoblado; sin residencia fija; indeciso; descompuesto; (*bills*) por pagar

unshackle [ʌn'ʃækəl] *tr* desherrar, desencadenar

unshaken [ʌn'ʃekən] *adj* imperturbado

unshapely [ʌn'ʃepli] *adj* desproporcionado, mal formado

unshatterable [ʌn'ʃætərəbəl] *adj* inastillable

unshaven [ʌn'ʃevən] *adj* sin afeitar

unsheathe [ʌn'ʃið] *tr* desenvainar

unshod [ʌn'ʃɑd] *adj* descalzo; (*horse*) desherrado

unshrinkable [ʌn'ʃrɪŋkəbəl] *adj* inencogible

unsightly [ʌn'saɪtli] *adj* feo, de aspecto malo, repugnante

unsinkable [ʌn'sɪŋkəbəl] *adj* insumergible

unskilled [ʌn'skɪld] *adj* inexperto

unskilled laborer *s* bracero, peón *m*

unskillful [ʌn'skɪlfəl] *adj* desmañado

unsnarl [ʌn'snɑrl] *tr* desenredar

unsociable [ʌn'soʃəbəl] *adj* insociable, huraño

unsold [ʌn'sold] *adj* invendido

unsolder [ʌn'sɑdər] *tr* desoldar; (fig) desunir, separar

unsophisticated [‚ʌnsə'fɪstɪ‚ketɪd] *adj* ingenuo, natural, sencillo

unsound [ʌn'saʊnd] *adj* poco firme; falso, erróneo; (*decayed*) podrido; (*sleep*) ligero

unsown [ʌn'son] *adj* yermo, no sembrado

unspeakable [ʌn'spikəbəl] *adj* indecible, inefable; (*atrocious, infamous*) incalificable

unsportsmanlike [ʌn'sportsmən‚laɪk] *adj* antideportivo

unstable [ʌn'stebəl] *adj* inestable

unsteady [ʌn'stɛdi] *adj* inseguro, inestable; irresoluto, inconstante; poco juicioso

unstinted [ʌn'stɪntɪd] *adj* no escatimado, generoso, liberal

unstitch [ʌn'stɪtʃ] *tr* descoser

un•stop [ʌn'stɑp] *v* (*pret & pp* **-stopped**; *ger* **-stopping**) *tr* destaponar

unstressed [ʌn'strɛst] *adj* sin énfasis; (*syllable*) inacentuado

un
un

unstrung [ʌn'strʌŋ] *adj* nervioso, trastornado

unsuccessful [,ʌnsək'sɛsfəl] *adj* (*person*) desairado; (*undertaking*) impróspero; **to be unsuccessful** no tener éxito

unsuitable [ʌn'sutəbəl] o [ʌn'sjutəbəl] *adj* inadecuado, inconveniente

unsurpassable [,ʌnsər'pæsəbəl] *adj* insuperable

unsuspected [,ʌnsəs'pɛktɪd] *adj* insospechado

unswerving [ʌn'swʌrvɪŋ] *adj* firme, inmutable, resoluto

unsymmetrical [,ʌnsɪ'mɛtrɪkəl] *adj* asimétrico, disimétrico

unsympathetic [,ʌnsɪmpə'θɛtɪk] *adj* incompasivo, indiferente

unsystematic(al) [,ʌnsɪstə'mætɪk(əl)] *adj* poco sistemático, sin sistema

untactful [ʌn'tæktfəl] *adj* indiscreto, falto de tacto

untamed [ʌn'temd] *adj* indomado, bravío

untangle [ʌn'tæŋgəl] *tr* desenredar, desenmarañar

unteachable [ʌn'titʃəbəl] *adj* indócil

untenable [ʌn'tɛnəbəl] *adj* insostenible

unthankful [ʌn'θæŋkfəl] *adj* ingrato, desagradecido

unthinkable [ʌn'θɪŋkəbəl] *adj* impensable

unthinking [ʌn'θɪŋkɪŋ] *adj* irreflexivo, desatento; irracional, instintivo

untidy [ʌn'taɪdi] *adj* desaseado, desaliñado; descachalandrado

un·tie [ʌn'taɪ] *v* (*pret & pp* **-tied;** *ger* **-tying**) *tr* desatar; deshacer (*un nudo, una cuerda*); (*to free from restraint*) soltar; resolver ‖ *intr* desatarse

until [ʌn'tɪl] *prep* hasta ‖ *conj* hasta que; **to wait until** aguardar a que, esperar a que

untillable [ʌn'tɪləbəl] *adj* incultivable

untimely [ʌn'taɪmli] *adj* intempestivo

untiring [ʌn'taɪrɪŋ] *adj* incansable

untold [ʌn'told] *adj* nunca dicho; (*uncounted*) innumerable, incalculable

untouchable [ʌn'tʌtʃəbəl] *adj* intangible ‖ *s* intocable *mf*

untouched [ʌn'tʌtʃt] *adj* intacto; íntegro; impasible; no mencionado

untoward [ʌn'tord] *adj* desfavorable; indecoroso

untrammeled o **untrammelled** [ʌn'træməld] *adj* libre, sin trabas

untried [ʌn'traɪd] *adj* no probado, no ensayado

untroubled [ʌn'trʌbləd] *adj* tranquilo, sosegado

untrue [ʌn'tru] *adj* falso; infiel

untrustworthy [ʌn'trʌst,wʌrði] *adj* indigno de confianza

untruth [ʌn'truθ] *s* falsedad, mentira

untruthful [ʌn'truθfəl] *adj* falso, mentiroso

untwist [ʌn'twɪst] *tr* destorcer ‖ *intr* destorcerse

unused [ʌn'juzd] *adj* inutilizado, no usado; nuevo; **unused to** [ʌn'juzdtʊ] o [ʌn'justʊ] *adj* no acostumbrado a

unusual [ʌn'juʒʊ·əl] *adj* inusual, insólito

unutterable [ʌn'ʌtərəbəl] *adj* indecible, inexpresable

unvanquished [ʌn'væŋkwɪʃt] *adj* invicto

unvarnished [ʌn'vɑrnɪʃt] *adj* sin barnizar; (fig) sencillo, sin adornos

unveil [ʌn'vel] *tr* quitar el velo a; descubrir, develar, inaugurar, (*una estatua*) ‖ *intr* quitarse el velo

unveiling [ʌn'velɪŋ] *s* develación, inauguración

unventilated [ʌn'vɛntɪ,letɪd] *adj* sin ventilar

unvoice [ʌn'vɔɪs] *tr* afonizar, ensordecer ‖ *intr* afonizarse, ensordecerse

unwanted [ʌn'wɑntɪd] *adj* indeseado

unwarranted [ʌn'wɑrəntɪd] *adj* injustificado; no autorizado; sin garantía

unwary [ʌn'wɛri] *adj* incauto, imprudente

unwavering [ʌn'wevərɪŋ] *adj* firme, determinado, resuelto

unwelcome [ʌn'wɛlkəm] *adj* mal acogido; importuno, molesto

unwell [ʌn'wɛl] *adj* indispuesto, enfermo; (coll) menstruante

unwholesome [ʌn'holsəm] *adj* insalubre

unwieldy [ʌn'wildi] *adj* inmanejable, abultado, pesado

unwilling [ʌn'wɪlɪŋ] *adj* desinclinado, maldispuesto, renuente

unwillingly [ʌn'wɪlɪŋli] *adv* de mala gana

un·wind [ʌn'waɪnd] *v* (*pret & pp* **-wound** ['waʊnd]) *tr* desenvolver; (*rewind*) rebobinar ‖ *intr* desenvolverse; distenderse (*el muelle del reloj*)

unwise [ʌn'waɪz] *adj* indiscreto, malaconsejado

unwished-for [ʌn'wɪʃt,fɔr] *adj* indeseado

unwitting [ʌn'wɪtɪŋ] *adj* inadvertido, inconsciente

unwonted [ʌn'wɑntɪd] *adj* poco común, raro, insólito

unworldly [ʌn'wʌrldi] *adj* no terrenal, no mundano, espiritual

unworthy [ʌn'wʌrði] *adj* indigno, desmerecedor

un·wrap [ʌn'ræp] *v* (*pret & pp* **-wrapped;** *ger* **wrapping**) *tr* desenvolver, desempapelar

unwrinkle [ʌn'rɪŋkəl] *tr* desarrugar ‖ *intr* desarrugarse

unwritten [ʌn'rɪtən] *adj* no escrito; (*blank*) en blanco; oral

unyielding [ʌn'jildɪŋ] *adj* firme, inflexible; terco, reacio

unyoke [ʌn'jok] *tr* desuncir

up [ʌp] *adj* ascendente; alto, elevado; derecho, en pie; terminado; cumplido; levantado de la cama; **to be up and about** estar levantado (*el que estaba enfermo*) ‖ *s* subida; **ups and downs** altibajos, vicisitudes ‖ *adv* arriba; en el aire; hacia arriba; al norte; **to be up** estar levantado; vencer (*un plazo*); **to be up in arms** estar sobre las armas; protestar vehementemente; **to be up to a person** tocarle a una persona; **to get up** levantarse; **to go up** subir; **to keep up** mantener; continuar; mantenerse firme; **to keep up with** correr parejas con; **up above**

allá arriba; **up against it** (slang) en apuros; **up to** hasta; (*capable of*) a la altura de; (*informed of*) al corriente de; (*scheming*) armando, tramando; **what is up?** ¿qué pasa? ‖ *prep* subiendo; **up the river** río arriba; **up the street** calle arriba

up-and-coming [ˈʌpənˈkʌmɪŋ] *adj* (coll) prometedor

up-and-doing [ˈʌpənˈdu•ɪŋ] *adj* (coll) emprendedor

up-and-up [ˈʌpənˈʌp] *s*—**on the up-and-up** (coll) mejorándose; (coll) abiertamente, sin dolo

up•braid' *tr* regañar, reprender

upbringing [ˈʌpˌbrɪŋɪŋ] *s* educación, crianza

UPC *abbr* **universal product code**

up'coun'try *adv* (coll) hacia el interior, tierra adentro ‖ *s* (coll) interior *m* del país

up•date' *tr* poner al día

upheaval [ʌpˈhivəl] *s* trastorno, cataclismo

up'hill' *adj* ascendente; arduo, difícil, penoso ‖ **up'hill'** *adv* cuesta arriba

up•hold' *v* (*pret* & *pp* **-held**) *tr* levantar; apoyar, sostener; defender

upholster [ʌpˈholstər] *tr* tapizar

upholsterer [ʌpˈholstərər] *s* tapicero

upholster•y [ʌpˈholstəri] *s* (*pl* **-ies**) tapicería

up'keep' *s* conservación, manutención; gastos de conservación, gastos de entretenimiento

upland [ˈʌplənd] o [ˈʌplænd] *adj* alto, elevado ‖ *s* tierra alta, terreno elevado

up'lift' *s* (*lifting*) elevación, levantamiento; mejora social; (*moral or spiritual improvement*) edificación ‖ **up•lift'** *tr* elevar, levantar; edificar

upon [əˈpɑn] *prep* en, sobre, encima de; **upon** + *ger* al + *inf*, p.ej., **upon arriving** al llegar; **upon my word!** ¡por mi palabra!

upper [ˈʌpər] *adj* alto, superior; (*country*) interior; (*clothing*) exterior ‖ *s* (*of shoe*) pala; **on one's uppers** con las suelas gastadas; (coll) andrajoso, pobre, sin blanca

upper berth *s* litera alta, cama alta

upper case *s* (typ) caja alta

upper classes *spl* altas clases

upper hand *s* dominio, ventaja; **to have the upper hand** tener vara alta

upper middle class *s* alta burguesía

up'per•most' *adj* (el) más alto; (el) principal ‖ *adv* en lo más alto primero, en primer lugar

uppish [ˈʌpɪʃ] *adj* (coll) copetudo, arrogante

up•raise' *tr* levantar

up'right' *adj* derecho, vertical; probo, recto ‖ *adv* verticalmente ‖ *s* montante *m*

uprising [ʌpˈraɪzɪŋ] [ˈʌpˌraɪzɪŋ] *s* insurrección, levantamiento

up'roar' *s* alboroto, conmoción, tumulto

uproarious [ʌpˈrorɪ•əs] *adj* tumultuoso; (*noisy*) ruidoso; (*funny*) muy cómico

up•root' *tr* desarraigar

up•set' o **up'set'** *adj* (*overturned*) volcado; trastornado; indispuesto ‖ **up'set'** *s* (*overturn*) vuelco; (*unexpected defeat*) contra-

tiempo; (*disturbance*) trastorno; (*illness*) indisposición, enfermedad ‖ **up•set'** *v* (*pret* & *pp* **-set**; *ger* **-setting**) *tr* volcar; trastornar; indisponer ‖ *intr* volcar

upset price *s* precio mínimo fijado en una subasta

upsetting [ʌpˈsɛtɪŋ] *adj* desconcertante

up'shot' *s* conclusión, resultado; esencia, quid *m*

up'side' *s* parte *f* superior, lado superior; **on the upside** (*said of prices*) subiendo

upside down *adv* alrevés, lo de arriba abajo, patas arriba; en confusión, revuelto; **to turn upside down** volcar; trastornar; volcarse; trastornarse

up'stage' *adj* situado al fondo de la escena; (coll) altanero, arrogante ‖ *adv* al fondo de la escena ‖ **up'stage'** *tr* (coll) mirar por encima del hombro, desairar

up'stairs' *adj* de arriba ‖ *adv* arriba ‖ *s* piso superior, pisos superiores

upstanding [ʌpˈstændɪŋ] *adj* derecho; gallardo; probo, recto

up'start' *adj* & *s* advenedizo

up'stream' *adv* aguas arriba, río arriba

up'stroke' *s* carrera ascendente

up'swing' *s* movimiento hacia arriba; mejora notable; **on the upswing** mejorando notablemente

up'-to-date' *adj* corriente; reciente, moderno; de última hora, de última moda

up'-to-the-min'ute *adj* al día, de actualidad

up'town' *adj* de la parte alta de la ciudad ‖ *adv* en la parte alta de la ciudad

up train *s* tren *m* ascendente

up'trend' *s* tendencia al alza

up'turn' *s* alza, subida, mejora

upturned [ʌpˈtʌrnd] *adj* revuelto; (*part of clothing*) arremangado; (*nose*) respingada

upward [ˈʌpwərd] *adj* ascendente ‖ *adv* hacia arriba; **upward of** más de

Ural [ˈjʊrəl] *adj* ural ‖ **Urals** *spl* Urales *mpl*

uranium [jʊˈrenɪ•əm] *s* uranio

urban [ˈʌrbən] *adj* urbano (*perteneciente a la ciudad*)

urbane [ʌrˈben] *adj* urbano (*atento, cortés*)

urban guerrilla *s* guerrillero urbano

urbanite [ˈʌrbə‚naɪt] *s* ciudadano

urbanity [ʌrˈbænɪti] *s* urbanidad

urbanize [ˈʌrbə‚naɪz] *tr* urbanizar

urchin [ˈʌrtʃɪn] *s* pilluelo, galopín *m*; patojo (CAm)

ure•thra [jʊˈriθrə] *s* (*pl* **-thras** o **-thrae** [θri]) uretra

urge [ʌrdʒ] *s* impulso, estímulo ‖ *tr* apremiar, impeler, estimular; pedir instantánedmente; (*to try to persuade*) instar ‖ *intr* instar

urgen•cy [ˈʌrdʒənsi] *s* (*pl* **-cies**) urgencia; instancia, apremio

urgent [ˈʌrdʒənt] *adj* urgente; apremiante

urinal [ˈjʊrɪnəl] *s* (*receptacle*) orinal *m*; (*place*) urinario

urinary [ˈjʊrɪ‚nɛri] *adj* urinario

urinate [ˈjʊrɪ‚net] *tr* orinar (*p.ej., sangre*) ‖ *intr* orinar, orinarse; (coll) hacer pipí

urine ['jʊrɪn] s orina, orines mpl; (coll) pipí m

urn [ʌrn] s (decorative vase) jarrón m; cafetera o tetera con grifo; (to hold ashes of the dead after cremation) urna

urology [jʊ'rɑlədʒi] s urología

Uruguay ['jʊrə,gwaɪ] s el Uruguay

Uruguayan [,jʊrə'gwaɪ•ən] adj & s uruguayo

us [ʌs] pron pers nos; nosotros; **to us** nos; a nosotros

U.S.A. abbr **United States of America, United States Army, Union of South Africa**

usable ['juzəbəl] adj aprovechable, utilizable

usage ['jusɪdʒ] o ['juzɪdʒ] s usanza; (e.g., of a language) uso

usage instructions spl modo de empleo

use [jus] s uso, empleo; utilidad; **in use** en uso; **out of use** desusado; **to be of no use** no servir para nada; **to have no use for** no necesitar; no servirse de; (coll) tener en poco; **to make use of** servirse de ‖ [juz] tr usar, emplear, servirse de; **to use badly** maltratar; **to use up** agotar, consumir ‖ intr (empléase sólo en el pretérito y se traduce al español con el pretérito imperfecto o el verbo **soler**), p.ej., **I used to go out for a walk every evening** salía de paseo todas las tardes o solía salir de paseo todas las tardes

used [juzd] adj (customarily employed; worn, partly worn-out; accustomed) usado; **used to** ['juzdtʊ] o ['justʊ] acostumbrado a

useful ['jusfəl] adj útil

usefulness ['jusfəlnɪs] s utilidad

useless ['juslɪs] adj inservible, inútil

user ['juzər] s usuario

usher ['ʌʃər] s (in a theater) acomodador m; (doorkeeper) ujier m, portero ‖ tr acomodar; **to usher in** anunciar, introducir

U.S.S.R. abbr **Union of Soviet Socialist Republics**

usual ['juʒʊ•əl] adj usual, acostumbrado; **as usual** como de costumbre

usually ['juʒʊ•əli] adj usualmente, de ordinario

usurp [ju'zʌrp] tr usurpar

usu•ry ['juʒəri] s (pl -ries) usura

utensil [ju'tɛnsɪl] s utensilio; **utensils** corotos mpl

uter•us ['jutərəs] s (pl -i [,aɪ]); útero

utilitarian [,jutɪlɪ'tɛrɪ•ən] adj utilitario

utili•ty [ju'tɪlɪti] s (pl -ties) utilidad; empresa de servicio público

utilize ['jutɪ,laɪz] tr utilizar

utmost ['ʌt,most] adj sumo, extremo, último; más grande, mayor posible; más lejano ‖ s— **the utmost** lo sumo, lo mayor, lo más; **to the utmost** a lo sumo, a más no poder; **to do one's utmost** hacer todo lo posible

utopia [ju'topɪ•ə] s utopía

utopian [ju'topɪ•ən] adj utópico, utopista ‖ s utopista mf

utter ['ʌtər] adj total, absoluto ‖ tr proferir, pronunciar; dar (un suspiro)

utterance ['ʌtərəns] s expresión, pronunciación; declaración

utterly ['ʌtərli] adj completamente, totalmente, absolutamente

uxoricide [ʌk'sɔrɪ,saɪd] s (husband) uxoricida m; (act) uxoricidio

uxorious [ʌk'sɔrɪ•əs] adj uxorio

V

V, v [vi] vigésima segunda letra del alfabeto inglés

v. abbr **verb, verse, versus, vide** (Lat) **see, voice, volt, volume**

V. abbr **Venerable, Vice, Viscount, Volunteer**

vacan•cy ['vekənsi] s (pl -cies) (emptiness; gap, opening) vacío; (unfilled position or job) vacancia, vacante f, vacío; piso vacante; cargo vacante

vacant ['vekənt] adj (empty) vacío; (having no occupant; untenanted) vacante; (expression, look) vago; distraído

vacate ['veket] tr dejar vacante; anular, invalidar, revocar ‖ intr (to move out) desalojar; (coll) irse, marcharse

vacation [ve'keʃən] s vacaciones; **on vacation** de vacaciones ‖ intr tomar vacaciones

vacationist [ve'keʃənɪst] s vacacionista mf

vacation with pay s vacaciones retribuídas

vaccinate ['væksɪ,net] tr vacunar

vaccination [,væksɪ'neʃən] s vacunación

vaccine [væk'sin] s vacuna

vacillate ['væsɪ,let] intr vacilar

vacillating ['væsɪ,letɪŋ] adj vacilante

vacui•ty [væ'kju•ɪti] s (pl -ties) vacuidad

vacu•um ['vækju•əm] s (pl -ums o -a [ə]) vacío ‖ tr (coll) limpiar

vacuum cleaner s aspirador m de polvo

vacuum tank s (aut) aspirador m de gasolina, nodriza

vacuum tube s tubo de vacío

vagabond ['vægə,bɑnd] adj & s vagabundo

vagar•y [və'gɛri] s (pl -ies) capricho

vagina [və'dʒaɪnə] s vagina

vagran•cy ['vegrənsi] s (pl -cies) vagabundaje m

vagrant ['vegrənt] adj & s vagabundo

vague [veg] adj vago; impreciso

vain [ven] adj vano; (conceited) vanidoso; **in vain** en vano

vainglorious [ven'glorɪ•əs] adj vanaglorioso

valance ['væləns] s (across the top of a window) guardamalleta; (drapery) doselera

vale [vel] *s* valle *m*

valedictorian [,vælɪdɪk'torɪ•ən] *s* alumno que pronuncia el discurso de despedida al fin del curso

valedicto•ry [,vælɪ'dɪktəri] *adj* de despedida ‖ *s* (*pl* **-ries**) discurso de despedida

valence ['veləns] *s* (chem) valencia

valentine ['vælən,taɪn] *s* tarjeta amorosa o jocosa del día de San Valentín

Valentine Day *s* día *m* de los corazones, día de los enamorados (*14 de febrero*)

vale of tears *s* valle *m* de lágrimas

valet ['vælɪt] o ['væle] *s* ayuda *m*, paje *m*

valiant ['væljənt] *adj* valiente, valeroso

valid ['vælɪd] *adj* válido, valedero

validate ['vælɪ,det] *tr* validar; (sport) homologar

validation [,vælɪ'defən] *s* validación; (sport) homologación

validi•ty [və'lɪdɪti] *s* (*pl* **-ties**) validez *f*

valise [və'lis] *s* maleta

valley ['væli] *s* valle *m*; (*of roof*) lima hoya

valor ['vælər] *s* valor *m*, ánimo

valorous ['vælərəs] *adj* valeroso

valuable ['vælju•əbəl] o ['væljəbəl] *adj* (*having monetary value*) valioso; (*highly thought of*) estimable ‖ **valuables** *spl* alhajas, objetos de valor

value ['vælju] *s* valor *m*; (*return for one's money in a purchase*) (coll) adquisición, inversión, p.ej., **an excellent value** una adquisición excelente ‖ *tr* (*to think highly of*) estimar; (*to set a price for*) valorar, valuar

val′ue-add′ed tax *s* impuesto sobre el valor añadido, impuesto al valor agregado

valueless ['væljulɪs] *adj* sin valor

valve [vælv] *s* válvula; (*of mollusk*) valva; (mus) llava *f*

valve cap *s* capuchón *m*

valve gears *spl* distribución

valve′-in-head′ engine *s* motor *m* con válvulas en cabeza

valve lifter ['lɪftər] *s* levantaválvulas *m*

valve seat *s* asiento de válvula

valve spring *s* muelle *m* de válvula

valve stem *s* vástago de válvula

vamp [væmp] *s* (*of shoe*) empella; (*patchwork*) remiendo; (*woman who preys on men*) (slang) mujer *f* fatal, vampiresa ‖ *tr* poner empella a (*un zapato*); remendar; (*to concoct*) componer, enmendar; (jazz) improvisar (*un acompañamiento*); (slang) seducir (*una mujer mundana a un hombre*)

vampire ['væmpaɪr] *s* vampiro; (*woman who preys on men*) mujer *f* fatal, vampiresa

van [væn] *s* carro de carga, camión *m* de mudanzas; (mil & fig) vanguardia; (Brit) furgón *m* de equipajes

vanadium [və'nedɪ•əm] *s* vanadio

vandal ['vændəl] *adj & s* vándalo ‖ **Vandal** *adj & s* vándalo

vandalism ['vændə,lɪzəm] *s* vandalismo

vane [ven] *s* (*weathervane*) veleta; (*of windmill*) aspa; (*of propeller or turbine*) paleta; (*of feather*) barba

vanguard ['væn,gɑrd] *s* (mil & fig) vanguardia; **in the vanguard** a vanguardia

vanilla [və'nɪlə] *s* vainilla

vanish ['vænɪʃ] *intr* desvanecerse

vanishing cream ['vænɪʃɪŋ] *s* crema desvanecedora

vani•ty ['vænɪti] *s* (*pl* **-ties**) vanidad; (*dressing table*) tocador *m*; (*vanity case*) estuche *m* de afeites

vanity case *s* estuche *m* de afeites, neceser *m* de belleza

vanquish ['væŋkwɪʃ] *tr* vencer, rendir

vantage ground ['væntɪdʒ] *s* posición ventajosa

vapid ['væpɪd] *adj* insípido

vapor ['vepər] *s* vapor *m* (*el visible; exhalación, vaho, niebla, etc.*)

vaporize ['vepə,raɪz] *tr* vaporizar ‖ *intr* vaporizarse

vaporous ['vepərəs] *adj* vaporoso

vapor trail *s* (aer) estela de vapor, rastro de condensación

var. *abbr* **variant**

variable ['vɛrɪ•əbəl] *adj & s* variable *f*

variance ['vɛrɪ•əns] *s* diferencia, variación; **at variance with** en desacuerdo con

variant ['vɛrɪ•ənt] *adj & s* variante *f*

variation [,vɛrɪ'eʃən] *s* variación

varicose ['vɛrɪ,kos] *adj* varicoso

varicose vein *s* (pathol) varice *f*

varied ['vɛrɪd] *adj* variado, vario

variegated ['vɛrɪ•ə,getɪd] o ['vɛrɪ,getɪd] *adj* abigarrado, variado

varie•ty [və'raɪ•ɪti] *s* (*pl* **-ties**) variedad

variety show *s* variedades

variola [və'raɪ•ələ] *s* (pathol) viruela

various ['vɛrɪ•əs] *adj* (*several; of different kinds*) varios; (*many-sided; many-colored*) vario

varnish ['vɑrnɪʃ] *s* barniz *m*; (fig) capa, apariencia ‖ *tr* barnizar; (fig) dar apariencia falsa a

varsi•ty ['vɑrsɪti] *adj* (sport) universitario ‖ *s* (*pl* **-ties**) (sport) equipo principal de la universidad

var•y ['vɛri] *v* (*pret & pp* **-ied**) *tr & intr* variar

vase [ves] o [vez] *s* florero, jarrón *m*

Vaseline ['væsə,lin] *s* (trademark) vaselina

vassal ['væsəl] *adj & s* vasallo

vast [væst] o [vɑst] *adj* vasto

vastly ['væstli] *adv* enormemente

vastness ['væstnɪs] *s* vastedad

vat [væt] *s* cuba, tina

vaudeville ['vodvɪl] o ['vɔdəvɪl] *s* variedades; (*light theatrical piece interspersed with songs*) zarzuela

vault [vɔlt] *s* (*underground chamber*) bodega; (*of a bank*) cámara acorazada; (*burial chamber*) sepultura, tumba; (*firmament*) bóveda celeste; (*leap*) salto; (archit) bóveda ‖ *tr* abovedar; saltar ‖ *intr* saltar

vaunt [vɔnt] *s* jactancia ‖ *tr* jactarse de ‖ *intr* jactarse

VCR *abbr* **video-cassette recorder**

veal [vil] *s* ternera, carne *f* de ternera

veal chop *s* chuleta de ternera

ur
ve

vedette [vɪ'dɛt] s buque m escucha; centinela m de avanzada

veer [vɪr] s viraje m ‖ tr virar ‖ intr virar; (naut) llamar (el viento)

vegetable ['vɛdʒɪtəbəl] adj vegetal ‖ s (plant) vegetal m; (edible part of plant) hortaliza, legumbre f

vegetable garden s huerto de hortalizas, huerto de verduras

vegetable soup s menestra, sopa de hortalizas

vegetarian [,vɛdʒɪ'tɛrɪ•ən] adj & s vegetariano

vehemence ['vi•ɪməns] s vehemencia

vehement ['vi•ɪmənt] adj vehemente

vehicle ['vi•ɪkəl] s vehículo

vehicular traffic [vɪ'hɪkjələr] s circulación rodada

veil [vel] s velo; **to take the veil** tomar el velo ‖ tr velar (cubrir con un velo; cubrir, disimular)

vein [ven] s vena; (streak) veta; (distinctive quality) rasgo ‖ tr vetear

velar ['vilər] adj & s velar f

vellum ['vɛləm] s vitela; papel m vitela

veloci•ty [vɪ'lɑsɪti] s (pl -ties) velocidad

velvet ['vɛlvɪt] adj de terciopelo ‖ s terciopelo; (slang) ganancia limpia

velveteen [,vɛlvɪ'tin] s velludillo

velvety ['vɛlvɪti] adj aterciopelado

Ven. abbr **Venerable**

vend [vɛnd] tr vender como buhonero

vending machine s distribuidor automático

vendor ['vɛndər] s vendedor m, buhonero

veneer [və'nɪr] s chapa, enchapado; (fig) apariencia ‖ tr enchapar

venerable ['vɛnərəbəl] adj venerable

venerate ['vɛnə,ret] tr venerar

venereal [vɪ'nɪrɪ•əl] adj venéreo

Venetia [vɪ'niʃɪ•ə] o [vɪ'niʃə] s Venecia (provincia)

Venetian [vɪ'niʃən] adj & s veneciano

Venetian blind s persiana

Venezuela [,vɛnɪ'zwilə] s Venezuela

Venezuelan [,vɛnɪzwilən] adj & s venezolano

vengeance ['vɛndʒəns] s venganza; **with a vengeance** con furia, con violencia; excesivamente, con creces

vengeful ['vɛndʒfəl] adj vengativo

Venice ['vɛnɪs] s Venecia (ciudad)

venire [vɪ'naɪri] s (law) auto de convocación del jurado

venison ['vɛnɪsən] o ['vɛnɪzən] s carne f de venado

venom ['vɛnəm] s veneno

venomous ['vɛnəməs] adj venenoso

vent [vɛnt] s agujero, orificio; (outlet) salida; **to give vent to** dar libre curso a ‖ tr proveer de abertura; desahogar, expresar; **to vent one's spleen** descargar la bilis

vent'hole' s respiradero

ventilate ['vɛntɪ,let] tr ventilar

ventilator ['vɛntɪ,letər] s ventilador m

ventricle ['vɛntrɪkəl] s ventrículo

ventriloquism [vɛn'trɪlə,kwɪzəm] s ventriloquia

ventriloquist [vɛn'trɪləkwɪst] s ventrílocuo

venture ['vɛntʃər] s empresa arriesgada; **at a venture** a la buena ventura ‖ tr aventurar ‖ intr aventurarse; **to venture on** arriesgarse en

venturesome ['vɛntʃərsəm] adj (bold, daring) aventurero; (hazardous) aventurado

venturous ['vɛntʃərəs] adj (bold, daring) aventurero; (hazardous) aventurado, arriesgado

venue ['vɛnju] s (law) lugar m del crimen; (law) lugar donde se reúne el jurado; **change of venue** (law) traslado de jurisdicción

Venus ['vinəs] s (astr) Venus m; (myth) Venus f; (very beautiful woman) Venus f

veracious [vɪ'reʃəs] adj veraz

veraci•ty [vɪ'ræsɪti] s (pl -ties) veracidad

veranda o **verandah** [və'rændə] s terraza, veranda, galería

verb [vʌrb] adj verbal ‖ s verbo

verbatim [vər'betɪm] adj textual ‖ adv palabra por palabra, al pie de la letra

verbena [vər'binə] s (bot) verbena

verbiage ['vʌrbɪ•ɪdʒ] s palabrería, verbosidad

verbose [vər'bos] adj verboso

verdant ['vʌrdənt] adj verde; cándido, sencillo

verdict ['vʌrdɪkt] s veredicto, fallo

verdigris ['vʌrdɪ,gris] s verdete m

verdure ['vʌrdʒər] s verdor m

verge [vʌrdʒ] s borde m, límite m; (of a column) fuste m; báculo; (eccl) cetro; **on the verge of** al borde de; a punto de; **within the verge of** al alcance de ‖ intr— **to verge on** o **upon** llegar casi hasta, rayar en

verification [,vɛrɪfɪ'keʃən] s verificatión

veri•fy ['vɛrɪ,faɪ] v (pret & pp -fied) tr verificar, comprobar; (law) afirmar bajo juramento

verily ['vɛrɪli] adv verdaderamente, en verdad

veritable ['vɛrɪtəbəl] adj verdadero

vermicelli [,vʌrmɪ'sɛli] s fideos

vermilion [vər'mɪljən] adj bermejo ‖ s bermellón m

vermin ['vʌrmɪn] ssg (objectionable person) sabandija; bichería (SAm) ‖ spl (objectionable animals or persons) sabandijas

vermouth [vər'muθ] o ['vʌrmuθ] s vermú m

vernacular [vər'nækjələr] adj vernáculo ‖ s lenguaje vernáculo; idioma m corriente; (language peculiar to a class or profession) jerga

veronica [və'rɑnɪkə] s (bot & taur) verónica; lienzo de la Verónica

Versailles [vɛr'saɪ] s Versalles

versatile ['vʌrsətɪl] adj versátil; (person) de muchas habilidades; (informed on many subjects) polifacético, universal; (device or tool) útil para muchas cosas

verse [vʌrs] s verso; (in the Bible) versículo

versed [vʌrst] adj versado; **to become versed in** versarse en

versification [,vʌrsɪfɪ'keʃən] s versificación

ver•si•fy [`vʌrsɪ,faɪ] v (pret & pp -fied) tr & intr versificar

er•sion [`vʌrʒən] s versión

ver•so [`vʌrso] s (pl -sos) (e.g., of a coin) reverso; (typ) verso

versus [`vʌrsəs] prep contra

verte•bra [`vʌrtɪbrə] s (pl -brae [,bri] o -bras) vértebra

vertebral disk [`vʌrtə,brəl] s disco vertebral

vertebrate [`vʌrtɪ,bret] adj & s vertebrado

ver•tex [`vʌrtɛks] s (pl -texes o -tices [tɪ,siz]) (top, summit) ápice m; (geom) vértice m

vertical [`vʌrtɪkəl] adj & s vertical f

vertical hold s (telv) bloqueo vertical

vertical rudder s (aer) timón m de dirección

vertical take-off m despegue m vertical

verti•go [`vʌrtɪ,go] s (pl -gos o -goes) vértigo

verve [vʌrv] s brío, ánimo, vigor m

very [`vɛri] adj mismísimo; (sheer, utter) mero, puro; (actual) verdadero ‖ adv muy; mucho, p.ej., **to be very hungry** tener mucha hambre

vesicle [`vɛsɪkəl] s vesícula

vesper [`vɛspər] s tarde f, caída de la tarde; oración de la tarde; canción de la tarde; **vespers** (eccl) vísperas ‖ **Vesper** s Véspero

vesper bell s campana que llama a vísperas

vessel [`vɛsəl] s vasija, recipiente m; (ship) bajel m, embarcación, buque m; (anat) vaso

vest [vɛst] s (of man's suit) chaleco; (jabot) chorrera; (undershirt) camiseta ‖ tr vestir; **to vest in** conceder (p.ej., poder) a; **to vest with** investir de ‖ intr vestirse; **to vest in** pasar a

vested interests spl intereses creados

vestibule [`vɛstɪ,bjul] s vestíbulo, zaguán m

vestige [`vɛstɪdʒ] s vestigio

vestment [`vɛstmənt] s vestidura

vest'-pock'et adj de bolsillo, en miniatura; diminuto

ves•try [`vɛstri] s (pl -tries) sacristía; (chapel) capilla; junta parroquial; reunión de la junta parroquial

vestry•man [`vɛstrimən] s (pl -men [mən]) miembro de la junta parroquial

Vesuvius [vɪ`suvi•əs] o [vɪ`sjuvi•əs] s el Vesubio

vet. abbr **veteran, veterinary**

vetch [vɛtʃ] s arveja, veza; (grass pea) almorta

veteran [`vɛtərən] adj & s veterano

veterinarian [,vɛtərɪ`nɛri•ən] s veterinario

veterinar•y [`vɛtəri,nɛri] adj veterinario ‖ s (pl -ies) veterinario

veterinary medicine s veterinaria, medicina veterinaria

ve•to [`vito] s (pl -toes) veto ‖ tr vetar

vex [vɛks] tr vejar, molestar

vexation [vɛk`seʃən] s vejación, molestia

v.g. abbr **verbi gratia** (Lat) **for example**

via [`vaɪ•ə] prep vía, p.ej., **via Lisbon** vía Lisboa

viaduct [`vaɪ•ə,dʌkt] s viaducto

vial [`vaɪ•əl] s redoma, frasco pequeño

viati•cum [vaɪ`ætɪkəm] s (pl -cums o -ca [kə]) (eccl) viático

viand [`vaɪ•ənd] s vianda, manjar m

vibrate [`vaɪbret] tr & intr vibrar

vibration [vaɪ`breʃən] s vibración

vicar [`vɪkər] s vicario

vicarage [`vɪkərɪdʒ] s casa del vicario; (duties of vicar) vicaría

vicarious [vaɪ`kɛri•əs] adj substituto; (punishment) sufrido por otro; (power, authority) delegado; (enjoyment) reflejado

vice [vaɪs] s vicio

vice'-ad'miral s vicealmirante m

vice'-pres'ident s vicepresidente m

viceroy [`vaɪsrɔɪ] s virrey m

vice versa [`vaɪsi `vʌrsə] o [`vaɪs `vʌrsə] adv viceversa

vicini•ty [vɪ`sɪnɪti] s (pl -ties) vecindad

vicious [`vɪʃəs] adj vicioso; malazo; (dog) bravo; (horse) arisco

victim [`vɪktɪm] s víctima

victimize [`vɪktɪ,maɪz] tr hacer víctima; engañar, estafar

victor [`vɪktər] s vencedor m

victorious [vɪk`tori•əs] adj victorioso

victo•ry [`vɪktəri] s (pl -ries) victoria

victuals [`vɪtəlz] spl vituallas, provisiones de boca

vid. abbr **vide** (Lat) **see**

video cassette s videocasete m

vid'e•o-cas•sette' recorder s videograbador m

video-cassette recording s videograbación

video disk s videodisco

video game s video-juego

video recorder s magnetoscopia

video signal [`vɪdɪ,o] s señal f de vídeo

video tape s cinta grabada de televisión

vid'eo-tape' recording s videograbación

vie [vaɪ] v (pret & pp **vied;** ger **vying**) intr competir, emular, rivalizar

Vien•nese [,vi•ə`niz] adj vienés ‖ s (pl -nese) vienés m

Vietnam•ese [vɪ,ɛtnə`miz] adj vietnamés ‖ s (pl -ese) vietnamés m

view [vju] s vista; (purpose) intento, propósito, vista; **to be on view** estar expuesto (p.ej., un cadáver); **to keep in view** no perder de vista; no olvidar, tener presente; **to take a dim view of** no entusiasmarse por, mirar escépticamente; **with a view to** con vistas a ‖ tr ver, mirar; considerar, contemplar; examinar, inspeccionar

viewer [`vju•ər] s espectador m; telespectador m, televidente mf; proyector m de transparencias; mirador m de transparencias

view finder s (phot) visor m

view'point' s punto de vista

vigil [`vɪdʒɪl] s vigilia; **to keep vigil** velar

vigilance [`vɪdʒɪləns] s vigilancia

vigilant [`vɪdʒɪlənt] adj vigilante

vignette [vɪn`jɛt] s viñeta

vigor [`vɪgər] s vigor m

vigorous [`vɪgərəs] adj vigoroso

vile [vaɪl] adj vil; (disgusting) asqueroso, repugnante; (weather) muy malo

vili·fy ['vɪlɪˌfaɪ] v (pret & pp **-fied**) tr difamar, denigrar

villa ['vɪlə] s villa, quinta

village ['vɪlɪdʒ] s aldea

villager ['vɪlɪdʒər] s aldeano

villain ['vɪlən] s malvado; (of a play) malo, traidor m

villainous ['vɪlənəs] adj malvado

villain·y ['vɪləni] s (pl **-ies**) maldad, perfidia

vim [vɪm] s fuerza, brío, vigor m

vinaigrette [ˌvɪnəˈɡrɛt] s vinagrera

vinaigrette sauce s vinagreta

vindicate ['vɪndɪˌket] tr vindicar, exculpar

vindictive [vɪnˈdɪktɪv] adj vengativo

vine [vaɪn] s (creeping or climbing plant) enredadera; (grape plant) vid f, parra

vine′dress′er s viñador m, viticultor m

vinegar ['vɪnɪɡər] s vinagre m

vinegarish ['vɪnɪɡərɪʃ] adj avinagrado

vinegary ['vɪnɪɡəri] adj vinagroso

vineyard ['vɪnjərd] s viña, viñedo

vineyardist ['vɪnjərdɪst] s viñador m, viticultor m

vintage ['vɪntɪdʒ] s vendimia; vino de buena cosecha; (coll) categoría, clase f

vintager ['vɪntɪdʒər] s vendimiador m

vintage wine s vino de buena cosecha

vintage year s año de buen vino

vintner ['vɪntnər] s vinatero

vinyl ['vaɪnɪl] s vinilo

violate ['vaɪəˌlet] tr violar

violence ['vaɪələns] s violencia

violent ['vaɪələnt] adj violento

violet ['vaɪəlɪt] adj violado ‖ s (color) violeta m, violado; (dye) violeta m; (bot) violeta f

violin [ˌvaɪəˈlɪn] s violín m

violinist [ˌvaɪəˈlɪnɪst] s violinista mf

violoncellist [ˌvaɪələnˈtʃɛlɪst] o [ˌvɪələnˈtʃɛlɪst] s violoncelista mf

violoncel·lo [ˌvaɪələnˈtʃɛlo] o [ˌvɪələnˈtʃɛlo] s (pl **-los**) violoncelo

viper ['vaɪpər] s víbora

VIPs ['viˌaɪˈpis] spl (letterword) notables mpl

vira·go [vɪˈreɡo] s (pl **-goes** o **-gos**) mujer de mal genio

virgin ['vɜrdʒɪn] adj & s virgen f

virgin birth s parto virginal de María Santísima; (zool) partenogénesis f

Virginia creeper [vərˈdʒɪnɪə] s (bot) guau m

virginity [vərˈdʒɪnɪti] s virginidad

Virgo ['vɜrɡo] s (astr) Virgo

virility [vɪˈrɪlɪti] s virilidad

virology [vaɪˈrɑlədʒi] s virología

virtual ['vɜrtʃuəl] adj virtual

virtue ['vɜrtʃu] s virtud

virtuosi·ty [ˌvɜrtʃuˈɑsɪti] s (pl **-ties**) virtuosismo

virtuo·so [ˌvɜrtʃuˈoso] s (pl **-sos** o **-si** [si]) virtuoso

virtuous ['vɜrtʃuəs] adj virtuoso

virulence ['vɪrjələns] s virulencia

virulent ['vɪrjələnt] adj virulento

virus ['vaɪrəs] s virus m

Vis. abbr **Viscount**

visa ['vizə] s visa ‖ tr visar

visage ['vɪzɪdʒ] s cara, semblante m; aspecto, apariencia

vis-à-vis [ˌvizəˈvi] adj enfrentados ‖ adv frente a frente ‖ prep enfrente de; respecto de

viscera ['vɪsərə] spl vísceras

viscount ['vaɪkaunt] s vizconde m

viscountess ['vaɪkauntɪs] s vizcondesa

viscous ['vɪskəs] adj viscoso

vise [vaɪs] s tornillo, torno

visé ['vize] o [viˈze] s & tr var de **visa**

visible ['vɪzɪbəl] adj visible

Visigoth ['vɪzɪˌɡɑθ] s visigodo

vision ['vɪʒən] s visión; (sense of sight) vista

visionar·y ['vɪʒəˌnɛri] adj visionario ‖ s (pl **-ies**) visionario

visit ['vɪzɪt] s visita ‖ tr visitar; afligir, acometer; enviar (p.ej., castigo, venganza) ‖ intr hacer visitas; visitarse (dos o más personas)

visitation [ˌvɪzɪˈteʃən] s visitación; gracia del cielo, castigo del cielo

visiting card s tarjeta de visita

visiting hours spl horas de visita

visiting nurse s enfermera ambulante

visitor ['vɪzɪtər] s visitante mf

visor ['vaɪzər] s visera; (disguise) máscara

vista ['vɪstə] s vista, panorama m

visual ['vɪʒuəl] adj visual

visual acuity s agudeza visual

visualize ['vɪʒuəˌlaɪz] tr representarse en la mente; hacer visible

vital ['vaɪtəl] adj vital; (deadly) mortal ‖ **vitals** spl partes fpl vitales, órganos vitales

vitality [vaɪˈtælɪti] s vitalidad

vitalize ['vaɪtəˌlaɪz] tr vitalizar

vitamin ['vaɪtəmɪn] s vitamina

vitiate ['vɪʃɪˌet] tr viciar

vitreous ['vɪtrɪəs] adj vítreo

vitriolic [ˌvɪtrɪˈɑlɪk] adj (chem) vitriólico; (fig) cáustico, mordaz

vituperable [vaɪˈtupərəbəl] o [vaɪˈtjupərəbəl] adj vituperable

vituperate [vaɪˈtupəˌret] o [vaɪˈtjupəˌret] tr vituperar

viva ['vivə] interj ¡viva! ‖ s viva m

vivacious [vɪˈveʃəs] o [vaɪˈveʃəs] adj vivaz, vivaracho

vivaci·ty [vɪˈvæsɪti] o [vaɪˈvæsɪti] s (pl **-ties**) vivacidad, animación

viva voce ['vaɪvə 'vosi] adv de viva voz

vivid ['vɪvɪd] adj vivo (intenso; brillante; expresivo)

vivi·fy ['vɪvɪˌfaɪ] v (pret & pp **-fied**) tr vivificar

vivisection [ˌvɪvɪˈsɛkʃən] s vivisección

vixen ['vɪksən] s vulpeja; mujer regañona y colérica

viz. abbr **videlicet** (Lat) **namely, to wit**

vizier [vɪˈzɪr] o ['vɪzjər] s visir m

vocabular·y [voˈkæbjəˌlɛri] s (pl **-ies**) vocabulario

vocal ['vokəl] adj vocal; (inclined to express oneself freely) expresivo

vocalist ['vokəlɪst] s vocalista mf

vocation [voˈkeʃən] s vocación; empleo, ocupación

vocative ['vakətɪv] s vocativo
vociferate [vo'sɪfə,ret] intr vociferar
vociferous [vo'sɪfərəs] adj clamoroso, voçinglero
vogue [vog] s boga, moda; **in vogue** en boga, de moda
voice [vɔɪs] s voz f; **in a loud voice** en alta voz; **in a low voice** en voz baja; **with one voice** a una voz || tr expresar; sonorizar (una consonante sorda) || intr sonorizarse
voiceless ['vɔɪslɪs] adj sin voz; mudo; silencioso; (phonet) sordo
void [vɔɪd] adj (empty) vacío; (useless) vano; (law) inválido, nulo; **void of** desprovisto de || s vacío; (gap) hueco || tr vaciar; evacuar (el vientre); anular || intr excretar
voile [vɔɪl] s espumilla
vol. abbr **volume**
volatile ['valətɪl] adj volátil
volatilize ['valətɪ,laɪz] tr volatilizar || intr volatilizarse
volcanic [val'kænɪk] adj volcánico
volca•no [val'keno] s (pl -noes o -nos) volcán m
volition [və'lɪʃən] s voluntad; **of one's own volition** por su propia voluntad
volley ['vali] s (of stones, bullets, etc.) descarga, lluvia; (mil) descarga; (tennis) voleo || tr & intr volear
vol•ley•ball s volibol m
volplane ['val,plen] s vuelo planeado || intr planear
volt [volt] s voltio
voltage ['voltɪdʒ] s voltaje m
voltage divider s (rad) divisor m de voltaje
voltaic [val'te•ɪk] adj voltaico
volte-face [vɔlt'fas] s cambio de dirección; cambio de opinión
volt'me'ter s voltímetro
voluble ['valjəbəl] adj locuaz, hablador
volume ['valjəm] s (book; bulk; mass, e.g., of water) volumen m; (each book in a set) tomo; (degree of loudness) volumen sonoro; (geom) volumen m; **to speak volumes** ser muy significativo; ser muy expresivo
voluminous [və'lumɪnəs] adj voluminoso
voluntar•y ['valən,tɛri] adj voluntario || s (pl -ties) (eccl) solo de órgano
volunteer [,valən'tɪr] adj & s voluntario || tr ofrecer (sus servicios) || intr ofrecerse; servir como voluntario; **to volunteer to +** inf ofrecerse a + inf
voluptuar•y [və'lʌptʃʊ,ɛri] adj voluptuoso || s (pl -ties) voluptuoso, sibarita mf
voluptuous [və'lʌptʃʊ•əs] adj voluptuoso
volute [və'lut] s voluta

vomit ['vamɪt] s vómito; (emetic) vomitivo || tr & intr vomitar
voodoo ['vudu] adj voduísta || s (practice) vodú m; (person) voduísta mf
voracious [və'reʃəs] adj voraz
voracity [və'ræsɪti] s voracidad
vor•tex ['vɔrtɛks] s (pl -texes o -tices [tɪ,siz]) vórtice m
vota•ry ['votəri] s (pl -ries) persona ligada por votos solemnes; aficionado, partidario
vote [vot] s (formal expression of choice; right to vote; person who votes) voto; (act of voting; votes considered together) votación; **to put to the vote** poner a votación; **to tally the votes** regular los votos || tr votar (sí, no); **to vote down** derrotar por votación; **to vote in** elegir por votación || intr votar
vote getter ['gɛtər] s acaparador m de votos; (slogan) consigna que gana votos
voter ['votər] s votante mf
voting machine ['votɪŋ] s máquina registradora de votos
votive ['votɪv] adj votivo
votive offering s voto, exvoto
vouch [vautʃ] tr garantizar || intr—**to vouch for** responder de.(una cosa); responder por (una persona)
voucher ['vautʃər] s garante mf; (certificate) comprobante m
vouch•safe' tr conceder, otorgar; permitir || intr— **to vouchsafe to +** inf dignarse + inf
voussoir [vu'swar] s dovela
vow [vau] s voto; **to take vows** tomar el hábito religioso || tr votar (p.ej., un cirio a la Virgen); jurar (venganza) || intr votar; **to vow to** hacer votos de
vowel ['vau•əl] s vocal f
voyage ['vɔɪ•ɪdʒ] s travesía, trayecto; (any journey) viaje m || tr atravesar (p.ej., el mar) || intr viajar
voyager ['vɔɪ•ɪdʒər] s pasajero, navegante mf, viajero
V.P. abbr **Vice-President**
vs. abbr **versus**
Vul. abbr **Vulgate**
vulcanize ['vʌlkə,naɪz] tr vulcanizar
vulg. abbr **vulgar**
Vulg. abbr **Vulgate**
vulgar ['vʌlgər] adj grosero; (popular, common; vernacular) vulgar
vulgari•ty [vʌl'gærɪti] s (pl -ties) grosería
Vulgar Latin s latín vulgar, latín rústico
Vulgate ['vʌlget] s Vulgata
vulnerable ['vʌlnərəbəl] adj vulnerable
vulture ['vʌltʃər] s buitre m; (American vulture) catartes m, aura (buitre americano)

W

W, w [ˈdʌbəl,ju] vigésima tercera letra del alfabeto inglés

w *abbr* **watt**

w. *abbr* **week, west, wide, wife**

W. *abbr* **Wednesday, west**

wad [wɑd] *s* (*of cotton*) bolita, tapón *m;* (*of papers*) fajo, lío; (*in a gun*) taco ‖ *v* (*pret & pp* **wadded;** *ger* **wadding**) *tr* emborrar, rellenar; atacar (*una escopeta*)

waddle [ˈwɑdəl] *s* anadeo ‖ *intr* anadear

wade [wed] *intr* andar sobre terreno cubierto de agua; andar.descalzo por la orilla; chapotear (*los niños*) con los pies desnudos; **to wade into** (coll) embestir con violencia; (coll) meter el hombro a; **to wade through** (coll) avanzar con dificultad por; (coll) leer con dificultad

wading bird [ˈwedɪŋ] *s* ave zancuda

wafer [ˈwefər] *s* (*for sealing letters; pill*) oblea; (*thin, crisp cake*) hostia; (eccl) hostia

waffle [ˈwɑfəl] *s* barquillo

waffle iron *s* barquillero

waft [wæft] o [wɑft] *tr* llevar por el aire; llevar por encima del agua ‖ *intr* flotar

wag [wæg] *s* (*of head*) meneo; (*of tail*) coleada; (*jester*) bromista *mf* ‖ *v* (*pret & pp* **wagged;** *ger* **wagging**) *tr* menear (*la cabeza, la cola*) ‖ *intr* menearse

wage [wedʒ] *s* salario; **wages** galardón *m,* premio ‖ *tr* hacer (*la guerra*)

wage earner [ˈʌrnər] *s* asalariado

wager [ˈwedʒər] *s* apuesta; **to lay a wager** hacer una apuesta ‖ *tr & intr* apostar

wage′work′er *s* asalariado

waggish [ˈwægɪʃ] *adj* divertido, gracioso; (*person*) bromista

Wagnerian [vɑgˈnɪrɪ•ən] *adj & s* vagneriano

wagon [ˈwægən] *s* carro, furgón *m,* carretón *m;* **on the wagon** (slang) sin tomar bebidas alcohólicas; **to hitch one's wagon to a star** poner el tiro muy alto

wag′tail′ *s* aguanieves *m,* aguzanieves *m*

waif [wef] *s* (*foundling*) expósito; animal extraviado o abandonado; (*stray child*) granuja *m*

wail [wel] *s* gemido, lamento ‖ *intr* gemir, lamentar

wain•scot [ˈwenskət] o [ˈwenskɑt] *s* arrimadillo, friso de madera ‖ *v* (*pret & pp* **-scoted** o **-scotted;** *ger* **-scoting** o **-scotting**) *tr* poner arrimadillo o friso de madera a

waist [west] *s* (*of human body; corresponding part of garment*) talle *m,* cintura; (*garment*) corpiño, jubón *m,* blusa

waist′band′ *s* pretina

waist′cloth′ *s* taparrabo

waistcoat [ˈwest,kot] o [ˈwɛskət] *s* chaleco

waist′line′ *s* cintura

wait [wet] *s* espera; **to have a good wait** (coll) esperar sentado; **to lie in wait for** acechar emboscado ‖ *tr*—**to wait one's turn** esperar vez ‖ *intr* esperar, aguardar; **to wait for** esperar, aguardar; **to wait on**

atender, despachar (*a los parroquianos en una tienda*); servir (*a una persona a la mesa*); **to wait until** esperar a que

waiter [ˈwetər] *s* camarero, mozo de restaurante; (*tray*) bandeja

waiting list *s* lista de espera

waiting room *s* (*of station*) sala de espera; (*of doctor's office*) antesala

waitress [ˈwetrɪs] *s* camarera, moza de restaurante

waive [wev] *tr* renunciar a (*un derecho*); diferir, poner a un lado

waiver [ˈwevər] *s* renuncia

wake [wek] *s* (*watch by the body of a dead person*) velatorio; (*of a boat or other moving object*) estela; **in the wake of** siguiendo inmediatamente; de resultas de ‖ *v* (*pret* **waked** o **woke** [wok]; *pp* **waked**) *tr* despertar ‖ *intr*— **to wake to** darse cuenta de; **to wake up** despertar

wakeful [ˈwekfəl] *adj* desvelado

wakefulness [ˈwekfəlnĩs] *s* desvelo

waken [ˈwekən] *tr & intr* despertar

wale [wel] *s* verdugón *m*

Wales [welz] *s* Gales, el país de Gales

walk [wɔk] *s* (*act*) paseo; (*distance*) caminata; (*way of walking, bearing*) andar *m,* paso; (*of a horse*) andadura; (*place to walk animals*) cercado; empleo, cargo, carrera; **at a walk** al paso de una persona; **to go for a walk** salir a pasear; **to take a walk** dar un paseo ‖ *tr* pasear (*a un niño, un caballo*); caminar (*recorrer caminando*); hacer ir al paso (*un caballo*); **to walk off** quitarse (*p.ej., un dolor de cabeza*) caminando ‖ *intr* andar, caminar, ir a pie; (*to stroll*) pasear; **to walk away from** alejarse caminando de; **to walk off with** cargar con, llevarse; **to walk out** salir repentinamente; declararse en huelga; **to walk out on** (coll) dejar airadamente

walkaway [ˈwɔkə,we] *s* (coll) triunfo fácil

walker [ˈwɔkər] *s* caminante *mf;* (*pedestrian*) peatón *m;* (*gocart*) andaderas

walkie-talkie [ˈwɔkiˈtɔki] *s* (rad) transmisorreceptor *m* portátil

walking papers *spl* (coll) despedida de un empleo

walking stick *s* bastón *m*

walk′-on′ *s* (theat) parte *f* de por medio

walk′out′ *s* (coll) huelga

walk′o′ver *s* (coll) triunfo fácil

wall [wɔl] *s* muro; (*between rooms; of a pipe, boiler, etc.*) pared *f;* (*of a fortification*) muralla; **to drive to the wall** poner entre la espada y la pared; **to go to the wall** rendirse; fracasar ‖ *tr* murar, amurallar (*una ciudad, un castillo*); emparedar (*a un criminal*); **to wall up** cerrar con muro

wall′board′ *s* cartón *m* tabla

wallet [ˈwɑlɪt] *s* cartera de bolsillo

wall′flow′er *s* alhelí *m;* **to be a wallflower** (coll) comer pavo, planchar el asiento

Walloon [wɑˈlun] *adj & s* valón *m*

wallop ['wɑləp] s (coll) golpaza, puñetazo || tr (coll) golpear fuertemente; (coll) vencer cabalmente

wallow ['wɑlo] s revuelco; (place) revolcadero || intr revolcarse; (e.g., in wealth) nadar

wall'pa'per s papel m de empapelar, papel pintado || tr empapelar

walnut ['wɔlnət] s (tree and wood) nogal m; nuez f de nogal

walrus ['wɔlrəs] o ['wɑlrəs] s morsa

Walter ['wɔltər] s Gualterio

waltz [wɔlts] s vals m || tr hacer valsar; (coll) conducir directamente || intr valsar

wan [wɑn] adj (comp **wanner**; super **wannest**) pálido, macilento; débil

wand [wɑnd] s vara; (of deviner or magician) varilla de virtudes

wander ['wɑndər] tr recorrer a la ventura || intr errar, vagar; extraviarse, perderse; **to wander around** errar de una parte a otra

wanderer ['wɑndərər] s vagabundo; peregrino

wan'der•lust' s ansia de viajar

wane [wen] s decadencia, declinación; menguante f de la luna; **on the wane** decayendo, declinando; menguando (la luna) || intr decaer, declinar; menguar (la luna)

wangle ['wɛŋɡəl] tr (to obtain by scheming) (coll) mamar o mamarse; (coll) adulterar, falsear (cuentas); **to wangle one's way out of** (coll) salir con maña de || intr (to get along by scheming) (coll) sacudirse

want [wɑnt] o [wɔnt] s deseo; necesidad; carencia; **for want of** a falta de; **to be in want** pasar necesidad || tr desear; necesitar; carecer de || intr desear; **to want for** necesitar; carecer de

want ad s anuncio clasificado

wanton ['wɑntən] adj inconsiderado, desconsiderado; insensible, perverso; disoluto, licencioso; lascivo; cabezudo

war [wɔr] s guerra; **to go to war** declarar la guerra; (as a soldier) ir a la guerra; **to wage war** hacer la guerra || v (pret & pp **warred**; ger **warring**) intr guerrear; **to war on** guerrear con, hacer la guerra a

warble ['wɔrbəl] s gorjeo, trino || intr gorjear, trinar

warbler ['wɔrblər] s pájaro cantor; curruca de cabeza negra

war cloud s amenaza de guerra

ward [wɔrd] s (person, usually a minor, under protection of another) pupilo; (guardianship) custodia, tutela; (of a city) barrio, distrito; (of a hospital) cuadra, crujía; (of a lock) guarda || tr— **to ward off** parar, desviar

warden ['wɔrdən] s guardián m; (of a jail) alcaide m, carcelero; (of a church) capiller m; (in charge of fire prevention) vigía m

ward heeler s muñidor m

ward'robe' s (closet or cabinet for holding clothes) guardarropa m; (stock of clothing for a person) vestuario; (theat) guardarropía

wardrobe trunk s baúl ropero

ward'room' s (nav) cámara de oficiales

ware [wɛr] s loza; **wares** efectos, artículos de comercio, mercancías

war effort s esfuerzo bélico

ware'house' s almacén m; (for furniture) guardamuebles m

warehouse•man ['wɛr,hausmən] s (pl **-men** [mən]) almacenista m; guardaalmacén m

war'fare' s guerra

war'head' s punta de combate

war horse s corcel m de guerra; (coll) veterano

warily ['wɛrɪli] adv cautelosamente

wariness ['wɛrɪnɪs] s cautela

war'like' adj guerrero

war loan s empréstito de guerra

war lord s jefe m militar

warm [wɔrm] adj (being moderately hot) caliente; (neither hot nor cold) templado; (clothing) abrigado; (climate, region) caluroso; (color) cálido; (fig) caluroso, cordial; **to be warm** (said of a person) tener calor; (said of the weather) hacer calor || tr calentar, acalorar; (fig) animar, acalorar; **to warm up** recalentar (p.ej., la comida); hacer más amistoso || intr calentarse; **to warm up** templar (el tiempo); (with work or exercise) acalorarse; **to warm up to** cobrar afecto a

warm-blooded ['wɔrm'blʌdɪd] adj apasionado, ardiente; (animals) de sangre caliente

war memorial s monumento a los caídos

warmer ['wɔrmər] s calentador m

warm-hearted ['wɔrm'hɑrtɪd] adj afectuoso, de buen corazón; cariñoso; simpático

warming pan s mundillo

warmonger ['wɔr,mʌŋɡər] s belicista mf

war mother s madrina de guerra

warmth [wɔrmθ] s calor m; ardor m, entusiasmo; cordialidad

warm'-up' s calentón m

warn [wɔrn] tr advertir, avisar; (to exhort) amonestar; (to advise) aconsejar

warning adj de aviso || s advertencia, aviso

War of the Roses s guerra de las dos Rosas

warp [wɔrp] s (of a fabric) urdimbre f; (of a board) comba, alabeo; aberración mental; (naut) espía || tr combar, alabear; pervertir (el juicio de una persona); (naut) move, con espía || intr combarse, alabearse; (naut) espiar

war'path' s—**to be on the warpath** prepararse para la guerra; estar buscando pendencia

war'plane' s avión m de guerra

warrant ['wɑrənt] o ['wɔrənt] s garantía, promesa; (for arrest) orden f de prisión; (before a judge) citación; cédula, certificado || tr garantizar, prometer; autorizar; justificar

warrantable ['wɑrəntəbəl] o ['wɔrəntəbəl] adj garantizable; justificable

warrant officer s suboficial m de las clases

w
wa

warren ['wɑrən] o ['wɔrən] s (where rabbits breed) conejera; barrio densamente poblado

warrior ['wɔrjər] s guerrero

Warsaw ['wɔrsɔ] s Varsovia

war'ship' s buque m de guerra

wart [wɔrt] s verruga

war'time' s tiempo de guerra

war'-torn' adj devastado por la guerra

war to the death s guerra a muerte

war•y [wɛri] adj (comp **-ier**; super **-iest**) cauteloso

wash [wɑʃ] o [wɔʃ] s lavado; (clothes washed or to be washed) jabonado; (dirty water) lavazas; loción; (place where surf breaks) batiente m; (aer) estela turbulenta ‖ tr lavar; fregar (los platos); bañar, mojar; **to wash away** quitar lavando; derrubiar (las aguas corrientes la tierra de las riberas) ‖ intr lavarse; lavar la ropa; batir (el agua); derrubiarse

washable ['wɑʃəbəl] o ['wɔʃəbəl] adj lavable

wash and wear adj de lava y pon

wash'ba'sin s jofaina, palangana

wash'bas'ket s cesto de la colada

wash'board' s lavadero, tabla de lavar; (baseboard) rodapié m

wash'bowl' s jofaina, palangana

wash'cloth' s paño para lavarse

wash'day' s día m de la colada

washed-out ['wɑʃt,aut] o ['wəʃt,aut] adj desteñido; (coll) debilitado, rendido

washed-up ['wɑʃt,ʌp] o ['wɔʃt,ʌp] adj (coll) agotado, deslomado

washer ['wɑʃər] o ['wɔʃər] s lavador m; (machine) lavadora; (ring of metal placed under head of bolt) arandela; (ring of rubber, etc., to keep a spigot from leaking) zapatilla; (phot) lavador

wash'er•wom'an s (pl **-wom'en**) lavandera

wash goods spl tejidos lavables

washing ['wɑʃɪŋ] o ['wɔʃɪŋ] s (act of washing; washed clothes or clothes to be washed) lavado; lavada; **washings** (dirty water; abraded material) lavadura

washing machine s lejiadora, lavadora mecánica

washing soda s sal f de sosa

wash'out' s derrubio; derrumbe m; (coll) desilusión, fracaso

wash'rag' s paño para lavarse; paño de cocina

wash'room' s gabinete m de aseo, lavabo

wash'stand' s lavamanos m

wash'tub' s cuba de colada, tina de lavar

wash water s lavazas

wasp [wɑsp] s avispa

waste [west] s derroche m, desgaste m; (garbage) basura, despojo; (wild region) despoblado, yermo; (of time) pérdida; (useless by-products) desperdicios; excremento; (for wiping machinery) hilacha de algodón; **to lay waste** devastar, poner a fuego y sangre ‖ tr malgastar, perder ‖ intr—**to waste away** consumirse

waste'bas'ket s papelera

wasteful ['westfəl] adj derrochador, manirroto; devastador, destructivo

waste'-land' s peladero

waste paper s papeles usados, papel de desecho, papel viejo

waste pipe s tubo de desagüe

waste products spl desperdicios; materia excretada

wastrel ['westrəl] s derrochador m, malgastador m; pródigo, perdido

watch [wɑtʃ] s reloj m (de bolsillo o de pulsera); (lookout) vigía m; (mil) vigilia; (naut) guardia; **to be on the watch for** estar a la mira de; **to keep watch over** velar ‖ tr (to look at) mirar; (to oversee) velar, vigilar; guardar; tener cuidado con ‖ intr mirar; (to keep awake) velar; **to watch for** acechar; **to watch out** tener cuidado; **to watch out for** estar a la mira de; tener cuidado con; guardarse de; **to watch over** velar, vigilar

watch'case' s caja de reloj

watch charm s dije m

watch crystal s cristal m de reloj

watch'dog' s perro de guarda, perro guardián; (fig) guardián m fiel

watchful ['wɑtʃfəl] adj desvelado, vigilante

watchfulness ['wɑtʃfəlnɪs] s desvelo, vigilancia

watch'mak'er s relojero

watch•man ['wɑtʃmən] s (pl **men** [mən]) vigilante m, velador m

watch night s noche vieja; oficio de noche vieja

watch pocket s relojera

watch strap s pulsera

watch'tow'er s atalaya, vigía

watch'word' s santo y seña; (slogan) lema m

water ['wɔtər] o ['wɑtər] s agua; **of the first water** de lo mejor; **to back water** ciar; **to carry water on both shoulders** nadar entre dos aguas; **to fish in troubled waters** pescar en río revuelto; **to hold water** (coll) ser bien fundado; **to make water** (to urinate) hacer aguas; (naut) hacer agua; **to pour** o **throw cold water on** echar un jarro de agua (fría) a ‖ tr regar, rociar; abrevar (el ganado); aguar (el vino); proveer de agua ‖ intr abrevarse (el ganado); tomar agua (una locomotora); llorar (los ojos)

water carrier s aguador m

water closet s excusado, retrete m, váter m

water color s acuarela

wa'ter•course' s corriente f de agua; lecho de corriente

water cress s berzo

water cure s cura de aguas

wa'ter•fall' s cascada, caída de agua

water front s terreno ribereño

water gap s garganta, hondonada

water hammer s golpe m de ariete

water heater s calentador m de agua

water ice s sorbete m

watering can s regadera

watering place s aguadero; balneario

watering pot s regadera

watering trough s abrevadero

water jacket s camisa de agua
water lily s ninfea, nenúfar m
water line s línea de agua, línea de flotación; nivel m de agua
water main s cañería de agua
wa'ter•mark' s (in paper) filigrana; marca de nivel de agua
wa'ter•mel'on s sandía
water meter s contador m de agua
water pipe s cañería de agua
water polo s polo de agua
water power s fuerza de agua, hulla blanca
wa'ter•proof' adj & s impermeable m
wa'ter•shed' s divisoria de aguas; (drainage area) cuenca
water ski s esquí acuático
wa'ter•spout' s (to carry water from roof) canalón m; (funnel of wet air extending from cloud to surface of water) manga de agua, tromba marina
wa'ter•sup•ply' system s fontanería
wa'ter•tight' adj estanco, hermético; (fig) seguro
water tower s arca de agua
water wagon s (mil) carro de agua; **on the water wagon** (slang) sin tomar bebidas alcohólicas
wa'ter•way' s vía de agua, vía fluvial; (naut) canalizo
water wheel s rueda de agua; turbina de agua; (of steamboat) rueda de paletas
water wings spl nadaderas
wa'ter•works' s estación de bombas
watery ['wɔtəri] o ['watəri] adj acuoso; (said of the eyes) lagrimoso, lloroso; insípido; húmedo, mojado
watt [wat] s vatio
wattage ['watıdʒ] s vatiaje m
watt'-hour' s (pl **watt-hours**) vatiohora
wattle ['watəl] s (of bird) barba; (of fish) barbilla
watt'me'ter s vatímetro
wave [wev] s onda; (of hair) onda, ondulación; (e.g., of heat or cold) ola; (e.g., of strikes) oleaje m; señal hecha con la mano ǁ tr blandir (la espada); ondear, ondular (el cabello); hacer señal con (la mano); decir (adiós) con la mano; **to wave aside** rechazar ǁ intr ondear u ondearse; hacer señal con la mano
wave motion s movimiento ondulatorio
waver ['wevər] intr oscilar; (to hesitate) vacilar, titubear; (to totter) tambalear
wave theory s teoría ondulatoria
wav•y ['wevi] adj (comp **-ier**; super **-iest**) undoso, ondoso; (water) ondulado; (hair) ondeado
wax [wæks] s cera; **to be wax in one's hands** ser como una cera ǁ tr encerar; cerotear (el hilo) ǁ intr hacerse, volverse; crecer (la luna)
wax paper s papel encerado, papel parafinado
wax taper s cerilla
wax'works' s museo de cera
way [we] s vía, camino; dirección, sentido; manera, modo; costumbre, hábito; **across**

the way enfrente; **a good way** un buen trecho; **all the way** hasta el fin del camino; **any way** de cualquier modo; **by the way** a propósito; **in a way** hasta cierto punto; **in every way** en todos respectos; **in this way** de este modo; **on the way to** camino de, rumbo a; **on the way out** saliendo; desapareciendo; **out of the way** hecho, despachado; inconveniente, impropio; a un lado, apartado; fuera de lo común; **that way** por allí; de ese modo; **this way** por aquí; de este modo; **to be in the way** estorbar; **to feel one's way** tantear el camino; proceder con tiento; **to force one's way** abrirse paso por fuerza; **to get out of the way** quitarse de en medio; (to finish) quitarse de encima; **to give way** ceder, retroceder; romperse (una cuerda); fracasar; **to give way to** entregarse a; **to go out of one's way** dar un rodeo; dar un rodeo innecesario; darse molestia; **to have one's way** salirse con la suya; **to keep out of the way** no obstruir el paso; **to know one's way around** saber entendérselas; **to know one's way to** conocer el camino a, saber ir a; **to lead the way** enseñar el camino; ir o entrar primero; **to lose one's way** perder el camino, extraviarse; **to make one's way** avanzar; hacer carrera, acreditarse; **to make way for** dar paso a, hacer lugar para; **to mend one's ways** mudar de vida; **to not know which way to turn** no saber dónde meterse; **to put out of the way** alejar, apartar; quitar de en medio; **to see one's way to** ver el modo de; **to take one's way** irse, marcharse; **to wend one's way** seguir camino; **to wind one's way through** serpentear por; **to wing one's way** ir volando; **under way** en marcha, en camino; **way in** entrada; **way out** salida; **ways** maneras, modales mpl; (for launching a ship) anguilas; **which way?** ¿por dónde?; ¿cómo?
way'bill' s hoja de ruta
wayfarer ['we,fɛrər] s caminante mf
way'lay' v (pret & pp **-laid'**) tr detener de improviso; (to attack from ambush) insidiar, asaltar
way'side' s borde m del camino; **to fall by the wayside** (to disappear) caer en el camino; fracasar
way station s apeadero
way train s tren m ómnibus
wayward ['wewərd] adj díscolo, voluntarioso; voltario, caprichoso
w.c. abbr **water closet, without charge**
we [wi] pron pers nosotros
weak [wik] adj débil, flaco, caedizo; (vowel; verb) débil
weaken ['wikən] tr debilitar, enflaquecer ǁ intr debilitarse, enflaquecerse
weakling ['wiklıŋ] s alfeñique m, canijo
weak-minded ['wik'maındıd] adj irresoluto; simple, mentecato
weakness ['wiknıs] s debilidad, flaqueza; caducidad; lado débil; afición, gusto
weal [wil] s verdugón m
wealth [wɛlθ] s riqueza

wa
we

wealth•y ['wɛlθi] *adj* (*comp* -ier; *super* -iest) rico

wean [win] *tr* destetar; **to wean away from** apartar gradualmente de

weanling ['winlɪŋ] *adj* & *s* destetado

weapon ['wɛpən] *s* arma

wear [wɛr] *s* (*act of wearing*) uso; (*clothing*) ropa; estilo, moda; (*wasting away from use*) desgaste *m*, deterioro; (*lasting quality*) durabilidad; **for all kinds of wear** a todo llevar; **for everyday wear** para todo trote || *v* (*pret* wore [wor]; *pp* worn [worn]) *tr* llevar, traer, llevar puesto; calzar (*cierto tamaño de zapato o guante*); (*to waste away by use*) desgastar, deteriorar; (*to tire*) agotar, cansar; **to wear out** consumir, gastar; agotar, cansar; abusar de (*la hospitalidad de una persona*) || *intr* desgastarse, deteriorarse; **to wear off** pasar, desaparecer; **to wear out** gastarse, usarse; **to wear well** durar, ser duradero

wear and tear *s* uso y desgaste

weariness ['wɪrɪnɪs] *s* cansancio; aburrimiento

wearing apparel ['wɛrɪŋ] *s* ropaje *m*, prendas de vestir

wearisome ['wɪrɪsəm] *adj* aburrido, cansado, fastidioso

wea•ry ['wɪri] *adj* (*comp* -rier; *super* -riest) cansado || *v* (*pret* & *pp* -ried) *tr* cansar || *intr* cansarse

weasel ['wizəl] *s* comadreja

weaseler ['wizələr] *s* pancista *mf*

weasel words *spl* palabras ambiguas

weather ['wɛðər] *s* tiempo; mal tiempo; **to be under the weather** (coll) no estar muy católico; (coll) estar borracho || *tr* aguantar (*el temporal, la adversidad*)

weather-beaten ['wɛðər,bitən] *adj* curtido por la intemperie

weather bureau *s* meteo *f*, servicio meteorológico

weath'er•cock' *s* veleta; (*fickle person*) (fig) veleta

weather forecasting *s* pronóstico del tiempo, previsión del tiempo

weather•man ['wɛðər,mæn] *s* (*pl* -men [,mɛn]) meteorologista *m*, pronosticador *m* del tiempo

weather report *s* parte meteorológico

weather station *s* estación meteorológica

weather stripping ['strɪpɪŋ] *s* burlete *m*, cierre hermético

weather vane *s* veleta

weave [wiv] *s* tejido || *v* (*pret* wove [wov] o weaved; *pp* wove o woven ['wovən]) *tr* tejer; **to weave one's way** avanzar zigzagueando || *intr* tejer; zigzaguear

weaver ['wivər] *s* tejedor *m*

web [wɛb] *s* tejido, tela; (*of spider*) tela; (*between toes of birds and other animals*) membrana; (*of an iron rail*) alma; (fig) tejido, tela, enredo

web-footed ['wɛb,fʊtɪd] *adj* palmípedo, de pie palmeado

wed [wɛd] *v* (*pret* & *pp* wed o wedded; *ger* wedding) *tr* (*to join in marriage*) casar; casarse con || *intr* casarse

wedding ['wɛdɪŋ] *adj* nupcial || *s* bodas, nupcias, matrimonio

wedding cake *s* pastel *m* de boda

wedding day *s* día *m* de bodas

wedding march *s* marcha nupcial

wedding night *s* noche *f* de bodas

wedding ring *s* anillo nupcial

wedge [wɛdʒ] *s* cuña || *tr* acuñar, apretar con cuña

wed'lock' *s* matrimonio

Wednesday ['wɛnzdi] *s* miércoles *m*

wee [wi] *adj* pequeñito, diminuto

weed [wid] *s* mala hierba; (coll) tabaco; **weeds** ropa de luto (*especialmente, de una viuda*) || *tr* desherbar, escardar

weeding hoe *s* escardillo

weed killer *s* matamalezas *m*, herbicida *m*

week [wik] *s* semana; **week in week out** semana tras semana

week'day' *s* día *m* laborable

week'days' *adv* entresemana (SAm)

week'end' *s* fin *m* de semana || *intr* pasar el fin de semana

week•ly ['wikli] *adj* semanal || *adv* cada semana || *s* (*pl* -lies) revista semanal, semanario

weep [wip] *v* (*pret* & *pp* wept [wɛpt]) *tr* llorar (*p.ej., la muerte de una persona*); derramar (*lágrimas*) || *intr* llorar

weeper ['wipər] *s* llorón *m*; (*hired mourner*) llorona, plañidera

weeping willow *s* sauce *m* llorón

weep•y ['wipi] *adj* (*comp* -ier; *super* -iest) (coll) lloroso

weevil ['wiyəl] *s* gorgojo

weft [wɛft] *s* (*yarns running across warp*) trama; (*fabric*) tejido

weigh [we] *tr* pesar; (naut) levantar (*el ancla*) || *intr* pesar; **to weigh in** pesarse (*un jockey*)

weight [wet] *s* peso; (*of scales, clock, gymnasium, etc.*) pesa; **to lose weight** rebajar de peso; **to put on weight** ponerse gordo; **tó throw one's weight around** (coll) hacer valer su poder || *tr* cargar, gravar; (*statistically*) ponderar

weightless ['wetlɪs] *adj* ingrávido

weightlessness ['wetlɪsnɪs] *s* ingravidez *f*; antigravedad

weight lifter *s* halterofilista *mf*

weight lifting *s* halterofilia

weight•y ['weti] *adj* (*comp* -ier; *super* -iest) (*heavy*) pesado; (*troublesome*) gravoso; importante, influyente

weir [wɪr] *s* presa, vertedero; (*for catching fish*) pescadera

weird [wɪrd] *adj* misterioso, sobrenatural, espectral; extraño, raro

welcome ['wɛlkəm] *adj* bienvenido; grato, agradable; **you are welcome** (*i.e., gladly received*) sea Vd. bienvenido; (*in answer to thanks*) no hay de qué; **you are welcome to it** está a la disposición de Vd.; **you are welcome to your opinion** piense Vd. lo que quiera || *interj* ¡bienvenido! || *s* bienvenida, buena acogida || *tr* dar la bienvenida a; acoger con gusto, recibir con amabilidad

weld [wɛld] *s* autógena; (bot) gualda || *tr* soldar con autógena; (fig) unir || *intr* soldarse

welder [ˈwɛldər] *s* soldador *m*; (*machine*) soldadora

welding [ˈwɛldɪŋ] *s* autógena, soldadura autógena

wel′fare′ *s* bienestar *m*; (*effort to improve living conditions of the underprivileged*) asistencia, beneficencia; **to be on welfare** vivir de la asistencia pública

welfare state *s* gobierno socializante, estado de beneficencia, estado asistencial

well [wɛl] *adj* bien; bien de salud; **get well!** ¡que se mejore! || *adv* bien; pues; pues bien; **as well** también; **as well as** así como; además de || *interj* ¡vaya! || *s* pozo; (*natural source of water*) fuente *f*, manantial *m* || *intr*—**to well up** salir a borbotones

well-appointed [ˈwɛləˈpɔɪntɪd] *adj* bien amueblado, bien equipado

well-attended [ˈwɛləˈtɛndɪd] *adj* muy concurrido

well-behaved [ˈwɛlbɪˈhevd] *adj* de buena conducta

well′-be′ing *s* bienestar *m*

well′born′ *adj* bien nacido

well-bred [ˈwɛlˈbrɛd] *adj* cortés, bien criado

well-disposed [ˈwɛldɪsˈpozd] *adj* bien dispuesto

well-done [ˈwɛlˈdʌn] *adj* bien hecho; (*meat*) bien asado

well-fixed [ˈwɛlˈfɪkst] *adj* (coll) acaudalado

well-formed [ˈwɛlˈfɔrmd] *adj* bien formado; (*nose*) perfilado

well-founded [ˈwɛlˈfaʊndɪd] *adj* bien fundado

well-groomed [ˈwɛlˈgrumd] *adj* de mucho aseo, atildado

well-heeled [ˈwɛlˈhild] *adj* (coll) acomodado; **to be well-heeled** (coll) tener bien cubierto el riñón

well-informed [ˈwɛlɪnˈfɔrmd] *adj* versado, bien enterado

well-intentioned [ˈwɛlɪnˈtɛnʃənd] *adj* bien intencionado

well-kept [ˈwɛlˈkɛpt] *adj* bien cuidado, bien atendido; (*secret*) bien guardado

well-known [ˈwɛlˈnon] *adj* bien conocido; familiar

well-meaning [ˈwɛlˈminɪŋ] *adj* bien intencionado

well-nigh [ˈwɛlˈnaɪ] *adv* casi

well′-off′ *adj* adinerado, acaudalado

well-preserved [ˈwɛlprɪˈzʌrvd] *adj* bien conservado

well-read [ˈwɛlˈrɛd] *adj* leído, muy leído

well-spent [ˈwɛlˈspɛnt] *adj* (*money, youth, life*) bien empleado

well-spoken [ˈwɛlˈspokən] *adj* (*person*) bienhablado; (*word*) bien dicho

well′spring′ *s* fuente *f*, manantial *m*; fuente inagotable

well sweep *s* cigoñal *m*

well-tempered [ˈwɛlˈtɛmpərd] *adj* bien templado

well-thought-of [ˈwɛlˈθɔt,ɑv] *adj* bien mirado

well-timed [ˈwɛlˈtaɪmd] *adj* oportuno

well-to-do [ˈwɛltəˈdu] *adj* adinerado, acaudalado; (coll) plateado

well-wisher [ˈwɛlˈwɪʃər] *s* amigo, favorecedor *m*

well-worn [ˈwɛlˈworn] *adj* trillado, vulgar

welsh [wɛlʃ] *intr* (slang) dejar de cumplir; **to welsh on** (slang) dejar de cumplir con || **Welsh** *adj* galés || *s* (*language*) galés *m*; **the Welsh** los galeses

Welsh•man [ˈwɛlʃmən] *s* (*pl* **-men** [mən]) galés *m*

Welsh rabbit o **rarebit** [ˈrɛrbɪt] *s* tostada cubierta de queso derretido en cerveza

welt [wɛlt] *s* (*finish along a seam*) ribete *m*; (*of a shoe*) vira; (*wale from a blow*) verdugón *m*

welter [ˈwɛltər] *s* confusión, conmoción; (*a tumbling about*) revuelco || *intr* revolcar

wel′ter•weight′ *s* (box) peso mediano ligero

wen [wɛn] *s* lobanillo

wench [wɛntʃ] *s* muchacha, jovencita; moza, criada

wend [wɛnd] *tr*—**to wend one′s way** dirigir sus pasos, seguir su camino

west [wɛst] *adj* occidental, del oeste || *adv* al oeste, hacia el oeste || *s* oeste *m*

western [ˈwɛstərn] *adj* occidental || *s* película del Oeste

West Indies [ˈɪndiz] *spl* Indias Occidentales

westward [ˈwɛstwərd] *adv* hacia el oeste

wet [wɛt] *adj* (*comp* **wetter;** *super* **wettest**) mojado; (*damp*) húmedo; (*paint*) fresco; (*weather*) lluvioso; (coll) antiprohibicionista || *s* (coll) antiprohibicionista *mf* || *v* (*pret* & *pp* **wet** o **wetted;** *ger* **wetting**) *tr* mojar || *intr* mojarse

wet′back′ *s* mojado

wet bar *s* bar *m* con agua corriente

wet battery *s* pila húmeda

wet blanket *s* aguafiestas *mf*

wet goods *spl* caldos

wet nurse *s* ama de cría o de leche

w.f. *abbr* **wrong font**

w.g. *abbr* **wire gauge**

whack [hwæk] *s* (coll) golpe ruidoso; (coll) prueba, tentativa || *tr* (coll) golpear ruidosamente

whale [hwel] *s* ballena; (*sperm whale*) cachalote *m*; **a whale at** (coll) un as de; **a whale for** (coll) un genio para; **a whale of a difference** (coll) una enorme diferencia; **a whale of a meal** (coll) una comida brutal || *tr* (coll) azotar || *intr* pescar ballenas

whale′bone′ *s* ballena

wharf [hwɔrf] *s* (*pl* **wharves** [hwɔrvz] o **wharfs**) muelle *m*, embarcadero

what [hwɑt] *pron interr* qué; cuál; **what else?** ¿qué más?; **what if . . . ?** ¿y si . . . ?; ¿qué le parece si?; **what of it?** ¿qué importa? || *pron rel* lo que; **what′s what** lo que hay, toda la verdad || *adj interr* qué ||

adj rel el . . . que, la . . . que, etc. ‖ *interj* qué; **what a . . .!** qué . . . más o tan, p.ej., **what a beautiful day!** ¡qué día más (o tan) hermoso!

what•ev′er *pron* cualquiera; todo lo que ‖ *adj* cualquier; cualquier . . . que

what′not′ *s* juguetero

what's-his-name [ˈhwɑtsɪz,nem] *s* (coll) el señor fulano

wheal [hwil] *s* roncha

wheat [hwit] *s* trigo

wheedle [ˈhwidəl] *tr* engatusar; conseguir por medio de halagos

wheel [hwil] *s* rueda; (coll) bicicleta; **at the wheel** en el volante ‖ *tr* pasear (*a un niño*) en un cochecito; conducir (*a un enfermo*) en una silla de ruedas ‖ *intr* (coll) ir en bicicleta; **to wheel about** o **around** dar una vuelta; cambiar de opinión

wheelbarrow [ˈhwil,bæro] *s* carretilla

wheel base *s* batalla, paso, distancia entre ejes

wheel chair *s* silla de ruedas, cochecillo para inválidos

wheeler-dealer [ˈhwilər′dilər] *s* (slang) negociante *m* de gran influencia e independencia

wheel horse *s* caballo de varas; (fig) esclavo (*el que trabaja mucho y cumple con sus obligaciones*)

wheelwright [ˈhwil,raɪt] *s* carpintero de carretas

wheeze [hwiz] *s* resuello ruidoso ‖ *intr* resollar produciendo un silbido

whelp [hwɛlp] *s* cachorro ‖ *intr* parir

when [hwɛn] *adv* cuándo ‖ *conj* cuando

whence [hwɛns] *adv* de dónde; por lo tanto ‖ *conj* de donde

when•ev′er *conj* siempre que, cada vez que

where [hwɛr] *adv* dónde; adónde ‖ *conj* donde; adonde

whereabouts [ˈhwɛrə,baʊts] *s* paradero

whereas [hwɛr′æz] *conj* mientras que, al paso que; considerando ‖ *s* considerando

where•by′ *adv* por medio del cual

wherefore [ˈhwɛrfor] *adv* por qué, para qué; por eso, por tanto ‖ *conj* por lo cual ‖ *s* motivo, razón *f*

where•from′ *adv* de donde

where•in′ *adv* donde, en qué ‖ *conj* donde; en el que; en lo cual

where•of′ *adv* de qué ‖ *conj* de que; de lo cual

where′up•on′ *adv* con lo cual, después de lo cual

wherever [hwɛr′ɛvər] *conj* dondequiera que

wherewithal [ˈhwɛrwɪð,ɔl] *s* cumquibus *m*, medios

whet [hwɛt] *v* (*pret & pp* **whetted;** *ger* **whetting**) *tr* afilar, aguzar; despertar, estimular; abrir (*el apetito*)

whether [ˈwɛðər] *conj* si; **whether or no** en todo caso, de todas maneras; **whether or not** si . . . o no, ya sea que . . . o no

whet′stone′ *s* piedra de afilar

whey [hwe] *s* suero de la leche

which [hwɪtʃ] *pron interr* cuál; **which is which** cuál es el uno y cuál el otro ‖ *pron rel* que, el (la, etc.) que ‖ *adj interr* qué; cuál, cuál de los (las) ‖ *adj rel* el (la, etc.) . . . que

which•ev′er *pron rel* cualquiera ‖ *adj rel* cualquier; **whichever ones** cualesquiera

whiff [hwɪf] *s* soplo; fumada; olorcillo; acceso, arranque *m;* **to get a whiff of** percibir un olor fugaz de ‖ *intr* soplar (*el viento*); echar bocanadas (*el que fuma*)

while [hwaɪl] *conj* mientras, mientras que ‖ *s* rato; **a long while** largo rato; **a while ago** hace un rato; **between whiles** de vez en cuando ‖ *tr* **to while away** entretener (*el tiempo*); pasar (*p.ej., la tarde*) de un modo entretenido

whim [hwɪm] *s* capricho, antojo

whimper [ˈhwɪmpər] *s* lloriqueo ‖ *tr* decir lloriqueando ‖ *intr* lloriquear

whimsical [ˈhwɪmzɪkəl] *adj* caprichoso, extravagante, fantástico

whine [hwaɪn] *s* gimoteo, quejido ‖ *intr* gimotear, quejarse

whin•ny [ˈhwɪni] *s* (*pl* **-nies**) relincho ‖ *v* (*pret & pp* **-nied**) *intr* relinchar

whip [hwɪp] *s* látigo, zurriago; huevos batidos con nata ‖ *v* (*pret & pp* **whipped** o **whipt;** *ger* **whipping**) *tr* azotar, zurriagar, fustigar; batir (*huevos y nata*); (coll) derrotar, vencer; **to whip off** (coll) escribir de prisa; **to whip out** sacar de repente; **to whip up** (coll) preparar de prisa; (coll) avivar, excitar

whip′cord′ *s* tralla; tejido fuerte con costurones diagonales

whip hand *s* mano *f* del látigo; (*upper hand*) vara alta

whip′lash′ *s* tralla

whipped cream *s* nata, crema batida

whipper-snapper [ˈhwɪpər,snæpər] *s* arrapiezo, mequetrefe *m*

whippet [ˈhwɪpɪt] *s* perro lebrel

whipping boy [ˈhwɪpɪŋ] *s* cabeza de turco, víctima inocente

whipping post *s* poste *m* de flagelación

whippoorwill [,hwɪpər′wɪl] *s* chotacabras norteamericano (*Caprimulgus vociferus*)

whir [hwʌr] *s* zumbido ‖ *v* (*pret & pp* **whirred;** *ger* **whirring**) *intr* girar zumbando

whirl [hwʌrl] *s* vuelta, giro; remolino; (*of events, parties, etc.*) serie *f* interminable ‖ *tr & intr* remolinear; **my head whirls** siento vértigo

whirligig [ˈhwʌrli,gɪg] *s* (ent) escribano del agua; tíovivo; (*pinwheel*) rehilandera, molinete *m;* peonza

whirl′pool′ *s* remolino, vorágine *f*

whirl′wind′ *s* torbellino, manga de viento

whirlybird [ˈhwʌrli,bʌrd] *s* (coll) helicóptero

whish [hwɪʃ] *s* zumbido suave ‖ *intr* zumbar suavemente

whisk [hwɪsk] *s* escobilla; toque ligero ‖ *tr* barrer, cepillar; **to whisk out of sight** escamotear ‖ *intr* moverse rápidamente

whisk broom *s* escobilla

whiskers [ˈhwɪskərz] *spl* barbas; (*on side of face*) patillas; (*of cat*) bigotes *mpl*

whiskey [ˈhwɪski] *adj* (*voice*) (coll) aguardentoso ‖ *s* whisky *m*

whisper [ˈhwɪspər] *s* cuchicheo; (*of leaves*) susurro; **in a whisper** en voz baja ‖ *tr* susurrar, decir al oído ‖ *intr* cuchichear, hablar al oído; susurrar (*p.ej., las hojas*); (*to gossip*) susurrar, murmurar

whisperer [ˈhwɪspərər] *s* susurrón *m*

whispering [ˈhwɪspərɪŋ] *adj & s* (*gossiping*) susurrón *m*

whist [hwɪst] *s* whist *m* (*juego de naipes*)

whistle [ˈhwɪsəl] *s* (*sound*) silbido, silbo; pitazo; (*device*) silbato, pito; **to wet one's whistle** (coll) remojar la palabra ‖ *tr* silbar (*p.ej., una canción* ‖ *intr* silbar; pitear; **to whistle for** llamar con un silbido; (coll) tener que componérselas sin

whistle stop *s* apeadero, pueblecito

whit [hwɪt] *s*—**not a whit** ni pizca; **to not care a whit** no importarle a (*uno*) un bledo

white [hwaɪt] *adj* blanco ‖ *s* blanco; (*of an egg*) clara; **whites** (pathol) pérdidas blancas, flujo blanco

white'caps' *spl* cabrillas, palomas

white coal *s* hulla blanca

white'-col'lar *adj* oficinesco

white-collar crime *s* crímenes *mpl* de oficinistas

white feather *s*—**to show the white feather** mostrarse cobarde

white goods *spl* tejidos de algodón; ropa blanca; aparatos electrodomésticos

white-haired [ˈhwaɪt,hɛrd] *adj* de pelo blanco; (*gray-haired*) cano; (coll) favorito, predilecto

white heat *s* blanco, calor blanco; (fig) viva agitación

white lead [lɛd] *s* albayalde *m*

white lie *s* mentirilla, mentira inocente u oficiosa

white meat *s* pechuga, carne *f* de la pechuga del ave

whiten [ˈhwaɪtən] *tr* blanquear, emblanquecer ‖ *intr* blanquear, emblanquecerse; palidecer

whiteness [ˈhwaɪtnɪs] *s* blancura

white plague *s* peste blanca (*tuberculosis*)

white slavery *s* trata de blancas

white tie *s* corbatín blanco; traje *m* de etiqueta

white'wash' *s* jalbegue *m*, lechada, blanqueadura; (*e.g., of a scandal*) encubrimiento ‖ *tr* jalbegar, enjalbegar, encalar; absolver sin justicia; encubrir (*un escándalo*)

whither [ˈhwɪðər] *adv* adónde ‖ *conj* adonde

whitish [ˈhwaɪtɪʃ] *adj* blanquecino, blancuzco

whitlow [ˈhwɪtlo] *s* panadizo, uñero

Whitsuntide [ˈhwɪtsən,taɪd] *s* semana de Pentecostés

whittle [ˈhwɪtəl] *tr* sacar pedazos a (*un trozo de madera*); **to whittle away** o **down** reducir poco a poco

whiz o **whizz** [hwɪz] *s* silbido, zumbido; (slang) perito, fenómeno ‖ *v* (*pret & pp*

whizzed; *ger* **whizzing**) *intr*—**to whiz by** rehilar, silbar; pasar como una flecha

who [hu] *pron interr* quién; **who else?** ¿quién más?; **who goes there?** (mil) ¿quién vive?; **who's who** quién es el uno y quién el otro; quiénes son gente de importancia ‖ *pron rel* que, quien; el (la, etc.) que

whoa [hwo] o [wo] *interj* ¡so!

who•ev'er *pron rel* quienquiera que, cualquiera que

whole [hol] *adj* todo, entero; (*intact*) ileso; (*not scattered or dispersed*) único, p.ej., **the whole interest for him was the child he was raising** el único interés para él era el niño que educaba; **made out of the whole cloth** enteramente falso o imaginario ‖ *s* conjunto, todo; **as a whole** en conjunto; **on the whole** en general; por la mayor parte

wholehearted [ˈhol,hartɪd] *adj* sincero, cordial

whole note *s* (mus) semibreve *f*

whole'sale' *adj & adv* al por mayor ‖ *s* venta ·al pormayor ‖ *tr* vender al por mayor ‖ *intr* vender al por mayor; venderse al por mayor

wholesaler [ˈhol,selər] *s* comerciante *mf* al por mayor

wholesome [ˈholsəm] *adj* (*conducive to good health*) saludable; (*in good health*) fresco, rollizo

wholly [ˈholi] *adv* enteramente, completamente

whole wheat *s* trigo entero

whom [hum] *pron interr* a quién ‖ *pron rel* que, a quien; al (a la, etc.) que

whom•ev'er *pron rel* a quienquiera que

whoop [hup] o [hwup] *s* ululato ‖ *tr*—**to whoop it up** (slang) armar una gritería ‖ *intr* ulular

whooping cough [ˈhupɪŋ] o [ˈhupɪŋ] *s* tos ferina, tos convulsiva

whopper [ˈhwapər] *s* (coll) enormidad; (coll) mentirón *m*

whopping [ˈhwapɪŋ] *adj* (coll) enorme, grandísimo

whore [hor] *s* puta ‖ *intr*—**to whore around** putañear, putear

whore'house' *s* burdel *m*; congal *m* (Mex)

whortleber•ry [ˈhwʌrtəl,bɛri] *s* (*pl* **-ries**) arándano

whose [huz] *pron interr* de quién ‖ *pron rel* de quien, cuyo

why [hwaɪ] *adv* por qué; **why not?** ¿cómo no? ‖ *s* (*pl* **whys**) porqué *m* ‖ *interj* ¡toma!; **why, certainly!** ¡desde luego!, ¡por supuesto!; **why, yes!** ¡claro!, ¡pues sí!

wick [wɪk] *s* mecha, pabilo

wicked [ˈwɪkɪd] *adj* malo; malazo; (*mischievous*) travieso, revoltoso; (*vicious*) arisco; ofensivo

wicker [ˈwɪkər] *adj* mimbroso ‖ *s* mimbre *m & f*

wicket [ˈwɪkɪt] *s* (*small door in a larger one*) portillo, postigo; (*small opening in a door*) ventanillo; (*ticket window*) taquilla; (*gate to regulate flow of water*) compuerta; (cricket) meta; (croquet) aro

wide [waɪd] *adj* ancho; de ancho; (*sense of a word*) amplio, lato ‖ *adv* de par en par; enteramente; lejos; **wide of the mark** lejos del blanco; fuera de propósito

wide'-an'gle *adj* granangular

wide'-a·wake' *adj* despabilado

widen [`waɪdən] *tr* ensanchar ‖ *intr* ensancharse

wide'-o'pen *adj* abierto de par en par; **to be wide-open** estar (*p.ej.*, *una ciudad*) abierta a los jugadores

wide'spread' *adj* (*arms, wings*) extendido; difundido, extenso

widow [`wɪdo] *s* viuda; (cards) baceta ‖ *tr* dejar viuda

widower [`wɪdo·ər] *s* viudo

widowhood [`wɪdo,hʊd] *s* viudez *f*

widow's mite *s* limosna que da un pobre

widow's pension *s* viudedad

widow's weeds *spl* luto de viuda

width [wɪdθ] *s* anchura

wield [wild] *tr* esgrimir, manejar (*la espada*); ejercer (*el poder*)

wife [waɪf] *s* (*pl* **wives** [waɪvz]) esposa, mujer *f*

wig [wɪg] *s* peluca

wiggle [`wɪgəl] *s* meneo rápido ‖ *tr* menear rápidamente ‖ *intr* menearse rápidamente

wig'wag' *s* comunicación con banderas ‖ *v* (*pret & pp* **-wagged**; *ger* **-wagging**) *tr* menear; mandar (*informes*) moviendo banderas ‖ *intr* menearse; señalar con banderas

wigwam [`wɪgwɑm] *s* choza cónica (*de los pieles rojas*)

wild [waɪld] *adj* (*not domesticated; growing without cultivation; uncivilized*) salvaje; (*unrestrained*) descabellado; (*frantic, mad*) frenético; (*riotous*) desenfrenado, revoltoso; extravagante; (*bullet, shot*) perdido; **wild about** loco por ‖ *adv* disparatadamente; **to run wild** crecer locamente; estar sin gobierno ‖ *s* desierto, yermo; **wilds** monte *m*, despoblado

wild boar *s* jabalí *m*

wild card *s* comodín *m*

wild'cat' *s* gato montés; lince *m;* empresa arriesgada

wildcat strike *s* huelga no autorizada por el sindicato

wilderness [`wɪldərnɪs] *s* desierto, yermo

wild'fire' *s* fuego fatuo; fucilazo; **to spread like wildfire** ser un reguero de pólvora, correr como pólvora en reguero

wild flower *s* flor *f* del campo

wild goose *s* ganso bravo

wild'-goose' chase *s* caza de grillos

wild'life' *s* animales *mf* salvajes

wild oats *spl* excesos de la juventud, mocedad; **to sow one's wild oats** llevar (*los mozos*) una vida de excesos

wild olive *s* acebuche *m*

wile [waɪl] *s* ardid *m* engaño; (*cunning*) astucia ‖ *tr* engatusar; **to wile away** entretener (*el tiempo*); pasar (*p.ej.*, *la tarde*)

will [wɪl] *s* voluntad; (law) testamento; **at will** a voluntad ‖ *tr* querer; (*to bequeath*) legar ‖ *intr* querer; **do as you will** haga

Vd. lo que quiera ‖ *v* (*pret & cond* **would**) *v aux* he **will arrive at six o'clock** llegará a las seis; **he will go for days without smoking** pasa días enteros sin fumar

willful [`wɪlfəl] *adj* voluntarioso

willfulness [`wɪlfəlnɪs] *s* voluntariedad

William [`wɪljəm] *s* Guillermo

willing [`wɪlɪŋ] *adj* dispuesto; gustoso, pronto; espontáneo; **willing or unwilling** que quiera, que no quiera

willingly [`wɪlɪŋli] *adv* de buena gana, de buena voluntad

willingness [`wɪlɪŋnɪs] *s* buena gana, buena voluntad

will-o'-the-wisp [`wɪləðə'wɪsp] *s* fuego fatuo; ilusión, quimera

willow [`wɪlo] *s* sauce *m*

willowy [`wɪlo·i] *adj* (*pliant*) juncal, mimbreño; (*slender, graceful*) juncal, cimbreño, esbelto; lleno de sauces

will power *s* fuerza de voluntad

willy-nilly [`wɪli'nɪli] *adv* de grado o por fuerza

wilt [wɪlt] *tr* marchitar ‖ *intr* marchitarse

wil·y [`waɪli] *adj* (*comp* **-ier**; *super* **-iest**) artero, engañoso; astuto

wimple [`wɪmpəl] *s* griñón *m*, impla

win [wɪn] *s* (coll) éxito, triunfo ‖ *v* (*pret & pp* **won** [wʌn]; *ger* **winning**) *tr* ganar; **to win over** ganar, conquistar ‖ *intr* ganar; **to win out** ganar; (coll) tener éxito

wince [wɪns] *s* sobresalto ‖ *intr* sobresaltarse

winch [wɪntʃ] *s* maquinilla, torno; (*handle, crank*) manubrio

wind [wɪnd] *s* viento; (*gas in intestines*) (coll) viento; (*breath*) respiración, resuello; **to break wind** ventosear; **to get wind of** saber de, tener noticia de; **to sail close to the wind** (naut) ceñir el viento; **to take the wind out of one's sails** apagarle a uno los fuegos ‖ *tr* dejar sin aliento ‖ [waɪnd] *v* (*pret & pp* **wound** [waʊnd]) *tr* (*to coil; to wrap up*) arrollar, envolver, devanar (*alambre*); ovillar (*hilo*); torcer (*hebras*); hacer girar (*un manubrio*); dar cuerda a (*un reloj*); **to wind one's way through** serpentear por; **to wind up** arrollar, envolver; (coll) poner punto final a ‖ *intr* serpentear (*un camino*)

windbag [`wɪnd,bæg] *s* (*of bagpipe*) odre *m*; (coll) charlatán *m*, palabrero, discursista *mf*

windbreak [`wɪnd,brek] *s* guardavientos *m*

wind cone [wɪnd] *s* (aer) cono de viento

winded [`wɪndɪd] *adj* falto de respiración, sin resuello

windfall [`wɪnd,fɔl] *s* fruta caída del árbol; fortunón *m*, cosa llovida del cielo

winding sheet [`waɪndɪŋ] *s* sudario, mortaja

winding stairs *spl* escalera de caracol

wind instrument [wɪnd] *s* (mus) instrumento de viento

windlass [`wɪndləs] *s* maquinilla, torno

windmill [`wɪnd,mɪl] *s* (*mill operated by wind*) molino de viento; (*modern wind-driven source of power*) aeromotor *m*; (*pinwheel*) molinete *m*; **to tilt at windmills** luchar con los molinos de viento

window [`wɪndo] *s* ventana; (*of ticket office; of envelope*) ventanilla; (*of coach, automobile*) ventanilla, portezuela
window dresser *s* escaparatista *mf*
window dressing *s* adorno de escaparates
window frame *s* marco de ventana
win'dow•pane' *s* cristal *m* o vidrio de ventana
window screen *s* alambrera, sobrevidriera
window shade *s* visillo, transparente *m* de resorte
win'dow•shop' *v* (*pret & pp* **-shopped;** *ger* **-shopping**) *intr* curiosear en las tiendas
window shutter *s* contraventana
window sill *s* repisa de ventana
windpipe [`wɪnd,paɪp] *s* tráquea
wind shear *s* (aer) ráfaga violenta
windshield [`wɪnd,ʃild] *s* parabrisa *m*
windshield washer *s* lavaparabrisas *m*
windshield wiper *s* limpiaparabrisas *m*
wind'shield-wip'er blade *s* escobilla de limpiaparabrisas
wind sock *s* (aer) cono de viento
windstorm [`wɪnd,stɔrm] *s* ventarrón *m*
wind-up [`waɪnd,ʌp] *s* conclusión; (sport) final *f* de partido
windward [`wɪndwərd] *s* barlovento; **to turn to windward** barloventear
Windward Islands *spl* islas de Barlovento
Windward Passage *s* paso de los Vientos
wind•y [`wɪndi] *adj* (*comp* **-ier;** *super* **-iest**) ventoso; (*unsubstantial*) vacío; palabrero, ampuloso, discursisto; **it is windy** hace viento
wine [waɪn] *s* vino ‖ *tr* obsequiar con vino ‖ *intr* beber vino
wine cellar *s* bodega
wine'glass' *s* copa para vino
winegrower [`waɪn,gro•ər] *s* vinicultor *m*
winegrowing [`waɪn,gro•ɪŋ] *s* vinicultura
wine making *s* enotecnia
wine press *s* lagar *m*
winer•y [`waɪnəri] *s* (*pl* **-ies**) lagar *m*
wine'skin' *s* odre *m*
winetaster [`waɪn,testər] *s* catavinos *m*
wing [wɪŋ] *s* ala; facción; bando; (theat) bastidor *m*; **to take wing** alzar el vuelo ‖ *tr* herir en el ala; **to wing one's way** avanzar volando
wing chair *s* sillón *m* de orejas
wing collar *s* cuello de pajarita
wing nut *s* tuerca de aletas
wing'spread' *s* envergadura
wink [wɪŋk] *s* guiño; **to not sleep a wink** no pegar los ojos; **to take forty winks** (coll) descabezar el sueño ‖ *tr* guiñar (*el ojo*) ‖ *intr* guiñar; (*to blink*) parpadear, pestañear; **to wink at** guiñar el ojo a; fingir no ver
winner [`wɪnər] *s* ganador *m*, vencedor *m*; premiado
winning [`wɪnɪŋ] *adj* triunfante, victorioso; atrayente, simpático ‖ **winnings** *spl* ganancias
winnow [`wɪno] *tr* aventar; entresacar ‖ *intr* aletear
winsome [`wɪnsəm] *adj* atrayente, simpático; engañador; alegre

winter [`wɪntər] *adj* invernal ‖ *s* invierno ‖ *intr* invernar
win'ter•green' *s* gaulteria, té *m* del Canadá; esencia de gaulteria
win•try [`wɪntri] *adj* (*comp* **-trier;** *super* **-triest**) invernal, invernizo; helado, frío
wipe [waɪp] *tr* frotar para limpiar; enjugar (*la cara, el sudor, las manos*); **to wipe away** enjugar (*lágrimas*); **to wipe off** quitar frotando; **to wipe out** (coll) borrar, cancelar; (coll) aniquilar, destruir; (coll) enjugar (*deudas, un déficit*)
wiper [`waɪpər] *s* paño, trapo; (elec) contacto deslizante
wire [waɪr] *s* (*thread of metal*) alambre *m*; telégrafo; telegrama *m*; teléfono; **to pull wires** (coll) tocar resortes ‖ *tr* alambrar; telegrafiar ‖ *intr* telegrafiar
wire cutter *s* cortaalambres *m*
wire entanglement *s* (mil) alambrado
wire gauge *s* calibrador *m* de alambre
wire-haired [`waɪr,hɛrd] *adj* de pelo áspero
wireless [`waɪrlɪs] *adj* inalámbrico, sin hilos
wire nail *s* punta de París, clavo de alambre
wire pulling [`pʊlɪŋ] *s* (coll) empleo de resortes; enchufismo
wire recorder *s* grabadora de alambre
wire screen *s* alambrera, tela de alambre
wire service *s* servicio telegráfrico y telefónico
wire'tap' *v* (*pret & pp* **-tapped;** *ger* **-tapping**) *tr* intervenir (*una conversación telefónica*)
wire tapping *s* escuchas telefónicas *fpl*
wiring [`waɪrɪŋ] *s* (elec) alambraje *m*
wir•y [`waɪri] *adj* (*comp* **-ier;** *super* **-iest**) alambrino; cimbreante; nervudo; vibrante
wisdom [`wɪzdəm] *s* sabiduría, cordura
wisdom tooth *s* muela cordal, muela del juicio
wise [waɪz] *adj* sabio, cuerdo; (*step, decision*) acertado, juicioso; **to be wise to** (slang) conocer el juego de; **to get wise** (coll) caer en el chiste ‖ *s* modo, manera; **in no wise** de ningún modo
wiseacre [`waɪz,ekər] *s* sabihondo
wise'crack' *s* (slang) cuchufleta ‖ *intr* (slang) cuchufletear
wise guy *s* (slang) sabelotodo
wish [wɪʃ] *s* deseo; **to make a wish** pensar algo que se desea ‖ *tr* desear; dar (*los buenos días*) ‖ *intr* desear; **to wish for** desear, anhelar
wish'bone' *s* espoleta, hueso de la suerte
wishful [`wɪʃfəl] *adj* deseoso
wishful thinking *s* optimismo a ultranza; **to indulge in wishful thinking** forjarse ilusiones
wistful [`wɪstfəl] *adj* melancólico, tristón, pensativo
wit [wɪt] *s* agudeza; (*person*) chistoso; (*keen mental power*) juicio; **to be at one's wits' end** no saber qué hacer; **to have the wit to** tener el tino de; **to live by one's wits** vivir del cuento
witch [wɪtʃ] *s* bruja, hechicera; (*old hag*) bruja

wi
wi

witch'craft' *s* brujería

witches' Sabbath *s* aquelarre *m*

witch hazel *s* (*shrub*) nogal *m* de la brujería, planta del sortilegio; (*liquid*) hamamelina, hazelina

with [wɪð] o [wɪθ] *prep* con; de

with·draw' *v* (*pret* -drew; *pp* -drawn) *tr* retirar ‖ *intr* retirarse

withdrawal [wɪð'drɔ·əl] o [wɪθ'drɔ·əl] *s* retirada

withdrawal symptom *s* síntoma *m* de abstinencia; (slang) mono

wither ['wɪðər] *tr* marchitar; (fig) aplastar, confundir ‖ *intr* marchitarse; confundirse

with·hold' *v* (*pret & pp* -held) *tr* retener; suspender (*pago*); negar (*un permiso*)

withholding tax *s* impuesto deducido del sueldo

with·in' *adv* dentro ‖ *prep* dentro de; al alcance de; poco menos de; con un margen de

with·out' *adv* fuera ‖ *prep* fuera de; (*lacking, not with*) sin; **to do without** pasar sin; **without** + *ger* sin + *inf*, p.ej., **he left without saying goodbye** salió sin despedirse; **sin que** + *subj*, p.ej., **he came in without anyone seeing him** entró sin que nadie le viese

with·stand' *v* (*pret & pp* -stood) *tr* aguantar, resistir

witness ['wɪtnɪs] *s* testigo *mf;* **in witness whereof** en fe de lo cual; **to bear witness** dar testimonio ‖ *tr* (*to be present at*) presenciar; (*to attest*) atestiguar, testimoniar; firmar como testigo

witness stand *s* banquillo o estrado de los testigos

witticism ['wɪtɪ,sɪzəm] *s* agudeza, dicho agudo, ocurrencia

wittingly ['wɪtɪŋli] *adv* a sabiendas

wit·ty ['wɪti] *adj* (*comp* -tier; *super* -tiest) agudo, ingenioso; (*person*) ocurrente, chistoso

wizard ['wɪzərd] *s* brujo, hechicero; (coll) as *m*, experto

wizardry ['wɪzərdri] *s* hechicería, magia

wizened ['wɪzənd] *adj* acartonado, arrugado

wk. *abbr* week

w.l. *abbr* wave length

woad [wod] *s* hierba pastel

wobble ['wɑbəl] *s* bamboleo, tambaleo ‖ *intr* bambolear, tambalear; bailar (*una silla*); (fig) vacilar, ser inconstante

wob·bly ['wɑbli] *adj* (*comp* -blier; *super* -bliest) bamboleante, inseguro; vacilante

woe [wo] *s* aflicción, miseria, infortunio ‖ *interj* —woe is me! ¡ay de mí!

woebegone ['wobɪ,gɔn] o ['wobɪ,gɑn] *adj* cariacontecido, triste

woeful ['wofəl] *adj* triste, miserable; (*of poor quality*) malo, pésimo

wolf [wʊlf] *s* (*pl* wolves [wʊlvz]) lobo; persona cruel, persona mañosa; (coll) tenorio; **to cry wolf** dar falsa alarma; **to keep the wolf from the door** ponerse a cubierto del hambre ‖ *tr & intr* comer vorazmente, engullir

wolf'hound' *s* galgo lobero

wolfram ['wʊlfrəm] *s* (*element*) volframio; (*mineral*) volframita

wolf's-bane o wolfsbane ['wʊlfs,ben] *s* matalobos *m*

woman ['wʊmən] *s* (*pl* women ['wɪmɪn]) mujer *f*

womanhood ['wʊmən,hʊd] *s* el sexo femenino; las mujeres

womanish ['wʊmənɪʃ] *adj* mujeril; (*effeminate*) afeminado

wom'an·kind' *s* el sexo femenino

womanly ['wʊmənli] *adj* (*comp* -lier; *super* -liest) femenil, mujeriego

woman suffrage *s* sufragismo

woman-suffragist ['wʊmən'sʌfrədʒɪst] *s* sufragista *mf*

womb [wʊm] *s* útero; (fig) seno

womenfolk ['wɪmɪn,fok] *spl* las mujeres

women's lib(eration movement) *s* movimiento feminista; feminismo

wonder ['wʌndər] *s* (*something strange or surprising*) maravilla; (*feeling of surprise*) admiración; (*something strange, miracle*) milagro; **for a wonder** cosa extraña; **no wonder that** . . . no es mucho que. . .; **to work wonders** hacer milagros ‖ *tr* preguntarse ‖ *intr* admirarse, maravillarse; **to wonder at** admirarse de, maravillarse con o de

wonder drugs *spl* drogas milagrosas

wonderful ['wʌndərfəl] *adj* maravilloso

won'der·land' *s* tierra de las maravillas; reino de las hadas

wonderment ['wʌndərmənt] *s* asombro, sorpresa

wont [wʌnt] o [wɔnt] *adj* acostumbrado; **to be wont to** acostumbrar ‖ *s* costumbre, hábito

wonted ['wʌntɪd] o ['wɔntɪd] *adj* acostumbrado, habitual

woo [wu] *tr* cortejar (*a una mujer*); tratar de conquistar; tratar de persuadir

wood [wʊd] *s* madera; (*for making a fire*) leña; barril *m* de madera; **out of the woods** (coll) fuera de peligro; (coll) libre de dificultades; **to take to the woods** andar a monte; **woods** bosque *m*

woodbine ['wʊd,baɪn] *s* (*honeysuckle*) madreselva; (*Virginia creeper*) guau *m*

wood carving *s* labrado de madera

wood'chuck' *s* marmota de América

wood'cock' *s* becada, coalla, chocha

wood'cut' *s* (typ) grabado en madera

wood'cut'ter *s* leñador *m*

wooded ['wʊdɪd] *adj* arbolado, enselvado

wooden ['wʊdən] *adj* de madera, hecho de madera; torpe, estúpido; sin ánimo

wood engraving *s* (typ) grabado en madera

wooden-headed ['wʊdən,hɛdɪd] *adj* (coll) torpe, estúpido

wooden leg *s* pata de palo

wooden shoe *s* zueco

wood grouse *s* gallo de bosque

woodland ['wʊdlənd] *adj* selvático ‖ *s* bosque *m*, monte *m*

woodland scene *s* (paint) boscaje *m*

wood·man ['wʊdmən] s (pl **-men** [mən]) leñador m

woodpecker ['wʊd,pɛkər] s carpintero, pájaro carpintero; (green woodpecker) picamaderos m

wood′pile′ s montón m de leña

wood screw s tirafondo

wood′shed′ s leñero

woods·man ['wʊdzmən] s (pl **-men** [mən]) leñador m

wood′wind′ s (mus) instrumento de viento de madera

wood′work′ s (working in wood) ebanistería, obra de carpintería; (things made of wood) maderaje m

wood′work′er s ebanista mf, carpintero

wood′worm′ s carcoma

wood·y ['wʊdi] adj (comp **-ier**; super **-iest**) arbolado, enselvado; (like wood) leñoso

wooer ['wu·ər] s pretendiente m, galán m

woof [wuf] s (yarns running across warp) trama; (fabric) tejido

woofer ['wufər] s altavoz m para audiofrecuencias bajas

wool [wʊl] s lana

woolen ['wʊlən] adj de lana, hecho de lana ‖ s tejido de lana; **woolens** lanerías

woolgrower ['wʊl ,gro·ər] s criador m de ganado lanar

wool·ly ['wʊli] adj (comp **-lier**; super **-liest**) lanoso, lanudo; borroso, confuso

Worcestershire sauce ['wʊstərʃər] s salsa inglesa

word [wʌrd] s palabra; **to be as good as one's word** cumplir lo prometido; **to have a word with** hablar cuatro palabras con; **to have word from** recibir noticias de; **to keep one's word** cumplir su palabra; **to leave word** dejar dicho; **to send word that** mandar decir que; **words** (a quarrel) palabras mayores; (text of a song) letra ‖ tr redactar, formular ‖ **Word** s (theol) Verbo

word count s recuento de vocabulario

word formation s (gram) formación de palabras

wording ['wʌrdɪŋ] s fraseología, estilo

word order s (gram) orden m de colocación

word processing s redacción por medios electrónicos

word′stock′ s vocabulario, léxico

word·y ['wʌrdi] adj (comp **-ier**; super **-iest**) verboso

work [wʌrk] s (exertion; labor, toil) trabajo; (result of exertion; human output; engineering structure) obra; (sew) labor f; **at work** trabajando; (not at home) en la oficina, en el taller, en la tienda; **out of work** sin trabajo, desempleado; **to shoot the works** (slang) echar el resto; **works** fábrica; mecanismo; (of clock) movimiento ‖ tr hacer trabajar; trabajar, obrar (la madera, el hierro); obrar (un milagro); explotar (una mina); **to work up** preparar; estimular, excitar ‖ intr trabajar; funcionar, marchar (un aparato, un motor); obrar (p.ej., un remedio); **to work loose** aflojarse; **to work out** resolverse

workable ['wʌrkəbəl] adj (feasible) practicable; (that can be worked) laborable

workaholic [,wʌrkə'hɔlɪk] s (coll) individuo con compulsión al trabajo

work′bench′ s banco de trabajo, banco de taller

work′book′ s (manual of instructions) libro de reglas; libro de ejercicios

work′box′ s caja de herramientas; (for needlework) caja de labor

work′day′ adj de cada día; ordinario, vulgar ‖ s día m de trabajo; (number of hours of work) jornada

work′days′ adv entresemana (SAm)

worked-up ['wʌrkt'ʌp] adj muy conmovido, sobreexcitado, exaltado

worker ['wʌrkər] s trabajador m, obrero

work force s mano f de obra, personal obrero

work′horse′ s caballo de carga; (tireless worker) yunque m

work′house′ s taller penitenciario; (Brit) asilo de pobres

working class s clase obrera

work′ing-girl′ s trabajadora joven

working hours spl horas de trabajo

working hypothesis s hipótesis f de guía

working·man ['wʌrkɪŋ,mæn] s (pl **-men** [,mɛn]) obrero, trabajador m

working·woman ['wʌrkɪŋ,wʊmən] s (pl **-women** [,wɪmɪn]) obrera, trabajadora

work·man ['wʌrkmən] s (pl **-men** [mən]) obrero, trabajador m; (skilled worker) artífice m

workmanship ['wʌrkmən,ʃɪp] s destreza en el trabajo; (work executed) hechura, obra

work of art s obra de arte

work′out′ s ensayo, prueba; (physical exercise) ejercicio

work′room′ s (for manual work) obrador m, taller m; (study) gabinete m de trabajo

work′shop′ s obrador m, taller m

work stoppage s paro

work therapy s laborterapia

world [wʌrld] adj mundial ‖ s mundo; **a world of** la mar de; **half the world** (a lot of people) medio mundo; **since the world began** desde que el mundo es mundo; **the other world** el otro mundo; **to bring into the world** echar al mundo; **to see the world** ver mundo; **to think the world of** tener un alto concepto de

world affairs spl asuntos internacionales

world′-class′ adj sobresaliente

world·ly ['wʌrldli] adj (comp **-lier**; super **-liest**) mundano

world′ly-wise′ adj que tiene mucho mundo

world's fair s exposición mundial

World War s Guerra Mundial

world′-wide′ adj global, mundial

worm [wʌrm] s gusano; **worms** (pathol) lombrices fpl ‖ tr limpiar de lombrices; **to worm a secret out of a person** arrancar mañosamente un secreto a una persona; **to worm one's way into** insinuarse en

worm-eaten ['wʌrm,itən] adj carcomido; (fig) decaído, desgastado

worm gear s engranaje m de tornillo sin fin

wi
wo

worm'wood' *s* (*Artemisia*) ajenjo; (*Artemisia absinthium*) ajenjo del campo o ajenjo mayor; (*something bitter or grievous*) (fig) ajenjo

worm•y ['wʌrmi] *adj* (*comp* -**ier**; *super* -**iest**) gusaniento, gusanoso; (*worm-eaten*) carcomido; (*groveling*) rastrero, servil

worn [worn] *adj* roto, raído, gastado

worn'-out' *adj* muy gastado, inservible; (*by toil, illness*) consumido, rendido

worrisome ['wʌrɪsəm] *adj* inquietante; (*inclined to worry*) aprensivo, inquieto

wor•ry ['wʌri] *s* (*pl* -**ries**) inquietud, preocupación; (*cause of anxiety*) molestia ‖ *v* (*pret & pp* -**ried**) *tr* inquietar, preocupar; (*to harass, pester*) acosar, molestar; **to be worried** estar inquieto ‖ *intr* inquietarse, preocuparse; **don't worry** pierda Vd. cuidado

worse [wʌrs] *adj & adv comp* peor; **worse and worse** de mal en peor

worsen ['wʌrsən] *tr & intr* empeorar ‖ *ref* gravarse

wor•ship ['wʌrʃɪp] *s* adoración, culto; **your worship** vuestra merced ‖ *v* (*pret & pp* -**shiped** o -**shipped**; *ger* -**shiping** o -**shipping**) *tr & intr* adorar, venerar

worshiper o **worshipper** ['wʌrʃɪpər] *s* adorador *m*, devoto

worst [wʌrst] *adj & adv super* peor ‖ *s* (lo) peor; **at worst** en las peores circunstancias; **if worst comes to worst** si pasa lo peor; **to get the worst of** llevar la peor parte, salir perdiendo

worsted ['wʊstɪd] *adj* de estambre ‖ *s* estambre *m*; tela de estambre

wort [wʌrt] *s* (bot) hierba, planta; mosto de cerveza

worth [wʌrθ] *adj* del valor de; digno de; **to be worth** valer; tener una fortuna de; **to be worth** + *ger* valer la pena de + *inf*; **to be worth while** valer la pena; ser de mérito ‖ *s* valor *m*; mérito; **a dollar's worth of** un dólar de

worthless ['wʌrθlɪs] *adj* sin valor, inútil, inservible; (*person*) despreciable

worth'while' *adj* de mérito, digno de atención

wor•thy ['wʌrði] *adj* (*comp* -**thier**; *super* -**thiest**) digno; benemérito, meritorio ‖ *s* (*pl* -**thies**) benemérito; (*hum & iron*) personaje *m*

would [wʊd] *v aux* **she said she would do it** dijo que lo haría; **he would come if he could** vendría si pudiese; **he would go for days without smoking** pasaba días enteros sin fumar; **would that . . .!** ¡ojalá que . . .!

would'-be' *adj* llamado; supuesto ‖ *s* presumido

wound [wund] *s* herida ‖ *tr* herir

wounded ['wundɪd] *adj* herido ‖ **the wounded** los heridos

wow [waʊ] *s* (*of phonograph record*) ululación; (slang) éxito rotundo ‖ *tr* (slang) entusiasmar ‖ *interj* ¡cielos!, ¡mecachis!

wrack [ræk] *s* naufragio; vestigio; (*fucaceous seaweed*) varec *m*; **to go to wrack and ruin** desvencijarse; ir al desastre

wraith [reθ] *s* fantasma *m*, espectro

wrangle ['ræŋgəl] *s* pendencia, riña ‖ *intr* pelotear, reñir

wrap [ræp] *s* abrigo, manto ‖ *v* (*pret & pp* **wrapped**; *ger* **wrapping**) *tr* envolver; **to be wrapped up in** (fig) estar prendado de; **to wrap up** envolver; (*in clothing*) arropar; (coll) concluir ‖ *intr*—**to wrap up** arroparse

wrapper ['ræpər] *s* bata, peinador *m*; (*of newspaper or magazine*) faja; (*of tobacco*) capa

wrapping paper ['ræpɪŋ] *s* papel *m* de envolver, papel de embalar

wrath [ræθ] o [rɑθ] *s* cólera, ira; venganza

wrathful ['ræθfəl] o ['rɑθfəl] *adj* colérico, iracundo

wreak [rik] *tr* descargar (*la cólera*); infligir (*venganza*)

wreath [riθ] *s* (*pl* **wreaths** [riðz]) guirnalda; corona funeraria; (*worn as a mark of honor or victory*) corona de laurel; (*of smoke*) espiral *f*

wreathe [rið] *tr* enguirnaldar; ceñir, envolver; tejer (*una guirnalda*) ‖ *intr* elevarse en espirales (*el humo*)

wreck [rɛk] *s* destrucción, ruina; naufragio; catástrofe *f*, desastre *m*; despojos, restos; (*of one's hopes*) naufragio; **to be a wreck** estar hecho un cascajo, estar hecho una ruina ‖ *tr* destruir, arruinar; hacer naufragar; hacer chocar, descarrilar (*un tren*)

wrecking ball *s* bola rompedora

wrecking car *s* (aut) camión *m* de auxilio; (rr) carro de grúa

wrecking crane *s* grúa de auxilio

wren [rɛn] *s* buscareta, coletero, rey *m* de zarza

wrench [rɛntʃ] *s* llave *f*; (*pull*) arranque *m*, tirón *m*; (*twist of a joint*) esguince *m* ‖ *tr* torcerse (*p.ej., la muñeca*); (fig) torcer (*el sentido de una oración*)

wrest [rɛst] *tr* arrebatar, arrancar violentamente

wrestle ['rɛsəl] *s* lucha; partido de lucha ‖ *intr* luchar

wrestling match ['rɛslɪŋ] *s* partido de lucha

wretch [rɛtʃ] *s* miserable *mf*

wretched ['rɛtʃɪd] *adj* miserable; (*poor, worthless*) malísimo, pésimo

wriggle ['rɪgəl] *s* culebreo, meneo serpentino ‖ *tr* menear rápidamente ‖ *intr* culebrear, ondular; **to wriggle out of** escabullirse de

wrig•gly ['rɪgli] *adj* (*comp* -**glier**; *super* -**gliest**) retorciéndose; (fig) evasivo, tramoyista

wring [rɪŋ] *v* (*pret & pp* **wrung** [rʌŋ]) *tr* torcer; retorcer (*las manos*); exprimir (*el zumo, la ropa, etc.*); sacar por fuerza (*la verdad*); arrancar (*dinero*); **to wring out** exprimir (*la ropa*)

wringer ['rɪŋər] *s* exprimidor *m*

rinkle ['rɪŋkəl] s arruga; (*clever trick or idea*) (coll) ardid *m*, truco ‖ *tr* arrugar ‖ *ntr* arrugarse

n•kly ['rɪŋkli] *adj* (*comp* **-klier;** *super* **-kliest**) arrugado

wrist [rɪst] *s* muñeca

wrist'band' *s* bocamanga, puño

wrist watch *s* reloj *m* de pulsera

writ [rɪt] *s* escrito, escritura; (law) mandato, orden *f*

write [raɪt] *v* (*pret* **wrote** [rot]; *pp* **written** ['rɪtən]) *tr* escribir; **to write down** poner por escrito; bajar el precio de; **to write off** cancelar (*una deuda*); **to write up** describir extensamente por escrito; (*to ballyhoo*) dar bombo a ‖ *intr* escribir; **to write back** contestar por carta

writer ['raɪtər] *s* escritor *m*

writer's cramp *s* grafospasmo

write'-up' *s* (*favorable report*) bombo; (com) valoración excesiva

writhe [raɪð] *intr* contorcerse, retorcerse

writing ['raɪtɪŋ] *s* el escribir; (*something written*) escrito; profesión de escritor; **at this writing** al escribir ésta; **in one's own writing** de su puño y letra; **to put in writing** poner por escrito

writing desk *s* escritorio

writing materials *spl* recado de escribir

writing paper *s* papel *m* de escribir, papel de cartas

written accent ['rɪtən] *s* acento ortográfico

wrong [rɔŋ] *adj* injusto; malo; erróneo, equivocado; impropio; no . . . que se busca,

p.ej., **this is the wrong house** ésta no es la casa que se busca; no . . . que se necesita, p.ej., **this is the wrong train** éste no es el tren que se necesita; no . . . que debe, p.ej., **he is going the wrong way** no sigue el camino que debe; **in the wrong place** mal colocado; **to be wrong** no tener razón; tener la culpa; **to be wrong with** pasar algo a, p.ej., **something is wrong with the motor** algo le pasa al motor ‖ *adv* mal; sin razón; al revés; **to go wrong** ir por mal camino; darse a la mala vida ‖ *s* daño, perjuicio; agravio, injusticia; error *m;* **to be in the wrong** no tener razón; tener la culpa; **to do wrong** obrar mal ‖ *tr* agraviar, hacer daño a, ofender, ser injusto con

wrongdoer ['rɔŋ,du•ər] *s* malhechor *m*

wrongdoing ['rɔŋ,du•ɪŋ] *s* malhecho, maldad

wrong number *s* (telp) número equivocado

wrong side *s* contrahaz *f*, revés *m;* (*of the street*) lado contrario; **to get out of bed on the wrong side** levantarse del lado izquierdo; **wrong side out** al revés

wrought iron [rɔt] *s* hierro dulce

wrought'-up' *adj* muy conmovido, sobreexcitado, exaltado

wry [raɪ] *adj* (*comp* **wrier;** *super* **wriest**) torcido; desviado, pervertido; irónico, burlón

wry'neck' *s* (orn) torcecuello; (pathol) torticolis *m*

wt. *abbr* **weight**

X

X, x [ɛks] vigésima cuarta letra del alfabeto inglés

Xanthippe [zæn'tɪpi] *s* Jantipa

Xavier ['zevɪ•ər] *s* Javier

xebec ['zibɛk] *s* (naut) jabeque *m*

xenia ['zɪnɪ•ə] *s* xenia

xenon ['zinɑn] o ['zɛnɑn] *s* xenón *m*

xenophobe ['zɛnə,fob] *s* xenófobo

xenophobia [,zɛnə'fobɪ•ə] *s* xenofobia

Xenophon ['zɛnəfən] *s* Jenofonte *m*

xerograph ['zɪrə,græf] *s* fotocopia instantánea en seco ‖ *tr & intr* xerografiar

xerography [zɪ'rɑgrəfi] *s* xerografía

Xerxes ['zʌrksiz] *s* Jerjes *m*

Xmas ['krɪsməs] *s* Navidad

X-rated ['ɛks,retɪd] *adj* (*film, etc.*) no recomendado; pornográfico

X ray *s* rayo X; (*photograph*) radiograma *m*

X-ray ['ɛks,re] *adj* radiográfico ‖ ['ɛks're] *tr* radiografiar; tratar por medio de los rayos X

xylograph ['zaɪlə,græf] *s* xilografía

xylography [zaɪ'lɑgrəfi] *s* xilografía

xylophone ['zaɪlə,fon] *s* (mus) xilófono

Y

Y, y [waɪ] vigésima quinta letra del alfabeto inglés

y. *abbr* **yard, year**

yacht [jɑt] *s* yate *m*

yacht club *s* club náutico

yak [jæk] *s* (zool) yac *m*

yam [jæm] *s* ñame *m;* (*sweet potato*) boniato, camote *m*

yank [jæŋk] s (coll) tirón m ‖ tr (coll) sacar de un tirón ‖ intr (coll) dar un tirón
Yankee ['jæŋki] adj & s yanqui mf
Yankeedom ['jæŋkidəm] s Yanquilandia; los yanquis
yap [jæp] s ladrido corto; (slang) charla necia y ruidosa ‖ v (pret & pp **yapped**; ger **yapping**) intr ladrar con ladrido corto; (slang) charlar necia y ruidosamente
yard [jɑrd] s cercado, patio; (measure) yarda; (naut) verga; (rr) patio
yard'arm' s (naut) penol m
yard goods spl géneros de pieza
yard'mas'ter s (rr) superintendente m de patio
yard'stick' s yarda, vara de medir; (fig) criterio, norma
yarn [jɑrn] s hilado, hilaza; (coll) cuento increíble, burlería
yarrow ['jæro] s milenrama
yaw [jɔ] s (naut) guiñada; **yaws** (pathol) frambesia ‖ intr (naut) guiñar
yawl [jɔl] s (naut) bote m; (naut) queche m
yawn [jɔn] s bostezo ‖ intr bostezar; abrirse desmesuradamente
yd. abbr **yard**
yea [je] adv & s sí m
yean [jin] intr parir (la oveja, la cabra, etc.)
year [jɪr] s año; **to be . . . years old** cumplir . . . años; **year in, year out** año tras año
year'book' s anuario
yearling ['jɪrlɪŋ] adj & s primal m
yearly ['jɪrli] adj anual ‖ adv anualmente
yearn [jʌrn] intr suspirar; **to yearn for** suspirar por, anhelar por
yearning ['jʌrnɪŋ] s anhelo, deseo ardiente
yeast [jist] s levadura
yeast cake s levadura comprimida, pastilla de levadura
yell [jɛl] s grito, voz f ‖ tr decir a gritos ‖ intr gritar, dar voces
yellow ['jɛlo] adj amarillo; (cowardly) (coll) blanco; (journalism) sensacional ‖ s amarillo; yema de huevo ‖ intr amarillecer
yellowish ['jɛlo·ɪʃ] adj amarillento
yellow jacket s avispón m
yellowness ['jɛlonɪs] s amarillez f
yellow press s prensa amarilla
yellow streak s vena de cobarde
yelp [jɛlp] s gañido ‖ intr gañir
yeo•man ['jomən] s (pl **-men** [mən]) (naut) pañolero; (naut) oficinista m de a bordo; (Brit) labrador acomodado
yeoman of the guard s (Brit) alabardero de palacio, continuo
yeoman's service s ayuda leal
yes [jɛs] adv sí ‖ s sí m; **to say yes** dar el sí ‖

v (pret & pp **yessed**; ger **yessing**) tr decir sí a ‖ intr decir sí
yes man s (coll) sacristán m de amén
yesterday ['jɛstərdi] o ['jɛstər,de] adj & s ayer m
yet [jɛt] adv todavía, aún; **as yet** hasta ahora; **not yet** todavía no ‖ conj sin embargo
yew tree [ju] s tejo
yield [jild] s producción, rendimiento; (crop) cosecha; (income produced) rédito ‖ tr producir, rendir, redituar ‖ intr entregarse, rendirse, someterse; acceder, ceder, consentir; producir
yodeling o **yodelling** ['jodəlɪŋ] s tirolesa
yoga ['jogə] s yoga
yogi ['jogi] s yogui m
yogurt ['jogərt] s yogurt m
yoke [jok] s (pair of draft animals) yunta; (device to join a pair of draft animals) yugo; (fig) yugo; (of a shirt) hombrillo; (elec) culata; **to throw off the yoke** sacudir el yugo ‖ tr uncir
yokel ['jokəl] s patán m
yolk [jok] s yema
yonder ['jɑndər] adj aquel, de más allá ‖ adv allá, más allá
yore [jor] s—**of yore** antaño, antiguamente
you [ju] pron pers usted, ustedes; le, la, les; **with you** consigo ‖ pron indef se, p.ej., **you go in this way** se entra por aquí
young [jʌŋ] adj (comp **younger** ['jʌŋgər]; super **youngest** ['jʌŋgɪst]) joven ‖ **the young** los jóvenes, la gente joven
young hopeful s joven m de esperanzas
young people spl jóvenes mpl, gente f joven
youngster ['jʌŋstər] s jovencito; (child) chico, chiquillo
your [jʊr] adj poss su, el (o su) de Vd. o de Vds.
Yours [jʊrz] pron poss suyo; de Vd., de Vds.; el suyo; el de Vd., el de Vds.; **of yours** suyo; de Vd., de Vds.; **yours truly** su seguro servidor; (coll) este cura (yo)
your•self [jʊr'sɛlf] pron pers (pl **-selves** ['sɛlvz]) usted mismo; sí, sí mismo; se, p.ej., **you enjoyed yourself** se divirtió Vd.
youth [juθ] s (pl **youths** [juθs] o [juðz]) juventud; (person) jovenzuelo; jovenzuelos, jóvenes mpl
youthful ['juθfəl] adj juvenil, mocil
yowl [jaʊl] s aullido, alarido ‖ intr aullar, dar alaridos
yr. abbr **year**
Yugoslav ['jugo'slɑv] adj & s yugoeslavo
Yugoslavia ['jugo'slɑvɪ·ə] s Yugoeslavia
Yule [jul] s la Navidad; la pascua de Navidad
Yule log s nochebueno, leño de nochebuena
Yuletide ['jul,taɪd] s la pascua de Navidad

Z

Z, z [zi] vigésima sexta letra del alfabeto inglés
za•ny ['zeni] adj (comp **-nier**; super **-niest**)

cómico, gracioso, chiflado ‖ s (pl **-nies**) bufón m, payaso; mentecato
zeal [zil] s celo, entusiasmo

zealot [ˈzɛlət] *s* fanático, entusiasta *mf*
zealotry [ˈzɛlətri] *s* fanatismo
zealous [ˈzɛləs] *adj* celoso, entusiasta
zebra [ˈzibrə] *s* cebra
zebu [ˈzibju] *s* cebú *m*
zenith [ˈzinɪθ] *s* cenit *m*
zephyr [ˈzɛfər] *s* céfiro
zeppelin [ˈzɛpəlɪn] *s* zepelín *m*
ze•ro [ˈzɪro] *s (pl* **-ros** o **-roes)** cero
zero gravity *s* gravedad nula
zero growth *s* crecimiento cero
ze′ro-growth′ *adj* sin aumento; estable
zero option *s* opción cero, opción nula
zest [zɛst] *s* entusiasmo; *(agreeable and piquant flavor)* gusto, sabor *m*
Zeus [zus] *s* Zeus *m*
zig•zig [ˈzɪg,zæg] *adj & adv* en zigzag ‖ *s* zigzag *m*, ziszas *m* ‖ *v (pret & pp* **-zagged;** *ger* **-zagging)** *intr* zigzaguear
zinc [zɪŋk] *s* cinc *m*
zinc etching *s* cincograbado
zinnia [ˈzɪnɪ•ə] *s* rascamoño
Zionism [ˈzaɪ•ə,nɪzəm] *s* sionismo
zip [zɪp] *s* (coll) silbido, zumbido; (coll)

energía, brío ‖ *v (pret & pp* **zipped;** *ger* **zipping)** *tr* cerrar con cierre relámpago, abrir con cierre relámpago; (coll) llevar con rapidez; **to zip up** dar gusto a ‖ *intr* silbar, zumbar; (coll) moverse con energía; **to zip by** (coll) pasar rápidamente
zip code *s* código postal
zipper [ˈzɪpər] *s* cierre *m* relámpago, cierre cremallera; chanclo con cierre relámpago; cíper (Mex)
zircon [ˈzʌrkɑn] *s* circón *m*
zirconium [zərˈkonɪ•əm] *s* circonio
zither [ˈzɪθər] *s* (mus) cítara
zodiac [ˈzodɪ,æk] *s* zodíaco
zone [zon] *s* zona; distrito postal ‖ *tr* dividir en zonas
zoölogic(al) [,zo•əˈlɑdʒɪk(əl)] *adj* zoológico
zoölogist [zoˈɑlədʒɪst] *s* zoólogo
zoölogy [zoˈɑlədʒi] *s* zoología
zoom [zum] *s* zumbido; (aer) empinada ‖ *tr* (aer) empinar ‖ *intr* zumbar; (aer) empinarse
zoöphyte [ˈzo•ə,faɪt] *s* zoófito
Zu•lu [ˈzulu] *adj* zulú ‖ *s (pl* **-lus)** zulú *mf*

ya
zu

SPANISH GRAMMAR

1. STRESS, PUNCTUATION, CAPITALIZATION

All Spanish words, except compound words and adverbs in **-mente,** have only one stress. The position of this stress is always shown by the spelling in accordance with the following rules:

(a) Words ending in a vowel sound or in **n** or **s** are stressed on the syllable next to the last, e.g., **ca-sa, a-gua, se-rio, ha-blan, co-sas.**

(b) Words ending in a consonant except **n** or **s** are stressed on the last syllable, e.g., **se-ñor, pa-pel, fe-liz, U-ru-guay, es-toy.**

(c) If the stress does not fall in accordance with either of the above rules, it is indicated by an acute accent placed above the stressed vowel, e.g., **ca-fé, a-pren-dí, na-ción, lá-piz, fá-cil, re-pú-bli-ca.** The acute accent is also used to distinguish between words spelled alike but having different meanings or parts of speech, e.g., **aun** (= even) and **aún** (= still, yet), **donde** (*conj*) and **dónde** (*adv*), **el** (*def art*) and **él** (*pron*).

Question marks and exclamation points are placed both before and after a word or sentence, and the first is inverted, e.g., **¿Que tal?** How's everything? **¡Que lástima!** What a pity!

Capital letters are used less in Spanish than in English, e.g., **un inglés** an Englishman, **el idioma español** the Spanish language, **domingo** Sunday, **enero** January.

Substantivos invariables: **craft, craft; deer, deer; fish, fish** (o **fishes**); **grouse, grouse; salmon, salmon; sheep, sheep; swine, swine; trout, trout**

2. GÉNERO

A diferencia de los substantivos en español, los nombres de cosas en inglés usualmente no tienen género.

NEUTROS:
Los nombres de cosas concretos o abstractos: **chair, idea** etc. **(the chair and *its* legs)**
Los de animales cuando no se especifica su sexo: **dog, kitten** etc. **(the dog and *its* tail)**
Los que significan niño o niño de pecho: **child, baby** etc. **(the baby and *its* smile)**

MASCULINOS: Los nombres que significan varón o animal macho: **actor, boy, buck, father, knight** etc. **(the actor and *his* voice)**

FEMININOS: Los nombres que significan mujer o animal hembra: **girl, cow, actress, mother, heroine** etc. **(the actress and *her* speech)** (también los nombres de barcos, máquinas y países)

COMUNES: **acquaintance, chairperson, poet, nurse, president, dentist** etc. **(Dr. Paul Miller is a dentist; *his* office is closed. Dr. Mary Miller is also a dentist; *her* office is open.)**

3. LA *S* DE POSESIÓN

Es posible expresar la «posesión» de los nombres substantivos utilizando un apóstrofe + s(**'s**): **my friend's car** el coche de mi amigo; **a month's vacation** unas vacaciones de un mes

Cuando el substantivo es plural, se añade **s** + un apóstrofe (**s'**): **the birds' nests** los nidos de los pájaros; **my friends' house** la casa de mis amigos

Pero se puede también expresar la posesión utilizando **of**: **the main street of Newark** o **Newark's main street** la calle principal de Newark; **the cover of the book** o **the book's cover** la cubierta del libro

Cuando se usa el nombre propio de una persona hay que añadir siempre un apóstrofe + s (**'s**) para expresar la posesión (o solamente un apóstrofe si el nombre propio de la persona termina en **s**): **Philip's brother** el hermano de Felipe; **Mary's book** el libro de María; **Williams' dictionary** el diccionario de Williams

4. REGLAS GENERALES PARA EL ADJETIVO Y EL ADVERBIO

LUGAR DEL ADJETIVO. Por regla general, el adjetivo (cuando no tiene función de predicado) precede al substantivo que califica o determina: **an intelligent student, a great country**

LUGAR DEL ADVERBIO. Por regla general, el adverbio va delante de la palabra que modifica: **seriously ill, very well**

GÉNERO Y NÚMERO. Los adjetivos y adverbios en inglés no tienen género o número; son invariables: **the very intelligent boy, the very intelligent girls**

5. FORMACIÓN DEL ADVERBIO

Por regla general, los adverbios se forman añadiendo **ly** al adjetivo: **quick, quickly; luxurious, luxuriously; faithful, faithfully**

Hay irregularidades:
(a) Los adjetivos terminados en **y** precedida de consonante cambian la **y** en **i** antes de añadir **ly: easy, easily**
(b) Los terminados en **ble** cambian la **e** en **y: probable, probably**
(c) Los terminados en **ue** pierden la **e** final antes de añadir **ly: true, truly**
(d) Muchos adjetivos que terminan en **ic** añaden **ally: poetic, poetically** (Pero otros añaden **ly: public, publicly**)

6. FORMACIÓN DEL COMPARATIVO Y DEL SUPERLATIVO

Para construir el comparativo y el superlativo de los adjetivos y de los adverbios de una sílaba se añaden **er** para el comparativo y **est** para el superlativo: **fast, faster, fastest**

Los adjetivos y adverbios que terminan en **e** muda omiten la **e** antes de añadir **er** o **est: late, later, latest**

The definite article is omitted before nouns in apposition, e.g., **Madrid, capital de España** Madrid, the capital of Spain, and in the numbered names of rulers and popes, e.g., **Luis catorce** Louis the Fourteenth.

5. INDEFINITE ARTICLE

The singulars of the indefinite article are **un,** masculine, and **una,** feminine; the plurals are **unos,** masculine, and **unas,** feminine, e.g., **un mes** a month, **unos meses** (some) months; **una calle** a street, **unas calles** (some) streets.

The form **un** is also commonly used before feminine singular nouns beginning with a stressed **a** or **ha,** e.g., **un arma** a weapon.

The plural forms **unos, unas,** when followed by a cardinal number, mean *about,* e.g., **unos cinco años** about five years.

The indefinite article is not used before a noun of nationality, religion, occupation, and the like, e.g., **Mi amigo es abogado** My friend is a lawyer. If the noun is modified, the indefinite article is generally used, e.g., **Mi hermano es un abogado excelente** My brother is an excellent lawyer. The indefinite article is omitted before **otro,** which therefore means both *other* and *another,* e.g., **Quiero otro libro** I want another book.

6. GENDER OF ADJECTIVES

Adjectives agree in gender and number with the noun they modify.

Adjectives ending in **-o** become feminine by changing **-o** to **-a,** e.g., **alto** and **alta** high. Adjectives ending in any other letter have the same form in the masculine and the feminine, e.g., **constante** constant, **fácil** easy, **belga** Belgian, except adjectives of nationality ending in **-l, -s,** or **-z** and adjectives ending in **-or, -án,** and **-ón,** which add **-a** to form their feminines, e.g., **español** and **española** Spanish, **inglés** and **inglesa** English, **conservador** and **conservadora** preservative, **barrigón** and **barrigona** big-bellied.

Comparatives ending in **-or** have the same form in the masculine and the feminine, e.g., **mejor** better, **superior** upper, superior.

7. PLURAL OF ADJECTIVES

Adjectives ending in a vowel form their plurals by adding **-s,** e.g., **alto** and **altos, alta** and **altas** high; **constante** and **constantes** constant.

Adjectives ending in a consonant form their plurals by adding **-es,** e.g., **fácil** and **fáciles** easy, **barrigón** and **barrigones** big-bellied. Those ending in **-z** change the **z** to **c** and add **-es,** e.g., **feliz** and **felices** happy.

(The acute accent found on the last syllable of the masculine singular of some adjectives ending in **-n** and **-s** is omitted in the feminine singular and in the plural, e.g., **inglés** and **inglesa,** *pl* **ingleses** English.)

8. POSITION OF ADJECTIVES

Adjectives generally follow the nouns they modify, e.g., **vino italiano** Italian wine. However, they precede the noun they modify when used in a figurative, derived, or unemphatic sense, e.g., **pobre hombre** poor (pitiable) man, but **un hombre pobre** a poor man; **cierta ciudad** a certain city, but **cosa cierta** sure thing.

9. SHORTENING OF ADJECTIVES

When **bueno** good, **malo** bad, **primero** first, **tercero** third, **alguno** some, any, and **ninguno** none, no, are used before a masculine singular noun, they drop their final **-o,** e.g., **buen libro** good book, **mal olor** bad odor, **primer capítulo** first chapter, **algun muchacho** some boy, **ningun soldado** no soldier.

When **grande** large, great, is used before a masculine or feminine singular noun, it drops **-de,** e.g., **gran nación** great nation. If the noun begins with a vowel or **h,** either **gran** or **grande** may be used, e.g., **grande amigo** or **gran amigo** great friend.

Ciento hundred, drops **-to** before a noun, e.g., **cien años** a hundred years, **cien dólares** a hundred dollars.

The masculine **santo** saint, becomes **san** before all names of saints except **Domingo** and **Tomás,** e.g., **San Francisco** Saint Francis. Before common nouns it is not shortened, e.g., **el santo papa** the Holy Father.

Los *adjetivos posesivos* son: **my, your, his, her, its, our, your, their**

Ejemplo del uso de pronombres personales y adjetivos posesivos: *We* gave *her his* **book** (o *We* gave *his* **book** *to her*), but *I* told *myself* that *she* wanted *theirs*. *Le* dimos *su* libro, pero *me* dije que *ella* quería *los suyos*.

El pronombre complemento indirecto puede usarse sin o con una preposición. Cuando no tiene una preposición, va delante del objeto directo (**his book**): **We gave *her* his book.** Cuando tiene una preposición, va después del objeto directo (**his book**): **We gave his book *to her*.**

Si el pronombre complemento es directo, no puede usarse una preposición: **We saw *her*.** La veíamos.

(Nótese que la misma regla se aplica cuando el objeto indirecto es un substantivo. Sin preposición: **We gave *our father* the book.** Con una preposición: **We gave the book *to our father*.** Dimos el libro a nuestro padre.)

11. CONJUGACIÓN REGULAR

PRESENTE **Simple present** (llego etc.)	PRETÉRITO **Simple past** (llegué etc.)	PRETÉRITO PERFECTO COMPUESTO **Present perfect** (he llegado etc.)	PRETÉRITO PLUSCUAM-PERFECTO **Past perfect** (había llegado etc.)
I arrive	I arrived	I have arrived	I had arrived
you arrive	you arrived	you have arrived	you had arrived
he arrives	he arrived	he *has* arrived	he had arrived
she arrives	she arrived	she *has* arrived	she had arrived
it arrives	it arrived	it *has* arrived	it had arrived
we arrive	we arrived	we have arrived	we had arrived
you arrive	you arrived	you have arrived	you had arrived
they arrive	they arrived	they have arrived	they had arrived

FUTURO **Future** (llegaré etc.)	CONDICIONAL **Conditional** (llegaría etc.)	CONJUGACIÓN CONTINUA **Present progressive** (estoy llegando etc.)
I will arrive	I would arrive	I am arriving
you will arrive	you would arrive	you are arriving (etc.)
he will arrive	he would arrive	
she will arrive	she would arrive	
it will arrive	it would arrive	**Past progressive**
we will arrive	we would arrive	(estaba llegando etc.)
you will arrive	you would arrive	I was arriving
they will arrive	they would arrive	you were arriving (etc.)

IMPERATIVO
Imperative
  arrive! ¡llega! ¡llegad! ¡llegue Vd.! ¡lleguen Vds.!
  let us arrive! ¡lleguemos!
  let him arrive! ¡que él llegue! **let her arrive!** ¡que ella llegue! **let it arrive!** ¡que llegue!
  let them arrive! ¡que lleguen!

Nótese que algunas veces en inglés la misma forma del verbo sirve para el pretérito y el imperfecto: **I arrived** llegaba, **you arrived** llegabas etc. Otras veces el imperfecto se expresa en inglés por medio de la conjugación continua: **I was arriving** estaba llegando etc.

12. FORMACIÓN DEL GERUNDIO

Por regla general, los verbos del inglés forman el gerundio añadiendo **ing** al infinitivo: **to land, landing**

Si el verbo termina en una **e** muda, se omite la **e: to arrive, arriving.** (Excepciones están indicadas para los verbos irregulares, p. 714.)

Si el verbo termina en una consonante simple precedida de una vocal corta acentuada, en general se dobla la consonante: **to star, starring; to rebel, rebelling.** (Estas consonantes dobladas están indicadas para los verbos irregulares, p. 714.)

	SINGULAR	PLURAL
masculine	**este** this (near me)	**estos** these (near me)
feminine	**esta** this (near me)	**estas** these (near me)
masculine	**ese** that (near you)	**esos** those (near you)
feminine	**esa** that (near you)	**esas** those (near you)
masculine	**aquel** that (yonder)	**aquellos** (yonder)
feminine	**aquella** that (yonder)	**aquellas** (yonder)

Examples: **este lápiz** this pencil; **ese lápiz** that pencil; **aquel lápiz** that pencil; **estos lápices** these pencils; **esos lápices** those pencils; **aquellos lápices** those pencils

14. FORMATION OF ADVERBS

Adverbs are formed from adjectives by adding **-mente** to the feminine form, e.g., **perfecto** perfect, **perfectamente** perfectly; **fácil** easy, **fácilmente** easily; **constante** constant, **constantemente** constantly. With two or more such adverbs in a series, **-mente** is added only to the last one, e.g., **Escribe clara y correctamente** He writes clearly and correctly.

15. COMPARISON OF ADVERBS

As with adjectives, the comparative and superlative of adverbs are formed by placing **más** more, and **menos** less, before the adverb, e.g., **despacio** slowly, **más despacio** more slowly.
The following adverbs have irregular comparatives and superlatives:

POSITIVE	COMPARATIVE AND SUPERLATIVE
bien well	**mejor** better, best
mal bad, badly	**peor** worse, worst
mucho much	**más** more, most
poco little	**menos** less, least

16. SUBJECT PRONOUNS

	SINGULAR	PLURAL
1st person	**yo** I	**nosotros, -as** we
2nd person (familiar)	**tu** thou, you	**vosotros, -as** you
2nd person (formal)	**usted** you	**ustedes** you
3rd person masculine	**él** he, it	**ellos** they
3rd person feminine	**ella** she, it	**ellas** they
3rd person neuter	**ello** it	

With the exception of **usted** and **ustedes,** which are regularly expressed, these pronouns are used only for emphasis, for contrast, or to avoid ambiguity, and when no verb is expressed, e.g., **Yo trabajo mucho** I work hard; **Él es aplicado pero ella es perezosa** He is diligent, but she is lazy; **¿Quién llama? Yo** Who is calling? I (or me).
When the 3rd-person subject is not a person, it is rarely expressed by a pronoun, e.g., **es larga** it (e.g., the table) is long; and it is never expressed with impersonal verbs, e.g., **llueve** it is raining.
The adjective **mismo,** *fem* **misma** self, is used with the subject pronouns to form the intensive subject pronoun: **yo mismo, -ma** I myself, **tú** (or **usted**) **mismo, -ma** you yourself, **él mismo** he himself, **ella misma** she herself, **nosotros mismos, -mas** we ourselves, **vosotros mismos, -mas** you yourselves, **ellos mismos,** *fem* **ellas mismas** they themselves, **ustedes mismos, -mas** you yourselves

17. PREPOSITIONAL PRONOUNS

	SINGULAR	PLURAL
1st person	**mí** me	**nosotros, -as** us
2nd person (familiar)	**ti** thee, you	**vosotros, -as** you
2nd person (formal)	**usted** you	**ustedes** you
3rd person masculine	**él** him, it	**ellos** them
3rd person feminine	**ella** her, it	**ellas** them
3rd person neuter	**ello** it	
3rd person reflexive	**sí** himself, herself, itself, yourself	**sí** themselves, yourselves

These pronouns are used as objects of prepositions, e.g., **Compró un libro para mí** He bought a book for me; **Compró un libro para sí** He bought a book for himself; **Vd. compró un libro para sí** You bought a book for yourself.

INFINITIVO	PRETÉRITO	PARTICIPIO PASADO
bend	bent	bent, *bended
bereave	bereaved, bereft	bereaved, *bereft
beseech (-es)	beseeched, besought	beseeched, besought
bet/-ting	bet, betted	bet, betted
bid/-ding	bade, bid	bidden
bide	bode, bided	bided
bind	bound	bound, *bounden
bite	bit	bit, bitten
bleed	bled	bled
blend	blended, blent	blended, blent
blow	blew	blown
break	broke	broken
breed	bred	bred
bring	brought	brought
build	built	built
burn	burned, burnt	burned, *burnt
burst	burst	burst
buy	bought	bought
can (AUXILIAR MODAL, INVARIABLE)		
canoe/-ing	canoed (REGULAR)	canoed
cast	cast	cast
catch (-es)	caught	caught
chide	chided, chid	chided, chid, chidden
choose	chose	chosen
cleave	cleaved, cleft	cleaved, *cleft, *cloven
cling	clung	clung
clothe	clothed	clothed, *clad
come	came	come
cost	cost	cost
could (AUXILIAR MODAL, INVARIABLE)		
creep	crept	crept
cut/-ting	cut	cut
deal	dealt	dealt
dig/-ging	dug, digged	dug, digged
dive	dived, dove	dived
do (-es) [dʌz]	did	done
draw	drew	drawn
dream	dreamed, dreamt	dreamed, dreamt
drink	drank	drunk, *drunken
drive	drove	driven
dwell	dwelled, dwelt	dwelled, dwelt
dye/-ing	dyed (REGULAR)	dyed
eat	ate	eaten
fall	fell	fallen
feed	fed	fed
feel	felt	felt
fight	fought	fought
find	found	found
flee/-ing	fled	fled
fling	flung	flung
fly (flies)	flew	flown
forbear	forbore	forborne
forbid/-ding	forbade, forbad	forbidden
forget/-ting	forgot	forgot, forgotten
forsake	forsook	forsaken
freeze	froze	frozen
get/-ting	got	got, gotten
gild	gilded, gilt	gilded, *gilt
gird	girt	girded
give	gave	given
go (-es)	went	gone

These pronouns agree in gender and number with the nouns for which they stand, e.g., **éste** this one (stands, for example, for **este libro** this book), **éstas** these (stands, for example, for **estas plumas** these pens). Their stressed vowel is always marked with an accent to distinguish them from the corresponding possessive adjectives (**esta, estas,** etc., without written accent).

22. RELATIVE PRONOUNS

The form **que,** meaning that, which, who, whom, is the most frequent relative pronoun and is invariable. It is used as both subject and object of the verb and refers to persons and things. For example, **El hombre que me conoce . . .** The man who knows me. . . ; **El hombre que conozco . . .** The man (whom) I know . . . ; **El libro que lee . . .** The book (that) he is reading . . . ; **El trabajo a que dedico mi tiempo . . .** The work to which I devote my time . . .

The form **quien** (*pl* **quienes**) who, whom, is inflected for number, refers only to persons, and takes the personal **a** as direct object, e.g., **El amigo con quien viajé por España . . .** The friend with whom I traveled in Spain . . . ; **La señora a quien vi en la estación . . .** The lady (whom) I saw at the station . . . ; **Los señores para quienes he traído estos libros . . .** The gentlemen for whom I brought these books . . .

The forms **el que** (*fem* **la que,** *pl* **los que, las que**) and **el cual** (*fem* **la cual,** *pl* **los cuales, las cuales**), both meaning who, which, that, agree in gender and number with their antecedent and are therefore used to replace **que** where the reference might be ambiguous, e.g., **El hijo de aquella señora, el cual vive en Nueva York, . . .** The son of that lady who (i.e., the son) lives in New York . . .

The forms **lo que** and **lo cual,** both meaning what, which, are invariable and refer to a previous statement, e.g., **No entiendo lo que él dice** I don't understand what he is saying; **Llegó a medianoche, lo que indicaba que había trabajado mucho** He arrived at midnight, which indicated (that) he had worked hard.

The form **cuanto** (*fem* **cuanta,** *pl* **cuantos, cuantas**) contains its own antecedent and it means: all that which, all those which, all those who (or whom), as much as, as many as. For example, **Eso es cuanto quiero decir** That is all (that) I want to say; **Dijo algo a cuantas personas se hallaban allí** He said something to all the people who were there.

23. REGULAR VERBS

Spanish verbs are classified into three conjugations: those ending in **-ar,** those ending in **-er,** and those ending in **-ir,** e.g., **hablar, comer, vivir.**

FIRST CONJUGATION	SECOND CONJUGATION	THIRD CONJUGATION
1. Simple Tenses		
	Infinitive:	
habl-ar to speak	**com-er** to eat	**viv-ir** to live
	Gerund:	
habl-ando speaking	**com-iendo** eating	**viv-iendo** living
	Past Participle:	
habl-ado spoken	**com-ido** eaten	**viv-ido** lived
	Indicative:	
PRESENT:		
habl-o I speak	**com-o** I eat	**viv-o** I live
habl-as	**com-es**	**viv-es**
habl-a	**com-e**	**viv-e**
habl-amos	**com-emos**	**viv-imos**
habl-áis	**com-éis**	**viv-ís**
habl-an	**com-en**	**viv-en**
IMPERFECT:		
habl-aba I was speaking	**com-ía** I was eating	**viv-ía** I was living
habl-abas	**com-ías**	**viv-ías**
habl-aba	**com-ía**	**viv-ía**
habl-ábamos	**com-íamos**	**viv-íamos**

FIRST CONJUGATION	SECOND CONJUGATION	THIRD CONJUGATION
habl-abals	com-íais	viv-íais
habl-aban	com-ían	viv-ían

PRETERIT:

habl-é I spoke	com-í I ate	viv-í I lived
habl-aste	com-iste	viv-iste
habl-ó	com-ió	viv-ió
habl-amos	com-imos	viv-imos
habl-asteis	com-isteis	viv-isteis
habl-aron	com-ieron	viv-ieron

FUTURE:

hablar-é I shall speak	comer-é I shall eat	vivir-é I shall live
hablar-ás	comer-ás	vivir-ás
hablar-á	comer-á	vivir-á
hablar-emos	comer-emos	vivir-emos
hablar-éis	comer-éis	vivir-éis
hablar-án	comer-án	vivir-án

CONDITIONAL:

hablar-ía I should speak	comer-ía I should eat	vivir-ía I should live
hablar-ías	comer-ías	vivir-ías
hablar-ía	comer-ía	vivir-ía
hablar-íamos	comer-íamos	vivir-íamos
hablar-íais	comer-íais	vivir-íais
hablar-ían	comer-ían	vivir-ían

Subjunctive:

PRESENT:

habl-e	com-a	viv-a
habl-es	com-as	viv-as
habl-e	com-a	viv-a
habl-emos	com-amos	viv-amos
habl-éis	com-áis	viv-áis
habl-en	com-an	viv-an

IMPERFECT S-FORM:

habla-se	comie-se	vivie-se
habla-ses	comie-ses	vivie-ses
habla-se	comie-se	vivie-se
hablá-semos	comié-semos	vivié-semos
habla-seis	comie-seis	vivie-seis
habla-sen	comie-sen	vivie-sen

IMPERFECT R-FORM:

habla-ra	comie-ra	vivie-ra
habla-ras	comie-ras	vivie-ras
habla-ra	comie-ra	vivie-ra
hablá-ramos	comié-ramos	vivié-ramos
habla-rais	comie-rais	vivie-rais
habla-ran	comie-ran	vivie-ran

FUTURE:

habla-re	comie-re	vivie-re
habla-res	comie-res	vivie-res
habla-re	comie-re	vivie-re
hablá-remos	comié-remos	vivié-remos
habla-reis	comie-reis	vivie-reis
habla-ren	comie-ren	vivie-ren

Imperative:

habl-a speak	com-e eat	viv-e live
habl-ad	com-ed	viv-id

INFINITIVO	PRETÉRITO	PARTICIPIO PASADO
understand	understood	understood
vie (vying)	vied (REGULAR)	vied
wake	waked, woke	waked
wear	wore	worn
weave (tejer)	wove	woven, wove
weave (zigzaguear)	weaved (REGULAR)	weaved
wed/-ding	wed, wedded	wed, wedded
weep	wept	wept
wet/-ting	wet, wetted	wet, wetted
will (AUXILIAR MODAL, INVARIABLE)		
win/-ning	won	won
wind	wound	wound
work	worked, wrought	worked, *wrought
would (AUXILIAR MODAL, INVARIABLE)		
wring	wrung	wrung
write	wrote	written

17. CONSTRUCCIÓN DE LA ORACIÓN INTERROGATIVA

La oración interrogativa en general se construye con el auxiliar **to do,** que va delante del sujeto; el verbo toma la forma invariable del infinitivo sin **to: do you see this tree?** ¿ves este árbol? **did your country win?** ¿ganó su país?

Si el verbo es **to be** o un auxiliar modal (**can, could, may, might, must, ought, shall, should, will, would**), la oración interrogativa se construye sin **to do;** el sujeto va inmediatamente después del verbo: **are the students ready?** ¿están listos los estudiantes? **shall we go?** ¿nos vamos?

18. CONSTRUCCIÓN DE LA NEGACIÓN

La negación en general se construye con el auxiliar **to do** seguido de **not;** el verbo toma la forma invariable del infinitivo sin **to: I do not see it** no lo veo; **he does not play** él no juega; **her father did not come** su padre no vino

Si el verbo es **to be** o un auxiliar modal (**can, could, may, might, must, ought, shall, should, will, would**), la negación se construye sin **to do,** poniendo **no** inmediatamente después del verbo: **they are not here** no están aquí; **John will not win** Juan no ganará

19. CONTRACCIONES

Las contracciones son muy corrientes en inglés, especialmente en el lenguaje coloquial y la escritura familiar.

Contracciones del pronombre y del verbo:

I am = I'm [aɪm]
you are = you're [jur]
he is = he's [hiz]
she is = she's [ʃ iz]
it is = it's [ɪts]
we are = we're [wir]
they are = they're [ðɛr]
who is = who's [huz]

I have = I've [aɪv]
you have = you've [juv]
he has = he's [hiz]
she has = she's [ʃ iz]
it has = it's [ɪts]
we have = we've [wiv]
they have = they've [ðev]
who has = who's [huz]

I will = I'll [aɪl]
you will = you'll [jul]
he will = he'll [hil]
she will = she'll [ʃ il]
it will = it'll [ɪtl]
we will = we'll [wil]
they will = they'll [ðel]
who will = who'll [hul]

I would = I'd [aɪd]
you would = you'd [jud]
he would = he'd [hid]
she would = she'd [ʃ id]
we would = we'd [wid]
they would = they'd [ðed]
who would = who'd [hud]

Nótese que se usan las contracciones del pronombre y del verbo **to have** solamente con los participios pasados, p.ej., **she's written a book.** (No se usa la contracción en casos como **she has a book.**)

hayamos hablado	hayamos comido	hayamos vivido
hayáis hablado	hayáis comido	hayáis vivido
hayan hablado	hayan comido	hayan vivido

PLUPERFECT S-FORM:

hubiese hablado	hubiese comido	hubiese vivido
hubieses hablado	hubieses comido	hubieses vivido
hubiese hablado	hubiese comido	hubiese vivido
hubiésemos hablado	hubiésemos comido	hubiésemos vivido
hubieseis hablado	hubieseis comido	hubieseis vivido
hubiesen hablado	hubiesen comido	hubiesen vivido

PLUPERFECT R-FORM:

hubiera hablado	hubiera comido	hubiera vivido
hubieras hablado	hubieras comido	hubieras vivido
hubiera hablado	hubiera comido	hubiera vivido
hubiéramos hablado	hubiéramos comido	hubiéramos vivido
hubierais hablado	hubierais comido	hubierais vivido
hubieran hablado	hubieran comido	hubieran vivido

FUTURE:

hubiere hablado	hubiere comido	hubiere vivido
hubieres hablado	hubieres comido	hubieres vivido
hubiere hablado	hubiere comido	hubiere vivido
hubiéremos hablado	hubiéremos comido	hubiéremos vivido
hubiereis hablado	hubiereis comido	hubiereis vivido
hubieren hablado	hubieren comido	hubieren vivido

24. IRREGULAR VERBS

See pages 343 to 350.

25. *SER* AND *ESTAR*

In Spanish there are two verbs that mean *to be*, **ser** and **estar**. Basically, **ser** expresses a permanent or characteristic state of being, while **estar** expresses a temporary or accidental state of being.

SER

pres ind	soy, eres, es, somos, sois, son
pres subj	sea, seas, sea, seamos, seáis, sean
imperf ind	era, eras, era, éramos, erais, eran
fut ind	seré, serás, será, seremos, seréis, serán
pret ind	fui, fuiste, fue, fuimos, fuisteis, fueron

ESTAR

pres ind	estoy, estás, está, estamos, estáis, están
pres subj	esté, estés, esté, estemos, estéis, estén
imperf ind	estaba, estabas, estaba, estábamos, estabais, estaban
fut ind	estaré, estarás, estará, estaremos, estaréis, estarán
pret ind	estuve, estuviste, estuvo, estuvimos, estuvisteis, estuvieron

The fundamental difference between these two verbs is found in their use with predicate adjectives:

SER—**El hierro es duro** Iron is hard; **El alumno es aplicado** The pupil is studious; **El muchacho es bueno** The boy is good.

ESTAR—**La puerta está cerrada** The door is closed; **La casa está llena** The house is full; **El muchacho está bueno** The boy is well.

The location of a person or thing, whether temporary or permanent, is expressed with **estar**, e.g., **La casa está en la esquina** The house is on the corner. The location of an event, however, is expressed by **ser**, e.g., **La escena es en Madrid** The scene is in Madrid; **La boda será en la catedral** The wedding will be in the cathedral.

Ser is used:

(a) when the predicate is a noun or pronoun, e.g., **Son médicos** They are doctors; **Es mi mejor amigo** He is my best friend.

(b) generally in impersonal expressions, e.g., **Es fácil aprender el español** It's easy to learn

	CARDINALES	ORDINALES
200	**two hundred**	**two-hundredth**
1000	**one (o a) thousand**	**(one o a) thousandth**
1001	**one thousand and one**	**(one) thousand and first**
1981	**one thousand nine hundred and eighty-one**	**(one) thousand nine hundred and eighty-first**
100,000	**one (o a) hundred thousand**	**(one o a) hundred thousandth**
1,000,000	**one (o a) million**	**(one o a) millionth**

Nótese que en inglés se usa el número cardinal para los tomos (**volume three** tomo tercero) y el número ordinal para las fechas (**July Fourth** el cuatro de julio). Si la fecha es un año, se dice, p.ej., **nineteen eighty-nine** o **nineteen hundred eighty-nine** (1989).

LA PRONUNCIACIÓN DEL INGLÉS

Los símbolos siguientes representan aproximadamente todos los sonidos del idioma inglés.

VOCALES

SÍMBOLO	SONIDO	EJEMPLO
[æ]	Más cerrado que la **a** de **caro**.	**hat** [hæt]
[ɑ]	Como la **a** de **bajo**.	**father** [ˈfɑðər] **proper** [ˈprɑpər]
[ɛ]	Como la **e** de **perro**.	**met** [mɛt]
[e]	Más cerrado que la **e** de **canté**. Suena como si fuese seguido de [ɪ].	**fate** [fet] **they** [ðe]
[ə]	Como la **e** de la palabra francesa **le**.	**heaven** [ˈhɛvən] **pardon** [ˈpɑrdən]
[i]	Como la **i** de **nido**.	**she** [ʃ i] **machine** [məˈʃ in]
[ɪ]	Menos cerrado que la **i** de **nido**. Como la **i** de **tilde**.	**fit** [fɪt] **beer** [bɪr]
[o]	Más cerrado que la **o** de **habló**. Suena como si fuese seguido de [ʊ].	**nose** [noz] **road** [rod]
[ɔ]	Menos cerrado que la **o** de **torre**.	**bought** [bɔt] **law** [lɔ]
[ʌ]	Más o menos como **eu** en la palabra francesa **peur**.	**cup** [kʌp] **come** [kʌm] **mother** [ˈmʌðər]
[ʊ]	Menos cerrado que la **u** de **bulto**.	**pull** [pʊl] **book** [bʊk] **wolf** [wʊlf]
[u]	Como la **u** de **agudo**.	**rude** [rud] **move** [muv] **tomb** [tum]

DIPTONGOS

SÍMBOLO	SONIDO	EJEMPLO
[aɪ]	Como **ai** de **amáis**.	**night** [naɪt] **eye** [aɪ]
[aʊ]	Como **au** de **causa**.	**found** [faʊnd] **cow** [kaʊ]
[ɔɪ]	Como **oy** de **estoy**.	**voice** [vɔɪs] **oil** [ɔɪl]

SPANISH PRONUNCIATION

The Spanish alphabet has twenty-eight letters. Note that **ch, ll,** and **ñ** are considered to be separate single letters and are so treated in the alphabetization of Spanish words. While **rr** is considered to be a distinct sign for a particular sound, it is not included in the alphabet and, except in syllabification—notably for the division of words at the end of a line—, is not treated as a separate letter, perhaps because words never begin with it.

LETTER	NAME	SOUND
a	a	Like **a** in English **father**, e.g., **casa, fácil.**
b	be	When initial or preceded by **m,** like **b** in English **book,** e.g., **boca, combate.** When standing between two vowels and when preceded by a vowel and followed by **l** or **r,** like **v** in English **voodoo** except that it is formed with both lips, e.g., **saber, hablar, sobre.** It is generally silent before **s** plus a consonant and often dropped in spelling, e.g., **oscuro** for **obscuro.**
c	ce	When followed by **e** or **i,** like **th** in English **think** in Castilian, and like **c** in English **cent** in American Spanish, e.g., **acento, cinco.** When followed by **a, o, u,** or a consonant, like **c** in English **come,** e.g., **cantar, como, cubo, acto, creer.**
ch	che	Like **ch** in English **much,** e.g., **escuchar.**
d	de	Generally, like **d** in **dog,** e.g., **diente, rendir.** When standing between two vowels, when preceded by a vowel and followed by **r,** and when final, like **th** in English **this,** e.g., **miedo, piedra, libertad.**
e	e	At the end of a syllable, like **a** in English **fate,** but without the glide the English sound sometimes has, e.g., **beso, menos.** When followed by a consonant in the same syllable, like **e** in English **met,** e.g., **perla, selva.**
f	efe	Like **f** in English **five,** e.g., **flor, efecto.**
g	ge	When followed by **e** or **i,** like **h** in English **home,** e.g., **gente, giro.** When followed by **a, o, u,** or a consonant, like **g** in English **go,** e.g., **gato, gota, agudo, grande.**
h	hache	Always silent, e.g., **hombre, alcohol.**
i	i	Like **i** in English **machine,** e.g., **camino, ida.** When preceded or followed by another vowel, it has the sound of English **y,** e.g., **tierra, reina.**
j	jota	Like **h** in English **home,** e.g., **jardín, junto.**
k	ka	Like English **k,** e.g., **kilociclo.**
l	ele	Like **l** in English **laugh,** e.g., **lado, ala.**
ll	elle	Somewhat like **lli** in **William** in Castilian and like **y** in English **yes** in American Spanish, e.g., **silla, llamar.**
m	eme	Like **m** in English **man,** e.g., **mesa, amar.**
n	ene	Generally, like **n** in English **name,** e.g., **andar, nube.** Before **v,** like **m** in English **man,** e.g., **invierno, enviar.** Before **c** [k] and **g** [g], like **n** in English **drink,** e.g., **finca, manga.**

[z]	Como la **s** de **mismo**. Sonido alveolar fricativo sonoro.	**zeal** [zil] **busy** [ˈbɪzi] **his** [hɪz]
[ʒ]	Como la **j** de la palabra francesa **jardin**. Sonido palatal fricativo sonoro.	**azure** [ˈeʒər] **measure** [ˈmɛʒər]

PRONUNCIACIÓN DE LA *S* DEL PLURAL

Las **s** del plural en general es sorda ([s]) como la **s** de **ser** después de los sonidos sordos, representados por los consonantes **f, k, p, t, th**[θ] etc.; p.ej.:

[f] **roo*f*s** [rufs], **laug*h*s** [læfs], **trium*ph*s** [ˈtraɪ·əmfs]
[k] **loo*k*s** [lʊks], **cli*ques*** [kliks]
[p] **ma*p*s** [mæps]
[t] **ha*t*s** [hæts]
[θ] **leng*th*s** [lɛŋθs]

Las **s** del plural es sonora ([z]) como la **s** de **mismo** después de los sonidos sonoros, representados por el mayor número de las consonantes y por las voçales; p.ej.:

[b] **ro*b*es** [robz]
[g] **do*g*s** [dɔgz], **ro*gues*** [rogz]
[l] **ha*ll*s** [hɔlz]
[ŋ] **thi*ng*s** [θɪŋz]
[r] **fu*r*s** [fʌrz]
[e] **da*y*s** [dez]
[o] **to*es*** [toz]
[u] **sho*es*** [ʃuz]
[aɪ] **li*es*** [laɪz], **sig*h*s** [saɪz]
[ə] **sofa*s*** [ˈsofəz]

(Por consiguiente, **wife** se pronuncia [waɪf], pero **wives** se pronuncia [waɪvz].)
La terminación **es** que se añade después de los sibilantes se pronuncia [ɪz]; p.ej.:

[s] **ki*ss*es** [ˈkɪsɪz]
[z] **ro*s*es** [ˈrozɪz]
[tʃ] **wa*tch*es** [ˈwɑtʃɪz]
[dʒ] **pa*ges*** [ˈpedʒɪz]

PRONUNCIACIÓN DE LOS PARTICIPIOS PASADOS

La terminación del participio pasado **ed** se pronuncia [d] si el infinitivo termina en el sonido de una vocal o en el sonido de una consonante sonora, excepto [d]: [b], [g], [l], [m], [n], [ŋ], [r], [v], [z], [ð], [ʒ] o [dʒ]; p.ej.:

ÚLTIMO SONIDO	INFINITIVO	PARTICIPIO PASADO Y PRETÉRITO
[b]	**ebb** [ɛb]	**ebbed** [ɛbd]
[r]	**fear** [fɪr]	**feared** [fɪrd]
[ð]	**smooth** [smuð]	**smoothed** [smuɔd]
sonido de vocal	**key** [ki]	**keyed** [kid]
	sigh [saɪ]	**sighed** [saɪd]

La terminación del participio pasado **ed** se pronuncia [t] si el infinitivo termina en el sonido de una consonante sorda: [f], [k], [p], [s], [θ], [ʃ] o [tʃ]; p.ej.:

[f]	**loaf** [lof]	**loafed** [loft]
[θ]	**lath** [læθ]	**lathed** [læθt]
[ʃ]	**mash** [mæʃ]	**mashed** [mæʃt]

La terminación del participio pasado **ed** se pronuncia [ɪd] o [əd] si el infinitivo termina en el sonido de una consonante dental: [t] o [d].

[t]	**wait** [wet]	**waited** [ˈwetɪd]
	mate [met]	**mated** [ˈmetɪd]
[d]	**mend** [mɛnd]	**mended** [ˈmɛndɪd]
	wade [wed]	**waded** [ˈwedɪd]

LA PRONUNCIACIÓN DEL INGLÉS

Los símbolos siguientes representan aproximadamente todos los sonidos del idioma inglés.

VOCALES

SÍMBOLO	SONIDO	EJEMPLO
[æ]	Más cerrado que la **a** de **caro**.	**hat** [hæt]
[ɑ]	Como la **a** de **bajo**.	**father** [ˈfɑðər]
		proper [ˈprɑpər]
[ɛ]	Como la **e** de **perro**.	**met** [mɛt]
[e]	Más cerrado que la **e** de **canté**. Suena como si fuese seguido de [ɪ].	**fate** [fet]
		they [ðe]
[ə]	Como la **e** de la palabra francesa **le**.	**heaven** [ˈhɛvən]
		pardon [ˈpɑrdən]
[i]	Como la **i** de **nido**.	**she** [ʃ i]
		machine [məˈʃ in]
[ɪ]	Como la **i** de **tilde**.	**fit** [fɪt]
		beer [bɪr]
[o]	Más cerrado que la **o** de **habló**. Suena como si fuese seguido de [ʊ].	**nose** [noz]
		road [rod]
[ɔ]	Menos cerrado que la **o** de **torre**.	**bought** [bɔt]
		law [lɔ]
[ʌ]	Más o menos como **eu** en la palabra francesa **peur**.	**cup** [kʌp]
		come [kʌm]
		mother [ˈmʌðər]
[ʊ]	Menos cerrado que la **u** de **bulto**.	**pull** [pʊl]
		book [bʊk]
		wolf [wʊlf]
[u]	Como la **u** de **agudo**.	**rude** [rud]
		move [muv]
		tomb [tum]

DIPTONGOS

SÍMBOLO	SONIDO	EJEMPLO
[aɪ]	Como **ai** de **amáis**.	**night** [naɪt]
		eye [aɪ]
[aʊ]	Como **au** de **causa**.	**found** [faʊnd]
		cow [kaʊ]
[ɔɪ]	Como **oy** de **estoy**.	**voice** [vɔɪs]
		oil [ɔɪl]

CONSONANTES

SÍMBOLO	SONIDO	EJEMPLO
[b]	Como la **b** de **hombre**. Sonido bilabial oclusivo sonoro.	**bed** [bɛd]
		robber [ˈrabər]
[d]	Como la **d** de **conde**. Sonido dental oclusivo sonoro.	**dead** [dɛd]
		add [æd]
[dʒ]	Como la **y** de **cónyuge**. Sonido palatal africado sonoro.	**gem** [dʒɛm]
		jail [dʒel]
[ð]	Como la **d** de **nada**. Sonido interdental fricativo sonoro.	**this** [ðɪs]
		father [ˈfɑðər]
[f]	Como la **f** de **fecha**. Sonido labiodental fricativo sordo.	**face** [fes]
		phone [fon]
[g]	Como la **g** de **gato**. Sonido velar oclusivo sonoro.	**go** [go]
		get [gɛt]
[h]	Sonido más aspirado pero menos áspero que el sonido velar fricativo sordo de la **j** de **junto**.	**hot** [hɑt]
		alcohol [ˈælkə,hɔl]
[j]	Como la **y** de **cuyo**. Sonido palatal semiconsonantal sonoro.	**yes** [jɛs]
		unit [ˈjunɪt]

ñ	eñe	Somewhat like **ni** in English **onion**, e.g.. **año, enseñar**.
o	o	At the end of a syllable, like **o** in English **note**, but without the glide the English sound sometimes has, e.g. **boca, como**. When followed by a consonant in the same syllable, like **o** in English **organ**, e.g.. **poste, norte.**
p	pe	Like **p** in English **pen**, e.g.. **poco, aplicar**. It is often silent in **septiembre** and **séptimo.**
q	cu	Like **c** in English **come**. It is always followed by **ue** or **ui**, in which the **u** is silent, e.g.. **querer, quitar**. The sound of English **qu** is represented in Spanish by **cu**, e.g.. **frecuente.**
r	ere	Strongly trilled, when initial and when preceded by **l, n,** or **s**, e.g.. **rico, alrededor, honra, israelí**. Pronounced with a single tap of the tongue in all other positions, e.g.. **caro, grande, amar.**
rr	erre	Strongly trilled, e.g.. **carro, tierra.**
s	ese	Generally, like **s** in English **say**, e.g.. **servir, casa, este.** Before a voiced consonant (**b, d, g** [g], **l, r, m, n**), like **z** in English **zero**, e.g.. **esbelto, desde, rasgar, eslabón, mismo, asno.**
t	te	Like **t** in English **stamp**, e.g.. **tiempo, matar.**
u	u	Like **u** in English **rude**, e.g.. **mudo, puño**. It is silent in **gue, gui, que,** and **qui**, but not in **güe** and **güi**, e.g.. **guerra, guisa, querer, quitar**, but **agüero, lingüístico**. When preceded or followed by another vowel, it has the sound of English **w**, e.g.. **fuego, deuda.**
v	ve or uve	Like Spanish **b** in all positions, e.g. **vengo, invierno, uva, huevo.**
x	equis	When followed by a consonant, like **s** in English **say**, e.g.. **expresar, sexto**. Between two vowels, like **gs**, e.g.. **examen, existencia, exótico**; and in some words, like **s** in **say**, e.g.. **auxilio, exacto**. In México (for Méjico), like Spanish **j**.
y	ye or i griega	In the conjunction **y**, like **i** in English **machine**. When standing next to a vowel or between two vowels, like **y** in English **yes**, e.g.. **yo, hoy, vaya.**
z	zeda or zeta	Like **th** in English **think** in Castilian and like **c** in English **cent** in American Spanish, e.g.. **zapato, zona.**

DIPHTHONG	SOUND
ai, ay	Like **i** in English **might**, e.g.. **baile, hay**
au	Like **ou** in English **pound**, e.g.. **causa**
ei, ey	Like **ey** in English **they**, e.g.. **reina, ley**
eu	Like **ayw** in English **hayward**, e.g.. **deuda**
oi, oy	Like **oy** in English **boy**, e.g.. **estoy**